DELUXE
ILLUSTRATED
ATLAS
OF THE WORLD

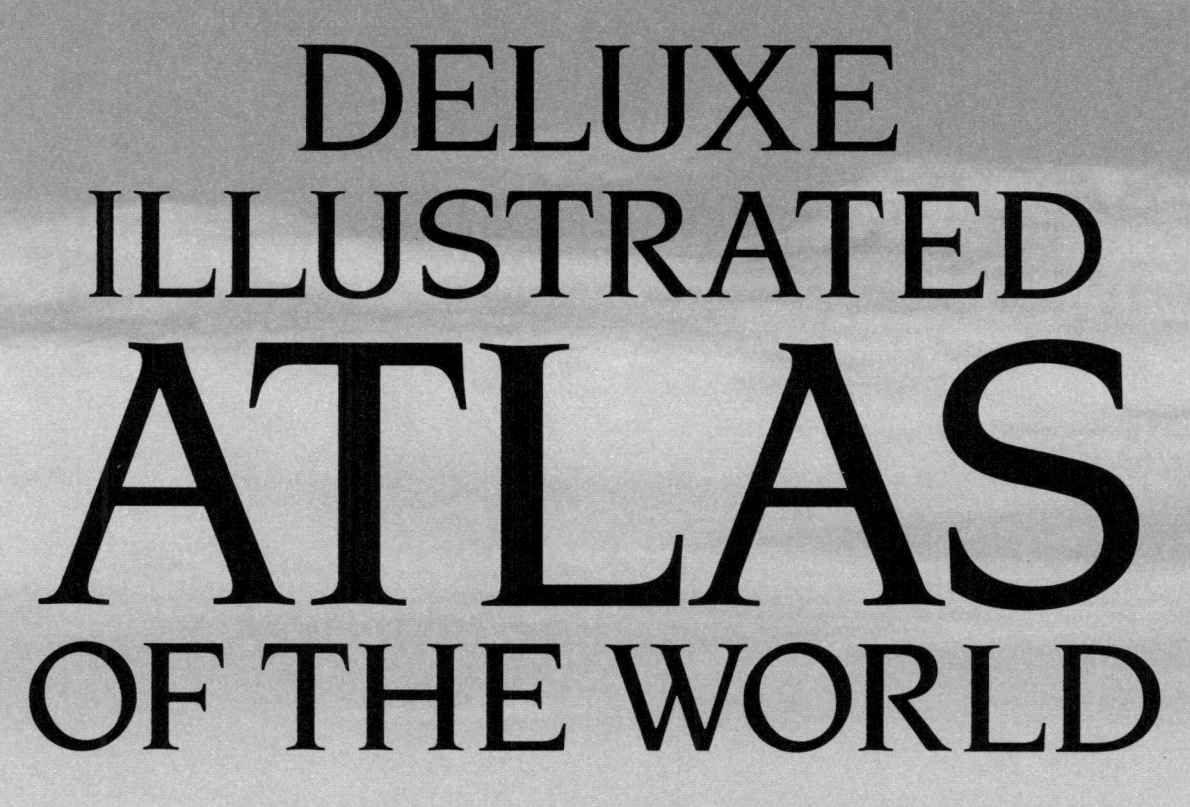

DELUXE
ILLUSTRATED
ATLAS
OF THE WORLD

RAND McNALLY

CHICAGO • NEW YORK • SAN FRANCISCO

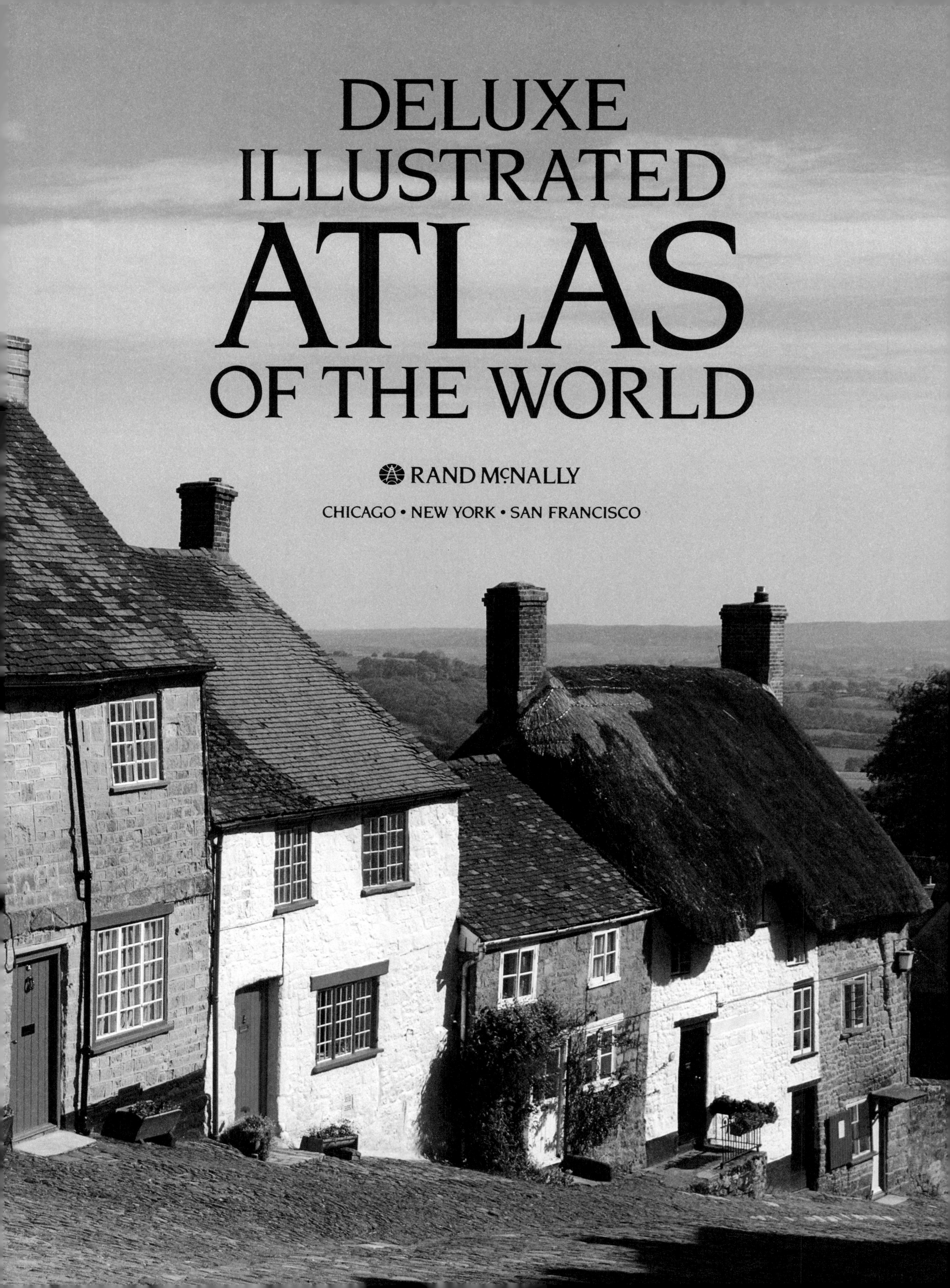

CONTENTS

**DELUXE
ILLUSTRATED ATLAS OF THE WORLD**
Copyright © 1989
Rand McNally & Company

Pages 1 through 240 and A·16 through A·144
Copyright © 1982
Istituto Geografico De Agostini
Revised, 1989

Pages 241 through 304
Copyright © 1983
Rand McNally & Company
Revised, 1989

ISBN: 528-83379-0

Library of Congress
Catalog Card Number: 89-40420

Printed in the United States of America by
Rand McNally & Company
Revised 1990 Edition

Jacket photo by David Muench
Title page photo by Ric Ergenbright

Our Planet
Earth Section

Maps

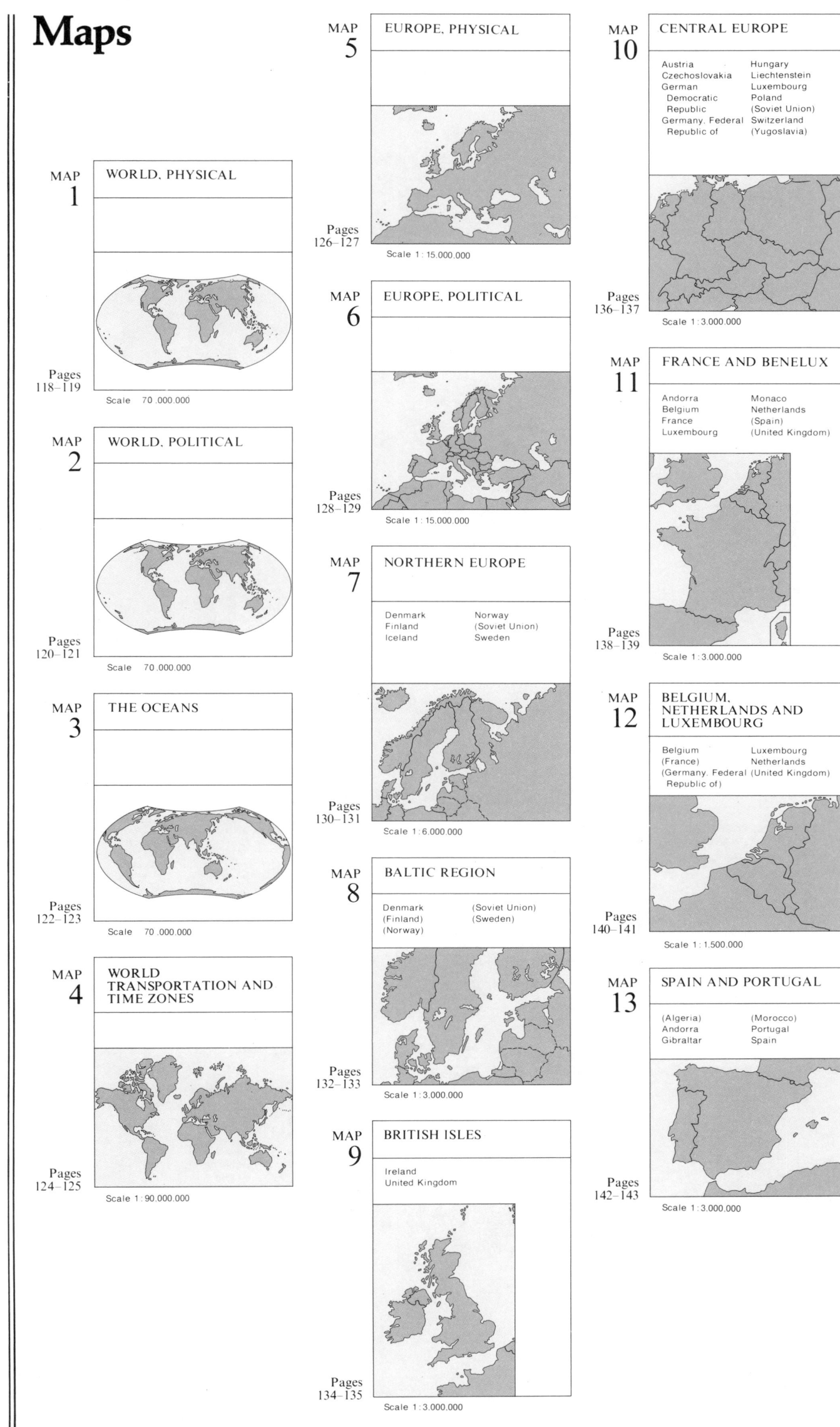

MAP 1 — WORLD, PHYSICAL
Pages 118–119
Scale 70,000,000

MAP 2 — WORLD, POLITICAL
Pages 120–121
Scale 70,000,000

MAP 3 — THE OCEANS
Pages 122–123
Scale 70,000,000

MAP 4 — WORLD TRANSPORTATION AND TIME ZONES
Pages 124–125
Scale 1:90,000,000

MAP 5 — EUROPE, PHYSICAL
Pages 126–127
Scale 1:15,000,000

MAP 6 — EUROPE, POLITICAL
Pages 128–129
Scale 1:15,000,000

MAP 7 — NORTHERN EUROPE
Denmark
Finland
Iceland
Norway
(Soviet Union)
Sweden
Pages 130–131
Scale 1:6,000,000

MAP 8 — BALTIC REGION
Denmark
(Finland)
(Norway)
(Soviet Union)
(Sweden)
Pages 132–133
Scale 1:3,000,000

MAP 9 — BRITISH ISLES
Ireland
United Kingdom
Pages 134–135
Scale 1:3,000,000

MAP 10 — CENTRAL EUROPE
Austria
Czechoslovakia
German Democratic Republic
Germany, Federal Republic of
Hungary
Liechtenstein
Luxembourg
Poland
(Soviet Union)
Switzerland
(Yugoslavia)
Pages 136–137
Scale 1:3,000,000

MAP 11 — FRANCE AND BENELUX
Andorra
Belgium
France
Luxembourg
Monaco
Netherlands
(Spain)
(United Kingdom)
Pages 138–139
Scale 1:3,000,000

MAP 12 — BELGIUM, NETHERLANDS AND LUXEMBOURG
Belgium
(France)
(Germany, Federal Republic of)
Luxembourg
Netherlands
(United Kingdom)
Pages 140–141
Scale 1:1,500,000

MAP 13 — SPAIN AND PORTUGAL
(Algeria)
Andorra
Gibraltar
(Morocco)
Portugal
Spain
Pages 142–143
Scale 1:3,000,000

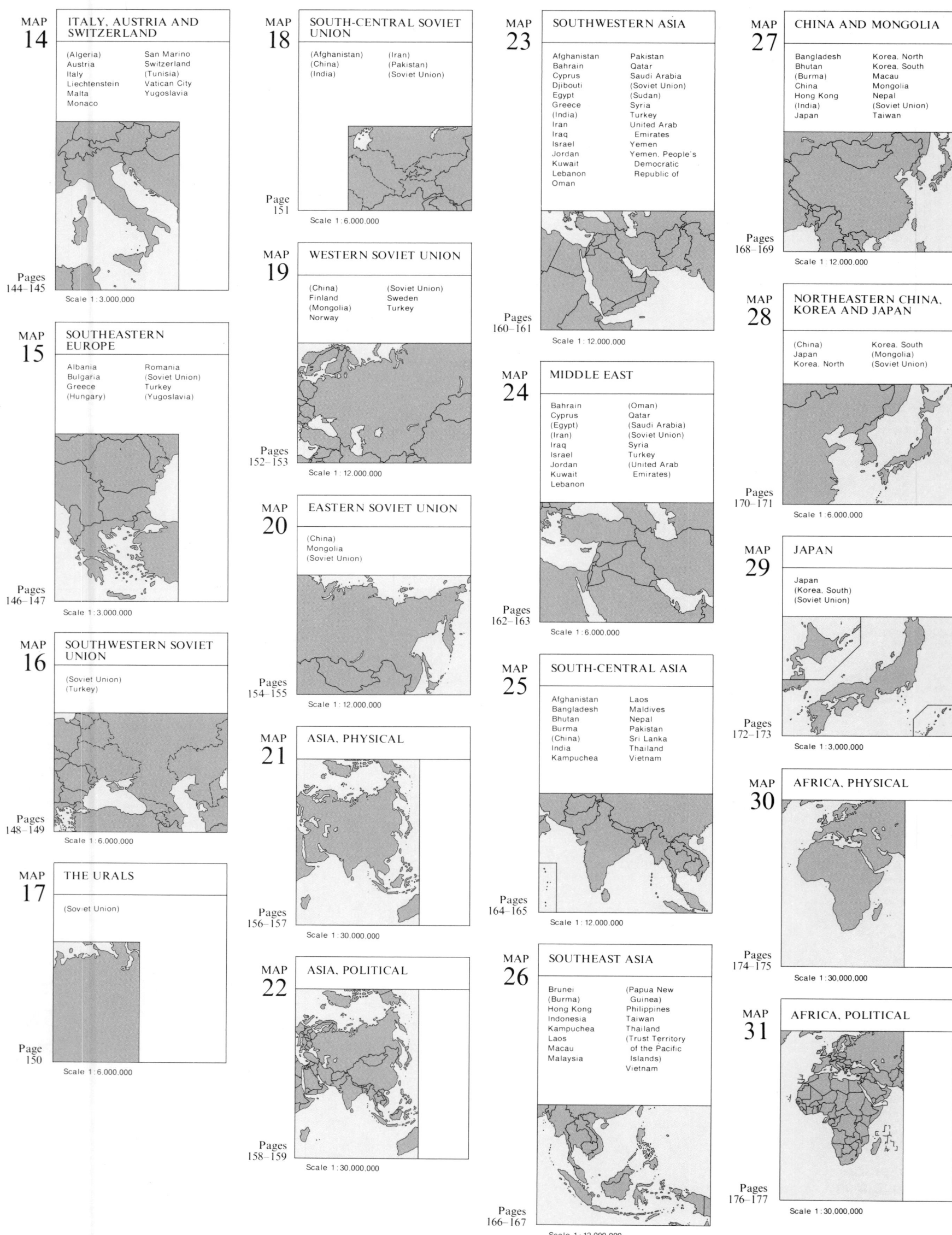

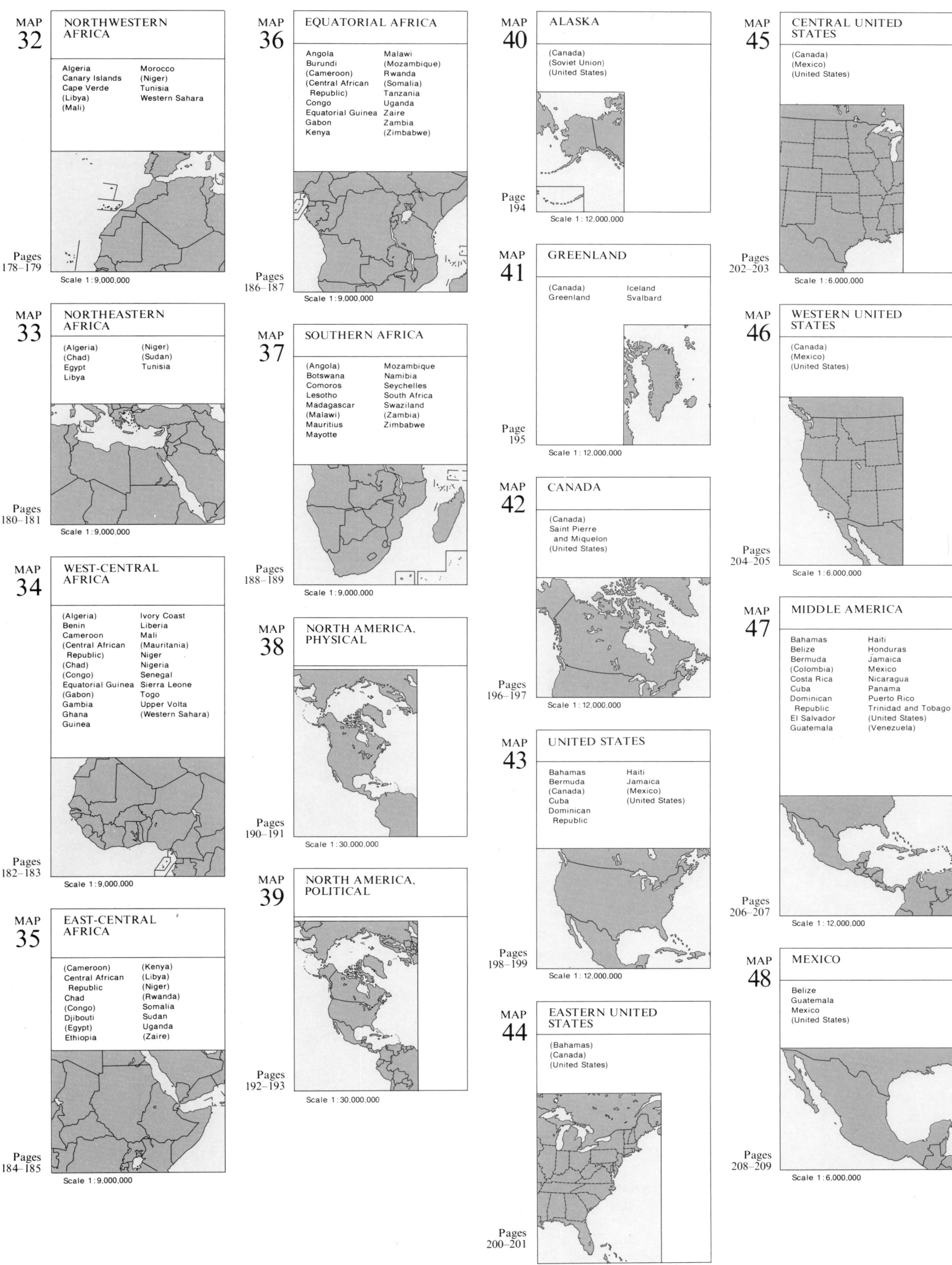

MAP 32 — NORTHWESTERN AFRICA

Algeria
Canary Islands
Cape Verde
(Libya)
(Mali)
Morocco
(Niger)
Tunisia
Western Sahara

Pages 178–179
Scale 1:9,000,000

MAP 33 — NORTHEASTERN AFRICA

(Algeria)
(Chad)
Egypt
Libya
(Niger)
(Sudan)
Tunisia

Pages 180–181
Scale 1:9,000,000

MAP 34 — WEST-CENTRAL AFRICA

(Algeria)
Benin
Cameroon
(Central African
 Republic)
(Chad)
(Congo)
Equatorial Guinea
(Gabon)
Gambia
Ghana
Guinea
Ivory Coast
Liberia
Mali
(Mauritania)
Niger
Nigeria
Senegal
Sierra Leone
Togo
Upper Volta
(Western Sahara)

Pages 182–183
Scale 1:9,000,000

MAP 35 — EAST-CENTRAL AFRICA

(Cameroon)
Central African
 Republic
Chad
(Congo)
Djibouti
(Egypt)
Ethiopia
(Kenya)
(Libya)
(Niger)
(Rwanda)
Somalia
Sudan
Uganda
(Zaire)

Pages 184–185
Scale 1:9,000,000

MAP 36 — EQUATORIAL AFRICA

Angola
Burundi
(Cameroon)
(Central African
 Republic)
Congo
Equatorial Guinea
Gabon
Kenya
Malawi
(Mozambique)
Rwanda
(Somalia)
Tanzania
Uganda
Zaire
Zambia
(Zimbabwe)

Pages 186–187
Scale 1:9,000,000

MAP 37 — SOUTHERN AFRICA

(Angola)
Botswana
Comoros
Lesotho
Madagascar
(Malawi)
Mauritius
Mayotte
Mozambique
Namibia
Seychelles
South Africa
Swaziland
(Zambia)
Zimbabwe

Pages 188–189
Scale 1:9,000,000

MAP 38 — NORTH AMERICA, PHYSICAL

Pages 190–191
Scale 1:30,000,000

MAP 39 — NORTH AMERICA, POLITICAL

Pages 192–193
Scale 1:30,000,000

MAP 40 — ALASKA

(Canada)
(Soviet Union)
(United States)

Page 194
Scale 1:12,000,000

MAP 41 — GREENLAND

(Canada)
Greenland
Iceland
Svalbard

Page 195
Scale 1:12,000,000

MAP 42 — CANADA

(Canada)
Saint Pierre
 and Miquelon
(United States)

Pages 196–197
Scale 1:12,000,000

MAP 43 — UNITED STATES

Bahamas
Bermuda
(Canada)
Cuba
Dominican
 Republic
Haiti
Jamaica
(Mexico)
(United States)

Pages 198–199
Scale 1:12,000,000

MAP 44 — EASTERN UNITED STATES

(Bahamas)
(Canada)
(United States)

Pages 200–201
Scale 1:6,000,000

MAP 45 — CENTRAL UNITED STATES

(Canada)
(Mexico)
(United States)

Pages 202–203
Scale 1:6,000,000

MAP 46 — WESTERN UNITED STATES

(Canada)
(Mexico)
(United States)

Pages 204–205
Scale 1:6,000,000

MAP 47 — MIDDLE AMERICA

Bahamas
Belize
Bermuda
(Colombia)
Costa Rica
Cuba
Dominican
 Republic
El Salvador
Guatemala
Haiti
Honduras
Jamaica
Mexico
Nicaragua
Panama
Puerto Rico
Trinidad and Tobago
(United States)
(Venezuela)

Pages 206–207
Scale 1:12,000,000

MAP 48 — MEXICO

Belize
Guatemala
Mexico
(United States)

Pages 208–209
Scale 1:6,000,000

Our Planet Earth Section

Part 1

THE EARTH AND THE UNIVERSE

How the universe began · Earth's place in the Solar System
How the Earth became fit for life
Man looks at Earth from outer space

CREATION AND DESTRUCTION

Violent activity pervades our universe and has done so ever since the primordial fireball of creation. Evidence of violence comes from radio telescopes scanning the farthest reaches: entire galaxies may be exploding, torn apart by gravitational forces of unimaginable power. Some very large stars may burst apart in supernovas, spraying interstellar space with cosmic debris. From this violence new stars and new planets are constantly being formed throughout the universe.

The Big Bang theory (left) of the origin of the universe envisages all matter originating from one point in time and space—a point of infinite density. In the intensely hot Big Bang all the material that goes to make up the planets, stars and galaxies that we see now began to expand outward in all directions. This expansion has been likened to someone blowing up a balloon on which spots have been painted. As the air fills and expands the balloon, the spots get farther away from each other. Likewise, clusters of galaxies that formed from the original superdense matter began, and continue, to move away from neighboring clusters. The Big Bang generated enormous temperatures and the remnants of the event still linger throughout space. A leftover, background radiation provides a uniform and measurable temperature of 3°C. It is generally believed that the universe will continue to expand into complete nothingness.

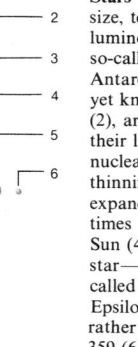

Stars vary enormously in size, temperature and luminosity. The largest, so-called red giants like Antares (1)—the biggest yet known—or Aldebaran (2), are nearing the end of their lives: diminishing nuclear "fuel" causes their thinning envelopes to expand. Rigel (3) is many times brighter than our Sun (4)—a middle-aged star—but both are so-called main-sequence stars. Epsilon Eridani (5) is rather like the Sun. Wolf 359 (6) is a red dwarf.

Our Solar System was formed from a collapsing cloud of gas and dust (A). Collapse made the center hotter and denser (B) until nuclear reactions started. Heat blew matter from the heart of the now flattened, spinning disc (C). Heavier materials condensed closest to the young Sun, now a hot star, eventually forming the inner ring of planets; the lighter ones accumulated farther out, making up the atmosphere and composition of the giant outer planets (D).

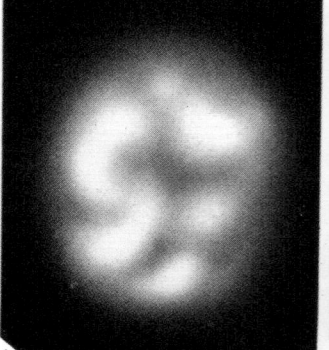
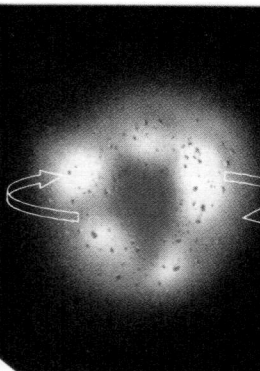

Billions of galaxies exist outside our own Milky Way, each thousands of light-years across and filled with millions of stars. Found in clusters, they are either elliptical or spiral in form. The clusters recede from each other following the space-time geometry, as established by Hubble in 1929, proving that the universe is expanding.

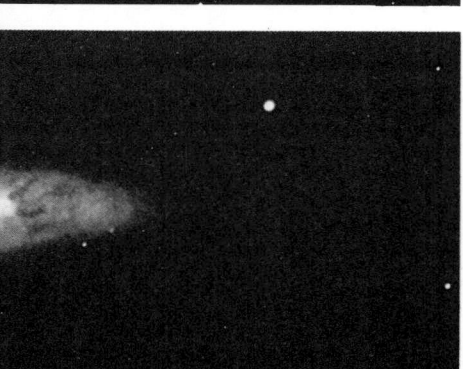

The "exploding" galaxy M82 may be an example of the violence of our universe. Clouds of hydrogen gas, equivalent in mass to 5,000,000 suns, have been ejected from the nucleus at 160 km (100 miles) per second. Black holes may cause the explosions, when gravity sucks in all matter, so that even light cannot escape.

Our own cluster of galaxies (below), the Local Group (A), consists of about 30 members, weakly linked by the force of gravity. Earth lies in the second-largest galaxy, the Milky Way (B)—here shown edge-on and at an angle—which is a spiral galaxy of about 100,000 million stars. Its rotating "arms" are great masses of clouds, dust and stars that sweep around a dense nucleus. In the course of this new stars are regularly created from dust and gas. Our Sun (S) lies 33,000 light-years from the nucleus and takes 225 million years to complete an orbit. The Andromeda Galaxy (C), known to astronomers as M31, is the largest of our Local Group. It too is a spiral, and lies about two million light-years away. Roughly 130,000 light-years in diameter, it appears as a flattened disc, and indicates how our galaxy would look if viewed from outside. Two smaller elliptical galaxies, M32 and NGC 205, can also be seen.

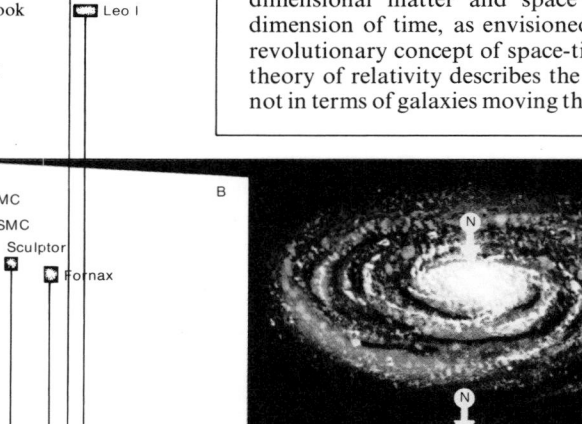

Nucleus (N)   Sun (S)

100,000 light-years

Stars are being born (left) in the Great Nebula of Orion, visible from Earth. The brilliant light comes from a cluster of very hot young stars, the Trapezium, surrounded by a glowing aura of hydrogen gas. Behind the visible nebula there is known to be a dense cloud where radio astronomers have detected emissions from interstellar molecules, and have identified high-density globules. These probably indicate that stars are starting to form.

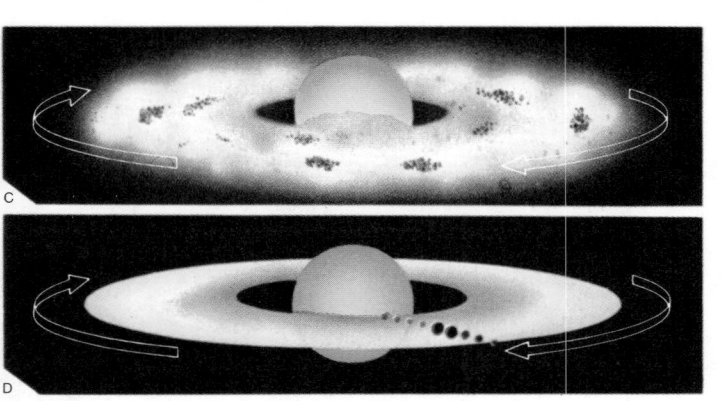

The Making of the Universe

Most astronomers believe that the universe began in a great explosion of matter and energy – the "Big Bang" – about 15,000 million years ago. This event was implied by Einstein's theory of general relativity, as well as by more recent astronomical observations and calculations. But the clinching evidence came in 1965, when two American radio astronomers discovered a faint, uniform, background radiation which permeated all space. This they identified as the remnants of the primordial Big Bang.

The generally accepted explanation for the so-called "cosmic microwave" background, detected by American astronomers Arno Penzias and Robert Wilson, is indeed that it is the echo of the Big Bang itself, the radio noise left over from the fireball of creation. In recognition of their discovery, Penzias and Wilson shared a Nobel Prize in 1978.

The Big Bang has also been identified by astronomers in other ways. All the evidence shows that the universe is expanding, and its constituent parts—clusters of galaxies, each containing thousands of millions of stars like our Sun—are moving away from each other at great speeds. From this and other evidence scientists deduce that long ago the galaxies must have been closer together, in a superdense phase, and that at some time in the remote past all the material in the universe must have started spreading out from a single point. But this "single point" includes not only all three-dimensional matter and space but also the dimension of time, as envisioned in Einstein's revolutionary concept of space-time. Einstein's theory of relativity describes the phenomenon, not in terms of galaxies moving through space in the expansion, but as being carried apart by the expansion of space-time itself. Space-time may be imagined as a rubber sheet speckled with paint blobs (galaxies), which move apart as the rubber sheet expands.

Galaxies consist of star systems, dust clouds and gases formed from the hot material exploding outward from the original cosmic fireball. Our own Milky Way system, the band of light that stretches across the night sky, is typical of many galaxies, containing millions of stars slowly rotating around a central nucleus.

Exploding space

The original material of the universe was hydrogen, the simplest of all elements. Nuclear reactions that occurred during the superdense phase of the Big Bang converted about 20 percent of the original hydrogen into helium, the next simplest element. So the first stars were formed from a mixture of about 80 percent hydrogen and 20 percent helium. All other matter in the universe, including the atoms of heavier elements such as carbon and oxygen—which help to make up the human body or the pages of this book—has been processed in further nuclear reactions. The explosion of a star—a relatively rare event called a supernova—scatters material across space, briefly radiating more energy than a trillion suns and ejecting matter into the cosmic reservoir of interstellar space. This is then reused to form new stars and planets.

Thus, from the debris of such explosions new stars can form to repeat the creative cycle, and at each stage more of the heavy elements are produced. Today's heavenly bodies are very much the products of stellar violence in the universe, and indeed the universe itself is now seen to be an area of violent activity. During the past two decades the old idea of the universe as a place of quiet stability has been increasingly superseded by evidence of intense activity on all scales. Astronomers have identified what appear to be vast explosions involving whole galaxies, as well as those of individual stars.

Black holes

The evidence of just why these huge explosions occur is often hard to obtain, because the exploding galaxies may be so far away that light from them takes millions of years to reach telescopes on Earth. But it is becoming increasingly accepted by astronomers that such violent events may be associated with the presence of black holes at the centers of some galaxies.

These black holes are regions in which matter has become so concentrated that the force of gravity makes it impossible for anything—even light itself—to escape. As stars are pulled into super-massive black holes they are torn apart by gravitational forces, and their material forms into a swirling maelstrom from which huge explosions can occur. Collapse into black holes, accompanied by violent outbursts from the maelstrom, may be the ultimate fate of all matter in the universe. For our own Solar System, however, such a fate is far in the future: the Sun in its present form is believed to have enough "fuel" to keep it going for at least another 5,000 million years.

A star is born

The origins of the Earth and the Solar System are intimately connected with the structure of our own galaxy, the Milky Way. There are two main types of galaxies: flattened, disc-shaped spiral galaxies (like the Milky Way), and the more rounded elliptical galaxies, which range in form from near spheres to cigar shapes. The most important feature of a spiral galaxy is that it is rotating, a great mass of stars sweeping around a common center. In our galaxy the Sun, located some way out from the galaxy's center, takes about 225 million years to complete one circuit, called a cosmic year.

New stars are born out of the twisting arms of a spiral galaxy, with each arm marking a region of debris left over from previous stellar explosions. These arms are in fact clouds of dust and gas, including nitrogen and oxygen. As the spiral galaxy rotates over a period of millions of years, the twisting arms are squeezed by a high-density pressure wave as they pass through the cycle of the cosmic year. With two main spiral arms twining around a galaxy such as our own, large, diffuse clouds get squeezed twice during each orbit around the center of the galaxy.

Even if one orbit takes as long as hundreds of millions of years, a score or more squeezes have probably occurred since the Milky Way was first formed thousands of millions of years ago. At a critical point, such repeated squeezing increases the density of a gas cloud so much that it begins to collapse rapidly under the inward pull of its own gravity. A typical cloud of this kind contains enough material to make many stars. As it breaks up it collapses into smaller clouds—which are also collapsing—and these become stars in their own right.

Our own Solar System may have been formed in this way from such a collapsing gas cloud, which went on to evolve into the system of planets that we know today.

Earth in the Solar System

The Sun is an ordinary, medium-sized star located some two-thirds of the way from the center of our galaxy, the Milky Way. Yet it comprises more than 99 percent of the Solar System's total mass and provides all the light and heat that make life possible on Earth. This energy comes from nuclear reactions that take place in the Sun's hot, dense interior. The reactions convert hydrogen into helium, with the release of vast amounts of energy – the energy that keeps the Sun shining.

Nuclear reactions in the Sun's core maintain a temperature of some 15,000,000°C and this heat prevents the star from shrinking. The surface temperature is comparatively much lower —a mere 6,000°C. Thermonuclear energy-generating processes cause the Sun to "lose" mass from the center at the rate of four million tonnes of hydrogen every second. This mass is turned into energy (heat), and each gram of matter "burnt" produces the heat equivalent of 100 trillion electric fires. The Sun's total mass is so great, however, that it contains enough matter to continue radiating at its present rate for several thousand million years before it runs out of "fuel."

The Sun's retinue

The Solar System emerged from a collapsing gas cloud. In addition to the Sun there are at least nine planets, their satellites, thousands of minor planets (asteroids), comets and meteors. Most stars occur in pairs, triplets or in even more complicated systems, and the Sun is among a minority of stars in being alone except for its planetary companions. It does seem, however, that a single star with a planetary system offers the greatest potential for the development of life. When there are two or more stars in the same system, any planets are likely to have unstable orbits and to suffer from wide extremes of temperature.

The Solar System's structure is thought to be typical of a star that formed in isolation. As the hot young Sun threw material outward, inner planets (Mercury, Venus, Earth and Mars) were left as small rocky bodies, whereas outer planets (Jupiter, Saturn, Uranus and Neptune) kept their lighter gases and became huge "gas giants." Jupiter has two and a half times the mass of all the other planets put together. Pluto, a small object with a strange orbit, which sometimes carries it within the orbit of Neptune, is usually regarded as a ninth planet, but some astronomers consider it to be an escaped moon of Neptune or a large asteroid.

Planetary relations

Several planets are accompanied by smaller bodies called moons or satellites. Jupiter and Saturn have at least 17 and 22 respectively, whereas Earth has its solitary Moon. Sizes vary enormously, from Ganymede, one of Jupiter's large, so-called Galilean satellites, which has a diameter of 5,000 km (3,100 miles), to Mars' tiny Deimos, which is only 8 km (5 miles) across.

The Earth's Moon is at an average distance of 384,000 km (239,000 miles) and has a diameter of 3,476 km (2,160 miles). Its mass is $\frac{1}{81}$ of the Earth's. Although it is referred to as the Earth's satellite, the Moon is large for a secondary body. Some astronomers have suggested that the Earth/Moon system is a double planet. Certain theories of the origins of the Moon propose that it was formed from the solar nebula in the same way as the Earth was and very close to it. The Moon takes 27.3 days to orbit the Earth—exactly the same time that it takes to rotate once on its axis. As a result, it presents the same face to the Earth all the time.

Our planet's orbit around the Sun is not a perfect circle but an ellipse and so its distance from the Sun varies slightly. More importantly, the Earth is tilted, so that at different times of the year one pole or another "leans" toward the Sun. Without this tilt there would be no seasons. The angle of tilt is not constant: over tens of thousands of years the axis of the Earth "wobbles" like a slowly spinning top, so that the pattern of the seasons varies over the ages. These changes have been linked to recent ice ages, which seem to occur when the northern hemisphere has relatively cool summers.

Patterns of time

The Earth's movements on its axis and around the Sun give us our basic measurements of time—the day and the year—as well as setting the rhythm of the seasons and the ice ages. One rotation of the Earth on its axis—the time from one sunrise to the next—originally defined the day, and the time taken for one complete orbit around the Sun defined the year. Today, however, scientists define both the day and the year in terms of time units "counted" by precision instruments called atomic clocks.

A third basic rhythm is set not by the Sun but by the Moon, which runs through a cycle of phases $29\frac{1}{2}$ days long. This is the basis of the calendar month. But just as the modern calendar cannot cope with months $29\frac{1}{2}$ days long, so too it would have trouble with the precise year, which is, inconveniently, just less than $365\frac{1}{4}$ days long. This is the reason for leap years, by means of which an extra day is added to the month of February every fourth year.

Even this system does not keep the calendar exactly in step with the Sun. Accordingly, the leap year is left out in the years which complete centuries, such as 1900, but retained when they divide exactly by 400. The year 2000 will, therefore, be a leap year. With all these corrections, the average length of the calendar year is within 26 seconds of the year defined by the Earth's movements around the Sun. Thus the calendar will be one day out of step with the heavens in the year 4906.

Cosmic rubble

The other planets are too small and too far away to produce noticeable effects on the Earth, but the smallest members of the Sun's family, the asteroids, can affect us directly. Some of them have orbits that cross the orbit of the Earth around the Sun. From time to time they penetrate the Earth's atmosphere: small fragments burn up high in the atmosphere as meteors, whereas larger pieces may survive to strike the ground as meteorites. These in fact provide an echo of times gone by. All the planets, as the battered face of the Moon shows, suffered collisions from many smaller bodies in the course of their evolution from the collapsing pre-solar gas cloud.

Eclipses occur because the Moon, smaller than the Sun, is closer to Earth and looks just as big. This means that when all three are lined up the Moon can blot out the Sun, causing a solar eclipse. When the Earth passes through the main shadow cone, or umbra, the eclipse is total; in the area of partial shadow, or penumbra, a partial eclipse is seen. A similar effect is produced when Earth passes between the Moon and the Sun, causing a lunar eclipse. At most full moons, eclipses do not occur; the Moon passes either above or below the Earth's shadow, because the Moon's orbit is inclined at an angle of 5° to the orbit of the Earth.

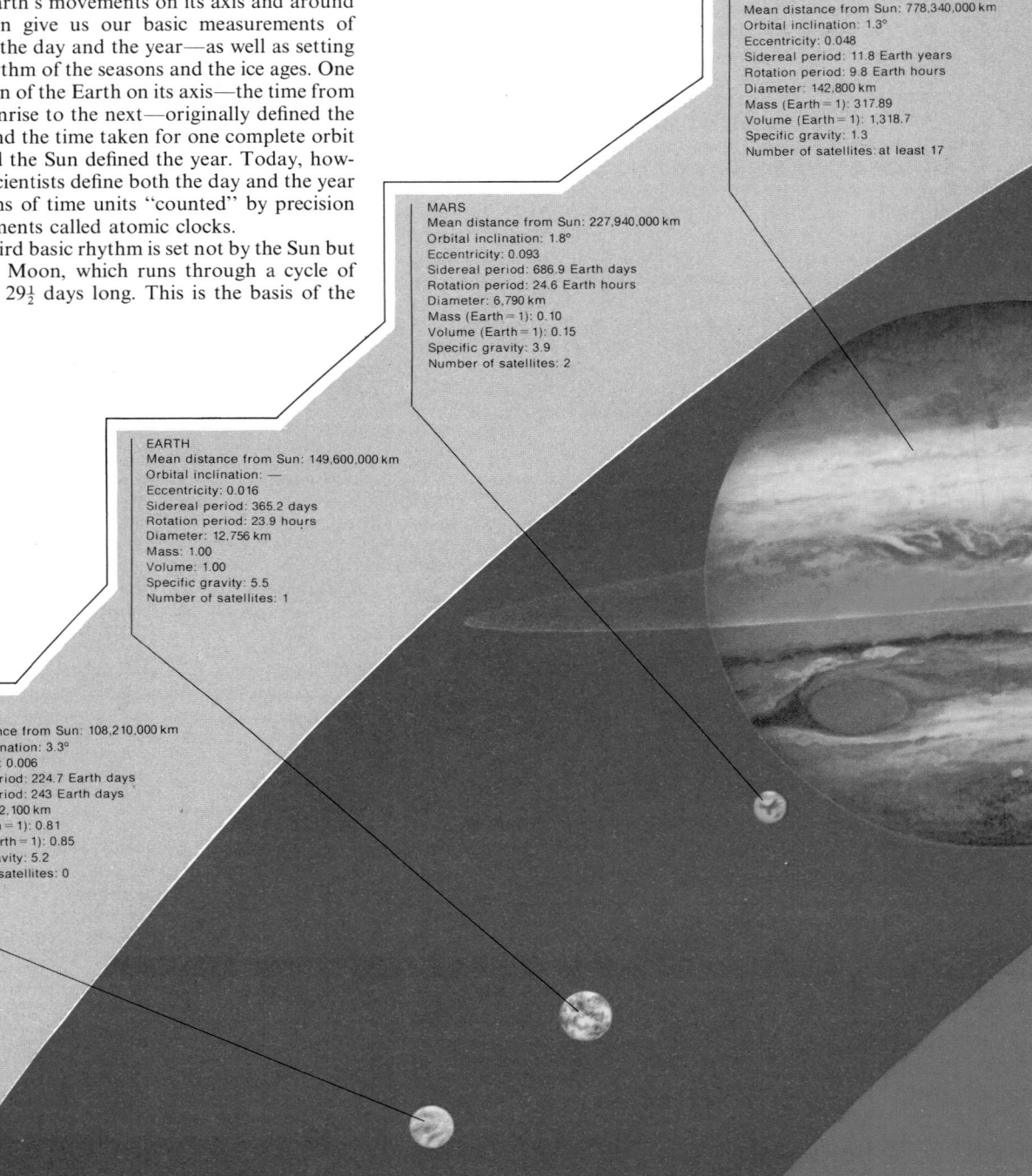

JUPITER
Mean distance from Sun: 778,340,000 km
Orbital inclination: 1.3°
Eccentricity: 0.048
Sidereal period: 11.8 Earth years
Rotation period: 9.8 Earth hours
Diameter: 142,800 km
Mass (Earth = 1): 317.89
Volume (Earth = 1): 1,318.7
Specific gravity: 1.3
Number of satellites: at least 17

MARS
Mean distance from Sun: 227,940,000 km
Orbital inclination: 1.8°
Eccentricity: 0.093
Sidereal period: 686.9 Earth days
Rotation period: 24.6 Earth hours
Diameter: 6,790 km
Mass (Earth = 1): 0.10
Volume (Earth = 1): 0.15
Specific gravity: 3.9
Number of satellites: 2

EARTH
Mean distance from Sun: 149,600,000 km
Orbital inclination: —
Eccentricity: 0.016
Sidereal period: 365.2 days
Rotation period: 23.9 hours
Diameter: 12,756 km
Mass: 1.00
Volume: 1.00
Specific gravity: 5.5
Number of satellites: 1

VENUS
Mean distance from Sun: 108,210,000 km
Orbital inclination: 3.3°
Eccentricity: 0.006
Sidereal period: 224.7 Earth days
Rotation period: 243 Earth days
Diameter: 12,100 km
Mass (Earth = 1): 0.81
Volume (Earth = 1): 0.85
Specific gravity: 5.2
Number of satellites: 0

MEMBERS OF THE SOLAR SYSTEM

The Sun has nine planetary attendants. They are best compared in terms of orbital data (distance from the Sun, inclination of orbit to the Earth's orbit, and eccentricity, which means the departure of a planet's orbit from circularity); planetary periods (the time for a planet to go around the Sun—sidereal periods, and the time it takes for one axial revolution—the rotation period); and physical data (equatorial diameter, mass, volume and density or specific gravity—the weight of a substance compared with the weight of an equal volume of water).

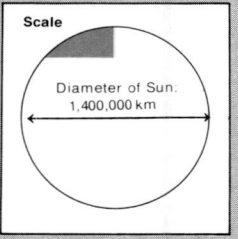

Scale
Diameter of Sun:
1,400,000 km

MERCURY
Mean distance from Sun: 57,910,000 km
Orbital inclination: 7°
Eccentricity: 0.205
Sidereal period: 87.9 Earth days
Rotation period: 58.7 Earth days
Diameter: 4,870 km
Mass (Earth = 1): 0.05
Volume (Earth = 1): 0.05
Specific gravity: 5.5
Number of satellites: 0

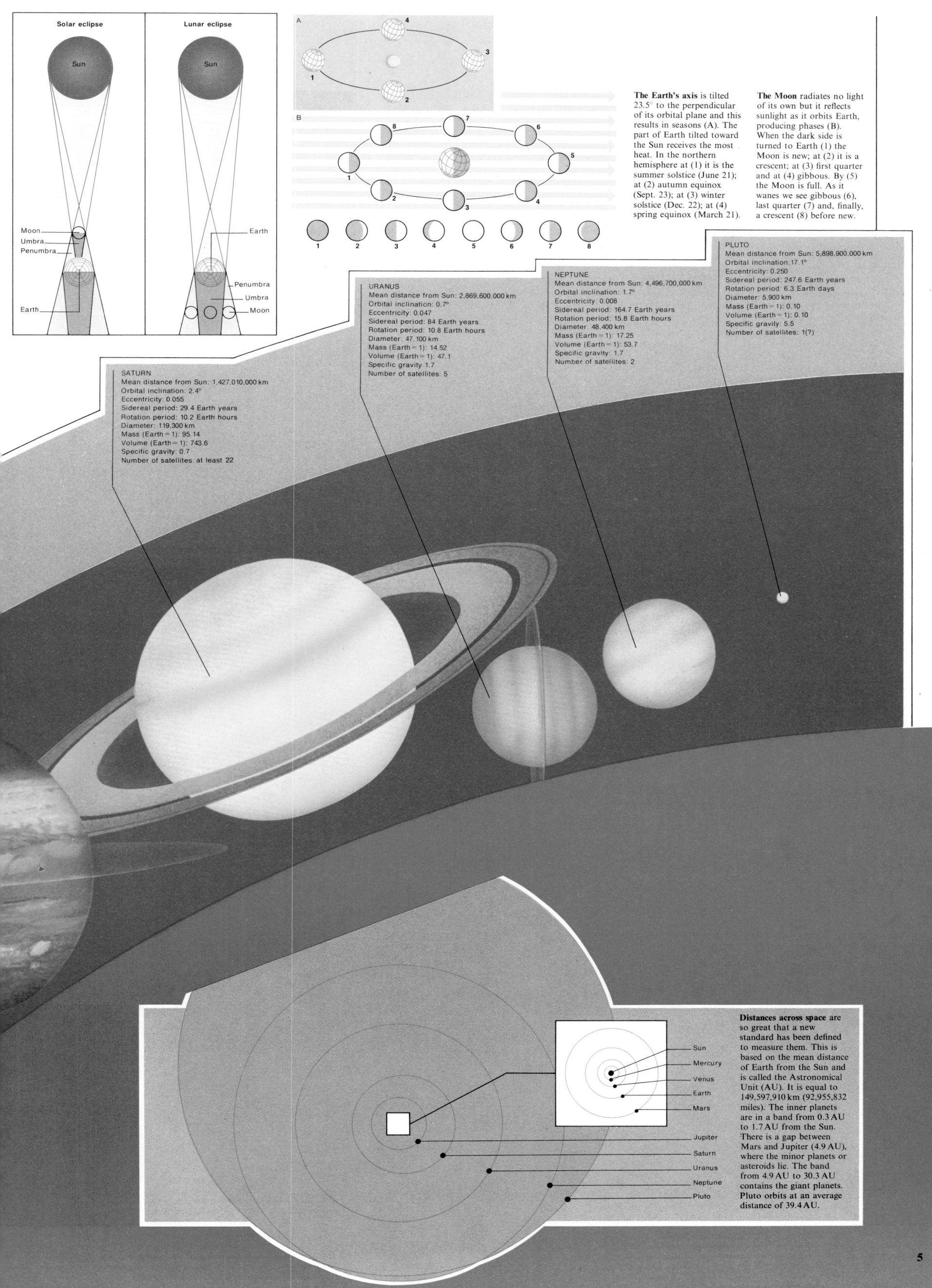

Solar eclipse

Lunar eclipse

Sun

Sun

Moon
Umbra
Penumbra

Earth

Earth

Penumbra
Umbra
Moon

A

4

3

1

2

B

8

7

6

1

5

2

3

4

1 2 3 4 5 6 7 8

The Earth's axis is tilted 23.5° to the perpendicular of its orbital plane and this results in seasons (A). The part of Earth tilted toward the Sun receives the most heat. In the northern hemisphere at (1) it is the summer solstice (June 21); at (2) autumn equinox (Sept. 23); at (3) winter solstice (Dec. 22); at (4) spring equinox (March 21).

The Moon radiates no light of its own but it reflects sunlight as it orbits Earth, producing phases (B). When the dark side is turned to Earth (1) the Moon is new; at (2) it is a crescent; at (3) first quarter and at (4) gibbous. By (5) the Moon is full. As it wanes we see gibbous (6), last quarter (7) and, finally, a crescent (8) before new.

PLUTO
Mean distance from Sun: 5,898,900,000 km
Orbital inclination: 17.1°
Eccentricity: 0.250
Sidereal period: 247.6 Earth years
Rotation period: 6.3 Earth days
Diameter: 5,900 km
Mass (Earth = 1): 0.10
Volume (Earth = 1): 0.10
Specific gravity: 5.5
Number of satellites: 1(?)

NEPTUNE
Mean distance from Sun: 4,496,700,000 km
Orbital inclination: 1.7°
Eccentricity: 0.008
Sidereal period: 164.7 Earth years
Rotation period: 15.8 Earth hours
Diameter: 48,400 km
Mass (Earth = 1): 17.25
Volume (Earth = 1): 53.7
Specific gravity: 1.7
Number of satellites: 2

URANUS
Mean distance from Sun: 2,869,600,000 km
Orbital inclination: 0.7°
Eccentricity: 0.047
Sidereal period: 84 Earth years
Rotation period: 10.8 Earth hours
Diameter: 47,100 km
Mass (Earth = 1): 14.52
Volume (Earth = 1): 47.1
Specific gravity 1.7
Number of satellites: 5

SATURN
Mean distance from Sun: 1,427,010,000 km
Orbital inclination: 2.4°
Eccentricity: 0.055
Sidereal period: 29.4 Earth years
Rotation period: 10.2 Earth hours
Diameter: 119,300 km
Mass (Earth = 1): 95.14
Volume (Earth = 1): 743.6
Specific gravity: 0.7
Number of satellites: at least 22

Sun
Mercury
Venus
Earth
Mars
Jupiter
Saturn
Uranus
Neptune
Pluto

Distances across space are so great that a new standard has been defined to measure them. This is based on the mean distance of Earth from the Sun and is called the Astronomical Unit (AU). It is equal to 149,597,910 km (92,955,832 miles). The inner planets are in a band from 0.3 AU to 1.7 AU from the Sun. There is a gap between Mars and Jupiter (4.9 AU), where the minor planets or asteroids lie. The band from 4.9 AU to 30.3 AU contains the giant planets. Pluto orbits at an average distance of 39.4 AU.

Earth as a Planet

Viewed from space, the Earth appears to be an ordinary member of the group of inner planets orbiting the Sun. But the Earth is unique in the Solar System because it has an atmosphere that contains oxygen. It is the nature of this surrounding blanket of air that has allowed higher life forms to evolve on Earth and provides their life-support system. At the same time the atmosphere acts as a shield to protect living things from the damaging effects of radiation from the Sun.

Any traces of gas that may have clung to the newly formed Earth were soon swept away into space by the heat of the Sun before it attained a stable state powered by nuclear fusion. Farther out in the Solar System, the Sun's heat was never strong enough to blow these gases away into space, so that even today the giant planets retain atmospheres composed of these primordial gases—mostly methane and ammonia.

The evolution of air
Until the Sun "settled down," Earth was a hot, airless ball of rock. The atmosphere and oceans—like the atmospheres of Venus and Mars—were produced by the "outgassing" of material from the hot interior of the planet as the crust cooled. Volcanoes erupted constantly and produced millions of tonnes of ash and lava. They also probably yielded, as they do today, great quantities of gas, chiefly carbon dioxide, and water vapor. A little nitrogen and various sulphur compounds were also released. Other things being equal, we would expect rocky planets, like the young Earth, to have atmospheres rich in carbon dioxide and water vapor. Venus and Mars do indeed have carbon dioxide atmospheres today, but the Earth now has a nitrogen/oxygen atmosphere. This results from the fact that life evolved on Earth, converting the carbon dioxide to oxygen and storing carbon in organic remains such as coal. Some carbon dioxide was also dissolved in the oceans. The Earth's oxygen atmosphere is a clear sign of life; the carbon dioxide atmospheres of Venus and Mars suggest the absence of life. Why did the Earth begin to evolve in a different way from the other inner planets?

When the Sun stabilized, Earth, Venus and Mars started off down the same evolutionary road, and carbon dioxide and water vapor were the chief constituents of the original atmospheres. On Venus the temperature was hot enough for the water to remain in a gaseous form, and both the water vapor and carbon dioxide in the Venusian atmosphere trapped heat by means of the so-called "greenhouse effect." In this process, radiant energy from the Sun passes through the atmospheric gases and warms the ground. The warmed ground re-radiates heat energy, but at infrared wavelengths, with the result that carbon dioxide and water molecules absorb it and stop it escaping from the planet. Instead of acting like a window, the atmosphere acts like a mirror for outgoing energy. As a result, the surface of Venus became hotter still. Today the surface temperature has stabilized at more than 500°C.

Mars, farther out from the Sun than Earth, was never hot enough for the greenhouse effect to dominate. The red planet once had a much thicker atmosphere than it does today, but, being smaller than the Earth, its gravity is too weak to retain a thick atmosphere. As a result, the planet cooled into a frozen desert as atmospheric gases escaped into space. Mars then, in fact, suffered a climatic change. At one time—hundreds of millions of years ago—there must have been running water because traces of old riverbeds still scar the Martian surface. Today, however, Mars has a thin atmosphere of carbon dioxide and surface temperatures below zero.

Earth—the ideal home
On Earth conditions were just right. Water stayed as a liquid and formed the oceans, while some carbon dioxide from outgassing went into the atmosphere, and some dissolved in the oceans. The resulting modest greenhouse effect

The thermosphere extends from 80 km (50 miles) up to 400 km (250 miles). Within this zone temperatures rise steadily with height to as much as 1,650°C (3,000°F), but the air is so thin that temperature is not a meaningful concept. At this height the air is mostly composed of nitrogen molecules to a height of 200 km (125 miles), when oxygen molecules become the dominant constituent.

The mesosphere is between 50 and 80 km (30 and 50 miles) above ground level. The stratopause is its lower limit and the mesopause its upper. This zone of the atmosphere is mainly distinguished by its ever decreasing temperatures and, unlike the stratosphere, it does not absorb solar energy.

The stratosphere is the level above the troposphere and extends as far as 50 km (30 miles). The chemical composition of the air up to this height is nearly constant and, in terms of volume, it is composed of nitrogen (78%) and oxygen (20%). The rest is mostly argon and other trace elements. The percentage of carbon dioxide (0.003) is small but crucial because this gas absorbs heat. There is virtually no water vapor or dust in this region of the atmosphere, but it does include the ozone layer, which is strongest between 20 km (12 miles) and 40 km (24 miles) high.

The troposphere extends from ground level to a height of between 10 and 15 km (6 and 9 miles). This height varies with latitude and season of the year: it is greater at the Equator than at the poles. Most weather phenomena occur in this zone. Mixed with the gases of the troposphere is water vapor and millions of tiny dust particles, around which vapor condenses to form clouds. The upper limit of this zone is called the tropopause.

EARTH'S OUTER SKIN
The Earth's atmosphere is wafer thin when compared with the size of the planet. Half of the atmosphere's mass lies in the 5.5 km (3½ miles) nearest the ground and more than 99 percent of it lies within 40 km (24 miles) of the Earth.

Scale

Atmosphere
Earth

Earth's radius: 6,378 km

Earth reduced by 90% in proportion to this scale

Stratosphere and Mesosphere
Troposphere

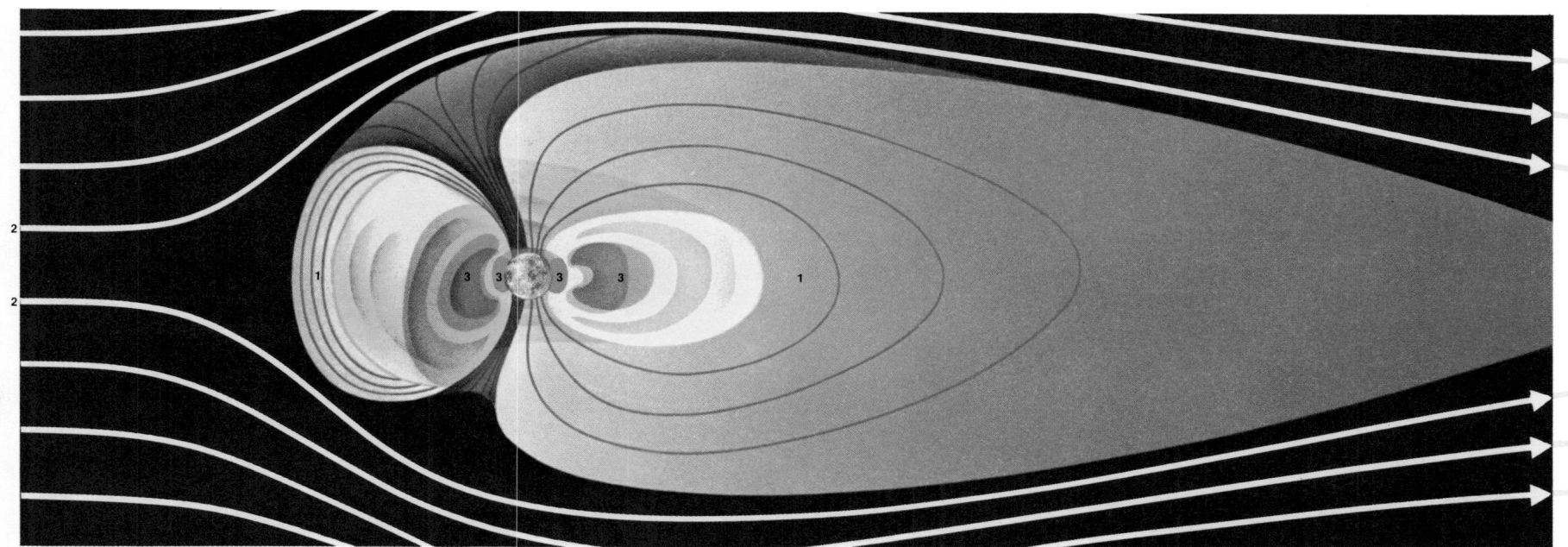

was compensated for by the formation of shiny white clouds of water droplets which reflected some of the Sun's radiation back into space. Our planet stabilized with an average temperature of 15°C. This proved ideal for the emergence of life, which evolved first in the seas and then moved onto land, converting carbon dioxide into oxygen as it did so.

In any view from space, planet Earth is dominated by water—in blue oceans and white clouds—and water is the key to life as we know it. Animal life—oxygen-breathing life—could only evolve after earlier forms of life had converted the atmosphere to an oxygen-rich state. The nature of the air today is a product of life as well as being vital to its existence.

An atmospheric layer cake

Starting at ground level, the first zone of the atmosphere is the troposphere, kept warm near the ground by the greenhouse effect but cooling to a chilly −60°C at an altitude of 15 km (9 miles). Above the troposphere is a warming layer, the stratosphere, in which energy from the Sun is absorbed and temperatures increase to reach 0°C at an altitude of 50 km (30 miles). The energy—in the form of ultraviolet radiation—is absorbed by molecules of ozone, a form of oxygen. Without the ozone layer in the atmosphere, ultraviolet rays would penetrate the

The Earth's magnetic field behaves as if there were a huge bar magnet placed inside the globe, with its magnetic axis tilted at a slight angle to the geographical north–south axis. The speed of rotation of the liquid core differs from that of the mantle, producing an effect like a dynamo (below). The region in which the magnetic field extends beyond the Earth is the magnetosphere (1). Streams of charged particles (2) from the Sun distort its shape into that of a teardrop. Zones of the magnetosphere include the Van Allen Belts (3), which are regions of intense radioactivity where magnetic particles are "trapped."

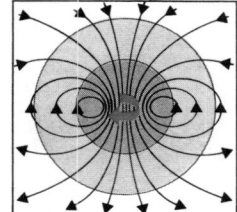

ground and sterilize the land surface: without life, there would be no oxygen from which an ozone layer could form.

Above the stratosphere, another cooling layer, the mesosphere, extends up to 80 km (50 miles), at which point the temperature has fallen to about −100°C. Above this level the gases of the atmosphere are so thin that the standard concept of temperature is no real guide to their behavior, and from the mesosphere outwards the atmosphere is best described in terms of its electrical properties.

In the outer layers of the atmosphere, the Sun's energy is absorbed by individual atoms in such a way that it strips electrons off them, leaving behind positively charged ions, which give the region its name—the ionosphere. A few hundred kilometers above the Earth's surface, gravity is so feeble that electromagnetic forces begin to determine the behavior of the charged particles, which are shepherded along the lines of force in the Earth's magnetic field. Above 500 km (300 miles), the magnetic field is so dominant that yet another region, the magnetosphere, is distinguished. This is the true boundary between Earth and interplanetary space.

The magnetosphere has been likened to the hull of "spaceship Earth." Charged particles (the solar wind) streaming out from the Sun are deflected around Earth by the magnetosphere

like water around a moving ship, while the region of the Earth's magnetic influence in space trails "downstream" away from the Sun like the wake of a ship. The Van Allen Belts, at altitudes of 3,000 and 15,000 km (1,850 and 9,300 miles) are regions of space high above the Equator where particles are trapped by the magnetic field. Particles spilling out of the belts spiral towards the polar regions of Earth, producing the spectacle of the auroras—the northern and southern lights. The Earth and Mercury are the only inner planets with magnetospheres such as this. The cause of the Earth's magnetism is almost certainly the planet's heavy molten core, which is composed of magnetic materials.

The Earth's atmosphere exhibits a great variety of characteristics on a vertical scale. As well as variations of temperature and the electrical properties of the air, there are differences in chemical composition—in the mixture of gases and water vapor—according to altitude. The Earth's gravitational pull means that air density and pressure decrease with altitude. Pressure of about 1,000 millibars at sea level falls to virtually nothing (10^{-42} millibars) by a height of 700 km (435 miles) above the Earth. All these factors, and their interrelationships, help to maintain the Earth's atmosphere as a protective outer covering or radiation shield and an essential life-support system.

The ionosphere is another name for the atmospheric layer beyond 80 km (50 miles). The region is best described in terms of the electrical properties of its constituents rather than by temperature. It is here that ionization occurs. Gamma and X-rays from the Sun are absorbed by atoms and molecules of nitrogen and oxygen and, as a result, each molecule or atom gives up one or more of its electrons, thus becoming a positively charged ion. These ions reflect radio waves and are used to bounce back radio waves transmitted from the surface of the Earth.

The exosphere is the layer above the thermosphere and it extends from 400 km (250 miles) up to about 700 km (435 miles), the point at which, it may be said, space begins. It is almost a complete vacuum because most of its atoms and molecules of oxygen escape the Earth's gravity.

The magnetosphere includes the exosphere, but it extends far beyond the atmosphere—to a distance of between 64,000 and 130,000 km (40,000 and 80,000 miles) above the Earth. It represents the Earth's external magnetic field and its outer limit is called the magnetopause.

The atmosphere protects the Earth from harmful solar radiation and also from bombardment by small particles from space. Most meteors (particles orbiting the Sun) burn up in the atmosphere, but meteorites (debris of minor planets) reach the ground. Of all incoming solar radiation, only visible light, radio waves and infrared rays reach the surface of Earth. X-rays are removed in the ionosphere, and ultraviolet and some infrared radiations are filtered out in the stratosphere. Studies of such radiations have, therefore, to be made from observatories in space.

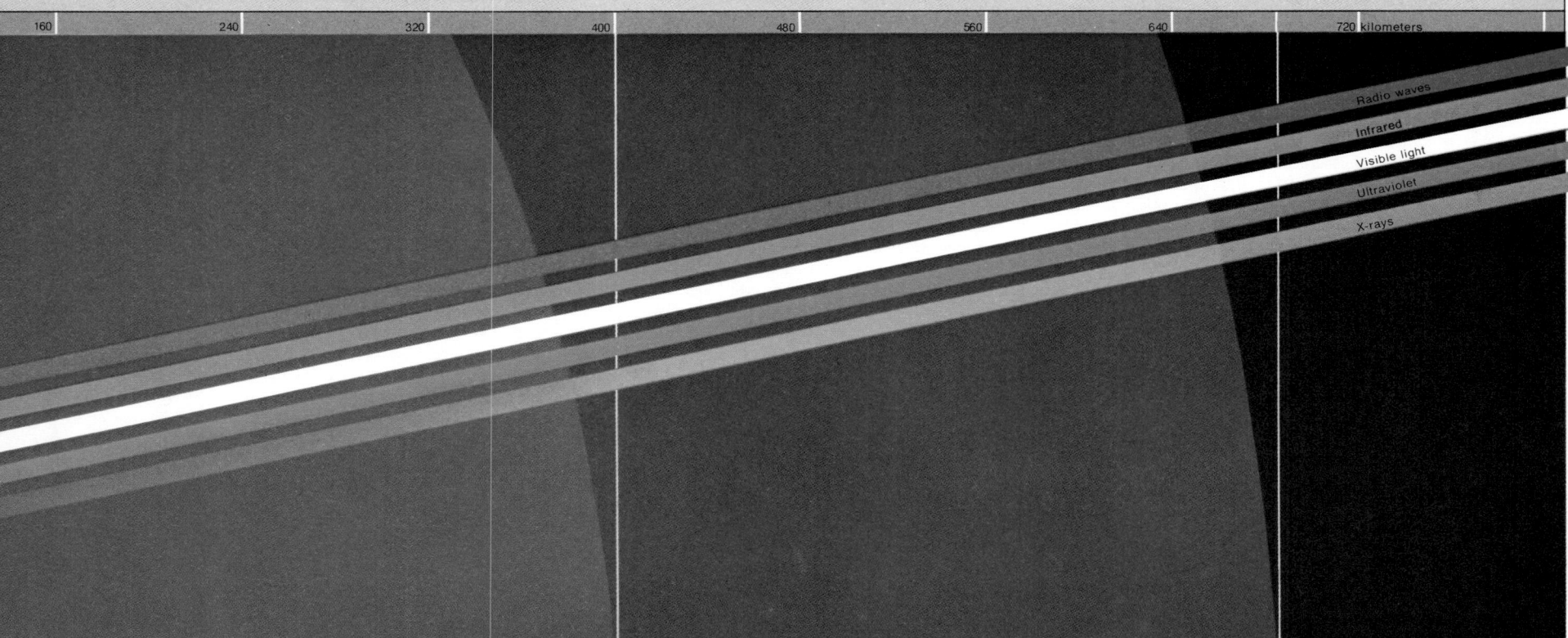

| 160 | 240 | 320 | 400 | 480 | 560 | 640 | 720 kilometers |

Radio waves

Infrared

Visible light

Ultraviolet

X-rays

Thermosphere/Ionosphere   Exosphere/Magnetosphere   Space

Man Looks at the Earth

Orbiting satellites keep a detailed watch on the Earth's land surface, oceans and atmosphere, feeding streams of data to meteorologists, geologists, oceanographers, farmers, fishermen and many others. Some information would be unobtainable by any other means. Surveys from orbit are quicker and less expensive than from aircraft, for example, because a satellite can scan a much larger area. And, surprisingly enough, certain features on the ground are easier to see from space.

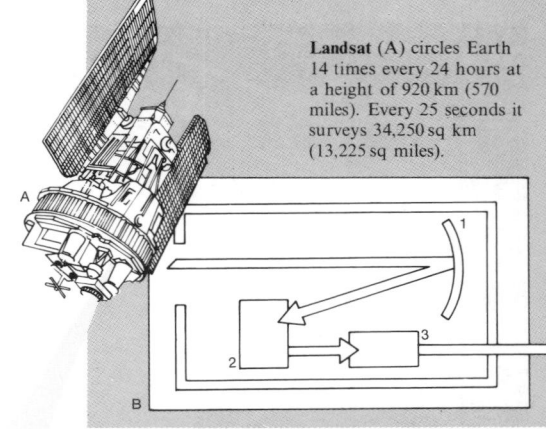

Landsat (A) circles Earth 14 times every 24 hours at a height of 920 km (570 miles). Every 25 seconds it surveys 34,250 sq km (13,225 sq miles).

MAPPING AND MEASURING

Man has been looking at Earth from satellites since the beginning of the 1960s, and has firmly established the value of surveys from space to those engaged in a variety of earthly pursuits. Chief of these activities are resource management, ranging from monitoring the spread of deserts and river silting to locating likely mineral deposits; environmental protection, which includes observing delicate ecosystems and natural disasters; and a whole range of mapping and land-use planning.

Satellites give us a greater overview of numerous aspects of life on Earth than any earthbound eye could see.

Of all the information gleaned from satellites, accurate weather forecasts are of particular social and economic value. The first weather satellite was Tiros 1 (Television and Infrared Observation Satellite), launched by the United States in 1960. By the time Tiros 10 ceased operations in 1967, the series had sent back more than half a million photographs, firmly establishing the value of satellite imagery.

Tiros was superseded by the ESSA (Environmental Science Services Administration) and the NOAA (National Oceanic and Atmospheric Administration) satellites. These orbited the Earth from pole to pole, and they covered the entire globe during the course of a day. Other weather satellites, such as the European Meteosat, are placed in geostationary orbit over the Equator, which means they stay in one place and continually monitor a single large region.

Watching the weather

In addition to photographing clouds, weather satellites monitor the extent of snow and ice cover, and they measure the temperature of the oceans and the composition of the atmosphere. Information about the overall heat balance of our planet gives clues to long-term climatic change, and includes the effects on climate of human activities such as the burning of fossil fuels and deforestation.

Infrared sensors allow pictures to be taken at night as well as during the day. The temperature of cloud tops, measured by infrared devices, is a guide to the height of the clouds. In a typical infrared image, high clouds appear white because they are the coldest, lower clouds and land areas appear gray, and oceans and lakes are black. Information on humidity in the atmosphere is provided by sensors tuned to wavelengths between 5.5 and 7 micrometers, at which water vapor strongly absorbs the radiation.

To "see" inside clouds, where infrared and visible light cannot penetrate, satellites use sensors tuned to short-wavelength radio waves (microwaves) around the 1.5 centimeter wavelength. These sensors can reveal whether or not clouds will give rise to heavy rainfall, snow or hail. Microwave sensors are also useful for locating ice floes in polar regions, making use of the different microwave reflections from land ice, sea ice and open water.

Satellites that send out such pictures are in relatively low orbits, at a height of about 1,000 km (620 miles), and they pass over each part of the Earth once every 12 hours. But to build up a global model of the Earth's weather and climate, meteorologists need continual information on wind speed and direction at

various levels in the atmosphere, together with temperature and humidity profiles. This data is provided by geostationary satellites. Cloud photographs taken every half-hour give information on winds, and computers combine this with temperature and humidity soundings to give as complete a model as is possible of the Earth's atmosphere.

Increasing attention is also being paid to the Earth's surface, notably by means of a series of satellites called Landsat (originally ERTS or Earth Resource Technology Satellites), the first of which was launched by the United States in 1972. The third and current Landsat is in a similar pole-to-pole orbit as the weather satellites, but its cameras are more powerful and they make more detailed surveys of the Earth. Landsat rephotographs each part of the Earth's surface every 18 days.

How to map resources

The satellite has two sensor systems: a television camera, which takes pictures of the Earth using visible light; and a device called a multispectral scanner, which scans the Earth at several distinct wavelengths, including visible light and infrared. Data from the various channels of the multispectral scanner can be combined to produce so-called false-color images, in which each wavelength band is assigned a color (not necessarily its real one) to emphasize features of interest.

An important use of Landsat photographs is for making maps, particularly of large countries with remote areas that have never been adequately surveyed from the ground. Several countries, including Brazil, Canada and China, have set up ground stations to receive Landsat data directly. Features previously unknown or incorrectly mapped, including rivers, lakes and glaciers, show up readily on Landsat images. Urban mapping and hence planning are aided by satellite pictures that can distinguish areas of industry, housing and open parkland.

Landsat photographs have also proved invaluable for agricultural land-use planning.

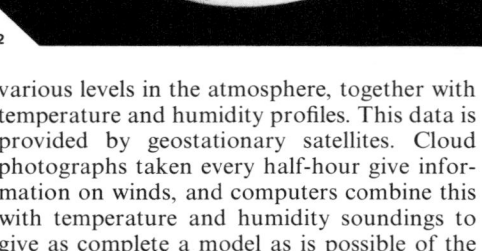

They are used for estimates of soil types and for determining land-use patterns. Areas of crop disease or dying vegetation are detectable by their different colors. Yields of certain crops such as wheat can now be accurately predicted from satellite imagery, so that at last it is becoming possible to keep track of the worldwide production of vital food crops. Fresh water, too, is one of our most valuable resources, and knowing its sources and seasonal variation is vital to irrigation projects.

Finally, the geologist and mineral prospector have benefited from remote sensing. Features such as fault lines and different types of sediments and rocks show up clearly on Landsat pictures. This allows geologists to select promising areas in which the prospector can look for mineral deposits.

Another way to study the Earth is by bouncing radar beams off it. Radar sensing indicates the nature of soil or rock on land and movement of water at sea, for example. This was not done by Landsat, but by equipment aboard the United States' Skylab and by a short-lived American satellite called Seasat. The Soviet Union has included Earth surveying in its Salyut program, and resource mapping is also a feature of the spacelab aboard the American space shuttle. All these activities help man to manage the limited resources on our planet and to preserve the environment.

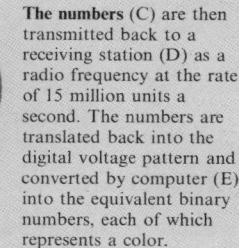

A multispectral scanner (B) has an oscillating mirror (1) that focuses visible and near infrared radiation on to a detector (2). This converts the intensity of the radiation into a voltage. An electronics unit (3) turns the voltage pattern into a series of digitized numbers that can be fed into a computer.

The numbers (C) are then transmitted back to a receiving station (D) as a radio frequency at the rate of 15 million units a second. The numbers are translated back into the digital voltage pattern and converted by computer (E) into the equivalent binary numbers, each of which represents a color.

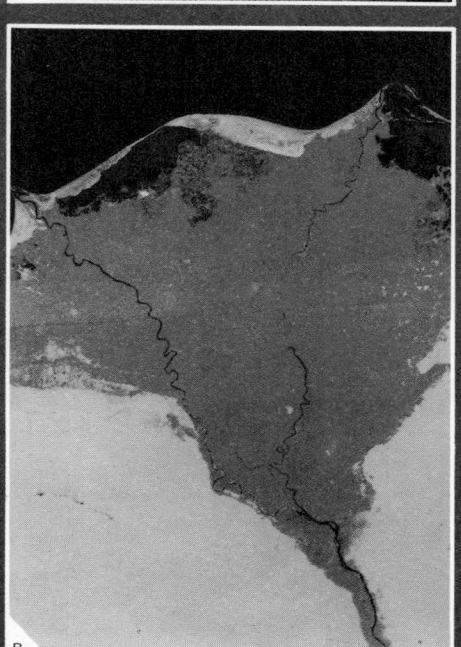

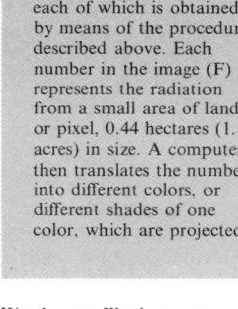

A Landsat image is made up of very many points, each of which is obtained by means of the procedure described above. Each number in the image (F) represents the radiation from a small area of land, or pixel, 0.44 hectares (1.1 acres) in size. A computer then translates the numbers into different colors, or different shades of one color, which are projected on to a TV screen (G) and the image is seen for the first time. Finally, photographs of this false-color image are produced (H). This picture, showing a forest fire in the Upper Peninsula, Michigan, is of use to those engaged in forest management. Other satellite data of use in forestry include types of trees, patterns of growth and the spread of disease.

Observation of waterways and coastal areas (above) shows pollution and deposition of sediments. This is of importance to the fishing industry. Fish congregate in areas where upwelling brings nutrients to the surface, for example. The large yellow-orange halo around Akimiski Island in James Bay (A)—a southern extension of Hudson Bay in Canada—is fine sediment resulting from wave action on a silty shore. Seeing the sediment in this way helps to determine current patterns in the Bay. In a predominantly desert area, the Nile delta (B) stands out dramatically. The red is an intensively cultivated area: cotton is the main crop. The larger irrigation canals can be seen on the photograph. Thermal imagery, or heat capacity mapping, is used to identify rocks, to study the effects of urban "heat islands," to estimate soil moisture and snow melt,

and to map shallow ground water. In this photograph of the northeast coast of North America (C) purple represents the coldest temperatures—in Lakes Erie and Ontario. The coldest parts of the Atlantic Ocean are deep blue, whereas warmer waters near the coast are light blue. Green is the warmer land, but also the Gulf Stream in the lower right part of the image. Brown, yellow and orange represent successively warmer land surface areas. Red is hot regions around cities and coal-mining regions found in eastern Pennsylvania (to the upper left of center in the picture); and, finally, gray and white are the very hottest areas—the urban heat islands of Baltimore, Philadelphia and New York City. Black areas in the upper left are cold clouds. The temperature range of the image is about 30°C (55°F).

The Earth seen from space shows phases just like the Moon, Mercury and Venus do to us. These dramatic photographs were taken from a satellite moving at

35,885 km (22,300 miles) above South America at 7.30 am (1), 10.30 am (2), noon (3), 3.30 pm (4) and at 10.30 pm (5), and clearly show the Earth in phase.

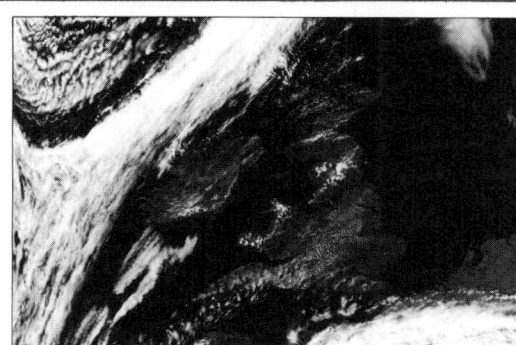
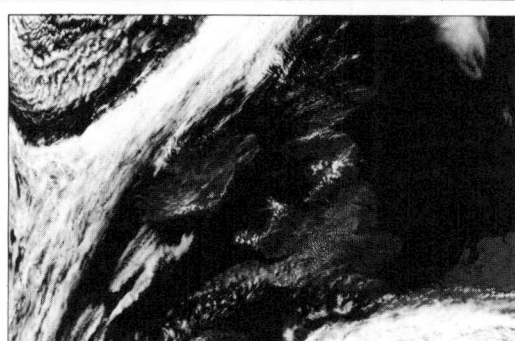

Weather satellite imagery can save lives and property by giving advance warning of bad weather conditions, as well as providing day-to-day forecasts. This Tiros image (left) shows a cold front moving west of Ireland with low-level wave clouds over southern and central England. There are low-pressure systems over northern France and to the northwest of Ireland.

LANDSAT AND THE FARMER

sown	grows		dormant			grows			ripe	harvest
Sep	Oct	Nov	Dec	Jan	Feb	Mar	Apr	May	Jun	Jul	Aug

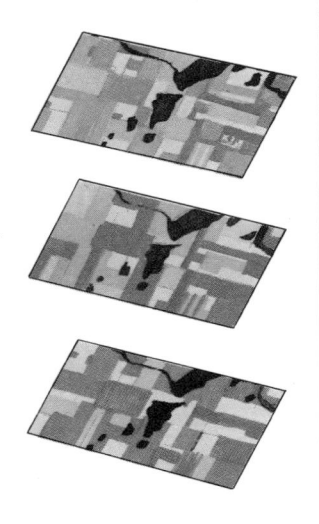

Agriculturists benefit from "multitemporal analysis" by satellites (left). This is the comparison of data from the same field recorded on two or more dates. It is also able to differentiate crops, which may have an identical appearance, or signature, on one day, but on another occasion exhibit different rates of growth. The pattern of growth is different for small grains than most other crops. A "biowindow" is the period of time in which vegetation is observed. These three biowindows (right) show the emergence and ripening (light blue to red to dark blue) of wheat in May, July and August.

Part 2

MAKING AND SHAPING THE EARTH

The structure and substance of the Earth
Forces that move continents · Forces that fashion Earth's landscapes
How man has changed the face of the Earth

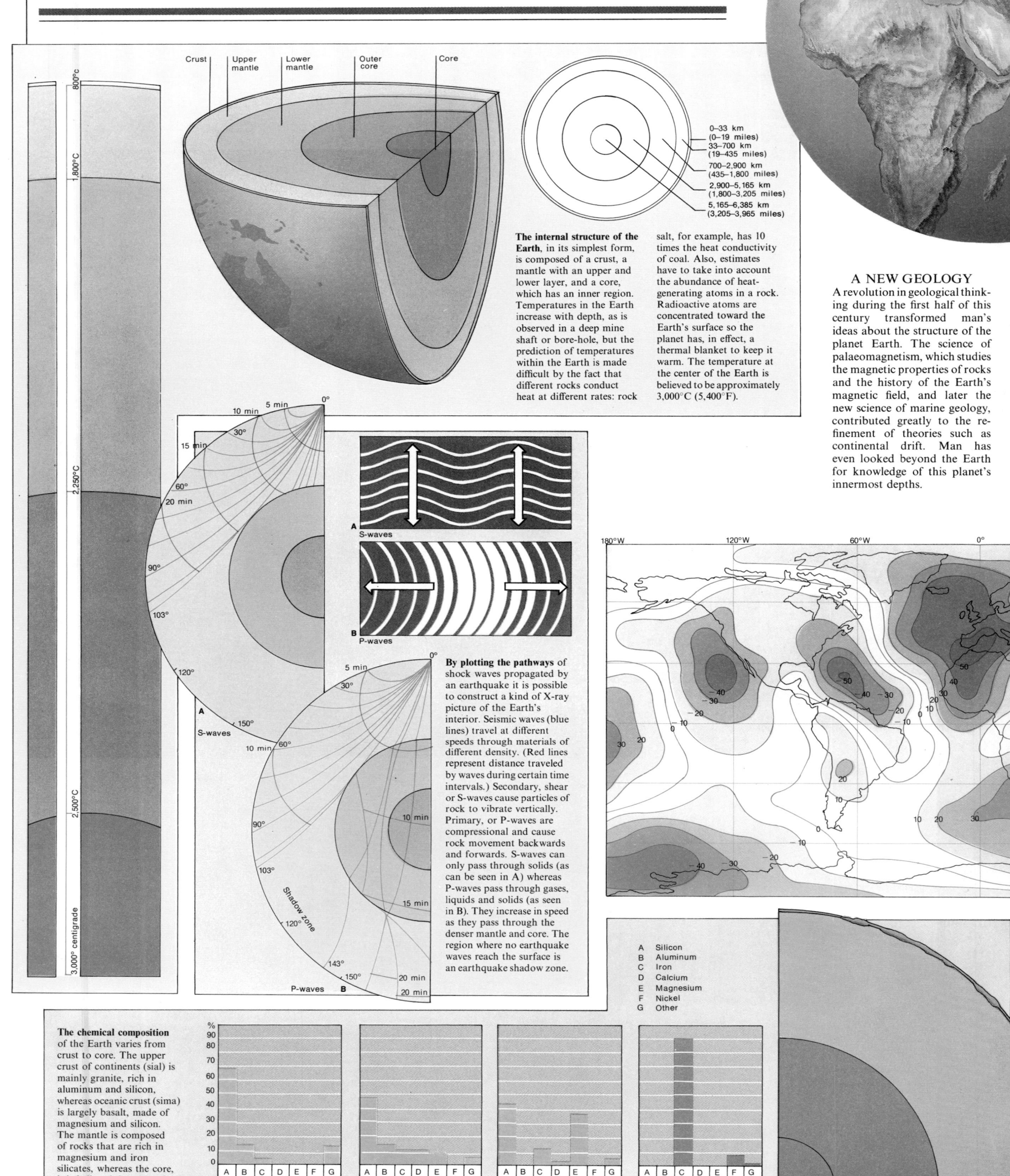

Crust | Upper mantle | Lower mantle | Outer core | Core

0–33 km
(0–19 miles)
33–700 km
(19–435 miles)
700–2,900 km
(435–1,800 miles)
2,900–5,165 km
(1,800–3,205 miles)
5,165–6,385 km
(3,205–3,965 miles)

The internal structure of the Earth, in its simplest form, is composed of a crust, a mantle with an upper and lower layer, and a core, which has an inner region. Temperatures in the Earth increase with depth, as is observed in a deep mine shaft or bore-hole, but the prediction of temperatures within the Earth is made difficult by the fact that different rocks conduct heat at different rates: rock salt, for example, has 10 times the heat conductivity of coal. Also, estimates have to take into account the abundance of heat-generating atoms in a rock. Radioactive atoms are concentrated toward the Earth's surface so the planet has, in effect, a thermal blanket to keep it warm. The temperature at the center of the Earth is believed to be approximately 3,000°C (5,400°F).

A NEW GEOLOGY
A revolution in geological thinking during the first half of this century transformed man's ideas about the structure of the planet Earth. The science of palaeomagnetism, which studies the magnetic properties of rocks and the history of the Earth's magnetic field, and later the new science of marine geology, contributed greatly to the refinement of theories such as continental drift. Man has even looked beyond the Earth for knowledge of this planet's innermost depths.

A S-waves

B P-waves

By plotting the pathways of shock waves propagated by an earthquake it is possible to construct a kind of X-ray picture of the Earth's interior. Seismic waves (blue lines) travel at different speeds through materials of different density. (Red lines represent distance traveled by waves during certain time intervals.) Secondary, shear or S-waves cause particles of rock to vibrate vertically. Primary, or P-waves are compressional and cause rock movement backwards and forwards. S-waves can only pass through solids (as can be seen in A) whereas P-waves pass through gases, liquids and solids (as seen in B). They increase in speed as they pass through the denser mantle and core. The region where no earthquake waves reach the surface is an earthquake shadow zone.

A S-waves

Shadow zone

P-waves B

A Silicon
B Aluminum
C Iron
D Calcium
E Magnesium
F Nickel
G Other

The chemical composition of the Earth varies from crust to core. The upper crust of continents (sial) is mainly granite, rich in aluminum and silicon, whereas oceanic crust (sima) is largely basalt, made of magnesium and silicon. The mantle is composed of rocks that are rich in magnesium and iron silicates, whereas the core, it is believed, is made of iron and nickel oxides.

Sial

Sima

Mantle

Core

Earth's Structure

The Earth is made up of concentric shells of different kinds of material. Immediately beneath us is the crust; below that is the mantle; and at the center of the globe is the core. Knowledge of the internal structure of Earth is the key to an understanding of the substances of Earth and an appreciation of the forces at work, not only deep in the center of the planet but also affecting the formation of surface features and large-scale landscapes. The workings of all these elements are inextricably linked.

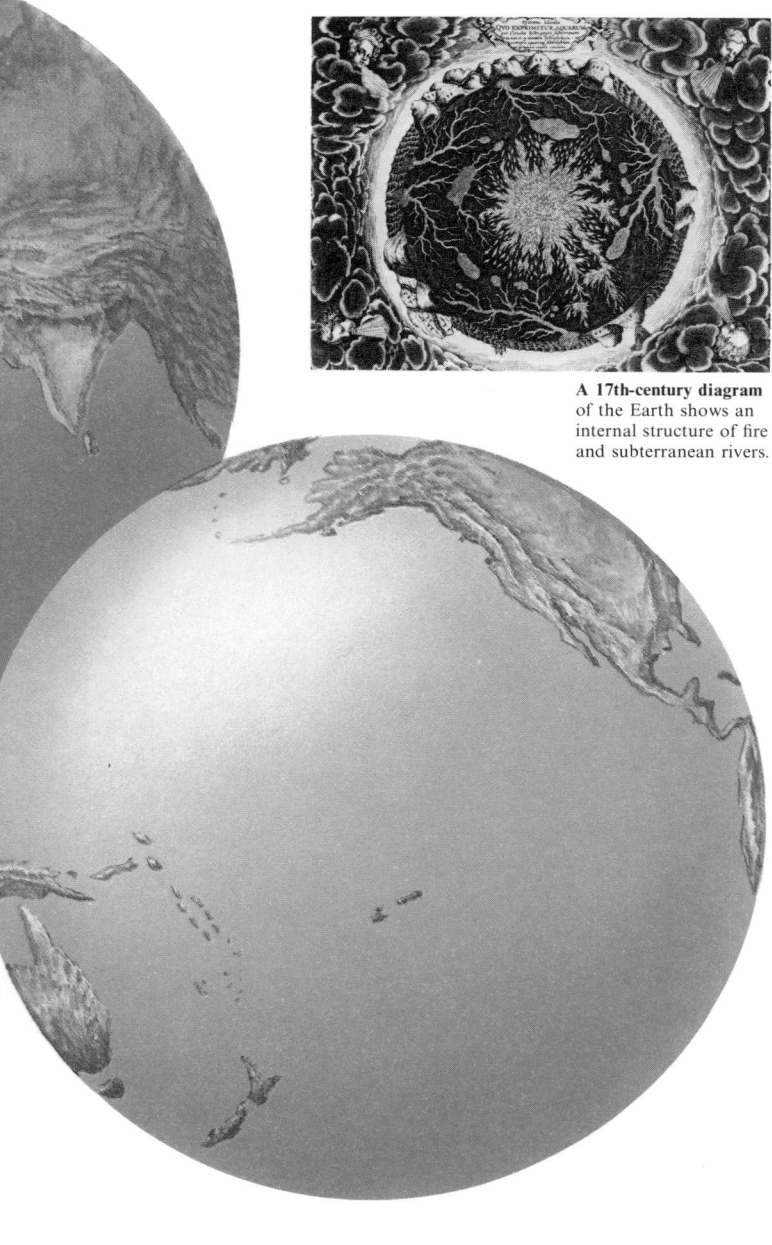

A 17th-century diagram of the Earth shows an internal structure of fire and subterranean rivers.

Our knowledge of the Earth is largely restricted to the outer crust. The deepest hole that man has drilled reaches only 10 km (6 miles)—less than 1/600th of the planet's radius—and so our knowledge about the rest of the Earth has had to come via indirect means: by the study of earthquake waves, and a comparison between rocks on Earth and those that make up meteorites—small fragments of asteroids and other minor planetary bodies that originated from similar materials to the Earth.

The Earth's crust

The outermost layer of the Earth is called the crust. The crust beneath the oceans is different from the material that makes up continental crust. Ocean crust is formed at mid-ocean ridges where melted rocks (magma) from the mantle rise up in great quantities and solidify to form a layer a few kilometers thick over the mantle. As this ocean crust spreads out from the ridge it becomes covered with deep-ocean sediments. The ocean crust was initially called "sima," a word made up from the first two letters of the characteristic elements—silicon and magnesium. Sima has a density of 2.9 gm/cc (1 gm/cc is the density of water).

Continental crust was named "sial"—from silicon and aluminum, the most abundant elements. Sial is lighter than sima with a density of 2.7 gm/cc. The continental crust is like a series of giant rafts, 17 to 70 km (9–43 miles) thick. As a result of numerous collisions and breakages, these continental rafts have been bulldozed into their present shape, but they have been forming for at least 4,000 million years. The oldest known rocks, in Greenland, are 3,750 million years old, which is only about 800 million years younger than the Earth itself. The complex history of the continents' evolution over this vast time span makes construction of an ideal cross section difficult, but the rocks of the lower two-thirds of the crust appear to be denser (2.9 gm/cc) than the upper levels.

The Moho, or Mohorovičić discontinuity, discovered in 1909, marks the base of the crust and the beginning of the mantle rocks, where the density increases from 2.9 to 3.3 gm/cc. The Moho is at an average depth of 10 km (6 miles) under the sea and 35 km (20 miles) below land.

The mantle

Our knowledge of the mantle comes from mantle rocks that are sometimes brought to the surface. These are even more enriched in magnesium oxides than the sima, with lesser amounts of iron and calcium oxides. The uppermost mantle to a depth of between 60 and 100 km (40–60 miles), together with the overlying crust, forms the rigid lithosphere, which is divided into plates. Below this is a pasty

layer, or asthenosphere, extending to a depth of 700 km (435 miles). The upper mantle is separated from the lower mantle by another discontinuity where the density of the rock increases from 3.3 to 4.3 gm/cc.

Scientists now believe that the mantle is the planetary motor force behind the movements of the continents. By studying in detail the chemistry of the volcanic rocks that have come directly from the mantle, they have gathered much information about this mantle motor. The rocks that come up along oceanic ridges and form new oceanic crust reveal by their chemical composition that they have formed from mantle that has undergone previous melting. By contrast, islands such as Hawaii and Iceland have formed from mantle material that, for the most part, has never been melted before. One explanation for these chemical observations is that, while the top 700 km (435 miles) of the mantle region is moving in accordance with movement of the plates, the mantle beneath it is moving independently and sending occasional rivers of unaltered material through the surface to form islands like volcanic Hawaii.

The core

Structurally, the most important boundary in the Earth lies at a depth of 2,900 km (1,800 miles) below the surface, where the rock density almost doubles from about 5.5 to 9.9 gm/cc. This is known as the Gutenberg discontinuity and was discovered in 1914. Below this level the material must have the properties of a liquid since certain earthquake waves cannot penetrate it. Scientists infer from the composition of meteorites, some of which are composed of iron and nickel, that this deep core material is composed largely of iron, with some nickel and perhaps lighter elements such as silicon. The processes involved in the formation of a planet have been compared to the separation of the metals (the core) from the slag (the mantle and crust) in a blast furnace.

The core has a radius of 3,485 km (2,165 miles) and makes up only one-sixth of the Earth's volume, yet it has one-third of its mass. In the middle of the liquid outer core there is an even denser ball with a radius of 1,220 km (760 miles)—two-thirds the size of the Moon—where, under intense pressure, the metals have solidified. The inner core is believed to be solid iron and nickel and is 20 percent denser (12–13 gm/cc) than the surrounding liquid.

Electric currents in the core are the only possible source of the Earth's magnetic field. This drifts and alters in a way which could arise only from some deeply buried fluid movement. At the top of the core, the pattern of the field moves about 100 m (330 ft) west each day. Every million years or so during the Earth's history, the north–south magnetic poles have switched so that compasses pointed south, not north.

The dynamo that generates magnetism and its strange variations is still not fully understood. Motion in the core may be powered by giant slabs of metal that crystallize out from the liquid and sink to join the inner core. Our knowledge of the Earth's structure has increased greatly over the last 50 years, but many intriguing questions remain to be answered.

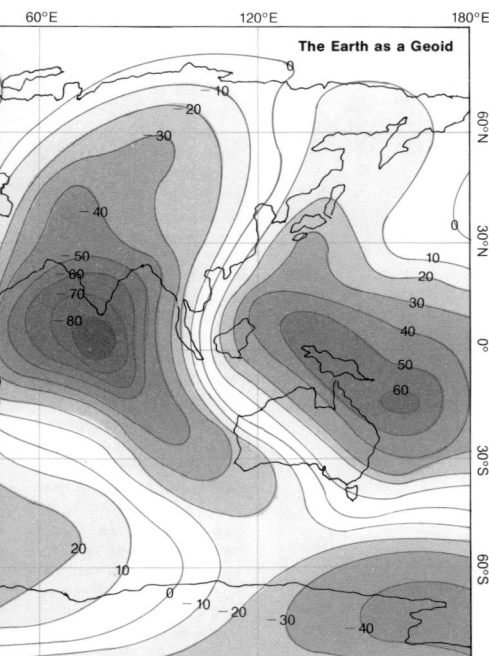

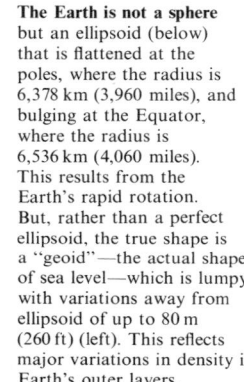

60°E   120°E   180°E

The Earth as a Geoid

The Earth is not a sphere but an ellipsoid (below) that is flattened at the poles, where the radius is 6,378 km (3,960 miles), and bulging at the Equator, where the radius is 6,536 km (4,060 miles). This results from the Earth's rapid rotation. But, rather than a perfect ellipsoid, the true shape is a "geoid"—the actual shape of sea level—which is lumpy, with variations away from ellipsoid of up to 80 m (260 ft) (left). This reflects major variations in density in Earth's outer layers.

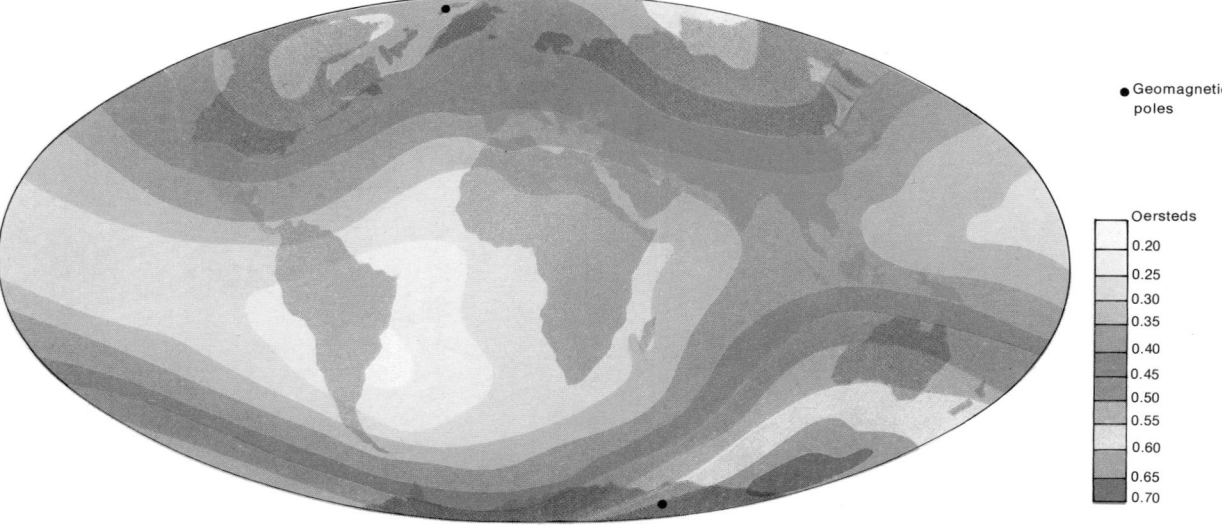

● Geomagnetic poles

Oersteds
0.20
0.25
0.30
0.35
0.40
0.45
0.50
0.55
0.60
0.65
0.70

The Earth's magnetic field is strongest at the poles and weakest in equatorial regions. If the field were simply like a bar magnet inside the globe, lines of intensity would mirror lines of latitude; but the field is inclined at an angle of 11° to the Earth's axis. The geomagnetic poles are similarly inclined and they do not coincide with the geographic poles. In reality, the field is much more complex than that of a bar magnet. In addition, over long periods of time, the magnetic poles and the north–south orientation of the field change slowly. The strength of the Earth's magnetic field is measured in units called oersteds.

Earth's Moving Crust

The top layer of the Earth is known as the lithosphere and is composed of the crust and the uppermost mantle. It is divided into six major rigid plates and several smaller platelets that move relative to each other, driven by movements that lie deep in the Earth's liquid mantle. The plate boundaries correspond to the zones of earthquakes and the sites of active volcanoes. The concept of plate tectonics – that the Earth's crust is mobile despite being rigid – emerged in the 1960s and helped to confirm the early twentieth-century theory of continental drift proposed by Alfred Wegener.

THE DYNAMIC EARTH

As early as the 17th century, the English philosopher Francis Bacon noted that the coasts on either side of the Atlantic were similar and could be fitted together like pieces of a jigsaw puzzle. Three hundred years later Alfred Wegener proposed the theory of continental drift, but no one would believe the Earth's rigid crust could move. Today, geological evidence has provided the basis for the theory of plate tectonics, which demonstrates that the Earth's crust is slowly but continually moving.

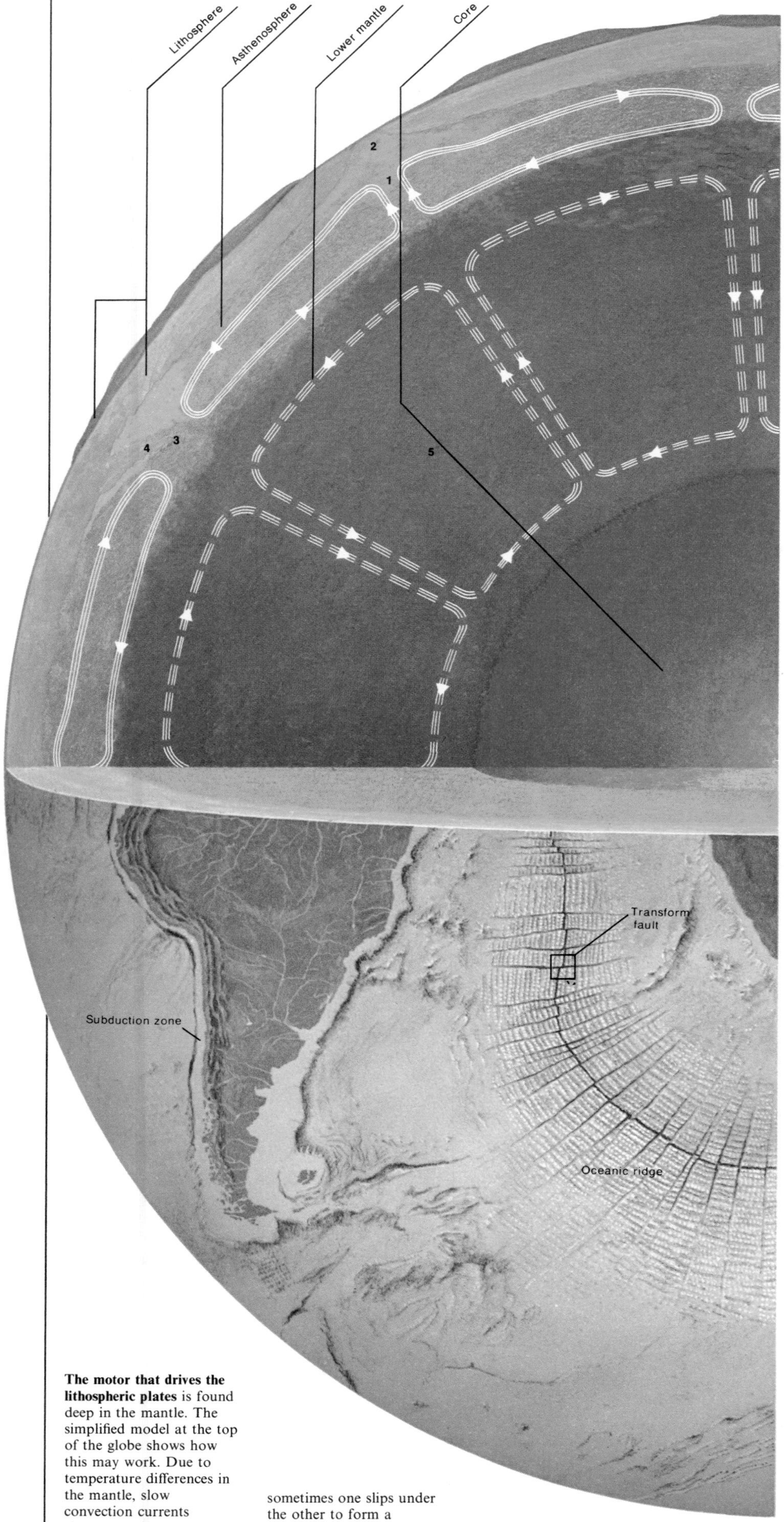

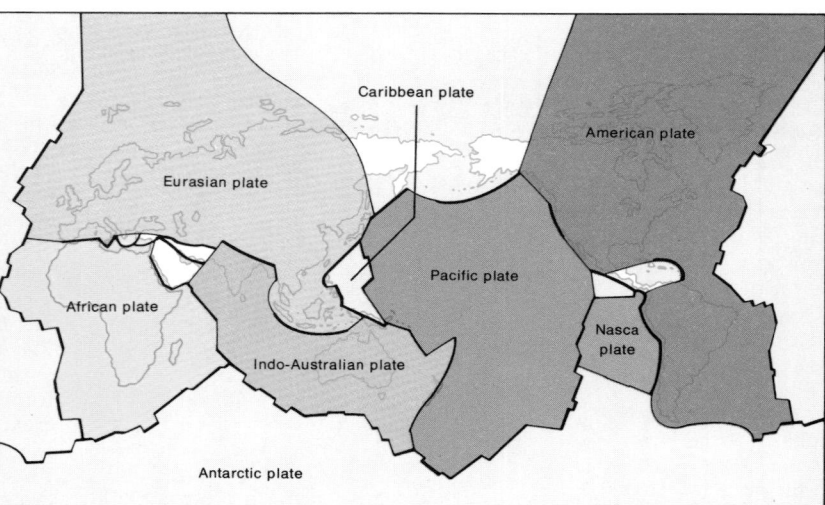

Earth's lithosphere—the rocky shell, or crust—is made up of six major plates and several smaller platelets, each separated from each other by ridges, subduction zones or transcurrent faults. The plates grow bigger by accretion along the mid-ocean ridges, are destroyed at subduction zones beneath the trenches, and slide beside each other along the transcurrent faults. The African and Antarctic plates have no trenches along their borders to destroy any of their crust, so they are growing bigger. This growth is compensated by the subduction zone that is developing to the north of the Tonga Islands and subduction zones in the Pacific. Conversely, the Pacific and Indo-Australian plates are shrinking. Along the plate boundaries magma wells up from the mantle to form volcanoes. Here, too, are the origins of earthquakes as the plates collide or slide slowly past each other.

The motor that drives the lithospheric plates is found deep in the mantle. The simplified model at the top of the globe shows how this may work. Due to temperature differences in the mantle, slow convection currents circulate. Where two current cycles move upwards together and separate (1), the plates bulge and move apart along mid-ocean ridges (2). Where there is a downward moving current (3), the plates move together and sometimes one slips under the other to form a subduction zone (4). Another model proposes that the convection currents are found deep in the mantle (5). Only time and more research, however, will reveal the true mechanism of plate movement.

Subduction zones are the sites of destruction of the ocean crust. As one plate passes beneath another down into the mantle, the ocean floor is pulled downward and a deep ocean trench is formed. The movement taking place along the length of the subduction zone causes earthquakes, while melting of the rock at depth produces magma that rises to create the volcanoes that form island arcs.

An oceanic ridge is formed when two plates move away from each other. As they move, molten magma from the mantle forces its way to the surface. This magma cools and is in turn injected with new magma. Thus the oceanic ridge is gradually forming the newest part of Earth's crust.

Transform, or transcurrent, faults are found where two plates slide past each other. They may, for example, link two parts of a ridge (A, B). A study of the magnetic properties of the seabed may suggest a motion shown by the white arrows, but the true movements of the plates are shown by the red arrows. The transform fault is active only between points (2) and (3). Between points (1) and (2) and between (3) and (4) the scar of the fault is healed and the line of the fault is no longer a plate boundary.

The early evidence for continental drift was gathered by Alfred Wegener, a German meteorologist. He noticed that the coastlines on each side of the Atlantic Ocean could be made to fit together, and that much of the geological history of the flanking continents—shown by fossils, structures and past climates—also seemed to match. Wegener compared the two sides of the Atlantic with a sheet of torn newspaper and reasoned that if not just one line of print but 10 lines match then there is a good case for arguing that the two sides were once joined. Yet for 50 years continental drift was generally considered to be a fanciful dream.

Seafloor spreading

In the 1950s the first geological surveys of the oceans began, and a 60,000 km (37,200 mile) long chain of mountains was discovered running down the center of the Atlantic Ocean, all round the Antarctic, up to the Indian Ocean, into the Red Sea and up the Eastern Pacific Ocean into Alaska. Along the axis of this mid-ocean ridge system there was often a narrow, deep rift valley. In places this ridge was offset along sharp fractures in the ocean floor.

The breakthrough in developing the global plate tectonic theory came with the first large-scale survey of the ocean floor. Magnetometers, which were developed during World War II for tracking submarines, showed the ocean floor to be magnetically striped. The ocean floor reveals magnetic characteristics because the ocean crust basalts are full of tiny crystals of the magnetic mineral magnetite. As the basalt cooled, the magnetic field of these crystals aligned itself with the Earth's magnetic field. This would be insignificant if it were not for the fact that the magnetic pole of the Earth has switched from north to south at different times in the past. Half the magnetite compasses of the ocean floor point south rather than north.

In the middle 1960s, two Cambridge geophysicists, Drummond Matthews and Fred Vine, noticed that the pattern of stripes was symmetrical around the mid-ocean ridge. Such an extraordinary and unlikely symmetry could mean only one thing—any two matching stripes must originally have been formed together at the mid-ocean ridge and then moved away from each other as newer crust formed between them to create new stripes. It was soon calculated that the North Atlantic Ocean was growing wider by about 2 cm ($\frac{3}{4}$ in) a year. At last, drifting continents was accepted.

Consumption of the seafloor

Seafloor spreading soon became included in an even more sensational model—plate tectonics. If the oceans are growing wider, then either the whole planet is expanding or the spreading ocean floor is consumed elsewhere. In the late 1950s a global network of seismic stations had been set up to monitor nuclear explosions and earthquakes. For the first time the positions of all earthquakes could be accurately defined.

It was found that the zones of earthquake activity were predominantly narrow, following the mid-ocean ridges and extending along the rim of the Pacific, beneath the island arcs of the West Pacific and beneath the continental margins in the East Pacific as well as underlying the Alpine-Himalayan Mountain Belt. The seismic zones around the Pacific dipped away from the ocean and continued to depths as great as 700 km (430 miles). They intercepted the surface at the curious arc-shaped deep-ocean trenches. It had been known for 20 years that the pull of gravity over these trenches is strangely reduced, so to survive they must continually be dragged downwards. Here was the site of ocean-floor consumption—now known as a subduction zone. Subduction zones must be efficient at consuming ocean crust because no known ocean crust is older than 200 million years—less than five percent of Earth's lifetime.

The oceanic lithosphere (the Earth's rocky crust) is extraordinarily rigid. Even where the oceanic lithosphere becomes consumed within subduction zones it still maintains its rigidity. As it bends down into the Earth it tends to corrugate, forming rise to the pattern of chains of deep-ocean trenches and chains of volcanic islands formed above the subduction zone.

As oceanic lithosphere grows older it cools, contracts and sinks. From the depth of the ocean floor it is possible to make an accurate estimate of the age of the crust beneath. Even the steepness of the subduction zone is a function of the age, and therefore the density, of the lithosphere. The oldest crust provides the strongest downward pull and hence the steepest angle of dip of the subduction zone.

As well as the spreading ridges (constructive margins) and the subduction zones (destructive margins) there is another kind of plate boundary (conservative margins), where the plates slip past one another along a major fault such as the San Andreas Fault of California.

The past positions of the continents

Continental drift is thus the result of the creation and destruction of oceanic lithosphere, but only the continents can record the oceanic plate motions taking place more than 200 million years ago. The discovery of ancient lines of subduction zone volcanoes can testify to the destruction of long-gone oceans. One particularly important technique for finding the positions of the continents is to study the magnetism of certain rocks, particularly lavas, that record the position of the north–south magnetic poles at the time when the rock cooled. If the rock "compass" points, for example, west, then the continent must have rotated by 90°. The vertical dip of the rock compass can reveal the approximate latitude of the rock at its formation (the dip increases from horizontal at the Equator to vertical at the magnetic poles).

As longitude is entirely arbitrary (defined on the position of Greenwich) one can only hope to gain the relative positions of the continents with regard to one another. The best additional information is provided by studies of fossils—if the remains of shallow-water marine organisms are very different they must have been separated by an ocean. The full impact of continental drift on the development of land animals and plants is only beginning to be realized.

THE DRIFTING CONTINENTS

It is now accepted that the continents have changed their positions during the past millions of years, and by studying the magnetism preserved in the rocks the configuration of the continents has been plotted for various geological times. The sequence of continental drifting, illustrated below, begins with one single landmass—the so-called supercontinent Pangaea—and the ancestral Pacific Ocean, called the Panthalassa Ocean. Pangaea first split into a northern landmass called Laurasia and a southern block called Gondwanaland, and subsequently into the continents we see today. The maps illustrate the positions of the continents in the past, where they are now and their predicted positions in 50 million years' time.

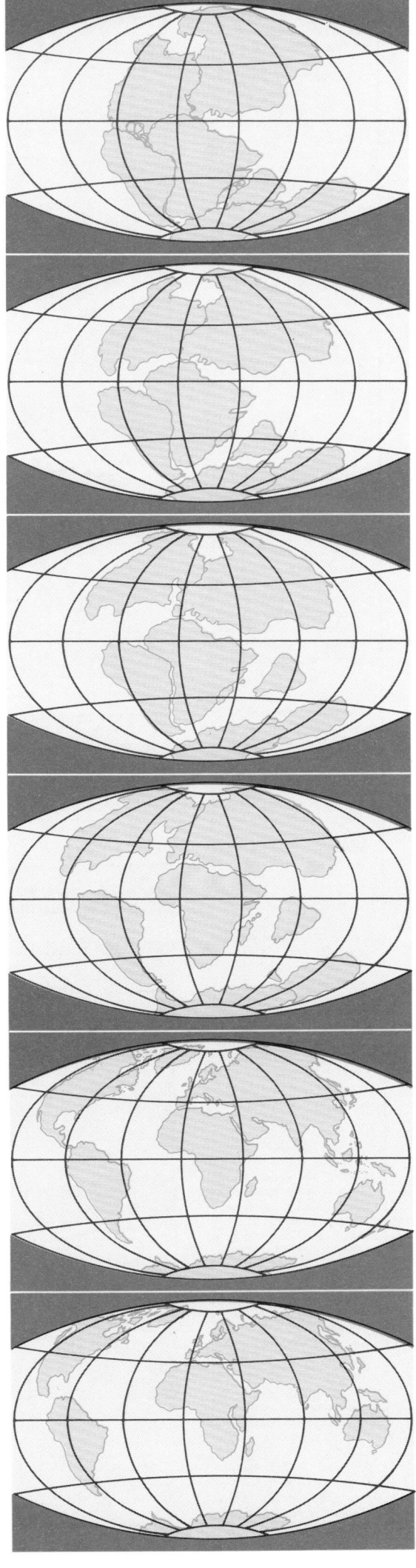

225 million years ago one large landmass, the supercontinent Pangaea, exists and Panthalassa forms the ancestral Pacific Ocean. The Tethys Sea separates Eurasia and Africa and forms an ancestor of the Mediterranean Sea.

180 million years ago Pangaea splits up, the northern block of continents, Laurasia, drifts northwards and the southern block, Gondwanaland, begins to break up. India separates and the South American–African block divides from Australia–Antarctica. New ocean floor is created between the continents.

135 million years ago the Indian plate continues its northward drift and Eurasia rotates to begin to close the eastern end of the Tethys Sea. The North Atlantic and the Indian Ocean have opened up and the South Atlantic is just beginning to form.

65 million years ago Madagascar has split from Africa and the Tethys Sea has closed, with the Mediterranean Sea opening behind it. The South Atlantic Ocean has opened up considerably, but Australia is still joined to the Antarctic and India is about to collide with Asia.

The present day: India has completed its northward migration and collided with Asia, Australia has set itself free from Antarctica, and North America has freed itself from Eurasia to leave Greenland between them. During the past 65 million years (a relatively short geological span of time) nearly half of the present-day ocean floor has been created.

50 million years in the future, Australia may continue its northward drift, part of East Africa will separate from the mainland, and California west of the San Andreas Fault will separate from North America and move northwards. The Pacific Ocean will become smaller, compensating for the increase in size of both the Atlantic and Indian oceans. The Mediterranean Sea will disappear as Africa moves to the north.

Magnetic surveys of the seabed helped build the plate tectonics theory. Research vessels equipped with magnetometers sailed back and forth over a mid-ocean ridge and recorded the varying magnetism of the seabed. The Earth's magnetic pole has switched from north to south at different times in the past, and this mapping revealed a striped magnetic pattern on the seabed. It was noticed that the stripes on either side of the ridge were symmetrical. The explanation was that the matching stripes must have formed together and moved apart as more crust was injected between them—a notion that was subsequently supported by dating of the seafloor.

3 2 1 0 1 3

Time in millions of years

Folds, Faults and Mountain Chains

The continents are great rafts of lighter rock that float in the mantle of the Earth. When drifting continents collide, great mountain chains are thrown up as the continental crust is forced to thicken to absorb the impact of the collision. The highest mountains are formed out of thick piles of sediment that are built up from the debris of erosion constantly washed off the land and deposited on the continental margins. Through the massive deformations of rock faults and folds these remains of old mountains become recycled, thus building new mountains from the remains of old ones.

For the formation of mountain ranges such as the Appalachians or the Himalayas, or the Caledonian mountain chain of Norway, Scotland and Newfoundland, the pattern of development is very much the same. First, a widening ocean with passive margins is located between two continents.

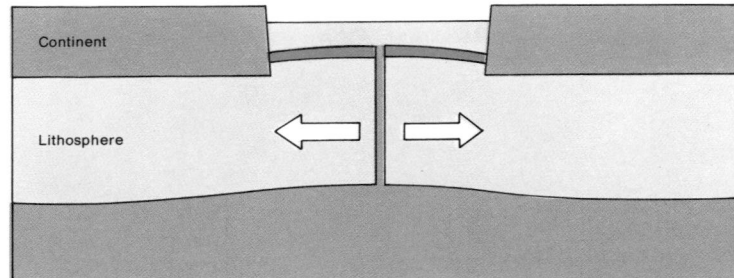

As more ocean floor is created the continents move farther apart, and at the edge of each continent sediment accumulates from the debris of erosion. These piles of thick sediment are known as sedimentary basins.

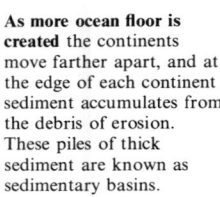
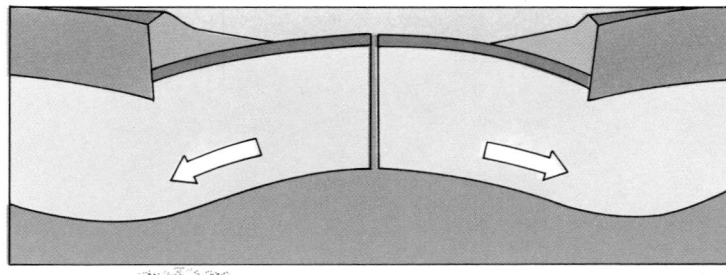

For the formation of the Appalachians, the ancestral Atlantic Ocean began to close, a subduction zone was formed at the ocean–continent boundary, and the oceanic lithosphere began to be absorbed into the mantle. Magma intruded to form granite "plutons" and volcanoes, and much of the sedimentary basin was metamorphosed.

The ocean continued to close until North America and Africa were joined together, further compressing the sediments in the sedimentary basin at the passive ocean margin. The two continents were joined like this between 350 and 225 million years ago.

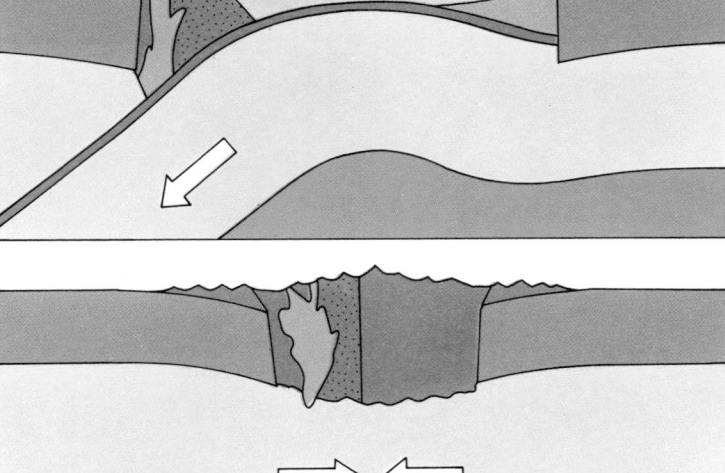

About 180 million years ago, after the original Appalachians had been worn down in size, the present Atlantic Ocean opened along a new break in the continental crust, offset from the line of the original mountains. As the continents split, so the crust became stretched along great curved faults.

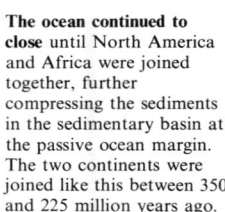
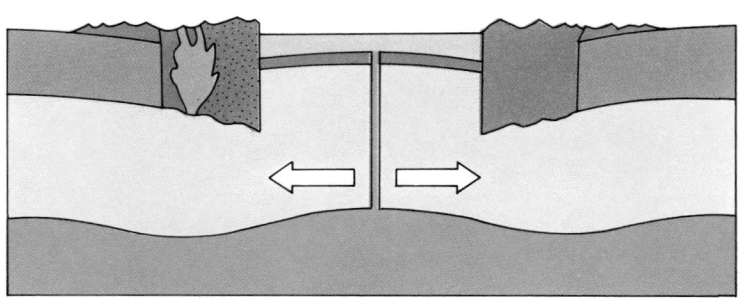

Parts of the ancient Appalachian mountains have been eroded to sea level, leaving the Appalachians, that formed on the edge of the old continent, inland.

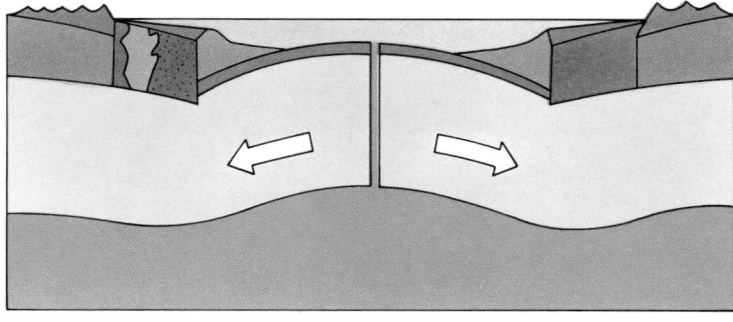

- Continental shelf
- Granite
- Metamorphic rock
- Sediment
- Ocean crust

BIRTH AND DEATH OF A MOUNTAIN

Mountains are thrust upward by the pressure exerted by the moving plates of the Earth's crust, and are formed out of the sediments that have been eroded from the continental masses. Young mountains are lofty and much folded, but the agents of erosion and weathering soon begin to reduce their height, and over many millions of years the mountain range is eroded to sea level. This eroded material accumulates in the sea at the edge of the continents and becomes the building material for another phase of mountain building.

ISOSTASY

The continents float in the Earth's mantle, and because they are only slightly less dense (2.67 g/cc compared to 3.27 g/cc), 85% of their bulk lies below sea level. Thus the higher the mountain the deeper the mountain root. And as the crust can exist only to a maximum depth of about 70 km (43 miles) before it is liquefied in the mantle, mountains can never rise above a maximum of 10 km (6 miles) above sea level.

Folds are generally related to underlying faults. The commonest simple folds are monoclines, formed when a single fault exhibits underlying movement. With continued movement a simple symmetrical anticline (1) may fold unevenly to form an asymmetric anticline (2). More movement bends the strata further into a recumbent fold (3) and eventually the strata break to form an overthrust fold (4). Over a long period an overthrust fold may be pushed many kilometers from its original position to form a nappe (5). Faults are generally of three kinds: faults of tension known as normal faults, when one block drops down (6); faults of horizontal shear (7), known as strike-slip faults; and faults of compression (8), known as thrust faults.

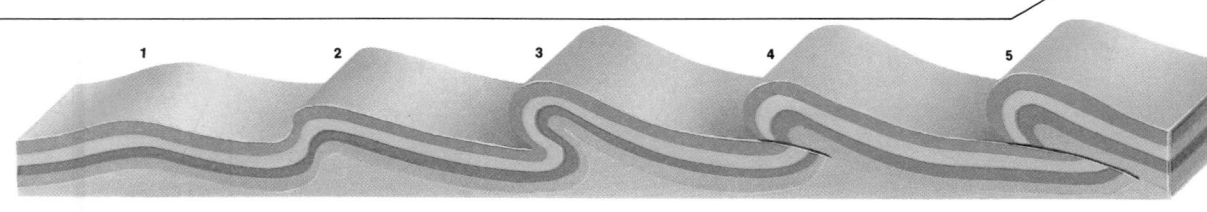

Continents float in the Earth's mantle like icebergs in the sea—more than four-fifths of their bulk lies beneath the surface. The continental crust is 28 km (17 miles) thick at sea level, and where mountains rise above this level there is a corresponding thickening in the crust beneath. The maximum thickness of crust is 70 km (43 miles), so mountains can only ever rise to a maximum height of approximately 10 km (6 miles) above sea level. This relation between upper and underlying crust is known as isostasy, or state of equal pressure.

As mountains become eroded, the process of isostatic rebound allows them to recover about 85 cm (34 in) for every 1 meter (40 in) removed. When, after about 100 million years, a major mountain range has been eroded down to sea level, the rocks exposed at the surface are those that were 15–25 km (9–15 miles) underground when the mountains were at their highest. Such rocks are coarsely crystalline, and make up the fabric of the old, tough continental crust.

Sedimentary basins
As early as the nineteenth century it was noticed that the biggest mountains formed where there had previously been the thickest pile of sediments. According to the principle of isostasy, a thick pile of sediments can form only where the Earth's crust is thin and sinking. The Aegean Sea in the eastern Mediterranean, for example, is at present being pulled apart, and therefore becoming thinner. Over the next few million years, as the Aegean crust sinks, a thick pile of sediments—a sedimentary basin—will accumulate. Most sedimentary basins are at present shallow seas, and form the continental shelves. The depth of water over these shelf seas has been determined by the erosion that accompanied the lowest sea levels of the past 100 million years—about 140 m (460 ft) below the present sea level.

Mountain building
When continents collide, it is the regions of stretched crust that are the first to absorb some of the impact. Such a former sedimentary basin is being turned into the Zagros Mountains of southwestern Iran as Arabia advances northeastward into Asia. The individual blocks of continental crust appear to be sliding back along curved faults, and the sediments that have built up over the thinned crust are now being forced into folds.

Early in the life of such a sedimentary basin sea water may become cut off from the ocean and evaporate to form extensive deposits of salt. Such salt deposits reduce friction and allow the folded pile of sediments overlying the continental blocks to become disconnected and to slide up to 100 km (62 miles) away from the collision zone. In the Zagros Mountains this process has only just begun, but in older mountain ranges, such as the Canadian Rockies or the European Alps, the formation of nappes—disconnected sediment piles forced ahead of the main compression zone—has been widespread.

As mountain ranges often form out of the sedimentary basins along the boundaries between a continent and the ocean, new mountains tend to add on to the fringes of the continents. In North America, for example, the oldest remnants of ranges that make up large tracts of the Canadian shield are found in the center of the continent, while the process of mountain building is continuing in the west.

Other continents show a more complex pattern of mountain ranges through subsequent phases of splitting and amalgamation, and the Himalayas and the Urals have formed where smaller continents have come together to make up the continent of Asia.

The boundary between the continent and the ocean along the western coast of the Atlantic Ocean is not a plate boundary and is therefore termed passive, in contrast to active boundaries such as the eastern coast of the Pacific Ocean, where the ocean plate is moving down into the mantle at a subduction zone beneath the Andean mountain chain. The highest Andean mountains are tall volcanoes of andesite (formed from magmas pouring off the underlying subduction zone). The bulk of the mountain range consists of enormous underground batholiths, in which the magma has solidified before being able to erupt, and compressed and uplifted sedimentary basins formed along the continental margin.

The crustal region immediately beyond the volcanoes that form above subduction zones, however, is very often in tension and in the process of being pulled apart. This appears to be caused by mantle material being dragged down with the oceanic lithosphere. Small ocean basins, such as the Sea of Japan, may open up under such conditions.

Folds and faults
When movement of the Earth's crust has taken place along a planar fracture through sedimentary rocks, it can be easily identified by the breaks in the layers, and such planes of movement are known as faults. Folds form where rock layers bend rather than break. Generally, faults form when rocks are brittle, and folds are found when rocks are plastic.

Sediments close to the surface are often so soft that they behave plastically, as do rocks at depths greater than 15–20 km (9–12 miles), where the continental crust is of sufficiently high temperature and pressure for slow rock flow to take place. Thus most continental faults are found between these levels. All major folds found in soft sediments apparently have a fault of some kind beneath them, and it is the failure of the fault to pass right through to the surface that creates the fold.

Folds are often extremely complicated and some geologists have tended to describe them in extraordinary detail, but in fact they are little more than brush strokes in the overall picture. Pre-existing faults beneath the folds tend to determine the folds' orientation. Once a continental fault has formed, it provides a plane of weakness wherever the continental crust is subject to stress. Many faults around the Mediterranean Sea came into existence during a period of tension, and these are now being reactivated and produce the large earthquakes associated with the continuing collision of Africa with Europe.

At the end of all the complications and intricacies of continental collision, the final phase of mountain building—that involving uplift—remains perhaps the least understood. In the last two million years, for example, while man has been increasingly active on Earth, 2,500,000 sq km (almost 1,000,000 sq miles) of Tibet has risen 4,000 m (2 miles). But the origin of such gigantic and rapid movement lies within the Earth's mantle.

The highest mountains are the product of continental collisions. As the rocks are squeezed, folded and faulted, the original continental crust becomes shortened and thickened. Although the overall extent and height of mountain chains is controlled by mountain building, the whole range can only be viewed from a spacecraft. For the earthbound mountain visitor the familiar shapes of peaks and valleys are those formed by mountain destruction (1). Snow at high altitudes consolidates to form ice that moves slowly downhill in the form of glaciers. To wear away a mountain range at an average of 5 km (3 miles) above sea level requires the removal of more than 20 km (12 miles) of rock, as the thick continental crust that floats in the underlying mantle rises to compensate for the loss of surface mass. Half-eroded mountains (2), such as the Appalachians, pictured above, may linger on for tens of millions of years until, like large regions of the Canadian interior, the mountains are all eroded away and only the hard crystalline surface rocks that were once buried 20 km (12 miles) underground remain (3).

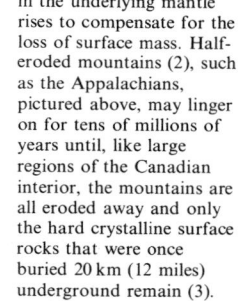

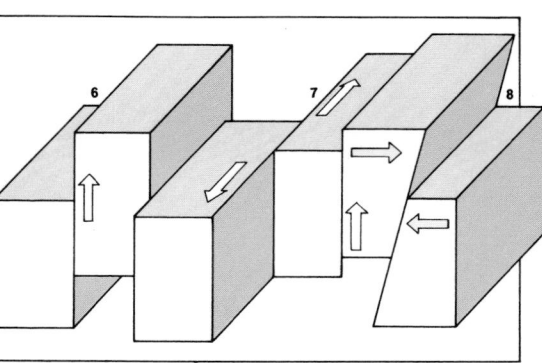

Rock Formation and History

All the rocks on Earth are interrelated through the rock cycle – a never-ending chain of processes that forms and modifies rocks and minerals on the Earth's surface, in its crust and in the mantle. These events are powered both by energy from the Sun and the heat of the Earth itself, and the processes include the forces of nature – from wind and water to the movements of the continents. This geological cycle of creation and destruction ·is one of the most distinctive features of our planet. Each feature of geological activity, each agent of landscape-making is but a stage of the continuing rock cycle.

CONSTANT CHANGE

The processes of formation and destruction of the three basic rock types—igneous, sedimentary and metamorphic—are linked in an interminable cycle of change. Igneous rocks are thrown up from inside the Earth, are eroded and eventually laid down as sediments. As accumulated sediments sink into the Earth, they are changed by heat and pressure—metamorphosed—before surfacing again in the processes of mountain building.

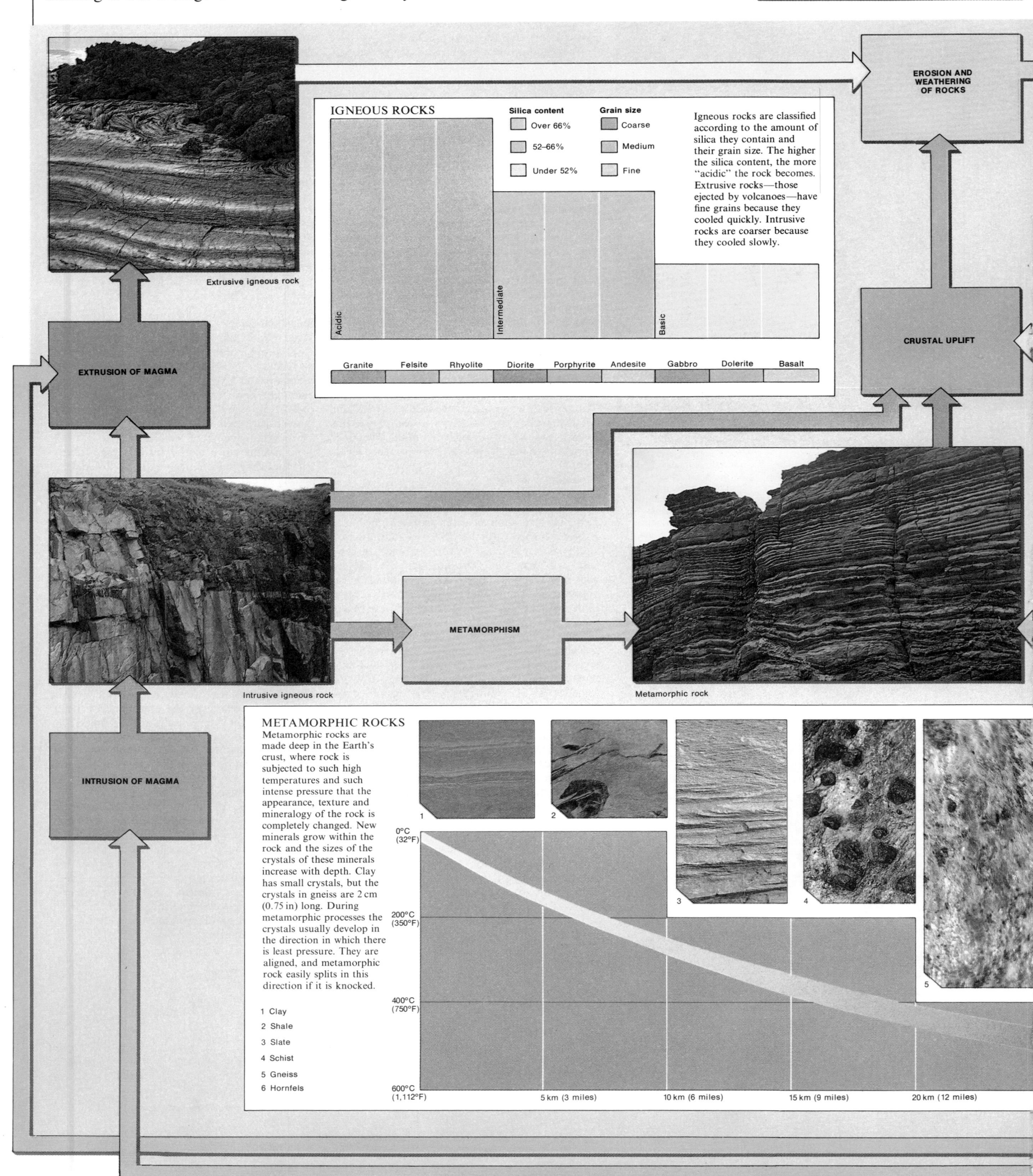

Extrusive igneous rock

EROSION AND WEATHERING OF ROCKS

IGNEOUS ROCKS

Silica content
- Over 66%
- 52–66%
- Under 52%

Grain size
- Coarse
- Medium
- Fine

Igneous rocks are classified according to the amount of silica they contain and their grain size. The higher the silica content, the more "acidic" the rock becomes. Extrusive rocks—those ejected by volcanoes—have fine grains because they cooled quickly. Intrusive rocks are coarser because they cooled slowly.

Acidic — Intermediate — Basic

Granite Felsite Rhyolite Diorite Porphyrite Andesite Gabbro Dolerite Basalt

EXTRUSION OF MAGMA

CRUSTAL UPLIFT

METAMORPHISM

Intrusive igneous rock

Metamorphic rock

INTRUSION OF MAGMA

METAMORPHIC ROCKS
Metamorphic rocks are made deep in the Earth's crust, where rock is subjected to such high temperatures and such intense pressure that the appearance, texture and mineralogy of the rock is completely changed. New minerals grow within the rock and the sizes of the crystals of these minerals increase with depth. Clay has small crystals, but the crystals in gneiss are 2 cm (0.75 in) long. During metamorphic processes the crystals usually develop in the direction in which there is least pressure. They are aligned, and metamorphic rock easily splits in this direction if it is knocked.

1 Clay
2 Shale
3 Slate
4 Schist
5 Gneiss
6 Hornfels

0°C (32°F)
200°C (350°F)
400°C (750°F)
600°C (1,112°F)

5 km (3 miles) 10 km (6 miles) 15 km (9 miles) 20 km (12 miles)

SEDIMENTARY ROCKS

Sediments can be turned into rock by means of three main processes. Cementation is the term used when water percolates between grains of sand. As it does so, any iron oxide, silica or calcium carbonate that were in solution are deposited in thin layers around the grains, thus cementing them into a hard sandstone (1). As more sediment is laid down, the increasing weight of the sediments on top exerts pressure on the underlying layers. Water is squeezed out and a dense rock is formed (2) by the process of compaction. This is the way clay becomes mudstone. Finally, during mountain-building processes forces are exerted on rock minerals that cause them to recrystallize into a solid mass of rock (3) that has no spaces between its mineral constituents.

TRANSPORTATION AND DEPOSITION OF SEDIMENTS

BURIAL AND FORMATION OF ROCK FROM SEDIMENTS (LITHIFICATION)

Sedimentary rock

METAMORPHISM

MELTING

6

25 km (15 miles)   30 km (18 miles)

All the rocks on Earth are formed at one stage or another in what is known as the rock cycle. All high ground on the continents suffers erosion; the eroded material is transported and deposited on lower ground; in time, these sediments may be elevated by mountain-building processes and so, in turn, become eroded. If, between their formation and destruction, sediments pass deep into the Earth's crust, they may be transformed by heat or pressure into metamorphic rock; or, at even greater depths, they may melt to form yet another kind of rock—igneous rock.

Materials at the bottom of a thick pile of sediments may be heated enough to melt. If this material then cools and solidifies underground, it is called plutonic rock. Sometimes, however, it escapes to the surface by means of a short cut— a volcano—to become part of the rock cycle. On the other hand, some sediments are lost off the edge of the continents on to the deep ocean floor, and they disappear into the mantle of the Earth by means of the downward movements of the oceanic crust. A measure of the difference between the input and the output of the continental rock cycle is a measure of how fast the continental crust is increasing or decreasing. Scientists believe it is increasing—at a rate of between 0.1 and 1.0 cu km a year.

Types of rock
The range of rock types found on the continents has been classified under three headings: sedimentary, igneous and metamorphic. Sedimentary rocks include all those formed at low temperatures on the Earth's surface; igneous rocks have all solidified from molten rock, or magma; and metamorphic rocks are sedimentary or igneous rocks that have changed their nature under conditions of high temperature and pressure.

There is a certain amount of difficulty in defining the boundaries between the different types. Ash formed from solidified magma falling out of the air after a volcanic eruption is igneous, but what if it should move downhill in a mudslide? If a metamorphic rock is deeply buried it may start to melt and form a "migmatite," which is part liquid and part solid. Is this igneous? And where does the boundary lie between a deeply buried sediment and a metamorphic rock? Coal seams that have been thoroughly metamorphosed from their original peat deposits are found as layers in unaltered sandstones. This classification does, however, provide a useful preliminary guide to understanding the nature of different types of rock.

Rock types are defined by studying their texture, the way they were formed, and their composition. There are interesting textural similarities between evaporites—salt deposits formed as an inland sea dries up—and some plutonic igneous rocks. Both have crystallized

directly from a liquid. There are similarities between sandstones and plutonic "cumulates," which form at the base of enormous magma reservoirs where strong magma currents deposit thick layers of crystals. So rock types must be defined in terms of more than just texture.

Rock formation
The simplest sedimentary rocks are those made up of whole fragments of eroded material. "Scree" deposits that accumulate at the base of a cliff or a steep valley side from angular rock fragments that have broken off the rock face above can make a sedimentary "breccia." A rock made from rounded stream pebbles is a "conglomerate." Further erosion reduces the rock into three components: dissolved ions (atoms with an electrical charge) such as those of calcium or magnesium; mineral grains (sand) that cannot be broken down chemically, such as quartz; and a variety of minerals containing sheet-like layers of silicate and alumina (silicon and aluminum oxides)—the minerals that are often the main constituents of clays.

A river carrying these minerals first deposits the sand, and then the clay, while the dissolved ions pass out into the sea, where some are absorbed by living organisms and used to construct protective shells and rigid skeletons. When the creatures die, the shells and bones again become part of the rock cycle, building up great thicknesses of limestone.

Igneous rocks are chemically far more complex than are sedimentary rocks, but are texturally simpler. The slower the magma cools, the larger are the crystals that form within it. If it cools too quickly it may not crystallize at all, forming instead a super-cooled liquid, or glass. A plutonic igneous rock—one cooled deep underground—is coarse grained; a volcanic rock is fine grained. A rock can, however, have both large and small crystals, testifying to a more complex history.

The most striking feature of Earth magmas is their uniformity. With few exceptions, they are all rich in silica. The greater the silica content, the higher their viscosity (resistance to flowing). Those rich in silica tend to solidify underground. The complex chemistry of magmas comes from the melting of the variety of minerals making up the mantle.

The chemistry of metamorphic rocks is like that of their igneous or sedimentary starting materials. As these become more deeply buried and heated, the constituent minerals grow larger. A mudstone metamorphoses to a slate, then to a schist and finally a gneiss. The "slatiness" or "schistosity" of these rocks is provided by micas and other sheet-shaped mineral grains. Such minerals require abundant alumina to form. If this is not present in the starting rock, it will be metamorphosed into more granular material.

A record in the rocks
Rocks contain an unwritten history of the Earth. Sedimentary rocks hold information about climates of the past and fossil relics of organisms that lived when the sediments were laid down. Igneous rocks record periods of crustal activity that relate to the movements of the continents; and metamorphic rocks indicate periods of uplift that exposed previously buried rock. From such information it is possible to construct a geological time scale. Although fossils are a useful means of correlating one pile of sediment with another, good fossils go back only 600 million years. Earlier organisms are believed to have been soft bodied and were not easily fossilized.

The only complete time scale comes from the radioactive "clocks" in many igneous and metamorphic rocks. Certain forms of natural elements, or isotopes, are unstable and emit energy. By measuring the amount of "daughter" atoms that have been formed by the radioactive decay of a larger "parent" atom, it is possible to determine the age of a rock and events in the history of its formation. The dating of rocks from radioactive decay has thus enabled a true time scale for the history of the Earth to be constructed.

Earth's Minerals

Minerals are the basic ingredients of the Earth, from crust to core. They make up not only the ores on which man has based much of his technology, and the gemstones which he values for their beauty or rarity, but also the components of rocks, pebbles and sands. Two million years ago minerals – in the form of stones – provided early man with his first tools. Today, man's use of minerals, such as uranium for nuclear power or silicon for microcomputers, is revolutionizing our lives.

SUBSTANCES OF THE EARTH
Minerals are made up of chemical elements, arranged according to various crystal structures. Man's chief interest in minerals has been as precious stones and, increasingly, as a resource in the form of useful metal ores. But of the 2,500 minerals so far identified, the majority are rock-forming substances—the material components of the Earth. Relatively infrequent geological processes over vast time spans are responsible for concentrating minerals dispersed through rocks into richer deposits, and it is these economically important ores that have provided man with his supply of workable mineral resources through the ages.

Minerals, and the metals derived from them, have always had an inherent fascination for man, as well as providing the basis for his technology. Gold in particular, which was worked in Egypt as early as 5000 BC, still retains its mysterious attraction. Because of its chemical inactivity it is imperishable, immutable and nontarnishing, and has served as the basis of world trade for almost 2,000 years. Copper has been smelted since the early part of the third millennium BC, to be replaced eventually by harder alloys. Arsenical bronze, for instance, bridged the gap between the Copper and Bronze ages (bronze is an alloy of copper and tin). More complex technology was needed for the working of iron, which began c.1100 BC, whereas brass (an alloy of copper and zinc) did not appear until Roman times.

Although the steel-making process had its roots in antiquity, it was not until the nineteenth century that new techniques changed man's attitude to minerals. Before the modern age of plastics, the capacity to produce steel was the hallmark of industrial development, and together with coal it formed the linchpin of western industrial progress. Today minerals have come to assume their greatest importance as exploitable—but nonrenewable—resources.

Components of the Earth

The terms "mineral," "rock" and "stone" are often used interchangeably, but in fact all rocks are made up of minerals, which are natural and usually inorganic substances with a particular chemical makeup and crystal structure.

Certain stones have properties that satisfy basic human needs for beauty and color. Some possess a flashing sparkle, others have special optical characteristics such as refraction and dispersion ("fire"), or contain inclusions that give rise to phenomena like the "asterism" found in opals and sapphires. About 100 such minerals are classified as gemstones and valued for their beauty, durability or rarity.

Most minerals occur as either pure (ore) deposits or mixed with other minerals in rocks—an economically important difference. Their exploitation has been vastly extended in recent decades through our greater understanding of the mineral-forming processes that take place in the Earth's crust. All mineral ores result from a separation process in which a mineral-rich solution separates into its various components according to the temperature, pressure and composition of the original mixture. Precipitation is the simplest kind of separation, as when calcium salts separate from circulating groundwater to yield stalactites and stalagmites in caves, in the form of calcite crystals.

Mineral formation

Most deposits of metallic ores originate in the intense physicochemical activity that takes place at the boundaries between the Earth's huge crustal plates. Very high concentrations of minerals occur in association with warm solutions coming from springs in the seabed, notably along the spreading zones in the southeastern Pacific Ocean, the Red Sea, the African Rift Valley and the Gulf of Aden. This process also occurs in shallow-water volcanic areas, as near the Mediterranean island of Thira and the submarine volcano of Bahu Wuhu, Indonesia. Cold seawater penetrates the crust and leaches out minerals from the basalts of these "hot spots," returning to the surface of the seabed as hot springs. The minerals then precipitate in the cold, oxygen-rich seawater.

Mineral separation may also occur when part of the deep-seated magma forces its way into the upper layers of the Earth's crust and begins to cool. The great plugs of magma that form the

MINERALS FROM THE OCEAN
Ocean sediments that originally came from land contain organic matter that absorbs the oxygen in the sediments. As a result, solutions of minerals such as manganese and iron are released, seeping upwards through the debris. When they come in contact with the oxygen in seawater they are precipitated, condensing into so-called "manganese" nodules in amounts that may eventually prove to be a valuable source of mineral wealth. Metallic elements also accumulate very slowly from the seawater itself.

rock kimberlite, in which diamonds are found, must have come from a depth of at least 100 km (62 miles). If the magma reaches the surface through fissures as extrusive rocks, the pattern of minerals in the surrounding rocks is also changed by a process called contact metamorphism, with various bands or zones of minerals occurring at various distances from the contact boundary.

As rocks become weathered, mineral concentrations that resist weathering may be left. Alternatively, all the weathered materials may be transported by running water, becoming concentrated as they are sorted out according to their different densities. Gold is the best-known example of this alluvial type of mineral deposit—known as a placer deposit. If the minerals are washed into the sea, they may be distributed over deltas or over the seafloor, but when this happens the concentrations of minerals are usually very low.

Mineral energy

Fossil fuels such as coal and petroleum are major mineral sources of energy. But with the twentieth-century discovery of nuclear fission, uranium also became an important energy resource. The richest deposits occur, as with other minerals, as veins deposited in fractures by hot-water movements. These deposits, consisting of a uranium oxide called pitchblende, were the first to be mined, for example at Joachimstal (Czechoslovakia), Great Bear Lake (Canada) and Katanga (Zaire). Weathered products of such rocks, redeposited as sandstones, also contain uranium, as in Wyoming (USA) and in the Niger basin. In many respects uranium is similar to silver: both occur with similar geological abundance, their ores are enriched about 2,000 times during processing, and the metals are recovered by using chemicals to dissolve the metal selectively and then by "stripping" the metal from the solution.

METAL-RICH BRINES
Scientists have recently discovered deep hollows on the floor of the Red Sea and other similar enclosed basins connected with rift valleys. These prevent normal circulation of water and form undersea pools of hot, high-density brines. The brines contain sulphur and other minerals in very high concentrations, and overlie sediments rich in metals such as zinc, copper, lead, silver and gold. Hot springs in fissures below the pools escape into them, carrying up solutions of the metallic minerals which combine with sulphur to create a concentrated broth rich in metals.

METALS FROM THE INTERIOR
Rift zones on the bed of the Pacific Ocean, where the Earth's crustal plates are slowly separating, provide sensational visual evidence of metallic ores in the actual process of creation. Seawater percolates through the fractured surface to the molten rock below, where it leaches out the soluble metallic components, erupting in superheated hydrothermal springs to form geysers of mineral-rich water. Oxygen in the cold water of the seafloor causes the minerals to condense out, precipitating in plumes of dark powder. Continental drift, collision and sedimentation over millions of years will eventually incorporate these deposits into the landmasses.

Uranium, chromium and many other minerals are widely distributed through the Earth's crust, but they are valuable as a resource only if the technology exists to extract them economically. In mineral development, the high-grade ores are worked out first, followed by the poorer deposits if demand remains or increases. With uranium, the low-grade deposits contain far more of the total quantity of the mineral, but these are worth exploiting because of uranium's importance and because the technology exists. Chromium, on the other hand, is currently extracted only from high-grade ores. Large deposits of low-grade ores do exist, but technology for exploiting them economically has not yet been developed.

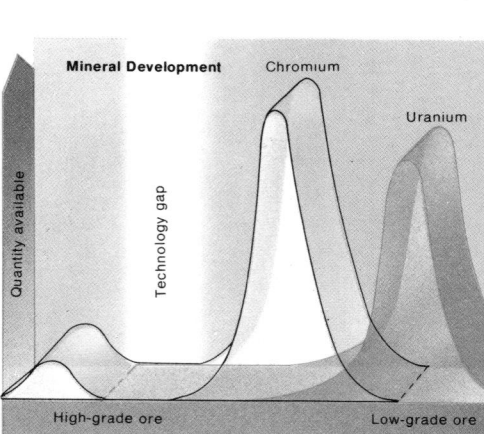

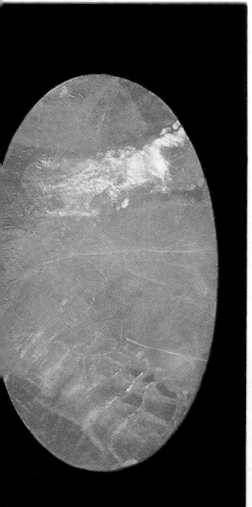

Opal (above), a silica mineral, often contains impurities which give it a range of colors. These flash and change according to the angle of vision, a result of the interference of light along minute internal cracks in the stone.

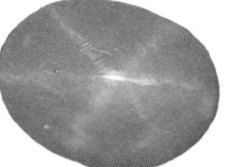

Sapphire gemstone (left), a form of the dull gray mineral carborundum (below), owes its color to inclusions of titanium and iron. If cut with a rounded top it gives a starry effect known as asterism.

MINERALS IN THE SERVICE OF MAN

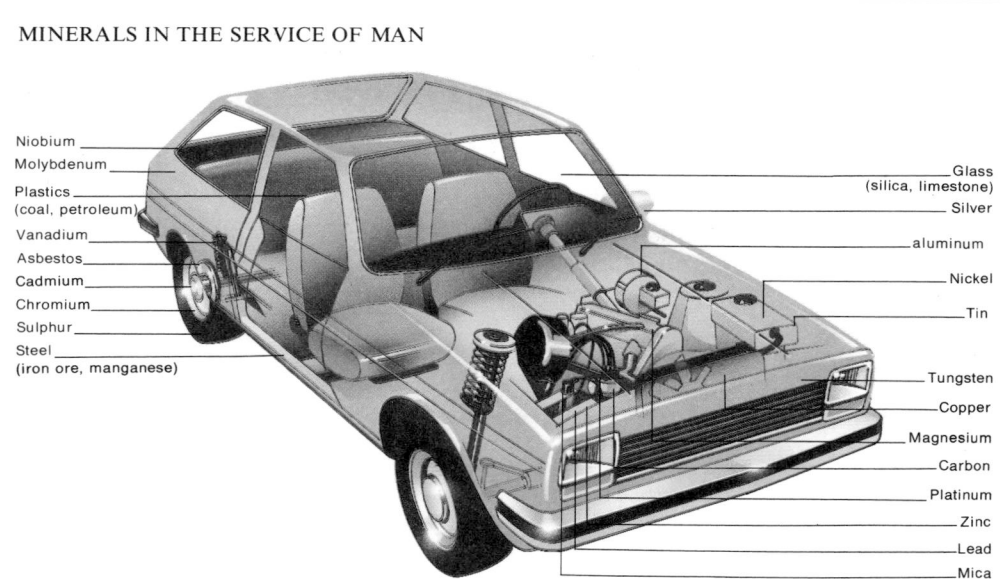

Niobium
Molybdenum
Plastics (coal, petroleum)
Vanadium
Asbestos
Cadmium
Chromium
Sulphur
Steel (iron ore, manganese)

Glass (silica, limestone)
Silver
aluminum
Nickel
Tin
Tungsten
Copper
Magnesium
Carbon
Platinum
Zinc
Lead
Mica

The modern automobile makes use of a whole alphabet of minerals in its composition, from aluminum to zinc. The importance of plastics, made from petroleum and coal, is constantly increasing, but the need for specialist metals is as great as ever. Cadmium, for example, is used in electro-plating; carbon goes into making electrodes and graphite seals; transistors and electric contact points require platinum; sulphur is present in vulcanizing rubber and lubricants; lamp filaments contain tungsten. Of basic metals, iron and steel still account for almost three-quarters of the total quantity of the metals used; lead for 1.19 percent and copper for only 0.94 percent. But the amount of useful metal is often a small fraction of the rock that has to be mined and processed. A copper ore, for instance, only yields about 0.7 percent of metal, so to equip a single car's radiator with copper well over one and a half tonnes of rock will have to be excavated, of which 99.3 percent will simply be discarded.

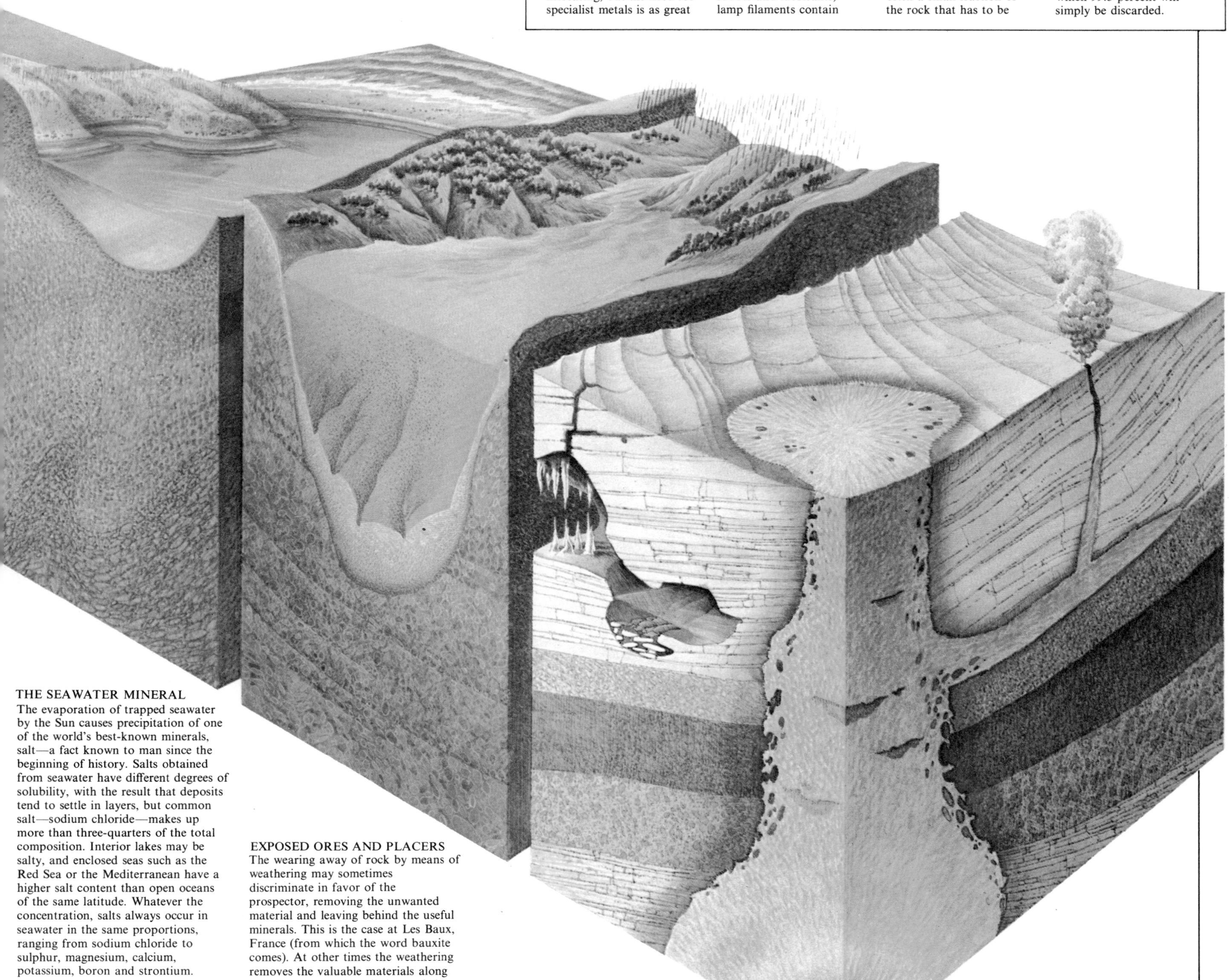

THE SEAWATER MINERAL
The evaporation of trapped seawater by the Sun causes precipitation of one of the world's best-known minerals, salt—a fact known to man since the beginning of history. Salts obtained from seawater have different degrees of solubility, with the result that deposits tend to settle in layers, but common salt—sodium chloride—makes up more than three-quarters of the total composition. Interior lakes may be salty, and enclosed seas such as the Red Sea or the Mediterranean have a higher salt content than open oceans of the same latitude. Whatever the concentration, salts always occur in seawater in the same proportions, ranging from sodium chloride to sulphur, magnesium, calcium, potassium, boron and strontium.

EXPOSED ORES AND PLACERS
The wearing away of rock by means of weathering may sometimes discriminate in favor of the prospector, removing the unwanted material and leaving behind the useful minerals. This is the case at Les Baux, France (from which the word bauxite comes). At other times the weathering removes the valuable materials along with the rest, so that all the eroded rock is carried down by the movement of water until it eventually reaches the sea. So-called "placer" deposits occur where the heavier particles of minerals have become separated, accumulating as deposits of mineral sand and concentrating in riverbeds or estuaries. Gold is the best-known example of this alluvial type of deposit, but tin and other minerals are also found as placers in many parts of the world.

UNDERGROUND PROCESSES
Limestone rock, formed from calcium carbonate, is dissolved by seeping water containing carbon dioxide from the air and the soil. The subsurface water may create vast networks of underground caverns in the limestone, and as the water slowly evaporates it leaves deposits of calcium carbonate, forming stalactites and stalagmites.

VOLCANOES AND MINERALS
Volcanic magma penetrating the Earth's crust may form important mineral deposits. On cooling, the heavy or "basic" minerals are the first to crystallize and sink to the bottom. The minerals may also separate out chemically. The intense heat affects surrounding rocks, causing mineral changes in banded zones.

Earthquakes and Volcanoes

Earthquakes and volcanic eruptions challenge man's faith in the stability of the world, but these violent releases of energy testify to our planet's ever-dynamic activity. Earthquakes are caused when the rigid crust is driven past or over itself by underlying movements that extend deep into the Earth's mantle. Stress builds up until it exceeds the strength of the rocks, when there follows a sudden movement. Volcanoes occur where molten rock, or magma, from the mantle forces its way to the surface through lines of weakness in the crust, often at the lithospheric plate boundaries.

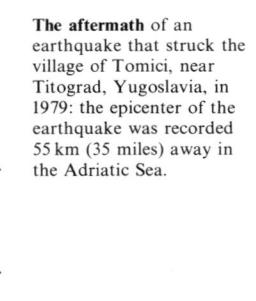

MODIFIED MERCALLI SCALE

I Earthquake not felt, except by a few.

II Felt on upper floors by few at rest. Swinging of suspended objects.

III Quite noticeable indoors, especially on upper floors. Standing cars may sway.

IV Felt indoors. Dishes and windows rattle, standing cars rock. Like a heavy truck hitting a building.

V Felt by nearly all, many wakened. Fragile objects broken, plaster cracked, trees and poles disturbed.

VI Felt by all, many run outdoors. Slight damage, heavy furniture moved, some fallen plaster.

VII People run outdoors. Average homes slightly damaged, substandard ones badly damaged. Noticed by car drivers.

VIII Well-built structures slightly damaged, others badly damaged. Chimneys and monuments collapse. Car drivers disturbed.

IX Well-designed buildings badly damaged, substantial ones greatly damaged, shifted off foundations. Conspicuous ground cracks open up.

X Well-built wood-structures destroyed, masonry structures destroyed. Rails bent, ground cracked, landslides. Rivers overflow.

XI Few masonry structures left standing. Bridges and underground pipes destroyed. Broad cracks in ground. Earth slumps.

XII Damage total. Ground waves seem like sea waves. Line of sight disturbed, objects thrown into the air.

The Earth's crust generally breaks along pre-existing planes of weakness, or faults. Such breakages give rise to an "explosive" release of stress that is familiar to surface dwellers as the vibrations of an earthquake.

Not all earthquakes, however, take place along pre-existing faults, otherwise no new faults would be generated. Many recent large earthquakes have been located immediately north of the Tonga Islands because a giant rent is developing through previously unbroken ocean crust. The crust to the south is being swallowed down into the mantle and that to the north continues at the surface to be subducted farther to the west. Once a fault has formed, however, it remains a plane of weakness even though the two sides tend to become partly resealed, so that when movement does occur there is a considerable release of energy.

Measuring earthquakes

Earthquakes are quantified in two ways. The actual energy release (magnitude) at the source of the earthquake (the focus) is measured on the Richter scale, a log scale where every unit of increase represents approximately 24 times the energy release. A magnitude 7 earthquake is roughly equivalent to the explosion of a one megaton nuclear bomb (one million tonnes of TNT). The strongest earthquake recorded this century was a magnitude 8.5 event in Alaska in 1964. Earthquakes as they are perceived are measured on the Modified Mercalli scale by their impact in terms of the amount of surface destruction. A medium-size earthquake under a town, such as that beneath Tangshan, China, in 1976 which killed more than a quarter of a million people, might record higher on the Mercalli scale than the Alaska event, which affected a large but sparsely populated region.

The magnitude of the earthquake depends on the frictional resistance that has to be overcome before movement can take place. This total frictional resistance, therefore, increases with the area of the fault plane. So the bigger the fault plane that moves, the bigger the earthquake. The largest earthquakes occur on wide fault planes that dip at a very shallow angle and can pass through a great deal of relatively shallow crust that will not deform plastically.

Earthquakes are unlikely to occur where rocks are plastic and can flow to accommodate the buildup of stress. Some faults, such as the San Andreas Fault in the western United States, pass from brittle rocks into a plastic zone at depths of only a few kilometers. Therefore, the next San Francisco earthquake cannot be as great as the 1964 Alaskan one, although this may be of little comfort to the potential victims. Along some sections of the San Andreas Fault the plastic zone comes directly to the surface, and motion occurs without large earthquakes.

Earthquake prediction is still in its infancy, although it is recognized that a number of phenomena may occur before a major earthquake—the ground may swell, the electrical conductivity of groundwater may change, and the water height of wells may rapidly alter.

How volcanoes are formed

Volcanoes, although spectacular, are safer than earthquakes. While an average of 20,000 people are killed each year in earthquakes, only about 400 are killed by volcanoes; and many of the victims die from starvation due to crop failure after heavy ash falls.

Volcanoes are formed when molten rock (magma) escapes through the Earth's crust to the Earth's surface. Most of this magma forms within the upper mantle between 30 and 100 km (20–60 miles) underground. The temperature increases with depth between 20° and 50°C per

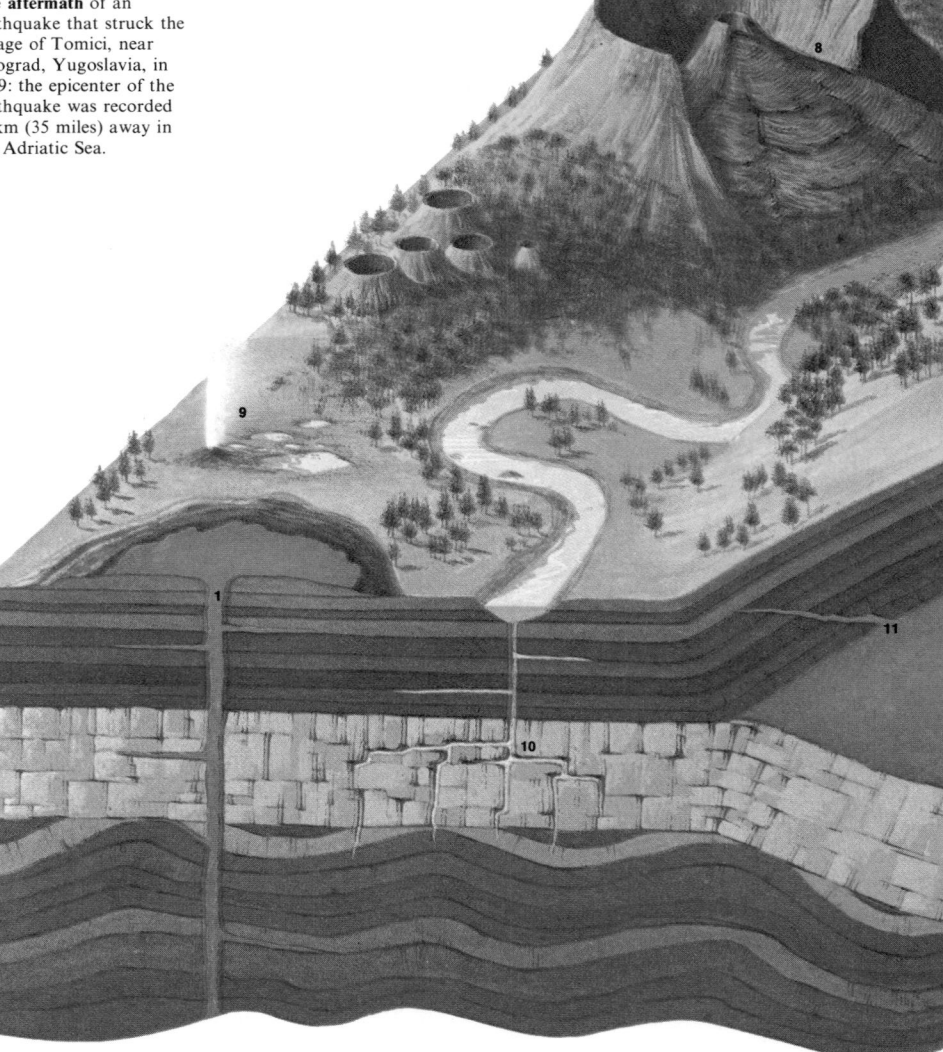

The aftermath of an earthquake that struck the village of Tomici, near Titograd, Yugoslavia, in 1979: the epicenter of the earthquake was recorded 55 km (35 miles) away in the Adriatic Sea.

Earthquakes occur when slabs of the Earth's crust move in relation to each other. The focus of the earthquake is the point where movement occurs (1), and the epicenter is the point on the surface directly above it (2). Blue lines represent zones of surface damage as measured on the Modified Mercalli scale.

km (35°–90°F per 3,250 ft) from the crust to the mantle, but even so the rocks are normally not hot enough to melt.

Basaltic magmas, found along mid-ocean spreading ridges and oceanic islands, are formed when hot, deep mantle rises and, on reduction of pressure, begins to melt. Such "basic" magmas generally have low silica and water content, a high temperature and flow easily—often, as in Hawaii, "quietly erupting" to form volcanoes with very gentle gradients known as shield volcanoes. Silica-rich magma forms under continental crust. Ocean crust sucks up water after it has formed at the oceanic spreading ridges and much of this water later becomes taken with the crust down a subduction zone, where it helps to lower the melting point of both mantle and ocean-crust rocks.

By the time these magmas reach the surface they are cooler and have a higher water content than basalts. These "intermediate" or andesite magmas are also more viscous (less willing to

flow) because they contain more silica. The eruptions are more explosive as the water and other gases dissolve out of the magma as it approaches the surface, and the lava remains close to the volcanic vent, building up the archetypal steep-sided conical stratified volcano, such as Mount Fujiyama in Japan. Sometimes the conical form may be destroyed in catastrophic eruptions, as has happened at Mount St Helens in the United States.

The most violent of all eruptions are found where magmas from the mantle have penetrated and melted a great thickness of continental rocks, so as to create highly viscous silica- and water-rich "acid" magmas. As such magmas approach the surface they may turn into a red-hot froth that blasts out from fissures to cover enormous areas in a volcanic material known as ignimbrite. The most extensive eruption known to have occurred in the past 2,000 years was probably on Mount Taupo, on North Island, New Zealand. In AD 150 it discharged some

THE VIOLENT EARTH

Large, destructive earthquakes occur somewhere in the world approximately every two weeks, but fortunately most take place under the sea, where they cause little harm. Most of the millions of small earthquakes that occur on Earth pass unnoticed. Volcanoes are the most impressive display of the Earth's dynamic activity and are also responsible for forming the starting materials of the Earth's crust.

ASH FALLOUT

Some volcanic eruptions are so violent that ash is thrown high into the atmosphere to be carried away on the prevailing winds. Krakatoa in 1883 distributed ash around the world. The map shows the limits of airborne ash deposited by the eruption of Quizapu in Chile in 1932, the bulk of which fell within 10 km (6 miles).

Volcanoes are fed by magma, or molten rock, that wells up from deep in the Earth's mantle. The magma can either rise directly to the surface through fissures in the Earth's crust (1) and pour forth gently and continuously to form a shield volcano, or lava plateau, or be stored in a magma chamber (2) that swells up before erupting to the surface. To form the traditional cone-shaped stratified volcano, magma reaches the surface through a vent (3) and spews forth as gases, ash and lava (4, 5). Eventually the conical shape is made up of alternate layers of ash consolidated by lava. As rock and other debris build up around the main vent, and pressure increases, flank vents (6) open up other pathways to the surface, thereby creating parasitic cones (7).

When a volcano erupts violently the surrounding countryside can be devastated. The power of the blast flattens trees, poisonous gases kill all forms of wildlife, ash falls damage property and crops and can create mudflows and avalanches, and lava pouring from the vent can dam rivers to create floods.

Other special features of a volcanic landscape include extinct craters, which sometimes fill with water to form lakes, and calderas (8). Calderas are created either by vast explosions or when the magma chamber and vent are emptied of magma and the volcano collapses in on itself. Magma may later force itself through the collapsed debris so as to form new active cones on the floor of the caldera.

In volcanic regions there are other forms of volcanic activity. Water may seep down to be heated by the hot magma and reach the surface some distance away as a geyser (9) or hot spring, or be mixed with soil and ejected as a mud volcano. Some vents emit gases and steam, and these are called fumaroles. Geysers are created when water is heated in underground passageways or caverns (10). Water is periodically converted to superheated steam, which builds up pressure until it is able to rush up a vent and throw steam and water great distances into the air.

Not all magma reaches the surface: some cools and solidifies underground to form volcanic intrusions. Dykes (11) are sheets of cooled magma that have cut through strata of overlying rock, sills (12) are magma sheets injected between strata, and laccoliths (13) are large lens-shaped pools of solidified magma. Years later, when weathering and erosion have removed the overlying rock, these intrusions become features of the landscape.

10 cu km ($2\frac{1}{2}$ cu miles) of ignimbrite in about 15 minutes—spreading across the landscape at more than 100 m (330 ft) per second.

Other more explosive eruptions, such as that of Krakatoa in 1883, or Santorini more than 3,000 years ago, can result in the collapse of the volcano into the underlying magma chamber after it has become partly emptied during an eruption to create a caldera. Many of the largest explosions are caused by the mixing of water with magma—at Krakatoa the cataclysm probably resulted from seawater breaking into the magma and flashing straight to steam, thereby allowing more seawater to enter until the chain reaction could set off more energy than the most powerful nuclear bomb.

Predicting at least the approximate time of an eruption is relatively easy. Small earthquakes indicate that a new batch of magma is rising toward the surface. Many volcanoes also swell prior to an eruption and release gases that indicate the arrival of new magma.

The Oceans

Earth is the water planet. Of all the planets of the solar system only the Earth has abundant liquid water, and 97 percent of this surface water is found in the seas and oceans. The water of the oceans appears to be passive and unchanging, whereas the rain and rivers seem active, but this is far from true. In reality the oceans are a turmoil of giant sluggish rivers – far larger than any of the land rivers – and of circulating surface currents that are driven by the prevailing winds.

No topographic map of the Earth can be drawn unless there is some kind of base line from which to measure depths and heights. This base line has always been taken as the level of the sea, yet the sea is perpetually changing level. One can choose some kind of average to call "sea level," but even today different countries have defined that base line in different ways. The currents found within the sea itself can also give the water surface a slope—the calm Sargasso Sea off the northern coast of South America is, for example, about 1.5 m (5 ft) higher than the water to the west adjacent to the Gulf Stream.

Waves

The changes in the level of the sea, at its surface, provide the most familiar image of motion within the waters. Various changes take place over many different time periods, but the most rapid are those that we call waves.

Waves are produced by the wind moving over the water and catching on the surface. They can move at between 15 and 100 km/hr (10–60 mph) and wave crests may be separated by up to 300 m (1,000 ft) in the open ocean. In general, the greater the wavelength, the faster the wave's speed and the farther the distance traveled by the wave. Waves that have traveled a long way from the winds that created them are known as swell. Without the wind continually pushing them they become symmetrical and smooth. Wind waves produce spilling breakers more like the rapids of a mountain torrent, whereas swell produces giant plunging breakers.

A combination of strong winds and low atmospheric pressure associated with storms can cause yet another kind of wave, known as a storm surge. A storm surge is formed by the water being driven ahead of the wind, and rising as the atmospheric pressure weighing down on the water decreases. Where storms drive water into funnel-shaped coasts, the water can rise more than 10 m (33 ft) above normal sea level, flooding large areas of low-lying land at the head of the bay. Venice, the Netherlands and Bangladesh have been particularly subject to destructive storm surges. Other catastrophic changes in sea level have their origins in the seabed. These are tsunamis (Japanese for "high-water in the harbor") and are generally triggered by underwater earthquakes that suddenly raise or lower large areas of the seafloor.

Tides

As the Earth orbits around the Sun the water in the oceans experiences a changing pull of gravity from both the Moon and the Sun. The Sun is overhead once a day, and because the Moon is itself orbiting the Earth, it is overhead once every 24 hours 50 minutes. The pull of gravity from the Sun is less than half that from the Moon, and so it is the Moon that sets the rhythm of the water movements we call tides. The variation in gravitational pull from the Moon is extremely small, however, and even if the whole of the Earth were covered with deep water a tide of only about 30 cm (12 in) would be produced, rushing around the world keeping pace with the circling Moon. Yet the tides in shallow coastal regions are often very much higher than this—for example, up to 18 m (60 ft) in the Bay of Fundy, Canada. The seas and bays with the highest tides are located where the whole mass of water is resonating—rebounding backwards and forwards like water in a bath, as the smaller tides in the outlying oceans push it twice each day.

The Bay of Fundy experiences a particularly high tidal range because it happens to have a resonant frequency—a range of movement— very close to the 12¼-hour frequency between tides. Large enclosed seas such as the Mediterranean have very small tides because there is no outside push from an ocean to set them resonating. In contrast, where water movement associated with the tides passes through a narrow channel it can produce tidal currents of up to 30 km/hr (19 mph), such as the famous maelstrom of northern Norway.

After these relatively short-lived disturbances the sea returns to its normal, or at least to its average, level again. When the total volume of free water at the Earth's surface alters, or when the shapes of the ocean basins vary, the sea level itself may start to wander.

How does the volume of water vary? It can be buried in rocks—but the steam clouds above volcanoes return such water so it is normally recycled rather than lost. Some vapor can be broken down through radiation in the upper atmosphere and the hydrogen lost to outer space, but this is relatively insignificant. Or it can be frozen and stacked up on land in the form of ice—this is significant as we are still living in an ice age. The lowest ice-age sea levels produced beaches at about 130 m (430 ft) below present sea level, and the low-lying coastal regions of that period have now become flooded to form the continental shelves.

The salt content of the oceans

Average ocean water contains about 35 parts per 1,000 of salts which include 14 elements in concentrations greater than 1 part per million— the most abundant being sodium and chlorine. Where there is considerable surface evaporation, for example in enclosed seas such as the Dead Sea, the salt concentration builds up and the water becomes denser. Where the sea-surface is turning to ice the salt also becomes concentrated in the water.

The coldest, saltiest ocean water comes from the Antarctic. As it is also the densest it hugs the ocean bottom as it flows northwards, reaching as far as the latitudes of Spain. A similar current from the Arctic is slightly lighter and therefore rides above it—but traveling southwards, as far as the southern Atlantic. A second slightly lighter body of Antarctic water rides above the Arctic water—again traveling northwards. Where these water movements meet each other they rise up, bringing to the surface oxygenated water that can support a profusion of life in oceans that have been compared to a desert because of their lack of biological activity. Unlikely as it seems, it is the icy, stormy, polar waters that provide the lungs of the oceans.

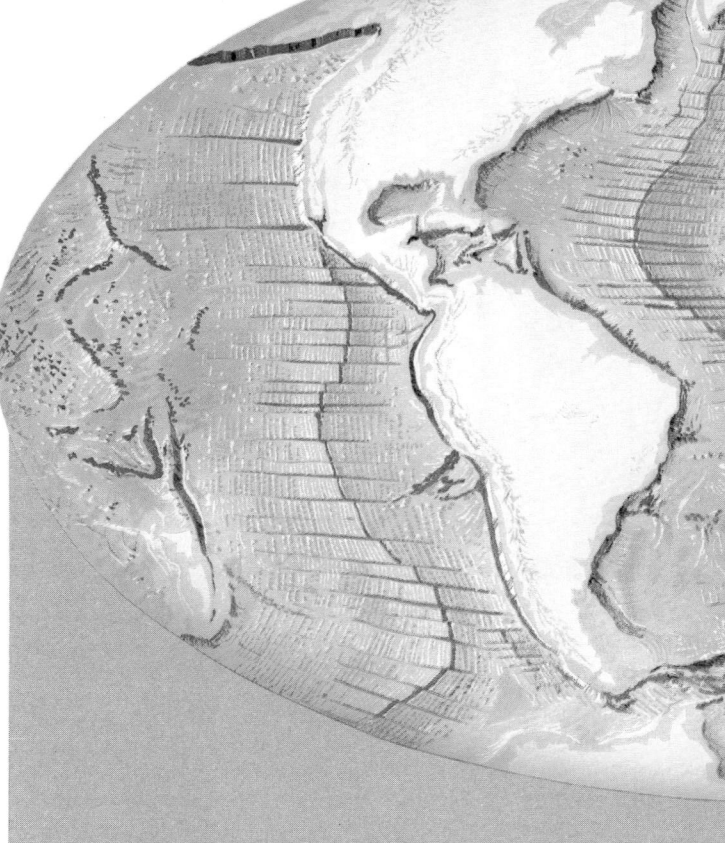

Both the Sun and the Moon exert gravitational pull on the water in the oceans, but the pull of the Sun is less than half that of the Moon. It is the Moon, therefore, that sets the rhythm of the tides. Because the Moon orbits the Earth every 24 hours and 50 minutes, the time of high or low tide advances approximately an hour each day. When the Moon is in its first and last quarters (1, 3) it forms a right angle with the Earth and the Sun and the gravitational fields are opposed, thus causing only a small difference between high and low tide. These are called neap tides. When the Sun, Moon and Earth lie in a straight line (2, 4), at the full and the new Moon, then the high tides become higher and the low tides lower. These are the spring tides. The graph illustrates tidal range over a period of a month.

Depth in meters
0 1 2 3 4 5 6 7 8

Neap tide

Spring tide

Neap tide

Spring tide

Depth in meters

0
1,000
2,000
3,000
4,000
5,000
6,000
7,000
8,000

1 Continent
2 Continental shelf
3 Continental slope
4 Continental rise
5 Submarine canyon
6 Abyssal plain
7 Abyssal hills
8 Mid-ocean ridge
9 Oceanic trench
10 Island arc
11 Continental sea

THE CHANGING OCEANS

Nearly two-thirds of the Earth's surface is covered by the seas and oceans and this great expanse of water is continually in movement. The most familiar movements are waves formed by the wind and the rising and falling tides that respond to the position of the Moon. But even greater movements take place. Currents driven by prevailing winds form whirlpools an ocean in width, and below the surface flow great rivers of colder water. Sea level is also rising as ice melts from the polar caps.

Cl 55.0%
Na 30.6%
SO₄ 7.7%
Mg 3.7%
Ca 1.5%
K 1.5%

Seawater is about 96% pure water and the rest is made up of dissolved salts. Many elements are present in minute quantities, but only chlorine (Cl), sodium (Na), sulphate (SO₄), magnesium (Mg), calcium (Ca) and potassium (K) appear in concentrations of more than 1% of the total dissolved salts.

Polar easterlies
Southwesterlies
Northeast trades
Southeast trades
Northwesterlies
Polar easterlies

60° N
30° N
0°
30° S
60° S

B

The surface currents of the world's oceans (A) are driven by the prevailing winds (B). The winds and the spinning motion of the Earth drive the currents into gyres—massive whirlpools the width of an ocean. These gyres draw warm water away from the Equator and pull cold polar waters towards it. The centers of gyres are characterized by areas of high pressure, around which winds circulate. Because the Earth is spinning, gyres formed in the northern hemisphere rotate in a clockwise direction, whereas those of the southern hemisphere turn anticlockwise. In all, there are five major gyres, made up of the 38 major named currents. The formation of warm (red) and cold (blue) surface currents is not difficult to understand, given the regions from which they flow. However, even in temperate and subtropical regions, the warm waters of the oceans' surfaces have a permanent layer of cold water beneath them. This cold layer has been formed in the polar regions, where, as the ocean waters have been chilled, they have sunk and then spread out into all the other major ocean basins of the world. The warm subtropical and temperate waters float like an oil slick, from 10 m to 550 m (33–1,900 ft) thick, on top of this cold layer. There is very little mixing between the two layers because the warm water is lighter than the cold water.

Much of the Earth's water is locked up as ice and stacked on the land. As the ice melts the sea level rises. Only 20,000 years ago the sea level was a full 100 m (330 ft) lower than it is today, and the continental shelves were dry land. About 10,000 years ago the sea level was rising as fast as 3 cm (1 in) each year. Today the melting ice is causing the sea level to rise about 1 mm (0.04 in) each year: only a small increment, but if all the ice melted, the sea level would rise by about 60 m (197 ft) and would flood many of the world's major cities.

< 60 m
> 60 m
• Major cities

The seabed, more uniform than the land surface, also contains a landscape of underwater features that resemble the plains, valleys and mountains of the continents. Off the edge of continents lie the flat, shallow continental shelves, which are bounded by the steeper incline of the continental slope, which meets the true ocean floor at the continental rise.

Here deep submarine canyons may be found. These seem to be in a process of continual erosion from turbidity currents. River water pouring into major estuaries and carrying sediment can also scour out the slope—especially during periods of low sea level. The abyssal plain is rarely interrupted by volcanic hills and

mountains. The largest chains are at the mid-ocean ridge, where two crustal plates are moving apart and new ocean floor is being created. At some ocean margins deep trough-shaped valleys or trenches are the sites of ocean floor consumption at a subduction zone. The volcanic island arcs that form behind it sometimes isolate a continental sea.

TSUNAMIS

Tsunamis are generated by massive underwater earthquakes (A) and are common around the Pacific. They can travel at more than 700 km/hr (435 mph) and individual waves may occur at intervals of 15 minutes, or 200 km (125 miles). Low-lying atolls of the Pacific have extremely steep sides underwater, and are generally unharmed, but the gently shelving islands such as Hawaii slow down the tsunami and build it into a giant wave 30 m (100 ft) or more in height. This map plots the hourly position of a tsunami that originated south of Alaska.

A

Landscape-makers: Water

Of all the natural agents of erosion at work on the Earth's surface, water is probably the most powerful. Many of the finer details of the landscape, from the contouring of hills and valleys to the broad spread of plains, are the work of water. In recent years we have come to understand more fully the subtle factors at work in a river, for example, as it deepens mountain gorges or builds up sedimentary layers in its approach to the sea. The full force of a waterfall, the instability of a meandering stream, the multiple layering of river terraces – all are features of this most versatile landscape-maker.

Ninety-seven percent of the world's water is in the oceans, another two percent is locked up in the ice caps of Greenland and Antarctica, which leaves one percent only on the surface of Earth, under the ground and in the air. The importance of this one percent is, however, inestimable: most life forms could not exist without it, and yet at the same time many are threatened by it, in the form of flood and storm.

The Sun's energy "powers" the evaporation of water from the oceans. Water vapor then circulates in the atmosphere and is precipitated as rain or snow over land, from which it eventually drains back to the oceans. This is the vast, never-ending water cycle. Water in the air that falls as, for example, rain is replaced on average every 12 days. The total water supply remains constant and is believed to be exactly the same as it was 3,000 million years ago.

From raindrops to rivers

Rain falling on to the surface of the land has a great deal of energy: large drops may hit the ground with a terminal velocity of about 35 km/hr (20 mph). If the rain falls on bare soil, it splashes upwards, breaking off and transporting tiny fragments of soil, which come to rest downhill. Vegetation-covered soil breaks the impact and some of the rain may evaporate without ever reaching the ground.

Soil is rather like a sponge. If the holes or pores are very small, rain finds it difficult to penetrate and water runs over the surface of the soil. If the pores are large, rain infiltrates, filling up the pore spaces. Soils that are thin, have low infiltration rates, or already have a lot of water in them, are very susceptible to overland flow. The water may then concentrate into a channel called a gully, and this can have a dramatic effect upon the landscape. The creation of gullies, together with the splash effect, leads to soil erosion. The problem is particularly severe in semiarid regions, where rainfall is sporadic but intense, vegetation is sparse and over-grazing is common. In extreme cases, badlands are formed and by this time recuperation of the land is impossible or is prohibitively expensive.

Where the infiltration rate is high, water percolates through the soil and eventually into the bedrock. There are two well-defined regions, the saturated and the unsaturated. The upper limit of the saturated zone is the water table. Beneath this, water moves at a rate of a few meters a day, but in rocks such as limestone it can move much more quickly along cracks and joints. In most rock types there are some soluble components which are removed as water continually flows through. In limestone regions, the dissolution of calcium salts results in spectacular cave formations.

Groundwater often provides a vital source for domestic consumption. In porous materials, especially chalk, water is stored in large quantities. Such strata are called aquifers and in some areas, notably North Africa, it is believed that water being pumped up now resulted from rainfall when the climate was wetter tens of thousands of years ago.

Water from a number of sources—from overland flow, soil seepage and springs draining aquifers—produces the flow in rivers. Groundwater appears days or even weeks after a heavy rainfall, but overland flow reaches the channel in hours, producing the sudden peak in flow that may cause flooding and occasionally great damage farther downstream. Flood waves usually rise quickly in mountain areas and the wave moves downstream as the river collects more and more water from its tributaries. Eventually, although the volume continues to increase downstream, the flood wave becomes broader and flatter, so it moves more slowly and causes less damage. The most serious floods occur after intense rainfall on already saturated soils where upland rivers issue on to plains.

Rivers at work

The work of a river from its source to its mouth involves three processes, the first of which is erosion. This includes corrasion, or abrasion— the grinding of rocks and stones against the river's banks and bed—which produces both

The hydrological cycle involves a vast transfer of water from sea to air to land, and back to sea again. Water evaporates from the world's oceans and is carried by maritime air masses towards land, where it condenses and is precipitated in the form of rain or snow. This water then evaporates from the ground surface; drains off the surface into lakes, rivers or seas; seeps as groundwater into rivers, lakes or seas; or is taken in by vegetation from the soil and then transpired.

When a river reaches the sea, providing the coast is sheltered and the sea is shallow with no strong currents, its speed is checked and material is deposited (1). The river then forms distributaries (2) in order to continue its flow to the sea. A delta forms its characteristic fan shape (3) as it grows sideways and seawards. A river needs active erosion in its upper course in order to form a delta.

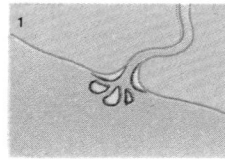
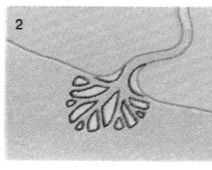
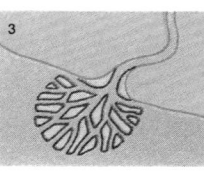

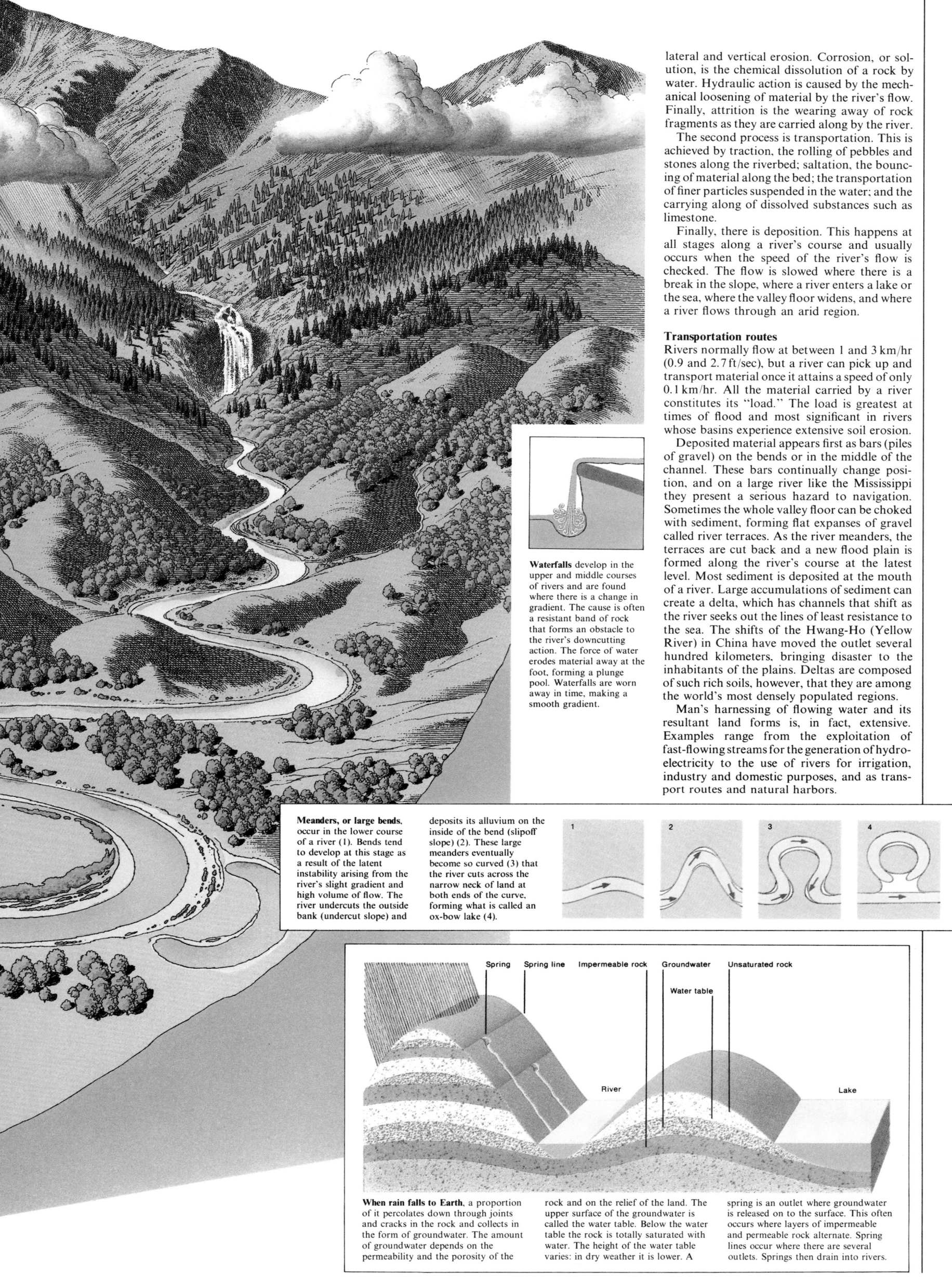

lateral and vertical erosion. Corrosion, or solution, is the chemical dissolution of a rock by water. Hydraulic action is caused by the mechanical loosening of material by the river's flow. Finally, attrition is the wearing away of rock fragments as they are carried along by the river.

The second process is transportation. This is achieved by traction, the rolling of pebbles and stones along the riverbed; saltation, the bouncing of material along the bed; the transportation of finer particles suspended in the water; and the carrying along of dissolved substances such as limestone.

Finally, there is deposition. This happens at all stages along a river's course and usually occurs when the speed of the river's flow is checked. The flow is slowed where there is a break in the slope, where a river enters a lake or the sea, where the valley floor widens, and where a river flows through an arid region.

Transportation routes

Rivers normally flow at between 1 and 3 km/hr (0.9 and 2.7 ft/sec), but a river can pick up and transport material once it attains a speed of only 0.1 km/hr. All the material carried by a river constitutes its "load." The load is greatest at times of flood and most significant in rivers whose basins experience extensive soil erosion.

Deposited material appears first as bars (piles of gravel) on the bends or in the middle of the channel. These bars continually change position, and on a large river like the Mississippi they present a serious hazard to navigation. Sometimes the whole valley floor can be choked with sediment, forming flat expanses of gravel called river terraces. As the river meanders, the terraces are cut back and a new flood plain is formed along the river's course at the latest level. Most sediment is deposited at the mouth of a river. Large accumulations of sediment can create a delta, which has channels that shift as the river seeks out the lines of least resistance to the sea. The shifts of the Hwang-Ho (Yellow River) in China have moved the outlet several hundred kilometers, bringing disaster to the inhabitants of the plains. Deltas are composed of such rich soils, however, that they are among the world's most densely populated regions.

Man's harnessing of flowing water and its resultant land forms is, in fact, extensive. Examples range from the exploitation of fast-flowing streams for the generation of hydroelectricity to the use of rivers for irrigation, industry and domestic purposes, and as transport routes and natural harbors.

Waterfalls develop in the upper and middle courses of rivers and are found where there is a change in gradient. The cause is often a resistant band of rock that forms an obstacle to the river's downcutting action. The force of water erodes material away at the foot, forming a plunge pool. Waterfalls are worn away in time, making a smooth gradient.

Meanders, or large bends, occur in the lower course of a river (1). Bends tend to develop at this stage as a result of the latent instability arising from the river's slight gradient and high volume of flow. The river undercuts the outside bank (undercut slope) and deposits its alluvium on the inside of the bend (slipoff slope) (2). These large meanders eventually become so curved (3) that the river cuts across the narrow neck of land at both ends of the curve, forming what is called an ox-bow lake (4).

When rain falls to Earth, a proportion of it percolates down through joints and cracks in the rock and collects in the form of groundwater. The amount of groundwater depends on the permeability and the porosity of the rock and on the relief of the land. The upper surface of the groundwater is called the water table. Below the water table the rock is totally saturated with water. The height of the water table varies: in dry weather it is lower. A spring is an outlet where groundwater is released on to the surface. This often occurs where layers of impermeable and permeable rock alternate. Spring lines occur where there are several outlets. Springs then drain into rivers.

Landscape-makers: Ice and Snow

A series of glacial periods has punctuated the Earth's history for the last two million years. During the last glacial, the ice covered an area nearly three times larger than that covered by ice sheets and glaciers today. Its remnants are still found in the ice caps of the world: most present-day glacial ice is in Antarctica and Greenland in two great ice sheets which together contain about 97 percent of all the Earth's ice. The rest is in glaciers in Iceland, the Alps and other high mountain chains.

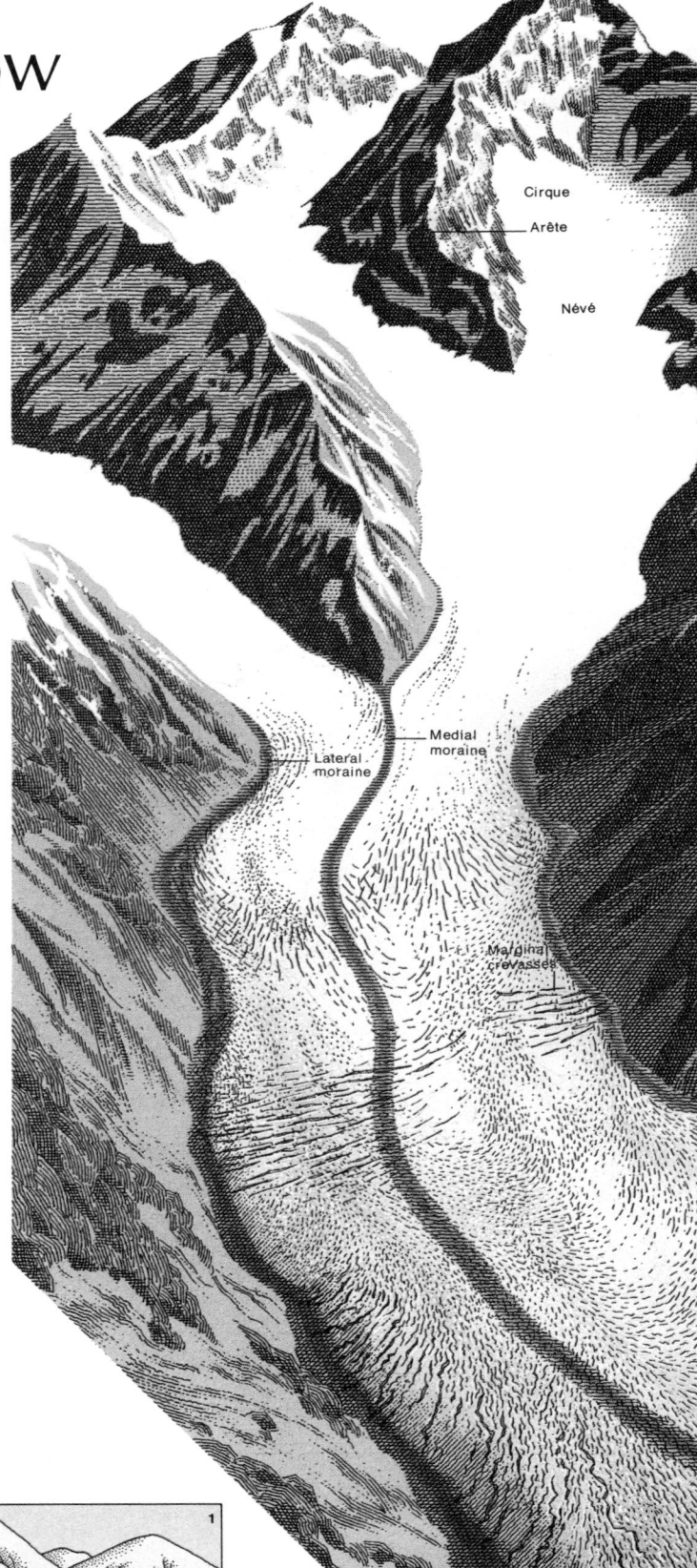

During the Earth's major glacial periods, ice sheets almost as big as that of present-day Antarctica spread over the northern part of North America, reaching as far south as the Ohio River, and over northern Europe as far south as southern England, the Netherlands and southern Poland. Today glacial activity is more restricted, but the mechanisms by which it carves dramatic features of the Earth's landscape remain the same.

Types of glacier

There are six main types of ice mass: cirque glaciers, which occupy basin-shaped depressions in mountain areas; valley glaciers; piedmont glaciers, in which the ice spreads in a lobe over a lowland; floating ice tongues and ice shelves; mountain ice caps; and ice sheets. Climate and relief are responsible for these differences, but glaciers can also be classified according to their internal temperatures.

Cold glaciers are those in which the ice temperature is below freezing point and they are frozen to the rock beneath. This condition, which hinders the movement of glaciers, exists in many parts of Antarctica and Greenland, where air temperatures are low, as well as at high altitudes in some lower-latitude mountain regions. Temperate glaciers, on the other hand, show internal temperatures at or close to the melting point of ice. Unlike cold glaciers, they are not frozen to the rock beneath and can therefore slide over it. Ice melts on the surface of the glacier when the weather is warm, and underneath the glacier as it is warmed by geothermal heat from inside the Earth. Streams collecting meltwater may flow over, through or under the ice and emerge at the ice edge. In other glaciers, cold ice may overlie temperate ice.

Glaciers are formed from snow that, as it accumulates year after year, becomes compacted, turning first into "névé" or "firn" and eventually, after several years or even decades, into glacial ice. This process of accumulation is offset by ablation, through which ice is lost by melting, evaporation or, in glaciers that end in the sea or in lakes, by calving. If accumulation exceeds ablation, the glacier increases in size; conversely, if ablation is higher, the glacier shrinks and eventually disappears.

Glaciers move because of the force of gravity. The fastest-moving glaciers, for example those of coastal Greenland which descend steeply from areas of great accumulation, move at speeds of more than 20 m (65 ft) a day. A few meters a day is more common, however. Some glaciers move exceptionally quickly in surges, which usually last for a few weeks; rates of more than 100 m (330 ft) a day have been recorded. At the other extreme, some glaciers or parts of glaciers—the central zones of ice sheets and ice caps for example—are virtually motionless. When the ice in a glacier is subject to pressure or tension—as it flows down a valley, for example—it behaves rather like a plastic substance and changes its shape to fit the contours of the valley. Part or all of the movement of a glacier is accomplished by means of this internal deformation. In temperate glaciers, or glaciers whose lower layers are temperate, there is also basal sliding. Movement of a glacier produces cracks or crevasses in areas where stress exceeds the strength of the ice.

The work of glaciers

Glaciers and ice sheets can profoundly modify the landscape by both erosion and deposition. Measured rates of erosion of bedrock may be as much as several millimeters a year. Rock surfaces are scratched, or striated, and worn down by the constant grinding action (abrasion) of rock fragments embedded in the base of the ice. The extreme pressure of thick glacial ice on a basal boulder has been known to rupture solid bedrock beneath it.

The products of bedrock erosion range from fine clays and silts produced by abrasion, to large boulders picked up and transported by the ice. Some rocks have been carried hundreds of kilometers, from southern Scandinavia to

A U-shaped valley, such as Langdale (below) in the English Lake District, is a clear indication of a glaciated past. The floor is quite flat and the valley sides rise steeply from it.

A crevasse (below left) is created by stress within a glacier. Internally, the ice is rather like plastic but its surface is rigid and brittle. This causes tension and cracking on the surface.

This erratic (below right) is made of Silurian grit, yet it sits on a limestone perch. Ice left Yorkshire 20,000 years ago, since when the limestone surface has been lowered by solution.

Before the onset of glaciation a mountain region is often sculpted largely by the work of rivers and the processes of weathering. The hills are rounded and the valleys are V-shaped (1). During a period of glacial activity, valleys become filled with snow and eventually glaciers and, after thousands of years, the region shows a typically glaciated landscape (2). When the ice has finally disappeared there remains a glacial trough (3) with hanging valleys, truncated spurs, waterfalls and all the landforms associated with deposition of material.

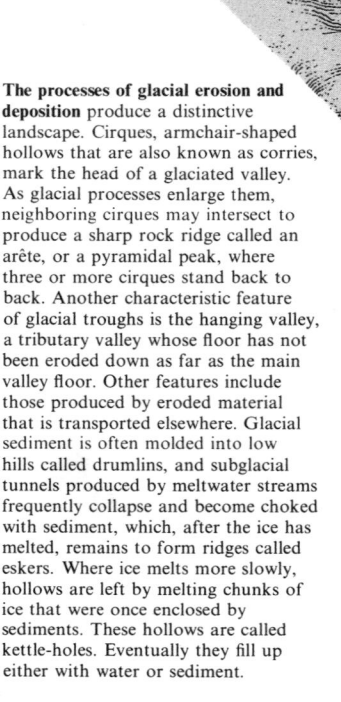

The processes of glacial erosion and deposition produce a distinctive landscape. Cirques, armchair-shaped hollows that are also known as corries, mark the head of a glaciated valley. As glacial processes enlarge them, neighboring cirques may intersect to produce a sharp rock ridge called an arête, or a pyramidal peak, where three or more cirques stand back to back. Another characteristic feature of glacial troughs is the hanging valley, a tributary valley whose floor has not been eroded down as far as the main valley floor. Other features include those produced by eroded material that is transported elsewhere. Glacial sediment is often molded into low hills called drumlins, and subglacial tunnels produced by meltwater streams frequently collapse and become choked with sediment, which, after the ice has melted, remains to form ridges called eskers. Where ice melts more slowly, hollows are left by melting chunks of ice that were once enclosed by sediments. These hollows are called kettle-holes. Eventually they fill up either with water or sediment.

eastern England, for example, and such far-traveled rocks are termed erratics. The finer sediments, compacted at the base of the glacier by the weight of the overlying ice, form till or boulder clay.

The surface of a glacier is often strewn with rock debris, which either rests on the ice or is within the glacier and revealed as the ice melts. Lateral moraines consist of rock debris that has accumulated along the sides of the glacier as a result of rockfall from, and erosion of, the valley sides. Where two glaciers join, the inner lateral moraines merge to form a medial moraine. In the ablation zone, the surface of the glacier becomes increasingly laden with debris "melting out" so that the ice may become completely buried. At the end of the glacier all rock debris is dumped, forming a terminal moraine.

Meltwater streams pouring out from glaciers or flowing in tunnels beneath them can be powerful agents of erosion and can transport large quantities of sediment. Bedrock surfaces become potholed and carved by channels that are eroded with great speed. As the streams emerge from the edge of the ice, they carry with them and deposit vast quantities of sand and gravel which form flood plains (outwash plains). Alternatively, meltwater streams may deposit sediment between the edge of the glacier and valley side, leaving a "kame terrace" when the ice finally melts. Meltwater streams feeding glacial lakes that are dammed by a glacier or moraine, for example, construct deltas of sand and gravel and lay down finer sediments (varved clays) on the lake floor.

Snow processes
Snow plays a smaller part than glacial ice in landform sculpture. Its most important role is in avalanches, which, in mountain regions, regularly bring down thousands of tonnes of rock debris. The mixture of snow, rock and other debris forms avalanche boulder tongues on the flat ground where the avalanche comes to rest and the snow melts. Gullies (avalanche chutes) on mountain slopes are swept clean of loose debris several times a year and they are gradually enlarged. Snow patches that remain stationary on more gentle slopes or in hollows encourage rock weathering under and around them. Such a process, termed nivation, may lead to deepening and enlargement of hollows and further snow accumulation. This is one way in which new glaciers are formed.

A glaciated valley exhibits a distinctive shape and profile. A cross section shows a U-shape, while longitudinally the valley floor is marked by a series of rocky steps and basins. The zone of accumulation is characterized by a cirque, in which snow collects to produce a firn field. A bergschrund is a type of crevasse that opens up near the top of the firn field where the head of the glacier is pulled away from the cirque walls. A rock step is where the gradient becomes much steeper. The speed of the ice flow is accelerated and consequent tension within the ice creates a number of deep crevasses called an ice fall. The zone of ablation has large accumulations of various kinds of rock debris.

Glacial erosion of rock surfaces is typified by a roche moutonnée, a resistant rock hummock that lies in the path of the ice. The upstream side is smooth as a result of abrasion by rock debris that is frozen into the base of the glacier. This debris scratches and scrapes rock, producing striations. The downstream side is rough as a result of ice plucking. Meltwater removes the small blocks of rock.

A great variety of material arrives at the terminus or snout of a glacier—ranging from large blocks of rock and boulders to very finely ground rock "flour." All the material is dropped in a haphazard way as the ice melts. The mixture of clay and boulders is termed glacial till. If the ice margin remains stationary, till accumulates to form a terminal moraine. If the snout recedes continuously, no ridge forms.

Landscape-makers: The Seas

The coastline is both the birthplace and the graveyard of the land. Over tens of thousands of years, geological uplift of a continent, or a fall in sea level, may create an emerging fringe of new land, whereas a period of submergence drowns the coasts and floods the adjacent river valleys, destroying land but producing some of the most attractive coastal landscapes. More rapid are the changes brought about by the sea itself. Erosion of coastal rocks or beaches can cut back the coastline at a rate of several meters a year, whereas other coastlines are built up at a comparable rate from marine sediments.

Changing coastlines are apparent on a human time scale. In temperate latitudes, beaches tend to be combed down and narrowed by winter waves, only to be restored during the calmer weather of summer. They may be lost one week and replenished the next, demonstrating an invaluable ability to recover from the wounds of all but the most devastating storms. Cliffs are generally much less dynamic, particularly if composed of resistant rock, but any loss that they suffer is permanent because there is no process that is capable of rebuilding them.

Coasts vary greatly around the world. Tropical areas often have wide beaches made up of fine material which in many cases forms broad mangrove swamps that collect sediment and build up the coast. In more exposed tropical zones coral reefs are common, either fringing the shore or (particularly where the sea level is rising) separated from the shore by a lagoon to give a barrier reef. Continued submergence of a small island surrounded by such a reef may produce an atoll. In contrast, Arctic beaches are narrow and coarse, and may be icebound for up to 10 months each year. Recession of soft rock cliffs results more from melting of ice in the ground than from wave erosion.

Waves at work

Across great expanses of open ocean energy is transferred from the wind to the sea surface to produce waves, thus fueling the machine that ultimately creates the coast. Originating as waves with heights of up to 20 or even 30 m (65–100 ft), they lose part of their energy quite rapidly as they travel, and once they have been reduced in height to the lower but more widely spaced ocean swell, they continue to travel across enormous distances.

The coasts of western Europe receive waves produced almost 10,000 km (6,200 miles) away off Cape Horn, and swell reaching California has sometimes crossed more than 11,000 km

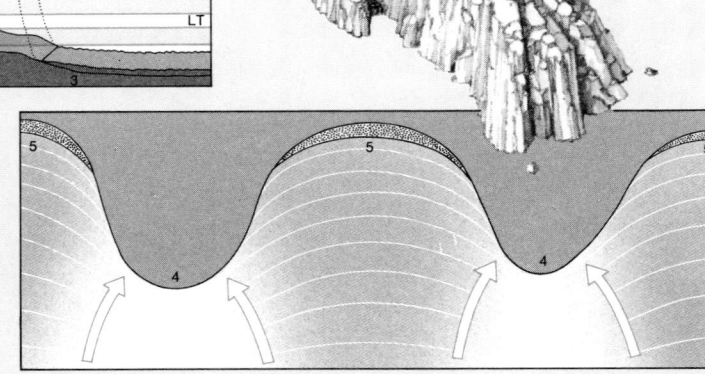

Cliffs are attacked by waves at the zone that lies between high tide (HT) and low tide (LT). The rate of erosion depends on the strength and jointing pattern of the rock and the angle at which the strata are presented to the sea. Erosion begins when water and rocks are hurled at the cliff and new fragments are broken off. The pressure of the water also compresses air in joints and cracks to shatter the rock face. As the base of the cliff is attacked, a notch (1) may be cut, and as this is made deeper the cliff above collapses. Eventually a wave-cut platform (2) is created, the top of which is exposed at low tide. The debris from the cliff is carried along the coast or deposited offshore (3). The shallow seabed now slows down incoming waves: they attack the cliff (4), but their energy is reduced. In calm water, for example at the head of a bay (5), wave energy is diffused and light material such as sand is deposited as beaches.

THE SEA COAST

The coastline is continually changing, whether day by day as the tides sift and sort the sand and shingle on the beaches, or over tens of thousands of years as the erosive power of waves carves out headlands and bays. And over millions of years the coastline is subjected to major changes of sea level, whether it is the land uplifting or sinking, or the sea itself rising or receding. Today, interference by man can damage the coast. Dam building and river-channel engineering drastically reduce the amount of sediment reaching the coast; and sea walls built to protect the coast and groynes constructed to retard sand removal both pose a long-term threat to adjacent coasts, which become starved of the sediment that previously supplied their beaches.

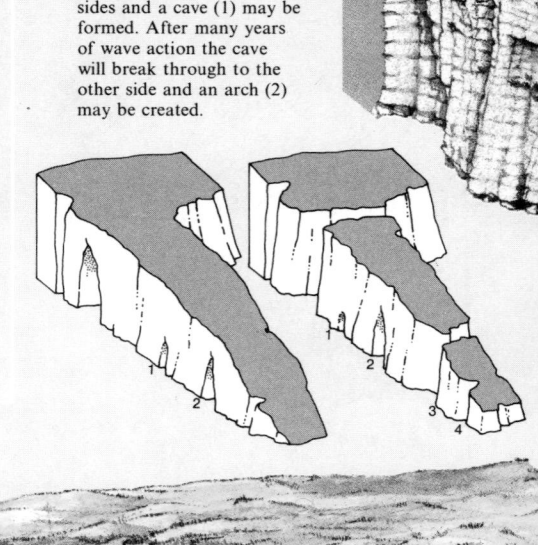

When a headland has been created (below), wave erosion continues on both sides and a cave (1) may be formed. After many years of wave action the cave will break through to the other side and an arch (2) may be created.

Light material such as mud, sand and shingle is carried by the sea. Waves tend to push the particles obliquely up a beach (right), but the backwash moves the material down again at right-angles to the shore. Thus the materials move in a zigzag fashion along the beach (1). This is known as longshore drift. When the load-carrying capacity of the waves is reduced for any reason, the material is deposited and forms a variety of features. The largest beaches (2) are found in the calmest waters such as in bays or at river mouths, with the finest grains sorted out nearest to the sea and larger pebbles stranded higher up. Spits (3) and bars (4) are sand ridges deposited across a bay or river mouth. When one end of the ridge is attached to the land it is called a spit. Spits are very often shaped like a hook as waves are refracted around the tip of land. Bars are formed where sand is deposited in shallow water offshore across the entrances to bays and run parallel to the coastline. Dunes, pictured above, are formed when sand on the beach is driven inland by onshore winds. Very often they isolate flooded land behind them to form coastal features such as salt marshes and mud flats.

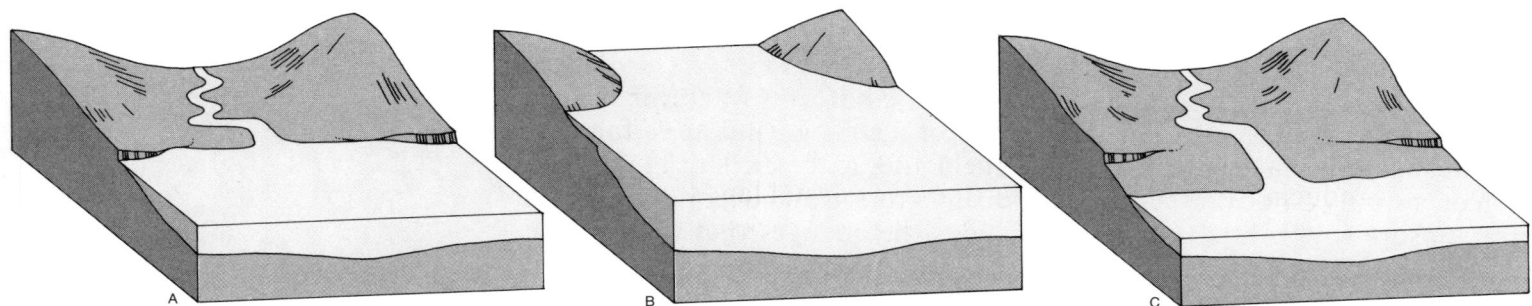

There are two major kinds of coastline—coastlines of submergence and coastlines of emergence. They are created by either a sinking or an uplift of the land, or by a change in sea level. A coastline with wave-cut cliffs and a river valley (A), for example, that experiences a rise in sea level will produce a new coastline (B) with a drowned estuary, coastal uplands isolated as islands, and a submerged coastal plain. The same coastline subjected to a drop in sea level (C) results in an extended river, abandoned cliffs far inland, and a raised beach that forms a new coastal plain.

(6,800 miles) of the Pacific from the storm belt south of New Zealand. The waves thus act as a giant conveyor for the energy that is finally used up in a few seconds of intense activity. Few other natural systems gather their energy so widely and then concentrate it so effectively.

A ball floating on the sea surface shows that, although a passing wave form moves forward, the water (and ball) follow a near-circular path and end up almost where they started. Beneath the surface the water follows similar orbits, but the amount of movement becomes progressively less with depth, until it dies out altogether. The greater the wavelength (the distance between crests) the greater is the depth of disturbance.

Long-swell waves approaching a gentle shore start disturbing the seabed far from the coast and these waves slow up, pack closer together and increase in height until they become unstable, thus producing the spilling white surf that carries much sediment to build up wide sandy beaches. Shorter local storm waves disturb the water to less depth, and thus reach much closer inshore before they interact with the seabed. Such waves do not therefore break until they plunge directly down on to the beach, leading to severe erosion, which results in the production of steep pebble beaches.

Waves slow up in shallow water, and so an undulating seabed causes their crests to bend and change their direction of approach. As a result, waves converge toward headlands (where their erosional attack is concentrated),

but they diverge as they enter bays, spreading out their energy and encouraging the deposition of the sediment they carry across the seabed close inshore. The high-energy waves at the headlands remove any rock fragments that become detached and transport them to the beaches that form at the bayheads.

Erosional coasts

Much of the local variability of coastal scenery results from differing rates of erosion on different types of rock. Bays are cut back rapidly into soft rocks such as clay, sand or gravel. Headlands are evidence that the sea takes longer to remove higher areas of harder rock such as granite or limestone. Despite the enormous power of storm waves, erosion of resistant rocks is slow and relies on any weakness that the sea can exploit.

Joints, faults and bedding planes are etched out by the water and by rock fragments hurled against them by breaking waves. Air compressed into such crevices by water pressure widens and deepens them into cracks and then into caves. In this way a solid cliff face can be eroded to form the great variety of features.

Resistant rocks can form steep, simple cliffs of great height—more than 600 m (2,000 ft) in some places—and the sea may have to undercut them to produce collapse and retreat. Cliffs of weaker rocks rarely reach 100 m (330 ft) in height and are more rapidly eroded by atmospheric processes, by running water and by

landslips. There the role of the sea is largely confined to removing the rock debris from the foot of the cliff. Soft rock cliffs are gently sloping but complex in form.

Coasts of deposition

Although waves bend as they approach the shore, they rarely become completely parallel to the coastline. Wave crests drive sediment obliquely toward the beach, whereas the troughs carry it back directly offshore down the beach slope. In this way, sand and pebbles are transported in a zigzag motion, called longshore drift, away from the areas where they are produced. One such source of material is cliff erosion, but on average about 95 percent of the material moving on to beaches was originally carried to the coast by rivers.

Beaches are built up wherever longshore drift is impeded (for example, by a headland) or where wave and current energy is reduced (as at the head of a bay). An abundant supply of sediment may build a sandbar across the mouth of a bay or in shallow water offshore. Where the coast changes direction, longshore drift may continue in its original direction and build a spit out from the land. Depositional features may become strengthened by vegetation. Plants may take root and bind together newly deposited sediments, but they constitute relatively delicate coasts that are vulnerable to erosion if for any reason they are not continually supplied with fresh deposits of sediment.

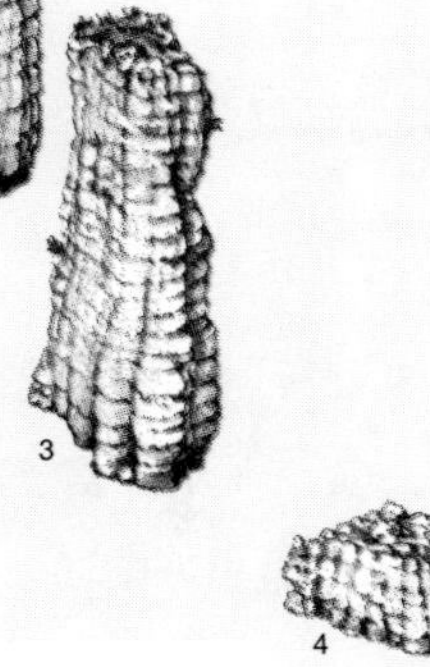

Further wave erosion (above) causes the roof of the arch to collapse, leaving an isolated column of rock called a stack (3). Another cave, and then an arch, may be formed behind the stack, which itself may be eroded to a short stump (4).

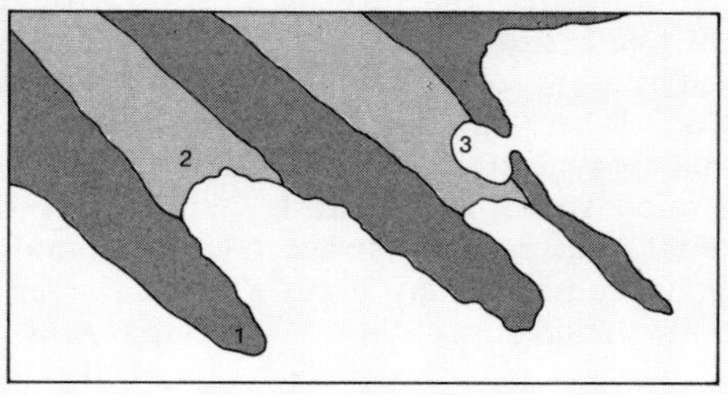

Headlands alternating with bays are found where bands of strong (1) and weak (2) rocks meet the coast at an angle and there is a varied resistance to erosion. The bays are first carved out of the softer rock, leaving the waves to attack the headlands of hard rock. If, in contrast, the strata lie parallel to the coast, then the hard rock has few irregular indentations except where the sea has broken through to the soft rock behind and has scoured out a cove (3).

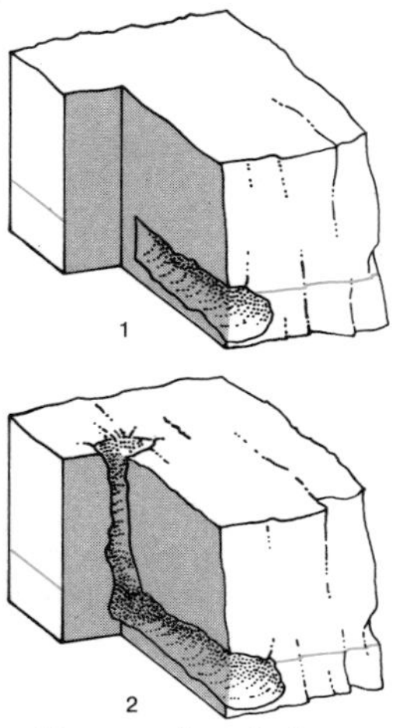

Gloups are formed when waves first erode a cave, then extend it backward as a long shaft running into the cliff (1). If the roof collapses at one point, a blowhole, or gloup (2), is formed. If the whole roof collapses, a deep cleft called a geo is created.

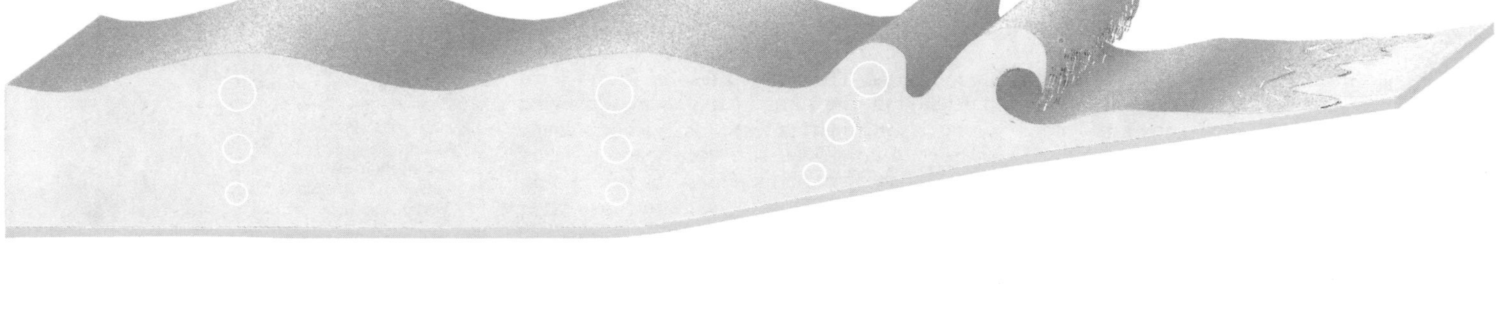

Waves are generated by wind on the surface of the sea. It is the shape of the wave that travels forward—the individual water particles move in near-circular orbits. Disturbance diminishes with depth to about half a wavelength. Waves break when they strike a sloping shore, and the wave height is about the same as the depth of the water.

Landscape-makers: Wind and Weathering

Winds are part of the global circulation of air and they can affect landforms wherever surface material is loose and unprotected by vegetation. The effects of a strong wind are a familiar sight—whether in the dust clouds that rise from a plowed field after a dry spell, or in the sand swept along the beach on a windy day. Weathering is the disintegration and decomposition of rocks through their exposure to the atmosphere. It includes the changes that destroy the original structure of rocks, and few on the Earth's surface have not been weathered at one time or another in the history of our evolving landscape.

Active and fixed dunes in Africa and western Asia

Most sand seas today are being actively molded by winds. The landscape has long been shaped by wind, and some dune fields produced in dry climates in the distant past may be "fossilized" now by soils and vegetation cover. Desertification often occurs where this vegetation is disturbed by man.

Fixed sand dunes

Active sand dunes

Sand dunes cover only 20 percent of the world's deserts, and tend to be concentrated in a small number of sand seas, or ergs, such as the Erg Bourharet in Algeria (above).

Longitudinal, or seif, dunes (below) are long, narrow ridges that lie parallel to the direction of prevailing winds. Surface heating and wind flow produce vertical spiraling motions of air.

Direction of wind

EROSION AND WEATHERING

Winds result from the differential heating of regions of the globe. They act indirectly as agents of erosion through water or waves, but they also directly affect the surface of the Earth, molding landforms either by erosion or deposition. The nature of weathering processes and the rate at which they operate depend upon climate, the properties of the rock and the conditions of the biosphere. Both wind erosion and the various weathering processes are significant landscape-makers.

Many rocks are formed deep in the Earth, where they are in equilibrium with the forces that created them. If they become exposed at the surface, they are in disequilibrium with atmospheric forces. This brings about the changes —adjustments to atmospheric and organic agents—that we call weathering. Products of weathering are moved by agents of erosion, one of which is the wind. Where the surface is protected, for example by vegetation, the wind has little effect, but where strong winds attack loose surface material that is unprotected, erosion, abrasion and deposition may occur, producing characteristic landforms.

How wind shapes the surface

Strong winds occur in many places, but nowhere are they more effective in forming the surface of the land than in deserts, where their work is largely unhindered by vegetation. There the wind can pick up material and then, charged with sand particles, blast away at the ground, carrying away the debris and depositing it. Many notorious desert winds are associated with sand movement and dust storms—the harmattan of West Africa and the sirocco of the Middle East, for example.

Wind erosion occurs where winds charged

with sand attack soils or rock. Dry soils may be broken up and the resulting debris, which includes soil nutrients, is carried away as dust. This poses a serious problem, especially when arid and semiarid lands experience drought. Wind erosion involving the lifting and blowing away of loose material from the ground surface is called deflation.

Erosion by sand and rock fragments carried by winds is called abrasion. In this way winds erode individual surface pebbles into distinctive shapes known as ventifacts. They can also mold larger rock masses into aerodynamic shapes known as yardangs—features that often look rather like upturned rowing boats. Some of these features are so large that they have been identified only since satellite photographs have become available. Finally, winds erode by attrition, which involves the mutual wearing down of particles as they are carried along.

Winds can transport material in three different ways. They can lift loose, sand-sized particles into the air and carry them downwind along trajectories that resemble those of ballistic missiles: the particles rise steeply and descend along gentle flight paths. This produces a bouncing movement known as saltation in a layer extending approximately 1 m (3 ft) above the

Direction of wind

Grain path

Rebound

Sand cloud

Surface creep

Loose sand surface

Sand particles move in a series of long jumps—a process called saltation. Particles describe a curved path (above), the height and length of which depends upon the mass of the grain, the wind velocity and the number of other particles moving around. Saltation only occurs in a layer extending up to approximately 1 m (3 ft) above the ground surface. Sand grains moving in this way are also responsible for the abraded base of features such as pedestal rocks (right). These landforms are weathered first—for example by the crystallization of salts—and are then eroded by the sand-laden winds.

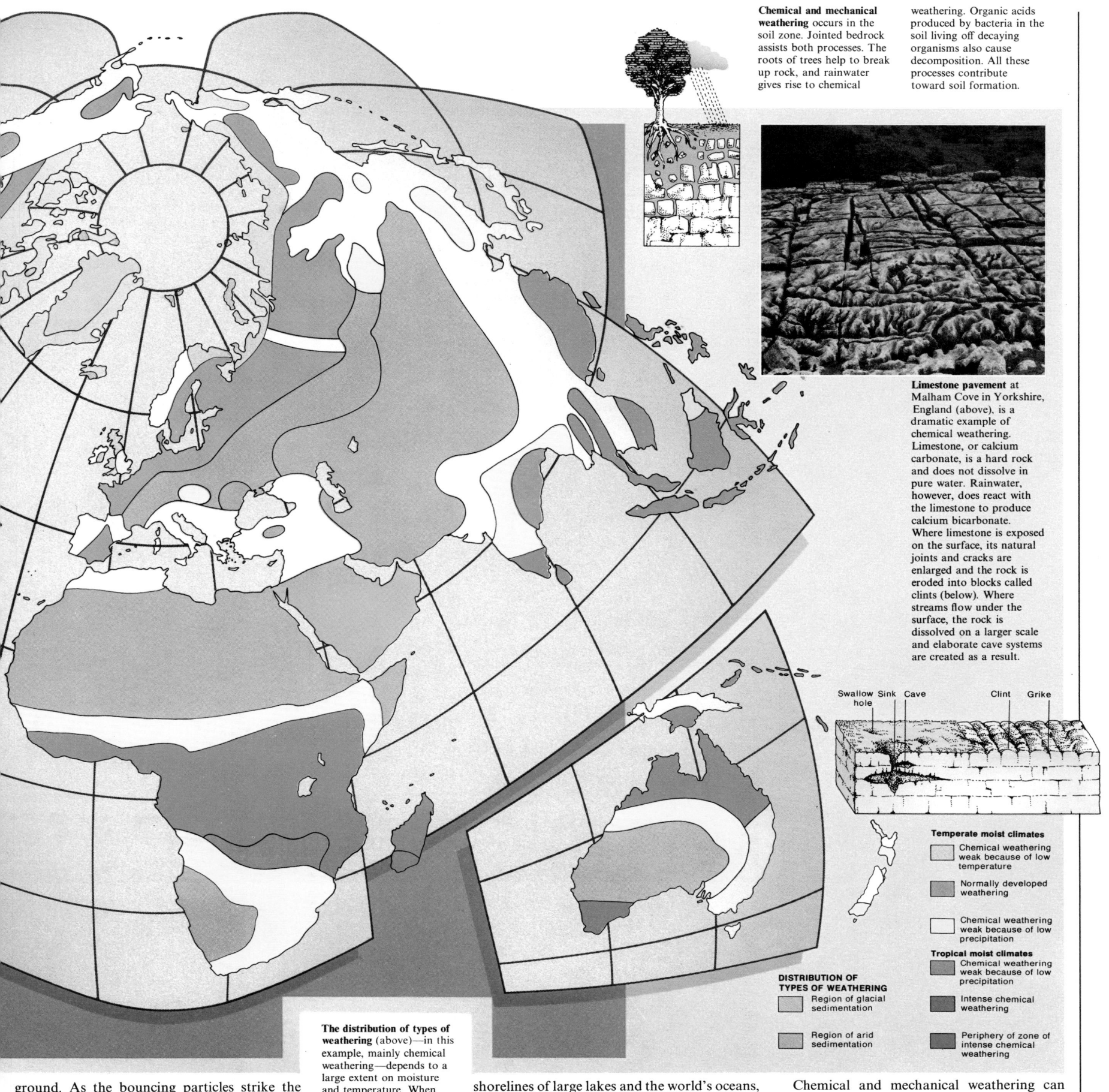

Chemical and mechanical weathering occurs in the soil zone. Jointed bedrock assists both processes. The roots of trees help to break up rock, and rainwater gives rise to chemical weathering. Organic acids produced by bacteria in the soil living off decaying organisms also cause decomposition. All these processes contribute toward soil formation.

Limestone pavement at Malham Cove in Yorkshire, England (above), is a dramatic example of chemical weathering. Limestone, or calcium carbonate, is a hard rock and does not dissolve in pure water. Rainwater, however, does react with the limestone to produce calcium bicarbonate. Where limestone is exposed on the surface, its natural joints and cracks are enlarged and the rock is eroded into blocks called clints (below). Where streams flow under the surface, the rock is dissolved on a larger scale and elaborate cave systems are created as a result.

Swallow hole Sink Cave Clint Grike

Temperate moist climates
- Chemical weathering weak because of low temperature
- Normally developed weathering
- Chemical weathering weak because of low precipitation

Tropical moist climates
- Chemical weathering weak because of low precipitation
- Intense chemical weathering
- Periphery of zone of intense chemical weathering

DISTRIBUTION OF TYPES OF WEATHERING
- Region of glacial sedimentation
- Region of arid sedimentation

The distribution of types of weathering (above)—in this example, mainly chemical weathering—depends to a large extent on moisture and temperature. When classifying regions with different rates of chemical weathering in terms of climatic zones, many areas of the world can be placed into one of two principal categories: tropical moist climates and temperate moist climates. The white areas on the map are mountain ranges or regions of tectonic activity where there is no appreciable weathering mantle.

ground. As the bouncing particles strike the surface, they push other particles along the ground (creep or drift). Fine particles that are disturbed by saltation rise up into the airflow and are carried away as dust (suspension).

The materials eroded and transported by winds must eventually come to rest in features of deposition, the most extensive of which are sand dunes. Sand seas at first sight appear to be random and complex, rather like a choppy ocean, but their features generally fall into three size groups: small ripples, which have a wavelength of up to 3 m (10 ft) and a height of 20 cm (8 in); dunes, with a wavelength of 20–300 m (65–1,000 ft) and a height of up to 30 m (68 ft); and sand mountains or "draa," which have a wavelength of 1–3 km (0.6–1.5 miles) and rise to a height of up to 200 m (650 ft). Within each size group various forms can be explained in terms of the nature of the sand and the kinds of winds that blow over it. Where winds blow consistently from one direction, long linear dunes form parallel or transverse to the wind direction. Where sand supply is limited, horned "barchan" dunes may form. If winds blow from several directions during a year, then star-shaped dunes and other complex patterns appear. Sand dunes are also common along the

shorelines of large lakes and the world's oceans, where onshore winds can pile quite extensive areas of loose drifting sand.

Agents of weathering

Weathering takes two forms: mechanical weathering breaks up rock without altering its mineral constituents, whereas chemical weathering changes in some way the nature of mineral crystals. One agent of mechanical weathering is temperature change. It used to be thought that rocks disintegrated as a result of a huge daily range of temperature (thermal weathering). Despite travelers' tales of rocks splitting in the desert night with cracks like pistol shots, there is little evidence to support this view. In the presence of water, however, alternate heating and cooling of rocks does result in fracture. Frost is also an effective rock breaker. The freezing of water and expansion of ice in the cracks and pores of rocks create disruptive pressures; alternate freezing and thawing eventually causes pieces of rock to break off in angular fragments. Finally, the roots of plants and trees grow into the joints of rock and widen them, thus loosening the structure of the rock. Animals burrowing through the soil can have a similar effect on rocks.

Chemical and mechanical weathering can work hand in hand. In arid regions, for example, the crystallization of salts results in the weathering of rock. As water evaporates from the rock surface, salt crystals grow (from minerals dissolved in the water) in small openings in the rock. In time these crystals bring to bear enough pressure to break off rock fragments from the parent block.

Chemical weathering is most effective in humid tropical climates, however, and it usually involves the decomposition of rocks as a result of their exposure to air and rainwater, which contains dissolved chemicals. Carbon dioxide from the air, for example, becomes dissolved in rainwater, making it into weak carbonic acid. This reacts with minerals such as calcite, which is found in many rocks. Similarly, rocks can be oxidized by oxygen in the air. This happens to rocks that contain iron, for example, if they are exposed on the surface: a reddish iron oxide is produced which causes the rocks to crumble.

Over many thousands, even millions, of years, the processes of mechanical and chemical weathering have affected many of the rocks on the Earth's surface. When rocks are weakened in such a way, they then fall prey to the agents of erosion—water, ice, winds and waves.

Landscape-makers: Man

Man has done much to reshape the face of the planet since his first appearance on Earth more than two million years ago. Early man did little to harm the environment but, with the rise of agriculture, the landscape began to change. An increasing population and the growth of urban settlements gradually created greater demands for agricultural land and living space. But industrialization during the last 200 years has had the biggest impact. Man's search for and exploitation of the Earth's resources has to a large extent transformed the natural landscape and at the same time created totally artificial man-made environments.

MAN THE GEOLOGICAL AGENT

In 1864 a conservationist named George Perkins Marsh introduced the thesis that "man in fact made the Earth" rather than the converse. The idea of man as a geological agent was further developed in the 1920s. Man modifies the landscape in many ways; sometimes he transforms the Earth completely—he even creates land where no land was before.

Man's major impact on the landscape has been through forest clearance. He made the first attack on natural forests about 8,000 years ago in Neolithic times in northern and western Europe, as revealed by the changing composition of tree pollen deposited in bogs. After Roman times, especially in the Mediterranean region, there was another spate of forest clearance, so that by the Middle Ages little original forest survived in the Old World. As population and emigration increased, it was the turn of trees in the New World and Africa to fall before the axe and plow. Man's present voracious appetite for timber and its products could, if unchecked, clear most of the Earth's great forests by the end of this century.

Forest clearance not only changes the appearance of the landscape but can alter the balance of nature within a region. The hydrological cycle may be affected, and soil erosion may be increased, which in turn chokes rivers with sediment and leads to the silting up of harbors and estuaries. The coastal area of Valencia in Spain, for example, has widened by nearly 4 km (2.5 miles) since Roman times, much of which can be accounted for by forest clearance, and subsequent soil erosion and the deposition of the material by rivers as they near the sea. Reafforestation of an area can reduce soil erosion and the threat of flooding. Landscape management can reduce wind speeds: for example, shelter belts in the Russian steppes have been planted over distances of more than 100 km (62 miles).

Water management

The second great impact of man has been on the waterways of the world. The most spectacular changes are caused by the construction of dams to make vast new lakes. Such projects have frequently had effects far beyond those originally anticipated. The Aswan High Dam on the River Nile was completed in 1970, creating Lake Nasser and making possible the irrigation of an additional 550,000 hectares (1,358,000 acres) in upper Egypt. But some would argue that the dam holds back silt from the rivers and stores it in the lake, a fact that has seriously reduced the rate of silting in the Nile delta. This has resulted in increased salinity and some loss of fertility of the soil, as well as changes to the delta's coastline. The storage of silt in Lake Nasser has caused increased erosion of the riverbed downstream and the undermining of the foundations of bridges and barrages.

Other man-made changes to rivers include straightening and canalization, usually for

Massive power plants (left) symbolize man's modifications to the landscape in modern, industrialized society. Demand for energy and mineral resources has led to the creation of huge holes in the ground like this borax mine (below left) in the Mojave desert in California. The open pit is 100 m (330 ft) deep, 1,460 m (4,800 ft) long and 915 m (3,000 ft) wide. In opening up resource areas in Brazil, the Trans-Amazonian highway has disturbed the forest (below).

flood protection, but also to prevent the channel from shifting. As long ago as the third millennium BC, during the reign of Emperor Yao, a hydraulic engineer was apparently appointed to control the wandering course of the Hwang-Ho (Yellow River), and the system he devised survived for at least 1,500 years. Even so, over the centuries, the river has changed course radically, and today measures are still being taken to control the fine sediment that the river carries and the flooding caused by its deposition. The Missouri River in the United States is estimated to erode material from an area of about 3,680 hectares (9,000 acres) annually over a length of 1,220 km (758 miles). It is little wonder that engineers attempt to control rivers by means of realignment or try to "train" a river's flow by using concrete stays.

New land from old

The continuing pressure of population on food resources and the need to create new agricultural land illustrate still further the impact of man as a landscape shaper. As part of irrigation projects land is often leveled and new waterways are created in the form of canals. Pakistan has one of the most extensive man-made irrigation systems in the world. It controls almost completely the flow of the Indus, Sutlej and Punjab rivers through some 640 km (400 miles) of linking canals.

A huge demand for rice in many parts of southeastern Asia has led to farmers terracing steep slopes on many mountainous islands. In the Netherlands, about one-third of the entire cultivated area of the country is land that has been reclaimed from the sea. In the future more grandiose schemes are likely. Any large-scale expansion of agricultural land in the Soviet Union will be mainly dependent on water supply. There have been plans since the 1930s to divert northward-flowing rivers to irrigated areas in the south and west. This idea, and it is believed that it might become a reality by the turn of the century, could have serious implications for the waters of the Arctic Ocean. If the amount of fresh water flowing into the ocean is reduced, salinity will increase, thus affecting the melting of ice floes and, consequently, sea level.

Man has also made his mark along the coastlines, from small-scale measures, such as the construction of groynes—wooden piles that reduce the amount of sand that is transported along the beach by wave action—to large-scale man-made harbors.

Modern man, the urban dweller of the machine age, has brought great changes to the face of the landscape. The need for materials for the construction of the urban fabric has led to the creation of huge quarries, in which building stone and road-building materials are extracted from the ground. Demand for energy and minerals leads to extensive modification of the landscape, especially where mineral deposits are near the surface and can be extracted by opencast mining. The largest holes on Earth (excluding ocean basins) are those that result from the extraction of fuel (coal) and minerals.

The side effects of mining can be detrimental to the environment. Land may subside and despoliation of the landscape by slag heaps, for example, is considerable. Escaping coal dust can suffocate vegetation in a mining area, and gases given off during some mining operations can also damage plant and animal life.

Reclamation of spoiled areas is obligatory in many countries. Old open-cast workings are often filled with water to be used for recreational facilities, and slag heaps are treated and planted with vegetation: research has produced certain strains of plants that will grow even in the most acidic soils.

The true impact of man

During the last hundred years or so man has become much more aware of his role as an agent of landscape creation and destruction. The significance of man the landscape-maker, in comparison with slow, natural changes, is the speed with which he effects transformation, the sheer amount of energy which he can apply to a relatively small area, and the selectiveness and determination with which he applies that energy. Man's increased impact has not been a smooth and continuous process: it has occurred at different rates in different places and at different times. While it can be argued that some landscapes have been constructed which themselves conserve and often beautify the natural environment, man's active role has primarily been destructive: he has transformed the Earth's surface, perhaps irreversibly.

THE DUTCH POLDERS

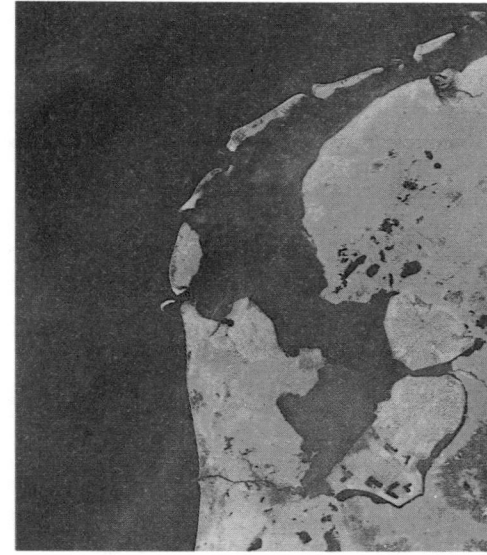

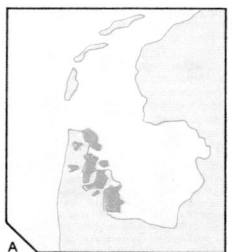

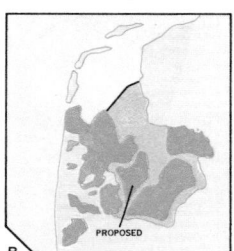

Reclamation of the Dutch polders from the North Sea is an example of man creating land. Many centuries ago a large part of what is now the western Netherlands was beneath the sea. From the 15th to the 17th centuries (A) dykes were constructed to enclose land and protect it against inundation from the sea, and enable it to be farmed. Later, windmills were used to drain away sea water. Further reclamation in the 19th and 20th centuries (B) has brought the total area to

165,000 hectares (408,000 acres). In 1932 a 40 km (25 mile) dam was completed, enclosing the Zuider Zee—which is now a freshwater lake that was renamed the IJsselmeer—and reducing Holland's vulnerable coastline by 320 km (200 miles). To create a polder, a dyke is built and the water pumped out. Reeds are grown to help dry out the soil. After a few years drains are put in to remove water remaining. Newly created polders (light blue) show up well on this satellite image (top).

Man-made environments have become increasingly complex and large scale. Highway construction—this vast interchange (left) is in Chicago—is typical of the extensive use of land for modern transport systems alone. The acreage of land use classified as urban continues to increase. Man's endeavors to make still more land available for his many purposes have extended to cultivating previously inhospitable desert lands (above). More than half the land in Israel is naturally unproductive because of its aridity. By means of elaborate water carriage and storage schemes and scientifically researched irrigation projects, the desert has been totally transformed from a barren wasteland into intensively cultivated fields. Output from agriculture can also be increased by terracing. In densely populated areas, or mountainous regions, as in Luzon in the Philippines (right), man's skillful landscaping has completely reshaped the topography.

Part 3

THE EMERGENCE OF LIFE

How life on Earth began and developed
How life has evolved and spread over the planet
How man came to inherit the Earth

THE STAGES OF LIFE
Simple organic molecules, the precursors of life, could certainly have evolved in Earth's primitive atmosphere. Energy from the Sun, volcanoes and electric storms had the power to combine the basic chemicals into the amino acids and other molecules that are the constituents of living matter, forming droplets of "pre-life" in pools and on shorelines. Concentrations of droplets collected around some minerals, coagulating in a "soup" of long-chain polymers—proteins and nucleic acids which together form the living cell. Thus far have scientists re-created life's origins, but the combining of proteins and nucleic acids into a living unit remains to be achieved.

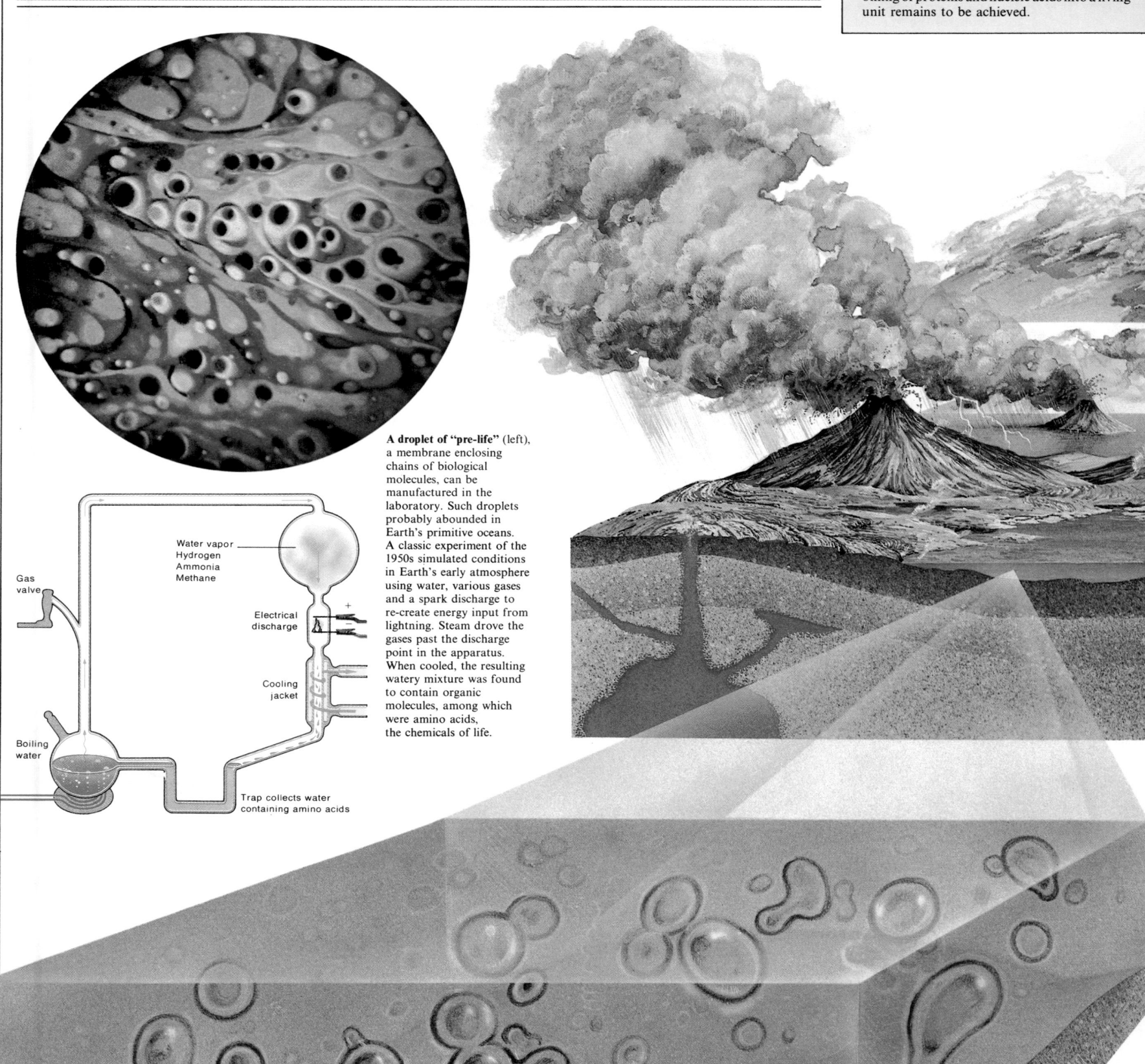

A droplet of "pre-life" (left), a membrane enclosing chains of biological molecules, can be manufactured in the laboratory. Such droplets probably abounded in Earth's primitive oceans. A classic experiment of the 1950s simulated conditions in Earth's early atmosphere using water, various gases and a spark discharge to re-create energy input from lightning. Steam drove the gases past the discharge point in the apparatus. When cooled, the resulting watery mixture was found to contain organic molecules, among which were amino acids, the chemicals of life.

Water vapor
Hydrogen
Ammonia
Methane

Gas valve

Electrical discharge

Cooling jacket

Boiling water

Trap collects water containing amino acids

LIFE BEGINS
A "primordial soup" of organic molecules, each separated from the water by a membrane, formed thick concentrations in Earth's shallow pools. From these evolved the long-chain polymers that form proteins and nucleic acids in every living cell.

The Source of Life

Life may have come to Earth from outer space – some meteorites contain life-like organic molecules – but the basic constituents of life, the biochemical structures called proteins and nucleic acids, could just as well have formed on Earth itself. By simulating possible primitive conditions on Earth, and applying a likely energy source, American scientists of the 1950s manufactured, from inorganic substances, the amino acids that form the subunits of all living things.

Water played a key part in the creation of life on Earth. At first the temperature of the newly formed planet was far too high for water to exist in a liquid state. Instead, it formed a dense atmosphere of steam, which, as the Earth cooled, condensed into droplets of rain that poured down for perhaps thousands of years. This torrential, thundery rain eroded the land and dissolved the minerals, which collected in pools on the surface.

Earth's original atmosphere was also very different from today's. Most importantly, it contained no free oxygen, the gas which makes air-breathing life possible; the primitive atmosphere was composed of carbon monoxide, carbon dioxide, hydrogen and nitrogen. But the absence of oxygen created two conditions that are essential if life is to evolve. First, without oxygen the atmosphere could have no layer of ozone (an oxygen compound), which now acts as a barrier to most of the Sun's high-energy radiation (mainly ultraviolet light). Second, the absence of free oxygen meant that any complex chemicals that might be formed would not immediately break down again. Thus the molecules of life could form.

The chemistry of life

Life may be distinguished from nonlife in three ways: living organisms are able to increase the complexity of their parts through synthetic, self-building reactions; they obtain and use energy by breaking down chemical compounds; and they can make new copies of themselves.

It is the combined properties of the chemicals

soup," and it is from this "soup" that life may have emerged.

Miller and Urey had shown that the basic substances of life can be derived from a primitive atmosphere. But there are still large gaps in our understanding of how these substances became more organized and self-regulating: in other words, how they became alive. More complex molecular structures somehow developed through the linking up of the basic units to form long, chain-like sequences of larger units, called polymers. But how this happened is still not fully understood.

The two most important classes of biological molecules are proteins and nucleic acids, both of which are polymers. Proteins are the building materials of living matter, the chief components of muscles, skin and hair. They also form enzymes—the chemicals that control biochemical reaction in living cells. Nucleic acids—DNA (deoxyribonucleic acid) and RNA (ribonucleic acid)—are so called because they are found in the central nuclei of cells. They are the cell's genetic material, the raw stuff of heredity. They act as the memories and the messengers of life, storing information in units called genes, and releasing that information to the cells when it is needed. Nucleic acids can reproduce themselves and, without this ability, life would not exist or continue.

The basic units that link together to form proteins are amino acids, and all proteins in living organisms are made up of just 20 different amino acids. In chemical terms, a protein molecule is a polymer consisting of a long chain of amino acid units joined together in a particular sequence, and the code to this sequence is held by DNA.

How living chemicals joined

Experiments with simulated primordial conditions have produced many amino acids other than the 20 commonly found in proteins. All amino acids (and other types of chemicals) tend to "stick" onto the surface of clay, but those 20 found in proteins stick particularly well to clays rich in the metal nickel. This suggests that the first proteins may have been formed in pools or on the fringes of seas, where the primordial soup was in contact with nickel-rich clays. There heat from the Sun or a volcano could have combined the amino acids to form a primitive protein.

The four classes of chemicals that form the basic components of nucleic acids have also, like the amino acids, been "cooked up" in a primordial soup, and they too will stick to clay to form long-chain polymers. And, just as nickel-rich clays are best at absorbing the amino acid constituents of protein, so clays rich in zinc absorb the building blocks of nucleic acids. This suggests that such clays could have been the birthplace of genes, which are the "messengers" of inheritance.

However, the coupling of proteins and nucleic acids, which together form the living cell, has yet to be explained, and it is improbable that proteins or nucleic acids alone could have provided the basis for life.

The Russian biochemist I. A. Oparin has shown that, in water, solutions of polymers (such as proteins) have a tendency to form droplets surrounded by an outer membrane very like that which encloses living cells. As these droplets grow by absorbing more polymers, some split in two when they become too large for stability. If such a droplet had protein enzymes to harness energy and make more polymers, and if it had nucleic acids with instructions for making those proteins, and if each new droplet received a complete copy of the nucleic acid instructions, the droplet would be alive—it would be a living cell.

THE RADIANT SUN
A dense atmosphere of water vapor and various gases—but not oxygen—formed round the cooling planet Earth after its creation 4,600 million years ago. Oxygen in the atmosphere would have prevented the evolution of life from nonliving organic matter by blocking the Sun's ultraviolet radiation (which may have provided energy for the forming of organic compounds), and free oxygen would also have destroyed such compounds as they began to accumulate.

THE PRIMITIVE ATMOSPHERE
Volcanic eruptions drove water vapor and gases into the atmosphere of the young Earth; lightning and other discharges of atmospheric electricity accompanied the torrential rain; dissolved minerals collected in the pools. These were some of the preconditions for life on Earth, whereby mixtures of organic compounds in water may have combined to form more complex units essential for life.

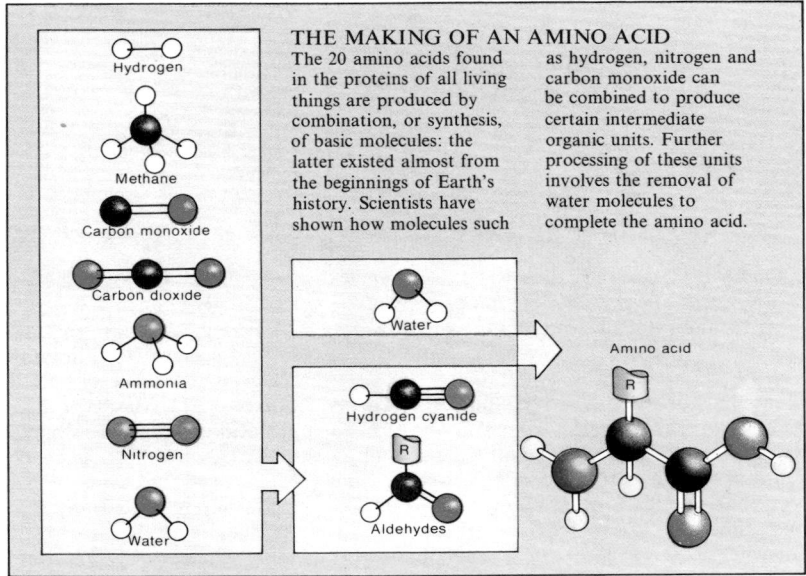

THE MAKING OF AN AMINO ACID
The 20 amino acids found in the proteins of all living things are produced by combination, or synthesis, of basic molecules: the latter existed almost from the beginnings of Earth's history. Scientists have shown how molecules such as hydrogen, nitrogen and carbon monoxide can be combined to produce certain intermediate organic units. Further processing of these units involves the removal of water molecules to complete the amino acid.

of life that make them so special, not just the chemicals themselves. Experiments in the last few decades have given us a very good idea of how life could have arisen from the simple, nonliving chemicals which compose it. In the early 1950s, Harold Urey and Stanley Miller simulated the atmosphere of a primitive world by filling a flask with water, ammonia, methane and hydrogen. They supplied it with energy in the form of heat and an electric spark—to simulate lightning—and the experiment was left to run for a week.

Analyzing the mixture formed, they found it contained many chemicals that are associated with living things, particularly nitrogen compounds called amino acids—the really important chemicals of life. Further experiments brought together other gas mixtures, including the one that is now thought to have covered the young Earth, and these gave similar results, as long as there was no free oxygen present. The resulting mixture of organic compounds in water came to be known as the "primordial

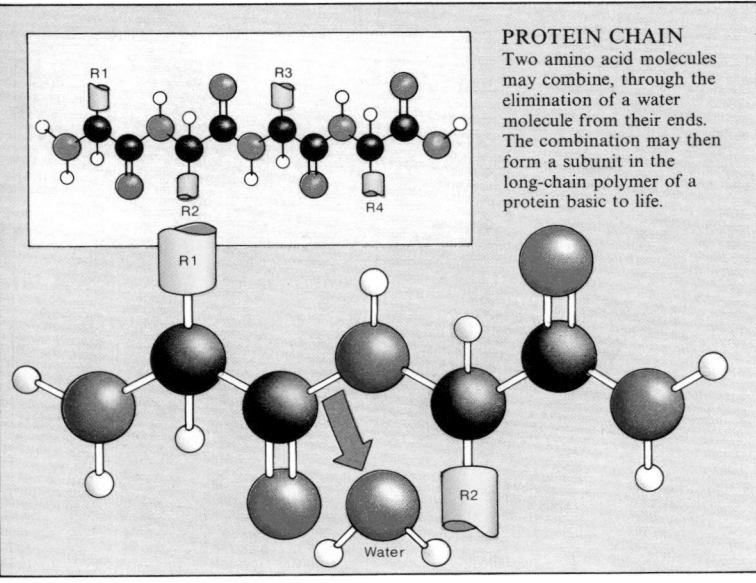

PROTEIN CHAIN
Two amino acid molecules may combine, through the elimination of a water molecule from their ends. The combination may then form a subunit in the long-chain polymer of a protein basic to life.

The Structure of Life

All life forms stem from a single cell, and every cell contains in its nucleus instructions for the re-creation of the organism of which it forms a part. These are encoded in chromosomes, which contain the miraculous molecular substance of DNA, sectioned into units of heredity called genes. The genetic code determines in detail the physical characteristics of an individual creature, so that variations in DNA cause variations in the individual. Scientists believe that it is the interaction of the individual variation with the environment that ultimately leads to the evolution of the similar, interbreeding groups of creatures that are known as species.

THE HIDDEN SECRET

Dramatic discoveries in recent decades have revolutionized biology, the primary life science. Scientists can now trace parts of the genetic blueprint that lays down the pattern for every form of life, linking the large-scale unfolding of species that we know as evolution with the ultramicroscopic activity of the molecules within the nucleus of every cell. This may be the secret behind the rich diversity of life on Earth.

Deoxyribonucleic acid (DNA) consists of a "backbone" of alternating sugar and phosphate molecules, and to each sugar is attached one of four nitrogenous bases (adenine, guanine, thymine and cytostine, or A, G, T, C). A single gene might contain 2,000 of these bases, and in the body cell of a human being the 46 chromosomes (thread-like bodies of DNA and protein) run to 3,000 million bases. The sequence of these bases stores the information for making amino acids into proteins, just as the sequence of letters in this sentence stores the information for making a particular verbal structure. But the DNA alphabet has only four letters (A, G, T, C).

The thread of life

DNA is a double molecule, resembling a twisted ladder, its two main strands twining around each other to form the famous double helix. The strands are linked by pairs of bases—A and T, or G and C—whose shape is such that each pair fits together neatly, like pieces of a jigsaw, to form the rungs of the DNA ladder. As a result, the information on the strands can be duplicated by "unzipping" the double helix and making new strands by using the old ones as templates. DNA stores, duplicates and passes on the information that makes life alive.

Cells multiply by splitting in two, and each newly made cell thus gets instructions for its existence by the mechanism of heredity, the gene. But heredity is a word more often applied to the passing on of DNA from an organism to its offspring. In sexual reproduction the offspring gets some of the DNA (usually half) from one parent, and the rest from the other, ending up with a unique mix all of its own.

The laws of heredity

Man has long known that characteristics can be passed on from one generation to the next, for he has been selectively breeding crops and animals for thousands of years. However, it was not until the mid-nineteenth century that an obscure Austrian monk, Gregor Mendel (1822–84), discovered the laws that govern inheritance, and his work was ignored until the beginning of the twentieth century, when more powerful microscopes made possible the direct observation of the cell.

Mendel experimented with pea plants because they had easily recognizable traits, and because, although normally self-fertilizing, they could be cross-fertilized with pollen from a different plant. Mendel made many crosses between different pure-bred plants and found that in the offspring, or hybrids, some characters always prevailed over others: red flowers over white, tall plants over short, and so on. He called the prevailing characters dominant, and the nonprevailing characters recessive. He then let the first-generation hybrids self-fertilize, and found not only that the recessive traits reappeared in the hybrids' offspring, but also that they reappeared in a constant proportion of three dominant to one recessive; the second generation contained three times as many red-flowered peas as white-flowered peas.

To explain his results, Mendel proposed that each plant had two hereditary "factors"— today called alleles—for each character, and that the dominant factor suppressed the recessive factor. If a plant inherited both a dominant and a recessive factor, the dominant one would prevail. Only if both factors were recessive would the recessive character be apparent. Mendel found many other pairs of traits where one form was dominant and the other recessive. He established that permutations arising from the crossing of the two first-generation hybrids allows the dominant gene to be present in three out of four crosses in the second generation; but in the fourth cross, only the two recessive alleles of the genes are present. So there is always a three-to-one ratio of dominant to recessive.

Theories of evolution

Mendel's work was of course unknown to his contemporaries, Charles Darwin and Alfred Russel Wallace, who even then were providing solutions to the major mystery of biology—the way that species evolve, change and develop over time. Evolution was not a new idea in Darwin's day. In 1809 the French naturalist Jean-Baptiste Lamarck had proposed a theory of the inheritance of acquired characteristics, suggesting that new habits learned by an organism in response to environmental change may become physically incorporated in the animal's descendants. For instance, the fact that the ancestral giraffe had to stretch its neck to reach food might give its offspring long necks to enable them to reach food more easily. Less satisfactory than the "natural selection" theory of Darwin and Wallace (who independently reached the same conclusion), Lamarckism founders on the fact that there is no genetic mechanism enabling acquired characters to pass on in this way.

Darwin's theory of natural selection has three key elements: all individuals vary, and some variations are passed on to the next generation; the gap between the potential and the actual number of offspring reproduced by organisms is very wide and implies that not all will survive; organisms best adapted to the environment will survive, their offspring will have been selected, and the favorable variation will spread through the population, perhaps eventually changing it.

Genetic variation, the mainspring of natural selection, is reflected in variations of DNA, the material substance of heredity. Changes in the order of DNA's nitrogenous bases—called mutations—produce changes in the proteins which are usually, but not always, harmful. More important than these is the effect of genes recombining in sexually reproduced offspring.

Sexual reproduction provides the offspring with two sets of DNA, one from each parent. The processes that give rise to a half-set of chromosomes in a sperm or egg shuffle and recombine the genes on each chromosome to provide new combinations. Then, when sperm and egg fuse together at fertilization, the half-sets come together and even more combinations are produced. The world's enormous diversity of life can be explained in terms of a struggle that favors certain genetic combinations.

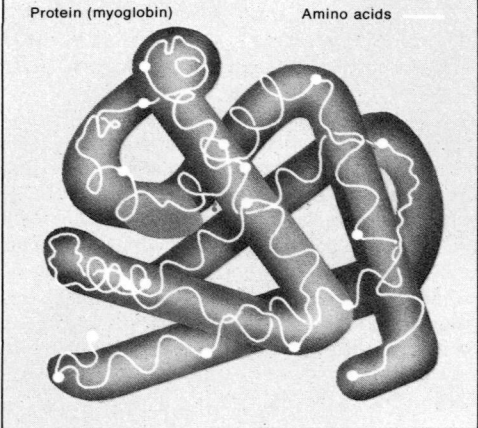

Protein (myoglobin) — Amino acids

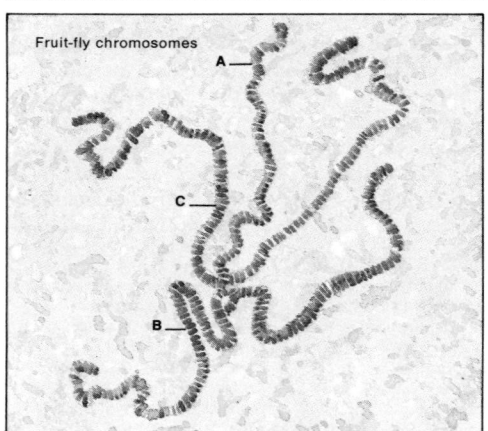

Fruit-fly chromosomes — A, C, B

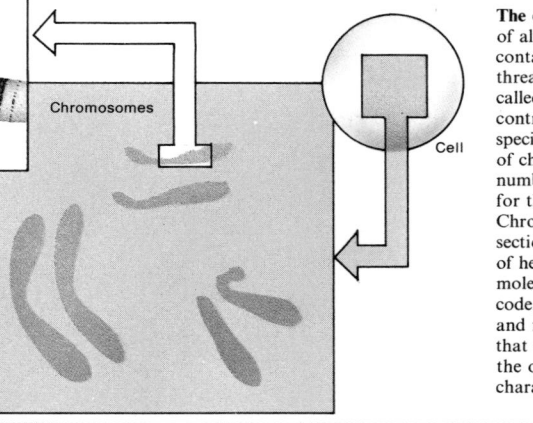

Genes — Chromosomes — Cell

The cell is the basic unit of all life, and every cell contains in its nucleus the thread-like structures, called chromosomes, that control heredity. Each species has its own number of chromosomes, and the number is always the same for that species. Chromosomes are sectioned into genes, units of heredity made of DNA molecules. DNA acts like a code, specifying the order and number of amino acids that make up proteins—the organic compounds characteristic of all life.

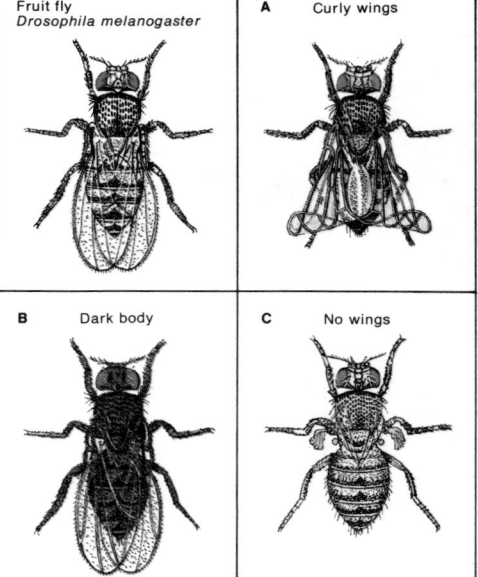

Fruit fly Drosophila melanogaster — A Curly wings — B Dark body — C No wings

Chromosomes (below left) of the fruit fly, much magnified, show bands of DNA arranged in sections that correspond exactly with specific genes, the chemical units of heredity. The proof of this correspondence came when the American geneticist Hermann Muller introduced the use of ionizing radiation to damage the fruit flies' chromosomes at ultramicroscopic points, causing precise point mutations in offspring of parents whose DNA had been damaged at the places indicated. Random mutations may occur in any organism, and not only as a result of radiation. A gradual accumulation of minor mutations may lead to evolutionary change.

Iiwi Vestiaria coccinea

Apapane Himatione sanguinea

Laysan finch Psittirostra cantans

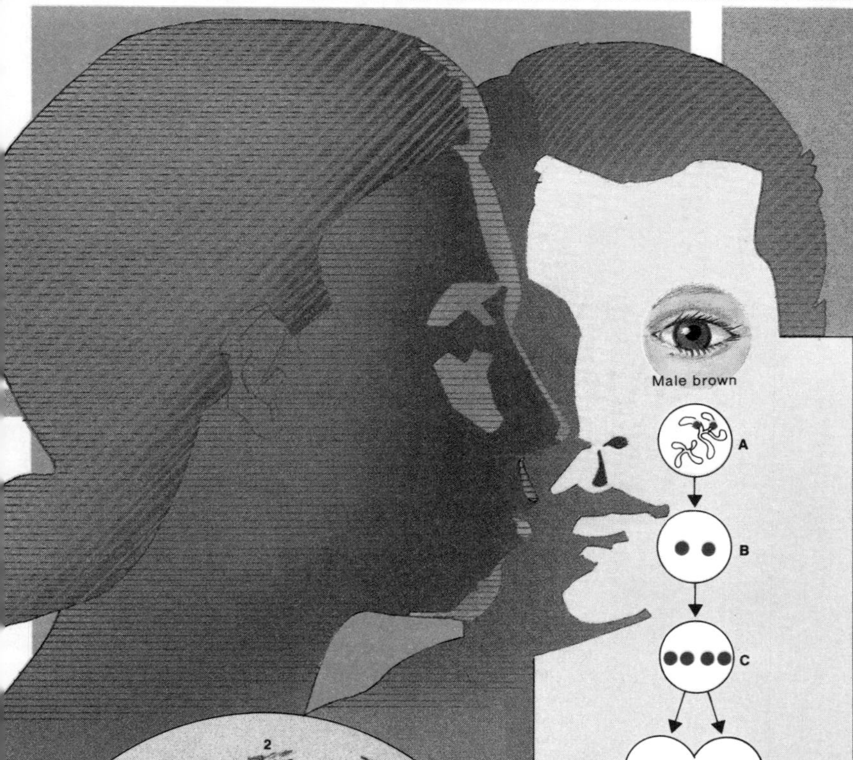

Some human traits, such as eye color, are inherited as single factors (below). In such cases one gene is dominant over the other, recessive, gene, and the gene giving a brown eye color is always dominant over that which gives a blue eye color. The chromosomes carrying eye-color genes (A) pair (B) and duplicate (C, D) before dividing twice (E, F) in the process known as meiosis, or reduction division. This ensures that the offspring gets half the chromosomes from the male and half from the female parent, so each new cell gets both genes when sperm and egg unite. But because brown-eye genes are dominant over blue, all offspring have brown eyes, with the blue-eye gene hidden. But if two brown-eyed parents carry recessive blue-eye genes, half the male sperm cells have blue-eye genes, and the female eggs carry a gene for either blue or brown eyes. So the two recessive genes have a one-in-four chance of being combined to produce a blue-eyed child, no brown-eye genes being present.

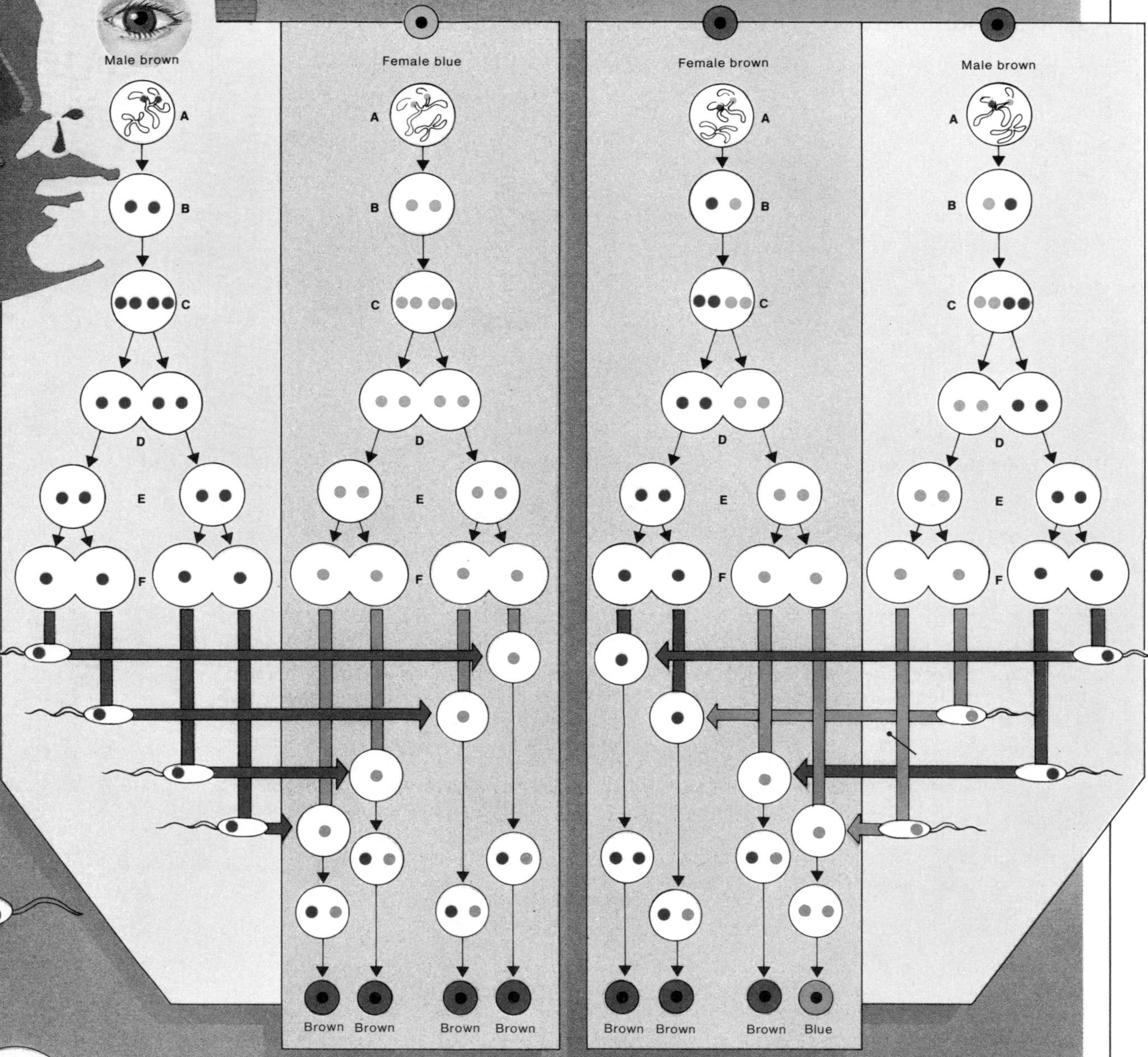

Male brown

Female blue

A

B

C

D

E

F

Brown Brown

Female brown

Male brown

A

B

C

D

E

F

Brown Brown

Brown Brown

Brown Blue

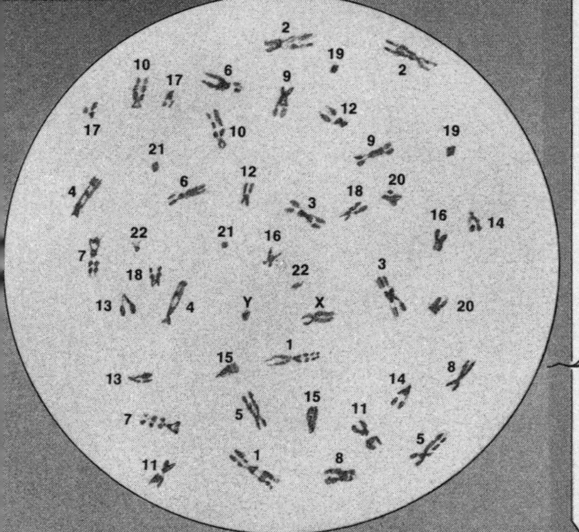

A human body cell (above) contains 46 chromosomes—22 matching pairs and the chromosomes (X, Y) which determine sex. Males have X and Y, females X and X. In sexual reproduction (right) traits carried by the male sperm and the female egg combine in the zygote, the fertilized egg from which new life starts. All growth is the result of repeated cell division, or mitosis, where the nucleus forms paired chromosomes that duplicate themselves; the cell splits, and the chromosomes re-form in the nucleus of the new cells. Sex cells are produced by reduction division, or meiosis, with each cell taking only one from each pair of chromosomes, which exchange corresponding segments in the process called recombination. The genes are thus reshuffled at each generation, so that new combinations of gene traits are available for selection each time meiosis takes place. The result is genetic diversity, with many possibilities for the species to adapt to a changing environment.

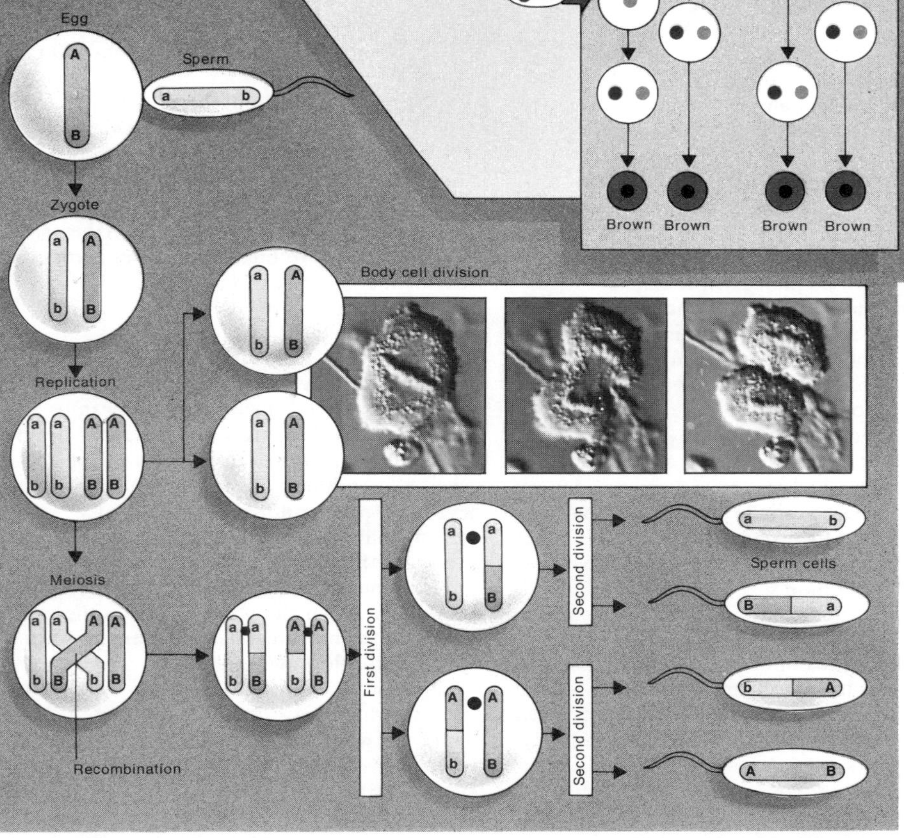

Egg

Sperm

Zygote

Replication

Meiosis

Recombination

Body cell division

First division

Second division

Second division

Sperm cells

A diversity of forms (left) has stemmed from a single ancestor of the Hawaiian honeycreeper, which now numbers 14 species. These have adapted in their mid-Pacific isolation to fill niches usually taken by other birds, ranging from the nectar-feeding iiwi to the Laysan finch with its thick beak for cracking seeds, and the short-billed apapane, which includes insects in its diet. But the honeycreepers' success in divergence may have led to overspecialization, with at least eight species now extinct. The Australian marsupial mouse and the Indian spiny mouse (right) look very similar, due to the fact that they fill similar ecological niches, but they belong to groups evolving separately for almost 100 million years.

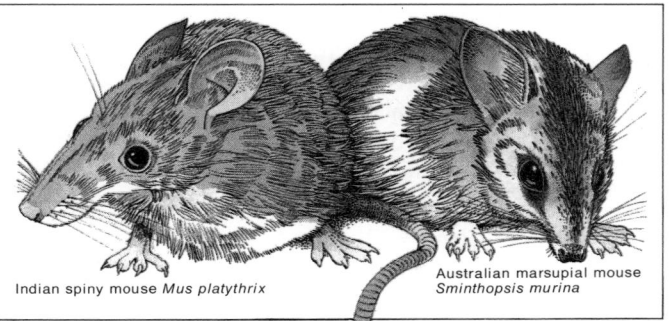

Indian spiny mouse *Mus platythrix*

Australian marsupial mouse *Sminthopsis murina*

VARIANT FORMS

Dark forms of many insects, such as the peppered moth *Biston betularia*, have developed widely in industrial areas of the world since the industrial age. The dark variant, resulting from a single genetic mutation, escapes the eye of predators against the black, lichen-free bark of soot-darkened trees (top), whereas the typical pale form is very conspicuous. In rural, unpolluted areas where tree trunks are light and lichen covered (bottom) the well-concealed pale form is much commoner. *Biston*'s rapid evolutionary response is remarkable: in 1849 only one dark example was recorded at Manchester, England, but by 1900 98% of the moths caught in the area were of the dark type. A similar change occurred in other industrial areas, during the period when the most coal was being burned and the population was most rapidly expanding. But with today's clean-air laws the number of pale moths in these areas is once again on the increase.

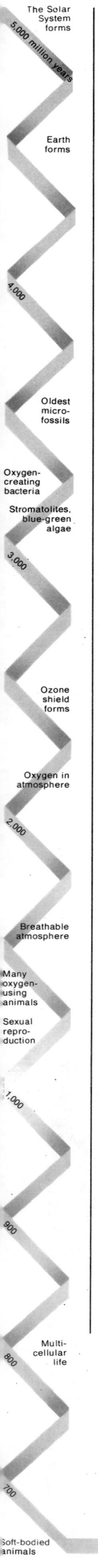
The Solar System forms
5,000 million years
Earth forms
4,000
Oldest micro-fossils
Oxygen-creating bacteria
Stromatolites, blue-green algae
3,000
Ozone shield forms
Oxygen in atmosphere
2,000
Breathable atmosphere
Many oxygen-using animals
Sexual reproduction
1,000
900
Multi-cellular life
800
700
Soft-bodied animals

Earliest Life Forms

Earth's original atmosphere lacked oxygen, without which there could be no survival for air-breathing creatures. This vital gas was supplied by life itself, in the form of microscopic organisms that flourished in the atmosphere of the time and emitted oxygen as "waste." In this way a breathable atmosphere built up; increasingly complex life forms were able to develop in the seas; early plants and insects gained a foothold on the shores; and, finally, larger animals could survive on land.

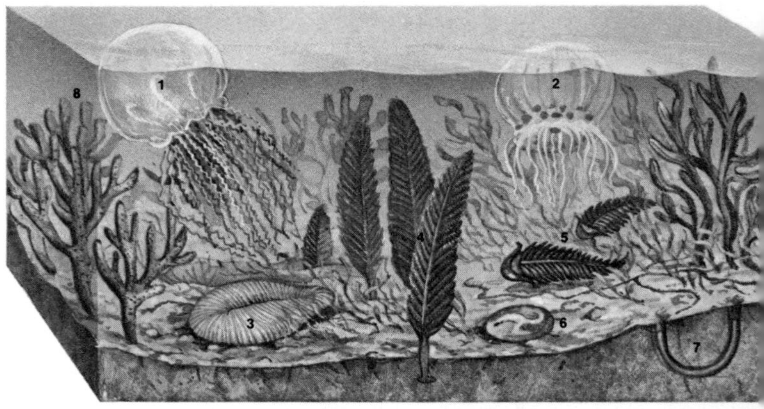

A BREATHABLE ATMOSPHERE

Without oxygen, life as we know it could not exist; yet Earth's original atmosphere contained practically none. The oxygenation of the atmosphere was the work of the planet's first life—primeval bacteria and algae. Of these, some released oxygen as waste while consuming carbon dioxide or nitrogen in photosynthesis. Colonies of algae forming stromatolites ("stony carpets") generated even more oxygen, but this was first taken up by ocean rocks, visible today as "banded iron formations." Once all the ocean rocks were oxidized, an oxygen-rich atmosphere could develop, with an ozone layer to filter out harmful radiation from the Sun.

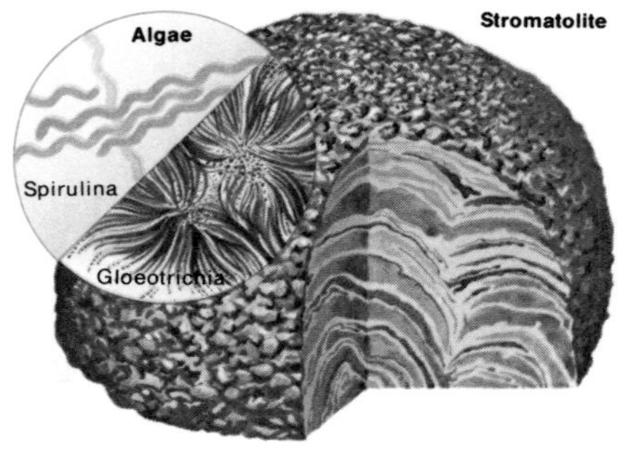
Stromatolite
Algae
Spirulina
Gloeotrichia

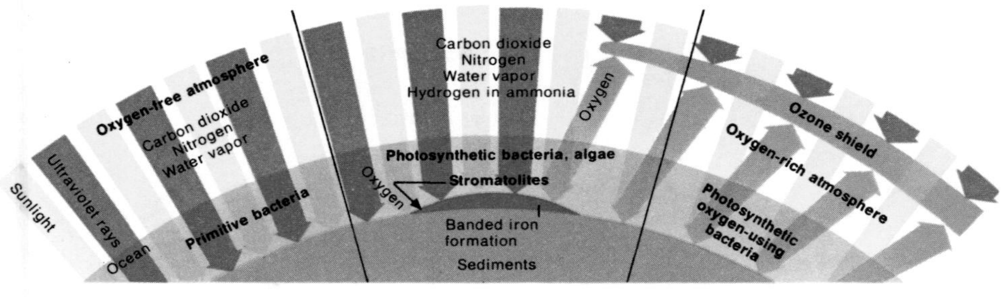
Oxygen-free atmosphere
Carbon dioxide
Nitrogen
Water vapor
Ultraviolet rays
Sunlight
Ocean
Primitive bacteria
Carbon dioxide
Nitrogen
Water vapor
Hydrogen in ammonia
Oxygen
Photosynthetic bacteria, algae
Oxygen
Stromatolites
Banded iron formation
Sediments
Ozone shield
Oxygen-rich atmosphere
Photosynthetic oxygen-using bacteria

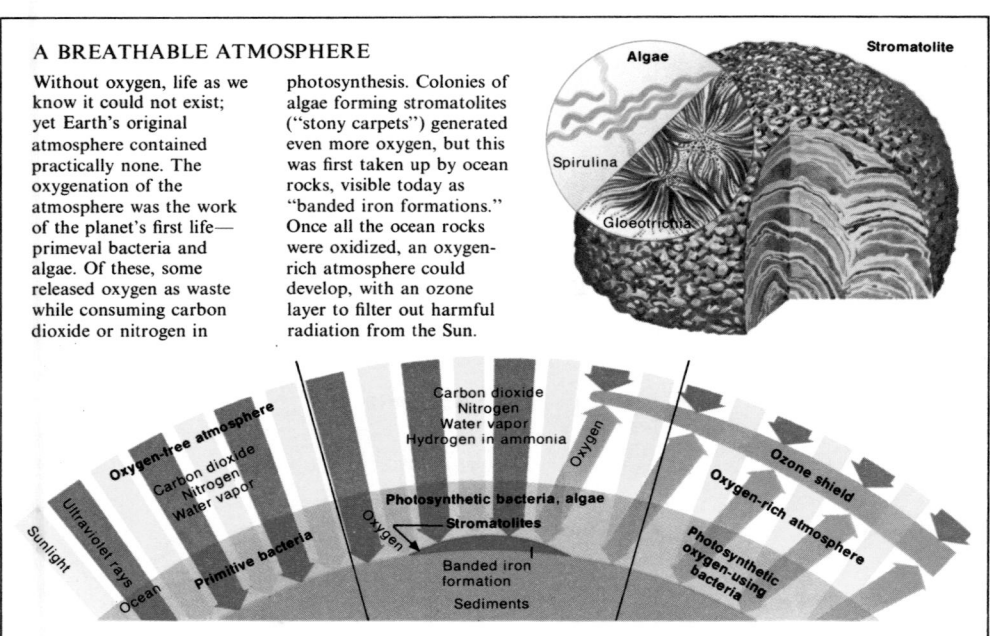

Scientists have identified bacteria-like microfossils in the rocks that were formed more than 3,500 million years ago. Some of these organisms appear to have been capable of photosynthesis—the process of utilizing sunlight, water and carbon dioxide for "food," with release of oxygen as the vitally important by-product. As a result, surplus oxygen very gradually accumulated in the Earth's atmosphere, forming an upper-atmosphere shield of ozone (which kept out damaging ultraviolet radiation from the Sun) and providing an oxygen-rich atmosphere in which breathing life could develop.

At least five types of microfossil have been found in ancient sediments of Western Australia, aged about 3,560 million years, and these provide the earliest evidence of life so far discovered. Other early proof of life comes from the so-called "stromatolites," some of which may date back as far as 3,400 million years. These curious columns, growing in warm, shallow waters, are formed of blue-green algae which have entrapped chalky sediments, bacteria and other microfossils. Their study is made easier by the fact that similar structures have developed at later geological times, and some are even being formed at the present day.

Living below the surface of the water and not initially reliant on oxygen for life, such bacteria and algae were shielded from the Sun's ultraviolet rays as they imperceptibly altered the Earth's atmosphere. For hundreds of millions of years life of this kind persisted, with few obvious developments or changes.

Breathing life

About 1,800 million years ago, the effects of these microscopic photosynthesizers became dramatically apparent in the "rusting" of the ocean sediments, when the red color of the rocks being formed at that time indicates that there was enough free oxygen on Earth to bring about the process known as oxidation. Once the ocean rocks capable of absorbing oxygen had done so, forming the red "banded iron formations" known to geologists, oxygen could enter the atmosphere in ever greater quantities.

It has been estimated that a breathable atmosphere existed on Earth about 1,700 million years ago, and aerobic (oxygen-using) organisms first became abundant not very long afterwards. These organisms were single celled, and it may have been almost 1,000 million years before multicellular animals evolved. The fossilized remains of animals alive 800 million years ago have been found in many parts of the world, but it is not yet known whether multicellular animals had a long history before these earliest known forms, or whether they had developed and radiated rapidly from a creature capable of feeding as well as photosynthesizing.

One of the earliest collections of animals of this type was discovered in the Ediacara Sandstones of the Flinders Range in Australia, where some 650 million years ago the rocks once formed part of an ancient beach. Here a spectacular collection of soft-bodied animals, similar to today's coelenterates (such as jellyfish) and worms, was washed ashore and preserved in silt from the nearby shallow sea. Comparable, mainly floating forms have been found in other parts of the world in rocks dating from between 650 and 580 million years ago.

The first vertebrates

One of the most important changes in animal life seems to have occurred about 580 million years ago. At that date many creatures evolved hard, protective shells, which also acted as areas of muscle attachment and as support for their bodies—in other words, as external skeletons. Hard shells were more easily preserved as fossils than the soft bodies of earlier animals, so rich collections have been recovered from rocks of the Cambrian Period, beginning 580 million years ago, as well as from later strata.

The first fish-like animals—the earliest true vertebrates—are found in rocks of the Ordovician Period, from about 500 million years ago, and these were in many ways very similar to the lampreys and hagfishes of today. But unlike them, these ancient creatures were heavily armored with external bone. They must have been poor swimmers, living mainly on the seabed and filtering edible particles from the sediments, which they sucked into their jawless mouths. From them arose true fishes, with backbones, jaws and teeth, and they came to replace the less efficient earlier forms.

During the Devonian Period, about 400 million years ago, the fishes diversified greatly, adapting to fit all kinds of aquatic environments. Some grew to a huge size, such as *Dunkleosteus*, which achieved a length of up to 9 m (29 ft 7 in), although it belonged to a group of fishes that retained heavy armor. Some of these curious creatures probably used their stilt-like pectoral fins to hitch themselves across the beds of the pools in which they lived.

From water to land

The fishes that teemed in the seas and fresh waters of the Devonian world found their way into difficult environments such as swamps and oasis pools, where there was a danger of drying out in the warmer weather. Many of these fishes had rudimentary lungs, and one group developed powerful jointed fins.

Such marginal habitats were not ideal for fishes, but they were nevertheless rich in species, and it is from them that the first land vertebrates developed. When the water dried up they survived, for their strong fins held them up so that they did not flop over helplessly.

They found themselves in a new, dry world, but one which was already inhabited, at least round the water's edges, with plants related to modern liverworts, mosses and club mosses. There were also numerous invertebrate animals such as millipedes, spiders and wingless insects. These plants and animals provided shelter and food, so that the environment was not wholly hostile to larger animals.

The first steps on land probably took the form of strong flexions of the body—desperate swimming movements which swung the fins forward, pegging the animal's position in the drying mud. But in a very short time geologically, animals had evolved in which the rays of the lobe fins had vanished, leaving stubby legs with which the animals—no longer fishes but amphibians—could haul themselves over land. But they still had to return to water to breed and lay eggs.

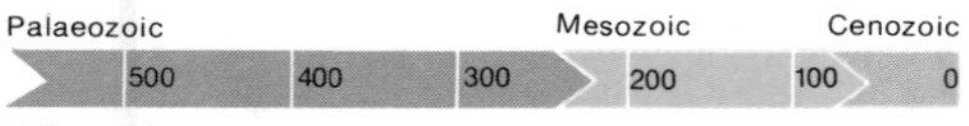
Palaeozoic
Mesozoic
Cenozoic
500
400
300
200
100
0
Millions of years ago

A timescale of life on Earth emerges from the record of fossils embedded in rock strata. Major breaks in faunas (animal assemblages) separate eras coinciding roughly with periods of intense mountain-building activity. These eras are broken down into geological periods, which are separated by lesser faunal breaks and which are generally named from the area where rocks of that age were first discovered. The geological eras and periods do not imply particular rock types.

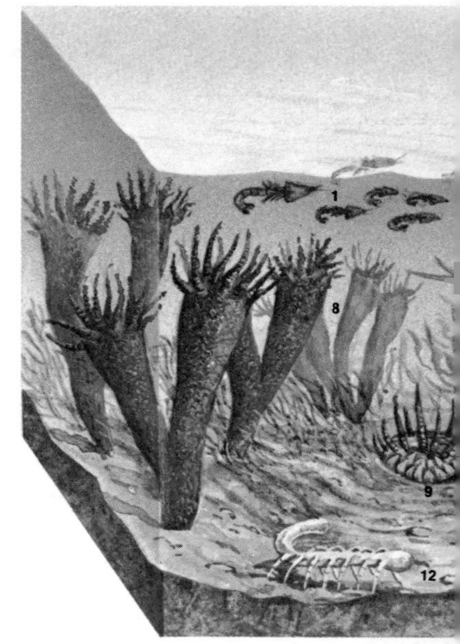

THE FIRST SHELLED CREATURES
These evolved (right) in the seas when conditions allowed soft-bodied life to form protective casings. In the fossil record of 550 million years ago, soft and shelled forms are found. The trilobites (1, 2, 3)—a now extinct order of woodlouse-like animals—dominated the scene, but other early arthropods (4) included a possible insect ancestor (5), and there may even have been an ancestor to fish (6). Sponges (7), crinoids (8), early moluscs (9), bristleworms (10) and lamp-shells (11) were plentiful, but other creatures (12) are bewilderingly strange.

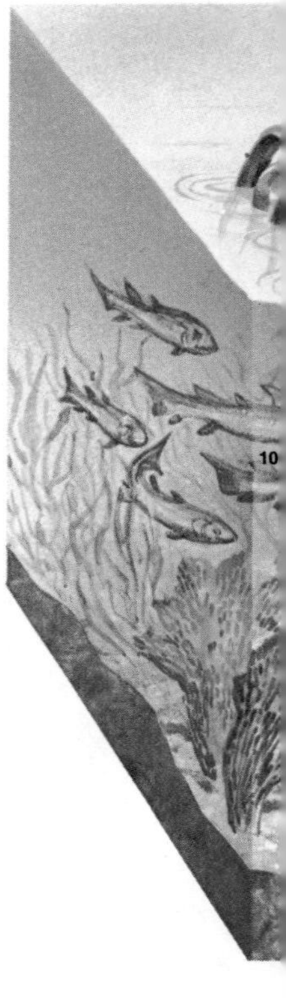

THE FIRST AMPHIBIANS
Amphibians (1) emerged some 345 million years ago (right), inhabiting swampy environments with luxuriant vegetation—club mosses and ferns (2, 3) that made up the early coal forests. Lungfish (4) were well adapted to life in oxygen-poor waters, but the move to land was probably made by related fish with a passage linking nostrils to throat—*Eusthenopteron* (5). Land offered food (6, 7, 8) and suitably damp conditions for a possibly stranded aquatic animal.

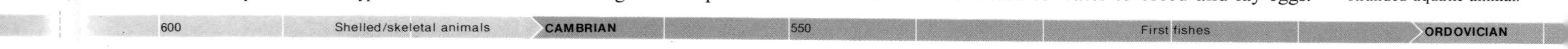
600
Shelled/skeletal animals
CAMBRIAN
550
First fishes
ORDOVICIAN

THE AGE OF JELLYFISH

Jellyfish (left) and other soft-bodied animals flourished in the pre-Cambrian seas, more than 600 million years ago. The forms of one group, imprinted on sand, have been preserved as fossils in the Australian Ediacara Sandstones. They include varieties similar to modern jellyfish (1, 2); worm-like crawlers (3); sea pens (4) very like modern types; segmented worms (5); "three-legged" creatures like no known animal (6); and sand casts of burrowing worms (7).

LIFE ON SEA AND LAND

For more than half the Earth's existence, its atmosphere has been hostile to air-breathing life. Then, about 1,600 million years ago, the photosynthesizing action of minute organisms built up enough free oxygen in the atmosphere for more complex oxygen-dependent forms to develop. The first multicellular life led to the soft-bodied animals of the pre-Cambrian time—worms, jellyfish and sea pens. About 580 million years ago many animals developed hard parts, including shells. Over 1,200 new marine species date from this period, and the evolutionary explosion came to fill the Earth's seas with fishes. Some of these had powerful jointed fins and rudimentary lungs, and lived in swamps where primitive plants and insects had already made the move to land. As the pools dwindled the stranded animals could survive by breathing air.

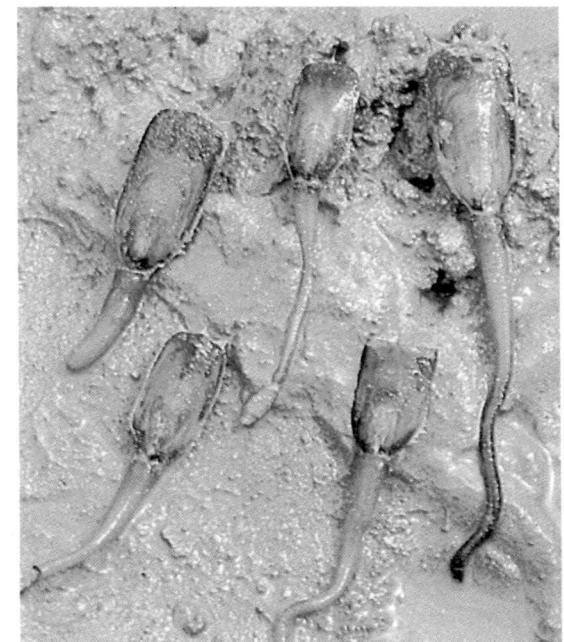

LIVING FOSSILS

Some life forms that emerged 570 million years ago have survived virtually unchanged to the present day. These "living fossils" include *Lingula* (left), today found in warm, brackish coastal waters, poor in oxygen and unsuited to most life, off the Pacific and Indian oceans. *Neopilina* (below), a primitive marine mollusc first found alive in 1952, has features unlike other molluscs but suggesting much closer affinities with the annelids (worms) and arthropods (insects, crabs, etc.).

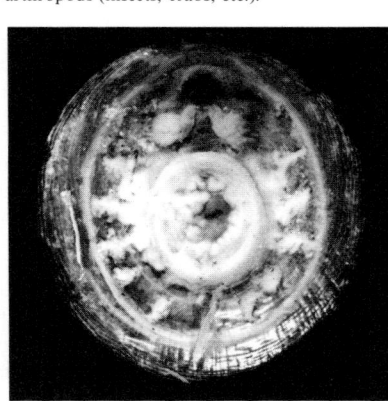

THE AGE OF JELLYFISH
1 Jellyfish (*Ediacaria*)
2 Jellyfish (*Medusina*)
3 Flatworm (*Dickinsonia costata*)
4 Sea pens (*Rangea, Charnia*)
5 Segmented worms (*Spriggina floundersi*)
6 Unknown animal (*Tribrachidium*)
7 Burrowing worm (fossil casts)
8 Sponges and algae (hypothetical)

THE FIRST SHELLED CREATURES
1 Trilobites (*Waptia*)
2 Trilobites (*Marella splendens*)
3 Trilobite (*Olenoides serratus*)
4 Primitive arthropod (*Perspicaris dictynna*)
5 Primitive arthropod (*Aysheaia pedunculata*)
6 Ancestral lancelet fish (*Branchiostoma*)
7 Sponge (*Vauxia*)
8 Crinoids (*Echmatocrinus*)
9 Mollusc (*Wiwaxia*)
10 Bristleworm (*Nereis*)
11 Brachiopod (*Lingulella*)
12 Unknown animal (*Hallucigenia sparsa*)

THE AGE OF FISHES
1 Primitive plant (*Nematophyton*)
2 Psilophite plant (*Asteroxylon*)
3 Psilophite plant (*Rhynia*)
4 Primitive insect (*Rhyniella*)
5 Placoderm fish (*Bothriolepis*)
6 Placoderm fish (*Phyllolepis*)
7 Placoderm fish (*Dunkleosteus*)
8 Early shark (*Cladoselache*)
9 Lungfish (*Dipterus*)
10 Lobe-fin fish (*Osteolepis*)
11 Crustacean (*Montecaris*)

THE FIRST AMPHIBIANS
1 Amphibian (*Ichthyostega*)
2 Club moss (*Cyclostigma*)
3 Fern (*Pseudosporochnus*)
4 Lungfish (*Scaumenacia*)
5 Rhipidistian fish (*Eusthenopteron*)
6 Millipede (*Acantherpestes ornatus*)
7 Early scorpion (*Palaeophonus*)
8 Spider-like creature (*Palaeocharinoides*)
9 Small plant (*Sciadophyton*)

THE AGE OF FISHES

Fishes (left) filled the brackish Devonian waters, about 350 million years ago, while primitive plants and insects had pioneered the land. Giant weeds (1) grew above muddy waters, and vascular plants (2, 3) colonized the shores, sheltering early insects (4). Primitive fishes (5, 6, 7) remained, but ray-finned types (8)—ancestors of modern fish—were dominant. However, it was from the lobe-finned fishes (9, 10) that the first land vertebrates emerged.

The Age of Reptiles

When the Carboniferous Period began, the world was already populated with animals and plants of many kinds. The oceans were full of fishes, invertebrates and aquatic plants. The land, meanwhile, was producing dramatic new species: giant mosses and ferns, spiders and insects and, most important of all, the rapidly evolving amphibians. These creatures were taking the first evolutionary steps on a path that would lead to some of the most remarkable creatures ever to live – the dinosaurs.

The broad, low-lying, swampy plains of the late Carboniferous provided ideal conditions for the world's early plants. They spread and diversified, and some of them grew to enormous size. Giant club mosses, huge horsetails and luxuriant tree ferns took on the proportions of modern-day trees and formed the world's first forests. These new forests were full of animal life: primitive spiders and scorpions hunting their prey, giant dragonflies hovering over the marshy waters and other insects scavenging or hunting on the mossy forest floor or in the branches of the "trees." In the huge coal-forest swamps, the most advanced of all animals, the amphibians, were rapidly evolving. Some of these would ultimately return to life in the water. But others were developing stronger legs and were becoming better able to cope with an existence on dry land.

It was from this second group that the reptiles evolved—the first animals to be equipped with waterproof skins. Unlike their amphibian ancestors, they could stay out of the water indefinitely without losing their body fluids through their skins. They were no longer tied to the water's edge and the pattern of life was revolutionized. The world was soon inhabited by the first wave of land vertebrates—reptiles, which then rapidly diversified.

Included among these first reptiles were creatures known as sailbacks. They had a row of long, bony spines that supported a great fin running down from the back of their heads to the base of their tails. This whole apparatus functioned as a heat-exchange organ: the fin absorbed heat from the atmosphere in the early, cooler parts of the day, when the animal was cold, and blushed off warmth later, when it became overheated. Unlike the cold-blooded reptiles, sailbacked reptiles could, to a certain extent, regulate their body temperatures.

Mammal-like reptiles

It was only about 50 million years later, however, that animals skeletally identical to mammals were found throughout the world. Almost certainly these creatures had a degree of warm-bloodedness. But they were all rather small—the biggest was no larger than a domestic cat—and this may account for their decline. They were destined to be overshadowed for many millions of years by the dinosaurs.

The late Triassic Period, about 200 million years ago, is marked by a sudden decline in the

THE RULING REPTILES

Seymouria and other advanced amphibians evolved to form the first reptiles, such as *Scutosaurus*. From these a multitude of adaptations evolved. Some herbivores, such as *Corythosaurus*, developed 2,000 or more teeth, to help them consume tough, fibrous food plants. Another herbivorous group attained enormous size—*Brachiosaurus* weighed as much as 80 tonnes—and this may have been an adaptation to regulate body temperature (large objects lose and gain heat more slowly than small objects). Another adaptation, but one that developed mainly in the carnivores, was that of offensive weaponry: *Deinonychus* had a huge sickle-shaped claw on each hind foot and the later *Tyrannosaurus* combined a massive body with a jagged mouthful of 60 teeth. Armor plating was a defensive adaptation, produced by herbivores such as *Triceratops*, whereas speed of movement was developed both by some herbivores and by small carnivores such as *Struthiomimus*.

Corythosaurus

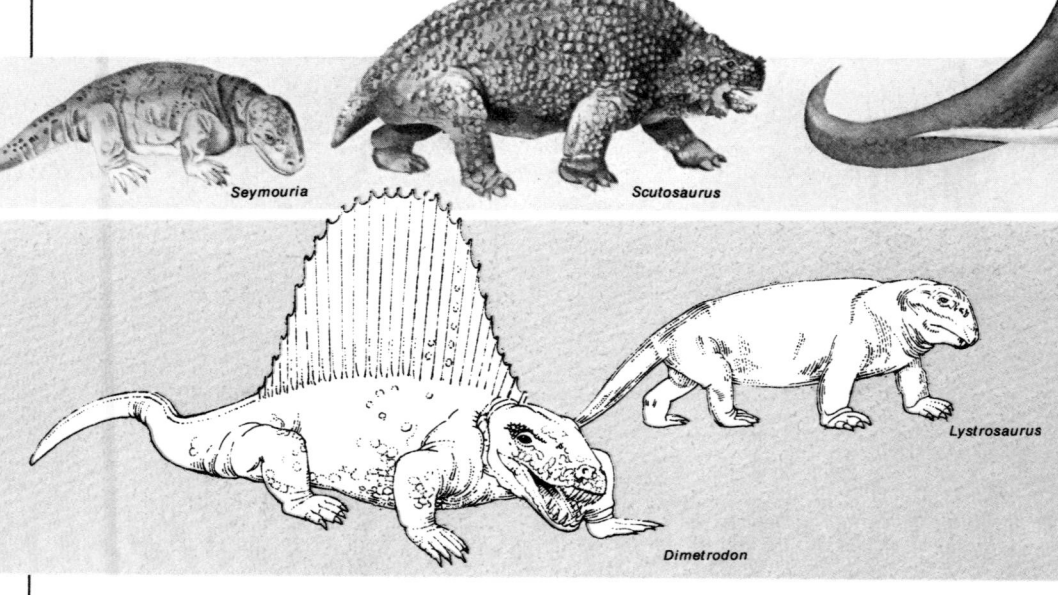

Seymouria

Scutosaurus

Deinonychus

Dimetrodon

Lystrosaurus

THE MAMMAL LINE

Sailbacks such as *Dimetrodon* mark the beginning of mammal history. These reptiles had developed the first method of regulating body temperature—each was equipped with a large fin on its back which acted as a heat-exchange organ, a living solar panel. From these strange creatures, para-mammals such as *Lystrosaurus* evolved, animals with many mammal-like features. Some of the later members of this group, such as *Thrinaxodon*, probably even had fur on their bodies. Then, about 200 million years ago, the first true warm-blooded mammals, such as *Morganucodon*, developed. But by this time the group as a whole was declining in response to reptilian competition. Mammals would have to wait 140 million years before becoming successful again.

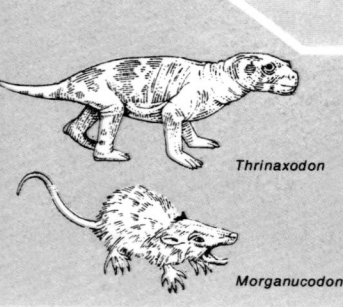

Thrinaxodon

Morganucodon

COAL FORMATION

Coal consists of carbon from plant remains and most of it was formed in the swamp-forests from which reptiles emerged. First, peat formed from rotted vegetation. Sea levels rose, ocean covered the peat bogs and marine sediments were laid down. The resulting pressure converted peat to coal. The cycle recurred and the deepest coal seams were compressed and hardened.

Coal-forming forest swamp
Peat layer
Lignite seam
Bituminous seam
Anthracite seam

Palaeozoic | Mesozoic | Cenozoic
500   400   300   200   100   0
Millions of years ago

Three geological eras mark the evolution of life on Earth. It was the Mesozoic era, beginning 230 million years ago, that spanned the age of reptiles. Until then, throughout the Palaeozoic era, life had been slowly evolving from the primitive organisms that appeared 400 million years earlier.

By the Mesozoic, the earliest reptiles had developed. Among their descendants were dinosaurs and early representatives of the mammalian line. Mammals, however, would have to wait another 165 million years, until the Cenozoic, before they achieved dominance.

The plant communities underwent as many developments in the course of the Mesozoic era as did the reptiles. The end of the Palaeozoic saw changes in climate—the Permian Period was much drier than the Carboniferous. Giant horsetails, ferns and club mosses that had formed the world's first forests gave way to other types of plant: early conifers and their relatives

(the gymnosperms) came to the fore. These new species, such as the Cycadales, had evolved a new, improved method of reproduction—using seeds not spores. By Jurassic times, the climate had changed again and the moist conditions supported dense forests of ferns and of conifers. The final major Mesozoic development took place in Cretaceous times, when the flowering plants evolved.

Cycadale

Gingko biloba

CARBONIFEROUS   300   Earliest reptiles   **PERMIAN**   Early conifers   250   First radiation of reptiles   **TRIASSIC**   First mammals

40

EVOLUTION AND ADAPTATION

Once their amphibian ancestors had crawled from the swamps, reptiles rapidly evolved and developed a remarkable range of adaptations: they took to the air, invaded the seas and held dominion over the land. By early Jurassic times, they had firmly established their claim to the title Ruling Reptiles. Another group of early reptile descendants led to the mammals, and although these were long overshadowed by the dinosaurs, they were destined to rise to dominance.

mammal-like reptiles and by the extraordinary evolutionary radiation of the so-called Archosaurs ("ruling reptiles"). These began to fill every available ecological niche. They evolved into carnivores, herbivores and omnivores. They included the Crocodilians, which adapted to a life in the water; the flying pterosaurs, which were the first vertebrates to fly, and, most important of all, the dinosaurs, whose evolutionary reign over the land was to endure for the next 140 million years.

Dinosaurs adapted well to life on the land. They developed "fully erect" limbs (not unlike those of the later higher mammals) rather than the splayed legs found in most other reptiles. The new position of their limbs, which gave them the necessary mobility on dry land, was also accompanied by a general increase in size. But the dinosaurs were not the only land reptiles of the time; many other forms, including tortoises, snakes and lizards, were also carving their niches during the Mesozoic era.

Similarly, the pterosaurs did not remain the only creatures of the sky. By 170 million years ago, birds in the form of claw-winged *Archaeopteryx* had evolved, and these were to prove a serious challenge to the primitive winged reptiles which had poor flying abilities.

Aquatic reptiles

Just as the land and the air were rapidly inhabited by newly evolving forms, so the water produced many new developments. Several of the Mesozoic reptiles began to adapt to aquatic life in ways often parallel to present-day mammals: the long-necked, fish-eating plesiosaurs led a life much like that of seals; the larger

pliosaurs had a streamlined shape similar to that of certain whales; some mollusc-eating placodonts could be likened to the walrus; and the elegant icthyosaurs were in many ways like dolphins. Large invertebrates were also found in the seas. The most dramatic of these were the ammonites—shelled relatives of the octopus— some of which grew to more than 2 m (6 ft) in size. Among fishes a new type emerged, the Teleosts, and these were destined to become the dominant fishes of the modern world.

Wholesale extinction

At the end of the Cretaceous Period, the reptiles were flourishing. Then suddenly, 65 million years ago, a catastrophe occurred. Virtually every species, including all the large animals, were wiped out. Throughout the Mesozoic, a series of dinosaurs and other reptiles had been evolving and slowly becoming extinct, but they were always replaced by other species. This wholesale extinction was unprecedented.

The cause of the catastrophe is unknown, but since the nature of the Earth itself was unchanged, it seems likely that some outside phenomenon was responsible. One theory suggests that a large meteorite collided with the Earth, throwing enough dust into the atmosphere to blot out the sun for several years—long enough to kill almost all the green plants on land and in the sea. If this was the case, only small animals that fed on carrion, decaying vegetation, seeds or nuts could hope to survive. Whatever the cause, the reign of the reptiles was at an end, leaving the small, adaptable mammals and birds to recolonize the virtually empty planet during the Cenozoic era.

Brachiosaurus

Tyrannosaurus rex

Struthiomimus

Triceratops

Rhamphorhynchus

Archaeopteryx

Plesiosaurus

Ichthyornis

Birds are relatives of the reptiles. The first bird, *Archaeopteryx*, evolving in Jurassic times, had many reptilian features—a long, bony tail, toothed mouth and clawed wings. By Cretaceous times, birds such as *Ichthyornis* had a more familiar form.

Plesiosaurs evolved at the same time as the dinosaurs and were as successful in their marine environment as were the dinosaurs on land. They were most common in Jurassic times.

Pterosaurs such as *Rhamphorhynchus* were the first vertebrates to take to the sky. They were not strong fliers and probably glided on air currents much of the time.

Norfolk Island pine
Araucaria heterophylla

Williamsonia

Common oak
Quercus robur

Fig tree
Ficus sp

Plane tree
Platanus sp

…liation of reptiles **JURASSIC** First birds 150 **CRETACEOUS** First flowering plants 100 First modern fishes Extinction of dinosaurs

41

The Age of Mammals

After the time of the great dying, 65 million years ago, reptiles never regained the importance they had achieved during the Mesozoic era. A new era, the Cenozoic, had begun. On the continental landmasses, mammals and birds, newly released from 160 million years of reptilian domination, began to occupy their niches in the rich, empty habitats. They flourished and diversified, and the cold-blooded reptiles became second-class citizens in a world of warm-blooded animals.

While reptiles still dominated the world, during the late Mesozoic, a new group of mammals had arisen. These were the first creatures on Earth to give birth to fully formed, live young. Until this time, the most advanced of the mammals had been marsupials whose young were still virtually embryos at birth and had to develop in the mother's pouch, or marsupium. The new mammals had evolved a more sophisticated system—the mother retained the fetus safely inside her body until it was fully formed, nourishing it during this time through a special organ, the placenta, developed during pregnancy. These mammals, the placentals, were destined to become the major mammalian group.

Although all the Mesozoic placentals were small, they had already evolved into a number of different forms that existed alongside the dinosaurs. Besides the insectivores, which were the ancestral type, they included early representatives of the Primates (precursors of modern monkeys and apes), the Carnivores, and the now extinct Condylarthrans (primitive hoofed mammals). When suddenly, 65 million years ago, there was no longer competition from the large land reptiles, these early groups rapidly evolved and extravagant forms developed.

But just as the first reptiles had passed through an early evolution, largely to be replaced by a second evolutionary wave, so the first large mammals were, in many cases, superseded by other, more successful lines. In the earliest part of the Cenozoic era, the different groups of placentals, although not closely related, all tended to be heavy limbed and heavy tailed and to walk on the whole length of their feet (as do modern bears) or on thick, stubby toes. These ungainly, thickset mammals soon died out. Some became extinct because their descendants, more efficiently adapted to their environment, overtook and replaced them. Others, such as the powerful taeniodonts and the large rodent-like tillodonts, seem to have been evolutionary blind alleys.

Spectacular developments

It was the Oligocene Period, 36 million years ago, that saw the end of most of these early essays in mammalian gigantism but, in many parts of the world, they were replaced by others just as spectacular. In South America, the giant sloths and glyptodonts (massive relatives of the armadillos) survived until comparatively recently. The ground sloths, at least, were contemporaries of the first men on the continent.

As each group of early mammals evolved, during the early and middle part of the Cenozoic era, many of their developments closely reflected changes taking place in their environment. The first horse-like creature, for example, was *Hyracotherium*, also called *Eohippus* or "dawn horse." It lived 54 million years ago and was a small, multi-toed creature, well adapted to its densely forested habitat. The teeth of its descendants gradually changed in size and complexity, but it was not until the Miocene Period, nearly 20 million years later, that any radical alterations took place. This was the time when grasses (the Gramineae), until then a rare family of plants, came to the fore. The world's plains suddenly became clothed in a food plant very suitable for the attention of grazing creatures such as the early horses.

Animals of the grasslands

Horses and many other animals moved from the forests to make use of this new and abundant food supply. Once on the plains, different adaptations for survival were required: high-crowned teeth to deal with tough grasses; limbs enabling the animal to run tirelessly without extra, unwanted weight from supporting side toes (which were lost); large eyes capable of seeing for long distances and placed far back on the head for detecting predators approaching from any direction (as a result of which, however, the ability to judge distances ahead had to be sacrificed). Thus, the modern horses are plains-dwelling animals, perfectly adapted to their present way of life.

Mammals reached the climax of diversity during the Pliocene Period, 10 million years ago. But in the following period, the Pleistocene, ice sheets swept down from the polar regions and from the high mountains of the north, bringing massive and sudden changes to the ecology of virtually every region in the world. This dramatic disturbance to the environment brought extinction to an enormous number of species.

The survivors consisted mainly of the smaller species. Unfortunately for many of them, however, they included *Homo sapiens*. Man rose to success at the end of the Pleistocene and has, in the last 10,000 years, taken dominion over virtually every part of the world. During this time, he has proved far more destructive to other animal species than any natural force has ever been. More than 5,000 years ago, the giant sloths may have been a dying species, but there is no doubt that early human hunters hurried on their extinction. Since then, the list of species eliminated by man has grown ever longer. Today the human race is causing the extinction of both animals and plants at a rate comparable to that of 65 million years ago, when some dramatic natural catastrophe swept the dinosaurs from the face of the world. Unless man, the super-efficient species, can curb his numbers and his destructive activities, a new age of dying may soon be upon the world.

By early Cenozoic times, many forms had evolved from the insectivorous mammals of the Mesozoic Period. *Miacis*, *Hyaenodon* and *Oxyaena* were flesh eaters. Plant-eating mammals, such as Taeniodonts, *Arsinoitherium* and *Phenacodus* (one of the first hoofed mammals), had also evolved, while other early forms, such as *Andrewsarchus*, were omnivorous. The early Primates, however, remained insect eaters for millions of years.

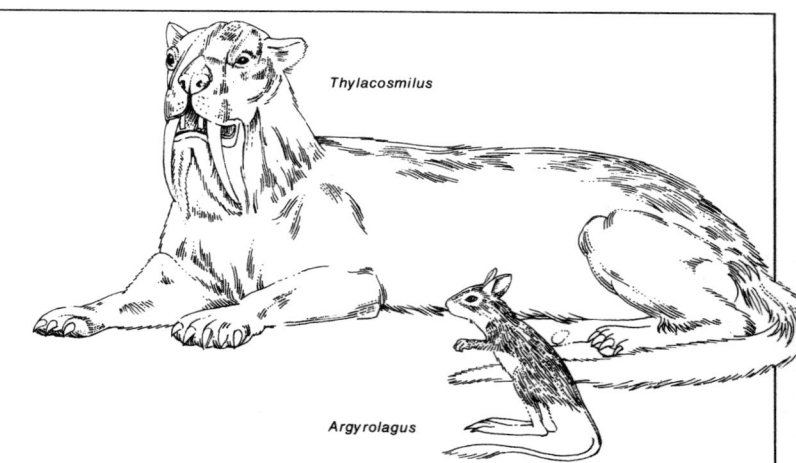

Miacis

EARLY STAGES

Andrewsarchus

Hyaenodon

Diatryma

Euryapteryx

CENOZOIC BIRDS

Giant flightless birds came to the fore more than once during the Cenozoic era. *Diatryma*, a massive, flesh-eating bird, ruled the North American grasslands in early Cenozoic times, while mammals were still small, fairly primitive and easily dominated. *Euryapteryx* and its relatives (the moas) evolved in New Zealand, where, because there were no mammals, they filled an empty ecological niche.

The Carnivores diversified into two major types—the cats and their kin (Aeluroidea), and the dogs and their relatives (Arctoidea). During the Oligocene Period, about 36 million years ago, Aeluroidea gave rise not only to early relatives of modern cats, such as sabre-toothed *Hoplophoneus*, but also to two other families, the civets and the hyenas. At the same time, Arctoidea also diversified and produced the dogs, weasels, bears and racoons. It was a complex group, with many forms that were later to become extinct—the massive bear-dogs, such as *Daphoenus*, for example, which lived during the Miocene Period. Cats and dogs evolved to exploit different habitats. The cats adapted to life in forests, and learned to hide and then stalk and ambush their prey. Dogs evolved as plains animals, and used pack-hunting techniques to catch fleet-footed, grassland animals.

Perissodactyls and Artiodactyls were two important groups that evolved from the primitive hoofed mammals; Perissodactyls had an odd number of toes on each foot, Artiodactyls had an even number. These two groups suffered very different fortunes. Artiodactyls are still at the height of their success; the early stock produced the modern pig, camel, deer, giraffe, hippopotamus, antelope, sheep, goat and cow. Perissodactyls, however, are in decline and the only survivors are the horse, rhinoceros and tapir. But they were once important and many, now-extinct, kinds such as *Moropus* and *Brontotherium* existed alongside more familiar types such as *Hyracotherium*. Few remained after the Pliocene Period, however. This was when the Artiodactyls came to the fore. They, too, had had casualties—the pig-like *Archaeotherium* was by then extinct—but many other Artiodactyls, such as the early giraffe, *Palaeotragus*, were evolving. Most important, however, was small *Archaeomeryx*, for it had developed the key to Artiodactyl success—it was a ruminant and this enabled it to make the best possible use of the world's new grasslands.

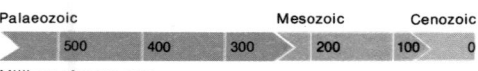

Palaeozoic		Mesozoic	Cenozoic	
500	400	300	200	100	0

Millions of years ago

Three geological eras mark the slow evolution of life on Earth. The Palaeozoic era, 570 million years ago, saw the appearance of the first primitive life forms. By the end of the era, 340 million years later, the reptiles had evolved and the following Mesozoic era was the age of reptilian domination. This reign over the land ended 65 million years ago as the Cenozoic era began. Then mammals came to the fore and the age of mammalian dominance of the world had dawned.

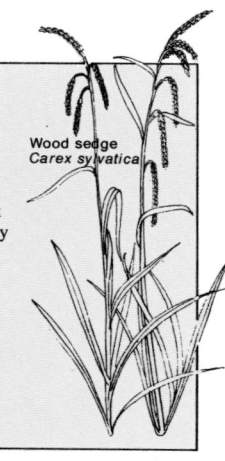

EARLY GRASSES

Grasses first appeared in the densely forested lands of 60 million years ago. Probably similar to the sedges (right) found in wet woodland areas today, they offered an attractive meal to many mammals. But it was not until the Miocene Period, when a change in climate reduced forest cover, that grasses became widespread. Then many forest creatures migrated to grassland areas.

Wood sedge
Carex sylvatica

THE MARSUPIALS

Thylacosmilus and mouse-like *Argyrolagus* were two of the many forms of marsupial mammal that evolved in Cenozoic times in South America. Almost everywhere else, the marsupials, unable to compete with their more efficient placental cousins, met with an early extinction. But in two remote regions—South America (then separate from North America) and Australia—there was no competition from placentals, and there the marsupials flourished.

Thylacosmilus

Argyrolagus

TERTIARY	First radiation of mammals and birds		Forest horses				Second radiation of mammals
Palaeocene	60	Eocene	50		40		Oligocene

42

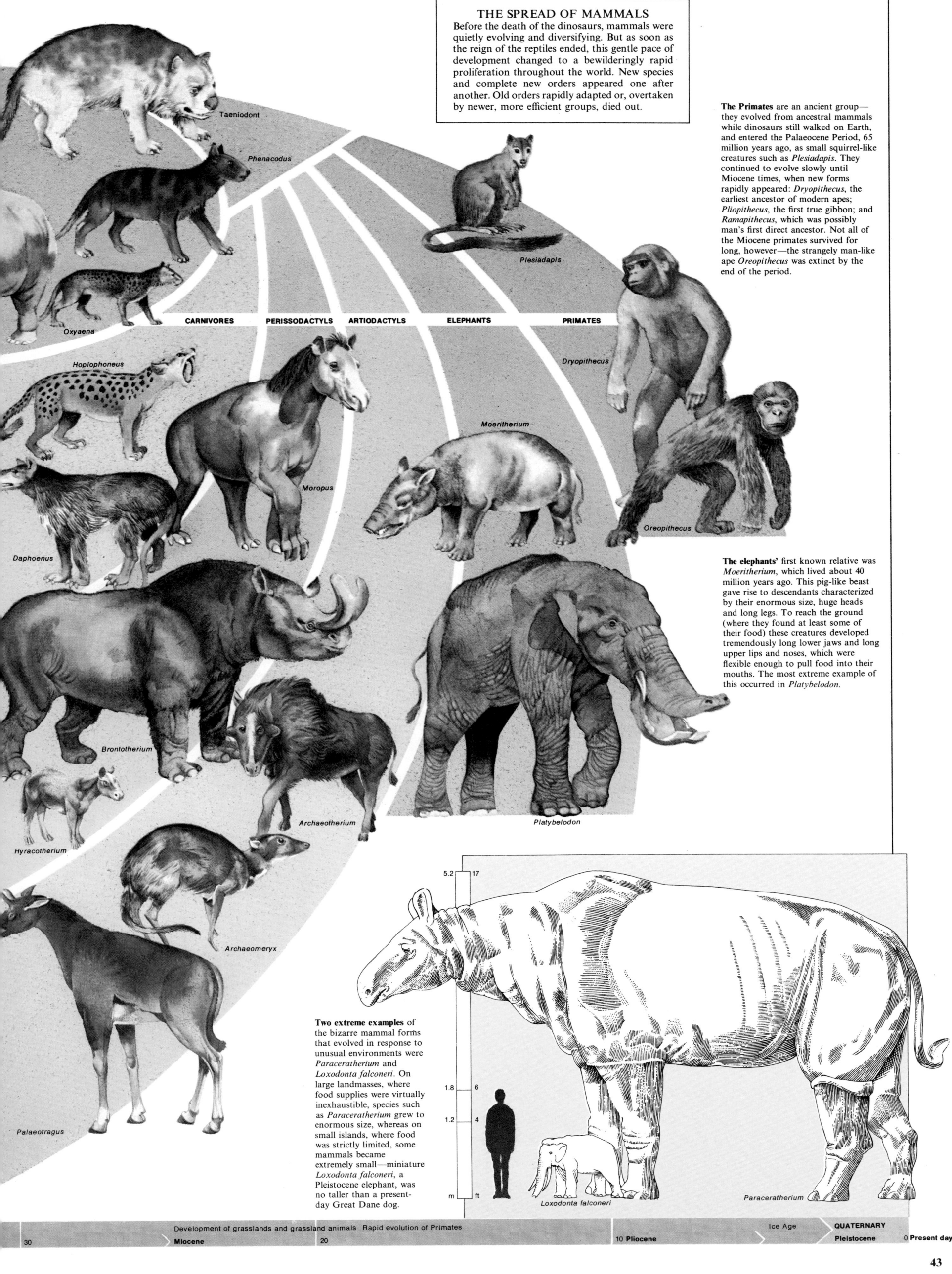

THE SPREAD OF MAMMALS

Before the death of the dinosaurs, mammals were quietly evolving and diversifying. But as soon as the reign of the reptiles ended, this gentle pace of development changed to a bewilderingly rapid proliferation throughout the world. New species and complete new orders appeared one after another. Old orders rapidly adapted or, overtaken by newer, more efficient groups, died out.

The Primates are an ancient group—they evolved from ancestral mammals while dinosaurs still walked on Earth, and entered the Palaeocene Period, 65 million years ago, as small squirrel-like creatures such as *Plesiadapis*. They continued to evolve slowly until Miocene times, when new forms rapidly appeared: *Dryopithecus*, the earliest ancestor of modern apes; *Pliopithecus*, the first true gibbon; and *Ramapithecus*, which was possibly man's first direct ancestor. Not all of the Miocene primates survived for long, however—the strangely man-like ape *Oreopithecus* was extinct by the end of the period.

Taeniodont

Phenacodus

Plesiadapis

Oxyaena

CARNIVORES   PERISSODACTYLS   ARTIODACTYLS   ELEPHANTS   PRIMATES

Hoplophoneus

Dryopithecus

Moeritherium

Moropus

Oreopithecus

Daphoenus

The elephants' first known relative was *Moeritherium*, which lived about 40 million years ago. This pig-like beast gave rise to descendants characterized by their enormous size, huge heads and long legs. To reach the ground (where they found at least some of their food) these creatures developed tremendously long lower jaws and long upper lips and noses, which were flexible enough to pull food into their mouths. The most extreme example of this occurred in *Platybelodon*.

Brontotherium

Hyracotherium

Archaeotherium

Platybelodon

Archaeomeryx

5.2 | 17

Two extreme examples of the bizarre mammal forms that evolved in response to unusual environments were *Paraceratherium* and *Loxodonta falconeri*. On large landmasses, where food supplies were virtually inexhaustible, species such as *Paraceratherium* grew to enormous size, whereas on small islands, where food was strictly limited, some mammals became extremely small—miniature *Loxodonta falconeri*, a Pleistocene elephant, was no taller than a present-day Great Dane dog.

1.8 | 6

1.2 | 4

m | ft

Palaeotragus

Loxodonta falconeri

Paraceratherium

Spread of Life

Different parts of the Earth have their own characteristic groups of animals, and this pattern of distribution caused nineteenth-century zoologists to divide the world into zoogeographical regions. Charles Darwin suggested how these assemblages of animals may have come about by the process of evolution. But we now know that movements of the Earth's land surfaces are also responsible for the present-day distribution of many of the world's animal species and groups.

The evolution of a major group of animals, such as the reptiles or the mammals, tends to follow a set pattern in five stages. First the original ancestral group spreads out, with each subgroup adapting to its environment. This process, called adaptive radiation, results in a variety of different kinds of animals, each suited to life in a particular niche or habitat— determined largely by food supply and environmental conditions. The different kinds then move into all of the areas they can reach in which the environment is right, producing the second stage of widespread distribution.

Competition for food or living space, or changes in climate may then cause some forms to decline and disappear from parts of the range, resulting in a third stage of discontinuous distribution. Any further reduction leads to isolated relict populations—the fourth stage— in which the animal exists only in one or two limited areas. The final stage is extinction.

In all distribution patterns, however, there is not only an ecological element but also a historical one, with past events determining where animals are and where they are not. There are thus two basic types of distribution: continuous, where the area is not interrupted by an insurmountable barrier (such as a mountain range), and discontinuous, where the area of distribution is subdivided and there is no way that members of one group can interchange with members of another.

One of these factors—the earliest and most important—is the (continuing) movement of the Earth's tectonic plates. This caused the supercontinent Pangaea to break up, probably in the Triassic Period (225–180 million years ago), and the continental masses to drift apart to their present positions. New oceans developed, separating the Americas from the Euro-African block and splitting both from Antarctica. Madagascar and Australia became islands, India moved north from Africa to join the Asian block, and mountain ranges such as the Alps, Andes, Rockies and Himalayas were thrown up. As a result, animal types that had already evolved on Pangaea or its fragments before they had significantly separated (i.e. all the major invertebrate groups and most of the earlier vertebrates) can be expected to exist on all the present-day continents.

Bridging the continents

Independently of these activities, ice ages occurred from time to time, resulting in the vast accumulations of ice at the poles and a consequent general lowering of the sea level by as much as 100 m (330 ft). This temporarily exposed the previously submerged continental shelves, providing additional land for colonization, and new corridors that linked existing areas, such as the land bridge that appeared between Alaska and Siberia.

Groups that had evolved after the breakup of Pangaea, e.g. the hare, squirrel and dog families, made use of land bridges as the climate allowed, and came to occupy more than one continent. Flying animals—birds and bats— also made intercontinental crossings and established themselves on both sides of oceans, although a surprising number of these have remained very restricted in distribution. But most animals have to stay where they are because of special dietary or environmental requirements, or because they are "trapped" on islands, such as Madagascar and Australia, and cannot get off. These areas have the most distinctive faunas in the world.

Barriers and corridors

The extent to which an expanding group can spread from its original area depends on whether there are barriers, such as mountain ranges, deserts or seas, or corridors that link major areas in which the animals can live. Different animals have different environmental requirements, and so a topographical feature that is a barrier for one may be a corridor for another.

The dispersal of many animals is achieved by "hopping" from lake to lake across a continent, or from island to island across a sea. Some, such as insects, are good at this, whereas others, such as land mammals, are bad. Thus a considerable range of weevils (Curculionidae) are found on islands from New Caledonia to the Marquesas, some 6,500 km (4,000 miles) across the southern Pacific Ocean, whereas the marsupials of the region are concentrated in Australia, Papua New Guinea and a few adjacent islands, with only one genus reaching the Celebes and none crossing Wallace's Line into Borneo.

An example of colonization by "hopping" is seen on the volcanic island of Krakatoa near Java, which exploded in 1883 destroying all life. Within 25 years there were 263 species of animals on the island. Most were insects, but there were three species of land snails, two species of reptiles and 16 of birds. In another 22 years, 46 species of vertebrates had arrived, including two species of rats.

The effect of man

Animal distribution cannot be considered merely as a natural phenomenon, because it has been greatly and increasingly modified by man's impact on the environment. Agricultural practice has made large sections of the land area unsuitable for many of the animals that originally lived there, notably through the clearing of forests and the draining of marshes.

Man has also introduced animals, either deliberately or accidentally, to regions where they were not endemic. The rabbit in Australia and the deer in New Zealand were both deliberately introduced, but rats, cockroaches and many other animals have been accidentally transported throughout the world on ships and aircraft. The enormous growth in human population has driven many animals from their natural homes and into more remote environments, such as mountains. Indeed, in the past century human interference has altered the pattern of animal distribution more drastically than any topographic or climatic change.

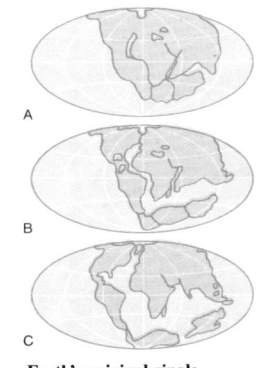
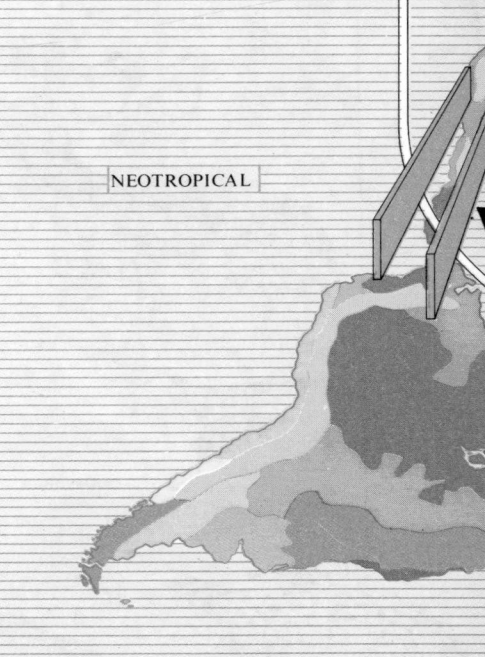

A

B

C

Earth's original single landmass, Pangaea (A), probably began to break up more than 200 million years ago. Species that had already evolved diversified on the Noah's Arks of the drifting supercontinents (B), called Laurasia and Gondwanaland. As the process continued (C), related animals flourished in the separated continents of the southern hemisphere.

PATTERNS OF ANIMALS

Over the ages the shape of the Earth has changed. Whole continents have moved; mountains and deserts have grown; land bridges between continents have opened and closed. These events, together with food supply, climate and other animals, account for the present natural pattern of life in the six zoogeographical regions, each containing a unique mix of animals. But man's activities have drastically affected this natural distribution in all parts of the world.

NEARCTIC

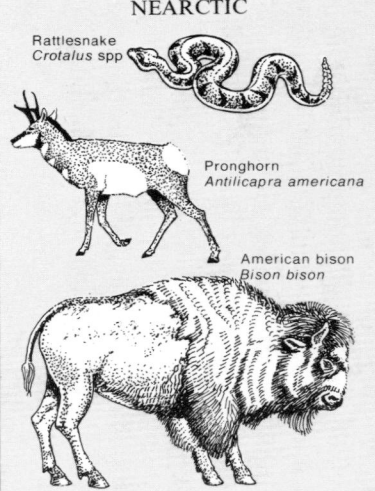

Rattlesnake
Crotalus spp

Pronghorn
Antilicapra americana

American bison
Bison bison

The Nearctic or "New North" region covers all of North America, from the highlands of Mexico in the south to Greenland and the Aleutian Islands in the north. Its climate and vegetation resemble that of the Palearctic region, and many of its mammals crossed over from the Nearctic via the Bering land bridge, which linked Siberia and Alaska when the sea level was lower. Animals unique to the Nearctic group include the pronghorn, an antelope-like mammal that inhabits the grasslands and plains of western and central America, and the bison, another large mammal that inhabits the prairies. Several species of rattlesnake also belong to the Nearctic group, although they are not exclusive to this region.

NEOTROPICAL

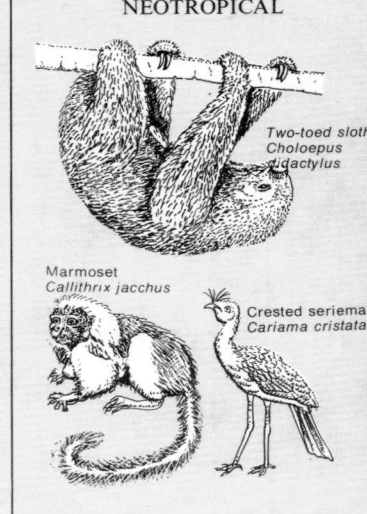

Two-toed sloth
Choloepus didactylus

Marmoset
Callithrix jacchus

Crested seriema
Cariama cristata

The Neotropical or "New Tropical" region consists of South America, the West Indies and most of Mexico. The climate and vegetation are mostly tropical—only the southern tip is in the temperate zone—and it is linked to the Nearctic by the Central American corridor. The Neotropical region has more distinctive families than any other. These include, among mammals, the sloth, which inhabits the tropical forests and has adapted to an upside-down existence. Among birds, the long-legged crested seriema is also unique to the region. Neotropical monkeys, such as the marmoset, have lateral-facing nostrils, which distinguish them from their downward-nosed relatives found in the Old World.

Land routes around the world have altered with the ages, sometimes allowing invaders to penetrate new lands, or closing to form natural sanctuaries for less efficient animals. The Central American isthmus (A) opened South America to placental mammals from the north. The Sahara desert closed most of Africa (B) to Eurasian species. Asia and Australia (C) share "island hoppers" in the transitional zones, but sea barriers have kept the regions separate.

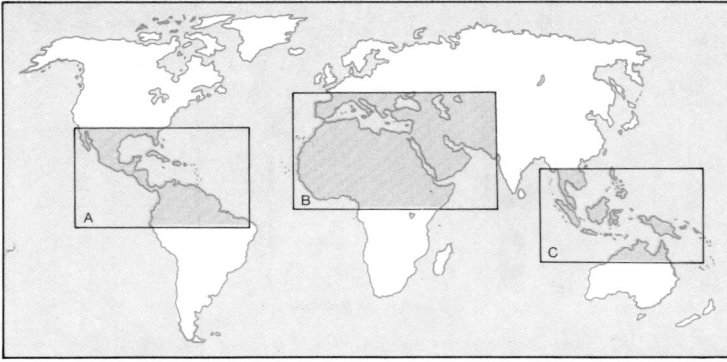

A land bridge between the Americas emerged about three million years ago, breaking the long isolation of the south. The primitive pouched mammals which had developed there were now threatened by more advanced mammals from the north, and many extinctions followed. Northern invaders included peccaries, raccoons and a llama-like camelid. But members of the armadillo and opossum families were successful in making their way to the northern region.

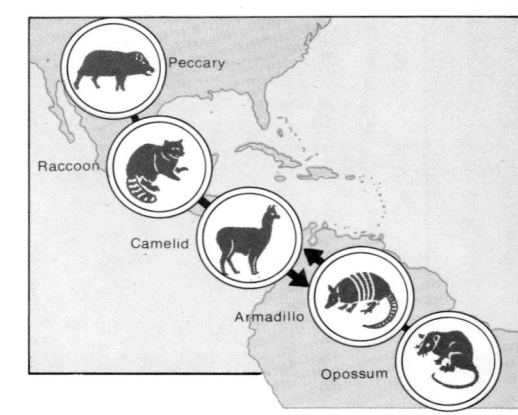

Peccary

Raccoon

Camelid

Armadillo

Opossum

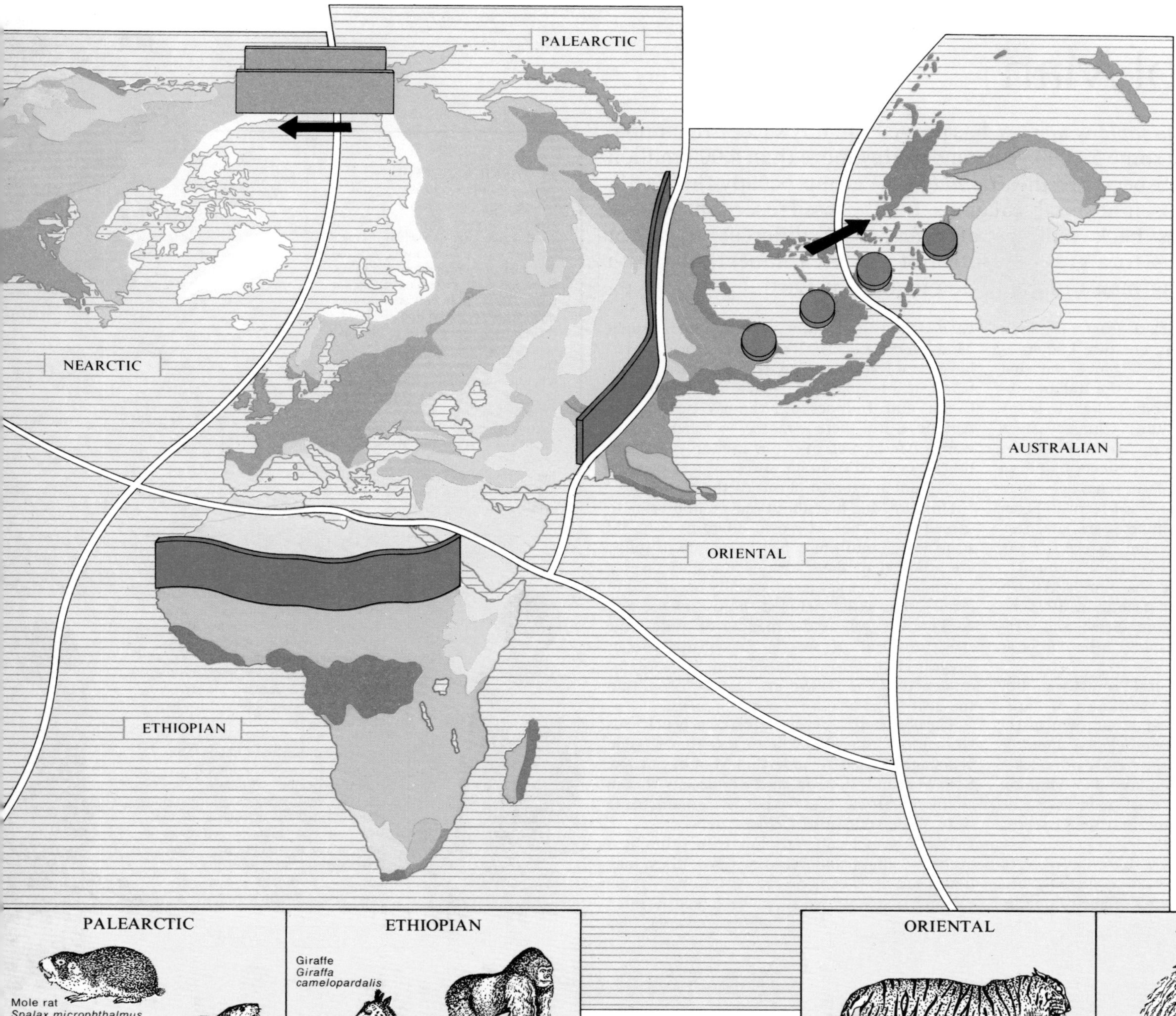

PALEARCTIC

NEARCTIC

AUSTRALIAN

ORIENTAL

ETHIOPIAN

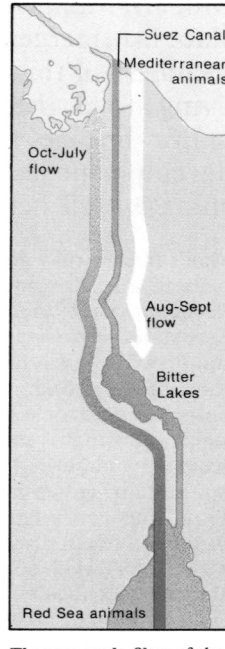

The man-made filter of the Suez Canal, cut in 1869, is an animal corridor between the Mediterranean and Red Sea. But movement is mainly from the latter, for the channel passes through the hot, salty Bitter Lakes, favoring animals adapted to these conditions, and the current flows northwards for 10 months of the year. However, not all the 130 invading species are likely to survive Mediterranean conditions.

PALEARCTIC

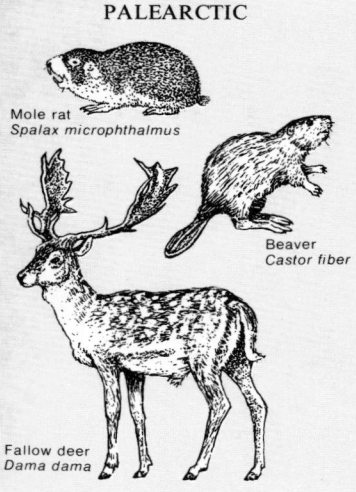

Mole rat
Spalax microphthalmus

Beaver
Castor fiber

Fallow deer
Dama dama

The Palearctic or "Old North" region covers the entire northerly part of the Old World, with seas to the north, east and west. To the south, the Sahara desert and the Himalaya mountains form barriers that separate the Palearctic from the Ethiopian and Oriental regions, although these regions are all part of the same landmass. One of the few species of mammals unique to the Palearctic is the Mediterranean mole rat, a thick-furred rodent. Another Palearctic rodent, the beaver, is shared with the Nearctic region. Fallow deer occur throughout Europe. They have been introduced by man into many other parts of the world, but their origin is almost certainly Mediterranean.

ETHIOPIAN

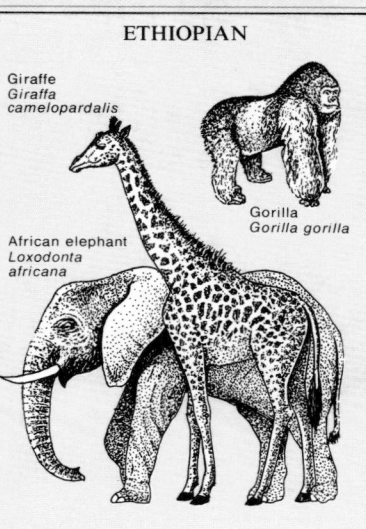

Giraffe
Giraffa camelopardalis

Gorilla
Gorilla gorilla

African elephant
Loxodonta africana

The Ethiopian region includes southern Arabia as well as all Africa south of the Sahara. It resembles in many ways the Neotropical region and is almost as rich in unique families. Its fauna also has much in common with the Oriental region. Unique mammals include the giraffe, at 5.5 m (18 ft) the tallest of living land animals, which inhabits the savanna. The region also supports two of the world's four great apes, the gorilla and the chimpanzee, which are found in the forests of western and central Africa. (The other great apes, the orangutan and the gibbon, are Oriental.) The African elephant is distinguished from its Indian relative by its greater size and by its huge ears and massive tusks.

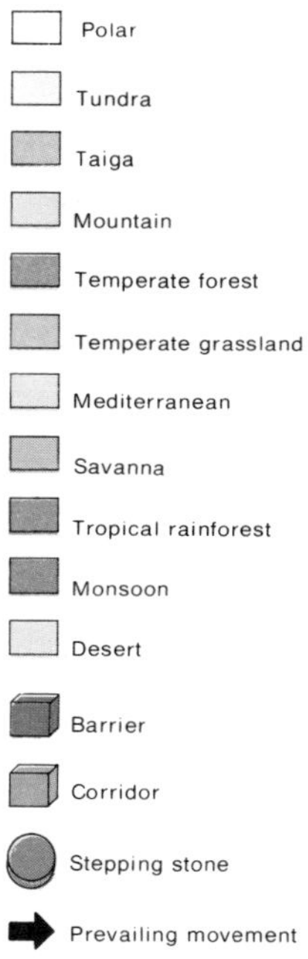

Polar
Tundra
Taiga
Mountain
Temperate forest
Temperate grassland
Mediterranean
Savanna
Tropical rainforest
Monsoon
Desert
Barrier
Corridor
Stepping stone
Prevailing movement

ORIENTAL

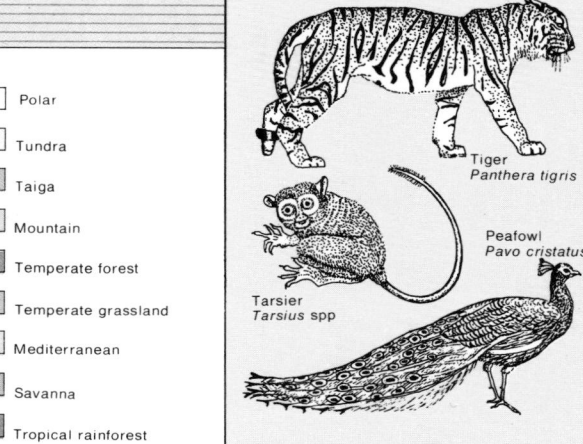

Tiger
Panthera tigris

Peafowl
Pavo cristatus

Tarsier
Tarsius spp

The Oriental region includes India, southern China, southeastern Asia and part of Malaysia. It is bounded to the north by the Himalayas and on either side by ocean, and is separated from the Australian region by a line known as Wallace's Line. It shares a quarter of its mammal families with Africa, but has more primates than any other region. The tarsier, a small relative of the monkey, is unique to southeastern Asia and represents an important early stage of primate evolution. The tiger was once widespread, but its natural habitats are steadily diminishing and the tiger itself is in danger of extinction by man. The peacock is one of the region's many brilliantly colored birds.

AUSTRALIAN

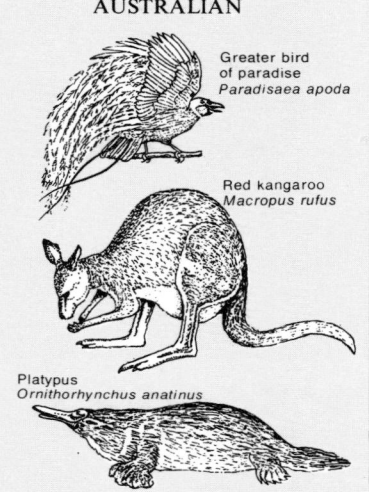

Greater bird of paradise
Paradisaea apoda

Red kangaroo
Macropus rufus

Platypus
Ornithorhynchus anatinus

The Australian region is unique in having no land connection with any other region. Its native fauna has developed in isolation from the rest of the world for at least 50 million years. Most of the mammals are marsupial—animals such as the kangaroo that carry their young in a pouch. Even more of a biological curiosity than the marsupials is the duckbilled platypus, a monotreme or egg-laying mammal. It lives along the banks of streams in Australia and Tasmania, and lays small, leathery eggs like those of snakes and turtles, but it is a true mammal and nurses its young with milk. Some 13 bird families are unique to the region, including the magnificent bird of paradise.

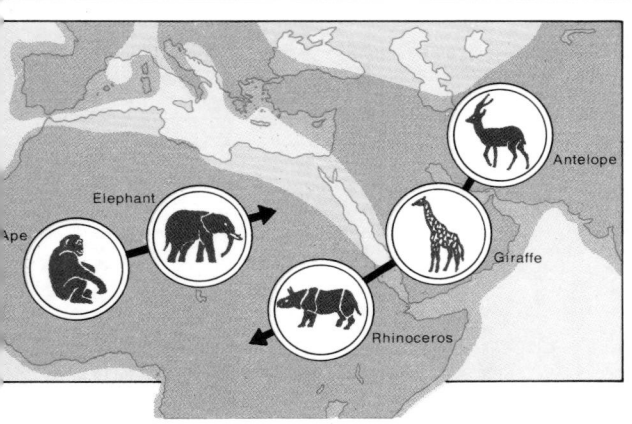

Ape

Elephant

Giraffe

Antelope

Rhinoceros

A desert barrier gradually began to form in northern Africa about nine million years ago, replacing the forest corridor between the Ethiopian and Palearctic regions. During the change, many animals typical of the African plains moved in from the north, including ancestors of today's antelopes, giraffes and rhinoceroses. But African animals also moved up north: early elephants and, much later, apes, which may have been precursors of modern man.

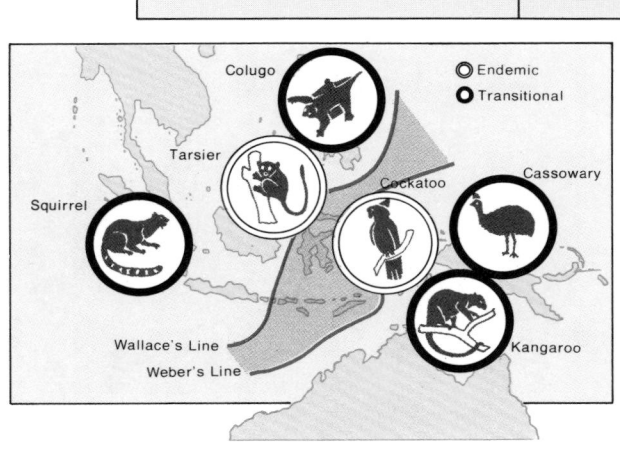

Colugo

Tarsier

Squirrel

Cockatoo

Cassowary

Kangaroo

Wallace's Line
Weber's Line

○ Endemic
◎ Transitional

The transitional area of "Wallacea" contains animals from both the Oriental and Australian regions, bounded by Wallace's and Weber's Lines, but few have crossed to the other region. Some Oriental mammals, such as tarsiers, are found in Wallacea, but the gliding colugo and varieties of squirrel are not. The Australian cockatoo has reached the transition area, but the flightless cassowary and the tree kangaroo have not.

Spread of Man

Modern Man, *Homo sapiens sapiens*, has proved a highly successful animal since his emergence some 50,000 years ago: today more than 4,000 million members of this subspecies of the *Homo* (Man) group occupy the Earth, living in even the most inhospitable regions. But the fossil record shows that man's lineage goes back millions of years, with different stages of development leading to a greater control of the environment, and with climate itself helping man's ultimate domination of Earth.

Man's lineage may go back at least 14 million years to a small woodland creature known as *Ramapithecus* (Rama's ape). Since the first discoveries of *Ramapithecus* in the Indian subcontinent, its fossils have come to light in many parts of the world, including China, eastern Europe, Turkey and eastern Africa. Fossil remains show that it survived for several million years until, about eight million years ago, there is a tantalizing gap in the fossil record. Then, about four and a half million years later (according to recent discoveries in eastern Africa), we have solid evidence of an upright hominid—a member of man's zoological family. This is "Lucy," a fossil skeleton found in 1973 by Donald Johanson and Tom Gray, and subsequently classified with many other finds as *Australopithecus afarensis*.

This may be man's ancestral "rootstock," but a little later there existed two kinds of "apeman" (*Australopithecus*), and our own direct ancestor Handy Man (*Homo habilis*). Datable volcanic ash found with the fossils provides a time scale and indicates that, about two million years ago, ape-man and "true" man lived side by side in the lush grassland that then covered the eastern African plains.

One and a half million years ago, according to the fossil evidence, there was again only one hominid species. The varieties of australopithecines had died out, and Handy Man (*Homo habilis*) had apparently evolved into Upright Man (*Homo erectus*). Remains of Upright Man have been found in many regions of the world, from various parts of Africa and Europe to China and Indonesia, although not in the Americas. But there is reason to believe that it was in Africa, well over one million years ago, that he evolved from his ancestor, and began a very gradual expansion out of the continent.

Upright Man had about one million years to spread across the Old World, adapting as he did so to local conditions, just as people of today are adapted in their various ways. He was a nomadic hunter gatherer, socially organized in groups. His skills included the use of fire and cooking, as well as the making of quite large structures out of wood. Recent discoveries suggest that, during the million years of his existence, *Homo erectus* gradually evolved into the next stage of man – *Homo sapiens*.

The next step is revealed most clearly in fossils from more than 100,000 to less than 50,000 years ago. Called Neanderthal Man in Europe, Solo Man in Indonesia, and Rhodesian Man in southern Africa, these types of human being were all descendants of *Homo erectus*.

Variable in brain size, but with prominent eyebrow ridges and receding jaws, they may have been dead ends on the evolutionary road; or some may have led to, or been incorporated in, Modern Man (*Homo sapiens sapiens*).

THE AFRICAN CRADLE
Handy Man (*Homo habilis*), who shared the East African grasslands two million years ago with a related "apeman" species, was a slender and agile creature with a human way of walking and a capacity for conceptual thought, as evidenced in systematic making of tools. Handy Man collected stones, often from far away, and reshaped them into purpose-made tools, using other stones. Fossil remains suggest that these earliest humans were efficient hunters as well as scavengers of larger predators' kills, and that they brought food to campsites, probably sharing it among the whole group, rather than eating it on the spot. Such specifically human characteristics as the sharing of food may have helped our ancestors to survive their more primitive hominid relations.

MAN THE FIRE-BRINGER
Upright Man (*Homo erectus*) emerged about 1.5 million years ago, evolving from his predecessor, Handy Man. For one million years these people developed and adapted, spreading over most of the Old World and following a nomadic hunter-gatherer life-style, assisted by a more sophisticated tool technology. The cooler climates of northern Asia and Europe may have encouraged their most impressive innovation—the use of fire for warmth, cooking and hunting game—and also their ability to construct quite elaborate shelters. It seems likely that they possessed language; and traces of ocher lumps at a campsite perhaps 400,000 years old suggest the possibility of ritual adornment or some kind of body painting.

THE HUMANIZING OF MAN
Modern man's predecessor, although called Wise Man (*Homo sapiens*), was long regarded as more brutish than human. But widespread finds have now changed this image, as can be seen in an old and an updated reconstruction of the same Neanderthal skull (right). Many scientists believe that these people showed a human concern for each other, burying their dead with ceremonial reverence, and looking after disabled members of the group. In their Neanderthal form they inhabited Europe and the Middle East from about 100,000 to 40,000 years ago, and were perhaps adapted to ice-age conditions. *Homo sapiens* counterparts of Neanderthal Man also occur in Africa and southeastern Asia.

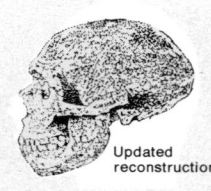

Updated reconstruction

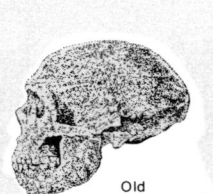

Old reconstruction

The burial of a Neanderthal man took place 60,000 years ago at Shanidar in the Iraq highlands. Fossil traces suggest that the body was laid on a bed of branches, and that flowers were brought to the grave and placed deliberately around the body. The flowers included many varieties still known locally for their medicinal properties. Ritual burials occur at many Neanderthal sites, from the Pyrenees to Soviet Asia, and indicate a sensitivity that contradicts Neanderthal Man's traditional image.

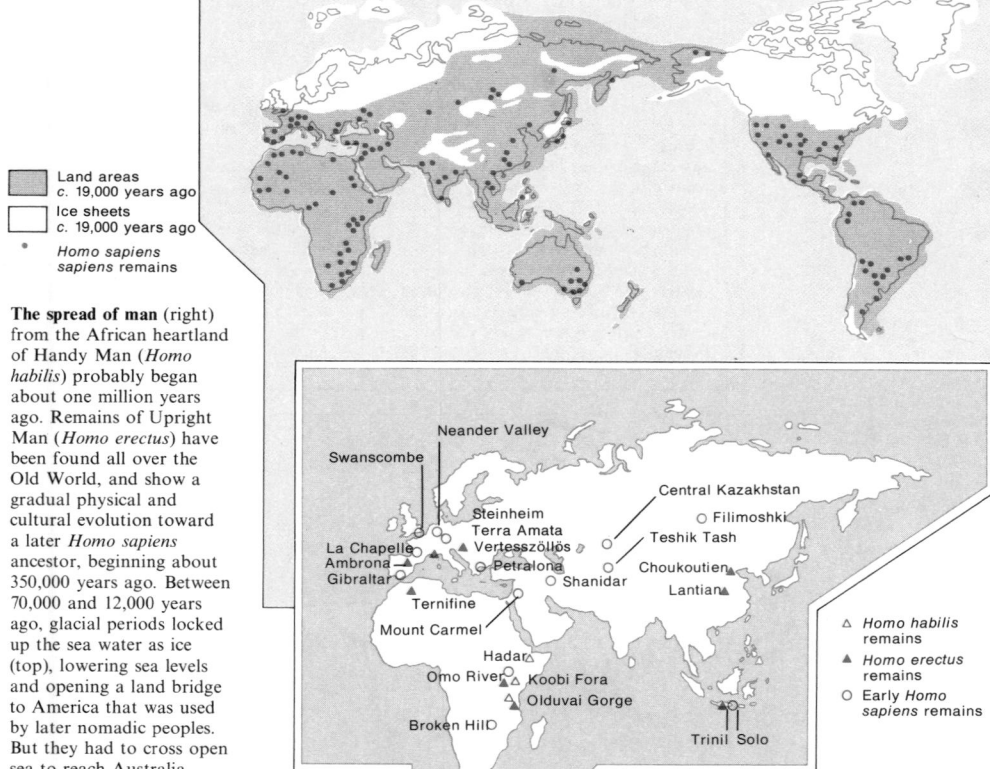

Land areas *c.* 19,000 years ago
Ice sheets *c.* 19,000 years ago
• *Homo sapiens sapiens* remains

The spread of man (right) from the African heartland of Handy Man (*Homo habilis*) probably began about one million years ago. Remains of Upright Man (*Homo erectus*) have been found all over the Old World, and show a gradual physical and cultural evolution toward a later *Homo sapiens* ancestor, beginning about 350,000 years ago. Between 70,000 and 12,000 years ago, glacial periods locked up the sea water as ice (top), lowering sea levels and opening a land bridge to America that was used by later nomadic peoples. But they had to cross open sea to reach Australia.

Neander Valley
Swanscombe
Steinheim
Terra Amata
Vertesszöllös
La Chapelle
Ambrona
Gibraltar
Petralona
Ternifine
Mount Carmel
Hadar
Omo River
Koobi Fora
Olduvai Gorge
Broken Hill
Central Kazakhstan
Filimoshki
Teshik Tash
Choukoutien
Lantian
Shanidar
Trinil Solo

△ *Homo habilis* remains
▲ *Homo erectus* remains
○ Early *Homo sapiens* remains

THE AGE OF ART
Toward the end of the last Ice Age, from about 35,000 years ago, truly modern humans began to depict their world in wonderfully vivid terms. The age of art may have reached its peak at Lascaux, France, some 15,000 years ago, but less well-preserved cave paintings from Africa show that the artistic impulse was equally present elsewhere. Called Cro-Magnon Man in Europe, these people spread to all parts of the world, crossing to the Americas by way of the Bering land bridge (when ice locked up the water of the straits), and even venturing over the seas to Australia. Physically these people were just like present-day humans. They led a nomadic, hunter-gathering life, living in large, organized groups, hunting such animals as mammoths, reindeer, bison and horses, and using a technology, as well as an artistry, far in advance of anything previously developed.

Fossils almost four million years old, found since 1973, may mark the ancestral "rootstock" of humanity, but the earliest form of true man is thought to be *Homo habilis*, who shared his African habitat with "apeman" relatives some two million years ago. His successor, *Homo erectus*, spread over Asia and Europe, evolving gradually into modern man's predecessors, creatures whose large brow ridges belie many typically human characteristics. These were replaced by Modern Man.

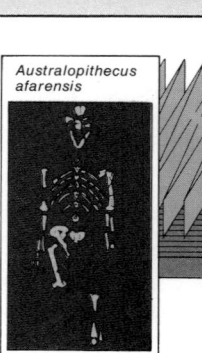

Australopithecus afarensis

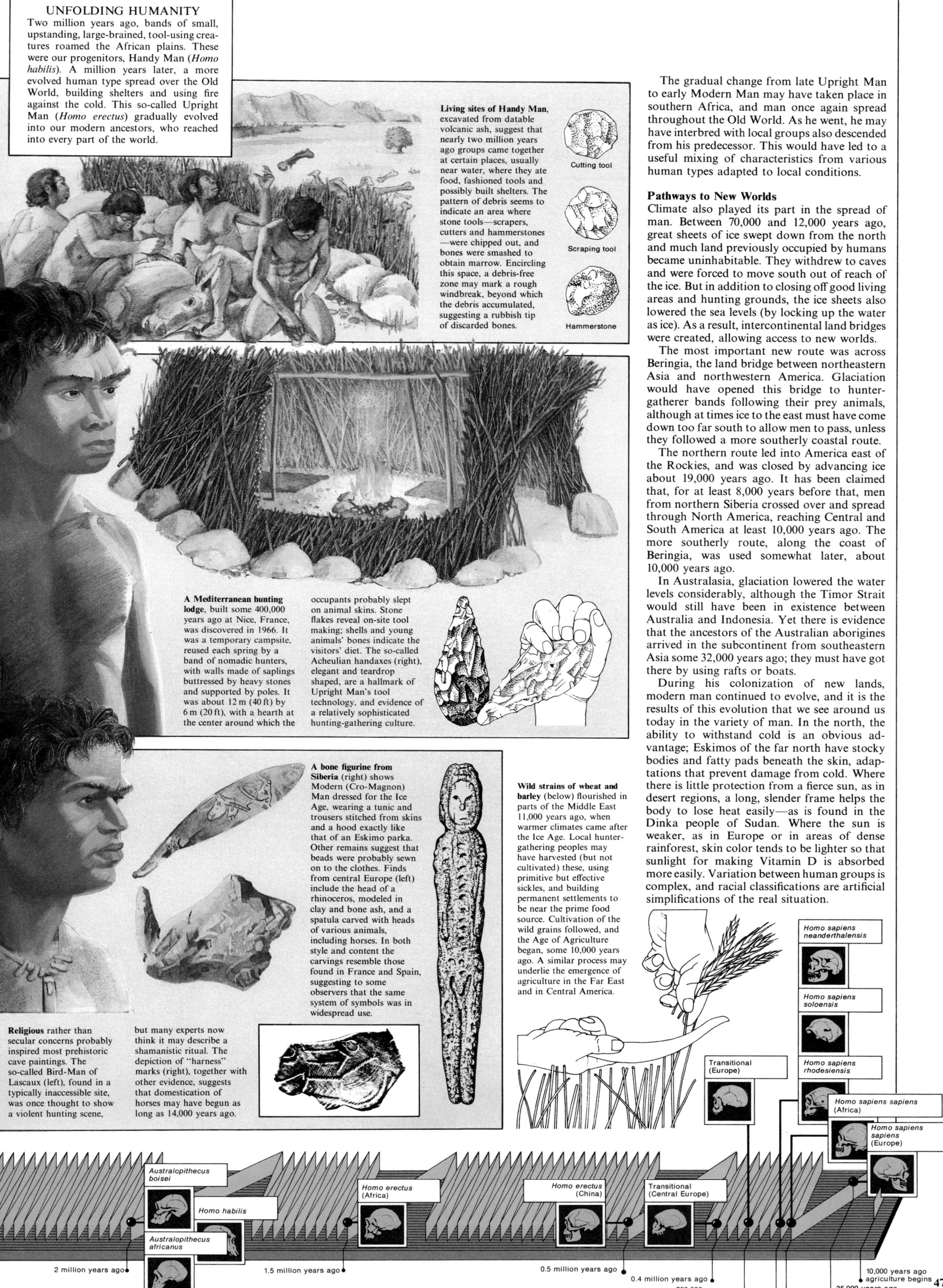

UNFOLDING HUMANITY

Two million years ago, bands of small, upstanding, large-brained, tool-using creatures roamed the African plains. These were our progenitors, Handy Man (*Homo habilis*). A million years later, a more evolved human type spread over the Old World, building shelters and using fire against the cold. This so-called Upright Man (*Homo erectus*) gradually evolved into our modern ancestors, who reached into every part of the world.

Living sites of Handy Man, excavated from datable volcanic ash, suggest that nearly two million years ago groups came together at certain places, usually near water, where they ate food, fashioned tools and possibly built shelters. The pattern of debris seems to indicate an area where stone tools—scrapers, cutters and hammerstones—were chipped out, and bones were smashed to obtain marrow. Encircling this space, a debris-free zone may mark a rough windbreak, beyond which the debris accumulated, suggesting a rubbish tip of discarded bones.

Cutting tool

Scraping tool

Hammerstone

A Mediterranean hunting lodge, built some 400,000 years ago at Nice, France, was discovered in 1966. It was a temporary campsite, reused each spring by a band of nomadic hunters, with walls made of saplings buttressed by heavy stones and supported by poles. It was about 12 m (40 ft) by 6 m (20 ft), with a hearth at the center around which the occupants probably slept on animal skins. Stone flakes reveal on-site tool making; shells and young animals' bones indicate the visitors' diet. The so-called Acheulian handaxes (right), elegant and teardrop shaped, are a hallmark of Upright Man's tool technology, and evidence of a relatively sophisticated hunting-gathering culture.

A bone figurine from Siberia (right) shows Modern (Cro-Magnon) Man dressed for the Ice Age, wearing a tunic and trousers stitched from skins and a hood exactly like that of an Eskimo parka. Other remains suggest that beads were probably sewn on to the clothes. Finds from central Europe (left) include the head of a rhinoceros, modeled in clay and bone ash, and a spatula carved with heads of various animals, including horses. In both style and content the carvings resemble those found in France and Spain, suggesting to some observers that the same system of symbols was in widespread use.

Wild strains of wheat and barley (below) flourished in parts of the Middle East 11,000 years ago, when warmer climates came after the Ice Age. Local hunter-gathering peoples may have harvested (but not cultivated) these, using primitive but effective sickles, and building permanent settlements to be near the prime food source. Cultivation of the wild grains followed, and the Age of Agriculture began, some 10,000 years ago. A similar process may underlie the emergence of agriculture in the Far East and in Central America.

Religious rather than secular concerns probably inspired most prehistoric cave paintings. The so-called Bird-Man of Lascaux (left), found in a typically inaccessible site, was once thought to show a violent hunting scene, but many experts now think it may describe a shamanistic ritual. The depiction of "harness" marks (right), together with other evidence, suggests that domestication of horses may have begun as long as 14,000 years ago.

The gradual change from late Upright Man to early Modern Man may have taken place in southern Africa, and man once again spread throughout the Old World. As he went, he may have interbred with local groups also descended from his predecessor. This would have led to a useful mixing of characteristics from various human types adapted to local conditions.

Pathways to New Worlds

Climate also played its part in the spread of man. Between 70,000 and 12,000 years ago, great sheets of ice swept down from the north and much land previously occupied by humans became uninhabitable. They withdrew to caves and were forced to move south out of reach of the ice. But in addition to closing off good living areas and hunting grounds, the ice sheets also lowered the sea levels (by locking up the water as ice). As a result, intercontinental land bridges were created, allowing access to new worlds.

The most important new route was across Beringia, the land bridge between northeastern Asia and northwestern America. Glaciation would have opened this bridge to hunter-gatherer bands following their prey animals, although at times ice to the east must have come down too far south to allow men to pass, unless they followed a more southerly coastal route.

The northern route led into America east of the Rockies, and was closed by advancing ice about 19,000 years ago. It has been claimed that, for at least 8,000 years before that, men from northern Siberia crossed over and spread through North America, reaching Central and South America at least 10,000 years ago. The more southerly route, along the coast of Beringia, was used somewhat later, about 10,000 years ago.

In Australasia, glaciation lowered the water levels considerably, although the Timor Strait would still have been in existence between Australia and Indonesia. Yet there is evidence that the ancestors of the Australian aborigines arrived in the subcontinent from southeastern Asia some 32,000 years ago; they must have got there by using rafts or boats.

During his colonization of new lands, modern man continued to evolve, and it is the results of this evolution that we see around us today in the variety of man. In the north, the ability to withstand cold is an obvious advantage; Eskimos of the far north have stocky bodies and fatty pads beneath the skin, adaptations that prevent damage from cold. Where there is little protection from a fierce sun, as in desert regions, a long, slender frame helps the body to lose heat easily—as is found in the Dinka people of Sudan. Where the sun is weaker, as in Europe or in areas of dense rainforest, skin color tends to be lighter so that sunlight for making Vitamin D is absorbed more easily. Variation between human groups is complex, and racial classifications are artificial simplifications of the real situation.

Homo sapiens neanderthalensis

Homo sapiens soloensis

Homo sapiens rhodesiensis

Transitional (Europe)

Homo sapiens sapiens (Africa)

Homo sapiens sapiens (Europe)

Australopithecus boisei

Homo habilis

Australopithecus africanus

Homo erectus (Africa)

Homo erectus (China)

Transitional (Central Europe)

2 million years ago

1.5 million years ago

0.5 million years ago

0.4 million years ago

250,000 years ago

100,000 years ago

50,000 years ago

35,000 years ago

10,000 years ago agriculture begins

Part 4

THE DIVERSITY OF LIFE

Earth's habitats from the Poles to the Equator
Plants and animals of the Earth's natural regions
Man the preserver and man the destroyer

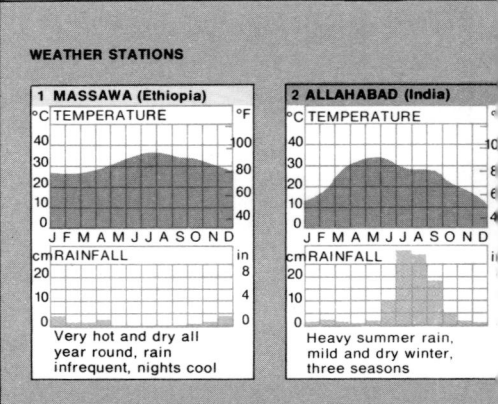

WEATHER STATIONS

1 MASSAWA (Ethiopia)
°C TEMPERATURE °F
Very hot and dry all year round, rain infrequent, nights cool

2 ALLAHABAD (India)
°C TEMPERATURE
Heavy summer rain, mild and dry winter, three seasons

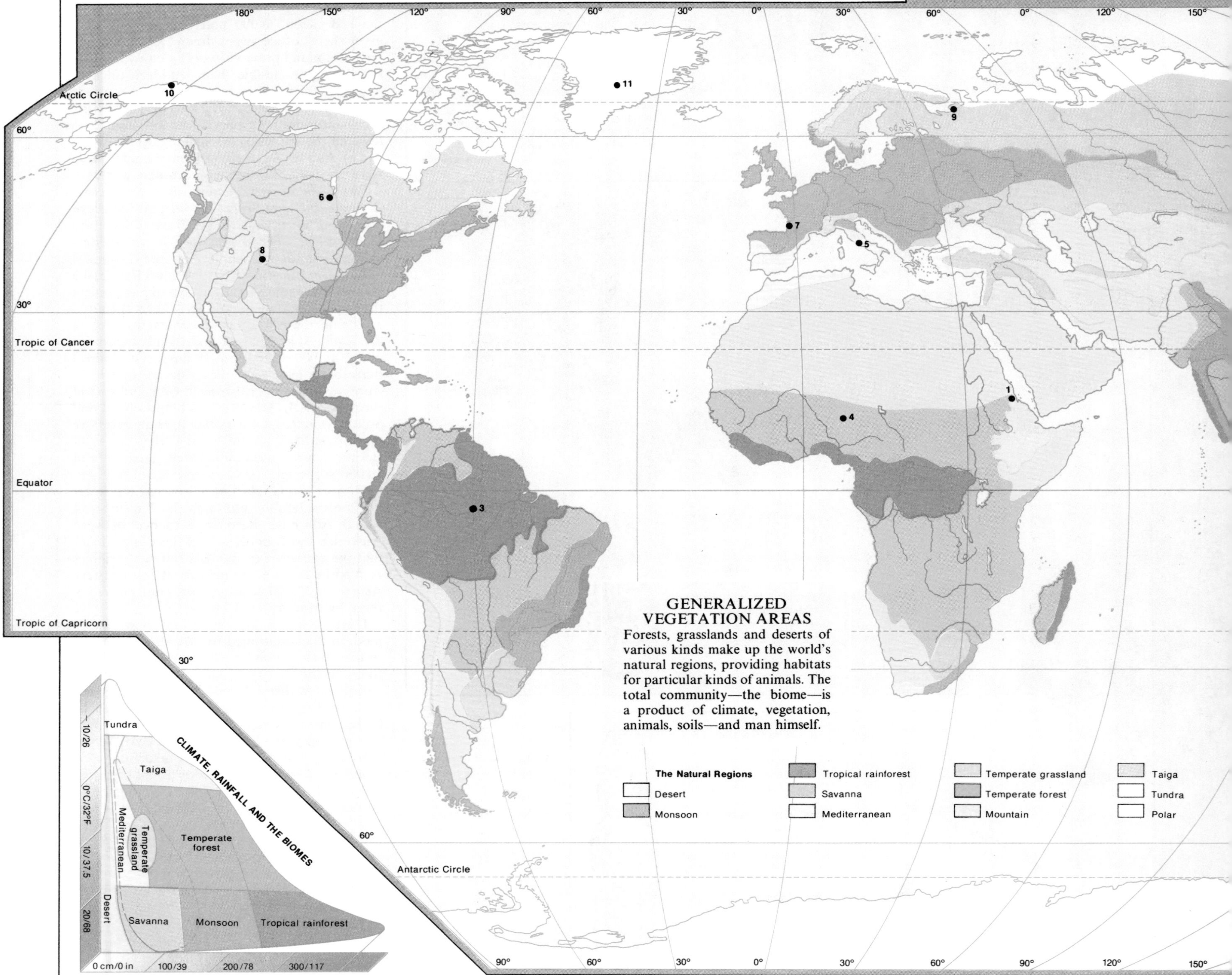

GENERALIZED VEGETATION AREAS

Forests, grasslands and deserts of various kinds make up the world's natural regions, providing habitats for particular kinds of animals. The total community—the biome—is a product of climate, vegetation, animals, soils—and man himself.

The Natural Regions

- Desert
- Monsoon
- Tropical rainforest
- Savanna
- Mediterranean
- Temperate grassland
- Temperate forest
- Mountain
- Taiga
- Tundra
- Polar

CLIMATE, RAINFALL AND THE BIOMES

Tundra
Taiga
Mediterranean
Temperate grassland
Temperate forest
Desert
Savanna
Monsoon
Tropical rainforest

Temperature and rainfall (above) govern the world's zones of plant and animal life. Dryness prevents tree growth both in icy tundra and in hot deserts. Wetter conditions cause savannas and grasslands to yield to forest biomes, tropical or temperate (the dotted line indicates zones within which variations occur).

A broad correlation (below) between soil types, climate and vegetation areas shows the interconnections that define the biomes. The soil of the biome is related to climatic conditions and is also modified by plant and animal activity, but soil types are not necessarily confined to any one particular biome.

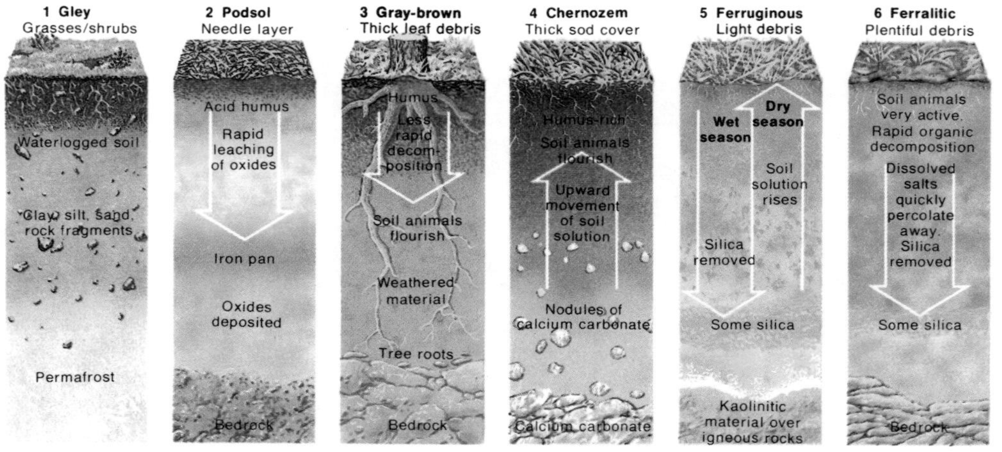

SOIL AND THE BIOMES

Cold — Cold
Tundra soils
High-latitude podsolic soils
Middle-latitude podsolic soils
Desertic soils
Middle-latitude chernozemic soils
Subtropical podsolic soils
Ferruginous soils
Ferralitic soils
Hot — Hot

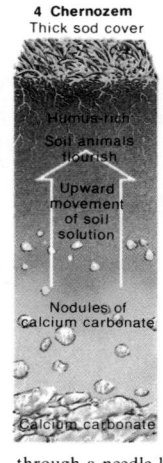

1 Gley
Grasses/shrubs
Waterlogged soil
Glay silt, sand, rock fragments
Permafrost

2 Podsol
Needle layer
Acid humus
Rapid leaching of oxides
Iron pan
Oxides deposited
Bedrock

3 Gray-brown
Thick leaf debris
Humus. Less rapid decomposition
Soil animals flourish
Weathered material
Tree roots
Bedrock

4 Chernozem
Thick sod cover
Humus-rich. Soil animals flourish
Upward movement of soil solution
Nodules of calcium carbonate
Calcium carbonate

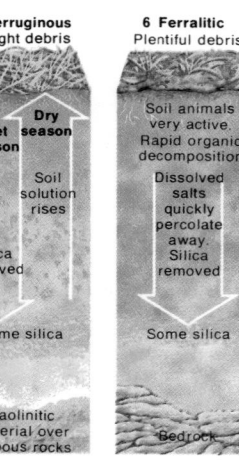

5 Ferruginous
Light debris
Wet season / Dry season
Soil animals very active. Rapid organic decomposition
Soil solution rises
Silica removed
Some silica
Kaolinitic material over igneous rocks

6 Ferralitic
Plentiful debris
Soil animals very active. Rapid organic decomposition
Dissolved salts quickly percolate away. Silica removed
Some silica
Bedrock

Soil profiles (above) from surface to bedrock reflect the influence of climate and vegetation on the rock. Depths vary from 1 m in the tundra to 30–40 m at the Equator. Waterlogged gley (1) may form above tundra permafrost. Podsol (2) is typical of taiga forests, where spring snow-melt is heavily leached through a needle layer, sometimes forming an iron "pan." Gray-brown forest soil (3) has rich, organic humus, as has chernozem (4), the typical temperate grassland soil. Ferruginous soils (5) occur in dry-season tropical climates (monsoon, savanna), and ferralitic soils (6) where there is constant rainfall.

ECOSYSTEM DYNAMICS

An ecosystem consists of a group of organisms and its physical environment. A marshland ecosystem from North America (right) shows the dynamic interactions between plant and animal communities and their habitats, which include climate, soil and water. The energy and food in the system initially derive from the Sun—the main energy source for living things, notably plants. Plants are food for herbivores, on land and in water; herbivores are food for carnivores; decomposers (bacteria and fungi) nourish plants, breaking down dead bodies into compounds.

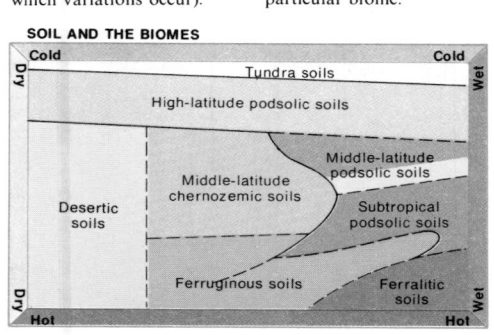

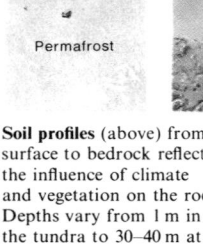

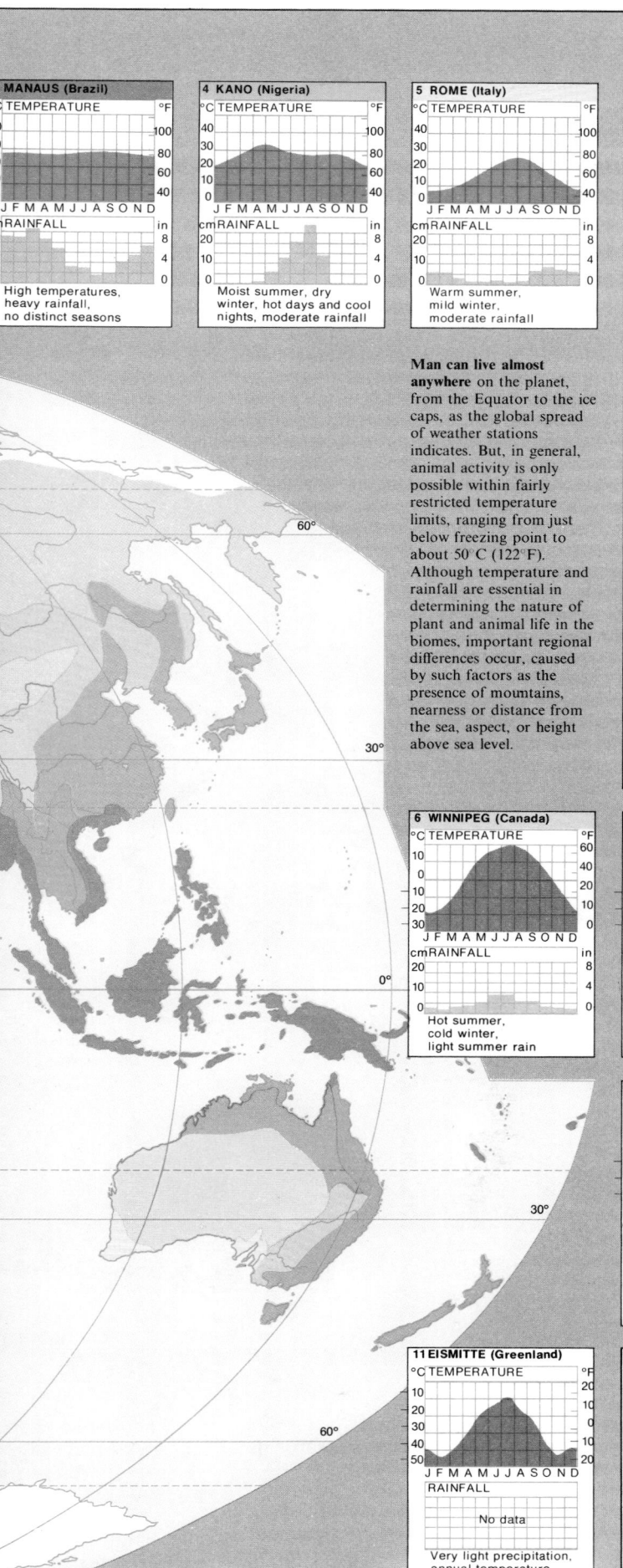

3 MANAUS (Brazil)
°C TEMPERATURE °F
High temperatures, heavy rainfall, no distinct seasons

4 KANO (Nigeria)
°C TEMPERATURE °F
Moist summer, dry winter, hot days and cool nights, moderate rainfall

5 ROME (Italy)
°C TEMPERATURE °F
Warm summer, mild winter, moderate rainfall

Man can live almost anywhere on the planet, from the Equator to the ice caps, as the global spread of weather stations indicates. But, in general, animal activity is only possible within fairly restricted temperature limits, ranging from just below freezing point to about 50°C (122°F). Although temperature and rainfall are essential in determining the nature of plant and animal life in the biomes, important regional differences occur, caused by such factors as the presence of mountains, nearness or distance from the sea, aspect, or height above sea level.

6 WINNIPEG (Canada)
°C TEMPERATURE °F
cm RAINFALL in
Hot summer, cold winter, light summer rain

7 BORDEAUX (France)
°C TEMPERATURE °F
cm RAINFALL in
Warm summer, mild winter, four distinct seasons

8 PIKE'S PEAK (USA)
°C TEMPERATURE °F
cm RAINFALL in
4,300 m (14,111ft) Temperature decreases with increasing altitude

9 ARKHANGELSK (USSR)
°C TEMPERATURE °F
cm RAINFALL in
Short summer, long and cold winter, light summer rain

10 BARROW (Alaska)
°C TEMPERATURE °F
cm RAINFALL in
Brief summer, very long and cold winter, very light rainfall

11 EISMITTE (Greenland)
°C TEMPERATURE °F
RAINFALL
No data
Very light precipitation, annual temperature variation 15.3°C/27.5°F

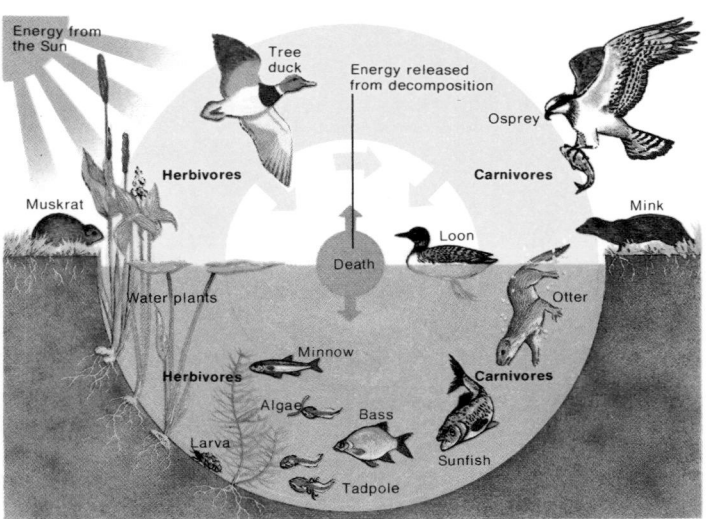

Energy from the Sun — Tree duck — Energy released from decomposition — Osprey — Herbivores — Carnivores — Muskrat — Mink — Loon — Otter — Death — Water plants — Minnow — Herbivores — Carnivores — Algae — Bass — Larva — Sunfish — Tadpole

Earth's Natural Regions

Geographers have long looked for ways of classifying conditions such as climate, soil and vegetation to describe the general similarities and differences from area to area throughout the world. By identifying distinctive patterns of climate and vegetation they have provided a convenient global division into natural regions or biomes. And recent developments in ecology – the study of plants and animals in relation to their environments – have given such divisions a greater depth.

Divisions according to climate were first suggested by the Greek philosopher Aristotle, and his ideas were still in use until about 100 years ago. Aristotle posited a number of climatic zones—called torrid, temperate and frigid —defined by latitude. But with time it became increasingly apparent that the complex distribution of atmospheric pressure, winds, rainfall and temperature could not be related to such a simple frame. Nineteenth-century scientists divided the world into 35 climatic provinces. Then in 1900 the German meteorologist Wladimir Köppen produced a more sophisticated climatic classification based on temperature and moisture conditions related to the needs of plants. At about the same time other scientists studied the distribution of vegetation types throughout the world. These studies together provided the basis for much of the later work on climatic regions.

An important step forward was made in 1904 by the British geographer A. J. Herbertson. He argued that subdivision of physical environments should take into account the distribution of the various phenomena as they related to each other. He conceived the idea of *natural regions*, each with "a certain unity of configuration (relief), climate and vegetation." His final classification contained four groups or regions: Polar Types, Cool Temperate Types, Warm Temperate Types and Tropical Hot Lands. Herbertson's scheme, controversial at first, was later much used for teaching geography.

Ecology

Meanwhile the study of environmental problems had been advanced by the idea of *ecology*, the relationship of living things between each other and their surroundings. The term was first used in 1868 by Ernst Haeckel, the German biologist, but it was not until the end of the nineteenth century that scientists really began to study life forms in relation to their habitat. In addition to the central ideas of interdependence between the members of plant and animal communities and between the community and the physical environment, there now came the suggestion that communities develop in a sequence that leads to a "climax"—a final step of equilibrium or balance. Their climax stage depends on conditions of climate or soil.

Later the British botanist A. G. Tansley, a leading exponent of ecological thinking, introduced the term *ecosystem* to describe a group of living organisms and its effective environment. Tansley's definition of 1935 referred to the whole system, including "not only the organism complex, but also the whole complex of physical factors forming what we call the environment of the biome." The idea became very influential and has been used in the social sciences as well as in the natural ones. But it is difficult to apply in practice, partly because of the highly complex and often diverse interactions that take place in different parts of the ecosystem.

Ecologists have developed special methods and have given particular attention to the ways in which energy is transferred within the system. The term *biome* refers to the whole complex of organisms, both animals and plants, that live together naturally as a society. By *environment* is meant all the external conditions that affect the life and development of an organism.

Biomes

The biomes shown on the map are broadly drawn generalizations. They should be regarded as idealized regions, within which many local variations may exist—for example, of climate or soil conditions. On a larger scale such features as mountain ranges may cause variations at a regional level. Scientists have tried to work out "hierarchies" that include many levels or orders of scale leading to the major climatic-vegetation realms or biomes. These realms give a broad picture that is useful at the world level of scale, and which forms a starting point for further analysis. Any map of the biomes has to have lines to indicate the boundaries of each region, but these too are generalizations. Although climate and vegetation do sometimes change abruptly from place to place, more often there are transitional zones, and the boundaries on the maps give the broad locations of these.

Herbertson's concept of natural regions attempted also to take account of the influence of man as an important factor in the environment. But he was not totally successful in including man in his analysis, no doubt because of the complexity of the problems involved and because of the immense influence that man has had upon the natural vegetation of the world. The cutting of forests, the drainage and reclamation of land, the introduction, use and spread of cultivated plants, the domestication of animals, the development of sophisticated systems of agriculture and many other actions all create, over large areas of the biomes, landscapes that are more man-made than natural.

Resource systems

An idea that clarifies the study of the interrelations of societies and environments, and the ways in which these change with the passage of time, is that of the *resource system*. This is a model of a population of human beings and their social and economic characteristics, including their technical skills and resources, together with those aspects of the natural environment that affect them and which they influence. The model includes the sequences by which natural materials are obtained, transformed and used. It tries to show how societies are organized according to their natural resources, the effects of that use, and the ways in which natural conditions limit or expand the life and work of the society. But it is easier to apply such a model to societies that have direct relations with natural conditions, through farming, fishing or forestry, than to great urban–industrial complexes.

The sections that follow present a picture of the diversity of habitats from ice caps to equatorial forests, the principal ways man has modified the environment and the problems of maintaining healthy resource systems.

Climate and Weather

The pattern of world climates depends largely on great circulations of air in the atmosphere. These movements of air are driven by energy from the Sun, and they transfer surplus heat from the tropics to the polar regions. Over a long period of time – such as months, seasons or years – they create the climate. Over a short period – day by day, or week by week – they form the weather. Together, climate and weather are among the most significant natural components of the world's diverse environments.

The world's tropical zones receive more heat from the Sun than they re-emit into space, and so their land and sea surfaces become warm. The polar regions, on the other hand, emit more radiation than they receive, and so they become cold. Warm air is less dense than cold air, and this means that atmospheric pressure becomes low at the Equator and high at the poles. As a result, a circulation of air—both vertical and horizontal—is set up. But because of the Earth's rotation and the distribution of land and sea there is not a simple air circulation pattern in each hemisphere; winds are deflected to the right in the northern hemisphere and to the left in the southern hemisphere, a phenomenon known as the Coriolis effect.

A climatic patchwork

When warm air rises it expands and cools and the water vapor it is carrying condenses to form clouds. For this reason heavy, showery rain is frequent in the belt of rising air near the Equator. In the subtropical zones (where the air is sinking), clouds evaporate and the weather is fine. Air moves out of the subtropical high-pressure belts in the lower atmosphere. Some of it flows towards the poles and meets colder air, flowing out of the polar high-pressure region, in a narrow zone called the polar front. This convergence of air is concentrated around low-pressure systems known as depressions.

The pattern of climates does not remain constant throughout the year because of seasonal changes in the amount of radiation from the Sun—the "fuel" of the atmospheric engine. In June, when the northern hemisphere is tilted towards the Sun, the radiation is at a maximum at latitude 23°N and all the climatic belts shift northwards. In December it is summer in the southern hemisphere and all the belts move southwards.

Climate is also affected by the distribution of land and sea across the globe. The temperature of the land changes more quickly than that of

TYPES OF WEATHER

There is a constant flow of air between the world's polar and tropical regions, and this has a prime effect on the weather in other regions. In the high and middle latitudes cold and warm fronts succeed each other, and along coasts sea fogs often form. In temperate and tropical regions thunderstorms are frequent, and the tropics are characterized by the turbulent storms known as hurricanes in the Caribbean area and typhoons in the Pacific.

POLAR WEATHER
Weather in high latitudes is marked by consistently low temperatures—on the ice caps temperatures are nearly always below freezing. At the poles the sun never rises for six months of the year and for the remaining six months it never sets. Even in summer it stays low on the horizon and its rays are so slanted that they bring very little warmth. On the tundra the temperature rises above freezing for a few months in summer, but severe frosts are likely to occur at any time. As well as being bitterly cold, polar weather is predominantly dry. The lower the temperature the less moisture the air can contain. Clouds, when they form, are high, thin sheets of cirrostratus. Composed of ice crystals, they often produce a halo effect around the sun. Snow, when it falls, is usually dry and powdery.

DEPRESSIONS
Low-pressure weather systems, or depressions, form when polar and subtropical air masses converge. Cloud and rain usually occur at the boundary, or front, of the different air masses. Seen in cross section, a fully developed depression shows both warm (A) and cold (B) fronts. As the wave of warm air rises over the cold, its moisture condenses into the "layered" clouds that usually precede a warm front. Behind the warm front, cold air forces under the warm air, producing the wedge-shaped cold front.

FOG
Fogs form as a result of the condensation of water vapor in the air; they may occur when warm, moist air is cooled by its passage over a cold surface. Off the coast of California, for example, air near the surface of the sea is cooled by the cold California current and sea fog is frequent. The air at higher levels is still warm and acts like a lid over the fog, and mountains prevent the fog from dispersing in an easterly direction. Fumes and smoke are trapped by this temperature inversion, creating the notorious Los Angeles smog.

THUNDERSTORMS
These develop when air is unstable to a great height. Particularly violent storms occur when cold, dry air masses meet warm, moist air, causing the latter to rise rapidly. As the warm air surges upwards it cools and its moisture condenses into cumulonimbus, or thunder, clouds. Flat cloud tops mark the level where stable air occurs again. Quickly moving raindrops and hail in the clouds become electrically charged and cause lightning, and the explosion of heated air along the path of the flash creates the sound wave that is heard as thunder.

HURRICANES
These are tropical storms on a vast scale that build up over warm oceans. Their core is an area of low pressure around which large quantities of warm, moist air are carried to the high atmosphere at great speed. The Earth's rotation is responsible for the huge swirling movement: in the northern hemisphere the movement is anticlockwise, in the southern hemisphere it is clockwise. Towering bands of clouds produce torrential rain. The central region, or "eye," of a hurricane, however, has light winds, clear skies and no rainfall.

THE WORLD'S CLIMATIC REGIONS

Climate is the characteristic weather of a region over a long period of time. It is often described in terms of average monthly and yearly temperatures and rainfall. These in turn depend largely on latitude, which determines whether a region is basically hot or cold and whether it has pronounced seasonal changes. Climate is also influenced by prevailing winds, by ocean currents and by geographical features such as the distribution of land and water. Highland climates are influenced by altitude and are always cooler than those of nearby lowland regions. Tropical climates are always warm. Near the Equator rain falls for most of the year, but towards the subtropics the wet and dry seasons are more marked. Temperate climates reflect the conflict between warm and cold air masses. They range from the Mediterranean type with hot, dry summers and mild, moist winters to the cooler, wetter climates of higher latitudes. The subarctic is mainly cold and humid; polar climates are always cold and mainly dry.

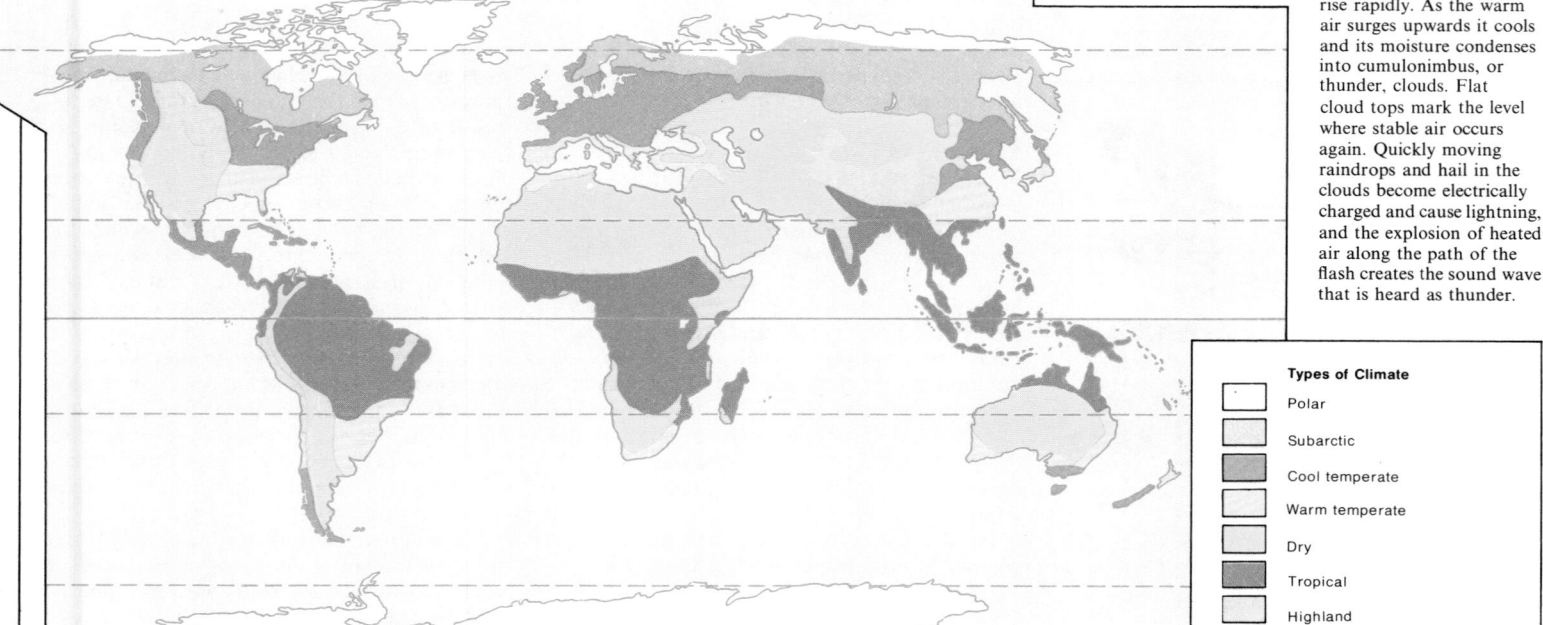

Types of Climate

- Polar
- Subarctic
- Cool temperate
- Warm temperate
- Dry
- Tropical
- Highland

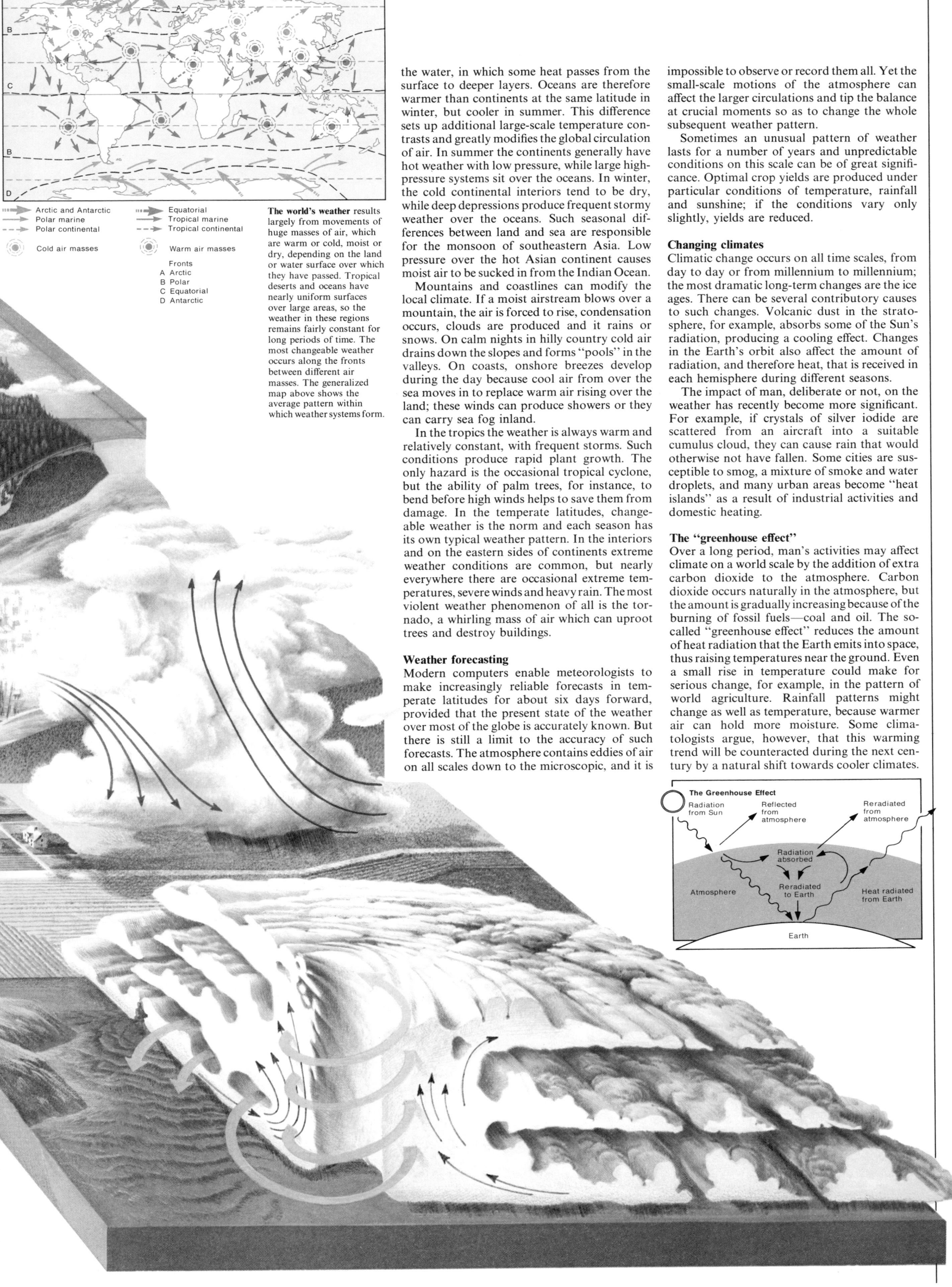

The world's weather results largely from movements of huge masses of air, which are warm or cold, moist or dry, depending on the land or water surface over which they have passed. Tropical deserts and oceans have nearly uniform surfaces over large areas, so the weather in these regions remains fairly constant for long periods of time. The most changeable weather occurs along the fronts between different air masses. The generalized map above shows the average pattern within which weather systems form.

the water, in which some heat passes from the surface to deeper layers. Oceans are therefore warmer than continents at the same latitude in winter, but cooler in summer. This difference sets up additional large-scale temperature contrasts and greatly modifies the global circulation of air. In summer the continents generally have hot weather with low pressure, while large high-pressure systems sit over the oceans. In winter, the cold continental interiors tend to be dry, while deep depressions produce frequent stormy weather over the oceans. Such seasonal differences between land and sea are responsible for the monsoon of southeastern Asia. Low pressure over the hot Asian continent causes moist air to be sucked in from the Indian Ocean.

Mountains and coastlines can modify the local climate. If a moist airstream blows over a mountain, the air is forced to rise, condensation occurs, clouds are produced and it rains or snows. On calm nights in hilly country cold air drains down the slopes and forms "pools" in the valleys. On coasts, onshore breezes develop during the day because cool air from over the sea moves in to replace warm air rising over the land; these winds can produce showers or they can carry sea fog inland.

In the tropics the weather is always warm and relatively constant, with frequent storms. Such conditions produce rapid plant growth. The only hazard is the occasional tropical cyclone, but the ability of palm trees, for instance, to bend before high winds helps to save them from damage. In the temperate latitudes, changeable weather is the norm and each season has its own typical weather pattern. In the interiors and on the eastern sides of continents extreme weather conditions are common, but nearly everywhere there are occasional extreme temperatures, severe winds and heavy rain. The most violent weather phenomenon of all is the tornado, a whirling mass of air which can uproot trees and destroy buildings.

Weather forecasting

Modern computers enable meteorologists to make increasingly reliable forecasts in temperate latitudes for about six days forward, provided that the present state of the weather over most of the globe is accurately known. But there is still a limit to the accuracy of such forecasts. The atmosphere contains eddies of air on all scales down to the microscopic, and it is

impossible to observe or record them all. Yet the small-scale motions of the atmosphere can affect the larger circulations and tip the balance at crucial moments so as to change the whole subsequent weather pattern.

Sometimes an unusual pattern of weather lasts for a number of years and unpredictable conditions on this scale can be of great significance. Optimal crop yields are produced under particular conditions of temperature, rainfall and sunshine; if the conditions vary only slightly, yields are reduced.

Changing climates

Climatic change occurs on all time scales, from day to day or from millennium to millennium; the most dramatic long-term changes are the ice ages. There can be several contributory causes to such changes. Volcanic dust in the stratosphere, for example, absorbs some of the Sun's radiation, producing a cooling effect. Changes in the Earth's orbit also affect the amount of radiation, and therefore heat, that is received in each hemisphere during different seasons.

The impact of man, deliberate or not, on the weather has recently become more significant. For example, if crystals of silver iodide are scattered from an aircraft into a suitable cumulus cloud, they can cause rain that would otherwise not have fallen. Some cities are susceptible to smog, a mixture of smoke and water droplets, and many urban areas become "heat islands" as a result of industrial activities and domestic heating.

The "greenhouse effect"

Over a long period, man's activities may affect climate on a world scale by the addition of extra carbon dioxide to the atmosphere. Carbon dioxide occurs naturally in the atmosphere, but the amount is gradually increasing because of the burning of fossil fuels—coal and oil. The so-called "greenhouse effect" reduces the amount of heat radiation that the Earth emits into space, thus raising temperatures near the ground. Even a small rise in temperature could make for serious change, for example, in the pattern of world agriculture. Rainfall patterns might change as well as temperature, because warmer air can hold more moisture. Some climatologists argue, however, that this warming trend will be counteracted during the next century by a natural shift towards cooler climates.

The Greenhouse Effect

Radiation from Sun
Reflected from atmosphere
Reradiated from atmosphere
Radiation absorbed
Atmosphere
Reradiated to Earth
Heat radiated from Earth
Earth

Resources and Energy

Resources, it has been said, comprise mankind's varying needs from generation to generation and are valued because of the uses societies can make of them. They represent human appraisals and are the products of man's ingenuity and experience. While natural resources remain vitally important in themselves, they must always be regarded as the rewards of human skill in locating, extracting and exploiting them. The development of resources depends on many factors, including the existence of a demand, adequate transport facilities, the availability of capital and the accessibility, quality and quantity of the resource itself.

The world's extraction of its resources highlights the inequality of their distribution. Each resource shown on the map is attributed to the three countries with the largest production percentages of that commodity. So, in 1976, the three leading bauxite producers were Australia (26.69%), Jamaica (14.19%) and Rep. of Guinea (13.9%). Usually, the larger and more wealthy a state the greater its monopoly of resources—although the tiny Pacific island of New Caledonia produces more than 14% of the world's nickel. China is reputed to mine 75% of the world's tungsten and to be increasing its oil supply rapidly. Energy consumption figures are for the year 1976, since when there have been some outstanding changes to patterns of availability, perhaps most noticeably in Britain's new-found oil and gas surplus. Bahrain and Tobago, too small to be shown on this map, also have surpluses of energy production.

A dictionary defines the term "resource" as "a means of aid or support," implying anything that lends support to life or activity. Man has always assessed nature with an eye to his own needs, and it is these varying needs that endow resources with their usefulness. Fossil fuels such as oil have lain long in the Earth, but it was not until about 1900 that the large-scale needs fostered by the rising demands of motor vehicles led to the development of new techniques for locating and extracting this raw material. Today oil has also become precious in the manufacture of a wide variety of industrial products, which themselves are resources that are much used by other industries.

The nature of resources
Resources can be most usefully classified in two groups: "renewable" and "nonrenewable." The latter is composed of materials found at or near the Earth's surface, which are sometimes known as "physical" resources. They include such essential minerals as uranium, iron, copper, nickel, bauxite, gold, silver, lead, mercury and tungsten. Oil, coal and natural gas are the principal nonrenewable fuel and energy resources, but after they have been used for producing heat or power their utility is lost and part of the geological capital of 325 million years of history is gone for ever. Some minerals such as iron and its product, steel, can be recycled and renewed, however. "Renewable" resources are basically biological, being the food and other vegetable matter which life needs to sustain human needs. Provided soil quality is maintained, their productivity may even be increased as better strains of plants and breeds of animals are developed.

Work has long been in progress to improve renewable resources, and has moved forward to manufacturing vegetable-flavored protein (VFP) from soybeans as a meat substitute and to viable experiments to extract protein from leaves. In Brazil, many cars have been converted to run successfully on alcohol extracted from sugar. One renewable resource—the tree—can be closely related to other resources: some conservationists are alarmed at the overuse of firewood as a source of fuel and energy in the semiarid areas of Africa. This may be an important factor in increasing the tendency for the deserts to spread in that continent, and in such a situation there is a new realization of the concept of closely managing resources such as soil, timber and fisheries. This is partly because we have a clearer understanding of the ecology of vegetation and the important interdependence of climate, soil, plants and animal life. Much, however, remains to be done.

The politics of nonrenewable resources
Today we are naturally troubled about the availability of natural resources. Oil is a prime cause for concern. Although many believe that production will grow until the mid-2020s and that new oil reserves will be discovered, oil's scarcity, based on a growing rate of demand and increasingly wasteful use, is now widely accepted. Because, like many resources, it is unevenly distributed, those countries with large and accessible supplies—such as the members of OPEC—have used their political power on a number of occasions to raise oil's price, with adverse effects on the economies of most importers. Ironically, these substantial price rises have had the effect of stimulating exploration and development in many new areas; there are already signs of increased production in China.

Other nonrenewable resources are also distributed unevenly, but have not been mined on any scale comparable with their availability; vast reserves of coal in the USSR and China have not been worked on any scale resembling their known extent.

New energy sources
As resources such as oil become less available and more expensive, the renewable resources of power such as water, wind, waves and solar energy, all of which are currently under study or development, will receive new injections of capital. Attention will also have to be paid to more widespread nuclear energy production. Energy has been called "the ultimate resource," and it is imperative that we make wise provisions for its future availability.

Future resources
It has been calculated that within four years of the launch of Sputnik I, more than 3,000 products resulting from space research were put into commercial production. These included new alloys, ceramics, plastics, fabrics and chemical compounds. Satellite developments have meant that land use can now be measured quickly and potential mineral sources closely identified. A satellite capable of converting solar power to electricity and contributing to the Earth's energy deficit has been widely discussed, while the Moon and planets have been mooted as future possible sources of minerals.

Conclusions
Resources are, in the main, the products of man's skill, ingenuity and expertise, and their widespread use, as in the case of timber and iron for shipbuilding, became apparent only as man's needs for them became clear. Our forebears were once concerned about the availability of flint, seaweed, charcoal and natural rubber; countries even went to war over supplies of spices. Today our requirements are slightly different—we no longer depend only on local sites for resources, and improved transport facilities and appropriate technologies have lowered the costs of obtaining materials for manufacture.

Nevertheless, the principles remain the same. A continual search for new resources capable of exploitation and wide application must be maintained, together with a close regard for the value of the renewable resources such as animal and vegetable products required to support man in his search for new resources. Perhaps the most vital consideration is the need for wise policies of conservation relating to the proven reserves of nonrenewable resources still in the ground, and the careful future use of such valuable deposits known or thought to exist.

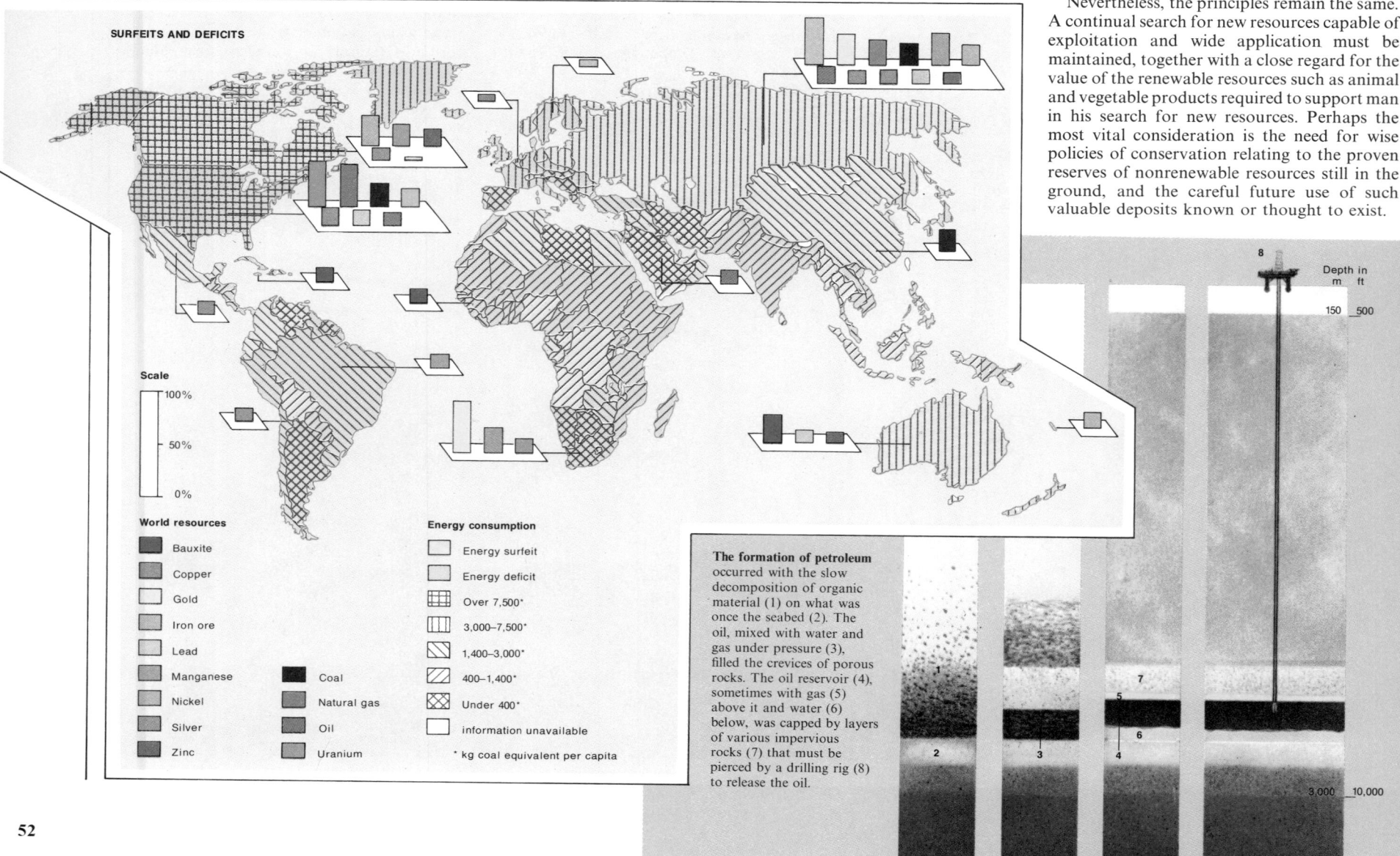

SURFEITS AND DEFICITS

Scale
100%
50%
0%

World resources
- Bauxite
- Copper
- Gold
- Iron ore
- Lead
- Manganese
- Nickel
- Silver
- Zinc
- Coal
- Natural gas
- Oil
- Uranium

Energy consumption
- Energy surfeit
- Energy deficit
- Over 7,500*
- 3,000–7,500*
- 1,400–3,000*
- 400–1,400*
- Under 400*
- information unavailable

* kg coal equivalent per capita

The formation of petroleum occurred with the slow decomposition of organic material (1) on what was once the seabed (2). The oil, mixed with water and gas under pressure (3), filled the crevices of porous rocks. The oil reservoir (4), sometimes with gas (5) above it and water (6) below, was capped by layers of various impervious rocks (7) that must be pierced by a drilling rig (8) to release the oil.

Depth in
m ft
150 500
3,000 10,000

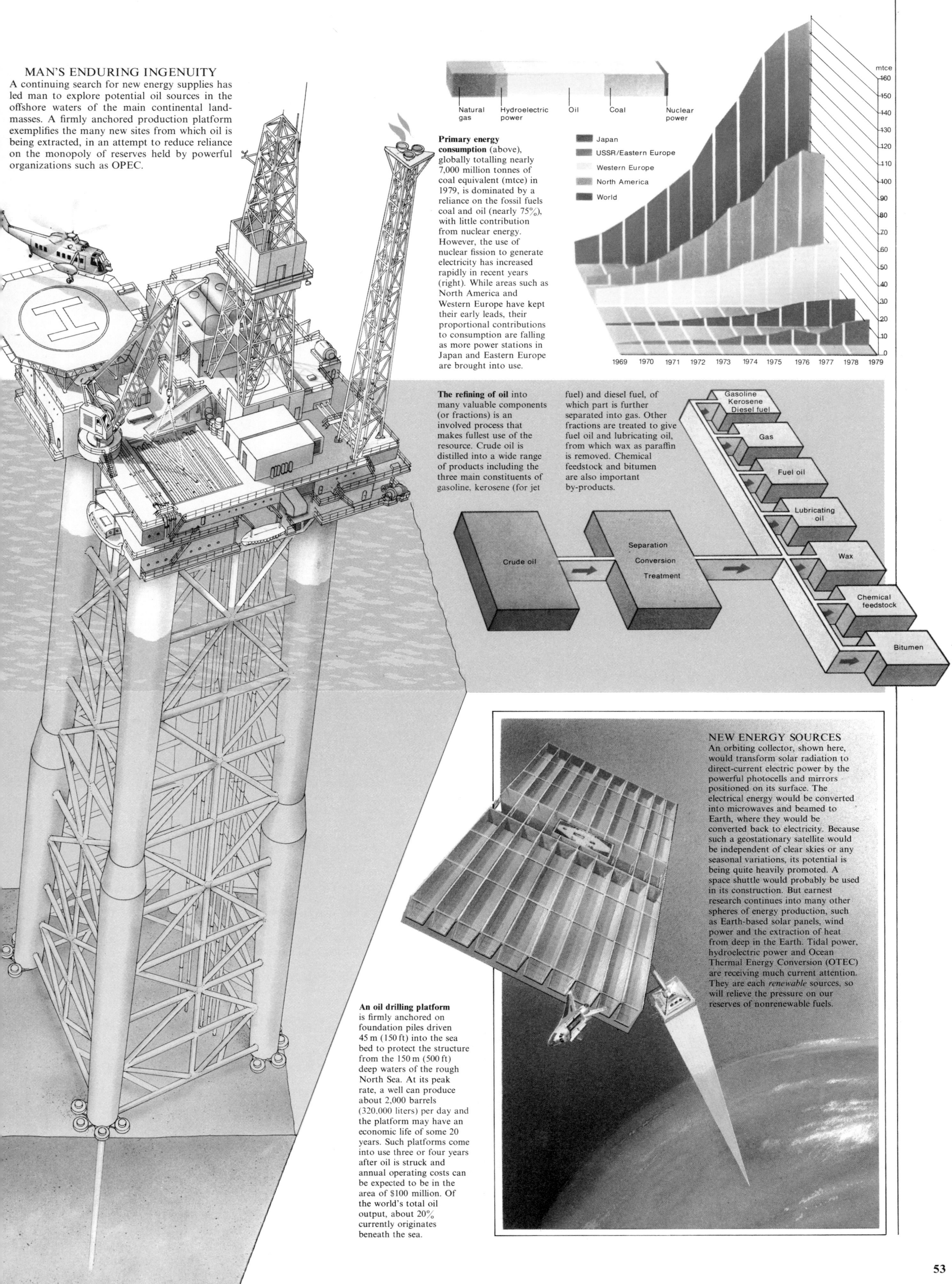

MAN'S ENDURING INGENUITY

A continuing search for new energy supplies has led man to explore potential oil sources in the offshore waters of the main continental land-masses. A firmly anchored production platform exemplifies the many new sites from which oil is being extracted, in an attempt to reduce reliance on the monopoly of reserves held by powerful organizations such as OPEC.

Natural gas   Hydroelectric power   Oil   Coal   Nuclear power

Japan
USSR/Eastern Europe
Western Europe
North America
World

mtce
160
150
140
130
120
110
100
90
80
70
60
50
40
30
20
10
0

1969 1970 1971 1972 1973 1974 1975 1976 1977 1978 1979

Primary energy consumption (above), globally totalling nearly 7,000 million tonnes of coal equivalent (mtce) in 1979, is dominated by a reliance on the fossil fuels coal and oil (nearly 75%), with little contribution from nuclear energy. However, the use of nuclear fission to generate electricity has increased rapidly in recent years (right). While areas such as North America and Western Europe have kept their early leads, their proportional contributions to consumption are falling as more power stations in Japan and Eastern Europe are brought into use.

The refining of oil into many valuable components (or fractions) is an involved process that makes fullest use of the resource. Crude oil is distilled into a wide range of products including the three main constituents of gasoline, kerosene (for jet fuel) and diesel fuel, of which part is further separated into gas. Other fractions are treated to give fuel oil and lubricating oil, from which wax as paraffin is removed. Chemical feedstock and bitumen are also important by-products.

Crude oil → Separation Conversion Treatment → Gasoline Kerosene Diesel fuel / Gas / Fuel oil / Lubricating oil / Wax / Chemical feedstock / Bitumen

NEW ENERGY SOURCES

An orbiting collector, shown here, would transform solar radiation to direct-current electric power by the powerful photocells and mirrors positioned on its surface. The electrical energy would be converted into microwaves and beamed to Earth, where they would be converted back to electricity. Because such a geostationary satellite would be independent of clear skies or any seasonal variations, its potential is being quite heavily promoted. A space shuttle would probably be used in its construction. But earnest research continues into many other spheres of energy production, such as Earth-based solar panels, wind power and the extraction of heat from deep in the Earth. Tidal power, hydroelectric power and Ocean Thermal Energy Conversion (OTEC) are receiving much current attention. They are each *renewable* sources, so will relieve the pressure on our reserves of nonrenewable fuels.

An oil drilling platform is firmly anchored on foundation piles driven 45 m (150 ft) into the sea bed to protect the structure from the 150 m (500 ft) deep waters of the rough North Sea. At its peak rate, a well can produce about 2,000 barrels (320,000 liters) per day and the platform may have an economic life of some 20 years. Such platforms come into use three or four years after oil is struck and annual operating costs can be expected to be in the area of $100 million. Of the world's total oil output, about 20% currently originates beneath the sea.

Population Growth

Every minute of every day, more than 250 children are born into the world. The Earth's population now stands at about 4,300 million and is continuing to grow extremely rapidly. The problems associated with such growth are enormous – already, about two-thirds of the world's people are underfed, according to United Nations' recommended standards of nutrition. And an even greater number live in very poor housing conditions, have inadequate access to medical facilities, receive little or no education and, at present, have no hope of improving their lot. As yet, there are no simple or immediate solutions.

World population (millions)

- World population
- Projected world population

If the world's population continues to grow at its present rate, by the year 2000 there could be more than 6,400 million people on Earth (above). Such growth rates are only a recent phenomenon—for most of mankind's existence on Earth the numbers grew slowly (right). Then in the late 18th century, scientific and industrial developments and the discovery of new food sources (the prairies of the New World) raised living standards. Death rates declined and populations grew rapidly.

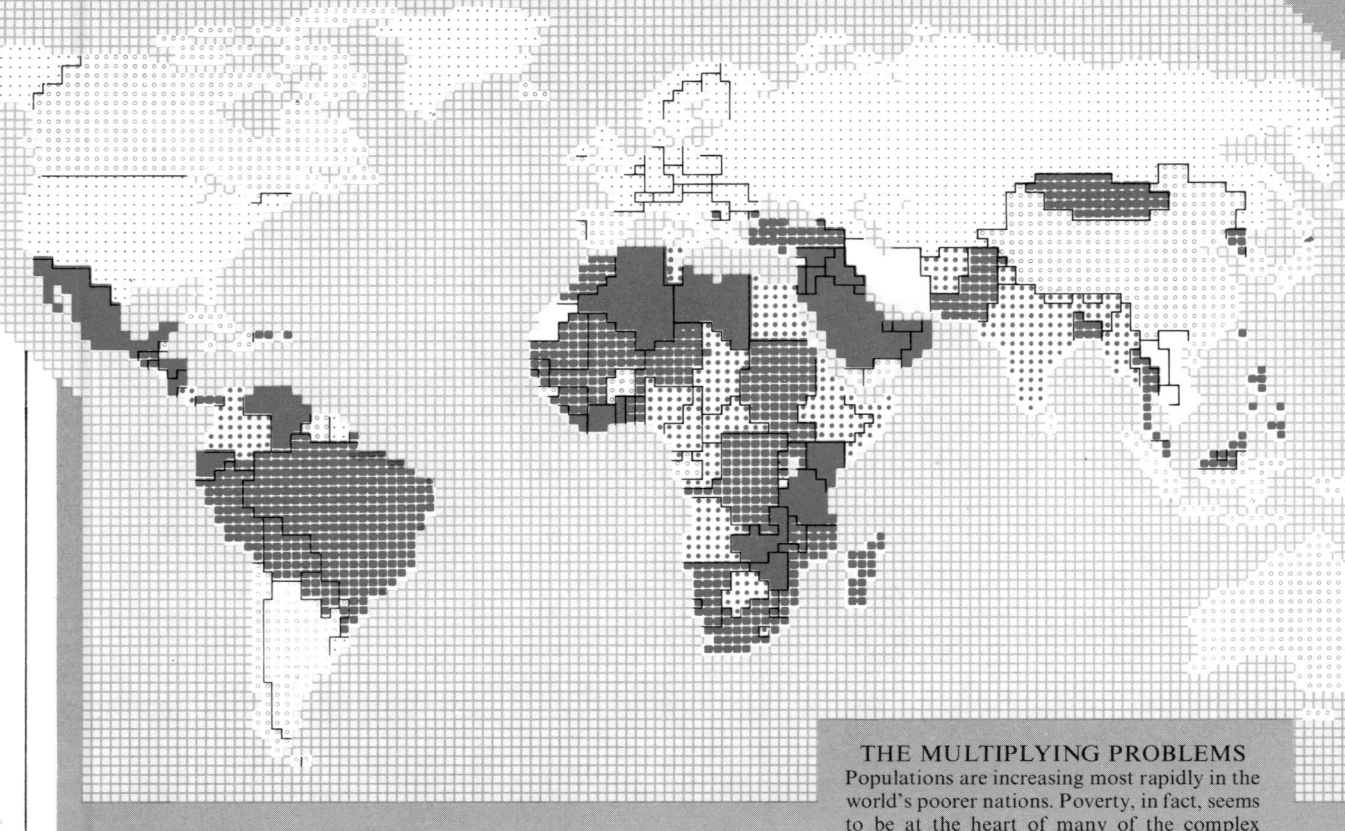

Average annual population growth rate 1970–1978

- 3% and over
- 2.5% to less than 3%
- 2% to less than 2.5%
- 1.0% to less than 2%
- Less than 1%
- Information unavailable

THE MULTIPLYING PROBLEMS
Populations are increasing most rapidly in the world's poorer nations. Poverty, in fact, seems to be at the heart of many of the complex interrelated problems created by rapid population growth. Poor countries, for example, are the least able to feed increasing numbers of people, while at the same time their lack of educational and medical facilities means that family planning is often inadequate and birth rates remain relatively high.

In 1830, there were only about 1,000 million people on Earth. By 1930, this figure had doubled. And by 1975, it had doubled again. If the present rate of increase continues, it will have doubled again by the year 2020.

This may not happen—it is extremely difficult to predict how world population will behave. What is certain is that it will continue to increase and, moreover, that this increase will not be evenly distributed. Since more than 50 percent of the human race lives in Asia, it is inevitable that the largest population increases will take place there. In fact, by the year 2000, the population of Asia may well have grown from about 2,000 million to more than 3,600 million. Substantial increases, of 400 million or more, will probably also occur in Africa, and Latin America is growing equally quickly.

In more prosperous North America and Europe, however, population growth seems to be stabilizing as women have fewer children and families become smaller—several countries, such as West Germany, now record a zero population growth rate. The poorer countries, the so-called Third World, are therefore gaining, and will probably continue to gain, an increasing share of the world's people. In 1930, about 64 percent of the human race lived in the poor countries of Asia, Africa and Latin America. By 1980, this proportion had increased to more than 75 percent. Population growth in these regions is creating enormous problems. It is estimated that there are now

more than 800 million people living in absolute poverty in the developing world, and these numbers can but increase as populations swell.

An obvious solution is to reduce birth rates, but this cannot be achieved quickly. In much of Africa and Asia, a very high proportion of the population is made up of young people who are, or soon will be, of childbearing age. Population increases are therefore inevitable. This will probably change as family planning becomes more widespread and women have fewer children, but such relief lies in the future and is likely to affect the poorest countries last. The most pressing problem for the growing numbers of impoverished people today is that of hunger.

Food – the fundamental problem
In theory, no food supply problem should exist—already enough food is produced in the world to feed a population of 5,500 million people. In fact, however, two-thirds of this food is consumed by the rich industrialized nations, and supplies are not reaching many of those in need. The developed nations dominate world food markets because developing nations, and people within those nations, are too poor to buy food, and are themselves unable to produce sufficient quantities to feed their growing populations. The answer to undernutrition and malnutrition lies largely in raising the incomes of poor peoples and improving distribution of supplies of food.

At a local level, food produced or imported

by developing countries must reach those in need at a price they can afford. One way of doing this is to encourage the rural poor to produce their own food. Small-scale, intensively farmed plots often prove to be the most efficient form of agriculture in areas where labor is plentiful. At present, many of the rural poor are either without land, or hold plots on extremely unfavorable terms of tenancy. By providing land, appropriate technology (small-scale, inexpensive farming equipment such as windpumps to draw water for irrigation), financial aid and information and education, small farmers could be helped to farm their land as effectively and efficiently as possible.

At a national level, too, developing countries must become more self-sufficient in food. This has already been achieved in some countries. India, although at one time heavily dependent upon imports of one of its staple foodstuffs—rice—has now increased production on such a scale that imports are no longer necessary. Unfortunately, for many developing countries this is not the case. Zaire, for example, was once an exporter of food. Today the country can no longer produce enough to keep pace with the demands of its own expanding population. At a world level, food production must be maintained as well, for unless production is kept high, prices are unstable and at times of bad harvests the poorer nations cannot afford to import essential supplies.

Food alone, however, is not enough to solve

FEEDING THE WORLD

How are the growing numbers of people on Earth to be fed when millions are already undernourished? In the short term, the food problem could be solved by improving distribution of supplies that are already available. But the world can also be made to produce more food. Fertilizers and pest control can make land more productive and genetic engineering could produce higher-yielding and more nutritious crops.

The world will have to produce more food than it does today (below) if future populations are to be fed. At present, large areas of the Earth's land surface cannot be farmed—they are either too cold, dry, marshy, mountainous or forested. Cultivatable areas could be extended, given the necessary investment.

THE HEALTH OF NATIONS

Many developing nations are severely short of medical and welfare facilities for their growing populations. Yet these are the very countries with high incidences of disease—mainly because of malnutrition, lack of clean water supplies, and inadequate and overcrowded housing. Furthermore, without health services family planning facilities are not widely available, and expanding populations continue to strain existing resources.

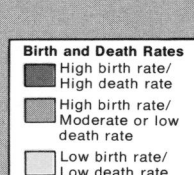

Birth and Death Rates
- High birth rate/ High death rate
- High birth rate/ Moderate or low death rate
- Low birth rate/ Low death rate
- Information unavailable

THE NONPRODUCTIVE LANDS

- Areas with no agricultural activity

PATTERNS OF POPULATION GROWTH

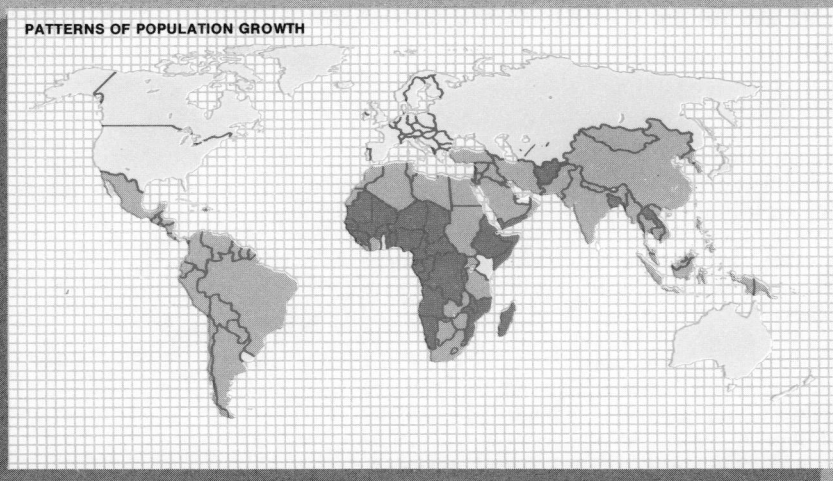

FOOD CONSUMPTION

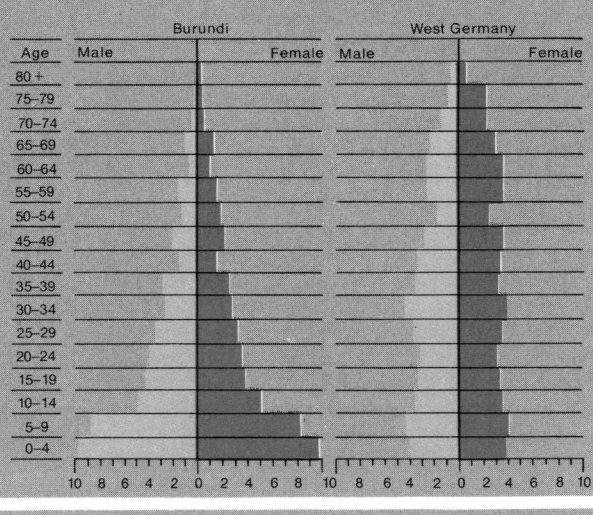

As a country's health facilities improve, its mortality rates decline. Birth rates, however, do not immediately fall (above). Thus, ironically, an improvement in facilities at first exacerbates the problem of rapid growth in population. A country with a declining death rate and a high birth rate gains an increasing percentage of young people who are, or will be, of child-bearing age. Population pyramids (right) plot the percentage balance between age and youth in a nation.

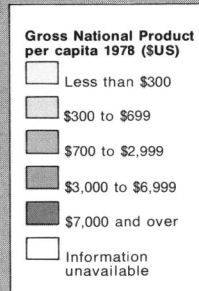

Calories per capita
- Less than 95% of needs
- 95% to 115% of needs
- More than 115% of needs
- Information unavailable

Malnutrition is widespread throughout the developing nations of Africa, Asia and South America. The problem is made worse by the fact that populations in these countries are growing more rapidly than anywhere else in the world.

the problems created by population growth. Broadly based economic development, such as in manufacturing and industry, is essential if developing countries are to have the income and other resources to enable them to cope with their evergrowing numbers of people.

INCOME

When the income level of a population is raised sufficiently, it seems that birth rates ultimately decline. This has been the pattern that has emerged in the Western world. If this is the case, then economic development of the Third World countries could eventually help to stabilize world population growth, as well as provide nations with the means to cope. It could also help provide for their growing numbers.

POVERTY AND WEALTH

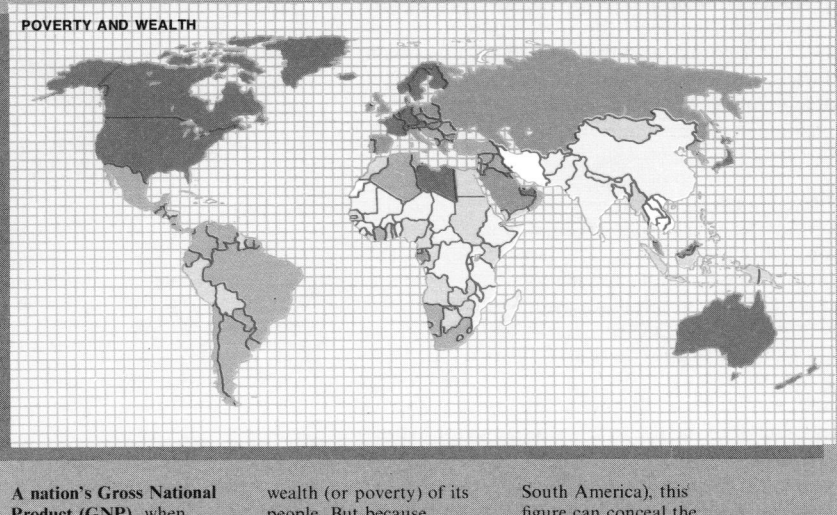

Economic growth

To achieve economic development, certain obstacles must be overcome. First, the Third World needs energy supplies at a price it can afford, for, with the exception of Nigeria and the now-rich Middle East, most developing regions are woefully short of the energy resources needed to fuel growth. Second, for sustained economic development a skilled labor force is required, as are educational facilities to provide the necessary skills from within the nations themselves. Third, investment is required to enable developing nations to exploit the resources they do have—minerals, for example. And this investment must be on terms that are as beneficial to the developing nations as they are to powerful multinational organizations that frequently fund such projects. Finally, and most important, more enlightened social and political outlooks are needed within many countries if their growing populations of impoverished people are to benefit from any economic development and consequent increase in national wealth.

It has been said that wealth is the best method of contraception and, judging by the history of population growth in the rich industrialized nations, this seems to be the case. If it is, economic development of the Third World may well alleviate many of the problems created by population growth.

Gross National Product per capita 1978 ($US)
- Less than $300
- $300 to $699
- $700 to $2,999
- $3,000 to $6,999
- $7,000 and over
- Information unavailable

A nation's Gross National Product (GNP), when divided by the number of its population, gives some indication of the relative wealth (or poverty) of its people. But because national wealth is not evenly distributed in many countries (particularly in South America), this figure can conceal the extreme poverty of very large numbers of a nation's people.

EDUCATIONAL RESOURCES

Education is essential if the people of the developing world are to be equipped to improve their lot. Basic education on health and hygiene could dramatically reduce the incidence of disease; education about birth control would help lower birth rates; agricultural advice could help the rural poor to produce more food. Finally, general schooling is required to provide skilled labor.

ILLITERACY

Illiteracy rate
- 80% and over
- 60% to less than 80%
- 40% to less than 60%
- 20% to less than 40%
- Less than 20%
- Information unavailable

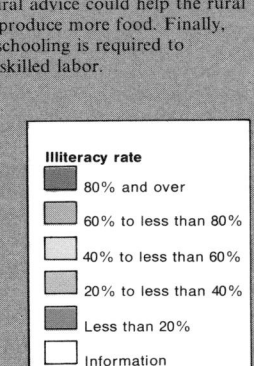

Literacy rates are in fact improving in developing countries and national expenditure on schools is growing more quickly than is population. Two major problems are, first, the social traditions that severely restrict the number of girls attending school and, second, the reluctance of many rural poor to send to school children who provide valuable manual labor on the land.

55

Human Settlement

Man is naturally a gregarious animal. As an agriculturist he first settled in small communities, but it was not long before the emergence of towns and cities. Now nearly half the world's people live in these larger settlements, and by the year 2000, for the first time in history, more people will live in cities than in the countryside. Cities have grown up for various reasons, and are unevenly distributed across the world; but it is in the developing countries that the most rapid rates of urban growth are today taking place.

City life has a long and varied history going back to the early population centers of the Tigris–Euphrates, Indus and Nile valleys. Administrative and political needs led to the development of capital cities. Some, like London and Paris, evolved on conveniently located river crossings; others, such as Canberra, Islamabad and Brasilia, have locations that were deliberately planned.

Types of towns and cities
Market towns were established to exchange produce and, as trade expanded, hierarchies of service centers became established. These ranged from small "central places" that supplied rural areas with simple goods and services from elsewhere, to large cities that provided highly specialized services. Through such centrally placed systems, rural areas became connected with major industrialized areas. Mining towns such as Johannesburg, South Africa, and Broken Hill, Australia, sprang up as man began to exploit the Earth's mineral resources, their locations determined by the presence of rich ore deposits. Fishing ports and settlements dependent on forestry fall into the same group.

Increasing specialization, exemplified by the Black Country, England, and the Ruhr, West Germany, was a feature of European industrial development in the eighteenth and nineteenth centuries, and was based on the availability of capital investment and the presence of sources of fuel and power, especially water and steam power. Such industrialized cities relied on newly developed forms of transport to bring in new materials and to carry away manufactured products. Chicago is a good example of the relationship between the development of rail and water routes and the growth of a city as a market, agricultural processing and manufacturing center. As transport developed, further specialized centers concentrated on locomotive, ship or aircraft construction.

Uneven settlement patterns
Across the world, density and distribution of population are uneven. The land surface of the Earth as a whole has a density of 28 people per sq km (73 per sq mile) although Manhattan, for example, has 26,000 per sq km (63,340 per sq mile) and Australia has only 1.5 per sq km (4 per sq mile). In Brazil, towns and cities are mostly sited in the rich southeast, in contrast to a sparseness of settlement in its interior. Contrasts also occur between Mediterranean North Africa and the deserted Sahara to the south; or Canada of the St. Lawrence and the Canadian Shield to the north. Here the causes are not hard to find: extremes of climate, terrain and vegetation form effective barriers to settlement. Geographers estimate that two-thirds of the world's population lives within 500 km (310 miles) of the sea.

Any true consideration of human settlements must, however, be placed within the context of the economic, political and social systems in which they have evolved. Physical considerations alone cannot fully explain the urban concentrations of Western Europe, Japan or the northeastern USA, or the comparative absence of cities elsewhere. Only 5 percent of Malawi's and 4.7 percent of New Guinea's populations live in towns; in Belgium the percentage is 87, in Australia 86, in the UK 78 and in the USA 73.5. The figure for Norway is only 42 percent. Urbanization is a varied phenomenon and cities grow for many reasons.

The attractions of the city
Cities have always acted as magnets to poor or unemployed rural populations, and migrations from the countryside have assisted high rates of city growth. Very large cities—Tokyo, New York and Los Angeles—are still found in the northern world, but many cities with far faster growth rates are sited in the Third World, especially in Asia. There the total number of inhabitants living in towns and cities is still much lower than in Europe, but centers such as Shanghai, Karachi, Bandung, New Delhi, Seoul, Jakarta and Manila are among the world's most rapidly expanding urban centers. Perhaps as many as a third of these city dwellers in Asia, Africa and Latin America put up with makeshift housing in shanty towns that present enormous problems of health, sanitation, education and unemployment: city growth in the developing world is a daunting prospect.

People on the move
In the past, one solution to population pressure on the land could be found in the migrations which occurred on a large scale from Asia into Europe, from Europe to the Americas and Australasia, and from China into southeastern Asia. But as claims are being made on almost every habitable area of the Earth, mass migrations have largely declined in importance. Many nations restrict movement to or from their countries. Australia has strict immigration quotas; Vietnam and the USSR restrict emigration for largely ideological reasons. Large movements of labor still take place, however, from the poorer regions of the Mediterranean to the industrial cities of France and Germany. Migrant workers from neighboring countries in Africa also play an essential part in the mining economy of South Africa.

New trends in urbanization
In many industrialized countries, a strong process of decentralization is leading to reductions in the populations of cities and corresponding increases in those of the suburbs and beyond. In 1951 the geographer Jean Gottman showed how groups of city regions tend to form chains of functionally linked cities, to which he gave the term "megalopolis." His prime example was Megalopolis, USA, stretching from north of Boston to south of Washington DC. Similar settlements occur in the Tokyo–Yokohama–Osaka area of Japan and the Ruhr megalopolis of northwestern Europe. Ultimately, equally drastic and large-scale patterns are likely to emerge in the already overcrowded human settlements of the Third World.

THE DISTRIBUTION OF POPULATION
Human settlement is highly uneven because it is related to many social and topographical factors. At first, man was tied to the sites of his crops and the grazing land of his cattle; life in nonrural centers only became a typical feature of population development as specialized services came into demand and towns and cities arose to support these needs. But during the 20th century there has been a vast increase in urban populations, particularly in Third World countries.

Oil and gas deposits
Iron ore railroads
Farming
● Towns
⊙ Hydroelectric projects
+++ Iron ore railroads
═══ Current oil and gas pipelines

Ciudad Guayana
Ciudad Bolivar
VENEZUELA
GUYANA

Expanding settlements (above) and new lines of communication are being developed in the poorly populated eastern lowlands of Venezuela in order fully to exploit the resources being discovered there. Huge deposits of iron ore and large supplies of oil and gas have been located, and Ciudad Bolivar and Ciudad Guayana have become steel-making and service centers. To feed the people of these new settlements, agriculture has been greatly expanded.

Immigration to the United States (below) from Europe was partly responsible for the growth of the vast Washington–Boston urban mass known as "Megalopolis." Since World War II, more immigrants have come from Puerto Rico and Mexico.

Boston
New York City
Philadelphia
Baltimore
Washington DC
Richmond

Immigrants in 000s
Year
1840 1860 1880 1900 1920 1940 1960 1980
1,000 2,000 3,000 4,000 5,000 (estimated) 6,000 7,000 8,000 9,000

Migrating refugees, the world total of which increases on average by 2,000–3,000 every day, can affect settlement patterns. The Ugandan children (below) fled to the northern province of Karamoja in the wake of the 1979 war with Tanzania and the resultant famine that occurred in much of Uganda.

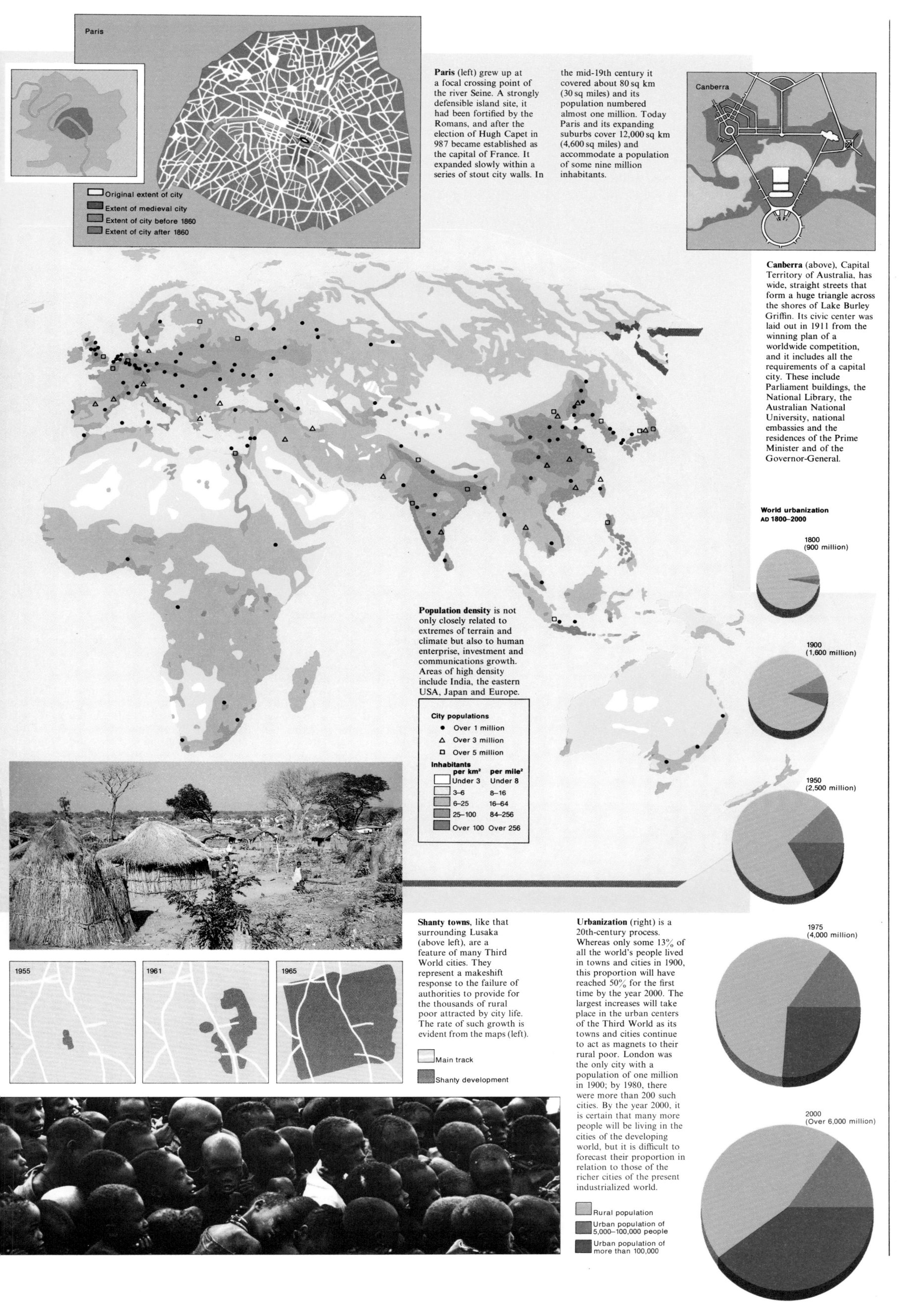

Paris

- ☐ Original extent of city
- Extent of medieval city
- Extent of city before 1860
- Extent of city after 1860

Paris (left) grew up at a focal crossing point of the river Seine. A strongly defensible island site, it had been fortified by the Romans, and after the election of Hugh Capet in 987 became established as the capital of France. It expanded slowly within a series of stout city walls. In the mid-19th century it covered about 80 sq km (30 sq miles) and its population numbered almost one million. Today Paris and its expanding suburbs cover 12,000 sq km (4,600 sq miles) and accommodate a population of some nine million inhabitants.

Canberra

Canberra (above), Capital Territory of Australia, has wide, straight streets that form a huge triangle across the shores of Lake Burley Griffin. Its civic center was laid out in 1911 from the winning plan of a worldwide competition, and it includes all the requirements of a capital city. These include Parliament buildings, the National Library, the Australian National University, national embassies and the residences of the Prime Minister and of the Governor-General.

Population density is not only closely related to extremes of terrain and climate but also to human enterprise, investment and communications growth. Areas of high density include India, the eastern USA, Japan and Europe.

City populations
- • Over 1 million
- △ Over 3 million
- ☐ Over 5 million

Inhabitants

per km²	per mile²
Under 3	Under 8
3–6	8–16
6–25	16–64
25–100	84–256
Over 100	Over 256

World urbanization
AD 1800–2000

1800
(900 million)

1900
(1,600 million)

1950
(2,500 million)

1975
(4,000 million)

2000
(Over 6,000 million)

Shanty towns, like that surrounding Lusaka (above left), are a feature of many Third World cities. They represent a makeshift response to the failure of authorities to provide for the thousands of rural poor attracted by city life. The rate of such growth is evident from the maps (left).

1955

1961

1965

- ☐ Main track
- Shanty development

Urbanization (right) is a 20th-century process. Whereas only some 13% of all the world's people lived in towns and cities in 1900, this proportion will have reached 50% for the first time by the year 2000. The largest increases will take place in the urban centers of the Third World as its towns and cities continue to act as magnets to their rural poor. London was the only city with a population of one million in 1900; by 1980, there were more than 200 such cities. By the year 2000, it is certain that many more people will be living in the cities of the developing world, but it is difficult to forecast their proportion in relation to those of the richer cities of the present industrialized world.

- Rural population
- Urban population of 5,000–100,000 people
- Urban population of more than 100,000

Trade and Transport

It is a commonplace that we live in a "shrinking" world. During the last century the development of communications has been so rapid that man appears almost to have conquered the challenge of distance; but such a concept depends on the kind of area to be covered and the cost of transporting goods in relation to their value, bulk and perishability. People, goods and services become accessible by trade. Transport makes trade possible: trade's demands lead to improvements in transport.

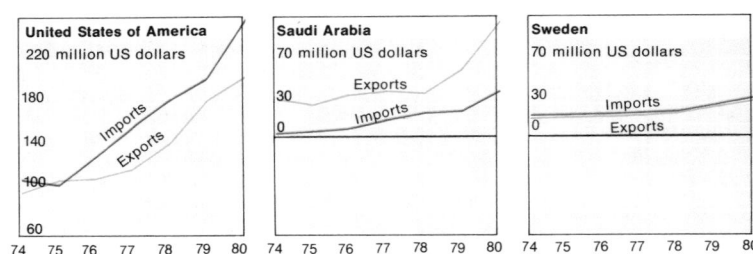

Exports in millions of US dollars (A)

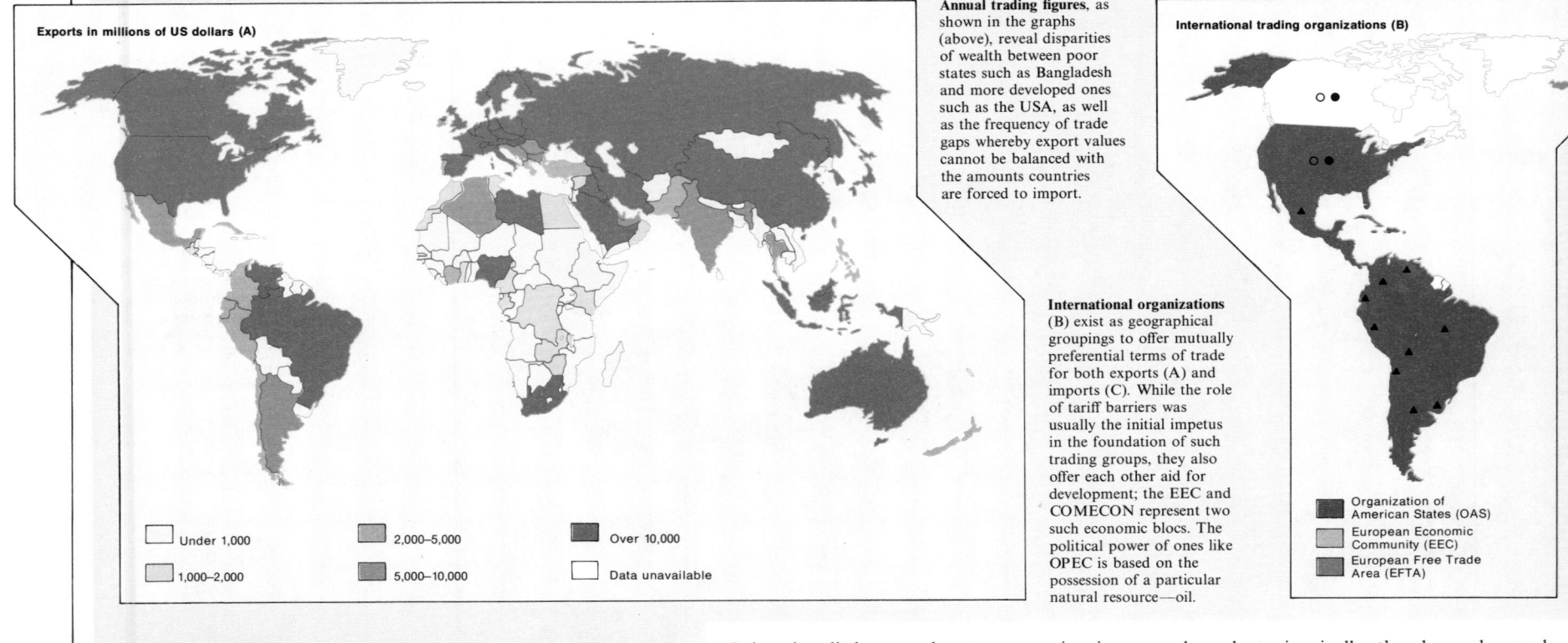

| Under 1,000 | 2,000–5,000 | Over 10,000 |
| 1,000–2,000 | 5,000–10,000 | Data unavailable |

Annual trading figures, as shown in the graphs (above), reveal disparities of wealth between poor states such as Bangladesh and more developed ones such as the USA, as well as the frequency of trade gaps whereby export values cannot be balanced with the amounts countries are forced to import.

International trading organizations (B)

International organizations (B) exist as geographical groupings to offer mutually preferential terms of trade for both exports (A) and imports (C). While the role of tariff barriers was usually the initial impetus in the foundation of such trading groups, they also offer each other aid for development; the EEC and COMECON represent two such economic blocs. The political power of ones like OPEC is based on the possession of a particular natural resource—oil.

- Organization of American States (OAS)
- European Economic Community (EEC)
- European Free Trade Area (EFTA)

Japanese export of electronic products (1979)

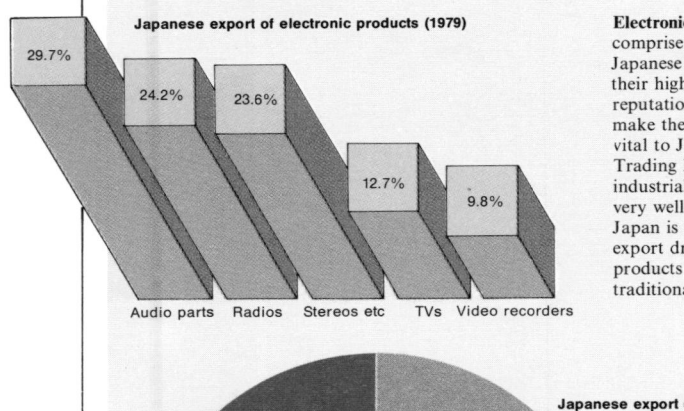

29.7% Audio parts
24.2% Radios
23.6% Stereos etc
12.7% TVs
9.8% Video recorders

Electronic products comprise only one-sixth of Japanese exports (left); their high export value and reputation for quality make their sales abroad vital to Japan's economy. Trading links (below) with industrialized countries are very well established; now Japan is mounting new export drives to sell its products to much less traditional markets.

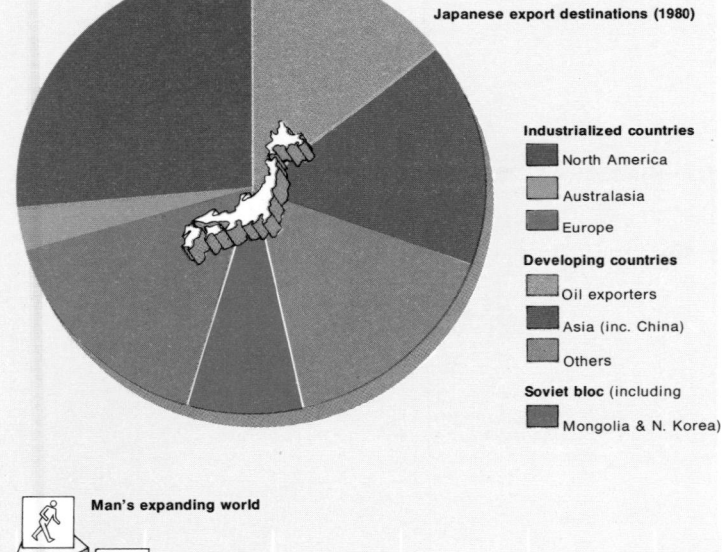

Japanese export destinations (1980)

Industrialized countries
- North America
- Australasia
- Europe

Developing countries
- Oil exporters
- Asia (inc. China)
- Others

Soviet bloc (including
- Mongolia & N. Korea)

It is only a little more than two centuries since navigators completed the mapping of the world's major landmasses and much less since the mapping of the continental interiors was completed—even today some gaps still remain. Canals like the Suez (1869) and Panama (1915) reduced the extent of long sea voyages—the Suez Canal shortened the distance from northwestern Europe to India by 15,000 km (9,300 miles)—so that in transport terms, the various parts of the world became more accessible, especially as steamships and motor vessels replaced sailing ships, and time distances were reduced still further by the airplane.

Locational advantages
Inland waterways, roads and railroads opened up new areas for mining or specialized agriculture, and created opportunities for the manufacture of goods and for the distribution of the finished products. The contrast, however, between locations such as London, Tokyo or Chicago (which are accessible to all forms of transport) and parts of South America where modern transport hardly penetrates, has become much more marked over the years. New transport developments tend to connect major centers first of all, and thus increase their already high locational status.

Such developments must nevertheless be seen in the light of the demand for communications and trade between different points, the nature of the goods being carried and the actual cost of transport. Transport improvements have allowed different parts of the world to share ideas

and products; ironically, they have also made such places more dissimilar, since each area of the Earth has had the chance to specialize in the services it can provide most efficiently.

Specialization of area
Before the widespread development of canals and railroads, road transport was expensive and towns and villages tended to be more self-sufficient. Railroads played a vital role in reducing transport costs in relation to distance and in providing an opportunity for different areas to specialize. After the emergence of railroad networks in North America, specialized areas of agricultural production quickly developed because they were well adjusted to the climatic conditions needed for growing maize (corn), cotton, fruit and fresh vegetables for the new urban markets. In the southern hemisphere, steamships and the introduction of refrigeration enabled meat, butter and cheese to be kept fresh on their journeys to the north.

This concept of specialization of area is basic to world trading patterns, since regions tend to concentrate on commodities and services that they can exchange for other specialized goods and products from other regional or world markets. Countries and areas do best when they concentrate on products for which they have comparative cost advantages in terms of the presence of natural resources, the availability of the skills to develop them, and a demand for the products. Enterprise in adapting natural conditions for the production of goods at competitive price levels is also important. Settlers in New

Man's expanding world

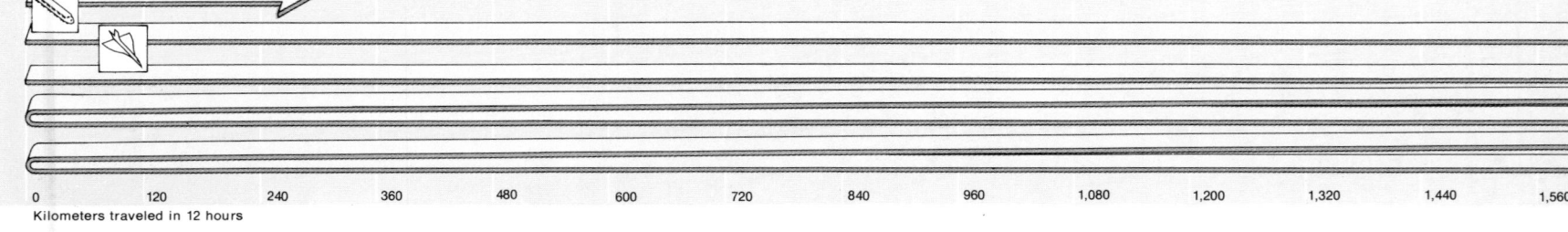

Technological change in transport has resulted in important reductions in the cost of trade. A man trading on foot might travel half the area a

draft horse could cover in a 12-hour day, but it was the acceptance of steam after *The Rocket* (1829) that made trade more reliable and greatly

expanded the potential for international commerce. Modern jet airliners can easily fly thousands of kilometers in half a day, and while they are being

used more and more for freight, most bulk freight is still carried by train or by specialized cargo vessel. The graph below plots changing transport technology.

0   120   240   360   480   600   720   840   960   1,080   1,200   1,320   1,440   1,560

Kilometers traveled in 12 hours

THE WEALTH OF NATIONS

Economists measure a country's richness in terms of Gross National Product (GNP), the value of the goods and services available for consumption and for adding to its wealth. The difference in value between its exported and imported goods is often an important aspect of a nation's economy, and effective systems to transport such goods must play a major role in overseas trade. The 1980 Brandt Report highlighted the huge gap between the income of the rich world and the poverty of many developing states, but solutions to such problems of inequality will be difficult to obtain.

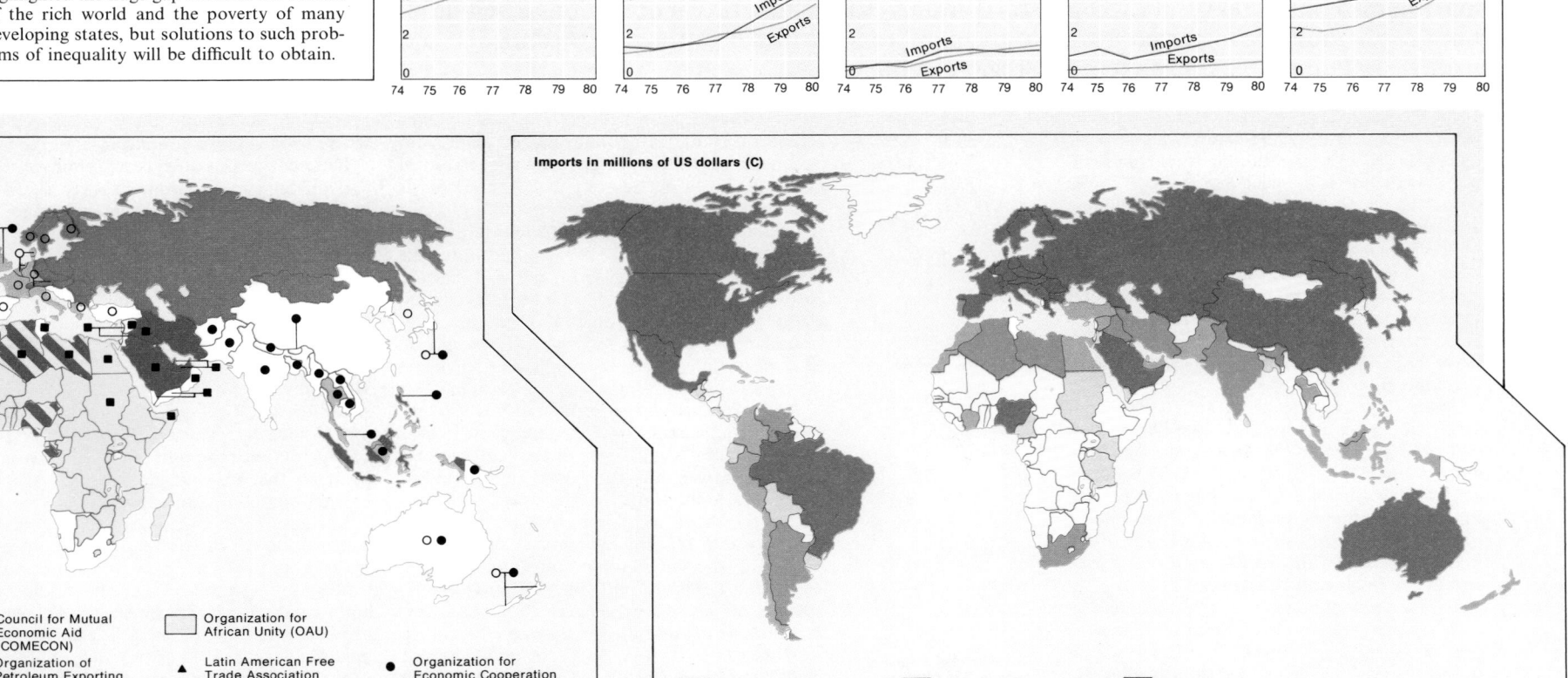

Imports in millions of US dollars (C)

| Under 1,000 | 2,000–5,000 | Over 10,000 |
| 1,000–2,000 | 5,000–10,000 | Data unavailable |

Council for Mutual Economic Aid (COMECON)
Organization of Petroleum Exporting Countries (OPEC)
Association of South-East Asian Nations (ASEAN)
Organization for African Unity (OAU)
Latin American Free Trade Association (LAFTA)
Arab League (AL)
Colombo Plan
Organization for Economic Cooperation and Development (OECD)

Zealand, for example, had little hesitation in clearing the prevailing tussock grass to create a new pastoral environment for their large-scale production of sheep and dairy products.

In the real world, however, there are many impediments to the operation of a free market system, and it is unwise for states like New Zealand to assume that they will always dominate Commonwealth dairy trade.

Impediments to free markets

Countries erect protectionist tariff barriers to assist their home industries and/or to obtain extra revenue. Import or export quotas may be imposed, and trade agreements with other countries give special preference to certain commodities. Problems arise from the exchange of currencies and their fluctuations in value. Tariff barriers may be erected for political, welfare or defense reasons. Sometimes special measures may be adopted to encourage the internal production of certain goods rather than obtaining them more cheaply from abroad, and such methods may be economically important to a new country that has always relied on the export of raw materials for its income but now wishes domestically to manufacture previously imported goods.

Political ties are vital to the groupings of certain countries. For reasons of international politics, countries such as those of the Soviet bloc trade with each other rather than with the outside world; and historical links, as between the UK and the Commonwealth, France and her ex-colonies, and Spain and Portugal with

Latin America, are also influential. The European Economic Community (EEC) is composed of countries that have formed a strong bloc among the developed countries.

Rich man, poor man

The developed countries of "the North" have more than 80 percent of the world's manufacturing income but only a quarter of its population, whereas the poorer peoples of "the South" number 3,000 million and receive only a fifth of world income. Attempts have been made to obtain a better economic balance. The 1948 General Agreement on Tariffs and Trade (GATT) and the United Nations Conference on Trade and Development (UNCTAD) provided mechanisms for multinational trade negotiations, and the World Bank and the International Monetary Fund (IMF) together with the 1960 International Development Association (IDA) have all provided easier loans for less developed states.

The widening gap between rich and poor countries has led to understandable demands for a new international order calling for basic changes in the structure of world production, aid and trade, and the transfer of resources. The 1980 Independent Commission on International Development Issues (The Brandt Commission) advocated just such a transfer to the Third World. But during a major world recession there seems little sign of any international political will strong enough to take action on the scale needed to solve the problems that contrasts in wealth and poverty involve.

Land over 1,000 meters
Trans-African highways
Major railroads
Copper belt

The weakness of African communications (above) results from the severe obstacles presented by its terrain and also from its very short period of economic development. Northern Zambia (below right) has copper which comprises some 90% of its exports and is much sought after by the industrialized world. But recent history has severely hampered its economic routes out of Africa; even though Zimbabwe and Mozambique no longer present export barriers, Zambia badly needs to invest in new track and rolling stock.

| 1,800 | 1,920 | 2,040 | 2,160 | 2,280 | 2,400 | 2,520 | 2,640 | 2,760 | 2,880 | 3,000 | 3,120 | 3,240 | 3,360 |

Polar Regions

Sunless in winter, and capped with permanent land ice and shifting sea ice, the world's polar regions present an image of intense and everlasting cold. But permanent ice caps have been the exception rather than the rule in the 4,600 million years of Earth's history. The most recent intensification of the present ice age (which began at least two million years ago) reached its maximum about 20,000 years ago and still continues to fluctuate. Polar conditions preclude all but the toughest life forms on land, but the plankton-rich waters attract many animals, and man is beginning to exploit the polar regions' potential.

There have been about a dozen ice ages since the world began. During the intervening periods there was still a zonal pattern of world temperatures, with hot equatorial regions and cooler poles. But the ice caps, which are both chilling and self-sustaining, were absent altogether—the poles being cold temperate rather than icebound. The shiny ice surfaces of today's poles reflect more than 90 percent of the solar radiation which reaches them from the low-angled summer sun, while in winter the sun never rises at all. Thus the regions are now permanently ice capped.

Antarctica, the great southern polar continent, lies under an ice mantle 14 million sq km (5.4 million sq miles) in area, and sometimes more than 4,000 m (13,000 ft) thick. Many of its neighboring islands also carry permanent ice. In the Arctic, the three islands of Greenland lie under a pall of ice of subcontinental size, more than 1.8 million sq km (700,000 sq miles) in area and up to 3,000 m (9,800 ft) thick.

The ice cover of polar seas varies. The central core of the Arctic Ocean carries a mass of permanent pack ice, slowly circulating within the polar basin, which is added to each winter by a belt of ice forming over the open sea. Currents and winds break this up to form pack ice that also circulates, gradually melting in summer or drifting south. Antarctica too is surrounded by fast ice, which breaks up in spring to form a broad belt of persistent pack ice. Circulating slowly about the continent, the pack ice forms huge gyres spreading far to the north, dotted with tabular bergs that have broken away from the continental ice sheet.

The frozen land
In the present glacial phase, the ice caps reached their farthest spread about 20,000 years ago, and then began the retreat which brought them, some 10,000 to 12,000 years ago, to their current position and size. Since then the climate of the polar regions has been both warmer and colder than it is at the present time.

The fluctuating nature of the polar climates creates very difficult conditions for plants and animals. Very little will grow on the terrestrial ice caps, but water scarcity rather than cold is the most important factor inhibiting plant growth: the small patches of lichens, algae and mosses that occur on rock faces and nunataks (points of rock jutting above the land ice) are usually in the path of a snowmelt runnel. Vegetation patches sometimes contain tiny populations of insects and mites, which may be active for only a few days each year when the sun warms them from a state of dormancy.

However, these tiny scattered plant communities appear all over Antarctica wherever rock surfaces break through the ice cap, and have been seen less than 300 km (190 miles) from the South Pole, and on peaks 2,000 m (6,600 ft) above sea level. Insects and mites occur within 600 km (380 miles) of the Pole itself. In specially favored positions on the Antarctic Peninsula and the offshore islands, carpets of moss and grasses may be seen. Conditions around the northern terrestrial ice cap are similar, with aridity, strong winds and cold discouraging all but the hardiest plants and the smallest, toughest animal colonies.

The frozen seas
The marine ice caps, by contrast, are relatively lively places, especially during summer, when days are long and the sea ice is patchy. Water-lanes between floes are often rich in microscopic algae and the minute zooplanktonic animals

that feed on them. These animals in turn attract fish, sea birds and seals in their thousands, as well as whales—including the largest baleen species. Some of the richest patches of sea are close to islands where strong currents stir the water and bring nutrients to the surface, and these attract semipermanent populations of seals and birds. The birds breed on the island cliffs and feed in the sheltered waters among the ice; the seals may breed on the ice itself, producing their pups on a floating nursery where food is close at hand.

Different species of seals are found on inshore and offshore ice environments. In the Arctic, bearded and ringed seals, which produce their young in spring as the inshore ice begins to break up, are often preyed upon by floe-riding polar bears; Eskimos too prize both species for their meat, blubber and skins. Farther out on the offshore pack ice live hooded and harp seals, where their pups are safe from all but the ship-borne commercial hunters. In the Antarctic, Weddell seals are the inshore species, whereas crabeater and Ross seals prefer the distant pack ice. Crabeaters, which feed largely on planktonic krill (once thought to be crab larvae), are probably the most numerous of all seal species, with a population estimated at 10 to 15 million.

Sea ice in the north provides a precarious platform on which coastal human populations of the Arctic, such as Eskimos, can extend their winter hunting range. When the land is snowbound and animals are scarce, the sea may still provide food for hunters skilled in fishing, and in stalking seals to their breathing holes.

Nonindigenous inhabitants of the ice caps have greatly increased in recent years, following the discovery and exploitation of oil in the north, as well as other valuable minerals in both the regions. Scientists and technicians today occupy bases and weather stations which in some cases, such as the Amundsen-Scott at the South Pole, are several decades old and have to be maintained by means of aircraft.

The coldness of the poles is caused by the tilt of the Earth's axis, which prevents sunlight from reaching them at all in the winter. Even in summer, little heat is received from the sun because of the low angle at which its rays reach the surface; much even of this is reflected away by the ice.

Arctic spring
Arctic summer
Arctic winter
Arctic autumn

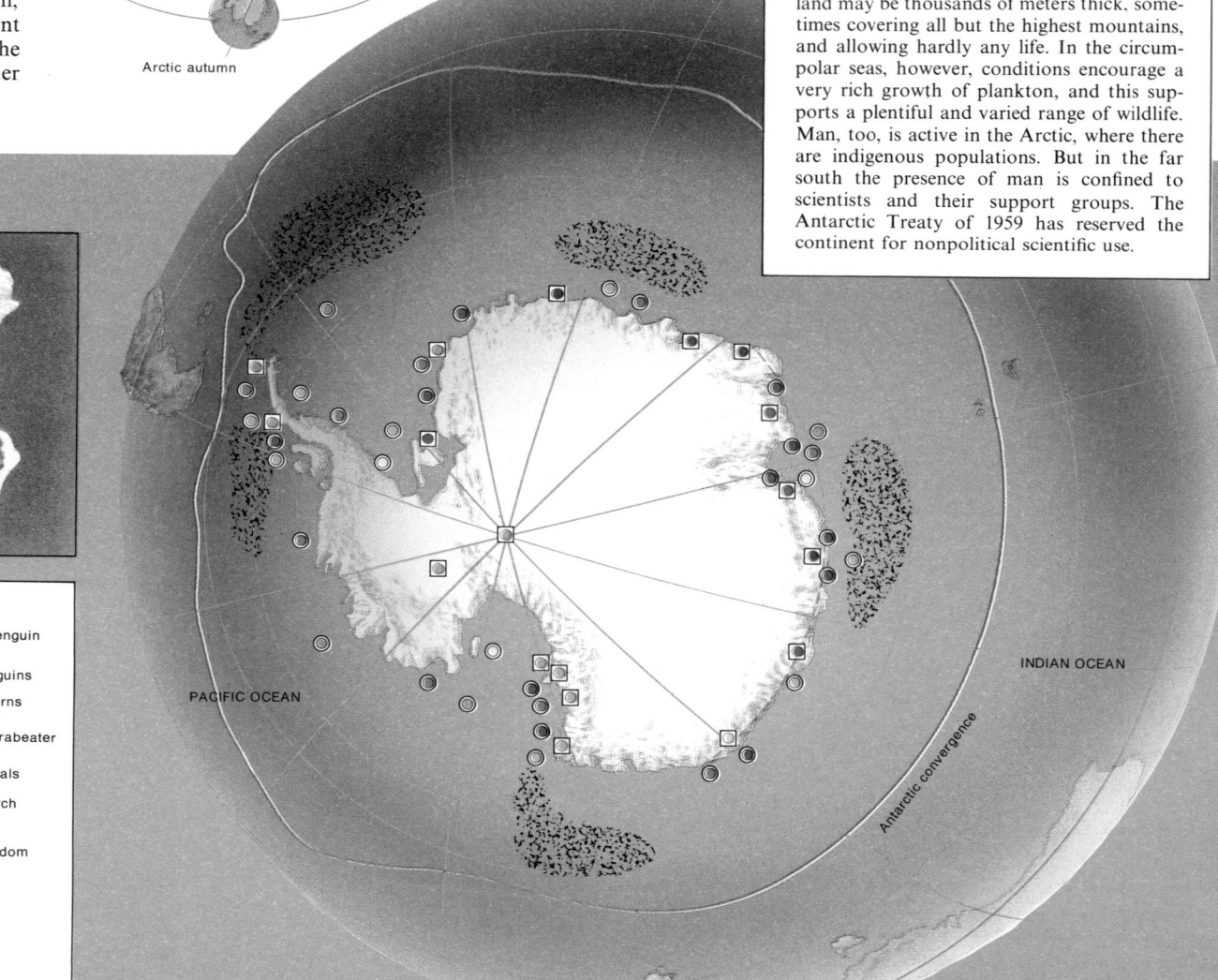

THE FAR SOUTH

A crushing weight of ice (above) permanently covers the continent and seas of Antarctica, forcing much of the land below sea level. The Antarctic convergence (right), the line at which northern and southern water masses meet, marks a sharp change in temperature and marine life. Especially in areas of upwelling, nutrients make these waters rich in plankton. This feeds a multitude of shrimp-like krill that provide food for a huge number of other animals—fish, penguins, flying birds, seals and whales. The Antarctic landmass allows little natural life, but since the 1959 Antarctic Treaty it has proved to be an area of international scientific cooperation.

Whales
Emperor penguin rookeries
Adélie penguins
Antarctic terns and petrels
Ross and crabeater seals
Leopard seals

Scientific research stations

United Kingdom
USSR
Japan
Australia
USA
Chile
France
New Zealand
Argentina

ATLANTIC OCEAN
PACIFIC OCEAN
INDIAN OCEAN
Antarctic convergence

Pleistocene ice sheet · Iceberg tracks · Limit of pack ice
Iceberg source · Approx. iceberg limit

An underground shelter against the winter is built by both men and bears in the polar regions. The bear's den (left) is prepared by a pregnant female for the delivery of her cubs, but may be used by other females and some males. The Inuit *igdlu* (below left) is a semipermanent winter house with an approaching passage and a sleeping platform cut from the earth. The largest roof slabs are then erected, the outside walls are built, and the structure is sealed with turfs to keep in the heat.

Hunting seals has always been an essential activity for indigenous Arctic peoples (above), who rely on them for food, fuel and clothing. Use of the gun for subsistence purposes has had a far less drastic effect than the industrial killing, or culling, of baby seals for their fur (left) in North America.

The frozen seas yield to modern technology as man develops the Arctic's vast potential. The Soviet nuclear icebreaker *Lenin* (left) clears a way for commercial shipping. The US nuclear submarine *Nautilus* has pioneered a shortened route under the North Pole (below).

Route of *Nautilus* 1958
Proposed submarine tanker routes

Huge sheets of sea ice cover the Arctic ocean basin; land ice covers most of Greenland and the northern edges of North America and Eurasia. Less than 20,000 years ago land ice extended as far south as London in the UK and New Jersey in the USA. Many scientists believe that we are still between two periods of glacial activity. Desolate in winter, the Arctic bursts into life during the short summer; but the breakup of ice may send bergs south into the path of transatlantic shipping.

MIGRATION
Of all migrant birds, the Arctic tern travels the farthest. It breeds in the high Arctic of Europe and North America and then, as winter approaches, migrates 17,000 km (11,000 miles) to the krill-rich waters of the Antarctic. It thus regularly packs two summers into a single year.

Krill
Euphausia superba

Blue whale
Balaenoptera musculus

Leopard seal
Hydrurga leptonyx

Emperor penguin
Aptenodytes forsteri

Killer whale
Orcinus orca

Crabeater seal
Lobodon carcinophagus

Countless tiny shrimp-like krill (above), yielding up to 1,350 million tonnes a year, are the chief food source of Antarctic waters and could possibly be used for human needs. Krill eaters include the blue whale, which can eat as much as three tonnes a day, and the crabeater seal. Among the Antarctic carnivores, the leopard seal preys mainly on penguins, and the killer whale on seals and penguins.

The South Pole, scene of Scott's tragic expedition of 1912 (left), is now the site of one of Antarctica's many scientific research stations (right). The bleak region may eventually yield a vast supply of mineral and other resources.

The emperor penguin (above) endures the rigors of the Antarctic winter on sea ice close to the continent in order to breed. Once the female has laid her single egg, the male starts the 64-day incubation through the midwinter darkness, carrying and incubating the egg on the top of his feet. This arduous regime ensures that young chicks, hatched in spring, avoid attacks from skuas, and benefit from better weather during their summer development. Penguins are one of the several kinds of wingless birds to have evolved in the southern hemisphere; but of all birds the emperor penguin is best adapted to the harsh polar environment of the Antarctic region.

Tundra and Taiga

Tundra is land that has been exposed for only about 8,000 years, since the retreat of the ice caps, and only relatively recently occupied by plants. In consequence, few plants and animals have yet had time to adapt to the virtually soilless and treeless environment. The less rigorous conditions of neighboring taiga forest allow a longer growing season and a somewhat wider range of species. The delicately balanced ecology of both areas is being increasingly threatened, however, by the activities of man.

"Tundra," from a Lapp word meaning "rolling, treeless plain," defines the narrow band of open, low ground that surrounds the Arctic Ocean. It lies north of the line beyond which the temperature of the warmest month usually fails to reach 10°C (50°F). North of this trees do not generally grow well, so the line forms a natural frontier between tundra and the broad band of coniferous forest that circles the northern hemisphere to its south between about 60°N and 48°N. This forest, forming the world's largest and most uninterrupted area of vegetation, is usually referred to by its Russian name of "taiga."

Cheerless landscapes

The tundra presents a desolate and restrictive environment for most of the year: in winter there are several months of semidarkness. While there is considerable variation in the climates of places at the same latitude, temperatures average only −5°C (23°F) and are well below freezing for many months of the year. Frost-free days are restricted to a few weeks in midsummer and even then, although days are warmer, the sun is never high in the sky. Nearly all tundra has been free from ice for only a few thousand years. As a result, it either has no soil at all or has developed only a thin covering of

sandy, muddy or peaty soil, successfully colonized by only a few types of plants.

Trimmed by such grazing animals as hares, musk oxen and reindeer or caribou, and by strong winds carrying abrasive rock dust and ice particles, typical tundra vegetation forms a low, patchy mat a few centimeters deep. Much of it grows on permafrost — ground that thaws superficially in summer but remains perennially frozen beneath the surface. Here drainage is poor, shallow ponds are frequent and the scanty soils tend to be waterlogged and acidic. Nevertheless, a small number of grasses, sedges, mosses and marsh plants may grow well and the summer tundra in flower can be an impressive sight. Knee-high forests of dwarf birch, willow and alder grow in valleys sheltered from the strong and biting wind.

The taiga also is a dark and monotonous habitat. Again, while there is a good deal of variation in climatic conditions, on average the region has somewhat milder summers than the tundra with mean average temperatures of 2–6°C (34–42°F), less wind and a slightly longer growing season. The taiga is mostly older than the tundra, and its soils have had longer to mature. They support a small number of tree species, with coniferous spruce, pine, fir and

larch predominating. Short-season broadleaves such as willows, alders, birches and poplars tend to occur on the better soils of river valleys and the edges of forest lakes.

Animals of the far north

The number of animal species supported throughout the year by tundra and taiga is also comparatively small, with interdependent populations that may fluctuate wildly from season to season. In winter both tundra and taiga are silent, although far from deserted. Mice, voles and lemmings remain active, living in tunnels under the snow, which keeps them well insulated from the wind and subzero temperatures. Above the snow Arctic hares forage; they tend to gather in snow-free areas where food can still be found. Arctic foxes are mainly tundra animals and the musk oxen, too, winter on high, exposed tundra where their dense, shaggy coats protect them from the worst

The circumpolar north that surrounds the permanently frozen ice cap is dominated by tundra—open plain that remains snowfree for only several months in the summer—and taiga, the vast coniferous forest stretching right round the northern hemisphere. The Siberian taiga, for example, is one-third larger than the entire United States.

☐ Tundra	☐ Taiga

Producers

■ USSR	
■ USA	

Pollution of Lake Baikal, the world's deepest freshwater lake, is being increasingly threatened by man's indifference to its unique position as a freshwater reservoir. Increasing exploitation of the Siberian taiga for minerals and timber has led to the pollution of the 300 or so rivers discharging effluents into the lake.

Man's pursuit of resources has accelerated in the past two decades, with the USSR drastically increasing its outflow of both oil and gas since 1970. North American output has lagged far behind, mainly because the need for exploration and exploitation has only recently become important. In all tundra and taiga areas, gas did not start flowing until the early 1960s. USSR coal output is rising steadily while that of North America has fluctuated. (In these figures, North America is composed of Alaska and the Yukon and Northwest territories. The USSR is more loosely defined as "regions of the far north".)

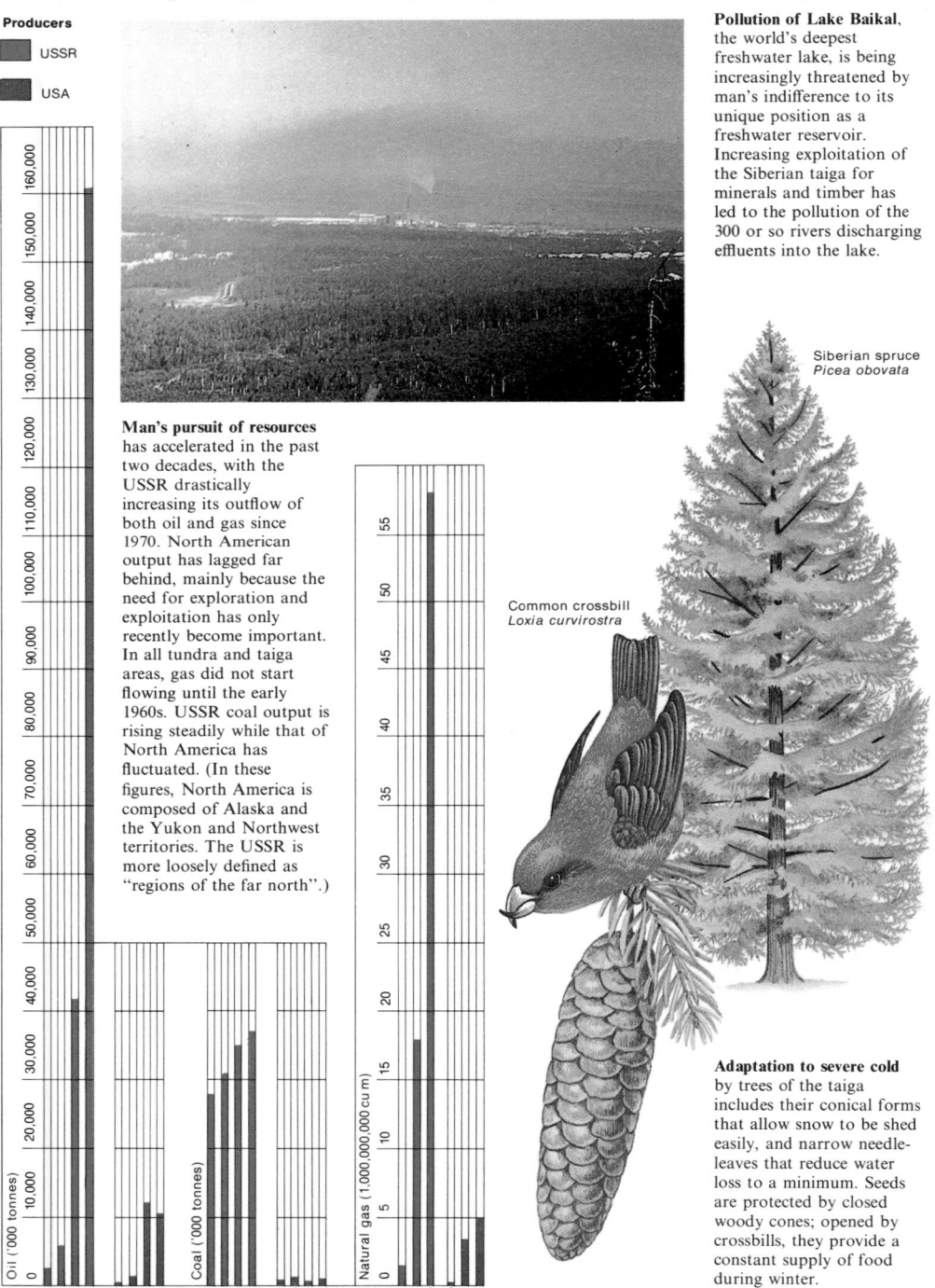

Siberian spruce *Picea obovata*

Common crossbill *Loxia curvirostra*

Adaptation to severe cold by trees of the taiga includes their conical forms that allow snow to be shed easily, and narrow needle-leaves that reduce water loss to a minimum. Seeds are protected by closed woody cones; opened by crossbills, they provide a constant supply of food during winter.

Oil ('000 tonnes)
Coal ('000 tonnes)
Natural gas (1,000,000,000 cu m)

Reindeer or caribou *Rangifer tarandus*

Raven *Corvus corax*

Arctic fox *Alopex lagopus*

January
February
March
April
May
June

Capercaillie *Tetrao urogallus*

Snowy owl *Nyctea scandiaca*

Brown lemming *Lemmus lemmus*

Arctic skua *Stercorarius parasiticus*

Movement in these regions takes many directions. The capercaillie spends all winter in the taiga, where it thrives on the abundant conifer needles, buds and shoots. Some move southward into deciduous woods during the summer months. The Arctic skua breeds on the tundra but moves to the warmer oceans in winter, while the tundra movements of the all-scavenging raven and the snowy owl are governed by those of their prey. The raven picks clean the carcasses left by other predators; the snowy owl feeds on small rodents such as mice and lemmings, as does the Arctic fox. Lemmings remain static and inconspicuous in normal years but some populations expand rapidly every third or fourth year, leading to mass local migration in every direction, possibly caused by an abundance of vegetation that encourages more frequent breeding.

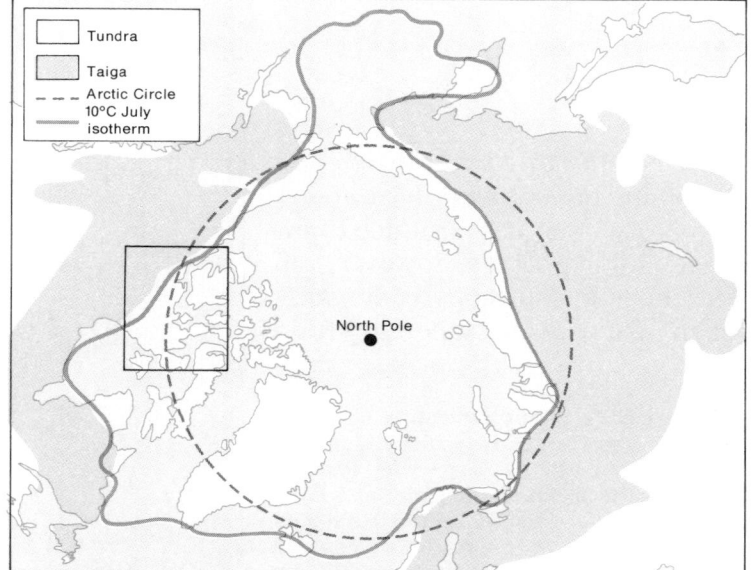

The rough boundary between the tundra and taiga—the tree line—approximates to the 10°C July isotherm, the climatic point north of which trees fail to grow successfully. Seasonal caribou migration in the Canadian barren grounds (boxed) is shown in the main diagram (below). Such migration is also undertaken by reindeer in northern Eurasia.

Legend:
- Tundra
- Taiga
- Arctic Circle
- 10°C July isotherm

North Pole

weather. Bears, badgers, beavers and squirrels are common taiga mammals. Elk and reindeer (in North America, moose and caribou) winter in the shelter of the taiga; wolves are mostly woodland animals in winter, following their prey to the open tundra in spring. Red foxes, coyotes, mink and wolverines also move to the tundra in summer.

Snow buntings, ptarmigans and snowy owls live on the tundra throughout the coldest months and are fully adapted to life there. Crossbills and capercaillies are among taiga residents, equipped to live on its abundant conifer buds, seeds and needles. Enormous populations of migrant birds, especially water birds and waders, fly north to both tundra and taiga with the spring thaw. Waxwings, bramblings, siskins and redpolls leave their temperate latitudes to feed on the lush and fast-growing vegetation and the profusion of insects that appear as soon as the snows begin to melt.

Many Norwegian Lapps (or Samer) derive their income from reindeer, which they domesticated many centuries ago to provide meat, milk and skins. Now they follow them through the seasons along well-worn and familiar routes. Such nomadic life styles are becoming rarer as Samer settle down.

Man in the northlands

These circumpolar regions act as a strategic buffer between the USA and the USSR. Situated between the world's greatest centers of population, they are now crisscrossed with air routes. A total population of about nine million people currently inhabits the tundra and taiga. Numbers have been increased by the immigration of technicians and administrators during the last few decades; oil prospecting and mining, forest exploitation and other activities of these newcomers is altering the seminomadic lives of the million or so aboriginal peoples such as the Khanty (Ostyaks) and Nentsy (Samoyeds) of the USSR, the Samer (Lapps) of Scandinavia and the Soviet Union, and the Inuit (formerly Eskimos) of North America. New roads, exploitation of minerals and forests, and pipeline construction have disrupted the migration of their reindeer (caribou) and their land has been appropriated for hydroelectric schemes.

In the taiga, the Soviets are constructing railroads and towns and extracting huge amounts of timber; they have prospected widely and successfully for gold, nickel, iron, tin, mica, diamonds and tungsten, and have discovered vast reserves of oil and natural gas in western Siberia. Alaskan oil, discovered in 1968, now flows across the state at 54–62°C (130–145°F), and to protect the permafrost from this heat the pipeline has had to be elevated for half its 1,300 km (800 mile) length. The pipe's route to the ice-free port of Valdez has interfered with the migration of caribou; hunting and other pressures have led to a drop in their population from three million to some 200,000 in about 30 years. Only official protection has saved the musk ox from a similar fate. These bleak areas are so vast and inhospitable that living space there will never be threatened. However, if only on a local scale, their ecologies are under increasing pressure from man.

The summer tundra—seen here in Swedish Lapland—provides a wide cover of low plants including "reindeer mosses" and other lichens. Grazing reindeer return minerals to the soil. Shallow ponds form as the frozen ground above the permafrost thaws for a few months in summer. Mountains stay partly snow covered in the warmest weather and are a prominent physical feature of the tundra.

Musk ox
Ovibos moschatus

MOVEMENT THROUGH THE SEASONS

Life on tundra and taiga is dominated by the mark of the seasons. In this diagrammatic representation of the north–south migration of the American caribou, each block represents the same area of terrain through the 12 months of the year. From February to April, the caribou move north in a steady file from the forest, emerging to eat the newly exposed lichen and moving to grounds where calving takes place in late May and early June. In the summer months they disperse freely before returning south in smaller groups on a broader front in late July and August. Rutting and mating take place in October/early November before the caribou regain the shelter of the taiga.

Rock ptarmigan
Lagopus mutus

Arctic hare
Lepus arcticus

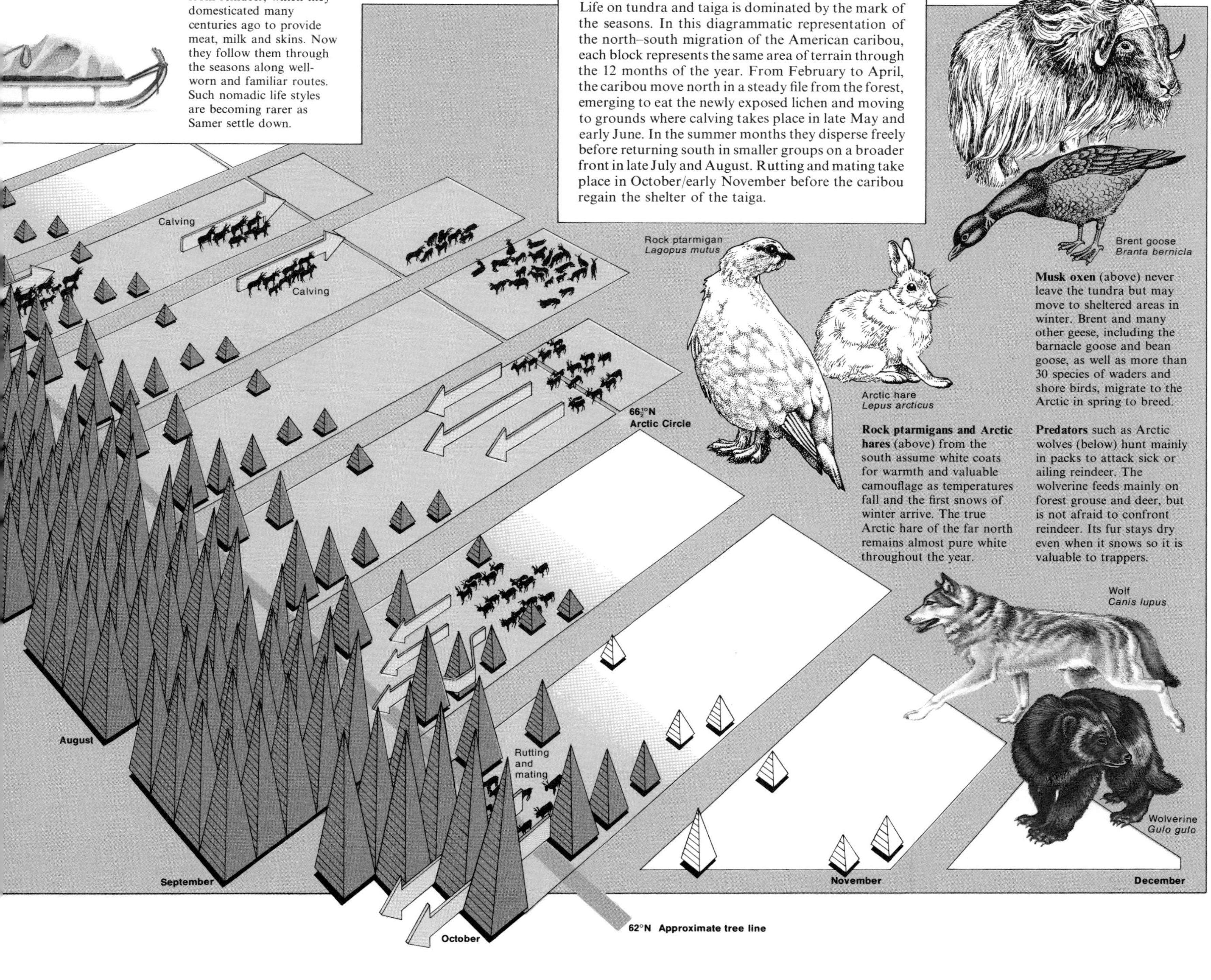

Musk oxen (above) never leave the tundra but may move to sheltered areas in winter. Brent and many other geese, including the barnacle goose and bean goose, as well as more than 30 species of waders and shore birds, migrate to the Arctic in spring to breed.

Rock ptarmigans and Arctic hares (above) from the south assume white coats for warmth and valuable camouflage as temperatures fall and the first snows of winter arrive. The true Arctic hare of the far north remains almost pure white throughout the year.

Predators such as Arctic wolves (below) hunt mainly in packs to attack sick or ailing reindeer. The wolverine feeds mainly on forest grouse and deer, but is not afraid to confront reindeer. Its fur stays dry even when it snows so it is valuable to trappers.

Brent goose
Branta bernicla

Wolf
Canis lupus

Wolverine
Gulo gulo

Calving

Calving

66½°N
Arctic Circle

August

September

October

Rutting and mating

November

December

62°N Approximate tree line

Temperate Forests

At one time, dense, primeval forests blanketed large areas of North America, Europe and eastern Asia. Almost all of the trees that flourished in these temperate regions were deciduous – they shed their leaves in autumn, stood bare branched through winter and produced new foliage every spring. Little of this forest now exists. The few remaining pockets, however, still provide habitats for a large range of shade-loving plants: lichens and fungi, tree-hugging mosses, scrambling creepers and shrubs. And this vegetation in turn provides sanctuary for a surprisingly wide variety of forest creatures.

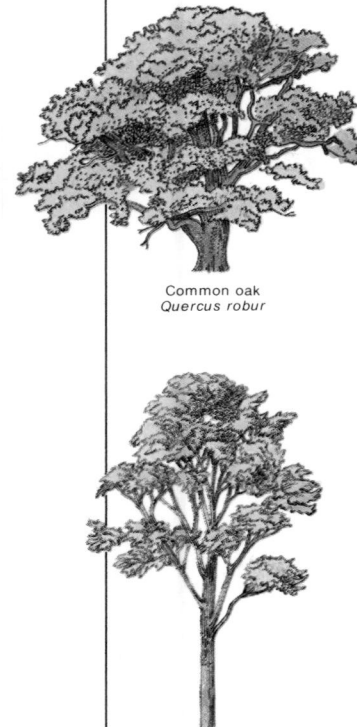

Common oak
Quercus robur

Silver beech
Nothofagus menziesii

Deciduous trees such as the oak (top) make up the temperate forests in cooler temperate regions. In milder, wetter climates, where the seasons are less distinct, evergreens such as southern beech (above) are typical temperate species.

The greater part of the temperate forest zone lies in the northern hemisphere, where winter soil temperatures reduce the ability of plants to absorb water. Hence the trees tend to shed their leaves, which use up moisture through evaporation. In the southern hemisphere, however, the temperate latitudes encourage a type of rainforest in such areas as southern Chile, Tasmania, New Zealand and parts of southeastern Australia. Here the climate is maritime, often with high rainfall and frequent fogs, and evergreen rather than deciduous types of trees grow. Temperate rainforests also occur in the northern hemisphere, in China and in northwestern and northeastern North America.

Deciduous forest consists of a mixture of trees, sometimes with one variety predominant. In central Europe, beech is the leading—and sometimes the only—tree species, whereas oaks mixed with other species made up the forest farther west and east. In North America, beech and maple were once extensive.

The climate in temperate forest zones varies sharply according to seasons—summers tend to be warm, winters moderately cold, and rainfall fairly regular. In fact, the seasonal rhythm is a central feature of temperate forests, and it affects the entire ecosystem—the whole community of plants and animals found there. Soils are generally of the fertile "brown earth" type: the leaf litter of deciduous forests in particular breaks down easily, and is quickly worked into the soil by burrowing animals such as earthworms. In wetter or rockier regions, the soil is more "podsolic"—bleached, sandy and less fertile than the true brown earths.

After the ice

Two million years ago, a series of ice sheets began to extend into the temperate latitudes. In Europe, species moving south before the advancing cold were cut off from the warmer climates by the east–west run of mountains. As a result, many varieties of plants and animals

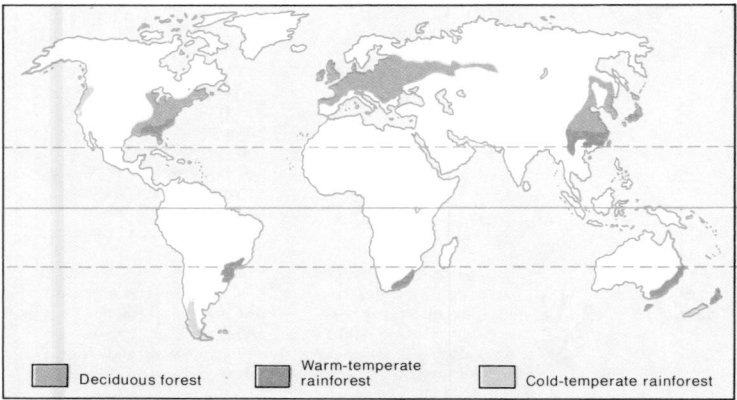

Deciduous forest   Warm-temperate rainforest   Cold-temperate rainforest

Natural distribution: in the northern hemisphere's temperate zone deciduous forests occur in the cooler areas—in eastern USA, northeastern China, Korea, the northern parts of Japan's Honshu island and western Europe. These forests only give way to evergreens in the warmer and wetter parts of the zone. In the southern hemisphere, the climate is generally rather milder throughout the temperate zone and so there are virtually no deciduous forests. Evergreen forests, however, can be found in southeastern South Africa, Chile, New Zealand, Australia and Tasmania.

were killed off. Species were reduced still further in islands such as Britain, where the newly formed barriers of the English Channel, Irish Sea and North Sea made recolonization even more difficult after the ice had retreated.

Eastern Asia was one of the few areas in the world that escaped the extreme climatic changes of the ice ages and therefore its temperate forests, unlike those of Europe, still contain an enormous variety of tree species. North America also fared better than Europe, for although glaciers at one time extended deep into the continent, the north–south direction of the mountain ranges allowed relatively easy migration of trees southwards as the climate worsened. Hence most species survived and were able to reoccupy their former territories when the ice retreated. As a result, some 40 species of deciduous trees occur in the North American forests, and contribute to the spectacular display of color during the autumn, notably in

the eastern USA. But a combination of climatic change and, more recently and importantly, of intense human activity, has meant that the remnants of temperate forest seen today differ greatly from the original forest in both composition and form. Only in remote regions such as the southern Appalachian Mountains do substantial areas of the original forest survive. Elsewhere, regrowth has occurred, but much of this is essentially scrub woodland.

The forest structure

Mature temperate deciduous forest is made up of distinct horizontal layers, particularly where the dominant tree is the oak, which allows enough light for a rich shrub layer to grow beneath it. The largest trees, such as oak, maple or ash, may be 25–50 m (80–160 ft) tall, and beneath them grows a prominent layer of smaller trees such as hazel, hornbeam or yew. Lower down again, a varied ground cover of perennial herbs, ferns, lichens and mosses flourishes in the comparative dampness of the forest floor. Because the trees are bare of leaves in winter, many of the plants growing on the forest floor take advantage of the warmth and light of spring to flower early in the year before the main trees come into full leaf and prevent the sun from reaching them. Various woody climbers, such as ivy and honeysuckle, are also present, growing over the trees and shrubs.

Much of the food supply in temperate forests is locked up in the trees themselves, but the annual fall of leaves in the deciduous forests produces a soil rich in nourishment. This supports a vast quantity of life, ranging in size from earthworms and insects to microscopic bacteria of the soil. The death of individual trees and branches also releases the food supply back to the earth. In shady, damp locations, insects, fungi, bacteria and other decomposing agents break down the leaves and other plant and animal debris more quickly, returning them to the soil as food for new plants.

Creatures of the forest

Temperate forests once contained many varieties of animal life, including several species of large animals. Herbivores such as wild oxen, wood bison, elk and moose ate grass and leaves; scavengers such as wild pigs rooted in the forest floor; predators such as wolves preyed on the other animals. Most of these have now been hunted to extinction by man or are extremely rare. Smaller animals still survive in comparatively large numbers, and include squirrels, chipmunks and raccoons, hedgehogs, wood mice, badgers and foxes.

The bird life of temperate forests is very diverse. Some species are insect eaters, exploring the bark and crevices for insects and grubs. Others, such as the wood pigeon, concentrate on seeds. Yet others, like the tawny owl, are predators. Complex interactions between predators and prey have developed at all levels of the forest, from the high canopy to the rotting ground litter, with each group evolving more efficient techniques of capture or escape in a kind of evolutionary race for survival.

The invertebrate insect life is also extremely varied and numerous, and forms a key component of the ecosystem. Oaks are particularly rich in insect life, and more than 100 species of moths feed on their leaves.

The plant and animal life of the temperate forest is remarkably rich and plentiful. And yet it is only a fraction of what once existed. Ever since man has occupied these regions he has found them so suited to his needs that he has long since cleared most of the original tree cover, replaced it with "civilization" and, in the process, destroyed innumerable species of forest wildlife.

THE SEASONAL CYCLE

It is the cycle of the four seasons that gives the temperate deciduous forest its distinctive character. All animals and plants have adapted their ways of life to cope with the seasonal changes in heat, light, moisture and food. The yearly shedding and regrowth of the forest's leaves is one of the most striking and important of adaptations to the seasonal cycle and one that affects all other life in the forest. In summer the leafy canopy of the trees blocks out the sunlight from the forest floor and creates unsuitable conditions for many other plants to flourish. When the leaves fall they form a layer over the soil and provide winter protection for the plant roots and hibernating animals beneath the ground. Finally, once the dead leaves have been broken down, they give fertility to the soil and provide food for future generations of plants.

SPRING

Between February and April, the low spring sun climbs steadily higher in the sky and, streaming through the still leafless branches of the trees, falls more directly on the forest floor, warming the soil and melting the last frosts. As soon as the days become warmer the sluggish sap in the trees begins to flow more quickly, carrying nutrients to the branches, where leaf buds start to form.

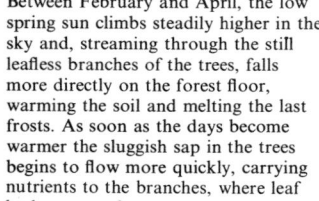

Small plants of the forest floor, such as European bluebells and hepaticas taking advantage of the warm soil and plentiful light, flower in spring.

Bluebell
Endymion non-scriptus

Hepatica
Hepatica nobilis

Forest insects emerge in spring, some, such as the emperor moth, from their winter cocoons, some from hibernation and some newly hatched from eggs.

Small emperor moth
Saturnia pavonia

European blackbird *Turdus merula*

Birds building nests in early spring make use of the forest's winter litter—broken twigs, dead leaves and dried grasses all serve as construction materials.

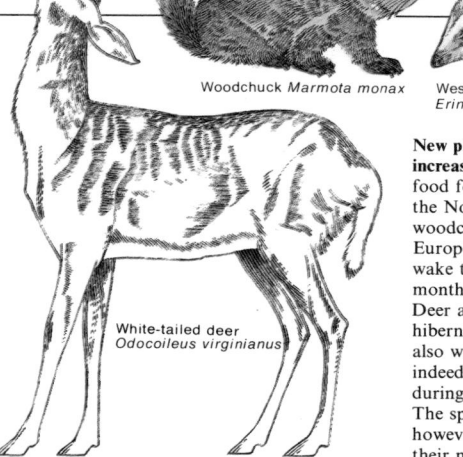

Woodchuck *Marmota monax*

Western European hedgehog
Erinaceus europaeus

White-tailed deer
Odocoileus virginianus

New plant growth and the increase in insects provide food for such animals as the North American woodchuck and the European hedgehog that wake thin and hungry from months of hibernation. Deer and other non-hibernating animals are also weak and thin—indeed many may have died during the harsh weather. The spring birth of young, however, soon restores their numbers.

SUMMER

By early summer the leaves of the trees are fully grown. They form a dense canopy, blocking out the sun and cooling the soil of the forest floor. Most of the small ground plants have long since finished flowering, but their leaves remain green and they continue actively storing food in their roots ready for their rapid spring growth.

Cranberry *Vaccinium oxycoccus*

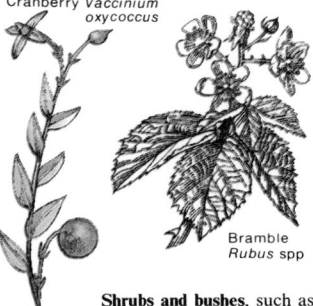

Bramble
Rubus spp

Shrubs and bushes, such as bramble and cranberry, form tangled flowering masses wherever sunlight manages to filter through the forest's gloomy canopy.

Hordes of insects inhabit the forest in summer, living off the vast supply of food plants. The European stag beetle feeds on the sap of chestnut and oak trees.

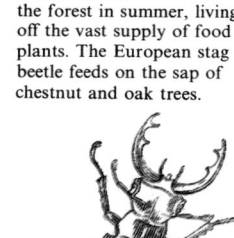

Stag beetle
Lucanus cervus

Willow warbler
Phylloscopus trochilus

The North American pewee and the willow warbler are two of the forest's many summer visitors that feed on the insect population. Some seed-eating birds, finches for example, also take advantage of this summer food supply.

Eastern wood pewee
Contopus virens

Hazel mouse
Muscardinus avellanarius

The hazel mouse protects its young by raising them in a summer nest, which it builds in a tree: almost every creature in the forest is viewed as a source of food by some other animal and the young litters are particularly at risk.

AUTUMN

As the autumn days grow shorter and cooler the forest foliage begins to turn color; the trees are responding to the drop in temperature and are cutting off the food supply to their leaves, which lose their green color and fall to the ground, forming a thick carpet on the forest's floor. Rain, frost, insects, earthworms and fungi then break down the leaves, making them part of the fertile forest soil.

Ripe fruits and seeds of the forest trees—acorns, beech nuts and hazel nuts—drop to the ground, where a few are buried in the layers of dead leaves and remain protected until they sprout in the early spring.

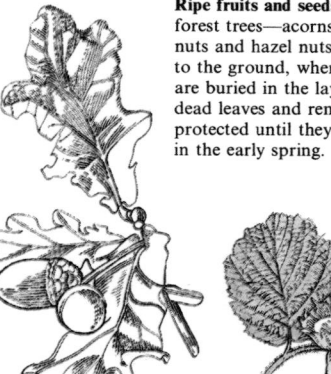

Common hazel
Corylus avellana

Oak
Quercus spp

Preparing for winter, the acorn woodpecker stores seeds in holes that it drills in tree trunks. Chipmunks hide supplies of nuts in their winter nests.

Acorn woodpecker
Melanerpes formicivorus

Eastern chipmunk
Tamias striatus

American black bear
Ursus americanus

The black bear of North America, like other winter hibernators, consumes vast quantities of food during autumn to build up its winter stores of food in the form of body fat.

WINTER

By winter, only evergreen shrubs and a few small hardy plants remain green. Many of the plants of the forest floor lose their green leaves during the first deep frost. The leaves of the trees still lie rotting on the bare ground, but within the soil, beneath the protective layers of leaf litter, plants are growing and spring flowers are developing buds.

Late-fruiting plants, such as holly, mistletoe and dog rose, provide food for winter residents of the temperate forest such as the European hawfinch.

Holly
Ilex spp

Hawfinch
Coccothraustes coccothraustes

European woodcock
Scolopax rusticola

Woodcocks are insect-eaters. They can survive winter by prizing insects from the soil with their long beaks, providing that the ground is not too deeply frozen.

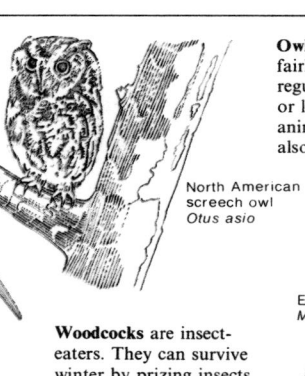

North American screech owl
Otus asio

Owls and foxes remain fairly active in winter, regularly leaving their nests or lairs to catch small animals or birds that are also in search of food.

Red fox
Vulpes vulpes

European badger
Meles meles

European badgers, like racoons, opossums, bears and skunks, are "shallow" hibernators. On mild winter days they wake and go to search for food.

THE EVERGREEN TEMPERATE RAINFORESTS

There are two main kinds of temperate rainforest, the warm temperate, such as can still be found on North Island, New Zealand (left), and the cold temperate, such as that of the Chilean coast. Both of these kinds of forest have one major feature in common: they have enough water for even the most moisture-greedy plants, such as mosses and ferns, to grow throughout the year. The animal life of the forest is also affected by the abundance of rain, so that snails, slugs, frogs and other water-loving creatures flourish. Most temperate rainforest is of the warm-temperate kind, normally found on the edges of subtropical regions, and the vegetation, with palms, lianas,

bamboos, as well as ferns and mosses, is similar to, although less rich than, the tropical rainforest's vegetation. The cold-temperate rainforests grow in cooler regions but their coastal position means that the climate is milder and wetter than inland (where deciduous trees dominate). Their vegetation is less lush and less varied than the warm-temperate forests, but mosses and ferns grow in abundance. Broad-leaved evergreens, such as New Zealand's southern beech, are the most common trees of these forests, although on the northwestern coast of North America Douglas firs and other conifers outnumber the broad-leaved evergreen species.

Man and the Temperate Forests

Temperate forests have suffered enormously at the hands of man. For the great civilizations of China, Europe and, later, North America the forests not only yielded cropland for expanding populations but also contributed materials and fuel for early technologies. More recently the demands of industry have reduced the forests still further. But today, scientists believe that this depleted resource could again play an important role in providing energy, food and materials for future generations.

PERMANENT SETTLEMENT
The Bronze Age and, later, the Iron Age laid the foundations of Chinese and Western civilizations. The forest shrank as permanent settlements grew (3) and, with the use of metals and improved technology, agricultural land was extended (4). But the forest was recognized as an important resource and areas were protected. Management techniques were introduced that, especially in medieval Europe, changed dense forest to coppice woods (5).

EARLY INDUSTRIAL TIMES
Sources of cropland and timber had been discovered in the New World, but in the Far East and Europe forests were drastically reduced. Virtually no Chinese forest remained, and in Europe nations began importing timber to serve growing industrial needs (6). To help solve shortages, plantations were established on country estates (7), which were often landscaped into parkland and planted with introduced species of trees (8).

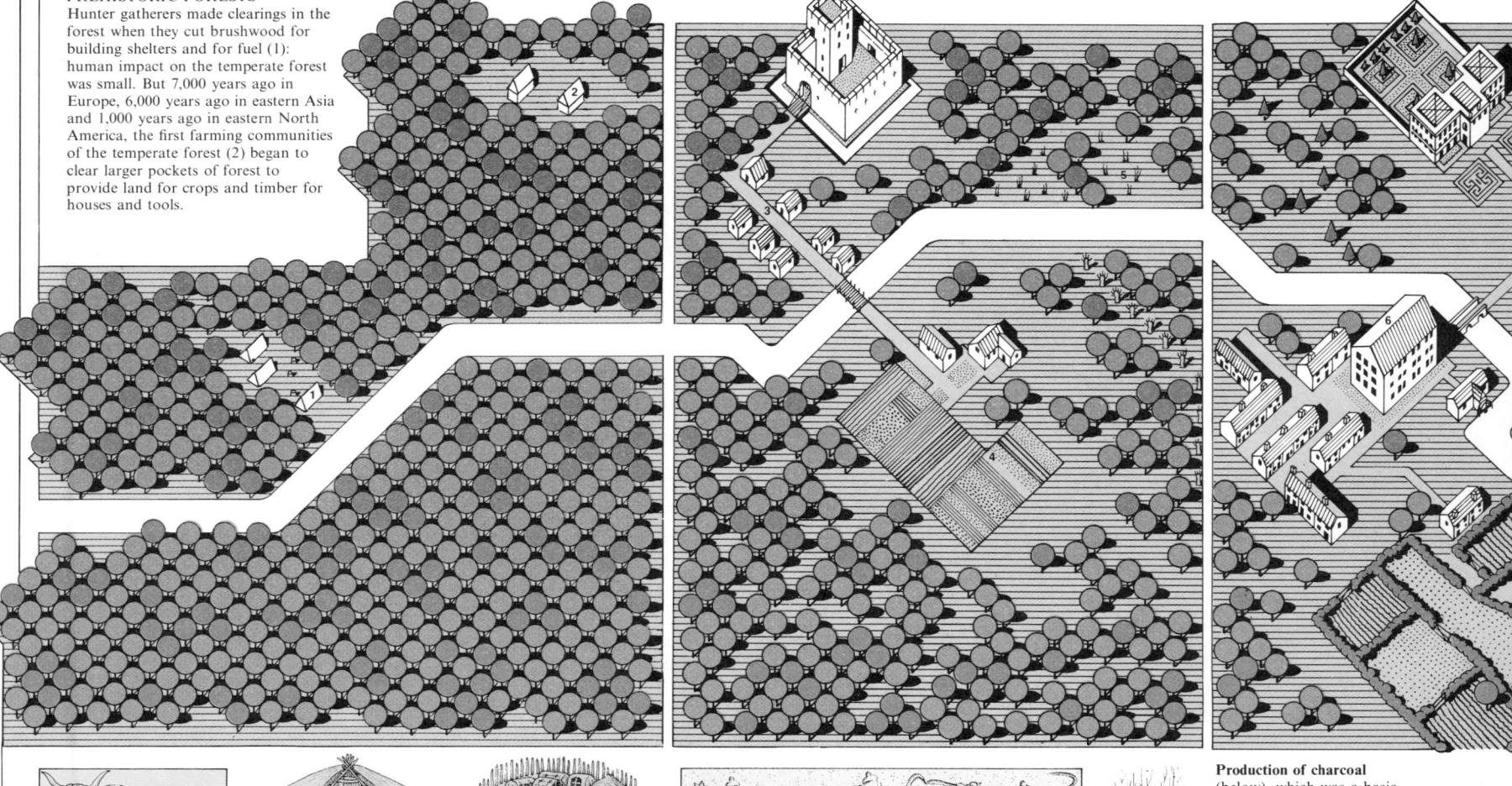

PREHISTORIC FORESTS
Hunter gatherers made clearings in the forest when they cut brushwood for building shelters and for fuel (1): human impact on the temperate forest was small. But 7,000 years ago in Europe, 6,000 years ago in eastern Asia and 1,000 years ago in eastern North America, the first farming communities of the temperate forest (2) began to clear larger pockets of forest to provide land for crops and timber for houses and tools.

 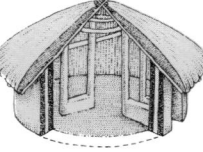   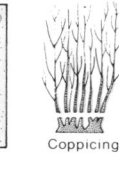 

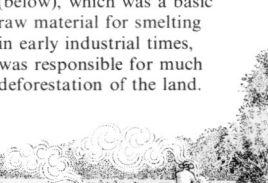

Production of charcoal (below), which was a basic raw material for smelting in early industrial times, was responsible for much deforestation of the land.

The aurochs, or wild ox, was one of the many forest animals that provided food for early hunter gatherers. Once man began to farm the land, he domesticated some of these animals—the wild boar, the aurochs and the wild turkey.

The dwellings of the late Neolithic Chinese were relatively sophisticated, reflecting an increasingly settled way of life that was soon to alter the landscape as forests were felled to provide building materials and land to plant crops.

The fortified villages and the farms of the Eastern Woodland Indians were set in semipermanent clearings cut in the North American forest. Before European settlement, however, human populations were small and deforestation was negligible.

Grain harvesting is depicted in a Chinese tomb image. By the 1st century AD, China contained nearly 60 million people, and agriculture, along with stock raising and metal mining, was drastically depleting the tree cover.

Coppicing and pollarding allowed continual cropping of forests. Branches were cut from trees, the bases of which were left to regrow shoots. This technique reduced the density of tree cover, encouraging a richer growth of ground plants.

Coppicing

Pollarding

Human interference with the forests goes back deep into prehistory. There is evidence that fire was used to stampede hunted animals in southern Europe as long as 400,000 years ago. Human populations, while they remained small, had only a slight effect on the vast stretches of primeval forest. Even so, hunting practices and the use of fire to clear land reduced some of the forests of Europe and Asia even before the invention of agriculture. In the New World, too, Eastern Woodland Indians had already affected the North American forests, and early Maori hunters had burned much of the tree cover of New Zealand by the time Europeans arrived.

Nevertheless it was the development of agriculture in Neolithic (New Stone Age) times that had the first really destructive effect on the temperate forests. Clearings were made for crops and the felled trees provided fuel and building material for the new communities. Large forest animals suffered as well, some (such as deer) being hunted for food and others (such as wolves) because they threatened grazing animals. But it was the population increase resulting from the new, settled way of life that caused the extension of man-made cropland deep into former forests.

With man's development of metals, more forests were destroyed: wood and charcoal were used for smelting and the new iron tools made tree clearance easier and more thorough. Firing of forests was also a familiar military ploy, used by such warriors as the Romans.

Medieval woodlands

By medieval times, large tracts of forest had been cleared in Europe and in the Far East, although in the former area there remained extensive royal hunting forest reserves. Local woodlands were carefully managed to serve the needs of the community; the techniques used included pollarding and coppicing.

Pollarding involved the cropping of main branches at a certain height above ground. In coppicing, the "coppice with standards" method was used to harvest the smaller species, such as hazel and hornbeam, whereas the standards (such as oaks) were cut on a longer rotation of 100 years or so. Alternatively, the oak itself could be part of the coppice crop, its stems being cut near ground level so that shoots arose from the stump, to be cut 10 to 20 years later. For local communities, industries and cities, forests provided a variety of materials for building, tanning and fencing, as well as dyestuffs, charcoal and domestic fuel.

The growth of the iron and shipbuilding industries in the sixteenth century devastated so much woodland and forest that in many regions good timber became scarce and had to be imported from considerable distances. The pressure on woodland continued until the production of coke and cheap coal brought some relaxation, but by the early twentieth century the coppice system had broken down and management of Europe's woodlands had largely been abandoned. In Europe the poor state of the deciduous forests was further worsened by two world wars. Many countries have since set up organizations with the specific task of building reserves of timber. Economic pressures, however, have led to the planting mainly of quick-growing conifers, rather than typical trees of the temperate deciduous forest.

New World forests

The migrants who settled in the New World were the descendants of the people who had largely destroyed the forests of Europe. Confronted by the temperate deciduous forests of eastern North America, they virtually continued where they had left off. Tracts were cleared to create arable and range land and to provide the massive amounts of timber needed for the colonization, industrialization and urbanization of North America. With the opening of the prairie lands for agriculture, however,

Disturbance to the natural vegetation has occurred throughout the temperate forest zone. Exploitation of this biome's greatest resource, its agricultural potential, has been one of the major causes of deforestation. The only forests that have escaped major disturbance are in remote areas, too rocky or too steep for cultivation. Today, intensive farming is still a major economic activity of the temperate forest regions. But farmland is not the only important resource to have disturbed the forests. Mining for key minerals such as copper, iron and coal, all of which made possible the development of Western and Chinese civilization, has also contributed to destruction of the forest cover. For centuries the forests provided man with food, fuel and materials, but, ironically, it has been the removal of the forest that has enabled man to exploit the most important of these regions' resources.

THE CHANGING LANDSCAPE

Mankind has been occupying the temperate forest regions for many thousands of years, at first with little effect on the natural forest ecology. But during the last 2,000 years human activity has destroyed the original tree cover at an accelerating pace. As populations increased and economies developed —at different rates in the three major regions— forests disappeared to be replaced by farms, cities, industries and communications networks. Today, scarcely any of the original forest cover remains.

THE 19TH CENTURY

The Industrial Revolution developed in Europe and the New World, large towns and cities sprang up (9), pushing back the woodlands and forests still farther. This process was aided by the spreading network of railroads (10). Coke, iron and other minerals were replacing timber products as raw materials for growing industries (11), but demands were still made on the forests to provide, for example, railway sleepers and mine pit props.

FORESTS TODAY

The 20th century has seen an increasing trend towards urbanization in areas that were once temperate forest. Housing complexes (12) and new factory sites (13) cover large areas, while roadbuilding (14), industrial agriculture (15) and open-cast mining (16) destroy remaining woodland. Leisure areas (17) and nature reserves protect some woods, but plantations of exotic conifers (18) do not always provide suitable wildlife habitats.

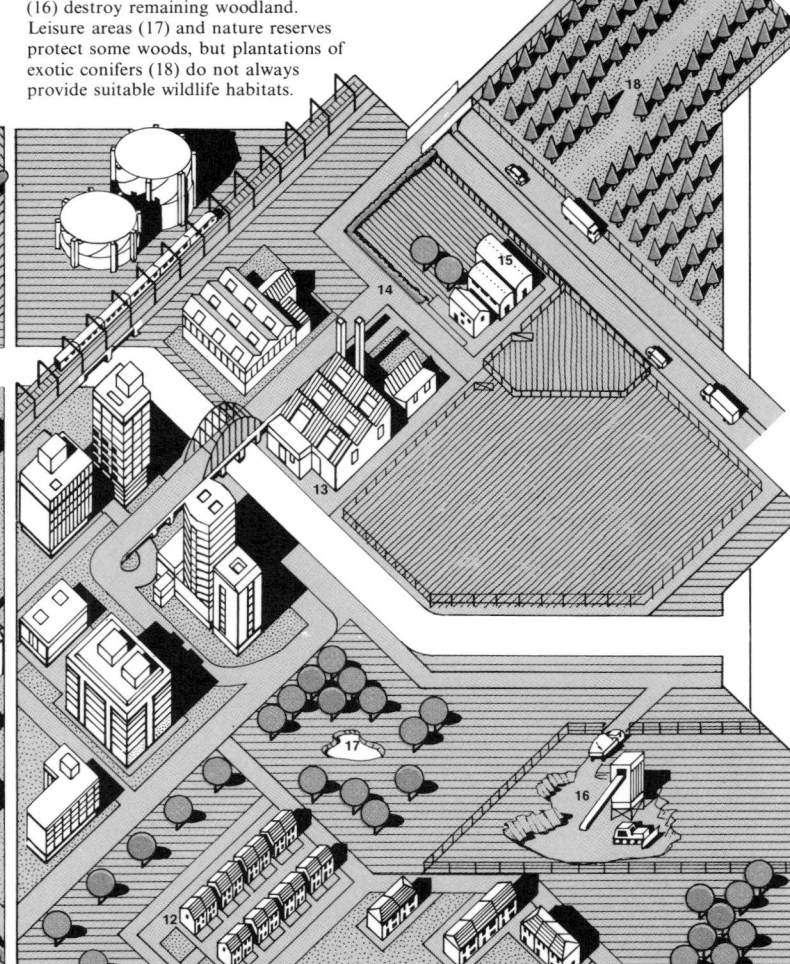
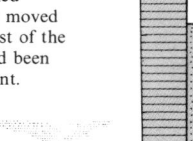
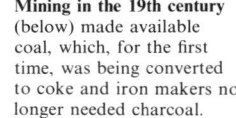
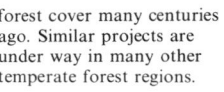

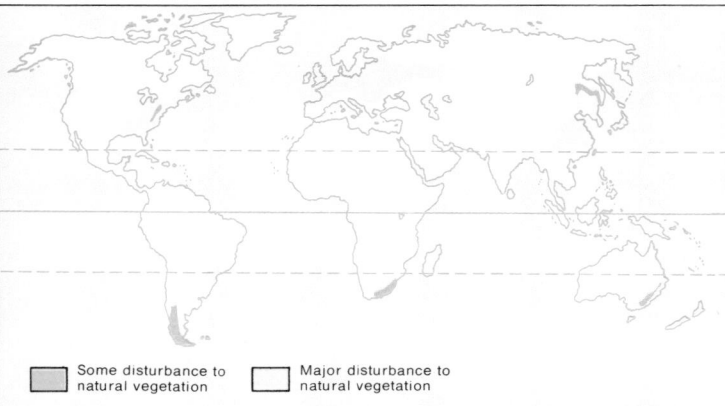

Early pioneers in the USA (below) transformed forestland as they moved west. By 1830 most of the eastern forests had been felled for settlement.

Mining in the 19th century (below) made available coal, which, for the first time, was being converted to coke and iron makers no longer needed charcoal.

Large department stores appeared in 19th-century Chicago, a town that, within 100 years, had been transformed from a remote fort to a city. This rapid growth reflected the huge population increase in many 19th-century towns.

A reafforestation scheme (below) was set up in China in 1950 to replant areas that lost their original forest cover many centuries ago. Similar projects are under way in many other temperate forest regions.

The European wood bison has escaped extinction because one herd of the animals has lived, for centuries, in a royal hunting reserve. Today, wildlife parks throughout temperate regions protect endangered forest species.

Some disturbance to natural vegetation

Major disturbance to natural vegetation

the pressures shifted, some of the east coast deciduous forest grew up again, and it is possible that parts of the eastern USA may have nearly as much forest cover now as when the settlers first arrived. Nevertheless, other areas of forestland have been destroyed in recent decades by strip mining and the creation of a vast road and rail network. In the southern hemisphere, especially in the last 200 years, the temperate rainforests of Australia and New Zealand have been subjected to much the same pattern of events, although on a smaller and somewhat less devastating scale.

Conservation

Today the general need to preserve and extend the woodlands is clearly recognized, but great uncertainty exists about their future. The demand for hardwoods for veneers, quality papermaking and furniture still exceeds supply. Oak is still the preferred material for some types of boat building and, especially in Europe, for joinery work. But one of the major difficulties with forestry as a land use is forecasting future trends within the industry, largely as a result of the long-term nature of the crop—hardwood trees planted today will not yield their timber until well into the next century. Government tax policies can be all important in deciding whether the majority of woodlands are, or will

continue to be, sound economic investments.

Temperate forests and woodlands still exist in sizeable quantities in central Europe and the USA, but many of today's plots, particularly in western Europe, are far too small for efficient conservation of plant and animal life, and are isolated from other woods. As a result, successful breeding and exchange of genetic material is very difficult, especially when modern agriculture is rapidly destroying the linking corridors of hedgerows. The use of woodlands for recreation is also presenting considerable problems. Controlling agencies have been formed to cope with leisure demands, and a start has been made in the multiple use of forests for recreation, conservation and timber felling, but progress still needs to be made in harmonizing these potentially conflicting interests. Meanwhile, natural expanses of woodland and forest are still being lost to agricultural and urban expansion and to plantations of nonnative conifers.

Temperate forests are a biologically efficient form of land use. In terms of biomass—the amount of living material (animal and plant) in any one area—they could still play an important role in the provision of food, materials and even renewable energy. Thus on scientific, economic and aesthetic grounds a strong case can be made for immediate conservation measures.

Mediterranean Regions

Forests of evergreen trees once covered much of the Mediterranean regions. They flourished in spite of the hot, rainless summer months – as the original plant life, they had evolved to survive such harsh conditions. Man, however, has proved to be a greater threat than the climate. He introduced domestic animals and cleared the land to grow crops; the natural vegetation was burned, browsed and plowed into nonexistence. Man's activities left behind tracts of impoverished soil which rapidly became scrubland. Today, scrub is the most typical vegetation in all the Mediterranean climate zones throughout the world.

Long, hot, dry summers and warm, moist winters form the seasonal rhythm of the "Mediterranean" year. This climatic pattern can be found in small areas of nearly every continent in the world, typically on the western side of landmasses and in the mild, temperate latitudes. North America's "Mediterranean" is in California, South America's occurs in Chile and Africa's lies at the southern tip of Cape Province. Australia has two small "Mediterranean" areas, one on the southern coast and one on the western. Europe's Mediterranean region, which has given its name to this climate, covers much of the southern part of the continent and extends into northern Africa.

Wherever Mediterranean conditions prevail, the native plant life has adapted to survive the scanty annual rainfall and the long summer droughts. Some species have developed deep root systems that can tap low summer water tables, and many of the ground plants—such as bulbs and aromatic herbs—grow vigorously only in early summer while rain still moistens the soil. But it is the broad-leaved evergreens with their drought-resistant leaves that are the most typical of the Mediterranean areas.

This natural pattern of vegetation has been drastically altered by man. In southern Europe in particular, almost all the original evergreen forests have long since been destroyed and thickets of fast-growing, tough scrub plants have grown up in their place. This scrub, which once probably covered only small areas, is now so widespread that it is considered the most typically Mediterranean of all kinds of vegetation. It is the *maquis* of France, the *macchia* of Italy and the *mattoral* of Spain. A similar type of vegetation (although containing different species) can also be found in South Africa's fynbos, in California's chapparal, and in Australia's tracts of natural mallee scrub.

Classical land use

Southern Europe, with its long history of human settlement, farming and pastoralism, is the most altered of all the Mediterranean regions. Over the centuries vast tracts of original vegetation have been removed, either by farmers (for crop growing) or by grazing animals. And, particularly on the steep slopes and rocky outcrops, this has resulted in extensive deterioration and erosion of the soil. Agriculture generally has less serious effects upon the vegetation than has animal grazing. Mankind has learned, over many hundreds of years, which are the most suitable crops for the various soils, terrain and climatic conditions of the region. The Mediterranean "triad" of wheat on the lowlands and olives and vines on the hills has been a successful combination since Classical times.

Pastoral plundering of the land, however, has more serious consequences. The virtually omnivorous goat is particularly damaging and can strip a whole forest of its foliage, bark, shrubs, ground plants and grass. After such an assault the vegetation rarely returns to its former condition; normally, a scrubby growth of kermes oak and shrubs springs up to form a typical maquis-type vegetation.

The rise and fall of each great Mediterranean civilization has seen forests destroyed in one area after another. The Greek colonization of southern Italy was provoked by deforestation and soil erosion in Attica. The Romans extended clearance north to the Po valley and into eastern Tunisia. From the seventh century onwards, Muslims made great inroads into the forests of North Africa as well as southern and eastern Spain; and in the north of Spain and southern France, medieval monks cleared forested valleys. During the seventeenth and eighteenth centuries large areas of Provence and Italy were cleared to plant vines and this process continued in the 1800s, when the great wine-producing areas of Languedoc and Algeria were established. During this time the iron industries of Spain and northern Italy, with their growing need for charcoal, were adding to the destruction. Recent reafforestation efforts have been puny compared to past degradation.

Protected species

But throughout this history of forest removal some tree species have been protected. These have been the natural tree crops that have, at times, supported complete peasant economies. The chestnut forests of Corsica, for example, sustained a large rural population until this century; the chestnuts provided flour for bread and fodder for pigs. In Portugal and Sardinia the cork-oak forests are still important today.

It is the olive, however, symbol of peace and of New Testament landscapes, that is the Mediterranean's most characteristic tree crop. Of all the Mediterranean plants, it is the most perfectly adapted to its environment, with its deep roots to search out scarce water and its hard, shiny leaves to conserve what it finds. In fact, the summer drought is essential to olive growers for it encourages the build-up of oil in the fruit. Paradoxically, however, the olive—like the vine, the fig and many other "Mediterranean" crops—did not originate in the Mediterranean but was introduced from Asia Minor.

In spite of massive destruction of the natural landscape, mankind has learned many valuable lessons during his occupation of this region. Ideas that were to become important in laying the foundations of sound land management policy were developed in the Mediterranean area. Hillside terracing, irrigation, crop rotation and manuring were all, from necessity, practiced from early times. The flourishing agricultural industries of the world's other Mediterranean regions—the wine industry of California, the vast soft-fruit plantations of Australia and the citrus industry of South Africa—all owe a considerable debt to the generations of farmers who learned to exploit the red soils of the Mediterranean basin.

CONVERGENCE
Isolated from each other by enormous areas of land and ocean, regions with a Mediterranean type of climate rarely have any plant species in common. But, by a process known as "convergent evolution," the plant communities in each of these areas have produced remarkably similar responses to their similar environments. This can be seen in the conifer communities, the broad-leaved evergreen trees, and in the various hardy shrubs and ground plants typical of each of the regions.

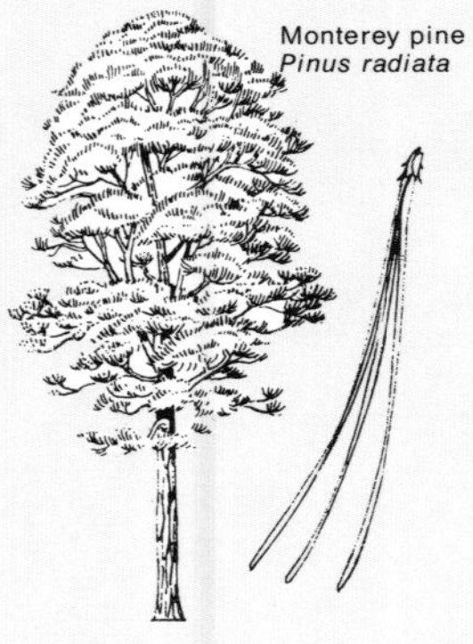

Monterey pine
Pinus radiata

California's Monterey pine and other Mediterranean conifers—South African podocarps and Chile pines, for example—have needle-shaped leaves that prevent rapid loss of water from such trees during drought.

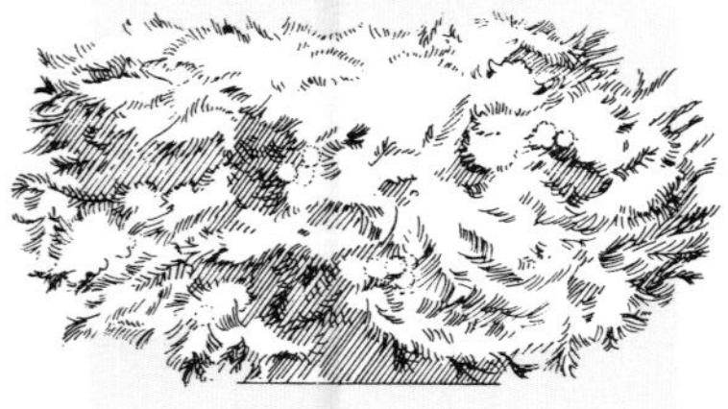

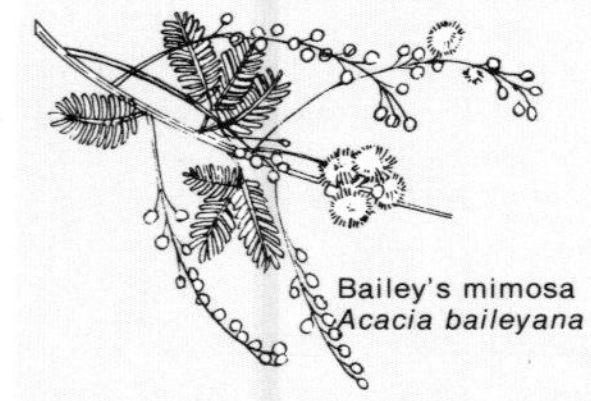

Bailey's mimosa
Acacia baileyana

Nonconiferous evergreens such as Australia's acacias and eucalypts, Chile's *quillajas* and California's evergreen oaks are typical Mediterranean trees. Their leathery leaves limit summer moisture loss.

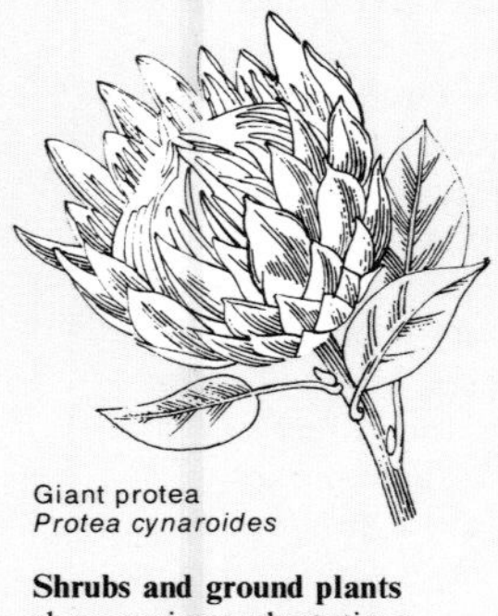

Giant protea
Protea cynaroides

Shrubs and ground plants show various adaptations to drought. South African proteas and Europe's laurel have thick evergreen leaves. Narrow leaves and water-storing roots are other common adaptations.

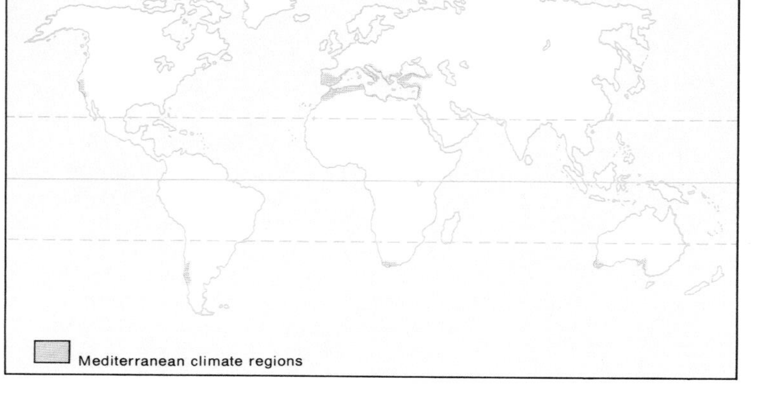

The Mediterranean regions occur between the latitudes 30° and 40°, on the western and southwestern sides of the continents. These areas are affected in summer by the high-pressure systems of nearby desert regions, and in winter by wet, low-pressure systems brought in from the oceans and over the land by the prevailing Westerlies. This distinct seasonal shifting of major influences on the climate produces the hot, waterless summers and warm, moist, sometimes stormy winters typical of the Mediterranean climate.

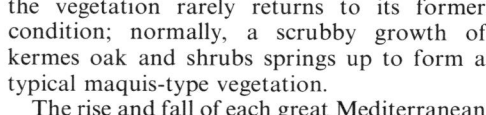

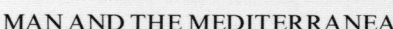

MAN AND THE MEDITERRANEAN
Even by Classical times, the once-forested lands fringing the Mediterranean Sea were suffering from massive deforestation and soil erosion. In the 5th century BC, Plato described the bare, dry hills of Attica, recently stripped of their woodlands. "What now remains," he wrote, "is like the skeleton of a sick man, all the fat and soft earth having been wasted away." By the end of the Classical period, irreparable damage had been done. At the same time, however, mankind was gradually learning through the mistakes he had already made. Suitable patterns of land use, better farming practices and improved land management techniques were slowly being adopted and were enabling man to make better use of the much-altered Mediterranean landscape.

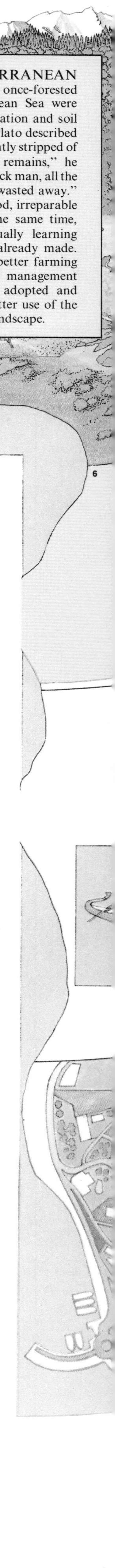

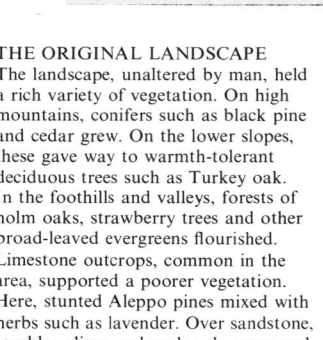

THE ORIGINAL LANDSCAPE
The landscape, unaltered by man, held a rich variety of vegetation. On high mountains, conifers such as black pine and cedar grew. On the lower slopes, these gave way to warmth-tolerant deciduous trees such as Turkey oak. In the foothills and valleys, forests of holm oaks, strawberry trees and other broad-leaved evergreens flourished. Limestone outcrops, common in the area, supported a poorer vegetation. Here, stunted Aleppo pines mixed with herbs such as lavender. Over sandstone, scrubby olives and cork oaks grew and by the sea stood isolated, wind-bent maritime pines.

THE CLASSICAL AGE
Civilizations followed one after another, each taking its toll of the environment. In the mountains, forests were felled, the tall, straight conifers sought after by shipbuilders such as the Phoenicians, and deciduous hardwood timber in demand for charcoal to fuel growing industries. Some replanting did take place, especially as groves of crop trees such as chestnuts. Below in the foothills, agriculture and the grazing of animals had destroyed vast areas of natural forest. Terracing techniques, however, helped to stop soil erosion, and irrigation reached the height of its Classical art with Roman aqueducts and canals. Tree crops, such as olives, were found best suited to the thin hill soils. On the plains, especially where alluvial soils had been deposited, cereals were grown. Meanwhile, towns sprang up and the coastline became densely populated as ships and ports were built and sea trade grew. Exotic food plants, such as pomegranate trees, citron trees and vines, were brought into the region by merchant seamen.

THE MEDITERRANEAN TODAY
The region today bears the scars of many centuries of human activity. The once-forested mountains will never return to their former state, although some regrowth and some replanting (mostly with introduced tree species) has occurred. As in Classical times, hillsides are terraced and planted with vines and fruit trees. But with modern irrigation and fertilizing, land is less readily exhausted and abandoned now. On the plains, native shrubs, such as lavender, are commercially cultivated and grain is widely grown, particularly durum wheat used for making pasta. Cork oaks are planted, especially over dry sandstone areas, but indigenous vegetation has not suffered by this—scrubby woodland is more widespread than ever and can be found throughout the landscape. Perhaps the single most important part of the Mediterranean basin today is the coastline, for this has produced the region's major modern industry—tourism.

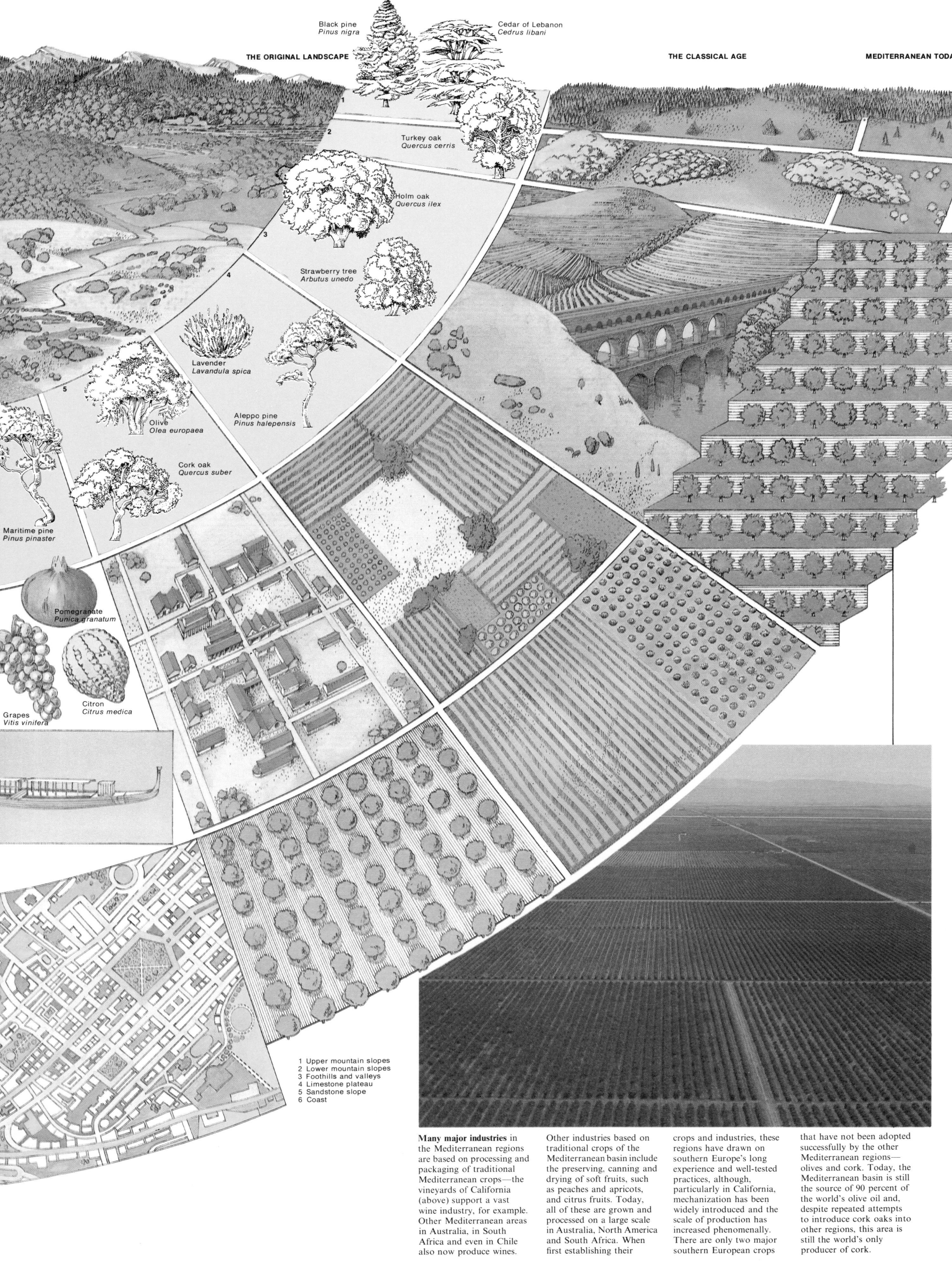

Black pine
Pinus nigra

Cedar of Lebanon
Cedrus libani

Turkey oak
Quercus cerris

Holm oak
Quercus ilex

Strawberry tree
Arbutus unedo

Lavender
Lavandula spica

Aleppo pine
Pinus halepensis

Olive
Olea europaea

Cork oak
Quercus suber

Maritime pine
Pinus pinaster

Pomegranate
Punica granatum

Citron
Citrus medica

Grapes
Vitis vinifera

1 Upper mountain slopes
2 Lower mountain slopes
3 Foothills and valleys
4 Limestone plateau
5 Sandstone slope
6 Coast

Many major industries in the Mediterranean regions are based on processing and packaging of traditional Mediterranean crops—the vineyards of California (above) support a vast wine industry, for example. Other Mediterranean areas in Australia, in South Africa and even in Chile also now produce wines.

Other industries based on traditional crops of the Mediterranean basin include the preserving, canning and drying of soft fruits, such as peaches and apricots, and citrus fruits. Today, all of these are grown and processed on a large scale in Australia, North America and South Africa. When first establishing their

crops and industries, these regions have drawn on southern Europe's long experience and well-tested practices, although, particularly in California, mechanization has been widely introduced and the scale of production has increased phenomenally. There are only two major southern European crops

that have not been adopted successfully by the other Mediterranean regions— olives and cork. Today, the Mediterranean basin is still the source of 90 percent of the world's olive oil and, despite repeated attempts to introduce cork oaks into other regions, this area is still the world's only producer of cork.

Temperate Grasslands

Compared with other flowering plants, grasses are newcomers to the Earth. They appeared only 60 million years ago, but since then they have proved to be an extremely successful family of plants. Today, the grasses dominate large areas of the world's natural vegetation and play a vital part in the intricate balance of plant and animal life in these regions. In spite of the inroads made by man, vast stretches of original grassland still cover the interiors of the North American and Eurasian landmasses.

The prairies of North America and the steppes of Eurasia extend far into the interiors of the northern continents. These are the best known and the most extensive of the world's temperate grasslands. The southern hemisphere, however, has examples in the veld of South Africa and the pampas of South America. Extensive grasslands also occur in southern Australia, although these are sometimes described as semiarid scrub because of the high average temperatures and the prolonged droughts in the region.

Temperate grasslands probably developed wherever the rainfall was too low to support forest and too high to result in semiarid regions, conditions found typically in the interiors of large continents. Continental interiors tend to be somewhat drier than coastal regions, but they are also characterized by extreme changes in temperature from one season to the next. In the North American grasslands, for example, winter temperatures may fall well below freezing whereas summer temperatures of 38°C (100°F) are not unusual. And these sharp fluctuations in seasonal temperature greatly influence how much of the rainfall is made available to plants. In summer particularly, when most of the rain falls, high temperatures, strong winds and lack of protective tree cover cause much of the moisture to evaporate before it can be absorbed into the soil.

Climatic conditions are not the only factor responsible for the distribution and form of the temperate grasslands. There are many pointers that indicate the importance of fire in determining their continuing existence and their extent. Natural fires, caused by lightning and fueled by the dry summer grasses, have always been a feature of these regions, but more recently, man-made fires have been crucial in fixing the boundary between forest and grassland.

Trees and shrubs frequently invade the margins of grasslands, but whenever there is a fire few of them survive. Grasses, however, have certain characteristics that enable them to withstand the potentially destructive impact of fire. The growing point of grasses is at the base of the leaves, close to the ground, and so destruction of the leaves above this point does not interrupt growth—in fact it may stimulate it. These same characteristics also serve to protect grasses from destruction by grazing animals. The large animals of these lands, such as the North American bison and the Eurasian horse, are able to crop the grasses without permanently damaging their food supply.

Grazers and predators

Large migrating herbivores with a strong herd instinct characterize one of the major types of temperate grassland animal. In the North American grasslands the bison (which may have numbered 60 million before being virtually exterminated by settlers) and the antelope-like pronghorn were the major examples of large herbivores. In Eurasia large herds of saiga antelopes, wild horses and asses at one time roamed the steppes, although they too have suffered from human activities, as has South America's largest grassland herd animal, the pampas deer. As these herds of grazing animals have been reduced, so have the carnivorous animals of the grasslands that preyed upon them. At one time, however, these predators played an important part in protecting the grasslands by continually keeping the numbers of grazing herd animals in check.

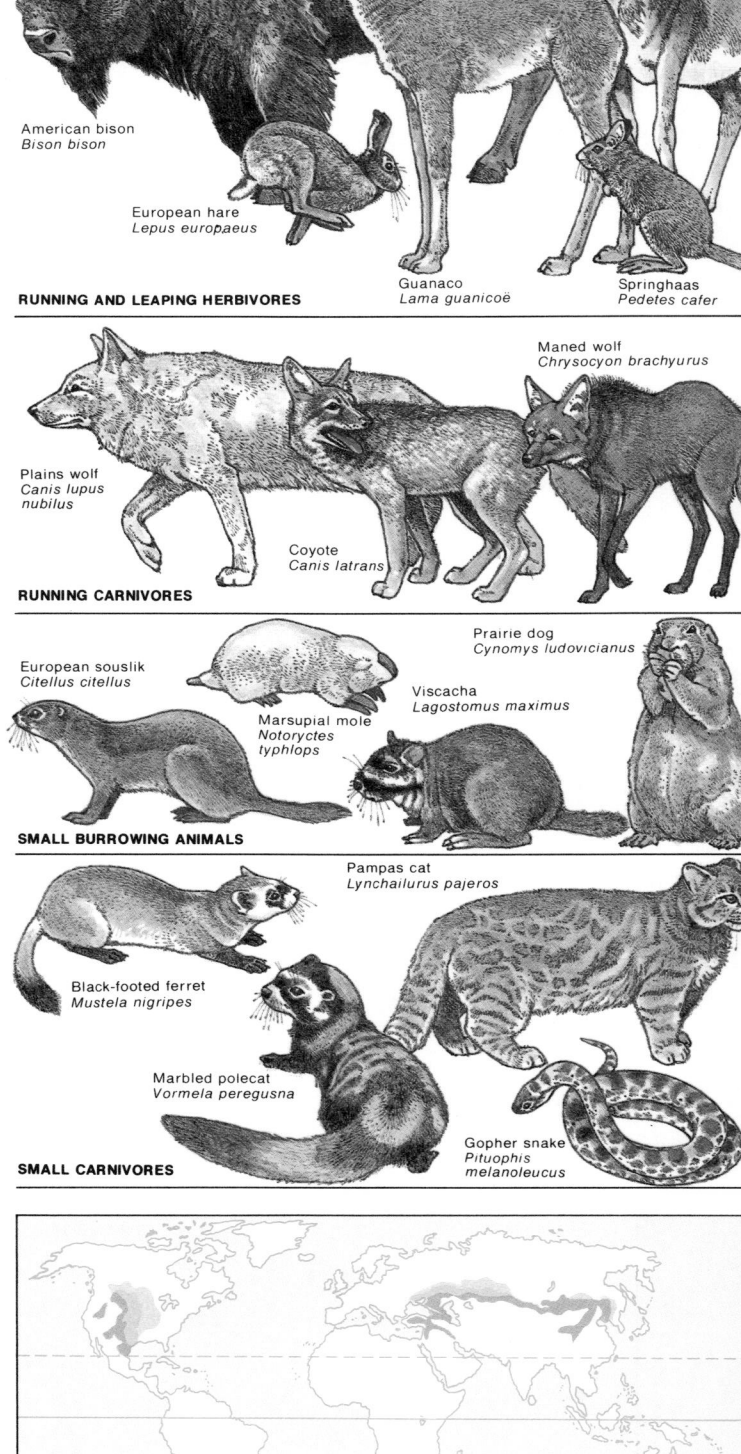

Saiga
Saiga tatarica

American bison
Bison bison

European hare
Lepus europaeus

Guanaco
Lama guanicoe

Springhaas
Pedetes cafer

RUNNING AND LEAPING HERBIVORES

Maned wolf
Chrysocyon brachyurus

Plains wolf
Canis lupus nubilus

Coyote
Canis latrans

RUNNING CARNIVORES

Prairie dog
Cynomys ludovicianus

European souslik
Citellus citellus

Viscacha
Lagostomus maximus

Marsupial mole
Notoryctes typhlops

SMALL BURROWING ANIMALS

Pampas cat
Lynchailurus pajeros

Black-footed ferret
Mustela nigripes

Marbled polecat
Vormela peregusna

Gopher snake
Pituophis melanoleucus

SMALL CARNIVORES

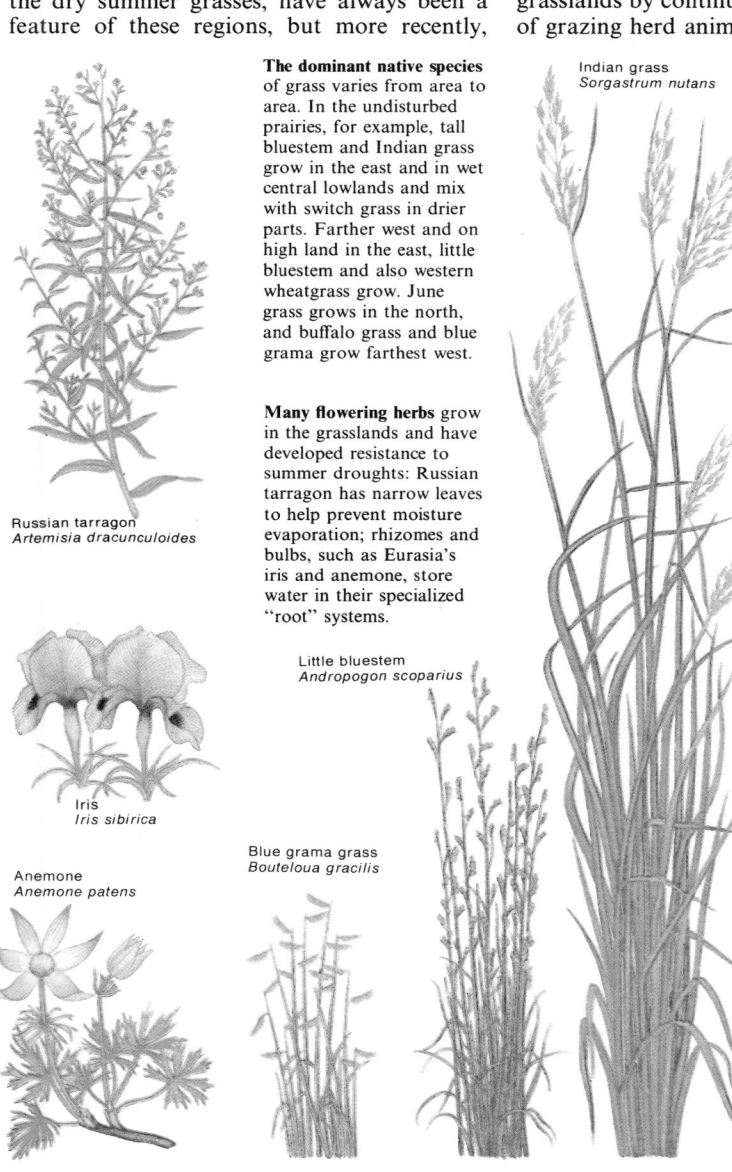

The dominant native species of grass varies from area to area. In the undisturbed prairies, for example, tall bluestem and Indian grass grow in the east and in wet central lowlands and mix with switch grass in drier parts. Farther west and on high land in the east, little bluestem and also western wheatgrass grow. June grass grows in the north, and buffalo grass and blue grama grow farthest west.

Many flowering herbs grow in the grasslands and have developed resistance to summer droughts: Russian tarragon has narrow leaves to help prevent moisture evaporation; rhizomes and bulbs, such as Eurasia's iris and anemone, store water in their specialized "root" systems.

Russian tarragon
Artemisia dracunculoides

Iris
Iris sibirica

Anemone
Anemone patens

Blue grama grass
Bouteloua gracilis

Little bluestem
Andropogon scoparius

Indian grass
Sorgastrum nutans

The natural distribution of the temperate grasslands is dictated mainly by rainfall: most occur in continental interiors where there is too little rain for forest but enough to prevent desert from forming. Between these limits the large range in rainfall allows three main types of grassland: tall grass in wetter areas, mid-grass, and short grass in drier parts. The largest grasslands exist in North America, Eurasia, South America, in Australia's Murray–Darling river basin and on the South African plateau.

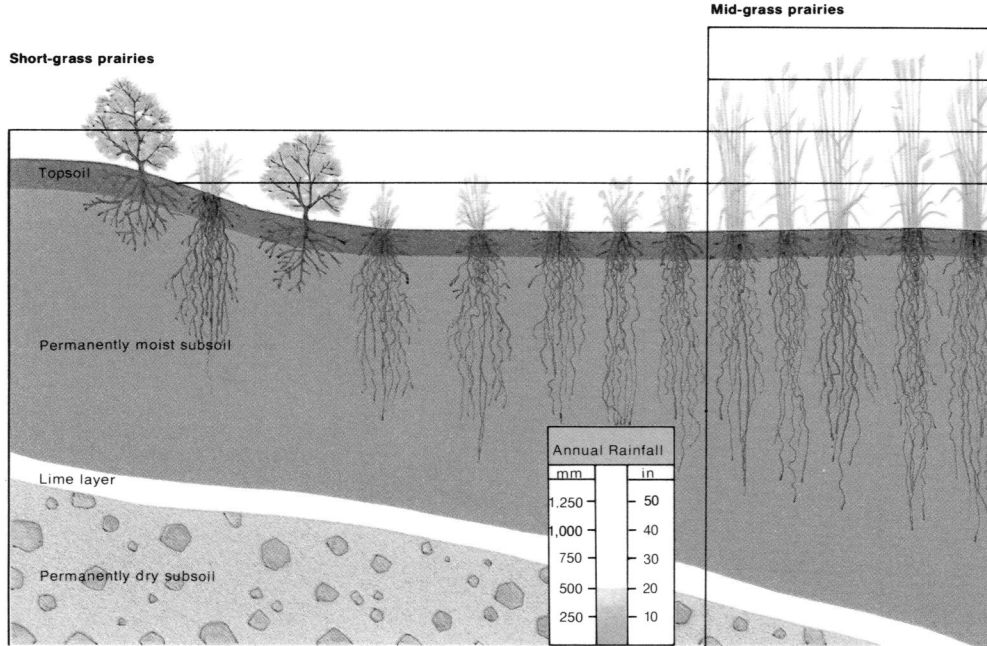

☐ Short-grass regions   ☐ Mid-grass regions   ☐ Tall-grass regions

Short-grass prairies

Mid-grass prairies

Topsoil

Permanently moist subsoil

Lime layer

Permanently dry subsoil

Annual Rainfall	
mm	in
1,250	50
1,000	40
750	30
500	20
250	10

GRASSLAND ADAPTATION

Animals of these regions have had to adapt to a difficult environment: vast, treeless expanses of grass offer little protection from harsh weather or predators. Different animals have found various answers to the problem and a clearly defined pattern of these adaptations can be traced throughout the grasslands.

Running and leaping herbivores survive because of their ability to move faster than a pursuer. The larger animals such as the Eurasian saiga, North America's bison and pronghorn and the guanaco of South America are runners. The leaping herbivores are usually smaller creatures that escape danger by bounding away to bolt-holes. They include the European hare and the African springhaas.

Running carnivores follow, and prey on, running and leaping herbivores. These animals, such as the coyote and the now extinct plains wolf of North America, and South America's maned wolf, also depend on speed—to enable them to catch their prey.

Small burrowing animals hide from predators by digging under the ground. Some, such as Australia's marsupial mole, spend most of their lives below ground. Others, such as the European souslik, South America's viscacha and North America's prairie dog, live and sleep under the ground but come to the surface to find food.

Small carnivores concentrate on the burrowers as their main source of food. They either, like the pampas cat, rely on surprise attack of their prey, or, like Eurasia's marbled polecat and the grasslands' many kinds of snake, depend on their long, lithe shape to follow creatures into their burrows.

Two distinctive types of grassland bird can be distinguished: the sky birds, which spend long periods of time on the wing, and the ground birds.

Birds of the sky include songbirds such as the skylark which, having no perch from which to proclaim its territory, sings in the sky, and birds of prey such as Eurasia's tawny eagle and North America's red-tailed hawk and prairie falcon, which ride the thermals scanning the ground for their prey.

Ground birds rarely take to the wing, although none has actually lost the ability to fly when necessary. They include birds such as the New World sage grouse and burrowing owl (which lives below ground in abandoned prairie dog burrows), the black grouse of Eurasia and songbirds such as North America's meadowlark.

Insects and other invertebrates have developed many different survival techniques. Some use camouflage: the praying mantis resembles a leaf bud and the tumble bug is the color of the dark grassland soil. Grasshoppers are miniature leaping herbivores and earthworms are small-scale versions of the grassland burrowers.

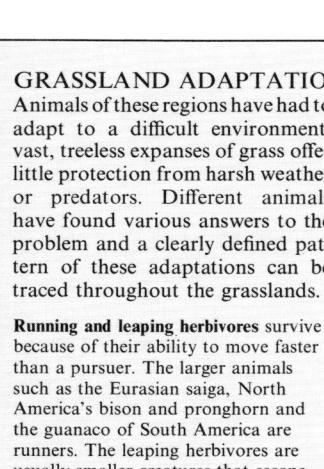
Skylark
Alauda arvensis

Red-tailed hawk
Buteo jamaicensis

Tawny eagle
Aquila rapax

Prairie falcon
Falco mexicanus

BIRDS OF THE SKY

Western meadowlark
Sturnella neglecta

Burrowing owl
Speotyto cunicularia

Sage grouse
Centrocercus urophasianus

Black grouse
Lyurus tetrix

GROUND BIRDS

Lubber grasshopper
Romalea microptera

Tumble bug
Canthonlaevis drury

Common earthworm
Lumbricus terrestris

Praying mantis
Mantis religiosa

INSECTS AND OTHER INVERTEBRATES

A typical cross section, based on the North American prairies, shows temperate grasslands in relation to rainfall. Annual rainfall determines the depth of the permanently moist subsoil, which in turn dictates the length to which grass roots can grow. Tall grasses have deep root systems and need a considerable depth of moist subsoil. As the rainfall decreases, they gradually give way to shorter grass species. Short grasses require less water and their shallower roots are well suited to drier regions. On dry margins, desert plants start to dominate, and on the wet margins, trees appear.

Tall-grass prairies

cm	ft
215	7
180	6
150	5
120	4
90	3
60	2
30	1
0	0

Annual Rainfall	
mm	in
1,250	50
1,000	40
750	30
500	20
250	10

Annual Rainfall	
mm	in
1,250	50
1,000	40
750	30
500	20
250	10

Another major type of animal found in the temperate grasslands, and one that is better adapted to survive man's activities, is the small, burrowing animal, for example the prairie dog and the gopher of North America, the viscacha of South America and the little ground squirrel known as the souslik in Eurasia.

Unlike the large herd animals, these creatures tend not to migrate. Many of them live together in complex, permanent, underground communities. The colonial "townships" of the prairie dog, for example, may house more than one million individuals, which each year excavate vast quantities of the grassland soil. This has considerable effect upon the structure of the soil. By bringing up earth from lower layers to the surface, these animals are responsible for changing the mineral content of certain areas of topsoil. This then encourages isolated pockets of different plant species to flourish.

A third group of grassland animals, consisting of insects and other invertebrates such as earthworms, has an even more important effect upon the soil. They live in or on the soil and play a vital role in maintaining grassland fertility. These creatures may be herbivores, carnivores or primary (first stage) decomposers (which break down such material as dead grass and animal remains). These three types of activity allow a complete range of organic matter to be processed and incorporated into the earth, where it is further broken down by the second-stage decomposers, the countless millions of soil bacteria. In this way nutrients continuously flow back to the earth and restore its fertility.

Fertile black earths

The topsoil of temperate grassland regions, therefore, contains large amounts of organic material, which is produced every year and is quickly incorporated into the soil. The low and intermittent rainfall and the protective cover of grasses mean that the topsoil undergoes little chemical leaching, a process in which minerals are removed and carried down to lower layers by rainfall percolating through the earth. The soils are thus dark in color, generally fertile and of the "black earth" type ("chernozem" in Russian) which is, at least at first, capable of producing high yields of crops.

The most suitable and most widely grown crops are, predictably, the cultivated grasses, and it is these grasses that provide more food for mankind (either directly as grain or indirectly as animal fodder) than any other source. The temperate grassland biome is therefore an important agricultural resource. Undisturbed natural grasslands, however, are also valuable resources. They need to be preserved both for the information that they can provide about how complex communities of wildlife function efficiently, and because, as a rich source of genetic material, they hold many of the answers to the major agricultural problems that probably lie ahead for the human race.

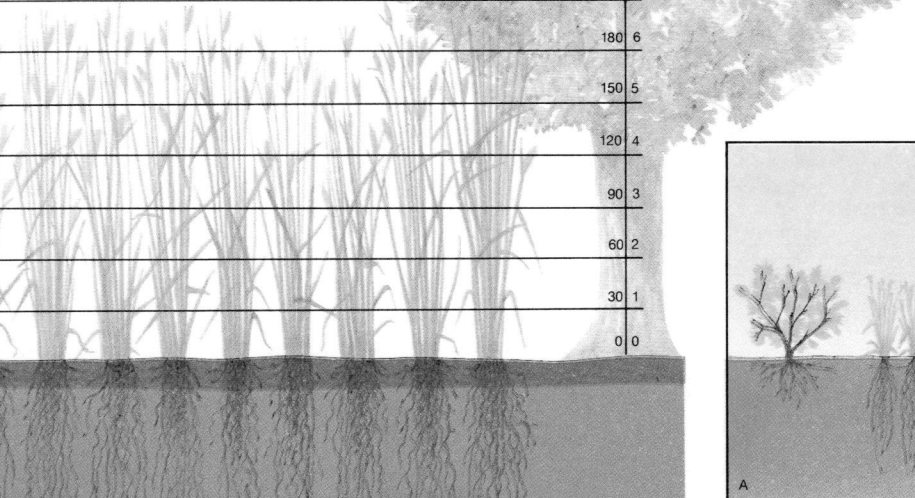

Fire plays a major part in fixing and maintaining the natural boundaries of the temperate grasslands, where tree saplings and shrubs are continually attempting to invade (A). Man-made fires are recent phenomena, natural fires have always occurred. In summer, low-pressure systems build up in continental interiors, causing violent electrical storms. The dry sward of summer grass is easily ignited by lightning and fire is quickly spread by wind. Shrubs and saplings are killed or badly damaged by fire, but grasses, with their growing points close to the soil, remain unharmed (B). They may even benefit from this "pruning" and grow more quickly. Some species grow new buds from their underground shoots. Removal of the main shoot may encourage growth of "tillers" (shoots growing out sideways), which then increase the spread of the grasses as they begin to invade the area left vacant by the dead, or slowly recuperating, shrubs (C).

Man and the Temperate Grasslands

The vast areas of temperate grassland lay virtually empty until the end of the eighteenth century. Over the next 125 years they were occupied by millions of people, most of them migrants from overcrowded Europe. By 1914, the grasslands had become the granaries and the stockyards of the world. Today, they are still the most important food-producing regions on Earth and their riches, properly distributed, are the world's first reserve against the possibility of a hungry future for the human race.

The great nineteenth-century migration to the grasslands proved of immense significance to the human race. It meant that, within a single century, the area of productive land available was suddenly enlarged by thousands of millions of hectares. In all of mankind's history, such a thing had never happened before.

But before the grasslands could be occupied a number of major problems had to be solved. First, in order to reach these regions it was almost always necessary to travel deep into the continental interiors, and there were few navigable rivers and no mechanized forms of transportation for early pioneers. Second, with virtually no indigenous population, newcomers had to learn by their mistakes how best to exploit the new and unfamiliar environment. Third, even if settlers succeeded in using the land, they still had to find markets for their produce.

A number of technological developments, however, that took place in the nineteenth century provided the right combination of circumstances for the opening up of the grasslands. The Industrial Revolution in Europe produced the steamship and the railway locomotive, which created both a means of travel to and from these distant parts and an internal transport system for moving produce to ports and markets. It also produced the kind of machinery needed to plow and farm the great new open spaces; it made it possible for one family to cultivate an area 50 times as large as that which most farmers had known in Europe. Industrialization also threw thousands of Europeans out of work, and therefore provided a large supply of eager migrants. And it crowded further thousands into cities, thus creating vast markets for the settlers' produce.

It was the coming together of these various circumstances that acted as the catalyst and converted, for example, the Russian penetration of the Eurasian steppes in the late eighteenth

THE CRADLE OF AGRICULTURE

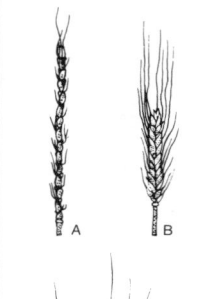
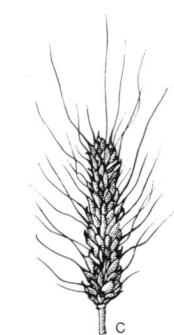

Stands of wild einkorn (A), emmer wheat (B) and wild barleys can be seen today in the grassy foothills that flank the Taurus and the Zagros mountains, and the uplands of northern Israel. It was in this region 10,000 years ago that the world's earliest farmers gathered seeds from these species and sowed the first crops. Wild einkorn is probably the oldest of all wheats and the parent of every modern variety—including the most important and most widely grown kind of grain in the world today, common bread wheat (C).

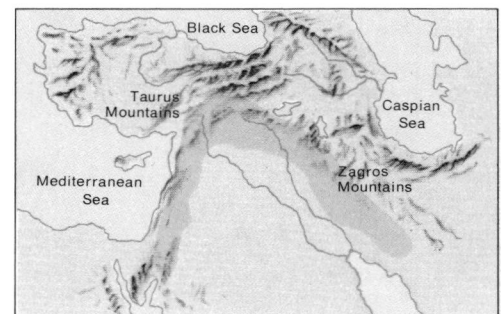

GRASSLAND EXPLOITATION

Today, temperate grasslands provide mankind with a superabundance of food. But the vast potential of these regions was not exploited until the mid-19th century, when mass migration by Europeans, combined with new technology, allowed full-scale development and settlement.

BEFORE EUROPEAN SETTLEMENT
The grasslands were sparsely populated. Most of the indigenous tribespeoples were nomadic hunters and gatherers. They wandered widely over the regions, making temporary camps (1) as they followed the movement of their quarry—the plentiful herds of grazing animals (2). These peoples made little impact on the natural grasslands.

GRASSLAND SETTLERS
Early pioneers relied on animal-drawn transport (3), primitive farm tools (4) and unpredictable free-range livestock grazing (5). During the 19th century, farming became more productive: better equipment cultivated larger areas (6); barbed wire made stock raising efficient (7); railways and the telegraph improved communication (8).

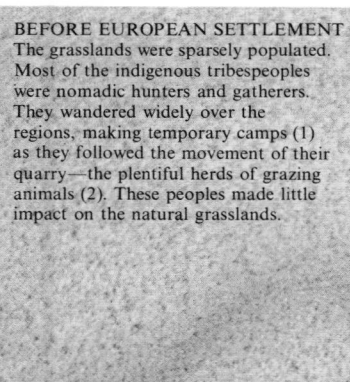

Tehuelche Indians (above) adopted horses for hunting from early Spanish settlers to the pampas. In South Africa and North America, too, the introduced horse became a valued asset for grassland hunters. For people of the Eurasian steppes, for example the Mongols (right), native horses have always been culturally important.

The South African veld was first settled by Europeans after 1836 (left). Dutch farmers (Boers), rejecting British rule of the Cape Colony, trekked north in search of new land. Moving into the Transvaal they discovered rich grassland, recently emptied of its original inhabitants, who had fled to escape the aggressive attentions of neighboring Zulus.

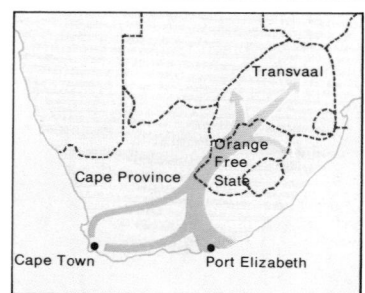

Vaqueros were the original cowboys (left). Tending herds of cattle for the missionaries in 18th-century California, they developed techniques and traditions that served hundreds of later cowboys working the prairie ranges. In other grassland regions, as free-range stock raising became important, similar "cowboy" professions evolved—the Australian stockman and the gaucho of South America.

century into the explosive movement of hundreds of thousands of settlers a few years later. In the USA, too, by the year 1850, settlement had reached and then rapidly crossed the Mississippi. In the Argentine, genuine colonization of the pampas had begun, in South Africa, the Boers had reached the high veld, and in Australia pioneer settlers were moving outwards from the various areas of coastal settlement into the scrub grasslands of the interior.

Farmers or ranchers?

The fundamental question posed for these settlers was whether their newly found land should be used for crops or for livestock. Most grasslands have a dry edge and a wet edge, and it was therefore sensible to use the drier parts for stock raising and the wetter parts for cultivation. But the question was complicated by the fact that most of the newcomers were cultivators, and also that the line dividing dry from wet was vague—worse, it shifted from year to year.

Early attempts to define the dividing line tended to be ignored by the settlers themselves, and they pushed the limit of cultivation into areas where plowing the soil led to its destruction. Several generations of farmers had to learn this bitter lesson, and they learned only slowly: the worst disasters on the American grasslands occurred in the 1930s and created the infamous

Dust Bowl region in the dry grasslands of the Midwest. Similarly, the Soviet Virgin Lands Program for growing cereal crops on the dry steppes was established in 1954 and is still experiencing difficulties.

Special methods are required both for farming and for ranching the grasslands successfully. Farming has to take account of the open, treeless surface, the scanty and variable rainfall and the comparatively shallow topsoil. To minimize the risk of soil erosion, farmers plant windbreaks, plow fields along the contour, and protect the soil with a covering of the previous year's stubble and by planting cover crops in rotation with cereals. Ranchers, too, have learned to live with variable rainfall. They build stock ponds, irrigate areas of fodder crops to be used as a reserve in dry years and avoid overstocking and consequent overgrazing, which destroys the quality of the grass.

Food for the world

Today, the world's principal trading supplies of cereals and meat flow from these lands, over the networks of railway which link the grasslands to mill towns, slaughter yards and ports of shipment such as Adelaide in Australia, Buenos Aires in Argentina and Montreal in Canada. Without these links to large towns, the grasslands would be of little value, for even

today their populations are sparse and the local markets are relatively insignificant.

Throughout most of the world, however, the human population continues to soar and it remains to be seen whether the grasslands can continue to supply these growing numbers with food. Undoubtedly, the output of cereals and meat can be increased, although at considerable cost in fertilizers, new crop strains, more irrigation and more machines. On the other hand, the problem at present is not mainly one of production, nor will it be in the near future. The land can produce more, but there is no point in doing so unless the yields can be made available where they are most needed.

The world's hungry people live in other regions, many of them in countries that are unable to afford imported food supplies, particularly during those years when prices are high. The major importers of temperate grassland produce are the rich industrialized nations, such as those of western Europe. Furthermore, much of the grain imported by these countries is not consumed by humans but used to feed stalled, beef-producing cattle—a highly inefficient way of using these supplies. Consequently, unless producer nations and wealthy importing nations can create a system for produce to reach those in need of it, extra output from the grasslands will be irrelevant.

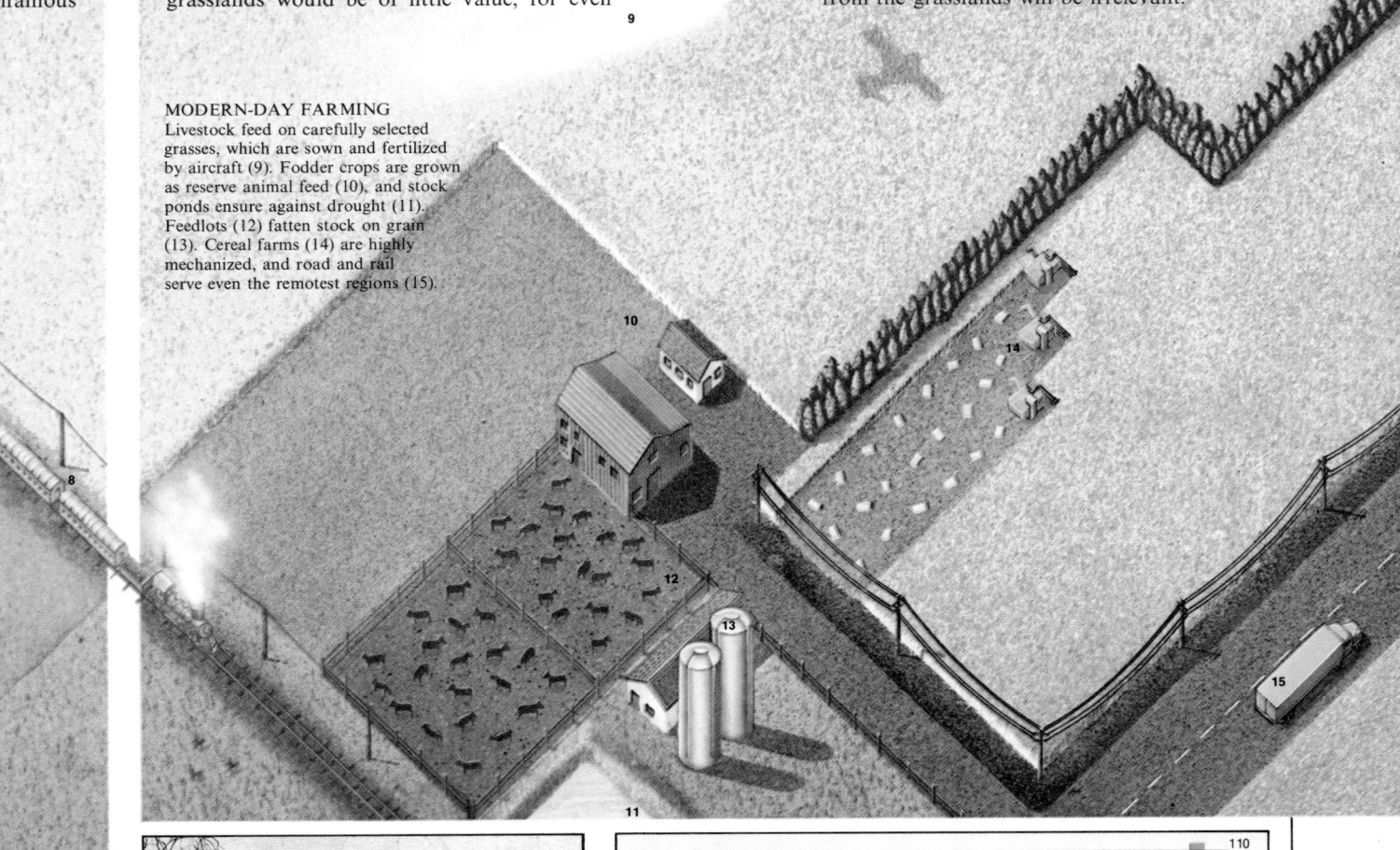

MODERN-DAY FARMING
Livestock feed on carefully selected grasses, which are sown and fertilized by aircraft (9). Fodder crops are grown as reserve animal feed (10), and stock ponds ensure against drought (11). Feedlots (12) fatten stock on grain (13). Cereal farms (14) are highly mechanized, and road and rail serve even the remotest regions (15).

The steam-driven plow (below) went through many developments to reduce its unwieldiness and heaviness. The version produced in 1858 used a traction engine and pulley wheel system. The plow was drawn back and forth between these by a power-driven cable. This design was, however, superseded by the steam tractor, which, although unsuited to small European fields, was ideal for drawing multifurrow plows across the grasslands.

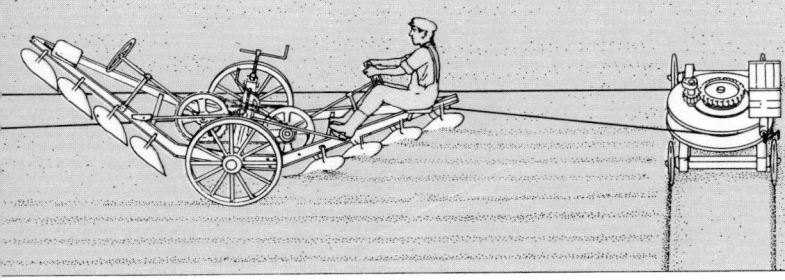

Sand-smothered farms in the heart of the Dust Bowl were rapidly abandoned during the 1930s and 40s (above). This was one costly lesson that man had to learn in the process of developing the grasslands. Traditionally grazing land, the western part of the prairies was first plowed this century. Years of drought arrived, crops died and the desert encroached.

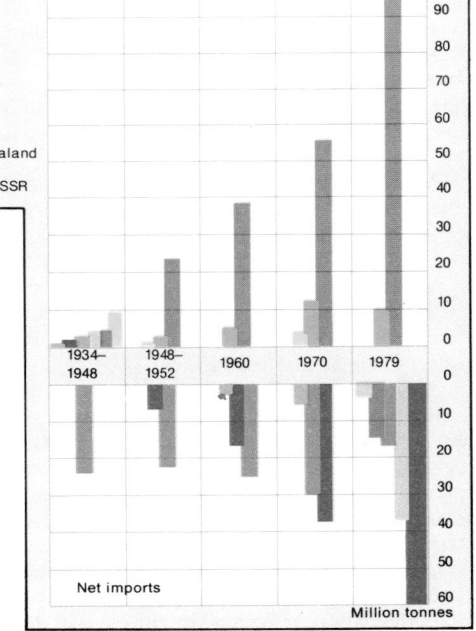

World grain-trading regions

- Africa
- North America
- South America
- Asia
- Western Europe
- Australia and New Zealand
- Eastern Europe and USSR

World cereal supplies flow from temperate grasslands (right). North America is the most important producing region, for although almost all nations produce grain, few can grow enough to feed their populations and even fewer have any surplus to export or hold in reserve against poor harvests. But North America, with its prairie cornfields and its small population, exports many millions of tonnes.

Net exports

1934–1948   1948–1952   1960   1970   1979

Net imports

Million tonnes

Deserts

Much of the Earth's land surface is so short of water that it is defined as desert. Not all deserts are hot, sandy wastelands; some are cold, some are rocky, but all lack moisture for most of the year. Even so, a surprising variety of plants and animals have adapted to these hostile environments. Plants have developed ingenious ways of surviving long periods of drought, and many desert animals shelter during the intense heat of the day, emerging only at night to feed.

LIFE IN THE DESERT

The overriding need to obtain and conserve water dictates the pattern of desert life. Many plants close their pores during the day and most daytime creatures limit their activity to early morning and late afternoon. At night the temperature drops sharply and dew provides welcome moisture. Some plants bloom at night, and the desert is alive with insects, night-hunting birds, reptiles and small mammals.

DESERTS BY DAY

Many birds are at home in the desert. The lanner falcon of Africa and Asia gets all the moisture it needs from its diet of small birds and rodents. Sandgrouse live in the open deserts of Eurasia and North Africa; mainly seed eaters, they must make long flights each day to find water. Roadrunners, in American deserts, hunt insects, lizards and small rattlesnakes.

Lanner falcon
Falco biarmicus

Pallas's sandgrouse
Syrrhaptes paradoxus

Roadrunner
Geococcyx californianus

Large mammals are nomadic and obtain most of the moisture they need from plants. Camels can go for long periods without food or water because their humped back stores fat which can be drawn on when food is scarce, and water stored in their body tissues prevents dehydration. Addax antelopes survive entirely on plants. They roam remote parts of the Sahara, their broad hooves enabling them to travel easily over soft sand. Gazelles rely on speed. Small and fleet footed, they are able to disperse quickly over great distances to find food and water.

Arabian camel
Camelus dromedarius

Asian camel
Camelus bactrianus

Dorcas gazelle
Gazella dorcas

Addax antelope
Addax nasomaculatus

Insects and reptiles are well adapted to desert life. Desert locusts, when overpopulation threatens their food supply, change from a solitary to a swarming migratory form. Harvester ants store seeds against times of drought; desert tortoises withstand drought by becoming torpid. Lizards are cold blooded and need the sun to warm them, but must shelter from the intense heat of midday. The thorny devil, a small Australian ant-eating lizard, is protected from potential predators by its prickly scales.

Desert locust
Schistocerca gregaria

swarming adult

solitary hopper

Harvester ants
Pogonomyrmex sp

Desert tortoise
Gopherus polyphemus

Gridiron-tailed lizard
Callisaurus draconoides

Thorny devil
Moloch horridus

Desert plants have evolved various ways of coping successfully with drought. The ocotillo of southwestern America sheds its leaves, reducing its need for water. Euphorbias, and cacti such as the prickly pear, store water in their stems. Blue kleinia, a South African succulent, has a waxy coating that limits water loss. Agaves mature very slowly, building up reserves of food and water in their leaves before they flower. Esparto, a needlegrass, is typical of many desert grasses.

Ocotillo
Fouquieria splendens

Euphorbia
Euphorbia obesa

Prickly pear
Opuntia ficus-indica

Blue kleinia
Senecio articulatus

Agave
Agave americana

Deserts occur where rainfall is low and infrequent and where any moisture quickly evaporates or disappears instantly into the parched ground. In the driest deserts, rainfall rarely exceeds 100 mm (4 in) a year, and is so unreliable that some places may have no rain for 10 years or more. These are deserts in the truest sense of the word: harsh wildernesses that are almost totally without life. Regions with less than 255 mm (10 in) of rain a year are generally classified as arid and those with less than 380 mm (15 in) as semiarid.

Hot deserts have very high daytime temperatures in summer, although they drop sharply at night, and the winters are relatively mild. In the so-called cold deserts the summers are hot but the winters are so cold that temperatures may fall as low as −30°C (−22°F).

Desert climates and landscapes

In the subtropical latitudes, swept by hot, drying winds, high-pressure weather systems prevent rain clouds from forming. In these regions, rain comes only from local storms or follows low-pressure weather systems (often seasonal) when they move in across the desert. Large areas of central Asia have become desert because they are so far from the sea that clouds have shed all their rain before they reach them. Other deserts occur because mountains cut them off from moisture-bearing winds. The Andes, for example, shelter the drylands of Argentina, and a high sierra stops rain from reaching the Mojave and Great Basin deserts of North America. Rain is also rare on the western sides of continents where cold ocean currents flow from the polar regions towards the Equator.

Desert climates vary not only from place to place but also with time. Over short periods rainfall is much less predictable than it is in temperate regions and droughts are frequent. Some droughts, such as those that occur along the southern fringe of the Sahara, are so severe that it may seem that the climate has changed permanently. But most droughts are short-lived and are followed by years of normal (although sparse) rainfall. Over longer periods of time, however, desert climates do change. Prehistoric cave drawings in the Saharan highlands, for example, show that elephants, rhinoceroses and even hippopotamuses—animals that are at home in wetter climates—lived in these now dry, barren uplands in a more moist period between 7,000 and 4,000 years ago.

Desert landscapes also vary enormously. They are as contrasted as the Colorado canyon country of the United States and the sandy wastes of the Middle East, but most include one or more of several basic features: steep, rocky mountain slopes, broad plains, basin floors dominated by dry lake beds or sand seas, and canyon-like valleys. In low-lying areas, evaporation sometimes leaves a glistening residue of salt. Where there is soil, it is often sandy or consists of little more than fragmented rock, and because plant life is usually sparse there is little or no humus to enrich the ground.

Where water is life

Plant growth depends on water, and desert plants are usually widely spaced to reduce competition for what little moisture is available. Many plants rely on short, sharp rainstorms; others make use of dew and grow in locations, such as crevices in rocks, where water can accumulate. Some complete their life cycle in a single wet season, producing seeds that lie dormant during the following drought and germinate only when enough moisture is available for them to grow. These are the ephemerals that carpet the desert with a brief but brilliant display of flowers shortly after rain has fallen.

Most desert plants, however, are able to tolerate or resist drought. These are the xerophytes ("dry plants") and phreatophytes ("deep-water plants"). Xerophytic trees and shrubs have a wide-spreading network of shallow roots that take in water from a large area of ground. Many xerophytes also limit the amount of water

Esparto grass
Stipa tenacissima

Adaptations to desert life: kangaroo rats, jerboas and gerbils (A) make prodigious leaps with their long back legs to escape predators, and some desert lizards (B) run at high speed on their hind legs when pursued, using their tail for balance. Spadefoot toads have scoop-like hind feet with which they dig burrows to avoid the intense heat of day. Skinks use flattened toes fringed with scales to "swim" through the sand. Fan-toed geckos have toes that spread into fans at the tips, enabling them to walk easily on sand dunes, and the Namib palmate gecko has webbed feet that support it on loose sand.

The saguaro dominates the desert landscapes of Mexico and southern America. Immensely slow growing, it can take 200 years to reach its full height, and more than four-fifths of its weight may be water stored in its stem to be used in times of drought. To minimize water loss, it opens its pores only at night to absorb carbon dioxide and to help radiate heat accumulated by day.

Five great arid regions are bordered by semi-arid steppe and scrub. Cold deserts—the Gobi in central Asia, the Great Basin in North America and the Patagonian Desert in South America—lie in the higher latitudes. Cold ocean currents also affect climate, causing fogs to form over coastal deserts in southwest Africa, South America and Baja California, Mexico.

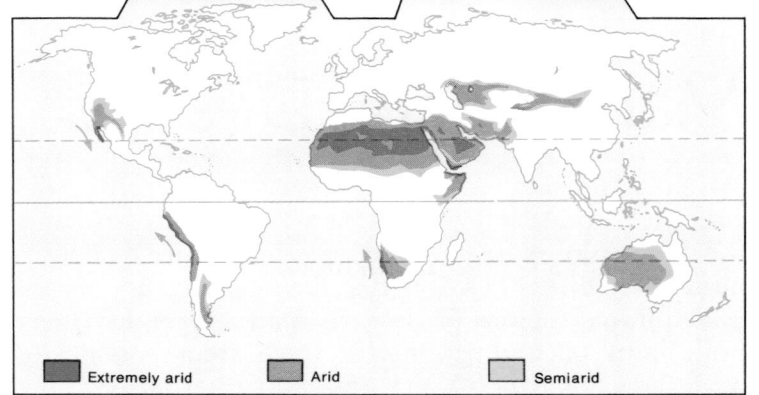

Extremely arid   Arid   Semiarid

DESERTS BY NIGHT

Owls and nightjars hunt under cover of darkness. Elf owls shelter by day, emerging at dusk to catch insects, and great horned owls often come into the desert at night to hunt. The poorwill, a small desert nightjar, is known to American Indians as "the sleeper." An insect eater, it sometimes survives the rigors of winter, when food is scarce, by hibernating.

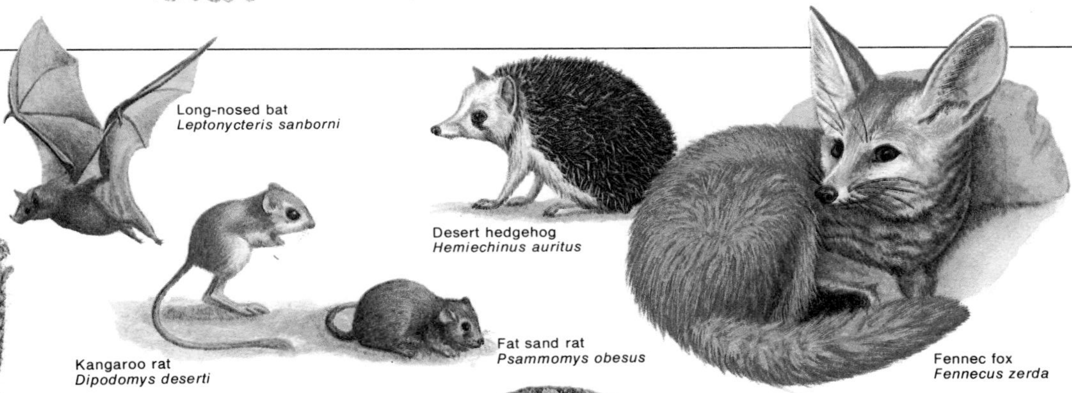

Elf owl
Micrathene whitneyi

Great horned owl
Bubo virginianus

White-throated poorwill
Phalaenoptilus nuttallii

Most small animals are active at night. Nectar-eating bats visit plants that blossom at night, pollinating the flowers while they feed. American kangaroo rats obtain water from a dry diet of seeds and conserve moisture by producing very concentrated urine. The sand rat of North Africa feeds on salty succulents and excretes great quantities of extremely salty urine. Hedgehogs are mainly insect eaters; the long ears of desert species help to disperse body heat. The Saharan fennec, the smallest type of desert fox, hunts lizards, rodents and locusts.

Long-nosed bat
Leptonycteris sanborni

Desert hedgehog
Hemiechinus auritus

Kangaroo rat
Dipodomys deserti

Fat sand rat
Psammomys obesus

Fennec fox
Fennecus zerda

Among insects and other invertebrates the hunt for food intensifies at night. Honey ants gather nectar; centipedes and camel spiders hunt insects. The gila monster, a poisonous American lizard, eats centipedes, eggs and sometimes other lizards, and uses its tail to store fat. The sidewinder, a small rattlesnake, is active mainly at night, leaving its distinctive parallel tracks in the sand. Scorpions emerge from their burrows to stalk insects and spiders, and darkling beetles feed on dry, decomposing vegetation.

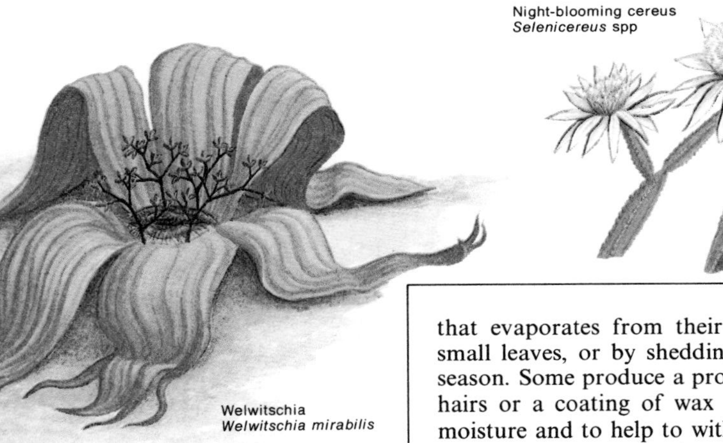

Gila monster
Heloderma suspectum

Scorpion
Buthus occitanus

Camel spider
Solifugae

Honey ants
Myrmecocystus melliger

Centipede
Chilopoda

Sidewinder rattlesnake
Crotalus cerastes

Darkling beetle
Tenebrionidae

Some desert plants are nocturnal, in the sense that they bloom only at night or make use of the dew that forms when the temperature falls. The welwitschia, unique to the Namib Desert in southwest Africa, has broad, sprawling leaves on which moisture condenses at night. The night-blooming cereus of the American deserts flowers for a single night in summer. Like other nocturnal plants, its flowers are luminously pale and strongly scented to attract pollinating night insects.

Night-blooming cereus
Selenicereus spp

Welwitschia
Welwitschia mirabilis

Saguaro cactus
Cereus giganteus

A

B

Skink
Scincus scincus

Fan-toed gecko
Ptyodactylus hasselquistii

Palmate gecko
Palmatogecko rangei

Spadefoot toad
Scaphiopus couchi

that evaporates from their leaves by having small leaves, or by shedding them in the dry season. Some produce a protective covering of hairs or a coating of wax to prevent loss of moisture and to help to withstand heat.

Succulent plants, such as cacti and euphorbias, store water in their thick stems. Their leaves are usually reduced to spines, and their round or cylindrical shape also helps to reduce water loss. Spines have the added advantage in the desert of discouraging foraging animals.

The drought-resisting phreatophytes—date palms, mesquite and cottonwood trees, for example—have a similar variety of adaptations to dry conditions, but their most typical feature is a long tap root that draws water from great depths. Many plants can also tolerate the presence of salt in the soil. These are the halophytes ("salt plants") such as saltbush and other small shrubs that grow in and around salt pans.

The struggle to survive

Animals, too, need to obtain and conserve water at all costs and to be able to adjust to extremes of temperature. Most are small enough to shelter under stones or in burrows during the intense heat of day; others survive adverse conditions by becoming dormant or by migrating. For most desert creatures it is also an advantage to be inconspicuous, and many are

pale in color so that they are hard to see against their light background of sand or stones.

Many animals, especially those that are active by day, show adaptations that are strikingly similar to those of desert plants. Frogs and toads are activated by rain, emerging from dormancy to feed and mate in temporary pools and then quickly burying themselves until the next rain falls. Mammals have hairy coats that reduce water loss and also help to keep their body temperature at a tolerable level. Most desert insects have a waxy coating that serves much the same purpose.

Some geckos and other lizards store food, in the form of fat, in their tails, and camels store fat in their humped backs to sustain them when food is scarce. Honey ants force-feed nectar to some members of the colony, creating living "honey pots" for the rest of the community to feed from in times of drought. Many creatures are able to survive on the moisture contained in their food, and rarely need to drink. Most desert dwellers also have extremely efficient kidneys that produce very concentrated urine, so that little or no moisture is lost in the process.

Man enjoys no such advantages. Nevertheless, he still seeks to live in deserts, as he has for thousands of years, and the pressures he exerts on the environment may well have irrevocably changed much of the world's desert landscapes.

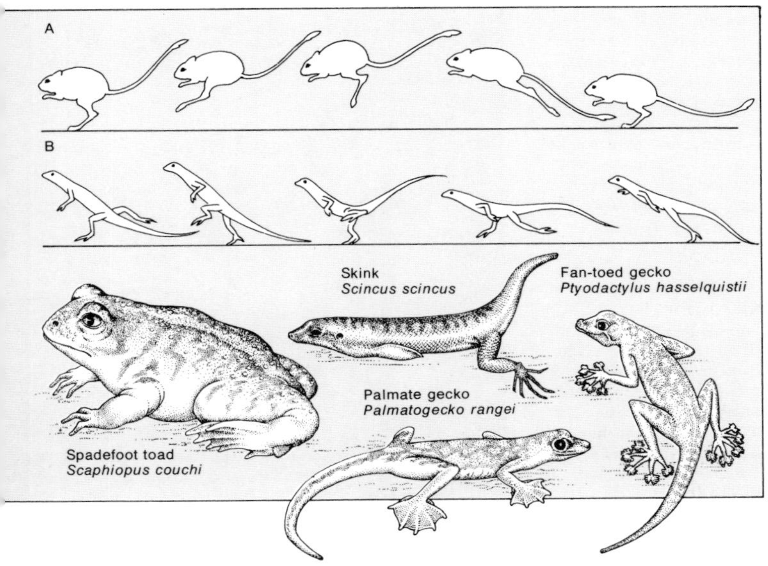

Man and the Deserts

Water is the key to man's survival in deserts: where water has been available, great civilizations have flourished, and man's dream of making the desert bloom has become a reality. More recently, discoveries of great mineral wealth have spurred the opening up of some of Earth's most inhospitable regions. But while man's ingenuity has made many deserts both habitable and productive, the human tendency to increase the extent of deserts has become a problem of international proportions.

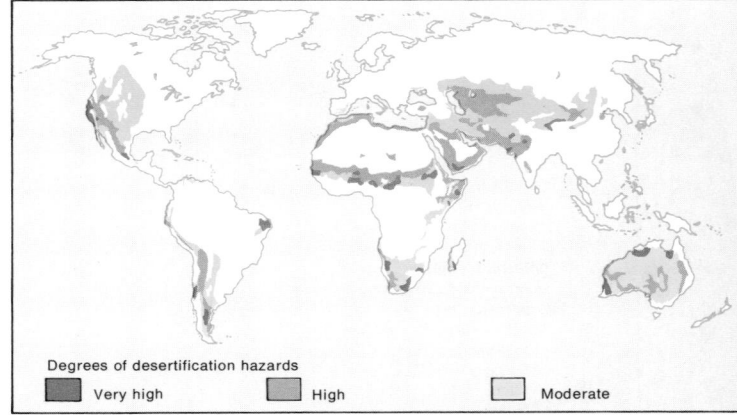

Degrees of desertification hazards

☐ Very high   ☐ High   ☐ Moderate

Given water, much is possible, and not surprisingly man has tended to settle where water is most readily available: along the courses of rivers (such as the Nile) that rise outside the desert, and around oases fed by springs or by wells that tap groundwater supplies. But desert rainfall is so unreliable that often runoff and spring flow are uncertain in quantity and timing. Much groundwater is either also unreliable or it is fossil water that has accumulated in the geological past and is not being replenished by today's rainfall. Thus in areas such as southern Libya and some of the oasis settlements of the Arabian Gulf, and in America's arid west, groundwater is a nonrenewable resource that is being rapidly depleted.

Making water go farther

Man has also used great ingenuity to secure water supplies and to transport them to where they are needed. Runoff from flash floods that follow rare desert storms may be collected in channels and distributed to crops in nearby fields, and terracing slopes to trap runoff is a traditional way of obtaining the maximum benefit from limited rainfall. Reservoirs, ranging from the small night tanks of the southern Atacama desert in Chile to the massive artificial lakes along the Colorado river in the United States, store seasonally or perennially unreliable runoff. Also, surface runoff may be increased by reducing the permeability of runoff surfaces, a

solution engineered by the Nabataeans in the Negev desert more than 2,000 years ago and being reemployed by the Israelis today.

The transport of water is a fundamental desert activity. Open canals are typical, usually carrying water to irrigated fields—a practice used throughout the fertile crescent of Mesopotamia more than 8,000 years ago and still widespread today. A striking alternative are the ancient qanats, which limit the evaporation of water while it is in transit. Qanats are still found in the Middle East, although today pipelines are increasingly used.

Ultimately the conversion of salt water to fresh water may ensure plentiful supplies for many desert regions. The process is expensive, but large-scale desalination has already become a reality in some affluent communities such as oil-rich Saudi Arabia and Kuwait. Increasing emphasis is also being placed on more efficient use of existing freshwater supplies: in Egypt and Israel, waste water from towns is being purified and recycled for use in agriculture.

Cultivating the desert

The successful control of water has enabled large areas of otherwise arid and semiarid land to be made productive. The Egyptian civilization along the Nile depended, and still depends, on the management of seasonal floodwaters. In North America, the large-scale, long-distance piping of water has made central

Desertification—the advance of desert areas across the Earth—now affects more than 30 million sq km (12 million sq miles) and deserts are continuing to expand at an alarming rate. In recent years, on the southern edge

of the Sahara alone, as much as 650,000 sq km (250,900 sq miles) of land that was once productive have been lost, and in places there is little left to show where the Sahara ends and the Sahel–Sudan region begins. Intense and

often inappropriate human pressures are major causes, frequently aggravated by drought: overcultivating vulnerable land, chopping down trees for fuelwood and grazing too many livestock, especially on the margins of arid lands.

THE SHIFTING SANDS

Recent decades have seen unprecedented changes in the world's deserts. Increasing pressure on the environment, especially from pastoralists and farmers, has caused extensive damage and a rapid expansion of barren land. In many desert regions, nomadism has long been the only way in which man could survive, except in oases. Today, even these traditional ways of life are changing as the exploitation of oil and other mineral resources, and the introduction of new agricultural techniques, are drawing many of the deserts into a spectacular new age of development.

The traditional pastoral response to limited water supplies and forage in desert regions is nomadic livestock herding, still practiced by the Tuareg of the northern Sahara (right) and by tribal groupings in Mongolia (left). The nomadic way of life has, however, become severely restricted in recent years. Long-distance migrations are often incompatible with the requirements of the modern state, and the poor rewards no longer match the incentives to settle in towns and cities.

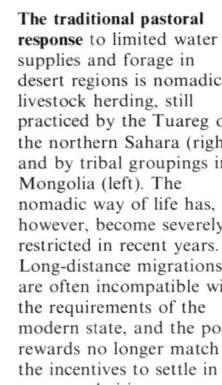

Oases have provided welcome refuges in deserts since ancient times. Secure water supplies from wells or springs make settled life possible in the midst of the most arid landscapes. Many oases are intensively cultivated with three tiers of vegetation: tall date palms shade orchards of citrus fruits, apricots, peaches, pomegranates and figs, and both palms and orchard trees shade the ground crops of vegetables and cereals. Irrigation channels distribute water to the desert soils, which are frequently rich in plant foods although they lack humus. Windbreaks help to protect cultivated land from erosion and from migrating dunes, although many oases are losing the battle with encroaching sands and the oasis people are leaving to find work in the oil fields.

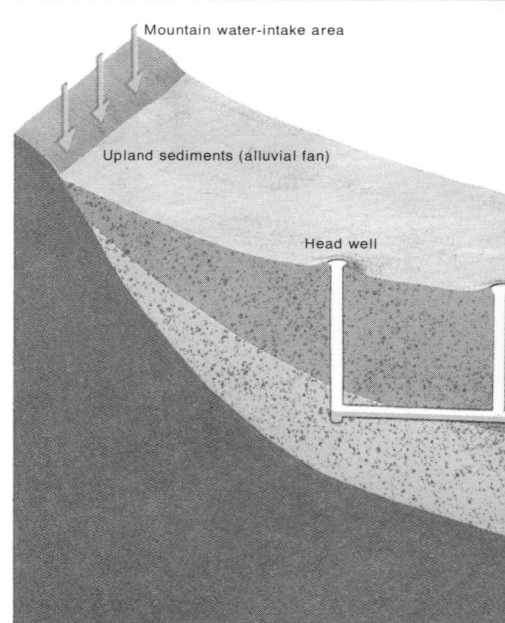

Mountain water-intake area

Upland sediments (alluvial fan)

Head well

California the most productive agricultural region in the world. But while irrigation can bring enormous benefits, it can also create problems. Too much water causes waterlogging of the land, and where water evaporates in the dry desert air, concentrations of dissolved salts build up in the soil.

Farming without irrigation is possible only where rainfall, although meager, is sufficient to sustain crops with a short growing season. Soil moisture is conserved by using dry surface mulches, by fallowing and crop rotation, by planting seeds sparsely and by controlling weeds. Geneticists are also producing new varieties of cereal crops that can survive for weeks without water. Dry farming, however, is precarious. Especially at times of drought it can cause serious problems of soil erosion, chiefly by the action of wind.

Man the desert maker

The extension of dry farming into unsuitable regions, and waterlogging and the accumulation of salts in irrigated areas, are major causes of desertification—the spread of deserts into formerly habitable land. Other major causes are the overgrazing of livestock on land with too little forage and the removal of trees and shrubs for firewood by communities that have no alternative fuel supply. A sequence of drier than normal years does the rest.

Many scientists believe that desertification can be reversed, provided the pressures on the land are reduced sufficiently to allow vegetation to recover. But desertification affects such huge areas, often crossing national frontiers, that broad-scale, international cooperation is needed to coordinate reductions in population and livestock pressures and to improve understanding of drought.

In some countries the battle against desertification has already begun. In China, extensive planting of drought-tolerant trees has created windbreaks to control sand movement and to protect farmland. In Algeria, a broad belt of trees has been planted to keep the Sahara at bay, and in Iran, advancing dunes have been halted by spraying them with petroleum residue: when the spray dries it forms a mulch that retains moisture and allows vegetation to grow, and much desert land has been reclaimed.

The deserts' riches

The exploitation of resources has also led to an "opening up" of many deserts. The rushes for precious metals in Arizona, Australia and South Africa started man's development of these regions in the nineteenth century. Some minerals, such as the evaporite deposits of Searles Basin in California and the nitrates of the Atacama desert in Chile, are actually products of the arid environment.

A resource that deserts also possess in abundance is solar power, and in many hot, dry regions the heat of the sun is used to evaporate mineral-rich solutions of salts, as well as being harnessed as a source of energy. Sunshine and the dry, clear air are also drawing ever-increasing numbers of tourists to the "sun cities" of the western United States and to Saharan oases, which were, until recently, only remote desert outposts.

No resource, however, has created as much attention or wealth as has oil. Oil has transformed the fortunes of several desert nations and provided an economic boom that has led to rapid industrialization and spectacular urban growth. The benefits of such growth in terms of affluence are substantial. The problems—the weakening of traditional desert societies, the submerging of traditional cities in the concrete labyrinths of modern complexes, and the precariousness of prosperity that is based on finite resources—are also clear.

Mineral wealth provides a powerful incentive for man's development of arid lands, and today the flow of oil rather than water is often a measure of a desert nation's prosperity. In some of the world's most desolate regions, flares signal the presence of modern "oases" where fossil fuels are being extracted—products, like the fossil waters that are sometimes trapped in the same sedimentary rocks, of the desert's geological past. Uranium, another mineral "fuel," also often lies beneath desert sands. Arid environments may also provide a rich harvest of other minerals: potash, phosphates and nitrates, valuable sources of commercial fertilizers; gypsum, manganese and salt; and borax, source of the element boron, used in nuclear reactors.

A "plastic" revolution has helped transform much of Israel's desert hinterland into productive farmland. Plastic cloches, plastic mulches and greenhouses trap moisture and reduce evaporation, and water trickled through thin plastic tubes irrigates the plants' roots with a minimum of wastage. Such innovative agricultural techniques enable Israel to produce most of its own food requirements, and fruit and vegetables grown in the relatively mild desert winters are also exported to Europe, where they command high prices.

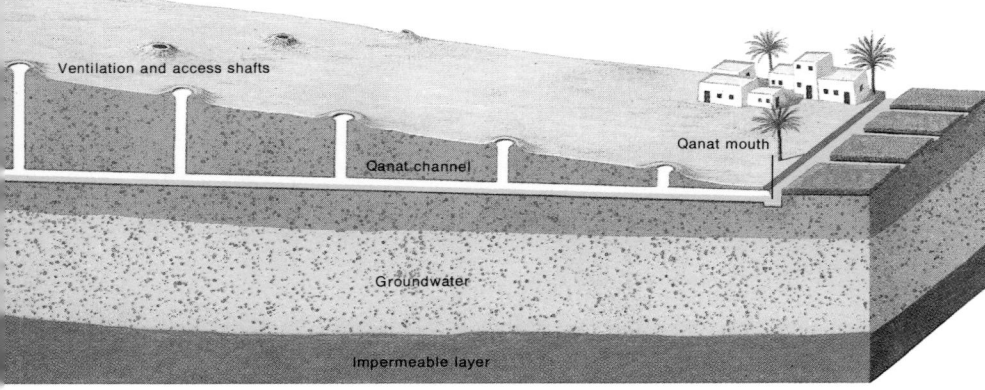

One of the most ingenious ways man has devised of bringing water to desert regions is by the ancient underground system known as the qanat. Invented by the Persians in the first millennium BC, qanats tap groundwater in upland sediments and carry it by gravity to the surface on lower land. The head well is dug first, sometimes to a depth of 100 m (330 ft), until water is reached. A line of shafts is then sunk to provide ventilation and to give access to the channel being tunneled below. Work begins at the mouth end, and a typical channel is 10–20 km (6–12 miles) long when completed, depending on the depth of the head well and the slope of the land. Its slight gradient ensures that water flows freely but gently down to ground level. Surface canals then divert the water to where it is needed. Thousands of such qanats are still in use, their routes marked by mounds of excavated debris.

Ventilation and access shafts

Qanat mouth

Qanat channel

Groundwater

Impermeable layer

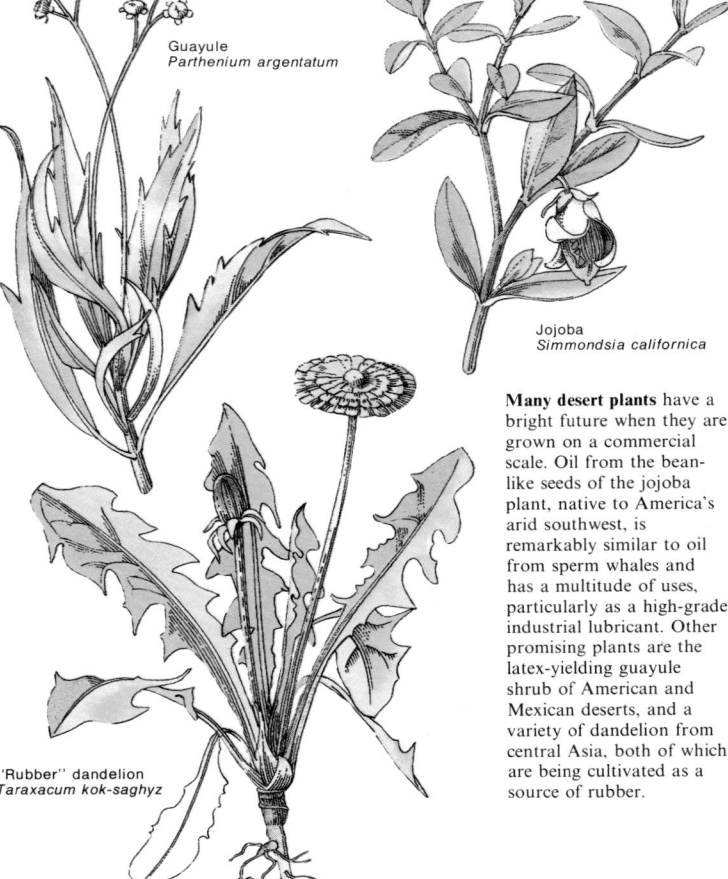

Guayule
Parthenium argentatum

Jojoba
Simmondsia californica

"Rubber" dandelion
Taraxacum kok-saghyz

Many desert plants have a bright future when they are grown on a commercial scale. Oil from the bean-like seeds of the jojoba plant, native to America's arid southwest, is remarkably similar to oil from sperm whales and has a multitude of uses, particularly as a high-grade industrial lubricant. Other promising plants are the latex-yielding guayule shrub of American and Mexican deserts, and a variety of dandelion from central Asia, both of which are being cultivated as a source of rubber.

Savannas

Between the tropical rainforest and desert regions lie large stretches of savanna, which are characterized by seasonal rainfall and long periods of drought. Those nearest to the forests usually take the form of open woodland, whereas those nearest to the deserts consist of widely scattered thorn scrub or tufts of grass. Unlike temperate grasslands, where the summers are hot but the winters are cold, savanna regions are always warm and in the wet season rain falls in heavy tropical downpours.

The most extensive areas of savanna are in Africa, north and south of the rainforest, and in South America, where the two main regions are the *llanos* of Venezuela, north of the Amazon rainforest, and the *campos* of Brazil in the south. Smaller areas of savanna also occur in Australia, India and southeastern Asia.

Savannas range from thickly wooded grasslands to almost treeless plains. Some are the result of man's destruction of the forest, and most are maintained in their present state by the high incidence of fire, both natural and manmade. The grasses tend to be taller and coarser than their temperate counterparts and they grow in tufts rather than as a uniform ground cover. In areas of high rainfall some grasses grow up to 4.5 m (15 ft) tall. Trees and bushes are usually widely spaced so that they do not compete with each other for water in the dry season. Humid, or moist, savannas experience 3 to 5 dry months a year, dry savannas 6 to 7 months, and thornbush savannas 8 to 10 months. Rainfall also varies widely, from more than 1,200 mm (47 in) a year in humid savannas to as little as 200 mm (8 in) where the savanna merges into desert.

Types of savannas
Humid woodland savanna presents an abrupt contrast to the rainforest. Trees tend to be scattered and some are so low growing that they are dwarfed by the tall grass that springs up during the summer rains. In the dry season the grass fuels fierce fires, which destroy all except thick-barked, large-leaved deciduous trees. Consequently, the proportion of fire-resistant trees and shrubs is large, and the grass quickly regenerates with the coming of the next rains.

In Africa this type of savanna is known as Guinea savanna north of the rainforest and as miombo savanna south of the rainforest. In South America it is known as *campo cerrado*, from the Portuguese words meaning field (*campo*) and dense. (*Campos sujos* are *campos* in which stretches of open grassland predominate and *campos limpos* are grasslands from which trees are entirely absent.) The *llanos*, or plains, of northern South America are grasslands interspersed with forests and swamps.

North of the Guinea savanna in Africa lies a belt known as Sudan savanna. The annual rainfall is in the range 500 to 1,000 mm (20–40 in) and the dry season lasts from October to April. This is typical dry savanna. Tall grasses between 1 and 1.5 m (3–5 ft) form an almost continuous ground cover and acacias and other thorny trees dot the landscape, together with branching dôm palms and massive water-storing baobab trees. Because of the interrupted tree cover the old name given to many savannas of this type was orchard steppe, and this description gives a good idea of the countryside. Like the humid woodland savannas it is maintained by regular burning of the grass in the dry season, and there is a delicate

balance and interaction between climate, soil, vegetation, animals and fire. On the desert margins the grasses grow in short tufts and the scattered acacias are seldom more than 3 m (10 ft) tall. The scrub and grasses are too widely dispersed for fires to spread, and this type of savanna is modified not by fire but by aridity and blistering heat.

Thorn-scrub and thorn-forest savannas frequently form transitional zones between tropical forests and grasslands. The *caatinga*, or "light forest," of northeastern Brazil is a typical thorn-forest savanna. Long, hot, dry seasons alternate with erratic downpours of rain, and the rate of evaporation is high. Drought-resisting trees and thorny shrubs mix with bromeliads, cacti and palm trees.

Abundance of life
No other environment supports animals so spectacular in size and so immense in numbers as do the African savannas. In spite of the concentration of animal life, however, competition for food is not severe. Each species has its own preferences and feeds from different levels of the vegetation. Giraffes and elephants can easily reach the upper branches of trees, antelopes feed on bushes at different heights from the ground, zebras and impalas eat the grasses and warthogs root for the underground parts of plants. With the onset of the dry season, massed herds assemble for the great migrations that are a major part of savanna life, moving to areas where rain has recently fallen and new grass is plentiful.

Following the grazing animals are the large predators: the lions, leopards and cheetahs. Wild dogs hunt in packs, and the scavengers—jackals, hyenas and vultures—move in to dispose of the remains of the kill.

The savannas of South America and Australia are much poorer in animal species. The only mammal of any size on the South American savanna is the elusive, nocturnal maned wolf, which eats almost anything from small animals to wild fruit. On the Australian savanna the largest inhabitant is the kangaroo, and the prime predator—apart from man—is the dingo, or native dog.

Many of the resident savanna birds are ground-living species such as the ostrich in Africa and its counterparts, the rhea in South America and the emu in Australia. The warm African climate attracts large numbers of visiting birds, which migrate each year across the Sahara to escape from the severe winter of the northern hemisphere.

For many thousands of years man has lived in harmony with the savanna. Within the last century, however, and in recent decades in particular, the savanna has come under increasing pressure. Inevitably, there is competition between the needs of the environment and those of the human population, and the future of the savanna is very much in the balance.

On each side of the Equator are broad tracts of tropical grassland known as savannas. In these regions there are distinct wet and dry seasons and temperatures are high all the year round, seldom falling below 21°C (70°F). Rain falls mainly in the hottest months, whereas the cooler months are generally dry. Thorn-scrub and thorn-forest savannas occur where the rainfall is more erratic; they have relatively little grass cover, and trees and bushes can tolerate long periods of drought.

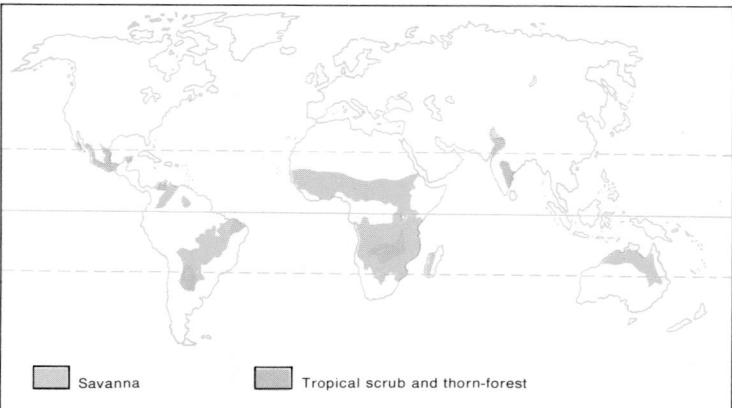

Savanna

Tropical scrub and thorn-forest

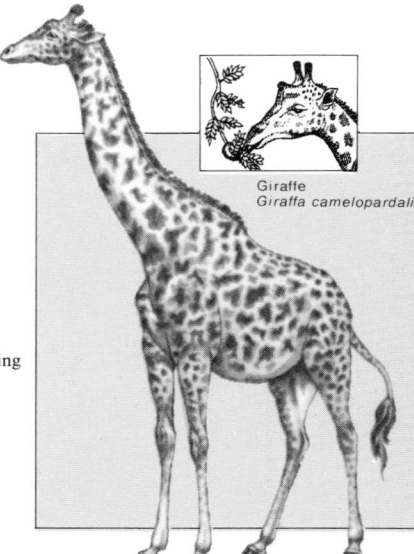

THE PLANT EATERS
Most plant eaters have adapted to feeding at a particular level of the vegetation. Giraffes browse on acacia tips that other animals cannot reach and elephants use their trunks to tear down succulent branches and leaves, although both feed on low-growing vegetation when it is easily available. Elephants will also uproot trees to gather leaves that are otherwise out of reach. The black rhinoceros plucks low-growing twigs and leaves by grasping them with its upper lip (the white rhinoceros has a broad, square mouth for grazing on grass). Eland often use their horns to collect twigs by twisting and breaking them. Zebra, wildebeest, topi and gazelle all graze on the same grasses, but at different stages of the plants' growth.

Giraffe
Giraffa camelopardalis

HUNTERS OF THE PLAINS
The plant eaters provide rich hunting for the carnivores. Lions kill the largest prey and hunt in family groups; the lioness usually makes the kill but the male is the first to eat. The leopard is a solitary hunter. It lies in ambush or stalks its prey, mainly at night, in brush country where it has ground cover. Cheetahs are the swiftest of all the hunters. They usually hunt in pairs in open grassland, stalking their prey and then charging in a lightning-fast sprint. Hunting dogs travel in well-organized packs. They exhaust their quarry by chasing it to a standstill and attacking as a team. Whereas lions, leopards and cheetahs usually kill by leaping for the neck or throat, packs of hunting dogs characteristically attack from the rear.

Lion
Panthera leo

THE SCAVENGERS
When the hunters have eaten, the scavengers move in. Jackals, small and quick, make darting runs to snatch titbits while packs of hyenas use their powerful bone-crushing jaws to demolish the bulk of the carcass. Hyenas are the most voracious of the carnivores, often driving the primary predator from its kill. Vultures are frequently the first to see a kill as they circle high in the sky, but must await their turn to feed on the skin and scraps because their descent attracts the more aggressive scavengers. Carrion beetles, carrion flies and the larvae of the horn-boring moth dispose of what is left. Most of the large scavengers, particularly the hyenas, also do their own hunting, singling out prey that is small, weak or sickly.

Jackal
Canis aureus

Plants in the savanna are remarkably well adapted to withstand drought, fire and the onslaughts of the animals that eat them. Acacias tolerate both drought and fire, and are armed with sharp thorns—although many animals do feed on them, thorns and all. Red oat grass survives fire because its seeds twist deep into the ground. Bermuda, or sawtooth, grass is a favorite food of many grazers, but it recovers quickly from close cropping because its growing point lies too flat against the ground to be eaten.

Acacia
Acacia sp

Red oat grass
Themeda triandra

Bermuda grass
Cynodon dactylon

Zebras

Wildebeest and topi

Gazelles

SAVANNA SWAMPS, LAKES AND MARSHES

Swamps, lakes and marshes are especially characteristic of the African savanna. Many are fringed with papyrus, the paper reed, *Cyperus papyrus* (1) which grows to a height of 3.5 m (12 ft) or more, and most are rich in microscopic organisms that play the same role in the water as grass does on the plains, supporting large numbers of birds and animals. Swamps and marshes also act as natural reservoirs, which collect and hold excess water during the rainy season, and provide welcome dry-season grazing for plains animals when other savanna productivity is at its lowest. The lakes of the Great Rift Valley, which form a chain down the northeastern side of the continent, are also rich with life. Many provide a refuge for crocodiles, their numbers seriously depleted by systematic hunting, and for multitudes of birds, including huge flocks of flamingos.

Many birds and animals have adapted to a semiaquatic way of life. The shoebill stork *Balaeniceps rex* (2) uses its feet and the hooked tip of its beak to stir up mud and dislodge the frogs, fish and soft-shelled turtles that form the bulk of its diet. The goliath heron *Ardea goliath* (3) is a shallow-water fisher. The sitatunga *Tragelaphus speki* (4) has long, splayed hooves that support its weight on soft mud. It hides by day among reeds on the edge of the swamp and moves to dry ground at night to feed. The jacana, or lily trotter, *Actophilornis africana* (5) relies on long toes and constant motion to walk on floating plants. The hippopotamus *Hippopotamus amphibius* (6) wallows in the water for most of the day and leaves the swamp at dusk to graze. It helps to fertilize the swamp with the enormous amounts of waste matter it excretes.

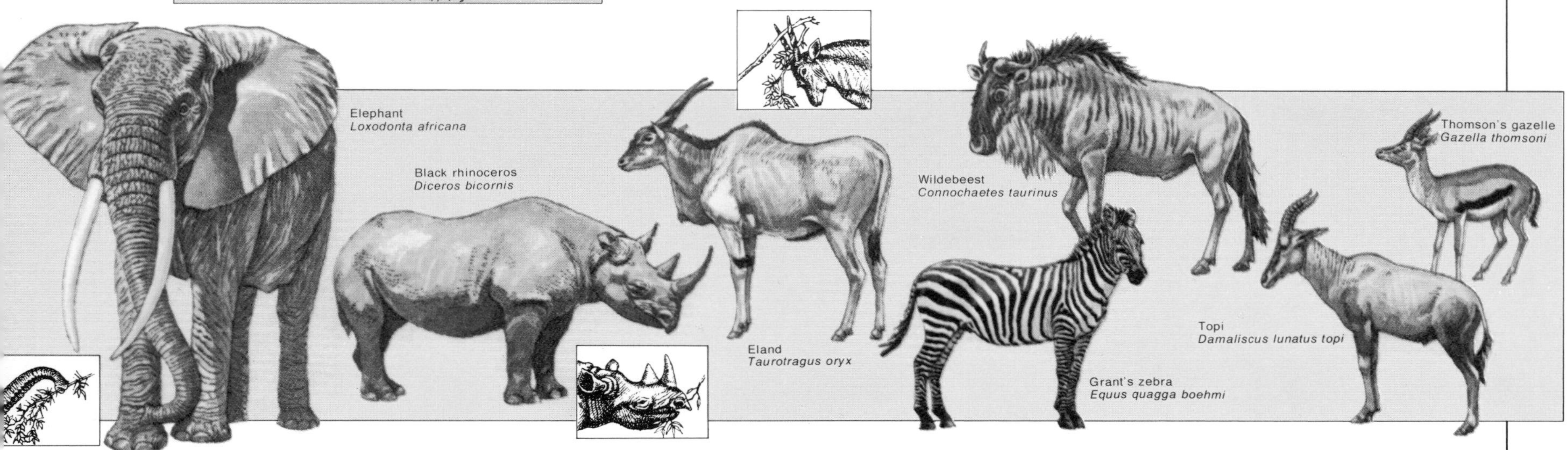

Elephant
Loxodonta africana

Black rhinoceros
Diceros bicornis

Eland
Taurotragus oryx

Wildebeest
Connochaetes taurinus

Grant's zebra
Equus quagga boehmi

Topi
Damaliscus lunatus topi

Thomson's gazelle
Gazella thomsoni

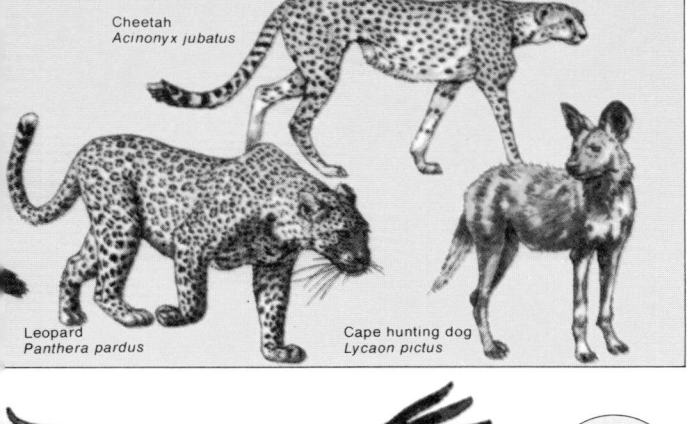

Cheetah
Acinonyx jubatus

Leopard
Panthera pardus

Cape hunting dog
Lycaon pictus

Ostrich
Struthio camelus

Secretary bird
Sagittarius serpentarius

LONG-LEGGED BIRDS
The ostrich, up to 2.4 m (8 ft) tall, can see for great distances across the plains and can outrun most of its enemies. Its territory is often shared with grazing animals, such as wildebeest, which take advantage of the ostrich's keen sight to alert them to danger. The secretary bird (so-called because of its quill-like crest) strides through the grass hunting small mammals, insects and snakes; it kills snakes by battering them with its powerful, long-clawed feet.

Large termite mounds are a distinctive feature of many savanna landscapes. The mounds, or termitaria, are made of soil excavated by the termites and bound with their saliva. Thick walls help to keep the interior at a constant temperature, and some species of termite cultivate fungus "gardens" as a source of food. The royal chamber deep inside the mound is occupied by the colony's queen, grossly distended with eggs, and her consort. Predators include the aardwolf and the aardvark. The aardwolf is related to the hyena but is smaller and has weak jaws; it digs the termites out of their mound and scoops them up with its long sticky tongue. The aardvark, distantly related to the elephant, uses its powerful hoof-like claws to break into termite nests.

Aardwolf
Proteles cristatus

Aardvark
Orycteropus afer

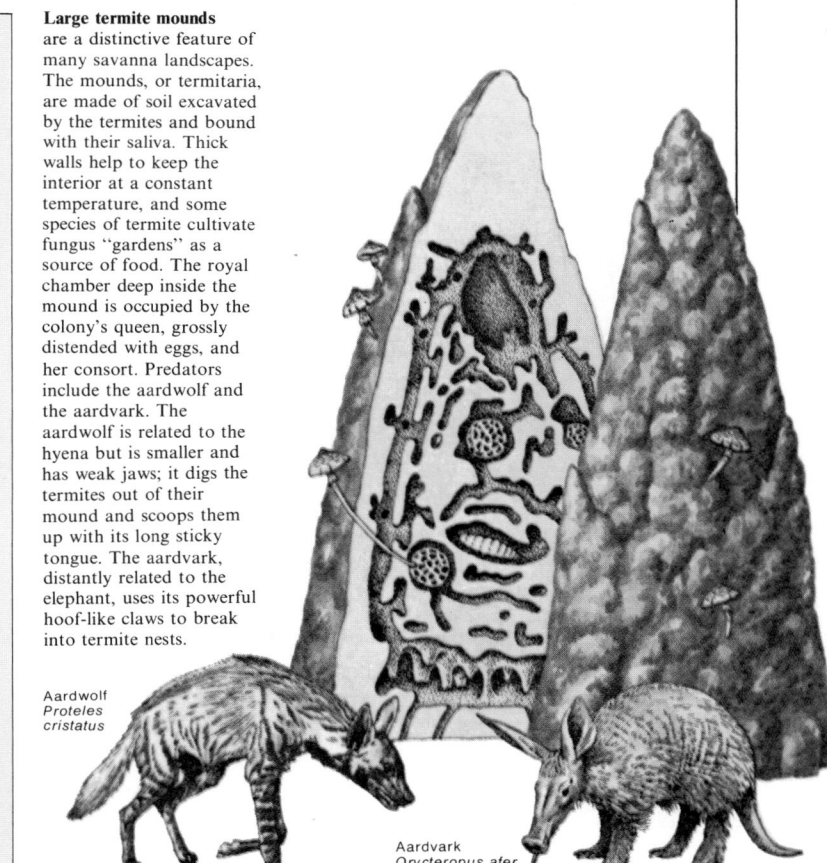

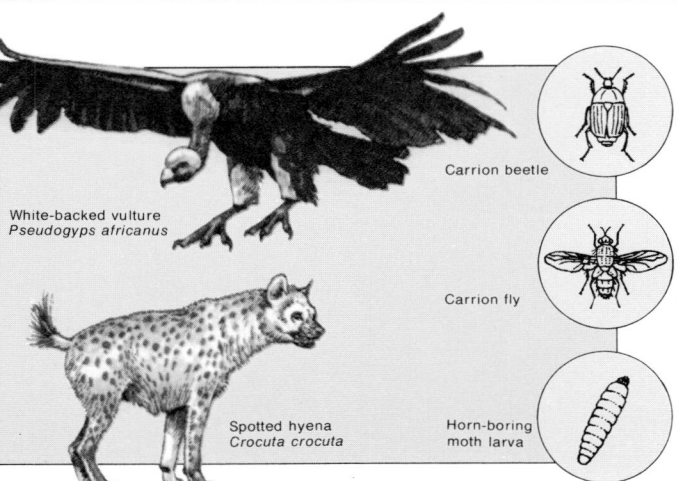

White-backed vulture
Pseudogyps africanus

Carrion beetle

Carrion fly

Horn-boring moth larva

Spotted hyena
Crocuta crocuta

Man and the Savannas

In their natural state, savannas are among the most strikingly productive of all Earth's regions. Before the coming of man they supported a wealth of animal life that has seldom been surpassed. As yet they are relatively undeveloped, but many of them lie in areas where the pressures of population growth are becoming increasingly acute. Wisely used, they offer great hope for the future, both as cattle lands and for the cultivation of food crops. But without proper management savannas can rapidly turn into wasteland, and man will be the poorer for the loss of such a great natural resource.

Throughout much of the savannas the climate is semiarid and the soils tend to be poor: stripped of their plant cover, they bake hard and crack during the long months of hot sunshine, and during the wet season they often become water-logged or are washed away by the rains. Man's indiscriminate use of fire, unwise agricultural methods and the unrestricted grazing of domestic animals have already led to much soil loss, and erosion is widespread in tropical Africa, Asia, South America and Australia.

Systematic burning has long been practiced by the people of the savannas. Large areas are burned each year to clear land for agriculture or to remove dead grass and encourage a fresh growth to feed livestock. The resulting ash provides much-needed nutrients for crops, and the grasses rapidly produce new green shoots that provide a rich pasture for domestic herds. But although the short-term effects may be beneficial, repeated burning is harmful to the vegetation, the animals and the soil.

Trees are always more or less damaged by fire. Their trunks become twisted and gnarled, fresh shoots are killed and young trees are prevented from growing. Constant burning can destroy some species altogether, and when they disappear so too does the wildlife that depends on them for food and shelter.

Grasses, on the other hand, may be encouraged by burning, and the lush new growth that springs up when the first rains break the long dry season provides welcome nourishment for domestic herds and game animals alike. But whereas game animals move freely over the range, cropping grasses at various stages of growth, cattle tend to feed on grass only in the neighborhood of wells and other sources of drinking water. They may trample the soil and continue to graze the same area until the grass is completely suppressed.

The hazards of large projects

Cultivation in marginal areas that are unsuited to intensive agriculture also contributes to the impoverishment of the savanna. The Sahel and Sudan savannas on the fringes of the Sahara are particularly vulnerable to large-scale development projects that fail to take account of local climate and soil. Mechanized agriculture in fragile areas bordering the desert may well lead to soil erosion and dustbowl conditions, and large-scale irrigation schemes often result in waterlogging and an accumulation of salts in the soil. Cultivation in the savannas requires understanding and care. Many smaller schemes are safer—and usually more productive—than a few large ones, but not all planners yet realize that agricultural methods that are effective in temperate regions seldom come up to expectations in tropical climates.

Man first inhabited the savannas, as he did many other regions of the world, as a hunter and gatherer. He took from the land only what he needed from day to day, and although he used fire as a hunting tool, his impact was little more than that of any other savanna inhabitant. In East Africa, groups of nomadic Hadza (left) still hunt game and collect roots, fruit and the honey of wild bees, building grass huts as temporary shelters.

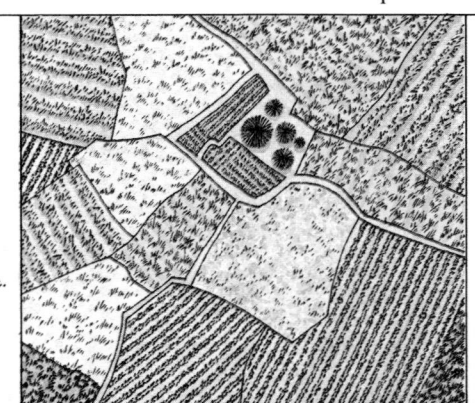

Small farms are scattered over much of the savannas. Plots close to houses are farmed continuously; beyond them lie the main fields, where periods of cultivation are usually followed by periods of fallow. Maize, millet and peanuts are the main food crops, and early and late crops are sometimes sown on the same plot to extend the growing season. Most of the work is done by hand, and any surplus to a family's needs is sold.

THE VULNERABLE WILDERNESS

Nowhere has man's impact on the tropical grasslands been felt more keenly than in Africa, although much of what is happening in Africa is happening also in savannas elsewhere. The majority of the people still live on the land, where the determining factor is the length and severity of the annual dry season. In the moister savannas the people are primarily cultivators, while in savannas that are too dry to sustain agriculture the main occupation is raising livestock. Most of the savannas are as yet sparsely settled, but competition is inevitably growing between man and wildlife, particularly in Africa, for the remaining tracts of relatively untouched wilderness.

The development of mineral resources and industries has led to an increasing movement of people—mainly young adults—from rural areas to towns and mining centers, attracted by opportunities for work—often at the expense of agriculture, since the heavy work of farming is left to the women, old people and children. Mining enterprises such as those in the Zambian Copper Belt (above), may recruit large labor forces from the surrounding countryside. Mining also dramatically alters the landscape, especially where the bedrock containing the ore reaches the surface and is quarried in huge terraces. The need for electricity to power mining and other industries leads, in turn, to the development of hydro-electric schemes, many of which entail resettling people whose villages are flooded by the creation of large artificial lakes.

Large areas of savanna have been set aside in East and Central Africa, and to a lesser extent in South America and Australia, as national parks and reserves where the landscape is kept intact and animals can be studied in their natural habitats. In Africa, observation platforms are frequently built close to waterholes where animals congregate to drink, and wardens use light aircraft to patrol the vast areas involved. Camel units are also used to patrol near-desert regions where much of the wildlife flourishes. Animals, such as elephants, whose numbers can grow out of control in the protected environment of the reserves are culled by licensed hunters to prevent the vegetation being destroyed. Culling maintains the health of the community as a whole and is also an economic source of meat in many countries where the people are short of protein foods.

Similarly, the introduction of European breeds of cattle into the savannas has not been an unqualified success. Not only are these breeds more susceptible to tropical pests and diseases than are the local varieties, but they are also adversely affected by the hot climate and their productivity is greatly reduced. In Africa and Brazil, native breeds are replacing more recent importations, and their productivity is being enhanced by selective breeding. In Australia, where most of the cattle are of British stock, tropical zebu, or humped cattle, are being introduced into the herds.

In the future, much more of the savanna may be developed as ranch lands, because the temperate grasslands will become less able to support enough animals to satisfy the world demand for meat. The *llanos* of Venezuela, the *campos* of Brazil and the tropical grasslands of Argentina and Australia already carry large herds of beef cattle. Throughout the savannas, however, ranching is still hampered by lack of water, poor natural pasture and remoteness from markets. In Africa, where herding is mainly nomadic, the sinking of wells by government organizations is changing the traditional ways of life, and cattle raising on a commercial scale is likely to become increasingly important. In Africa, too, the conservation and controlled cropping of game animals could become one of the most productive—and constructive—forms of land use.

Game as a resource

The value of game animals as a source of food is considerable. Buffaloes, for example, and kangaroos in Australia, can thrive on natural grasses that will not even maintain the weight of domestic stock, and they show greater gains in weight than African and European cattle on most forms of vegetation, while several species of antelopes can survive on a water ration that is wholly inadequate for cattle.

In recent years attention has been directed toward the economics of controlled cropping of wild game, and of ranching animals such as eland, which can be kept as if they were domesticated stock and can convert poor pasture into excellent meat. Game animals are also more resistant than cattle to the tsetse fly, which infests large areas of Africa and transmits the disease trypanosomiasis (known as nagana in cattle and as sleeping sickness in man).

But for the most part game animals are still considered to be a nuisance by man, and it is perhaps fortunate that by denying much of the savanna to domestic animals—and to man— the tsetse fly has preserved these regions from exploitation at the expense of the game. Many countries have also set aside large tracts of savanna as national parks and game reserves, where the natural environment is preserved and the wildlife can thrive.

Safeguarding the savanna

At a time when the pressure of the expanding human population calls for the development of areas hitherto uninhabited or only sparsely populated, it may seem paradoxical to maintain that the development of national parks and nature reserves is essential to the welfare of mankind. The aim of game conservation, however, is not simply to preserve rare or unusual animals for the enjoyment of posterity, or even for their scientific interest. It is to ensure that the land is put to its most economic and efficient use. The next few decades will show whether the savannas of the world will be developed into major sources of food and revenue for the countries that own them, or whether they will be misused and degraded into desert.

Commercial agriculture is important to the economies of many savanna countries. Cotton and coffee are major cash crops in Africa and Brazil, together with maize, tobacco, sisal and peanuts—crops that need a cycle of wet and dry seasons and year-round warmth. But large-scale cultivation of one crop tends to attract pests and diseases, and dependence on a single crop makes the economy vulnerable to fluctuating world prices.

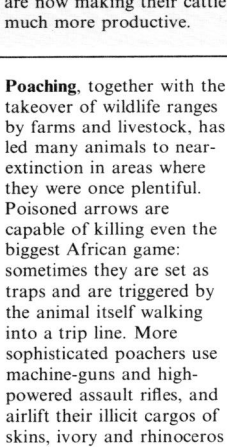

Cattle rearing takes the place of cultivation in areas that are too dry to be cropped successfully. In Africa, people such as the Masai are nomadic herders, moving their cattle long distances in search of pasture. Wealth is counted in terms of the numbers rather than the quality of the cattle they own, but improved management of their herds and better control of animal diseases are now making their cattle much more productive.

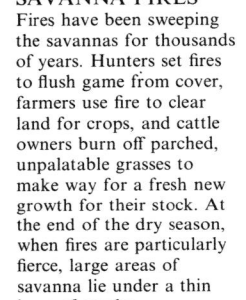

SAVANNA FIRES

Fires have been sweeping the savannas for thousands of years. Hunters set fires to flush game from cover, farmers use fire to clear land for crops, and cattle owners burn off parched, unpalatable grasses to make way for a fresh new growth for their stock. At the end of the dry season, when fires are particularly fierce, large areas of savanna lie under a thin haze of smoke.

Poaching, together with the takeover of wildlife ranges by farms and livestock, has led many animals to near-extinction in areas where they were once plentiful. Poisoned arrows are capable of killing even the biggest African game: sometimes they are set as traps and are triggered by the animal itself walking into a trip line. More sophisticated poachers use machine-guns and high-powered assault rifles, and airlift their illicit cargos of skins, ivory and rhinoceros horn. Illegal hunting for meat, which is dried and sold, has also become a large, highly organized and very profitable business in many areas.

Game animals also provide the spectacular displays that attract tourists and make tourism an important source of income for many developing nations. Today, most tourists pursue game with cameras instead of guns. The hunting that led to the wholesale slaughter of wildlife in previous years is banned, and so is the traffic in trophies, although even in the sanctuary provided by parks and reserves animals still fall prey to poachers.

Animals are frequently transferred from areas where they are at risk to safer areas such as game parks and reserves. In Kenya, helicopters came to the rescue of a herd of rare antelopes when their range was threatened by a proposed irrigation scheme and moved them to Tsavo National Park. Animals are also moved to introduce new blood to small, isolated herds or to restock areas from which they have been lost.

Tropical Rainforests

Tropical rainforests, extremely rich in both plant and animal life, consist of a series of layered or stratified habitats. These range from the dark and humid forest floor through a layer of shrubs to the emerging tops of the scattered giant trees towering above the dense main canopy of the forest. Each layer of vegetation is a miniature life zone containing a wide selection of animal species. These can be divided into a number of ecological groups according to their various ways of life, and many have evolved special adaptations to enable them to make maximum use of the plentiful food supply surrounding them.

Crested tree swift
Hemiprocne longipennis

Crowned eagle
Stephanoaetus coronatus

Tropical rainforests occur only in the regions close to the Equator; they have a heavy rainfall and a uniformly hot and moist climate. There are slightly more of these forests in the northern half of the world than in the southern half and they occur at altitudes of up to 1,500 m (5,000 ft). Temperatures are normally between 24°C and 30°C (77°–86°F) and rarely fall below 21°C (70°F) or rise above 32°C (90°F). The skies are often cloudy and the rain falls more or less evenly throughout the year. Rainfall is usually more than 2,000 mm (78 in) a year and is never less than 1,500 mm (59 in). A distinctive feature of this tropical, humid climate is that the average daily temperature range is much greater than the range between the hottest and coolest months.

A stratified habitat
There are usually three to five overlapping layers in the mature tropical rainforest. The tallest trees (called "emergents") rise above a closed, dense canopy formed by the crowns of less tall trees, which nevertheless can reach more than 40 m (130 ft) tall. Below this canopy is a third or middle layer of trees—the understory; their crowns do not meet but they still form a dense layer of growth about 5–20 m (16–65 ft) tall. The fourth layer consists of woody shrubs of varying heights between 1–5 m (3–16 ft). The bottom layer comprises decomposers (fungi) that rarely reach 50 cm (20 in) in height.

Although the trees are so tall, few of them have really thick trunks. Nearly all are evergreens, shedding their dark, leathery leaves and growing new ones continuously. Many of the larger species grow buttresses—thin, triangular slabs of hardwood that spread out from the bases of their trunks. These support the trees, so removing the need for a heavy outlay of energy and resources on deep root systems. Hanging lianas (vines), thin and strong as rope, vanish like cables into the mass of foliage. They are especially abundant on riverbanks, where the canopy of trees is thinner; their leaves and flowers appear only among the treetops.

Epiphytes—plants that grow on other plants but do not take their nourishment from them—festoon the trunks and branches of trees, and up to 80 may grow on a single tree. They include many kinds of orchid and bromeliad. Their aerial roots make use of a humus substitute derived from the remains of other plants, often

Moth orchid
Phalaenopsis sanderana

Tropical rainforests are located in the hot and wet equatorial lands of Latin America, West Africa, Madagascar and Asia. These areas have consistently high temperatures throughout the year and receive high rainfall from the moist and unstable winds blowing in from the oceans.

The hummingbird numbers about 300 species, most of which are confined to the forests of South America. It is renowned for its ability to hover while gathering nectar, a feat achieved by the almost 180° rotations of its wings, which beat rapidly more than 80 times per second.

Tropical rainforests

brought together by ants. The bases of their leaves may be broad and bowl shaped and collect and hold water; they also provide homes for a variety of insects and reptiles.

Rainforest soils are not as fertile as might be supposed by the luxuriance of their vegetation. On the contrary, the silicates and compounds necessary for plant growth are leached away by the rain to leave red or yellow soils of poor quality. This process, known as laterization, is widespread in the humid tropics. Humus is rapidly broken down by bacteria, fungi and termites, while earthworms, which in more temperate regions normally contribute to the mixing of humus with mineral particles, are usually absent.

In rainforests there are often up to 25 different tree species on a single hectare of land (60 species to the acre). Most temperate forests have only a fifth of this number, with nothing like the abundance of plants that grow in the tropics. This incredible variety supports—directly or indirectly—a corresponding variety of animal species which has an abundant food supply because the forest never ceases to be productive. This is why most mammals do not move far; they stay where their food grows.

Life in the canopy
The dense leaves and branches of the canopy provide the most food and so support the greatest number of species. Macaws and toucans (from the American tropics) and parrots and trogons (which live in forests throughout the tropics) eat the fruit growing in the

Flowering plants of the forest include epiphytes such as bromeliads and orchids like the species of *Phalaenopsis* illustrated here. Epiphytes grow on other plants such as trees where they can receive sunlight and are nourished by humus in the bark. Many epiphytic orchids have swellings in their roots or at the bases of their leaves where water can be stored. Seventy species of *Phalaenopsis* grow in southeast Asian forests and *P. sanderana*, one of the most beautiful, was first discovered in the Philippines in 1882.

THE LAYERS OF THE FOREST
Stratification—the existence of distinct layers of forest vegetation—is especially pronounced in the tropics, where there are usually five main storys. These can overlap greatly and may vary in height from area to area. The large differences between the layers present many varied habitats and ecological niches for a very wide range of animals.

CANOPY LAYER
This dense story exerts a powerful influence on the levels below since its trees, which grow between 20 m (65 ft) and 40 m (130 ft) tall, form such a thick layer of vegetation that they cut off sunlight from the forest below. The canopy is noted for the diversity of its fauna. Many birds and animals are adapted to running along branches to get the flowers, fruits or nuts that form their diets. The pointed tips of canopy leaves encourage rapid drainage.

Sacred langur
Presbytis entel

Tree shrew
Tupaia glis

MIDDLE LAYER
This understory comprises trees from 5 m (16 ft) to 20 m (65 ft) tall whose long, narrow crowns do not become quite so dense as those of the canopy. There is very often no clear distinction, however, between this level and the canopy. Middle-layer trees are strong enough to bear large animals such as leopards that spend part of their lives on the ground. Epiphytes are plentiful in this layer.

Leopard
Panthera pardu

Pouched tree frog
Gastrotheca ovifera

Orang-utan
Pongo pygmaeus

SHRUB LAYER
The vegetation of this level is sparse in comparison with that above it and consists of treelets and woody shrubs that rarely reach 5 m (16 ft). These grow up in any available space between the abundant boles of large trees. Life in this story exists equally well at ground level.

Four-striped squirrel
Funisciurus lemniscatus

Oriental civet
Viverra tangalunga

Tree pangolin
Manis tricuspis

GROUND LAYER
Shade-tolerant herbs, ferns and tree seedlings represent the only flora at ground level; there is no grass there. Light is less than one percent of full daylight so that many mammals are well camouflaged in the gloom, whereas others have compact bodies to facilitate movement through the undergrowth. Ants and termites are well adapted to the high humidity and darkness of the forest floor. Fungi and a host of invertebrates quickly break down the litter of rotting leaves, fruit and fallen branches to provide vital nutrients for the fast-growing trees of the tropical rainforest.

Okapi
Okapia johnstoni

Forest buffalo
Syncerus caffer nanus

Congo forest mouse
Deomys ferrugineus

Short-eared elephant shrew
Macroscelides proboscideus

Orange-rumped agouti
Dasyprocta aguti

Mandrill
Mandrillus sphinx

Indian tiger
Panthera tigris tigris

Malayan tapir
Tapirus indicus

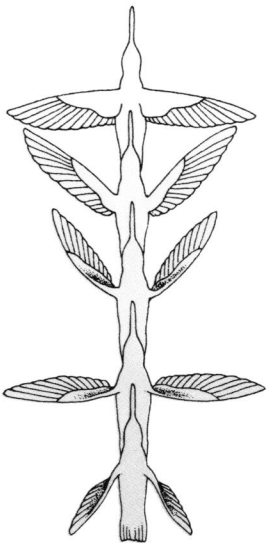

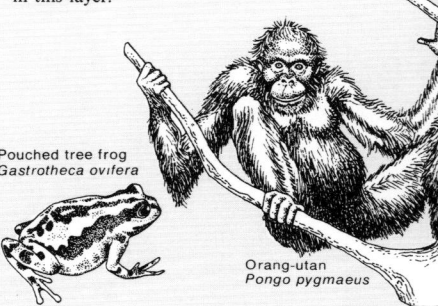

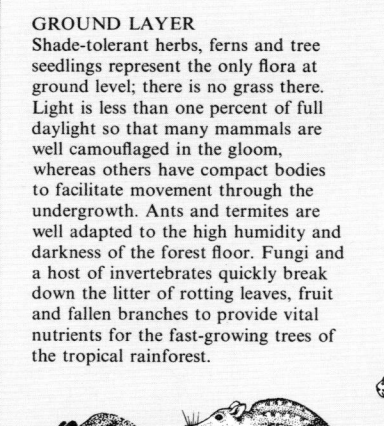

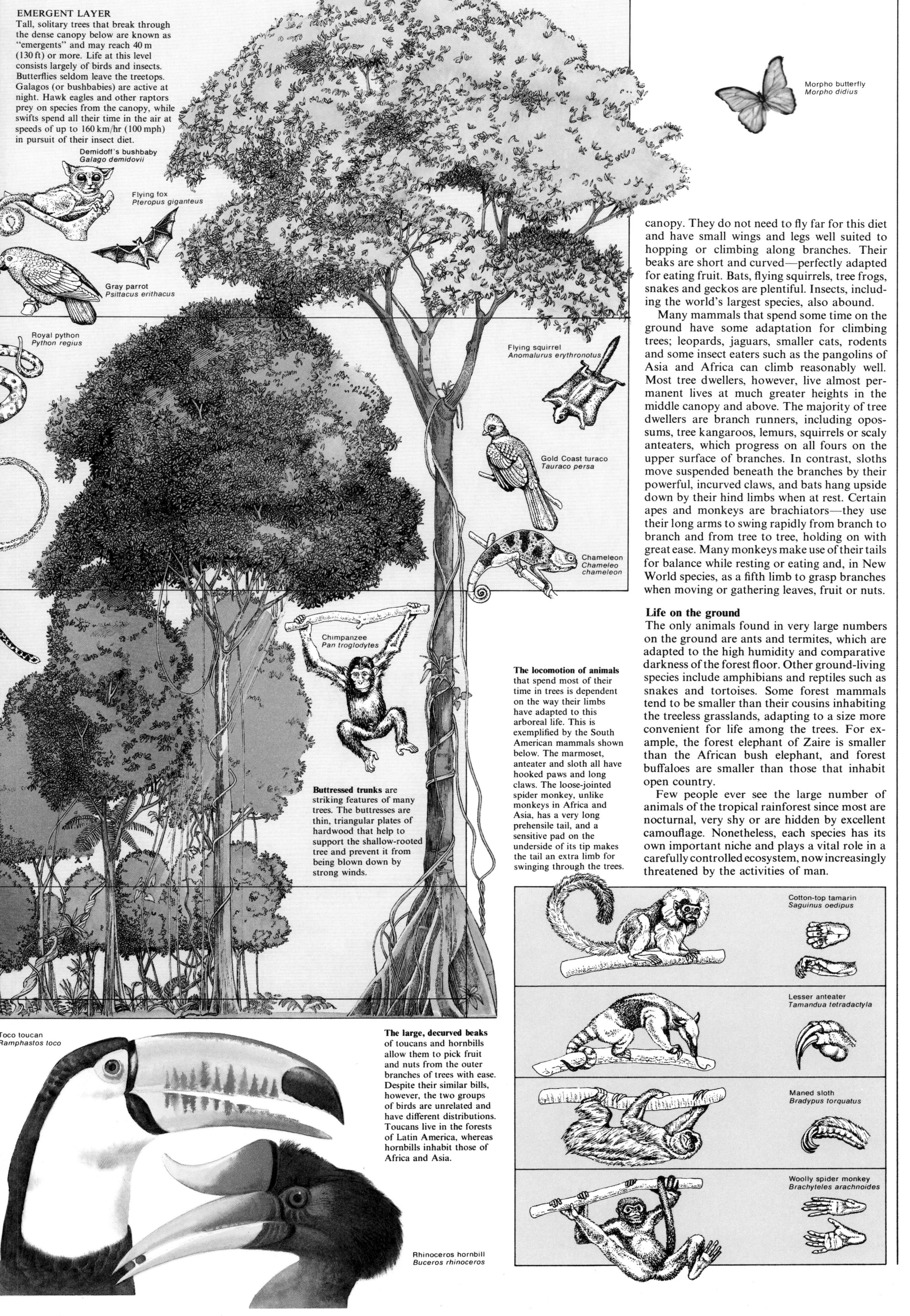

EMERGENT LAYER
Tall, solitary trees that break through the dense canopy below are known as "emergents" and may reach 40 m (130 ft) or more. Life at this level consists largely of birds and insects. Butterflies seldom leave the treetops. Galagos (or bushbabies) are active at night. Hawk eagles and other raptors prey on species from the canopy, while swifts spend all their time in the air at speeds of up to 160 km/hr (100 mph) in pursuit of their insect diet.

Morpho butterfly
Morpho didius

Demidoff's bushbaby
Galago demidovii

Flying fox
Pteropus giganteus

Gray parrot
Psittacus erithacus

Royal python
Python regius

Flying squirrel
Anomalurus erythronotus

Gold Coast turaco
Tauraco persa

Chameleon
Chameleo chameleon

Chimpanzee
Pan troglodytes

Buttressed trunks are striking features of many trees. The buttresses are thin, triangular plates of hardwood that help to support the shallow-rooted tree and prevent it from being blown down by strong winds.

The locomotion of animals that spend most of their time in trees is dependent on the way their limbs have adapted to this arboreal life. This is exemplified by the South American mammals shown below. The marmoset, anteater and sloth all have hooked paws and long claws. The loose-jointed spider monkey, unlike monkeys in Africa and Asia, has a very long prehensile tail, and a sensitive pad on the underside of its tip makes the tail an extra limb for swinging through the trees.

Toco toucan
Ramphastos toco

The large, decurved beaks of toucans and hornbills allow them to pick fruit and nuts from the outer branches of trees with ease. Despite their similar bills, however, the two groups of birds are unrelated and have different distributions. Toucans live in the forests of Latin America, whereas hornbills inhabit those of Africa and Asia.

Rhinoceros hornbill
Buceros rhinoceros

Cotton-top tamarin
Saguinus oedipus

Lesser anteater
Tamandua tetradactyla

Maned sloth
Bradypus torquatus

Woolly spider monkey
Brachyteles arachnoides

canopy. They do not need to fly far for this diet and have small wings and legs well suited to hopping or climbing along branches. Their beaks are short and curved—perfectly adapted for eating fruit. Bats, flying squirrels, tree frogs, snakes and geckos are plentiful. Insects, including the world's largest species, also abound.

Many mammals that spend some time on the ground have some adaptation for climbing trees; leopards, jaguars, smaller cats, rodents and some insect eaters such as the pangolins of Asia and Africa can climb reasonably well. Most tree dwellers, however, live almost permanent lives at much greater heights in the middle canopy and above. The majority of tree dwellers are branch runners, including opossums, tree kangaroos, lemurs, squirrels or scaly anteaters, which progress on all fours on the upper surface of branches. In contrast, sloths move suspended beneath the branches by their powerful, incurved claws, and bats hang upside down by their hind limbs when at rest. Certain apes and monkeys are brachiators—they use their long arms to swing rapidly from branch to branch and from tree to tree, holding on with great ease. Many monkeys make use of their tails for balance while resting or eating and, in New World species, as a fifth limb to grasp branches when moving or gathering leaves, fruit or nuts.

Life on the ground
The only animals found in very large numbers on the ground are ants and termites, which are adapted to the high humidity and comparative darkness of the forest floor. Other ground-living species include amphibians and reptiles such as snakes and tortoises. Some forest mammals tend to be smaller than their cousins inhabiting the treeless grasslands, adapting to a size more convenient for life among the trees. For example, the forest elephant of Zaire is smaller than the African bush elephant, and forest buffaloes are smaller than those that inhabit open country.

Few people ever see the large number of animals of the tropical rainforest since most are nocturnal, very shy or are hidden by excellent camouflage. Nonetheless, each species has its own important niche and plays a vital role in a carefully controlled ecosystem, now increasingly threatened by the activities of man.

Man and the Tropical Rainforests

Every three seconds a portion of original rainforest the size of a football field disappears as man fells the trees and extends his cultivation. Although tropical conditions allow rapid regrowth of secondary forest, the loss of primary forest is destroying thousands of plant and animal species that will never again be seen on Earth. Even by conservative estimates, it is likely that all the world's primary tropical forest will have disappeared within 85 years unless the trend is reversed.

The activities of man have only recently begun to threaten the tropical rainforest. Since pre-historic times, forests have offered shelter to people who, lacking any knowledge of agriculture, have existed as hunters and gatherers. They used only stone and wooden weapons such as bows and arrows to kill their animal prey, and collected berries, fruit and honey from their surroundings. Their influence on the forest environment was minimal and today a few races such as African pygmies and the Punans of Borneo still live in such a simple state of balance with nature. The Punans, for example, have no permanent homes, but use leaves and branches to construct temporary shelters that are used for only a few weeks before being abandoned. The pygmies build similar homes.

Shifting agriculture

Most forest dwellers, however, live in more permanent settlements and grow most of their food in forest clearings they have made. Such people are expert at chopping down trees in order to set fire to them, and this "slash-and-burn" farming results in small areas littered with charred logs and stumps whose ashes enrich the ground. Crops such as wild tapioca (cassava or manioc) are widely grown, but after a year or two the soil loses the little fertility it once had so that a new tract of forest has to be cleared and burned. Such shifting agriculture provides food for more than 200 million inhabitants of the Third World. As a farming system it has been used throughout the world for more than 2,000 years. When there were few farmers per kilometer the land was allowed to lie fallow for at least 10 years so that the soil could recover. Today, however, population pressures are so great that fallow periods have been drastically reduced and a swift repetition of slash-and-burn degrades and removes nutrients from the soil.

Effects on world climate

Tropical forest floors seldom have deep layers of humus so that, once trees are removed, the shallow topsoil is exposed and soon becomes eroded. In turn, this reduces the capacity of the ground to retain moisture, and without this sponge-like effect runoff can become very erratic and lead to floods, such as those that frequently occur in India and Bangladesh. Estuary sedimentation is often greatly increased

A DIMINISHING RESOURCE
This idealized tract of rainforest includes many of the activities of man that are daily endangering the survival of the forest. Shifting "slash-and-burn" cultivation and excessive logging present the greatest threats. Antidotes such as reafforestation have so far made very little headway.

Living in harmony with the forest are small groups of hunter gatherers who mainly live on a flesh diet, killing their prey with bows and arrows. Nuts and berries supplement this diet, and leaves gathered from the immediate jungle cover their temporary dome-shaped shelters. These are abandoned as an area becomes exhausted and the tribe moves on. Twenty or so pygmies need about 500 sq km (200 sq miles) to support themselves.

Selective logging by gangs of men seeking out the straightest and most valuable hardwood species has been the most common form of tree extraction, even though 75 percent of the canopy might have to be destroyed to remove just a few important trees. Today heavy axes are being replaced by power saws that have no difficulty in cutting down the large buttresses that were once left behind.

Plantation forestry has made increasing inroads into the forests over the decades. The commercial advantage of products that can be cropped several times during the hardwoods' maturation period is becoming increasingly apparent to farmers in the regions. Many rubber plantations in southeastern Asia consist of small holdings that have tended to encroach upon the forest, and intercropping now takes place between the long-established trees.

Shifting cultivation converts thousands of square kilometers of primary forest to substandard cultivation every year. Forest is cleared by slash-and-burn, the resulting fertile clearing is cropped with staples such as manioc, and then left to degrade to secondary forest once the ash-strewn ground has lost its poor fertility. Inevitably, the ground becomes permanently degraded. One encouraging antidote to the futility of such shifting agriculture is the recent strategy of agroforestry (as used by countries such as Nigeria and Thailand), which encourages the planting of fast-growing trees at the same time as the farmer's normal crops. Such intercropping offers considerable financial incentives to the small itinerant farmer.

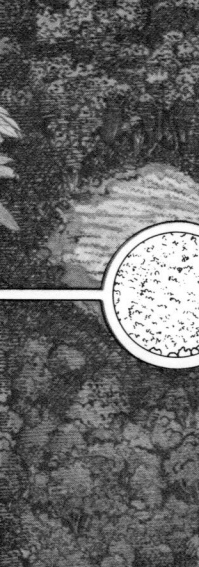

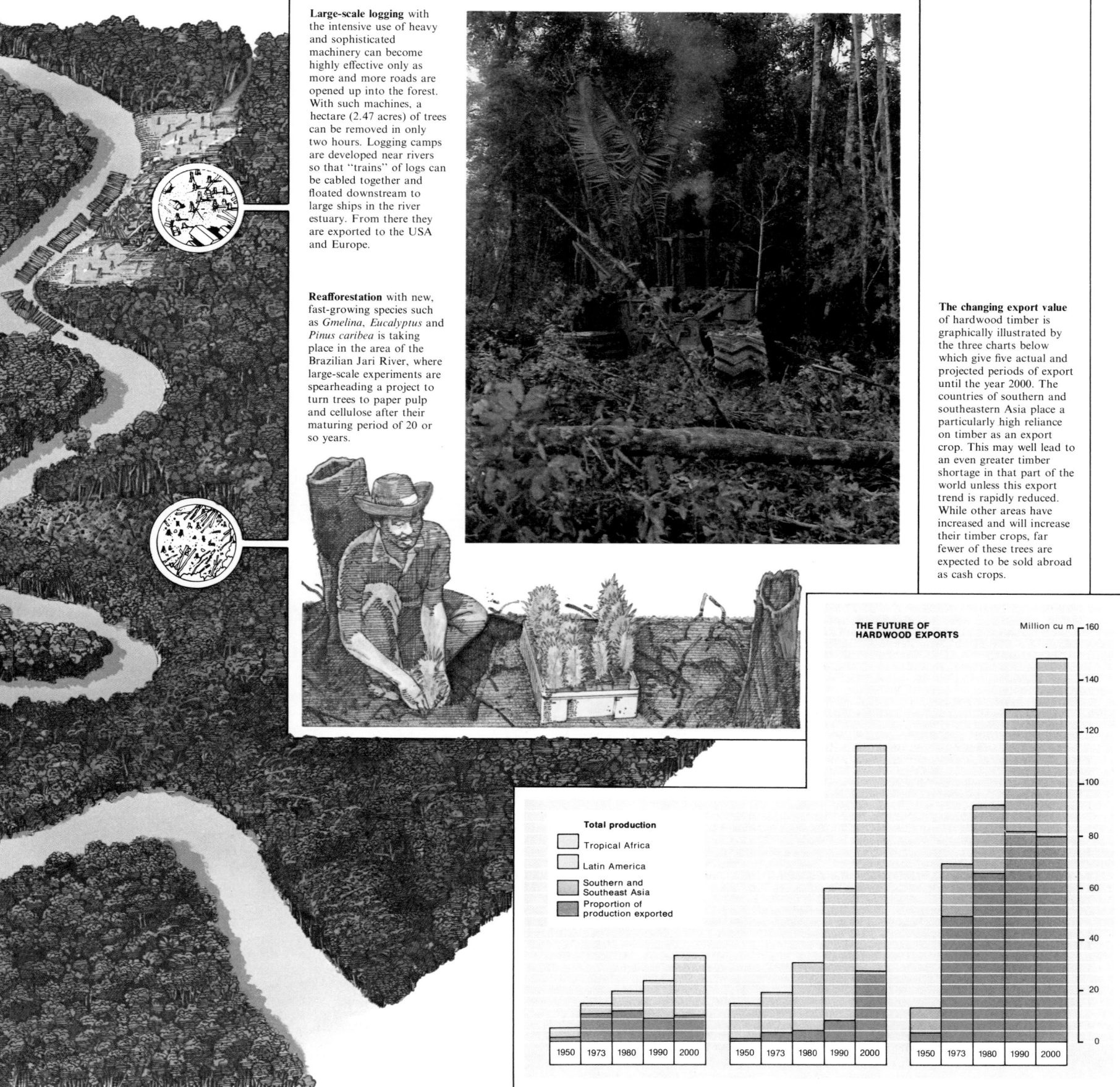

Large-scale logging with the intensive use of heavy and sophisticated machinery can become highly effective only as more and more roads are opened up into the forest. With such machines, a hectare (2.47 acres) of trees can be removed in only two hours. Logging camps are developed near rivers so that "trains" of logs can be cabled together and floated downstream to large ships in the river estuary. From there they are exported to the USA and Europe.

Reafforestation with new, fast-growing species such as *Gmelina*, *Eucalyptus* and *Pinus caribea* is taking place in the area of the Brazilian Jari River, where large-scale experiments are spearheading a project to turn trees to paper pulp and cellulose after their maturing period of 20 or so years.

The changing export value of hardwood timber is graphically illustrated by the three charts below which give five actual and projected periods of export until the year 2000. The countries of southern and southeastern Asia place a particularly high reliance on timber as an export crop. This may well lead to an even greater timber shortage in that part of the world unless this export trend is rapidly reduced. While other areas have increased and will increase their timber crops, far fewer of these trees are expected to be sold abroad as cash crops.

THE FUTURE OF HARDWOOD EXPORTS   Million cu m

Total production
- Tropical Africa
- Latin America
- Southern and Southeast Asia
- Proportion of production exported

1950 1973 1980 1990 2000   1950 1973 1980 1990 2000   1950 1973 1980 1990 2000

as the forest topsoil is simply washed away by torrential rain. In parts of Asia, deforestation has caused changes in water flow that have interfered with the production of new high-yield rice crops.

Tropical forests contain an enormous store of carbon, and some authorities believe that its release into the air (as carbon dioxide) when the forest is burned down may be as great in volume as that released by the rest of the world's fossil fuels. The higher proportion of carbon dioxide in the atmosphere may lead to an increase in global temperatures, especially at the poles. Trees also release oxygen into the air through photosynthesis, and some scientists have estimated that half of the world's oxygen is derived from this source. Others estimate that half of the rainfall of the Amazon basin is generated by the forest itself, so that any great reduction in tree cover would turn Amazonia into a much drier region.

Threats to Amazonia

Much attention has been paid to the situation of Amazonia, covering as it does some 6.5 million sq km (2½ million sq miles). In an attempt to give better access to timber and mineral reserves, the Brazilian government's building of the TransAmazonian Highway (3,000 km or 1,860 miles long) has opened the way to deforestation, and settlers have been encouraged to make small holdings on the cleared forest beside the road. Between 1966 and 1978, the government calculated that farmers and big business interests had turned 80,000 sq km (31,000 sq miles) of forest into grazing land for 6 million cattle intended for hamburgers. However, like the wholesale extraction of timber, this has proved to be of doubtful economic value. Because costs rise steeply as less accessible areas are tapped, expenses tend to eliminate logging profits.

Threats in Africa

Even greater threats to tropical forest land have come from less cautious and realistic governments, such as that of Ivory Coast. There neither shifting agriculture nor excessive logging for valuable export sales appear to be under any sort of control. Accordingly, between 1966 and 1974, the area of forest declined from 156,000 sq km (60,000 sq miles) to 54,000 sq km (20,000 sq miles), much of the latter being secondary forest that can never be returned to its original status. Like many other developing countries, Ivory Coast has been more keen to cut down and export its profitable timbers than to think about protecting its invaluable forest environment. Inevitably, forest farmers move into cleared areas and often establish plantation cash crops such as coffee, cocoa and rubber, while the establishment of national parks to curtail depletion has often had very little profitable effect. The Malaysian rainforest is also disappearing rapidly, through widescale logging and open-cast mining for bauxite (aluminum ore).

A large proportion of the world's rainforest occurs in tropical countries faced with severe problems of population control. It is therefore inevitable that the pressures on such forests will be great. Human interference does more than merely destroy the primary forest, to be replaced in time by secondary growth; more importantly, the wholesale removal of trees also drastically reduces the vast genetic reservoir contained in the number of plant and animal species the forests harbor. This in itself is a sound ecological argument for preserving forests and for reversing current trends towards monoculture in the tropics. All the warnings about forest depletion appear to be clear, yet there seems little hope that man will heed them until it is too late.

Monsoon Regions

The word monsoon often conjures up the image of torrential rain and steaming tropical jungles. Yet such a view is misleading, for very great contrasts occur in the regions of the tropical world with a monsoon climate. What distinguishes monsoon regions is not so much the amount of rainfall or the permanently high temperatures, but the dramatic contrast between seasons, with an extended dry season as an essential feature. And in fact the word monsoon derives from the Arabic word for season.

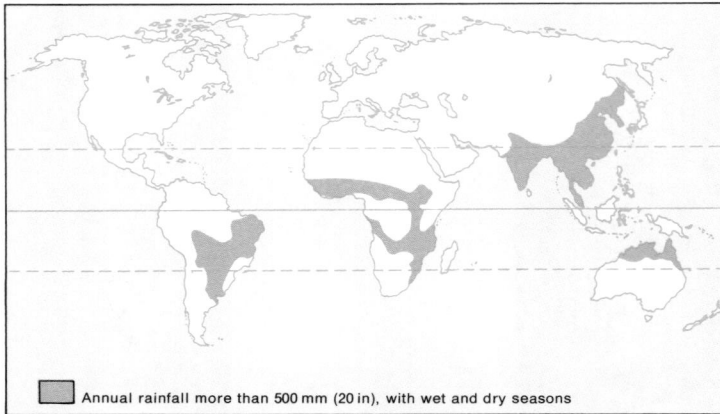

THE SEASON OF RAIN
Life in the monsoon regions balances on the expectation of seasonal heavy rain. In much of India, for instance, 85 percent of the annual rainfall occurs during the limited monsoon periods, and humans as well as plants and animals depend on it wholly. About half the world's people live in these regions, in communities whose rhythm of life necessarily reflects the rains' seasonal nature.

This contrast between wet and dry seasons reflects the reversals of winds over sea and land, which in the northern hemisphere blow from the northeast in the dry winter season, and from the southwest in the wet summer periods.

The monsoon regions occur most widely in southern, southeastern and eastern Asia to the south of latitude 25°N, and in western and central Africa north of the Equator, but there are also smaller regions with a characteristically monsoon climate in eastern Africa, northern Australia and central America. Despite the similar overall climatic pattern, however, the monsoon regions are otherwise very diverse.

Before human settlement the original vegetation of the monsoon regions reflected the dominance of an extended dry season followed by a period of violent rainfall. Typical forest cover was provided by the sal (*Shorea robusta*) deciduous forest, which adjusts to extended periods of moisture deficiency by shedding its leaves. However, within the monsoon region rainfall varies from 200 mm (8 in) a year to more than 20,000 mm (800 in), and the rainy periods may vary between three and nine months.

The range of vegetation found in the monsoon regions reflects this diversity. Where tropical rainforest alters to monsoon forest, as in eastern Java, there is a sharp fall in the total number of plant and animal species, and species adapted to endure seasonal drought begin to be seen. At the other extreme of rainfall the forest thins and shades into semidesert vegetation in India's northwest. But if there is a "type" of monsoon vegetation it is tropical deciduous forest, with sal as the dominant species.

As well as contrasts in climate, the monsoon regions also exhibit pronounced changes in temperature and vegetation as a result of variations in altitude. The Western Ghats of India and the foothills of the Himalayas in Assam both rise to more than 2,500 m (8,200 ft). Temperatures decrease sharply at such altitudes with corresponding changes in vegetation. In southern India on the Nilgiri Hills a wet temperate forest is characteristic, with an intermingling of temperate and tropical species. Magnolias, planes and elms all grow there.

Agriculture in monsoon regions
Despite its extensive area there is no part of the monsoon world that is untouched by man and by man's activities. In southern Asia, agricultural activity can be traced back at least 5,000 years, and there have been agricultural settlements throughout the monsoon regions for at least 1,500 years. Man's activity and the grazing of domesticated animals have interfered with, and progressively modified, the natural vegetation. The range of species indicates that, in the whole of the monsoon biome, there is now virtually no primary forest left. The pace of man's interference has speeded up considerably over the last 100 years. As a result, less than 10 percent of the land in southern Asia is now forested, and other parts of the monsoon

Many parts of the world experience "monsoon" winds, blowing from sea to land in summer, and from land to sea in winter; but typical monsoon vegetation is most clearly seen in the regions of southeastern Asia and the Indian subcontinent. In climatic terms, however, the monsoon circulation of seasonal wind reversals, with wetter summers and dry winters, also affects considerable areas of Africa, South America and northern Australia.

☐ Annual rainfall more than 500 mm (20 in), with wet and dry seasons

regions are similarly losing their forest cover.

Many of today's farming methods incorporate traditional cultivation practices, but there have also been very significant changes in recent decades. Traditional agriculture in the monsoon regions has been developed to take into account the seasonal nature of its rainfall pattern and the total rainfall received. The fundamental role of water throughout the region and the absence of low temperatures have placed great importance on either cultivating crops that can tolerate the seasonal rainfall pattern, or on providing irrigation.

Through most of southern Asia, overwhelmingly the most populous of the monsoon regions, the most important single crop is rice, which covers about one-third of the total cultivated area. Rice needs a great deal of water and for this reason is grown mainly in areas of high irrigation, such as the delta lands of the southern and eastern coasts of India, and in areas where rainfall is more than 1,500 mm (59 in) a year. Its cultivation creates a very distinctive landscape as a result of the fact that rice must spend much of its growing period with a few centimeters of water over the soil.

Rice cultivation gives the monsoon regions their characteristic pattern of paddy fields, but other cereal crops such as wheat, the millets and sorghum are also very important. These can tolerate far drier conditions than can rice and occur in areas such as central India or upland Thailand, where uncertain and less abundant rainfall puts a premium on drought tolerance.

Even with traditional crops, man has often interfered extensively with the environment in order to increase yields and attempt to guarantee successful cropping. Traditional irrigation schemes range from diverting rivers at times of flood, in order to lead water to dry land, to digging wells and building small reservoirs. But recent technological developments have brought a new dimension to agricultural activity in the monsoon regions. Large-scale dam and irrigation canal schemes have become important in Africa as well as in monsoon Asia. The introduction and speed of electric or diesel "pumpsets" have transformed well irrigation in regions with extensive groundwater. The

Heat differences in the atmosphere cause the seasonal wind reversals (left) characteristic of monsoon circulation. In January the northern hemisphere is tilted away from the sun, and cold, dry winds blow from the central Asian landmass toward the Equator. Here they change direction (an effect of the Earth's rotation), converge with other winds, and drop their rain. In July the situation is reversed when the heated Asian landmass attracts a flow of cooler air from the equatorial oceans, which moves northward with the sun. The moist air condenses on reaching land, and the monsoon rains descend.

Wind convergence zone
January

Wind convergence zone
July

reliable water supply that irrigation can give has brought in its train the opportunity for farmers to adopt a wide range of new farming practices. Chemical fertilizers and new strains of seed have made possible great increases in the productivity of the land in many parts of the monsoon regions, but their use is generally restricted to areas of reliable water supply.

Subsistence cultivation over thousands of years has been by far the most important element in the transformation of the landscape and vegetation of the monsoon world, but the introduction of plantation cultivation during the last centuries has also had a major effect. Tea plantations, for instance, have led to the almost total replacement of natural vegetation in the hills of southern India and Sri Lanka.

Populations in all of the countries of the monsoon regions are rapidly increasing, and demands for economic development are constantly growing, placing increasing pressures on the environment, pressures which to date have seemed almost irresistible.

DISAPPEARING ANIMALS
The dwindling wildlife of southeastern Asia includes species that may be regarded locally as pests—a fact that makes their protection difficult outside game reserves. Animals such as the tiger and the wild pig are doubly threatened as human cultivation spreads into the natural habitat: their hunting and foraging grounds are reduced, and their destruction of crops or livestock provides villagers with an obvious incentive for killing them in order to protect their own livelihoods.

Tiger
Panthera tigris

Wild pig
Sus scrofa

SELF-SUFFICIENCY IN CHINA
Local materials are turned into saleable products at a ratan factory in southern China. This factory is not owned by the state but by the village-sized brigade responsible for the manufacturing. The brigade functions as a smaller economic unit within the Ting Chow people's commune of 20 to 30 villages, but is encouraged to act independently, owning what it creates. The commune takes care of such matters as waterways—it contains 82 km (51 miles) of canals.

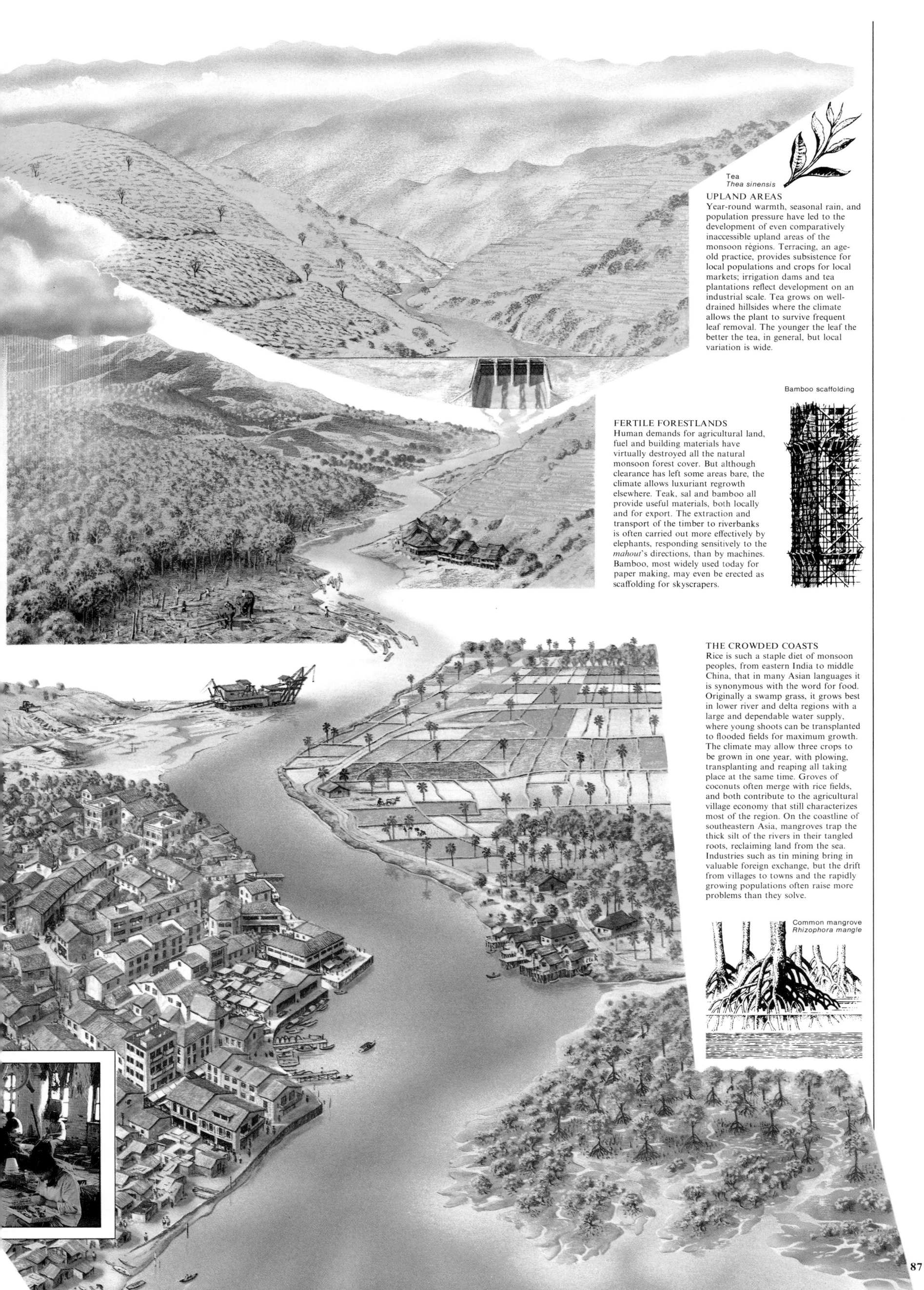

Tea
Thea sinensis

UPLAND AREAS

Year-round warmth, seasonal rain, and population pressure have led to the development of even comparatively inaccessible upland areas of the monsoon régions. Terracing, an age-old practice, provides subsistence for local populations and crops for local markets; irrigation dams and tea plantations reflect development on an industrial scale. Tea grows on well-drained hillsides where the climate allows the plant to survive frequent leaf removal. The younger the leaf the better the tea, in general, but local variation is wide.

Bamboo scaffolding

FERTILE FORESTLANDS

Human demands for agricultural land, fuel and building materials have virtually destroyed all the natural monsoon forest cover. But although clearance has left some areas bare, the climate allows luxuriant regrowth elsewhere. Teak, sal and bamboo all provide useful materials, both locally and for export. The extraction and transport of the timber to riverbanks is often carried out more effectively by elephants, responding sensitively to the *mahout*'s directions, than by machines. Bamboo, most widely used today for paper making, may even be erected as scaffolding for skyscrapers.

THE CROWDED COASTS

Rice is such a staple diet of monsoon peoples, from eastern India to middle China, that in many Asian languages it is synonymous with the word for food. Originally a swamp grass, it grows best in lower river and delta regions with a large and dependable water supply, where young shoots can be transplanted to flooded fields for maximum growth. The climate may allow three crops to be grown in one year, with plowing, transplanting and reaping all taking place at the same time. Groves of coconuts often merge with rice fields, and both contribute to the agricultural village economy that still characterizes most of the region. On the coastline of southeastern Asia, mangroves trap the thick silt of the rivers in their tangled roots, reclaiming land from the sea. Industries such as tin mining bring in valuable foreign exchange, but the drift from villages to towns and the rapidly growing populations often raise more problems than they solve.

Common mangrove
Rhizophora mangle

87

Mountain Regions

A quarter of Earth's land surface lies at heights of 1,000 m (3,300 ft) or more above sea level. But the highland regions are thinly populated by man, who is, generally speaking, a lowland dweller (most major population centers are less than 100 m (330 ft) above sea level). Some formerly lowland animals have fled from man to the harsh refuge of the mountains, joining with specially adapted plants and wildlife, but today man himself is finding the highland regions increasingly useful and desirable.

The world's highest mountain peaks rise to almost 9.6 km (6 miles) above sea level, but these heights are small compared to the total diameter of the Earth. The rough surface of an orange would have mountains higher than the Himalayas if scaled up to world size. But mountain environments, although they vary enormously from system to system, all tend to demand remarkable endurance and adaptability from the plants and animals that inhabit them.

Altitude rather than geological variation determines conditions of life on mountains. The temperature falls by 2°C with every 300 m (3.4°F every 1,000 ft)—hence the snowcapped beauty of the heights—and life forms must be adapted to increasingly harsh conditions as height increases. As a result, zones of different life occur at different levels, from tropical forests (at the base of low-latitude mountains) to arctic-type life in the zone of ice and snow at the summit. The latitude of the mountain affects the heights to which these zones extend: trees occur at 2,300 m (7,500 ft) in the southern Alps, whereas farther north, in central Sweden, trees cannot survive above 1,000 m (3,300 ft).

Life at the top

The specially adapted plant and animal life of the mountains occurs above the tree line, for here the variations in living conditions reach their greatest extremes. A plant that has found a foothold on a bare rock face may have to endure intense heat, even where the average temperature is low, when the summer sun blazing through the clear air warms the slabs to tropical temperatures. But when that part of the mountain falls into shadow, the temperature decreases very rapidly, often assisted by the high winds that blow almost constantly throughout the year in many mountain areas.

Soil necessary for plant life develops with the breakdown of the rock through the agency of water, frost and ice. Lichens, whose acids may aid in this destruction, can survive at very high levels, and as they die may add some humus to the newly forming soil. This may first accumulate in sheltered places where plants requiring high humidity, such as mosses and filmy ferns, are found. Flowering plants follow where a greater depth of soil has formed, although some grow in cracks between rocks.

Flowering plants of the mountains all tend to be small (to avoid harsh, drying winds), deep rooted (to anchor the plant firmly), and abundantly flowering (to benefit from the short growing season). Many unrelated species have independently developed a similar cushion form. This enables them to shed excess rainwater easily and to retain heat better in a tight tangle of stems and leaves, where the temperature may be more than 10°C (18°F) higher than that of the outside air. Insects sheltering there are well placed to perform the vital task of pollination. But pollinating insects are relatively rare at high altitudes, and some mountain plants are wind pollinated. The brilliant color of many others may be to increase their attractiveness for the insects. Nearly all upland plants are very slow-growing perennials, and many are evergreen, with leaves that exploit all available light.

Some large animals, such as the ibex or the Rocky Mountain goat, are adapted to spend their lives among the rocks and slopes. These stocky creatures, with hooves that act rather like suction cups, produce their summer young in the security of the heights, although in winter they descend to the shelter of the upper forests. Among smaller mammals, most of which are rodents, some dig burrows in which they hibernate through the winter. Others have very thick insulating coats, and may stay awake through the coldest weather in burrows under the snow.

Refugees from the lowlands

Some mountain animals, particularly carnivorous mammals and birds, have been driven by human persecution into remote mountain fastnesses. Many birds of prey, which could otherwise survive well in lowland areas, have their last strongholds among the mountains. They survive by feeding on small rodents, many of which are extremely wary. Some upland birds feed on insects or on seeds, but their number is comparatively small. The Alpine chough is one of the most interesting of mountain birds, for it has learned to find food among the scraps provided by climbers and skiers, whom it often follows to very high altitudes.

Insects and other small invertebrates, like their Arctic counterparts, may take several years to mature. Some are wingless, and many tend to fly low in order not to be blown away from their home range. Jumping spiders have been seen at heights of 6,700 m (22,000 ft) on the slopes of Mount Everest, where they exist on small flies and springtails, but even above this level springtails and glacier "fleas" occur where there are no plants, apparently surviving on wind-blown insects and pollen grains.

Man and the mountains

The remote beauty of the mountains has led many peoples to identify them as the abode of the gods, but man himself prefers to live in the more convenient lowlands. The rarefied atmosphere of the heights makes physical work difficult, although some mountain-dwelling peoples have developed adaptations of the blood system to enable them to carry scarce oxygen more efficiently. The short growing season prevents cultivation of all but the hardiest cereal crops, and most uplanders rely on their livestock—cattle, sheep, llamas or yaks—for their existence. The animals are often driven to high pasture during the summer, descending to the valleys in the winter.

Modern, urbanized man finds the beauty and freshness of mountains increasingly attractive. Climbers have invaded most of the world's mountain regions, and in winter hosts of skiers flock to the resorts. Many important wildlife sanctuaries and national parks, particularly in the United States, are in mountain areas.

Lowland populations often rely on the pure mountain streams for both water and energy. Whole upland valleys are sometimes flooded to store water for distant conurbations. And the forceful flow of the water as it descends from the snow-fed heights is frequently harnessed to produce electricity for entire regions hundreds of kilometers away. The clear mountain air also offers the best conditions for astronomical observation, and most observatories today are built in dry, cloudless mountain areas.

LIFE ON THE HEIGHTS

Mountain climates become colder the higher one goes. This change in conditions creates distinctive horizontal zones of plant and animal life, although the pattern may vary according to the latitude and aspect of a mountain. Some life forms manage to eke out a precarious existence even on the roof of the world. Lower down, the brief growing season encourages a short burst of plant and animal activity above the timber line, conspicuous for the brightly colored summer flowers. Man mainly inhabits the lower slopes and valleys. He exploits mountain resources but rarely lives on the inhospitable heights.

Many peoples have believed that the gods have their abodes in the high places of the world. Tibet (above), one of the highest and most mountainous of all countries, has a large number of religious sites. Modern man also finds the clear, dry air suitable for the study of heavenly bodies: most modern observatories, such as Kitt Peak, USA (right), are built on mountain sites far from cities.

Activity in Earth's crust has produced mountains in every continent (left). Some thrust up sharply, while older mountains have been eroded to rounded shapes. The Scottish Highlands were made by mountain-building forces 400 million years ago (170 million years before the Appalachians and the Urals). The Rockies are 70 million years old and the Alps 15 million years old.

Ancient mountains (Caledonian orogenesis)	Intermediate mountains (Hercynian orogenesis)	Recent mountains (Alpine orogenesis)

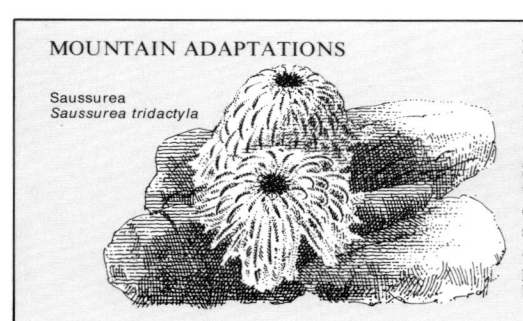

MOUNTAIN ADAPTATIONS

Saussurea
Saussurea tridactyla

Alpine soldanella
Soldanella alpina

Ingenious adaptations to harsh mountain conditions have been evolved by many plants, most of which have tiny cells with thick sap that does not freeze easily. Saussurea masks itself with white hair to reduce evaporation from the leaf surface. Alpine soldanellas are active even under snow, pushing up their flowers before the thaw.

| 7,600 m |
| 25,000 ft |

SNOWBOUND PEAKS

Perpetual snow, violent winds and atmospheric dryness impose harsh conditions on life in the high Himalayas. But wind-blown organic debris from the plains does support some life forms—springtails, flies and jumping spiders—where the air is too dry to allow even lichens to survive. Lower down, a cushion plant may take root in a rock-base niche, but there is little other vegetation. Among birds, the Alpine chough is a scavenger that has followed Everest expeditions to heights of 7,900 m (26,000 ft).

Jumping spider
Salticus scenicus

Alpine chough
Pyrrhocorax graculus

Cushion pink
Parrya lanuginosa

| 4,900 m |
| 16,000 ft |

Fly
Diptera sp

Primula
Primula rosea

Royle's pika
Ochotona roylei

Blue sheep
Pseudois nayaur

| 4,300 m |
| 14,000 ft |

Himalayan blue poppy
Meconopsis horridula

MOUNTAIN MEADOWS

Between the snow line and the zone of coniferous trees, the Himalayan slopes exhibit a glorious variety of flowering plants during summer. Small and slow growing, these often have bright flowers which attract pollinating insects such as fly-like *Diptera*. The pika and other small, thick-furred rodents are the most common animals, although larger creatures, such as blue (bharal) sheep and yaks, also find summer pasturage at these heights. Snow leopards tend to inhabit the coniferous forests, but they travel up to higher parts to prey on the grazing herds. Few people live within the zone, but some Sherpas take their yak herds as high as 4,600 m (15,000 ft) for summer grazing, and even grow crops of potatoes at this height. Their permanent villages, however, are on the lower alpine slopes.

Domestic yak
Bos grunniens

| 3,700 m |
| 12,000 ft |

Snow leopard
Panthera uncia

| 3,000 m |
| 10,000 ft |

FORESTED SLOPES

Isolated birches mark the tree line—the transition from meadow to coniferous and rhododendron forest. In the upper parts of the forest, trees are dwarfed by cold and lack of moisture, and are twisted and bent from the wind. These low and tangled masses provide shelter for animals such as the Asian black bear and the red panda. Below the conifers lies a zone of broad-leaved evergreens, and in the foothills these in turn give way to tropical monsoon forests of sal trees (*Shorea robusta*) and thickets of bamboo. The raucous flocks of hill mynahs represent just one of the many kinds of birds found in this zone, which has the widest range of wildlife of all the kinds of mountain vegetation. Unfortunately, many species are in danger of extinction, for here man has settled, cut down forests and terraced hillsides to grow crops.

Rhododendron
Rhododendron sp

| 2,400 m |
| 8,000 ft |

Asiatic black bear
Selenarctos thibetanus

| 1,800 m |
| 6,000 ft |

Red panda
Ailurus fulgens

Hill mynah bird
Gracula religiosa

| 1,200 m |
| 4,000 ft |

☐ Permanent snow
☐ Alpine meadows
☒ Isolated birches
■ Coniferous forest
▨ Rhododendron groves
☐ Broadleaved evergreen forest
▨ Bamboo
☐ Tropical monsoon forest

Rocky Mountain goat
Oreamnos americanus

Animals and humans adapt to mountain conditions in many ways. The Rocky Mountain goat (left) has evolved a fleecy undercoat and hooves with concave pads to grip on any surface. Comparison of the blood counts (right) of a lowlander (A) and an Andean (B) shows how the latter has a higher total content and more red cells.

liters   pints

The golden eagle *Aquila chrysaetos* (left) epitomizes the grandeur of the heights. Although it lives and nests in remote regions, it could equally well find its food in the lowlands were it not for human competition. An eagle's territory may cover 130 sq km (50 sq miles): it preys on small mammals and even (it is believed) on young deer and lambs. It mates for life and returns each year to the same nest.

Freshwater Environments

Broad, muddy rivers, fast-running streams, miniature ponds and deep, ancient lakes all provide their own distinctive environments for populations of animals and colonies of aquatic plants. And in spite of the fact that these, the world's freshwater systems, contain only a minute proportion of the Earth's total supplies of water, the remarkable variety and richness of the wildlife they support make them among the most valuable and significant of all the world's natural habitats.

Fresh water is never really pure for, like sea water, and indeed like all other natural waters, it contains various dissolved minerals. Fresh water differs from seawater only in the relatively low concentrations of the minerals it contains. But these mineral traces are extremely important; they provide essential nutrients without which freshwater plants could not exist. And without plant life, there would be virtually no animal life either.

Not all parts of every freshwater system are rich in both plants and animals. Large, deep lakes are very similar to oceans—no light can penetrate their gloomy depths, and few plants can live in these conditions. The surface waters, on the other hand, where light is plentiful, teem with microscopic floating plants, mainly single-celled algae such as desmids and diatoms. The edges of lakes provide a different set of conditions again, for here the water is shallow and light can penetrate right through it. Plants can take root in the silt on the bottom, grow up through the water and thrust their leaves out into the light and air. Edges of lakes and, for the same reasons, the waters of small ponds are usually full of such plant life, which in turn supports many freshwater animals.

Running waters
Just as the still waters of lakes and ponds offer a variety of habitats, so the running waters of rivers support many different forms of life, each adapted to the particular conditions of its environment. In the upper reaches, where rivers are scarcely more than upland streams, water is fast flowing and clear of silt. Few plants, except close-clinging mosses, can gain a hold on the bare stony bottom and most of the fish are well muscled and strong bodied to enable them to withstand the constant tug of the current. As a river swells to form a mature lowland water course, however, it becomes slower moving and the water is warmer and richer in nutrients. Plants grow readily in these lower reaches and provide a supply of food for aquatic animals.

With such a wide range of conditions, freshwater environments support an enormous variety of animal life—insects, fishes, amphibians, reptiles, mammals and birds. In some ways insects are the most important of all these creatures: freshwater systems contain more insects and other invertebrates, representing a greater variety of species, than any other kind of animal. Furthermore, these, the smallest representatives of the freshwater animal world, provide one of the most important links in the complex freshwater food chain.

Insects may be the most numerous, but fishes are probably the most familiar of all freshwater creatures, and they certainly show some of the greatest varieties of adaptations to the many different habitats. Their sizes vary from the tiny, 14 mm ($\frac{1}{2}$ in) of the virtually transparent dwarf goby fish found in small streams and lakes in the Philippines to the 4 m (14 ft) of the arapaima found in deep rivers in tropical South America. Their feeding habits vary from those of the ferocious carnivorous piranha of South America to those of the North American paddle fish which, although more than three times the size of the largest piranha, feed solely on microscopic organisms which they filter from the water with their specially adapted throats.

The breeding habits of freshwater fish also vary widely, from the carefully maternal instincts of the African mouthbreeding cichlids—these retain the developing eggs safely in their mouths until the offspring hatch—to the rather more common ejection of eggs into the water, where their fertilization and survival is simply left to chance. Other adaptations include the ability to breathe air (as does the African lungfish), to leap waterfalls (a common practice among migrating salmon) and to emit an electric shock of up to 600 volts (an adaptation of the South American electric eel).

Creatures of the water's edge
Of all the other major groups of animals, amphibians (such as frogs and toads) are probably the most reliant on freshwater systems. Because their skins must not dry out and they have to lay their eggs in water, few amphibians can venture far from the water's edge. And because they cannot tolerate the salt in seawater (it causes them to lose their body fluids through their skins) they are totally dependent upon fresh water for their existence. Reptiles, rather less typical of freshwater environments, range in size from miniature North American terrapins to the giant crocodiles that live along the banks of the Nile. Freshwater mammals, on the other hand, with the considerable exception of the hippopotamus, all tend to be rather small creatures such as otters, beavers, coypus, aquatic moles and water shrews.

Birds are another important group of freshwater creatures. Although few birds are truly aquatic an enormous number of species live in or near freshwater systems and take advantage of the various food supplies: the plants and fish within the waters; the bankside vegetation and small animal life; and the many forms of freshwater insects. Marshes and swamps, for example, provide some of the richest bird habitats in the world.

Also numbered among the species dependent on Earth's freshwater systems is man. And although strictly a nonaquatic, land-living animal, man uses more fresh water than any other creature. His needs seem to be inexhaustible as he harnesses, channels, diverts and often pollutes freshwater systems throughout the world. Unfortunately, the vast requirements of the human race are not always compatible with the rather more humble needs of all other species that depend upon fresh water.

Volume of Lakes in cu km (cu miles)	Discharge of Rivers in cu m (cu ft) per second
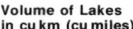Huron, North America 3,447 (827)	Ganges, Asia 18,689 (660,000)
Nyasa, Africa 8,373 (2,009)	Brahmaputra, Asia 19,822 (700,000)
Superior, North America 12,153 (2,916)	Yangtze, Asia 21,804 (770,000)
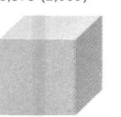Tanganyika, Africa 19,418 (4,659)	Congo, Africa 39,644 (1,400,000)
Baikal, Asia 23,260 (5,581)	Amazon, South America 212,376 (7,500,000)

The five largest lakes in the world hold more than 53% of all fresh water that flows over the land. The rest of the world's lakes account for another 45%.

The world's largest river, the Amazon, discharges more than one-fifth of all fresh water that flows from the mouths of the world's rivers into the oceans.

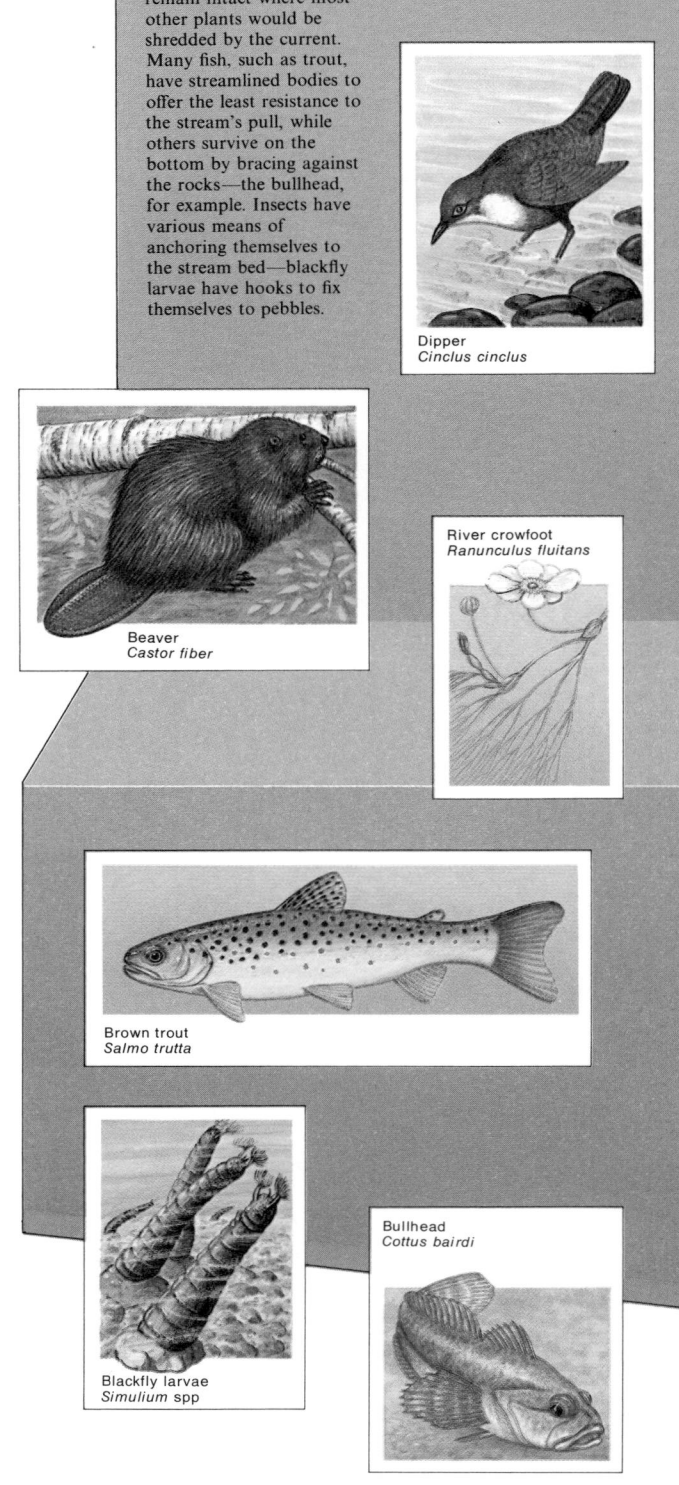

THE UPPER REACHES
Here, water flows rapidly. Tumbling over bare rocks and stones, it is chilly, oxygen-rich and free of silt. Bird life attracted to these reaches includes the sure-footed dipper, which walks the stream bed hunting for caddis larvae. Slightly farther downstream, but where the river is still narrow and easily dammed, beavers are found. Few plants can live within the water, but river crowfoot has feathery underwater leaves that remain intact where most other plants would be shredded by the current. Many fish, such as trout, have streamlined bodies to offer the least resistance to the stream's pull, while others survive on the bottom by bracing against the rocks—the bullhead, for example. Insects have various means of anchoring themselves to the stream bed—blackfly larvae have hooks to fix themselves to pebbles.

Dipper
Cinclus cinclus

Beaver
Castor fiber

River crowfoot
Ranunculus fluitans

Brown trout
Salmo trutta

Blackfly larvae
Simulium spp

Bullhead
Cottus bairdi

Crayfish
Procambarus sp

Blindfish
Typhlichthys sp

Cave salamander
Proteus anguinus

THE LIFE OF A RIVER

As a river makes its way from its upland source to the sea, it gradually changes its character. And at every stage in its progress, the animals and plants that inhabit the riverbanks and the waters reflect these changes by their adaptations to their environments. Most distinctive and dramatic are those adaptations produced in the wildlife of the upper and lower river reaches.

African spoonbill
Platalea alba

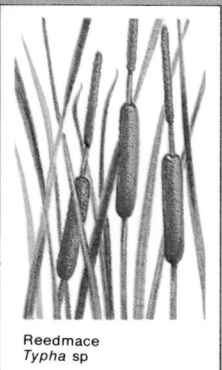

Reedmace
Typha sp

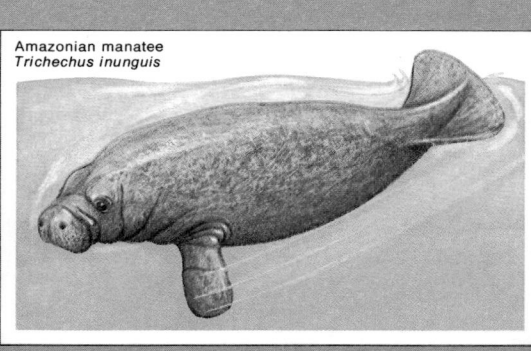

Amazonian manatee
Trichechus inunguis

White ramshorn snail
Planorbis albus

DARK WATERS

Underground rivers that flow through many of the world's cave systems support surprising numbers of creatures that have adapted to the permanent darkness. Many of these, such as the American cave crayfish, have lost the coloration of their surface-living kin. Some, such as Kentucky blind fishes, no longer possess eyes. Some salamanders are sighted and black when born, but become blind and colorless by adulthood.

THE LOWER REACHES

The slowly flowing river and its muddy banks are rich in animals and plants. Many birds live along the water's edge; spoonbills wade in the shallows, filtering food from the water with their beaks. The banks, fringed with reedmaces and other plants, provide habitats for many reptiles, such as the American painted turtle, and mammals, such as the platypus. Plants also grow on the water—they range from large waterlilies to tiny algae that are food for river fishes: Africa's upside-down-feeding catfish, for example. In these waters, mammals as well as fish are to be found—Amazonian manatees live entirely aquatic lives. The plentiful river plants, such as curled pondweed, provide food for water snails and other herbivores, and cover for predators such as pike. Crustacea and insects living in the silt of the riverbed are food for bottom-feeding fish such as the strange-looking North American paddle fish.

Southern painted turtle
Chrysemys picta dorsalis

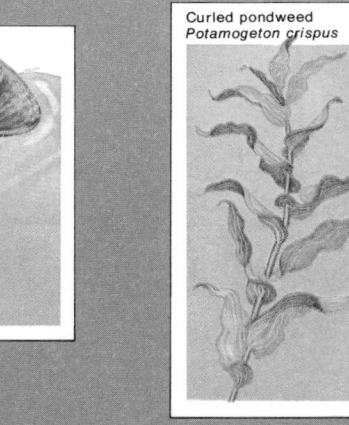

Platypus
Ornithorhynchus anatinus

Curled pondweed
Potamogeton crispus

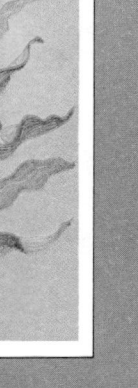

Pike
Esox lucius

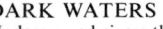

Paddle fish
Polydon spathula

LAKES: CHANGE AND EVOLUTION

No two lakes are alike: each is virtually a self-contained world for its population of aquatic animals and plants. Furthermore, no individual lake remains the same for long: in every lake, slow, inexorable changes in conditions are gradually but constantly changing the balance of species inhabiting the lake bed, the bankside and the water.

Changing conditions may be caused by one of several processes. Accumulating sediments, one of the most common of these processes, may eliminate a lake altogether. The water becomes shallower as sediments thicken (1) and these sediments are then added to and consolidated by water plants taking root. Ultimately, land plants (2) invade the area.

Lakes develop their own peculiar species when the aquatic wildlife that evolves within them has no means of migrating to other freshwater systems to interbreed. The world's only existing species of freshwater seal, for example, is found in just one lake—isolated Lake Baikal in Asia.

Baikal seal
Phoca sibirica

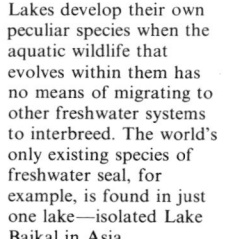

Waterlily
Nymphaea sp

African catfish
Synodontis batensoda

WETLANDS

Marshes and swamps are the richest of freshwater habitats. Wading birds, such as Asia's painted stork *Ibis leucocephalus* (above), are particularly common. Reptiles include caimans, which lay their eggs in swamps' warm, rotting vegetation. Of the many insects, mosquitoes are probably the most numerous, and of the many fishes, African lungfish are perhaps best adapted to life in wetlands. They survive drought, when marshes dry up, by their ability to breathe air.

Spectacled caiman
Caiman crocodilus

African lungfish
Protopterus annectens

Mosquito
Aedes impiger

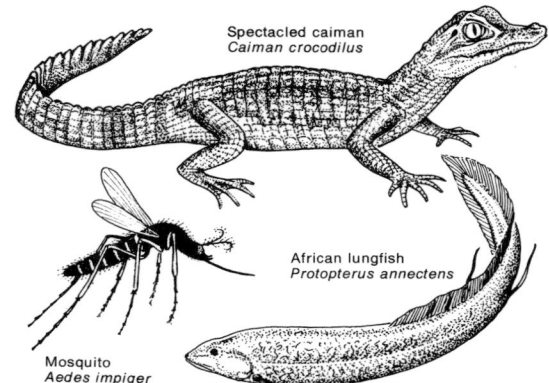

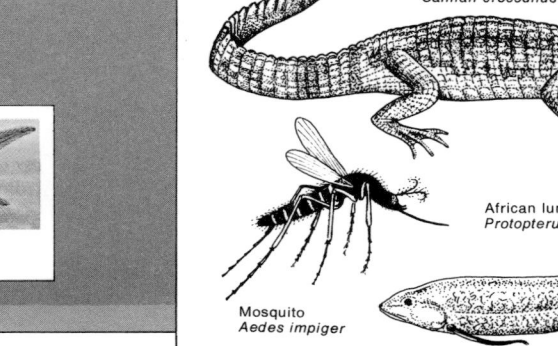

Man and the Freshwater Environments

From earliest times, man has been finding new uses for and making new demands upon the world's freshwater resources. Today, the whole of modern society depends upon a vast supply to serve its agricultural, industrial, domestic and other needs. To meet the ever-growing demand for water, man has performed remarkable engineering feats: altering the courses of rivers, creating and destroying lakes, drowning valleys and tapping water sources that lie deep within the Earth.

Water is essential to human life. Simply to remain alive, an active adult living in a temperate climate needs a liquid intake of about two liters (3½ pints) every day. In warmer climates, the body's fluid requirements are even greater. Consequently, man has always been tied to reliable sources of drinking water—rivers, springs, lakes and ponds—and the availability of these, until very recently, has dictated the routes of all his wanderings and determined the sites of all his settlements.

From the time of the earliest human settlements, however, man has looked upon freshwater systems not simply as a source of drinking water but also as an increasingly useful resource for a multitude of other purposes. Today, water enters into virtually every aspect of modern life, and enormous quantities are used in agriculture, in industry, in the home, in the production of energy, for transport and for recreation.

The farmer's resource

Of all the major activities that rely on fresh water, agriculture is by far the world's largest consumer. In much of Europe and North America, rainfall is usually plentiful and lack of sufficient water for crops is rarely a problem. But in other parts of the world the climate simply does not produce enough rainfall and water shortages are a perennial problem. There, irrigation is not just a sophisticated technique to improve the yields and increase the varieties of crops grown; it is, and always has been, an essential element of agriculture.

Methods of irrigation range from small-scale devices—such as miniature windpumps—used in many developing countries simply to lift water from rivers for bankside crops, to vast dams, reservoirs and canal systems such as the Indus River project in Pakistan, which irrigates 10 million hectares (25 million acres) of land.

Traditional irrigation techniques usually involve using open channels or furrows for conducting water to fields. But one of the major problems with these, particularly in hot climates, is that much of the water evaporates and is lost before it can be used. Several new techniques, such as sprinklers and drip-feed systems, have recently been developed, however, to help make more efficient use of available supplies.

Although the most severe water deficiencies are experienced in the dry subtropical and tropical regions of the world, the temperate regions of North America and Europe, in spite of their relatively wet climates, do suffer shortages. Large towns and cities rarely have enough locally available rainfall or river flow to satisfy both domestic demand and the insatiable needs of industry. In the developed nations, industry consumes more water than any other activity.

Industrial demands

Fresh water is not only an integral part of almost every manufacturing process, it has other important industrial uses. As a source of power, it has been used since the early days of civilization—water wheels were one of man's first industrial inventions. Today, these simple devices are rarely seen in industrial societies, but water power is more important than ever before. Giant dams allow enormous volumes of water to be controlled and the power harnessed to drive turbines and generate electricity.

Freshwater systems have also, for centuries, provided industry with an important means of transporting its goods, and canal systems are still an essential part of industrial infrastructure in many countries of the world: the Europa Canal, when completed, will link three of Europe's major rivers, the Rhine, Main and Danube, and so form a continuous waterway running east–west across the breadth of Europe.

Already, the finished sections of the canal are carrying oil, chemicals, fertilizers, coal, coke and building materials to and from some of Europe's major industrial regions.

Many of Europe's waterways date back to the great canal-building days of the Industrial Revolution. Although a few of these are still used for commerce, many are today considered too narrow to transport economical quantities of goods. Some, however, are now finding a role to play in one of the world's fastest-growing new industries—the leisure market. Today, canals provide a wide range of aquatic activities for holiday makers, tourists and sportsmen.

Recreation and sport

Freshwater systems throughout the world, in fact, are rapidly being recognized and developed as major recreational resources. Lakes and reservoirs are stocked with fish for anglers, silted waterways are dredged to provide sailing and swimming facilities, and old quarries and open-cast workings are landscaped and flooded to provide entirely new freshwater systems purely for leisure pursuits. The projects not only help to rejuvenate previously misused land, they also provide significant incomes to otherwise underdeveloped areas, especially highland regions that are too remote to attract other industries, and are unsuitable for farming.

Unfortunately, however, few of the world's freshwater systems can continue indefinitely to absorb the ever-growing demands that are being made upon them. Overuse of water resources is already a problem and has led to the pollution and destruction of many water systems—in some places overtapping has lowered water tables so drastically that rivers and lakes have been permanently destroyed. Although steps have been taken to protect certain waterways, legislation to guard against misuse and overuse is costly, time consuming and, inevitably, comes up against vested interests. Nevertheless, stringent conservation measures are becoming increasingly necessary if society is to maintain one of its most precious resources.

INDUSTRY	19.5%
DOMESTIC	4.4%
AGRICULTURE	73.8%
RESERVOIRS	2.3%

Man obtains fresh water by trapping it as it passes through one of the stages in the hydrological cycle— the never-ending circulation of Earth's waters from the ocean, to the atmosphere, to land. This cycle can be traced from the point at which water evaporates from the sea. The water vapor is blown across the land and falls as rain, hail or snow. Some then evaporates, but the rest completes the cycle by flowing over the land or through the soil or rocks back to the sea. It is at this point in its journey that man obtains his water supplies—from lakes (1), boreholes and wells (2) and dammed rivers (3). These supplies are then either used locally, or are transported by pipe or canal (4) to reservoirs (5) where they are stored ready for distribution.

→ Movement of water in the hydrological cycle

▦ Water-bearing rock

RESERVOIRS

About 70 trillion liters (15 trillion gallons) of fresh water are held in storage during any one year. Reservoirs ensure a continuous supply of water in spite of the inevitable seasonal fluctuations in demand and in the natural supply from rivers and rainfall. And where reservoirs are formed by damming rivers, there are additional benefits—the vast quantities of water held can be controlled and the power used to generate electricity. The Kariba Dam in Zimbabwe (right) has the potential for producing 8,500 million kilowatt hours of electrical power every year.

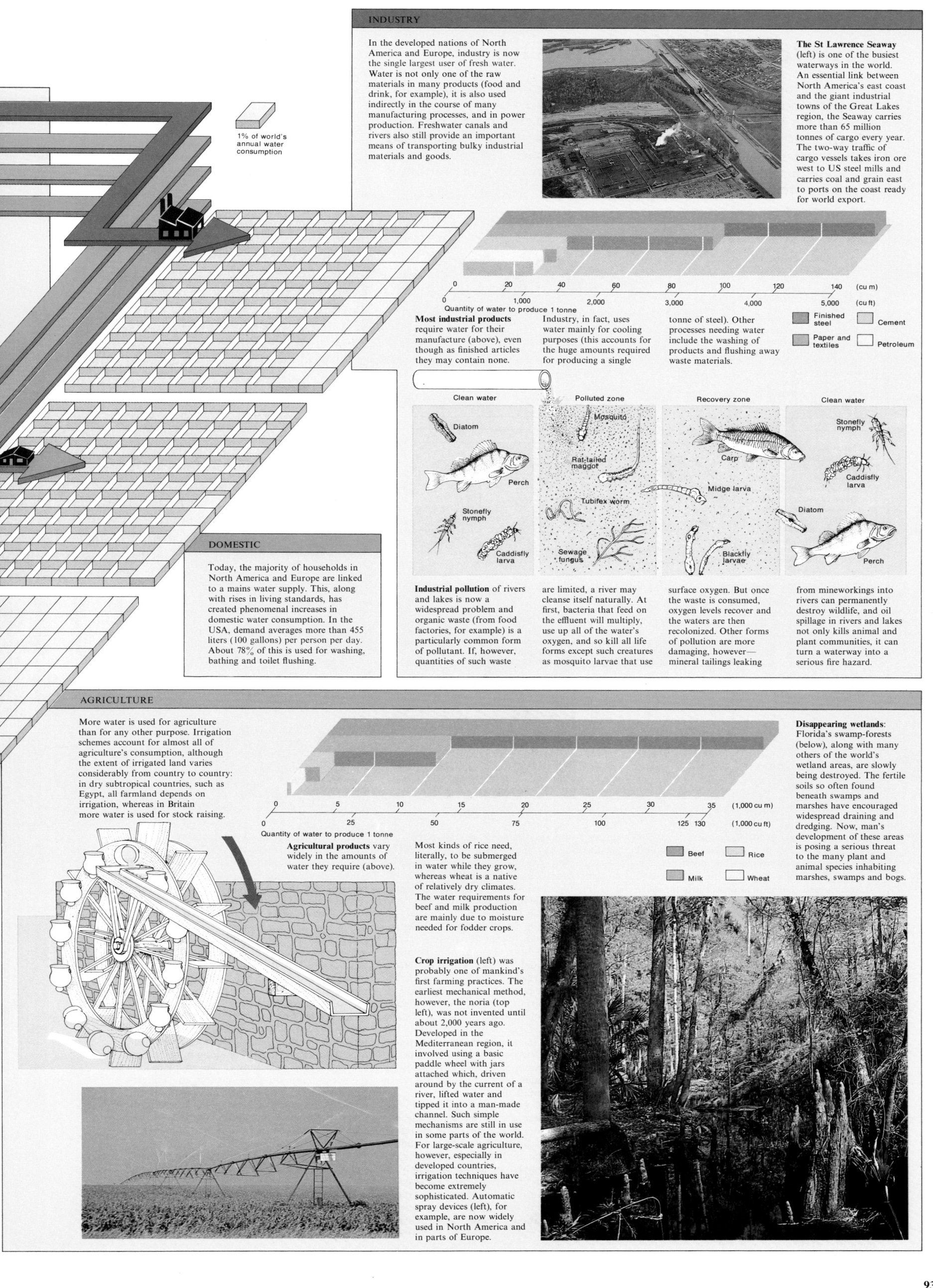

1% of world's annual water consumption

INDUSTRY

In the developed nations of North America and Europe, industry is now the single largest user of fresh water. Water is not only one of the raw materials in many products (food and drink, for example), it is also used indirectly in the course of many manufacturing processes, and in power production. Freshwater canals and rivers also still provide an important means of transporting bulky industrial materials and goods.

The St Lawrence Seaway (left) is one of the busiest waterways in the world. An essential link between North America's east coast and the giant industrial towns of the Great Lakes region, the Seaway carries more than 65 million tonnes of cargo every year. The two-way traffic of cargo vessels takes iron ore west to US steel mills and carries coal and grain east to ports on the coast ready for world export.

Quantity of water to produce 1 tonne

0   20   40   60   80   100   120   140   (cu m)
0   1,000   2,000   3,000   4,000   5,000   (cu ft)

Finished steel
Paper and textiles
Cement
Petroleum

Most industrial products require water for their manufacture (above), even though as finished articles they may contain none.

Industry, in fact, uses water mainly for cooling purposes (this accounts for the huge amounts required for producing a single tonne of steel). Other processes needing water include the washing of products and flushing away waste materials.

Clean water
Diatom
Perch
Stonefly nymph
Caddisfly larva

Polluted zone
Mosquito
Rat-tailed maggot
Tubifex worm
Sewage fungus

Recovery zone
Carp
Midge larva
Blackfly larvae

Clean water
Stonefly nymph
Caddisfly larva
Diatom
Perch

Industrial pollution of rivers and lakes is now a widespread problem and organic waste (from food factories, for example) is a particularly common form of pollutant. If, however, quantities of such waste are limited, a river may cleanse itself naturally. At first, bacteria that feed on the effluent will multiply, use up all of the water's oxygen, and so kill all life forms except such creatures as mosquito larvae that use surface oxygen. But once the waste is consumed, oxygen levels recover and the waters are then recolonized. Other forms of pollution are more damaging, however—mineral tailings leaking from mineworkings into rivers can permanently destroy wildlife, and oil spillage in rivers and lakes not only kills animal and plant communities, it can turn a waterway into a serious fire hazard.

DOMESTIC

Today, the majority of households in North America and Europe are linked to a mains water supply. This, along with rises in living standards, has created phenomenal increases in domestic water consumption. In the USA, demand averages more than 455 liters (100 gallons) per person per day. About 78% of this is used for washing, bathing and toilet flushing.

AGRICULTURE

More water is used for agriculture than for any other purpose. Irrigation schemes account for almost all of agriculture's consumption, although the extent of irrigated land varies considerably from country to country: in dry subtropical countries, such as Egypt, all farmland depends on irrigation, whereas in Britain more water is used for stock raising.

Quantity of water to produce 1 tonne

0   5   10   15   20   25   30   35   (1,000 cu m)
0   25   50   75   100   125   130   (1,000 cu ft)

Agricultural products vary widely in the amounts of water they require (above).

Most kinds of rice need, literally, to be submerged in water while they grow, whereas wheat is a native of relatively dry climates. The water requirements for beef and milk production are mainly due to moisture needed for fodder crops.

Beef
Milk
Rice
Wheat

Disappearing wetlands: Florida's swamp-forests (below), along with many others of the world's wetland areas, are slowly being destroyed. The fertile soils so often found beneath swamps and marshes have encouraged widespread draining and dredging. Now, man's development of these areas is posing a serious threat to the many plant and animal species inhabiting marshes, swamps and bogs.

Crop irrigation (left) was probably one of mankind's first farming practices. The earliest mechanical method, however, the noria (top left), was not invented until about 2,000 years ago. Developed in the Mediterranean region, it involved using a basic paddle wheel with jars attached which, driven around by the current of a river, lifted water and tipped it into a man-made channel. Such simple mechanisms are still in use in some parts of the world. For large-scale agriculture, however, especially in developed countries, irrigation techniques have become extremely sophisticated. Automatic spray devices (left), for example, are now widely used in North America and in parts of Europe.

Seawater Environments

The oceans form by far the largest of the world's habitable environments, covering almost three-quarters of the Earth's surface at an average depth of more than 3,500 m (11,500 ft). Little more than a century ago, scientists believed that the deep sea's low temperatures, perpetual darkness and immense pressures made life in these regions completely untenable. But we now know that animals live at all depths in the ocean, even at the bottom of trenches more than 11,000 m (36,000 ft) deep.

THE PATTERN OF MARINE LIFE
The distribution of life in the seas is like an inverted pyramid whose broad base is formed by billions of minute single-celled plants—the phytoplankton. Plants need sunlight and nutrient salts, so phytoplankton occurs only in the upper, sunlit layers and where salts are present. Elsewhere, the distribution of marine life thins out rapidly.

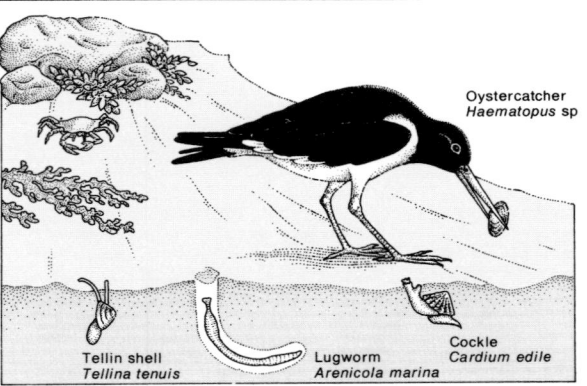

Shore life belongs to both land and sea, and thus has to cope with a wide range of conditions. Seaweeds get all their food from the sea and are quite unlike land plants. Many animals take refuge below the surface: tellin shell molluscs sift food particles through special "lips"; lugworms swallow sand, digesting any organic matter; cockles take in food and eject waste through two siphons. Some birds have bills adapted for opening bivalve molluscs.

Oystercatcher
Haematopus sp

Tellin shell
Tellina tenuis

Lugworm
Arenicola marina

Cockle
Cardium edile

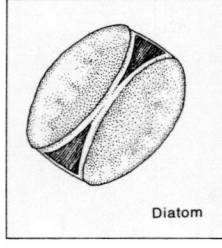
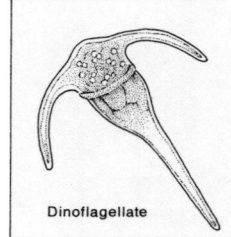
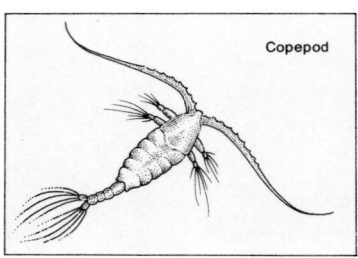

Marine plant life consists largely of diatoms—minute single-celled specks, each enclosed in a lidded box of silicon. Dinoflagellates, classed as plants but able to swim, dominate warmer waters. Both are food for copepods, the flea-sized grazers whose total weight, in the North Sea alone, is some seven million tonnes.

Diatom

Dinoflagellate

Copepod

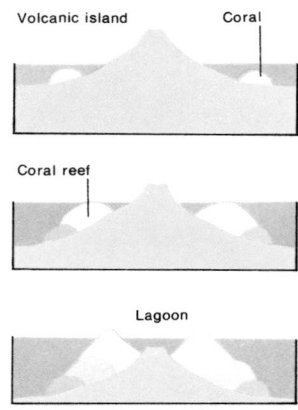

A coral atoll, forming in warm shallow water round an extinct volcano, makes up a living aquarium for thousands of tropical marine life forms. Countless billions of tiny polyps, each secreting a hard, calcareous skeleton, form the first layer of the reef, but die as the volcano gradually sinks. Their skeletons provide a base for further layers of corals, which enclose the sinking island to create a shallow, salt water lagoon. Different coral species in the same reef provide homes for a great variety of life.

Volcanic island   Coral

Coral reef

Lagoon

Life is by no means evenly distributed throughout the oceans, either vertically or horizontally. The great majority of marine creatures are concentrated in the upper few hundred meters, for the biological organization of life in the seas, as on land, depends on photosynthesis (the process by which plants use the Sun's energy to combine carbon dioxide and water to produce more complex compounds). This near-surface layer is the euphotic ("well-lighted") zone.

Some of the Sun's rays are reflected from the surface of the sea, and those that penetrate are scattered and absorbed as they pass through the water, so that even in the clearest oceanic water there is insufficient light to support photosynthesis at depths greater than about 100 m (330 ft). In turbid inshore regions, where the water is less clear, this near-surface layer may be reduced to a very few meters. So the large seaweeds that anchor themselves to the seabed are restricted to the small areas of the sea where the water is sufficiently shallow to allow them to photosynthesize. Of much greater importance over most of the oceans are the tiny floating plants of the phytoplankton, which live suspended in the sunlit surface layers.

Pastures of the sea
Phytoplankton, like all plant life, requires not only sunlight for survival but also adequate supplies of nutrient salts and chemical trace elements. River waters carry down considerable quantities of dissolved mineral salts and other matter, so that high levels of phytoplankton production may occur locally around major estuaries. But a far more important source of nutrient supply to the euphotic zone is the recycling of salts that have sunk into the deeper layers, locked up in the bodies of plants and animals or in their fecal pellets.

In those areas of the oceans that overlie the continental shelves (about six percent of the total), the depth is nowhere more than about 200 m (650 ft), and the nutrient-rich bottom water is fairly readily brought back to the surface by currents and the stirring effect of storms. This stirring can reach much greater depths in near-polar latitudes, where the "water column" is not layered by temperature but remains more or less uniformly cold from top to bottom. In the Antarctic, cold (and therefore heavy) surface water sinks and is replaced by nutrient-rich water that may surface from depths of 1,000 m (3,300 ft).

In subtropical and tropical regions of the open ocean, where the warm surface layer is only a few tens of meters deep, the temperature falls rapidly with depth. There is little exchange between deep and shallow layers, and the euphotic zone receives an adequate supply of nutrient salts only in certain areas. These occur between westward-flowing and eastward-flowing currents in each of the major oceans. The Earth's rotation causes these currents to diverge so as to create an upwelling of nutrient-rich water along their common boundaries.

Finally, in restricted coastal regions of the tropics and subtropics the local climatic conditions cause an offshore movement of surface water, which is again replaced by upwelling nutrient-rich deep water. The central oceanic regions, including the deep blue subtropical waters, are in effect the deserts of the sea.

Sea grazers and carnivores
The abundance of animals in the oceans closely follows that of the plants. But very few of the larger marine animals can feed directly on the phytoplankton because the individual plants are so small—often only a fraction of a millimeter across. Instead, the phytoplankton supports an amazingly diverse community of planktonic animals, which also spend their lives in mid-water and are swept along by the ocean currents. This community, the zooplankton, includes many different protozoans (single-celled animals), crustaceans, worms and molluscs, and also the juvenile stages of fishes and of many invertebrate animals that live as adults on the seabed. Most members of the zooplankton are very small and many of them graze on the phytoplankton. But some planktonic animals, particularly among the jellyfish and salps, may be a meter or more across and are voracious carnivores feeding on their planktonic neighbors. In turn, the zooplankton provides food for many of the active swimmers such as the fishes and baleen whales, while at the top of the food chain are larger carnivores including

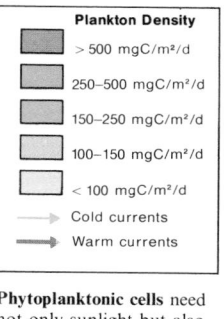

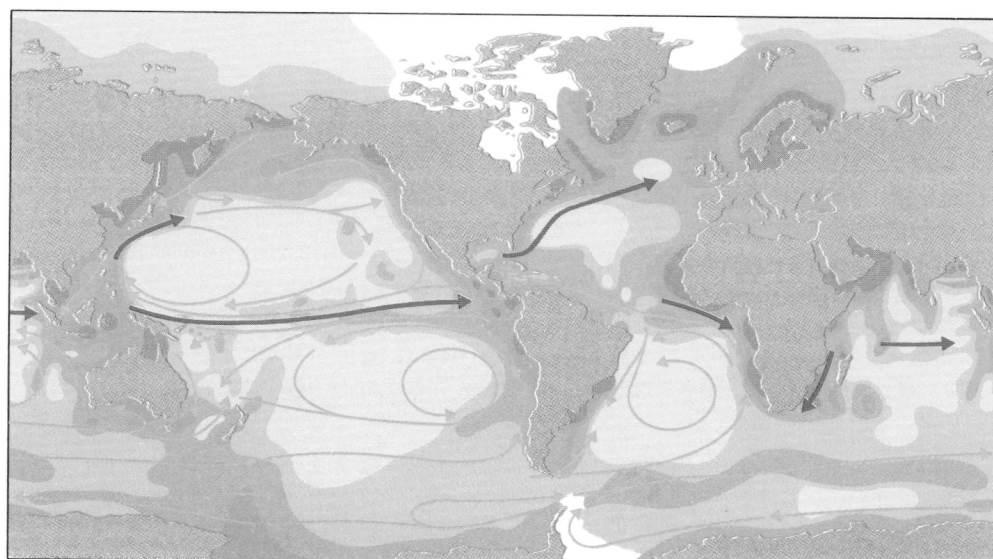

The by-the-wind sailor, *Velella,* is a so-called colonial animal, consisting of a whole collection of animals that function as a single individual. The gas-filled float of its body carries a vertical sail to catch the wind, and below dangle a group of modified polyps specialized for particular roles such as deterrence, reproduction, feeding and digesting.

Phytoplanktonic cells need not only sunlight but also nutrient salts, and so they are restricted to areas where these are available: coastal regions, high latitudes (particularly the Antarctic), narrow tongues extending across the tropical regions of the main ocean basins, and a number of subtropical upwelling regions.

Zones of life (below) extend from the teeming euphotic ("well-lighted") layer to the sparsely populated bathypelagic ("deep-sea") depths, while benthic ("bottom") life occurs at all seabed levels. Phytoplankton (plant life) (1) dictates the pattern of the rest, flourishing where surface conditions allow nutrient salts to well up from lower depths. Herbivores such as minute zooplankton (2) provide food for a host of surface-layer life, which in turn feeds larger predators. Dead animals and fecal pellets fall to lower levels, where they sustain life, but in far smaller quantity.

1 Phytoplankton
2 Zooplankton
3 Blue whale *Balaenoptera musculus*
4 Herring *Clupea harengus*
5 Gray seal *Halichoerus grypus*
6 Bluefin tuna *Thunnus thynnus*
7 Bottlenosed dolphin *Tursiops truncatus*
8 Mackerel *Scomber scomber*
9 Common squid *Loligo* spp
10 White shark *Carcharodon carcharias*
11 Hatchet fish *Argyropelecus hemigymnus*
12 Giant squid *Architeuthis* spp
13 Sea anemone *Cerianthus orientalis*
14 Tripod fish *Benthosaurus grallator*
15 Scarlet shrimp *Notostomus longirostris*
16 Angler fish *Linophryne bicornis*
17 Brittle star *Ophiothrix fragilis*
18 Sea cucumber class Holothuroidea

Offshore wind

Euphotic zone

500 m (1,650 ft)

Mesopelagic zone

1,000 m (3,300 ft)

Bathypelagic zone

Benthic zone

4,000 m (13,200 ft)

Bizarre life forms new to science live in the sunless depths, where plumes of hot mineral-rich water gush through deep-sea vents in the Earth's crust. These oases of life support huge, gutless tubeworms more than 1.5 m (5 ft) long, which appear to take food particles from the hot vents through blood-red tentacles. Other creatures include blind crabs and large white clams.

sharks, tuna-like fishes and toothed whales.

Beneath the euphotic zone, of course, there can be no herbivores at all, although some animals that spend the daylight hours in the deeper layers move upwards at night to feed in the plankton-rich surface waters. All of the permanent members of the deep-living communities are dependent for food upon material that sinks or is carried downwards from the euphotic zone. Many of them feed on dead animal remains and fecal material as it sinks through the water column or after it reaches the seabed. These detritus eaters in turn support the predatory carnivores that feed upon the detritivores or upon each other.

In shallow areas the food material that reaches the bottom supports complex communities, notably the rich and varied groups of invertebrates and fishes associated with coral reefs. In the deep sea, however, where the euphotic zone is separated from the seabed by several kilometers of water, much of the sinking material is recycled within the water column and relatively little reaches the bottom. Life on the deep-sea floor therefore becomes more and more sparse with increasing depth, but in recent years scientists have discovered that this community includes a surprising number of fishes, some many meters in length. So far man's knowledge of these deep-sea communities is relatively meager, but with our increasing use of the deep oceans we may need to know much more about the life in this environment.

Man and the Seawater Environments

For thousands of years man has used the oceans as a source of food and other materials, and as a repository for wastes. But only in the last 100 years have technological advances and fast-growing human populations had a significant effect, to a point where overfishing and pollution are becoming a cause for concern. Harvesting of krill and seaweeds may ease the pressure on traditional seafoods, but legal restrictions on dumping of wastes or on overfishing are notoriously hard to enforce.

Until about the middle of the nineteenth century the seas had always seemed to be a boundless source of food and of income for fishermen who were brave enough to face the elements with their relatively small sailing ships and primitive gear. But once fishing vessels began to be fitted with steam engines in the 1880s they became relatively independent of the weather, while improvements in the fishing gear itself, such as steam-powered winches in trawling and harpoon guns in whaling, made the whole business of fishing much more efficient.

At first these advances resulted in enormous increases in catches, but in many fisheries this was rapidly followed by a distressing fall in the catch per unit of effort—that is, it was becoming more and more difficult in successive years to catch the same amount of fish as before. In most fisheries the initial response to this situation was to increase the size and number of fishing vessels and to search for new fishing grounds. But as the fishing pressure on the stocks increased, with smaller fish being captured, often before they were able to reproduce, the catch per unit of effort frequently continued to fall.

In many cases attempts were made to counter the effects of overfishing by introducing regulations to control the mesh size of the nets, so allowing the small fish to escape; by establishing closed seasons or quotas of fish which might legitimately be taken from a particular fishing ground in any one year; or even, as in the case of the British herring fishery in the late 1970s, by imposing a complete ban on fishing. Moral questions also sometimes intervene, as in whaling operations, which, many conservationists believe, have driven some species close to extinction despite attempts to rationalize the fisheries.

Fisheries in decline

The North Sea trawl fishery, the first to be affected by the new technology in the nineteenth century, has been declining in terms of catch per unit of effort since the early decades of this century. Dramatic but short-lived improvements after the "closed seasons" of the two world wars proved that fishing pressure had a serious effect on stocks, but by the 1970s many North Sea fishing ports had become almost deserted. This decline put pressure on more distant fishing grounds used by European fishermen, and recent decades have been marked by a series of fishing disputes, with nations fighting for the continued existence of their fisheries despite clear evidence that there are not enough catchable fish to satisfy everyone.

A similar story of declining catches during the present century could be told of many of the old-established fisheries around the world, but at the same time the demand for fish in a protein-hungry world has increased. To satisfy this demand the total annual world catch increased by about seven percent from the end of World War II until the early 1970s, by this time reaching a figure of around 60–70 million tonnes. But this increase was achieved only by exploiting previously unfished stocks or new geographical areas. Such an increase cannot go on indefinitely, for we are rapidly running out of "new" areas and some of the new fisheries have already shown the same symptoms of over-fishing as the older ones—and sometimes even more dramatically.

New foods from the sea

The indications are that the present total catch is close to the maximum that can be obtained from relatively conventional fisheries even with careful management, and that, to increase the total, or even to sustain it, we must look to completely new sources such as krill, the shrimp-like food of the whalebone whales.

Estimates of the sustainable annual catch of krill in the Antarctic range from about 50 to 500 million tonnes, that is up to about seven times as much as the current total from all other fisheries put together. Of course, the use of such an enormous quantity of small crustaceans would present considerable problems. Part of it might be converted into a protein-rich paste for human consumption, but much would be used indirectly as a feed for farm animals.

Many larger seaweeds are already cropped in several parts of the world, particularly in Japan, and are used not only for human food but also for animal food and in many industrial processes. About one million tonnes of seaweed are taken each year, but because seaweeds grow naturally only in relatively shallow areas of the oceans this figure could probably not be significantly increased using natural populations. However, seaweeds can be grown artificially on frames floating over deep water. Experiments suggest that, by enriching the surface layers through artificial upwelling of nutrient-rich deep water, each square kilometer of such a floating seaweed farm could produce enough food to feed 1,000–2,000 people, and enough energy and other products to satisfy the needs of a further 1,000. With an estimated 260 million sq km (100 million sq miles) of "arable" surface, the seas might thus support up to 10 times the present world population.

Polluted waters

Of course, the present century has seen an increase not only in what man takes out of the sea but also in the harmful substances that he throws into it. Not only oil but many other substances are dumped into the seas accidentally or intentionally, usually either in the discharged effluent from industrial plant or as a result of agricultural chemicals being leached into rivers and thence into the ocean. In many cases the amounts are very small compared with the amounts present in the oceans as a whole; the problem is that they are usually released, and accumulate, in restricted inshore areas near which we live and from which we obtain most of our sea-caught food.

Since the 1930s there have been both national and international attempts to control pollution by legislation, and since 1958 a series of United Nations conferences has sought agreement on many aspects of international maritime law, including pollution. Despite many prophecies of imminent doom, it does not seem that marine pollution yet poses any general threat to humanity. Nevertheless, with ever-increasing industrialization and the production of more and more toxic materials, including radioactive wastes, it is essential that we monitor the effects of man's activities on the ocean.

THE MARINE RESOURCES
Modern technology has enabled man to expand his age-old exploitation of the seas to the limit in some areas, and a need for the careful management of our marine resource is imperative. But in some fields, such as energy and the extraction of fresh water, the seas may yield inexhaustible riches.

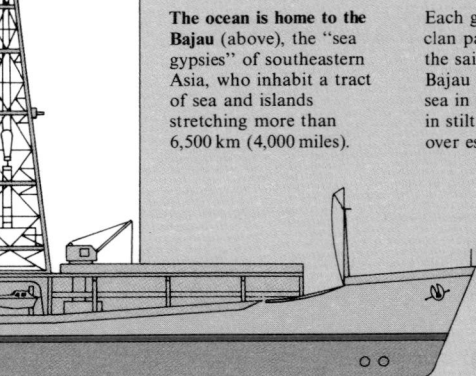

Drilling derrick

Hydrophones

The ocean is home to the **Bajau** (above), the "sea gypsies" of southeastern Asia, who inhabit a tract of sea and islands stretching more than 6,500 km (4,000 miles).

Each group has its own clan pattern, blazoned on the sails of their *praus*. The Bajau may live on the open sea in clusters of boats, or in stilt-house villages built over estuaries.

The deep-sea drilling ship *Glomar Challenger* (above) plays an important role in surveying and prospecting the oceans. It can drill in water depths of 7,000 m (23,000 ft) and obtain core samples 1,200 m (4,000 ft) below the ocean bed. The ship is positioned over the drill hole through signals from a sonar beacon to hydrophones in the hull.

Sonar beacons

Core sample tube

Drilling head

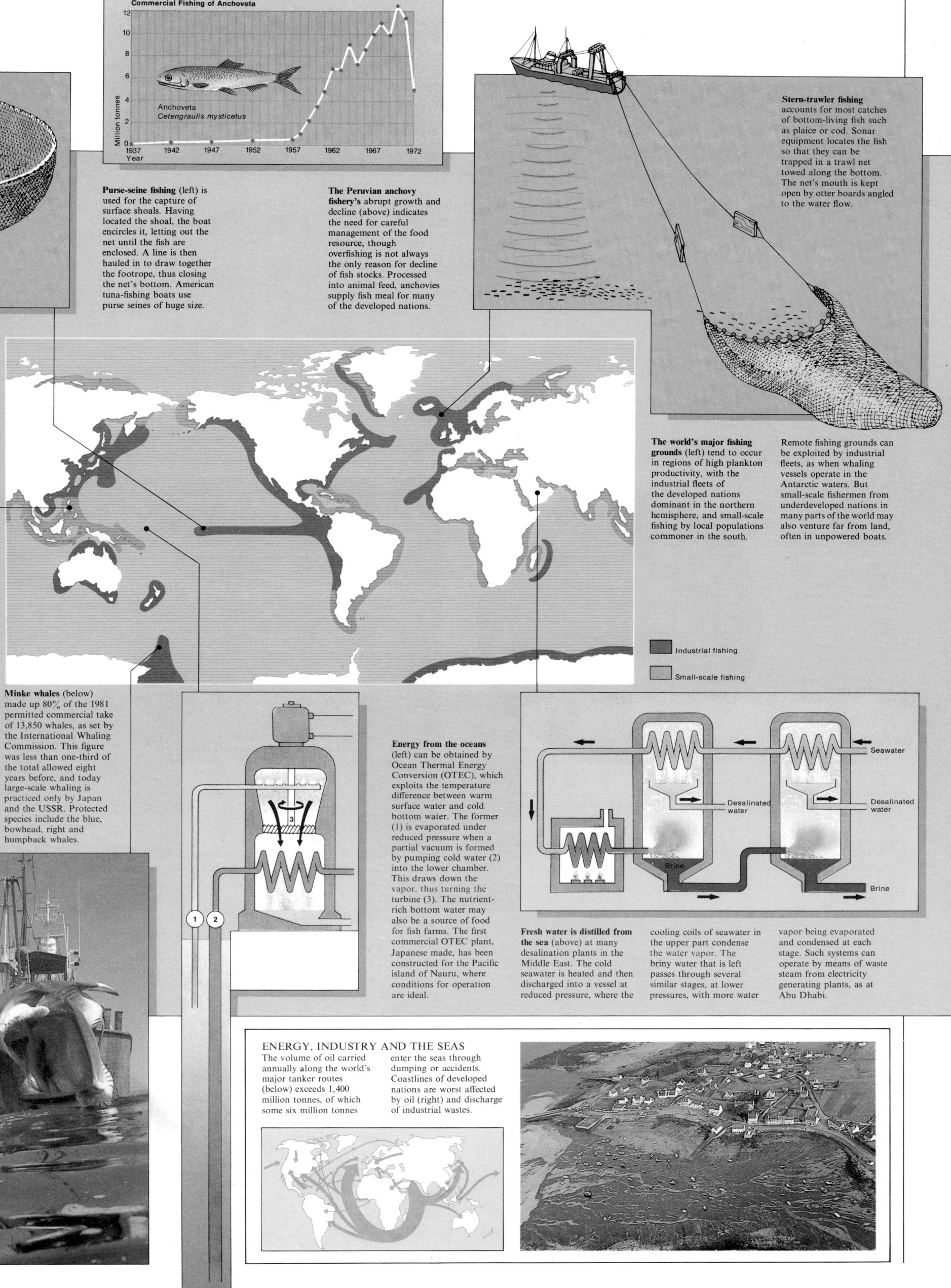

Commercial Fishing of Anchoveta

Anchoveta
Cetengraulis mysticetus

Million tonnes

1937 1942 1947 1952 1957 1962 1967 1972
Year

Purse-seine fishing (left) is used for the capture of surface shoals. Having located the shoal, the boat encircles it, letting out the net until the fish are enclosed. A line is then hauled in to draw together the footrope, thus closing the net's bottom. American tuna-fishing boats use purse seines of huge size.

The Peruvian anchovy fishery's abrupt growth and decline (above) indicates the need for careful management of the food resource, though overfishing is not always the only reason for decline of fish stocks. Processed into animal feed, anchovies supply fish meal for many of the developed nations.

Stern-trawler fishing accounts for most catches of bottom-living fish such as plaice or cod. Sonar equipment locates the fish so that they can be trapped in a trawl net towed along the bottom. The net's mouth is kept open by otter boards angled to the water flow.

The world's major fishing grounds (left) tend to occur in regions of high plankton productivity, with the industrial fleets of the developed nations dominant in the northern hemisphere, and small-scale fishing by local populations commoner in the south.

Remote fishing grounds can be exploited by industrial fleets, as when whaling vessels operate in the Antarctic waters. But small-scale fishermen from underdeveloped nations in many parts of the world may also venture far from land, often in unpowered boats.

Industrial fishing

Small-scale fishing

Minke whales (below) made up 80% of the 1981 permitted commercial take of 13,850 whales, as set by the International Whaling Commission. This figure was less than one-third of the total allowed eight years before, and today large-scale whaling is practiced only by Japan and the USSR. Protected species include the blue, bowhead, right and humpback whales.

Energy from the oceans (left) can be obtained by Ocean Thermal Energy Conversion (OTEC), which exploits the temperature difference between warm surface water and cold bottom water. The former (1) is evaporated under reduced pressure when a partial vacuum is formed by pumping cold water (2) into the lower chamber. This draws down the vapor, thus turning the turbine (3). The nutrient-rich bottom water may also be a source of food for fish farms. The first commercial OTEC plant, Japanese made, has been constructed for the Pacific island of Nauru, where conditions for operation are ideal.

Seawater

Desalinated water

Desalinated water

Brine

Brine

Fresh water is distilled from the sea (above) at many desalination plants in the Middle East. The cold seawater is heated and then discharged into a vessel at reduced pressure, where the cooling coils of seawater in the upper part condense the water vapor. The briny water that is left passes through several similar stages, at lower pressures, with more water vapor being evaporated and condensed at each stage. Such systems can operate by means of waste steam from electricity generating plants, as at Abu Dhabi.

ENERGY, INDUSTRY AND THE SEAS

The volume of oil carried annually along the world's major tanker routes (below) exceeds 1,400 million tonnes, of which some six million tonnes enter the seas through dumping or accidents. Coastlines of developed nations are worst affected by oil (right) and discharge of industrial wastes.

Part 5

UNDERSTANDING MAPS

What maps are and how they are made
New horizons and latest developments in maps and mapmaking
How to read the language of maps

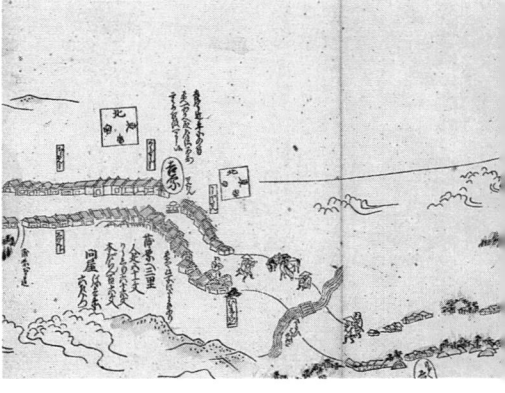

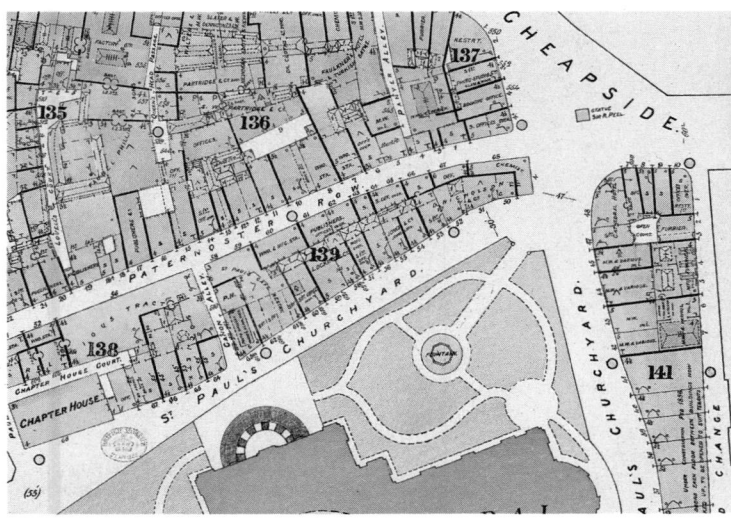

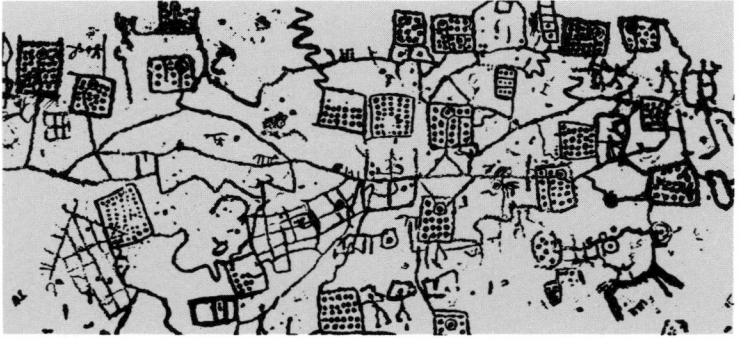

Elegant road maps with pictorial and geographical features have been produced by many different cultures. The woodcut map of the Tōkaidō (detail above), the great Japanese highway, 555 km (345 miles) long, between Edo (Tokyo) and Kyoto, was drawn as a panorama by the famous artist Moronobu in 1690. Its pictorial details do not prevent it being an accurate representation of the road's track. A Mexican map of the Tepetlaoztoc valley (right) drawn in 1583 marks roads with footprints between parallel lines, and hill ranges with wavy lines. Symbols in panels represent place-names.

Maps defining territory and ownership are almost as old as the human territorial instinct itself. The rock-carving maps of the Val Camonica, Italy (above), dating from the second and first millennia BC, show stippled square fields, paths, river lines, houses, and even humans and animals. It is uncertain whether their purpose was legal, but the need to establish ownership is a basic function of many maps, as seen in a detail from Goad's 19th-century insurance map of London (left), where every occupation is recorded.

America first appears as a separate continent (below) in an inset to Martin Waldseemüller's world map of 1507, with the two hemispheres facing each other. Presiding over the Old World is Claudius Ptolemy, the 2nd-century geographer whose remarkably scientific maps, copied and recopied over a thousand years, were revised and emended by Waldseemüller to show some of the results of Portuguese exploration. His New World counterpart is the Italian Amerigo Vespucci, one of the early explorers of the continent, after whom it was named. This is the first map to show the Pacific (not yet named) as an ocean between America and Asia. The west coast of South America, still to be explored by Europeans, seems to be inspired guesswork. The island between the landmasses is Cipango (Japan) known from Marco Polo.

The earliest surviving Chinese globe (above) was made in 1623 by two Jesuit missionaries, probably for the emperor of China. The long legend in Chinese expresses terms and ideas derived from early Chinese cosmology. It describes the Earth as "floating in the Heavens like the yolk of an egg . . . with all objects having mass tending toward its center"—one of the first known references to gravity.

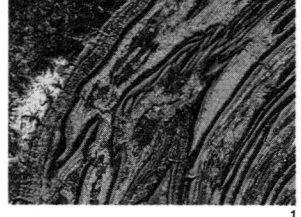

High-altitude photography (left) allows accurate updating of topographic maps (right), while data gathering by satellites (above) expands the range. Landsat satellites carry electronic remote-sensing equipment that detects the energy emitted by surface materials and translates it into images. Healthy plants may show as bright red, sparse vegetation as pink, barren lands as light gray, and urban areas as green or dark gray. The folded shape of the Appalachians (1) is clearly seen; the Canada–US border (2) is revealed by land-use patterns; silt from the Mississippi (3) builds up the delta. Sudan irrigation (4) shows up as brilliant red.

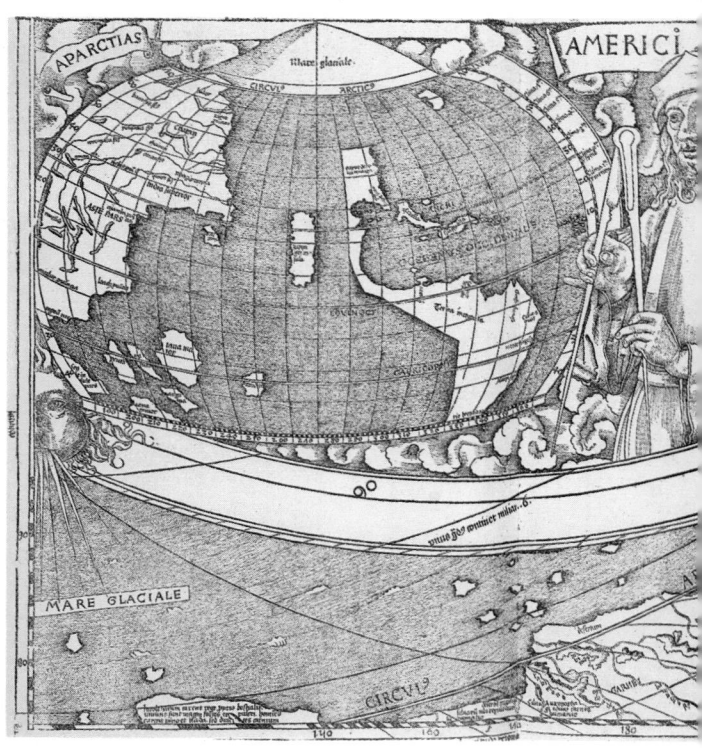

Mapping, Old and New

Mapmaking must have its origins in the earliest ages of human history, since people of preliterate as well as literate cultures possess an innate skill in map drawing. This innate capacity is further indicated by the ease with which almost anyone can sketch in the sand or on paper simple directions for showing the way. But maps may also define territory and express man's idea of the world in graphic representation. Today, modern technology has vastly extended the scope of cartography.

Many non-European cultures developed ingenious route-map techniques: the North American Indians, for example, made sketch maps of routes on birch bark. These were diagrammatic maps in which directions and distances were not accurate but relationships were true, as in New York Subway or London Underground maps. The people of the Marshall Islands in the western Pacific made route maps over the seas, depicting the direction of the main seasonal wave swells in relation to the islands.

Although maps of routes are the simplest type of map in concept, they developed complex forms as cartography progressed. A road map of the whole Roman Empire, drawn about AD 280, survives today in a thirteenth-century copy known as the Peutinger Table. Hernando Cortes, the Spanish conqueror, made his way across Mexico in the 1520s with the help of preconquest Mexican maps painted on cloth. These showed roads with double lines or colored bands marked with footprints. Another type of map is the strip map depicting a single road along its entire length. Pictorial maps of the Tōkaidō highway from Edo to Kyoto in Japan, made from a survey of 1651, were popular in the Edo period of Japanese history.

Nautical charts evolved as a special type of direction-finding map to meet the needs of seamen. Those of the late Middle Ages came to be known as "portolan" charts, from the word "portolani," or sailing directions. They showed the sea and adjacent coasts superimposed on a network of radiating compass lines.

Territorial maps

Another basic type of map derives from man's sense of territorial possession. The earliest example of a "cadastral" plan (a map showing land parcels and property boundaries) appears to be that preserved as rock carvings at Bedolina in Val Camonica in northern Italy. However, in the ancient civilizations of Mesopotamia and Egypt, land surveying had become an established profession by 2000 BC. An idea of what Egyptian surveyors' plans of 1000 BC were like can be seen from the "Fields of the Dead" representing the Egyptians' idea of life after death. These show plots of land surrounded by water and intersected by canals. The Romans used cadastral surveys to determine land ownership and assess tax liability.

Another form of map showing territorial demarcations is the map of administrative units. The Chinese in the thirteenth century AD were making official district maps to help in the organization of grain supplies and the collection of taxes. Many of their gazetteers (*fang chih*), written in the form of local geographies and

histories from the eleventh century onward, were illustrated with maps. Political maps showing the boundaries of states were increasingly significant in European cartography from the sixteenth century onward.

A third major class of map is the general or topographical map expressing man's perception of the world, its regions and its place in the universe. A Babylonian world map of the seventh century BC is drawn on a clay tablet and shows the Earth as a circular disc surrounded by the Earthly Ocean. With the ancient Greeks, geography developed on scientific principles. The treatise on mapmaking by Claudius Ptolemy (AD 87–150), later known as the *Geographia*, was the most famous cartographic text of the period. It influenced the Arabic geographers of the Middle Ages, notably Muhammad Ibn Muhammad, Al-Idrisi (1099–1164), and with the revival of Ptolemy in fifteenth-century Europe became one of the major works of the Renaissance. Published, with engraved maps, at Bologna in 1477, the *Geographia* ranks as the first printed atlas in the western world. The invention of techniques of engraving in wood and copper facilitated a wide diffusion of geographical knowledge through the map-publishing trade. The first atlas made up of modern maps to a uniform design was Abraham Ortelius's *Theatrum Orbis Terrarum* published at Antwerp in 1570. From 1492, when Martin Behaim made his "Erdapfel" at Nürnberg, globes also became popular, and globemakers vied with each other to make larger and more elaborate ones to keep pace with the growth of knowledge about the world.

Over the last two hundred years cartography has made rapid and remarkable advances. Observatories built in Paris in 1671 and at Greenwich in 1675 enabled the location of places to be established more exactly with the use of astronomical tables. Improvements in surveying instruments facilitated more accurate and rapid land survey. France was the pioneer in establishing (from 1679 onward) a national survey on a geometrical basis of triangulation. By the end of the eighteenth century national surveys on small and medium scales had been begun by most European countries. In the United States the Geological Survey was set up in 1879 to undertake the topographical and geological mapping of the country.

Mapping today

Since World War II cartographic techniques have undergone a revolution. The use of air survey and photogrammetry has made it possible to map most of the Earth's surface. Electronic distance measurement by laser or light beams in surveying, and digital computers in mapping, are among the most recent advances in methods. Mosaics or air photography are used to produce orthophoto maps which can supplement or substitute for the conventional topographic map. Artificial satellites and manned space craft make it possible to provide a world-wide framework of geodetic networks.

Earth Resource Technology Satellites (ERTS) imagery has made it possible to map mountain ranges in Africa and features on the surface of Antarctica that were hitherto unknown. The imagery is made available by means of remote-sensing instruments, carried by the satellites, that are sensitive to invisible portions of the electromagnetic spectrum—longer and shorter wavelengths than can be sensed by the human eye. Remote-sensing instruments usually work in the infrared bands. They can also pick up the energy emitted by all types of surface material—rocks, soils, vegetation, water and man-made structures—and produce photographs or images from it.

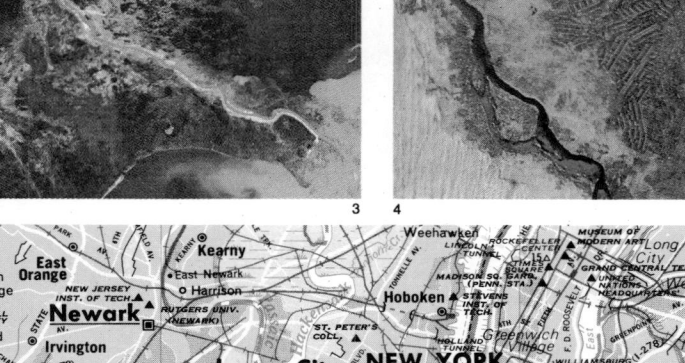

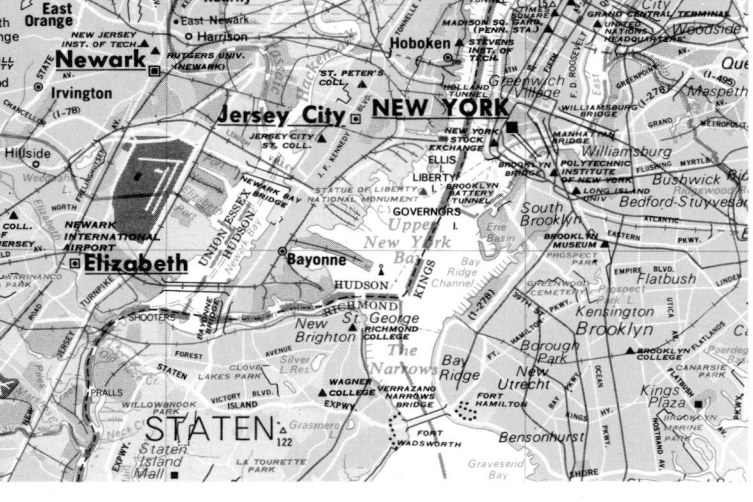

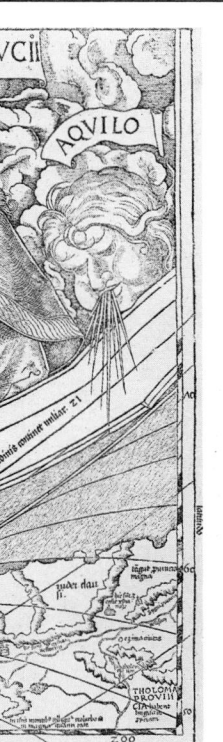

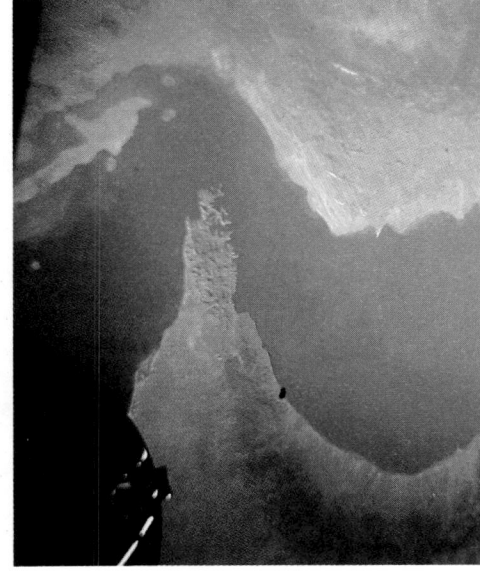

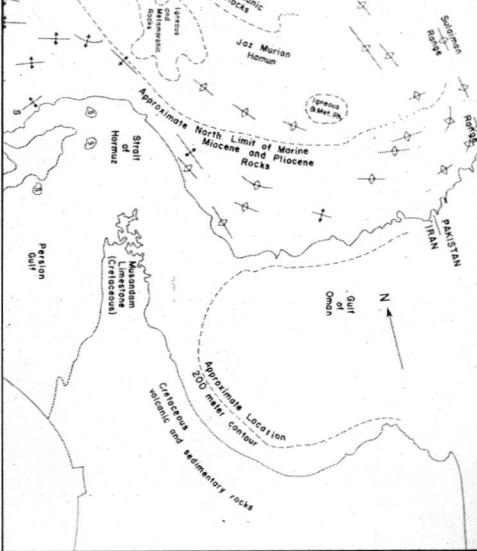

Space technology helps cartographers to map even interior details of the planet: its geology and mineral wealth. A photo (below) taken from Gemini 12 at an altitude of 272 km (168 miles) forms the basis of a geologic sketch map of SW Asia (below right), showing the oil-rich area around the region between the Persian Gulf and the Gulf of Oman. The symbol S on the map indicates salt plugs; diamonds show fold trends; double-headed arrows anticlines.

The Language of Maps

Mapmakers for more than 4,000 years have tried to find the best way to represent the shape and features of the three-dimensional Earth on two-dimensional paper, parchment and cloth. The measurement of distance and direction is a basic requirement for accurate surveys, but until about 1800 theoretical understanding of the method was well in advance of the technical equipment available. Today the use of lasers and light beams sometimes takes the place of direct measurement on the ground.

A reference system must be used to show distance and direction correctly in the construction of maps. The simplest type is the rectangular or square grid. The Chinese mapmaker Pei Xin made a map with a grid in about AD 270, and this system remained in continuous use in China until modern times. The Roman system of centuriation, a form of division of public lands on a square or rectangular basis, was also a "coordinate" system starting from a point of origin at the intersection of two perpendicular axes. Roman surveyors' maps, dating from the first century AD, are the earliest known European maps based on a grid system.

Latitude and longitude

Makers of small-scale regional maps and of world maps in early times also had to take account of the fact that the Earth is a sphere. The Greeks derived from the Babylonians the idea of dividing a circle into 360 degrees. In the second century BC the Greek geographer Eratosthenes (c. 276–194 BC) was the first to calculate the circumference of the globe and was reported to have made a world map based on the concept of the Earth's sphericity. From this the Greeks went on to develop the system of spherical coordinates which remains in use today. The poles at each end of the Earth's axis provide reference points for the Earth in its rotation in relation to the celestial sphere. Parallel circles around the Earth are degrees of latitude and express the idea of distance north or south of the Equator. Lines of longitude running north and south through the poles express east–west distances. One meridian is chosen as the meridian of origin, known as the prime meridian.

Whereas latitude from early times could be observed from the height of the Sun or (in the northern hemisphere) from the position of the Pole Star at night, accurate observations of longitude were not possible until the middle of the eighteenth century, when the chronometer was invented and more accurate astronomical tables were provided. In 1884 most countries agreed, at an international conference in Washington DC, to adopt the prime meridian through the Royal Greenwich Observatory in England and to calculate longitude to 180 degrees east and west of Greenwich.

Projection and distortion

The mathematical system by which the spherical surface of the Earth is transferred to the plane surface of a map is called a map projection. The Greek geographer Ptolemy gave instructions in his geographical treatise of AD 150 for the construction of two projections. When the *Geographia* was revised in Europe in the fifteenth century, and navigators began sailing across the oceans, mapmakers devised new projections more appropriate to the expanding geographical knowledge of the world. The Dutch geographer Gerard Mercator invented the projection named after him, applying it to his world chart of 1569. This cylindrical projection, in which all points are at true compass courses from each other, was of great benefit to navigators and is still one of the most commonly

used projections. Another advance was made when Johann Heinrich Lambert of Alsace (1728–1777) invented the azimuthal equal-area projection, in which the sizes of all areas are represented on the projection in correct proportion to one another, and the conformal projection, in which at any point on the map the scale is constant in all directions.

Since all projections involve deformation of the geometry of the globe, the cartographer has to choose the one that best suits the purpose of his map. "Conformal" or "orthomorphic" projections, in which angular relations (or shape) are preserved, are widely used for the construction of topographical maps. "Equivalent" or "equal-area" projections retain relative sizes and are particularly useful for general reference maps displaying economic, historical, political and other geographical phenomena.

Since the mid-fifteenth century, European mapmakers have generally arranged their maps with north at the top of the sheet. Earlier maps, however, were not standardized in this way. The circular world maps of the Middle Ages were orientated with east at the top, because this was where the terrestrial paradise was traditionally sited. Indeed, the word "orientation" originally meant the arrangement of something so as to face east.

Map scale

Scale is another basic property of a map. The scale of a map is the ratio of the distance on the map to the actual distance represented. Whereas the Babylonians, Egyptians, Greeks and Romans drew surveys to scale, in medieval Europe mapmakers used customary methods of estimating. The earliest known local map since Roman times which is drawn to scale (it displays a scale bar) is a plan of Vienna, 1422.

Projection, grid, orientation and scale form the framework of a map. The language of maps in concept and content is much more complex. To represent the surface of the Earth on a map, the cartographer must select and generalize from a vast quantity of material, using symbols and conventional signs as codes.

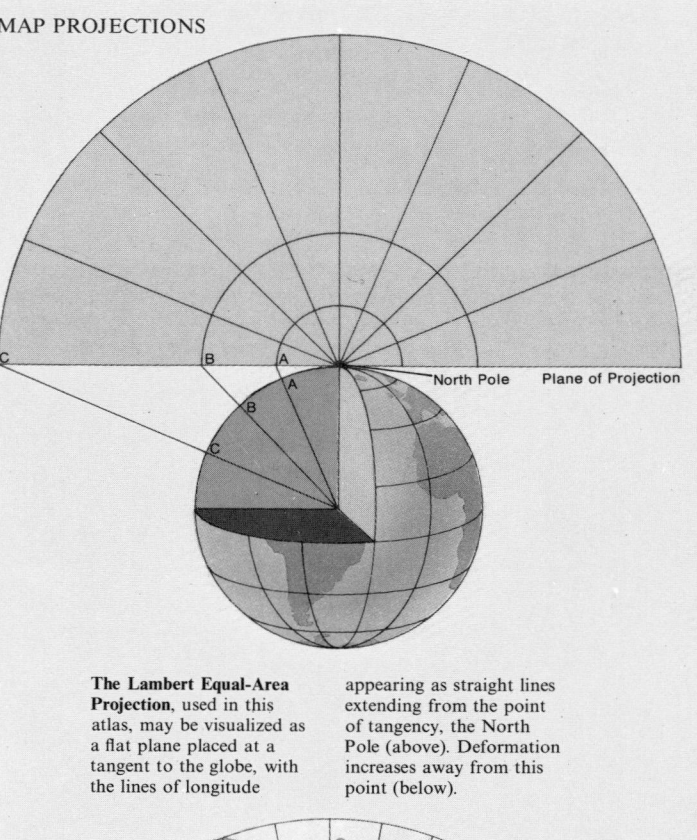

The Lambert Equal-Area Projection, used in this atlas, may be visualized as a flat plane placed at a tangent to the globe, with the lines of longitude appearing as straight lines extending from the point of tangency, the North Pole (above). Deformation increases away from this point (below).

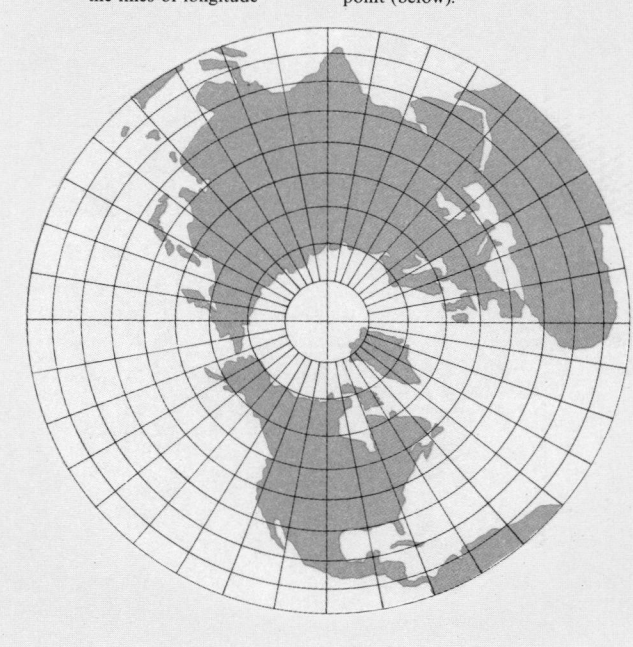

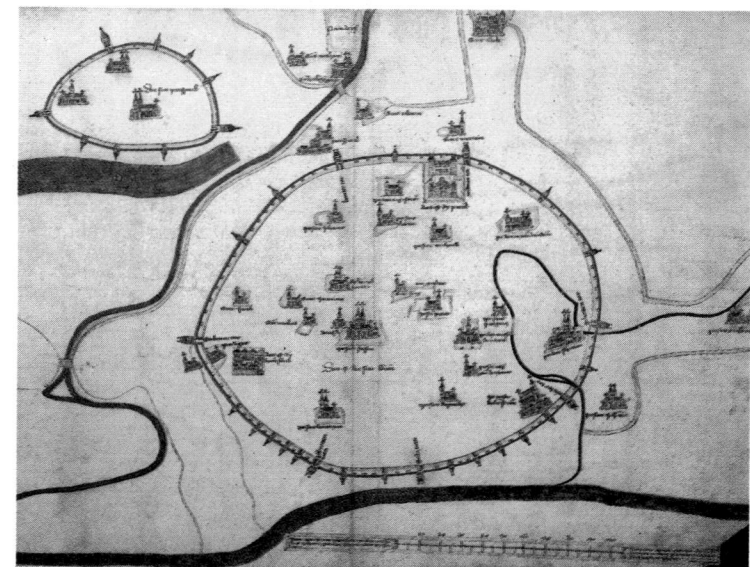

Map scales express the relationship between a distance measured on the map and the true distance on the ground. A plan of Vienna (left), originally made in 1422, is drawn in the bird's-eye-view style typical of early medieval town plans. But the scale bar at its foot shows that it has been explicitly drawn to scale, indicating that the concept of a uniform scale had been grasped in medieval Europe.

Direction and distance are concepts used in the relative location of two or more points (below). These concepts are organized according to a general frame of reference, with direction following the grid system of coordinates. Thus places shown in (A) can be precisely located in terms of longitude and of latitude (B), with the degrees further subdivided into one-sixtieths of minutes.

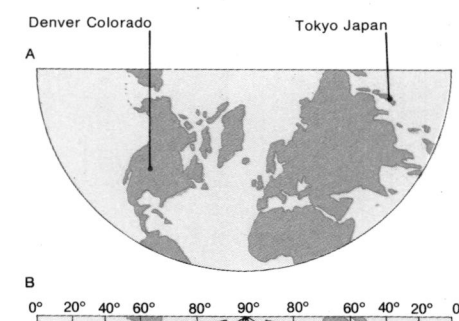
Denver Colorado   Tokyo Japan
A

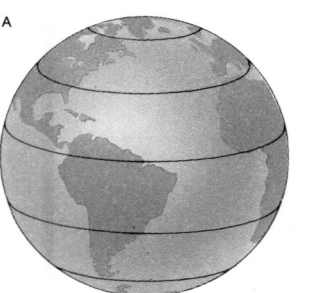

A

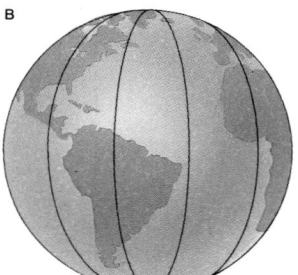

B

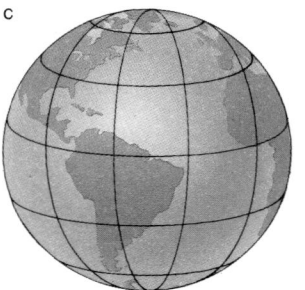

C

Superimposed on the globe (left), lines of latitude (A) and longitude (B) allow every place to be exactly located in terms of a coordinate system (C). The parallels of latitude measure distance from 0° to 90° north and south of the Equator. The meridians of longitude measure distance from 0° to 180° east and west of a "prime meridian" at Greenwich.

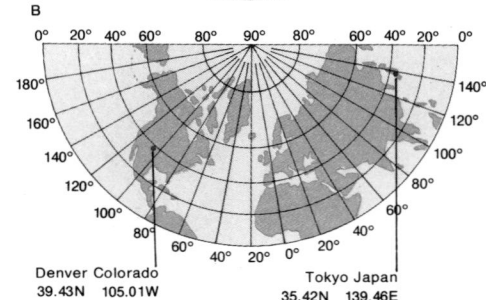

Denver Colorado 39.43N 105.01W

Tokyo Japan 35.42N 139.46E

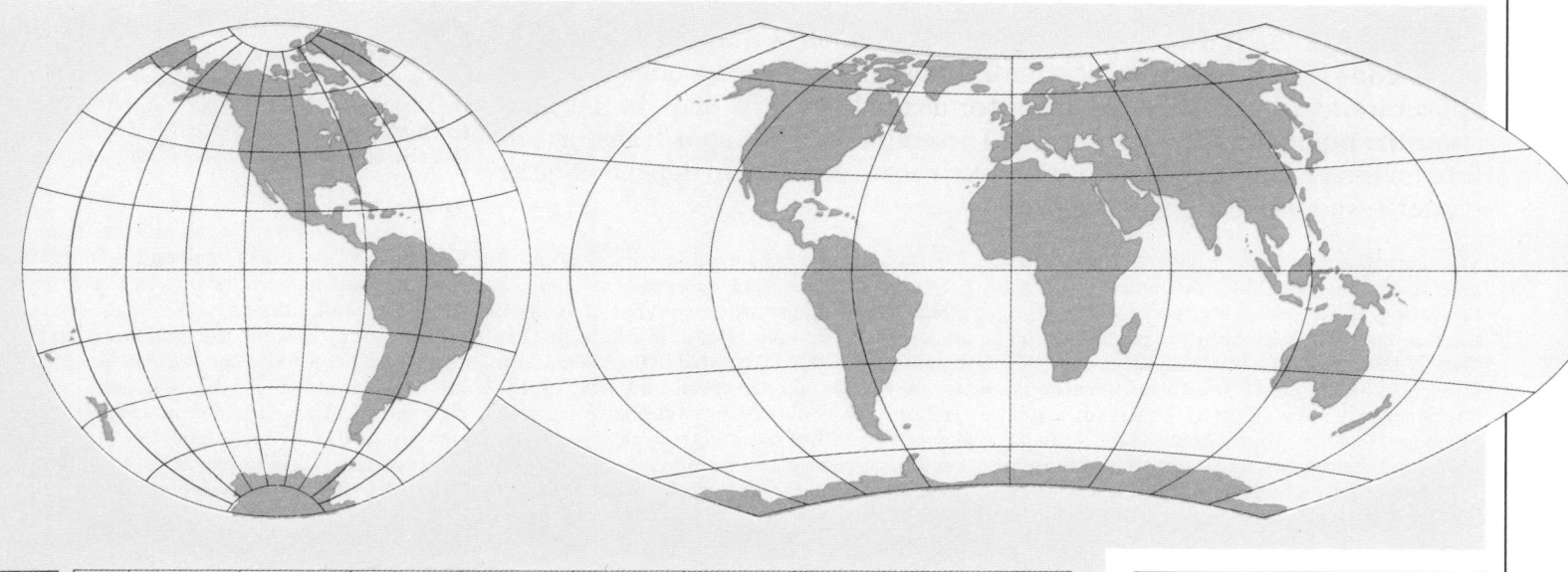

The Hammer Projection (far right), developed from the Lambert Projection of one hemisphere (right), is designed to show the whole world in a single view, and is used in this atlas in a version modified by Wagner and known as the Hammer-Wagner Projection. The Earth appears as an ellipse because the lines of longitude are plotted at twice their horizontal distance from the center line, and numbered at twice their previous values. The central meridian is half the length of the Equator.

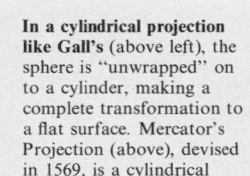

Delisle's Conic Projection (right), used in this atlas, intersects the globe at two points (above). Distortion is least at the parallels where the cone "touches" the globe, increasing with distance from them. Thus it is good for mid-latitudes.

In a cylindrical projection like Gall's (above left), the sphere is "unwrapped" on to a cylinder, making a complete transformation to a flat surface. Mercator's Projection (above), devised in 1569, is a cylindrical projection that aids navigation by showing all compass directions as straight lines. A projection (below), based on Peters', distorts shape to show land surface area ratios, emphasizing the Third World.

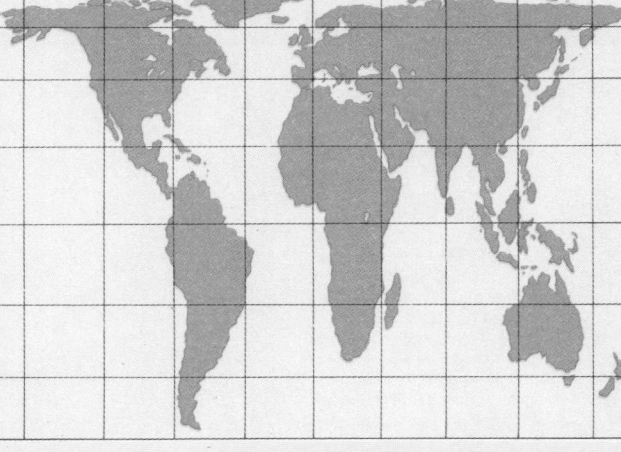

Photogrammetric plotting instruments (above) are now used in the preparation of large-scale accurate topographic maps. These are sophisticated machines that provide very precise measurements, plotting the map data in orthogonal projection.

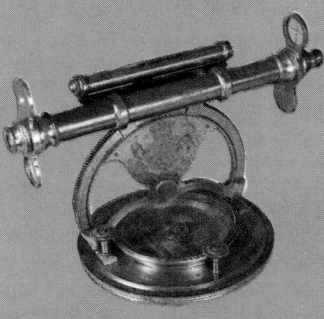

The theodolite (above), a basic surveying instrument dating back to the 16th century, can measure angles and directions horizontally and vertically. A swivel telescope with cross-hairs inside it permits accurate alignment, and it may be used in the field.

EARTH MEASUREMENT THROUGH THE AGES

Surveying—the technique of making accurate measurements of the Earth's surface—is as old as civilization and has been an essential element in mankind's development of his environment. The need to establish land boundaries arose at least 3,500 years ago in the fertile valleys of the Nile, Tigris and Euphrates rivers. Man's urge to explore and to describe the world also led to the development of instruments determining position, distance and direction. The astrolabe, sometimes called the world's oldest scientific instrument, may date to the 3rd century BC. Today's techniques make increasing use of computers.

An Egyptian wall painting (left) from the middle of the second millennium BC shows what appears to be the measurement of a grain field by means of a rope with knots at regular intervals on its length.

The astrolabe (right), used in classical times to observe the positions of celestial bodies, became a navigational instrument in the Middle Ages, when it was developed to permit establishment of latitude.

How to Use Maps

Today maps play a role more important than ever before in increasing our knowledge of the Earth, its regions and peoples. How maps communicate knowledge is now a subject of scientific study. The process comprises the collection and mapping of the data and the reading of the map. In this final stage the map user is all important. Through him the map is transformed into an image in the mind, and the effectiveness of the map depends on the reader being able to understand it.

The cartographer's map has to convey an objective picture of reality. To compile the map the cartographer selects and generalizes information, taking into account the purpose of his map. If he is making a topographical reference map, he has to reduce the three-dimensional landforms of the Earth on to the flat surface of the map. He adds cultural detail such as towns, roads and railroads, and features not apparent to the eye, such as administrative boundaries. On the topographical base map he adds appropriate place-names, using typefaces which reflect their class and significance. All this requires the classification of phenomena, with emphasis to direct the reader's attention.

Themes and symbolization

The cartographer who seeks not merely to represent visible features but to convey geographical ideas about specific phenomena uses the techniques of thematic cartography, where the emphasis is on one or two elements, or themes. Maps today provide one of the most effective means of communicating many kinds of data and ideas relating to the world and its peoples. Their extensive use makes them an important force in education, planning, recreation and in many other human affairs.

The map is designed in code, with symbols to represent features, and a legend, or key, to explain them. There are three types of symbol: point, line and area. Point symbols usually denote places, which may be distinguished into classes by the shape, color and size of the symbol. Line symbols express connections, such as roads or traffic flow, and they may also define and distinguish areas. Area symbols in which variations of color are often combined with patterns of lines or dots are used to depict spatial phenomena, such as types of soil, vegetation and density of population.

How much detail can be shown on a map will depend on its scale, which controls the process of generalization. Scale expresses the relationship of the distance on the map to the distance on the Earth, with the distance on the map always given as the unit 1. It is denoted in various ways: as a representative fraction such as 1:1,000,000; as a written statement; or by means of a graph or bar. Some map scales have become widely used and are generally familiar to map users. The scale 1:25,000 is ideal for walkers and relief can be shown in detail. That of 1:50,000 is a typical medium scale for national surveys. The publication of an international map of the world on a scale of one to

one million (1:1,000,000) has been in progress since 1909. On this scale 1 mm represents 1 km on the ground. The regional maps of countries in this atlas are drawn on scales of 1:6,000,000, 1:3,000,000 and 1:1,500,000; those of the continents are at 1:30,000,000 and 1:15,000,000. The Map Section index maps show the arrangement.

Terrain depiction

Since the early days of map making in ancient Chinese and classical Greek and Roman civilizations, map makers have been concerned to show the configuration of the land. For many centuries they symbolized mountains and hills by pictorial features often looking like caterpillars or sugar loaves. As topographical mapping developed in Europe from the seventeenth century onward, new techniques were devised to improve the visual impression of the features and to depict them accurately in terms of height and location. The system of hachuring (shading with fine parallel or crossed lines), first used in 1674, gives a good idea of relief but not of height. The use of contours, which became general from the nineteenth century onward, is more exact in representing actual elevation, but for many regions, especially those of irregular relief, the appearance of the land is lost.

The addition of hypsometric tints (tints between contours which show elevation) helps clarify the elevation. Applying shadows to the form of the land through the process called hill shading or relief shading creates a visual impression of the configuration of the land surface. Hypsometric tints combined with hill shading gives both elevation information and surface form of the area being depicted, leading to an almost three-dimensional effect.

Maps are classed (right) as either general (A) or thematic (B,C). The purpose of a general reference map is to provide locational information, showing how the positions of various geographical phenomena relate to each other. Thematic maps concentrate on a particular type of information, or theme, such as the distribution of people (B) or rainfall (C), and are generally based on statistical data.

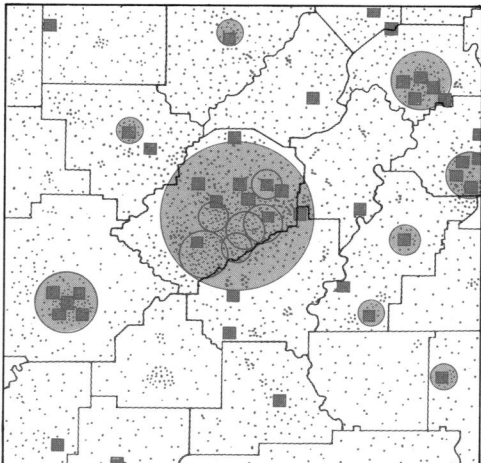

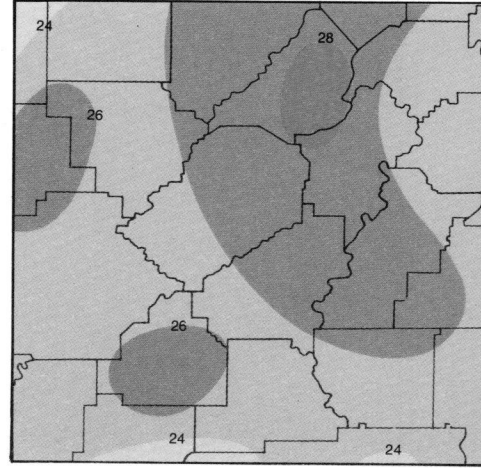

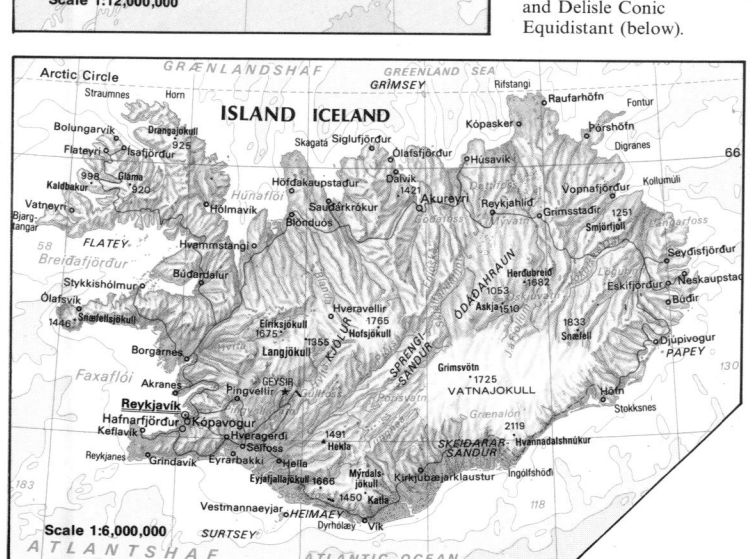

The ratio between a map's dimensions and those of the physical world is defined by the map scale (left and below), with the map distance always given as the unit 1. The larger the reduction, the smaller the scale, so that a scale of 1:6,000,000—1 mm (.04 in) to 6 km (3.74 miles)—is twice that of 1:12,000,000 (.04 in to 7.5 miles). The size of the scale reflects the amount of detail that needs to be shown. The projections are the Lambert Azimuthal Equal-Area (left) and Delisle Conic Equidistant (below).

Scale 1:12,000,000

Scale 1:6,000,000

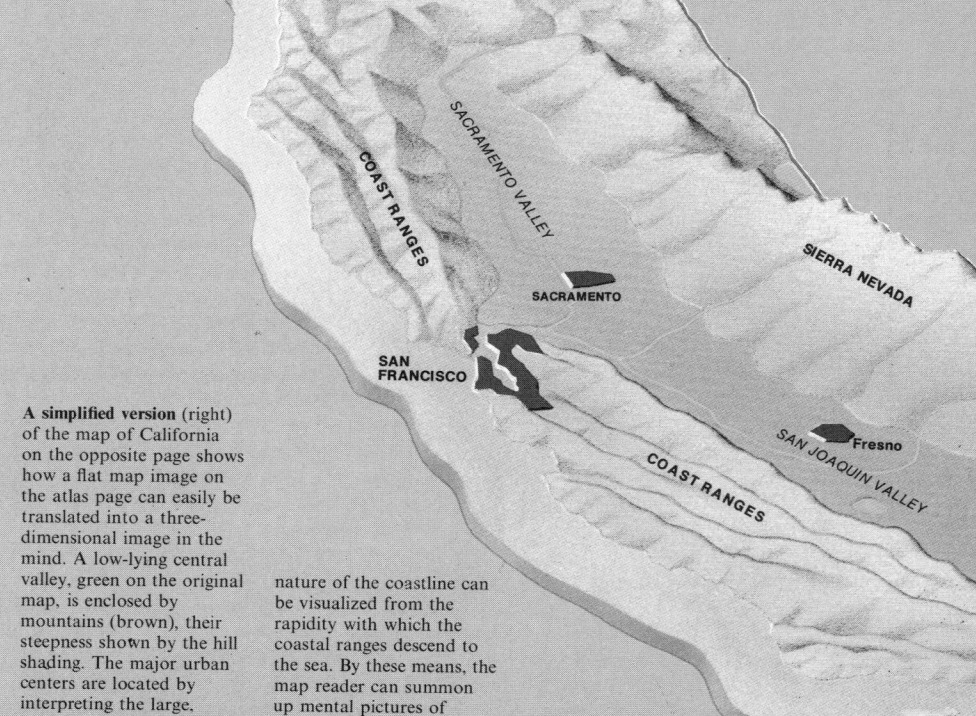

A simplified version (right) of the map of California on the opposite page shows how a flat map image on the atlas page can easily be translated into a three-dimensional image in the mind. A low-lying central valley, green on the original map, is enclosed by mountains (brown), their steepness shown by the hill shading. The major urban centers are located by interpreting the large, bold typeface, and the nature of the coastline can be visualized from the rapidity with which the coastal ranges descend to the sea. By these means, the map reader can summon up mental pictures of utterly unfamiliar lands.

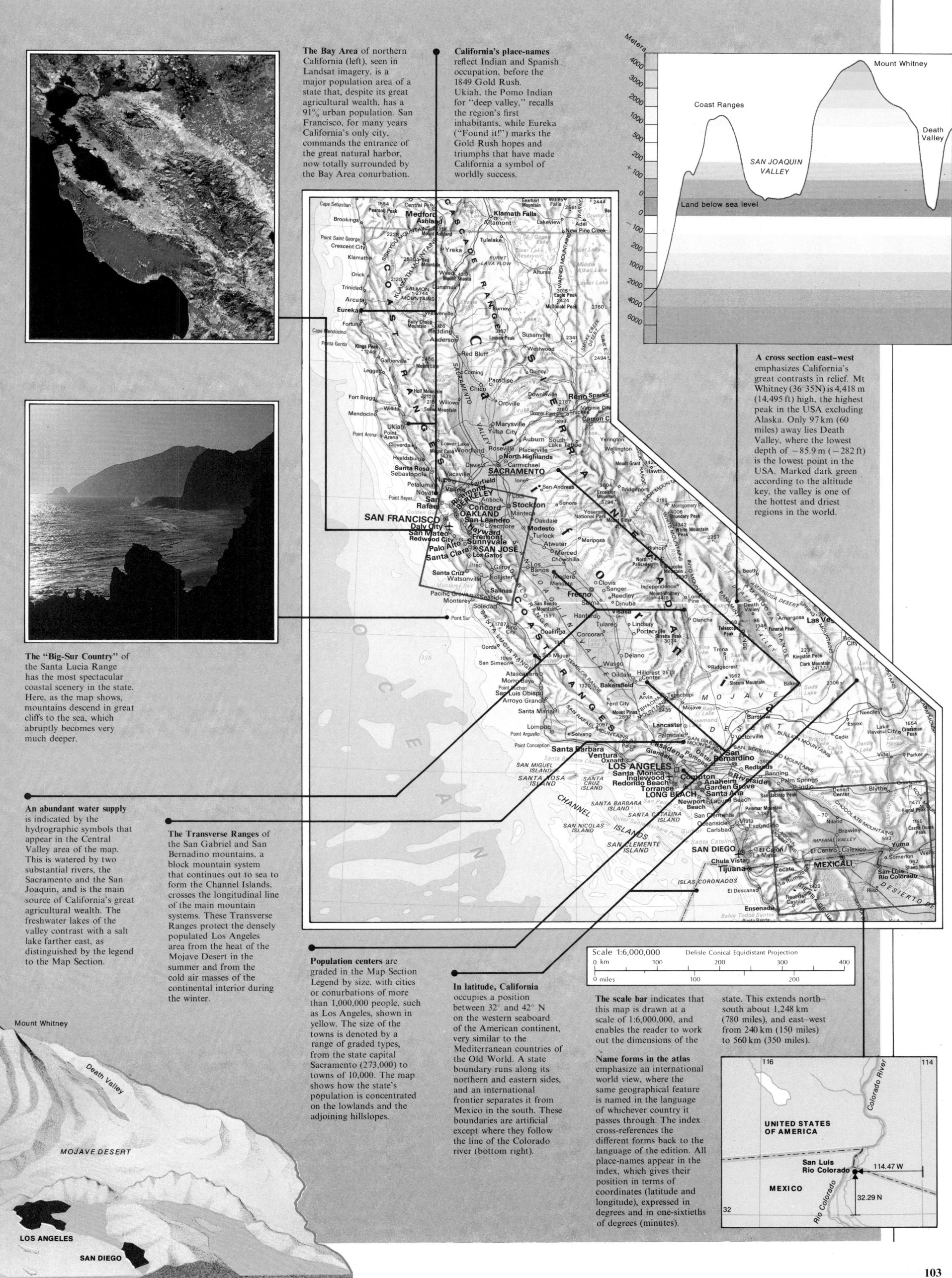

The Bay Area of northern California (left), seen in Landsat imagery, is a major population area of a state that, despite its great agricultural wealth, has a 91% urban population. San Francisco, for many years California's only city, commands the entrance of the great natural harbor, now totally surrounded by the Bay Area conurbation.

California's place-names reflect Indian and Spanish occupation, before the 1849 Gold Rush. Ukiah, the Pomo Indian for "deep valley," recalls the region's first inhabitants, while Eureka ("Found it!") marks the Gold Rush hopes and triumphs that have made California a symbol of worldly success.

A cross section east–west emphasizes California's great contrasts in relief. Mt Whitney (36°35N) is 4,418 m (14,495 ft) high, the highest peak in the USA excluding Alaska. Only 97 km (60 miles) away lies Death Valley, where the lowest depth of −85.9 m (−282 ft) is the lowest point in the USA. Marked dark green according to the altitude key, the valley is one of the hottest and driest regions in the world.

The "Big-Sur Country" of the Santa Lucia Range has the most spectacular coastal scenery in the state. Here, as the map shows, mountains descend in great cliffs to the sea, which abruptly becomes very much deeper.

An abundant water supply is indicated by the hydrographic symbols that appear in the Central Valley area of the map. This is watered by two substantial rivers, the Sacramento and the San Joaquin, and is the main source of California's great agricultural wealth. The freshwater lakes of the valley contrast with a salt lake farther east, as distinguished by the legend to the Map Section.

The Transverse Ranges of the San Gabriel and San Bernadino mountains, a block mountain system that continues out to sea to form the Channel Islands, crosses the longitudinal line of the main mountain systems. These Transverse Ranges protect the densely populated Los Angeles area from the heat of the Mojave Desert in the summer and from the cold air masses of the continental interior during the winter.

Population centers are graded in the Map Section Legend by size, with cities or conurbations of more than 1,000,000 people, such as Los Angeles, shown in yellow. The size of the towns is denoted by a range of graded types, from the state capital Sacramento (273,000) to towns of 10,000. The map shows how the state's population is concentrated on the lowlands and the adjoining hillslopes.

In latitude, California occupies a position between 32° and 42° N on the western seaboard of the American continent, very similar to the Mediterranean countries of the Old World. A state boundary runs along its northern and eastern sides, and an international frontier separates it from Mexico in the south. These boundaries are artificial except where they follow the line of the Colorado river (bottom right).

The scale bar indicates that this map is drawn at a scale of 1:6,000,000, and enables the reader to work out the dimensions of the state. This extends north–south about 1,248 km (780 miles), and east–west from 240 km (150 miles) to 560 km (350 miles).

Name forms in the atlas emphasize an international world view, where the same geographical feature is named in the language of whichever country it passes through. The index cross-references the different forms back to the language of the edition. All place-names appear in the index, which gives their position in terms of coordinates (latitude and longitude), expressed in degrees and in one-sixtieths of degrees (minutes).

Scale 1:6,000,000   Delisle Conical Equidistant Projection

ACKNOWLEDGMENTS

Senior Executive Art Editor
Michael McGuinness

Executive Editor
James Hughes

Coordinating Editor
Dian Taylor

Editors
Lesley Ellis
Judy Garlick
Ken Hewis

Art Editor
Mike Brown

Designers
Sue Rawkins
Lisa Tai

Picture Researcher
Flavia Howard

Researchers
Nicholas Law
Nigel Morrison
Alicia Smith

Editorial Assistant
Barbara Gish

Proofreader
Kathie Gill

Indexers
Hilary and Richard Bird

Production Controller
Barry Baker

Typesetting by Servis Filmsetting
Limited, Manchester, England

Reproduction by Gilchrist
Brothers Limited, Leeds, England

CONTRIBUTORS AND CONSULTANTS

GENERAL CONSULTANT
Professor Michael Wise, CBE, MC, BA, PhD, D.Univ, Professor of
Geography, London School of Economics and Political Science

EDITORIAL CONSULTANT
John Clark

Frances Atkinson, BSc

British Museum (Natural History), Botany Library

Robert W. Bradnock, MA, PhD, Lecturer in Geography with special
reference to South Asia at the School of Oriental and African
Studies, University of London

Michael J. Bradshaw, MA, Principal Lecturer in Geography, College
of St Mark and St John, Plymouth

Dr J. M. Chapman, BSc, ARCS, PhD, MIBiol, Lecturer in Biology,
Queen Elizabeth College, University of London

Dr Jeremy Cherfas, Departmental Demonstrator in Zoology, Oxford
University

Dr M. J. Clark, Senior Lecturer in Geomorphology, Geography
Department, Southampton University

J. L. Cloudsley-Thompson, MA, PhD(Cantab), DSc(Lond),
Hon DSc(Khartoum), Professor of Zoology, Birkbeck College,
University of London

Professor R. U. Cooke, Department of Geography, University
College, London

Professor Clifford Embleton, MA, PhD, Department of Geography,
King's College, University of London

Dr John Gribbin, Physics Consultant to *New Scientist* magazine

Dr John M. Hellawell, BSc, PhD, FIBiol, MIWES, Principal,
Environmental Aspects, Severn Trent Water Authority, Birmingham

Dr Garry E. Hunt, BSc, PhD, DSc, FRAS, FRMetS, FIMA, MBCS,
Head of Atmospheric Physics, Imperial College, London

David K. C. Jones, Lecturer in Geography, London School of
Economics and Political Science

Dr Russell King, Department of Geography, University of Leicester

Dr D. McNally, Assistant Director, University of London
Observatory

Meteorological Office, Berkshire

Dr Robert Muir Wood, PhD

Dr B. O'Connor, Department of Geography, University of London

J. H. Paterson, MA, Professor of Geography in the University of
Leicester

Dr Nigel Pears, Department of Geography, University of Leicester

Joyce Pope, BA

Dr A. L. Rice, Institute of Oceanographic Sciences, Wormley, Surrey

Ian Ridpath, science writer and broadcaster

Royal Geographical Society

Helen Scoging, BSc, Department of Geography, London School of
Economics and Political Science

Bernard Stonehouse, DPhil, MA, BSc, Chairman, Post-Graduate
School of Environmental Science, University of Bradford

Dr Christopher B. Stringer, PhD, Senior Scientific Officer,
Palaeontology Department, British Museum (Natural History)

J. B. Thornes, Professor of Physical Geography and Head of
Department, Bedford College, University of London

UN Information Office and Library

Professor J. E. Webb, DSc, *Emeritus*, Department of Zoology,
Westfield College, University of London

Peter B. Wright, BSc, MPhil

UNDERSTANDING MAPS
Helen Wallis, MA, DPhil, FSA, The Map Librarian, British Library

A great many other individuals, organizations, and institutions have
given invaluable advice and assistance during the preparation of this
Our Planet Earth Section and the publishers wish to extend their
thanks to them all.

ILLUSTRATION CREDITS

Maps in the Our Planet Earth Section by Creative Cartography Limited
unless otherwise specified. Map of the world's climatic regions, page 50,
adapted from *An Introduction to Climate* 4th edition by Trewartha/
Elements of Geography by G. T. Trewartha, A. H. Robinson and
E. H. Hammond © McGraw-Hill Book Co., N.Y., 1967. Used with
permission of McGraw-Hill Book Co. Map diagram page 101 (bottom)
courtesy Doctor Arno Peters.

2–3 *Exploding universe* Product Support (Graphics); *others* Quill.
4–5 Bob Chapman. **6–7** Bob Chapman. **8–9** Mick Saunders;
Landsat diagrams Gary Marsh; *biowindows* Chris Forsey. **10–11**
Mick Saunders. **12–13** Bob Chapman. **14–15** *Diagrams* Chris Forsey;
mountain sequence Donald Myall. **16–17** Colin Salmon. **18–19** Peter
Morter; *graph* Mick Saunders; *car* Peter Owen. **20–21** Bob
Chapman; *diagram* Chris Forsey; *map* Colin Salmon. **22–23** Chris
Forsey (*including maps*). **24–25** Brian Delf. **26–27** Brian Delf.
28–29 Dave Etchell/John Ridyard. **30–31** Creative Cartography Ltd.
32–33 Mick Saunders. **34–35** Chris Forsey; *experiment* Gary Hincks;
others Mick Saunders. **36–37** Chris Forsey; *fruit flies, birds and mice*
Donald Myall. **38–39** Chris Forsey; *time scale* Mick Saunders;
stromatolite and diagram Garry Hincks. **40–41** Donald Myall;
time scale Mick Saunders. **42–43** Donald Myall; *time scale* Mick
Saunders. **44–45** Creative Cartography Ltd. **46–47** Donald Myall;
diagram Kai Choi; *skulls* Jim Robins. **48–49** Creative Cartography
Ltd. **50–51** Peter Morter; *diagram* Marilyn Clark. **52–53** Kai Choi.
54–55 Creative Cartography Ltd. **56–57** Creative Cartography Ltd.
58–59 Creative Cartography Ltd. **60–61** Creative Cartography Ltd;
illustrations Jim Robins. **62–63** *Migration diagram and graph* Kai
Choi; *illustrations* Coral Mula. **64–65** Donald Myall. **66–67**
Landscape diagram Bill le Fever; *illustrations* Russell Barnett. **68–69**
Donald Myall. **70–71** Jim Robins; *plants, bottom left* Andrew
Macdonald. **72–73** Rory Kee; *bottom left* Russell Barnett; *plow*
Kai Choi; *grains and graph* Creative Cartography Ltd. **74–75** Bob
Bampton/The Garden Studio; *animal adaptations* Russell Barnett.
76–77 Donald Myall. **78–79** David Ashby.
80–81 David Ashby. **82–83** Coral Mula. **84–85** Jim Robins. **86–87** Creative
Cartography Ltd. **88–89** Brian Delf; *blood counts diagram* Colin
Salmon. **90–91** Bob Chapman; *animals and plants* Rod Sutterby.
92–93 Kai Choi; *hydrological cycle* Bob Chapman. **94–95** Andy
Farmer; *shore and plant life* Russell Barnett; *coral atoll* Colin
Salmon. **96–97** Creative Cartography Ltd. **98–99** *Topographic maps*
Rand McNally; *sketch map* Space Frontiers Ltd. **100–101** *Diagrams*
Creative Cartography Ltd. **102–103** *Maps* Istituto Geografico De
Agostini; Rand McNally; *diagrams* Creative Cartography Ltd.

PICTURE CREDITS

Credits read from top to bottom and from left to right on each page. Images that extend over two pages are credited to the left-hand page only.

2 US Naval Observatory; California Institute of Technology and Carnegie Institution of Washington. **3** Both pictures from Royal Observatory, Edinburgh. **8** All pictures from NASA. **9** All pictures from NASA except top and top right, courtesy of Garry Hunt, Laboratory of Planetary Atmospheres, University College, London. **14–15** Maurice and Sally Landre/Colorific! **16–17** All pictures courtesy of Dr Basil Booth, Geoscience Features. **18** Institute of Geological Sciences. **19** Paul Brierley; Institute of Geological Sciences. **20** Camera Press, London. **26** Barnaby's Picture Library; Barnaby's Picture Library; Institute of Geological Sciences. **28** Dr Alan Beaumont. **30** Tom Sheppard/Robert Harding Picture Library; Professor Ronald Cooke. **31** Institute of Geological Sciences. **32** Stuart Windsor; Sefton Photo Library, Manchester; Rio Tinto Zinc; Douglas Botting; Aspect Picture Library. **33** NASA; Mireille Vautier; Explorer/Vision International. **34** Paul Brierley. **37** Paediatric Research Unit, Guy's Hospital Medical School; Dr Laurence Cook, Zoology Department, University of Manchester. **39** Both pictures from British Museum (Natural History). **46** Colophoto Hans Hinz. **47** Dr P. G. Bahn, School of Archaeology and Oriental Studies, University of Liverpool/Musée des Antiquités Nationales, St. Germain-en-Laye. **56** UNICEF (Photo no. 8675 by H. Dalrymple). **57** Dr A. M. O'Connor, Department of Geography, University College, London. **61** International Fund for Animal Welfare; K. Kunov/Novosti Press Agency; Popperfoto; Charles Swithinbank. **62** Alan Robson. **63** Gösta Hakansson/Frank Lane Agency. **65** G. R. Roberts. **67** Anglo-Chinese Educational Trust; Aerofilms. **69** Ted Streshinsky. **72** Engraving from *At Home with the Patagonians*. **73** The Mansell Collection. **76** J. Bitsch/Zefa; Penny Tweedie/Colorific! **77** Alan Hutchison Library; Bill Holden/Zefa. **80** Syndication International; Gerald Cubitt/Bruce Coleman Ltd; Bruce Coleman Ltd. **81** Alan Hutchison Library; R. and M. Borland/Bruce Coleman Ltd; M. P. Kahl/Bruce Coleman Ltd; Jan and Des Bartlett/Bruce Coleman Ltd. **84** J. von Puttkamer/Alan Hutchison Library. **85** Marion Morrison. **86–87** Richard and Sally Greenhill. **88** Alan Hutchison Library; The Association of Universities for Research in Astronomy, Inc. **89** Gunter Ziesler/Bruce Coleman Ltd. **91** Mike Price/Bruce Coleman Ltd. **92** Ian Murphy. **93** Paolo Koch/Vision International; J. Allan Cash; M. Timothy O'Keefe/Bruce Coleman Ltd. **94** Heather Angel. **95** Institute of Oceanographic Sciences. **96** Fritz Prenzel/Bruce Coleman Ltd; Gordon Williamson/Bruce Coleman Ltd. **97** Martin Rogers/Susan Griggs Agency. **98** British Library; British Museum; Centro Camuno di Studi Preistorici; British Library; NASA; NASA; Rand McNally; British Museum; British Museum. **99** British Museum; NASA; NASA; Rand McNally; Space Frontiers Ltd; Paul G. Lowman/NASA Goddard SFC/Space Frontiers Ltd. **100** Historisches Museum, Vienna. **101** Hunting Surveys Ltd; Michael Holford/Science Museum, London; Michael Holford; Michael Holford/Science Museum, London. **103** Space Frontiers Ltd; F. Damm/Zefa.

Page numbers in *italic* refer to the illustrations and their captions.

Cartographic and Geographic Director
Giuseppe Motta

Geographic Research
G. Baselli
M. Colombo

Toponymy and Translation
C. Carpine
M. Colombo
H. R. Fischer
R. Nuñez de las Cuevas
Rand McNally
Cartographic Research Staff
I. Straube

Computerized Data Organization
C. Bardesono
E. Ciano
G. Comoglio
E. Di Costanzo

Index
S. Osnaghi
T. Tomasini

Cartographic Editor
V. Castelli

Cartographic Compilation
G. Albera
L. Cairo
C. Camera
G. Conti
G. Fizzotti
G. Gambaro
M. Mochetti
O. Passarelli
M. Peretti
G. Rassiga
A. Saino
F. Valsecchi

Terrain Illustration
S. Andenna
E. Ferrari

Cartographic Production
F. Tosi
G. Capitini
A. Carnero

Filmsetting
S. Fiorini
P. L. Gatta
E. Geranio
G. Ghezzi
L. Lorena
R. Martelli
E. Morchio
M. Morganti
C. Pezzana
P. Uglietti
D. Varalli

Photographic Processing
G. Fracassina
G. Klaus
L. Mella

Coordination
S. Binda
L. Pasquali
G. Zanetta

The editors wish to thank the many organizations, institutions and individuals who have given their valuable help and advice during the preparation of this International Map Section. Special thanks are extended to the following:

Agenzia Novosti, Rome, Italy
D. Arnold, Acting Chief of Documentation and Terminology Section, United Nations, New York, USA
Australian Bureau of Statistics, Brisbane, Australia
J. Breu, United Nations Group of Experts on Geographical Names, Vienna, Austria
Bureau Hydrographique International, Monaco, Principality of Monaco
Canada Map Office, Ottawa, Canada
Cartactual, Budapest, Hungary
Census and Statistical Department, Tripoli, Libya
Central Bureau of Statistics, Accra, Ghana
Central Bureau of Statistics, Jerusalem, Israel
Central Bureau of Statistics, Ministry of Economic Planning and Development, Nairobi, Kenya
Central Department of Statistics, Riyadh, Saudi Arabia
Central Statistical Board of the USSR, Moscow, USSR
Central Statistical Office, London, UK
Centro de Informaçao e Documentaçao Estadística, Rio de Janeiro, Brazil
Committee for the Reform of Chinese Written Language, Peking, China
Danmark Statistik, Copenhagen, Denmark
Defense Mapping Agency, Distribution Office for Latin America, Miami, USA
Defense Mapping Agency, Washington DC, USA
Department of National Development and Energy, Division of National Mapping, Belconnen ACT, Australia
Department of State Coordinator for Maps and Publications, Washington DC, USA
Department of State Map Division, Sofia, Bulgaria
Department of Statistics, Wellington, New Zealand
Direcçao Nacional de Estadística, Maputo, Mozambique
Dirección de Cartografia Naciónal, Caracas, Venezuela
Dirección de Estadística y Censo de la Repubblica de Panamá, Panama
Dirección General de Estadística, Mexico City, Mexico
Dirección General de Estadística y Censos, San Salvador, El Salvador
Direcţia Centrala de Statistică, Bucharest, Romania
Directorate of National Mapping, Kuala Lumpur, Malaysia
Directorate of Overseas Surveys, London, UK
Elaborazione Dati e Disegno Automatico, Torino, Italy
Federal Office of Statistics, Lagos, Nigeria
Federal Office of Statistics, Prague, Czechoslovakia
Geographical Research Institute, Hungarian Academy of Sciences, Budapest, Hungary
Geological Map Service, New York, USA
G. Gomez de Silva, Chief Conference Services Section, United Nations Environment Programme, New York, USA
Government of the People's Republic of Bangladesh, Statistics Division, Ministry of Planning, Dacca, Bangladesh
High Commissioner for Trinidad and Tobago, London, UK
L. Iarotski, World Health Organization, Geneva, Switzerland Information Division, Valletta, Malta
Institut für Angewandte Geodäsie, Frankfurt, West Germany
Institut Géographique, Abidjan, Ivory Coast
Institut Géographique du Zaïre, Kinshasa, Zaïre
Institut Géographique National, Brussels, Belgium
Institut Géographique National, Paris, France
Institut Haïtien de Statistique, Port-au-Prince, Haiti
Institut National de Géodésie et Cartographie, Antananarivo, Madagascar
Institut National de la Statistique, Tunis, Tunisia
Institute of Geography, Polish Academy of Sciences, Warsaw, Poland
Instituto Geográfico Militar, Buenos Aires, Argentina
Instituto Nacional de Estadística, La Paz, Bolivia
Instituto Nacional de Estadística, Madrid, Spain
Istituto Centrale di Statistica, Rome, Italy
Istituto Geografico Militare, Florence, Italy
Istituto Idrografico della Marina, Genoa, Italy
Landesverwaltung des Fürstentums, Vaduz, Liechtenstein
Ministère des Affaires Economiques, Brussels, Belgium
Ministère des Ressources Naturelles, des Mines et des Carrières, Kigali, Rwanda
Ministère des Travaux Publics, des Transports et de l'Urbanisme, Ouagadougou, Upper Volta
Ministry of Finance, Department of Statistics and Research, Nicosia, Cyprus

Ministry of Lands, Housing and Urban Development, Surveys and Mapping Division, Dar es Salaam, Tanzania
Ministry of the Interior, Jerusalem, Israel
National Census and Statistics Office, Manila, Philippines
National Central Bureau of Statistics, Stockholm, Sweden
National Geographic Society, Washington DC, USA
National Institute of Polar Research, Tokyo, Japan
National Ocean Survey, Riverdale, Maryland, USA
National Statistical Institute, Lisbon, Portugal
National Statistical Office, Zomba, Malawi
National Statistical Service of Greece, Athens, Greece
J. Novotny, Prague, Czechoslovakia
Office Nationale de la Recherche Scientifique et Technique, Yaoundé, Cameroon
Officina Comercial del Gobierno de Colombia, Rome, Italy
Ordnance Survey of Ireland, Dublin, Ireland
Österreichisches Statistisches Zentralamt, Vienna, Austria
Państwowe Przedsiebiorstwo Wydawnictw Kartograficznych, Warsaw, Poland
Scott Polar Research Institute, University of Cambridge, Cambridge, UK
Secrétariat d'Etat au Plan, Algiers, Algeria
Servicio Geografico Militar, Montevideo, Uruguay
Z. Shiying, Research Institute of Surveying and Mapping, Peking, China
Statistisches Bundesamt, Wiesbaden, West Germany
Statistisk Sentralbyrå, Oslo, Norway
Survey and National Mapping Department, Kuala Lumpur, Malaysia
Ufficio Turismo e Informazioni della Turchia, Rome, Italy
United States Board on Geographic Names, Washington DC, USA
M. C. Wu, Chinese Translation Service, United Nations, New York, USA
Z. Youguang, Committee for the Reform of Chinese Written Language, Peking, China

The editors are also grateful for the assistance provided by the following embassies, consulates and official state representatives:

Angolan Embassy, Rome
Australian Embassy, Rome
Austrian Embassy, Rome
Embassy of Bangladesh, Rome
Embassy of Botswana, Brussels
Brazilian Embassy, Rome
British Embassy, Rome
Burmese Embassy, Rome
Embassy of Cameroon, Rome
Embassy of Cape Verde, Lisbon
Consulate of Chad, Rome
Chilean Embassy, Rome
Embassy of the People's Republic of China in Italy, Rome
Danish Embassy, Rome
Embassy of El Salvador, Rome
Ethiopian Embassy, Rome
Finnish Embassy, Rome
Embassy of the German Democratic Republic, Rome
Greek Embassy, Rome
Honduras Republic Embassy, Rome
Hungarian Embassy, Rome
Consulate General of Iceland, Rome
Embassy of India, Rome
Embassy of the Republic of Indonesia, Rome
Embassy of the Islamic Republic of Iran, Rome
Irish Embassy, Rome
Embassy of Israel, Rome
Japanese Embassy, Rome
Korean Embassy, Rome
Luxembourg Embassy, Rome
Embassy of Malta, Rome
Mexican Embassy, Rome
Moroccan Embassy, Rome
Netherlands Embassy, Rome
Embassy of New Zealand, Rome
Embassy of Niger, Rome
Embassy of Pakistan, Rome
Peruvian Embassy, Rome
Philippine Embassy, Rome
Romanian Embassy, Rome
Somali Embassy, Rome
South African Embassy, Rome
Spanish Embassy, Rome
Consulate General of Switzerland, Milan
Royal Thai Embassy, Rome
Consulate of Upper Volta, Rome
Uruguay Embassy, Rome
Embassy of the Socialist Republic of Vietnam in Italy, Rome
Permanent Mission of Yemen to United Nations Educational, Scientific and Cultural Organization, Paris

INTERNATIONAL MAP SECTION

Hydrographic and Topographic Features
Symboles hydrographiques et morphologiques
Gewässer- und Geländeformen
Idrografia, Morfologia
Hidrografía y morfología

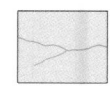
River, Stream
Cours d'eau permanent
Ständig wasserführender Fluß
Corso d'acqua perenne
Corriente de agua de régimen permanente

Lake
Lac d'eau douce
Süßwassersee
Lago d'acqua dolce
Lago de agua dulce

Rocks
Ecueils, Roches
Klippen, Felsriffe
Scogli, Rocce
Escollos, Rocas

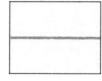
Summer Limit of Pack Ice
Limite du pack en été
Packeisgrenze im Sommer
Limite estivo del pack ghiacciato
Límite estival de banco de hielo

Intermittent Stream
Cours d'eau intermittent
Zeitweilig wasserführender Fluß
Corso d'acqua periodico
Corriente de agua intermitente

Intermittent Lake
Lac d'eau douce temporaire
Zeitweiliger Süßwassersee
Lago d'acqua dolce periodico
Lago de agua dulce intermitente

Reef, Atoll
Barrière, Atoll
Riff, Atoll
Barriera, Atollo
Barrera de arrecifes

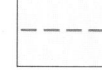
Winter Limit of Pack Ice
Limite du pack en hiver
Packeisgrenze im Winter
Limite invernale del pack ghiacciato
Límite invernal de banco de hielo

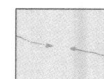
Disappearing Stream
Perte de cours d'eau
Versickernder Fluß
Corso d'acqua che si inabissa
Corriente de agua que desaparece

Salt Lake
Lac d'eau salée
Salzsee
Lago d'acqua salata
Lago de agua salada

Mangrove
Mangrove
Mangrove
Mangrovie
Manglar

Limit of Icebergs
Limite des glaces flottantes
Treibeisgrenze
Limite dei ghiacci alla deriva
Límite de hielo a la deriva

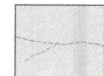
Undefined or Fluctuating River Course
Cours d'eau incertain
Fluß mit veränderlichem Lauf
Fiume dal corso incerto
Corriente de agua incerta

Intermittent Salt Lake
Lac d'eau salée temporaire
Zeitweiliger Salzsee
Lago d'acqua salata periodico
Lago de agua salada intermitente

Continental Ice-cap
Glacier continental
Inlandeis, Gletscher
Ghiacciaio continentale
Glaciar continental

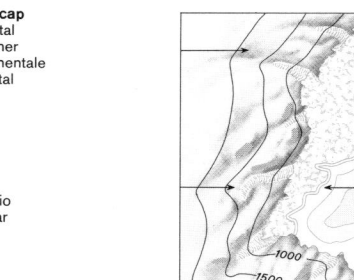

Ice Shelf
Banquise
Schelfeis oder Eisschelf
Banchisa polare (Ice-shelf)
Banquisa

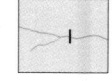
Waterfall, Rapids, Cataract
Chute, Rapide, Cataracte
Wasserfall, Stromschnelle, Katarakt
Cascata, Rapida, Cateratta
Cascada, Rapido, Catarata

Dry Lake Bed
Lac asséché
Trockener Seeboden
Alveo di lago asciutto
Lecho de lago seco

Glacial Tongue
Langue glaciaire
Gletscherzunge
Lingua di ghiaccio
Lengua de glaciar

Limit of Ice Shelf
Limite de la banquise
Schelfeisgrenze
Limite della banchisa
Límite de la banquisa

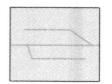
Canal
Canal
Kanal
Canale
Canal

Lake Surface Elevation
Cote du lac au-dessus du niveau de la mer
Höhe des Seespiegels
Altitudine del lago
Elevación de lago sobre el nivel del mar

Rocky Areas (Antarctica)
Région de roches (Antarctique)
Eisfreie Gebiete, Gebirge (Antarktika)
Aree rocciose (Antartide)
Area rocosa (Antártida)

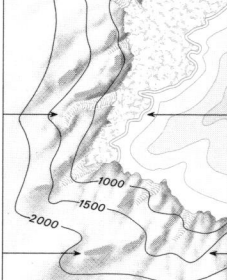

Contour Lines in Continental Ice
Courbes de niveau dans les régions glaciaires
Höhenlinien auf vergletschertem Gebiet
Curve altimetriche nelle aree ghiacciate
Curvas de nivel en áreas heladas

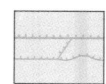
Navigable Canal
Canal navigable
Schiffbarer Kanal
Canale navigabile
Canal navegable

Lake Depth
Profondeur du lac
Seetiefe
Profondità del lago
Profundidad del lago

Defined Shoreline
Trait de côte définie
Küsten- oder Uferlinie
Linea di costa definita
Línea de costa definida

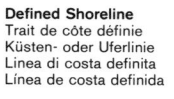

Bathymetric Contour
Courbe bathymétrique
Tiefenlinie
Curva batimetrica
Curva batimétrica

Swamp
Marais
Sumpf
Palude d'acqua dolce
Pantano

Sand Area
Région de sable, Désert
Sandgebiet, Sandwüste
Area sabbiosa, Deserto
Zona arenosa, desierto

Undefined or Fluctuating Shoreline
Trait de côte indéfinie
Unbestimmte oder veränderliche Uferlinie
Linea di costa indefinita
Línea de costa indefinida

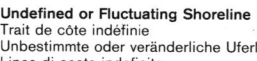 

Depth of Water
Valeur de sonde
Tiefenzahl
Quota batimetrica
Cota batimétrica

Salt Marsh
Marais d'eau salée
Salzsumpf
Palude d'acqua salata
Pantano de agua salada

Sandbank, Sandbar
Banc de sable
Sandbank
Bassofondo sabbioso
Banco submarino de arena

Mountain Range
Chaîne de montagnes
Bergkette
Catena di monti
Cadena montañosa

Mountain
Mont
Berg, Bergmassiv
Monte
Monte

Salt Pan
Marais salant
Salzpfanne
Salina
Salina

Port Facilities
Installations portuaires
Hafenanlagen
Impianti portuali
Instalaciones portuarias

Elevation
Cote, Altitude
Höhenzahl
Quota altimetrica
Cota altimétrica

Mountain Pass, Gap
Passage, Col, Port
Paß, Joch, Sattel
Passo, Colle, Valico
Paso, Collado, Puerto de montaña

Key to Elevation and Depth Tints
Hypsométrie, Bathymétrie
Höhenstufen, Tiefenstufen
Altimetria, Batimetria
Altimetría, Batimetría

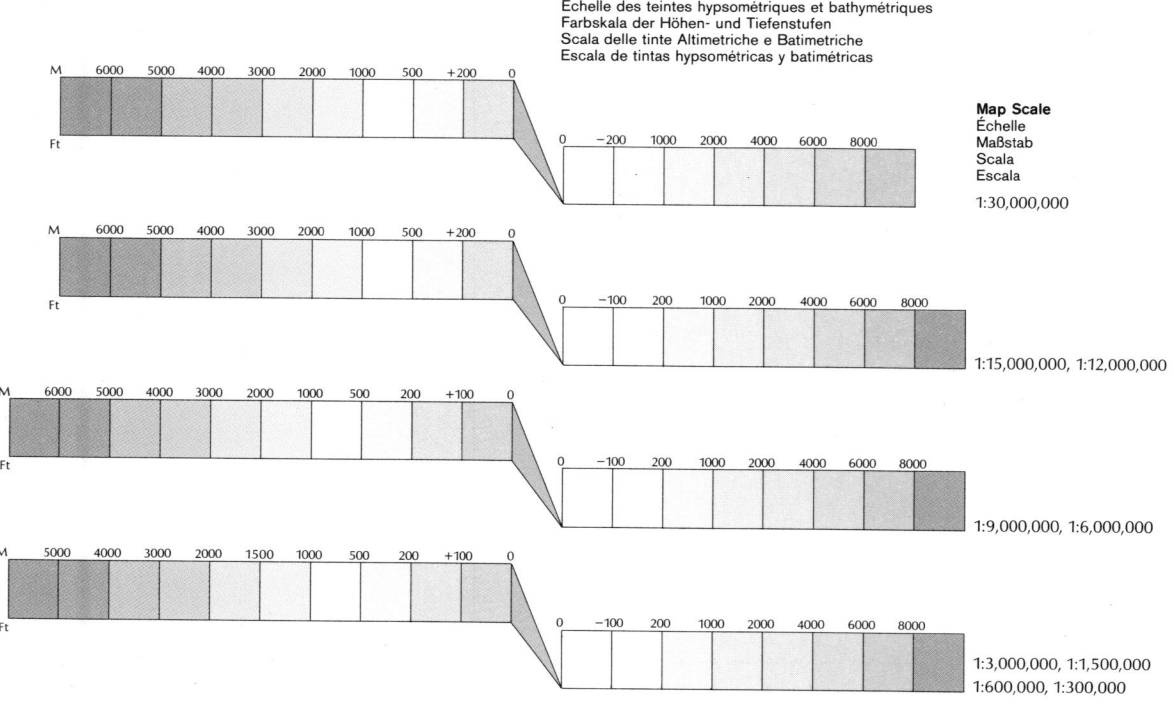

Scales in Metric and English Measures
Échelle des teintes hypsométriques et bathymétriques
Farbskala der Höhen- und Tiefenstufen
Scala delle tinte Altimetriche e Batimetriche
Escala de tintas hypsométricas y batimétricas

Map Scale
Échelle
Maßstab
Scala
Escala

1:30,000,000

1:15,000,000, 1:12,000,000

1:9,000,000, 1:6,000,000

1:3,000,000, 1:1,500,000
1:600,000, 1:300,000

Land Elevation Below Sea Level
Dépression et cote au-dessous du niveau de la mer
Senke mit Tiefenzahl unter dem Meeresspiegel
Depressione e quota sotto il livello del mare
Depresión y elevación bajo el nivel del mar

Map Projections
Projections cartographiques
Kartennetzentwürfe
Proiezioni cartografiche
Proyecciones cartográficas

The projections appearing in this atlas have been plotted by computer

Les réseaux des projections ont été obtenus par élaboration automatique à partir de formules mathématiques

Die Kartennetze aller im Atlas vorkommenden Abbildungen wurden mit Hilfe der Datenverarbeitung (EDV) völlig neu errechnet

I disegni delle proiezioni presenti in quest'opera sono stati realizzati interamente ex-novo con l'uso del computer e del plotter a partire dalle formule matematiche

El reticulado de las proyecciones (redes geográficas) incluidas en esta obra han sido obtenidas por proceso automático a partir de las formulas matemáticas

The meanings of the symbols on the Legend pages are in English, French, German, Italian, and Spanish languages to permit the interpretation of the maps by a broad readership.

Boundaries, Capitals
Frontières, Soulignements   Confini, Sottolineature
Grenzen, Unterstreichungen   Límites, Subrayados

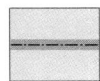
Defined International Boundary
Frontière internationale définie
Staatsgrenze
Confine di Stato definito
Límite de Nación definido

Second-order Political Boundary
Frontière d'État fédéré, Région
Bundesstaats-, Regionsgrenze
Confine di Stato federato, Regione
Límite de Estado federado, Región

International Boundary (Continent Maps)
Frontière internationale (Continents)
Staatsgrenze (Erdteilkarten)
Confine di Stato (Carte dei Continenti)
Límite de Nación (Continentes)

Third-order Political Boundary
Frontière de Province, Comté, Bezirk
Provinz-, Grafschafts-, Bezirksgrenze
Confine di Provincia, Contea, Bezirk
Límite de Provincia, Condado, Bezirk

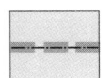
Undefined International Boundary
Frontière internationale indéfinie
Nicht genau festgelegte Staatsgrenze
Confine di Stato indefinito
Límite de Nación indefinido

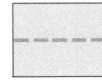
Administrative District Boundary (U.S.S.R.)
Frontière de Circonscription
Kreisgrenze
Confine di Circondario
Límite de Circunscripción administrativa

International Ocean Floor Boundary Defined by Treaty or Bilateral Agreement
Frontière d'état en mer définie par traités et conventions bilatéraux
Durch Verträge festgelegte Staatsgrenze im Meeresgebiet
Confine di Stato nel mare definito da trattati e convenzioni bilaterali
Límite de Nación en el Mar definido por los tratados bilaterales

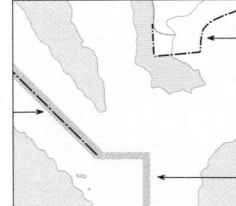

International Ocean Floor Boundary
Frontière d'état en mer
Staatsgrenze im Meeresgebiet
Confine di Stato nel mare
Límite de Nación en el mar

Undefined Ocean Floor Boundary
Frontière indéfinie d'état tracée en meer
Unbstimmte Staatsgrenze im Meeresgebiet
Confine di Stato indefinito nel mare
Límite indefinido de Nación en el mar

 **ROMA**
National Capital
Capitale d'État
Hauptstadt eines unabhängigen Staates
Capitale di Stato
Capital de Nación

Kristiansand
Third - order Capital
Capitale de Province, Comté, Bezirk
Provinz-, Grafschafts-, Bezirkshauptstadt
Capoluogo di Provincia, Contea, Bezirk
Capital de Provincia, Condado, Bezirk

RIGA
Dependency or Second-order Capital
Capitale d'État fédéré, Région
Bundesstaats-, Regionshauptstadt
Capitale di Stato federato, Regione
Capital de Estado federado, Región

Anadyr
Administrative District Capital (U.S.S.R.)
Capitale de Circonscription
Kreishauptstadt
Capoluogo di Circondario
Capital de Circunscripción administrativa

Other Symbols
Symboles divers   Simboli vari
Sonstige Zeichen   Signos varios

 LUTON AIRPORT
International Airport
Aéroport international
Internationaler Flughafen
Aeroporto internazionale
Aeropuerto internacional

SANTAS CREUS
Church, Monastery, Abbey
Monastère, Église, Abbaye
Kloster, Kirche, Abtei
Monastero, Chiesa, Abbazia
Monasterio, Iglesia, Abadía

Lighthouse
Phare
Leuchtturm
Faro
Faro

DAMPIERRE
Castle
Château
Burg, Schloß
Castello
Castillo

BUI DAM
Dam
Barrage
Staudamm, Staumauer
Diga artificiale, Sbarramento
Presa

PAESTUM
Ruin, Archeological Site
Ruine, Centre archéologique
Ruine, Archäologisches Zentrum
Rovina, Zona archeologica
Ruina, Zona arqueológica

L-GREENWICH · V-IJmuiden
Section of a City
Faubourg
Stadt- oder Ortsteil
Sobborgo urbano
Suburbio

MOLENS VAN KINDERDIJK
Monument, Historic Site, etc.
Monument
Denkmal
Monumento
Monumento

Bidon V
Uninhabited Locality, Hamlet
Ville inhabitée, Ferme, Hameau
Unbewohnte Stadt, Gehöft, Weiler
Città disabitata, Fattoria, Nucleo di case
Ciudad despoblada, Granja, Casar

HADRIAN'S WALL
Wall
Muraille
Wall, Mauer
Vallo, Muraglia
Muralla

Bi'r Nāhid
Periodically Inhabited Oasis
Oasis habitées périodiquement
Zeitweilig bewohnte Oase
Oasi periodicamente abitate
Oasis periodicamente habitados

GIANT'S CAUSEWAY
Point of Interest
Curiosité
Sehenswürdigkeit
Curiosità
Curiosidad

Casey (Australia)
Scientific Station
Base géophysique
Geophysikalische Beobachtungsstation
Base geofisica
Base geofísica

CUEVAS DE ARTÁ
Cave
Grotte, Caverne
Höhle
Grotta, Caverna
Cueva, Gruta

Populated Places
Population   Popolazione
Bevölkerung   Población

Continent Maps
Cartes des Continents   Carte dei Continenti
Erdteilkarten   Mapas de Continentes
- < 25 000
- 25 000-100 000
- 100 000-250 000
- 250 000-1 000 000
- > 1 000 000

Regional Maps
Cartes à plus grande échelle   Carte di sviluppo
Karten größeren Maßstabs   Mapas a gran escala
- < 10 000
- 10 000-25 000
- 25 000-100 000
- 100 000-250 000
- 250 000-1 000 000
- > 1 000 000

Symbols represent population of inhabited localities
Les symboles représentent le nombre d'habitants des localités
Die Signaturen entsprechen der Einwohnerzahl des Ortes
I simboli sono relativi al valore demografico dei centri abitati
Los simbolos son proporcionales a la población del lugar

Town area symbol represents the shape of the urban area
Le petit plan de la ville reproduit la configuration de l'aire urbaine
Die Plansignatur stellt die Gestalt des Stadtgebietes dar
La piantina della città rappresenta la configurazione dell'area urbana
El pequeño plano de la ciudad representa la forma del area urbana

Transportation
Communications   Comunicazioni
Verkehrsnetz   Comunicaciones

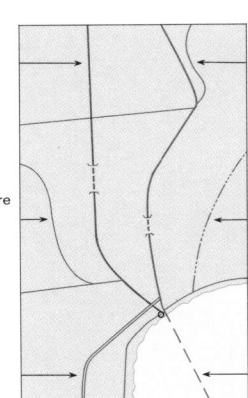

Primary Railway
Chemin de fer principal
Hauptbahn
Ferrovia principale
Ferrocarril principal

Road
Route de grande communication, Autres Routes
Fernverkehrsstraße, andere Straßen
Strada principale, Altre Strade
Carretera principal, Otras Carreteras

Secondary Railway
Chemin de fer secondaire
Sonstige Bahn
Ferrovia secondaria
Ferrocarril secundario

Trail, Caravan Route
Piste, Voie caravanière
Wüstenpiste, Karawanenweg
Pista nel deserto, Carovaniera
Pista en el desierto, Vía de Carabanas

Motorway, Expressway
Autoroute
Autobahn
Autostrada
Autopista

Ferry, Shipping Lane
Bac, Ligne maritime
Fähre, Schiffahrtslinie
Traghetto, Linea di navigazione
Transbordador (Ferry), Línea de navegación

Type Styles
Caractères utilisés pour la toponymie   Caratteri usati per la toponomastica
Zur Namenschreibung verwendete Schriftarten   Caracteres utilizados para la toponimia

ITALY
Hessen   RIBE
Political Units
Etat, Dépendance, Division administrative
Staat, abhängiges Gebiet, Verwaltungsgliederung
Stato, Dipendenza, Divisione amministrativa
Nación, Dependencia, Division administrativa

Ankaratra   Monte Bianco
Tsiafajavona   Ngorongoro Crater
Nevado del Tolima   Kings Peak
Small Mountain Range, Mountain, Peak
Petit massif, Mont, Cime
Bergmassiv, Berg, Gipfel
Piccolo gruppo montuoso, Monte, Vetta
Macizo pequeño, Monte, Cima

LABRADOR SEA
Gulf of Alaska   *Hudson Bay*
Estrecho de Magallanes
Sea, Gulf, Bay, Strait
Mer, Golfe, Baie, Détroit
Meer, Golf, Bucht, Meeresstraße
Mare, Golfo, Baia, Stretto
Mar, Golfo, Bahía, Estrecho

SAXONY
THRACE   *SUSSEX*
Historical or Cultural Region
Région historique ou culturelle
Historische oder Kulturlandschaft
Regione storico - culturale
Región histórica y cultural

Cabo de São Vicente   Land's End
Mizen Head   Point Conception
Col de la Perche   Passo della Cisa
Cape, Point, Pass
Cap, Pointe, Passe
Kap, Landspitze, Paß
Capo, Punta, Passo
Cabo, Punta, Paso

West Mariana Basin
Galapagos Fracture Zone
Mid-Atlantic Ridge
Undersea Features
Formes du relief sous-marin
Formen des Meeresbodens
Forme del rilievo sottomarino
Formas del relieve submarino

PATAGONIA
BASSIN DE RENNES
PENÍNSULA DE YUCATÁN
Physical Region (plain, peninsula)
Région physique (plaine, péninsule)
Landschaft (Ebene, Halbinsel)
Regione fisica (pianura, penisola)
Región natural (llanura, península)

MAHÉ   *ALDABRA ISLANDS*
CORSE   *CHANNEL ISLANDS*
SULU ARCHIPELAGO
Island, Archipelago
Ile, Archipel
Insel, Archipel
Isola, Arcipelago
Isla, Archipiélago

Tarfaya
Tombouctou
Agadir
Nouakchott
BRAZZAVILLE
CASABLANCA
Size of type indicates relative importance of inhabited localities
La dimension des caractères indique l'importance d'une localité
Die Schriftgröße entspricht der Gesamtbedeutung des Ortes
La grandezza del carattere è proporzionale all'importanza della località
La dimensión de los caracteres de imprenta indica la importancia de la localidad

PYRENEES
CUMBRIAN MOUNTAINS
SIERRA DE GÁDOR   LA SILA
Mountain Range
Chaîne de montagnes
Bergkette, Gebirge
Catena di monti
Cadena montañosa

Thames   *Po*   *Victoria Falls*
Lotagipi Swamp   *Göta kanal*
Lago Maggiore
River, Waterfall, Cataract, Canal, Lake
Fleuve, Chute d'eau, Cataracte, Canal, Lac
Fluß, Wasserfall, Katarakt, Kanal, See
Fiume, Cascata, Cateratta, Canale, Lago
Rio, Cascada, Catarata, Canal, Lago

INDEX MAPS

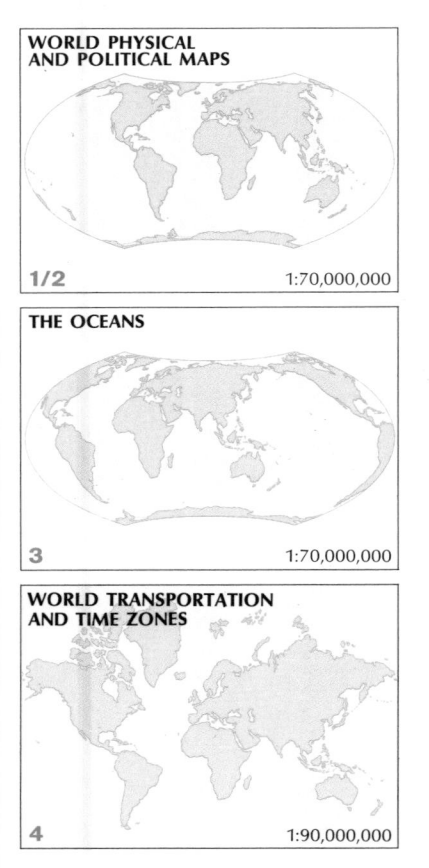
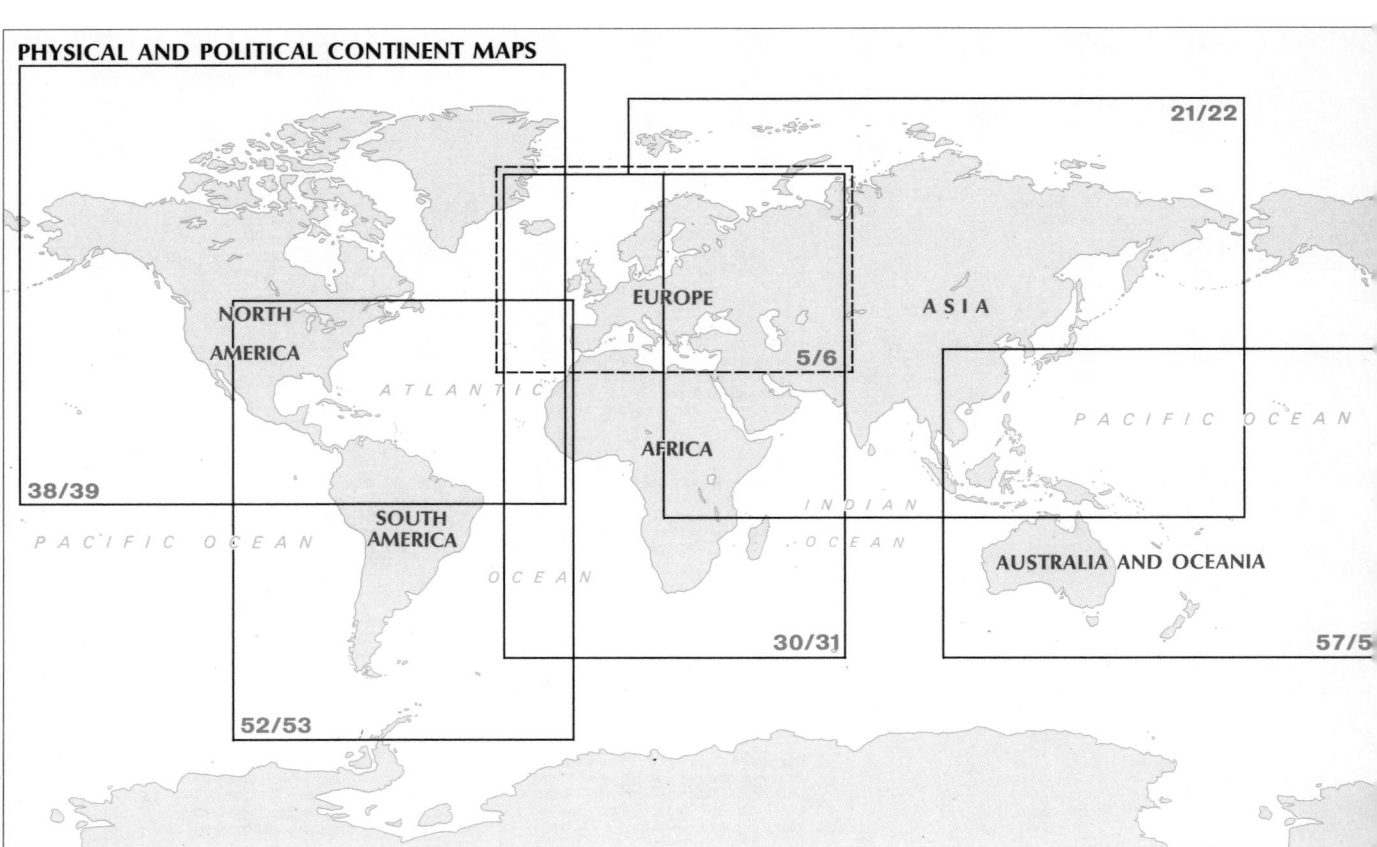

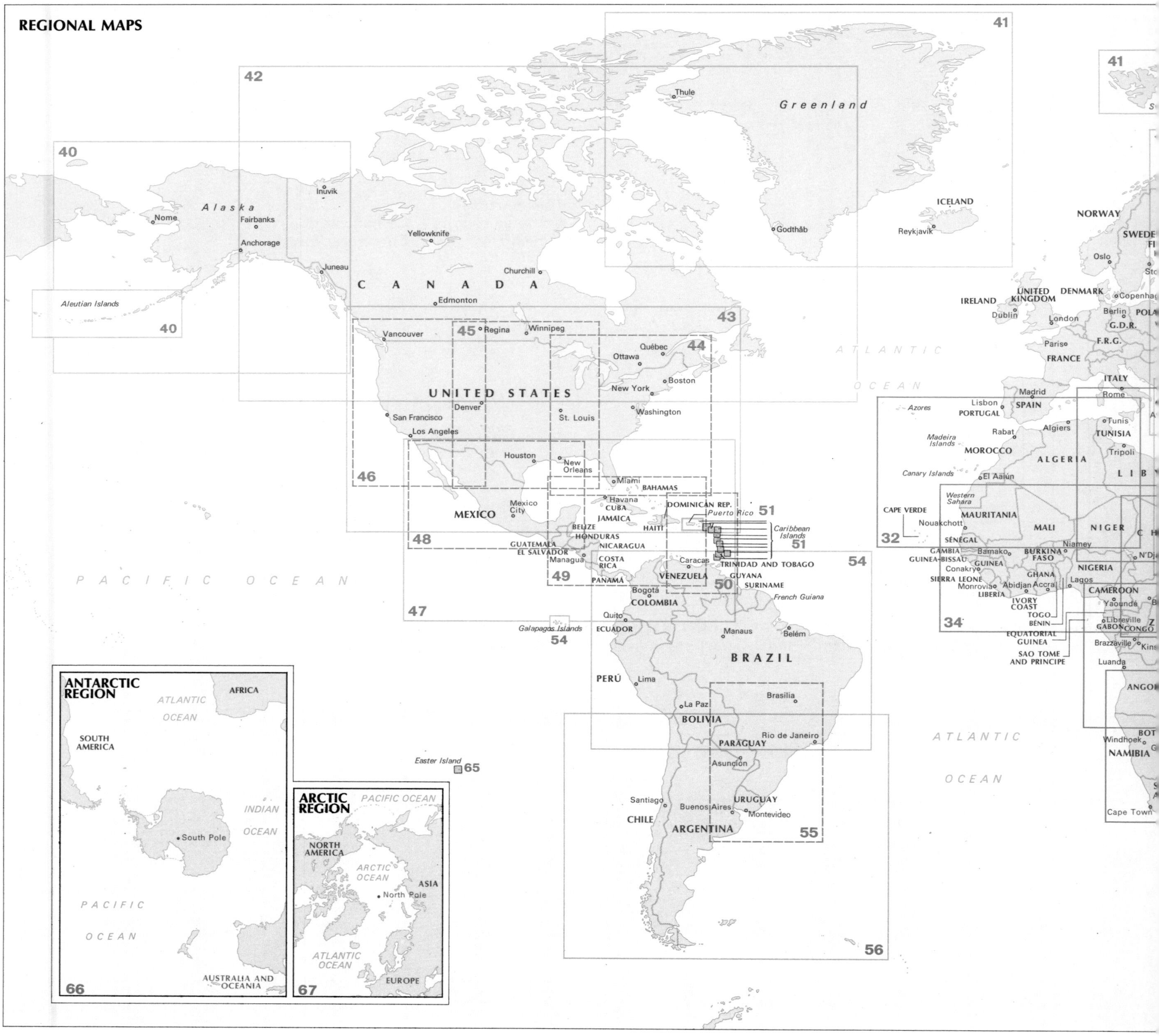

REGISTERED MAPS

REGIONAL MAPS

116

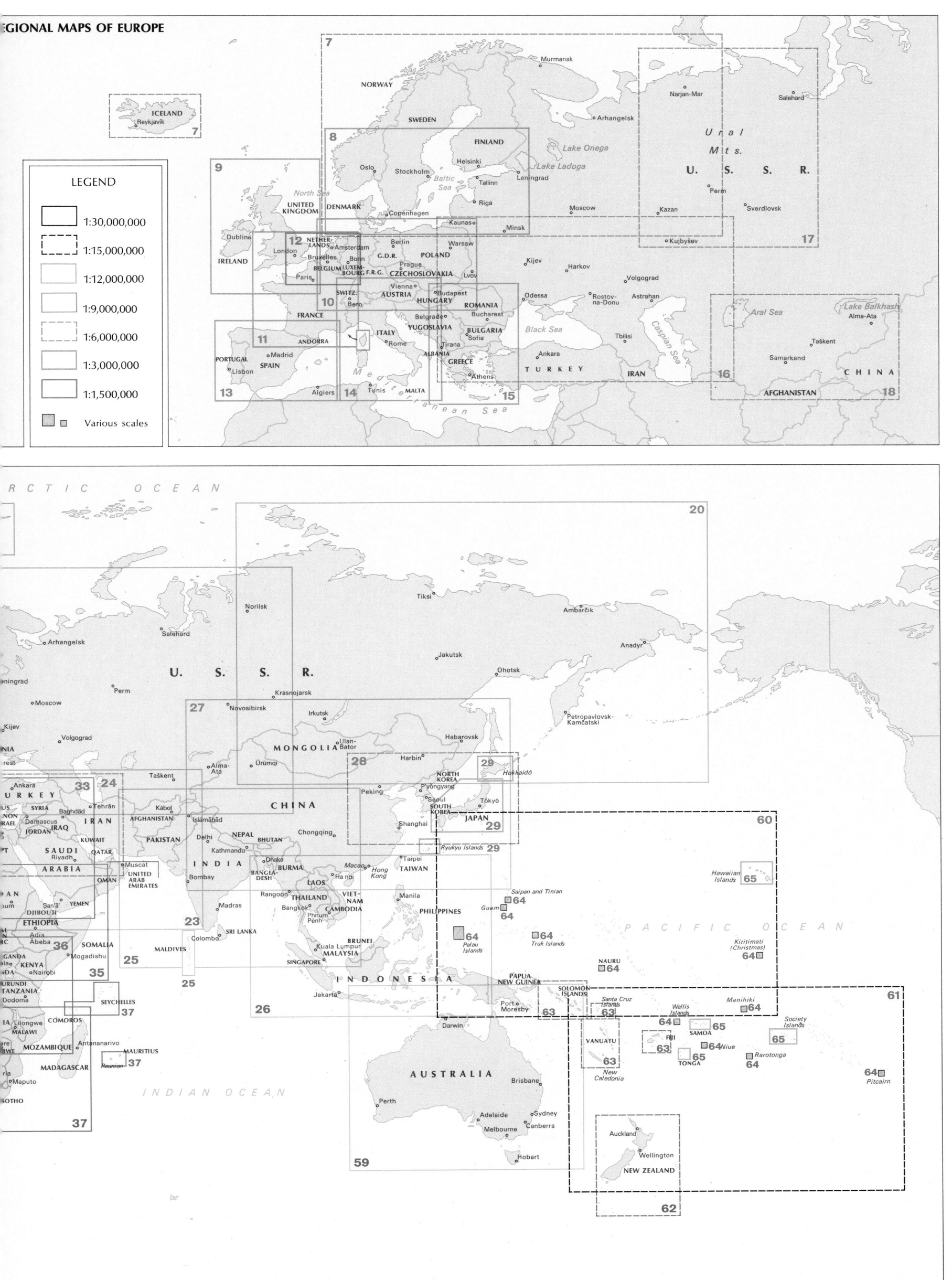

REGIONAL MAPS OF EUROPE

LEGEND

▭	1:30,000,000
▭	1:15,000,000
▭	1:12,000,000
▭	1:9,000,000
▭	1:6,000,000
▭	1:3,000,000
▭	1:1,500,000
▨ ▫	Various scales

Map 1 **WORLD, PHYSICAL**

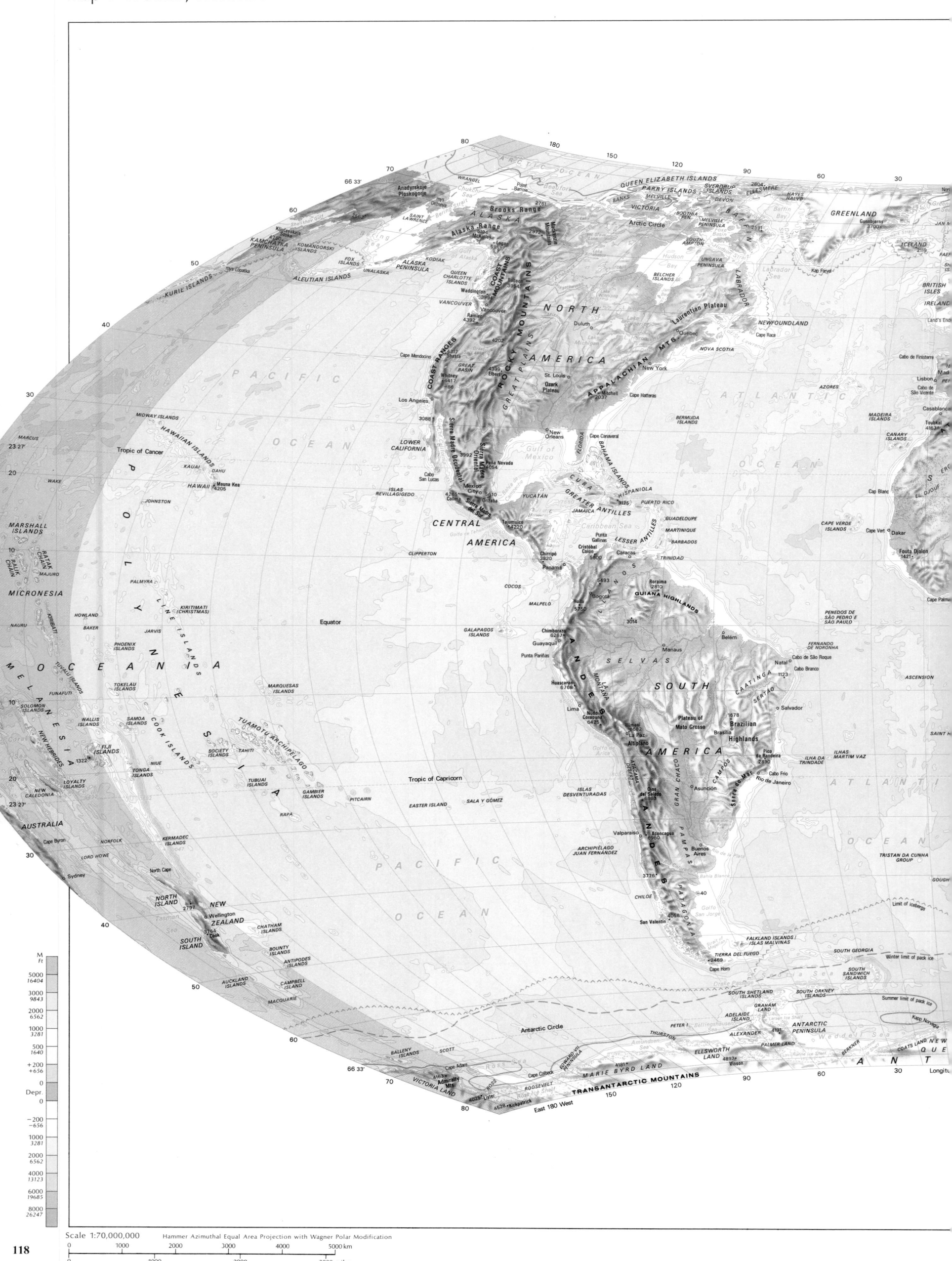

Scale 1:70,000,000   Hammer Azimuthal Equal Area Projection with Wagner Polar Modification

M	Ft
5000	16404
3000	9843
2000	6562
1000	3281
500	1640
+200	+656
0	0
Depr.	0
0	
−200	−656
1000	3281
2000	6562
4000	13123
6000	19685
8000	26247

0   1000   2000   3000   4000   5000 km

0   1000   2000   3000 miles

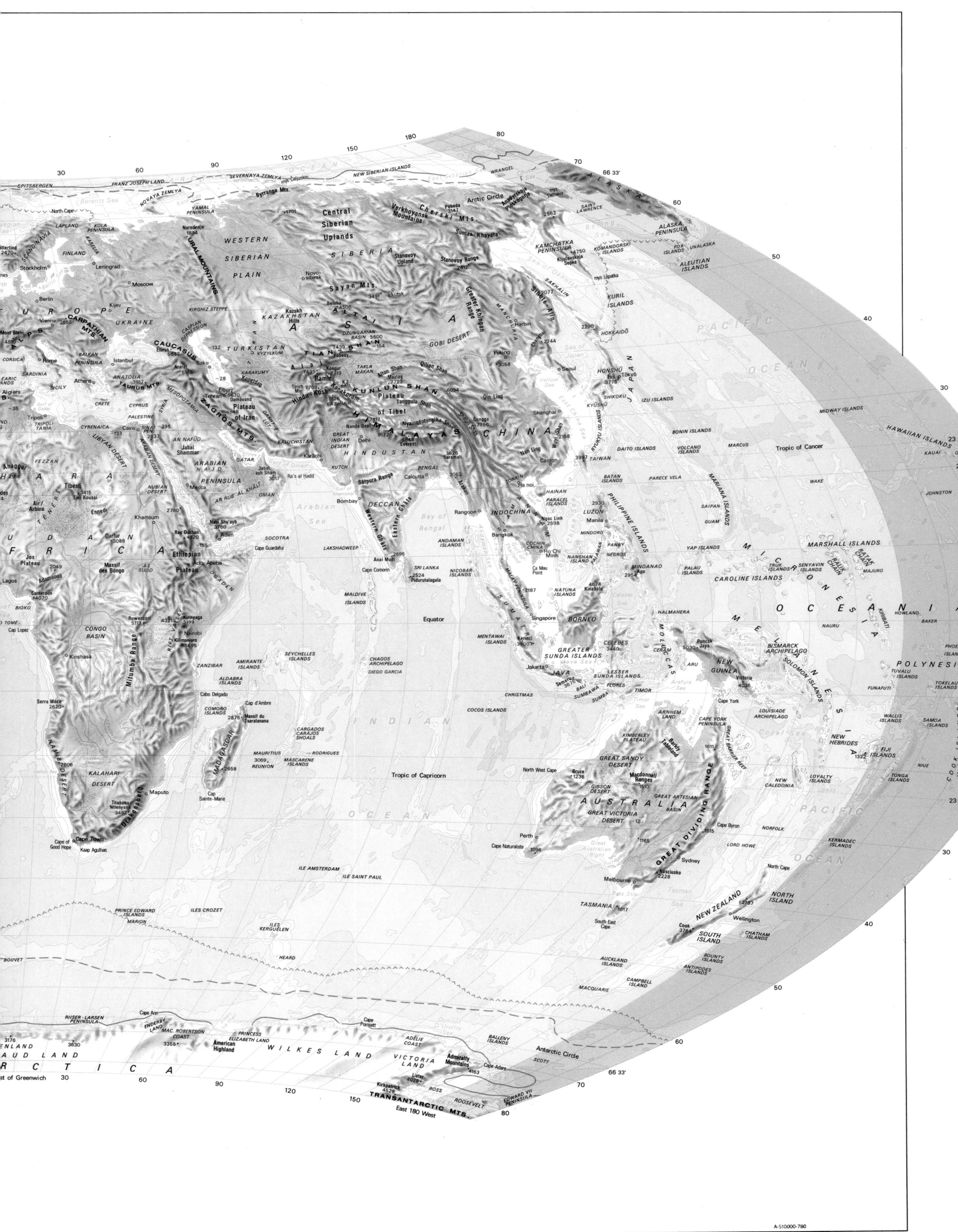

Map 2 **WORLD, POLITICAL**

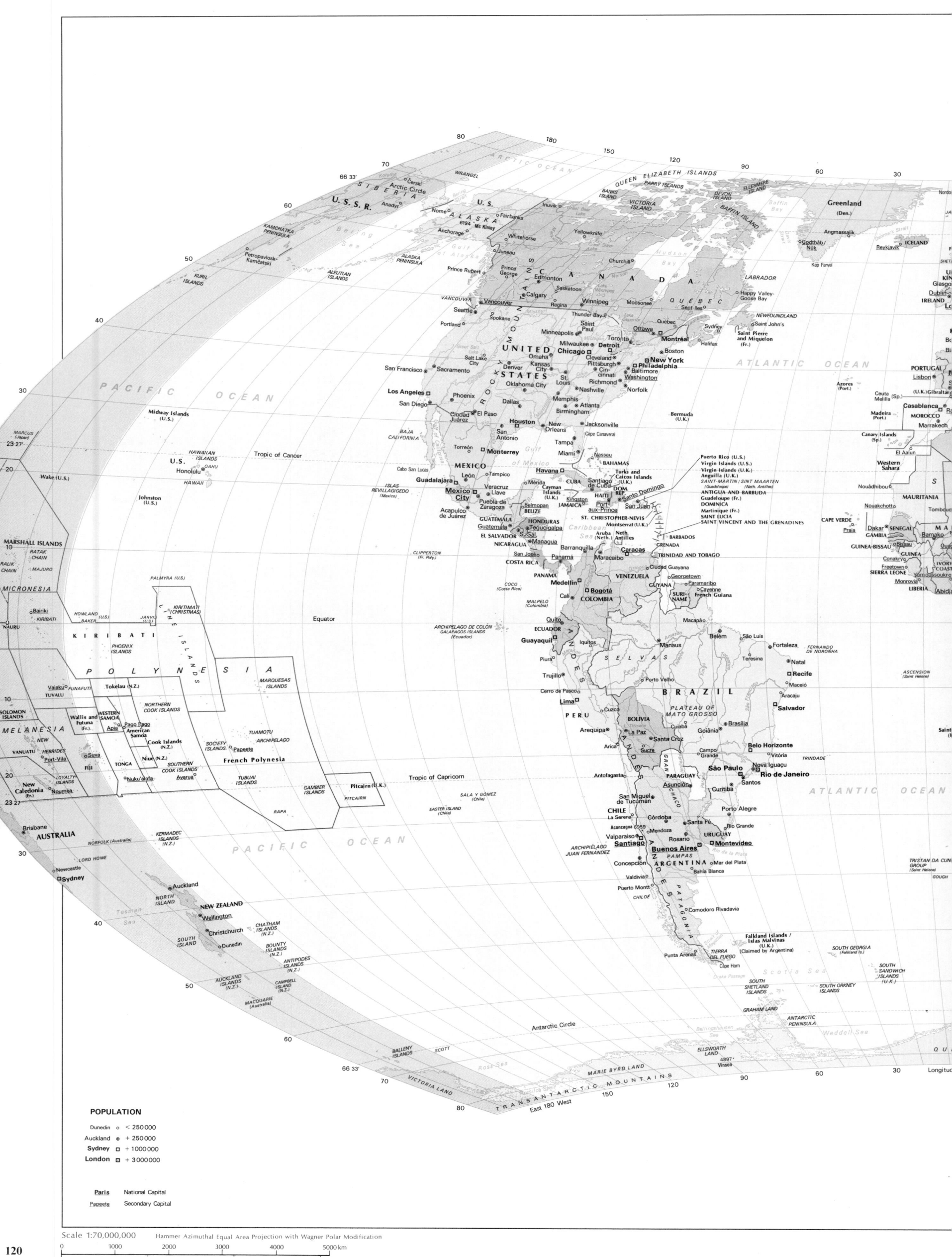

Scale 1:70,000,000   Hammer Azimuthal Equal Area Projection with Wagner Polar Modification

POPULATION

Dunedin	∘	< 250 000
Auckland	⊛	+ 250 000
Sydney	▫	+ 1 000 000
London	▣	+ 3 000 000

<u>Paris</u>   National Capital

<u>Papeete</u>   Secondary Capital

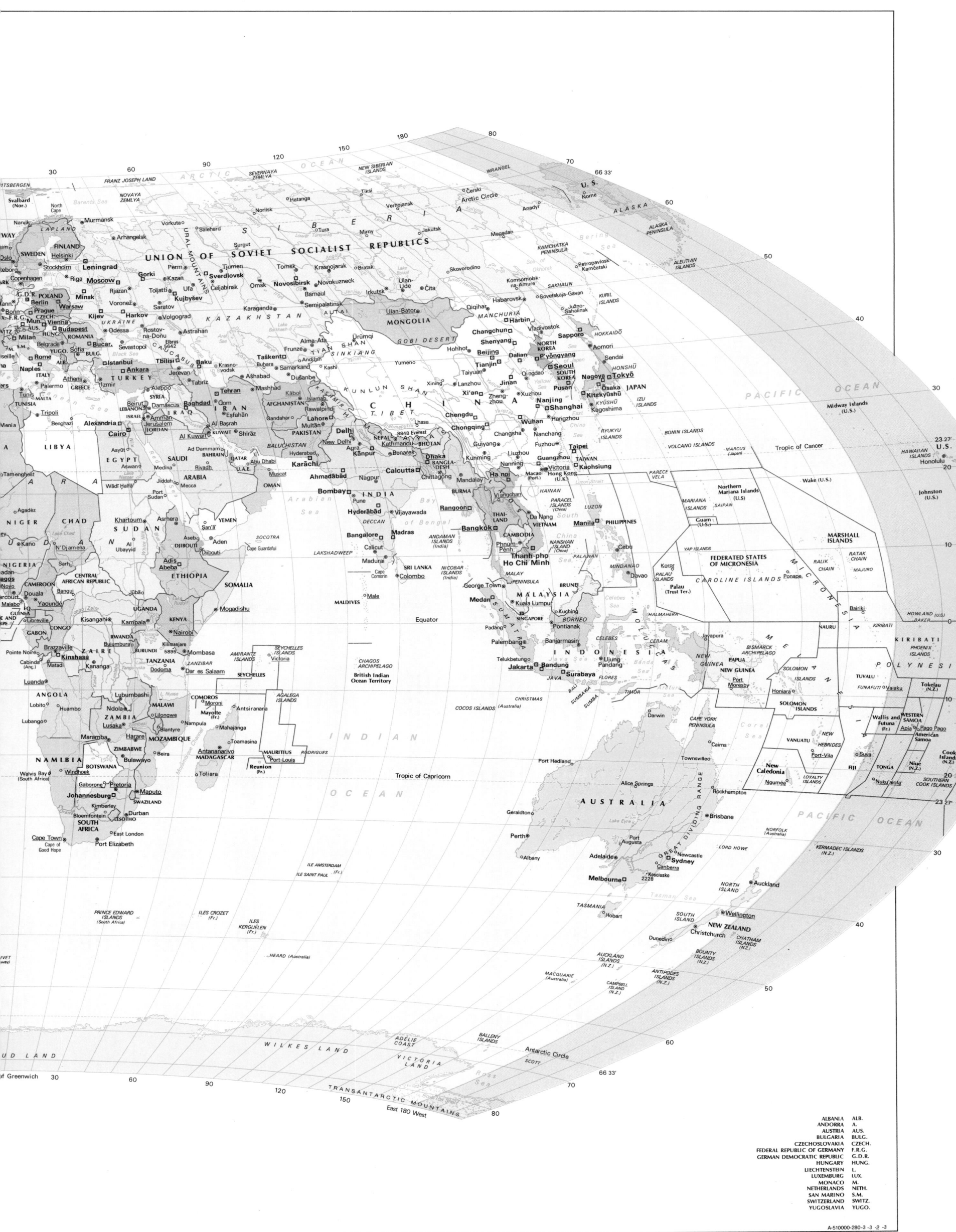

A-510000-280-3 -3 -2 -3

Map 3 **THE OCEANS**

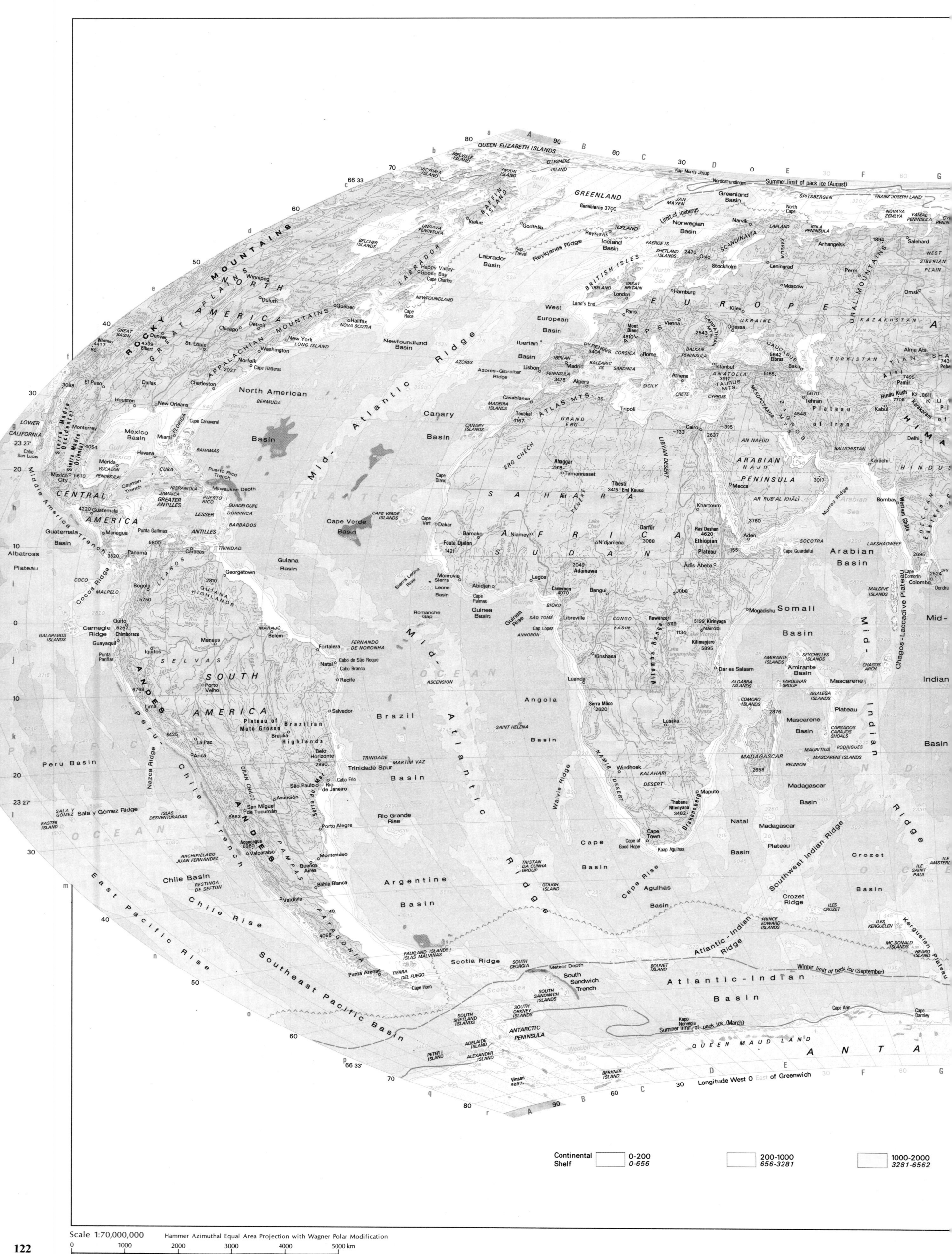

Continental Shelf
| | 0-200 / 0-656 | | 200-1000 / 656-3281 | | 1000-2000 / 3281-6562 |

Scale 1:70,000,000   Hammer Azimuthal Equal Area Projection with Wagner Polar Modification

0   1000   2000   3000   4000   5000 km

0   1000   2000   3000 miles

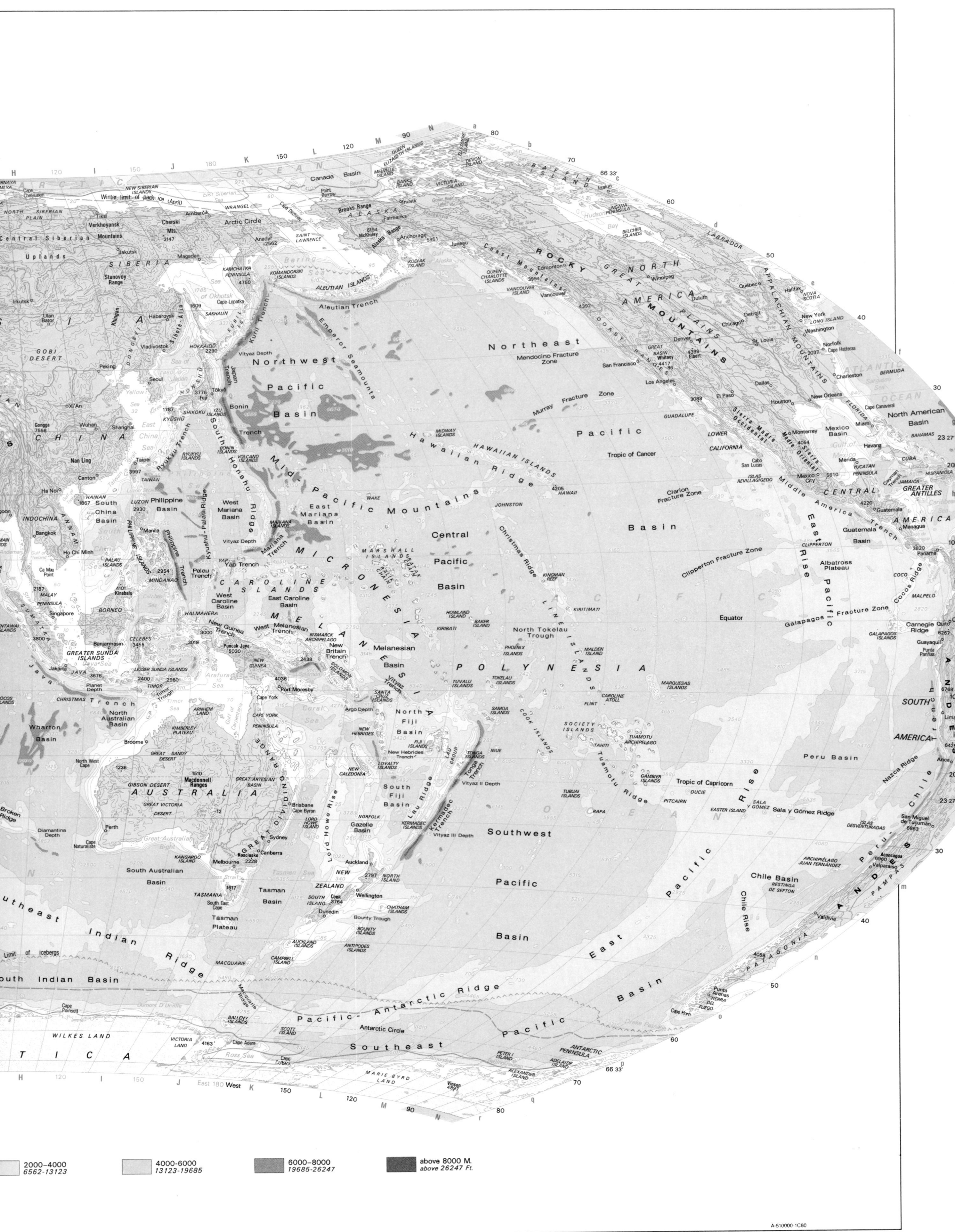

2000–4000	4000–6000	6000–8000	above 8000 M.
6562-13123	13123-19685	19685-26247	above 26247 Ft.

A-510000 1C80

Map 4 **WORLD TRANSPORTATION AND TIME ZONES**

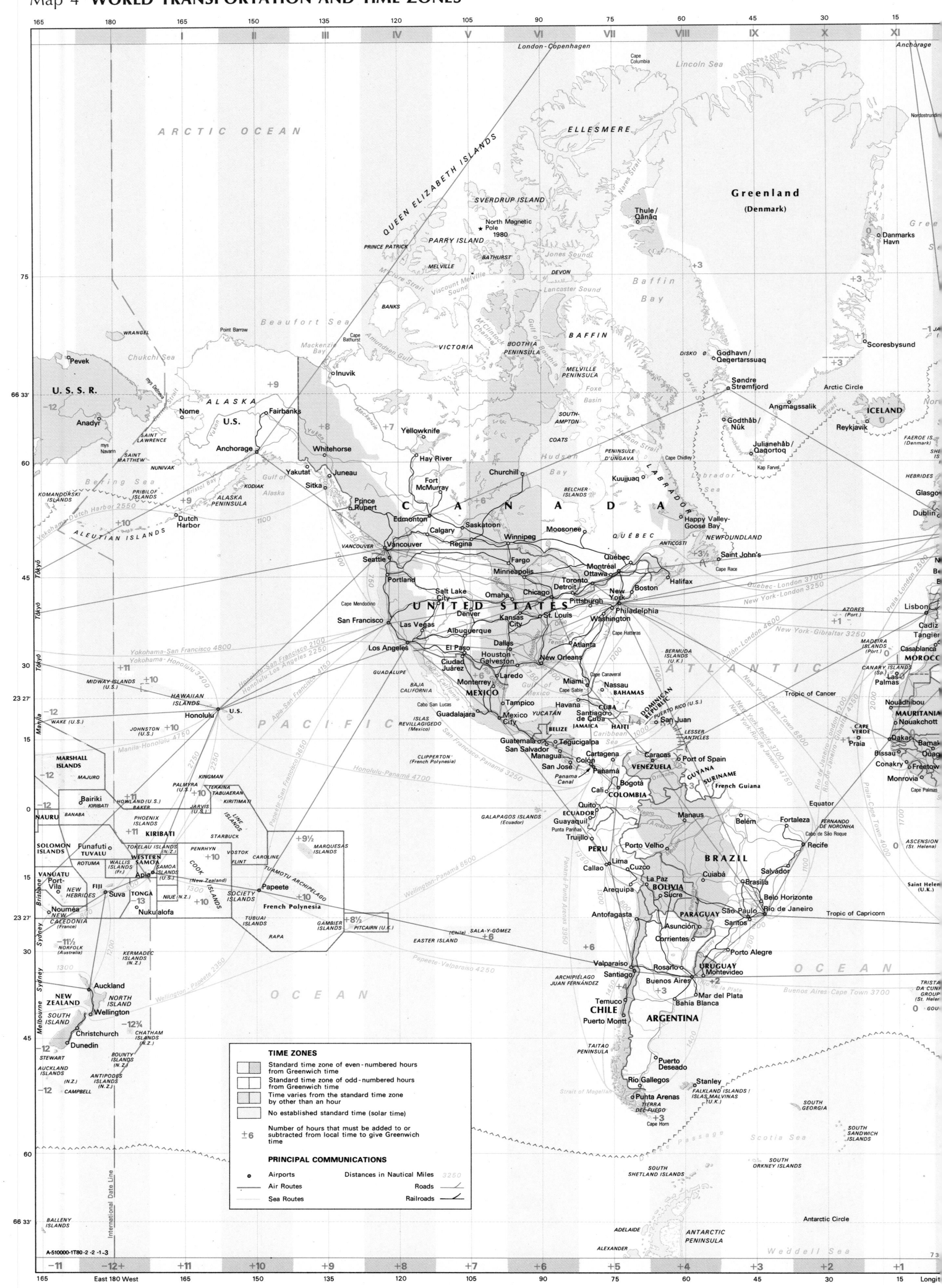

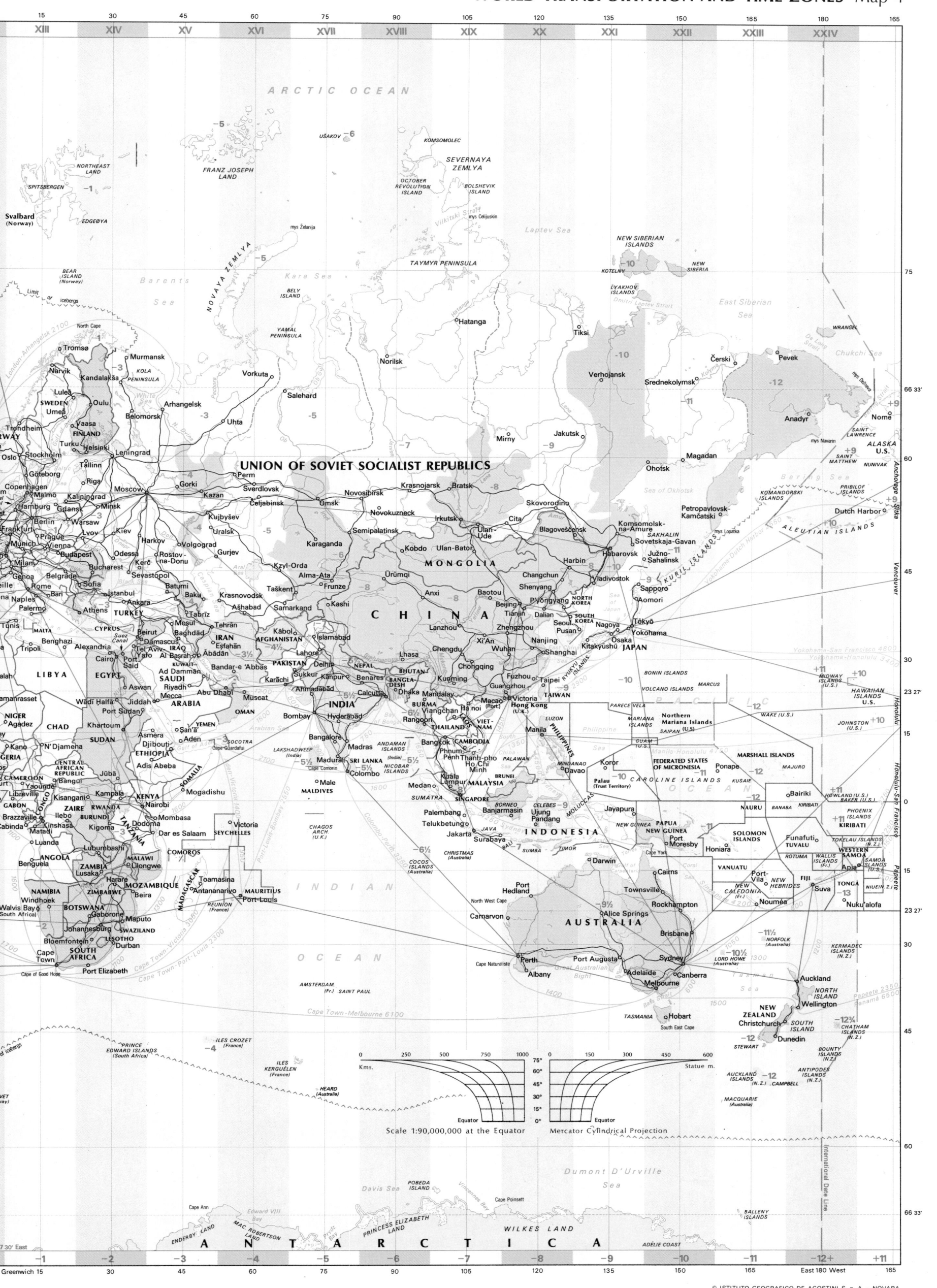

Scale 1:90,000,000 at the Equator   Mercator Cylindrical Projection

© ISTITUTO GEOGRAFICO DE AGOSTINI S. p. A. - NOVARA

Map 5 **EUROPE, PHYSICAL**

GREENLAND

KING FREDERIK VI COAST

KING CHRISTIAN IX LAND

GREENLAND SEA

Denmark Strait

Limit of icebergs

ICELAND

VATNAJÖKULL

Reykjavík

Reykjanes Ridge

Iceland Basin

Iceland-Faeroe Ridge

FAEROE ISLANDS

JAN MAYEN

Mohns Ridge

Lofoten Basin

Arctic Circle

NORWEGIAN SEA

Norwegian Basin

VESTERÅLEN

LOFOTEN

HINNØY

Trondheim

SCANDINAVIA

Mid-Atlantic Ridge

ATLANTIC OCEAN

Rockall

Rockall Rise

Ireland Trough

SHETLAND ISLANDS

ORKNEY ISLANDS

NORTH SEA

Ålesund

Jotunheimen

Bergen

Oslo

SVEALAND

GÖTALAND

Göteborg

BRITISH ISLES

HEBRIDES

Cape Wrath

Duncansby Head

GRAMPIAN MTS.

Aberdeen

Glasgow

Edinburgh

Southern Uplands

GREAT BRITAIN

Porcupine Bank

IRELAND

Dublin

Galway Bay

Cork

MAN

ANGLESEY

Liverpool

PENNINES

ENGLAND

WALES

Birmingham

Bristol

London

CELTIC SEA

CORNWALL

Land's End

ISLES OF SCILLY

Lizard Point

ENGLISH CHANNEL

West European Basin

Iberian Basin

AZORES

GRACIOSA

SÃO JORGE

PICO

TERCEIRA

SÃO MIGUEL

SANTA MARIA

Azores-Gibraltar Ridge

Josephine Seamount

Ampère Seamount

Seine Seamount

Dacia Seamount

MADEIRA ISLANDS

Funchal

PORTO SANTO

ILHAS DESERTAS

CANARY ISLANDS

LA PALMA

GOMERA

HIERRO

TENERIFE

GRAN CANARIA

LANZAROTE

FUERTEVENTURA

STRAIT of Dover

Calais

NORTH SEA

Amsterdam

Rotterdam

FRISIAN ISLANDS

Hamburg

Kiel

København Copenhagen

Malmö

RÜGEN

BORNHOLM

GERMAN PLAIN

Berlin

POMERANIA

Poznań

SILESIA

Wrocław Breslau

Leipzig

HARZ

Frankfurt

RHENISH SLATE MOUNTAINS

ARDENNES

Luxembourg

PARIS BASIN

Paris

Orléans

CHAMPAGNE

VOSGES

BLACK FOREST

JURA

ALPS

BOHEMIA

Praha Prague

MORAVIA

BAVARIA

München Munich

SWABIAN-BAVARIAN PLATEAU

Wien Vienna

Bern

NORMANDY

BRITTANY

Armorican Massif

Nantes

ÎLE DE RÉ

ÎLE D'OLÉRON

Bordeaux

AQUITAINE BASIN

Bay of Biscay

Toulouse

PYRENEES

MASSIF CENTRAL

Lyon

CÉVENNES

LANGUEDOC

PROVENCE

Marseille

La Coruña

Cabo de Finisterre

GALICIA

CANTABRIAN MTS.

Bilbao

SUBMESETA NORTE

IBERIAN PENINSULA

Lisboa Lisbon

ARAGON

SISTEMA CENTRAL

SUBMESETA SUR

LA MANCHA

Valencia

CATALONIA

Barcelona

Cabo de Creus

BALEARIC ISLANDS

MINORCA

MAJORCA

IBIZA

FORMENTERA

Palma

SIERRA MORENA

ANDALUSIA

SIERRA NEVADA

SISTEMAS BÉTICOS

Sevilla Seville

Málaga

Cádiz

Cabo de Gata

Cabo de Palos

CORSICA

Ajaccio

SARDINIA

Cagliari

TUSCAN ARCHIPELAGO

ELBA

APENNINES

Genova Genoa

Milano Milan

Torino Turin

PO VALLEY

Venezia Venice

Bologna

Firenze Florence

Roma Rome

Napoli Naples

Vesuvius

SICILY

Palermo

Messina

Etna

TYRRHENIAN SEA

Tyrrhenian Basin

MEDITERRANEAN SEA

Algerian Basin

Rabat

Casablanca

Marrakech

HIGH ATLAS

MIDDLE ATLAS

ANTI ATLAS

ATLAS MOUNTAINS

SAHARAN ATLAS

TELL ATLAS

HAUTS PLATEAUX

Oran

Algiers

Constantine

Tunis

GRAND ERG OCCIDENTAL

GRAND ERG ORIENTAL

TRIPOLITANIA

Tripoli

Gulf of Sidra

MALTA

GOZO

PANTELLERIA

KERKENNAH ISLANDS

Gulf of Gabès

DJERBA

Scale 1:15,000,000 Lambert Azimuthal Equal Area Projection

0 200 400 600 800 1000 km

0 250 500 miles

Longitude East 0 of Greenwich

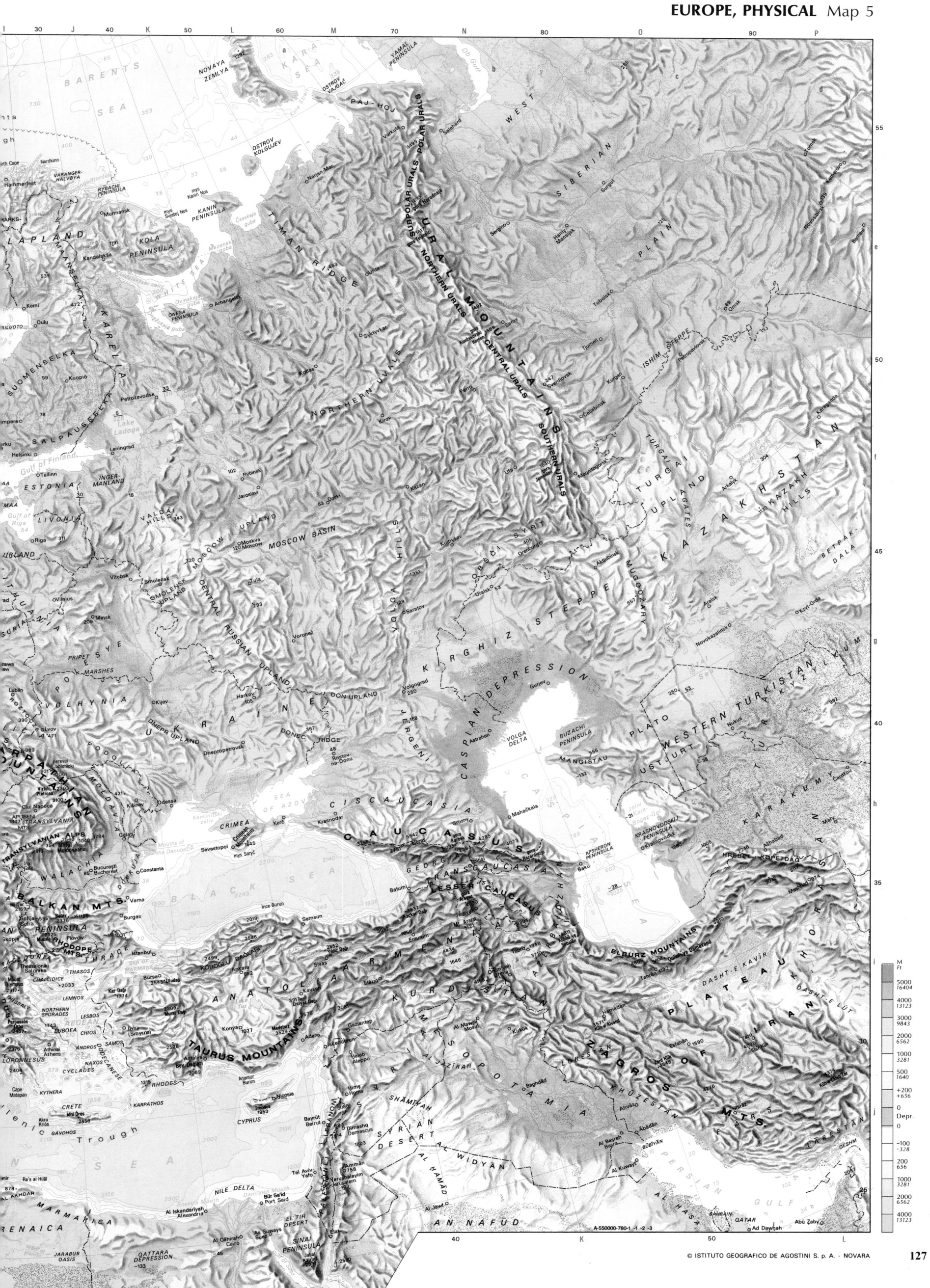

Map 6 EUROPE, POLITICAL

GREENLAND
KING FREDERIK VI COAST
Ammassalik
KING CHRISTIAN IX LAND
Greenland Sea
Greenland (Den.)
Scoresbysund
3700
Nanortalik
Skjoldungen
Frederiksdal
Kap Farvel
Umanarssuak
GREENLAND SEA
JAN MAYEN (Norway)

ICELAND
Reykjavik
Akureyri
Isafjördur
Hofn
VATNAJÖKULL
Hvannadalshnúkur
Seydisfjördur

Arctic Circle

Denmark Strait

Norwegian Sea

VESTERÅLEN
LOFOTEN
Bodø
Mo i Rana

NORWAY
Namsos
Kristiansund
Trondheim
Ålesund
Molde
Dombås
Glittertinden 2472
Lillehammer
SWEDEN
Östersund
Sundsvall
Gävle
Bergen
Gjøvik
Hamar
Falun
Haugesund
Oslo
Drammen
Skien
Moss
Västerås
Stavanger
Karlstad
Örebro
Kristiansand
Lindesnes
Göteborg
Norrköping
Linköping

Faeroe Islands (Den.)
Thorshavn
FØROYAR / FÆRØERNE

SHETLAND ISLANDS

ROCKALL

ORKNEY ISLANDS
Thurso
Inverness
Aberdeen
HEBRIDES
Dundee
Glasgow
Edinburgh
Londonderry
Belfast
Carlisle
Newcastle upon Tyne
IRELAND
Sligo
Galway
Middlesbrough
Limerick
Dublin
Manchester
Liverpool
Leeds
UNITED KINGDOM
Kingston-upon-Hull
Waterford
Wexford
Sheffield
Nottingham
Cork
Fishguard
Leicester
Norwich
Mizen Head
Birmingham
Ipswich
Swansea
Oxford
Cardiff
Bristol
London
Celtic Sea
Land's End
ISLES OF SCILLY
Southampton
Brighton
Dover
Penzance
Exeter
Plymouth

North Sea

DENMARK
Herning
Esbjerg
Århus
Kolding
Flensburg
Odense
København
Copenhagen
Helsingborg
Malmö
Trelleborg
Ålborg
Frederikshavn
Kattegat
Kalmar
ÖLAND
Växjö
Karlskrona
BORNHOLM (Den.)
Gdynia
Szczecin Stettin
Gdansk Danzig

Bremerhaven
Kiel
Lübeck
Rostock
Stralsund
Groningen
Amsterdam
Bremen
Hamburg
GERMAN
s-Gravenhage
Den Haag
Utrecht
Osnabrück
Hannover
Magdeburg
Berlin
FED. REP.
DEM. REP.
POZNAN
Rotterdam
Antwerpen
Essen
Dortmund
Leipzig
Dresden
Wroclaw Breslau
Antwerp
Düsseldorf
Köln Cologne
Bonn
Kassel
Karl-Marx-Stadt
Walbrzych
Czestochowa
NETHERLANDS
BELGIUM
Brussel
Bruxelles
Liège
Luxembourg
Wiesbaden
Frankfurt
Würzburg
Praha Prague
Katowice
Ostrava
CZECHOSLOVAKIA
Lille
Amiens
Reims
LUXEMBOURG
Mannheim
Nürnberg
Plzen
Brno

Cherbourg
Le Havre
Rouen
Metz
Saarbrücken
Nancy
GERMANY
Stuttgart
Regensburg
München Munich
Linz
Wien Vienna
Bratislava
Pointe de Saint-Mathieu
Brest
Saint-Malo
Caen
Paris
Troyes
Strasbourg
Augsburg
Salzburg
AUSTRIA
Györ
Székesfehérvár
Rennes
Le Mans
Angers
Orléans
Freiburg
Basel
Innsbruck
Klagenfurt
Graz
Balaton
Pécs
Nantes
Tours
Dijon
Besançon
Zürich
Bern
LIECHTENSTEIN
Bolzano
Ljubljana
Zagreb
FRANCE
Bourges
Poitiers
Mulhouse
SWITZERLAND
Lausanne
Genève Geneva
Trieste
Rijeka
Osijek
YUGOSLAVIA
La Rochelle
Limoges
Clermont-Ferrand
Saint-Étienne
Mont Dore 1885
Mont Blanc 4807
Lyon
Grenoble
Milano Milan
Brescia
Verona
Venezia Venice
Parma
La Coruña
Cabo de Finisterre
Bordeaux
Torino Turin
Genova Genoa
Bologna
Split
Vigo
Oviedo
Santander
San Sebastián
Bayonne
Toulouse
Montpellier
Nîmes
Avignon
Nice
La Spezia
Firenze Florence
Livorno Leghorn
Ancona
Dubrovnik
León
Pau
PYRENEES
Marseille
MONACO
Perugia
PORTO
Braga
Burgos
Pamplona
Pico de Aneto 3404
ANDORRA
Andorra la Vella
Cabo de Creus
Toulon
CORSICA (Fr.)
Bastia
SAN MARINO
ITALY
PORTUGAL
Coimbra
Valladolid
Salamanca
Zaragoza Saragossa
Tarragona
Barcelona
Ajaccio
VATICAN CITY
Roma Rome
Pescara
Foggia
ALBANIA
Lisboa Lisbon
SPAIN
Madrid
Toledo
Castellón de la Plana
LIGURIAN SEA
Sassari
Olbia
L'Aquila
Napoli Naples
Bari
Brindisi
Setúbal
Évora
Badajoz
Valencia
BALEARIC ISLANDS
Nuoro
SARDINIA
Salerno
Taranto
Lecce
Cabo de São Vicente
Córdoba
Albacete
MINORCA
Palma
MAJORCA
TYRRHENIAN SEA
Cagliari
Cosenza
Catanzaro
IONIAN SEA
Huelva
Sevilla
Murcia
Alicante
IBIZA
Faro
Granada
Mulhacén 3482
Cartagena
Palermo
Messina
Cádiz
Algeciras
Málaga
Almería
Reggio di Calabria
Gibraltar (U.K.)
ISLA DE ALBORÁN (Spain)
Mt. Etna 3323
SICILY
Catania
Siracusa Syracuse
Tanger Tangier
Ceuta (Spain)
Tétouan
Melilla (Spain)
Oran
Mostaganem
Algiers
Al Jazā'ir
Blida
PANTELLERIA (Italy)
Trapani
Agrigento
Capo delle Correnti
Valletta
MALTA
Casablanca
Rabat
Kenitra
Ksar el Kebir
Sidi Bel Abbès
Relizane
Tizi Ouzou
Jijel
Skikda
Annaba
Bizerte
Cap Bon
Nabül
Tūnis
Meknès
Fès
Taza
Oujda
Saïda
Chlef
Sétif
Constantine
Sousse
DJERBA
MOROCCO
Beni Mellal
Marrakech
ATLAS MOUNTAINS
Djelfa
Batna
Tébessa
Al Qayrawān
Safāqis
TUNISIA
El Jadida
Safi
Oued Zem
Laghouat
Biskra
Qafsah
Qābis
Essaouira
Agadir
Aïn Sefra
ALGERIA
Touggourt
Tarābulus Tripoli
Al Khums
Tiznit
Béchar
Ghardaïa
Ouargla
Adh Dhahibāt
Al Zāwiyah
Banī Walīd
Gharyān
Tindouf
Abadla
El Goléa
Hassi Messaoud
Madaniyīn
TRIPOLITANIA
Mizdah
Nālūt
LIBYA

Western Sahara
El Aaiún
Tarfaya
Goulimine
Zagora
GRAND ERG OCCIDENTAL
Timimoun
GRAND ERG ORIENTAL
In Salah

ATLANTIC OCEAN

Azores (Portugal)
GRACIOSA
SÃO JORGE
TERCEIRA
Angra do Heróismo
PICO
Ponta Delgada
SÃO MIGUEL
SANTA MARIA

MADEIRA ISLANDS
Funchal
PORTO SANTO
ILHAS DESERTAS
Madeira (Portugal)
ILHAS SELVAGENS

LA PALMA
Santa Cruz de Tenerife
TENERIFE
GOMERA
HIERRO
Canary Islands (Spain)
Las Palmas de Gran Canaria
GRAN CANARIA
FUERTEVENTURA
LANZAROTE

Scale 1:15,000,000   Lambert Azimuthal Equal Area Projection
0   200   400   600   800   1000 km
0   250   500 miles

Longitude East 10 of Greenwich

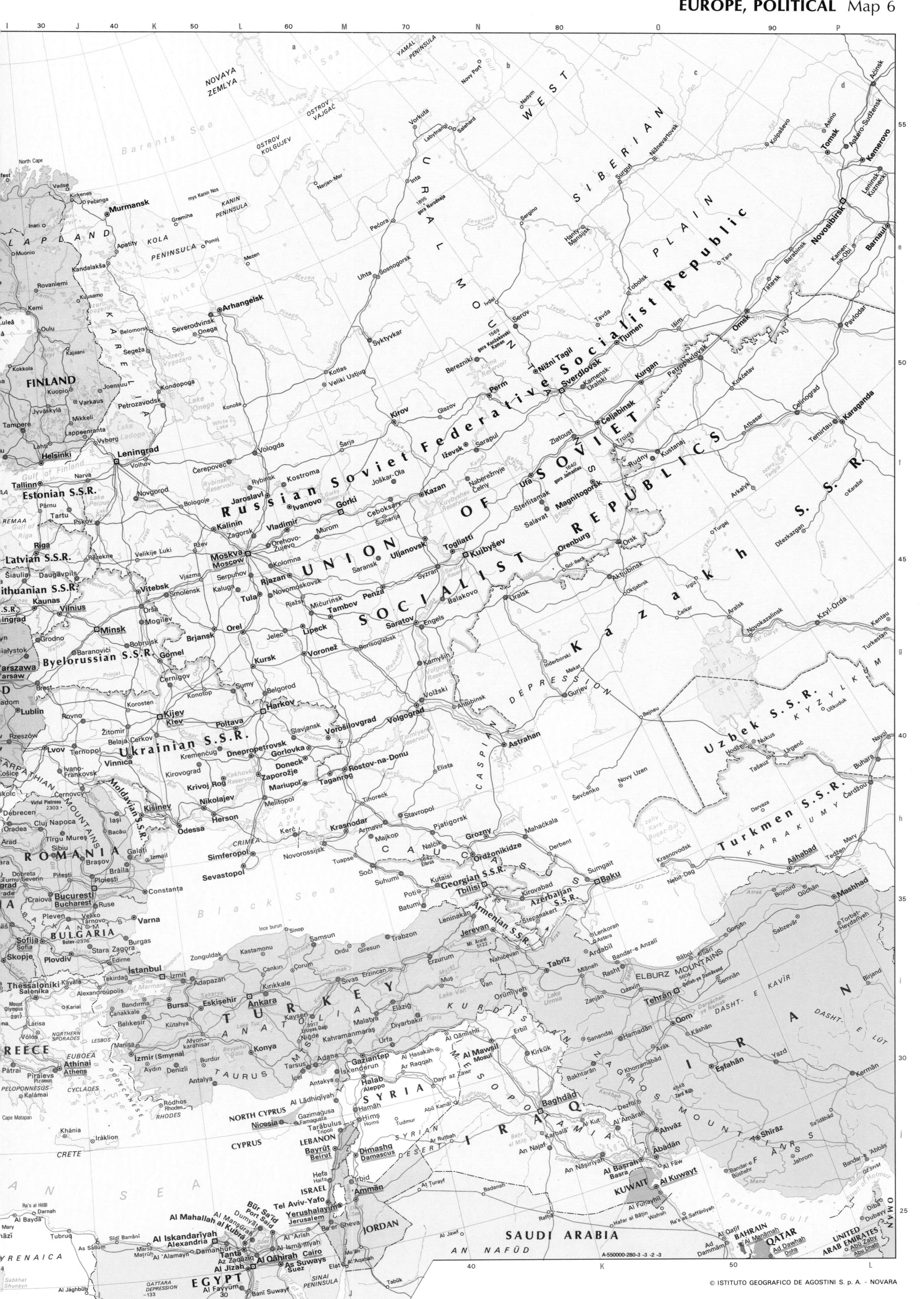

Map 7 **NORTHERN EUROPE**

ÌSLAND ICELAND

Long. West 20 of Greenwich

West 0 East

NORGE
NORWAY

SVERIGE
SWEDEN

SUOMI
FINLAND

DANMARK
DENMARK

BUNDESREPUBLIK
DEUTSCHLAND
FEDERAL REPUBLIC OF GERMANY

DEUTSCHE
DEMOKRATISCHE REPUBLIK
GERMAN DEMOCRATIC REPUBLIC

POLSKA POLAND

Scale 1:6,000,000

Delisle Conic Equidistant Projection

0   100   200   300   400 km

0   100   200 miles

SOJUZ SOVETSKIH
SOCIALISTIČESKIH
RESPUBLIK (SSSR)

UNION OF SOVIET
SOCIALIST
REPUBLICS (USSR)

Rossijskaja Sovetskaja
Federativnaja
Socialističeskaja
Respublika (RSFSR)

Russian Soviet
Federative Socialist
Republic (RSFSR)

8 Arhangelskaja
  oblast
8A Nanecki nac. okrug
11 Brjanskaja oblast
14 Gorkovskaja oblast
15 Ivanovskaja oblast
17 Jaroslavskaja oblast
18 Kaliningradskaja
  oblast
19 Kalininskaja oblast
20 Kalužskaja oblast
21 Kirovskaja oblast
24 Kostromskaja
  oblast
25 Kujbyševskaja
  oblast
28 Leningradskaja
  oblast
29 Lipeckaja oblast
31 Moskovskaja oblast
32 Murmanskaja
  oblast
33 Novgorodskaja
  oblast
36 Orenburgskaja
  oblast
37 Orlovskaja oblast
38 Penzenskaja oblast
39 Permskaja oblast
39A Komi-Permjacki nac.
  okrug

40 Pskovskaja oblast
42 Rjazanskaja oblast
44 Saratovskaja oblast
45 Smolenskaja oblast
47 Tambovskaja oblast
48 Tjumenskaja oblast
48A Hanty-Mansijsko
  nac. okrug
50 Tulskaja oblast
51 Uljanovskaja oblast
52 Vladimirskaja oblast
54 Vologodskaja oblast

Belorusskaja SSR

Byelorussian SSR

3 Grodnenskaja oblast
4 Minskaja oblast
5 Mogilevskaja oblast
6 Vitebskaja oblast

Map 8 **BALTIC REGION**

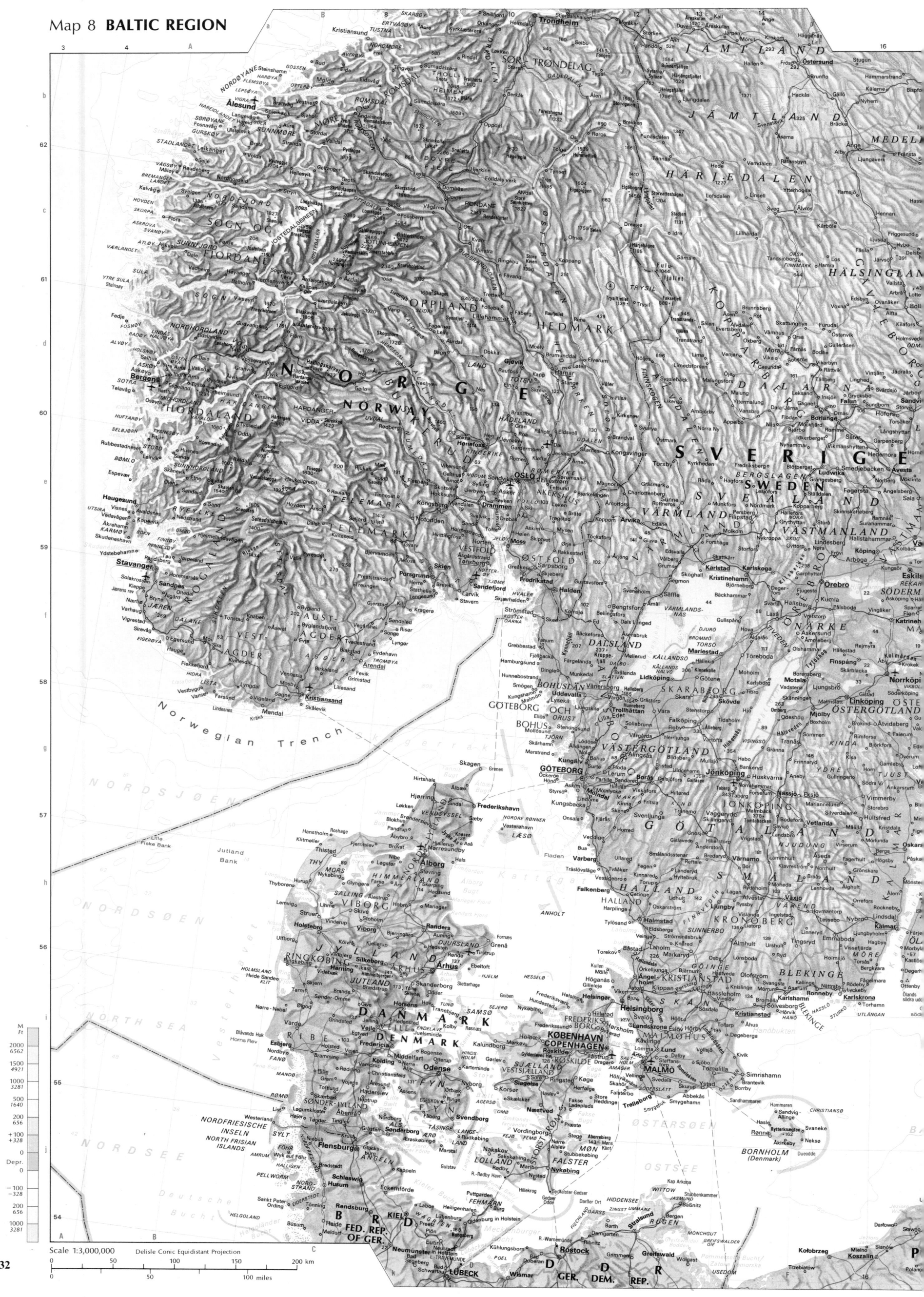

Scale 1:3,000,000   Delisle Conic Equidistant Projection

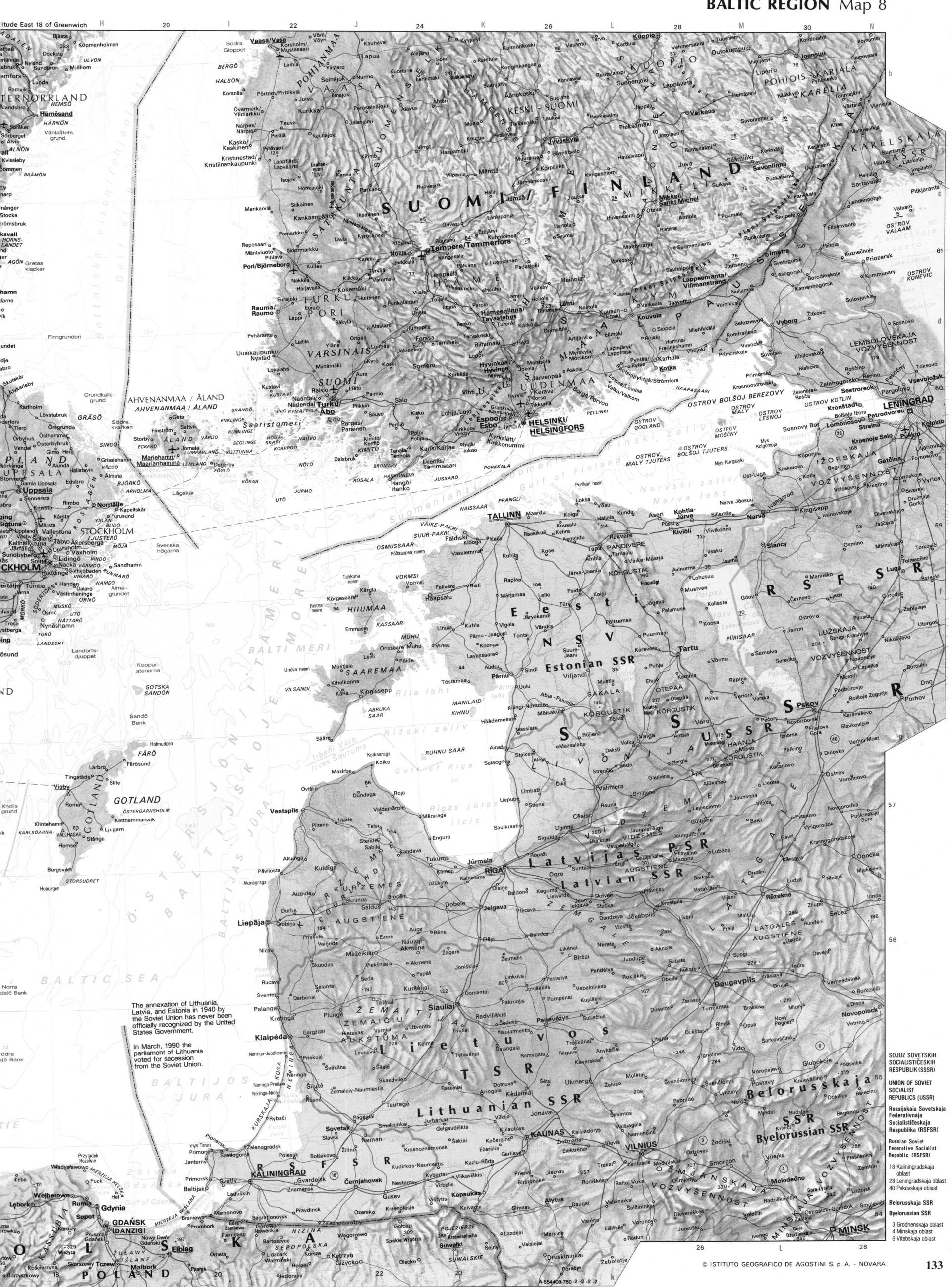

The annexation of Lithuania, Latvia, and Estonia in 1940 by the Soviet Union has never been officially recognized by the United States Government.

In March, 1990 the parliament of Lithuania voted for secession from the Soviet Union.

SOJUZ SOVETSKIH SOCIALISTIČESKIH RESPUBLIK (SSSR)

UNION OF SOVIET SOCIALIST REPUBLICS (USSR)

Rossijskaja Sovetskaja Federativnaja Socialističeskaja Respublika (RSFSR)

Russian Soviet Federative Socialist Republic (RSFSR)

18 Kaliningradskaja oblast
28 Leningradskaja oblast
40 Pskovskaja oblast

Belorusskaja SSR
Byelorussian SSR

3 Grodnenskaja oblast
4 Minskaja oblast
6 Vitebskaja oblast

© ISTITUTO GEOGRAFICO DE AGOSTINI S. p. A. - NOVARA

A-554400-780-2 -2 -2 -2

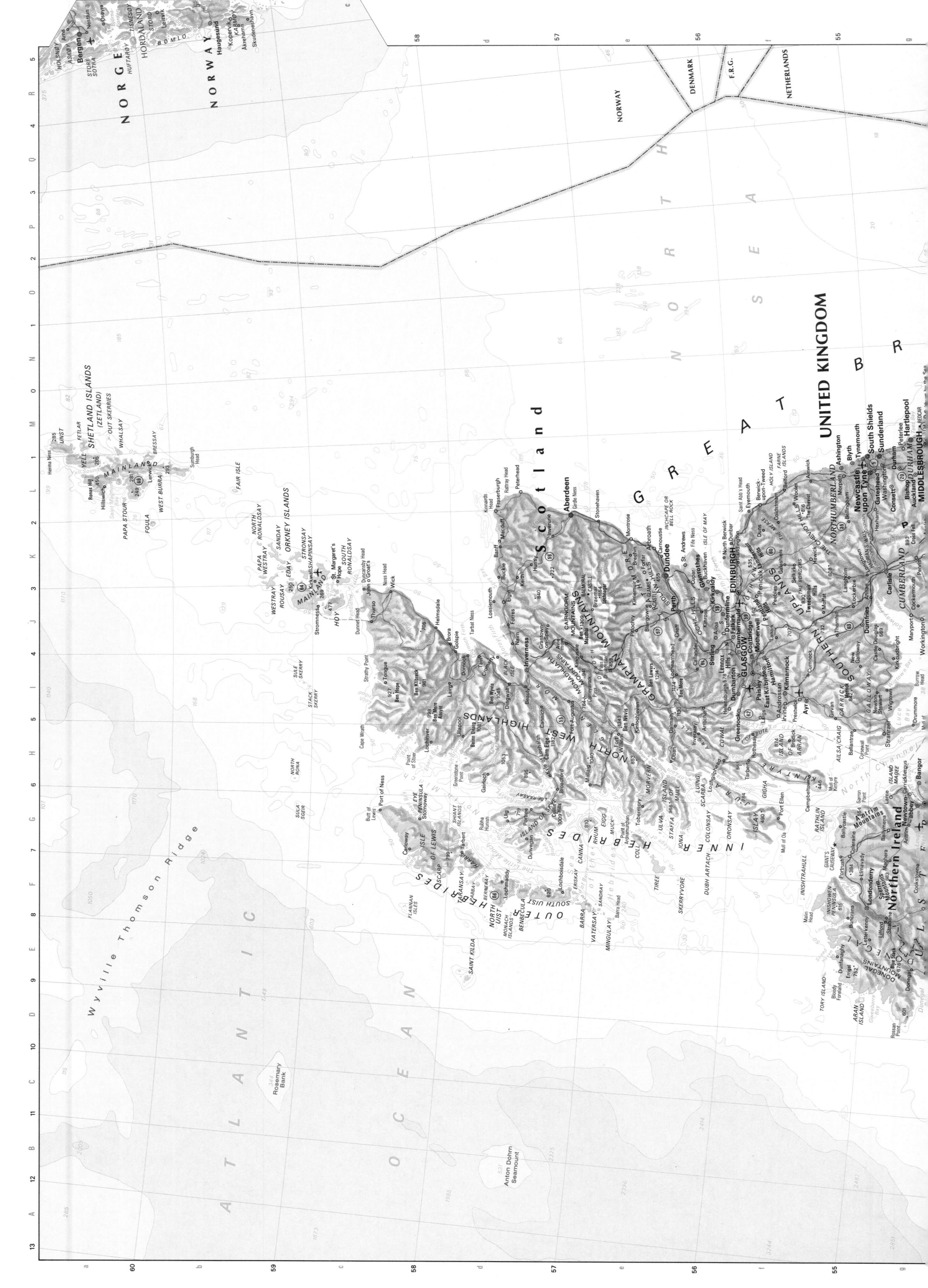

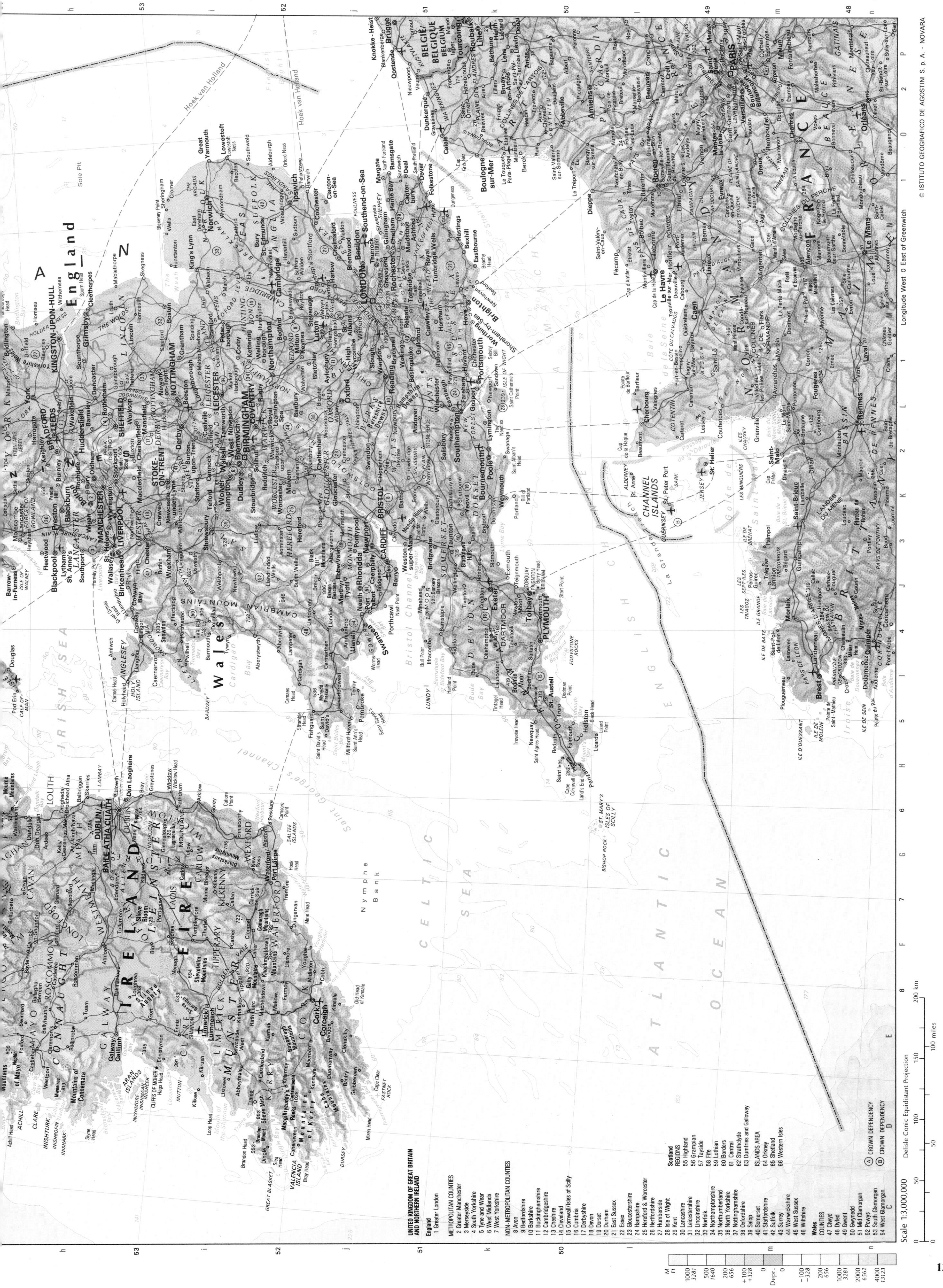

© ISTITUTO GEOGRAFICO DE AGOSTINI S. p. A. - NOVARA

Longitude West 0 East of Greenwich

Scale 1:3,000,000

Delisle Conic Equidistant Projection

UNITED KINGDOM OF GREAT BRITAIN
AND NORTHERN IRELAND

England

METROPOLITAN COUNTIES
1 Greater London
2 Greater Manchester
3 Merseyside
4 South Yorkshire
5 Tyne and Wear
6 West Midlands
7 West Yorkshire

NON-METROPOLITAN COUNTIES
8 Avon
9 Bedfordshire
10 Berkshire
11 Buckinghamshire
12 Cambridgeshire
13 Cheshire
14 Cleveland
15 Cornwall/Isles of Scilly
16 Cumbria
17 Derbyshire
18 Devon
19 Dorset
20 Durham
21 East Sussex
22 Essex
23 Gloucestershire
24 Hampshire
25 Hereford & Worcester
26 Hertfordshire
27 Humberside
28 Isle of Wight
29 Kent
30 Lancashire
31 Leicestershire
32 Lincolnshire
33 Norfolk
34 Northamptonshire
35 Northumberland
36 North Yorkshire
37 Nottinghamshire
38 Oxfordshire
39 Salop
40 Somerset
41 Staffordshire
42 Suffolk
43 Surrey
44 Warwickshire
45 West Sussex
46 Wiltshire

Wales
COUNTIES
47 Clwyd
48 Dyfed
49 Gwent
50 Gwynedd
51 Powys
52 Mid Glamorgan
53 South Glamorgan
54 West Glamorgan

Scotland
REGIONS
55 Highland
56 Grampian
57 Tayside
58 Fife
59 Lothian
60 Borders
61 Strathclyde
62 Central
63 Dumfries and Galloway
ISLANDS AREA
64 Orkney
65 Shetland
66 Western Isles

Ⓓ CROWN DEPENDENCY
Ⓒ CROWN DEPENDENCY

200 km
100 miles

135

Map 10 **CENTRAL EUROPE**

Scale 1:3,000,000   Delisle Conic Equidistant Projection

J Longitude East 14 of Greenwich K

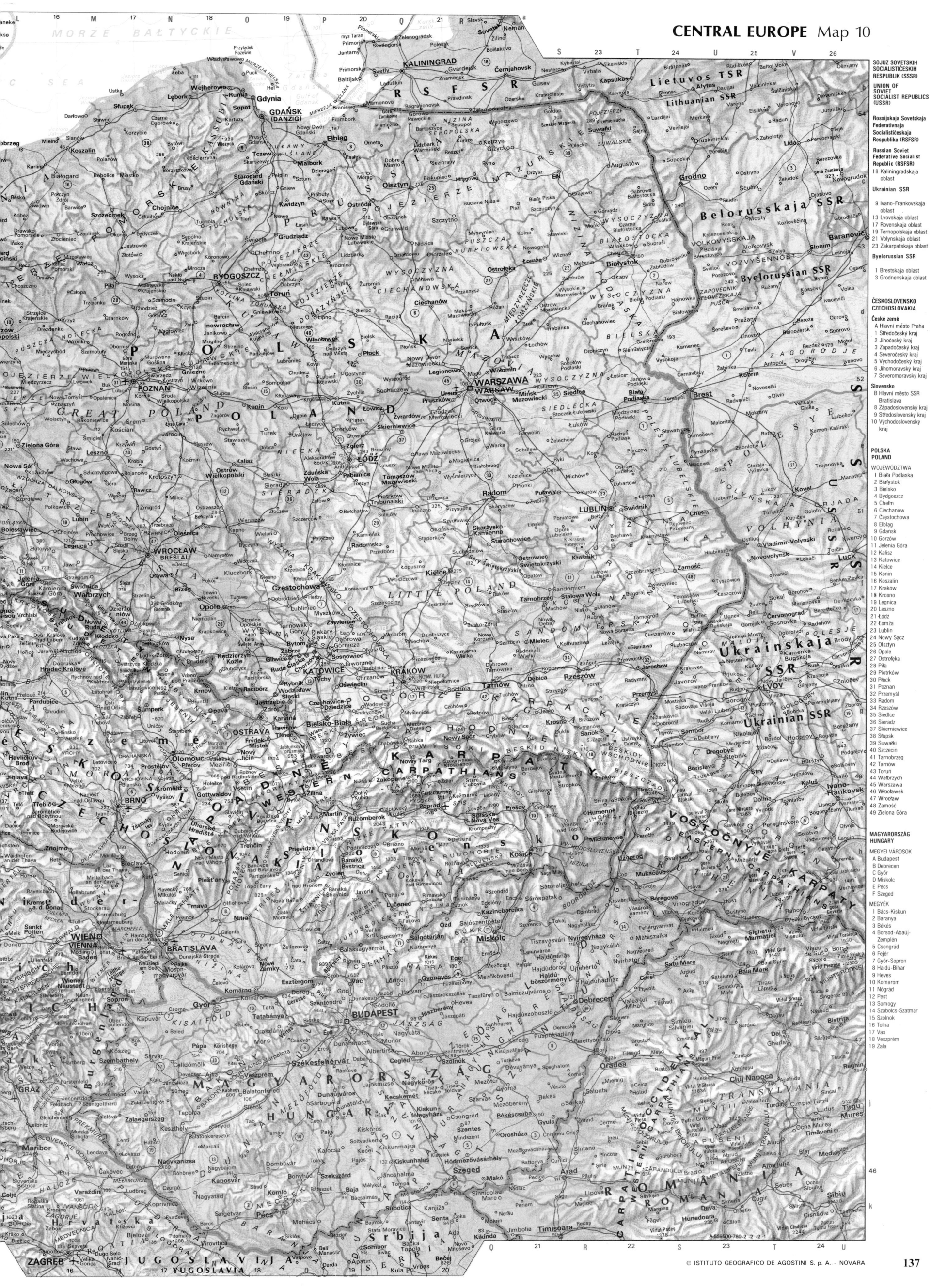

SOJUZ SOVETSKICH
SOCIALISTIČESKICH
RESPUBLIK (SSSR)

UNION OF
SOVIET
SOCIALIST REPUBLICS (USSR)

Rossijskaja Sovetskaja
Federativnaja
Socialističeskaja
Respublika (RSFSR)

Russian Soviet Federal Socialist
Republic (RSFSR)
18 Kaliningradskaja
oblast

Ukrainian SSR
9 Ivano-Frankovskaja
oblast
13 Lvovskaja oblast
17 Rovenskaja oblast
19 Ternopolskaja oblast
21 Volynskaja oblast
23 Zakarpatskaja oblast

Byelorussian SSR
1 Brestskaja oblast
3 Grodnenskaja oblast

ČESKOSLOVENSKO
CZECHOSLOVAKIA

České země
A Hlavní město Praha
1 Středočeský kraj
2 Jihočeský kraj
3 Západočeský kraj
4 Severočeský kraj
5 Východočeský kraj
6 Jihomoravský kraj
7 Severomoravský kraj

Slovensko
B Hlavní město SSR
  Bratislava
8 Západoslovenský kraj
9 Stredoslovenský kraj
10 Východoslovenský kraj

POLSKA
POLAND

WOJEWÓDZTWA
1 Biała Podlaska
2 Białystok
3 Bielsko
4 Bydgoszcz
5 Chełm
6 Ciechanów
7 Częstochowa
8 Elbląg
9 Gdańsk
10 Gorzów
11 Jelenia Góra
12 Kalisz
13 Katowice
14 Kielce
15 Konin
16 Koszalin
17 Kraków
18 Krosno
19 Legnica
20 Leszno
21 Łódź
22 Łomża
23 Lublin
24 Nowy Sącz
25 Olsztyn
26 Opole
27 Ostrołęka
28 Piła
29 Płock
30 Płock
31 Poznań
32 Przemyśl
33 Radom
34 Rzeszów
35 Siedlce
36 Sieradz
37 Skierniewice
38 Słupsk
39 Suwałki
40 Szczecin
41 Tarnobrzeg
42 Tarnów
43 Toruń
44 Wałbrzych
45 Warszawa
46 Włocławek
47 Wrocław
48 Zamość
49 Zielona Góra

MAGYARORSZÁG
HUNGARY

MEGYEI VÁROSOK
A Budapest
B Debrecen
C Győr
D Miskolc
E Pécs
F Szeged

MEGYÉK
1 Bács-Kiskun
2 Baranya
3 Békés
4 Borsod-Abaúj-
  Zemplén
5 Csongrád
6 Fejér
7 Győr-Sopron
8 Hajdú-Bihar
9 Heves
10 Komárom
11 Nógrád
12 Pest
13 Somogy
14 Szabolcs-Szatmár
15 Szolnok
16 Tolna
17 Vas
18 Veszprém
19 Zala

Map 11 **FRANCE AND BENELUX**

FRANCE
DÉPARTEMENTS
01 Ain
02 Aisne
2A Corse-du-Sud
2B Haute-Corse
03 Allier
04 Alpes-de-
    Haute-
    Provence
05 Hautes-Alpes
06 Alpes-
    Maritimes
07 Ardèche
08 Ardennes
09 Ariège
10 Aube
11 Aude
12 Aveyron
13 Bouches-du-
    Rhône

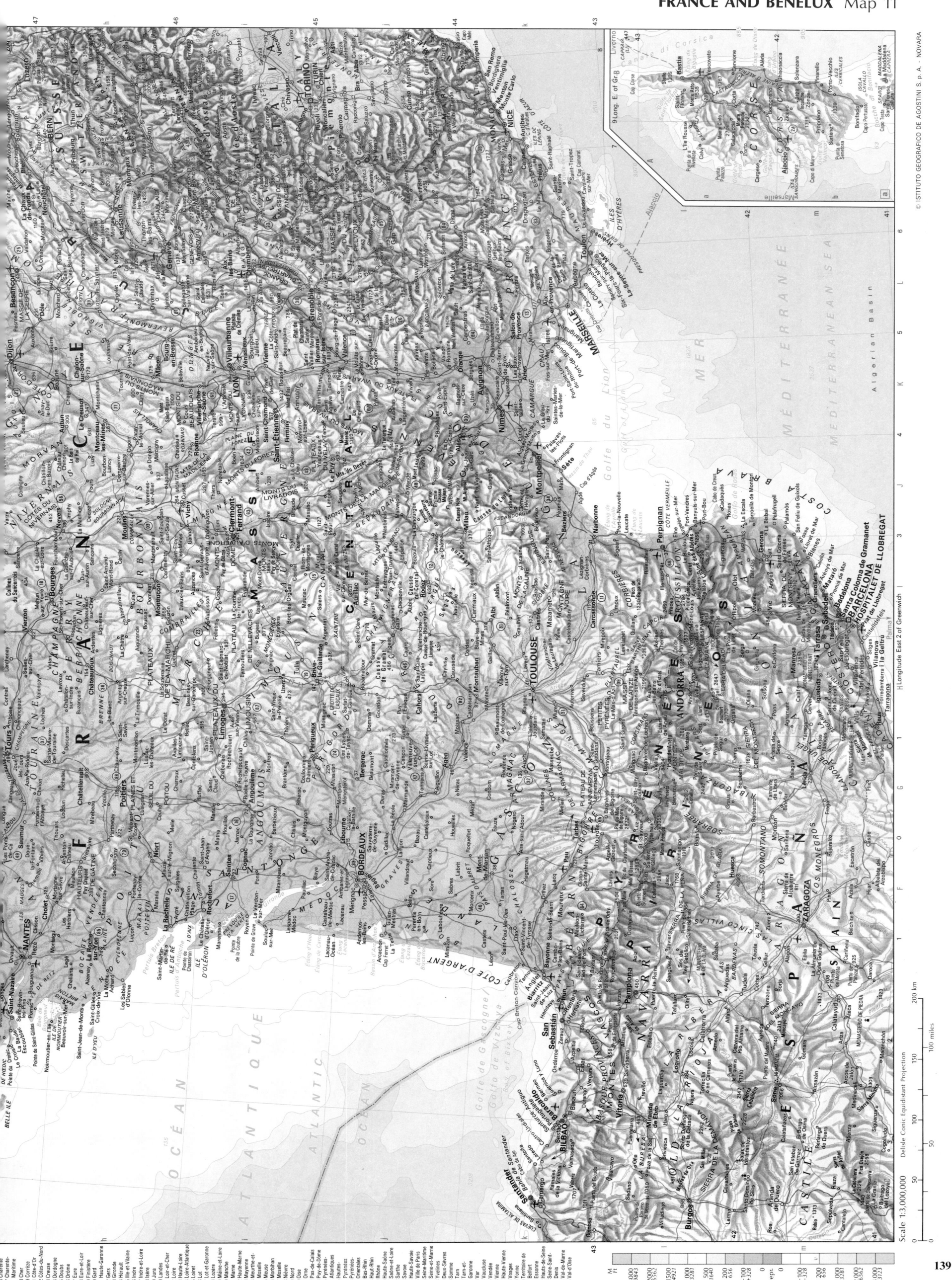

Scale 1:3,000,000

Delisle Conic Equidistant Projection

© ISTITUTO GEOGRAFICO DE AGOSTINI S. p. A. · NOVARA

139

Map 12 **BELGIUM, NETHERLANDS AND LUXEMBOURG**

Scale 1:1,500,000   Delisle Conic Equidistant Projection

Map 12

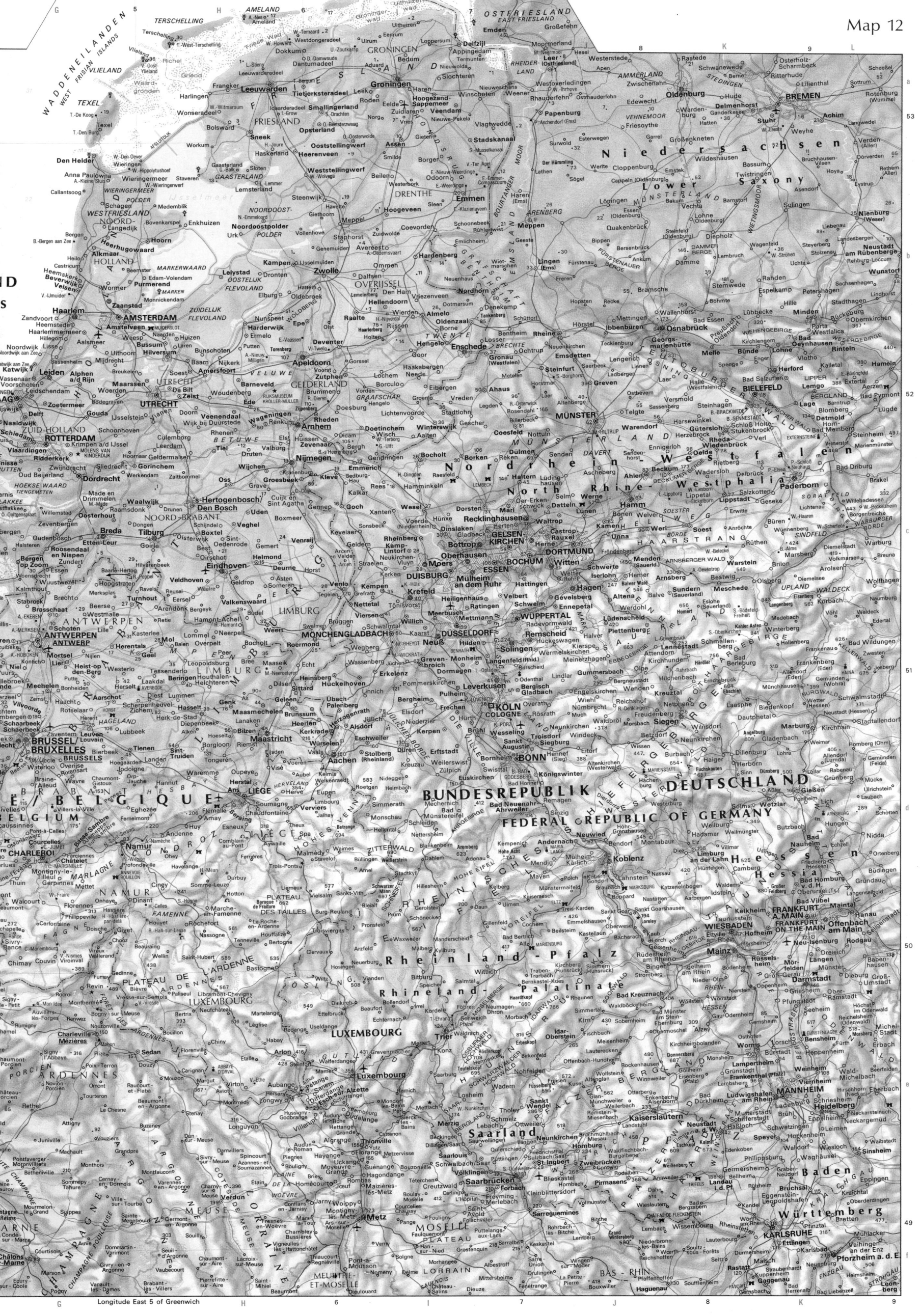

Map 13 **SPAIN AND PORTUGAL**

Scale 1:3,000,000   Delisle Conic Equidistant Projection

Map 14 **ITALY, AUSTRIA AND SWITZERLAND**

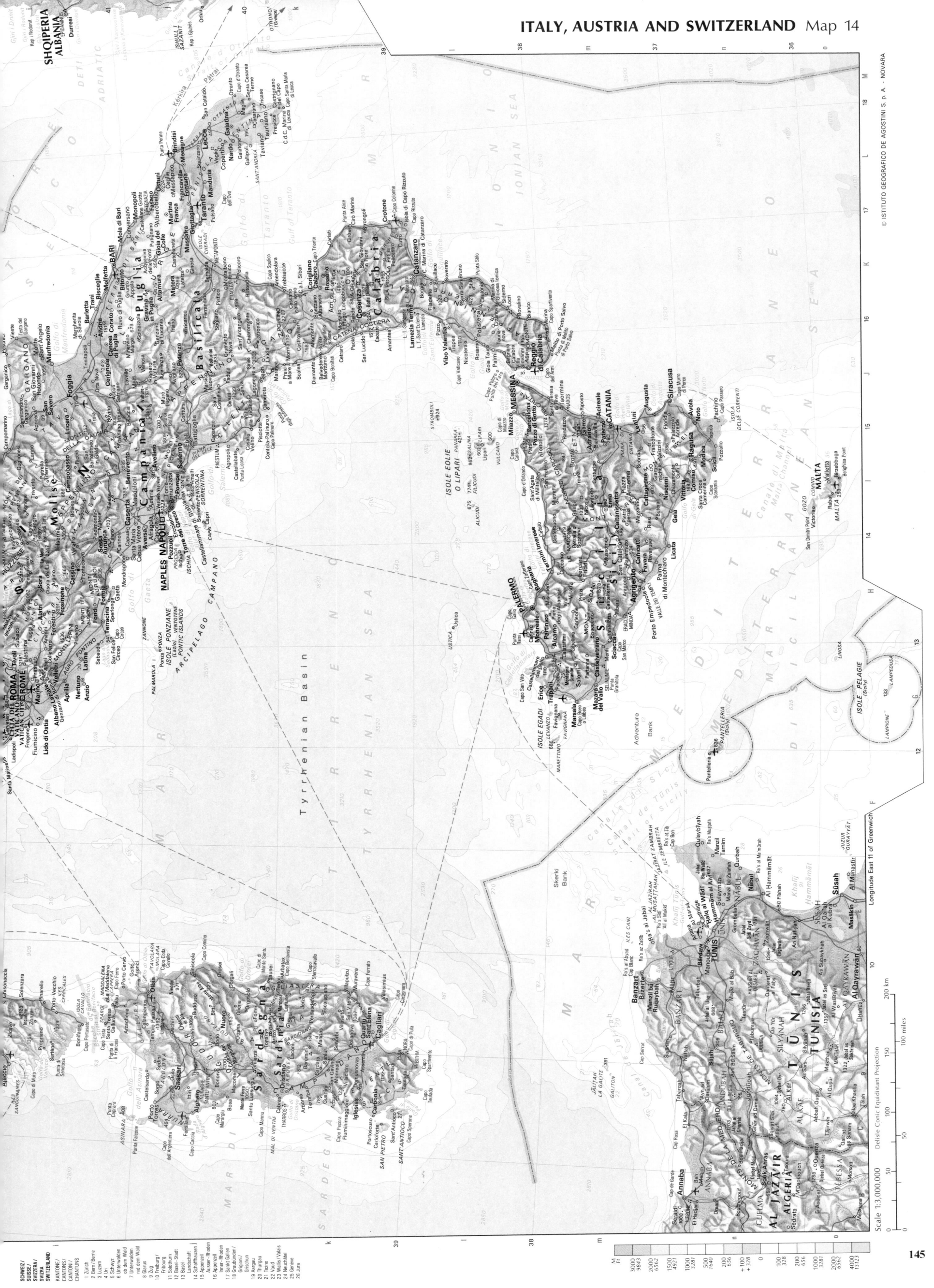

Scale 1:3,000,000

Delisle Conic Equidistant Projection

Longitude East 11 of Greenwich

© ISTITUTO GEOGRAFICO DE AGOSTINI S. p. A. - NOVARA

145

Map 15 **SOUTHEASTERN EUROPE**

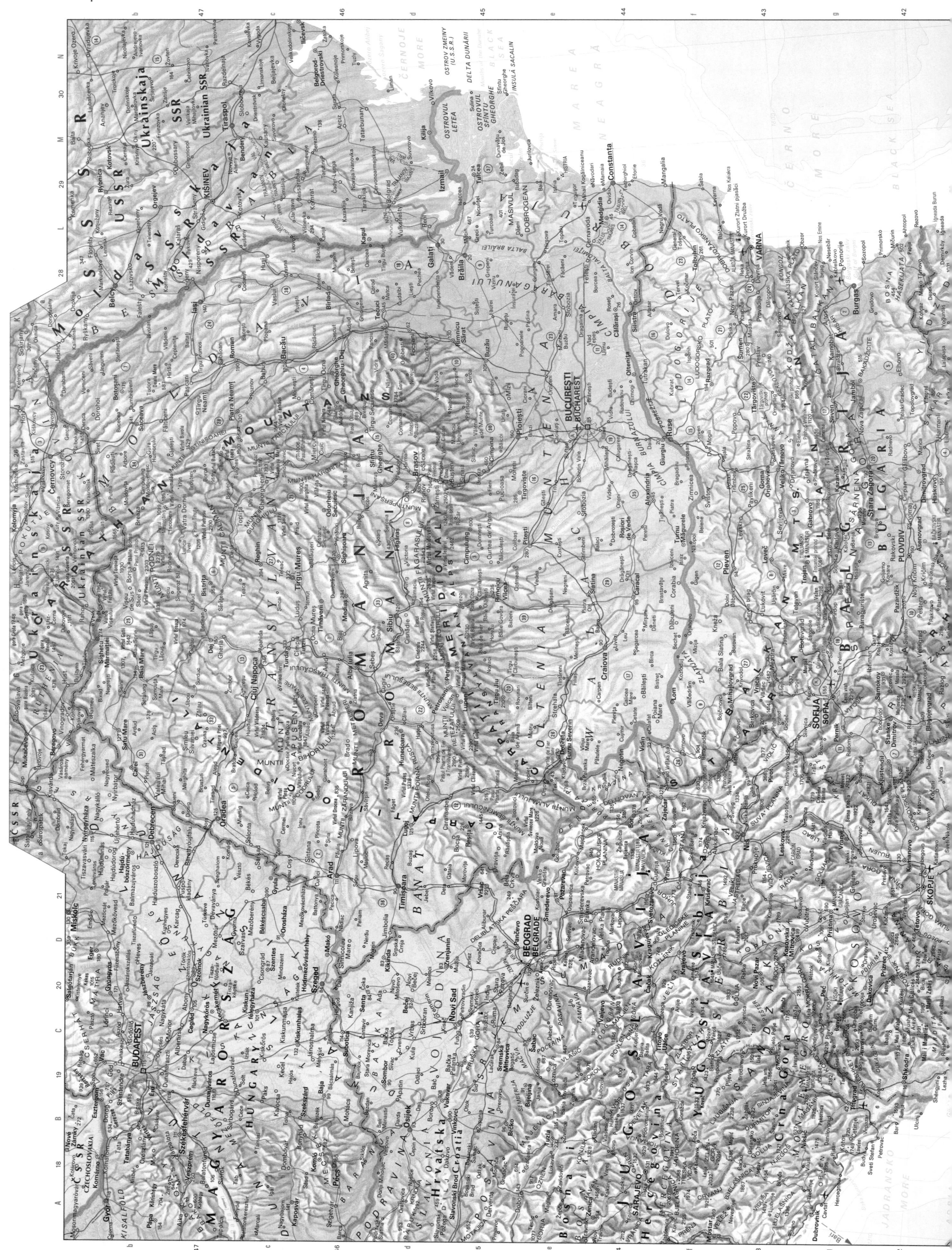

Map 15

© ISTITUTO GEOGRAFICO DE AGOSTINI S. p. A. - NOVARA

Scale 1:3,000,000

Delisle Conic Equidistant Projection

Map 16 **SOUTHWESTERN SOVIET UNION**

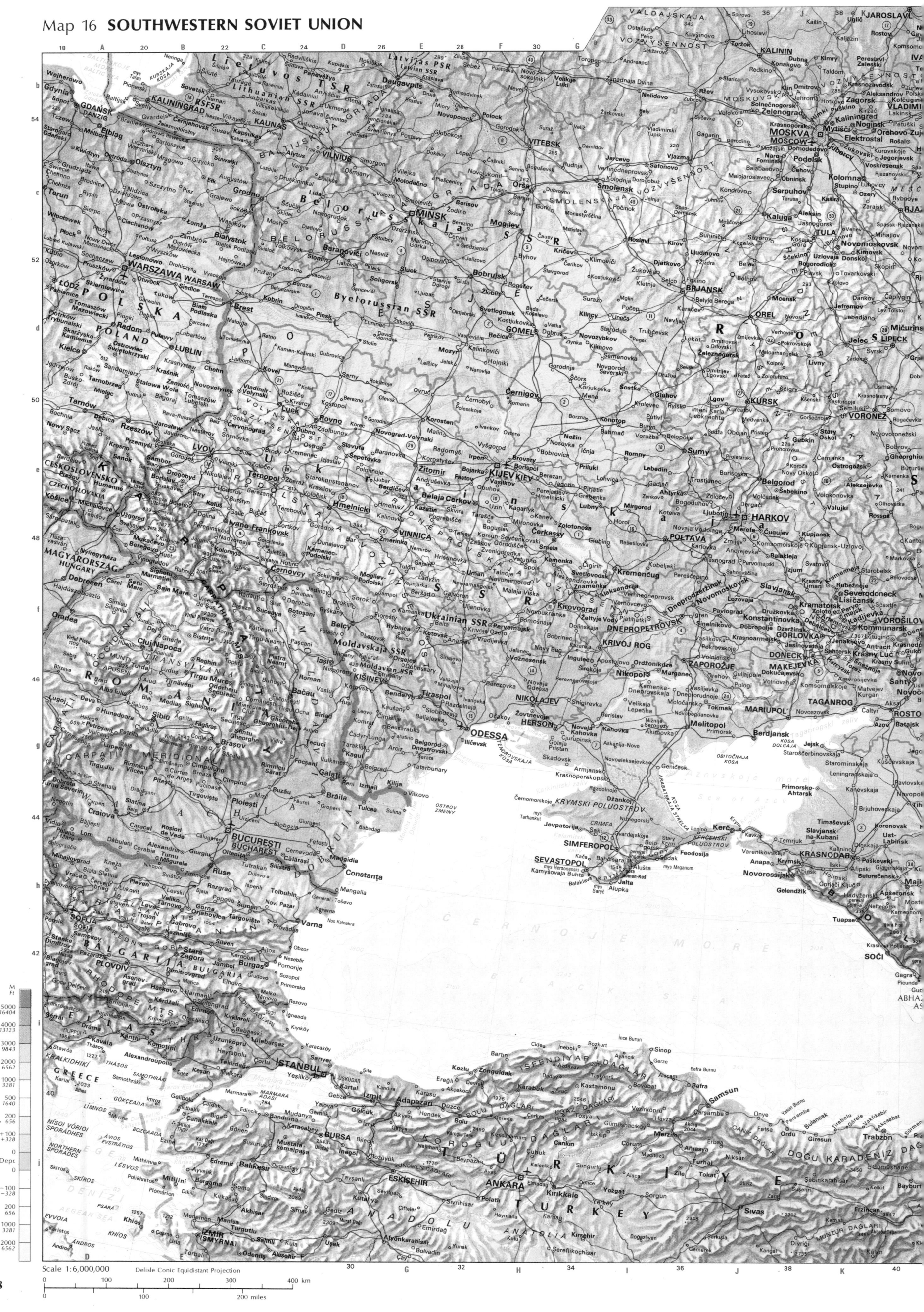

Scale 1:6,000,000   Delisle Conic Equidistant Projection

SOJUZ SOVETSKIH
SOCIALISTIČESKIH
RESPUBLIK (SSSR)

UNION OF
SOVIET
SOCIALIST
REPUBLICS (USSR)

Rossijskaja Sovetskaja
Federativnaja
Socialističeskaja
Respublika (RSFSR)

Russian Soviet
Federative Socialist
Republic (RSFSR)

3 Krasnodarskij kraj
3A Adygejskaja
  avtonomnaja oblast
6 Stavropolski kraj
6A Karačajevo-
  Čerkesskaja
  avtonomnaja oblast
9 Astrahanskaja oblast
10 Belgorodskaja oblast
11 Brjanskaja oblast
12 Čeljabinskaja oblast
14 Gorkovskaja oblast
15 Ivanovskaja oblast
17 Jaroslavskaja oblast
18 Kaliningradskaja oblast
19 Kalininskaja oblast
20 Kalužskaja oblast
23 Kirovskaja oblast
24 Kostromskaja oblast
25 Kujbyševskaja oblast
26 Kurganskaja oblast
27 Kurskaja oblast
30 Lipeckaja oblast
31 Moskovskaja oblast
35 Novgorodskaja oblast
36 Orenburgskaja oblast
37 Orlovskaja oblast
38 Penzenskaja oblast
40 Pskovskaja oblast
41 Rostovskaja oblast
42 Rjazanskaja oblast
44 Saratovskaja oblast
45 Smolenskaja oblast
47 Tambovskaja oblast
50 Tulskaja oblast
51 Uljanovskaja oblast
52 Vladimirskaja oblast
53 Volgogradskaja oblast
55 Voronežskaja oblast

Ukrainskaja SSR

Ukrainian SSR

1 Čerkasskaja oblast
2 Černigovskaja oblast
3 Černovickaja oblast
4 Dnepropetrovskaja
  oblast
5 Doneckaja oblast
6 Harkovskaja oblast
7 Hersonskaja oblast
8 Hmelnickaja oblast
9 Ivano-Frankovskaja
  oblast
10 Kijevskaja oblast
11 Kirovogradskaja oblast
12 Krymskaja oblast
13 Lvovskaja oblast
14 Nikolajevskaja oblast
15 Odesskaja oblast
16 Poltavskaja oblast
17 Rovenskaja oblast
18 Sumskaja oblast
19 Ternopolskaja oblast
20 Vinnickaja oblast
21 Vinynskaja oblast
22 Vorošilovgradskaja
  oblast
23 Zakarpatskaja oblast
24 Zaporožskaja oblast
25 Žitomirskaja oblast

Belorusskaja SSR

Byelorussian SSR

1 Brestskaja oblast
2 Gomelskaja oblast
3 Grodnenskaja oblast
4 Minskaja oblast
5 Mogilevskaja oblast
6 Vitebskaja oblast

Kazahskaja SSR

Kazakh SSR

1 Aktjubinskaja oblast
7 Gurjevskaja oblast
9 Kzyl-Ordinskaja oblast
11 Kustanajskaja oblast
12 Mangyšlakskaja
  oblast
18 Uralskaja oblast

Gruzinskaja SSR

Georgian SSR

1 Jugo-Osetinskaja
  avtonomnaja oblast

Azerbajdžanskaja SSR

Azerbaijan SSR

1 Nagorno-Karabahskaja
  avtonomnaja oblast

Turkmenskaja SSR

Turkmen SSR

1 Ašhabadskaja oblast
3 Krasnovodskaja oblast
5 Tašauzskaja oblast

Map 17 THE URALS

SOJUZ SOVETSKIH
SOCIALISTIČESKIH
RESPUBLIK (SSSR)

UNION OF
SOVIET
SOCIALIST
REPUBLICS

Rossijskaja Sovetskaja
Federativnaja
Socialistićeskaja
Respublika (RSFSR)

Russian Soviet
Federated Socialist
Republic

8 Arhangelskaja oblast
8A Nenecki nac. okrug
12 Čeljabinskaja oblast
14 Gorkovskaja oblast
23 Kirovskaja oblast
24 Kostromskaja oblast
25 Kujbyševskaja oblast
26 Kurganskaja oblast
35 Omskaja oblast
36 Orenburgskaja oblast
39 Permskaja oblast
39A Komi-Permjacki nac. okrug
44 Saratovskaja oblast
46 Sverdlovskaja oblast
48 Tjumenskaja oblast
48A Hanty-Mansijski nac. okrug
48B Jamalo-Neneci nac. okrug
51 Uljanovskaja oblast
54 Vologodskaja oblast

Kazahskaja SSR

Kazakh SSR

3 Celinogradskaja oblast
10 Kokčetavskaja oblast
11 Kustanajskaja oblast
15 Severo-Kazahstanskaja oblast
17 Turgajskaja oblast

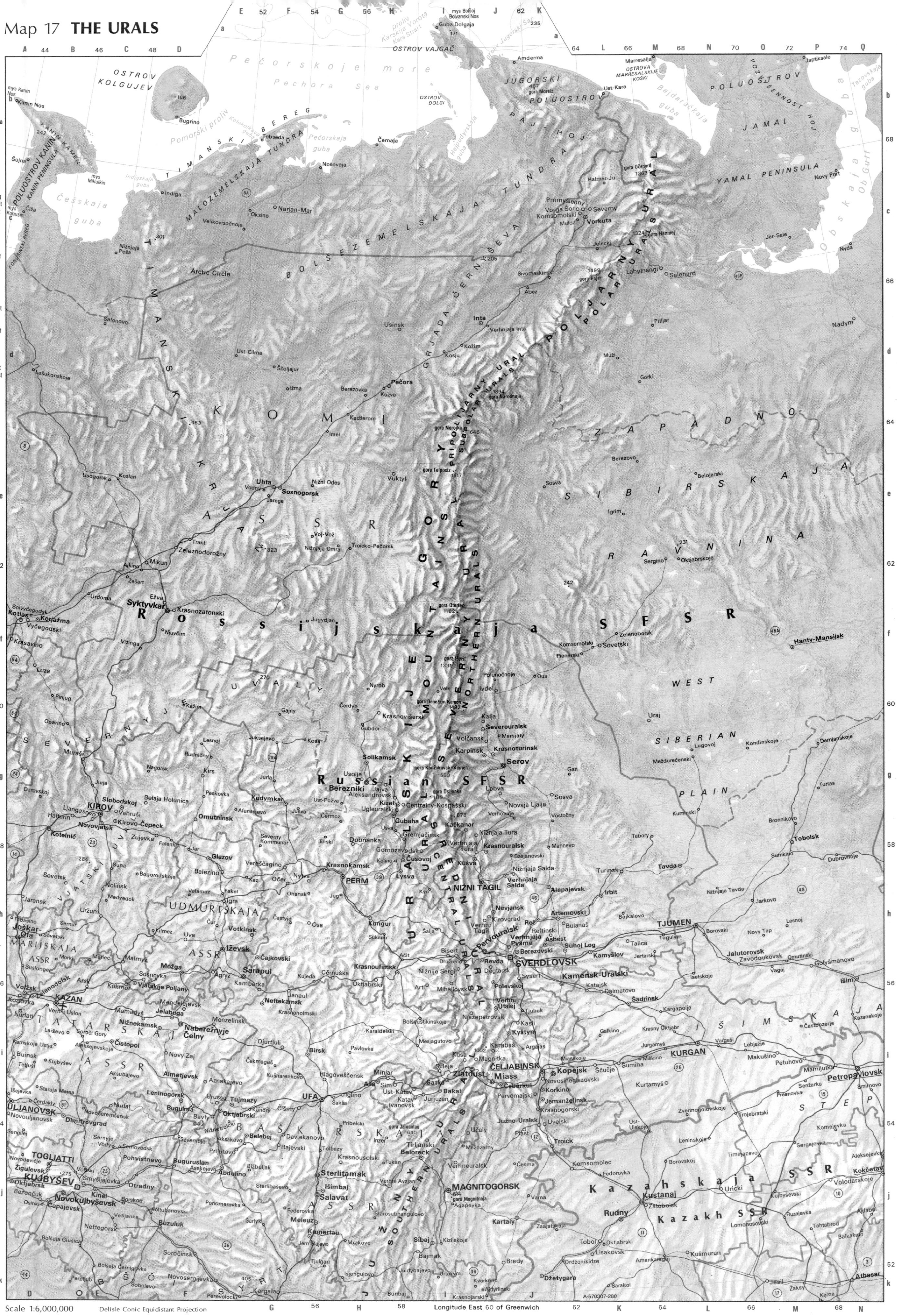

Scale 1:6,000,000

Delisle Conic Equidistant Projection

0   100   200   300   400 km

0   100   200 miles

Longitude East 60 of Greenwich

150

© ISTITUTO GEOGRAFICO DE AGOSTINI S. p. A. - NOVARA

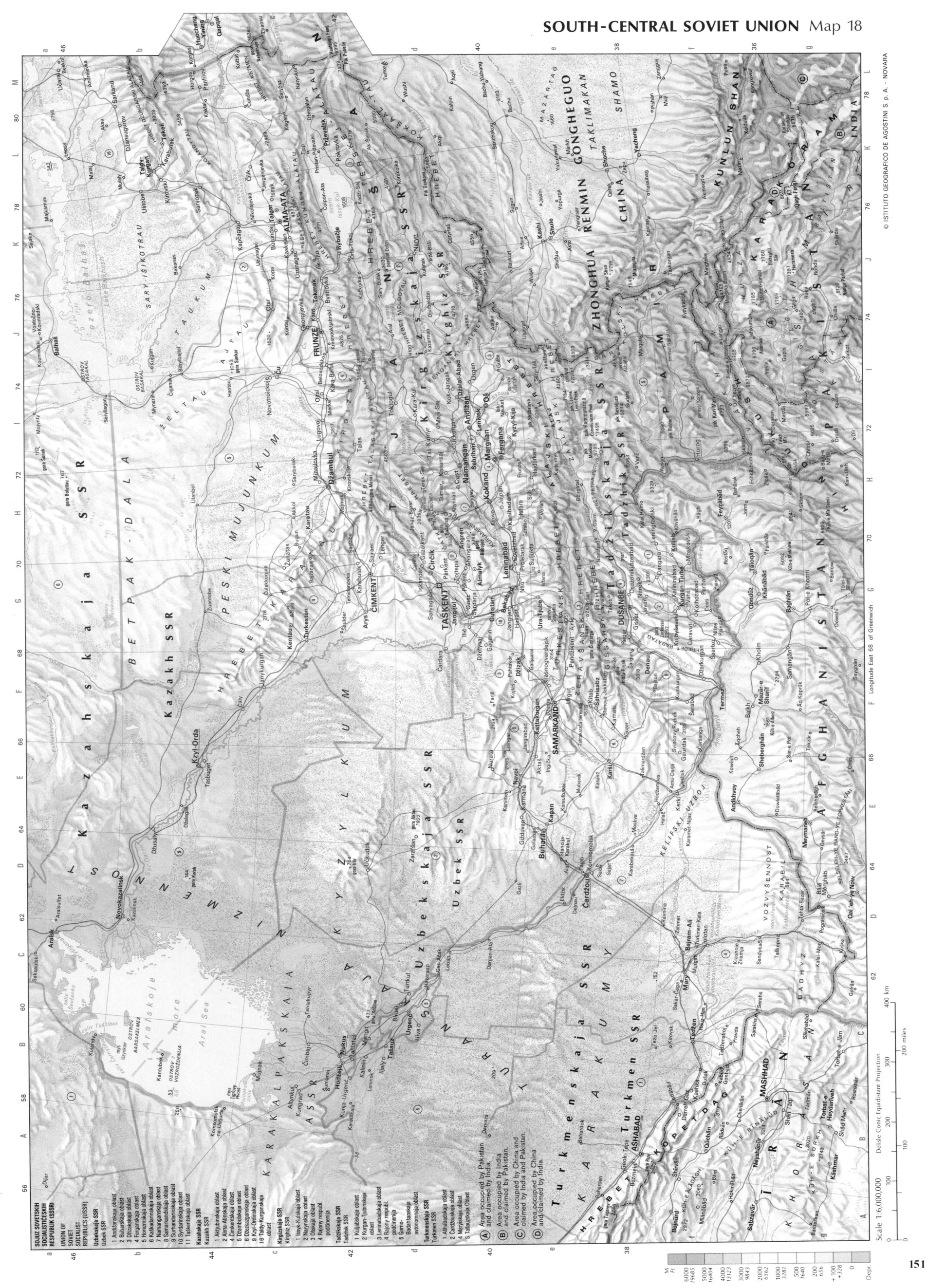

© ISTITUTO GEOGRAFICO DE AGOSTINI S. p. A. - NOVARA

Scale 1:6,000,000

Delsle Conic Equidistant Projection

Map 19

Sojuz Sovetskih
Socialističeskih
Respublik (SSSR)
UNION OF SOVIET
SOCIALIST
REPUBLICS (USSR)

Rossijskaja Sovetskaja
Federativnaja
Socialistićeskaja
Respublika (RSFSR)

Russian Soviet
Federative Socialist
Republic (RSFSR)

3   Krasnodarski kraj
3A Adygejskaja
    avt. oblast
6   Stavropolski kraj
6A Karačajevo-
    Čerkesskaja
    avt. oblast
8   Arhangelskaja
    oblast
8A Nemecki nac. okr.
9   Astrahanskaja
    oblast
10 Belgorodskaja
    oblast
11 Brjanskaja obl.
13 Čeljabinskaja obl.
14 Gorkovskaja obl.
15 Ivanovskaja obl.
17 Jaroslavskaja obl.
18 Kaliningradskaja
    oblast
19 Kalininskaja obl.
22 Kalužskaja obl.
23 Kirovskaja obl.
24 Kostromskaja obl.
25 Kujbyševskaja
    oblast
26 Kurganskaja obl.
27 Kurskaja obl.
28 Leningradskaja
    oblast
29 Lipeckaja obl.
31 Moskovskaja obl.
32 Murmanskaja obl.
33 Novgorodskaja
    oblast
35 Omskaja obl.
36 Orenburgskaja
    oblast
37 Orlovskaja obl.
38 Penzenskaja obl.
39 Permskaja obl.
39A Komi-Permjacki
    nac. okr.
40 Pskovskaja obl.
42 Rostovskaja obl.
43 Rjazanskaja obl.
44 Saratovskaja obl.
45 Smolenskaja obl.
46 Sverdlovskaja obl.
47 Tambovskaja obl.
48 Tjumenskaja obl.
48A Hanty-Mansijski
    nac. okr.

50 Tulskaja obl.
51 Uljanovskaja obl.
52 Vladimirskaja obl.
53 Volgogradskaja obl.
54 Vologodskaja obl.
55 Voronežskaja obl.

Ukrainskaja SSR
Ukrainian SSR

1   Čerkasskaja obl.
2   Černigovskaja obl.
3   Černovickaja obl.
4   Dnepropetrovskaja
    oblast
5   Doneckaja obl.
6   Harkovskaja obl.
7   Hersonskaja obl.
8   Hmelnickaja obl.
9   Ivano-Frankovskaja
    oblast
10 Kijevskaja obl.

Scale 1:12,000,000
Delisle Conic Equidistant Projection

0   200   400   600   800 km
0   200   400 miles

Longitude East 55 of Greenwich

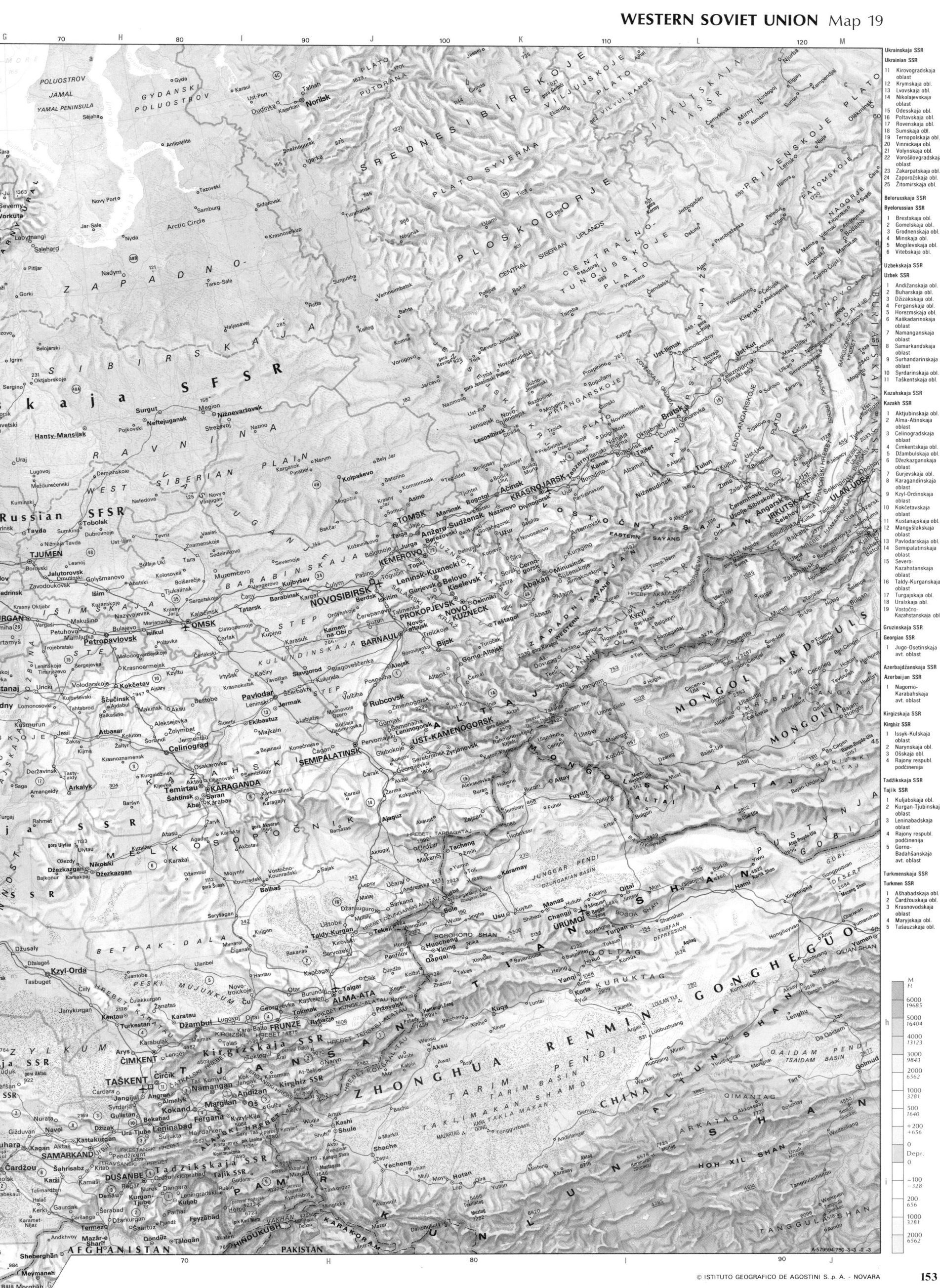

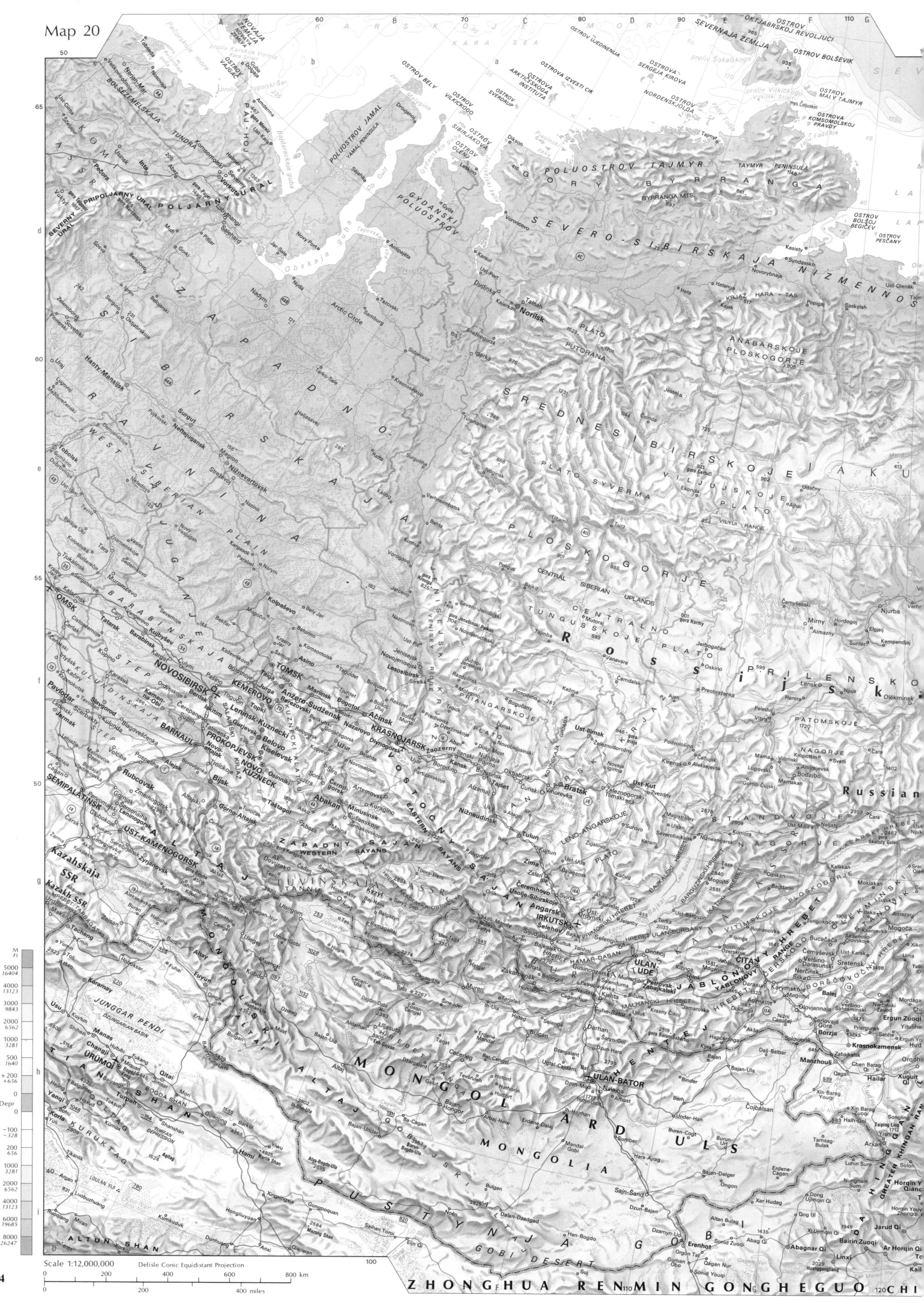

Map 20

Scale 1:12,000,000   Delisle Conic Equidistant Projection

0   200   400   600   800 km

0   200   400 miles

ZHONGHUA RENMIN GONGHEGUO CHI

© ISTITUTO GEOGRAFICO DE AGOSTINI S. p A. - NOVARA

Map 21 **ASIA, PHYSICAL**

Scale 1:30,000,000

Lambert Azimuthal Equal Area Projection

Longitude East 80 of Greenwich

Map 22 **ASIA, POLITICAL**

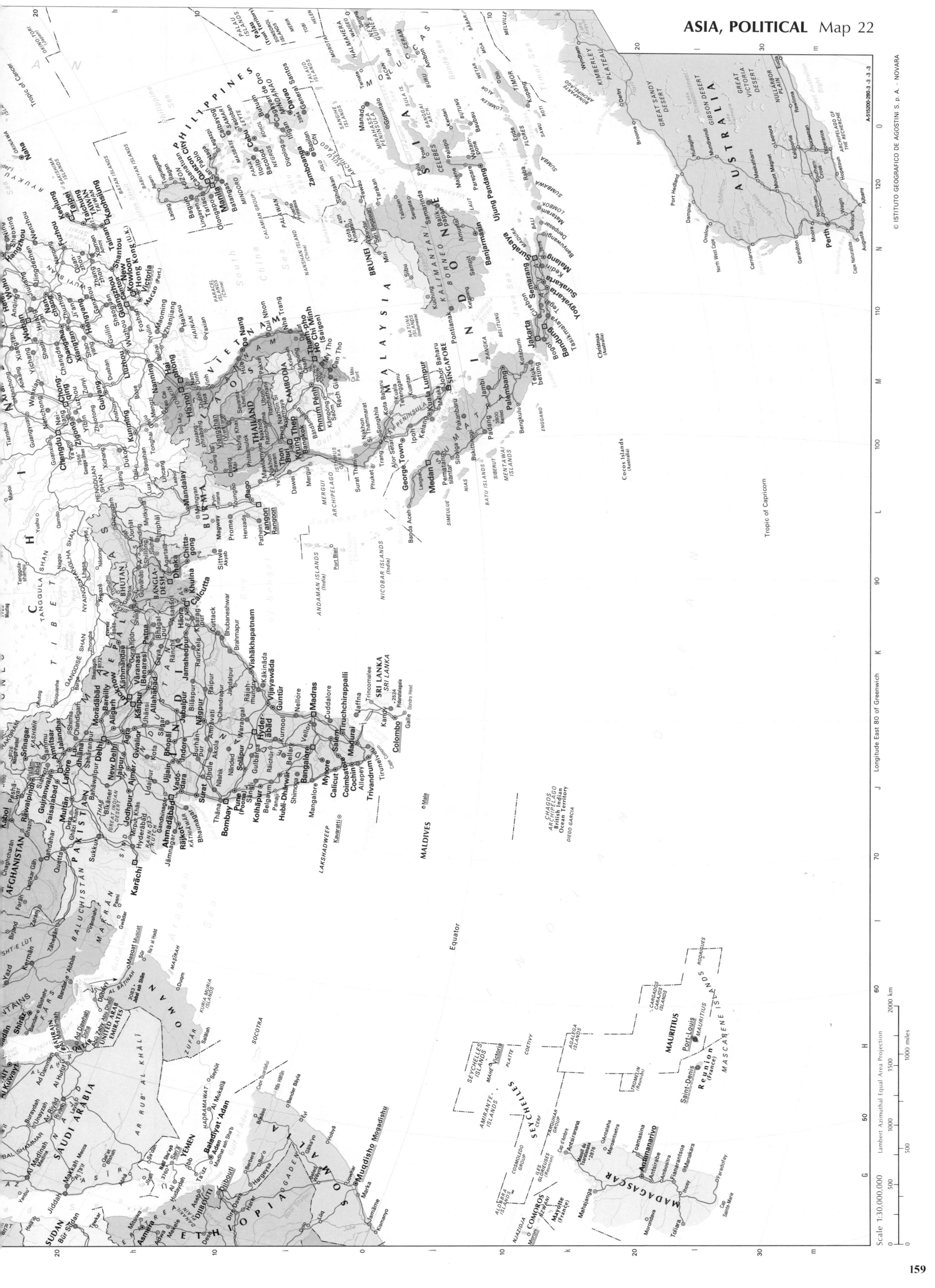

Map 23 **SOUTHWESTERN ASIA**

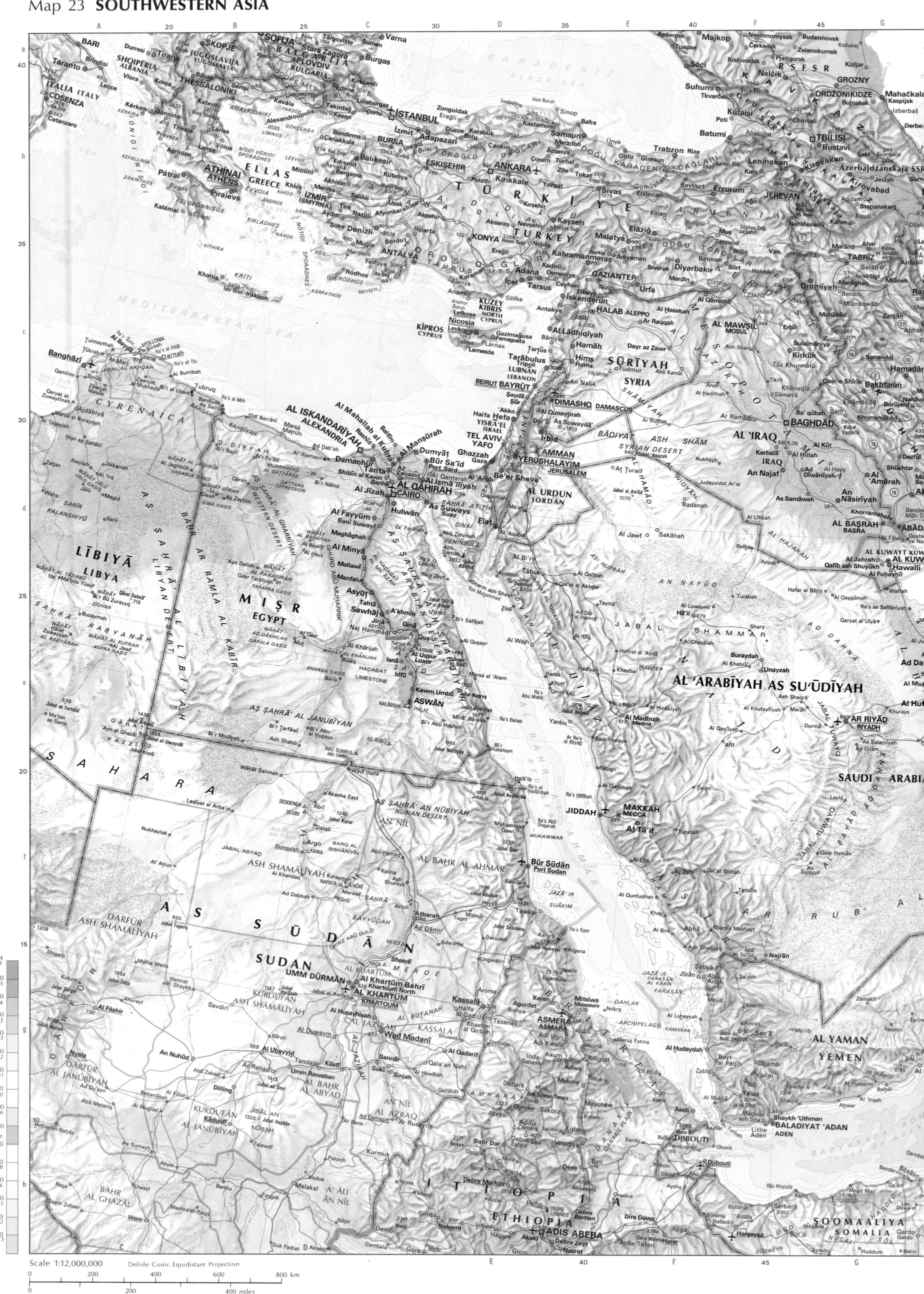

Scale 1:12,000,000   Delisle Conic Equidistant Projection

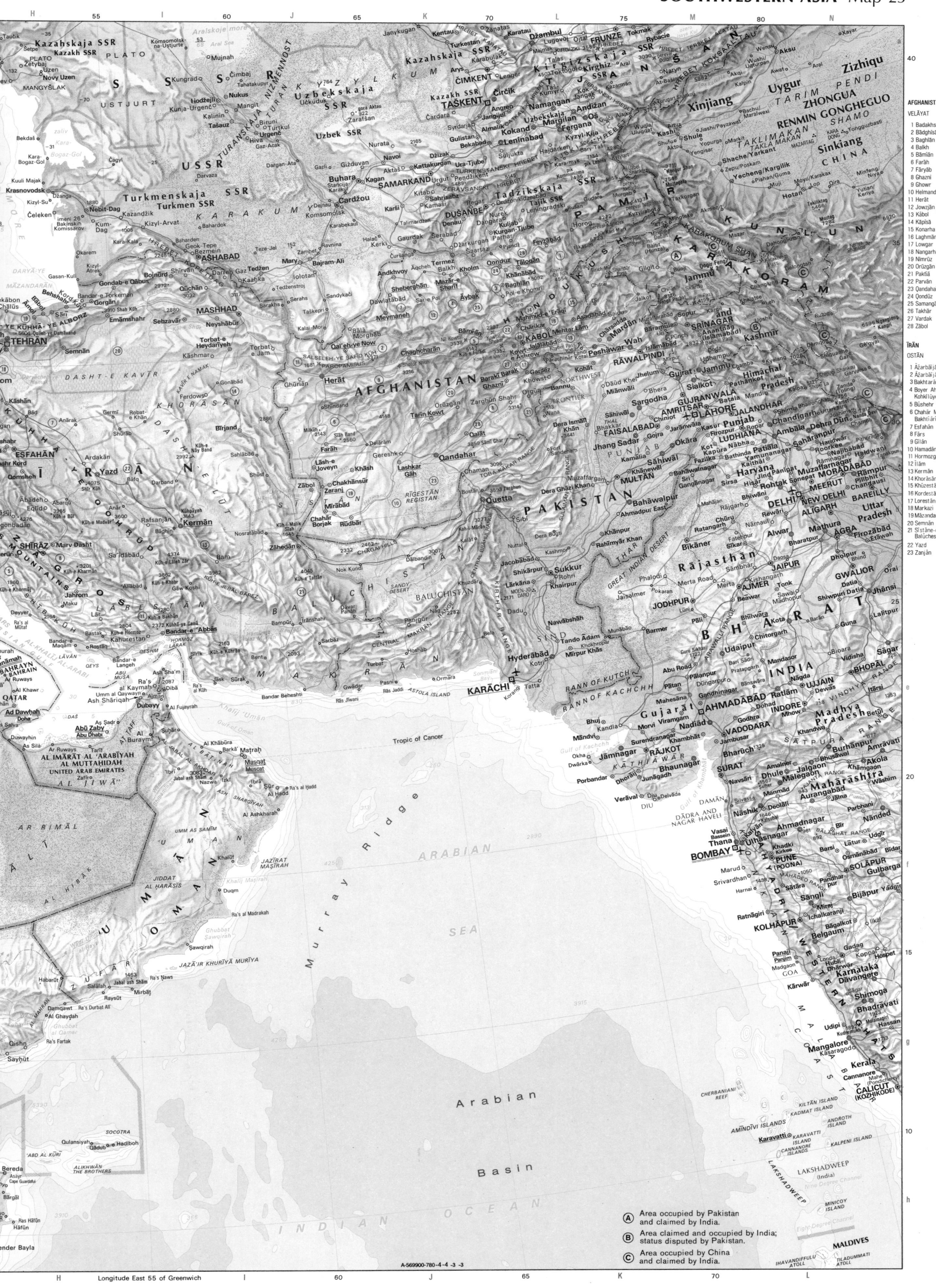

AFGHANISTAN

VELĀYAT

1 Badakhshān
2 Bādghīsāt
3 Baghlān
4 Balkh
5 Bāmiān
6 Farāh
7 Fāryāb
8 Ghazni
9 Ghowr
10 Helmand
11 Herāt
12 Jowzjān
13 Kābol
14 Kāpīsā
15 Konarha
16 Laghmān
17 Lowgar
18 Nangarhār
19 Nīmrūz
20 Orūzgān
21 Paktiā
22 Parvān
23 Qandahār
24 Qonduz
25 Samangān
26 Takhār
27 Vardak
28 Zābol

ĪRĀN

OSTĀN

1 Āzarbāījān-e Gharbī
2 Āzarbāījān-e Sharqī
3 Bakhtarān
4 Boyer Ahmadi -e
   Kohkī lūyeh
5 Chahār Mahāl-e
   Bakhtī ārī
6 Esfahān
7 Fārs
8 Gīlān
9 Gīlān
10 Hamadān
11 Hormozgān
12 Īlam
13 Kermān
14 Khorāsān
15 Khūzestān
16 Kordestān
17 Lorestān
18 Markazi
19 Māzandarān
20 Semnān
21 Sīstāne-e Balūchestān
22 Yazd
23 Zanjān

Area occupied by Pakistan and claimed by India.

Area claimed and occupied by India; status disputed by Pakistan.

Area occupied by China and claimed by India.

MALDIVES

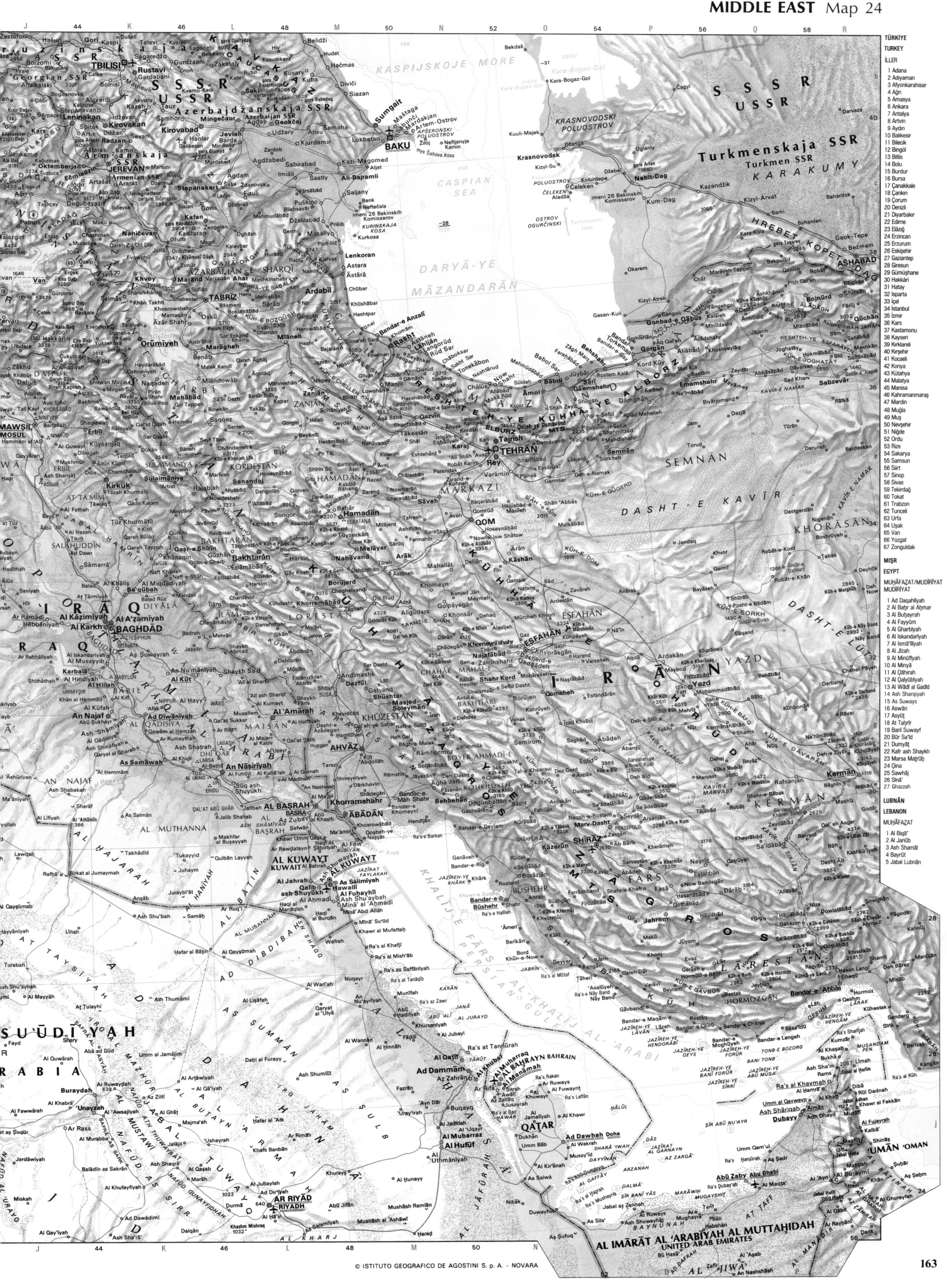

TÜRKİYE
TURKEY
İLLER

1 Adana
2 Adıyaman
3 Afyonkarahisar
4 Ağrı
5 Amasya
6 Ankara
7 Antalya
8 Artvin
9 Aydın
10 Balıkesir
11 Bilecik
12 Bingöl
13 Bitlis
14 Bolu
15 Burdur
16 Bursa
17 Çanakkale
18 Çankırı
19 Çorum
20 Denizli
21 Diyarbakır
22 Edirne
23 Elâzığ
24 Erzincan
25 Erzurum
26 Eskişehir
27 Gaziantep
28 Giresun
29 Gümüşhane
30 Hakkâri
31 Hatay
32 Isparta
33 İçel
34 İstanbul
35 İzmir
36 Kars
37 Kastamonu
38 Kayseri
39 Kırklareli
40 Kırşehir
41 Kocaeli
42 Konya
43 Kütahya
44 Malatya
45 Manisa
46 Kahramanmaraş
47 Mardin
48 Muğla
49 Muş
50 Nevşehir
51 Niğde
52 Ordu
53 Rize
54 Sakarya
55 Samsun
56 Siirt
57 Sinop
58 Sivas
59 Tekirdağ
60 Tokat
61 Trabzon
62 Tunceli
63 Urfa
64 Uşak
65 Van
66 Yozgat
67 Zonguldak

MISR
EGYPT
MUḤĀFAZĀT/MUDĪRĪYAT
MUDĪRĪYAT

1 Ad Daqahlīyah
2 Al Baḥr al Aḥmar
3 Al Buḥayrah
4 Al Fayyūm
5 Al Gharbīyah
6 Al Iskandarīyah
7 Ismā'īlīyah
8 Al Jīzah
9 Al Minūfīyah
10 Al Minya
11 Al Qāhirah
12 Al Qalyūbīyah
13 Al Wādī al Gadīd
14 Ash Sharqīyah
15 As Suways
16 Aswān
17 Asyūṭ
18 At Taḥrīr
19 Banī Suwayf
20 Būr Sa'īd
21 Dumyāṭ
22 Kafr ash Shaykh
23 Marsá Maṭrūḥ
24 Qinā
25 Sawhāj
26 Sīnā'
27 Ghazzah

LUBNĀN
LEBANON
MUḤĀFAZĀT

1 Al Biqā'
2 Al Janūb
3 Ash Shamāl
4 Bayrūt
5 Jabal Lubnān

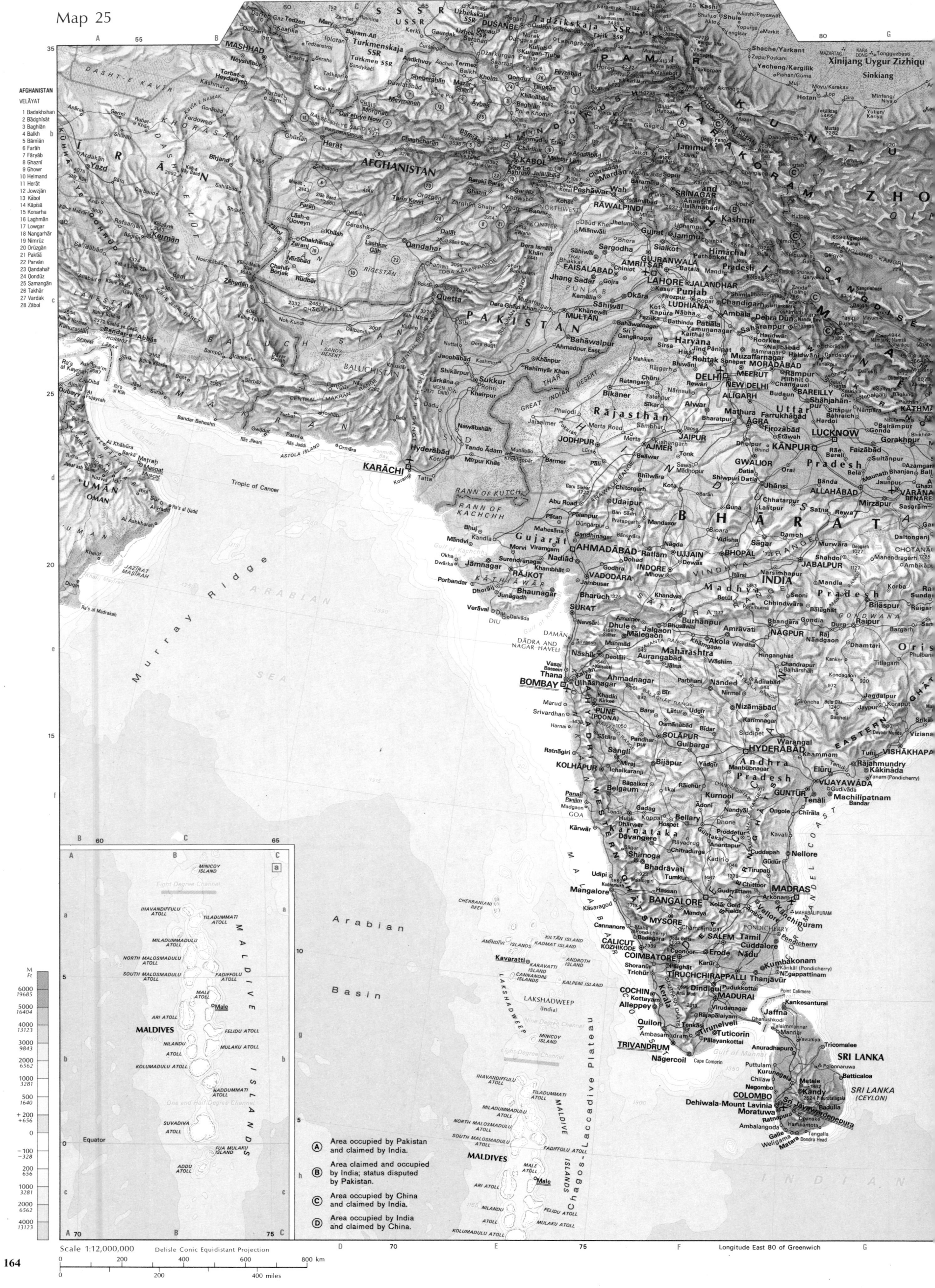

Map 25

AFGHANISTAN

VELĀYAT

1 Badakhshān
2 Bādghīsāt
3 Baghlān
4 Balkh
5 Bāmiān
6 Farāh
7 Fāryāb
8 Ghazni
9 Ghowr
10 Helmand
11 Herāt
12 Jowzjān
13 Kābol
14 Kāpīsā
15 Konarha
16 Laghmān
17 Lowgar
18 Nangarhār
19 Nīmrūz
20 Orūzgān
21 Paktiā
22 Parvān
23 Qandahār
24 Qondūz
25 Samangān
26 Takhār
27 Vardak
28 Zābol

MALDIVES

MALDIVES

Scale 1:12,000,000   Delisle Conic Equidistant Projection

0   200   400   600   800 km

0   200   400 miles

Ⓐ Area occupied by Pakistan and claimed by India.

Ⓑ Area claimed and occupied by India; status disputed by Pakistan.

Ⓒ Area occupied by China and claimed by India.

Ⓓ Area occupied by India and claimed by China.

Longitude East 80 of Greenwich

Map 26 SOUTHEAST ASIA

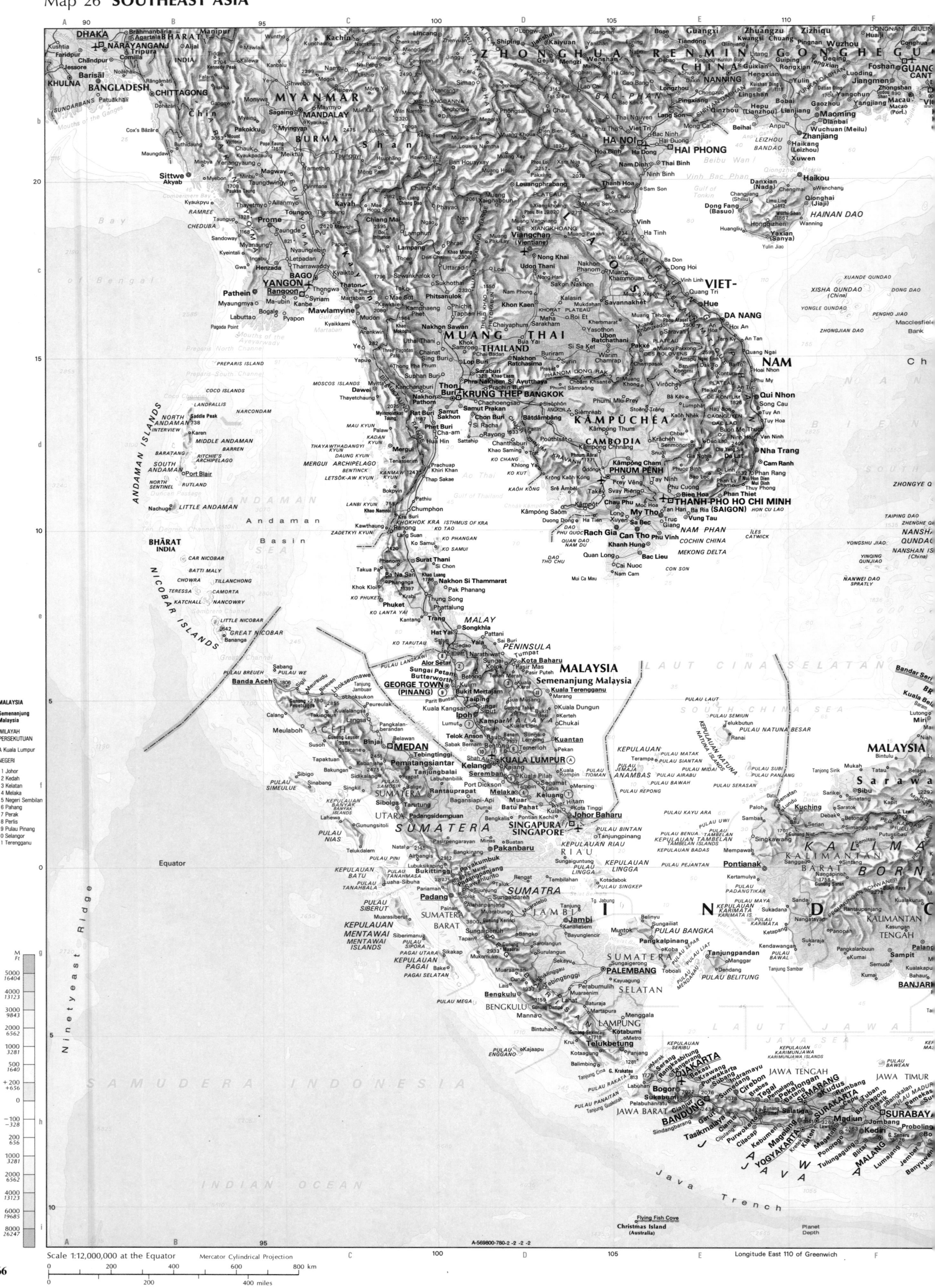

Scale 1:12,000,000 at the Equator   Mercator Cylindrical Projection   Longitude East 110 of Greenwich

Zhangping
Longyan *1493
Hui'an
Quanzhou
Xiamen Amoy
Zhangzhou
Chao'an
Zhao'an Yunxiao
Huilai
ufeng
SHANTOU
LOON

120
Taoyuan
Fukueichiao
KEELUNG
WUCHIU HSU
(Taiwan)
Hsinchu
TAIPEI
TAICHUNG
Changhua
Nantou Hualien
Yunlin
CHIAYI
Hsinying
TAINAN
KAOHSIUNG
Pingtung
Fangliao
Checheng
Tapanlieh

SAKISHIMA - SHOTŌ
Hirara
MIYAKO-
RETTŌ
YAEYAMA-SHOTŌ
Ishigaki
YONAGUNI JIMA
NIPPON JAPAN
125
NANSEI-SHOTŌ
RYUKYU IS.

Tropic of Cancer

TAIWAN
CHINMEN
QUEMOY
PENGHU
LIEHTAO
PESCADORES
Makung
Taitung
LU TAO
LAN HSU
Okanbi

Bashi Channel

DONGSHA QUNDAO

HUANGYAN
DAO
ITBAYAT
BATAN ISLANDS
Basco
BATAN
SABTANG

Luzon Strait

Balintang Channel

BABUYAN ISLANDS
CALAYAN
BABUYAN
DALUPIRI
FUGA
CAMIGUIN

Mayraira Point
Bangui
Aparri
Escarpada Point
San Vicente
Laoag
Bangued
Mount Mammanot
Tuguegarao
Vigan
Tabuk
Bontoc
Ilagan
San Fernando
Bayombong
Baguio
Alaminos
Lingayen
Dagupan
San Carlos
Camiling
Tarlac
Iba
Cabanatuan
Angeles
San Fernando
Olongapo
MANILA
QUEZON CITY

LUZON

West
Mariana
Basin

PHILIPPINE BASIN

PHILIPPINE SEA

OKINO-TORI-SHIMA
PARECE VELA
(Japan)

20

b

c

15

PACIFIC

Santa Cruz
Balayan
Lipa
San Pablo
Lucena
Batangas
Calapan
Boac
MINDORO
Mamburao
Bongabong
San Jose

PILIPINAS
CATANDUANES
Naga
Virac
Daet
Legazpi
Mount Mayon 2462
Sorsogon
Bulan
Catarman

PHILIPPINES

BUSUANGA
Coron
Culion
CALAMIAN GROUP
CUYO
ISLANDS
San Jose
de Buenavista
Iloilo
Bacolod
San Carlos

PANAY

MASBATE
Masbate
Roxas
Kalibo
Pandan

TABLAS
SIBUYAN
Romblon
TICAO
BURIAS

Mandaon

SAMAR
Calbayog
Catbalogan
Borongan
Basey
Tacloban
LEYTE
Ormoc
Baybay
Maasin
HOMONHON

DINAGAT
SIARGAO
Surigao
Numancia

BUTUAN

OCEAN

FEDERATED STATES
OF MICRONESIA

ULITHI ATOLL

YAP ISLANDS
Colonia

NGULU ATOLL

FAIS

SOROL ATOLL

10

PALAWAN
Taytay
Roxas
Puerto Princesa
Aborlan

NEGROS
La Carlota
Dumaguete
Sipalay
Bayawan
Santander
Siquijor
Tagbilaran
BOHOL

CEBU
Toledo
Carcar

Dipolog
Oroquieta
Ozamiz
Iligan
**Cagayan
de Oro**
Malaybalay

Gingoog

Cabadbaran
Tandag

KAYANGEL ISLANDS

YAP TRENCH

BABELTHUAP
Koror
PALAU ISLANDS
PELELIU
ANGAUR

CAROLINE ISLANDS

Palau

Belau

(Trust Territory)

e

Sabah
Kudat
Sandakan
Lahad Datu
Tawau

ZAMBOANGA
Basilan City
Isabela
BASILAN
Jolo
Luuk
SULU ARCHIPELAGO
TAWI-TAWI
SIBUTU IS.

ZAMBOANGA
PENINSULA
Kabasalan
Pagadian
Marawi
Cotabato
Maganoy
Datu
Piang
Isulan
Koronadal
Kiamba
DAVAO
Mati

**General
Santos**

Tinaca Point

MINDANAO

PULAU MIANGAS
(Indonesia)

SARANGANI
ISLANDS

SONSOROL
ISLANDS

PULO ANNA

MERIR

TOBI
HELEN REEF

West

Caroline

Basin

5

KEPULAUAN
KAWIO
Beo
TALAUD ISLANDS
PULAU KARAKELANG
PULAU
KABURUANG

PULAU
NANUSA

0

Celebes Basin

CELEBES SEA

Tahuna
PULAU SANGIHE
PULAU SIAU
PULAU
TAHULANDANG
PULAU BIARO

Manado
Tondano
Bitung
GUNUNG KLABAT
MINAHASSA
SULAWESI UTARA

Galela
Tobelo
Akelamo
PULAU MOROTAI

Tanjung Sopi

HALMAHERA
Ternate
Tidore
Weda
Patani

KEPULAUAN
ASIA

KEPULAUAN
MAPIA

f

Equator

New Guinea Trench

CELEBES

SULAWESI TENGAH
Palu

Samarinda

KALIMANTAN
TIMUR
Balikpapan

Manokwari
PULAU BIAK
PULAU
SUPIORI
PULAU
NUMFOOR
MIOS NUM
Nabire
PEGUNUNGAN VAN REES
PULAU YAPEN
TARIKU - TARITATU
Jayapura
IRIAN JAYA
PEGUNUNGAN
MAOKE
PEGUNUNGAN JAYAWIJAYA
Wamena

N

D

O

N

E

S

I

A

MALUKU
KEP. KAI
MOLUCCA SEA

SERAM CERAM
Ambon
PULAU BURU

LAUT SERAM

Fakfak
JAZIRAH
BOMBERAI

PULAU MISOOL

PAPUA
NEW GUINEA

NEW GUINEA

g

Makale
Palopo

SULAWESI
TENGGARA
Kendari

PULAU BUTUNG
PULAU MUNA
Baubau

UJUNG PANDANG
(MAKASAR)

MALUKU

PULAU ARU
ARU

KEPULAUAN
KAI
BESAR

PULAU
KOLA

PULAU IRIAN

PULAU DOLAK

PULAU
KOMORAN

h

BANDA SEA

KEPULAUAN
TANIMBAR
Saumlaki

LAUT ARAFURA

ARAFURA SEA

140

Mataram
PULAU BALI
PULAU LOMBOK
PULAU SUMBAWA
NUSA TENGGARA
BARAT

PULAU FLORES
Ende
NUSA TENGGARA
TIMUR
PULAU SUMBA
Waingapu

PULAU
WETAR
Kupang
PULAU TIMOR
TIMOR TIMUR
Dili

TIMOR SEA

LAUT TIMOR

TIMOR TROUGH

MULGRAVE
ISLAND

i

120
125
130
Darwin
AUSTRALIA
135
Nhulunbuy

167

Map 27 **CHINA AND MONGOLIA**

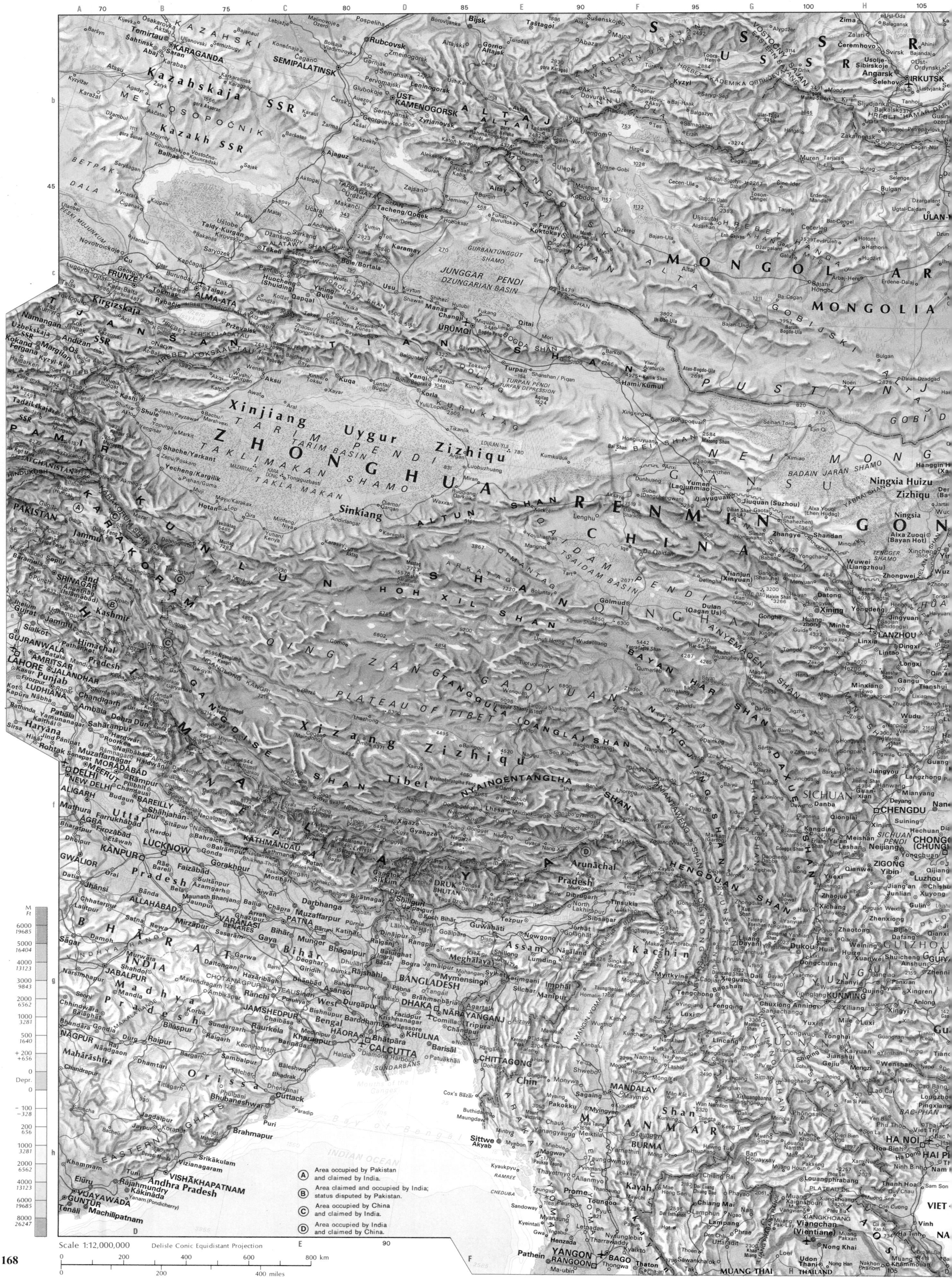

(A) Area occupied by Pakistan and claimed by India.

(B) Area claimed and occupied by India; status disputed by Pakistan.

(C) Area occupied by China and claimed by India.

(D) Area occupied by India and claimed by China.

Scale 1:12,000,000

Delisle Conic Equidistant Projection

0   200   400   600   800 km

0   200   400 miles

M	Ft
6000	19685
5000	16404
4000	13123
3000	9843
2000	6562
1000	3281
500	1640
+200	+656
0	0
Depr.	
−100	−328
200	656
1000	3281
2000	6562
4000	13123
6000	19685
8000	26247

ZHONGHUA
RENMIN
GONGHEGUO

CHINA

1 Beijing Shi
2 Shanghai Shi
3 Tianjin Shi

A-569700-780-1 -1 -2 -3

Map 28   **NORTHEASTERN CHINA, KOREA AND JAPAN**

Scale 1:6,000,000   Delisle Conic Equidistant Projection

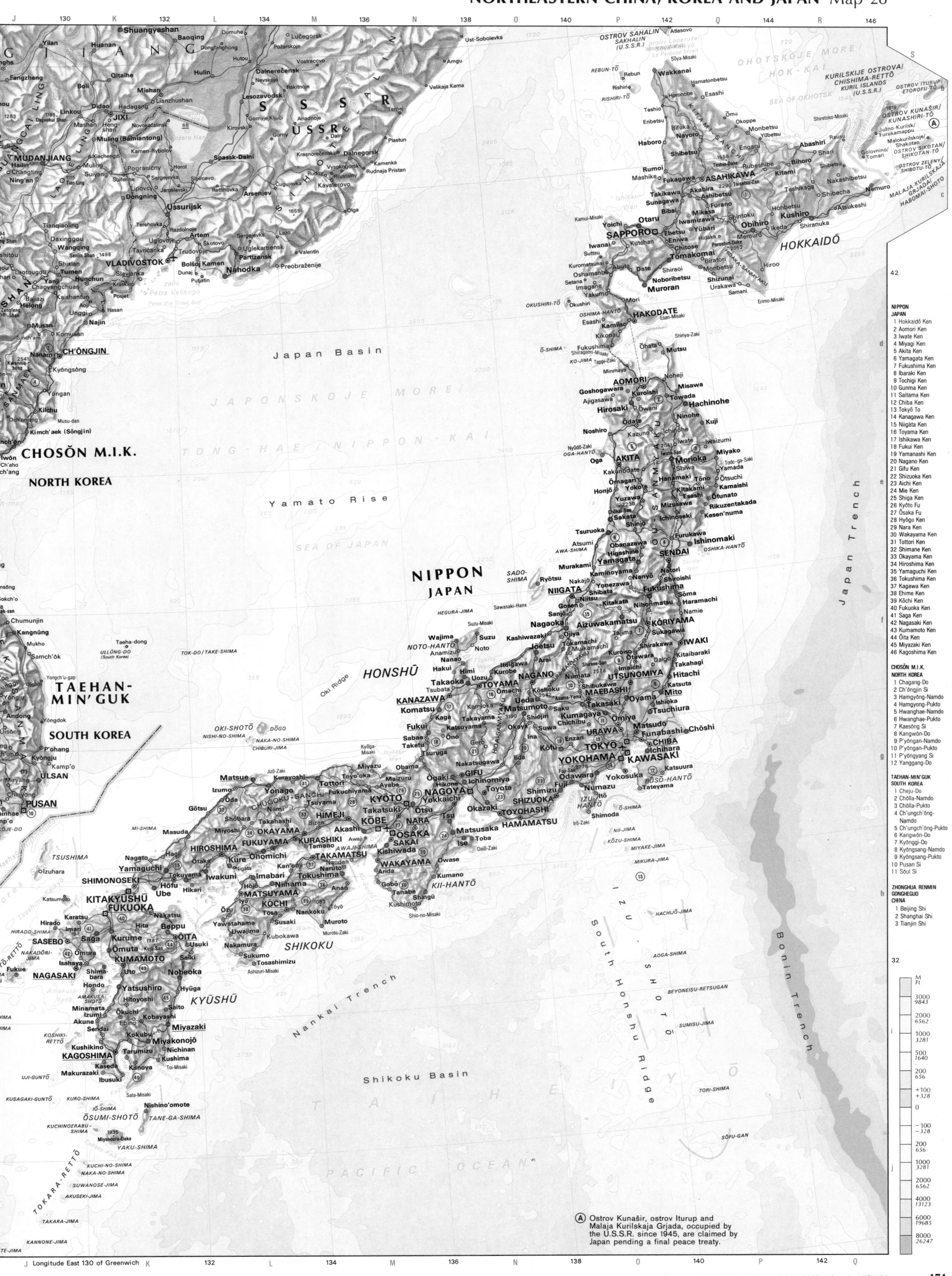

Map 29 **JAPAN**

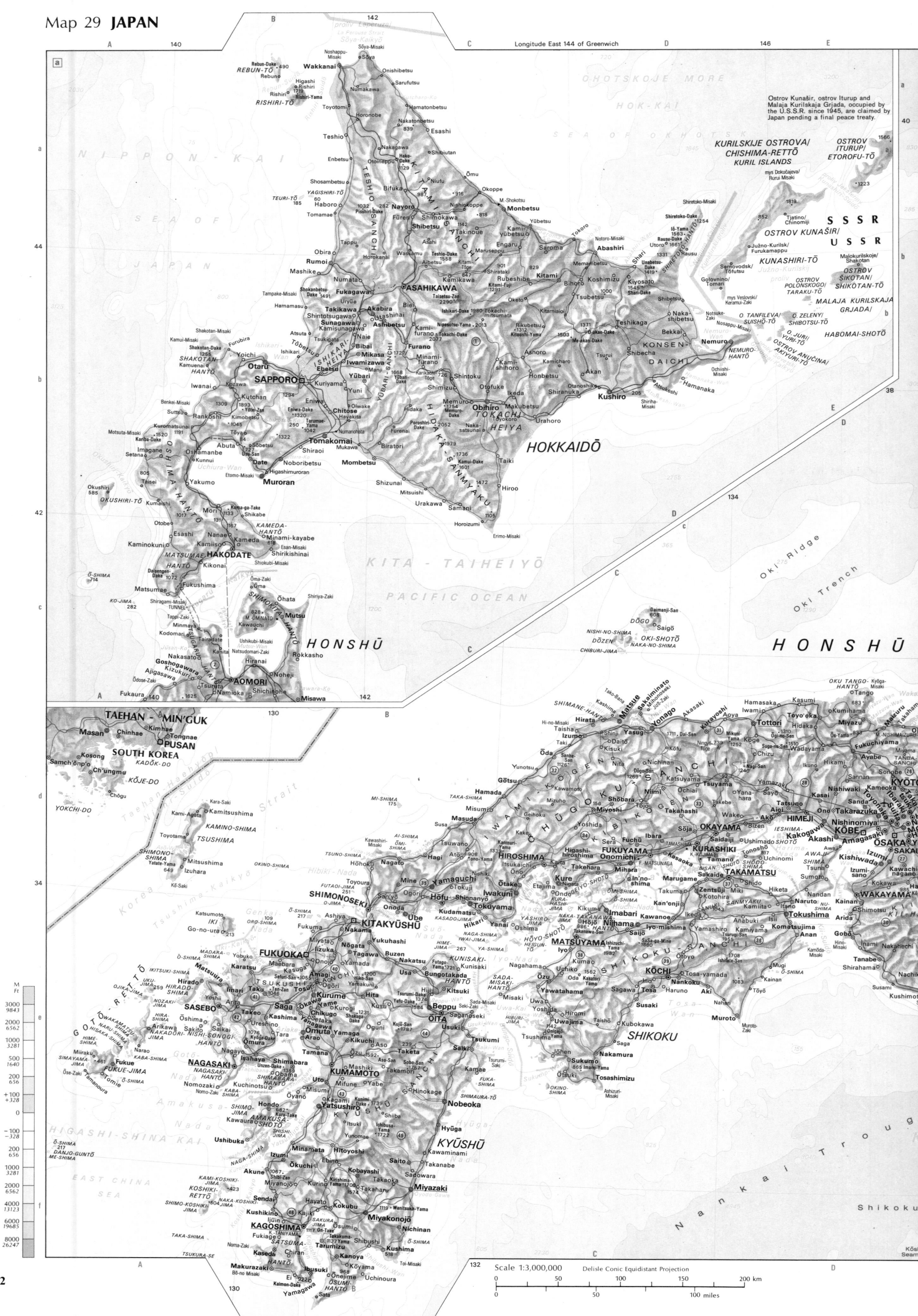

Ostrov Kunašir, ostrov Iturup and
Malaja Kurilskaja Grjada, occupied by
the U.S.S.R. since 1945, are claimed by
Japan pending a final peace treaty.

KURILSKIJE OSTROVA/
CHISHIMA-RETTŌ
KURIL ISLANDS

OSTROV
ITURUP/
ETOROFU-TŌ

SSSR
OSTROV KUNAŠIR
USSR

KUNASHIRI-TŌ

OSTROV
ŠIKOTAN/
SHIKOTAN-TŌ

MALAJA KURILSKAJA
GRJADA/
HABOMAI-SHOTŌ

HOKKAIDŌ

NIPPON-KAI

SEA OF
JAPAN

KITA - TAIHEIYŌ

PACIFIC OCEAN

HONSHŪ

HONSHŪ

Oki Ridge

Oki Trench

TAEHAN - MIN'GUK

SOUTH KOREA

PUSAN

TSUSHIMA

Korea Strait

CHŪGOKU - SANCHI

KYOTO

HIMEJI

KŌBE

OSAKA

SAKAI

WAKAYAMA

HIROSHIMA

OKAYAMA

KURASHIKI

TAKAMATSU

SHIMONOSEKI

KITAKYŪSHŪ

FUKUOKA

SHIKOKU - SANCHI

MATSUYAMA

KŌCHI

SASEBO

SAGA

KURUME

ŌITA

BEPPU

SHIKOKU

NAGASAKI

KUMAMOTO

KYŪSHŪ

MIYAZAKI

EAST CHINA
SEA

KAGOSHIMA

Nankai Trough

Shikoku

M
Ft
3000
9843
2000
6562
1000
3281
500
1640
200
656
+ 100
+ 328
— 0
— 0
200
656
2000
6562
4000
13123
6000
19685
8000
26247

Scale 1:3,000,000   Delisle Conic Equidistant Projection

0   50   100   150   200 km

0   50   100 miles

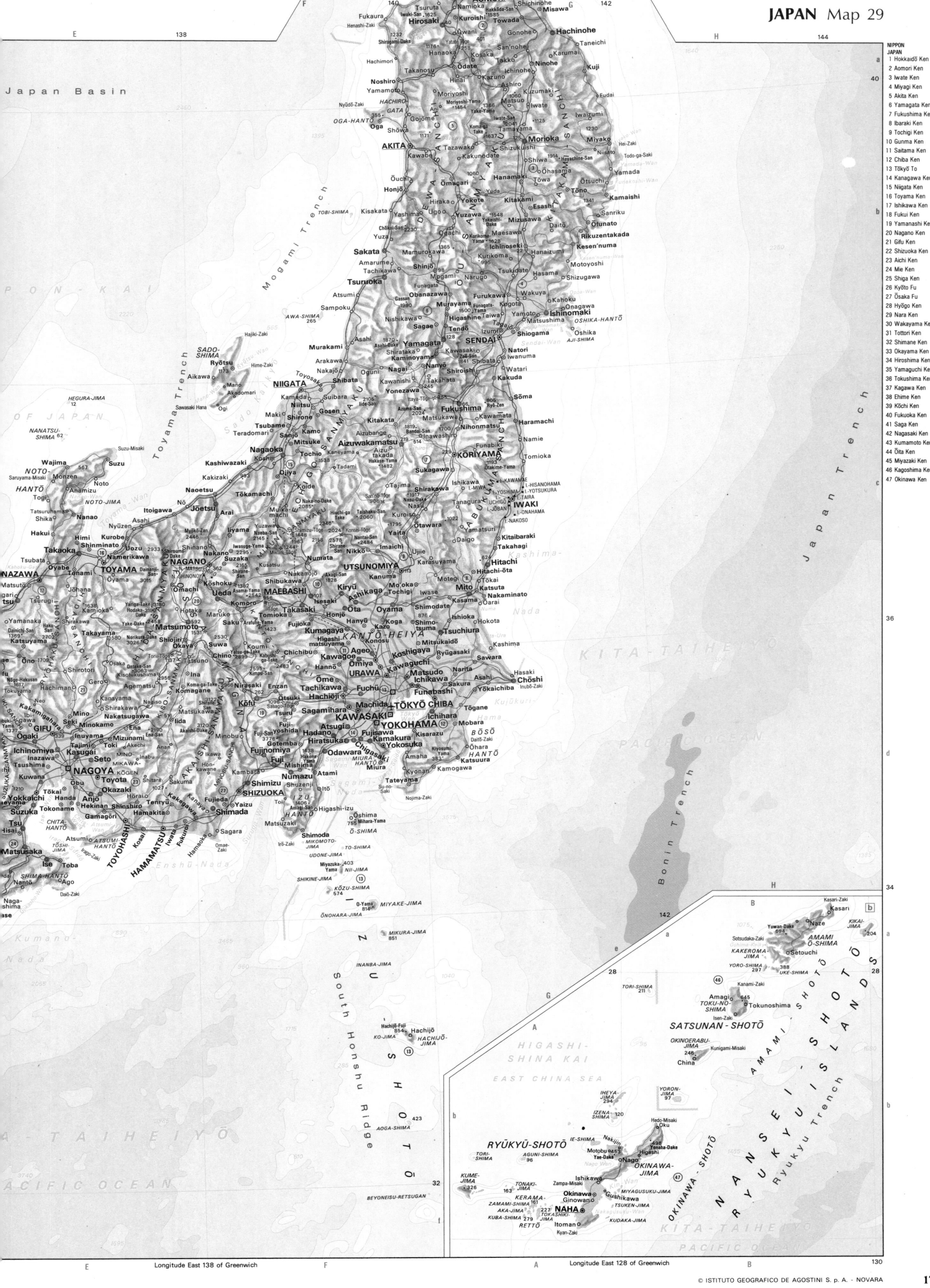

NIPPON
JAPAN
1 Hokkaidō Ken
2 Aomori Ken
3 Iwate Ken
4 Miyagi Ken
5 Akita Ken
6 Yamagata Ken
7 Fukushima Ken
8 Ibaraki Ken
9 Tochigi Ken
10 Gunma Ken
11 Saitama Ken
12 Chiba Ken
13 Tōkyō To
14 Kanagawa Ken
15 Niigata Ken
16 Toyama Ken
17 Ishikawa Ken
18 Fukui Ken
19 Yamanashi Ken
20 Nagano Ken
21 Gifu Ken
22 Shizuoka Ken
23 Aichi Ken
24 Mie Ken
25 Shiga Ken
26 Kyōto Fu
27 Ōsaka Fu
28 Hyōgo Ken
29 Nara Ken
30 Wakayama Ken
31 Tottori Ken
32 Shimane Ken
33 Okayama Ken
34 Hiroshima Ken
35 Yamaguchi Ken
36 Tokushima Ken
37 Kagawa Ken
38 Ehime Ken
39 Kōchi Ken
40 Fukuoka Ken
41 Saga Ken
42 Nagasaki Ken
43 Kumamoto Ken
44 Ōita Ken
45 Miyazaki Ken
46 Kagoshima Ken
47 Okinawa Ken

Map 30 **AFRICA, PHYSICAL**

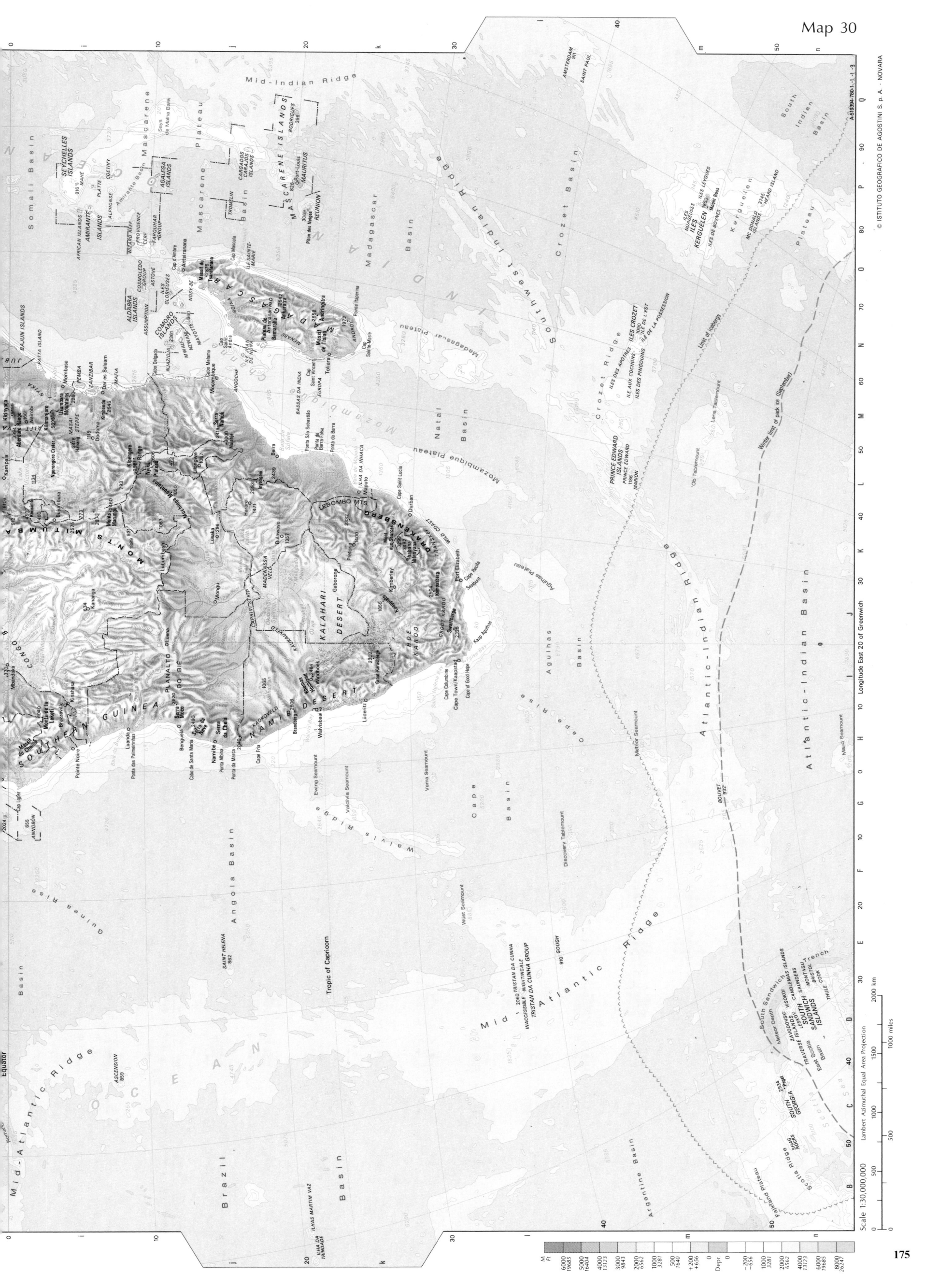

Map 30

© ISTITUTO GEOGRAFICO DE AGOSTINI S. p. A. - NOVARA

A-519384-760-1.-1.-3.

Scale 1:30,000,000   Lambert Azimuthal Equal Area Projection

175

Map 31 **AFRICA, POLITICAL**

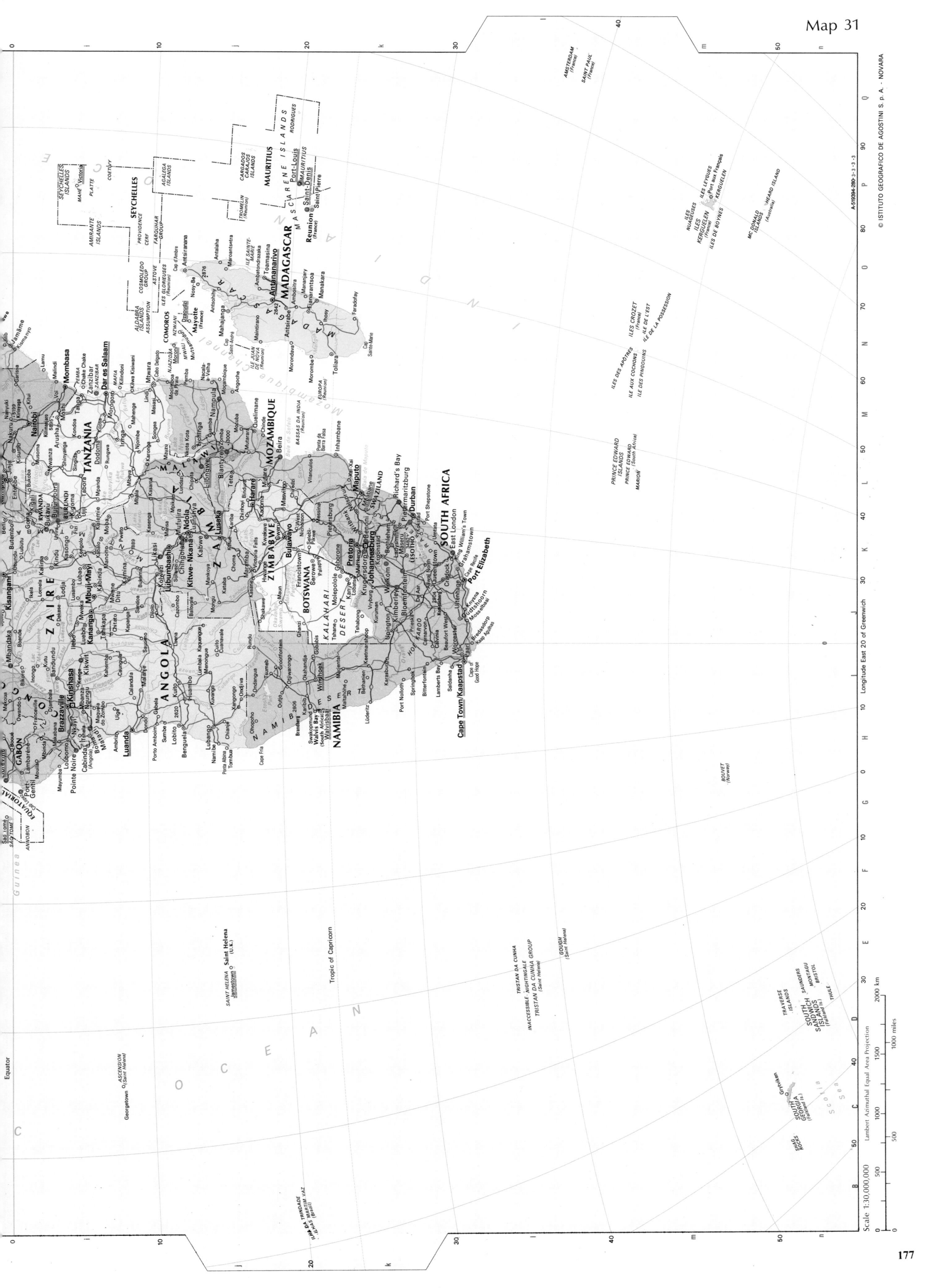

Map 31

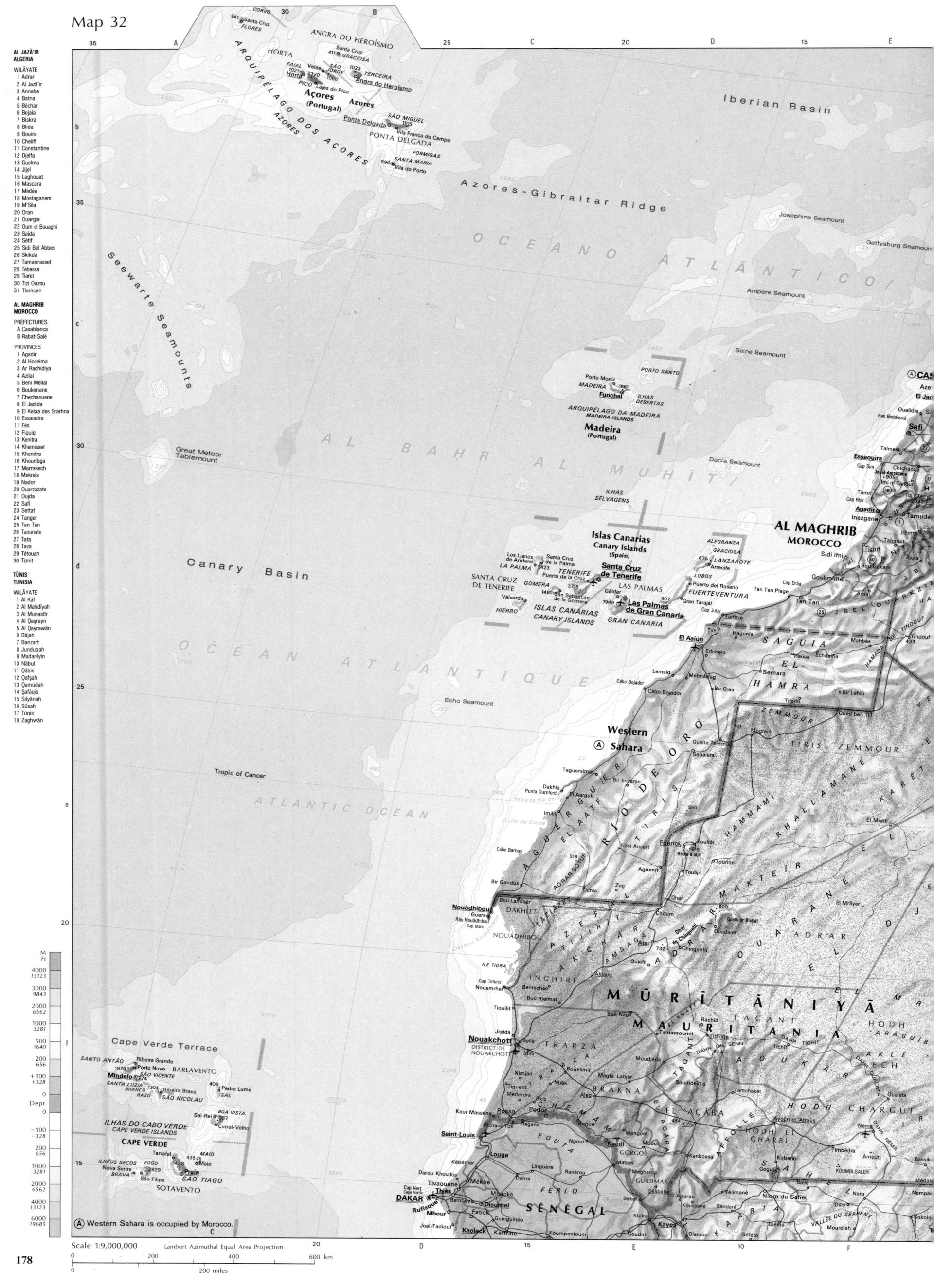

Map 32

AL JAZĀ'IR
ALGERIA
WILĀYATE
1 Adrar
2 Al Jazā'ir
3 Annaba
4 Batna
5 Bechar
6 Bejaia
7 Biskra
8 Blida
9 Bouira
10 Cheliff
11 Constantine
12 Djelfa
13 Guelma
14 Jijel
15 Laghouat
16 Mascara
17 Médéa
18 Mostaganem
19 M'Sila
20 Oran
21 Ouargla
22 Oum el Bouaghi
23 Saida
24 Setif
25 Sidi Bel Abbes
26 Skikda
27 Tamanrasset
28 Tebessa
29 Tiaret
30 Tizi Ouzou
31 Tiemcen

AL MAGHRIB
MOROCCO
PRÉFECTURES
A Casablanca
B Rabat-Salé
PROVINCES
1 Agadir
2 Al Hoceima
3 Ar Rachidiya
4 Azilal
5 Beni Mellal
6 Boulemane
7 Chechaouene
8 El Jadida
9 El Kelaa des Srarhna
10 Essaouira
11 Fès
12 Figuig
13 Kenitra
14 Khemisset
15 Khenifra
16 Khouribga
17 Marrakech
18 Meknès
19 Nador
20 Ouarzazate
21 Oujda
22 Safi
23 Settat
24 Tanger
25 Tan Tan
26 Taounate
27 Tata
28 Taza
29 Tétouan
30 Tiznit

TŪNIS
TUNISIA
WILĀYATE
1 Al Kāf
2 Al Mahdīyah
3 Al Munastīr
4 Al Qaṣrayn
5 Al Qayrawān
6 Bājah
7 Banzart
8 Jundubah
9 Madanīyīn
10 Nābul
11 Qābis
12 Qafṣah
13 Qamūdah
14 Ṣafāqis
15 Sillyānah
16 Sūsah
17 Tūnis
18 Zaghwān

Ⓐ Western Sahara is occupied by Morocco.

Scale 1:9,000,000   Lambert Azimuthal Equal Area Projection

0   200   400   600 km

0   200 miles

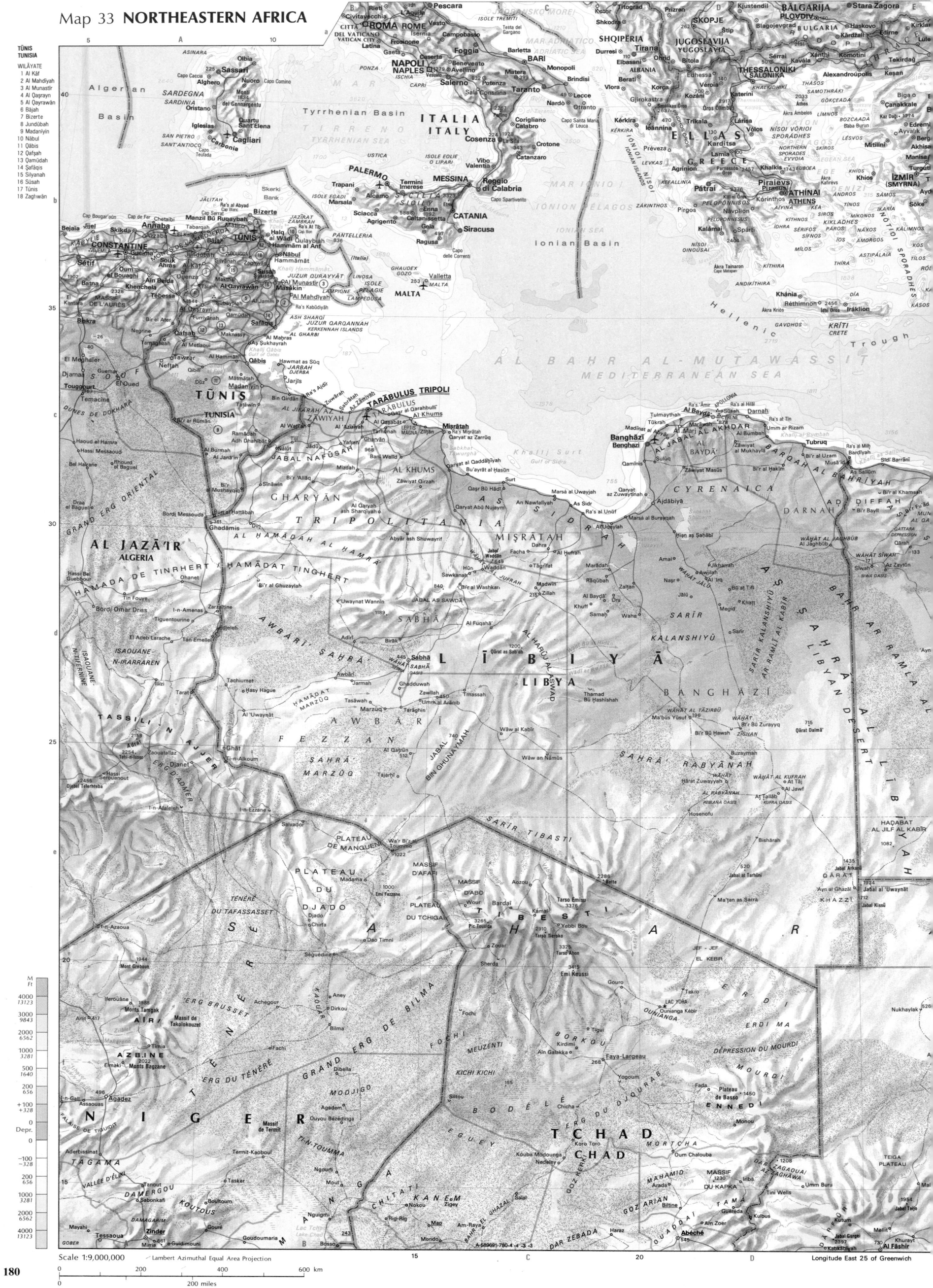

Map 33 NORTHEASTERN AFRICA

TÛNIS
TUNISIA

WILĀYATE
1 Al Kāf
2 Al Mahdīyah
3 Al Munastīr
4 Al Qaşrayn
5 Al Qayrawān
6 Bājah
7 Bizerte
8 Jundūbah
9 Madanīyīn
10 Nābul
11 Qābis
12 Qafşah
13 Qamūdah
14 Şafāqis
15 Silyanah
16 Sūsah
17 Tūnis
18 Zaghwān

Scale 1:9,000,000 — Lambert Azimuthal Equal Area Projection

0   200   400   600 km

0   200 miles

Longitude East 25 of Greenwich

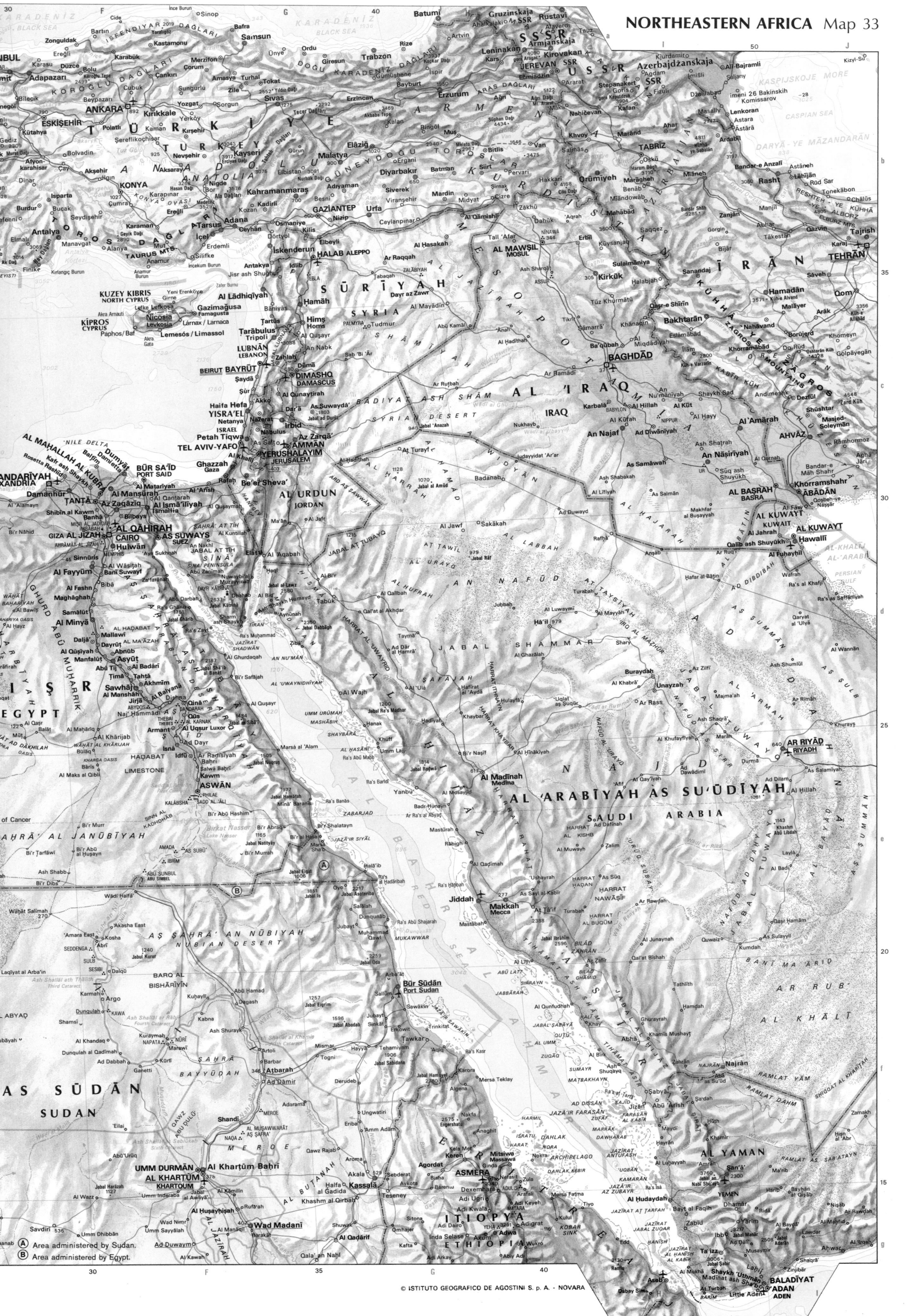

Ⓐ Area administered by Sudan.
Ⓑ Area administered by Egypt.

Map 34 **WEST-CENTRAL AFRICA**

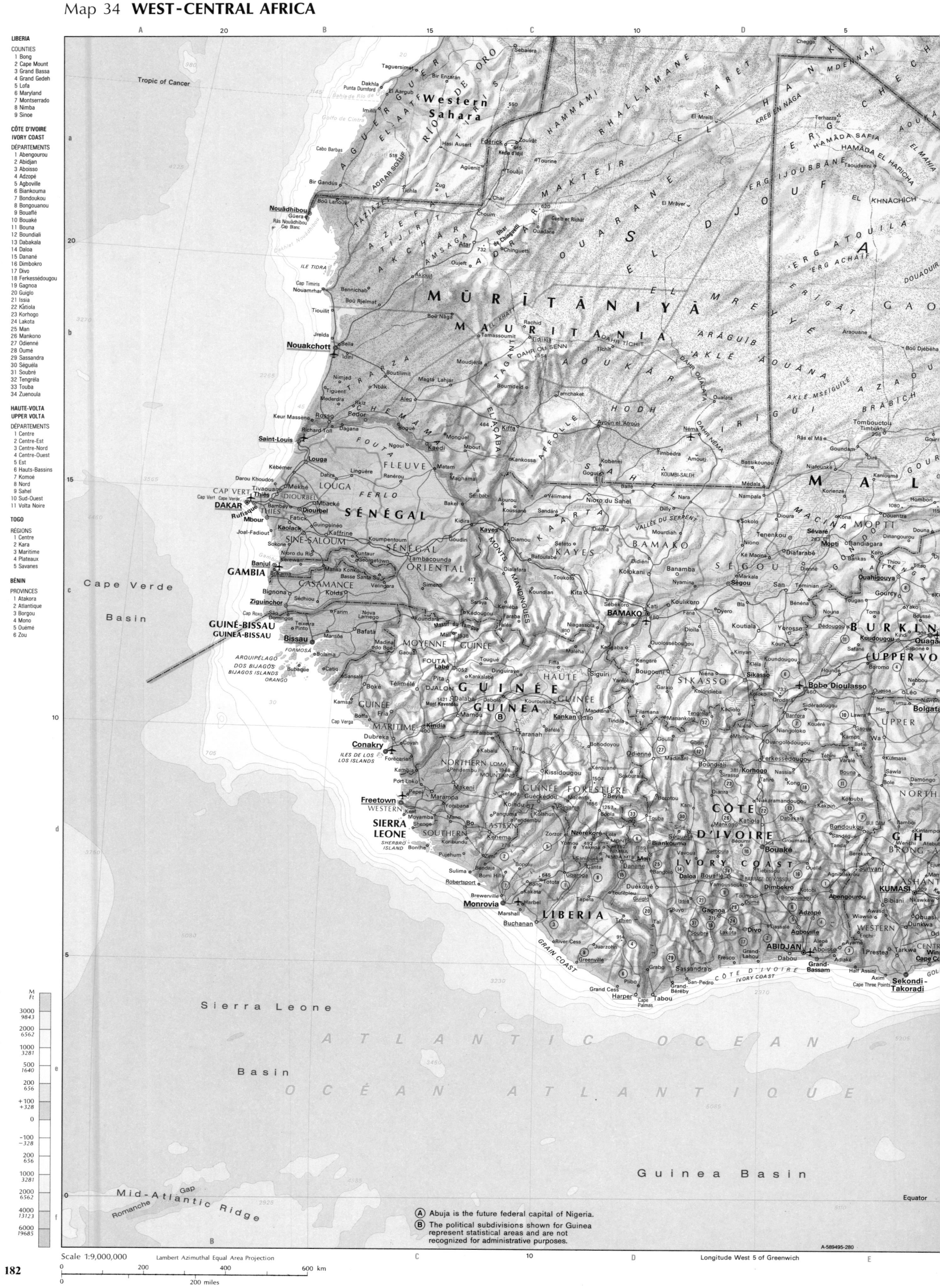

LIBERIA
COUNTIES
1 Bong
2 Cape Mount
3 Grand Bassa
4 Grand Gedeh
5 Lofa
6 Maryland
7 Montserrado
8 Nimba
9 Sinoe

**CÔTE D'IVOIRE
IVORY COAST**
DÉPARTEMENTS
1 Abengourou
2 Abidjan
3 Aboisso
4 Adzopé
5 Agboville
6 Biankouma
7 Bondoukou
8 Bongouanou
9 Bouaflé
10 Bouaké
11 Bouna
12 Boundiali
13 Dabakala
14 Daloa
15 Danané
16 Dimbokro
17 Divo
18 Ferkessédougou
19 Gagnoa
20 Guiglo
21 Issia
22 Katiola
23 Korhogo
24 Lakota
25 Man
26 Mankono
27 Odienné
28 Oumé
29 Sassandra
30 Séguéla
31 Soubré
32 Tengréla
33 Touba
34 Zuenoula

**HAUTE-VOLTA
UPPER VOLTA**
DÉPARTEMENTS
1 Centre
2 Centre-Est
3 Centre-Nord
4 Centre-Ouest
5 Est
6 Hauts-Bassins
7 Komoé
8 Nord
9 Sahel
10 Sud-Ouest
11 Volta Noire

TOGO
RÉGIONS
1 Centre
2 Kara
3 Maritime
4 Plateaux
5 Savanes

BÉNIN
PROVINCES
1 Atakora
2 Atlantique
3 Borgou
4 Mono
5 Ouémé
6 Zou

(A) Abuja is the future federal capital of Nigeria.

(B) The political subdivisions shown for Guinea represent statistical areas and are not recognized for administrative purposes.

Scale 1:9,000,000   Lambert Azimuthal Equal Area Projection

0   200   400   600 km

0   200 miles

Longitude West 5 of Greenwich

A-589495-280

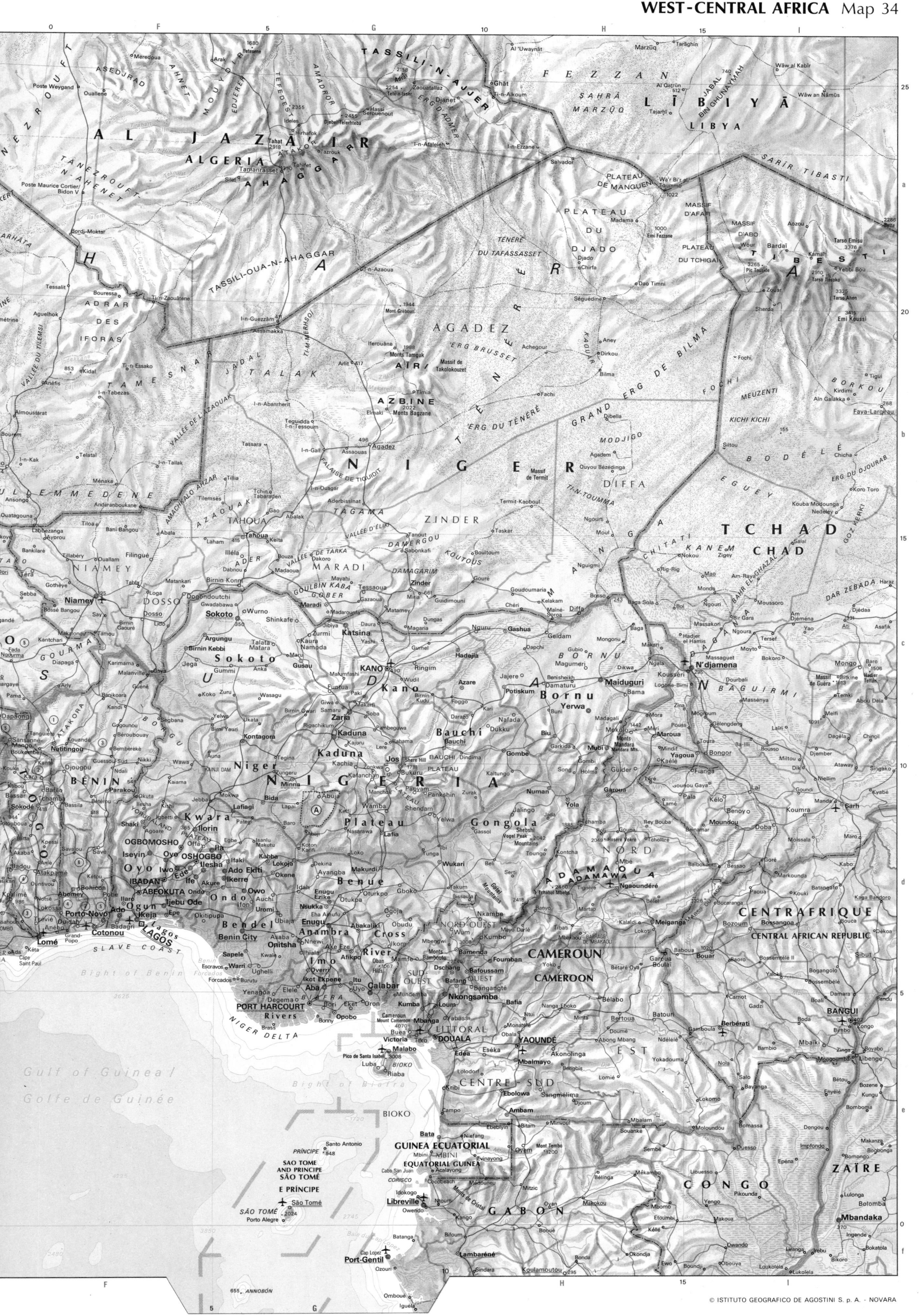

Map 35 **EAST-CENTRAL AFRICA**

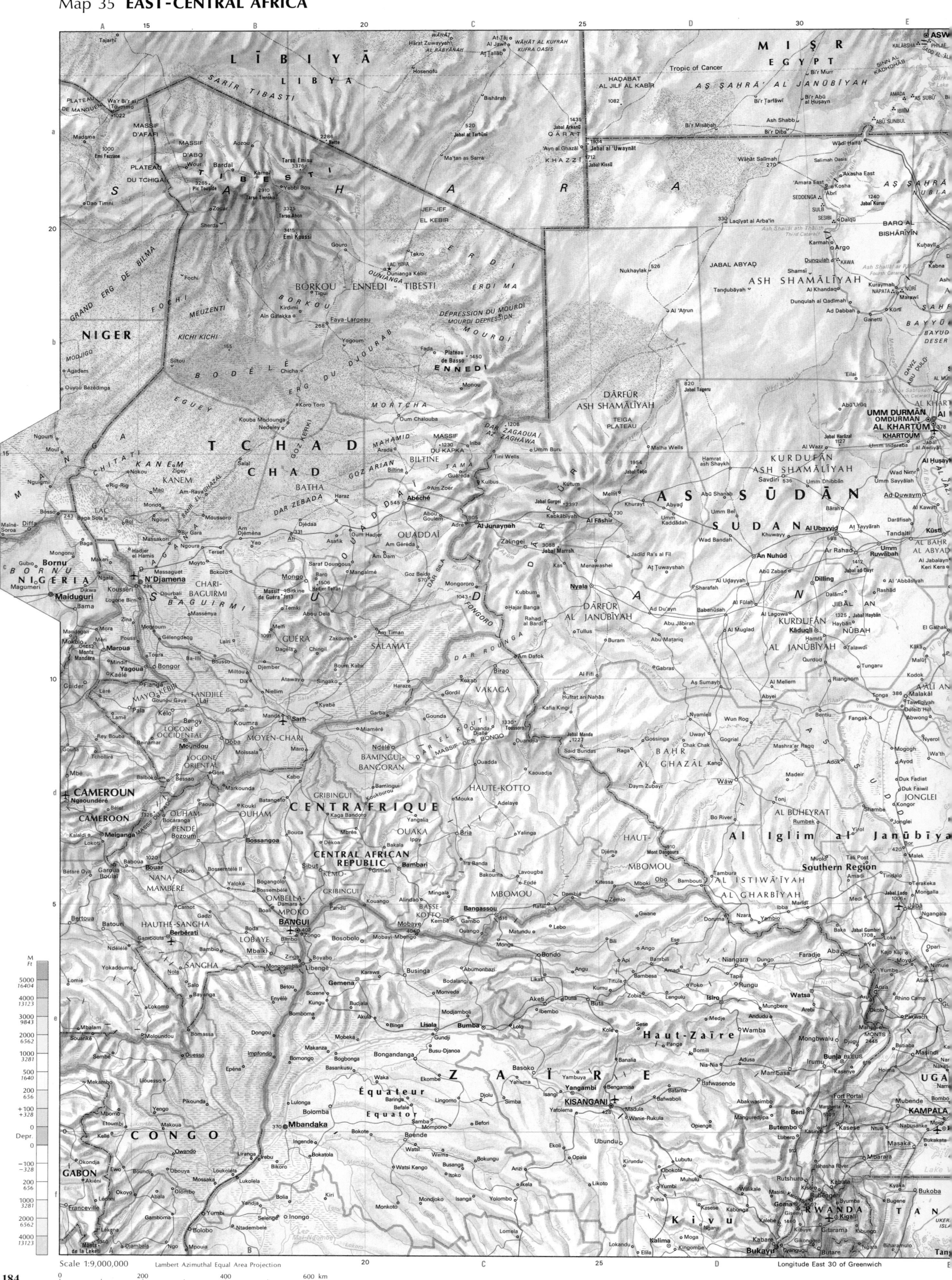

Scale 1:9,000,000

Lambert Azimuthal Equal Area Projection

Longitude East 30 of Greenwich

0   200   400   600 km

0   200 miles

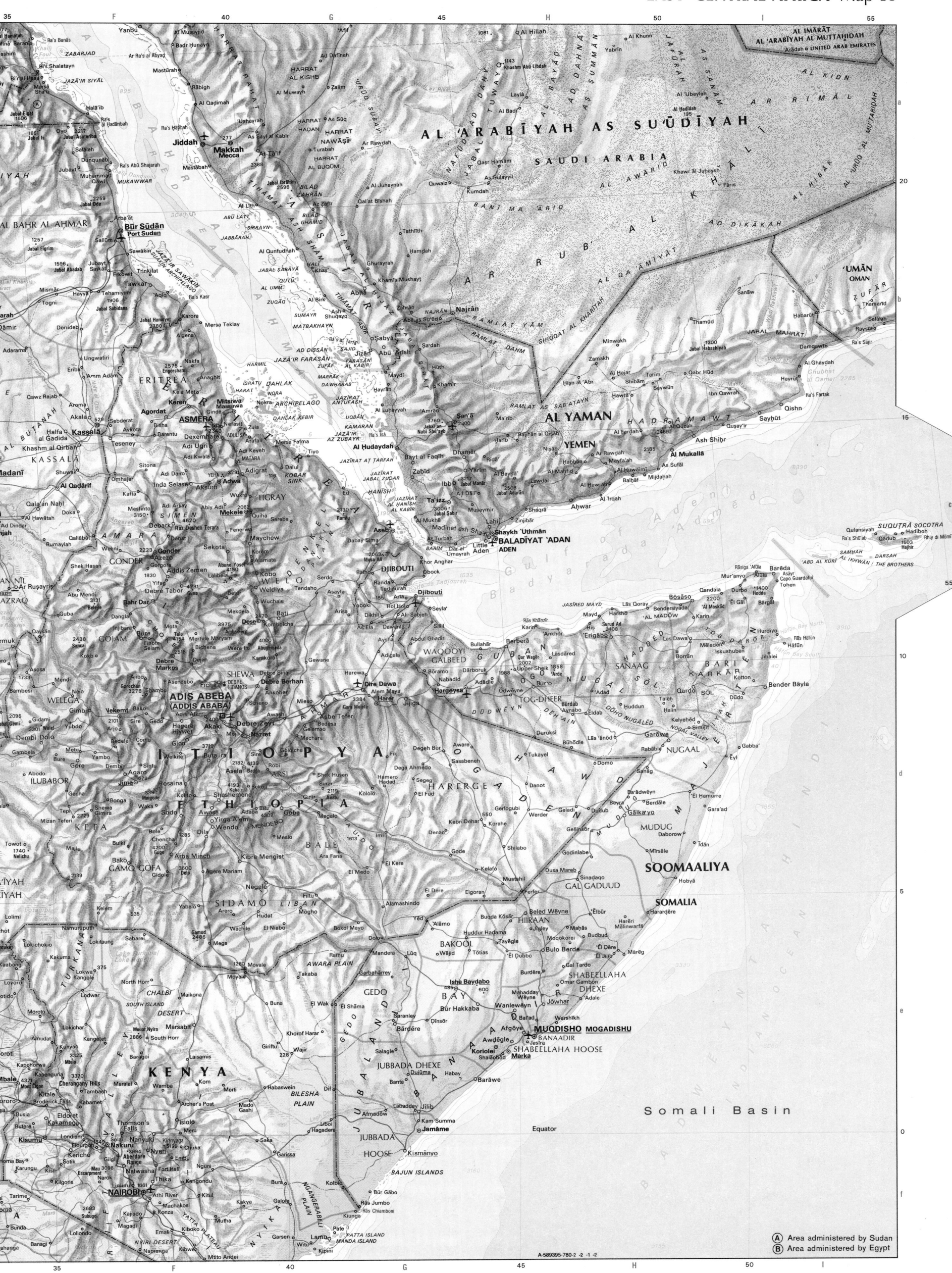

A Area administered by Sudan
B Area administered by Egypt

A-589395-780-2 -2 -1 -2

Map 36 **EQUATORIAL AFRICA**

Scale 1:9,000,000   Lambert Azimuthal Equal Area Projection

Map 37 **SOUTHERN AFRICA**

Angola Basin

ANGOLA

ZAÏRE

LUBUMBASHI
Likasi
Kolwezi
Chililabombwe
Chingola
KITWE-NKANA
Mufulira
NDOLA
Luanshya

ZAMBIA

Kabwe
LUSAKA

Lobito
Benguela
Huambo
Kuito
Malanje

BAROTSELAND
LIUWA PLAIN
SILOANA PLAINS

Namibe
Lubango

NAMIBIA

SKELETON COAST
KAOKOVELD
KAOKOVELD DESERT
NAMIB DESERT

OVAMBOLAND
Ondangua

CAPRIVI ZIPFEL
CAPRIVI STRIP
OKAVANGO
Rundu

Victoria Falls
Hwange
ZIMBABWE
BULAWAYO
MATABELELAND NORTH

KAUKAUVELD
NGAMILAND
Maun
Lake Ngami

BOTSWANA
GHANZI
Ghanzi

SANDVELD

Tsumeb
Grootfontein
Otjiwarongo
OMARURU
Omaruru
DAMARALAND
Okahandja
GOBABIS
Gobabis

SWAKOPMUND
KARIBIB
Karibib
WINDHOEK
Windhoek

Walvisbaai
Walvis Bay (South Africa)

Tropic of Capricorn

REHOBOTH

KALAHARI DESERT
KWENENG
KGATLENG
Molepolole
Gaborone
NGWAKETSE

NAMIBDESERT

GREAT NAMALAND / GROOT NAMALAND
Maltahöhe
Mariental
GIBEON
Gibeon

KGALAGADI

ATLANTIC OCEAN
ATLANTIESE OSEAAN

HOLLANDSBIRD ISLAND (South Africa)

LÜDERITZ
Lüderitz
POSSESSION ISLAND (South Africa)

KEETMANSHOOP
Keetmanshoop
BETHANIEN
Bethanien
FISH RIVER CANYON

WARMBAD
Warmbad

Upington
Kuruman
Kimberley

Transvaal
PRETORIA
Rustenburg
Krugersdorp
JOHANNESBURG
Benoni
Springs
Germiston
Vereeniging
Vanderbijl Park

BOPHUTHATSWANA

Klerksdorp

Orange Free State
Oranje Vrystaat
Welkom
Virginia
Kroonstad
Bloemfontein

LESOTHO
Maseru

Port Nolloth
Springbok

BOESMANLAND
BUSHMAN LAND

NAMAQUALAND

Namaqua Seamount

Oranjemund
Alexanderbaai

HOÉ KAROO
Cape Province / Kaapprovinsie

De Aar
Colesberg

TRANSKEI
Umtata
WILD COAST
East London

GREAT KAROO
GROOT KAROO

Beaufort West
Graaff-Reinet
Cradock

Grahamstown
Uitenhage
PORT ELIZABETH

SOUTH AFRICA
SUID-AFRIKA

Worcester
Stellenbosch
CAPE TOWN / KAAPSTAD
Simonstown
Cape of Good Hope / Kaap die Goeie Hoop

George
Knysna
Mosselbaai

Cape Agulhas

Cape Basin

Agulhas Bank

M ft
3000 9843
2000 6562
1000 3281
500 1640
200 656
+100 +328
0
−100 −328
−200 −656
1000 3281
2000 6562
4000 13123

Scale 1:9 000 000 Lambert Azimuthal Equal Area Projection

0   200   400   600 km
0   200 miles

Longitude East 25 of Greenwich

A-589200-780-1 -1 -1 -2

Map 38 **NORTH AMERICA, PHYSICAL**

Map 39 **NORTH AMERICA, POLITICAL**

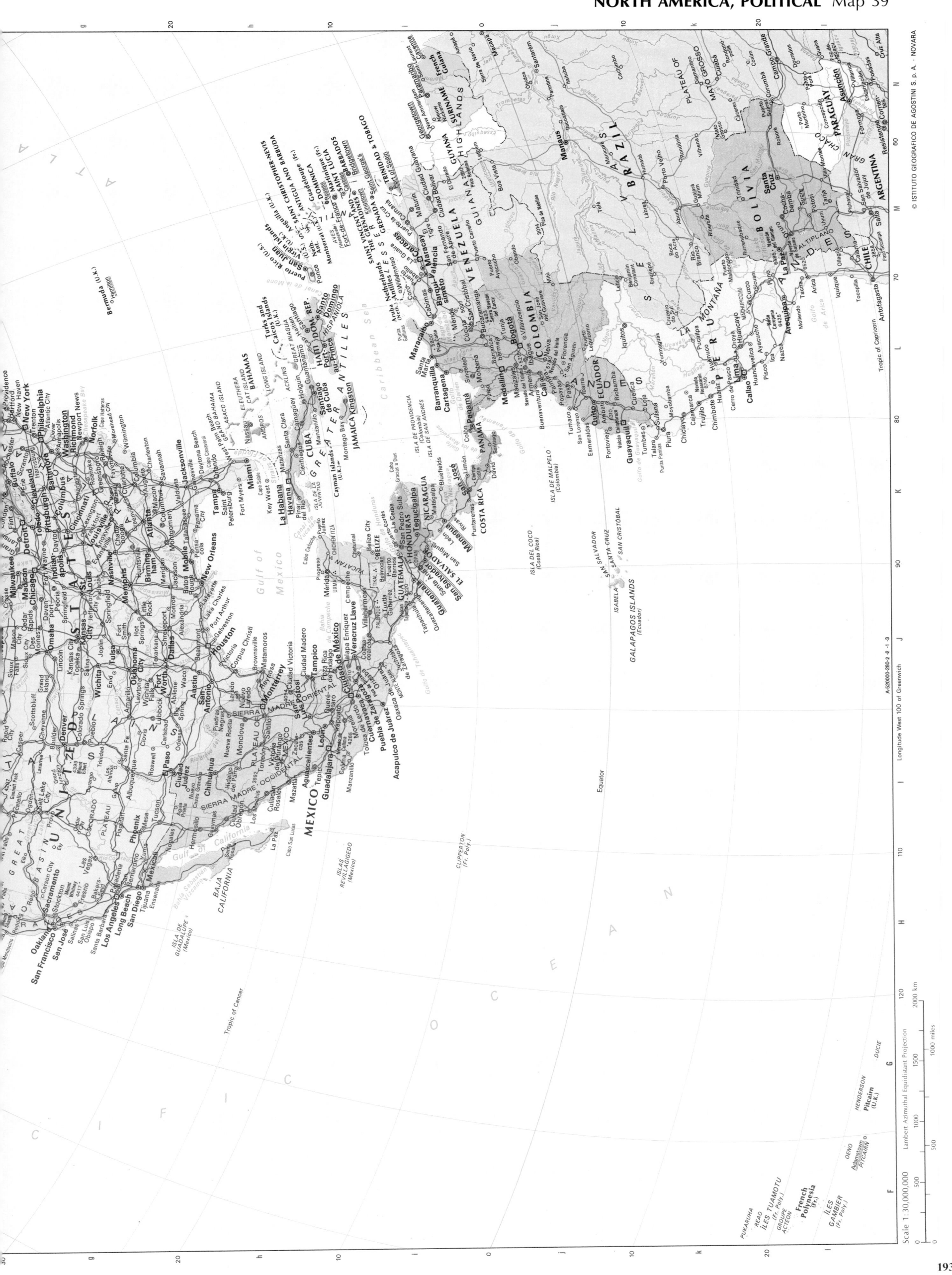

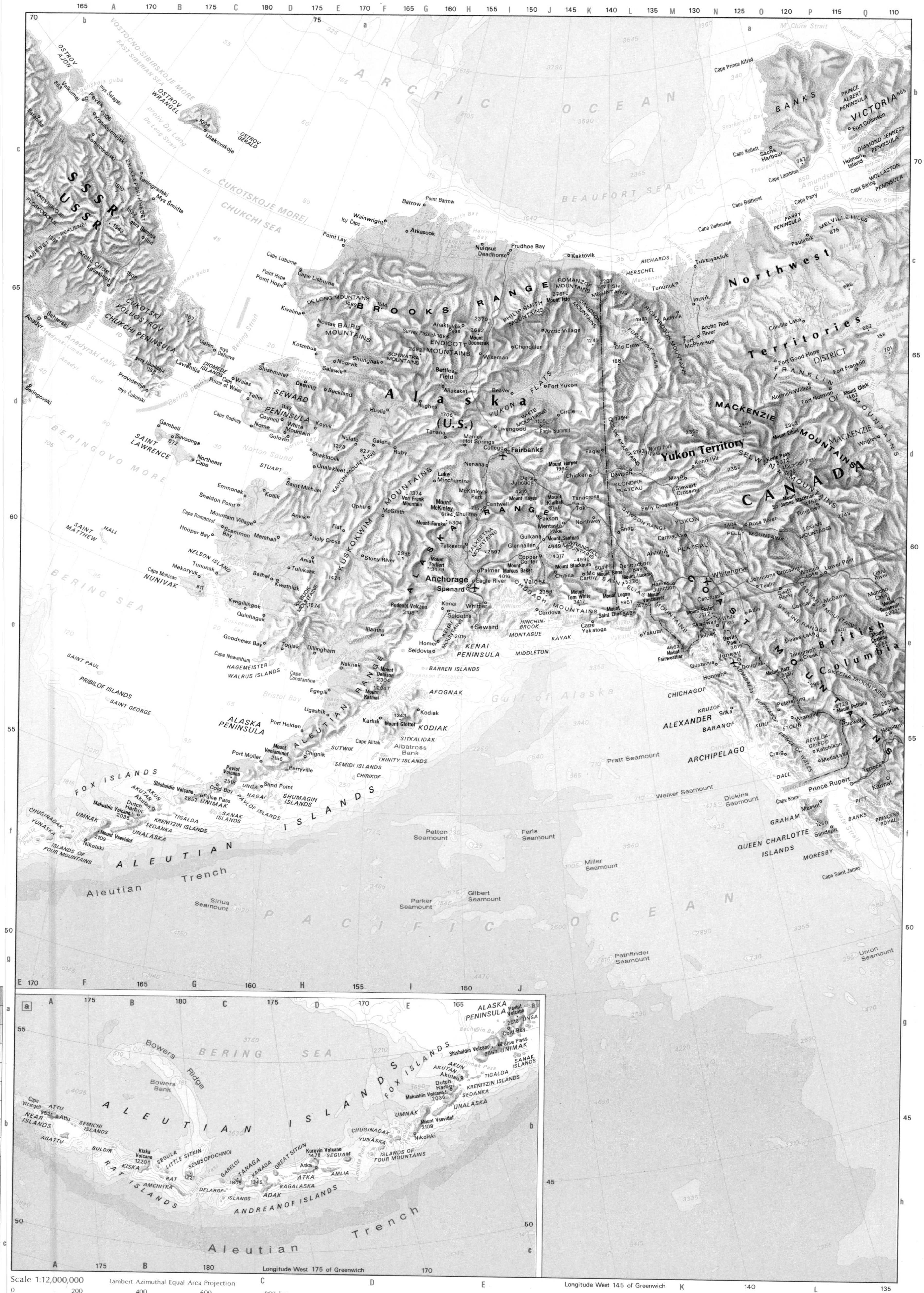

Map 40 **ALASKA**

ARCTIC OCEAN

BEAUFORT SEA

CHUKCHI SEA

CUKOTSKOJE MORE

VOSTOCNO-SIBIRSKOJE MORE
EAST SIBERIAN SEA

SSSR
USSR

CUKOTSKI POLUOSTROV
CHUKCHI PENINSULA

Arctic Circle

BANKS

VICTORIA

PRINCE ALBERT PENINSULA

DIAMOND JENNESS PENINSULA

WOLLASTON PENINSULA

MELVILLE HILLS

Northwest Territories

FRANKLIN DISTRICT

MACKENZIE MOUNTAINS

CANADA

Yukon Territory

Dawson

KLONDIKE PLATEAU

DAWSON RANGE

PELLY MOUNTAINS

LOGAN MOUNTAINS

Whitehorse

COAST MOUNTAINS

British Columbia

BROOKS RANGE

DE LONG MOUNTAINS

BAIRD MOUNTAINS

ENDICOTT MOUNTAINS

SCHWATKA MOUNTAINS

PHILIP SMITH MOUNTAINS

ROMANZOF MOUNTAINS

DAVIDSON MOUNTAINS

BRITISH MOUNTAINS

RICHARDSON MOUNTAINS

PORCUPINE MOUNTAINS

Barrow
Point Barrow
Wainwright
Icy Cape
Atkasook
Point Lay
Nuiqsut
Deadhorse
Prudhoe Bay
Kaktovik
Cape Lisburne
Point Hope
Kivalina
Noatak
Kotzebue
Shungnak
Noorvik
Selawik
Bettles Field
Wiseman
Anaktuvuk
Arctic Village
Chandalar
Old Crow
Fort Yukon
Beaver
Circle
Eagle

Alaska (U.S.)

YUKON FLATS

WHITE MOUNTAINS

SEWARD PENINSULA

Nome
Teller
Wales
Shishmaref
Deering
Buckland
Koyuk
Golovin
Council
White Mountain
Shaktoolik
Unalakleet
Galena
Ruby
Tanana
Manley Hot Springs
Livengood
Eagle Summit
College
Fairbanks
Nenana
Chicken

SAINT LAWRENCE

Gambell
Savoonga
Northeast Cape

NORTON SOUND

STUART

Saint Michael
Emmonak
Kotlik
Sheldon Point
Mountain Village
Scammon Bay
Hooper Bay
Marshall
Russian Mission
Holy Cross
Anvik
Flat
Ophir
McGrath
Aniak
Bethel
Kwethluk
Tuluksak

NELSON ISLAND
NUNIVAK

BERING SEA

SAINT MATTHEW
HALL

SAINT PAUL
PRIBILOF ISLANDS
SAINT GEORGE

KUSKOKWIM MOUNTAINS

KUSKOKWIM

Kwigillingok
Quinhagak
Goodnews Bay
Togiak
Dillingham
Naknek
Egegik
Ugashik
Port Heiden

ALASKA RANGE

Mount McKinley 6194
Mount Foraker 5304
Denali
McKinley Park
Cantwell
Mount Hayes
Delta Junction
Tok
Northway

TALKEETNA MOUNTAINS

Talkeetna
Palmer
Anchorage
Spenard
Eagle River
Whittier

CHUGACH MOUNTAINS

WRANGELL MOUNTAINS

Copper Center
Glennallen
Gulkana
Paxson
Chitina
McCarthy
Mount Sanford
Mount Wrangell
Mount Blackburn
Mount Bona
Mount Logan
Mount Saint Elias 5489

Redoubt Volcano 3106
Kenai
Soldotna
Homer
Seldovia
Seward
Cordova
Valdez
Yakutat
Gustavus

KENAI PENINSULA

MONTAGUE
KAYAK
MIDDLETON

Gulf of Alaska

KODIAK
Kodiak
Karluk
Chignik
Perryville
Sand Point
Cold Bay
False Pass
Port Moller

ALASKA PENINSULA

Mount Katmai
Mount Denison 2304
Mount Veniaminof 2156

ALEUTIAN RANGE

SHUMAGIN ISLANDS
SANAK ISLANDS
PAVLOF ISLANDS

Pavlof Volcano 2516
Shishaldin Volcano 2857
UNIMAK
AKUTAN
Dutch Harbor
Makushin Volcano 2036
UNALASKA
UMNAK
Mount Vsevidof 2109
Nikolski

FOX ISLANDS

CHUGINADAK
YUNASKA
ISLANDS OF FOUR MOUNTAINS

ALEUTIAN ISLANDS

Aleutian Trench

PACIFIC OCEAN

Patton Seamount
Miller Seamount
Gilbert Seamount
Parker Seamount
Sirius Seamount
Welker Seamount
Dickins Seamount
Pratt Seamount
Pathfinder Seamount
Union Seamount

CHICHAGOF
KRUZOF
Sitka
BARANOF
ALEXANDER ARCHIPELAGO
Petersburg
Wrangell
Ketchikan
Prince Rupert
Craig
Metlakatla

QUEEN CHARLOTTE ISLANDS
GRAHAM
MORESBY
Cape Saint James

M Ft
5000 16404
4000 13123
3000 9843
2000 6562
1000 3281
500 1640
200 656
0
100 328
200 656
1000 3281
2000 6562
4000 13123
6000 19685

Scale 1:12,000,000
Lambert Azimuthal Equal Area Projection

0 200 400 600 800 km
0 200 400 miles

Inset map (a) — Aleutian Islands

BERING SEA
Bowers Ridge
Bowers Bank

NEAR ISLANDS
Cape Wrangell
ATTU
Attu
AGATTU
SEMICHI ISLANDS

RAT ISLANDS
KISKA
Kiska Volcano 1201
BULDIR
LITTLE SITKIN
SEGULA
SEMISOPOCHNOI
AMCHITKA

ANDREANOF ISLANDS
GARELOI
TANAGA
Tanaga Volcano 1805
KANAGA
Kanaga Volcano 1345
ADAK
Atka
ATKA 1533
Great Sitkin
Korovin Volcano 1478
SEGUAM
AMLIA
KAGALASKA
DELAROF

ISLANDS OF FOUR MOUNTAINS

ALEUTIAN ISLANDS

Aleutian Trench

Longitude West 175 of Greenwich

Inset — Alaska Peninsula / Fox Islands

ALASKA PENINSULA
Pavlof Volcano 2516
UNGA
Cold Bay
False Pass
UNIMAK
SANAK ISLANDS
Shishaldin Volcano
TIGALDA
AKUN
AKUTAN
Dutch Harbor
Makushin Volcano 2036
KRENITZIN ISLANDS
SEDANKA
UNALASKA
UMNAK
Mount Vsevidof 2109
Nikolski
CHUGINADAK
YUNASKA
ISLANDS OF FOUR MOUNTAINS

FOX ISLANDS

Longitude West 145 of Greenwich

Longitude West 175 of Greenwich

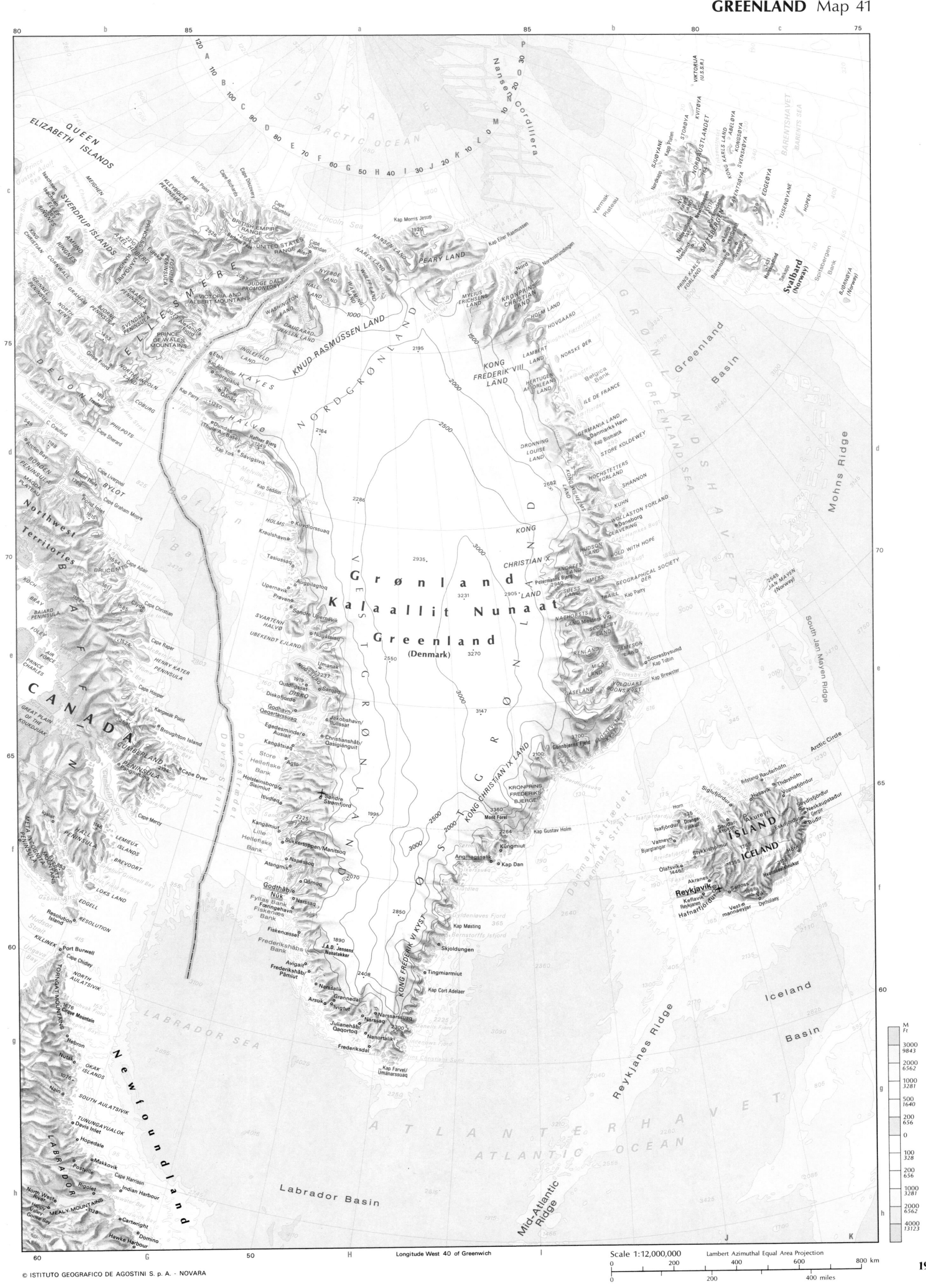

© ISTITUTO GEOGRAFICO DE AGOSTINI S. p. A. - NOVARA

Longitude West 40 of Greenwich

Scale 1:12,000,000   Lambert Azimuthal Equal Area Projection

0   200   400   600   800 km

0   200   400 miles

Map 42 **CANADA**

Scale 1:12,000,000   Lambert Azimuthal Equal Area Projection

0   200   400   600   800 km

0   200   400 miles

Longitude West 100 of Greenwich

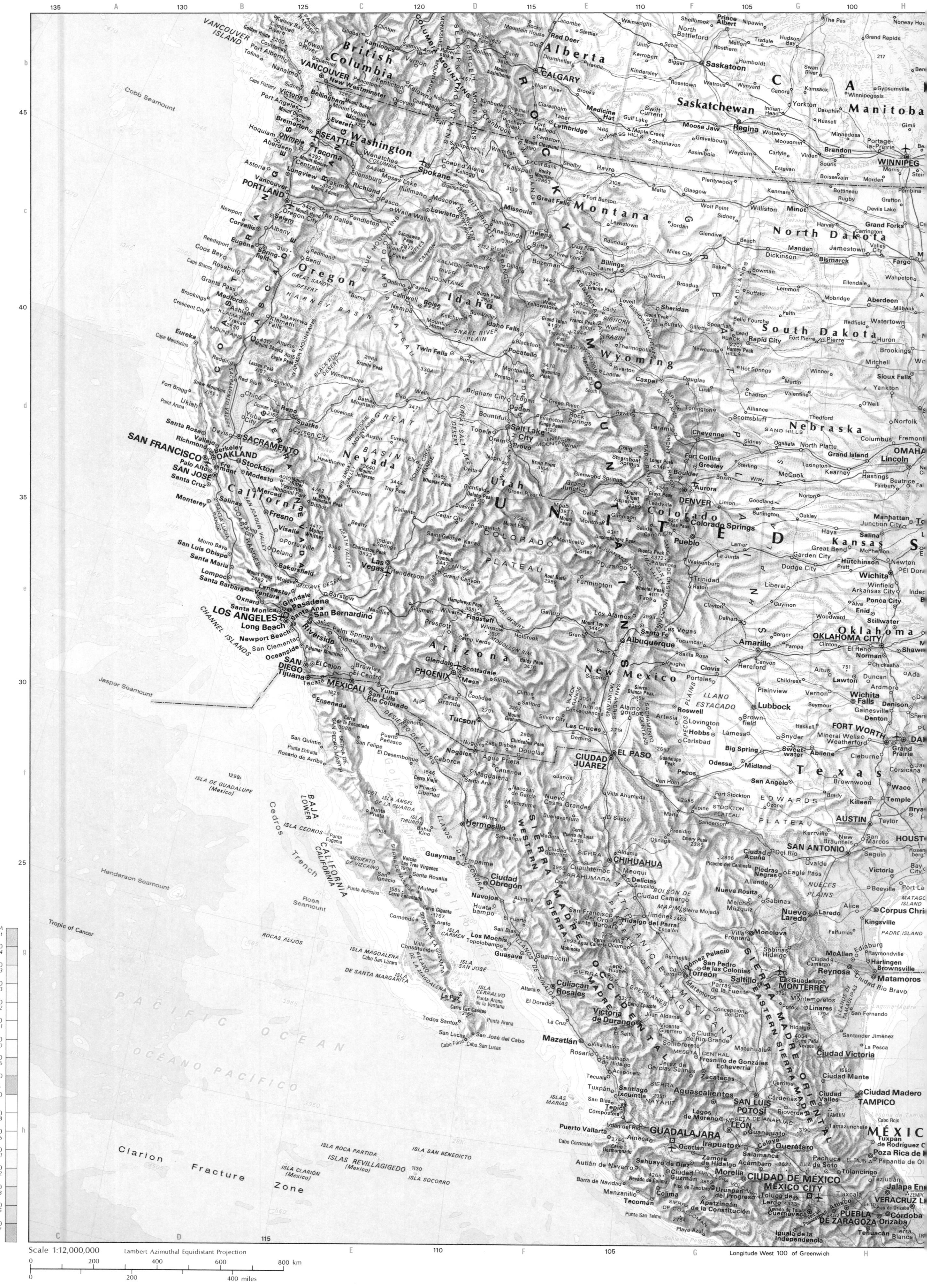

Map 43 **UNITED STATES**

Scale 1:12,000,000   Lambert Azimuthal Equidistant Projection

Longitude West 100 of Greenwich

0	200	400	600	800 km
0		200		400 miles

M / Ft
5000 / 16404
4000 / 13123
3000 / 9843
2000 / 6562
1000 / 3281
500 / 1640
200 / +656
0
Depr. / 0
−100 / −328
200 / 656
1000 / 3281
2000 / 6562
4000 / 13123
6000 / 19685
8000 / 26247

Map 44

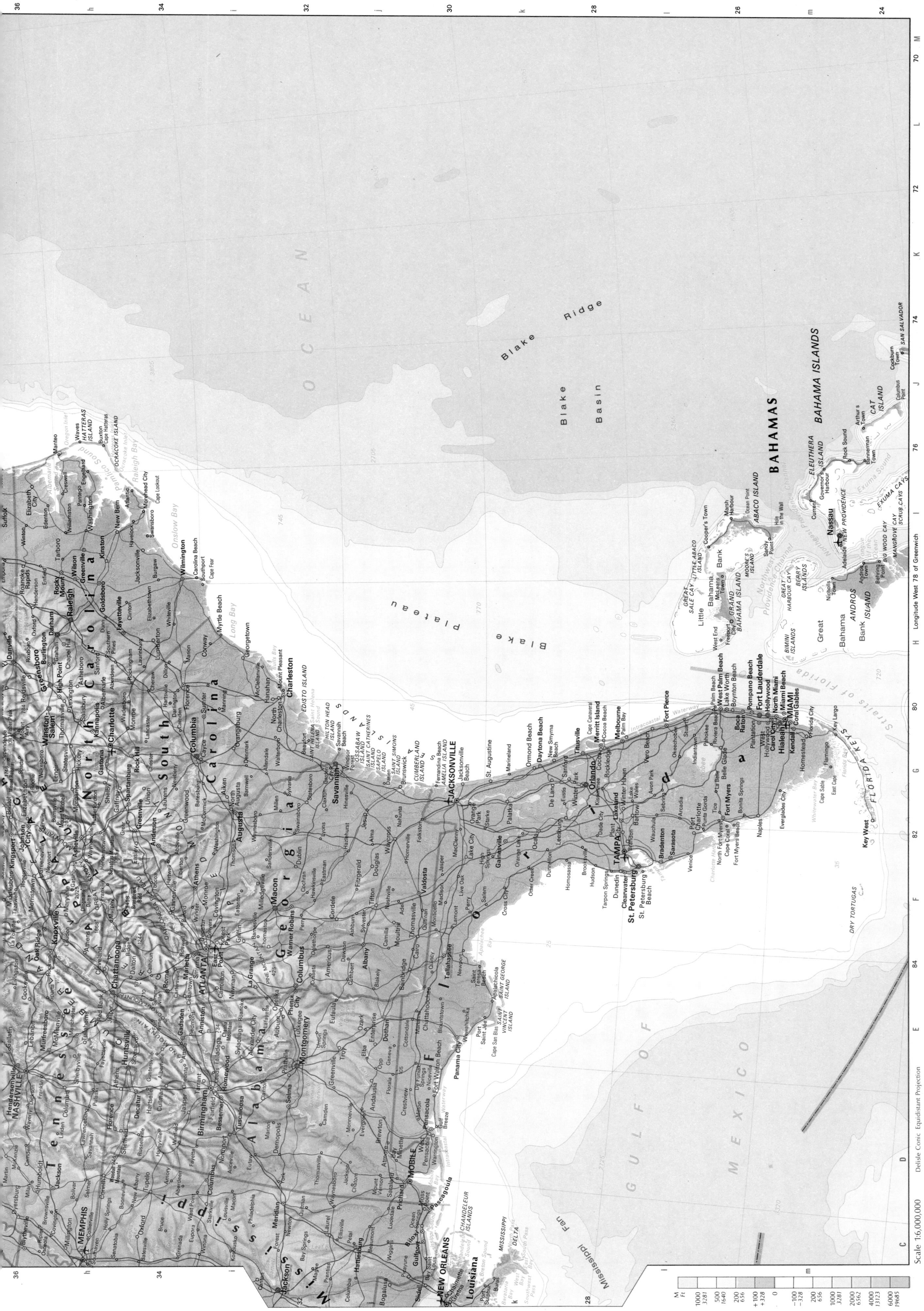

BAHAMAS

BAHAMA ISLANDS

Blake Ridge

Blake Basin

Blake Plateau

ATLANTIC OCEAN

GULF OF MEXICO

Straits of Florida

FLORIDA KEYS

Tennessee

Alabama

Georgia

Mississippi

Louisiana

Florida

North Carolina

South Carolina

MEMPHIS
NASHVILLE
Knoxville
Chattanooga
ATLANTA
Columbus
Montgomery
Birmingham
MOBILE
NEW ORLEANS
Jackson
Macon
Savannah
Columbia
Charlotte
Greensboro
Winston-Salem
Raleigh
Durham
Wilmington
JACKSONVILLE
Orlando
TAMPA
St. Petersburg
Clearwater
Fort Myers
MIAMI
Fort Lauderdale
West Palm Beach
Daytona Beach
Key West
Tallahassee
Panama City
Pensacola
Augusta
Columbus
Nassau
ANDROS ISLAND
ELEUTHERA
GRAND BAHAMA ISLAND
ABACO ISLAND
CAT ISLAND
SAN SALVADOR
NEW PROVIDENCE
Freeport
DRY TORTUGAS

Longitude West 78 of Greenwich

Scale 1:6,000,000

Delisle Conic Equidistant Projection

© ISTITUTO GEOGRAFICO DE AGOSTINI S. p. A. - NOVARA

m	ft
1000	3281
500	1640
200	656
0	0
+100	+328
−100	−328
200	656
1000	3281
2000	6562
4000	13123
6000	19685

0 100 200 300 400 km
0 100 200 miles

Map 45

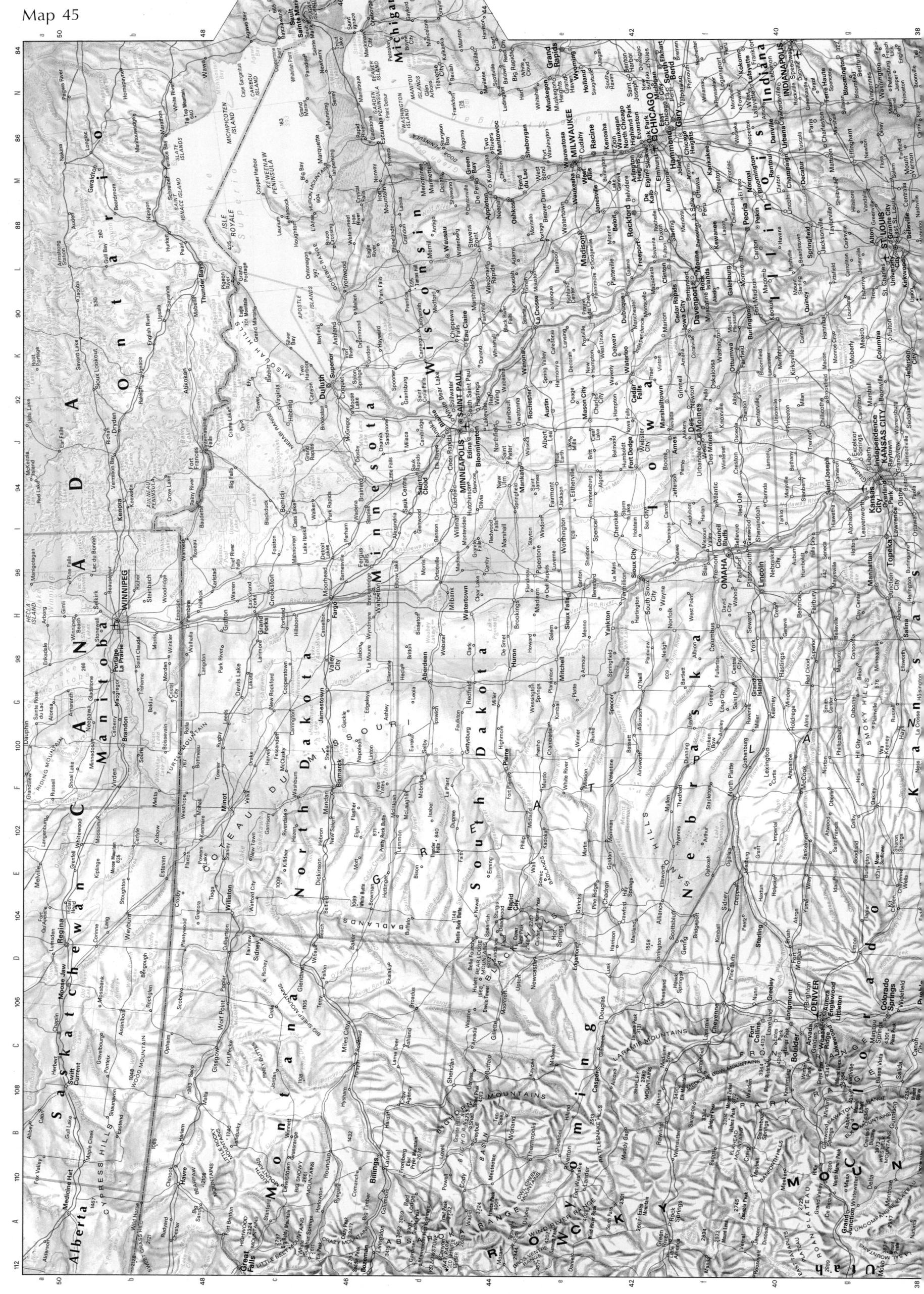

Scale 16,000,000

Delisle Conic Equidistant Projection

Longitude West 98 of Greenwich

Map 46 **WESTERN UNITED STATES**

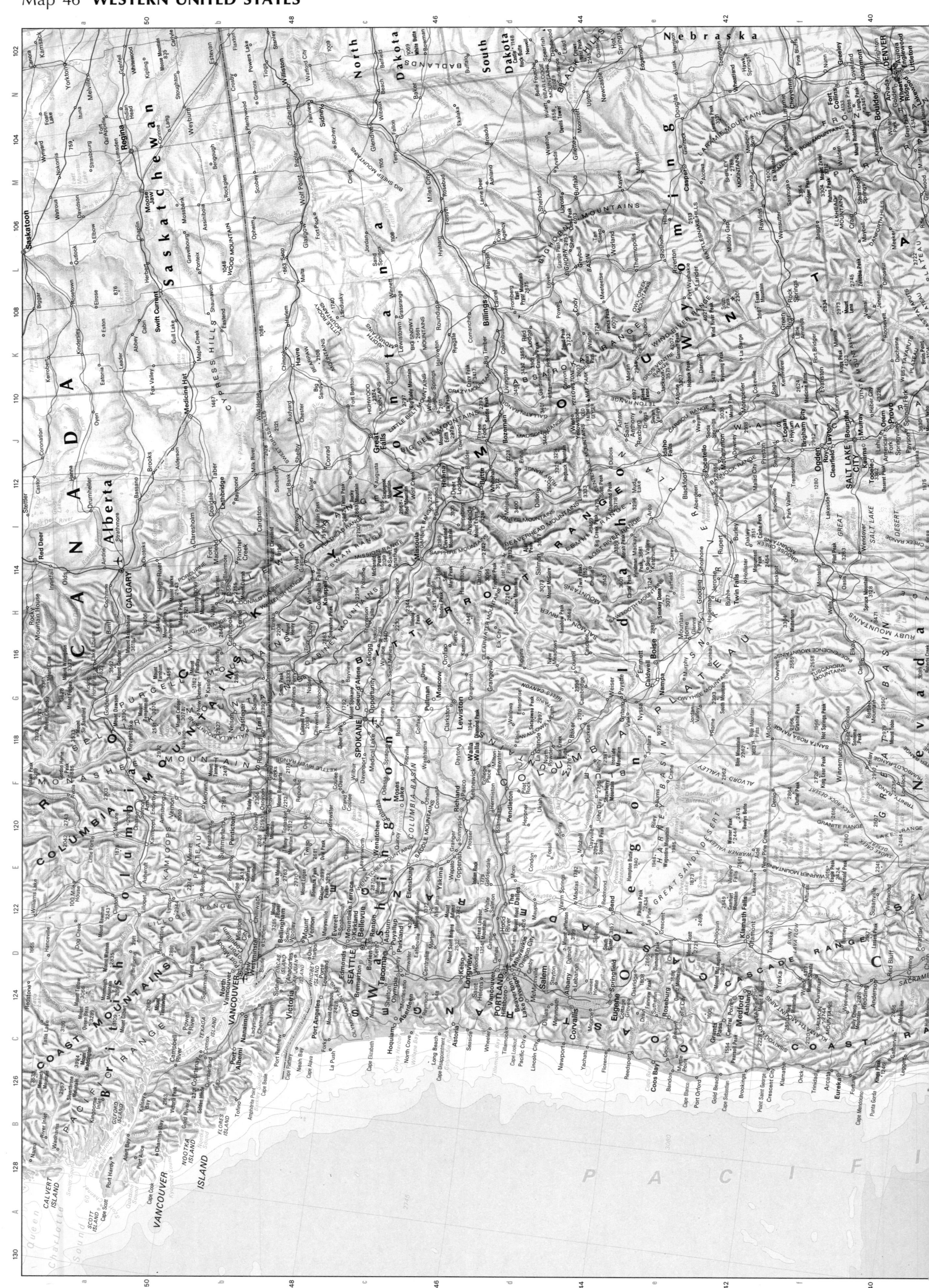

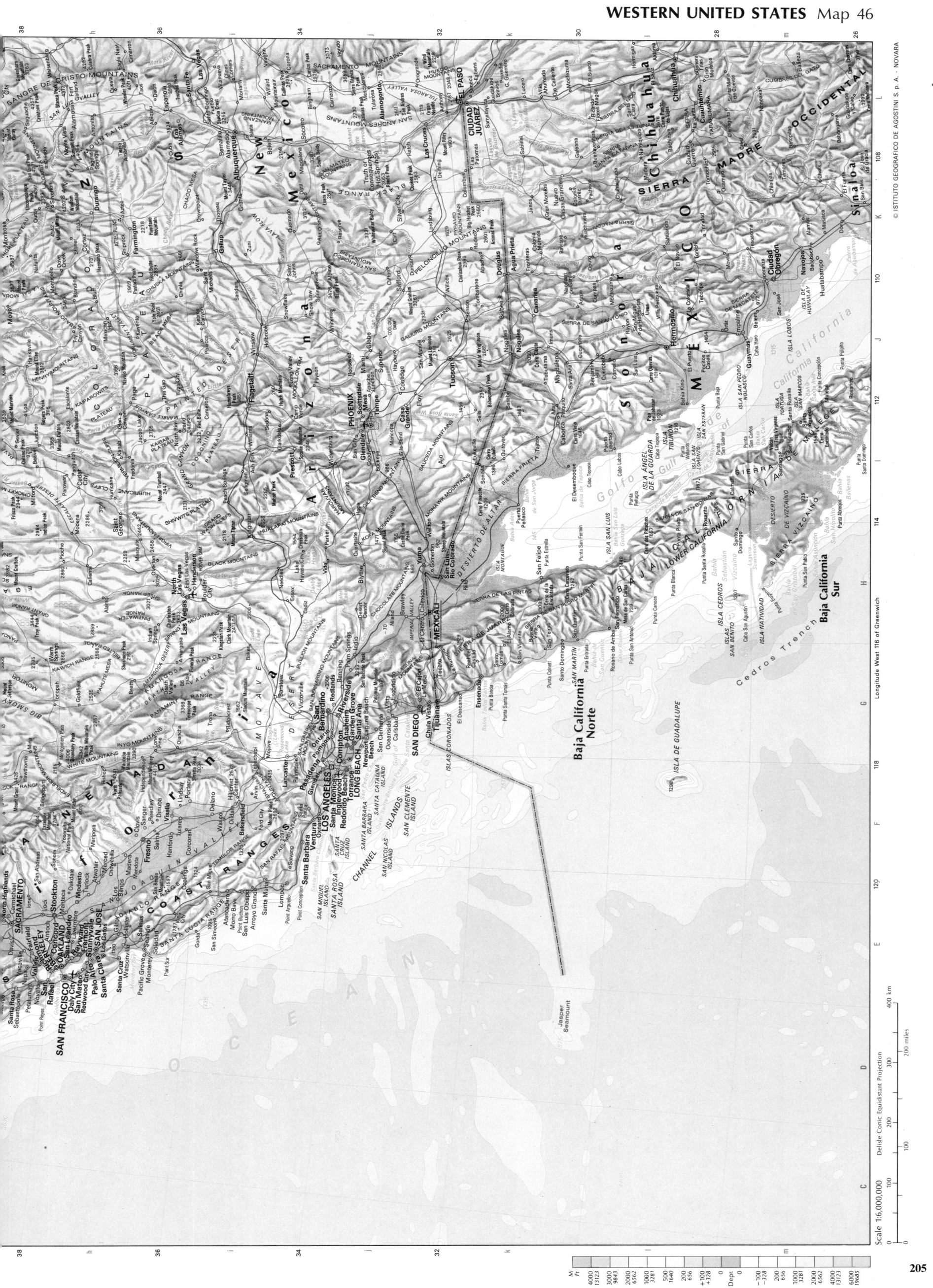

Scale 1:6,000,000

Delisle Conic Equidistant Projection

Longitude West 116 of Greenwich

Map 47 **MIDDLE AMERICA**

MÉXICO
ESTADOS

D.F. Distrito Federal
1 Aguascalientes
2 Baja California Norte
3 Baja California Sur
4 Campeche
5 Coahuila
6 Colima
7 Chiapas
8 Chihuahua
9 Durango
10 Guanajuato
11 Guerrero
12 Hidalgo
13 Jalisco
14 México
15 Michoacán
16 Morelos
17 Nayarit
18 Nuevo León
19 Oaxaca
20 Puebla
21 Querétaro
22 Quintana Roo
23 San Luis Potosí
24 Sinaloa
25 Sonora
26 Tabasco
27 Tamaulipas
28 Tlaxcala
29 Veracruz
30 Yucatán
31 Zacatecas

M / Ft
5000 / 16404
4000 / 13123
3000 / 9843
2000 / 6562
1000 / 3281
500 / 1640
+200 / +656
Depr.
0
−100 / −328
200 / 656
1000 / 3281
2000 / 6562
4000 / 13123
6000 / 19685
8000 / 26247

Scale 1:12,000,000
Lambert Azimuthal Equal Area Projection
0 200 400 600 800 km
0 200 400 miles

Longitude West 90 of Greenwich

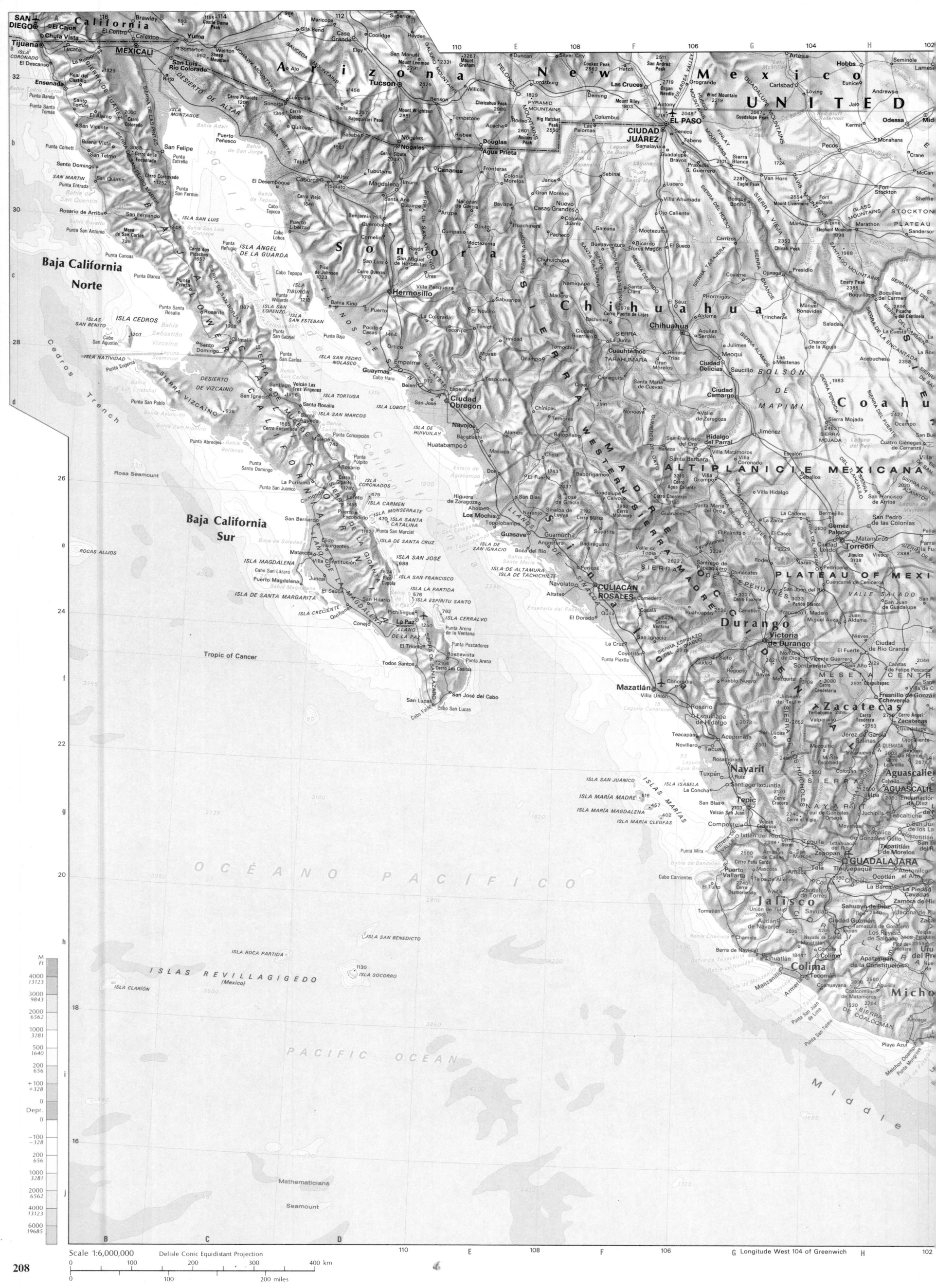

Scale 1:6,000,000   Delisle Conic Equidistant Projection

Longitude West 104 of Greenwich

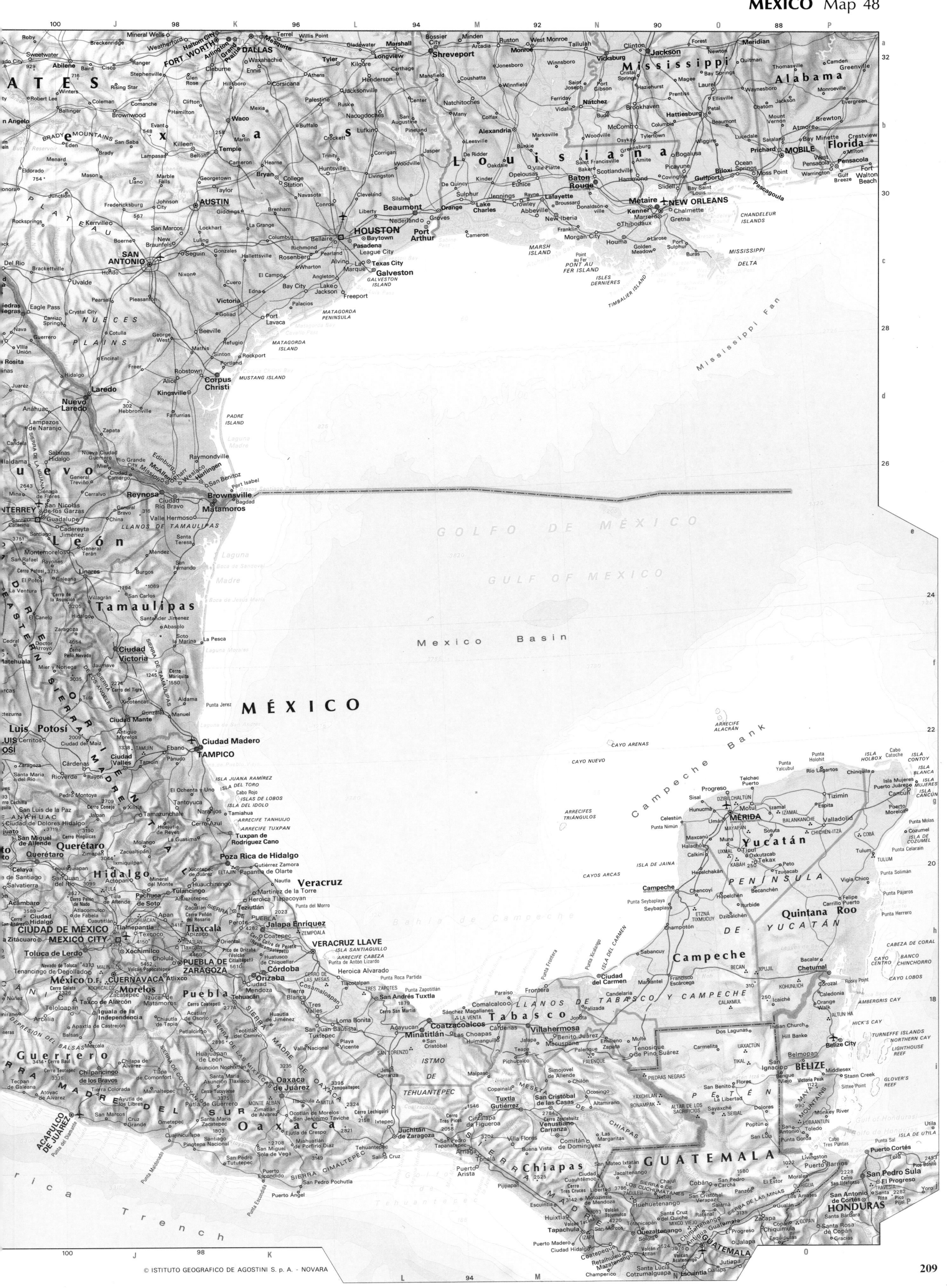

ATES

TEXAS

Roby · Sweetwater · Mineral Wells · Haltom City · Terrell · Willis Point · Gladewater · Marshall · Bossier City · Minden · Ruston · West Monroe · Tallulah · Clinton · Forest · Newton · Meridian
Robert Lee · Abilene · Baird · Cisco · Weatherford · FORT WORTH · Arlington · DALLAS · Mesquite · Tyler · Kilgore · Longview · Shreveport · Monroe · Vicksburg · Jackson · Quitman · Thomasville · Camden · Greenville
929 · Winters · Rising Star · Stephenville · Cleburne · Waxahachie · Corsicana · Athens · Jacksonville · Carthage · Mansfield · Winnfield · Saint Joseph · Port Gibson · Hazlehurst · Magee · Laurel · Waynesboro · Jackson · Evergreen
Del Rio · Brackettville · Eagle Pass

MÉXICO

Tamaulipas

GOLFO DE MÉXICO

GULF OF MEXICO

Mexico Basin

MÉXICO

TAMPICO

Ciudad Madero

Luis Potosí

Querétaro
Hidalgo

CIUDAD DE MÉXICO
MEXICO CITY
Toluca de Lerdo

México D.F.
CUERNAVACA
Morelos
PUEBLA DE ZARAGOZA
Puebla

Veracruz

VERACRUZ LLAVE

Coatzacoalcos
Minatitlán

Guerrero

ACAPULCO DE JUÁREZ

Oaxaca de Juárez

Oaxaca

Villahermosa
Tabasco

LLANOS DE TABASCO Y CAMPECHE

Chiapas

Tuxtla Gutiérrez

GUATEMALA

HONDURAS

Campeche

MÉRIDA

Yucatán

PENÍNSULA DE YUCATÁN

Quintana Roo

Chetumal

BELIZE

Belize City

Mississippi

Alabama

Louisiana

MOBILE
Florida

NEW ORLEANS

Map 49 CENTRAL AMERICA AND WESTERN CARIBBEAN

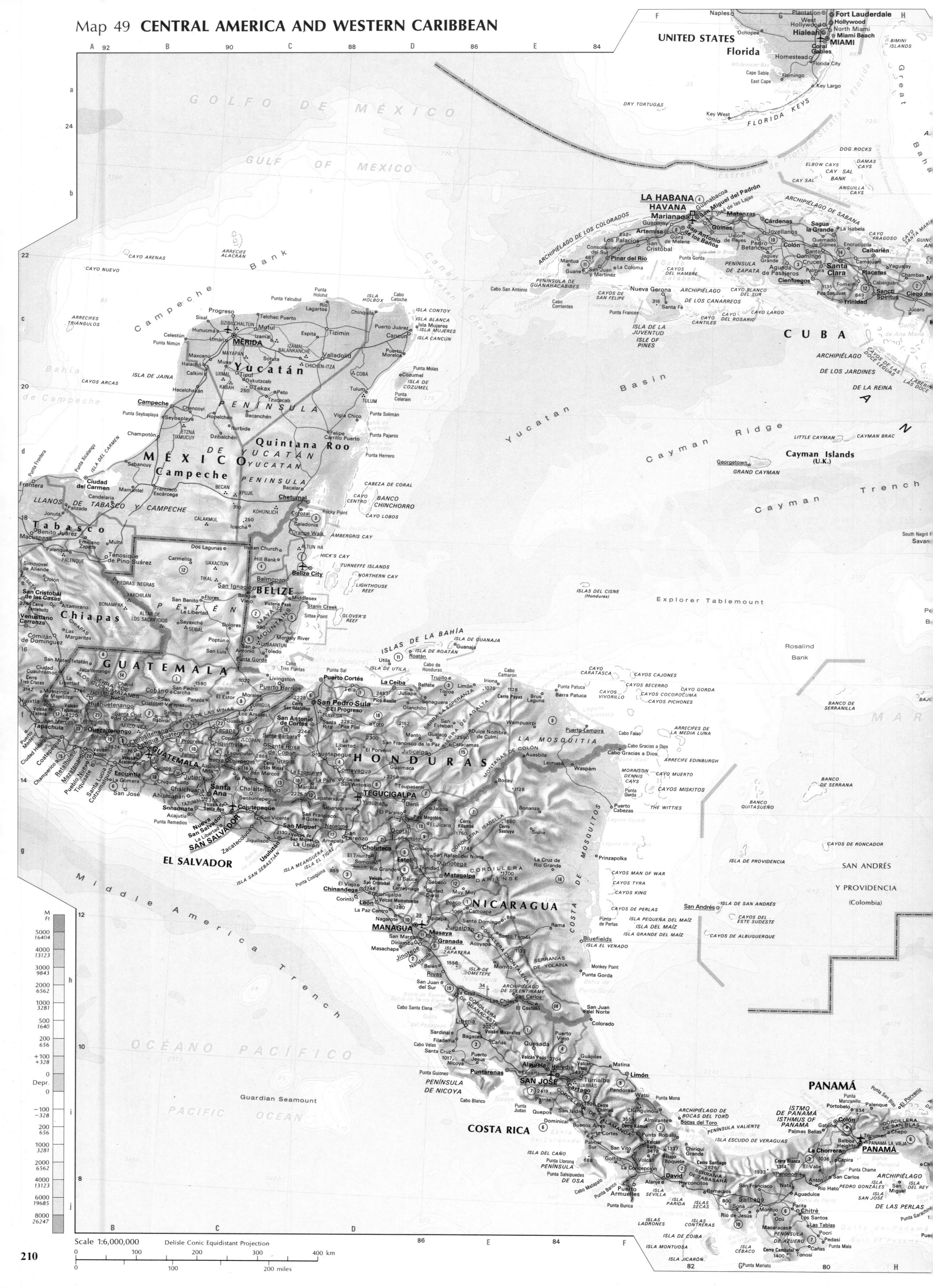

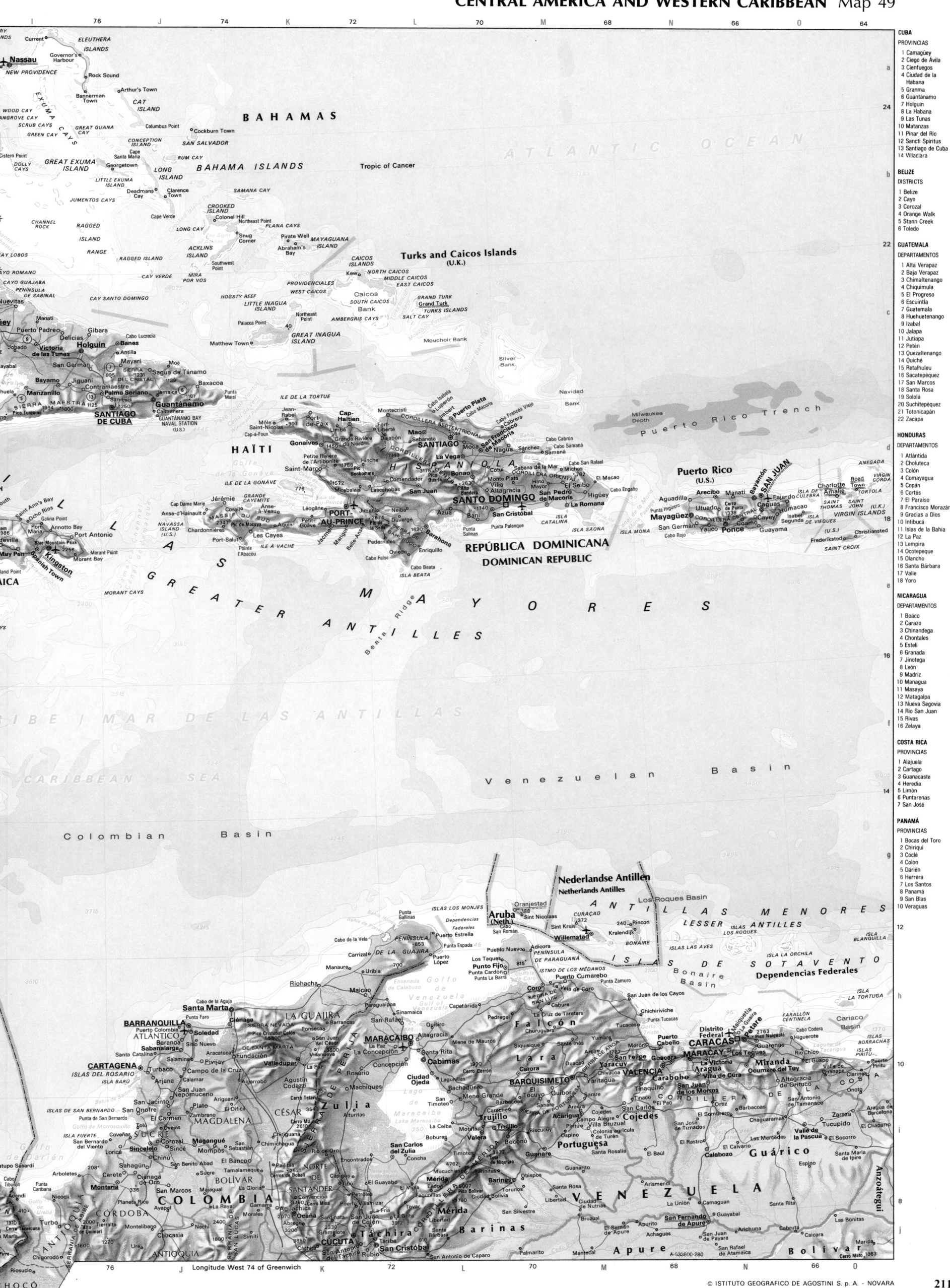

Map 50 EASTERN CARIBBEAN

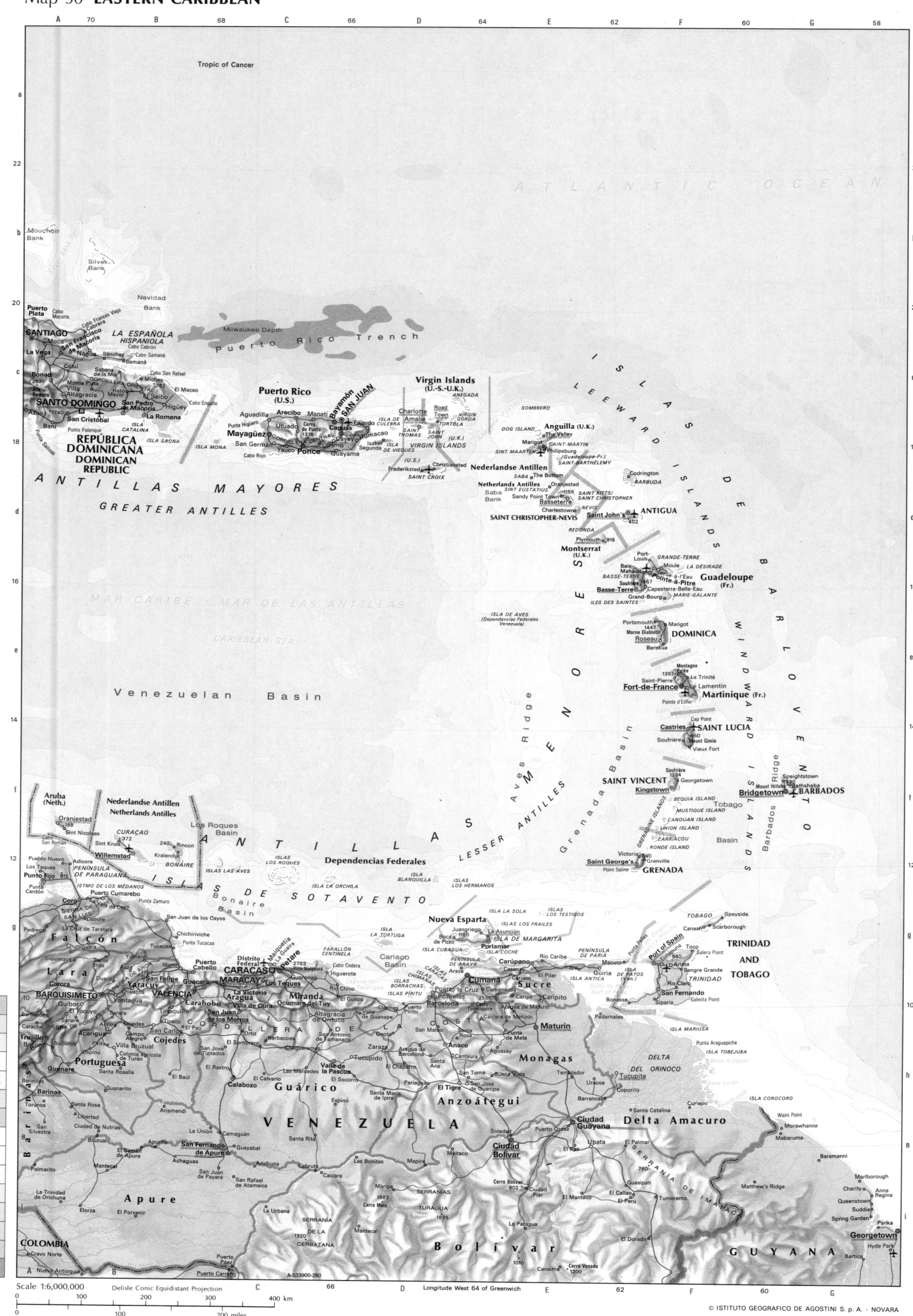

Scale 1:6,000,000   Delisle Conic Equidistant Projection

0   100   200   300   400 km

0   100   200 miles

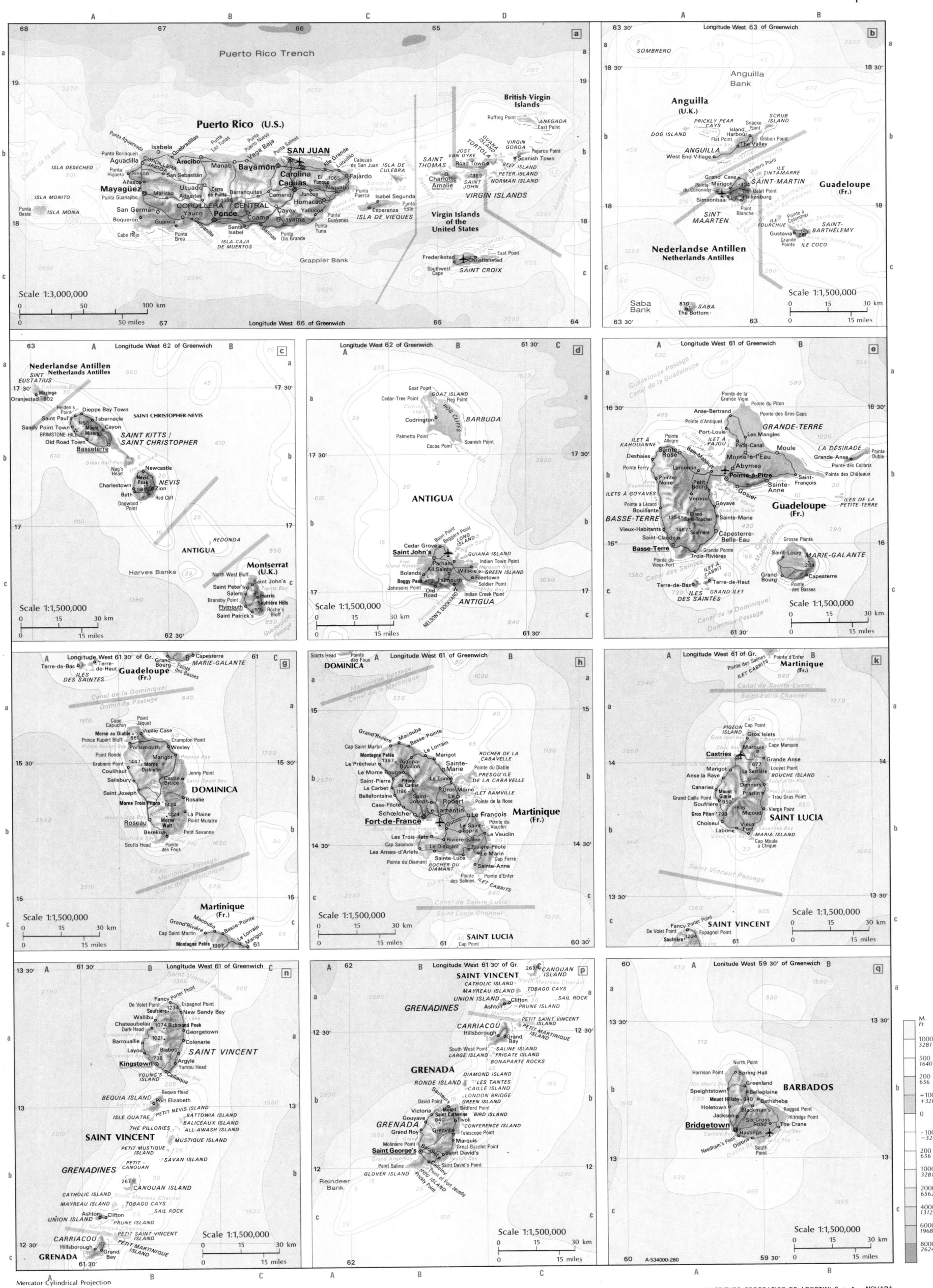

Map [a] — Puerto Rico

Puerto Rico Trench

Puerto Rico (U.S.)

Isla Desecheo
Isla Monito
Isla Mona
Isla Caja de Muertos

Punta Aguentaes, Isabela, Quebradillas, Punta Las Tunas, Punta Vega Baja, Punta Puerto Nuevo
Aguadilla, Arecibo, **SAN JUAN**, Manati, **BAYAMÓN**
Punta Borinquen, CORDILLERA, El, 1065, **Carolina**
Mayagüez, Rincón, San Sebastián, Utuado, Adjuntas, **Caguas**, Humacao
Punta Higuero, Añasco, Maricao, Cerro de Punta, Barranquitas, Comerio, Juncos, Yabucoa
San Germán, Yauco, Coamo, Cayey, Guayama, Punta Guayanes
Boquerón, Guánica, CENTRAL, **Ponce**, Salinas
Cabo Rojo, Santa Isabel, Punta Tuna
Punta Brea, Isla de Vieques

British Virgin Islands
Anegada, East Point
Ruffing Point, VIRGIN GORDA, Spanish Town, Pajaros Point
JOST VAN DYKE, TORTOLA, Road Town, Beef Island
SAINT THOMAS, Charlotte Amalie, SAINT JOHN, PETER ISLAND, NORMAN ISLAND
VIRGIN ISLANDS
Virgin Islands of the United States

Frederiksted, Christiansted
Southwest Cape, **SAINT CROIX**, East Point

Grappler Bank
Scale 1:3,000,000
0 50 100 km
0 50 miles
Longitude West 66 of Greenwich

Map [b] — Anguilla

SOMBRERO
Longitude West 63 of Greenwich
Anguilla Bank
Anguilla (U.K.)
PRICKLY PEAR CAYS, SCRUB ISLAND
DOG ISLAND, Island Harbour, Snacke Point, Flat Point
ANGUILLA, The Valley, Gibbon Point
West End Village, Eastern Point
Grand Case, ILE TINTAMARRE
SAINT-MARTIN, Marigot
SINT MAARTEN, Simsonbaai, Philipsburg
Point Blanche, ILE FOURCHUE, SAINT-BARTHÉLEMY, Gustavia, ILE COCO
Guadeloupe (Fr.)
Pointe à Colombier, Grande Pointe, Pointe du Grand Fond
Nederlandse Antillen / Netherlands Antilles
Saba Bank, SABA, The Bottom
Scale 1:1,500,000
0 15 30 km
0 15 miles

Map [c] — Saint Kitts / Nevis

Nederlandse Antillen / Netherlands Antilles
SINT EUSTATIUS, Oranjestad, 602
Helden's Point, Dieppe Bay Town, SAINT CHRISTOPHER-NEVIS
Saint Paul's, Tabernacle
Sandy Point Town, Mount Misery 1156, Cayon
BRIMSTONE HILL, Old Road Town, **SAINT KITTS / SAINT CHRISTOPHER**
Basseterre
Nag's Head, Newcastle
Nevis Peak 985, Zion, **NEVIS**
Charlestown, Bath, Red Cliff
Dogwood Point
REDONDA
ANTIGUA
Harves Banks
Montserrat (U.K.)
North West Bluff, Saint Peter's, Saint John's
Salem, Harris
Bransby Point, Soufrière Hills 915, Roche's Bluff
Plymouth, Saint Patrick's
Scale 1:1,500,000
0 15 30 km
0 15 miles

Map [d] — Antigua

Longitude West 62 of Greenwich
Goat Point
Cedar-Tree Point, GOAT ISLAND
Codrington, **BARBUDA**
Palmetto Point, Cocoa Point, Spanish Point
ANTIGUA
Boon Point, Beggars Point
Cedar Grove, LONG ISLAND
Saint John's, Parham, GUIANA ISLAND
All Saints, Willikie, GREEN ISLAND, Indian Town Point
Bolands, Freetown
Boggy Peak, Falmouth, Soldier Point
Johnsons Point, Indian Creek Point
Old Road
NELSON'S DOCKYARD
Scale 1:1,500,000
0 15 30 km
0 15 miles

Map [e] — Guadeloupe

Longitude West 61 of Greenwich
Pointe de la Grande Vigie
Anse-Bertrand, Pointe des Gros Caps
Port-Louis, **GRANDE-TERRE**, Les Mangles
ILET À KAHOUANNE, ILET À FAJOU, Petit-Canal, Moule, LA DÉSIRADE
Deshaies, Sainte-Rose, Baie-Mahault, Grande-Anse, Pointe des Colibris
Pointe Noire, Lamentin, Morne-à-l'Eau, Abymes, Pointe des Châteaux
ILETS À GOYAVES, **Pointe-à-Pitre**, Sainte-Anne, Saint-François
BASSE-TERRE, Petit-Bourg, Vernou, Gosier
Vieux-Habitants, Grand-Sans-Toucher 1354, Sainte-Marie, ILES DE LA PETITE-TERRE
Saint-Claude, Soufrière 1467, Capesterre-Belle-Eau
Basse-Terre, Grande Pointe, Trois-Rivières, Saint-Louis
Pointe du Vieux-Fort, ILET À CABRIT, **MARIE-GALANTE**
Terre-de-Bas, ILES DES SAINTES, Terre-de-Haut, Grand-Bourg, Capesterre
GRAND ILET, Pointe des Basses
Scale 1:1,500,000
0 15 30 km
0 15 miles

Map [g] — Guadeloupe / Dominica

Longitude West 61° of Gr.
Terre-de-Bas, Terre-de-Haut, **Guadeloupe (Fr.)**, Grand-Bourg, **MARIE-GALANTE**, Capesterre
ILES DES SAINTES, Pointe des Basses
DOMINICA
Cape Capuchin, Point Jaquet
Morne au Diable 861, Vieille Case
Prince Rupert Bluff, Portsmouth, Crumpton Point, Wesley
Grabiere Point, Morne Diablotin 1447, Jenny Point
Coulihaut, Salisbury, Castle Bruce
Saint Joseph, Morne Trois Pitons 1424, **DOMINICA**, Rosalie
Roseau, Morne Watt 1224, La Plaine
Berekua, Petit Mulatre
Scotts Head, Petit Savanne, Pointe des Fous
Martinique (Fr.)
Grand'Rivière, Macouba, Basse-Pointe
Cap Saint Martin, Le Lorrain, Marigot
Montagne Pelée 1397
Scale 1:1,500,000
0 15 30 km
0 15 miles

Map [h] — Martinique

Scotts Head, Pointe des Fous, **DOMINICA**
Longitude West 61 of Greenwich
Martinique Passage
Grand'Rivière, Macouba, Basse-Pointe
Cap Saint Martin, Le Lorrain, Marigot
Montagne Pelée 1397, Morne Rouge, Ajoupa-Bouillon, Sainte-Marie
Le Prêcheur, Le Morne Rouge, La Trinité
Saint-Pierre, Pitons du Carbet 1196, Gros Morne, ROCHER DE LA CARAVELLE
Le Carbet, PRESQU'ÎLE DE LA CARAVELLE, Pointe du Diable
Bellefontaine, Saint-Joseph, Robert, ILET RAMVILLE
Case-Pilote, Le Lamentin, Pointe de la Rose
Schoelcher, Le François
Fort-de-France, Ducos, Le Saint-Esprit, Le Vauclin, **Martinique (Fr.)**
Les Trois-Îlets, Rivière-Salée, Le Vauclin
Cap Salomon, Le Diamant, Rivière-Pilote, Le Marin
Les Anses-d'Arlets, Sainte-Luce, Sainte-Anne
Pointe du Diamant, ROCHER DU DIAMANT, Pointe des Salines, Pointe d'Enfer, ILET CABRITS
SAINT LUCIA, Cap Point
Scale 1:1,500,000
0 15 30 km
0 15 miles

Map [k] — Saint Lucia

Longitude West 61 of Gr.
Pointe d'Enfer, **Martinique (Fr.)**
Pointe des Salines, ILET CABRITS
Canal de Sainte-Lucie / Saint Lucia Channel
PIGEON ISLAND, Gros Islets
Castries, Marquis, Cape Marquis
Grande Anse, Louvet Point
Marigot, La Sorcière 677, BOUCHE ISLAND
Anse la Raye, Dennery
Canaries, Mount Gimie 950, Praslin, Trou Gras Point
Grand Caille Point, Soufrière, Micoud, Vierge Point
Gros Piton 798, **SAINT LUCIA**
Choiseul, Vieux-Fort
Laborie, MARIA ISLAND, Cap Moule à Chique
SAINT VINCENT
De Volet Point, Espagnol Point
Soufrière 1234
Scale 1:1,500,000
0 15 30 km
0 15 miles

Map [n] — Saint Vincent

Longitude West 61 of Greenwich
Saint Vincent Passage
Fancy Porter Point
De Volet Point, Espagnol Point
Fancy, New Sandy Bay
Soufrière 1234, Richmond Peak 1074, Georgetown
Chateaubelair, Dark Head, Colonarie
Wallibu, **SAINT VINCENT**
Barrouallie, 1021, Biabou
Layou, Yambu Head
Kingstown, Argyle, Calliaqua
YOUNG'S ISLAND, 715
BEQUIA ISLAND, Port Elizabeth
Bequia Head, PETIT NEVIS ISLAND
ISLE QUATRE, BATTOWIA ISLAND
SAINT VINCENT, THE PILLORIES, BALICEAUX ISLAND, ALL-AWASH ISLAND
MUSTIQUE ISLAND
GRENADINES
PETIT MUSTIQUE ISLAND
SAVAN ISLAND
PETIT CANOUAN
CATHOLIC ISLAND, 267 CANOUAN ISLAND
MAYREAU ISLAND, TOBAGO CAYS, SAIL ROCK
UNION ISLAND, Ashton, Clifton, PRUNE ISLAND
PETIT SAINT VINCENT ISLAND
CARRIACOU, PETIT MARTINIQUE ISLAND
Hillsborough, Grand Bay
GRENADA
Scale 1:1,500,000
0 15 30 km
0 15 miles

Map [p] — Grenada

SAINT VINCENT
CATHOLIC ISLAND, 267 CANOUAN ISLAND
MAYREAU ISLAND, TOBAGO CAYS
GRENADINES
UNION ISLAND, Ashton, Clifton, SAIL ROCK, PRUNE ISLAND
PETIT SAINT VINCENT ISLAND
CARRIACOU, PETIT MARTINIQUE ISLAND
Hillsborough, Grand Bay
South West Point, SALINE ISLAND, FRIGATE ISLAND
LARGE ISLAND, BONAPARTE ROCKS
DIAMOND ISLAND, LES TANTES
RONDE ISLAND, CAILLE ISLAND
London Bridge, GREEN ISLAND
David Point, Bedford Point, BIRD ISLAND
Victoria, Saint Catherine 840, Tivoli, CONFERENCE ISLAND
Gouyave, Grenville, Telescope Point
Grand Roy, Marquis, Great Bacolet Point
Moliniere Point, **GRENADA**
Saint George's, Saint David's Point
Point Saline, HOG ISLAND
GLOVER ISLAND, Point of Fort Jeudy, FROG ISLAND
Reindeer Bank
Scale 1:1,500,000
0 15 30 km
0 15 miles

Map [q] — Barbados

Lonitude West 59 30' of Greenwich
North Point
Harrison Point, Spring Hall
Greenland
Speightstown, Belleplaine
BARBADOS
Mount Hillaby 340, Bathsheba
Holetown, Blackman's, Ragged Point
Jackson, Six Cross Road, Kirtage Point
Bridgetown, Hastings, The Crane
Needham's Point, Oistins, South Point
Scale 1:1,500,000
0 15 30 km
0 15 miles

Elevation scale
M / Ft
1000 / 3281
500 / 1640
200 / 656
+100 / +328
0
-100 / -328
200 / 656
1000 / 3281
2000 / 6562
4000 / 13123
6000 / 19685
8000 / 26247

Mercator Cylindrical Projection

A-534000-280

© ISTITUTO GEOGRAFICO DE AGOSTINI S. p. A. - NOVARA

Map 52   SOUTH AMERICA, PHYSICAL

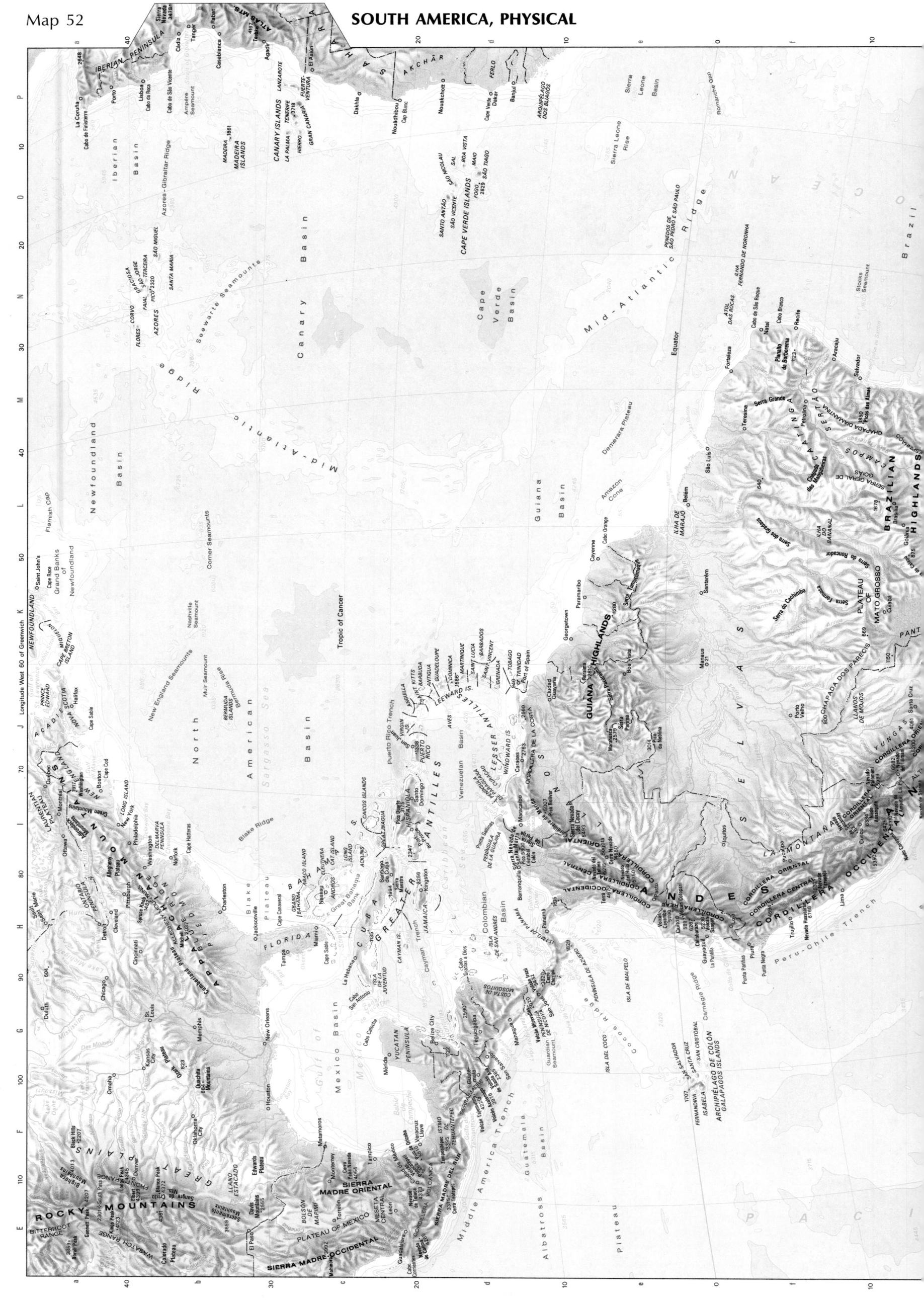

© ISTITUTO GEOGRAFICO DE AGOSTINI S. p. A. - NOVARA

Scale 1:30,000,000

Lambert Azimuthal Equal Area Projection

M Ft		
6000 19685		
5000 16404		
4000 13123		
3000 9843		
2000 6562		
1000 3281		
500 1640		
200 +656		
Depr. 0		
-200 -656		
1000 3281		
2000 6562		
4000 13123		
6000 19685		
8000 26247		

Map 53

SOUTH AMERICA, POLITICAL

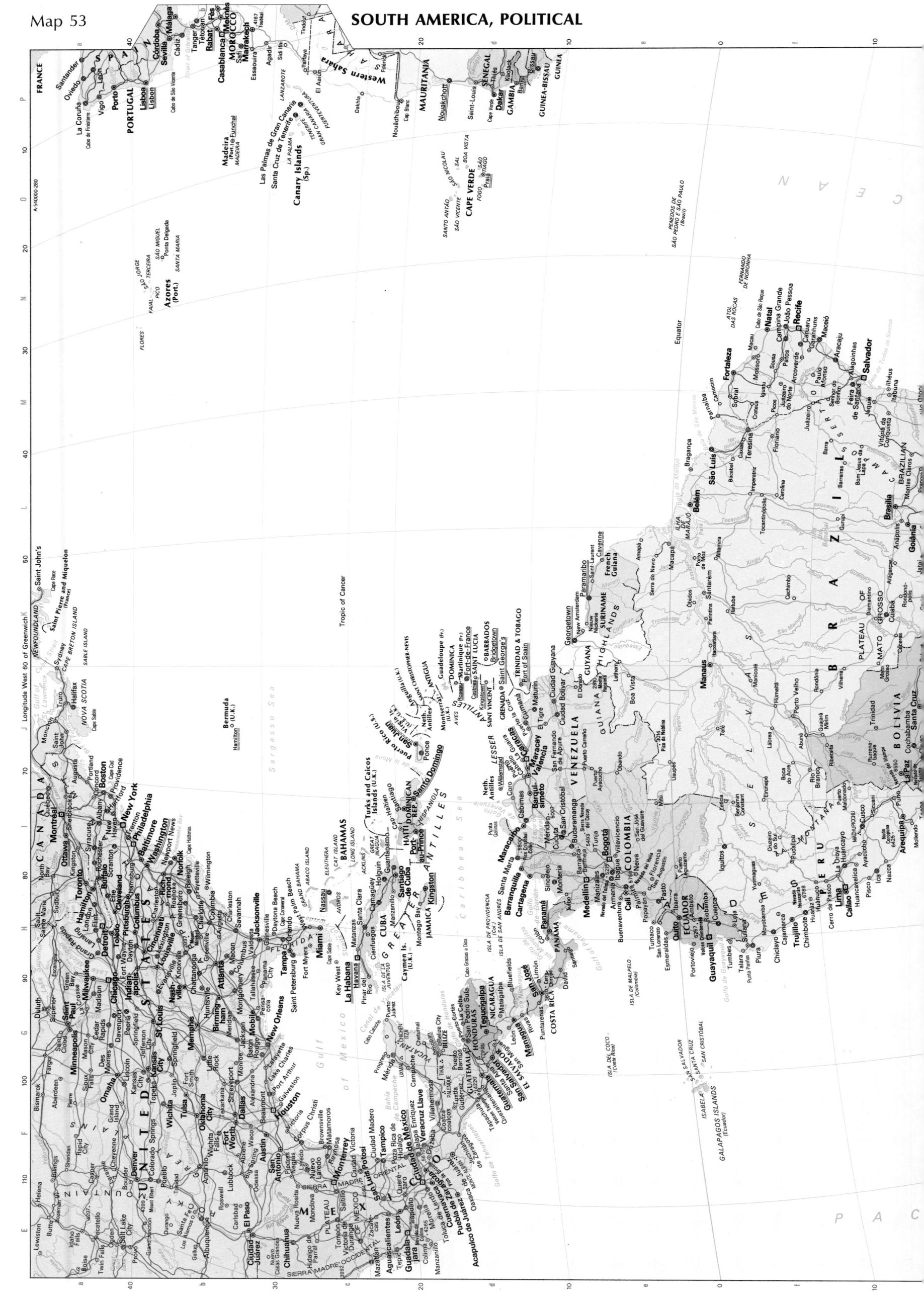

ILHAS MARTIM VAZ (Brazil)

ILHA DA TRINDADE (Brazil)

TRISTAN DA CUNHA GROUP (St. Helena)

GOUGH ISLAND (St. Helena)

BOUVET (Norway)

A T L A N T I C

Juiz de Fora
Volta Redonda
Petrópolis
Campos
Cabo Frio
Rio de Janeiro
Niterói
Nova Iguaçu
Taubaté
Campinas
Santos
São Paulo
Sorocaba
Bauru
Ourinhos
Londrina
Paranaguá
Maringá
Ponta Grossa
Curitiba
Joinville
Itajaí
Florianópolis
Criciúma
Lajes
Caxias do Sul
Passo Fundo
Santa Maria
Porto Alegre
Passo
Rio Grande
Pelotas
Bagé

PARAGUAY
Asunción
Villarrica
Encarnación
Formosa
Posadas
Corrientes
Resistencia
Goya
Presidencia Roque Sáenz Peña
MESOPOTAMIA
Paraná
Santa Fe
Rosario
Rafaela

Uruguaiana
Salto
Paysandú
Mercedes
URUGUAY
Minas
Montevideo
La Plata
Punta del Este
Mar del Plata

Jujuy
San Salvador de Jujuy
Salta
San Miguel de Tucumán
Catamarca
La Rioja
Santiago del Estero
Córdoba
Villa María
Río Cuarto
San Luis
Mendoza
San Juan
San Rafael

Buenos Aires
Zárate
Junín
Tandil
Azul
Olavarría
Bahía Blanca
Tres Arroyos
Necochea
Punta Alta

CHILE
Santiago
Valparaíso
Viña del Mar
Rancagua
San Antonio
Curicó
Talca
Linares
Chillán
Concepción
Talcahuano
Los Ángeles
Temuco
Valdivia
Osorno
Puerto Montt

Tocopilla
Calama
Antofagasta
Taltal
Copiapó
Vallenar
La Serena
Coquimbo
Ovalle

Paso de la Cumbre
Aconcagua 6960

Neuquén
San Carlos de Bariloche
Zapala
Esquel

Las Plumas
Rawson
Trelew
Comodoro Rivadavia

San Julián
Puerto Deseado
Puerto Santa Cruz
Río Gallegos

PATAGONIA

Viedma
Carmen de Patagones

PENÍNSULA VALDÉS
Golfo San Matías
Golfo San Jorge

Bahía Grande

ISLA DE CHILOÉ
Golfo de Corcovado
ARCHIPIÉLAGO DE LOS CHONOS
PENÍNSULA DE TAITAO
Golfo de Penas
ISLA WELLINGTON
ISLA
ISLA INÉS
Estrecho de Magallanes
Punta Arenas
Porvenir

TIERRA DEL FUEGO
Río Grande
Ushuaia
Cape Horn

ISLA DE LOS ESTADOS
WEST FALKLAND
EAST FALKLAND
Stanley
Falkland Islands / Islas Malvinas (U.K.) (Claimed by Argentina)

ISLA HOSTE
ISLA NAVARINO
SANTA INÉS

Drake Passage

SHAG ROCKS

SOUTH GEORGIA (Falkland Is.)
Grytviken

TRAVERSE ISLANDS
SAUNDERS
MONTAGU
BRISTOL
THULE
SOUTH SANDWICH ISLANDS (Falkland Is.)

Scotia Sea

SOUTH ORKNEY ISLANDS
CORONATION

ELEPHANT ISLAND
JOINVILLE
SOUTH SHETLAND ISLANDS
KING GEORGE ISLAND
LIVINGSTON ISLAND
PALMER ARCHIPELAGO
ANVERS ISLAND
RENAUD ISLAND
BISCOE ISLANDS
ADELAIDE ISLAND
CHARCOT ISLAND
ALEXANDER ISLAND

ROSS
JASON PENINSULA
GRAHAM LAND
ANTARCTIC PENINSULA
PALMER LAND
PENINSULA

Weddell Sea

Larsen Ice Shelf
Ronne Ice Shelf
Filchner Ice Shelf
BERKNER
LUITPOLD COAST
COATS LAND
CAIRD COAST

QUEEN MAUD LAND
NEW SCHWABENLAND
PRINCESS MARTHA COAST
Cape Norvegia
PRINCESS ASTRID COAST
PRINCESS RAGNHILD COAST
PRINCE OLAV COAST
RIISER-LARSEN PENINSULA

ANTARCTICA

South Pole

ELLSWORTH LAND
ENGLISH COAST
BRYAN COAST
EIGHTS COAST
MARIE BYRD LAND
WALGREEN COAST
Vinson Massif 4897

Bellingshausen Ice Shelf
THURSTON ISLAND
PETER I (Norway)
FARWELL COAST
Pine Island Bay
Cape Flying Fish
Cape Dart
BEAR PENINSULA
MARTIN PENINSULA
CARNEY ISLAND
GOULD COAST
SIPLE COAST
SHIRASE COAST
EDWARD VII PENINSULA
GUEST PENINSULA
Sulzberger Ice Shelf
Cape Colbeck
SAUNDERS COAST
ROOSEVELT
HOBBS COAST

Ross Ice Shelf
Land Bay
Wrigley Gulf
Amundsen Sea
Getz Ice Shelf

Bellingshausen Sea
Marguerite Bay
George VI Sound
Wilkins Sound

Antarctic Circle

YOSEMITE ROCK
ISLAS DESVENTURADAS (Chile)
ARCHIPIÉLAGO JUAN FERNÁNDEZ
ISLA ROBINSON CRUSOE
ISLA ALEJANDRO SELKIRK
ISLA RESTINGA DE SEFTON
EMILY ROCK

SALA Y GÓMEZ (Chile)
EASTER ISLAND

Tropic of Capricorn

P A C I F I C   O C E A N

Scale 1:30,000,000   Lambert Azimuthal Equal Area Projection

0   500   1000   1500   2000 km
0   500   1000 miles

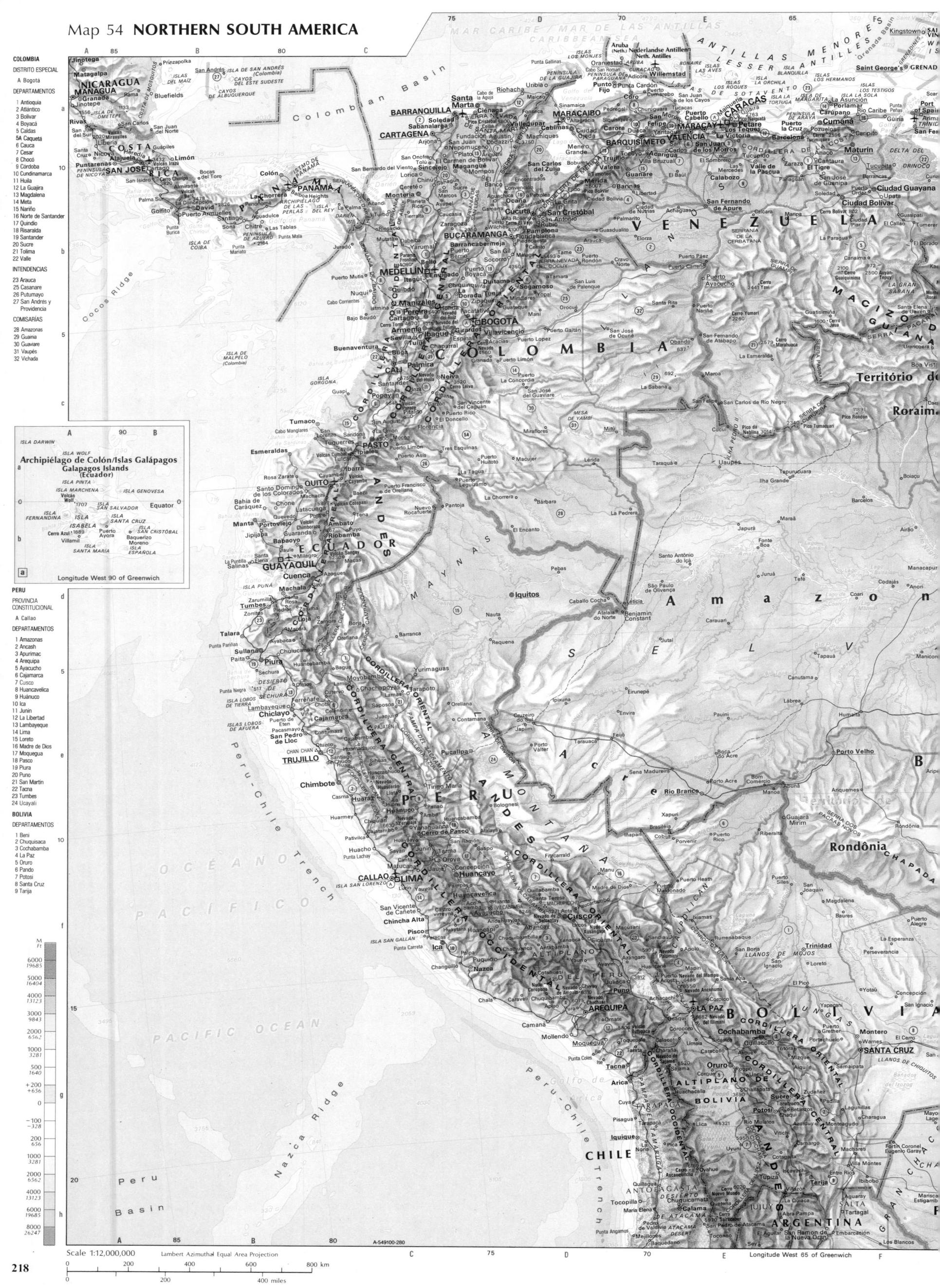

Map 54 NORTHERN SOUTH AMERICA

COLOMBIA

DISTRITO ESPECIAL
A Bogotá

DEPARTAMENTOS
1 Antioquia
2 Atlántico
3 Bolívar
4 Boyacá
5 Caldas
5A Caquetá
6 Cauca
7 Cesar
8 Chocó
9 Córdoba
10 Cundinamarca
11 Huila
12 La Guajira
13 Magdalena
14 Meta
15 Nariño
16 Norte de Santander
17 Quindío
18 Risaralda
19 Santander
20 Sucre
21 Tolima
22 Valle

INTENDENCIAS
23 Arauca
25 Casanare
26 Putumayo
27 San Andrés y
    Providencia

COMISARÍAS
28 Amazonas
29 Guainía
30 Guaviare
31 Vaupés
32 Vichada

PERU

PROVINCIA
CONSTITUCIONAL
A Callao

DEPARTAMENTOS
1 Amazonas
2 Ancash
3 Apurímac
4 Arequipa
5 Ayacucho
6 Cajamarca
7 Cusco
8 Huancavelica
9 Huánuco
10 Ica
11 Junín
12 La Libertad
13 Lambayeque
14 Lima
15 Loreto
16 Madre de Dios
17 Moquegua
18 Pasco
19 Piura
20 Puno
21 San Martín
22 Tacna
23 Tumbes
24 Ucayali

BOLIVIA

DEPARTAMENTOS
1 Beni
2 Chuquisaca
3 Cochabamba
4 La Paz
5 Oruro
6 Pando
7 Potosí
8 Santa Cruz
9 Tarija

Archipiélago de Colón/Islas Galápagos
Galapagos Islands
(Ecuador)

Longitude West 90 of Greenwich

Scale 1:12,000,000

Lambert Azimuthal Equal Area Projection

A-549100-280

Longitude West 65 of Greenwich

Mid-Atlantic Ridge

Guiana Basin

OCEANO ATLÂNTICO

ATLANTIC OCEAN

SURINAME

Guyane Française
French Guiana

Território do Amapá

Pará

Maranhão

Ceará

Piauí

Bahia

Goiás

Mato Grosso

Planalto do Mato Grosso

B R A Z I L

B R A S I L

Minas Gerais

Brazilian Highlands

BRASÍLIA
Distrito Federal

GOIÂNIA

BELO HORIZONTE

RIO DE JANEIRO

SÃO PAULO

SANTOS

Território de Fernando de Noronha

FORTALEZA

NATAL

RECIFE

MACEIÓ

Aracaju

SALVADOR

Tropic of Capricorn

© ISTITUTO GEOGRAFICO DE AGOSTINI S.p.A. - NOVARA

219

Map 55 **EAST-CENTRAL SOUTH AMERICA**

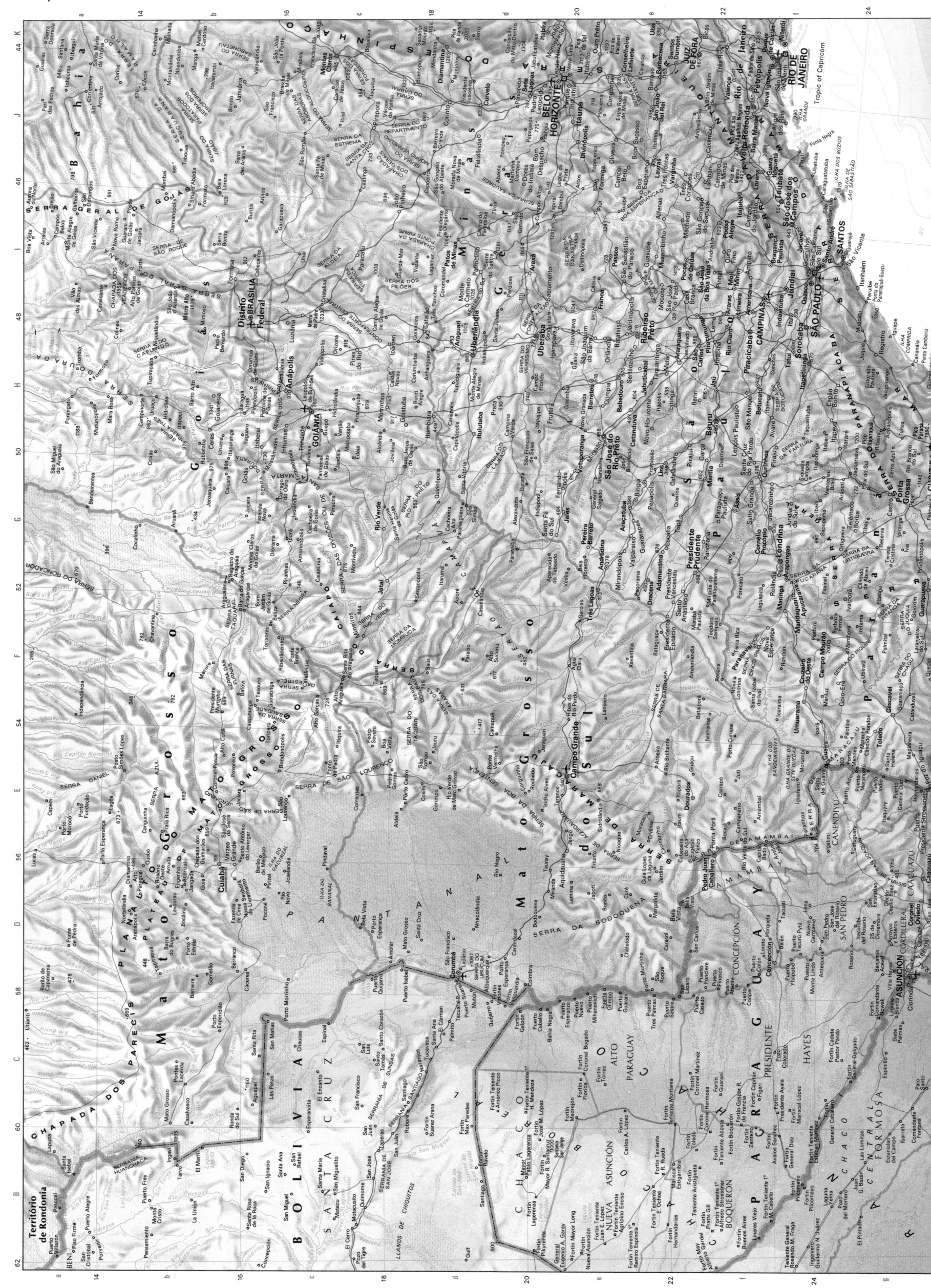

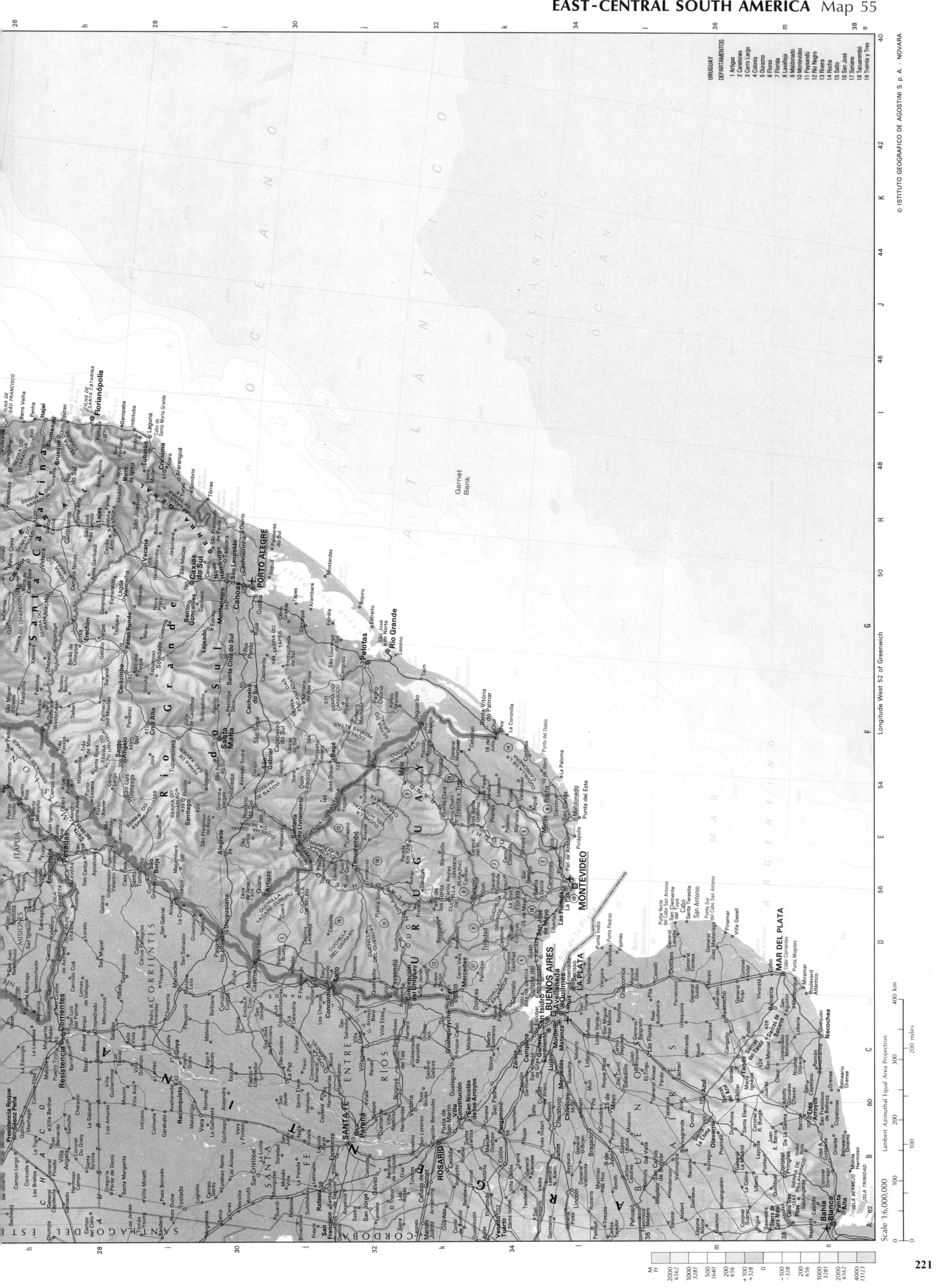

URUGUAY
DEPARTAMENTOS
1 Artigas
2 Canelones
3 Cerro Largo
4 Colonia
5 Durazno
6 Flores
7 Florida
8 Lavalleja
9 Maldonado
10 Montevideo
11 Paysandú
12 Río Negro
13 Rivera
14 Rocha
15 Salto
16 San José
17 Soriano
18 Tacuarembó
19 Treinta y Tres

Scale 1:6,000,000

Lambert Azimuthal Equal Area Projection

Longitude West 52 of Greenwich

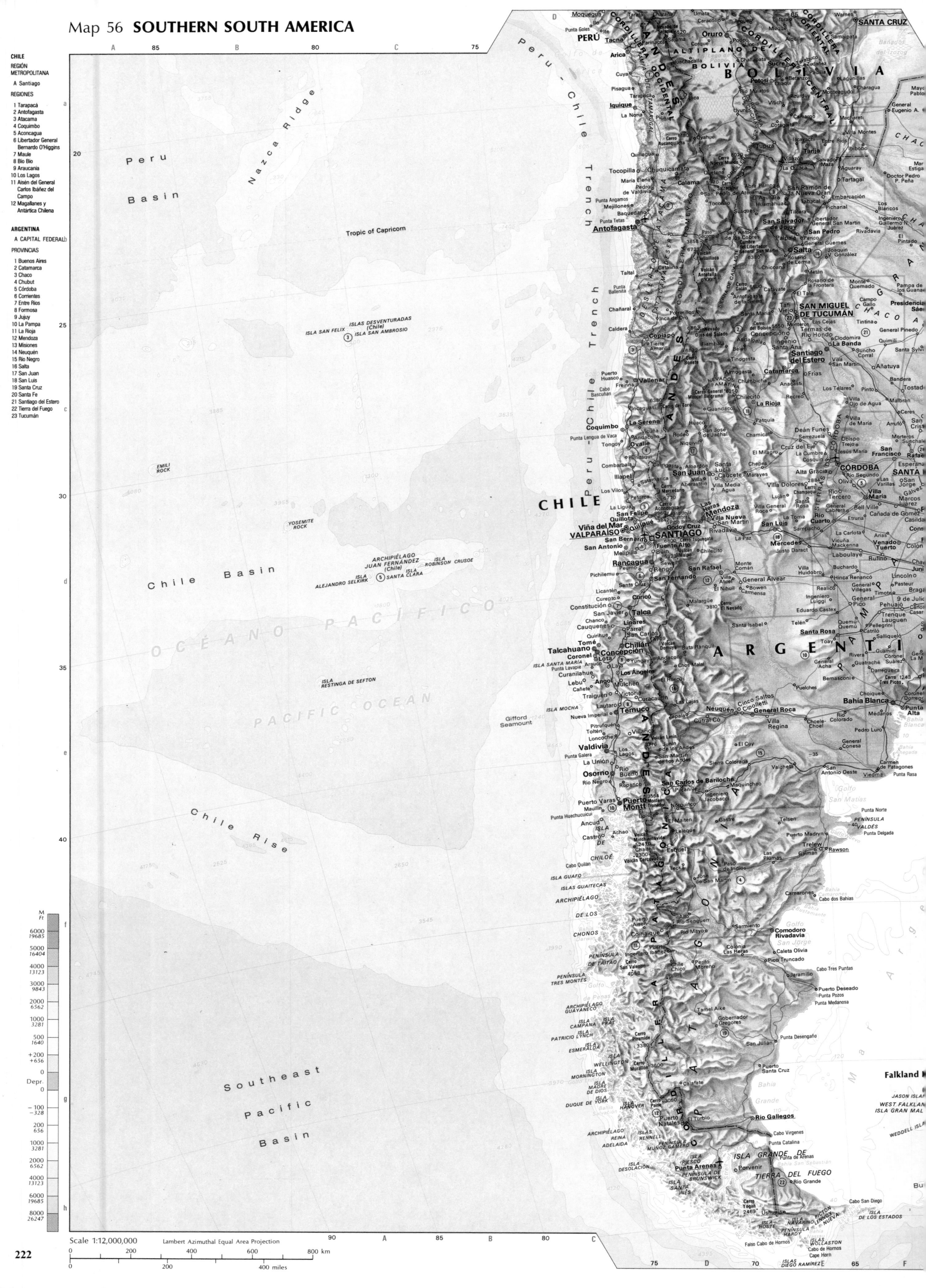

Map 56 SOUTHERN SOUTH AMERICA

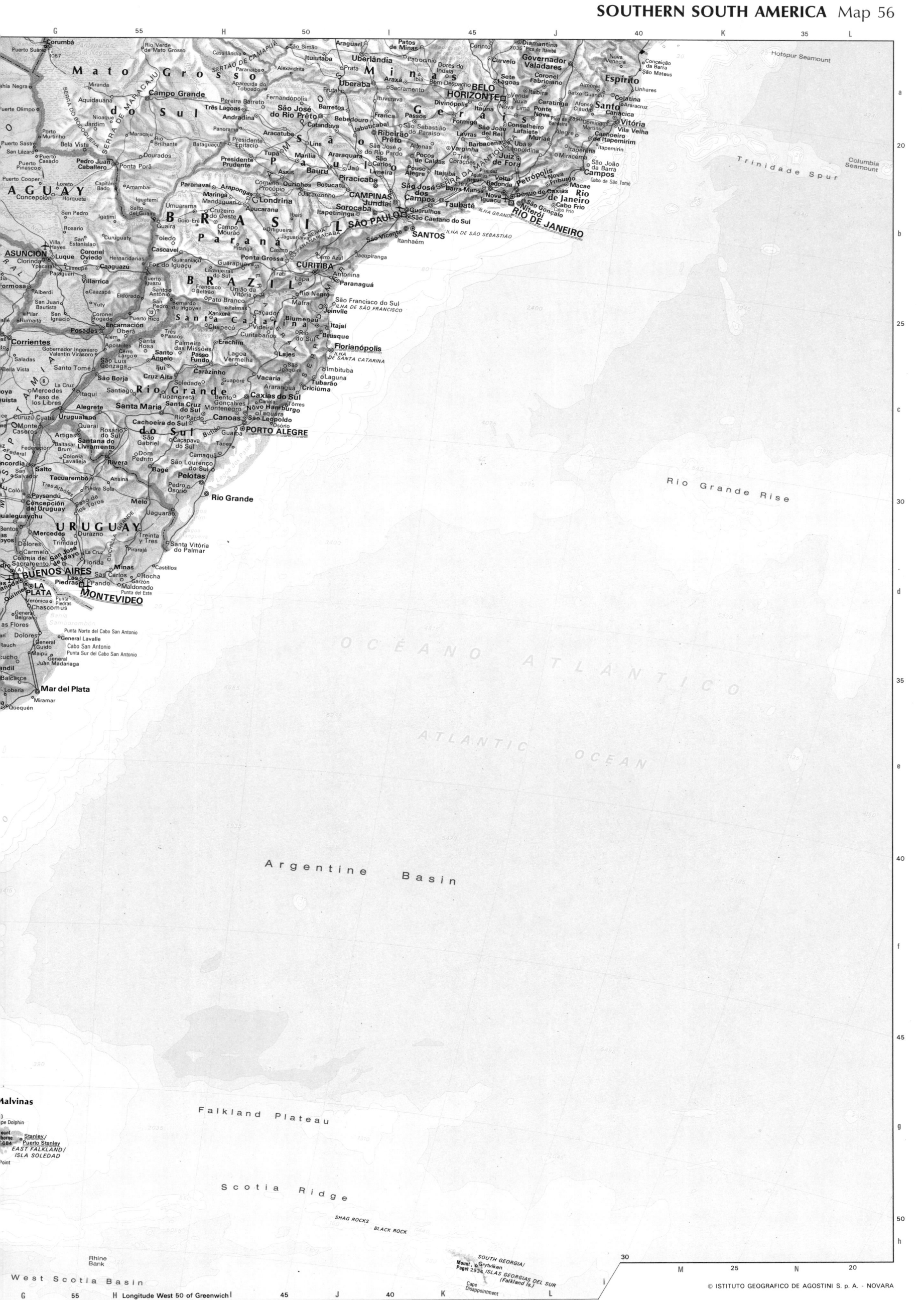

Map 57 **AUSTRALIA AND OCEANIA, PHYSICAL**

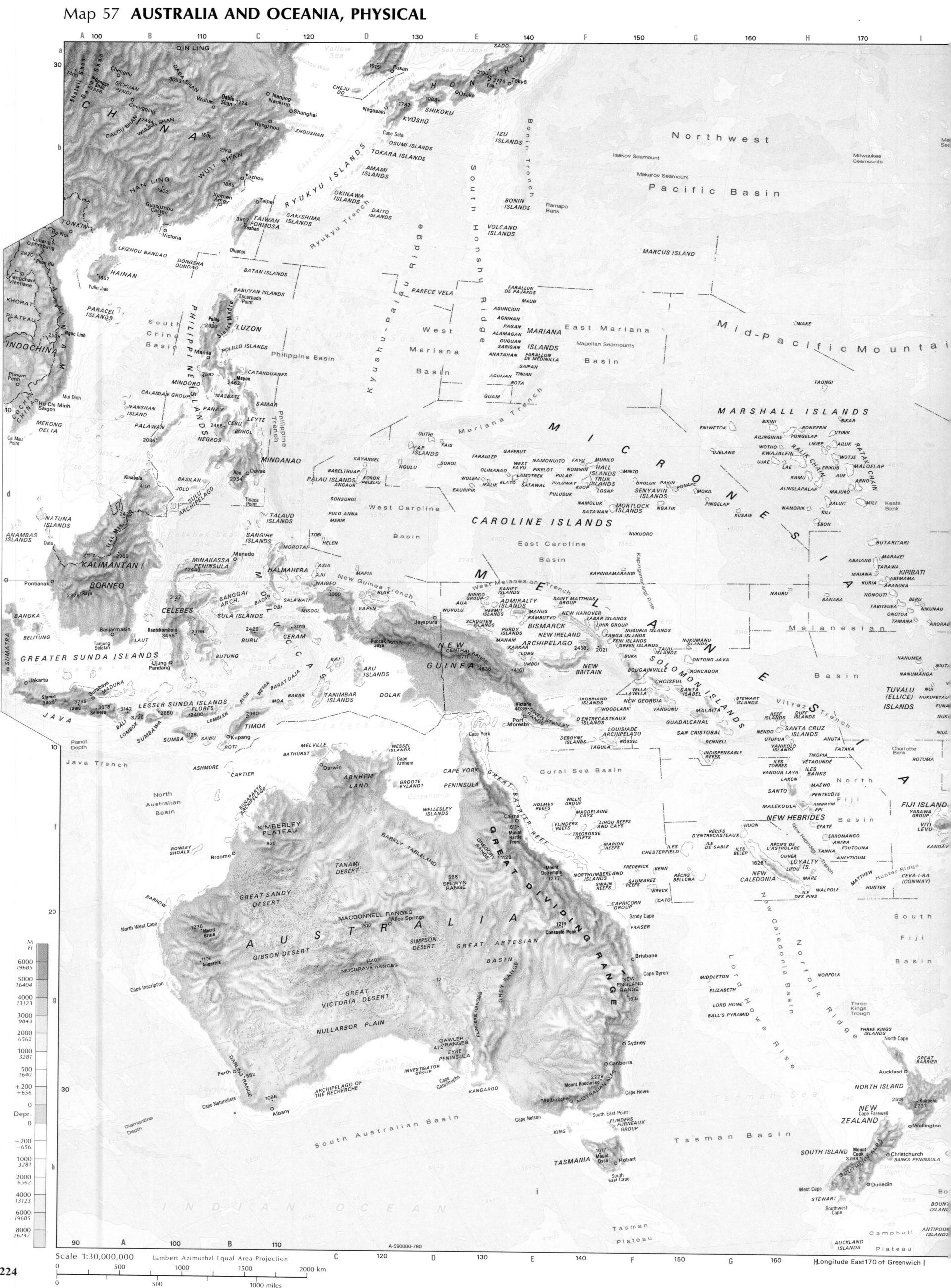

Scale 1:30,000,000   Lambert Azimuthal Equal Area Projection

A-590000-780

Longitude East 170 of Greenwich

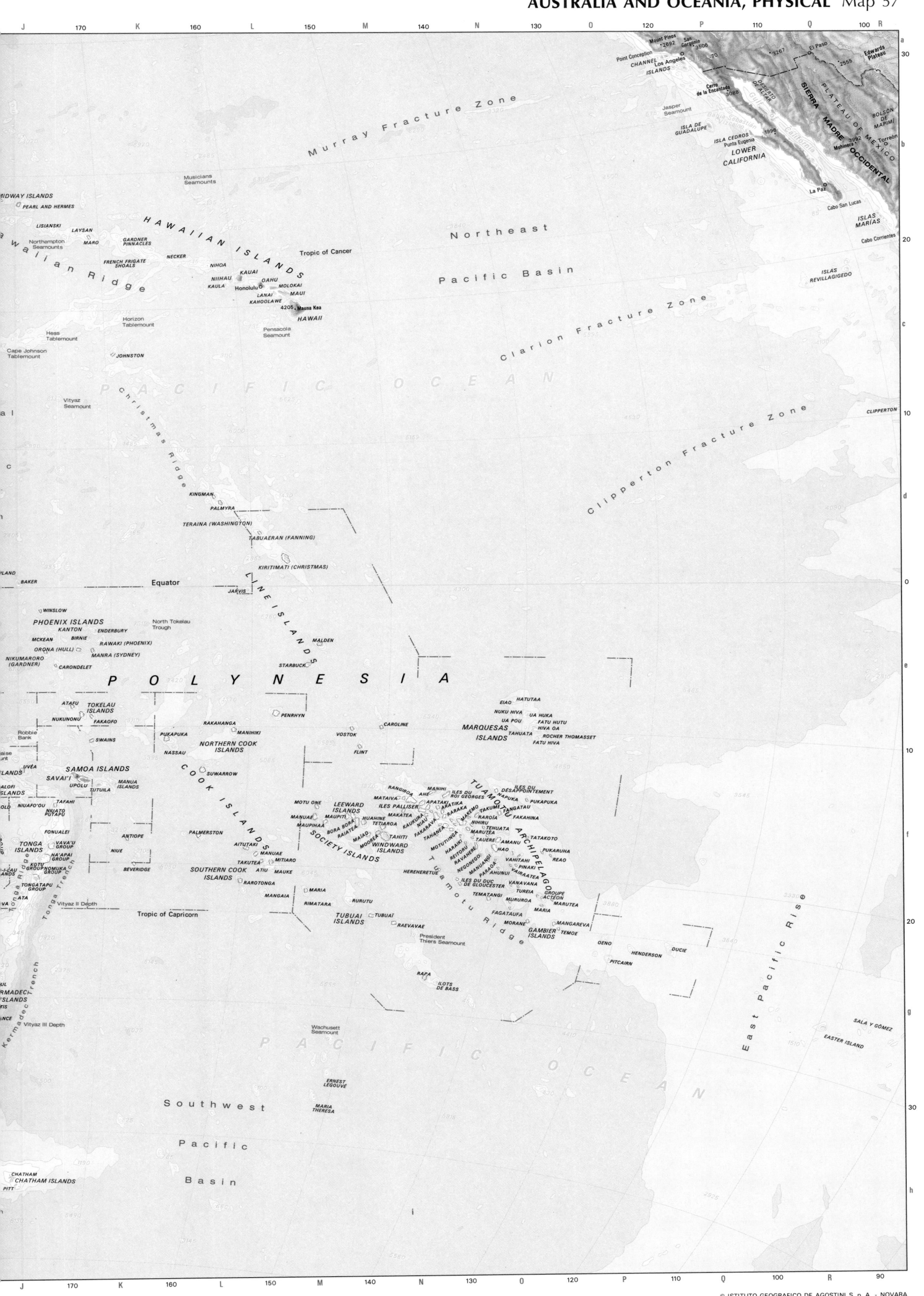

Map 58 **AUSTRALIA AND OCEANIA, POLITICAL**

CHINA

Chengdu Guanxian Nanchong Gyangyuan
Zigong Luzhou Nei Chong Mianyang
Xichang Panzhi Zhaotong Yibin Zunyi
Kunming Anshun Dushan **Guiyang** Hengyang
Nanning **Guangzhou** Guilin Liuzhou
Beihai Yulin Zhanjiang Maoming
Haiphong Ha noi Nam Dinh Thanh Hoa Vinh
HAINAN Haikou

Chengdu Chongqing Yichang **Wuhan** Hefei Nanjing
Xuzhou Kaifeng Lianyungang
Xiangfan Changde **Changsha Xiangtan** Nanchang
Jiujiang Hangzhou **Shanghai Wuxi Suzhou**
Wenzhou Fuzhou **Keelung**
Taipei Taichung TAIWAN Kaohsiung
Hong Kong (U.K.) **New Kowloon** Victoria **Macau** (Port.)

SOUTH KOREA Taejŏn Taegu Kwangju Mokp'o **Pusan** CHEJU-DO

Nagoya Toyama Niigata Sendai **Iwaki**
Kanazawa Gifu Utsunomiya **Tōkyō Yokohama**
JAPAN Hiroshima Okayama Ōsaka Kyōto Shizuoka
Nagasaki Kumamoto Wakayama KYŪSHŪ SHIKOKU
Fukuoka Kitakyūshū Masuyama Kagoshima
OSUMI ISLANDS

RYŪKYŪ ISLANDS (Japan) AMAMI **Naha** OKINAWA
TOKARA ISLANDS SAKISHIMA ISLANDS DAITO ISLANDS (Japan)

East China Sea
South China Sea
Philippine Sea
Celebes Sea
Sulu Sea
Java Sea
Banda Sea
Flores Sea
Timor Sea
Arafura Sea
Coral Sea
Tasman Sea

VIET-NAM Da Nang Qui Nhon Nha Trang
CAMBODIA Phnum Penh **Ho Chi Minh (Saigon)** My Tho Can Tho
THAILAND Ubon Bangkok
LAOS Viangchan (Vientiane)

PHILIPPINES Laoag Aparri Ilagan Baguio LUZON
Cabanatuan **Quezon City Manila** San Pablo
Batangas Naga Legazpi MINDORO PANAY
Iloilo SAMAR LEYTE **Cebu** BOHOL NEGROS
PALAWAN Puerto Princesa Dipolog Butuan
Cagayan de Oro Iligan **Zamboanga** MINDANAO
Basilan City **Davao** General Santos
SULU ARCHIPELAGO JOLO Sandakan **Tawau**

BRUNEI Bandar Seri Begawan Miri Kota Kinabalu
MALAYSIA Kuching Sibu
KALIMANTAN / BORNEO Pontianak Samarinda Balikpapan Banjarmasin
SUMATRA Palu Poso CELEBES Ujung Pandang
Jakarta Bandung Bogor Cirebon Semarang **Surabaya**
Yogyakarta Surakarta Malang Kediri MADURA BALI
INDONESIA LOMBOK SUMBAWA FLORES TIMOR Kupang ROTI

MARIANA ISLANDS (U.S.) Northern Mariana Islands (U.S.)
FARALLON DE PAJAROS MAUG ASUNCION AGRIHAN PAGAN
ALAMAGAN GUGUAN SAIPAN Administrative Center
Agana Guam (U.S.) ROTA TINIAN ANATAHAN

Wake (U.S.) MINAMI-TORI (Japan)

MARSHALL ISLANDS ENEWETAK BIKINI RONGERIK
AILINGHINAE RONGELAP UTIRIK BIKAR TAONGI
WOTHO LIKIEP AILUK MEJIT WOTJE MALOELAP ERIKUB
UJELANG LAE NAMU KWAJALEIN **Majuro** AUR ARNO
JALUIT KILI EBON MILI

FEDERATED STATES OF MICRONESIA YAP ISLANDS
ULITHI FAIS GAFERUT FARAULEP NGULU SOROL
NAMONUITO FAYU PIKELOT HALL ISLANDS MINTO
OROLUK PONAPE MOKIL NGATIK PINGELAP KOSRAE (KUSAIE)
PALAU ISLANDS Koror BELAU (Trust Territory) ANGAUR
SONSOROL PULO ANNA MERIR HELEN TOBI
NUKUORO KAPINGAMARANGI
CAROLINE ISLANDS

MICRONESIA

NAURU / NAORO BANABA

KIRIBATI BUTARITARI MARAKEI ABAIANG
TARAWA Bairiki MAIANA ABEMAMA KURIA ARANUKA
NONOUTI TABITEUEA ONOTOA TAMANA

MELANESIA
BISMARCK ARCHIPELAGO NEW IRELAND NEW HANOVER
ADMIRALTY ISLANDS MANUS NEW BRITAIN Rabaul
PAPUA NEW GUINEA Madang Goroka Lae **Port Moresby**
NEW GUINEA Jayapura Wewak
SOLOMON ISLANDS BOUGAINVILLE CHOISEUL Buka
NEW GEORGIA SANTA ISABEL Auki MALAITA **Honiara**
GUADALCANAL SAN CRISTOBAL RENNELL

VANUATU NEW HEBRIDES ESPÍRITU SANTO Luganville
MALEKOULA EFATE **Port-Vila** ERROMANGO TANNA ANEITYUM

NEW CALEDONIA (France) **Nouméa** Koumac LOYALTY ISLANDS

TUVALU NANUMEA NANUMANGA

FIJI YASAWA GROUP VITI LEVU VANUA LEVU

Norfolk (Australia) Kingston
LORD HOWE BALL'S PYRAMID
MIDDLETON REEF ELIZABETH (Australia)

AUSTRALIA
GREAT SANDY DESERT GIBSON DESERT GREAT VICTORIA DESERT
TANAMI DESERT SIMPSON DESERT NULLARBOR PLAIN
ARNHEM LAND KIMBERLEY CAPE YORK PENINSULA
Darwin Katherine Wyndham Derby Broome Port Hedland
Dampier Karratha Onslow Carnarvon Geraldton **Perth**
Bunbury Albany Esperance Norseman Kalgoorlie
Alice Springs Tennant Creek Mount Isa Cloncurry
Cairns Townsville Mackay Rockhampton Gladstone
Bundaberg Maryborough Gympie **Brisbane** Gold Coast
Toowoomba Ipswich Lismore Coffs Harbour Tamworth
Dubbo Orange Bathurst **Newcastle**
Sydney Wollongong **Canberra** Wagga Wagga
Adelaide Port Augusta Port Pirie Mildura
Melbourne Ballarat Geelong Bendigo Shepparton

TASMANIA Launceston **Hobart** Devonport Smithton Zeehan

NEW ZEALAND **Auckland** Manukau Hamilton NORTH ISLAND
New-Plymouth Whangarei Nelson Blenheim
SOUTH ISLAND Westport Hokitika Timaru **Christchurch**
Mount Cook Wanaka Haast Queenstown Dunedin
Invercargill STEWART AUCKLAND ISLANDS (New Zealand)

INDIAN OCEAN

Scale 1:30,000,000   Lambert Azimuthal Equal Area Projection
0   500   1000   1500   2000 km
0   500   1000 miles

Longitude East 170 of Greenwich

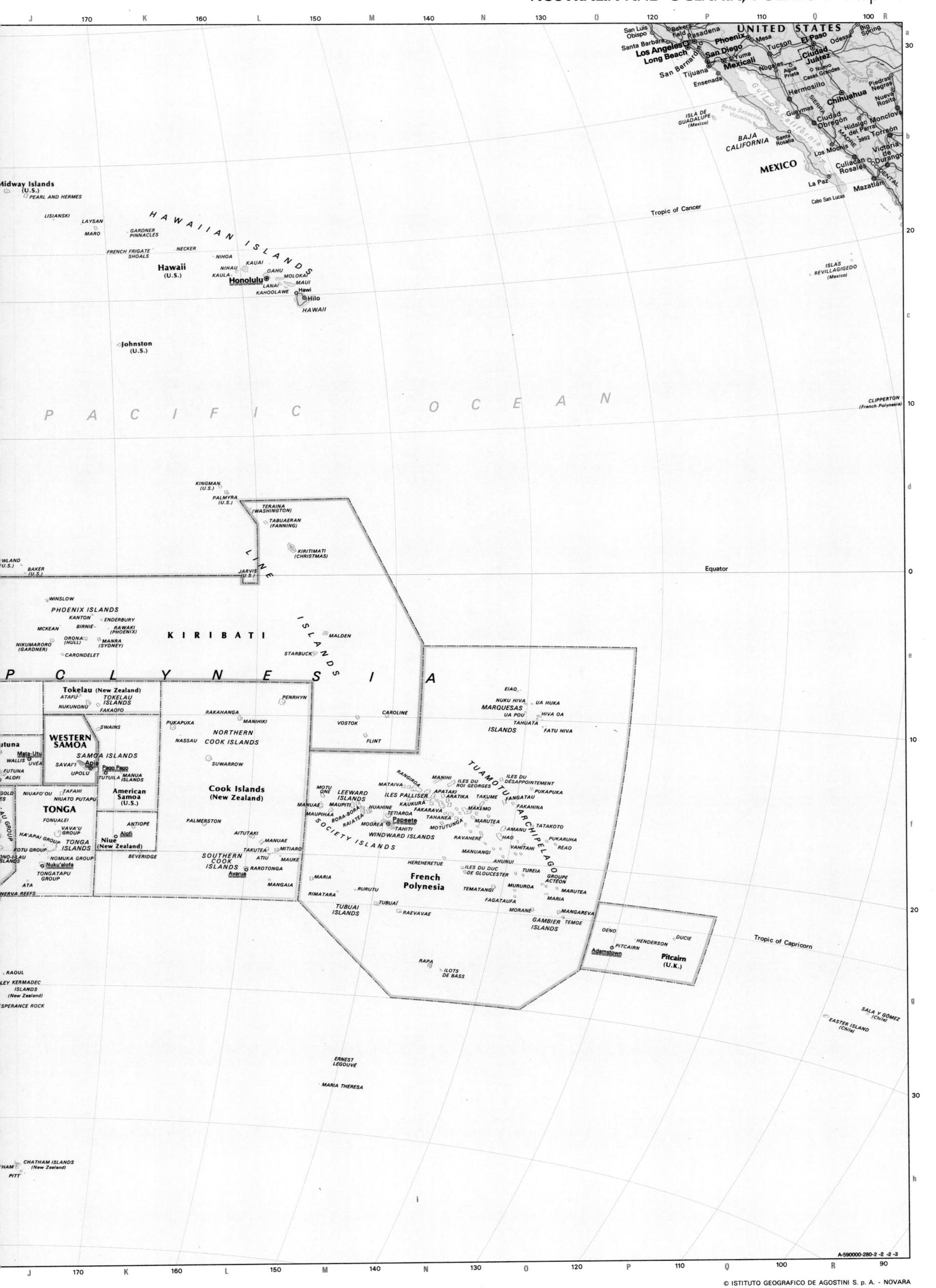

Map 59 AUSTRALIA

Grid references (top)
C · 115 · D · 120 · E · 125 · F · 130 · G

INDONESIA

LAUT JAWA (Java Sea)
Pulau Bawean
Rembang · Tuban · Gresik
Kudus · Lasem
SEMARANG · SURABAYA
Magelang · Madiun · Kediri · Bangkalan · Sumenep
Probolinggo · Bondowoso
SURAKARTA · MALANG · Jember
YOGYAKARTA · Tulungagung · Lumajang · Banjuwang
JAWA (Java)
NUSA PENIDA · PULAU LOMBOK · PULAU SUMBAWA
Tanjung Bungkuk
KEPULAUAN KANGEAN
KEPULAUAN TENGAH
PULAU MOYO · Sumbawa Besar · Raba
Gunung Tambora
PULAU SUMBAWA
Mataram · Denpasar · Singaraja
BALI
Waikabubak · Waingapu · Baing
PULAU SUMBA
KEPULAUAN SAWU · PULAU SAWU
Baa · PULAU ROTI
KEPULAUAN LIUKANG TENGGAYA
KEPULAUAN BONE RATE
LAUT FLORES (Flores Sea)
PULAU KOMODO · Ruteng · Ende
PULAU FLORES · Larantuka
LAUT SAWU
KEPULAUAN SOLOR
PULAU LOMBLEN · PULAU ALOR
Kalabahi
Kupang · Soe · Atambua
Gunung Mutis
PULAU TIMOR
Dili · Manatuto
Tala Mailau
KEPULAUAN BARAT DAYA
PULAU WETAR · Iwaki
PULAU ROMANG
PULAU LETI · KEPULAUAN LETI
KEPULAUAN SERMATA
PULAU BABAR
PULAU SELARU
KEPULAUAN TANIMBAR
PULAU YAMDENA
Saumlaki
KEPULAUAN KAI
PULAU TRANGAN

TIMOR SEA
Timor Trough
ARAFURA SEA

Ocean and undersea features (west)
INDIAN OCEAN
North Australian Basin
Java Trench
Planet Deep
Corona Bank
Exmouth Plateau
Cuvier Basin
South Australian Basin
Diamantina Deep
Diamantina Trench
ROWLEY SHOALS
Rowley Shoals

Northern Australia
Cape Van Diemen
BATHURST ISLAND
MELVILLE ISLAND
Snake Bay Settlement
COBOURG PENINSULA
Croker Island
Darwin
Rum Jungle · Batchelor
Adelaide River
Pine Creek · Katherine
Mataranka · Larrimah
Willeroo · Birdum · Daly Waters
ARNHEM LAND
Cape Scott
Cape Londonderry
Kalumburu Mission
Wyndham · Kununurra
KIMBERLEY
Mount Hann · Gibb River
Kuri Bay
Mount Ord · Mount Wells · Turkey Creek
KING LEOPOLD RANGES
KIMBERLEY PLATEAU
Derby · Fitzroy Crossing · Halls Creek
Mount Amherst
DAMPIER LAND
Broome
Christmas Creek
Victoria River Downs
Top Springs
Newcastle Waters
Wave Hill · Elliot
TANAMI DESERT
Tanami · The Granites
Barrow Creek · Tea Tree
NORTHERN TERRITORY
STUART BLUFF
MACDONNELL RANGES
Mount Liebig · Mount Zeil
Henbury
Mount Olga · Erldunda
Kulgera · De Rose

Western Australia coast and interior
Port Hedland · Goldsworthy
Marble Bar · Nullagine
EIGHTY MILE BEACH
Larrey Point · Pardoo
CANNING BASIN
GREAT SANDY DESERT
PATERSON RANGE
DAMPIER ARCHIPELAGO
Dampier · Roebourne
Onslow · MONTE BELLO ISLANDS
BARROW ISLAND
MUIRON ISLANDS
NORTH WEST CAPE
Exmouth · Learmonth
Point Cloates
HAMERSLEY RANGE
CHICHESTER RANGE
Pannawonica · Wittenoom
Tom Price · Mount Bruce · Mount Meharry
Paraburdoo
OPHTHALMIA RANGE
Newman · Roy Hill
ROBERTSON RANGE
ROBINSON RANGE
Mundiwindi
GIBSON DESERT
Docker River
RAWLINSON RANGES
Warburton Mission
Giles Meteorological Station
PETERMANN RANGES
TOMKINSON RANGES
MUSGRAVE RANGES
Mount Aloysius
BIRKSGATE RANGE
Mount Sir Thomas
EVERARD RANGES

WESTERN AUSTRALIA

Cape Farquhar
Minilya
BARLEE RANGE
KENNEDY RANGE
Mount Augustus · Mount Vernon · Mount Egerton
Cape Cuvier
Carnarvon · Gascoyne Junction
CARNARVON RANGE
Mount Essenden
BERNIER ISLAND · DORRE ISLAND
Shark Bay
DIRK HARTOG ISLAND · Denham
Cape Inscription
Wooramel
Mount Hale · Mount Narryer
Murchison · Meekatharra · Wiluna
NICHOLSON RANGE
Cue · Sandstone
Mount Magnet · Agnew · Leonora
GREAT VICTORIA DESERT
Mount Shenton · Laverton
Mount Redcliffe
Simpson Hill
Yalgoo · Mount Singleton · Menzies
Sandstone
Mount Wymaando
Mount Dalgaranga
Bluff Point
Northampton · Mullewa
Geraldton
Dongara · Morawa · Perenjori
Mount Jackson
HOUTMAN ABROLHOS
Carnamah · Watheroo
Coorow · Koorda · Mukinbudin
Dalwallinu · Mukinbudin
Kalgoorlie · Coolgardie · Kambalda
Southern Cross · Widgiemooltha
Lancelin · Moora · Wongan Hills
Goomalling · Wyalkatchem
Northam · Merredin · Nungarin
Kellerberrin
Norseman
FRASER RANGE
Zanthus · Rawlinna · Forrest
NULLARBOR PLAIN
Cook · Ooldea
Maralinga
SOUTH AUSTRALIA

Perth region / Southwest
PERTH
FREMANTLE · ROTTNEST ISLAND
ARMADALE
Rockingham · Mandurah
Cunderdin · Quairading · York · Beverley
Brookton · Corrigin · Pingelly
Waroona · Harvey
Wickepin · Narrogin
Kondinin · Lake King
Bunbury · Collie · Wagin
Ravensthorpe
Donnybrook · Katanning · Nyabing
Gnowangerup · Hopetoun
Busselton · Bridgetown · Kojonup
Cape Naturaliste
Margaret River · Nannup · Kojonup
Augusta · Cape Leeuwin · Pemberton
Manjimup · Cranbrook · Mount Barker
STIRLING RANGE
Denmark · Albany
Bald Head
Point D'Entrecasteaux
Hood Point
ARCHIPELAGO OF THE RECHERCHE
Esperance · Cape Arid
Point Culver
Balladonia
Eucla · Nullarbor
GREAT AUSTRALIAN BIGHT
INVESTIGATOR GROUP
Streaky Bay · Smoky Bay
Penong · Ceduna
Great Australian Bight
Tropic of Capricorn

Scale box (lower left)
M / Ft
4000 / 13123
3000 / 9843
2000 / 6562
1000 / 3281
500 / 1640
+200 / +656
0 / 0
Depr. / 0
−100 / −328
200 / 656
1000 / 3281
2000 / 6562
4000 / 13123
6000 / 19685
8000 / 26247

Scale 1:12,000,000 Delisle Conic Equidistant Projection
0   200   400   600   800 km
0   200   400 miles

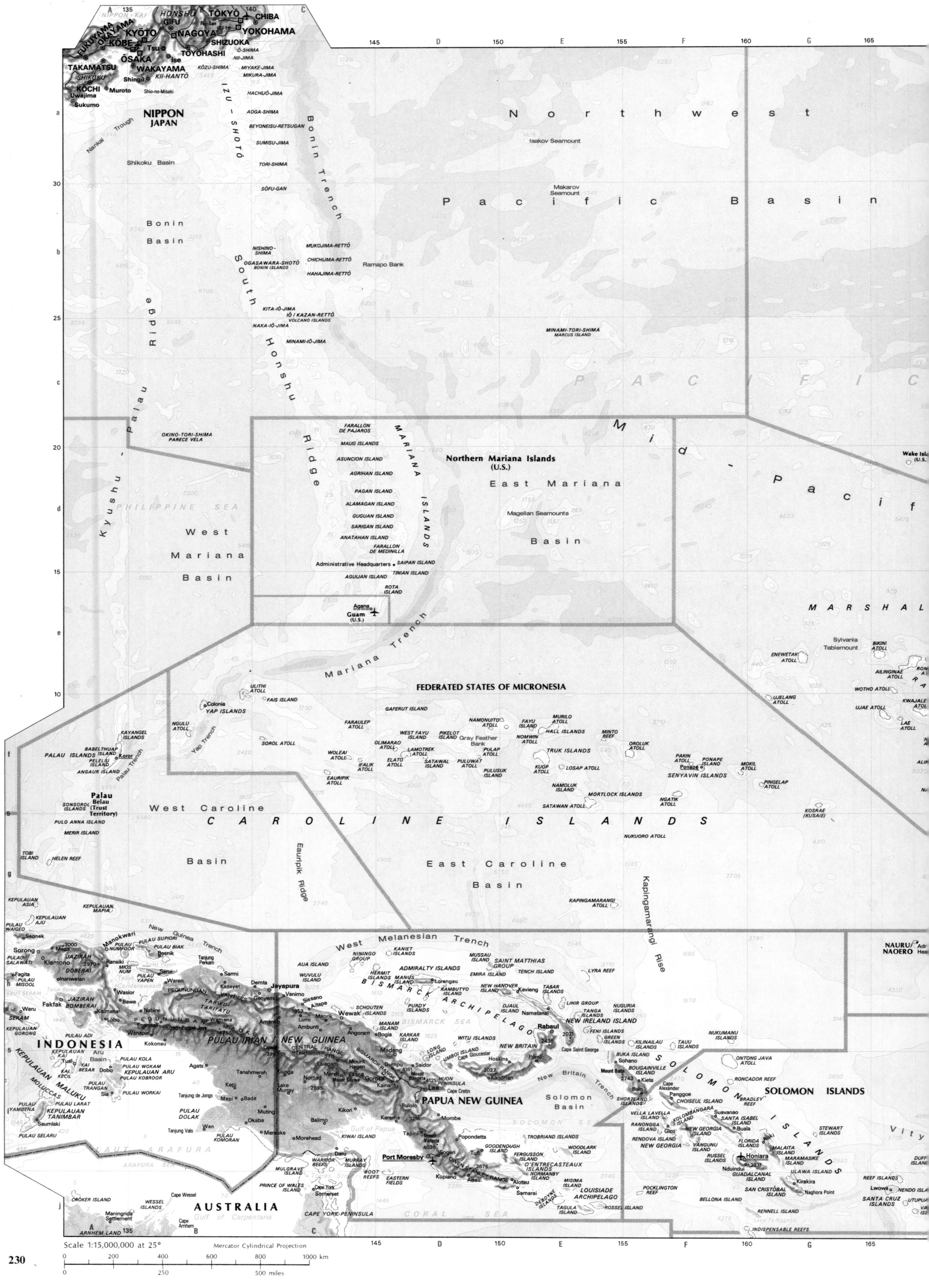

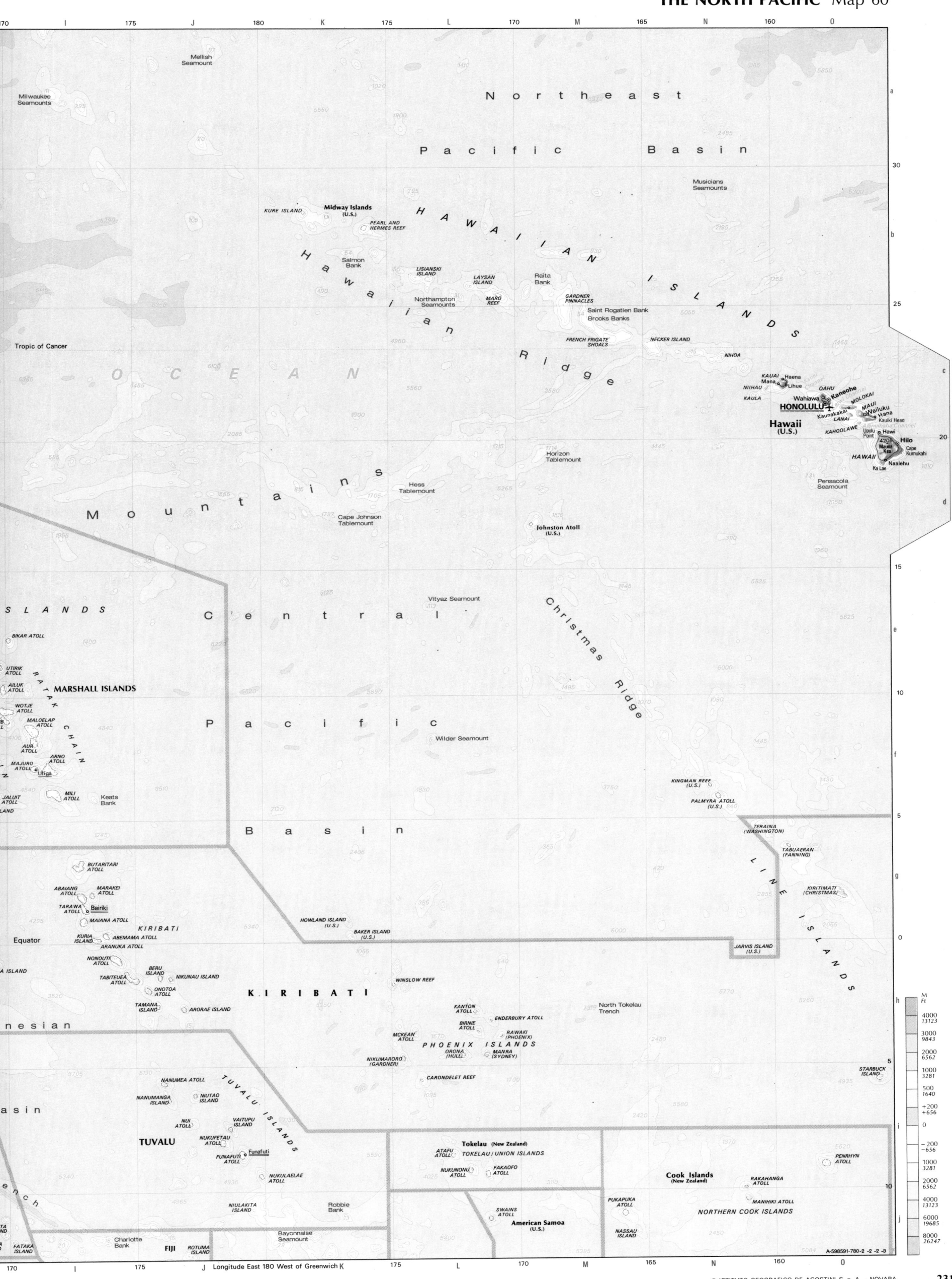

Northeast

Pacific   Basin

a

30

Musicians
Seamounts

Mellish
Seamount

Milwaukee
Seamounts

b

HAWAIIAN

KURE ISLAND
Midway Islands (U.S.)
PEARL AND
HERMES REEF

Salmon
Bank

LISIANSKI
ISLAND

LAYSAN
ISLAND

Raita
Bank

HAWAIIAN ISLANDS

25

Hawaiian

Northampton
Seamounts

MARO
REEF

GARDNER
PINNACLES

Saint Rogatien Bank
Brooks Banks

5055

Tropic of Cancer

O   C   E   A   N

Ridge

FRENCH FRIGATE
SHOALS

NECKER ISLAND

NIHOA

KAUAI Haena
Mana Lihue
NIIHAU   OAHU   Kaneohe
KAULA   Wahiawa   MOLOKAI
HONOLULU   Kaunakakai   MAUI
LANAI   Wailuku
Hana
Kauiki Head

c

Hawaii
(U.S.)

KAHOOLAWE   Upolu
Point   Hawi
Hilo
Cape
Kumukahi

20

Horizon
Tablemount

Mauna
Kea

HAWAII   Naalehu

Ka Lae

M   o   u   n   t   a   i   n   s

Hess
Tablemount

Pensacola
Seamount

d

Cape Johnson
Tablemount

Johnston Atoll
(U.S.)

15

ISLANDS

Vityaz Seamount

C   e   n   t   r   a   l

Christmas

e

BIKAR ATOLL

UTIRIK
ATOLL

AILUK
ATOLL
MARSHALL ISLANDS

WOTJE
ATOLL

R   A   T   A   K   C   H   A   I   N

P   a   c   i   f   i   c

Ridge

10

MALOELAP
ATOLL

AUR
ATOLL

ARNO
ATOLL

MAJURO
ATOLL
Uliga

Wilder Seamount

f

JALUIT
ATOLL

MILI
ATOLL

Keats
Bank

KINGMAN REEF
(U.S.)

PALMYRA ATOLL
(U.S.)

B   a   s   i   n

5

TERAINA
(WASHINGTON)

TABUAERAN
(FANNING)

L   I   N   E

BUTARITARI
ATOLL

g

ABAIANG
ATOLL

MARAKEI
ATOLL

KIRITIMATI
(CHRISTMAS)

TARAWA
ATOLL   Bairiki

MAIANA ATOLL

K   I   R   I   B   A   T   I

HOWLAND ISLAND
(U.S.)

0

Equator

KURIA
ISLAND

ABEMAMA ATOLL

ARANUKA ATOLL

BAKER ISLAND
(U.S.)

JARVIS ISLAND
(U.S.)

I   S   L   A   N   D   S

NONOUTI
ATOLL

BERU
ISLAND

NIKUNAU ISLAND

TABITEUEA
ATOLL

ONOTOA
ATOLL

WINSLOW REEF

K.IRIBATI

North Tokelau
Trench

5

TAMANA
ISLAND

ARORAE ISLAND

KANTON
ATOLL

ENDERBURY ATOLL

nesian

MCKEAN
ATOLL

BIRNIE
ATOLL

RAWAKI
(PHOENIX)

MANRA
(SYDNEY)

PHOENIX ISLANDS

ORONA
(HULL)

h

NUKUMARORO
(GARDNER)

CARONDELET REEF

STARBUCK
ISLAND

5

NANUMEA ATOLL

TUVALU ISLANDS

NANUMANGA
ISLAND

NIUTAO
ISLAND

i

asin

NUI
ATOLL

VAITUPU
ISLAND

TUVALU

NUKUFETAU
ATOLL

Tokelau (New Zealand)
ATAFU
ATOLL   TOKELAU / UNION ISLANDS

FUNAFUTI
ATOLL   Funafuti

NUKUNONU
ATOLL

FAKAOFO
ATOLL

PENRHYN
ATOLL

10

NUKULAELAE
ATOLL

NIULAKITA
ISLAND

Robbie
Bank

RAKAHANGA
ATOLL

Cook Islands
(New Zealand)

MANIHIKI ATOLL

nch

SWAINS
ATOLL

PUKAPUKA
ATOLL

NORTHERN COOK ISLANDS

FATAKA
ISLAND

Charlotte
Bank

FIJI

ROTUMA
ISLAND

Bayonnaise
Seamount

American Samoa
(U.S.)

NASSAU
ISLAND

A-598591-780-2 -2 -2 -3

j

M
Ft

4000
13123

3000
9843

2000
6562

1000
3281

500
1640

+200
+656

0

- 200
-656

1000
3281

2000
6562

4000
13123

6000
19685

8000
26247

Map 61 **THE SOUTH PACIFIC**

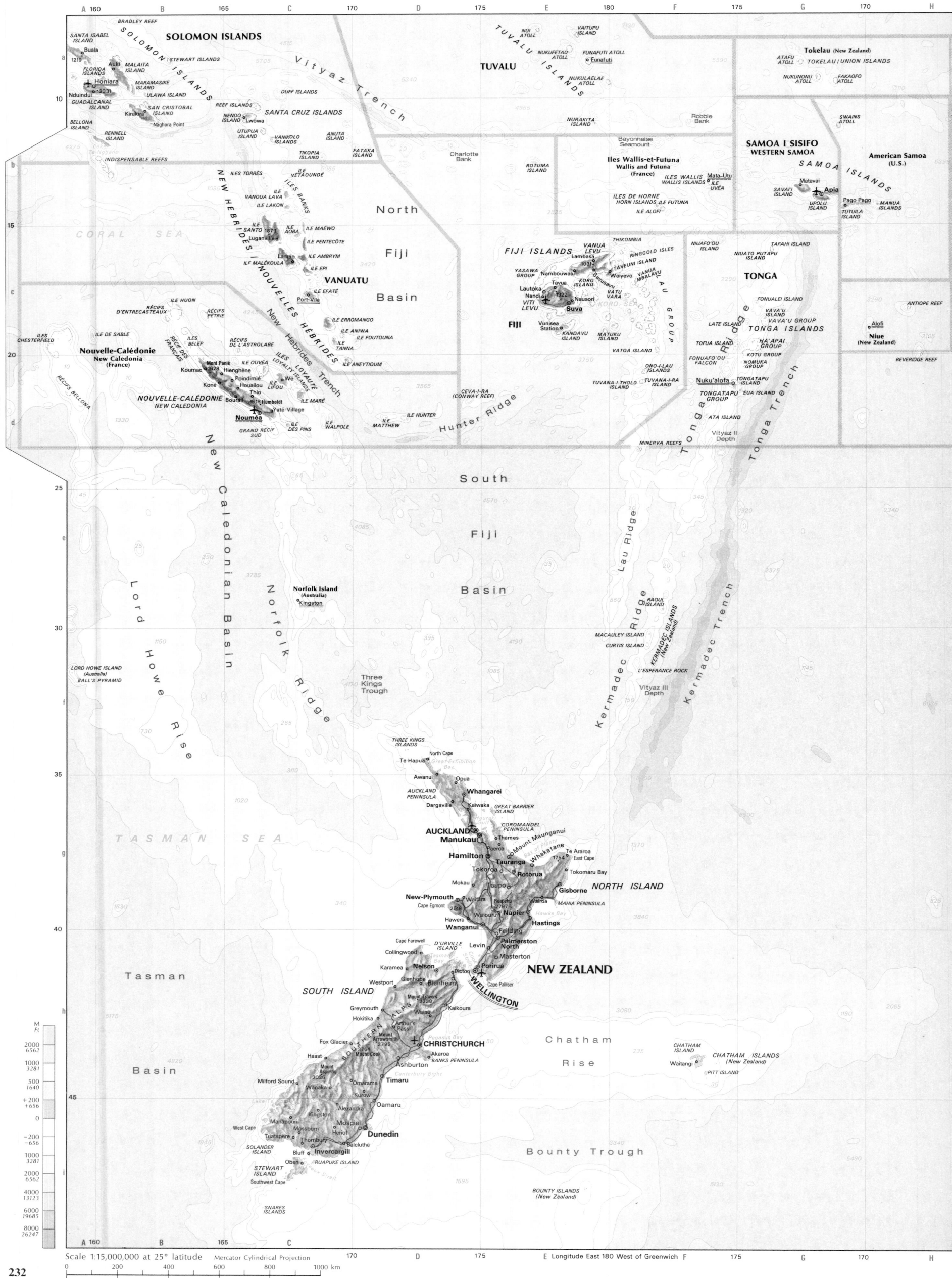

Scale 1:15,000,000 at 25° latitude   Mercator Cylindrical Projection

Longitude East 180 West of Greenwich

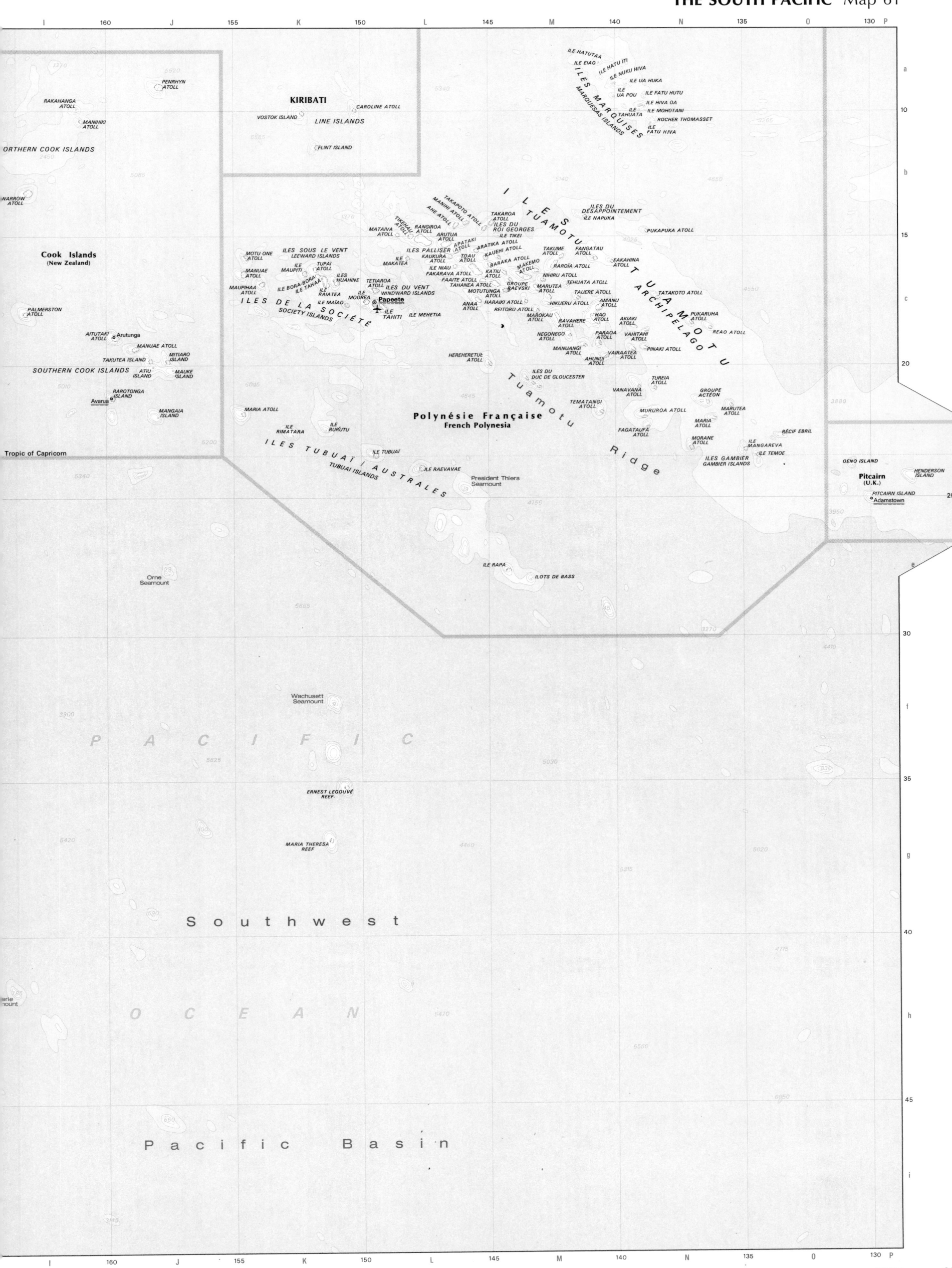

KIRIBATI

Caroline Atoll

Vostok Island

LINE ISLANDS

Flint Island

ILE HATUTAA
ILE EIAO
ILE HATU ITI
ILE NUKU HIVA
ILE UA HUKA
ILE UA POU
ILE FATU HUTU
ILE HIVA OA
ILE MOHOTANI
ROCHER THOMASSET
ILE TAHUATA
ILE FATU HIVA

ILES MARQUISES
MARQUESAS ISLANDS

RAKAHANGA ATOLL

PENRHYN ATOLL

MANIHIKI ATOLL

ORTHERN COOK ISLANDS

NARROW ATOLL

Cook Islands
(New Zealand)

PALMERSTON ATOLL

AITUTAKI ATOLL — Arutunga

MANUAE ATOLL

TAKUTEA ISLAND

MITIARO ISLAND

ATIU ISLAND

MAUKE ISLAND

SOUTHERN COOK ISLANDS

RAROTONGA ISLAND

Avarua

MANGAIA ISLAND

Tropic of Capricorn

TAKAPOTO ATOLL
MANIHI ATOLL
ANE ATOLL
TAKAROA ATOLL

I L E S   T U A M O T U

ILES DU ROI GEORGES
ILES DU DESAPPOINTEMENT
ILE NAPUKA

PUKAPUKA ATOLL

MATAIVA ATOLL
TIKEHAU ATOLL
RANGIROA ATOLL
ARUTUA ATOLL
ILE TIKEI

MOTU ONE ATOLL

ILES SOUS LE VENT
LEEWARD ISLANDS

APATAKI ATOLL
ARATIKA ATOLL
KAUEHI ATOLL
TAKUME ATOLL
FANGATAU ATOLL

MANUAE ATOLL

ILE MAUPITI

ILE TUPAI

ILE MAKATEA

KAUKURA ATOLL
TOAU ATOLL
BARAKA ATOLL
MAKEMO ATOLL
RAROÏA ATOLL
FAKAHINA ATOLL

MAUPIHAA ATOLL

ILE BORA-BORA
ILE TAHAA

ILES HUAHINE

ILE NIAU
FAKARAVA ATOLL
KATIU ATOLL
MARUTEA ATOLL
TEHUATA ATOLL

U A M O T U

TATAKOTO ATOLL

ILE RAIATEA

TETIAROA ATOLL

ILES DU VENT
WINDWARD ISLANDS

FAAITE ATOLL
TAHANEA ATOLL
MOTUTUNGA ATOLL

GROUPE RAEVSKI
NIHIRU ATOLL
TAUERE ATOLL
HIKUERU ATOLL
AMANU ATOLL

A R C H I P E L A G O

PUKARUHA ATOLL

ILE MOOREA

Papeete

ANAA ATOLL
HARAIKI ATOLL
REITORU ATOLL
MAROKAU ATOLL
HAO ATOLL
AKIAKI ATOLL

REAO ATOLL

ILES DE LA SOCIÉTÉ
SOCIETY ISLANDS

ILE TAHITI

ILE MEHETIA

RAVAHERE ATOLL

VAHITAHI ATOLL

NEGONEGO ATOLL
PARAOA ATOLL
PINAKI ATOLL

HEREHERETUE ATOLL

MANUANGI ATOLL

VAIRAATEA ATOLL

AHUNUI ATOLL

ILES DU DUC DE GLOUCESTER

TUREIA ATOLL

Tuamotu Ridge

VANAVANA ATOLL

GROUPE ACTÉON

MARIA ATOLL

TEMATANGI ATOLL

MURUROA ATOLL

MARUTEA ATOLL

Polynésie Française
French Polynesia

ILE RIMATARA

ILE RURUTU

FAGATAUFA ATOLL

MARIA ATOLL

RÉCIF EBRIL

MORANE ATOLL

ILE MANGAREVA

ILES GAMBIER
GAMBIER ISLANDS

ILE TEMOE

ILES TUBUAÏ AUSTRALES
TUBUAI ISLANDS

ILE TUBUAÏ

ILE RAEVAVAE

President Thiers
Seamount

OENO ISLAND

Pitcairn
(U.K.)

PITCAIRN ISLAND
Adamstown

HENDERSON ISLAND

Orne
Seamount

ILE RAPA

ILOTS DE BASS

P   A   C   I   F   I   C

Wachusett
Seamount

S o u t h w e s t

ERNEST LEGOUVÉ
REEF

O   C   E   A   N

MARIA THERESA
REEF

P a c i f i c   B a s i n

Map 62 **NEW ZEALAND**

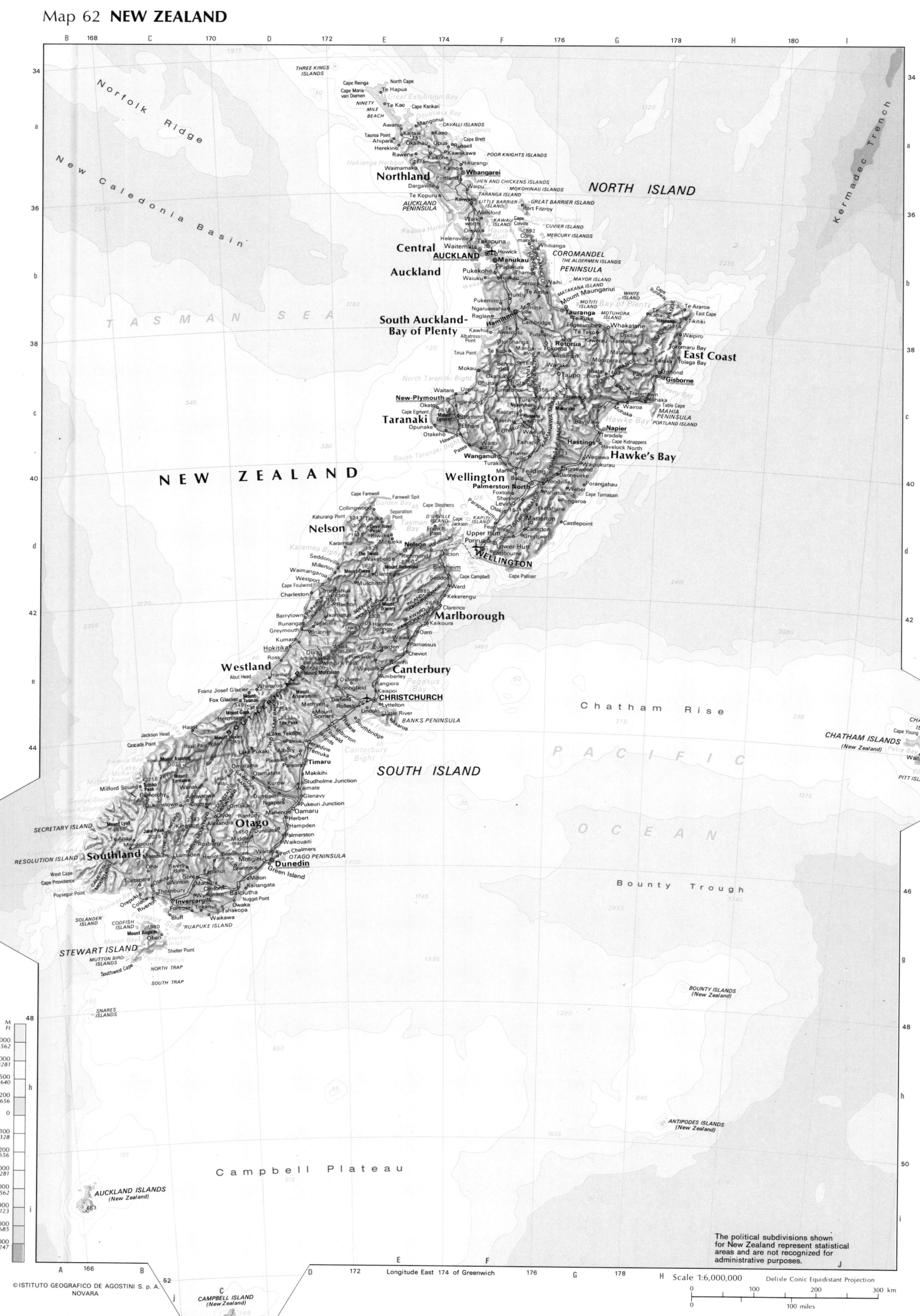

The political subdivisions shown
for New Zealand represent statistical
areas and are not recognized for
administrative purposes.

Longitude East 174 of Greenwich

Scale 1:6,000,000   Delisle Conic Equidistant Projection

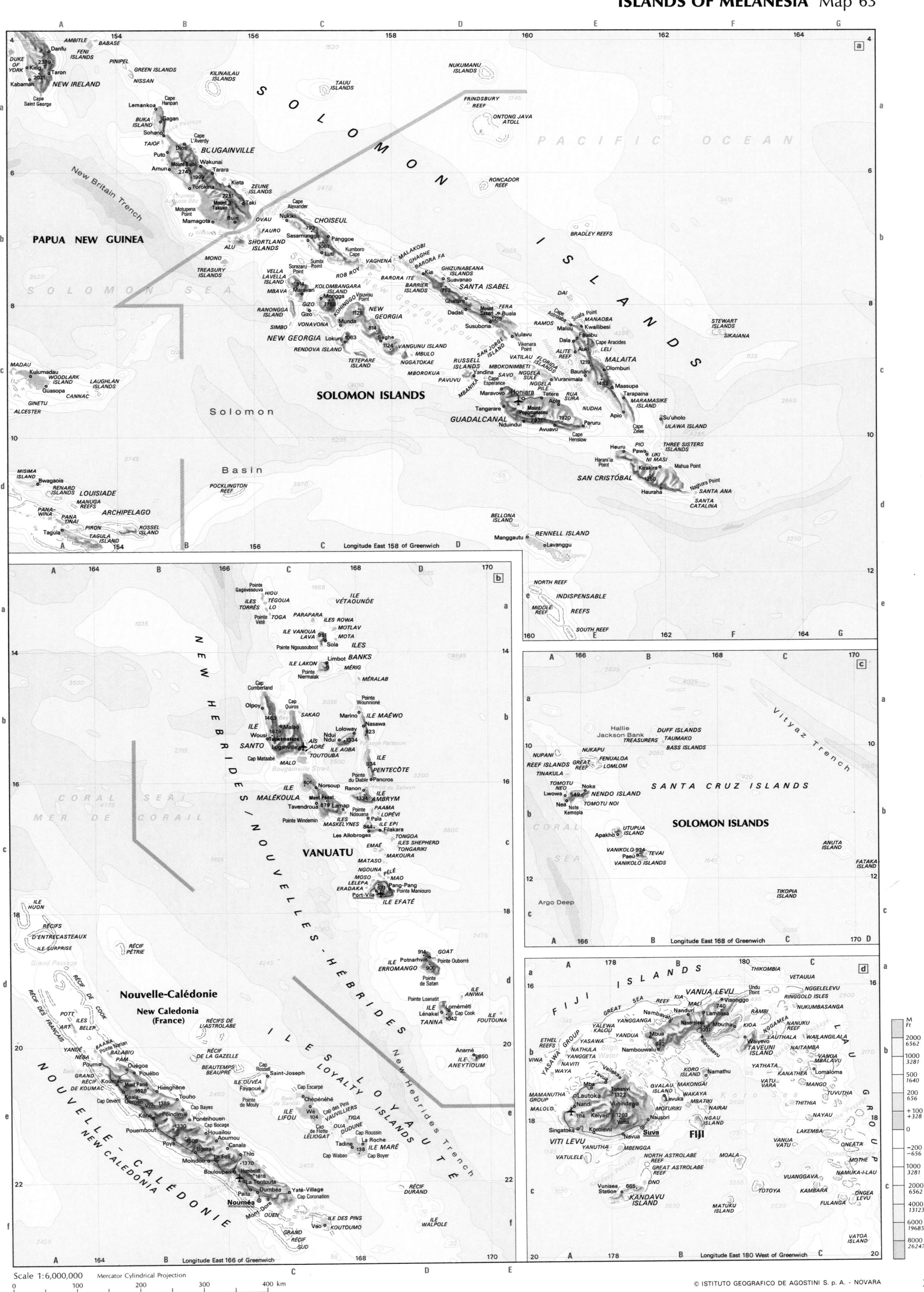

Scale 1:6,000,000   Mercator Cylindrical Projection

Map 64 **ISLANDS OF MICRONESIA-POLYNESIA**

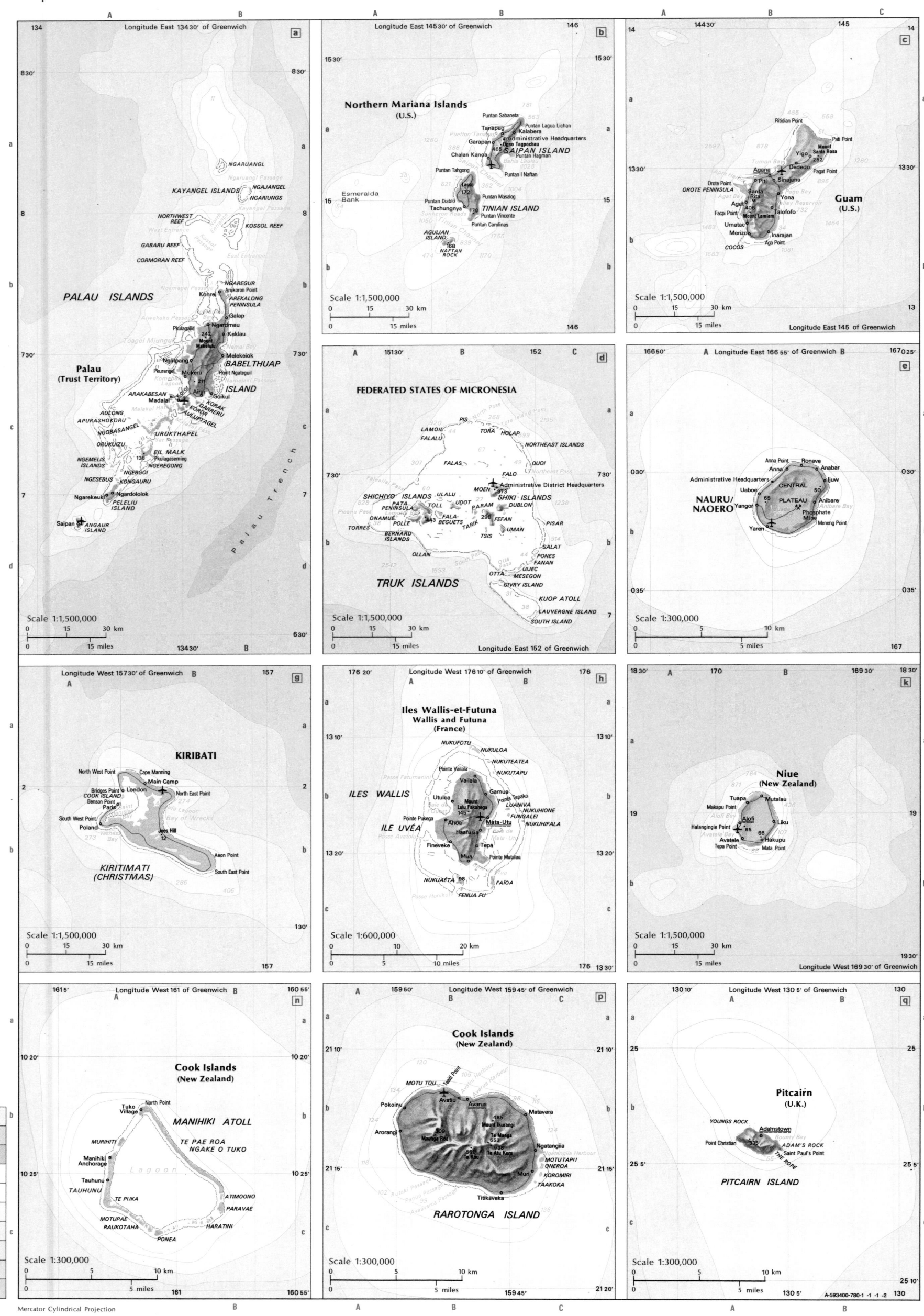

Mercator Cylindrical Projection

© ISTITUTO GEOGRAFICO DE AGOSTINI S. p. A. - NOVARA

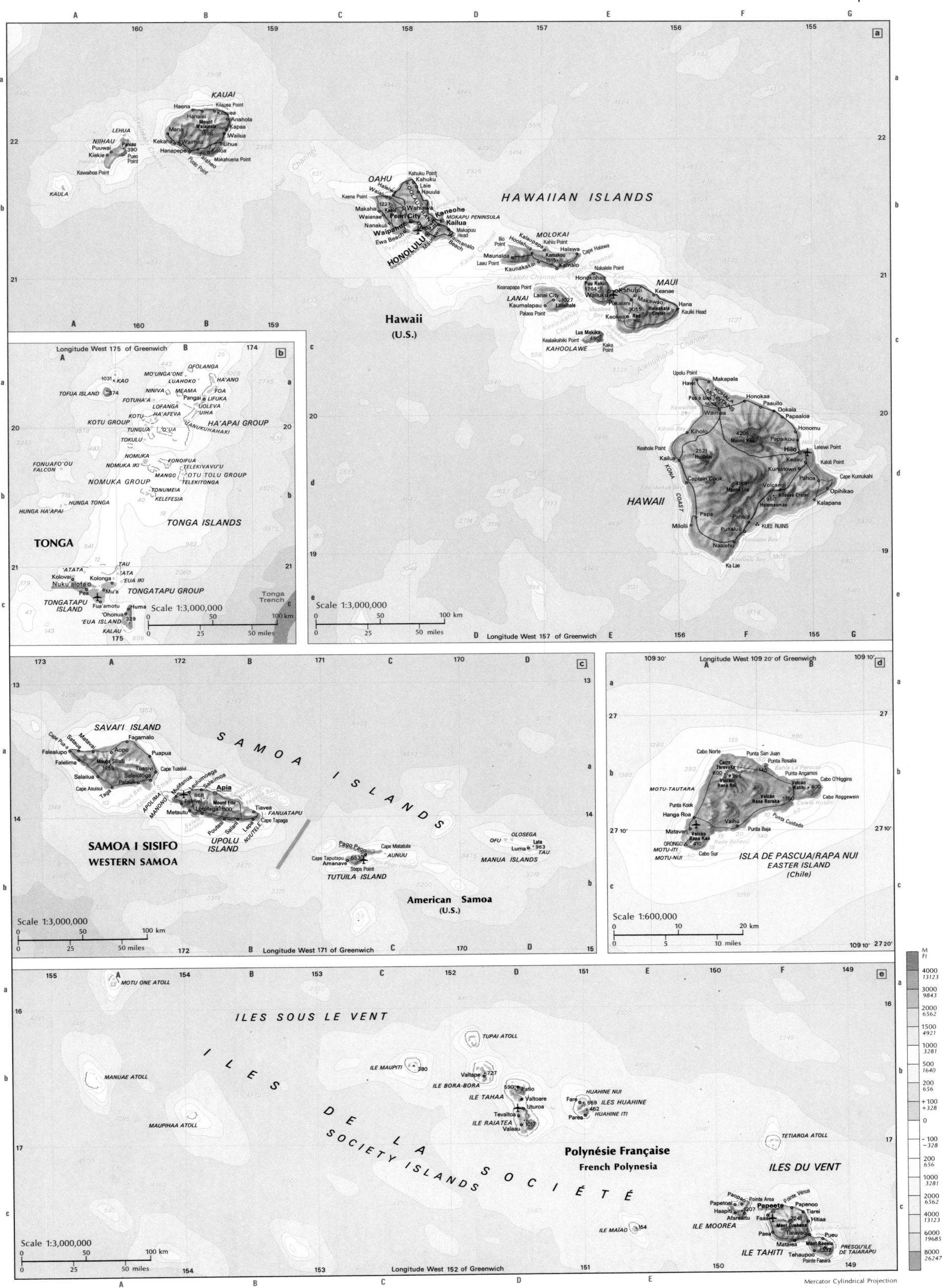

Map 66 **ANTARCTIC REGION**

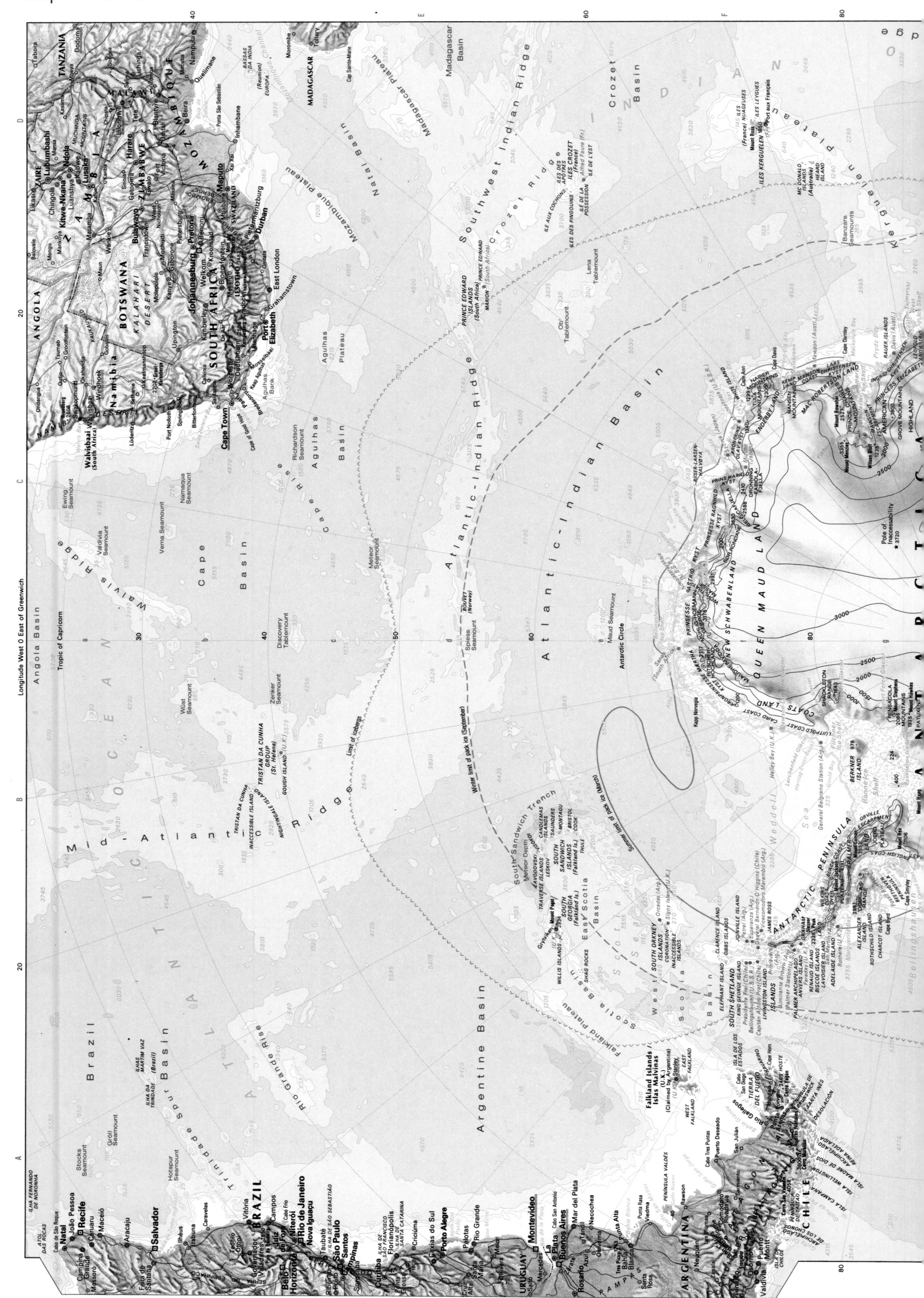

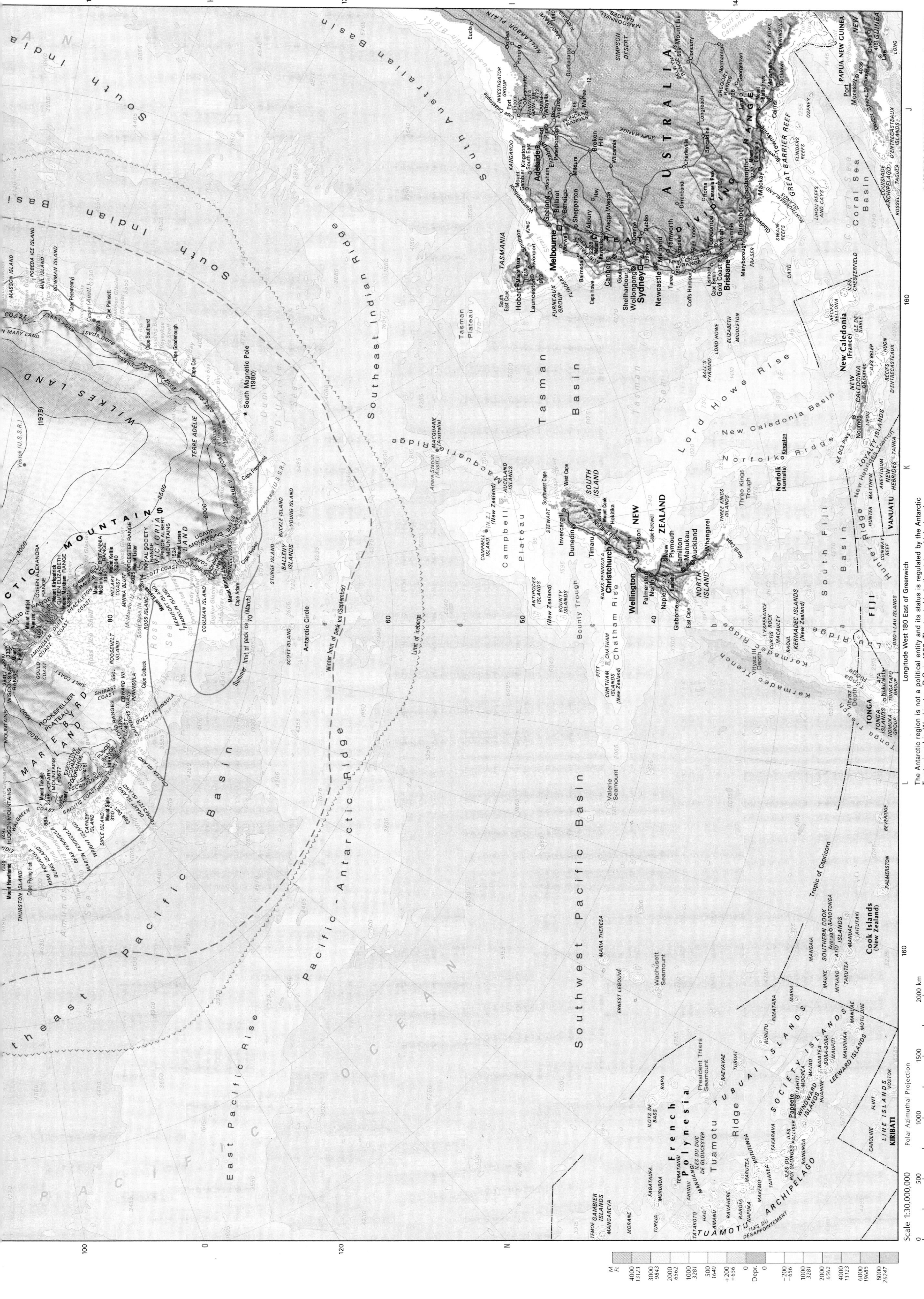

The Antarctic region is not a political entity and its status is regulated by the Antarctic Treaty signed in Washington, D.C. in 1959. The treaty binds the states which signed the agreement to use the region solely for peaceful purposes and scientific research.
Longitude West 180 East of Greenwich
Scale 1:30,000,000
Polar Azimuthal Projection
© ISTITUTO GEOGRAFICO DE AGOSTINI S. p. A. - NOVARA
AUSTRALIA
NEW ZEALAND
TASMANIA
NORTH ISLAND
SOUTH ISLAND
Tasman Basin
Southeast Indian Ridge
South Australian Basin
Southwest Pacific Basin
Pacific - Antarctic Ridge
East Pacific Rise
PACIFIC OCEAN
French Polynesia
Tuamotu Ridge
Lord Howe Rise
New Caledonia Basin
Norfolk Ridge
Campbell Plateau
Chatham Rise
Bounty Trough
Kermadec Trench
Tonga Trench
South Fiji Basin
Coral Sea Basin
Antarctic Circle
Limit of icebergs
Winter limit of pack ice (September)
Summer limit of pack ice (March)
WILKES LAND
MARIE BYRD LAND
TERRE ADÉLIE
South Magnetic Pole (1980)
Ross Sea
Melbourne
Sydney
Canberra
Brisbane
Adelaide
Hobart
Wellington
Auckland
Christchurch
Dunedin
Nouméa
Cook Islands (New Zealand)
TONGA
FIJI
VANUATU
KIRIBATI
Tropic of Capricorn

Map 67 **ARCTIC REGION**

PACIFIC OCEAN

Suiko Seamount
Papanin Seamount

Aleutian Trench
ALEUTIAN ISLANDS
ATKA ANDREANOF ISLANDS
RAT ISLANDS
NEAR ISLANDS
FOX ISLANDS
Bowers Bank
Bowers Ridge
Obruchev Rise
Kuril Trench
JAPAN
Aomori Hakodate
HONSHŪ
HOKKAIDO Asahikawa Sapporo
SIMUŠIR URUP ITURUP
KUNAŠIR
KURIL ISLANDS
ONEKOTAN PARAMUŠIR
mys Lopatka
Petropavlovsk-Kamčatski
Južno-Sahalinsk Holmsk
Wakkanai
SAKHALIN
Sovetskaja Gavan
Vladivostok
SIHOTE-ALIN
Habarovsk
Komsomolsk-na-Amure Birobidžan
Nikolajevsk-na-Amure
SHANTAR ISLANDS
Magadan
Ust-Kamčatsk
KAMCHATKA PENINSULA
Komandorskiye
KOMANDORSKI ISLANDS
Shirshov Ridge
Bering Sea
PRIBILOF ISLANDS
KORYAK RANGE
SREDINNY RANGE
KOLYMA RANGE
Anadyr
ANADYR RANGE
SAINT MATTHEW
NUNIVAK
Cape Romanzof
SAINT LAWRENCE
CHUKCHI PENINSULA
Uelen
SEWARD PENINSULA
Nome
Kotzebue
Point Hope
Barrow
Point Barrow
Prudhoe Bay
Pevek
WRANGEL
BEAR ISLANDS
KOLYMA PLAIN
ČERSKI RANGE
VERKHOYANSK RANGE
STANOVOY
Jakutsk
SIBERIA
CHINA
ALASKA PENINSULA
Patton Seamount
KODIAK
KENAI PENINSULA
Seward Kenai
Anchorage
Valdez Cordova
Homer
SAINT ELIAS MOUNTAINS
McKinley
Fairbanks
Old Crow
Fort Yukon
BROOKS RANGE
Alaska (U.S.)
ALASKA RANGE
YUKON PLATEAU
Dawson
Whitehorse
Skagway
Juneau
Sitka
Ketchikan
Prince Rupert
Wrangell
ALEXANDER ARCHIPELAGO
QUEEN CHARLOTTE ISLANDS
VANCOUVER ISLAND
Victoria Vancouver
Seattle
COAST MOUNTAINS
Prince George
CASSIAR MOUNTAINS
COLUMBIA MOUNTAINS
ROCKY MOUNTAINS
Jasper
Calgary
Edmonton
Grande Prairie
Peace River
Fort St John
Fort Nelson
Fort Liard
Watson Lake
Keele Peak
MACKENZIE MOUNTAINS
SELWYN MOUNTAINS
Norman Wells
Fort Good Hope
Inuvik
Tuktoyaktuk
Cape Bathurst
RICHARDSON MOUNTAINS
Fort McPherson
Fort Franklin
Fort Norman
Fort Simpson
Fort Providence
Yellowknife
Hay River
Fort Smith
CARIBOU MOUNTAINS
Fort McMurray
North Battleford
Uranium City
Flin Flon
Lynn Lake
CANADA
Reliance
Coppermine
Paulatuk
WOLLASTON PENINSULA
Cambridge Bay
VICTORIA
BANKS
PRINCE PATRICK
MELVILLE
MACKENZIE KING
QUEEN ELIZABETH ISLANDS
ELLEF RINGNES ISLAND
AXEL HEIBERG
North Magnetic Pole 1980
ELLESMERE
Resolute
Eskimo Point
Bathurst Inlet
KING WILLIAM
BOOTHIA PENINSULA
SOMERSET
PRINCE OF WALES
Spence Bay
Pelly Bay
Repulse Bay
Chesterfield Inlet
Rankin Inlet
BRODEUR PENINSULA
DEVON
Grise Fiord
Barbeau Peak 2604
Cape Columbia
Alert
PEARY LAND
Kap Morris Jesup
KNUD RASMUSSEN LAND
HAYES HALVØ
Kap York
Thule/Qânâq
Clyde
Pond Inlet
BYLOT
Igloolik
Arctic Bay
BORDEN PENINSULA
BAFFIN
CUMBERLAND PENINSULA
Broughton Island
Cape Dyer
PRINCE CHARLES
FOXE PENINSULA
Cape Dorset
MELVILLE PENINSULA
SOUTHAMPTON
MANSEL
COATS
OTTAWA ISLANDS
BELCHER ISLANDS
Churchill
Fort Severn
Winisk
Inukjuak
Povungnituk
Chisasibi
HUDSON BAY
PÉNINSULE D'UNGAVA
Kangirsuk
Kuujjuaq
Kangiqsualujjuaq
TORNGAT MOUNTAINS
Nain
LABRADOR
Happy Valley Goose Bay
Schefferville
Labrador City
LAURENTIAN PLATEAU
Battle Harbour
Corner Brook
Grand Falls
Saint John's
NEWFOUNDLAND
Cape Race

ARCTIC OCEAN
Canada Basin
Chukchi Plateau
Makarov Basin
Lomonosov Ridge
Eurasia Basin
Alpha Cordillera
North Pole
Beta Cordillera
Nansen Basin
Fram Basin
Amundsen Basin
NEW SIBERIA
GREAT LYAKHOV
ANJOU ISLANDS
LITTLE LYAKHOV
NEW SIBERIAN ISLANDS
KOTELNY
BELKOVSKI
East Siberian Sea
Laptev Sea
Tiksi
DE LONG ISLANDS
SEVERNAYA ZEMLYA
BOLSHEVIK ISLAND
KOMSOMOLEC
OCTOBER REVOLUTION ISLAND
PIONER
SMIDTA
Voronin Trough
NORTH SIBERIAN PLAIN
TAYMYR PENINSULA
BYRRANGA MTS
CENTRAL SIBERIAN UPLANDS
PUTORANA
Norilsk
Dudinka
Turuhansk
UNION OF SOVIET SOCIALIST REPUBLICS
WEST SIBERIAN PLAIN
Krasnojarsk
GYDA PENINSULA
YAMAL PENINSULA
Nadym
Salehard
Labytnangi
Vorkuta
NOVAYA ZEMLYA
Kara Sea
FRANZ JOSEPH LAND
ZEMLJA ALEKSANDRY
ZEMLJA GEORGA
KVITØYA
NORDAUSTLANDET
SPITSBERGEN
Barentsburg
Longyearbyen
EDGEØYA
Svalbard (Norway)
BEAR ISLAND (Norway)
Greenland
Greenland Sea
Summer limit of pack ice (August)
Winter limit of pack ice (April)
KOLGUJEV
KANIN PENINSULA
Barents Sea
Barents Trough
KOLA PENINSULA
Murmansk
Arhangelsk
Hammerfest
Tromsø
Narvik
North Cape
LAPLAND
KARELIA
NORWAY
SWEDEN
FINLAND
VESTERÅLEN
LOFOTEN
Bodø
Luleå
Kemi
Oulu
Vaasa
Helsinki
Leningrad
Novgorod
Vologda
Gorki
Kirov
Perm
Sverdlovsk
URAL MOUNTAINS
TIMAN RIDGE
Syktyvkar
Narjan-Mar
Kotlas
Naryan-Mar
Sergino
Hanty-Mansijsk
Nižnevartovsk
Novosibirsk
Tomsk
SIBERIA
Tjumen
Kurgan
Celjabinsk
Ufa
Kazan
Togliatti
Kujbyšev
Uljanovsk
Penza
Saratov
Volgograd
Rostov-na-Donu
CAUCASUS
Novorossijsk
Trondheim
Ålesund
Bergen
Oslo
Stavanger
Kristiansand
Göteborg
Stockholm
Uppsala
Örebro
Norrköping
GOTLAND
ÅLAND ISLANDS
Turku
Tallinn
Pskov
Riga
Kaunas
Vilnius
Minsk
Gomel
Kiev
Vitebsk
Smolensk
Moskva
Vladimir
Rjazan
Tula
Orel
Voronež
Kalinin
Jaroslavl
SHETLAND ISLANDS
ORKNEY ISLANDS
HEBRIDES
BRITISH ISLES
Aberdeen
Glasgow
Edinburgh
Belfast
IRELAND
Dublin
Wexford
Cork
UNITED KINGDOM
Liverpool
Manchester
Birmingham
Bristol
London
Plymouth
NETHERLANDS
Amsterdam
Rotterdam
BELGIUM
Bruxelles
LUXEMBOURG
Le Havre
Paris
Brest
Nantes
FRANCE
Dijon
Lyon
Bordeaux
MASSIF CENTRAL
Bern
Zürich
Genève
SWITZERLAND
Milano
Torino
Genova
ITALY
Firenze
Venezia
Trieste
DENMARK
København
Malmö
BORNHOLM
Kiel
Hamburg
Hannover
Berlin
Bonn
F.R.G.
G.D.R.
Leipzig
Frankfurt
Nürnberg
München
Praha
CZECHOSLOVAKIA
Ostrava
Wien
AUSTRIA
Graz
Zagreb
YUGOSLAVIA
Beograd
Sarajevo
Split
Gdańsk
Warszawa
Poznań
Katowice
POLAND
Brest
Žitomir
Vinnica
Odessa
Nikolajev
Sevastopol
CRIMEA
HUNGARY
Budapest
Timişoara
ROMANIA
Cluj-Napoca
Bucureşti
Constanţa
BULGARIA
Sofija
Varna
ALBANIA
Tirana
GREECE
Thessaloníki
TURKEY
Istanbul
Ankara
ANATOLIAN PLATEAU
Izmir
Eskişehir
CYPRUS
Lefkosia / Lefkoşa
Kaunas
Kaliningrad
Hárkov
Dnepropetrovsk
UKRAINE
Kišinev

ATLANTIC OCEAN
Mid-Atlantic Ridge
Reykjanes Ridge
ICELAND
Reykjavik
Hvannadalshnúkur
Denmark Strait
Kap Farvel / Umánarsuaq
KING FREDERIK VI COAST
Julianehåb / Qaqortoq
Angmagssalik
Mont Forel 3700
Gunnbjørns Field
KING CHRISTIAN IX LAND
KING CHRISTIAN X LAND
KING FREDERIK VIII LAND
Scoresbysund
Kap Brewster
JAN MAYEN (Norway)
Mohns Ridge
Greenland Basin
Danmarks Havn
Nordostrundingen
Belgica Bank
Newtontoppen
KING FREDERIK VIII LAND
Godthåb / Nûk
Holsteinsborg / Sisimiut
Søndre Strømfjord
Egedesminde / Ausiait
Jakobshavn / Ilulissat
Godhavn / Qeqertarsuaq
DISKO Ø
Greenland (Den.)
Ümanaq
Melville Bugt
Reykjanes Ridge
Labrador Basin
Labrador Sea
Newfoundland Basin
Rockall Rise
Porcupine Bank
Iceland Basin
Faroe Bank
SHETLAND ISLANDS
Rockall
West European Basin
AZORES (Port.)
Mid-Atlantic Ridge
Arctic Circle
Limit of icebergs
Horn
Rifstangi
Norwegian Sea
Norwegian Basin
Jan Mayen Ridge

Longitude West 0 East of Greenwich

Scale 1:30,000,000
Polar Azimuthal Projection
0   500   1000   1500   2000 km
0   500   1000 miles
240
© ISTITUTO GEOGRAFICO DE AGOSTINI S.p.A. - NOVARA

UNITED STATES AND CANADA MAP SECTION

MAP LEGEND

CULTURAL FEATURES

Political Boundaries

International

Secondary (State)

County

Populated Places

Cities, towns, and villages

 Symbol size represents population of the place

Chicago
Gary
Racine
Glenview
Edgewood

Type size represents relative importance of the place

 **Major Urban Areas**
Area of continuous commercial, industrial, and residential development in and around a major city

○ Community within a city

⊛ Capital of major political unit

✪ Capital of U.S. state

○ County Seat

▲ Military Installation

Transportation

Major Highway

Railroad

Tunnel

Miscellaneous

 National Park

National Monument

Indian Reservation

△ Point of Interest

Dam

Bridge

 Pier

LAND FEATURES

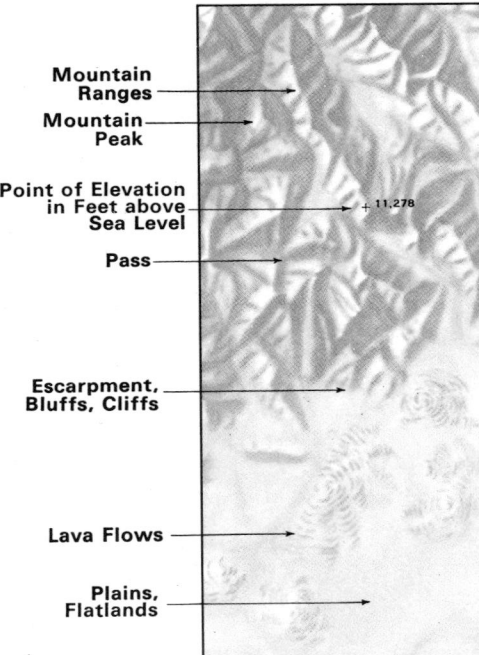

Mountain Ranges

Mountain Peak

Point of Elevation in Feet above Sea Level — 11,278

Pass

Escarpment, Bluffs, Cliffs

Lava Flows

Plains, Flatlands

WATER FEATURES

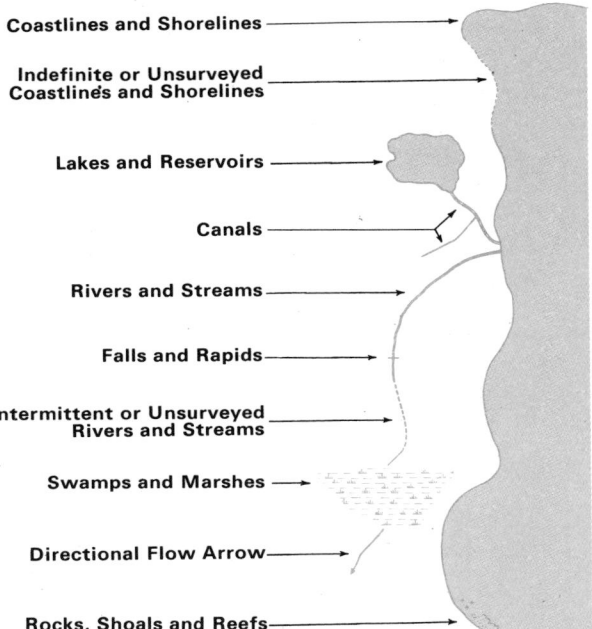

Coastlines and Shorelines

Indefinite or Unsurveyed Coastlines and Shorelines

Lakes and Reservoirs

Canals

Rivers and Streams

Falls and Rapids

Intermittent or Unsurveyed Rivers and Streams

Swamps and Marshes

Directional Flow Arrow

Rocks, Shoals and Reefs

TYPE STYLES USED TO NAME FEATURES

Note: Size of type varies according to importance and available space. Letters for names of major features are spread across the extent of the feature.

CANADA	Country, State, or Province	*U I N T A* / *DESERT*	Major Terrain Features
Naval Air Station	Military Installation	MT. MORIAH	Individual Mountain
CROCKETT	County	*MESA VERDE* / *SAN XAVIER*	National Park or Monument, Indian Res.
		NUNIVAK	Island or Coastal Feature
		Ocean / *Lake* / *River* / *Canal*	Hydrographic Features

Lambert Conformal Conic Projection
SCALE 1:12,000,000   1 Inch = 189 Statute Miles

ALABAMA

Statute Miles

Kilometers

A-520501-71   7-10-12
COSMO SERIES ALABAMA
Copyright by
RAND McNALLY & COMPANY
Made in U.S.A.

Lambert Conformal Conic Projection
SCALE 1:1,831,000 1 Inch = 29 Statute Miles

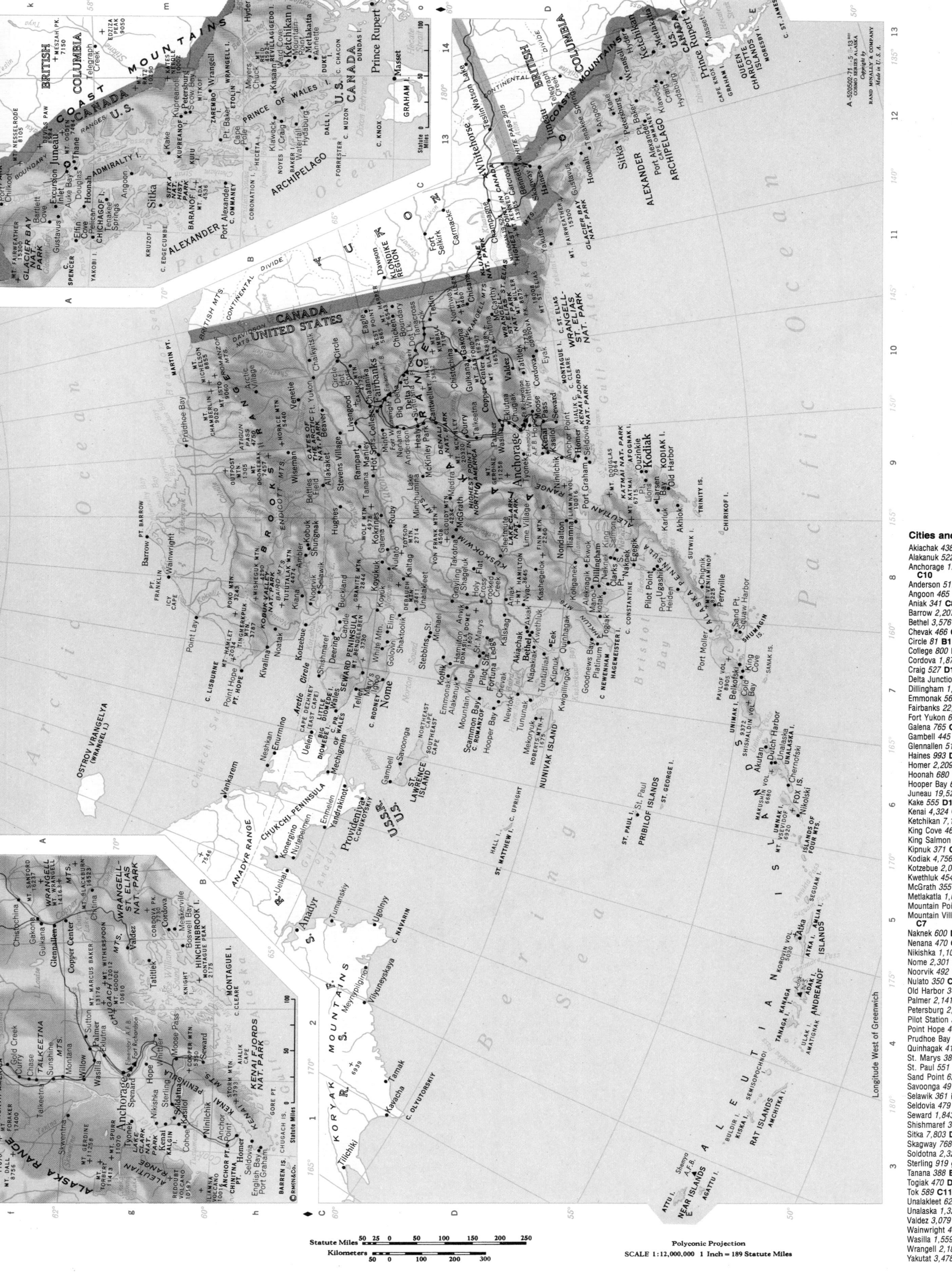

Polyconic Projection
SCALE 1:12,000,000 1 Inch = 189 Statute Miles

Statute Miles 50 25 0 50 100 150 200 250
Kilometers 50 0 100 200 300

Cities and Towns

Ajo 5,189 **E3**
Apache Junction 9,935 **m9**
Avondale 8,168 **D3**
Bagdad 2,331 **C2**
Benson 4,190 **F5**
Bisbee 7,154 **F6**
Buckeye 3,434 **D3**
Bullhead City 5,000 **B1**
Casa Grande 14,971 **E4**
Casas Adobes 5,300 **E5**
Chandler 29,673 **D4**
Chinle 2,815 **A6**
Chino Valley 2,858 **C3**
Claypool 2,362 **D5**
Clifton 4,245 **D6**
Coolidge 6,851 **E4**
Cottonwood 4,550 **C3**
Douglas 13,058 **F6**
Eagar 2,791 **C6**
Eloy 6,240 **E4**
Flagstaff 34,743 **B4**
Florence 3,391 **D4**
Fort Defiance 3,431 **B6**
Gila Bend 1,585 **E3**
Gilbert 5,717 **D4**
Glendale 97,172 **D3**
Globe 6,886 **D5**
Green Valley 7,999 **F5**
Holbrook 5,785 **C5**
Kayenta 3,343 **A5**
Kearny 2,646 **D5**
Kingman 9,257 **B1**
Lake Havasu City 15,909 **C1**
Mammoth 1,906 **E5**
Mesa 152,453 **D4**
Miami 2,716 **D5**
Nogales 15,683 **F5**
Oracle 2,484 **E5**
Page 4,907 **A4**
Paradise Valley 11,085 **k9**
Parker 2,542 **C1**
Payson 5,068 **C4**
Peoria 12,307 **D3**
Phoenix 789,704 **D3**
Prescott 20,055 **C3**
Riviera 4,500 **B1**
Sacaton 1,951 **D4**
Safford 7,010 **E6**
St. Johns 3,368 **C6**
San Carlos 2,668 **D5**
San Luis 1,946 **E1**
San Manuel 5,443 **E5**
Scottsdale 88,622 **D4**
Sedona 5,368 **C4**
Sells 1,864 **F4**
Show Low 4,298 **C5**
Sierra Vista 24,937 **F5**
Snowflake 3,510 **C5**
Somerton 5,761 **E1**
South Tucson 6,554 **E5**
Sun City 40,505 **k8**
Superior 4,600 **D4**
Taylor 1,915 **C5**
Tempe 106,743 **D4**
Thatcher 3,374 **E6**
Tombstone 1,632 **F5**
Tuba City 5,041 **A4**
Tucson 330,537 **E5**
Wickenburg 3,535 **D3**
Willcox 3,243 **E6**
Williams 2,266 **B3**
Window Rock 2,230 **B6**
Winslow 7,921 **C5**
Yuma 42,481 **E1**

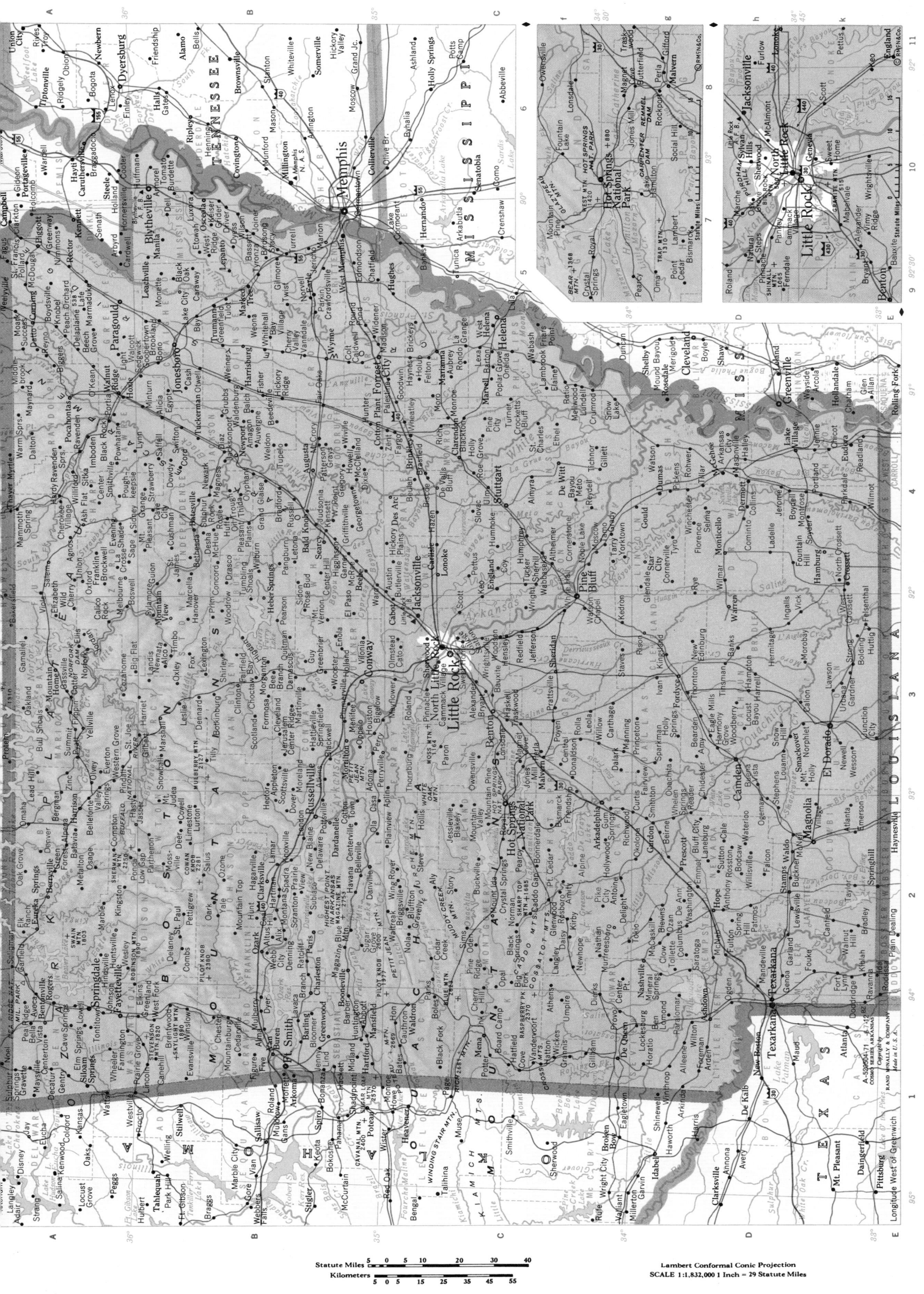

Statute Miles 5 0 5 10 20 30 40
Kilometers 5 0 5 15 25 35 45 55

Lambert Conformal Conic Projection
SCALE 1:1,832,000 1 Inch = 29 Statute Miles

CALIFORNIA

Statute Miles
Kilometers

Lambert Conformal Conic Projection
SCALE 1:2,186,000   1 Inch = 34.5 Statute Miles

CONNECTICUT

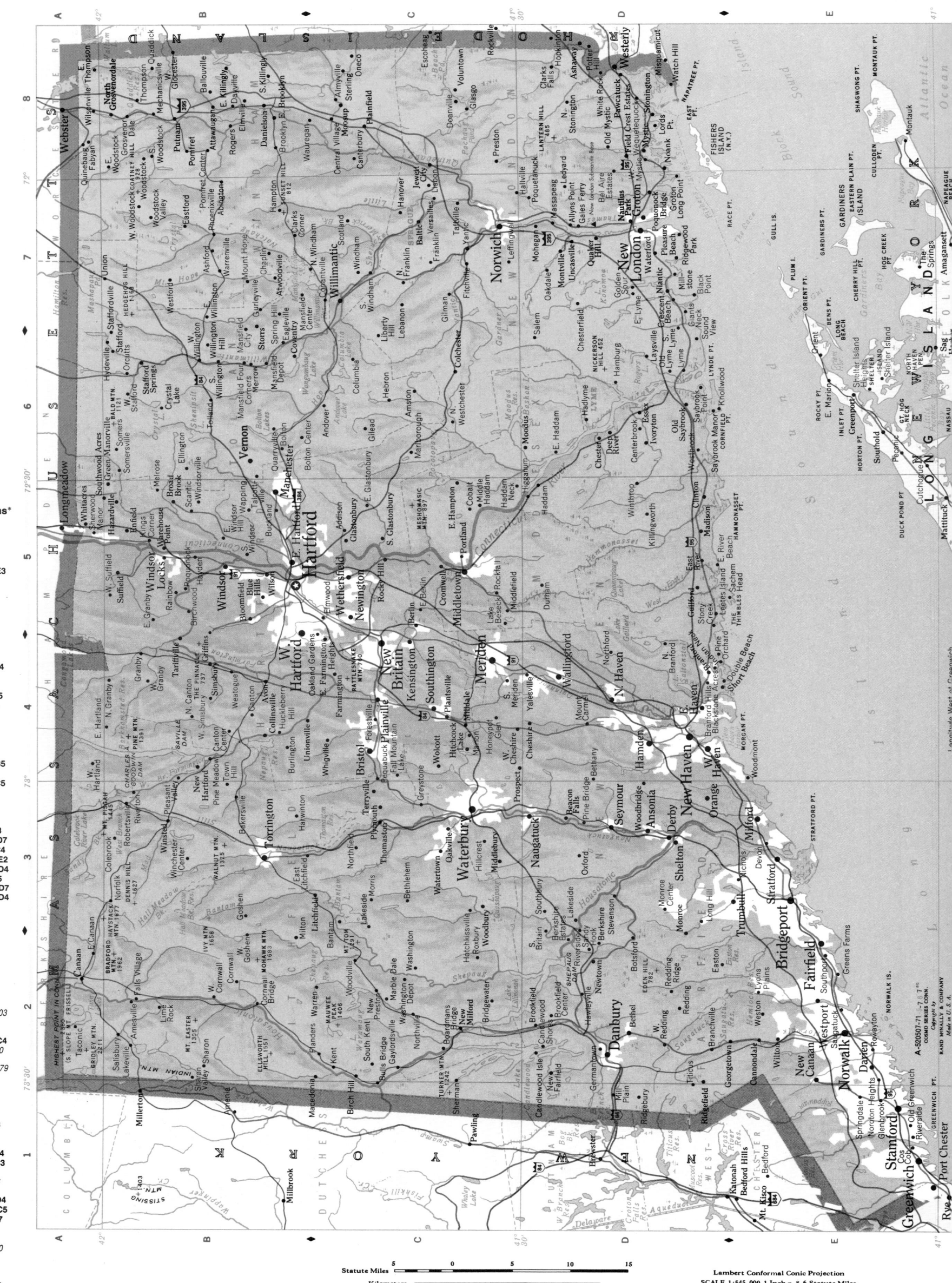

*Populations are for localities, not incorporated towns.

Statute Miles
Kilometers

Lambert Conformal Conic Projection
SCALE 1:545.000 1 Inch = 8.6 Statute Miles

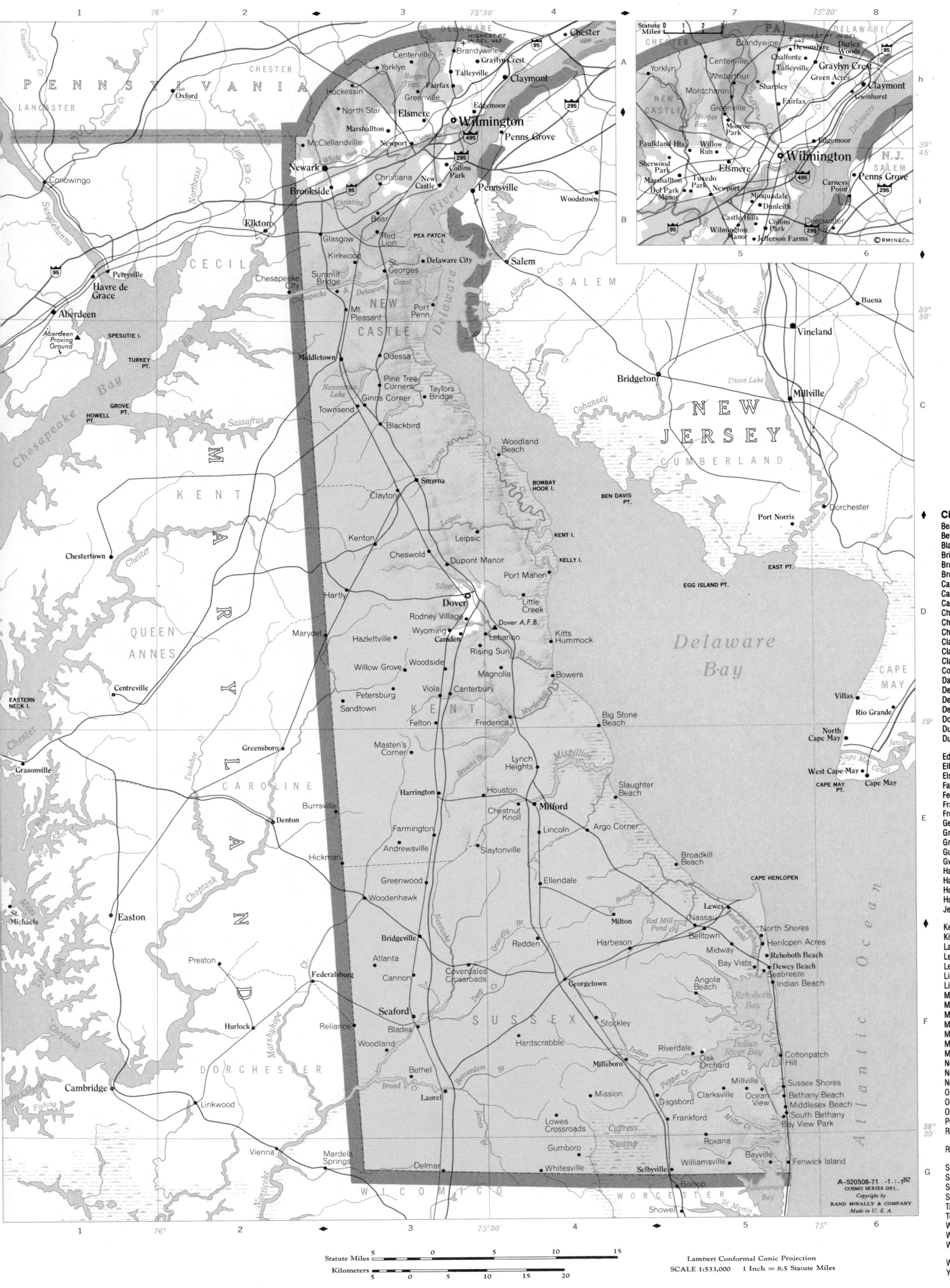

Lambert Conformal Conic Projection
SCALE 1:533,000   1 Inch = 8.5 Statute Miles

Statute Miles
Kilometers

Cities and Towns

Bear 950 **B3**
Bethany Beach 330 **F5**
Blades 664 **F3**
Bridgeville 1,238 **F3**
Broadkill Beach 200 **E5**
Brookside 15,255 **B3**
Camden 1,757 **D3**
Canterbury 500 **D3**
Castle Hills 1,950 **I7**
Chalfonte 2,200 **h7**
Cheswold 269 **D3**
Christiana 500 **B3**
Clarksville 450 **F5**
Claymont 10,022 **A4**
Clayton 1,216 **C3**
Collins Park 2,850 **B3**
Dagsboro 344 **F5**
Delaware City 1,858 **B3**
Delmar 948 **G3**
Dewey Beach 1,500 **F5**
Dover 23,507 **D3**
Dunleith 2,700 **I7**
Dupont Manor 1,059 **D3**
Edgemoor 7,397 **A3**
Ellendale 361 **E4**
Elsmere 6,493 **B3**
Fairfax 2,850 **A3**
Felton 547 **D3**
Frankford 828 **F5**
Frederica 864 **D4**
Georgetown 1,710 **F4**
Graylyn Crest 5,000 **A3**
Greenwood 578 **E3**
Gumboro 200 **G4**
Gwinhurst 1,400 **h8**
Harbeson 250 **F4**
Harrington 2,405 **E3**
Hockessin 950 **A3**
Houston 357 **E3**
Jefferson Farms 2,400 **I7**
Kenton 243 **D3**
Kirkwood 400 **B3**
Laurel 3,052 **F3**
Leipsic 228 **D3**
Lewes 2,197 **E5**
Lincoln 500 **E4**
Little Creek 230 **D4**
Marshallton 3,950 **B3**
Middletown 2,946 **C3**
Midway 500 **F5**
Milford 5,366 **E4**
Millsboro 1,233 **F4**
Milton 1,359 **E4**
Minquadale 1,700 **I7**
Newark 25,247 **B2**
New Castle 4,907 **B3**
Newport 1,167 **B3**
Oak Orchard 250 **F5**
Ocean View 495 **F5**
Odessa 384 **C3**
Port Penn 300 **B3**
Rehoboth Beach 1,730 **F5**
Rodney Village 1,100 **D3**
St. Georges 500 **B3**
Seaford 5,256 **F3**
Selbyville 1,251 **G5**
Smyrna 4,750 **C3**
Talleyville 6,880 **A3**
Townsend 386 **C3**
Willow Run 1,950 **I7**
Wilmington 70,195 **B3**
Wilmington Manor 2,000 **I7**
Wyoming 960 **D3**
Yorklyn 600 **A3**

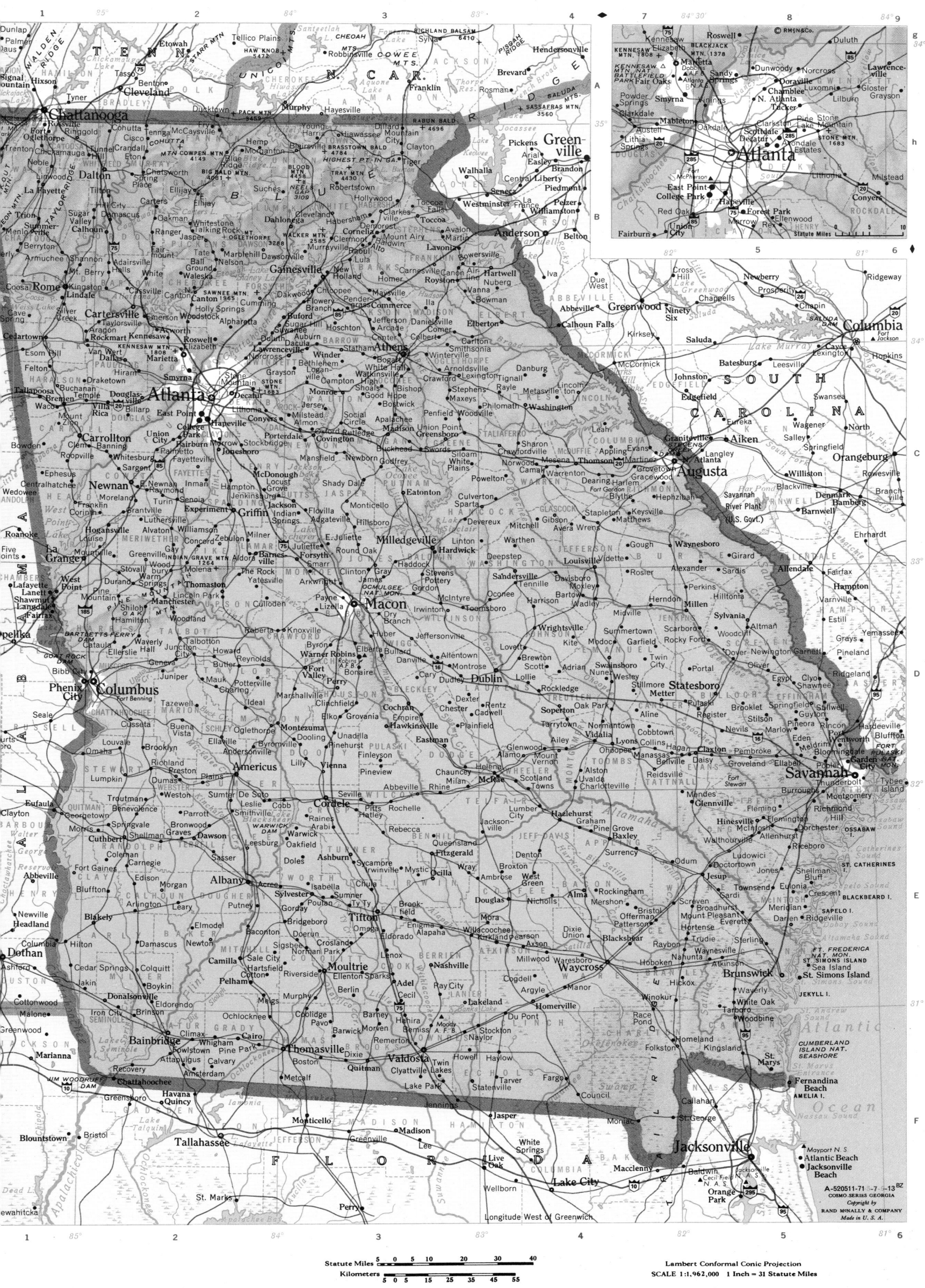

Cities and Towns

Adel 5,592 **E3**
Albany 74,550 **E2**
Americus 16,120 **E2**
Athens 42,549 **C3**
Atlanta 425,022 **C2**
Augusta 47,532 **C5**
Bainbridge 10,553 **F2**
Blakely 5,880 **E2**
Brunswick 17,605 **E5**
Buford 6,578 **B2**
Cairo 8,777 **F2**
Calhoun 5,563 **B2**
Camilla 5,414 **E2**
Carrollton 14,078 **C1**
Cartersville 9,247 **B2**
Cedartown 8,619 **B1**
Cochran 5,121 **D3**
College Park 24,632 **C2**
Columbus 169,441 **D2**
Cordele 10,733 **E3**
Covington 10,586 **C3**
Dalton 20,939 **B2**
Dawson 5,699 **E2**
Decatur 18,404 **C2**
Douglas 10,980 **E4**
Douglasville 7,641 **C2**
Dublin 16,083 **D4**
Eastman 5,330 **D3**
East Point 37,486 **C2**
Elberton 5,686 **B4**
Fitzgerald 10,187 **E3**
Forest Park 18,782 **h8**
Fort Oglethorpe 5,443 **B1**
Fort Valley 9,000 **D3**
Gainesville 15,280 **B3**
Griffin 20,728 **C2**
Hinesville 11,309 **E5**
Kennesaw 5,095 **B2**
La Fayette 6,517 **B1**
La Grange 24,204 **C1**
Lawrenceville 8,928 **C3**
Mableton 20,200 **h7**
Macon 116,896 **D3**
Marietta 30,829 **C2**
Martinez 16,472 **C4**
Milledgeville 12,176 **C3**
Monroe 8,854 **C3**
Moultrie 15,708 **E3**
Newnan 11,449 **C2**
North Atlanta 22,800 **h8**
Perry 9,453 **D3**
Quitman 5,188 **F3**
Rome 29,654 **B1**
Roswell 23,337 **B2**
St. Simons Island 6,566 **E5**
Sandersville 6,137 **D4**
Sandy Springs 20,300 **h8**
Savannah 141,390 **D5**
Smyrna 20,312 **C2**
Statesboro 14,866 **D5**
Stone Mountain 4,867 **C2**
Swainsboro 7,602 **D4**
Sylvester 5,860 **E3**
Thomaston 9,682 **D2**
Thomasville 18,463 **F3**
Thomson 7,001 **C4**
Tifton 13,749 **E3**
Toccoa 9,104 **B3**
Tucker 18,200 **h8**
Valdosta 37,596 **F3**
Vidalia 10,393 **D4**
Warner Robins 39,893 **D3**
Waycross 19,371 **E4**
Waynesboro 5,760 **C4**

253

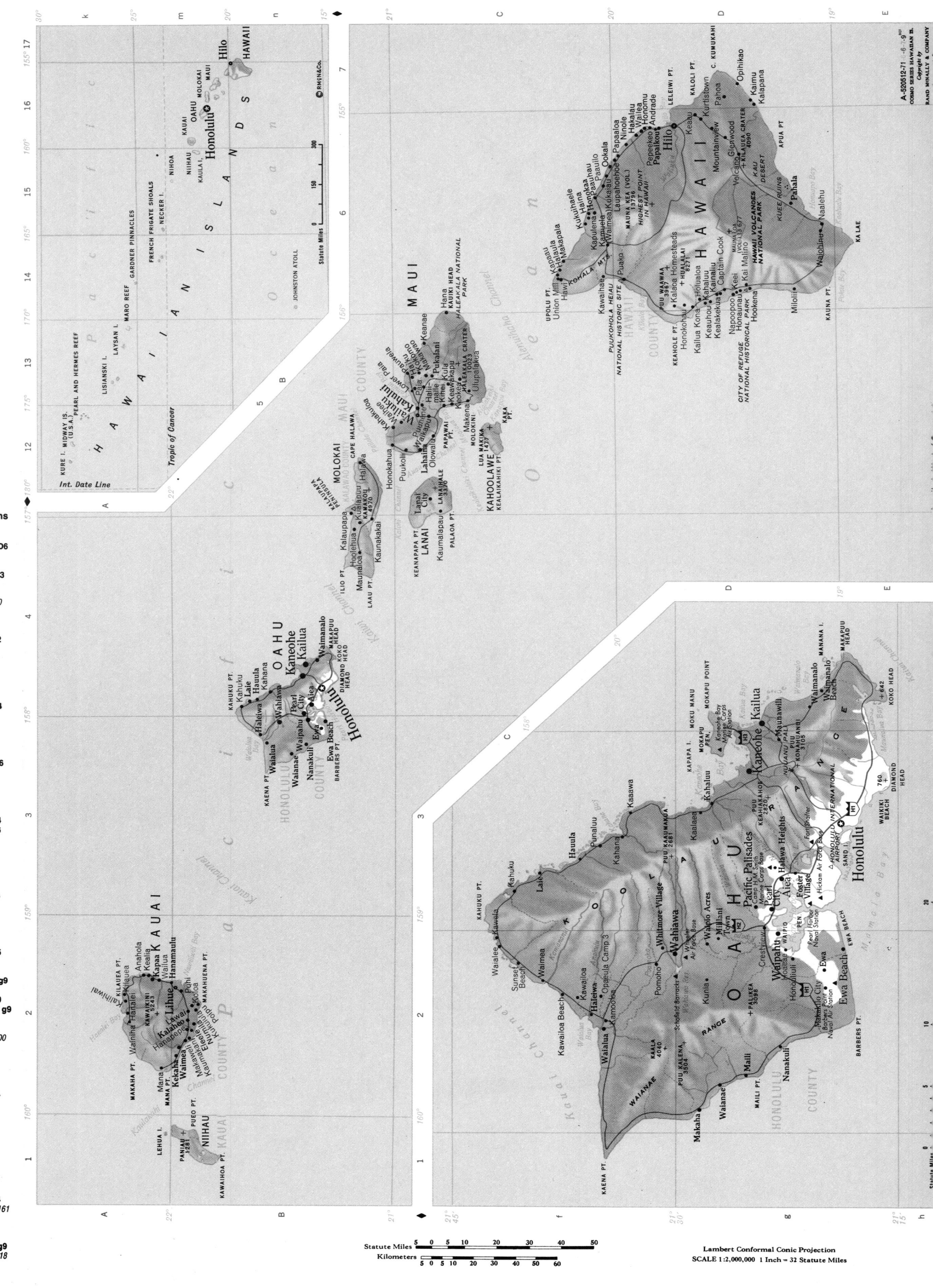

Cities and Towns

Aiea *15,200* **B4**
Anahola *915* **A2**
Captain Cook *2,008* **D6**
Crestview *1,000* **g10**
Ewa *2,637* **B3**
Ewa Beach *14,369* **B3**
Foster Village *3,700*
　g10
Halawa Heights *7,000*
　g10
Haleiwa *2,412* **B3**
Haliimaile *741* **C5**
Hanamaulu *3,227* **B2**
Hanapepe *1,417* **B2**
Hauula *2,997* **B4**
Hawi *795* **C6**
Hilo *35,269* **D6**
Holualoa *1,243* **D6**
Honokaa *1,936* **C6**
Honolulu *365,048* **B4**
Hookena *959* **f10**
Kahaluu *2,925* **g10**
Kahuku *935* **B4**
Kahului *12,978* **C5**
Kailua *35,812* **B4**
Kailua Kona *4,751* **D6**
Kalaheo *2,500* **B2**
Kamuela *1,179* **C6**
Kapaa *4,467* **A2**
Kaumakani *888* **B2**
Kaunakakai *2,231* **B4**
Kealakekua *1,033* **D6**
Kekaha *3,260* **B2**
Keokea *900* **C5**
Kihei *5,644* **C5**
Kilauea *895* **A2**
Koloa *1,457* **B2**
Kula *1,300* **C5**
Kurtistown *1,200* **D6**
Lahaina *6,095* **C5**
Laie *4,643* **B4**
Lanai City *2,092* **C5**
Lawai *950* **B2**
Lihue *4,000* **B2**
Lower Paia *1,500* **C5**
Maili *5,026* **g9**
Makaha *7,905* **g9**
Makakilo City *7,691* **g9**
Makawao *1,066* **C5**
Maunawili *2,200* **g10**
Mililani Town *20,351* **g9**
Naalehu *1,168* **D6**
Nanakuli *8,185* **B3**
Pacific Palisades *9,500*
　g10
Pahala *1,619* **D6**
Pahoa *923* **D7**
Paia *1,000* **C5**
Papaikou *1,567* **D6**
Pearl City *33,000* **B4**
Pepeekeo *1,800* **D6**
Puhi *991* **B2**
Pukalani *3,950* **C5**
Sunset Beach *800* **f9**
Volcano *900* **D6**
Wahiawa *16,911* **B3**
Waialua *4,051* **B3**
Waianae *5,000* **B3**
Wailua *1,587* **A2**
Wailuku *10,260* **C5**
Waimanalo *3,562* **B4**
Waimanalo Beach *4,161*
　g11
Waimea *1,569* **B2**
Waipahu *29,139* **B3**
Waipio Acres *4,091* **g9**
Whitmore Village *2,318*
　f9

Statute Miles
Kilometers

Lambert Conformal Conic Projection
SCALE 1:2,000,000   1 Inch = 32 Statute Miles

A-520512-71 -6 - 9³¹
COSMO SERIES HAWAIIAN B.
Copyright
RAND M℠NALLY & COMPANY

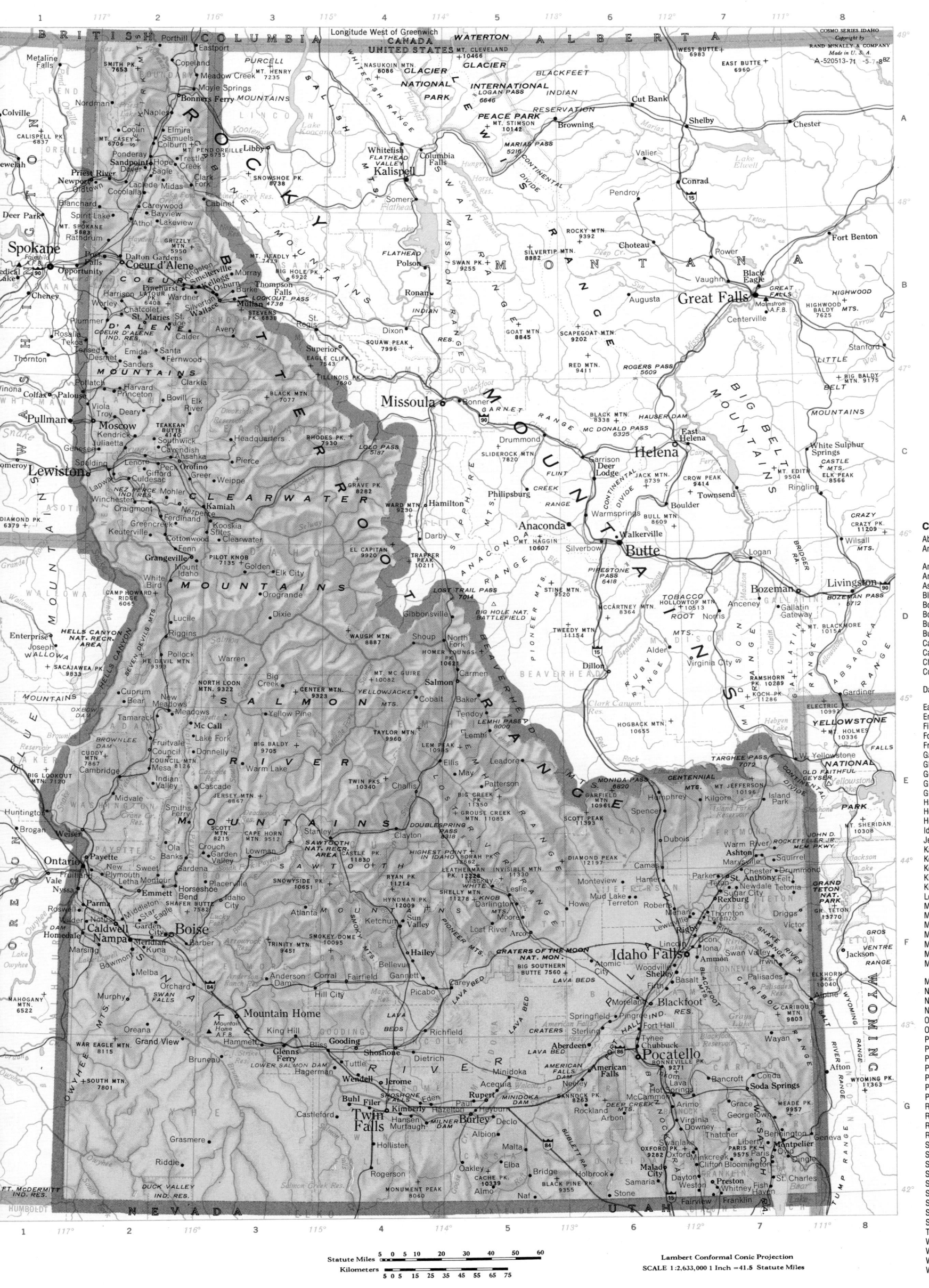

COSMO SERIES IDAHO
Copyright by
RAND McNALLY & COMPANY
Made in U. S. A.
A-520513-71 -5-7-8BZ

Cities and Towns

Aberdeen 1,528 **G6**
American Falls 3,626 **G6**
Ammon 4,669 **F7**
Arco 1,241 **F5**
Ashton 1,219 **E7**
Blackfoot 10,065 **F6**
Boise 102,160 **F2**
Bonners Ferry 1,906 **A2**
Buhl 3,629 **G4**
Burley 8,761 **G5**
Caldwell 17,699 **F2**
Cascade 945 **E2**
Chubbuck 7,052 **G6**
Coeur d'Alene 20,054 **B2**
Dalton Gardens 1,795 **B2**
Eagle 2,620 **F2**
Emmett 4,605 **F2**
Filer 1,645 **G4**
Fort Hall 900 **F6**
Fruitland 2,559 **F2**
Garden City 4,571 **F2**
Glenns Ferry 1,374 **G3**
Gooding 2,949 **G4**
Grace 1,216 **G7**
Grangeville 3,666 **D2**
Hailey 2,109 **F4**
Heyburn 2,889 **G5**
Homedale 2,078 **F2**
Idaho Falls 39,590 **F6**
Jerome 6,891 **G4**
Kamiah 1,478 **C2**
Kellogg 3,417 **B2**
Ketchum 2,200 **F4**
Kimberly 2,307 **G4**
Kuna 1,767 **F2**
Lewiston 27,986 **C1**
McCall 2,188 **E2**
Malad City 1,915 **G6**
Meridian 6,658 **F2**
Middleton 1,901 **F2**
Montpelier 3,107 **G7**
Moscow 16,513 **C2**
Mountain Home 7,540 **F3**
Mullan 1,269 **B3**
Nampa 25,112 **F2**
New Plymouth 1,186 **F2**
Nezperce 517 **C2**
Orofino 3,711 **C2**
Osburn 2,220 **B3**
Parma 1,820 **F2**
Payette 5,448 **E2**
Pierce 1,060 **C3**
Pocatello 46,340 **G6**
Post Falls 5,736 **B2**
Preston 3,759 **G7**
Priest River 1,639 **A2**
Rathdrum 1,369 **B2**
Rexburg 11,559 **F7**
Rigby 2,624 **F7**
Rupert 5,476 **G5**
St. Anthony 3,212 **F7**
St. Maries 2,794 **B2**
Salmon 3,308 **D5**
Sandpoint 4,460 **A2**
Shelley 3,300 **F6**
Shoshone 1,242 **G4**
Soda Springs 4,051 **G7**
Sugar City 1,022 **F7**
Sun Valley 545 **F4**
Twin Falls 26,209 **G4**
Wallace 1,736 **B3**
Weiser 4,771 **E2**
Wendell 1,974 **G4**
Wilder 1,260 **F2**

Lambert Conformal Conic Projection
SCALE 1:2,633,000 1 Inch = 41.5 Statute Miles

Statute Miles 5 0 5 10 20 30 40 50 60
Kilometers 5 0 5 15 25 35 45 55 65 75

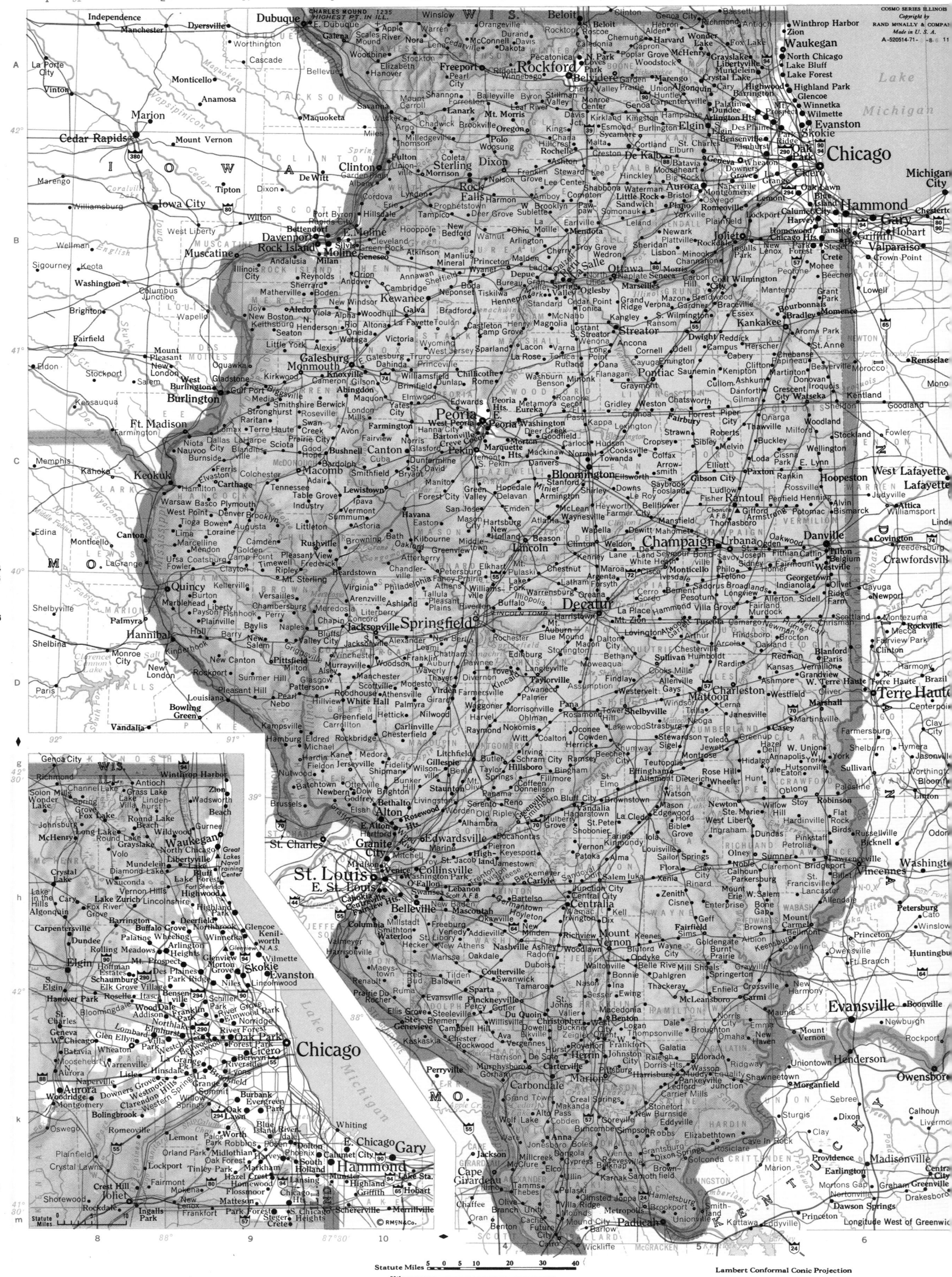

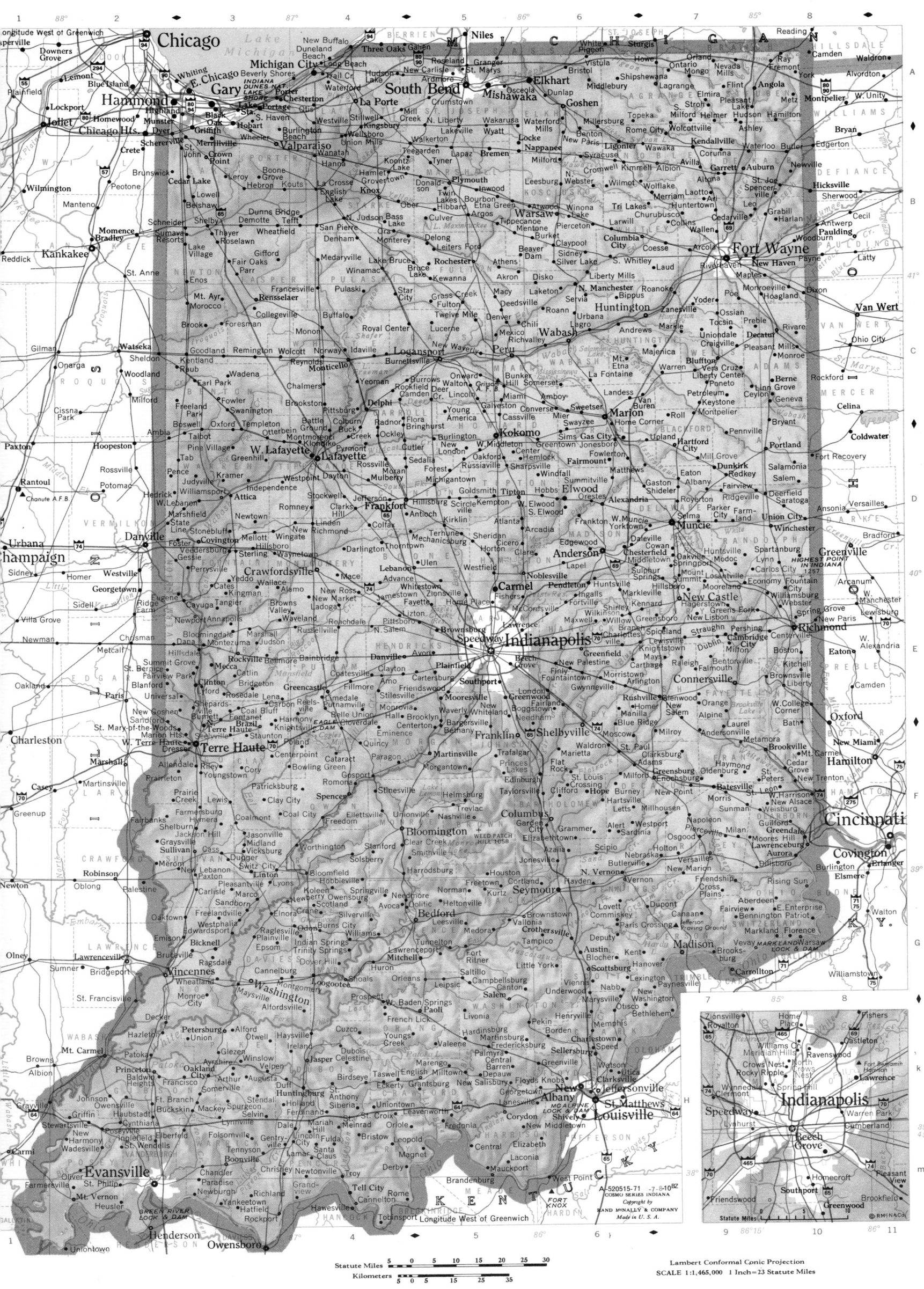

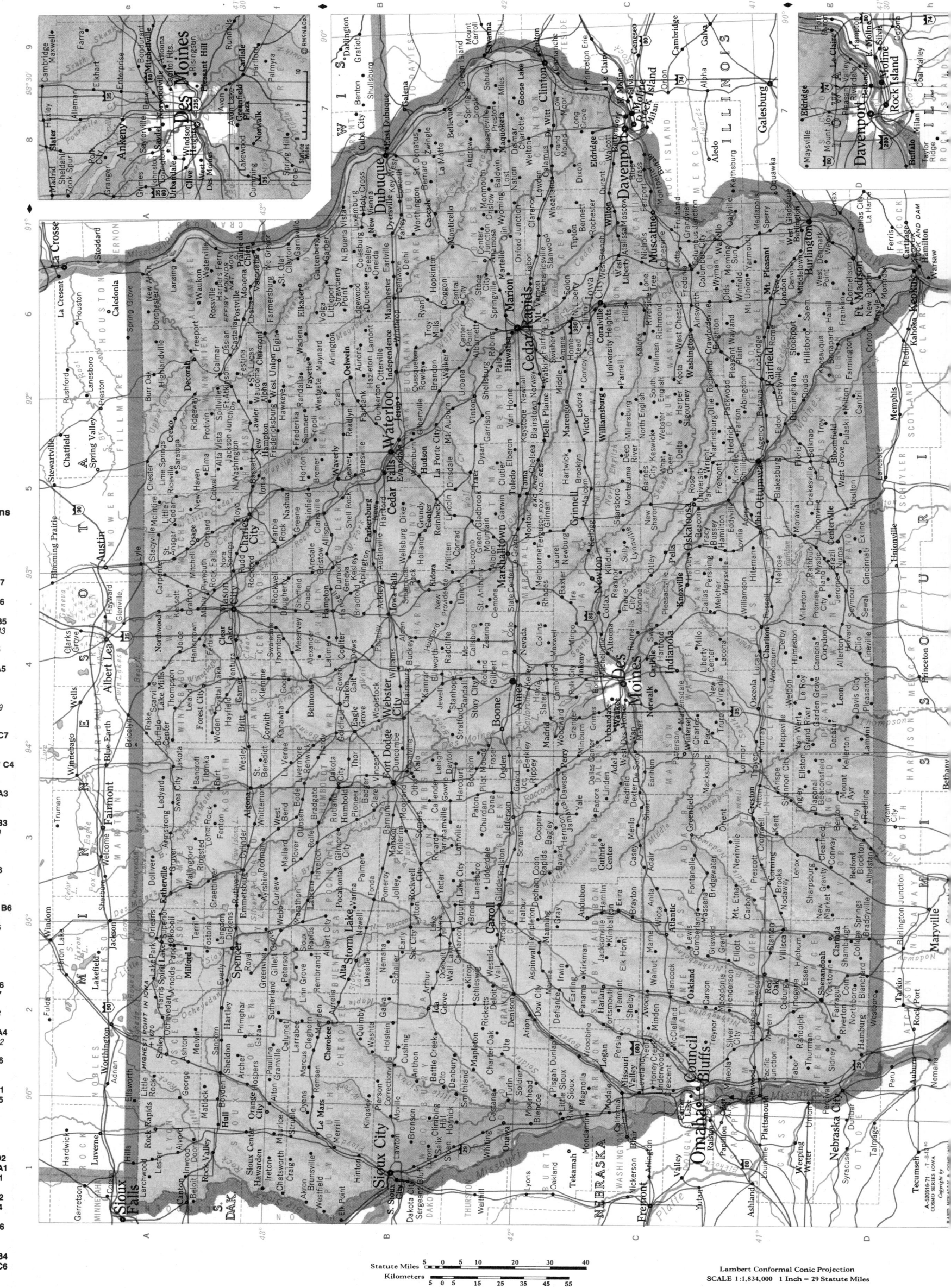

Statute Miles
Kilometers

Lambert Conformal Conic Projection
SCALE 1:1,834,000 1 Inch = 29 Statute Miles

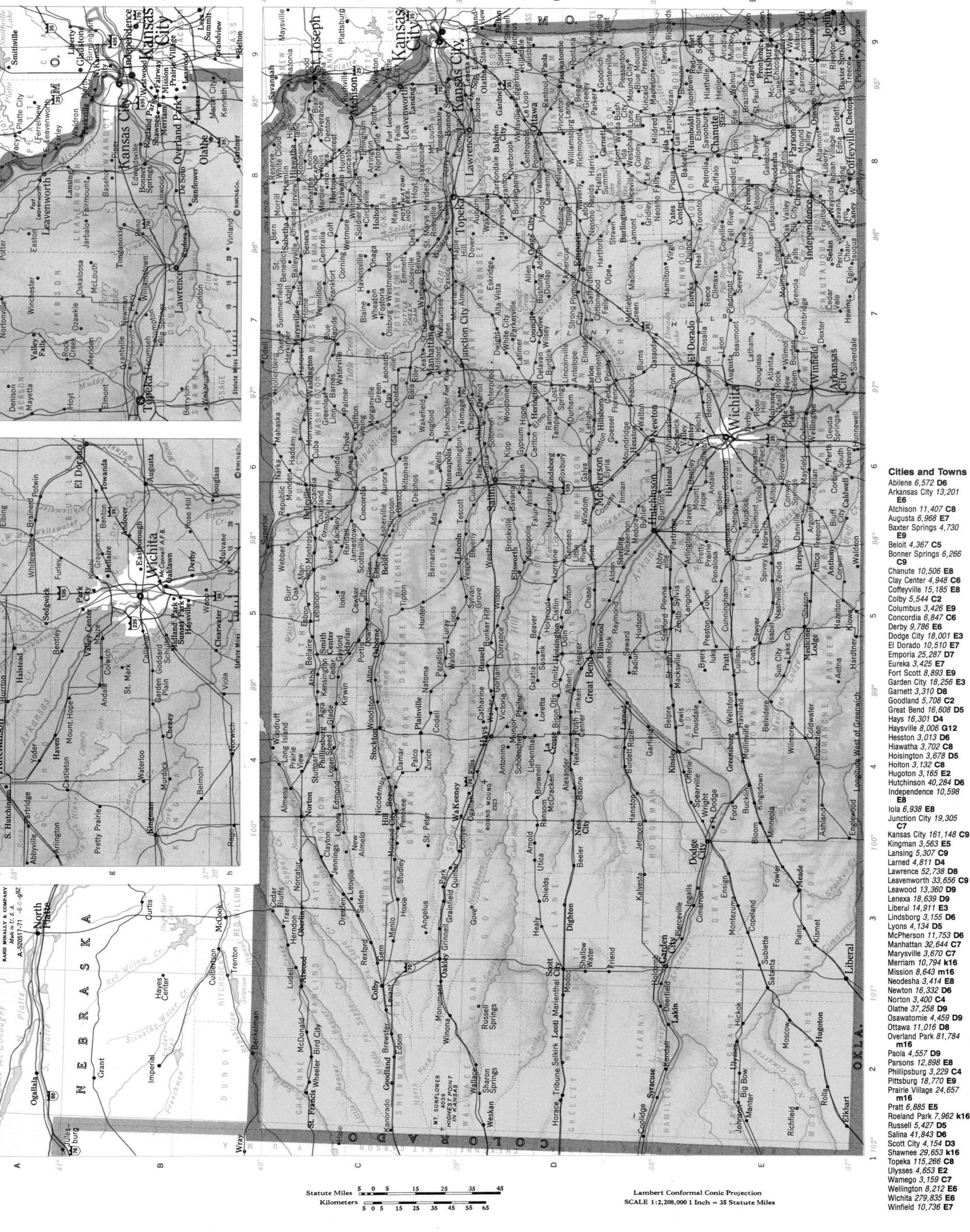

Statute Miles 5 0 5 15 25 35 45
Kilometers 5 0 5 15 25 35 45 55 65

Lambert Conformal Conic Projection
SCALE 1:2,208,000 1 Inch = 35 Statute Miles

Cities and Towns

Abilene 6,572 **D6**
Arkansas City 13,201 **E6**
Atchison 11,407 **C8**
Augusta 6,968 **E7**
Baxter Springs 4,730 **E9**
Beloit 4,367 **C5**
Bonner Springs 6,266 **C9**
Chanute 10,506 **E8**
Clay Center 4,948 **C6**
Coffeyville 15,185 **E8**
Colby 5,544 **C2**
Columbus 3,426 **E9**
Concordia 6,847 **C6**
Derby 9,786 **E6**
Dodge City 18,001 **E3**
El Dorado 10,510 **E7**
Emporia 25,287 **D7**
Eureka 3,425 **E7**
Fort Scott 8,893 **E9**
Garden City 18,256 **E3**
Garnett 3,310 **D8**
Goodland 5,708 **C2**
Great Bend 16,608 **D5**
Hays 16,301 **D4**
Haysville 8,006 **G12**
Hesston 3,013 **D6**
Hiawatha 3,702 **C8**
Hoisington 3,678 **D5**
Holton 3,132 **C8**
Hugoton 3,165 **E2**
Hutchinson 40,284 **D6**
Independence 10,598 **E8**
Iola 6,938 **E8**
Junction City 19,305 **C7**
Kansas City 161,148 **C9**
Kingman 3,563 **E5**
Lansing 5,307 **C9**
Larned 4,811 **D4**
Lawrence 52,738 **D8**
Leavenworth 33,656 **C9**
Leawood 13,360 **D9**
Lenexa 18,639 **D9**
Liberal 14,911 **E3**
Lindsborg 3,155 **D6**
Lyons 4,134 **D5**
McPherson 11,753 **D6**
Manhattan 32,644 **C7**
Marysville 3,670 **C7**
Merriam 10,794 **k16**
Mission 8,643 **m16**
Neodesha 3,414 **E8**
Newton 16,332 **D6**
Norton 3,400 **C4**
Olathe 37,258 **D9**
Osawatomie 4,459 **D9**
Ottawa 11,016 **D8**
Overland Park 81,784 **m16**
Paola 4,557 **D9**
Parsons 12,898 **E8**
Phillipsburg 3,229 **C4**
Pittsburg 18,770 **E9**
Prairie Village 24,657 **m16**
Pratt 6,885 **E5**
Roeland Park 7,962 **k16**
Russell 5,427 **D5**
Salina 41,843 **D6**
Scott City 4,154 **D3**
Shawnee 29,653 **k16**
Topeka 115,266 **C8**
Ulysses 4,653 **E2**
Wamego 3,159 **C7**
Wellington 8,212 **E6**
Wichita 279,835 **E6**
Winfield 10,736 **E7**

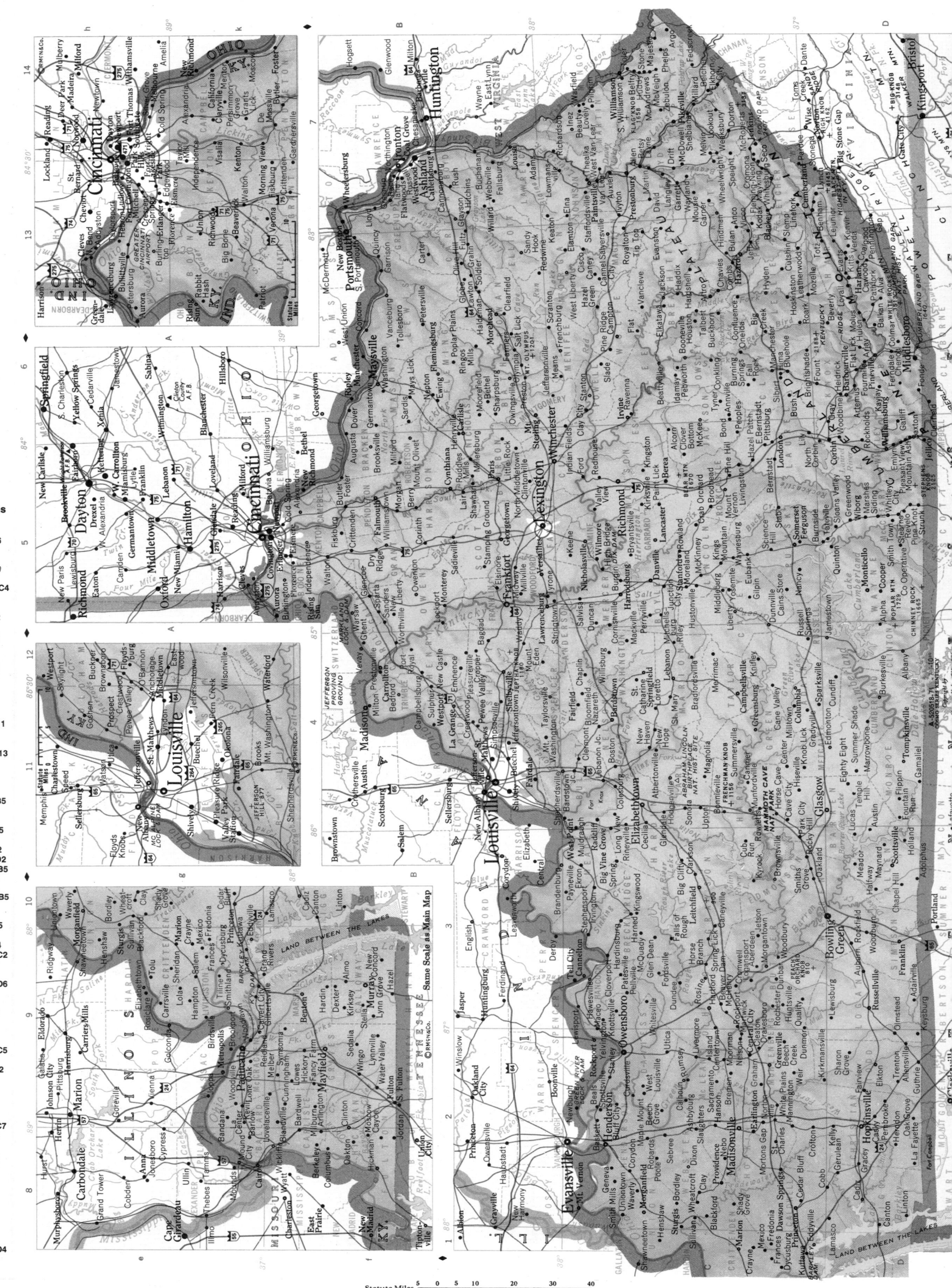

Statute Miles
Kilometers

Lambert Conformal Conic Projection
SCALE 1:1,738,000 1 Inch = 27 Statute Miles

Lambert Conformal Conic Projection

SCALE 1:2,083,000   1 Inch = 33 Statute Miles

Statute Miles   5 0 5   10   20   30   40

Kilometers   5 0 5   15   25   35   45   55

MAINE

A-520520-71 -6 -9 BZ
COSMO SERIES MAINE
Copyright by
RAND McNALLY & COMPANY
Made in U.S.A.

Statute Miles 5 0 5 10 20 30
Kilometers 5 0 5 10 40

Lambert Conformal Conic Projection
SCALE 1:1,581,000 1 Inch = 25 Statute Miles

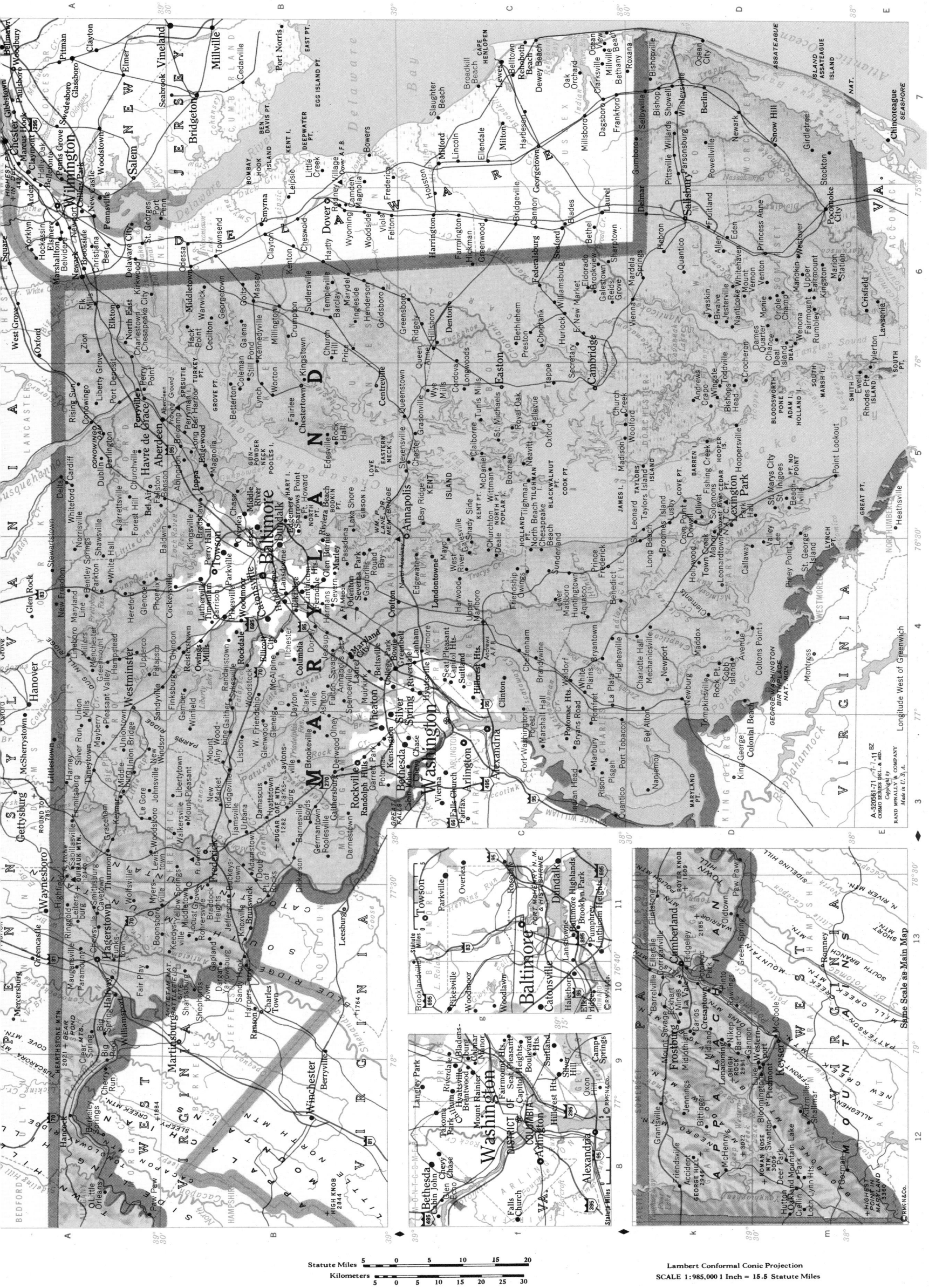

Statute Miles 5 0 5 10 15 20
Kilometers 5 0 5 10 15 20 25 30

Lambert Conformal Conic Projection
SCALE 1:985,000 1 Inch = 15.5 Statute Miles

263

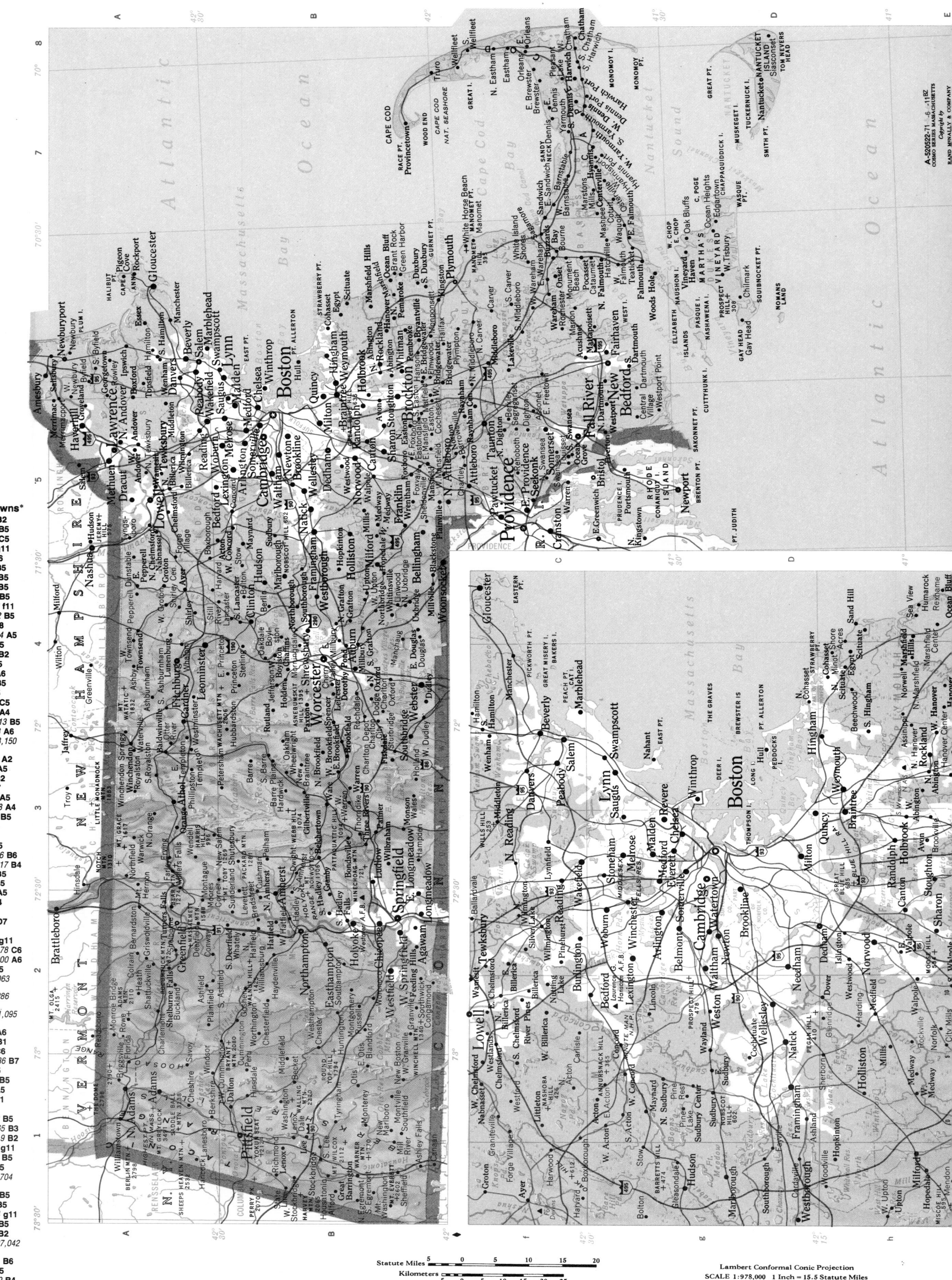

Cities and Towns*

Amherst 26,300 **B2**
Arlington 48,219 **B5**
Attleboro 34,196 **C5**
Belmont 26,100 **g11**
Beverly 37,655 **A6**
Boston 562,994 **B5**
Braintree 36,337 **B5**
Brockton 95,172 **B5**
Brookline 55,062 **B5**
Burlington 23,486 **f11**
Cambridge 95,322 **B5**
Chatham 1,922 **C8**
Chelmsford 31,174 **A5**
Chelsea 25,431 **B5**
Chicopee 55,112 **B2**
Concord 6,400 **B5**
Danvers 24,100 **A6**
Dedham 25,298 **B5**
Dracut 21,249 **A5**
Fall River 92,574 **C5**
Fitchburg 39,580 **A4**
Framingham 65,113 **B5**
Gloucester 27,768 **A6**
Great Barrington 3,150
B1
Greenfield 14,198 **A2**
Haverhill 46,865 **A5**
Holyoke 44,678 **B2**
Hyannis 8,000 **C7**
Lawrence 63,175 **A5**
Leominster 34,508 **A4**
Lexington 29,479 **B5**
Lowell 92,418 **A5**
Lynn 78,471 **B6**
Malden 53,386 **B5**
Marblehead 20,126 **B6**
Marlborough 30,617 **B4**
Medford 64,397 **B5**
Melrose 30,055 **B5**
Methuen 35,701 **A5**
Milford 23,390 **B4**
Milton 25,860 **B5**
Nantucket 3,229 **D7**
Natick 29,461 **B5**
Needham 27,901 **g11**
New Bedford 98,478 **C6**
Newburyport 15,900 **A6**
Newton 83,622 **B5**
North Adams 18,063
A1
Northampton 29,286
B2
North Attleboro 21,095
C5
Peabody 45,976 **A6**
Pittsfield 51,974 **B1**
Plymouth 7,232 **C6**
Provincetown 3,536 **B7**
Quincy 84,743 **B5**
Randolph 22,218 **B5**
Reading 22,678 **A5**
Revere 42,423 **g11**
Salem 38,220 **A6**
Somerville 77,372 **B5**
Southbridge 16,665 **B3**
Springfield 152,319 **B2**
Stoneham 21,424 **g11**
Stoughton 26,710 **B5**
Taunton 45,001 **C5**
Vineyard Haven 1,704
D6
Wakefield 24,895 **B5**
Waltham 58,200 **B5**
Watertown 34,384 **g11**
Wellesley 27,209 **B5**
Westfield 36,465 **B2**
West Springfield 27,042
B2
Weymouth 55,601 **B6**
Woburn 36,626 **B5**
Worcester 161,799 **B4**

*Populations are for localities, not incorporated towns.

Statute Miles

Kilometers

Lambert Conformal Conic Projection
SCALE 1:978,000   1 Inch = 15.5 Statute Miles

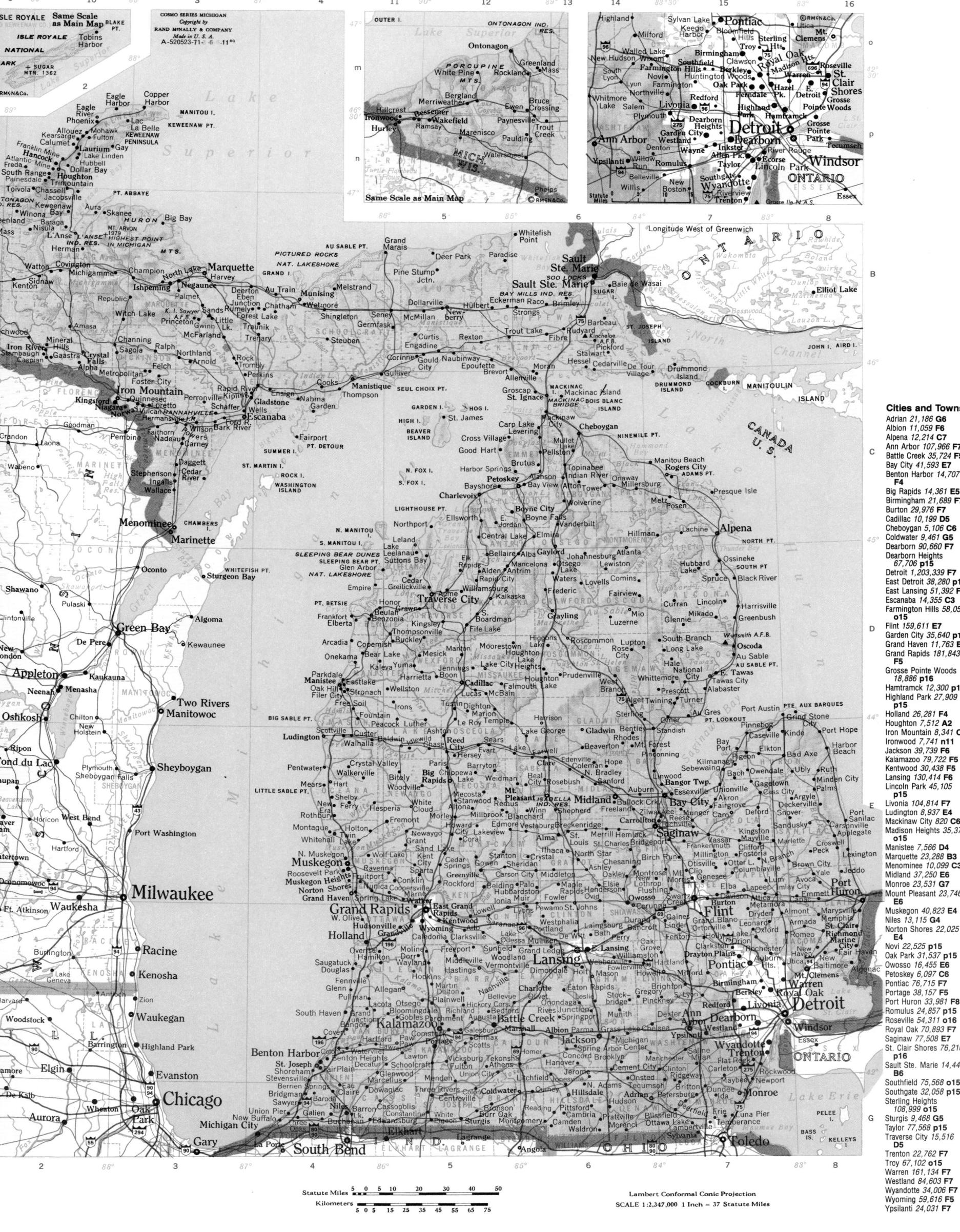

MINNESOTA

266

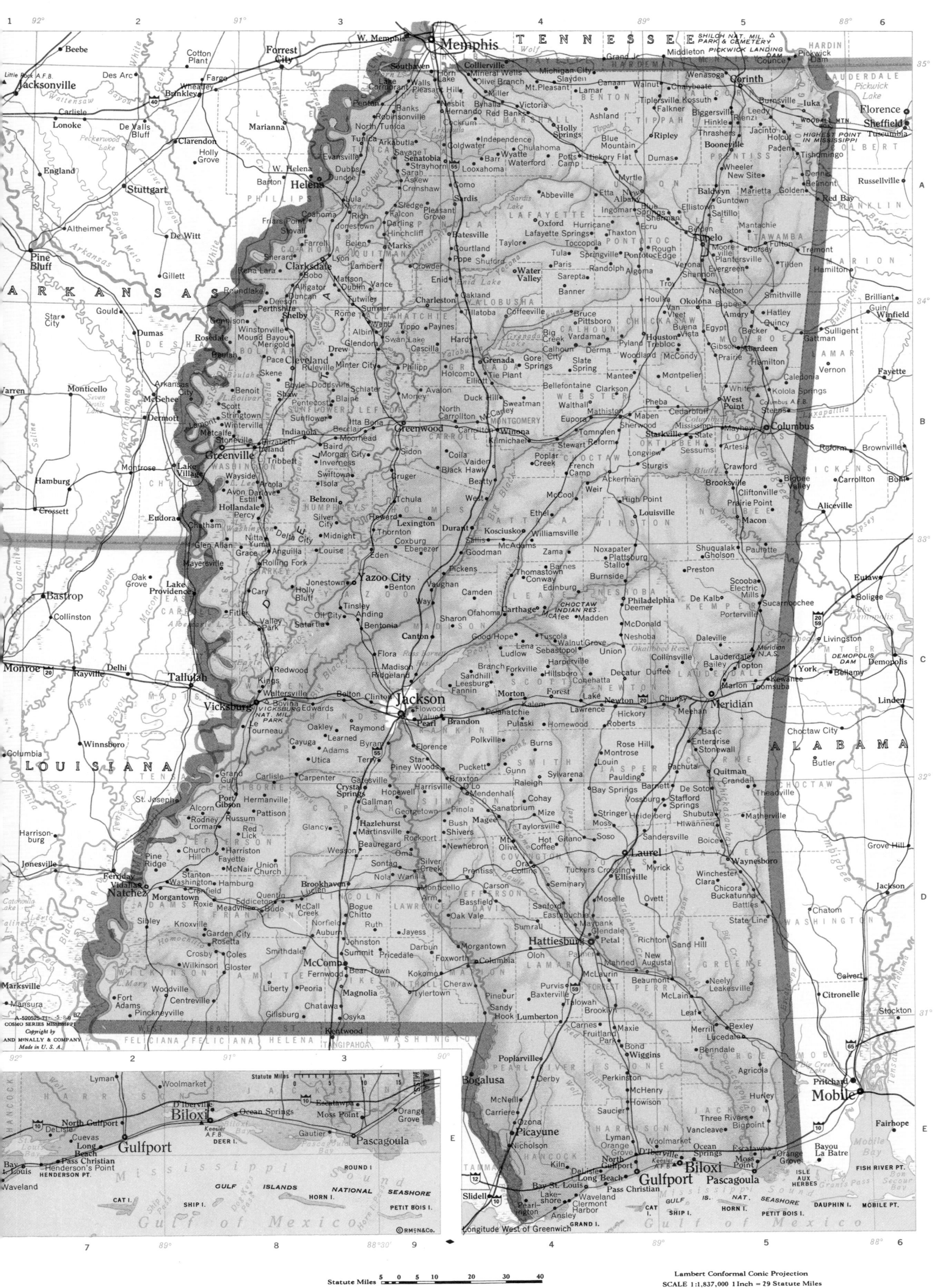

Lambert Conformal Conic Projection
SCALE 1:1,837,000 1 Inch = 29 Statute Miles

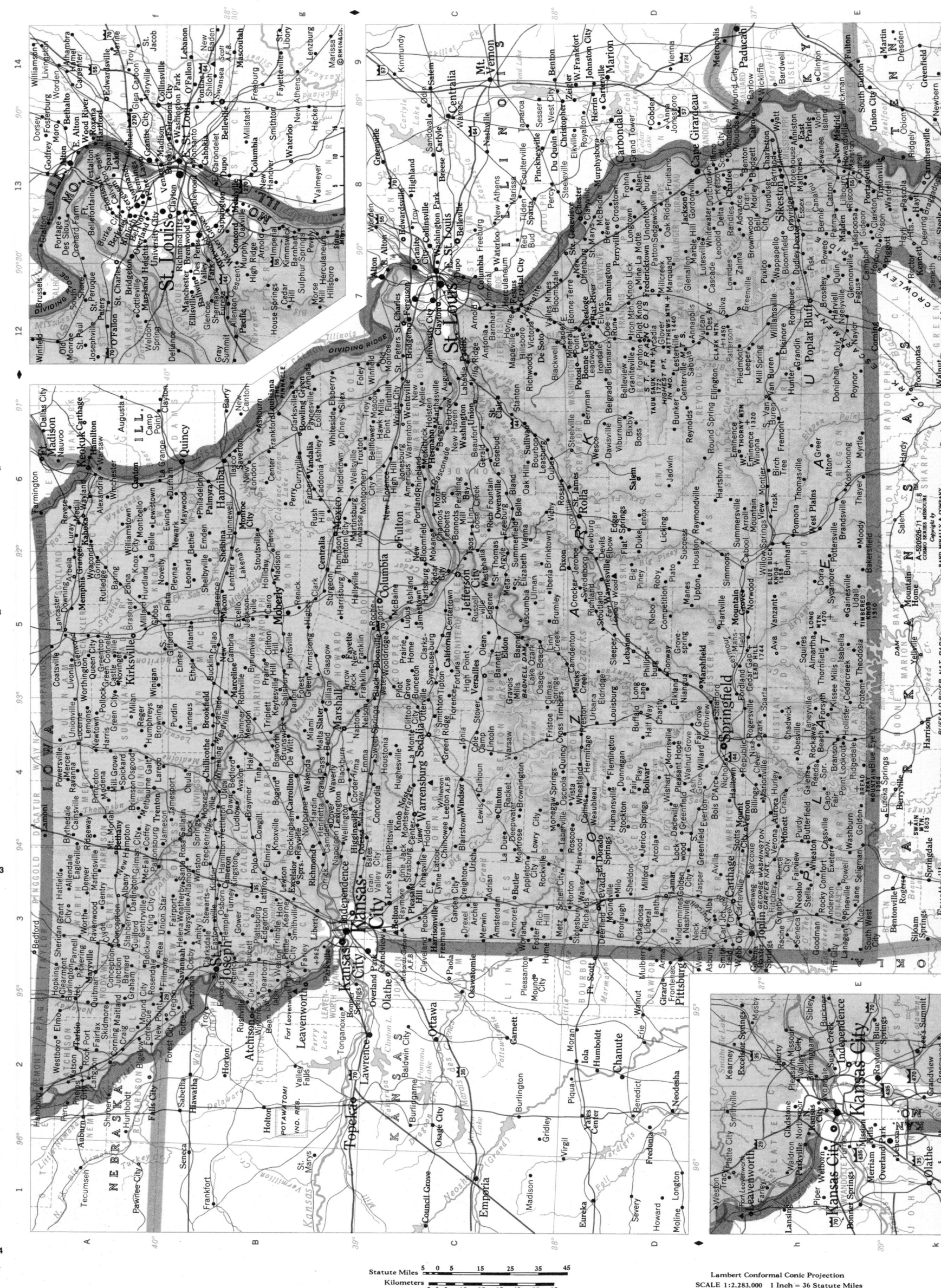

Statute Miles

Kilometers

Lambert Conformal Conic Projection
SCALE 1:2,283,000   1 Inch = 36 Statute Miles

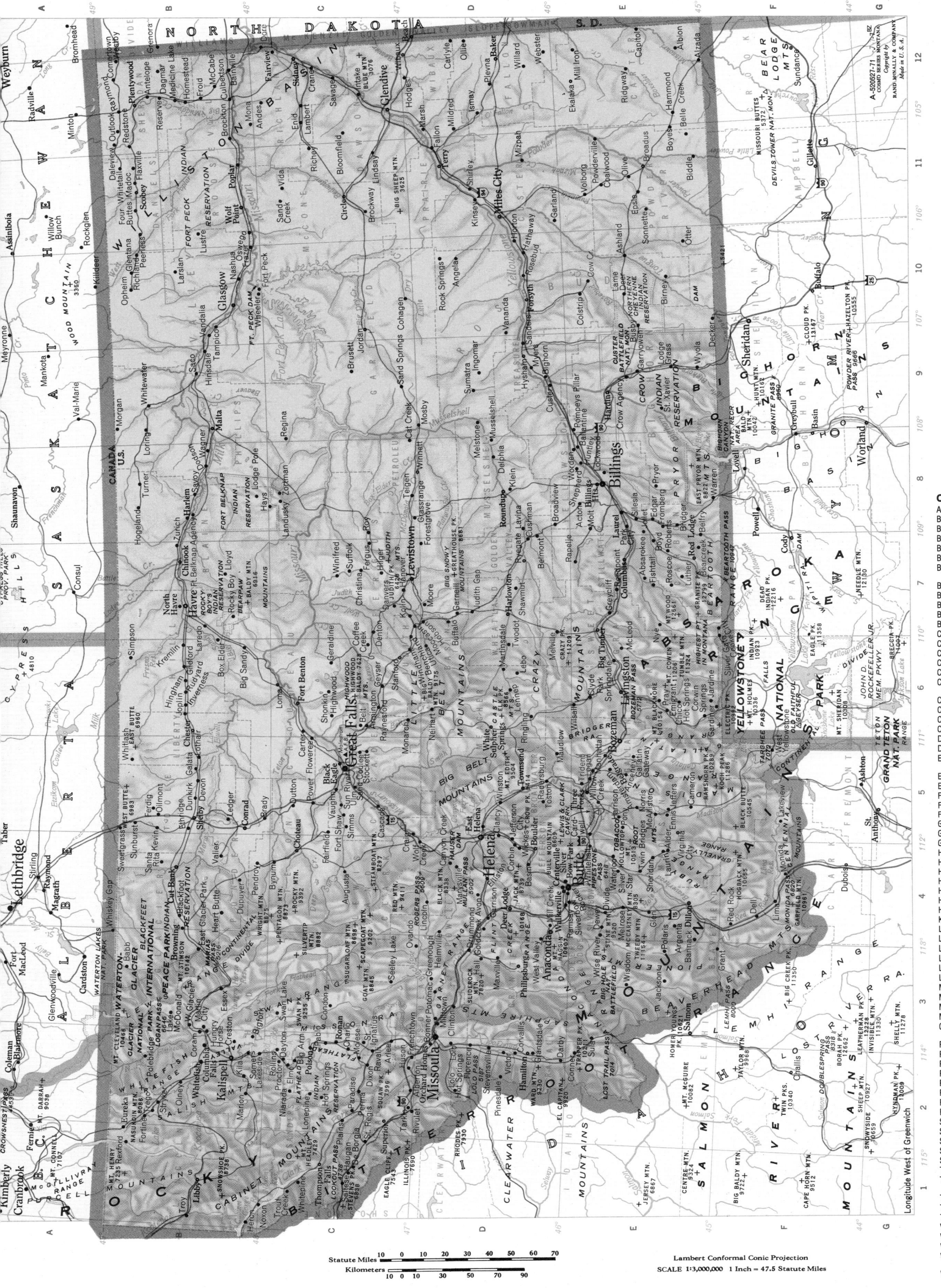

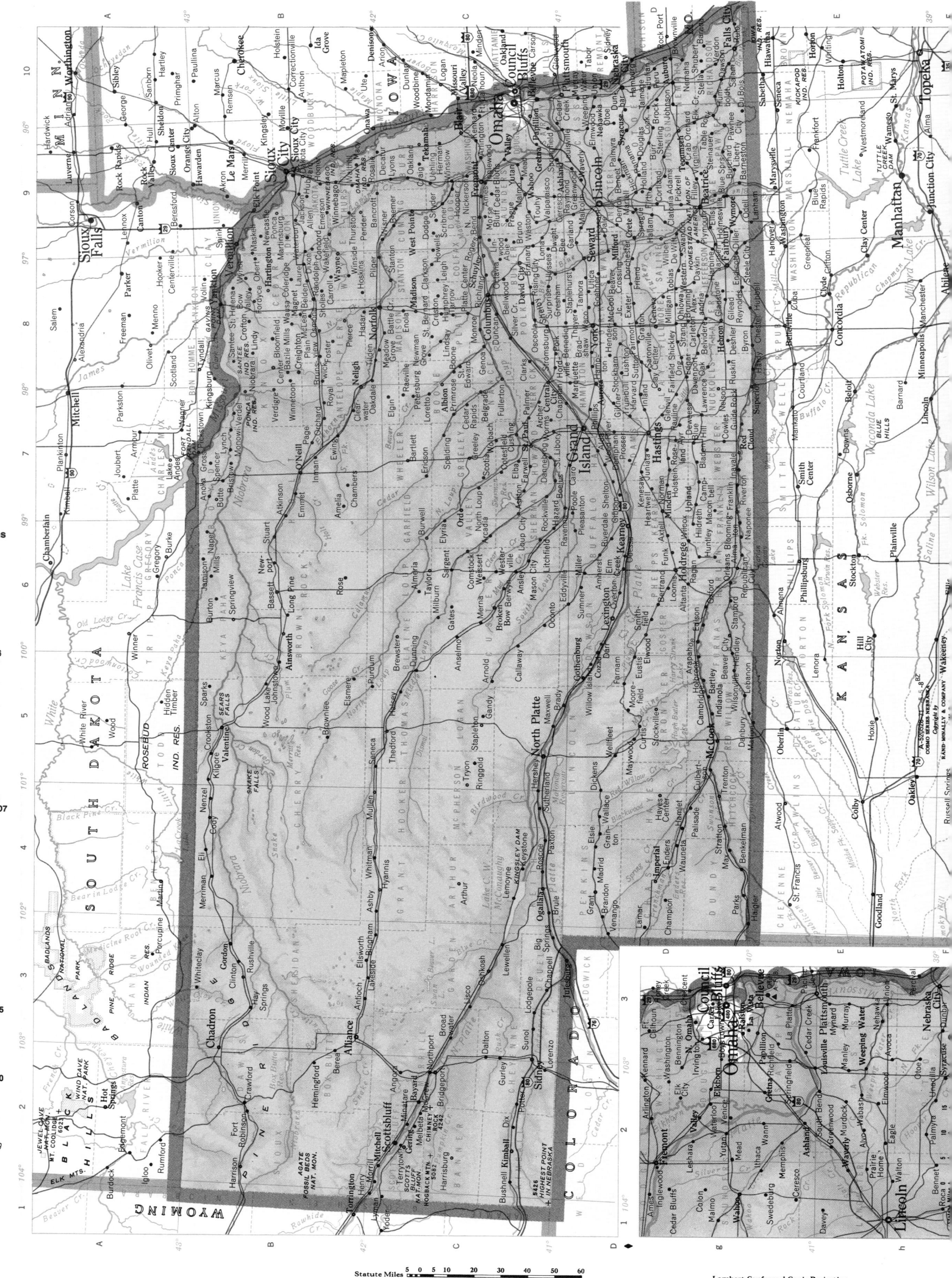

Statute Miles 5 0 5 10 20 30 40 50 60
Kilometers 5 0 5 15 35 55 75 95

Lambert Conformal Conic Projection
SCALE 1:2,460,000 1 Inch = 39 Statute Miles

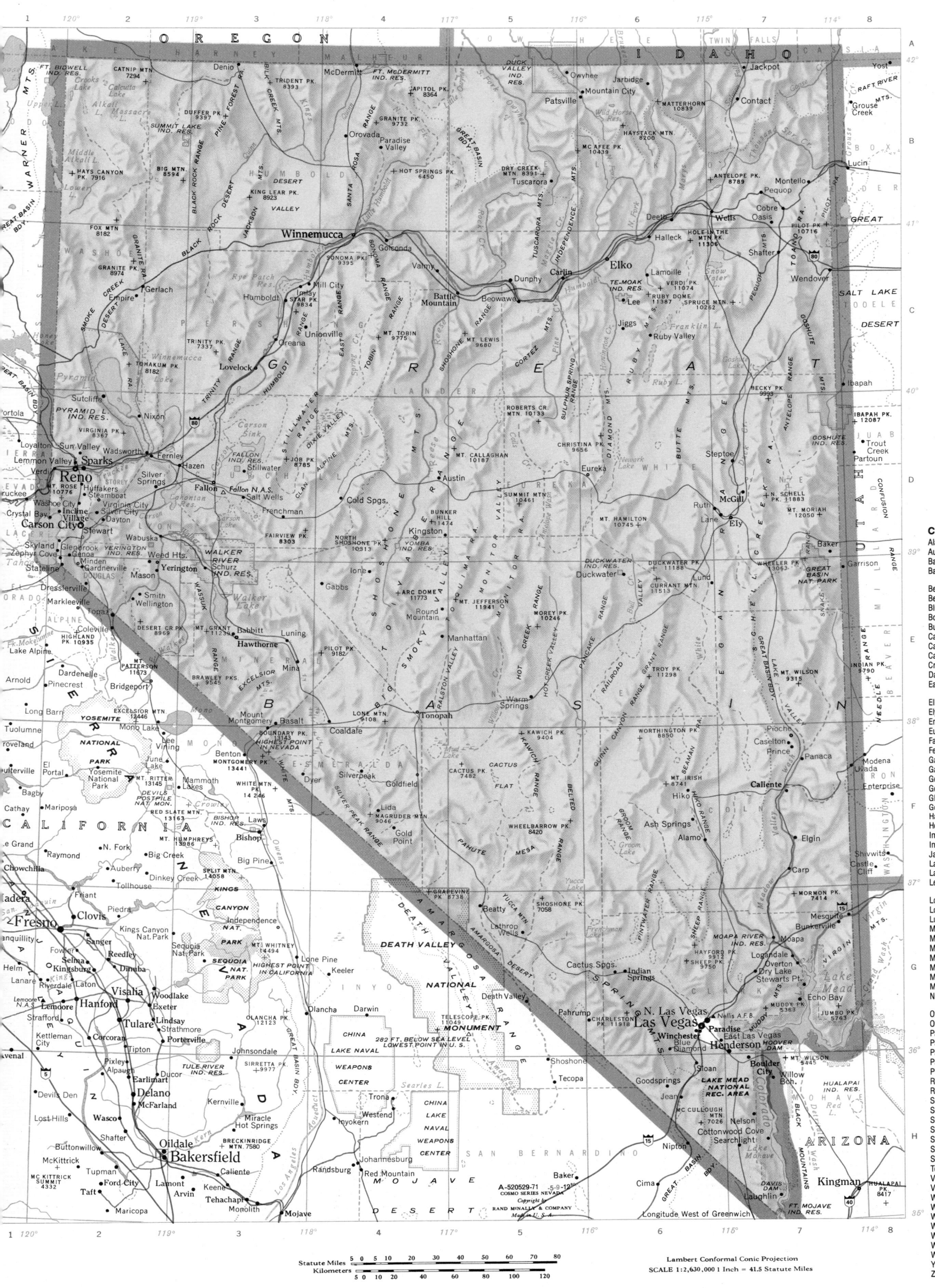

Lambert Conformal Conic Projection
SCALE 1:2,630,000 1 Inch = 41.5 Statute Miles

Statute Miles 5 0 5 10 20 30 40 50 60 70 80
Kilometers 5 0 10 20 40 60 80 100 120

A-520529-71   5-8-12½
COSMO SERIES NEVADA
Copyright by
RAND MCNALLY & COMPANY
Made in U.S.A.

Cities and Towns

Alamo 250 **F6**
Austin 350 **D4**
Babbitt 1,800 **E3**
Battle Mountain 2,755 **C5**
Beatty 900 **G5**
Beowawe 250 **C5**
Blue Diamond 300 **G6**
Boulder, City 9,590 **H7**
Bunkerville 180 **G7**
Caliente 982 **F7**
Carlin 1,232 **C5**
Carson City 32,022 **D2**
Crystal Bay 1,200 **D1**
Dayton 300 **D2**
East Las Vegas 6,449 **G6**
Elko 8,758 **C6**
Ely 4,882 **D7**
Empire 300 **C2**
Eureka 500 **D6**
Fallon 4,262 **D3**
Fernley 1,200 **D2**
Gabbs 811 **E4**
Gardnerville 2,800 **E2**
Genoa 145 **D2**
Gerlach 200 **C2**
Glenbrook 300 **D2**
Goldfield 300 **F4**
Hawthorne 3,741 **E3**
Henderson 24,363 **G7**
Imlay 200 **C3**
Indian Springs 900 **G6**
Jackpot 500 **B7**
Las Vegas 164,674 **G6**
Lathrop Wells 250 **G5**
Lemmon Valley 2,000 **D2**
Logandale 375 **G7**
Lovelock 1,680 **C3**
Lund 300 **E6**
McDermitt 200 **B4**
McGill 1,419 **D7**
Mason 200 **E2**
Mesquite 700 **G7**
Mina 425 **E3**
Minden 1,300 **E2**
Montello 180 **B7**
North Las Vegas 42,739 **G6**
Overton 1,111 **G7**
Owyhee 700 **B5**
Pahrump 1,000 **G6**
Panaca 550 **F7**
Paradise 45,000 **G6**
Paradise Valley 150 **B4**
Pioche 700 **F7**
Reno 100,756 **D2**
Ruth 735 **D6**
Schurz 325 **E3**
Searchlight 300 **H7**
Silver Springs 300 **D2**
Skyland 500 **D2**
Sparks 40,780 **D2**
Stateline 1,500 **E2**
Sun Valley 8,822 **D2**
Tonopah 1,952 **E4**
Verdi 800 **D2**
Virginia City 600 **D2**
Wadsworth 350 **D2**
Washoe City 400 **D2**
Weed Heights 650 **E2**
Wellington 200 **E2**
Wells 1,218 **B7**
Winchester 19,728 **G6**
Winnemucca 4,140 **C4**
Yerington 2,021 **E2**
Zephyr Cove 1,300 **E2**

*Populations are for localities, not incorporated towns.

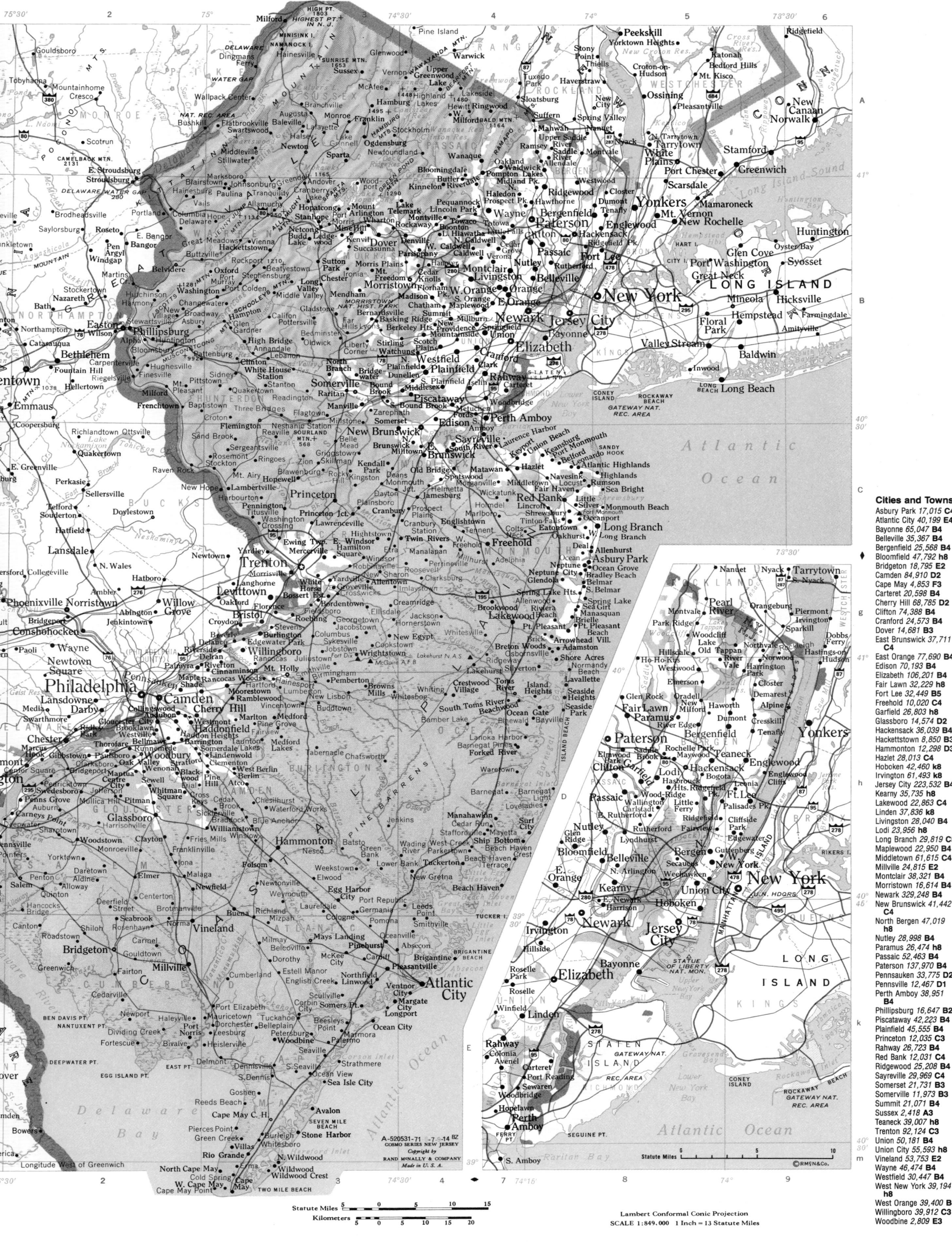

NEW MEXICO

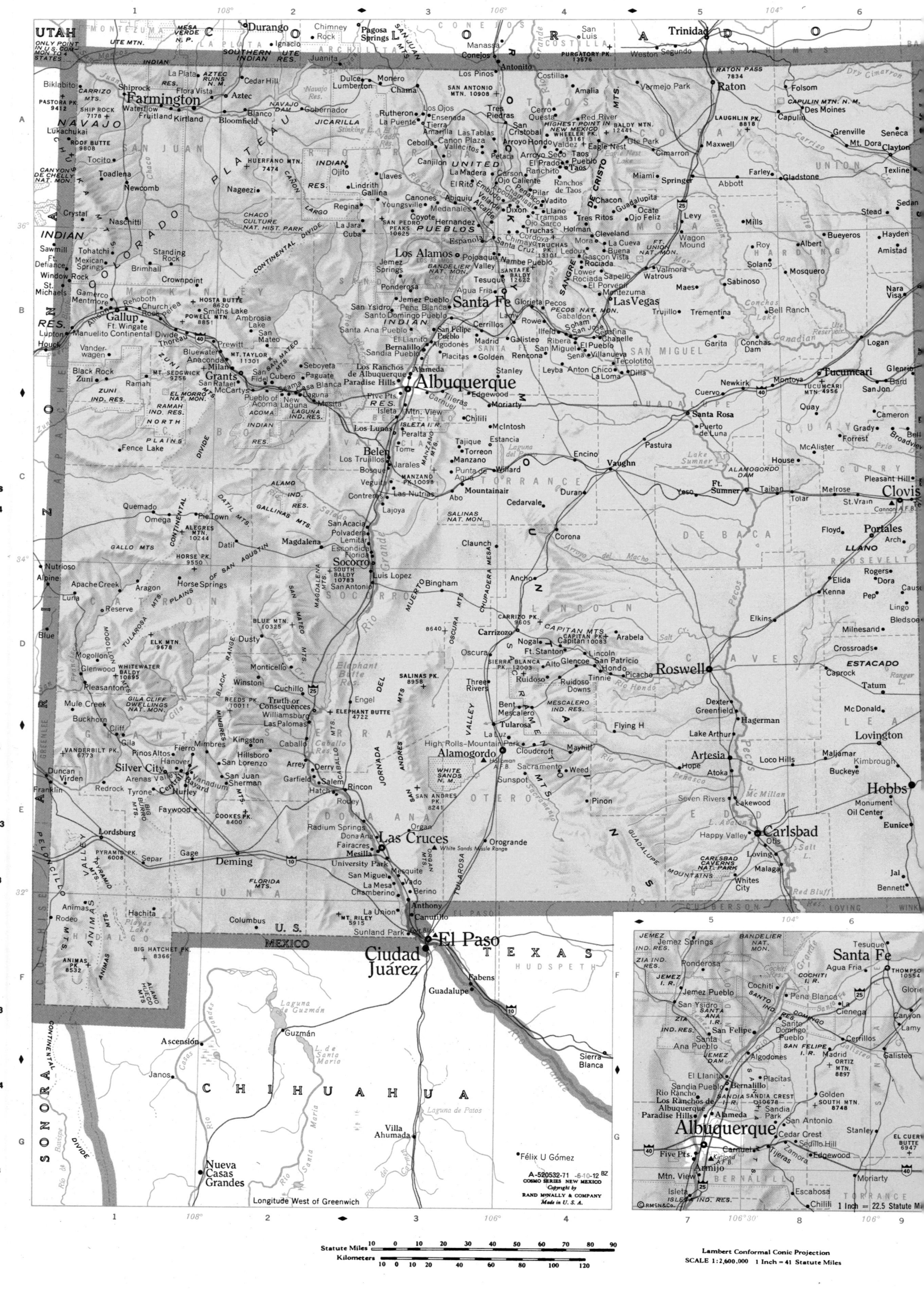

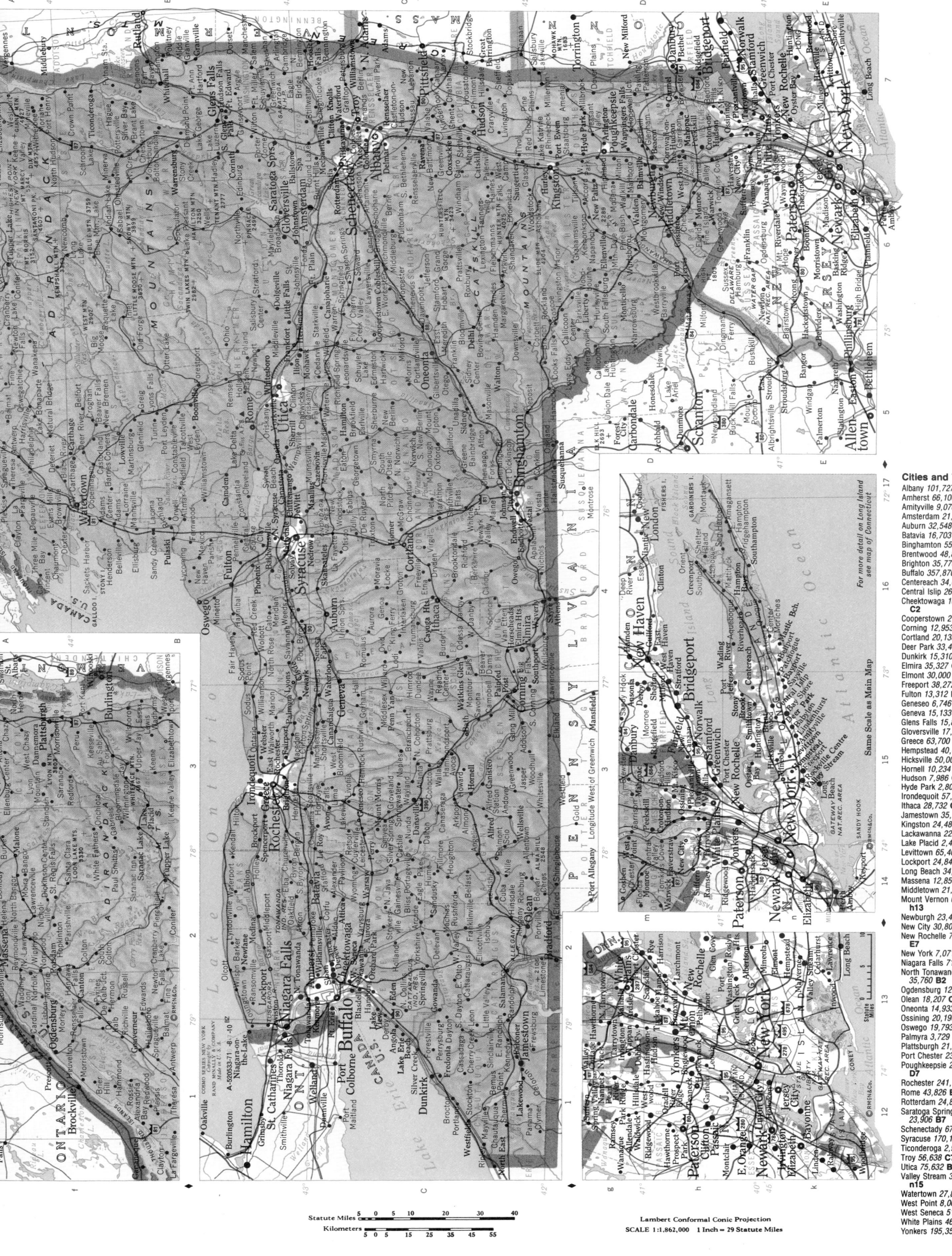

For more detail on Long Island
see map of Connecticut

Same Scale as Main Map

Statute Miles 5 0 5 10 20 30 40
Kilometers 5 0 5 15 25 35 45 55

Lambert Conformal Conic Projection
SCALE 1:1,862,000   1 Inch = 29 Statute Miles

Cities and Towns

Albemarle 15,110 **B2**
Archdale 5,326 **B3**
Asheboro 15,252 **B3**
Asheville 53,583 **f10**
Boone 10,191 **A1**
Brevard 5,323 **f10**
Burlington 37,266 **A3**
Carrboro 7,336 **B3**
Chapel Hill 32,421 **B3**
Charlotte 314,447 **B2**
Clemmons 7,401 **A2**
Clinton 7,552 **C4**
Concord 16,942 **B2**
Dunn 8,962 **B4**
Durham 100,538 **B4**
Eden 15,672 **A3**
Edenton 5,357 **A6**
Elizabeth City 13,784 **A6**
Fayetteville 59,507 **B4**
Forest City 7,688 **B1**
Garner 10,073 **B4**
Gastonia 47,333 **B1**
Goldsboro 31,871 **B5**
Graham 8,674 **A3**
Greensboro 155,642 **A3**
Greenville 35,740 **B5**
Havelock 17,718 **C6**
Henderson 13,522 **A4**
Hendersonville 6,862 **f10**
Hickory 20,757 **B1**
High Point 63,808 **B2**
Jacksonville 18,237 **C5**
Kannapolis 34,564 **B2**
Kernersville 6,802 **A2**
Kings Mountain 9,080 **B1**
Kinston 25,234 **B5**
Laurinburg 11,480 **C3**
Lenoir 13,748 **B1**
Lexington 15,711 **B2**
Lincolnton 4,879 **B1**
Lumberton 18,241 **C3**
Monroe 12,639 **C2**
Mooresville 8,575 **B2**
Morehead City 4,359 **C6**
Morganton 13,763 **B1**
Mount Airy 6,862 **A2**
Mount Olive 4,876 **B4**
Nags Head 1,020 **B7**
New Bern 14,557 **B5**
Newton 7,624 **B1**
Oxford 7,603 **A4**
Plymouth 4,571 **B6**
Raleigh 150,255 **B4**
Reidsville 12,492 **A3**
Roanoke Rapids 14,702 **A5**
Rockingham 8,300 **C3**
Rocky Mount 41,283 **B5**
Roxboro 7,532 **A4**
Salisbury 22,677 **B2**
Sanford 14,773 **B3**
Selma 4,762 **B4**
Shelby 15,310 **B1**
Smithfield 7,288 **B4**
Southern Pines 8,620 **B3**
Statesville 18,622 **B2**
Swannanoa 5,586 **f10**
Tarboro 8,634 **B5**
Thomasville 14,144 **B2**
Washington 8,418 **B5**
Whiteville 5,565 **C4**
Williamston 6,159 **B5**
Wilmington 44,000 **C5**
Wilson 34,424 **B5**
Winston-Salem 131,885 **A2**

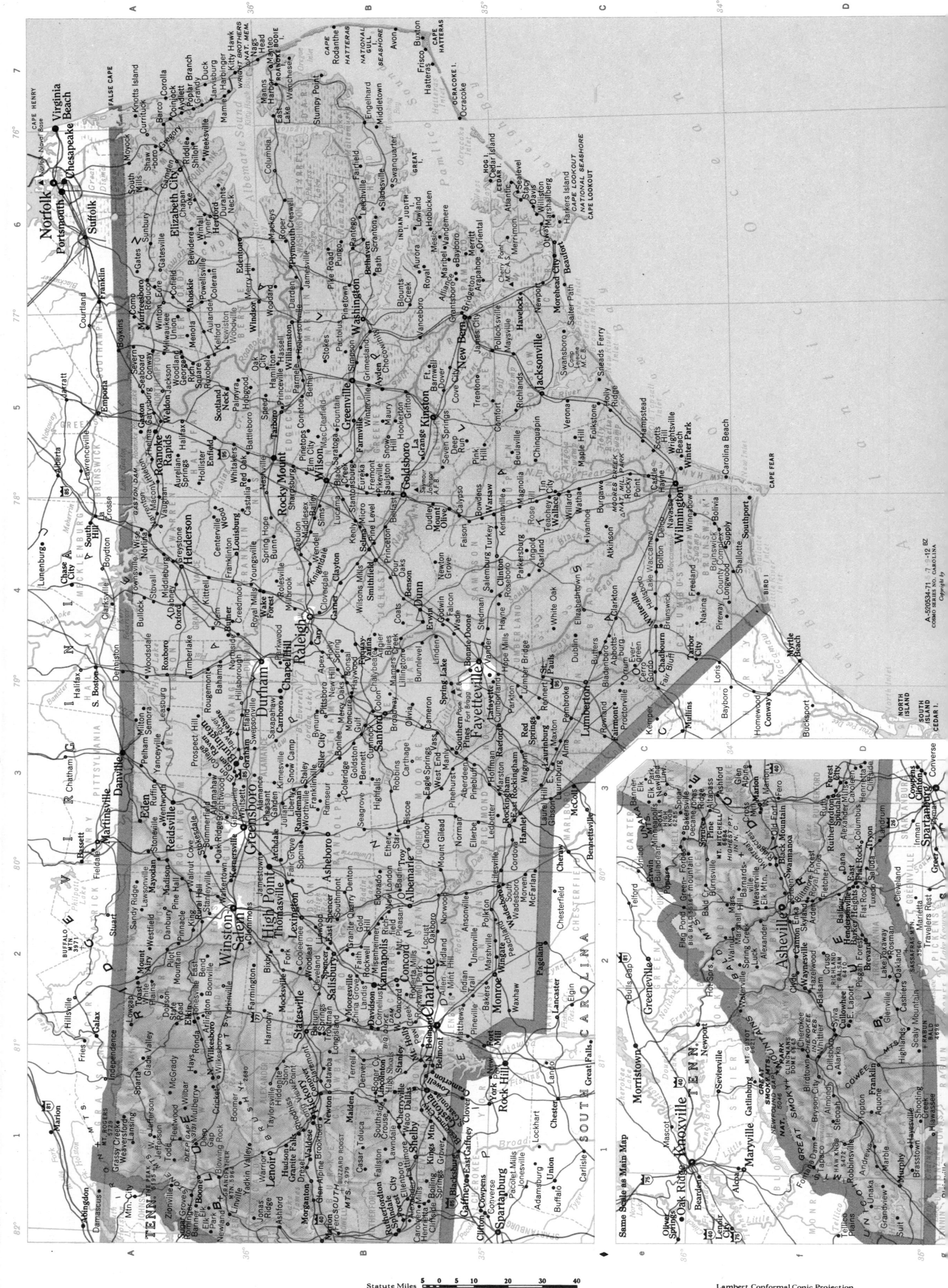

A-520534-71 .7 9-12 BZ
COSMO SERIES NO. CAROLINA
Copyright by

Statute Miles
Kilometers

Lambert Conformal Conic Projection
SCALE 1:1,950,000 1 Inch = 31 Statute Miles

Same Scale as Main Map

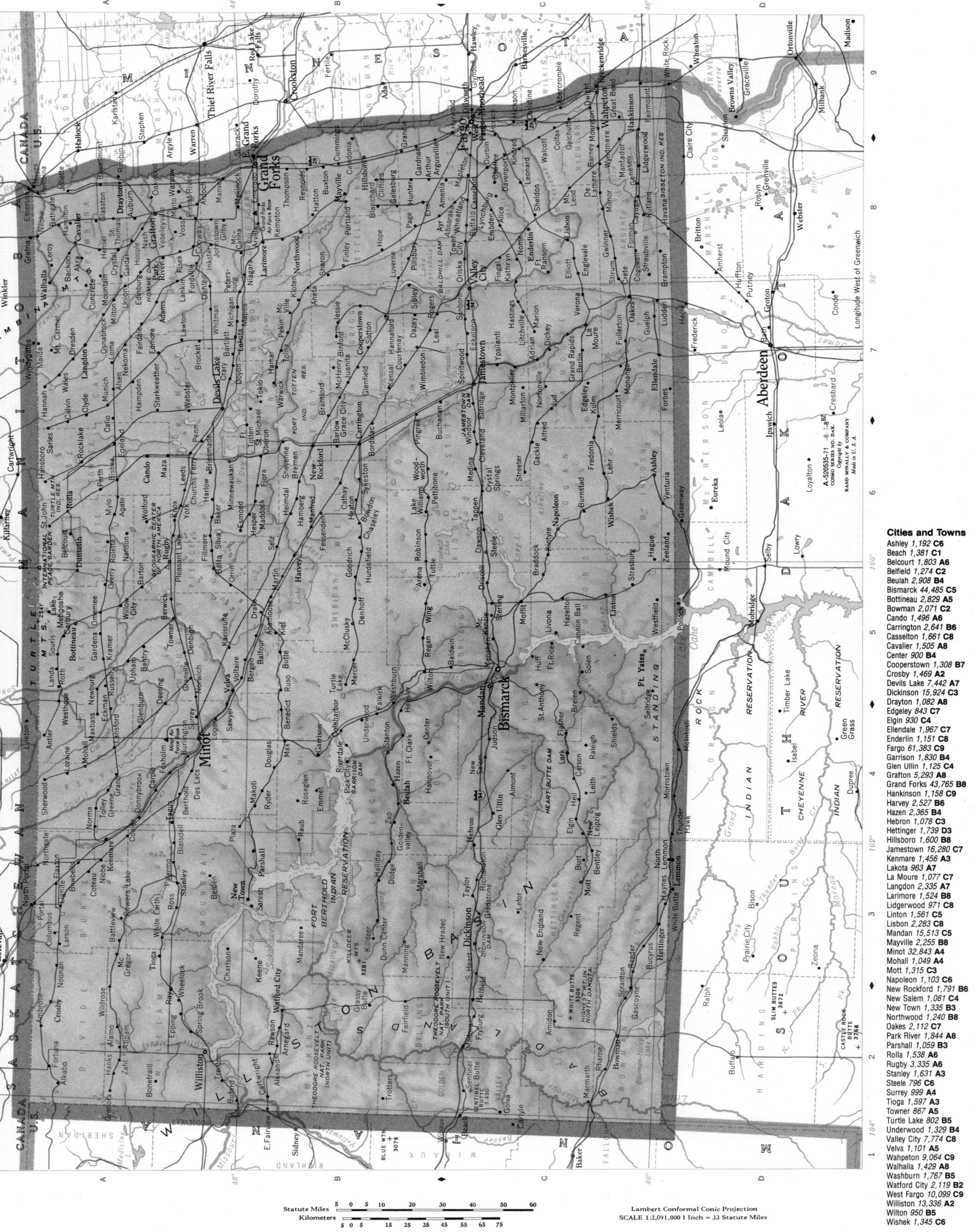

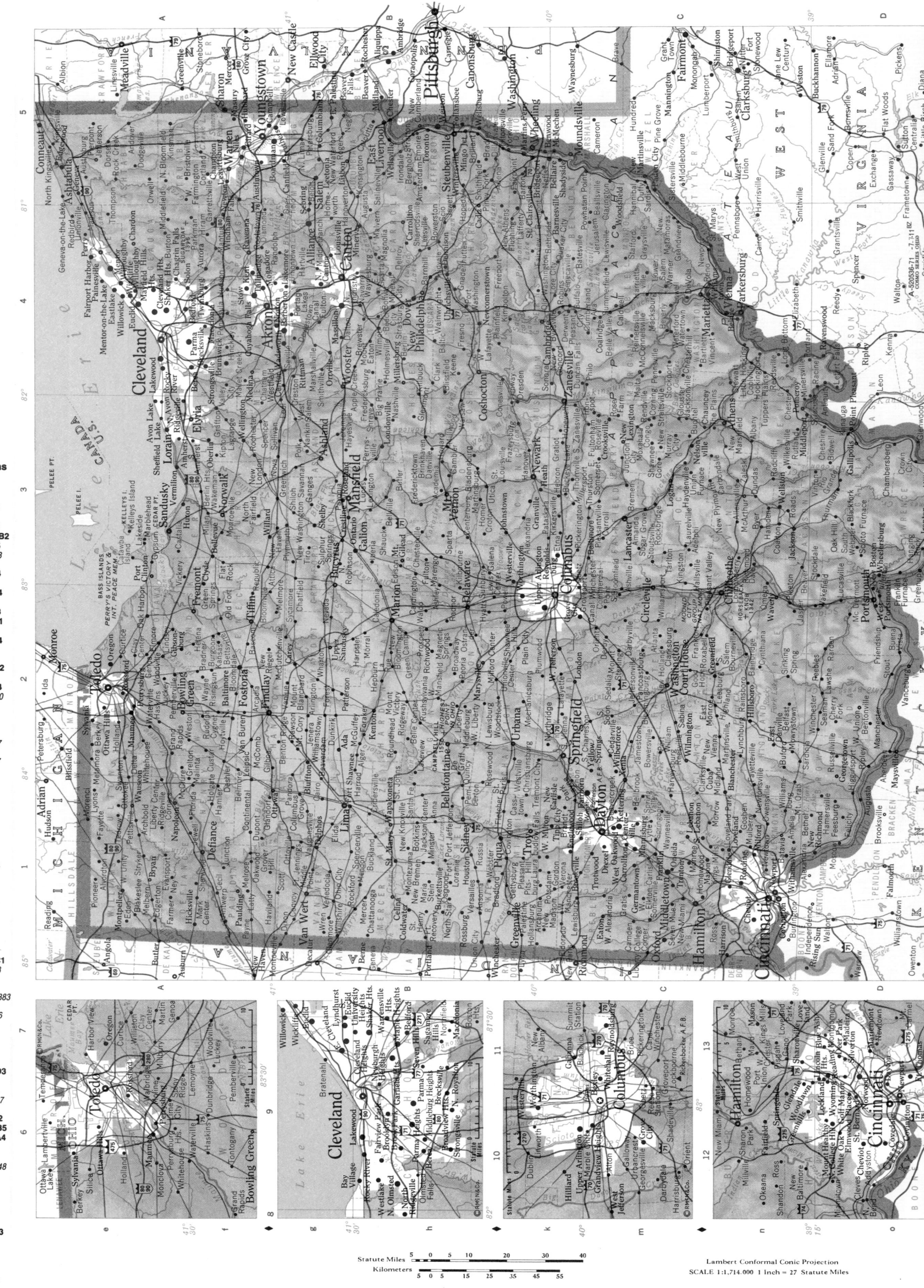

Cities and Towns

Akron 237,177 **A4**
Alliance 24,315 **B4**
Ashland 20,326 **B3**
Ashtabula 23,449 **A5**
Athens 19,743 **C3**
Barberton 29,751 **A4**
Bellefontaine 11,888 **B2**
Boardman 39,161 **A5**
Bowling Green 25,728 **A2**
Brunswick 28,104 **A4**
Bucyrus 13,433 **B3**
Cambridge 13,573 **B4**
Canton 93,077 **B4**
Chillicothe 23,420 **C3**
Cincinnati 385,457 **C1**
Circleville 11,700 **C3**
Cleveland 573,822 **A4**
Cleveland Heights 56,438 **A4**
Columbus 565,032 **C2**
Conneaut 13,835 **A5**
Coshocton 13,405 **B4**
Cuyahoga Falls 43,890 **A4**
Dayton 193,444 **C1**
Defiance 16,810 **A1**
Delaware 18,780 **B2**
East Cleveland 36,957 **g9**
East Liverpool 16,687 **B5**
Elyria 57,538 **A3**
Euclid 59,999 **A4**
Findlay 35,594 **A2**
Fostoria 15,743 **A2**
Fremont 17,834 **A2**
Greenville 12,999 **B1**
Hamilton 63,189 **C1**
Ironton 14,290 **D3**
Kettering 61,186 **C1**
Lakewood 61,963 **A4**
Lancaster 34,953 **C3**
Lima 47,381 **B1**
Lorain 75,416 **A3**
Mansfield 53,927 **B3**
Marietta 16,467 **C4**
Marion 37,040 **B2**
Massillon 30,557 **B4**
Medina 15,268 **A4**
Mentor 42,065 **A4**
Middletown 43,719 **C1**
Mount Vernon 14,323 **B3**
Newark 41,200 **B3**
New Philadelphia 16,883 **B4**
North Olmsted 36,486 **h9**
Norwalk 14,358 **A3**
Oxford 17,655 **C1**
Parma 92,548 **A4**
Piqua 20,480 **B1**
Portsmouth 25,943 **D3**
Salem 12,869 **B5**
Sandusky 31,360 **A3**
Shaker Heights 32,487 **A4**
Springfield 72,563 **C2**
Steubenville 26,400 **B5**
Strongsville 28,577 **A4**
Tiffin 19,549 **A2**
Toledo 354,635 **A2**
Upper Arlington 35,648 **B2**
Urbana 10,762 **B2**
Van Wert 11,035 **B1**
Warren 56,629 **A5**
Washington Court House 12,682 **C2**
Westerville 23,414 **B3**
Wooster 29,289 **B4**
Xenia 24,653 **C2**
Youngstown 115,436 **A5**
Zanesville 28,655 **C4**

Statute Miles

Kilometers

Lambert Conformal Conic Projection
SCALE 1:1,714,000 1 Inch = 27 Statute Miles

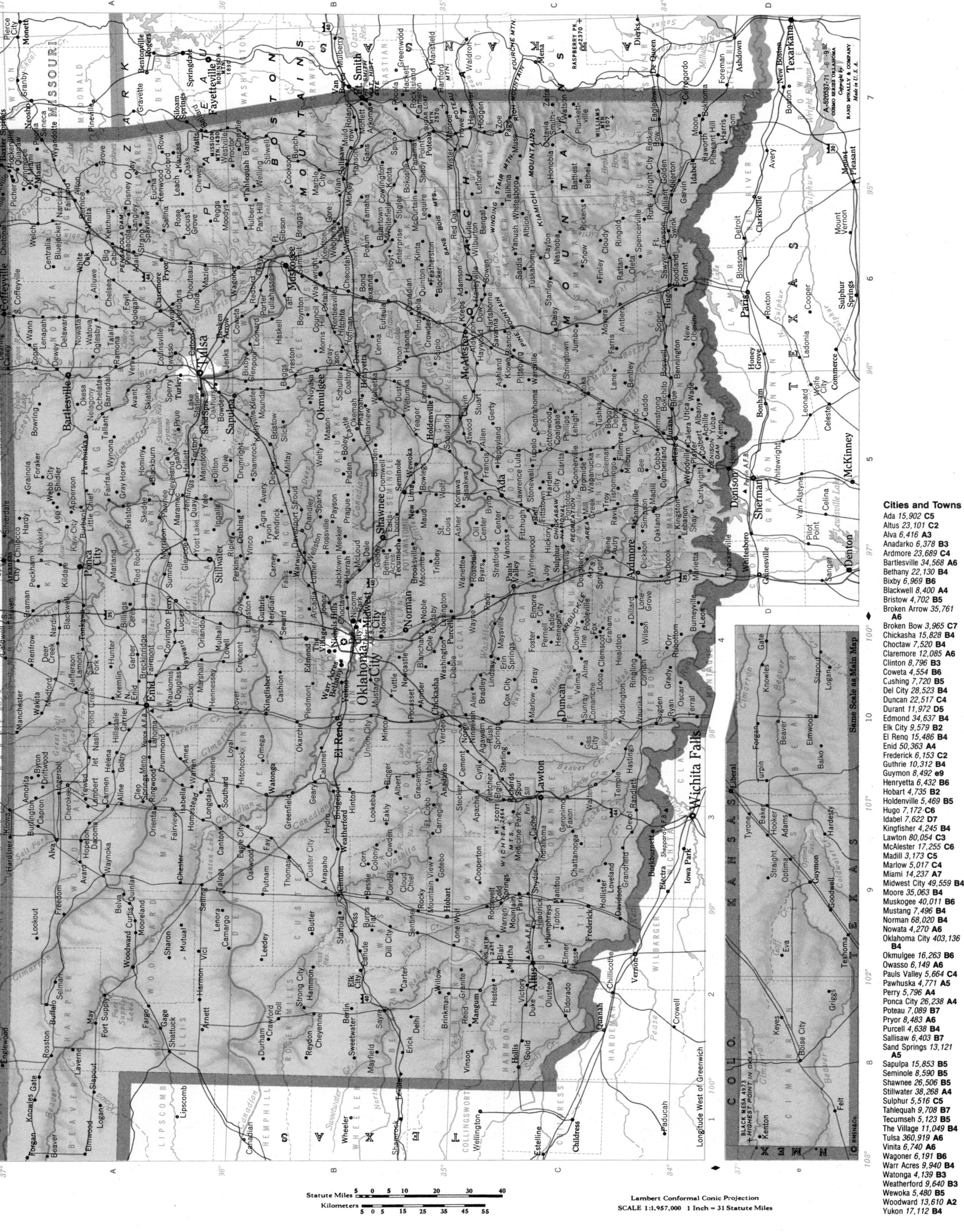

Statute Miles 5 0 5 10 20 30 40
Kilometers 5 0 5 15 25 35 45 55

Lambert Conformal Conic Projection
SCALE 1:1,957,000   1 Inch = 31 Statute Miles

Cities and Towns

Albany 26,678 **C3**
Aloha 10,000 **h12**
Altamont 19,805 **E5**
Ashland 14,943 **E4**
Astoria 9,998 **A3**
Baker 9,471 **C9**
Beaverton 30,582 **B4**
Bend 17,263 **C5**
Burns 3,579 **D7**
Canby 7,659 **B4**
Central Point 6,357 **E4**
Coos Bay 14,424 **D2**
Coquille 4,481 **D2**
Corvallis 40,960 **C3**
Cottage Grove 7,148 **D3**
Crater Lake 25 **E4**
Dallas 8,530 **C3**
Eugene 105,624 **C3**
Florence 4,411 **D2**
Forest Grove 11,499 **B3**
Gladstone 9,500 **B4**
Grants Pass 15,032 **E3**
Gresham 33,005 **B4**
Hermiston 9,408 **B7**
Hillsboro 27,664 **B4**
Hood River 4,329 **B5**
Independence 4,024 **C3**
John Day 2,012 **C8**
Keizer 18,592 **C3**
Klamath Falls 16,661 **E5**
La Grande 11,354 **B8**
Lake Oswego 22,527 **B4**
Lakeview 2,770 **E6**
Lebanon 10,413 **C4**
Lincoln City 5,469 **C3**
McMinnville 14,080 **B3**
Medford 39,603 **E4**
Metzger 5,544 **h12**
Milton-Freewater 5,086 **B8**
Milwaukie 17,931 **B4**
Monmouth 5,594 **C3**
Myrtle Creek 3,365 **D2**
Newberg 10,394 **B4**
Newport 7,519 **C2**
North Bend 9,779 **D2**
Oak Grove 11,640 **B4**
Ontario 8,814 **C10**
Oregon City 14,673 **B4**
Parkrose 21,103 **B4**
Pendleton 14,521 **B8**
Portland 366,383 **B4**
Prineville 5,276 **C6**
Redmond 6,452 **C5**
Reedsport 4,984 **D2**
River Road 10,370 **C3**
Roseburg 16,644 **D3**
St. Helens 7,064 **B4**
Salem 89,233 **C4**
Scappoose 3,213 **B4**
Seaside 5,193 **B3**
Silverton 5,168 **C4**
Springfield 41,621 **C4**
Stayton 4,396 **C4**
Sutherlin 4,560 **D3**
Sweet Home 6,921 **C4**
The Dalles 10,820 **B5**
Tigard 14,286 **h12**
Tillamook 3,981 **B3**
Tri City 3,439 **E3**
Umatilla 3,199 **B7**
West Linn 12,956 **B4**
West Slope 5,364 **g12**
White City 5,445 **E4**
Woodburn 11,196 **B4**

Statute Miles 5 0 5 10 20 30 40 50
Kilometers 5 0 5 15 25 35 45 55 65 75

Lambert Conformal Conic Projection
SCALE 1:2,329,000   1 Inch = 37 Statute Miles

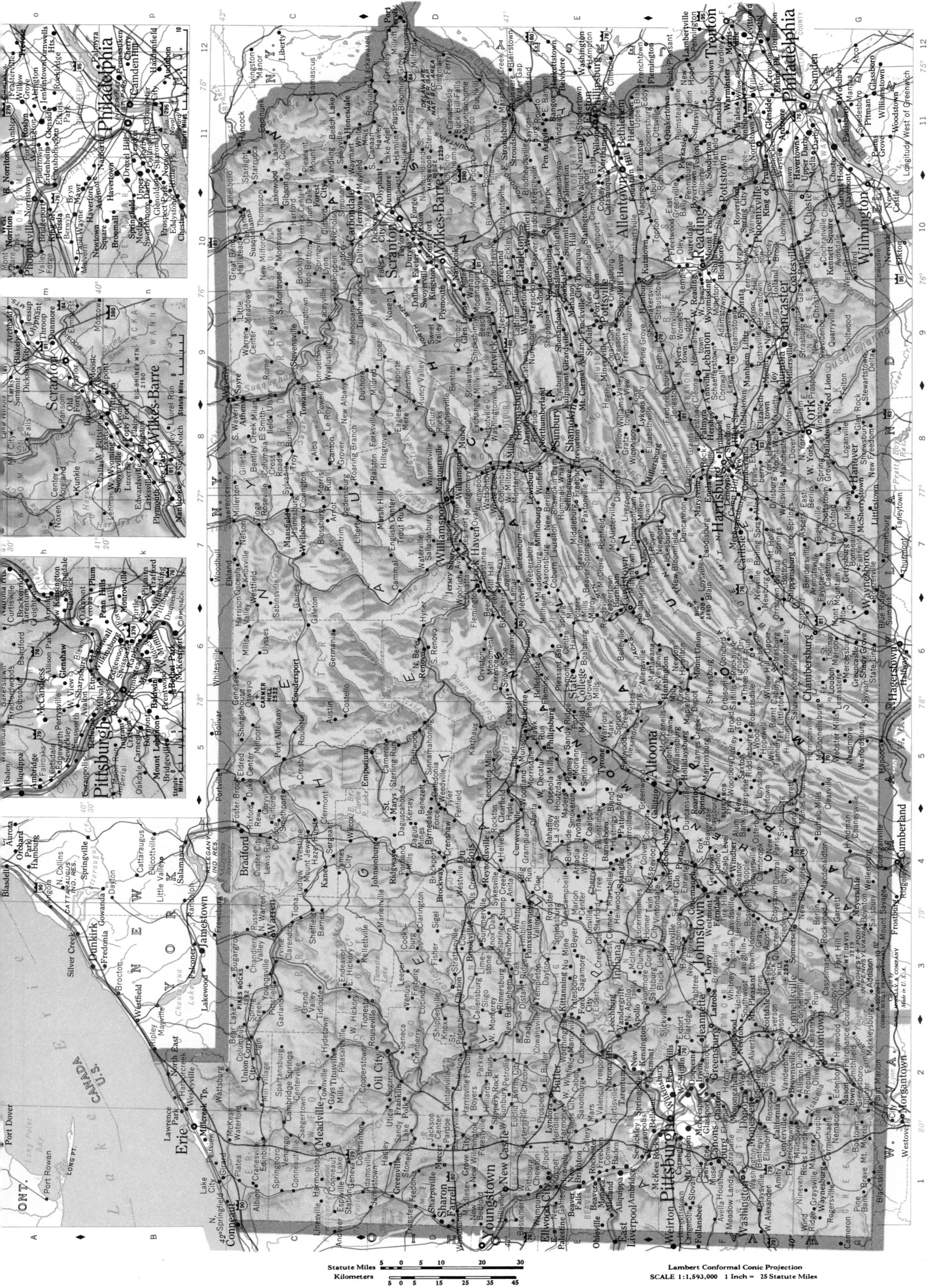

Statute Miles
Kilometers

Lambert Conformal Conic Projection
SCALE 1:1,593,000   1 Inch = 25 Statute Miles

Cities and Towns

Aliquippa 17,094 **E1**
Allentown 103,758 **E11**
Altoona 57,078 **E5**
Beaver Falls 12,525 **E1**
Berwick 11,850 **D9**
Bethel Park 34,755 **k14**
Bethlehem 70,419 **E11**
Bloomsburg 11,717 **E9**
Bradford 11,211 **C4**
Broomall 23,642 **p20**
Butler 17,026 **E2**
Carbondale 11,255 **C10**
Carlisle 18,314 **F7**
Chambersburg 16,174 **G6**
Chester 45,794 **G11**
Coatesville 10,698 **G10**
Connellsville 10,319 **F2**
Du Bois 9,290 **D4**
Easton 26,027 **E11**
Ephrata 11,095 **F9**
Erie 119,123 **B1**
Gettysburg 7,194 **G7**
Greensburg 17,558 **F2**
Hanover 14,890 **G8**
Harrisburg 53,264 **F8**
Havertown 36,000 **G11**
Hazleton 27,318 **E10**
Hershey 9,000 **F8**
Indiana 16,051 **E3**
Jeannette 13,106 **F2**
Johnstown 35,496 **F4**
King of Prussia 18,200 **F11**
Lancaster 54,725 **F9**
Lansdale 16,526 **F11**
Latrobe 10,799 **F3**
Lebanon 25,711 **F9**
Levittown 78,600 **F12**
Lewistown 9,830 **E6**
Lock Haven 9,617 **D7**
McKeesport 31,012 **F2**
Meadville 15,544 **C1**
Middletown 10,122 **F8**
Millcreek Township 44,303 **B1**
Monroeville 30,977 **k14**
Mount Lebanon 34,414 **F1**
New Castle 33,621 **D1**
Norristown 34,684 **F11**
Oil City 13,881 **D2**
Penn Hills 57,632 **F2**
Philadelphia 1,688,210 **G11**
Pittsburgh 423,959 **F1**
Plum 25,390 **k14**
Pottstown 22,729 **F10**
Pottsville 18,195 **E9**
Punxsutawney 7,479 **E4**
Reading 78,686 **F10**
Scranton 88,117 **D10**
Shamokin 10,357 **E8**
Sharon 19,057 **D1**
Springfield 25,326 **p20**
State College 36,130 **E6**
Sunbury 12,292 **E8**
Uniontown 14,510 **G2**
Upper Darby 50,200 **G11**
Warminster 35,543 **F11**
Warren 12,146 **C3**
Washington 18,363 **F1**
Waynesboro 9,726 **G6**
West Chester 17,435 **G11**
West Mifflin 26,552 **F2**
Wilkes-Barre 51,551 **D10**
Wilkinsburg 23,669 **F2**
Williamsport 33,401 **D7**
Willow Grove 21,300 **F11**
York 44,619 **G8**

RHODE ISLAND

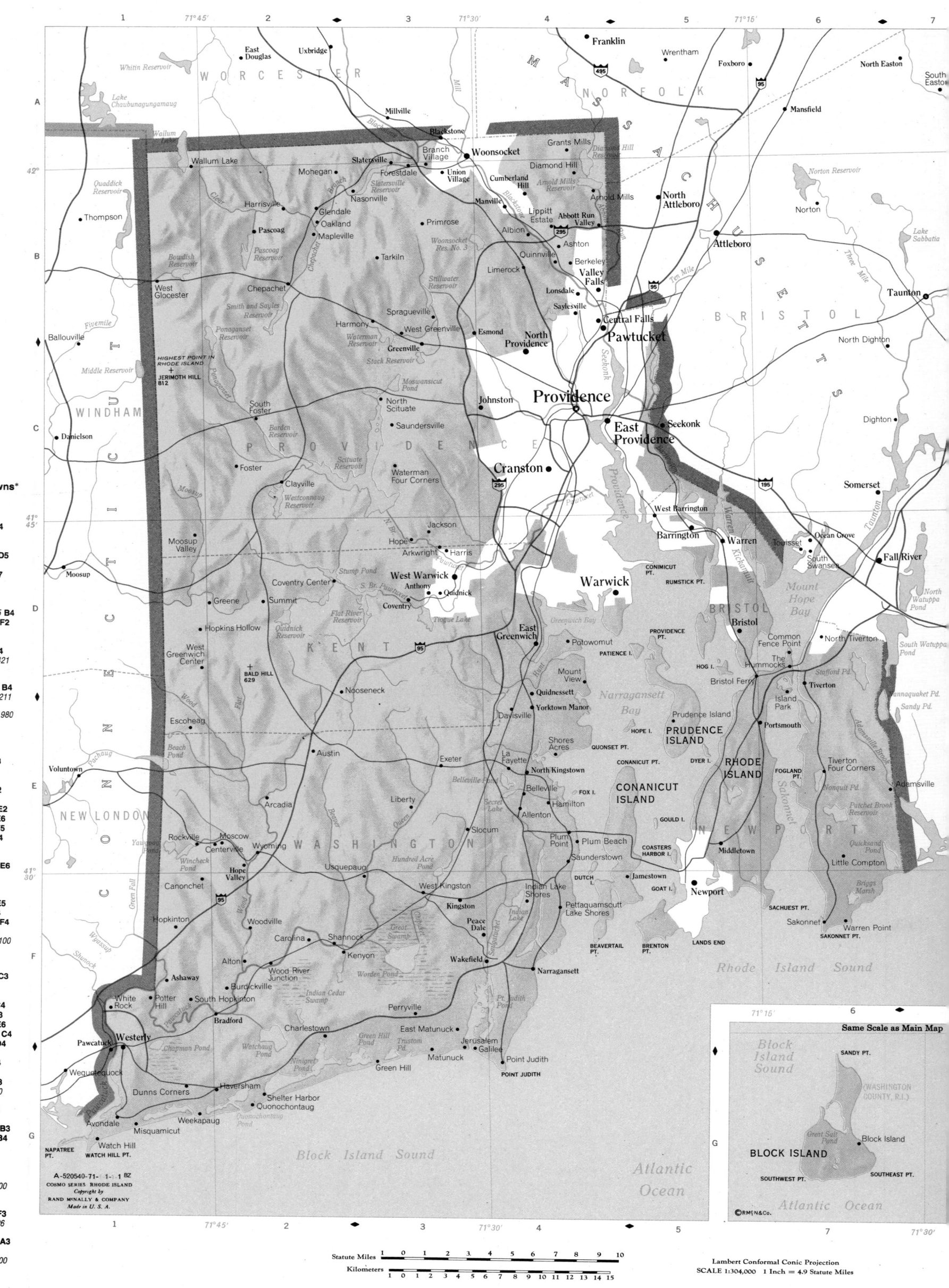

Cities and Towns*

Albion 1,200 **B4**
Allenton 600 **E4**
Anthony 4,500 **D3**
Arnold Mills 600 **B4**
Ashaway 1,747 **F1**
Ashton 875 **B4**
Barrington 16,174 **D5**
Berkeley 930 **B4**
Block Island 620 **h7**
Bradford 1,354 **F1**
Bristol 20,128 **D5**
Carolina 500 **F2**
Central Falls 16,995 **B4**
Charlestown 1,200 **F2**
Chepachet 900 **B2**
Coventry 8,000 **D3**
Cranston 71,992 **C4**
Cumberland Hill 5,421 **B4**
Davisville 550 **E4**
Diamond Hill 1,150 **B4**
East Greenwich 10,211 **D4**
East Providence 50,980 **C4**
Esmond 3,500 **B4**
Forestdale 450 **B4**
Glendale 600 **B2**
Greenville 7,576 **C3**
Harmony 800 **B3**
Harris 1,000 **D3**
Harrisville 1,224 **B2**
Hope 490 **D3**
Hope Valley 1,414 **E2**
Island Park 1,000 **E6**
Jamestown 4,040 **F5**
Johnston 24,907 **C4**
Kingston 5,419 **F3**
La Fayette 680 **E4**
Little Compton 300 **E6**
Lonsdale 4,100 **B4**
Manville 3,100 **B4**
Mapleville 900 **B2**
Middletown 3,350 **E5**
Mount View 560 **D4**
Narragansett 3,342 **F4**
Newport 29,259 **F5**
North Kingstown 3,100 **E4**
North Providence 29,188 **C4**
North Scituate 325 **C3**
Oakland 500 **B2**
Pascoag 3,807 **B2**
Pawtucket 71,204 **C4**
Peace Dale 3,100 **F3**
Portsmouth 4,300 **E6**
Providence 156,804 **C4**
Quidnessett 3,300 **D4**
Quidnick 2,300 **D3**
Saylesville 3,200 **B4**
Shannock 600 **D2**
Slatersville 2,000 **A3**
South Hopkinton 500 **F1**
Spragueville 430 **B3**
Tiverton 7,653 **D6**
Union Village 2,400 **B3**
Valley Falls 10,892 **B4**
Wakefield 3,400 **F3**
Warren 10,640 **D5**
Warwick 87,123 **D4**
Watch Hill 500 **G1**
West Barrington 3,700 **C5**
Westerly 14,093 **F1**
West Kingston 700 **F3**
West Warwick 27,026 **D3**
Woonsocket 45,914 **A3**
Wyoming 600 **E2**
Yorktown Manor 2,500 **E4**

*Populations are for localities, not incorporated towns.

Statute Miles
Kilometers

A-520540-71- 1- 1 BZ
COSMO SERIES RHODE ISLAND
Copyright by
RAND McNALLY & COMPANY
Made in U.S.A.

Same Scale as Main Map

BLOCK ISLAND

Lambert Conformal Conic Projection
SCALE 1:304,000   1 Inch = 4.9 Statute Miles

282

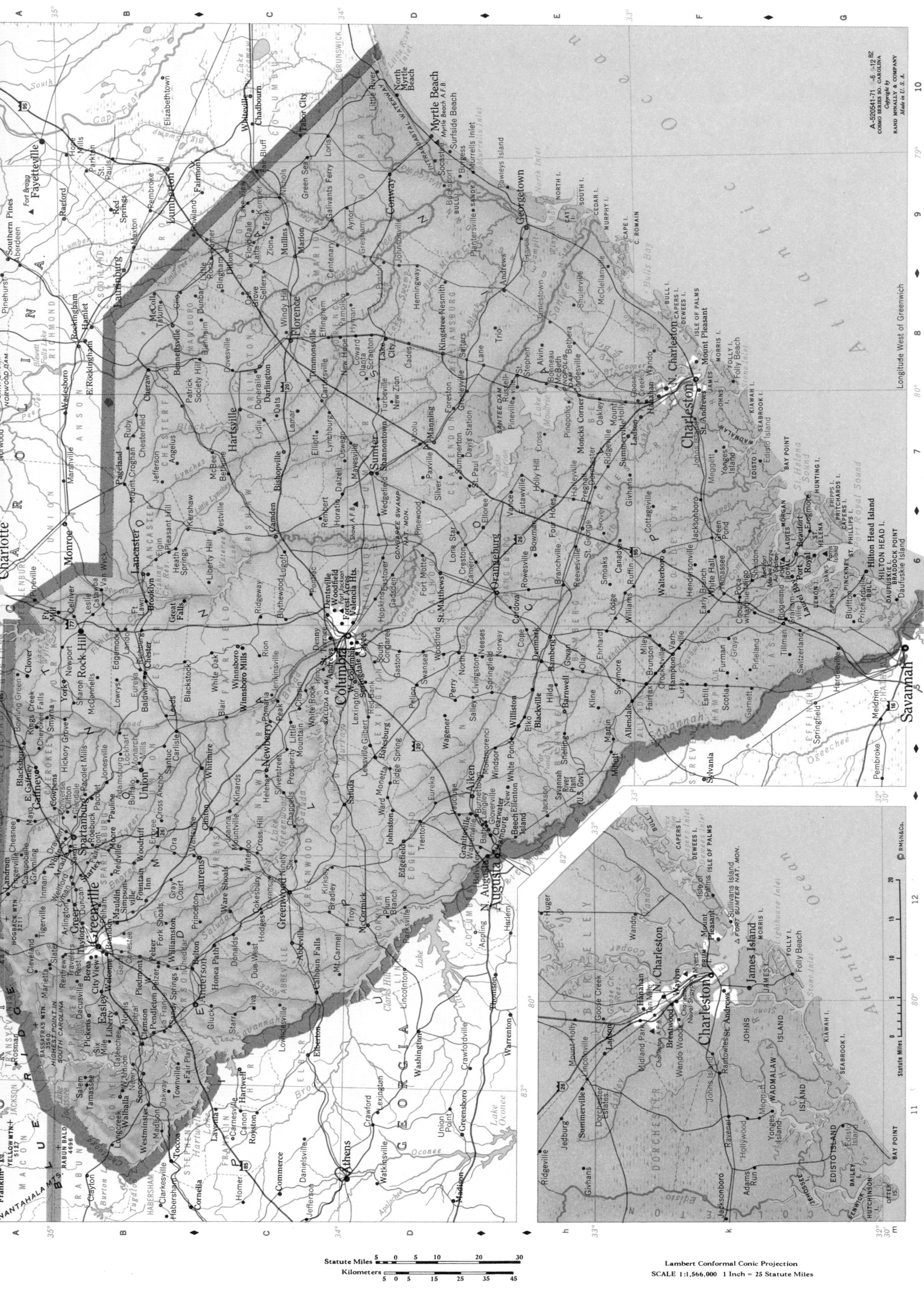

Cities and Towns

Abbeville 5,833 C3
Aiken 14,978 D4
Allendale 4,400 E5
Anderson 27,965 B2
Barnwell 5,572 E5
Batesburg 4,023 D4
Beaufort 8,634 G6
Belton 5,312 B3
Belvedere 6,859 D4
Bennettsville 8,774 B8
Berea 7,500 B3
Bishopville 3,429 C7
Camden 7,462 C6
Cayce 11,701 D5
Charleston 69,510 F8
Cheraw 5,654 B8
Chester 6,820 B5
Clemson 8,118 B2
Clinton 8,596 C4
Columbia 100,385 C5
Conway 10,240 C9
Cowpens 2,023 A4
Darlington 7,989 C8
Denmark 4,434 E5
Dillon 7,060 C9
Easley 14,264 B2
Florence 29,176 C8
Fort Mill 4,162 A6
Fountain Inn 4,226 B3
Gaffney 13,453 A4
Georgetown 10,144 E9
Goose Creek 17,811 F7
Greenville 58,242 B3
Greenwood 21,613 C3
Greer 10,525 B3
Hanahan 13,224 F7
Hartsville 7,631 C7
Hilton Head Island
   11,344 G6
Honea Path 4,114 C3
James Island 24,124
   k12
Kingstree 4,147 D8
Ladson 13,246 F7
Lake City 6,731 C8
Lancaster 9,703 B6
Laurel Bay 5,238 G6
Laurens 10,587 C3
Manning 4,746 D7
Marion 7,700 C9
Mauldin 8,143 B3
Moncks Corner 3,699
   E7
Mount Pleasant 14,209
   F8
Mullins 6,068 C9
Myrtle Beach 18,446
   D10
Newberry 9,866 C4
North Augusta 13,593
   D4
North Charleston 62,534
   F8
North Myrtle Beach
   3,960 D10
Orangeburg 14,933 E6
Rock Hill 35,344 B5
St. Andrews 9,908 F7
St. Andrews 20,245 C5
Seneca 7,436 B2
Shannontown 7,900 D7
Simpsonville 9,037 B3
Spartanburg 43,826 B4
Summerville 6,706 E7
Sumter 24,890 D7
Taylors 12,100 B3
Union 10,523 B4
Walhalla 3,977 B1
West Columbia 10,409
   D5
Williamston 4,310 B3
Woodruff 5,171 B3
York 6,412 B5

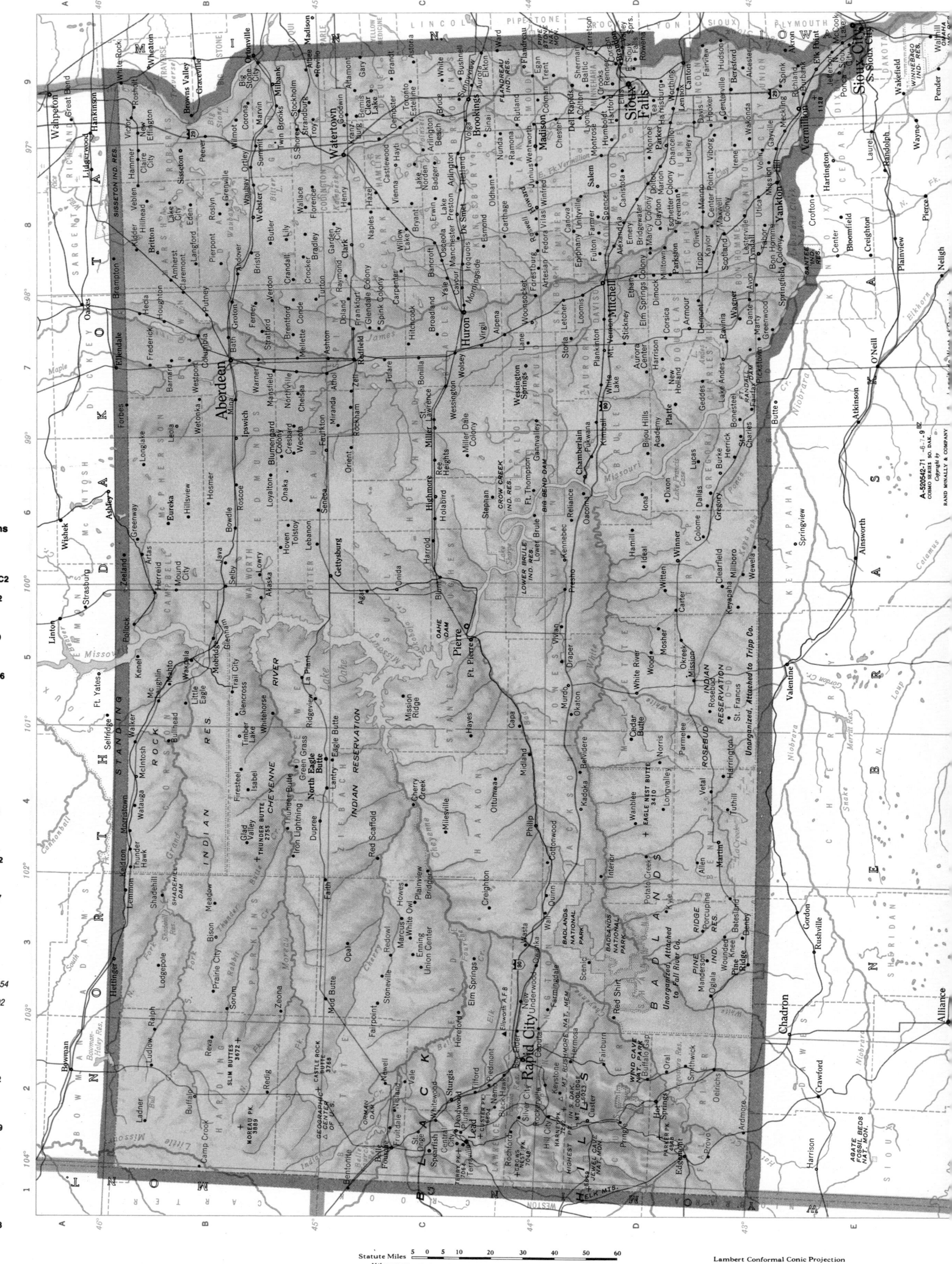

Cities and Towns

Aberdeen 25,851 **B7**
Alcester 885 **D9**
Arlington 991 **C8**
Armour 819 **D7**
Belle Fourche 4,692 **C2**
Beresford 1,865 **D9**
Black Hawk 1,608 **C2**
Box Elder 3,186 **C2**
Brandon 2,589 **D9**
Britton 1,590 **B8**
Brookings 14,951 **C9**
Burke 859 **D6**
Canton 2,886 **D9**
Centerville 892 **D9**
Chamberlain 2,258 **D6**
Clark 1,351 **C8**
Clear Lake 1,310 **C9**
Custer 1,830 **D2**
De Smet 1,237 **C8**
Deadwood 2,035 **C2**
Edgemont 1,468 **D2**
Elk Point 1,661 **E9**
Eureka 1,360 **B6**
Faulkton 981 **B6**
Flandreau 2,114 **C9**
Fort Pierre 1,789 **C5**
Freeman 1,462 **D8**
Garretson 963 **D9**
Gettysburg 1,623 **C6**
Gregory 1,503 **D6**
Groton 1,230 **B7**
Hartford 1,207 **D9**
Highmore 1,055 **C6**
Hot Springs 4,742 **D2**
Howard 1,169 **C8**
Huron 13,000 **C7**
Ipswich 1,153 **B6**
Lake Andes 1,029 **D7**
Lead 4,330 **C2**
Lemmon 1,871 **B3**
Lennox 1,827 **D9**
Martin 1,018 **D4**
Milbank 4,120 **B9**
Miller 1,931 **C7**
Mitchell 13,916 **D7**
Mobridge 4,174 **B5**
North Eagle Butte 1,354 **B4**
North Sioux City 1,992 **E9**
Parker 999 **D8**
Parkston 1,545 **D8**
Philip 1,088 **C4**
Pierre 11,973 **C5**
Pine Ridge 3,059 **D3**
Platte 1,334 **D7**
Rapid City 46,492 **C2**
Redfield 3,027 **C7**
Salem 1,486 **D8**
Scotland 1,022 **D8**
Selby 884 **B5**
Sioux Falls 81,343 **D9**
Sisseton 2,789 **B8**
Spearfish 5,251 **C2**
Springfield 1,377 **E8**
Sturgis 5,184 **C2**
Tyndall 1,253 **E8**
Vermillion 10,136 **E9**
Volga 1,221 **C9**
Wagner 1,453 **D7**
Wall 770 **D3**
Watertown 15,649 **C8**
Webster 2,417 **B8**
Wessington Springs 1,203 **C7**
Winner 3,472 **D6**
Yankton 12,011 **E8**

Statute Miles 5 0 5 10 20 30 40 50 60
Kilometers 5 0 15 25 35 45 55 75

Lambert Conformal Conic Projection
SCALE 1:2,091,000   1 Inch = 33 Statute Miles

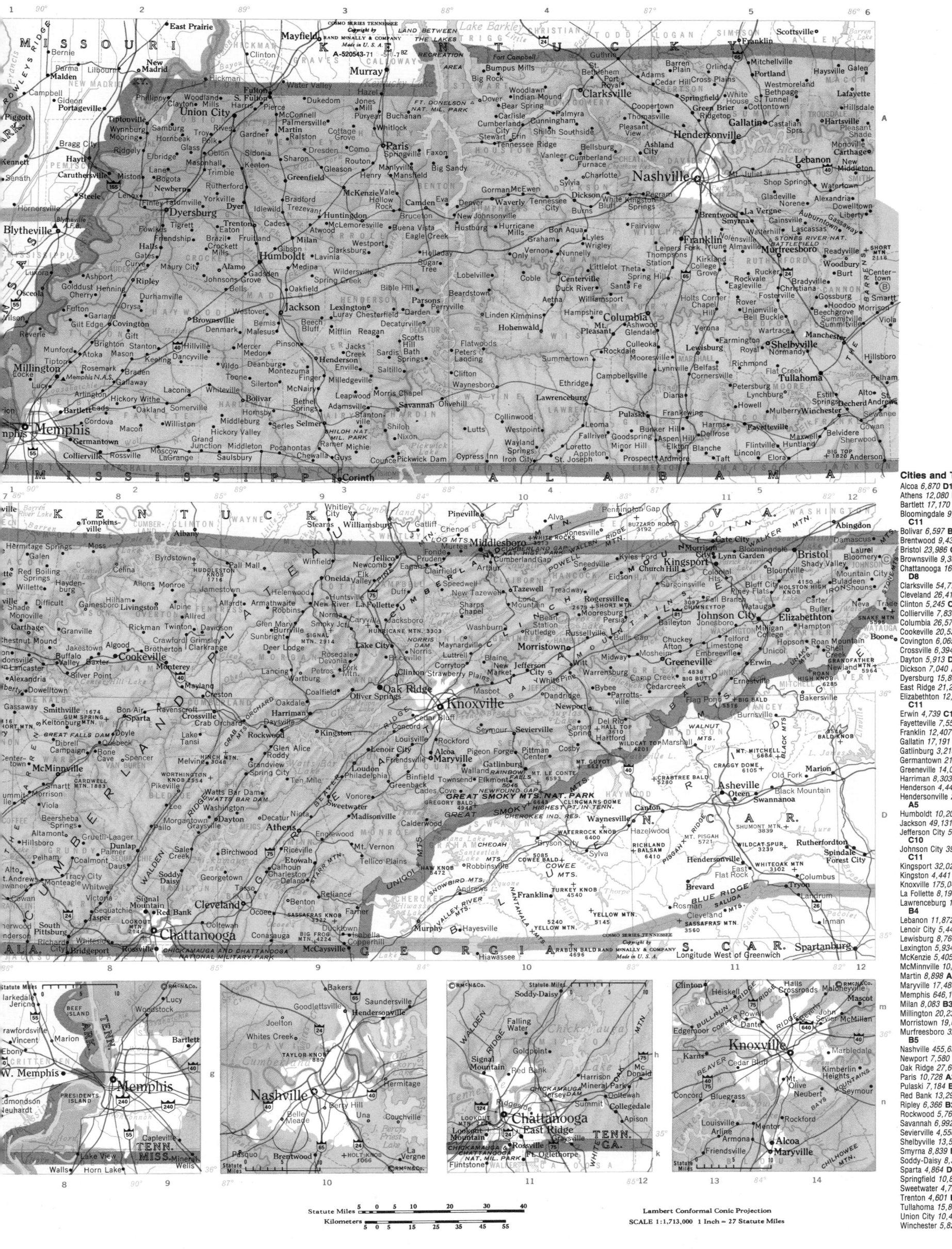

Lambert Conformal Conic Projection
SCALE 1:1,713,000   1 Inch = 27 Statute Miles

Statute Miles 5 0 5 10 20 30 40
Kilometers 5 0 5 15 25 35 45 55

TEXAS

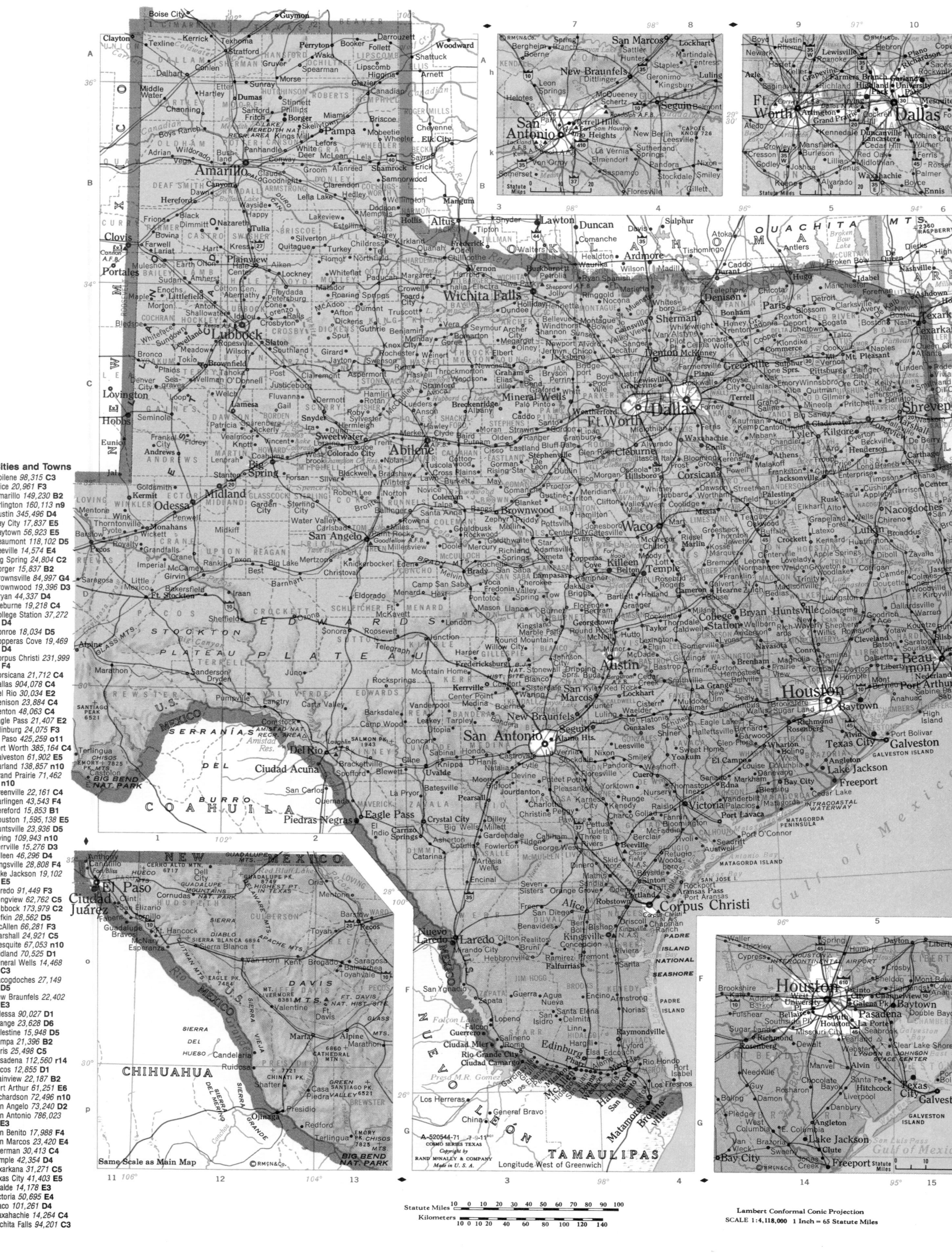

Statute Miles 10 0 10 20 30 40 50 60 70 80 90 100

Kilometers 10 0 10 20 40 60 80 100 120 140

Lambert Conformal Conic Projection
SCALE 1:4,118,000 1 Inch = 65 Statute Miles

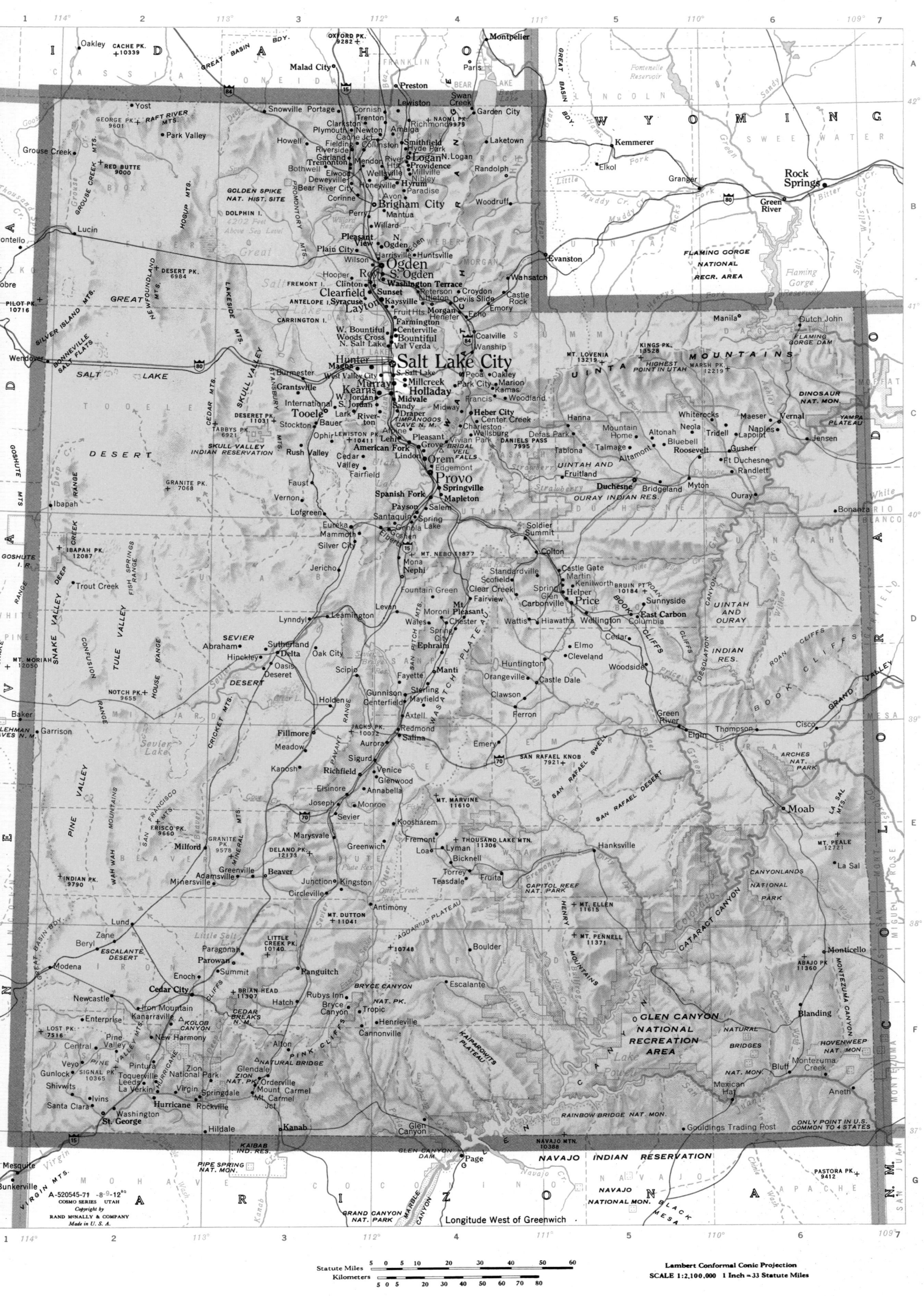

Statute Miles
Kilometers

Lambert Conformal Conic Projection
SCALE 1:2,100,000   1 Inch ≈ 33 Statute Miles

Cities and Towns

American Fork 12,693 **C4**
Beaver 1,792 **E3**
Blanding 3,118 **F6**
Bountiful 32,877 **C4**
Brigham City 15,596 **B3**
Cedar City 10,972 **F2**
Centerville 8,069 **C4**
Clearfield 17,982 **B3**
Clinton 5,777 **B3**
Delta 1,930 **D3**
Draper 5,521 **C4**
Ephraim 2,810 **D4**
Farmington 4,691 **C4**
Fillmore 2,083 **E3**
Fruit Heights 2,728 **B4**
Grantsville 4,419 **C3**
Heber City 4,362 **C4**
Helper 2,724 **D5**
Holladay 28,700 **C4**
Huntington 2,316 **D5**
Hurricane 2,361 **F2**
Hyrum 3,952 **B4**
Kanab 2,148 **F3**
Kaysville 9,811 **B4**
Kearns 17,000 **C4**
Layton 26,393 **B4**
Lehi 6,848 **C4**
Logan 26,844 **B4**
Magna 8,600 **C3**
Manti 2,080 **D4**
Midvale 10,146 **C4**
Moab 5,333 **E6**
Monticello 1,929 **F6**
Mount Pleasant 2,049 **D4**
Murray 25,750 **C4**
Nephi 3,285 **D4**
North Ogden 9,309 **B4**
North Salt Lake 5,548 **C4**
Ogden 64,407 **B4**
Orem 52,399 **C4**
Panguitch 1,343 **F3**
Payson 8,246 **C4**
Pleasant Grove 10,833 **C4**
Price 9,086 **D5**
Providence 2,675 **B4**
Provo 74,108 **C4**
Richfield 5,482 **E3**
Riverton 7,293 **C4**
Roosevelt 3,842 **C5**
Roy 19,694 **B3**
St. George 11,350 **F2**
Salem 2,233 **C4**
Salina 1,992 **E4**
Salt Lake City 163,697 **C4**
Sandy 52,210 **C4**
Santaquin 2,175 **D4**
Smithfield 4,993 **B4**
South Jordan 7,492 **C3**
South Ogden 11,366 **B4**
Spanish Fork 9,825 **C4**
Springville 12,101 **C4**
Sunset 5,733 **B3**
Syracuse 3,702 **B3**
Tooele 14,335 **C3**
Tremonton 3,464 **B3**
Val Verda 6,500 **C4**
Vernal 6,600 **C6**
Washington 3,092 **F2**
Washington Terrace 8,212 **B4**
Wendover 1,099 **C1**
West Bountiful 3,556 **C4**
West Jordan 27,192 **C4**
West Valley City 72,511 **C4**
Woods Cross 4,263 **C4**

287

VERMONT

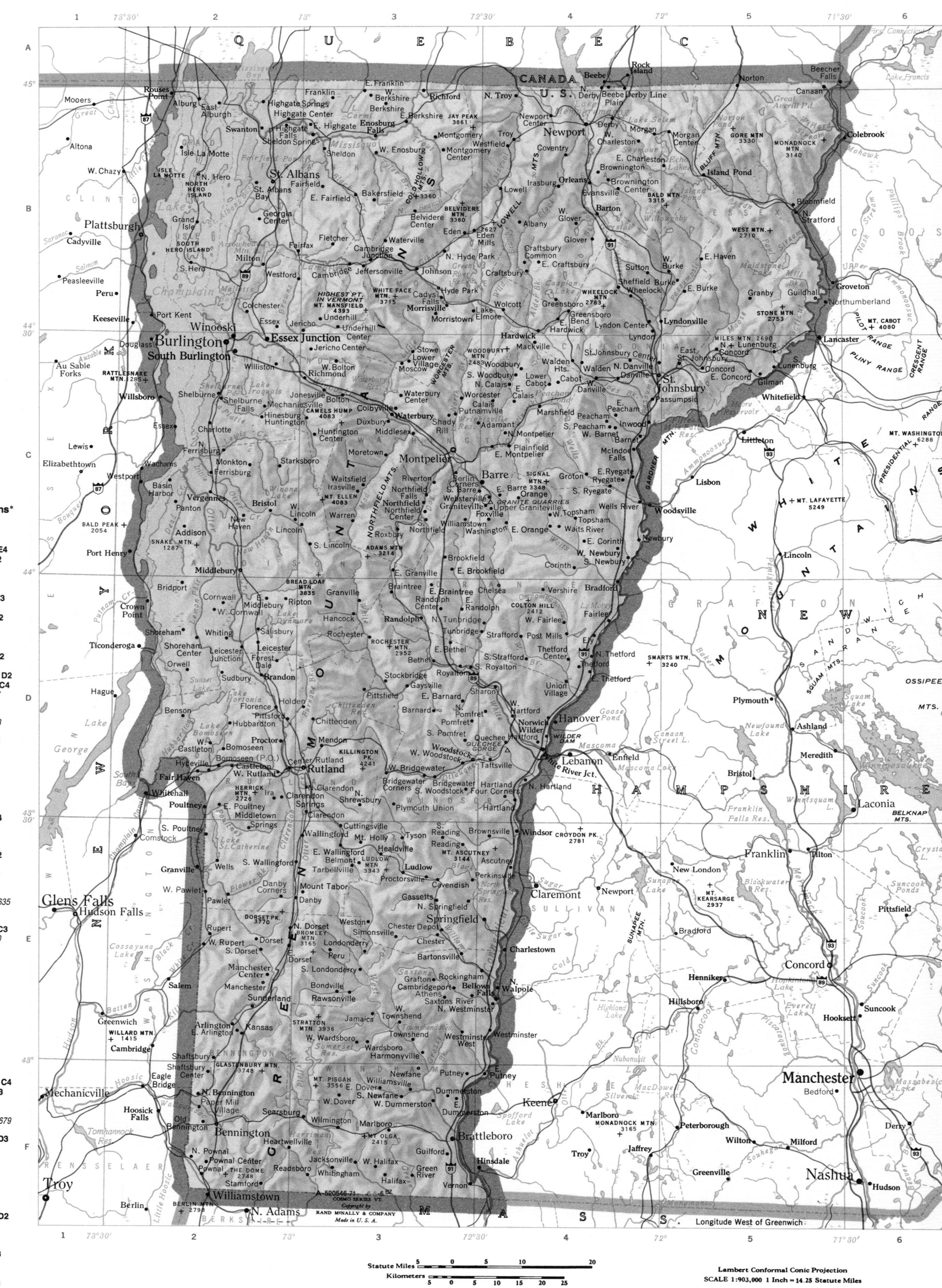

Lambert Conformal Conic Projection
SCALE 1:1,822,000 1 Inch = 29 Statute Miles

Statute Miles 5 0 5 10 20 30 40
Kilometers 5 0 5 15 25 35 45 55

Cities and Towns

Alexandria 103,217 **B5**
Annandale 35,300 **g12**
Appomattox 1,345 **C4**
Arlington 152,700 **B5**
Bedford 5,991 **C3**
Big Stone Gap 4,748 **f9**
Blacksburg 30,638 **C2**
Bluefield 5,946 **C1**
Bon Air 13,000 **C5**
Bristol 19,042 **f9**
Buena Vista 6,717 **C3**
Charlottesville 39,916
　B4
Chesapeake 114,486 **D6**
Chester 7,000 **C5**
Chincoteague 1,607 **C7**
Christiansburg 10,345
　C2
Clifton Forge 5,046 **C3**
Collinsville 7,400 **D3**
Colonial Heights 16,509
　C5
Covington 9,063 **C3**
Culpepper 6,621 **B5**
Dale City 23,000 **B5**
Danville 45,642 **D3**
Emporia 4,840 **D5**
Engleside 21,400 **g12**
Fairfax 19,390 **B5**
Farmville 6,067 **C4**
Franklin 7,308 **D6**
Fredericksburg 15,322
　B5
Front Royal 11,126 **B4**
Galax 6,524 **D2**
Hampton 122,617 **C6**
Harrisonburg 19,671 **B4**
Herndon 11,449 **B5**
Highland Springs 7,500
　C5
Hollins 11,000 **C3**
Hopewell 23,397 **C5**
Leesburg 8,357 **A5**
Lexington 7,292 **C3**
Lynchburg 66,743 **C4**
McLean 22,000 **g12**
Manassas 15,438 **B5**
Manassas Park 6,524
　B5
Marion 7,029 **f10**
Martinsville 18,149 **D3**
Mechanicsville 9,000
　C5
Newport News 144,903
　D6
Norfolk 266,979 **D6**
Norton 4,757 **f9**
Petersburg 41,055 **C5**
Poquoson 8,726 **C6**
Portsmouth 104,577 **D6**
Pulaski 10,106 **C2**
Radford 13,225 **C2**
Reston 32,000 **B5**
Richlands 5,796 **e10**
Richmond 219,214 **C5**
Roanoke 100,220 **C3**
Salem 23,958 **C2**
Shenandoah 1,861 **B4**
South Boston 7,093 **D4**
Springfield 12,500 **g12**
Staunton 21,857 **B3**
Sterling 12,000 **A5**
Suffolk 47,621 **D6**
Tazewell 4,468 **e10**
Vienna 15,469 **B5**
Vinton 8,027 **C3**
Virginia Beach 262,199
　D7
Waynesboro 15,329 **B4**
West Springfield 16,000
　g12
Williamsburg 9,870 **C6**
Winchester 20,217 **A4**
Woodbridge 35,000 **B5**
Wytheville 7,135 **D1**
Yorktown 390 **C6**

WASHINGTON

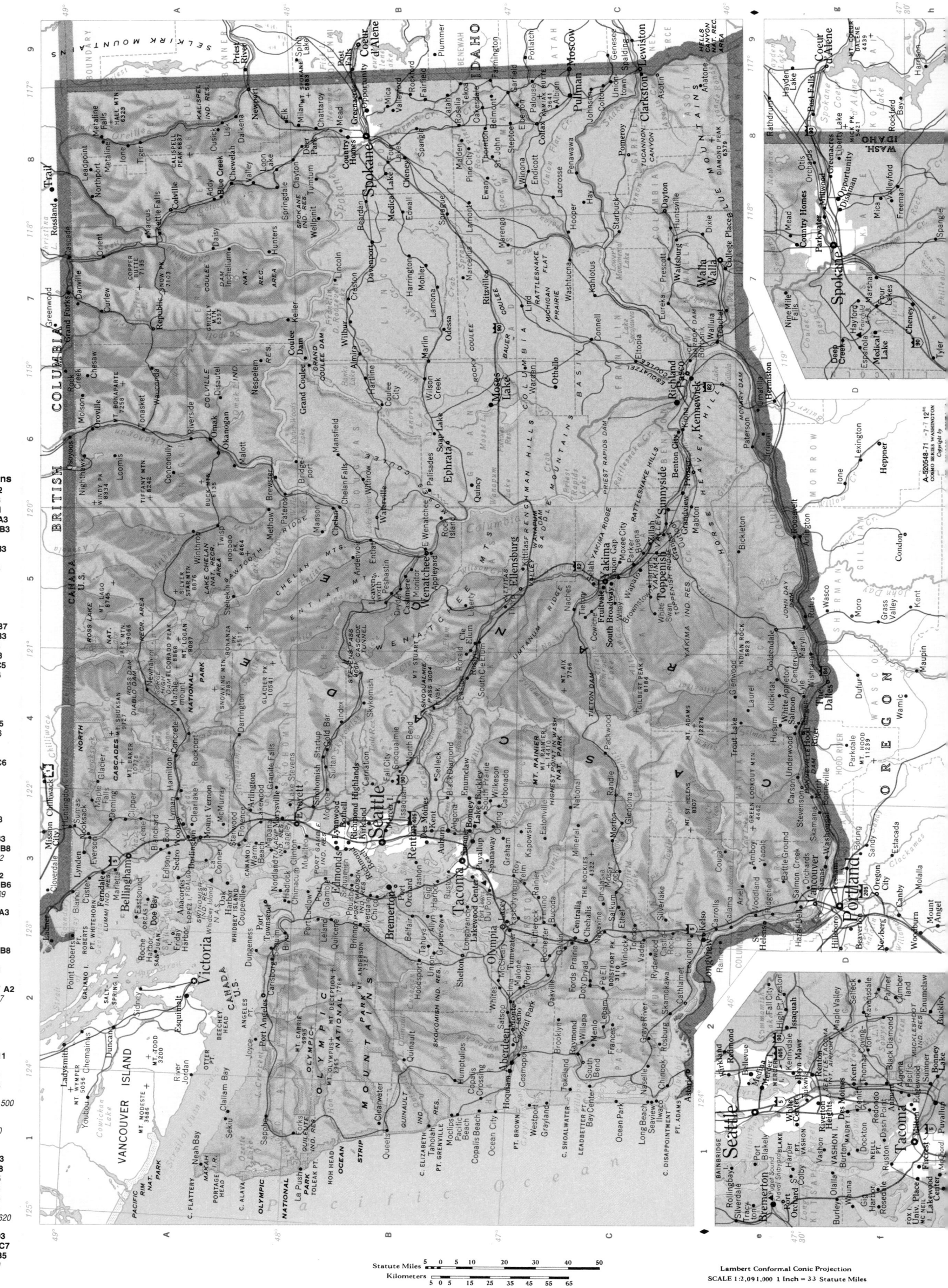

Statute Miles
Kilometers

Lambert Conformal Conic Projection
SCALE 1:2,091,000 1 Inch = 33 Statute Miles

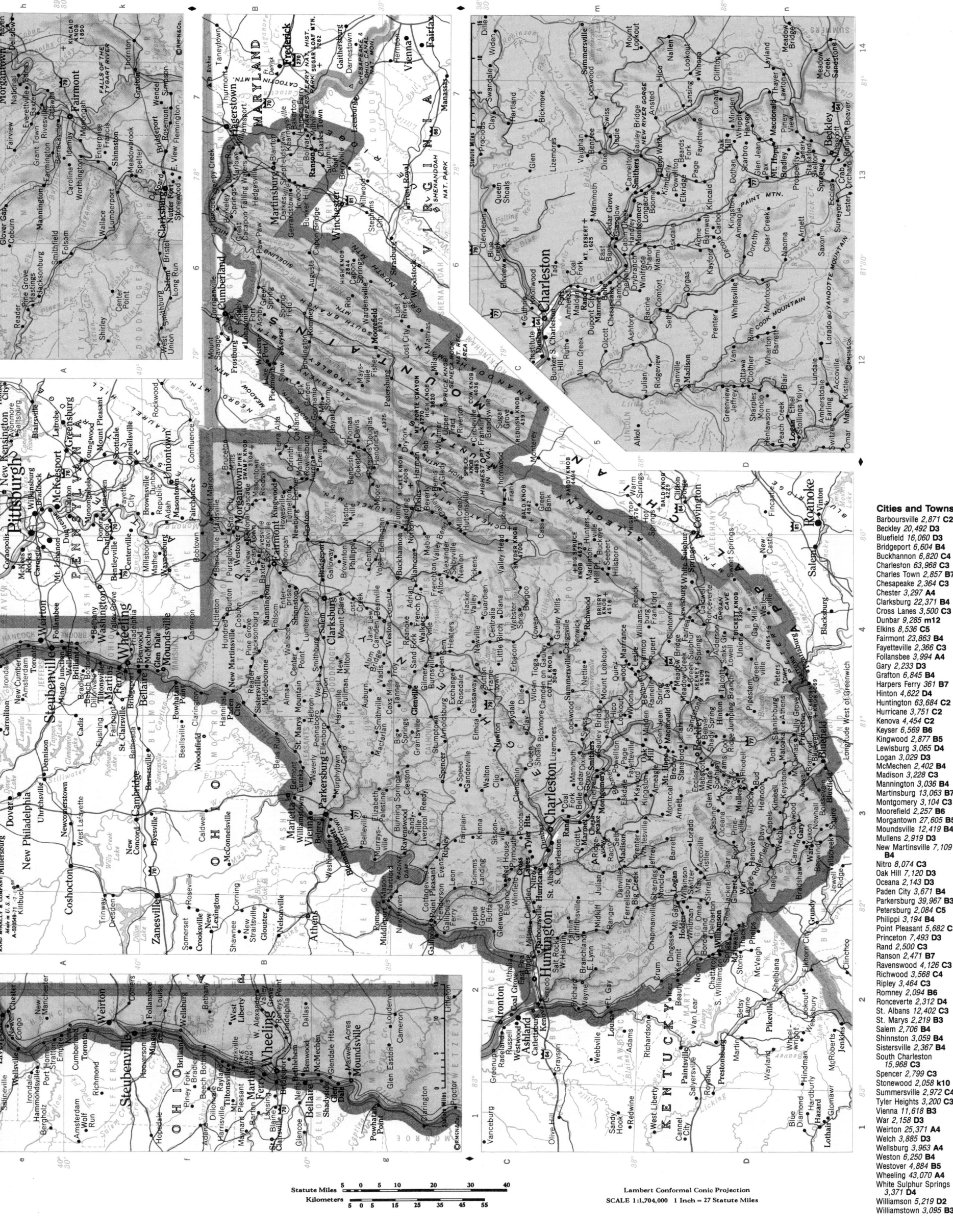

Statute Miles 5 0 5 10 20 30 40
Kilometers 5 0 5 15 25 35 45 55

Lambert Conformal Conic Projection
SCALE 1:1,704,000 1 Inch = 27 Statute Miles

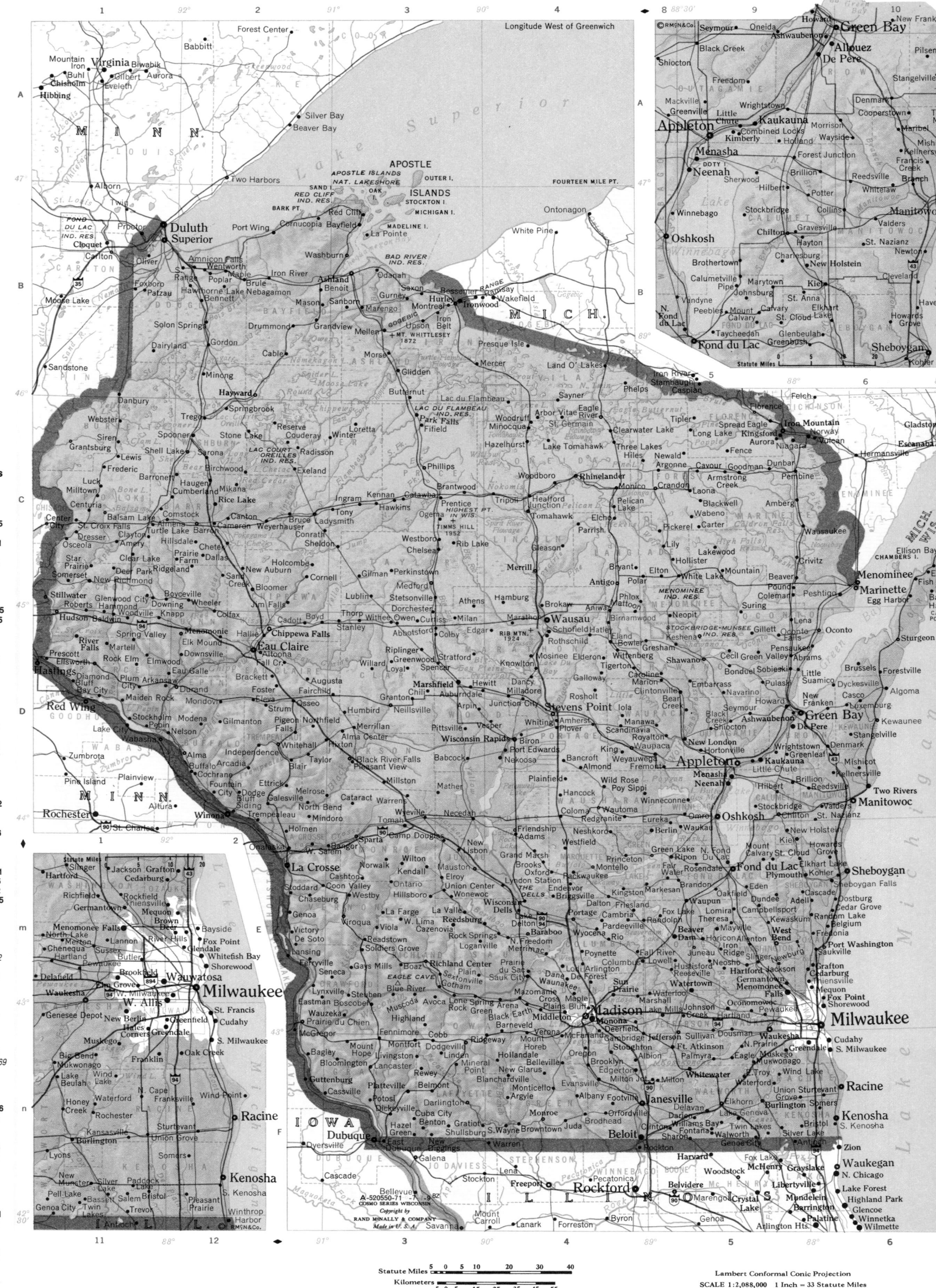

Longitude West of Greenwich

Cities and Towns

Antigo 8,653 **C4**
Appleton 58,913 **D5**
Ashland 9,115 **B3**
Baraboo 8,081 **E4**
Beaver Dam 14,149 **E5**
Beloit 35,207 **F4**
Brookfield 34,035 **m11**
Burlington 8,385 **F5**
Chippewa Falls 12,270 **D2**
Cudahy 19,547 **F6**
De Pere 14,892 **D5**
Eau Claire 51,509 **D2**
Fond du Lac 35,863 **E5**
Fort Atkinson 9,785 **F5**
Franklin 16,871 **n11**
Green Bay 87,899 **D6**
Greendale 16,928 **F5**
Greenfield 31,467 **n11**
Hayward 1,698 **B2**
Hudson 5,434 **D1**
Janesville 51,071 **F4**
Kaukauna 11,310 **D5**
Kenosha 77,685 **F6**
La Crosse 48,347 **E2**
Lake Geneva 5,612 **F5**
Madison 170,616 **E4**
Manitowoc 32,547 **D6**
Marinette 11,965 **C6**
Marshfield 18,290 **D3**
Menasha 14,728 **D5**
Menomonee Falls 27,845 **E5**
Menomonie 12,769 **D2**
Mequon 16,193 **E6**
Merrill 9,578 **C4**
Milwaukee 636,236 **E6**
Monroe 10,027 **F4**
Muskego 15,277 **F5**
Neenah 22,432 **D5**
New Berlin 30,529 **n11**
New London 6,210 **D5**
Oak Creek 16,932 **n12**
Oconomowoc 9,909 **E5**
Oconto 4,505 **D6**
Oshkosh 49,620 **D5**
Park Falls 3,192 **C3**
Platteville 9,580 **F3**
Portage 7,896 **E4**
Port Washington 8,612 **E6**
Prairie du Chien 5,859 **E2**
Racine 85,725 **F6**
Reedsburg 5,038 **E3**
Rhinelander 7,873 **C4**
Rice Lake 7,691 **C2**
River Falls 9,019 **D1**
Shawano 7,013 **D5**
Sheboygan 48,085 **E6**
South Milwaukee 21,069 **F6**
Stevens Point 22,970 **D4**
Stoughton 7,589 **F4**
Sturgeon Bay 8,847 **D6**
Sun Prairie 12,931 **E4**
Tomah 7,204 **E3**
Two Rivers 13,354 **D6**
Watertown 18,113 **E5**
Waukesha 50,365 **E5**
Waupun 8,132 **E5**
Wausau 32,426 **D4**
Wauwatosa 51,308 **m11**
West Allis 63,982 **m11**
West Bend 21,484 **E5**
Whitefish Bay 14,930 **m12**
Whitewater 11,520 **F5**
Wisconsin Dells 2,521 **E4**
Wisconsin Rapids 17,995 **D4**

Statute Miles 5 0 5 10 20 30 40
Kilometers 5 0 5 15 25 35 45 55

Lambert Conformal Conic Projection
SCALE 1:2,088,000 1 Inch = 33 Statute Miles

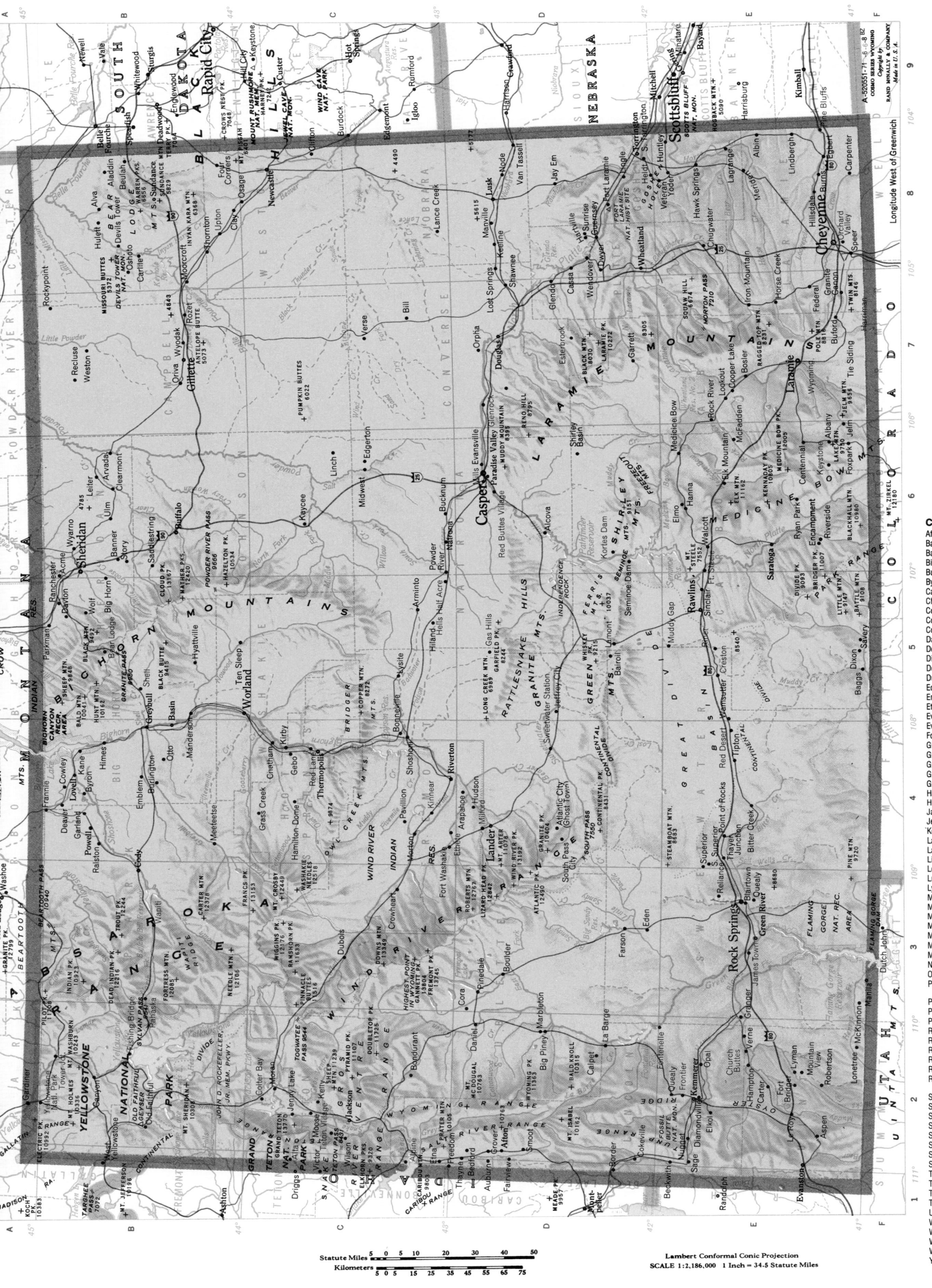

A-520551-71 -6-8 82
COSMO SERIES WYOMING
Compiled by
RAND McNALLY COMPANY
Made in U.S.A.

Cities and Towns

Afton 1,481 **D2**
Baggs 433 **E5**
Basin 1,349 **B4**
Big Piney 530 **D2**
Buffalo 3,799 **B6**
Byron 633 **B4**
Casper 51,016 **D6**
Cheyenne 47,283 **E8**
Cody 6,790 **B3**
Cokeville 515 **D2**
Cowley 455 **B4**
Dayton 701 **B5**
Devils Tower 40 **B8**
Diamondville 1,000 **E2**
Douglas 6,030 **D7**
Dubois 1,067 **C3**
Edgerton 510 **C6**
Encampment 611 **E6**
Etna 400 **C1**
Evanston 6,421 **E2**
Evansville 2,335 **D6**
Fort Laramie 356 **D8**
Gillette 12,134 **B7**
Glenrock 2,736 **D7**
Green River 12,807 **E3**
Greybull 2,277 **B4**
Guernsey 1,512 **D8**
Hanna 2,288 **E6**
Hudson 514 **D4**
Jackson 4,511 **C2**
Jeffrey City 400 **D5**
Kemmerer 3,273 **E2**
Lander 7,867 **D4**
Laramie 24,410 **E7**
Lingle 475 **D8**
Lovell 2,447 **B4**
Lusk 1,650 **D8**
Lyman 2,284 **E2**
Marbleton 537 **D2**
Medicine Bow 953 **E6**
Meeteetse 512 **B4**
Midwest 638 **C6**
Mills 2,139 **D6**
Moorcroft 1,014 **B8**
Mountain View 628 **E2**
Newcastle 3,596 **C8**
Orchard Valley 800 **E8**
Paradise Valley 2,300 **D6**
Pine Bluffs 1,077 **E8**
Pinedale 1,066 **D3**
Powell 5,310 **B4**
Ranchester 655 **B5**
Rawlins 11,547 **E5**
Reliance 500 **E3**
Riverton 9,247 **C4**
Rock River 415 **E7**
Rock Springs 19,458 **E3**
Saratoga 2,410 **E6**
Sheridan 15,146 **B6**
Shirley Basin 450 **D6**
Shoshoni 879 **C4**
Sinclair 586 **E5**
South Superior 586 **E4**
Story 700 **B6**
Sundance 1,087 **B8**
Ten Sleep 407 **B5**
Teton Village 200 **C2**
Thermopolis 3,852 **C4**
Torrington 5,441 **D8**
Upton 1,193 **B8**
Wamsutter 681 **E5**
West Laramie 2,000 **E7**
Wheatland 5,816 **D8**
Worland 6,391 **B5**
Yellowstone National Park 350 **B2**

Statute Miles 5 0 5 10 20 30 40 50
Kilometers 5 0 5 15 25 35 45 55 65 75

Lambert Conformal Conic Projection
SCALE 1:2,186,000 1 Inch = 34.5 Statute Miles

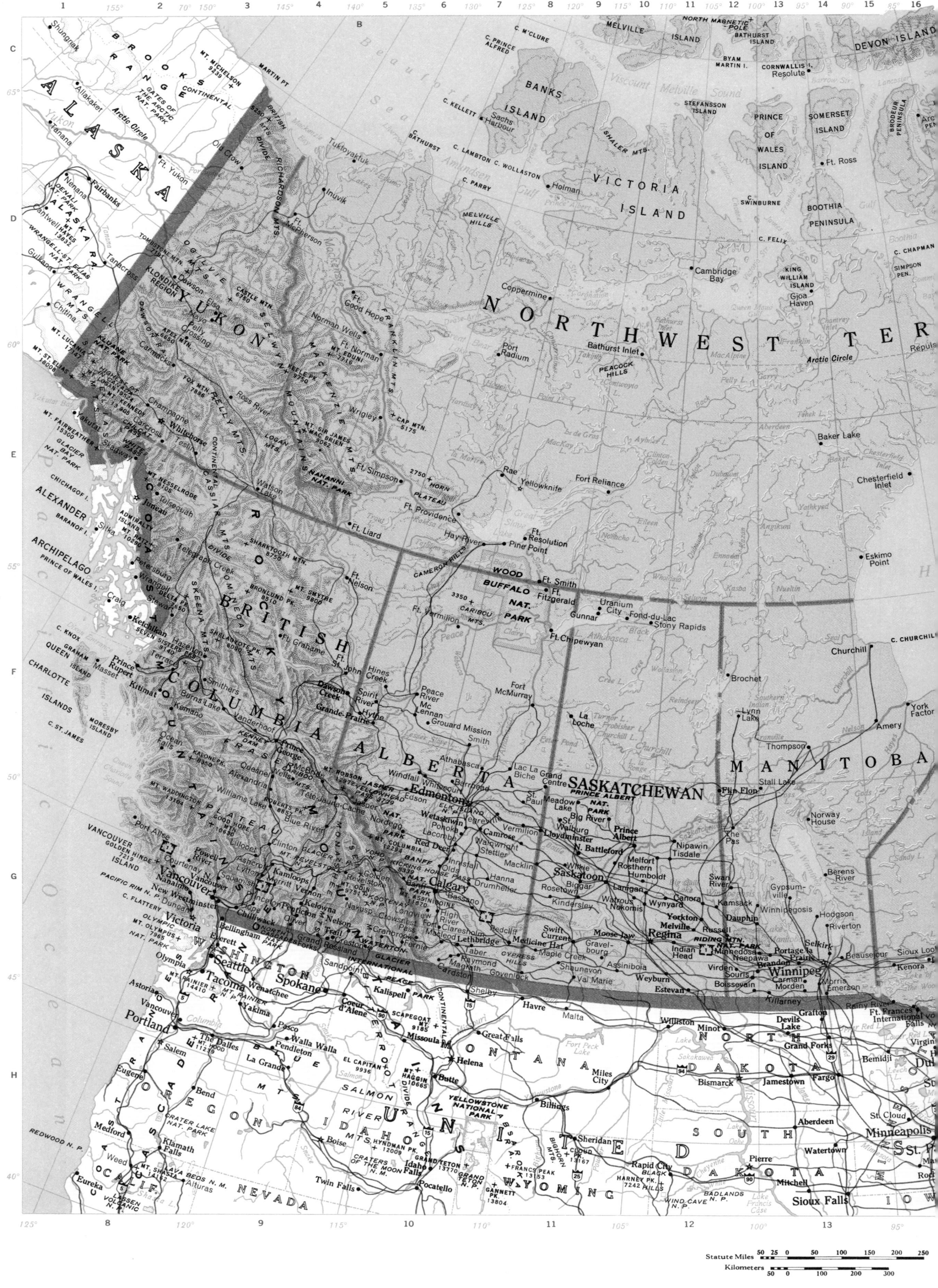

Northwest Territories

Cities and Towns
Alert **k9**
Arctic Bay 375 **B16**
Baker Lake 954 **D13**
Bathurst Inlet 20 **C11**
Cambridge Bay 815 **C12**
Chesterfield Inlet 249 **D14**
Coppermine 352 **C15**
Eskimo Point 1,022 **D14**
Eureka **m34**
Ft. Franklin 521 **C8**
Ft. Good Hope 463 **C7**
Ft. Laird 405 **D8**
Ft. McPherson 632 **C6**
Ft. Norman 286 **D7**
Ft. Providence 605 **D9**
Ft. Resolution 480 **D10**
Ft. Simpson 980 **D8**
Ft. Smith 2,298 **D10**
Gjoa Haven 523 **C13**
Hay River 2,863 **D9**
Inuvik 3,147 **C6**
Norman Wells 420 **C7**
Pine Point 1,861 **D10**
Rae 1,378 **D9**
Rankin Inlet 1,109 **D14**
Repulse Bay 352 **C15**
Snowdrift 253 **D10**
Spence Bay 431 **C14**
Yellowknife 9,483 **D10**

Yukon

Cities and Towns
Carmacks 256 **D5**
Carcross 216 **D6**
Dawson 697 **D5**
Destruction Bay 45 **D5**
Elas 336 **D5**
Faro 1,652 **D6**
Haines Junction 366 **D5**
Mayo 398 **D5**
Old Crow 243 **C5**
Pelly Crossing 182 **D5**
Ross River 294 **D6**
Teslin 310 **D6**
Watson Lake 748 **D7**
Whitehorse 14,814 **D6**

Lambert Conformal Conic Projection
SCALE 1:12,000,000 1 Inch = 189 Statute Miles

295

ALBERTA

Statute Miles 10 0 10 20 30 40 50 60 70
Kilometers 10 0 10 20 40 60 80 100

Oblique Cylindrical Projection
SCALE 1:3,110,600 1 Inch = 49 Statute Miles

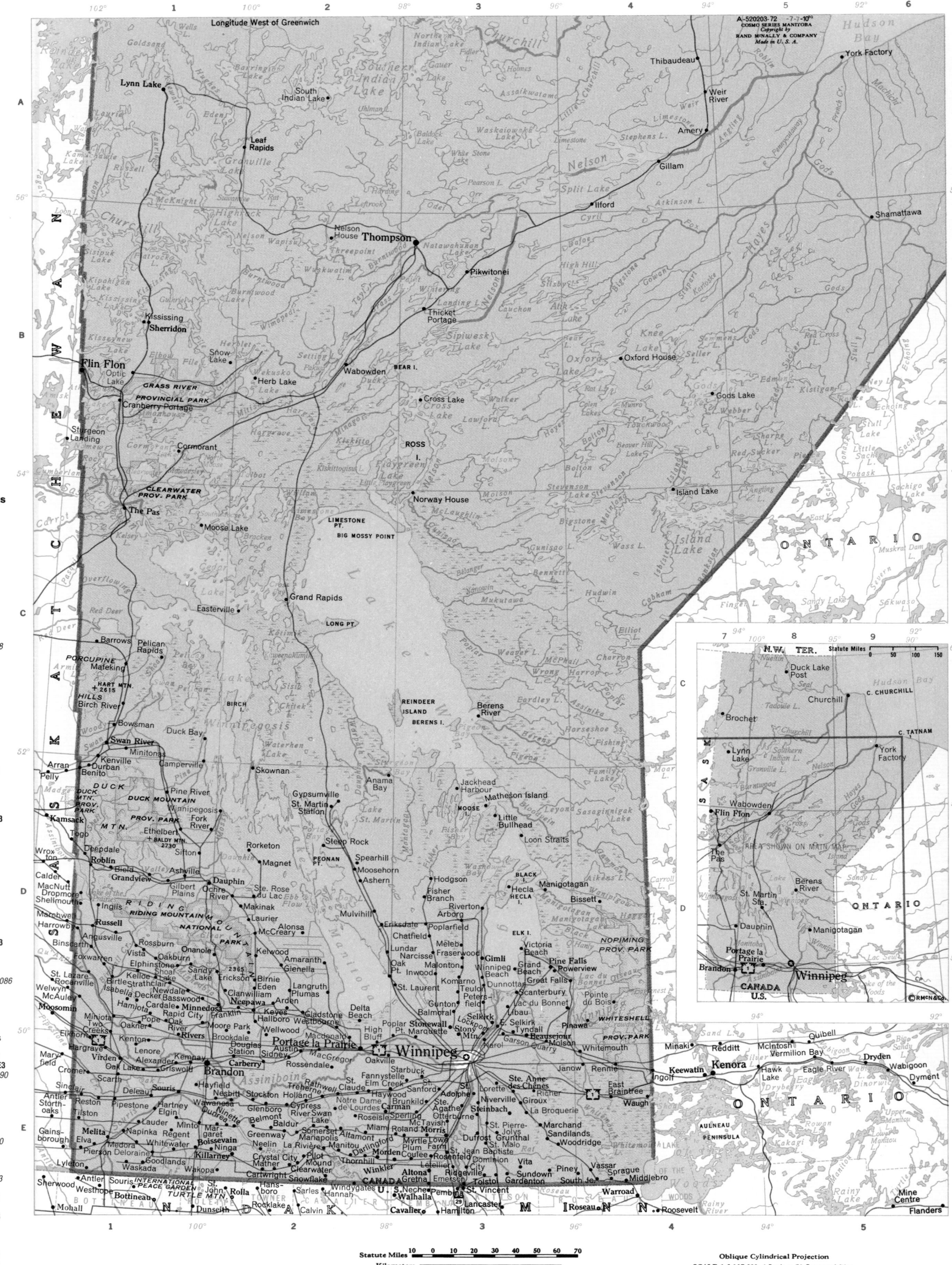

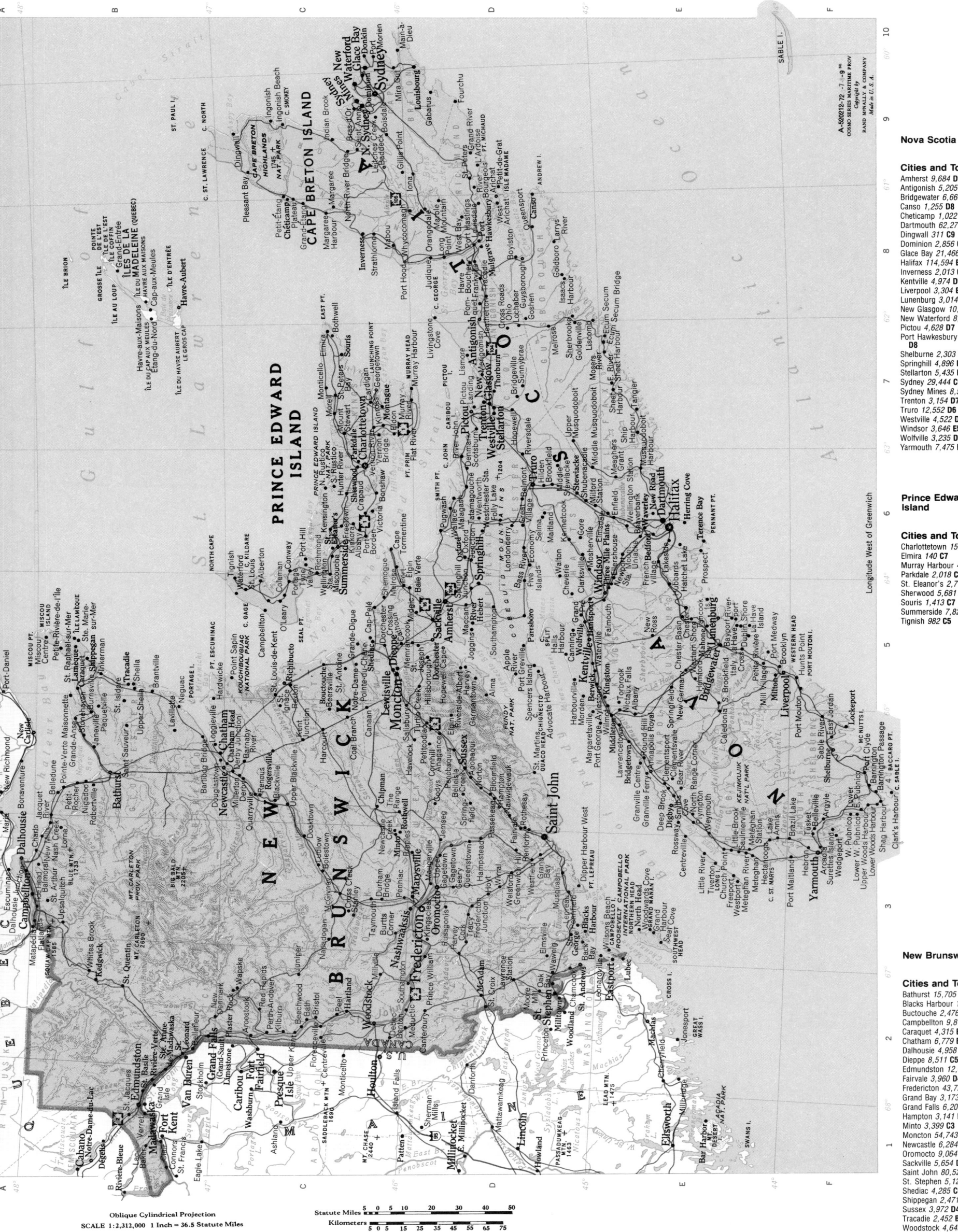

NEWFOUNDLAND

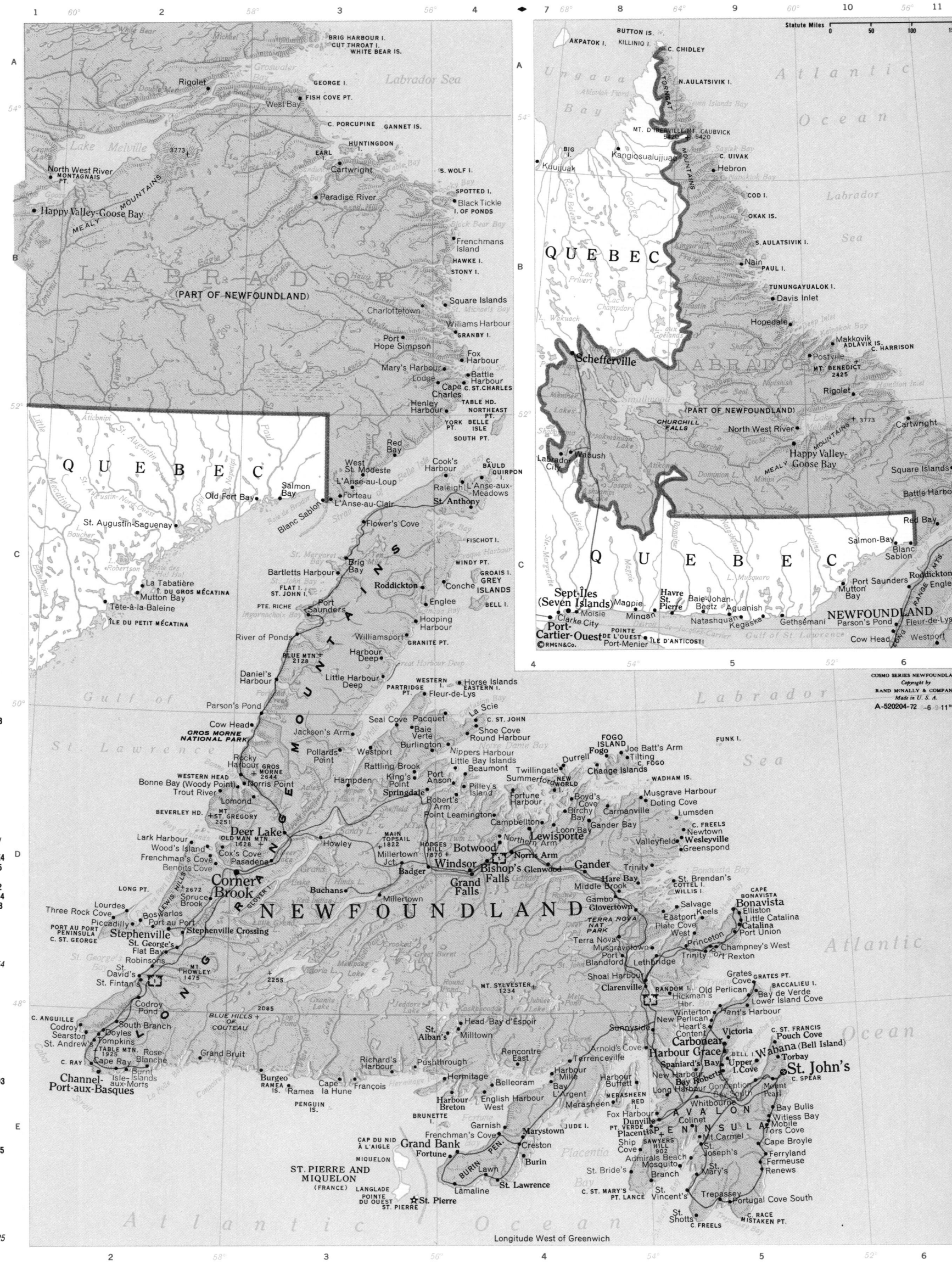

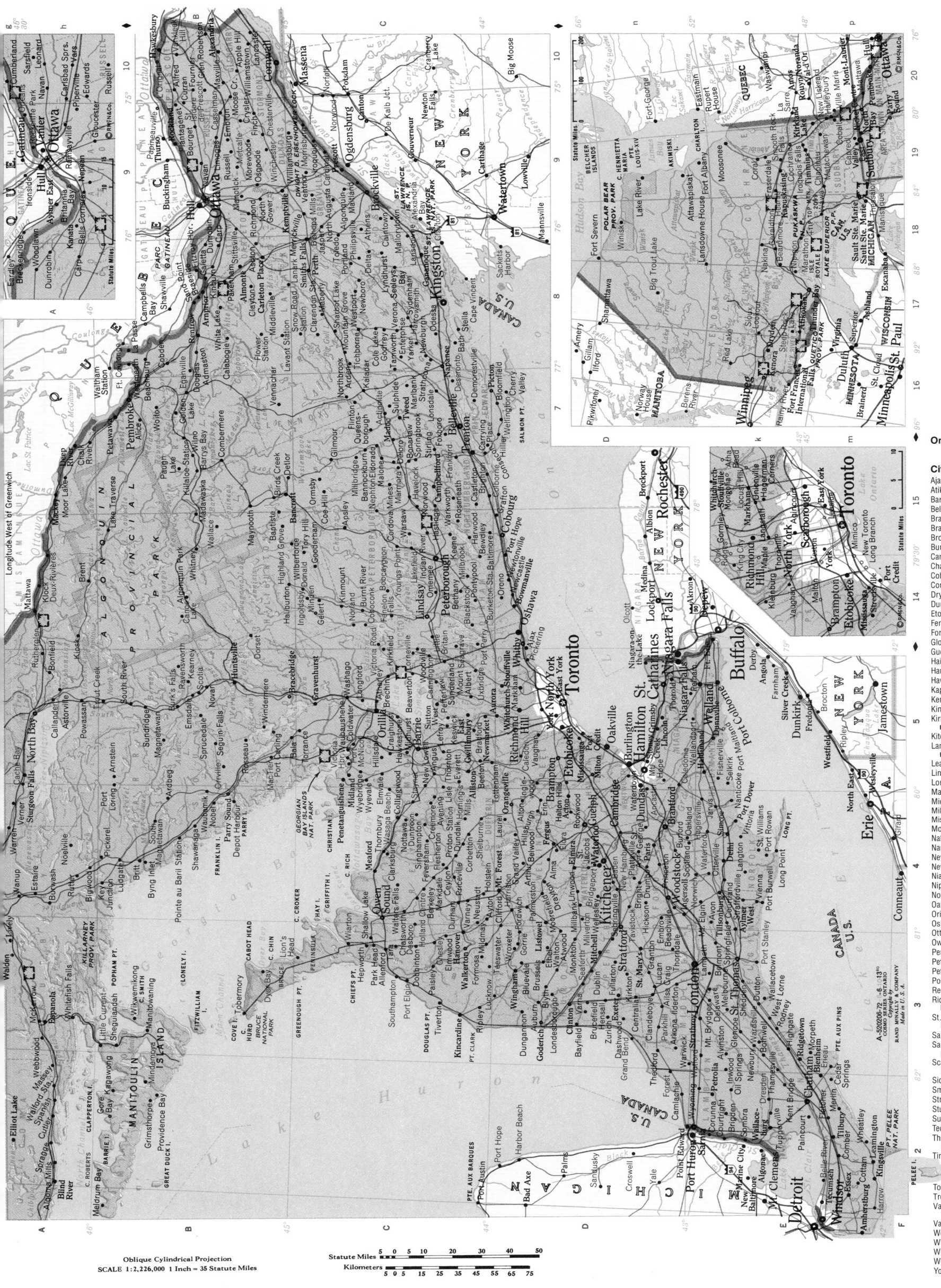

Oblique Cylindrical Projection
SCALE 1:2,226,000 1 Inch = 35 Statute Miles

Statute Miles

Kilometers

A-520206-72, -6, -13'80
COSMO/CONTROL
Copyright by
RAND McNALLY & COMPANY
Made in U.S.

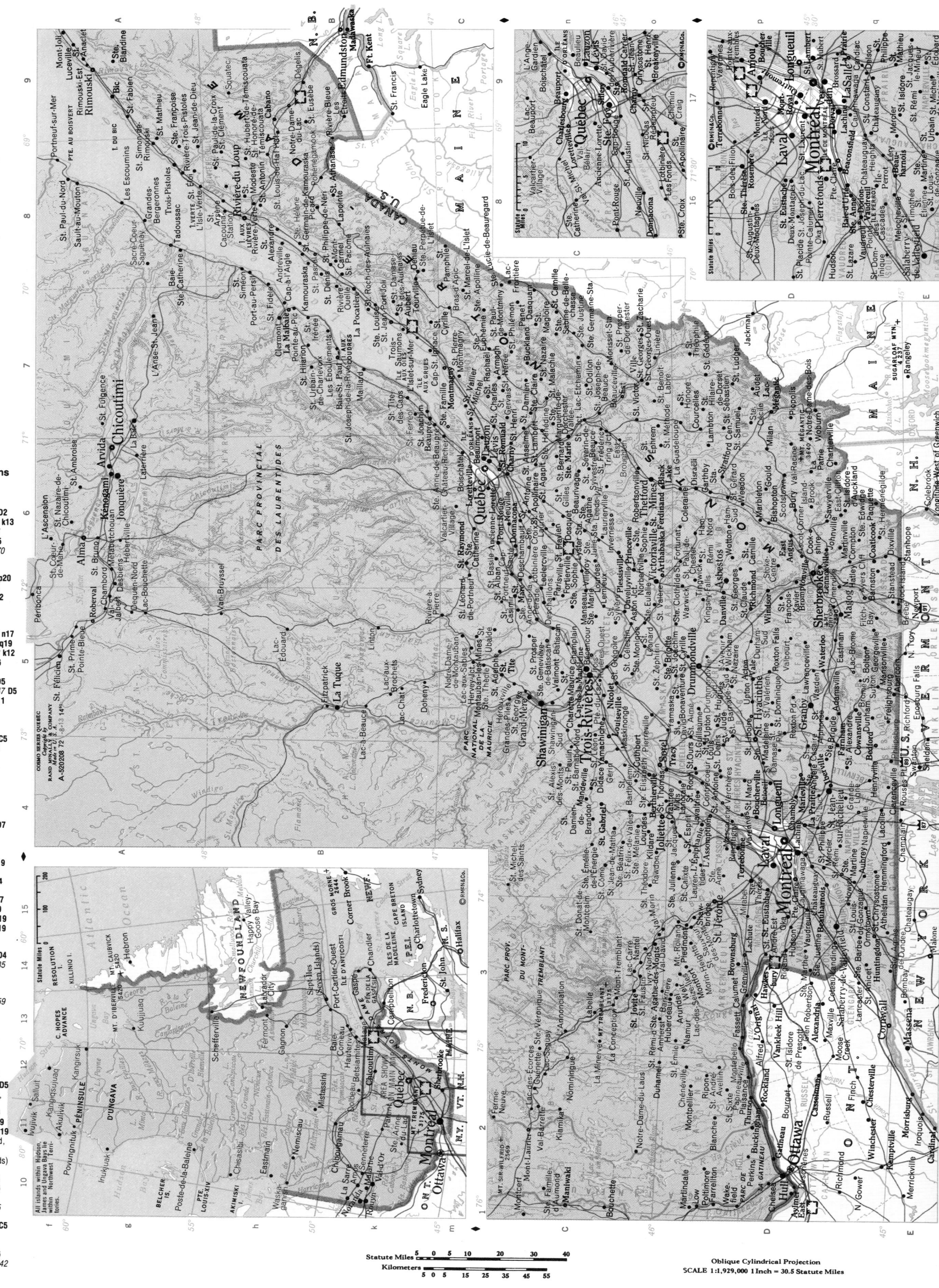

Oblique Cylindrical Projection
SCALE 1:1,929,000 1 Inch = 30.5 Statute Miles

Statute Miles
Kilometers

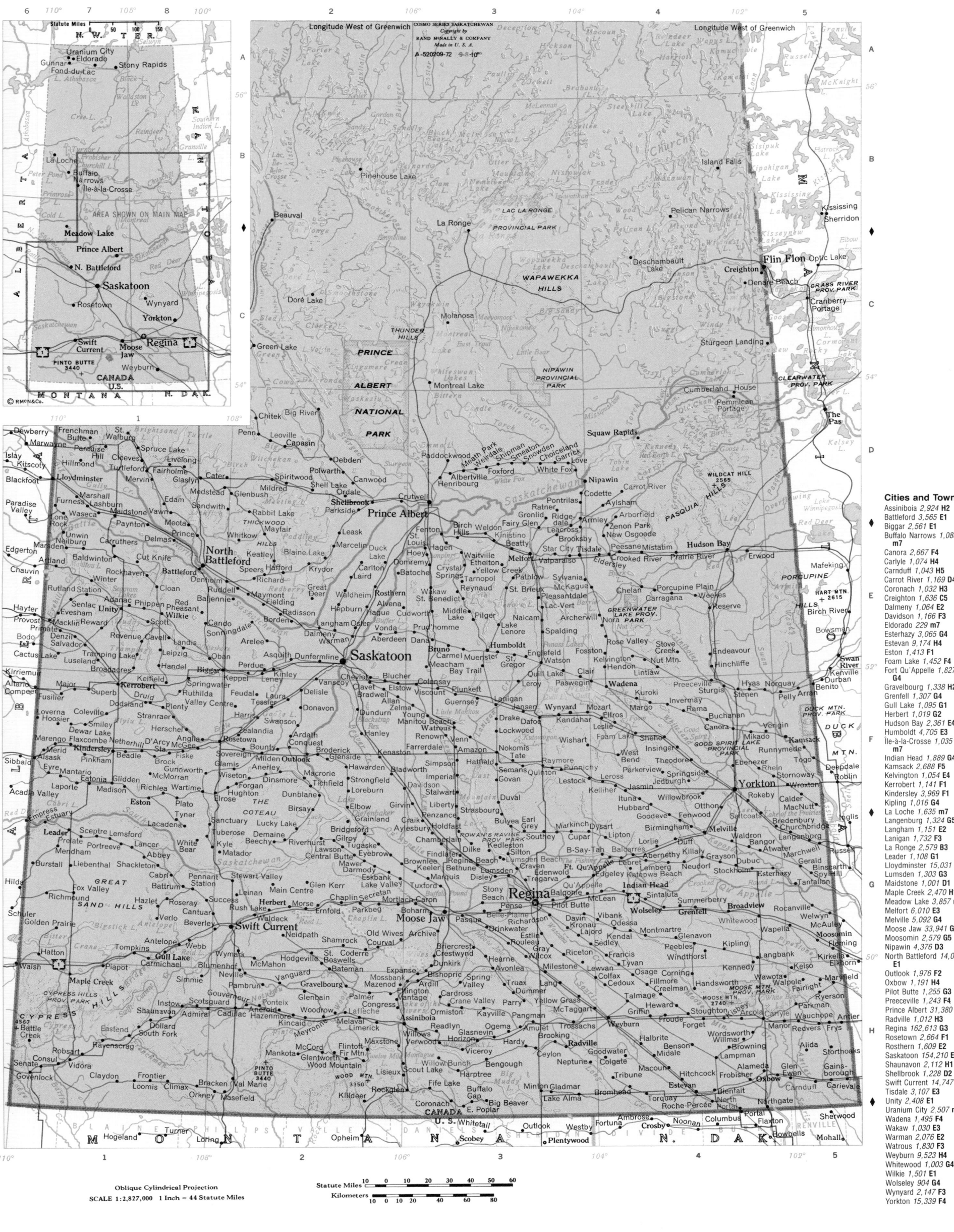

Cities and Towns

Assiniboia 2,924 **H2**
Battleford 3,565 **E1**
Biggar 2,561 **E1**
Buffalo Narrows 1,088 **m7**
Canora 2,667 **F4**
Carlyle 1,074 **H4**
Carnduff 1,043 **H5**
Carrot River 1,169 **D4**
Coronach 1,032 **H3**
Creighton 1,636 **C5**
Dalmeny 1,064 **E2**
Davidson 1,166 **F3**
Eldorado 229 **m7**
Esterhazy 3,065 **G4**
Estevan 9,174 **H4**
Eston 1,413 **F1**
Foam Lake 1,452 **F4**
Fort Qu'Appelle 1,827 **G4**
Gravelbourg 1,338 **H2**
Grenfell 1,307 **G4**
Gull Lake 1,095 **G1**
Herbert 1,019 **G2**
Hudson Bay 2,361 **E4**
Humboldt 4,705 **E3**
Île-à-la-Crosse 1,035 **m7**
Indian Head 1,889 **G4**
Kamsack 2,688 **F5**
Kelvington 1,054 **E4**
Kerrobert 1,141 **F1**
Kindersley 3,969 **F1**
Kipling 1,016 **G4**
La Loche 1,635 **m7**
Langenburg 1,324 **G5**
Langham 1,151 **E2**
Lanigan 1,732 **F3**
La Ronge 2,579 **B3**
Leader 1,108 **G1**
Lloydminster 15,031 **D1**
Lumsden 1,303 **G3**
Maidstone 1,001 **D1**
Maple Creek 2,470 **H1**
Meadow Lake 3,857 **m7**
Melfort 6,010 **E3**
Melville 5,092 **G4**
Moose Jaw 33,941 **G3**
Moosomin 2,579 **G5**
Nipawin 4,376 **D3**
North Battleford 14,030 **E1**
Outlook 1,976 **F2**
Oxbow 1,191 **H4**
Pilot Butte 1,255 **G3**
Preeceville 1,243 **F4**
Prince Albert 31,380 **D3**
Radville 1,012 **H3**
Regina 162,613 **H4**
Rosetown 2,664 **F2**
Rosthern 1,609 **E2**
Saskatoon 154,210 **E2**
Shaunavon 2,112 **H1**
Shellbrook 1,228 **D2**
Swift Current 14,747 **G2**
Tisdale 3,107 **E3**
Unity 2,408 **E1**
Uranium City 2,507 **m7**
Wadena 1,495 **F4**
Wakaw 1,030 **E3**
Warman 2,076 **E2**
Watrous 1,830 **F3**
Weyburn 9,523 **H4**
Whitewood 1,003 **G4**
Wilkie 1,501 **E1**
Wolseley 904 **G4**
Wynyard 2,147 **F3**
Yorkton 15,339 **F4**

United States and Canada Information Table

United States

STATE	CAPITAL	LARGEST CITY	ENTERED UNION AS STATE		GREATEST MEASUREMENT				HIGHEST POINT	Altitude		OFFICIAL FLOWER
			Date of Entry	Rank of Entry	N-S km	N-S mi	E-W km	E-W mi	Location	m	ft	
Alabama	Montgomery	Birmingham	Dec. 14, 1819	22	531	330	322	200	Cheaha Mtn.	734	2,407	Camellia
Alaska	Juneau	Anchorage	Jan. 3, 1959	49	2,144	1,332	3,621	2,250	McKinley, Mt.	6,194	20,320	Forget-me-not
Arizona	Phoenix	Phoenix	Feb. 14, 1912	48	628	390	539	335	Humphreys Pk.	3,851	12,633	Saguaro Cactus Blossom
Arkansas	Little Rock	Little Rock	June 15, 1836	25	386	240	443	275	Magazine Mtn.	839	2,753	Apple Blossom
California	Sacramento	Los Angeles	Sept. 9, 1850	31	1,287	800	604	375	Whitney, Mt.	4,417	14,491	Golden Poppy
Colorado	Denver	Denver	Aug. 1, 1876	38	435	270	612	380	Elbert, Mt.	4,399	14,433	Rocky Mountain Columbine
Connecticut	Hartford	Bridgeport	Jan. 9, 1788	5	121	75	145	90	Frissell, Mt.	725	2,380	Mountain Laurel
Delaware	Dover	Wilmington	Dec. 7, 1787	1	153	95	56	35	In New Castle County	137	448	Peach Blossom
District of Columbia	Washington	Washington	January, 1791	. . .	24	15	24	15	Unnamed	125	410	American Beauty Rose
Florida	Tallahassee	Jacksonville	March 3, 1845	27	740	460	644	400	In Walton County	105	345	Orange Blossom
Georgia	Atlanta	Atlanta	Jan. 2, 1788	4	507	315	402	250	Brasstown Bald	1,458	4,784	Cherokee Rose
Hawaii	Honolulu	Honolulu	Aug. 21, 1959	50	1,070	665	2,575	1,600	Mauna Kea	4,205	13,796	Hibiscus
Idaho	Boise	Boise	July 3, 1890	43	772	480	491	305	Borah Pk.	3,859	12,662	Syringa
Illinois	Springfield	Chicago	Dec. 3, 1818	21	612	380	330	205	Charles Mound	376	1,235	Native Violet
Indiana	Indianapolis	Indianapolis	Dec. 11, 1816	19	426	265	257	160	In Wayne County	383	1,257	Peony
Iowa	Des Moines	Des Moines	Dec. 28, 1846	29	330	205	499	310	In Osceola County	509	1,670	Wild Rose
Kansas	Topeka	Wichita	Jan. 29, 1861	34	330	205	660	410	Sunflower, Mt.	1,231	4,039	Native Sunflower
Kentucky	Frankfort	Louisville	June 1, 1792	15	282	175	563	350	Black Mtn.	1,263	4,145	Goldenrod
Louisiana	Baton Rouge	New Orleans	April 30, 1812	18	443	275	483	300	Driskill Mtn.	163	535	Magnolia
Maine	Augusta	Portland	March 15, 1820	23	499	310	338	210	Katahdin, Mt.	1,606	5,268	White Pine Cone and Tassel
Maryland	Annapolis	Baltimore	April 28, 1788	7	193	120	322	200	Backbone Mtn.	1,024	3,360	Black-eyed Susan
Massachusetts	Boston	Boston	Feb. 6, 1788	6	177	110	306	190	Greylock, Mt	1,064	3,491	Mayflower
Michigan	Lansing	Detroit	Jan. 26, 1837	26	644	400	499	310	Arvon, Mt.	603	1,979	Apple Blossom
Minnesota	St. Paul	Minneapolis	May 11, 1858	32	644	400	563	350	Eagle Mtn.	701	2,301	Pink and White Lady's-slipper
Mississippi	Jackson	Jackson	Dec. 10, 1817	20	547	340	290	180	Woodall Mtn.	246	806	Magnolia
Missouri	Jefferson City	Kansas City	Aug. 10, 1821	24	451	280	483	300	Taum Sauk Mtn.	540	1,772	Hawthorn
Montana	Helena	Billings	Nov. 8, 1889	41	507	315	917	570	Granite Pk.	3,901	12,799	Bitterroot
Nebraska	Lincoln	Omaha	March 1, 1867	37	338	210	668	415	In Kimball County	1,654	5,426	Goldenrod
Nevada	Carson City	Las Vegas	Oct. 31, 1864	36	781	485	507	315	Boundary Pk.	4,005	13,140	Sagebrush
New Hampshire	Concord	Manchester	June 21, 1788	9	298	185	145	90	Washington, Mt.	1,917	6,288	Purple Lilac
New Jersey	Trenton	Newark	Dec. 18, 1787	3	267	166	113	70	High Point	550	1,803	Purple Violet
New Mexico	Santa Fe	Albuquerque	Jan. 6, 1912	47	628	390	563	350	Wheeler Pk.	4,011	13,161	Yucca
New York	Albany	New York	July 26, 1788	11	499	310	531	330	Marcy, Mt.	1,629	5,344	Rose
North Carolina	Raleigh	Charlotte	Nov. 21, 1789	12	322	200	837	520	Mitchell, Mt.	2,037	6,684	Dogwood
North Dakota	Bismarck	Fargo	Nov. 2, 1889	39	338	210	579	360	White Butte	1,069	3,506	Wild Prairie Rose
Ohio	Columbus	Columbus	March 1, 1803	17	370	230	330	205	Campbell Hill	472	1,550	Scarlet Carnation
Oklahoma	Oklahoma City	Oklahoma City	Nov. 16, 1907	46	338	210	740	460	Black Mesa	1,516	4,973	Mistletoe
Oregon	Salem	Portland	Feb. 14, 1859	33	467	290	604	375	Hood, Mt.	3,426	11,239	Oregon Grape
Pennsylvania	Harrisburg	Philadelphia	Dec. 12, 1787	2	290	180	499	310	Davis, Mt.	979	3,213	Mountain Laurel
Rhode Island	Providence	Providence	May 29, 1790	13	80	50	56	35	Jerimoth Hill	247	812	Violet
South Carolina	Columbia	Columbia	May 23, 1788	8	346	215	459	285	Sassafras Mtn.	1,085	3,560	Carolina Jessamine
South Dakota	Pierre	Sioux Falls	Nov. 2, 1889	40	386	240	579	360	Harney Pk.	2,207	7,242	Pasque Flower
Tennessee	Nashville	Memphis	June 1, 1796	16	193	120	692	430	Clingmans Dome	2,025	6,643	Iris
Texas	Austin	Houston	Dec. 29, 1845	28	1,143	710	1,223	760	Guadalupe Pk.	2,667	8,749	Bluebonnet
Utah	Salt Lake City	Salt Lake City	Jan. 4, 1896	45	555	345	443	275	Kings Pk.	4,123	13,528	Sego Lily
Vermont	Montpelier	Burlington	March 4, 1791	14	249	155	145	90	Mansfield, Mt.	1,339	4,393	Red Clover
Virginia	Richmond	Virginia Beach	June 25, 1788	10	330	205	684	425	Rogers, Mt.	1,746	5,729	Dogwood
Washington	Olympia	Seattle	Nov. 11, 1889	42	370	230	547	340	Rainier, Mt.	4,392	14,410	Western Rhododendron
West Virginia	Charleston	Charleston	June 20, 1863	35	322	200	362	225	Spruce Knob	1,482	4,862	Big Rhododendron
Wisconsin	Madison	Milwaukee	May 29, 1848	30	483	300	467	290	Timms Hill	595	1,951	Wood Violet
Wyoming	Cheyenne	Cheyenne	July 10, 1890	44	443	275	587	365	Gannett Pk.	4,207	13,804	Indian Paintbrush
UNITED STATES	Washington, D.C.	New York	. . .	. . .	. . .	. . .	. . .	. . .	McKinley, Mt.	6,194	20,320	. . .

Canada

PROVINCE	CAPITAL	LARGEST CITY	ENTERED CONFEDERATION		GREATEST MEASUREMENT				HIGHEST POINT	Altitude		FLORAL EMBLEM
			Date of Entry	Rank of Entry	N-S km	N-S mi	E-W km	E-W mi	Location	m	ft	
Alberta	Edmonton	Edmonton	Sept. 1, 1905	8	1,207	750	644	400	Columbia, Mt.	3,747	12,293	Wild Rose
British Columbia	Victoria	Vancouver	July 20, 1871	6	1,263	785	1,022	635	Fairweather, Mt.	4,663	15,300	Dogwood
Manitoba	Winnipeg	Winnipeg	July 15, 1870	5	1,207	750	740	460	Baldy Mtn.	832	2,730	Pasque Flower
New Brunswick	Fredericton	St. John	July 1, 1867	1	378	235	314	195	Carleton, Mt.	820	2,690	Purple Violet
Newfoundland	St. John's	St. John's	March 31, 1949	10	1,545	960	1,022	635	Caubvick, Mt. (Mont d'Iberville)	1,652	5,420	Pitcher Plant
Northwest Territories	Yellowknife	Yellowknife	. . .	. . .	2,414	1,500	3,219	2,000	Unnamed	2,773	9,098	Mountain Avens
Nova Scotia	Halifax	Halifax	July 1, 1867	1	177	110	314	195	White Hill	532	1,745	Trailing Arbutus
Ontario	Toronto	Toronto	July 1, 1867	1	1,489	925	1,682	1,045	Ishpatina Ridge	693	2,274	White Trillium
Prince Edward Island	Charlottetown	Charlottetown	July 1, 1873	7	80	50	177	110	Unnamed	142	466	Lady's-slipper
Québec	Québec	Montréal	July 1, 1867	1	1,915	1,190	1,545	960	d'Iberville, Mont (Mt. Caubvick)	1,652	5,420	White Garden Lily
Saskatchewan	Regina	Saskatoon	Sep. 1, 1905	8	1,207	750	636	395	Unnamed	1,392	4,567	Prairie Lily
Yukon Territory	Whitehorse	Whitehorse	. . .	. . .	1,054	655	909	565	Logan, Mt.	5,951	19,524	Fireweed
CANADA	Ottawa	Toronto	. . .	. . .	. . .	. . .	. . .	. . .	Logan, Mt.	5,951	19,524	. . .

GEOGRAPHICAL INFORMATION AND INTERNATIONAL MAP INDEX

World Nations

This table gives the area, population, population density, form of government, capital and location of every country in the world.

Area figures include inland water.

The populations are estimates made by Rand McNally on the basis of official data, United Nations estimates and other available information.

Besides specifying the form of government for all political areas, the table classifies them into five groups according to their political status. Units labeled

A are independent sovereign nations. Units labeled *B* are independent as regards internal affairs, but for purposes of foreign affairs they are under the protection of another country. Units labeled *C* are colonies, overseas territories, dependencies, etc. of other countries. Units labeled *D* are states, provinces or other major administrative subdivisions of important countries. Units in the table with no letter designations are regions, islands or other areas that do not constitute separate political units by themselves.

Map Plate numbers refer to the International Map section of the atlas.

Country, Division, or Region English (Conventional)	Local Name	Area km²	Area sq mi	Population 1/1/89	Population Density per km²	Population Density per sq mi	Form of Government and Political Status		Capital	Continent and Map Plate	
Afars and Issas, *see* Djibouti	...			...							
†AFGHANISTAN	Afghānestān	652,225	251,826	14,655,000	22	58	Republic	A	Kābol	Asia	23
Africa	...	30,300,000	11,700,000	642,100,000	21	55			...	Africa	30-31
Alabama	Alabama	133,913	51,704	4,125,000	31	80	State (U.S.)	D	Montgomery	N. Amer	44
Alaska	Alaska	1,530,693	591,004	558,000	0.4	0.9	State (U.S.)	D	Juneau	N. Amer	40
†ALBANIA	Shqiperia	28,748	11,100	3,181,000	111	287	Socialist republic	A	Tirana	Europe	15
Alberta	Alberta	661,190	255,287	2,450,000	3.7	9.6	Province (Canada)	D	Edmonton	N. Amer	42
†ALGERIA	Al Jazā'ir	2,381,741	919,595	24,215,000	10	26	Socialist republic	A	Al Jazā'ir (Algiers)	Africa	32
American Samoa	American Samoa (English) / Amerika Samoa (Samoan)	199	77	40,000	201	519	Unincorporated territory (U.S.)	C	Pago Pago	Oceania	65
Andaman and Nicobar Islands	Andaman and Nicobar Islands	8,293	3,202	. . . (1)	...	...	Territory (India)	D	Port Blair	Asia	25
ANDORRA	Andorra	453	175	51,000	113	291	Coprincipality (Spanish and French protection)	B	Andorra la Vella	Europe	13
†ANGOLA	Angola	1,246,700	481,354	8,385,000	6.7	17	Socialist republic	A	Luanda	Africa	36
ANGUILLA	Anguilla	91	35	7,000	77	200	Dependent territory (U.K. protection)	B	The Valley	N. Amer	51
Anhui	Anhui	140,000	54,054	53,970,000	386	998	Province (China)	D	Hefei	Asia	28
Antarctica	...	14,000,000	5,400,000	. . . (1)	...	...			...	Antarctica	66
†ANTIGUA AND BARBUDA	Antigua	443	171	84,000	190	491	Parliamentary state	A	St. John's	N. Amer	51
Arabian Peninsula	...	3,010,000	1,112,000	34,630,000	12	31			...	Asia	23
†ARGENTINA	Argentina	2,780,092	1,073,400	32,205,000	12	30	Republic	A	Buenos Aires	S. Amer	56
Arizona	Arizona	295,264	114,002	3,558,000	12	31	State (U.S.)	D	Phoenix	N. Amer	46
Arkansas	Arkansas	137,764	53,191	2,410,000	17	45	State (U.S.)	D	Little Rock	N. Amer	45
Armenian S.S.R.	Armjanskaja S.S.R.	29,800	11,506	3,505,000	118	305	Soviet socialist republic (U.S.S.R.)	D	Jerevan	Asia	16
ARUBA	Aruba	193	75	66,000	342	880	Self-governing territory (Netherlands protection)	B	Oranjestad	N. Amer	49
Ascension	Ascension	88	34	1,800	20	53	Dependency (St. Helena)	C	Georgetown	Africa	30-31
Asia	...	45,000,000	17,400,000	3,130,600,000	70	180			...	Asia	21-22
†AUSTRALIA	Australia	7,682,300	2,966,155	16,955,000	2.2	5.7	Federal parliamentary state	A	Canberra	Oceania	59
Australian Capital Territory	Australian Capital Territory	2,400	927	281,000	117	303	Territory (Australia)	D	Canberra	Oceania	59
†AUSTRIA	Österreich	83,855	32,377	7,584,000	90	234	Federal republic	A	Wien (Vienna)	Europe	14
Azerbaijan S.S.R.	Azerbajdžanskaja S.S.R.	86,600	33,436	7,020,000	81	210	Soviet socialist republic (U.S.S.R.)	D	Baku	Asia	16
Azores	Açores	2,247	868	260,000	116	300	Autonomous region (Portugal)	D	Ponta Delgada	Europe	32
Baden-Wurttemberg	Baden-Württemberg	35,751	13,804	9,445,000	264	684	State (Fed. Rep. of Germany)	D	Stuttgart	Europe	10
†BAHAMAS	Bahamas	13,939	5,382	243,000	17	45	Parliamentary state	A	Nassau	N. Amer	47
†BAHRAIN	Al Baḥrayn	662	256	458,000	692	1,789	Monarchy	A	Al Manāmah (Manama)	Asia	24
Balearic Islands	Islas Baleares	5,014	1,936	771,000	154	398	Province (Spain)	D	Palma	Europe	13
Baltic Republics	...	174,000	67,182	7,995,000	46	119			...	Europe	
†BANGLADESH	Bangladesh	143,998	55,598	111,390,000	774	2,003	Republic	A	Dhaka	Asia	25
†BARBADOS	Barbados	430	166	255,000	593	1,536	Parliamentary state	A	Bridgetown	N. Amer	51
Bavaria	Bayern	70,553	27,241	11,135,000	158	409	State (Fed. Rep. of Germany)	D	München (Munich)	Europe	10
†BELGIUM	Belgique (French) / België (Flemish)	30,518	11,783	9,862,000	323	837	Constitutional monarchy	A	Bruxelles (Brussels)	Europe	12
†BELIZE	Belize	22,963	8,866	184,000	8.0	21	Parliamentary state	A	Belmopan	N. Amer	49
Benelux	...	74,889	28,914	25,045,000	334	866			...	Europe	12
†BENIN	Bénin	112,622	43,484	4,725,000	42	109	Socialist republic	A	Porto-Novo and Cotonou	Africa	34
Berlin (West)	Berlin (West)	480	185	1,925,000	4,010	10,405	State (Fed. Rep. of Germany)	D	Berlin (West)	Europe	10
Bermuda	Bermuda	54	21	56,000	1,037	2,667	Dependent territory (U.K.)	C	Hamilton	N. Amer	47
†BHUTAN	Druk	46,500	17,954	1,519,000	33	85	Monarchy (Indian protection)	B	Thimphu	Asia	25
Bioko	Bioko	2,034	785	83,000	41	106	Province of Equatorial Guinea	D	Malabo	Africa	34
†BOLIVIA	Bolivia	1,098,581	424,165	7,184,000	6.5	17	Republic	A	La Paz and Sucre	S. Amer	54
BOPHUTHATSWANA (2)	Bophuthatswana	40,509	15,641	2,202,000	54	141	National state (South African protection)	B	Mmabatho	Africa	37
Borneo, Indonesian	Kalimantan	539,460	208,287	8,480,000	16	41	Part of Indonesia (4 provinces)		...	Asia	26
†BOTSWANA	Botswana	582,000	224,711	1,230,000	2.1	5.5	Republic	A	Gaborone	Africa	37
†BRAZIL	Brasil	8,511,965	3,286,488	145,930,000	17	44	Federal republic	A	Brasília	S. Amer	54-56
Bremen	Bremen	404	156	645,000	1,597	4,135	State (Fed. Rep. of Germany)	D	Bremen	Europe	10
British Columbia	British Columbia (English) / Columbie-Britannique (French)	947,800	365,948	2,965,000	3.1	8.1	Province (Canada)	D	Victoria	N. Amer	42
British Indian Ocean Territory	British Indian Ocean Territory	60	23	. . . (1)	...	...	Dependent territory (U.K.)	C	...	Africa	22
†BRUNEI	Brunei	5,765	2,226	247,000	43	111	Monarchy	A	Bandar Seri Begawan	Asia	26
†BULGARIA	Balgarija	110,912	42,823	8,997,000	81	210	Socialist republic	A	Sofija (Sofia)	Europe	15
†BURKINA FASO	Burkina Faso	274,200	105,869	8,596,000	31	81	Provisional military government	A	Ouagadougou	Africa	34
†BURMA	Myanmar	676,577	261,228	41,860,000	62	160	Socialist republic	A	Yangon (Rangoon)	Asia	25
†BURUNDI	Burundi	27,830	10,745	5,200,000	187	484	Provisional military government	A	Bujumbura	Africa	36
†Byelorussian S.S.R.	Belorusskaja S.S.R.	207,600	80,155	10,215,000	49	127	Soviet socialist republic (U.S.S.R.)	D	Minsk	Europe	16
California	California	411,041	158,704	28,630,000	70	180	State (U.S.)	D	Sacramento	N. Amer	46
†CAMBODIA	Kâmpŭchéa	181,035	69,898	6,760,000	37	97	Socialist republic	A	Phnum Pénh (Phnom Penh)	Asia	26
†CAMEROON	Cameroon (English) / Cameroun (French)	475,442	183,569	11,495,000	24	63	Republic	A	Yaoundé	Africa	34
†CANADA	Canada	9,970,610	3,849,674	25,895,000	2.6	6.7	Federal parliamentary state	A	Ottawa	N. Amer	42
Canary Islands	Islas Canarias	7,273	2,808	1,535,000	211	547	Part of Spain (2 provinces)		...	Africa	32
†CAPE VERDE	Cabo Verde	4,033	1,557	359,000	89	231	Republic	A	Praia	Africa	32
Cayman Islands	Cayman Islands	259	100	25,000	97	250	Dependent territory (U.K.)	C	Georgetown	N. Amer	49
Celebes	Sulawesi	189,216	73,057	12,405,000	66	170	Part of Indonesia (4 provinces)		...	Asia	26
†CENTRAL AFRICAN REPUBLIC	Centrafrique	622,984	240,535	3,089,000	5.0	13	Republic	A	Bangui	Africa	35
Central America	...	520,000	200,000	28,195,000	54	141			...	N. Amer	49
Central Asia, Soviet	...	1,277,100	493,090	33,145,000	26	67			...	Asia	19
Ceylon, *see* Sri Lanka	...			...							
†CHAD	Tchad	1,284,000	495,755	4,845,000	3.8	9.8	Republic	A	N'Djamena	Africa	35

Country, Division, or Region English (Conventional)	Local Name	Area km²	Area sq mi	Population 1/1/89	Population Density per km²	Population Density per sq mi	Form of Government and Political Status	Capital	Continent	Map Plate
Channel Islands	...	194	*75*	137,000	706	*1,827*	...	...	Europe	9
†CHILE	Chile	756,626	*292,135*	12,925,000	17	*44*	Provisional military government	A Santiago	S. Amer	56
†CHINA (excl. Taiwan)	Zhongguo Renmin Gongheguo	9,631,600	*3,718,782*	1,094,700,000	114	*294*	Socialist republic	A Beijing (Peking)	Asia	27
China (Nationalist), *see* Taiwan	...	...	...	...	...	...	...	...	...	...
Christmas Island	Christmas Island	135	*52*	2,000	15	*38*	External territory (Australia)	C Flying Fish Cove	Oceania	26
CISKEI (2)	Ciskei	7,790	*3,008*	1,006,000	129	*334*	National state (South African protection)	B Bisho	Africa	37
Cocos (Keeling) Islands	Cocos (Keeling) Islands	14	*5.4*	600	43	*111*	Part of Australia	...	Oceania	22
†COLOMBIA	Colombia	1,141,748	*440,831*	30,465,000	27	*69*	Republic	A Bogotá	S. Amer	54
Colorado	Colorado	269,602	*104,094*	3,392,000	13	*33*	State (U.S.)	D Denver	N. Amer	45
†COMOROS (excl. Mayotte)	Al-Qumur (Arabic) / Comores (French)	2,171	*838*	436,000	201	*520*	Federal islamic republic	A Moroni	Africa	37
†CONGO	Congo	342,000	*132,047*	2,191,000	6.4	*17*	Socialist republic	A Brazzaville	Africa	36
Connecticut	Connecticut	12,999	*5,019*	3,233,000	249	*644*	State (U.S)	D Hartford	N. Amer	44
COOK ISLANDS	Cook Islands	236	*91*	17,000	72	*187*	Self-governing territory (New Zealand protection)	B Avarua	Oceania	61
Coral Sea Islands Territory	Coral Sea Islands Territory	2.6	*1.0*	(1)	...	...	External territory (Australia)	C ...	Oceania	59
Corsica	Corse	8,681	*3,352*	253,000	29	*75*	Part of France (2 departments)	D ...	Europe	11
†COSTA RICA	Costa Rica	51,100	*19,730*	2,990,000	59	*152*	Republic	A San José	N. Amer	49
†CUBA	Cuba	110,861	*42,804*	10,440,000	94	*244*	Socialist republic	A La Habana (Havana)	N. Amer	49
Curacao	Curaçao	444	*171*	167,000	376	*977*	Division of Netherlands Antilles (Neth.)	D Willemstad	N. Amer	49
†CYPRUS	Kípros (Greek) / Kıbrıs (Turkish)	5,896	*2,276*	573,000	97	*252*	Republic	A Nicosia (Levkosía)	Asia	24
CYPRUS, NORTH	Kuzey Kıbrıs	3,355	*1,295*	172,000	51	*133*	Republic	A Nicosia (Lefkoşa)	Asia	24
†CZECHOSLOVAKIA	Československo	127,905	*49,384*	15,605,000	122	*316*	Federal socialist republic	A Praha (Prague)	Europe	10
Delaware	Delaware	5,297	*2,045*	655,000	124	*320*	State (U.S.)	D Dover	N. Amer	44
†DENMARK	Danmark	43,092	*16,638*	5,135,000	119	*309*	Constitutional monarchy	A København (Copenhagen)	Europe	8
Denmark and Possessions	...	2,220,091	*857,182*	5,238,000	2.4	*6.1*	...	...	...	...
District of Columbia	District of Columbia	179	*69*	619,000	3,458	*8,971*	Federal district (U.S.)	D Washington	N. Amer	44
†DJIBOUTI	Djibouti	23,200	*8,958*	324,000	14	*36*	Republic	A Djibouti	Africa	35
†DOMINICA	Dominica	752	*290*	100,000	133	*345*	Republic	A Roseau	N. Amer	51
†DOMINICAN REPUBLIC	República Dominicana	48,442	*18,704*	7,069,000	146	*378*	Republic	A Santo Domingo	N. Amer	49
†ECUADOR	Ecuador	283,561	*109,484*	10,345,000	36	*94*	Republic	A Quito	S. Amer	54
†EGYPT	Mişr	1,001,450	*386,662*	52,490,000	52	*136*	Socialist republic	A Al Qāhirah (Cairo)	Africa	33
Ellis Islands, *see* Tuvalu	...	...	...	...	...	...	...	...	...	...
†EL SALVADOR	El Salvador	21,041	*8,124*	5,122,000	243	*630*	Republic	A San Salvador	N. Amer	49
England	England	130,439	*50,363*	47,510,000	364	*943*	Administrative division (U.K.)	D London	Europe	9
†EQUATORIAL GUINEA	Guinea Ecuatorial	28,051	*10,831*	438,000	16	*40*	Republic	A Malabo	Africa	36
Estonian S.S.R.	Eesti N.S.V.	45,100	*17,413*	1,585,000	35	*91*	Soviet socialist republic (U.S.S.R.)	D Tallinn	Europe	8
†ETHIOPIA	Ītiopya	1,251,282	*483,123*	48,470,000	39	*100*	Socialist republic	A Ādīs Ābeba (Addis Ababa)	Africa	35
Eurasia	...	54,900,000	*21,200,000*	3,816,000,000	70	*180*	...	...	...	...
Europe	...	9,900,000	*3,800,000*	685,400,000	69	*180*	...	...	Europe	5-6
FAEROE ISLANDS	Føroyar	1,399	*540*	48,000	34	*89*	Self-governing territory (Danish protection)	B Thorshavn	Europe	6
Falkland Islands (3)	Falkland Islands (English) / Islas Malvinas (Spanish)	12,173	*4,700*	2,000	0.2	*0.4*	Dependent territory (U.K.)	C Stanley	S. Amer	56
†FIJI	Fiji (French) / Viti (Fijian)	18,333	*7,078*	749,000	41	*106*	Republic	A Suva	Oceania	63
†FINLAND	Suomi (Finnish) / Finland (Swedish)	338,145	*130,559*	4,949,000	15	*38*	Republic	A Helsinki (Helsingfors)	Europe	7
Florida	Florida	151,949	*58,668*	12,605,000	83	*215*	State (U.S.)	D Tallahassee	N. Amer	44
†FRANCE (excl. Overseas Departments)	France	547,026	*211,208*	55,970,000	102	*265*	Republic	A Paris	Europe	11
France and Possessions	...	667,359	*257,667*	57,780,000	87	*224*	...	... Paris	...	...
French Guiana	Guyane Française	91,000	*35,135*	93,000	1.0	*2.6*	Overseas department (France)	C Cayenne	S. Amer	54
French Polynesia	Polynésie Française	4,000	*1,544*	194,000	49	*126*	Overseas territory (France)	C Papeete	Oceania	61
French West Indies	...	2,880	*1,112*	678,000	235	*610*	...	...	N. Amer	50
Fujian	Fujian	123,000	*47,491*	28,355,000	231	*597*	Province (China)	D Fuzhou	Asia	27
†GABON	Gabon	267,667	*103,347*	1,056,000	3.9	*10*	Republic	A Libreville	Africa	36
Galapagos Islands	Archipiélago de Colón (Islas Galápagos)	7,964	*3,075*	10,000	1.3	*3.3*	Province (Ecuador)	D Baquerizo Moreno	S. Amer	54
†GAMBIA	Gambia	11,295	*4,361*	789,000	70	*181*	Republic	A Banjul	Africa	34
Gansu	Gansu	390,000	*150,580*	21,345,000	55	*142*	Province (China)	D Lanzhou	Asia	27
Georgia	Georgia	152,587	*58,914*	6,401,000	42	*109*	State (U.S.)	D Atlanta	N. Amer	44
Georgian S.S.R.	Gruzinskaja S.S.R.	69,700	*26,911*	5,330,000	76	*198*	Soviet socialist republic (U.S.S.R.)	D Tbilisi	Asia	16
†GERMAN DEMOCRATIC REPUBLIC (EAST GERMANY)	Deutsche Demokratische Republik	108,333	*41,828*	16,582,000	153	*396*	Socialist republic	A Berlin (Ost-) (East Berlin)	Europe	10
†GERMANY, FEDERAL REPUBLIC OF (WEST GERMANY)	Bundesrepublik Deutschland	248,707	*96,027*	61,380,000	247	*639*	Federal republic	A Bonn	Europe	10
Germany (entire)	...	357,040	*137,855*	77,960,000	218	*566*	...	...	Europe	10
†GHANA	Ghana	238,533	*92,098*	14,575,000	61	*158*	Provisional military government	A Accra	Africa	34
Gibraltar	Gibraltar	6.0	*2*	31,000	5,167	*13,478*	Dependent territory (U.K.)	C Gibraltar	Europe	13
Gilbert Islands, *see* Tuvalu	...	...	...	...	...	...	...	...	...	...
Great Britain, *see* United Kingdom	...	...	...	...	...	...	...	...	...	...
†GREECE	Ellas	131,944	*50,944*	10,030,000	76	*197*	Republic	A Athínai (Athens)	Europe	15
GREENLAND	Kalaallit Nunaat (Inuit) / Grønland (Danish)	2,175,600	*840,004*	55,000	0.1	*0.1*	Self-governing territory (Danish protection)	B Godthåb (Nûk)	N. Amer	41
†GRENADA	Grenada	344	*133*	95,000	276	*714*	Parliamentary state	A St. George's	N. Amer	51
Guadeloupe (incl. Dependencies)	Guadeloupe	1,780	*687*	340,000	191	*495*	Overseas department (France)	C Basse-Terre	N. Amer	51
Guam	Guam	541	*209*	137,000	253	*656*	Unincorporated territory (U.S.)	C Agana	Oceania	64
Guangdong	Guangdong	197,000	*76,062*	58,730,000	298	*772*	Province (China)	D Guangzhou (Canton)	Asia	27
†GUATEMALA	Guatemala	108,889	*42,042*	8,818,000	81	*210*	Republic	A Guatemala	N. Amer	49
Guernsey (incl. Dependencies)	Guernsey	78	*30*	56,000	718	*1,867*	Bailiwick (Channel Islands)	C St. Peter Port	Europe	9
†GUINEA	Guinée	245,857	*94,926*	6,999,000	28	*74*	Provisional military government	A Conakry	Africa	34
†GUINEA-BISSAU	Guiné-Bissau	36,125	*13,948*	962,000	27	*69*	Republic	A Bissau	Africa	34
Guizhou	Guizhou	174,000	*67,182*	30,980,000	178	*461*	Province (China)	D Guiyang	Asia	27
†GUYANA	Guyana	214,969	*83,000*	765,000	3.6	*9.2*	Republic	A Georgetown	S. Amer	54
Hainan	Hainan	34,000	*13,127*	6,520,000	192	*497*	Province (China)	D Haikou	Asia	27
†HAITI	Haïti	27,750	*10,714*	6,346,000	229	*592*	Provisional military government	A Port-au-Prince	N. Amer	49
Hamburg	Hamburg	755	*292*	1,555,000	2,060	*5,325*	State (Fed. Rep. of Germany)	D Hamburg	Europe	10
Hawaii	Hawaii	16,765	*6,473*	1,110,000	66	*171*	State (U.S.)	D Honolulu	N. Amer	60
Hebei	Hebei	203,000	*78,379*	58,020,000	286	*740*	Province (China)	D Shijiazhuang	Asia	28
Heilongjiang	Heilongjiang	460,000	*177,607*	34,810,000	76	*196*	Province (China)	D Harbin	Asia	27
Henan	Henan	167,000	*64,479*	80,900,000	484	*1,255*	Province (China)	D Zhengzhou	Asia	27
Hesse	Hessen	21,114	*8,152*	5,575,000	264	*684*	State (Fed. Rep. of Germany)	D Wiesbaden	Europe	10

Country, Division, or Region English (Conventional)	Local Name	Area km²	Area sq mi	Population 1/1/89	Population Density per km²	Population Density per sq mi	Form of Government and Political Status	Capital	Continent and Map Plate
Hispaniola	La Española	76,192	29,418	13,415,000	176	456	. . . .	. . . . . .	N. Amer . . . 49
Holland, see Netherlands	. . .	. . .	. . .	. . .	. . .	. . .	. . . .	. . . . . .	. . . .
† HONDURAS	Honduras	112,088	43,277	5,047,000	45	117	Republic	A Tegucigalpa	N. Amer . . . 49
Hong Kong	Hong Kong (English) / Xianggang (Chinese)	1,068	412	5,731,000	5,366	13,910	Dependent territory (U.K.)	C Victoria (Hong Kong)	Asia 27
Hubei	Hubei	188,000	72,587	51,560,000	274	710	Province (China)	D Wuhan	Asia 27
Hunan	Hunan	211,000	81,468	58,790,000	279	722	Province (China)	D Changsha	Asia 27
† HUNGARY	Magyarország	93,033	35,920	10,580,000	114	295	Socialist republic	A Budapest	Europe . . . 10
† ICELAND	Ísland	103,000	39,769	248,000	2.4	6.2	Republic	A Reykjavik	Europe . . . 7
Idaho	Idaho	216,435	83,566	1,010,000	4.7	12	State (U.S.)	D Boise	N. Amer . . . 46
Illinois	Illinois	149,888	57,872	11,615,000	77	201	State (U.S.)	D Springfield	N. Amer . . . 45
† INDIA (incl. part of Jammu and Kashmir)	India (English) / Bhārat (Hindi)	3,203,975	1,237,062	825,000,000	257	667	Federal republic	A New Delhi	Asia 25
Indiana	Indiana	94,320	36,417	5,539,000	59	152	State (U.S.)	D Indianapolis	N. Amer . . . 44
† INDONESIA	Indonesia	1,919,443	741,101	185,860,000	97	251	Republic	A Jakarta	Asia 26
Inner Mongolia	Nei Mongol Gaoyuan	1,200,000	463,323	20,020,000	17	43	Autonomous region (China)	D Hohhot	Asia 27
Iowa	Iowa	145,752	56,275	2,818,000	19	50	State (U.S.)	D Des Moines	N. Amer . . . 45
† IRAN	Īrān	1,648,000	636,296	52,760,000	32	83	Islamic republic	A Tehrān	Asia 23
† IRAQ	Al 'Irāq	438,317	169,235	17,900,000	41	106	Republic	A Baghdād	Asia 24
† IRELAND	Ireland (English) / Éire (Gaelic)	70,283	27,136	3,524,000	50	130	Republic	A Dublin (Baile Átha Cliath)	Europe . . . 9
ISLE OF MAN	Isle of Man	572	221	62,000	108	281	Self-governing territory (U.K. protection)	B Douglas	Europe . . . 9
† ISRAEL (excl. Occupied Areas)	Yisra'el (Hebrew) / Isrā'īl (Arabic)	20,770	8,019	4,374,000	211	545	Republic	A Yerushalayim (Jerusalem)	Asia 24
Israeli Occupied Areas [4]	. . .	7,632	2,947	1,728,000	226	586	. . . .	. . . . . .	Asia 24
† ITALY	Italia	301,268	116,320	57,500,000	191	494	Republic	A Roma (Rome)	Europe . . . 14
† IVORY COAST	Côte d'Ivoire	320,763	123,847	11,400,000	36	92	Republic	A Abidjan and Yamoussoukro [5]	Africa 34
† JAMAICA	Jamaica	10,991	4,244	2,470,000	225	582	Parliamentary state	A Kingston	N. Amer . . . 49
† JAPAN	Nippon	377,801	145,870	123,010,000	326	843	Constitutional monarchy	A Tōkyō	Asia 29
Java	Jawa	132,187	51,038	106,140,000	803	2,080	Part of Indonesia (5 provinces) . . .	. . . . . .	Asia 26
Jersey	Jersey	116	45	81,000	698	1,800	Bailiwick (Channel Islands)	C St. Helier	Europe . . . 9
Jiangsu	Jiangsu	102,000	39,382	65,240,000	640	1,657	Province (China)	D Nanjing (Nanking)	Asia 28
Jiangxi	Jiangxi	165,000	63,707	36,235,000	220	569	Province (China)	D Nanchang	Asia 27
Jilin	Jilin	187,000	72,201	24,195,000	129	335	Province (China)	D Changchun	Asia 27
Johnston Atoll	Johnston Atoll	1.3	0.5	300	231	600	Unincorporated territory (U.S.) . . .	C . . .	Oceania . . . 60
† JORDAN (excl. West Bank)	Al Urdun	91,000	35,135	2,904,000	32	83	Constitutional monarchy	A 'Ammān	Asia 24
Kansas	Kansas	213,109	82,282	2,500,000	12	30	State (U.S.)	D Topeka	N. Amer . . . 45
Kashmir, Jammu and	Jammu and Kashmir	222,801	86,024	8,960,000	40	104	Disputed territory (India and Pakistan)	D . . .	Asia 25
Kazakh S.S.R.	Kazahskaja S.S.R.	2,717,300	1,049,156	16,680,000	6.1	16	Soviet socialist republic (U.S.S.R.)	D Alma-Ata	Asia 19
Kentucky	Kentucky	104,672	40,414	3,741,000	36	93	State (U.S.)	D Frankfort	N. Amer . . . 44
† KENYA	Kenya	582,646	224,961	25,825,000	44	115	Republic	A Nairobi	Africa 36
Kerguelen Islands	Iles Kerguélen	6,993	2,700	100	. . .	. . .	Part of French Southern and Antarctic Territories	C . . .	S. Amer . . . 30-31
Kirghiz S.S.R.	Kirgizskaja S.S.R.	198,500	76,641	4,330,000	22	56	Soviet socialist republic (U.S.S.R.)	D Frunze	Asia 18
KIRIBATI	Kiribati	726	280	69,000	95	246	Republic	A Bairiki	Oceania . . . 60
KOREA, NORTH	Chosŏn Minjujuŭi Inmin Konghwaguk	120,538	46,540	22,250,000	185	478	Socialist republic	A P'yŏngyang	Asia 28
KOREA, SOUTH	Taehan-min'guk	98,484	38,025	42,840,000	435	1,127	Republic	A Sŏul (Seoul)	Asia 28
Korea (entire)	. . .	219,022	84,565	65,090,000	297	770	. . . .	. . . . . .	Asia 28
† KUWAIT	Al Kuwayt	17,818	6,880	2,002,000	112	291	Constitutional monarchy	A Al Kuwayt (Kuwait)	Asia 24
Kwangsi	Guangxi Zhuangzu Zizhiqu	237,000	91,506	40,285,000	170	440	Autonomous region (China)	D Nanning	Asia 27
Labrador	Labrador	292,218	112,826	31,000	0.1	0.3	Part of Newfoundland province (Canada)	. . . . . .	N. Amer . . . 42
† LAOS	Lao	236,800	91,429	3,892,000	16	43	Socialist republic	A Viangchan (Vientiane)	Asia 26
Latin America	. . .	20,500,000	8,000,000	372,800,000	18	47	. . . .	. . . . . .	N.A., S.A. 52-53
Latvian S.S.R.	Latvijas P.S.R.	63,700	24,595	2,695,000	42	110	Soviet socialist republic (U.S.S.R.)	D Rīga	Europe . . . 8
† LEBANON	Lubnān	10,400	4,015	3,351,000	322	835	Republic	A Bayrūt (Beirut)	Asia 24
† LESOTHO	Lesotho	30,355	11,720	1,689,000	56	144	Constitutional monarchy	A Maseru	Africa 37
Liaoning	Liaoning	151,000	58,301	38,645,000	256	663	Province (China)	D Shenyang (Mukden)	Asia 28
† LIBERIA	Liberia	99,067	38,250	2,553,000	26	67	Republic	A Monrovia	Africa 34
† LIBYA	Lībiya	1,759,540	679,362	4,019,000	2.3	5.9	Socialist republic	A Ṭarābulus (Tripoli)	Africa 33
LIECHTENSTEIN	Liechtenstein	160	62	29,000	181	468	Constitutional monarchy	A Vaduz	Europe . . . 14
Lithuanian S.S.R. [6]	Lietuvos T.S.R.	65,200	25,174	3,715,000	57	148	Soviet socialist republic (U.S.S.R.)	D Vilnius	Europe . . . 8
Louisiana	Louisiana	123,672	47,750	4,517,000	37	95	State (U.S.)	D Baton Rouge	N. Amer . . . 45
Lower Saxony	Niedersachsen	47,438	18,316	7,195,000	152	393	State (Fed. Rep. of Germany) . . .	D Hannover	Europe . . . 10
† LUXEMBOURG	Luxembourg (French) / Lezebuurg (Luxembourgish)	2,586	998	368,000	142	369	Constitutional monarchy	A Luxembourg	Europe . . . 12
Macao	Macau	17	6.6	432,000	25,412	65,455	Chinese territory under Portuguese administration	C Macau	Asia 27
† MADAGASCAR	Madagasikara	587,041	226,658	11,250,000	19	50	Republic	A Antananarivo	Africa 37
Madeira	Madeira	794	307	277,000	349	902	Autonomous region (Portugal) . . .	D Funchal	Europe . . . 32
Maine	Maine	86,156	33,265	1,205,000	14	36	State (U.S.)	D Augusta	N. Amer . . . 44
† MALAWI	Malaŵi	118,484	45,747	8,440,000	71	184	Republic	A Lilongwe	Africa 36
Malaya	Semenanjung Malaysia	131,312	50,700	14,240,000	108	281	Part of Malaysia (11 states)	D . . .	Asia 26
† MALAYSIA	Malaysia	330,228	127,502	17,255,000	52	135	Federal constitutional monarchy . .	A Kuala Lumpur	Asia 26
† MALDIVES	Maldives	298	115	209,000	701	1,817	Republic	A Male	Asia 25
† MALI	Mali	1,240,000	478,767	9,039,000	7.3	19	Republic	A Bamako	Africa 34
† MALTA	Malta	316	122	370,000	1,171	3,033	Republic	A Valletta	Europe . . . 14
Manitoba	Manitoba	649,950	250,947	1,095,000	1.7	4.4	Province (Canada)	D Winnipeg	N. Amer . . . 42
Maritime Provinces	. . .	134,590	51,965	1,734,000	13	33	. . . .	. . . . . .	N. Amer . . . 42
MARSHALL ISLANDS	Marshall Islands	181	70	40,000	221	571	Republic (U.S. protection)	B Uliga	Oceania . . . 60
Martinique	Martinique	1,100	425	338,000	307	795	Overseas department (France) . . .	C Fort-de-France	N. Amer . . . 51
Maryland	Maryland	27,094	10,461	4,605,000	170	440	State (U.S.)	D Annapolis	N. Amer . . . 44
Massachusetts	Massachusetts	21,461	8,286	5,880,000	274	710	State (U.S.)	D Boston	N. Amer . . . 44
† MAURITANIA	Mūritāniya (Arabic) / Mauritanie (French)	1,030,700	397,956	1,948,000	1.9	4.9	Provisional military government . . .	A Nouakchott	Africa 32
† MAURITIUS (incl. Dependencies)	Mauritius	2,040	788	1,057,000	518	1,341	Parliamentary state	A Port-Louis	Africa 37
Mayotte [7]	Mayotte	373	144	79,000	212	549	Territorial collectivity (France) . . .	C Dzaoudzi and Mamoudzou [5]	Africa 37
† MEXICO	México	1,972,547	761,605	85,300,000	43	112	Federal republic	A Ciudad de México (Mexico City)	N. Amer . . . 48

Country, Division, or Region English (Conventional)	Local Name	Area km²	sq mi	Population 1/1/89	Population Density per km²	sq mi	Form of Government and Political Status	Capital	Continent and Map Plate
Michigan	Michigan	251,506	97,107	9,186,000	37	95	State (U.S.)	D Lansing	N. Amer . . . 44
MICRONESIA, FEDERATED STATES OF	Federated States of Micronesia	702	271	108,000	154	399	Republic (U.S. protection)	B Ponape	Oceania . . . 60
Middle America	. . .	2,730,000	1,050,000	85,300,000	31	81	. . . .	. . . .	N. Amer . . . 47
Midway Islands	Midway Islands	5.2	2.0	500	96	250	Unincorporated territory (U.S.)	C . . .	Oceania . . . 60
Minnesota	Minnesota	224,329	86,614	4,283,000	19	49	State (U.S.)	D St. Paul	N. Amer . . . 45
Mississippi	Mississippi	123,519	47,691	2,647,000	21	56	State (U.S.)	D Jackson	N. Amer . . . 45
Missouri	Missouri	180,514	69,697	5,145,000	29	74	State (U.S.)	D Jefferson City	N. Amer . . . 45
Moldavian S.S.R.	Moldavskaja S.S.R.	33,700	13,012	4,260,000	126	327	Soviet socialist republic (U.S.S.R.) .	D Kišinev (Kishinev)	Europe . . . 16
MONACO	Monaco	1.9	0.7	29,000	15,263	41,429	Constitutional monarchy	A Monaco	Europe . . . 11
†MONGOLIA	Mongol Ard Uls	1,565,000	604,250	2,097,000	1.3	3.5	Socialist republic	A Ulan-Bator (Ulaanbaatar)	Asia 27
Montana	Montana	380,845	147,045	814,000	2.1	5.5	State (U.S.)	D Helena	N. Amer . . . 46
Montserrat	Montserrat	103	40	12,000	117	300	Dependent territory (U.K.)	C Plymouth	N. Amer . . . 51
†MOROCCO (excl. Western Sahara)	Al Maghrib	446,550	172,414	25,600,000	57	148	Consitutional monarchy	A Rabat	Africa . . . 32
†MOZAMBIQUE	Moçambique	799,379	308,642	17,660,000	22	57	Socialist republic	A Maputo	Africa . . . 37
NAMIBIA (excl. Walvis Bay)	Namibia	823,144	317,818	1,337,000	1.6	4.2	Republic	A Windhoek	Africa . . . 37
NAURU	Nauru (English) / Naoero (Nauruan)	21	8.1	9,000	429	1,111	Republic	A Domaneab	Oceania . . . 64
Navassa Island	Navassa Island	4.9	1.9	. . .(1)	. . .	. . .	Unincorporated territory (U.S.) . . .	C . . .	N. Amer . . . 49
Nebraska	Nebraska	200,336	77,350	1,599,000	8.0	21	State (U.S.)	D Lincoln	N. Amer . . . 45
†NEPAL	Nepāl	147,181	56,827	18,415,000	125	324	Constitutional monarchy	A Kathmandū	Asia 25
†NETHERLANDS	Nederland	41,785	16,133	14,815,000	355	918	Constitutional monarchy	A Amsterdam and 's-Gravenhage (The Hague)	Europe . . . 12
NETHERLANDS ANTILLES	Nederlandse Antillen	800	309	194,000	243	628	Self-governing territory (Netherlands protection)	B Willemstad	N. Amer . . . 50
Nevada	Nevada	286,354	110,562	1,061,000	3.7	9.6	State (U.S.)	D Carson City	N. Amer . . . 46
New Brunswick	New Brunswick (English) / Nouveau-Brusnwick (French)	73,440	28,355	718,000	9.8	25	Province (Canada)	D Fredericton	N. Amer . . . 42
New Caledonia	Nouvelle-Calédonie	19,079	7,366	161,000	8.4	22	Overseas territory (France)	C Nouméa	Oceania . . . 63
New England	New England	172,685	66,674	12,955,000	75	194	Part of U.S. (6 states)	. . . .	N. Amer . . . 43
Newfoundland	Newfoundland (English) / Terre-Neuve (French)	405,720	156,649	571,000	1.4	3.6	Province (Canada)	D St. John's	N. Amer . . . 42
Newfoundland (island)	Newfoundland (English) / Terre-Neuve (French)	108,860	42,031	540,000	5.0	13	Part of Newfoundland province (Canada)		N. Amer . . . 42
New Hampshire	New Hampshire	24,030	9,278	1,089,000	45	117	State (U.S.)	D Concord	N. Amer . . . 44
New Hebrides, see Vanuatu	. . .	. . .	. . .	. . . .	. . .	. . .	. . . .	. . . .	. . . .
New Jersey	New Jersey	20,168	7,787	7,739,000	384	994	State (U.S.)	D Trenton	N. Amer . . . 44
New Mexico	New Mexico	314,927	121,594	1,547,000	4.9	13	State (U.S.)	D Santa Fe	N. Amer . . . 45
New South Wales	New South Wales	801,600	309,500	5,820,000	7.3	19	State (Australia)	D Sydney	Oceania . . . 59
New York	New York	136,588	52,737	17,880,000	131	339	State (U.S.)	D Albany	N. Amer . . . 44
†NEW ZEALAND	New Zealand	268,112	103,519	3,391,000	13	33	Parliamentary state	A Wellington	Oceania . . . 62
†NICARAGUA	Nicaragua	130,000	50,193	3,689,000	28	73	Republic	A Managua	N. Amer . . . 49
†NIGER	Niger	1,267,000	489,191	7,329,000	5.8	15	Provisional military government . . .	A Niamey	Africa 34
†NIGERIA	Nigeria	923,768	356,669	113,580,000	123	318	Provisional military government . . .	A Lagos and Abuja (5)	Africa 34
Ningsia	Ningxia Huizu Zizhiqu	66,000	25,483	4,270,000	65	168	Autonomous region (China)	D Yinchuan	Asia 27
NIUE	Niue	263	102	2,400	9.1	24	Self-governing territory (New Zealand protection)	B Alofi	Oceania . . . 64
Norfolk Island	Norfolk Island	36	14	2,000	56	143	External territory (Australia)	C Kingston	Oceania . . . 61
North America	. . .	24,400,000	9,400,000	420,100,000	17	45	. . . .		N. Amer . . . 38-39
North Borneo, see Sabah	. . .	. . .	. . .	. . . .	. . .	. . .	. . . .	. . . .	. . . .
North Carolina	North Carolina	136,412	52,669	6,532,000	48	124	State (U.S.)	D Raleigh	N. Amer . . . 44
North Dakota	North Dakota	183,117	70,702	676,000	3.7	9.6	State (U.S.)	D Bismarck	N. Amer . . . 45
Northern Ireland	Northern Ireland	14,122	5,453	1,575,000	112	289	Administrative division (U.K.)	D Belfast	Europe . . . 9
NORTHERN MARIANA ISLANDS	Northern Mariana Islands	477	184	22,000	46	120	Commonwealth (U.S. protection) . .	B Saipan (island)	Oceania . . . 60
Northern Territory	Northern Territory	1,346,200	519,771	168,000	0.1	0.3	Territory (Australia)	D Darwin	Oceania . . . 59
North Rhine-Westphalia	Nordrhein-Westfalen	34,068	13,154	16,685,000	490	1,268	State (Fed. Rep. of Germany) . . .	D Düsseldorf	Europe . . . 10
Northwest Territories	Northwest Territories (English) / Territoires du Nord-Ouest (French)	3,426,320	1,322,910	56,000	. . .	. . .	Territory (Canada)	D Yellowknife	N. Amer . . . 42
†NORWAY (incl. Svalbard and Jan Mayen)	Norge	386,975	149,412	4,221,000	11	28	Constitutional monarchy	A Oslo	Europe . . . 7
Nova Scotia	Nova Scotia (English) / Nouvelle-Écosse (French)	55,490	21,425	886,000	16	41	Province (Canada)	D Halifax	N. Amer . . . 42
Oceania (incl. Australia)	. . .	8,500,000	3,300,000	26,300,000	3.1	8.0	. . . .		Oceania . . . 57-58
Ohio	Ohio	115,995	44,786	10,780,000	93	241	State (U.S.)	D Columbus	N. Amer . . . 44
Oklahoma	Oklahoma	181,188	69,957	3,327,000	18	48	State (U.S.)	D Oklahoma City	N. Amer . . . 45
†OMAN	'Umān	212,457	82,030	1,284,000	6.0	16	Monarchy	A Masqaṭ (Muscat)	Asia 23
Ontario	Ontario	1,068,580	412,581	9,375,000	8.8	23	Province (Canada)	D Toronto	N. Amer . . . 42
Oregon	Oregon	251,426	97,076	2,743,000	11	28	State (U.S.)	D Salem	N. Amer . . . 46
Orkney Islands	Orkney Islands	976	377	19,000	19	50	Part of Scotland (U.K.)	D Kirkwall	Europe . . . 9
PACIFIC ISLANDS, TRUST TERRITORY OF THE	Trust Territory of the Pacific Islands	508	196	15,000	30	77	United Nations trusteeship (U.S. administration)	B Saipan (island)	Oceania . . . 60
†PAKISTAN (incl. part of Jammu and Kashmir)	Pākistān	879,902	339,732	108,990,000	124	321	Federal Islamic republic	A Islāmābād	Asia 25
PALAU	Palau (English) / Belau (Palauan)	508	196	15,000	30	77	Part of Trust Territory of the Pacific Islands	B Koror	Oceania . . . 60
†PANAMA	Panamá	77,082	29,762	2,346,000	30	79	Republic	A Panamá	N. Amer . . . 49
†PAPUA NEW GUINEA	Papua New Guinea	462,840	178,704	3,639,000	7.9	20	Parliamentary state	A Port Moresby	Oceania . . . 60
†PARAGUAY	Paraguay	406,752	157,048	4,210,000	10	27	Republic	A Asunción	S. Amer . . . 56
Peking	Beijing	16,800	6,487	10,070,000	599	1,552	Autonomous city (China)	D Beijing (Peking)	Asia 28
Pennsylvania	Pennsylvania	119,261	46,047	11,950,000	100	260	State (U.S.)	D Harrisburg	N. Amer . . . 44
†PERU	Perú	1,285,216	496,225	21,535,000	17	43	Republic	A Lima	S. Amer . . . 54
†PHILIPPINES	Pilipinas (Tagalog) / Philippines (English)	300,000	115,831	60,110,000	200	519	Republic	A Manila	Asia 26
Pitcairn (incl. Dependencies)	Pitcairn	49	19	70	1.4	3.7	Dependent territory (U.K.)	C Adamstown	Oceania . . . 61
†POLAND	Polska	312,683	120,728	37,955,000	121	314	Socialist republic	A Warszawa (Warsaw)	Europe . . . 10
†PORTUGAL	Portugal	91,985	35,516	10,445,000	114	294	Republic	A Lisboa (Lisbon)	Europe . . . 13
Prairie Provinces	Prairie Provinces	1,963,470	758,100	4,575,000	2.3	6.0	Part of Canada (3 provinces)		N. Amer . . . 42
Prince Edward Island	Prince Edward Island / Île-du Prince-Édouard (French)	5,660	2,185	130,000	23	59	Province (Canada)	D Charlottetown	N. Amer . . . 42

A • 5

Country, Division, or Region English (Conventional)	Local Name	Area km²	Area sq mi	Population 1/1/89	Population Density per km²	Population Density per sq mi	Form of Government and Political Status	Capital	Continent and Map Plate
PUERTO RICO	Puerto Rico	9,104	3,515	3,301,000	363	939	Commonwealth (U.S. protection)	B San Juan	N. Amer . . . 51
† QATAR	Qaṭar	11,437	4,416	400,000	35	91	Monarchy	A Ad Dawḥah (Doha)	Asia 24
Qinghai	Qinghai	721,000	278,380	4,270,000	5.9	15	Province (China)	D Xining	Asia 27
Quebec	Québec	1,540,680	594,860	6,595,000	4.3	11	Province (Canada)	D Québec	N. Amer . . . 42
Queensland	Queensland	1,727,200	666,876	2,849,000	1.6	4.3	State (Australia)	D Brisbane	Oceania . . . 59
Reunion	Réunion	2,504	967	580,000	232	600	Overseas department (France) . . .	C Saint-Denis	Africa 37
Rhineland-Palatinate	Rheinland-Pfalz	19,848	7,663	3,605,000	182	470	State (Fed. Rep. of Germany) . . .	D Mainz	Europe . . . 10
Rhode Island	Rhode Island	3,139	1,212	994,000	317	820	State (U.S.)	D Providence	N. Amer . . . 44
Rhodesia, see Zimbabwe	. . .	. . .	. . .	. . .	. . .	. . .		. . . .	
Rodrigues	Rodrigues	104	40	35,000	337	875	Part of Mauritius		Africa 30-31
† ROMANIA	România	237,500	91,699	23,085,000	97	252	Socialist republic	A București (Bucharest)	Europe . . . 15
Russian Soviet Federative Socialist Republic	Rossijskaja Sovetskaja Federativnaja Socialističeskaja Respublika	17,075,400	6,592,849	147,780,000	8.7	22	Soviet socialist republic (U.S.S.R.)	D Moskva (Moscow)	Eur.-Asia . . 19-20
Russian S.F.S.R. in Europe	Rossijskaja S.F.S.R.	3,955,818	1,527,350	107,940,000	27	71	. . . .		Europe . . . 19
† RWANDA	Rwanda	26,338	10,169	7,192,000	273	707	Republic	A Kigali	Africa 36
Saarland	Saar	2,569	992	1,035,000	403	1,043	State (Fed. Rep. of Germany) . . .	D Saarbrücken	Europe . . . 10
Sabah	Sabah	73,711	28,460	1,405,000	19	49	State (Malaysia)	D Kota Kinabalu	Asia 26
† ST. CHRISTOPHER-NEVIS	St. Christopher-Nevis	269	104	47,000	175	452	Parliamentary state	A Basseterre	N. Amer . . . 51
St. Helena (incl. Dependencies)	St. Helena	419	162	7,800	19	48	Dependent territory (U.K.)	C Jamestown	Africa 31
† ST. LUCIA	St. Lucia	616	238	148,000	240	622	Parliamentary state	A Castries	N. Amer . . . 51
St. Pierre and Miquelon	St.-Pierre et Miquelon	242	93	6,500	27	70	Overseas department (France) . . .	C Saint-Pierre	N. Amer . . . 42
† ST. VINCENT AND THE GRENADINES	St. Vincent	388	150	125,000	322	833	Parliamentary state	A Kingstown	N. Amer . . . 51
SAN MARINO	San Marino	61	24	24,000	393	1,000	Republic	A San Marino	Europe . . . 14
† SAO TOME AND PRINCIPE	São Tomé e Príncipe	964	372	119,000	123	320	Republic	A São Tomé	Africa 34
Sarawak	Sarawak	125,205	48,342	1,610,000	13	33	State (Malaysia)	D Kuching	Asia 26
Sardinia	Sardegna	24,090	9,301	1,665,000	69	179	Autonomous region (Italy)	D Cagliari	Europe . . . 14
Saskatchewan	Saskatchewan	652,330	251,866	1,030,000	1.6	4.1	Province (Canada)	D Regina	N. Amer . . . 42
† SAUDI ARABIA	Al 'Arabīyah as Su'ūdīyah	2,240,000	864,869	15,775,000	7.0	18	Monarchy	A Ar Riyāḍ (Riyadh)	Asia 23
Scandinavia	. . .	1,320,000	510,000	23,045,000	17	45	. . . .		Europe . . . 7
Schleswig-Holstein	Schleswig-Holstein	15,727	6,072	2,580,000	164	425	State (Fed. Rep. of Germany) . . .	D Kiel	Europe . . . 10
Scotland	Scotland	77,167	29,794	5,150,000	67	173	Administrative division (U.K.)	D Edinburgh	Europe . . . 9
† SENEGAL	Sénégal	196,722	75,955	7,394,000	38	97	Republic	A Dakar	Africa 34
† SEYCHELLES	Seychelles	453	175	70,000	155	400	Republic	A Victoria	Africa 37
Shaanxi	Shaanxi	196,000	75,676	31,420,000	160	415	Province (China)	D Xi'an (Sian)	Asia 27
Shandong	Shandong	153,000	59,074	80,790,000	528	1,368	Province (China)	D Jinan	Asia 27
Shanghai	Shanghai	5,800	2,239	12,700,000	2,190	5,672	Autonomous city (China)	D Shanghai	Asia 28
Shanxi	Shanxi	157,000	60,618	27,475,000	175	453	Province (China)	D Taiyuan	Asia 27
Shetland Islands	Shetland Islands	1,433	553	24,000	17	43	Part of Scotland (U.K.)	D Lerwick	Europe . . . 9
Sichuan	Sichuan	569,000	219,692	106,950,000	188	487	Province (China)	D Chengdu	Asia 27
Sicily	Sicilia	25,708	9,926	5,195,000	202	523	Autonomous region (Italy)	D Palermo	Europe . . . 14
† SIERRA LEONE	Sierra Leone	72,325	27,925	4,015,000	56	144	Republic	A Freetown	Africa 34
† SINGAPORE	Singapore (English) / Singapura (Malay)	636	236	2,663,000	4,187	11,284	Republic	A Singapore	Asia 26
Sinkiang	Xinjiang Uygur Zizhiqu	1,647,000	635,910	14,230,000	8.6	22	Autonomous region (China)	D Ürümqi	Asia 27
† SOLOMON ISLANDS	Solomon Islands	28,369	10,953	295,000	10	27	Parliamentary state	A Honiara	Oceania . . . 63
† SOMALIA	Soomaaliya	637,657	246,201	8,118,000	13	33	Socialist republic	A Muqdisho (Mogadishu)	Africa 35
† SOUTH AFRICA (incl. Walvis Bay)	South Africa (English) / Suid-Afrika (Afrikaans)	1,123,226	433,680	35,480,000	32	82	Republic	A Pretoria, Cape Town, and Bloemfontein	Africa 37
South America	. . .	17,800,000	6,900,000	287,500,000	16	42	. . . .		S. Amer . . . 52-53
South Australia	South Australia	984,000	379,925	1,435,000	1.5	3.8	State (Australia)	D Adelaide	Oceania . . . 59
South Carolina	South Carolina	80,590	31,116	3,494,000	43	112	State (U.S.)	D Columbia	N. Amer . . . 44
South Dakota	South Dakota	199,740	77,120	713,000	3.6	9.2	State (U.S.)	D Pierre	N. Amer . . . 45
South Georgia (incl. Dependencies)	South Georgia	3,755	1,450	. . .(1)	. . .	. . .	Dependent territory (U.K.)	C . . .	S. Amer . . . 56
South West Africa, see Namibia	. . .	. . .	. . .	. . .	. . .	. . .			
Soviet Union, see Union of Soviet Socialist Republics	. . .	. . .	. . .	. . .	. . .	. . .			
† SPAIN	España	504,750	194,885	39,330,000	78	202	Constitutional monarchy	A Madrid	Europe . . . 13
Spanish North Africa (8)	Plazas de Soberanía en el Norte de África	32	12	100,000	3,125	8,333	Five possessions (Spain)	C . . .	Africa 13
Spanish Sahara, see Western Sahara	. . .	. . .	. . .	. . .	. . .	. . .			
† SRI LANKA	Sri Lanka	64,652	24,962	16,730,000	259	670	Socialist republic	A Colombo and Sri Jayawardenapura	Asia 25
† SUDAN	As Sūdān	2,505,813	967,500	24,255,000	9.7	25	Republic	A Al Kharṭūm (Khartoum)	Africa 35
Sumatra	Sumatera	473,606	182,860	36,140,000	76	198	Part of Indonesia (7 provinces) . . .		Asia 26
† SURINAME	Suriname	163,820	63,251	398,000	2.4	6.3	Provisional military government	A Paramaribo	S. Amer . . . 54
† SWAZILAND	Swaziland	17,364	6,704	727,000	42	108	Monarchy	A Mbabane and Lobamba (5)	Africa 37
† SWEDEN	Sverige	449,964	173,732	8,444,000	19	49	Constitutional monarchy	A Stockholm	Europe . . . 7
SWITZERLAND	Schweiz (German) / Suisse (French) / Svizzera (Italian)	41,293	15,943	6,590,000	160	413	Federal republic	A Bern (Berne)	Europe . . . 14
† SYRIA	Sūrīyah	185,180	71,498	11,530,000	62	161	Socialist republic	A Dimashq (Damascus)	Asia 24
TAIWAN	Taiwan	36,002	13,900	20,125,000	559	1,448	Republic	A Taipei	Asia 27
Tajik S.S.R.	Tadžikskaja S.S.R.	143,100	55,251	5,135,000	36	93	Soviet socialist republic (U.S.S.R.)	D Dušanbe (Dushanbe)	Asia 18
† TANZANIA	Tanzania	945,087	364,900	24,055,000	25	66	Republic	A Dar es Salaam and Dodoma (5)	Africa 36
Tasmania	Tasmania	67,800	26,178	452,000	6.7	17	State (Austl.)	D Hobart	Oceania . . . 59
Tennessee	Tennessee	109,150	42,143	4,913,000	45	117	State (U.S.)	D Nashville	N. Amer . . . 44
Texas	Texas	691,022	266,805	17,415,000	25	65	State (U.S.)	D Austin	N. Amer . . . 45
† THAILAND	Muang Thai	513,115	198,115	55,375,000	108	280	Constitutional monarchy	A Krung Thep (Bangkok)	Asia 26
Tibet	Xizang Zizhiqu	1,222,000	471,817	2,080,000	1.7	4.4	Autonomous region (China)	D Lhasa	Asia 27
Tientsin	Tianjin	11,000	4,247	8,430,000	766	1,985	Autonomous city (China)	D Tianjin (Tientsin)	Asia 28
† TOGO	Togo	56,785	21,925	3,393,000	60	155	Republic	A Lomé	Africa 34
Tokelau	Tokelau	12	4.6	1,700	142	370	Island territory (New Zealand) . . .	C . . .	Oceania . . . 61
TONGA	Tonga	699	270	100,000	143	370	Constitutional monarchy	A Nuku'alofa	Oceania . . . 61
Transcaucasia	. . .	186,100	71,853	15,855,000	85	221	. . . .		Asia 16
TRANSKEI (2)	Transkei	42,000	16,216	3,900,000	93	241	National state (South African protection)	B Umtata	Africa 37
† TRINIDAD AND TOBAGO	Trinidad and Tobago	5,128	1,980	1,295,000	253	654	Republic	A Port of Spain	N. Amer . . . 50
Tristan da Cunha	Tristan da Cunha	104	40	300	2.9	7.5	Dependency (St. Helena)	C Edinburgh	Africa 30-31

Country, Division, or Region English (Conventional)	Local Name	Area km²	Area sq mi	Population 1/1/89	Population Density per km²	per sq mi	Form of Government and Political Status	Capital	Continent and Map Plate
†TUNISIA	Tunisie (French) / Tūnis (Arabic)	163,610	63,170	7,876,000	48	125	Republic	A Tūnis	Africa 32
†TURKEY	Türkiye	779,452	300,948	51,970,000	67	173	Republic	A Ankara	Eur.-Asia . . 24
Turkey in Europe	. . .	23,764	9,175	5,025,000	211	548	. . . .	Europe . . . 24
Turkmen S.S.R.	Turkmenskaja S.S.R.	488,100	188,456	3,545,000	7.3	19	Soviet socialist republic (U.S.S.R.)	D Ašhabad	Asia 19
Turks and Caicos Islands	Turks and Caicos Islands	430	166	10,000	23	60	Dependent territory (U.K.)	C Grand Turk	N. Amer . . . 49
TUVALU	Tuvalu	26	10	8,700	335	870	Parliamentary state	A Funafuti	Oceania . . . 60
†UGANDA	Uganda	241,139	93,104	16,725,000	69	180	Republic	A Kampala	Africa 36
†Ukrainian S.S.R.	Ukrainskaja S.S.R.	603,700	233,090	51,620,000	86	221	Soviet socialist republic (U.S.S.R.)	D Kijev (Kiev)	Europe . . . 16
†UNION OF SOVIET SOCIALIST REPUBLICS	Sojuz Sovetskich Socialističeskich Respublik	22,274,900	8,600,387	287,550,000	13	33	Federal socialist republic	A Moskva (Moscow)	Eur.-Asia 19-20
U.S.S.R. in Europe		4,974,818	1,920,789	182,030,000	37	95	. . . .	. . . . .	Europe . . . . . .
†UNITED ARAB EMIRATES	Al Imārāt al 'Arabīyah al Muttaḥidah	83,600	32,278	2,047,000	24	63	Federation of monarchs	A Abū Ẓaby (Abu Dhabi)	Asia 23
†UNITED KINGDOM	United Kingdom	242,496	93,629	57,090,000	235	610	Constitutional monarchy	A London	Europe . . . 9
United Kingdom and Possessions	. . .	258,127	99,664	63,180,000	245	634	. . . .	. . . .	. . . .
†UNITED STATES	United States	9,529,202	3,679,245	247,410,000	26	67	Federal republic	A Washington	N. Amer . . . 43
United States and Possessions	. . .	9,541,271	3,683,905	251,180,000	26	68	. . . .	. . . .	. . . .
Upper Volta, see Burkina Faso		. . .	. . .	. . .	. . .	. . .			
†URUGUAY	Uruguay	175,016	67,574	3,184,000	18	47	Republic	A Montevideo	S. Amer . . . 55
Utah	Utah	219,895	84,902	1,732,000	7.9	20	State (U.S.)	D Salt Lake City	N. Amer . . . 46
Uzbek S.S.R.	Uzbekskaja S.S.R.	447,400	172,742	20,135,000	45	117	Soviet socialist republic (U.S.S.R.)	D Taškent (Tashkent)	Asia 19
†VANUATU	Vanuatu	12,189	4,706	155,000	13	33	Republic	A Port-Vila	Oceania . . . 63
VATICAN CITY	Città del Vaticano	0.4	0.2	800	2,000	4,000	Ecclesiastical city-state	A Vatican City	Europe . . . 14
VENDA (2)	Venda	6,875	2,654	556,000	81	209	National state (South African protection)	B Thohoyandou	Africa 37
†VENEZUELA	Venezuela	912,050	352,145	19,010,000	21	54	Federal republic	A Caracas	S. Amer . . . 54
Vermont	Vermont	24,900	9,614	556,000	22	58	State (U.S.)	D Montpelier	N. Amer . . . 44
Victoria	Victoria	227,600	87,877	4,325,000	19	49	State (Australia)	D Melbourne	Oceania . . . 59
†VIETNAM	Viet Nam	329,556	127,242	66,030,000	200	519	Socialist republic	A Ha Noi	Asia 26
Virginia	Virginia	105,576	40,763	6,031,000	57	148	State (U.S.)	D Richmond	N. Amer . . . 44
Virgin Islands of the United States	Virgin Islands of the United States	344	133	106,000	308	797	Unincorporated territory (U.S.) . . .	C Charlotte Amalie	N. Amer . . . 51
Virgin Islands, British	British Virgin Islands	153	59	13,000	85	220	Dependent territory (U.K.)	C Road Town	N. Amer . . . 51
Wake Island	Wake Island	7.8	3.0	300	38	100	Unincorporated territory (U.S.) . . .	C . . .	Oceania . . . 60
Wales	Wales	20,768	8,019	2,855,000	137	356	Administrative Division (U.K.)	D Cardiff	Europe . . . 9
Wallis and Futuna	Îles Wallis et Futuna	255	98	15,000	59	153	Overseas territory (France)	C Mata-Utu	Oceania . . . 61
Washington	Washington	176,479	68,139	4,630,000	26	68	State (U.S.)	D Olympia	N. Amer . . . 46
Western Australia	Western Australia	2,525,500	975,101	1,625,000	0.6	1.7	State (Australia)	D Perth	Oceania . . . 59
Western Sahara	. . .	266,000	102,703	97,000	0.4	0.9	Occupied by Morocco	C El Aaiún	Africa 32
†WESTERN SAMOA	Western Samoa (English) / Samoa i Sisifo (Samoan)	2,842	1,097	180,000	63	164	Constitutional monarchy	A Apia	Oceania . . . 65
West Indies	West Indies (English) / Indias Occidentales (Spanish)	235,000	91,000	33,130,000	141	364	. . . .	. . . .	N. Amer . . . 47
West Virginia	West Virginia	62,771	24,236	1,886,000	30	78	State (U.S.)	D Charleston	N. Amer . . . 44
Wisconsin	Wisconsin	171,491	66,213	4,828,000	28	73	State (U.S.)	D Madison	N. Amer . . . 45
Wyoming	Wyoming	253,322	97,808	494,000	2.0	5.1	State (U.S.)	D Cheyenne	N. Amer . . . 46
†YEMEN	Al Yaman	531,869	205,356	12,661,000	24	62	Islamic republic	A Şan'ā'	Asia 23
†YUGOSLAVIA	Jugoslavija	255,804	98,766	23,970,000	94	243	Federal socialist republic	A Beograd (Belgrade)	Europe . . . 14-15
Yukon Territory	Yukon Territory	483,450	186,661	24,000	0.1	0.1	Territory (Canada)	D Whitehorse	N. Amer . . . 42
Yunnan	Yunnan	436,000	168,341	35,580,000	82	211	Province (China)	D Kunming	Asia 27
†ZAIRE	Zaire	2,345,409	905,568	33,795,000	14	37	Republic	A Kinshasa	Africa 36
†ZAMBIA	Zambia	752,614	290,586	7,682,000	10	26	Republic	A Lusaka	Africa 36
Zanzibar	Zanzibar	1,660	641	634,000	382	989	Part of Tanzania	. . . Zanzibar	Africa 36
Zhejiang	Zhejiang	102,000	39,382	42,255,000	414	1,073	Province (China)	D Hangzhou	Asia 27
†ZIMBABWE	Zimbabwe	390,759	150,873	9,003,000	23	60	Republic	A Harare	Africa 37
WORLD	. . .	149,900,000	57,900,000	5,192,000,000	35	90	. . . .	. . . .	 1-2

† Member of the United Nations (1988).
. . . None, or not applicable.
(1) No permanent population.
(2) Bophuthatswana, Ciskei, Transkei, and Venda are not recognized by the United Nations.
(3) Claimed by Argentina.
(4) Includes West Bank, Golan Heights, and Gaza Strip.
(5) Future capital.
(6) On March 11, 1990 Lithuania unilaterally declared its independence from the Soviet Union.
(7) Claimed by Comoros.
(8) Comprises Ceuta, Melilla, and several small islands.

World Geographical Tables

The Earth: Land and Water

	Total Area km²	Total Area sq mi	Area of Land km²	Area of Land sq mi	%	Area of Oceans and Seas km²	Area of Oceans and Seas sq mi	%
Earth	510,100,000	197,000,000	149,900,000	57,900,000	29.4	360,200,000	139,100,000	70.6
N. Hemisphere	255,050,000	98,500,000	106,429,000	41,109,000	41.6	148,762,600	57,448,300	58.4
S. Hemisphere	255,050,000	98,500,000	43,471,000	16,791,000	17.0	211,437,400	81,651,700	83.0

The Continents

Continent	Area km² / sq mi	Population Estimate (1/1/89)	Population per km² / sq mi	Mean Eleva-tion m / ft	Highest Elevation m/ft	Lowest Elevation m/ft (below sea level)	Highest Recorded Temperature °C/°F	Lowest Recorded Temperature °C/°F
Europe	9,900,000 / 3,800,000	685,400,000	69 / 180	300 / 980	gora Elbrus, U.S.S.R. 5,642/18,510	Caspian Sea, U.S.S.R.-Iran −28/−92	Sevilla, Spain 50°/122°	Ust-Ščugor, U.S.S.R. −55°/−67°
Asia	45,000,000 / 17,400,000	3,130,600,000	70 / 180	910 / 3,000	Everest, China-Nepal 8,848/29,028	Dead Sea, Israel-Jordan −403/−1,322	Tirat Zevi, Israel 54°/129°	Ojmjakon and Verkhoyansk, U.S.S.R. −68°/−90°
Africa	30,300,000 / 11,700,000	642,100,000	21 / 55	580 / 1,900	Kilimanjaro, Tanzania 5,895/19,340	Lac Assal, Djibouti −155/−509	Al ʿAzīzīyah, Libya 58°/136°	Ifrane, Morocco −24°/−11°
North America	24,400,000 / 9,400,000	420,100,000	17 / 45	610 / 2,000	Mt. McKinley, U.S. 6,194/20,320	Death Valley, U.S. −86/−282	Death Valley, U.S. 57°/134°	Northice, Greenland −66°/−87°
South America	17,800,000 / 6,900,000	287,500,000	16 / 42	550 / 1,800	Cerro Aconcagua, Argentina 6,960/22,835	Salinas Chicas −42/−138	Rivadavia, Argentina 49°/120°	Sarmiento, Argentina −33°/−27°
Oceania, incl. Australia	8,500,000 / 3,300,000	26,300,000	3 / 8	.... /	Mt. Wilhelm, Papua New Guinea 4,509/14,793	Lake Eyre, Australia −12/−39	Cloncurry, Australia 53°/128°	Charlotte Pass, Australia −22°/−8°
Australia	7,682,300 / 2,966,155	16,955,000	2 / 6	300 / 1,000	Mt. Kosciusko, Australia 2,228/7,310	Lake Eyre, Australia −12/−39	Cloncurry, Australia 53°/128°	Charlotte Pass, Australia −22°/−8°
Antarctica	14,000,000 / 5,400,000	....	... / ...	1,830 / 6,000	Vinson Massif 4,897/116,06	sea level	Vanda Station 15°/59°	Vostok −89°/−129°
World	149,900,000 / 57,900,000	5,192,000,000	35 / 90	.... /	Everest, China-Nepal 8,848/29,028	Dead Sea, Israel-Jordan −403/−1,322	Al ʿAzīzīyah, Libya 58°/136°	Vostok −89°/−129°

Principal Mountains

Mountain	Country	Height M	Height Ft
Europe			
Elbrus, gora	U.S.S.R.	5,642	18,510
Dyhtau, gora	U.S.S.R.	5,204	17,073
Blanc, Mont	△France-△Italy	4,807	15,771
Rosa, Monte	Italy-△Switzerland	4,634	15,203
Matterhorn	Italy-Switzerland	4,478	14,692
Grossglockner	△Austria	3,797	12,457
Teide, Pico de	△Spain (Canary Is.)	3,718	12,198
Aneto, Pico de	Spain	3,404	11,168
Etna	Italy	3,323	10,902
Zugspitze	Austria-△Germany, Fed. Rep. of	2,963	9,721
Ólimbos, Óros	△Greece	2,917	9,570
Corno Grande	Italy	2,912	9,554
Gerlachovský štít	△Czechoslovakia	2,663	8,737
Glittertind	△Norway	2,472	8,110
Kebnekaise	△Sweden	2,111	6,926
Narodnaja, gora	U.S.S.R.	1,895	6,217
Nevis, Ben	△United Kingdom	1,343	4,406
Asia			
Everest	△China-△Nepal	8,848	29,028
K2 (Qogir Feng)	China-△Pakistan	8,611	28,250
Kānchenjunga	△India-Nepal	8,598	28,208
Makālu	China-Nepal	8,481	27,825
Dhaulāgiri	Nepal	8,172	26,810
Annapurna	Nepal	8,078	26,504
Muztag	China	7,723	25,338
Tirich Mīr	Pakistan	7,690	25,230
Kommunizma, pik (Communism Peak)	△U.S.S.R.	7,495	24,590
Pobedy, pik	China-U.S.S.R.	7,439	24,406
Damāvand, Qolleh-ye	△Iran	5,604	18,386
Ağrı Dağı, Büyük (Mt. Ararat)	△Turkey	5,122	16,804
Jaya, Puncak	△Indonesia	5,030	16,503
Ključevskaja Sopka, vulkan	U.S.S.R.	4,750	15,584
Kinabalu, Gunong	△Malaysia	4,101	13,455
Yushan	△Taiwan	3,997	13,114
Fuji-San	△Japan	3,776	12,388
Nabī Shuʿayb, Jabal an	△Yemen	3,760	12,336
Apo, Mt.	△Philippines	2,954	9,692
Shaykh, Jabal ash- (Mt. Hermon)	Lebanon-△Syria	2,814	9,232
Mayon, Mt.	Philippines	2,462	8,077
Chili-san	△South Korea	1,915	6,283
Meron, Hare	△Israel	1,208	3,963

Mountain	Country	Height M	Height Ft
Africa			
Kilimanjaro	△Tanzania	5,895	19,340
Kirinyaga (Mt. Kenya)	△Kenya	5,199	17,058
Margherita	△Uganda-△Zaire	5,109	16,762
Ras Dashan Terara	△Ethiopia	4,620	15,158
Toubkal, Jebel	△Morocco	4,165	13,665
Cameroon, Mt.	△Cameroon	4,100	13,451
North America			
McKinley, Mt.	△United States	6,194	20,320
Logan, Mt.	△Canada	5,951	19,524
Orizaba, Pico de	△Mexico	5,610	18,406
Popocatépetl, Volcán	Mexico	5,452	17,887
Whitney, Mt.	United States	4,417	14,491
Elbert, Mt.	United States	4,399	14,433
Rainier, Mt.	United States	4,392	14,410
Shasta, Mt.	United States	4,317	14,162
Pikes Pk.	United States	4,301	14,110
Tajumulco, Volcán	△Guatemala	4,220	13,845
Mauna Kea	United States	4,205	13,796
Grand Teton	United States	4,197	13,770
Waddington, Mt.	Canada	3,994	13,104
Robson, Mt.	Canada	3,954	12,972
Chirripó, Cerro	△Costa Rica	3,819	12,530
Gunnbjørns Fjeld	△Greenland	3,700	12,139
Duarte, Pico	△Dominican Rep.	3,175	10,417
Mitchell, Mt.	United States	2,037	6,684
Marcy, Mt.	United States	1,629	5,344
South America			
Aconcagua, Cerro	△Argentina	6,960	22,835
Ojos del Salado, Nevado	Argentina-△Chile	6,863	22,516
Huascarán, Nevado	△Peru	6,746	22,133
Illimani, Nevado del	△Bolivia	6,682	21,923
Chimborazo, Volcán	△Ecuador	6,310	20,702
Cristóbal Colón, Pico	△Colombia	5,800	19,029
Neblina, Pico da	△Brazil-Venezuela	3,014	9,888
Oceania			
Wilhelm, Mt.	△Papua New Guinea	4,509	14,793
Cook, Mt.	△New Zealand	3,764	12,349
Kosciusko, Mt.	△Australia	2,228	7,310
Antarctica			
Vinson Massif	△Antarctica	4,897	16,066
Kirkpatrick, Mt.	Antarctica	4,528	14,856

△ Highest mountain in country.

Oceans, Seas, and Gulfs

Name	Area km²	sq mi	Greatest Depth m	ft
Pacific Ocean	165,200,000	63,800,000	11,020	36,155
Atlantic Ocean	82,400,000	31,800,000	9,220	30,249
Indian Ocean	74,900,000	28,900,000	7,450	24,442
Arctic Ocean	14,000,000	5,400,000	5,450	17,881
Arabian Sea	3,864,000	1,492,000	5,800	19,029
South China Sea	3,447,000	1,331,000	5,560	18,241
Caribbean Sea	2,753,000	1,063,000	7,680	25,197
Mediterranean Sea	2,505,000	967,000	5,020	16,470
Bering Sea	2,269,000	876,000	4,096	13,438
Bengal, Bay of	2,173,000	839,000	5,258	17,251
Okhotsk, Sea of	1,603,000	619,000	3,372	11,063
Norwegian Sea	1,546,000	597,000	4,020	13,189
Mexico, Gulf of	1,544,000	596,000	4,380	14,370
East China Sea	1,248,000	482,000	4,424	14,514
Hudson Bay	1,230,000	475,000	259	850

Waterfalls

Waterfall	Country	River	Height m	ft
Angel	Venezuela	Churún	972	3,189
Tugela	South Africa	Tugela	948	3,110
Yosemite	United States	Yosemite Creek	739	2,425
Sutherland	New Zealand	Arthur	579	1,900
Gavarnie	France	Gave de Pau	421	1,381
Lofoi	Zaire	Lofoi	384	1,260
Krimml	Austria	Krimml	381	1,250
Takakkaw	Canada	Yoho	380	1,248
Staubbach	Switzerland	Staubbach	305	1,001
Mardalsfoss	Norway	. . .	297	974
Gersoppa	India	Sharavati	253	830
Kaieteur	Guyana	Potaro	247	810

Principal Rivers

River	Continent	Length km	mi
Nile	Africa	6,671	4,145
Amazon-Ucayali	South America	6,400	4,000
Yangtze (Chang Jiang)	Asia	6,300	3,900
Yellow (Huang He)	Asia	5,464	3,395
Ob-Irtyš	Asia	5,410	3,362
Río de la Plata-Paraná	South America	4,876	3,030
Congo (Zaïre)	Africa	4,700	2,900
Paraná	South America	4,500	2,800
Amur (Heilong Jiang)	Asia	4,416	2,744
Lena	Asia	4,400	2,700
Mekong	Asia	4,200	2,600
Niger	Africa	4,200	2,600
Jenisej	Asia	4,092	2,543
Mississippi	North America	3,779	2,348
Missouri	North America	3,726	2,315
Volga	Europe	3,531	2,194
São Francisco	South America	3,199	1,988
Rio Grande	North America	3,034	1,885
Indus	Asia	2,900	1,800
Danube	Europe	2,858	1,776
Yukon	North America	2,849	1,770
Brahmaputra	Asia	2,849	1,770
Salween (Thanlwin)	Asia	2,816	1,750
Zambezi	Africa	2,700	1,700
Tocantins	South America	2,639	1,640
Orinoco	South America	2,600	1,600
Paraguay	South America	2,591	1,610
Amudarja	Asia	2,540	1,578
Murray	Australia	2,520	1,566
Ganges	Asia	2,511	1,560
Euphrates	Asia	2,430	1,510
Ural	Asia	2,428	1,509
Arkansas	North America	2,348	1,459
Colorado	North America (U.S.-Mex.)	2,334	1,450
Syrdarja	Asia	2,205	1,370
Tarim	Asia	2,137	1,328
Orange	Africa	2,100	1,300
Negro	South America	2,100	1,300
Irrawaddy (Ayeyarwady)	Asia	2,100	1,300
Red	North America	2,044	1,270
Columbia	North America	2,000	1,200
Xingu	South America	1,979	1,230
Ucayali	South America	1,963	1,220
Saskatchewan-Bow	North America	1,939	1,205
Peace	North America	1,923	1,195
Tigris	Asia	1,899	1,180
Sungari	Asia	1,835	1,140
Pechora	Europe	1,809	1,124
Limpopo	Africa	1,800	1,100
Snake	North America	1,670	1,038

Principal Islands

Island	Area km²	sq mi	Name	Highest Point m	ft
Grønland (Greenland)	2,175,600	840,000	Gunnbjørns Fjeld	3,700	12,139
New Guinea	800,000	309,000	Puncak Jaya	5,030	16,503
Borneo	744,100	287,300	Gunong Kinabalu	4,101	13,455
Madagascar	587,000	227,000	Maromokotro	2,876	9,436
Baffin Island	507,451	195,928	Unnamed	2,591	8,501
Sumatera (Sumatra)	473,606	182,860	Gunung Kerinci	3,800	12,467
Honshū	230,966	89,176	Fuji-San	3,776	12,388
Great Britain	229,978	88,795	Ben Nevis	1,343	4,406
Victoria Island	217,291	83,897	Mt. Bumpus	655	2,149
Ellesmere Island	196,236	75,767	Barbeau Peak	2,604	8,543
Sulawesi (Celebes)	189,216	73,057	Bulu Rantekombola	3,455	11,335
South Island	149,883	57,870	Mt. Cook	3,764	12,349
Jawa (Java)	132,187	51,038	Gunung Semeru	3,676	12,060
Seram (Ceram)	118,625	45,801	Gunung Binaiya	3,019	9,905
North Island	114,669	44,274	Mt. Ruapehu	2,797	9,177
Cuba	110,800	42,800	Pico Turquino	1,994	6,542
Newfoundland	108,860	42,031	Unnamed	814	2,670
Luzon	104,688	40,420	Mt. Pulog	2,930	9,613
Ísland (Iceland)	103,000	39,800	Hvannadalshnúkur	2,119	6,952
Mindanao	94,630	36,537	Mt. Apo	2,954	9,692
Ireland	84,400	32,600	Carrauntoohil	1,038	3,406
Hokkaidō	83,515	32,245	Taisetsu-Zan	2,290	7,513
Novaja Zemlja (Novaya Zemlya)	82,600	31,900	Unnamed	1,547	5,075
Sahalin, ostrov (Sakhalin)	76,400	29,500	gora Lopatina	1,609	5,279
Hispaniola	76,000	29,300	Pico Duarte	3,175	10,417
Banks Island	70,028	27,038	Unnamed	747	2,451
Tasmania	67,800	26,200	Mt. Ossa	1,617	5,305
Sri Lanka	64,600	24,900	Pidurutalagala	2,524	8,281
Devon Island	55,247	21,331	Unnamed	1,887	6,191
Tierra del Fuego, Isla Grande de	48,200	18,600	Cerro Yogan	2,469	8,100

Major Lakes

Lake	Location	Area km²	sq mi	Depth m	ft
Caspian Sea	Iran-U.S.S.R.	370,990	143,240	1,025	3,363
Superior, L.	Canada-U.S.	82,100	31,700	406	1,332
Victoria, L.	Africa	69,463	26,820	85	279
Aral'skoje more (Aral Sea)	U.S.S.R.	64,100	24,700	68	223
Huron, L.	Canada-U.S.	60,000	23,000	229	750
Michigan, L.	U.S.	57,800	22,300	282	924
Tanganyika. L.	Africa	31,986	12,350	1,463	4,800
Bajkal, ozero (L. Baikal)	U.S.S.R.	31,500	12,200	1,620	5,315
Great Bear Lake	Canada	31,326	12,095	413	1,356
Nyasa, L.	Africa	28,878	11,150	695	2,280
Great Slave Lake	Canada	28,568	11,030	614	2,015
Erie, L.	Canada-U.S.	25,667	9,910	62	204
Winnipeg, L.	Canada	24,387	9,416	28	92
Ontario, L.	Canada-U.S.	19,529	7,540	243	798
Balhaš, ozero (L. Balkhash)	U.S.S.R.	18,300	7,100	26	85
Chad, L.	Africa	16,300	6,300	7	24
Onežskoje ozero (L. Onega)	U.S.S.R.	9,720	3,753	127	417
Eyre, L.	Australia	9,500	3,700	1	4
Titicaca, Lago	Bolivia-Peru	8,300	3,200	302	990
Nicaragua, Lago de	Nicaragua	8,158	3,150	70	230
Mai-Ndombe, Lac	Zaire	8,000	3,100	11	36
Athabasca, L.	Canada	7,935	3,064	124	407
Reindeer Lake	Canada	6,650	2,568	219	720
Tônlé Sab, Bœng	Cambodia	6,500	2,500	12	39
Rudolf, L.	Ethiopia-Kenya	6,405	2,473	219	720
Torrens, L.	Australia	5,900	2,300	*	*
Albert, L.	Uganda-Zaire	5,594	2,160	51	168
Vänern	Sweden	5,584	2,156	99	325

* Intermittently dry lake

Drainage Basins

Name	Continent	Area km²	sq mi
Amazon	South America	6,151,000	2,375,000
Congo (Zaïre)	Africa	3,823,000	1,476,000
Mississippi-Missouri	North America	3,230,000	1,247,000
Río de la Plata-Paraná	South America	3,100,000	1,197,000
Ob'-Irtyš	Asia	2,989,000	1,154,000
Nile	Africa	2,802,000	1,082,000
Lena	Asia	2,489,000	961,000
Amur-Argun	Asia	2,051,000	792,000
Niger	Africa	1,891,000	730,000
Yangtze (Chang Jiang)	Asia	1,826,000	705,000
Mackenzie	North America	1,572,000	607,000
Volga	Europe	1,360,000	525,000
Zambezi	Africa	1,331,000	514,000
St. Lawrence	North America	1,303,000	503,000

World Geographical Tables

Historical Population of the World

AREA	1650	1750	1800	1850	1900	1914	1920	1939	1950	1989
Europe	100,000,000	140,000,000	190,000,000	265,000,000	400,000,000	470,000,000	453,000,000	526,000,000	530,000,000	685,400,000
Asia	335,000,000	476,000,000	593,000,000	754,000,000	932,000,000	1,006,000,000	1,000,000,000	1,247,000,000	1,418,000,000	3,130,600,000
Africa	100,000,000	95,000,000	90,000,000	95,000,000	118,000,000	130,000,000	140,000,000	170,000,000	199,000,000	642,100,000
North America	5,000,000	5,000,000	13,000,000	39,000,000	106,000,000	141,000,000	147,000,000	186,000,000	219,000,000	420,100,000
South America	8,000,000	7,000,000	12,000,000	20,000,000	38,000,000	55,000,000	61,000,000	90,000,000	111,000,000	287,500,000
Oceania, incl. Australia	2,000,000	2,000,000	2,000,000	2,000,000	6,000,000	8,000,000	9,000,000	11,000,000	13,000,000	26,300,000
Australia					4,000,000	5,000,000	6,000,000	7,000,000	8,000,000	16,955,000
World	550,000,000	725,000,000	900,000,000	1,175,000,000	1,600,000,000	1,810,000,000	1,810,000,000	2,230,000,000	2,490,000,000	5,192,000,000

Figures in italics represent very rough estimates.

Largest Countries: Population

	Country	Population 1/1/89
1.	China	1,094,700,000
2.	India	825,000,000
3.	U.S.S.R.	287,550,000
4.	United States	247,410,000
5.	Indonesia	185,860,000
6.	Brazil	145,930,000
7.	Japan	123,010,000
8.	Nigeria	113,580,000
9.	Bangladesh	111,390,000
10.	Pakistan	108,990,000
11.	Mexico	85,300,000
12.	Vietnam	66,030,000
13.	Germany, Fed. Rep.	61,380,000
14.	Philippines	60,110,000
15.	Italy	57,500,000
16.	United Kingdom	57,090,000
17.	France	55,970,000
18.	Thailand	55,375,000
19.	Iran	52,760,000
20.	Egypt	52,490,000
21.	Turkey	51,970,000
22.	Ethiopia	48,470,000
23.	South Korea	42,840,000
24.	Burma	41,860,000
25.	Spain	39,330,000
26.	Poland	37,955,000
27.	South Africa	35,480,000
28.	Zaire	33,795,000
29.	Argentina	32,205,000
30.	Colombia	30,465,000
31.	Canada	25,895,000
32.	Kenya	25,825,000
33.	Morocco	25,600,000
34.	Sudan	24,255,000
35.	Algeria	24,215,000
36.	Tanzania	24,055,000
37.	Yugoslavia	23,970,000
38.	Romania	23,085,000
39.	North Korea	22,250,000
40.	Peru	21,535,000
41.	Taiwan	20,125,000
42.	Venezuela	19,010,000
43.	Nepal	18,415,000
44.	Iraq	17,900,000
45.	Mozambique	17,660,000

Largest Countries: Area

	Country	Area km²	Area sq mi
1.	U.S.S.R.	22,274,900	8,600,387
2.	Canada	9,970,610	3,849,674
3.	China	9,631,600	3,718,782
4.	United States	9,529,202	3,679,245
5.	Brazil	8,511,965	3,286,488
6.	Australia	7,682,300	2,966,155
7.	India	3,203,975	1,237,062
8.	Argentina	2,780,092	1,073,400
9.	Sudan	2,505,813	967,500
10.	Algeria	2,381,741	919,595
11.	Zaire	2,345,409	905,568
12.	Saudi Arabia	2,240,000	864,869
13.	Greenland	2,175,600	840,004
14.	Mexico	1,972,547	761,605
15.	Indonesia	1,919,443	741,101
16.	Libya	1,759,540	679,362
17.	Iran	1,648,000	636,296
18.	Mongolia	1,565,000	604,250
19.	Peru	1,285,216	496,225
20.	Chad	1,284,000	495,755
21.	Niger	1,267,000	489,191
22.	Ethiopia	1,251,282	483,123
23.	Angola	1,246,700	481,354
24.	Mali	1,240,000	478,767
25.	Colombia	1,141,748	440,831
26.	South Africa	1,123,226	433,680
27.	Bolivia	1,098,581	424,165
28.	Mauritania	1,030,700	397,956
29.	Egypt	1,001,450	386,662
30.	Tanzania	945,087	364,900
31.	Nigeria	923,768	356,669
32.	Venezuela	912,050	352,145
33.	Pakistan	879,902	339,732
34.	Mozambique	799,379	308,642
35.	Turkey	779,452	300,948
36.	Chile	756,626	292,135
37.	Zambia	752,614	290,586
38.	Burma	676,577	261,228
39.	Afghanistan	652,225	251,826
40.	Somalia	637,657	246,201
41.	Central African Republic	622,984	240,535
42.	Madagascar	587,041	226,658
43.	Kenya	582,646	224,961
44.	Botswana	582,000	224,711
45.	France	547,026	211,208

Smallest Countries: Population

	Country	Population 1/1/89
1.	Vatican City	800
2.	Niue	2,400
3.	Anguilla	7,000
4.	Tuvalu	8,700
5.	Nauru	9,000
6.	Palau	15,000
7.	Cook Islands	17,000
8.	Northern Mariana Is.	22,000
9.	San Marino	24,000
10.	Liechtenstein	29,000
	Monaco	29,000
11.	Marshall Islands	40,000
12.	St. Christopher-Nevis	47,000
13.	Faeroe Islands	48,000
14.	Andorra	51,000
15.	Greenland	55,000
16.	Isle of Man	62,000
17.	Aruba	66,000
18.	Kiribati	69,000
19.	Seychelles	70,000
20.	Antigua	84,000
21.	Grenada	95,000
22.	Dominica	100,000
	Tonga	100,000
23.	Micronesia, Federated States of	108,000
24.	Sao Tome and Principe	119,000
25.	St. Vincent	125,000
26.	St. Lucia	148,000
27.	Vanuatu	155,000
28.	Cyprus, North	172,000
29.	Western Samoa	180,000
30.	Belize	184,000
31.	Netherlands Antilles	194,000
32.	Maldives	209,000
33.	Bahamas	243,000
34.	Brunei	247,000
35.	Iceland	248,000
36.	Barbados	255,000
37.	Solomon Islands	295,000
38.	Djibouti	324,000
39.	Cape Verde	359,000
40.	Luxembourg	368,000
41.	Malta	370,000
42.	Suriname	398,000

Smallest Countries: Area

	Country	Area km²	Area sq mi
1.	Vatican City	0.4	0.2
2.	Monaco	1.9	0.7
3.	Nauru	21	8.1
4.	Tuvalu	26	10
5.	San Marino	61	24
6.	Anguilla	91	35
7.	Liechtenstein	160	62
8.	Marshall Islands	181	70
9.	Aruba	193	75
10.	Cook Islands	236	91
11.	Niue	263	102
12.	St. Christopher-Nevis	269	104
13.	Maldives	298	115
14.	Malta	316	122
15.	Grenada	344	133
16.	St. Vincent	388	150
17.	Barbados	430	166
18.	Antigua	443	171
	Andorra	453	175
19.	Seychelles	453	175
20.	Northern Mariana Is.	477	184
21.	Palau	508	196
22.	Isle of Man	572	221
23.	St. Lucia	616	238
24.	Singapore	636	236
25.	Bahrain	662	256
26.	Tonga	699	270
27.	Micronesia, Federated States of	702	271
28.	Kiribati	726	280
29.	Dominica	752	290
30.	Netherlands Antilles	800	309
31.	Sao Tome and Principe	964	372
32.	Faeroe Islands	1,399	540
33.	Mauritius	2,040	788
34.	Comoros	2,171	838
35.	Luxembourg	2,586	998
36.	Western Samoa	2,842	1,097
37.	Cyprus, North	3,355	1,295
38.	Cape Verde	4,033	1,557
39.	Trinidad and Tobago	5,128	1,980
40.	Brunei	5,765	2,226
41.	Cyprus	5,896	2,276
42.	Venda	6,875	2,654
43.	Ciskei	7,790	3,008

Highest Population Densities

	Country	Density per km²	Density per sq mi			Country	Density per km²	Density per sq mi
1.	Monaco	15,263	41,429		16.	Aruba	342	880
2.	Singapore	4,187	11,284		17.	Tuvalu	335	870
3.	Vatican City	2,000	4,000		18.	Japan	326	843
4.	Malta	1,171	3,033		19.	Belgium	323	837
5.	Bangladesh	774	2,003		20.	Lebanon	322	835
6.	Maldives	701	1,817		21.	St. Vincent	322	833
7.	Bahrain	692	1,789		22.	Grenada	276	714
8.	Barbados	593	1,536		23.	Rwanda	273	707
9.	Taiwan	559	1,448		24.	Sri Lanka	259	670
10.	Mauritius	518	1,341		25.	India	257	667
11.	South Korea	435	1,127		26.	Trinidad and Tobago	253	654
12.	Nauru	429	1,111		27.	Germany, Fed. Rep. of	247	639
13.	San Marino	393	1,000		28.	El Salvador	243	630
14.	Puerto Rico	363	939		29.	Netherlands Antilles	243	628
15.	Netherlands	355	918		30.	St. Lucia	240	622

Lowest Population Densities

	Country	Density per km²	Density per sq mi			Country	Density per km²	Density per sq mi
1.	Greenland	...	0.1		16.	Congo	6.4	17
2.	Mongolia	1.3	3.5			Bolivia	6.5	17
3.	Mauritania	1.9	4.9			Angola	6.7	17
4.	Botswana	2.1	5.5		17.	Saudi Arabia	7.0	18
5.	Australia	2.2	5.7		18.	Mali	7.3	19
6.	Libya	2.3	5.9		19.	Papua New Guinea	7.9	20
7.	Iceland	2.4	6.2		20.	Belize	8.0	21
8.	Suriname	2.4	6.3		21.	Niue	9.1	24
9.	Canada	2.6	6.7		22.	Sudan	9.7	25
10.	Guyana	3.6	9.2		23.	Algeria	10	26
11.	Chad	3.8	9.8			Zambia	10	26
12.	Gabon	3.9	10		24.	Paraguay	10	27
13.	Central African Republic	5.0	13			Solomon Islands	10	27
14.	Niger	5.8	15		25.	Norway	11	28
15.	Oman	6.0	16					

... Less than 0.1

Major Metropolitan Areas of the World

This table lists the major metropolitan areas of the world according to their estimated population on January l, 1989. For convenience in reference, the areas are grouped by major region with the total for each region given. The number of areas by population classification is given in parentheses with each size group.

For ease of comparison, each metropolitan area has been defined by Rand McNally according to consistent rules. A metropolitan area includes a central city, neighboring communities linked to it by continuous built-up areas, and more distant communities if the bulk of their population is supported by commuters to the central city. Some metropolitan areas have more than one central city; in such cases each central city is listed.

SIZE	ANGLO-AMERICA	LATIN AMERICA	EUROPE	U.S.S.R.	WEST ASIA	EAST ASIA	AFRICA-OCEANIA
Over 15,000,000 (6)	New York	Ciudad de México (Mexico City) São Paulo				Ōsaka-Kōbe-Kyōto Sŏul (Seoul) Tōkyō-Yokohama	
10,000,000-15,000,000 (9)	Los Angeles	Buenos Aires Rio de Janeiro	London Paris	Moskva (Moscow)	Bombay Calcutta		Al Qāhirah (Cairo)
5,000,000-10,000,000 (18)	Chicago Philadelphia-Trenton-Wilmington San Francisco-Oakland-San Jose	Lima		Leningrad	Delhi-New Delhi İstanbul Karāchi Madras Tehrān	Beijing (Peking) Jakarta Krung Thep (Bangkok) Manila Shanghai Taipei Tianjin (Tientsin) Victoria (Hong Kong)	
3,000,000-5,000,000 (38)	Boston Dallas-Fort Worth Detroit-Windsor Houston Miami-Fort Lauderdale Toronto Washington	Belo Horizonte Bogotá Caracas Guadalajara Santiago	Athínai (Athens) Barcelona Berlin Essen-Dortmund-Duisburg (Ruhr Area) Madrid Milano (Milan) Roma (Rome)		Baghdād Bangalore Dhaka (Dacca) Hyderābād, India Lahore	Guangzhou (Canton) Nagoya Pusan Yangon (Rangoon) Shenyang (Mukden) Singapore Ho Chi Minh (Saigon) Wuhan	Al Iskandarīyah (Alexandria) Johannesburg Kinshasa Lagos Melbourne Sydney
2,000,000-3,000,000 (49)	Atlanta Baltimore Cleveland Minneapolis-St. Paul Montréal Phoenix Pittsburgh St. Louis San Diego-Tijuana Seattle-Tacoma	Fortaleza La Habana (Havana) Medellín Monterrey Porto Alegre Recife Salvador	Birmingham Bruxelles (Brussels) Bucureşti (Bucharest) Budapest Hamburg Katowice-Bytom-Gliwice Lisboa (Lisbon) Manchester Napoli (Naples) Warszawa (Warsaw)	Baku Doneck-Makejevka Gorki Kijev (Kiev) Taškent	Ahmadābād Ankara Colombo Kānpur Pune (Poona)	Bandung Chongqing (Chungking) Harbin Kuala Lumpur Nanjing (Nanking) Sapporo-Otaru Surabaya Taegu Xi'an (Sian)	Cape Town Casablanca Al Jazā'ir (Algiers)
1,500,000-2,000,000 (57)	Cincinnati Denver	Brasília Cali Curitiba Guayaquil Montevideo San Juan Santo Domingo	Amsterdam Beograd (Belgrade) Frankfurt am Main Glasgow København (Copenhagen) Köln (Cologne) Leeds-Bradford Liverpool München (Munich) Stuttgart Torino (Turin) Wien (Vienna)	Char'kov (Kharkov) Dnepropetrovsk Kujbyšev (Kuybyshev) Minsk Novosibirsk Sverdlovsk	Al Kuwayt (Kuwait) 'Amman Ar Riyāḍ (Riyadh) Bayrūt (Beirut) Chittagong Dimashq (Damascus) İzmir Jīddah Mashhad Nāgpur Tel Aviv-Yafo	Changchun (Hsinking) Chengdu (Chengtu) Dalian (Lüda) Fukuoka Ha Noi Hiroshima-Kure Jinan (Tsinan) Kaohsiung Kitakyūshū-Shimonoseki Medan P'yŏngyang Semarang Taiyuan	Abidjan Adis Abeba Al Kharṭūm-Umm Durmān (Khartoum-Omdurman) Dakar Dar es Salaam Durban
1,000,000-1,500,000 (105)	Buffalo-Niagara Falls-St. Catharines Columbus El Paso-Ciudad Juárez Hartford-New Britain Indianapolis Kansas City Milwaukee New Orleans Portland Riverside-San Bernardino Sacramento St. Petersburg-Clearwater San Antonio Vancouver	Barranquilla Belém Campinas Córdoba Goiânia Guatemala La Paz Maracaibo Puebla Quito Rosario Santos	Antwerpen (Antwerp) Dublin (Baile Átha Cliath) Düsseldorf Hannover Lille-Roubaix Łódź Lyon Mannheim Marseille Newcastle-Sunderland Nürnberg Porto Praha (Prague) Rotterdam Sofija (Sofia) Stockholm Valencia	Alma-Ata Čeljabinsk (Chelyabinsk) Jerevan Kazan Odessa Omsk Perm Rīga Rostov-na-Donu Saratov Tbilisi Ufa Volgograd	Asansol Coimbatore Eşfahān Faisalabad Halab (Aleppo) Indore Jaipur Kābol Lucknow Madurai Patna Rāwalpindi-Islāmābād Surat Tabrīz Vārānasi (Benares)	Anshan Baotou Changsha Fushun Guiyang (Kweiyang) Hangzhou (Hangchow) Jilin (Kirin) Kunming Kwangju Lanzhou (Lanchow) Nanchang Palembang Qingdao (Tsingtao) Qiqihar (Tsitsihar) Sendai Shijiazhuang Tangshan Ujung Pandang (Makasar) Ürümqi Zhengzhou (Chengchow)	Accra Adelaide Brisbane Douala Harare Ibadan Luanda Maputo Nairobi Perth Pretoria Rabat-Salé Ṭarābulus (Tripoli) Tūnis
Total by region (282)	38	36	48	26	43	61	30

Populations of Major Cities

The largest and most important of the world's major cities are listed in the following table. Also included are some smaller cities because of their regional significance.

Local official name forms have been used throughout the table. When a commonly used "conventional" name form exists, it has been featured within parentheses, following the official name. Each city name is followed by the English name of its country. Names in the United States, the United Kingdom, and Canada are further distinguished by the name of the state, region, or province in which they are located.

Many cities have population figures within parentheses following the country name. These are metropolitan populations, comprising the central city and its suburbs. When a city is within the metropolitan area of another city the name of the metropolitan central city is specified in parentheses preceded by a *. The symbol † identifies a political district population which includes some rural population. For these cities the estimated city population has been based upon the district figure.

The population of each city has been dated for ease of comparison. The date is followed by a letter designating: Census (C) or Official Estimate (E).

City and Country	Population	Date
Aachen, Fed. Rep. of Ger. (535,000)	239,170	87E
Ābādān, Iran	296,081	76C
Abidjan, Ivory Coast	1,500,000	83E
Abū Ẓaby (Abu Dhabi), United Arab Emirates	242,975	80C
Acapulco [de Juárez], Mexico	301,900	80C
Accra, Ghana (1,250,000)	859,640	84C
Adana, Turkey	777,550	85C
Ad Dawḥah (Doha), Qatar (310,000)	217,294	86E
Addis Ababa, see Ādīs Ābeba		
Adelaide, Australia (977,721)	14,157	86C
Aden, see Baladiyad 'Adan		
Ādīs Ābeba (Addis Ababa), Ethiopia (1,500,000)	1,412,575	84C
Agana, Guam (44,000)	896	80C
Āgra, India (747,318)	694,190	81C
Aguascalientes, Mexico	293,152	80C
Ahmadābād, India (2,400,000)	2,059,725	81C
Ahvāz, Iran	471,000	82E
Akita, Japan	296,400	85C
Akron, Oh., U.S. (614,100)	237,177	80C
Albany, N.Y., U.S. (729,100)	101,727	80C
Al Baṣrah, Iraq	616,700	85E
Albuquerque, N.M., U.S. (453,200)	332,336	80C
Aleppo, see Halab		
Alexandria, see Al Iskandarīyah		
Algiers, see Al Jazā'ir		
Al Iskandarīyah (Alexandria), Egypt (3,350,000)	2,821,000	85E
Al Jazā'ir (Algiers), Algeria (2,300,000)	1,721,607	83E
Al Jīzah (Giza), Egypt (*Al Qāhirah)	1,608,400	85E
Al Kharṭūm (Khartoum), Sudan (1,450,000)	476,218	83C
Al Kuwayt (Kuwait), Kuwait (1,375,000)	44,335	85C
Allahābād, India (650,070)	616,050	81C
Alma-Ata, U.S.S.R. (1,170,000)	1,108,000	87E
Al Madīnah (Medina), Saudi Arabia	290,000	80E
Al Maḥallah al Kubrā, Egypt (375,000)	328,700	85E
Al Manāmah (Manama), Bahrain (224,643)	108,684	81C
Al Manṣurah, Egypt (375,000)	328,700	85E
Al Mawṣil (Mosul), Iraq	570,920	85E
Al Qāhirah (Cairo), Egypt (9,300,000)	6,205,000	85E
Amagasaki, Japan (*Ōsaka)	509,110	85C
'Ammān, Jordan (1,250,000)	833,500	86E
Amritsar, India	594,840	81C
Amsterdam, Netherlands (1,860,000)	679,140	86E
Anchorage, Ak., U.S. (184,300)	174,431	80C
Andorra la Vella, Andorra	14,928	82C
Ankara, Turkey (2,400,000)	2,235,035	85C
Annaba (Bône), Algeria (†348,322)	302,700	83E
Anshan, China	1,300,000	87E
Antananarivo, Madagascar	663,000	85E
Antwerpen (Antwerp), Belgium (1,100,000)	490,524	83E
Apia, Western Samoa	33,170	81C
Arequipa, Peru (446,942)	108,020	81C
Arhangelsk, U.S.S.R.	416,000	87E
Arnhem, Netherlands (294,085)	127,960	86E
Ar Riyāḍ (Riyadh), Saudi Arabia	1,250,000	80E
Asansol, India (1,050,000)	183,370	81C
As Suways (Suez), Egypt	254,000	85E
Astrahan, U.S.S.R.	509,000	87E
Asunción, Paraguay (700,000)	455,517	82C
Athínai (Athens), Greece (3,027,331)	885,737	81C
Atlanta, Ga., U.S. (1,962,500)	425,022	80C
Auckland, New Zealand (850,000)	149,046	86C
Augsburg, Fed. Rep. of Ger. (405,000)	245,960	87E
Austin, Tx., U.S. (430,200)	345,890	80C
Baghdād, Iraq (4,000,000)	2,200,000	85E
Bakhtarān, Iran	532,000	82E
Baku, U.S.S.R. (2,005,000)	1,115,000	87E
Baladiyat 'Adan (Aden), Yemen (318,000)	176,100	84E
Balikpapan, Indonesia (†279,852)	208,040	80C
Baltimore, Md., U.S. (1,960,400)	786,741	80C
Bamako, Mali	600,000	80E
Bandar Seri Begawan, Brunei	63,868	81C
Bandung, Indonesia (1,800,000)	1,461,407	80C
Bangalore, India (2,950,000)	2,476,355	81C
Banghāzī (Benghazi), Libya	367,600	81E
Bangkok, see Krung Thep		
Bangui, Cen. Afr. Rep.	473,800	84E
Banjul, Gambia (95,000)	44,536	83C
Barcelona, Spain (4,040,000)	1,694,064	86E
Barnaul, U.S.S.R. (655,000)	596,000	87E
Barquisimeto, Venezuela	497,630	81C
Barranquilla, Colombia	1,140,000	85C
Basel, Switzerland (575,000)	173,160	87E
Basse-Terre, Guadeloupe (26,000)	13,656	82C
Basseterre, St. Chris.-Nevis	14,725	80C
Baton Rouge, La., U.S. (434,400)	238,876	80C
Bayrūt (Beirut), Lebanon (1,675,000)	509,000	82
Beijing (Peking), China (6,450,000)	5,970,000	87E
Beirut, see Bayrūt		
Belém, Brazil (1,200,000)	1,116,578	85E
Belfast, N. Ire., U.K. (685,000)	318,600	84E
Belgrade, see Beograd		
Belize City, Belize	39,041	80C
Belmopan, Belize	2,907	80C
Belo Horizonte, Brazil (2,950,000)	2,114,429	85E
Benares, see Vārānasi		
Bengbu, China (†612,600)	403,900	86E
Benxi, China	840,000	87E
Beograd (Belgrade), Yugoslavia (1,400,000)	936,200	81C
Bergamo, Italy (340,000)	121,840	81C
Berlin, Ost- (East), Ger. Dem. Rep. (*Berlin, West)	1,236,248	87E
Berlin, West, Fed. Rep. of Ger. (3,825,000)	1,879,225	87E
Bern (Berne), Switzerland (298,800)	137,134	87E
Bhopāl, India	671,010	81C
Bielefeld, Fed. Rep. of Ger. (515,000)	299,360	87E
Bilbao, Spain (985,000)	378,221	86E
Billings, Mt., U.S. (96,100)	66,842	80C
Birmingham, Eng., U.K. (2,675,000)	1,013,995	81C
Birmingham, Al., U.S. (747,400)	286,799	80C
Bissau, Guinea-Bissau	109,486	79C
Blackpool, Eng., U.K. (280,000)	146,290	81C
Bloemfontein, South Africa (235,000)	104,380	85C
Bogor, India (560,000)	246,940	80C
Bogotá, Colombia (4,550,000)	4,260,000	85C
Boise, Id., U.S. (164,200)	102,160	80C
Bologna, Italy (530,000)	455,850	81C
Bombay, India (9,950,000)	8,243,405	81C
Bonn, Fed. Rep. of Ger. (570,000)	291,439	87E
Bordeaux, France (640,012)	208,150	82C
Boston, Ma., U.S. (3,971,700)	562,994	80C
Brasília, Brazil	1,567,709	85E
Bratislava, Czechoslovakia	417,100	86E
Braunschweig, Fed. Rep. of Ger. (330,000)	247,830	87E
Brazzaville, Congo	595,102	84C
Bremen, Fed. Rep. of Ger. (800,000)	521,976	87E
Brest, France (201,145)	156,060	82C
Bridgetown, Barbados (115,000)	7,466	80C
Brighton, Eng., U.K. (420,000)	134,580	81C
Brisbane, Australia (1,149,401)	705,755	86C
Bristol, Eng., U.K. (1,630,000)	413,860	8IC
Bruxelles / Brussel (Brussels), Belgium (2,395,000)	137,738	83E
Bucaramanga, Colombia	550,000	85C
Bucureşti (Bucharest), Romania (2,250,000)	1,989,823	86E
Budapest, Hungary (2,565,000)	2,104,700	88E
Buenos Aires, Argentina (10,750,000)	2,922,829	80C
Buffalo, N.Y., U.S. (1,483,000)	357,870	80C
Bujumbura, Burundi	229,980	83E
Bulawayo, Zimbabwe	413,810	82C
Burlington, Vt., U.S. (115,300)	37,712	80C
Bursa, Turkey	612,510	85C
Būr Saʿīd (Port Said), Egypt	374,000	85E
Cádiz, Spain (240,000)	160,839	84E
Cagliari, Italy (300,000)	232,780	81C
Cairo, see Al Qāhirah		
Calcutta, India (11,100,000)	3,305,006	81C
Calgary, Alta., Can. (671,326)	636,100	86C
Cali, Colombia (1,400,000)	1,350,565	85C
Calicut (Kozhikode), India (546,058)	394,440	81C
Callao, Peru (*Lima)	264,133	81C
Campinas, Brazil (1,125,000)	841,010	85E
Canberra, Australia (271,362)	247,194	86C
Cannes, France (295,525)	72,250	82C
Canton, see Guangzhou		
Cape Town, South Africa (1,790,000)	776,617	85C
Caracas, Venezuela (3,600,000)	3,041,000	81E
Cardiff, Wales, U.K. (625,000)	262,310	81C
Cartagena, Colombia	531,420	85C
Casablanca, Morocco (2,475,000)	2,139,204	82C
Castries, St. Lucia	50,798	84E
Catania, Italy (515,000)	378,520	81C
Cayenne, French Guiana	38,093	82C
Cebu, Philippines (600,000)	490,280	80C
Čeljabinsk (Chelyabinsk), U.S.S.R. (1,300,000)	1,119,000	87E
Chandīgarh, India (422,841)	373,780	81C
Changchun, China (†1,910,000)	1,740,000	87E
Changshu, China (†998,000)	281,300	86E
Changzhou, China	522,700	86E
Chao'an, China (†1,214,500)	265,400	86E
Charleston, W.V., U.S. (236,300)	63,968	80C
Charlotte, N.C., U.S. (479,200)	315,473	80C
Chattanooga, Tn., U.S. (359,200)	169,728	80C
Chengdu, China (†2,640,000)	1,810,000	87E
Chiba, Japan (*Tōkyō)	788,930	85C
Chicago, Il., U.S. (7,717,100)	3,005,072	80C
Chiclayo, Peru (279,527)	213,090	81C
Chihuahua, Mexico	385,600	80C

City and Country	Population	Date
Chittagong, Bangladesh (1,391,877)	980,000	81C
Ch'ŏngjin, N. Korea	490,000	81E
Chongqing (Chungking), China (†2,830,000)	2,450,000	87E
Chŏnju, S. Korea	426,470	85C
Christchurch, New Zealand (320,000)	168,200	86C
Chungking, see Chongqing		
Cincinnati, Oh., U.S. (1,480,100)	385,457	80C
Ciudad de México, Mexico (14,100,000)	8,831,079	80C
Ciudad Juárez, Mexico (*El Paso)	544,490	80C
Clermont-Ferrand, France (256,189)	147,360	82C
Cleveland, Oh., U.S. (2,218,400)	573,822	80C
Cochin, India (685,836)	513,240	81C
Coimbatore, India (965,000)	704,510	81C
Cologne, see Köln		
Colombo, Sri Lanka (2,050,000)	623,000	83E
Columbia, S.C., U.S. (375,900)	101,229	80C
Columbus, Oh., U.S. (963,600)	565,032	80C
Conakry, Guinea	705,280	83C
Concepción, Chile (535,000)	267,890	82C
Constanţa, Romania	327,670	86E
Constantine, Algeria	448,570	83E
Córdoba, Argentina (1,070,000)	993,050	80C
Córdoba, Spain	291,370	84E
Cotonou, Benin	215,000	80E
Coventry, Eng., U.K. (645,000)	318,710	81C
Cúcuta, Colombia (440,000)	445,000	85C
Cuernavaca, Mexico	192,770	80C
Curitiba, Brazil (1,700,000)	1,279,205	85E
Cusco, Peru (184,550)	89,563	81C
Dakar, Senegal	1,428,084	85E
Dalian (Lüda), China	1,680,000	87E
Dallas, Tx., U.S. (2,727,300)	904,078	80C
Dandong, China	579,800	86E
Danzig, see Gdańsk		
Daqing, China (†850,000)	620,000	87E
Dar es Salaam, Tanzania	757,346	78C
Darmstadt, Fed. Rep. of Ger. (305,000)	133,570	87E
Datong, China (†1,020,000)	790,000	87E
Davao, Philippines (†610,375)	408,770	80C
Dayton, Oh., U.S. (768,200)	193,536	80C
Delhi, India (7,200,000)	4,884,234	81C
Denver, Co., U.S. (1,405,300)	492,365	80C
Des Moines, Ia., U.S. (320,400)	191,003	80C
Detroit, Mi., U.S. (4,691,900)	1,202,463	80C
Dhaka, Bangladesh (3,430,312)	2,365,695	81C
Dhānbād, India (825,000)	120,220	81C
Dimashq (Damascus), Syria (1,850,000)	1,259,000	86E
Djibouti, Djibouti	120,000	76E
Dnepropetrovsk, U.S.S.R. (1,600,000)	1,182,000	87E
Doneck, U.S.S.R. (2,220,000)	1,090,000	87E
Dongguan, China (†1,208,500)	254,900	86E
Dortmund, Fed. Rep. of Ger. (*Essen)	568,160	87E
Douala, Cameroon	853,000	85E
Dresden, Ger. Dem. Rep. (670,000)	519,810	87E
Dublin (Baile Átha Cliath), Ireland (1,140,000)	502,749	86C
Duisburg, Fed. Rep. of Ger. (*Essen)	514,620	87E
Durban, South Africa (1,550,000)	634,301	85C
Dušanbe, U.S.S.R.	582,000	87E
Düsseldorf, Fed. Rep. of Ger. (1,190,000)	560,572	87E
Ecatepec de Morelos, Mexico (*Ciudad de México)	741,820	80C
Edinburgh, Scot., U.K. (630,000)	408,822	81C
Edmonton, Alta., Can. (785,465)	573,980	86C
El Paso, Tx., U.S. (1,037,700)	425,259	80C
Enschede, Netherlands (288,000)	144,040	86E
Erbīl, Iraq	333,900	85E
Eşfahān (Isfahan), Iran	927,000	82E
Essen, Fed. Rep. of Ger. (4,950,000)	615,421	87E
Faisalabad, Pakistan	1,104,209	81C
Fargo, N.D., U.S (108,800)	61,383	80C
Fès, Morocco (535,000)	448,820	82C
Firenze (Florence), Italy (650,000)	453,293	81C
Florianópolis, Brazil (365,000)	178,400	85E
Fortaleza, Brazil (1,825,000)	1,582,414	85E

City and Country	Population	Date
Fort-de-France, Martinique (116,017)	99,844	82C
Fort Worth, Tx., U.S. (*Dallas)	385,164	80C
Frankfurt am Main, Fed. Rep. of Ger. (1,855,000)	592,411	87E
Freetown, Sierra Leone (315,000)	276,600	74C
Frunze, U.S.S.R.	632,000	87E
Fukuoka, Japan (1,750,000)	1,160,440	85C
Funabashi, Japan (*Tōkyō)	506,960	85C
Funafuti, Tuvalu	2,191	79C
Fushun, China	1,270,000	87E
Fuxian, China (†960,700)	246,200	86E
Fuxin, China	690,000	87E
Fuzhou, China (†1,210,000)	890,000	87E
Gaborone, Botswana	95,163	86E
Gdańsk (Danzig), Poland (909,000)	468,400	87E
General Sarmiento, Argentina (*Buenos Aires)	502,920	80C
Genève (Geneva), Switzerland (460,000)	160,645	87E
Genova (Genoa), Italy (830,000)	760,300	81C
Gent (Ghent), Belgium (465,000)	236,540	83E
Georgetown, Cayman Islands	11,500	87E
Georgetown, Guyana (188,000)	78,500	83E
George Town (Pinang), Malaysia (495,000)	248,240	80C
Gifu, Japan	411,740	85C
Giza, see Al Jīzah		
Glasgow, Scot., U.K. (1,800,000)	754,586	81C
Godthåb (Nûk), Greenland	10,972	86E
Goiânia, Brazil (990,000)	923,330	85E
Gorki, U.S.S.R. (2,005,000)	1,425,000	87E
Göteborg, Sweden (710,894)	429,330	87E
Granada, Spain	280,590	86E
Graz, Austria (325,000)	243,160	81C
Grenoble, France (392,021)	156,640	82C
Guadalajara, Mexico (2,325,000)	1,626,152	80C
Guadalupe, Mexico (*Monterrey)	370,520	80C
Guangzhou (Canton), China (†3,360,000)	3,050,000	87E
Guarulhos, Brazil (*São Paulo)	571,700	86E
Guatemala, Guatemala (1,100,000)	754,243	81C
Guayaquil, Ecuador (1,255,000)	1,204,532	82C
Guilin, China (†457,500)	342,200	86E
Guiyang, China (†1,400,000)	1,010,000	87E
Gujranwala, Pakistan (658,753)	600,990	81C
Gwalior, India (555,862)	539,010	81C
Haicheng, China (†984,800)	210,700	86E
Haikou, China (†289,600)	209,200	86E
Hai Phong, Vietnam (†1,279,067)	385,210	79C
Halab (Aleppo), Syria (1,115,000)	1,060,002	83E
Halifax, N.S., Can. (295,990)	113,570	86C
Hamamatsu, Japan	514,110	85C
Hamburg, Fed. Rep. of Ger. (2,225,000)	1,571,267	87E
Hamilton, Bermuda (15,000)	1,676	85E
Hamilton, Ont., Can. (557,029)	306,720	86C
Handan, China (†1,010,000)	850,000	87E
Hannover, Fed. Rep. of Ger. (1,000,000)	505,718	87E
Ha Noi (Hanoi), Vietnam (1,500,000)	897,500	79C
Hāora (Howrah), India (*Calcutta)	744,420	81C
Harare, Zimbabwe (890,000)	656,011	82C
Harbin, China	2,670,000	87E
Harkov, U.S.S.R. (1,905,000)	1,587,000	87E
Hartford, Ct., U.S. (1,013,600)	136,392	80C
Havana, see La Habana		
Hefa (Haifa), Israel (435,000)	223,400	87E
Hefei, China (†900,000)	720,000	87E
Hegang, China	588,300	86E
Helsinki, Finland (900,000)	484,263	84E
Hibli, India	527,100	81C
Ḩims (Homs), Syria	346,870	81C
Hiroshima, Japan (1,575,000)	1,044,118	85C
Hohhot, China (†810,000)	650,000	87E
Hong Kong, see Victoria		
Honiara, Solomon Is.	30,499	86C
Honolulu, Ha., U.S. (762,600)	365,048	80C
Houston, Tx., U.S. (2,755,100)	1,595,138	80C
Huainan, China (†1,090,000)	690,000	87E
Hyderābād, India (2,750,000)	2,187,262	81C
Ibadan, Nigeria	1,144,000	87E
Ilorin, Nigeria	380,000	87E

City and Country	Population	Date
Inch'ŏn, S. Korea (*Seoul)	1,386,991	85C
Indianapolis, In., U.S. (1,072,500)	700,807	80C
Indore, India (850,000)	829,320	81C
Irkutsk, U.S.S.R.	609,000	87E
Isfahan, see Eşfahān		
Isīamādād, Pakistan (*Rāwalpindi)	204,364	81C
İstanbul, Turkey (5,750,000)	5,475,982	85C
İževsk, U.S.S.R.	631,000	87E
İzmir, Turkey (1,550,000)	1,489,772	85C
Jabalpur, India (757,303)	614,160	81C
Jackson, Ms., U.S. (306,900)	202,895	80C
Jacksonville, Fl., U.S. (635,900)	540,920	80C
Jaipur, India (1,025,000)	977,160	81C
Jakarta, Indonesia (8,600,000)	6,503,449	80C
Jamshedpur, India (669,580)	438,380	81C
Jaroslavl, U.S.S.R.	634,000	87E
Jerevan, U.S.S.R. (1,280,000)	1,168,000	87E
Jiaozuo, China (†509,900)	335,400	86E
Jīddah, Saudi Arabia	1,300,000	80E
Jinan, China	1,460,000	87E
Jinzhou, China (†790,000)	690,000	87E
Jixi, China (†820,000)	700,000	87E
João Pessoa, Brazil (550,000)	348,500	85E
Jodhpur, India	506,340	81C
Johannesburg, South Africa (3,650,000)	632,369	85C
Kābol, Afghanistan	972,836	81E
Kagoshima, Japan	530,500	80C
Kaifeng, China (†629,100)	458,800	86E
Kalinin, U.S.S.R.	447,000	87E
Kaliningrad, U.S.S.R.	394,000	87E
Kampala, Uganda	460,000	82E
Kano, Nigeria	538,300	87E
Kānpur, India (1,875,000)	1,481,789	81C
Kansas City, Mo., U.S. (1,272,400)	448,033	80C
Kaohsiung, Taiwan (1,785,000)	1,302,849	85E
Karāchi, Pakistan (5,300,000)	4,901,627	81C
Karaganda, U.S.S.R.	633,000	87E
Karl-Marx-Stadt, Ger. Dem. Rep. (450,000)	313,790	87E
Kāṭhmāṇḍāu, Nepal (320,000)	235,160	81C
Katowice, Poland (2,778,000)	367,300	87E
Kawasaki, Japan (*Tōkyō)	1,088,624	85C
Kayseri, Turkey	373,930	85C
Kazan, U.S.S.R. (1,120,000)	1,068,000	87E
Keelung (Chilung), Taiwan	351,520	85E
Kemerovo, U.S.S.R.	520,000	87E
Khartoum, see Al Kharṭūm		
Khulna, Bangladesh	648,350	81C
Kiel, Fed. Rep. of Ger. (335,000)	245,682	86E
Kigali, Rwanda	181,600	83E
Kijev (Kiev), U.S.S.R. (2,850,000)	2,544,000	87E
Kingston, Jamaica (770,000)	586,930	82C
Kingston-upon-Hull, Eng., U.K. (350,000)	322,140	81C
Kingstown, St. Vin. and the Gren. (27,948)	18,378	84E
Kinshasa, Zaire	3,000,000	86E
Kisangani (Stanleyville), Zaire	282,650	84C
Kišinev, U.S.S.R.	663,000	87E
Kitakyūshū, Japan (1,525,000)	1,056,402	85C
Kitchener, Ont., Can. (311,195)	150,600	86C
Kitwe-Nkana, Zambia (283,962)	207,500	80C
Knoxville, Tn., U.S. (490,000)	175,045	80C
Kōbe, Japan (*Ōsaka)	1,410,834	85C
København (Copenhagen), Denmark (1,685,000)	473,000	86E
Köln (Cologne), Fed. Rep. of Ger. (1,760,000)	914,336	87E
Kowloon, Hong Kong (*Victoria)	799,123	81C
Kraków, Poland (828,000)	744,000	87E
Krasnodar, U.S.S.R.	623,000	87E
Krasnojarsk, U.S.S.R.	899,000	87E
Krivoj Rog, U.S.S.R.	698,000	87E
Krung Thep (Bangkok), Thailand (6,450,000)	5,446,708	86E
Kuala Lumpur, Malaysia (1,475,000)	919,610	80C
Kujbyšev, U.S.S.R. (1,510,000)	1,280,000	87E
Kumamoto, Japan	555,710	85C
Kumasi, Ghana (600,000)	348,880	84C
Kunming, China (†1,520,000)	1,280,000	87E
Kuwait, see Al Kuwayt		
Kwangju, S. Korea (975,000)	905,890	85C
Kyōto, Japan (*Ōsaka)	1,479,218	85C
Lagos, Nigeria (3,800,000)	1,213,000	87E

Metropolitan area populations are shown in parentheses.
★ City is located within the metropolitan area of another city; for example, Kyōto, Japan, is located in the Ōsaka metropolitan area.
† Population of entire municipality or district, including rural area.

C Census
E Official estimate

City and Country	Population	Date
La Habana (Havana), Cuba (1,975,000)	1,914,466	81C
Lahore, Pakistan (3,025,000)	2,707,215	81C
Lansing, Mi., U.S. (352,600)	130,414	80C
Lanzhou, China (†1,390,000)	1,270,000	87E
La Paz, Bolivia	992,592	85E
La Plata, Argentina (*Buenos Aires)	477,170	80C
Las Palmas de Gran Canaria, Spain	372,270	86E
Las Vegas, Nv., U.S. (453,800)	164,674	80C
Lausanne, Switzerland (259,900)	124,200	87E
Leeds, Eng., U.K. (1,540,000)	445,242	81C
Le Havre, France (254,595)	199,380	82C
Leicester, Eng., U.K. (495,000)	324,390	81C
Leipzig, Ger. Dem. Rep. (700,000)	550,641	87E
Leningrad, U.S.S.R. (5,750,000)	4,393,000	87E
León, Mexico	593,000	80C
Leshan, China (†972,300)	307,300	86E
Lexington, Ky., U.S. (255,600)	204,165	80C
Libreville, Gabon	235,700	85E
Liège, Belgium (755,000)	207,496	83E
Lille, France (1,020,000)	168,424	82C
Lilongwe, Malawi	175,000	85E
Lima, Peru (4,608,010)	371,122	81C
Linyi, China (†1,365,000)	190,000	86E
Linz, Austria (355,000)	199,910	81C
Lisboa (Lisbon), Portugal (2,250,000)	807,167	81C
Little Rock, Ar., U.S. (382,000)	167,744	80C
Liuzhou, China	660,000	87E
Liverpool, Eng., U.K. (1,525,000)	538,809	81C
Ljubljana, Yugoslavia (†305,211)	205,600	81C
Łódź, Poland (1,061,000)	847,400	87E
Lomas de Zamora, Argentina (*Buenos Aires)	510,130	80C
Lomé, Togo	369,926	81C
London, Ont., Can. (342,302)	269,140	86C
London, Eng., U.K. (11,100,000)	6,851,400	81C
Los Angeles, Ca., U.S. (9,763,600)	2,968,579	80C
Louisville, Ky., U.S. (891,400)	298,694	80C
Luanda, Angola	1,200,000	82E
Lubumbashi, Zaire	543,260	84C
Lucknow, India (1,060,000)	895,721	81C
Ludhiāna, India	607,050	81C
Luoyang, China (1,060,000)	740,000	87E
Lusaka, Zambia	535,830	80C
Luxembourg, Luxembourg (133,000)	78,924	81C
Lvov, U.S.S.R.	767,000	87E
Lyon, France (1,275,000)	413,095	82C
Madison, Wi., U.S. (294,300)	170,616	80C
Madras, India (4,475,000)	3,276,622	81C
Madrid, Spain (4,650,000)	3,123,713	86E
Madurai, India (960,000)	820,890	81C
Magdeburg, Ger. Dem. Rep. (400,000)	288,970	87E
Magnitogorsk, U.S.S.R.	430,000	87E
Makkah (Mecca), Saudi Arabia	550,000	80E
Malabo, Equatorial Guinea	30,710	83C
Málaga, Spain	595,260	86E
Malang, Indonesia	511,780	80C
Male, Maldives	46,334	85E
Malmö, Sweden (445,000)	230,050	87E
Managua, Nicaragua	644,588	81E
Manama, see Al Manāmah		
Manaus, Brazil	809,910	85E
Manchester, Eng., U.K. (2,775,000)	437,612	81C
Manchester, N.H., U.S. (129,300)	90,936	80C
Mandalay, Burma	532,890	83C
Manila, Philippines (6,800,000)	1,630,485	80C
Manizales, Colombia	330,000	85C
Mannheim, Fed. Rep. of Ger. (1,400,000)	294,648	87E
Maputo, Mozambique	755,300	80C
Maracaibo, Venezuela	929,000	81E
Mar del Plata, Argentina	414,690	80C
Mariupol', U.S.S.R.	529,000	87E
Marrakech, Morocco (535,000)	439,720	82C
Marseille, France (1,225,000)	874,436	82C
Maseru, Lesotho	14,686	76C
Masqaṭ (Muscat), Oman	50,000	81E
Mbabane, Swaziland	53,000	84E
Mbuji-Mayi, Zaire	423,360	84C
Medan, Indonesia	1,208,678	80C
Medellín, Colombia	2,095,000	85C
Medina, see Al Madīndah		
Meknès, Morocco (375,000)	319,780	82C

City and Country	Population	Date
Melbourne, Australia (2,832,893)	60,828	86C
Memphis, Tn., U.S. (852,900)	646,174	80C
Mendoza, Argentina (650,000)	119,080	80C
Mexicali, Mexico (365,000)	341,550	80C
Mexico City, see Ciudad de México		
Miami, Fl., U.S. (2,827,300)	346,865	80C
Middlesbrough (Teesside), Eng., U.K. (580,000)	158,510	81C
Milano (Milan), Italy (3,775,000)	1,634,638	81C
Milwaukee, Wi., U.S. (1,374,700)	636,297	80C
Minneapolis, Mn., U.S. (2,012,400)	370,951	80C
Minsk, U.S.S.R. (1,600,000)	1,543,000	87E
Mobile, Al., U.S. (361,900)	200,452	80C
Mombasa, Kenya	425,600	84E
Mönchengladbach, Fed. Rep. of Ger. (410,000)	255,080	87E
Monrovia, Liberia	425,000	84E
Monterrey, Mexico (2,015,000)	1,090,009	80C
Montevideo, Uruguay (1,550,000)	1,246,500	85C
Montgomery, Al., U.S. (225,000)	177,857	80C
Montréal, Que., Can. (2,921,357)	1,015,420	86C
Morón, Argentina (*Buenos Aires)	598,420	80C
Moroni, Comoros	20,112	80C
Moskva (Moscow), U.S.S.R. (12,900,000)	8,614,000	87E
Mudanjiang, China	630,000	87E
Multān, Pakistan (732,070)	696,310	81C
München (Munich), Fed. Rep. of Ger. (1,955,000)	1,274,716	87E
Münster, Fed. Rep. of Ger.	267,620	87E
Muqdisho (Mogadishu), Somalia	600,000	83E
Murcia, Spain (†305,221)	200,300	84E
Murmansk, U.S.S.R.	432,000	87E
Mysore, India (479,081)	441,750	81C
Naberežnyje Čelny (Brežnev), U.S.S.R.	480,000	87E
Nagasaki, Japan	449,380	85C
Nagoya, Japan (4,800,000)	2,116,381	85C
Nāgpur, India (1,302,066)	1,219,461	81C
Nairobi, Kenya	1,103,600	84E
Nanchang, China (†1,190,000)	1,030,000	87E
Nancy, France (306,982)	96,310	82C
Nanjing (Nanking), China	2,290,000	87E
Nanning, China (†960,000)	690,000	87E
Nantes, France (464,857)	240,530	82C
Napoli (Naples), Italy (2,765,000)	1,210,503	81C
Nashville, Tn., U.S. (633,900)	455,651	80C
Nassau, Bahamas	135,000	82E
Natal, Brazil	510,100	85E
N'Djamena, Chad	303,000	79E
Netzahualcóyotl, Mexico (*Ciudad de México)	1,341,230	80C
Newark, N.J., U.S. (*New York)	329,248	80C
Newcastle, Australia (405,089)	129,490	86C
Newcastle upon Tyne, Eng., U.K. (1,300,000)	199,064	81C
New Delhi, India (*Delhi)	273,036	81C
New Kowloon, Hong Kong (*Victoria)	1,651,064	81C
New Orleans, La., U.S. (1,185,000)	557,927	80C
Newport, Wales, U.K. (310,000)	115,890	81C
New York, N.Y., U.S. (16,800,900)	7,071,639	80C
Niamey, Niger	399,100	83C
Nice, France (449,496)	337,080	82C
Nicosia, Cyprus (185,000)	48,221	82E
Nikolajev, U.S.S.R.	501,000	87E
Ningbo, China (†1,030,000)	560,000	87E
Niterói, Brazil (*Rio de Janeiro)	441,680	85E
Norfolk, Va., U.S. (795,600)	266,979	80C
North York, Ont., Can. (*Toronto)	556,290	86C
Nottingham, Eng., U.K. (655,000)	273,300	81C
Nouakchott, Mauritania	285,000	87E
Nouméa, New Caledonia (83,000)	60,112	83C
Nova Iguaçu, Brazil (*Rio de Janeiro)	592,800	85E
Novokuzneck, U.S.S.R.	589,000	87E
Novosibirsk, U.S.S.R. (1,580,000)	1,423,000	87E
Nuku'alofa, Tonga	21,265	86C
Nürnberg, Fed. Rep. of Ger. (1,030,000)	467,392	87E
Odessa, U.S.S.R. (1,210,000)	1,141,000	87E
Ogbomosho, Nigeria	582,900	87E
Okayama, Japan	572,470	85C
Oklahoma City, Ok., U.S. (742,000)	403,484	80C
Omaha, Nb., U.S. (538,600)	322,133	80C

City and Country	Population	Date
Omdurman, see Umm Durmān		
Omsk, U.S.S.R. (1,160,000)	1,134,000	87E
Oran, Algeria	663,500	83E
Orenburg, U.S.S.R.	537,000	87E
Orlando, Fl., U.S. (619,300)	128,291	80C
Orūmīyeh, Iran	263,000	82E
Ōsaka, Japan (16,450,000)	263,624	85C
Osasco, Brazil (*São Paulo)	591,560	85E
Oshogbo, Nigeria	380,800	87E
Oslo, Norway (720,000)	448,747	83E
Ostrava, Czechoslovakia (755,000)	327,790	86E
Ottawa, Ont., Can. (819,263)	300,763	86C
Ouagadougou, Burkina Faso	442,223	85C
Palembang, Indonesia	786,600	80C
Palermo, Italy	699,690	81C
Palma, Spain	311,197	84E
Panamá, Panama (625,000)	413,992	82E
Papeete, French Polynesia (80,000)	23,496	83C
Paramaribo, Suriname (192,810)	67,905	80C
Paris, France (9,775,000)	2,127,100	86E
Patna, India (1,025,000)	776,370	81C
Peking, see Beijing		
Penza, U.S.S.R.	540,000	87E
Perm, U.S.S.R. (1,145,000)	1,075,000	87E
Perth, Australia (994,472)	79,409	86C
Peshāwar, Pakistan (566,248)	506,890	81C
Philadelphia, Pa., U.S. (5,208,600)	1,688,210	80C
Phnum Pénh, Cambodia	700,000	86E
Phoenix, Az., U.S. (1,482,400)	790,044	80C
Pingxiang, China (†1,286,700)	368,700	86E
Pittsburgh, Pa., U.S. (2,218,800)	423,959	80C
Ploiești, Romania (300,000)	234,880	86E
Plovdiv, Bulgaria	349,140	86E
Pointe-à-Pitre, Guadeloupe (83,000)	25,310	82C
Port-au-Prince, Haiti (760,000)	684,284	82C
Port Elizabeth, South Africa (690,000)	272,840	85C
Port Harcourt, Nigeria	327,300	87E
Portland, Me., U.S. (193,800)	61,572	80C
Portland, Or., U.S. (1,227,200)	368,139	80C
Port-Louis, Mauritius (415,000)	138,272	86E
Port Moresby, Papua New Guinea	123,624	80C
Porto (Oporto), Portugal (1,225,000)	327,368	81C
Porto Alegre, Brazil (2,600,000)	1,272,121	85E
Port of Spain, Trinidad and Tobago (370,000)	55,800	80C
Porto-Novo, Benin	123,000	80E
Port Said, see Būr Sa'īd		
Portsmouth, Eng., U.K. (485,000)	174,210	81C
Port-Vila, Vanuatu (18,000)	13,067	86E
Poznań, Poland (672,000)	578,100	87E
Praha (Prague), Czechoslovakia (1,310,000)	1,193,513	86E
Praia, Cape Verde	37,480	80C
Pretoria, South Africa (960,000)	443,059	85C
Providence, R.I., U.S. (921,800)	156,804	80C
Puebla [de Zaragoza], Mexico (1,055,000)	835,750	80C
Pune, India (1,775,000)	1,203,351	81C
Pusan, S. Korea (3,550,000)	3,514,798	85C
P'yŏngyang, N. Korea (1,600,000)	1,283,000	80C
Qingdao, China	1,270,000	87E
Qiqihar, China (†1,300,000)	1,150,000	87E
Qom, Iran	424,000	82E
Québec, Que., Can. (603,267)	164,580	86C
Quetta, Pakistan (285,791)	244,840	81C
Quezon City, Philippines (*Manila)	1,165,865	80C
Quilmes, Argentina (*Buenos Aires)	446,580	80C
Quito, Ecuador (1,050,000)	890,355	82C
Rabat, Morocco (980,000)	518,616	82C
Rājkot, India	445,070	81C
Raleigh, N.C., U.S. (282,800)	150,255	80C
Rānchī, India (502,771)	489,620	81C
Rangoon, see Yangon		
Rāwalpindi, Pakistan (1,040,000)	457,091	81C
Recife, Brazil (2,625,000)	1,287,623	85E
Reno, Nv., U.S. (176,200)	100,756	80C
Reykjavík, Iceland (130,722)	88,745	84E
Ribeirão Prêto, Brazil	383,120	85E
Richmond, Va., U.S. (690,600)	219,214	80C
Rīga, U.S.S.R. (990,000)	900,000	87E

City and Country	Population	Date
Rio de Janeiro, Brazil (10,150,000)	5,603,388	85E
Riverside, Ca., U.S. (768,300)	170,591	80C
Riyadh, see Ar Riyāḍ		
Rjazan, U.S.S.R.	508,000	87E
Rochester, N.Y., U.S. (816,200)	241,741	80C
Roma (Rome), Italy (3,115,000)	2,830,569	81C
Rosario, Argentina (1,045,000)	938,120	80C
Rostov-na-Donu, U.S.S.R. (1,145,000)	1,004,000	87E
Rotterdam, Netherlands (1,110,000)	571,372	86E
Rouen, France (379,879)	101,945	82C
Rouseau, Dominica	9,348	84E
Sacramento, Ca., U.S. (866,400)	275,741	80C
Safāqis, Tunisia (310,000)	231,910	84C
Saigon, see Ho Chi Minh		
St. Catharines, Ont., Can. (343,258)	123,450	86C
St.-Étienne, France (317,228)	204,950	82C
St. George's, Grenada (25,000)	4,788	81C
St. John's, Antigua and Barbuda	24,359	77C
St. Louis, Mo., U.S. (2,203,000)	452,801	80C
St. Paul, Mn., U.S. (*Minneapolis)	270,230	80C
St. Petersburg, Fl., U.S. (852,300)	238,647	80C
Sakai, Japan (*Ōsaka)	818,270	85C
Salem, India (518,615)	361,390	81C
Salt Lake City, Ut., U.S. (682,400)	163,034	80C
Salvador, Brazil (2,050,000)	1,804,438	85E
Samarkand, U.S.S.R.	388,000	87E
Şan'ā', Yemen	277,818	81C
San Antonio, Tx., U.S. (968,200)	786,023	80C
San Diego, Ca., U.S. (2,098,500)	875,538	80C
San Francisco, Ca., U.S. (4,683,200)	678,974	80C
San José, Costa Rica (670,000)	241,464	84C
San José, Ca., U.S. (*San Francisco)	629,400	80C
San Juan, Puerto Rico (1,775,260)	424,600	80C
San Luis Potosí, Mexico (470,000)	362,370	80C
San Miguel de Tucumán, Argentina (525,000)	392,880	80C
San Salvador, El Salvador (920,000)	459,902	85E
San Sebastián, Spain (285,000)	180,040	86E
Santiago, Chile (4,025,000)	425,924	82C
Santo André, Brazil (São Paulo)	635,120	85E
Santo Domingo, Dominican Rep.	1,313,172	81C
Santos, Brazil (1,065,000)	460,100	85E
São Bernardo do Campo, Brazil (*São Paulo)	562,480	85E
São Luís, Brazil (600,000)	227,900	85E
São Paulo, Brazil (15,175,000)	10,063,110	85E
São Tomé, Sao Tome and Prin.	17,380	70C
Sapporo, Japan (1,900,000)	1,542,979	85C
Sarajevo, Yugoslavia (†448,500)	374,500	81C
Saratov, U.S.S.R. (1,170,000)	918,000	87E
Sargodha, Pakistan (291,362)	231,890	81C
Savannah, Ga., U.S. (212,800)	141,651	80C
Scarborough, Ont., Can. (*Toronto)	484,670	86C
Seattle, Wa., U.S. (2,077,100)	493,846	80C
Semarang, Indonesia	820,140	80C
Semipalatinsk, U.S.S.R.	330,000	87E
Sendai, Japan (1,175,000)	700,250	85C
Seoul, see Sŏul		
Sevilla (Seville), Spain (945,000)	668,350	86E
's-Gravenhage (The Hague), Netherlands (770,000)	443,961	86E
Shanghai, China (9,300,000)	7,100,000	87E
Shantou, China (†770,000)	550,000	87E
Sheffield, Eng., U.K. (710,000)	470,680	81C
Shenyang (Mukden), China (†4,290,000)	3,840,000	87E
Shīrāz, Iran	800,000	82E
Shubrā al Khaymah, Egypt (*Al Qāhirah)	515,500	85E
Sialkot, Pakistan (302,009)	258,140	81C
Singapore, Singapore (3,000,000)	2,631,000	88E
Sioux Falls, S.D., U.S. (92,200)	81,343	80C
Sofija (Sofia), Bulgaria (1,205,000)	1,119,152	86E
Solāpur, India (514,860)	511,100	81C
Sŏul (Seoul), S. Korea (14,100,000)	9,639,110	85C
Southampton, Eng., U.K. (415,000)	211,320	81C
Soweto, South Africa (*Johannesburg)	521,940	85C
Springfield, Il., U.S. (154,200)	100,054	80C
Springfield, Ma., U.S. (485,900)	152,319	80C
Srīnagar, India (606,002)	594,770	81C
Stalingrad, see Volgograd		
Stockholm, Sweden (1,449,972)	663,217	87E
Stoke-on-Trent, Eng., U.K. (440,000)	272,440	81C
Strasbourg, France (400,000)	248,710	82C
Stuttgart, Fed. Rep. of Ger. (1,925,000)	565,486	87E
Suez, see As Suways		
Suichang, China (†2,216,500)	363,500	86E
Suixian, China (†1,281,600)	187,700	86E
Surabaya, Indonesia	2,027,913	80C
Surakarta, Indonesia (575,000)	469,530	80C
Surat, India (913,806)	776,580	81C
Suva, Fiji (141,273)	69,665	86C
Suzhou, China	720,000	87E
Sverdlovsk, U.S.S.R. (1,575,000)	1,331,000	87E
Swansea, Wales, U.K. (275,000)	172,430	81C
Sydney, Australia (3,364,858)	86,311	86C
Syracuse, N.Y., U.S. (518,600)	170,105	80C
Szczecin, Poland (449,000)	395,000	87E
Tabrīz, Iran	852,000	82E
Tacoma, Wa., U.S. (*Seattle)	158,501	80C
Taegu, S. Korea	2,029,853	85C
Taejŏn, S. Korea	866,140	85C
Tai'an, China (†1,325,400)	215,900	86E
Taichung, Taiwan	674,930	85E
Tainan, Taiwan	639,880	85E
Taipei, Taiwan (5,725,000)	2,507,620	85E
Taiyuan, China (†1,930,000)	1,660,000	87E
Tallinn, U.S.S.R.	478,000	87E
Tampa, Fl., U.S. (594,500)	271,598	80C
Tampico, Mexico (435,000)	267,950	80C
Tanger (Tangier), Morocco (370,000)	266,340	82C
Tangshan, China (†1,410,000)	1,060,000	87E
Tantā, Egypt	364,700	85E
Ṭarābulus (Tripoli), Libya	858,500	81E
Taškent (Tashkent), U.S.S.R. (2,370,000)	2,124,000	87E
Tbilisi, U.S.S.R. (1,380,000)	1,194,000	87E
Tegucigalpa, Honduras	597,500	85E
Tehrān, Iran (6,400,000)	5,734,199	82C
Tel Aviv-Yafo, Israel (1,670,000)	320,300	87E
Teresina, Brazil (525,000)	425,300	85E
Thanh Pho Ho Chi Minh (Saigon), Vietnam (3,100,000)	2,700,849	79C
The Hague, see s'-Gravenhage		
Thessaloníki, Greece (706,180)	406,410	81C
Thimphu, Bhutan	12,000	82E
Thunder Bay, Ont., Can. (122,217)	112,272	86C
Tianjin (Tientsin), China (†5,460,000)	4,880,000	87E
Tianshui, China (†953,200)	209,500	86E
Tijuana, Mexico (*San Diego)	429,500	80C
Tirana, Albania	210,800	84E
Tiruchchirāppalli, India (609,548)	362,040	81C
Tlalnepantla, Mexico (*Ciudad de México)	778,170	80C
Togliatti (Stavropol), U.S.S.R.	627,000	87E
Tōkyō, Japan (27,700,000)	8,354,615	85C
Tomsk, U.S.S.R.	489,000	87E
Torino (Turin), Italy (1,600,000)	1,103,520	81C
Toronto, Ont., Can. (3,427,168)	612,289	86C
Torreón, Mexico (575,000)	328,080	80C
Toulon, France (410,393)	179,420	82C
Toulouse, France (541,271)	347,990	82C
Tours, France (262,786)	132,209	82C
Tripoli, see Ṭarābulus		
Trivandrum, India (520,125)	483,080	81C
Trujillo, Peru (354,301)	202,460	81C
Tsun Wan, Hong Kong (*Victoria)	599,010	81C
Tucson, Az., U.S. (495,600)	336,503	80C
Tula, U.S.S.R. (635,000)	538,000	87E
Tulsa, Ok., U.S. (742,000)	360,919	80C
Tūnis, Tunisia (1,225,000)	596,654	84C
Ufa, U.S.S.R. (1,110,000)	1,092,000	87E
Ujung Pandang (Makasar), Indonesia	708,460	80C
Ulan-Bator, Mongolia	488,200	85E
Ulsan, S. Korea	551,010	85C
Umm Durmān (Omdurman), Sudan (*Khartoum)	526,280	83C
Utrecht, Netherlands (511,195)	229,930	86E
Vadodara (Baroda), India (744,881)	734,470	81C
Vaduz, Liechtenstein	4,920	87E
Valencia, Spain (1,270,000)	738,575	86E
Valletta, Malta (215,000)	9,263	87E
Valparaíso, Chile (700,000)	265,350	82C
Vancouver, B.C., Can. (1,380,729)	431,147	86C
Vārānasi (Benares), India (925,000)	708,640	81C
Venezia (Venice), Italy (415,000)	332,770	81C
Veracruz [Llave], Mexico (385,000)	284,820	80C
Vereeniging, South Africa (525,000)	60,580	85C
Verona, Italy	261,208	81C
Viangchan (Vientiane), Laos	377,000	85C
Victoria, B.C., Can. (255,547)	66,300	86C
Victoria, Hong Kong (4,515,000)	1,183,621	81C
Victoria, Seychelles	23,000	74C
Vienna, see Wien		
Vientiane, see Viangchan		
Vilnius, U.S.S.R.	566,000	87E
Vishākhapatnam, India (603,530)	565,320	81C
Vitória, Brazil (735,000)	201,500	85E
Vladivostok, U.S.S.R.	615,000	87E
Volgograd (Stalingrad), U.S.S.R. (1,335,000)	988,000	87E
Volta Redonda, Brazil (375,000)	219,260	85E
Voronež, U.S.S.R.	872,000	87E
Vorošilovgrad, U.S.S.R.	509,000	87E
Warszawa (Warsaw), Poland (2,323,000)	1,664,700	87E
Washington, D.C., U.S. (3,221,400)	638,432	80C
Weifang, China (†1,042,200)	312,500	86E
Wellington, New Zealand (350,000)	137,495	86C
Wichita, Ks., U.S. (372,200)	279,835	80C
Wien (Vienna), Austria (1,875,000)	1,489,153	85E
Wiesbaden, Fed. Rep. of Ger. (795,000)	266,540	87E
Willemstad, Netherlands Antilles (130,000)	31,883	81C
Wilmington, De., U.S. (*Philadelphia)	70,195	80C
Windhoek, Namibia	120,000	84E
Windsor, Ont., Can. (253,988)	193,110	86C
Winnipeg, Man., Can. (625,304)	594,550	86C
Wrocław, Poland	640,000	87E
Wuhan, China	3,490,000	87E
Wuppertal, Fed. Rep. of Ger. (830,000)	374,217	87E
Wuxi, China	860,000	87E
Wuxing (Huzhou), China (†964,400)	208,500	86E
Xiamen, China (†546,400)	343,700	86E
Xi'an, China (†2,390,000)	2,050,000	87E
Xiaogan, China (†1,204,400)	125,500	86E
Xining, China	610,000	87E
Xuzhou, China	840,000	87E
Yancheng, China (†1,251,400)	258,400	86E
Yangon (Rangoon), Burma (2,800,000)	2,458,712	83C
Yaoundé, Cameroon	583,000	85E
Yerushalayim (Jerusalem), Israel (490,000)	468,900	87E
Yichun, China	830,000	87E
Yokohama, Japan (*Tōkyō)	2,992,926	85C
Yulin, China (†1,228,800)	115,600	86E
Zagreb, Yugoslavia	768,700	81C
Zanzibar, Tanzania	110,669	78C
Zaozhuang, China (†1,592,000)	292,200	86E
Zaporožje, U.S.S.R.	875,000	87E
Zaragoza (Saragossa), Spain	596,080	86E
Zhangjiakou, China (†626,500)	492,800	86E
Zhengzhou, China (†1,610,000)	1,170,000	87E
Zhongshan, China (†1,059,700)	238,700	86E
Zibo, China (†2,330,000)	830,000	87E
Zurich, Switzerland (860,000)	349,549	87E

Metropolitan area populations are shown in parentheses.
★ City is located within the metropolitan area of another city; for example, Kyōto, Japan is located in the Ōsaka metropolitan area.
† Population of entire municipality or district, including rural area.

C Census
E Official estimate

A • 15

Transliteration Systems

Toponymy: Criteria Used for the Writing of Names on the Maps

The language of geography is a language which defines geographic features in universally recognized terms. In creating this language, toponymy experts and cartographers have confronted complex problems in finding terms which are universally acceptable. So that the reader can fully understand the maps in this atlas, here is a brief explanation of how the toponyms (place-names for geographic features) have been written, particularly those relating to regions or countries where the Roman alphabet is not used. Among these are the Slavic-speaking nations such as the Soviet Union, Yugoslavia and Bulgaria; and China and Japan, which use ideographic characters. Of the European countries, Greece has its own alphabet, which is totally different from the Roman alphabet. Many of the Islamic countries use Arabic, with variations derived from local dialects.

There are two basic systems for Romanizing writing. The first is by phonetic transcription, using combinations of different alphabetical signs for each language when the phonetic sound in other languages should be maintained. For example, the Italian sound "sc" (which must be followed by an "e" or "i" to remain soft) in French is "ch," in English is "sh," and in German is "sch."

The second system is transliteration, in which the words, letters or characters of one language are represented or spelled in the letters or characters of another language.

Chinese, Japanese and Arabic Languages

Various Asian and African countries use non-Roman forms in their writing. For example, the Chinese and Japanese languages use ideographic characters instead of an alphabet, and these ideographic characters are transformed into the Roman alphabet through phonetic transcription. Until recently, one of the methods used for transforming Chinese was the Wade-Giles system, named for its English authors. Used in this atlas is the Pinyin system, which was approved by the Chinese government in 1958 and has been incorporated into the official maps of the People's Republic of China. The Pinyin system also has been adopted by the United States Board on Geographic Names and is used in official United Nations documents. The Pinyin names, however, often are accompanied by the Wade-Giles form, as the latter was widely known.

In Japan, ideographic characters are used, although the Roman alphabet is used in many Japanese scientific works. Japan uses two principal systems for standardizing names. They are the Kunreisiki, used by the government in official publications, and the Hepburn method. Adopted for this atlas is the Hepburn method, the system used in international English-language publications and by the United States Board on Geographic Names.

Romanization of the Arabic alphabet, which is used in many Islamic countries, is by transliteration. Since English and French are still used as an international language in many Arab countries, the name forms proposed by the major English and French sources have been taken into consideration. Generally, the systems proposed by the United States Board on Geographic Names and the Permanent Committee on Geographical Names have been used for most Asian countries and Arab-speaking countries.

Greek, Russian and Other Slavic Languages

Practically all written languages in Europe use the Roman alphabet. The differences in phonetics and grammar are shown by the use of diacritical marks and by groupings of consonants, vocals and syllables which give meaning to the various tones in the language. According to a centuries-old tradition, each written language maintains its formal characters, using the translated form rather than the phonetic transcription when a geographical term must be given in another language. This system, therefore, makes it more a translation than a transliteration.

In the Aegean area, Greek and the Greek alphabet are particularly significant because of historical links to the beginning of European civilization. The 1962 United States Board on Geographic Names and the Permanent Committee on Geographical Names systems, based on modern Greek pronunciation, have been used in transcribing toponyms from official sources for these maps. (The table that follows has an example indicating essential norms for Romanizing the modern Greek alphabet.)

A different situation arises in countries using the Cyrillic alphabet. Six principal Slavic languages using this alphabet are Russian, Byelorussian, Ukrainian, Bulgarian, Serbian, and Macedonian. The Cyrillic alphabet also is used by the non-Slavic people of the central Soviet Union. The nomenclature of these regions has been transliterated in accordance with the system proposed by the International Organization for Standardization, taking into consideration sounds and letters and uses of the diacritical marks normal in Slavic languages. The International Organization for Standardization method is accepted and used in bibliographical works and international documents. (The table which follows gives the relationship between the letters of the Cyrillic and Roman alphabets for the above six languages.) An exception to this transliteration is made by the Soviet Balkan republics of Estonia, Latvia and Lithuania. Here the name forms deriving from the national languages have been adopted, using the Roman alphabet.

Special Cases: Conventional Forms and Multilinguals

Cartographic nomenclature generally derives from the official nomenclature of the sovereign and nonsovereign countries, although a number of cases need an explanation.

In numerous situations, English conventional forms are used along with the local or conventional name in referring to a geographical entity used outside the official language area. For example, Vienna, Prague, Copenhagen and Moscow are English forms for Wien, Praha, København and Moskva, respectively. There have been cases, however, where the conventional or historical form commonly used in English cartography has been applied with the same meaning. Thus, Peking and Nanking are the English conventional forms for Beijing and Nanjing, while Tsinan, Tientsin and Mukden are the former conventional spellings or names for Jinan, Tianjin and Shenyang, respectively. Other examples are Saigon, the former name for Ho Chi Minh, Vietnam; and Bangkok, the name for Krung Thep, which is used in Thailand.

The lack of reliable data for countries, especially ex-colonies without a firm national cartographic tradition, has made it necessary to utilize mapping skills of former colonist nations such as France, the United Kingdom and Belgium. A lack of data has led to the adoption of French and British forms in many areas, as these two languages are widely used for official purposes.

Another special case is that of the multilingual areas. Many countries and areas officially recognize two or more written and spoken languages; therefore, all of the principal written forms appear on the maps. This is true, for example, of Belgium where the official languages are French and Dutch (e.g. Bruxelles/ Brussel) and of Italian regions such as Valle d'Aosta and Alto Adige, where French, German and Italian are used (e.g. Aosta/Aoste) (Bolzano/Bozen).

In preparing this atlas, each of these special cases has been taken into full consideration within the limits of the scale, space and readability of the maps.

Transliteration of the Cyrillic Alphabet
(International System—ISO)

Cyrillic Letter		Roman Letter		Cyrillic Letter		Roman Letter	
А	а	a		О	о	o	
Б	б	b		П	п	p	
В	в	v		Р	р	r	
Г	г	g		С	с	s	
Д	д	d		Т	т	t	
Е	е	e	initially, after a vowel or after the mute sign "Ъ", becomes "je"	У	у	u	
				Ф	ф	f	
				Х	х	h	
Ё	ё	ë		Ц	ц	c	
Ж	ж	ž		Ч	ч	č	
З	з	z		Ш	ш	š	
И	и	i		Щ	щ	šč	
Й	й	j	not written if preceded by "И" or "Ы"	Ъ	ъ	—	not written
				Ы	ы	y	
К	к	k		Ь	ь	—	not written
Л	л	l		Э	э	e	
М	м	m		Ю	ю	ju	
Н	н	n		Я	я	ja	

Transcription of Modern Greek
(U.S. B. G. N. / P.C.G.N.)

Greek Letter (or combination)		Roman Letter (or combination)		Greek Letter (or combination)		Roman Letter (or combination)	
Α	α	a			μπ	b	beginning a word
	αι	ai				mb	within a word
	αυ	av		Ν	ν	n	
Β	β	v			ντ	d	beginning a word
Γ	γ	g				nd	within a word
	γγ	ng		Ξ	ξ	x	
	γκ	g	beginning a word	Ο	ο	o	
					οι	oi	
		ng	within a word		ου	ou	
Δ	δ	d		Π	π	p	
Ε	ε	e		Ρ	ρ	r	
	ει	i		Σ	σ	s	
	ευ	ev			ς	s	ending a word
Ζ	ζ	z		Τ	τ	t	
Η	η	i			τζ	tz	
	ηυ	iv		Υ	υ	i	
Θ	θ	th			υι	i	
Ι	ι	i		Φ	φ	f	
Κ	κ	k		Χ	χ	kh	
Λ	λ	l		Ψ	ψ	ps	
Μ	μ	m		Ω	ω	o	

The "Geographical Glossary" lists the principal geographical terms used on the maps. All of these terms, including abbreviations, prefixes and suffixes, appear in the cartographic table as they appear on the maps. Terms are listed in accordance with the English alphabet, without consideration of diacritical marks on letters or of particular groups of letters.

Prefixes and suffixes relating to principal names or forming part of geographical toponyms are followed or preceded by a dash and the language to which they refer: e.g. Chi-/*Dan.* (Chi, a Danish prefix, means large); -bor/*Slvn.* (-bor, a Slovakian suffix, means city). Suffixes can also appear as words in themselves. In this case, the suffix and primary word are coupled together: e.g. Berg, -berg (Berg, which means mountain, can be used alone or as part of another word, such as Hapsberg).

Certain terms are followed or preceded by their abbreviation used on the maps. Both instances are listed: e.g. Fjord, Fj. and Fj., Fjord.

All geographical terms are identified by the language or languages to which each belongs. The language or languages in italics follows the term: e.g. Abbey/*Eng.*; -bad/*Nor., Dut., Swed., Germ.* Each term is translated into a corresponding English term or terms.

Below is a table identifying the abbreviations of various language names used on the maps. Note that certain abbreviations represent a group of languages, instead of one language: e.g. Ural. is the abbreviation for Uralic, a group word for Udmurt, Komi, and Nenets.

Alt. = Altaic (Turkmen, Tatar, Bashkir, Kazakh, Karalpak, Nogai, Kirghiz, Uzbek, Uigur, Altaic, Yakut, Khakass)

Ban. = Bantu (KiSwahili, ChiLuba, Lingala, KiKongo)

Cauc. = Caucasian (Chechen, Ingush, Kalmuck, Georgian)
Iran. = Iranian (Baluchi, Tagus)
Mel. = Melanesian (Fijian, New Caledonian, Micronesian, Nauruan)
Mong. = Mongolian (Buryat, Khalka Mongol)
Poly. = Polynesian (Maori, Samoan, Tongan, Tahitian, Hawaiian)
Sah. = Saharan (Kanuri, Tubu)
Som. = Somalian (Somali, Galla)
Sud. = Sudanese (Peul, Ehoué, Mossi, Yoruba, Ibo)
Ural. = Uralic (Udmurt, Komi, Nenets).

Because of their technical application to geography, some geographical terms may not fully correspond with the meaning given for them in some dictionaries.

Abbreviations of Language Names

Abbreviations in English	English	Abbreviations in English	English	Abbreviations in English	English	Abbreviations in English	English	Abbreviations in English	English	Abbreviations in English	English
Afr.	Afrikaans	Bulg.	Bulgarian	Fr.	French	Khm.	Khmer	Pers.	Persian	Som.	Somalian
A.I.	American Indian	Burm.	Burmese	Gae.	Gaelic	Kor.	Korean	Pol.	Polish	Sp.	Spanish
Alb.	Albanian	Cat.	Catalan	Georg.	Georgian	K.S.	Khoi-San	Poly.	Polynesian	Sud.	Sudanese
Alt.	Altaic	Cauc.	Caucasian	Germ.	German	Laot.	Laotian	Port.	Portuguese	Swa.	Swahili
Amh.	Amharic	Chin.	Chinese	Gr.	Greek	Lapp.	Lappish	Prov.	Provençal	Swed.	Swedish
Ar.	Arabic	Cz.	Czech	Hebr.	Hebrew	Latv.	Latvian	Rmsh.	Romansh	Tam.	Tamil
Arm.	Armenian	Dan.	Danish	Hin.	Hindi	Lith.	Lithuanian	Rom.	Romanian	Thai	Thai
Az.	Azerbaidzhani	Dut.	Dutch	Hung.	Hungarian	Mal.	Malay	Rus.	Russian	Tib.	Tibetan
Ban.	Bantu	Eng.	English	Icel.	Icelandic	Malag.	Malagasy	Sah.	Saharan	Tur.	Turkish
Bas.	Basque	Esk.	Eskimo	Indon.	Indonesian	Mel.	Melanesian	S.C.	Serbo-Croatian	Ural.	Uralic
Beng.	Bengali	Est.	Estonian	Ir.	Irish	Mong.	Mongolian			Urdu	Urdu
Ber.	Berber	Far.	Faroese	Iran.	Iranian	Nep.	Nepalese	Sin.	Sinhalese	Viet.	Vietnamese
Br.	Breton	Finn.	Finnish	It.	Italian	Nor.	Norwegian	Slvk.	Slovak	Wall.	Walloon
		Fle.	Flemish	Jap.	Japanese	Pash.	Pashto	Slvn.	Slovene	Wel.	Welsh

Glossary of Geographical Terms

Local Form	English	Local Form	English	Local Form	English	Local Form	English
A		Ait / *Ar.; Ber.*	sons	Ard- / *Gae.*	high	Badwëynta / *Som.*	ocean
		Aivi, -aivi / *Lapp.*	mountain	Areg / *Ar.*	dune	Badyarada / *Som.*	gulf
A- / *Ban.*	people	Ak / *Tur.*	white	Areia / *Port.*	beach	Baeg / *Kor.*	white
A' / *Icel.*	river	'Aklé / *Ar.*	dunes	Arena / *Sp.*	beach	Bæk / *Dan.*	brook
Å / *Dan.; Nor.; Swed.*	stream	Akmeŋs / *Latv.*	stone	Argent / *Fr.*	silver	Bælt / *Dan.*	strait
a., an / *Germ.*	on	Ákra / *Gr.*	point	Arhipelag / *Rus.*	archipelago	Bagni / *It.*	thermal springs
Aa / *Germ.*	stream	Akti / *Gr.*	coast	Arkhaios / *Gr.*	old, antique	Baharu / *Mal.*	new
Aache / *Germ.*	stream	Ala / *Malag.*	forest	Arm / *Eng.; Germ.*	branch	Bahia / *Port.*	bay
Aaiún / *Ar.*	springs	Ala / *Finn.*	low, lower	Arquipélago / *Port.*	archipelago	Bahía / *Sp.*	bay
Aan / *Dut.; Fle.*	on	Alan / *Tur.*	field	Arr., Arroyo / *Sp.*	stream	Bahir / *Ar.*	river, lake, sea
Āb / *Pers.*	stream	Alb / *Rom.*	white	Arrecife / *Sp.*	reef	Bahnhof / *Germ.*	railway station
Ābād / *Pers.*	city, town	Albo / *Sp.*	white	Arroio / *Port.*	stream	Bahr / *Ar.*	wadi
Abad, -abad / *Pers.*	city, town	Albufera / *Sp.*	lagoon	Art / *Tur.*	pass, watershed	Baḥr / *Ar.*	river, lake, sea
Ābār / *Ar.*	spring	Alcalá / *Sp.*	castle	Aru / *Sin.; Tam.*	river	Baḥrat / *Ar.*	lake
Abbadia / *It.*	abbey	Alcázar / *Sp.*	castle	Ås / *Dan.; Nor.; Swed.*	hills	Bahri / *Ar.*	north, northern
Abbaye / *Fr.*	abbey	Aldea / *Sp.*	village	Asfar / *Ar.*	yellow	Baḥrī / *Ar.*	north
Abbazia / *It.*	abbey	Alföld / *Hung.*	lowland	Asif / *Ber.*	river	Bahrīyah / *Ar.*	northern
Abbi / *Amh.*	great	Ali / *Amh.*	mountain	Asky / *Alt.*	lower	Bai / *Chin.*	white
Abd / *Ar.*	servant	Alia / *Poly.*	stream	Áspros / *Gr.*	white	Băi / *Rom.*	thermal springs
Abeba / *Amh.*	flower	Alin / *Mong.*	range	Assa / *Ber.*	wadi	Baia / *Port.*	bay
Aber / *Br.; Wel.*	estuary	Alm / *Germ.*	mountain pasture	Atalaya / *Sp.*	frontier	Baie / *Fr.*	bay
Abhang / *Germ.*	slope			Áth / *Gae.*	ford	Baigne / *Fr.*	seaside resort
Abū / *Ar.*	father, master	Alor / *Mal.*	river	Átha / *Gae.*	ford	Baile / *Gae.*	city, town
Abyad / *Ar.*	white	Alp / *Germ.*	mountain pasture	Atol / *Port.*	atoll	Bain / *Fr.*	thermal springs
Abyaḍ / *Ar.*	white			Au / *Germ.*	meadow	Bains / *Fr.*	thermal springs
Abyār / *Ar.*	well	Alpe / *Germ.; Fr.; It.*	mountain pasture	Aue / *Germ.*	irrigated field	Baixo / *Port.*	low, lower
Abyss / *Eng.*	ocean depth, deep			Aust / *Nor.*	east	Bajan / *Mong.*	rich
		Alps / *Eng.*	mountains	Austur / *Icel.*	east	Bajo / *Sp.*	low
Ach / *Germ.*	stream	Alsó / *Hung.*	low, lower	Ava / *Poly.*	canal	Bajrak / *Alb.*	tribe
Achaïf / *Ar.*	dunes	Alt / *Germ.*	old	Aven / *Fr.*	doline, sink	Bakhtīyārī / *Pers.*	western
Ache / *Germ.*	stream	Altin / *Tur.*	lower	Awa / *Poly.*	bay	Bakki / *Icel.*	hill
Acqua / *It.*	water	Altiplano / *Sp.*	plateau	Àyios / *Gr.*	saint	Bālā / *Pers.*	high
Açu / *A.I.*	great	Alto / *Sp.; It.; Port.*	high	'Ayn / *Ar.*	spring, well	Bald / *Eng.*	peak
Açude / *Port.*	reservoir, dam	Altopiano / *It.*	plateau	'Ayoún / *Ar.*	springs, wells	Balka / *Rus.*	gorge
Ada / *Tur.*	island	Älv / *Swed.*	river	'Ayoûn / *Ar.*	spring	Balkan / *Bulg.; Tur.*	mountain range
Adalar / *Tur.*	archipelago	Am / *Kor.*	mountain, peak	Aza / *Ber.*	wadi	Ballin / *Gae.*	mouth
Adasr / *Tur.*	island	Amane / *Ber.*	water	Azraq / *Ar.*	light blue	Ballon / *Fr.*	dome
Addis / *Amh.*	new	Amba / *Amh.*	mountain	Azul / *Port.; Sp.*	light blue	Bally / *Gae.*	city, town
Adi / *Amh.*	village	Ambato / *Malag.*	rock	Azur / *Fr.*	light blue	Balta / *Rom.*	marsh
Adrar / *Ber.*	mount, mountains	An / *Gae.*	of			Báltos / *Gr.*	marsh
		An, a. / *Germ.*	on			Ban / *Laot.*	village
Aéroport / *Fr.*	airport	Ana / *Poly.*	grotto	**B**		Bana / *Jap.*	promontory
Aeroporto / *It.; Port.*	airport	Anatolikós / *Gr.*	eastern			Baña / *Slvk.*	mine
Aeropuerto / *Sp.*	airport	Äng / *Swed.*	meadow	B., Bay / *Eng.*	bay	Bañados / *Sp.*	marsh
Af / *Som.*	mouth, gorge	Angra / *Port.*	bay, anchorage	b., bei / *Germ.*	by	Banc / *Fr.*	bank
Afsluitdijk / *Dut.*	dam	Ani- / *Malag.*	center	B., Bucht / *Germ.*	bay	Banco / *It.; Sp.*	bank
Agadir / *Ber.*	castle	Áno / *Gr.*	upper	Ba / *Sud.*	river	Band / *Pers.*	dam, mountain range
Aġiz / *Tur.*	mouth	Ánou / *Gr.*	well	Ba- / *Ban.*	people		
Agro / *Sp.; It.*	plain	Anse / *Fr.*	inlet	Ba / *Mel.*	hill, mountain	Bandao / *Chin.*	peninsula
Agua / *Sp.*	water	Ant- / *Malag.*	center	Baai / *Afr.*	bay	Bandar / *Ar.; Mal.; Pers.*	port, market
Aguja / *Sp.*	needle	Ao / *Chin.; Khm.; Thai*	gulf	Bab / *Ar.*	gate	Bang / *Indon.; Mal.*	stream
Agulha / *Port.*	needle, promontory	'Áouána / *Ar.*	well	Bac / *Viet.*	north	Bangou / *Sah.*	well
Ahal / *Georg.*	new	Apă / *Rom.*	water	Bach / *Germ.*	brook, torrent	Banhado / *Port.*	marsh
Aḥmar / *Ar.*	red	'Aqabat / *Ar.*	pass	Bacino / *It.*	reservoir	Bani / *Ar.*	sons
Ahrāmāt / *Ar.*	pyramids	Aqueduc / *Fr.*	aqueduct	Back / *Eng.*	ridge	Banja / *Bulg.; S.C.; Slvn.*	thermal springs
Ahzar / *Ber.*	wadi	Ar / *Mong.*	north	Back / *Eng.*	brook	Banjaran / *Mal.*	mountain range
Aigialós / *Gr.*	coast	Ar / *Sin.; Tam.*	river	Bäck / *Swed.*	brook	Banka / *Rus.*	sandbank
Aigue / *Prov.*	water	'Aráguib / *Ar.*	hills	Backe / *Swed.*	hill	Banke / *Dan.*	bank
Aiguille / *Fr.*	needle	Arba / *Amh.*	mount	Bad, -bad / *Dan.; Germ.; Nor.; Swed.*	thermal springs	Baño / *Sp.*	thermal springs
Ain / *Ar.*	spring	Arbore / *Rom.*	tree			Banský / *Cz.*	upper
		Archipiélago / *Sp.*	archipelago	Baden, -baden / *Germ.*	thermal springs	Bánya / *Hung.*	mine
		Arcipelago / *It.*	archipelago	Bādiyat / *Ar.*	desert	Bar / *Gae.*	peak
		Ard / *Ar.*	region			Bar / *Eng.*	sandbar

Geographical Glossary

Local Form	English
Bar / Hin.	great
Bāra / Hin.	great
Bara / S.C.	pond
Barā / Urdu	great
Baraj / Tur.	dam
Baraju / Indon.; Mal.	west, western
Barkas / Lith.	castle, city, town
Barlovento / Sp.	windward
Barq / Ar.	hill
Barra / Port.; Sp.	bar, bank
Barrage / Fr.	dam
Barragem / Port.	reservoir
Barranca / Sp.	gorge
Barranco / Port.; Sp.	gorge
Barre / Fr.	bar
Barun / Mong.	western
Bas / Fr.	low
-bas / Rus.	reservoir
Bassa / Port.	flat
Bassejn / Rus.	reservoir
Bassin / Fr.	basin
Bassure / Fr.	flat
Bassurelle / Fr.	flat
Bašta / S.C.	garden
Bataille / Fr.	battle
Batalha / Port.	battle
Batang / Indon.; Mal.	river
Batha / Sah.	stream
Baţin / Ar.	depression
Bāţlāq / Pers.	marsh
Batu / Mal.	rock
Bayan / Mong.	rich
Bayır / Tur.	mountain, slope
Bayou / Fr.	branch, stream
Bayt / Ar.	house
Bazar / Pers.	market
Be / Malag.	great
Beau / Fr.	beautiful
Becken / Germ.	basin
Bed / Eng.	river bed
Beek / Dut.	creek
Be'er / Hebr.	spring
Bei / Chin.	north
Bei, b. / Germ.	by
Beida / Ar.	white
Beinn / Gae.	mount
Bel / Ar.	son
Bel / Bulg.	white
Bel / Tur.	pass
Beled / Ar.	village
Belen / Tur.	mount
Belet / Ar.	village
Beli / S.C.; Slvn.	white
Beli / Tur.	pass
Bellah / Sah.	well
Belogorje / Rus.	mountains
Belt / Dan.; Germ.	strait
Bely / Rus.	white
Bělý / Cz.	white
Ben / Ar.	son
Ben / Gae.	mount
Bender / Pers.	port, market
Bendi / Tur.	dam
Beni / Ar.	son
Beo / S.C.	white
Bereg / Rus.	bank
Berg, -berg / Afr.; Dut.; Fle.; Germ.; Nor.; Swed.	mount
Berge / Afr.	mountain
Bergen / Dut.; Fle.	dunes
Bergland / Germ.	upland
Bermejo / Sp.	red
Besar / Mal.	great
Betsu / Jap.	river
Betta / Tam.	mountain
Bhani / Hin.	community
Bharu / Mal.	new
Bheag / Gae.	little
Bīābān / Pers.	desert
Biały / Pol.	white
Bianco / It.	white
Bien / Viet.	lake
Bight / Eng.	bay
Bijeli / S.C.	white
Bill / Eng.	promontory
Bilo / S.C.	range
Bílý / Cz.	white
Binnen / Dut.; Fle.; Germ.	inner
Biqā' / Ar.	valley
Bir / Ar.	well
Bi'r / Ar.	well
Birkat / Ar.	pond
Bistrica / Bulg.; S.C.; Slvn.	stream
Bjarg / Icel.	rock
Bjerg / Dan.	mount
Bjeshkët / Alb.	mountain pasture
Blaauw / Afr.	blue
Blanc / Fr.	white
Blanco / Sp.	white
Blau / Germ.	blue
Bleu / Fr.	blue
Bluff / Eng.	cliff
Bo- / Ban.	people
Bo / Chin.	white
Bo / Swed.	habitation
Boca / Sp.	gap, mouth

Local Form	English
Bôca / Port.	gap, mouth
Bocage / Fr.	forest
Bocca / It.	gap, pass
Bocchetta / It.	gap, pass
Bodden / Germ.	bay, lagoon
Boden / Germ.	soil
Bœng / Khm.	lake, marsh
Bog / Eng.	marsh
Bogaz / Alt.; Az.; Tur.	strait
Bogāzi / Tur.	strait
Bogdo / Mong.	high
Bogen / Nor.	bay
Bois / Fr.	forest
Boka / S.C.	channel
Boloto / Rus.	marsh
Bolšoj / Rus.	great
Bolsón / Sp.	basin
Bom / Port.	good
Bong / Kor.	peak
Bongo / Malag.	upland
Bor / Cz.; Rus.	coniferous forest
Bór / Pol.	forest
-bor / Slvn.	city, town
Bóras / Gr.	north
Börde / Germ.	fertile plain
Bordj / Ar.	fort
Bóreios / Gr.	northern
Borg, -borg / Dan.; Nor.; Swed.	castle
Borgo / It.	village
Born / Germ.	spring
Bory / Pol.	forest
Bosch / Dut.; Fle.	forest
Bosco / It.	wood
Bosque / Sp.	forest
Bosse / Fr.	hill
Botn / Nor.	bay
Bou / Ar.	father, master
Bouche / Fr.	mouth
Boula / Sud.	well
Bourg / Fr.	city, town
Bourne, - bourne / Eng.	frontier
Boven / Afr.	upper
Boz / Tur.	grey
Bozorg / Pers.	great
Brána / Cz.	gate
Braña / Sp.	mountain pasture
Branche / Fr.	branch
Branco / Port.	white
Braţul / Rom.	branch
Bravo / Sp.	wild
Brazo / Sp.	branch
Brdo / Cz.; S.C.	hill
Bre / Nor.	glacier
Bredning / Dan.	bay
Breg / Alb.; Bulg.; S.C.	hill, coast
Brjag / Bulg.	bank
Bro / Dan.; Nor.; Swed.	bridge
Brod / Bulg.; Cz.; Rus.; S.C.; Slvk.; Slvn.	ford
Bród / Pol.	ford
Bron / Afr.	spring
Bronn / Germ.	spring
Bru / Nor.	bridge
Bruch / Germ.	peat-bog
Bruchzone / Germ.	fracture zone
Bruck, -bruck / Germ.	bridge
Brücke / Germ.	bridge
Brug / Dut.; Fle.	bridge
Brugge / Dut.; Fle.	bridge
Bruk / Nor.	factory
Brunn / Swed.	spring
-brunn / Swed.	spring
Brunnen / Germ.	spring
Brygg / Swed.	bridge
Brzeg / Pol.	coast
Bū / Ar.	father, master
Bucht, B. / Germ.	bay
Bugt / Dan.	bay
Buḩayrat / Ar.	lake, lagoon
Bühel / Germ.	hill
Bühl / Germ.	hill
Buhta / Rus.	bay
Bukit / Mal.	mountain, peak
Bukt / Nor.; Swed.	bay
Buku / Indon.	hill, mountain
Bulag / Mong.; Tur.	spring
Bulak / Mong.; Tur.	spring
Būlāq / Tur.	spring
Bult / Afr.	hill
Bulu / Indon.	mountain
Bur / Som.	mount
Bür / Ar.	port
Burg, - burg / Afr.; Ar.; Dut.; Eng.; Germ.	castle
Burgh / Eng.	city, town
Burgo / Sp.	village
Burha / Hin.	old
Buri / Thai	city, town
Burj / Ar.	village
Burn / Eng.	stream
Burnu / Tur.	promontory
Burqat / Ar.	mount, marsh
Burun / Tur.	cape
Busen / Germ.	bay
Busu / Ban.	land
Būtat / Ar.	lake, pond
Butte / Eng.; Fr.	flat-topped hill

Local Form	English
Büyük / Tur.	great
By / Eng.	near
By, -by / Dan.; Nor.; Swed.	city, town
Bystrica / Cz.; Slvk.	stream
Bystrzyca / Pol.	stream

C

Local Form	English
C., Cap / Cat.; Fr.; Rom.	cape
C., Cape / Eng.	cape
C., Colle / It.	pass
Caatinga / A.I.	forest
Cabeça / Port.	peak
Cabeço / Port.	peak
Cabeza / Sp.	peak
Cabezo / Sp.	peak, mountain
Cabo / Port.; Sp.	cape
Cachoeira / Port.	waterfall, rapids
Cachopo / Port.	reef
Cadena / Sp.	range
Caer / Wel.	castle
Cagan / Cauc.; Mong.	white
Cairn / Gae.	hill
Čāj / Az.; Tur.	river
Cajdam / Mong.	salt marsh
Caka / Chin.	lake
Cala / Sp.; It.	inlet
Calar / Sp.	plateau
Caldas / Sp.; Port.	thermal springs
Caleta / Sp.	inlet
Camp / Cat.; Fr.; Eng.	field
Campagna / It.	plain
Campagne / Fr.	plain
Campo / Sp.; It.; Port.	field
Cañada / Sp.	gorge, ravine
Canale / It.	canal, channel
Caño / Sp.	branch
Cañón / Sp.	gorge
Canyon / Eng.	gorge
Cao / Viet.	mountain
Cap, C. / Cat.; Fr.; Rom.	cape
Càrn / Gae.	peak
Carrera / Sp.	road
Carrick / Gae.	rock
Casale / It.	hamlet
Cascada / Sp.	waterfall
Cascata / It.	waterfall
Castel / It.	castle
Castell / Cat.	castle
Castello / It.	castle
Castelo / Port.	castle
Castillo / Sp.	castle
Castro / Sp.; It.	village
Catarata / Sp.	cataract
Catena / It.	mountain range
Catinga / Port.	degraded forest
Cauce / Sp.	river bed
Causse / Fr.	highland
Cava / It.	stone quarry
Çay / Tur.	river
Cay / Eng.	islet, island
Caye / Fr.	island
Cayo / Sp.	islet, island
Ceann / Gae.	promontory
Centralny / Rus.	middle
Čeren / Alb.	black
Černi / Bulg.	black
Černý / Cz.	black
Čërny / Rus.	black
Cerrillo / Sp.	hill
Cerrito / Sp.	hill
Cerro / Sp.; Port.	hill, mountain
Cêrro / Port.	hill, mountain
Červen / Bulg.	red
Červony / Rus.	red
Cetate / Rom.	city, town
Chaco / Sp.	scrubland
Chāh / Pers.	well
Chaïf / Ar.	dunes
Chaîne / Fr.	mountain range
Champ / Fr.	field
Chang / Chin.	highland
Chapada / Port.	highland
Chapadão / Port.	highland
Château / Fr.	castle
Châtel / Fr.	castle
Chây / Tur.	river
Chedo / Kor.	archipelago
Chenal / Fr.	canal
Cheng / Chin.	city, town, wall
Cheon / Kor.	city, river
Chergui / Ar.	eastern
Cherry, -cherry / Hin.; Tam.	city, town
Chew / Amh.	salt mine, salt
Chhǎk / Khm.	bay
Chhotla / Hin.	little
Chi- / Ban.	great
Chi / Chin.	marsh, lake
Chi / Kor.	lake, pond
Chi- / Swa.	land
Chiang / Thai	city, town
Chico / Sp.	little
Chine / Eng.	ridge
Ch'on / Kor.	station

Local Form	English
Ch'ŏn / Kor.	river
Chôsuji / Kor.	reservoir
Chott / Ar.	salt marsh
Chu / Chin.; Viet.	mountain, hill
Chuŏr phnum / Khm.	mountain range
Chute / Fr.	waterfall
Chutes / Fr.	waterfalls
Cidade / Port.	city, town
Ciems / Latv.	village
Čierny / Slvk.	black
Cime / It.	peak
Cîmp / Rom.	field
Cîmpie / Rom.	plain
Cinco / Sp.; Port.	five
Citeli / Georg.	red
Città / It.	city, town
Ciudad / Sp.	city, town
Ckali / Georg.	water
Ckaro / Georg.	spring
Co / Chin.	lake
Col / Cat.; Fr.	pass
Colina / Port.; Sp.	hill
Coll / Cat.	hill
Collado / Sp.	pass
Colle, C. / It.	pass
Collina / It.	hill
Colline / Fr.	hill
Colonia / Sp.; It.	colony
Coma / Sp.	hill country
Comb / Eng.	basin
Comba / Sp.	basin
Combe / Fr.	basin
Comtė / Fr.	county, shire
Con / Viet.	island
Conca / It.	depression
Condado / Sp.	county, shire
Cone / Eng.	volcanic cone
Cône / Fr.	volcanic cone
Contraforte / Port.	front range
Cordal / Sp.	crest
Cordilheira / Port.	mountain range
Cordillera / Sp.	mountain range
Coring / Chin.	lake
Corixa / A.I.	stream
Corno / It.	peak
Cornone / It.	peak
Corrente / It.; Port.	stream
Corriente / Sp.	stream
Costa / Sp.; It.; Port.	coast
Côte / Fr.	coast
Coteau / Fr.	height, slope
Coxilha / Port.	ridge
Craig / Gae.	rock
Cratère / Fr.	crater
Cresta / Sp.; It.	crest
Crêt / Fr.	crest
Crête / Fr.	crest
Crkva / S.C.	church
Crni / S.C.; Slvn.	black
Crven / S.C.	red
Csatorna / Hung.	canal
Cuchilla / Sp.	ridge
Cuenca / Sp.	basin
Cuesta / Sp.	escarpment
Cueva / Sp.	cave
Čuka / Bulg.; S.C.	peak
Çukur / Tur.	well
Cu Lao / Viet.	island
Cumbre / Sp.	peak
Cun / Chin.	village
Cura / A.I.	stone
Curr / Alb.	rock
Cy., City / Eng.	city, town
Czarny / Pol.	black

D

Local Form	English
Da / Chin.	great
Da / Viet.	mountain, peak
Daal / Dut.; Fle.	valley
Daba / Mong.	pass
Daba / Som.	hill
Daban / Chin.; Mong.	pass
Dae / Kor.	great
Dağ / Tur.	mountain
Dağ., Dağı / Tur.	mountain
Dāgh / Pers.; Tur.	mountain
Dağı, Dağ. / Tur.	mountain
Dağları / Tur.	mountain range
Dahar / Ar.	hill
Dahr / Ar.	plateau, escarpment
Dai / Chin.; Jap.	great
Daiet / Ar.	marsh
Dak / Viet.	stream
Dake / Jap.	mountain
Dakhla / Ar.	depression
Dakhlet / Ar.	depression, bay
Dal, -dal / Afr.; Dan.; Dut.; Fle.; Nor.; Swed.	valley
Dala / Alt.	steppe, plain
Dalaj / Mong.	lake, sea
Dalan / Mong.	wall
Dallol / Sud.	valley, torrent
Dalur / Icel.	valley
Damm / Germ.	dam
Dan / Kor.	point

Local Form	English
Danau / Indon.	lake
Danda / Nep.	mountains
Dao / Chin.	island, peninsula
Dao / Viet.	island
Dar / Ar.	house, region
Dar / Swa.	port
Dara / Tur.	torrent, valley
Darb / Ar.	track
Darja / Alt.	river, sea
Darya, Daryā / Pers.	river, sea
Daryācheh / Pers.	lake, sea
Daš / Alt.; Az.	rock
Dasht / Pers.	desert, plain
Dawḥat / Ar.	bay
Dayr / Ar.	convent
De / Sp.; Fr.	of
Deal / Rom.	hill
Dearg / Gae.	red
Debre / Amh.	hill, monastery
Dega / Som.	stone
Deh / Pers.	village
Dêḥ / Som.	stream
Deich / Germ.	dike
Dél / Hung.	south
Delft / Dut.; Fle.	deep
Delger / Mong.	wide, market
-den / Eng.	city, town
Deniz / Tur.	sea
Denizi / Tur.	sea
Dent / Fr.	peak
Deo / Laot.; Viet.	pass
Dépression / Fr.	depression
Depressione / It.	depression
Der / Som.	high
Dera / Hin.; Urdu	temple
Derbent / Tur.	gorge, pass
Dere / Tur.	river, valley
Désert / Fr.	desert
Desfiladero / Sp.	pass
Desh / Hin.	land, country
Desierto / Sp.	desert
Det / Alb.	sea
Détroit / Fr.	strait
Deux / Fr.	two
Dezh / Pers.	castle
Dhar / Ar.	heights, hills
Dhār / Hin.; Urdu	mountain
Dhitikós / Gr.	western
Dien / Khm.; Viet.	rice-field
Diep / Dut.; Fle.	deep, strait
Dijk, -dijk / Dut.; Fle.	dam
Ding / Chin.	mountain, peak
Dique / Sp.	dam
Di Sopra / It.	upper
Di Sotto / It.	lower
Distrito / Sp.; Port.	district
Diu / Hin.	island
Diz / Pers.	castle
Djebel / Ar.	mountain
Dji / Ban.	water
Djup / Swed.	deep
Do / Kor.	Island
Do / S.C.	valley
Dō / Jap.	island, administrative division
Dōho / Som.	valley
Doi / Thai	mountain, peak
Dol / Bulg.; Cz.; Rus.; S.C.	valley
Dol / Pol.	valley
Dolen / Bulg.	low
Dolgi / Rus.	long
Dolina / Bulg.; Cz.; Pol.; Rus.; S.C.; Slvn.	valley
Dolni / Bulg.	low
Dolni / Pol.	lower
Dolny / Pol.	lower
Domb / Hung.	hill
Dôme / Fr.	dome
Dong / Chin.; Viet.	east
Dong / Kor.	city, town
Dong / Thai	mountain
Dong / Viet.	marsh, plain
Donji / S.C.	low, lower
Dorf, -dorf / Germ.	village
Doroga / Rus.	road
Dorp, -dorp / Afr.; Dut.; Fle.	village
Dos / Rom.	ridge
Dos / Sp.	two
Douarn / Br.	land
Dougou / Sud.	settlement
Doukou / Sud.	settlement
Down / Eng.	hill
Drâa / Ar.	dunes, hills
Dracht / Germ.	sandbank
Draw / Eng.	ravine, valley
Drif / Afr.	ford
Drift / Afr.	ford
Droichead / Gae.	bridge
Droûs / Ar.	crest
Dry / Pash.	river
Dubh / Gae.	black
Dugi / S.C.	long
Dugu / Sud.	settlement
Dun / Gae.	castle
Duna / Sp.; It.	dune
Düne / Germ.	dune
Dungar / Hin.	mountain
Düngar / Hin.	mountain
Duong / Viet.	stream
Durchbruch / Germ.	gorge
Ḍurg / Hin.	castle
-durga / Hin.	castle
Duży / Pol.	great
Dvor / Cz.	court
Dvorec / Rus.	castle
Dvůr / Cz.	castle
Dwór / Pol.	court
Džebel / Bulg.	mountain
Dzong / Tib.	fort, monastery

E

Local Form	English
Ea / Thai	river
Eau / Fr.	water
Ebe / Ban.	forest
Ebene / Germ.	plain
Eck / Germ.	point
Eclusa / Sp.	lock
Écluse / Fr.	lock
Écueil / Fr.	cliff
Edeien / Ber.	sand desert
Edjérir / Ber.	wadi
Egg / Germ.; Nor.	crest, point
Eglab / Ar.	hills
Ehi / Sah.	mountain
Eid / Nor.	isthmus
Eiland / Afr.	island
Eisen / Germ.	iron
Eisenerz / Germ.	iron ore
El / Amh.	well
Elv, -elv / Nor.	river
Embalse / Sp.	reservoir
Embouchure / Fr.	mouth
Emi / Sah.	mountain
En / Fr.	in
Ende / Germ.	end
Enneri / Sah.	stream
Ennis / Gae.	island
Enseada / Port.	Bay, inlet
Ensenada / Sp.	bay, inlet
Ér / Hung.	stream
Erdö / Hung.	forest
Erg / Ar.	sand desert
Erz / Germ.	ore
Espigão / Port.	plateau
Êstān / Pers.	land
Este / Sp.	east
Estero / Sp.	estuary, marsh
Estrecho / Sp.	strait
Estreito / Port.	strait
Estuaire / Fr.	estuary
Estuário / Port.	estuary
Estuario / Sp.; It.	estuary
Észak / Hung.	north
Étang / Fr.	pond
Ewaso / Ban.	river
Ey / Icel.	island
Eyja / Icel.	island
Eyjar / Icel.	islands
Eylandt / Dut.	island
Ežeras / Lith.	lake
Ezers / Latv.	lake

F

Local Form	English
Fa / Mel.	stream
Falaise / Fr.	cliff
Fall, -fall / Germ.; Eng.; Swed.	waterfall
Falls / Eng.	waterfall
Falu / Hung.	village
-falva / Hung.	village
Fan / Sah.	village
Faraglione / It.	cliff
Farallón / Sp.	cliff
Faro / Sp.; It.	lighthouse
Farvand / Dan.	strait
Fehér / Hung.	white
Fehn / Germ.	peat fen, peat-bog
Fekete / Hung.	black
Feld / Dan.; Germ.	field
Fell / Eng.	upland moor
Fell / Bas.	torrent
Fell / Icel.	mountain
Fels / Germ.	rock
Fen / Eng.	marsh, peat-bog
Feng / Chin.	mountain, peak
Feste / Germ.	fort
Festung / Germ.	fort
Fier / Rom.	iron
Firn / Germ.	snow-field
Firth / Eng.	estuary, fjord
Fiume / It.	river
Fjäll / Swed.	mountain
Fjärd / Swed.	fjord
Fjell / Nor.	mountain
Fjöll / Icel.	mountain
Fjord, Fj. / Dan.; Nor.; Swed.	fjord
Fjörður / Icel.	fjord, bay
Fleuve / Fr.	river
Fließ / Germ.	torrent
Fljót / Icel.	river
Flój / Icel.	bay, gulf
Floresta / Sp.; Port.	forest
Flow / Eng.	strait
Flughafen / Germ.	airport
Fluß / Germ.	river
Fo / Mel.	stream
Foa / Mel.	stream
Foa / Poly.	cove
Foce / It.	mouth
Föld / Hung.	plain
Fonn / Nor.	glacier
Fontaine / Fr.	fountain
Fonte / It.; Port.	spring
Fontein / Afr.; Dut.	spring
Foort / Afr.; Dut.	ford
Forca / It.	pass
Forcella / It.	defile
Ford / Rus.	fjord
Förde / Germ.	fjord, gulf
Foreland / Eng.	promontory
Foresta / It.	forest
Forêt / Fr.	forest
Fors / Swed.	rapids, waterfall
Forst / Germ.; Dut.	forest
Forte / It.; Port.	fort
Fortin / Sp.	fort
Fosa / Sp.	trench
Foss / Icel.; Nor.	rapids, waterfall
Fossé / Fr.	trench
Foum / Ar.	pass
Fourche / Fr.	pass
Foz / Sp.; Port.	mouth
Frei / Germ.	free
Fronteira / Port.	frontier
Frontera / Sp.	frontier
Frontón / Sp.	promontory
Fuente / Sp.	spring
Fuerte / Sp.	fort
Fuji / Jap.	mountain
Fūlat / Ar.	marsh
Furt / Germ.	ford
Fushë / Alb.	plain

G

Local Form	English
G., Gora / Bulg.; Rus.; S.C.	mountain, hill
G., Gunung / Indon.	mountain
Ga / Jap.	bay
Ga / Mel.	mountain, peak
Gabel / Germ.	pass
Gaissa / Lapp.	mountain
Gala / Sin.; Tam.	mountain
Gam / Hin.; Urdu	village
Gamle / Nor.; Swed.	old
Gana / Sud.	little
Gang / Germ.	passage
Gang / Chin.	port, bay
Gang / Kor.	stream, bay
Gang / Tib.	glacier
Ganga / Hin.	river
Ganj / Hin.; Urdu	market
-gaon / Hin.	city, town
Gaoyuan / Chin.	plateau
Gap / Kor.	point
Gar / Hin.	house
Gara / Bulg.	station
Gara / Ar.	hills, range
Gară / Rom.	station
Garaet / Ar.	marsh, intermittent lake
Garam / Beng.; Hin.; Urdu	village
-gard / Pol.	city, town
Gård, -gård / Dan.; Nor.; Swed.	farmhouse
Gardaneh / Pers.	pass
Gare / Fr.	railway station
Garet / Ar.	hill
Garh, -garh / Hin.; Urdu	castle
Garhi / Hin.; Nep.; Urdu	fort
Garten / Germ.	garden
Gat / Dan.; Fle.; Dut.	strait
Gata / Jap.	bay, lake
Gau / Germ.	district
Gau, -gau / Germ.	district
Gău, -gău / Germ.	district
Gavan / Rus.	port
Gave / Bas.	torrent
Gawa / Jap.	river
Geb., Gebirge / Germ.	mountain range
Gebergte / Afr.; Dut.	mountain range
Gebirge, Geb. / Germ.	mountain range
Geç., Geçit / Tur.	pass
Geçidi / Tur.	pass
Geçit, Geç. / Tur.	pass
Geysir / Icel.	geyser
Ghar / Hin.; Urdu	house
Ghar / Pash.	mountain, mountain range
Gharbīyah / Ar.	western
Ghat / Hin.; Nep.; Urdu	pass
Ghubbat / Ar.	bay
Ghurd / Ar.	dune
Gi / Kor.	peninsula
Giang / Viet.	stream
Giri / Hin.; Urdu	mountain, hill
Girlo / Rus.	branch
Gjebel / Ar.	mountain
Gji / Alb.	bay
Glace / Fr.	ice
Glaciar / Sp.	glacier
Glacier / Eng.; Fr.	glacier
Glen / Gae.	valley
Gletscher / Germ.	glacier
Gobi / Mong.	desert
Godār / Pers.	ford
Gok / Kor.	river
Gök / Tur.	blue
Gol / Cauc.; Mong.	river
Göl / Tur.	lake
Gola / It.	gorge
Gold / Germ.; Eng.	gold
Golet / S.C.	mountain
Golf / Germ.	gulf
Golfe / Fr.	gulf
Golfete / Sp.	inlet
Golfo / Sp.; It.; Port.	gulf
Goljam / Bulg.	great
Gölü / Tur.	lake
Gong / Tib.	high
Gonggar / Tib.	mountain
Gongo / Ban.	mountain
Góra / Pol.	mountain
Gora, G. / Bulg.; Rus.; S.C.	mountain, hill
Gorica / S.C.; Slvn.	hill
Gorje / S.C.	mountain range
Gorlo / Rus.	gorge
Gorm / Gae.	blue
Gorni / Bulg.; S.C.; Slvn.	upper
Gornji / S.C.; Slvn.	upper
Górny / Pol.	high
Gorod / Rus.	city, town
Gorodok / Rus.	village
Gorski / Bulg.	upper
Gory / Rus.	mountains
-gou / Chin.	river
Goulbi / Sud.	river, lake
Goulbin / Sud.	wadi
Goulet / Fr.	gap
Gour / Ar.	hills, range
Gourou / Sud.	wadi
Goz / Sah.	dune
Graafschap / Dut.	county, shire
Graben / Germ.	ditch, canal
Gracht / Dut.	canal
Grad, -grad / Bulg.; Rus.; S.C.; Slvn.	city, town, castle
Gradac / S.C.	castle
Gradec / Bulg.	village
Gradec / S.C.	castle
Græn / Icel.	green
Gran / Sp.; It.	great
Grande / Sp.; It.; Port.	great
Grao / Cat.; Sp.	gap
Grat / Germ.	crest
Grève / Fr.	beach
Grind / Germ.	peak
Grjada / Rus.	range
Gród, -gród / Pol.	castle, city, town
Grön / Icel.	green
Grond / Afr.	soil
Gronden / Dut.; Fle.	flat
Groot / Afr.; Dut.; Fle.	great
Groß / Germ.	great
Grotta / It.	grotto
Grotte / Fr.; Germ.	grotto
Grube / Germ.	mine
Grün / Germ.	green
Grunn / Nor.	ground
Gruppe / Germ.	mountain system
Gruppo / It.	mountain system
Gua / Mal.	cave
Guaçu / A.I.	great
Guan / Chin.	pass
Guazú / A.I.	great
Guba / Rus.	bay
Guchi / Jap.	strait
Guelb / Ar.	hill, mountain
Guelta / Ar.	well
Guic / Br.	village
Güney / Tur.	south, southern
Gunong / Mal.	mountain
Guntō / Jap.	archipelago
Gunung, G. / Indon.	mountain
Guo / Chin.	state, land
Gur / Mong.	mountain
Guri / Jap.	cliff
Gurud / Ar.	hills, dunes
Gyár / Hung.	factory

H

Local Form	English
Haag / Dut.; Fle.	hedge
-hâb / Dan.	port
Ḥaḍabat / Ar.	highland
Hadd / Ar.	point
Hadjer / Ar.	hill, mountain
Hae / Kor.	bay, sea
Haehyeop / Kor.	strait

Geographical Glossary

Local Form	English
Haf / *Icel.*	sea
Ḩafar / *Ar.*	well
Hafen / *Germ.*	port
Haff / *Germ.*	lagoon
Hafir / *Ar.*	spring, ditch
Hafnar / *Icel.*	port
Hāfūn / *Som.*	bay
Hage / *Dan.*	point
Hage / *Dut.; Fle.*	hedge
Hågna / *Swed.*	peak
Hai / *Chin.*	sea, lake, bay
Hain / *Germ.*	forest
Haixia / *Chin.*	strait
Ḩajar / *Ar.*	hill, mountain
Hajar / *Ar.*	hill country
Halbinsel / *Germ.*	peninsula
Halma / *Hung.*	hill
Halom / *Hung.*	hill
Halq / *Ar.*	gap
Hals / *Nor.*	peninsula
Halvø / *Dan.*	peninsula
Halvøy / *Nor.*	peninsula
Hama / *Jap.*	beach
Hamāda / *Ar.*	rocky desert
Ḩamādah / *Ar.*	plateau
Ḩamādat / *Ar.*	plateau
Hammam / *Ar.*	thermal springs
Ḩammām / *Ar.*	well
Hamn / *Nor.; Swed.*	port
Hamrā' / *Ar.*	red
Hāmūn / *Jap.*	salt lake
Hana / *Jap.*	cape
Hana / *Poly.*	bay
Hane / *Tur.*	house
Hang / *Kor.*	port
Hank / *Ar.*	escarpment, plateau
Hantō / *Jap.*	peninsula
Har / *Hebr.*	mountain
Hara / *Mong.*	black
Harar / *Swa.*	well
Ḩarrah / *Ar.*	lava field
Ḩarrat / *Ar.*	lava field
Hasi / *Ar.*	well
Ḩasi / *Ar.*	well
Hassi / *Ar.*	well
Ḩasy / *Ar.*	well
Haug / *Nor.*	hill
Haupt- / *Germ.*	principal
Haure / *Lapp.*	lake
Haus / *Germ.*	house
Hausen / *Germ.*	village
Haut / *Fr.*	high
Hauteur / *Fr.*	hill
Hauts Plateaux / *Fr.*	highlands
Hauz / *Pers.*	reservoir
Hav / *Dan.; Nor.; Swed.*	sea, gulf
Haven / *Eng.; Fle.; Dut.*	port
Havn / *Dan.; Nor.*	port
Havre / *Fr.*	port
Hawr / *Ar.*	lake, marsh
Ház / *Hung.*	house
-háza / *Hung.*	house
Hazm / *Ar.*	height, mountain range
He / *Chin.*	river
Head / *Eng.*	headland
Hed / *Dan.; Swed.*	heath
Hegy / *Hung.*	mountain
Hegység / *Hung.*	mountain
Hei / *Nor.*	heath
Heide / *Germ.*	heath
Heijde / *Dut.; Fle.*	heath
Heilig / *Germ.*	saint
Heim, -heim / *Germ.; Nor.*	house
Heiya / *Jap.*	plain
-hely / *Hung.*	locality
Hem / *Swed.*	home
Hen / *Br.*	old
Higashi / *Jap.*	east, eastern
Hima / *Hin.*	ice
Himal / *Nep.*	peak
Hisar / *Tur.*	castle
Ho / *Chin.*	reservoir, river
Ho / *Kor.*	river, reservoir
Hō / *Jap.*	mountain
Hoch / *Germ.*	high, upper
Hochland / *Germ.*	highland
Hochplato / *Afr.*	highland
Hodna / *Ar.*	highland
Hoek / *Dut.; Fle.*	cape
Hof / *Dut.; Germ.*	court
Höfn / *Icel.*	port
Høg / *Nor.*	peak
Hög / *Swed.*	mountain
Hogna / *Nor.*	peak
Höhe / *Germ.*	peak
Høj / *Dan.*	hill
Hoj / *Ural.*	mountain range
Hok / *Jap.*	north
Hoku / *Jap.*	north, northern
Holm / *Dan.; Nor.; Swed.*	island
Holz / *Germ.*	forest
Hon / *Viet.*	island, point
Hong / *Chin.; Viet.*	red
Hono / *Poly.*	bay, anchorage
Hoog / *Afr.; Dut.; Fle.*	high
Hook / *Eng.*	point
Hoorn / *Afr.; Dut.; Fle.*	cape, point
Hora / *Cz.; Slvk.*	point
Horn / *Eng.; Germ.; Icel.; Nor.; Swed.*	point
Horni / *Cz.*	high
Horný / *Slvk.*	upper
Horst / *Germ.*	mountain
Horvot / *Hebr.*	ruins
Hory / *Cz.; Slvk.*	mountain range
Hout / *Dut.; Fle.*	forest
Hovd, -hovd / *Dan.; Nor.*	cape
Ḩowz / *Pers.*	basin
Hrad / *Cz.; Slvk.*	castle, city, town
Hradiště / *Cz.*	citadel
Hřeben / *Cz.*	crest
Hrebet / *Rus.*	mountain range
Hu / *Rmsh.*	lake
Huang / *Chin.*	yellow
Hude / *Germ.*	pasture
Huerta / *Sp.*	market garden
Hügel / *Germ.*	hill
Hügelland / *Germ.*	hill country
Huis, -huis / *Afr.; Dut.; Fle.*	house
Huisie / *Afr.*	house
Huizen, -huizen / *Dut.*	houses
Huk / *Afr.; Dan.; Swed.*	cape
Hum / *S.C.*	hill
Hurst / *Eng.*	grove
Hus / *Dut.; Nor.; Swed.*	house
Huta / *Pol.; Slvk.*	hut
Hütte / *Germ.*	hut
Hver / *Icel.*	crater
Hvit / *Icel.*	white
Hvost / *Rus.*	spit

I

Local Form	English
I., Island / *Eng.*	island
Ierós / *Gr.*	holy
Igarapé / *A.I.*	river
Ighazer / *Ber.*	torrent
Ighil / *Ber.*	hill
Iguidi / *Ber.*	dunes
Ih / *Mong.*	great
Ike / *Jap.*	pond
Ile / *Fr.*	island
Ilha / *Port.*	island
Iller / *Tur.*	administrative division
Ilot / *Fr.*	islet
Imi / *Ar.*	spring
I-n / *Ber.*	well
Inch / *Gae.*	island
Inder / *Dan.; Nor.*	inner
Indre / *Nor.*	inner
Inferiore / *It.*	lower
Inish / *Gae.*	island
Insel / *Germ.*	island
Insulă / *Rom.*	island
Inver / *Gae.*	mouth
Irhazér / *Ber.*	wadi
Irmak / *Tur.*	river
'Irq / *Ar.*	dunes
Is / *Nor.*	glacier
Ís / *Icel.*	ice
Isblink / *Dan.*	glacier
Ishi / *Jap.*	rock
Iske / *Alt.*	old
Isla / *Sp.*	island
Iso / *Finn.*	great
Iso / *Jap.*	cliff
Isola / *It.*	island
Isthmós / *Gr.*	isthmus
Istmo / *Sp.; It.*	isthmus
Ita / *A.I.*	stone
Itä / *Finn.*	east
Itivdleq / *Esk.*	isthmus
Iwa / *Jap.*	rock, cliff
Iztočni / *Bulg.*	eastern
Izvor / *Bulg.; Rom.; S.C.; Slvn.*	spring

J

Local Form	English
J., Jazīrat / *Ar.*	island
J., Jiang / *Chin.*	river
Jabal / *Ar.*	mountain
Jaha / *Ural.*	river
Jam / *Ural.*	lake, river
Jama / *Rus.*	cave
Jan / *Alt.*	great
Janga / *Tur.*	north
Jangi / *Alt.; Iran.*	new
Janūbīyah / *Ar.*	southern
Jar / *Rus.*	bank
Järv / *Est.*	lake
Järve / *Finn.*	lake
Järvi / *Finn.*	lake
Jasirēd / *Som.*	island
Jaun / *Latv.*	new
Jaur / *Lapp.*	lake
Jaure / *Lapp.*	lake
Javr / *Lapp.*	lake
Javrre / *Lapp.*	lake
Jazā'ir / *Ar.*	islands
Jazīrat, J. / *Ar.*	island
Jazovir / *Bulg.*	reservoir
Jbel / *Ar.*	mountain
Jebel / *Ar.*	mountain
Jedid / *Ar.*	new
Jedo / *Kor.*	archipelago
Jezero / *S.C.; Slvn.*	lake
Jezioro / *Pol.*	lake
Jhil / *Hin.; Urdu*	lake
Jian / *Chin.*	mountain
Jiang, J. / *Chin.*	river
Jiao / *Chin.*	cape, cliff
Jibāl / *Ar.*	mountain
Jih / *Cz.*	south
Jima / *Jap.*	island
Jin / *Kor.*	cove
Jing / *Chin.*	spring
Jisr / *Ar.*	bridge
Joch / *Germ.*	pass
Jõgi / *Est.*	river
Jøkel / *Nor.*	glacier
Joki / *Finn.*	river
Jokka / *Lapp.*	river
Jökull / *Icel.*	glacier
Jord, -jord / *Nor.*	earth
Ju / *Ural.*	river
Judeţ / *Rom.*	district
Jugan / *Ural.*	river
Jura / *Lith.*	sea
Jūra / *Latv.*	sea
Jūras Līcis / *Latv.*	bay
Jūrmala / *Latv.*	beach
Jurt / *Cauc.*	village
Južni / *Bulg.; S.C.; Slvn.*	southern
Južny / *Rus.*	southern
Juzur / *Ar.*	islands

K

Local Form	English
Ka / *Poly.*	lake
Kaap / *Afr.*	cape
Kabīr / *Ar.*	great
Kae / *Kor.*	inlet
Kāf / *Ar.*	peak, mountain
Kafr / *Ar.*	village
Kaga / *Ban.*	hills, mountain range
Kahal / *Ar.*	plateau, escarpment
Kai / *Jap.*	sea
Kaikyō / *Jap.*	strait
Kaise / *Lapp.*	mountain
Kal / *Pers.*	stream
Kala / *Az.; Kor.*	fort
Kala / *Finn.*	river
Kala / *Hin.*	black
Kala / *Tur.*	castle
Kalaa / *Ar.*	castle
Kalaki / *Georg.*	city, town
Kale / *Tur.*	castle
Kali / *Hin.*	black
Kali / *Indon.; Mal.*	bay, river
Kallio / *Finn.*	rock
Kaln / *Latv.*	mountain
Kalós / *Gr.*	beautiful, good
Kamen / *Bulg.; Rus.; S.C.; Slvn.*	mountain, peak
Kámen / *Cz.*	rock
Kameň / *Slvk.*	rock
Kami / *Jap.*	upper
Kamień / *Pol.*	rock
Kamm / *Germ.*	crest
Kamp / *Germ.*	field
Kâmpóng / *Khm.*	village
Kámpos / *Gr.*	field
Kampung / *Indon.; Mal.*	village
Kan., Kanal / *Alb.; Dan.; Germ.; Nor.; Rus.; S.C.; Slvn.; Swed.; Tur.*	canal, channel
Kanaal / *Dut.; Fle.*	canal
Kanał / *Pol.*	canal
Kanal, Kan. / *Alb.; Dan.; Germ.; Nor.; Rus.; S.C.; Slvn.; Swed.; Tur.*	canal, channel
Kand, -kand / *Pers.; Tur.*	city, town
Kang / *Chin.; Kor.*	bay, river
Kangas / *Fle.*	heath
Kange / *Esk.*	east
Kangri / *Tib.*	snow-capped mountain
Kantara / *Ar.*	bridge
Kaôh / *Khm.*	island
Kap / *Dan.; Germ.*	cape
Kapija / *S.C.*	gate, gorge
Kapp / *Nor.*	cape
Kar / *Tib.*	white
Kar / *Ural.*	city, town
Kara / *Tur.*	black
Karang / *Indon.; Mal.*	sandbank, cliff
Kari / *Finn.*	cliff
Kariba / *Ban.*	gorge
Kariet / *Ar.*	village
Karki / *Finn.*	peninsula
Kastel / *Germ.*	castle
Kástron / *Gr.*	fort, city, town
Káto / *Gr.*	lower
Kaupstadur / *Icel.*	city, town
Kaupunki / *Finn.*	city, town
Kavīr / *Pers.*	salt desert
Kawa / *Jap.*	river
Kawm / *Ar.*	hill
Kebir / *Ar.*	great
Kedi / *Georg.*	mountain range
Kédia / *Ar.*	mountain, plateau
Kedim / *Ar.*	old
Kef / *Ar.*	mountain
Kefála / *Gr.*	mountain, peak
Kefar / *Hebr.*	village
Kei / *Jap.*	river
Kelet / *Hung.*	east
Ken / *Gae.*	cape
Kent / *Alt.; Iran.; Tur.*	city, town
Kenya / *Swa.*	fog
Kep / *Alb.*	cape
Kep., Kepulauan / *Mal.*	archipelago
Kepulauan, Kep. / *Mal.*	archipelago
Kereszt / *Hung.*	cross
Kerk / *Dut.; Fle.*	church
Keski / *Finn.*	middle
Kette / *Germ.*	mountain range
Keur / *Sud.*	village
Key / *Eng.*	coral island
Kha / *Tib.*	valley
Khal / *Hin.*	canal
Khalīj / *Ar.*	gulf
Khand / *Hin.*	district
Khao / *Thai*	hill, mountain
Kharābeh / *Pers.*	ruins
Khashm / *Ar.*	promontory
Khatt / *Ar.*	wadi
Khawr / *Ar.*	mouth, bay
Khazzān / *Ar.*	dam
Khemis / *Ar.*	fifth
Khersónisos / *Gr.*	peninsula
Khirbat / *Ar.*	ruins
Khlong / *Thai*	stream, mouth
Khokhok / *Thai*	isthmus
Khor / *Ar.*	mouth, bay
Khóra / *Gr.*	land
Khorion / *Gr.*	village
Khowr / *Pers.*	bay
Khrisós / *Gr.*	gold
Ki- / *Ban.*	little
Kibali / *Sud.*	river
Kil / *Gae.*	church
Kilde / *Dan.*	spring
Kilima / *Swa.*	mountain
Kill / *Gae.*	strait
Kilwa / *Ban.*	lake
Kin / *Gae.*	cape
Kinn / *Nor.*	cape, point
Kirche / *Germ.*	church
Kirk / *Eng.*	church
Kis / *Hung.*	little
Kisiwa / *Swa.*	island
Kita / *Jap.*	north, northern
Kızıl / *Tur.*	red
Klein / *Afr.; Dut.; Germ.*	little
Kliff / *Germ.*	cliff
Klint / *Dan.*	reef
Klip / *Afr.; Dut.*	rock, cliff
Klit / *Dan.*	dune
Kloof / *Afr.; Dut.*	gorge
Kloster / *Dan.; Germ.; Nor.; Swed.*	convent
Knob / *Eng.*	mountain
Knock / *Gae.*	mountain, hill
Ko / *Jap.*	bay, lake, little
Ko / *Sud.*	stream
Ko / *Thai*	island, point
Købing / *Dan.*	town
Kogel / *Germ.*	dome
Kōgen / *Jap.*	plateau
Koh / *Hin.; Pers.*	mountain, mountain range
Kol / *Alt.*	river, valley
Kol / *Alt.; Tur.*	lake
Koll / *Nor.*	peak
Kólpos / *Gr.*	gulf
Kong / *Dan.; Nor.; Swed.*	king
Kong / *Indon.; Mal.*	mountain
Kong / *Viet.*	mountain, hill
Konge / *Ban.*	river
König / *Germ.*	king
Koog / *Germ.*	polder
Kop / *Afr.*	hill
Kopec / *Cz.; Slvk.*	hill
Kopf / *Germ.*	peak
Köping / *Swed.*	town
Köprü / *Tur.*	bridge
Körfezi / *Tur.*	gulf
Korfi / *Gr.*	rock
Koro / *Mel.*	mountain, island
Koro / *Sud.*	old
Koru / *Tur.*	forest
Kosa / *Rus.*	spit
Koška / *Rus.*	cliff
Koski / *Finn.*	rapids
Kosui / *Jap.*	lake
Kot / *Urdu*	castle
Kota / *Mal.*	city, town
Kotal / *Pash.; Pers.*	pass
Kotar / *S.C.*	cultivated area
Kotlina / *Pol.*	basin

Local Form	English
Kotlovina / *Rus.*	basin, plain
Kou / *Chin.*	mouth, pass
Kourou / *Sud.*	well
Kowr / *Pers.*	river
Kowtal / *Pers.*	pass
Koy / *Tur.*	bay
Köy / *Tur.*	village
Kraal / *Afr.*	village
Kraina / *Pol.*	land
Kraj / *Rus.; S.C.*	land
Kraj / *Rus.*	administrative division
Krajina / *S.C.*	land
Krak / *Ar.*	hill, castle
Krans / *Afr.*	mountain
Kras / *S.C.; Slvn.*	karst landscape
Krasny / *Rus.*	red
Kreb / *Ar.*	hills, mountain range
Kriaž / *Ar.*	mountain range
Krš / *S.C.*	karst area, limestone area
Krung / *Thai*	city, town
Ksar / *Ar.*	castle
Ksour / *Ar.*	fortified village
Ku- / *Ban.*	river branch
Kuala / *Mal.*	river, mouth
Kubra / *Ar.*	bridge
Küçük / *Tur.*	little
Kuduk / *Tur.*	spring
Kūh / *Pers.*	mountain
Kūhhā / *Pers.*	mountain range
Kul / *Alt.; Iran.; Tur.*	lake
Kulam, -kulam / *Hin.; Tam.*	pond
Kulle / *Swed.*	hill
Kulm / *Germ.*	peak
Kultuk / *Rus.*	bay
Kum / *Tur.*	dunes, sand desert
Kuppe / *Germ.*	dome, seamount
Kurayb / *Ar.*	hill
Kurgan / *Alt.*	hill
Kurgan / *Tur.*	fort
Kuro / *Jap.*	black
Kurort / *Bulg.; Germ.; Rus.*	spa
Kust / *Dut.; Fle.*	coast
Kust- / *Swed.*	coast
Küste / *Germ.*	coast
Kút / *Hung.*	spring
Kuyu / *Tur.*	spring
Kvemo / *Georg.*	low, lower
Kwa / *Ban.*	village
Kylä / *Finn.*	village
Kyle / *Gae.*	strait, channel
Kyō / *Jap.*	strait
Kyrka / *Swed.*	church
Kyst / *Dan.; Nor.*	coast
Kyun / *Burm.*	island
Kyūryō / *Jap.*	hills, mountains
Kyzyl / *Tur.*	red
Kzyl / *Tur.*	red

L

Local Form	English
L., Lake, Lago / *Eng.; It.; Port.; Sp.*	lake
La / *Tib.*	pass
Laagte / *Afr.*	stream, valley
Labuan / *Indon.; Mal.*	bay, port
Lac / *Fr.*	lake
Lach / *Som.*	stream, wadi
Lacul / *Rom.*	lake
Lae / *Poly.*	cape, point
Laem / *Thai*	bay, port
Låg / *Nor.; Swed.*	low, lower
Lag / *Swed.*	stream, wadi
Läge / *Swed.*	beach
Lagh / *Som.*	stream, wadi
Lago, L. / *It.; Port.; Sp.*	lake
Lagoa / *Port.*	lagoon
Laguna / *Alb.; It.; Rus.; Sp.*	lagoon, lake
Lagune / *Fr.*	lagoon
Laht / *Est.*	bay
Lahti / *Finn.*	bay, gulf
Laks / *Finn.*	bay
Lalla / *Ar.*	saint
Lampi / *Finn.*	pond
Lande / *Fr.*	heath
Lang / *Afr.; Dut.; Germ.*	long
Lang / *Viet.*	village
Lao / *Chin.*	old
Lapa / *Poly.*	mountain range, peak
Largo / *Port.; Sp.*	basin
Las / *Pol.*	forest
Las, Lās / *Som.*	well
Laut / *Mal.*	sea
Law / *Gae.*	hill, mountain
Lázně / *Cz.*	thermal springs
Lednik / *Rus.*	glacier
Leite / *Germ.*	coast
Lekh / *Nep.*	mountain range
Les / *Bulg.; Cz.; Rus.; Slvk.*	forest
Leso / *Rus.*	forested
Levante / *It.; Sp.*	eastern
Levkós / *Gr.*	white
Levy / *Rus.*	left
Lha / *Tib.*	temple
Lhari / *Hin.; Nep.*	mountain
Lho / *Tib.*	south
Lido / *It.*	sandbar
Liedao / *Chin.*	archipelago
Liehtao / *Chin.*	archipelago
Liels / *Latv.*	great
Lilla / *Swed.*	little
Lille / *Dan.; Nor.*	little
Liman / *Alb.; Rus.; Tur.*	lagoon, bay
Liman / *Tur.*	bay, port
Limin / *Gr.*	port
Limni / *Gr.*	lake
Ling / *Chin.*	mountain range, peak
Linna / *Finn.*	castle
Liqen / *Alb.*	lake
Lithos / *Gr.*	stone
Litoral / *Port.; Sp.*	littoral
Litorale / *It.*	littoral
Llan / *Wel.*	church
Llano / *Sp.*	plain
Llanura / *Sp.*	plain
Lo- / *Ban.*	river
Loch / *Gae.*	lake, inlet
Loch / *Germ.*	grotto
Loka / *Slvn.*	forest
Loma / *Sp.*	hill
Long / *Indon.*	stream
Loo / *Dut.; Fle.*	clearing
Lough / *Gae.*	lake
Loutrá / *Gr.*	thermal springs
Ložbina / *Rus.*	depression
Lu- / *Ban.*	river
Lua / *Ban.*	river
Lua / *Mel.*	island, reef
Lua / *Poly.*	crater
Luang / *Thai*	yellow
Luch / *Germ.*	peat-bog
Lücke / *Germ.*	pass
Lug / *Rus.*	meadow
Luka / *S.C.; Slvn.*	port
Lule / *Lapp.*	east, eastern
Lum / *Alb.*	river
Lund / *Dan.; Swed.*	forest
Lung / *Rom.*	long
Lung / *Tib.*	valley
Luoto / *Finn.*	shoal
Lurg / *Pers.*	salt flat
Lut / *Pers.*	desert

M

Local Form	English
M., Monte / *It.; Port.; Sp.*	mountain
Ma / *Ar.*	water
Ma- / *Ban.*	people
Maa / *Est.; Finn.*	island, land
Ma'arrat / *Ar.*	height
Machi / *Jap.*	district
Macizo / *Sp.*	massif
Madhya / *Hin.*	central
Madīnah / *Ar.*	city, town
Madīq / *Ar.*	strait
Mado / *Swa.*	well
Madu / *Tam.*	pond
Mae / *Thai*	stream
Mae nam / *Thai*	stream, mouth
Magh / *Gae.*	plain
Mägi / *Est.*	mountain
Măgura / *Rom.*	height
Mahā / *Hin.*	great
Mahal / *Hin.; Urdu*	palace
Mai / *Amh.; Ban.*	stream
Majdan / *S.C.*	quarry
Mäki / *Finn.*	mountain, hill
Makrós / *Gr.*	long
Mala / *Hin.; Tam.*	mountain
Malai / *Hin.; Tam.*	mountain
Malal / *A.I.*	fence
Malhão / *Port.*	dome
Mali / *Alb.*	mountain
Mali / *S.C.; Slvn.*	little
Malki / *Bulg.*	little
Malla / *Tam.*	mountain
Maly / *Rus.*	little
Malý / *Cz.; Slvk.*	little
Mały / *Pol.*	little
Man / *Kor.*	bay
Manastir / *Bulg.; S.C.*	monastery
Manche / *Fr.*	channel
Mar / *It.; Port.; Sp.*	sea
Mar / *Tib.*	red
Mar / *Ural.*	city, town
Marais / *Fr.*	marsh
Marché / *Fr.*	market
Mare / *Fr.*	pond
Mare / *It.; Rom.*	sea
Mare / *Rom.*	great
Marea / *Rom.*	sea
Marécage / *Fr.*	marsh
Marios / *Lith.*	reservoir
Marisma / *Sp.*	marsh
Mark / *Dan.; Nor.; Swed.*	land
Markt / *Germ.*	market
Marsa / *Ar.*	anchorage, bay
Marsch / *Germ.*	marsh
Maru / *Jap.*	mountain
Mas / *Prov.*	farmhouse
Maşabb / *Ar.*	mouth
Mashra' / *Ar.*	landing, pier
Masivul / *Rom.*	massif
Massiv / *Germ.; Rus.*	massif
Mata / *Poly.*	point
Mata / *Port.; Sp.*	forest
Mata / *Som.*	waterfall
Mato / *Port.; Sp.*	forest
Matsu / *Jap.*	point
Mauna / *Poly.*	mountain
Mávros / *Gr.*	black
Mayo / *Sud.*	river
Maza / *Lith.*	little
Mazar / *Pers.; Tur.*	sanctuary
Mazs / *Latv.*	little
Me / *Khm.*	river
Me / *Mel.*	hill, mountain
Me / *Thai*	great
Medina / *Ar.*	city, town
Medjez / *Ar.*	ford
Meer / *Dut.; Fle.*	lake
Meer / *Germ.*	lake, sea
Megálos / *Gr.*	great
Mégas / *Gr.*	great
Megye / *Hung.*	district
Mélas / *Gr.*	black
Melkosopočnik / *Rus.*	hill country
Mellan / *Swed.*	central
Men / *Chin.*	gate, channel
Ménez / *Br.*	mountain
Menzel / *Ar.*	bivouac
Meos / *Indon.*	island
Mer / *Fr.*	sea
Mercato / *It.*	market
Merdja / *Ar.*	lagoon, marsh
Meri / *Est.; Finn.*	sea
Meridional / *Rom.; Sp.*	southern
Merin / *A.I.*	little
Merja / *Ar.*	lagoon, marsh
Mers / *Ar.*	port
Mersa / *Ar.*	port
Mesa / *Sp.*	mesa, tableland
Meseta / *Sp.*	plateau
Mésos / *Gr.*	central
Mesto / *Bulg.; S.C.; Slvk.; Slvn.*	city, town
Město / *Cz.*	city, town
Mestre / *Port.*	principal
Meydan / *Tur.*	square
Meẓad / *Hebr.*	castle
Mezö / *Hung.*	field
Mgne., Montagne / *Fr.*	mountain
Mgnes., Montagnes / *Fr.*	mountains
Miao / *Chin.*	temple
Miasto / *Pol.*	city, town
Mic / *Rom.*	little
Middel / *Afr.; Dut.; Fle.*	middle
Midi / *Fr.*	noon, south
Między / *Pol.*	central
Miedzyrzecze / *Pol.*	interfluve
Mierzeja / *Pol.*	sand spit
Mifraz / *Hebr.*	bay, gulf
Miftah / *Ar.*	gorge
Mikrós / *Gr.*	little
Mina / *Port.; Sp.*	mine
Mīnā' / *Ar.*	port
Minami / *Jap.*	south, southern
Minamoto / *Jap.*	spring
Minato / *Jap.*	port
Mine / *Jap.*	peak
Mirim / *A.I.*	little
Misaki / *Jap.*	cape
Mittel- / *Germ.*	middle
Mo / *Chin.*	sand desert
Mo / *Nor.; Swed.*	heath
Moana / *Poly.*	lake
Mogila / *Bulg.; Rus.*	hill
Moku / *Poly.*	island
Mølle / *Dan.*	mill
Monasterio / *Sp.*	monastery
Mond / *Afr.; Dut.; Fle.*	mouth
Mong / *Burm.; Thai; Viet.*	city, town
Moni / *Gr.*	monastery
Mont / *Cat.; Fr.*	mountain
Montagna / *It.*	mountain
Montagne, Mgne. / *Fr.*	mountain
Montagnes, Mgnes. / *Fr.*	mountains
Montaña / *Sp.*	mountain
Monte, M. / *It.; Port.; Sp.*	mountain
Monts, Mts. / *Fr.*	mountains
Moos / *Germ.*	moor
Mór / *Gae.*	great
More / *Bulg.; Rus.; S.C.*	sea
More / *Gae.*	great
Mori / *Jap.*	mountain, forest
Morne / *Fr.*	mountain
Moron / *Mong.*	river
Morro / *Port.; Germ.*	hill, peak
Morrón / *Sp.*	mountain
Morze / *Pol.*	sea
Most / *Bulg.; Cz.; Pol.; Rus.; S.C.; Slvn.*	bridge
Moto / *Jap.*	spring
Motte / *Fr.*	hill
Motu / *Mel.; Poly.*	island, rock
Moutier / *Fr.*	monastery
Movilă / *Rom.*	hill
Moyen / *Fr.*	central
Mta / *Georg.*	mountain
Mts., Monts, Mountains / *Eng.; Fr.*	mountains
Muang / *Laot.; Thai*	city, town, land
Muara / *Indon.; Mal.*	mouth
Muela / *Sp.*	mountain
Mühle / *Germ.*	mill
Mui / *Mel.*	point
Mui / *Viet.*	point, cape
Muiden / *Dut.; Fle.*	mouth
Muir / *Gae.*	sea
Mukh / *Hin.*	mouth
Mull / *Gae.*	promontory
Münde / *Germ.*	mouth
Mündung / *Germ.*	mouth
Municipiul / *Rom.*	commune
Munkhafaḍ / *Ar.*	depression
Münster / *Germ.*	monastery
Munte / *Rom.*	mountain
Muntele / *Rom.*	mountain
Munții / *Rom.*	mountain range
Muren / *Mong.*	river
Mushāsh / *Ar.*	spring
Muz / *Tur.*	ice
Muztagh / *Tur.*	snow-capped mountain
Mwambo / *Ban.*	rock, cliff
Myit / *Burm.*	stream
Mynydd / *Wel.*	mountain
Myo / *Burm.*	city, town
Mýri / *Icel.*	marsh
Mys / *Rus.*	cape

N

Local Form	English
Na / *Cz.; Pol.; Rus.; S.C.; Slvn.*	on
Nab / *Ar.*	spring
Nad / *Cz.; Pol.; Rus.*	on
Nada / *Jap.*	bay, sea
Nadi, -nadi / *Hin.; Urdu*	river
Næs / *Dan.*	point
Nafūd / *Ar.*	dunes
Nag / *Tib.*	black
Nagar, -nagar / *Hin.; Tib.*	city, town
Nagaram / *Hin.; Tam.*	city, town
Nagorje / *Rus.*	plateau, mountains
Nagy / *Hung.*	great
Nahr / *Ar.*	river
Naikai / *Jap.*	sea
Naka / *Jap.*	central
Nakhon / *Thai*	city, town
Nam / *Burm.; Laot.; Thai*	river
Nam / *Kor.*	south
Namakzar / *Pers.*	salt desert
Nan / *Chin.*	south
Narrows / *Eng.*	strait
Narssaq / *Esk.*	plain, valley
Näs / *Swed.*	cape
Nationalpark / *Swed.; Germ.*	national park
Nau / *Lith.*	new
Nauja / *Lith.*	new
Navolok / *Rus.*	cape, promontory
Ne / *Jap.*	cliff
Neder / *Fle.; Dut.*	low
Neem / *Est.*	cape
Negro / *Port.; Sp.*	black
Negru / *Rom.*	black
Nehir / *Tur.*	river
Nei / *Chin.*	inner
Nene, -nene / *Ban.*	great
Néos / *Gr.*	new
Nero / *It.*	black
Nes / *Icel.; Nor.*	cape
Ness / *Gae.*	promontory
Neu / *Germ.*	new
Neuf / *Fr.*	new
Nevado / *Sp.*	snow-capped mountain
Nez / *Fr.*	cape
Ngok / *Viet.*	mountain, peak
Ngolo / *Ber.*	great
Ni / *Kor.*	village
Niecka / *Pol.*	basin
Niemi / *Finn.*	peninsula
Nieuw / *Fle.; Dut.*	new
Nij / *Dut.*	new
Nīl / *Hin.*	blue
Nishi / *Jap.*	west
Niski / *Pol.*	lower
Nisko / *S.C.*	low
Nisoi / *Gr.*	islands
Nisos / *Gr.*	island
Nizina / *Pol.*	lowland
Nížina / *Cz.*	depression
Nízký / *Cz.*	low, lower

Geographical Glossary

Local Form	English
Nizmennost / Rus.	lowland, depression
Nižni / Rus.	low, lower
Nižný / Slvk.	low, lower
No / Mel.	stream
Nock / Gae.	ridge
Noir / Fr.	black
Non / Thai	hill
Nong / Thai	lake, marsh
Noord / Afr.; Fle.; Dut.	north
Noordoost / Afr.; Fle.; Dut.	northeast
Nor / Arm.	new
Nord / Fr.; It.; Germ.	north
Nördlich / Germ.	northern
Nørdre / Dan.; Nor.	northern
Norra / Swed.	northern
Nørre / Dan.	northern
Norte / Sp.	north
Nos / Bulg.; Rus.; S.C.; Slvn.	cape
Nosy / Malag.	island
Nótios / Gr.	southern
Nou / Rom.	new
Novi / Bulg.; S.C.; Slvn.	new
Novo / Port.	new
Novy / Rus.	new
Nový / Cz.; Slvk.	new
Now / Pers.	new
Nowy / Pol.	new
Nudo / Sp.	mountain
Nuevo / Sp.	new
Nui / Viet.	mountain
Numa / Jap.	marsh, lake
Nummi / Finn.	heath
Nunatak / Esk.	peak
Nuovo / It.	new
Nur / Chin.	lake
Nusa / Mal.	island
Nut, -nut / Nor.	peak
Nuwara / Sin.; Tam.	city, town
Nuwe / Afr.	new
Nyanza / Ban.	water, river, lake
Nyasa / Ban.	lake
Nyeong / Kor.	pass
Nyika / Ban.	upland
Nyŏng / Kor.	mount, pass
Nyugat / Hung.	west

O

Local Form	English
Ō / Jap.	great
Ó / Hung.	old
Ö / Swed.	island
Ø, -ø / Dan.; Nor.	island
Öar / Swed.	islands
Ober / Germ.	upper
Oblast / Rus.	province
Obo / Mong.	mountain, hill
Occidental / Fr.; Rom.; Sp.	western
Océan / Fr.	ocean
Océano / Sp.	ocean
Oceano / It.; Port.	ocean
Ocnă / Rom.	salt mine
Odde / Dan.; Nor.	promontory
Oeste / Port.; Sp.	west
Oever / Fle.; Dut.	bank
Oewer / Afr.	bank
Oie / Germ.	islet
Ojos / Sp.	spring
Oka / Jap.	coast
Oke / Sud.	height
Okean / Rus.	ocean
Oki / Jap.	bay
Okrug / Rus.	district
Ola / Alt.	city, town
Omuramba / K.S.	stream
Onder / Afr.	under
Oni / Malag.	river
Oos / Afr.	east
Oost / Fle.; Dut.	east
Oostelijk / Dut.	eastern
Opatija / Slvn.	abbey
Or / Fr.	gold
Oraş / Rom.	city, town
Óri / Gr.	mountains
Oriental / Fr.; Port.; Rom.; Sp.	eastern
Orientale / It.	eastern
Orilla / Sp.	bank
Órmos / Gr.	bay
Óros / Gr.	mountain
Ország / Hung.	land
Ort / Germ.	cape
Orta / Tur.	central
Orto / Alt.	central
Oseaan / Afr.	ocean
Ōshima / Jap.	large island
Ost / Dan.; Germ.	east
Öst / Swed.	east
Ostān, -ostān / Pers.	province
Øster / Dan.; Nor.	east, eastern
Öster / Swed.	east, eastern
Östlich / Germ.	eastern
Ostrog / Rus.	castle

Local Form	English
Ostrov / Rus.	island
Ostrovul / Rom.	island
Ostrów / Pol.	island
Ostrvo / S.C.	island
Otok / S.C.; Slvn.	island
Otrog / Rus.	front range (mountains)
Oua / Mel.	stream
Ouar / Ar.	rocky desert
Oud / Fle.; Dut.	old
Oued / Ar.	wadi
Ouest / Fr.	west
Ouled / Ar.	son
Oum / Ar.	mother
Ouro / Port.	gold
Outu / Poly.	cape
Ova / Ban.	people
Ova / Tur.	plain
Ovasi / Tur.	plain
Øver / Nor.	over
Över / Swed.	over
Övre / Swed.	over
Øy / Dan.; Nor.	island
oz., Ozero / Rus.	lake
Ozek / Alt.	hollow
Ozera / Rus.	lakes
Ozero, oz. / Rus.	lake

P

Local Form	English
P., Pulau / Mal.; Indon.	island
Pää / Finn.	principal
Pad / Rus.	valley
Padang / Indon.	plain
Padiş / Rom.	upland
Padół / Pol.	valley
Pădure / Rom.	forest
Pahorek / Cz.	hill
Pahorkatina / Cz.	plateau, hills
Pais / Port.; Sp.	land, country
Pak / Thai	mouth
Pala / It.	peak
Palaiós / Gr.	old
Palanka / S.C.	village
Pali / Poly.	cliff
-palli / Hin.	village
Pampa / Sp.	plain, prairie
Panda / Swa.	junction
Panev / Cz.	basin
Pantanal / Sp.	swamp
Pantano / Sp.	swamp, lake
Pao / Mel.	hill
Pará / A.I.	river
Paramera / Sp.	desert highland
Páramo / Sp.	moor
Paraná / A.I.	river
Parbat / Hin.; Urdu	mountain
Parc / Fr.	park
Parco / It.	park
Parco Nazionale / It.	national park
Pardo / Port.	grey
Parque / Sp.	park
Parque Nacional / Sp.; Port.	national park
Pas / Fr.; Rom.	pass, strait
Pasaje / Sp.	passage
Pasir / Mal.	sand, beach
Paso / Sp.	pass
Passágem / Port.	passage
Passe / Fr.	pass
Passo / It.; Port.	pass
Pasul / Rom.	pass
Patak / Hung.	stream
Patam, -patam / Hin.	city, town
Patnã / Hin.	city, town
Patnam, -patnam / Hin.	city, town
Pattinam, -pattinam / Hin.	city, town
Pays / Fr.	land, country
Pazar / Tur.	market
Pea / Est.	cape
Pech / Cat.	hill
Pedhiás / Gr.	plain
Pedra / Port.	rock, mountain
Peg., Pegunungan / Mal.; Indon.	mountain range
Pegunungan, Peg. / Mal.; Indon.	mountain range
Pélagos / Gr.	sea
Pele / Poly.	peak, hill
Pen / Br.	principal
Pen / Br.; Gae.	cape, mountain
Peña / Sp.	peak
Pendi / Chin.	basin
Pendiente / Sp.	slope
Penha / Port.	peak
Peninsula / Port.; Sp.	peninsula
Péninsule / Fr.	peninsula
Penisola / It.	peninsula
Peñon / Sp.	rock, island
Pente / Fr.	slope
Perekop / Rus.	channel
Pereval / Rus.	pass
Perevoz / Rus.	ford
Pertuis / Fr.	strait
Peščara / S.C.	sandy soil
Peski / Rus.	sand desert

Local Form	English
Petit / Fr.	little
Pétra / Gr.	rock
Phanom / Thai; Khm.	mountain range, mountain
Phau / Laot.	mountain
Phnum / Khm.	hill, mountain
Phu / Viet.	mountain, hill
Phum / Thai	forest
Phumĭ / Khm.	village
Pi / Chin.	cape
Piana, Pianura / It.	plain
Piano / It.	plain
Piatră / Rom.	stone
Pic / Cat.; Fr.	peak
Picacho / Sp.	peak
Piccolo / It.	little
Pico / Port.; Sp.	peak
Piedra / Sp.	rock, cliff
Pietra / It.	stone
Pieve / It.	parish
Pik / Rus.	peak
Pils / Latv.	city, town
Pinar / Sp.	pine forest
Pingyuan / Chin.	plain
Pioda / It.	crest
Pirgos / Gr.	tower, peak
Pīsh / Pers.	anterior, before
Pitkä / Finn.	great
Piton / Fr.	mountain, peak
Piz / Rmsh.	peak
Pizzo / It.	peak
Pjasăci / Bulg.	beach
Plaat / Fle.; Dut.	sandbank
Plage / Fr.	beach
Plaine / Fr.	plain
Plan / Fr.	plain
Planalto / Port.	plateau
Planina / Bulg.	mountain
Plano / Sp.	plain
Plas / Dut.; Fle.	lake, marsh
Plato / Bulg.; Rus.	plateau
Platosu / Tur.	plateau
Platte / Germ.	plain, plateau
Plav / S.C.	blue
Plavnja / Rus.	marsh
Playa / Sp.	beach
Ploskogorje / Rus.	plateau
Plou / Br.	church
Po / Kor.	port
Po / Chin.	lake, white
P'o / Kor.	bay, lake
Poa / Mel.	hill
Poarta / Rom.	pass
Poartă / Rom.	gate
Pobla / Cat.	village
Pobrzeże / Pol.	littoral, coast
Poço / Port.	well
Poço / Port.	point
Pod / Cz.; Pol.; Rus.; S.C.; Slvn.	bridge
Podkamenny / Rus.	stony
Poggio / It.	hill
Pohja / Finn.	north, northern
Pohjois- / Finn.	north
Pojezierze / Pol.	lake region
Pol / Pers.	bridge
Pol, -pol / Rus.	city, town
Pola / Port.; Sp.	village
Polder / Fle.; Dut.	reclaimed land
Pole / Pol.	field
Pólis / Gr.	city, town
Poljana / Bulg.; Rus.; S.C.; Slvn.	field, terrace
Poljarny / Rus.	polar
Polje / S.C.; Slvn.	valley, field, basin
Poluostrov / Rus.	peninsula
Pomorije / Bulg.	littoral
Pomorze / Pol.	littoral
Ponente / It.	western
Pont / Cat.; Fr.	bridge
Ponta / Port.	point
Ponte / It.; Port.	bridge
Póntos / Gr.	sea
Poort / Afr.; Fle.; Dut.	pass
Pore, -pore / Hin.; Urdu	city, town
Porog / Rus.	rapids
Porte / Fr.	gate
Portile / Rom.	gorge
Portillo / Sp.	pass
Portiţa / Rom.	small gate
Porto / It.	port
Pôrto / Port.	port
Posht / Pers.	back, posterior
Potjo / Indon.	peak
Potok / Bulg.; Cz.; Pol.; Rus.; S.C.; Slvn.	stream
Póvoa / Port.	village
Pozo / Sp.	well
Pozzo / It.	well
Pradesh / Hin.	region, state
Prado / Sp.	meadow
Praia / Port.	beach
Prato / It.	meadow
Pré / Fr.	meadow
Prealpi / It.	prealps
Presa / Sp.	reservoir
Presqu'île / Fr.	peninsula
Prêto / Port.	black

Local Form	English
Priehradní nádrž / Cz.	reservoir
Pripoljarny / Rus.	subpolar
Pristan / Rus.	port
Prohod / Bulg.	pass
Proliv / Rus.	strait
Promontoire / Fr.	promontory
Průchod / Cz.	pass
Przedgorze / Pol.	front range (mountains)
Przełęcz / Pol.	pass
Przemysł / Pol.	industry
Przylądek / Pol.	cape
Pua / Mel.	hill
Puebla / Sp.	village
Puente / Sp.	bridge
Puerto / Sp.	port, pass
Puig / Cat.	peak
Puits / Fr.	well
Pul / Pash.	bridge
Pulau, P. / Mal.; Indon.	island
Pulau Pulau / Mal.	islands
Pulo / Mal.; Indon.	island
Puna / A.I.	upland
Puncak / Indon.	mountain
Punjung / Mal.; Indon.	mountain
Punt / Afr.	point
Punta / It.; Sp.	point
Pur, -pur / Hin.; Urdu	city, town
-pura / Hin.; Urdu	city, town
Pura / Indon.	city, town, temple
Puri, -puri / Hin.; Urdu	city, town
Pus / Alb.	spring
Pušča / Rus.	forest
Pustynja / Rus.	desert
Puszcza / Pol.	heath
Puszta / Hung.	lowland
Put / Afr.	well
Put / Rus.; S.C.	road
Putra, -putra / Hin.	son
Puu / Poly.	mountain, volcano
Puy / Fr.	peak
Pwell / Wel.	pond
Pyeong / Kor.	plain
Pyhä / Finn.	saint

Q

Local Form	English
Qagan / Mong.	white
Qala / Pash.	fortified town
Qal'at / Ar.	castle
Qalb / Ar.	hill
Qalīb / Ar.	spring
Qalīş / Ar.	spring
Qanāt / Ar.	canal
Qantara / Ar.	bridge
Qaqortoq / Esk.	white
Qar / Som.	mountain
Qara / Pers.	black
Qarah / Tur.	black
Qārat / Ar.	height, mountain
Qāret / Ar.	village, hill
Qaryah / Ar.	village
Qaryat / Ar.	village
Qaşr / Ar.	castle
Qawz / Ar.	dunes
Qeqertarssuaq / Esk.	peninsula
Qezel / Tur.	red
Qi / Chin.	river
Qing / Chin.	blue, green
Qiryat / Hebr.	city, town
Qolleh / Pers.	mountain, peak
Qu / Chin.	river, canal
Quan dao / Viet.	islands
Quebracho / Sp.	stream
Quebrada / Sp.	gorge, stream
Quedas / Port.	waterfalls
Qulbān / Ar.	well
Qundao / Chin.	archipelago
Qūr / Ar.	height, hill
Qytet / Alb.	city, town
Qyteti / Alb.	city, town

R

Local Form	English
R., Rio, River / Eng.; Sp.	river
Rada / It.; Sp.	anchorage
Rade / Fr.	anchorage
Rags / Latv.	cape
Rahad / Ar.	lake, pond
Rajon / Rus.	district
Rak / Fle.; Dut.	strait
Rakai / Poly.	reef
Ramla / Ar.	sand
Rancho / Port.; Sp.	farm, ranch
Rand / Afr.; Germ.	escarpment
Range / Eng.	mountain range
Rann / Urdu	marsh
Rano / Malag.	water
Ranta / Finn.	bank, beach
Rapide / Fr.	rapids
Ras / Amh.	peak
Räs / Ar.	point, cape

Local Form	English
Ras, Ràs / Ar.	promontory, peak
Rāsiga / Som.	promontory
Rass / Ar.	promontory, peak
Rassa / Lapp.	mountain
Ráth / Gae.	castle
Raunina / Bulg.; Rus.	plain
Raz / Fr.	strait
Razliv / Rus.	flood plain
Récif / Fr.	reef
Recife / Port.	reef
Reede / Germ.; Dut.; Slvn.	anchorage
Reek / Afr.; Gae.	mountain range
Reg / Pash.	dunes
Région / Fr.	region
Rei / Port.	king
Reka / Bulg.; Rus.; S.C.; Slvn.	river
Řeka / Cz.	river
Réma / Gr.	torrent
Renne / Dan.; Nor.	deep
Reprêsa / Port.	dam, reservoir
Represa / Sp.	dam, reservoir
República / Port.; Sp.	republic
République / Fr.	republic
Rés., Réservoir / Fr.	reservoir
Res., Reservoir / Eng.	reservoir
Réservoir, Rés. / Fr.	reservoir
Reshteh / Pers.	mountain range
Respublika / Rus.	republic
Restinga / Port.	cliff, sandbank
Retsugan / Jap.	reef
Rettō / Jap.	archipelago
Rev / Dan.; Nor.; Swed.	reef
Rey / Sp.	king
Ri / Tib.	mountain
Ria / Sp.	estuary
Riacho / Port.	stream
Rialto / It.	plateau
Rialto / It.	rise
Riba / Port.	bank
Ribeira / Port.	river
Ribeirão / Port.	stream
Ribeiro / Port.	stream
Ribera / Sp.	coast
Ribnik / Slvn.	pond
Rid / Bulg.	mountain range
Rif / Icel.	cliff
Riff / Germ.	reef
Rīg / Pash.	dunes
Rijeka / S.C.	river
Rimāl / Ar.	sand desert
Rincón / Sp.	peninsula between two rivers
Ring / Tib.	long
Rinne / Germ.	trench
Rio / Port.	river
Rio, R. / Sp.	river
Riu / Rom.	river
Riva / It.	bank
Rive / Fr.	bank
Rivera / Sp.	brook, stream
Rivier, -rivier / Afr.; Dut.; Fle.	river
Riviera / It.	coast
Rivière / Fr.	river
Roads / Eng.	anchorage
Roc / Fr.	rock
Roca / Port.; Sp.	rock
Rocca / It.	castle
Roche / Fr.	rock
Rocher / Fr.	rock
Rock / Eng.	rock
Rod / Pash.	river
Rode / Germ.	tilled soil
Rodnik / Rus.	spring
Rog / Rus.; S.C.; Slvn.	peak
Roi / Fr.	king
Rojo / Sp.	red
Roque / Sp.	rock
Rot / Germ.	red
Roto / Poly.	lake
Rouge / Fr.	red
Równina / Pol.	plain
Rt / S.C.; Slvn.	cape
Ru / Tib.	mountain
Ruck / Germ.	ridge
Rücken / Germ.	ridge
Rud / Pers.	river
Ruda / Cz.; Slvk.	mine
Ruda / Pol.	ore
Rūdbār / Pers.	river
Rudha / Gae.	point
Rudnik / Rus.; S.C.; Slvn.	mine
Rug / Fle.; Dut.	ridge
Ruggen / Afr.	ridge
Ruina / Sp.	ruins
Ruine / Fr.; Dut.; Germ.	ruins
Rujm / Ar.	hill
Run / Eng.	stream

S

Local Form	English
S., See / Germ.	lake, sea
Saar / Est.	island
Saari / Finn.	island
Sabbia / It.	sand
Sabkhat / Ar.	salt flat, salt marsh
Sable / Fr.; Eng.	beach
Sacca / It.	anchorage
Saco / Port.	bay
Sad / Cz.; Slvk.	park
Sad / Pers.	wall
Sadd / Ar.; Pers.	cataract, dam
Safid / Pash.; Urdu; Hin.	white
Şafrā' / Ar.	desert
Sāgar / Hin.	reservoir
Saguia / Ar.	irrigation canal
Sahara / Ar.	desert
Sahel / Ar.	plain, coast
Sahr / Iran.	city, town
Şaḩrā' / Ar.	desert
Said / Ar.	sweet
Saj / Alt.	stream, valley
Saki / Jap.	point
Sala / Latv.; Lith.	island
Saladillo / Sp.	salt desert
Salar / Sp.	salt lake
Sale / Ural.	village
Salina / It.; Sp.	salt flat, salt marsh
Saline / Dut.; Fr.; Germ.	salt flat, salt marsh
Salmi / Finn.	strait
Salseleh-ye Kūh / Pers.	mountain range
Salto / Port.; Sp.	waterfall, rapids
Salz / Germ.	salt
Samudera / Indon.	ocean
Samudra / Hin.	lake
Samut / Thai	sea
San / Jap.; Kor.	mountain
San / It.; Sp.	saint
Sanchi / Jap.	mountain range
Sand / Dan.; Eng.; Nor.; Swed.; Afr.	beach
Šand / Mong.	spring
Sandur / Icel.	sand
Sank / Pers.	rock
Sankt, St. / Germ.; Swed.	saint
Sanmaeg / Kor.	mountain range
Sanmyaku / Jap.	mountain range
Sansanné / Sud.	campsite
Santo / It.; Port.; Sp.	saint
Santuario / It.	sanctuary
São / Port.	saint
Sar / Pers.	cape; peak
Šar / Rus.; Tur.	strait
Saraf / Ar.	well
Sari / Finn.	island
Sari / Tur.	yellow
Sarīr / Ar.	rocky desert
Sary / Tur.	yellow
Sasso / It.	stone
Sat / Rom.	village
Sattel / Germ.	pass
Saurum / Latv.	strait
Schleuse / Germ.	lock
Schloß / Germ.	castle
Schlucht / Germ.	gorge
Schnee / Germ.	snow
Schwarz / Germ.	black
Scoglio / It.	cliff
Se / Jap.	bank, shoal
Sebkha / Ar.	salt flat
Sebkhet / Ar.	salt flat
Sed / Ar.	dam
Seda / Ural.	mountain
See, S. / Germ.	lake, sea
Sefra / Ar.	yellow
Segara / Indon.	lagoon
Şehir / Tur.	city, town
Seki / Jap.	dam
Selat / Mal.; Indon.	strait
Selatan / Indon.	southern
Selkä / Finn.	ridge, lake
Sella / It.	pass
Selo / Bulg.; Rus.; S.C.; Slvn.	village
Selsela Kohe / Pers.	mountain range
Selva / It.; Sp.	forest
Semenanjung / Mal.	peninsula
Sen / Jap.	mountain
Seong / Kor.	castle
Sep / Alt.	canal
Serīr / Ar.	rocky desert
Serra / Cat.; Port.	mountain range
Serra / It.	mountain
Serrania / Sp.	mountain range
Sertão / Port.	steppe
Seto / Jap.	strait
Sett., Settentrionale / It.	northern
Settentrionale, Sett. / It.	northern
Seuil / Fr.	sill
Sev / Arm.	black
Sever / Rus.	north
Severny / Rus.	northern
Sfint / Rom.	saint
Sfintu / Rom.	saint
Sgeir / Gae.	cliff
Sha'b / Ar.	cliff
Shahr / Pers.; Hin.	city, town
Sha'īb / Ar.	stream
Shallāl / Ar.	cataract

Local Form	English
Shām / Ar.	north; northern
Shamo / Chin.	sand desert
Shan / Chin.	mountain, mountain range
Shan / Gae.	old
Shand / Mong.	spring
Shankou / Chin.	pass
Shaqq / Ar.	wadi
Sharm / Ar.	bay
Sharqī / Ar.	east, eastern
Sharqīyah / Ar.	eastern
Shatt / Ar.	river, salt lake
Shatt / Tur.	stream
Shēn / Alb.	saint
Sheng / Chin.	province
Shi / Chin.	city, town
Shibīn / Ar.	village
Shih / Chin.	rock
Shima / Jap.	island
Shimo / Jap.	lower
Shin / Jap.	new
Shō / Jap.	island
Shotō / Jap.	archipelago
Shū / Jap.	administrative division
Shui / Chin.	river
Shuiku / Chin.	reservoir
Shur / Pers.	salt
Sidhiros / Gr.	iron
Sidi / Ar.	master
Sieben / Germ.	seven
Sierra / Sp.	mountain range
Sikt / Ural.	village
Sillon / Fr.	furrow
Šine / Mong.	new
Sink / Eng.	depression
Sinn / Ar.	point
Sint / Dut.; Fle.	saint
Sirt / Tur.	mountain range
Sirtlar / Tur.	mountain range
Sistema / It.; Sp.	mountain system
Sīyāh / Pers.	black
Sjø / Nor.	lake
Sjö / Swed.	lake, sea
Skag / Icel.	peninsula
Skala / Bulg.; Rus.	rock
Skála / Slvk.	rock
Skar / Nor.	pass
Skär / Swed.	cliff
Skeir / Gae.	cliff
Skerry / Gae.	cliff
Skog / Nor.; Swed.	forest
Skóg / Icel.	forest
Skov / Dan.; Nor.	forest
Slatina / S.C.; Slvn.	mineral water
Slätt / Swed.	plain
Slieve / Gae.	mountain
Slot / Dut.; Fle.	castle
Slott / Nor.; Swed.	castle
Slough / Eng.	creek, pond, marsh
Sluis / Dut.; Fle.	sluice
Små / Swed.	little
Sne / Nor.	snow
Sneeuw / Afr.; Dut.	snow
Snežny / Rus.	snowy
Snø / Nor.	snow
So / Kor.	little
Sø / Dan.; Nor.	lake; sea
So / Ural.	passage
Söder / Swed.	south
Södra / Swed.	southern
Solončak / Rus.	salt flat
Sommet / Fr.	peak
Son / Viet.	mountain
Sønder / Dan.; Nor.	southern
Søndre / Dan.	southern
Sone / Jap.	bank
Song / Viet.	river
Sopka / Rus.	volcano
Sopočnik / Rus.	mountain system
Soprana / It.	upper
Šor, Sor / Alt.	salt marsh
Sos / Sp.	upon
Sotavento / Sp.	leeward
Sotoviento / Sp.	leeward
Sottana / It.	lower
Souk / Ar.	market
Souq / Ar.	market
Sour / Ar.	rampart
Source / Eng.; Fr.	spring
Souto / Port.	forest
Spitze / Germ.	peak
Spruit / Afr.	current
Sreden / Bulg.	central
Sredni / Rus.	central
Średni / Pol.	central
Srednji / S.C.; Slvn.	central
St., Saint, Sankt / Eng.; Fr.; Germ.; Swed.	saint
Stadhur / Icel.	city, town
Stadt, -stadt / Germ.	city, town
Stag / Eng.	city, town
Stagno / It.	pond
-stan / Hin.; Pers.; Urdu	land
Star / Bulg.	old
Stari / S.C.; Slvn.	old

Local Form	English
Stary / Pol.; Rus.	old
Starý / Cz.; Slvk.	old
Stat / Afr.; Dan.; Fle.; Nor.; Dut.; Swed.	city, town
Stathmós / Gr.	railway station
Stausee / Germ.	reservoir
Stavrós / Gr.	cross
Sted / Dan.; Nor.	place
Stedt / Germ.	place
Stein, -stein / Nor.; Germ.	stone
Sten / Nor.; Swed.	stone
Stena / S.C.; Slvn.	rock
Stěna / Cz.	mountain range
Stenón / Gr.	strait, pass
Step / Rus.	steppe
-sthān / Hin.; Pers.; Urdu	land
Stift / Germ.	foundation
Štít / Cz.; Slvk.	peak
Stock / Germ.	massif
Stok / Pol.	slope
Stor / Dan.; Nor.; Swed.	great
Store / Dan.	great
Stræde / Dan.	strait
Strana / Rus.	land
Strand / Germ.; Nor.; Swed.; Afr.; Dan.	beach
Straße / Germ.	street, road
Strath / Gae.	valley
Straum / Nor.; Swed.	stream
Střední / Cz.	central
Středný / Slvk.	central
Strelka / Rus.	spit
Stret / Nor.	strait
Stretto / It.	strait
Strom / Germ.	stream
Strøm / Nor.	stream
Ström / Swed.	stream
Stroom / Dut.	stream
Su / Jap.	sandbank
Su / Tur.	river
Suando / Finn.	pond
Suid / Afr.	south
Suidō / Jap.	strait
Sul / Port.	south
Sund / Dan.; Nor.; Swed.; Germ.	strait
Sungai / Mal.	river
Sunn / Nor.	south
Süq / Ar.	market
Sur / Fr.	on
Sur / Sp.	south
Surkh / Pers.	red
Suu / Finn.	mouth, river mouth
Suur / Cat.	great
Svart / Nor.; Swed.	black
Sveti / S.C.; Slvn.	saint
Swa / Ban.	great
Swart / Afr.	black
Świety / Pol.	saint
Syrt / Alt.	ridge
Szállás / Hung.	village
Szczyt / Pol.	peak
Szeg / Hung.	bend
Székes / Hung.	residence
Szent / Hung.	saint
Sziget / Hung.	river island

T

Local Form	English
Tadi / Ban.	rock, cliff
Tae / Kor.	great
Tafua / Poly.	mountain
Tag / Alt.; Tur.	mountain
Tahta / Ar.	lower
Tahti / Ar.	lower
Tai / Chin.; Jap.	great
Taipale / Finn.	isthmus
Tajga / Rus.	forest
Take / Jap.	mountain
Tal / Germ.	valley
Tala / Mong.	plain, steppe
Tala / Ber.	spring
Tall / Ar.	hill
Talsperre / Germ.	dam
Tam / It.	stream
Tamgout / Ber.	peak
Tan / Chin.; Kor.	sandbank
Tana / Malag.	city, town
Tanana / Malag.	city, town
Tandjung / Mal.	cape, point
Tanezrouft / Ber.	desert
Tang / Tib.	upland
Tangeh / Pers.	strait
Tanjong / Mal.	cape, point
Tanjung, Tg. / Indon.	cape, point
Tanout / Ber.	well
Tao / Chin.	island
Taourirt / Ber.	peak
Targ / Pol.	market
Tărg / Bulg.	market
Tarn / Eng.	glacial lake
Tarso / Sah.	crater
Taš / Alt.	stone

Geographical Glossary

Local Form	English
Tassili / *Ber.*	upland
Tau / *Tur.*	mountain
Taung / *Burm.*	mountain
Ţawil / *Ar.*	hill
Tégi / *Sah.*	hill
Teguidda / *Ber.*	well
Tehi / *Ber.*	pass, mountain
Teich / *Germ.*	pond
Tell / *Tur.*	hill
Telok / *Mal.*	bay, port
Teluk / *Mal.*	bay, port
Tempio / *It.*	temple
Ténéré / *Ber.*	rocky desert
Tengah / *Indon.; Mal.*	central
Tepe / *Tur.*	hill
Tepesi / *Tur.*	hill
Termas / *Sp.*	thermal springs
Terme / *It.*	thermal springs
Terra / *It.; Dut.*	land, earth
Terrazzo / *It.*	guyot, tablemount
Terre / *Fr.*	land, earth
Teso / *Cat.*	hill
Téssa / *Ber.*	wadi, depression
Testa / *It.*	point
Tête / *Fr.*	peak
Tetri / *Georg.*	white
Teu / *Poly.*	reef
Teze / *Alt.*	new
Tg., Tanjung / *Indon.*	cape, point
Thaba / *Ban.*	mountain
Thabana / *Ban.*	mountain
Thal / *Germ.*	valley
Thálassa / *Gr.*	sea
Thale / *Thai*	lagoon
Thamad / *Ar.*	well
Theós / *Gr.*	god
Thermes / *Fr.*	thermal springs
Thog / *Tib.*	high, upper
Tian / *Chin.*	field
Tiefe / *Germ.*	deep
Tierra / *Sp.*	land, earth
Timur / *Indon.; Mal.*	eastern
Tind / *Nor.*	mountain
Tinto / *Sp.*	black
Tirg / *Rom.*	market
Tis / *Amh.*	new
Tizgui / *Ber.*	forest
Tizi / *Ber.*	pass
Tjåkko / *Lapp.*	mountain
Tjärn / *Swed.*	tarn, glacial lake
Tji / *Mal.*	stream
To / *Kor.*	island
To / *Mel.*	stream
Tō / *Jap.*	island
Tó / *Hung.*	lake
To / *Ural.*	lake
Tobe / *Tur.*	hill
Tofua / *Poly.*	mountain
Tog / *Som.*	valley
Tōge / *Jap.*	pass
Tokoj / *Alt.*	forest
Tônle / *Khm.*	stream, lake
Tope / *Dut.*	peak
Toplice / *S.C.; Slvn.*	thermal springs
Topp / *Nor.*	peak
Tor / *Gae.*	rock
Tor / *Germ.*	gate
Torbat / *Pers.*	tomb
Törl / *Germ.*	pass
Torp / *Swed.*	hut
Torre / *Cat.; It.; Sp.; Port.*	tower
Torrente / *It.; Sp.*	torrent, stream
Tossa / *Cat.*	mountain, peak
Tota / *Sin.*	port
Tour / *Fr.*	tower
Traforo / *It.*	tunnel
Träsk / *Swed.*	lake
Trg / *S.C.*	market
Trog / *Germ.*	trough, trench
Trois / *Fr.*	three
Trung / *Viet.*	central
Tse / *Tib.*	peak, point
Tsi / *Chin.*	pond
Tskali / *Georg.*	river
Tsu / *Jap.*	bay
Tulül / *Ar.*	hills
Tünel / *Pers.*	tunnel
Tunturi / *Lapp.*	mountain, tundra
Tur'ah / *Ar.*	irrigation canal
Turm / *Germ.*	tower
Turn / *Rom.*	tower
Turó / *Cat.*	dome
Tuz / *Tur.*	salt
Týn / *Cz.*	fortress

U

Local Form	English
U., Unter-, Upon / *Eng.; Germ.*	under, lower
Uaimh / *Gae.*	cave
Uchi / *Jap.*	bay
Udde / *Swed.*	cape
Údolní nádrž / *Cz.*	reservoir

Local Form	English
Uebi / *Som.*	river
Új- / *Hung.*	new
Ujście / *Pol.*	mouth
Ujung / *Indon.*	point, cape
Ul / *Chin.; Mong.*	mountain, mountain range
Ula / *Mong.*	mountain range
Ulan / *Mong.*	red
Uls / *Mong.*	state
Umi / *Jap.*	bay
Umm / *Ar.*	mother, spring
Umne / *Mong.*	south
Under / *Mong.*	mountain, peak
Ungur / *Alt.*	cave
Unter-, U. / *Germ.*	under, lower
Upar / *Hin.*	river
'Uqlat / *Ar.*	well
Ür / *Tam.*	city, town
Ura / *Jap.*	bay, coast
Ura / *Alt.*	depression
Urd / *Mong.*	south
Uru / *Tam.*	city, town
Ušće / *S.C.*	mouth
Uske / *Alt.*	upper
Ust / *Rus.*	mouth
Ústi / *Cz.*	mouth
Ustup / *Rus.*	terrace
Utan / *Indon.; Mal.*	forest
Utara / *Indon.*	north, northern
Uusi / *Finn.*	new
Uval / *Rus.*	height
Úval / *Cz.*	mountain
'Uwaynāt / *Ar.*	well
Uzboj / *Alt.*	river bed
Uzun / *Tur.*	long
Užürekis / *Lith.*	gulf

V

Local Form	English
Va / *Alb.*	ford
Va / *Ural.*	water, river
Vaara / *Finn.*	mountain
Väärti / *Finn.*	bay
Vad / *Rom.*	ford
Vær / *Nor.*	port
Våg / *Nor.*	bay
Vähä / *Finn.*	little
Väike / *Est.*	little
Väin / *Est.*	strait
Val / *Fr.; It.*	valley
Val / *Rom.; Rus.*	wall
Valico / *It.*	pass
Vall / *Cat.*	valley
Vall / *Swed.*	pasture
Valle / *It.; Sp.*	valley
Valiée / *Fr.*	valley
Vallei / *Afr.*	valley
Vallo / *It.*	wall
Valta / *Finn.*	cape
Váltos / *Gr.*	marsh
Valul / *Rom.*	wall
Vann / *Dan.; Nor.*	water, lake
Vanua / *Mel.*	land
Vár / *Hung.*	fort
Vara / *Finn.*	mountain
Varoš / *S.C.*	city, town
Város / *Hung.*	city, town
Varre / *Lapp.*	mountain
Vary / *Cz.*	spring
Vas / *S.C.; Slvn.*	village
Vásár / *Hung.*	market
Väst / *Swed.*	west
Väster / *Swed.*	western
Vatn / *Icel.; Nor.*	lake
Vatten / *Swed.*	water, lake
Vatu / *Mel.; Poly.*	island, reef
Vdhr., Vodohranilišče / *Rus.*	reservoir
Vechiu / *Rom.*	old
Vecs / *Latv.*	old
Veen / *Dut.; Fle.*	moor
Vega / *Sp.*	irrigated crops
Veld / *Afr.; Dut.; Fle.*	field
Veli / *S.C.; Slvn.*	great
Velik / *Bulg.*	great
Veliki / *Rus.; S.C.; Slvn.*	great
Veliký / *Cz.*	great
Velký / *Cz.*	great
Vel'ky / *Slvk.*	great
Vella / *Cat.*	old
Ver / *Ural.*	forest
Verde / *It.; Sp.*	green
Verh / *Rus.*	peak
Verhni / *Rus.*	upper
Verk / *Swed.*	factory
Vermelho / *Port.*	red
Vert / *Fr.*	green
Ves / *Cz.*	village
Vesi / *Finn.*	water, lake
Vest / *Dan.; Nor.*	west
Vester / *Dan.; Nor.*	western
Vestur / *Icel.*	west
Vetta / *It.*	summit
Viaduc / *Fr.*	viaduct

Local Form	English
Vidda / *Nor.*	upland
Vidde / *Nor.*	upland
Viejo / *Sp.*	old
Vier / *Germ.*	four
Viertel / *Germ.*	quarter
Vieux / *Fr.*	old
Vig / *Dan.*	bay
Vík / *Icel.; Nor.; Swed.*	gulf, bay
Vila / *Port.*	city, town
Villa / *Sp.*	city, town
Ville, -ville / *Eng.; Fr.*	city, town
Vinh / *Viet.*	bay
Virful / *Rom.*	peak, mountain
Virta / *Finn.*	river
Višni / *Rus.*	high
Visok / *S.C.*	high
Viz / *Hung.*	water
Viztároló / *Hung.*	reservoir
Vlakte / *Dut.; Fle.*	plain
Vlei / *Afr.*	pond
Vliet / *Dut.; Fle.*	river
Vloer / *Afr.*	depression
Voda / *Bulg.; Cz.; Rus.; S.C.; Slvn.*	water
Vodny put / *Rus.*	stream, canal
Vodohranilišče, vdhr. / *Rus.*	reservoir
Vodopad / *Rus.*	waterfall
Volcan / *Fr.*	volcano
Volcán / *Sp.*	volcano
Voll / *Nor.*	meadow
Vórios / *Gr.*	northern
Vorota / *Rus.*	gate
Vorrás / *Gr.*	north
Vostočny / *Rus.*	eastern
Vostok / *Rus.*	east
Vötn / *Icel.*	lake, water
Vož / *Ural.*	mouth
Vozvyšennost / *Rus.*	upland
Vpadina / *Rus.*	depression
Vrah / *Bulg.*	peak
Vrata / *Bulg.; S.C.; Slvn.*	pass
Vrch / *Cz.; Slvk.*	mountain
Vrch / *S.C.; Slvn.*	peak
Vrchni / *Cz.*	upper
Vrchovina / *Cz.*	upland
Vulcan / *Rom.; Rus.*	volcano
Vulcano / *It.*	volcano
Vulkan / *Germ.; Rus.*	volcano
Vuopio / *Lapp.*	bend
Vuori / *Finn.*	rock
Východný / *Cz.*	eastern
Vyšný / *Slvk.*	upper
Vysoki / *Rus.*	high
Vysoky / *Cz.; Slvk.*	high
Vyšši / *Cz.*	high

W

Local Form	English
W., Wādī / *Ar.*	wadi
Wa / *Ban.*	people
Wabe / *Amh.*	stream
Wad / *Ar.*	wadi
Wad / *Dut.*	tidal flat
Wādī, W. / *Ar.*	wadi
Wāḥāt / *Ar.*	oasis
Wai / *Mel.; Poly.*	stream
Wal / *Afr.*	wall
Wala / *Hin.*	mountain range
Wald / *Germ.*	forest
Wan / *Burm.*	village
Wan / *Chin.; Jap.*	bay
Wand / *Germ.*	bluff
War / *Som.*	pond
Wār / *Ar.*	desert
-waram / *Hin.; Tam.*	village
Wasser / *Germ.*	water
Wat / *Rus.*	wall
Wat / *Thai*	church
Waterval / *Afr.; Dut.*	waterfall
Watt / *Germ.*	tidal flat
Wāw / *Ar.*	oasis
Weald / *Eng.*	wooded country
Webi / *Som.*	stream
Weg / *Germ.*	way, road
Wei / *Chin.*	cape, point
Weide / *Germ.*	pasture
Weiler / *Germ.*	village
Weiß / *Germ.*	white
Weon / *Kor.*	field
Wer / *Som.*	pond
Werder / *Germ.*	river island
Werk / *Germ.*	factory
Wes / *Afr.*	west
Westlich / *Germ.*	western
Westr- / *Sca.*	western
Wēyn / *Som.*	great
Wēyne / *Som.*	great
Wick / *Eng.*	village
Wiek / *Germ.*	bay
Wielki / *Pol.*	great
Wies / *Germ.*	village
Wijk / *Dut.; Fle.*	quarter, district
-willer / *Germ.*	village

Local Form	English
Woda / *Pol.*	water
Woestyn / *Afr.*	desert
Wold / *Dut.; Fle.; Eng.*	forest
Wörth / *Germ.*	river island
Woud / *Dut.; Fle.*	forest
Wschodni / *Pol.*	eastern
Wysoczyzna / *Pol.*	upland
Wysoki / *Pol.*	upper
Wyspa / *Pol.*	island
Wyżyna / *Pol.*	highland
Wzgórze / *Pol.*	hill

X

Local Form	English
Xi / *Chin.*	west
Xia / *Chin.*	gorge, strait
Xian / *Chin.*	county, shire
Xiang / *Chin.*	village
Xiao / *Chin.*	little
Xin / *Chin.*	new
Xu / *Chin.*	island

Y

Local Form	English
Yam / *Hebr.*	lake, sea
Yama / *Jap.*	mountain
Yan / *Chin.*	mountain
Yang / *Chin.*	strait, ocean
Yani / *Tur.*	new
Yar / *Tur.*	gorge
Yarimada / *Tur.*	peninsula
Yazı / *Tur.*	plain
Yegge / *Sah.*	well
Yeni / *Tur.*	new
Yeon / *Kor.*	sea
Yeong / *Kor.*	mountain
Yeşil / *Tur.*	green
Ylä / *Finn.*	upper
Yli- / *Finn.*	upper
Yō / *Jap.*	ocean
Yobe / *Sud.*	great
Yŏm / *Kor.*	island
Yoma / *Burm.*	mountain range
Yŏn / *Kor.*	lake, pond
Yŏng / *Kor.*	mountain, peak
Ytter / *Nor.; Swed.*	outer
Yttre / *Swed.*	outer
Yu / *Chin.*	old
Yu / *Chin.*	island
Yu / *Jap.*	thermal spring
Yüan / *Chin.*	spring, river
Yunhe / *Chin.*	canal

Z

Local Form	English
Zāb / *Ar.*	river
Zachodni / *Pol.*	western
Zaki / *Jap.*	cape
Zalew / *Pol.*	gulf
Zaliv / *Bulg.; Rus.; S.C.; Slvn.*	gulf
Zaljev / *Slvn.*	bay
Zámek / *Cz.*	castle
Zan / *Jap.*	mountain
Zand / *Dut.; Fle.*	sand
Zandt / *Dut.; Fle.*	sand
Zangbo / *Chin.*	river
Zapad / *Rus.*	west
Zapaden / *Bulg.*	western
Zapadni / *S.C.; Slvn.*	western
Západní / *Cz.*	western
Zapadny / *Rus.*	western
Zapovednik / *Rus.*	reserve
Zatoka / *Pol.*	gulf
Zavod / *Rus.*	roadstead
Zāwiyat / *Ar.*	monastery
Zdrój / *Pol.*	thermal springs
Ze / *Jap.*	islet
Zee / *Dut.; Fle.*	sea
Zelëny / *Rus.*	green
Žem / *Lith.*	land, country
Zemé / *Cz.; Slvk.*	land, country
Zemlja / *Rus.*	land
Zen / *Jap.*	mountain
Zhan / *Chin.*	mountain
Zhen / *Chin.*	market
Zhong / *Chin.*	central
Zhou / *Chin.*	quarter, district
Zhuang / *Chin.*	village
Ziemia / *Pol.*	land
Zigos / *Gr.*	pass
Zipfel / *Germ.*	tip, point
Ziwa / *Swa.*	marsh
Zizhiqu / *Chin.*	autonomous region
Zlato / *Bulg.*	gold
Zuid / *Dut.; Fle.*	south
Zuidelijk / *Dut.*	southern
Żuława / *Pol.*	marsh
Zun / *Mong.*	east
Zwart / *Dut.*	black
Zwei / *Germ.*	two

International Map Index

All of the toponyms (place-names) which appear on the maps are listed in the International Map Index. Each entry includes the following: Place-name and, where applicable, other forms by which it is written or known; a symbol, where applicable, indicating what kind of feature it is; the number of the map on which it appears; and the map-reference letters and geographical coordinates indicating its location on the map.

Toponyms

Each toponym, or place-name, is written in full, with accents and diacritical marks. Since many countries have more than one official language, many of these forms are included on the maps. For example, many Belgian place-names are listed as follows: Bruxelles/Brussel; Antwerpen/Anvers, and vice versa, Brussel/Bruxelles; Anvers/Antwerpen. In Italy, certain regions have a special status—they are largely autonomous and officially bilingual. As a result, Index listings appear as follows: Aosta/Aoste; Alto Adige/Sud Tirol, and vice versa. One name, however, may be the only name on the map.

In China, the written forms of commonly used regional languages have been taken into account. These forms are enclosed in parenthesis following the official name: e.g. Xiangshan (Dancheng). However, when the regional is listed first, it is linked to the official name with an→: e.g. Dancheng→Xiangshan. The same style is used for former or historical name forms: e.g. Rhodesia→Zimbabwe and Zimbabwe (Rhodesia).

Place-names for major features (countries, major cities, and large physical features), where applicable, include the English conventional form identified by (EN) and linked in the local name or names with an = sign: e.g. Italia=Italy (EN), and vice versa, Italy (EN)=Italia. Former English names are linked in the Index to the conventional form by an→.

Symbols

The last component with the place-name is a symbol, where applicable, specifying the broad category of the feature named. A table preceding the Index lists all of the symbols used and their meanings; this information also appears as a footnote on each page of the Index. Place-names without symbols are cities and towns.

Alphabetization

Place-names are listed in English alphabetical order—26 letters, from A to Z—because of its international usage. Names including two or more words are listed alphabetically according to the first letter of the word: e.g. De Ruyter is listed under D; Le Havre is listed under L. Names with the prefix Mc are listed as if spelled Mac. The generic portion of a name (lake, sierra, mountain, etc.) is placed after the name: e.g. Lake Erie is listed as Erie, Lake; Sierra Morena is listed as Morena, Sierra. In Spanish, "ch" and "ll" groups and the letter "ñ" are included respectively under C, L, and N, without any distinction.

The same place-name sometimes is listed in the Index several times. It may because of the various translations of a name, or it may be that several places have the same name.

Various translations of a name appear as follows:

Danube (EN)=Dunav   Danube (EN)=Donau
Danube (EN)=Dunărea   Danube (EN)=Dunaj

Several places with the same name appear as follows; however, only in these cases is the location—abbreviated and enclosed in brackets—included. A table of these abbreviations precedes the Index.

Abbeville [U.S.]   Aberdeen [Scot.-U.K.]
Abbeville [Fr.]   Aberdeen [N.C.-U.S.]
Aberdeen [S. Afr.]

Map Number

Each map in the atlas is identified by a number. Where multiple maps are on one page, each map is additionally identified by a boxed letter in the upper-right-hand corner of the map. In the Index listing following the place-name and its variations in language and spelling, where applicable, is the number of the map on which it appears. If the map is one of several on a page, the Index listing includes the map number and letter.

Although a place-name may appear on one or more maps, it is indexed to only one map. Most places are indexed to the regional maps. However, if a place-name appears on either the physical or political continental maps, it is indexed to one of the two types of map. For example, a river or mountain would be indexed to a physical continental map; a city or state would be indexed to a political continental map.

Map-Reference Letters and Geographical Coordinates

The next elements in the Index listing are the map-reference letters and the geographical coordinates, respectively, locating the place on the map.

Map-reference letters consist of a capital and a lowercase letter. Capital letters are across the top and bottom of the maps; lowercase letters are down the sides. The map-reference letters assigned to each place-name refer to the location of the name within the area formed by grid lines connecting the geographical coordinates on either sides of the letters.

Geographical coordinates are the latitude (N for North, S for South) and longitude (E for East, W for West) expressed in degrees and minutes and based on the prime meridian, Greenwich.

Map-reference letters and coordinates for extensive geographical features, such as mountain ranges and countries, are given for the approximate central point of the area. Those for waterways, such as canals and rivers, are given for the mouth of the river, the point where it enters another river or where the feature reaches the map margin. On this page are sample maps showing points to which features are indexed according to map-reference letters and coordinates.

On most maps there is not enough space to place all of the names of administrative subdivisions. In these cases the location of the place is shown on the map by a circled letter or number and the place-name and circled letter or number are listed in the map margin. The map-reference numbers and coordinates for these places refer to the location of the circled letter or number on the map.

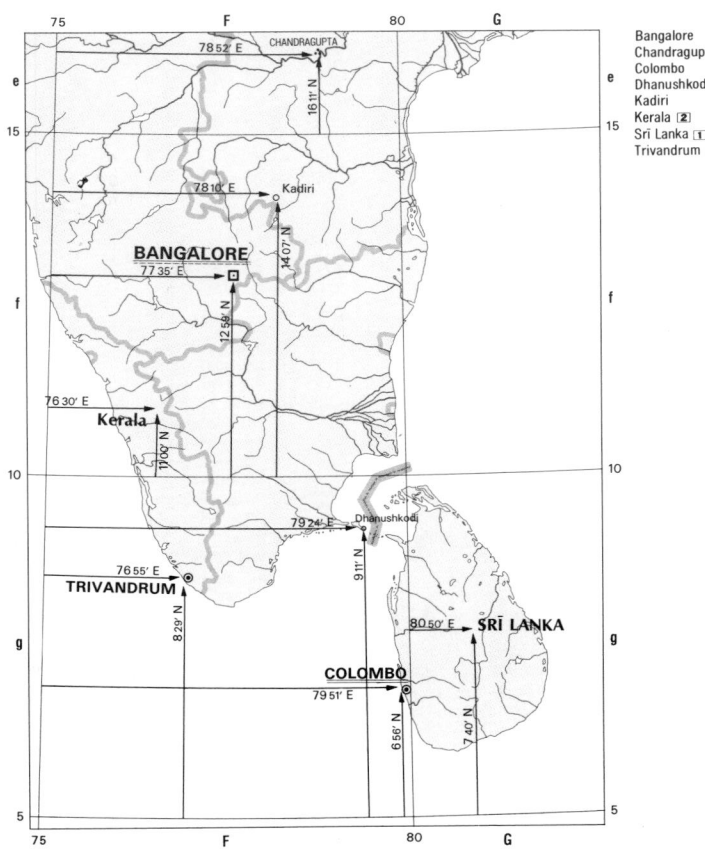

Bangalore	25	Ff	12°59'N	77°35'E
Chandragupta ⌂	35	Fe	16°11'N	78°52'E
Colombo	25	Fg	6°56'N	79°51'E
Dhanushkodi	25	Fg	9°11'N	79°24'E
Kadiri	25	Ff	14°07'N	78°10'E
Kerala [2]	25	Ff	11°00'N	76°30'E
Sri Lanka [1]	25	Gg	7°40'N	80°50'E
Trivandrum	25	Fg	8°29'N	76°55'E

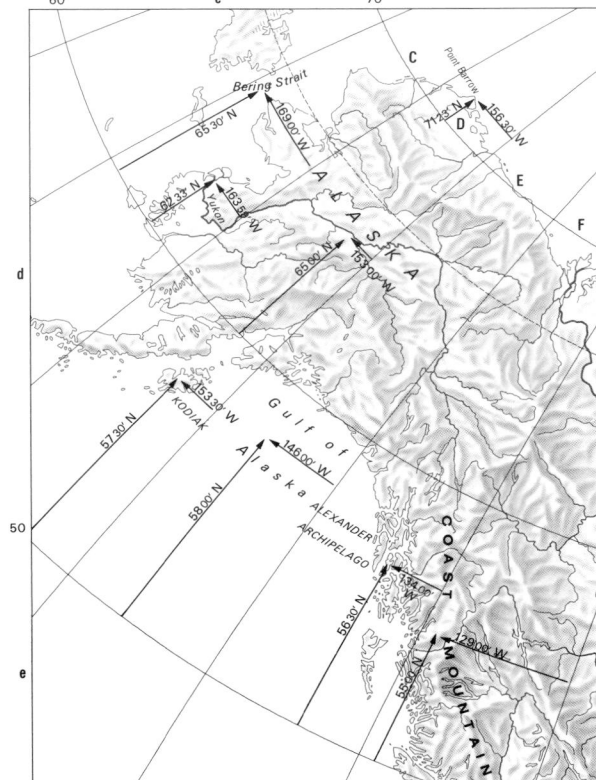

Alaska	38	Dc	65°00'N	153°00'W
Alaska, Gulf of-	38	Ed	58°00'N	146°00'W
Alexander Archipelago	38	Fd	56°30'N	134°00'W
Barrow, Point-	38	Db	71°23'N	156°30'W
Bering Strait	38	Cc	65°30'N	169°00'W
Coast Mountains	38	Gd	55°00'N	129°00'W
Kodiak	38	Dd	57°30'N	153°30'W
Yukon	38	Cc	62°33'N	163°59'W

List of Abbreviations

Abz.-U.S.S.R. Azerbaijan S.S.R., U.S.S.R.
Afg. Afghanistan
Afr. Africa
Agl. Anguilla
Ak.-U.S. Alaska, U.S.
Alb. Albania
Alg. Algeria
Alta.-Can. Alberta, Canada
Am. Sam. American Samoa
And. Andorra
Ang. Angola
Ant. Antarctica
Ar.-U.S. Arkansas, U.S.
Arg. Argentina
Arm.-U.S.S.R. Armenian S.S.R., U.S.S.R.
Asia Asia
Atg. Antigua and Barbuda
Aus. Austria
Austl. Australia
Az.-U.S. Arizona, U.S.
Azr. Azores
Bah. Bahamas
Bar. Barbados
B.A.T. British Antarctic Territory
B.C.-Can. British Columbia, Canada
Bel. Belgium
Ben. Benin
Ber. Bermuda
Bhr. Bahrain
Bhu. Bhutan
Blz. Belize
Bnd. Burundi
Bngl. Bangladesh
Bol. Bolivia
Bots. Botswana
Braz. Brazil
Bru. Brunei
Bul. Bulgaria
Bur. Burma
Burkina Burkina Faso
B.V.I. British Virgin Islands
Bye.-U.S.S.R. Byelorussian S.S.R., U.S.S.R.
Ca.-U.S. California, U.S.
Cam. Cameroon
C. Amer. Central America
Can. Canada
Can. Is. Canary Islands
C.A.R. Central African Republic
Cay. Is Cayman Islands
Chad Chad
Chan. Is. Channel Islands
Chile Chile
China China
Co.-U.S. Colorado, U.S.
Cocos Is. Cocos Islands
Col. Colombia
Con. Congo
Cook Cook Islands
Cor. Sea Is. Coral Sea Islands
C.R. Costa Rica
Ct.-U.S. Connecticut, U.S.
Cuba Cuba
C.V. Cape Verde
Cyp. Cyprus
Czech. Czechoslovakia

D.C.-U.S. District of Columbia, U.S.
De.-U.S. Delaware, U.S.
Den. Denmark
Dji. Djibouti
Dom. Dominica
Dom. Rep. Dominican Republic
Ec. Ecuador
Eg. Egypt
El Sal. El Salvador
Eng.-U.K. England, U.K.
Eq. Gui. Equatorial Guinea
Est.-U.S.S.R. Estonian S.S.R., U.S.S.R.
Eth. Ethiopia
Eur. Europe
Falk. Is. Falkland Islands
Far. Is. Faeroe Islands
Fiji Fiji
Fin. Finland
Fl.-U.S. Florida, U.S.
Fr. France
F.R.G. Federal Republic of Germany
Fr. Gui. French Guiana
Fr. Poly. French Polynesia
F.S.M. Federated States of Micronesia
Ga.-U.S. Georgia, U.S.
Gabon Gabon
Gam. Gambia
G.D.R. German Democratic Republic
Geo.-U.S.S.R. Georgian S.S.R., U.S.S.R.
Ghana Ghana
Gib. Gibraltar
Grc. Greece
Gren. Grenada
Grld. Greenland
Guad. Guadeloupe
Guam Guam
Guat. Guatemala
Gui. Guinea
Gui. Bis. Guinea Bissau
Guy. Guyana
Haiti Haiti
Hi.-U.S. Hawaii, U.S.
H.K. Hong Kong
Hond. Honduras
Hun. Hungary
Ia.-U.S. Iowa, U.S.
I.C. Ivory Coast
Ice. Iceland
Id.-U.S. Idaho, U.S.
Il.-U.S. Illinois, U.S.
In.-U.S. Indiana, U.S.
India India
Indon. Indonesia
I. of M. Isle of Man
Iran Iran
Iraq Iraq
Ire. Ireland
Isr. Israel
It. Italy
Jam. Jamaica
Jap. Japan
Jor. Jordan
Kam. Cambodia
Kaz.-U.S.S.R. Kazakh S.S.R., U.S.S.R.
Kenya Kenya

Ker. Is. Kermadec Islands
Kir. Kiribati
Kirg.-U.S.S.R. Kirghiz S.S.R., U.S.S.R.
Ks.-U.S. Kansas, U.S.
Kuw. Kuwait
Ky.-U.S. Kentucky, U.S.
La.-U.S. Louisiana, U.S.
Laos Laos
Lat.-U.S.S.R. Latvian S.S.R., U.S.S.R.
Lbr. Liberia
Leb. Lebanon
Les. Lesotho
Lib. Libya
Liech. Liechtenstein
Lith.-U.S.S.R. Lithuanian S.S.R., U.S.S.R.
Lux. Luxembourg
Ma.-U.S. Massachusetts, U.S.
Mac. Macao
Mad. Madagascar
Mala. Malaysia
Mald. Maldives
Mali Mali
Malta Malta
Man.-Can. Manitoba, Canada
Mar. Is. Marshall Islands
Mart. Martinique
Maur. Mauritius
May. Mayotte
Mco. Monaco
Md.-U.S. Maryland, U.S.
Me.-U.S. Maine, U.S.
Mex. Mexico
Mi.-U.S. Michigan, U.S.
Mid. Is. Midway Islands
Mn.-U.S. Minnesota, U.S.
Mo.-U.S. Missouri, U.S.
Mold.-U.S.S.R. Moldavian S.S.R., U.S.S.R.
Mong. Mongolia
Mont. Montserrat
Mor. Morocco
Moz. Mozambique
Ms.-U.S. Mississippi, U.S.
Mt.-U.S. Montana, U.S.
Mtna. Mauritania
Mwi. Malawi
Nam. Namibia
N. Amer. North America
Nauru Nauru
N.B.-Can. New Brunswick, Canada
Nb.-U.S. Nebraska, U.S.
N.C.-U.S. North Carolina, U.S.
N. Cal. New Caledonia
N.D.-U.S. North Dakota, U.S.
Nep. Nepal
Neth. Netherlands
Neth. Ant. Netherlands Antilles
Newf.-Can. Newfoundland, Canada
N.H.-U.S. New Hampshire, U.S.
Nic. Nicaragua
Nig. Nigeria
Niger Niger

N. Ire.-U.K. Northern Ireland, U.K.
N.J.-U.S. New Jersey, U.S.
N. Kor. North Korea
N.M.-U.S. New Mexico, U.S.
N. M. Is. Northern Mariana Islands
Nor. Norway
Nor. I. Norfolk Island
N.S.-Canada Nova Scotia, Canada
Nv.-U.S. Nevada, U.S.
N.W.T.-Can. Northwest Territories, Canada
N.Y.-U.S. New York, U.S.
N.Z. New Zealand
Ocn. Oceania
Oh.-U.S. Ohio, U.S.
Ok.-U.S. Oklahoma, U.S.
Oman Oman
Ont.-Ont. Ontario, Canada
Or.-U.S. Oregon, U.S.
Pa.-U.S. Pennsylvania, U.S.
Pak. Pakistan
Pal. Palau
Pan. Panama
Pap. N. Gui. Papua New Guinea
Par. Paraguay
Pas. Pascua
P.D.R.Y. Yemen
P.E.I.-Can. Prince Edward Island, Canada
Peru Peru
Phil. Philippines
Pit. Pitcairn
Pol. Poland
Port. Portugal
P.R. Puerto Rico
Qatar Qatar
Que.-Can. Quebec, Canada
Reu. Reunion
R.I.-U.S. Rhode Island, U.S.
Rom. Romania
R.S.F.S.R.-U.S.S.R. Russian Soviet Federative Socialist Republic, U.S.S.R.
Rwn. Rwanda
S. Afr. South Africa
S. Amer. South America
Sao T.P. Sao Tome and Principe
Sask.-Can. Saskatchewan, Canada
Sau. Ar. Saudi Arabia
S.C.-U.S. South Carolina, U.S.
Scot.-U.K. Scotland, U.K.
S.D.-U.S. South Dakota, U.S.
Sen. Senegal
Sey. Seychelles
Sing. Singapore
S. Kor. South Korea
S.L. Sierra Leone
S. Lan. Sri Lanka
S.M. San Marino
S.N.A. Spanish North Africa
Sol. Is. Solomon Islands
Som. Somalia
Sp. Spain
St. C.N. Saint Christopher-Nevis

St. Hel. Saint Helena
St. Luc. Saint Lucia
St. P.M. Saint Pierre and Miquelon
St. Vin. Saint Vincent and the Grenadines
Sud. Sudan
Sur. Suriname
Sval. Svalbard
Swe. Sweden
Switz. Switzerland
Syr. Syria
Tad.-U.S.S.R. Tajik S.S.R., U.S.S.R.
Tai. Taiwan
Tan. Tanzania
T.C. Is. Turks and Caicos Islands
Thai. Thailand
Tn.-U.S. Tennessee, U.S.
Togo Togo
Ton. Tonga
Trin. Trinidad and Tobago
T.T.P.I. Trust Territory of the Pacific Islands
Tun. Tunisia
Tur. Turkey
Tur.-U.S.S.R. Turkmen S.S.R., U.S.S.R.
Tuv. Tuvalu
Tx.-U.S. Texas, U.S.
U.A.E. United Arab Emirates
Ug. Uganda
U.K. United Kingdom
Ukr.-U.S.S.R. Ukrainian S.S.R., U.S.S.R.
Ur. Uruguay
U.S. United States
U.S.S.R. Union of Soviet Socialist Republics
Ut.-U.S. Utah, U.S.
Uzb.-U.S.S.R. Uzbek S.S.R., U.S.S.R.
Va.-U.S. Virginia, U.S.
Van. Vanuatu
V.C. Vatican City
Ven. Venezuela
Viet. Vietnam
V.I.U.S. Virgin Islands of the U.S.
Vt.-U.S. Vermont, U.S.
Wa.-U.S. Washington, U.S.
Wake Wake Island
Wales-U.K. Wales, U.K.
W.F. Wallis and Futuna
Wi.-U.S. Wisconsin, U.S.
W. Sah. Western Sahara
W. Sam. Western Samoa
W.V.-U.S. West Virginia, U.S.
Wy.-U.S. Wyoming, U.S.
Yem. Yemen
Yugo. Yugoslavia
Yuk.-Can. Yukon, Canada
Zaire Zaire
Zam. Zambia
Zimb. Zimbabwe

List of Symbols

Plains and Associated Features
Plain, Basin, Lowland
Delta
Salt Flat

Valleys and Depressions
Valley, Gorge, Ravine, Canyon
Cave, Crater, Quarry
Karst Features
Depression
Polder, Reclaimed Marsh

Vegetational Features
Desert, Dunes
Forest, Woods
Heath, Steppe, Tundra, Moor
Oasis

Political/Administrative Units
1 Independent Nation
2 State, Canton, Region
3 Province, Department, County, Territory, District
4 Municipality
5 Colony, Dependency, Administered Territory

Geographical Regions
Continent
Physical Region
Historical or Cultural Region

Mountain Features
Mount, Mountain, Peak
Volcano
Hill
Mountains, Mountain Range
Hills, Escarpment
Plateau, Highland, Upland
Pass, Gap

Coastal Features
Cape, Point
Coast, Beach
Cliff
Peninsula, Promontory
Isthmus
Sandbank, Tombolo, Sandbar

Islands Rocks, Reefs
Island
Atoll
Rock, Reef
Islands, Archipelago
Rocks, Reefs
Coral Reef

Hydrographic Features
Well, Spring
Geyser, Fumarole
River, Stream, Brook
Waterfall, Rapids, Cataract
River Mouth, Estuary
Lake
Salt Lake
Intermittent Lake, Dry Lake Bed
Reservoir, Artificial Lake
Swamp, Marsh, Pond
Irrigation Canal, Navigable Canal, Ditch, Aqueduct

Ice Features
Glacier, Snowfield
Ice Shelf, Pack Ice

Marine Features
Ocean
Sea
Gulf, Bay
Strait, Fjord, Sea Channel
Lagoon, Anchorage

Submarine Features
Bank, Shoal
Seamount
Rise, Plateau, Tablemount
Seamount Chain, Ridge
Platform, Shelf
Basin, Depression
Escarpment, Slope, Sea Scarp
Fracture
Trench, Abyss, Valley, Canyon

Other Features
National Park, Nature Reserve
Scenic Area, Point of Interest
Recreation Site, Sports Arena
Cave, Cavern
Historic Site, Memorial, Mausoleum, Museum
Ruins
Wall, Walls, Tower, Castle, Fortress
Church, Abbey, Cathedral, Sanctuary
Temple, Synagogue, Mosque
Research or Scientific Station
Airport, Heliport
Port, Dock
Lighthouse
Mine
Tunnel
Dam, Bridge

A

Å 7 Cc 67.53N 12.59 E
Aa [Eur.] 12 Ic 51.50N 6.25 E
Aa [Fr.] 11 Ic 51.01N 2.06 E
Aa [Fr.] 12 Dd 50.44N 2.18 E
Aa [F.R.G.] 12 Kb 52.07N 8.41 E
Aa [F.R.G.] 12 Jb 52.15N 7.18 E
Aachen 10 Cf 50.46N 6.06 E
Aalen 10 Gh 48.50N 10.06 E
A'ālī an Nīl [3] 35 Ed 9.15N 33.00 E
Aalsmeer 12 Gb 52.15N 4.45 E
Aalst/Alost 11 Kd 50.56N 4.02 E
Aalten 12 Ic 51.55N 6.35 E
Aalter 12 Fc 51.05N 3.27 E
Äänekoski 7 Fe 62.36N 25.44 E
Aa of Weerijs 12 Gc 51.35N 4.46 E
Aar 12 Kd 50.23N 8.00 E
Aarau 14 Cc 47.25N 8.02 E
Aarbergen 12 Kd 50.13N 8.03 E
Aare 14 Cc 47.37N 8.13 E
Aargau [2] 14 Cc 47.30N 8.10 E
Aarlen/Arlon 11 Le 49.41N 5.49 E
Aarschot 11 Kd 50.59N 4.50 E
Aat/Ath 11 Jd 50.38N 3.47 E
Aazanèn 13 Ii 35.06N 3.02W
Āb 24 Md 36.00N 48.05 E
Aba [Nig.] 31 Hh 5.07N 7.22 E
Aba [Zaire] 31 Hk 3.52N 30.14 E
Aba/Ngawa 27 He 32.55N 101.45 E
Abā ad Dūd 24 Ki 27.02N 44.04 E
Abā as Su'ūd 23 Ff 17.28N 44.06 E
Abacaxis, Rio- 54 Gd 3.54S 58.50W
Abaco Island 38 Lg 26.25N 77.10W
Abacou, Pointe l'- 49 Kd 18.03N 73.47W
Abadab, Jabal- 35 Fb 18.53N 35.59 E
Ābādān 22 Gf 30.10N 48.50 E
Ābādeh [Iran] 23 Hc 31.10N 52.37 E
Ābādeh [Iran] 24 Oh 29.08N 52.52 E
Abadiânia 55 Hc 16.06S 48.48W
Abadla 31 Ge 31.01N 2.43W
Abaeté 55 Jd 19.09S 45.27W
Abaeté, Rio- 55 Jd 18.02S 45.12W
Abaetetuba 54 Id 1.42S 48.54W
Abagnar Qi (Xilin Hot) 22 Ne 43.58N 116.08 E
Abag Qi (Xin Hot) 27 Jc 44.01N 114.59 E
Abai 55 Eh 26.01S 55.57W
Abaiang Atoll 57 Id 1.51N 172.58 E
Abaj 19 Hf 49.38N 72.50 E
Abaji 34 Gd 8.28N 6.57 E
Abajo Mountains 46 Kh 37.50N 109.25W
Abakaliki 34 Gd 6.20N 8.03 E
Abakan 20 Ef 53.43N 91.30 E
Abakan 22 Ld 53.43N 91.26 E
Abakwasimbo 36 Eb 0.36N 28.43 E
Abala [Con.] 36 Cc 1.21S 15.30 E
Abala [Niger] 34 Fc 14.56N 3.26 E
Abalak 34 Gb 15.27N 6.17 E
Aban 20 Ee 56.40N 96.10 E
Abancay 54 Df 13.35S 72.55W
Abancourt 12 De 49.42N 1.46 E
Abanga 36 Bb 0.13N 10.28 E
Abano Terme 14 Fe 45.21N 11.47 E
Ābār al Jidd 24 Hf 32.50N 39.50 E
Abarqū 23 Hc 31.08N 53.17 E
Abarqu, Kavīr-e- 24 Og 31.00N 53.50 E
Abashiri 27 Pc 44.01N 144.17 E
Abashiri-Gawa 29a Db 43.56N 144.09 E
Abashiri-Ko 29a Da 44.00N 144.10 E
Abashiri-Wan 29a Da 44.00N 144.35 E
Abasolo 48 Je 24.04N 98.22W
Abatski 19 Hd 56.18N 70.28 E
Abau 60 Dj 10.11S 148.42 E
Abava 7 Eh 57.06N 21.54 E
Abay=Blue Nile (EN) 30 Kg 15.38N 32.31 E
Abaya, Lake- 30 Kh 6.20N 37.55 E
Abaza 20 Ef 52.39N 90.06 E
Abbadia San Salvatore 14 Fh 42.53N 11.41 E
Abbah Quşūr 14 Co 35.57N 8.50 E
Āb Bārīk 24 Oh 29.45N 52.37 E
'Abbāsābād 24 Qd 36.20N 56.25 E
Abbekås 8 Ei 55.24N 13.36 E
Abberton Reservoir 12 Cc 51.50N 0.55 E
Abbeville [Fr.] 11 Hd 50.06N 1.50 E
Abbeville [La.-U.S.] 45 Jl 29.58N 92.08W
Abbeville [S.C.-U.S.] 44 Fh 34.10N 82.23W
Abbey 46 Ka 50.43N 108.45W
Abbeyfeale/Mainistir na Féile 9 Di 52.24N 9.18W
Abbiategrasso 14 Ce 45.24N 8.54 E
Abbot, Mount- 59 Jd 20.03S 147.45 E
Abbot Ice Shelf 66 Pf 72.45S 96.00W
'Abd Al 'Azīz, Jabal- 24 Id 36.25N 40.20 E
'Abd al Kūrī 21 Hh 12.12N 52.13 E
Ābdānān 24 Lf 32.57N 47.26 E
Abdul Ghadir 35 Gc 10.42N 42.59 E
Abdulino 19 Fe 53.42N 53.38 E
Abe, Lake- 35 Gc 11.10N 41.45 E
Abéché 31 Jg 13.49N 20.49 E
Abeek 12 Hc 51.15N 6.00 E
Abe-Gawa 29 Fd 34.55N 138.22 E
Abeløya 41 Pc 79.00N 30.15 E
Abelvær 7 Cd 64.44N 11.11 E
Abemama Atoll 57 Id 0.21N 173.51 E
Abenab 37 Bc 19.12S 18.06 E
Abengourou [3] 34 Ed 6.35N 3.25W
Abengourou 31 Gh 6.44N 3.29W
Åbenrå 7 Bi 55.02N 9.26 E
Åbenrå Fjord 8 Ci 55.05N 9.35 E
Abeokuta 31 Hh 7.09N 3.21 E
Āb-e-Pany 23 If 37.06N 68.20 E
Aberayron 9 Ii 52.15N 4.15W
Aberdare Range 30 Ki 0.25S 36.38 E
Aberdeen [Id.-U.S.] 46 Ie 42.57N 112.50W
Aberdeen [Md.-U.S.] 44 If 39.30N 76.14W
Aberdeen [Ms.-U.S.] 45 Lj 33.49N 88.33W
Aberdeen [N.C.-U.S.] 44 Hh 35.08N 79.26W
Aberdeen [S.Afr.] 37 Cf 32.29S 24.03 E
Aberdeen [Scot.-U.K.] 6 Fd 57.10N 2.04W
Aberdeen [S.D.-U.S.] 39 Je 45.28N 98.29W
Aberdeen [Wa.-U.S.] 43 Cb 46.59N 123.50W
Aberdeen Lake 42 Hd 64.28N 99.00W
Abergavenny 9 Kj 51.50N 3.00W
Aberystwyth 9 Ii 52.25N 4.05W
Abetone 14 Ef 44.08N 10.40 E
Abez 19 Gb 66.32N 61.46 E
Abhā 22 Gh 18.13N 42.30 E
Abhainn an Chláir/Clare 9 Dh 53.20N 9.03W
Abhainn an Lagáin/Lagan 9 Hg 54.37N 5.53W
Abhainn na Bandan/Bandon 9 Ej 51.40N 8.30W
Abhainn na Deirge/Derg 9 Fg 54.40N 7.25W
Abhar 24 Md 36.02N 49.45 E
Abhar 23 Gb 36.09N 49.13 E
Abhazskaja ASSR [3] 19 Eg 43.00N 41.10 E
Abibe, Serrania de- 54 Cb 8.00N 76.30W
Abidjan 31 Gh 5.19N 4.02W
Abidjan [3] 34 Ed 5.30N 4.30W
Abilene [Ks.-U.S.] 45 Hg 38.55N 97.13W
Abilene [Tx.-U.S.] 39 Jf 32.27N 99.44W
Abingdon 9 Lj 51.41N 1.17W
Abinsk 16 Kg 44.52N 38.10 E
Abiquiu 45 Ch 36.12N 106.19W
Abiquiu Reservoir 45 Ch 36.18N 106.32W
Abisko 7 Eb 68.20N 18.51 E
Abitibi 42 Jf 51.04N 80.55W
Abitibi, Lake- 38 Le 48.42N 79.45W
Abiy Adi 35 Fc 13.37N 39.01 E
Abiyata, Lake- 35 Fd 7.38N 38.36 E
Abja-Paluoja 8 Kf 58.02N 25.14 E
Abnūb 33 Fd 27.16N 31.09 E
Åbo/Turku 6 Ic 60.27N 22.17 E
Abo, Massif d'- 35 Ba 21.41N 16.08 E
Abóboras, Serra das- 55 Jc 16.12S 44.35W
Abodo 35 Ed 7.50N 34.25 E
Aboisso [3] 34 Ed 5.28N 3.02W
Aboisso 34 Ed 5.28N 3.12W
Abomey 31 Hh 7.11N 1.59 E
Abong Mbang 34 He 3.59N 13.11 E
Abony 10 Pi 47.11N 20.00 E
Aborigen, Pik- 20 Jd 62.05N 149.10 E
Aborlar 26 Ge 9.26N 118.33 E
Aborrebierg 8 Ej 54.59N 12.32 E
Abou Deia 35 Bc 11.27N 19.17 E
Abou Goulem 35 Cc 13.37N 21.38 E
Abovjan 16 Ni 40.14N 44.37 E
Abrād, Wādī- 23 Gf 15.51N 46.05 E
Abraham's Bay 49 Kb 22.21N 72.55W
Abramovski Bereg 7 Kc 66.25N 43.05 E
Abrántes 13 De 39.28N 8.12W
Abra Pampa 56 Gb 22.43S 65.42W
Abrego 49 Ki 8.04N 73.14W
Abreojos, Punta- 47 Bc 26.42N 113.35W
'Abrī 35 Ea 20.48N 30.20 E
Abrolhos, Arquipélago dos- 54 Kg 18.00S 38.40W
Abrud 15 Gc 46.16N 23.04 E
Abruka, Ostrov-/Abruka Saar 8 Jf 58.08N 22.25 E
Abruka Saar/Abruka, Ostrov- 8 Jf 58.08N 22.25 E
Abruzzi [2] 14 Hh 42.20N 13.45 E
Absaroka Range 43 Fc 44.45N 109.50W
Abtenau 14 Hc 47.33N 13.21 E
Abū, Ḩād, Wādī- 24 Ei 27.46N 33.30 E
Abū ad Duhūr 24 Ge 35.44N 37.02 E
Abū 'Alī 24 Mi 27.20N 49.33 E
Abū al Khaşīb 24 Lg 30.27N 47.59 E
Abū an Na'am 24 Hj 25.14N 38.49 E
Abū 'Arīsh 23 Ff 16.58N 42.50 E
Abū Ballaş 33 Ee 24.26N 27.39 E
Abū Daghmah 24 Hd 36.25N 38.15 E
Abū Darbah 33 Fd 28.29N 33.20 E
Abu Dhabi (EN)=Abū Zaby 22 Hg 24.28N 54.22 E
Abū Ḩadrīyah 24 Mi 27.20N 48.58 E
Abū Ḩamad 31 Kg 19.32N 33.19 E
Abū Ḩammād 24 Dg 30.32N 31.40 E
Abū Ḩarbah, Jabal- 24 Ei 27.17N 33.13 E
Abū Ḩashā'ifah, Khalīj- 24 Bg 31.16N 27.25 E
Abuja 31 Hh 9.10N 7.11 E
Abu Jābirah 35 Dc 11.04N 26.51 E
Abū Jifān 24 Lj 24.31N 47.43 E
Abū Kabīr 24 Dg 30.44N 31.40 E
Abū Kamāl 23 Fc 34.27N 40.55 E
Abukuma-Gawa 29 Gb 38.06N 140.52 E
Abukuma-Sanchi 29 Gc 37.20N 140.45 E
Abū Latt 33 Hf 19.58N 40.08 E
Abū Libdah, Khashm- 33 Ie 22.58N 46.13 E
Abū Maţāriq 35 Dc 10.58N 26.17 E
Abu Mendi 35 Fc 11.47N 35.42 E
Abumonbazi 36 Db 3.42N 22.10 E
Abū Muḩarrik, Ghurd- 33 Ed 27.00N 30.00 E
Abū Musā, Jazīreh-ye- 23 Id 25.52N 55.03 E
Abunã 53 Jf 9.42S 65.23W
Abunã, Rio- 52 Jf 9.41S 65.23W
Abune Yosef 35 Fc 12.09N 39.12 E
Abū Qīr 24 Dg 31.19N 30.04 E
Abū Qīr, Khalīj- 24 Dg 31.20N 30.15 E
Abū Qumayyis, Ra's- 24 Nj 24.34N 51.30 E
Abu Road 25 Ed 24.29N 72.47 E
Abū Sawmah, Ra's- 24 Ei 26.51N 33.59 E
Abū Shanab 35 Dc 13.57N 27.47 E
Abu Simbel (EN)=Abū Sumbul 33 Fe 22.22N 31.38 E
Abū Şukhayr 24 Kg 31.52N 44.27 E
Abū Sumbul=Abu Simbel (EN) 33 Fe 22.22N 31.38 E
Abuta 28 Pc 42.31N 140.46 E
Abut Head 62 De 43.06S 170.15 E
Abū Tīj 33 Fd 27.02N 31.19 E
Abū Ţurţūr, Jabal- 24 Cj 25.20N 30.00 E
Abū'Urūq 35 Eb 15.54N 30.27 E
Abuyemeda 35 Fc 10.38N 39.43 E
Abū Zabad 35 Dc 12.21N 29.15 E
Abū Zaby=Abu Dhabi (EN) 22 Hg 24.28N 54.22 E
Abū Zanīmah 33 Fd 29.03N 33.06 E
Abwong 35 Ed 9.07N 32.12 E
Åby 8 Gf 58.40N 16.11 E
Abyaḑ 35 Dc 13.46N 26.28 E
Abyaḑ, Al Baḩr al-=White Nile (EN) 30 Kg 15.38N 32.31 E
Abyaḑ, Al Baḩr al-=White Nile (EN) [3] 35 Ec 12.40N 32.30 E
Abyaḑ, Ar Ra's al- 23 Ee 23.32N 38.32 E
Abyaḑ, Jabal- 35 Db 18.55N 28.40 E
Abyaḑ, Ra's al-=Blanc, Cape- (EN) 30 He 37.20N 9.50 E
Abyār Alī 24 Hj 24.25N 39.33 E
Abyār ash Shuwayrif 33 Bd 29.59N 14.16 E
Åbybro 7 Bh 57.09N 9.45 E
Abydos 33 Fd 26.11N 31.55 E
Abyei 35 Dd 9.36N 28.26 E
Ābyek 24 Nd 36.02N 50.31 E
Abymes 51e Ab 16.16N 61.31W
Acacias 54 Dc 3.59N 73.47W
Academy Gletscher 41 Ib 81.45N 33.35W
Acadie 38 Me 46.00N 65.00W
Acaill/Achill 9 Dh 54.00N 10.00W
Acajutla 49 Cg 13.36N 89.50W
Acalayong 34 Ge 1.05N 9.40 E
Acámbaro 47 Dd 20.02N 100.44W
Acandí 54 Cb 8.31N 77.17W
Acaponeta 47 Cd 22.30N 105.22W
Acaponeta, Rio- 48 Gf 22.20N 105.37W
Acapulco de Juárez 39 Jh 16.51N 99.55W
Acará 54 Id 1.57S 48.11W
Acarai, Serra- 54 Gc 1.50N 57.40W
Acaraú 54 Jd 2.53S 40.07W
Acaray, Rio- 55 Eg 25.29S 54.42W
Acari, Rio- [Braz.] 54 Ge 5.18S 59.42W
Acari, Rio- [Braz.] 55 Jb 16.00S 45.03W
Acarigua 54 Eb 9.33N 69.12W
Acatenango, Volcán- 38 Jh 14.30N 91.40W
Acatlán de Osorio 48 Jh 18.12N 98.03W
Acayucan 47 Fe 17.57N 94.55W
Accéglio 14 Af 44.28N 7.00 E
Aččitau, Gora- 18 Cc 42.07N 60.31 E
Accomac 44 Jg 37.43N 75.40W
Accra 31 Gh 5.33N 0.13W
Acebal 55 Bk 33.14S 60.50W
Acebuches 48 Hc 28.15N 102.43W
Aceguá [Braz.] 55 Ej 31.52S 54.09W
Aceguá [Ur.] 55 Ej 31.52S 54.12W
Aceh [3] 26 Cf 4.10N 96.50 E
Acerenza 14 Jj 40.48N 15.56 E
Acerra 14 Ij 40.57N 14.22 E
Achacachi 54 Eg 16.03S 68.43W
Achaguas 54 Eb 7.46N 68.14W
Achaïf, 'Erg- 34 Ea 20.49N 4.34W
Achao 56 Ff 42.28S 73.30W
Achegour 34 Hb 19.03N 11.53 E
Acheng 27 Mb 45.32N 126.56 E
Acheux-en-Amiénois 12 Ed 50.04N 2.32 E
Achiet-le-Grand 12 Ed 50.08N 2.47 E
Achill/Acaill 9 Dh 54.00N 10.00W
Achilleion 15 Cj 39.34N 19.55 E
Achill Head/Ceann Acla 9 Ch 53.59N 10.13W
Achim 10 Fc 53.02N 9.01 E
Achim 35 Bb 15.53N 19.31 E
Achterwasser 10 Jb 54.00N 13.57 E
Acı Gölü 24 Cd 37.50N 29.54 E
Ačinsk 22 Ld 56.17N 90.30 E
Acıpayam 24 Cd 37.25N 29.22 E
Acireale 14 Jm 37.37N 15.10 E
Aciş 15 Fb 47.32N 22.47 E
Ačisaj 18 Gc 43.33N 68.53 E
Ačit 17 Hh 56.48N 57.54 E
Ačit-Nur 27 Fb 49.30N 90.30 E
Acklins 38 Lg 22.25N 74.00W
Acklins, The Bight of- 49 Jb 22.30N 74.15W
Acle 12 Db 52.38N 1.33 E
Acobamba 54 Df 12.48S 74.34W
Acolin 11 Jh 46.49N 3.23 E
Aconcagua [2] 56 Fd 32.15S 70.50W
Aconcagua, Cerro- 52 Ji 32.39S 70.00W
Açor, Serra de- 13 Ed 40.13N 7.48W
Açores=Azores (EN) [5] 31 Ee 38.30N 28.00W
Açores, Arquipélago dos-=Azores (EN) 30 Ee 38.30N 28.00W
Acorizal 55 Dc 15.12S 56.22W
Acoyapa 49 Eh 11.58N 85.10W
Acquapendente 14 Fh 42.44N 11.52 E
Acquasanta Terme 14 Hh 42.46N 13.24 E
Acquasparta 14 Gh 42.41N 12.33 E
Acquaviva delle Fonti 14 Kj 40.54N 16.50 E
Acqui Terme 14 Cf 44.41N 8.28 E
Acraman, Lake- 59 Hf 32.05S 135.25 E
Acre [2] 54 Ee 9.00S 70.00W
Acre, Rio- 52 Jf 8.45S 67.22W
Acri 14 Kk 39.29N 16.23 E
Actéon, Groupe- 57 Ng 21.20S 136.30W
Actopan 48 Jg 20.16N 98.56W
Açu 54 Ke 5.34S 36.54W
Acuña 55 Di 29.55S 57.58W
Ada [Ghana] 34 Fd 5.47N 0.38 E
Ada [Ok.-U.S.] 43 He 34.46N 96.41W
Ada [Yugo.] 15 Dd 45.48N 20.08 E
Adaba 35 Fd 7.03N 39.31 E
'Adād 35 Hb 8.23N 46.48 E
'Adādle 35 Gd 9.45N 44.41 E
Adair, Bahia- 48 Cb 31.30N 113.50W
Adair, Cape- 42 Kb 71.31N 71.24W
Adaja 13 Hc 41.32N 4.52W
Adak 40a Cb 51.45N 176.40W
Adalar 15 Mi 40.52N 29.07 E
'Adale 35 He 2.46N 46.20 E
Ådalen 8 Ga 63.20N 17.30 E
Adalselv 8 Dd 60.04N 10.11 E
Adam, Mount- 56 Hh 51.34S 60.04W
Adamantina 55 Ge 21.42S 51.04W
Adamaoua=Adamawa (EN) 30 Ih 7.00N 15.00 E
Adamawa (EN)= Adamaoua 30 Ih 7.00N 15.00 E
Adamello 14 Ed 46.09N 10.30 E
Adamovka 16 Ud 51.32N 59.59 E
Adams 45 Le 43.58N 89.49W
Adams, Mount- 43 Cb 46.12N 121.28W
Adams Lake 46 Fa 51.13N 119.33W
Adams River 42 Ff 50.54N 119.33W
Adam's Rock 64q Ab 25.04S 130.05W
Adamstown 58 Ng 25.04S 130.05W
Adamuz 13 Hf 38.02N 4.31W
Adana 22 Ff 37.01N 35.18 E
Adapazarı 24 Db 40.46N 30.24 E
Adarama 35 Eb 17.05N 34.54 E
Adarân, Jabal- 33 Ig 13.46N 45.08 E
Adare, Cape- 66 Kf 71.17S 170.14 E
Adavale 59 Ie 25.55S 144.36 E
Adda [It.] 5 Gf 45.08N 9.53 E
Adda [Sud.] 35 Cd 9.51N 24.50 E
Aḑ Ḑab'ah 33 Ec 31.02N 28.26 E
Ad Dabbah 35 Eb 18.03N 30.57 E
Ad Dafinah 33 He 23.18N 41.58 E
Aḑ Ḑafrah 24 Ok 23.25N 53.25 E
Ad Dahnā' 21 Gg 24.30N 48.10 E
Addala-Šuhgelmeer, Gora- 16 Oh 42.20N 46.15 E
Aḑ Ḑāli' 33 Hg 13.42N 44.44 E
Ad Damazin 35 Ec 11.49N 34.23 E
Ad Dāmir 35 Eb 17.35N 33.58 E
Ad Dammām 22 Hg 26.26N 50.07 E
Ad Dār al Ḩamrā' 23 Ed 27.19N 37.44 E
Ad Dawādimī 23 Fe 24.28N 44.18 E
Ad Dawḩah=Doha (EN) 22 Hg 25.17N 51.32 E
Ad Dawr 24 Je 34.27N 43.47 E
Ad Dayr 33 Fd 25.20N 32.35 E
Ad Dibdibah 24 Lh 28.00N 46.30 E
Aḑ Ḑiffah 33 Ec 30.30N 25.30 E
Ad Dikākah 35 Ib 19.25N 51.30 E
Ad Dilam 23 Ge 23.59N 47.10 E
Ad Dindar 35 Ec 13.20N 34.05 E
Ad Dir'īyah 24 Lj 24.48N 46.32 E
Ad Dissān 33 Hf 16.56N 41.41 E
Addis Zemen 35 Fc 12.05N 37.44 E
Ad Dīwānīya 23 Fc 31.59N 44.56 E
Addu Atoll 21 Jj 0.25S 73.10 E
Ad Du'ayn 35 Dc 11.26N 26.09 E
Ad Duwayd 24 Jg 30.13N 42.18 E
Ad Duwaym 35 Ec 14.00N 32.19 E
Adel [Ga.-U.S.] 44 Fj 31.18N 83.25W
Adel [Or.-U.S.] 46 Fe 42.11N 119.54W
Adelaide [Austl.] 58 Eh 34.56S 138.36 E
Adelaide [Bah.] 44 Im 25.00N 77.31W
Adelaide [S.Afr.] 37 Df 32.42S 26.20 E
Adelaide Island 66 Qe 67.15S 68.30W
Adelaide Peninsula 42 Hc 68.05N 97.50W
Adelaide River 58 Ef 13.15S 131.06 E
Adelaye 35 Cd 7.07N 22.49 E
Adelboden 14 Bd 46.30N 7.33 E
Adèle Island 59 Ec 15.30S 123.10 E
Adélie, Terre- 66 Ie 67.00S 139.00 E
Ademuz 13 Kd 40.04N 1.17W
Aden (EN)=Baladiyat 'Adan 22 Gh 12.46N 45.01 E
Aden, Gulf of- (EN) 30 Lg 12.00N 48.00 E
Aden, Gulf of- (EN)= 'Admēd, Badyarada- 30 Lg 12.00N 48.00 E
Adenau 12 Id 50.23N 6.56 E
Ader 30 Hg 14.10N 5.05 E
Aderbissinat 34 Gb 15.37N 7.52 E
Adhan, Jabal- 24 Qj 25.27N 56.13 E
Adh Dhahībāt 32 Jc 32.01N 10.42 E
Adh Dhayd 24 Pj 25.17N 55.53 E
Adhélfi 15 Gj 39.08N 23.59 E
Adhelfoi 15 Jm 36.25N 26.37 E
'Adhriyāt, Jibāl- al- 24 Gg 30.25N 36.48 E
Adi, Pulau- 26 Jg 4.18S 133.26 E
Adiaké 34 Ed 5.16N 3.17W
Adi Arkay 35 Fc 13.31N 38.00 E
Adicora 54 Ea 11.57N 69.48W
Adi Dairo 35 Fc 14.21N 38.12 E
Adigala 35 Gc 10.24N 42.18 E
Adige/Etsch 5 Hf 45.10N 12.20 E
Adigrat 35 Fc 14.16N 39.28 E
Adi Keyeh 35 Fc 14.48N 39.23 E
Adi Kwala 35 Fc 14.37N 38.51 E
Ādilābād 25 Fe 19.40N 78.32 E
Adīrī 31 If 27.30N 13.16 E
Adirondack Mountains 38 Le 44.00N 74.00W
Adis Abeba 31 Kh 9.01N 38.46 E
Adis Alem 35 Fd 9.03N 38.24 E
Adi Ugri 35 Fc 14.53N 38.49 E
Adiyaman 23 Eb 37.46N 38.17 E
Adjud 15 Kc 46.06N 27.10 E
Adjuntas 51a Bb 18.09N 66.43W
'Admēd, Badyarada-=Aden, Gulf of- (EN) 30 Lg 12.00N 48.00 E
Admer, Erg d'- 32 Ie 24.12N 9.10 E
Admiralty 40 Me 57.50N 134.30W
Admiralty Bay 51n Ba 13.00N 61.16W
Admiralty Gulf 59 Fb 14.20S 125.50 E
Admiralty Inlet 42 Ib 72.30N 86.00W
Admiralty Islands 57 Fe 2.10S 147.00 E
Admiralty Mountains 66 Kf 71.45S 168.30 E
Admont 14 Ic 47.34N 14.27 E
Ado 34 Fd 6.36N 2.56 E
Ado Ekiti 34 Gd 7.38N 5.13 E
Adok 35 Ed 8.11N 30.19 E
Adolfo Gonzales Chaves 55 Bn 38.02S 60.06W
Adolfo López Mateos, Presa- 48 Fe 25.05N 107.20W
Adonara, Pulau- 26 Hh 8.20S 123.10 E
Ādoni 25 Fe 15.38N 77.17 E
Adra 13 Ih 36.44N 3.01W
Adrano 14 Im 37.40N 14.50 E
Adrar 30 Ff 20.30N 13.30W
Adrar 31 Gf 27.54N 0.17W
Adrar 30 Hf 25.12N 8.10 E
Adrar [Alg.] [3] 32 Gd 27.00N 1.00W
Adrar [Mtna.] [3] 32 Ee 21.00N 11.00W
Adré 35 Cc 13.28N 22.12 E
Adria 14 Ge 45.03N 12.03 E
Adrian 44 Ee 41.54N 84.02W
Adrianópolis 55 Hg 24.41S 48.50W
Adriatic, Deti-=Adriatic Sea (EN) 5 Hg 43.00N 16.00 E
Adriatico, Mar-=Adriatic Sea (EN) 5 Hg 43.00N 16.00 E
Adriatic Sea (EN)=Adriatic, Deti- 5 Hg 43.00N 16.00 E
Adriatic Sea (EN)= Adriatico, Mar- 5 Hg 43.00N 16.00 E
Adriatic Sea (EN)= Jadransko More 5 Hg 43.00N 16.00 E
Aduard 12 Ia 53.15N 6.25 E
Adula 14 Dd 46.30N 9.05 E
Adulis 35 Fb 15.15N 39.37 E
Adur 12 Bd 50.49N 0.16W
Adusa 36 Eb 1.23N 28.01 E
Adventure Bank (EN) 14 Gm 37.20N 12.10 E
Adwa 31 Kg 14.10N 38.55 E
Adyča 21 Pc 68.13N 135.03 E
Adygalah 20 Jd 62.57N 146.25 E
Adygejskaja Avt. Oblast [3] 19 Eg 44.30N 40.05 E
Adžarskaja ASSR [3] 19 Eg 41.40N 42.10 E
Adzopé [3] 34 Ed 6.15N 3.45W
Adzopé 34 Ed 6.06N 3.52W
Adzva 17 Ic 66.36N 59.28 E
Aegean Sea (EN)=Aiyaion Pélagos 5 Ih 39.00N 25.00 E
Aegean Sea (EN)=Ege Denizi 5 Ih 39.00N 25.00 E
Aegina (EN) = Aiyina 15 Gl 37.40N 23.30 E
Aegviidu 8 Ke 59.17N 25.37 E
Aeon Point 64g Bb 1.46N 157.11W
Aerfort na Sionainne/Shannon 9 Ei 52.42N 8.57W
Ærø 8 Dj 54.55N 10.20 E
Ærøskøbing 8 Dj 54.53N 10.25 E
Aerzen 12 Lb 52.02N 9.16 E
Afafi, Massif d'- 34 Ha 22.15N 15.00 E
'Afak 24 Kf 32.04N 45.15 E
Afanasjevo 7 Mg 58.54N 53.16 E
Afareaitu 65e Fc 17.33S 149.47W
Afars and Issas→Djibouti [1] 31 Lg 11.30N 43.00 E
Aff 11 Dg 47.43N 2.07W
Affollé 30 Fg 16.55N 10.25W
Affrica, Scoglio d'- 14 Eh 42.20N 10.05 E
Afghanistan [1] 22 If 33.00N 65.00 E
Afgōye 35 He 2.09N 45.07 E
'Afīf 23 Fe 23.55N 42.56 E
Afikpo 34 Gd 5.53N 7.55 E
Afipski 16 Kg 44.52N 38.50 E
Aflou 32 Hc 34.07N 2.06 E
Afmadōw 35 Ge 0.29N 42.06 E
Afognak 40 Ie 58.15N 152.30W
Afonso Cláudio 54 Jh 20.05S 41.08W
Afon Teifi 9 Ii 52.06N 4.43W
Afon Tywi 9 Ij 51.40N 4.15W
Afragola 14 Ij 40.55N 14.18 E
Āfrēra, Lake- 35 Gc 13.20N 41.03 E
Africa 30 Jh 10.00N 22.00 E
African Islands 30 Mi 4.53S 43.24 E
Afşin 24 Gc 38.36N 36.55 E
Afsluitdijk 11 La 53.00N 5.15 E
Afton 46 Je 42.44N 110.56W
Afuá 54 Hd 0.10S 50.23W
'Afula 24 Ff 32.36N 35.17 E
Afyonkarahisar 22 Ff 38.45N 30.40 E
Agadem 31 Ig 16.50N 13.17 E
Agadez 31 Hg 16.58N 7.59 E
Agadez [2] 34 Hb 19.45N 10.15 E
Agadir 31 Ge 30.25N 9.37W
Agadir [3] 32 Fc 30.00N 9.00W
Agadyr 19 Hf 48.17N 72.53 E
Agalega Islands 30 Mj 10.24S 56.30 E
Agalta, Sierra de- 47 Ge 15.00N 85.53W
Agan 19 Hc 61.23N 74.35 E
Agana 58 Fc 13.28N 144.45 E
Agano-Gawa 28 Of 37.57N 139.07 E
Aga Point 64c Bb 13.14N 144.43 E
Agapovka 17 Ij 53.18N 59.10 E
Agaro 35 Fd 7.53N 36.36 E
Agartala 22 Lg 23.49N 91.16 E
Agassiz Pool 45 Ib 48.20N 95.58W
Agat 64c Bb 13.23N 144.39 E
Agat Bay 64c Bb 13.24N 144.39 E
Agats 58 Ee 5.33S 138.08 E
Agattu 40a Ab 52.25N 173.35 E
Agawa Bay 44 Eb 47.22N 84.33W
Agawa Bay 44 Eb 47.20N 84.42W
Agboville 34 Ed 5.56N 4.13W
Agboville [3] 34 Ed 6.00N 4.15W
Agdam 19 Eh 39.58N 46.57 E
Agdaš 16 Oi 40.38N 47.29 E
Agde 11 Jk 43.19N 3.28 E
Agde, Cap d'- 11 Jk 43.16N 3.30 E
Agder 8 Cf 58.25N 8.15 E
Agdz 32 Fc 30.27N 7.56W
Agdžabedi 16 Oi 40.03N 47.28 E
Agematsu 29 Ed 35.47N 137.41 E
Agen 11 Gj 44.12N 0.38 E
Ageo 29 Fd 35.58N 139.35 E
Agepsta, Gora- 16 Lh 43.32N 40.30 E
Ager 14 Hb 48.05N 13.51 E
Agere Mariam 35 Fd 5.39N 38.15 E
Agersø 8 Di 55.10N 11.10 E
Agger 12 Jd 50.48N 7.11 E
Āghā Jārī 23 Gc 30.42N 49.50 E
Aghireşu 15 Gc 46.53N 23.15 E
Agiabampo, Estero de- 48 Ed 26.15N 109.15W
Ağın 24 Hc 38.57N 38.43 E

Index Symbols

[1] Independent Nation
[2] State, Region
[3] District, County
[4] Municipality
[5] Colony, Dependency
Continent
Physical Region
Historical or Cultural Region
Mount, Mountain
Volcano
Hill
Mountains, Mountain Range
Hills, Escarpment
Plateau, Upland
Pass, Gap
Plain, Lowland
Delta
Salt Flat
Valley, Canyon
Crater, Cave
Karst Features
Depression
Polder
Desert, Dunes
Forest, Woods
Heath, Steppe
Oasis
Cape, Point
Coast, Beach
Cliff
Peninsula
Isthmus
Sandbank
Island
Atoll
Rock, Reef
Islands, Archipelago
Rocks, Reefs
Coral Reef
Well, Spring
Geyser
River, Stream
Waterfall Rapids
River Mouth, Estuary
Lake
Salt Lake
Intermittent Lake
Reservoir
Swamp, Pond
Canal
Glacier
Ice Shelf, Pack Ice
Ocean
Sea
Gulf, Bay
Strait, Fjord
Lagoon
Bank
Seamount
Tablemount
Ridge
Shelf
Basin
Escarpment, Sea Scarp
Fracture
Trench, Abyss
National Park, Reserve
Point of Interest
Recreation Site
Cave, Cavern
Historic Site
Ruins
Wall, Walls
Church, Abbey
Temple
Scientific Station
Airport
Port
Lighthouse
Mine
Tunnel
Dam, Bridge

Aginski Burjatski Nacionalny Okrug [3] 20 Gf 51.00N 114.30 E
Aginskoje 20 Gf 51.03N 114.33 E
Agnew 59 Ee 28.01S 120.30 E
Agnibilékrou 34 Ed 7.08N 3.12W
Agnitá 15 Hd 45.58N 24.37 E
Agno 14 Fe 45.32N 11.21 E
Agnone 14 Ii 41.48N 14.22 E
Ago 29 Ed 34.19N 136.50 E
Agoare 34 Fd 8.30N 3.25 E
Agogna 14 Ce 45.04N 8.54 E
Agön 8 Gc 61.35N 17.25 E
Agordat 31 Kg 15.32N 37.53 E
Agordo 14 Gd 46.17N 12.02 E
Agout 11 Hk 43.47N 1.41 E
Āgra 22 Jg 27.11N 78.01 E
Agrahanski Poluostrov 16 Oh 43.45N 47.35 E
Agramunt 13 Nc 41.47N 1.06 E
Agreda 13 Kc 41.51N 1.56W
Ağrı 23 Fb 39.44N 43.03 E
Ağrı Dağı = Mount Ararat (EN) 21 Gf 39.40N 44.24 E
Agričaj 16 Oi 41.17N 46.43 E
Agrigento 6 Hh 37.19N 13.34 E
Agrihan Island 57 Fc 18.46N 145.40 E
Agrij 15 Gb 47.15N 23.16 E
Agrínion 15 Ek 38.38N 21.25 E
Agropoli 14 Ij 40.21N 14.59 E
Agro Pontino 14 Gi 41.25N 12.55 E
Agryz 7 Mh 56.31N 53.01 E
Agto 41 Ge 67.37N 53.49W
Agua Brava, Laguna- 48 Gf 22.10N 105.32W
Agua Caliente, Cerro- 47 Cc 26.27N 106.12W
Aguachica 54 Db 8.18N 73.38W
Agua Clara 55 Fe 20.27S 52.52W
Aguada de Pasajeros 49 Gb 22.23N 80.51W
Aguadez, Irhazer Oua-n- 34 Gb 17.28N 6.26 E
Aguadilla 49 Nd 18.26N 67.09W
Aguadulce 49 Gi 8.15N 80.33W
Agua Fria River 46 Ij 33.23N 112.21W
Agua Limpa, Rio- 55 Gb 14.58S 51.20W
Aguán, Río- 49 Ef 15.57N 85.44W
Aguanaval, Río- 48 Hf 25.28N 102.53W
Aguapeí 55 Cc 16.12S 59.43W
Aguapeí, Rio- 56 Jb 21.03S 51.47W
Aguapeí, Rio- 55 Cb 15.53S 58.25W
Agua Prieta 39 If 31.18N 109.34W
Aguaray 56 Hb 22.16S 63.44W
Aguaray Guazú, Río- [Par.] 55 Dg 24.05S 56.40W
Aguaray Guazú, Río- [Par.] 55 Dg 24.47S 57.19W
Aguasay 50 Eh 9.25N 63.44W
Aguascalientes 39 Ig 21.53N 102.18W
Aguascalientes [2] 47 Dd 22.00N 102.30W
Aguasvivas 13 Lc 41.20N 0.25W
Água Verde, Rio- 55 Da 13.42S 56.43W
Agua Vermelha, Reprêsa- 56 Ja 19.53S 50.17W
Agudo [Braz.] 55 Fi 29.38S 53.15W
Agudo [Sp.] 13 Hf 38.59N 4.52W
Agueda 13 Fc 41.02N 6.56W
Águeda 13 Dd 40.34N 8.27W
Aguelhok 34 Fb 19.28N 0.51 E
Agüenit 32 Ee 22.11N 13.08W
Aguerguer 30 Ff 23.09N 16.01W
Aguijan Island 57 Fc 14.51N 145.34 E
Aguilar de Campóo 13 Hb 42.48N 4.16W
Aguilar de la Frontera 13 Hg 37.31N 4.39W
Aguilas 13 Kg 37.24N 1.35W
Aguililla 48 Hh 18.44N 102.44W
Aguirre, Río- 50 Fh 8.28N 61.02W
Aguja, Cabo de la- 54 Da 11.21N 73.59W
Agujereada, Punta- 51a Ab 18.31N 67.08W
Agul 20 Ee 55.40N 95.45 E
Agulhas, Cape-(EN) = Agulhas, Kaap- 30 Jl 34.50S 20.00 E
Agulhas, Kaap- = Agulhas, Cape-(EN) 30 Jl 34.50S 20.00 E
Agulhas Negras, Pico das- 52 Lh 22.23S 44.38W
Agulhas Plateau (EN) 30 Jm 40.00S 26.00 E
Agung, Gunung- 26 Gh 8.21S 115.30 E
Aguni-Shima 27 Mf 26.35N 127.15 E
Agupey, Río- 55 Di 29.07S 56.36W
Agustin Codazzi 54 Da 10.02N 73.15W
Ağva 24 Cb 41.05N 29.50 E
Ahaggar 30 Hf 23.10N 5.50 E
Ahaggar, Tassili-oua-n- 30 Hf 20.30N 5.00 E
Aha Hills 37 Cc 19.45S 21.10 E
Ahalcihe 19 Eg 41.38N 42.59 E
Ahalkalaki 19 Eg 41.25N 43.29 E
Ahangaran 18 Gd 40.57N 69.37 E
Ahar 23 Gb 38.28N 47.04 E
Ahat 15 Mk 38.39N 29.47 E
Ahaus 10 Cd 52.04N 7.00 E
Ahe Atoll 57 Mf 14.30S 146.18W
Ahenet, Tanezrouft-n- 32 He 22.00N 1.00 E
Ahini 20 Ff 53.18N 105.01 E
Ahipara 62 Ea 35.10S 173.09 E
Ahja Jōgi 8 Lf 58.19N 27.15 E
Ahlat 24 Jc 38.45N 42.29 E
Ahlen 10 De 51.45N 7.55 E
Ahmadābād 22 Jg 23.02N 72.37 E
Aḩmadī 24 Qi 27.56N 56.42 E
Ahmadnagar 25 Ee 19.05N 74.44 E
Ahmadpur East 25 Ec 29.09N 71.16 E
Ahmar 30 Lh 9.23N 41.13 E
Aḩmar, Al Baḩr al- = Red Sea (EN) 30 Kf 25.00N 38.00 E
Ahmeta 16 Nh 42.02N 45.11 E
Ahmetli 15 Kk 38.31N 27.57 E
Ahnet 32 He 24.35N 3.15 E
Ahoa 64h Ab 13.17S 176.12W
Ahome 48 Ee 25.55N 109.11W
Ahon, Tarso- 35 Ba 20.23N 18.18 E
Ahr 10 Df 50.33N 7.17 E
Ahram 24 Nh 28.52N 51.16 E
Ahrāmāt al Jīzah 33 Fd 29.55N 31.05 E
Ahrensburg 10 Gc 53.41N 10.15 E
Ahrgebirge 12 Id 50.31N 6.54 E
Ahse 12 Jc 51.42N 7.51 E
Ahsu 16 Pi 40.35N 48.26 E
Ähtäri 7 Ee 62.02N 21.20 E
Ahtärinjarvi 8 Kb 62.40N 24.05 E
Ähtävänjoki 7 Fe 63.38N 22.48 E
Ahtopol 15 Kg 42.06N 27.57 E
Ahtuba 5 Kf 46.42N 48.00 E
Ahtubinsk 6 Kf 48.14N 46.14 E
Ahtyrka 19 De 50.19N 34.55 E
Ahuacapán 49 Cg 13.55N 89.51W
Ahuazotepec 48 Jg 20.03N 98.09W
Ahunui Atoll 57 Mf 19.35S 140.28W
Åhus 7 Di 55.55N 14.17 E
Ahvāz 22 Gf 31.19N 48.42 E
Ahvenanmaa/Åland [2] 7 Ef 60.15N 20.00 E
Ahvenanmaa/Åland = Aland Islands (EN) 5 Hc 60.15N 20.00 E
Ahvenanmeri 8 Hd 60.00N 19.30 E
Aḩwar 23 Gg 13.31N 46.42 E
Aibag Gol 28 Ad 41.42N 110.24 E
Aibetsu 29a Cb 43.55N 142.33 E
Aichach 10 Hh 48.28N 11.08 E
Aichi Ken [2] 28 Ng 35.00N 137.07 E
Aiea 65a Db 21.23N 157.56W
Aigle 14 Ad 46.20N 6.59 E
Aigoual, Mont- 11 Jj 44.07N 3.35 E
Aiguá 55 El 34.12S 54.45W
Aigues 11 Kj 44.07N 4.43 E
Aigues-Mortes 11 Kk 43.34N 4.11 E
Aiguilles 11 Mj 44.47N 6.52 E
Aiguillon 11 Gj 44.18N 0.21 E
Aigurande 11 Hh 46.26N 1.50 E
Ai He 28 Hd 40.13N 124.30 E
Aihui (Heihe) 22 Od 50.13N 127.26 E
Aikawa 29 Fb 38.02N 138.14 E
Aiken 43 Ke 33.34N 81.44W
Ailao Shan 27 Hg 23.15N 102.20 E
Aîlette 12 Fe 49.35N 3.10 E
Ailinginae Atoll 57 Hc 11.08N 166.24 E
Aillte an Mhothair/Moher, Cliffs of- 9 Di 52.58N 9.27W
Ailly-le-Haut-Clocher 12 Dd 50.05N 1.59 E
Ailly-sur-Noye 12 Ee 49.45N 2.22 E
Ailsa Craig 9 Hf 55.16N 5.07W
Ailuk Atoll 57 Hc 10.20N 169.56 E
Aim 20 Ie 58.48N 134.12 E
Aimogasta 56 Gc 28.33S 66.49W
Aimorés 54 Jg 19.30S 41.04W
Ain [3] 11 Lh 46.10N 5.20 E
Ain 11 Li 45.48N 5.10 E
Ainazi/Ajnazi 7 Fh 57.52N 24.25 E
Aïn Beïda 32 Ib 35.48N 7.24 E
Aïn Beni Mathar 32 Gc 34.01N 2.01W
Aïn Bessem 13 Ph 36.18N 3.40 E
Aïn Boucif 13 Pi 35.53N 3.09 E
Aïn Defla 13 Nh 36.16N 1.58 E
Aïn el Berd 13 Li 35.21N 0.31W
Aïn el Hammam 13 Qh 36.34N 4.19 E
Aïn el Turck 13 Li 35.44N 0.46W
Aïn Galakka 35 Bb 18.05N 18.31 E
Aínos Óros 15 Dk 38.07N 20.40 E
Aïn Oulmene 13 Ri 35.55N 5.18 E
Aïn Oussera 13 Oi 35.27N 2.54 E
Aïn Sefra 31 Ge 32.45N 0.35W
Ainsworth 45 Ge 42.33N 99.52W
Aïn Taghrout 13 Rh 36.08N 5.05 E
Aïn Tedeles 13 Mh 36.00N 0.18 E
Ain Témouchent 32 Gb 35.18N 1.08W
Aïn Tolba 13 Ki 35.15N 1.15W
Aioi 29 Dd 34.49N 134.28 E
Aiquile 54 Eg 18.10S 65.10W
Aïr/Azbine 30 Hg 18.00N 8.30 E
Airabu, Pulau- 26 Ef 2.46N 106.14 E
Airai 64a Bc 7.21N 134.34 E
Airaines 12 De 49.58N 1.57 E
Airão 54 Fd 1.56S 61.22W
Airbangis 26 Cf 0.12N 99.23 E
Airdrie 46 Ha 51.18N 114.02W
Aire 11 Id 50.38N 2.24 E
Aire [Eng.-U.K.] 9 Mh 53.44N 0.54W
Aire [Fr.] 11 Ke 49.19N 4.49 E
Aire, Canal d'- 11 Id 50.38N 2.25 E
Aire, Isla del- 13 Qe 39.47N 4.16 E
Aire-sur-l'Adour 11 Fk 43.42N 0.16W
Air Force 42 Kc 67.55N 74.05W
Airolo 14 Cd 46.33N 8.35 E
Aïs 63b Cb 15.26S 167.15 E
Aisch 10 Hg 49.46N 11.01 E
Aisén del General Carlos Ibáñez del Campo [2] 56 Fg 46.00S 73.00W
Aishihik 42 Dd 61.34N 137.30W
Ai-Shima 29 Bd 34.30N 131.18 E
Aisne [3] 11 Je 49.30N 3.30 E
Aisne 11 Ie 49.26N 2.50 E
Aisne à la Marne, Canal de l'- 11 Je 49.24N 3.55 E
Aïssa, Djebel- 32 Gc 32.51N 0.30W
Aitana, Pico- 13 Lf 38.39N 0.16W
Aitape 60 Ch 3.08S 142.21 E
Aitolikón 15 Ek 38.26N 21.21 E
Aitutaki Atoll 57 Lf 18.52S 159.45W
Ait Youssef ou Ali 13 Ii 35.09N 3.55W
Aiud 15 Gc 46.18N 23.43 E
Aiviekste 7 Fh 56.36N 25.44 E
Aiviekste/Ajviekste 7 Fh 56.36N 25.44 E
Aiwokako Passage 64a Bb 7.39N 134.33 E
Aix, Ile d'- 11 Eh 46.01N 1.10W
Aix-en-Provence 11 Lk 43.32N 5.26 E
Aixe-sur-Vienne 11 Hi 45.48N 1.08 E
Aix-les-Bains 11 Li 45.42N 5.55 E
Aiyaíon Pélagos = Aegean Sea (EN) 5 Ih 39.00N 25.00 E
Aiyina 15 Gl 37.45N 23.26 E
Aiyina = Aegina (EN) 15 Gl 37.40N 23.30 E
Aiyínion 15 Fi 40.30N 22.33 E
Aiyion 15 Fk 38.15N 22.05 E
Aizawl 25 Id 23.44N 92.43 E
Aizenay 11 Eh 46.44N 1.37W
Aizpute/Ajzpute 7 Eh 56.45N 21.39 E
Aizubange 29 Fc 37.34N 139.49 E
Aizutakada 29 Fc 37.29N 139.48 E
Aizuwakamatsu 28 Of 37.30N 139.56 E
Ajā', Jabal- 24 Ii 27.30N 41.30 E
'Ajab Shīr 24 Kd 37.28N 45.54 E
Ajaccio 6 Gg 41.55N 8.44 E
Ajaccio, Golfe d'- 11a Ab 41.50N 8.41 E
Ajaguz 22 Ke 47.58N 80.27 E
Ajakli 20 Eb 70.13N 95.55 E
Ajan [R.S.F.S.R.] 20 Fe 59.38N 106.45 E
Ajan [R.S.F.S.R.] 20 Ie 56.27N 138.10 E
Ajanka 20 Ld 63.40N 167.30 E
Ajanta Range 25 Fd 20.30N 76.00 E
Ajat 17 Kj 52.54N 62.50 E
Ajax Peak 46 Id 45.20N 113.40W
Ajdābiyā 31 Je 30.46N 20.14 E
Ajdabul 19 Ge 52.42N 69.01 E
Ajdar 16 Ke 48.42N 39.13 E
Ajdar, Soloncak- 18 Fd 40.50N 66.50 E
Ajdovščina 14 He 45.53N 13.53 E
Ajdyrlinski 17 Ij 52.03N 59.50 E
Ajhal 20 Gc 66.00N 111.32 E
Ajigasawa 28 Pd 40.47N 140.12 E
Aji-Shima 29 Gb 38.15N 141.30 E
Ajjer, Tassili-n- 30 Hf 25.30N 9.00 E
Ajka 10 Ni 47.06N 17.34 E
Ajke, Ozero- 16 Vd 50.55N 61.35 E
Ajkino 17 De 62.15N 49.56 E
'Ajlūn 24 Ff 32.20N 35.45 E
'Ajmah, Jabal al- 24 Fh 29.12N 34.02 E
'Ajmān 23 Id 25.25N 55.27 E
Ajmer 22 Jg 26.27N 74.38 E
Ajnaži/Ainaži 7 Fh 57.52N 24.25 E
Ajni 18 Ge 39.23N 68.36 E
Ajo 43 Ee 32.22N 112.52W
Ajo, Cabo de- 13 Ia 43.31N 3.35W
Ajon, Ostrov- 21 Sc 69.50N 168.40 E
Ajoupa-Bouillon 51h Ab 14.50N 61.08W
Ajsary 19 He 53.05N 71.00 E
Ajtos 15 Kg 42.42N 27.15 E
Aju, Kepulauan- 26 Jf 0.28N 131.03 E
'Ajūz, Jabal al- 24 Dj 25.49N 30.43 E
Ajviekste 7 Fh 56.36N 25.44 E
Ajviekste/Aiviekste 7 Fh 56.36N 25.44 E
Ajzpute/Aizpute 7 Eh 56.45N 21.39 E
Akaba 34 Fd 7.57N 1.03 E
Akabira 28 Qc 43.30N 142.04 E
Akabli 32 Hd 26.42N 1.22 E
Akademika Obručeva, Hrebet- 20 Ef 51.30N 96.45 E
Akadomari 29 Fc 37.54N 138.24 E
Aka-Gawa 29 Fb 38.54N 139.50 E
Akagi-San 29 Fc 36.33N 139.11 E
Akaishi-Dake 29 Fd 35.27N 138.09 E
Akaishi-Sanmyaku 29 Fd 35.25N 138.10 E
Akajaure 7 Dc 67.42N 17.30 E
Aka-Jima 29b Ab 26.14N 127.17 E
Akaki 35 Fd 8.51N 38.48 E
Akala 35 Fb 15.38N 36.12 E
Akan 29a Db 43.08N 144.07 E
Akan-Gawa 29a Db 43.00N 144.16 E
Akar 24 Dc 38.38N 31.06 E
Akarnaniká Óri 15 Dk 38.45N 21.00 E
Akaroa 61 Dh 43.48S 172.59 E
Akasaki 29 Cd 35.31N 133.38 E
'Akasha East 35 Ea 21.05N 30.43 E
Akashi 28 Mg 34.38N 134.59 E
Akbaba Tepe 24 Hc 39.32N 39.33 E
Akbajtal, Pereval- 19 Hh 38.31N 73.41 E
Akbou 13 Qh 36.28N 4.32 E
Akbulak 19 Fe 51.03N 55.37 E
Akbura 18 Id 40.34N 72.45 E
Akçaabat 24 Hb 40.59N 39.34 E
Akçadağ 24 Gc 38.21N 37.59 E
Akçakale 24 Hd 36.41N 38.56 E
Akçakara Dağı 24 Ic 38.40N 40.52 E
Akçakoca 24 Db 41.05N 31.09 E
Akçaova [Tur.] 15 Mh 41.03N 29.57 E
Akçaova [Tur.] 15 Ll 37.30N 28.02 E
Akčatau 19 Hf 47.59N 74.02 E
Akçay 15 Ll 37.50N 28.15 E
Akçay 15 Mm 36.36N 29.45 E
Akchâr 30 Ff 20.20N 14.28W
Ak Dağ [Tur.] 24 Ib 40.35N 41.46 E
Ak Dağ [Tur.] 23 Cb 36.32N 29.34 E
Akdağ [Tur.] 24 Gd 37.53N 37.56 E
Akdağ [Tur.] 24 Fb 40.57N 35.55 E
Akdağ [Tur.] 24 Cc 39.15N 28.49 E
Akdağ [Tur.] 15 Ll 37.42N 28.56 E
Akdağ [Tur.] 15 Mk 38.18N 29.58 E
Akdağ [Tur.] 15 Jk 38.33N 26.30 E
Ak Dağlar 24 Gc 39.30N 36.00 E
Ak Dağları 24 Ic 38.40N 40.12 E
Akdağmadeni 24 Fc 39.40N 35.54 E
Akdeniz = Mediterranean Sea (EN) 5 Hh 35.00N 20.00 E
Ak-Dovurak 20 Ef 51.10N 90.40 E
Akechi 29 Ed 35.18N 137.22 E
Ake Eze 34 Gd 5.55N 7.40 E
Akera 16 Oj 39.09N 46.48 E
Åkersberga 8 He 59.29N 18.18 E
Akershus [2] 7 Cf 60.00N 11.10 E
Aketi 31 Jh 2.44N 23.46 E
Akharnai 15 Gk 38.05N 23.44 E
Akhdar, al Jabal al- 21 Hg 23.30N 57.00 E
Akhḑar, Al Jabal al- 30 Je 32.30N 21.30 E
Akhḑar, Wādī al- 24 Gh 28.35N 36.35 E
Akhelóös 15 Ej 38.18N 21.10 E
Akhisar 23 Cb 38.55N 27.51 E
Akhmīm 33 Fd 26.34N 31.44 E
Akhtarīn 24 Gd 36.31N 37.20 E
Aki 29 Ce 33.30N 133.53 E
Akiaki Atoll 61 Nc 18.30S 139.12W
Akiéni 36 Bc 1.11S 13.53 E
Akimiski 38 Kd 53.00N 81.20W
Akimovka 16 If 46.42N 35.09 E
Aki-Nada 29 Cd 34.05N 132.40 E
Åkirkeby 8 Fi 55.04N 14.56 E
Akita 22 Qf 39.43N 140.07 E
Akita Ken [2] 28 Pe 39.45N 140.20 E
Akjoujt 31 Fg 19.44N 14.22W
Akka 32 Fd 29.25N 8.15W
Akkanburluk 17 Mj 52.46N 66.35 E
'Akko 23 Ec 32.55N 35.05 E
Akkol 18 Hc 43.25N 70.47 E
Akköy 24 Bd 37.29N 27.15 E
Akkystau 19 Ff 47.17N 51.03 E
Aklavik 42 Dc 68.14N 135.02W
Aklé Mseïguîlé 34 Eb 16.20N 4.45W
Akmenė/Akmene 8 Jh 56.14N 22.43 E
Akmene/Akmenė 8 Jh 56.14N 22.43 E
Akmenrags/Akmeņrags 8 Ih 56.54N 20.55 E
Akmeņrags/Akmenrags 8 Ih 56.54N 20.55 E
Akmeqit 27 Cd 37.05N 76.55 E
Akniste 8 Kh 56.10N 25.54 E
Akō 29 Dd 34.45N 134.23 E
Akobo 30 Kh 7.48N 33.03 E
Akobo 31 Kh 7.47N 33.01 E
Akola 22 Jg 20.44N 77.00 E
Akonolinga 34 He 3.46N 12.15 E
Akosombo Dam 34 Fd 6.16N 0.03 E
Akpatok 42 Kd 60.24N 68.05W
Akqi 27 Cc 40.50N 78.01 E
Ákra Ámbelos 15 Gj 39.56N 23.56 E
Ákra Kambanós 15 Hl 37.59N 24.45 E
Akranes 7a Ab 64.19N 22.06W
Ákra Spathí 15 Gl 37.27N 23.31 E
Åkrehamn 7 Ag 59.16N 5.11 E
Akritas, Ákra- = Akritas, Cape- (EN) 15 Em 36.43N 21.53 E
Akritas Cape- (EN) = Akritas, Ákra- 15 Em 36.43N 21.53 E
Akron [Co.-U.S.] 45 Ef 40.10N 103.13W
Akron [Oh.-U.S.] 43 Kc 41.04N 81.31W
Akrotiri 24 Ee 34.36N 32.57 E
Akša 20 Gf 50.17N 113.17 E
Aksaj 16 Oh 43.32N 46.55 E
Aksaj [Kaz.-U.S.S.R.] 19 Fe 51.13N 53.01 E
Aksaj [R.S.F.S.R.] 16 Kf 47.15N 39.52 E
Aksakal 15 Li 40.09N 28.07 E
Aksakovo 17 Gi 54.02N 54.09 E
Aksaray 23 Db 38.23N 34.03 E
Aksay 27 Fd 39.28N 94.15 E
Akşehir 23 Db 38.21N 31.25 E
Aksehir Gölü 24 Dc 38.30N 31.28 E
Akseki 24 Dd 37.02N 31.48 E
Aksenovo-Zilovskoje 20 Gf 53.00N 117.35 E
'Aks-e Rostam 24 Ph 28.23N 54.52 E
Aksoran, Gora 19 Hf 48.25N 75.30 E
Akstafa 16 Ni 41.13N 45.27 E
Akstafa 16 Ni 41.06N 45.28 E
Aksu [China] 22 Ke 41.09N 80.15 E
Aksu [Kaz.-U.S.S.R.] 19 He 52.28N 71.59 E
Aksu [Kaz.-U.S.S.R.] 18 Lb 45.34N 79.30 E
Aksu [Kaz.-U.S.S.R.] 19 Hf 46.20N 78.15 E
Aksu [Tur.] 15 Ll 37.56N 28.56 E
Aksu [Tur.] 24 Dd 36.51N 30.54 E
Aksuat 19 If 47.48N 82.50 E
Aksubajevo 7 Mi 54.52N 50.50 E
Aksu He 21 Ke 40.28N 80.52 E
Aksum 35 Fc 14.07N 38.44 E
Ak-Šyjrak 18 Ld 41.49N 78.44 E
Aktag 27 Dd 36.45N 84.40 E
Aktaš [R.S.F.S.R.] 20 Df 50.18N 87.44 E
Aktaš [Uzb.-U.S.S.R.] 19 Gh 39.55N 65.53 E
Aktau 19 He 50.16N 73.07 E
Aktau, Gora- 19 Gg 41.45N 64.30 E
Aktjubinsk 6 Le 50.17N 57.10 E
Aktjubinskaja Oblast [3] 19 Ff 48.00N 58.00 E
Ak-Tjuz 18 Kc 42.50N 76.07 E
Akto 27 Cd 39.05N 76.02 E
Aktogaj 19 Hf 47.01N 79.40 E
Akula 36 Db 2.22N 20.11 E
Akun 40a Eb 54.12N 165.35W
Akune 28 Kh 32.01N 130.11 E
Akure 34 Gd 7.15N 5.12 E
Akureyri 6 Eb 65.40N 18.06W
Akuseki-Jima 28 Jj 29.28N 129.33 E
Akutan 40a Eb 54.10N 165.55W
Akutan 40a Eb 54.08N 165.46W
Akyab → Sittwe 22 Lg 20.09N 92.54 E
Akyazı 24 Db 40.41N 30.37 E
Akžajkyn, Ozero- 18 Fb 44.55N 67.45 E
Akzäl 19 If 49.13N 81.30 E
Ål 8 Cd 60.38N 8.34 E
Alà, Monti di- 14 Dj 40.35N 9.16 E
Alabama 38 Kf 31.08N 87.57W
Alabama [2] 43 Je 32.50N 87.30W
Al'Abbāsīyah 35 Ec 12.10N 31.18 E
Alaca 24 Fb 40.10N 34.51 E
Alaçam Dağlari 15 Lj 39.20N 28.32 E
Alaçan 24 Fb 41.37N 35.37 E
Alaçati 15 Jk 38.16N 26.23 E
Aladağ 24 Jc 43.35N 39.20 E
Ala Dağ [Tur.] 24 Jb 40.11N 42.49 E
Ala Dağ [Tur.] 24 Ed 37.58N 32.04 E
Alādāgh, Kūh-e- 24 Qd 37.13N 57.30 E
Ala Dağları 24 Fd 37.55N 35.13 E
Aladža 16 Rj 39.21N 53.12 E
Aladža Manastir 15 Lf 43.17N 28.01 E
Alagir 16 Nh 43.01N 44.12 E
Alagna Valsesia 14 Be 45.51N 7.56 E
Alagnon 11 Ji 45.27N 3.19 E
Alagoas [2] 54 Ke 9.30S 36.30W
Alagoinhas 53 Mg 12.07S 38.26W
Alagón 13 Kc 41.46N 1.07W
Alagón 13 Fe 39.44N 6.53W
Ala Gou 27 Ec 42.42N 89.12 E
Alahanpanjang 26 Dg 1.05S 100.47 E
Alahärmä 7 Fe 63.14N 22.51 E
Al Aḩmadī 24 Mh 29.05N 48.04 E
Alaid, Vulkan 20 Kf 50.50N 155.33 E
Alajärvi 7 Fe 63.00N 23.49 E
Alajku 19 Hg 40.18N 74.29 E
Alajski Hrebet 21 Jf 39.45N 72.30 E
Alajuela [3] 49 Eh 10.30N 84.30W
Alajuela 47 Hf 10.01N 84.13W
Alajuela, Lago- 49 Hi 9.05N 79.24W
Alakol, Ozero- 21 Ke 46.05N 81.50 E
Alakurtti 7 Hc 66.59N 30.20 E
Alalakeiki Channel 65a Ec 20.35N 156.30W
Al 'Alamayn 31 Je 30.49N 28.57 E
Alalau, Rio- 54 Fd 0.30S 61.10W
Al Amādīyah 24 Jd 37.06N 43.29 E
Alamagan Island 57 Fc 17.36N 145.50 E
Al 'Amārah 23 Gc 31.50N 47.09 E
'Alam ar Rūm, Ra's- 24 Bg 31.22N 27.21 E
Alāmarvdasht 24 Oi 27.52N 52.34 E
Alamashindo 35 Ge 4.51N 42.04 E
Alamata 35 Fc 12.25N 39.37 E
Alameda 45 Ci 35.11N 106.37W
Alaminos 26 Gc 16.10N 119.59 E
Al 'Āmirīyah 24 Cg 31.01N 29.48 E
Alamito Creek 45 Dl 29.31N 104.17W
Alamitos, Sierra de los- 48 Hd 26.20N 102.15W
'Alāmo 35 Ge 4.23N 43.09 E
Alamo 46 Hh 37.22N 115.10W
Alamogordo 43 Fe 32.54N 105.57W
Alamos 47 Cc 27.01N 108.56W
Alamos, Sierra- 48 Gc 28.25N 105.00W
Alamosa 43 Fd 37.28N 105.52W
Al Anbār [3] 24 If 34.00N 42.00 E
Åland/Ahvenanmaa [2] 7 Ef 60.15N 20.00 E
Åland/Ahvenanmaa = Aland Islands (EN) 5 Hc 60.15N 20.00 E
Aland Islands (EN) = Ahvenanmaa/Åland 5 Hc 60.15N 20.00 E
Aland Islands (EN) = Åland/Ahvenanmaa 5 Hc 60.15N 20.00 E
Älandsbro 8 Gb 62.40N 17.50 E
Ålandshav 8 Hd 60.00N 19.30 E
Alange 13 Ff 38.47N 6.15W
Alanje 49 Fi 8.24N 82.33W
Alanya 23 Db 36.33N 32.01 E
Alaotra, Lac- 37 Hc 17.30S 48.30 E
Alapaha River 44 Fj 30.26N 83.06W
Alapajevsk 19 Gd 57.52N 61.42 E
Alaplı 24 Db 41.08N 31.25 E
Al 'Aqabah = Aqaba (EN) 23 Dd 29.31N 35.00 E
Al 'Aqabah aş Şaghīrah 24 Ej 24.14N 32.53 E
Al 'Arabīyah As-Su'ūdīyah = Saudi Arabia (EN) [1] 22 Gg 25.00N 45.00 E
Alarcón, Embalse de- 13 Je 39.45N 2.20W
Al 'Arīsh 33 Fc 31.08N 33.48 E
Al 'Armah 24 Lj 25.30N 46.30 E
Al Arţāwīyah 24 Ki 26.30N 45.20 E
Alas, Selat- 26 Gh 8.40S 116.40 E
Al 'Aşab 24 Pk 23.20N 54.10 E
Alaşehir 24 Cc 38.21N 28.32 E
Al Ashkharah 23 Ie 21.47N 59.30 E
Al 'Āshūrīyah 24 Jg 31.02N 43.05 E
Alaska [2] 40 Ic 65.00N 153.00W
Alaska 38 Dc 65.00N 153.00W
Alaska, Gulf of- 38 Ed 58.00N 146.00W
Alaska Peninsula 38 Dd 57.00N 158.00W
Alaska Range 38 Ec 62.30N 150.00W
Alassio 14 Cf 44.00N 8.10 E
Alastaro 8 Jd 60.57N 22.51 E
Alat 18 De 39.26N 63.48 E
Alataw Shan 27 Cb 45.00N 80.00 E
Alataw Shankou = Dzungarian Gate (EN) 21 Ke 45.25N 82.25 E
Al 'Athāmīn 24 Jg 30.35N 43.40 E
Alatri 14 Hi 41.43N 13.21 E
Al 'Aţrun 31 Jg 18.11N 26.36 E
Alatyr 7 Li 54.52N 46.36 E
Alatyr 19 Ee 54.50N 46.36 E
Álava [3] 13 Jb 42.50N 2.45W
Alava, Cape- 46 Cb 48.10N 124.43W
Alaverdi 19 Eg 41.08N 44.37 E
Alavījeh 24 Nf 33.03N 51.05 E
Alavo/Alavus 7 Fe 62.35N 23.37 E
Alavus/Alavo 7 Fe 62.35N 23.37 E
Al 'Awāliq 23 Gg 14.15N 46.30 E
Al 'Awāriq 35 Ha 20.25N 48.40 E
Al 'Awsajīyah 24 Ki 26.04N 44.08 E
'Ālayh 24 Ff 33.48N 35.36 E
Al 'Ayn [Sau.Ar.] 24 Hj 25.04N 38.06 E
Al 'Ayn [U.A.E.] 24 Pj 24.13N 55.45 E
Alayor 13 Qe 39.56N 4.08 E
Al 'Ayyōţ 24 Dh 29.37N 31.15 E
Al A'ẓamīyah 24 Kf 33.23N 44.22 E
Alazani 16 Oi 41.03N 46.40 E
Alazeja 20 Kb 70.55N 153.40 E
Al'Azīzīyah 33 Bc 32.32N 13.01 E
Alazores, Puerto de los- 13 Hg 37.05N 4.15W
Alb [Eur.] 10 Ei 47.35N 8.08 E
Alb [F.R.G.] 12 Ke 49.04N 8.20 E
Alba [2] 15 Gc 46.08N 23.30 E
Alba 14 Cf 44.42N 8.02 E
Alba Adriatica 14 Hh 42.50N 13.56 E
Al Bāb 24 Gd 36.22N 37.31 E
Albac 15 Fc 46.27N 22.58 E
Albacete 6 Fh 38.59N 1.51W
Albacete [3] 13 Kf 38.50N 2.00W
Al Badārī 33 Fd 26.59N 31.25 E
Alba de Tormes 13 Gd 40.49N 5.31W
Al Badi 33 Ie 22.02N 46.34 E
Al Bādi 24 Ie 35.56N 41.32 E
Ålbæk 8 Dg 57.36N 10.25 E
Ålbæk Bugt 8 Dg 57.35N 10.30 E
Al Bahrah 24 Lh 29.40N 47.52 E
Al Baḩr al Aḩmar [3] 35 Fb 19.50N 35.30 E
Al Baḩrayn 21 Hg 26.00N 50.30 E

Index Symbols

[1] Independent Nation
[2] State, Region
[3] District, County
[4] Municipality
[5] Colony, Dependency
Continent
Physical Region
Historical or Cultural Region
Mount, Mountain
Volcano
Hill
Mountains, Mountain Range
Hills, Escarpment
Plateau, Upland
Pass, Gap
Plain, Lowland
Delta
Salt Flat
Valley, Canyon
Crater, Cave
Karst Features
Depression
Polder
Desert, Dunes
Forest, Woods
Heath, Steppe
Oasis
Cape, Point
Coast, Beach
Cliff
Peninsula
Isthmus
Sandbank
Island
Atoll
Rock, Reef
Islands, Archipelago
Rocks, Reefs
Coral Reef
Well, Spring
Geyser
River, Stream
Waterfall Rapids
River Mouth, Estuary
Lake
Salt Lake
Intermittent Lake
Reservoir
Swamp, Pond
Canal
Glacier
Ice Shelf, Pack Ice
Ocean
Sea
Gulf, Bay
Strait, Fjord
Lagoon
Bank
Seamount
Tablemount
Ridge
Shelf
Basin
Escarpment, Sea Scarp
Fracture
Trench, Abyss
National Park, Reserve
Point of Interest
Recreation Site
Cave, Cavern
Historic Site
Ruins
Wall, Walls
Church, Abbey
Temple
Scientific Station
Airport
Port
Lighthouse
Mine
Tunnel
Dam, Bridge

Al Baḩrayn=Bahrain (EN) [1] 22 Hg 26.00N 50.29 E
Albaida 13 Lf 38.51N 0.31W
Alba Iulia 15 Gc 46.04N 23.35 E
Albalate del Arzobispo 13 Lc 41.07N 0.31W
Al Balyanā 33 Fd 26.14N 32.00 E
Alban 11 Ik 43.54N 2.28 E
Albanel, Lac- 42 Kf 51.05N 73.05W
Albani, Colli- 14 Gi 41.45N 12.45 E
Albania (EN)=Shqipëria [1] 6 Hg 41.00N 20.00 E
Albano, Lago- 14 Gi 41.45N 12.40 E
Albano Laziale 14 Gi 41.44N 12.39 E
Albany 38 Kd 52.17N 81.31W
Albany [Austl.] 58 Ch 35.02S 117.53 E
Albany [Ga.-U.S.] 43 Ke 31.35N 84.10W
Albany [Ky.-U.S.] 44 Eg 36.42N 85.08W
Albany [N.Y.-U.S.] 39 Le 42.39N 73.45W
Albany [Or.-U.S.] 43 Cc 44.38N 123.06W
Alba Posse 55 Eh 27.33S 54.42W
Albarche 13 He 39.58N 4.46W
Albardón 56 Gd 31.26S 68.32W
Albarracín 13 Kd 40.25N 1.26W
Albarracín, Sierra de- 13 Kd 40.30N 1.30W
Al Başalīyah Qiblī 24 Ej 25.06N 32.47 E
Al Başrah [3] 24 Lg 30.30N 47.27 E
Al Başrah=Basra (EN) 22 Gf 30.30N 47.47 E
Al Baţḩā' 24 Kg 31.07N 45.54 E
Al Bāţın 24 Lh 29.00N 46.35 E
Al Bāţinah 21 Hg 23.45N 57.20 E
Albatross Bank (EN) 40 Ie 56.10N 152.20W
Albatross Bay 59 Ib 12.45S 141.43 E
Albatross Plateau (EN) 3 Mi 10.00N 103.00W
Albatross Point 62 Fc 38.07S 174.40 E
Al Batrūn 24 Fe 34.15N 35.39 E
Al Bawīţī 33 Ed 28.21N 28.52 E
Al Bayāḑ 21 Gg 22.00N 47.00 E
Al Bayḑā' [3] 33 Dc 32.00N 21.30 E
Al Bayḑā' 33 Cd 28.21N 18.58 E
Al Bayḑā' 31 Je 32.46N 21.43 E
Al Bayḑā' 33 Ig 13.58N 45.35 E
Albegna 14 Fh 42.30N 11.11 E
Albemarle 44 Gh 35.21N 80.12W
Albemarle Sound 43 Ld 36.03N 76.12W
Albenga 14 Cf 44.03N 8.13 E
Alberdi 56 Ic 26.10S 58.09W
Albères, Chaîne des- 11 Il 42.28N 2.56 E
Albères, Montes-/Les Alberes 11 Il 42.28N 2.56 E
Albergaria-a-Velha 13 Dd 40.42N 8.29W
Alberique 13 Le 39.07N 0.31W
Alberobello 14 Lj 40.47N 17.16 E
Albert 11 Id 50.00N 2.39 E
Albert, Canal-/Albert Kanaal =Albert Canal (EN) 11 Ld 50.39N 5.37 E
Albert, Lake- [Afr.] 30 Kh 1.40N 31.00 E
Albert, Lake- [Or.-U.S.] 46 Ee 42.38N 120.13W
Albert, Lake- (EN)=Mobuto Sese Seko, Lac- 30 Kh 1.40N 31.00 E
Alberta [3] 42 Gf 55.00N 115.00W
Albert Canal (EN)=Albert, Canal-/Albert Kanaal 11 Ld 50.39N 5.37 E
Albert Canal (EN)=Albert Kanaal/Albert, Canal- 11 Ld 50.39N 5.37 E
Albert Edward, Mount- 59 Ja 8.23S 147.27 E
Albert Edward Bay 42 Hc 69.35N 103.10W
Alberti 56 He 35.02S 60.16W
Albertirsa 10 Pi 47.15N 19.37 E
Albert Kanaal/Albert, Canal- =Albert Canal (EN) 11 Ld 50.39N 5.37 E
Albert Lea 43 Ic 43.39N 93.22W
Albert Nile 30 Kh 3.36N 32.02 E
Albertville [Al.-U.S.] 44 Dh 34.16N 86.12W
Albertville [Fr.] 11 Mi 45.41N 6.23 E
Albestroff 12 If 48.56N 6.51 E
Albi 11 Ik 43.56N 2.09 E
Albia 45 Jf 41.02N 92.48W
Al Bid' 24 Fh 28.28N 35.01 E
Albina 54 Hb 5.30N 54.03W
Albina, Ponta- 30 Ij 15.51S 11.44 E
Albino 14 De 45.46N 9.47 E
Albion [Mi.-U.S.] 44 Ed 42.15N 84.45W
Albion [Nb.-U.S.] 45 Hf 41.42N 98.00W
Albion [N.Y.-U.S.] 44 Hd 43.15N 78.12W
Al Biqa' 24 Ge 34.10N 36.10 E
Al Bi'r 23 Ed 28.51N 36.15 E
Al Bi'r al Jadīd 23 Ed 26.01N 38.29 E
Al Birk 23 Ff 18.13N 41.33 E
Albis 14 Cc 47.20N 8.30 E
Albo, Monte- 14 Dj 40.32N 9.35 E
Albocácer/Albocasser 13 Md 40.21N 0.02 E
Albocasser/Albocácer 13 Md 40.21N 0.02 E
Alborán, Isla de- 5 Fh 35.58N 3.02W
Alboran Basin (EN) 13 Ii 36.00N 4.00W
Ålborg 6 Gd 57.03N 9.56 E
Ålborg Bugt 7 Ch 56.45N 10.30 E
Alborz, Reshteh-ye Kūhhā-ye-=Elburz Mountains (EN) 21 Hf 36.00N 53.00 E
Albox 13 Jg 37.23N 2.08W
Albret, Pays d'- 11 Fj 44.10N 0.20W
Ālbū 'Alī 24 Je 34.49N 43.35 E
Albufeira 13 Dg 37.05N 8.15W
Albū Gharz, Sabkhat- 24 Ie 34.45N 41.15 E
Al Buheyrat [3] 35 Dd 7.00N 29.30 E
Al Bumbah 33 Dc 32.13N 23.00 E
Albuñol 13 Ih 36.47N 3.12W
Albuquerque [Braz.] 55 Dd 19.23S 57.26W
Albuquerque [N.M.-U.S.] 39 If 35.05N 106.40W
Albuquerque, Cayos de- 47 Hf 12.10N 81.50W
Al Burayj 24 Ge 34.15N 36.46 E
Al Buraymī 23 Ie 24.15N 55.45 E
Al Burmah 32 Ic 31.45N 9.02 E
Alburquerque 13 Fe 39.13N 7.00W
Albury [Austl.] 58 Fh 36.05S 146.55 E
Albury [N.Z.] 62 Df 44.14S 170.53 E
Al Buţanah 30 Kg 15.00N 35.00 E
Al Buţayn 24 Kj 25.52N 45.50 E
Alby 8 Fb 62.30N 15.28 E
Alcácer do Sal 13 Df 38.22N 8.30W
Alcáçovar 13 Df 38.25N 8.13W
Alcalá de Chivert 13 Md 40.18N 0.14 E
Alcalá de Guadaira 13 Gg 37.20N 5.50W
Alcalá de Henares 13 Id 40.29N 3.22W
Alcalá del Júcar 13 Ke 39.12N 1.26W
Alcalá de los Gazules 13 Gh 36.28N 5.44W
Alcalá del Río 13 Gg 37.31N 5.59W
Alcalá la Real 13 Ig 37.28N 3.56W
Alcamo 14 Gm 37.59N 12.58 E
Alcanandre 13 Mc 41.37N 0.12 E
Alcañices 13 Fc 41.42N 6.21W
Alcañiz 13 Lc 41.03N 0.08W
Alcántara 13 Fe 39.43N 6.53W
Alcântara 54 Jd 2.24S 44.24W
Alcantara 14 Jm 37.49N 15.16 E
Alcántara, Embalse de- 13 Fe 39.45N 6.48W
Alcantarilla 13 Kg 37.58N 1.13W
Alcaraz 13 Jf 38.40N 2.29W
Alcaraz, Sierra de- 13 Jf 38.35N 2.25W
Alcaudete 13 Hg 37.36N 4.05W
Alcázar de San Juan 13 Ie 39.24N 3.12W
Alcester 63a Ac 9.33S 152.25 E
Alcira/Alzira 13 Le 39.09N 0.26W
Alcobaça [Braz.] 54 Kg 17.30S 39.13W
Alcobaça [Port.] 13 De 39.33N 8.59W
Alcobendas 13 Id 40.32N 3.38W
Alcoi/Alcoy 13 Lf 38.42N 0.28W
Alcolea del Pinar 13 Jc 41.02N 2.28W
Alcorta 55 Bk 33.32S 61.07W
Alcoutim 13 Eg 37.28N 7.28W
Alcova 46 Le 42.37N 106.36W
Alcoy/Alcoi 13 Lf 38.42N 0.28W
Alcubierre, Sierra de- 13 Lc 41.44N 0.29W
Alcudia 13 Pe 39.52N 3.07 E
Alcúdia, Badia d'-/Alcudia, Bahía de- 13 Pe 39.48N 3.13 E
Alcudia, Bahía de-/Alcúdia, Badia d'- 13 Pe 39.48N 3.13 E
Alcudia, Sierra de- 13 Hf 38.35N 4.35W
Aldabra Group 37b Ab 9.25S 46.22 E
Aldabra Islands 30 Li 9.25S 46.22 E
Aldama [Mex.] 48 Jf 22.55N 98.04W
Aldama [Mex.] 47 Cc 28.51N 105.54W
Aldan 22 Od 58.37N 125.24 E
Aldan [R.S.F.S.R.] 20 Hd 63.20N 129.25 E
Aldan [U.S.S.R.] 21 Oc 63.28N 129.35 E
Aldan Plateau (EN)=Aldanskoje Nagorje 21 Od 57.30N 127.30 E
Aldanskoje Nagorje=Aldan Plateau (EN) 21 Od 57.30N 127.30 E
Aldarhan 27 Gb 47.42N 96.36 E
Alde 12 Db 52.10N 1.32 E
Aldeburgh 9 Oi 52.09N 1.35 E
Aldeia 55 Ed 18.12S 55.10W
Aldeia, Serra da- 55 Ic 17.00S 46.50W
Alderney 9 Kl 49.43N 2.12W
Aldershot 12 Bc 51.15N 0.46W
Alderson 46 Ja 50.18N 111.26W
Aledo 45 Kf 41.12N 90.45W
Aleg 31 Fg 17.03N 13.53W
Alegranza 32 Ed 29.23N 13.30W
Alegre 54 Jh 20.46S 41.32W
Alegre, Rio- 55 Cb 15.14S 59.58W
Alegrete 56 Ic 29.46S 55.46W
Alej 20 Df 52.50N 83.35 E
Alejandra 55 Ci 29.54S 59.50W
Alejandro Selkirk, Isla- 52 Hi 33.45S 80.46W
Alejsk 20 Df 52.28N 82.45 E
Aleksandrija 16 He 48.40N 33.07 E
Aleksandrov 19 Dd 56.25N 38.42 E
Aleksandrov Gaj 19 Ee 50.08N 48.32 E
Aleksandrovka 16 He 48.59N 32.13 E
Aleksandrovsk 17 Hg 59.10N 57.35 E
Aleksandrovskoje 16 Mg 44.39N 43.00 E
Aleksandrovsk-Sahalinsk 22 Qd 50.54N 142.10 E
Aleksandrów Kujawski 10 Od 52.52N 18.42 E
Aleksandrów Łódzki 10 Pe 51.49N 19.19 E
Aleksandry, Zemlja- 21 Ga 80.45N 46.00 E
Aleksejevka [Kaz.-U.S.S.R.] 19 If 48.26N 85.40 E
Aleksejevka [Kaz.-U.S.S.R.] 19 He 51.58N 70.59 E
Aleksejevka [Kaz.-U.S.S.R.] 17 Nj 53.31N 69.28 E
Aleksejevka [R.S.F.S.R.] 19 De 50.39N 38.42 E
Aleksejevsk 20 Fe 57.50N 108.23 E
Aleksejevskoje 7 Mi 55.19N 50.03 E
Aleksin 16 Jb 54.31N 37.07 E
Aleksinac 15 Ef 43.32N 21.43 E
Alem 56 Ic 27.31S 55.15W
Ålem 7 Dh 56.57N 16.23 E
Alem Maya 35 Gd 9.27N 41.58 E
Ålen 8 Db 62.51N 11.17 E
Alençon 11 Gf 48.26N 0.05 E
Alenquer 54 Hd 1.56S 54.46W
Alenuihaha Channel 60 Oc 20.26N 156.00W
Alépé 34 Ed 5.30N 3.39W
Aleppo (EN)=Ḩalab 22 Ff 36.12N 37.10 E
Aléria 11a Ba 42.06N 9.31 E
Aléria, Plaine d'- 11a Ba 42.05N 9.30 E
Alert 39 Ma 82.30N 62.00W
Alert Bay 46 Ba 50.35N 126.55W
Alès 11 Kj 44.08N 4.05 E
Aleşd 15 Fb 47.04N 22.25 E
Alessandria 14 Cf 44.54N 8.37 E
Ålestrup 8 Ch 56.42N 9.30 E
Ålesund 6 Gc 62.28N 6.09 E
Aleutian Basin (EN) 38 Ad 57.00N 177.00 E
Aleutian Islands 38 Bd 52.00N 176.00W
Aleutian Range 38 Dd 59.00N 155.00W
Aleutian Trench (EN) 3 Je 51.00N 179.00 E
Alexander, Cape- 60 Fi 6.35S 156.30 E
Alexander, Kap- 41 Ec 78.10N 72.45W
Alexander Archipelago 38 Fd 56.30N 134.00W
Alexanderbaai 37 Be 28.40S 16.30 E
Alexander City 43 Je 32.56N 85.57W
Alexander Island 66 Qe 71.00S 70.00W
Alexandra 61 Ci 45.15S 169.24 E
Alexandra Fiord 42 Ka 79.17N 75.00W
Alexandretta (EN)=İskenderun 22 Ff 36.37N 36.07 E
Alexandretta, Gulf of- (EN) =İskenderun Körfezi 23 Eb 36.30N 35.40 E
Alexándria 15 Fi 40.38N 22.27 E
Alexandria [Austl.] 59 Hc 19.05S 136.40 E
Alexandria [La.-U.S.] 39 Jf 31.18N 92.27W
Alexandria [Mn.-U.S.] 43 Hb 45.53N 95.22W
Alexandria [Rom.] 15 If 43.59N 25.20 E
Alexandria [S.Afr.] 37 Df 33.39S 26.24 E
Alexandria [Va.-U.S.] 44 If 38.49N 77.06W
Alexandria (EN)=Al Iskandarīyah [Eg.] 31 Je 31.12N 29.54 E
Alexandria Bay 44 Jc 44.20N 75.55W
Alexandrina, Lake- 59 Hg 35.25S 139.10 E
Alexandrita 54 Hg 19.42S 50.27W
Alexandroúpolis 6 Ig 40.51N 25.52 E
'Aleyak, Godār-e- 24 Qd 36.30N 57.45 E
Alf 10 Df 50.03N 7.07 E
Alfabia, Sierra de- 13 Oe 39.45N 2.48 E
Alfambra 13 Kd 40.21N 1.07W
Al Fardah 35 Hc 14.51N 48.26 E
Alfaro 13 Kb 42.11N 1.45W
Al Fāshir 31 Jg 13.38N 25.21 E
Al Fashn 33 Fd 28.49N 30.54 E
Alfatar 15 Kf 43.57N 27.17 E
Al Fathah 24 Je 35.04N 43.34 E
Al Fāw 23 Gd 29.58N 48.29 E
Al Fawwārah 24 Ji 26.03N 43.05 E
Al Fayyūm 31 Kf 29.19N 30.58 E
Alfbach 12 Jd 50.03N 7.08 E
Alfeld 10 Fe 51.59N 9.50 E
Alfenas 54 Ih 21.26S 45.57W
Al Fifi 35 Dc 10.03N 25.01 E
Alfiós 15 El 37.37N 21.27 E
Alföld 5 If 47.15N 20.25 E
Alfonsine 14 Gf 44.30N 12.03 E
Alford 12 Ca 53.15N 0.11 E
Ålfotbreen 8 Ac 61.45N 5.40 E
Alfreton 12 Aa 53.06N 1.23W
Alfta 7 Df 61.21N 16.05 E
Al Fuḩayḩīl 23 Gd 29.05N 48.08 E
Al Fuhūd 24 Lg 30.58N 46.43 E
Al Fujayrah 23 Id 25.06N 56.21 E
Al Fūlah 35 Dc 11.48N 28.24 E
Al Fuqahā' 33 Cd 27.50N 16.21 E
Al Furāt=Euphrates (EN) 21 Gf 31.00N 47.25 E
Al Fuwayriţ 24 Ni 26.02N 51.22 E
Alga 19 Ff 49.55N 57.20 E
Algador 13 Ie 39.55N 3.53W
Al Gārah 24 Ih 29.52N 40.15 E
Algarås 8 Ff 58.48N 14.14 E
Ålgård 8 Af 58.46N 5.51 E
Algarrobo 49 Jh 10.12N 74.04W
Algarve 13 Dg 37.10N 8.15W
Algarve 5 Fh 37.10N 8.15W
Algeciras 6 Fh 36.08N 5.30W
Algeciras, Bahía de- 13 Gh 36.09N 5.25W
Algena 35 Fb 17.20N 38.34 E
Algeria (EN)=Al Jazā'ir [1] 31 Hf 28.00N 3.00 E
Algerian Basin (EN) 5 Gh 39.00N 5.00 E
Al Gharaq as Sulţānī 24 Dh 29.08N 30.42 E
Al Gharbi 32 Jc 34.40N 11.13 E
Al Ghāţ 24 Ki 26.00N 45.03 E
Al Ghaydah 23 Hf 16.12N 52.15 E
Alghero 14 Cj 40.33N 8.19 E
Alghero, Rada d'- 14 Cj 40.35N 8.20 E
Älghult 8 Fg 57.01N 15.34 E
Al Ghurāb 24 Dj 25.20N 30.20 E
Al Ghurayfah 24 Qk 23.59N 56.29 E
Al Ghurdaqah 33 Fd 27.14N 33.50 E
Algiers (EN)=Al Jazā'ir 31 He 36.47N 3.03 E
Algiers (EN)=Al Jazā'ir [3] 32 Hb 36.35N 3.00 E
Algoa Bay 30 Jl 33.50S 25.50 E
Algodoeiro, Serra do- 55 Jc 16.30S 44.45W
Algoma 45 Md 44.36N 87.27W
Algoma Uplands 44 Fb 47.00N 83.35W
Algona 45 Ie 43.04N 94.14W
Algonquin Park 44 Hc 45.27N 78.26W
Algrange 12 Ie 49.21N 6.03 E
Al Ḩabakah 24 Jh 29.51N 42.16 E
Al Ḩadd 23 Ie 22.29N 59.58 E
Al Ḩadīdah 35 Ia 21.31N 50.28 E
Al Ḩadīthah 23 Fc 34.07N 42.23 E
Al Ḩadithah 24 Gg 31.28N 37.08 E
Al Ḩaḑr 24 Je 35.35N 42.44 E
Al Haffah 24 Ge 35.35N 36.02 E
Al Ḩahjarah 23 Fc 30.25N 44.30 E
Al Ḩā'ır 24 Lj 24.23N 46.50 E
Al Ḩajar 35 Hb 16.08N 47.50 E
Al Hajar 23 Ie 23.15N 57.30 E
Al Halfāyah 24 Lg 31.49N 47.26 E
Alhama 13 Kb 42.11N 1.45W
Al Ḩamād 21 Ff 32.00N 39.30 E
Alhama de Granada 13 Ih 37.00N 3.59W
Alhama de Murcia 13 Kg 37.51N 1.25W
Alhamilla, Sierra- 13 Jh 36.58N 2.20W
Al Ḩammāh 32 Ic 33.54N 9.48 E
Al Ḩammām [Eg.] 24 Cg 30.50N 29.23 E
Al Ḩammām [Iraq] 24 Kg 31.08N 44.04 E
Al Ḩamrā 24 Pj 25.42N 55.47 E
Al Hanīyah 24 Kh 29.10N 45.50 E
Al Ḩarrah 24 Ch 28.20N 29.07 E
Al Ḩarrah 24 Hg 31.00N 38.40 E
Al Harūj al Aswad 30 If 27.00N 17.10 E
Al Ḩasā 24 Fg 30.49N 35.59 E
Al Hasā' 21 Gg 26.35N 48.10 E
Al Ḩasakah 23 Fb 36.29N 40.45 E
Al Ḩasan 24 Je 34.39N 43.43 E
Al Ḩasānī 24 Gj 24.58N 37.05 E
Alhaurín el Grande 13 Hh 36.38N 4.41W
Al Ḩawāmidīyah 24 Dh 29.54N 31.15 E
Al Ḩawātah 35 Ec 13.25N 34.38 E
Al Ḩawjā' 24 Hh 28.59N 38.34 E
Al Ḩawrah 35 Hc 13.49N 47.35 E
Al Hayy 23 Gc 32.10N 46.03 E
Al Ḩayz 33 Ed 28.02N 28.39 E
Al Hibāk 23 He 20.20N 53.10 E
Al Ḩijāz 21 Fg 24.30N 38.30 E
Al Hillah 33 Ie 23.50N 46.51 E
Al Ḩillah 23 Fc 32.29N 44.25 E
Al Ḩinākīyah 23 Fe 24.51N 40.31 E
Al Hindiyah 24 Kf 32.32N 44.13 E
Al Ḩınnāh 24 Mi 26.56N 48.45 E
Al Hirmil 24 Ge 34.23N 36.23 E
Al Hoceima 32 Gb 35.15N 3.55W
Al Hoceima [3] 32 Gb 35.00N 4.15W
Alhucemas, Peñón de- 13 Ii 35.13N 3.53W
Al Ḩudaydah 22 Gh 14.48N 42.57 E
Al Ḩufrah 33 Cd 29.30N 17.55 E
Al Hufrah 23 Ed 28.49N 38.15 E
Al Hufūf 22 Gg 25.22N 49.34 E
Al Hūj 24 Hh 29.00N 38.25 E
Al Ḩunayy 24 Mj 24.48N 48.45 E
Al Ḩuşayḩişah 35 Ec 14.44N 33.18 E
Al Ḩuwaimī 23 Fg 13.58N 47.40 E
Al Ḩuwayyiţ 24 Ij 25.36N 40.23 E
Al Ḩyyānīyah 24 Jh 28.42N 42.18 E
'Alīābād [Iran] 23 Id 28.37N 55.51 E
'Alīābād [Iran] 24 Le 35.04N 46.58 E
'Alīābād [Iran] 24 Nd 36.37N 51.33 E
Aliābād 24 Pd 36.56N 54.50 E
Alīābād, Kūh-e- 23 Hc 34.13N 50.46 E
Aliaga 13 Ld 40.40N 0.42W
Aliağa 24 Bc 38.48N 26.59 E
Aliákmon 15 Fi 40.30N 22.40 E
'Alī al Gharbī 24 Lf 32.27N 46.41 E
'Alī ash Sharqī 24 Lf 32.07N 46.44 E
Ali-Bajramly 19 Eh 39.55N 48.57 E
Alibej, Ozero- 15 Nd 45.50N 30.00 E
Alibey Adasi 15 Jj 39.20N 26.38 E
Alibo 35 Fd 9.53N 37.05 E
Alibori 34 Fc 11.56N 3.17 E
Alibunar 15 Dd 45.04N 20.58 E
Alicante 6 Fh 38.21N 0.29W
Alicante [3] 13 Lf 38.30N 0.30W
Alicante, Golfo de- 13 Lf 38.20N 0.15W
Alice [S.Afr.] 37 Df 32.47S 26.50 E
Alice [Tx.-U.S.] 43 Hf 27.45N 98.04W
Alice, Punta- 14 Lk 39.12N 17.09 E
Alice Springs 58 Eg 23.42S 133.53 E
Aliceville 44 Ci 33.08N 88.09W
Alicudi 14 Il 38.30N 14.20 E
Alīgarh 22 Jg 28.02N 78.17 E
Alīgūdarz 24 Mf 33.24N 49.41 E
Alihe → Oroqen Zizhiqi 27 La 50.35N 123.42 E
Alijó 13 Ec 41.16N 7.28W
Alijos, Rocas- 47 Ad 24.57N 115.44W
'Al Ijūq, Kūh-e- 24 Ng 31.30N 51.45 E
Al Ikhwan 21 Hh 12.08N 53.10 E
Al Ikhwān 24 Fi 26.19N 34.52 E
Alima 30 Ii 1.36S 16.36 E
Al Imārāt al 'Arabīyah al Muttaḩidah=United Arab Emirates (EN) [1] 22 Hg 24.00N 54.00 E
Alimiá 15 Km 36.16N 27.43 E
Alindao 35 Cd 5.02N 21.13 E
Alinglapalap Atoll 57 Hd 7.08N 168.16 E
Alingsås 7 Ch 57.56N 12.31 E
Aliquippa 44 Ge 40.38N 80.16W
Al 'Irāq=Iraq (EN) [1] 22 Gf 33.00N 44.00 E
Al'Irq 33 Dd 29.01N 21.31 E
Al 'Irqah 23 Gg 13.40N 47.18 E
Ali-Sabjeh 35 Gc 11.08N 42.43 E
'Alī Shāh 'Avaz 24 Ne 35.39N 51.04 E
Al Iskandarīyah [Eg.] = Alexandria (EN) 31 Je 31.12N 29.54 E
Al Iskandarīyah [Iraq] 24 Kf 32.53N 44.21 E
Aliskerovo 20 Lc 67.52N 167.40 E
Al Ismā'īlīyah=Ismailia (EN) 33 Fc 30.35N 32.16 E
Al Istiwā'īyah al Gharbīyah [3] 35 Dd 5.20N 28.30 E
Al Istiwā'īyah al Sharkīyah [3] 35 Ed 5.20N 33.50 E
Alistráti 15 Gh 41.04N 23.58 E
Alitak, Cape- 40 Ie 56.51N 154.21W
Alite Reef 63a Ec 8.53S 160.38 E
Alitus/Alytus 19 Ce 54.25N 24.08 E
Alivérion 15 Hk 38.25N 24.02 E
Aliwal North 31 Jl 30.44S 26.40 E
Al Jabalayn 35 Ec 12.36N 32.48 E
Al Jadīdah [Eg.] 24 Cj 25.34N 28.51 E
Al Jadīdah [Sau.Ar.] 24 Mj 25.39N 49.32 E
Al Jafr 24 Gg 30.18N 36.13 E
Al Jāfūrah 35 Ia 23.25N 50.17 E
Al Jāfūrah 24 Nj 25.00N 50.15 E
Al Jaghbūb 31 Jf 29.45N 24.31 E
Al Jahrah 23 Gc 29.20N 47.40 E
Al Jalāmīd 24 Ig 31.17N 40.06 E
Al Jamalīyah 24 Nj 25.37N 51.05 E
Al Jamm 32 Jb 35.18N 10.43 E
Al Janā'in 32 Jc 31.44N 10.09 E
Aljat 16 Pj 39.58N 49.27 E
Al Jawf [Lib.] 31 Jf 24.12N 23.18 E
Al Jawf [Sau.Ar.] 22 Fg 29.50N 39.52 E
Al Jazā'ir=Algeria (EN) [1] 31 Hf 28.00N 3.00 E
Al Jazā'ir=Algiers (EN) [3] 32 Hb 36.35N 3.00 E
Al Jazā'ir=Algiers (EN) 31 He 36.47N 3.03 E
Al Jazā'ir-El Harrach 13 Ph 36.43N 3.08 E
Al Jazīrah [3] 35 Ec 14.40N 33.30 E
Al Jazīrah [Asia] 21 Gf 35.10N 42.00 E
Al Jazīrah [Sud.] 30 Kg 14.25N 33.00 E
Aljezur 13 Dg 37.19N 8.48W
Aljibe 13 Gh 36.31N 5.37W
Al Jifārah 30 Ie 32.30N 11.45 E
Al Jiwā' 23 He 23.00N 54.00 E
Al Jīzah=Giza (EN) 31 Ke 30.01N 31.13 E
Al Jubayl 23 Gd 27.01N 49.40 E
Al Jubaylah 24 Lj 24.54N 46.27 E
Al Junaynah [Sau.Ar.] 33 He 20.17N 42.48 E
Al Junaynah [Sud.] 31 Jg 13.27N 22.27 E
Al Juraid 24 Mi 27.11N 49.52 E
Aljustrel 13 Dg 37.52N 8.10W
Alkạ 40a Db 52.15N 174.30W
Al Kaba'ish 24 Lg 30.58N 47.00 E
Al Kāf [3] 32 Ib 36.00N 9.00 E
Al Kāf 32 Ib 36.11N 8.43 E
Alkali Lake 46 Ff 41.42N 119.50W
Al Kamāsin 23 Fe 20.25N 44.48 E
Al Kāmilīn 35 Eb 15.05N 33.11 E
Al Karak 24 Fg 31.11N 35.42 E
Al Karkh 24 Kf 33.20N 44.20 E
Al Karnak 33 Fd 25.43N 32.39 E
Al Kawah 35 Ec 13.44N 32.30 E
Al Kāẓimīyah 24 Kf 33.22N 44.20 E
Alken 12 Hd 50.52N 5.18 E
Al Khabrā' 23 Fd 26.04N 43.33 E
Al Khābūra 23 Ie 23.50N 57.18 E
Al-Khalīj al- 'Arabi=Persian Gulf (EN) 21 Hg 27.00N 51.00 E
Al Khalīl 24 Fg 31.32N 35.06 E
Al Khālis 24 Kf 33.51N 44.32 E
Al Khandaq 35 Eb 18.36N 30.34 E
Al Khārijah 31 Kf 25.26N 30.33 E
Al Kharj 24 Lj 24.10N 47.30 E
Al Kharţūm=Khartoum (EN) [3] 35 Eb 15.50N 33.00 E
Al Kharţūm=Khartoum (EN) 31 Kg 15.36N 32.32 E
Al Kharţūm Baḩrī= Khartoum North (EN) 31 Kg 15.38N 32.33 E
Al Khaşab 24 Qi 26.12N 56.15 E
Al Khaţţ 24 Qk 25.37N 56.01 E
Al Khawr 23 Hd 25.40N 51.30 E
Al Khidr 24 Kg 31.12N 45.33 E
Al Khubar 23 Hd 26.17N 50.12 E
Al Khufayfīyah 23 Fe 24.55N 44.42 E
Al Khums [3] 33 Bc 31.20N 14.10 E
Al Khums 31 Ie 32.39N 14.16 E
Al Khunn 35 Ha 23.18N 49.15 E
Al Khuwayr 24 Ni 26.04N 51.05 E
Al Kidn 35 Ia 22.30N 54.00 E
Al Kilḩ Sharq 24 Ej 25.03N 32.52 E
Alkionídhon, Kólpos- 15 Fk 38.05N 23.00 E
Al Kır'ānah 24 Nj 25.00N 51.03 E
Alkmaar 11 Kb 52.37N 4.44 E
Al Kūfah 24 Kf 32.02N 44.24 E
Al Kumayt 24 Lf 32.02N 46.52 E
Al Kuntillah 33 Fc 30.00N 34.41 E
Al Kushḩ 24 Ei 26.14N 32.05 E
Al Kut 23 Gc 32.30N 45.49 E
Al Kuwayt=Kuwait (EN) [1] 22 Gg 29.30N 47.45 E
Al Kuwayt=Kuwait (EN) 22 Gg 29.20N 47.59 E
Al Labbah 24 Ih 29.20N 41.30 E
Al Lādhiqīyah=Latakia (EN) 22 Ff 35.31N 35.07 E
Allagash River 44 Mb 47.05N 69.20W
Al Lagowa 35 Dc 11.24N 29.08 E
Allahābād 22 Kg 25.27N 81.51 E
Allah-Jun 20 Id 60.27N 134.57 E
Allah-Jun 20 Id 61.08N 137.59 E
Allahüekber DaGı 24 Jb 40.35N 42.32 E
Allakaket 40 Ic 66.34N 152.41W
Allanmyo 25 Je 19.22N 95.13 E
Allariz 13 Eb 42.11N 7.48W
All-Awash Island 51n Bb 12.55N 61.10W
Alldays 37 Dd 22.41S 29.06 E
Ålleberg 8 Ef 58.08N 13.36 E
Allegan 44 Ed 42.32N 85.51W
Allegheny Mountains 38 Lf 38.30N 80.00W
Allegheny Plateau 38 Le 41.30N 78.00W
Allegheny Reservoir 44 He 42.00N 78.56W
Allegheny River 43 Lc 40.27N 80.00W
Allègre, Pointe- 51e Ab 16.22N 61.45W
Allen 26 Hd 12.30N 124.17 E
Allen, Bog of- 9 Gh 53.20N 7.00W
Allen, Lough-/Loch Aillionn 9 Eg 54.08N 8.08W
Allendale 44 Gi 33.01N 81.19W
Allende 47 Dc 28.20N 100.51W
Allendorf (Eder) 12 Kc 51.02N 8.40 E
Allendorf (Lumda) 12 Kd 50.41N 8.50 E
Allentown 43 Lc 40.37N 75.30W
Alleppey 22 Ji 9.29N 76.19 E
Aller 10 Fd 52.57N 9.11 E
Allevard 11 Mi 45.24N 6.04 E
Allgäuer Alpen 10 Gi 47.20N 10.25 E
Alliance [Nb.-U.S.] 43 Gc 42.06N 102.52W
Alliance [Oh.-U.S.] 44 Ge 40.56N 81.06W
Allier [3] 11 Ih 46.30N 3.00 E
Allier 5 Gf 46.57N 3.05 E
Al Līfīyah 23 Fc 30.35N 43.09 E
Al Lişāfah 24 Li 27.37N 46.52 E
Alliston 44 Hc 44.09N 79.52W
Al Līth 23 Fe 20.09N 40.16 E
Alloa 9 Je 56.07N 3.49W
Allonnes 11 Gg 47.58N 0.09 E
Allos 11 Mj 44.14N 6.38 E
All Saints 51d Bb 17.03N 61.48W
Al Luḩayyah 23 Ff 15.43N 42.42 E
Al Luwaymī 23 Fd 27.54N 42.22 E
Alm 14 Hb 48.05N 13.55 E
Alma [Ga.-U.S.] 44 Fj 31.33N 82.28W
Alma [Mi.-U.S.] 44 Ed 43.23N 84.39W
Alma [Nb.-U.S.] 45 Gf 40.06N 99.22W
Alma [Que.-Can.] 42 Kg 48.32N 71.40W
Alma-Ata 22 Je 43.15N 76.57 E
Alma-Atinskaja Oblast [3] 19 Hg 44.00N 77.00 E
Almada 13 Cf 38.41N 9.09W
Almadén 13 Hf 38.46N 4.50W
Al Madīnah [Iraq] 24 Lg 30.57N 47.16 E
Al Madīnah [Sau.Ar.] = Medina (EN) 22 Fg 24.28N 39.36 E
Al Madīnah al Fikrīyah 24 Di 27.56N 30.49 E
'Al Madōw 35 Hc 10.59N 48.42 E
Al Mafraq 24 Gf 32.21N 36.12 E
Al Maghrib=Morocco (EN) [1] 31 Ge 32.00N 5.50W
Almagro 13 If 38.53N 3.43W
Almagrundet 8 He 59.06N 19.00 E

Index Symbols

[1] Independent Nation
[2] State, Region
[3] District, County
[4] Municipality
[5] Colony, Dependency
Continent
Physical Region
Historical or Cultural Region
Mount, Mountain
Volcano
Hill
Mountains, Mountain Range
Hills, Escarpment
Plateau, Upland
Pass, Gap
Plain, Lowland
Delta
Salt Flat
Valley, Canyon
Crater, Cave
Karst Features
Depression
Polder
Desert, Dunes
Forest, Woods
Heath, Steppe
Oasis
Cape, Point
Coast, Beach
Cliff
Peninsula
Isthmus
Sandbank
Island
Atoll
Rock, Reef
Islands, Archipelago
Rocks, Reefs
Coral Reef
Well, Spring
Geyser
River, Stream
Waterfall Rapids
River Mouth, Estuary
Lake
Salt Lake
Intermittent Lake
Reservoir
Swamp, Pond
Canal
Glacier
Ice Shelf, Pack Ice
Ocean
Sea
Gulf, Bay
Strait, Fjord
Lagoon
Bank
Seamount
Tablemount
Ridge
Shelf
Basin
Escarpment, Sea Scarp
Fracture
Trench, Abyss
National Park, Reserve
Point of Interest
Recreation Site
Cave, Cavern
Historic Site
Ruins
Wall, Walls
Church, Abbey
Temple
Scientific Station
Airport
Port
Lighthouse
Mine
Tunnel
Dam, Bridge

Index Symbols

[1] Independent Nation
[2] State, Region
[3] District, County
[4] Municipality
[5] Colony, Dependency
■ Continent
⊠ Physical Region

Historical or Cultural Region
Mount, Mountain
Volcano
Hill
Mountains, Mountain Range
Hills, Escarpment
Plateau, Upland

Pass, Gap
Plain, Lowland
Delta
Salt Flat
Valley, Canyon
Crater, Cave
Karst Features

Depression
Polder
Desert, Dunes
Forest, Woods
Heath, Steppe
Oasis
Cape, Point

Coast, Beach
Cliff
Peninsula
Isthmus
Sandbank
Island
Atoll

Rock, Reef
Islands, Archipelago
Rocks, Reefs
Coral Reef
Well, Spring
Geyser
River, Stream

Waterfall Rapids
River Mouth, Estuary
Lake
Salt Lake
Intermittent Lake
Reservoir
Swamp, Pond

Canal
Glacier
Ice Shelf, Pack Ice
Ocean
Sea
Gulf, Bay
Strait, Fjord

Lagoon
Bank
Seamount
Tablemount
Ridge
Shelf
Basin

Escarpment, Sea Scarp
Fracture
Trench, Abyss
National Park, Reserve
Point of Interest
Recreation Site
Cave, Cavern

Historic Site
Ruins
Wall, Walls
Church, Abbey
Temple
Scientific Station
Airport

Port
Lighthouse
Mine
Tunnel
Dam, Bridge

Index Symbols

[1] Independent Nation
[2] State, Province
[3] District, County
[4] Municipality
[5] Colony, Dependency
Continent
Physical Region
Historical or Cultural Region
Mount, Mountain
Volcano
Hill
Mountains, Mountain Range
Hills, Escarpment
Plateau, Upland
Pass, Gap
Plain, Lowland
Delta
Salt Flat
Valley, Canyon
Crater, Cave
Karst Features
Depression
Polder
Desert, Dunes
Forest, Woods
Heath, Steppe
Oasis
Cape, Point
Coast, Beach
Cliff
Peninsula
Isthmus
Sandbank
Island
Atoll
Rock, Reef
Islands, Archipelago
Rocks, Reefs
Coral Reef
Well, Spring
Waterfall Rapids
River Mouth, Estuary
Lake
Salt Lake
Intermittent Lake
Reservoir
Swamp, Pond
Canal
Glacier
Ice Shelf, Pack Ice
Ocean
Sea
Gulf, Bay
Strait, Fjord
Lagoon
Bank
Seamount
Tableland
Ridge
Shelf
Basin
Escarpment, Sea Scarp
Fracture
Trench, Abyss
National Park, Reserve
Point of Interest
Recreation Site
Cave, Cavern
Historic Site
Ruins
Wall, Walls
Church, Abbey
Temple
Scientific Station
Airport
Port
Lighthouse
Mine
Tunnel
Dam, Bridge

Antabamba 54 Df 14.19S 72.55W
Antakya=Antioch (EN) 23 Eb 36.14N 36.07 E
Antalaha 31 Mj 14.55S 50.15 E
Antalya 22 Ff 36.53N 30.42 E
Antalya, Gulf of- (EN)= Antalya Körfezi 23 Db 36.30N 31.00 E
Antalya Körfezi=Antalya, Gulf of- (EN) 23 Db 36.30N 31.00 E
An Tan 25 Le 15.26N 108.39 E
Antananarivo 31 Lj 18.55S 47.30 E
Antananarivo [3] 37 Hc 19.00S 46.40 E
Antanimora 37 Hd 24.48S 45.39 E
An tAonach/Nenagh 9 Ei 52.52N 8.12W
Antarctica (EN) 66 Bg 90.00S 0.00
Antarctic Peninsula (EN) 66 Qe 69.30S 65.00W
Antas, Cachoeira das- 55 Ha 13.06S 48.09W
Antas, Rio das- 55 Gi 29.04S 51.21W
An Teampall Mór/Templemore 9 Fi 52.48N 7.50W
Antela, Laguna de- 13 Eb 42.07N 7.41W
Antelao 14 Gd 46.27N 12.16 E
Antelope Creek 46 Me 43.29N 105.23W
Anten 8 Ef 58.03N 12.30 E
Antequera [Par.] 55 Dg 24.08S 57.07W
Antequera [Sp.] 13 Hg 37.01N 4.33W
Anthony 45 Cj 32.00N 106.34W
Anti-Atlas 30 Ge 30.00N 8.30W
Antibes 11 Nk 43.35N 7.07 E
Antibes, Cap d'- 11 Nk 43.32N 7.07 E
Antica, Isla- 50 Eg 10.24N 62.43W
Anticosti, Ile d'- 38 Me 49.30N 63.00W
Antigo 45 Ld 45.09N 89.09W
Antigonish 42 Lg 45.37N 61.58W
Antigua 38 Mh 17.03N 61.48W
Antigua and Barbuda 39 Mh 17.03N 61.48W
Antigua Guatemala 47 Ff 14.34N 90.44W
Antiguo Cauce del Río Bermejo 56 Hc 25.39S 60.11W
Antiguo Morelos 48 Jf 22.30N 99.05W
Antilla 49 Jc 20.50N 75.45W
Antillas, Mar de las-/Caribe, Mar-=Caribbean Sea (EN) 38 Lh 15.00N 73.00W
Antillas Mayores=Greater Antilles (EN) 38 Lh 20.00N 74.00W
Antillas Menores=Lesser Antilles (EN) 38 Mh 15.00N 61.00W
Antilles, Mer des-/Caraïbe, Mer-=Caribbean Sea (EN) 38 Lh 15.00N 73.00W
An tInbhear Mór/Arklow 9 Gi 52.48N 6.09W
Antioch 46 Eg 38.00N 121.49W
Antioch (EN)=Antakya 23 Eb 36.14N 36.07 E
Antioche, Pertuis d'- 11 Eh 46.05N 1.20W
Antipe Reef 57 Kf 18.18S 168.40W
Antioquia [2] 54 Cb 7.00N 75.30W
Antipajëta 20 Cc 69.09N 77.00 E
Antipodes Islands 57 Ii 49.40S 178.50 E
Antiques, Pointe d'- 51e Ab 16.26N 61.33W
An t-Iúr/Newry 9 Gg 54.11N 6.20W
Antler River 45 Fb 49.08N 101.00W
Antlers 45 Ii 34.14N 95.37W
Antofagasta [2] 56 Gb 23.30S 69.00W
Antofagasta 53 Ih 23.39S 70.24W
Antofagasta de la Sierra 56 Gc 26.04S 67.25W
Antofalla, Salar de- 56 Gc 25.44S 67.45W
Antofalla, Volcán- 56 Gc 25.34S 67.55W
Antoing 12 Fd 50.34N 3.27 E
Antón 49 Gi 8.24N 80.16W
Anton Dohrn Seamount (EN) 9 Cd 57.30N 11.00W
Antongil, Baie d'- 30 Lj 15.45S 49.50 E
Antonina 56 Kc 25.27S 48.43W
Antônio João 55 Ef 23.15S 55.31W
Antonito 45 Dh 37.05N 106.00W
Antón Lizardo, Punta de- 48 Lh 19.03N 95.58W
Antony 12 Ef 48.45N 2.18 E
Antopol 10 Ud 52.12N 24.53 E
Antracit 16 Ke 48.06N 39.06 E
Antreff 12 Ld 50.52N 9.15 E
Antrim/Aontroim 9 Gg 54.43N 6.13W
Antrim Mountains 9 Gf 55.00N 6.10W
Antrodoco 14 Hh 42.25N 13.05 E
Antsakabary 37 Hc 15.03S 48.56 E
Antsalova 37 Gc 18.42S 44.33 E
Antseranana [3] 37 Hb 13.40S 49.15 E
An tSionainn/Shannon 5 Fe 52.36N 9.41W
Antsirabe 31 Lj 19.51S 47.01 E
Antsiranana 31 Lj 12.17S 49.17 E
An tSiúir/Suir 9 Gi 52.15N 7.00W
Antsla 7 Gh 57.52N 26.33 E
An tSláine/Slaney 9 Gi 52.21N 6.30W
Antsohihy 31 Lj 14.52S 47.58 E
An tSuca/Suck 9 Eh 53.16N 8.03W
Anttola 8 Lc 61.35N 27.39 E
Antu (Songjiang) 28 Jc 42.33N 128.20 E
An Tuc 25 Lf 13.57N 108.39 E
Antufash, Jazīrat- 33 Hf 15.42N 42.25 E
An Tulach/Tullow 9 Gi 52.48N 6.44W
An Tulach Mhór/Tullamore 9 Fh 53.16N 7.30W
Antwerp (EN)=Antwerpen/Anvers 6 Ge 50.38N 5.34 E
Antwerp (EN)=Anvers/Antwerpen 6 Ge 50.38N 5.34 E
Antwerpen [3] 12 Gc 51.10N 4.30 E
Antwerpen/Anvers=Antwerp (EN) 6 Ge 50.38N 5.34 E
Antwerpen-Ekeren 11 Kc 51.17N 4.25 E
Antwerpen-Hoboken 12 Gc 51.10N 4.21 E
Antwerpen-Merksem 12 Gc 51.15N 4.27 E
Antykan 20 If 54.55N 135.13 E
An Uaimh/Navan 9 Gh 53.39N 6.41W
Anuradhapura 25 Gg 8.21N 80.23 E
Anuta Island 57 Hf 11.38S 169.50 E
Anvers/Antwerpen=Antwerp (EN) 6 Ge 50.38N 5.34 E
Anvers Island 66 Qe 64.33S 63.35W
Anvik 40 Gd 62.40N 160.12W
Anxi 22 Le 40.30N 96.00 E
Anxiang 27 Jf 29.26N 112.11 E
Anxin 28 Ce 38.55N 115.56 E
Anxious Bay 59 Gf 33.25S 134.35 E
Anyang (Zhangde) 22 Nf 36.01N 114.25 E
A'nyêmaqen Shan 21 Lf 34.30N 100.00 E
Anyi 28 Cj 28.50N 115.31 E
Anykščiai/Anikščjaj 7 Fi 55.31N 25.08 E
Anyva, Mys- 20 Jg 46.00N 143.25 E
Anza 14 Ce 46.00N 8.17 E
Anze 28 Bf 36.09N 112.14 E
Anzegem 12 Fd 50.50N 3.28 E
Anžero-Sudžensk 22 Kd 56.07N 86.00 E
Anzi 36 Dc 0.52S 23.24 E
Anzio 14 Gi 41.27N 12.37 E
Anzoátegui [2] 54 Fb 9.00N 64.30W
Anzob, Pereval- 18 Ge 39.07N 68.53 E
Aoba, Ile- 61 Cc 15.25S 167.50 E
Ao Ban Don 25 Jg 9.20N 99.25 E
Aoga-Shima 27 Oe 32.30N 139.50 E
Aohan Qi (Xinhui) 28 Ec 42.18N 119.53 E
Aoiz 13 Kb 42.47N 1.22W
Aoji 28 Kc 42.31N 130.24 E
Aola 63a Ec 9.32S 160.29 E
Aomen/Macau=Macao (EN) [5] 22 Ng 22.10N 113.33 E
Aomen/Macau=Macao (EN) 27 Jg 22.12N 113.33 E
Aomori 22 Qe 40.49N 140.45 E
Aomori Ken [2] 28 Pd 40.40N 140.40 E
Aono-Yama 29 Bd 34.27N 131.48 E
Aontroim/Antrim 9 Gg 54.43N 6.13W
Aopo 65c Aa 13.29S 172.30W
Aôral, Phnum- 25 Kf 12.02N 104.10 E
Aoré 63b Cb 15.35S 167.10 E
Aosta / Aoste 14 Be 45.44N 7.20 E
Aosta, Val d'- 14 Be 45.45N 7.20 E
Aoste / Aosta 14 Be 45.44N 7.20 E
Aouk, Bahr- 30 Ih 8.51N 18.53 E
Aoukalé 35 Cd 9.10N 20.30 E
Aoukâr [Afr.] 32 Ge 24.00N 2.30W
Aoukâr [Mtna.] 30 Gg 17.30N 9.30W
Aoulef 32 Hd 26.58N 1.05 E
Aoumou 63b Be 21.24S 165.49 E
Aourou 34 Cc 14.28N 11.34W
Aoya 29 Cd 35.32N 133.59 E
Aozou 31 If 21.49N 17.25 E
Apa, Rio- 56 Ib 22.06S 58.00W
Apača 20 Kf 52.50N 157.10 E
Apache 46 Kh 31.44N 109.07W
Apache Junction 46 Jj 33.26N 111.32W
Apahida 15 Gc 46.49N 23.45 E
Apakho 63c Bb 11.25S 166.32 E
Apalachee Bay 38 Kg 29.30N 84.00W
Apalachicola 44 Ek 29.44N 84.59W
Apalachicola River 44 Ek 29.44N 84.59W
Apan 48 Jh 19.43N 98.25W
Apaporis, Rio- 52 Jf 1.23S 69.25W
Aparecida do Taboado 54 Hg 20.05S 51.05W
Aparri 22 Oh 18.22N 121.39 E
Apataki Atoll 57 Mf 15.26S 146.20W
Apatin 15 Bd 45.40N 18.59 E
Apatity 6 Jb 67.34N 33.18 E
Apatzingán de la Constitucion 47 De 19.05N 102.21W
Apaxtla de Castrejón 48 Jh 18.09N 99.52W
Ape 7 Gh 57.32N 26.42 E
Apeldoorn 11 Lb 52.13N 5.58 E
Apeldoorn-Nieuw Milligen 12 Hb 52.14N 5.45 E
Apen 12 Ja 53.13N 7.48 E
Apennines (EN) = Appennini 5 Hg 43.00N 13.00 E
Apere, Rio- 54 Ef 13.44S 65.18W
Aphrodisias 24 Cd 37.45N 28.40 E
Api 21 Kf 30.00N 80.57 E
Api 36 Eb 3.40N 25.26 E
Apia 58 Jf 13.50S 171.44W
Apiacás, Serra dos- 54 Gf 10.15S 57.15W
Apio 63a Ec 9.39S 161.23 E
Apipé Grande, Isla- 55 Di 27.30S 56.54W
Apizaco 48 Jh 19.25N 98.09W
Aplao 54 Dc 16.05S 72.31W
Apo, Mount- 21 Oi 6.59N 125.16 E
Apodi 54 Ke 5.39S 37.48W
Apolda 10 He 51.01N 11.30 E
Apolima 65c Aa 13.49S 172.07W
Apolima Strait 65c Aa 13.50S 172.10W
Apollo Bay 59 Ig 38.45S 143.40 E
Apollonia [Alb.] 15 Ci 40.43N 19.27 E
Apollonia [Lib.] 33 Dc 32.54N 21.58 E
Apolo 54 Ef 14.43S 68.31W
Apón, Rio- 49 Kh 10.06N 72.23W
Apopka, Lake- 44 Gk 28.37N 81.38W
Aporé 55 Fd 18.58S 52.01W
Aporé, Rio- 52 Kg 19.27S 50.57W
Apostle Islands 43 Ib 46.50N 90.30W
Apostoles 56 Ic 27.55S 55.46W
Apostolovo 16 Hf 47.39N 33.43 E
Apoteri 54 Gc 4.02N 58.34W
Apôtres, Iles des- 30 Mm 45.40S 50.20 E
Appalachia 44 Fg 36.54N 82.48W
Appalachian Mountains 38 Lc 41.00N 77.00W
Äppelbo 8 Ed 60.30N 14.00 E
Appennini = Apennines (EN) 5 Hg 43.00N 13.00 E
Appennino Abruzzese 14 Hh 42.00N 13.55 E
Appennino Calabro 14 Kl 39.00N 16.30 E
Appennino Campano 14 Ii 40.50N 14.45 E
Appennino Ligure 14 Cf 44.30N 9.00 E
Appennino Lucano 14 Jj 40.30N 16.00 E
Appennino Tosco-Emiliano 14 Fg 44.00N 11.30 E
Appennino Umbro-Marchigiano 14 Gg 43.20N 12.55 E
Appenzell 14 Dc 47.20N 9.25 E
Appenzell Ausser-Rhoden [2] 14 Dc 47.20N 9.20 E
Appenzell Inner-Rhoden [2] 14 Dc 47.15N 9.25 E
Appingedam 12 Ia 53.19N 6.52 E
Appleby 9 Kg 54.36N 2.29W
Appleton 43 Jc 44.16N 88.25W
Appomattox 44 Hg 37.21N 78.51W
Apra Harbor 64c Bb 13.27N 144.38 E
Apricena 14 Ji 41.47N 15.27 E
Aprilia 14 Gi 41.36N 12.39 E
Apšeronsk 19 Dg 44.27N 39.44 E
Apšeronskij Poluostrov=Apsheron Peninsula (EN) 5 Lg 41.00N 50.50 E
Apsheron Peninsula (EN)=Apšeronskij Poluostrov 5 Lg 41.00N 50.50 E
Apt 11 Lk 43.53N 5.24 E
Apucarana 56 Jb 23.33S 51.29W
Apuoarana, Serra da- 55 Gf 23.50S 51.20W
Apuka 20 Ld 60.23N 169.45 E
Apuka 20 Ld 60.25N 169.35 E
Apulia (EN) = Puglia [2] 14 Ki 41.15N 16.15 E
Apurashokoru 64a Ac 7.17N 134.18 E
Apure [2] 54 Eb 7.10N 68.50W
Apure, Rio- 52 Je 7.37N 66.25W
Apurimac [2] 54 Df 14.00S 73.00W
Apurimac, Rio- 52 Ig 12.17S 73.56W
Apurito 50 Bi 7.56N 68.27W
Apuseni, Munţii-=Apuseni Mountains (EN) 5 If 46.30N 22.30 E
Apuseni Mountains (EN)=Apuseni, Munţii- 5 If 46.30N 22.30 E
Āq 24 Kc 38.59N 45.27 E
Āqā 24 Me 35.00N 47.00 E
Aqaba (EN)=Al 'Aqabah 23 Dd 29.31N 35.00 E
Aqaba, Gulf of- (EN)='Aqabah, Khalij al- 30 Kf 29.00N 34.40 E
Āqā Bāba 24 Md 36.20N 49.46 E
'Aqabah, Khalij al-=Aqaba, Gulf of- (EN) 30 Kf 29.00N 34.40 E
Āqcheh 23 Kb 36.56N 66.11 E
'Aqdā 24 Of 32.26N 53.37 E
'Aqīq 35 Fb 18.14N 38.12 E
Aqitag 27 Fc 41.49N 90.38 E
Āqotāq 24 Ld 37.10N 47.05 E
Āq Qal'eh 24 Pd 37.01N 54.30 E
Aqqikkol Hu 27 Ed 37.00N 88.20 E
'Aqrah 24 Jd 36.45N 43.54 E
Aqrin, Jabal- 24 Hg 31.32N 38.18 E
Āq Şū 24 Ke 34.35N 44.31 E
Aquidabã, Rio- 55 De 20.58S 57.50W
Aquidabán, Rio- 55 Df 23.11S 57.32W
Aquidauana 54 Gh 20.28S 55.48W
Aquidauana, Rio- 54 Gg 19.44S 56.50W
Aquidauna, Serra de- 55 Ee 20.50S 55.30W
Aquiles Serdán 48 Gc 28.36N 105.53W
Aquin 49 Kd 18.16N 73.24W
Aquitaine, Bassin d'-=Aquitaine Basin (EN) 5 Fg 44.00N 0.10W
Aquitaine Basin (EN)=Aquitaine, Bassin d'- 5 Fg 44.00N 0.10W
Ara 13 Mb 42.25N 0.09 E
'Arab, Bahr al- 30 Jh 9.02N 29.28 E
'Arab, Khalij al- 33 Ec 30.55N 29.05 E
'Arab, Shaṭṭ al- 21 Gf 30.28N 47.59 E
'Arabah, Wādī- 24 Eh 29.07N 32.39 E
'Arabah, Wādī al- 24 Fg 30.58N 32.24 E
Arabatskaja Strelka, Kosa- 16 Ig 45.40N 35.05 E
'Arabestān 24 Mg 30.30N 50.00 E
Arabian Basin (EN) 3 Gh 11.30N 65.00 E
Arabian Desert (EN)=Sharqīyah, Aş Şaḩrā' ash- 30 Kf 28.00N 32.00 E
Arabian Peninsula (EN) 21 Gg 25.00N 45.00 E
Arabian Sea (EN) 21 Ih 15.00N 65.00 E
Araç 24 Eb 41.15N 33.21 E
Aracá, Rio- 54 Fd 0.25S 62.55W
Aracaju 53 Mg 10.55S 37.04W
Aracataca 49 Jh 10.35N 74.13W
Aracati 54 Kd 4.34S 37.46W
Araçatuba 53 Kh 21.12S 50.25W
Aracena 13 Fg 37.53N 6.33W
Aracena, Sierra de- 13 Fg 37.56N 6.50W
Aracides, Cape- 63a Ec 8.39S 161.01 E
Aracruz 54 Jg 19.49S 40.16W
Araçuai 54 Jg 16.52S 42.04W
Arad 6 If 46.11N 21.19 E
'Arad 24 Fg 31.15N 35.13 E
Arad [2] 15 Ec 46.11N 21.25 E
Arada 35 Cb 15.01N 20.40 E
'Arādah 35 Ia 22.59N 53.26 E
Arafali 35 Fb 15.04N 39.45 E
Ara Fana 35 Gd 6.01N 41.11 E
Arafune-Yama 29 Fc 36.12N 138.38 E
Arafura, Laut-=Arafura Sea (EN) 57 Ee 9.00S 133.00 E
Arafura, Sea (EN)=Arafura, Laut- 57 Ee 9.00S 133.00 E
Aragac, Gora- 5 Kg 40.31N 44.10 E
Aragarças 53 Kg 15.55S 52.15W
Aragón [3] 13 Kb 42.13N 1.44W
Aragón 5 Fg 41.00N 1.00W
Aragón 13 Lc 41.00N 1.00W
Aragona 14 Hm 37.24N 13.37 E
Aragua [2] 54 Eb 10.00N 67.10W
Araguacema 54 Ie 8.50S 49.34W
Aragua de Barcelona 50 Dh 9.28N 64.49W
Aragua de Maturin 50 Eh 9.58N 63.29W
Araguaia, Rio- 52 Lf 5.21S 48.41W
Araguaiana 55 Gb 16.49S 53.05W
Araguaina 54 Ie 7.12S 48.12W
Araguao, Boca- 54 Fb 9.17N 60.48W
Araguao, Caño- 50 Fh 9.15N 60.50W
Araguapiche, Punta- 50 Fh 9.29N 60.56W
Araguari 54 Ig 18.38S 48.11W
Araguari, Rio- [Braz.] 52 Le 1.15N 49.55W
Araguari, Rio- [Braz.] 55 Hd 18.21S 48.40W
Araguatins 54 Ie 5.38S 48.07W
'Arāguīb 32 Ff 18.50N 7.45W
Aragvi 16 Ni 41.50N 44.43 E
Arai 28 Of 37.09N 138.06 E
Árainn/Inishmore 9 Dh 53.07N 9.45W
Árainn Mhór/Aran Island 9 Ef 55.00N 8.30W
Araioses 54 Jd 2.53S 41.55W
Arāk 22 Gf 34.05N 49.41 E
Arak 32 Hd 25.18N 3.45 E
Arakabesan 64a Ac 7.21N 134.27 E
Arakan [2] 25 Ie 19.00N 94.15 E
Arakan Yoma 21 Lh 19.00N 94.40 E
Arakawa 29 Fb 38.09N 139.25 E
Ara-Kawa [Jap.] 29 Fb 38.09N 139.23 E
Ara-Kawa [Jap.] 29 Fc 37.11N 138.15 E
Árakhthos 15 Ej 39.01N 21.03 E
Araks 21 Gf 39.56N 48.20 E
Aral [China] 27 Dc 40.38N 81.24 E
Aral [Kirg.-U.S.S.R.] 19 Hg 41.48N 74.25 E
Aral Sea (EN)=Aralskoje More 21 He 45.00N 60.00 E
Aralsk 22 Ie 46.48N 61.40 E
Aralskoje More=Aral Sea (EN) 21 He 45.00N 60.00 E
Aralsor, Ozero- 16 Pe 49.05N 48.15 E
Aralsulfat 19 Gf 46.50N 61.59 E
Aramac 59 Jd 22.59S 145.14 E
Arambaré 55 Gj 30.55S 51.29W
Ārān 24 Ne 34.03N 51.30 E
Aranda de Duero 13 Ic 41.41N 3.41W
Arandelovac 15 De 44.18N 20.35 E
Arandilla 13 Ic 41.40N 3.41W
Aran Island/Arainn Mhór 9 Dh 53.07N 9.43W
Aran Islands 9 Ef 55.00N 8.30W
Aranjunez 13 Id 40.02N 3.36W
Aranos 37 Bd 24.09S 19.09 E
Arañuelo, Campo- 13 Ge 39.55N 5.30W
Aranuka Atoll 57 Id 0.11N 173.36 E
Arao 29 Be 32.59N 130.27 E
Araouane 31 Gg 18.53N 3.35W
Arapahoe 45 Gf 40.18N 99.54W
Arapey Grande, Rio- 55 Dj 30.55S 57.49W
Arapiraca 54 Ke 9.45S 36.39W
Arápis, Ákra- 15 Gi 40.27N 24.00 E
Arapkir 24 Hc 39.03N 38.30 E
Arapoim, Rio- 55 Kb 15.45S 43.39W
Arapongas 56 Jb 23.23S 51.27W
Arapoti 55 Hg 24.08S 49.50W
'Ar'ar 24 Ig 30.59N 41.02 E
'Ar'ar, Wādī 24 Jg 31.23N 42.26 E
Araranguá 56 Kc 28.56S 49.29W
Araraquara 53 Lh 21.47S 48.10W
Araras 55 If 22.22S 47.23W
Araras, Açude- 54 Jd 4.20S 40.30W
Araras, Serra das- 55 Fd 18.45S 53.30W
Ararat [Arm.-U.S.S.R.] 19 Eh 39.50N 44.43 E
Ararat [Austl.] 59 Ig 37.17S 142.56 E
Ararat, Mount- (EN)=Büyük Ağri Daği 21 Gf 39.40N 44.24 E
Arari 54 Jd 3.28S 44.47W
Arari, Lago- 54 Id 0.37S 49.07W
Aras 21 Gf 39.56N 48.20 E
Aras Dağlari 24 Jc 40.00N 43.00 E
Aratika Atoll 57 Mf 15.32S 145.32W
Aratürük/Yiwu 27 Fc 43.15N 94.35 E
Arauca [2] 54 Db 6.30N 71.00W
Arauca 54 Db 7.03N 70.47W
Arauca, Rio- 52 Je 7.24N 66.35W
Araucania [2] 56 Fe 37.50S 73.15W
Arauco 56 Fe 37.15S 73.19W
Araure 50 Bh 9.38N 69.15W
Aravaca, Madrid- 13 Id 40.27N 3.47W
Aravis 11 Mi 45.53N 6.28 E
Arawalli Range 21 Jg 25.00N 73.30 E
Araxá 54 Ig 19.35S 46.55W
Araxos, Ákra- 15 Ek 38.10N 21.23 E
Araya 50 Dg 10.34N 64.15W
Araya, Peninsula de- 54 Fa 10.35N 64.00W
Arba 13 Kc 41.52N 1.18W
Arba'āt 35 Fb 19.50N 37.03 E
Arba'īn, Darb al- 24 Di 26.40N 30.50 E
Arbaj-Here 27 Hb 46.15N 102.48 E
Arba Minch 31 Kh 5.59N 37.38 E
'Arbat 24 Ke 35.25N 45.35 E
Arbatax 14 Dk 39.56N 9.42 E
Arboga 7 Dg 59.24N 15.50 E
Arbogaån 8 Ge 59.26N 16.04 E
Arbois 11 Lh 46.54N 5.46 E
Arboletes 49 Ii 8.52N 76.25W
Arbolito 55 Ek 32.39S 54.15W
Arbon 14 Dc 47.30N 9.25 E
Arbore 15 Ib 47.44N 25.56 E
Arborea 14 Ck 39.46N 8.35 E
Arborea 14 Ck 39.50N 8.50 E
Arborg 45 Ha 50.55N 97.15W
Arbrå 7 Dc 61.29N 16.23 E
Arbroath 9 Ke 56.34N 2.35W
Arbus 14 Ck 39.32N 8.36 E
Arc [Fr.] 11 Mi 45.34N 6.12 E
Arc [Fr.] 11 Lk 43.31N 5.07 E
Arcachon 11 Ej 44.39N 1.10W
Arcachon, Bassin d'- 11 Ej 44.42N 1.09W
Arcadia [Fl.-U.S.] 44 Gl 27.14N 81.52W
Arcadia [La.-U.S.] 45 Jj 32.33N 92.55W
Arcagly-Ajat 17 Jj 53.00N 61.50 E
Arcas, Cayos- 47 Fd 20.12N 91.58W
Arcata 46 Cf 40.52N 124.05W
Arcelia 48 Ih 18.17N 100.16W
Arcen, Areen en Velden- 12 Ic 51.28N 6.11 E
Arcevia 14 Gg 43.30N 12.56 E
Archangel (EN)=Arhangelsk 6 Kc 64.34N 40.32 E
Archaringa Creek 59 He 28.15S 135.15 E
Archer River 59 Ib 13.28S 141.41 E
Archer's Post 36 Gb 0.39N 37.41 E
Archidona 13 Hg 37.05N 4.23W
Arcidosso 14 Fh 42.52N 11.33 E
Arcipelago Campano 5 Hg 40.30N 13.20 E
Arcipelago Toscano=Tuscan Archipelago (EN) 5 Hg 42.45N 10.20 E
Arcis-sur-Aube 11 Kf 48.32N 4.08 E
Arciz 16 Fg 45.59N 29.27 E
Arco [Id.-U.S.] 46 Ie 43.38N 113.18W
Arco [It.] 14 Ee 45.55N 10.53 E
Arconce 11 Jh 46.27N 4.00 E
Arcos 55 Je 20.17S 45.32W
Arcos de Jalón 13 Jc 41.13N 2.16W
Arcos de la Frontera 13 Gh 36.45N 5.48W
Arcos de Valdevez 13 Dc 41.51N 8.25W
Arcoverde 53 Mf 8.25S 37.04W
Arctic Bay 39 Kb 73.02N 85.11W
Arctic Ocean 67 Be 85.00N 170.00 E
Arctic Ocean (EN)=Ishavet 67 Be 85.00N 170.00 E
Arctic Ocean (EN)=Severny Ledovity Okean 67 Be 85.00N 170.00 E
Arctic Red River 42 Ec 67.27N 133.45W
Arctic Red River 42 Ec 67.22N 133.30W
Arctic Village 40 Jc 68.08N 145.19W
Arda [Eur.] 15 Jh 41.39N 26.29 E
Arda [It.] 14 Ee 45.02N 10.02 E
Ardabīl [Iran] 22 Gf 38.15N 48.18 E
Ardabīl [Iraq] 24 Ie 34.24N 40.59 E
Ardahan 24 Jb 41.07N 42.41 E
Ardakāh 23 Hc 32.19N 53.59 E
Ardakān 24 Og 30.16N 52.01 E
Ardal 24 Ng 31.59N 50.39 E
Ardales 13 Hh 36.52N 4.51W
Ardalsfjorden 8 Bc 61.15N 7.30 E
Årdalstangen 7 Bf 61.14N 7.43 E
Ardanuç 24 Jb 41.08N 42.03 E
Ardatov [R.S.F.S.R.] 7 Ki 55.17N 43.12 E
Ardatov [R.S.F.S.R.] 7 Li 54.53N 46.13 E
'Arde 35 Hd 9.58N 46.04 E
Ardèche 11 Kj 44.16N 4.39 E
Ardèche [3] 11 Kj 44.40N 4.20 E
Ardee/Béal Átha Fhirdhia 9 Gh 53.52N 6.33W
Ardencaple Fjord 41 Jd 75.15N 20.10W
Ardenne, Plateau de l'-/Ardennen, Plateau van der-=Ardennes (EN) 5 Ge 50.10N 5.45 E
Ardennen, Plateau van der-/Ardenne, Plateau de l'-=Ardennes (EN) 5 Ge 50.10N 5.45 E
Ardennes [3] 11 Ke 49.40N 4.40 E
Ardennes (EN)=Ardenne, Plateau de l'-/Ardennen, Plateau van der- 5 Ge 50.10N 5.45 E
Ardennes (EN)=Ardennen, Plateau van der-/Ardenne, Plateau de l'- 5 Ge 50.10N 5.45 E
Ardennes, Canal des- 11 Ke 49.26N 4.02 E
Ardennes, Forêt des- 12 Ge 49.48N 4.50 E
Ardentes 11 Hh 46.45N 1.50 E
Ardeşen 24 Ib 41.12N 41.00 E
Ardestān 24 Of 33.22N 52.23 E
Árdhas 15 Jh 41.39N 26.29 E
Ardila 13 Ef 38.12N 7.28W
Ard Mhacha/Armagh 9 Gg 54.21N 6.39W
Ardmore 43 He 34.10N 97.08W
Ardnamurchan, Point of- 9 Ge 56.45N 6.30W
Ardon 16 Nh 43.07N 44.13 E
Ardooie 12 Fd 50.59N 3.12 E
Ardre 12 Fe 49.18N 3.40 E
Ardres 12 Dd 50.51N 1.59 E
Ards Peninsula/An Aird 9 Hg 54.30N 5.30W
Ar Dub'al Khālī 21 Hg 21.00N 51.00 E
Ardud 15 Fb 47.38N 22.53 E
Arebi 36 Eb 2.50N 29.38 E
Arecibo 47 Ke 18.28N 66.43W
Areen en Valden 12 Ic 51.28N 6.11 E
Areen en Velden-Arcen 12 Ic 51.28N 6.11 E
Arėgala/Ariogala 8 Ji 55.13N 23.30 E
Areia, Ribeirão da- 55 Jc 16.07S 45.52W
Areia Branca 54 Kd 4.57S 37.08W
Arekalong Peninsula 64a Bb 7.40N 134.38 E
Aremberg 12 Id 50.25N 6.49 E
Arena 26 He 9.14N 120.46 E
Arena, Point- 43 Cd 38.57N 123.44W
Arena, Punta- 47 Cd 23.30N 109.30W
Arena de la Ventana, Punta- 47 Cd 24.04N 109.52W
Arenápolis 54 Gf 14.26S 56.49W
Arenas, Cayo- 47 Fd 22.08N 91.24W
Arenas, Punta de- 56 Gh 53.09S 68.13W
Arenas de San Pedro 13 Gd 40.12N 5.05W
Arenberg 12 Jb 52.42N 7.20 E
Arendal 7 Bg 58.27N 8.48 E
Arendonk 12 Hc 51.19N 5.05 E
Arénys de Mar/Arenys de Mar 13 Oc 41.35N 2.33 E
Arenys de Mar/Arénys de Mar 13 Oc 41.35N 2.33 E
Areópolis 15 Fm 36.40N 22.23 E
Areq, Sebkha bou- 13 Ji 35.10N 2.45W
Arequipa 53 Ig 16.24S 71.33W
Arequipa [2] 54 Dg 16.00S 72.30W
Arequito 55 Bk 33.09S 61.28W
Arero 35 Fe 4.44N 38.50 E
Ares, Muela de- 13 Ld 40.28N 0.07W
Åreskutan 8 Ea 63.26N 13.06 E
Åreskutan 7 Ce 63.24N 13.06 E
Arévalo 13 Hc 41.04N 4.43W
Arezzo 14 Fg 43.25N 11.53 E
Arga 13 Kb 42.18N 1.47W
Argajas 17 Ji 55.31N 60.55 E
Argamasilla de Alba 13 Ie 39.07N 3.06W
Argan 27 Ec 40.09N 88.22 E
Arganda 13 Id 40.18N 3.26W
Arga-Sala 20 Gc 68.37N 112.05 E
Argelès-Gazost 11 Fk 43.01N 0.06W
Argelès-sur-Mer 11 Jl 42.33N 3.01 E
Argens 11 Mk 43.24N 6.44 E

Index Symbols

[1] Independent Nation
[2] State, Region
[3] District, County
[4] Municipality
[5] Colony, Dependency
Continent
Physical Region
Historical or Cultural Region
Mount, Mountain
Volcano
Hill
Mountains, Mountain Range
Hills, Escarpment
Plateau, Upland
Pass, Gap
Plain, Lowland
Delta
Salt Flat
Valley, Canyon
Crater, Cave
Karst Features
Depression
Polder
Desert, Dunes
Forest, Woods
Heath, Steppe
Oasis
Cape, Point
Coast, Beach
Cliff
Peninsula
Isthmus
Sandbank
Island
Atoll
Rock, Reef
Islands, Archipelago
Rocks, Reefs
Coral Reef
Well, Spring
Geyser
River, Stream
Waterfall Rapids
River Mouth, Estuary
Lake
Salt Lake
Intermittent Lake
Reservoir
Swamp, Pond
Canal
Glacier
Ice Shelf, Pack Ice
Ocean
Sea
Gulf, Bay
Strait, Fjord
Lagoon
Bank
Seamount
Tablemount
Ridge
Shelf
Basin
Escarpment, Sea Scarp
Fracture
Trench, Abyss
National Park, Reserve
Point of Interest
Recreation Site
Cave, Cavern
Historic Site
Ruins
Wall, Walls
Church, Abbey
Temple
Scientific Station
Airport
Port
Lighthouse
Mine
Tunnel
Dam, Bridge

Index Symbols

① Independent Nation	◫ Historical or Cultural Region	Pass, Gap	Depression	Coast, Beach
② State, Region	▲ Mount, Mountain	Plain, Lowland	Polder	Cliff
③ District, County	Volcano	Delta	Desert, Dunes	Peninsula
④ Municipality	Hill	Salt Flat	Forest, Woods	Isthmus
⑤ Colony, Dependency	Mountains, Mountain Range	Valley, Canyon	Heath, Steppe	Sandbank
Continent	Hills, Escarpment	Crater, Cave	Oasis	Island
Physical Region	Plateau, Upland	Karst Features	Cape, Point	Atoll

Rock, Reef	Waterfall Rapids	Canal	Lagoon	Escarpment, Sea Scarp	Historic Site
Islands, Archipelago	River Mouth, Estuary	Bank	Seamount	Fracture	Ruins
Rocks, Reefs	Lake	Ice Shelf, Pack Ice	Trench, Abyss	Wall, Walls
Coral Reef	Salt Lake	Ocean	Tablemount	National Park, Reserve	Church, Abbey
Well, Spring	Intermittent Lake	Sea	Ridge	Point of Interest	Temple
Geyser	Reservoir	Gulf, Bay	Shelf	Recreation Site	Scientific Station
River, Stream	Swamp, Pond	Strait, Fjord	Basin	Cave, Cavern	Airport
					Port
					Lighthouse
					Mine
					Tunnel
					Dam, Bridge

Index Symbols

[1] Independent Nation	Historical or Cultural Region	Pass, Gap
[2] State, Region	Mount, Mountain	Plain, Lowland
[3] District, County	Volcano	Delta
[4] Municipality	Hill	Salt Flat
[5] Colony, Dependency	Mountains, Mountain Range	Valley, Canyon
Continent	Hills, Escarpment	Crater, Cave
Physical Region	Plateau, Upland	Karst Features

Depression	Coast, Beach	Rock, Reef
Polder	Cliff	Islands, Archipelago
Desert, Dunes	Peninsula	Rocks, Reefs
Forest, Woods	Isthmus	Coral Reef
Heath, Steppe	Sandbank	Well, Spring
Oasis	Island	Geyser
Cape, Point	Atoll	River, Stream

Waterfall Rapids	Canal	Lagoon
River Mouth, Estuary	Glacier	Bank
Lake	Ice Shelf, Pack Ice	Seamount
Salt Lake	Ocean	Tablemount
Sea	Ridge	Point of Interest
Gulf, Bay	Shelf	Recreation Site
Swamp, Pond	Strait, Fjord	Basin

Escarpment, Sea Scarp	Historic Site	Port
Fracture	Ruins	Lighthouse
Trench, Abyss	Wall, Walls	Mine
National Park, Reserve	Church, Abbey	Tunnel
Scientific Station	Dam, Bridge	
Airport		
Cave, Cavern		

Ayeyarwady	25	Ie	17.00N	95.00 E
Ayeyarwady = Irrawaddy (EN)	21	Lg	15.50N	95.06 E
Ayiá	15	Fj	39.43N	22.46 E
Ayía Marína	15	Jl	37.09N	26.52 E
Ayiásos	15	Jj	39.06N	26.22 E
Áyion Óros=Athos, Mount- (EN) [2]	15	Hi	40.15N	24.15 E
Áyios Evstrátios	15	Hj	39.31N	25.00 E
Áyios Ioánnis, Ákra-	15	In	35.20N	25.46 E
Áyios Kírikos	15	Jl	37.35N	26.14 E
Áyios Minás	15	Jl	37.36N	26.34 E
Áyios Nikólaos	15	In	35.11N	25.43 E
Áyios Yeóryios	15	Gl	37.28N	23.56 E
Aykota	35	Fb	15.10N	37.03 E
Aylesbury	9	Mj	51.50N	0.50W
Ayllón, Sierra de-	13	Ic	41.15N	3.25W
Aylmer Lake	42	Gd	64.05N	108.30W
Aylsham	12	Db	52.47N	1.15 E
Ayna	13	Jf	38.33N	2.05W
'Aynabo	35	Hd	8.57N	46.30 E
'Ayn ad Darāhim	14	Cn	36.47N	8.42 E
'Ayn al Baydā	24	Ge	34.32N	37.55 E
'Ayn al Ghazāl [Eg.]	24	Dj	25.46N	30.38 E
'Ayn al Ghazāl [Lib.]	31	Jf	21.50N	24.55 E
'Ayn al Shigi	24	Ci	27.01N	28.02 E
'Ayn al Wādī	24	Ci	27.23N	28.13 E
'Ayn Bū Sālim	14	Cn	36.37N	8.59 E
'Ayn Dāllah	33	Ed	27.19N	27.20 E
'Ayn Dār	24	Mj	25.58N	49.14 E
'Ayn Dīwār	24	Jd	37.17N	42.11 E
'Ayn Ilwān	24	Dj	25.44N	30.25 E
'Ayn Khalīfah	24	Bi	26.46N	27.47 E
'Ayn Sifnī	24	Jd	36.42N	43.21 E
'Ayn Sukhnah	33	Fd	29.30N	32.10 E
'Aynūnah	23	Ed	28.05N	35.08 E
Ayod	35	Ed	8.08N	31.24 E
Ayora	13	Ke	39.04N	1.03W
Ayorou	34	Fc	14.44N	0.55 E
'Ayoûn el 'Atroûs	31	Gg	16.38N	9.36W
Ayr	9	If	55.29N	4.28W
Ayr [Austl.]	59	Jc	19.35 S	147.24 E
Ayr [Scot.-U.K.]	9	If	55.28N	4.38W
Ayre, Point of-	9	Ig	54.26N	4.22W
Ayrolle, Étang de l'-	11	Jk	43.16N	3.30 E
Aysha	35	Gc	10.45N	42.35 E
Aytré	11	Eh	46.08N	1.06W
Ayutla	48	Gg	20.07N	104.22W
Ayutla de los Libres	48	Ji	16.54N	99.13W
Ayvacık	24	Gb	41.00N	36.45 E
Ayvacik	15	Jj	39.36N	26.24 E
Ayvalık	23	Cb	39.18N	26.41 E
Aywaille	12	Hd	50.28N	5.40 E
Āzādshahr	24	Pd	37.05N	55.08 E
Azahar, Costa del-	13	Me	39.58N	0.01 E
Azaila	13	Lc	41.17N	0.29W
Azambuja	13	De	39.04N	8.52W
Azamgarh	25	Gc	26.04N	83.11 E
Azángaro	54	Df	14.55 S	70.13W
Azannes-et-Soumazannes	12	He	49.18N	5.28 E
Azaouâd=Azaouad (EN)	30	Gg	19.00N	3.00W
Azaouad (EN)=Azaouâd	30	Gg	19.00N	3.00W
Azaouak	34	Fb	15.30N	3.18 E
Azaouak	30	Hg	15.20N	4.55 E
Azaouak, Vallée de l'-	30	Hg	17.30N	3.40 E
Azar	34	Fb	16.02N	4.04 E
Āžarbāījān-e Gharbī [3]	23	Fb	37.00N	45.00 E
Āžarbāījān-e Sharqī [3]	23	Gb	37.00N	47.00 E
Azarbaijčan Sovet Socialistik Respublicasy/ Azerbajdžanskaja SSR [2]	19	Eg	40.30N	47.30 E
Azare	34	Hc	11.41N	10.12 E
Āzār Shahr	24	Kd	37.45N	45.59 E
Azay-le-Rideau	11	Gg	47.16N	0.28 E
A 'zāz	24	Gd	36.35N	37.03 E
Azazga	13	Qh	36.44N	4.22 E
Azbine/Aïr	30	Hg	18.00N	8.30 E
Azdaak, Gora-	16	Ni	40.13N	44.59 E
Azdavay	24	Eb	41.39N	33.18 E
Azefal	30	Ff	21.00N	14.45W
Azeffoun	13	Qh	36.53N	4.25 E
Azemmour	32	Fc	33.17N	8.21W
Azerbaijan (EN)	21	Gf	37.00N	46.00 E
Azerbaijan SSR (EN) = Azerbajdžanskaja SSR [2]	19	Eg	40.30N	47.30 E
Azerbajdžanskaja Sovetskaja Socialističeskaja Respublika [2]	19	Eg	40.30N	47.30 E
Azerbajdžanskaja SSR/ Azarbaijčan Sovet Socialistik Respublicasy [2]	19	Eg	40.30N	47.30 E
Azerbajdžanskaja SSR= Azerbaijan SSR (EN)	19	Eg	40.30N	47.30 E
Azeri/Aseri	7	Gg	59.29N	26.51 E
Azevedo Sodré	55	Ej	30.04S	54.36W
Azezo	35	Fc	12.33N	37.25 E
Azilal [3]	32	Fc	32.09N	6.05W
Azilal	32	Fc	31.58N	6.35W
Aznā	24	Mf	33.56N	49.24 E
Aznakajevo	7	Mi	54.56N	53.04 E
Azogues	54	Cd	2.44 S	78.48W
Azores (EN)=Açores [5]	31	Ee	38.30N	28.00W
Azores (EN)=Açores, Arquipélago dos-	30	Ee	38.30N	28.00W
Azores-Gibraltar Ridge (EN)	3	Df	37.00N	16.00W
Azoum, Bahr-	30	Jg	10.53N	20.15 E
Azov	19	Df	47.05N	39.25 E
Azov, Sea of- (EN)= Azovskoje More	5	Jf	46.00N	36.00 E
Azovskoje More=Azov, Sea of- (EN)	5	Jf	46.00N	36.00 E
Azpeitia	13	Ja	43.11N	2.16W
Azrak, Bahr-	35	Bc	10.50N	19.50 E
Azraq, Al Baḩr al-=Blue Nile (EN)	30	Kg	15.38N	32.31 E
Azraq ash Shīshān	24	Gg	31.50N	36.49 E
Azrou	32	Fc	33.26N	5.13W
Aztec	45	Ch	36.49N	107.59W
Aztec Ruins	46	Kh	36.51N	108.10W
Azua	49	Ld	18.27N	70.44W
Azuaga	13	Gf	38.16N	5.41W
Azuar	13	Ie	39.08N	3.36W
Azuero, Peninsula de-= Azuero Peninsula (EN)	38	Ki	7.40N	80.30W
Azuero Peninsula (EN)= Azuero, Península de-	38	Ki	7.40N	80.30W
Azul	53	Ki	36.45 S	59.50W
Azul, Arroyo del-	55	Cm	36.15 S	59.07W
Azul, Cerro-	54a	Ab	0.54 S	91.21W
Azul, Cordillera-	54	Ce	8.30 S	76.00W
Azul, Río-	48	Oi	17.54N	88.52W
Azul, Serra-	55	Eb	14.50 S	54.50W
Azul, Sierras del-	55	Cm	37.02 S	59.55W
Azūm	35	Cc	10.53N	20.15 E
Azuma-San	29	Gc	37.44N	140.08 E
Azur, Côte d'-	11	Mk	43.30N	7.00 E
Azurduy	54	Fg	19.59 S	64.29W
Azzaba	32	Ib	36.44N	7.06 E
Az Zāb al Kabīr	23	Fb	36.00N	43.21 E
Az Zāb aş Şaghīr	23	Fb	35.12N	43.25 E
Az Zabdānī	24	Gf	33.43N	36.05 E
Az Zabū	24	Ch	28.22N	28.56 E
Aẓ Ẓafīr	23	Ff	19.57N	41.30 E
Az Zaghāwa	35	Cb	15.15N	23.14 E
Aẓ Ẓāhirah	24	Qk	23.30N	56.15 E
Az Zallāq	24	Ni	26.03N	50.29 E
Az Zaqāzīq	33	Fc	30.35N	31.31 E
Az Zarqā'	24	Oj	24.53N	53.04 E
Az Zarqā'	24	Gf	32.05N	36.06 E
Az Zāwiyah [3]	33	Bc	32.40N	12.10 E
Az Zāwiyah	33	Bc	32.45N	12.44 E
Az Zaytūn	33	Ed	29.09N	25.47 E
Azzel Matti, Sebkha-	30	Hf	26.00N	0.55 E
Az Zilfī	24	Ki	26.18N	44.48 E
Az Zubayr	24	Lg	30.23N	47.43 E

B

Baa	26	Hi	10.43 S	123.03 E
Baaba	63b	Ae	20.03 S	163.58 E
Ba'ādwēyn	35	Hd	7.12N	47.24 E
Bá an Daingin/Dingle Bay	9	Ci	52.05N	10.15W
Baar	10	Ei	48.00N	8.30 E
Baarle-Hertog	12	Gc	51.27N	4.56 E
Baarn	12	Hb	52.14N	5.17 E
Baas, Bassure de-	12	Dd	50.30N	1.15 E
Bāb	24	Ok	23.55N	53.45 E
Baba	35	Bd	6.25N	17.07 E
Baba	15	Ei	40.55N	21.10 E
Baba Burun [Tur.]	24	Db	41.18N	31.26 E
Baba Burun [Tur.]	24	Bc	39.29N	26.04 E
Babadağ	15	Ll	37.48N	28.52 E
Baba Dağ	15	Mm	36.32N	29.10 E
Babadag	15	Le	44.54N	28.43 E
Babadag, Gora-	16	Pi	41.01N	48.29 E
Babaeski	24	Bb	41.26N	27.06 E
Bābā-Ḩeydar	24	Nf	32.20N	50.28 E
Babajevo	19	Dd	59.24N	35.55 E
Babajtag, Gora-	18	Hd	41.13N	70.16 E
Babajurt	16	Oh	43.35N	46.47 E
Bāb al Māndab=Bab el Mandeb (EN)	30	Lg	12.35N	43.25 E
Babanūsah	35	Dc	11.20N	27.48 E
Babao → Qilian	27	Hd	38.14N	100.15 E
Babaoyo	54	Cd	1.50 S	79.30W
Babar, Kepulauan-	26	Ih	7.50 S	129.45 E
Babar, Pulau-	57	De	7.55 S	129.45 E
Babase	63a	Aa	4.01 S	153.42 E
Babatag, Hrebet-	18	Ge	38.00N	68.10 E
Babati	36	Gc	4.13 S	35.45 E
Babbitt	45	Kc	47.43N	91.57W
B'abdā	24	Ff	33.50N	35.32 E
Bab el Mandeb (EN)=Bāb al Māndab	30	Lg	12.35N	43.25 E
Babelthuap Island	57	Ed	7.30N	134.36 E
Babenhausen [F.R.G.]	12	Ke	49.58N	8.57 E
Babenhausen [F.R.G.]	10	Gh	48.09N	10.15 E
Babeni	15	He	44.59N	24.15 E
Baberton	44	Ge	41.02N	81.38W
Bá Bheanntraí/Bantry Bay	9	Dj	51.38N	9.48W
Babian Jiang=Black River (EN)	21	Mg	20.17N	106.34 E
Babil [3]	24	Kf	32.40N	44.50 E
Babine Lake	42	Ef	54.45N	126.00W
Babino Polje	14	Lh	42.43N	17.33 E
Babit Point	51b	Ab	18.03N	63.02W
Babo	26	Jg	2.33 S	133.25 E
Bābol	23	Hb	36.34N	52.42 E
Babol Sar	24	Od	36.43N	52.39 E
Baboquivari Peak	46	Jk	31.46N	111.35W
Babor, Djebel-	13	Rh	36.32N	5.28 E
Baborigame	48	Fd	26.27N	107.16W
Baboua	35	Ad	5.48N	14.49 E
Babozero, Ozero-	7	Ic	66.30N	37.25 E
Babu → Hexian	27	Jg	24.28N	111.34 E
Babuna	15	Eh	41.30N	21.40 E
Babuyan	26	Hc	19.32N	121.57 E
Babuyan	26	Gd	10.01N	118.58 E
Babuyan Channel	26	Hc	18.44N	121.40 E
Babuyan Islands	21	Oh	19.15N	121.40 E
Babylon	23	Fc	32.32N	44.25 E
Bač	15	Cd	45.23N	19.14 E
Bacabachi	48	Ed	26.55N	109.24W
Bacabal	53	Lf	4.14 S	44.47W
Ba-Cagan	27	Gb	45.40N	99.30 E
Bacajá, Rio-	54	Hd	3.25 S	51.50W
Bacalar	48	Oh	18.43N	88.27W
Bacalar, Laguna de-	48	Oh	18.43N	88.22W
Bacalar Chico, Boca-	49	Dd	18.12N	87.53W
Bacan, Kepulauan-	26	Ig	0.35 S	127.30 E
Bacan, Pulau-	26	Ig	0.35 S	127.30 E
Bacău [2]	15	Jc	46.36N	27.00 E
Bacău	6	If	46.34N	26.54 E
Baccarat	11	Mf	48.27N	6.45 E
Bacchiglione	14	Ge	45.11N	12.14 E
Baceşti	15	Kc	46.51N	27.14 E
Bachaquero	49	Li	9.56N	71.08W
Bacharach	12	Jd	50.04N	7.46 E
Bacheli	25	Ge	18.40N	81.15 E
Bachiniva	48	Fc	28.45N	107.15W
Bachu/Maralwexi	27	Cd	39.46N	78.15 E
Back	38	Jd	67.15N	95.15W
Bačka	15	Cd	45.50N	19.30 E
Bac Kan	25	Ld	22.08N	105.49 E
Bačka Palanka	15	Cd	45.15N	19.22 E
Bačka Topola	15	Cd	45.49N	19.39 E
Bäckefors	8	Ef	58.48N	12.10 E
Bäckhammar	8	Fe	59.10N	14.11 E
Backnang	10	Fh	48.57N	9.26 E
Bačkovski Manastir	15	Hh	41.56N	24.51 E
Bac Lieu	25	Lg	9.17N	105.43 E
Bac Ninh	25	Ld	21.11N	106.03 E
Bacolet	51p	Bb	12.02N	61.41W
Bacolod	22	Oh	10.40N	122.57 E
Bac-Phan=Tonkin (EN)	21	Mg	22.00N	105.00 E
Bacqueville, Lac-	42	Ke	58.00N	74.00W
Bacqueville-en Caux	12	Ce	49.47N	1.00 E
Bácsalmás	10	Pj	46.08N	19.20 E
Bács-Kiskun [2]	10	Pj	46.30N	19.25 E
Bacton	12	Db	52.51N	1.28 E
Bād	23	Hc	33.41N	52.01 E
Badagara	25	Ff	11.36N	75.35 E
Badagri	34	Fd	6.25N	2.53 E
Badain Jaran Shamo	21	Me	40.20N	101.40 E
Badajós, Lago-	54	Fd	3.15 S	62.45W
Badajoz	6	Fh	38.53N	6.58W
Badajoz [3]	13	Ff	38.40N	6.10W
Badakhshan [3]	23	Lb	36.45N	72.00 E
Badalona	13	Oc	41.27N	2.15 E
Badanah	23	Fc	30.59N	41.02 E
Badaohao	28	Fd	41.50N	121.59 E
Badas, Kepulauan-	26	Ef	0.35N	107.06 E
Bad Aussee	14	Hc	47.36N	13.47 E
Bad Axe	44	Fd	43.48N	83.00W
Bad Bergzabern	10	Dg	49.06N	8.00 E
Bad Berleburg	12	Kc	51.04N	8.24 E
Bad Bertrich	12	Jd	50.03N	7.02 E
Bad Bramstedt	10	Fc	53.55N	9.53 E
Bad Brückenau	10	Ff	50.18N	9.45 E
Badda	35	Fd	7.55N	39.23 E
Baddo	25	Cc	27.59N	64.21 E
Bad Doberan	10	Hb	54.06N	11.54 E
Bad Driburg	12	Lc	51.44N	9.01 E
Bad Düben	10	Ie	51.36N	12.35 E
Bad Dürkheim	12	Ke	49.28N.	8.12 E
Bade	26	Kh	7.10 S	139.35 E
Bademli	15	Lk	38.04N	28.04 E
Baden [Aus.]	14	Kb	48.01N	16.14 E
Baden [Switz.]	14	Cc	47.28N	8.18 E
Baden-Baden	10	Eh	48.45N	8.15 E
Badenoch	9	Je	56.50N	4.00W
Baden-Württemberg [2]	10	Eh	48.30N	9.00 E
Bad Essen	12	Kb	52.19N	8.20 E
Bad Freienwalde	10	Kd	52.47N	14.02 E
Badgastein	14	Hc	47.07N	13.08 E
Bādghīsat [3]	23	Jc	35.00N	63.45 E
Bad Gleichenberg	14	Jd	46.52N	15.54 E
Bad Godesberg, Bonn-	10	Df	50.41N	7.09 E
Bad Hall	14	ib	48.02N	14.12 E
Bad Harzburg	10	Ge	51.53N	10.34 E
Bad Herrenalb	12	Kf	48.48N	8.25 E
Bad Hersfeld	10	Ff	50.52N	9.42 E
Bad Homburg	10	Ef	50.13N	8.37 E
Bad Honnef	12	Jd	50.38N	7.12 E
Bá Dhún na nGall/Donegal Bay	5	Fe	54.30N	8.30W
Badhyz	18	Cg	35.50N	62.00 E
Badiraguato	48	Fe	25.22N	107.31W
Bad Ischl	14	Hc	47.43N	13.37 E
Bad Kissingen	10	Gf	50.12N	10.05 E
Bad Kreuznach	10	Dg	49.50N	7.52 E
Badlands [S.D.-U.S.]	45	Ee	43.30N	102.20W
Badlands [U.S.]	43	Gb	46.45N	103.30W
Bad Langensalza	10	Ge	51.06N	10.39 E
Bad Lautenberg am Harz	10	Ge	51.38N	10.28 E
Bad Liebenwerda	10	Je	51.31N	13.24 E
Bad Liebenzel	12	Kf	48.46N	8.44 E
Bad Mergentheim	10	Fg	49.29N	9.46 E
Bad Mondorf/Mondorf-les-Bains	12	Ie	49.30N	6.17 E
Bad Münster am Stein Ebernburg	12	Je	49.49N	7.51 E
Bad Münstereifel	12	Id	50.34N	6.45 E
Bad Muskau	10	Ke	51.33N	14.43 E
Bad Nauheim	12	Kd	50.22N	8.45 E
Bad Neuenahr-Ahweiler	10	Df	50.33N	7.08 E
Bad Neustadt an der Saale	10	Gf	50.20N	10.13 E
Bad Oeynhausen	12	Kb	52.12N	8.48 E
Bad Oldesloe	10	Gc	53.49N	10.23 E
Ba Don	25	Le	17.45N	106.27 E
Badou [China]	28	Df	36.27N	117.56 E
Badou [Togo]	34	Fd	7.35N	0.36 E
Bad Pyrmont	10	Fe	51.59N	9.15 E
Bad Ragaz	14	Dc	47.00N	9.30 E
Badrah	24	Kf	33.06N	45.58 E
Bad Reichenhall	10	Ii	47.44N	12.53 E
Badr Ḩunayn	23	Ee	23.44N	38.46 E
Bad River	45	Fd	44.22N	100.22W
Bad Salzuflen	12	Kb	52.05N	8.46 E
Bad Salzungen	10	Gf	50.49N	10.14 E
Bad Schwartau	10	Gc	53.55N	10.42 E
Bad Segeberg	10	Gc	53.56N	10.19 E
Bad Tölz	10	Hi	47.46N	11.34 E
Badulla	25	Gg	6.59N	81.03 E
Bad Wildungen	10	Fe	51.07N	9.07 E
Bad Wimpfen	10	Fg	49.14N	9.08 E
Baena	13	Hg	37.37N	4.19W
Baeza [Ec.]	54	Cd	0.28S	77.53W
Baeza [Sp.]	13	Ig	37.59N	3.28W
Baf/Paphos	24	Ee	34.50N	32.35 E
Bafang	34	Hd	5.09N	10.11 E
Bafatà	31	Fg	12.10N	14.40W
Bafélé	34	Cc	10.09N	10.08W
Baffin	38	Mc	68.00N	70.00W
Baffin Bay	38	Mb	73.00N	65.00W
Bafia	34	He	4.45N	11.14 E
Bafilo	34	Fd	9.21N	1.16 E
Bafing [Afr.]	30	Fg	13.49N	10.50W
Bafing [I.C.]	34	Dd	7.52N	7.07W
Bafoulabé	34	Cc	13.48N	10.50W
Bafoussam	31	Ih	5.28N	10.25 E
Bāfq	23	Ic	31.35N	55.24 E
Bāfq, Kūh-e-	24	Pg	31.20N	55.10 E
Bafra	23	Ea	41.34N	35.56 E
Bafra Burnu	24	Fb	41.44N	35.58 E
Bāft	24	Qh	29.14N	56.38 E
Bafwaboli	36	Eb	0.39N	26.10 E
Bafwasende	36	Eb	1.05N	27.16 E
Baga	34	Hc	13.06N	13.50 E
Bagaces	49	Eh	10.31N	85.15W
Bagagem, Rio-	55	Ha	13.58 S	48.21W
Bagajevski	16	Lf	47.19N	40.25 E
Bāgalkot	25	Fe	16.11N	75.42 E
Bagamoyo	36	Gd	6.26 S	38.54 E
Bagansiapi-Api	26	Df	2.09N	100.49 E
Bağarasi	15	Kl	37.42N	27.33 E
Baga Sola	35	Ac	13.32N	14.19 E
Bagata	36	Cc	3.44 S	17.57 E
Bagdad	48	Ke	25.57N	97.09W
Bagdarin	20	Gf	54.30N	113.36 E
Bağdere	24	Ic	38.10N	40.45 E
Bagé	53	Ki	31.20 S	54.06W
Bages et de Sigean, Étang de-	11	Jk	43.05N	3.01 E
Baggs	46	Lf	41.02N	107.39W
Bågh Baile na Sgealg/ Ballinskelligs Bay	9	Cj	51.50N	10.15W
Baghdād [3]	24	Kf	33.18N	44.36 E
Baghdād	22	Gf	33.21N	44.23 E
Baghdādī, Ra's-	24	Fj	24.40N	35.06 E
Bāgh-e Chenār	24	Qh	28.11N	56.54 E
Bāgh-e-Malek	24	Mg	31.32N	49.55 E
Bagheria	14	Hl	38.05N	13.30 E
Bāghīn	23	Ic	30.12N	56.48 E
Baghlān [3]	23	Kb	35.45N	69.00 E
Baghlān	23	Kb	36.13N	68.46 E
Bāglung	25	Gc	28.16N	83.36 E
Bagn	8	Cd	60.49N	9.34 E
Bagnara Calabra	14	Jl	38.17N	15.48 E
Bagnères-de-Bigorre	11	Gk	43.04N	0.09 E
Bagnères-de-Luchon	11	Gl	42.47N	0.36 E
Bagni di Lucca	14	Ef	44.01N	10.35 E
Bagno di Romagna	14	Fg	43.50N	11.57 E
Bagnolo Mella	14	Ee	45.26N	10.10 E
Bagnols-sur-Cèze	11	Kj	44.10N	4.37 E
Bago	22	Lh	17.30N	96.30 E
Bagoé	30	Gg	12.36N	6.34W
Bagolino	14	Ee	45.49N	10.28 E
Bagrationovsk	8	Ij	54.23N	20.40 E
Bagrax/Bohu	27	Ec	41.58N	86.29 E
Bagrax Hu/Bosten	21	Ke	42.00N	87.00 E
Bagua	54	Ce	5.40 S	78.31W
Baguio	22	Oh	16.25N	120.36 E
Baguirmi	30	Ig	11.40N	16.20 E
Bagzane, Monts-	30	Hg	17.43N	8.45 E
Bahama Islands	38	Lg	24.15N	76.00W
Bahamas [1]	39	Lg	24.15N	76.00W
Bahamas, Canal Viejo de-= Old Bahama Channel (EN)	49	Ib	22.30N	78.05W
Bahār	24	Me	34.54N	48.26 E
Baharampur	25	Hd	24.06N	88.15 E
Baharden	19	Fh	38.28N	57.28 E
Bahardok	19	Fh	38.51N	58.24 E
Baharīyah, Wāḩāt al-	33	Ed	28.10N	29.00 E
Bahariya Oasis (EN)= Baḩarīyah, Wāḩāt al-	33	Ed	28.15N	28.57 E
Bahaur	26	Fg	3.20N	114.00 E
Bahāwalnagar	25	Ec	29.59N	73.16 E
Bahāwalpur	22	Jg	29.24N	71.41 E
Bahčisaraj	16	Hg	44.45N	33.51 E
Bahę	24	Gd	37.14N	36.34 E
Bahi	36	Gd	5.39 S	35.19 E
Bahia [2]	54	Jf	12.00 S	42.00W
Bahía, Islas de la-	47	Ge	16.20N	86.30W
Bahía Blanca	53	Ji	38.44 S	62.16W
Bahía de Caráquez	54	Bd	0.37 S	80.25W
Bahía Kino	47	Bc	28.50N	111.55W
Bahía Negra	56	Ib	20.15 S	58.12W
Bahías, Cabo dos-	52	Jj	44.55 S	65.32W
Bahīj	24	Cg	30.56N	29.35 E
Bahinga	36	Ed	5.57 S	27.06 E
Bahi Swamp	36	Gd	6.05 S	35.10 E
Bahlui	15	Kb	47.08N	27.44 E
Bahmač	19	De	51.11N	32.50 E
Bahoruco, Sierra de-	49	Ld	18.10N	71.25W
Bahraich	25	Gc	27.35N	81.36 E
Bahrain (EN)=Al Baḩrayn [1]	22	Hg	26.00N	50.29 E
Baḩr al Ghazāl [3]	35	Dd	8.15N	26.50 E
Bahr ar Ramla al Kabīr	33	Ed	27.00N	26.00 E
Baḩrayn, Khalij al-	24	Nj	25.45N	50.40 E
Bahr Dar	31	Kg	11.36N	37.22 E
Bahta	20	Dd	62.20N	89.15 E
Bahusi	15	Jc	46.43N	26.42 E
Baia	15	Le	44.43N	28.40 E
Baia de Aramă	15	Fe	45.00N	22.50 E
Baia de Fier	15	Gd	45.10N	23.46 E
Baia dos Tigres	36	Bf	16.35 S	11.43 E
Baia Farta	36	Be	12.37 S	13.26 E
Baia Mare	15	Gb	47.40N	23.35 E
Baião	54	Id	2.41 S	49.41W
Baia Sprie	15	Gb	47.40N	23.42 E
Baibiene	55	Ci	29.36 S	58.10W
Baïbokoum	35	Bd	7.45N	15.41 E
Baicheng	22	Oe	45.34N	122.49 E
Baicheng/Bay	27	Dc	41.46N	81.52 E
Băicoi	15	Id	45.02N	25.51 E
Băiculeşti	15	Hd	45.04N	24.42 E
Baïdou	35	Cd	5.52N	20.41 E
Baie-Comeau	39	Me	49.13N	68.10W
Baie-Mahault	50	Fd	16.16N	61.35W
Baie-Saint-Paul	42	Kg	47.27N	70.30W
Baie-Trinité	44	Na	49.24N	67.19W
Baie Verte	42	Lg	49.55N	56.11W
Baiguan → Shangyu	28	Fi	30.01N	120.53 E
Baihe	27	Je	32.46N	110.06 E
Bai He [China]	28	Bh	32.10N	112.20 E
Bai He [China]	28	Dd	40.43N	116.33 E
Baikal, Lake- (EN)=Bajkal, Ozero-	21	Md	53.00N	107.40 E
Baikal Range (EN)= Bajkalski Hrebet	21	Md	55.00N	108.40 E
Baile an Chaistil/ Ballycastle	118	Gf	55.12N	6.15W
Baile an Róba/Ballinrobe	118	Dh	53.37N	9.13W
Baile Átha Cliath/Dublin [2]	9	Gh	53.20N	6.15W
Baile Átha Cliath/Dublin	6	Fe	53.20N	6.15W
Baile Átha Luain/Athlone	9	Fh	53.25N	7.56W
Baile Átha Troim/Trim	9	Gh	53.34N	6.47W
Băile Borşa	15	Hb	47.41N	24.43 E
Baile Brigín/Balbriggan	9	Gh	53.37N	6.11W
Băile Govora	15	Hd	45.05N	24.11 E
Baile Locha Riach/Loughrea	9	Eh	53.12N	8.34W
Baile Mhistéala/ Mitchelstown	9	Ei	52.16N	8.16W
Bailén	13	If	38.06N	3.46W
Baile na Mainistreach/ Newtownabbey	9	Hg	54.42N	5.54W
Baile Nua na hArda/ Newtownards	9	Hg	54.36N	5.41W
Băile Olăneşti	15	Hd	45.12N	24.14 E
Băileşti	15	Ge	44.01N	23.21 E
Bailleul	12	Ce	49.12N	0.26 E
Bailleul	12	Ed	50.44N	2.44 E
Ba Illi	35	Bc	10.31N	16.29 E
Bailong Jiang	27	Ie	32.42N	105.15 E
Bailundo	36	Ce	12.10 S	15.56 E
Baima	27	He	33.05N	100.29 E
Bain	12	Ba	53.04N	0.12W
Bainbridge	43	Ke	30.54N	84.34W
Bain-de-Bretagne	11	Eg	47.50N	1.41W
Baines Drift	37	Dd	22.30 S	28.43 E
Baing	26	Hi	10.14 S	120.34 E
Baingoin	27	Ee	31.36N	89.48 E
Baiquan	27	Mb	47.38N	126.04 E
Bā'ir	24	Gg	30.46N	36.41 E
Bā'ir, Wādī-	24	Gg	31.12N	37.31 E
Baird	45	Gj	32.24N	99.24W
Baird Inlet	40	Gd	60.45N	164.00W
Baird Mountains	40	Gc	67.35N	161.30W
Baird Peninsula	42	Jc	69.00N	75.15W
Bairiki	58	Id	1.20N	173.01 E
Bairin Youqi (Daban)	27	Kc	43.30N	118.37 E
Bairin Zuoqi (Lindong)	27	Kc	43.59N	119.22 E
Bairnsdale	58	Fh	37.50 S	147.38 E
Bais	26	He	9.35N	123.07 E
Bai Shan	27	Fc	40.53N	93.48 E
Baisogala/Bajsogala	8	Ji	55.35N	23.44 E
Baitou Shan	21	Oe	42.00N	128.00 E
Baitoushan Tian Chi	28	Jc	42.00N	128.03 E
Baixiang	28	Cf	37.29N	114.44 E
Baixo Alentejo	13	Dg	37.55N	8.10W
Baixo Guandu	54	Jg	19.31 S	41.01W
Baixo Longa	36	Cf	15.42 S	18.38 E
Baiyanghe	27	Ec	43.12N	88.28 E
Baiyü	27	Ge	31.13N	98.51 E
Baja	10	Oj	46.11N	18.58 E
Baja, Punta- [Mex.]	48	Dc	28.25N	111.45W
Baja, Punta- [Pas.]	65d	Ab	27.10 S	109.22W
Baja California=Lower California (EN)	38	Hg	28.00N	112.00W
Baja California Norte [2]	47	Ac	30.00N	115.00W
Baja California Sur [2]	47	Bd	25.50N	111.50W
Bājah [3]	32	Ib	36.30N	9.30 E
Bājah	32	Ib	36.44N	9.11 E
Bajalān	24	Md	37.18N	48.47 E
Bajan	27	Jb	49.15N	111.58 E
Bajanaul	19	He	50.47N	75.42 E
Bajandaj	20	Ff	53.04N	105.30 E
Bajan-Delger	27	Jb	45.55N	112.15 E
Bajangol	20	Ff	50.40N	103.25 E
Bajan-Hongor	22	Me	46.20N	100.40 E
Bajan-Ula [Mong.]	27	Jb	49.07N	112.45 E
Bajan-Ula [Mong.]	27	Gb	47.05N	95.15 E
Bajan-Under	27	Gc	44.45N	98.45 E
Baja Verapaz [3]	49	Bf	15.05N	90.20W
Bajawa	26	Hh	8.47 S	120.59 E
Bajčunas	16	Rf	47.17N	53.03 E
Bajdarackaja Guba	20	Bc	69.00N	67.30 E
Bajdarata	17	Nb	68.12N	68.18 E
Bajdrag Gol	27	Hb	45.10N	100.45 E
Bājgīrān	24	Rd	37.36N	58.24 E
Baj-Haak	20	Ef	51.07N	94.34 E
Bajiazi	28	Jc	42.41N	129.13 E
Bajina Bašta	15	Cf	43.58N	19.34 E
Bajkal	20	Ff	51.53N	104.47 E
Bajkal, Ozero-=Baikal, Lake- (EN)	21	Md	53.00N	107.40 E
Bajkalovo	17	Kh	57.24N	63.40 E
Bajkalsk	20	Ff	51.30N	104.05 E
Bajkalski Hrebet=Baikal Range (EN)	21	Md	55.00N	108.40 E
Bajkit	20	Ed	61.41N	96.25 E
Bajkonur	19	Gf	47.50N	66.07 E
Bajmak	19	Fe	52.36N	58.19 E
Bajmba, Mount-	59	Ke	29.20 S	152.05 E
Bajmok	15	Cd	45.58N	19.26 E
Bajo Baudó	54	Cc	4.58N	77.22W

Index Symbols

[1] Independent Nation
[2] State, Region
[3] District, County
[4] Municipality
[5] Colony, Dependency
Continent
Physical Region
Historical or Cultural Region
Mount, Mountain
Volcano
Hill
Mountains, Mountain Range
Hills, Escarpment
Plateau, Upland
Pass, Gap
Plain, Lowland
Delta
Salt Flat
Valley, Canyon
Crater, Cave
Karst Features
Depression
Polder
Desert, Dunes
Forest, Woods
Heath, Steppe
Oasis
Cape, Point
Coast, Beach
Cliff
Peninsula
Isthmus
Sandbank
Island
Atoll
Rock, Reef
Islands, Archipelago
Rocks, Reefs
Coral Reef
Well, Spring
Geyser
River, Stream
Waterfall Rapids
River Mouth, Estuary
Lake
Salt Lake
Intermittent Lake
Reservoir
Swamp, Pond
Canal
Glacier
Ice Shelf, Pack Ice
Ocean
Sea
Gulf, Bay
Strait, Fjord
Lagoon
Bank
Seamount
Tablemount
Ridge
Shelf
Basin
Escarpment, Sea Scarp
Fracture
Trench, Abyss
National Park, Reserve
Point of Interest
Recreation Site
Cave, Cavern
Historic Site
Ruins
Wall, Walls
Church, Abbey
Temple
Scientific Station
Airport
Port
Lighthouse
Mine
Tunnel
Dam, Bridge

Index Symbols

[1] Independent Nation	Historical or Cultural Region
[2] State, Region	Mount, Mountain
[3] District, County	Volcano
[4] Municipality	Hill
[5] Colony, Dependency	Mountains, Mountain Range
■ Continent	Hills, Escarpment
Physical Region	Plateau, Upland

Pass, Gap	Depression	Coast, Beach
Plain, Lowland	Polder	Cliff
Delta	Desert, Dunes	Peninsula
Salt Flat	Forest, Woods	Isthmus
Valley, Canyon	Heath, Steppe	Sandbank
Crater, Cave	Oasis	Island
Karst Features	Cape, Point	

Rock, Reef	Waterfall Rapids	Canal
Islands, Archipelago	River Mouth, Estuary	Glacier
Rocks, Reefs	Lake	Ice Shelf, Pack Ice
Coral Reef	Salt Lake	Ocean
Well, Spring	Intermittent Lake	Sea
Geyser	Reservoir	Gulf, Bay
Atoll	River, Stream	Strait, Fjord
		Swamp, Pond

Lagoon	Escarpment, Sea Scarp	Historic Site	Port
Bank	Fracture	Ruins	Lighthouse
Seamount	Trench, Abyss	Wall, Walls	Mine
Tablemount	National Park, Reserve	Church, Abbey	Tunnel
Ridge	Point of Interest	Temple	Dam, Bridge
Shelf	Recreation Site	Scientific Station	
Basin	Cave, Cavern	Airport	

Baranoviči 6 Ie 53.08N 26.02 E
Baranovka 16 Ed 50.18N 27.41 E
Baranya [2] 10 Oj 46.05N 18.15 E
Barão de Capanema 55 Da 13.19S 57.52W
Barão de Cotegipe 55 Fh 27.37S 52.23W
Barão de Grajaú 54 Je 6.45S 43.01W
Barão de Melgaço 54 Gg 16.13S 55.58W
Baraque de Fraiture 11 Ld 50.15N 5.45 E
Baratang 25 If 12.13N 92.45 E
Barataria Bay 45 Ll 29.22N 89.57W
Barat Daya, Kepulauan- 21 Oj 7.25S 128.00 E
Barāwe 31 Lh 1.09N 44.03 E
Barbacena 53 Lh 21.14S 43.46 E
Barbacoas [Ven.] 49 Li 9.49N 70.03W
Barbacoas [Ven.] 50 Ch 9.29N 66.58W
Barbacoas, Bahía de- 49 Jh 10.10N 75.35W
Barbado, Rio- 55 Cb 15.12S 58.58W
Barbados [1] 39 Nh 13.10N 59.32W
Barbados 38 Nh 13.10N 59.32W
Barbados Ridge (EN) 50 Gf 12.45N 59.35W
Barbagia 14 Dj 40.10N 9.10 E
Barbar 35 Eb 18.01N 33.59 E
Bárbara 54 Dd 0.52S 72.30W
Barbaros 15 Ki 40.54N 27.27 E
Barbas, Cabo- 32 De 22.18N 16.41W
Barbastro 13 Mb 42.02N 0.08 E
Barbate de Franco 13 Gh 36.12N 5.55W
Barbeau Peak 38 La 81.54N 75.01W
Barbeton 37 Ee 25.48S 31.03 E
Barbezieux 11 Fi 45.28N 0.09W
Barbourville 44 Fg 36.52N 83.53W
Barboza Ferraz 55 Fg 24.04S 52.03W
Barbuda 38 Mh 17.38N 61.48W
Barcaldine 58 Fg 23.33S 145.17 E
Barcarrota 13 Ff 38.31N 6.51W
Barcău 15 Ec 46.59N 21.07 E
Barcellona Pozzo di Gotto 14 Jl 38.09N 15.13 E
Barcelona [3] 13 Nc 41.40N 2.00 E
Barcelona [Sp.] 6 Gg 41.23N 2.11 E
Barcelona [Ven.] 54 Fa 10.08N 64.42W
Barcelonnette 11 Mj 44.23N 6.39 E
Barcelos [Braz.] 54 Fd 0.58S 62.57W
Barcelos [Port.] 13 Dc 41.32N 8.37W
Barcin 10 Nd 52.52N 17.57 E
Barcoo River 59 Ie 25.30S 142.50 E
Barcs 10 Nk 45.58N 17.28 E
Barda 16 Oi 40.25N 47.05 E
Bardagé 35 Ba 22.06N 16.28 E
Bardaï 31 If 21.21N 16.59 E
Bardār Shāh 24 Ld 36.45N 47.15 E
Bārdaw 14 En 36.49N 10.08 E
Barddhamān 25 Hd 23.15N 87.51 E
Bardejov 10 Rg 49.18N 21.16 E
Bārḍēre 31 Lh 2.20N 42.20 E
Bardeskan 24 Qe 35.12N 57.58 E
Bardīyah 33 Ed 31.46N 25.06 E
Bardonecchia 14 Ae 45.05N 6.42 E
Bardsey 9 Ii 52.45N 4.45W
Bardstown 44 Eg 37.49N 85.28W
Barēda 31 Mg 11.52N 51.03 E
Bareilly 22 Jg 28.25N 79.23 E
Barencevo More = Barents Sea (EN) 67 Jd 74.00N 36.00 E
Barentin 11 Ge 49.33N 0.57 E
Barentsburg 67 Kd 78.04N 14.14 E
Barentshav = Barents Sea (EN) 67 Jd 74.00N 36.00 E
Barentsøya 41 Oc 78.27N 21.15 E
Barents Sea (EN) = Barencevo More 67 Jd 74.00N 36.00 E
Barents Sea (EN) = Barentshav 67 Jd 74.00N 36.00 E
Barents Trough (EN) 5 Ia 73.00N 29.00 E
Barentu 35 Fb 15.06N 37.36 E
Barfleur 11 Ee 49.40N 1.15W
Barfleur, Pointe de- 11 Ee 49.42N 1.16W
Barga 22 Kf 30.48N 81.17 E
Bārgāl 35 Ic 11.18N 51.07 E
Bargarh 25 Gd 21.20N 83.37 E
Barguelonne 11 Gj 44.07N 0.50 E
Barguzin 20 Ff 53.27N 108.58 E
Barguzinski Hrebet 20 Ff 54.30N 110.00 E
Bar Harbor 44 Mc 44.23N 68.13W
Barhi 25 Hd 24.18N 85.25 E
Bari [3] 35 Hd 10.00N 50.00 E
Bari 6 Hg 41.08N 16.51 E
Bari, Terra di- 14 Kj 41.05N 16.50 E
Ba Ria 25 Lf 10.30N 107.10 E
Barīdī, Ra's- 24 Gj 24.17N 37.31 E
Barika 13 Ri 35.22N 5.05 E
Barīm 33 Hg 12.39N 43.25 E
Barima, Río- 50 Fh 8.35N 60.25W
Barima River 50 Fh 8.35N 60.25W
Barinas 54 Db 8.38N 70.12W
Barinas [2] 54 Eb 8.10N 70.00W
Baring, Cape- 42 Fb 70.01N 117.28W
Baringa 36 Db 0.45N 20.52 E
Barinitas 49 Li 8.45N 70.25W
Baripāda 25 Hd 21.56N 86.43 E
Bariri 55 Hf 22.04S 48.44W
Bariri, Represa- 55 Hf 22.21S 48.39W
Bārīs 33 Fe 24.40N 30.36 E
Bari Sādri 25 Ed 24.25N 74.28 E
Barisāl 25 Id 22.42N 90.22 E
Barisan, Pegunungan- = Barisan Mountains (EN) 21 Mj 3.00S 102.15 E
Barisan Mountains (EN) = Barisan, Pegunungan- 21 Mj 3.00S 102.15 E
Barito 21 Nj 3.32S 114.29 E
Barjols 11 Lk 43.33N 6.00 E
Barkā' 23 Ie 23.35N 57.55 E
Barkam 27 He 31.45N 102.32 E
Barkan, Ra's-e- 24 Mg 30.01N 49.35 E
Barkava 8 Lh 56.40N 26.45 E
Barkley, Lake- 43 Jd 36.40N 87.55W
Barkley Sound 46 Cb 48.53N 125.20W
Barkly East 37 Df 30.58S 27.33 E
Barkly Tableland 57 Ef 19.00S 138.00 E
Barkly West 37 Ce 28.05S 24.31 E
Barkol 27 Fc 43.35N 92.51 E
Barkol Hu 27 Fc 43.40N 92.39 E
Barlavento [3] 32 Cf 16.10N 24.40W
Bar-le-Duc 11 Lf 48.47N 5.10 E
Barlee, Lake- 57 Cg 29.10S 119.30 E
Barlee Range 59 Dd 23.35S 116.00 E
Barletta 14 Ki 41.19N 16.17 E
Barlinek 10 Lc 53.00N 15.12 E
Barlovento, Islas de- = Windward Islands (EN) 38 Mh 15.00N 61.00W
Barma 26 Jg 1.54S 133.00 E
Barmer 25 Ec 25.45N 71.23 E
Barmera 59 If 34.15S 140.28 E
Barmouth 9 Ii 52.43N 4.03W
Barnard Castle 9 Lg 54.33N 1.55W
Barnaul 22 Kd 53.22N 83.45 E
Barnes Ice Cap 42 Kc 70.00N 73.30W
Barnesville [Ga.-U.S.] 44 Ei 33.04N 84.09W
Barnesville [Mn.-U.S.] 45 Hc 46.39N 96.25W
Barnet, London- 12 Bc 51.39N 0.12W
Barneveld 12 Hb 52.08N 5.34 E
Barnim 10 Jd 52.40N 13.45 E
Barnsley 9 Lh 53.34N 1.28W
Barnstaple 9 Ij 51.05N 4.04W
Barnstaple (Bideford Bay) 9 Ij 51.05N 4.20W
Barnstorf 12 Kb 52.43N 8.30 E
Barntrup 12 Lc 51.59N 9.07 E
Barnwell 44 Gi 33.14N 81.21W
Baro 30 Kh 8.26N 33.14 E
Baro [Chad] 35 Bc 12.12N 18.58 E
Baro [Nig.] 34 Gd 8.36N 6.25 E
Baronnies 11 Lj 44.15N 5.30 E
Barora Fa 63a Db 7.30S 158.20 E
Barora Ite 63a Db 7.36S 158.24 E
Barotseland 36 Df 15.05S 24.00 E
Barqah = Cyrenaica (EN) 33 Dc 31.00N 22.30 E
Barqah = Cyrenaica (EN) 30 Je 31.00N 23.00 E
Barqah, Jabal al- 24 Ej 24.24N 32.34 E
Barqah al Bahrīyah = Marmarica (EN) 30 Je 31.40N 24.30 E
Barqū, Jabal- 14 Dn 36.04N 9.37 E
Barques, Pointe aux- 44 Fc 44.04N 82.58W
Barquisimeto 53 Jd 10.04N 69.19W
Barr 11 Nf 48.24N 7.27 E
Barr, Ra's al- 24 Nj 25.47N 50.34 E
Barra 53 Lg 11.05S 43.10W
Barra 9 Fd 57.00N 7.30W
Barra, Ponta da- 30 Kk 23.47S 35.32 E
Barra, Sound of- 9 Fd 57.10N 7.20W
Barraba 59 Kf 30.22S 150.36 E
Barra Bonita, Represa- 55 Hf 22.38S 48.20W
Barra de Navidad 47 De 19.12N 104.41W
Barra do Bugres 54 Gg 15.05S 57.11W
Barra do Corda 54 Ie 5.30S 45.15W
Barra do Cuanza 36 Bd 9.18S 13.09 E
Barra do Dande 36 Bd 8.28S 13.22 E
Barra do Garças 54 Hg 15.53S 52.15W
Barra Falsa, Ponta da- 30 Kk 22.55S 35.37 E
Barra Head 9 Fe 56.46N 7.36W
Barra Mansa 54 Jh 22.32S 44.11W
Barrāmīyah, Wādī al- 24 Ej 25.00N 33.23 E
Barranca 54 Cd 4.50S 76.42W
Barrancabermeja 53 Ie 7.03N 73.52W
Barrancas [Col.] 49 Kh 10.57N 72.50W
Barrancas [Ven.] 54 Fb 8.42N 62.11W
Barrancas, Arroyo- 55 Cj 30.19S 59.25W
Barranco 55 Db 15.56S 57.41W
Barrancos 13 Ff 38.08N 6.59W
Barranqueras 56 Ic 27.29S 58.56W
Barranquilla 53 Id 10.59N 74.48W
Barranquitas 51a Bb 18.12N 66.23W
Barra Patuca 49 Ef 15.50N 84.17W
Barras 54 Jd 4.15S 42.18W
Barra Velha 55 Hh 26.39S 48.43W
Barre 44 Kc 44.12N 72.30W
Barreira 55 Db 15.24S 57.52W
Barreiras 53 Lg 12.08S 45.00W
Barreirinha 54 Gd 2.47S 57.03W
Barreirinhas 54 Jd 2.45S 42.50W
Barreiro 13 Cf 38.40N 9.04W
Barreiro, Rio- 55 Fb 15.43S 52.45W
Barreiro Grande 55 Jd 18.12S 45.10W
Barreiros 54 Ke 8.49S 35.12W
Barren 25 If 12.16N 93.51 E
Barren, Iles- 37 Gc 18.25S 43.40 E
Barren Islands 40 Ie 58.55N 152.15W
Barretos 56 Kb 20.33S 48.33W
Barrie 42 Jh 44.24N 79.40W
Barrier Bay 66 Ge 67.45S 81.10 E
Barrier Islands 63a Db 7.44S 158.32 E
Barrington Tops 59 Kf 32.00S 151.28 E
Barro Alto 55 Hb 15.04S 48.58W
Barrois, Plateau du- 11 Kf 48.45N 5.00 E
Barros, Lagoa dos- 55 Gi 29.56S 50.23W
Barros, Tierra de- 13 Ff 38.40N 6.25W
Barroso 55 Ke 21.11S 43.58W
Barrouallie 51n Ba 13.14N 61.17W
Barrow [Ak.-U.S.] 39 Db 71.17N 156.47W
Barrow [Arg.] 55 Bn 38.18S 60.14W
Barrow/An Bhearú 9 Gi 52.10N 7.00W
Barrow, Point- 38 Db 71.23N 156.30W
Barrow Creek 58 Eg 21.33S 133.53 E
Barrow-in-Furness 9 Jg 54.07N 3.14W
Barrow Island 57 Cg 20.50S 115.25 E
Barrow Range 59 Fe 26.05S 127.30 E
Barrow Strait 38 Jb 74.21N 94.10W
Barru 26 Gg 4.25S 119.37 E
Barry 9 Jj 51.24N 3.18W
Barrytown 62 De 42.14S 171.20 E
Barsakelmes, Ostrov- 18 Bb 45.40N 59.55 E
Barsalogo 34 Ec 13.25N 1.03W
Barsatas 19 Hf 48.13N 78.33 E
Baršć/Forst 10 Ke 51.44N 14.38 E
Bārsi 25 Fe 18.14N 75.42 E
Barsinghausen 10 Fd 52.18N 9.27 E
Barstow 43 De 34.54N 117.01W
Bar-sur-Aube 11 Kf 48.14N 4.43 E
Bar-sur-Seine 11 Kf 48.07N 4.22 E
Baršyn 19 Gf 49.45N 69.36 E
Bārta/Barta 8 Ih 56.57N 20.57 E
Barta/Bārta 8 Ih 56.57N 20.57 E
Barṯallah 24 Jd 36.23N 43.25 E
Bartang 18 Hf 37.55N 71.33 E
Barth 10 Ib 54.22N 12.44 E
Bartholomew, Bayou- 45 Jj 32.43N 92.04W
Bartica 54 Gb 6.24N 58.37W
Bartın 24 Eb 41.38N 32.21 E
Bartle Frere, Mount- 57 Ff 17.23S 145.49 E
Bartlesville 43 Hd 36.45N 95.59W
Bartlett 45 Gf 41.53N 98.33W
Bartoszyce 10 Qb 54.16N 20.49 E
Bartow 44 Gl 27.54N 81.50W
Barú, Isla- 49 Jh 10.26N 75.35W
Barú, Volcán 47 Hg 8.48N 82.33W
Bārūd, Ra's- 24 Ei 26.47N 33.39 E
Barumini 14 Dk 39.42N 9.01 E
Barun-Bogdo-Ula 27 Hb 45.00N 100.20 E
Bāruni 25 Hc 25.29N 85.59 E
Barun-Šabartuj, Gora- 20 Fg 49.43N 109.58 E
Barun-Urt 27 Jb 46.40N 113.12 E
Barwice 10 Mc 53.45N 16.22 E
Barwon River 57 Fg 30.00S 148.05 E
Barycz 10 Me 51.42N 16.15 E
Baryš 7 Lj 53.40N 47.08 E
Baryš 7 Li 54.35N 46.47 E
Bāsa'īdū 24 Pi 26.39N 55.17 E
Basail 55 Ch 27.52S 59.18W
Basankusu 36 Cb 1.14N 19.48 E
Basaral, Ostrov- 18 Ib 45.25N 73.45 E
Basauri 13 Ja 43.13N 2.53W
Basavilbaso 55 Ck 32.22S 58.53W
Bas Champs 12 Dd 50.20N 1.41 E
Basco 26 Hb 20.27N 121.58 E
Bascuñán, Cabo- 56 Fc 28.51S 71.30W
Base 11 Gj 44.17N 0.18 E
Basel [2] 14 Bc 47.35N 7.40 E
Basel/Bâle 6 Gf 47.30N 7.30 E
Baselland [2] 14 Bc 47.30N 7.45 E
Basentello 14 Kj 40.40N 16.23 E
Basento 14 Kj 40.20N 16.49 E
Başeu 15 Kb 47.44N 27.15 E
Basey 26 Id 11.17N 125.04 E
Bashi Channel (EN) = Bashi Haixia 27 Lg 22.00N 121.00 E
Bashi Haixia = Bashi Channel (EN) 27 Lg 22.00N 121.00 E
Bāsht 24 Ng 30.21N 51.09 E
Ba Shui 28 Ci 30.25N 115.02 E
Basilan 21 Oi 6.34N 122.03 E
Basilan City (Isabela) 22 Oi 6.42N 121.58 E
Basilan Strait 26 He 6.49N 122.05 E
Basildon 9 Nj 51.34N 0.25 E
Basilicata [2] 14 Kj 40.30N 16.30 E
Basingstoke 9 Lj 51.16N 1.05W
Basjanovski 17 Jg 58.19N 60.44 E
Başkale 24 Jc 38.02N 44.00 E
Baskatong, Réservoir- 42 Jg 46.47N 75.50W
Baškaus 20 Df 51.09N 87.43 E
Baskil 24 Hc 38.35N 38.40 E
Baškirskaja ASSR [3] 19 Fe 55.00N 56.00 E
Baskunčak, Ozero- 16 Oe 48.10N 46.55 E
Bašmakovo 16 Mc 53.12N 43.03 E
Bāsmenj 24 Ld 37.59N 46.29 E
Basoko 36 Db 1.14N 23.36 E
Basongo 36 Dc 4.20S 20.24 E
Basque Provinces (EN) = Euzkadi/Vascongadas 13 Ja 43.00N 2.30W
Basque Provinces (EN) = Vascongadas/Euzkadi 13 Ja 43.00N 2.30W
Basra (EN) = Al Başrah 22 Gf 30.30N 47.47 E
Bas Rhin [3] 11 Nf 48.35N 7.40 E
Bass, Ilots de- 57 Mg 27.55S 143.26W
Bassano 46 Ia 50.47N 112.28W
Bassano del Grappa 14 Fe 45.46N 11.44 E
Bassar 34 Fd 9.15N 0.47 E
Bassas da India 30 Lk 21.25S 39.42 E
Bassein → Pathein 22 Lh 16.47N 94.44 E
Bassein → Vasai 25 Ee 19.21N 72.48 E
Basse-Kotto [3] 35 Ce 5.00N 21.30 E
Basse-Pointe 51h Ab 14.52N 61.07W
Basses, Pointe des- 51e Bc 15.52N 61.17W
Basse-Sambre 12 Gd 50.27N 4.37 E
Basse Santa Su 34 Cc 13.19N 14.13W
Basse-Terre 50 Fd 16.10N 61.40W
Basse-Terre 47 Le 16.00N 61.44W
Basseterre 47 Le 17.18N 62.43W
Bassett 45 Ge 42.35N 99.32W
Bassigny 11 Lf 48.00N 5.30 E
Bassikounou 32 Ff 15.52N 5.58W
Bassila 34 Fd 9.01N 1.40 E
Bass Islands 63c Ba 9.58S 167.17 E
Basso, Plateau de- 30 Jg 17.20N 22.40 E
Bass Strait 57 Fh 39.20S 145.30 E
Bassum 12 Kb 52.51N 8.44 E
Basswood Lake 45 Kb 48.05N 91.35W
Båstad 7 Ch 56.26N 12.51 E
Bastak 24 Pi 27.14N 54.22 E
Bastām 24 Pd 36.29N 55.04 E
Bastenaken/Bastogne 11 Le 50.00N 5.43 E
Bastia [Fr.] 6 Gg 42.42N 9.27 E
Bastia [It.] 14 Gg 43.04N 12.33 E
Bastogne/Bastenaken 11 Le 50.00N 5.43 E
Bastrop 45 Kj 32.47N 91.55W
Basudan Ula 27 Fe 33.05N 91.00 E
Basuo → Dongfang 27 Ih 19.14N 108.39 E
Basuto 37 Dc 19.52S 26.32 E
Bas-Zaïre [2] 36 Bd 5.30S 14.30 E
Bata 31 Hh 1.51N 9.45 E
Batabanó, Golfo de- 47 Hd 22.15N 82.30W
Batagaj 20 Ic 67.38N 134.38 E
Batagaj-Alyta 20 Ic 67.53N 130.31 E
Bataguaçu 54 Hh 21.42S 52.22W
Bataiporã 55 Ff 22.20S 53.17W
Batajnica 15 De 44.54N 20.17 E
Batajsk 19 Df 47.05N 39.46 E
Batak 15 Hh 41.57N 24.13 E
Bataklık Gölü 24 Ed 37.42N 33.07 E
Batala 25 Fb 31.48N 75.12 E
Batalha 13 De 39.39N 8.50W
Batama 36 Eb 0.56N 26.39 E
Batamaj 20 Hd 63.30N 129.25 E
Batamšinski 19 Fe 50.36N 58.17 E
Batan 26 Hb 20.30N 121.50 E
Batang 27 Ge 30.02N 99.10 E
Batanga 36 Ac 0.21S 9.18 E
Batangafo 35 Bd 7.18N 18.18 E
Batangas 22 Oh 13.45N 121.03 E
Batanghari 26 Mj 1.00S 104.00 E
Batan Islands 21 Og 20.30N 121.50 E
Batanta, Pulau- 26 Jg 0.50S 130.40 E
Bátaszék 10 Oj 46.11N 18.44 E
Batatais 55 Ie 20.53S 47.37W
Batavia 44 Hd 43.00N 78.11W
Bat-Cengel 27 Hb 47.47N 101.58 E
Batchawana 44 Eb 46.58N 84.34W
Batchelor 59 Gb 13.04S 131.01 E
Bătdâmbâng 22 Mh 13.06N 103.12 E
Batéké, Plateaux- 36 Cc 3.30S 15.45 E
Batel, Esteros del- 55 Ci 28.30S 58.20W
Batemans Bay 59 Kg 35.43S 150.11 E
Batesburg 44 Gi 33.56N 81.33W
Batesville [Ar.-U.S.] 45 Ki 35.46N 91.39W
Batesville [Ms.-U.S.] 45 Li 34.18N 90.00W
Bath [Eng.-U.K.] 9 Kj 51.23N 2.22W
Bath [Me.-U.S.] 44 Md 43.55N 69.49W
Bath [N.B.-Can.] 44 Nb 46.32N 67.33W
Bath [St.C.N.] 51c Ab 17.08N 62.37W
Batha 35 Bc 14.00N 19.00 E
Bathinda 25 Fb 30.12N 74.57 E
Bá Thrá Lí/Tralee Bay 9 Di 52.15N 9.59W
Bathsheba 50 Gf 13.13N 59.31W
Bá Thuath Reanna/Liscannor Bay 9 Di 52.55N 9.25W
Bathurst 38 Ib 76.00N 100.30W
Bathurst [Austl.] 59 Jf 33.25S 149.35 E
Bathurst [N.B.-Can.] 39 Me 47.36N 65.39W
Bathurst, Cape- 38 Gb 70.35N 128.00W
Bathurst Inlet 38 Ic 68.10N 108.50W
Bathurst Inlet 39 Ic 66.50N 108.01W
Bathurst Island 57 Ef 11.35S 130.25 E
Bati 35 Gc 11.13N 40.01 E
Batié 34 Ed 9.53N 2.55W
Bāṯin, Wādī al- 23 Gc 30.25N 47.35 E
Batman 23 Fb 37.52N 41.07 E
Batman 24 Id 37.45N 41.00 E
Batna [3] 32 Ib 35.10N 6.00 E
Batna 31 He 35.34N 6.11 E
Ba To 25 Lf 14.46N 108.44 E
Bato Bato 26 Ge 5.06N 119.50 E
Batoka 36 Ef 16.47S 27.15 E
Baton Rouge 39 Jf 30.23N 91.11W
Batopilas 48 Fd 27.01N 107.44W
Batouri 34 He 4.26N 14.22 E
Batovi 55 Fb 15.53S 53.24W
Batovi, Coxilha de- 55 Ej 30.33S 54.27W
Båtsfjord 7 Ga 70.38N 29.44 E
Bat-Sumber 27 Ib 48.25N 106.42 E
Batticaloa 25 Gg 7.43N 81.42 E
Batti Maly 25 Ig 8.50N 92.51 E
Battipaglia 14 Ij 40.37N 14.58 E
Battle 12 Cd 50.55N 0.30 E
Battle 42 Gf 52.42N 108.15W
Battle Creek 46 Kb 48.36N 109.11W
Battle Creek 43 Jc 42.19N 85.11W
Battle Harbour 39 Nd 52.17N 55.35W
Battle Mountain 43 Dc 40.38N 116.56W
Battonya 10 Rj 46.17N 21.01 E
Battowia Island 51n Bb 12.58N 61.09W
Batu 35 Fd 6.59N 39.37 E
Batu, Kepulauan- = Batu Islands (EN) 21 Lj 0.18S 98.28 E
Batuasa 26 Jg 3.32S 130.08 E
Batuata, Pulau- 26 Hh 6.12S 122.42 E
Batudaka, Pulau- 26 Hg 0.28S 121.48 E
Batui 26 Hg 1.17S 122.33 E
Batu Islands (EN) = Batu, Kepulauan- 21 Lj 0.18S 98.28 E
Batumi 6 Kg 41.38N 41.38 E
Batu Pahat 26 Df 1.51N 102.56 E
Baturaja 26 Dg 4.08S 104.10 E
Baturino 20 De 57.45N 85.12 E
Baturité 54 Kd 4.20S 38.53W
Batz, Ile de- 11 Bf 48.45N 4.01W
Bau 26 Ff 1.25N 110.09 E
Baubau 22 Oj 5.28S 122.38 E
Baucau 26 Ih 8.27S 126.27 E
Bauchi 31 Hg 10.19N 9.50 E
Bauchi [2] 34 Hc 10.40N 10.00 E
Bauchi Plateau 34 Gc 10.00N 9.30 E
Baud 11 Cg 47.52N 3.01W
Baudette 45 Ib 48.43N 94.36W
Baudo, Serrania de- 54 Cb 6.00N 77.05W
Baudour, Saint-Ghislain- 12 Fd 50.29N 3.49 E
Baugé 11 Fg 47.33N 0.06W
Bauges 11 Mi 45.38N 6.10 E
Baúl, Cerro- 48 Ii 17.38N 100.19W
Baula 26 Hg 4.09S 121.41 E
Bauld, Cape- 38 Nd 51.38N 55.25W
Bauman Fiord 42 Ia 77.45N 86.00W
Baume-les-Dames 11 Mg 47.21N 6.22 E
Baunach 10 Gg 49.59N 10.51 E
Baunani 63a Ec 9.08S 160.51 E
Baunei 14 Dj 40.02N 9.40 E
Baures 54 Ff 13.35S 63.35W
Bauru 53 Lh 22.19S 49.04W
Baús 55 Fd 18.19S 53.10W
Baús, Serra dos- 55 Fd 18.20S 53.25W
Bauska 7 Fh 56.24N 24.13 E
Bautzen/Budyšin 10 Ke 51.11N 14.26 E
Bavaria (EN) = Bayern [2] 10 Hg 49.00N 11.30 E
Bavaria (EN) = Bayern 5 Hf 49.00N 11.30 E
Bavarian Forest (EN) = Bayerischer Wald 10 Ig 49.00N 12.55 E
Bavay 12 Fd 50.18N 3.47 E
Båven 8 Ge 59.00N 16.55 E
Bavispe 48 Eb 30.24N 108.50W
Bavispe, Río de- 48 Ec 29.15N 109.11W
Bavly 7 Mi 54.26N 53.18 E
Bawah, Pulau- 26 Ef 2.31N 106.03 E
Bawal, Pulau- 26 Fg 2.44S 110.06 E
Bawe 58 Ee 2.59S 134.43 E
Bawean, Pulau- 26 Fh 5.46S 112.40 E
Bawku 34 Ec 11.03N 0.15W
Baxian 27 Kd 39.03N 116.24 E
Baxol 27 Ge 30.07N 96.56 E
Bay [3] 35 Ge 2.50N 43.30 E
Bay/Baicheng 27 Dc 41.46N 81.52 E
Bayamo 47 Id 20.23N 76.39W
Bayamón 49 Nd 18.24N 66.09W
Bayan 28 Ia 46.05N 127.24 E
Bayanbulak 27 Dc 43.05N 84.05 E
Bayanga 35 Be 2.53N 16.19 E
Bayan Gol 27 Gd 37.18N 96.50 E
Bayan Gol → Dengkou 22 Me 40.25N 106.59 E
Bayan Har Shan 21 Lf 34.20N 97.00 E
Bayan Har Shankou 27 Ge 34.06N 97.38 E
Bayan Hot → Alxa Zuoqi 27 Id 38.50N 105.32 E
Bayan Hure → Chen Barag Qi 27 Kb 49.21N 119.25 E
Bayan Huxu → Horqin Youyi Zhongqi 27 Lb 45.04N 121.27 E
Bayano, Lago de- 49 Hi 9.00N 78.30W
Bayan Obo 27 Ic 41.50N 109.58 E
Bayan Qagan 28 Ga 46.11N 123.59 E
Bayan Qagan → Qahar Youyi Houqi 28 Bd 41.28N 113.10 E
Bayan Ul Hot → Xi Ujimqin Qi 27 Kc 44.31N 117.33 E
Bayas 48 Gf 23.32N 104.50W
Bayat 24 Fb 40.39N 34.15 E
Bayauca 55 Bl 34.51S 61.18W
Bayawan 26 He 9.20N 123.00 E
Bayāẕ 24 Pg 30.42N 55.28 E
Bayāzeh 24 Pf 30.42N 55.28 E
Baybay 26 Hd 10.41N 124.48 E
Bayburt 23 Fa 40.16N 40.15 E
Bay City [Mi.-U.S.] 43 Kc 43.36N 83.53W
Bay City [Tx.-U.S.] 43 Hf 29.09N 95.39W
Bayerische Alpen 10 Hi 47.30N 11.30 E
Bayerischer Wald = Bavarian Forest (EN) 10 Ig 49.00N 12.55 E
Bayern = Bavaria (EN) 5 Hf 49.00N 11.30 E
Bayern = Bavaria (EN) [2] 10 Hg 49.00N 11.30 E
Bayes, Cap- 63b Be 20.57S 165.25 E
Bayeux 11 Fe 49.16N 0.42W
Bayfield 45 Kc 46.49N 90.49W
Bay Fiord 42 Ja 79.00N 84.00W
Baygorria 55 Dk 32.52S 56.44W
Baygorria, Lago Artificial de- 55 Dk 33.05S 57.00W
Bayḥān al Qişāb 33 Ig 14.48N 45.44 E
Bayındır 24 Bc 38.13N 27.40 E
Bayjī 24 Je 34.56N 43.29 E
Bay Minette 44 Dj 30.53N 87.47W
Baynūnah 24 Ok 23.50N 52.50 E
Bayombong 26 Hc 16.29N 121.09 E
Bayona 13 Db 42.07N 8.51W
Bayonnaise Seamount (EN) 57 Jf 12.00S 179.30W
Bayonne 6 Fg 43.29N 1.29W
Bayou Bodcau Lake 45 Jj 32.58N 93.30W
Bayou D'Arbonne Lake 45 Jj 32.45N 92.27W
Bayramiç 15 Jj 39.48N 26.37 E
Bayreuth 10 Hg 49.57N 11.35 E
Bayrūt = Beirut (EN) 22 Ff 33.53N 35.30 E
Bay Saint Louis 45 Lk 30.19N 89.20W
Bay Springs 45 Lk 31.59N 89.17W
Bayt al Faqīh 23 Fg 14.31N 43.17 E
Baytik Shan 27 Fb 45.15N 90.50 E
Bayt Laḥm = Bethlehem (EN) 24 Fg 31.43N 35.12 E
Baytown 43 If 29.44N 94.58W
Bayuda Desert (EN) = Bayyūḍah, Şaḥrā'- 30 Kg 18.00N 33.00 E
Bayunglencir 26 Dg 2.03S 103.41 E
Bayview 46 Gc 48.00N 116.30W
Bay View 62 Gc 39.26S 176.52 E
Bayy al Kabīr 33 Cc 31.11N 15.53 E
Bayyūḍah, Şaḥrā'- = Bayuda Desert (EN) 30 Kg 18.00N 33.00 E
Baza 13 Jg 37.29N 2.46W
Baza, Sierra de- 13 Jg 37.15N 2.45W
Bazardjuzju, Gora- 5 Kg 41.13N 47.51 E
Bazaruto, Ilha do- 37 Fd 21.40S 35.25 E
Bazas 11 Fj 44.26N 0.13W
Bazhong 27 Ie 31.54N 106.42 E
Bazoches-sur-Vesle 12 Fe 49.19N 3.37 E
Baztán 13 Ka 43.09N 1.31W
Beach 43 Gb 46.55N 103.52W
Beachy Head 9 Nk 50.44N 0.16 E
Beacon 44 Ke 41.31N 73.59W
Beaconsfield [Austl.] 59 Jh 41.12S 146.48 E
Beaconsfield [Eng.-U.K.] 12 Bc 51.36N 0.38W
Beagle, Canal- 56 Gh 54.53S 68.10W
Beagle Gulf 59 Gb 12.00S 130.20 E
Bealach an Doirin/Ballaghaderreen 9 Eh 53.55N 8.35W
Béalanana 37 Hb 14.33S 48.44 E
Béal an Átha/Ballina 9 Dg 54.07N 9.09W
Béal an Bheara/Gweebarra Bay 9 Eg 54.52N 8.20W
Béal Átha Fhirdhia/Ardee 9 Gh 53.52N 6.33W
Béal Átha hAmhnais/Ballyhaunis 9 Eh 53.46N 8.46W

Index Symbols

[1] Independent Nation
[2] State, Region
[3] District, County
[4] Municipality
[5] Colony, Dependency
Continent
Physical Region
Historical or Cultural Region
Mount, Mountain
Volcano
Hill
Mountains, Mountain Range
Hills, Escarpment
Plateau, Upland
Pass, Gap
Plain, Lowland
Delta
Salt Flat
Valley, Canyon
Crater, Cave
Karst Features
Depression
Polder
Desert, Dunes
Forest, Woods
Heath, Steppe
Oasis
Cape, Point
Coast, Beach
Cliff
Peninsula
Isthmus
Sandbank
Island
Atoll
Rock, Reef
Islands, Archipelago
Rocks, Reefs
Coral Reef
Well, Spring
Geyser
River, Stream
Waterfall Rapids
River Mouth, Estuary
Lake
Salt Lake
Intermittent Lake
Reservoir
Swamp, Pond
Canal
Glacier
Ice Shelf, Pack Ice
Ocean
Sea
Gulf, Bay
Strait, Fjord
Lagoon
Bank
Seamount
Tablemount
Ridge
Shelf
Basin
Escarpment, Sea Scarp
Fracture
Trench, Abyss
National Park, Reserve
Point of Interest
Recreation Site
Cave, Cavern
Historic Site
Ruins
Wall, Walls
Church, Abbey
Temple
Scientific Station
Airport
Port
Lighthouse
Mine
Tunnel
Dam, Bridge

Béal Atha na Muice/ Swinford 9 Eh 53.57N 8.57W
Béal Átha na Sluaighe/ Ballinasloe 9 Eh 53.20N 8.13W
Béal Átha Seanaidh/ Ballyshannon 9 Eg 54.30N 8.11W
Beale, Cape- 46 Cb 48.44N 125.20W
Béal Easa/Foxford 9 Dh 53.59N 9.07W
Béal Feirste/Belfast 6 Fe 54.35N 5.55W
Beal Range 59 Ie 25.30S 141.30 E
Béal Tairbirt/Belturbet 9 Fg 54.06N 7.26W
Beanna Boirche/Mourne Mountains 9 Gg 54.10N 6.04W
Beannchar/Bangor 9 Hg 54.40N 5.40W
Beanntrai/Bantry 9 Dj 51.41N 9.27W
Bear Bay 42 Ia 75.45N 86.30W
Beardmore 45 Mb 49.36N 87.57W
Beardstown 45 Kg 39.59N 90.26W
Bear Island (EN) = Bjørnöya 5 Ha 74.30N 19.00 E
Bear Islands (EN) = Medveži, Ostrova- 21 Sb 70.52N 161.26 E
Bear Lake 43 Ec 42.00N 111.20W
Bear Lodge Mountains 45 Dd 44.35N 104.15W
Béarn 11 Fk 43.20N 0.45W
Bearpaw Mountains 46 Kb 48.15N 109.30W
Bear Peninsula 66 Of 74.36S 110.50W
Bear River 46 If 41.30N 112.08W
Bearskin Lake 42 If 53.57N 90.59W
Beās 25 Eb 31.10N 74.59 E
Beas de Segura 13 Jf 38.15N 2.53W
Beata, Cabo- 47 Je 17.36N 71.25W
Beata, Isla- 49 Le 17.35N 71.31W
Beata Ridge (EN) 47 Je 16.00N 72.30W
Beatrice 43 Hc 40.16N 96.44W
Beatrice, Cape- 59 Hb 14.15S 137.00 E
Beatton 42 Fe 56.06N 120.22W
Beatton River 42 Fe 56.10N 120.25W
Beatty 43 Dd 36.54N 116.46W
Beattyville 44 Ia 48.52N 77.10W
Beatys Butte 46 Fe 42.23N 119.20W
Beau-Bassin 37a Bb 20.13S 57.27 E
Beaucaire 11 Kk 43.48N 4.38 E
Beaucamps-le-Vieux 12 De 49.50N 1.47 E
Beaucanton 44 Ha 49.05N 79.15W
Beauce 11 Hf 48.22N 1.50 E
Beaudesert 59 Ke 27.59S 153.00 E
Beaufort [Mala.] 26 Ge 5.20N 115.45 E
Beaufort [S.C.-U.S.] 44 Gi 32.26N 80.40W
Beaufort/Befort 12 Ie 49.50N 6.18 E
Beaufort, Massif de- 11 Mi 45.50N 6.40 E
Beaufort Island 66 Kf 76.57S 166.56 E
Beaufort Sea 67 Eb 73.00N 140.00W
Beaufort West 31 Jl 32.20S 22.33 E
Beaugency 11 Hg 47.47N 1.38 E
Beaujolais, Monts du- 11 Kh 46.00N 4.22 E
Beauly 9 Id 57.29N 4.29W
Beaumesnil 12 Ce 49.01N 0.43 E
Beaumetz-lès-Loges 12 Ed 50.14N 2.39 E
Beaumont [Bel.] 12 Gd 50.14N 4.14 E
Beaumont [Fr.] 11 Gj 44.46N 0.46 E
Beaumont [Fr.] 11 Ee 49.40N 1.51W
Beaumont [Fr.] 12 Hf 48.51N 5.47 E
Beaumont [Ms.-U.S.] 45 Lk 31.11N 88.55W
Beaumont [N.Z.] 62 Cf 45.49S 169.32 E
Beaumont [Tx.-U.S.] 39 Jf 30.05N 94.06W
Beaumont-de-Lomagne 11 Gk 43.53N 0.59 E
Beaumont-en-Argonne 12 He 49.32N 5.03 E
Beaumont-le-Roger 12 Ce 49.05N 0.47 E
Beaumont-sur-Oise 12 Ee 49.08N 2.17 E
Beaumont-sur-Sarthe 11 Gf 48.13N 0.08 E
Beaune 11 Kg 47.02N 4.50 E
Beaupré 44 Lb 47.03N 70.53W
Beauraing 12 Gd 50.07N 4.48 E
Beaurepaire 11 Li 45.20N 5.03 E
Beausejour 42 Hf 50.04N 96.33W
Beautemps Beaupré 63b Ce 20.25S 166.08 E
Beauvais 11 Ie 49.26N 2.05 E
Beauval 12 Ed 50.06N 2.20 E
Beauvoir-sur-Mer 11 Dh 46.55N 2.03W
Beaver [Ak.-U.S.] 40 Jc 66.22N 147.24W
Beaver [Ok.-U.S.] 45 Fh 36.48N 100.30W
Beaver [Ut.-U.S.] 43 Ed 38.17N 112.38W
Beaver Creek [Co.-U.S.] 45 Ef 40.20N 103.33W
Beaver Creek [U.S.] 45 Ec 47.20N 103.39W
Beaver Creek [U.S.] 45 Gf 40.04N 99.20W
Beaver Creek [U.S.] 45 Ee 43.25N 103.59W
Beaver Dam 45 Le 43.28N 88.50W
Beaver Falls 44 Ge 40.45N 80.21W
Beaverhead Mountains 46 Id 45.00N 113.20W
Beaver Island 44 Ec 45.40N 85.31W
Beaver Lake 45 Jh 36.20N 93.55W
Beaver River [U.S.] 45 Gh 36.10N 98.45W
Beaver River [Ut.-U.S.] 46 Ig 39.10N 112.57W
Beaverton 46 Dd 45.29N 122.48W
Beāwar 25 Ec 26.06N 74.19 E
Bebedouro 56 Kb 20.56S 48.28W
Becan 48 Oh 18.37N 89.35W
Becanchén 48 Oh 19.50N 89.22W
Beccles 9 Oi 52.28N 1.34 E
Bečej 15 Dd 45.37N 20.03 E
Beceni 15 Jd 45.23N 26.47 E
Becerreá 13 Eb 42.51N 7.10W
Becerro, Cayos- 49 Ff 15.57N 83.17W
Béchar 31 Ge 31.37N 2.13W
Béchar [3] 32 Gd 30.00N 2.00W
Becharof Lake 40 He 58.00N 156.30W
Bechet 15 Gf 43.46N 23.57 E
Bechevin Bay 40 Ge 55.00N 163.27W
Bechyně 10 Kg 49.18N 14.28 E
Beckingen 12 Ie 49.24N 6.42 E
Beckley 43 Kd 37.46N 81.12W
Beckum 10 Ee 51.45N 8.02 E
Beckumer Berge 12 Kc 51.43N 8.10 E
Beclean 15 Hb 47.11N 24.11 E
Bédarieux 11 Jk 43.37N 3.09 E
Bedburg-Hau 12 Ic 51.46N 6.11 E
Bedele 35 Fd 8.27N 36.22 E
Bedesa 35 Gd 8.53N 40.46 E
Bedford 9 Mi 52.10N 0.50W
Bedford [Eng.-U.K.] 9 Mi 52.08N 0.29W
Bedford [In.-U.S.] 44 Df 38.52N 86.29W
Bedford [Pa.-U.S.] 44 He 40.00N 78.31W
Bedford [Va.-U.S.] 44 Hg 37.20N 79.31W
Bedford Level 9 Ni 52.30N 0.05 E
Bedford Point 51p Bb 12.13N 61.36W
Bedfordshire [3] 9 Mi 52.05N 0.20W
Bednja 14 Kd 46.18N 16.45 E
Bednodemjanovsk 16 Mc 53.55N 43.12 E
Bedourie 59 Hd 24.21S 139.28 E
Bedum 12 Ia 53.18N 6.39 E
Beech Grove 44 Df 39.43N 86.03W
Beecroft Head 59 Kg 35.01S 150.50 E
Beef Island 51a Db 18.27N 64.31W
Beelitz 10 Id 52.14N 12.58 E
Beemster 12 Gb 52.34N 4.56 E
Beerfelden 12 Ke 49.34N 8.59 E
Beernem 12 Fc 51.09N 3.20 E
Beerse 12 Gc 51.19N 4.52 E
Beersel 12 Gd 50.46N 4.18 E
Beersheba (EN) = Be'er Shevà 23 Dc 31.14N 34.47 E
Be'er Shevà = Beersheba (EN) 23 Dc 31.14N 34.47 E
Beerze 12 Hc 51.36N 5.19 E
Beeskow 10 Kd 52.10N 14.14 E
Beestekraal 37 De 25.23S 27.38 E
Beeston 9 Li 52.56N 1.12W
Beethoven Peninsula 66 Qf 71.40S 73.45W
Beetsterzwaag, Opsterland- 12 Ia 53.03N 6.04 E
Beeville 43 Hf 28.24N 97.45W
Befale 36 Db 0.28N 20.58 E
Befandriana Nord 37 Hc 15.15S 48.32 E
Befandriana Sud 37 Gd 22.06S 43.54 E
Befori 36 Db 0.06N 22.17 E
Befort/Beaufort 12 Ie 49.50N 6.18 E
Bega 15 Dd 45.13N 20.19 E
Bega 58 Fh 36.40S 149.50 E
Bégard 11 Cf 48.38N 3.18W
Begejski kanal 15 Dd 45.27N 20.27 E
Beggars Point 51d Bb 17.10N 61.48W
Bègle 11 Fj 44.48N 0.32W
Begna 7 Bf 60.35N 10.00 E
Begoml 8 Mj 54.46N 28.14 E
Begunicy 8 Me 59.31N 29.30 E
Behābād 24 Pg 31.52N 55.57 E
Behbehān 23 Hc 30.35N 50.14 E
Behring Point 49 Ia 24.27N 77.43W
Behshahr 23 Hb 36.43N 53.34 E
Bei'an 22 Oe 48.16N 126.29 E
Beibu Wan = Tonkin, Gulf of- (EN) 21 Mh 20.00N 108.00 E
Beida He 27 Gc 40.18N 99.01 E
Beihai 22 Mg 21.31N 109.07 E
Bei Hulsan Hu 27 Gd 36.55N 95.55 E
Bei Jiang 27 Jg 23.02N 112.58 E
Beijing = Peking (EN) 22 Nf 39.55N 116.23 E
Beijing Shi (Pei-ching Shih) [4] 27 Kc 40.15N 116.30 E
Beïla 32 Df 18.10N 15.53W
Beilen 12 Ib 52.52N 6.32 E
Beiliutang He 28 Eg 34.12N 119.33 E
Beilrstroom 12 Ib 52.41N 6.12 E
Beilsteim 12 Jd 50.07N 7.15 E
Beilu He 27 Fe 34.34N 94.00 E
Beinamar 35 Bd 8.40N 15.23 E
Beine-Nauroy 12 Ge 49.15N 4.13 E
Beipiao 27 Lc 41.49N 120.45 E
Beira 31 Kj 19.50S 34.52 E
Beira Alta 13 Ed 40.40N 7.35W
Beira Baixa 13 Ee 39.55N 7.30W
Beira Litoral 13 Dd 40.15N 8.25W
Beiru He 28 Bh 33.40N 113.35 E
Beirut (EN) = Bayrūt 22 Ff 33.53N 35.30 E
Bei Shan 21 Le 41.30N 96.00 E
Beitstad 7 Cd 64.05N 11.22 E
Beiuş 15 Fc 46.40N 22.21 E
Beiwei Tan 27 Kg 21.10N 116.10 E
Beizhen [China] 27 Kd 37.24N 117.59 E
Beizhen [China] 27 Fd 41.36N 121.47 E
Beja 13 Ef 38.01N 7.52W
Beja [2] 13 Eg 37.58N 7.50W
Bejaïa [3] 32 Ib 36.40N 5.10 E
Bejaïa 31 He 36.45N 5.05 E
Bejaia, Golfe de- 13 Rh 36.45N 5.20 E
Béjar 13 Gd 40.23N 5.46W
Beji 25 Dc 29.47N 67.58 E
Bejneu 19 Ff 45.15N 55.05 E
Bejsug 16 Kf 46.02N 38.35 E
Bejsugski Liman 16 Kf 46.05N 38.25 E
Bekabad 19 Gg 40.13N 69.14 E
Bekasi 26 Eh 6.14S 106.59 E
Bekdaš 19 Fg 41.31N 52.40 E
Békés 10 Rj 46.46N 21.08 E
Békés [2] 10 Qj 46.45N 21.10 E
Békéscsaba 10 Rj 46.41N 21.06 E
Bekilli 15 Mk 38.14N 29.26 E
Bekily 37 Hd 24.12S 45.18 E
Bekkai 29a Db 43.25N 145.07 E
Bekoji 35 Fd 7.32N 39.15 E
Bekopaka 37 Gc 19.08S 44.45 E
Bekovo 16 Mc 52.29N 43.43 E
Bela [India] 25 Gc 25.56N 81.59 E
Bela [Pak.] 25 Dc 26.14N 66.19 E
Bélabo 34 He 4.52N 13.10 E
Bela Crkva 15 Ee 44.54N 21.26 E
Bela Dila 25 Ge 18.40N 80.55 E
Bela Floresta 55 Ge 20.36S 51.16W
Belaga 26 Ff 2.42N 113.47 E
Belaja [R.S.F.S.R.] 20 Mc 65.30N 173.15 E
Belaja [R.S.F.S.R.] 5 Ld 56.00N 54.32 E
Belaja [R.S.F.S.R.] 16 Kg 45.03N 39.25 E
Belaja Cerkov 6 Jf 49.49N 30.07 E
Belaja Gora 20 Jc 68.30N 146.15 E
Belaja Holunica 19 Fd 58.53N 50.50 E
Belaja Kalitva 19 Ef 48.09N 40.49 E
Bela Krajina 14 Je 45.35N 15.15 E
Bela Lorena 55 Ib 15.13S 46.01W
Belang 26 Hf 0.57N 124.47 E
Bela Palanka 15 Ff 43.13N 22.19 E
Belarbi 13 Li 35.09N 0.27W
Belaruskaja Sovetskaja Socialističnaja Respublika /Belorusskaja SSR [2] 19 Ce 53.50N 28.00 E
Belasica 15 Fh 41.21N 22.50 E
Belau = Palau (EN) 14 Di 41.11N 9.23 E
Bela Vista [Braz.] 54 Gh 22.06S 56.31W
Bela Vista [Braz.] 55 Dc 17.37S 57.01W
Bela Vista [Moz.] 37 Ee 26.20S 32.40 E
Belawan 26 Cf 3.47N 98.41 E
Běła Woda/Weißwasser 10 Ke 51.31N 14.38 E
Belayan 26 Gg 0.14S 116.36 E
Belbo 14 Cf 44.54N 8.31 E
Bełchatów 10 Pe 51.22N 19.21 E
Belcher Channel 42 Ia 77.20N 94.30W
Belcher Islands 38 Ld 56.20N 79.30W
Belchite 13 Lc 41.18N 0.45W
Belcy 19 Cf 47.46N 27.55 E
Bełczyna 10 Ne 51.25N 17.50 E
Belebej 19 Fe 54.10N 54.07 E
Belecke, Warstein- 12 Kc 51.29N 8.20 E
Beled 10 Ni 47.28N 17.06 E
Beled Wēyne 31 Lh 4.47N 45.12 E
Bélel 34 Hd 7.03N 14.26 E
Belém [Moz.] 37 Fb 14.08S 35.58 E
Belém [Braz.] 53 Lf 1.27S 48.29W
Belem [Mex.] 48 Dd 27.45N 110.28W
Belém de São Francisco 54 Ke 8.46S 38.58W
Belen 43 Fe 34.40N 106.46W
Belén [Arg.] 56 Gc 27.39S 67.02W
Belén [Nic.] 49 Eh 11.30N 85.53W
Belén [Par.] 55 Df 23.30S 57.06W
Belén [Ur.] 55 Dj 30.47S 57.47W
Belén, Cuchilla de- 55 Dj 30.55S 56.30W
Belén de Escobar 55 Cl 34.21S 58.47W
Belene 15 If 43.39N 25.07 E
Bélep, Iles- 57 Hf 19.45S 163.40 E
Beles 35 Fc 10.55N 35.10 E
Belev 16 Jc 53.50N 36.10 E
Beleye 35 Fc 11.24N 36.10 E
Belfast [Me.-U.S.] 44 Mc 44.27N 69.01W
Belfast [S.Afr.] 37 Ee 25.43S 30.03 E
Belfast/Béal Feirste 6 Fe 54.35N 5.55W
Belfast Lough/Loch Lao 9 Hg 54.40N 5.50W
Belfield 45 Ec 46.53N 103.12W
Belford 9 Lf 55.36N 1.49W
Belfort 11 Mg 47.45N 7.00 E
Belgaum 22 Jh 15.52N 74.30 E
Belgica Bank (EN) 67 Ld 78.28N 15.00W
Belgicafjella 66 Df 72.35S 31.10 E
België/Belgique = Belgium (EN) [1] 6 Ge 50.30N 4.30 E
Belgique/België = Belgium (EN) [1] 6 Ge 50.30N 4.30 E
Belgium (EN) = België/Belgique [1] 6 Ge 50.30N 4.30 E
Belgium (EN) = Belgique/België [1] 6 Ge 50.30N 4.30 E
Belgorod 6 Je 50.36N 36.35 E
Belgorod-Dnestrovski 19 Df 46.12N 30.17 E
Belgorodskaja Oblast [3] 19 De 50.45N 37.30 E
Belgrade (EN) = Beograd 6 Ig 44.50N 20.30 E
Bel Hairane 32 Ic 31.17N 6.20 E
Beli 34 Hd 7.52N 10.58 E
Belice 14 Gm 37.35N 12.52 E
Beli Drim 15 Dg 42.05N 20.20 E
Belidži 16 Pi 41.53N 48.20 E
Beli Lom 15 Jf 43.41N 26.00 E
Beli Manastir 14 Me 45.46N 18.37 E
Belimbegovo 15 Eh 42.00N 21.35 E
Belin 11 Fj 44.30N 0.47W
Belinga 36 Bb 1.04N 13.12 E
Belinski 16 Mc 52.58N 43.29 E
Belinyu 26 Eg 1.38S 105.46 E
Beliş 15 Gc 46.39N 23.02 E
Beli Timok 15 Ff 43.55N 22.18 E
Belize [1] 39 Kh 17.15N 88.45W
Belize (British Honduras) 49 Ce 17.35N 88.35W
Belize City 39 Kh 17.30N 88.12W
Belize River 49 Ce 17.32N 88.14W
Beljajevka 16 Gf 46.29N 30.14 E
Beljanica 15 Ee 44.07N 21.43 E
Belka 8 Mg 57.40N 29.47 E
Belkovski, Ostrov- 20 Ia 75.30N 136.00 E
Bellac 11 Hh 46.07N 1.03 E
Bella Coola 42 Ef 52.22N 126.46W
Bellagio 14 De 45.59N 9.15 E
Bellaire [Oh.-U.S.] 44 Ge 40.02N 80.46W
Bellaire [Tx.-U.S.] 45 Il 29.43N 95.28W
Bellaria-Igea Marina 14 Gf 44.09N 12.28 E
Bellary 22 Jh 15.09N 76.56 E
Bella Unión 55 Dj 30.15S 57.35W
Bella Vista [Arg.] 56 Ic 28.30S 59.03W
Bella Vista [Par.] 55 Df 22.08S 56.31W
Bellavista, Capo- 14 Dk 39.56N 9.43 E
Bell Bay 42 Jb 71.10N 84.55W
Belle-Anse 49 Kd 18.14N 72.04W
Belledonne 11 Mi 45.18N 6.08 E
Bellefontaine [Mart.] 51h Ab 14.40N 61.10W
Bellefontaine [Oh.-U.S.] 44 Fe 40.22N 83.45W
Belle Fourche 43 Gc 44.40N 103.51W
Belle Fourche River 45 Ed 44.26N 102.19W
Bellegarde 11 If 47.59N 2.26 E
Bellegarde-sur-Valserine 11 Lh 46.06N 5.49 E
Belle Glade 44 Gl 26.41N 80.40W
Belle Ile 5 Ff 47.19N 3.11W
Belle Isle 42 Lf 51.55N 55.20W
Belle Isle, Strait of- 38 Nd 51.35N 56.30W
Bellencombre 12 De 49.42N 1.14 E
Belleplaine 51q Ab 13.15N 59.34W
Belleville [Fr.] 11 Kh 46.06N 4.45 E
Belleville [Il.-U.S.] 45 Lg 38.31N 90.00W
Belleville [Ks.-U.S.] 45 Hg 39.49N 97.38W
Belleville [Ont.-Can.] 42 Jh 44.10N 77.23W
Bellevue [Nb.-U.S.] 45 If 41.09N 95.54W
Bellevue [Wa.-U.S.] 46 Dc 47.37N 122.12W
Belley 11 Li 45.46N 5.41 E
Bellheim 12 Ke 49.12N 8.17 E
Bellin → Kangirsuk 39 Lc 60.00N 70.01W
Bellingham [Eng.-U.K.] 9 Kf 55.09N 2.16W
Bellingham [Wa.-U.S.] 39 Ge 48.46N 122.29W
Bellingsfors 8 Ef 58.59N 12.15 E
Bellingshausen 66 Re 62.12S 58.56W
Bellingshausen Ice Shelf 66 Ce 71.00S 89.00W
Bellingshausen Sea (EN) 66 Pf 71.00S 85.00W
Bellinzona 14 Dd 46.11N 9.02 E
Bello 54 Cb 6.19N 75.34W
Bellocq 55 Bl 35.55S 61.32W
Bellona, Récifs- 57 Gg 21.00S 159.00 E
Bellona Island 60 Fj 11.17S 159.47 E
Bellot Strait 42 Ib 72.00N 94.30W
Bellow Falls 44 Kd 43.08N 72.28W
Bell Peninsula 42 Jd 63.45N 81.30W
Bell River 42 Jg 49.49N 77.39W
Bell Rock → Inchcape 9 Ke 56.26N 2.24W
Bellsund 41 Nc 77.39N 14.15 E
Belluno 14 Gd 46.09N 12.13 E
Bell Ville 56 Hd 32.37S 62.42W
Bellville 37 Bf 33.53S 18.36 E
Belmond 45 Je 42.51N 93.37W
Belmont 44 Hd 42.14N 78.02W
Belmonte [Braz.] 54 Kg 15.51S 38.54W
Belmonte [Port.] 13 Ed 40.21N 7.21W
Belmonte [Sp.] 13 Je 39.34N 2.42W
Belmopan 39 Kh 17.15N 88.46W
Beloeil 12 Fd 50.35N 3.43 E
Belogorsk [R.S.F.S.R.] 22 Od 50.57N 128.25 E
Belogorsk [Ukr.-U.S.S.R.] 16 Ig 45.01N 34.33 E
Belogradčik 15 Ff 43.38N 22.41 E
Belogradčiški 15 Ff 43.38N 22.28 E
Belo Horizonte 53 Lg 19.55S 43.56W
Beloit [Ks.-U.S.] 45 Gg 39.28N 98.06W
Beloit [Wi.-U.S.] 43 Jc 42.31N 89.02W
Belojarovo 20 Hf 51.35N 128.55 E
Belojarski 19 Gc 63.40N 66.45 E
Beloje More = White Sea (EN) 5 Kb 66.00N 44.00 E
Beloje Ozero = White Lake (EN) 5 Jc 60.11N 37.35 E
Belokany 16 Oi 41.43N 46.28 E
Belomorsk 6 Jc 64.29N 34.43 E
Belomorsko-Baltijski Kanal = White Sea-Baltic Canal (EN) 5 Jc 63.30N 34.48 E
Belomorsko-Kulojskoje Plato 7 Jd 65.20N 41.50 E
Beloozersk 16 Dc 52.28N 25.13 E
Belopolje 19 De 51.09N 34.18 E
Belorečensk 16 Kg 44.43N 39.52 E
Beloreck 19 Fe 53.58N 58.24 E
Belorusskaja Grjada 16 Ec 53.50N 27.00 E
Belorusskaja Sovetskaja Socialističeskaja Respublika [2] 19 Ce 53.50N 28.00 E
Belorusskaja SSR/ Belaruskaja Sovetskaja Socialistyčnaja Respublika [2] 19 Ce 53.50N 28.00 E
Belorusskaja SSR = Byelorussian SSR (EN) [2] 19 Ce 53.50N 28.00 E
Belo-sur-Mer 37 Gd 20.44S 44.00 E
Belo-sur-Tsiribihina 37 Gc 19.39S 44.32 E
Belot, Lac- 42 Ec 66.50N 126.20W
Belovo 20 Df 54.25N 86.18 E
Belovodsk 16 Ke 49.10N 39.33 E
Belovodskoe 18 Jc 42.47N 74.13 E
Belozersk 19 Dd 60.03N 37.48 E
Belper 12 Aa 53.02N 1.28W
Belted Range 46 Gh 37.25N 116.10W
Belton [Mo.-U.S.] 45 Ig 38.49N 94.32W
Belton [Tx.-U.S.] 45 Hk 31.04N 97.28W
Belton Lake 45 Hk 31.08N 97.32W
Belturbet/Béal Tairbirt 9 Fg 54.06N 7.26W
Beluha 21 Ke 49.48N 86.35 E
Belvedere Marittimo 14 Jk 39.37N 15.52 E
Belvidere 45 Le 42.15N 88.50W
Bely 7 Hi 55.50N 32.58 E
Bely, Ostrov- = Bely Island (EN) 21 Jb 73.10N 70.45 E
Belyando River 59 Jd 21.38S 146.50 E
Bely Čeremoš 15 Ia 48.06N 25.04 E
Bely Island (EN) = Bely, Ostrov- 21 Jb 73.10N 70.45 E
Bely Jar 20 De 58.26N 85.03 E
Belyje Berega 16 Ic 53.12N 34.42 E
Belz 16 Dd 50.23N 24.03 E
Bełżec 10 Tf 50.24N 23.26 E
Belzoni 45 Kj 33.11N 90.29W
Bełżyce 10 Se 51.11N 22.18 E
Bemaraha, Plateau de- 30 Lj 19.00S 45.15 E
Bembe 36 Bd 7.02S 14.18 E
Bembéréké 34 Fc 10.13N 2.40 E
Bembézar 13 Gg 37.45N 5.13W
Bembridge 12 Ad 50.41N 1.05W
Bemidji 43 Ib 47.29N 94.53W
Ben 24 Nf 32.32N 50.45 E
Benāb 23 Gb 37.18N 46.05 E
Benabarre/Benavarn 13 Mb 42.07N 0.29 E
Bena Dibele 36 Dc 4.07S 22.50 E
Bénaize 11 Hh 46.34N 1.04 E
Benalla 59 Jg 36.33S 145.59 E
Benares → Vārānasi 22 Kg 25.20N 83.00 E
Benasc/Benasque 13 Mb 42.36N 0.32 E
Benasque/Benasc 13 Mb 42.36N 0.32 E
Benavarn/Benabarre 13 Mb 42.07N 0.29 E
Benavente 13 Gc 42.00N 5.41W
Benbecula 9 Fd 57.27N 7.20W
Bencheng → Luannan 28 Ee 39.30N 118.42 E
Ben-Chicao, Col de- 13 Oh 36.12N 2.51 E
Bend 43 Cc 44.03N 121.19W
Bendaja 34 Cd 7.10N 11.15W
Bendel [2] 34 Gd 6.00N 5.50 E
Bendela 36 Cc 3.18S 17.36 E
Bender Bäyla 31 Mh 9.30N 50.30 E
Bendersiyada 35 Hc 11.14N 48.57 E
Bendery 19 Cf 46.48N 29.22 E
Bendigo 58 Fh 36.46S 144.17 E
Bendorf 12 Jd 50.26N 7.34 E
Bène/Bene 8 Jh 56.28N 23.01 E
Bene/Bène 8 Jh 56.28N 23.01 E
Bénéna 34 Ec 13.06N 4.22W
Benepú, Rada- 65d Ac 27.10S 109.25W
Benešov 10 Kg 49.47N 14.40 E
Benevento 14 Ii 41.08N 14.45 E
Bengal 21 Kg 24.00N 90.00 E
Bengal, Bay of- (EN) 21 Kh 15.00N 90.00 E
Bengamisa 36 Eb 0.57N 25.10 E
Bengbis 34 He 3.27N 12.27 E
Bengbu 22 Nf 32.47N 117.23 E
Benghazi (EN) = Banghāzī 31 Je 32.07N 20.04 E
Benghazi (EN) = Banghāzī [3] 33 Dd 27.00N 20.30 E
Benghisa Point 14 Io 35.50N 14.35 E
Bengkalis 26 Df 1.28N 102.08 E
Bengkulu [3] 26 Dg 3.48S 102.16 E
Bengkulu 22 Mj 3.48S 102.16 E
Bengo, Baia do- 30 Ii 8.43S 13.21 E
Bengo He 28 Eg 35.04N 118.22 E
Bengough 46 Mb 49.24N 105.08W
Bengtsfors 7 Cg 59.02N 12.13 E
Benguela 31 Ij 12.35S 13.26 E
Benguela [3] 36 Be 12.00S 15.00 E
Benguerir 32 Fc 32.14N 7.57W
Benguérua, Ilha- 37 Fd 21.53S 35.26 E
Bengue Viejo 49 Ce 17.05N 89.08W
Bengut, Cap- 32 Hb 36.55N 3.54 E
Beni 31 Jh 0.30N 29.28 E
Beni [2] 54 Ef 14.00S 65.30W
Beni, Rio- 52 Jg 10.23S 65.24W
Beni Abbes 32 Gc 30.08N 2.10W
Beni Baufrah 13 Hi 35.05N 4.18W
Benicarló 13 Md 40.25N 0.26 E
Benicasim 13 Md 40.03N 0.04 E
Beni Chougran, Monts des- 13 Mi 35.30N 0.15 E
Benidorm 13 Lf 38.32N 0.08W
Beni Enzar 13 Ji 35.14N 2.57W
Beni Haoua 13 Nh 36.32N 1.34 E
Beni Mellal 31 Ge 32.20N 6.21W
Beni Mellal [3] 32 Fc 32.30N 6.30W
Benin 34 Gd 5.45N 5.04 E
Bénin = Benin (EN) [1] 31 Hh 9.30N 2.15 E
Bénin (Dahomey) [1] 31 Hh 9.30N 2.15 E
Benin (EN) = Bénin [1] 31 Hh 9.30N 2.15 E
Benin, Bight of- 30 Hh 5.30N 4.00 E
Benin City 31 Hh 6.20N 5.38 E
Beni Ounif 32 Gc 32.03N 1.15W
Benisa 13 Mf 38.43N 0.03 E
Beni Saf 13 Ki 35.19N 1.23W
Benisheikh 34 Hc 11.48N 12.29 E
Benito Juárez 48 Mi 17.50N 92.32W
Benito Juárez, Presa- 48 Li 16.27N 95.30W
Benjamen Island 37b Bb 5.27S 53.21 E
Benjamin 45 Gj 33.35N 99.48W
Benjamín Aceval 55 Dg 24.58S 57.34W
Benjamin Constant 53 If 4.22S 70.02W
Benjamin Hill 48 Db 30.10N 111.10W
Benkei-Misaki 29a Bb 42.50N 140.11 E
Benkelman 45 Ff 40.03N 101.32W
Benkovac 14 Jf 44.02N 15.37 E
Ben Mehidi 14 Bn 36.46N 7.54 E
Bennett, Lake- 59 Gd 23.50S 131.00 E
Bennett, Ostrov- 20 Ja 76.45N 149.00 E
Benneydale 62 Fc 38.31S 175.21 E
Bennichab 32 Df 19.26N 15.21W
Bennington 44 Kd 42.53N 73.12W
Benom 26 Df 3.50N 102.06 E
Benoni 31 Jk 26.19S 28.27 E
Bénoué = Benue (EN) 30 Hh 7.48N 6.46 E
Benoy 35 Bd 8.59N 16.19 E
Benrath 12 Ic 51.10N 6.52 E
Bensekrane 13 Ki 35.04N 1.13W
Bensheim 10 Eg 49.41N 8.37 E
Ben Slimane 32 Fc 33.37N 7.07W
Benson [Az.-U.S.] 46 Jk 31.58N 110.18W
Benson [Mn.-U.S.] 45 Id 45.19N 95.36W
Benson Point 64g Ab 1.56N 157.30W
Bent 23 Id 26.17N 59.31 E
Benteng [Indon.] 26 Hg 0.24S 121.59 E
Benteng [Indon.] 26 Hh 6.08N 120.27 E
Bentheim 10 Dd 52.19N 7.10 E
Bentiaba 36 Be 14.29S 12.50 E
Bentinck 25 Jf 11.45N 98.03 E
Bentinck Island 59 Hc 17.05S 139.30 E
Bentiu 35 Dd 9.14N 29.50 E
Bento Conçalves 56 Jc 29.10S 51.31W
Bento Gomes, Rio- 55 Dc 16.40S 57.12W
Benton [Ar.-U.S.] 45 Ji 34.34N 92.35W
Benton [Il.-U.S.] 45 Lg 38.01N 88.55W
Bentong 26 Df 3.32N 101.55 E
Benton Harbor 44 Dd 42.07N 86.27W
Bentonville 45 Ih 36.22N 94.13W
Benua, Pulau- 26 Ef 0.56N 107.27 E
Benue [2] 34 Gd 7.15N 8.20 E
Benue 30 Hh 7.48N 6.46 E
Benue (EN) = Bénoué 30 Hh 7.48N 6.46 E
Benwee Head/An Bhinn Bhuí 9 Dg 54.21N 9.48W
Benxi 22 Oe 41.16N 123.48 E
Beo 26 If 4.15N 126.48 E
Beograd = Belgrade (EN) 6 Ig 44.50N 20.30 E
Beograd-Krnjača 15 De 44.52N 20.28 E
Beograd-Zemun 15 De 44.53N 20.25 E
Béoumi 34 Dd 7.40N 5.34W

Index Symbols

[1] Independent Nation
[2] State, Region
[3] District, County
[4] Municipality
[5] Colony, Dependency
Continent
Physical Region
Historical or Cultural Region
Mount, Mountain
Volcano
Hill
Mountains, Mountain Range
Hills, Escarpment
Plateau, Upland
Pass, Gap
Plain, Lowland
Delta
Salt Flat
Valley, Canyon
Crater, Cave
Karst Features
Depression
Polder
Desert, Dunes
Forest, Woods
Heath, Steppe
Oasis
Cape, Point
Coast, Beach
Cliff
Peninsula
Isthmus
Sandbank
Island
Atoll
Rock, Reef
Islands, Archipelago
Rocks, Reefs
Coral Reef
Well, Spring
Geyser
River, Stream
Waterfall Rapids
River Mouth, Estuary
Lake
Salt Lake
Intermittent Lake
Reservoir
Swamp, Pond
Canal
Glacier
Ice Shelf, Pack Ice
Ocean
Sea
Gulf, Bay
Strait, Fjord
Lagoon
Bank
Seamount
Tablemount
Ridge
Shelf
Basin
Escarpment, Sea Scarp
Fracture
Trench, Abyss
National Park, Reserve
Point of Interest
Recreation Site
Cave, Cavern
Historic Site
Ruins
Wall, Walls
Church, Abbey
Temple
Scientific Station
Airport
Port
Lighthouse
Mine
Tunnel
Dam, Bridge

Beppu 27 Ne 33.17N 131.30 E
Beppu-Wan 29 Be 33.20N 131.35 E
Bequia Head 51n Ba 13.03N 61.12W
Bequia Island 50 Ff 13.01N 61.13W
Beraketa 37 Hd 24.11S 45.42 E
Berati 15 Ci 40.42N 19.57 E
Beratus, Gunung- 26 Gg 1.02S 116.20 E
Berau, Teluk-=McCluer Gulf (EN) 26 Jg 2.30S 132.30 E
Berberá 31 Lg 10.25N 45.02 E
Berbérati 31 Ih 4.16N 15.47 E
Berberia, Cabo- 13 Nf 38.38N 1.23 E
Berbice River 54 Gb 6.17N 57.32W
Berca 15 Jd 45.17N 26.41 E
Berchères-sur-Vesgre 12 Df 48.51N 1.33 E
Berchtesgaden 10 Ii 47.38N 13.00 E
Berck [Fr.] 12 Dd 50.24N 1.36 E
Berck [Fr.] 11 Hd 50.24N 1.34 E
Berck- Berck Plage 12 Dd 50.24N 1.34 E
Berck-Plage, Berck- 12 Dd 50.24N 1.34 E
Berda 16 Jf 46.47N 36.52 E
Berdåle 35 Hd 7.04N 47.51 E
Berdičev 19 Cf 49.53N 28.36 E
Berdigestjah 20 Hd 62.03N 126.50 E
Berdjansk 19 Df 46.43N 36.48 E
Berdsk 20 Df 54.47N 83.05 E
Beregomet 15 Ia 48.10N 25.24 E
Beregovo 19 Cf 48.13N 22.41 E
Bereku 36 Gc 4.27S 35.44 E
Berekua 50 Fe 15.14N 61.19W
Berekum 34 Ed 7.27N 2.35W
Berens 42 Hf 52.21N 97.01W
Berens River 42 Hf 52.22N 97.02W
Beresford 45 He 43.05N 96.47W
Berestečko 10 Vf 50.16N 25.14 E
Bereşti 15 Kc 46.06N 27.53 E
Berettyó 15 Ec 46.59N 21.07 E
Berettyóújfalu 10 Ri 47.13N 21.33 E
Bereza 19 Ce 52.33N 24.58 E
Berezan 16 Gd 50.19N 31.31 E
Berežany 16 De 49.29N 25.00 E
Berezina [Bye.-U.S.S.R.] 16 Dc 53.48N 25.59 E
Berezina [U.S.S.R.] 5 Je 52.33N 30.14 E
Berezino [Bye.-U.S.S.R.] 16 Fc 53.51N 29.00 E
Berezino [Bye.-U.S.S.R.] 8 Mj 54.55N 28.16 E
Berezino [Ukr.-U.S.S.R.] 15 Mc 46.16N 29.11 E
Bereznegovatoje 16 Hf 47.20N 32.49 E
Bereznik 19 Ec 62.53N 42.42 E
Berezniki 6 Ld 59.24N 56.46 E
Berezno 16 Ed 51.01N 26.45 E
Berezovka [Bye.-U.S.S.R.] 10 Vc 53.40N 25.37 E
Berezovka [R.S.F.S.R.] 17 Hd 64.59N 56.29 E
Berezovka [Ukr.-U.S.S.R.] 19 Df 47.12N 30.56 E
Berezovka Višerka 17 Hf 60.55N 56.50 E
Berezovo 19 Gc 63.58N 65.00 E
Berezovski [R.S.F.S.R.] 17 Jh 56.55N 60.50 E
Berezovski [R.S.F.S.R.] 20 De 55.39N 86.16 E
Berezovy 20 If 51.41N 135.52 E
Berga [Sp.] 13 Nb 42.06N 1.51 E
Berga [Swe.] 8 Gg 57.13N 16.02 E
Bergama 23 Cb 39.07N 27.10 E
Bergamo 14 De 45.41N 9.43 E
Bergantiños 13 Da 43.20N 8.45W
Bergby 7 Df 60.56N 17.02 E
Bergen [G.D.R.] 10 Jb 54.25N 13.26 E
Bergen [Neth.] 12 Gb 52.40N 4.42 E
Bergen [Nor.] 6 Gc 60.23N 5.20 E
Bergen/Mons 11 Jd 50.27N 3.56 E
Bergen aan Zee, Bergen- 12 Gb 52.40N 4.38 E
Bergen-Bergen aan Zee 12 Gb 52.40N 4.38 E
Bergen op Zoom 11 Kc 51.30N 4.17 E
Bergerac 11 Gj 44.51N 0.29 E
Bergeyk 12 Hc 51.19N 5.22 E
Bergh 12 Ic 51.53N 6.16 E
Bergheim 10 Cf 50.58N 6.39 E
Bergh-s'Heerenberg 12 Ic 51.53N 6.16 E
Bergisches Land 10 De 51.07N 7.10 E
Bergisch Gladbach 10 Df 50.59N 7.08 E
Bergkvara 8 Gh 56.23N 16.05 E
Bergneustadt 12 Jc 51.02N 7.39 E
Bergö 8 Ib 62.55N 21.10 E
Bergsjö 7 Df 61.59N 17.04 E
Bergslagen 8 Fd 60.05N 14.30 E
Bergstraße 12 Ke 49.40N 8.40 E
Bergues 12 Ed 50.58N 2.26 E
Bergum, Tietjerksteradeel- 12 Ha 53.12N 6.00 E
Bergviken 8 Gc 61.10N 16.45 E
Bergville 37 De 28.52S 29.18 E
Berh 27 Jb 47.45N 111.07 E
Berhala, Selat- 26 Dg 0.48S 104.25 E
Berici, Monti- 14 Fe 45.26N 11.31 E
Berīkān 24 Nh 28.17N 51.14 E
Berikulski 20 De 55.32N 88.08 E
Beringa, Ostrov-=Bering Island (EN) 20 Lf 55.00N 166.10 E
Beringen 12 Hc 51.03N 5.13 E
Bering Glacier 40 Kd 60.15N 143.30W
Bering Island (EN)=Beringa, Ostrov- 20 Lf 55.00N 166.10 E
Beringovo More=Bering Sea (EN) 38 Bd 60.00N 175.00W
Beringovski 22 Tc 63.07N 179.19 E
Bering Proliv=Bering Strait (EN) 38 Cc 65.30N 169.00W
Bering Sea 38 Bd 60.00N 175.00W
Bering Sea (EN)=Beringovo More 38 Bd 60.00N 175.00W
Bering Strait 38 Cc 65.30N 169.00W
Bering Strait (EN)=Bering Proliv 38 Cc 65.30N 169.00W
Berislav 16 Hf 46.51N 33.29 E
Berisso 55 Dl 34.52S 57.53W
Berit Dağı 24 Gc 38.01N 36.52 E
Berīzak 24 Qi 26.06N 57.15 E
Berja 13 Jh 36.51N 2.57W
Berkåk 7 Be 62.50N 10.00 E
Berkane 32 Gc 34.56N 2.20W
Berkel 10 Cd 52.09N 6.12 E
Berkeley 43 Cd 37.57N 122.18W
Berkhamsted 12 Bc 51.45N 0.33W
Berkner Island 66 Rf 79.30S 49.30W
Berkovica 15 Gf 43.14N 23.07 E
Berks 9 Lj 51.15N 1.20W
Berkshire [3] 9 Lj 51.30N 1.10W
Berkshire Downs 9 Lj 51.35N 1.25W
Berkshire Hills 44 Kd 42.20N 73.10W
Berlaimont 12 Fd 50.12N 3.49 E
Berlanga de Duero 13 Jc 41.28N 2.51W
Berlengas, Ilhas- 13 Ce 39.25N 9.30W
Berlevåg 7 Ga 70.51N 29.06 E
Berlin 43 Mc 44.29N 71.10W
Berlin (Ost)=East Berlin (EN) [2] 10 Jd 52.30N 13.25 E
Berlin (Ost)=East Berlin (EN) 6 He 52.31N 13.24 E
Berlin (West)=West Berlin (EN) 6 He 52.31N 13.24 E
Berlin-Pankow 10 Jd 52.34N 13.24 E
Bermeja, Sierra- 13 Gh 36.30N 5.15W
Bermejillo 47 Dc 25.53N 103.37W
Bermejito, Río- 55 Bg 25.39S 60.11W
Bermejo, Isla- 55 An 39.01S 62.01W
Bermejo, Paso-/Cumbre, Paso de la- 52 Ii 32.50S 70.05W
Bermejo, Río- [Arg.] 52 Ji 31.52S 67.22W
Bermejo, Río- [S.Amer.] 52 Kh 26.52S 58.23W
Bermen, lac- 42 Kf 53.35N 68.55W
Bermeo 13 Ja 43.26N 2.43W
Bermillo de Sayago 13 Fc 41.22N 6.06W
Bermuda [5] 39 Mf 32.20N 64.45W
Bermuda Islands 39 Mf 32.20N 64.45W
Bermuda Rise (EN) 38 Mf 32.30N 65.00W
Bern [2] 14 Bd 46.55N 7.40 E
Bern/Berne 6 Gf 46.55N 7.30 E
Bernalda 14 Kj 40.24N 16.41 E
Bernalillo 45 Ci 35.18N 106.33W
Bernard Islands 64d Bb 7.18N 151.32 E
Bernardo de Irigoyen 55 Bk 32.10S 61.09W
Bernardo de Irigoyen 56 Jc 26.15S 53.39W
Bernasconi 56 He 37.54S 63.43W
Bernau bei Berlin 10 Jd 52.40N 13.35 E
Bernaville 12 Ed 50.08N 2.10 E
Bernay 11 Ge 49.06N 0.36 E
Bernburg 10 He 51.48N 11.44 E
Berndorf 14 Kc 47.57N 16.06 E
Berne [F.R.G.] 12 Ka 53.11N 8.29 E
Berne [In.-U.S.] 44 Ee 40.39N 84.57W
Berne/Bern 6 Gf 46.55N 7.30 E
Berner Alpen/Alpes Bernoises=Bernese Alps (EN) 14 Bd 46.25N 7.30 E
Berneray 9 Fd 57.43N 7.15W
Bernese Alps (EN)=Alpes Bernoises/Berner Alpen 14 Bd 46.25N 7.30 E
Bernese Alps (EN)=Berner Alpen/Alpes Bernoises 14 Bd 46.25N 7.30 E
Bernesga 13 Gb 42.28N 5.31W
Bernesq 12 Be 49.16N 0.56W
Bernier Bay 42 Ib 71.08N 88.00W
Bernier Island 59 Cd 24.50S 113.10 E
Bernina 14 Ed 46.25N 10.01 E
Bernina 5 Gf 46.22N 9.50 E
Berninapaß 14 Ed 46.25N 10.01 E
Bernissart 12 Fd 50.28N 3.38 E
Bernkastel-Kues 12 Je 49.55N 7.04 E
Bernstorffs Isfjord 41 Hf 63.10N 40.45W
Berón de Astrada 55 Dh 27.33S 57.32W
Beroroha 37 Hd 21.39S 45.10 E
Bérouboua y 34 Fc 10.32N 2.44 E
Beroun 10 Kg 49.58N 14.04 E
Berounka 10 Kg 50.00N 14.24 E
Berovo 15 Fh 41.43N 22.51 E
Berre, Étang de- 11 Lk 43.27N 5.08 E
Berriane 32 Hc 32.50N 3.46 E
Berrouaghia 13 Oh 36.08N 2.55 E
Berry 11 Hh 47.00N 2.00 E
Berry-au-Bac 12 Fe 49.24N 3.54 E
Berryessa, Lake- 46 Dg 38.37N 122.16W
Berry Head 9 Jk 50.24N 3.29W
Berry Islands 47 Ic 25.34N 77.45W
Berry River 46 Ja 50.50N 111.36W
Beršad 19 Cf 48.23N 29.33 E
Berseba 37 Be 26.01S 17.41 E
Bersenbrück 12 Jb 52.33N 7.56 E
Berthierville 44 Kb 46.05N 73.11W
Bertincourt 12 Ed 50.05N 2.59 E
Bertogne 12 Hd 50.05N 5.40 E
Bertolinia 54 Je 7.38S 43.57W
Bertoua 31 Ih 4.35N 13.41 E
Bertraghboy Bay 9 Dh 53.23N 9.50W
Bertrix 12 He 49.51N 5.15 E
Beru Island 57 Ie 1.20S 176.00 E
Berwick-upon-Tweed 9 Lf 55.46N 2.00W
Berwyn 9 Ji 52.53N 3.24W
Besalampy 37 Gc 16.44S 44.24 E
Besançon 6 Gf 47.15N 6.02 E
Besar, Gunung- 26 Gg 1.25S 115.39 E
Besbre 11 Jh 46.33N 3.44 E
Besed 16 Gc 52.38N 31.11 E
Besikama 26 Hh 9.36S 124.57 E
Beskid Mountains (EN) 5 Hf 49.40N 20.00 E
Beskid Niski 10 Rg 49.20N 21.30 E
Beskid Średni 10 Pg 49.45N 19.20 E
Beskid Wysoki 10 Pg 49.32N 20.00 E
Beskidy Wschodnie 10 Sg 49.20N 22.30 E
Beskidy Zachodnie 10 Pg 49.30N 19.30 E
Beskol 18 Ma 46.06N 81.01 E
Beslan 19 Eg 43.10N 44.35 E
Besna Kobila 15 Fg 42.32N 22.14 E
Besni 24 Gd 37.41N 37.52 E
Besparmak Dağ 15 Kl 37.30N 27.35 E
Bessao 35 Bd 7.53N 15.59 E
Bessarabia (EN)=Bessarabija 15 Lb 47.00N 28.30 E
Bessarabija=Bessarabia (EN) 15 Lb 47.00N 28.30 E
Bessarabka 16 Ff 46.20N 28.59 E
Bességes 11 Kj 44.17N 4.06 E
Bessemer 43 Je 33.25N 86.57W
Bessin 11 Fe 49.10N 1.00W
Bessines-sur-Gartempe 11 Hh 46.06N 1.22 E
Besšoki, Gora- 16 Rh 43.57N 52.30 E
Best 12 Hc 51.30N 5.24 E
Bestjah [R.S.F.S.R.] 20 Hc 66.00N 123.35 E
Bestjah [R.S.F.S.R.] 20 Hd 61.17N 128.50 E
Bestobe 19 He 52.30N 73.05 E
Bestwig 12 Kc 51.22N 8.24 E
Betafo 37 Hc 19.49S 46.50 E
Betanzos [Bol.] 54 Eg 19.34S 65.27W
Betanzos [Sp.] 13 Da 43.17N 8.12W
Betanzos, Ría de- 13 Da 43.23N 8.15W
Bétaré Oya 34 Hd 5.36N 14.05 E
Bétérou 34 Fd 9.12N 2.16 E
Beteta 13 Jd 40.34N 2.04W
Bethal 37 De 26.27S 29.28 E
Bethanien [3] 37 Be 26.30S 17.00 E
Bethanien 31 Ik 26.32S 17.11 E
Bethany [Mo.-U.S.] 45 If 40.16N 94.02W
Bethany [Ok.-U.S.] 45 Hi 35.31N 97.38W
Bethel 39 Cc 60.48N 161.46W
Béthenville 12 Ge 49.18N 4.22 E
Bethlehem [Pa.-U.S.] 44 Je 40.36N 75.22W
Bethlehem [S.Afr.] 31 Jk 28.15S 28.15 E
Bethlehem (EN)=Bayt Laḩm 24 Fg 31.43N 35.12 E
Bethulie 37 Df 30.32S 25.59 E
Béthune 11 Id 50.32N 2.38 E
Béthune 11 He 49.53N 1.09 E
Betioky 37 Gd 23.42S 44.22 E
Betong 25 Kg 5.45N 101.05 E
Betor 35 Fc 11.37N 39.00 E
Bétou 36 Cb 3.03N 18.31 E
Betpak-Dala 21 Ie 46.00N 70.00 E
Betroka 37 Hd 23.15S 46.05 E
Bet She'an 24 Ff 32.30N 35.30 E
Betsiamites, Rivière- 42 Kg 48.56N 68.38W
Betsiboka 30 Lj 16.03S 46.36 E
Bette 30 If 22.00N 19.12 E
Bettembourg/Bettemburg 12 Ie 49.31N 6.06 E
Bettemburg/Bettembourg 12 Ie 49.31N 6.06 E
Bettendorf 45 Kf 41.32N 90.30W
Bettles Field 40 Ic 66.53N 151.51W
Bettna 8 Gf 58.55N 16.38 E
Bettola 14 Df 44.47N 9.36 E
Betül 25 Fd 21.55N 77.54 E
Betuwe 11 Lc 51.55N 5.30 E
Betwa 25 Hc 25.55N 80.12 E
Betz 12 Ee 49.09N 2.57 E
Betzdorf 10 Df 50.47N 7.53 E
Beulah 44 Dc 44.38N 86.06W
Beult 12 Cc 51.13N 0.26 E
Beuvron 11 Hg 47.29N 1.15 E
Beuzeville 12 Ce 49.20N 0.21 E
Beveland 11 Jc 51.30N 3.40 E
Beveren 12 Gc 51.13N 4.15 E
Beveridge Reef 57 Kg 20.00S 168.00W
Beverley [Austl.] 59 Df 32.06S 116.56 E
Beverley [Eng.-U.K.] 9 Mh 53.51N 0.26W
Beverwijk 11 Kb 52.28N 4.40 E
Bewsher, Mount- 66 Ff 70.54S 65.28 E
Bexhill 9 Nk 50.50N 0.29 E
Bexley, London- 12 Cc 51.26N 0.09 E
Beyağaç 15 Ll 37.13N 28.57 E
Beyänlü 24 Ld 36.02N 47.53 E
Bey Dağı 24 Hc 38.15N 38.22 E
Bey Dağlari 23 Db 36.40N 30.15 E
Beykoz 24 Cb 41.08N 29.05 E
Beyla 34 Dd 8.41N 8.38W
Beyoğlu, İstanbul 15 Lh 41.02N 28.59 E
Beyoneisu-Retsugan 27 Oe 31.55N 139.55 E
Beypazari 24 Db 40.10N 31.55 E
Beyra 35 Hd 6.57N 47.19 E
Beyram 24 Oi 27.26N 53.31 E
Beyşehir 24 Dd 37.41N 31.43 E
Beyşehir Gölü 23 Db 37.40N 31.30 E
Bezaha 37 Gd 23.29S 44.30 E
Bežanickaja Vozvyšennost 7 Gh 56.45N 29.30 E
Bežanicy 7 Gh 56.58N 29.57 E
Bezdan 15 Bd 45.51N 18.56 E
Bezděz 10 Kf 50.32N 14.43 E
Bezdež 10 Vd 52.18N 25.20 E
Bežeck 19 Dd 57.50N 36.41 E
Bezenčuk 7 Lj 53.01N 49.24 E
Bezerra, Rio- 55 Ia 13.16S 47.31W
Bezerros 54 Ke 8.14S 35.45W
Beziers 11 Jk 43.21N 3.15 E
Bezmein 19 Fh 38.05N 58.12 E
Bežta 19 Eg 42.08N 46.08 E
Bhadrak 25 Hd 21.04N 86.30 E
Bhadrāvati 25 Ff 13.52N 75.43 E
Bhāgalpur 22 Kg 25.15N 87.00 E
Bhairawa 25 Gc 27.31N 83.24 E
Bhaironghati 25 Fb 31.01N 78.53 E
Bhakkar 25 Eb 31.38N 71.04 E
Bhamo 25 Jd 24.16N 97.14 E
Bhandāra 25 Fd 21.10N 79.39 E
Bhanjan 25 Gc 25.47N 83.36 E
Bhārat Juktarashtra=India (EN) [1] 22 Jh 20.00N 77.00 E
Bharatpur 25 Fc 27.13N 77.29 E
Bharūch 25 Ed 21.46N 72.54 E
Bhatinda → Bathinda 25 Eb 30.12N 74.57 E
Bhātpāra 25 Hd 22.52N 88.24 E
Bhaunagar 22 Jg 21.46N 72.09 E
Bhera 25 Eb 32.29N 72.55 E
Bheri 25 Gc 28.44N 81.16 E
Bhīlwāra 25 Ec 25.21N 74.38 E
Bhīma 21 Jh 16.25N 77.17 E
Bhind 25 Fc 26.34N 78.48 E
Bhiwāni 25 Fc 28.47N 76.08 E
Bhopāl 22 Jg 23.16N 77.24 E
Bhubaneshwar 22 Kg 20.14N 85.50 E
Bhuj 25 Dd 23.16N 69.40 E
Bhusāwal 25 Fd 21.03N 75.46 E
Bhutan (Druk-Yul) [1] 22 Lg 27.30N 90.30 E
Bia 34 Ed 5.21N 3.11W
Bia, Phou- 21 Mh 18.36N 103.01 E
Biá, Rio- 54 Ed 3.28S 67.23W
Bīābān, Kūh-e- 24 Qi 26.30N 57.25 E
Biabou 51n Ba 13.12N 61.09W
Biafra 30 Hh 5.00N 7.30 E
Biafra, Bight of- 30 Hh 3.20N 9.20 E
Biak 26 Kg 1.10S 136.06 E
Biak, Pulau- 57 Ee 1.00S 136.00 E
Biała Piska 10 Sc 53.37N 22.04 E
Biała Podlaska [2] 10 Td 52.00N 23.05 E
Biała Podlaska 10 Td 52.02N 23.06 E
Białobrzegi 10 Qe 51.40N 20.57 E
Białogard 10 Lb 54.01N 16.00 E
Białostocka, Wysoczyzna- 10 Tc 53.23N 23.10 E
Białowieża 10 Td 52.41N 23.50 E
Białystok 6 Ie 53.09N 23.09 E
Białystok [2] 10 Tc 53.10N 23.10 E
Biancavilla 14 Im 37.38N 14.52 E
Bianco 14 Kl 38.05N 16.09 E
Bianco, Monte- 5 Gf 45.50N 6.52 E
Biankouma 34 Dd 7.44N 7.37W
Biankouma [3] 34 Dd 7.43N 7.40W
Bianzhuang → Cangshan 28 Eg 34.51N 118.03 E
Biaro, Pulau- 26 If 2.05N 125.20 E
Biarritz 11 Ek 43.29N 1.34W
Biasca 14 Cd 46.22N 8.57 E
Bibā 33 Fd 28.55N 30.59 E
Bibai 27 Pc 43.19N 141.52 E
Bibala 36 Be 14.50S 13.30 E
Biban, Chaine des- 13 Qh 36.12N 4.25 E
Bibbiena 14 Fg 43.42N 11.49 E
Biberach an der Riß 10 Fh 48.06N 9.48 E
Bibiani 34 Ed 6.28N 2.20W
Bic 44 Ma 48.22N 68.42W
Bicaj 15 Dh 41.59N 20.25 E
Bicas 55 Ke 21.43S 43.04W
Bicaz 15 Jc 46.55N 26.04 E
Bicaz, Pasul- 15 Ic 46.49N 25.52 E
Bičenekski, Pereval- 16 Nj 39.33N 45.48 E
Bicester 9 Lj 51.54N 1.09W
Bichena 35 Fc 10.21N 38.14 E
Bickerton Island 59 Hb 13.45S 136.10 E
Bicske 10 Oi 47.29N 18.38 E
Bičura 20 Ff 50.36N 107.35 E
Bīd 24 Qd 36.33N 57.35 E
Bida 31 Hh 9.05N 6.01 E
Bīdar 25 Fe 17.54N 77.33 E
Bidasoa 13 Ka 43.22N 1.47W
Biddeford 43 Mc 43.30N 70.26W
Bideford 9 Ij 51.01N 4.13W
Bideford Bay → Barnstaple Bay 9 Ij 51.05N 4.20W
Bidon V/Poste Maurice Cortier 32 He 22.18N 1.05 E
Bié [3] 36 Ce 13.00S 17.30 E
Bié, Planalto do- 30 Ij 13.30S 17.02 E
Biebrza 10 Sc 53.13N 22.28 E
Biecz 10 Rg 49.44N 21.14 E
Biedenkopf 12 Kd 50.55N 8.32 E
Biei 29a Cb 43.35N 142.28 E
Biel/Bienne 14 Bc 47.10N 7.15 E
Bielefeld 10 Ed 52.02N 8.32 E
Bielefeld-Brackwede 12 Kc 51.59N 8.31 E
Bielefeld-Sennestadt 12 Kc 51.57N 8.35 E
Biella 14 Ce 45.34N 8.03 E
Bielsk 10 Pd 52.40N 19.49 E
Bielska, Wysoczyzna- 10 Sd 52.35N 23.00 E
Bielsko [2] 10 Og 49.50N 19.00 E
Bielsko-Biała 10 Pg 49.49N 19.02 E
Bielsk Podlaski 10 Td 52.47N 23.12 E
Bien Dong=South China Sea (EN) 21 Ni 10.00N 113.00 E
Bien Hoa 25 Lf 10.57N 106.49 E
Bienne 11 Lh 46.20N 5.38 E
Bienne/Biel 14 Bc 47.10N 7.15 E
Bienvenida 13 Jd 40.30N 2.30W
Bienville, Lac- 42 Ke 55.20N 72.40W
Bierbeek 12 Gd 50.50N 4.46 E
Bieszczady 10 Sg 49.10N 22.35 E
Bièvre 12 He 49.56N 5.01 E
Biferno 14 Ji 41.59N 15.02 E
Bifoum 36 Bc 0.20S 10.23 E
Bifuka 28 Qb 44.29N 142.21 E
Biga 24 Bb 40.13N 27.14 E
Bigadiç 24 Cc 39.23N 28.08 E
Big Bald Mountain 44 Nb 47.37N 66.38W
Big Baldy Mountain 46 Jc 46.58N 110.37W
Big Bay [Mi.-U.S.] 44 Db 46.49N 87.44W
Big Bay [Van.] 63b Cb 15.05S 166.54 E
Big Beaver House 42 If 52.58N 89.57W
Big Belt Mountains 46 Jc 46.40N 111.25W
Big Black River 45 Kj 32.00N 91.05W
Big Blue River 43 Hd 39.11N 96.32W
Big Creek Peak 46 Id 44.28N 113.32W
Big Dry Creek 46 Lc 47.30N 106.19W
Big Falls 45 Jb 48.11N 93.46W
Biggar 42 Gf 52.04N 108.00W
Biggenden 59 Ke 25.30S 152.00 E
Biggleswade 9 Mi 52.05N 0.17W
Big Hatchet Peak 45 Bk 31.37N 108.20W
Big Hole River 46 Id 45.34N 112.20W
Bighorn Basin 43 Fc 44.15N 108.10W
Bighorn Lake 46 Kd 45.08N 108.10W
Bighorn Mountains 38 Ie 44.00N 107.30W
Bighorn River 43 Fb 46.09N 107.28W
Bight, Head of- 59 Gf 31.30S 131.10 E
Big Island 42 Kd 62.43N 70.40W
Big Lake 44 Nc 45.10N 67.40W
Big Lake 45 Fk 31.12N 101.28W
Big Lost River 46 Ie 43.50N 112.44W
Big Muddy Creek 46 Mb 48.08N 104.36W
Big Muddy Lake 46 Mb 49.08N 104.54W
Bignona 34 Bc 12.49N 16.14W
Bigorre 11 Gk 43.06N 0.05 E
Big Porcupine Creek 46 Lc 46.17N 106.47W
Big Quill Lake 42 Hf 51.51N 104.18W
Big Rapids 44 Ed 43.42N 85.29W
Big River 42 Gf 53.50N 107.01W
Big River 42 Fb 72.50N 125.00W
Big Sand Lake 42 He 57.45N 99.45W
Big Sandy 46 Jb 48.11N 110.07W
Big Sandy Creek 45 Eg 38.06N 102.29W
Big Sandy River [Az.-U.S.] 46 Ii 34.19N 113.31W
Big Sandy River [Wy.-U.S.] 46 Kf 41.50N 109.48W
Big Sheep Mountains 46 Mc 47.03N 105.43W
Big Sioux River 43 Hc 42.30N 96.25W
Big Smoky Valley 43 Dd 38.30N 117.15W
Big Snowy Mountains 46 Kc 46.50N 109.30W
Big Spring 39 If 32.15N 101.28W
Big Spruce Knob 44 Gf 38.16N 80.12W
Big Stone Lake 45 Hd 45.25N 96.40W
Big Timber 46 Kd 45.50N 109.57W
Big Trout Lake 42 If 53.45N 90.00W
Biguglia, Étang de- 11a Ba 42.36N 9.29 E
Big Wood Cay 49 Ia 24.21N 77.44W
Big Wood River 46 He 42.52N 114.55W
Bihać 14 Jf 44.49N 15.52 E
Bihār [3] 25 Hd 25.00N 86.00 E
Bihār 25 Hc 25.11N 85.31 E
Biharamulo 36 Fc 2.38S 31.20 E
Bihor [2] 15 Fc 47.00N 22.00 E
Bihoro 27 Pc 43.49N 144.07 E
Bihorului, Munţii- 15 Fc 46.40N 22.45 E
Bija 21 Kd 52.25N 85.05 E
Bijagós, Arquipélago dos-=Bijagos Islands (EN) 30 Fg 11.15N 16.05W
Bijagós Islands (EN)=Bijagós, Arquipélago dos- 30 Fg 11.15N 16.05W
Bijapur 25 Fe 16.50N 75.42 E
Bijār 23 Gb 35.52N 47.36 E
Bijeljina 14 Nf 44.45N 19.13 E
Bijelo Polje 15 Cf 43.02N 19.45 E
Bijiang (Zhiziluo) 27 Gf 26.39N 99.00 E
Bijie 27 If 27.15N 105.16 E
Bijlikol, Ozero- 18 Hc 43.05N 70.40 E
Bijou Creek 45 Ef 40.17N 103.52W
Bijoutier Island 37b Bb 7.04S 52.45 E
Bijsk 22 Kd 52.34N 85.15 E
Bikāner 22 Jg 28.01N 73.18 E
Bikar Atoll 57 Ic 12.15N 170.06 E
Bikeqi 28 Ad 40.45N 111.17 E
Bikin 20 Ig 46.43N 134.02 E
Bikin 20 Ig 46.51N 134.02 E
Bikini Atoll 57 Hc 11.35N 165.23 E
Bikoro 31 Ii 0.45S 18.07 E
Bilād Ghāmid 33 Hf 19.58N 41.38 E
Bilād Zahrān 33 He 20.15N 41.15 E
Bilāspur 22 Kg 22.03N 82.10 E
Bilate 35 Fd 6.34N 38.01 E
Bilauktaung Range 21 Lh 13.00N 99.00 E
Bilbao 6 Fg 43.15N 2.58W
Bilbays 33 Fc 30.25N 31.34 E
Bileća 14 Mh 42.53N 18.26 E
Bilecik 23 Ca 40.09N 29.59 E
Bilehsavār 24 Mc 39.28N 48.20 E
Bilé Karpaty=White Carpathians (EN) 10 Nh 48.55N 17.50 E
Bilesha Plain 36 Hb 0.35N 40.45 E
Biłgoraj 10 Sf 50.34N 22.43 E
Bili 36 Db 4.50N 22.29 E
Bili 36 Eb 4.09N 25.10 E
Bilibino 22 Sc 68.03N 166.20 E
Biliran 26 Hd 11.35N 124.28 E
Bilishti 15 Di 40.37N 20.59 E
Biliu He 28 Ge 39.30N 122.36 E
Bill Baileys Bank (EN) 9 Ca 60.40N 10.20W
Billerbeck 12 Jc 51.58N 7.18 E
Billericay 12 Cc 51.37N 0.35 E
Billingen 8 Ef 58.24N 13.45 E
Billings 39 Jf 37.04N 93.33W
Billings, Represa- 55 If 23.45S 46.40W
Billingshurst 12 Bc 51.01N 0.27W
Bill Williams River 46 Hi 34.17N 114.03W
Billy Chinook, Lake- 46 Ed 44.33N 121.20W
Bilma 13 Ig 18.41N 12.56 E
Biloela 59 Kd 24.24S 150.30 E
Bilo Gora 14 Le 45.50N 17.10 E
Biloku 54 Gc 1.46N 58.33W
Biloxi 43 Je 30.24N 88.53W
Bilqās Qism Awwal 24 Dg 31.13N 31.21 E
Bilteni 15 Ge 44.52N 23.17 E
Biltine 35 Cc 14.32N 20.55 E
Biltine [3] 35 Cc 15.00N 21.00 E
Bilzen 12 Hd 50.51N 5.31 E
Bima 36 Eb 3.23N 25.09 E
Bimbān 24 Ej 24.26N 32.53 E
Bimberi Peak 59 Jg 35.40S 148.47 E
Bimbila 34 Fd 8.51N 0.04 E
Bimbo 35 Be 4.18N 18.33 E
Bimini Islands 47 Ic 25.44N 79.15W
Bināb 24 Md 36.35N 48.41 E
Binačka Morava 15 Eg 42.27N 21.47 E
Binaiya, Gunung- 26 Ig 3.11S 129.26 E
Binatang 26 Ff 2.10N 111.38 E
Binboga Daği 24 Gc 38.21N 36.32 E
Binche 12 Gd 50.24N 4.10 E
Binder 27 Jb 48.35N 110.36 E
Bindura 31 Kj 17.17S 31.20 E
Bine el Ouidane 32 Fc 32.08N 6.28W
Binéfar 13 Mc 41.51N 0.18 E
Binem 35 Bb 18.43N 19.40 E
Binga [Zaire] 36 Db 2.20N 20.30 E
Binga [Zimb.] 37 Dc 17.37S 27.20 E

Index Symbols

[1] Independent Nation
[2] State, Region
[3] District, County
[4] Municipality
[5] Colony, Dependency
Continent
Physical Region
Historical or Cultural Region
Mount, Mountain
Volcano
Hill
Mountains, Mountain Range
Hills, Escarpment
Plateau, Upland
Pass, Gap
Plain, Lowland
Delta
Salt Flat
Valley, Canyon
Crater, Cave
Karst Features
Depression
Polder
Desert, Dunes
Forest, Woods
Heath, Steppe
Oasis
Cape, Point
Coast, Beach
Cliff
Peninsula
Isthmus
Sandbank
Island
Atoll
Rock, Reef
Islands, Archipelago
Rocks, Reefs
Coral Reef
Well, Spring
Geyser
River, Stream
Waterfall Rapids
River Mouth, Estuary
Lake
Salt Lake
Intermittent Lake
Reservoir
Swamp, Pond
Canal
Glacier
Ice Shelf, Pack Ice
Ocean
Sea
Gulf, Bay
Strait, Fjord
Lagoon
Bank
Seamount
Tablemount
Ridge
Shelf
Basin
Escarpment, Sea Scarp
Fracture
Trench, Abyss
National Park, Reserve
Point of Interest
Recreation Site
Cave, Cavern
Historic Site
Ruins
Wall, Walls
Church, Abbey
Temple
Scientific Station
Airport
Port
Lighthouse
Mine
Tunnel
Dam, Bridge

Index Symbols

[1] Independent Nation	Historical or Cultural Region	Pass, Gap	Depression	Coast, Beach	Rock, Reef	Waterfall Rapids	Canal	Lagoon	Escarpment, Sea Scarp	Historic Site	Port
[2] State, Region	Mount, Mountain	Plain, Lowland	Polder	Cliff	Islands, Archipelago	River Mouth, Estuary	Glacier	Bank	Fracture	Ruins	Lighthouse
[3] District, County	Volcano	Delta	Desert, Dunes	Peninsula	Rocks, Reefs	Ice Shelf, Pack Ice	Seamount	Trench, Abyss	Wall, Walls	Mine
[4] Municipality	Hill	Salt Flat	Forest, Woods	Isthmus	Coral Reef	Lake	Ocean	Tableland	National Park, Reserve	Church, Abbey	Tunnel
[5] Colony, Dependency	Mountains, Mountain Range	Valley, Canyon	Heath, Steppe	Sandbank	Well, Spring	Salt Lake	Sea	Ridge	Point of Interest	Temple	Dam, Bridge
Continent	Hills, Escarpment	Crater, Cave	Oasis	Island	Geyser	Intermittent Lake	Shelf	Recreation Site	Scientific Station	Airport
Physical Region	Plateau, Upland	Karst Features	Cape, Point	Atoll	River, Stream	Reservoir	Gulf, Bay	Basin	Cave, Cavern	
						Swamp, Pond	Strait, Fjord			

Bogcang Zangbo 27 Ee 31.56N 87.24 E
Bogda Feng 27 Ec 43.45N 88.32 E
Bogdan 15 Hg 42.37N 24.28 E
Bogdanovka 16 Mi 41.15N 43.36 E
Bogda Shan 21 Ke 43.35N 90.00 E
Bogen 7 Db 68.32N 17.00 E
Bogenfels 37 Be 27.23S 15.22 E
Bogense 8 Di 55.34N 10.06 E
Boggeragh Mountains/An Bhograch 9 Ei 52.05N 9.00W
Boggy Peak 51d Bb 17.03N 61.51W
Boghar 13 Oi 35.55N 2.43 E
Boghni 13 Ph 36.32N 3.57 E
Bogia 60 Ch 4.16S 144.58 E
Bognor Regis 12 Bd 50.47N 0.39W
Bogny-sur-Meuse 12 Ge 49.54N 4.43 E
Bogoduhov 16 Id 50.12N 35.31 E
Bogomila 15 Eh 41.36N 21.28 E
Bogor 22 Mj 6.35S 106.47 E
Bogoridick 19 De 53.50N 38.08 E
Bogorodčany 10 Uh 48.45N 24.40 E
Bogorodsk 7 Kh 56.09N 43.32 E
Bogorodskoje [R.S.F.S.R.] 7 Mh 57.51N 50.48 E
Bogorodskoje [R.S.F.S.R.] 20 Jf 52.22N 140.30 E
Bogotá 53 Ie 4.36N 74.05W
Bogotol 20 De 56.17N 89.43 E
Bogøy 7 Dc 67.54N 15.11 E
Bogra 25 Hd 24.51N 89.22 E
Bogučany 20 Ee 58.23N 97.39 E
Bogučar 16 Le 49.57N 40.33 E
Bogué 32 Ef 16.36N 14.15W
Boguševsk 7 Hi 54.50N 30.13 E
Boguslav 19 Df 49.33N 30.54 E
Bo Hai=Chihli, Gulf of- (EN) 21 Nf 38.30N 120.00 E
Bohai Haixia 27 Ld 38.00N 121.30 E
Bohain-en-Vermandois 12 Fe 49.59N 3.27 E
Bohemia (EN)=Čechy 5 Hf 50.00N 14.30 E
Bohemia (EN)=Čechy 10 Kf 50.00N 14.30 E
Bohemian Forest (EN)= Böhmerwald 5 Hf 49.00N 13.30 E
Bohemian Forest (EN)= Český Les 10 Ig 49.50N 12.30 E
Bohemian Forest (EN)= Oberpfälzer Wald 10 Ig 49.50N 12.30 E
Bohemian Forest (EN)= Šumava 5 Hf 49.00N 13.30 E
Bohicon 34 Fd 7.12N 2.04 E
Böhmerwald=Bohemian Forest (EN) 5 Hf 49.00N 13.30 E
Bohmte 12 Kb 52.22N 8.19 E
Bohodoyou 34 Dd 9.46N 9.04W
Bohol 21 Oi 9.50N 124.10 E
Böhönye 10 Nj 46.24N 17.24 E
Bohor 14 Jd 46.04N 15.26 E
Bohu/Bagrax 27 Ec 41.58N 86.29 E
Bohus 8 Eg 57.51N 12.01 E
Bohuslän 8 Df 58.15N 11.50 E
Boiaçu 54 Fd 0.27S 61.46W
Boiano 14 Ii 41.29N 14.29 E
Boina 30 Lj 16.00S 46.30 E
Bois, Lac des- 42 Ec 66.50N 125.15W
Bois, Rio dos- [Braz.] 55 Gd 18.35S 50.02W
Bois, Rio dos- [Braz.] 55 Ha 13.55S 49.51W
Bois Blanc Island 44 Ec 45.45N 84.28W
Boischaut 11 Hh 46.40N 1.45 E
Boise 39 He 43.37N 116.13W
Boise City 45 Eh 36.44N 102.31W
Boise River 46 Ge 43.49N 117.01W
Boissay 12 De 49.31N 1.21 E
Boissevain 42 Hg 49.14N 100.03W
Boizenburg 10 Gc 53.23N 10.43 E
Bojador, Cabo- 30 Ff 26.08N 14.30W
Bojana 15 Ch 41.52N 19.22 E
Bojanowo 10 Me 51.42N 16.44 E
Bojarka 19 De 50.19N 30.20 E
Bojčinovci 15 Gf 43.28N 23.20 E
Bojnūrd 23 Ib 37.28N 57.19 E
Bojonegoro 26 Fh 7.09S 111.52 E
Bojuru 55 Gj 31.38S 51.26W
Bokatola 36 Cc 0.38S 18.46 E
Boké 34 Cc 10.56N 14.13W
Bokhara River 59 Je 29.55S 146.42 E
Bokn 8 Ae 59.15N 5.25 E
Boknafjorden 5 Gd 59.10N 5.35 E
Boko 36 Bc 4.47S 14.38 E
Bokol Mayo 35 Ge 4.31N 41.32 E
Bokoro 35 Bc 12.23N 17.03 E
Bokote 36 Dc 0.05S 20.08 E
Bokpyin 25 Jf 11.16N 98.46 E
Boksitogorsk 19 Dd 59.29N 33.52 E
Bokungu 36 Dc 0.41S 22.19 E
Bol [Chad] 35 Ac 13.30N 14.41 E
Bol [Yugo.] 14 Kg 43.16N 16.40 E
Bola, Bahr- 35 Bd 9.50N 18.59 E
Bolama 34 Bc 11.35N 15.28W
Bolands 51d Bb 17.02N 61.53W
Bolaños, Rio- 48 Gg 21.14N 104.08W
Bolattau, Gora- 18 Ha 46.44N 71.54 E
Bolayir 15 Ji 40.31N 26.45 E
Bolbec 11 Ge 49.34N 0.29 E
Bolda 16 Pg 45.58N 48.35 E
Bole [Eth.] 35 Fd 6.37N 37.22 E
Bole [Ghana] 34 Ed 9.02N 2.29W
Bole/Bortala 27 Dc 44.59N 81.57 E
Bolehov 16 Ce 49.03N 23.50 E
Bolesławiec 10 Le 51.16N 15.34 E
Bolgatanga 31 Gg 10.47N 0.51W
Bolgrad 16 Fg 45.40N 28.38 E
Bolhov 19 De 53.30N 36.01 E
Boli 27 Nb 45.46N 130.31 E
Bolia 36 Cc 1.36S 18.23 E
Boliden 7 Ed 64.52N 20.23 E
Bolinao, Cape- 26 Gc 16.22N 119.50 E
Bolintin Vale 15 Ie 44.27N 25.46 E
Bolívar [Col.] [2] 54 Db 9.00N 74.40W
Bolivar [Mo.-U.S.] 45 Jh 37.37N 93.25W
Bolivar [Tn.-U.S.] 44 Ch 35.15N 88.59W
Bolívar [Ven.] [2] 54 Fb 6.20N 63.30W
Bolívar, Cerro- 54 Fb 7.28N 63.25W
Bolívar, Pico- 52 Ie 8.30N 71.02W
Bolivia [1] 53 Jg 17.00S 65.00W
Bolivia, Altiplano de- 52 Jg 18.00S 68.00W
Boljevac 15 Ef 43.50N 21.58 E
Bollendorf 12 Ie 49.51N 6.22 E
Bollène 11 Kj 44.17N 4.45 E
Bollnäs 7 Df 61.21N 16.25 E
Bollon 59 Je 28.02S 147.28 E
Bollstabruk 8 Ga 63.00N 17.41 E
Bollullos par del Condado 13 Fg 37.20N 6.32W
Bolmen 7 Ch 56.55N 13.40 E
Bolnisi 16 Ni 41.28N 44.31 E
Bolobo 36 Cc 2.10S 16.14 E
Bolodek 20 If 53.43N 133.09 E
Bologna 6 Hg 44.29N 11.20 E
Bolognesi 54 Df 10.01S 74.05W
Bologoje 6 Jd 57.54N 34.02 E
Bolohovo 16 Jb 54.05N 37.52 E
Bolomba 36 Cb 0.29N 19.12 E
Bolombo 36 Dc 3.59S 21.22 E
Bolon 20 Ig 49.58N 136.04 E
Bolotnoje 20 De 55.41N 84.33 E
Bolovens, Plateau des- 25 Le 15.20N 106.20 E
Bolšaja Balahnja 20 Fb 73.37N 107.05 E
Bolšaja Berestovica 10 Uc 53.09N 24.02 E
Bolšaja Černigovka 7 Mj 52.08N 50.48 E
Bolšaja Glušica 7 Mj 52.24N 50.29 E
Bolšaja Ižora 8 Me 59.55N 29.40 E
Bolšaja Kinel 7 Mj 53.14N 50.32 E
Bolšaja Koksaga 7 Lh 56.07N 47.48 E
Bolšaja Kuonamka 20 Gc 70.50N 113.20 E
Bolšaja Oju 17 Jb 69.42N 60.42 E
Bolšaja Rogovaja 17 Jc 66.30N 60.40 E
Bolšaja Synja 17 Jd 65.58N 58.01 E
Bolšaja Tap 17 Lg 59.55N 65.42 E
Bolšaja Ussurka 20 Ig 46.00N 133.30 E
Bolšaja Vladimirovka 19 He 50.53N 79.30 E
Bolšakovo 8 Ij 54.50N 21.36 E
Bolsena 14 Fh 42.39N 11.59 E
Bolsena, Lago di- 14 Fh 42.35N 11.55 E
Bolšerečje 19 Hd 56.06N 74.38 E
Bolšereck 20 Kf 52.22N 156.24 E
Bolšeustikinskoje 17 Ii 55.57N 58.20 E
Bolševik 20 Jd 62.40N 147.30 E
Bolševik, Ostrov-=Bolshevik Island (EN) 21 Mb 78.40N 102.30 E
Bolšezemelskaja Tundra 19 Fb 67.30N 58.30 E
Bolshevik Island (EN)= Bolševik, Ostrov- 21 Mb 78.40N 102.30 E
Bolšije Uki 19 Hd 56.57N 72.37 E
Bolšoj Anjuj 20 Lc 68.30N 160.50 E
Bolšoj Begičev, Ostrov- 20 Gb 74.20N 112.30 E
Bolšoj Berezovy, Ostrov- 8 Md 60.15N 28.35 E
Bolšoj Boktybaj, Gora- [Kaz.-U.S.S.R.] 19 Ff 48.30N 58.20 E
Bolšoj Boktybaj, Gora- [U.S.S.R.] 16 Ue 48.30N 58.25 E
Bolšoj Bolvanski Nos, Mys- 17 Ia 70.27N 59.05 E
Bolšoj Čeremšan 7 Li 54.12N 49.40 E
Bolšoje Muraškino 7 Ki 55.47N 44.46 E
Bolšoje Vlasjevo 20 Jf 53.25N 140.55 E
Bolšoje Zagorje 8 Mg 57.47N 28.58 E
Bolšoj Gašun 16 Mf 47.22N 42.42 E
Bolšoj Ik 17 Hj 51.47N 56.20 E
Bolšoj Irgiz 19 Ee 52.01N 47.24 E
Bolšoj Jenisej 20 Ef 51.40N 94.26 E
Bolšoj Jugan 19 Hc 60.55N 73.40 E
Bolšoj Kamen 20 Ih 43.08N 132.28 E
Bolšoj Klimecki, Ostrov- 7 Ie 62.00N 35.15 E
Bolšoj Kujalnik 16 Gf 46.46N 30.38 E
Bolšoj Kumak 16 Ud 51.22N 58.55 E
Bolšoj Ljahovski, Ostrov- 20 Jb 73.35N 142.00 E
Bolšoj Murta 20 Ee 56.55N 93.10 E
Bolšoj Nimnyr 20 He 58.08N 125.45 E
Bolšoj Pit 20 Ee 59.02N 91.40 E
Bolšoj Tjuters, Ostrov- 8 Le 59.50N 27.10 E
Bolšoj Uluj 20 Ee 56.45N 90.46 E
Bolšoj Uvat, Ozero- 17 Oh 57.35N 70.30 E
Bolšoj Uzen 5 Kf 48.50N 49.40 E
Bolsón, Cerro del- 52 Jh 27.13S 66.06W
Bolšovcy 10 Ug 49.08N 24.47 E
Bolsward 12 Ha 53.04N 5.30 E
Boltaña 13 Mb 42.27N 0.04 E
Bolton 9 Kh 53.35N 2.26W
Bolu 23 Da 40.44N 31.37 E
Bolu Dağları 24 Eb 41.05N 32.05 E
Bolungarvik 7a Aa 66.09N 23.15W
Boluntay 27 Fd 36.29N 92.18 E
Bolva 16 Ic 53.17N 34.20 E
Bolvadin 24 Dc 38.42N 31.04 E
Bolzano/Bozen 6 Hf 46.31N 11.22 E
Bom, Rio- 55 Gf 23.56S 51.44W
Boma 31 Ii 5.51S 13.03 E
Bomassa 36 Cb 2.12N 16.12 E
Bombala 59 Jg 36.54S 149.14 E
Bombarral 13 Ce 39.16N 9.09W
Bombay 22 Jh 18.58N 72.50 E
Bomberai, Jazirah- 26 Jg 3.00S 133.00 E
Bombo 36 Fb 0.35N 32.32 E
Bomboma 36 Cb 2.26N 18.57 E
Bom Comércio 54 Ee 9.45S 65.54W
Bom Conselho 54 Ke 9.10S 36.41W
Bom Despacho 54 Ig 19.43S 45.15W
Bomdila 25 Ic 27.16N 92.23 E
Bomi/Bowo 27 Ge 30.02N 95.39 E
Bomi Hills 31 Fh 6.52N 10.45W
Bomili 36 Eb 1.40N 27.01 E
Bom Jardim de Goiás 55 Fc 16.17S 52.07W
Bom Jardim de Minas 55 Je 21.57S 44.11W
Bom Jesus 53 Gi 28.42S 50.24W
Bom Jesus da Lapa 53 Lg 13.15S 43.25W
Bom Jesus de Goiás 55 Hd 18.12S 49.37W
Bømlafjorden 8 Ae 59.40N 5.20 E
Bømlo 7 Ag 59.45N 5.10 E
Bomokandi 36 Eb 3.30N 26.08 E
Bomongo 36 Cb 1.22N 18.21 E
Bom Retiro 55 Hh 27.48S 49.31W
Bom Sucesso 55 Je 21.02S 44.46W
Bomu 30 Jh 4.08N 22.26 E
Bomu (EN)=Mbomou 30 Jh 4.08N 22.26 E
Bomu (EN)=Mbomou [3] 35 Cd 5.30N 23.30 E
Bon, Cape- (EN)=Ṭīb, Ra's Aṭ- 30 Ie 37.05N 11.03 E
Bona, Mount- 40 Kd 61.20N 141.50W
Bonaire 54 Ea 12.10N 68.15W
Bonaire Basin (EN) 50 Cg 11.25N 67.30W
Bonampak 48 Ni 16.43N 91.05W
Bonanza 49 Ef 14.01N 84.35W
Bonanza Peak 46 Eb 48.14N 120.52W
Bonao 49 Ld 18.56N 70.25W
Bonaparte, Mount- 46 Fb 48.45N 119.08W
Bonaparte Archipelago 57 Df 14.20S 125.20 E
Bonaparte Lake 46 Ea 51.16N 120.35W
Bonaparte Rocks 51p Cb 12.24N 61.30W
Bonasse 50 Fg 10.05N 61.52W
Bonavista 42 Mg 48.39N 53.07W
Bonavista Bay 42 Mg 49.00N 53.20W
Bon-Cagan-Nur 27 Gb 45.35N 99.15 E
Bondeno 14 Ff 44.53N 11.25 E
Bondo 31 Jh 3.49N 23.40 E
Bondoukou 34 Ed 8.02N 2.48W
Bondoukou [3] 34 Ed 8.20N 2.55W
Bondowoso 26 Fh 7.55S 113.49 E
Bone, Gulf of- (EN)=Bone, Teluk- 21 Oj 4.00S 120.40 E
Bone, Teluk-=Bone, Gulf of- (EN) 21 Oj 4.00S 120.40 E
Bone Bay 51a Db 18.45N 64.22W
Bonelohe 26 Hh 5.48S 120.27 E
Bönen 12 Jc 51.36N 7.46 E
Bone Rate, Kepulauan- 26 Hh 7.00S 121.00 E
Bone Rate, Pulau- 26 Hh 7.22S 121.08 E
Bonete, Cerro- 56 Gc 27.51S 68.47W
Bong 34 Cd 6.49N 10.19W
Bong [3] 34 Dd 7.00N 9.40W
Bonga 35 Fd 7.16N 36.14 E
Bongabong 26 Hd 12.45N 121.29 E
Bongandanga 36 Db 1.30N 21.03 E
Bongo, Massif des- 30 Jh 8.40N 22.25 E
Bongolava 37 Hc 18.35S 45.20 E
Bongor 31 Ig 10.17N 15.22 E
Bongouanou [3] 34 Ed 6.43N 4.12W
Bongouanou 34 Ed 6.39N 4.12W
Bonham 45 Hj 33.35N 96.11W
Bonheiden 12 Gc 51.02N 4.32 E
Bonhomme, Col du- 11 Nf 48.10N 7.06 E
Bonhomme, Pic- 49 Kd 19.05N 72.15W
Bonifacio 11a Bb 41.23N 9.09 E
Bonifacio, Bocche di-= Bonifacio, Strait of- (EN) 5 Gg 41.18N 9.15 E
Bonifacio, Strait of- (EN)= Bonifacio, Bocche di- 5 Gg 41.18N 9.15 E
Bonifati, Capo- 14 Jk 39.33N 15.52 E
Bonin Basin (EN) 60 Bb 29.00N 137.00 E
Bonin Islands (EN)= Ogasawara-Shotō 21 Qg 27.00N 142.10 E
Bonin Trench (EN) 3 If 30.00N 145.00 E
Bonita Springs 44 Gl 26.21N 81.47W
Bonito [Braz.] 55 Jb 15.20S 44.46W
Bonito [Braz.] 55 De 21.08S 56.28W
Bonito, Pico- 47 Ge 15.38N 86.55W
Bonito, Rio- [Braz.] 55 Hb 15.18S 49.36W
Bonito, Rio- [Braz.] 55 Gc 16.31S 51.23W
Bonn 6 Ge 50.44N 7.06 E
Bonn-Bad Godesberg 10 Df 50.41N 7.09 E
Bonnebosq 12 Ce 49.12N 0.05 E
Bonnechère River 44 Ic 45.31N 76.33W
Bonners Ferry 46 Gb 48.41N 116.18W
Bonnet, Lac du- 45 Ia 50.22N 95.55W
Bonnétable 11 Gf 48.11N 0.26 E
Bonnet Plume 42 Ec 65.53N 134.58W
Bonneval 11 Hf 48.11N 1.24 E
Bonneville 11 Mh 46.05N 6.25 E
Bonneville Salt Flats 46 If 40.45N 113.50W
Bonnières-sur-Seine 12 De 49.02N 1.35 E
Bonningues-lès-Ardres 12 Ed 50.47N 2.01 E
Bonny 34 Ge 4.25N 7.10 E
Bono 14 Dj 40.25N 9.02 E
Bō-no-Misaki 29 Bf 31.15N 130.13 E
Bonorva 14 Cj 40.25N 8.46 E
Bontang 26 Gf 0.08N 117.30 E
Bonthain 26 Gh 5.32S 119.56 E
Bonthe 34 Cd 7.32N 12.30W
Bontoc 26 Hc 17.05N 120.58 E
Bonyhád 10 Oj 46.18N 18.32 E
Boo, Kepulauan- 26 Ig 1.12S 129.24 E
Boola 34 Dd 8.22N 8.43W
Booligal 59 If 33.52S 144.53 E
Boone [Ia.-U.S.] 45 Je 42.04N 93.53W
Boone [N.C.-U.S.] 44 Gg 36.13N 81.41W
Booneville [Ar.-U.S.] 45 Ji 35.08N 93.55W
Booneville [Ms.-U.S.] 45 Li 34.39N 88.34W
Boon Point 51d Bb 17.10N 61.50W
Boonville [In.-U.S.] 44 Df 38.03N 87.16W
Boonville [Mo.-U.S.] 45 Jg 38.58N 92.44W
Boos 12 De 49.23N 1.12 E
Boothia, Gulf of- 38 Jb 71.00N 91.00W
Boothia Peninsula 38 Jb 70.30N 95.00W
Boot Reefs 60 Cj 10.00S 144.35 E
Booué 31 Ii 0.06S 11.56 E
Bophuthatswana 37 De 26.00S 25.30 E
Bopolu 34 Cd 7.04N 10.29W
Boppard 12 Jd 50.14N 7.36 E
Boquerón [3] 55 Bf 23.00S 61.00W
Boquerón 51a Ab 18.03N 67.09W
Boquilla, Presa de la- 48 Gd 27.30N 105.30W
Boquillas del Carmen 48 Hc 29.17N 102.53W
Bor [Czech.] 10 Ig 49.43N 12.47 E
Bor [R.S.F.S.R.] 19 Ed 56.23N 44.07 E
Bor [Sud.] 31 Kh 6.12N 31.33 E
Bor [Swe.] 8 Fg 57.07N 14.10 E
Bor [Tur.] 24 Fd 37.54N 34.34 E
Bor [Yugo.] 15 Fe 44.06N 22.06 E
Bora-Bora, Ile- 57 Lf 16.30S 151.45W
Borah Peak 38 He 44.08N 113.14W
Boraldaj 18 Gc 42.30N 69.05 E
Bora Marina 14 Jm 37.56N 15.55 E
Böramo 35 Gd 9.58N 43.07 E
Borås 7 Ch 57.43N 12.55 E
Borāzjān 24 Nh 29.16N 51.12 E
Borba [Braz.] 54 Gd 4.24S 59.35W
Borba [Port.] 13 Ef 38.48N 7.27W
Borborema, Planalto da- 52 Mf 7.00S 37.00W
Borca 15 Ib 47.11N 25.46 E
Borcea 15 Ke 44.20N 27.45 E
Borcea, Braţul- 15 Ke 44.40N 27.53 E
Borchgrevink Coast 66 Kf 73.00S 171.00 E
Borçka 24 Ib 41.22N 41.40 E
Borculo 12 Ib 52.07N 6.31 E
Borda da Mata, Serra- 55 Ie 21.18S 47.06W
Bordeaux 6 Fg 44.50N 0.34W
Borden 42 Ga 78.30N 110.30W
Borden Peninsula 38 Kb 73.00N 83.00W
Borders [3] 9 Kf 55.35N 3.00W
Bordertown 58 Fh 36.19S 140.47 E
Bordighera 14 Bg 43.46N 7.39 E
Bordj Bou Arreridj 32 Hb 36.04N 4.46 E
Bordj el Emir Abdelkader 13 Oi 35.52N 2.16 E
Bordj Fly Sainte Marie 32 Gd 27.18N 2.59W
Bordj-Menaïel 13 Ph 36.44N 3.43 E
Bordj Messouda 32 Ic 30.12N 9.25 E
Bordj Moktar 31 Hf 21.20N 0.56 E
Bordj Omar Driss 31 Hf 28.09N 6.49 E
Bord Khūn-e Now 24 Nh 28.03N 51.28 E
Bordon Camp 12 Bc 51.07N 0.51W
Boreal, Chaco- 52 Kh 23.00S 60.00W
Boren 8 Ff 58.35N 15.10 E
Borensberg 8 Ff 58.34N 15.17 E
Borgå/Porvoo 7 Ff 60.24N 25.40 E
Borgarnes 7a Bb 64.32N 21.55W
Børgefjell 7 Cd 65.23N 13.50 E
Borgentreich 12 Lc 51.34N 9.15 E
Borger [Neth.] 12 Ib 52.55N 6.48 E
Borger [Tx.-U.S.] 43 Gd 35.39N 101.24W
Borgholm 7 Dh 56.53N 16.39 E
Borghorst, Steinfurt- 12 Jb 52.08N 7.25 E
Borgia 14 Kl 38.49N 16.30 E
Borgloon 12 Hd 50.48N 5.20 E
Borgomanero 14 Ce 45.42N 8.28 E
Borgorose 14 Hh 42.11N 13.15 E
Borgo San Dalmazzo 14 Bf 44.20N 7.30 E
Borgo San Lorenzo 14 Fg 43.57N 11.23 E
Borgosesia 14 Ce 45.43N 8.16 E
Borgou [3] 34 Fc 10.30N 2.50 E
Borgo Val di Taro 14 Df 44.29N 9.46 E
Borgo Valsugana 14 Fd 46.03N 11.27 E
Borgu 30 Hg 10.35N 3.40 E
Borgworm/Waremme 11 Ld 50.42N 5.15 E
Bori 34 Ge 4.42N 7.21 E
Borinquen, Punta- 51a Ab 18.30N 67.10W
Borislav 19 Cf 49.18N 23.27 E
Borisoglebsk 6 Ke 51.23N 42.06 E
Borisov 19 Ce 54.15N 28.30 E
Borisovka 16 Jd 50.36N 36.06 E
Borispol 19 De 50.23N 30.59 E
Bo River 35 Dd 6.48N 27.55 E
Borja 14 Lf 44.31N 17.44 E
Borja [Peru] 54 Cd 4.26S 77.33W
Borja [Sp.] 13 Kc 41.50N 1.32W
Borjas Blancas/Les Borges Blanques 13 Mc 41.31N 0.52 E
Borken 10 Ce 51.51N 6.52 E
Borkou 30 Ig 18.15N 18.50 E
Borkou-Ennedi-Tibesti [3] 35 Bb 18.00N 19.00 E
Borkoviči 8 Mi 55.38N 28.23 E
Borkum 10 Cc 53.35N 6.41 E
Borlänge 7 Df 60.29N 15.25 E
Borlu 24 Cc 38.44N 28.27 E
Bormida 14 Cf 44.56N 8.40 E
Bormio 14 Ed 46.28N 10.22 E
Born 11 Fj 44.30N 1.00W
Borna 10 Ie 51.07N 12.30 E
Borndiep 12 Ha 53.25N 5.35 E
Borne 12 Ib 52.18N 6.45 E
Borneo/Kalimantan 21 Ni 1.00N 114.00 E
Bornheim 12 Id 50.46N 7.00 E
Bornholm 5 Hd 55.10N 15.00 E
Bornholm [2] 8 Fi 55.10N 15.00 E
Bornos 13 Gh 36.48N 5.44W
Bornova, İzmir- 24 Bc 38.27N 27.14 E
Bornu [2] 34 Hc 12.00N 12.40 E
Bornu 30 Ig 12.30N 13.00 E
Boro 30 Jh 8.52N 26.11 E
Borodino [R.S.F.S.R.] 7 Ii 55.32N 35.49 E
Borodino [R.S.F.S.R.] 20 Ee 55.57N 95.03 E
Borodinskoje 8 Md 61.00N 29.29 E
Borogoncy 20 Id 62.39N 131.08 E
Borohoro Shan 21 Ke 42.00N 85.00 E
Boromo 34 Ec 11.45N 2.56W
Borongan 26 Id 11.37N 125.26 E
Borotou 34 Dd 8.44N 7.30W
Borovan 15 Gf 43.26N 23.45 E
Borovec 15 Gg 42.16N 23.35 E
Boroviči 19 Dd 58.24N 33.56 E
Borovici 8 Mg 57.58N 29.47 E
Borovljanka 20 Df 52.38N 84.35 E
Borovo 14 Me 45.24N 18.59 E
Borovski 19 Gd 57.03N 65.44 E
Borovskoj 19 Ge 53.48N 64.17 E
Borrachas, Islas- 50 Dg 10.18N 64.44W
Borrān 35 Hc 10.11N 48.53 E
Borrby 8 Fi 55.27N 14.10 E
Borroloola 58 Ef 16.04S 136.17 E
Borş 15 Eb 47.07N 21.49 E
Borşa 15 Hb 47.39N 24.40 E
Borščovočny Hrebet= Borshchovochny Range (EN) 20 Gf 52.00N 118.30 E
Borsec 15 Ic 46.57N 25.34 E
Borshchovochny Range (EN) =Borščovočny Hrebet 20 Gf 52.00N 118.30 E
Borsod-Abaúj-Zemplén [2] 10 Qh 48.15N 21.00 E
Bortala/Bole 27 Dc 44.59N 81.57 E
Bortala He 27 Dc 44.53N 82.45 E
Bort-les-Orgues 11 Ii 45.24N 2.30 E
Borūjen 24 Ng 31.59N 51.18 E
Borūjerd 23 Gc 33.54N 48.46 E
Borzja 22 Nd 50.24N 116.31 E
Borzna 16 Hd 51.15N 32.29 E
Boržomi 16 Mi 41.50N 43.25 E
Borzsöny 10 Oi 47.55N 19.00 E
Borzyszkowy 10 Nb 54.03N 17.22 E
Bosa 14 Cj 40.18N 8.30 E
Bosanska Dubica 14 Ke 45.11N 16.48 E
Bosanska Gradiška 14 Le 45.09N 17.15 E
Bosanska Krupa 14 Kf 44.53N 16.10 E
Bosanski Brod 14 Me 45.08N 18.01 E
Bosanski Novi 14 Ke 45.03N 16.22 E
Bosanski Petrovac 14 Kf 44.34N 16.21 E
Bosanski Šamac 14 Me 45.04N 18.28 E
Bosansko Grahovo 23 Ff 44.11N 16.22 E
Bösäso 31 Lg 11.13N 49.08 E
Bosavi, Mount- 59 Ia 6.35S 142.50 E
Bosbeek 12 Hc 51.06N 5.48 E
Bose 22 Mg 24.01N 106.32 E
Boshan 27 Kd 36.30N 117.50 E
Boshrūyeh 24 Qf 33.53N 57.26 E
Bosilegrad 15 Fg 42.30N 22.28 E
Bosingfeld, Extertal- 12 Lb 52.04N 9.07 E
Bosna 14 Me 45.04N 18.28 E
Bosna 15 Kg 42.11N 27.27 E
Bosna=Bosnia (EN) 5 Hg 44.00N 18.00 E
Bosna = Bosnia (EN) 14 Lf 44.00N 18.00 E
Bosna i Hercegovina = Bosnia-Hercegovina (EN) [2] 14 Lf 44.15N 17.50 E
Bosnia (EN) = Bosna 14 Lf 44.00N 18.00 E
Bosnia (EN)=Bosna 5 Hg 44.00N 18.00 E
Bosnia-Hercegovina (EN) = Bosna i Hercegovina [2] 14 Lf 44.15N 17.50 E
Bosnik 26 Kg 1.10S 136.14 E
Bošnjakovo 20 Jg 49.41N 142.10 E
Bosobolo 36 Cb 4.11N 19.54 E
Bōsō-Hantō 28 Pg 35.20N 140.10 E
Bosporus (EN)=İstanbul Boğazi 5 Ig 41.00N 29.00 E
Bosque Bonito 48 Gb 30.42N 105.06W
Bossangoa 31 Ih 6.29N 17.27 E
Bossé Bangou 34 Fc 13.21N 1.18 E
Bossembélé 35 Bd 5.16N 17.39 E
Bossembélé II 35 Bd 5.41N 16.38 E
Bossier City 43 Ie 32.31N 93.43W
Bosso 34 Hc 13.42N 13.19 E
Bosso, Dallol- 30 Hg 12.25N 2.50 E
Bossut, Cape- 59 Ec 18.43S 121.38 E
Bostān 25 Db 30.26N 67.02 E
Bostānābād 24 Ld 37.50N 46.50 E
Bosten/Bagrax Hu 21 Ke 42.00N 87.00 E
Boston [Eng.-U.K.] 9 Mi 52.59N 0.01W
Boston [Ma.-U.S.] 39 Le 42.21N 71.04W
Boston Bar 46 Eb 49.52N 121.26W
Boston Deeps 12 Ca 53.00N 0.15 E
Boston Mountains 43 Id 35.50N 93.20W
Botan 24 Id 37.44N 41.48 E
Botas, Ribeirão das- 55 Fe 20.26S 53.43W
Botesdale 12 Db 52.20N 1.01 E
Botev 5 Ig 42.43N 24.55 E
Botevgrad 15 Gg 42.54N 23.47 E
Bothnia, Gulf of- (EN)= Bottniska viken 5 Hc 63.00N 20.00 E
Bothnia, Gulf of- (EN)= Pohjanlahti 5 Hc 63.00N 20.00 E
Boticas 13 Ec 41.41N 7.40W
Botletle 37 Cd 21.07S 24.42 E
Botlih 16 Oh 42.41N 46.13 E
Botna 15 Mc 46.48N 29.30 E
Botoşani [2] 15 Jb 47.40N 26.43 E
Botoşani 15 Jb 47.45N 26.40 E
Botrange 11 Md 50.30N 6.08 E
Botswana [1] 31 Jk 22.00S 24.00 E
Botte Donato 14 Kk 39.17N 16.27 E
Bottineau 43 Gb 48.50N 100.27W
Bottniska viken=Bothnia, Gulf of- (EN) 5 Hc 63.00N 20.00 E
Bottrop 10 Ce 51.31N 6.55 E
Botucatu 56 Kb 22.52S 48.26W
Botucatu, Serra de- 55 Hf 23.00S 48.20W
Botwood 42 Lg 49.08N 55.21W
Bouaflé 34 Dd 6.59N 5.45W
Bouaflé [3] 34 Dd 7.03N 5.48W
Bouaké 31 Gh 7.41N 5.02W
Bouaké [3] 34 Dd 7.45N 5.02W
Bou Anane 32 Gc 32.02N 3.03W
Bouar 31 Ih 5.57N 15.36 E
Bou Arfa 32 Gc 32.32N 1.57W
Boubin 10 Jh 48.58N 13.50 E
Bouca 31 Ih 6.30N 18.17 E
Bouchain 12 Fd 50.17N 3.19 E
Bouchegouf 14 Bn 36.28N 7.44 E
Bouche Island 51k Bb 13.57N 60.53W
Bouches-du-Rhône [3] 11 Kk 43.30N 5.00 E
Boudenib 32 Gc 31.57N 3.36W
Boudeuse Cay 37b Bb 6.05S 52.51 E
Boû Djébéha 34 Eb 18.33N 2.45W
Bouenza [3] 36 Bc 3.00S 13.00 E
Boufarik 13 Oh 36.34N 2.55 E
Bougaa 13 Rh 36.20N 5.05 E
Bougainville Island 57 Ge 6.00S 155.00 E
Bougainville Reef 59 Jc 15.30S 147.05 E
Bougainville Strait [Ocn.] 63a Cb 6.40S 156.10 E
Bougainville Strait [Van.] 63b Cb 15.50S 167.10 E
Bougouni 31 Gg 11.25N 7.28W

Index Symbols

[1] Independent Nation
[2] State, Region
[3] District, County
[4] Municipality
[5] Colony, Dependency
Continent
Physical Region
Historical or Cultural Region
Mount, Mountain
Volcano
Hill
Mountains, Mountain Range
Hills, Escarpment
Plateau, Upland
Pass, Gap
Plain, Lowland
Delta
Salt Flat
Valley, Canyon
Crater, Cave
Karst Features
Depression
Polder
Desert, Dunes
Forest, Woods
Heath, Steppe
Oasis
Cape, Point
Coast, Beach
Cliff
Peninsula
Isthmus
Sandbank
Island
Atoll
Rock, Reef
Islands, Archipelago
Rocks, Reefs
Coral Reef
Well, Spring
Geyser
River, Stream
Waterfall Rapids
River Mouth, Estuary
Lake
Salt Lake
Intermittent Lake
Reservoir
Swamp, Pond
Canal
Glacier
Ice Shelf, Pack Ice
Ocean
Sea
Gulf, Bay
Strait, Fjord
Lagoon
Bank
Seamount
Tablemount
Ridge
Shelf
Basin
Escarpment, Sea Scarp
Fracture
Trench, Abyss
National Park, Reserve
Point of Interest
Recreation Site
Cave, Cavern
Historic Site
Ruins
Wall, Walls
Church, Abbey
Temple
Scientific Station
Airport
Port
Lighthouse
Mine
Tunnel
Dam, Bridge

Bougtob	32	Hc	34.02N	0.05 E
Bouguenais	11	Eg	47.11N	1.37W
Bougzoul	13	Oi	35.42N	2.51 E
Bou Hadjar	14	Cn	36.30N	8.06 E
Bouhalla, Jbel- ▲	13	Gi	35.06N	5.07W
Bou Hamed	13	Hi	35.19N	4.58W
Bouillante	51e	Ab	16.08N	61.46W
Bouillon	11	Le	49.48N	5.04 E
Bouira	32	Hb	36.23N	3.54 E
Bouira [3]	32	Hb	36.15N	4.10 E
Bou Ismaïl	13	Oh	36.38N	2.41 E
Bou Izakarn	32	Fd	29.10N	9.44W
Bou Kadir	13	Nh	36.04N	1.07 E
Boukombé	34	Fc	10.11N	1.06 E
Boû Lanouâr	32	De	21.16N	16.30W
Boulay-Moselle	12	Ie	49.11N	6.30 E
Boulder [Co.-U.S.]	39	Ie	40.01N	105.17W
Boulder [Mt.-U.S.]	46	Ic	46.14N	112.07W
Boulder City	46	Hi	35.59N	114.50W
Boulemane	32	Gc	33.22N	4.45W
Boulemane [3]	32	Gc	33.02N	4.04W
Boulevard Atlántico	55	Dn	38.19S	57.59W
Boulia	59	Hd	22.54S	139.54 E
Bouligny	11	Le	49.17N	5.45 E
Boulogne ⟍	11	Eg	47.05N	1.40W
Boulogne-Billancourt	11	If	48.50N	2.15 E
Boulogne-sur-Mer	11	Hd	50.43N	1.37 E
Boulonnais ⊠	11	Hd	50.42N	1.40 E
Bouloupari	63b	Ce	21.52S	166.03 E
Boulsa	34	Ec	12.39N	0.34W
Boultoum	34	Hc	14.40N	10.18 E
Bou Maad, Djebel- ▲	13	Oh	36.26N	2.08 E
Boumba ⟍	34	Ie	2.02N	15.12 E
Boumdeïd	32	Ef	17.26N	11.21W
Boum Kabir	35	Bc	10.11N	19.24 E
Boumort ▲	13	Nb	42.14N	1.08 E
Bouna	31	Gh	9.16N	3.00W
Bouna [3]	34	Ed	9.15N	3.20W
Boû Nâga	32	Ef	19.00N	13.13W
Bou Nasser, Adrar- ▲	32	Gc	33.35N	3.53W
Boundary Peak ▲	46	Fh	37.51N	118.21W
Boundiali [3]	34	Dd	9.23N	6.32W
Boundiali	34	Dd	9.31N	6.29W
Boundji	36	Cc	1.03S	15.22 E
Boungou ⟍	35	Cd	6.45N	22.06 E
Bountiful	43	Ec	40.53N	111.53W
Bounty Bay ◐	64q	Ab	25.03S	130.05W
Bounty Islands ❖	57	Ii	47.45S	179.05 E
Bounty Trough (EN) ⋁	3	Jn	46.00S	178.00 E
Bourail	61	Cd	21.34S	165.30 E
Bourbon-Lancy	11	Jh	46.37N	3.47 E
Bourbonnais ▣	11	Ih	46.30N	3.00 E
Bourbonne-les-Bains	11	Lg	47.57N	5.45 E
Bourbourg	12	Ed	50.57N	2.12 E
Bourbre ⟍	11	Li	45.47N	5.11 E
Bourem	34	Eb	16.58N	0.21W
Bouressa	34	Fa	20.01N	2.18 E
Bourg-Achard	12	Ce	49.21N	0.49 E
Bourganeuf	11	Hi	45.57N	1.45 E
Bourgar'oûn, Cap- ►	32	Ib	37.06N	6.28 E
Bourg-de-Péage	11	Li	45.02N	5.03 E
Bourg-en-Bresse	11	Lh	46.12N	5.13 E
Bourges	6	Gf	47.05N	2.24 E
Bourget, Lac du- ◒	11	Li	45.44N	5.52 E
Bourgneuf, Baie de- ◐	11	Dg	47.05N	2.13W
Bourgogne	12	Ge	49.21N	4.04 E
Bourgogne=Burgundy (EN) ⊠	5	Gf	47.00N	4.30 E
Bourgogne=Burgundy (EN) ▣	11	Kg	47.00N	4.30 E
Bourgogne, Canal de- ⊟	11	Jg	47.58N	3.30 E
Bourgogne, Porte de- ⛰	11	Mg	47.38N	6.52 E
Bourgoin-Jallieu	11	Li	45.35N	5.17 E
Bourgtheroulde-Infreville	12	Ce	49.18N	0.53 E
Bourguébus	12	Be	49.07N	0.18W
Boû Rjeïmat	32	Df	19.04N	15.08W
Bourke	58	Fh	30.05S	145.56 E
Bourne	12	Bb	52.46N	0.23W
Bournemouth	9	Lk	50.43N	1.54W
Bourtanger Moor ⩸	12	Jb	52.50N	7.06 E
Bourth	12	Cf	48.46N	0.49 E
Bou Saâda	32	Hb	35.12N	4.11 E
Bou Sellam ⟍	13	Qh	36.26N	4.34 E
Boussac	11	Ih	46.21N	2.13 E
Boussé	34	Ec	12.39N	1.53W
Boussens	11	Gk	43.11N	0.58 E
Bousso	35	Bc	10.29N	16.43 E
Bouthaleb, Djebel- ▲	13	Ri	35.48N	5.12 E
Boutilimit	32	Ef	17.33N	14.42W
Bou-Tlélis	13	Li	35.34N	0.54W
Boutonne ⟍	11	Fi	45.55N	0.49W
Bouvet ❖	66	Cd	54.26S	3.24 E
Bouxwiller	12	Jf	48.49N	7.29 E
Bouza	34	Gc	14.25N	6.02 E
Bouzanne ⟍	11	Hh	46.38N	1.28 E
Bouzghaïa	13	Nh	36.20N	1.15 E
Bouzonville	12	Ie	49.18N	6.32 E
Bovalino	14	Kl	38.09N	16.11 E
Bovec	14	Hd	46.20N	13.33 E
Bovenkarspel	12	Hb	52.42N	5.17 E
Boves	12	Ee	49.51N	2.23 E
Bovino	14	Ji	41.15N	15.20 E
Bovril	55	Cj	31.21S	59.26W
Bowa → Muli	27	Hf	27.55N	101.13 E
Bowen [Arg.]	56	Ge	35.02S	67.31W
Bowen [Austl.]	58	Fg	20.01S	148.15 E
Bowers Bank (EN) ⊞	40a	Bb	54.00N	180.00
Bowers Ridge (EN) ⋀	40a	Bb	54.30N	180.00
Bowie	45	Hj	33.34N	97.51W
Bowkān	24	Ld	36.31N	46.12 E
Bowland, Forest of- ♣	9	Kh	54.00N	2.35W
Bowling Green [Ky.-U.S.]	43	Jd	37.00N	86.27W
Bowling Green [Oh.-U.S.]	44	Fe	41.22N	83.40W
Bowman	43	Gb	46.11N	103.24W
Bowman Bay ◐	42	Kc	65.33N	73.40W
Bowman Island ◆	66	He	65.17S	103.08 E
Bowman. Mount- ▲	46	Ea	51.10N	121.55W

Bowo/Bomi	27	Ge	30.02N	95.39 E
Bowokan, Kepulauan- ❖	26	Hg	2.05S	123.35 E
Bowral	59	Kf	34.28S	150.25 E
Bow River ⟍	42	Gg	49.56N	111.42W
Box Elder Creek ⟍	46	Kc	46.57N	108.04W
Boxelder Creek ⟍	46	Nd	45.59N	103.57W
Boxholm	7	Dg	58.12N	15.03 E
Boxian	27	Ke	33.46N	115.44 E
Boxing	27	Kd	37.07N	118.04 E
Boxmeer	12	Hc	51.39N	5.57 E
Boxtel	11	Lc	51.35N	5.20 E
Boyabat	24	Fb	41.28N	34.47 E
Boyabo	36	Cb	3.43N	18.46 E
Boyacá [2]	54	Db	5.30N	72.50W
Boyang	27	Kf	29.00N	116.41 E
Boyer, Cap- ►	63b	De	21.37S	168.07 E
Boyer Ahmadī-e Kohkīlūyeh [3]	23	Hc	31.00N	50.30 E
Boyle/Mainistir na Búille	9	Eh	53.58N	8.18W
Boyne/An Bhóinn ⟍	9	Gh	53.43N	6.15W
Boyne City	44	Ec	45.13N	85.01W
Boynes, Iles de- ❖	30	Nm	49.58S	69.59 E
Boynton Beach	44	Gl	26.32N	80.03W
Boysen Reservoir ⊡	46	Ke	43.19N	108.11W
Boz, Kūh-e- ▲	24	Pi	27.46N	55.54 E
Bozburun ►	15	Li	40.32N	28.46 E
Bozburun	15	Lm	36.41N	28.04 E
Bozburun Dağı ▲	24	Dd	37.18N	31.03 E
Bozcaada	24	Bc	39.50N	26.04 E
Bozcaada ◆	24	Bc	39.49N	26.03 E
Bozdağ	15	Lk	38.20N	28.06 E
Boz Dağı [Tur.] ▲	24	Cd	37.18N	29.12 E
Boz Dağı [Tur.] ▲	24	Cc	38.19N	28.08 E
Boz Dağlari ⛰	15	Kj	38.20N	27.45 E
Bozdoğan	15	Ll	37.40N	28.19 E
Bozeman	39	He	45.41N	111.02W
Bozen / Bolzano	6	Hf	46.31N	11.22 E
Bozene	36	Cb	2.56N	19.12 E
Bozhen	28	De	38.04N	116.34 E
Bozkol, Zaliv- ◐	18	Cb	45.20N	61.45 E
Bozkurt	24	Fb	41.57N	34.01 E
Bozok Platosu ▭	24	Fc	39.05N	35.05 E
Bozouls	11	Ij	44.28N	2.43 E
Bozoum	31	Ih	6.19N	16.23 E
Bozova	24	Hd	37.22N	38.31 E
Bozovici	15	Ee	44.56N	22.00 E
Bozqūsh, Kūh-e- ⛰	24	Ld	37.45N	47.40 E
Bra	14	Bf	44.42N	7.51 E
Braås	8	Fg	57.04N	15.03 E
Braathen, Cape- ►	66	Pf	71.48S	96.05W
Brabant ▣	11	Lc	51.10N	5.05 E
Brabant [3]	12	Gd	50.45N	4.30 E
Brabant-les-Villers	12	Gf	48.51N	4.59 E
Brâbîch ⊠	34	Eb	17.30N	3.00W
Brač ◆	14	Kg	43.19N	16.40 E
Bracadale, Loch- ⇌	9	Gd	57.20N	6.35W
Bracciano	14	Gh	42.06N	12.40 E
Bracciano, Lago di- ◒	14	Gh	42.05N	12.15 E
Bräcke	7	De	62.43N	15.27 E
Brackettville	45	Fl	29.19N	100.24W
Brački Kanal ⇌	14	Kg	43.24N	16.40 E
Brackley	12	Ab	52.02N	1.09W
Bracknell	9	Mj	51.26N	0.46W
Brackwede, Bielefeld-	12	Kc	51.59N	8.31 E
Brad	15	Fc	46.08N	22.47 E
Bradano ⟍	14	Kj	40.23N	16.51 E
Bradenton	43	Kf	27.29N	82.34W
Bradford [Eng.-U.K.]	9	Lh	53.48N	1.45W
Bradford [Pa.-U.S.]	44	He	41.57N	78.39W
Bradley Reef ✿	60	Gi	6.52S	160.48 E
Brady	43	He	31.08N	99.20W
Brady Mountains ⛰	45	Gk	31.20N	99.40W
Brædstrup	8	Ci	55.58N	9.37 E
Braemar	9	Jd	57.01N	3.24W
Braga [2]	13	Dc	41.35N	8.25W
Braga	6	Fg	41.33N	8.26W
Bragadiru	15	If	43.46N	25.31 E
Bragado	56	He	35.08S	60.30W
Braganca [2]	13	Fc	41.30N	6.45W
Bragança [Braz.]	53	Lf	1.03S	46.46W
Bragança [Port.]	13	Fc	41.49N	6.45W
Bragança Paulista	55	If	22.57S	46.34W
Brahestad/Raahe	7	Fd	64.41N	24.29 E
Brāhmanbāria	25	Id	23.59N	91.07 E
Brahmapur	22	Kh	19.19N	84.47 E
Brahmaputra ⟍	21	Lg	24.02N	90.59 E
Brăila [2]	15	Kd	45.13N	27.48 E
Brăila	6	If	45.16N	27.59 E
Brăilei, Balta- ⩸	15	Ke	45.00N	28.00 E
Braine	12	Fe	49.20N	3.32 E
Braine-l'Alleud/Eigenbrakel	12	Gd	50.41N	4.22 E
Brainerd	43	Ib	46.21N	94.12W
Braintree	12	Cc	51.53N	0.34 E
Braithwaite Point ►	59	Gb	11.58S	134.00 E
Brake	10	Ec	53.20N	8.29 E
Brakel [Bel.]	12	Fd	50.47N	3.45 E
Brakel [F.R.G.]	12	Lc	51.43N	9.11 E
Brakna [3]	32	Ef	17.30N	13.30W
Brålanda	8	Ef	58.34N	12.22 E
Bralorne	46	Da	50.47N	122.49W
Bramming	8	Ci	55.28N	8.42 E
Brämön ◆	8	Gb	62.10N	17.40 E
Brampton	44	Hd	43.41N	79.46W
Bramsche	10	Dd	52.24N	7.59 E
Bran, Pasul- ⩂	15	Id	45.26N	25.17 E
Branco ◆	32	Cf	16.39N	24.41W
Branco, Cabo- ►	52	Mf	7.09S	34.47W
Branco, Rio- [Braz.] ⟍	52	Jf	1.24S	61.51W
Branco, Rio- [Braz.] ⟍	55	De	21.00S	57.48W
Branco ou Cabixi, Rio- ⟍	55	Ba	13.55S	60.10W
Brandberg ▲	30	Ik	21.08S	14.35 E
Brandbu	7	Cf	60.26N	10.28 E
Brande	7	Bi	55.57N	9.07 E
Brandenburg	10	Id	52.25N	12.33 E
Brandenburg ▣	10	Jd	52.10N	13.30 E
Brändö ◆	8	Id	60.25N	21.05 E
Brandon [Eng.-U.K.]	12	Cb	52.27N	0.37 E

Brandon [Fl.-U.S.]	44	Fl	27.56N	82.17W
Brandon [Man.-Can.]	39	Je	49.50N	99.57W
Brandon [Vt.-U.S.]	44	Kd	43.47N	73.05W
Brandon Head/Na Machairí ►	9	Ci	52.16N	10.15W
Brandon Mount/Cnoc Bréanainn ▲	9	Ci	52.14N	10.15W
Brandval	8	Ed	60.19N	12.02 E
Brandvlei	37	Cf	30.25S	20.30 E
Brandýs nad Labem-Stará Boleslav	10	Kf	50.11N	14.40 E
Brăneşti	15	Je	44.27N	26.20 E
Braniewo	10	Pb	54.24N	19.50 E
Bransby Point ►	51c	Bc	16.43N	62.14W
Bransfield Strait ⇌	66	Re	63.00S	59.00W
Brańsk	10	Sd	52.45N	22.51 E
Branson	•45	Jh	36.39N	93.13W
Brantevik	8	Fi	55.31N	14.21 E
Brantford	42	Jh	43.08N	80.16W
Brantôme	11	Gi	45.22N	0.39 E
Bras d'Or Lake ◒	42	Lg	45.50N	60.50W
Brasil=Brazil (EN) [1]	53	Kf	9.00S	53.00W
Brasil, Planalto do- = Brazilian Highlands (EN) ▭	52	Lg	17.00S	45.00W
Brasiléia	54	Ef	11.00S	68.44W
Brasília	53	Lg	15.47S	47.55W
Brasília de Minas	55	Jc	16.12S	44.26W
Brasla ⟍	8	Kg	57.08N	24.50 E
Braslav	7	Gi	55.37N	27.05 E
Braşov [2]	15	Id	45.40N	25.10 E
Braşov	6	If	45.38N	25.35 E
Brass	34	Ge	4.19N	6.14 E
Brassac	11	Ik	43.38N	2.30 E
Brasschaat	12	Gc	51.17N	4.27 E
Brasstown Bald ▲	44	Fh	34.52N	83.48W
Brastavăţu	15	Hf	43.55N	24.24 E
Brataj	15	Ci	40.16N	19.40 E
Bråte	8	De	59.43N	11.27 E
Bratea	15	Fc	46.56N	22.37 E
Bratislava	6	Hf	48.09N	17.07 E
Bratsk	22	Md	56.05N	101.48 E
Bratskoje Vodohranilišče= Bratsk Reservoir (EN) ⊡	20	Fe	56.30N	102.00 E
Bratsk Reservoir (EN)= Bratskoje Vodohranilišče ⊡	20	Fe	56.30N	102.00 E
Brattleboro	43	Mc	42.51N	72.36W
Brattvåg	8	Bb	62.36N	6.27 E
Braubach	12	Jd	50.17N	7.40 E
Braunau am Inn	14	Hb	48.16N	13.02 E
Braunschweig	10	Gd	52.16N	10.32 E
Brava ◆	30	Eg	14.52N	24.43W
Brava, Costa- ☰	13	Pc	41.45N	3.04 E
Bråviken ◐	8	Gf	58.40N	16.30 E
Bravo del Norte, Río-= Grande, Rio- (EN) ⟍	38	Jg	25.57N	97.09W
Brawley	43	De	32.59N	115.34W
Bray ◆	42	Jc	69.20N	77.00W
Bray	37	Ce	25.26S	23.38 E
Bray/Brè	9	Gh	53.12N	6.06W
Bray, Pays de- ⊠	11	He	49.46N	1.26 E
Bray-Dunes	12	Ec	51.05N	2.31 E
Braye ⟍	11	Gg	47.45N	0.42 E
Bray Head ►	9	Cj	51.53N	10.25W
Bray-sur-Somme	12	Ee	49.56N	2.43 E
Brazi	15	Je	44.52N	26.01 E
Brazil	44	Df	39.32N	87.08W
Brazil (EN)=Brasil [1]	53	Kf	9.00S	53.00W
Brazil Basin (EN) ⌣	3	Dk	15.00S	25.00W
Brazilian Highlands (EN) = Brasil, Planalto do- ▭	52	Lg	17.00S	45.00W
Brazos ⟍	38	Jg	28.53N	95.23W
Brazos Santiago Pass ⇌	45	Hm	26.05N	97.16W
Brazzaville	31	Ii	4.16S	15.17 E
Brčko	14	Mf	44.52N	18.49 E
Brda ⟍	10	Oc	53.07N	18.08 E
Brdy ⛰	10	Jg	49.35N	13.50 E
Bré/Bray	9	Gh	53.12N	6.06W
Brea, Punta- ►	51a	Bc	17.54N	66.55W
Breaden, Lake- ◒	59	Fe	25.45S	125.40 E
Breaksea Sound ⇌	62	Bf	45.35S	166.40 E
Breaza [Rom.]	15	Id	45.11N	25.40 E
Breaza [Rom.]	15	Ib	47.37N	25.20 E
Breaza, Vîrful- ▲	15	Hb	47.22N	24.02 E
Brebes	26	Eh	6.53S	109.03 E
Brêche ⟍	12	Ee	49.16N	2.30 E
Brechin	9	Ke	56.44N	2.40W
Brecht	12	Gc	51.21N	4.38 E
Brechte ⊠	12	Jb	52.15N	7.10 E
Breckenridge [Mn.-U.S.]	45	Hc	46.16N	96.35W
Breckenridge [Tx.-U.S.]	45	Gj	32.45N	98.54W
Breckland ⊠	9	Ni	52.30N	0.35 E
Břeclav	10	Mh	48.46N	16.54 E
Brecon	9	Jj	51.57N	3.24W
Brecon Beacons ⛰	9	Jj	51.53N	3.31W
Breda	11	Kc	51.35N	4.46 E
Bredaryd	8	Eg	57.10N	13.44 E
Bredasdorp	31	Jl	34.32S	20.02 E
Brede ⟍	12	Cd	50.55N	0.43 E
Bredene	12	Ec	51.14N	2.58 E
Bredstedt	10	Eb	54.37N	8.59 E
Bredy	19	Ge	52.26N	60.21 E
Bree	12	Hc	51.08N	5.36 E
Breg ⟍	10	Ei	47.57N	8.31 E
Bregalnica ⟍	15	Eh	41.36N	21.56 E
Bregenz	14	Dc	47.30N	9.46 E
Bréhat, Ile de- ◆	11	Df	48.51N	3.00W
Breiðafjörður ◐	5	Db	65.15N	23.15W
Breimsvatnet ◒	8	Bc	61.40N	6.25 E
Breisach am Rhein	10	Dh	48.02N	7.35 E
Breisund ⇌	8	Ab	62.30N	6.00 E
Breit Bridge	37	Dd	22.12S	29.59 E
Breivikbotn	7	Fa	70.37N	22.29 E
Brejão	55	Ia	12.59S	46.28W
Brekken	7	Ce	62.39N	11.53 E
Brekstad	7	Be	63.41N	9.41 E

Bremangerlandet ◆	7	Af	61.50N	5.00 E
Brembana, Val- ∨	14	De	45.55N	9.40 E
Brembo ⟍	14	De	45.35N	9.32 E
Bremen [2]	10	Ec	53.05N	8.50 E
Bremen [F.R.G.]	6	Ge	53.05N	8.48 E
Bremen [In.-U.S.]	44	De	41.27N	86.09W
Bremerhaven	6	Ge	53.33N	8.35 E
Bremerton	43	Cb	47.34N	122.38W
Bremervörde	10	Fc	53.29N	9.08 E
Brendel	46	Kg	38.57N	109.50W
Brenham	45	Hk	30.10N	96.24W
Brenne ⊠	11	Hh	46.44N	1.14 E
Brennero, Passo del-= Brenner Pass (EN) ⩂	5	Hf	47.00N	11.30 E
Brennerpaß=Brenner Pass (EN) ⩂	5	Hf	47.00N	11.30 E
Brenner Pass (EN)= Brennero, Passo del- ⩂	5	Hf	47.00N	11.30 E
Brenner Pass (EN)= Brennerpaß ⩂	5	Hf	47.00N	11.30 E
Brenta ⟍	14	Ge	45.11N	12.18 E
Brentwood	9	Nj	51.38N	0.18 E
Brescia	6	Hf	45.33N	10.15 E
Breskens	12	Fc	51.24N	3.33 E
Breslau (EN)=Wrocław	6	He	51.06N	17.00 E
Bresle ⟍	11	Hd	50.04N	1.22 E
Bressanone / Brixen	14	Fd	46.43N	11.39 E
Bressay ◆	9	La	60.08N	1.05W
Bresse ⊠	11	Lh	46.30N	5.15 E
Bressuire	11	Fh	46.51N	0.29W
Brest [Bye.-U.S.S.R.]	6	Ie	52.06N	23.42 E
Brest [Fr.]	6	Ff	48.24N	4.29W
Brestova	14	Ie	45.08N	14.14 E
Brestskaja Oblast [3]	19	Ce	52.20N	25.30 E
Bretagne=Brittany (EN) ▣	11	Df	48.00N	3.00W
Bretagne=Brittany (EN) ⊠	5	Ff	48.00N	3.00W
Bretçu	15	Jc	46.03N	26.18 E
Breteuil [Fr.]	12	Cf	48.50N	0.55 E
Breteuil [Fr.]	11	Ie	49.38N	2.18 E
Breton, Marais- ⩸	11	Eh	46.56N	2.00W
Breton, Pertuis- ⇌	11	Eh	46.16N	1.22W
Breton Sound ⇌	45	Ll	29.30N	89.30W
Brett ⟍	12	Cc	51.58N	0.57 E
Brett, Cape- ►	62	Fa	35.10S	174.20 E
Bretten	12	Ke	49.03N	8.42 E
Bretteville-sur-Laize	12	Be	49.03N	0.20W
Breueh, Pulau- ◆	26	Be	5.41N	95.05 E
Breuil Cervinia	14	Be	45.56N	7.38 E
Breukelen	12	Db	52.10N	5.01 E
Breuna	12	Lc	51.25N	9.11 E
Breves	54	Hd	1.40S	50.29W
Brevik	7	Bg	59.04N	9.42 E
Brevoort ◆	42	Ld	63.30N	64.20W
Brewarrina	59	Je	29.57S	146.52 E
Brewerville	34	Cd	6.25N	10.47W
Brewster	46	Fb	48.06N	119.47W
Brewster, Kap- ►	67	Md	70.10N	21.30W
Brewton	43	Je	31.07N	87.04W
Brežiče	14	Je	45.54N	15.35 E
Brézina	32	Hc	33.05N	1.16 E
Březnice	10	Jg	49.33N	13.57 E
Breznik	15	Fg	42,44B	22.54 E
Brezno	10	Ph	48.49N	19.39 E
Brezoi	15	Hd	45.21N	24.15 E
Brezolles	12	Df	48.41N	1.04 E
Brezovo	15	Ig	42.21N	25.05 E
Bria	31	Jh	6.32N	21.59 E
Briance ⟍	11	Hi	45.47N	1.12 E
Briançon	11	Mj	44.54N	6.39 E
Brianza ⊠	14	De	45.45N	9.15 E
Briare, Canal de- ⊟	11	If	48.02N	2.43 E
Bribie Island ◆	59	Ke	27.00S	153.05 E
Bričany	15	Ka	48.18N	27.04 E
Bride ⟍	9	Fi	52.05N	7.50W
Bridgend	9	Jj	51.31N	3.35W
Bridgeport [Ca.-U.S.]	46	Fg	38.10N	119.13W
Bridgeport [Ct.-U.S.]	43	Mc	41.11N	73.11W
Bridgeport [Nb.-U.S.]	45	Ef	41.40N	103.06W
Bridge River ⟍	46	Ea	50.45N	121.55W
Bridger Peak ▲	46	Lf	41.12N	107.02W
Bridges Point ►	64g	Bb	1.58N	157.28W
Bridgeton	44	Jf	39.26N	75.14W
Bridgetown [Austl.]	59	Df	33.57S	116.08 E
Bridgetown [Bar.]	39	Nh	13.06N	59.37W
Bridgewater	42	Lh	44.23N	64.31W
Bridgwater	9	Kj	51.08N	3.00W
Bridgwater Bay ◐	9	Jj	51.16N	3.12W
Bridlington	9	Mg	54.05N	0.12W
Bridlington Bay ◐	9	Mg	54.04N	0.08W
Bridport	9	Kk	50.44N	2.46W
Brie ⊠	11	Jf	48.40N	3.30 E
Brielle	12	Gc	51.54N	4.10 E
Brienzer-See ◒	14	Bd	46.45N	7.55 E
Briey	11	Le	49.15N	5.56 E
Brig	14	Bd	46.20N	8.00 E
Brigach ⟍	10	Ei	47.58N	8.30 E
Brigham City	43	Ec	41.31N	112.01W
Brighstone	12	Ad	50.38N	1.23W
Bright	59	Jg	36.44S	146.58 E
Brightlingsea	12	Dc	51.48N	1.02 E
Brighton [Co.-U.S.]	45	Dg	39.59N	104.49W
Brighton [Eng.-U.K.]	6	Fe	50.50N	0.10W
Brignoles	11	Mk	43.24N	6.04 E
Brihuega	13	Jd	40.45N	2.52W
Brijuni ❖	14	Hf	44.55N	13.46 E
Brikama	34	Bc	13.16N	16.39W
Brilhante, Rio- ⟍	54	Hh	21.58S	54.18W
Brilon	12	Kc	51.24N	8.35 E
Brilon-Alme	12	Kc	51.27N	8.37 E
Brimstone Hill ∴	51c	Ab	17.21N	62.49W
Brindisi	6	Hg	40.38N	17.56 E
Brinkley	45	Ki	34.53N	91.12W
Brinkmann	55	Aj	30.52S	62.02W
Brionne	12	Ce	49.12N	0.43 E
Brioude	11	Ji	45.18N	3.24 E
Brisbane	58	Gg	27.28S	153.02 E
Brisighella	14	Ff	44.13N	11.46 E

Bristol ◆	66	Ad	59.02S	26.31W
Bristol [Eng.-U.K.]	6	Fe	51.27N	2.35W
Bristol [Tn.-U.S.]	44	Fg	36.36N	82.11W
Bristol Bay ◐	38	Dd	58.00N	159.00W
Bristol Channel ⇌	5	Fe	51.20N	4.00W
Bristol Lake ⩸	46	Hi	34.28N	115.41W
Bristow	45	Hi	35.50N	96.23W
Britannia Range ⛰	66	Jf	80.00S	158.00 E
British Columbia [3]	42	Fe	55.00N	125.00W
British Honduras → Belize	49	Ce	17.35N	88.35W
British Indian Ocean Territory [5]	22	Jj	7.00S	72.00 E
British Isles ❖	5	Fd	54.00N	4.00W
British Mountains ⛰	40	Kc	69.20N	140.20W
British Solomon Islands → Solomon Islands [1]	58	Ge	8.00S	159.00 E
British Virgin Islands [5]	39	Mh	18.20N	64.50W
Brits	37	De	25.40S	27.46 E
Britstown	37	Cf	30.37S	23.30 E
Britt	45	Je	43.06N	93.48W
Brittany (EN)=Bretagne ⊠	5	Ff	48.00N	3.00W
Brittany (EN)=Bretagne ▣	11	Df	48.00N	3.00W
Britton	45	Hd	45.48N	97.45W
Brive-la-Gaillarde	11	Hi	45.09N	1.32 E
Briviesca	13	Ib	42.33N	3.19W
Brixen / Bressanone	14	Fd	46.43N	11.39 E
Brixham	9	Jk	50.24N	3.30W
Brjansk	6	Je	53.15N	34.22 E
Brjanskaja Oblast [3]	19	De	52.50N	33.20 E
Brjuhoveckaja	16	Kg	45.46N	39.01 E
Brjukoviči	10	Jg	49.52N	24.00 E
Brno	6	Hf	49.12N	16.37 E
Broa, Ensenada de la- ◐	49	Fb	22.35N	82.00W
Broad Bay ◐	9	Gc	58.15N	6.15W
Broadford	9	Hd	57.14N	5.54W
Broad Sound ⇌	59	Jd	22.10S	149.45 E
Broadstairs	12	Dc	51.22N	1.27 E
Broadus	43	Fb	45.27N	105.25W
Brocēni/Broceny	8	Jh	56.41N	22.30 E
Broceny/Brocēni	8	Jh	56.41N	22.30 E
Brochet	42	He	57.53N	101.40W
Brochu, Lac- ◒	44	Ja	48.26N	74.15W
Brock ◆	42	Ga	77.55N	114.30W
Brocken ▲	10	Ge	51.48N	10.36 E
Brockman, Mount- ▲	59	Dd	22.28S	117.18 E
Brockton	44	Ld	42.05N	71.01W
Brockville	42	Jh	44.35N	75.41W
Brod	15	Eh	41.31N	21.14 E
Brodarevo	15	Cf	43.14N	19.43 E
Broderick Falls	36	Fb	0.37N	34.46 E
Brodeur Peninsula ⊢	38	Kb	73.00N	88.00W
Brodick	9	Hf	55.35N	5.09W
Brodnica	10	Pc	53.16N	19.23 E
Brody	16	Dd	50.04N	25.12 E
Broglie	12	Ce	49.01N	0.32 E
Brok	10	Rd	52.43N	21.52 E
Brok ⟍	10	Rd	52.38N	21.55 E
Broken Arrow	45	Ih	36.03N	95.48W
Broken Bow	45	Gf	41.24N	99.38W
Broken Bow Lake ⊡	45	Ii	34.10N	94.40W
Broken Hill	58	Fh	31.57S	141.27 E
Broken Ridge (EN) ⋀	3	Hm	31.30S	95.00 E
Brokind	8	Ff	58.13N	15.40 E
Brokopondo	54	Hb	5.04N	55.00W
Bromarv ⊢	8	Je	59.55N	23.00 E
Bromley, London-	12	Cc	51.25N	0.01 E
Bromölla	7	Dh	56.04N	14.28 E
Brønderslev	8	Cg	57.16N	9.58 E
Brong-Ahafo [3]	34	Ed	7.45N	1.30W
Bronnikovo	17	Ng	58.29N	68.27 E
Brønnøysund	7	Cd	65.28N	12.13 E
Bronte	14	Im	37.47N	14.50 E
Brooke's Point	26	Ge	8.47N	117.50 E
Brookfield	45	Jg	39.47N	93.04W
Brookhaven	45	Kk	31.35N	90.26W
Brookings [Or.-U.S.]	43	Cc	42.03N	124.17W
Brookings [S.D.-U.S.]	43	Hc	44.19N	96.48W
Brooks	42	Gf	50.35N	111.53W
Brooks Banks (EN) ⊞	60	Mc	24.05N	166.50W
Brooks Range ⛰	38	Dc	68.00N	154.00W
Brookston	45	Jc	46.50N	92.32W
Brooksville	44	Fk	28.33N	82.23W
Brookton	59	Df	32.22S	117.01 E
Brookville [In.-U.S.]	44	Ef	39.25N	85.01W
Brookville [Pa.-U.S.]	44	He	41.10N	79.06W
Broom ⟍	9	Hd	57.45N	5.05W
Broom, Loch- ◐	9	Hd	57.55N	5.15W
Broome	58	Df	17.58S	122.14 E
Brora ⟍	9	Jc	58.00N	3.50W
Brora	9	Jc	58.01N	3.51W
Brosna/An Bhrosnach ⟍	9	Fh	53.13N	7.58W
Broşteni	15	Ib	47.14N	25.42 E
Brou	11	Hf	48.13N	1.11 E
Brough	9	Kg	54.32N	2.19W
Broughton Island	39	Mc	67.35N	63.50W
Broussard	45	Kk	30.09N	91.58W
Brovary	16	Gd	50.32N	30.48 E
Brovst	8	Cg	57.06N	9.32 E
Brown Bank (EN)=Bruine Bank ⊞	12	Fb	52.35N	3.20 E
Brownfield	43	Ge	33.11N	102.16W
Browning	46	Ib	48.34N	113.01W
Browns Bank (EN) ⊞	42	Kh	42.40N	66.05W
Brownsville [Tn.-U.S.]	44	Ch	35.36N	89.15W
Brownsville [Tx.-U.S.]	39	Jg	25.54N	97.30W
Brownwood	43	He	31.43N	98.59W
Browse Island ◆	59	Eb	14.05S	123.35 E
Broye ⟍	14	Bd	46.55N	7.02 E
Bruay-en-Artois	11	Id	50.29N	2.33 E
Bruay-sur-l'Escaut	12	Fd	50.23N	3.32 E
Bruce	45	Lj	33.59N	89.21W
Bruce, Mount- ▲	57	Cg	22.36S	118.08 E
Bruce Crossing	44	Cb	46.32N	89.10W
Bruce Peninsula ⊢	42	Jh	44.59N	81.20W
Bruce Rock	59	Df	31.53S	118.09 E
Bruche ⟍	11	Nf	48.34N	7.43 E

Index Symbols

- [1] Independent Nation
- [2] State, Region
- [3] District, County
- [4] Municipality
- [5] Colony, Dependency
- ■ Continent
- ⊠ Physical Region
- ▣ Historical or Cultural Region
- ▲ Mount, Mountain
- △ Volcano
- ⌒ Hill
- ⛰ Mountains, Mountain Range
- ⌓ Hills, Escarpment
- ▭ Plateau, Upland
- ⩂ Pass, Gap
- ▁ Plain, Lowland
- ◣ Delta
- ▤ Salt Flat
- ∨ Valley, Canyon
- ◡ Crater, Cave
- ✲ Karst Features
- ⊔ Depression
- ⊓ Polder
- ◢ Desert, Dunes
- ♣ Forest, Woods
- ≀ Heath, Steppe
- ✳ Oasis
- ► Cape, Point
- ☰ Coast, Beach
- ◧ Cliff
- ⊢ Peninsula
- ⧓ Isthmus
- ░ Sandbank
- ◆ Island
- ⊙ Atoll
- ✱ Rock, Reef
- ❖ Islands, Archipelago
- ⁂ Rocks, Reefs
- ✿ Coral Reef
- ⊚ Well, Spring
- ⫯ Geyser
- ⟍ River, Stream
- ⟋ Waterfall Rapids
- ⋎ River Mouth, Estuary
- ◒ Lake
- ◓ Salt Lake
- ◌ Intermittent Lake
- ⊡ Reservoir
- ⩸ Swamp, Pond
- ⊟ Canal
- ❄ Glacier
- ❅ Ice Shelf, Pack Ice
- ≋ Ocean
- ≈ Sea
- ◐ Gulf, Bay
- ⇌ Strait, Fjord
- ◎ Lagoon
- ⊞ Bank
- ⩑ Seamount
- ⏏ Tablemount
- ⋀ Ridge
- ▔ Shelf
- ⌣ Basin
- ⌐ Escarpment, Sea Scarp
- ⚡ Fracture
- ⋁ Trench, Abyss
- ⚑ National Park, Reserve
- ✓ Point of Interest
- ↑ Recreation Site
- ◖ Cave, Cavern
- ⛫ Historic Site
- ∴ Ruins
- ⊓⊓ Wall, Walls
- ✝ Church, Abbey
- ⛩ Temple
- ⊗ Scientific Station
- ✈ Airport
- ⚓ Port
- ⛯ Lighthouse
- ⚒ Mine
- ∩ Tunnel
- ⌿ Dam, Bridge

Bruchhausen Vilsen 12 Lb 52.50N 9.01 E
Bruchmühlbach Miesau 12 Je 49.23N 7.28 E
Bruchsal 10 Eg 49.08N 8.36 E
Bruck an der Leitha 14 Kb 48.01N 16.46 E
Bruck an der Mur 14 Jc 47.25N 15.17 E
Brue 9 Kj 51.13N 3.00W
Bruges/Brugge 11 Jc 51.13N 3.14 E
Brugg 14 Cc 47.29N 8.12 E
Brugge/Bruges 11 Jc 51.13N 3.14 E
Brugge-Assebroek 12 Fc 51.12N 3.16 E
Brüggen 12 Ic 51.15N 6.11 E
Brugge-Sint-Andries 12 Fc 51.12N 3.10 E
Brühl [F.R.G.] 12 Id 50.50N 6.54 E
Brühl [F.R.G.] 12 Ke 49.24N 8.32 E
Bruine Bank=Brown Bank (EN) 12 Fb 52.35N 3.20 E
Bruin Point 43 Ed 39.39N 110.22W
Brule River 44 Cc 45.57N 88.12W
Brumado 54 Jf 14.13S 41.40W
Brummen 12 Ib 52.06N 6.10 E
Brummo 8 Ef 58.50N 13.40 E
Brumunddal 7 Cf 60.53N 10.56 E
Bruna 14 Eh 42.45N 10.53 E
Brune 12 Fe 49.45N 3.47 E
Bruneau 46 He 42.53N 115.48W
Bruneau River 46 He 42.57N 115.58W
Bruneck / Brunico 14 Fd 46.48N 11.56 E
Brunehamel 12 Ge 49.46N 4.11 E
Brunei 22 Ni 4.30N 114.40 E
Brunei, Teluk- 21 Ni 5.05N 115.18 E
Brunette Downs 59 Hc 18.38S 135.57 E
Brunflo 8 Fa 63.05N 14.49 E
Brunico / Bruneck 14 Fd 46.48N 11.56 E
Brunna 8 Ge 59.52N 17.25 E
Brunner 62 De 42.26S 171.19 E
Brunner, Lake- 62 De 42.35S 171.25 E
Brunnsberg 8 Ec 61.17N 13.55 E
Brunsbüttel 10 Fc 53.54N 9.07 E
Brunssum 12 Hd 50.57N 5.57 E
Brunswick [Ga.-U.S.] 43 Ke 31.10N 81.29W
Brunswick [Me.-U.S.] 43 Nc 43.55N 69.58W
Brunswick, Peninsula de- 52 Ik 53.30S 71.25W
Brunswick Lake 44 Fa 49.00N 83.23W
Bruntál 10 Ng 49.59N 17.28 E
Bruny Island 59 Jh 43.30S 147.05 E
Brus 15 Ef 43.23N 21.02 E
Brus, Laguna de- 49 Ef 15.50N 84.35W
Brush 43 Gc 40.15N 103.37W
Brus Laguna 49 Ef 15.47N 84.35W
Brusque 56 Kc 27.06S 48.56W
Brussel/Bruxelles=Brussels (EN) 6 Ge 50.50N 4.20 E
Brussels (EN)=Brussel/Bruxelles 6 Ge 50.50N 4.20 E
Brussels (EN)=Bruxelles/Brussel 6 Ge 50.50N 4.20 E
Brusset, 'Erg- 34 Hb 18.55N 10.30 E
Brusturi 15 Fb 47.09N 22.15 E
Brusy 10 Nc 53.53N 17.45 E
Bruxelles/Brussel=Brussels (EN) 6 Ge 50.50N 4.20 E
Bruzual 50 Bh 8.03N 69.19W
Bryan [Oh.-U.S.] 44 Ee 41.30N 84.34W
Bryan [Tx.-U.S.] 43 He 30.40N 96.22W
Bryan Coast 66 Pf 73.35S 84.00W
Bryne 7 Ag 58.44N 5.39 E
Brza Palanka 15 Fe 44.28N 22.27 E
Brzava kanal 15 Dd 45.16N 20.49 E
Brzeg 10 Nf 50.52N 17.27 E
Brzeg Dolny 10 Me 51.15N 16.40 E
Brzeziny 10 Pe 51.48N 19.46 E
Brzozów 10 Sg 49.42N 22.02 E
Bsharrī 24 Ge 34.15N 36.01 E
Bû 12 Df 48.48N 1.30 E
Bua 8 Eg 57.14N 12.07 E
Buada Lagoon 64e Ab 0.32S 166.54 E
Buala 63a Ge 8.10S 159.35 E
Bū al Ḩidān, Wādī- 33 Cd 27.25N 19.22 E
Buapinang 26 Hg 4.46S 121.34 E
Buatan 26 Df 0.44N 101.51 E
Bū aţ Tifl 33 Dd 28.54N 22.30 E
Bua Yai 25 Ke 15.34N 102.24 E
Bu'ayrāt al Ḩasūn 33 Cc 31.24N 15.44 E
Bubanza 36 Ec 3.06S 29.23 E
Bubaque 34 Bc 11.17N 15.50W
Būbīyan 24 Mh 29.45N 48.15 E
Bubu 36 Gd 6.03S 35.19 E
Bubye 37 Ed 22.20S 31.07 E
Buca 15 Kk 38.22N 27.11 E
Bučač 16 De 49.04N 25.23 E
Bucačača 20 Gf 52.59N 116.55 E
Bucak 24 Dd 37.28N 30.36 E
Bucaramanga 53 Ie 7.08N 73.09W
Bucas Grande 26 Ie 9.40N 125.58 E
Buccament Bay 51n Ba 13.12N 61.17W
Buccaneer Archipelago 59 Ec 16.17S 123.20 E
Bucecea 15 Jb 47.46N 26.26 E
Buchanan 31 Fh 5.53N 10.03W
Buchanan, Lake- [Austl.] 59 Jd 21.30S 145.50 E
Buchanan, Lake- [Tx.-U.S.] 45 Gk 30.48N 98.25W
Buchanan Bay 42 Ka 78.55N 75.00W
Buchan Gulf 42 Kb 71.48N 74.06W
Buchardo 56 Hd 34.43S 63.31W
Bucharest (EN)=Bucureşti 6 Ig 44.26N 26.06 E
Buchen 10 Fg 49.31N 9.20 E
Buchholz in der Nordheide 10 Fc 53.20N 9.52 E
Buchon, Point- 46 Ei 35.15N 120.54W
Buchs 14 Dc 47.10N 9.30 E
Buchy 12 De 49.35N 1.22 E
Bückeburg 12 Lb 52.16N 9.03 E
Buckeye 46 Ij 33.22N 112.35W
Buckhaven 9 Je 56.11N 3.03W
Buckie 9 Kd 57.40N 2.58W
Buckingham [Eng.-U.K.] 12 Bb 52.00N 0.59W
Buckingham [Que.-Can.] 44 Jc 45.35N 75.25W
Buckingham Bay 59 Hb 12.10S 135.46 E
Buckinghamshire 9 Mj 51.50N 0.55W
Buckland 40 Gc 66.16N 161.20W
Buckle Island 66 Ke 66.47S 163.14 E
Buckley Bay 66 Je 68.16S 148.12 E
Bucks 9 Mj 51.50N 0.55W
Bucksport 44 Mc 44.34N 68.48W
Buco Zau 36 Bc 4.50S 12.33 E
Bu Craa 32 Ed 26.17N 12.46W
Bucureşti 15 Je 44.30N 26.05 E
Bucureşti=Bucharest (EN) 6 Ig 44.26N 26.06 E
Bucy-lès-Pierrepont 12 Fe 49.39N 3.54 E
Bucyrus 44 Fe 40.47N 82.57W
Bud 7 Be 62.55N 6.55 E
Budacu, Virful- 15 Ib 47.07N 25.41 E
Buda-Koševelo 16 Gc 52.43N 30.39 E
Budapest 10 Pi 47.30N 19.05 E
Budapest 6 Hf 47.30N 19.05 E
Búdardalur 7a Bb 65.07N 21.46W
Budaun 25 Fc 28.03N 79.07 E
Budbud 35 He 4.13N 46.31 E
Budd Coast 66 He 66.30S 113.00 E
Buddusò 14 Di 40.35N 9.15 E
Bude [Eng.-U.K.] 9 Ik 50.50N 4.33W
Bude [Ms.-U.S.] 45 Kk 31.28N 90.51W
Bude Bay 9 Ik 50.50N 4.37W
Budel 12 Hc 51.16N 5.30 E
Budennovsk 19 Eg 44.45N 44.08 E
Budeşti 15 Je 44.14N 26.27 E
Budia 13 Jd 40.38N 2.45W
Büdingen 10 Ff 50.18N 9.07 E
Búdir 7a Cb 64.56N 14.01W
Budjala 36 Cb 2.39N 19.42 E
Budkowiczanka 10 Nf 50.52N 17.33 E
Budogošč 7 Hg 59.19N 32.29 E
Budrio 14 Ff 44.32N 11.32 E
Budslav 8 Lj 54.49N 27.32 E
Budva 15 Bg 42.17N 18.51 E
Budyšin/Bautzen 10 Ke 51.11N 14.26 E
Budžjak 15 Lc 46.15N 28.45 E
Buea 34 Ge 4.09N 9.14 E
Buech 11 Lj 44.12N 5.57 E
Buenaventura [Col.] 53 Ie 3.53N 77.04W
Buenaventura [Mex.] 47 Cc 29.51N 107.29W
Buenaventura, Bahia de- 54 Cc 3.45N 77.15W
Buenavista 48 Ef 23.39N 109.42W
Buena Vista [Co.-U.S.] 45 Cg 38.50N 106.08W
Buena Vista [Mex.] 48 Mi 16.05N 93.00W
Buena Vista [Mex.] 48 Bb 31.10N 115.40W
Buena Vista [Ven.] 50 Eh 9.02N 63.49W
Buenavista, Bahía de- 49 Hb 22.30N 79.08W
Buendia, Embalse de- 13 Jd 40.25N 2.43W
Buenópolis 55 Jc 17.54S 44.11W
Buenos Aires 56 Ie 36.00S 60.00W
Buenos Aires [Arg.] 53 Ki 34.36S 58.27W
Buenos Aires [C.R.] 49 Fi 10.04N 84.26W
Buenos Aires, Lago- 52 Ij 46.30S 72.00W
Buffalo 42 Fe 60.52N 115.03W
Buffalo [N.Y.-U.S.] 39 Le 42.54N 78.53W
Buffalo [Ok.-U.S.] 45 Gh 36.50N 99.38W
Buffalo [S.D.-U.S.] 43 Gb 45.35N 103.33W
Buffalo [Tx.-U.S.] 45 Hk 31.28N 96.04W
Buffalo [Wy.-U.S.] 43 Fc 44.21N 106.42W
Buffalo Bill Reservoir 46 Kd 44.29N 109.13W
Buffalo Lake 42 Fd 60.12N 115.25W
Buffalo Narrows 42 Ge 55.51N 108.30W
Buffalo Pound Lake 46 Ma 50.38N 105.20W
Buffels 37 Be 29.36S 17.04 E
Bū Fishah 14 En 36.18N 10.28 E
Buford 44 Fh 34.07N 84.00W
Buftea 15 Ie 44.34N 25.57 E
Bug 5 Ie 52.31N 21.05 E
Buga 54 Cc 3.55N 76.18W
Bugarach, Pech de- 11 Il 42.52N 2.23 E
Bugeat 11 Hi 45.36N 1.56 E
Bugene 36 Fc 1.35S 31.08 E
Bugey 11 Li 45.48N 5.30 E
Bugojno 23 Ff 44.03N 17.27 E
Bugøynes 7 Gb 69.58N 29.39 E
Bugrino 17 Db 68.48N 49.09 E
Bugsuk 26 Ge 8.15N 117.18 E
Bugt 27 Lb 48.47N 121.55 E
Bugulma 19 Fe 54.33N 52.48 E
Bugun 18 Hc 43.22N 70.10 E
Bugun 18 Gc 42.56N 68.36 E
Bügür/Luntai 27 Dc 41.46N 84.10 E
Buguruslan 19 Fe 53.39N 52.30 E
Buhara 22 If 39.49N 64.25 E
Buharskaja Oblast 19 Gg 41.20N 64.20 E
Bū Ḩaşā' 24 Ok 23.20N 53.20 E
Buhera 37 Ec 19.18S 31.29 E
Buh He 27 Gd 36.58N 99.48 E
Buhl 46 He 42.36N 114.46W
Bühl 10 Eh 48.42N 8.09 E
Bühödle 35 Hd 8.15N 46.20 E
Buhtarminskoje Vodohranilišče 19 If 49.10N 84.00 E
Bui Dam 34 Ed 8.22N 2.10W
Builth Wells 9 Ji 52.09N 3.24W
Buin [Chile] 56 Fd 33.44S 70.44W
Buin [Pap.N.Gui.] 60 Fi 6.50S 155.44 E
Buinsk 19 Ee 54.59N 48.17 E
Buir Nur 27 Kb 47.48N 117.42 E
Buitrago del Lozoya 13 Id 41.00N 3.38W
Buj 17 Gh 56.15N 54.12 E
Buj 19 Ed 58.29N 41.31 E
Bujalance 13 Hg 37.54N 4.22W
Bujanovac 15 Eg 42.28N 21.47 E
Bujaraloz 13 Lc 41.30N 0.09W
Buje 14 He 45.24N 13.40 E
Bujnaksk 19 Eg 42.49N 47.07 E
Bujukly 20 Jg 49.33N 142.55 E
Bujumbura 31 Ji 3.23S 29.22 E
Bujunda 20 Kd 62.00N 153.30 E
Buk 10 Md 52.22N 16.31 E
Bük 10 Mi 47.23N 16.45 E
Buk 10 Hb 54.10N 11.42 E
Buka Island 57 Ge 5.15S 154.35 E
Bukakata 36 Fc 0.18S 32.02 E
Bukama 31 Ji 9.12S 25.51 E
Buka Passage 63a Ba 5.25S 154.41 E
Bukavu 31 Ji 2.30S 28.52 E
Bukene 36 Fc 4.14S 32.53 E
Bukhā 24 Qi 26.10N 56.09 E
Bukit Besi 26 Df 4.46N 103.12 E
Bukit Mertajam 26 De 5.22N 100.28 E
Bukittinggi 22 Mj 0.19S 100.22 E
Bükk 10 Qh 48.05N 20.30 E
Bukoba 31 Ki 1.20S 31.49 E
Bukovina 15 Ia 48.00N 25.30 E
Bukowiec 10 Ld 52.23N 15.20 E
Bukuru 34 Gd 9.48N 8.52 E
Bül, Küh-e- 23 Hc 30.48N 52.45 E
Bulajevo 19 He 54.53N 70.26 E
Bulan 26 Hd 12.40N 123.52 E
Bulanaš 17 Kh 57.16N 62.02 E
Bulancak 24 Hb 40.57N 38.14 E
Bulanık 24 Jc 39.05N 42.15 E
Būlāq 33 Fd 25.12N 30.32 E
Bulawayo 31 Jk 20.09S 28.34 E
Buldan 24 Cc 38.03N 28.51 E
Buldir 40a Bb 52.21N 175.54 E
Bulgan [Mong.] 27 Hc 44.05N 103.32 E
Bulgan [Mong.] 27 Hb 48.45N 103.34 E
Bulgan [Mong.] 27 Fb 46.05N 91.34 E
Bulgaria (EN)=Bâlgarija 6 Ig 43.00N 25.00 E
Buli 26 If 0.53N 128.18 E
Buli, Teluk- 26 If 0.45N 128.30 E
Buliluyan, Cape- 26 Ge 8.20N 117.11 E
Bulki 35 Fd 6.01N 36.36 E
Bullahār 35 Gc 10.23N 44.27 E
Bullange/Büllingen 12 Id 50.25N 6.16 E
Bullaque 13 Hf 38.59N 4.17W
Bulla Regia 14 Cn 36.33N 8.45 E
Bullas 13 Kf 38.03N 1.40W
Bulle 14 Bd 46.37N 7.04 E
Buller 62 Dd 41.44S 171.35 E
Bullfinch 59 Df 30.59S 119.06 E
Büllingen/Bullange 12 Id 50.25N 6.16 E
Bullion Mountains 46 Hi 34.25N 116.00W
Bulloo River 57 Fg 28.43S 142.30 E
Bull Point [Eng.-U.K.] 9 Ij 51.12N 4.10W
Bull Point [Falk.Is.] 56 Ih 52.19S 59.18W
Bulls 62 Fd 40.10S 175.23 E
Bulls Bay 44 Hi 32.59N 79.33W
Bull Shoals Lake 45 Jh 36.30N 92.50W
Bully Choop Mountain 46 Df 40.35N 122.45W
Bully-les-Mines 12 Ed 50.26N 2.43 E
Bulo Berde 35 He 3.52N 45.40 E
Bulolo 60 Di 7.12S 146.39 E
Bulqiza 15 Dh 41.30N 20.21 E
Bulter 45 Ig 38.16N 94.20W
Bultfontein 37 De 28.20S 26.05 E
Bulukumba 26 Hh 5.33S 120.11 E
Bulungu [Zaire] 36 Cc 4.33S 18.36 E
Bulungu [Zaire] 36 Dd 6.04S 21.54 E
Bumba 31 Jh 2.11N 22.28 E
Bumbah, Khalīj al- 33 Dc 32.25N 23.06 E
Buna 15 Ch 41.52N 19.22 E
Buna 36 Gb 2.47N 39.31 E
Bunbury 58 Ch 33.19S 115.38 E
Buncrana/Bun Cranncha 9 Ff 55.08N 7.27W
Bun Cranncha/Buncrana 9 Ff 55.08N 7.27W
Bunda 36 Fc 2.03S 33.52 E
Bundaberg 58 Gg 24.52S 152.21 E
Bünde 12 Kb 52.12N 8.35 E
Bundesrepublik Deutschland =Germany, Federal Republic of- (EN) 6 Ge 51.00N 9.00 E
Bun Dobhráin/Bundoran 9 Eg 54.28N 8.17W
Bundoran/Bun Dobhráin 9 Eg 54.28N 8.17W
Bungay 12 Db 52.27N 1.27 E
Bungku 26 Hg 2.33S 121.58 E
Bungo 36 Cd 7.26S 15.24 E
Bungo Strait (EN)=Bungo-Suidō 28 Lh 32.40N 132.18 E
Bungo-Suidō=Bungo Strait (EN) 28 Lh 32.40N 132.18 E
Bungotakada 29 Be 33.33N 131.27 E
Bungsberg 10 Gb 54.12N 10.43 E
Buni 34 Hc 11.12N 12.02 E
Bunja 31 Kh 1.34N 30.15 E
Bunji 25 Ea 35.40N 74.36 E
Bunker 45 Kh 37.27N 91.13W
Bunker Group 59 Kd 23.50S 152.20 E
Bunkeya 36 Ee 10.24S 26.58 E
Bunkie 45 Jk 30.57N 92.11W
Bunnerfjällen 8 Ea 63.10N 12.34 E
Buñol 13 Le 39.25N 0.47W
Bunschoten 12 Hb 52.14N 5.24 E
Buntingford 12 Bc 51.57N 0.01W
Buntok 26 Fg 1.42S 114.48 E
Bünyan 24 Fc 38.51N 35.52 E
Bunyu, Pulau- 26 Gf 3.30N 117.50 E
Buon Me Thuot 25 Lf 12.40N 108.03 E
Buor-Haja, Guba- 20 Ib 71.00N 131.00 E
Buotama 20 Hd 61.17N 128.55 E
Buqayaq 23 Gd 25.56N 49.40 E
Buqda Kōsār 35 Ge 4.31N 44.49 E
Bur 20 Hb 71.40N 123.40 E
Bura 36 Gc 1.06S 39.57 E
Buram 31 Jg 10.49N 25.10 E
Buran 19 If 48.04N 85.15 E
Burang 27 De 30.18N 81.08 E
Burāq 24 Gf 33.10N 36.29 E
Buras 45 Ll 29.21N 89.32W
Buraydah 22 Gg 26.20N 43.59 E
Burbach 12 Kd 50.43N 8.03 E
Burdab 35 Hd 9.05N 46.30 E
Burdekin River 59 Jc 19.39S 147.30 E
Burdère 35 He 3.30N 45.37 E
Burdur 23 Db 37.43N 30.17 E
Burdur Gölü 24 Dd 37.44N 30.12 E
Burdwood Bank (EN) 56 Ih 54.15S 59.00W
Bure 12 Db 52.38N 1.45 E
Bure [Eth.] 35 Fd 8.20N 35.08 E
Bure [Eth.] 35 Fc 10.43N 37.03 E
Bureå 7 Ed 64.37N 21.12 E
Bureinski Hrebet=Bureya Range (EN) 21 Pd 50.40N 134.00 E
Bureja 20 Hg 49.43N 129.51 E
Bureja 21 Oe 49.25N 129.35 E
Büren 10 Ee 51.33N 8.34 E
Buren-Cogt 27 Jb 46.45N 111.30 E
Bureya Range (EN)= Bureinski Hrebet 21 Pd 50.40N 134.00 E
Burfjord 7 Fb 69.56N 22.03 E
Bür Gābo 35 Gf 1.10S 41.50 E
Burgas 6 Ig 42.30N 27.28 E
Burgas 15 Kg 42.30N 27.20 E
Burgas, Gulf of- (EN)= Burgaski Zaliv 15 Kg 42.30N 27.33 E
Burgaski Zaliv=Burgas, Gulf of- (EN) 15 Kg 42.30N 27.33 E
Burg auf Fehmarn 10 Hb 54.26N 11.12 E
Burg auf Fehmarn-Puttgarden 10 Hb 54.30N 11.13 E
Burgaw 44 Ih 34.33N 77.56W
Burgaz Dağı 15 Mk 38.25N 29.46 E
Burg bei Magdeburg 10 Hd 52.16N 11.51 E
Burgdorf [F.R.G.] 10 Gd 52.27N 10.01 E
Burgdorf [Switz.] 14 Bc 47.04N 7.37 E
Burgenland 14 Kc 47.30N 16.25 E
Burgersdorp 37 Df 31.00S 26.20 E
Burgess Hill 12 Bd 50.58N 0.08W
Burgfjället 7 Dd 64.56N 15.03 E
Burghausen 10 Ih 48.10N 12.50 E
Burghūth, Sabkhat al- 24 Ie 34.58N 41.06 E
Burglengenfeld 10 Ig 49.12N 12.02 E
Burgos 13 Ib 42.20N 3.40W
Burgos [Mex.] 48 Je 24.57N 98.57W
Burgos [Sp.] 6 Fg 42.21N 3.42W
Burg-Reuland 12 Id 50.12N 6.09 E
Burgsvik 7 Eh 57.03N 18.16 E
Burgundy (EN)= Bourgogne 5 Gf 47.00N 4.30 E
Burgundy (EN)= Bourgogne 11 Kg 47.00N 4.30 E
Burgwald 12 Kd 50.57N 8.48 E
Bür Hakkaba 35 Ge 2.43N 44.10 E
Burhaniye 24 Bc 39.30N 26.58 E
Burhānpur 22 Jg 21.18N 76.14 E
Burias 26 Hd 12.57N 123.08 E
Buribaj 17 Ij 51.57N 58.11 E
Burica, Punta- 47 Hg 8.03N 82.53W
Burien 46 Dc 47.27N 122.21W
Burin Peninsula 42 Lg 47.00N 55.40W
Buriram 25 Kf 14.59N 103.08 E
Buriti, Rio- 55 Ca 12.50S 58.28W
Buriti Alegre 55 Hd 18.09S 49.03W
Buriti Bravo 54 Je 5.50S 43.50W
Buriti dos Lopes 54 Jd 3.10S 41.52W
Buritis 55 Ib 15.37S 46.26W
Burj al Ḩaţţābah 32 Ic 30.20N 9.30 E
Burjasot 13 Le 39.31N 0.25W
Burjatskaja ASSR 20 Ff 53.00N 110.00 E
Burj Şāfitā 24 Ge 34.49N 36.07 E
Burkandja 20 Jd 63.27N 147.27 E
Burkburnett 45 Gi 34.06N 98.34W
Burke 45 Ge 43.11N 99.18W
Burke, Mount- 46 Ha 50.18N 114.30W
Burke Island 66 Of 73.08S 105.06W
Burke River 59 Hd 23.12S 139.33 E
Burketown 58 Ef 17.44S 139.22 E
Burkina Faso 31 Gg 13.00N 2.00W
Burley 43 Ec 42.32N 113.48W
Burli 16 Rd 51.28N 52.44 E
Burlingame 45 Ig 38.45N 95.50W
Burlington [Co.-U.S.] 43 Gd 39.18N 102.16W
Burlington [Ia.-U.S.] 43 Ic 40.49N 91.07W
Burlington [Ks.-U.S.] 45 Ig 38.12N 95.45W
Burlington [N.C.-U.S.] 44 Hg 36.06N 79.26W
Burlington [Ont.-Can.] 44 Hd 43.19N 79.43W
Burlington [Vt.-U.S.] 43 Mc 44.28N 73.14W
Burlington [Wi.-U.S.] 45 Le 42.41N 88.17W
Burma 22 Lg 22.00N 98.00 E
Burma (Myanmar-Nainggan-Daw) 22 Lg 22.00N 98.00 E
Burnazului, Cîmpia- 15 Ie 44.10N 25.50 E
Burnett River 59 Kd 24.46S 152.25 E
Burney 46 Ef 40.53N 121.40W
Burnham Market 12 Cb 52.57N 0.44 E
Burnham-on-Crouch 12 Cc 51.37N 0.50 E
Burnie 59 Jh 41.04S 145.54 E
Burnley 9 Kh 53.48N 2.14W
Burns 43 Dc 43.35N 119.03W
Burnside 42 Gc 66.51N 108.04W
Burnside, Lake- 59 Ee 25.20S 123.10 E
Burns Lake 42 Ef 54.14N 125.46W
Burnsville 44 Fh 35.55N 82.18W
Burnt Lava Flow 46 Ef 41.35N 121.35W
Burnt River 44 Hc 44.35N 78.46W
Burntwood 42 He 56.08N 96.33W
Bur'o 31 Lh 9.30N 45.34 E
Burqin 27 Eb 47.43N 86.53 E
Burqin He 27 Eb 47.42N 86.50 E
Burqūm, Ḩarrat al- 33 He 20.54N 42.00 E
Burra 59 Hf 33.40S 138.56 E
Burragorang Lake 59 Kf 34.00S 150.25 E
Burreli 15 Ch 41.37N 20.00 E
Burrendong Reservoir 59 Jf 32.40S 149.10 E
Burriana 13 Le 39.53N 0.05W
Burro, Serranias del 48 Ic 28.50N 101.35W
Burrow Head 9 Ig 54.41N 4.24W
Bursa 22 Ee 40.11N 29.04 E
Būr Sa'īd=Port Said (EN) 31 Ke 31.16N 32.18 E
Burscheid 12 Jc 51.06N 7.07 E
Bürstadt 12 Ke 49.38N 8.27 E
Burštyn 16 De 49.16N 24.37 E
Būr Sūdān=Port Sudan (EN) 31 Kg 19.37N 37.14 E
Burt Lake 44 Ec 45.27N 84.40W
Burtnieku, Ozero- 8 Kg 57.35N 25.10 E
Burtnieku, Ozero-/Burtnieku Ezers 8 Kg 57.35N 25.10 E
Burtnieku Ezers 8 Kg 57.35N 25.10 E
Burtnieku Ezers/Burtnieku, Ozero- 8 Kg 57.35N 25.10 E
Burton 44 Fd 43.02N 83.36W
Burton Latimer 12 Bb 52.21N 0.40W
Burton-upon-Trent 9 Li 52.49N 1.36W
Burträsk 7 Ed 64.31N 20.39 E
Buru, Pulau- 57 De 3.24S 126.40 E
Burullus, Buḩayrat al- 24 Dg 31.30N 30.50 E
Burultokay/Fuhai 27 Eb 47.06N 87.23 E
Burum Gana 34 Hc 13.00N 11.57 E
Burūn, Ra's- 24 Eg 31.14N 33.04 E
Burundaj 19 Hg 43.20N 76.49 E
Burundi 31 Ki 3.15S 30.00 E
Bururi 36 Ec 3.57S 29.37 E
Burutu 34 Gd 5.21N 5.31 E
Bury 9 Kh 53.36N 2.17W
Burylbajtal 18 Ib 44.56N 73.59 E
Buryn 16 Hd 51.13N 33.48 E
Bury Saint Edmunds 9 Ni 52.15N 0.43 E
Burzil Pass 25 Ff 34.54N 75.06 E
Busalla 14 Cf 44.34N 8.57 E
Busanga [Zaire] 36 Ee 10.12S 25.23 E
Busanga [Zaire] 36 Dc 0.51S 22.04 E
Busanga Swamp 36 Ee 14.10S 25.50 E
Bušayrah 24 Ie 35.09N 40.26 E
Büsh 24 Dh 29.09N 31.08 E
Būshehr 23 Hd 28.00N 52.00 E
Büshgān 24 Nh 28.48N 51.42 E
Bushimaie 29 Ji 6.02S 23.45 E
Bushmanland (EN) = Boesmanland 37 Be 29.30S 19.00 E
Busia 36 Fb 0.28N 34.06 E
Busigny 12 Fd 50.02N 3.28 E
Businga 36 Db 3.20N 20.53 E
Busira 30 Ii 0.15S 18.59 E
Busk 16 Dd 50.01N 24.37 E
Buskerud 7 Bf 60.30N 9.10 E
Busko-Zdrój 10 Qf 50.28N 20.44 E
Busoga 36 Fb 0.45N 33.30 E
Buşrá ash Shām 24 Gf 32.31N 36.29 E
Busselton 59 Df 33.39S 115.20 E
Bussum 11 Lb 52.16N 5.10 E
Bustamante, Bahía- 56 Gg 45.07S 66.27W
Bušteni 15 Id 45.24N 25.32 E
Busto Arsizio 14 Ce 45.37N 8.51 E
Buštyna 10 Th 48.03N 23.28 E
Busuanga 26 Hd 12.05N 120.05 E
Busu-Djanoa 36 Db 1.43N 21.23 E
Büsum 10 Eb 54.08N 8.51 E
Buta 31 Jh 2.48N 24.44 E
Butajira 35 Fd 8.08N 38.27 E
Buta Ranquil 56 Ge 37.03S 69.50W
Butare 36 Ec 2.36S 29.44 E
Butaritari Atoll 57 Id 3.03N 172.49 E
Bute, Island of- 9 Hf 55.50N 5.05W
Bute Inlet 46 Ca 50.37N 124.53W
Butembo 31 Jh 0.09N 29.17 E
Butera 14 Im 37.11N 14.11 E
Butere 36 Fb 0.13N 34.30 E
Butha Qi (Zalantum) 27 Lb 48.02N 122.42 E
Buthidaung 25 Id 20.52N 92.32 E
Butiá 55 Jd 30.07S 51.58W
Butiaba 36 Fb 1.49N 31.19 E
Butler 44 He 40.51N 79.55W
Butler Hill 12 Bd 50.57N 0.59W
Butte 39 He 46.00N 112.32W
Butterworth [Mala.] 26 Df 5.25N 100.24 E
Butterworth [S.Afr.] 37 Df 32.23S 28.04 E
Button Bay 42 Ie 58.45N 94.25W
Butuan 22 Oi 8.57N 125.33 E
Butung, Palau- 21 Oj 5.00S 122.55 E
Buturlinovka 16 Ld 50.48N 40.45 E
Butzbach 12 Kd 50.26N 8.41 E
Bützow 10 Hc 53.50N 11.59 E
Buxtehude 10 Fc 53.27N 9.42 E
Buxton [Eng.-U.K.] 9 Lh 53.15N 1.55W
Buxton [N.C.-U.S.] 44 Jh 35.16N 75.32W
Buyo 34 Dd 6.16N 7.03W
Büyük Ağri Daği=Ararat, Mount- (EN) 21 Gf 39.40N 44.24 E
Büyükanafarta 15 Ji 40.17N 26.22 E
Büyükçekmece 15 Lh 41.01N 28.34 E
Büyükkariştiran 15 Kh 41.18N 27.32 E
Büyük Kemikli Burun 15 Ji 40.18N 26.14 E
Büyük Mahya 15 Kh 41.47N 27.36 E
Büyük Menderes 23 Cb 37.57N 28.58 E
Büyükorhan 15 Lj 39.45N 28.55 E
Buyun Shan 27 Lc 40.06N 122.42 E
Buzači, Poluostrov- 19 Ff 45.00N 52.00 E
Buzan 16 Pf 46.18N 49.06 E
Buzançais 11 Hh 46.53N 1.25 E
Buzancy 12 Ge 49.25N 4.57 E
Buzău 15 Jd 45.09N 26.50 E
Buzău 15 Jd 45.09N 26.50 E
Buzău 15 Jd 45.26N 27.44 E
Buzaymah 33 De 24.55N 22.02 E
Buzen 29 Be 33.37N 131.08 E
Buzet 14 He 45.24N 13.59 E
Büzhān 24 Lf 34.09N 47.05 E
Búzi 37 Ec 19.51S 34.30 E
Búzi 37 Ec 19.52S 34.46 E
Buziaş 15 Ed 45.39N 21.36 E
Búzios, Ilha dos- 55 Jf 23.48S 45.08W
Bužora, Gora- 10 Th 48.24N 23.15 E
Buzuluk 19 Fe 52.47N 52.17 E
Buzuluk [R.S.F.S.R.] 16 Md 50.13N 42.12 E
Buzuluk [R.S.F.S.R.] 16 Rc 52.47N 52.16 E
Buzzards Bay 44 Le 41.33N 70.47W

Index Symbols

Independent Nation; State, Region; District, County; Municipality; Colony, Dependency; Continent; Physical Region; Historical or Cultural Region; Mount, Mountain; Volcano; Hill; Mountains, Mountain Range; Hills, Escarpment; Plateau, Upland; Pass, Gap; Plain, Lowland; Delta; Salt Flat; Valley, Canyon; Crater, Cave; Karst Features; Depression; Polder; Desert, Dunes; Forest, Woods; Heath, Steppe; Oasis; Cape, Point; Coast, Beach; Cliff; Peninsula; Isthmus; Sandbank; Island; Atoll; Rock, Reef; Islands, Archipelago; Rocks, Reefs; Coral Reef; Well, Spring; Geyser; River, Stream; Waterfall Rapids; River Mouth, Estuary; Lake; Salt Lake; Intermittent Lake; Reservoir; Swamp, Pond; Canal; Glacier; Ice Shelf, Pack Ice; Ocean; Sea; Gulf, Bay; Strait, Fjord; Lagoon; Bank; Seamount; Tablemount; Ridge; Shelf; Basin; Escarpment, Sea Scarp; Fracture; Trench, Abyss; National Park, Reserve; Point of Interest; Recreation Site; Cave, Cavern; Historic Site; Ruins; Wall, Walls; Church, Abbey; Temple; Scientific Station; Airport; Port; Lighthouse; Mine; Tunnel; Dam, Bridge

Bwagaoia	63a	Ad	10.42 S	152.50 E
Byälven	8	Ee	59.06 N	12.54 E
Byam Martin	42	Ha	75.15 N	104.15 W
Byam Martin Channel	42	Ha	76.00 N	105.00 W
Bychawa	10	Se	51.01 N	22.32 E
Byczyna	10	Oe	51.07 N	18.11 E
Bydgoszcz [2]	10	Nc	53.10 N	18.00 E
Bydgoszcz	6	He	53.08 N	18.00 E
Byelorussian SSR (EN) = Belorusskaja SSR [2]	19	Ce	53.50 N	28.00 E
Bygdin	8	Cc	61.20 N	8.35 E
Bygland [Nor.]	7	Bg	58.51 N	7.51 E
Bygland [Nor.]	8	Bf	58.41 N	7.48 E
Byglandsfjorden	8	Bf	58.50 N	7.50 E
Byhov	19	De	53.31 N	30.15 E
Byk	15	Mc	46.55 N	29.25 E
Bykovec	15	Lb	47.12 N	28.18 E
Bykovo	16	Ne	49.47 N	45.25 E
Bykovski	20	Hb	71.56 N	129.05 E
Bylot	38	Lb	73.13 N	78.34 W
Byrd, Cape-	66	Qe	69.38 S	76.07 W
Byrdbreen	66	Df	71.35 S	26.00 E
Byrd Glacier	66	Jg	80.15 S	160.20 E
Byron, Cape-	57	Gg	28.39 S	153.38 E
Byron Bay	42	Gc	68.55 N	108.25 W
Byron Bay	59	Ke	28.39 S	153.37 E
Byrranga Gory = Byrranga Mountains (EN)	21	Mb	75.00 N	104.00 E
Byrranga Mountains (EN) = Byrranga Gory	21	Mb	75.00 N	104.00 E
Bystraja	20	Kf	52.40 N	156.10 E
Bystreyca	10	Se	51.40 N	22.33 E
Bystřice	10	Lf	50.11 N	15.30 E
Bystrovka	18	Jc	42.45 N	75.43 E
Bystrzyca [Pol.]	10	Se	51.16 N	22.45 E
Bystrzyca [Pol.]	10	Me	51.13 N	16.54 E
Bystrzyca Kłodzka	10	Mf	50.19 N	16.39 E
Bytantaj	20	Ic	68.40 N	134.50 E
Bytča	10	Og	49.14 N	18.35 E
Byten	10	Vd	52.49 N	25.33 E
Bytom	10	Of	50.22 N	18.54 E
Bytów	10	Nb	54.11 N	17.30 E
Byumba	36	Fc	1.35 S	30.04 E
Byxelkrok	7	Dh	57.20 N	17.00 E
Bzura	10	Qd	52.23 N	20.09 E
Bzyb	16	Lh	43.12 N	40.15 E

C

Cà, Sông-	25	Le	18.40 N	105.40 E
Caacupé	56	Ic	25.23 S	57.09 W
Čaadajevka	16	Nc	53.09 N	45.56 E
Caaguazú	56	Ic	25.26 S	56.02 W
Caaguazú [3]	55	Eg	25.00 S	55.45 W
Caála	36	Ce	12.55 S	15.35 E
Caapucú	55	Dh	26.13 S	57.12 W
Caarapó	55	Ef	22.38 S	54.48 W
Caatinga	54	Ig	17.10 S	45.53 W
Caatinga	52	Lf	9.00 S	42.00 W
Caatinga, Rio-	55	Jc	17.10 S	45.52 W
Caazapá [3]	55	Dh	26.10 S	56.00 W
Caazapá	56	Ic	26.09 S	56.24 W
Cabaçal, Rio-	55	Db	16.00 S	57.42 W
Cabadbaran	26	Ie	9.10 N	125.38 E
Cabaiguán	49	Hb	22.05 N	79.30 W
Caballeria, Cabo de-	13	Qd	40.05 N	4.05 E
Caballo Cocha	54	Dd	3.54 S	70.32 W
Caballo Reservoir	45	Cj	32.58 N	107.18 W
Cabañas	13	Jg	37.40 N	3.00 W
Cabanatuan	22	Oh	15.29 N	120.58 E
Cabano	44	Mb	47.41 N	68.54 W
Čabar	14	Ie	45.36 N	14.39 E
Cabeceira do Apa	55	Ef	22.01 S	55.46 W
Cabeceiras	55	Ib	15.48 S	46.59 W
Cabeceiras de Basto	13	Ec	41.31 N	7.59 W
Cabeza, Arrecife-	48	Lh	19.04 N	95.50 W
Cabeza de Buey	13	Gf	38.43 N	5.13 W
Cabildo	55	Bn	38.29 S	61.54 W
Cabimas	53	Id	10.23 N	71.28 W
Cabinda	31	Ii	5.35 S	12.13 E
Cabinda [3]	36	Bd	5.00 S	12.30 E
Cabinet Mountains	46	Hb	48.08 N	115.46 W
Cabo Bojador	32	Ed	26.08 N	14.30 W
Cabo Frio	53	Lh	22.53 S	42.01 W
Cabo Gracias a Dios	49	Ff	14.59 N	83.10 W
Cabonga, Réservoir-	42	Jg	47.20 N	76.35 W
Caboolture	59	Ke	27.05 S	152.50 E
Cabora Bassa, Dique de-	37	Ec	15.34 S	32.42 E
Cabora Bassa, Lago- = Cabora Bassa, Lake-(EN)	30	Kj	15.40 S	31.40 E
Cabora Bassa, Lake-(EN) = Cabora Bassa, Lago-	30	Kj	15.40 S	31.40 E
Caborca	47	Bb	30.37 N	112.06 W
Cabot Strait	38	Ne	47.20 N	59.30 W
Cabourg	11	Fe	49.17 N	0.08 W
Cabo Verde = Cape Verde (EN) [1]	31	Eg	16.00 N	24.00 W
Cabo Verde, Ilhas do- = Cape Verde Islands (EN)	30	Eg	16.00 N	24.10 W
Cabra	13	Hg	37.28 N	4.27 W
Cabral, Serra do-	55	Jc	17.45 S	44.22 W
Cabras	14	Ck	39.56 N	8.32 E
Cabras, Stagno di-	14	Ck	39.55 N	8.30 E
Cabreira	13	Dc	41.39 N	8.04 W
Cabrejas, Puerto de-	13	Jd	40.08 N	2.25 W
Cabrera	49	Md	19.38 N	69.54 W
Cabrera, Isla-	13	Oe	39.09 N	2.56 E
Cabrera, Sierra de la-	13	Fb	42.10 N	6.25 W
Cabri	46	Ka	50.37 N	108.28 W
Cabriel	13	Ke	39.14 N	1.03 W
Cabrit, Ilet 'a-	51e	Ac	15.53 N	61.36 W
Cabrits, Ilet-	51h	Bc	14.23 N	60.52 W
Cabrón, Cabo-	49	Md	19.22 N	69.12 W
Cabruta	50	Ci	7.38 N	66.15 W
Čabulja	14	Lg	43.30 N	17.35 E
Cabure	49	Mh	11.08 N	69.38 W
Cacacas, Islas-	50	Dg	10.22 N	64.26 W
Caçador	56	Jc	26.47 S	51.00 W
Čačak	15	Df	43.54 N	20.21 E
Caçapava dó Sul	56	Jd	30.30 S	53.30 W
Caccamo	14	Hm	37.56 N	13.40 E
Caccia, Capo-	14	Cj	40.34 N	8.09 E
Cacequi	55	Ei	29.53 S	54.49 W
Cáceres [3]	13	Ge	39.40 N	6.00 W
Cáceres [Braz.]	53	Kg	16.04 S	57.41 W
Cáceres [Sp.]	13	Fe	39.29 N	6.22 W
Cáceres, Laguna-	55	Dd	18.56 S	57.48 W
Cachari	56	Ie	36.24 S	59.32 W
Cache Peak	46	Ie	42.11 N	113.40 W
Cacheu	34	Bc	12.10 N	16.21 W
Cachimbo	53	Kf	9.08 S	55.10 W
Cachimbo, Serra do-	52	Kf	8.30 S	55.50 W
Cachimo	36	Dd	8.20 S	21.21 E
Cáchira	49	Kj	7.46 N	73.03 W
Cáchira, Río-	49	Kj	7.52 N	73.40 W
Cachoeira	54	Kf	12.36 S	38.58 W
Cachoeira Alta	55	Gd	18.48 S	50.58 W
Cachoeira de Goiás	55	Gc	16.44 S	50.38 W
Cachoeira do Arari	54	Id	1.01 S	48.58 W
Cachoeira do Sul	56	Jc	29.58 S	52.54 W
Cachoeira Dourada, Reprêsa de-	54	Ig	18.30 S	49.00 W
Cachoeirinha	55	Gi	29.57 S	51.05 W
Cachoeiro de Itapemirim	54	Jh	20.51 S	41.06 W
Cacinbinho	55	Ee	21.50 S	55.43 W
Căciulaţi	15	Je	44.38 N	26.10 E
Cacolo	36	Ce	10.08 S	19.18 E
Caconda	36	Ce	13.45 S	15.05 E
Cacuaco	36	Bd	8.47 S	13.21 E
Cacuchi	36	Ce	14.23 S	16.59 E
Cacula	36	Be	14.29 S	14.10 E
Caculé	54	Jf	14.30 S	42.13 W
Caculuvar	36	Bf	16.46 S	14.56 E
Cacuso	36	Cd	9.26 S	15.45 E
Čadan	20	Ef	51.17 N	91.40 E
Cadaqués	13	Pb	42.17 N	3.17 E
Čadca	10	Og	49.26 N	18.48 E
Caddo Lake	45	Ij	32.42 N	94.01 W
Cadena Costero Catalana/Serralada Litoral Catalana = Catalan Coastal Range (EN)	5	Gg	41.35 N	1.40 E
Cadereyta Jiménez	48	Ie	25.36 N	100.00 W
Cadí, Serra del-/Cadí, Sierra del-	13	Nb	42.17 N	1.42 E
Cadibarrawirracanna, Lake-	59	He	28.50 S	135.25 E
Cadibona, Colle di-	14	Cf	44.20 N	8.22 E
Cadillac [Fr.]	11	Fj	44.38 N	0.19 W
Cadillac [Mi.-U.S.]	43	Jc	44.15 N	85.24 W
Cadí, Sierra del/Cadí, Serra del-	13	Nb	42.17 N	1.42 E
Cadiz	26	Hd	10.57 N	123.18 E
Cádiz [3]	13	Gh	36.30 N	5.45 W
Cádiz	6	Fh	36.32 N	6.18 W
Cadiz [Ca.-U.S.]	46	Hi	34.30 N	115.30 W
Cadiz [Ky.-U.S.]	44	Dg	36.52 N	87.50 W
Cádiz, Bahía de-	13	Fh	36.32 N	6.16 W
Cádiz, Golfo de-	5	Fh	36.50 N	7.10 W
Cadiz Lake	46	Hi	34.18 N	115.24 W
Cadore	14	Gd	46.30 N	12.20 E
Cadwell	43	Dc	43.40 N	116.41 W
Čadyr-Lunga	16	Ff	46.04 N	28.52 E
Caen	6	Ff	49.11 N	0.21 W
Caen, Campagne de-	11	Fe	49.05 N	0.20 W
Caernarvon	9	Ih	53.08 N	4.16 W
Caernarvon Bay	9	Ih	53.05 N	4.30 W
Caerphilly	9	Jj	51.35 N	3.14 W
Caetité	54	Jf	14.04 S	42.29 W
Cafayate	56	Gc	26.05 S	65.58 W
Cafelândia [Braz.]	55	Fc	16.40 S	53.25 W
Cafelândia [Braz.]	55	Ie	21.49 S	49.35 W
Cafundó, Serra do-	55	Hb	14.40 S	48.23 W
Čagan	19	He	50.30 N	79.10 E
Cagan-Aman	19	Ef	47.32 N	46.43 E
Cagan-Nur [Mong.]	27	Eb	49.40 N	89.55 E
Cagan-Nur [Mong.]	27	Ia	50.25 N	105.15 E
Cagan-Ula	27	Gb	49.35 N	98.25 E
Cagatá, Arroyo-	55	Df	23.26 S	56.36 W
Cagayan	26	Hc	18.22 N	121.37 E
Cagayan de Oro	22	Oi	8.29 N	124.39 E
Cagayan Islands	26	He	9.40 N	121.16 E
Cagayan Sulu	26	Ge	7.01 N	118.30 E
Čagda	20	Ie	58.42 N	130.37 E
Cageri	16	Mh	42.39 N	42.42 E
Çağiş	15	Lj	39.30 N	28.01 E
Cagli	14	Gg	43.33 N	12.39 E
Cagliari	6	Gh	39.13 N	9.07 E
Cagliari, Golfo di-	14	Dk	39.10 N	9.10 E
Cagliari, Stagno di-	14	Dk	39.15 N	9.05 E
Čaglinka	17	Nj	53.59 N	69.47 E
Cagnes-sur-Mer	11	Nk	43.40 N	7.09 E
Čagoda	7	Ig	59.12 N	35.13 E
Čagodošča	7	Ig	58.58 N	36.37 E
Caguas	47	Ke	18.14 N	66.02 W
Čagyl	19	Fg	40.43 N	55.25 E
Cahama	36	Bf	16.16 S	14.17 E
Caha Mountains/An Cheacha	9	Dj	51.45 N	9.45 W
Caher/An Chathair	9	Fi	52.22 N	7.55 W
Cahersiveen/Cathair Saidhbhín	9	Cj	51.57 N	10.13 W
Cahore Point/Rinn Chathóir	9	Gi	52.34 N	6.11 W
Cahors	11	Hj	44.26 N	1.26 E
Caí, Rio-	55	Gi	29.56 S	51.16 W
Caia	37	Fc	17.49 S	35.20 E
Caia	13	Ef	38.50 N	7.05 W
Caiabis, Serra dos-	54	Gf	11.40 S	56.30 W
Caiapó, Rio-	55	Gb	15.49 S	51.53 W
Caiapó, Serra do-	52	Kg	17.00 S	52.00 W
Caiapônia	55	Gc	16.57 S	51.49 W
Caibarién	47	Id	22.31 N	79.28 W
Caiçara	55	Gb	15.34 S	50.12 W
Caicara	54	Eb	7.37 N	66.10 W
Caicara de Maturín	50	Eh	9.49 N	63.36 W
Caicó	54	Ke	6.27 S	37.06 W
Caicos Bank (EN)	47	Jd	21.35 N	71.55 W
Caicos Islands	38	Lg	21.45 N	71.35 W
Caicos Passage	47	Jd	22.00 N	72.30 W
Caille Island	51p	Bb	12.17 N	61.35 W
Caimanera	49	Jd	19.59 N	75.09 W
Caine, Río-	54	Eg	18.23 S	65.21 W
Cai Nuoc	25	Lg	8.56 N	105.01 E
Caird Coast	66	Af	76.00 S	24.30 W
Cairngorms Mountains	9	Jd	57.06 N	3.30 W
Cairns	58	Ff	16.55 S	145.46 E
Cairo [Ga.-U.S.]	44	Ej	30.53 N	84.12 W
Cairo [Il.-U.S.]	43	Jd	37.00 N	89.11 W
Cairo (EN) = Al Qāhirah	31	Ke	30.03 N	31.15 E
Cairo Montenotte	14	Cf	44.24 N	8.16 E
Caiseal/Cashel	9	Fi	52.31 N	7.53 W
Caisleán an Bharraigh/Castlebar	9	Dh	53.52 N	9.17 W
Caister-on-Sea	12	Db	52.40 N	1.45 E
Caiundo	36	Cf	15.42 S	17.27 E
Caiúva, Lagoa-	55	Fk	32.24 S	52.30 W
Caiyuanzhen → Shengsi	28	Gi	30.42 N	122.29 E
Caizi Hu	28	Di	30.48 N	117.05 E
Čaja	20	De	58.17 N	82.45 E
Cajabamba	54	Ce	7.58 S	77.59 W
Caja de Muertos, Isla-	51a	Bc	17.53 N	66.31 W
Cajamarca	53	If	7.10 S	78.31 W
Cajamarca [2]	54	Ce	6.15 S	78.50 W
Cajapió	54	Jd	2.58 S	44.48 W
Cajarc	11	Hj	44.29 N	1.51 E
Cajatambo	54	Cf	10.29 S	77.02 W
Čajkovski	19	Fd	56.47 N	54.09 E
Çakırgöl Dağ	24	Hb	40.34 N	39.42 E
Cakmak	24	Fd	37.37 N	34.19 E
Çakmak Dağı	24	Jc	39.46 N	42.12 E
Čakor	15	Dg	42.40 N	20.02 E
Čakovec	14	Kd	46.23 N	16.26 E
Cakrani	15	Ci	40.36 N	19.37 E
Çal	24	Cc	38.05 N	29.24 E
Cal, Río de la-	55	Cc	17.27 S	58.15 W
Calabar	31	Hh	4.57 N	8.19 E
Calabozo	54	Eb	8.56 N	67.26 W
Calabozo, Ensenada de-	49	Lh	11.30 N	71.45 W
Calabria [2]	14	Kl	39.00 N	16.30 E
Calaburras, Punta de-	13	Hh	36.30 N	4.38 W
Calacoto	54	Eg	17.18 S	68.39 W
Calacuccia	11a	Ba	42.20 N	9.01 E
Calaf	13	Nc	41.44 N	1.31 E
Calafat	15	Ff	43.59 N	22.56 E
Calafate	53	Ik	50.20 S	72.16 W
Cala Figuera, Cabo de-	13	Oe	39.27 N	2.31 E
Calagua Islands	26	Hd	14.27 N	122.55 E
Calahorra	13	Kb	42.18 N	1.58 W
Calai	36	Cf	17.50 S	19.20 E
Calais [Fr.]	6	Ge	50.57 N	1.50 E
Calais [Me.-U.S.]	44	Nc	45.11 N	67.17 W
Calais, Pas de- = Dover, Strait of- (EN)	5	Ge	51.00 N	1.30 E
Calakmul	48	Oh	18.05 N	89.55 W
Calalaste, Sierra de-	56	Gc	25.30 S	67.30 W
Calama	53	Jh	22.28 S	68.56 W
Calamar	49	Jh	10.14 N	74.56 W
Calamian Group	21	Nh	12.00 N	120.00 E
Calamocha	13	Kd	40.55 N	1.18 W
Călan	15	Fd	45.44 N	22.59 E
Calanda	13	Ld	40.56 N	0.14 W
Calang	26	Cf	4.30 N	95.40 E
Calangiánus	14	Dj	40.56 N	9.11 E
Calapan	26	Hd	13.25 N	121.10 E
Calar Alto	13	Jg	37.15 N	2.25 W
Călăraşi	15	Ke	44.12 N	27.20 E
Cala Ratjada	13	Pe	39.42 N	3.25 E
Calar del Mundo	13	Jf	38.31 N	2.28 W
Calatafimi	14	Gm	37.55 N	12.52 E
Calatañazor	13	Jc	41.42 N	2.49 W
Calatayud	13	Kc	41.21 N	1.38 W
Calatrava	13	If	38.35 N	3.48 W
Calatrava, Campo de-	13	Hf	38.50 N	4.15 W
Calavà, Capo-	14	Il	38.10 N	14.55 E
Calavon	11	Kk	43.51 N	5.00 E
Calayan	26	Hc	19.20 N	121.27 E
Calbayog	22	Oh	12.04 N	124.36 E
Calchaquí	56	Hc	29.54 S	60.18 W
Calçoene	54	Hc	2.30 N	50.57 W
Calcutta	22	Kg	22.32 N	88.22 E
Caldaro / Kaltern	14	Fd	46.25 N	11.14 E
Caldas [2]	54	Cb	5.15 N	75.30 W
Caldas da Rainha	13	Ce	39.24 N	9.08 W
Caldas Novas	55	Hc	17.45 S	48.38 W
Caldeirão, Serra de-	13	Dg	37.19 N	8.04 W
Calder	9	Lh	53.44 N	1.21 W
Caldera	56	Fc	27.04 S	70.50 W
Calderina, Sierra de la-	13	Ie	39.19 N	3.48 W
Caldes de Mombúy	13	Oc	41.38 N	2.10 E
Caldwell	44	Gf	39.44 N	81.32 W
Caledon	37	Bf	34.12 S	19.23 E
Caledon	30	Jl	30.32 S	26.05 E
Caledonia [Blz.]	49	Cd	18.14 N	88.29 W
Caledonia [Mn.-U.S.]	45	Ke	43.38 N	91.29 W
Caledonian Canal	9	Id	57.20 N	4.30 W
Calella	13	Oc	41.37 N	2.40 E
Caleta Olivia	56	Gg	46.26 S	67.32 W
Calexico	46	Hj	32.40 N	115.30 W
Çalgal Dağı	24	Hc	39.06 N	38.05 E
Calgary	39	Hd	51.03 N	114.05 W
Calhoun	44	Eh	34.30 N	84.57 W
Cali	53	Ie	3.27 N	76.31 W
Calicut (Kozhikode)	22	Jh	11.19 N	75.46 E
Caliente	43	Ed	37.37 N	114.31 W
California [2]	43	Dd	37.30 N	119.30 W
California, Golfo de- = California, Gulf of- (EN)	38	Hg	28.00 N	112.00 W
California, Gulf of- (EN) = California, Golfo de-	38	Hg	28.00 N	112.00 W
Căliman, Munţii-	15	Ib	47.07 N	25.03 E
Călimăneşti	15	Hd	45.14 N	24.20 E
Calimere, Point-	25	Ff	10.18 N	79.52 E
Calingasta	56	Gd	31.19 S	69.25 W
Calispell Peak	46	Gb	48.26 N	117.30 W
Calitri	14	Jj	40.54 N	15.26 E
Calitzdorp	37	Cf	33.33 S	21.42 E
Caliviny	51p	Bb	12.01 N	61.43 W
Calixtlahuaca	48	Jh	19.15 N	99.45 W
Calka	16	Ni	41.35 N	44.05 E
Calkiní	48	Ng	20.22 N	90.03 W
Callabonna, Lake-	59	Ie	29.45 S	140.05 E
Callac	11	Cf	48.24 N	3.26 W
Callaghan, Mount-	46	Gg	39.42 N	116.57 W
Callainn/Callan	9	Fi	52.33 N	7.23 W
Callan/Callainn	9	Fi	52.33 N	7.23 W
Callander [Ont.-Can.]	44	Hb	46.13 N	79.23 W
Callander [Scot.-U.K.]	9	Ie	56.15 N	4.13 W
Callantsoog	12	Gb	52.50 N	4.41 E
Callao	53	Ig	12.02 S	77.05 W
Callao [2]	54	Cf	2.04 S	77.09 W
Calliaqua	51n	Ba	13.08 N	61.12 W
Callosa de Ensarriá	13	Lf	38.39 N	0.07 W
Callosa de Segura	13	Lf	38.08 N	0.52 W
Calmalli	48	Cc	28.14 N	113.33 W
Călmăţui [Rom.]	15	If	43.46 N	25.10 E
Călmăţui [Rom.]	15	Ke	44.50 N	27.50 E
Calonne	12	Ce	49.17 N	0.12 E
Calore	14	Ii	41.11 N	14.28 E
Čalovo	10	Ni	47.52 N	17.47 E
Calpe	13	Mf	38.39 N	0.03 E
Caltabellotta	14	Hm	37.34 N	13.13 E
Caltagirone	14	Im	37.14 N	14.31 E
Caltanissetta	14	Im	37.29 N	14.04 E
Caltilibük	15	Lj	39.57 N	28.36 E
Čaltyr	16	Kf	47.17 N	39.29 E
Caluago	36	Cd	8.15 S	19.38 E
Calucinga	36	Ce	11.19 S	16.13 E
Călugareni	15	Ie	44.11 N	25.59 E
Calulo	36	Bd	9.59 S	14.54 E
Caluquembe	36	Be	13.46 S	14.41 E
Calvados [3]	11	Fe	49.10 N	0.30 W
Calvados, Côte du-	11	Fe	49.22 N	0.30 W
Calvert Island	46	Ba	51.35 N	128.00 W
Calvert River	59	Hc	16.17 S	137.44 E
Calvi	11a	Aa	42.34 N	8.45 E
Calvillo	48	Hg	21.51 N	102.43 W
Calvinia	31	Il	31.25 S	19.45 E
Calvitero	13	Gd	40.20 N	5.43 W
Cam	9	Ni	52.21 N	0.15 E
Camabatela	36	Cd	8.13 S	15.23 E
Camacá	54	Kg	15.24 S	39.30 W
Camacupa	36	Ce	12.01 S	17.22 E
Camaguán	50	Ch	8.06 N	67.36 W
Camagüey [3]	49	Ic	21.30 N	78.10 W
Camagüey	39	Lg	21.23 N	77.55 W
Camagüey, Archipiélago de-	47	Id	22.18 N	78.00 W
Camaiore	14	Eg	43.56 N	10.18 E
Camajuaní	49	Hb	22.28 N	79.44 W
Camamu	54	Kf	13.57 S	39.07 W
Camaná	54	Dg	16.37 S	72.42 W
Camapuã	55	Ed	19.30 S	54.05 W
Camapuã, Sertão de-	52	Kg	19.00 S	51.30 W
Camaquã	56	Jd	30.51 S	51.49 W
Camaquã, Rio-	55	Gj	31.17 S	51.47 W
Camarat, Cap-	11	Mk	43.12 N	6.41 E
Camargo [Bol.]	54	Eh	20.39 S	65.13 W
Camargo [Sp.]	13	Ia	43.24 N	3.54 W
Camargos, Reprêsa-	55	Je	21.20 S	44.30 W
Camargue	11	Kk	43.31 N	4.34 E
Camariñas	13	Ca	43.07 N	9.10 W
Camarón, Cabo-	47	He	16.00 N	85.04 W
Camarones	56	Gf	44.48 S	65.42 W
Camarones, Bahía-	56	Gf	44.45 S	65.34 W
Camas [Sp.]	13	Fg	37.24 N	6.02 W
Camas [Wa.-U.S.]	46	Dd	45.35 N	122.24 W
Camatagua, Embalse de-	50	Ch	9.48 N	66.55 W
Ca Mau, Mui- = Ca Mau Point (EN)	21	Mi	8.38 N	104.44 E
Ca Mau Point (EN) = Ca Mau, Mui-	21	Mi	8.38 N	104.44 E
Cambados	13	Db	42.30 N	8.48 W
Camberg	12	Kd	50.18 N	8.16 E
Camberley	12	Bc	51.21 N	0.44 W
Cambo	36	Cd	7.40 S	17.17 E
Cambodia (EN) = Kampuchea	22	Mh	13.00 N	105.00 E
Cambo-les-Bains	11	Ek	43.22 N	1.24 W
Cambrai	11	Jd	50.10 N	3.14 E
Cambremer	12	Ce	49.09 N	0.03 E
Cambrésis	12	Fd	50.15 N	3.05 E
Cambrian Mountains	5	Fe	52.35 N	3.35 W
Cambridge	9	Ni	52.25 N	0.10 E
Cambridge [Eng.-U.K.]	9	Ni	52.12 N	0.07 E
Cambridge [Id.-U.S.]	46	Gd	44.34 N	116.41 W
Cambridge [Ma.-U.S.]	44	Ld	42.22 N	71.06 W
Cambridge [Md.-U.S.]	44	If	38.34 N	76.04 W
Cambridge [Mn.-U.S.]	45	Jd	45.31 N	93.14 W
Cambridge [N.Z.]	62	Fb	37.53 S	175.28 E
Cambridge [Oh.-U.S.]	44	Ge	40.02 N	81.36 W
Cambridge Airport	12	Cb	52.10 N	0.08 E
Cambridge Bay	39	Ic	69.03 N	105.05 W
Cambridge Gulf	59	Fb	14.55 S	128.15 E
Cambridgeshire [3]	9	Mi	52.25 N	0.05 W
Cambutal, Cerro-	49	Gj	7.16 N	80.36 W
Camden [Al.-U.S.]	44	Dj	32.00 N	87.17 W
Camden [Ar.-U.S.]	43	Ie	33.35 N	92.50 W
Camden [N.J.-U.S.]	44	Jf	39.57 N	75.07 W
Camden [S.C.-U.S.]	44	Gh	34.16 N	80.36 W
Camden [Tn.-U.S.]	44	Cg	36.04 N	88.06 W
Camden Bay	40	Kb	70.00 N	145.00 W
Camdenton	45	Jg	38.00 N	92.45 W
Camel	9	Ik	50.33 N	4.55 W
Çameli	24	Cd	37.05 N	29.20 E
Camerino	14	Hg	43.08 N	13.04 E
Cameron	42	Ha	76.15 N	104.00 W
Cameron [Az.-U.S.]	46	Ji	35.51 N	111.25 W
Cameron [La.-U.S.]	45	Jl	29.48 N	93.19 W
Cameron [Mo.-U.S.]	45	Ig	39.44 N	94.14 W
Cameron [Tx.-U.S.]	45	Hk	30.51 N	96.59 W
Cameron [Wi.-U.S.]	45	Kd	45.25 N	91.44 W
Cameron Hills	42	Fe	60.00 N	118.00 W
Cameron Mountains	62	Bf	46.00 S	166.55 E
Cameroon (EN) = Cameroun [1]	31	Ih	6.00 N	12.00 E
Cameroon, Mount- (EN) = Cameroun	30	Hh	4.12 N	9.11 E
Camerota	14	Jj	40.02 N	15.22 E
Cameroun = Cameroon (EN) [1]	31	Ih	6.00 N	12.00 E
Cameroun = Cameroon, Mount-(EN)	30	Hh	4.12 N	9.11 E
Cametá	54	Id	2.15 S	49.30 W
Camiguin [Phil.]	26	Hc	18.56 N	121.55 E
Camiling	26	Hc	15.42 N	120.24 E
Camilla	44	Ej	31.14 N	84.12 W
Caminha	13	Dc	41.52 N	8.50 W
Camissombo	36	Dd	8.10 S	20.39 E
Camoapa	49	Eg	12.23 N	85.31 W
Camocim	53	Lf	2.54 S	40.50 W
Camonica, Val-	14	Ed	46.00 N	10.20 E
Camooweal	59	Hc	19.55 S	138.07 E
Camopi	54	Hc	3.13 N	52.28 W
Camorta	25	Ig	8.08 N	93.30 E
Campagne-lès-Hesdin	12	Dd	50.24 N	1.52 E
Campana	55	Cl	34.10 S	58.57 W
Campana, Isla-	52	Ij	48.20 S	75.15 W
Campanario	13	Gf	38.52 N	5.37 W
Campanário	55	Ef	22.48 S	55.03 W
Campania [2]	14	Ii	41.00 N	14.30 E
Campanquiz, Cerros-	54	Cd	4.30 S	77.40 W
Campbell, Cape-	62	Fd	41.44 S	174.16 E
Campbell Island	62	Ci	52.30 S	169.10 E
Campbell Plateau (EN)	57	Ij	51.00 S	170.00 E
Campbell River	42	Ef	50.01 N	125.15 W
Campbellsville	44	Eg	37.21 N	85.20 W
Campbellton	42	Kg	48.00 N	66.40 W
Campbelltown, Sydney-	59	Kf	34.04 S	150.49 E
Campbeltown	9	Hf	55.26 N	5.36 W
Campeche	39	Jh	19.51 N	90.32 W
Campeche [2]	47	Fe	19.00 N	90.30 W
Campeche, Bahía de- = Campeche, Gulf of- (EN)	38	Jg	20.00 N	94.00 W
Campeche, Gulf of- (EN) = Campeche, Bahía de-	38	Jg	20.00 N	94.00 W
Campeche Bank (EN)	47	Fd	22.00 N	90.00 W
Campechuela	49	Ic	20.14 N	77.17 W
Camperdown	59	Ig	38.14 S	143.09 E
Campidano	14	Ck	39.30 N	8.45 E
Campiglia Marittima	14	Eg	43.03 N	10.37 E
Campillos	13	Hg	37.03 N	4.51 W
Campina Grande	53	Mf	7.13 S	35.53 W
Campinas	53	Lh	22.54 S	47.05 W
Campina Verde	55	Hd	19.31 S	49.28 W
Campine/Kempen	11	Lc	51.10 N	5.20 E
Campinorte	55	Hb	14.20 S	49.08 W
Campione d'Italia	14	Ce	45.59 N	8.59 E
Campo	34	Ge	2.22 N	9.49 E
Campo Alegre	50	Bh	9.15 N	68.25 W
Campo Alegre de Goiás	55	Ic	17.36 S	47.46 W
Campobasso	14	Ii	41.34 N	14.39 E
Campo Belo	55	Je	20.53 S	45.16 W
Campo de Criptana	13	Ie	39.24 N	3.07 W
Campo de la Cruz	49	Jh	10.23 N	74.52 W
Campo del Cielo	55	Bh	27.53 S	61.49 W
Campo Florido	55	Hd	19.46 S	48.34 W
Campo Formoso	54	Jf	10.31 S	40.20 W
Campo Gallo	56	Hc	26.35 S	62.51 W
Campo Garay	55	Bi	29.41 S	61.37 W
Campo Grande [Arg.]	55	Eh	27.13 S	54.58 W
Campo Grande [Braz.]	53	Kh	20.27 S	54.37 W
Campo Largo [Arg.]	55	Bh	26.48 S	60.50 W
Campo Largo [Braz.]	55	Hg	25.26 S	49.32 W
Campo Maior [Braz.]	54	Jd	4.49 S	42.10 W
Campo Maior [Port.]	13	Ee	39.01 N	7.04 W
Campomarino	14	Ji	41.57 N	15.02 E
Campo Mourão	56	Jb	24.03 S	52.22 W
Campos	53	Lh	21.45 S	41.18 W
Campos [Braz.]	52	Lg	15.00 S	44.30 W
Campos [Braz.]	52	Kh	21.00 S	51.00 W
Campos, Laguna-	55	Be	20.50 S	61.31 W
Campos, Tierra de-	13	Hb	42.10 N	4.50 W
Campos Altos	55	Id	19.41 S	46.10 W
Campos Belos	55	Ia	13.03 S	46.53 W
Campos do Jordão	55	Jf	22.44 S	45.35 W
Campos Novos	55	Gh	27.24 S	51.12 W
Campos Sales	54	Je	7.04 S	40.23 W
Campo Tures / Sand in Taufers	14	Fd	46.55 N	11.57 E
Camp Verde	43	Ee	34.34 N	111.51 W
Cam Ranh	25	Lf	11.54 N	109.13 E
Camrose	42	Gf	53.01 N	112.50 W
Camseil	42	Fc	65.40 N	118.07 W
Camsell Portage	42	Ge	59.38 N	109.42 W
Çan	24	Bb	40.02 N	27.03 E
Canaan [Ct.-U.S.]	44	Kd	42.02 N	73.20 W
Canaan [Trin.]	50	Fg	11.09 N	60.49 W
Canaan Mountain	46	Jh	37.45 N	111.51 W
Cana Brava, Ribeirão-	55	Ic	16.35 S	46.34 W
Cana Brava, Rio- [Braz.]	55	Ib	14.40 S	47.07 W
Cana Brava, Rio- [Braz.]	55	Ha	12.12 S	48.40 W
Cana Brava, Rio- [Braz.]	55	Ha	13.11 S	48.11 W
Canada [1]	39	Jc	60.00 N	95.00 W
Cañada	13	Fb	42.50 N	6.05 W
Canada Basin (EN)	67	Ad	80.00 N	145.00 W
Cañada de Gomez	56	Hd	32.49 S	61.24 W
Canadian	45	Fi	35.55 N	100.23 W
Canadian River	38	Jf	35.27 N	95.03 W
Canaguá, Río-	49	Mj	7.57 N	69.36 W
Canaima	54	Db	9.49 N	70.56 W

Index Symbols

[1] Independent Nation
[2] State, Region
[3] District, County
[4] Municipality
[5] Colony, Dependency
Continent
Physical Region
Historical or Cultural Region
Mount, Mountain
Volcano
Hill
Mountains, Mountain Range
Hills, Escarpment
Plateau, Upland
Pass, Gap
Plain, Lowland
Delta
Salt Flat
Valley, Canyon
Crater, Cave
Karst Features
Depression
Polder
Desert, Dunes
Forest, Woods
Heath, Steppe
Oasis
Cape, Point
Coast, Beach
Cliff
Peninsula
Isthmus
Sandbank
Island
Atoll
Rock, Reef
Islands, Archipelago
Rocks, Reefs
Coral Reef
Well, Spring
Geyser
River, Stream
Waterfall Rapids
River Mouth, Estuary
Lake
Salt Lake
Intermittent Lake
Reservoir
Swamp, Pond
Canal
Glacier
Ice Shelf, Pack Ice
Ocean
Sea
Gulf, Bay
Strait, Fjord
Lagoon
Bank
Seamount
Tablemount
Ridge
Shelf
Basin
Escarpment, Sea Scarp
Fracture
Trench, Abyss
National Park, Reserve
Point of Interest
Recreation Site
Cave, Cavern
Historic Site
Ruins
Wall, Walls
Church, Abbey
Temple
Scientific Station
Airport
Port
Lighthouse
Mine
Tunnel
Dam, Bridge

Canakkale Boğazi= Dardanelles (EN) 5 Ig 40.15N 26.25 E
Canala 63b Be 21.32S 165.57 E
Canandaigua 44 Id 42.53N 77.19W
Cananea 47 Bb 30.57N 110.18W
Cananéia 55 Ig 25.01S 47.57W
Canapolis 55 Hd 18.44S 49.13W
Canarias, Islas-=Canary Islands (EN) [5] 31 Ff 28.00N 15.30W
Canarias, Islas-=Canary Islands (EN) 30 Ff 28.00N 15.30W
Canaries 51k Ab 13.55N 61.04W
Canaronero, Laguna- 48 Ff 23.00N 106.15W
Canarreos, Archipiélago de los- 47 Hd 21.50N 82.30W
Canary Basin (EN) 3 Dg 30.00N 25.00W
Canary Islands (EN)= Canarias, Islas- 30 Ff 28.00N 15.30W
Canary Islands (EN)= Canarias, Islas- [5] 31 Ff 28.00N 15.30W
Cañas [C.R.] 49 Eh 10.25N 85.07W
Cañas [Pan.] 49 Gj 7.27N 80.16W
Canastra, Serra da- 55 Ie 20.00S 46.20W
Canatlán 48 Ge 24.31N 104.47W
Cañaveral 13 Fe 39.47N 6.23W
Canaveral, Cape- 38 Kg 28.30N 80.35W
Canavese 14 Be 45.20N 7.40 E
Canavieiras 54 Kg 15.39S 38.57W
Canazei 14 Fd 46.28N 11.46 E
Canberra 58 Fh 35.17S 149.08 E
Canby [Mn.-U.S.] 45 Hd 44.43N 96.16W
Canby [Or.-U.S.] 46 Dd 45.16N 122.42W
Cance 11 Ki 45.12N 4.48 E
Canche 11 Hd 50.31N 1.39 E
Cancon 11 Gj 44.32N 0.37 E
Cancún 47 Gd 21.05N 86.46W
Cancún, Isla- 48 Pg 21.05N 86.46W
Çandarli 15 Jk 38.56N 26.56 E
Çandarli Körfezi 15 Jk 38.52N 26.55 E
Candé 11 Eg 47.34N 1.02W
Candela 48 Id 26.50N 100.40W
Candelaria 48 Nh 18.18N 91.21W
Candelaria, Cerro- 48 Hf 23.25N 103.43W
Candelaria, Río- [Bol.] 55 Cc 17.17S 58.39W
Candelaria, Río- [Mex.] 48 Nh 18.38N 91.15W
Candelaro 14 Ji 41.34N 15.53 E
Cândido de Abreu 55 Gg 24.35S 51.20W
Cândido Mendes 54 Id 1.27S 45.43W
Candlemas Islands 66 Ad 57.03S 26.40W
Candói 55 Fg 25.43S 52.11W
Čandyr 16 Jj 38.13N 55.44 E
Canela 56 Jc 29.22S 50.50W
Canelli 14 Cf 44.43N 8.17 E
Canelones [2] 55 El 34.35S 56.00W
Canelones 55 Dl 34.32S 56.17W
Canendiyu [3] 55 Eg 24.20S 55.00W
Cañete [Chile] 56 Fe 37.48S 73.24W
Cañete [Sp.] 13 Kd 40.03N 1.35W
Cangallo 55 Cm 37.13S 58.42W
Cangamba 36 Ce 13.44S 19.53 E
Cangas 13 Db 42.16N 8.47W
Cangas de Narcea 13 Fa 43.11N 6.33W
Cangas de Onís 13 Ga 43.21N 5.07W
Cangola 36 Cd 7.58S 15.53 E
Cangombe 36 Ce 14.24S 19.59 E
Cangshan (Bianzhuang) 28 Eg 34.51N 118.03 E
Canguçu 55 Fj 31.24S 52.41W
Canguçu, Serra do- 55 Fj 31.20S 52.40W
Canguinha 55 Eb 14.42S 55.40W
Cangumbe 36 Ce 12.00S 19.09 E
Cangyuan 27 Gg 23.10N 99.15 E
Cangzhou 27 Kd 38.14N 116.58 E
Cani, Iles- 14 Em 37.21N 10.07 E
Caniapiscau 38 Md 57.40N 69.30W
Caniapiscau, Lac- 42 Kf 54.00N 70.10W
Canicattì 14 Hm 37.21N 13.51 E
Canigou, Pic du- 11 Il 42.31N 2.27 E
Canik Dağlari 24 Gb 40.50N 37.10 E
Canim Lake 46 Ea 51.52N 120.45W
Canindé 54 Kd 4.22S 39.19W
Canindé, Rio- 54 Je 6.15S 42.52W
Cañitas de Felipe Pescador 48 Hf 23.36N 102.43W
Çankaya 24 Ec 39.56N 32.52 E
Çankırı 23 Da 40.36N 33.37 E
Canna 9 Gd 57.03N 6.33W
Cannac 63a Ac 9.15S 153.29 E
Cannakale 23 Ca 40.09N 26.24 E
Cannanore 25 Ff 11.51N 75.22 E
Cannanore Islands 25 Ef 10.05N 72.10 E
Cannes 11 Nk 43.33N 7.01 E
Cannich 9 Id 57.20N 4.45W
Canning Basin 59 Ed 20.10S 123.00 E
Cannobio 14 Cd 46.04N 8.42 E
Cannock 9 Ki 52.42N 2.01W
Cannonball River 45 Fc 46.26N 100.38W
Cann River 59 Jg 37.34S 149.10 E
Caño, Isla del- 49 Fi 8.44N 83.53W
Canoas 56 Jc 29.56S 51.11W
Canoas, Punta- 48 Bc 29.25N 115.10W
Canoas, Rio- 56 Jc 27.36S 51.25W
Canoeiros 54 Ig 18.02S 45.31W
Canoinhas 55 Gh 26.10S 50.24W
Canoinhas, Rio- 55 Gh 26.07S 50.22W
Cañoles 13 Le 39.02N 0.29W
Canon City 43 Fd 38.27N 105.14W
Canon Fiord 42 Ja 80.15N 83.00W
Canonnier, Pointe du- 51b Ab 18.04N 63.10W
Canora 42 Hf 51.37N 102.26W
Canosa di Puglia 14 Ki 41.13N 16.04 E
Canouan Island 50 Ff 12.43N 61.20W
Canourgue 11 Jj 44.25N 3.13 E
Canso, Strait of - 42 Lg 45.35N 61.23W
Canta 54 Cf 11.25S 76.38W
Cantabrian Mountains (EN) =Cantábrica, Cordillera- 5 Fg 43.00N 5.00W
Cantábrica, Cordillera-= Cantabrian Mountains (EN) 5 Fg 43.00N 5.00W
Cantal 5 Gf 45.10N 2.50 E
Cantal [3] 11 Ii 45.05N 2.40 E
Cantalejo 13 Ic 41.15N 3.55W
Cantanhede 13 Dd 40.21N 8.36W
Cantaura 54 Fb 9.19N 64.21W
Cantavieja 13 Ld 40.32N 0.24W
Cantavir 15 Cd 45.55N 19.46 E
Canterbury [2] 62 De 43.30S 171.50 E
Canterbury 9 Oj 51.17N 1.05 E
Canterbury Bight 57 Ii 44.10S 172.00 E
Can Tho 22 Mi 10.02N 105.47 E
Cantiles, Cayo- 49 Fc 21.36N 82.02W
Canto do Buriti 54 Je 8.07S 42.58W
Canton [Il.-U.S.] 45 Kf 40.33N 90.02W
Canton [Mo.-U.S.] 45 Kf 40.08N 91.32W
Canton [Ms.-U.S.] 45 Kj 32.37N 90.02W
Canton [N.Y.-U.S.] 44 Jc 44.37N 75.11W
Canton [Oh.-U.S.] 43 Kc 40.48N 81.23W
Canton [S.D.-U.S.] 45 He 43.18N 96.35W
Canton (EN)=Guangzhou 22 Ng 23.07N 113.18 E
Cantù 14 De 45.44N 9.08 E
Cantwell 40 Jd 63.23N 148.57W
Cañuelas 55 Cl 35.03S 58.44W
Canumã, Rio- 52 Kf 3.55S 59.10W
Canutama 54 Fe 6.32S 64.20W
Canvey 12 Cc 51.31N 0.36 E
Čany 20 Ce 55.19N 76.56 E
Čany, Ozero- 21 Jd 54.50N 77.30 E
Cany-Barville 12 Ce 49.47N 0.38 E
Canyon [Mn.-U.S.] 45 Jc 47.02N 92.29W
Canyon [Tx.-U.S.] 43 Ge 34.59N 101.55W
Canyon [Wy.-U.S.] 46 Jd 44.44N 110.30W
Canyon Lake 45 Gl 29.52N 98.16W
Canzar 36 Dd 7.36S 21.33 E
Cao Bang 25 Ld 22.40N 106.15 E
Caojiahe → Qichun 28 Ci 30.15N 115.26 E
Caojian 27 Gf 25.38N 99.07 E
Caombo 36 Cd 8.42S 16.33 E
Caorle 14 Ge 45.36N 12.53 E
Caoxian 28 Cg 34.49N 115.33 E
Caozhou → Heze 27 Kd 35.14N 115.28 E
Capaccio 14 Jj 40.25N 15.05 E
Čapajev 19 Fe 50.14N 51.08 E
Čapajevsk 19 Ee 53.01N 49.36 E
Capanaparo, Río- 54 Eb 7.01N 67.07W
Capanema [Braz.] 54 Id 1.12S 47.11W
Capanema [Braz.] 55 Fg 25.40S 53.48W
Capanema, Serra do- 55 Fh 26.05S 53.16W
Capão Alto 55 Gh 27.56S 50.30W
Capão Bonito 55 Hf 24.01S 48.20W
Capão Doce, Morro do- 55 Gh 26.43S 51.25W
Caparo, Río- 49 Lj 7.46N 70.23W
Capatárida 49 Lh 11.11N 70.37W
Capbreton 11 Ek 43.38N 1.26W
Cap Breton Canyon (EN) 11 Ek 43.40N 1.50W
Čapčama, Pereval- 18 Hd 41.34N 70.50 E
Cap-Chat 44 Na 49.06N 66.42W
Capcir 11 Il 42.45N 2.10 E
Cap-de-la-Madeleine 42 Kg 46.22N 72.32W
Capdenac-Gare 11 Ij 44.34N 2.05 E
Cape Barren Island 59 Jh 40.25S 148.10 E
Cape Basin (EN) 3 Em 37.00S 7.00 E
Cape Breton Island 38 Me 46.00N 60.30W
Cape Charles 44 Jg 37.17N 76.00W
Cape Coast 31 Gh 5.06N 1.15W
Cape Cod Bay 44 Le 41.52N 70.22W
Cape Coral 44 Gl 26.33N 81.58W
Cape Dorset 39 Lc 64.14N 76.32W
Cape Dyer 39 Mc 66.30N 61.18W
Cape Fear River 44 Ii 33.53N 78.00W
Cape Girardeau 43 Jd 37.19N 89.32W
Cape Johnson Tablemount (EN) 57 Jc 17.08N 177.15W
Capel 12 Bc 51.08N 0.19W
Cape Lisburne 40 Fc 68.52N 166.05W
Capelka 8 Mf 58.02N 29.07 E
Capelongo 36 Ce 14.54S 15.05 E
Capem 55 Ea 13.14S 55.14W
Cape May 44 Jf 38.56N 74.54W
Cape Mount [3] 34 Cd 7.05N 10.50W
Cape Province/ Kaapprovinsie [2] 37 Cf 32.00S 22.00 E
Cape Rise (EN) 3 En 42.00S 15.00 E
Cape Smith 42 Jd 60.44N 78.29W
Capesterre 51e Bc 15.54N 61.13W
Capesterre-Belle-Eau 50 Fd 16.03N 61.34W
Cape Town / Kaapstad 31 Il 33.55S 18.22 E
Cape Verde (EN)=Cabo Verde [1] 31 Eg 16.00N 24.00W
Cape Verde (EN)=Cap Vert 34 Bc 14.45N 17.20W
Cape Verde Basin (EN) 3 Ch 15.00N 30.00W
Cape Verde Islands (EN)= Cabo Verde, Ilhas do- 30 Eg 16.00N 24.10W
Cape Yakataga 40 Kd 60.04N 142.26W
Cape York Peninsula 57 Ff 14.00S 142.30 E
Cap-Haïtien 39 Lh 19.45N 72.15W
Capiibary, Arroyo- 55 Dg 24.06S 56.26W
Capiibary, Río- 55 Eg 25.30S 55.33W
Capim, Rio- 52 Lf 1.40S 47.47W
Capinópolis 55 Hd 18.41S 49.35W
Capira 49 Hi 8.45N 79.53W
Capital Federal [2] 56 Id 34.36S 58.27W
Capitán Arturo Prat 66 Re 62.29S 59.39W
Capitán Bado 56 Ib 23.16S 55.32W
Capitán Bermúdez 55 Bk 32.49S 60.43W
Capitán Sarmiento 55 Cl 34.10S 59.48W
Capitão Noronha, Rio- 55 Ea 13.19S 54.36W
Capivara, Represa da- 55 Gf 22.40S 50.57W
Capivari, Rio- 55 Dd 19.16S 57.10W
Capivarita 55 Fj 30.18S 52.19W
Cap Lopez, Baie du- 36 Ac 0.40S 9.00 E
Čaplygin 16 Kc 53.17N 39.59 E
Cappeln (Oldenburg) 12 Kb 52.49N 8.07 E
Cap Point 50 Fe 14.07N 60.57W
Capraia 14 Dg 43.05N 9.50 E
Caprara, Punta- 14 Ci 41.07N 8.19 E
Capreol 44 Gb 46.43N 80.56W
Caprera 14 Di 41.10N 9.30 E
Capri 14 Ij 40.35N 14.15 E
Capri 14 Ij 40.33N 14.14 E
Capricorn, Cape- 59 Kd 23.30S 151.15 E
Capricorn Channel 59 Kd 22.15S 151.30 E
Capricorn Group 57 Gg 23.30S 152.00 E
Caprivi Strip (EN)=Caprivi Zipfel 30 Jj 18.00S 23.00 E
Caprivi Zipfel=Caprivi Strip (EN) 30 Jj 18.00S 23.00 E
Captain Cook 65a Fd 19.30N 155.55W
Captains Flat 59 Jg 35.35S 149.27 E
Captieux 11 Fj 44.17N 0.15W
Capua 14 Ii 41.06N 14.12 E
Capuchin, Cape- 51g Ba 15.38N 61.28W
Capunda 36 Ce 10.41S 17.23 E
Cap Vert=Cape Verde (EN) [3] 34 Bc 14.45N 17.20W
Caquetá [2] 54 Dc 1.00N 74.00W
Čara 21 Oc 60.17N 120.40 E
Čara [R.S.F.S.R.] 20 Ge 56.58N 118.17 E
Čara [R.S.F.S.R.] 20 Ge 56.54N 118.12 E
Carabobo [2] 54 Ea 10.10N 68.05W
Caracal 15 He 44.07N 24.21 E
Caracaraí 54 Fc 1.50N 61.08W
Caracas 53 Jd 10.30N 66.56W
Carache 49 Li 9.38N 70.14W
Caracol 55 De 21.59S 57.02W
Caracol, Rio- 55 Df 22.13S 57.03W
Caracollo 54 Eg 17.39S 67.10W
Cara Droma Rúisc/Carrick-on-Shannon 9 Eh 53.57N 8.05W
Caraguatá, Cuchilla- 55 Ek 32.05S 54.54W
Caraguatatuba 55 Jf 23.37S 45.25W
Caraïbe, Mer-/Antilles, Mer des-=Caribbean Sea (EN) 38 Lh 15.00N 73.00W
Carajas, Serra dos- 54 He 6.00S 51.20W
Caramoan Peninsula 26 Hd 13.48N 123.40 E
Caramulo, Serra do- 13 Dd 40.34N 8.11W
Caraná, Rio- 55 Ca 13.20S 59.17W
Carandai 55 Ke 20.57S 43.48W
Carandazal 55 Dd 19.50S 57.09W
Caransebeş 15 Fd 45.25N 22.13 E
Carapá, Río- 55 Eg 24.30S 54.20W
Carapelle 14 Ji 41.30N 15.55 E
Caraş 15 Ee 44.49N 21.20 E
Caraş Severin [2] 15 Ed 45.20N 22.00 E
Caratasca, Cayo- 49 Fe 16.02N 83.20W
Caratasca, Laguna de- 47 He 15.20N 83.50W
Caratinga 54 Jg 19.47S 42.08W
Carauari 54 Ed 4.52S 66.54W
Caraúbas 54 Ke 5.47S 37.34W
Caravaca 13 Kf 38.06N 1.51W
Caravelas 53 Mg 17.45S 39.15W
Caraveli 54 Dg 15.46S 73.22W
Caravelle, Presqu'île de la- 51h Bb 14.45N 60.55W
Caravelle, Rocher de la- 51h Bb 14.48N 60.53W
Caràzinho 56 Jc 28.18S 52.48W
Carazo [3] 49 Dh 11.45N 86.15W
Carballino 13 Db 42.26N 8.04W
Carballo 13 Da 43.13N 8.41W
Carberry 45 Gb 49.52N 99.20W
Carbet, Pitons du- 51h Ab 14.42N 61.07W
Carbon, Cap- [Alg.] 13 Rh 36.47N 5.06 E
Carbon, Cap- [Alg.] 13 Li 35.54N 0.20W
Carbonara, Capo- 14 Dk 39.06N 9.31 E
Carbondale [Il.-U.S.] 43 Jd 37.44N 89.13W
Carbondale [Pa.-U.S.] 44 Je 41.35N 75.31W
Carbonera, Cuchilla de la- 55 El 34.10S 54.00W
Carboneras 13 Kh 36.59N 1.54W
Carboneras, Cerro- 48 Ih 18.10N 101.10W
Carbones 13 Gg 37.36N 5.39W
Carbonia 14 Ck 39.10N 8.31 E
Carcans, Étang de- 11 Ei 45.06N 1.07W
Carcar 26 Hd 10.06N 123.38 E
Carcarañá, Río- 55 Bk 32.27S 60.48W
Carcassonne 11 Ik 43.13N 2.21 E
Carcross 42 Ed 60.10N 134.42W
Çardak [Tur.] 15 Ji 40.22N 26.43 E
Çardak [Tur.] 24 Cd 37.48N 29.40 E
Čardara 19 Gg 41.15N 68.01 E
Čardarinskoje Vodohranilišče 18 Gd 41.05N 68.15 E
Cárdenas [Cuba] 47 Hd 23.02N 81.12W
Cárdenas [Mex.] 47 Ed 22.00N 99.40W
Cárdenas [Mex.] 48 Mi 17.59N 93.22W
Cárdenas, Bahía de- 49 Gb 23.05N 81.10W
Cardener/Cardoner 13 Nc 41.41N 1.51 E
Cardiel, Lago- 56 Fg 48.55S 71.15W
Cardiff 6 Fe 51.30N 3.13W
Cardigan 9 Ii 52.06N 4.40W
Cardigan Bay 5 Fe 52.30N 4.20W
Cardona [Sp.] 13 Nc 41.55N 1.41 E
Cardona [Ur.] 55 Dk 33.54S 57.22W
Cardoner/Cardener 13 Nc 41.41N 1.51 E
Cardozo 55 Dk 32.38S 56.21W
Cardston 42 Gg 49.12N 113.18W
Čardžou 22 If 39.06N 63.34 E
Čardžouskaja Oblast [3] 19 Gh 39.00N 63.00 E
Carei 15 Fb 47.41N 22.28 E
Careiro 54 Gd 3.12S 59.45W
Carentan 11 Ee 49.18N 1.14W
Carey 46 Ie 43.20N 113.58W
Carey, Lake- 57 Dg 29.05S 122.15 E
Cargados Carajos Islands 30 Mj 16.35S 59.40 E
Cargèse 11a Aa 42.08N 8.35 E
Carhaix-Plouguer 11 Cf 48.17N 3.35W
Cari 14 Hi 41.23N 13.50 E
Caria 15 Ll 37.30N 29.00 E
Cariacica 54 Jh 20.16S 40.25W
Cariaco 50 Eg 10.29N 63.33W
Cariaco, Golfo de- 50 Eg 10.30N 64.00W
Cariaco Basin (EN) 50 Dg 10.37N 65.10W
Cariati 14 Kk 39.30N 16.57 E
Caribana, Punta- 49 Ii 8.37N 76.52W
Caribbean Sea 38 Lh 15.00N 73.00W
Caribbean Sea (EN)= Antillas, Mar de las-/ Caribe, Mar- 38 Lh 15.00N 73.00W
Caribbean Sea (EN)= Antilles, Mer des-/Caraïbe, Mer- 38 Lh 15.00N 73.00W
Caribbean Sea (EN)= Caribe, Mar-/Antillas, Mar de las- 38 Lh 15.00N 73.00W
Caribe, Mar-/Antillas, Mar de las-=Caribbean Sea (EN) 38 Lh 15.00N 73.00W
Cariboo Mountains 42 Ff 53.00N 121.00W
Caribou 42 Ie 59.20N 94.45W
Caribou 44 Mb 46.52N 68.01W
Caribou Island 44 Eb 47.27N 85.52W
Caribou Lake 45 La 50.25N 89.00W
Caribou Mountains 38 Hd 59.12N 115.40W
Caribou Range 46 Je 43.05N 111.15W
Caričin Grad 15 Eg 42.57N 21.45 E
Carignan 11 Le 49.38N 5.10 E
Carignano 14 Bf 44.55N 7.40 E
Cariñena 13 Kc 41.20N 1.13W
Carinhanha 54 Jf 14.08S 43.47W
Carinhanha, Rio- 55 Kb 14.20S 43.47W
Carini 14 Hl 38.08N 13.11 E
Carinola 14 Hi 41.11N 13.58 E
Carinthia (EN) = Kärnten [2] 14 Hd 46.45N 14.00 E
Carinthia (EN) = Kärnten 14 Hd 46.45N 14.00 E
Caripe 50 Eg 10.21N 63.29W
Caripito 54 Fa 10.08N 63.06W
Caris, Rio- 50 Eh 8.09N 63.46W
Carlet 13 Le 39.14N 0.31W
Carleton Place 44 Ic 45.07N 76.08W
Carletonville 37 De 26.23S 27.22 E
Carlin 46 Gf 40.43N 116.07W
Carling 12 Ie 49.10N 6.43 E
Carlingford Lough/Loch Cairlinn 9 Gg 54.05N 6.14W
Carlinville 45 Lg 39.17N 89.53W
Carlisle [Eng.-U.K.] 6 Fe 54.54N 2.55W
Carlisle [Pa.-U.S.] 44 Ie 40.12N 77.12W
Carlisle Bay 51q Ab 13.05N 59.37W
Carloforte 14 Ck 39.08N 8.18 E
Carlos Beguerie 55 Ck 35.29S 59.06W
Carlos Casares 56 He 35.38S 61.21W
Carlos Chagas 54 Jg 17.43S 40.45W
Carlos Reyles 55 Dk 33.03S 56.29W
Carlos Tejedor 55 Al 35.23S 62.25W
Carlow/Ceatharlach 9 Gi 52.50N 6.55W
Carlow/Ceatharlach [2] 9 Gi 52.50N 7.00W
Carloway 9 Gc 58.17N 6.47W
Carlsbad [Ca.-U.S.] 46 Gj 33.10N 117.21W
Carlsbad [N.M.-U.S.] 39 If 32.25N 104.14W
Carlyle 42 Hg 49.38N 102.16W
Carlyle Lake 45 Lg 38.40N 89.18W
Carmacks 42 Dd 62.05N 136.18W
Carmagnola 14 Bf 44.51N 7.43 E
Carmarthen 9 Ij 51.52N 4.19W
Carmarthen Bay 9 Ij 51.40N 4.30W
Carmaux 11 Ij 44.03N 2.09 E
Carmel Head 9 Ih 53.24N 4.34W
Carmelita 49 Be 17.21N 90.10W
Carmelo 56 Id 34.00S 58.17W
Carmen 55 Dk 33.15S 56.01W
Carmen, Isla- 47 Bc 25.57N 111.12W
Carmen, Isla del- 48 Nh 18.42N 91.40W
Carmen, Laguna del- 48 Mh 18.15N 93.50W
Carmen, Río del- 48 Fb 30.42N 106.29W
Carmen, Sierra del- 48 Hc 29.00N 102.30W
Carmen de Patagones 56 Hf 40.48S 62.59W
Carmensa 56 Ge 35.08S 67.38W
Carmi 45 Lg 38.07N 88.10W
Carmichael 46 Eg 38.38N 121.19W
Carmo de Minas 55 Jf 22.07S 45.08W
Carmo do Paranaíba 55 Id 18.59S 46.21W
Carmona 13 Gg 37.28N 5.38W
Carnac 11 Cg 47.35N 3.05W
Carnamah 59 De 29.42S 115.53 E
Carnarvon [Austl.] 58 Cg 24.53S 113.40 E
Carnarvon [S.Afr.] 31 Jl 30.56S 22.08 E
Carnarvon Range 59 Ee 25.10S 121.00 E
Carnatic (EN) 21 Jh 10.30N 79.00 E
Carnegie, Lake- 57 Dg 26.10S 122.30 E
Carnegie Ridge (EN) 3 Nj 1.00S 85.00W
Carn Eige 9 Hd 57.30N 5.05W
Carney Island 66 Nf 73.57S 121.00W
Carnia 14 Gd 46.25N 13.00 E
Car Nicobar 25 Ig 9.10N 92.47 E
Carnot 35 Be 4.48N 16.03 E
Carnoustie 9 Ke 56.30N 2.44W
Carnsore Point/Ceann an Chairn 9 Gi 52.10N 6.22W
Carn Uí Néid/Mizen Head 5 Fe 51.27N 9.49W
Caro 44 Fd 43.29N 83.24W
Carol City 44 Gm 25.56N 80.16W
Carolina [Braz.] 53 Lf 7.20S 47.28W
Carolina [P.R.] 51a Cb 18.24N 65.57W
Carolina [S.Afr.] 37 Ee 26.05S 30.06 E
Carolina Beach 44 Ih 34.02N 77.54W
Carolinas, Puntan- 64b Bb 14.54N 145.38 E
Caroline Atoll 57 Le 9.58S 150.13W
Caroline Islands 57 Fd 8.00N 147.00 E
Carondelet Reef 57 Je 5.34S 173.51W
Caroni, Rio- 52 Je 8.21N 62.43W
Caronie → Nebrodi 14 Im 37.55N 14.35 E
Carora 54 Da 10.11N 70.05W
Carpathian Mountains (EN) 5 If 48.00N 24.00 E
Carpathian Mountains (EN) =Carpații Occidentali 15 Fc 46.30N 22.10 E
Carpathian Mountains (EN) =Carpații Orientali 15 Ib 47.30N 25.30 E
Carpații Meridionali= Transylvanian Alps (EN) 5 If 45.30N 22.10 E
Carpații Occidentali = Carpathian Mountains (EN) 15 Fc 46.30N 22.10 E
Carpații Orientali= Carpathian Mountains (EN) 15 Ib 47.30N 25.30 E
Carpen 15 Ge 44.20N 23.15 E
Carpentaria, Gulf of- 57 Ef 14.00S 139.00 E
Carpentras 11 Lj 44.03N 5.03 E
Carpi 14 Ef 44.47N 10.53 E
Carpina 54 Ke 7.51S 35.15W
Carr, Cape- 66 Ie 66.07S 130.51 E
Carraig Fhearghais/ Carrickfergus 9 Hg 54.43N 5.44W
Carraig na Siúire/Carrick-on-Suir
Carrara 14 Ef 44.05N 10.06 E
Carrauntoohil 5 Fe 52.00N 9.45W
Carreiro, Rio- 55 Gi 29.07S 51.43W
Carreño 13 Ga 43.35N 5.46W
Carreta, Punta- 54 Cf 14.13S 76.18W
Carretero, Puerto- 13 Ig 37.28N 3.40W
Carriacou 50 Ff 12.30N 61.27W
Carrick 9 If 55.15N 4.40W
Carrickfergus/Carraig Fhearghais 9 Hg 54.43N 5.44W
Carrick-on-Shannon/cara Droma Rúisc 9 Eh 53.57N 8.05W
Carrick-on-Suir/Carraig na Siúire 9 Fi 52.21N 7.25W
Carrington 43 Hb 47.27N 99.08W
Carrión 13 Hc 41.53N 4.32W
Carrión de los Condes 13 Hb 42.20N 4.36W
Carrizal 49 Kh 11.58N 72.12W
Carrizo Peak 45 Dj 33.20N 105.38W
Carrizos 48 Gc 29.58N 105.16W
Carrizo Springs 45 Gl 28.31N 99.52W
Carrizo Wash 46 Ki 34.36N 109.26W
Carrizozo 45 Dj 33.38N 105.53W
Carroll 45 Ie 42.04N 94.52W
Carroll Inlet 66 Qf 73.18S 78.30W
Carrollton [Ga.-U.S.] 44 Ei 33.35N 85.05W
Carrollton [Il.-U.S.] 45 Kg 39.18N 90.24W
Carrollton [Ky.-U.S.] 44 Ef 38.41N 85.11W
Carrollton [Mo.-U.S.] 45 Jg 39.22N 93.30W
Carron, Loch- 9 Hd 57.30N 5.40W
Carrot 42 Hf 53.50N 101.18W
Carrowmore Lough 9 Dg 54.12N 9.47W
Çarşamba 24 Gb 41.12N 36.44 E
Çarşamba 24 Ed 37.53N 32.37 E
Čaršanga 19 Gh 37.31N 66.03 E
Čarsk 19 If 49.35N 81.05 E
Carson 46 Ed 45.44N 121.49W
Carson City 39 Hf 39.10N 119.46W
Carson Lake 46 Fg 39.19N 118.43W
Carson Sink 46 Fg 39.45N 118.30W
Cartagena [Col.] 53 Id 10.25N 75.32W
Cartagena [Sp.] 6 Fh 37.36N 0.59W
Cartago [3] 49 Fi 9.50N 83.45W
Cartago [Col.] 54 Cc 4.46N 75.56W
Cartago [C.R.] 47 Hg 9.52N 83.55W
Cartaxo 13 De 39.09N 8.47W
Carter, Mount- 59 Ib 13.05S 143.15 E
Carteret 11 Ee 49.23N 1.47W
Cartersville 44 Eh 34.10N 85.05W
Carterton 62 Fd 41.01S 175.31 E
Carthage [Mo.-U.S.] 45 Ih 37.11N 94.19W
Carthage [Tx.-U.S.] 45 Ij 32.09N 94.20W
Cartier 44 Gb 46.42N 81.32W
Cartier Island 57 Df 12.30S 123.30 E
Caruaru 53 Mf 8.17S 35.58W
Carúpano 54 Fa 10.40N 63.14W
Carutapera 54 Id 1.13S 46.01W
Čarvak 18 Gd 41.38N 69.56 E
Carvin 12 Ed 50.29N 2.58 E
Carvoeiro, Cabo- 13 Ce 39.21N 9.24W
Čaryn 18 Lc 43.50N 79.12 E
Čaryš 20 Df 52.22N 83.45 E
Casablanca [2] 32 Fc 33.37N 7.35W
Casablanca 31 Ge 33.36N 7.37W
Casa Branca 55 Ie 21.46S 47.05W
Casa Grande 43 Ee 32.53N 111.45W
Casalbordino 14 Ih 42.09N 14.35 E
Casale Monferrato 14 Ce 45.08N 8.27 E
Casalmaggiore 14 Ef 44.59N 10.26 E
Casalvasco 55 Cb 15.19S 59.59W
Casal Velino 14 Jj 40.11N 15.06 E
Casamance 34 Bc 12.33N 16.46W
Casamance [3] 34 Bc 12.50N 15.00W
Casanare [2] 54 Db 5.20N 72.00W
Casanare, Rio- 54 Eb 6.02N 69.51W
Casanay 50 Eg 10.30N 63.25W
Casa Nova 54 Je 9.25S 41.08W
Casarano 14 Mj 40.00N 18.10 E
Casas Grandes, Rio- 48 Eb 30.22N 107.31W
Casas-Ibáñez 13 Ke 39.17N 1.28W
Casca, Rio da- 55 Eb 14.52S 55.52W
Cascade 46 Hd 44.31N 115.59W
Cascade Point 62 Cf 44.01S 168.22 E
Cascade Range 38 Ge 45.00N 121.30W
Cascais 13 Cf 38.42N 9.25W
Cascavel 56 Jb 24.57S 53.28W
Cascia 14 Hh 42.43N 13.01 E
Casciana Terme 14 Eg 43.32N 10.38 E
Cascina 14 Eg 43.41N 10.33 E
Casentino 14 Fg 43.40N 11.50 E

Index Symbols

[1] Independent Nation
[2] State, Region
[3] District, County
[4] Municipality
[5] Colony, Dependency
Continent
Physical Region
Historical or Cultural Region
Mount, Mountain
Volcano
Hill
Mountains, Mountain Range
Hills, Escarpment
Plateau, Upland
Pass, Gap
Plain, Lowland
Delta
Salt Flat
Valley, Canyon
Crater, Cave
Karst Features
Depression
Polder
Desert, Dunes
Forest, Woods
Heath, Steppe
Oasis
Cape, Point
Coast, Beach
Cliff
Peninsula
Isthmus
Sandbank
Island
Atoll
Rock, Reef
Islands, Archipelago
Rocks, Reefs
Coral Reef
Well, Spring
Geyser
River, Stream
Waterfall Rapids
River Mouth, Estuary
Lake
Salt Lake
Intermittent Lake
Reservoir
Swamp, Pond
Canal
Glacier
Ice Shelf, Pack Ice
Ocean
Sea
Gulf, Bay
Strait, Fjord
Lagoon
Bank
Seamount
Tablemount
Ridge
Shelf
Basin
Escarpment, Sea Scarp
Fracture
Trench, Abyss
National Park, Reserve
Point of Interest
Recreation Site
Cave, Cavern
Historic Site
Ruins
Wall, Walls
Church, Abbey
Temple
Scientific Station
Airport
Port
Lighthouse
Mine
Tunnel
Dam, Bridge

Name	Page	Grid	Lat.	Long.
Case-Pilote	51h	Ab	14.38N	61.08W
Caserta	14	Ii	41.04N	14.20 E
Casey	66	He	66.17S	110.32 E
Casey Bay	66	Ee	67.00S	48.00 E
Cashel/Caiseal	9	Fi	52.31N	7.53W
Casigua	49	Ki	8.46N	72.30W
Casilda	56	Hd	33.03S	61.10W
Casimcea	15	Le	44.24N	28.33 E
Casino	59	Ke	28.52S	153.03 E
Casiquiare, Brazo-	54	Ec	2.01N	67.07W
Čáslav	10	Lg	49.55N	15.25 E
Casma	54	Ce	9.28S	78.19W
Časnačorr, Gora-	7	Hc	67.45N	33.29 E
Čašniki	7	Gi	54.52N	29.08 E
Casoli	14	Ih	42.07N	14.18 E
Casoria	14	Ij	40.54N	14.17 E
Caspe	13	Lc	41.14N	0.02W
Casper	39	Ie	42.51N	106.19W
Caspian Depression (EN)= Prikaspijskaja Nizmennost	5	Lf	48.00N	52.00 E
Caspian Sea (EN)= Kaspijskoje More	5	Lg	42.00N	50.30 E
Caspian Sea (EN)= Māzandarān, Daryā-ye-	5	Lg	42.00N	50.30 E
Cassai	30	Ii	3.02S	16.57 E
Cassamba	36	De	13.04S	20.25 E
Cassange, Rio-	55	Dc	17.06S	57.23W
Cassano allo Ionio	14	Kk	39.47N	16.19 E
Cass City	44	Fd	43.36N	83.10W
Cassel	12	Ed	50.47N	2.29 E
Casselton	45	Hc	46.54N	97.13W
Cássia	55	Ie	20.36S	46.56W
Cassiar	42	Ee	59.16N	129.40W
Cassiar Mountains	38	Gd	59.00N	129.00W
Cassilândia	54	Hg	19.09S	51.45W
Cassino [Braz.]	55	Fk	32.11S	52.10W
Cassino [It.]	14	Hi	41.30N	13.49 E
Cassis	11	Lk	43.13N	5.32 E
Cass Lake	45	Ic	47.23N	94.36W
Cass River	44	Fd	43.23N	83.59W
Cassununga	55	Fc	16.03S	53.38W
Castagneto Carducci	14	Eg	43.10N	10.36 E
Castagniccia	11a	Ba	42.25N	9.30 E
Castañar, Sierra del-	13	He	39.35N	4.10W
Castanhal	54	Id	1.18S	47.55W
Castaños	48	Id	26.47N	101.25W
Castelbuono	14	Im	37.56N	14.05 E
Castel di Sangro	14	Ii	41.47N	14.06 E
Castelfidardo	14	Hg	43.28N	13.33 E
Castelfranco Veneto	14	Fe	45.40N	11.55 E
Casteljaloux	11	Gj	44.19N	0.06 E
Castellabate	14	Ij	40.17N	14.57 E
Castellammare, Golfo di-	14	Gl	38.10N	12.55 E
Castellammare del Golfo	14	Gl	38.01N	12.53 E
Castellammare di Stabia	14	Ij	40.42N	14.29 E
Castellana Grotte	14	Lj	40.53N	17.10 E
Castellane	11	Mk	43.51N	6.31 E
Castellaneta	14	Kj	40.38N	16.56 E
Castelldefels	13	Nc	41.17N	1.58 E
Castelli [Arg.]	56	Hc	25.57S	60.37W
Castelli [Arg.]	55	Dm	36.06S	57.47W
Castelló de la Plana/ Castellón de la Plana	6	Fh	39.59N	0.02W
Castellón [3]	13	Ld	40.10N	0.10W
Castellón de la Plana/ Castelló de la Plana	6	Fh	39.59N	0.02W
Castellón de la Plana-El Grao	13	Me	39.58N	0.01 E
Castellote	13	Ld	40.48N	0.19W
Castelnaudary	11	Hk	43.19N	1.57 E
Castelnau-de-Médoc	11	Fi	45.02N	0.48W
Castelnovo ne' Monti	14	Ef	44.26N	10.24 E
Castelo Branco [2]	13	Ee	40.00N	7.30W
Castelo Branco	13	Ee	39.49N	7.30W
Castelo de Vide	13	Ee	39.25N	7.27W
Castelo do Piauí	54	Je	5.20S	41.33W
Castel San Giovanni	14	De	45.04N	9.26 E
Castelsardo	14	Cj	40.55N	8.43 E
Castelsarrasin	11	Hj	44.02N	1.06 E
Casteltermini	14	Hm	37.32N	13.39 E
Castelvetrano	14	Gm	37.41N	12.47 E
Castets	11	Ek	43.53N	1.09W
Castiglione del Lago	14	Gg	43.07N	12.03 E
Castiglione della Pescaia	14	Eh	42.46N	10.53 E
Castiglion Fiorentino	14	Fg	43.20N	11.55 E
Castilla la Nueva=New Castile (EN)	13	Id	40.00N	3.45W
Castilla la Vieja=Old Castile (EN)	13	Ic	41.30N	4.00W
Castillejo	13	Gc	41.14N	5.30W
Castillon-la-Bataille	11	Fj	44.51N	0.02W
Castillonnès	11	Gj	44.39N	0.36 E
Castillos	56	Jd	34.12S	53.50W
Castillos, Laguna de-	55	Fl	34.20S	53.54W
Castlebar/Caisleán an Bharraigh	9	Dh	53.52N	9.17W
Castle Bruce	51g	Bb	15.26N	61.16W
Castle Dome Peak	46	Hj	33.05N	114.08W
Castle Douglas	9	Jg	54.57N	3.56W
Castlegar	42	Fg	49.19N	117.40W
Castleisland/Oileán Ciarraí	9	Di	52.14N	9.27W
Castlemaine	59	Ig	37.04S	144.13 E
Castle Peak	46	Hd	44.03N	114.32W
Castlepoint	62	Gd	40.55S	176.13 E
Castlepollard	9	Fh	53.41N	7.17W
Castlerea/An Caisleán Riabhach	9	Eh	53.46N	8.29W
Castlereagh Bay	59	Hb	12.10S	135.10 E
Castle Rock Butte	45	Ed	45.00N	103.27W
Castle Rock Lake	45	Le	43.56N	89.58W
Častoozerje	17	Mi	55.34N	67.53 E
Castor	46	Ja	52.13N	111.53W
Castres	11	Ik	43.36N	2.15 E
Castricum	12	Gb	52.33N	4.42 E
Castries	39	Mh	14.01N	61.00W
Castrignano del Capo	14	Mk	39.50N	18.20 E
Castro [Braz.]	56	Jb	24.47S	50.03W
Castro [Chile]	56	Ff	42.29S	73.46W
Castro Alves	54	Kf	12.45S	39.26W
Castrocaro Terme e Terra del Sole	14	Ff	44.10N	11.57 E
Castro Daire	13	Ed	40.54N	7.56W
Castro del Río	13	Hg	37.41N	4.28W
Castrojeriz	13	Hb	42.17N	4.08W
Castropol	13	Ea	43.32N	7.02W
Castrop-Rauxel	12	Jc	51.33N	7.19 E
Castro Urdiales	13	Ia	43.23N	3.13W
Castro Verde	13	Dg	37.42N	8.05W
Castrovillari	14	Kk	39.49N	16.12 E
Castrovirreyna	54	Cf	13.16S	75.19W
Castuera	13	Gf	38.43N	5.33W
Častyje	17	Gh	57.19N	54.59 E
Casupá	55	El	34.09S	55.38W
Caswell Sound	62	Bf	45.00S	167.10 E
Çat	24	Ic	39.40N	41.02 E
Čata	10	Oi	47.58N	18.40 E
Catacamas	49	Ef	14.54N	85.56W
Catahoula Lake	45	Jk	31.30N	92.06W
Çatak	24	Jc	38.01N	43.07 E
Çatak	24	Jd	37.53N	42.39 E
Catalan Coastal Range (EN) =Cadena Costero Catalana /Serralada Litoral Catalana	5	Gg	41.35N	1.40 E
Catalan Coastal Range (EN) =Serralada Litoral Catalana/Cadena Costero Catalana	5	Gg	41.35N	1.40 E
Catalão	54	Ig	18.10S	47.57W
Čatal Balkan	15	Jg	42.46N	27.00 E
Çatalca	15	Lh	41.09N	28.27 E
Çatal Dağ	15	Lj	39.51N	28.20 E
Catalina	56	Gc	25.13S	69.43W
Catalina, Isla-	49	Md	18.21N	69.00W
Catalina, Punta-	56	Gh	52.32S	68.47W
Catalonia (EN)=Cataluña/ Catalunya	5	Gg	42.00N	2.00 E
Catalonia (EN)=Cataluña/ Catalunya	13	Nc	42.00N	2.00 E
Catalonia (EN)=Catalunya/ Cataluña	5	Gg	42.00N	2.00 E
Catalonia (EN)=Catalunya/ Cataluña	13	Nc	42.00N	2.00 E
Cataluña/Catalunya= Catalonia (EN)	5	Gg	42.00N	2.00 E
Cataluña/Catalunya= Catalonia (EN)	13	Nc	42.00N	2.00 E
Catalunya/Cataluña= Catalonia (EN)	13	Nc	42.00N	2.00 E
Catalunya/Cataluña= Catalonia (EN)	5	Gg	42.00N	2.00 E
Çatalzeytin	24	Fb	41.57N	34.13 E
Catamarca	53	Jh	28.30S	65.45W
Catamarca [2]	56	Gc	27.00S	67.00W
Catanduanes	21	Oh	13.45N	124.15 E
Catanduva	56	Kb	21.08S	48.58W
Catanduvas	55	Fg	25.12S	53.08W
Catania	6	Hh	37.30N	15.06 E
Catania, Golfo di-	14	Jm	37.25N	15.10 E
Catania, Piana di-	14	Im	37.25N	14.50 E
Catanzaro	6	Hh	38.54N	16.35 E
Catarman	26	Hd	12.30N	124.38 E
Catastrophe, Cape-	57	Eh	35.00S	136.00 E
Catatumbo, Río-	49	Li	9.21N	71.45W
Catbalogan	26	Hd	11.46N	124.53 E
Catemaco, Lago-	48	Lh	18.25N	95.05W
Catete	36	Bd	9.07S	13.41 E
Cathair na Mart/Westport	9	Dh	53.48N	9.32W
Cathair Saidhbhín/ Cahersiveen	9	Cj	51.57N	10.13W
Cathcart	37	Df	32.18S	27.09 E
Catherine, Mount-	46	Ig	39.05N	112.04W
Catholic Island	51n	Bb	12.40N	61.24W
Catio	34	Bc	11.17N	15.15W
Cat Island	38	Lg	24.30N	75.30W
Čatkal	18	Hd	41.36N	70.05 E
Čatkalski Hrebet	19	Hg	41.30N	70.50 E
Cat Lake	42	If	51.40N	91.52W
Catoche, Cabo-	38	Kg	21.36N	87.07W
Cato Island	57	Gg	23.15S	155.35 E
Catolé do Rocha	54	Ke	6.21S	37.45W
Catoute	13	Fb	42.45N	6.20W
Catria	14	Gg	43.28N	12.42 E
Catriló	56	He	36.26S	63.24W
Catrimani, Rio-	54	Fc	0.28N	61.44W
Catskill Mountains	44	Jd	42.10N	74.30W
Cattenom	12	Ie	49.25N	6.15 E
Cattolica	14	Gg	43.58N	12.44 E
Catu	54	Kf	12.21S	38.23W
Catuane	37	Ee	26.48S	32.14 E
Catumbela	36	Be	12.27S	13.29 E
Catur	37	Fb	13.45S	35.37 E
Catwick, Iles-	25	Lg	10.00N	109.00 E
Catwright	39	Nd	53.50N	56.45W
Catyrkël, Ozero-	18	Jd	40.35N	75.20 E
Catyrtaš	18	Kd	40.52N	76.23 E
Cauca [2]	54	Cc	2.30N	77.00W
Cauca, Río-	52	Ie	8.54N	74.28W
Caucasia	54	Cb	7.59N	75.13W
Caucasus (EN)=Kavkaz, Bolšoj-	5	Kg	42.30N	45.00 E
Caucete	56	Gd	31.38S	68.16W
Caudebec-en-Caux	12	Ce	49.32N	0.44 E
Caudete	13	Lf	38.42N	0.59W
Caudry	11	Jd	50.08N	3.25 E
Caulonia	14	Kl	38.23N	16.24 E
Caumont-l'Eventé	12	Be	49.05N	0.48W
Caungula	31	Ii	8.26S	18.37 E
Čaunskaja Guba	20	Lc	69.30N	170.00 E
Caupolican	54	Ef	13.30S	68.30W
Cauquenes	56	Fe	35.58S	72.21W
Caura, Río-	52	Je	7.38N	64.53W
Causapscal	44	Na	48.22N	67.14W
Caussade	11	Hj	44.10N	1.32 E
Čausy	16	Gc	53.50N	30.59 E
Cauterets	11	Fl	42.53N	0.07W
Cauto, Río-	49	Ic	20.33N	77.15W
Cauvery	21	Jh	11.09N	78.52 E
Caux, Pays de-	11	Ge	49.40N	0.40 E
Cávado	13	Dc	41.32N	8.48W
Cavaillon	11	Lk	43.50N	5.02 E
Cavalcante	55	Ia	13.48S	47.30W
Cavalese	14	Fd	46.17N	11.27 E
Cavalli Islands	62	Ea	35.00S	173.55 E
Cavallo, Isola-	11a	Bb	41.22N	9.16 E
Cavallo Pass	45	Hl	28.25N	96.26W
Cavally	30	Gh	4.22N	7.32W
Cavan/An Cabhán	9	Fg	54.00N	7.21W
Cavan/An Cabhán [2]	9	Fh	53.55N	7.30W
Cavarzere	14	Ge	45.08N	12.05 E
Çavdarhisar	15	Mj	39.12N	29.37 E
Çavdir	15	Ml	37.09N	29.42 E
Caviana, Ilha-	54	Hc	0.10N	50.05W
Cavili	26	He	9.17N	120.50 E
Cavour, Canale-	14	Be	45.11N	7.54 E
Cavtat	14	Mh	42.35N	18.13 E
Caxambu	55	Je	21.59S	44.56W
Caxias	53	Lf	4.50S	43.21W
Caxias do Sul	53	Kh	29.10S	51.11W
Caxito	36	Bd	8.34S	13.40 E
Çay	24	Dc	38.35N	31.02 E
Cayambe	54	Cc	0.05N	78.08W
Cayambe, Volcán-	52	Ie	0.02N	77.59W
Cayastá	55	Bj	31.12S	60.10W
Cayce	44	Gi	33.59N	81.04W
Çaycuma	24	Eb	41:25N	32.05 E
Çayeli	24	Ib	41.05N	40.44 E
Cayenne	53	Ke	4.56N	52.20W
Cayeux-Sur-Mer	12	Dd	50.11N	1.29 E
Cayey	49	Nd	18.07N	66.10W
Çayırlı	24	Ic	39.48N	40.01 E
Çaykara	24	Ib	40.45N	40.19 E
Caylus	11	Hj	44.14N	1.47 E
Cayman Brac	47	Ie	19.43N	79.49W
Cayman Islands [5]	39	Kh	19.30N	80.30W
Cayman Islands	38	Kh	19.30N	80.30W
Cayman Ridge (EN)	47	He	19.30N	80.30W
Cayman Trench (EN)	3	Bh	19.00N	80.00W
Cayo	49	Ce	17.10N	88.50W
Cayon	51c	Ab	17.21N	62.43W
Cayones, Cayos-	49	Fe	16.05N	83.12W
Cay Sal Bank	47	Hd	23.45N	80.00W
Cayuga Lake	44	Id	42.45N	76.45W
Cazalla de la Sierra	13	Gg	37.56N	5.45W
Caza Pava	55	Di	28.17S	56.07W
Cazaux, Étang de-	11	Ej	44.29N	1.10W
Cazombo	31	Jj	11.54S	22.53 E
Cazorla	13	Jg	37.55N	3.00W
Cazorla, Sierra de-	13	Jf	37.55N	2.55W
Cea	13	Gb	42.00N	5.36W
Ceahlău	15	Ib	47.03N	25.58 E
Ceanannas Mór/Kells	9	Gh	53.44N	6.53W
Ceanna Caillighe/Hags Head	9	Di	52.57N	9.28W
Ceann Acla/Achill Head	9	Ch	53.59N	10.13W
Ceann an Chairn/Carnsore Point	9	Gi	52.10N	6.22W
Ceann Chill Mhantáin/ Wicklow Head	9	Hi	52.58N	6.00W
Ceann Gólaim/Slyne Head	9	Ch	53.24N	10.13W
Ceann Iorrais/Erris Head	5	Fe	54.19N	10.00W
Ceann Léime/Loop Head	9	Di	52.34N	9.56W
Ceann Ros Eoghain/Rossan Point	9	Eg	54.42N	8.48W
Ceann Sléibhe/Slea Head	9	Ci	52.06N	10.27W
Ceann Toirc/Kanturk	9	Ei	52.10N	8.55W
Ceará [2]	54	Kd	5.00S	39.30W
Ceará-Mirim	54	Ke	5.38S	35.26W
Ceatharlach/Carlow [2]	9	Gi	52.50N	7.00W
Ceatharlach/Carlow	9	Gi	52.50N	6.55W
Cébaco, Isla-	49	Gj	7.32N	81.09W
Ceballos	48	Gd	26.32N	104.09W
Čebarkul	17	Ji	54.58N	60.25 E
Čeboksary	6	Kd	56.09N	47.15 E
Cebollati	55	Fk	33.16S	53.47W
Cebollati, Río-	55	Fk	33.09S	53.38W
Cebollera, Sierra-	13	Jc	42.00N	2.40W
Ceboruco, Volcán-	48	Gg	21.09N	104.30W
Cebreros	13	Hd	40.27N	4.28W
Cebrikovo	15	Nb	47.09N	30.02 E
Cebu	21	Oh	10.20N	123.45 E
Cebu	22	Oh	10.18N	123.54 E
Cece	10	Oj	46.46N	18.39 E
Čečen, Ostrov-	16	Og	44.00N	47.45 E
Čečeno-Ingušskaja ASSR [3]	19	Eg	43.15N	45.30 E
Cecen-Ula	27	Gb	48.45N	95.55 E
Cecerleg	22	Me	47.30N	101.27 E
Čečersk	16	Gc	52.56N	30.58 E
Čechy=Bohemia (EN)	5	Hf	50.00N	14.30 E
Čechy=Bohemia (EN)	10	Kf	50.00N	14.30 E
Cecina	14	Eg	43.18N	10.29 E
Cecina	14	Eg	43.10N	10.31 E
Čečuisk	20	Fe	58.07N	108.32 E
Cedar City	39	Hf	37.41N	113.04W
Cedar Creek	45	Fc	46.07N	101.18W
Cedar Creek Reservoir	45	Hj	32.20N	96.10W
Cedar Falls	43	Ic	42.32N	92.27W
Cedar Grove	51d	Bb	17.10N	61.49W
Cedar Lake	42	Hf	53.25N	100.00W
Cedar Rapids	39	Je	41.59N	91.40W
Cedar River [Nb.-U.S.]	45	Hf	41.22N	97.57W
Cedar River [U.S.]	43	Ic	41.17N	91.20W
Cedartown	44	Eh	34.01N	85.15W
Cedar-Tree Point	51d	Ba	17.42N	61.53W
Cedeira	13	Da	43.39N	8.03W
Cedral	48	If	23.48N	100.44W
Cedrino	14	Dj	40.23N	9.44 E
Cedro	54	Ke	6.36S	39.03W
Cedrón	13	Ie	39.48N	3.33W
Cedros, Isla- [Mex.]	47	Ac	28.12N	115.15W
Cedros, Isla [Mex.] =Cedros Island (EN)	38	Hg	28.10N	115.15W
Cedros Island (EN)=Cedros, Isla [Mex.]	38	Hg	28.10N	115.15W
Cedros Trench (EN)	47	Ac	27.45N	115.45W
Ceduna	59	Gf	32.07S	133.40 E
Cedynia	10	Kd	52.50N	14.14 E
Cefalù	14	Il	38.02N	14.01 E
Cega	13	Hc	41.33N	4.46W
Čegdomyn	22	Pd	51.07N	133.05 E
Čegem	16	Mh	43.36N	43.48 E
Cegléd	10	Pi	47.10N	19.48 E
Ceglie Messapico	14	Lj	40.39N	17.31 E
Cehegin	13	Kf	38.06N	1.48W
Cehotina	15	Bf	43.31N	18.45 E
Čehov [R.S.F.S.R.]	7	Ii	55.11N	37.29 E
Čehov [R.S.F.S.R.]	20	Jg	47.24N	142.05 E
Ceica	15	Fc	46.51N	22.11 E
Çekerek	24	Fb	40.34N	35.46 E
Çekerek	24	Fb	40.04N	35.31 E
Čekmaguš	17	Gi	55.10N	54.40 E
Celano	14	Hh	42.05N	13.33 E
Celaya	47	Dd	20.31N	100.37W
Čelbas	16	Kf	46.06N	38.59 E
Célé	11	Hj	44.28N	1.38 E
Celebes/Sulawesi	21	Oj	2.00S	121.10 E
Celebes Basin (EN)	26	Hf	4.00N	122.00 E
Celebes Sea (EN)= Sulawesi, Laut-	21	Oj	3.00N	122.00 E
Čeleken	19	Fh	39.27N	53.10 E
Čeleken, Poluostrov-	16	Rj	39.25N	53.35 E
Celendín	54	Ce	6.52S	78.09W
Celerain, Punta-	48	Pg	20.16N	86.59W
Celeste	55	Dj	31.18S	57.04W
Celestún	48	Ng	20.52N	90.24W
Celinograd	22	Jd	51.10N	71.30 E
Celinogradskaja Oblast [3]	19	Gh	51.00N	70.00 E
Čeljabinsk	22	Id	55.10N	61.24 E
Čeljabinskaja Oblast [3]	19	Ge	54.00N	61.00 E
Celje	14	Jd	46.14N	15.16 E
Celjuskin, Mys-	21	Mb	77.45N	104.20 E
Čelkar	19	Ff	47.50N	59.29 E
Celldömölk	10	Ni	47.15N	17.09 E
Celle	10	Gd	52.37N	10.05 E
Celles	12	Fd	50.43N	3.27 E
Celles, Houyet-	12	Hd	50.19N	5.01 E
Cellina	14	Ge	46.02N	12.47 E
Celone	14	Ji	41.36N	15.41 E
Celorico da Beira	13	Ed	40.38N	7.23W
Celtic Sea	5	Fe	51.00N	7.00W
Celtic Sea (EN)=An Mhuir Cheilteach	5	Fe	51.00N	7.00W
Cemaes Head	9	Ii	52.07N	4.44W
Čemal	20	Df	51.25N	86.05 E
Čemdalsk	20	Fe	59.45N	103.18 E
Cemernica	14	Lf	44.30N	17.15 E
Cemerno	15	Df	43.36N	20.26 E
Çemişkezek	24	Hc	39.04N	38.55 E
Cenajo, Embalse de-	13	Kf	38.20N	1.55W
Cenderawasih, Teluk-	26	Kg	2.25S	135.10 E
Cengel	27	Eb	48.56N	89.10 E
Çengel Geçidi	24	Kc	39.45N	44.02 E
Ceno	14	Ef	44.41N	10.05 E
Centenary	37	Ec	16.44S	31.07 E
Centennial	46	Lf	41.51N	106.07W
Centennial Lake	44	Ic	45.15N	77.00W
Centennial Mountains	46	Jd	44.35N	111.55W
Center	45	Ik	31.48N	94.11W
Center Hill Lake	44	Eg	36.00N	85.45W
Centerville	45	Jf	40.43N	92.52W
Centinela, Farallón-	50	Cg	10.49N	66.05W
Centinela, Picacho del-	47	Dc	29.07N	102.27W
Cento	14	Ff	44.43N	11.17 E
Centrafrique=Central African Republic (EN) [1]	31	Jh	7.00N	21.00 E
Central [Bots.] [3]	37	Dd	21.30S	26.00 E
Central [Ghana] [3]	34	Ed	5.30N	1.00W
Central [Kenya] [3]	36	Gc	0.45S	37.00 E
Central [Mwi.] [3]	36	Fe	13.30S	34.00 E
Central [Par.] [3]	55	Dg	25.30S	57.30W
Central [Scot.-U.K.] [3]	9	Ie	56.15N	4.10W
Central [Ug.] [3]	36	Fb	0.10N	32.05 E
Central [Zam.] [3]	36	Ee	15.00S	29.00 E
Central, Chaco-	52	Kh	25.00S	59.45W
Central, Cordillera- [Dom.Rep.]	47	Je	18.45N	70.30W
Central, Cordillera- [P.R.]	49	Nd	18.10N	66.35W
Central, Massif-	5	Gf	45.00N	3.10 E
Central, Meseta-	38	Ig	23.00N	103.00W
Central African Republic (EN)=Centrafrique [1]	31	Jh	7.00N	21.00 E
Central Auckland [2]	62	Fb	36.45S	174.40 E
Central Brāhui Range	25	Dc	29.20N	66.55 E
Central City	45	Hf	41.07N	98.00W
Centralia [Il.-U.S.]	45	Lg	38.31N	89.08W
Centralia [Wa.-U.S.]	43	Cb	46.43N	122.58W
Central Lowland	38	Ke	40.20N	90.00W
Central Makrān Range	21	Ig	26.40N	64.30 E
Centralno Tungusskoje Plato	20	Fd	61.15N	102.00 E
Centralny-Kospašski	17	Hg	59.03N	57.50 E
Central Pacific Basin (EN)	3	Ki	5.00N	175.00W
Central Plateau	64e	Bb	0.32S	166.56 E
Central Point	46	De	42.23N	122.57W
Central Range	57	Fe	5.00S	142.30 E
Central Russian Uplands (EN)=Srednerusskaja Vozvyšennost	5	Je	52.00N	38.00 E
Central Siberian Uplands (EN)=Srednesibirskoje Ploskogorje	21	Mc	65.00N	105.00 E
Central Urals (EN)=Sredni Ural	5	Ld	58.00N	59.00 E
Centre [Togo] [3]	34	Fd	9.15N	1.00 E
Centre [U.V.] [3]	34	Ec	12.00N	1.00W
Centre, Canal du-	11	Jh	46.28N	3.59 E
Centre-Est [3]	34	Ec	11.30N	0.20W
Centre-Nord [3]	34	Ec	13.20N	0.55W
Centre-Ouest [3]	34	Ec	12.00N	2.20W
Centre-Sud [3]	34	He	3.30N	11.50 E
Centro, Cayo-	48	Ph	18.35N	87.20W
Centuripe	14	Im	37.37N	14.44 E
Čepca	19	Fd	58.35N	50.05 E
Čepelare	15	Hh	41.44N	24.41 E
Cephalonia (EN)= Kefallinia	5	Ih	38.15N	20.35 E
Čepin	14	Me	45.32N	18.34 E
Ceplenița	15	Jb	47.23N	26.58 E
Cepu	26	Fh	7.09S	111.35 E
Cer	15	Ce	44.37N	19.28 E
Ceram Sea (EN)=Seram, Laut-	57	De	2.30S	128.00 E
Cerbatana, Serranía de la-	54	Eb	6.50N	66.15W
Cerbicales, Iles-	11a	Bb	41.33N	9.22 E
Cercal	13	Dg	37.47N	8.42W
Čerchov	10	Rg	49.10N	21.05 E
Čerdakly	7	Li	54.23N	48.51 E
Čerdyn	17	Hf	60.25N	56.29 E
Cère	11	Hj	44.55N	1.49 E
Čereha	7	Gh	57.47N	28.22 E
Čeremhovo	22	Md	53.09N	103.05 E
Čerepanovo	20	Df	54.13N	83.32 E
Čerepovec	6	Jd	59.08N	37.54 E
Ceres [Arg.]	56	Hc	29.53S	61.57W
Ceres [Braz.]	54	Ig	15.17S	49.35W
Ceres [S.Afr.]	37	Bf	33.21S	19.18 E
Céret	11	Il	42.29N	2.45 E
Cereté	54	Cb	8.53N	75.47W
Cerf Island	30	Mi	9.31S	51.01 E
Cerfontaine	12	Gd	50.10N	4.25 E
Cergy	12	Ee	49.02N	2.04 E
Cerignola	14	Ji	41.16N	15.54 E
Čerikov	16	Gc	53.35N	31.25 E
Cérilly	11	Ih	46.37N	2.50 E
Čerkasskaja Oblast [3]	19	Df	49.15N	31.15 E
Čerkassy	19	Df	49.26N	32.04 E
Çerkeş	24	Eb	40.50N	32.54 E
Čerkessk	19	Eg	44.14N	42.04 E
Çerkezköy	15	Kh	41.17N	28.00 E
Čerlak	19	He	54.09N	74.58 E
Čerlakski	19	He	53.47N	74.31 E
Čermasàn	17	Gi	55.10N	55.20 E
Cermei	15	Ec	46.33N	21.51 E
Çermenika	15	Dh	41.03N	20.20 E
Čermoz	17	Hg	58.47N	56.10 E
Cerna [Rom.]	15	Ge	44.37N	23.57 E
Cerna [Rom.]	15	Fd	44.42N	22.25 E
Cerna [Rom.]	15	Fe	45.53N	22.58 E
Černaja	17	Hb	68.35N	56.31 E
Černaja [R.S.F.S.R.]	17	Hb	68.35N	56.30 E
Černaja [Ukr.-U.S.S.R.]	15	Mb	47.39N	29.11 E
Černa Skala, Prohod-	15	Fg	42.02N	22.47 E
Černatica	15	Hh	41.53N	24.33 E
Černavčicy	10	Td	52.11N	23.47 E
Cernavoda	15	Le	44.22N	28.01 E
Cernay	11	Ng	47.49N	7.10 E
Cernay-en-Dormois	12	Ge	49.13N	4.46 E
Černevo	8	Mf	58.35N	28.23 E
Černigov	6	Je	51.30N	31.18 E
Černigovskaja Oblast [3]	19	De	51.20N	32.00 E
Černi Lom	15	If	43.33N	25.57 E
Černi vrăh	15	Gg	42.35N	23.15 E
Černjahovsk	19	Ce	54.38N	21.48 E
Černjanka	16	Jd	50.55N	37.49 E
Černobyl	19	De	51.17N	30.13 E
Černogorsk	20	Ef	53.45N	91.18 E
Černoje More=Black Sea (EN)	5	Jg	43.00N	35.00 E
Černo More=Black Sea (EN)	5	Jg	43.00N	35.00 E
Černomorskoje	16	Hg	45.31N	32.42 E
Černovcy	6	If	48.18N	25.56 E
Černovickaja Oblast [3]	19	Cf	48.20N	26.10 E
Černuška	19	Fd	56.31N	56.03 E
Černy Jar	16	Oe	48.03N	46.05 E
Černyje Zemli	16	Nf	45.55N	46.00 E
Černyšëva, Grjada-	17	Ic	66.20N	59.45 E
Černyševa, Zaliv-	18	Bb	45.50N	59.10 E
Černyševsk	20	Gf	52.35N	117.02 E
Černyševski	20	Gd	62.58N	112.15 E
Černyškovski	16	Me	48.27N	42.14 E
Cérou	11	Hj	44.08N	1.52 E
Cerralvo	48	Jd	26.06N	99.37W
Cerralvo, Isla-	47	Cd	24.15N	109.55W
Cerredo, Torre de-	13	Ha	43.13N	4.50W
Cerriku	15	Ch	41.02N	19.57 E
Cerrito [Col.]	54	Db	6.51N	72.42W
Cerrito [Par.]	55	Dh	27.19S	57.40W
Cerritos	47	Dd	22.26N	100.17W
Cerro Azul	48	Kg	21.12N	97.44W
Cêrro Azul	56	Kb	24.50S	49.15W
Cerro Chato	55	Ek	33.06S	55.08W
Cerro Colorado	55	Ek	33.52S	55.33W
Cerro de las Mesas	48	Kh	18.47N	96.05W
Cerro de Pasco	53	Ig	10.41S	76.16W
Cêrro Grande	55	Gj	30.36S	51.45W
Cerro Largo	56	Jc	28.09S	54.45W
Cerro Largo [2]	55	Ek	32.20S	54.20W
Cerron, Cerro-	49	Lh	10.19N	70.39W
Cerro San Valentín	52	Ij	46.36S	73.20W
Cerros Colorados, Embalse-	56	Ge	38.35S	68.40W
Cerro Vera	55	Dk	33.11S	57.28W
Cerrudo Cué	55	Dh	27.34S	57.57W
Čerski	22	Sc	68.45N	161.45 E
Čerskogo, Hrebet- [R.S.F.S.R.]	20	Gf	52.00N	114.00 E
Čerskogo, Hrebet- [R.S.F.S.R.] =Cherski Mountains (EN)	21	Qc	65.00N	145.00 E

Index Symbols

- [1] Independent Nation
- [2] State, Region
- [3] District, County
- [5] Municipality
- [6] Colony, Dependency
- Continent
- Physical Region
- Historical or Cultural Region
- Mount, Mountain
- Volcano
- Hill
- Mountains, Mountain Range
- Hills, Escarpment
- Plateau, Upland
- Pass, Gap
- Plain, Lowland
- Delta
- Salt Flat
- Valley, Canyon
- Crater, Cave
- Karst Features
- Depression
- Polder
- Desert, Dunes
- Forest, Woods
- Heath, Steppe
- Oasis
- Cape, Point
- Coast, Beach
- Cliff
- Peninsula
- Isthmus
- Sandbank
- Island
- Atoll
- Rock, Reef
- Islands, Archipelago
- Rocks, Reefs
- Coral Reef
- Well, Spring
- Geyser
- River, Stream
- Waterfall Rapids
- River Mouth, Estuary
- Lake
- Salt Lake
- Intermittent Lake
- Reservoir
- Swamp, Pond
- Canal
- Glacier
- Ice Shelf, Pack Ice
- Ocean
- Sea
- Gulf, Bay
- Strait, Fjord
- Lagoon
- Bank
- Seamount
- Tablemount
- Ridge
- Shelf
- Basin
- Escarpment, Sea Scarp
- Fracture
- Trench, Abyss
- National Park, Reserve
- Point of Interest
- Recreation Site
- Cave, Cavern
- Historic Site
- Ruins
- Wall, Walls
- Church, Abbey
- Temple
- Scientific Station
- Airport
- Port
- Lighthouse
- Mine
- Tunnel
- Dam, Bridge

Cheyenne [Wy.-U.S.]	39	Ie	41.08N	104.49W
Cheyenne River	43	Gc	44.40N	101.15W
Cheyenne Wells	45	Eg	38.51N	102.11W
Cheyne Bay	59	Df	34.35S	118.50 E
Chhatarpur	25	Fd	24.54N	79.36 E
Chhindwāra	25	Fd	22.04N	78.56 E
Chi	25	Ke	15.11N	104.43 E
Chiamboni, Rās-	35	Gf	1.38S	41.36 E
Chiana, Val di-	14	Fg	43.15N	11.50 E
Chianciano Terme	14	Fg	43.02N	11.49 E
Chiang-hsi Sheng→Jangxi Sheng=Kiangsi (EN) [2]	27	Kf	28.00N	116.00 E
Chiang Mai	22	Lh	18.46N	98.58 E
Chiang Rai	22	Lh	19.54N	99.50 E
Chiang-su Sheng→Jiangsu Sheng=Kiangsu (EN) [2]	27	Ke	33.00N	120.00 E
Chiani	14	Gh	42.44N	12.07 E
Chianje	31	Ij	15.45S	13.54 E
Chianti	14	Fg	43.30N	11.25 E
Chiapa, Río-	48	Mj	16.30N	93.10W
Chiapas [2]	47	Fe	16.30N	92.30W
Chiapas, Meseta de-	47	Fe	16.30N	92.00W
Chiaramonte Gulfi	14	Im	37.02N	14.42 E
Chiaravalle	14	Hg	43.36N	13.19 E
Chiaromonte	14	Kj	40.07N	16.13 E
Chiautla de Tapia	48	Jh	18.17N	98.36W
Chiavari	14	Df	44.19N	9.19 E
Chiavenna	14	Dd	46.19N	9.24 E
Chiayi	27	Lg	23.29N	120.27 E
Chiba	27	Pd	35.36N	140.07 E
Chiba Ken [2]	28	Pg	35.40N	140.20 E
Chibemba	36	Bf	15.45S	14.06 E
Chibia	36	Bf	15.11S	13.41 E
Chibougamau	39	Le	49.53N	74.21W
Chibougamau, Lac-	44	Ja	49.50N	74.15W
Chibougamau, Rivière-	44	Ja	49.50N	74.25W
Chiburi-Jima	28	Lf	36.00N	133.02 E
Chibuto	37	Ed	24.42S	33.33 E
Chicago	39	Ke	41.53N	87.38W
Chicago Heights	45	Mf	41.30N	87.38W
Chicala	36	Ce	11.59S	19.30 E
Chicapa	30	Ji	6.25S	20.48 E
Chic-Chocs, Monts-	44	Na	48.55N	66.45W
Chicha	35	Bb	16.52N	18.33 E
Chichagof	40	Le	57.30N	135.30W
Chichancanab, Laguna de-	48	Oh	19.54N	88.46W
Chichaoua	32	Fc	31.32N	8.46W
Chichas, Cordillera de-	54	Eh	20.30S	66.30W
Chicheng	27	Kc	40.55N	115.47 E
Chichén Itzá	39	Kg	20.40N	88.35W
Chichester	9	Mk	50.50N	0.48W
Chichester Range	59	Dd	22.20S	119.20 E
Chichibu	28	Og	35.59N	139.05 E
Chichigalpa	49	Dg	12.34N	87.02W
Chichijma-Rettō	60	Cb	27.06N	142.12 E
Chichilla de Monte-Aragón	13	Kf	38.55N	1.43W
Chichiriviche	49	Mh	10.56N	68.16W
Chickasawhay River	45	Lk	31.00N	88.45W
Chickasha	43	Hd	35.02N	97.58W
Chicken	40	Kd	64.04N	141.56W
Chiclana de la Frontera	13	Fh	36.25N	6.08W
Chiclayo	53	If	6.46S	79.50W
Chico	43	Cd	39.44N	121.50W
Chico, Río- [Arg.]	52	Jj	43.48S	66.25W
Chico, Río- [Arg.]	52	Jj	49.56S	68.32W
Chicoana	56	Gc	25.06S	65.33W
Chicomo	37	Ed	24.31S	34.17 E
Chicononо	37	Fb	12.57S	35.45 E
Chicopee	44	Kd	42.10N	72.36W
Chicote	36	Df	16.01S	21.48 E
Chicoutimi	39	Le	48.26N	71.04W
Chicoutimi Nord	44	La	48.29N	71.02W
Chicualacuala	37	Ed	22.05S	31.42 E
Chidenguele	37	Ed	24.55S	34.10 E
Chidley, Cape-	38	Mc	60.25N	64.30W
Chiemsee	10	Ii	47.54N	12.29 E
Chiengi	36	Ed	8.39S	29.10 E
Chienti	14	Hg	43.18N	13.45 E
Chieri	14	Be	45.01N	7.49 E
Chiers	12	He	49.39N	5.00 E
Chiese	14	Ee	45.08N	10.25 E
Chieti	14	Ih	42.21N	14.10 E
Chièvres	12	Fd	50.35N	3.48 E
Chifeng/Ulanhad	27	Kc	42.16N	118.57 E
Chifumage	36	De	12.10S	22.30 E
Chifwefwe	36	Fe	13.35S	29.35 E
Chigasaki	29	Fd	35.19N	139.24 E
Chignik	40	He	56.18N	158.23W
Chigombe	37	Ed	23.26S	33.19 E
Chigorodó	49	Ij	7.41N	76.41W
Chigubo	37	Ed	22.50S	33.31 E
Chigu Co	27	Ff	28.40N	91.50 E
Chi He	28	Dh	32.51N	117.59 E
Chihli, Gulf of- (EN)=Bo Hai	21	Nf	38.30N	120.00 E
Chihuahua [2]	47	Cc	28.30N	106.00W
Chihuahua	39	Ig	28.38N	106.05W
Chii-san	28	Ig	35.20N	127.44 E
Chikaskia River	45	Hh	36.37N	97.15W
Chikugo	29	Be	33.13N	130.30 E
Chikugo-Gawa	29	Be	33.10N	130.21 E
Chikuma-Gawa	29	Fc	37.00N	138.35 E
Chikwana	36	Ff	16.03S	34.48 E
Chilapa de Alvarez	48	Ji	17.36N	99.10W
Chilās	25	Ea	35.26N	74.05 E
Chilaw	25	Fg	7.34N	79.47 E
Chilcotin	42	Ff	51.46N	122.22W
Childers	59	Ke	25.14S	152.17 E
Childress	43	Ge	34.25N	100.13W
Chile [1]	53	Ii	30.00S	71.00W
Chile Basin (EN)	3	Mm	33.00S	90.00W
Chile Chico	56	Fg	46.33S	71.44W
Chilecito [Arg.]	56	Gd	33.53S	69.03W
Chilecito [Arg.]	56	Gc	29.10S	67.30W
Chile Rise (EN)	3	Mm	40.00S	90.00W
Chili	35	Cb	16.44N	20.53 E
Chilia, Braţul-	15	Md	45.13N	29.43 E
Chililabombwe	36	Ee	12.22S	27.50 E
Chi-lin Sheng→Jilin Sheng =Kirin (EN) [2]	27	Mc	43.00N	126.00 E
Chilko Lake	46	Ca	51.20N	124.05W
Chilko River	46	Da	52.00N	123.40W
Chillán	53	Ii	36.36S	72.07W
Chillar	56	Ie	37.18S	59.59W
Chillicothe [Il.-U.S.]	45	Lf	40.55N	89.29W
Chillicothe [Mo.-U.S.]	45	Jg	39.48N	93.33W
Chillicothe [Oh.-U.S.]	43	Kd	38.20N	82.59W
Chilliwack	46	Eb	49.10N	121.57W
Chiloé, Isla de-	52	Ij	42.30S	73.55W
Chilón	48	Mi	17.14N	92.25W
Chiloquin	46	Ee	42.35N	121.52W
Chilpancingo de los Bravos	47	Ee	17.33N	99.30W
Chiltern Hills	9	Mj	51.42N	0.48W
Chilton	45	Ld	44.02N	88.10W
Chiluage	36	Dd	9.31S	21.46 E
Chilumba	36	Fe	10.27S	34.16 E
Chilwa, Lake-	36	Fc	15.12S	35.50 E
Chimala	36	Fd	8.51S	34.01 E
Chimaltenango	49	Bf	14.39N	90.49W
Chimaltenango [3]	49	Bf	14.40N	90.55W
Chimán	49	Hi	8.42N	78.37W
Chimanas, Islas-	50	Dg	10.17N	64.38W
Chimay	12	Gd	50.03N	4.19 E
Chimborazo, Volcán-	52	If	1.28S	78.48W
Chimbote	53	If	9.05S	78.36W
Chimichagua	49	Ki	9.16N	73.49W
Chimoio	37	Ec	19.00S	33.23 E
Chimorra	13	Hf	38.18N	4.53W
Chin [2]	25	Id	22.00N	93.30 E
China [Jap.]	29b	Bb	27.20N	128.36 E
China [Mex.]	48	Je	25.42N	99.14W
China (EN)=Zhonghua Renmin Gongheguo [1]	22	Mf	35.00N	105.00 E
Chinacates	48	Ge	25.00N	105.13W
China Lake	46	Gi	35.46N	117.39W
Chinandega	47	Gf	12.37N	87.09W
Chinandega [3]	49	Dg	12.45N	87.05W
Chinati Peak	45	Dl	29.57N	104.29W
Chincha Alta	54	Cf	13.27S	76.08W
Chinchaga	42	Fe	58.52N	118.19W
Chinchilla	59	Ke	26.45S	150.38 E
Chinchón	13	Id	40.08N	3.25W
Chinchorro, Banco-	47	Ge	18.35N	87.20W
Chincoteague	44	Jg	37.55N	75.23W
Chinde	31	Kj	18.34S	36.27 E
Chin-Do	28	Ig	34.25N	126.15 E
Chindu	27	Ge	33.30N	96.31 E
Chindwinn	21	Lg	21.26N	95.15 E
Ch'ing-hai Sheng → Qinghai Sheng=Tsinghai (EN) [2]	27	Gd	36.00N	96.00 E
Chingil	35	Bc	10.33N	18.57 E
Chingola	31	Jj	12.32S	27.52 E
Chinguar	36	Ce	12.33S	16.22 E
Chinguetti	32	Ee	20.27N	12.21W
Chinguetti, Dahr de-	32	Ee	20.43N	12.20W
Chinhae	28	Jg	35.08N	128.40 E
Chiniot	25	Eb	31.43N	72.59 E
Chínipas	48	Ed	27.23N	108.32W
Chinju	27	Md	35.11N	128.05 E
Chinko	30	Jh	4.50N	23.53 E
Chinle	46	Kh	36.09N	109.33W
Chinle Creek	46	Kh	37.12N	109.43W
Chinmen	27	Kg	24.25N	118.25 E
Chino	29	Fd	36.00N	138.09 E
Chinon	11	Gg	47.10N	0.15 E
Chinook	46	Kb	48.35N	109.14W
Chinquila	48	Pg	21.30N	87.25W
Chinsali	36	Fe	10.33S	32.04 E
Chinteche	36	Fe	11.50S	34.10 E
Chinú	54	Cb	9.06N	75.24W
Chinvali	19	Eg	42.13N	43.57 E
Chiny	12	He	49.44N	5.20 E
Chinyŏng	28	Jg	35.18N	128.44 E
Chioco	37	Ec	16.25S	32.50 E
Chioggia	14	Ge	45.13N	12.17 E
Chios (EN)=Khíos	5	Ih	38.22N	26.00 E
Chipata	31	Kj	13.39S	32.40 E
Chipepo	36	Ef	16.49S	27.50 E
Chipindo	36	Ce	13.48S	15.48 E
Chiping	28	Df	36.35N	116.16 E
Chipinge	37	Ed	20.12S	32.38 E
Chipman	44	Ob	46.11N	65.53W
Chippenham	9	Kj	51.28N	2.07W
Chippewa, Lake-	45	Kd	45.56N	91.13W
Chippewa Falls	43	Ic	44.56N	91.24W
Chippewa River [Wi.-U.S.]	45	Id	44.56N	95.44W
Chippewa River [U.S.]	45	Jd	44.25N	92.10W
Chipping Ongar	12	Cc	51.42N	0.15 E
Chiputneticook Lakes	44	Mc	45.45N	68.45W
Chiquián	54	Cf	10.09S	77.11W
Chiquimula [3]	49	Cf	14.40N	89.25W
Chiquimula	49	Cf	14.48N	89.33W
Chiquimulilla	49	Bf	14.05N	90.23W
Chiquinquirá	54	Db	5.37N	73.50W
Chiquitos, Llanos de-	54	Fg	18.00S	61.30W
Chīrāla	25	Ge	15.49N	80.21 E
Chiran	29	Bf	31.22N	130.27 E
Chiredzi	31	Kk	21.03S	31.45 E
Chirfa	34	Ha	20.57N	12.21 E
Chirgua, Río-	50	Bh	8.30N	68.01W
Chiricahua Peak	43	Fe	31.52N	109.20W
Chiriguaná	49	Ki	9.22N	73.37W
Chirikof	40	He	55.50N	155.35W
Chiriquí [3]	49	Fi	8.30N	82.00W
Chiriquí, Golfo de-	38	Ki	8.00N	82.20W
Chiriquí, Laguna de-	47	Hg	9.03N	82.00W
Chiriquí Grande	49	Fi	8.57N	82.07W
Chirnogi	15	Je	44.07N	26.84 E
Chiromo	36	Gf	16.33S	35.08 E
Chirripó, Cerro-	38	Ki	9.29N	83.29W
Chirripó, Río- [C.R.]	49	Fh	10.03N	83.16W
Chirripó, Río- [C.R.]	49	Fh	10.41N	83.41W
Chirundu	37	Dc	15.59S	28.54 E
Chisamba	36	Ee	14.59S	28.23 E
Chisāpāni Garhi	25	Hc	27.34N	85.08 E
Chisenga	36	Fd	9.56S	33.26 E
Chisasibi	39	Ld	53.50N	79.00W
Chishui	27	If	28.30N	105.44 E
Chişineu Criş	15	Ec	46.32N	21.31 E
Chisone	14	Bf	44.49N	7.25 E
Chitado	36	Bf	17.18S	13.54 E
Chita-Hantō	29	Ed	34.50N	136.50 E
Chitati	35	Ac	14.40N	14.30 E
Chitato	31	Jl	7.22S	20.49 E
Chita-Wan	29	Ed	34.50N	136.55 E
Chitembo	36	Ce	13.31S	16.45 E
Chitina	40	Kd	61.31N	144.27W
Chitipa	36	Fd	9.43S	33.16 E
Chitorgarh	25	Ed	24.53N	74.38 E
Chitose	28	Pc	42.49N	141.39 E
Chitradurga	25	Ff	14.14N	76.24 E
Chitrāl	25	Ea	35.51N	71.47 E
Chitré	47	Hg	7.58N	80.26W
Chittagong	22	Lg	22.20N	91.50 E
Chittoor	25	Ff	13.12N	79.07 E
Chiumbe	30	Ji	6.59S	21.12 E
Chiume	36	Df	15.08S	21.12 E
Chiusi	14	Fg	43.01N	11.57 E
Chiusi, Lago di-	14	Fg	43.05N	12.00 E
Chiva	13	Le	39.28N	0.43W
Chivacoa	50	Bg	10.10N	68.54W
Chivapuri, Río-	50	Ci	6.25N	66.23W
Chivasso	14	Be	45.11N	7.53 E
Chivay	54	Dg	15.38S	71.36W
Chivilcoy	56	Hd	34.53S	60.01W
Chixoy o Negro, Río-	49	Be	16.28N	90.33W
Chizou → Guichi	27	Ke	30.38N	117.30 E
Chizu	29	Dd	35.15N	134.14 E
Chŏâm Khsant	25	Kf	14.13N	104.56 E
Choapa, Río-	56	Fd	31.38S	71.34W
Chobe	30	Jj	17.47S	25.10 E
Choc Bay	51k	Ba	14.03N	60.59W
Choch'iwŏn	28	If	36.36N	127.18 E
Chocó [2]	54	Cb	6.00N	77.00W
Chocolate Mountains	46	Hj	33.25N	114.10W
Chodecz	10	Pd	52.24N	19.01 E
Chodov	10	If	50.15N	12.45 E
Chodzież	10	Md	52.59N	16.56 E
Choele-Choel	56	Ge	39.16S	65.41W
Choique	56	He	38.28S	62.43W
Choiseul	51k	Ab	13.47N	61.03W
Choiseul Island	57	Ge	7.00S	157.00 E
Choix	48	Ed	26.43N	108.17W
Chojna	10	Kd	52.58N	14.28 E
Chojnice	10	Nc	53.42N	17.34 E
Chojnów	10	Le	51.17N	15.56 E
Chōkai-San	21	Qf	39.10N	140.02 E
Choke	30	Kg	10.45N	37.35 E
Chókué	37	Ed	24.27S	32.55 E
Cho La	27	Ge	31.52N	98.51 E
Cholet	11	Fg	47.04N	0.53W
Chŏlla-Namdo [2]	28	Ig	34.45N	127.00 E
Chŏlla-Pukto [2]	28	Ig	35.45N	127.15 E
Cholo	36	Gf	16.04S	35.08 E
Cholula	48	Jh	19.04N	98.18W
Choluteca	47	Gf	13.18N	87.12W
Choluteca [3]	49	Dg	13.20N	87.10W
Choluteca, Río-	49	Dg	13.07N	87.19W
Choma	31	Jj	16.49S	26.59 E
Chomo/Yadong	27	Ef	27.38N	89.03 E
Chomo Lhari	27	Ef	27.50N	89.16 E
Chomutov	10	Jf	50.28N	13.25 E
Ch'ŏnan	27	Md	36.48N	127.09 E
Chon Buri	25	Kf	13.22N	100.59 E
Chone	54	Bd	0.42S	80.07W
Ch'ŏngch'ŏn-gang	28	He	39.35N	125.28 E
Ch'ŏngjin	22	Oe	41.46N	129.49 E
Ch'ŏngjin Si [2]	28	Jd	41.45N	129.45 E
Chŏngju	27	Md	39.51N	125.15 E
Ch'ŏngju	27	Md	36.38N	127.30 E
Chongli (Xiwanzi)	28	Cd	40.57N	115.12 E
Chongming	28	Fi	31.38N	121.24 E
Chongming Dao	28	Fi	31.36N	121.33 E
Chongoroi	36	Be	13.34S	13.55 E
Chongqing (Yuzhou)= Chungking (EN)	22	Mg	29.34N	106.27 E
Chongqing→Yuzhou= Chungking (EN)	22	Mg	29.34N	106.27 E
Ch'ŏngsan-Do	28	Ig	34.11N	126.54 E
Chŏngŭp	28	Ig	35.34N	126.51 E
Chongyang	28	Cj	29.32N	114.02 E
Chongzuo	27	Ig	22.29N	107.22 E
Chŏnju	27	Md	35.49N	127.09 E
Chonos, Archipiélago de los-	52	Ij	45.00S	74.00W
Chontaleña, Cordillera-	49	Eh	11.50N	85.00W
Chontales [3]	49	Eg	12.05N	85.10W
Chopim, Río-	55	Fg	25.35S	53.05W
Chopinzinho	55	Fg	25.51S	52.30W
Chorito, Sierra del-	13	He	39.25N	4.25W
Choroszcz	10	Sc	53.09N	22.59 E
Chorreras, Cerro-	48	Fd	26.02N	106.21W
Ch'ŏrwŏn	27	Md	38.15N	127.13 E
Chorzele	10	Qc	53.16N	20.55 E
Chorzów	10	Of	50.19N	18.57 E
Ch'osan	28	Hd	40.45N	125.50 E
Chośebuz/Cottbus	10	Ke	51.46N	14.20 E
Chōshi	28	Pg	35.44N	140.50 E
Chos Malal	56	Fe	37.23S	70.16W
Chosŏn M.I.K.=North Korea (EN) [1]	22	Oe	40.00N	127.30 E
Chosŏn Minjuju-Inmin-Konghwaguk=Chosŏn M.I.K. [1]	22	Oe	40.00N	127.30 E
Choszczno	10	Lc	53.10N	15.26 E
Chota	54	Ce	6.33S	78.39W
Chotanagpur Plateau	21	Kg	22.00N	86.00 E
Choteau	46	Ic	47.49N	112.11W
Chotla, Cerro de-	48	Ii	17.55N	101.31W
Choukchot, Djebel-	13	Qh	36.01N	4.11 E
Choum	32	Ee	21.18N	12.59W
Chovd→Kobdo	27	Fb	48.06N	92.11 E
Chövsgöl nuur→Hubsugul Nur	21	Md	51.00N	100.30 E
Chowchilla	46	Eh	37.07N	120.16W
Chowra	25	Ig	8.27N	93.02 E
Chréa	13	Oh	36.25N	2.53 E
Chřiby	10	Ng	49.10N	17.20 E
Christchurch	58	Ii	43.32S	172.37 E
Christian, Cape -	42	Kb	70.32N	68.18W
Christian, Point-	64q	Ab	25.04S	130.07W
Christiana	37	De	27.52S	25.08 E
Christian IV Gletscher	41	Ie	68.40N	30.20W
Christiansburg	44	Gg	37.07N	80.26W
Christiansfeld	8	Ci	55.21N	9.29 E
Christianshåb/Qasigiánguit	41	Ge	68.45N	51.30W
Christiansø	8	Fi	55.20N	15.10 E
Christian Sound	40	Me	55.56N	134.40W
Christiansted	50	Dd	17.45N	64.40W
Christiansted Harbor	51a	Dc	17.46N	64.42W
Christie Bay	42	Gd	62.45N	110.15W
Christmas→Kiritimati Atoll	57	Ld	1.52N	157.20W
Christmas Creek	59	Fc	18.29S	125.23 E
Christmas Creek	59	Fc	18.53S	125.55 E
Christmas Island [5]	22	Mk	10.30S	105.40 E
Christmas Ridge (EN)	3	Ki	10.00N	165.00W
Chrudim	10	Lg	49.57N	15.47 E
Chrzanów	10	Pf	50.09N	19.24 E
Chrząstowa	10	Mc	53.35N	16.58 E
Chuansha	28	Fi	31.11N	121.42 E
Chūbar	24	Mc	38.11N	48.51 E
Chubut [2]	56	Gf	44.00S	69.00W
Chubut, Río-	52	Jj	43.20S	65.03W
Chucunague, Río-	49	Ii	8.09N	77.44W
Chugach Mountains	40	Jd	61.00N	145.00W
Chuginadak	40	Ef	52.49N	169.50W
Chugoku-Sanchi	21	Pf	35.15N	133.30 E
Chu He	28	Eh	32.15N	119.03 E
Chuhuichupa	48	Ec	29.38N	108.22W
Chuí	55	Fk	33.41S	53.27W
Chuka	36	Gc	0.20S	37.39 E
Chukai	26	Df	4.15N	103.25 E
Chukchi Peninsula (EN)= Čukotski Poluostrov	21	Uc	66.00N	175.00W
Chukchi Plateau (EN)	67	Bd	78.00N	165.00W
Chukchi Sea	67	Bd	69.00N	171.00W
Chukchi Sea (EN)= Čukotskoje More	67	Bd	69.00N	171.00W
Chula Vista	46	Gj	32.39N	117.05W
Chulitna	40	Jd	62.55N	149.39W
Chullo	13	Jg	37.10N	2.57W
Chulucanas	54	Be	5.06S	80.10W
Chumbicha	56	Gc	28.52S	66.14W
Chumphon	25	Jf	10.32N	99.13 E
Chumunjin	28	Jf	37.53N	128.49 E
Ch'unch'ŏn	27	Md	37.52N	127.44 E
Chunga	36	Ef	15.03S	26.00 E
Ch'ungch'ŏng-Namdo [2]	28	If	36.30N	127.00 E
Ch'ungch'ŏng-Pukto [2]	28	Jf	36.45N	128.00 E
Ch'ungju	27	Md	36.58N	127.56 E
Chungking (EN)= Chongqing (Yuzhou)	22	Mg	29.34N	106.27 E
Chungking (EN)= Yuzhou→Chongqing	22	Mg	29.34N	106.27 E
Ch'ungmu	28	Jg	34.51N	128.26 E
Chunya	36	Fd	8.32S	33.25 E
Chuquibamba	54	Dg	15.50S	72.39W
Chuquibambilla	54	Df	14.07S	72.43W
Chuquicamata	56	Gb	22.19S	68.56W
Chuquisaca [2]	54	Fg	20.00S	64.20W
Chur/Cuera	14	Dd	46.50N	9.35 E
Churchill	39	Jd	58.46N	94.10W
Churchill [Can.]	38	Md	53.30N	60.10W
Churchill [Can.]	38	Jd	58.47N	94.12W
Churchill, Cape -	42	Ie	58.46N	93.12W
Churchill Falls	42	Lf	53.30N	64.10W
Churchill Lake	42	Ge	56.05N	108.15W
Churchill Peak	42	Ee	58.20N	125.02W
Churchill Range	66	Jg	81.30S	158.30 E
Chūru	25	Ec	28.18N	74.57 E
Churuguara	54	Ea	10.49N	69.32W
Churún Merú=Angel Falls (EN)	52	Je	5.57N	62.30W
Chuska Mountains	46	Kh	36.15N	108.50W
Chute-des Passes	42	Kg	49.50N	71.00W
Chuxian	27	Ke	32.16N	118.15 E
Chuxiong	27	Hf	25.02N	101.32 E
Chuy	55	Fk	33.41S	53.27W
Ciamis	26	Eh	7.20S	108.21 E
Cianjur	26	Eh	6.49S	107.08 E
Ciarraí/Kerry [2]	9	Di	52.10N	9.30W
Čiatura	16	Mh	42.17N	43.15 E
Cibuta, Cerro-	48	Db	31.02N	110.58W
Ćićarija	14	He	45.28N	13.54 E
Ćićevac	15	Ef	43.43N	21.27 E
Cicicleja	15	Nb	47.23N	30.50 E
Cicolano	14	Hh	42.15N	13.10 E
Cidacos	13	Kb	42.19N	1.55W
Cide	24	Eb	41.54N	33.00 E
Cidlina	10	Lf	50.09N	15.12 E
Ciechanów	10	Qd	52.53N	20.38 E
Ciechanów [2]	10	Qd	52.55N	20.40 E
Ciechanowiec	10	Sd	52.42N	22.31 E
Ciechanowska, Wysoczyzna-	10	Qc	53.10N	20.30 E
Ciego de Ávila	47	Id	21.51N	78.46W
Ciego de Ávila [3]	49	Hb	22.00N	78.40W
Ciénaga	54	Da	11.00N	74.14W
Ciénaga de Flores	48	Ie	25.57N	100.11W
Ciénaga de Oro	49	Ji	8.53N	75.38W
Cieneguita	48	Fd	27.57N	106.59W
Cienfuegos [3]	49	Gb	22.15N	80.30W
Cienfuegos	39	Kg	22.09N	80.27W
Cíes, Islas de-	13	Db	42.13N	8.54W
Cieszanów	10	Tf	50.16N	23.08 E
Cieza	13	Kf	38.14N	1.25W
Çifteler	24	Dc	39.22N	31.03 E
Cifuentes	13	Jd	40.47N	2.37W
Čiganak	19	Hf	45.05N	73.58 E
Čigirin	16	He	49.03N	32.42 E
Cigüela	13	Ie	39.08N	3.44W
Cihanbeyli	24	Ec	38.40N	32.56 E
Cihanbeyli Platosu	24	Ec	38.40N	32.45 E
Čihareši	16	Mh	42.47N	43.02 E
Cihuatlán	48	Gh	19.14N	104.35W
Čiily	19	Gg	44.13N	66.46 E
Cijara, Embalse de-	13	He	39.18N	4.52W
Cijulang	26	Eh	7.44S	108.27 E
Čik	15	Dd	45.42N	20.04 E
Čikoj	20	Ff	51.02N	106.39 E
Cikurački, Vulkan-	20	Kf	50.15N	155.29 E
Cilacap	26	Eh	7.44S	109.00 E
Çıldır	24	Jb	41.08N	43.07 E
Çıldır Gölü	24	Jb	41.04N	43.15 E
Cilento	14	Jj	40.20N	15.20 E
Čilik	18	Lc	43.42N	78.14 E
Čilik	19	Hg	43.35N	78.12 E
Cill Airne/Killarney	9	Di	52.03N	9.30W
Cill Chainnigh/Kilkenny	9	Fi	52.39N	7.15W
Cill Chainnigh/Kilkenny [2]	9	Fi	52.40N	7.20W
Cill Chaoi/Kilkee	9	Di	52.41N	9.38W
Cill Dara/Kildare [2]	9	Gh	53.15N	6.45W
Cill Dara/Kildare	9	Gh	53.10N	6.55W
Cill Mhantáin/Wicklow	9	Gi	52.59N	6.03W
Cill Mhantain/Wicklow [2]	9	Gi	53.00N	6.30W
Cill Mocheallóg/Kilmallock	9	Ei	52.25N	8.35W
Cill Rois/Kilrush	9	Di	52.39N	9.29W
Cilma	17	Fd	65.25N	52.05 E
Cilo Dağı	24	Kd	37.30N	44.00 E
Cimaltepec, Sierra-	47	Ee	16.00N	96.40W
Cimarron	38	Jf	36.10N	96.17W
Cimarron	45	Dh	36.31N	104.55W
Čimbaj	19	Fg	42.59N	59.47 E
Cimini, Monti-	14	Gh	42.24N	12.12 E
Čimišlija	16	Ff	46.32N	28.46 E
Čimkent	22	Ie	42.18N	69.36 E
Čimkentskaja Oblast [3]	19	Gg	43.00N	68.40 E
Cimljansk	19	Ef	47.37N	42.04 E
Cimljanskoje Vodohranilišče =Tsimlyansk Reservoir (EN)	5	Kf	48.00N	43.00 E
Cimone	5	Hg	44.12N	10.40 E
Cîmpeni	15	Gc	46.22N	23.03 E
Cîmpia Turzii	15	Gc	46.33N	23.53 E
Cîmpina	15	Id	45.08N	25.44 E
Cîmpulung	15	Id	45.16N	25.03 E
Cîmpulung Moldovenesc	15	Ib	47.32N	25.34 E
Čimtarga, Gora-	18	Ge	39.14N	68.12 E
Cina, Tanjung-	26	Dh	5.55S	104.35 E
Çinar	24	Id	37.39N	40.06 E
Cinarcik	15	Mi	40.39N	29.06 E
Cinaruco, Río-	50	Ci	6.41N	67.07W
Cina Selatan, Laut-=South China Sea (EN)	21	Ni	10.00N	113.00 E
Cinaz	18	Gd	40.56N	68.45 E
Cinca	13	Mc	41.26N	0.21 E
Cincar	14	Lg	43.54N	17.04 E
Cincinnati	39	Kf	39.06N	84.31W
Cinco Irmãos, Serra dos-	55	Ff	22.55S	52.50W
Cinco Saltos	56	Ge	38.49S	68.04W
Cindrelu, Vîrful-	15	Gd	45.35N	23.48 E
Çine	24	Cd	37.36N	28.04 E
Çine	15	Kl	37.46N	27.49 E
Ciney	11	Ld	50.18N	5.06 E
Čingirlau	19	Fe	51.07N	54.05 E
Cingoli	14	Hg	43.22N	13.13 E
Cintalapa de Figueroa	48	Mi	16.44N	93.43W
Cinto, Monte-	5	Gg	42.23N	8.56 E
Cintra, Golfo de-	32	De	23.00N	16.15W
Cinzas, Rio das-	55	Gf	22.56S	50.32W
Ciociaria	14	Hi	41.45N	13.15 E
Cionn Mhálanna/Malin Head	5	Fd	55.23N	7.24W
Cionn tSáile/Kinsale	9	Ej	51.42N	8.32W
Ciorani	15	Je	44.49N	26.25 E
Čiovo	14	Kg	43.30N	16.18 E
Cipa	20	Ge	55.20N	115.55 E
Cipikan	20	Gf	54.58N	113.21 E
Cipó	54	Kf	11.06S	38.31W
Cipolletti	56	Ge	38.56S	67.59W
Čiprovci	15	Ff	43.23N	22.53 E
Čir	16	Me	48.35N	42.55 E
Circeo, Capo-	14	Hi	41.14N	13.03 E
Čirčik	19	Gg	41.28N	69.35 E
Circle [Ak.-U.S.]	40	Kc	65.50N	144.04W
Circle [Mt.-U.S.]	46	Mc	47.25N	105.35W
Circleville	44	Ff	39.36N	82.57W
Cirebon	22	Mj	6.44S	108.34 E
Cirencester	9	Lj	51.44N	1.59W
Ciriè	14	Be	45.14N	7.36 E
Čirinda	20	Fc	67.30N	100.35 E
Čirip, Vulkan-	20	Jg	45.20N	147.58 E
Čirka-Kem	7	Hd	64.45N	32.10 E
Cirò	14	Lk	39.23N	17.04 E
Cirò Marina	14	Lk	39.22N	17.08 E
Ciron	11	Fj	44.36N	0.18W
Čirpan	15	Ig	42.12N	25.20 E
Cirque Mountain	42	Le	58.55N	63.33W
Cisa, Passo della-	14	Df	44.28N	9.55 E
Ciscaucasia (EN)	5	Kf	45.00N	43.00 E
Cisco	45	Gj	32.23N	98.59W
Ciskei	37	Df	31.30S	26.40 E
Čišmy	19	Fe	54.35N	55.25 E
Cisnădie	15	Hd	45.43N	24.09 E
Cisne, Islas del-	47	He	17.22N	83.51W
Cistern Point	49	Ib	24.40N	77.45W
Cistierna	13	Gb	42.48N	5.07W
Čistoozernoje	20	Cf	54.43N	76.43 E
Čistopol	19	Fd	55.23N	50.39 E
Čita	22	Nd	52.03N	113.30 E
Çitak	15	Mk	38.08N	29.39 E

Index Symbols

[1] Independent Nation
[2] State, Region
[3] District, County
[4] Municipality
[5] Colony, Dependency
Continent
Physical Region
Historical or Cultural Region
Mount, Mountain
Volcano
Hill
Mountains, Mountain Range
Hills, Escarpment
Plateau, Upland
Pass, Gap
Plain, Lowland
Delta
Salt Flat
Valley, Canyon
Crater, Cave
Karst Features
Depression
Polder
Desert, Dunes
Forest, Woods
Heath, Steppe
Oasis
Cape, Point
Coast, Beach
Cliff
Peninsula
Isthmus
Sandbank
Island
Atoll
Rock, Reef
Islands, Archipelago
Rocks, Reefs
Coral Reef
Well, Spring
Geyser
River, Stream
Waterfall Rapids
River Mouth, Estuary
Lake
Salt Lake
Intermittent Lake
Reservoir
Swamp, Pond
Canal
Glacier
Ice Shelf, Pack Ice
Ocean
Sea
Gulf, Bay
Strait, Fjord
Lagoon
Bank
Seamount
Tablemount
Ridge
Shelf
Basin
Escarpment, Sea Scarp
Fracture
Trench, Abyss
National Park, Reserve
Point of Interest
Recreation Site
Cave, Cavern
Historic Site
Ruins
Wall, Walls
Church, Abbey
Temple
Scientific Station
Airport
Port
Lighthouse
Mine
Tunnel
Dam, Bridge

Index Symbols

- [1] Independent Nation
- [2] State, Region
- [3] District, County
- [4] Municipality
- [5] Colony, Dependency
- [▲] Continent
- [X] Physical Region

- Historical or Cultural Region
- Mount, Mountain
- Volcano
- Hill
- Mountains, Mountain Range
- Hills, Escarpment
- Plateau, Upland

- Pass, Gap
- Plain, Lowland
- Delta
- Salt Flat
- Valley, Canyon
- Crater, Cave
- Karst Features

- Depression
- Polder
- Desert, Dunes
- Forest, Woods
- Heath, Steppe
- Oasis
- Cape, Point

- Coast, Beach
- Cliff
- Peninsula
- Isthmus
- Sandbank
- Island
- Atoll

- Rock, Reef
- Islands, Archipelago
- Rocks, Reefs
- Coral Reef
- Well, Spring
- Geyser
- River, Stream

- Waterfall Rapids
- River Mouth, Estuary
- Lake
- Salt Lake
- Intermittent Lake
- Reservoir
- Swamp, Pond

- Canal
- Glacier
- Ice Shelf, Pack Ice
- Ocean
- Sea
- Gulf, Bay
- Strait, Fjord

- Lagoon
- Bank
- Seamount
- Tablemount
- Ridge
- Shelf
- Basin

- Escarpment, Sea Scarp
- Fracture
- Trench, Fracture
- National Park, Reserve
- Point of Interest
- Recreation Site
- Cave, Cavern

- Historic Site
- Ruins
- Wall, Walls
- Church, Abbey
- Temple
- Scientific Station
- Airport

- Port
- Lighthouse
- Mine
- Tunnel
- Dam, Bridge

Index Symbols

- [1] Independent Nation
- [2] State, Region
- [3] District, County
- [4] Municipality
- [5] Colony, Dependency
- Continent
- Physical Region
- Historical or Cultural Region
- Mount, Mountain
- Volcano
- Hill
- Mountains, Mountain Range
- Hills, Escarpment
- Plateau, Upland
- Pass, Gap
- Plain, Lowland
- Delta
- Salt Flat
- Valley, Canyon
- Karst Features
- Depression
- Polder
- Desert, Dunes
- Forest, Woods
- Heath, Steppe
- Oasis
- Cape, Point
- Coast, Beach
- Cliff
- Peninsula
- Isthmus
- Sandbank
- Island
- Atoll
- Rock, Reef
- Islands, Archipelago
- Rocks, Reefs
- Coral Reef
- Well, Spring
- Geyser
- River, Stream
- Waterfall Rapids
- River Mouth, Estuary
- Lake
- Salt Lake
- Intermittent Lake
- Reservoir
- Swamp, Pond
- Canal
- Glacier
- Ice Shelf, Pack Ice
- Ocean
- Sea
- Gulf, Bay
- Strait, Fjord
- Basin
- Lagoon
- Bank
- Seamount
- Tablemount
- Ridge
- Shelf
- Escarpment, Sea Scarp
- Fracture
- Trench, Abyss
- National Park, Reserve
- Point of Interest
- Recreation Site
- Scientific Station
- Airport
- Cave, Cavern
- Historic Site
- Ruins
- Wall, Walls
- Church, Abbey
- Temple
- Port
- Lighthouse
- Mine
- Tunnel
- Dam, Bridge

A · 51

Dainanji-San ▲	29	Ec	36.36N	137.42 E
Dainichi-San ▲	29	Ec	36.09N	136.30 E
Dainkog	27	Ge	32.31N	97.59 E
Daiō-Zaki ►	28	Ng	34.22N	136.53 E
Dairan (EN)=Dalian (Luda)	22	Of	38.55N	121.39 E
Dairan (EN) = Lüda→Dalian	22	Of	38.55N	121.39 E
Dairbhre/Valentia ◈	9	Cj	51.55N	10.20W
Daireaux	55	Bm	36.36 S	61.45W
Dai-Sen ▲	29	Cd	35.24N	133.34 E
Daisengen-Dake ▲	29a	Bc	41.35N	140.09 E
Daishan (Gaotingzhen)	28	Gi	30.15N	122.13 E
Daitō [Jap.]	29	Cd	35.19N	132.58 E
Daitō [Jap.]	29	Gb	39.02N	141.22 E
Daito Islands (EN)=Daitō Shotō ⧈	21	Pg	25.00N	131.15 E
Daitō Shotō=Daito Islands (EN) ⧈	21	Pg	25.00N	131.15 E
Daitō-Zaki ►	29	Gd	35.18N	140.24 E
Daixian	28	Be	39.03N	112.57 E
Daiyue→Shanyin	28	Be	39.30N	112.48 E
Dajabón	49	Ld	19.33N	71.42W
Dajarra	58	Eg	21.42 S	139.31 E
Dajtit, Mali i- ▲	15	Ch	41.22N	19.55 E
Daka ∿	34	Ed	8.19N	0.13W
Dakar	31	Fg	14.40N	17.26W
Dākhilah, Wāḩāt al-= Dakhla Oasis (EN) 🌴	30	Jf	25.30N	29.10 E
Dakhla Oasis (EN)= Dākhilah, Wāḩāt al- 🌴	30	Jf	25.30N	29.10 E
Dakhlet Nouâdhibou ③	32	De	20.30N	16.00W
Dakla	31	Ff	23.42N	15.56W
Dakoro	34	Gc	14.30N	6.25 E
Đakovo	14	Me	45.19N	18.25 E
Daksti	8	Kg	57.38N	25.32 E
Dak To	25	Lf	14.42N	107.51 E
Dal	8	Dd	60.15N	11.12 E
Dal, Jökulsá á- ∿	7a	Cb	65.40N	14.20W
Đala	15	Dc	46.09N	20.07 E
Dala [Ang.]	36	De	11.03 S	20.17 E
Dala [Sol.Is.]	63a	c	8.36 S	160.41 E
Dalaba	34	Cc	10.42N	12.15W
Dalai → Da'an	27	Lb	45.35N	124.16 E
Dalai Nur ◫	27	Kc	43.18N	116.15 E
Dala-Järna	8	Fd	60.33N	14.21 E
Dālakī ∿	24	Nh	29.19N	51.06 E
Dalälven ∿	5	Hc	60.38N	17.27 E
Dalaman ∿	24	Cd	36.40N	28.45 E
Dalaman	15	Lm	36.44N	28.49 E
Dalāmī	35	Ec	11.52N	30.28 E
Dalān	24	Kj	24.15N	45.47 E
Dalan-Dzadgad	22	Me	43.47N	104.29 E
Dalane ⌧	8	Bf	58.35N	6.20 E
Dalarna ▣	8	Fd	61.00N	14.05 E
Dalarö	8	He	59.08N	18.24 E
Da Lat	22	Mh	11.56N	108.25 E
Dālbandin	25	Cc	28.53N	64.25 E
Dalbosjön ◫	8	Ef	58.45N	12.50 E
Dalboslätten ⌧	8	Ef	58.35N	12.25 E
Dalby	59	Ke	27.11 S	151.16 E
Dale [Nor.]	7	Af	60.35N	5.49 E
Dale [Nor.]	7	Af	61.22N	5.25 E
Dale Hollow Lake ◫	44	Eg	36.36N	85.19W
Dalen	7	Bg	59.27N	8.00 E
Dalfsen	12	Ib	52.30N	6.14 E
Dalgaranger, Mount- ▲	59	De	27.51 S	117.06 E
Dălgopol	15	Kf	43.03N	27.21 E
Dalhart	43	Gd	36.04N	102.31W
Dalhousie	42	Kg	48.04N	66.23W
Dalhousie, Cape - ►	42	Eb	70.15N	129.41W
Dali [China]	22	Mg	25.43N	100.07 E
Dali [China]	27	Ie	34.55N	110.00 E
Dalian (Lüda) = Dairan (EN)	22	Of	38.55N	121.39 E
Dalías	13	Jh	36.49N	2.52W
Daling He ∿	28	Fd	40.56N	121.44 E
Dalizi	27	Mc	41.45N	126.50 E
Dalj	14	Me	45.29N	18.59 E
Daljā'	33	Fd	27.39N	30.42 E
Dalkowskie, Wzgórza- ⛰	10	Le	51.35N	15.50 E
Dall [Ak.-U.S.] ◈	40	Mf	54.50N	132.55W
Dall [Can.] ◈	2	Ef	55.00N	133.00W
Dallas [Or.-U.S.]	46	Dd	44.55N	123.19W
Dallas [Tx.-U.S.]	39	Jf	32.47N	96.48W
Dalmā' ◈	24	Oj	24.30N	52.20 E
Dalmā', Qārat- ▲	33	Dd	25.32N	23.57 E
Dalmacija ▣	14	Kg	43.00N	17.00 E
Dalmacija = Dalmatia (EN) ⌧	5	Hg	43.00N	17.00 E
Dalmaj, Hawr- ◫	24	Kf	32.20N	45.28 E
Dalmally	9	Ie	56.24N	4.58W
Dalmatia (EN) = Dalmacija ⌧	5	Hg	43.00N	17.00 E
Dalmatovo	17	Kh	56.16N	63.00 E
Dalnegorsk	22	Pe	44.31N	135.31 E
Dalnerečensk	22	Pe	45.55N	133.45 E
Dalni [R.S.F.S.R.]	20	Kf	53.15N	157.30 E
Dalni [R.S.F.S.R.]	20	Ih	44.57N	135.03 E
Dalnjaja, Gora- ▲	20	Mc	68.08N	179.53 E
Daloa ③	34	Dd	6.58N	6.23W
Daloa	31	Gh	6.53N	6.27W
Dalou Shan ⛰	21	Mg	28.00N	106.40 E
Dalqū	35	Ea	20.07N	30.35 E
Dalrymple, Mount- ▲	57	Fg	21.02 S	148.38 E
Dalsbruk	8	Jd	60.02N	22.31 E
Dalsbruk/Taalintendas	8	Jd	60.02N	22.31 E
Dalsfjorden ⇌	8	Ac	61.20N	5.05 E
Dalsjöfors	8	Eg	57.43N	13.05 E
Dalsland ▣	8	Ef	58.35N	12.55 E
Dalslands kanal ⊟	8	Ef	58.50N	12.25 E
Dals Långed	7	Cg	58.55N	12.18 E
Dalton	44	Eh	34.47N	84.58W
Daltonganj	25	Gd	24.02N	84.04 E
Dalul	35	Gc	14.22N	40.21 E
Daluo	27	Hg	21.38N	100.15 E
Dalupiri ◈	26	Hc	19.05N	121.12 E
Dalvík	7a	Bb	65.58N	18.32W
Dalwallinu	59	Df	30.17 S	116.40 E
Dalyan	15	Lm	36.50N	28.39 E
Daly Bay ◖	42	Id	64.00N	89.40W
Daly City	46	Dh	37.42N	122.29W
Daly River ∿	57	Ef	13.20 S	130.19 E
Daly Waters	59	Gc	16.15 S	133.22 E
Damā, Wādī- ∿	24	Fi	27.09N	35.47 E
Damagarim ⌧	34	Gc	13.42N	9.00 E
Damān ③	25	Ed	20.10N	73.00 E
Damanhūr	33	Fc	31.02N	30.28 E
Damar, Pulau- ◈	26	Ih	7.09 S	128.40 E
Damara	35	Be	4.58N	18.42 E
Damaraland ▣	37	Bd	21.00 S	17.30 E
Damas Cays ⧈	49	Hb	23.58N	79.55W
Damascus (EN)=Dimashq	22	Ff	33.30N	36.15 E
Dāmāsh	24	Md	36.46N	49.46 E
Damaturu	34	Hc	11.45N	11.58 E
Damāvand	24	He	35.56N	52.08 E
Damāvand, Qolleh-ye- ▲	21	Hf	35.56N	52.08 E
Damba	36	Cd	6.50 S	15.07 E
Dambaslar	15	Kh	41.13N	27.14 E
Dame Marie, Cap- ►	47	Je	18.36N	74.26W
Damergou ⌧	30	Hg	15.00N	9.00 E
Dāmghān	24	Pd	36.09N	54.22 E
Damianópolis	55	Ib	14.33 S	46.10W
Damiao	27	He	30.52N	104.38 E
Damietta (EN)=Dumyāţ	31	Ke	31.25N	31.48 E
Daming	28	Cf	36.17N	115.09 E
Daming Shan ▲	27	Ig	23.23N	108.30 E
Damīr Qābū	24	Id	36.54N	41.47 E
Dammartin en Goële	12	Ee	49.03N	2.41 E
Dammastock ▲	14	Cd	46.38N	8.25 E
Damme [Bel.]	12	Fc	51.15N	3.17 E
Damme [F.R.G.]	12	Kb	52.31N	8.12 E
Dammer Berge ⌓	12	Kb	52.35N	8.17 E
Damoh	25	Fd	23.50N	79.27 E
Damongo	34	Ed	9.05N	1.49W
Damous	13	Nh	36.33N	1.42 E
Dampier	58	Cg	20.39 S	116.45 E
Dampier, Selat-=Dampier Strait (EN) ⇌	26	Jg	0.40 S	130.40 E
Dampier Archipelago ⧈	59	Dd	20.35 S	116.35 E
Dampier Land ⌧	59	Ec	17.30 S	122.55 E
Dampierre ⌓	12	Df	48.42N	1.59 E
Dampier Strait ⇌	59	Ja	5.36 S	148.12 E
Dampier Strait (EN)= Dampier, Selat- ⇌	26	Jg	0.40 S	130.40 E
Damqawt	23	Hf	16.34N	52.50 E
Damqog Kanbab/Maquan He ∿	27	Df	29.36N	84.09 E
Dam Qu ∿	27	Fe	33.56N	92.41 E
Damville	12	Df	48.52N	1.04 E
Damvillers	12	He	49.20N	5.24 E
Damwoude, Dantumadeel-	12	Ha	53.18N	5.59 E
Damxoi → Comai	27	Ff	28.26N	91.32 E
Damxung	27	Fe	30.34N	91.16 E
Danakil=Danakil Plain (EN) ⌧	30	Lg	12.25N	40.30 E
Danakil Plain (EN)= Danakil ⌧	30	Lg	12.25N	40.30 E
Danané ③	34	Dd	7.25N	8.10W
Danané	34	Dd	7.16N	8.09W
Da Nang	22	Mh	16.04N	108.13 E
Danba/Rongzhag	27	He	30.48N	101.54 E
Danbury	44	Ke	41.23N	73.27W
Danby Lake ⩩	46	Hi	34.14N	115.07W
Dancheng	28	Ch	33.36N	115.14 E
Dancheng→Xiangshan	27	Lf	29.29N	121.52 E
Dandarah ∵	33	Fd	26.10N	32.39 E
Dandeldhura	25	Gc	29.18N	80.35 E
Dandenong, Melbourne-	59	Jg	37.59 S	145.12 E
Dandong	22	Oe	40.10N	124.15 E
Daneborg	41	Jd	74.25N	20.10W
Danells Fjord ⇌	41	Hf	60.45N	42.45W
Daneţi	15	Hf	43.59N	24.03 E
Danfeng (Longjuzhai)	27	Je	33.44N	110.22 E
Danforth Hills ⛰	45	Cf	40.15N	108.00W
Danfu	63a	Aa	4.12 S	153.04 E
Dangara	19	Gh	38.09N	69.22 E
Dangchengwan → Subei	27	Fd	39.36N	94.58 E
Dang He ∿	27	Fc	40.30N	94.42 E
Dangjin Shankou ⊔	21	Lf	39.15N	94.30 E
Dangla	35	Fc	11.16N	36.50 E
Dangla Shan→Tanggula Shan ⛰	21	Lf	33.00N	92.00 E
Dangoura, Mount- ▲	35	Dd	6.12N	26.27 E
Dangrek Range (EN)=Dong Rak, Phanom- ⛰	21	Mh	14.25N	104.30 E
Dangshan	27	Ke	34.22N	116.21 E
Dangtu	28	Ei	31.33N	118.30 E
Dangu	12	De	49.15N	1.42 E
Dangyang	28	Ai	30.49N	111.47 E
Dan He ∿	28	Bg	35.05N	112.59 E
Daniel	46	Je	42.52N	110.04W
Daniel, Serra- ⛰	55	Ea	13.40 S	54.55W
Danielskuil	37	Ce	28.11 S	23.33 E
Danilov	19	Ed	58.12N	40.13 E
Danilovgrad	15	Cg	42.33N	19.07 E
Danilovka	16	Nd	50.21N	44.06 E
Daning	27	Jd	36.31N	110.45 E
Danjiang → Junxian	27	Je	32.31N	111.32 E
Danjiangkou Shuiku ⊞	27	Je	32.37N	111.30 E
Danjo-Guntō ⧈	27	Me	32.00N	128.20 E
Ḑank	24	Qk	23.33N	56.16 E
Dankov	16	Kc	53.16N	39.07 E
Danlí	49	Df	14.00N	86.35W
Danmark=Denmark (EN) ①	6	Gd	56.00N	10.00 E
Danmark Fjord ⇌	67	Me	81.10N	23.20W
Danmarks Havn	67	Ld	76.50N	18.30W
Danmarksstraedet= Denmark Strait (EN) ⇌	38	Qc	67.00N	25.00W
Dannenberg	10	Hc	53.06N	11.06 E
Dannevirke	62	Gd	40.12 S	176.06 E
Danot	35	Hd	7.33N	45.17 E
Dantumadeel	12	Ha	53.18N	5.59 E
Dantumadeel-Damwoude	12	Ha	53.18N	5.59 E
Danube (EN)=Donau ∿	5	If	45.20N	29.40 E
Danube (EN)=Duna ∿	5	If	45.20N	29.40 E
Danube (EN)=Dunaj ∿	5	If	45.20N	29.40 E
Danube (EN)=Dunărea ∿	5	If	45.20N	29.40 E
Danube (EN)=Dunav ∿	5	If	45.20N	29.40 E
Danube, Mouths of the- (EN) = Dunării, Delta- ⊻	5	If	45.30N	29.45 E
Danville [Ar.-U.S.]	45	Ji	35.03N	93.24W
Danville [Il.-U.S.]	43	Jc	40.08N	87.37W
Danville [In.-U.S.]	44	Df	39.46N	86.32W
Danville [Ky.-U.S.]	43	Kd	37.39N	84.46W
Danville [Va.-U.S.]	43	Ld	36.34N	79.25W
Danxian (Nada)	27	Ih	19.38N	109.32 E
Danyang	28	Eh	32.00N	119.33 E
Danzig (EN)=Gdańsk	6	He	54.23N	18.40 E
Dao	26	Hd	10.31N	121.57 E
Dão ∿	13	Dd	40.20N	8.11W
Daocheng/Dabba	27	Hf	29.01N	100.26 E
Daokou → Huaxian	28	Cg	35.33N	114.30 E
Daosa	25	Fc	26.53N	76.20 E
Dao Shui ∿	28	Ci	30.42N	114.40 E
Dao Timni	34	Ha	20.38N	13.39 E
Daoura ∿	32	Gd	29.03N	4.33W
Daoxian	27	Jf	25.37N	111.36 E
Dapaong	34	Fc	10.52N	0.12 E
Dapchi	34	Hc	12.29N	11.29 E
Daqing Shan ⛰	28	Ad	41.00N	111.00 E
Daqin Tal→Naiman Qi	27	Lc	42.49N	120.38 E
Daquing Shan ▲	28	Ed	40.30N	119.38 E
Dar'ā	23	Ec	32.37N	36.06 E
Dārāb	24	Ph	28.45N	54.34 E
Darabani	15	Ja	48.11N	26.35 E
Daraçya Yarimadasi ⊏	15	Lm	36.40N	28.10 E
Darāfisah	35	Ec	13.23N	31.59 E
Dārān	24	Nf	32.59N	50.24 E
Darasun	20	Gf	51.39N	113.59 E
Đaravica ▲	15	Dg	42.32N	20.08 E
Darāw	24	Ej	24.25N	32.56 E
Darazo	34	Hc	11.00N	10.25 E
Darband	23	Ic	31.38N	57.02 E
Darband, Kūh-e- ▲	24	Qg	31.34N	57.08 E
Darbandī Khān, Sad ad- ⌿	24	Ke	35.07N	45.50 E
Darbat Alī, Ra's- ►	23	Hf	16.43N	53.33 E
Darbėnai/Darbenaj	8	Ih	56.02N	21.08 E
Dar Ben Karriche el Bahri	13	Gi	35.51N	5.21W
Darbhanga	25	Hc	26.10N	85.54 E
Dārboruk	35	Gd	9.44N	44.31 E
Darby	46	Hc	46.01N	114.11W
Darchan→Darhan	22	Me	49.33N	106.21 E
Darda	14	Me	45.38N	18.42 E
Dardanelle Lake ◫	45	Ji	35.25N	93.20W
Dardanelles (EN)= Çanakkale Boğazi ⇌	5	Ig	40.15N	26.25 E
Dardo/Kangding	27	He	30.01N	101.58 E
Dar el Kouti ⌧	30	Jh	8.50N	21.50 E
Darende	24	Gc	38.34N	37.30 E
Dar es Salaam ③	36	Gd	6.50 S	39.02 E
Dar es Salaam	31	Ki	6.48 S	39.17 E
Darfield	62	Ee	43.29 S	172.07 E
Darfo Boario Terme	14	Ee	45.53N	10.11 E
Dārfūr	30	Jg	12.40 N	24.20 E
Dārfūr al Janūbīyah ③	35	Dc	11.30N	25.10 E
Dārfūr ash Shamālīyah ③	35	Db	16.00N	25.30 E
Dargan-Ata	19	Gg	40.29N	62.12 E
Dargaville	61	Dg	35.56 S	173.52 E
Darhan (Darchan)	22	Me	49.33N	106.21 E
Darhan Muminggan Lianheqi	27	Jc	41.45N	110.24 E
Darica [Tur.]	15	Kj	40.00N	27.50 E
Darica [Tur.]	15	Mi	40.45N	29.23 E
Darién ⌧	47	Ig	8.30N	77.30W
Darien	44	Gj	31.22N	81.26W
Darién ③	49	Ii	8.10N	77.45W
Darién, Golfo de- ◖	52	Ie	8.25N	76.53W
Darién, Serranía del- ⛰	47	Ig	8.30N	77.30W
Dariense, Cordillera- ⛰	49	Eg	12.55N	85.30W
Darja ∿	18	Ee	38.13N	65.46 E
Darjeeling → Dārjiling	25	Hc	27.02N	88.16 E
Dārjiling	25	Hc	27.02N	88.16 E
Dar-Kebdani	13	Ii	35.07N	3.21W
Dark Head ►	51n	Ba	13.17N	61.17W
Ḑārkhovīn	24	Mg	30.45N	48.25 E
Darlag	27	Ge	33.49N	99.08 E
Darling	37	Bf	33.23 S	18.23 E
Darling Downs ⛰	59	Ke	27.30 S	150.30 E
Darling Range ⛰	57	Ch	32.00 S	116.30 E
Darling River ∿	57	Fh	34.07 S	141.55 E
Darlington [Eng.-U.K.]	9	Lg	54.31N	1.34W
Darlington [S.C.-U.S.]	44	Hh	34.19N	79.53W
Darłowo	10	Mb	54.26N	16.23 E
Darmouth	9	Jk	50.21N	3.35W
Darmstadt	10	Eg	49.52N	8.39 E
Darnah	31	Je	32.46N	22.39 E
Darnah ③	33	Dc	31.00N	23.40 E
Darnétal	12	De	49.27N	1.09 E
Darney	11	Mf	48.05N	6.03 E
Darnley, Cape- ►	66	Fe	67.43 S	69.30 E
Darnley Bay ◖	42	Fc	69.45N	123.45W
Daroca	13	Kc	41.07N	1.25W
Darou Khoudos	34	Bb	15.06N	16.50W
Darovskoj	7	Lg	58.47N	47.59 E
Darrah, Mount- ▲	46	Hb	49.28N	114.35W
Darregueira	56	He	37.42 S	63.10W
Darrehshahr	24	Lf	33.10N	47.18 E
D'Arros Island ◈	37b	Bb	5.24 S	53.18 E
Dar Rounga ⌧	30	Jg	10.45N	22.20 E
Dar Sila ▭	35	Cc	12.11N	21.21 E
Darss ⊏	10	Ib	54.25N	12.31 E
Darßer Ort ►	10	Ib	54.29N	12.31 E
Dart ∿	9	Jk	50.20N	3.33W
Dart, Cape- ►	66	Nf	73.06 S	126.20W
D'Artagnan Bank (EN) ▦	59	Eb	13.00 S	121.00 E
Dartang → Baqên	27	Fe	31.58N	94.00 E
Dartford	12	Cc	51.27N	0.13 E
Dartmoor ⛰	9	Jk	50.35N	4.00W
Dartmouth	42	Lh	44.40N	63.34W
Dartuch, Cabo- ►	13	Pe	39.56N	3.48 E
Daru	60	Ci	9.04 S	143.12 E
Daruneh	24	Qe	35.10N	57.18 E
Daruvar	14	Le	45.35N	17.14 E
Darvaza	19	Fg	40.15N	58.24 E
Darvel, Teluk- ◖	26	Gf	4.50N	118.30 E
Darwin	58	Ef	12.28 S	130.50 E
Darwin, Bahía- ◖	56	Fg	45.27 S	74.40W
Darwin, Isla- ◈	54a	Aa	1.39N	92.00W
Darwin, Port- ◖	59	Gb	12.20 S	130.40 E
Dar Zagaoua ⌧	35	Cb	15.15N	23.14 E
Dar Zebada ⌧	35	Bc	13.45N	18.50 E
Dās ◈	24	Oj	25.09N	52.53 E
Dašava	10	Ug	49.13N	24.05 E
Daš-Balbar	27	Jb	49.31N	114.21 E
Dasha He ∿	28	Ce	38.27N	114.39 E
Dashengtang Shan ▲	28	Dc	42.07N	117.12 E
Dashennongjia ⊔	27	Je	31.47N	114.12 E
Dashennongjia ▲	27	Je	31.26N	110.18 E
Dashiqiao → Yingkou	28	Gd	40.39N	122.31 E
Dashitou	28	Jc	43.18N	128.29 E
Dasht	24	Qd	37.17N	56.04 E
Dasht Āb	24	Qh	28.59N	56.32 E
Dashtak	24	Og	30.23N	52.30 E
Dasht-e-Āzādegan	24	Mg	31.32N	48.10 E
Daškesan	16	Oi	40.30N	46.03 E
Dasseneiland ◈	37	Bf	33.26 S	18.05 E
Dastgardān	24	Qe	34.19N	56.51 E
Dastjerd-e Qaddādeh	24	Nf	32.44N	51.32 E
Datça	24	Bd	36.45N	27.40 E
Date	28	Pc	42.27N	140.51 E
Dāth, Sha'īb ad- ∿	24	Jj	25.45N	43.10 E
Datia	25	Fc	25.40N	78.28 E
Datian Ding ▲	27	Jg	22.17N	111.13 E
Datil	45	Ci	34.09N	107.47W
Datong [China]	27	Hd	36.56N	101.40 E
Datong [China]	22	Ne	40.09N	113.17 E
Datteln	12	Jc	51.40N	7.23 E
Datteln-Hamm Kanal ⊟	12	Jc	51.39N	7.21 E
Datu ►	21	Mi	2.05N	109.39 E
Datu, Teluk ◖	21	Ni	2.00N	111.00 E
Datu Plang	26	He	6.58N	124.40 E
Dāūd Khel	25	Eb	32.53N	71.34 E
Daudzeva	8	Kh	56.28N	25.18 E
Daugaard-Jensen Land ⌧	41	Fb	80.10N	63.30W
Daugaj/Daugai	8	Kj	54.20N	24.28 E
Daugava=Dvina(EN) ∿	19	Cd	57.04N	24.03 E
Daugavpils ∿	6	Id	55.53N	26.32 E
Daule	54	Cd	1.50 S	79.57W
Daun	10	Cf	50.12N	6.50 E
Daung Kyun ◈	25	Jf	12.14N	98.05 E
Daunia, Monti della- ⛰	14	Ji	41.25N	15.05 E
Dauphin	42	Hf	51.09N	100.03W
Dauphiné ▣	11	Lj	44.50N	6.00 E
Dauphin Lake ◫	42	Hf	51.15N	99.45W
Daura	34	Gc	13.02N	8.18 E
Dautphetal	12	Kd	50.52N	8.33 E
Dāvangere	25	Ff	14.28N	75.55 E
Davao	22	Oi	7.04N	125.36 E
Davao Gulf ◖	21	Oi	6.40N	125.55 E
Dāvarān, Kūh-e- ⛰	24	Qg	30.40N	56.15 E
Dāvar Panāh	23	Jd	27.21N	62.21 E
Dāvarzan	24	Qd	36.23N	56.50 E
Đavat ⊔	15	Eh	41.04N	21.06 E
Davenport [Ia.-U.S.]	39	Je	41.32N	90.41W
Davenport [Wa.-U.S.]	46	Fc	47.39N	118.09W
Davenport Range ⛰	59	Gd	20.45 S	134.50 E
Daventry	12	Ab	52.15N	1.10W
Davert ⌧	12	Jc	51.51N	7.36 E
Davey, Port- ◖	59	Jh	43.20 S	145.55 E
David	39	Ki	8.25N	82.27W
David City	45	Hf	41.15N	97.08W
David-Gorodok	16	Ec	52.03N	27.13 E
David Point ►	51p	Bb	12.14N	61.39W
Davidson	46	Ma	51.18N	105.59W
Davidson Mountains ⛰	40	Kc	68.45N	142.10W
Davies, Mount- ▲	59	Fe	26.14 S	129.16 E
Davis	43	Cd	38.33N	121.44W
Davis ⊗	66	Fe	68.35 S	77.58 E
Davis, Cape- ►	66	Ee	66.24 S	56.50 E
Davis, Mount- ▲	44	Hf	39.47N	79.10W
Davis Bay ◖	66	Ie	66.08 S	134.05 E
Davis Inlet	42	Le	56.00N	61.30W
Davis Mountains ⛰	45	Ek	30.35N	104.00W
Davis Sea (EN) ≋	66	Ge	66.00 S	92.00 E
Davisstrædet = Davis, Strait (EN) ⇌	38	Nc	68.00N	58.00W
Davis Strait ⇌	38	Nc	68.00N	58.00W
Davis Strait (EN) = Davisstrædet ⇌	38	Nc	68.00N	58.00W
Davlekanovo	19	Fe	54.13N	55.03 E
Davo ∿	34	Dd	5.00N	6.08W
Davos/Tavau	14	Dd	46.47N	9.50 E
Davutlar	15	Kl	37.43N	27.17 E
Dawa	28	Gd	40.58N	122.01 E
Dawanlē	35	Gc	11.06N	42.38 E
Dawāsir, Wādī ad-	21	Gg	20.24N	46.29 E
Dawei	22	Lh	14.05N	98.12 E
Dawen He ∿	28	Dg	35.37N	116.23 E
Dawes Range ⛰	59	Kd	24.30 S	151.10 E
Dawḩarab ◈	33	Hf	16.17N	41.57 E
Dawson [Ga.-U.S.]	44	Ej	31.47N	84.26W
Dawson [Yuk.-Can.]	39	Fc	64.04N	139.25W
Dawson, Mount- ▲	46	Ga	51.09N	117.25W
Dawson Creek	39	Gd	55.45N	120.07W
Dawson-Lambton Glacier ❄	66	Af	76.15 S	27.30W
Dawson Range ⛰	42	Dd	65.15N	137.45W
Dawson River ∿	59	Jd	23.38 S	149.46 E
Dawu	27	He	30.45N	101.11 E
Dawu (Erlangdian)	28	Ci	31.33N	114.07 E
Dawu→Maqên	27	He	34.29N	100.01 E
Dawukou → Shizuishan	27	Id	39.03N	106.24 E
Dax	11	Ek	43.43N	1.03W
Da Xi ∿	27	Lf	28.10N	120.14 E
Daxian	27	Ie	31.15N	107.28 E
Daxin	27	Ig	22.52N	107.14 E
Daxing	28	De	39.45N	116.19 E
Daxinggou	28	Jc	43.23N	129.39 E
Daxue Shan ⛰	21	Mf	30.30N	101.30 E
Dayan→Lijiang	22	Mg	26.56N	100.15 E
Dayang He ∿	28	Ge	39.52N	123.40 E
Dayao	27	Hf	25.49N	101.18 E
Daye	28	Ci	30.05N	114.58 E
Dayishan→Guanyun	28	Eg	34.18N	119.14 E
Daymán, Cuchilla del- ⛰	55	Dj	31.38 S	57.10W
Daymán, Río- ⛰	55	Dj	31.40 S	58.02W
Daym Zubayr	35	Dd	7.43N	26.13 E
Dayong	27	Jf	29.09N	110.30 E
Dayr, Jabal ad- ▲	35	Ec	12.27N	30.45 E
Dayr az Zawr	22	Gf	35.20N	40.09 E
Dayr Hāfir	24	Gd	36.09N	37.42 E
Dayr Kātrīnā = Saint Catherine Monastery of- (EN) ⌘	33	Fd	28.31N	33.57 E
Dayr Mawās	24	Di	27.38N	30.51 E
Dayrūţ	33	Fd	27.33N	30.49 E
Dayton [Oh.-U.S.]	39	Kf	39.45N	84.15W
Dayton [Wa.-U.S.]	46	Gc	46.19N	117.59W
Daytona Beach	39	Kg	29.12N	80.59W
Dayu	27	Jf	25.29N	114.22 E
Da Yunhe=Grand Canal (EN) ⊟	21	Nf	39.54N	116.44 E
Dayville	46	Fd	44.28N	119.32W
Dayyīnah ◈	24	Oj	24.57N	52.24 E
Dazhongji → Dafeng	28	Fh	33.11N	120.27 E
Dazhu	27	Ie	30.42N	107.12 E
Dazjā	24	Pe	35.50N	55.46 E
Dazkırı	24	Cd	37.54N	29.42 E
De Aar	31	Jl	30.39 S	24.00 E
Dead ∿	9	Ei	52.40N	8.30W
Deadhorse	40	Jb	70.11N	148.27W
Deadmans Cay	49	Jb	23.14N	75.14W
Dead Sea (EN)=Mayyit, Al Baḩr al- ◫	21	Ff	31.30N	35.30 E
Deadwood	45	Ed	44.23N	103.44W
Deal	12	Dc	51.13N	1.24 E
Dealu Mare ▲	15	Jb	47.27N	26.40 E
De'an	28	Cj	29.18N	115.45 E
Deán Funes	56	Hd	30.26 S	64.21W
Dearborn	44	Fd	42.18N	83.10W
Dearg, Beinn- ▲	9	Id	57.48N	4.57W
Deary	46	Gc	46.52N	116.31W
Dease ∿	42	Ee	59.55N	128.29W
Dease Arm ◖	42	Fc	66.50N	120.00W
Dease Lake	39	Fd	58.35N	130.02W
Dease Strait ⇌	42	Gc	69.00N	107.00W
Death Valley ▽	38	Hf	36.30N	117.00W
Death Valley	46	Gh	36.20N	116.50W
Deauville	11	Ge	49.22N	0.04 E
Debak	26	Ff	1.34N	111.25 E
Debalcevo	16	Ke	48.20N	38.29 E
Debao	27	Ig	23.17N	106.21 E
Debar	15	Dh	41.32N	20.32 E
Debark	35	Fc	13.08N	37.53 E
Debdou	32	Gc	33.59N	3.03W
Debed ∿	16	Ni	41.22N	44.58 E
Deben ∿	12	Db	52.01N	1.22 E
De Beque	45	Bg	39.20N	108.13W
Dębica	10	Rf	50.04N	21.24 E
De Bilt	12	Hb	52.06N	5.11 E
Debin	20	Kd	62.18N	150.47 E
Dęblin	10	Re	51.35N	21.50 E
Dębno	10	Kd	52.45N	14.40 E
Débo, Lac- ◫	34	Eb	15.18N	4.09W
Deborah East, Lake- ◫	59	Df	30.45 S	119.10 E
Deborah West, Lake- ◫	59	Df	30.45 S	119.05 E
Deboyne Islands ⧈	57	Gf	10.43 S	152.22 E
Debrc	15	Ce	44.37N	19.54 E
Debre Berhan	35	Fd	9.41N	39.33 E
Debrecen	6	If	47.32N	21.38 E
Debrecen ②	10	Ri	47.31N	21.40 E
Debre Libanos ⌘	35	Fd	9.43N	38.52 E
Debre Markós	31	Kg	10.10 N	37.36 E
Debre Sina	35	Fd	9.51N	39.46 E
Debre Tabor	35	Fc	11.51N	38.00 E
Debre Zeyt	31	Kh	8.47N	39.00 E
De-Buka, Glacier- ❄	66	Nf	76.00 S	131.00W
Decatur [Al.-U.S.]	43	Je	34.36N	86.59W
Decatur [Ga.-U.S.]	44	Ei	33.46N	84.18W
Decatur [Il.-U.S.]	43	Jd	39.51N	89.32W
Decatur [In.-U.S.]	44	Ee	40.50N	84.56W
Decatur [Tx.-U.S.]	45	Hj	33.14N	97.35W
Decazeville	11	Ij	44.33N	2.15 E
Deccan ⌧	21	Jh	14.00N	77.00 E
Decelles, Reservoir- ⊞	44	Hb	47.40N	78.08W
Deception Bay ◖	59	Ia	7.07 S	144.05 E
Dechang	27	Hf	27.22N	102.12 E
Děčín	10	Kf	50.47N	14.13 E
Decize	11	Jh	46.50N	3.28 E
Decorah	45	Ke	43.18N	91.48W
Deda	15	Hc	46.56N	24.54 E
Dededo	64c	Ba	13.31N	144.49 E
Dedegöl Dağı ▲	24	Dd	37.39N	31.17 E
Dedemsvaart, Avereest-	12	Ib	52.37N	6.27 E
Dédougou	34	Ec	12.28N	3.28W
Dedoviči	7	Gh	57.33N	29.58 E
Dedza	36	Fe	14.22 S	34.20 E
Dee [Eng.-U.K.] ∿	9	Jh	53.19N	3.11W
Dee [Scot.-U.K.] ∿	9	Kd	57.08N	2.04W
Dee [Scot.-U.K.] ∿	9	Ig	54.50N	4.03W
Deep Creek Range ⛰	46	If	40.00N	113.57W
Deering	40	Gc	66.05N	162.43W
Deer Isle ◈	44	Mc	44.13N	68.41W
Deer Lake [Newf.-Can.]	42	Lg	49.10N	57.25W
Deer Lake [Ont.-Can.]	42	If	52.40N	94.30W
Deer Park	46	Gc	47.57N	117.28W
Defiance	44	Ee	41.17N	84.21W
Defla ∿	13	Qi	35.14N	4.26 E
De Funiak Springs	44	Dj	30.43N	86.07W
Dega Ahmedo	35	Gd	7.50N	42.53 E
Dêgê	27	Ge	31.52N	98.36 E
Degebe ∿	13	Ef	38.13N	7.29W
Degeh Bur	35	Gd	8.13N	43.34 E
Degema	34	Ge	4.45N	6.46 E
Degerby	8	Id	60.02N	20.23 E
Degerfors	7	Dg	59.14N	14.26 E
Degerhamn	7	Dh	56.21N	16.24 E
Deggendorf	10	Ih	48.50N	12.58 E

Index Symbols

① Independent Nation
② State, Region
③ District, County
④ Municipality
⑤ Colony, Dependency
■ Continent
⌧ Physical Region
▣ Historical or Cultural Region
▲ Mount, Mountain
⩓ Volcano
⌒ Hill
⛰ Mountains, Mountain Range
⌓ Hills, Escarpment
▭ Plateau, Upland
⊔ Pass, Gap
▁ Plain, Lowland
◣ Delta
▤ Salt Flat
▽ Valley, Canyon
◒ Crater, Cave
⊡ Karst Features
◡ Depression
▟ Polder
∴ Desert, Dunes
♣ Forest, Woods
⁖ Heath, Steppe
🌴 Oasis
► Cape, Point
⌇ Coast, Beach
▌ Cliff
⊏ Peninsula
⋈ Isthmus
▒ Sandbank
◈ Island
◎ Atoll
✲ Rock, Reef
⧈ Islands, Archipelago
⁂ Rocks, Reefs
✺ Coral Reef
⊙ Well, Spring
⊥ Geyser
∿ River, Stream
⋎ Waterfall Rapids
⊻ River Mouth, Estuary
◫ Lake
◪ Salt Lake
◻ Intermittent Lake
⊞ Reservoir
⩩ Swamp, Pond
⊟ Canal
❄ Glacier
◩ Ice Shelf, Pack Ice
≈ Ocean
≋ Sea
◖ Gulf, Bay
⇌ Strait, Fjord
◍ Lagoon
▦ Bank
⊼ Seamount
⊓ Tablemount
⋀ Ridge
⊐ Shelf
◛ Basin
⩚ Escarpment, Sea Scarp
⊘ Fracture
⩡ Trench, Abyss
⚑ National Park, Reserve
✦ Point of Interest
✚ Recreation Site
◓ Cave, Cavern
⌘ Historic Site
∵ Ruins
⊓⊓ Wall, Walls
✝ Church, Abbey
⛩ Temple
⊗ Scientific Station
✈ Airport
⚓ Port
⛯ Lighthouse
⚒ Mine
⌒⌒ Tunnel
⌿ Dam, Bridge

Index Symbols

[1] Independent Nation	◉ Historical or Cultural Region	⊃ Pass, Gap
[2] State, Region	▲ Mount, Mountain	⌒ Plain, Lowland
[3] District, County	▲ Volcano	▽ Delta
[4] Municipality	⌂ Hill	▭ Salt Flat
[5] Colony, Dependency	▲ Mountains, Mountain Range	⋎ Valley, Canyon
■ Continent	⌓ Hills, Escarpment	⌔ Crater, Cave
◇ Physical Region	⏚ Plateau, Upland	✳ Karst Features

▽ Depression	≈ Coast, Beach	⊗ Rock, Reef
▭ Polder	⌐ Cliff	⊕ Islands, Archipelago
∴ Desert, Dunes	▸ Peninsula	⊙ Rocks, Reefs
♣ Forest, Woods	⊃ Isthmus	⌇ Coral Reef
⋰ Heath, Steppe	⌒ Sandbank	○ Well, Spring
⊛ Oasis	● Island	✦ Geyser
▸ Cape, Point	⊙ Atoll	⌇ River, Stream

⌇ Waterfall Rapids	⊂ Canal	⌒ Lagoon
⌇ River Mouth, Estuary	✶ Glacier	⌒ Bank
⬭ Lake	⊞ Ice Shelf, Pack Ice	▲ Seamount
⬚ Salt Lake	≋ Ocean	⌒ Ridge
⬚ Intermittent Lake	⌒ Tablemount	⌒ Shelf
≈ Sea	◉ Point of Interest	⌒ Basin
⬭ Reservoir	⊕ Recreation Site	
⬚ Swamp, Pond	⌔ Cave, Cavern	
⊐ Strait, Fjord		
⊃ Gulf, Bay		

⌒ Escarpment, Sea Scarp	▲ Historic Site	⚓ Port
⌒ Fracture	⌂ Ruins	⛫ Lighthouse
⌄ Trench, Abyss	⊞ Wall, Walls	⚒ Mine
⊡ National Park, Reserve	✞ Church, Abbey	⌇ Tunnel
	⛩ Temple	⌇ Dam, Bridge
	⚑ Scientific Station	
	✈ Airport	

Index Symbols

[1]	Independent Nation
[2]	State, Region
[3]	District, County
[4]	Municipality
[5]	Colony, Dependency
■	Continent
▨	Physical Region
⊠	Historical or Cultural Region
▲	Mount, Mountain
▲	Volcano
▲	Hill
▲	Mountains, Mountain Range
▨	Hills, Escarpment
▨	Plateau, Upland
	Pass, Gap
	Plain, Lowland
	Delta
	Salt Flat
	Valley, Canyon
	Crater, Cave
	Karst Features
	Depression
	Polder
	Desert, Dunes
	Forest, Woods
	Heath, Steppe
	Oasis
	Cape, Point
	Coast, Beach
	Cliff
	Peninsula
	Isthmus
	Coral Reef
	Well, Spring
	Geyser
	Atoll
	Rock, Reef
	Islands, Archipelago
	Rocks, Reefs
	Coral Reef
	Sandbank
	Island
	River, Stream
	Waterfall Rapids
	River Mouth, Estuary
	Lake
	Salt Lake
	Ocean
	Sea
	Gulf, Bay
	Strait, Fjord
	Canal
	Glacier
	Ice Shelf, Pack Ice
	Tableland
	Ridge
	Shelf
	Basin
	Lagoon
	Bank
	Seamount
	National Park, Reserve
	Point of Interest
	Recreation Site
	Scientific Station
	Airport
	Escarpment, Sea Scarp
	Fracture
	Trench, Abyss
	Historic Site
	Ruins
	Wall, Walls
	Church, Abbey
	Temple
	Port
	Lighthouse
	Mine
	Tunnel
	Dam, Bridge

Dragon's Mouths/Dragón, Bocas del- 54 Fa 10.45N 61.46W
Dragør 8 Ei 55.36N 12.41 E
Draguignan 11 Mk 43.32N 6.28 E
Drahanska vrchovina 10 Mg 49.30N 16.45 E
Drain 46 De 43.40N 123.19W
Drake 45 Fc 47.55N 100.23W
Drake, Estrecho de-=Drake Passage (EN) 52 Jk 58.00S 70.00W
Drakensberg 30 Jk 29.00S 29.00 E
Drake Passage (EN)=Drake, Estrecho de- 52 Jk 58.00S 70.00W
Dráma 15 Hh 41.09N 24.09 E
Drammen 6 Hd 59.44N 10.15 E
Dramselva 8 De 59.44N 10.14 E
Drangajokull 7a Aa 66.09N 22.15W
Dranse 11 Mh 46.24N 6.30 E
Drau=Drava (EN) 5 Hf 45.33N 18.55 E
Dráva=Drava (EN) 5 Hf 45.33N 18.55 E
Drava (EN)=Drau 5 Hf 45.33N 18.55 E
Drava (EN)=Dráva 5 Hf 45.33N 18.55 E
Dravograd 14 Jd 46.35N 15.01 E
Drawa 10 Ld 52.52N 15.59 E
Drawno 10 Lc 53.13N 15.45 E
Drawsko, Jezioro- 10 Mc 53.33N 16.10 E
Drawsko Pomorskie 10 Lc 53.32N 15.48 E
Drayton Valley 42 Gf 53.13N 115.00W
Drean 14 Bn 36.41N 7.45 E
Dreieich 12 Ke 50.01N 8.43 E
Drenovci 14 Mf 44.55N 18.55 E
Drenthe [3] 12 Ib 52.45N 6.30 E
Dresden [2] 10 Je 51.10N 14.00 E
Dresden 6 He 51.03N 13.45 E
Dreux 11 Hf 48.44N 1.22 E
Drevsjø 7 Cf 61.54N 12.02 E
Drezdenko 10 Ld 52.51N 15.50 E
Dricēni/Driceni 8 Lh 56.39N 27.11 E
Driceni/Dricēni 8 Lh 56.39N 27.11 E
Driffield 9 Mg 54.01N 0.26W
Driggs 46 Je 43.44N 111.14W
Drina 5 Hg 44.53N 19.21 E
Drincea 15 Fe 44.07N 22.59 E
Drin Gulf (EN)=Drinit, Gjiri i- 15 Ch 41.45N 19.28 E
Drini 5 Hg 41.45N 19.34 E
Drini i Zi 15 Dg 42.05N 20.23 E
Drinit, Gjiri i-=Drin Gulf (EN) 15 Ch 41.45N 19.28 E
Drinjača 14 Nf 44.17N 19.10 E
Drinosi 15 Di 40.17N 20.02 E
Drissa 7 Gi 55.47N 27.57 E
Drisvjaty, Ozero-/Drūkšiu Ežeras 8 Lj 55.37N 26.45 E
Driva 8 Cb 62.40N 8.34 E
Drjanovo 15 Ig 42.58N 25.28 E
Drniš 14 Kg 43.52N 16.09 E
Drøbak 7 Cg 59.39N 10.39 E
Drocea, Virful- 15 Fc 46.12N 22.14 E
Drogheda/Droichead Átha 9 Gh 53.43N 6.21W
Drogičin 16 Dc 52.13N 25.10 E
Drogobyč 16 Ce 49.22N 23.33 E
Drohiczyn 10 Sd 52.24N 22.41 E
Droichead Átha/Drogheda 9 Gh 53.43N 6.21W
Droichead na Bandan/Bandon 9 Ej 51.45N 8.45W
Droichead na Banna/Banbridge 9 Gg 54.21N 6.16W
Drokija 16 Ee 48.01N 27.53 E
Drôme 12 Be 49.19N 0.45W
Drôme [3] 11 Lj 44.35N 5.10 E
Drömling 10 Hd 52.29N 11.04 E
Dronero 14 Bf 44.28N 7.22 E
Dronne 11 Fi 45.02N 0.09W
Dronning Fabiola-Fjella 66 Df 71.30S 35.40 E
Dronning Louise Land 41 Jc 76.45N 24.00W
Dronten 11 Lb 52.31N 5.42 E
Dropt 11 Fj 44.35N 0.06W
Drovjanoj 20 Cb 72.25N 72.45 E
Drowning River 45 Na 50.55N 84.35W
Druja 7 Gi 55.47N 27.29 E
Drūkšiu Ežeras/Drisvjaty, Ozero- 8 Lj 55.37N 26.45 E
Druk-Yul→Bhutan [1] 22 Lg 27.30N 90.30 E
Drulingen 12 Jf 48.52N 7.11 E
Drumheller 42 Gf 51.28N 112.42W
Drummond [Mt.-U.S.] 46 Ic 46.40N 113.09W
Drummond [Wi.-U.S.] 45 Kc 46.20N 91.15W
Drummond Island 44 Fb 46.00N 83.40W
Drummond Range 59 Jd 23.30S 147.15 E
Drummondville 42 Kg 45.50N 72.20W
Drummore 9 Ig 54.42N 4.54W
Drumochter, Pass of- 9 Ie 56.50N 4.12W
Drunen 12 Hc 51.41N 5.10 E
Druskininkaj/Druskininkai 7 Fi 54.04N 24.06 E
Druskininkai/Druskininkaj 7 Fi 54.04N 24.06 E
Drut 16 Gc 53.04N 30.35 E
Druten 12 Hc 51.54N 5.38 E
Družba 16 Hc 52.02N 33.59 E
Družba 19 If 45.18N 82.29 E
Družkovka 16 Je 48.36N 37.33 E
Družnaja Gorka 8 Ne 59.11N 30.10 E
Družnino 17 Ih 56.48N 59.29 E
Družno, Jezioro- 10 Pb 54.08N 19.30 E
Drvar 14 Kf 44.22N 16.23 E
Drvenik 14 Lg 43.09N 17.15 E
Drwęca 10 Oc 53.00N 18.42 E
Dryden 42 Ig 49.47N 92.50W
Dry Fork 46 Me 43.30N 105.24W
Drygalski Ice Tongue 66 Kf 75.24S 163.30 E
Drygalski Island 66 Ge 65.45S 92.30 E
Drysdale River 59 Fb 13.59S 126.51 E
Dry Tortugas 43 Kg 24.38N 82.55W
Drzewica 10 Qe 51.27N 20.28 E
Drzewiczka 10 Qe 51.33N 20.35 E
Dschang 34 Hd 5.27N 10.04 E
Dua 36 Db 3.20N 20.53 E
Duaca 54 Ea 10.18N 69.10W
Duancun → Wuxiang 28 Bf 36.50N 112.51 E
Duarte, Pico- 38 Lh 19.00N 71.00W
Duartina 55 Hf 22.24S 49.25W
Dubawnt 42 Hd 64.30N 100.06W
Dubawnt Lake 38 Ic 63.08N 101.30W
Ḑubay'ah, Ra's- 24 Pj 24.20N 54.09 E
Dubayy 22 Hg 25.18N 55.18 E
Dubbo 58 Fh 32.15S 148.36 E
Dübener Heide 10 Ie 51.40N 12.40 E
Dubenski 16 Td 51.29N 56.38 E
Dubh Artach 9 Ge 56.08N 6.39W
Dubica 14 Ke 45.13N 16.48 E
Dublin 43 Ke 32.32N 82.54W
Dublin/Baile Átha Cliath [2] 9 Gh 53.20N 6.15W
Dublin/Baile Átha Cliath 6 Fe 53.20N 6.15W
Dublin Bay/Cuan Bhaile Átha Cliath 9 Gh 53.20N 6.06W
Dubljany 10 Tg 49.26N 23.16 E
Dublon 64d Bb 7.23N 151.53 E
Dubna 8 Lh 56.20N 26.31 E
Dubna 19 Dd 56.47N 37.10 E
Dubnica nad Váhom 10 Oh 48.58N 18.10 E
Dubno 19 Ce 50.29N 25.46 E
Du Bois 44 He 41.06N 78.46W
Dubois [Id.-U.S.] 46 Id 44.10N 112.14W
Dubois [Wy.-U.S.] 46 Ke 43.33N 109.38W
Dubossary 16 Ff 47.17N 29.10 E
Dubovka 19 Ef 49.03N 44.50 E
Dubovoje 10 Ih 48.08N 23.59 E
Dubreka 34 Cd 9.48N 13.31W
Dubrovica 16 Ed 51.34N 26.34 E
Dubrovnik 6 Hg 42.39N 18.07 E
Dubrovno 7 Hi 54.33N 30.41 E
Dubrovnoje 19 Gd 57.58N 69.25 E
Dubuque 43 Ic 42.30N 90.41W
Dubysa 8 Ji 55.02N 23.27 E
Duc de Gloucester, Iles du-=Duke of Gloucester, Islands (En) 57 Mg 20.38S 143.20W
Duchang 28 Dj 29.16N 116.11 E
Duchesne 46 Jf 40.10N 110.24W
Duchess 59 Hd 21.22S 139.52 E
Ducie Atoll 57 Og 24.40S 124.47W
Duck River 44 Dg 36.02N 87.52W
Duckwater Peak 46 Hg 38.58N 115.26W
Duclair 12 Ce 49.29N 0.53 E
Duc Lap 25 Lf 12.27N 107.38 E
Ducos 51h Bb 14.34N 60.58W
Dudelange/Düdelingen 12 Ie 49.28N 6.06 E
Duderstadt 10 Ge 51.31N 10.16 E
Dudinka 22 Kc 69.25N 86.15 E
Dudley 9 Ki 52.30N 2.05W
Dūdo 35 Id 9.20N 50.14 E
Dudub 35 Hd 6.55N 46.42 E
Dudune 63b Ce 21.21S 167.44 E
Dudváh 10 Ni 47.58N 17.50 E
Dudweiler, Saarbrücken- 12 Je 49.17N 7.02 E
Düdwēyn 35 Gd 9.19N 44.53 E
Dudypta 20 Db 70.55N 89.50 E
Duékoué 34 Dd 6.45N 7.21W
Dueodde 8 Fj 54.59N 15.05 E
Duerna 13 Gb 42.19N 5.54W
Duero 5 Fg 41.08N 8.40W
Dufek Coast 66 Lg 84.30S 179.00W
Duffer Peak 46 Ff 41.40N 118.44W
Duff Islands 57 He 9.50S 167.10 E
Dugi Otok 14 Ii 44.00N 15.00 E
Dugo Selo 14 Ke 45.48N 16.15 E
Du Gué, Rivière- 42 Ke 57.20N 70.46W
Duhovnickoje 16 Pc 52.29N 48.15 E
Duijan Yan 27 He 31.01N 103.28 E
Duiru → Wuchuan 27 If 28.28N 107.57 E
Duisburg 10 Ce 51.26N 6.45 E
Duitama 54 Db 5.50N 73.02W
Dujūma 35 Ge 1.14N 42.34 E
Dukagjini 15 Cg 42.18N 19.45 E
Dūkān 24 Ke 35.56N 44.58 E
Dukan, Sad ad- 24 Kd 36.10N 44.56 E
Dukat 15 Fg 42.26N 22.21 E
Duke of Gloucester Islands (EN)=Duc de Gloucester, Iles du- 57 Mg 20.38S 143.20W
Duke of York 63a Aa 4.10S 152.28 E
Duke of York Bay 42 Jc 65.25N 84.50W
Duk Fadiat 35 Ed 7.45N 31.25 E
Duk Faiwil 35 Ed 7.30N 31.29 E
Dukielska, Przełęcz- 10 Rg 49.25N 21.42 E
Dukku 34 Hc 10.49N 10.46 E
Dukla 10 Rg 49.34N 21.41 E
Dukou 22 Mg 26.31N 101.44 E
Dūkštas/Dukštas 8 Li 55.32N 26.28 E
Dukštas/Dūkštas 8 Li 55.32N 26.28 E
Dulan (Qagan Us) 22 Lf 36.29N 98.29 E
Dulce, Bahía- 48 Ji 16.30N 98.50W
Dulce, Golfo- 47 Hg 8.36N 83.15W
Dulce, Río- 52 Ji 30.31S 62.32W
Dulce Nombre de Culmi 49 Ef 15.09N 85.37W
Duldurga 20 Gf 50.38N 113.35 E
Dulgalah 20 Pc 67.30N 133.20 E
Dulia 36 Db 2.57N 24.08 E
Dülmen 10 De 51.50N 7.18 E
Dulovka 8 Mg 57.27N 28.29 E
Dulovo 15 Kf 43.49N 27.09 E
Duluth 39 Je 46.47N 92.06W
Dūmā 24 Gf 33.35N 36.24 E
Dumaguete 26 He 9.18N 123.18 E
Dumai 26 Df 1.41N 101.27 E
Dumaran 26 Gd 10.33N 119.51 E
Dumaresq River 59 Ke 28.40S 150.28 E
Dumas [Ar.-U.S.] 45 Kj 33.53N 91.29W
Dumas [Tx.-U.S.] 45 Fi 35.52N 101.58W
Dumayr 24 Gf 33.38N 36.40 E
Dumbarton 9 If 55.57N 4.35W
Dumbéa 63b Cf 22.09S 166.27 E
Dumbrăveni [Rom.] 15 Jb 47.39N 26.25 E
Dumbrăveni [Rom.] 15 Hc 46.14N 24.34 E
Dumfries 9 Jf 55.04N 3.37W
Dumfries and Galloway [3] 9 Jf 55.10N 3.35W
Dumka 25 Hd 24.16N 87.15 E
Dumlupinar 15 Mk 38.52N 30.00 E
Dümmer 10 Ed 52.31N 8.19 E
Dumoine, Lac- 44 Ib 46.52N 77.52W
Dumoine, Rivière- 44 Ib 46.13N 77.50W
Dumont d'Urville 66 Je 66.40S 140.01 E
Dumont D'Urville Sea (EN) 66 Je 63.00S 140.00 E
Dumpu 58 Fe 5.52S 145.46 E
Dümrek 15 Lk 38.40N 28.24 E
Dumuhe 28 La 46.21N 133.33 E
Dumyāṭ=Damietta (EN) 31 Ke 31.25N 31.48 E
Dumyāṭ, Maṣabb- 24 Dg 31.27N 31.51 E
Duna=Danube (EN) 5 If 45.20N 29.40 E
Dunaföldvár 10 Oi 46.48N 18.56 E
Dunaharaszti 10 Pi 47.21N 19.05 E
Dunaj 20 Ih 42.57N 132.20 E
Dunaj=Danube (EN) 5 If 45.20N 29.40 E
Dunajec 10 Qf 50.15N 20.44 E
Dunajevcy 16 Ee 48.51N 26.44 E
Dunajská Streda 10 Ni 47.01N 17.38 E
Dunakeszi 10 Pi 47.38N 19.08 E
Dunántúl 10 Nj 47.00N 18.00 E
Dunărea=Danube (EN) 5 If 45.20N 29.40 E
Dunărea Veche 15 Ld 45.17N 28.02 E
Dunării, Delta-=Danube, Mouths of the- (EN) 5 If 45.30N 29.45 E
Duna-Tisza Köze 10 Pj 46.45N 19.30 E
Dunaújváros 10 Oj 46.58N 18.56 E
Dunav=Danube (EN) 5 If 45.20N 29.40 E
Dunavățu de Jos 15 Me 44.59N 29.13 E
Dunav-Tisa-Dunav kanal 15 Dd 45.10N 20.50 E
Dunback 62 Df 45.23S 170.38 E
Dunbar 9 Kf 56.00N 2.31W
Duncan [Az.-U.S.] 46 Kj 32.43N 109.06W
Duncan [B.C.-Can.] 46 Db 48.47N 123.42W
Duncan [Ok.-U.S.] 43 He 34.30N 97.57W
Duncan Passage 25 If 11.00N 92.00 E
Duncansby Head 5 Fd 58.39N 3.01W
Dundaga 8 Jg 57.31N 22.14 E
Dundalk 44 If 39.15N 76.31W
Dundalk/Dún Dealgan 9 Gg 54.01N 6.25W
Dundalk Bay/Cuan Dhun Dealgan 9 Gh 53.57N 6.17W
Dundas [Grld.] 41 Fc 76.30N 69.00W
Dundas [Ont.-Can.] 44 Hd 43.16N 79.58W
Dundas, Lake- 59 Ef 32.35S 121.50 E
Dundas Peninsula 42 Gb 74.40N 113.00W
Dundas Strait 59 Gb 11.20S 131.35 E
Dún Dealgan/Dundalk 9 Gg 54.01N 6.25W
Dundee [S.Afr.] 37 Ee 28.12S 30.16 E
Dundee [Scot.-U.K.] 6 Fd 56.28N 3.00W
Dund Hot → Zhenglan Qi 28 Cc 42.14N 115.59 E
Dundrum Bay/Cuan Dhún Droma 9 Hg 54.13N 5.45W
Dunedin [Fl.-U.S.] 44 Fk 28.02N 82.47W
Dunedin [N.Z.] 58 Ii 45.53S 170.31 E
Dunfanaghy 9 Ff 55.11N 7.59W
Dunfermline 9 Je 56.04N 3.29W
Dungannon/Dún Geanainn 9 Gg 54.31N 6.46W
Dún Garbhán/Dungarvan 9 Fi 52.05N 7.37W
Dūngarpur 25 Ed 23.50N 73.43 E
Dungarvan/Dún Garbhán 9 Fi 52.05N 7.37W
Dungas 34 Gc 13.04N 9.20 E
Dungau 10 Ih 48.45N 12.30 E
Dún Geanainn/Dungannon 9 Gg 54.31N 6.46W
Dungeness 9 Nk 50.55N 0.58 E
Dungu 36 Eb 3.42N 28.40 E
Dungu 36 Eb 3.37N 28.34 E
Dunhua 27 Mc 43.22N 128.12 E
Dunhuang 27 Fc 40.10N 94.50 E
Dunkerque 11 Ic 51.03N 2.22 E
Dunkery Beacon 9 Jj 51.11N 3.35W
Dunkirk 43 Lc 42.29N 79.21W
Dunkwa 34 Ed 5.58N 1.47W
Dún Laoghaire 9 Gh 53.17N 6.08W
Dún Mánmhai/Dunmanway 9 Dj 51.43N 9.07W
Dunmanway/Dún Mánmhai 9 Dj 51.43N 9.07W
Dunn 44 Hh 35.19N 78.37W
Dún na nGall/Donegal [2] 9 Fg 54.50N 8.00W
Dún na nGall/Donegal 9 Eg 54.39N 8.06W
Dunnellon 44 Fk 29.03N 82.28W
Dunnet Head 9 Jc 58.39N 3.23W
Dunning 45 Ff 41.50N 100.06W
Dún Pádraig/Downpatrick 9 Hg 54.20N 5.43W
Dunqulah=Dongola (EN) 31 Kg 19.10N 30.29 E
Dunqulah al Qadīmah 35 Eb 18.13N 30.45 E
Dunqunāb 35 Fa 21.06N 37.05 E
Dunqunāb, Khalīj- 35 Fa 21.05N 37.08 E
Dunrankin 44 Fa 48.39N 83.04W
Duns 9 Kf 55.47N 2.20W
Dünsberg 12 Kd 50.39N 8.35 E
Dunsmuir 46 Df 41.13N 122.16W
Dunstable 12 Bc 51.53N 0.31W
Dunstan Mountains 62 Cf 44.55S 169.30 E
Dun-sur-Auron 11 Ih 46.53N 2.34 E
Dun-sur-Meuse 12 He 49.23N 5.11 E
Duntroon 62 Df 44.51S 170.41 E
Dunvegan 9 Gd 57.26N 6.35W
Duobukur 27 La 50.19N 124.57 E
Duolun (Dolonnur) 27 Kc 42.10N 116.30 E
Duong Dong 25 Kf 10.13N 103.58 E
Dupree 45 Fd 45.03N 101.36W
Duqm 22 Hf 19.41N 57.32 E
Duque de Bragança, Quedas- 30 Ii 9.05S 16.10 E
Duque de Caxias 54 Jh 22.47S 43.18W
Duque de York, Isla- 56 Eh 50.40S 75.20W
Du Quoin 45 Lg 38.01N 89.14W
Durack Range 59 Fc 17.00S 128.00 E
Durack River 59 Fc 15.33S 127.52 E
Durağan 24 Fb 41.25N 35.04 E
Durance 5 Gg 43.55N 4.44 E
Durand 45 Kd 44.38N 91.58W
Durand, Récif- 63b Df 22.02S 168.39 E
Durango [2] 47 Dd 24.50N 104.50W
Durango [Co.-U.S.] 39 If 37.16N 107.53W
Durango [Sp.] 13 Ja 43.10N 2.37W
Durañona 55 Bm 37.15S 60.31W
Durant 43 He 33.59N 96.23W
Duras 11 Gj 44.40N 0.11 E
Duratón 13 Hc 41.37N 4.07W
Durazno 56 Id 33.22S 56.31W
Durazno [2] 55 Dk 33.05S 56.05W
Durazno, Cuchilla Grande del- 55 Dk 33.15S 56.15W
Durazzo (EN)=Durresi 15 Ch 41.19N 19.26 E
Durban 31 Kk 29.55S 30.56 E
Durbe 8 Ih 56.39N 21.14 E
Durbet-Daba, Pereval- 27 Eb 49.37N 89.25 E
Ḑurbo 35 Ic 11.30N 50.18 E
Durbuy 12 Hd 50.21N 5.28 E
Đurđevac 14 Ld 46.02N 17.04 E
Düren 10 Cf 50.48N 6.29 E
Durg 25 Gd 21.11N 81.17 E
Durgāpur 25 Hd 23.30N 87.15 E
Durgen-Nur 27 Fb 47.40N 93.30 E
Durham 9 Lg 54.45N 1.45W
Durham [3] 9 Lg 54.45N 1.40W
Durham [Eng.-U.K.] 9 Lg 54.47N 1.34W
Durham [N.C.-U.S.] 43 Ld 35.59N 78.54W
Durkee 46 Gd 44.36N 117.28W
Durlas/Thurles 9 Fi 52.41N 7.49W
Ḑurmā 23 Ge 24.37N 46.08 E
Durmersheim 12 Kf 48.56N 8.16 E
Durmitor 5 Hg 43.09N 19.02 E
Durnford, Punta- 32 De 23.37N 16.00W
Durresi=Durazzo (EN) 15 Ch 41.19N 19.26 E
Durrësit, Gjiri- 15 Ch 41.16N 19.28 E
Dursey/Oileán Baoi 9 Cj 51.36N 10.12W
Dursunbey 24 Cc 39.35N 28.38 E
Durtal 11 Fg 47.40N 0.15W
Duru → Wuchuan 27 If 28.28N 107.57 E
Duruksi 35 Hd 8.29N 45.38 E
Durusu Gölü 15 Lh 41.20N 28.38 E
Durūz, Jabal ad- 24 Gf 32.40N 36.44 E
D'Urville Island 61 Dh 40.50S 173.50 E
Dušak 18 Cf 37.15N 60.01 E
Dusa Mareb 35 Hd 5.31N 46.24 E
Dušanbe 22 If 38.35N 68.48 E
Dušeti 16 Nh 42.05N 44.42 E
Dusetos 8 Li 55.42N 26.02 E
Dushan 22 Mg 25.55N 107.36 E
Dushan Hu 28 Dg 35.06N 116.48 E
Dusios Ežeras/Dusja, Ozero- 8 Jj 54.15N 23.45 E
Dusja, Ozero-/Dusios Ežeras 8 Jj 54.15N 23.45 E
Dusky Sound 62 Bf 45.45S 166.30 E
Düsseldorf 6 Ge 51.13N 6.46 E
Dusti 18 Gf 37.22N 68.43 E
Dutch Harbor 40a Eb 53.53N 166.32W
Dutlwe 37 Cd 23.58S 23.54 E
Dutton, Mount- 46 Ig 38.01N 112.13W
Duved 8 Ea 63.24N 12.52 E
Duvergé 49 Ld 18.22N 71.31W
Düvertepe 15 Lj 39.14N 28.27 E
Duvno 14 Lg 43.43N 17.14 E
Duwayhin 23 He 24.16N 51.20 E
Duwayhin, Khawr- 24 Nj 24.20N 51.25 E
Duyfken Point 59 Ib 12.35S 141.40 E
Duyun 27 If 26.20N 107.28 E
Düz 32 Ic 33.28N 9.01 E
Düzce 23 Da 40.50N 31.10 E
Dve Mogili 15 If 43.36N 25.52 E
Dvina (EN)=Daugava 19 Cd 57.04N 24.03 E
Dvina Gulf (EN)=Dvinskaja Guba 5 Jb 65.00N 39.45 E
Dvinskaja Guba=Dvina Gulf (EN) 5 Jb 65.00N 39.45 E
Dvor 14 Ke 45.04N 16.23 E
Dvuh Cirkov, Gora- 20 Lc 67.31N 168.20 E
Dvůr Králové nad Labem 10 Lf 50.26N 15.48 E
Dwārka 25 Dd 22.14N 68.58 E
Dworshak Reservoir 46 Hc 46.45N 116.00W
Dyer, Cape- 38 Mc 66.37N 61.18W
Dyero 34 Dc 12.50N 6.30W
Dyer Plateau 66 Qf 70.45S 65.30W
Dyersburg 43 Jd 36.03N 89.23W
Dyfed [3] 9 Ji 52.05N 4.00W
Dyhtau, Gora- 16 Mh 43.05N 43.12 E
Dyje 10 Mh 48.37N 16.56 E
Dyjsko-Svratecký úval 10 Mh 48.55N 16.25 E
Dyle 12 Gd 50.57N 4.40 E
Dylewska Góra 10 Pc 53.34N 19.57 E
Dynów 10 Sg 49.49N 22.14 E
Dyr, Djebel- 14 Cn 36.13N 8.46 E
Dyrhólaey 5 Ec 63.24N 19.08W
Dysnų Ežeras/Disnaj, Ozero- 7 Gi 55.35N 26.32 E
Dytike Rodhópi 15 Hh 41.45N 24.05 E
Dzabhan 21 Le 48.54N 93.23 E
Džagdy, Hrebet- 20 If 53.40N 131.00 E
Džalagaš 19 Gf 45.05N 64.40 E
Džalal-Abad 18 Id 40.56N 73.05 E
Džalilabad 19 Eh 39.12N 48.31 E
Džalinda 20 Hf 53.31N 123.59 E
Džambejty 16 Rd 50.14N 52.38 E
Džambul [Kaz.-U.S.S.R.] 22 Je 42.54N 71.22 E
Džambul [Kaz.-U.S.S.R.] 19 Hf 47.17N 71.42 E
Džambulskaja Oblast [3] 19 Hg 44.30N 72.30 E
Dzamyn-Ud 27 Jb 43.50N 111.45 E
Džanak 16 Si 40.30N 55.35 E
Džanga 19 Fg 40.01N 53.10 E
Džankoj 19 Df 45.42N 34.22 E
Džansugurov 19 Hf 45.23N 79.29 E
Džanybek 19 Ef 49.24N 46.50 E
Dzaoudzi 31 Lj 12.47S 45.17 E
Džardžan 20 Hc 68.55N 124.05 E
Džargalant 27 Gb 47.20N 99.35 E
Dzargalant 27 Ib 48.35N 105.50 E
Džarkurgan 19 Gh 37.29N 67.25 E
Džava 16 Mh 42.24N 43.53 E
Džebariki-Haja 20 Id 62.23N 135.50 E
Džebel [Bul.] 15 Ih 41.30N 25.18 E
Džebel [Tur.-U.S.S.R.] 16 Sj 39.37N 54.18 E
Džebrail 16 Oj 39.23N 47.01 E
Dzereg 27 Fb 47.08N 92.50 E
Džergalan 18 Lc 42.33N 79.02 E
Dzermuk 16 Nj 39.48N 45.39 E
Dzeržinsk [Bye.-U.S.S.R.] 16 Ec 53.44N 27.08 E
Dzeržinsk [R.S.F.S.R.] 19 Ed 56.16N 43.32 E
Dzeržinsk [Ukr.-U.S.S.R.] 16 Je 48.22N 37.50 E
Dzeržinskaja, Gora- 8 Lk 53.53N 27.10 E
Dzeržinskoje 20 Ee 56.49N 95.18 E
Džetygara 22 Id 52.11N 61.12 E
Džetysaj 18 Gd 40.49N 68.20 E
Džezkazgan [Kaz.-U.S.S.R.] 19 Gf 47.53N 67.27 E
Džezkazgan [Kaz.-U.S.S.R.] 22 Ie 47.47N 67.46 E
Džezkazganskaja Oblast [3] 19 Gf 47.30N 70.00 E
Dzhugdzhur Range (EN)=Džugdžur, Hrebet- 21 Pd 58.00N 136.00 E
Działdówka 10 Qd 52.58N 20.05 E
Działdowo 10 Qc 53.15N 20.10 E
Działoszyce 10 Qf 50.22N 20.21 E
Dzibalchén 48 Oh 19.31N 89.45W
Dzibilchaltún 48 Og 21.05N 89.36W
Dzierzgoń 10 Pc 53.56N 19.21 E
Dzierżoniów 10 Mf 50.44N 16.39 E
Džirgatal 18 He 39.13N 71.12 E
Džizak 19 Gg 40.07N 67.52 E
Džizakskaja Oblast [3] 19 Gg 40.20N 67.40 E
Džugdžur, Hrebet-=Dzhugdzhur Range (EN) 21 Pd 58.00N 136.00 E
Džūkste/Dzukste 8 Jh 56.45N 23.10 E
Dzukste/Džūkste 8 Jh 56.45N 23.10 E
Džulfa 16 Nj 38.59N 45.35 E
Džuma 18 Fe 39.44N 66.39 E
Dzun-Bajan 27 Jc 44.26N 110.03 E
Dzungarian Basin (EN)=Junggar Pendi 21 Ke 45.00N 88.00 E
Dzungarian Gate (EN)=Alataw Shankou 21 Ke 45.25N 82.25 E
Dzungarian Gate (EN)=Džungarskije Vorota 21 Ke 45.25N 82.25 E
Džungarski Alatau, Hrebet- 21 Ke 45.00N 81.00 E
Džungarskije Vorota=Dzungarian Gate (EN) 21 Ke 45.25N 82.25 E
Dzun-Hara 27 Ib 48.40N 106.40 E
Dzun-Mod 27 Ib 47.50N 106.57 E
Džurak-Sal 16 Mf 47.18N 43.36 E
Džusaly 19 Gf 45.29N 64.05 E
Dzvari 16 Mh 42.42N 42.02 E

E

Éadan Doire/Edenderry 9 Fh 53.21N 7.03W
Eads 45 Eg 38.29N 102.47W
Eagle 40 Kd 64.46N 141.16W
Eagle 42 Lf 53.35N 57.25W
Eagle Creek 46 La 52.22N 107.24W
Eagle Lake 44 Mb 47.02N 68.36W
Eagle Lake [Ca.-U.S.] 46 Ef 40.39N 120.44W
Eagle Lake [Me.-U.S.] 44 Mb 46.20N 69.20W
Eagle Lake [Ont.-Can.] 45 Jb 49.42N 93.13W
Eagle Mountain 45 Kc 47.54N 90.33W
Eagle Nest 45 Dh 36.35N 105.14W
Eagle Pass 43 Gf 28.43N 100.30W
Eagle Peak [Ca.-U.S.] 46 Cc 41.17N 120.12W
Eagle Peak [Tx.-U.S.] 45 Dk 30.56N 105.01W
Eagle River [Ak.-U.S.] 40 Jd 61.19N 149.34W
Eagle River [Wi.-U.S.] 45 Ld 45.55N 89.15W
Eagle Summit 40 Jc 65.30N 145.38W
Ealing, London- 12 Bc 51.30N 0.19W
Ear Falls 45 Ja 50.38N 93.13W
Earn 9 Je 56.25N 3.30W
Earn, Loch- 9 Ie 56.25N 4.10W
Earnslaw, Mount- 62 Cf 44.37S 168.25 E
Easley 44 Fh 34.50N 82.36W
East Alligator River 59 Gb 12.08S 132.42 E
East Anglia 9 Ni 52.25N 1.00 E
East Angus 44 Lc 45.29N 71.40W
East Bay [Can.] 42 Jd 64.05N 81.30W
East Bay [U.S.] 45 Ll 29.05N 89.15W
East Berlin (EN)=Berlin (Ost) [2] 10 Jd 52.30N 13.25 E
East Berlin (EN)=Berlin (Ost) 6 He 52.31N 13.24 E
Eastbourne [Eng.-U.K.] 9 Nk 50.46N 0.17 E
Eastbourne [N.Z.] 62 Fd 41.17S 174.54 E
East Caicos 49 Lc 21.41N 71.30W
East Cape [Fl.-U.S.] 44 Gm 25.07N 81.05W
East Cape [N.Z.] 57 Ih 37.41S 178.33 E
East Caroline Basin (EN) 3 Ii 4.00N 146.45 E
East Chicago 44 De 41.38N 87.27W
East China Sea (EN)=Dong Hai 21 Og 29.00N 125.00 E
East China Sea (EN)=Higashi-Shina-Kai 21 Og 29.00N 125.00 E
East Coast [2] 62 Gc 38.20S 177.50 E
East Dereham 9 Ni 52.41N 0.56 E
Eastend 46 Kb 49.31N 108.48W
East Entrance 64a Bb 7.50N 134.40 E
Easter Island (EN)=Pascua, Isla de-/Rapa Nui 57 Qg 27.07S 109.22W
Easter Island (EN)=Rapa Nui/Pascua, Isla de- 57 Qg 27.07S 109.22W
Eastern [Ghana] [3] 34 Ed 6.30N 0.30W
Eastern [Kenya] [3] 36 Gb 0.05N 38.00 E
Eastern [S.L.] [3] 34 Cd 8.15N 11.00W
Eastern [Ug.] [3] 36 Fb 1.30N 33.50 E
Eastern [Zam.] [3] 36 Fe 13.00S 32.15 E
Eastern Fields 60 Dj 10.03S 145.22 E

Index Symbols

[1] Independent Nation
[2] State, Region
[3] District, County
[4] Municipality
[5] Colony, Dependency
Continent
Physical Region
Historical or Cultural Region
Mount, Mountain
Volcano
Hill
Mountains, Mountain Range
Hills, Escarpment
Plateau, Upland
Pass, Gap
Plain, Lowland
Delta
Salt Flat
Valley, Canyon
Crater, Cave
Karst Features
Depression
Polder
Desert, Dunes
Forest, Woods
Heath, Steppe
Oasis
Cape, Point
Coast, Beach
Cliff
Peninsula
Isthmus
Sandbank
Island
Atoll
Rock, Reef
Islands, Archipelago
Rocks, Reefs
Coral Reef
Well, Spring
Geyser
River, Stream
Waterfall Rapids
River Mouth, Estuary
Lake
Salt Lake
Intermittent Lake
Reservoir
Swamp, Pond
Canal
Glacier
Ice Shelf, Pack Ice
Ocean
Sea
Gulf, Bay
Strait, Fjord
Lagoon
Bank
Seamount
Tablemount
Ridge
Shelf
Basin
Escarpment, Sea Scarp
Fracture
Trench, Abyss
National Park, Reserve
Point of Interest
Recreation Site
Cave, Cavern
Historic Site
Ruins
Wall, Walls
Church, Abbey
Temple
Scientific Station
Airport
Port
Lighthouse
Mine
Tunnel
Dam, Bridge

Index Symbols

[1] Independent Nation
[2] State, Region
[3] District, County
[4] Municipality
[5] Colony, Dependency
■ Continent
Physical Region

Pass, Gap
Mount, Mountain
Volcano
Hill
Mountains, Mountain Range
Hills, Escarpment
Plateau, Upland

Plain, Lowland
Delta
Salt Flat
Valley, Canyon
Crater, Cave
Karst Features

Depression
Polder
Desert, Dunes
Forest, Woods
Heath, Steppe
Oasis
Cape, Point

Coast, Beach
Cliff
Peninsula
Isthmus
Sandbank
Island
Atoll

Rock, Reef
Islands, Archipelago
Rocks, Reefs
Coral Reef
Well, Spring
Geyser
River, Stream

Waterfall Rapids
River Mouth, Estuary
Lake
Salt Lake
Ice Shelf, Pack Ice
Ocean
Sea
Gulf, Bay
Strait, Fjord

Canal
Glacier
Bank
Seamount
Tablemount
Ridge
Shelf
Basin

Lagoon
Escarpment, Sea Scarp
Fracture
Trench, Abyss
National Park, Reserve
Point of Interest
Recreation Site
Cave, Cavern

Historic Site
Ruins
Wall, Walls
Church, Abbey
Temple
Scientific Station
Airport

Port
Lighthouse
Mine
Tunnel
Dam, Bridge

Elm 10 Gd 52.09N 10.53 E
El Macao 49 Md 18.46N 68.33W
Elmadağ 24 Ec 39.55N 33.15 E
Elma Daği 15 Mk 38.46N 29.32 E
El Maestrat/El Maestrazgo 13 Ld 40.30N 0.10W
El Maestrazgo/El Maestrat 13 Ld 40.30N 0.10W
El Mahia 34 Ea 22.30N 2.30W
El Maitén 56 Ff 42.03S 71.10W
Elmaki 34 Gb 17.55N 8.20 E
El Malah 13 Ph 36.18N 3.14 E
Elmalı 24 Ic 39.25N 40.35 E
Elmali 24 Cd 36.44N 29.56 E
El Manteco 50 Ei 7.27N 62.32W
El Marfil 55 Bb 15.35S 60.19W
El Marsa 13 Mh 36.24N 0.55 E
El Medo 35 Gd 5.41N 41.46 E
El Meghaier 32 Ic 33.57N 5.56 E
Elmhurst 45 Mf 41.53N 87.56W
El Milagro 56 Gd 31.01S 65.59W
Elmira 43 Lc 42.06N 76.50W
El Mrâyer 32 Fe 21.30N 8.10W
El Mreïti 32 Fe 23.29N 7.52W
El Mreyyé 30 Gg 19.30N 7.00W
Elmshorn 10 Fc 53.45N 9.39 E
Elmstein 12 Je 49.22N 7.56 E
Elne 11 Il 42.36N 2.58 E
El Nevado, Cerro- 56 Ge 35.35S 68.30W
El Niabo 35 Fe 4.33N 39.59 E
El Nihuil 56 Gd 34.58S 68.40W
El Novillo 48 Ec 28.40N 109.30W
El Novillo, Presa- 48 Ec 29.05N 109.45W
El Ochenta y Uno 48 Kg 21.35N 97.57W
Elorn 11 Bf 48.27N 4.16W
Elortondo 55 Bk 33.42S 61.37W
Elorza 54 Eb 7.03N 69.31W
Elota, Rio- 48 Ff 23.52N 106.56W
El Oued 32 Ic 33.20N 6.53 E
Eloy 46 Jj 32.45N 111.33W
El Palmar 50 Fh 8.01N 61.53W
El Palmito 48 Ge 25.40N 104.59W
El Panadés/El Penedès 13 Nc 41.25N 1.30 E
El Pao [Ven.] 50 Eh 8.06N 62.33W
El Pao [Ven.] 50 Bh 9.38N 68.08W
El Paraíso 49 Df 14.10N 86.30W
El Paraíso 49 Dg 13.51N 86.34W
El Páramo 13 Gb 42.25N 5.45W
El Pardo, Madrid- 13 Id 40.32N 3.46W
El Paso [Il.-U.S.] 45 Lf 40.44N 89.01W
El Paso [Tx.-U.S.] 39 If 31.45N 106.29W
El Penedès/El Panadés 13 Nc 41.25N 1.30 E
El Perú 50 Fi 7.19N 61.49W
El Pico 54 Fg 15.57S 64.42W
El Pilar 50 Eg 10.32N 63.09W
El Pintado 56 Hb 24.38S 61.27W
El Porvenir [Hond.] 49 Df 14.41N 87.11W
El Porvenir [Pan.] 49 Hi 9.12N 80.08W
El Porvenir [Ven.] 50 Bi 6.55N 68.42W
El Potosí 48 Ie 24.51N 100.19W
El Prat de Llobregat/Prat de Llobregat 13 Oc 41.20N 2.06 E
El Priorat/El Priorato 13 Mc 41.10N 1.00 E
El Priorato/El Priorat 13 Mc 41.10N 1.00 E
El Progreso 49 Cf 14.50N 90.00W
El Progreso [Guat.] 49 Bf 14.51N 90.04W
El Progreso [Hond.] 47 Ge 15.21N 87.49W
El Puente del Arzobispo 13 Ge 39.48N 5.10W
El Puerto 48 Dc 28.45N 111.20W
El Puerto de Santa María 13 Fh 36.36N 6.13W
El Rastro 50 Ch 9.03N 67.27W
El Real de Santa María 49 Ii 8.08N 77.43W
El Reno 43 Hd 35.32N 97.57W
El Ribeiro 13 Db 42.25N 8.10W
Elrose 46 Ka 51.13N 108.01W
El Saler 13 Le 39.23N 0.20W
El Salto 47 Cd 23.47N 105.23W
El Salvador 39 Kh 13.50N 88.55W
El Samán de Apure 50 Bi 7.55N 68.44W
El Sauce [Mex.] 48 De 24.34N 111.29W
El Sauce [Nic.] 49 Dg 12.53N 86.32W
El Sáuz 48 Fc 29.03N 106.15W
Elsberry 45 Kg 39.10N 90.47W
Elsdorf 12 Id 50.56N 6.34 E
Else 12 Kb 52.12N 8.40 E
El Seibo 49 Md 18.46N 68.52W
Elsen, Paderborn- 12 Kc 51.44N 8.41 E
Elsen Nur 27 Fd 35.08N 92.20 E
'Êl Shâma 35 Ge 2.46N 41.03 E
El Socorro 50 Dh 8.59N 65.44W
El Sombrero 54 Eb 9.23N 67.03W
Elst 12 Hc 51.55N 5.52 E
Elsterwerda 10 Je 51.27N 13.32 E
El Sueco 47 Cc 29.54N 106.24W
El-Taht 13 Mi 35.27N 0.46 E
El Tajín 47 Ed 20.27N 97.23W
El Tala 56 Gc 26.07S 65.17W
Eltanin Bay 66 Pf 73.40S 82.00W
Eltham 62 Fc 39.26S 174.18 E
El Tigre 53 Je 8.55N 64.15W
El Tigre, Isla- 49 Dg 13.16N 87.38W
El Toboso 13 Je 39.31N 3.00W
El Tocuyo 54 Eb 9.47N 69.48W
Elton 16 Oe 49.08N 46.50 E
Elton, Ozero- 19 Ef 49.10N 46.40 E
El Torcal 13 Hh 36.55N 4.35W
El Trébol 55 Bk 32.12S 61.42W
El Trigo 55 Cl 35.52S 59.24W
El Triunfo [Hond.] 49 Dg 13.06N 87.00W
El Triunfo [Mex.] 48 Df 23.47N 110.08W
El Tuito 48 Gg 20.19N 105.22W
El Turbio 56 Fh 51.41S 72.05W
Eltville am Rhein 12 Kd 50.02N 8.07 E
Eltz 12 Jd 50.12N 7.18 E
Elūru 25 Ge 17.05N 82.15 E
Elva 7 Gg 58.13N 26.25 E
El Valle 49 Gi 8.31N 80.08W
El Valles/Valles 13 Oc 41.35N 2.15 E
Elvas 13 Ef 38.53N 7.10W
El Vejo, Cerro- 54 Db 7.30N 73.05W
El Venado, Isla- 49 Fh 11.57N 83.44W
El Vendrell/Vendrell 13 Nc 41.13N 1.32 E
Elverum 7 Cf 60.53N 11.34 E
El Viejo 49 Dg 12.40N 87.10W
El Viejo, Volcán 38 Kh 12.38N 87.11W
El Vigia 49 Li 8.38N 71.39W
El Vigia, Cerro- 48 Gg 21.25N 104.00W
El Wak 36 Hb 2.49N 40.56 E
Elwell, Lake- 46 Jb 48.22N 111.17W
Elwood 44 Ee 40.17N 85.50W
Ely [Eng.-U.K.] 9 Ni 52.24N 0.16 E
Ely [Mn.-U.S.] 43 Ib 47.54N 91.51W
Ely [Nv.-U.S.] 39 Hf 39.15N 114.53W
Elyria 44 Fe 41.22N 82.06W
El Yunque 51a Cb 18.18N 65.47W
Elz 12 Kd 50.25N 8.02 E
Elzbach 12 Jd 50.12N 7.22 E
Emaé 63b Dc 17.04S 168.22 E
Ema Jõgi/Emajygi 8 Lf 58.20N 27.15 E
Emajygi/Ema Jõgi 8 Lf 58.20N 27.15 E
Emali 36 Gc 2.05S 37.28 E
Emāmshahr [Iran] 23 Ib 36.25N 55.01 E
Emāmshahr [Iran] 22 Hf 36.50N 54.29 E
Emāmzādeh 'Abbās 24 Lf 32.25N 47.55 E
Emån 7 Dh 57.08N 16.30 E
Emba 19 Ff 48.50N 58.10 E
Emba 5 Lf 46.38N 53.04 E
Embaracai, Rio- 55 Ff 23.27S 53.58W
Embarcación 56 Hb 23.13S 64.06W
Embarras Portage 42 Ge 58.25N 111.27W
Embarras River 45 Mg 38.39N 87.37W
Embira, Rio- 54 De 7.19S 70.15W
Embrun 11 Mj 44.34N 6.30 E
Embu 36 Gc 0.32S 37.27 E
Emden 10 Dc 53.22N 7.13 E
Emeldžak 20 He 58.27N 126.57 E
Emerald 58 Fg 23.32S 148.10 E
Emerald 42 Ga 76.50N 114.00W
Emerson 45 Hb 49.00N 97.12W
Emet 24 Cc 39.20N 29.15 E
Emiliano Zapata 48 Ni 17.45N 91.46W
Emilia-Romagna 14 Ef 44.45N 11.00 E
Emilio R. Coni 55 Cj 30.04S 58.16W
Emili Rock 52 Hh 29.40S 87.25W
Emin/Dorbiljin 27 Db 46.32N 83.39 E
Emine, Nos- 15 Kg 42.42N 27.54 E
Emira Island 60 Dh 1.40S 150.00 E
Emirdağ 23 Db 39.01N 31.10 E
Emisu, Tarso- 30 If 21.13N 18.32 E
Emlichheim 10 Cd 52.37N 6.51 E
Emmaboda 7 Dh 56.38N 15.32 E
Emmaste 7 Fg 58.43N 22.36 E
Emme 14 Bd 47.10N 7.35 E
Emmeloord, Noordoostpolder- 12 Hb 52.42N 5.44 E
Emmelshausen 12 Jd 50.09N 7.34 E
Emmen 11 Mb 52.47N 6.55 E
Emmendingen 10 Dh 48.08N 7.51 E
Emmen-Emmer-Compascuum 12 Jb 52.49N 7.03 E
Emmen-Klazienaveen 12 Jb 52.44N 7.01 E
Emmen-Nieuw Weerdinge 12 Jb 52.52N 7.01 E
Emmental 14 Bd 46.55N 7.45 E
Emmen-Weerdinge 12 Ib 52.49N 6.57 E
Emmer 12 Lb 52.03N 9.23 E
Emmer-Compascuum, Emmen- 12 Jb 52.49N 7.03 E
Emmerich 10 Ce 51.50N 6.15 E
Emmet 59 Id 24.40S 144.28 E
Emmetsburg 45 Ie 43.07N 94.41W
Emmett 46 Ge 43.52N 116.30W
Emmonak 40 Gd 62.46N 164.30W
Emőd 10 Qi 47.56N 20.49 E
Emory 46 Jf 41.05N 111.16W
Emory Peak 43 Gf 29.13N 103.17W
Empalme 47 Bc 27.58N 110.51W
Empangeni 37 Ee 28.50S 31.48 E
Empedrado 56 Ic 27.57S 58.48W
Emperor Seamounts (EN) 3 Je 40.00N 171.00 E
Empoli 14 Eg 43.43N 10.57 E
Emporia [Ks.-U.S.] 43 Hd 38.24N 96.11W
Emporia [Va.-U.S.] 44 Ig 36.42N 77.33W
Emporium 44 He 41.31N 78.14W
Empress Augusta Bay 63a Bb 6.25S 155.05 E
Empress Mine 37 Dc 18.27S 29.27 E
Ems 11 Na 53.19N 7.03 E
Emsbach 12 Kd 50.24N 8.06 E
Emsdetten 10 Dd 52.11N 7.32 E
Ems-Jade-Kanal 10 Dc 53.19N 7.10 E
Emsland 10 Dd 52.50N 7.20 E
Emstek 12 Kb 52.50N 8.09 E
Emumägi/Emumjagi 8 Lf 58.54N 26.23 E
Emumjagi/Emumägi 8 Lf 58.54N 26.23 E
Ena 29 Ed 35.27N 137.24 E
Enånger 7 Df 61.32N 17.00 E
Enaratoli 26 Kg 3.55S 136.21 E
Enard Bay 9 Hc 58.06N 5.20W
Ena-San 29 Ed 35.26N 137.36 E
Enbetsu 28 Pb 44.44N 141.47 E
Encantada, Cerro de la- 38 Hf 31.00N 115.23W
Encantada, Sierra de la- 48 Hc 28.30N 102.20W
Encantadas, Serra das 55 Fj 30.40S 53.00W
Encantado, Cerro- 47 Bc 27.03N 112.30W
Encarnación 53 Kh 27.20S 55.54W
Encarnación de Díaz 48 Hg 21.31N 102.14W
Enchi 34 Ed 5.49N 2.49W
Encinal 45 Gl 28.02N 99.21W
Encinasola 13 Ff 38.08N 6.52W
Encontrados 54 Db 8.46N 72.30W
Encounter Bay 59 Hg 35.35S 138.45 E
Encrucijada 49 Hb 22.37N 79.52W
Encruzilhada do Sul 55 Fj 30.32S 52.31W
Encs 10 Rh 48.20N 21.08 E
Ende 22 Oj 8.50S 121.39 E
Endeavour Strait 59 Ib 10.50S 142.15 E
Endelave 8 Di 55.45N 10.15 E
Enderbury Atoll 57 Je 3.08S 171.05W
Enderby 46 Fa 50.33N 119.08W
Enderby Land 66 Ee 67.30S 53.00 E
Endicott Mountains 40 Ic 67.50N 152.00W
Ené, Rio- 54 Df 11.09S 74.19W
Energetik 19 Fe 51.44N 58.48 E
Enez 24 Bb 40.44N 26.04 E
Enez Körfezi 15 Ii 40.45N 26.00 E
Enfer, Portes d'- 36 Ed 5.05S 27.30 E
Enfield 44 Ig 36.11N 77.47W
Enfield, London- 12 Bc 51.40N 0.04W
Engadin/Engiadin'ota/Engadina 14 Dd 46.35N 10.00 E
Engadina/Engadin/Engiadin'ota 14 Dd 46.35N 10.00 E
Engaño, Cabo- 47 Ke 18.37N 68.20W
Engaru 28 Qb 44.03N 143.31 E
Engelberg 14 Cd 46.50N 8.24 E
Engelhard 44 Jh 35.31N 76.00W
Engels 6 Ke 51.30N 46.07 E
Engelskirchen 12 Jd 50.59N 7.24 E
Engenho 55 Db 15.10S 56.25W
Enger 12 Kb 52.08N 8.34 E
Engeren 8 Ec 61.35N 12.05 E
Engershatu 35 Fb 16.34N 38.15 E
Enggano, Pulau- 21 Mj 5.24S 102.16 E
Enghien/Edingen 12 Gd 50.42N 4.02 E
Engiadin'ota/Engadina/Engadin 14 Dd 46.35N 10.00 E
England 5 Fe 52.30N 1.30W
England 9 Li 52.30N 1.30W
Englehart 42 Jg 47.49N 79.52W
Englewood 45 Dg 39.39N 104.59W
English 44 Df 38.20N 86.28W
English Channel 5 Fe 50.20N 1.00W
English Coast 66 Qf 73.30S 73.00W
English River 45 Ia 50.12N 95.00W
English River 45 Kb 49.13N 90.58W
Engozero, Ozero- 7 Hd 65.45N 33.30 E
Enguera 13 Lf 38.59N 0.41W
Engure/Engures 8 Jg 57.09N 23.06 E
Engures/Engure 8 Jg 57.09N 23.06 E
Engures, Ozero-/Engures Ezers 8 Jg 57.15N 23.10 E
Engures Ezers/Engures, Ozero- 8 Jg 57.15N 23.10 E
Enh-Gajvan 27 Gb 48.05N 97.35 E
Enid 39 Jf 36.19N 97.48W
Enid Lake 45 Li 34.10N 89.50W
Eniwa 28 Pc 42.53N 141.14 E
Eniwa-Dake 29a Bb 42.47N 141.17 E
Eniwetok Atoll 57 Hc 11.30N 162.15 E
Enkenbach Alsenborn 12 Je 49.29N 7.53 E
Enkhuizen 11 Lb 52.42N 5.17 E
Enklinge 8 Id 60.20N 20.45 E
Enköping 7 Dg 59.38N 17.04 E
Enna 14 Im 37.34N 14.16 E
Ennadai 42 Hd 61.10N 101.00W
Ennadei Lake 42 Hd 60.55N 101.20W
Enné 35 Bc 14.24N 18.45 E
Ennedi 30 Jg 17.15N 22.00 E
Ennell, Lough-/Loch Ainninn 9 Fh 53.28N 7.24W
Ennepetal 12 Jc 51.18N 7.21 E
Ennigerloh 12 Kc 51.50N 8.01 E
Enning 45 Ed 44.37N 102.31W
Ennis [Mt.-U.S.] 46 Jd 45.21N 111.44W
Ennis [Tx.-U.S.] 45 Hj 32.20N 96.38W
Ennis/Inis 9 Ei 52.50N 8.59W
Enniscorthy/Inis Córthaidh 9 Gi 52.30N 6.34W
Enniskillen/Inis Ceithleann 9 Fg 54.21N 7.38W
Ennistymon/Inis Díomáin 9 Di 52.57N 9.13W
Enns 14 Ib 48.12N 14.28 E
Enns 5 Hf 48.14N 14.30 E
Ennstaler Alpen 14 Ic 47.37N 14.35 E
Eno 7 He 62.48N 30.09 E
Enontekiö 7 Fb 68.23N 23.38 E
Enonvesi [Fin.] 8 Mb 62.10N 28.55 E
Enonvesi [Fin.] 8 Lc 61.20N 26.30 E
Enozero, Ozero- 7 Ib 68.10N 38.00 E
Enrekang 26 Gg 3.34S 119.47 E
Enrique Carbó 55 Ck 33.08S 59.14W
Enriquillo 49 Le 17.54N 71.14W
Enriquillo, Lago- 47 Je 18.27N 71.39W
Enschede 11 Mb 52.12N 6.53 E
Ensenada [Arg.] 55 Dl 34.51S 57.55W
Ensenada [Mex.] 39 Hf 31.52N 116.37W
Enshi 27 Ie 30.16N 109.26 E
Enshū-Nada 29 Ed 34.30N 138.00 E
Entebbe 31 Kh 0.04N 32.28 E
Entenbühl 10 Ig 49.46N 12.24 E
Enterprise [Al.-U.S.] 44 Ej 31.19N 85.51W
Enterprise [N.W.T.-Can.] 42 Fd 60.39N 116.08W
Enterprise [Or.-U.S.] 46 Gd 45.25N 117.17W
Entinas, Punta- 13 Jh 36.41N 2.46W
Entrada, Punta- 47 Ab 30.22N 115.59W
Entraygues-sur-Truyère 11 Ij 44.39N 2.34 E
Entrecasteaux, Récifs d'- 57 Hf 18.20S 163.00 E
Entrepeñas, Embalse de- 13 Jd 40.34N 2.42W
Entre Rios 56 Id 32.00S 59.00W
Entre Rios 54 Fh 21.32S 64.25W
Entre Rios de Minas 55 Je 20.41S 44.04W
Entrevaux 11 Mk 43.57N 6.49 E
Entroncamento 13 De 39.28N 8.28W
Enugu 31 Hh 6.26N 7.29 E
Enugu Ezike 34 Gd 6.59N 7.27 E
Envermeu 12 De 49.54N 1.16 E
Envigado 54 Cb 6.08N 75.39W
Envira 54 De 7.18S 70.13W
Enyamba 36 Dc 3.40S 24.58 E
Enyélé 36 Cb 2.49N 18.06 E
Enz 10 Fh 49.00N 9.10 E
Enza 14 Ef 44.54N 10.31 E
Enzan 28 Og 34.52N 138.44 E
Enzgau 12 Kf 48.48N 8.37 E
Eo 13 Ea 43.28N 7.03W
Eochaill/Youghal 9 Fj 51.57N 7.50W
Eolie o Lipari, Isole-=Lipari Islands (EN) 5 Hh 38.35N 14.55 E
Epanomi 15 Fi 40.26N 22.56 E
Epazote, Cerro- 47 Cd 24.35N 105.07W
Epe [Neth.] 12 Hb 52.21N 5.59 E
Epe [Nig.] 34 Fd 6.35N 3.59 E
Epéna 36 Cb 1.22N 17.29 E
Épernay 11 Je 49.03N 3.57 E
Epe-Vaassen 12 Hb 52.17N 5.58 E
Ephesus (EN)=Efes 15 Kl 37.55N 27.20 E
Ephraim 46 Jg 39.22N 111.35W
Ephrata 46 Fc 47.19N 119.33W
Epi, Ile- 57 Hf 16.43S 168.15 E
Epidamnus 15 Ch 41.19N 19.26 E
Epidaurus (EN) = Epídhavros 15 Gl 37.38N 23.09 E
Epídhavros = Epidaurus (EN) 15 Gl 37.38N 23.09 E
Epila 13 Kc 41.36N 1.17W
Épinal 11 Mf 48.11N 6.27 E
Epirus (EN)=Ipiros 5 Ih 39.30N 20.40 E
Epirus (EN)=Ipiros 15 Dj 39.30N 20.40 E
Episkopi 24 Ee 34.40N 32.54 E
Epping 12 Cc 51.42N 0.07 E
Eppingen 12 Ke 49.08N 8.54 E
Epsom 9 Mj 51.20N 0.16W
Epte 11 He 49.04N 1.31 E
Epukiro 37 Bd 21.41S 19.08 E
Epukiro 37 Bd 21.28S 19.59 E
Epulu 36 Eb 1.15N 28.21 E
Eqlīd 23 Hc 30.55N 52.39 E
Équateur=Equator (EN) 36 Eb 1.00N 20.00 E
Equator (EN)=Équateur 36 Eb 1.00N 20.00 E
Equatorial Guinea (EN)=Guinea Ecuatorial 1 Hh 2.00N 9.00 E
Equinox Mountain 44 Kd 43.15N 73.10W
Era [It.] 14 Eg 43.40N 10.38 E
Era [Sud.] 35 Dd 5.30N 29.50 E
Eraclea 14 Kj 40.15N 16.40 E
Eraclea Minoa 14 Hm 37.25N 13.18 E
Eradaka 63b Dc 17.39S 168.08 E
Eräjärvi 8 Kc 61.35N 24.34 E
Eratini 15 Fk 38.22N 22.14 E
Erbaa 24 Gb 40.42N 36.36 E
Erbach 10 Eg 49.39N 9.00 E
Erbeskopf 10 Dg 49.44N 7.05 E
Erbil 24 Ke 36.10N 44.00 E
Erbīl 22 Gf 36.11N 44.01 E
Ercek 24 Jc 38.39N 43.36 E
Erçek Gölü 24 Jc 38.39N 43.32 E
Erciş 24 Jc 39.00N 43.19 E
Erciyas Daği 21 Ff 38.32N 35.28 E
Ercolano 14 Ij 40.48N 14.21 E
Ercsi 10 Oi 47.15N 18.54 E
Érd 10 Oi 47.22N 18.56 E
Erdaobaihe 27 Mc 42.28N 128.05 E
Erdao Jiang 28 Ic 42.35N 127.10 E
Erdek 24 Bb 40.24N 27.48 E
Erdek Körfezi 24 Bb 40.25N 27.45 E
Erdemli 24 Fd 36.37N 34.18 E
Erdene-Cagan 27 Kb 45.55N 115.30 E
Erdene-Dalaj 27 Hb 46.02N 104.55 E
Erdene-Mandal 27 Hb 48.30N 101.21 E
Erdi 30 Jg 19.05N 22.40 E
Erdi Ma 35 Cb 18.35N 23.30 E
Erding 10 Hh 48.18N 11.56 E
Erdinger Moos 10 Hh 48.20N 11.50 E
Erdre 11 Eg 47.13N 1.32W
Erebus, Mount- 66 Kf 77.32S 167.09 E
Erechim 56 Jc 27.38S 52.17W
Ereğli [Tur.] 23 Db 37.31N 34.04 E
Ereğli [Tur.] 23 Da 41.17N 31.25 E
Erei, Monti- 14 Im 37.35N 14.20 E
Ereke 26 Hg 4.45S 123.10 E
Eren 24 Dd 37.25N 30.05 E
Erenhot 22 Ne 43.35N 112.00 E
Erepecu, Lago do- 54 Gd 1.20S 56.35W
Eresma 13 Hc 41.26N 4.45W
Erétria 15 Gk 38.25N 23.48 E
Erfelek 24 Fb 41.55N 34.57 E
Erfengshan 28 Ag 35.50N 111.47 E
Erfoud 32 Gc 31.26N 4.14W
Erft 10 Ce 51.11N 6.44 E
Erftstadt 12 Id 50.48N 6.49 E
Erfurt 6 He 50.59N 11.02 E
Erfurt 10 Gf 51.00N 11.00 E
Ergani 24 Hc 38.17N 39.46 E
Ergene 24 Bb 41.01N 26.22 E
Erges 13 Ee 39.40N 7.01W
Ergig, Bahr- 35 Bc 11.22N 15.24 E
Ērgļi/Ergli 7 Fh 56.55N 25.41 E
Ergli/Ērgļi 7 Fh 56.55N 25.41 E
Ergun He 21 Od 53.20N 121.28 E
Ergun Youqi (Labudalin) 27 La 50.16N 120.09 E
Ergun Zuoqi (Genhe) 22 Od 50.47N 121.32 E
Er Hai 27 Hf 25.45N 100.10 E
Eria 13 Gb 42.03N 5.44W
Eriba 35 Fb 16.37N 36.04 E
Eriboll, Loch- 9 Ic 58.30N 4.40W
Eric 42 Kf 51.52N 65.45W
Erice 14 Gl 38.02N 12.35 E
Ericeira 13 Cf 38.59N 9.25W
Erichsen Lake 42 Jb 70.38N 80.20W
Ericht, Loch- 9 Ie 56.50N 4.25W
Erick 45 Gi 35.13N 99.52W
Eridu 24 Lg 36.00N 44.00 E
Erie 39 Ke 42.08N 80.04W
Erie, Lake- 38 Ke 42.15N 81.00W
'Erigābo 35 Hc 10.37N 47.24 E
Erigât 30 Gg 19.40N 4.50W
Erikoússa 15 Cj 39.53N 19.35 E
Eriksdale 45 Ga 50.52N 98.06W
Eriksenstretet 41 Oc 79.00N 26.00 E
Erikub Atoll 57 Id 9.08N 170.02 E
Erímanthos Óros 15 El 37.58N 21.48 E
Erimo-Misaki 27 Pc 41.55N 143.15 E
Eriskay 9 Fd 57.04N 7.13W
Eritrea 30 Kg 15.00N 40.00 E
Eritrea 35 Fb 15.00N 39.00 E
Eritrea 35 Fb 15.00N 40.00 E
Erjas 13 Ee 39.40N 7.01W
Erkelenz 12 Ic 51.05N 6.19 E
Erken 8 He 59.50N 18.35 E
Erkowit 35 Fb 18.46N 37.07 E
Erlangdian → Dawu 28 Ci 31.33N 114.07 E
Erlangen 10 Hg 49.36N 11.01 E
Erlang Shan 27 Hf 29.58N 102.20 E
Erlauf 14 Jb 48.12N 15.11 E
Erldunda 59 Ge 25.14S 133.12 E
Erlenbach 12 Ke 49.07N 8.11 E
Erlong Shan 27 Mc 43.30N 128.44 E
Ermelo [Neth.] 12 Hb 52.19N 5.37 E
Ermelo [S.Afr.] 37 De 26.34S 29.58 E
Ermenek 24 Ed 36.38N 32.54 E
Ermenistan=Armenia (EN) 23 Fb 39.10N 43.00 E
Ermenistan=Armenia (EN) 21 Gf 39.10N 43.00 E
Ermenonville 12 Ee 49.08N 2.42 E
Ermesinde 13 Dc 41.13N 8.33W
Ermoúpolis 15 Hl 37.27N 24.56 E
Erndtebrück 12 Kd 50.59N 8.16 E
Erne/An Éirne 9 Eg 54.30N 8.15W
Ernée 11 Ff 48.18N 0.56W
Ernest Legouvé Reef 57 Lh 35.12S 150.35W
Ernici, Monti- 14 Hi 41.50N 13.20 E
Erode 25 Ff 11.21N 77.44 E
Eromanga 59 Ie 26.40S 143.16 E
Erongoberg 37 Bd 21.40S 15.40 E
Erpengdianzi 28 Hd 41.12N 125.29 E
Errego 37 Fc 16.02S 37.10 E
Errigal/An Ea agail 9 Ef 55.02N 8.07W
Erris Head/Ceann Iorrais 5 Fe 54.19N 10.00W
Erromango, Ile- 57 Hf 18.48S 169.05 E
Erseka 15 Di 40.20N 20.41 E
Erstein 11 Nf 48.26N 7.40 E
Ertai 27 Fb 46.02N 90.10 E
Ertil 19 Ee 51.50N 40.51 E
Ertix He 21 Ke 47.52N 84.16 E
Erts 37 De 25.08S 29.55 E
Ertvågøy 8 Ca 63.15N 8.25 E
Eruh 24 Jd 37.46N 42.15 E
Ervânia 55 Ee 21.43S 55.32W
Erve 11 Fg 47.50N 0.20W
Ervy-le-Châtel 11 Jf 48.02N 3.55 E
Erwin 44 Fg 36.09N 82.25W
Erwitte 12 Kc 51.37N 8.21 E
Eryuan 27 Gf 26.09N 99.56 E
Erzeni 15 Ch 41.26N 19.27 E
Erzgebirge=Ore Mountains (EN) 5 He 50.30N 13.15 E
Erzin 20 Ef 50.17N 95.10 E
Erzincan 23 Eb 39.44N 39.29 E
Erzurum 22 Gf 39.55N 41.17 E
Esan-Misaki 28 Pd 41.48N 141.12 E
Esashi [Jap.] 28 Pd 41.52N 140.07 E
Esashi [Jap.] 28 Qb 44.56N 142.35 E
Esashi [Jap.] 28 Pe 39.12N 141.09 E
Esbjerg 6 Gd 55.28N 8.27 E
Esbo/Espoo 7 Ff 60.13N 24.40 E
Escalante 46 Jh 37.47N 111.36W
Escalante Desert 46 Ih 37.50N 113.30W
Escalante River 46 Jh 37.17N 110.53W
Escalaplano 14 Dk 39.37N 9.21 E
Escalón 47 Dc 26.45N 104.20W
Escalona 13 Hd 40.10N 4.24W
Escanaba 39 Ke 45.45N 87.04W
Escanaba River 45 Mc 45.47N 87.04W
Escandón, Puerto de- 13 Ld 40.17N 1.00W
Escandorgue 11 Jk 43.46N 3.14 E
Escarpada Point 21 Oh 18.31N 122.13 E
Escarpé, Cap- 63b 20.41S 167.13 E
Escatrón 13 Lc 41.17N 0.19W
Escaut=Schelde (EN) 11 Kc 51.22N 4.15 E
Esch an der Alzette/Esch-sur-Alzette 11 Le 49.30N 5.59 E
Eschkopf 12 Je 49.19N 7.51 E
Esch-sur-Alzette/Esch an der Alzette 11 Le 49.30N 5.59 E
Eschwege 10 Ge 51.11N 10.04 E
Eschweiler 10 Cf 50.49N 6.17 E
Escocesa, Bahía- 49 Md 19.25N 69.45W
Escondida, Punta- 48 Kj 15.49N 97.03W
Escondido 46 Gj 33.07N 117.05W
Escondido, Rio- 49 Fg 12.04N 83.45W
Escravos 34 Gd 5.36N 5.11 E
Escudo, Puerto del- 13 Ia 43.05N 3.50W
Escudo de Veraguas, Isla- 49 Gi 9.06N 81.33W
Escuintla 49 Bf 14.10N 91.00W
Escuintla [Guat.] 47 Ff 14.18N 90.47W
Escuintla [Mex.] 48 Mj 15.20N 92.38W
Escuro, Rio- [Braz.] 55 Ic 17.31S 46.39W
Escuro, Rio- [Braz.] 55 Ha 12.50S 49.28W
Ese 36 Eb 4.04N 26.40 E
Ese-Hajja 20 Ic 67.35N 134.55 E
Eséka 34 He 3.39N 10.46 E
Eşen 24 Cd 36.27N 29.16 E
Esendere 24 Kd 37.46N 44.40 E
Esera 13 Mb 42.06N 0.15 E
Esfahān 23 Hc 32.50N 51.50 E
Esfahān=Isfahan (EN) 22 Hf 32.40N 51.38 E
Esfandārān 24 Qg 31.52N 52.32 E
Esfarāyen, Reshteh-ye- 24 Qd 36.46N 57.10 E
Esgueva 13 Hc 41.40N 4.43W

Index Symbols

- Independent Nation
- State, Region
- District, County
- Municipality
- Colony, Dependency
- Continent
- Physical Region
- Historical or Cultural Region
- Mount, Mountain
- Volcano
- Hill
- Mountains, Mountain Range
- Hills, Escarpment
- Plateau, Upland
- Pass, Gap
- Plain, Lowland
- Delta
- Salt Flat
- Valley, Canyon
- Crater, Cave
- Karst Features
- Depression
- Polder
- Desert, Dunes
- Forest, Woods
- Heath, Steppe
- Oasis
- Cape, Point
- Coast, Beach
- Cliff
- Peninsula
- Isthmus
- Sandbank
- Island
- Atoll
- Rock, Reef
- Islands, Archipelago
- Rocks, Reefs
- Coral Reef
- Well, Spring
- Geyser
- River, Stream
- Waterfall Rapids
- River Mouth, Estuary
- Lake
- Salt Lake
- Intermittent Lake
- Reservoir
- Swamp, Pond
- Canal
- Glacier
- Ice Shelf, Pack Ice
- Ocean
- Sea
- Gulf, Bay
- Strait, Fjord
- Lagoon
- Bank
- Seamount
- Tablemount
- Ridge
- Shelf
- Basin
- Escarpment, Sea Scarp
- Fracture
- Trench, Abyss
- National Park, Reserve
- Point of Interest
- Recreation Site
- Cave, Cavern
- Historic Site
- Ruins
- Wall, Walls
- Church, Abbey
- Temple
- Scientific Station
- Airport
- Port
- Lighthouse
- Mine
- Tunnel
- Dam, Bridge

Eshowe	37	Ee	28.50S	31.29 E
Eshetehärd	24	Ne	35.44N	50.23 E
Esigodini	37	Dd	20.18S	28.56 E
Esino	14	Hg	43.39N	13.22 E
Esk	9	Jg	54.58N	3.04W
Eskifjördur	7a	Cb	65.04N	14.01W
Eskilstuna	7	Dg	59.22N	16.30 E
Eskimo Point	39	Jc	61.07N	94.03W
Eskişehir	22	Ff	39.46N	30.32 E
Esla	13	Fc	41.29N	6.03W
Eslāmābād	23	Gc	34.11N	46.35 E
Eşler Daği	15	Ml	37.24N	29.43 E
Eslohe (Sauerland)	12	Kc	51.15N	8.10 E
Eslöv	7	Ci	55.50N	13.20 E
Eşme	24	Cc	38.24N	28.59 E
Esmeralda [Braz.]	55	Gi	28.03S	51.12W
Esmeralda [Cuba]	49	Hc	21.51N	78.07W
Esmeralda, Isla-	56	Eg	48.57S	75.25W
Esmeralda Bank (EN)	65b	Ab	14.57N	145.15 E
Esmeraldas	53	Ie	0.59N	79.42W
Esnagami Lake	45	Ma	50.21N	86.48W
Esneux	12	Hd	50.32N	5.34 E
Espada, Punta-	49	Lg	12.05N	71.07W
Espagnol Point	51n	Ba	13.22N	61.09W
Espalion	11	Ij	44.31N	2.46 E
Espalmador, Isla-	13	Nf	38.47N	1.26 E
España=Spain (EN) (1)	6	Fg	40.00N	4.00W
Espanola [N.M.-U.S.]	45	Ch	36.06N	106.02W
Espanola [Ont.-Can.]	44	Gb	46.15N	81.46W
Española, Isla-	54a	Bb	1.25S	89.42W
Espardell, Isla-	13	Nf	38.47N	1.27 E
Esparta	49	Ei	9.59N	84.40W
Espeland	8	Ad	60.23N	5.28 E
Espelkamp	10	Ed	52.25N	8.37 E
Esperance	58	Dh	33.51S	121.53 E
Esperance, Cape-	63a	Dc	9.15S	159.43 E
Esperance Bay	59	Ef	33.50S	121.55 E
Esperance Harbour	51k	Ba	14.04N	60.55W
Esperancita	55	Bc	16.55S	60.06W
Esperantina	54	Jd	3.54S	42.14W
Esperanza	66	Re	63.26S	57.00W
Esperanza [Arg.]	56	Hd	31.27S	60.56W
Esperanza [Mex.]	48	Ed	27.35N	109.56W
Esperanza [P.R.]	51a	Cb	18.06N	65.29W
Esperanza, Sierra la-	49	Ef	15.40N	85.45W
Espevær	7	Ag	59.36N	5.10 E
Espichel, Cabo-	13	Cf	38.25N	9.13W
Espiel	13	Gf	38.12N	5.01W
Espigão Serra do-	55	Gh	26.55S	50.25W
Espinal [Bol.]	55	Cc	17.13S	58.43W
Espinal [Col.]	54	Dc	4.10N	74.54W
Espinazo del Diablo, Sierra-	48	Ff	24.00N	106.00W
Espinhaço, Serra do-	52	Lg	17.30S	43.30W
Espinho	13	Dc	41.01N	8.38W
Espinilho, Serra do-	55	Ei	28.30S	55.06W
Espinillo	55	Cg	24.58S	58.34W
Espino	50	Dh	8.34N	66.01W
Espinosa	54	Jf	14.56S	42.50W
Espinouse	11	Ik	43.32N	2.46 E
Espírito Santo (2)	54	Jg	20.00S	40.30W
Espiritu Santo, Bahia del-	48	Ph	19.20N	87.35W
Espíritu Santo, Isla-	48	De	24.30N	110.22W
Espita	48	Og	21.01N	88.19W
Esplanada	54	Kf	11.47S	37.57W
Espoo/Esbo	7	Ff	60.13N	24.40 E
Espoo-Tapiola	8	Kd	60.11N	24.49 E
Esposende	13	Dc	41.32N	8.47W
Espumoso	55	Fi	28.44S	52.51W
Espuña, Sierra de-	13	Kg	37.52N	1.34W
Espungabera	37	Ed	20.28S	32.46 E
Esquel	53	Ij	42.55S	71.20W
Esquina	56	Id	30.01S	59.32W
Esquinapa de Hidalgo	47	Cd	22.51N	105.48W
Esquipular	49	Cf	14.34N	89.21W
Essandsjøen	8	Da	63.05N	12.00 E
Essaouira	31	Ge	31.31N	9.46W
Essaouira (3)	32	Fc	31.04N	9.03W
Essen [Bel.]	12	Gc	51.28N	4.28 E
Essen [F.R.G.]	6	Ge	51.27N	7.01 E
Essen (Oldenburg)	12	Jb	52.42N	7.55 E
Essendon, Mount-	59	Ed	24.59S	120.28 E
Essequibo River	52	Ke	6.50N	58.30W
Essex	46	Hi	34.42N	115.12W
Essex	9	Nj	51.50N	0.30 E
Essex (3)	9	Mj	51.50N	0.35W
Essex Mountain	46	Ke	42.02N	109.13W
Esslingen am Neckar	10	Fh	48.45N	9.18 E
Esso	20	Ke	55.55N	158.40 E
Essonne	11	If	48.37N	2.29 E
Essonne (3)	11	If	48.36N	2.20 E
Est [Cam.] (3)	34	He	4.00N	14.00 E
Est [U.V.] (3)	34	Fc	12.00N	1.00 E
Est, Canal de l'-	11	Lf	48.45N	5.35 E
Est, Cap-	37	Ic	15.16S	50.29 E
Est, Ile de l'-	30	Mm	46.15S	52.05 E
Est, Pointe de l'-	42	Lg	49.08N	61.41W
Estaca de Bares, Punta de la-	5	Fg	43.46N	7.42W
Estados, Isla de los-=Staten Island (EN)	52	Jk	54.47S	64.15W
Estados Unidos Mexicanos (1)	39	Ig	23.00N	102.00W
Eşţahbān	24	Ph	29.08N	54.04 E
Estaimpuis	12	Fd	50.42N	3.15 E
Estância	54	Kf	11.16S	37.26W
Estancias, Sierra de las-	13	Jg	37.35N	2.20W
Estanislao del Campo	55	Bg	25.03S	60.06W
Estarreja	13	Dd	40.45N	8.34W
Estats, Pica d'-	11	Hn	42.40N	1.24 E
Estats, Pica d'-/Estats, Pico d'-	11	Hn	42.40N	1.24 E
Estats, Pic d'-	11	Hn	42.40N	1.24 E
Estats, Pico d'-	11	Hn	42.40N	1.24 E
Estats, Pico d'-/Estats, Pica d'-	11	Hn	42.40N	1.24 E
Estcourt	37	De	29.01S	29.52 E
Este	14	Fe	45.14N	11.39 E
Este, Punta-	51a	Cb	18.08N	65.16W
Este, Punta del-	56	Jd	34.59S	54.57W
Esteban Rams	55	Bi	29.47S	61.29W
Estelí	47	Gf	13.05N	86.23W
Estelí (3)	49	Dg	13.10N	86.20W
Estella	13	Jb	42.40N	2.02W
Estepa	13	Hg	37.18N	4.54W
Estepona	13	Gh	36.26N	5.08W
Estérel	11	Mk	43.30N	6.50 E
Esternay	12	Ff	48.44N	3.34 E
Esterri d'Aneu/Esterri de Aneu	13	Nb	42.38N	1.08 E
Esterri de Aneu/Esterri d'Aneu	13	Nb	42.38N	1.08 E
Esterwegen	12	Jb	52.59N	7.37 E
Estes Park	45	Df	40.23N	105.31W
Este Sudeste, Cayos del-	47	Hf	12.26N	81.27W
Estevan	42	Hg	49.07N	103.05W
Estherville	45	Ie	43.24N	94.50W
Estissac	11	Jf	48.16N	3.49 E
Eston	46	Ka	51.10N	108.46W
Estonia (EN)	5	Id	59.00N	26.00 E
Estonian SSR (EN)=Eesti NSV (2)	19	Cd	59.00N	26.00 E
Estonskaja Sovetskaja Socialističeskaja Respublika (2)	19	Cd	59.00N	26.00 E
Estonskaja SSR/Eesti Nõukogude Socialistlik Vabarijk (2)	19	Cd	59.00N	26.00 E
Estoril	13	Cf	38.42N	9.24W
Estrées-Saint-Denis	12	Ee	49.26N	2.39 E
Estreito	55	Gj	31.50S	51.44W
Estreito, Reprêsa do-	55	Ie	20.15S	47.09W
Estrêla [Braz.]	55	Gi	29.29S	51.58W
Estrêla [Braz.]	55	Gj	31.15S	21.45W
Estrela, Arroyo-	55	Df	22.05S	56.25W
Estrela, Serra da-	55	Fc	16.27S	53.24W
Estrêla, Serra da-	5	Fg	40.20N	7.38W
Estrêla do Sul	55	Id	18.21S	47.49W
Estrella	13	If	38.28N	3.35W
Estrella, Punta-	48	Bb	30.55N	114.40W
Estrema, Serra da-	55	Jc	16.50S	45.07W
Estremadura	13	Ce	39.15N	9.10W
Estremoz	13	Ef	38.51N	7.35W
Estrondo, Serra do-	54	Ie	9.00S	48.45W
Estry	12	Bf	48.54N	0.44W
Estuaire (3)	36	Ab	0.10N	10.00 E
Esztergom	10	Oi	47.48N	18.45 E
Etah	41	Ec	78.19N	72.38W
Étain	11	Le	49.13N	5.38 E
Etajima	29	Cd	34.15N	132.29 E
Etalle	12	He	49.41N	5.36 E
Étampes	11	If	48.26N	2.09 E
Étaples	11	Hd	50.31N	1.39 E
Etāwah	25	Fc	26.46N	79.02 E
Ethe, Virton-	12	He	49.35N	5.35 E
Ethel Reefs	63d	Ab	16.56S	177.13 E
Ethiopia (EN)=Itiopya (1)	31	Kh	9.00N	39.00 E
Ethiopian Plateau (EN)	30	Kg	10.00N	38.10 E
Etive, Loch-	9	He	56.35N	5.15W
Etna	8	Dd	60.50N	10.03 E
Etna	5	Hh	37.50N	14.55 E
Etne	8	Ae	59.40N	5.56 E
Etoile Cay	37b	Bb	5.53S	53.01 E
Etolin Island	40	Me	56.08N	132.26W
Etolin Strait	40	Fd	60.20N	165.15W
Etomo-Misaki	29a	Bb	42.20N	140.55 E
Etorofu Tō/Iturup, Ostrov-	21	Qe	44.54N	147.30 E
Etosha Pan	30	Ij	18.50S	16.20 E
Etoumbi	36	Bb	0.01N	14.57 E
Etrépagny	12	De	49.18N	1.37 E
Étretat	11	Ge	49.42N	0.12 E
Etropole	15	Gg	42.50N	24.00 E
Etruria	56	Hd	32.56S	63.15W
Etsch/Adige	5	Hf	45.10N	12.20 E
Ettelbrüch/Ettelbruck	12	Ie	49.51N	6.07 E
Ettelbruck/Ettelbrüch	12	Ie	49.51N	6.07 E
Etten-Leur	12	Gc	51.35N	4.39 E
Ettersberg	10	He	51.03N	11.15 E
Ettlingen	12	Kf	48.57N	8.24 E
Etzna Tixmucuy	48	Nh	19.35N	90.13W
Eu	11	Hd	50.03N	1.25 E
'Eua Iki	65b	Bc	21.07S	174.59W
Eua Island	61	Gd	21.22S	174.56W
Euboea (EN)=Évvoia	5	Ih	38.30N	24.00 E
Eucla	58	Dh	31.43S	128.52 E
Euclid	44	Ge	41.34N	81.33W
Euclides da Cunha	54	Kf	10.31S	39.01W
Eucumbene, Lake-	59	Jg	36.05S	148.45 E
Eudora	45	Kj	33.07N	91.16W
Eufaula	44	Ej	31.54N	85.09W
Eufaula Lake	45	Ii	35.17N	95.31W
Euganei, Colli-	14	Fe	45.19N	11.40 E
Eugene	39	Ge	44.02N	123.05W
Eugenia, Punta-	38	Hg	27.50N	115.03W
Eugênio Penzo	55	Ef	22.13S	55.53W
Eugmo	7	Fe	63.49N	22.45 E
Eume	13	Da	43.25N	8.08W
Eunice [La.-U.S.]	45	Jk	30.30N	92.26W
Eunice [N.M.-U.S.]	45	Ej	32.26N	103.09W
Eupen	11	Md	50.38N	6.02 E
Euphrates (EN)=Al Furāt	21	Gf	31.00N	47.25 E
Euphrates (EN)=Firat	21	Gf	31.00N	47.25 E
Eupora	45	Lj	33.32N	89.16W
Eura	7	Ff	61.08N	22.08 E
Eurajoki	8	Ic	61.12N	21.44 E
Eurasia Basin (EN)	67	Ge	87.00N	80.00 E
Eure (3)	11	Ge	49.10N	1.00 E
Eure	11	He	49.18N	1.12 E
Eure-et-Loir (3)	11	Hf	48.30N	1.30 E
Eureka [Ca.-U.S.]	39	Ge	40.47N	124.09W
Eureka [Ks.-U.S.]	45	Hh	37.49N	96.17W
Eureka [Mt.-U.S.]	46	Hb	48.53N	115.03W
Eureka [Nv.-U.S.]	43	Dd	39.31N	115.58W
Eureka [N.W.T.-Can.]	42	Ia	80.00N	85.59W
Eureka [S.D.-U.S.]	45	Gd	45.46N	99.38W
Eureka [Ut.-U.S.]	46	Ig	39.57N	112.07W
Eureka Sound	42	Ia	79.00N	87.00W
Europa	30	Lk	22.20S	40.22 E
Europa, Picos de-	5	Fg	43.12N	4.48W
Europe	5	Ie	50.00N	20.00 E
Europoort	11	Jc	51.58N	4.00 E
Euskirchen	10	Cf	50.40N	6.47 E
Eustis	44	Gk	28.51N	81.41W
Eutaw	44	Di	32.50N	87.53W
Eutin	10	Gb	54.08N	10.37 E
Euzkadi/Vascongadas=Basque Provinces (EN)	13	Ja	43.00N	2.30W
Evale	36	Cf	16.33S	15.44 E
Evans, Lac-	42	Jf	50.50N	77.00W
Evans, Mount-	46	Ic	46.05N	113.07W
Evans Strait	42	Jd	63.20N	82.00W
Evanston [Il.-U.S.]	45	Me	42.03N	87.42W
Evanston [Wy.-U.S.]	43	Ec	41.16N	110.58 E
Evansville	39	Kf	37.58N	87.35W
Evant	45	Gk	31.29N	98.09W
Evart	44	Ed	43.54N	85.14W
Evaux-les-Bains	11	Ih	46.10N	2.29 E
Evaz	24	Oi	27.46N	53.59 E
Evciler [Tur.]	15	Jj	39.46N	26.46 E
Evciler [Tur.]	15	Mk	38.03N	29.54 E
Evelyn, Mount-	59	Gb	13.36S	132.53 E
Evenkijski Nac. okrug (3)	20	Ed	65.00N	98.00 E
Evensk	22	Rc	61.57N	159.14 E
Everard, Lake-	59	Hf	31.25S	135.05 E
Everard Ranges	59	Ge	27.05S	132.30 E
Everest, Mount- (EN)=Qomolangma Feng	21	Kg	27.59N	86.56 E
Everest, Mount- (EN)=Saragmatha	21	Kg	27.59N	86.56 E
Everett	43	Cb	47.59N	122.13W
Everett Mountains	42	Kd	62.45N	67.10W
Evergem	12	Fc	51.07N	3.42 E
Evergem-Sleidinge	12	Fc	51.08N	3.41 E
Everglades City	44	Gm	25.52N	81.23W
Evergreen	44	Dj	31.26N	86.57W
Evertsberg	8	Ec	61.08N	13.57 E
Evesham	9	Li	52.05N	1.56W
Evesham, Vale of-	9	Li	52.05N	1.50W
Evian-les-Bains	11	Mh	46.23N	6.35 E
Evijärvi	7	Fe	63.22N	23.29 E
Evinayong	34	He	1.27N	10.34 E
Évinos	15	Ek	38.19N	21.32 E
Evje	7	Bg	58.36N	7.51 E
Évora	6	Fh	38.34N	7.54W
Évora (2)	13	Ef	38.35N	7.50W
Evoron	20	If	51.23N	136.23 E
Evowghlī	24	Kc	38.43N	45.13 E
Evre	11	Eg	47.22N	1.02W
Evrecy	12	Be	49.06N	0.30W
Evreux	11	He	49.01N	1.09 E
Evron	11	Ff	48.10N	0.24W
Évros	15	Ji	40.52N	26.12 E
Evrótas	15	Fm	36.48N	22.41 E
Evry	11	If	48.38N	2.27 E
Évvoia=Euboea (EN)	5	Ih	38.30N	24.00 E
Évvoia, Gulf of- (EN)=Vórios Evvoïkós Kólpos	15	Gk	38.45N	23.10 E
Evzonoi	15	Fh	41.06N	22.33 E
Ewa Beach	65a	Cb	21.19N	158.00W
Ewing Seamount (EN)	30	Hk	23.20S	8.45 E
Ewo	36	Bc	0.55S	14.49 E
Excelsior Mountain	46	Fg	38.02N	119.18W
Excelsior Mountains	46	Fg	38.10N	118.30W
Excelsior Springs	45	Ig	39.20N	94.13W
Exe	9	Jk	50.37N	3.25W
Executive Committee Range	66	Nf	76.50S	126.00W
Exeter [Eng.-U.K.]	6	Fe	50.43N	3.31W
Exeter [N.H.-U.S.]	44	Ld	42.59N	70.56W
Exeter Sound	42	Lc	66.10N	62.00W
Exmoor	9	Jj	51.10N	3.45W
Exmouth [Austl.]	59	Cd	21.55S	114.07 E
Exmouth [Eng.-U.K.]	9	Jk	50.37N	3.25W
Exmouth Gulf	57	Cg	22.00S	114.20 E
Exmouth Plateau (EN)	59	Cc	16.00S	114.00 E
Expedition Range	59	Jd	24.30S	149.05 E
Explorer Tablemount (EN)	47	He	16.55N	83.15W
Externsteine	12	Kc	51.52N	8.55 E
Extertal	12	Lb	52.04N	9.07 E
Extertal-Bösingfeld	12	Lb	52.04N	9.07 E
Extremadura	13	Ge	39.00N	6.00W
Exuma Cays	47	Id	24.00N	76.20W
Exuma Cays	49	Ia	24.20N	76.40W
Exuma Sound	47	Id	24.15N	76.00W
Eyasi, Lake-	30	Ki	3.40S	35.05 E
Eydehavn	8	Cf	58.31N	8.53 E
Eye	12	Db	52.19N	1.09 E
Eyemouth	9	Kf	55.52N	2.06W
Eye Peninsula	9	Gc	58.13N	6.05W
Eygurande	11	Ii	45.40N	2.28 E
Eyjafjallajökull	7a	Bc	63.38N	19.36W
Ēyl	31	Lh	8.00N	49.51 E
Eymoutiers	11	Hi	45.44N	1.44 E
Eynesil	24	Hb	41.03N	39.08 E
Eyrarbakki	7a	Bc	63.52N	21.09W
Eyre	59	Ff	32.15S	126.18 E
Eyre, Lake-	57	Eg	28.43S	137.11 E
Eyre Creek	57	Eg	26.40S	139.00 E
Eyre Mountains	62	Cf	45.20S	168.20 E
Eyre North, Lake-	59	He	28.40S	137.10 E
Eyre Peninsula	57	Ef	34.00S	135.45 E
Eyre South, Lake-	59	He	29.30S	137.20 E
Eyrieux	11	Kj	44.48N	4.48 E
Eystrup	12	Lb	52.47N	9.13 E
Eythorne	12	Dc	51.11N	1.17 E
Eyvānakī	24	Oe	35.24N	51.56 E
Ezequiel Ramos Mexia, Embalse-	56	Ge	39.30S	69.00W
Ezere	8	Jh	56.27N	22.17 E
Ežerelis	8	Jj	54.50N	23.38 E
Ezine	24	Bc	39.47N	26.20 E
Eznas/Jieznas	8	Kj	54.34N	24.17 E
Ežva	17	Ef	61.47N	50.40 E

F

Faaa	65e	Fc	17.33S	149.36W
Faaite Atoll	61	Lc	16.45S	145.14W
Fabens	45	Ck	31.30N	106.10W
Fåberg	8	Dc	61.10N	10.24 E
Faber Lake	42	Fd	63.55N	117.15W
Fåborg	7	Ci	55.06N	10.15 E
Fabriano	14	Gg	43.20N	12.54 E
Făcăeni	15	Ke	44.34N	27.54 E
Facatativá	54	Dc	4.49N	74.22W
Facha	33	Cd	29.30N	17.20 E
Fachi	31	Ig	18.06N	11.34 E
Facpi Point	64c	Bb	13.20N	144.38 E
Fada	31	Jg	17.14N	21.33 E
Fada N'Gourma	31	Hg	12.04N	0.21 E
Faddeja, Zaliv-	20	Fa	76.30N	107.30 E
Faddejevski, Ostrov-	20	Ja	75.30N	144.00 E
Fadiffolu Atoll	25a	Ba	5.25N	73.30 E
Fāḑilī	24	Mi	26.58N	49.15 E
Faeara, Pointe-	65e	Fc	17.52S	149.11W
Faenza	14	Ff	44.17N	11.53 E
Færœ Bank (EN)	9	Ea	60.55N	8.40W
Faeroe-Iceland Ridge (EN)	5	Fc	64.00N	10.00W
Faeroe Islands (EN)=Færøerne/Föroyar	5	Fc	62.00N	7.00W
Faeroe Islands (EN)=Færøerne/Föroyar (5)	6	Fc	62.00N	7.00W
Faeroe Islands (EN)=Föroyar/Færøerne (5)	6	Fc	62.00N	7.00W
Faeroe Islands (EN)=Föroyar/Færøerne	5	Fc	62.00N	7.00W
Færøerne/Föroyar=Faeroe Islands (EN)	5	Fc	62.00N	7.00W
Færøerne/Föroyar=Faeroe Islands (EN) (5)	6	Fc	62.00N	7.00W
Fafa	35	Bd	7.18N	18.16 E
Fafe	13	Dc	41.27N	8.10W
Fafen	30	Lh	5.47N	44.11 E
Faga	34	Fc	13.45N	0.58 E
Fagaloa Bay	65c	Ba	13.54S	171.28W
Fagamalo	65c	Aa	13.25S	172.21W
Făgăraş	15	Hd	45.51N	24.58 E
Făgarasului, Munţii-	15	Hd	45.35N	25.00 E
Fagataufa Atoll	57	Ng	22.14S	138.45W
Fågelmara	8	Fh	56.15N	15.57 E
Fagerhult	8	Fg	57.09N	15.40 E
Fagernes	7	Bf	60.59N	9.15 E
Fagersta	7	Df	60.00N	15.47 E
Făget	15	Fd	45.51N	22.11 E
Fagita	26	Jg	1.48S	130.25 E
Fagnano, Lago-	56	Gh	54.38S	68.00W
Fagne	11	Kd	50.10N	4.25 E
Faguibine, Lac-	30	Gg	16.45N	3.54W
Fahliān	24	Ng	30.12N	51.28 E
Fahner Höhe	10	Ge	51.10N	10.45 E
Faial	30	Ee	38.34N	28.42W
Fā'id	24	Eg	30.19N	32.19 E
Faïoa	64h	Bc	13.23S	176.08W
Fairbairn Reservoir	59	Jd	23.40S	148.00 E
Fairbanks	39	Ec	64.51N	147.43W
Fairborn	44	Ef	39.48N	84.03W
Fairbury	43	Hc	40.08N	97.11W
Fairchild	45	Kd	44.36N	90.58W
Fairfield [Al.-U.S.]	44	Di	33.29N	86.55W
Fairfield [Ca.-U.S.]	46	Dg	38.15N	122.01W
Fairfield [Ia.-U.S.]	45	Kf	40.59N	91.57W
Fairfield [Id.-U.S.]	46	He	43.21N	114.48W
Fairfield [Il.-U.S.]	45	Lg	38.23N	88.22W
Fair Isle	9	Lb	59.30N	1.40W
Fairlie	62	Df	44.06S	170.50 E
Fairmont [Mn.-U.S.]	43	Ic	43.39N	94.28W
Fairmont [W.V.-U.S.]	43	Ld	39.28N	80.08W
Fair Ness	42	Kd	63.24N	72.05W
Fairview [Mt.-U.S.]	46	Mc	47.51N	104.03W
Fairview [Ok.-U.S.]	45	Gh	36.16N	98.29W
Fairview Peak	46	De	43.35N	122.39W
Fairweather, Mount-	38	Fd	58.54N	137.32W
Fais Island	57	Fd	9.46N	140.31 E
Faistós	15	Hn	35.03N	24.48 E
Faith	43	Gb	45.02N	102.02W
Faizābād	25	Gc	26.47N	82.08 E
Fajardo	49	Od	18.20N	65.39W
Fajou, Ilet 'a-	51e	Ab	16.21N	61.35W
Fakahina Atoll	57	Mf	15.59S	140.08W
Fakaofo Atoll	57	Je	9.22S	171.14W
Fakarava Atoll	57	Mf	16.20S	145.37W
Fakaura	29	Fa	40.38N	139.55 E
Fakel	7	Mh	57.40N	53.05 E
Fakenham	12	Cb	52.50N	0.50 E
Fakfak	26	Jg	2.55S	132.18 E
Fakhr	24	Pg	31.25N	54.01 E
Fakse Bugt	8	Ei	55.10N	12.15 E
Faksefjell	8	Ec	61.20N	12.52 E
Fakse Ladeplads	8	Ei	55.15N	12.08 E
Faku	28	Gc	42.30N	123.24 E
Falaba	34	Cd	9.51N	11.19W
Fala-Beguets	64d	Bb	7.21N	151.40 E
Falaise	11	Ff	48.54N	0.12W
Falaise de Tiguidit	34	Gb	16.22N	7.45 E
Falakrón Óros	5	Gh	41.19N	24.00 E
Falalu	4d	Ba	7.38N	151.41 E
Falam	25	Id	22.55N	93.41 E
Falas	64d	Ba	7.32N	151.46 E
Fălciu	15	Lc	46.18N	28.08 E
Falcón (2)	54	Ea	11.00N	69.50W
Falcon, Cap	13	Li	35.46N	0.48W
Falcon, Presa-	45	Gm	26.37N	99.11W
Falconara Marittima	14	Hg	43.37N	13.24 E
Falcone, Punta-	14	Cj	40.58N	8.12 E
Falcon Reservoir	43	Hf	26.37N	99.11W
Faléa	34	Cc	12.16N	11.15W
Faleallej Pass	64d	Bb	7.26N	151.34 E
Falealupo	65c	Aa	13.30S	172.48W
Falelima	65c	Aa	13.32S	172.41W
Falémé	30	Fg	14.46N	12.14W
Falenki	7	Mg	58.23N	51.36 E
Falerum	8	Gf	58.09N	16.13 E
Faleşty	16	Ef	47.35N	27.44 E
Falevai	65c	Ba	13.55S	171.59W
Falfurrias	43	Hf	27.14N	98.09W
Falkenberg	7	Ch	56.54N	12.28 E
Falkensee	10	Jd	52.34N	13.05 E
Falkirk	9	Jf	56.00N	3.48W
Falkland Islands/Malvinas, Islas- (5)	53	Kk	51.45S	59.00W
Falkland Islands/Malvinas, Islas-	52	Kk	51.45S	59.00W
Falkland Plateau (EN)	52	Lk	51.00S	50.00W
Falkland Sound	56	Ih	51.45S	59.25W
Falkonéra	15	Gm	36.50N	23.53 E
Falköping	7	Cg	58.10N	13.31 E
Fallingbostel	10	Fd	52.52N	9.42 E
Fallon [Mt.-U.S.]	46	Mc	46.48N	105.00W
Fallon [Nv.-U.S.]	46	Fg	39.28N	118.47W
Fall River	43	Mc	41.43N	71.08W
Falls City	43	Hc	40.03N	95.36W
Falmouth [Atg.]	51d	Bb	17.01N	61.46W
Falmouth [Eng.-U.K.]	9	Hk	50.08N	5.04W
Falmouth [Jam.]	49	Id	18.30N	77.39W
Falmouth [Ky.-U.S.]	44	Ef	38.40N	84.20W
Falmouth Bay	9	Hk	50.10N	5.05W
Falmouth Harbour	51d	Bb	17.01N	61.46W
Falo	64d	Bb	7.29N	151.53 E
False Bay	30	Il	34.15S	18.35 E
False Pass	40	Gf	54.52N	163.24W
Falset	13	Mc	41.08N	0.49 E
Falso, Cabo- [Dom.Rep.]	49	Le	17.47N	71.41W
Falso, Cabo- [Hond.]	49	Ff	15.12N	83.20W
Falso, Cabo- [Mex.]	47	Cd	22.52N	109.58W
Falso Cabo de Hornos	56	Gi	55.43S	68.05W
Falster	7	Ci	54.50N	12.00 E
Falsterbo	8	Ei	55.24N	12.50 E
Falterona	14	Fg	43.52N	11.42 E
Fălticeni	15	Jb	47.27N	26.18 E
Falun	6	Hc	60.36N	15.38 E
Fama	35	Cb	15.22N	20.34 E
Famagusta (EN)=Gazimağusa	23	Dc	35.07N	33.57 E
Famatina, Nevados de-	56	Gc	29.00S	67.51W
Famenne	11	Ld	50.15N	5.15 E
Fana	34	Dc	12.45N	6.57W
Fanan	64d	Bb	7.11N	151.59 E
Fanchang	27	Ke	31.00N	118.11 E
Fancy	51n	Ba	13.22N	61.12W
Fandriana	37	Hd	20.13S	47.20 E
Fangak	35	Ed	9.04N	30.53 E
Fangatau Atoll	57	Mf	15.50S	140.52W
Fangcheng	27	Je	33.09N	113.05 E
Fangliao	27	Lg	22.22N	120.25 E
Fangshan	28	Ce	39.43N	115.58 E
Fangxian	27	Je	32.03N	110.41 E
Fangzheng	27	Mb	45.50N	128.49 E
Fangzi	28	Ef	36.36N	119.08 E
Fanjiatun	28	Hc	43.42N	125.05 E
Fanjing Shan	27	If	27.57N	108.50 E
Fannaråken	8	Bc	61.31N	7.55 E
Fanning→Tabuaeran Atoll	57	Ld	3.52N	159.20W
Fano	14	Hg	43.50N	13.01 E
Fanø	8	Ci	55.25N	8.25 E
Fanø Bugt	8	Ci	55.25N	8.10 E
Fanshi	28	Be	39.11N	113.16 E
Fan Si Pan	21	Mg	22.15N	103.50 E
Fan Si Pan	25	Kd	22.18N	103.46 E
Fanuatapu	65c	Ba	13.59S	171.20W
Fanxian	28	Cg	35.53N	115.29 E
Fāqūs	24	Dg	30.44N	31.48 E
Farab	18	De	39.12N	63.38 E
Faraba	34	Cc	12.52N	11.23W
Faraday	66	Qe	65.15S	64.15W
Faraday Seamounts (EN)	5	Df	49.30N	28.30W
Faradje	36	Eb	3.44N	29.43 E
Faradofay	31	Lk	25.01S	46.59 E
Farafangana	37	Hd	22.48S	47.50 E
Farāfirah, Wāḩāt al-=Farafra Oasis (EN)	30	Jf	27.15N	28.10 E
Farafra Oasis (EN)=Farāfirah, Wāḩāt al-	30	Jf	27.15N	28.10 E
Farāh	21	If	31.29N	61.24 E
Farāh	22	If	32.22N	62.07 E
Farāh (3)	23	Jc	33.00N	62.30 E
Far'ah, Wādī al-	24	Hj	24.02N	38.09 E
Faraḩābād	24	Od	36.47N	53.06 E
Faranah	34	Cc	10.02N	10.44W
Farasan	23	Ff	16.42N	42.00 E
Farasan, Jazā'ir-	23	Ff	16.48N	41.54 E
Farasān al Kabīr	33	Hf	16.42N	42.00 E
Faraulep Atoll	57	Fd	8.36N	144.33 E
Farcău, Vîrful-	15	Hb	47.55N	24.27 E
Farciennes	12	Gd	50.26N	4.33 E
Fardes	13	Jg	37.35N	3.00W
Fare	65e	Db	16.42S	151.01W
Fareham	9	Lk	50.51N	1.10W
Farewell, Cape-	57	Ii	40.30S	172.43 E
Farewell Spit	62	Ed	40.30S	172.50 E
Färgelanda	8	Df	58.34N	11.59 E
Fargo	39	Je	46.52N	96.48W
Faribault	45	Jd	44.18N	93.16W
Faribault, Lac-	42	Ke	58.00N	72.00W

Index Symbols

(1) Independent Nation
(2) State, Region
(3) District, County
(5) Municipality
Colony, Dependency
Continent
Physical Region
Historical or Cultural Region
Mount, Mountain
Volcano
Hill
Mountains, Mountain Range
Hills, Escarpment
Plateau, Upland
Pass, Gap
Plain, Lowland
Delta
Salt Flat
Valley, Canyon
Crater, Cave
Karst Features
Depression
Polder
Desert, Dunes
Forest, Woods
Heath, Steppe
Oasis
Cape, Point
Coast, Beach
Cliff
Peninsula
Isthmus
Sandbank
Island
Atoll
Rock, Reef
Islands, Archipelago
Rocks, Reefs
Coral Reef
Well, Spring
Geyser
River, Stream
Waterfall Rapids
River Mouth, Estuary
Lake
Salt Lake
Intermittent Lake
Reservoir
Swamp, Pond
Canal
Glacier
Ice Shelf, Pack Ice
Ocean
Sea
Gulf, Bay
Strait, Fjord
Lagoon
Bank
Seamount
Tablemount
Ridge
Shelf
Basin
Escarpment, Sea Scarp
Fracture
Trench, Abyss
National Park, Reserve
Point of Interest
Recreation Site
Cave, Cavern
Historic Site
Ruins
Wall, Walls
Church, Abbey
Temple
Scientific Station
Airport
Port
Lighthouse
Mine
Tunnel
Dam, Bridge

Farīd, Qarāt al- 24 Ch 28.43N 28.21 E
Faridpur 25 Hd 23.36N 89.50 E
Fārila 7 Df 61.48N 15.51 E
Farilhões, Ilhas- 13 Ce 39.28N 9.34W
Farim 34 Bc 12.29N 15.13W
Farini d'Olmo 14 Df 44.43N 9.34 E
Fāris 24 Ej 24.37N 32.54 E
Fariš 18 Fd 40.33N 66.52 E
Fāris 35 Ia 20.11N 50.56 E
Faris Seamount (EN) 40 Jf 54.30N 147.15W
Färjestaden 7 Dh 56.39N 16.27 E
Farkadhón 15 Fj 39.36N 22.04 E
Farmahīn 24 Me 34.30N 49.41 E
Farmakonisi 15 Kl 37.18N 27.08 E
Farmerville 45 Jj 32.47N 92.24W
Farmington [Me.-U.S.] 44 Lc 44.40N 70.09W
Farmington [Mo.-U.S.] 45 Kh 37.47N 90.25W
Farmington [N.M.-U.S.] 43 Fd 36.44N 108.12W
Farmville 44 Hg 37.17N 78.25W
Färnäs 8 Fc 61.00N 14.38 E
Farnborough 12 Bc 51.16N 0.44W
Farne Deep 9 Mf 55.30N 0.50W
Farne Islands 9 Lf 55.38N 1.38W
Farnham [Eng.-U.K.] 12 Bc 51.12N 0.48W
Farnham [Que.-Can.] 44 Kc 45.17N 72.59W
Farnham, Mount- 46 Ga 50.29N 116.30W
Fårö 7 Eh 57.55N 19.10 E
Faro 34 Hd 9.21N 12.55 E
Faro [2] 13 Dg 37.12N 8.10W
Faro 6 Fh 37.01N 7.56W
Faro, Punta- 49 Jh 11.07N 74.51W
Faro, Sierra del- 13 Eb 42.37N 7.55W
Faro de Avión 13 Db 42.18N 8.16W
Faro de Chantada 13 Eb 42.37N 7.55W
Farofa, Serra da- 55 Gh 28.00S 50.10W
Farosund 8 Hg 57.55N 19.05 E
Fårösund 7 Eh 57.52N 19.03 E
Farquhar, Cape- 59 Cd 23.35S 113.35 E
Farquhar Group 30 Mj 10.10S 51.10 E
Farrar 9 Id 57.27N 4.35W
Farrāshband 24 Oh 28.53N 52.06 E
Farris 8 Ce 59.05N 10.00 E
Farruch, Cabo- 13 Pe 39.47N 3.21 E
Farrukhābād 25 Fc 27.24N 79.34 E
Fārs 21 Hg 29.00N 53.00 E
Fārs [3] 23 Hd 29.00N 53.00 E
Fārsābād 24 Mc 39.30N 48.05 E
Fársala 15 Fj 39.18N 22.23 E
Farshūţ 24 Ei 26.03N 32.09 E
Farsø 8 Ch 56.47N 9.21 E
Farsund 7 Bg 58.05N 6.48 E
Fartak, Ra's- 23 Hf 15.38N 52.15 E
Fartura, Rio- 55 Gc 16.29S 50.33W
Fartura, Serra da- [Braz.] 55 Hf 23.20S 49.25W
Fartura, Serra da- [Braz.] 55 Fh 26.21S 52.52W
Fārūj 24 Rd 37.14N 58.14 E
Farvel, Kap-/
Ūmánarssuaq 67 Nb 59.50N 43.50W
Farwell Island 66 Pf 72.49S 91.10W
Fāryāb [3] 23 Jb 36.00N 65.00 E
Fasā 24 Oh 28.56N 53.42 E
Fasano 14 Lj 40.50N 17.22 E
Fastnet Rock 9 Dj 51.24N 9.35W
Fastov 19 De 50.06N 30.01 E
Fataka Island 57 If 11.55S 170.12 E
Fatala 34 Cc 10.13N 14.00W
Fatehpur 25 Ec 28.01N 74.58 E
Fatež 16 Ic 52.06N 35.52 E
Father Lake 44 Ja 49.24N 75.18W
Fatick 34 Bc 14.20N 16.25W
Fátima 13 De 39.37N 8.39W
Fatīrah, Wādī- 24 Ei 26.39N 32.58 E
Fatsa 24 Gb 40.59N 37.24 E
Fatu Hiva, Ile- 57 Nf 10.28S 138.38W
Fatu Hutu, Ile- 57 Ne 9.00S 138.50W
Fatumanini, Passe- 64h Ab 13.14S 176.13W
Fatunda 36 Cc 4.08S 17.13 E
Fauabu 63a Ec 8.34S 160.43 E
Faucigny 11 Mh 46.05N 6.35 E
Faucille, Col de la- 11 Mh 46.22N 6.02 E
Faulkton 45 Gd 45.02N 99.08W
Faulquemont 12 Ie 49.03N 6.36 E
Fauquembergues 12 Ed 50.36N 2.05 E
Făurei 15 Kd 45.04N 27.14 E
Fauro 63a Cb 6.55S 156.07 E
Fauske 7 Dc 67.15N 15.24 E
Fauville-en-Caux 12 Ce 49.39N 0.35 E
Faux-Lap 37 He 25.32S 45.30 E
Fåvang 8 Dc 61.26N 10.13 E
Favara 14 Hm 37.19N 13.39 E
Faversham 12 Cc 51.19N 0.54 E
Favignana 14 Gm 37.55N 12.19 E
Favignana 14 Gm 37.56N 12.20 E
Favorite 12 Kf 48.49N 8.16 E
Fawley 12 Ad 50.49N 1.21W
Fawn 42 Ie 55.22N 88.20W
Fa'w Qiblī 24 Ei 26.07N 32.24 E
Faxaflói 5 Dc 64.24N 23.00W
Faxinal 55 Gf 23.59S 51.22W
Faya-Largeau 31 Ig 17.55N 19.07 E
Fayaoué 63b Ce 20.39S 166.32 E
Fayd 24 Ji 27.07N 42.31 E
Fayette [Al.-U.S.] 44 Di 33.42N 87.50W
Fayette [Oh.-U.S.] 44 Ee 41.41N 84.20W
Fayetteville [Ar.-U.S.] 43 Id 36.04N 94.10W
Fayetteville [N.C.-U.S.] 39 Lf 35.03N 78.54W
Fayetteville [Tn.-U.S.] 44 Dh 35.09N 86.35W
Faylakah, Jazīrat- 24 Mh 29.27N 48.20 E
Faysh Khābūr 24 Jd 37.04N 42.23 E
Fayu Island 57 Gd 8.35N 151.22 E
Fazenda de Cima 55 Db 15.56S 56.37W
Fazenda Nova 55 Gc 16.11S 50.48W
Fāzilka 25 Eb 30.24N 74.02 E
Fazrān 24 Mi 26.13N 49.12 E
Fazzān = Fezzan (EN) 33 Bd 25.30N 14.00 E
Fazzān = Fezzan (EN) 30 If 26.00N 14.00 E
Fdérick 31 Ff 22.39N 12.43W
Feale/An Fhéil 9 Di 52.28N 9.40W
Fear, Cape- 43 Le 33.50N 77.58W
Featherston 62 Fd 41.07S 175.19 E
Feathertop, Mount- 59 Jg 36.54S 147.08 E
Fécamp 11 Ge 49.45N 0.22 E
Fecht 11 Nf 48.11N 7.26 E
Federacion 56 Id 31.00S 57.54W
Federal 56 Id 30.55S 58.45W
Federated States of
Micronesia [5] 58 Gd 6.30N 152.00 E
Federovka [Kaz.-U.S.S.R.] 19 Ge 53.38N 62.42 E
Federovka [R.S.F.S.R.] 17 Gj 53.10N 55.10 E
Federsee 10 Fh 48.05N 9.38 E
Fedje 7 Af 60.47N 4.42 E
Fedorovka 16 Qd 51.16N 52.00 E
Fefan 64d Bb 7.21N 151.51 E
Fegen 8 Eg 57.11N 13.09 E
Fegen 8 Eg 57.06N 13.02 E
Fehérgyarmat 10 Si 47.59N 22.31 E
Fehmarn 10 Hb 54.30N 11.10 E
Fehmarnbelt 8 Dj 54.35N 11.15 E
Fehrbellin 10 Id 52.48N 12.46 E
Feicheng 28 Df 36.15N 116.46 E
Feidong (Dianbu) 28 Di 31.53N 117.29 E
Fei Huang He 28 Fg 34.15N 120.17 E
Feijó 54 De 8.09S 70.21W
Feilding 61 Eh 40.12S 175.35 E
Feira 36 Ff 15.37S 30.25 E
Feira de Santana 53 Mg 12.15S 38.57W
Feiran Oasis 24 Eh 28.42N 33.38 E
Feistritz 14 Kc 47.01N 16.08 E
Feixi (Shangpaihe) 28 Di 31.42N 117.09 E
Feixian 28 Dg 35.16N 117.59 E
Feixiang 28 Cf 36.32N 114.47 E
Fejão Prêto ou Furtado, Rio-
55 Dc 17.33S 57.23W
Fejér [2] 10 Oi 47.10N 18.35 E
Fejø 8 Dj 54.55N 11.25 E
Feke 24 Fd 37.53N 35.58 E
Fekete-viz 10 Ok 45.47N 18.13 E
Felanitx 13 Pe 39.28N 3.08 E
Feldbach 14 Jd 46.57N 15.53 E
Feldioara 15 Id 45.49N 25.36 E
Feldkirch 14 Dc 47.14N 9.36 E
Feldkirchen 14 Id 46.43N 14.06 E
Feliciano, Arroyo- 55 Cj 31.06S 59.54W
Felidu Atoll 25a Bb 3.30N 73.30 E
Felipe Carrillo Puerto 47 Ge 19.35N 88.03W
Felix, Cape - 42 Hc 69.55N 97.47W
Felixlândia 55 Jd 18.47S 44.55W
Felixstowe 9 Oj 51.58N 1.20 E
Felletin 11 Ii 45.53N 2.11 E
Feltre 14 Fd 46.01N 11.54 E
Femer Bælt 8 Dj 54.35N 11.15 E
Femø 8 Dj 54.55N 11.35 E
Femund 7 Ce 62.15N 11.50 E
Fena Valley Reservoir 64c Bb 13.20N 144.45 E
Fener Burnu 24 Hb 41.07N 39.25 E
Fénérive 37 Hc 17.22S 49.25 E
Fenerwa 35 Fc 13.05N 39.01 E
Fénétrange 12 Jf 48.51N 7.01 E
Fengcheng [China] 27 Lc 40.28N 124.01 E
Fengcheng [China] 28 Cj 28.11N 115.47 E
Fengdu 27 If 29.58N 107.39 E
Fenghua 28 Fj 29.40N 121.24 E
Fengjie 27 He 31.06N 104.30 E
Fenglingdu 27 Je 34.40N 110.19 E
Fengnan (Xugezhuang) 28 Ee 39.34N 118.05 E
Fengning (Dagezhen) 28 Dd 41.12N 116.39 E
Fengqing 27 Gg 24.41N 99.53 E
Fengqiu 28 Cg 35.02N 114.25 E
Fengrun 28 Ee 39.50N 118.09 E
Fengshui Shan 27 La 52.15N 123.30 E
Fengtai [China] 28 Dh 32.43N 116.43 E
Fengtai [China] 28 De 39.51N 116.17 E
Fengweiba → Zhenkang 27 Gg 23.54N 99.00 E
Fengxian 28 Dg 34.42N 116.35 E
Fengxian (Nanqiao) 28 Fi 30.55N 121.27 E
Fengxiang 27 Ie 34.32N 107.34 E
Fengxiang → Luobei 27 Nb 47.36N 130.58 E
Fengxin 28 Cj 28.42N 115.23 E
Fengyang 28 Dh 32.53N 117.33 E
Fengzhen 27 Jc 40.28N 113.09 E
Fen He [China] 27 Jd 35.36N 110.42 E
Fen He [China] 28 Ae 38.06N 111.52 E
Feni Islands 57 Ge 4.05S 153.42 E
Fennimore 45 Ke 42.59N 90.39W
Fensfjorden 8 Ad 60.50N 4.50 E
Fenshui Guan 27 Kf 27.56N 117.50 E
Fenton 44 Fd 42.48N 83.42W
Fenua Fu 64h Ac 13.23S 176.11W
Fenualoa 63c Bb 10.16S 166.15 E
Fenyang 27 Jd 37.17N 111.45 E
Feodosija 19 Df 45.02N 35.23 E
Fer, Cap de- 32 Ib 37.05N 7.10 E
Fer, Point au- 45 Kl 29.20N 91.21W
Feragen 8 Db 62.30N 11.55 E
Férai 15 Ji 40.54N 26.10 E
Ferdows 23 Ic 34.00N 58.09 E
Fère-Champenoise 11 Jf 48.45N 3.59 E
Fère-en-Tardenois 12 Fe 49.12N 3.31 E
Feren 8 Da 63.34N 11.50 E
Ferentino 14 Hi 41.42N 13.15 E
Ferfer [Eth.] 35 Hd 5.06N 45.09 E
Ferfer [Som.] 35 Hd 5.07N 45.07 E
Fergana 22 Je 40.23N 71.46 E
Fergana 21 Je 40.30N 71.00 E
Ferganskaja Oblast [3] 19 Hg 40.30N 71.20 E
Ferganski Hrebet 19 Hg 41.00N 74.00 E
Fergus Falls 43 Hb 46.17N 96.04W
Ferguson Lake 42 Hc 69.00N 105.00W
Fergusson Island 60 Ei 9.30S 150.40 E
Ferkéssédougou [3] 34 Ed 9.20N 4.55W
Ferkéssédougou 34 Dd 9.36N 5.12W
Ferlo 30 Fg 15.00N 14.00W
Ferlo 30 Fg 15.42N 15.30W
Fermo 14 Hg 43.09N 13.43 E
Fermoselle 13 Fc 41.19N 6.23W
Fermoy/Mainistir Fhear Mai 9 Ei 52.08N 8.16W
Fernandina, Isla- 52 Gf 0.25S 91.30W
Fernandina Beach 44 Gj 30.40N 81.27W
Fernando de Noronha, Ilha- 52 Mf 3.51S 32.25W
Fernando de Noronha,
Território de- [2] 54 Ld 3.50S 33.00W
Fernandópolis 56 Kb 20.16S 50.00W
Fernán-Núñez 13 Hg 37.40N 4.43W
Fernelmont 12 Hd 50.35N 5.02 E
Fernie 46 Hb 49.30N 115.03W
Ferrandina 14 Kj 40.29N 16.27 E
Ferrara 14 Ff 44.50N 11.35 E
Ferrat, Cap- 13 Li 35.54N 0.23W
Ferrato, Capo- 14 Dk 39.18N 9.38 E
Ferré 55 Bl 34.08S 61.08W
Ferré, Cap- 51h Bc 14.28N 60.49W
Ferreira do Alentejo 13 Df 38.03N 8.07W
Ferreñafe 54 Ce 6.38S 79.48W
Ferret, Cap- 11 Ej 44.37N 1.15W
Ferriday 45 Kk 31.38N 91.33W
Ferrières 12 Hd 50.24N 5.36 E
Ferro, Capo- 14 Di 41.09N 9.31 E
Ferro, Rio- 55 Ea 12.27S 54.31W
Ferru, Monte- 14 Cj 40.08N 8.36 E
Ferry, Pointe- 51e Ab 16.17N 61.49W
Fertilia 14 Cj 40.36N 8.17 E
Fertő → Neusiedler See 10 Mi 47.50N 16.45 E
Fès 31 Ge 34.02N 4.59W
Fès [3] 32 Gc 34.00N 5.00W
Feshi 36 Cd 6.07S 18.10 E
Fessenden 45 Gc 47.39N 99.38W
Festieux 12 Fe 49.31N 3.45 E
Festus 45 Kg 38.13N 90.24W
Feteşti 15 Ke 44.23N 27.50 E
Fethiye 23 Cb 36.37N 29.07 E
Fethiye Körfezi 24 Cd 36.40N 29.00 E
Fetlar 9 Ma 60.37N 0.52W
Fetsund 7 Cg 59.56N 11.10 E
Feuchtwangen 10 Gg 49.10N 10.20 E
Feuilles, Baie aux - 42 Ke 58.55N 69.15W
Feuilles, Rivière aux- 42 Ke 58.46N 70.05W
Feurs 11 Ki 45.45N 4.14 E
Fevik 8 Cf 58.23N 8.42 E
Feyzābād 22 Jf 37.06N 70.34 E
Fezzan (EN) = Fazzān 33 Bd 25.30N 14.00 E
Fezzan (EN) = Fazzān 30 If 26.00N 14.00 E
Fezzane, Emi- 34 Ha 21.42N 14.15 E
Ffestiniog 9 Ji 52.58N 3.55W
Fiambalá 56 Gc 27.41S 67.38W
Fianarantsoa 31 Lk 21.28S 47.05 E
Fianarantsoa [3] 37 Hd 21.30S 47.05 E
Fianga 35 Bd 9.55N 15.09 E
Fiche 35 Fd 9.48N 38.44 E
Fichtelgebirge 5 He 50.00N 12.00 E
Ficksburg 37 De 28.57S 27.50 E
Fidenza 14 Ef 44.52N 10.03 E
Fieni 15 Id 45.08N 25.25 E
Fier 11 Li 45.56N 5.50 E
Fieri 15 Ci 40.43N 19.34 E
Fife [3] 9 Je 56.05N 3.15W
Fife Ness 9 Ke 56.17N 2.36W
Fiffa 34 Dc 11.27N 9.52W
Fifth Cataract (EN) =
Khāmis, Ash Shallāl al- 30 Kg 18.23N 33.47 E
Figalo, Cap- 13 Ki 35.35N 1.12W
Figeac 11 Ij 44.36N 2.02 E
Figeholm 8 Gg 57.22N 16.33 E
Figtree 37 Dd 20.22S 28.20 E
Figueira, Baia da- 55 Dc 16.33S 57.25W
Figueira da Foz 13 Dd 40.09N 8.52W
Figueira de Castelo Rodrigo 13 Fd 40.54N 6.58W
Figueras 13 Ob 42.16N 2.58 E
Figueras/Figueres 13 Ob 42.16N 2.58 E
Figueres 13 Ob 42.16N 2.58 E
Figueres/Figueras 13 Ob 42.16N 2.58 E
Figuig [3] 32 Gc 33.00N 2.01W
Figuig 32 Gc 32.06N 1.14W
Fiherenana 37 Gd 23.19S 43.37 E
Fijāj, Shaţţ al- 32 Ic 33.55N 9.10 E
Fiji [1] 58 If 18.00S 178.00 E
Fiji Islands 57 If 18.00S 178.00 E
Fik 35 Gd 8.08N 42.18 E
Filabres, Sierra de los- 13 Jg 37.15N 2.20W
Filabusi 37 Dd 20.32S 29.16 E
Filadélfia 54 Ie 7.21S 47.30W
Filadelfia [C.R.] 49 Eh 10.26N 85.34W
Filadelfia [It.] 14 Kl 38.47N 16.17 E
Filakara 63b Dc 16.49S 168.24 E
Filákovo 10 Ph 48.16N 19.50 E
Filamana 34 Dc 10.30N 7.57W
Filatova Gora 8 Mg 57.39N 28.21 E
Filchner Ice Shelf 66 Af 79.00S 40.00W
Filey 9 Mg 54.12N 0.17W
Filiaşi 15 Ge 44.33N 23.31 E
Filiátai 15 Dj 39.36N 20.49 E
Filiatrá 15 El 37.09N 21.35 E
Filicudi 14 Il 38.35N 14.35 E
Filingué 34 Fc 14.21N 3.19 E
Filiouri 15 Ii 40.57N 25.20 E
Filippiás 15 Dj 39.12N 20.53 E
Filippoi 15 Hh 41.02N 24.20 E
Filippoi = Philippi (EN) 15 Hh 41.02N 24.18 E
Filipstad 7 Dg 59.43N 14.10 E
Fillefjell 8 Cc 61.09N 8.15 E
Filliévres 12 Ed 50.19N 2.10 E
Fillmore 46 Ig 38.58N 112.20W
Fils 10 Fh 48.35N 9.29 E
Filtu 35 Gd 5.06N 40.40 E
Fimaina 15 Jl 37.35N 26.26 E
Fimi 36 Cc 3.01S 16.58 E
Fin [Iran] 24 Pi 27.38N 55.55 E
Fin [Iran] 24 Nf 33.57N 51.24 E
Finale Emilia 14 Ff 44.50N 11.17 E
Finale Ligure 14 Cf 44.10N 8.20 E
Findhorn 9 Jd 57.41N 3.32W
Fındıklı 24 Ib 41.17N 41.09 E
Findlay 43 Kc 41.02N 83.40W
Findlay, Mount- 46 Ga 50.04N 116.28W
Findlay Group 42 Ha 77.15N 104.00W
Fineveke 64h Ab 13.19S 176.12W
Fingoé 37 Ec 15.10S 31.53 E
Finike 24 Dd 36.18N 30.09 E
Finistère [3] 11 Cf 48.20N 4.00W
Finisterre, Cabo de- 5 Fg 42.53N 9.16W
Finisterre Range 59 Ja 5.50S 146.05 E
Finke 58 Eg 25.34S 134.35 E
Finke, Mount- 59 Gf 30.55S 134.02 E
Finke River 57 Eg 27.00S 136.10 E
Finland/Suomi [1] 6 Ic 64.00N 26.00 E
Finland, Gulf of- (EN) =
Finski Zaliv 5 Ic 60.00N 27.00 E
Finland, Gulf of- (EN) =
Soomenlaht 5 Ic 60.00N 27.00 E
Finland, Gulf of- (EN) =
Suomenlahti 5 Ic 60.00N 27.00 E
Finlay 42 Fe 55.59N 123.50W
Finlay Mountains 45 Dk 31.30N 105.35W
Finne 10 He 51.13N 11.19 E
Finngrunden 8 Hc 61.00N 18.19 E
Finnigan, Mount- 59 Jc 15.50S 145.20 E
Finniss, Cape- 59 Gf 33.38S 134.51 E
Finnmark 8 Fc 61.40N 14.45 E
Finnmark [3] 7 Fb 69.50N 24.10 E
Finnmarksvidda 5 Ib 69.30N 24.20 E
Finnøy 8 Ae 59.10N 5.50 E
Finnskogen 8 Ed 60.40N 12.40 E
Finnsnes 7 Eb 69.14N 18.02 E
Finnveden 8 Eh 56.50N 13.40 E
Finote Selam 35 Fc 10.42N 37.12 E
Finschhafen 59 Ja 6.35S 147.50 E
Finse 8 Bd 60.36N 7.30 E
Finski Zaliv = Finland, Gulf
of- (EN) 5 Ic 60.00N 27.00 E
Finspång 7 Dg 58.43N 15.47 E
Finstadåa 8 Dc 61.47N 11.10 E
Finsteraarhorn 14 Cd 46.32N 8.08 E
Finsterwalde 10 Je 51.38N 13.43 E
Finström 8 Hd 60.16N 19.50 E
Fiora 14 Fh 42.20N 11.34 E
Fiorenzuola d'Arda 14 Df 44.56N 9.55 E
Firat = Euphrates (EN) 21 Gf 31.00N 47.25 E
Firenze = Florence (EN) 6 Hg 43.46N 11.15 E
Firenzuola 14 Ff 44.07N 11.23 E
Firmat 55 Bk 33.27S 61.29W
Firminópolis 55 Gc 16.40S 50.19W
Firminy 11 Ki 45.23N 4.18 E
Firozābād 25 Fc 27.09N 78.25 E
Firozpur 25 Eb 30.55N 74.36 E
First Cataract (EN) = Aswān,
Sadd al- 30 Kf 24.01N 32.52 E
Firūzābād 24 Oh 28.50N 52.36 E
Firūzābād 24 Pg 31.59N 54.20 E
Firūzābād 24 Le 34.09N 46.25 E
Firūz Kūk 24 Oe 35.45N 52.47 E
Fischbach 12 Je 49.44N 7.24 E
Fischbacher Alpen 14 Jc 47.25N 15.30 E
Fischland 10 Ib 54.22N 12.25 E
Fish [Nam.] 30 Ik 17.11S 28.08 E
Fish [S.Afr.] 37 Cf 31.14S 20.15 E
Fisher Glacier 66 Ef 73.15S 66.00 E
Fisher Peak 44 Gg 36.33N 80.50W
Fisher Strait 42 Jd 63.00N 84.00W
Fishguard 6 Fe 51.59N 4.59W
Fish River Canyon 37 Be 27.35S 17.35 E
Fiskárdhon 15 Dk 38.28N 20.35 E
Fiskenaes Bank (EN) 41 Gf 63.18N 52.10W
Fiskenæsset 41 Gf 63.10N 50.45W
Fismes 11 Je 49.18N 3.41 E
Fišt, Gora- 19 Dg 43.57N 39.55 E
Fitchburg 44 Ld 42.35N 71.48W
Fitjar 7 Ag 59.55N 5.20 E
Fito, Mount- 65c Ba 13.55S 171.44W
Fitri, Lac- 35 Bc 12.50N 17.28 E
Fitzcarrald 54 Df 11.49S 71.48W
Fitzgerald [Alta.-Can.] 42 Ge 59.52N 111.40W
Fitzgerald [Ga.-U.S.] 44 Fj 31.43N 83.15W
Fitzroy Crossing 58 Ff 18.11S 125.35 E
Fitzroy River [Austl.] 59 Kc 23.32S 150.52 E
Fitzroy River [Austl.] 57 Df 17.31S 123.35 E
Fitzwilliam Island 44 Gc 45.30N 81.45W
Fiuggi 14 Hi 41.48N 13.13 E
Fiumicino 14 Gi 41.46N 12.14 E
Five Island Harbour 51d Bb 17.06N 61.54W
Fivizzano 14 Ef 44.14N 10.08 E
Fizi 31 Ji 4.18S 28.57 E
Fizuli 19 Eh 39.35N 47.11 E
Fjærlandsfjorden 8 Bc 61.15N 6.40 E
Fjällbacka 8 Df 58.36N 11.17 E
Fjärås 7 Ch 57.26N 12.09 E
Fjerritslev 8 Cg 57.05N 9.16 E
Fjöllum, Jökulsá á- 7a Ca 66.02N 16.27W
Fjugesta 8 Fe 59.10N 14.52 E
Flacq 37a Bb 20.12S 57.43 E
Flade Isblink 41 Kb 81.25N 16.00W
Fladen 8 Dg 57.09N 11.35 E
Fladen 8 Dg 57.10N 11.45 E
Flagler 45 Eg 39.18N 103.04W
Flagstaff 39 Hf 35.12N 111.39W
Flåm 7 Bf 60.50N 7.07 E
Flamborough Head 9 Mg 54.07N 0.04W
Fläming 10 Ie 52.00N 13.00 E
Flaming Gorge Reservoir 46 Kf 41.15N 109.30W
Flamingo 44 Gm 25.09N 80.56W
Flamingo, Teluk- 26 Kh 5.33S 138.00 E
Flanders (EN) = Flandres/
Vlaanderen 5 Ge 51.00N 3.20 E
Flanders (EN) = Flandres/
Vlaanderen 11 Jc 51.00N 3.20 E
Flanders (EN) = Vlaanderen/
Flandres 5 Ge 51.00N 3.20 E
Flanders (EN) = Vlaanderen/
Flandres 11 Jc 51.00N 3.20 E
Flanders Plain (EN) =
Flandres, Plaine des- 11 Id 50.40N 2.50 E
Flanders Plain (EN) =
Vlamse Vlakte 11 Id 50.40N 2.50 E
Flandreau 45 Hd 44.03N 96.36W
Flandres/Vlaanderen =
Flanders (EN) 11 Jc 51.00N 3.20 E
Flandres/Vlaanderen =
Flanders (EN) 5 Ge 51.00N 3.20 E
Flandres, Plaine des- =
Flanders Plain (EN) 11 Id 50.40N 2.50 E
Flannan Isles 9 Fc 58.20N 7.35W
Flåren 8 Fh 57.00N 14.05 E
Flasher 45 Fc 46.27N 101.14W
Fläsjön 7 Dd 64.06N 15.51 E
Flat 40 Hd 62.27N 158.01W
Flatey 7a Ab 65.22N 22.56W
Flateyri 7a Aa 66.03N 23.31W
Flathead Lake 43 Eb 47.52N 114.08W
Flathead Range 46 Ib 48.05N 113.28W
Flathead River 46 Hc 47.22N 114.47W
Flat Point 51b Ab 18.15N 63.05W
Flat River 45 Kh 37.51N 90.31W
Flattery, Cape- 38 Ge 48.23N 124.43W
Flåvatnet 8 Ce 59.20N 8.50 E
Flaxton 45 Eb 48.54N 102.24W
Flaygreen Lake 42 Hf 53.50N 97.20W
Fleckenstein, Château de-
12 Je 49.05N 7.48 E
Fleet 12 Bc 51.17N 0.50W
Fleetwood 9 Jh 53.56N 3.01W
Flekkefjord 7 Bg 58.17N 6.41 E
Flémalle 12 Hd 50.36N 5.29 E
Flemish Bight [Eur.] 11 Dc 51.44N 2.30W
Flemish Bight [U.K.] 9 Pi 52.10N 2.50 E
Flemish Cap (EN) 38 Oe 47.00N 45.00W
Flemsøya 8 Bb 62.40N 6.20 E
Flen 7 Dg 59.04N 16.35 E
Flensborg Fjord 8 Cj 54.50N 9.45 E
Flensburg 6 Ge 54.47N 9.26 E
Flensburger Förde 8 Cj 54.50N 9.45 E
Flers 11 Ff 48.45N 0.34W
Flesberg 8 Ce 59.51N 9.27 E
Fleurance 11 Gk 43.50N 0.40 E
Fleury-sur-Andelle 12 De 49.22N 1.21 E
Fleuve [3] 34 Cb 16.00N 13.50W
Flevoland 11 Lb 52.25N 5.30 E
Flian 8 Ef 58.27N 13.05 E
Flims 14 Dd 46.50N 9.16 E
Flinders Bay 59 Df 34.25S 115.19 E
Flinders Island 57 Fi 40.00S 148.00 E
Flinders Passage 59 Jc 18.50S 149.00 E
Flinders Ranges 57 Eh 31.25S 138.45 E
Flinders Reefs 57 Ff 17.40S 148.30 E
Flinders River 57 Ff 17.36S 140.36 E
Flin Flon 39 Id 54.56N 101.53W
Flint [Mi.-U.S.] 39 Ke 43.01N 83.41W
Flint [Wales-U.K.] 9 Jh 53.15N 3.07W
Flint Hills 45 Hh 37.20N 96.35W
Flint Island 57 Lf 11.26S 151.48W
Flint River 44 Ee 30.52N 84.38W
Flisa 7 Cf 60.37N 12.04 E
Flisa 8 Ed 60.36N 12.01 E
Flisegga 8 Be 59.50N 7.50 E
Flitwick 12 Bb 52.00N 0.29W
Flix 13 Mc 41.14N 0.33 E
Flixecourt 12 Ed 50.01N 2.05 E
Flize 12 Ge 49.42N 4.46 E
Flobecq/Vloesberg 12 Fd 50.44N 3.44 E
Floby 8 Ef 58.08N 13.20 E
Floda [Swe.] 8 Fd 60.26N 14.49 E
Floda [Swe.] 8 Eg 57.48N 12.22 E
Flood Range 66 Nf 76.03S 134.00W
Flora [Il.-U.S.] 45 Lg 38.40N 88.29W
Flora [Nor.] 7 Af 61.36N 5.00 E
Florac 11 Jj 44.19N 3.36 E
Florala 44 Dj 31.00N 86.20W
Florange 12 Ie 49.20N 6.07 E
Florence [Al.-U.S.] 43 Je 34.49N 87.40W
Florence [Ks.-U.S.] 45 Hg 38.15N 96.56W
Florence [Or.-U.S.] 46 Cd 44.01N 124.07W
Florence [S.C.-U.S.] 43 Le 34.12N 79.44W
Florence (EN) = Firenze 6 Hg 43.46N 11.15 E
Florencia [Arg.] 55 Ci 28.02S 59.15W
Florencia [Col.] 53 Ie 1.36N 75.36W
Florencio Sánchez 55 Dk 33.53S 57.24W
Florennes 12 Gd 50.15N 4.37 E
Florentino Ameghino,
Embalse- 56 Gf 43.48S 66.25W
Florenville 11 Le 49.42N 5.18 E
Flores [2] 55 Dk 33.35S 56.50W
Flores 30 De 39.26N 31.13W
Flores [Guat.] 49 Ce 16.56N 89.53W
Flores [Guat.] 47 Ge 16.58N 89.50W
Flores, Arroyo de las- 55 Cl 35.36S 59.01W
Flores, Laut- = Flores Sea
(EN) 21 Oj 8.00S 121.00 E
Flores, Pulau- 21 Oj 8.30S 121.00 E
Flores Island 46 Bb 49.20N 126.10W
Flores Sea (EN) = Flores,
Laut- 21 Oj 8.00S 121.00 E
Floreşty 16 Ff 47.55N 28.18 E
Floriano 53 Lf 6.47S 43.01W
Florianópolis 53 Lh 27.35S 48.34W
Florida 53 Kg 28.00N 82.00W
Florida [Braz.] 55 Ei 29.15S 54.36W
Florida [Cuba] 47 Id 21.32N 78.14W
Florida [U.S.] [2] 43 Kf 28.00N 82.00W
Florida [Ur.] 56 Ek 33.50S 55.55W
Florida [Ur.] 56 Id 34.06S 56.13W
Florida, Estrecho de- =
Florida, Straits of- (EN) 38 Kg 24.00N 81.00W
Florida, Straits of- 38 Kg 24.00N 81.00W
Florida, Straits of- (EN) =
Florida, Estrecho de- 38 Kg 24.00N 81.00W
Florida Bay 44 Gm 25.00N 80.45W
Floridablanca 54 Db 7.04N 73.06W

Index Symbols

[1] Independent Nation
[2] State, Region
[3] District, County
[4] Municipality
[5] Colony, Dependency
Continent
Physical Region
Historical or Cultural Region
Mount, Mountain
Volcano
Hill
Mountains, Mountain Range
Hills, Escarpment
Plateau, Upland
Pass, Gap
Plain, Lowland
Delta
Salt Flat
Valley, Canyon
Crater, Cave
Karst Features
Depression
Polder
Desert, Dunes
Forest, Woods
Heath, Steppe
Oasis
Cape, Point
Coast, Beach
Cliff
Peninsula
Isthmus
Sandbank
Island
Atoll
Rock, Reef
Islands, Archipelago
Rocks, Reefs
Coral Reef
Well, Spring
Geyser
River, Stream
Waterfall Rapids
River Mouth, Estuary
Lake
Salt Lake
Intermittent Lake
Reservoir
Swamp, Pond
Canal
Glacier
Ice Shelf, Pack Ice
Ocean
Sea
Gulf, Bay
Strait, Fjord
Lagoon
Bank
Seamount
Tablemount
Ridge
Shelf
Basin
Escarpment, Sea Scarp
Fracture
Trench, Abyss
National Park, Reserve
Point of Interest
Recreation Site
Cave, Cavern
Historic Site
Ruins
Wall, Walls
Church, Abbey
Temple
Scientific Station
Airport
Port
Lighthouse
Mine
Tunnel
Dam, Bridge

Index Symbols

[1] Independent Nation	Historical or Cultural Region	Pass, Gap	Depression	Coast, Beach
[2] State, Region	Mount, Mountain	Plain, Lowland	Polder	Cliff
[3] District, County	Volcano	Delta	Desert, Dunes	Peninsula
[4] Municipality	Hill	Salt Flat	Forest, Woods	Isthmus
[5] Colony, Dependency	Mountains, Mountain Range	Valley, Canyon	Heath, Steppe	Sandbank
Continent	Hills, Escarpment	Crater, Cave	Oasis	Island
Physical Region	Plateau, Upland	Karst Features	Cape, Point	Atoll

Rock, Reef	Waterfall Rapids	Canal	Lagoon	Escarpment, Sea Scarp
Islands, Archipelago	River Mouth, Estuary	Glacier	Bank	Fracture
Rocks, Reefs	Lake	Ice Shelf, Pack Ice	Seamount	Trench, Abyss
Coral Reef	Salt Lake	Ocean	Tablemount	National Park, Reserve
Well, Spring	Intermittent Lake	Sea	Ridge	Point of Interest
Geyser	Reservoir	Gulf, Bay	Shelf	Recreation Site
River, Stream	Swamp, Pond	Strait, Fjord	Basin	Cave, Cavern

Historic Site	Port
Ruins	Lighthouse
Wall, Walls	Mine
Church, Abbey	Tunnel
Temple	Dam, Bridge
Scientific Station	
Airport	

Friesoythe 10 Dc 53.01N 7.51 E
Frigate Island 51p Cb 12.25N 61.29W
Friggesund 8 Gc 61.54N 16.32 E
Frignano 14 Ef 44.20N 10.50 E
Frindsbury Reef 63a Da 5.00S 159.07 E
Frinnaryd 8 Fg 57.56N 14.49 E
Frinton-on-Sea 12 Dc 51.50N 1.15 E
Frio, Cabo- 52 Lh 22.53S 42.00W
Frio, Rio- 49 Eh 11.08N 84.46W
Frio Draw 45 Ei 34.50N 102.08W
Friona 45 Ei 34.38N 102.43W
Frio River 45 Gl 28.30N 98.10W
Frisco Peak 46 Ig 38.31N 113.14W
Frisian Islands (EN) 5 Ge 54.00N 7.00 E
Fristad 8 Eg 57.50N 13.01 E
Fritsla 8 Eg 57.33N 12.47 E
Fritzlar 10 Fe 51.08N 9.17 E
Friuli 14 Ge 46.00N 13.00 E
Friuli-Venezia Giulia [2] 14 Gd 46.00N 13.00 E
Frobisher Bay 38 Mc 62.30N 66.00W
Frobisher Lake 42 Ge 56.20N 108.20W
Froidchapelle 12 Gd 50.09N 4.20 E
Froissy 12 Ee 49.34N 2.13 E
Frolovo 19 Ef 49.45N 43.39 E
Fromberg 46 Kd 45.23N 108.54W
Frombork 10 Pb 54.22N 19.41 E
Frome 9 Kj 51.14N 2.20W
Frome, Lake- 57 Eh 30.50S 139.50 E
Frondenberg 12 Jc 51.28N 7.46 E
Fronteira 13 Ee 39.03N 7.39W
Fronteiras 54 Je 7.05S 40.37W
Frontera 48 Mh 18.32N 92.38W
Frontera, Punta- 48 Mh 19.36N 92.42W
Fronteras 48 Eb 30.56N 109.31W
Frontignan 11 Jk 43.27N 3.45 E
Frontino, Paramo- 54 Cb 6.28N 76.04W
Front Range 38 If 39.45N 105.45W
Front Royal 44 Hf 38.56N 78.13W
Frosinone 14 Hi 41.38N 13.19 E
Frösö 8 Fa 63.11N 14.32 E
Frostburg 44 Hf 39.39N 78.56W
Frost Glacier 66 Ie 67.05S 129.00 E
Frövi 8 Fe 59.28N 15.22 E
Frøya 7 Be 63.43N 8.42 E
Frøysjøen 8 Ac 61.50N 5.05 E
Frozen Strait 42 Jc 65.50N 84.30W
Fruges 11 Id 50.31N 2.08 E
Frunze [Kirg.-U.S.S.R.] 18 Hd 40.06N 71.45 E
Frunze [Kirg.-U.S.S.R.] 22 Je 42.54N 74.36 E
Frunzovka 15 Mb 47.20N 29.37 E
Fruška Gora 15 Cd 45.10N 19.35 E
Frutal 54 Ih 20.02S 48.55W
Frutigen 14 Bd 46.35N 7.40 E
Fry Canyon 46 Jh 37.38N 110.08W
Frýdek Mistek 10 Og 49.41N 18.22 E
Frylinckspan 37 Ce 26.46S 22.28 E
Ftéri 15 Ej 39.09N 21.33 E
Fua'amotu 65b Ac 21.15S 175.08W
Fua Mulaku Island 25a Bc 0.15S 73.30 E
Fu'an 27 Kf 27.10N 119.44 E
Fu-chien Sheng → Fujian Sheng = Fukien (EN) [2] 27 Kf 26.00N 118.00 E
Fuchskauten 10 Ef 50.40N 8.05 E
Fuchū [Jap.] 29 Cd 34.34N 133.14 E
Fuchū [Jap.] 29 Fd 35.41N 139.28 E
Fuchun-Jiang 28 Fi 30.15N 120.15 E
Fuchunjiang-Shuiku 28 Ej 29.29N 119.31 E
Fucino, Conca del- 14 Hj 42.01N 13.31 E
Fudai 29 Ga 40.01N 141.52 E
Fuding 27 Lf 27.19N 120.08 E
Fuengirola 13 Hh 36.32N 4.37W
Fuente Alto 56 Fd 33.37S 70.35W
Fuente del Maestre 13 Ff 38.32N 6.27W
Fuente-Obejuna 13 Gf 38.16N 5.25W
Fuentesaúco 13 Gc 41.14N 5.30W
Fuentes de Andalucia 13 Gg 37.28N 5.21W
Fuentes de Cantos 13 Ff 38.15N 6.18W
Fuerte 47 Cc 25.54N 109.22W
Fuerte, Isla- 49 Ii 9.23N 76.11W
Fuerte, Sierra del- 48 Hd 27.30N 102.45W
Fuerte Olimpo 56 Ib 21.02S 57.54W
Fuerteventura 30 Ff 28.20N 14.00W
Fuga 26 Hc 18.52N 121.22 E
Fugong 27 Gf 27.03N 98.57 E
Fugou 28 Cg 34.04N 114.23 E
Fugu 27 Jd 39.02N 111.03 E
Fuguo → Zhanhua 28 Ef 37.42N 118.08 E
Fuhai/Burultokay 27 Eb 47.06N 87.23 E
Fuhayrī, Wādī- 23 Hf 16.04N 52.11 E
Fu He 28 Dj 28.36N 116.04 E
Fuji 28 Og 35.09N 138.38 E
Fujian Sheng (Fu-chien Sheng) = Fukien (EN) [2] 27 Kf 26.00N 118.00 E
Fujieda 29 Fd 34.51N 138.15 E
Fuji-Gawa 29 Fd 35.07N 138.38 E
Fujin 27 Nb 47.15N 132.01 E
Fujinomiya 29 Fd 35.12N 138.38 E
Fujioka 29 Fc 36.15N 139.03 E
Fuji-San 21 Pf 35.26N 138.43 E
Fujisawa 29 Fd 35.21N 139.27 E
Fuji-yoshida 29 Fd 35.29N 138.47 E
Fukagawa 27 Pc 43.43N 142.03 E
Fūkah 24 Bg 31.04N 27.55 E
Fukang 27 Ec 44.10N 87.59 E
Fuka-Shima 29 Be 32.43N 131.56 E
Fukiage 29 Bf 31.30N 130.20 E
Fukien (EN) = Fu-chien Sheng → Fujian Sheng [2] 27 Kf 26.00N 118.00 E
Fukien (EN) = Fujian Sheng (Fu-chien Sheng) [2] 27 Kf 26.00N 118.00 E
Fukuchiyama 28 Mg 35.18N 135.07 E
Fukue 28 Jh 32.41N 128.50 E
Fukueichiao 27 Lf 25.19N 121.34 E
Fukue-Jima 28 Jh 32.41N 128.48 E
Fukui 27 Od 36.04N 136.13 E
Fukui Ken [2] 28 Ng 36.00N 136.20 E
Fukuma 29 Be 33.47N 130.28 E
Fukuoka 22 Pf 33.35N 130.24 E
Fukuoka Ken [2] 28 Kh 33.28N 130.45 E
Fukuroi 29 Ed 34.45N 137.54 E
Fukushima [Jap.] 27 Pd 37.45N 140.28 E
Fukushima [Jap.] 27 Pc 41.29N 140.15 E
Fukushima Ken [2] 28 Pf 37.25N 140.10 E
Fukuyama 27 Ne 34.29N 133.22 E
Fūlādī, Kūh-e- 23 Kc 34.38N 67.32 E
Fūlād Mahalleh 24 Od 36.02N 53.44 E
Fulanga 63d Cc 19.08S 178.34W
Fulda 5 Ge 51.25N 9.39 E
Fulda 10 Ff 50.33N 9.40 E
Fuliji 28 Dh 33.47N 116.59 E
Fulin → Hanyuan 27 Hf 29.25N 102.12 E
Fuling 27 If 29.40N 107.21 E
Fullerton 45 Hf 41.22N 97.58W
Fulton [Arg.] 55 Cm 37.25S 58.48W
Fulton [Il.-U.S.] 45 Kf 41.52N 90.11W
Fulton [Ky.-U.S.] 44 Cg 36.30N 88.53W
Fulton [Mo.-U.S.] 45 Kg 38.52N 91.57W
Fulton [N.Y.-U.S.] 44 Id 43.20N 76.26W
Fulufjället 8 Ec 61.33N 12.43 E
Fumaiolo 14 Gg 43.47N 12.04 E
Fumay 11 Kd 50.00N 4.42 E
Fumel 11 Gj 44.30N 0.58 E
Funabasi 28 Og 35.42N 139.59 E
Funabiki 29 Gc 37.26N 140.35 E
Funafuti 58 Ie 8.01S 178.00 E
Funafuti Atoll 57 Ie 8.31S 179.08 E
Funagata 29 Gb 38.42N 140.18 E
Funagata-Yama 29 Gb 38.27N 140.37 E
Funakoshi-Wan 29 Hb 39.25N 142.00 E
Funan 28 Ch 32.38N 115.35 E
Funäsdalen 7 Ce 62.32N 12.33 E
Funchal 31 Fe 32.38N 16.54W
Fundación 54 Da 10.29N 74.12W
Fundão 13 Ed 40.08N 7.30W
Fundy, Bay of- 38 Me 45.00N 66.00W
Funeral Peak 46 Gh 36.08N 116.37W
Fungalei 64h Bb 13.17S 176.07W
Funhalouro 37 Ed 23.05S 34.24 E
Funing [China] 27 Ig 23.39N 105.33 E
Funing [China] 28 Eh 33.48N 119.47 E
Funing [China] 28 Ee 39.56N 119.15 E
Funiu Shan 27 Je 33.40N 112.10 E
Funtua 34 Gc 11.32N 7.19 E
Fuping 28 Ce 38.49N 114.15 E
Fuqing 27 Kf 25.47N 119.24 E
Furancungo 37 Eb 14.54S 33.37 E
Furano 28 Qc 43.21N 142.23 E
Füren 29a Ca 44.17N 142.25 E
Furenai 29a Cb 42.43N 142.15 E
Füren-Ko 29a Db 43.20N 145.20 E
Fürg 24 Ph 28.18N 55.13 E
Fur Jiang 28 Hc 42.37N 125.33 E
Furmanov 7 Jh 57.16N 41.07 E
Furnas, Represa de- 54 Ih 21.20S 45.50W
Furnas, Serra das- 55 Fb 15.45S 53.20W
Furneaux Group 57 Fi 40.10S 148.05 E
Furnes/Veurne 11 Ic 51.04N 2.40 E
Furqlus 24 Ge 34.36N 37.05 E
Furriyānah 32 Ic 34.57N 8.34 E
Fürstenau 12 Jb 52.31N 7.43 E
Fürstenauer Berge 12 Jb 52.35N 7.45 E
Fürstenfeld 14 Kc 47.03N 16.05 E
Fürstenfeldbruck 10 Hh 48.11N 11.15 E
Fürstenlager 12 Ke 49.42N 8.38 E
Fürstenwalde 10 Kd 52.22N 14.04 E
Fürth [F.R.G.] 10 Gg 49.28N 11.00 E
Fürth [F.R.G.] 12 Ke 49.39N 8.47 E
Furth im Wald 10 Ig 49.18N 12.51 E
Furubira 29a Bb 43.16N 140.39 E
Furudal 7 Df 61.10N 15.08 E
Furukawa 27 Pd 38.34N 140.58 E
Furusund 8 He 59.40N 18.55 E
Fury and Hecla Strait 42 Jc 69.55N 84.00W
Fushan [China] 28 Ff 37.30N 121.15 E
Fushan [China] 28 Ag 35.58N 111.51 E
Fushë-Arëzi 15 Dg 42.04N 20.02 E
Fushë-Lura 15 Dh 41.48N 20.13 E
Fu Shui 28 Cj 29.52N 115.26 E
Fushun 22 Oe 41.46N 123.56 E
Fusong 27 Mc 42.20N 127.17 E
Füsselberg 12 Je 49.32N 7.14 E
Füssen 10 Gi 47.34N 10.42 E
Futa, Passo della- 14 Ff 44.05N 11.17 E
Futago-Yama 29 Be 33.35N 131.38 E
Futaoi-Jima 29 Bd 34.06N 130.47 E
Futog 15 Cd 45.15N 19.42 E
Futuna, Ile- 57 Jf 14.17S 178.09W
Fuwah 24 Dg 31.12N 30.33 E
Fuxian (Wafangdian) 27 Ld 39.38N 121.59 E
Fuxian Hu 27 Hg 24.30N 102.55 E
Fuxin 22 Oe 41.59N 121.38 E
Fuxin Monggolzu Zizhixian 28 Fc 42.06N 121.46 E
Fuyang 27 Ke 32.47N 115.46 E
Fuyang He 28 Dg 38.14N 116.05 E
Fuyang Zhan 28 Ch 32.56N 115.53 E
Fuyu [China] 27 Lb 45.10N 124.52 E
Fuyu [China] 27 Lb 47.48N 124.26 E
Fuyuan [China] 27 Lc 42.44N 124.57 E
Fuyuan [China] 27 Nb 48.21N 134.18 E
Fuyuan [China] 27 Hf 25.43N 104.20 E
Fuyun/Koktokay 22 Ke 47.13N 89.39 E
Füzesabony 10 Qi 47.45N 20.25 E
Fuzhou [China] 22 Ng 26.10N 119.20 E
Fuzhou [China] 27 Kf 27.58N 116.20 E
Fuzhou He 28 Fe 39.36N 121.35 E
Fyllas Bank (EN) 41 Gf 64.00N 53.00W
Fyn 5 Hd 55.20N 10.30 E
Fyn [2] 8 Di 55.20N 10.30 E
Fyne, Loch- 9 He 56.10N 5.20W
Fyresdal 7 Bg 59.11N 8.06 E
Fyresvatn 8 Ce 59.05N 8.10 E
Fzâra, Garaʿet- 14 Bn 36.47N 7.30 E

G

Gaasbeek 12 Gd 50.48N 4.10 E
Gaasterland 12 Hb 52.54N 5.36 E
Gaasterland 12 Hb 52.53N 5.35 E
Gaasterland-Balk 12 Hb 52.54N 5.36 E
Gabaru Reef 64a Bb 7.53N 134.31 E
Gabas 11 Fk 43.46N 0.42W
Gabba' 35 Id 8.02N 50.08 E
Gabbs 46 Gg 38.52N 117.55W
Gabela 31 Ij 10.52S 14.23 E
Gabès, Gulf of-(EN) = Qābis, Khalīj- 30 Ie 34.00N 10.25 E
Gabon 36 Ab 0.25N 9.20 E
Gabon [1] 31 Ii 1.00S 11.45 E
Gaborone 31 Jk 24.40S 25.55 E
Gabras 35 Dc 10.16N 26.14 E
Gabriel Strait 42 Kd 61.50N 65.40W
Gabriel y Galán, Embalse de- 13 Fd 40.15N 6.15W
Gabrovo 15 Ig 42.52N 25.19 E
Gabrovo [2] 15 Ig 42.52N 25.19 E
Gacé 11 Gf 48.48N 0.18 E
Gachsārān 24 Ng 30.12N 50.47 E
Gackle 45 Gc 46.38N 99.09W
Gacko 14 Mg 43.10N 18.32 E
Gadag 25 Fe 15.25N 75.37 E
Gäddede 7 Dd 64.30N 14.09 E
Gadê 27 Ge 34.13N 99.29 E
Gadjač 16 Id 50.22N 34.01 E
Gádor, Sierra de- 13 Jh 36.55N 2.45W
Gadsden 43 Je 34.02N 86.02W
Gadūk, Gardaneh-ye- 24 Oe 35.55N 52.55 E
Gadzi 35 Be 4.47N 16.42 E
Gael Hamkes Bugt 41 Jd 74.00N 22.00W
Găeşti 15 Ie 44.43N 25.19 E
Gaeta 14 Hi 41.12N 13.35 E
Gaeta, Golfo di- 14 Hi 41.05N 13.30 E
Gaferut Island 57 Fd 9.14N 145.23 E
Gaffney 44 Gh 35.05N 81.39W
Gagan 63a Ba 5.14S 154.37 E
Gagarin [R.S.F.S.R.] 19 Dd 55.35N 35.01 E
Gagarin [Uzb.-U.S.S.R.] 18 Gd 40.40N 68.05 E
Gagévésouva, Pointe- 63b Ca 13.04S 166.32 E
Gaggenau 12 Kf 48.48N 8.20 E
Gagnef 7 Df 60.35N 15.04 E
Gagnoa 31 Gh 6.08N 5.56W
Gagnoa [3] 34 Dd 6.03N 6.00W
Gagnon 42 Kf 51.55N 68.10W
Gagra 19 Eg 43.17N 40.15 E
Gahkom 24 Ph 28.12N 55.50 E
Gahkom, Kūh-e- 24 Ph 28.10N 55.57 E
Gaiba, Laguna- 55 Dc 17.45S 57.43W
Gail 14 Hd 46.36N 13.53 E
Gaillac 11 Hk 43.54N 1.55 E
Gaillefontaine 12 De 49.39N 1.37 E
Gaillimh/Galway 6 Fe 53.16N 9.03W
Gaillimh/Galway [2] 9 Eh 53.20N 9.00W
Gaillon 12 De 49.10N 1.20 E
Gailtaler Alpen 14 Gd 46.40N 13.00 E
Gaiman 56 Gf 43.17S 65.29W
Găineşti 15 Ib 47.25N 25.55 E
Gainesville [Fl.-U.S.] 39 Kg 29.40N 82.20W
Gainesville [Ga.-U.S.] 43 Ke 34.18N 83.50W
Gainesville [Mo.-U.S.] 45 Jh 36.36N 92.26W
Gainesville [Tx.-U.S.] 43 He 33.37N 97.08W
Gainsborough 9 Mh 53.24N 0.46W
Gairdner, Lake- 57 Eh 31.35S 136.00 E
Gairloch 9 Hd 57.43N 5.40W
Gaizina Kalns/Gajzinkalns 8 Kh 56.50N 25.59 E
Gaj 19 Fe 51.31N 58.30 E
Gajny 19 Fc 60.20N 54.15 E
Gajsin 19 Cf 48.50N 29.27 E
Gajvoron 16 Fe 48.22N 29.52 E
Gajzinkalns/Gaizina Kalns 8 Kh 56.50N 25.59 E
Galaasija 18 Ee 39.52N 64.27 E
Gălăbovo 15 Ig 42.08N 25.51 E
Gala Gölü 15 Ji 40.45N 26.12 E
Galaico, Macizo- 13 Eb 42.30N 7.20W
Galán, Cerro- 56 Gc 25.55S 66.52W
Galana 30 Li 3.09S 40.08 E
Galanta 10 Nh 48.12N 17.44 E
Galap 64a Bb 7.38N 134.39 E
Galápagos, Islas-/Colón, Archipiélago de- = Galapagos Islands (EN) 52 Gf 0.30S 90.30W
Galapagos Fracture Zone (EN) 3 Mi 0.00 100.00W
Galapagos Islands (EN) = Colon, Archipiélago de-/Galápagos, Islas- 52 Gf 0.30S 90.30W
Galapagos Islands (EN) = Galápagos, Islas-/Colón, Archipiélago de- 52 Gf 0.30S 90.30W
Galarza 55 Di 28.06S 56.41W
Galashiels 9 Kf 55.37N 2.49W
Galaţi [2] 15 Kd 45.33N 27.56 E
Galaţi 6 If 45.27N 28.03 E
Galatina 14 Mj 40.10N 18.10 E
Galatone 14 Mj 40.09N 18.04 E
Galatzó 13 Oe 39.38N 2.29 E
Galdar 32 Dd 28.09N 15.39W
Galdhøpiggen 7 Bf 61.37N 8.17 E
Galeana [Mex.] 48 Fb 30.07N 107.38W
Galeana [Mex.] 48 Ie 24.50N 100.04W
Galeh Dār 24 Oi 27.38N 52.42 E
Galela 58 Dd 1.50N 127.50 E
Galena [Ak.-U.S.] 40 Hd 64.44N 156.57W
Galena [Il.-U.S.] 45 Ke 42.25N 90.26W
Galeota Point 50 Fg 10.08N 60.59W
Galera, Punta- 56 Fe 39.59S 73.43W
Galera, Rio- 55 Bb 14.25S 60.07W
Galera Point 50 Fg 10.49N 60.55W
Galesburg 43 Ic 40.57N 90.22W
Galga 10 Pi 47.33N 19.43 E
Gal Gaduud [3] 35 Hd 5.00N 47.00 E
Galheirão, Rio- 55 Ja 12.23S 45.05W
Galheiros 55 Ia 13.18S 46.25W
Gali 16 Lh 42.36N 41.42 E
Galič [R.S.F.S.R.] 19 Ed 58.23N 42.21 E
Galič [Ukr.-U.S.S.R.] 16 De 49.06N 24.43 E
Galicea Mare 15 Ge 44.06N 23.18 E
Galicia 5 Fg 43.00N 8.00W
Galicia 13 Eb 43.00N 8.00W
Galicia (EN) = Galicija 5 If 49.50N 21.00 E
Galicia (EN) = Galicija [Eur.] 10 Qg 49.50N 21.00 E
Galicia (EN) = Galicja 10 Qg 49.50N 21.00 E
Galicia (EN) = Galicja 5 If 49.50N 21.00 E
Galicija [Eur.] = Galicia (EN) 10 Qg 49.50N 21.00 E
Galicija [Ukr.-U.S.S.R.] 10 Jg 49.00N 24.00 E
Galicija = Galicia (EN) 5 If 49.50N 21.00 E
Galicja = Galicia (EN) 5 If 49.50N 21.00 E
Galicja = Galicia (EN) 10 Qg 49.50N 21.00 E
Galilee, Lake- 59 Jd 22.20S 145.55 E
Galimy 20 Kd 62.19N 156.00 E
Galina Point 49 Id 18.24N 76.53W
Galion 44 Fe 40.44N 82.46W
Galion, Baie du- 51h Bb 14.44N 60.57W
Galiton 14 Cm 37.30N 8.52 E
Galiuro Mountains 46 Jj 32.40N 110.20W
Gälka'yo 31 Lh 6.49N 47.23 E
Galkino 17 Ki 55.40N 62.55 E
Gallarate 14 Ce 45.40N 8.47 E
Gallatin 44 Dg 36.24N 86.27W
Gallatin Range 46 Jd 45.15N 111.05W
Gallatin River 46 Jd 45.56N 111.29W
Galle 22 Ki 6.02N 80.13 E
Gällego 13 Lc 41.39N 0.51W
Gallegos, Rio- 52 Jk 51.36S 68.59W
Gallinas, Punta- 52 Id 12.25N 71.40W
Gallinas Peak 45 Di 34.15N 105.45W
Gallipoli 14 Lj 40.03N 17.58 E
Gallipoli Peninsula (EN) = Gelibolu Yarimadası 15 Ji 40.20N 26.30 E
Gallipolis 44 Ff 38.49N 82.14W
Gällivare 6 Ib 67.08N 20.42 E
Galljaaral 18 Fd 40.02N 67.35 E
Gallo 13 Jd 40.48N 2.09W
Gällö 7 De 62.55N 15.14 E
Gallo, Capo- 14 Hl 38.15N 13.19 E
Gallo Mountains 45 Bi 34.00N 108.15W
Galloway 9 If 55.00N 4.25W
Galloway, Mull of- 9 Ig 54.38N 4.50W
Gallup 39 If 35.32N 108.44W
Gallur 13 Kc 41.52N 1.19W
Gallura 14 Dj 41.00N 9.15 E
Galmaarden/Gammerages 12 Fd 50.45N 3.58 E
Galole 36 Hc 1.30S 40.02 E
Galt 44 Gd 43.22N 80.19W
Gal Tardo 35 He 3.37N 45.58 E
Galtasen 8 Eg 57.48N 13.30 E
Galty Mountains/Na Gaibhlte 9 Ei 52.23N 8.11W
Galut 27 Hb 46.43N 100.08 E
Galveston 39 Jg 29.18N 94.48W
Galveston Bay 38 Jg 29.36N 94.57W
Galveston Island 45 Il 29.13N 94.55W
Gálvez 56 Hd 32.02S 61.13W
Galway/Gaillimh [2] 9 Eh 53.20N 9.00W
Galway/Gaillimh 6 Fe 53.16N 9.03W
Galway Bay/Cuan na Gaillimhe 5 Fe 53.10N 9.15W
Gamaches 12 De 49.59N 1.33 E
Gamagōri 29 Ed 34.49N 137.13 E
Gamarra 54 Db 8.19N 73.44W
Gamba [China] 27 Ef 28.17N 88.31 E
Gamba [Gabon] 36 Ac 2.37S 10.00 E
Gambaga 34 Ec 10.32N 0.26W
Gambela 31 Kh 8.15N 34.36 E
Gambell 40 Ed 63.46N 171.46W
Gambia 30 Fg 13.28N 16.34W
Gambia [1] 31 Fg 13.25N 16.00W
Gambie 34 Bc 13.28N 16.34W
Gambier, Iles- = Gambier Islands (EN) 57 Ng 23.09S 134.58W
Gambier Islands (EN) = Gambier, Iles- 57 Ng 23.09S 134.58W
Gambo 35 Ce 4.39N 22.16 E
Gamboma 36 Cc 1.53S 15.51 E
Gamboula 35 Be 4.08N 15.09 E
Gamda → Zamtang 27 He 32.23N 101.05 E
Gamelão 55 Db 15.29S 57.50W
Gamkonora, Gunung- 26 If 1.21N 127.31 E
Gamlakarleby/Kokkola 6 Ic 63.50N 23.07 E
Gamla Uppsala 8 Ge 59.54N 17.38 E
Gamleby 7 Dh 57.54N 16.24 E
Gamo Gofa [3] 35 Fd 5.45N 37.20 E
Gamua 64h Bb 13.15S 176.08W
Gamud 35 Fe 4.05N 38.06 E
Gamvik 7 Ga 71.03N 28.14 E
Ganāne, Webi- = Juba (EN) 30 Lh 0.15S 42.38 E
Gananoque 44 Ic 44.20N 76.10W
Ganāveh 24 Nh 29.32N 50.31 E
Gancedo 55 Bh 27.30S 61.42W
Gancevići 16 Ec 52.45N 26.29 E
Gand/Gent = Ghent (EN) 11 Jc 51.03N 3.43 E
Ganda 36 Be 12.59S 14.40 E
Gandadiwata, Bulu- 26 Gg 2.42S 119.27 E
Gandajika 36 Dd 6.45S 23.57 E
Gandak 25 Hc 25.39N 85.13 E
Gander 39 Ne 48.57N 54.34W
Ganderkesee 12 Ka 53.04N 8.33 E
Gandesa 13 Mc 41.03N 0.26 E
Gandhinagar 22 Jg 23.21N 72.40 E
Gāndhi Sāgar 25 Fd 24.30N 75.30 E
Gandia 13 Lf 38.58N 0.11W
Gandia-Grao de Gandia 13 Lf 38.59N 0.09W
Gandisê Shan 21 Kf 31.00N 83.00 E
Gandu 54 Kf 13.45S 39.30W
Ganetti 35 Eb 17.58N 31.13 E
Ganga = Ganges (EN) 21 Lg 23.20N 90.30 E
Gangaw 25 Id 22.10N 94.08 E
Gangca (Shaliuhe) 27 Hd 37.30N 100.14 E
Ganges 11 Jk 43.56N 3.42 E
Ganges (EN) = Ganga 21 Lg 23.20N 90.30 E
Ganges, Mouths of the- (EN) 21 Lg 23.20N 90.30 E
Gangi 14 Im 37.48N 14.12 E
Gango 36 Cd 9.48S 15.40 E
Gangtok 22 Kg 27.20N 88.37 E
Gangu 27 Ie 34.45N 105.12 E
Gangziyao 28 Cf 36.17N 114.06 E
Gan He 27 Mb 49.12N 125.14 E
Ganhe 27 La 50.43N 123.00 E
Gani 26 Ig 0.47S 128.13 E
Ganjgah 24 Md 37.42N 48.16 E
Gan Jiang 21 Ng 29.12N 116.00 E
Ganjig → Horqin Zuoyi Houqi 27 Lc 42.57N 122.14 E
Gannan 27 Lb 47.53N 123.26 E
Gannat 11 Jh 46.06N 3.12 E
Gannett Peak 38 Ie 43.10N 109.40W
Gansbaai 37 Bf 34.35S 19.22 E
Gansu Sheng (Kan-su Sheng) = Kansu (EN) [2] 27 Hd 38.00N 102.00 E
Ganta 34 Dd 7.14N 8.59W
Gantang → Taiping 28 Ei 30.18N 118.07 E
Ganyu (Qingkou) 28 Eg 34.50N 119.07 E
Ganzhou 22 Ng 25.49N 114.56 E
Gao [3] 34 Eb 18.15N 1.00W
Gao [Mali] 31 Hg 16.15N 0.01 E
Gao [Niger] 34 Gb 15.25N 5.45 E
Gao'an 27 Kf 28.27N 115.24 E
Gaobeidian → Xincheng 28 Ce 39.20N 115.50 E
Gaocheng 28 Ce 38.02N 114.50 E
Gaolan (Shidongsi) 27 Hd 36.23N 103.55 E
Gaoliangjian → Hongze 27 Ke 33.10N 119.58 E
Gaoligong Shan 27 Gf 25.45N 98.45 E
Gaolou Ling 27 Ig 24.47N 106.48 E
Gaomi 28 Ef 36.23N 119.45 E
Gaoping 27 Jd 35.46N 112.55 E
Gaoqing (Tianzhen) 28 Df 37.10N 117.50 E
Gaotai 27 Gd 39.20N 99.58 E
Gaotingzhen → Daishan 28 Gi 30.15N 122.13 E
Gaoua 34 Ec 10.20N 3.11W
Gaoual 34 Cc 11.45N 13.12W
Gaoyang 28 Ce 38.42N 115.47 E
Gaoyi 28 Cf 37.37N 114.37 E
Gaoyou 28 Eh 32.46N 119.27 E
Gaoyou Hu 27 Ke 32.50N 119.15 E
Gaozhou 27 Jg 21.56N 110.47 E
Gap 11 Mj 44.34N 6.05 E
Gar 27 Ce 32.12N 79.57 E
Gara, Lough-/Loch Ui Ghadra 9 Eh 53.55N 8.30W
Gara'ad 35 Hd 6.54N 49.20 E
Garabato 55 Bi 28.56S 60.09W
Garachiné 49 Hi 8.04N 78.22W
Garachiné, Punta- 49 Hi 8.06N 78.25W
Gara Dragoman 15 Fg 42.55N 22.56 E
Ga'raet el Oubeira 14 Cn 36.50N 8.23 E
Gara Kostenec 15 Gg 42.18N 23.52 E
Garalo 34 Dc 11.00N 7.26W
Gara Muleta 35 Gd 9.05N 41.43 E
Garanhuns 53 Mf 8.54S 36.29W
Garapan 64b Ba 15.12N 145.43 E
Garapuava 55 Ic 16.06S 46.33W
Garavuti 18 Gf 37.36N 68.29 E
Garba 35 Cd 9.12N 20.30 E
Garbahārrey 35 Ge 3.20N 42.17 E
Garberville 46 Df 40.06N 123.48W
Gārbosh, Kūh-e- 24 Nf 32.36N 50.04 E
Garça 55 Hf 22.14S 49.37W
Garças, Rio das- 55 Fb 15.54S 52.16W
Garcias 55 Fe 20.34S 52.13W
Gard [3] 11 Jj 44.00N 4.00 E
Gard 11 Kk 43.51N 4.37 E
Garda 14 Ee 45.34N 10.42 E
Garda, Lago di- = Garda, Lake- (EN) 5 Hf 45.35N 10.35 E
Garda, Lake- (EN) = Garda, Lago di- 5 Hf 45.35N 10.35 E
Gardabani 16 Ni 41.29N 45.05 E
Garde, Cap de- 14 Bn 36.58N 7.47 E
Gardelegen 10 Hd 52.32N 11.22 E
Garden City [Ga.-U.S.] 44 Gi 32.06N 81.09W
Garden City [Ks.-U.S.] 43 Gd 37.58N 100.53W
Garden Grove 46 Gj 33.46N 117.57W
Garden Peninsula 44 Dc 45.40N 86.35W
Gardermoen 8 Dd 60.13N 11.06 E
Gardey 55 Cm 37.17S 59.21W
Gardēz 23 Kc 33.37N 69.07 E
Gardiner 46 Jd 45.02N 110.42W
Gardiner Range 59 Fc 19.15S 128.50 E
Gardner → Nikumaroro Atoll 57 Je 4.40S 174.32W
Gardner Pinnacles 57 Kb 25.00N 167.55W
Gardno, Jezioro- 10 Nb 54.43N 17.05 E
Gardone Riviera 14 Ee 45.37N 10.34 E
Gardždai/Gargždaj 7 Ei 55.43N 21.24 E
Gareloi 40a Cb 51.47N 178.48W
Garessio 14 Cf 44.12N 8.02 E
Garfagnana 14 Ef 44.05N 10.30 E
Gargaliánoi 15 El 37.04N 21.38 E
Gargano 5 Hg 41.50N 16.00 E
Gargano, Testa del- 14 Ki 41.35N 16.12 E
Gargantua, Cape- 44 Eb 47.36N 85.02W
Gargždai/Gargždaj 7 Ei 55.43N 21.24 E
Gari 19 Gd 59.28N 62.25 E
Garibaldi 55 Gi 29.15S 51.32W
Garibaldi, Mount- 46 Db 49.51N 123.01W
Garies 37 Bf 30.30S 18.00 E
Garigliano 14 Hi 41.13N 13.45 E
Garimpo 55 Ed 18.41S 54.50W
Garissa 31 Ki 0.28S 39.38 E

Index Symbols

[1] Independent Nation
[2] State, Region
[3] District, County
[4] Municipality
[5] Colony, Dependency
Continent
Physical Region
Historical or Cultural Region
Mount, Mountain
Volcano
Hill
Mountains, Mountain Range
Hills, Escarpment
Plateau, Upland
Pass, Gap
Plain, Lowland
Delta
Salt Flat
Valley, Canyon
Crater, Cave
Karst Features
Depression
Polder
Desert, Dunes
Forest, Woods
Heath, Steppe
Oasis
Cape, Point
Coast, Beach
Cliff
Peninsula
Isthmus
Sandbank
Island
Atoll
Rock, Reef
Islands, Archipelago
Rocks, Reefs
Coral Reef
Well, Spring
Geyser
River, Stream
Waterfall Rapids
River Mouth, Estuary
Lake
Salt Lake
Intermittent Lake
Reservoir
Swamp, Pond
Canal
Glacier
Ice Shelf, Pack Ice
Ocean
Sea
Gulf, Bay
Strait, Fjord
Lagoon
Bank
Seamount
Tablemount
Ridge
Shelf
Basin
Escarpment, Sea Scarp
Fracture
Trench, Abyss
National Park, Reserve
Point of Interest
Recreation Site
Cave, Cavern
Historic Site
Ruins
Wall, Walls
Church, Abbey
Temple
Scientific Station
Airport
Port
Lighthouse
Mine
Tunnel
Dam, Bridge

Garkida 34 Hc 10.25N 12.34 E
Garland 45 Hj 32.54N 96.39W
Garlasco 14 Ce 45.12N 8.55 E
Garliava/Garljava 8 Jj 54.49N 23.55 E
Garljava/Garliava 8 Jj 54.46N 23.55 E
Garm 18 He 39.02N 70.18 E
Garmisch-Partenkirchen 10 Hi 47.30N 11.06 E
Garmsar 24 Oe 35.20N 52.13 E
Garnet Bank (EN) 55 Hk 33.05S 49.25W
Garnet Range 46 Ic 46.45N 113.15W
Garnett 45 Ig 38.17N 95.14W
Garonne 5 Ff 45.02N 0.36W
Garonne, Canal latéral à la- 11 Fj 44.34N 0.09W
Garopába 55 Hi 28.04S 48.40W
Garoua 31 Ih 9.18N 13.24 E
Garoua Boulai 35 Ad 5.53N 14.33 E
Garoubi 34 Fc 13.07N 2.18 E
Garōwe 31 Lh 8.25N 48.33 E
Garpenberg 8 Gd 60.19N 16.12 E
Garphyttan 8 Fe 59.19N 14.56 E
Garrel 12 Kb 52.57N 8.01 E
Garreru 64a Bc 7.20N 134.33 E
Garri, Kūh-e- 24 Mf 33.59N 48.25 E
Garrigues 11 Kj 44.10N 4.30 E
Garrison 45 Fc 47.40N 101.25W
Garron Point/An Gearrath 9 Hf 55.05N 5.58W
Garrovillas 13 Fe 39.43N 6.33W
Garruchos 55 Ei 28.11S 55.39W
Garry 9 Je 56.45N 3.45W
Garry Bay 42 Ic 69.00N 85.10W
Garry Lake 38 Jc 66.00N 100.00W
Garsen 36 Hc 2.16S 40.07 E
Gartar/Qianning 27 He 30.27N 101.29 E
Gartempe 11 Gh 46.47N 0.50 E
Gartog → Markam 27 Gf 29.32N 98.33 E
Garut 26 Eh 7.13S 107.54 E
Garuva 55 Hh 26.01S 48.51W
Garvie Mountains 62 Cf 45.30S 168.50 E
Garwa 25 Gd 24.11N 83.49 E
Garwolin 10 Re 51.54N 21.37 E
Gary 43 Jc 41.36N 87.20W
Garyarsa 27 De 31.40N 80.26 E
Garzê 27 Ge 31.42N 99.58 E
Garzón [Col.] 54 Cc 2.13N 75.38W
Garzón [Ur.] 56 Jd 34.36S 54.33W
Gasan-Kuli 19 Fh 37.29N 53.59 E
Gascogne = Gascony (EN) 11 Gk 43.30N 0.10 E
Gasconade River 45 Kg 38.40N 91.33W
Gascony (EN) = Gascogne 11 Gk 43.30N 0.10 E
Gascoyne Junction 59 De 25.03S 115.12 E
Gascoyne River 57 Cg 24.52S 113.37 E
Gasefjord 41 Je 70.00N 27.30W
Gaseland 41 Jd 70.20N 29.00W
Gash 30 Kg 16.48N 35.51 E
Gas Hu 27 Fd 38.08N 90.45 E
Gashua 31 Ig 12.52N 11.03 E
Gaspar Strait (EN)=Kelasa, Selat- 26 Eg 2.40S 107.15 E
Gaspé 39 Me 48.50N 64.29W
Gaspé, Cap de- 42 Lg 48.45N 64.10W
Gaspé, Péninsule de-= Gaspe Peninsula (EN) 38 Me 48.30N 65.00W
Gaspe Peninsula (EN)= Gaspé, Péninsule de- 38 Me 48.30N 65.00W
Gassan 29 Gb 38.34N 140.01 E
Gassol 34 Hd 8.32N 10.28 E
Gaston, Lake- 44 Ig 36.35N 78.00W
Gastonia 43 Kd 35.16N 81.11W
Gastoúni 15 El 37.51N 21.15 E
Gastre 56 Gf 42.17S 69.14W
Gästrikland 8 Gd 60.30N 16.30 E
Gata, Akrotérion- 24 Ee 34.34N 33.02 E
Gata, Cabo de- 5 Fh 36.43N 2.12W
Gata, Sierra de- 13 Fd 40.15N 6.45W
Gătaia 15 Ed 45.26N 21.26 E
Gatčina 19 Dd 59.34N 30.09 E
Gate 45 Fh 36.51N 100.01W
Gate City 44 Fg 36.38N 82.37W
Gateshead 9 Lg 54.58N 1.37W
Gateshead 42 Hb 70.35N 100.15W
Gathemo 12 Bf 48.46N 0.58W
Gâtinais 11 If 48.00N 2.20 E
Gâtine, Hauteurs de- 11 Fh 46.38N 0.38W
Gatineau, Rivière- 42 Jg 45.27N 75.42W
Gatlinburg 44 Fh 35.43N 83.31W
Gato, Cumbres del- 48 Fd 27.00N 106.35W
Gattinara 14 Ce 45.37N 8.22 E
Gatún 49 Hi 9.16N 79.55W
Gatún, Lago-=Gatun Lake (EN) 47 Ig 9.12N 79.55W
Gatun Lake (EN)=Gatún, Lago- 47 Ig 9.12N 79.55W
Gatvand 24 Mf 32.15N 48.50 E
Gatwick Airport 12 Bc 51.08N 0.12W
Gaucín 13 Gh 36.31N 5.19W
Gauhati → Guwāhāti 22 Lg 26.11N 91.44 E
Gauiena/Gaujiena 8 Lg 57.25N 26.28 E
Gauja 7 Fh 57.10N 24.16 E
Gaujiena/Gauiena 8 Lg 57.25N 26.28 E
Gaula [Nor.] 8 Da 63.21N 10.14 E
Gaula [Nor.] 8 Ac 61.22N 5.41 E
Gauldalen 8 Db 63.00N 11.00 E
Gauley River 44 Gf 38.10N 81.12W
Gau-Odernheim 12 Ke 49.46N 8.12 E
Gaurdak 19 Gh 37.49N 66.01 E
Gausdal 8 Cc 61.20N 9.55 E
Gausta 7 Bg 59.50N 8.39 E
Gāvbandī 24 Oi 27.12N 53.04 E
Gāvbūs, Kūh-e- 24 Oi 27.10N 54.00 E
Gavdhopoúla 15 Go 34.56N 24.00 E
Gávdhos 5 Ii 34.50N 24.05 E
Gāveh 24 Le 35.00N 46.58 E
Gavere 12 Fd 50.56N 3.40 E
Gavkhūnī, Bāţlāq-e- 24 Of 32.06N 52.52 E
Gāv Kosh 24 Le 34.00N 48.00 E
Gävle 6 Hc 60.40N 17.10 E
Gävleborg [2] 7 Df 61.30N 16.15 E
Gävlebukten 8 Gd 60.40N 17.20 E
Gavorrano 14 Eh 42.55N 10.54 E
Gavri 8 Lh 56.49N 27.58 E
Gavrilov-Jam 7 Jh 57.19N 39.51 E
Gāw Koshi 23 Id 28.38N 57.12 E
Gawler 59 Hf 34.37S 138.44 E
Gawler Ranges 57 Eh 32.30S 136.00 E
Gaxun Nur 21 Me 42.25N 101.00 E
Gaya [India] 22 Kg 24.47N 85.00 E
Gaya [Niger] 34 Fc 11.53N 3.27 E
Gaya He 28 Jc 42.58N 129.52 E
Gaylord 44 Ec 45.02N 84.40W
Gayndah 59 Ke 25.37S 151.36 E
Gaz 24 Nf 32.48N 51.37 E
Gaza [3] 37 Ed 23.30S 33.00 E
Gaz-Ačak 19 Gg 41.11N 61.27 E
Gazalkent 18 Gd 41.33N 69.46 E
Gazaoua 34 Gc 13.32N 7.55 E
Gazelle, Récif de la- 63b Be 20.11S 165.27 E
Gaziantep 22 Ff 37.05N 37.22 E
Gaziemir 15 Kk 38.19N 27.10 E
Gazimağusa = Famagusta (EN) 23 Dc 35.07N 33.57 E
Gazipaşa 24 Ed 36.17N 32.20 E
Gazli 19 Gg 40.09N 63.23 E
Gbarnga 31 Gh 7.00N 9.29W
Gboko 34 Gd 7.21N 8.58 E
Gbon 34 Dd 9.50N 6.27W
Gdańsk [2] 10 Ob 54.25N 18.40 E
Gdańsk=Danzig (EN) 6 He 54.23N 18.40 E
Gdansk, Gulf of- (EN)= Gdanska, Zatoka- 5 He 54.40N 19.15 E
Gdov 7 Gg 58.47N 27.54 E
Gdynia 6 He 54.32N 18.33 E
Gearhart Mountain 46 Ee 42.30N 120.53W
Gêba 34 Bc 11.58N 15.00W
Gebe, Pulau- 26 Ig 0.05S 129.20 E
Gebze 24 Cb 40.48N 29.25 E
Gecha 35 Fd 7.29N 35.25 E
Geçitkale 25 Ee 35.15N 33.45 E
Gedi 36 Hc 3.18S 40.01 E
Gedinne 12 Ge 49.59N 4.56 E
Gediz 24 Cc 39.02N 29.25 E
Gedo 35 Ge 2.20N 41.20 E
Gedo [3] 35 Ge 3.00N 42.00 E
Gedo 35 Fd 9.00N 37.29 E
Gedser, Sydfalster- 7 Ci 54.35N 11.57 E
Gedser Odde 8 Dj 54.34N 11.59 E
Geel 11 Kc 51.10N 5.00 E
Geelong 58 Fh 38.08S 144.21 E
Geelvink Channel 59 Ce 28.30S 114.10 E
Geer 12 Hd 50.51N 5.42 E
Geeste 12 Jb 52.36N 7.16 E
Geesthacht 10 Gc 53.26N 10.22 E
Gê'gyai 27 De 32.29N 80.52 E
Ge Hu 28 Ei 31.36N 119.51 E
Geidam 34 Hc 12.53N 11.56 E
Geigar 35 Ec 11.59N 32.46 E
Geihoku 29 Cd 34.44N 132.17 E
Geikie 42 He 57.48N 103.46W
Geilo 7 Bf 60.31N 8.12 E
Geiranger 8 Bb 62.06N 7.12 E
Geisenheim 12 Je 49.59N 7.58 E
Geislingen an der Steige 10 Fh 48.37N 9.51 E
Geita 36 Fc 2.52S 32.10 E
Geithus 7 Bg 59.57N 9.59 E
Geiyo-Shotō 24 Cd 34.15N 132.45 E
Gejiu 22 Mg 23.22N 103.14 E
Gel [Sud.] 30 Jh 7.46N 29.36 E
Gel [Sud.] 35 Ed 6.08N 31.17 E
Gela 14 Im 37.04N 14.15 E
Gela, Golfo di- 14 Im 37.05N 14.10 E
Geladi 35 Hd 6.57N 46.25 E
Geldenaken/Jodoigne 12 Gd 50.43N 4.52 E
Gelderland [3] 12 Hb 52.10N 5.50 E
Geldermalsen 12 Hc 51.53N 5.19 E
Geldern 10 Ce 51.31N 6.20 E
Geldrop 12 Hc 51.25N 5.33 E
Geleen 11 Ld 50.58N 5.52 E
Gelembe 15 Kj 39.10N 27.50 E
Gelemso 35 Gd 8.48N 40.32 E
Gelendžik 19 Dg 44.33N 38.06 E
Gelengdeng 35 Bc 10.56N 15.32 E
Gelgaudiškis 8 Ji 55.02N 22.58 E
Gelibolu 24 Bb 40.24N 26.40 E
Gelibolu Yarimadası = Gallipoli Peninsula (EN) 15 Ji 40.20N 26.30 E
Gélise 11 Gj 44.11N 0.17 E
Gellinsör 35 Hd 6.24N 46.46 E
Gelnhausen 10 Ff 50.12N 9.11 E
Gelsenkirchen 10 De 51.31N 7.06 E
Gemena 31 Ih 3.15N 19.46 E
Gemerek 24 Gc 39.11N 36.05 E
Gemert 12 Hc 51.33N 5.41 E
Gemi, Jabal- 35 Ed 9.01N 34.09 E
Gemlik 24 Cb 40.26N 29.09 E
Gemlik Körfezi 24 Cb 40.25N 28.55 E
Gemona del Friuli 14 Hd 46.16N 13.09 E
Gemünden (Felda) 12 Ld 50.42N 9.03 E
Gemünden (Wohra) 12 Kd 50.58N 8.58 E
Gemünden am Main 10 Ff 50.03N 9.42 E
Genale 30 Lh 0.15S 42.38 E
Genç 24 Ic 38.46N 40.35 E
Gendringen 12 Ic 51.52N 6.23 E
Gendringen-Ulft 12 Ic 51.54N 6.24 E
Genemuiden 12 Ib 52.37N 6.02 E
General Acha 56 He 37.23S 64.36W
General Alvear [Arg.] 56 Gd 34.58S 67.42W
General Alvear [Arg.] 56 He 36.03S 60.01W
General Arenales 55 Bl 34.18S 61.18W
General Artigas 55 Dh 26.53S 56.17W
General Belgrano 56 Ie 35.46S 58.30W
General Belgrano Station 66 Af 77.50S 38.00W
General Bernardo O'Higgins 66 Re 63.19S 57.54W
General Bravo 48 Je 25.48N 99.10W
General Cabrera 56 Hd 32.48S 63.52W
General Capdevila 55 Bh 27.26S 61.28W
General Carneiro 55 Gh 26.28S 51.25W
General Carrera, Lago- 52 Ij 46.30S 72.00W
General Cepeda 48 Ie 25.23N 101.27W
General Conesa [Arg.] 55 Dm 36.30S 57.20W
General Conesa [Arg.] 56 Hf 40.06S 64.26W
General Enrique Martinez 55 Fk 33.12S 53.50W
General Galarza 55 Ck 32.43S 59.24W
General Güemes 56 Hb 24.40S 65.00W
General Guide 56 Ie 36.40S 57.46W
General José de San Martín 55 Ch 26.33S 59.21W
General Juan Madariaga 56 Ie 37.00S 57.09W
General La Madrid 56 He 37.16S 61.17W
General Lavalle 56 Ie 36.24S 56.58W
General Manuel Belgrano, Cerro- 52 Jh 29.01S 67.49W
General O'Brien 55 Bl 34.54S 60.45W
General Pico 56 He 35.40S 63.44W
General Pinedo 56 Hc 27.19S 61.17W
General Pinto 55 Bl 34.46S 61.53W
General Pirán 55 Dm 37.16S 57.45W
General Roca 56 Ge 39.02S 67.35W
General Salgado 55 Ge 20.39S 50.22W
General Santos 22 Oi 6.05N 125.10 E
General Sarmiento 55 Cl 34.33S 58.43W
General Terán 48 Je 25.16N 99.41W
General-Toševo 15 Lf 43.42N 28.02 E
General Treviño 48 Jd 26.14N 99.29W
General Trías 48 Fc 28.21N 106.22W
General Vargas 55 Ei 29.42S 54.40W
General Viamonte 55 Bl 35.01S 61.01W
General Villegas 56 He 35.02S 63.01W
Genesee River 44 Id 43.16N 77.36W
Geneseo 44 Id 42.46N 77.49W
Geneva [Al.-U.S.] 44 Ej 31.02N 85.52W
Geneva [Nb.-U.S.] 45 Hf 40.32N 97.36W
Geneva [N.Y.-U.S.] 44 Id 42.53N 76.59W
Geneva (EN) = Genève 6 Gf 46.10N 6.10 E
Geneva, Lake- (EN) = Léman, Lac- 5 Gf 46.25N 6.30 E
Genève [2] 14 Ad 46.10N 6.15 E
Genève = Geneva (EN) 6 Gf 46.10N 6.10 E
Genevois 11 Mh 46.00N 6.10 E
Genhe → Ergun Zuoqi 22 Od 50.47N 121.32 E
Geni 35 Ed 8.31N 33.10 E
Geničesk 19 Df 46.12N 34.48 E
Genil 13 Gg 37.42N 5.19W
Genk 11 Ld 50.58N 5.30 E
Genkai-Nada 29 Ae 33.45N 130.00 E
Gennargentu 5 Gg 40.00N 9.20 E
Gennep 12 Hc 51.42N 5.59 E
Genoa (EN) = Genova 6 Gg 44.25N 8.57 E
Genoa, Gulf of- (EN) = Genova, Golfo di- 5 Gg 44.10N 8.55 E
Genova = Genoa (EN) 6 Gg 44.25N 8.57 E
Genova, Golfo di- = Genoa, Gulf of- (EN) 5 Gg 44.10N 8.55 E
Genova-Nervi 14 Df 44.23N 9.02 E
Genova-Voltri 14 Cf 44.26N 8.45 E
Genovesa, Isla- 54a Ba 0.20N 89.58W
Gent/Gand=Ghent (EN) 11 Jc 51.03N 3.43 E
Gentbrugge, Gent- 12 Fc 51.03N 3.45 E
Gent-Gentbrugge 12 Fc 51.03N 3.45 E
Genthin 10 Id 52.24N 12.10 E
Gent-Sint-Amandsberg 12 Fc 51.04N 3.45 E
Genū, Kūhhā-ye- 23 Id 27.25N 56.09 E
Genyem 26 Lg 2.46S 140.12 E
Genzano di Lucania 14 Kj 40.51N 16.02 E
Genzano di Roma 14 Fi 41.42N 11.41 E
Geographe Bay 57 Ch 33.35S 115.15 E
Geographe Channel 59 Cd 24.40S 113.20 E
Geographical Society Øer 41 Jd 72.40N 22.20W
Geokčaj 16 Oi 40.40N 47.42 E
Geok-Tepe 19 Fh 38.10N 57.58 E
Geomagnetic Pole (1975) (EN) 66 Hf 78.40S 109.33 E
Georga, Zemlja- 21 Ga 80.30N 49.00 E
George 38 Md 58.30N 66.00W
George 37 Cf 33.58S 22.24 E
George, Lake- [Austl.] 59 Jg 35.05S 149.25 E
George, Lake- [Fl.-U.S.] 44 Gk 29.17N 81.36W
George, Lake- [Ug.] 36 Fc 0.00 30.12 E
George, Lake- [U.S.] 44 Kd 43.35N 73.35W
George Gill Range 59 Gd 24.15S 131.35 E
Georges Bank (EN) 43 Nc 41.15N 67.30W
George Sound 62 Bf 44.50S 167.20 E
George Town 58 Fi 41.06S 146.50 E
Georgetown 45 Hk 30.38N 97.41W
George Town 22 Mi 5.25N 100.20 E
Georgetown [Austl.] 58 Ff 18.18S 143.33 E
Georgetown [Bah.] 49 Jb 23.30N 75.46W
Georgetown [Cay.Is.] 47 He 19.18N 81.23W
Georgetown [De.-U.S.] 44 Jf 38.42N 75.23W
Georgetown [Gam.] 31 Fg 13.32N 14.46W
Georgetown [Guy.] 53 Ke 6.48N 58.10W
Georgetown [Ky.-U.S.] 44 Ef 38.13N 84.33W
Georgetown [Oh.-U.S.] 44 Ff 38.52N 83.54W
Georgetown [S.C.-U.S.] 43 Le 33.23N 79.18W
Georgetown [St.Hel.] 31 Fi 7.56S 14.25W
Georgetown [St.Vin.] 50 Ff 13.16N 61.08W
George V Coast 66 Je 68.30S 147.30 E
George VI Sound 66 Qf 71.00S 68.00W
George West 45 Gl 28.20N 98.07W
Georgia [2] 43 Ke 32.50N 83.15W
Georgia (EN) 5 Kg 42.00N 44.00 E
Georgia, Strait of- 42 Fg 49.00N 123.20W
Georgia del Sur, Islas-/ South Georgia 66 Ad 54.15S 36.45W
Georgian Bay 38 Ke 45.15N 80.50W
Georgian SSR (EN)= Gruzinskaja SSR [2] 19 Eg 42.00N 44.00 E
Georgijevka [Kaz.-U.S.S.R.] 19 Hg 43.02N 74.43 E
Georgijevka [Kaz.-U.S.S.R.] 19 If 49.19N 81.35 E
Georgijevsk 16 Mg 44.09N 43.28 E
Georgina River 57 Eg 23.30S 139.47 E
Georgsmarienhütte 10 Ed 52.16N 8.02 E
Gera 10 Ge 51.08N 10.56 E
Gera 10 If 50.52N 12.05 E
Gera [2] 10 Hf 50.45N 11.55 E
Geraardsbergen/Grammont 12 Fd 50.46N 3.52 E
Gerais, Chapadão dos- 55 Jc 17.40S 45.35W
Geral, Serra- [Braz.] 55 Gi 29.10S 50.15W
Geral, Serra- [Braz.] 52 Kh 26.30S 50.30W
Geral, Serra- [Braz.] 55 Gf 23.54S 50.46W
Geral da Serra, Coxilha- 55 Ej 30.20S 55.15W
Geral de Goiás, Serra- 52 Lg 13.00S 46.15W
Geraldine 62 Df 44.05S 171.15 E
Geral do Paraná, Serra- 55 Ib 14.45S 47.30W
Geraldton [Austl.] 58 Cg 28.46S 114.36 E
Geraldton [Ont.-Can.] 42 Ig 49.44N 86.57W
Gérardmer 11 Mf 48.04N 6.53 E
Gerāsh 24 Pi 27.40N 54.06 E
Gerbiči, Gora- 20 Fc 66.39N 105.02 E
Gerca 15 Ja 48.10N 26.17 E
Gercüş 24 Id 37.34N 41.23 E
Gerecse 10 Oi 47.41N 18.29 E
Gerede 24 Eb 40.52N 32.39 E
Gerede 24 Eb 40.48N 32.12 E
Gerês, Serra do- 13 Ec 41.48N 8.00W
Gereshk 23 Jc 31.48N 64.34 E
Gérgal 13 Jg 37.07N 2.33W
Gering 45 Ef 41.50N 103.40W
Gerlachovský štít 10 Qg 49.12N 20.09 E
Gerlogubi 35 Hd 6.56N 45.03 E
Gerlos 14 Gc 47.14N 12.02 E
Gerlovo 15 Kf 43.03N 27.35 E
German Democratic Republic (EN)=Deutsche Demokratische Republik [1] 6 He 52.00N 12.30 E
Germania 55 Al 34.34S 62.03W
Germania Land 41 Kc 76.50N 20.00W
Germany, Federal Republic of- (EN)=Bundesrepublik Deutschland [1] 6 Ge 51.00N 9.00 E
Germencik 15 Kl 37.51N 27.37 E
Germersheim 12 Ke 49.13N 8.22 E
Germī 23 Hc 33.32N 54.58 E
Germi 24 Mc 39.01N 48.03 E
Germiston 37 De 26.15S 28.05 E
Gernsbach 12 Kf 48.46N 8.19 E
Gernsheim 12 Ke 49.45N 8.29 E
Gero 28 Ng 35.48N 137.14 E
Gerolstein 12 Id 50.13N 6.40 E
Gerona [3] 13 Ob 42.10N 2.40 E
Gerona/Girona 13 Oc 41.59N 2.49 E
Gerpinnes 12 Gd 50.20N 4.31 E
Gers 11 Gj 44.09N 0.39 E
Gers [3] 11 Gk 43.40N 0.30 E
Gersprenz 12 Le 49.59N 9.04 E
Gêrzê 27 De 32.20N 84.04 E
Gerze 24 Fb 41.48N 35.12 E
Gescher 12 Jc 51.57N 7.00 E
Geseke 12 Kc 51.39N 8.31 E
Geser 26 Jg 3.53S 130.54 E
Gesunda 8 Fd 60.54N 14.32 E
Gesunden 8 Fa 63.10N 15.55 E
Geta 7 Ef 60.23N 19.50 E
Getafe 13 Id 40.18N 3.43W
Gete 11 Ld 50.55N 5.08 E
Getinge 7 Ch 56.49N 12.44 E
Gettysburg 45 Gd 45.01N 99.57W
Gettysburg Seamount (EN) 32 Eb 36.32N 11.37W
Getúlio Vargas 55 Fh 27.50S 52.16W
Getz Ice Shelf 66 Nf 74.15S 125.00W
Geul 12 Hd 50.40N 5.43 E
Gévaudan 11 Jj 44.27N 3.30 E
Gevelsberg 12 Jc 51.19N 7.20 E
Gevgelija 15 Fh 41.08N 22.31 E
Gévora 13 Ff 38.53N 6.57W
Gevsjön 8 Ea 63.25N 12.40 E
Gewane 35 Gc 10.10N 40.39 E
Gex 11 Mh 46.20N 6.04 E
Gexianzhuang → Qinghe 28 Cf 37.03N 115.39 E
Geyersberg 10 Fg 49.50N 9.30 E
Geyik Dağı 24 Ed 36.54N 32.10 E
Geyikli 15 Jj 39.48N 26.12 E
Geyser, Banc du- 37 Hb 12.25S 46.25 E
Geysir 5 Dc 64.19N 20.18W
Geyve 24 Db 40.30N 30.18 E
Ghabāri, Darb al- 24 Cj 25.10N 29.50 E
Ghadāmis 31 He 30.08N 9.30 E
Ghadduwah 33 Bd 26.26N 14.18 E
Ghaghara 21 Kg 24.52N 84.55 E
Ghaghe 63a Db 7.23S 158.12 E
Ghallah, Wādī al- 30 Jg 10.25N 27.32 E
Ghamrah, Wādī al- 24 Hj 25.47N 38.45 E
Ghana [1] 31 Gh 8.00N 2.00W
Ghanzi 31 Jk 21.42S 21.38 E
Ghanzi [3] 37 Cd 22.00S 23.00 E
Ghār ad Dimā' 14 Cn 36.27N 8.26 E
Gharaqābād 24 Me 35.06N 49.50 E
Gharbī, Al Hajar al- 24 Qj 24.10N 56.15 E
Gharbīyah, Aş Şahrā' al-= Western Desert (EN) 30 Jf 27.30N 28.00 E
Ghardaïa 31 He 32.29N 3.40 E
Ghārib, Jabal- 33 Fd 28.07N 32.54 E
Gharrāf, Shatt al- 24 Kf 32.30N 45.48 E
Gharsah, Shatt al- 32 Ic 34.06N 7.50 E
Gharyān 33 Bc 32.10N 13.01 E
Gharyān [3] 33 Bc 30.35N 12.00 E
Ghāt 31 If 24.58N 10.11 E
Ghatere 63a Db 7.58S 159.01 E
Ghattī 24 Gg 31.16N 37.31 E
Ghazāl, Bahr al- 35 Ed 9.31N 30.25 E
Ghazal, Bahr el- 30 Ig 13.01N 15.28 E
Ghazal, Bahr el- 35 Bc 14.00N 16.30 E
Ghazaouet 32 Gb 35.06N 1.51W
Ghazipur 25 Gc 25.35N 83.34 E
Ghaznī 22 If 33.33N 68.26 E
Ghaznī [3] 23 Kc 33.00N 68.00 E
Ghent (EN)=Gand/Gent 11 Jc 51.03N 3.43 E
Ghent (EN)=Gent/Gand 11 Jc 51.03N 3.43 E
Gheorghe Gheorghiu-Dej 15 Jc 46.12N 26.46 E
Gheorghieni 15 Ic 46.43N 25.37 E
Gheorghiu-Dej 19 De 51.00N 39.31 E
Gherla 15 Gb 47.02N 23.55 E
Ghidigeni 15 Kc 46.03N 27.30 E
Ghidole (EN)=Gidole 35 Fd 5.37N 37.29 E
Ghilarza 14 Cj 40.07N 8.50 E
Ghimeş, Pasul- 15 Jc 46.33N 26.07 E
Ghisonaccia 11a Ba 42.00N 9.24 E
Ghizunabeana Islands 63a Db 7.33S 158.45 E
Ghowr [3] 23 Jc 34.00N 65.00 E
Ghriss 13 Mi 35.15N 0.10 E
Ghubbat al Qamar 21 Hh 16.00N 52.30 E
Ghudāf, Wādī al- 24 Jf 32.56N 43.30 E
Ghurāb, Jabal al- 24 Hf 34.00N 38.42 E
Ghurayrah 33 Hf 18.37N 42.41 E
Ghūriān 23 Jc 34.21N 61.30 E
Ghurrah, Jabal al- 14 Cn 36.36N 8.23 E
Ghuzayyil, Sabkhat- 33 Dd 29.50N 19.45 E
Giaginskaja 16 Lg 44.52N 40.05 E
Giala, Jabal- 24 Ei 27.20N 32.57 E
Gialo Oasis (EN)=Jālū, Wāhāt- 30 Jf 29.00N 21.20 E
Gialoúsa 24 Fe 35.35N 34.15 E
Gia Nghia 25 Lf 11.59N 107.42 E
Giannutri 14 Fh 42.15N 11.05 E
Giant's Causeway/Clochán an Aifir 9 Gf 55.15N 6.35W
Giarre 14 Jm 37.43N 15.11 E
Gibara 49 Ic 21.07N 76.08W
Gibbon Point 51b Bb 18.14N 63.00W
Gibb River 59 Fc 16.25S 126.25 E
Gibbs Islands 66 Re 61.30S 55.31W
Gibellina 14 Gm 37.47N 12.58 E
Gibeon [3] 37 Bd 25.00S 18.30 E
Gibeon 37 Be 25.09S 17.43 E
Gibostad 7 Db 69.21N 18.00 E
Gibraleón 13 Fg 37.23N 6.58W
Gibraltar 6 Fh 36.11N 5.22W
Gibraltar [5] 6 Fh 36.11N 5.22W
Gibraltar, Estrecho de-= Gibraltar, Strait of- (EN) 5 Fh 35.57N 5.36W
Gibraltar, Strait of- (EN)= Djebel Ţāriq, El Bōghāz- 5 Fh 35.57N 5.36W
Gibraltar, Strait of- (EN)= Gibraltar, Estrecho de- 5 Fh 35.57N 5.36W
Gibson Desert 57 Dg 24.30S 126.00 E
Gidami 35 Ed 8.58N 34.40 E
Giddings 45 Hk 30.11N 96.56W
Gidigič 15 Lb 47.04N 28.38 E
Gidole=Ghidole (EN) 35 Fd 5.37N 37.29 E
Gien 11 Ig 47.42N 2.38 E
Giens, Presqu'île de- 11 Mk 43.02N 6.08 E
Gier 11 Ki 45.35N 4.46 E
Gießen 10 Ef 50.35N 8.39 E
Gieten 12 Ia 53.01N 6.48 E
Giethoorn 12 Ib 52.43N 6.07 E
Gifford 42 Jb 70.21N 83.05W
Gifford Seamount (EN) 52 Hi 39.00S 82.00W
Gifhorn 10 Gd 52.29N 10.33 E
Gift Lake 42 Fe 55.49N 115.57W
Gifu 22 Pf 35.25N 136.45 E
Gifu Ken [2] 28 Ng 35.50N 137.00 E
Gigant 16 Lf 46.29N 41.20 E
Giganta, Cerro- 47 Bc 26.07N 111.36W
Giganta, Sierra de la- 47 Bc 26.18N 111.39W
Gigante 54 Cc 2.24N 75.34W
Gigen 15 Hf 43.42N 24.29 E
Gigha 9 Hf 55.41N 5.44W
Giglio 14 Eh 42.20N 10.55 E
Gijón 6 Fg 43.32N 5.40W
Gikongoro 36 Ec 2.30S 29.35 E
Gila Bend 46 Ij 32.57N 112.43W
Gila Bend Mountains 46 Ij 33.10N 113.10W
Gīlān [3] 23 Gb 37.00N 49.50 E
Gīlān-e Gharb 24 Ke 34.08N 45.55 E
Gila River 43 Ee 32.43N 114.33W
Gilbert, Mount- 46 Ca 50.51N 124.20W
Gilbert River 59 Ic 16.35S 141.15 E
Gilbert Seamount (EN) 40 If 52.50N 150.10W
Gilbués 54 Ie 9.50S 45.21W
Gilé 37 Fc 16.09S 38.19 E
Giles Meteorological Station 59 Fe 25.02S 128.18 E
Gilford Island 46 Ba 50.45N 126.25W
Gilgandra 59 Jf 31.42S 148.39 E
Gilgău 15 Gb 47.17N 23.43 E
Gilgil 36 Gc 0.30S 36.19 E
Gilgit 25 Ea 35.44N 74.38 E
Gilgit 22 Jf 35.55N 74.18 E
Giljuj 20 Hf 54.17N 127.05 E
Gillam 42 Ie 56.21N 94.43W
Gilleleje 8 Eh 56.07N 12.19 E
Gillen, Lake- 59 Ee 26.10S 124.40 E
Gillenfeld 12 Id 50.07N 6.54 E
Gillette 43 Fc 44.18N 105.30W
Gillian, Lake - 42 Jc 69.30N 75.30W
Gillingham 9 Nj 51.24N 0.33 E
Gilo 35 Ed 8.10N 33.15 E
Gilort 15 Ge 44.36N 23.27 E
Gilroy 46 Eh 37.00N 121.34W
Giluwe, Mount- 60 Ci 6.04S 143.53 E
Gilvān 24 Md 36.47N 49.08 E
Gimån 8 Gb 62.28N 16.20 E
Gimbi 35 Fd 9.10N 35.51 E
Gimie, Mount- 50 Ff 13.52N 61.01W
Gimli 42 Hf 50.39N 97.00W
Gimo 8 Hd 60.11N 18.11 E
Gimolskoje, Ozero- 7 He 63.00N 32.15 E
Gimone 11 Hk 44.00N 1.06 E
Ginda 35 Fb 15.27N 39.06 E
Ginetu 63a Ac 9.30S 152.43 E

Index Symbols

[1] Independent Nation
[2] State, Region
[3] District, County
[4] Municipality
[5] Colony, Dependency
Continent
Physical Region
Historical or Cultural Region
Mount, Mountain
Volcano
Hill
Mountains, Mountain Range
Hills, Escarpment
Plateau, Upland
Pass, Gap
Plain, Lowland
Delta
Salt Flat
Valley, Canyon
Crater, Cave
Karst Features
Depression
Polder
Desert, Dunes
Forest, Woods
Heath, Steppe
Oasis
Cape, Point
Coast, Beach
Cliff
Peninsula
Isthmus
Sandbank
Island
Atoll
Rock, Reef
Islands, Archipelago
Rocks, Reefs
Coral Reef
Well, Spring
Geyser
River, Stream
Waterfall Rapids
River Mouth, Estuary
Lake
Salt Lake
Intermittent Lake
Reservoir
Swamp, Pond
Canal
Glacier
Ice Shelf, Pack Ice
Ocean
Sea
Gulf, Bay
Strait, Fjord
Lagoon
Bank
Seamount
Tablemount
Ridge
Shelf
Basin
Escarpment, Sea Scarp
Fracture
Trench, Abyss
National Park, Reserve
Point of Interest
Recreation Site
Cave, Cavern
Historic Site
Ruins
Wall, Walls
Church, Abbey
Temple
Scientific Station
Airport
Port
Lighthouse
Mine
Tunnel
Dam, Bridge

Index Symbols

[1]	Independent Nation
[2]	State, Region
[3]	District, County
[4]	Municipality
[5]	Colony, Dependency
	Continent
	Physical Region
	Historical or Cultural Region
	Mount, Mountain
	Volcano
	Hill
	Mountains, Mountain Range
	Hills, Escarpment
	Plateau, Upland
	Pass, Gap
	Plain, Lowland
	Delta
	Salt Flat
	Valley, Canyon
	Oasis
	Karst Features
	Depression
	Polder
	Desert, Dunes
	Forest, Woods
	Heath, Steppe
	Oasis
	Cape, Point
	Coast, Beach
	Cliff
	Peninsula
	Isthmus
	Sandbank
	Island
	Atoll
	Rock, Reef
	Islands, Archipelago
	Rocks, Reefs
	Coral Reef
	Well, Spring
	Geyser
	River, Stream
	Waterfall Rapids
	River Mouth, Estuary
	Lake
	Salt Lake
	Intermittent Lake
	Reservoir
	Swamp, Pond
	Canal
	Glacier
	Ice Shelf, Pack Ice
	Ocean
	Sea
	Gulf, Bay
	Strait, Fjord
	Lagoon
	Bank
	Seamount
	Tableland
	Ridge
	Shelf
	Basin
	Escarpment, Sea Scarp
	Fracture
	Trench, Abyss
	National Park, Reserve
	Point of Interest
	Recreation Site
	Cave, Cavern
	Historic Site
	Ruins
	Wall, Walls
	Church, Abbey
	Temple
	Scientific Station
	Airport
	Port
	Lighthouse
	Mine
	Tunnel
	Dam, Bridge

Index Symbols

[1] Independent Nation	≍ Historical or Cultural Region	⧢ Pass, Gap	⊐ Depression
[2] State, Region	▲ Mount, Mountain	⊐ Plain, Lowland	⊡ Polder
[3] District, County	▲ Volcano	⊠ Delta	⊐ Desert, Dunes
[4] Municipality	⬠ Hill	⊠ Salt Flat	⊡ Forest, Woods
[5] Colony, Dependency	▲ Mountains, Mountain Range	▨ Valley, Canyon	⊡ Heath, Steppe
▣ Continent	⬛ Hills, Escarpment	⊡ Crater, Cave	⊡ Oasis
▭ Physical Region	⬢ Plateau, Upland	⊡ Karst Features	⊡ Cape, Point

⊐ Coast, Beach	⬚ Rock, Reef	⬚ Waterfall Rapids	⊐ Canal
⬚ Cliff	⬚ Islands, Archipelago	⬚ River Mouth, Estuary	⬚ Glacier
⬚ Peninsula	⬚ Rocks, Reefs	⬚ Lake	⬚ Ice Shelf, Pack Ice
⬚ Isthmus	⬚ Coral Reef	⬚ Salt Lake	⬚ Ocean
⬚ Sandbank	⬚ Well, Spring	⬚ Intermittent Lake	⬚ Sea
⬚ Island	⬚ Geyser	⬚ Reservoir	⬚ Ridge
⬚ Atoll	⬚ River, Stream	⬚ Swamp, Pond	⬚ Gulf, Bay

⬚ Strait, Fjord	⬚ Basin		
⬚ Lagoon	⬚ Escarpment, Sea Scarp	⬚ Historic Site	⬚ Port
⬚ Bank	⬚ Fracture	⬚ Ruins	⬚ Lighthouse
⬚ Seamount	⬚ Trench, Abyss	⬚ Wall, Walls	⬚ Mine
⬚ Tablemount	⬚ National Park, Reserve	⬚ Church, Abbey	⬚ Tunnel
⬚ Shelf	⬚ Point of Interest	⬚ Temple	⬚ Dam, Bridge
	⬚ Recreation Site	⬚ Scientific Station	
	⬚ Cave, Cavern	⬚ Airport	

Groenlo	12	Ib	52.04N	6.39 E
Groesbeek	12	Hc	51.47N	5.56 E
Grofa, Gora-	15	Ha	48.34N	24.03 E
Groix	11	Cg	47.38N	3.28W
Groix, Ile de-	11	Cg	47.38N	3.28W
Grójec	10	Qe	51.52N	20.52 E
Gröll Seamount (EN)	54	Lf	14.00S	32.00W
Gromnik	10	Nf	50.42N	17.07 E
Gronau (Westfalen)	10	Dd	52.12N	7.02 E
Grong	7	Cd	64.30N	12.27 E
Groningen [3]	12	Ia	53.13N	6.33 E
Groningen [Neth.]	6	Ge	53.13N	6.33 E
Groningen [Sur.]	54	Gb	5.48N	55.28W
Groninger-wad	12	Ia	53.27N	6.25 E
Groningerwad	12	Ia	53.25N	6.30 E
Grønland/Kalaallit Nunaat= Greenland (EN)	38	Pb	70.00N	40.00W
Grønland/Kalaallit Nunaat= Greenland (EN) [5]	67	Nd	70.00N	40.00W
Grønlandshavet=Greenland Sea (EN)	67	Ld	77.00N	1.00W
Grønnedal	41	Hf	61.20N	47.45W
Grönskara	8	Fg	57.05N	15.44 E
Groot	30	Jl	33.45S	24.58 E
Groot Baai	51b	Ab	18.01N	63.04W
Groote Eylandt	57	Ef	14.00S	136.40 E
Grootfontein	31	Ij	19.32S	18.05 E
Grootfontein [3]	37	Bc	19.00S	19.00 E
Groot-Karasberge=Great Karasberge (EN)	30	Ik	27.20S	18.45 E
Groot Karoo=Great Karroo (EN)	30	Jl	33.00S	22.00 E
Grootlaagte	37	Cd	20.55S	21.27 E
Groot Namaland/Great Namaland	37	Be	26.00S	17.00 E
Grootvloer	37	Ce	30.00S	20.40 E
Gropeni	15	Kd	45.05N	27.54 E
Gros Caps, Pointe des-	51e	Bb	16.28N	61.25W
Gros Islet Bay	51k	Ba	14.05N	60.58W
Gros Islets	51k	Ba	14.05N	60.58W
Gros-Morne	51h	Ab	14.43N	61.01W
Gros-Morne	42	Lg	49.00N	57.22W
Grosne	11	Kh	46.42N	4.56 E
Gros Piton	51k	Ab	13.49N	61.04W
Große Aa	12	Jb	52.25N	7.23 E
Große Aue	12	Kb	52.30N	8.38 E
Großefehn	12	Ja	53.24N	7.33 E
Große Laaber	10	Ih	48.50N	12.30 E
Großenhain	10	Je	51.17N	13.33 E
Großenkneten	12	Kb	52.57N	8.16 E
Grosse Pointe	51e	Bb	16.01N	61.17W
Großer Arber	10	Jg	49.07N	13.07 E
Großer Gleichberg	10	Gf	50.23N	10.35 E
Großer Inselsberg	10	Gf	50.52N	10.28 E
Grosseto	14	Fh	42.46N	11.08 E
Grosseto, Formiche di-	14	Eh	42.40N	10.55 E
Groß-Gerau	10	Eg	49.55N	8.29 E
Großglockner	5	Hf	47.04N	12.42 E
Großräschen	10	Je	51.35N	14.00 E
Groß-Umstadt	12	Ke	49.52N	8.56 E
Großvenediger	14	Gc	47.06N	12.21 E
Grostenquin	12	If	48.59N	6.44 E
Gros Ventre Range	46	Je	43.30N	110.15W
Groswater Bay	38	Nd	54.20N	57.30W
Grøtavær	7	Db	68.58N	16.16 E
Grote Nete	12	Gc	51.07N	4.34 E
Grotli	7	Be	62.01N	7.40 E
Grottaglie	14	Lj	40.32N	17.26 E
Grottammare	14	Hh	42.59N	13.52 E
Groumania	34	Ed	7.55N	4.00W
Groundhog River	44	Ga	49.43N	81.58W
Grouse Creek Montains	46	If	41.55N	113.50W
Grove Mountains	66	Ff	72.53S	74.53 E
Groves	45	Jl	29.57N	93.55W
Grovfjord	7	Db	68.41N	17.09 E
Grow, Idaarderadeel-	12	Ha	53.06N	5.50 E
Grozny	6	Kg	43.20N	45.42 E
Grubišno Polje	14	Le	45.42N	17.10 E
Grudovo	15	Kg	42.21N	27.10 E
Grudziądz	10	Oc	53.29N	18.45 E
Grumento Nova	14	Jj	40.17N	15.53 E
Grumo Appula	14	Ki	41.01N	16.42 E
Grums	8	Ee	59.21N	13.06 E
Grünau	37	Be	27.47S	18.23 E
Grünberg	12	Kd	50.36N	8.57 E
Gründau	12	Ld	50.14N	9.05 E
Grundy	44	Fg	37.17N	82.06W
Gruñidera	48	Ie	24.15N	101.58W
Grünstadt	12	Ke	49.34N	8.10 E
Grunwald	10	Qc	53.30N	20.05 E
Gruppo di Brenta	14	Ed	46.10N	10.55 E
Gruyère	14	Bd	46.40N	7.10 E
Gruža	15	Df	43.54N	20.47 E
Gruzinskaja Sovetskaja Socialističeskaja Respublika [2]	19	Eg	42.00N	44.00 E
Gruzinskaja SSR/ Sakartvelos Sabčata Socialisturi Respublica [2]	19	Eg	42.00N	44.00 E
Gruzinskaja SSR=Georgian SSR (EN) [2]	19	Eg	42.00N	44.00 E
Grybów	10	Qg	49.38N	20.56 E
Grycksbo	8	Fd	60.41N	15.28 E
Gryfice	10	Lc	53.56N	15.12 E
Gryfino	10	Kc	53.15N	14.30 E
Grythyttan	8	Fe	59.42N	14.32 E
Grytviken	66	Ad	54.17S	36.31W
Gstaad	14	Bd	46.28N	7.17 E
Guacanayabo, Golfo de-	47	Id	20.28N	77.30W
Guacara	50	Cg	10.14N	67.53W
Guaçu	55	Ef	22.11S	54.31W
Guadaioz	13	Hg	37.50N	4.51W
Guadaira	13	Fg	37.20N	6.01W
Guadalajara [3]	13	Jd	40.50N	2.30W
Guadalajara [Mex.]	39	Ig	20.40N	103.20W
Guadalajara [Sp.]	13	Id	40.38N	3.10W
Guadalaviar	13	Kd	40.21N	1.08W
Guadalbullón	13	Ig	37.59N	3.47W
Guadalcanal	13	Gf	38.06N	5.49W
Guadalcanal Island	57	He	9.32S	160.12 E
Guadalén	13	If	38.05N	3.32W
Guadalentín o Sangonera	13	Kg	37.59N	1.04W
Guadalete	13	Fh	36.35N	6.13W
Guadalfeo	13	Ih	36.43N	3.35W
Guadalimar	13	Ig	37.59N	3.44W
Guadalmena	13	Jf	38.20N	2.55W
Guadalmez	13	Gf	38.46N	5.04W
Guadalope	13	Lc	41.15N	0.03W
Guadalquivir	5	Fh	36.47N	6.22W
Guadalupe [Mex.]	47	Dc	25.41N	100.15W
Guadalupe [Mex.]	48	Hf	22.45N	102.31W
Guadalupe [Mex.]	48	Id	26.12N	101.23W
Guadalupe [Sp.]	13	Ge	39.27N	5.19W
Guadalupe, Isla de-	38	Hg	29.00N	118.16W
Guadalupe, Sierra de-	13	Ge	39.25N	5.25W
Guadalupe Bravos	48	Fb	31.23N	106.07W
Guadalupe Mountains	45	Dj	32.20N	105.00W
Guadalupe Peak	43	Ge	31.50N	104.52W
Guadalupe River	45	Hl	28.30 N	96.53 W
Guadalupe Victoria, Presa-	48	Gf	23.50N	104.55W
Guadalupe y Calvo	48	Fd	26.06N	106.58W
Guadarrama	13	He	39.53N	4.10W
Guadarrama, Puerto de-	13	Hd	40.43N	4.10W
Guadarrama, Sierra de-	13	Id	40.55N	4.00W
Guadazaón	13	Ke	39.42N	1.36W
Guadeloupe	38	Mh	16.15N	61.35W
Guadeloupe [5]	39	Mh	16.15N	61.35W
Guadeloupe, Canal de la-= Guadeloupe Passage (EN)	47	Le	16.40N	61.50W
Guadeloupe Passage	50	Fd	16.40N	61.50W
Guadeloupe Passage (EN)= Guadeloupe, Canal de la-	47	Le	16.40N	61.50W
Guadiana	5	Fh	37.14N	7.22W
Guadiana, Canal del-	13	Ie	39.20N	3.20W
Guadiana, Ojos del-	13	Ie	39.08N	3.31W
Guadiana Menor	13	Ig	37.56N	3.15W
Guadiaro	13	Gh	36.17N	5.17W
Guadiela	13	Jd	40.22N	2.49W
Guadix	13	Ig	37.18N	3.08W
Guafo, Boca del-	56	Ff	43.40S	74.15W
Guafo, Isla-	56	Ff	43.36S	74.43W
Guaíba	56	Jd	30.06S	51.19W
Guaíba, Rio-	55	Gj	30.15S	51.12W
Guaimaca	49	Df	14.52N	86.51W
Guaimorato, Laguna de-	49	Ef	15.58N	85.55W
Guainía [2]	54	Ec	2.30N	69.00W
Guainía, Río-	52	Je	2.01N	67.07W
Guaiquinima, Cerro-	54	Fb	5.49N	63.40W
Guaira [3]	55	Dg	25.45S	56.30W
Guaíra [Braz.]	56	Jb	24.04S	54.15W
Guaira [Braz.]	55	He	20.19S	48.18W
Guaira Falls (EN) = Sete Quedas, Saltos das-	56	Jb	24.02S	54.16W
Guaíras	55	Ja	12.39S	44.16W
Guaire/Gorey	9	Gi	52.40N	6.18W
Guaitecas, Islas-	56	Ff	43.57S	73.50W
Guajaba, Cayo-	49	Ic	21.50N	77.30W
Guajará Mirim	53	Jg	10.48S	65.22W
Guajira, Península de la-	52	Id	12.00N	71.30W
Guajolotes, Sierra del-	48	Ge	26.00N	105.15W
Guakolak, Tanjung-	26	Eh	6.50S	105.14 E
Gualaco	49	Df	15.06N	86.07W
Gualán	49	Cf	15.08N	89.22W
Gualdo Tadino	14	Gg	43.14N	12.47 E
Gualeguay	55	Ck	33.09S	59.20W
Gualeguay, Río-	55	Ck	33.19S	59.39W
Gualeguaychu	56	Id	33.01S	58.31W
Gualeguaychú, Río-	55	Ck	33.05S	58.25W
Gualicho, Salina del-	56	Gf	40.24S	65.15W
Guam [5]	58	Fc	13.28N	144.47 E
Guam	57	Fc	13.28N	144.47 E
Guaminí	56	He	37.02S	62.25W
Guampi, Sierra de-	54	Eb	6.00N	65.35W
Guamuchil	47	Cc	25.22N	108.22W
Gua Musang	26	Df	4.53N	101.58 E
Gu'an	28	De	39.24N	116.10 E
Guanabacoa	49	Fb	23.07N	82.18W
Guanabara, Baía de-	55	Kf	22.50S	43.10W
Guanacaste [3]	49	Eh	10.30N	85.15W
Guanacaste, Cordillera de-	49	Eh	10.45N	85.05W
Guanacevi	48	Ge	25.56N	105.57W
Guanahacabibes, Golfo de-	49	Eb	22.08N	84.35W
Guanahacabibes, Península de-	49	Ec	21.57N	84.35W
Guana Island	51a	Db	18.29N	64.34W
Guanaja	49	Ee	16.27N	85.54W
Guanaja, Isla de-	49	Ee	16.30N	85.55W
Guanajay	49	Fb	22.55N	82.42W
Guanajibo	51a	Ab	18.10N	67.09W
Guanajibo, Punta-	51a	Ab	18.12N	67.10W
Guanajuato	47	Dd	21.01N	101.15W
Guanajuato [2]	47	Dd	21.00N	101.00W
Guanambi	54	Jf	14.13S	42.47W
Guanare	54	Eb	9.03N	69.45W
Guanare, Río-	50	Ch	8.13N	67.46W
Guanare Viejo, Río-	49	Mi	8.19N	68.10W
Guanarito	50	Bh	8.42N	69.12W
Guandacol	56	Gc	29.31S	68.32W
Guandi Shan	27	Jd	38.09N	111.27 E
Guane	47	Hd	22.12N	84.05W
Guangde	27	Ke	30.51N	119.26 E
Guangdong Sheng (Kuang-tung Sheng)= Kwangtung (EN) [2]	27	Jg	23.00N	113.00 E
Guangfeng	28	Ej	28.27N	118.12 E
Guanghua	27	Je	32.18N	111.45 E
Guangji (Wuxue)	27	Kf	29.58N	115.32 E
Guangling	28	Ce	39.46N	114.16 E
Guangmao Shan	27	Hf	26.48N	100.56 E
Guangming Ding	28	Ei	30.09N	118.11 E
Guangnan	27	Ig	24.02N	105.04 E
Guangrao	28	Ef	37.03N	118.25 E
Guangshan	28	Ci	32.02N	114.53 E
Guangshui	28	Ci	31.37N	114.01 E
Guangxi Zhuangzu Zizhiqu (Kuang-hsi-chuang-tsu Tzu-chih-ch'ü)=Kwangsi Chuang (EN) [2]	27	Ig	24.00N	109.00 E
Guangyuan	22	Mf	32.27N	105.55 E
Guangzhou=Canton (EN)	22	Ng	23.07N	113.18 E
Guan He	28	Ch	32.18N	115.44 E
Guánica	51a	Bc	17.59N	66.56W
Guanipa, Río-	50	Eh	9.56N	62.26W
Guannan (Xin'anzhen)	28	Eg	34.04N	119.21 E
Guantánamo [3]	49	Jc	20.10N	75.00W
Guantanamo	39	Lg	20.08N	75.12W
Guantánamo, Bahía de-	49	Jd	20.00N	75.10W
Guantánamo Bay	47	Id	20.00N	75.10W
Guantanamo Bay Naval Station	49	Jd	20.00N	75.08W
Guantao (Nanguantao)	28	Cf	36.33N	115.18 E
Guanting Shuiku	28	Cd	40.13N	115.36 E
Guanxian	22	Mf	31.00N	103.38 E
Guanyun (Dayishan)	28	Eg	34.18N	119.14 E
Guapé	55	Je	20.47S	45.55W
Guapí	54	Cc	2.35N	77.55W
Guápiles	49	Fh	10.13N	83.46W
Guapó	55	Hc	16.51S	49.33W
Guaporé	55	Gi	29.10S	51.54W
Guaporé	56	Jc	28.51S	51.54W
Guaporé, Rio-	52	Jg	11.55S	65.04W
Guaqui	54	Eg	16.35S	68.51W
Guará	55	Gg	25.23S	51.17W
Guara, Sierra de-	13	Lb	42.17N	0.10W
Guarabira	54	Ke	6.51S	35.29W
Guaranda	54	Cd	1.35S	78.59W
Guaraniacu	56	Jc	25.06S	52.52W
Guarani de Goiás	55	Ia	13.57S	46.28W
Guarapiche, Río-	50	Eh	9.57N	62.52W
Guarapuava	56	Jc	25.23S	51.27W
Guaraqueçaba	55	Hg	25.17S	48.21W
Guararapes	55	Ge	21.15S	50.38W
Guaratinguetá	55	Jf	22.49S	45.13W
Guaratuba	55	Hg	25.54S	48.34W
Guarayos, Río-	55	Bb	14.38S	62.11W
Guarda	13	Ed	40.32N	7.16W
Guarda [2]	13	Ed	40.40N	7.10W
Guardafui, Cape-(EN)= 'Asäyr	30	Mg	11.49N	51.15 E
Guardal	13	Jg	37.36N	2.45W
Guarda-Mor	55	Ic	17.47S	47.06W
Guardiagrele	14	Ih	42.11N	14.13 E
Guardian Seamount (EN)	38	Ki	9.32N	87.40W
Guardo	13	Hb	42.47N	4.50W
Guardunha, Serra da-	13	Ed	40.05N	7.31W
Guareí, Rio-	55	Ff	22.40S	53.34W
Guareña	13	Gc	41.29N	5.23W
Guarenas	50	Cg	10.28N	66.37W
Guaribas, Rio-	55	Jc	16.22S	45.03W
Guaribe, Río-	50	Dh	9.53N	65.11W
Guárico [2]	54	Eb	8.40N	66.35W
Guárico, Embalse del-	50	Ch	9.00N	67.20W
Guarico, Río-	54	Eb	7.55N	67.23W
Guariquito, Río-	50	Ci	7.40N	66.18W
Guarita, Rio-	55	Fh	27.11S	53.44W
Guaritico, Caño-	50	Bi	7.52N	68.53W
Guaritire, Rio-	55	Ba	13.43S	60.38W
Guarujá	55	If	24.00S	46.16W
Guarulhos	56	Kb	23.28S	46.32W
Guasave	47	Cc	25.34N	108.27W
Guasdualito	54	Db	7.15N	70.44W
Guasipati	54	Fb	7.28N	61.54W
Guasopa	63a	Ac	9.14S	152.55 E
Guastalla	14	Ef	44.55N	10.39 E
Guatemala	39	Jh	14.38N	90.31W
Guatemala [3]	49	Bf	14.40N	90.30W
Guatemala [1]	39	Jh	14.38N	90.31W
Guatemala Basin (EN)	3	Mh	11.00N	95.00W
Guateque [Col.]	54	Db	5.05N	73.30W
Guateque [Col.]	54	Db	5.00N	73.28W
Guatimozín	55	Ak	33.27S	62.27W
Guatisimiña	54	Fc	4.33N	63.57W
Guatraché	56	He	37.40S	63.32W
Guaviare, Río-	52	Je	4.03N	67.44W
Guaviravi	55	Di	29.22S	56.50W
Guaxupé	55	Ie	21.18S	46.42W
Guayabal [Cuba]	49	Ic	20.42N	77.36W
Guayabal [Ven.]	50	Ci	8.00N	67.24W
Guayabero, Río-	52	Je	4.03N	67.44W
Guayalejo, Río-	48	Kf	22.13N	97.52W
Guayama	49	Ne	17.59N	66.07W
Guayana, Macizo de la- = Guiana Highlands (EN)	52	Ke	5.00N	60.00W
Guayana Basin (EN)	3	Ci	10.00N	52.00W
Guayaneco, Archipiélago-	56	Eg	47.45S	75.10W
Guayanés, Punta-	51a	Cb	18.04N	65.48W
Guayanilla	51a	Bb	18.02N	66.47W
Guayanilla, Bahia de-	51a	Bc	17.58N	66.45W
Guayape, Río-	49	Df	14.26N	86.02W
Guayaquil	53	If	2.10S	79.50W
Guayaquil, Golfo de-	52	Hf	3.00S	80.30W
Guaycurú, Río-	55	Ch	27.19S	58.45W
Guaymas	39	Hg	27.56N	110.54W
Guayquiraró, Río-	55	Cj	30.10S	58.34W
Guba [Eth.]	35	Fc	11.15N	35.20 E
Guba [Zaire]	36	Ee	10.38S	26.25 E
Guba Dolgaja	19	Fa	70.19N	58.45 E
Gubaha	19	Fd	58.52N	57.36 E
Guban	30	Lg	10.15N	44.26 E
Gubbio	14	Gg	43.21N	12.25 E
Gubdor	17	Hf	60.15N	56.35 E
Guber	10	Rb	54.13N	21.02 E
Gubin	10	Ke	51.56N	14.45 E
Gubio	34	Hc	12.30N	12.47 E
Gubkin	19	De	51.17N	37.33 E
Gúdar, Sierra de-	13	Ld	40.27N	0.42W
Gudara	19	Hh	38.23N	72.42 E
Gudauta	16	Lh	43.07N	40.37 E
Gudbrandsdalen	7	Bf	61.30N	10.00 E
Gudenå	8	Dh	56.29N	10.13 E
Gudermes	19	Eg	43.22N	46.08 E
Gudivāda	25	Ge	16.27N	80.59 E
Gudiyāttam	25	Ff	12.57N	78.52 E
Gudou Shan	27	Jg	22.12N	112.57 E
Güdül	24	Eb	40.13N	32.15 E
Gūdūr	25	Ff	14.08N	79.51 E
Gudvangen	8	Bd	60.52N	6.50 E
Guebwiller	11	Ng	47.55N	7.12 E
Guéckédou	34	Cd	8.33N	10.09W
Guelma [3]	32	Ib	36.15N	7.30 E
Guelma	32	Ib	36.28N	7.26 E
Guelph	42	Jh	43.33N	80.15W
Guelta Zemmur	32	Ed	25.08N	12.22W
Guemar	32	Ic	33.29N	6.48 E
Guéméné-Penfao	11	Eg	47.38N	1.50W
Guénange	12	Ie	49.18N	6.11 E
Guéné	34	Fc	11.44N	3.13 E
Guer	11	Dg	47.54N	2.07W
Guéra [3]	35	Bc	11.30N	18.30 E
Güera	32	De	20.52N	17.03W
Guéra, Massif de-	30	Ig	11.55N	18.12 E
Guérande	11	Dg	47.20N	2.26W
Guerara	32	Hc	32.48N	4.30 E
Guercif	32	Gc	34.14N	3.22W
Guerdjoumane, Djebel-	13	Oh	36.25N	2.51 E
Güere, Río-	50	Dh	9.50N	65.08W
Guéréda	35	Cc	14.31N	22.05 E
Guéret	11	Hh	46.10N	1.52 E
Guérin-Kouka	34	Fd	9.41N	0.37 E
Guernica y Luno	13	Ja	43.19N	2.41W
Guernsey	9	Kl	49.27N	2.35W
Guerrero [2]	47	De	17.40N	100.00W
Guerrero	48	Ic	28.20N	100.26W
Guessou-Sud	34	Fc	10.03N	2.38 E
Guest Peninsula	66	Mf	76.18S	148.00W
Guge	35	Fd	6.12N	37.30 E
Gügerd, Kūh-e-	24	Oe	34.50N	53.00 E
Guglionesi	14	Ii	41.55N	14.55 E
Guguan Island	57	Fc	17.19N	145.51 E
Guia	55	Db	15.22S	56.14W
Guia Lopes da Laguna	55	De	21.26S	56.07W
Guiana Highlands (EN) = Guayana, Macizo de la-	52	Ke	5.00N	60.00W
Guiana Island	51d	Bb	17.06N	61.44W
Guichi (Chizhou)	27	Ke	30.38N	117.30 E
Guichón	55	Dk	32.21S	57.12W
Guide	27	Hd	36.00N	101.30 E
Guider	34	Hd	9.56N	13.57 E
Guidimaka [3]	32	Ef	15.30N	12.00W
Guidimouni	34	Gc	13.42N	9.30 E
Guiding	27	If	26.33N	107.16 E
Guidong	27	Jf	26.11N	113.58 E
Guiers	11	Li	45.37N	5.37 E
Guiglo	34	Dd	6.33N	7.29W
Guiglo [3]	34	Dd	6.30N	7.40W
Guijá	37	Ed	24.29S	33.00 E
Güija, Lago de-	49	Cf	14.13N	89.34W
Gui Jiang	21	Ng	23.28N	111.18 E
Guijk en Sint Agatha	12	Hc	51.44N	5.52 E
Guijuelo	13	Gd	40.33N	5.40W
Guil	11	Mj	44.40N	6.36 E
Guildford	9	Mj	51.14N	0.35W
Guiler Gol	28	Ga	46.03N	122.06 E
Guilin	22	Ng	25.21N	110.15 E
Guillaume Delisle, Lac-	42	Je	56.25N	76.00W
Guillestre	11	Mj	44.40N	6.39 E
Guilvinec	11	Bg	47.47N	4.17W
Guimarães [Braz.]	54	Jd	2.08S	44.36W
Guimarães [Port.]	13	Dc	41.27N	8.18W
Guimaras	26	Hd	10.35N	122.37 E
Guinchos Cay	49	Hb	22.45N	78.06W
Guinea (EN)=Guinée [1]	31	Fg	11.00N	10.00W
Guinea, Gulf of-	30	Hh	2.00N	2.30 E
Guinea, Gulf of- (EN)= Guinée, Golfe de-	30	Hh	2.00N	2.30 E
Guinea Basin (EN)	3	Di	0.00	5.00W
Guinea-Bissau (EN)=Guiné-Bissau [1]	31	Fg	12.00N	15.00W
Guinea Ecuatorial= Equatorial Guinea (EN) [1]	31	Hh	2.00N	9.00 E
Guinea Rise (EN)	3	Dj	4.00S	0.00
Guiné-Bissau=Guinea-Bissau (EN) [1]	31	Fg	12.00N	15.00W
Guinée=Guinea (EN) [1]	31	Fg	11.00N	10.00W
Guinée, Golfe de-=Guinea, Gulf of- (EN)	30	Hh	2.00N	2.30 E
Guinée Forestière [3]	34	Dd	8.40N	9.50W
Guinée Maritime [3]	34	Cc	10.00N	14.00W
Guînes	12	Dd	50.52N	1.52 E
Güines	47	Hd	22.50N	82.02W
Guingamp	11	Cf	48.33N	3.09W
Guinguinéo	34	Bc	14.16N	15.57W
Guiones, Punta-	49	Eh	9.54N	85.41W
Guiping	27	Ig	23.23N	110.00 E
Guipúzcoa [3]	13	Ja	43.10N	2.10W
Guir, Hamada du-	30	Ge	31.00N	3.20W
Güira de Melena	49	Fb	22.48N	82.30W
Guiratinga	54	Hg	16.21S	53.45W
Güiria	54	Fa	10.34N	62.18W
Guiscard	12	Fe	49.39N	3.03 E
Guise	11	Je	49.54N	3.38 E
Guitiriz	13	Ea	43.11N	7.54W
Guiuan	26	Id	11.02N	125.43 E
Guixi	27	Kf	28.18N	117.15 E
Guixian	27	Ig	23.10N	109.35 E
Guiyang	22	Mg	26.38N	106.43 E
Guizhou Sheng (Kuei-chou Sheng)=Kweichow (EN) [2]	27	If	27.00N	107.00 E
Gujan-Mestras	11	Ej	44.38N	1.04W
Gujarāt [3]	25	Ed	22.51N	71.30 E
Gujarāt	21	Jg	22.51N	71.30 E
Gujranwala	22	Jf	32.09N	74.11 E
Gujrāt	25	Eb	32.34N	74.05 E
Gukovo	16	Ke	48.04N	39.58 E
Gulang	27	Hd	37.30N	102.54 E
Gulbarga	22	Jh	17.20N	76.50 E
Gulbene	19	Cd	57.12N	26.49 E
Gulča	19	Hg	40.19N	73.33 E
Gulf	55	Ad	19.08S	62.01W
Gulf Breeze	44	Dj	30.22N	87.07W
Gulf Coastal Plain	38	Jf	31.00N	92.00W
Gulfport	43	Je	30.22N	89.06W
Gulian	27	La	52.58N	122.09 E
Gulin	27	If	28.02N	105.47 E
Gulistan	19	Gg	40.30N	68.45 E
Guliya Shan	27	Lb	49.48N	122.25 E
Gulja	20	Hf	54.43N	121.03 E
Gulja/Yining	27	Dc	43.54N	81.21 E
Guljajpole	16	Jf	47.37N	36.18 E
Gulkana	40	Jd	62.16N	145.23W
Gulkeviči	16	Lg	45.19N	40.44 E
Gull Bay	45	Lb	49.47N	89.02W
Gulleråsen	8	Fc	61.04N	15.11 E
Gullfoss	7a	Bb	64.20N	20.08W
Gullkronafjärd	8	Jd	60.05N	22.15 E
Gull Lake	42	Gf	50.08N	108.27W
Gullringen	8	Fg	57.48N	15.42 E
Gull River	45	Lb	49.50N	89.04W
Gullspång	8	Ff	58.59N	14.06 E
Güllü	15	Mk	38.16N	29.07 E
Güllük	24	Bd	37.14N	27.36 E
Gülpinar	15	Jj	39.32N	26.07 E
Gülşehir	24	Fc	38.45N	34.38 E
Gulstav	8	Dj	54.43N	10.41 E
Gulu	31	Kh	2.47N	32.18 E
Guma /Pishan	27	Cd	37.38N	78.19 E
Gumbiri, Jabal-	35	Ee	4.18N	30.57 E
Gumel	34	Gc	12.38N	9.23 E
Gummersbach	10	De	51.02N	7.33 E
Gummi	34	Gc	12.09N	5.07 E
Gümüşçey	15	Ki	40.17N	27.17 E
Gümüşhacıköy	24	Fb	40.53N	35.14 E
Gümüşhane	23	Ea	40.27N	39.29 E
Gümüşsu	15	Nk	38.14N	30.01 E
Guna	35	Fc	11.44N	38.15 E
Guna	25	Fd	24.19N	77.19 E
Gundagai	59	Jg	35.04S	148.07 E
Gundji	36	Db	2.05N	21.27 E
Gündoğdu	15	Ki	40.15N	27.07 E
Gündoğmuş	24	Ed	36.48N	32.01 E
Güney	15	Mk	38.09N	29.05 E
Güneydoğu Toroslar	21	Gf	38.30N	41.00 E
Gungu	36	Cd	5.44S	19.19 E
Gunma Ken [2]	28	Of	36.20N	139.05 E
Gunnar	42	Ge	59.23N	108.53W
Gunnbjørns Fjeld	67	Mc	68.55N	29.20W
Gunnedah	59	Kf	30.59S	150.15 E
Gunnison	43	Fd	38.33N	106.56W
Gunt	18	Hf	37.30N	71.03 E
Guntakal	25	Fe	15.10N	77.23 E
Guntersville	44	Dh	34.21N	86.18W
Guntersville Lake	44	Dh	34.45N	86.03W
Guntūr	22	Kh	16.18N	80.27 E
Gunungapi, Pulau-	26	Ih	6.38S	126.40 E
Gunungsitoli	26	Cf	1.17N	97.37 E
Günz	10	Gh	48.27N	10.16 E
Günzburg	10	Gh	48.27N	10.16 E
Gunzenhausen	10	Gg	49.06N	10.45 E
Guo He	28	Dh	32.58N	117.13 E
Guojiadian	28	Hc	43.20N	124.37 E
Guoyang	28	Dh	33.31N	116.12 E
Guozhen	28	Bj	29.24N	113.09 E
Gurahonţ	15	Fc	46.16N	22.21 E
Gura Humorului	15	Ib	47.33N	25.54 E
Gurban Obo	27	Jc	43.06N	112.28 E
Gurbantünggüt Shamo	27	Eb	45.30N	87.30 E
Gurdžaani	16	Ni	41.43N	45.48 E
Güre	15	Mk	38.39N	29.10 E
Gurgei, Jabal-	35	Cc	13.50N	24.19 E
Gurghiului, Munţii-	15	Ic	46.41N	25.12 E
Gurgueia, Rio-	52	Lf	6.50S	43.24W
Guri — Raúl Leoni, Represa-	54	Fb	7.30N	63.00W
Gurjev	6	Lf	47.07N	51.56 E
Gurjevsk	20	Df	54.20N	86.00 E
Gurjevskaja Oblast [3]	19	Ff	47.30N	52.00 E
Gurk	14	Id	46.36N	14.31 E
Gurk	14	Id	46.52N	14.18 E
Gurktaler Alpen	14	Hd	46.55N	14.00 E
Guro	37	Ec	17.26S	33.20 E
Gürpınar	24	Jc	38.18N	43.25 E
Gurskoje	20	If	50.20N	138.05 E
Gurskøy	7	Ae	62.15N	5.40 E
Gürsu	15	Mi	40.13N	29.12 E
Gurué	37	Fc	15.28S	36.59 E
Gurumeti	36	Fc	2.05S	33.57 E
Gürün	24	Gc	38.43N	37.17 E
Gurupá	54	Hd	1.25S	51.39W
Gurupi	53	Lg	11.43S	49.04W
Gurupi, Rio-	52	Lf	1.13S	46.06W
Gurupi, Serra do-	54	Id	5.00S	47.30W
Guru Sikhar	25	Ed	24.39N	72.46 E
Gus	7	Ji	55.00N	41.12 E
Gusau	31	Hg	12.10N	6.40 E
Gusev	19	Ce	54.37N	22.12 E
Gushan	28	Ge	39.54N	123.36 E
Gushi	27	Ke	32.02N	115.39 E
Gushikawa	29b	Ab	26.21N	127.52 E
Gūshk	24	Ph	28.13N	55.52 E
Gus-Hrustalny	7	Ji	55.38N	40.40 E
Gusinaja, Guba-	20	Kb	72.00N	150.00 E
Gusinaja Zemlja, Poluostrov-	19	Fa	71.50N	52.00 E
Gusinje	15	Cg	42.34N	19.50 E
Gusinoozersk	20	Ff	51.17N	106.30 E
Guspini	14	Ck	39.32N	8.37 E
Güssing	14	Kc	47.04N	16.20 E
Gustav Holm, Kap-	41	Ie	66.45N	34.00W
Gustavia	51b	Bc	17.54N	62.52W

Index Symbols

[1] Independent Nation; [2] State, Region; [3] District, County; [4] Municipality; [5] Colony, Dependency; Continent; Physical Region; Historical or Cultural Region; Mount, Mountain; Volcano; Hill; Mountains, Mountain Range; Hills, Escarpment; Plateau, Upland; Pass, Gap; Plain, Lowland; Delta; Salt Flat; Valley, Canyon; Crater, Cave; Karst Features; Depression; Polder; Desert, Dunes; Forest, Woods; Heath, Steppe; Oasis; Cape, Point; Coast, Beach; Cliff; Peninsula; Isthmus; Sandbank; Island; Atoll; Rock, Reef; Islands, Archipelago; Rocks, Reefs; Coral Reef; Well, Spring; Geyser; River, Stream; Waterfall Rapids; River Mouth, Estuary; Lake; Salt Lake; Intermittent Lake; Reservoir; Swamp, Pond; Canal; Glacier; Ice Shelf, Pack Ice; Ocean; Sea; Gulf, Bay; Strait, Fjord; Lagoon; Bank; Seamount; Tablemount; Ridge; Shelf; Basin; Escarpment, Sea Scarp; Fracture; Trench, Abyss; National Park, Reserve; Point of Interest; Recreation Site; Cave, Cavern; Historic Site; Ruins; Wall, Walls; Church, Abbey; Temple; Scientific Station; Airport; Port; Lighthouse; Mine; Tunnel; Dam, Bridge

Gustavs/Kustavi	8	Id	60.30N	21.25 E
Gustavs/Kustavi	8	Id	60.33N	21.21 E
Gustavsfors	8	Ee	59.12N	12.06 E
Gustavus	40	Le	58.25N	135.44W
Güstrow	10	Ic	53.48N	12.10 E
Gusum	8	Gf	58.16N	16.29 E
Gütersloh	10	Ee	51.54N	8.23 E
Guthrie [Ok.-U.S.]	45	Hi	35.53N	97.25W
Guthrie [Tx.-U.S.]	45	Fj	33.37N	100.19W
Gutian	27	Kf	26.40N	118.42 E
Gutiérrez Zamora	48	Kg	20.27N	97.05W
Gutii, Vîrful-	15	Gb	47.42N	23.52 E
Guting → Yutai	28	Dg	35.00N	116.40 E
Gutu	37	Ec	19.39S	31.10 E
Guwāhāti	22	Lg	26.11N	91.44 E
Guyana	53	Ke	5.00N	59.00W
Guyane Française = French Guiana (EN) [5]	53	Ke	4.00N	53.00W
Guyang	27	Jc	41.02N	110.04 E
Guyenne	11	Gj	44.35N	1.00 E
Guymon	43	Gd	36.41N	101.29W
Guyonneau, Anse-	51e	Ab	16.14N	61.47W
Guyuan	27	Id	36.01N	106.17 E
Guyuan (Pingdingbu)	28	Cd	41.40N	115.41 E
Guzar	18	Fe	38.37N	66.18 E
Güzelyurt	24	Ee	35.12N	32.59 E
Gūzhān	24	Le	34.20N	46.57 E
Guzhen	28	Dh	33.20N	117.19 E
Guzhou → Rongjiang	27	If	25.58N	108.30 E
Guzmán, Laguna de-	48	Fb	31.20N	107.30W
Gvardejsk	7	Ei	54.40N	21.03 E
Gvardejskoje	16	Hg	45.06N	33.59 E
Gvary	8	Ce	59.23N	9.09 E
Gwa	25	Ie	17.36N	94.35 E
Gwadabawa	34	Gc	13.22N	5.14 E
Gwādar	22	Ig	25.07N	62.19 E
Gwai	30	Jj	17.59S	26.52 E
Gwai	37	Dc	19.17S	27.39 E
Gwalior	22	Jg	26.13N	78.10 E
Gwanda	37	Dd	20.56S	29.00 E
Gwane	36	Eb	4.43N	25.50 E
Gwda	10	Mc	53.04N	16.44 E
Gweebarra Bay/Béal an Bheara	9	Eg	54.52N	8.20W
Gwent	9	Kj	51.45N	2.55W
Gweru	31	Jj	19.27S	29.49 E
Gweta	37	Dd	20.13S	25.14 E
Gwydir River	59	Je	29.27S	149.48 E
Gwynedd [3]	9	Ji	52.50N	3.50W
Gyaca	27	Ff	29.09N	92.38 E
Gya'gya → Saga	27	Ef	29.22N	85.15 E
Gyai Qu	27	Fe	31.30N	94.40 E
Gyaisi/Jiulong	27	Hf	28.58N	101.33 E
Gya La	27	Gf	29.05N	98.41 E
Gyala Shankou	27	Gf	29.05N	98.41 E
Gyangzê	27	Ef	29.00N	89.38 E
Gyaring Co	27	Ee	31.10N	88.15 E
Gyaring Hu	27	Ge	34.55N	98.00 E
Gyda	20	Cb	70.52N	78.30 E
Gydanskaja Guba	20	Cb	71.20N	76.30 E
Gydanski Poluostrov = Gyda Peninsula (EN)	21	Jb	70.50N	79.00 E
Gyda Peninsula (EN) = Gydanski Poluostrov	21	Jb	70.50N	79.00 E
Gyigang → Zayü	27	Gf	28.43N	97.25 E
Gyirong (Zongga)	27	Ef	28.57N	85.12 E
Gyldenløves Fjord	41	Hf	64.10N	40.30W
Gyldenløves Høj	8	Di	55.33N	11.52 E
Gympie	58	Gg	26.11S	152.40 E
Gyoma	10	Qj	46.56N	20.50 E
Gyöngyös	10	Pi	47.47N	19.56 E
Györ	6	Hf	47.41N	17.38 E
Győr [2]	10	Ni	47.40N	17.39 E
Győr-Sopron [2]	10	Ni	47.40N	17.15 E
Gypsumville	42	Hf	51.45N	98.35W
Gysinge	8	Gd	60.17N	16.53 E
Gyttorp	8	Fe	59.31N	14.58 E
Gyula	10	Rj	46.39N	21.17 E

H

Haacht	12	Gd	50.59N	4.38 E
Häädemeeste/Hjademeste	8	Uf	58.00N	24.28 E
Ha'afeva	65b	Ba	19.57S	174.43W
Haafusia	64h	Bb	13.18S	176.09W
Haag, Mount-	66	Qf	77.40S	79.00W
Haaksbergen	12	Ib	52.09N	6.45 E
Haamstede, Westerschouwen-	12	Fc	51.42N	3.45 E
Haanja Körgustik	8	Lg	57.30N	27.30 E
Ha'ano	65b	Ba	19.40S	174.17W
Ha'apai Group	57	Jf	19.47S	174.27W
Haapajärvi	7	Fe	63.45N	25.20 E
Haapamäki	8	Kb	62.15N	24.28 E
Haapasaari	8	Ld	60.15N	27.10 E
Haapaselkä [Fin.]	8	Mc	61.35N	28.15 E
Haapaselkä [Fin.]	8	Mb	62.10N	28.10 E
Haapiti	65e	Fc	17.34S	149.52W
Haapsalu	19	Cd	58.57N	23.32 E
Ḥa'arava	24	Fg	30.58N	32.24 E
Haardt	10	Dg	49.15N	8.00 E
Haardtkopf	12	Je	49.51N	7.04 E
Haaren, Wünnenberg-	12	Kc	51.34N	8.44 E
Haarlem	11	Kb	52.23N	4.38 E
Haarlemmermeer	12	Gb	52.20N	4.41 E
Haarlerberg	12	Ib	52.20N	6.25 E
Haarstrang	12	Kc	51.30N	8.20 E
Haast	58	Hi	43.52S	169.01 E
Haast Pass	62	Cf	44.06S	169.21 E
Habahe/Kaba	27	Eb	47.53N	86.12 E
Habarovsk	22	Pe	48.27N	135.06 E
Habarovski Kraj [3]	20	If	53.00N	137.00 E
Ḩabarūt	23	Hf	17.22N	52.42 E
Ḩabashīyah, Jabal-	35	Ib	16.45N	50.05 E
Habaswein	36	Gb	1.01N	39.29 E
Habay [Alta.-Can.]	42	Fe	58.52N	118.45W
Habay [Bel.]	12	He	49.45N	5.38 E
Habay [Som.]	35	Ge	1.08N	43.46 E
Ḩabbān	35	Hc	14.21N	47.05 E
Ḩabbānīyah, Hawr al-	24	Jf	33.17N	43.29 E
Habibas, Iles-	13	Ki	35.44N	1.08W
Habichtswald	10	Fe	51.20N	9.25 E
Habo	8	Fg	57.55N	14.04 E
Haboro	27	Pc	44.22N	141.42 E
Ḩabshān	24	Ok	23.50N	53.37 E
Hache	10	Ec	53.05N	8.50 E
Hachenburg	12	Jd	50.39N	7.50 E
Hachijō	29	Fe	35.15N	139.45 E
Hachijō-Fuji	29	Fe	33.08N	139.46 E
Hachijō-Jima	27	Oe	33.05N	139.50 E
Hachiman	29	Ed	35.46N	136.57 E
Hachimori	29	Fa	40.22N	140.00 E
Hachinohe	22	Qe	40.30N	141.29 E
Hạchiōji	29	Fd	35.39N	139.18 E
Hachiro-Gata	29	Fa	40.00N	140.00 E
Hacibey De	24	Kd	36.58N	44.18 E
Hackar Dağı	24	Ib	40.50N	41.10 E
Hackås	7	De	62.55N	14.31 E
Håckren	8	Ea	63.10N	13.35 E
Hačmas	19	Eg	41.25N	48.52 E
Hadagang	28	Kb	45.24N	131.12 E
Hadamar	12	Kd	50.27N	8.03 E
Ḩaḑan, Ḩarrat-	33	He	21.30N	41.23 E
Hadano	29	Fd	35.22N	139.14 E
Ḩadāribah, Ra's al-	35	Fa	22.04N	36.54 E
Hadd, Ra's al-	21	Hg	22.32N	59.59 E
Haddad	30	Ig	14.40N	18.46 E
Ḩadded	35	Hc	10.10N	48.28 E
Haddington	9	Kf	55.58N	2.47W
Haddummati Atoll	25a	Bb	1.45N	73.30 E
Hadejia	34	Hc	12.27N	10.03 E
Hadejia	34	Hc	12.50N	10.51 E
Hadeland	8	Dd	60.25N	10.35 E
Hadeln	10	Ec	53.45N	8.45 E
Hadera	24	Ff	32.26N	34.55 E
Haderslev	7	Bi	55.15N	9.30 E
Hadībah	23	Hg	12.39N	54.02 E
Hadım	24	Ed	36.59N	32.28 E
Hadimköy	24	Cb	41.09N	28.37 E
Hadīyah	23	Ed	25.34N	38.41 E
Hadjer el Hamis	35	Ac	12.51N	14.50 E
Hadjout	13	Oh	36.31N	2.25 E
Hadleigh	12	Cb	52.03N	0.56 E
Hadley Bay	42	Gb	72.30N	108.30W
Ha Dong	25	Ld	20.58N	105.46 E
Ḩaḑramawt	21	Gh	15.00N	50.00 E
Hadrian's Wall	9	Kg	54.59N	2.26W
Hadsten	8	Dh	56.20N	10.03 E
Hadsund	8	Dh	56.43N	10.07 E
Hadytajaha	17	Nc	66.57N	69.12 E
Hadyžensk	16	Kg	44.25N	39.31 E
Hadzibeiski Liman	15	Nc	46.40N	30.30 E
Haedo, Cuchilla de-	55	Dj	31.40S	56.18W
Haeju	28	He	38.02N	125.42 E
Haena	60	Oc	22.13N	159.34W
Ḩafar al 'Atk	24	Lj	25.56N	46.47 E
Ḩafar al Bāţin	23	Gd	28.27N	46.00 E
Haffner Bjerg	41	Fc	76.30N	63.00W
Ḩaffūz	14	Do	35.38N	9.40 E
Hafik	24	Gc	39.52N	37.24 E
Ḩafīrat al 'Aydā	23	Ed	26.26N	39.12 E
Ḩafīt	24	Pk	23.59N	55.49 E
Ḩafīt, Jabal-	24	Pj	24.03N	55.46 E
Hafnarfjördur	7a	Bb	64.04N	21.57W
Haft Gel	24	Mg	31.27N	49.27 E
Hāfūn	35	Ic	10.10N	51.05 E
Hāfūn, Rās- = Hafun, Ras- (EN)	30	Mg	10.27N	51.24 E
Hafun, Ras- (EN) = Hāfūn, Rās-	30	Mg	10.27N	51.24 E
Hāfūn Bay North	35	Ic	10.37N	51.15 E
Hāfūn Bay South	35	Ic	10.15N	51.05 E
Hagadera	36	Hb	0.02N	40.17 E
Hagby	8	Gh	56.33N	16.10 E
Hageland	12	Gd	50.55N	4.45 E
Hagemeister	40	Ge	58.40N	161.00W
Hagen	10	De	51.21N	7.28 E
Hagenow	10	Hc	53.26N	11.12 E
Hagere Hiywet	35	Fd	8.58N	37.53 E
Hagerman	46	He	42.49N	114.54W
Hagerstown	43	Ld	39.39N	77.43W
Hagetmau	11	Fk	43.40N	0.35W
Hagfors	7	Cf	60.02N	13.42 E
Häggenås	8	Fa	63.24N	14.55 E
Hagi	28	Kg	34.24N	131.25 E
Ha Giang	25	Kd	22.50N	104.59 E
Hágios Theódóros	24	Fe	35.20N	34.01 E
Hagman, Puntan-	64b	Ba	15.09N	145.48 E
Hagondange	11	Me	49.15N	6.10 E
Hags Head/Ceanna Caillighe	9	Di	52.57N	9.28W
Hague, Cap de la-	5	Ff	49.43N	1.57W
Haguenau	11	Nf	48.49N	7.47 E
Hagunia	32	Ed	27.26N	12.24W
Hahajima-Rettō	60	Cb	26.37N	142.10 E
Hahns Peak	45	Cf	40.56N	107.01W
Hahót	10	Mj	46.38N	16.56 E
Hai'an	28	Fh	32.33N	120.26 E
Haicheng	27	Lc	40.51N	122.43 E
Haidenaab	10	Ig	49.35N	12.08 E
Hai Duong	25	Ld	20.56N	106.19 E
Haifa (EN) = Hefa	22	Ff	32.50N	35.00 E
Haifeng	27	Kg	22.58N	115.21 E
Haiger	12	Kd	50.45N	8.13 E
Hai He	28	De	38.57N	117.43 E
Haikakan Sovetakan Socialistakan Respublika/Armjanskaja SSR [2]	19	Eg	40.00N	45.00 E
Haikang (Leizhou)	27	Jg	20.56N	110.06 E
Haikou	22	Ng	20.05N	110.20 E
Ḩā'il	22	Gg	27.33N	41.42 E
Hailang He	28	Jb	44.33N	129.33 E
Hailar	22	Ne	49.14N	119.42 E
Hailar He	21	Ne	49.30N	117.50 E
Hailin	27	Mc	44.35N	129.22 E
Hailong (Meihekou)	27	Mc	42.32N	125.37 E
Hailsham	12	Cd	50.52N	0.16 E
Hailun	27	Mb	47.29N	126.55 E
Hailuoto/Karlö	5	Ib	65.02N	24.42 E
Haima Tan	27	Kd	10.52N	116.53 E
Haimen [China]	28	Fi	31.53N	121.10 E
Haimen [China]	28	Fj	28.40N	121.27 E
Haina	12	Kc	51.03N	8.56 E
Hainan Dao	21	Mh	19.00N	109.00 E
Hainaut	11	Jd	50.20N	3.50 E
Hainaut [3]	12	Fd	50.30N	4.00 E
Hainburg an der Donau	14	Kb	48.09N	16.56 E
Haines	39	Fd	59.14N	135.27W
Haines Junction	42	Dd	60.45N	137.30W
Hainich	10	Ge	51.05N	10.27 E
Hainleite	10	Ge	51.20N	10.48 E
Hai Phong	22	Mg	20.52N	106.41 E
Haïti = Haiti (EN) [1]	39	Lh	19.00N	72.25W
Haiti (EN) = Haïti [1]	39	Lh	19.00N	72.25W
Haixing (Suji)	28	De	38.10N	117.29 E
Haixin Shan	27	Hd	37.00N	100.03 E
Haiyan (Sanjiaocheng)	27	Hd	36.58N	100.50 E
Haiyan (Wuyuanzhen)	28	Fi	30.31N	120.56 E
Haiyang (Dongoun)	28	Ff	36.46N	121.09 E
Haiyang Dao	28	Ge	39.03N	123.12 E
Haiyou → Sanmen	27	Lf	29.08N	121.22 E
Haiyuan	27	Id	36.35N	105.40 E
Haizhou	28	Eg	34.34N	119.08 E
Haizhou Wan	21	Nf	35.00N	119.30 E
Ḩajar Banga	35	Cc	11.30N	23.00 E
Hajdarken	19	Hh	39.55N	71.24 E
Hajdú-Bihar [2]	10	Ri	47.25N	21.30 E
Hajdúböszörmény	10	Ri	47.40N	21.31 E
Hajdúhadház	10	Ri	47.41N	21.40 E
Hajdúnánás	10	Ri	47.51N	21.26 E
Hajdúság	10	Ri	47.35N	21.30 E
Hajdúszoboszló	10	Ri	47.27N	21.24 E
Hajihi-Zaki	29	Fb	38.19N	138.31 E
Ḩājjīābād [Iran]	24	Ph	28.19N	55.55 E
Ḩājjīābād [Iran]	24	Ph	28.21N	54.27 E
Ḩājjīabād-e Māsīleh	24	Ne	34.49N	51.13 E
Hajnówka	10	Td	52.45N	23.36 E
Hajós	10	Pj	46.24N	19.07 E
Hajpudyrskaja Guba	17	Ib	68.40N	59.30 E
Hakase-Yama	29	Fc	37.22N	139.43 E
Hakasskaja Avtonomnaja Oblast [3]	20	Df	53.30N	90.00 E
Hakata-Wan	29	Be	33.40N	130.20 E
Hakefjord	8	Dg	57.41N	11.44 E
Hakha	25	Id	22.39N	93.37 E
Hakkâri	23	Fb	37.34N	43.45 E
Hakken-Zan	29	Dd	34.10N	135.54 E
Hakkōda San	29	Ga	40.40N	140.53 E
Hako-Dake	29a	Ca	44.40N	142.25 E
Hakodate	22	Qe	41.45N	140.43 E
Hakone-Yama	29	Fd	35.13N	139.00 E
Hakui	28	Nf	36.53N	136.47 E
Hakupu	64k	Bb	19.06S	169.50W
Haku-San	29	Ec	36.09N	136.45 E
Hal/Halle	11	Kd	50.44N	4.14 E
Halab	24	Md	36.17N	48.03 E
Ḩalab = Aleppo (EN)	22	Ff	36.12N	37.10 E
Ḩalabjah	24	Ke	35.10N	45.59 E
Halač	19	Gh	39.04N	64.53 E
Halachó	48	Ng	20.29N	90.05W
Halahei	28	Ga	46.11N	122.46 E
Ḩalā'ib	31	Kf	22.13N	36.38 E
Halalii Lake	65a	Ab	21.52N	160.11W
Halangingie Point	64k	Bb	19.03S	169.58W
Hålaveden	8	Ff	58.05N	14.45 E
Halawa	65a	Eb	21.10N	156.44W
Halawa, Cape-	65a	Eb	21.10N	156.43W
Ḩalbā	24	Ge	34.33N	36.05 E
Halberstadt	10	He	51.54N	11.03 E
Halcon, Mount-	26	Hd	13.16N	121.00 E
Haldean-Sogotyn-Daba	27	Gb	49.05N	97.55 E
Halden	7	Cg	59.09N	11.23 E
Haldensleben	10	Hd	52.18N	11.25 E
Haldia	25	Hd	22.08N	88.05 E
Haldwani	25	Fc	29.13N	79.31 E
Hale, Mount-	59	De	26.00S	117.10 E
Haleakala Crater	65a	Ec	20.43N	156.12W
Haleiwa	65a	Cb	21.36N	158.06W
Halemaumau	65a	Fd	19.24N	155.17W
Hale River	59	Hd	24.56S	135.53 E
Halesworth	12	Db	52.21N	1.30 E
Haleyville	44	Dh	34.14N	87.37W
Ḩalfā al Gadida	31	Kg	15.19N	35.34 E
Half Assini	34	Ed	5.03N	2.53W
Halfeti	24	Gd	37.15N	37.52 E
Halfway	42	Fe	56.13N	121.26W
Halh-Gol	27	Kb	48.01N	118.10 E
Haliburton	44	Hc	45.03N	78.33W
Halifax	39	Me	44.39N	63.36W
Halifax, Mount-	59	Jc	19.05S	146.20 E
Halifax Bay	59	Jc	18.50S	146.30 E
Hālīl	23	Id	27.28N	58.44 E
Halīleh, Ra's-e-	24	Nh	28.46N	50.56 E
Halilovo	16	Ud	51.27N	58.10 E
Ḩalin	35	Hd	9.08N	48.47 E
Haliut → Urad Zhonghou Lianheqi	27	Ic	41.34N	108.32 E
Haljala	8	Le	59.22N	26.09 E
Haljasavej	20	Cd	63.20N	78.30 E
Hall	40	Ed	60.40N	173.05W
Halladale	9	Jc	58.30N	3.50W
Hallam Peak	46	Fa	52.11N	118.46W
Halland	8	Eh	57.00N	12.45 E
Halland [2]	7	Ch	56.45N	13.00 E
Hallandsås	8	Eh	56.23N	13.00 E
Halla-san	28	Ih	33.22N	126.32 E
Ḩallat 'Ammār	24	Gh	29.08N	36.02 E
Hall Beach	42	Jc	68.10N	81.56W
Halle	10	He	51.30N	12.00 E
Halle [2]	10	He	51.30N	11.50 E
Halle/Hal	11	Kd	50.44N	4.14 E
Halle (Westfalen)	12	Kb	52.05N	8.22 E
Halleberg	8	Ef	58.23N	12.25 E
Hällefors	8	Fe	59.47N	14.30 E
Hälleforsnäs	8	Ge	59.10N	16.30 E
Halleim	14	Hc	47.41N	13.06 E
Hällekis	8	Ef	58.38N	13.25 E
Hallen	7	De	63.11N	14.05 E
Hallenberg	12	Kc	51.07N	8.38 E
Hallencourt	12	De	49.59N	1.53 E
Halle-Neustadt	10	He	51.31N	11.53 E
Hallertau	10	Hh	48.35N	11.50 E
Hällestad	8	Ff	58.44N	15.34 E
Hallettsville	45	Hl	29.27N	96.57W
Halley Bay	66	Af	75.31S	26.38W
Halli	8	Kc	61.52N	24.50 E
Hallie-Jackson Bank (EN)	63c	Ba	9.45S	166.10 E
Halligen	10	Eb	54.35N	8.35 E
Hallingdal	7	Bf	60.40N	9.15 E
Hallingdalselva	8	Cd	60.23N	9.35 E
Hallingskarvet	5	Gc	60.37N	7.45 E
Hall Islands	57	Gd	8.37N	152.00 E
Halliste Jõgi	8	Kf	58.23N	24.25 E
Hall Lake	42	Jc	68.40N	82.20W
Hall Land	41	Fb	81.12N	61.10W
Hallock	45	Hb	48.47N	96.57W
Hall Peninsula	38	Mc	63.30N	66.00W
Hallsberg	7	Dg	59.04N	15.07 E
Halls Creek	58	Df	18.13S	127.40 E
Hallstahammar	7	Dg	59.37N	16.13 E
Hallstatt	14	Hb	47.33N	13.39 E
Hallstavik	7	Ef	60.03N	18.36 E
Halluin	12	Fd	50.47N	3.08 E
Halmahera	57	Dd	1.00N	128.00 E
Halmahera, Laut- = Halmahera Sea (EN)	57	De	1.00S	129.00 E
Halmahera Sea (EN) = Halmahera, Laut-	57	De	1.00S	129.00 E
Halmer-Ju	19	Gb	67.58N	64.40 E
Halmeu	15	Gb	47.58N	23.01 E
Halmstad	6	Hd	56.39N	12.50 E
Haloze	14	Jd	46.20N	15.50 E
Ḩalq al Wādī	32	Jb	36.49N	10.18 E
Hals	7	Cg	57.00N	10.19 E
Hälsingland	8	Gc	61.30N	17.00 E
Halsön	8	Ib	62.50N	21.10 E
Halstead	12	Cc	51.57N	0.38 E
Halsteren	12	Gc	51.32N	4.16 E
Haltang He	27	Fd	39.00N	94.40 E
Halten Bank (EN)	7	Bd	64.45N	8.45 E
Haltern	12	Jc	51.44N	7.11 E
Haltiatunturi	7	Eb	69.18N	21.16 E
Haltom City	45	Hj	32.48N	97.16W
Halturin	19	Ed	58.35N	48.55 E
Hālūl	24	Oj	25.40N	52.25 E
Halver	12	Jc	51.12N	7.29 E
Ham	11	Je	49.45N	3.04 E
Ham, Roches de-	12	Ae	49.02N	1.02W
Hamada	29	Cd	34.53N	132.03 E
Hamadān	22	Gf	34.48N	48.30 E
Hamadān [3]	23	Gb	35.00N	48.40 E
Hamadia	13	Ni	35.28N	1.52 E
Hamaguir	32	Gc	30.54N	3.02W
Hamāh	23	Eb	35.08N	36.45 E
Hamakita	29	Ed	34.49N	137.45 E
Hamamasu	29a	Bb	43.36N	141.21 E
Hamamatsu	27	Oe	34.42N	137.44 E
Hamanaka	29a	Db	43.05N	145.05 E
Hamanaka-Wan	29a	Db	43.07N	145.10 E
Hamana-Ko	29	Ed	34.45N	137.34 E
Hamanen, Oued el-	32	Hd	25.52N	1.26 E
Hamaoka	29	Fd	34.39N	138.07 E
Hamar	6	Hc	60.48N	11.06 E
Hamar-Daran, Hrebet-	20	Ff	51.10N	105.00 E
Hamasaka	29	Dd	35.38N	134.27 E
Ḩamāţah, Jabal-	33	Ge	24.12N	35.00 E
Hamatonbetsu	28	Qb	45.07N	142.23 E
Hambantota	25	Gg	6.10N	81.07 E
Hambre, Cayos del-	49	Fb	22.15N	82.47W
Hamburg [2]	10	Fc	53.35N	10.00 E
Hamburg [F.R.G.]	6	Ge	53.33N	10.00 E
Hamburg [S.Afr.]	37	Df	33.18S	27.28 E
Hamburg-Altona	10	Fc	53.33N	9.57 E
Hamburg-Harburg	10	Fc	53.28N	10.00 E
Hamburgsund	8	Df	58.33N	11.16 E
Ḩamḑah	33	Hf	19.02N	43.36 E
Ḩamḑh, Wādī al-	21	Fg	25.58N	36.42 E
Häme [2]	7	Ff	61.30N	24.30 E
Häme	8	Kc	61.30N	25.30 E
Hämeenkangas	8	Jc	61.45N	22.40 E
Hämeenlinna/Tavastehus	7	Ff	61.00N	24.27 E
Hämeenselkä	8	Kb	62.30N	25.00 E
Hamelin Pool	59	Ce	26.15S	114.05 E
Hameln	10	Fd	52.06N	9.21 E
Hamero Hadad	35	Gd	7.28N	42.13 E
Hamersley Range	59	Dd	21.55S	116.45 E
Hamgyŏng-Namdo [2]	28	Id	40.00N	127.30 E
Hamgyŏng-Pukto [2]	28	Jd	41.45N	129.50 E
Hamgyŏng-Sanmaek	28	Jd	41.00N	128.45 E
Hamhŭng	22	Of	39.54N	127.32 E
Hami/Kumul	22	Le	42.48N	93.27 E
Ḩamīdīyeh	24	Mg	31.29N	48.26 E
Hamilton [Austl.]	59	Ig	37.45S	142.02 E
Hamilton [Ber.]	39	Mf	32.17N	64.46W
Hamilton [Mt.-U.S.]	43	Eb	46.15N	114.09W
Hamilton [N.Z.]	58	Ih	37.47S	175.17 E
Hamilton [Oh.-U.S.]	43	Kd	39.23N	84.33W
Hamilton [Ont.-Can.]	39	Le	43.15N	79.51W
Hamilton [Scot.-U.K.]	9	If	55.47N	4.03W
Hamilton [Tx.-U.S.]	45	Gk	31.42N	98.07W
Hamilton, Lake-	45	Ji	34.30N	93.05W
Hamilton, Mount-	46	Hg	39.14N	115.32W
Hamilton River	59	Hd	23.30S	139.47 E
Ḩamīn, Wādī al-	33	Dc	30.28N	22.00 E
Hamina/Fredrikshamn	7	Gf	60.34N	27.12 E
Hamm	10	De	51.41N	7.48 E
Ḩammām al 'Alīl	24	Jd	36.10N	43.16 E
Ḩammām al Anf	32	Jb	36.44N	10.20 E
Ḩammāmāt	32	Jb	36.24N	10.37 E
Ḩammāmāt, Khalīj-	32	Jb	36.05N	10.40 E
Hammam Bou Hadjar	13	Li	35.23N	0.58W
Hammami	30	Ff	23.03N	11.30W
Hammam Righa	13	Oh	36.23N	2.24 E
Ḩammār, Hawr al-	23	Gc	30.50N	47.10 E
Hammarstrand	8	Ga	63.06N	16.21 E
Hamme	12	Gc	51.06N	4.08 E
Hammelburg	10	Ff	50.07N	9.54 E
Hammerdal	7	De	63.36N	15.21 E
Hammeren	8	Fi	55.18N	14.47 E
Hammerfest	6	Ia	70.40N	23.45 E
Hamminkeln	12	Ic	51.44N	6.35 E
Hamminkeln-Dingden	12	Ic	51.46N	6.37 E
Hammond [In.-U.S.]	44	De	41.36N	87.30W
Hammond [La.-U.S.]	43	Ie	30.30N	90.28W
Hammonton	44	Jf	39.38N	74.48W
Hamont, Hamont-Achel-	12	Hc	51.15N	5.33 E
Hamont-Achel	12	Hc	51.15N	5.33 E
Hamont-Achel-Hamont	12	Hc	51.15N	5.33 E
Hamoyet, Jabal-	30	Kg	17.33N	38.02 E
Hampden	62	Df	45.20S	170.49 E
Hampshire [3]	9	Lk	51.00N	1.10W
Hampshire Downs	9	Lj	51.15N	1.15W
Hampton [Ia.-U.S.]	45	Je	42.45N	93.12W
Hampton [Va.-U.S.]	44	Ig	37.02N	76.23W
Hampton Butte	46	Ee	43.46N	120.17W
Hamp'yong	28	Ig	35.04N	126.31 E
Ḩamrā'	35	Dc	10.54N	29.54 E
Hamra [R.S.F.S.R.]	20	Gd	60.17N	114.10 E
Hamra [Swe.]	8	Fc	61.39N	15.00 E
Ḩamrā', Al Ḩamādah al-	30	If	29.30N	12.00 E
Hamra, Saguia el-	30	Ff	27.24N	13.43W
Hamrān	24	Kd	36.22N	45.44 E
Ḩamrat ash Shaykh	35	Dc	14.35N	27.58 E
Ḩamrīn, Jabal-	24	Ke	34.30N	44.30 E
Hāmūn-e Hirmand, Daryācheh-ye-	23	Jc	31.30N	61.20 E
Han	34	Ec	10.41N	2.27W
Hana	60	Oc	20.45N	155.59W
Hanahan	44	Hi	32.55N	80.00W
Hanaizum	29	Gb	38.51N	141.12 E
Ḩanak	23	Ed	25.33N	36.56 E
Hanalei	65a	Ba	22.13N	159.30W
Hanamaki	28	Pe	39.23N	141.07 E
Hanang	30	Ki	4.26S	35.24 E
Hanaoka	29	Ga	40.21N	140.34 E
Hanapepe	65a	Bb	21.55N	159.35W
Hanau	10	Ef	50.08N	8.55 E
Han-Bogdo	27	Ic	43.12N	107.10 E
Hanceville	42	Ff	51.55N	123.02W
Hancheng	27	Jd	35.30N	110.25 E
Hanchuan	28	Bi	30.39N	113.46 E
Hancock	44	Cb	47.07N	88.35W
Handa	29	Ed	34.53N	136.56 E
Handan	22	Nf	36.35N	114.28 E
Handen	8	He	59.10N	18.08 E
Handeni	36	Gd	5.26S	38.01 E
Handlová	10	Oh	48.44N	18.46 E
Handöl	8	Ea	63.16N	12.26 E
Handyga	22	Pc	62.40N	135.36 E
Ḩānegev = Negev Desert (EN)	24	Fg	30.30N	34.55 E
Hanford	46	Fh	36.20N	119.39W
Hangaj, Hrebet- (Changajn Nuruu) = Khangai Mountains (EN)	21	Le	47.30N	100.00 E
Han-gang	27	Md	37.45N	126.11 E
Hanga Roa	65d	Ab	27.09S	109.26W
Hang'bu He	28	Di	31.33N	117.05 E
Hanggin Houqi (Xamba)	27	Ic	40.59N	107.07 E
Hanggin Qi (Xin Zhen)	27	Id	39.54N	108.55 E
Hangö/Hanko	7	Fg	59.50N	22.57 E
Hangöudde/Hankoniemi	8	Je	59.50N	23.10 E
Hangu	28	De	39.16N	117.50 E
Hangzhou	22	Of	30.18N	120.11 E
Hangzhou Wan	28	Fi	30.25N	121.00 E
Ḩanīsh	33	Hg	13.45N	42.45 E
Ḩanīsh al Kabīr, Jazīrat al-	33	Hg	13.43N	42.45 E
Hanja, Vozvyšennost-	8	Lg	57.30N	27.30 E
Ḩanjūrah, Ra's-	24	Pj	24.44N	54.39 E
Hanka, Ozero- = Khanka Lake (EN)	21	Pe	45.00N	132.24 E
Hankasalmi	8	Lb	62.23N	26.26 E
Hankensbüttel	10	Gd	52.44N	10.36 E
Hanko/Hangö	7	Fg	59.50N	22.57 E
Hankoniemi/Hangöudde	8	Je	59.50N	23.10 E
Hankou, Wuhan-	28	Ci	30.35N	114.16 E
Hanksville	46	Jg	38.25N	110.10W
Hanlar	16	Oi	40.34N	46.20 E
Hanmej, Gora-	17	Lc	67.08N	66.00 E
Hanmer Springs	62	Ee	42.31S	172.50 E
Hann, Mount-	59	Fc	15.50S	125.50 E
Hanna [Alta.-Can.]	42	Gf	51.38N	111.54W
Hanna [Wy.-U.S.]	46	Lf	41.52N	106.34W
Hannah Bay	42	Jf	51.15N	79.50W
Hannibal	43	Id	39.42N	91.22W
Hanningfield Reservoir	12	Cc	51.37N	0.28 E
Hannō	29	Fd	35.53N	139.17 E
Hannover	6	Ge	52.22N	9.43 E
Hann River	59	Fc	17.10S	126.10 E
Hannuit/Hannut	12	Hd	50.40N	5.05 E
Hannut/Hannuit	12	Hd	50.40N	5.05 E
Hano	8	Fi	56.00N	14.50 E
Hanöbukten	8	Fi	55.45N	14.30 E
Ha Noi	22	Mg	21.02N	105.51 E
Hanover [N.H.-U.S.]	44	Kd	43.42N	72.17W
Hanover [Ont.-Can.]	44	Gc	44.09N	81.02W
Hanover [Pa.-U.S.]	44	If	39.47N	76.59W
Hanover [S.Afr.]	37	Cf	31.04S	24.29 E
Hanover, Isla-	56	Fh	51.00S	74.40W
Hanpan, Cape-	59	Ka	5.01S	154.37 E
Han Pijesak	14	Mf	44.05N	18.57 E

Index Symbols

- [1] Independent Nation
- [2] State, Region
- [3] District, County
- [4] Municipality
- [5] Colony, Dependency
- Continent
- Physical Region
- Historical or Cultural Region
- Mount, Mountain
- Volcano
- Hill
- Mountains, Mountain Range
- Hills, Escarpment
- Plateau, Upland
- Pass, Gap
- Plain, Lowland
- Delta
- Salt Flat
- Valley, Canyon
- Crater, Cave
- Karst Features
- Depression
- Polder
- Desert, Dunes
- Forest, Woods
- Heath, Steppe
- Oasis
- Cape, Point
- Coast, Beach
- Cliff
- Peninsula
- Isthmus
- Sandbank
- Island
- Atoll
- Rock, Reef
- Islands, Archipelago
- Rocks, Reefs
- Coral Reef
- Well, Spring
- Geyser
- River, Stream
- Waterfall Rapids
- River Mouth, Estuary
- Lake
- Salt Lake
- Intermittent Lake
- Reservoir
- Swamp, Pond
- Canal
- Glacier
- Ice Shelf, Pack Ice
- Ocean
- Sea
- Gulf, Bay
- Strait, Fjord
- Lagoon
- Bank
- Seamount
- Tablemount
- Ridge
- Shelf
- Basin
- Escarpment, Sea Scarp
- Fracture
- Trench, Abyss
- National Park, Reserve
- Point of Interest
- Recreation Site
- Cave, Cavern
- Historic Site
- Ruins
- Wall, Walls
- Church, Abbey
- Temple
- Scientific Station
- Airport
- Port
- Lighthouse
- Mine
- Tunnel
- Dam, Bridge

Index Symbols

[1] Independent Nation	[A] Mount, Mountain	[=] Pass, Gap	[=] Depression	[=] Coast, Beach	[::] Rock, Reef
[2] State, Region	[A] Mount, Mountain	[=] Plain, Lowland	[=] Polder	[=] Cliff	[::] Islands, Archipelago
[3] District, County	[A] Volcano	[=] Delta	[=] Desert, Dunes	[=] Peninsula	[::] Rocks, Reefs
[4] Municipality	[A] Hill	[=] Salt Flat	[=] Forest, Woods	[=] Isthmus	[::] Coral Reef
[5] Colony, Dependency	[A] Mountains, Mountain Range	[=] Valley, Canyon	[=] Heath, Steppe	[=] Sandbank	[=] Well, Spring
[■] Continent	[A] Hills, Escarpment	[=] Crater, Cave	[=] Oasis	[=] Island	[=] Geyser
[■] Physical Region	[A] Plateau, Upland	[=] Karst Features	[=] Cape, Point	[o] Atoll	[=] River, Stream

[=] Waterfall Rapids	[=] Canal	[=] Lagoon	[=] Escarpment, Sea Scarp
[=] River Mouth, Estuary	[=] Glacier	[=] Bank	[=] Fracture
[=] Lake	[=] Ice Shelf, Pack Ice	[=] Seamount	[=] Trench, Abyss
[=] Salt Lake	[=] Ocean	[=] Tablemount	[=] National Park, Reserve
[=] Intermittent Lake	[=] Sea	[=] Ridge	[=] Point of Interest
[=] Reservoir	[=] Gulf, Bay	[=] Shelf	[=] Recreation Site
[=] Swamp, Pond	[=] Strait, Fjord	[=] Basin	[=] Cave, Cavern

[=] Historic Site	[=] Port
[=] Ruins	[=] Lighthouse
[=] Wall, Walls	[=] Mine
[=] Church, Abbey	[=] Tunnel
[=] Temple	[=] Dam, Bridge
[=] Scientific Station	
[=] Airport	

Helgoländer Bucht	10	Eb	54.10N	8.04 E
Helikón Óros	15	Fk	38.20N	22.50 E
Helixi	28	Ei	30.39N	119.01 E
Heljulja	8	Nc	61.37N	30.38 E
Hella	7a	Bc	63.50N	20.24W
Hellberge	10	Hd	52.34N	11.17 E
Hélleh	24	Nh	29.10N	50.40 E
Hellendoorn	11	Mb	52.24N	6.26 E
Hellendoorn-Nijverdal	12	Ib	52.22N	6.27 E
Hellenic Trough (EN)	5	Ii	35.00N	24.00 E
Hellental	12	Id	50.29N	6.26 E
Hellesylt	7	Be	62.05N	6.54 E
Hellin	13	Kf	38.31N	1.41W
Hells Canyon	43	Db	45.20N	116.45W
Hellweg	12	Kc	51.40N	8.00 E
Helmand	21	If	31.12N	61.34 E
Helmand [3]	23	Jc	31.00N	64.00 E
Helme	10	He	51.20N	11.20 E
Helmeringhausen	37	Be	25.54S	16.57 E
Helmond	11	Lc	51.29N	5.40 E
Helmsdale	9	Jc	58.10N	3.40W
Helmsdale	9	Jc	58.07N	3.40W
Helmstedt	10	Gd	52.14N	11.00 E
Helong	27	Mc	42.32N	129.00 E
Helpe Majeure	12	Fd	50.11N	3.47 E
Helpringham	12	Bb	52.56N	0.18W
Helpter Berge	10	Jc	53.30N	13.36 E
Helsingborg	6	Hd	56.03N	12.42 E
Helsinge	8	Eh	56.01N	12.12 E
Helsingfors/Helsinki	6	Ic	60.10N	24.58 E
Helsingør	7	Ch	56.02N	12.37 E
Helsinki/Helsingfors	6	Ic	60.10N	24.58 E
Helska, Mierzeja-	10	Ob	54.45N	18.39 E
Helston	9	Hk	50.05N	5.16W
Helvecia	55	Bj	31.06S	60.05W
Helwân (EN)=Ḩulwān	33	Fd	29.51N	31.20 E
Ḩemār	24	Qg	31.42N	57.31 E
Hemčik	20	Ef	51.40N	92.10 E
Hemel Hempstead	9	Mj	51.46N	0.28W
Hemer	12	Jc	51.23N	7.46 E
Hemnesberget	7	Cc	66.14N	13.38 E
Hemsby	12	Db	52.41N	1.42 E
Hemse	8	Hg	57.14N	18.22 E
Hemsedal	8	Cd	60.50N	8.40 E
Hemsö	7	Ee	62.45N	18.05 E
Hen	8	Dd	60.13N	10.14 E
Henan	27	He	34.33N	101.55 E
Hen and Chickens Islands	62	Fa	35.55S	174.45 E
Henan Sheng (Ho-nan Sheng)=Honan (EN) [2]	27	Je	34.00N	114.00 E
Henares	13	Id	40.24N	3.30W
Henashi-Zaki	29	Fa	40.37N	139.51 E
Henbury	59	Gd	24.35S	133.15 E
Hendaye	11	Ek	43.22N	1.47W
Hendek	24	Db	40.48N	30.45 E
Henderson [Arg.]	55	Bm	36.18S	61.43W
Henderson [Ky.-U.S.]	44	Dg	37.50N	87.35W
Henderson [N.C.-U.S.]	44	Hg	36.20N	78.25W
Henderson [Nv.-U.S.]	43	Dd	36.02N	115.01W
Henderson [Tx.-U.S.]	45	Ij	32.09N	94.48W
Henderson Island	57	Og	24.22S	128.19W
Henderson Seamount (EN)	43	Df	25.34N	119.33W
Hendersonville [N.C.-U.S.]	44	Fh	35.19N	82.28W
Hendersonville [Tn.-U.S.]	44	Dg	36.18N	86.37W
Hendījān	24	Mg	30.14N	49.43 E
Hendorābī, Jazīreh-ye-	24	Oi	26.40N	53.37 E
Hendrik Verwerddam	30	Km	46.36S	37.55 E
Hengām, Jazīreh-ye-	24	Pi	26.39N	55.53 E
Hengduan Shan	21	Lg	27.30N	99.00 E
Hengelo [Neth.]	11	Mb	52.15N	6.45 E
Hengelo [Neth.]	12	Ib	52.03N	6.20 E
Heng Shan [China]	27	Jd	39.42N	113.45 E
Hengshan [China]	27	Jf	27.16N	112.51 E
Heng Shan [China]	27	Jf	27.18N	112.41 E
Hengshan [China]	27	Id	37.51N	109.20 E
Hengshan [China]	28	Kb	45.24N	131.01 E
Hengshui	27	Kd	37.39N	115.46 E
Hengxian	27	Ig	22.46N	109.15 E
Hengyang	22	Ng	26.56N	112.35 E
Henik Lakes	42	Hd	61.05N	97.20W
Hénin-Liétard	11	Id	50.25N	2.56 E
Henley-on-Thames	12	Bc	51.32N	0.54W
Hennan	8	Fb	62.05N	15.45 E
Hennan	7	De	62.02N	15.54 E
Hennebont	11	Cg	47.48N	3.17W
Hennef (Sieg)	12	Jd	50.47N	7.17 E
Hennigsdorf bei Berlin	10	Jd	52.38N	13.12 E
Henrietta Maria, Cape-	42	Je	55.09N	82.19W
Henrietty, Ostrov-	20	Ka	77.00N	157.00 E
Henry, Mount-	46	Hb	48.53N	115.31W
Henry Bay	66	Ie	66.40S	120.40 E
Henryetta	45	Ii	35.27N	95.59W
Henry Kater Peninsula	42	Kc	69.15N	67.30W
Henry Mountains	46	Jh	37.55N	110.50W
Henrys Fork River	46	Je	43.45N	111.56W
Henslow, Cape-	63a	Ec	9.56S	160.38 E
Hentej	21	Me	48.50N	109.00 E
Hentiesbaai	37	Ad	22.08S	14.18 E
Henzada	22	Lh	17.38N	95.28 E
Heping→Yanhe	27	If	28.31N	108.28 E
Heppenheim (Bergstraße)	12	Ke	49.38N	8.39 E
Heppner	46	Fd	45.21N	119.33W
Hepu (Lianzhou)	27	Ig	21.40N	109.12 E
Hequ	27	Jd	39.22N	111.15 E
Herakol Dağı	24	Id	37.45N	42.35 E
Heralds Cays	59	Jc	16.55S	149.10 E
Herāt [3]	23	Jc	34.30N	62.00 E
Herāt	22	If	34.20N	62.12 E
Hérault [3]	11	Jk	43.40N	3.30 E
Hérault	11	Jk	43.17N	3.26 E
Herbert [N.Z.]	62	Df	45.13S	170.46 E
Herbert [Sask.-Can.]	46	La	50.26N	107.12W
Herberton	59	Jc	17.23S	145.23 E
Herbert River	59	Jc	18.32S	146.17 E
Herborn	10	Ef	50.41N	8.19 E
Herby	10	Of	50.45N	18.40 E
Hercegnovi	15	Bg	42.27N	18.32 E
Hercegovina	14	Lg	43.00N	17.50 E
Hercegovina	5	Hg	43.00N	17.50 E
Herdubreid	7a	Cb	65.11N	16.21W
Heredia [3]	49	Fh	10.30N	84.00W
Heredia	47	Hf	10.00N	84.07W
Hereford	9	Ki	52.15N	2.50W
Hereford [Eng.-U.K.]	9	Ki	52.04N	2.43W
Hereford [Tx.-U.S.]	43	Ge	34.49N	102.24W
Hereford and Worcester [3]	9	Ki	52.10N	2.35W
Hereheretue Atoll	57	Mf	19.54S	144.58W
Hereke	15	Mi	40.48N	29.39 E
Herekino	62	Ea	35.16S	173.13 E
Herent	12	Gd	50.54N	4.40 E
Herentals	12	Gc	51.11N	4.50 E
Herfølge	8	Ei	55.25N	12.10 E
Herford	10	Ed	52.08N	8.41 E
Héricourt	11	Mg	47.35N	6.45 E
Herington	45	Hg	38.40N	96.57W
Heriot	61	Ci	45.51S	169.16 E
Heris	24	Lc	38.14N	47.07 E
Herisau	14	Dc	47.24N	9.16 E
Herk	12	Hd	50.58N	5.07 E
Herk-de-Stad	12	Hd	50.56N	5.10 E
Herkimer	44	Jd	43.02N	74.59W
Herlen He	27	Kb	48.48N	117.00 E
Hermagor	14	Hd	46.37N	13.22 E
Hermanas	48	Id	27.14N	101.14W
Herma Ness	9	Ma	60.50N	0.54W
Hermano Peak	45	Bh	37.17N	108.48W
Hermansverk	8	Bc	61.11N	6.51 E
Hermanus	37	Bf	34.25S	19.16 E
Hermeskeil	12	Ie	49.39N	6.57 E
Hermiston	46	Fd	45.51N	119.17W
Hermitage	62	De	43.44S	170.05 E
Hermit Islands	57	Fe	1.32S	145.05 E
Hermosa de Santa Rosa, Sierra-	48	Id	28.00N	101.45W
Hermosillo	39	Hg	29.04N	110.58W
Hermoso Campo	55	Bh	27.36S	61.21W
Hérnad	10	Qh	48.00N	20.58 E
Hernandarias	56	Jc	25.22S	54.45W
Hernández [Arg.]	55	Bk	32.21S	60.02W
Hernández [Mex.]	48	Hf	23.02N	102.02W
Hernani	13	Ka	43.16N	1.58W
Herne	10	De	51.33N	7.13 E
Herne Bay	9	Oj	51.23N	1.08 E
Herning	6	Gd	56.08N	8.59 E
Heroica Alvarado	48	Lh	18.46N	95.46W
Heroica Tlapacoyan	48	Kh	19.58N	97.13W
Heroica Zitácuaro	48	Ih	19.24N	100.22W
Herouville-Saint-Clair	12	Be	49.12N	0.19W
Herowābād	24	Md	37.37N	48.32 E
Herradura	55	Ch	26.29S	58.18W
Herre	8	Ce	59.06N	9.34 E
Herrera	55	Ck	32.26S	58.38W
Herrera [3]	49	Gj	7.54N	80.38W
Herrera del Duque	13	Ge	39.10N	5.03W
Herrera de Pisuerga	13	Hb	42.36N	4.20W
Herrero, Punta-	48	Ph	19.10N	87.30W
Herrljunga	8	Ef	58.05N	13.02 E
Hers	11	Hk	43.47N	1.20 E
Herschel	42	Dc	69.35N	139.05W
Herselt	12	Gc	51.03N	4.53 E
Herserange	12	He	49.31N	5.47 E
Hershey	44	Ie	40.17N	76.39W
Hersilia	55	Bj	30.00S	61.51W
Herson	6	Jf	46.38N	32.35 E
Hersonesskí, Mys-	16	Hg	44.33N	33.25 E
Hersonskaja Oblast [3]	19	Df	46.40N	33.30 E
Herstal	11	Ld	50.40N	5.38 E
Herten	12	Jc	51.36N	7.08 E
Hertford	9	Mj	51.50N	0.05W
Hertford	9	Mj	51.48N	0.05W
Hertfordshire [3]	9	Mj	51.45N	0.20W
Hertugen Af Orleans Land	41	Jc	78.15N	21.12W
Hervás	13	Gd	40.16N	5.51W
Herve	12	Hd	50.38N	5.48 E
Herve, Plateau van-/Herveland	12	Hd	50.40N	5.50 E
Herveland/Herve, Plateau van-	12	Hd	50.40N	5.50 E
Hervey Bay	59	Ke	25.15S	152.50 E
Herzberg	10	Je	51.41N	13.14 E
Herzberg am Harz	10	Ge	51.39N	10.20 E
Herzebrock	12	Kc	51.53N	8.15 E
Herzele	12	Fd	50.53N	3.53 E
Herzliyya	24	Ff	32.10N	34.51 E
Herzogenrath	12	Id	50.52N	6.06 E
Herzog-Ernst-Bucht (Vahsel Bay)	66	Af	77.48S	34.39W
Hesāmābād	24	Me	35.52N	48.25 E
Hesbaye/Haspengouws Plateau	11	Ld	50.35N	5.10 E
Hesdin	11	Id	50.22N	2.02 E
Hesel	12	Ja	53.18N	7.36 E
Heshī	24	Md	37.30N	48.15 E
Heshun	27	Jd	37.18N	113.32 E
Hesse (EN)=Hessen [2]	10	Ff	50.30N	9.15 E
Hesselberg	10	Gg	49.05N	10.35 E
Hesselø	8	Dh	56.10N	11.45 E
Hessen	12	Ke	49.47N	8.08 E
Hessen=Hesse (EN) [2]	10	Ff	50.30N	9.15 E
Hess Tablemount (EN)	57	Jc	17.50N	174.15W
Heta	21	Mb	71.54N	102.00 E
Heta	20	Eb	71.35N	99.45 E
Hettange-Grande	12	Ie	49.24N	6.09 E
Hettinger	45	Ec	46.00N	102.39W
Heuberg	10	Eh	48.06N	8.55 E
Heuchin	12	Ed	50.28N	2.16 E
Heuru	63a	Ed	10.12S	161.25 E
Hève, Cap de la-	11	Fe	49.31N	0.04W
Heves	10	Qi	47.36N	20.17 E
Heves [2]	10	Qi	47.50N	20.15 E
Hexham	9	Kg	54.58N	2.06W
Hexi	27	Hf	27.44N	102.09 E
Hexian	28	Ei	31.43N	118.22 E
Hexian (Babu)	27	Jg	24.28N	111.34 E
Hexigten Qi (Jingfeng)	27	Kc	43.15N	117.31 E
Heydarābād	24	Kd	37.06N	45.27 E
Heysham	9	Kg	54.02N	2.54W
Heyuan	27	Jg	23.41N	114.43 E
Heywood	59	Ig	38.08S	141.38 E
Heze (Caozhou)	27	Kd	35.14N	115.28 E
Hezuo	27	Hd	35.02N	102.57 E
Hialeah	44	Gm	25.49N	80.17W
Hiawatha	45	Ig	39.51N	95.32W
Hibara-Ko	29	Gc	37.42N	140.03 E
Hibbing	43	Ib	47.25N	92.56W
Hibernia Reef	59	Eb	12.00S	123.25 E
Hibiki-Nada	29	Bd	34.15N	130.40 E
Hibiny	7	Hc	67.40N	33.35 E
Hiburi-Jima	29	Ce	33.10N	132.18 E
Hickman	44	Cg	36.34N	89.11W
Hickory	44	Gh	35.44N	81.21W
Hick's Cay	49	Ce	17.39N	88.08W
Hida-Gawa	28	Ng	35.25N	137.03 E
Hidaka [Jap.]	28	Qc	42.53N	142.28 E
Hidaka [Jap.]	29	Dd	35.28N	134.47 E
Hidaka-Gawa	29	De	33.53N	135.08 E
Hidaka Sanmyaku	28	Qc	42.25N	142.50 E
Hidalgo [3]	47	Ed	20.30N	99.00W
Hidalgo [Mex.]	47	Ed	24.15N	99.26W
Hidalgo [Mex.]	48	Jd	27.47N	99.52W
Hidalgo del Parral	39	Ig	26.56N	105.40W
Hida-Sanchi	29	Ec	36.20N	137.00 E
Hida-Sanmyaku	28	Nf	36.10N	137.30 E
Hiddensee	10	Jb	54.33N	13.07 E
Hidra	8	Bf	58.15N	6.35 E
Hidrolândia	55	Hc	16.58S	49.16W
Hidrolina	55	Hb	14.37S	49.25W
Hieflau	14	Ic	47.36N	14.44 E
Hiei-Zan	29	Dd	35.05N	135.50 E
Hienghène	61	Cd	20.35S	164.56 E
Hierro	30	Ff	27.45N	18.00W
Higashi	29b	b	26.38N	128.08 E
Higashihiroshima	29	Cd	34.25N	132.43 E
Higashi-izu	29	Fd	34.48N	139.02 E
Higashi-matsuyama	29	Fc	36.02N	139.22 E
Higashimuroran	29a	Bb	42.21N	141.02 E
Higashine	28	Pe	38.26N	140.24 E
Higashiōsaka	29	Dd	34.40N	135.37 E
Higashi Rishiri	29a	Ba	45.16N	141.15 E
Higashi-Shina-Kai=East China Sea (EN)	21	Og	29.00N	125.00 E
Higgins	45	Fh	36.07N	100.02W
Higham Ferrers	12	Bb	52.18N	0.35W
High Atlas (EN)=Haut Atlas	30	Ge	32.00N	6.00W
Highland [3]	9	Id	57.30N	5.00W
Highland Park	45	Me	42.11N	87.48W
High Level	42	Fe	58.30N	117.05W
Highmore	45	Gd	44.31N	99.27W
High Plains	38	If	38.30N	103.00W
High Point	43	Ld	35.58N	79.59W
High Prairie	42	Fe	55.27N	116.30W
High River	42	Gf	50.35N	113.52W
Highrock Lake	42	He	55.49N	100.23W
High Springs	44	Fk	29.50N	82.36W
High Tatra (EN)=Vysoké Tatry	10	Pg	49.10N	20.00 E
High Willhays	9	Jk	50.41N	3.59W
Highwood Mountains	46	Jc	47.25N	110.30W
High Wycombe	9	Mj	51.38N	0.46W
Higuera de Zaragoza	48	Ee	25.59N	109.16W
Higüero, Punta-	49	Nd	18.22N	67.16W
Higuerote	50	Cg	10.29N	66.06W
Higüey	49	Md	18.37N	68.43W
Hiidenvesi	8	Kd	60.20N	24.10 E
Hii-Gawa	29	Cd	35.26N	132.52 E
Hiiraan [3]	35	He	4.00N	45.30 E
Hiitola	7	Gf	61.16N	29.42 E
Hiiumaa/Hiiuma	5	Id	58.50N	22.40 E
Hijar	13	Lc	41.10N	0.27W
Ḩijāz	23	Ee	24.30N	38.30 E
Hijāz, Jabal al-	33	Hf	19.45N	41.55 E
Hiji	29	Be	33.22N	131.32 E
Hiji-Gawa	29	Ce	33.36N	132.29 E
Hikami	29	Dd	35.11N	135.02 E
Hikari	28	Kh	33.58N	131.56 E
Hiketa	29	Dd	34.13N	134.24 E
Hikiä	8	Kd	60.45N	24.55 E
Hiki-Gawa	29	De	33.35N	135.26 E
Ḩikmah, Ra's al-	24	Bg	31.17N	27.44 E
Hikone	28	Ng	35.15N	136.15 E
Hiko-San	29	Be	33.29N	130.56 E
Hikueru Atoll	61	Mc	17.36S	142.37W
Hikurangi	62	Hb	37.55S	178.04 E
Hikurangi	62	Fa	35.36S	174.17 E
Hila	26	Ih	7.35S	127.24 E
Hilāl, Ra's al-	33	Dc	32.55N	22.11 E
Hiland	46	Le	43.08N	107.18W
Hilchenbach	12	Kc	51.00N	8.06 E
Hildburghausen	10	Gf	50.25N	10.45 E
Hilden	12	Ic	51.10N	6.56 E
Hildesheim	10	Fd	52.09N	9.58 E
Hillaby, Mount-	50	Gf	13.12N	59.35W
Hillared	8	Eg	57.38N	13.09 E
Hillary Coast	66	Kf	79.00S	161.00 E
Hill Bank	49	Ce	17.35N	88.42W
Hill City	45	Gg	39.22N	99.51W
Hillcrest Center	46	Fi	35.23N	118.57W
Hille	12	Kb	52.20N	8.45 E
Hillegom	12	Gb	52.18N	4.35 E
Hillekrog	8	Dj	54.36N	11.30 E
Hillerød	8	Ei	55.56N	12.19 E
Hillerstorp	8	Eg	57.19N	13.52 E
Hillesheim	12	Id	50.19N	6.41 E
Hillingdon, London-	12	Bc	51.31N	0.27W
Hillsboro [Il.-U.S.]	45	Lg	39.09N	89.29W
Hillsboro [N.D.-U.S.]	45	Hc	47.26N	97.03W
Hillsboro [Oh.-U.S.]	44	Ff	39.12N	83.37W
Hillsboro [Or.-U.S.]	46	Dd	45.31N	122.59W
Hillsboro [Tx.-U.S.]	45	Hj	32.01N	97.08W
Hillsborough	51p	Cb	12.29N	61.26W
Hillsdale	44	Ee	41.55N	84.38W
Hillsville	44	Gg	36.46N	80.44W
Hillswich	9	La	60.28N	1.30W
Hilo	58	Lc	19.44N	155.05W
Hilo Bay	65a	Fd	19.44N	155.05W
Hilok	21	Md	51.19N	106.59 E
Hilok	20	Gf	51.22N	110.30 E
Hilton Head Island	44	Gi	32.12N	80.45W
Hiltrup, Münster-	12	Jc	51.54N	7.38 E
Hilvan	24	Hd	37.30N	38.58 E
Hilvarenbeek	12	Hc	51.29N	5.08 E
Hilversum	11	Lb	52.14N	5.10 E
Himāchal Prādesh [3]	25	Fb	31.00N	78.00 E
Himalaya=Himalayas (EN)	21	Kg	29.00N	83.00 E
Himalayas (EN)=Himalaya	21	Kg	29.00N	83.00 E
Himara	15	Ci	40.07N	19.44 E
Himeji	27	Ne	34.49N	134.42 E
Hime-Jima	29	Be	33.43N	131.40 E
Hime-Kawa	29	Ec	37.02N	137.50 E
Hime-Shima	29	Ae	32.49N	128.41 E
Hime-Zaki	29	Fb	38.05N	138.34 E
Himi	28	Nf	36.51N	136.59 E
Himki	7	Ii	55.56N	37.28 E
Himmelbjerget	8	Ch	56.06N	9.42 E
Himmerfjärden	8	Ge	59.00N	17.43 E
Himmerland	8	Ch	56.50N	9.45 E
Himo	36	Gc	3.23S	37.33 E
Ḩimş=Homs (E)	22	Ff	34.44N	36.43 E
Hims, Bahrat-	24	Ge	34.39N	36.34 E
Hinai	29	Ga	40.13N	140.35 E
Hinca Renancó	56	Hd	34.50S	64.23W
Hinche	49	Kd	19.09N	72.01W
Hinchinbrook	40	Jd	60.22N	146.30W
Hinchinbrook Island	59	Jc	18.25S	146.15 E
Hinckley	12	Ab	52.32N	1.22W
Hindås	8	Eg	57.42N	12.27 E
Hindhead	12	Bc	51.06N	0.44W
Ḩindī, Badwēynta-=Indian Ocean (EN)	3	Gl	21.00S	82.00 E
Hindmarsh, Lake-	59	Ig	36.05S	141.55 E
Hinds	62	Df	44.00S	171.34 E
Hindsholm	8	Di	55.33N	10.40 E
Hindukush	21	Jf	35.00N	71.00 E
Hindustan	21	Jg	25.00N	79.00 E
Hinesville	44	Gj	31.51N	81.36W
Hinganghāt	25	Fd	20.34N	78.50 E
Hınıs	24	Ic	39.22N	41.44 E
Hınıs	24	Jc	39.18N	42.12 E
Hinlopenstretet	41	Oc	79.15N	21.00 E
Hinnøya	5	Hb	68.30N	16.00 E
Hino-Gawa	29	Cd	35.27N	133.22 E
Hinojosa del Duque	13	Gf	38.30N	5.09W
Hinokage	29	Be	32.39N	131.24 E
Hi-no-Misaki	29	Cd	35.26N	132.38 E
Hino-Misaki	29	De	33.53N	135.04 E
Hinterrhein	14	Dd	46.49N	9.25 E
Hinton	42	Ff	53.25N	117.34W
Hi-Numa	29	Gc	36.16N	140.30 E
Hınzır Burun	24	Fb	36.22N	35.45 E
Hiou	63b	Ca	13.08S	166.33 E
Hipólito	48	Ie	25.41N	101.26W
Hippolytushoef, Wieringen-	12	Gb	52.54N	4.59 E
Hippone	14	Bn	36.52N	7.44 E
Hirado	28	Jh	33.22N	129.33 E
Hirado-Shima	28	Jh	33.19N	129.32 E
Hiraka	29	Gb	39.16N	140.29 E
Hirakata	29	Dd	34.48N	135.38 E
Hīrākud	25	Gd	21.15N	84.15 E
Hiraman	36	Gc	1.07S	39.55 E
Hiranai	29a	Bc	40.54N	140.57 E
Hirara	27	Mg	24.48N	125.17 E
Hira-Shima	29	Ae	33.01N	129.15 E
Hirata	29	Cd	35.26N	132.49 E
Hiratsuka	29	Fd	35.19N	139.19 E
Hirfanlı barajı Gölü	24	Ec	39.10N	33.32 E
Hirgis	27	Fb	49.32N	93.48 E
Hirgis-Nur	21	Le	49.12N	93.24 E
Hirhafok	32	Ie	23.29N	5.45 E
Hîrlău	15	Jb	47.26N	26.54 E
Hiromi	29	Ce	33.15N	132.38 E
Hiroo	27	Pc	42.17N	143.19 E
Hirosaki	27	Pc	40.35N	140.28 E
Hiroshima	22	Pf	34.24N	132.27 E
Hiroshima Ken [2]	28	Lg	34.35N	132.50 E
Hiroshima-Wan	29	Cd	34.10N	132.20 E
Hirschhorn (Neckar)	12	Ke	49.27N	8.54 E
Hirson	11	Ke	49.55N	4.05 E
Hîrşova	15	Ke	44.41N	27.56 E
Hîrtibaciu	15	Hd	45.44N	24.14 E
Hirtshals	7	Bh	57.35N	9.58 E
Hirvensalmi	8	Lc	61.38N	26.48 E
Ḩīs	35	Hc	10.50N	46.54 E
Hisai	29	Ed	34.40N	136.28 E
Hisaka-Shima	29	Ae	32.48N	128.52 E
Hisar	15	Jg	42.35N	27.00 E
Hisar	25	Fc	29.10N	75.43 E
Hisarcık	15	Mj	39.15N	29.15 E
Hisarja	15	Hg	42.30N	24.42 E
Ḩismā	24	Fh	28.30N	35.50 E
Ḩişn al 'Abr	33	If	16.08N	47.14 E
Ḩişn aş Şaḩābī	33	Dc	30.01N	20.48 E
Hispaniola (EN)=La Española	38	Lh	19.00N	71.00W
Histon	12	Cb	52.15N	0.06 E
Histria	15	Le	44.30N	28.45 E
Hit	24	Jf	33.38N	42.49 E
Hita	28	Kh	33.19N	130.56 E
Hitachi	28	Pf	36.36N	140.39 E
Hitachi-ōta	29	Gc	36.32N	140.31 E
Hitchin	12	Bc	51.57N	0.16W
Hitiaa	65e	Fc	17.36S	149.18W
Hitotsuse-Gawa	29	Be	32.03N	131.31 E
Hitoyoshi	28	Kh	32.15N	130.45 E
Hitra	5	Gc	63.30N	8.45 E
Hiuchi-ga-Take	29	Fc	36.57N	139.17 E
Hiuchi-Nada	29	Cd	34.05N	133.15 E
Hiuma/Hiiumaa	5	Id	58.50N	22.40 E
Hiv	16	Oi	41.46N	47.57 E
Hiva	19	Gg	41.25N	60.23 E
Hiva Oa, Ile-	57	Ne	9.45S	139.00W
Hiw	24	Ei	26.01N	32.16 E
Hjademeste/Häädemeeste	8	Kf	58.00N	24.28 E
Hjallerup	8	Dg	57.10N	10.09 E
Hjälmare kanal	8	Fe	59.25N	15.55 E
Hjälmaren	5	Hd	59.15N	15.45 E
Hjelm	8	Dh	56.10N	10.50 E
Hjelmelandsvågen	7	Bg	59.15N	6.10 E
Hjelmsøya	7	Fa	71.05N	24.43 E
Hjerkinn	8	Cb	62.13N	9.32 E
Hjo	7	Dg	58.18N	14.17 E
Hjørring	7	Bh	57.28N	9.59 E
Hlatikulu	37	Ee	26.58S	31.19 E
Hlavní město Praha [3]	10	Kf	50.05N	14.25 E
Hlavní město SSR Bratislava [3]	10	Nh	48.10N	17.10 E
Hlinsko	10	Lg	49.46N	15.54 E
Hlohovec	10	Nh	48.25N	17.48 E
Hluhluwe	37	Ee	28.02S	32.17 E
Hmelnickaja Oblast [3]	19	Cf	49.30N	27.00 E
Hmelnicki	19	Cf	49.24N	26.57 E
Hmelnik	16	Ee	49.33N	27.59 E
Hnilec	10	Rh	48.53N	21.01 E
Ho	34	Fd	6.36N	0.28 E
Hoa Binh	25	Ld	20.50N	105.20 E
Hoai Nhon	25	Lf	14.26N	109.01 E
Hoanib	37	Ac	19.23S	13.06 E
Hoare Bay	42	Lc	65.30N	63.10W
Hoback Peak	46	Je	43.10N	110.33W
Hobart [Austl.]	58	Fi	42.53S	147.19 E
Hobart [Ok.-U.S.]	45	Gi	35.01N	99.06W
Hobbs	43	Ge	32.42N	103.08W
Hobbs Coast	66	Nf	74.50S	131.00W
Hoboda	16	Sd	50.55N	54.38 E
Hoboken, Antwerpen-	12	Gc	51.10N	4.21 E
Hoboksar	27	Eb	46.47N	85.43 E
Hobq Shamo	27	Ic	40.30N	108.00 E
Hobro	7	Bh	56.38N	9.48 E
Hoburgen	7	Eh	56.55N	18.07 E
Hobyā	31	Lh	5.20N	48.38 E
Hocalar	15	Mk	38.37N	29.57 E
Hochalmspitze	14	Hc	47.01N	13.19 E
Hochfeiler/Gran Pilastro	14	Fd	46.58N	11.44 E
Hochgolling	14	Hc	47.16N	13.45 E
Hochschwab	14	Jc	47.36N	15.05 E
Höchstadt an der Aisch	10	Gg	49.42N	10.44 E
Hochstetters Forland	41	Kc	75.45N	20.00W
Höchst im Odenwald	12	Ke	49.48N	9.00 E
Hochtor	14	Gc	47.05N	12.48 E
Hockenheim	12	Ke	49.19N	8.33 E
Hodaka-Dake	29	Ec	36.17N	137.39 E
Hodda	35	Ic	11.30N	50.45 E
Hoddesdon	12	Cc	51.45N	0.00
Hodgenville	44	Eg	37.34N	85.44W
Hodh	30	Gg	16.10N	8.40W
Hodh ech Chargui [3]	32	Ff	17.00N	7.15W
Hodh el Gharbi [3]	32	Ff	16.30N	10.00W
Hódmezővásárhely	10	Qj	46.25N	20.20 E
Hodna, Chott el-	32	Hb	35.25N	4.45 E
Hodna, Monts du-	32	Hb	35.50N	4.50 E
Hodna, Plaine du-	13	Qi	35.35N	4.35 E
Hodonin	10	Nh	48.52N	17.08 E
Hodorov	16	De	49.25N	24.18 E
Hodžambas	19	Gh	38.06N	65.01 E
Hodža-Pirjah, Gora-	18	Fe	38.47N	67.35 E
Hodžejli	19	Fg	42.23N	59.20 E
Hœdic, Ile de-	11	Dg	47.20N	2.52W
Hoegaarden	12	Gd	50.47N	4.53 E
Hoei/Huy	11	Ld	50.31N	5.14 E
Hoë Karoo	30	Jl	30.00S	21.30 E
Hoek van Holland	11	Kc	51.59N	4.09 E
Hoeselt	12	Hd	50.51N	5.29 E
Hof	10	Hf	50.19N	11.55 E
Höfdakaupstadur	7a	Bb	65.50N	20.19W
Hofgeismar	10	Fe	51.29N	9.24 E
Hofheim	12	Kd	50.05N	8.27 E
Hofmeyr	37	Df	31.39S	25.50 E
Höfn	7a	Cb	64.15N	15.13W
Hofsjökull	5	Ec	64.49N	18.48W
Höfu	28	Kg	34.03N	131.34 E
Höganäs	8	Eh	56.12N	12.33 E
Hogarth, Mount-	59	Hd	21.48S	136.58 E
Hogback Mountain	46	Id	44.54N	112.07W
Hog Cliffs	51d	Ba	17.38N	61.44W
Hoge Venen/Hautes Fagnes	10	Bf	50.30N	6.00 E
Högfors/Karkkila	7	Ff	60.32N	24.11 E
Hog Island	51p	Bb	12.00N	61.44W
Hogne, Somme-Leuze-	12	Hd	50.15N	5.17 E
Hog Point	51d	Ba	17.43N	61.48W
Högsby	7	Dh	57.10N	16.02 E
Høgste Breakulen	8	Bc	61.41N	7.02 E
Høgstegia	8	Db	62.23N	10.08 E
Hogsty Reef	49	Kc	21.41N	73.49W
Höhang-nyöng	28	Jd	41.48N	128.20 E
Hohe Acht	10	Cf	50.23N	7.00 E
Hohe Eifel	12	Id	50.16N	6.50 E
Hohenau	55	Eh	27.05S	55.45W
Hohenems	14	Dc	47.22N	9.41 E
Hohenloher Ebene	10	Fg	49.20N	9.40 E
Hohes Venn	10	Bf	50.30N	6.00 E
Hohe Tauern	14	Gc	47.10N	12.30 E
Hohhot	22	Ne	40.51N	111.38 E
Höhoku	29	Bd	34.17N	130.57 E
Höhr-Grenzhausen	12	Jd	50.26N	7.40 E
Höhtiäinen	8	Mb	62.50N	29.40 E
Hoh Xil Hu	27	Fd	35.35N	91.06 E
Hoh Xil Shan	21	Lf	35.20N	91.00 E
Hoi An	25	Le	15.52N	108.19 E

Index Symbols

- [1] Independent Nation
- [2] State, Region
- [3] District, County
- [4] Municipality
- [5] Colony, Dependency
- Continent
- Physical Region
- Historical or Cultural Region
- Mount, Mountain
- Volcano
- Hill
- Mountains, Mountain Range
- Hills, Escarpment
- Plateau, Upland
- Pass, Gap
- Plain, Lowland
- Delta
- Salt Flat
- Valley, Canyon
- Crater, Cave
- Karst Features
- Depression
- Polder
- Desert, Dunes
- Forest, Woods
- Heath, Steppe
- Oasis
- Cape, Point
- Coast, Beach
- Cliff
- Peninsula
- Isthmus
- Sandbank
- Island
- Atoll
- Rock, Reef
- Islands, Archipelago
- Rocks, Reefs
- Coral Reef
- Well, Spring
- Geyser
- River, Stream
- Waterfall Rapids
- River Mouth, Estuary
- Lake
- Salt Lake
- Intermittent Lake
- Reservoir
- Swamp, Pond
- Canal
- Glacier
- Ice Shelf, Pack Ice
- Ocean
- Sea
- Gulf, Bay
- Strait, Fjord
- Lagoon
- Bank
- Seamount
- Tablemount
- Ridge
- Shelf
- Basin
- Escarpment, Sea Scarp
- Fracture
- Trench, Abyss
- National Park, Reserve
- Point of Interest
- Recreation Site
- Cave, Cavern
- Historic Site
- Ruins
- Wall, Walls
- Church, Abbey
- Temple
- Scientific Station
- Airport
- Port
- Lighthouse
- Mine
- Tunnel
- Dam, Bridge

Hoima	36	Fb	1.26N	31.21 E
Hoisington	45	Gg	38.31N	98.47W
Hoj, Vozvyšennost-	17	Ob	68.50N	71.30 E
Højer	8	Cj	54.58N	8.43 E
Hojniki	19	Ce	51.54N	29.56 E
Hōjō	28	Lh	33.58N	132.46 E
Hökensås	8	Ff	58.11N	14.08 E
Hokianga Harbour	62	Ea	35.30S	173.20 E
Hokitika	58	Ii	42.43S	170.58 E
Hok-Kai=Okhotsk, Sea of- (EN)	21	Qd	53.00N	150.00 E
Hokkaidō	21	Qe	43.00N	143.00 E
Hokkaidō Ken [2]	28	Qc	43.00N	143.00 E
Hokksund	7	Bg	59.47N	9.59 E
Hokmābād	24	Qd	36.37N	57.36 E
Hokota	29	Gc	36.10N	140.30 E
Hol	8	Cd	60.36N	8.22 E
Holap	64d	Ba	7.39N	151.54 E
Holbæk	8	Di	55.43N	11.43 E
Holbeach	12	Cb	52.48N	0.01 E
Holbeach Marsh	12	Cb	52.52N	0.02 E
Holbox, Isla-	48	Pg	21.33N	87.15W
Holbrook	43	Ee	34.54N	110.10W
Holdenville	45	Hi	35.05N	96.24W
Holderness	9	Mh	53.47N	0.10W
Holdrege	45	Gf	40.26N	99.22W
Hold With Hope	41	Jd	73.40N	21.45W
Hole in the Wall	44	Im	25.51N	77.12W
Hølen	8	De	59.32N	10.45 E
Holešov	10	Ng	49.20N	17.33 E
Holetown	51q	Ab	13.11N	59.39W
Holguín	39	Lg	20.53N	76.15W
Holguín [3]	49	Jc	20.40N	75.50W
Hol Hol	35	Gc	11.20N	42.50 E
Holitna	40	Hd	61.40N	157.12W
Höljes	7	Cf	60.54N	12.36 E
Hollabrunn	14	Kb	48.33N	16.05 E
Holland	44	Dd	42.47N	86.07W
Holland [Eng.-U.K.]	12	Bb	52.52N	0.10W
Holland [Neth.]	5	Ge	52.20N	4.45 E
Hollandale	45	Kj	33.10N	90.58W
Hollandsbird Island	37	Ad	24.45S	14.34 E
Hollands Diep	12	Gc	51.40N	4.30 E
Hollesley Bay	12	Db	52.04N	1.33 E
Hollick-Kenyon Plateau	66	Pf	79.00S	97.00W
Hollis	45	Gi	34.41N	99.55W
Hollister [Ca.-U.S.]	46	Eh	36.51N	121.24W
Hollister [Id.-U.S.]	46	He	42.23N	114.35W
Hollola	8	Kc	61.03N	25.26 E
Höllviksnäs	8	Ei	55.25N	12.57 E
Holly Springs	45	Li	34.41N	89.26W
Hollywood	43	Kf	26.00N	80.09W
Holm	7	Hh	57.09N	31.12 E
Holma	34	Hd	9.54N	13.03 E
Holman Island	42	Fb	70.40N	117.35W
Hólmavík	7a	Bb	65.43N	21.41W
Holmes Reefs	57	Ff	16.30S	148.00 E
Holmestrand	8	De	59.29N	10.18 E
Holm Land	41	Kb	80.16N	18.20W
Holms	41	Gd	74.30N	57.00W
Holmsjö	8	Fh	56.25N	15.32 E
Holmsjön [Swe.]	7	De	62.25N	15.20 E
Holmsjön [Swe.]	8	Gb	62.40N	16.35 E
Holmsk	20	Jg	47.00N	142.03 E
Holmski	16	Kg	44.50N	38.24 E
Holmsland Klit	8	Ch	56.00N	8.10 E
Holmsund	7	Ee	63.42N	20.21 E
Holmsveden	8	Gc	61.07N	16.43 E
Holmudden	8	Hg	57.57N	19.21 E
Holod	15	Fc	46.47N	22.08 E
Holohit, Punta-	48	Og	21.37N	88.08W
Holothuria Banks (EN)	59	Fb	13.25S	126.00 E
Holsnøy	8	Ad	60.35N	5.05 E
Holstebro	7	Bh	56.21N	8.38 E
Holsted	8	Ci	55.30N	8.55 E
Holstein	45	Ie	42.29N	95.33W
Holsteinsborg/ Sisimiut	67	Nc	67.05N	53.45W
Holt	12	Db	52.54N	1.05 E
Holten	12	Ib	52.17N	6.27 E
Holton	45	Ig	39.28N	95.44W
Holtoson	20	Ff	50.18N	103.20 E
Holtyn-Daba	27	Ib	47.40N	107.20 E
Holwerd, Westdongeradeel-	12	Ha	53.22N	5.54 E
Holy Cross	40	Hd	62.12N	159.47W
Holyhead	9	Ih	53.20N	4.38W
Holy Island [Eng.-U.K.]	9	Lf	55.41N	1.48W
Holy Island [Wales-U.K.]	9	Ih	53.18N	4.37W
Holyoke [Co.-U.S.]	45	Ef	40.35N	102.18W
Holyoke [Ma.-U.S.]	44	Kd	42.12N	72.37W
Holýšov	10	Jg	49.36N	13.07 E
Homa Bay	36	Fc	0.31S	34.27 E
Homalin	25	Id	24.52N	94.55 E
Homathko River	46	Ca	50.55N	124.50W
Homberg (Ohm)	12	Kd	50.44N	8.59 E
Hombori	34	Eb	15.17N	1.42W
Hombre Muerto, Salar del-	56	Gc	25.23S	67.06W
Homburg	10	Dg	49.19N	7.20 E
Home Bay	38	Mc	68.45N	67.10W
Homecourt	12	He	49.14N	5.59 E
Home Hill	59	Jc	19.40S	147.25 E
Homer [Ak.-U.S.]	39	Dd	59.39N	151.33W
Homer [La.-U.S.]	45	Jj	32.48N	93.04W
Homert	12	Kc	51.16N	8.06 E
Homerville	44	Fj	31.02N	82.45W
Homestead	44	Gm	25.29N	80.29W
Homewood	44	Di	33.29N	86.48W
Hommelstø	7	Cd	65.25N	12.30 E
Hommersåk	8	Af	58.55N	5.50 E
Homoine	37	Fd	23.52S	35.08 E
Homoljske Planina	15	Ee	44.20N	21.45 E
Homonhon	26	Id	10.44N	125.43 E
Homosassa	44	Fk	28.47N	82.37W
Homs (EN)=Ḥimş	22	Ff	34.44N	36.43 E
Honan (EN)=Henan Sheng (Ho-nan Sheng) [2]	27	Je	34.00N	114.00 E
Honan (EN)=Ho-nan Sheng→Henan Sheng [2]	27	Je	34.00N	114.00 E
Ho-nan Sheng→Henan Sheng=Honan (EN) [2]	27	Je	34.00N	114.00 E
Honaz	15	Ml	37.45N	29.17 E
Honaz Dağı	15	Ml	37.41N	29.18 E
Honbetsu	28	Qc	43.18N	143.33 E
Honda	54	Db	5.13N	74.45W
Honda, Bahía-	49	Lg	12.21N	71.47W
Hondeklipbaai	37	Bf	30.20S	17.18 E
Hòn Diên, Núi-	25	Lf	11.33N	108.38 E
Hondo	47	Ge	18.29N	88.19W
Hondo [Jap.]	28	Kh	32.27N	130.12 E
Hondo [N.M.-U.S.]	45	Dj	33.23N	105.16W
Hondo [Tx.-U.S.]	45	Gl	29.21N	99.09W
Hondo, Rio-	45	Dj	33.22N	104.24W
Hondschoote	12	Ed	50.59N	2.35 E
Hondsrug	11	Mb	52.50N	6.50 E
Honduras [1]	39	Kh	15.00N	86.30W
Honduras, Cabo de-	49	De	16.01N	86.01W
Honduras, Golfo de-= Honduras, Gulf of- (EN)	38	Kh	16.10N	87.50W
Honduras, Gulf of-	38	Kh	16.10N	87.50W
Honduras, Gulf of- (EN)= Honduras, Golfo de-	38	Kh	16.10N	87.50W
Hønefoss	7	Cf	60.10N	10.18 E
Honey Lake	46	Ef	40.16N	120.19W
Honfleur	11	Ge	49.25N	0.14 E
Hông, Sông-=Red River (EN)	21	Mg	20.17N	106.34 E
Hong'an (Huang'an)	28	Ci	31.17N	114.37 E
Hongch'ŏn	28	If	37.41N	127.52 E
Hong-Do	28	Hg	34.41N	125.13 E
Hong He	28	Ch	32.24N	115.32 E
Honghton Lake	44	Ec	44.22N	84.43W
Hong Hu	27	Je	30.00N	113.25 E
Honghu (Xindi)	28	Bj	29.50N	113.28 E
Honghui	27	Id	36.46N	105.05 E
Hong Kong/Xianggang [5]	22	Ng	22.15N	114.10 E
Hongliuyuan	27	Gc	41.02N	95.24 E
Hongluoxian	28	Fd	41.01N	120.52 E
Hongning → Wulian	28	Eg	35.45N	119.13 E
Hongor	28	Bb	45.48N	112.45 E
Hongqizhen	27	Ih	18.48N	109.30 E
Hongshui He	21	Mg	23.47N	109.33 E
Hongsŏng	28	If	36.36N	126.40 E
Hongtong	28	Af	36.15N	111.41 E
Hongū	29	De	33.50N	135.46 E
Honguedo, Détroit d'-	42	Lg	49.30N	65.00W
Hongwansi → Sunan	27	Gd	38.59N	99.25 E
Hongwŏn	28	Id	40.02N	127.58 E
Hongyuan (Hurama)	27	He	32.45N	102.38 E
Hongze (Gaoliangjian)	27	Ke	33.10N	119.58 E
Hongze Hu	27	Ke	33.20N	118.40 E
Honiara	58	Ge	9.27S	159.57 E
Honikulu, Passe-	64h	Ac	13.23S	176.11W
Honiton	9	Jk	50.48N	3.13W
Honjō	28	Pe	39.23N	140.03 E
Honkajoki	8	Jb	61.59N	22.16 E
Hon-kawane	29	Fd	35.07N	138.06 E
Honningsvåg	7	Ga	70.59N	26.01 E
Hönö	8	Dg	57.42N	11.39 E
Honokaa	65a	Fc	20.05N	155.28W
Honokohau	65a	Eb	21.01N	156.37W
Honolulu	58	Lb	21.19N	157.52W
Honomu	65a	Fd	19.52N	155.07W
Honrubia	13	Je	39.37N	2.16W
Honshū	21	Pf	36.00N	136.00 E
Hontenisse	12	Gc	51.23N	4.00 E
Hontenisse-Kloosterzande	12	Gc	51.23N	4.00 E
Honuapo Bay	65a	Fd	19.05N	155.33W
Honuu	20	Jc	66.27N	143.06 E
Honyō	29	Fc	36.14N	139.10 E
Hood	42	Gc	67.25N	108.53W
Hood, Mount-	38	Ge	45.23N	121.41W
Hood Point	59	Df	34.23S	119.34 E
Hood River	46	Ed	45.43N	121.31W
Hoogeveen	11	Mb	52.43N	6.29 E
Hoogezand-Sappemeer	12	Ia	53.09N	6.48 E
Hooglede	12	Fd	50.59N	3.05 E
Hoogstraten	12	Gc	51.24N	4.46 E
Hooker	45	Fh	36.52N	101.13W
Hooker, Cape-	66	Kf	70.38S	166.45 E
Hook Head/Rinn Duáin	9	Gi	52.07N	6.55W
Hook Island	59	Jc	20.10S	148.55 E
Hoolehua	65a	Db	21.10N	157.05W
Hoonah	40	Le	58.07N	135.26W
Hooper, Cape-	42	Kc	68.24N	66.43W
Hooper Bay	40	Fd	61.31N	166.06W
Hoopeston	45	Mf	40.28N	87.40W
Höör	8	Ei	55.56N	13.32 E
Hoorn	11	Lb	52.38N	5.04 E
Hoornaar	12	Gc	51.53N	4.57 E
Hoover Dam	46	Hi	36.00N	114.27W
Hopa	24	Ib	41.25N	41.24 E
Hope [Ar.-U.S.]	45	Jj	33.40N	93.36W
Hope [Az.-U.S.]	46	Ij	33.44N	113.42W
Hope [B.C.-Can.]	46	Eb	49.23N	121.26W
Hope, Ben-	9	Ic	58.24N	4.36W
Hope, Lake-	59	Ef	32.50S	121.40 E
Hope, Point-	38	Cc	68.21N	166.50W
Hopedale	42	Le	55.50N	60.10W
Hopefield	37	Bf	33.04S	18.21 E
Hopeh (EN)=Hebei Sheng (Ho-pei Sheng) [2]	27	Kd	39.00N	116.00 E
Hopeh (EN)=Ho-pei Sheng→Hebei Sheng [2]	27	Kd	39.00N	116.00 E
Hopeh (EN)=Hu-pei Sheng→Hubei Sheng [2]	27	Je	31.00N	112.00 E
Ho-pei Sheng→Hebei Sheng =Hopeh (EN) [2]	27	Kd	39.00N	116.00 E
Hopelchén	48	Oh	19.46N	89.51W
Hopen	41	Oc	76.35N	25.10 E
Hopër	5	Kf	49.36N	42.19 E
Hopes Advance, Cap -	42	Kd	61.05N	69.33W
Hopetoun [Austl.]	59	Ig	35.44S	142.22 E
Hopetoun [Austl.]	58	Dh	33.57S	120.07 E
Hopetown	37	Ce	29.34S	24.03 E
Hopewell	44	Ig	37.17N	77.19W
Hopewell Islands	42	Je	58.20N	78.10W
Hopin	25	Jd	24.59N	96.31 E
Hopkins, Lake-	59	Fd	24.15S	128.50 E
Hopkinsville	43	Jd	36.52N	87.29W
Hopsten	12	Jb	52.23N	7.37 E
Hoptrup	8	Ci	55.11N	9.28 E
Hoquiam	43	Cb	46.59N	123.53W
Hor	20	Ig	47.48N	134.43 E
Hor	20	Ig	47.55N	135.01 E
Hōrai	29	Ed	34.55N	137.34 E
Hōrai-San	29	Dd	35.13N	135.53 E
Horasan	24	Jb	40.03N	42.11 E
Horaždovice	10	Jg	49.20N	13.42 E
Horb am Neckar	10	Eh	48.26N	8.41 E
Horconcitos	49	Fi	8.19N	82.10W
Hordaland [2]	7	Bf	60.15N	6.30 E
Hordogoj	20	Gd	62.32N	115.38 E
Horezmskaja Oblast [3]	19	Gg	41.30N	60.40 E
Horfors	7	Df	60.33N	16.17 E
Horgen	14	Cc	47.15N	8.36 E
Horgoš	15	Cc	46.09N	19.58 E
Horgos	19	Ig	44.10N	80.20 E
Hořice	10	Lf	50.22N	15.38 E
Horinger	28	Ad	40.24N	111.46 E
Horizon Tablemount (EN)	57	Kc	19.40N	168.30W
Horizontina	55	Eh	27.37S	54.19W
Horley	12	Bc	51.10N	0.10W
Horlick Mountains	66	Og	85.23S	121.00W
Hormigas	48	Gc	29.12N	105.45W
Hormoz [Iran]	24	Pi	27.32N	54.57 E
Hormoz [Iran]	23	Id	27.06N	56.28 E
Hormoz, Kūh-e-	23	Id	27.27N	55.10 E
Hormoz, Tangeh-ye-= Hormuz, Strait of- (EN)	21	Hg	26.34N	56.15 E
Hormozgān [3]	23	Id	27.30N	56.00 E
Hormūd-e Bāgh	24	Pi	27.30N	54.18 E
Hormuz, Strait of- (EN)= Hormoz, Tangeh-ye-	21	Hg	26.34N	56.15 E
Horn	42	Fd	61.30N	118.00W
Horn	5	Db	66.28N	22.30W
Horn [Aus.]	14	Jb	48.39N	15.39 E
Horn [Swe.]	8	Fg	57.54N	15.50 E
Horn, Cape- (EN)=Hornos, Cabo de-	52	Jk	55.59N	67.16W
Hornád	10	Qh	48.00N	20.58 E
Hornaday	42	Fc	69.22N	123.56W
Hornavan	7	Dc	66.14N	17.30 E
Hornbach	12	Je	49.12N	7.22 E
Horn-Bad Meinberg	12	Kc	51.54N	8.57 E
Hornby Bay	42	Fc	66.35N	117.50W
Horncastle	9	Mh	53.13N	0.07W
Horndal	8	Gd	60.18N	16.25 E
Horndean	12	Bd	50.55N	0.59W
Hörnefors	7	Ee	63.38N	19.54 E
Hornell	44	Id	42.19N	77.39W
Hornepayne	42	Jg	49.13N	84.47W
Hornindalsvatn	8	Bc	61.55N	6.25 E
Hornisgrinde	10	Eh	48.36N	8.12 E
Horn Islands (EN)=Horne, Iles de-	57	Jf	14.19S	178.05W
Hörnli	14	Cc	47.23N	8.56 E
Hornomoravský úval	10	Ng	49.25N	17.20 E
Hornos, Cabo de-=Horn, Cape- (EN)	52	Jk	55.59S	67.16W
Hornoy-le-Bourg	12	De	49.51N	1.54 E
Horn Plateau	42	Fd	62.10N	119.30W
Hornsea	9	Mh	53.55N	0.10W
Hornslandet	8	Gc	61.40N	17.30 E
Horns Rev	8	Bi	55.30N	8.00 E
Horns Rev	8	Bi	55.30N	7.45 E
Hornsund	41	Nc	76.58N	15.28 E
Hornsundtind	41	Nc	76.55N	16.10 E
Horog	22	Jf	37.31N	71.33 E
Horokanai	29a	Ca	44.02N	142.09 E
Horol	16	He	49.29N	33.49 E
Horol [R.S.F.S.R.]	28	Lb	44.30N	132.03 E
Horol [Ukr.-U.S.S.R.]	16	He	49.47N	33.16 E
Horonobe	28	Pb	45.00N	141.51 E
Hořovice	10	Jg	49.50N	13.54 E
Horqin Youyi Qianqi (Ulan Hot)	22	Oe	46.04N	122.00 E
Horqin Youyi Zhongqi (Bayan Huxu)	27	Lb	45.04N	121.27 E
Horqin Zuoyi Houqi (Ganjig)	27	Lc	42.57N	122.14 E
Horqin Zuoyi Zhongqi (Baokang)	27	Lc	44.06N	123.19 E
Horqueta	56	Ib	23.24S	56.53W
Horred	8	Eg	57.21N	12.28 E
Horse Creek [Co.-U.S.]	45	Eg	38.05N	103.19W
Horse Creek [U.S.]	46	Nf	41.57N	103.58W
Horsehead Lake	45	Gc	47.02N	99.47W
Horsens	7	Bi	55.52N	9.52 E
Horsham [Austl.]	58	Fh	36.43S	142.13 E
Horsham [Eng.-U.K.]	9	Mj	51.04N	0.21W
Hørsholm	8	Ei	55.53N	12.30 E
Horšovský Týn	10	Ig	49.32N	12.57 E
Horst	12	Gd	50.56N	4.44 E
Horst	12	Ic	51.28N	6.03 E
Hörstel	12	Jb	52.19N	7.35 E
Horstmar	12	Jb	52.05N	7.19 E
Horsunlu	15	Ll	37.55N	28.36 E
Horta	32	Bb	38.32N	28.28W
Horta [3]	32	Bb	38.35N	28.40W
Horten	8	De	59.25N	10.30 E
Horton	42	Ec	70.01N	126.42W
Hörvik	8	Fh	56.03N	14.46 E
Ḥorvot 'Avedat	24	Fg	30.48N	34.46 E
Ḥorvot Meẓada	24	Fg	31.19N	35.21 E
Horwood Lake	44	Fa	48.03N	82.20W
Hosaina	35	Fd	7.33N	37.52 E
Hose Mountains	26	Ff	2.00N	114.10 E
Hosenofu	33	De	23.34N	21.15 E
Hoseynābād [Iran]	24	Ne	34.30N	50.59 E
Hoseynābād [Iran]	24	Le	35.33N	47.08 E
Hoseynīyeh	24	Mg	32.42N	48.14 E
Hoshāb	25	Cc	26.01N	63.56 E
Hosingen	12	Id	50.01N	6.05 E
Hoskins	60	Ei	5.30S	150.32 E
Hospet	25	Fe	15.16N	76.24 E
Hospital, Cuchilla del-	55	Ej	31.40S	54.53W
Hospitalet	13	Oc	41.22N	2.08 E
Hospitalet del Infante/ L'Hospitalet de l'Infant	13	Md	40.59N	0.56 E
Hoste, Isla-	52	Jk	55.15S	69.00W
Hot	25	Je	18.06N	98.35 E
Hotagen	7	De	63.53N	14.29 E
Hotaka	29	Ec	36.20N	137.53 E
Hotan	22	Jf	37.07N	79.55 E
Hotan He	21	Ke	40.30N	80.48 E
Hotazel	37	Ce	27.15S	23.00 E
Hotin	16	Ee	48.29N	26.29 E
Hoting	7	Dd	64.07N	16.10 E
Hotkovo	7	Ih	56.18N	38.00 E
Hotont	27	Hb	47.23N	102.30 E
Hot Springs	43	Gc	43.26N	103.29W
Hot Springs→Truth or Consequences	43	Fe	33.08N	107.15W
Hot Springs National Park	39	Jf	34.30N	93.03W
Hot Springs Peak	46	Gf	41.22N	117.26W
Hotspur Seamount (EN)	54	Kg	18.00S	36.00W
Hottah Lake	42	Fc	65.05N	118.36W
Hottentot Bay	37	Ae	26.07S	14.57 E
Hotton	12	Hd	50.16N	5.27 E
Hottstedt	10	He	51.39N	11.30 E
Houailou	61	Cd	21.17S	165.38 E
Houat, Ile de-	11	Dg	47.24N	2.58W
Houdan	11	Hf	48.47N	1.36 E
Houeillès	11	Gj	44.12N	0.02 E
Houffalize	12	Hd	50.08N	5.47 E
Houghton	43	Jb	47.06N	88.34W
Houillères, Canal des-	12	If	48.42N	6.55 E
Houji → Liangshan	28	Dg	35.48N	116.07 E
Houlgate	12	Be	49.18N	0.04W
Houlton	43	Nb	46.08N	67.51W
Houma [China]	27	Jd	35.36N	111.23 E
Houma [La.-U.S.]	43	If	29.36N	90.43W
Houndé	34	Ec	11.30N	3.31W
Hourtin, Étang d'-	11	Ei	45.10N	1.06W
House Range	46	Ig	39.30N	113.15W
Houston [Mo.-U.S.]	45	Kh	37.22N	91.58W
Houston [Tx.-U.S.]	39	Jg	29.46N	95.22W
Houthalen-Helchteren	12	Hc	51.02N	5.22 E
Houthulst	12	Ed	50.59N	2.57 E
Houthulst-Merkem	12	Ed	50.57N	2.51 E
Houtman Abrolhos	59	Ce	28.40S	113.50 E
Houtskär/Houtskari	8	Id	60.15N	21.20 E
Houtskari/Houtskär	8	Id	60.15N	21.20 E
Houyet	12	Hd	50.11N	5.01 E
Houyet-Celles	12	Hd	50.19N	5.01 E
Hov	8	Di	55.55N	10.16 E
Hova	8	Ff	58.52N	14.13 E
Hovden	8	Ac	61.40N	4.50 E
Hovden	8	Be	59.32N	7.21 E
Hove	9	Mk	50.49N	0.10W
Hovgaard	41	Kc	80.00N	18.45W
Hovmantorp	8	Fh	56.47N	15.08 E
Hovu-Aksy	20	Ef	51.01N	93.43 E
Howa	35	Db	17.30N	27.08 E
Howar	30	Jg	17.30N	27.08 E
Howard	45	Hd	44.01N	97.32W
Howe, Cape-	57	Fh	37.31S	149.59 E
Howell	44	Fd	42.36N	83.55W
Howick [N.Z.]	62	Fb	36.54S	174.56 E
Howick [S.Afr.]	37	Ee	29.28S	30.14 E
Howland	44	Mc	45.14N	68.40W
Howland Island	57	Jd	0.48N	176.38W
Howrah → Hāora	22	Kg	22.35N	88.20 E
Howth	9	Gh	53.23N	6.04W
Ḩowz Soltān	24	Ne	35.06N	51.06 E
Hoxie	45	Fg	39.21N	100.26W
Höxter	10	Fe	51.46N	9.23 E
Hoxud	27	Ec	42.16N	86.51 E
Hoy	9	Jc	58.52N	3.18W
Hoya	12	Lb	52.48N	9.09 E
Høyanger	7	Bf	61.13N	6.05 E
Hoyerswerda/Wojerecy	10	Ke	51.26N	14.15 E
Hoyos	13	Fd	40.10N	6.43W
Hōyo-Shotō	29	Ce	33.50N	132.30 E
Hoytiäinen	7	Ge	62.48N	29.39 E
Hozat	24	Hc	39.07N	39.14 E
Hpunhpu	25	Jc	26.42N	97.17 E
Hradec Králové	10	Lf	50.13N	15.50 E
Hradiště	10	Jf	50.13N	13.08 E
Hrami	16	Ni	41.20N	45.07 E
Hrastnik	14	Jd	46.09N	15.06 E
Hřebeny	10	Kg	49.50N	14.10 E
Hristinovka	16	Fe	48.53N	29.56 E
Hroma	20	Jb	71.30N	144.49 E
Hromtau	19	Fe	50.18N	58.35 E
Hron	10	Oi	47.49N	18.45 E
Hrubieszów	10	Tf	50.49N	23.55 E
Hrubý Jeseník	10	Nf	50.05N	17.10 E
Hrustalny	28	Lb	44.24N	135.06 E
Hrvatska=Croatia (EN) [2]	14	Jf	45.00N	15.30 E
Hrvatska=Croatia (EN) [2]	14	Je	45.00N	15.30 E
Hrvatska=Croatia (EN)	5	Hf	45.00N	15.30 E
Ḥrvot Shivta	24	Fg	30.53N	34.38 E
Hsin-chiang-wei-wu-erh Tzu-chih-ch'ü→Xinjiang Uygur Zizhiqu=Sinkiang (EN) [2]	27	Ec	42.00N	86.00 E
Hsinchu	27	Lg	24.48N	120.58 E
Hsinying	27	Lg	23.25N	120.20 E
Hsipaw	25	Jd	22.37N	97.18 E
Hsi-tsang Tzu-chih-ch'ü→Xizang Zizhiqu [2]	27	Ee	32.00N	90.00 E
Hsuphāng	25	Jd	20.18N	98.42 E
Huab	37	Ad	20.49S	13.24 E
Huabei Pingyuan	21	Nf	37.00N	117.00 E
Huachacalla	54	Eg	18.45S	68.17W
Huachinera	48	Eb	30.15N	108.50W
Huacho	54	Cf	11.07S	77.37W
Huaco	56	Gd	30.09S	68.31W
Huacrachuco	54	Ce	8.39S	77.05W
Huade	27	Jc	41.50N	114.00 E
Huadian	27	Mc	42.59N	126.38 E
Hua Hin	25	Jf	12.34N	99.58 E
Huahine, Iles-	57	Lf	16.45S	151.00W
Huahine Iti	65e	Eb	16.45S	151.00W
Huahine Nui	65e	Eb	16.43S	151.00W
Huahuapán	48	Ge	24.31N	105.57W
Huai'an	28	Eh	33.30N	119.08 E
Huai'an (Chaigoubu)	28	Cd	40.40N	114.25 E
Huaibei	27	Ke	33.56N	116.48 E
Huaibin (Wulongji)	28	Ci	32.27N	115.23 E
Huaide (Gongzhuling)	27	Lc	43.30N	124.52 E
Huaidian → Shenqiu	27	Ke	33.27N	115.05 E
Huai He	21	Nf	33.12N	118.33 E
Huaiji	27	Jg	23.57N	112.12 E
Huailai (Shacheng)	27	Kc	40.29N	115.30 E
Huainan	22	Nf	32.32N	116.59 E
Huaining (Shipai)	28	Di	30.25N	116.39 E
Huairen	27	Jd	39.50N	113.07 E
Huairou	28	Dd	40.20N	116.37 E
Huaiyang	28	Ch	33.44N	114.52 E
Huaiyin (Wangying)	28	Eh	33.35N	119.02 E
Huaiyuan	28	Dh	32.58N	117.10 E
Huajuapan de León	47	Ee	17.48N	97.46W
Hualalai	65a	Fd	19.41N	155.52W
Hualapai Mountains	46	Ii	34.45N	113.45W
Hualien	27	Lg	23.58N	121.36 E
Huallaga, Río-	52	If	5.07S	75.30W
Huallanca	54	Ce	8.49S	77.52W
Huamachuco	54	Ce	7.48S	78.04W
Huamahuaca	56	Gb	23.13S	65.23W
Huambo [3]	36	Ce	12.30S	15.40 E
Huambo	31	Ij	12.47S	15.43 E
Huanan	27	Nb	46.14N	130.33 E
Huancabamba [Peru]	54	Cf	10.21S	75.32W
Huancabamba [Peru]	54	Ce	5.14S	79.28W
Huancané	54	Eg	15.12S	69.46W
Huancapi	54	Df	13.41S	74.04W
Huancavelica [2]	54	Df	13.00S	75.00W
Huancavelica	53	Ig	12.46S	75.02W
Huancayo	53	Ig	12.04S	75.14W
Huanchaca, Serrania-	55	Bb	14.30S	60.39W
Huang'an→Hong'an	28	Ci	31.17N	114.37 E
Huangcaoba→Xingyi	27	Hf	25.03N	104.55 E
Huangchuan	27	Ke	32.00N	115.02 E
Huanggang	28	Ci	30.27N	114.53 E
Huanggangliang	27	Kc	43.33N	117.32 E
Huanggang Shan	27	Kf	27.50N	117.47 E
Huanggi Hai	28	Bd	40.51N	113.17 E
Huang Hai=Yellow Sea (EN)	21	Of	36.00N	124.00 E
Huang He=Yellow River (EN)	21	Nf	37.32N	118.19 E
Huanghe Kou	28	Ef	37.54N	118.48 E
Huangheyan→Madoi	22	Lf	35.00N	98.56 E
Huanghua	28	De	38.23N	117.21 E
Huanghuashi	28	Bj	28.14N	113.11 E
Huangliu	27	Ih	18.41N	108.46 E
Huangmao Jian	27	Kf	27.55N	119.11 E
Huangmei	28	Ci	30.05N	115.56 E
Huangnihe	28	Ic	43.33N	127.28 E
Huangpi	28	Ci	30.53N	114.22 E
Huangpu	27	Jg	23.05N	113.25 E
Huang Shan	27	Ke	30.10N	118.10 E
Huangshi	22	Nf	30.12N	115.00 E
Huang Shui	27	Hd	36.05N	103.20 E
Huangtu Gaoyuan	21	Mf	37.00N	108.00 E
Huanguelén	55	Bm	37.02S	61.57W
Huangxian	27	Ld	37.38N	120.30 E
Huangyan	27	Lf	28.39N	121.17 E
Huangyuan	27	Hd	36.40N	101.12 E
Huangzhai → Yangqu	28	Be	38.05N	112.37 E
Huangzhong	27	Hd	36.30N	101.30 E
Huanren	27	Mc	41.16N	125.22 E
Huan Shui	28	Ci	30.40N	114.21 E
Huanta	54	Df	12.56S	74.15W
Huantai (Suozhen)	28	Ef	36.57N	118.05 E
Huánuco [2]	54	Ce	9.30S	75.50W
Huánuco	53	If	9.55S	76.14W
Huanxian	27	Id	36.36N	107.06 E
Huaráz	53	If	9.32S	77.32W
Huarmey	54	Cf	10.04S	78.10W
Huarong	28	Bj	29.31N	112.33 E
Huascarán, Nevado-	52	If	9.07S	77.37W
Hua Shan	27	Je	34.27N	110.05 E
Huatabampo	47	Cc	26.50N	109.38W
Huatong	28	Fd	40.03N	121.56 E
Huatusco de Chiquellar	48	Kh	19.09N	96.57W
Huauchinango	48	Jg	20.11N	98.03W
Huautla de Jiménez	48	Kh	18.08N	96.51W
Huaxian (Daokou)	28	Cg	35.33N	114.30 E
Huayllay	54	Cf	11.01S	76.21W
Huaynamota, Río-	48	Gg	21.51N	104.42W
Huaytara	54	Cf	13.36S	75.22W
Hubbard Creek Lake	45	Gj	32.45N	99.00W
Hubbard Lake	44	Fc	44.49N	83.34W
Hubei Sheng (Hu-pei Sheng) = Hupeh (EN) [2]	27	Je	31.00N	112.00 E
Hubli-Dhārwār	22	Jh	15.21N	75.10 E
Hubsugul Nur (Chövsgöl nuur)	21	Md	51.00N	100.30 E
Hückelhoven	12	Ic	51.03N	6.13 E
Hückeswagen	12	Jc	51.09N	7.21 E
Hucknall	9	Lh	53.02N	1.11W
Hucqueliers	12	Dd	55.03N	1.54 E
Huczwa	10	Tf	50.49N	23.59 E
Hudat [Abz.-U.S.S.R.]	16	Pi	41.34N	48.43 E
Hudat [Eth.]	35	Fe	4.45N	39.27 E
Huddersfield	9	Lh	53.39N	1.47W
Huddinge	8	Ge	59.14N	17.59 E
Ḥuddun	35	Hd	9.08N	47.32 E
Huddur Hadama	35	Ge	4.07N	43.55 E

Index Symbols

- [1] Independent Nation
- [2] State, Region
- [3] District, County
- [4] Municipality
- [5] Colony, Dependency
- Continent
- Physical Region
- Historical or Cultural Region
- Mount, Mountain
- Volcano
- Hill
- Mountains, Mountain Range
- Hills, Escarpment
- Plateau, Upland
- Pass, Gap
- Plain, Lowland
- Delta
- Salt Flat
- Valley, Canyon
- Crater, Cave
- Karst Features
- Depression
- Polder
- Desert, Dunes
- Forest, Woods
- Heath, Steppe
- Oasis
- Cape, Point
- Coast, Beach
- Cliff
- Peninsula
- Isthmus
- Sandbank
- Island
- Atoll
- Rock, Reef
- Islands, Archipelago
- Rocks, Reefs
- Coral Reef
- Well, Spring
- Geyser
- River, Stream
- Waterfall Rapids
- River Mouth, Estuary
- Lake
- Salt Lake
- Intermittent Lake
- Reservoir
- Swamp, Pond
- Canal
- Glacier
- Ice Shelf, Pack Ice
- Ocean
- Sea
- Gulf, Bay
- Strait, Fjord
- Lagoon
- Bank
- Seamount
- Tablemount
- Ridge
- Shelf
- Basin
- Escarpment, Sea Scarp
- Fracture
- Trench, Abyss
- National Park, Reserve
- Point of Interest
- Recreation Site
- Cave, Cavern
- Historic Site
- Ruins
- Wall, Walls
- Church, Abbey
- Temple
- Scientific Station
- Airport
- Port
- Lighthouse
- Mine
- Tunnel
- Dam, Bridge

Hude (Oldenburg) 12 Ka 53.07N 8.28 E
Huder 27 Lb 49.59N 121.30 E
Hudiksvall 6 Hc 61.44N 17.07 E
Hudson 38 Le 40.42N 74.02W
Hudson [Fl.-U.S.] 44 Fk 28.22N 82.42W
Hudson [N.Y.-U.S.] 44 Kd 42.15N 73.47W
Hudson, Lake- 45 Ih 36.20N 95.05W
Hudson Bay 42 Hf 52.52N 102.23W
Hudson Bay 38 Kd 60.00N 86.00W
Hudson Canyon (EN) 44 Kf 39.27N 72.12W
Hudson Hope 42 Fe 56.02N 121.55W
Hudson Land 41 Jd 73.45N 22.30W
Hudson Mountains 66 Pf 74.32S 99.20W
Hudson Strait 38 Lc 62.30N 72.00W
Hudžirt 27 Hb 47.05N 102.45 E
Hue 22 Mh 16.28N 107.36 E
Huebra 13 Fc 41.02N 6.48W
Huechucuicui, Punta- 56 Ff 41.47S 74.02W
Hueco Montains 45 Dj 32.05N 105.55W
Huedin 15 Gc 46.52N 23.03 E
Huehuetenango [3] 49 Bf 15.40N 91.35W
Huehuetenango 47 Fe 15.20N 91.28W
Huejutla de Reyes 48 Jg 21.08N 98.25W
Huelgoat 11 Cf 48.22N 3.45W
Huelma 13 Ig 37.39N 3.27W
Huelva [3] 13 Fg 37.40N 7.00W
Huelva 6 Fh 37.16N 6.57W
Huelva, Ribera de- 13 Gg 37.27N 6.00W
Huércal Overa 13 Kg 37.23N 1.57W
Huerfano Mountain 45 Bh 36.30N 108.10W
Huertas, Cabo de- 13 Lf 38.21N 0.24W
Huerva 13 Lc 41.39N 0.52W
Huesca 13 Lb 42.08N 0.25W
Huesca [3] 13 Lb 42.10N 0.10W
Huéscar 13 Jg 37.49N 2.32W
Hueso, Sierra del- 48 Gb 30.15N 105.20W
Huesos, Arroyo de los- 55 Cm 36.30S 59.09W
Huetamo de Núñez 48 Ih 18.35N 100.53W
Huete 13 Jd 40.08N 2.41W
Ḩufrat an Naḩās 35 Cd 9.45N 24.19 E
Huftarøy 8 Ad 60.05N 5.15 E
Hugh Butler Lake 45 Ff 40.22N 100.42W
Hughenden 58 Fg 20.51S 144.12 E
Hughes 40 Ic 66.03N 154.16W
Hughes Range 46 Hb 49.55N 115.28W
Hugo 45 Ii 34.01N 95.31W
Huguan 28 Bf 36.05N 113.12 E
Huhur He 28 Fc 43.55N 120.47 E
Hui'an 27 Kf 25.07N 118.47 E
Huiarau Range 62 Gc 38.35S 177.10 E
Huib-Hochplato 37 Be 27.10S 16.50 E
Huichang 27 Kf 25.33N 115.45 E
Huicheng → Shexian 28 Ej 29.53N 118.27 E
Huicholes, Sierra de los- 48 Gf 22.00N 104.00W
Huich'ŏn 27 Mc 40.10N 126.17 E
Huifa He 28 Ic 43.06N 126.53 E
Hui He [China] 27 Kb 48.51N 119.12 E
Hui He [China] 28 Be 39.21N 112.37 E
Huiji He 28 Ch 33.53N 115.37 E
Huila [2] 54 Cc 2.30N 75.45W
Huila [3] 36 Ce 15.00S 15.00 E
Huila, Nevado del- 52 Ie 3.00N 76.00W
Huilai 27 Kg 23.05N 116.18 E
Huili 27 Hf 26.37N 102.19 E
Huimanguillo 48 Mi 17.51N 93.23W
Huimin 27 Kd 37.29N 117.30 E
Huinan (Chaoyang) 28 Ic 42.41N 126.03 E
Huisne 11 Gg 47.59N 0.11 E
Huissen 12 Hc 51.56N 5.55 E
Huiten Nur 27 Fd 35.30N 91.55 E
Huittinen 8 Jc 61.11N 22.42 E
Huivulay, Isla de- 48 Dd 27.03N 110.01W
Huixian [China] 28 Bg 35.27N 113.47 E
Huixian [China] 27 Ie 33.46N 106.06 E
Huixtla 47 Fe 15.09N 92.28W
Huize 27 Hf 26.28N 103.18 E
Huizen 12 Hb 52.18N 5.16 E
Huizhou 27 Jg 23.02N 114.28 E
Hukou 28 Dj 29.44N 116.14 E
Hu Kou 27 Jd 36.09N 110.20 E
Hŭksan-Chedo 27 Me 34.30N 125.20 E
Hukuntsi 37 Cd 23.59S 21.44 E
Hulan 27 Mb 46.03N 126.36 E
Hulan He 27 Mb 45.54N 126.42 E
Ḩulayfā' 23 Fd 26.00N 40.47 E
Hulett 46 Md 44.41N 104.36W
Hulga 17 Jd 64.15N 60.58 E
Hulin 27 Nb 45.52N 132.58 E
Hulin He 28 Hb 45.19N 124.06 E
Hull 42 Jg 45.26N 75.43W
Hull → Kingston-upon-Hull 6 Fe 53.45N 0.20W
Hull → Orona Atoll 57 Je 4.29S 172.10W
Hull Bay 66 Nf 74.55S 137.40W
Hull Glacier 66 Nf 75.05S 137.15W
Hull Mountain 46 Dg 39.31N 122.59W
Hüls, Krefeld- 12 Ic 51.22N 6.31 E
Hultsfred 7 Dh 57.29N 15.50 E
Huludao 27 Lc 40.44N 120.59 E
Hulun Nur 21 Ne 49.00N 117.30 E
Ḩulwān=Helwān (EN) 33 Fd 29.51N 31.20 E
Hulwāt, Qūr al- 24 Hh 28.49N 38.50 E
Huma [China] 27 Ma 51.44N 126.36 E
Huma [Ton.] 65b Bc 21.19S 174.56W
Humacao 49 Od 18.09N 65.50W
Huma He 27 Ma 51.42N 126.42 E
Humaitá [Braz.] 53 Jf 7.31S 63.02W
Humaitá [Par.] 56 Ic 27.03S 58.33W
Humansdorp 37 Cf 34.02S 24.46 E
Humbe 36 Bf 16.42S 14.54 E
Humber 5 Fe 53.40N 0.10W
Humberside [3] 9 Mh 53.55N 0.30W
Humbolat River 38 He 40.02N 118.31W
Humboldt 61 Cd 21.53S 166.25 E
Humboldt [Ia.-U.S.] 45 Ie 42.43N 94.13W
Humboldt [Nb.-U.S.] 45 If 40.10N 95.57W
Humboldt [Sask.-Can.] 42 Gf 52.12N 105.07W
Humboldt [Tn.-U.S.] 44 Ch 35.49N 88.55W
Humboldt Gletscher 41 Fc 79.40N 63.45W
Humboldt Range 46 Ff 40.15N 118.10W
Hume, Lake- 59 Jg 36.05S 147.05 E
Humenné 10 Rh 48.56N 21.55 E
Hummelfjell 8 Db 62.27N 11.17 E
Hümmling, Der- 10 Dd 52.52N 7.31 E
Humphreys Peak 38 Hf 35.20N 111.40W
Humppila 7 Ff 60.56N 23.22 E
Humuya, Río- 49 Df 15.13N 87.57W
Hūn 31 If 29.07N 15.56 E
Húnaflói 5 Db 65.50N 20.50W
Hunan Sheng (Hu-nan Sheng) [3] 27 Jf 28.00N 112.00 E
Hu-nan Sheng → Hunan Sheng [3] 27 Jf 28.00N 112.00 E
Hunchun 28 Kc 42.52N 130.21 E
Hundested 8 Di 55.58N 11.52 E
Hunedoara [2] 15 Fd 45.45N 22.52 E
Hünfeld 10 Ff 50.40N 9.46 E
Hünfelden 12 Kd 50.19N 8.11 E
Hunga Ha'apai 65b Ab 20.33S 175.24W
Hungary (EN)= Magyarország [1] 6 Hf 47.00N 20.00 E
Hunga Tonga 65b Ab 20.32S 175.23W
Hungen 12 Kd 50.28N 8.54 E
Hŭngnam 27 Md 39.50N 127.38 E
Hungry Horse Reservoir 46 Ib 48.15N 113.50W
Hun He [China] 28 Be 39.47N 113.15 E
Hun He [China] 28 Gd 40.41N 122.12 E
Hunhedoara 15 Fd 45.45N 22.54 E
Hunish, Rubha- 9 Gd 57.43N 6.20W
Hun Jiang 28 Hd 40.52N 125.42 E
Hunjiang 27 Mc 41.55N 126.27 E
Hunneberg 8 Ef 58.20N 12.27 E
Hunnebostrand 8 Df 58.27N 11.18 E
Hunsrück 10 Cg 49.50N 6.40 E
Hunstanton 9 Ni 52.57N 0.30 E
Hunte 10 Ed 52.30N 8.19 E
Hunter, Ile- 57 Ig 22.24S 172.03 E
Hunter Island 59 Ih 40.30S 144.45 E
Hunter Ridge (EN) 57 Ig 21.30S 174.30 E
Hunter River 59 Kf 32.30S 151.42 E
Hunterville 62 Fc 39.56S 175.34 E
Huntingdon 9 Mi 52.30N 0.10W
Huntingdon [Eng.-U.K.] 9 Mi 52.20N 0.12W
Huntingdon [Pa.-U.S.] 44 He 40.31N 78.02W
Huntingdon [Que.-Can.] 44 Jc 45.05N 74.08W
Huntington [In.-U.S.] 44 Ee 40.53N 85.30W
Huntington [W.V.-U.S.] 43 Kd 38.24N 82.26W
Huntly [N.Z.] 62 Fb 37.33S 175.10 E
Huntly [Scot.-U.K.] 9 Kd 57.27N 2.47W
Huntsville [Al.-U.S.] 39 Kf 34.44N 86.35W
Huntsville [Ont.-Can.] 42 Jg 45.20N 79.13W
Huntsville [Tx.-U.S.] 43 He 30.43N 95.33W
Hunucmá 48 Oj 21.01N 89.52W
Hünxe 12 Ic 51.39N 6.47 E
Hunyani 37 Ec 15.37S 30.39 E
Hunyuan 27 Jd 39.38N 113.44 E
Hunza → Baltit 25 Ea 36.20N 74.40 E
Hunze 11 Ma 53.13N 6.40 E
Huocheng (Shuiding) 27 Dc 44.03N 80.49 E
Huojia 28 Bg 35.16N 113.39 E
Huolongmen 27 Mb 49.49N 125.49 E
Huolu 28 Ce 38.05N 114.18 E
Huon, Ile- 57 Hf 18.01S 162.57 E
Huon Gulf 59 Ja 7.10S 147.25 E
Huon Peninsula 60 Di 6.25S 147.30 E
Huonville 59 Jh 43.01S 147.02 E
Huoqin 28 Dh 32.21N 116.17 E
Huoshan 27 Ke 31.19N 116.20 E
Huo Shan [China] 27 Jd 37.00N 111.52 E
Huo Shan [China] 27 Ke 31.06N 116.12 E
Huoxian 27 Jd 36.39N 111.47 E
Hupeh (EN)=Hubei Sheng (Hu-pei Sheng) [2] 27 Je 31.00N 112.00 E
Hu-pei Sheng → Hubei Sheng=Hopeh (EN) [2] 27 Je 31.00N 112.00 E
Hür 24 Qg 30.50N 57.07 E
Hurama → Hongyuan 27 He 32.45N 102.38 E
Huránd 24 Lc 38.40N 47.20 E
Hurd, Cape- 44 Gc 45.13N 81.44W
Hurdalssjøen 8 Dd 60.20N 11.05 E
Hurd Deep=La Grande Trench (EN) 9 Kl 49.40N 3.00W
Hurdiyo 35 Ic 10.32N 51.08 E
Hurepoix 11 If 48.30N 2.10 E
Hure Qi 28 Fc 42.44N 121.44 E
Hurkett 45 Lb 48.50N 88.29W
Hurmuli 20 If 51.01N 136.56 E
Huroizumi 29a Cb 42.01N 143.07 E
Huron 43 Hc 44.22N 98.13W
Huron, Lake- 38 Ke 44.30N 82.15W
Huron Mountains 44 Db 46.45N 87.45W
Hurricane 46 Ih 37.11N 113.17W
Hurricane Cliffs 46 Ih 37.00N 113.05W
Hurrungane 8 Bc 61.27N 7.51 E
Hursley 12 Ac 51.01N 1.24W
Hurst 45 Hj 32.49N 97.09W
Hurstpierpoint 12 Bd 50.55N 0.10W
Hürth 10 Cf 50.52N 6.52 E
Hurum 8 De 59.35N 10.35 E
Hurunui 62 Ee 42.54S 173.18 E
Hurup 8 Ch 56.45N 8.25 E
Huş 15 Lc 46.41N 28.04 E
Húsavík 7a Ca 66.03N 17.21W
Hushan → Cixi 28 Fi 30.10N 121.14 E
Huskvarna 8 Fg 57.48N 14.16 E
Huslia 40 Hc 65.42N 156.25W
Husnes 8 Ae 59.52N 5.46 E
Husnesfjorden 8 Ae 59.50N 5.35 E
Hussigny-Godbrange 12 He 49.29N 5.52 E
Hust 16 Ce 48.10N 23.17 E
Hustadvika 8 Ba 63.00N 7.05 E
Husum [F.R.G.] 10 Fb 54.28N 9.03 E
Husum [Swe.] 7 Ee 63.20N 19.10 E
Hutag 27 Hb 49.23N 102.43 E
Hutchinson [Ks.-U.S.] 43 Hd 38.05N 97.56W
Hutchinson [Mn.-U.S.] 45 Id 44.54N 94.22W
Hutch Mountain 46 Ji 34.47N 111.22W
Hüth 33 Hf 16.14N 43.58 E
Hutou 27 Nb 46.00N 133.36 E
Hutte Sauvage, Lac de la- 42 Ke 55.57N 65.45W
Hutton, Mount- 59 Je 25.51S 148.20 E
Hutubi 27 Ec 44.07N 86.57 E
Hutuiti, Caleta- 65d Bb 27.07S 109.17W
Hutuo He 28 De 38.14N 116.05 E
Huvhojtun, Gora- 20 Le 57.44N 160.45 E
Huxley, Mount- 62 Cf 44.04S 169.41 E
Huy 10 Ge 51.55N 10.55 E
Huy/Hoei 11 Ld 50.31N 5.14 E
Huzhou → Wuxing 27 Le 30.47N 120.07 E
Hvaler 8 De 59.05N 11.00 E
Hvalynsk 19 Ee 52.30N 48.07 E
Hvammstangi 7a Bb 65.24N 20.57W
Hvannadalshnúkur 5 Ec 64.01N 16.41W
Hvar 14 Kg 43.07N 16.45 E
Hvar 14 Kg 43.11N 16.27 E
Hvarski kanal 14 Kg 43.15N 16.37 E
Hvatovka 16 Oc 52.21N 46.36 E
Hveragerdi 7a Bb 64.00N 21.12W
Hveravellir 7a Bb 64.54N 19.35W
Hvide Sande 8 Ci 55.59N 8.08 E
Hvitá [Ice.] 7a Bb 64.35N 21.46W
Hvitá [Ice.] 7a Bb 64.00N 20.58W
Hvittingfoss 8 De 59.29N 10.01 E
Hvojnaja 7 Ig 58.56N 34.31 E
Hwach'on-ni 28 Ie 38.58N 126.02 E
Hwang-Hae=Yellow Sea (EN) 21 Of 36.00N 124.00 E
Hwanghae-Namdo [2] 28 He 38.15N 125.30 E
Hwanghae-Pukto [2] 28 Ie 38.30N 126.25 E
Hwangju 28 He 38.40N 125.45 E
Hyannis [Ma.-U.S.] 44 Le 41.39N 70.17W
Hyannis [Nb.-U.S.] 45 Ff 42.00N 101.44W
Hybo 8 Gc 61.48N 16.12 E
Hyde Park 50 Gi 6.30N 58.16W
Hyderābād [India] 22 Jh 17.23N 78.28 E
Hyderābād [Pak.] 22 Ig 25.22N 68.22 E
Hyères 11 Mk 43.07N 6.07 E
Hyères, Iles d'- 11 Ml 43.00N 6.20 E
Hyesan 27 Mc 41.24N 128.10 E
Hyltebruk 7 Ch 57.00N 13.14 E
Hyndman Peak 46 He 43.50N 114.10W
Hyōgo Ken [2] 28 Mg 34.50N 134.48 E
Hyrov 10 Sg 49.32N 22.48 E
Hyrulä 8 Kd 60.24N 25.02 E
Hyrum 46 Jf 41.38N 111.51W
Hyrynsalmi 7 Gd 64.40N 28.32 E
Hysham 46 Lc 46.18N 107.14W
Hythe [Eng.-U.K.] 12 Ad 50.52N 1.24W
Hythe [Eng.-U.K.] 9 Oj 51.05N 1.05 E
Hyūga 28 Kh 32.25N 131.38 E
Hyūga-Nada 29 Be 32.25N 131.45 E
Hyvinge/Hyvinkää 7 Ff 60.38N 24.52 E
Hyvinkää/Hyvinge 7 Ff 60.38N 24.52 E

I

Iaco, Rio- 54 Ee 9.03S 68.35W
Iacobeni 15 Ib 47.26N 25.19 E
Iakora 37 Hd 23.08S 46.38 E
Ialomiţa [2] 15 Ke 44.30N 27.30 E
Ialomiţa 15 Kd 44.42N 27.51 E
Ialomiţei, Balta- 15 Ke 44.30N 28.00 E
Iapó, Rio- 55 Gg 24.30S 50.24W
Iaşi 6 If 47.10N 27.36 E
Iaşi [2] 15 Kb 47.07N 27.39 E
Iba 26 Gc 15.20N 119.58 E
Ibadan 31 Hh 7.23N 3.54 E
Ibague 53 Ie 4.27N 75.14W
Ibaiti 56 Jb 23.50S 50.10W
Iballja 15 Cg 42.11N 20.00 E
Ibans, Laguna de- 49 Ef 15.53N 84.52W
Ibar 15 Df 43.44N 20.45 E
Ibara 29 Cd 34.36N 133.28 E
Ibaraki 29 Dd 34.49N 135.34 E
Ibaraki Ken [2] 28 Pf 36.25N 140.30 E
Ibaré 55 Ej 30.49S 54.16W
Ibarra 53 Ie 0.21N 78.07W
Ibarreta 56 Ic 25.13S 59.51W
Ibb 22 Gh 13.58N 44.12 E
Ibba 35 De 4.48N 29.06 E
Ibba 35 Dd 7.09N 28.41 E
Ibbenbüren 10 Dd 52.16N 7.44 E
Ibdekkene 34 Fb 18.28N 0.38 E
Ibembo 36 Db 2.38N 23.37 E
Ibenga 36 Cb 2.20N 18.08 E
Iberá, Esteros del- 55 Di 28.05S 57.05W
Iberá, Laguna- 55 Di 28.30S 57.09W
Iberian Basin (EN) 3 De 40.00N 16.00W
Iberian Mountains (EN)= Sistema Ibérico 5 Fg 41.30N 2.30W
Iberian Peninsula (EN)= Península Ibérica 5 Fg 40.00N 4.00W
Iberville, Lac d'- 42 Ke 56.00N 73.10W
Ibestad 7 Db 68.48N 17.08 E
Ibi [Nig.] 34 Gd 8.11N 9.45 E
Ibi [Sp.] 13 Lf 38.38N 0.34W
Ibiá 54 Ig 19.29S 46.32W
Ibiagui 55 Ja 13.03S 44.12W
Ibiai 55 Jc 16.51S 44.55W
Ibibobo 54 Fh 21.35S 62.58W
Ibicaraí 54 Kf 14.51S 39.36W
Ibicuí, Rio- 52 Kh 29.25S 56.47W
Ibicuí da Armada, Rio- 55 Ej 30.16S 54.54W
Ibicuy 55 Ck 33.44S 59.10W
Ibicuy, Rio- 55 Ck 33.48S 59.10W
Ibigawa 29 Ed 35.29N 136.34 E
Ibipetuba 54 Jf 11.00S 44.32W
Ibiraiaras 55 Gi 28.22S 51.39W
Ibirama 55 Hh 27.04S 49.31W
Ibirapuitã, Rio- 55 Ei 29.22S 55.57W
Ibirocaí, Arroio- 55 Di 29.26S 56.43W
Ibiruba 55 Fi 28.38S 53.06W
Ibitinga 55 He 21.45S 48.49W
Ibitinga, Represa- 55 He 21.41S 49.05W
Ibity 37 Hd 20.10S 46.58 E
Ibiza 13 Nf 38.54N 1.26 E
Ibiza/Eivissa=Iviza (EN) 5 Gh 39.00N 1.25 E
Iblei, Monti- 14 Im 37.10N 14.55 E
Ibn Hāni', Ra's- 24 Fe 35.35N 35.43 E
Ibn Qawrah 35 Ib 15.43N 50.32 E
Ibo 37 Gb 12.22S 40.36 E
Ibo-Gawa 29 Dd 34.46N 134.35 E
Iboundji, Mont- 36 Bc 1.08S 11.48 E
Ibrā' 23 Ie 22.38N 58.40 E
Ibrah 35 Dc 10.36N 25.20 E
Ibrāhīm, Jabal- 21 Gg 20.27N 41.09 E
Ibresi 7 Li 55.18N 47.05 E
'Ibrī 23 Ie 23.16N 56.32 E
Ibrim 33 Fe 22.39N 32.05 E
Ibshawāy 24 Dh 29.22N 30.41 E
Ibuki-Sanchi 29 Ed 35.35N 136.25 E
Ibuki-Yama 29 Ed 35.25N 136.24 E
Ibusuki 28 Ki 31.16N 130.39 E
Iča 20 Ke 55.28N 155.58 E
Ica [2] 54 Cf 14.20S 75.30W
Ica 53 Ig 14.04S 75.42W
Iça, Rio- 52 Jf 3.07S 67.58W
Icaiché 48 Oh 18.05N 89.10W
Içamaquã, Rio- 55 Ei 28.34S 56.00W
Içana, Rio- 54 Ec 0.26N 67.19W
Icara 55 Hi 28.42S 49.18W
Icaraima 55 Ff 23.23S 53.41W
İçel 23 Db 36.48N 34.38 E
Iceland (EN) = Island 5 Eb 65.00N 18.00W
Iceland Basin (EN) 3 Dc 60.00N 20.00W
Ichalkaranji 25 Ee 16.42N 74.28 E
Ichibusa-Yama 29 Be 32.19N 131.06 E
Ichihara 28 Pg 35.31N 140.05 E
Ichi-Kawa 29 Dd 34.46N 134.43 E
Ichikawa 29 Fd 35.44N 139.55 E
Ichinohe 28 Pd 40.13N 141.17 E
Ichinomiya 28 Ng 35.18N 136.48 E
Ichinoseki 28 Pe 38.55N 141.08 E
Ich'ŏn [N.Kor.] 28 Ie 38.29N 126.53 E
Ich'ŏn [S.Kor.] 28 If 37.17N 127.27 E
Ichtegem 12 Fc 51.06N 3.00 E
Ičigemskij Hrebet 20 Ld 63.30N 164.00 E
Ičinskaja Sopka, Vulkan- 21 Rd 55.39N 157.40 E
Ičnja 19 De 50.52N 32.25 E
Icó 54 Ke 6.24S 38.51W
Icy Cape 40 Gb 70.20N 161.52W
Idaarderadeel 12 Ha 53.06N 5.50 E
Idaarderadeel-Grow 12 Ha 53.06N 5.50 E
Idabel 45 Ij 33.54N 94.50W
Idah 34 Gd 7.06N 6.44 E
Idaho [2] 43 Ec 45.00N 115.00W
Idaho Falls 39 He 43.30N 112.02W
Idalia 45 Eg 39.43N 102.14W
Idān 35 Hd 6.03N 49.01 E
Idanha-a-Nova 13 Ee 39.55N 7.14W
Idar-Oberstein 10 Dg 49.42N 7.18 E
Idarwald 12 Je 49.50N 7.13 E
Idel 7 Id 64.08N 34.12 E
Ideles 32 Ie 23.49N 5.55 E
Ider 27 Hb 49.16N 100.41 E
Idfū 33 Fe 24.58N 32.52 E
Idhi Óros 5 Ih 35.15N 24.45 E
Idhra 15 Gl 37.20N 23.30 E
Idhra 15 Gl 37.21N 23.28 E
Idhras, Kólpos- 15 Gl 37.22N 23.22 E
Idice 14 Ff 44.35N 11.49 E
Idil 24 Id 37.21N 41.54 E
Idini 32 Df 17.58N 15.40W
Idiofa 36 Cc 4.59S 19.36 E
Idjil, Kédia d'- 32 Ee 22.38N 12.33W
Idkerberget 8 Fd 60.23N 15.14 E
Idle 9 Mh 53.27N 0.48W
Idlib 23 Eb 35.55N 36.38 E
Idokogo 36 Ab 0.35N 9.19 E
Idolo, Isla del- 48 Kg 21.25N 97.27W
Idre 8 Ec 61.52N 12.43 E
Idrica 8 Mh 56.18N 28.55 E
Idrija 14 Id 46.00N 14.02 E
Idro, Lago d'- 14 Ee 45.47N 10.30 E
Idstein 10 Ef 50.14N 8.16 E
Idževan 16 Ni 40.52N 45.04 E
Iecava 8 Jh 56.40N 23.40 E
Iecava 8 Kh 56.33N 24.11 E
Iepê 55 Gf 22.40S 51.05W
Ieper/Ypres 11 Id 50.51N 2.53 E
Ierápetra 15 In 35.01N 25.45 E
Ierisós 15 Gi 40.24N 23.53 E
Ierisoú, Kólpos- 15 Gi 40.26N 23.55 E
Iernut 15 Hc 46.27N 24.15 E
Ie-Shima 29b Ab 26.43N 127.47 E
Ieshima-Shotō 29 Dd 34.40N 134.30 E
Iesolo 14 Ge 45.32N 12.38 E
Iezerul, Vîrful- 15 Hd 45.28N 24.57 E
Ifakara 36 Gd 8.08S 36.41 E
Ifaki 34 Gd 7.48N 5.14 E
'Ifāl, Wādī al- 24 Fh 28.07N 35.02 E
Ifalik Atoll 57 Fd 7.15N 144.27 E
Ifanadiana 37 Hd 21.17S 47.35 E
Ife 34 Fd 7.28N 4.34 E
Iferouâne 31 Hg 19.04N 8.24 E
Ifetesene 32 Hd 25.30N 4.33 E
Ifni 32 Ed 29.15N 10.08W
Ifon 34 Gd 6.58N 5.55 E
Iforas, Adrar des- 30 Hg 19.00N 2.00 E
Iga 29 Ed 34.49N 136.12 E
Igal 10 Nj 46.32N 17.57 E
Iganga 36 Fb 0.37N 33.29 E
Igara Paraná, Rio- 54 Dd 2.09N 71.47W
Igarapava 55 Ie 20.03S 47.47W
Igarapé-Açu 54 Id 1.07S 47.37W
Igarapé-Miri 54 Id 1.59S 48.58W
Igarka 22 Kc 67.28N 86.35 E
Igatimi 56 Ib 24.05S 55.30W
Igawa 36 Fd 8.46S 34.23 E
Igbetti 34 Fd 8.45N 4.08 E
Iğdır 24 Kc 39.56N 44.02 E
Iggesund 7 Df 61.38N 17.04 E
Iglesias 14 Ck 39.19N 8.32 E
Iglesiente 14 Ck 39.20N 8.40 E
Igli 32 Gc 30.27N 2.18W
Iglim al Janūbīyah = Southern Region (EN) [2] 35 Dd 6.00N 30.00 E
Iglino 17 Hi 54.50N 56.28 E
Igloolik 39 Kc 69.24N 81.49W
Ignace 42 Ig 49.26N 91.41W
Ignalina 7 Gi 55.22N 26.13 E
Ignatovo 7 If 60.49N 37.48 E
Iğneada 24 Bb 41.50N 27.58 E
Iğneada Burun 15 Lh 41.54N 28.03 E
Igombe 36 Fc 4.25S 31.58 E
Igoumenitsa 15 Dj 39.30N 20.16 E
Igra 19 Fd 57.33N 53.10 E
Igreja, Morro de- 55 Hi 28.08S 49.30W
Igren 16 Ie 48.29N 35.13 E
Igrim 19 Gc 63.12N 64.29 E
Iguaçu, Rio- 52 Kh 25.36S 54.36W
Igualada 13 Nc 41.35N 1.38 E
Iguala de la Independencia 47 Ee 18.21N 99.32W
Iguana, Sierra de la- 48 Id 26.30N 100.15W
Iguape 55 Ig 24.43S 47.33W
Iguariaça, Serra do- 55 Ei 29.03S 55.15W
Iguassu Falls (EN)=Iguazú, Cataratas del- 52 Kh 25.41S 54.26W
Iguatemi 54 If 14.35S 49.02W
Iguatemi, Rio- 55 Ef 23.55S 54.10W
Iguatu 53 Mf 6.22S 39.18W
Iguazú, Cataratas del- = Iguassu Falls (EN) 52 Kh 25.41S 54.26W
Iguéla 36 Ac 1.55S 9.19 E
Iguidi, 'Erg- 30 Gf 27.00N 6.00W
Ihavandiffulu Atoll 25a Ba 7.00N 72.55 E
Iheya-Jima 29b Ab 27.03N 127.57 E
Ih-Hajrhan 27 Ib 46.56N 105.56 E
Ihiala 34 Gd 5.51N 6.51 E
Ihirene 32 He 20.28N 4.37 E
Ihnāsiyat al Madīnah 24 Dh 29.05N 30.56 E
Ih-Obo-Ula 27 Gc 44.55N 95.20 E
Ihosy 31 Lk 22.25S 46.07 E
Ihotry, Lac- 37 Gd 21.56S 43.41 E
Ihrhove, Westoverledingen- 12 Ja 53.10N 7.27 E
Ihsaniye 24 Dc 36.55N 34.46 E
Ihtiman 15 Gg 42.26N 23.49 E
Ih-Ula 27 Hb 49.27N 101.27 E
Ii 7 Fd 65.19N 25.27 E
Iida 28 Ng 35.31N 137.50 E
Iide-San 29 Fc 37.52N 139.41 E
Iijoki 7 Fd 65.20N 25.17 E
Iisaku/Isaku 8 Le 59.14N 27.41 E
Iisalmi 7 Ge 63.34N 27.11 E
Iisvesi 8 Lb 62.45N 26.50 E
Iittala 8 Kc 61.04N 24.10 E
Iivaara 7 Gd 65.47N 29.40 E
Iiyama 29 Fc 36.52N 138.20 E
Iizuka 29 Be 33.38N 130.41 E
Ija 20 Fe 55.02N 101.00 E
Ijebu Ode 34 Fd 6.49N 3.56 E
IJmuiden, Velsen- 12 Gb 52.28N 4.35 E
Ijoubbâne, 'Erg- 34 Da 22.30N 6.00W
IJssel 11 Lb 52.30N 6.00 E
IJsselmeer 11 Lb 52.45N 5.25 E
IJsselmuiden 12 Hb 52.34N 5.56 E
IJsselstein 12 Hb 52.01N 5.02 E
Ijui 56 Jc 28.23S 53.55W
Ijui, Rio- 55 Eh 27.58S 55.20W
Ijūin 29 Bf 31.37N 130.24 E
Ijuizinho, Rio- 55 Ei 28.20S 54.28W
Ijuw 64e Bb 0.31S 166.57 E
Ijzendijke 12 Fc 51.20N 3.37 E
IJzer 11 Ic 51.09N 2.43 E
Ik [R.S.F.S.R.] 5 Ld 55.55N 52.36 E
Ikaalinen 7 Ff 61.46N 23.03 E
Ikalamavony 37 Hd 21.10S 46.32 E
Ikamatua 62 De 42.17S 171.42 E
Ikaria 15 Jl 37.35N 26.10 E
Ikarion Pélagos 15 Jl 37.30N 26.35 E
Ikast 8 Ch 56.08N 9.10 E
Ikatski Hrebet 20 Gf 54.00N 111.15 E
Ikawa 29 Fd 35.13N 138.14 E
Ikeda [Jap.] 29 Cd 34.01N 133.48 E
Ikeda [Jap.] 27 Pc 42.55N 143.27 E
Ikeda-Ko 29 Bf 31.14N 130.34 E
Ikej 20 Ff 54.12N 100.04 E
Ikeja 34 Fd 6.36N 3.21 E
Ikela 31 Ji 1.11S 23.16 E
Ikelemba 36 Cb 0.07N 18.17 E
Ikerre 34 Gd 7.30N 5.14 E
Ikerssuaq 41 Ie 65.10N 39.45W
Iki 29 Ae 33.45N 129.45 E
Iki-Kaikyō 28 Jh 33.45N 129.50 E
Ikitsuki-Shima 29 Ae 33.25N 129.25 E
İkizdere 24 Ib 40.47N 40.33 E
Ikom 34 Gd 5.58N 8.42 E
Ikongo 36 Gd 9.04S 36.51 E
Ikopa 37 Hc 16.50S 46.50 E
Ikot Ekpene 34 Gd 5.10N 7.43 E
Ikuno 29 Dd 35.10N 134.48 E
Ikurangi, Mount- 64p Bb 21.12S 159.45W
Ila 34 Fd 7.40N 4.40 E
Ilaferh 32 He 21.50N 1.20 E
Ilagan 22 Oh 17.10N 121.54 E
Ilām 25 Hc 26.54N 87.56 E
Ilam 23 Gc 33.38N 46.26 E
Ilām 23 Gc 33.00N 47.00 E
Ilan 27 Lg 24.45N 121.44 E
Ilanski 20 Ee 56.10N 96.03 E
Ilaro 34 Fd 6.53N 3.01 E
Ilawa 10 Pc 53.37N 19.33 E

Index Symbols

[1] Independent Nation
[2] State, Region
[3] District, County
[4] Municipality
[5] Colony, Dependency
Continent
Physical Region
Historical or Cultural Region
Mount, Mountain
Volcano
Hill
Mountains, Mountain Range
Hills, Escarpment
Plateau, Upland
Pass, Gap
Plain, Lowland
Delta
Salt Flat
Valley, Canyon
Crater, Cave
Karst Features
Depression
Polder
Desert, Dunes
Forest, Woods
Heath, Steppe
Oasis
Cape, Point
Coast, Beach
Cliff
Peninsula
Isthmus
Sandbank
Island
Atoll
Rock, Reef
Islands, Archipelago
Rocks, Reefs
Coral Reef
Well, Spring
Geyser
River, Stream
Waterfall Rapids
River Mouth, Estuary
Lake
Salt Lake
Intermittent Lake
Reservoir
Swamp, Pond
Canal
Glacier
Ice Shelf, Pack Ice
Ocean
Sea
Gulf, Bay
Strait, Fjord
Lagoon
Bank
Seamount
Tablemount
Ridge
Shelf
Basin
Escarpment, Sea Scarp
Fracture
Trench, Abyss
National Park, Reserve
Point of Interest
Recreation Site
Cave, Cavern
Historic Site
Ruins
Wall, Walls
Church, Abbey
Temple
Scientific Station
Airport
Port
Lighthouse
Mine
Tunnel
Dam, Bridge

Irpen 19 De 50.31N 30.16 E
Irpinia 14 Ij 40.55N 15.00 E
Irrawaddy → Ayeyarwady 25 Ie 17.00N 95.00 E
Irrawaddy (EN) = Ayeyarwady 21 Lg 15.50N 95.06 E
Irrel 12 Ie 49.51N 6.28 E
Irsâva 10 Th 48.15N 23.05 E
Irsina 14 Kj 40.45N 16.14 E
Irtek 16 Rd 51.29N 52.42 E
Irthlingborough 12 Bb 52.19N 0.36W
Irtyš 21 Ic 61.04N 68.52 E
Irtyšsk 19 He 53.21N 75.27 E
Irumu 36 Eb 1.27N 29.52 E
Irún 13 Ka 43.21N 1.47W
Irurzun 13 Kb 42.55N 1.50W
Irves Šaurums 8 Ig 57.48N 22.05 E
Irvine 9 If 55.37N 4.40W
Irving 45 Hj 32.49N 96.56W
Is, Jabal- 35 Fa 21.49N 35.39 E
Isa, Ra's- 33 Hf 15.11N 42.39 E
Isabel 45 Fd 45.24N 101.26W
Isabel, Bahía- 54a Ab 0.38 S 91.25W
Isabela 51a Ab 18.31N 67.07W
Isabela → Basilan City 26 He 6.42N 121.58 E
Isabela, Cabo- 49 Ld 19.56N 71.01W
Isabela, Isla- [Ec.] 52 Gf 0.30 S 91.06W
Isabela, Isla- [Mex.] 48 Gg 21.51N 105.55W
Isabella, Cordillera- 47 Gf 13.30N 85.30W
Isabel Segunda 49 Od 18.09N 65.27W
Isabey 15 Ml 38.00N 29.24 E
Isaccea 15 Ld 45.16N 28.28 E
Isachsen 39 Ib 78.50N 103.30W
Isafjörour 6 Db 66.03N 23.09W
Isahaya 28 Jh 32.50N 130.03 E
Isakov, Seamount (EN) 57 Ga 31.35N 151.07 E
Isana, Rio- 54 Ec 0.26N 67.19W
Isandja 36 Dc 2.59 S 22.00 E
Isanga 36 Dc 1.26 S 22.18 E
Isangi 36 Db 0.46N 24.15 E
Isanlu Makutu 34 Gd 8.16N 5.48 E
Isaouane-n-Irarraren 32 Id 27.15N 8.00 E
Isaouane-n-Tifernine 32 Id 27.00N 7.30 E
Isar 10 Ih 48.49N 12.58 E
Isarco/Eisack 14 Fd 46.27N 11.18 E
Isarco, Valle-/Eisacktal 14 Fd 46.45N 11.35 E
Isbergues 12 Ed 50.37N 2.27 E
Iscayachi 54 Eh 21.31 S 65.03W
Ischgl 14 Ec 47.01N 10.17 E
Ischia 14 Hj 40.45N 13.55 E
Ischia 14 Hj 40.44N 13.57 E
Ise 27 Oe 34.29N 136.42 E
Isefjord 8 Di 55.50N 11.50 E
Išejevka 7 Li 54.28N 48.17 E
Isen 10 Ih 48.20N 12.45 E
Isenach 12 Ke 49.38N 8.28 E
Isen-Zaki 29b Bb 27.39N 128.55 E
Iseo, Lago d'- 14 Ee 45.45N 10.05 E
Iseran, Col de l'- 11 Ni 45.25N 7.02 E
Isère 11 Kj 44.59N 4.51 E
Isère [3] 11 Li 45.10N 5.50 E
Išerit, Gora- 17 If 61.08N 59.10 E
Iserlohn 10 De 51.22N 7.42 E
Isernia 14 Ii 41.36N 14.14 E
Isesaki 29 Fc 36.19N 139.12 E
Iset 21 Id 56.36N 66.24 E
Isetskoje 17 Lh 56.29N 65.21 E
Ise-Wan 28 Ng 34.40N 136.42 E
Iseyin 34 Fd 7.58N 3.36 E
Isfahan (EN) = Eşfahān 22 Hf 32.40N 51.38 E
Isfana 18 Ge 39.51N 69.32 E
Isfara 18 Hd 40.07N 70.38 E
Isfendiyar Dağları 23 Da 41.45N 34.10 E
Isfjorden 41 Nc 78.15N 15.00 E
Isha Baydabo 31 Lh 3.04N 43.48 E
Ishasha River 36 Ec 0.50 S 29.40 E
Ishavet = Arctic Ocean (EN) 67 Be 85.00N 170.00 E
Isherton 54 Gc 2.19N 59.22W
Ishigaki 27 Lg 24.20N 124.09 E
Ishikari 29a Bb 43.13N 141.18 E
Ishikari-Dake 29a Cb 43.33N 143.00 E
Ishikari-Gawa 29a Bb 43.15N 141.20 E
Ishikari-Heiya 29a Bb 43.00N 141.40 E
Ishikari-Wan 27 Pc 43.25N 141.00 E
Ishikawa [Jap.] 27 Mf 26.27N 127.50 E
Ishikawa [Jap.] 29 Gc 37.09N 140.27 E
Ishikawa Ken [2] 28 Nf 36.35N 136.40 E
Ishim Steppe (EN) = Išimskaja Step 21 Id 55.00N 67.30 E
Ishinomaki 27 Pd 38.25N 141.18 E
Ishinomaki-Wan 29 Gb 38.20N 141.15 E
Ishioka 28 Pf 36.11N 140.16 E
Ishitate-San 29 De 33.44N 134.03 E
Ishizuchi-Yama 29 Ce 33.45N 133.05 E
Ishodnaja, Gora- 20 Nd 64.50N 173.26W
Ishpeming 44 Db 46.30N 87.40W
Isidro Alves 55 Ee 20.09 S 55.12W
Isigny-sur-Mer 11 Ee 49.19N 1.06W
Isii 29 Dd 34.04N 134.26 E
Işıklar Dağı 24 Bb 40.50N 27.05 E
Işıkli 15 Mk 38.19N 29.51 E
Isikli Göl 15 Mk 38.14N 29.55 E
Isili 14 Dk 39.44N 9.06 E
Isilkul 19 He 54.55N 71.16 E
Išim 22 Id 56.09N 69.27 E
Išim 21 Jd 57.45N 71.12 E
Išimbaj 19 Fe 53.28N 56.02 E
Išimskaja Step = Ishim Steppe (EN) 21 Id 55.00N 67.30 E
Isinga 20 Gf 52.55N 112.00 E
Isiolo 36 Gb 0.21N 37.35 E
Isiro 31 Jh 2.48N 27.41 E
Isisford 59 Id 24.16 S 144.26 E
Isjangulovo 17 Hj 52.12N 56.36 E
Iskandar 18 Gd 41.35N 69.43 E
Iskăr 15 Hf 43.44N 24.27 E
Iskăr, Jazovir- 15 Gg 42.25N 23.35 E
Iškašim 19 Hh 36.44N 71.39 E
İskenderun = Alexandretta 22 Ff 36.37N 36.07 E
İskenderun Körfezi = Alexandretta, Gulf of- (EN) 23 Eb 36.30N 35.40 E
İskilip 24 Fb 40.45N 34.29 E
Iski-Naukat 18 Id 40.14N 72.41 E
Iskininski 16 Rf 47.13N 52.36 E
Iskitim 20 Df 54.38N 83.18 E
Iskushuban 35 Ic 10.13N 50.14 E
Iskut 42 Ee 56.45N 131.48W
Isla-Cristina 13 Eg 37.12N 7.19W
İslâhiye 24 Gd 37.26N 36.41 E
Islāmābād 22 Jf 33.42N 73.10 E
Islāmābād → Anantnāg 25 Fb 33.44N 75.09 E
Isla Mujeres 48 Pg 21.12N 86.43W
Island = Iceland (EN) 6 Eb 65.00N 18.00W
Island = Iceland (EN) 5 Eb 65.00N 18.00W
Island Harbour 51b Ab 18.16N 63.02W
Island Lagoon 59 Hf 31.30 S 136.40 E
Island Lake 42 If 53.45N 94.30W
Island Lake 42 If 53.58N 94.46W
Island Pond 44 Lc 44.50N 71.53W
Islands, Bay of - [Can.] 42 Lg 49.10N 58.15W
Islands, Bay of- [N.Z.] 62 Fa 35.10 S 174.10 E
Islao, Massif de l'- 30 Lk 22.30 S 45.20 E
Islas de la Bahia [3] 49 De 16.20N 86.30W
Islay 5 Fd 55.46N 6.10W
Islaz 15 Hf 43.44N 24.45 E
Isle 11 Fj 44.55N 0.15W
Isle of Man [5] 9 Ig 54.15N 4.30W
Isle of Wight [3] 9 Lk 50.40N 1.15W
Isleta 45 Ci 34.55N 106.42W
Isle-Verte 44 Ma 48.01N 69.22W
Ismael Cortinas 55 Dk 33.56 S 57.08W
Ismailia (EN) = Al Ismā'īlīyah 33 Fc 30.35N 32.16 E
Ismailly 16 Pi 40.47N 48.13 E
Ismantorps Borg 8 Gh 56.45N 16.40 E
Isnā 31 Kf 25.18N 32.33 E
Isny im Allgäu 10 Gi 47.42N 10.02 E
Isojärvi 8 Ic 61.45N 21.45 E
Isojoki 7 Ee 62.07N 21.58 E
Isojoki/Storå 7 Ee 62.07N 21.58 E
Isoka 36 Fe 10.08 S 32.38 E
Isola del Liri 14 Hi 41.41N 13.34 E
Isola di Capo Rizzuto 14 Ll 38.58N 17.05 E
Isonzo 14 He 45.43N 13.33 E
Isonzo (EN) = Soča 14 He 45.43N 13.33 E
Isosyöte 7 Gd 65.37N 27.35 E
Isparta 23 Db 37.46N 30.33 E
Isperih 15 Jf 43.43N 26.50 E
Ispica 14 In 36.47N 14.55 E
İspir 24 Ib 40.29N 41.00 E
İspiriz Dağı 24 Jc 38.03N 43.55 E
Israel (EN) = Yisra'el 22 Ff 31.30N 35.00 E
Isratu 35 Fb 16.20N 39.55 E
Issa 8 Mh 56.55N 28.50 E
Issano 54 Gb 5.49N 59.25W
Issaran, Ra's- 24 Eh 28.50N 32.56 E
Issel 10 Cd 52.00N 6.10 E
Isser 13 Ph 36.51N 3.40 E
Issia [3] 34 Dd 6.30N 6.35W
Issia 34 Dd 6.29N 6.35W
Issoire 11 Ji 45.33N 3.15 E
Issoudun 11 Hh 46.57N 2.00 E
Issyk 18 Kc 43.20N 77.28 E
Issyk-Kul, Ozero- 21 Je 42.25N 77.15 E
Issyk-Kulskaja Oblast [3] 19 Hg 42.10N 78.00 E
Ist 14 If 44.17N 14.47 E
İstanbul 22 Ee 41.01N 28.58 E
İstanbul-Bakırköy 15 Lj 40.59N 28.52 E
İstanbul-Beyoğlu 15 Lh 41.02N 28.59 E
İstanbul Boğazi = Bosporus (EN) 5 Ig 41.00N 29.00 E
İstanbul-Kadıköy 15 Mi 40.59N 29.01 E
Isteren 8 Db 62.00N 11.50 E
Istgāh-e Eqbālīyeh 24 Ne 35.50N 50.45 E
Isthilart 55 Dj 31.11 S 57.58W
Istiaia 15 Gk 38.57N 23.09 E
Istisu 16 Nj 39.57N 46.00 E
Istmina 54 Cb 5.09N 76.42W
Isto, Mount- 38 Ec 69.12N 143.48W
Istok 15 Dg 42.47N 20.29 E
Istokpoga, Lake- 44 Gl 27.22N 81.17W
Istra = Istria (EN) 5 Hf 45.00N 14.00 E
Istres 11 Kk 43.31N 4.59 E
Istria 15 Le 44.34N 28.43 E
Istria (EN) = Istra 5 Hf 45.00N 14.00 E
Isulan 26 He 7.02N 124.29 E
Itabaiana 54 Kf 10.41 S 37.26W
Itabaianinha 54 Kf 11.16 S 37.47W
Itaberá 55 Hf 23.51 S 49.09W
Itaberaba 54 Jf 12.32 S 40.18W
Itaberai 54 Ig 16.02 S 49.48W
Itabira 54 Jg 19.37 S 43.13W
Itabirito 55 Ke 20.15 S 43.48W
Itabuna 53 Mg 14.48 S 39.16W
Itacaiúna, Rio- 54 Ie 5.21 S 49.08W
Itacarambi 55 Jb 15.01 S 44.03W
Itacoatiara 53 Kf 3.08 S 58.25W
Itacolomi, Pico do- 55 Ke 20.26 S 43.29W
Itacuai, Rio- 54 Dd 4.20 S 70.12W
Itacumbi 55 Ei 28.44 S 55.08W
Itacurubí del Rosario 55 Dg 24.29 S 56.41W
Itaguari, Rio- 55 Jb 14.11 S 44.40W
Itaguaru 55 Hb 15.44 S 49.37W
Itagüí 54 Cb 6.12N 75.40W
Itaimbèzinho 55 Gi 28.38 S 50.34W
Itaituba 53 Kf 4.17 S 55.59W
Itajaí 53 Lh 26.53 S 48.39W
Itajaí Açu, Rio- 55 Hh 26.54 S 48.33W
Itajubá 54 Ih 22.26 S 45.27W
Itajuípe 54 Kf 14.41 S 39.22W
Itaka 20 Gf 53.54N 118.42 E
Italia = Italy (EN) 6 Hg 42.50N 12.50 E
Itálica 13 Fg 37.25N 6.05W
Italy (EN) = Italia 6 Hg 42.50N 12.50 E
Itambacuri 54 Jg 18.01 S 41.42W
Itambé, Pico de- 52 Lg 18.23 S 43.21W
Itämeri = Baltic, Sea (EN) 5 Hd 57.00N 19.00 E
Itampolo 37 Gd 24.41 S 43.57 E
Itanagar 25 Ic 26.57N 93.15 E
Itanará, Rio- 55 Eg 24.00 S 55.53W
Itanhaém 56 Kb 24.11 S 46.47W
Itano 29 Dd 34.09N 134.28 E
Itapaci 55 Hb 14.57 S 49.34W
Itapagé 54 Kd 3.41 S 39.34W
Itapajipe 55 Hd 19.54 S 49.22W
Itaparaná, Rio- 54 Fe 5.47 S 63.03W
Itapebi 54 Kg 15.56 S 39.32W
Itapecerica 55 Je 20.28 S 45.07W
Itapecuru-Mirim 54 Jd 3.24 S 44.20W
Itapemirim 54 Jh 21.01 S 40.50W
Itaperina, Pointe- 30 Lk 24.59 S 47.06 E
Itaperuna 54 Jh 21.12 S 41.54W
Itapetinga 54 Jg 15.15 S 40.15W
Itapetininga 56 Kb 23.36 S 48.03W
Itapetininga, Rio- 55 Hf 23.35 S 48.27W
Itapeva 55 Hf 23.58 S 48.52W
Itapeva, Lagoa- 55 Hi 29.30 S 49.55W
Itapicuru, Rio- [Braz.] 54 Kf 11.47 S 37.32W
Itapicuru, Rio- [Braz.] 52 Lf 2.52 S 44.12W
Itapipoca 54 Kd 3.31 S 39.33W
Itapiranga [Braz.] 54 Gd 2.45 S 58.01W
Itapiranga [Braz.] 55 Fh 27.08 S 53.43W
Itapirapuã, Pico- 55 Hg 24.17 S 49.12W
Itápolis 55 He 21.35 S 48.46W
Itaporã 55 Ef 22.01 S 54.54W
Itaporanga [Braz.] 55 Hf 23.42 S 49.29W
Itaporanga [Braz.] 54 Ke 7.18 S 38.10W
Itapúa [3] 55 Eh 26.50 S 55.50W
Itapuã 55 Gj 30.16 S 51.01W
Itapuranga 54 Ig 15.35 S 49.59W
Itaqui 56 Ic 29.08 S 56.33W
Itaquyry 55 Eg 24.56 S 55.13W
Itararé 55 Hg 24.07 S 49.20W
Itararé, Rio- 55 Hf 23.10 S 49.42W
Itārsi 25 Fd 22.37N 77.45 E
Itarumã 55 Gd 18.42 S 51.25W
Itati 55 Ch 27.16 S 58.15W
Itatinga 55 Hf 23.07 S 48.36W
Itatski 20 De 56.07N 89.20 E
Itaum 55 Ef 22.00 S 55.20W
Itaúna 54 Jh 20.04 S 44.34W
Itaya-Tōge 29 Gc 37.50N 140.13 E
Itbāy 30 Kf 22.00N 35.30 E
Itbayat 26 Hb 20.46N 121.50 E
Itchen 12 Ad 50.57N 1.22W
Ite 54 Dg 17.50 S 70.58W
Itéa 15 Fk 38.26N 22.25 E
Ithaca 43 Lc 42.26N 76.30W
Ithaca (EN) = Itháki 15 Dk 38.24N 20.40 E
Itháki 15 Dk 38.22N 20.43 E
Itháki = Ithaca (EN) 15 Dk 38.24N 20.40 E
Ith Hils 10 Fd 52.05N 9.35 E
Ithnayn, Harrat- 24 Ii 26.40N 40.10 E
Itigi 36 Fd 5.42 S 34.29 E
Itimbiri 30 Jh 2.02N 22.44 E
Itiopya = Ethiopia (EN) 31 Kh 9.00N 39.00 E
Itiquira 54 Hg 17.05 S 54.56W
Itiquira, Rio- 52 Kg 17.18 S 56.44W
Itirapina 55 If 22.15 S 47.49W
Itiúba 54 Kf 10.43 S 39.51W
Itivdleq 41 Ge 66.38N 53.51W
Itō 28 Og 34.58N 139.05 E
Itoigawa 28 Nf 37.02N 137.51 E
Itoko 36 Dc 1.00 S 21.45 E
Itoman 29b Ab 26.07N 127.40 E
Iton 11 Hf 49.09N 1.12 E
Itremo, Massif de l'- 37 Hd 20.45 S 46.30 E
Itšā 24 Dh 29.15N 30.48 E
Itsukaichi 29 Cd 34.22N 132.22 E
Itsuki 29 Be 32.24N 130.50 E
Ittiri 14 Cj 40.36N 8.34 E
Itu [Braz.] 55 If 23.16 S 47.19W
Itu [Nig.] 34 Gd 5.12N 7.59 E
Itu, Rio- 55 Ei 29.25 S 55.51W
Itui, Rio- 54 Dd 4.38 S 70.19W
Ituiutaba 54 Ig 18.58 S 49.28W
Itula 36 Ec 3.29 S 27.52 E
Itumbiara 54 Ig 18.25 S 49.13W
Itumkale 16 Nh 42.43N 45.35 E
Ituna 46 Na 51.10N 103.30W
Itungi Port 36 Fd 9.35 S 33.56 E
Itupiranga 54 Ie 5.09 S 49.20W
Iturama 55 Gd 19.44 S 50.11W
Iturbide 48 Oh 19.40N 89.37W
Ituri 30 Jh 1.40N 27.01 E
Iturregui 55 Bm 36.50 S 61.08W
Iturup, Ostrov- 21 Qe 44.54N 147.30 E
Iturup, Ostrov-/Etorofu Tō 21 Qe 44.54N 147.30 E
Itutinga 55 Je 21.18 S 44.40W
Ituverava 56 Kb 20.20 S 47.47W
Ituxi, Rio- 54 Ee 7.18 S 64.51W
Ituzaingó 55 Dh 27.36 S 56.41W
Itz 10 Gg 49.58N 10.52 E
Itzehoe 10 Fc 53.55N 9.31 E
Ivacevići 16 Dc 52.43N 25.21 E
Ivai 55 Gg 25.01 S 50.52W
Ivai, Rio- [Braz.] 55 Fi 29.08 S 53.16W
Ivai, Rio- [Braz.] 52 Kh 23.18 S 53.42W
Ivaiporã 55 Gg 24.15 S 51.45W
Ivajlovgrad 15 Jh 41.32N 26.08 E
Ivakoany, Massif de l'- 37 Hd 23.50 S 46.25 E
Ivalojoki 7 Gc 68.43N 27.36 E
Ivančice 10 Mg 49.06N 16.22 E
Ivangorod 7 Gg 59.23N 28.20 E
Ivangrad 15 Cg 42.51N 19.52 E
Ivanhoe 58 Fh 32.54 S 144.18 E
Ivanić-Grad 14 Ke 45.42N 16.24 E
Ivaniči 10 Uf 50.38N 24.24 E
Ivanjica 15 Df 43.35N 20.14 E
Ivanjska 14 Lf 44.55N 17.04 E
Ivankov 16 Fd 50.57N 29.58 E
Ivano-Frankovo 10 Tg 49.52N 23.46 E
Ivano-Frankovsk 6 If 48.55N 24.43 E
Ivano-Frankovskaja Oblast [3] 19 Cf 48.40N 24.40 E
Ivanovka [R.S.F.S.R.] 20 Hf 50.18N 127.59 E
Ivanovka [Ukr.-U.S.S.R.] 16 Gf 46.57N 30.28 E
Ivanovo [Bye.-U.S.S.R.] 16 Dc 52.10N 25.32 E
Ivanovo [R.S.F.S.R.] 6 Kd 57.00N 40.59 E
Ivanovskaja Oblast [3] 19 Ed 57.00N 41.50 E
Ivanovskoje 8 Me 59.12N 28.59 E
Ivanščica 14 Kd 46.11N 16.10 E
Ivdel 19 Gc 60.42N 60.28 E
Ivenec 8 Lk 53.55N 26.49 E
Ivigtut 41 Hf 61.15N 48.00W
Ivindo 30 Ii 0.09 S 12.09 E
Ivinheima 55 Ff 22.10 S 53.37W
Ivinheima, Rio- 54 Hh 23.14 S 53.42W
Ivinski razliv 7 If 61.10N 35.00 E
Iviza (EN) = Eivissa/Ibiza 5 Gh 39.00N 1.25 E
Iviza (EN) = Ibiza/Eivissa 5 Gh 39.00N 1.25 E
Ivje 10 Vc 53.55N 25.51 E
Ivohibe 37 Hd 22.29 S 46.52 E
Ivoire, Côte d'- = Ivory Coast (EN) 30 Gh 5.00N 5.00W
Ivolândia 55 Gc 16.34 S 50.51W
Ivory Coast (EN) = Côte d'Ivoire [1] 31 Gh 8.00N 5.00W
Ivory Coast (EN) = Ivoire, Côte d'- 30 Gh 5.00N 5.00W
Ivösjön 8 Fh 56.05N 14.25 E
Ivrea 14 Be 45.28N 7.52 E
Ivrindi 15 Kj 39.34N 27.29 E
Ivry-la-Bataille 12 Df 48.53N 1.28 E
Ivry-sur-Seine 12 Ef 48.49N 2.23 E
Ivujivik 39 Lc 62.25N 77.54W
Iwai-Shima 29 Be 33.47N 131.58 E
Iwaizumi 28 Pe 39.50N 141.48 E
Iwaki 22 Qf 36.55N 140.48 E
Iwaki-Gawa 29 Ga 41.01N 140.22 E
Iwaki-Hisanohama 29 Gc 37.09N 140.59 E
Iwaki-Jōban 29 Gc 37.02N 140.50 E
Iwaki-Kawamae 29 Gc 37.12N 140.45 E
Iwaki-Miwa 29 Gc 37.09N 140.42 E
Iwaki-Nakoso 29 Gc 36.56N 140.48 E
Iwaki-Onahama 29 Gc 36.57N 140.53 E
Iwaki-San 29 Ga 40.40N 140.20 E
Iwaki-Taira 29 Gc 37.05N 140.55 E
Iwaki-Uchigō 29 Gc 37.04N 140.50 E
Iwaki-Yoshima 29 Gc 37.05N 140.50 E
Iwaki-Yotsukura 29 Gc 37.07N 140.58 E
Iwakuni 27 Ne 34.09N 132.11 E
Iwami 29 Dd 35.35N 134.20 E
Iwami-Kōgen 29 Cd 35.00N 132.30 E
Iwamizawa 27 Pc 43.12N 141.46 E
Iwanai 28 Pc 42.58N 140.30 E
Iwanuma 29 Gb 38.07N 140.52 E
Iwase 29 Gc 36.21N 140.06 E
Iwasuge-Yama 29 Fc 36.44N 138.32 E
Iwata 29 Ed 34.42N 137.48 E
Iwate 28 Pe 39.30N 141.30 E
Iwate Ken [2] 28 Pe 39.30N 141.15 E
Iwate San 28 Pe 39.49N 141.26 E
Iwo 34 Fd 7.38N 4.11 E
Iwŏn 27 Mc 40.19N 128.37 E
Iwuy 12 Fd 50.14N 3.19 E
Ixiamas 54 Ef 13.45 S 68.09W
Ixmiquilpan 48 Jg 20.29N 99.14W
Ixopo 37 Ef 30.08 S 30.00 E
Ixtapa, Punta- 48 Ii 17.39N 101.40W
Ixtepec 47 Ee 16.34N 95.06W
Ixtlahuacán del Rio 48 Hg 20.52N 103.15W
Ixtlán del Rio 47 Dd 21.02N 104.22W
Iyah 35 Hd 9.00N 49.38 E
Iyo 28 Lh 33.46N 132.42 E
Iyo-mishima 29 Ce 33.58N 133.33 E
Iyo-Nada 29 Ce 33.40N 132.15 E
Iž 7 Mh 56.00N 52.41 E
Iž 14 Jf 44.03N 15.06 E
Izabal [3] 49 Cf 15.30N 89.00W
Izabal, Lago de- 47 Ge 15.30N 89.10W
Izad Khvāst 24 Og 31.31N 52.07 E
Izamal 47 Gd 20.56N 89.01W
Izamal 48 Og 20.56N 89.01W
Izapa 47 Ff 14.55N 92.10W
'Izbat al Jājah 24 Dj 24.48N 30.35 E
'Izbat Dush 24 Dj 24.34N 30.42 E
Izberbaš 19 Eg 42.33N 47.52 E
Izbiceni 15 Hf 43.50N 24.39 E
Izborsk 8 Mg 57.39N 28.01 E
Izegem 12 Fd 50.55N 3.13 E
Izeh 24 Mg 31.50N 49.50 E
Izena-Shima 29b Ab 26.56N 127.56 E
Iževsk 6 Ld 56.51N 53.14 E
Izjaslav 16 Ed 50.09N 26.51 E
Izjum 19 Df 49.12N 37.17 E
Izkī 23 Ie 22.57N 57.49 E
Izma 5 Lb 65.19N 52.54 E
Izma 17 Fd 65.02N 53.55 E
Izmail 6 If 45.21N 28.50 E
İzmir = Smyrna (EN) 22 Ef 38.25N 27.09 E
İzmir, Gulf of- (EN) = İzmir Körfezi 24 Bc 38.30N 26.50 E
İzmir-Bornova 24 Bc 38.27N 27.14 E
İzmir Körfezi = İzmir, Gulf of- (EN) 24 Bc 38.30N 26.50 E
İzmit 22 Ee 40.46N 29.55 E
İzmit Körfezi 24 Cb 40.45N 29.35 E
İzmor 24 Ab 40.11N 25.55 E
Iznajar, Embalse de- 13 Hg 37.15N 4.30W
Iznalloz 13 Ig 37.23N 3.31W
İznik 24 Cb 40.26N 29.43 E
İznik Gölü 23 Ca 40.26N 29.30 E
Izobilny 16 Lg 45.19N 41.42 E
Izola 14 He 45.32N 13.40 E
Izôrskaja Vozvyšennost 8 Me 59.35N 29.30 E
Izozog, Bañados del- 54 Fg 18.50 S 62.10W
Izra' 24 Gf 32.51N 36.15 E
Izsák 10 Pj 46.48N 19.22 E
Iztočni Rodopi 15 Ih 41.44N 25.31 E
Izúcar de Matamoros 48 Jh 18.36N 98.28W
Izu-Hantō 28 Og 34.55N 138.55 E
Izuhara 28 Jg 34.12N 129.17 E
Izu Islands (EN) = Izu-shotō 21 Pf 32.00N 140.00 E
Izumi [Jap.] 28 Kh 32.05N 130.22 E
Izumi [Jap.] 29 Dd 34.29N 135.26 E
Izumi [Jap.] 29 Gb 38.19N 140.51 E
Izumi-sano 29 Dd 34.24N 135.18 E
Izumo 28 Lg 35.22N 132.46 E
Izu-Shotō = Izu Islands (EN) 21 Pf 32.00N 140.00 E
Izvesti CIK, Ostrova- = Izvestiya Tsik Islands (EN) 20 Da 75.55N 82.30 E
Izvestiya Tsik Islands (EN) = Izvesti CIK, Ostrova- 20 Da 75.55N 82.30 E

J

Jaala 8 Lc 61.03N 26.29 E
Jaama/Jama 8 Lf 58.59N 27.45 E
Jääsjärvi 8 Lc 61.35N 26.05 E
Jaba 24 Qe 35.55N 56.35 E
Jabal, Baḩr al- = Mountain Nile (EN) 30 Kh 9.30N 30.30 E
Jabal Abū Rujmayn 24 Ge 34.50N 37.56 E
Jabal al Awliyā' 35 Eb 15.14N 32.30 E
Jabal az Zannah 24 Oj 24.11N 52.38 E
Jabalón 13 Hf 38.53N 4.05W
Jabalpur 22 Jg 23.10N 79.57 E
Jabal Şabāyā 33 Hf 18.35N 41.03 E
Jabālyah 24 Fg 31.32N 34.29 E
Jabal Zuqar, Jazīrat- 33 Hg 14.00N 42.45 E
Jabbārah 33 Hf 19.27N 40.03 E
Jabbeke 12 Fc 51.11N 3.05 E
Jabjabah, Wādī- 35 Ea 22.37N 33.17 E
Jablah 24 Fe 35.21N 35.55 E
Jablanac 14 If 44.42N 14.53 E
Jablanica 15 Dh 41.15N 20.30 E
Jablanica [Bul.] 15 Hf 43.01N 24.06 E
Jablanica [Yugo.] 14 Lg 43.39N 17.45 E
Jabločny 20 Jg 47.09N 142.03 E
Jablonec nad Nisou 10 Lf 50.44N 15.10 E
Jablonicki, Pereval- 5 If 48.18N 24.28 E
Jablonovo 20 Gf 51.51N 112.50 E
Jablonovy Hrebet = Yablonovy Range (EN) 21 Nd 53.30N 115.00 E
Jablunkovský průsmyk 10 Og 49.31N 18.45 E
Jaboatão 54 Ke 8.07 S 35.01W
Jaboti 55 De 20.48 S 56.23W
Jabrīn 24 Ni 27.51N 51.26 E
Jabuka 14 Jg 43.05N 15.28 E
Jabung, Tanjung- 26 Dg 1.01 S 104.22 E
Jabuticabal 56 Kb 21.16 S 48.19W
Jabuticatubas 55 Kd 19.30 S 43.45W
Jaca 13 Lb 42.34N 0.33W
Jacaltenango 49 Bf 15.40N 91.44W
Jacaré, Rio- 55 Je 21.03 S 45.16W
Jacarei 55 Jf 23.19 S 45.58W
Jacarezinho 56 Kb 23.09 S 49.59W
Jáchal, Rio- 52 Ji 30.44 S 68.08W
Jaciara [Braz.] 55 Ib 14.12 S 46.41W
Jaciara [Braz.] 55 Eb 15.59 S 54.57W
Jackman 44 Lc 45.38N 70.16W
Jack Mountain 46 Eb 48.47N 120.57W
Jackpot 46 Hf 41.59N 114.09W
Jacksboro 45 Gj 33.13N 98.10W
Jacks Mountain 44 Ie 40.45N 77.30W
Jackson [Al.-U.S.] 44 Dj 31.31N 87.53W
Jackson [Bar.] 51q Ab 13.10N 59.43W
Jackson [Ky.-U.S.] 44 Fg 37.33N 83.23W
Jackson [Mi.-U.S.] 43 Kc 42.15N 84.24W
Jackson [Mn.-U.S.] 45 Ie 43.37N 94.59W
Jackson [Mo.-U.S.] 45 Lh 37.23N 89.40W
Jackson [Ms.-U.S.] 39 Jf 32.18N 90.12W
Jackson [Oh.-U.S.] 44 Ff 39.03N 82.40W
Jackson [Tn.-U.S.] 43 Jd 35.37N 88.49W
Jackson [Wy.-U.S.] 46 Je 43.29N 110.38W
Jackson, Cape- 62 Fd 40.59 S 174.19 E
Jackson, Mount- [Ant.] 66 Qf 71.23 S 63.22W
Jackson, Mount- [Austl.] 59 Df 30.15 S 119.16 E
Jackson Bay 62 Ce 43.55 S 168.40 E
Jackson Head 62 Ce 43.58 S 168.37 E
Jackson Lake 46 Je 43.55N 110.40W
Jacksonville [Ar.-U.S.] 45 Ji 34.52N 92.07W
Jacksonville [Fl.-U.S.] 39 Kf 30.20N 81.40W
Jacksonville [Il.-U.S.] 45 Kg 39.44N 90.14W
Jacksonville [N.C.-U.S.] 44 Le 34.45N 77.26W
Jacksonville [Tx.-U.S.] 43 He 31.58N 95.17W
Jacksonville Beach 44 Ke 30.18N 81.24W
Jacmel 47 Je 18.14N 72.32W
Jacobābād 25 Dc 28.17N 68.26 E
Jacobina 54 Jf 11.11 S 40.31W
Jacob Lake 46 Ih 36.45N 112.13W
Jacobs 45 La 50.15N 89.46W
Jacona de Plancarte 48 Hh 19.57N 102.16W
Jacques-Cartier, Détroit de - 42 Lg 50.00N 63.30W
Jacques Cartier, Mont - 42 Kg 48.58N 65.57W
Jacuba, Rio- 55 Fd 18.25 S 52.28W
Jacuí, Rio- 52 Ki 30.02 S 51.15W
Jacuí-Mirim, Rio- 55 Fi 28.51 S 53.07W
Jacundá 54 Id 4.33 S 49.28W
Jacundá, Rio- 54 Hd 1.57 S 50.26W
Jacupiranga 56 Kb 24.42 S 48.00W
Jada 34 Hd 8.46N 12.09 E
Jadal 34 Fb 18.37N 5.00 E

Index Symbols

[1] Independent Nation
[2] State, Region
[3] District, County
[4] Municipality
[5] Colony, Dependency
Continent
Physical Region
Historical or Cultural Region
Mount, Mountain
Volcano
Hill
Mountains, Mountain Range
Hills, Escarpment
Plateau, Upland
Pass, Gap
Plain, Lowland
Delta
Salt Flat
Valley, Canyon
Crater, Cave
Karst Features
Depression
Polder
Desert, Dunes
Forest, Woods
Heath, Steppe
Oasis
Cape, Point
Coast, Beach
Cliff
Peninsula
Isthmus
Sandbank
Island
Atoll
Rock, Reef
Islands, Archipelago
Rocks, Reefs
Coral Reef
Well, Spring
Geyser
River, Stream
Waterfall Rapids
River Mouth, Estuary
Lake
Salt Lake
Intermittent Lake
Reservoir
Swamp, Pond
Canal
Glacier
Ice Shelf, Pack Ice
Ocean
Sea
Gulf, Bay
Strait, Fjord
Lagoon
Bank
Seamount
Tablemount
Ridge
Shelf
Basin
Escarpment, Sea Scarp
Fracture
Trench, Abyss
National Park, Reserve
Point of Interest
Recreation Site
Cave, Cavern
Historic Site
Ruins
Wall, Walls
Church, Abbey
Temple
Scientific Station
Airport
Port
Lighthouse
Mine
Tunnel
Dam, Bridge

Jadar [Yugo.] 15 Ce 44.38N 19.16 E
Jaddi, Râs- 25 Cc 25.14N 63.31 E
Jade 10 Ec 53.25N 8.05 E
Jadebusen 10 Ec 53.30N 8.10 E
Jadīd Ra's al Fīl 35 Dc 12.40N 25.43 E
Jadito Wash 46 Ji 35.22N 110.50W
J.A.D. Jensens Nunatakker 41 Hf 62.45N 48.20W
Jädraås 8 Gd 60.51N 16.28 E
Jadransko More=Adriatic Sea (EN) 5 Hg 43.00N 16.00 E
Jadrin 7 Li 55.57N 46.11 E
Jādū 35 Bc 31.57N 12.01 E
Ja'ēl 35 Ic 10.56N 51.09 E
Jaén [3] 13 If 38.00N 3.30W
Jaén 13 Ig 37.46N 3.47W
Jæren 8 Af 58.45N 5.45 E
Jærens rev 8 Af 58.45N 5.29 E
Jaffa, Cape- 59 Hg 36.58S 139.40 E
Jaffna 22 Ji 9.40N 80.00 E
Jafr, Qā' al- 24 Gg 30.17N 36.20 E
Jägala Jõgi 8 Ke 59.28N 25.04 E
Jagdalpur 22 Kh 19.04N 82.02 E
Jagdaqi 27 La 50.26N 124.02 E
Jaghbūb, Wāḥāt al-=Jarabub Oasis (EN) 30 Jf 29.41N 24.43 E
Jagotin 16 Gd 50.17N 31.47 E
Jagst 10 Fg 49.14N 9.11 E
Jaguapitã 55 Gf 23.07S 51.33W
Jaguaquara 54 Kf 13.32S 39.58W
Jaguarão 56 Jd 32.34S 53.23W
Jaguarão, Rio- 55 Fk 32.39S 53.12W
Jaguarari 54 Jf 10.16S 40.12W
Jaguari 55 Ei 29.30S 54.41W
Jaguari, Rio- [Braz.] 55 Ei 29.42S 55.07W
Jaguari, Rio- [Braz.] 55 If 22.41S 47.17W
Jaguariaiva 56 Kb 24.15S 49.42W
Jaguaribe 54 Ke 5.53S 38.37W
Jaguaribe, Rio 52 Mf 4.25S 37.45W
Jaguaruana 54 Kd 4.50S 37.47W
Jagüey Grande 49 Gb 22.32N 81.08W
Jahadyjaha 17 Pc 67.03N 72.01 E
Jahām, 'Irq- 24 Li 26.12N 47.00 E
Jahorina 14 Mg 43.42N 18.35 E
Jahrom 23 Hd 28.31N 53.33 E
Jahroma 7 Ih 56.20N 37.29 E
Jaice 23 Ff 44.21N 17.17 E
Jaicoa, Cordillera- 51a Ab 18.25N 67.05W
Jaicós 54 Je 7.21S 41.08W
Jailolo 26 If 1.05N 127.30 E
Jailolo, Selat- 26 If 0.05N 129.05 E
Jaina, Isla de- 48 Ng 20.14N 90.40W
Jainca 27 Hd 35.57N 102.00 E
Jaipur 22 Jg 26.55N 75.49 E
Jaisalmer 25 Ec 26.55N 70.54 E
Jaja 20 De 56.12N 86.26 E
Jājarm 24 Qd 36.58N 56.27 E
Jajdúdorog 10 Ri 47.49N 21.30 E
Jajere 34 Hc 11.59N 11.26 E
Jajpan 18 Hd 40.23N 70.50 E
Jajsan 16 Td 50.51N 56.14 E
Jajva 19 Fd 59.20N 57.16 E
Jajva 17 Hg 59.16N 56.42 E
Jakarta 22 Mj 6.10S 106.46 E
Jakobshavn/Ilulissat 67 Nc 69.20N 50.50W
Jakobstad/Pietarsaari 7 Fe 63.40N 22.42 E
Jakoruda 15 Gg 42.02N 23.40 E
Jakupica 15 Eh 41.43N 21.26 E
Jakutsk 22 Oc 62.13N 129.49 E
Jakutskaja ASSR [3] 20 Hc 67.00N 130.00 E
Jal 45 Ej 32.07N 103.12W
Jalaid Qi (Inder) 27 Lb 46.41N 122.52 E
Jalājil 24 Kj 25.41N 45.28 E
Jalālābād 23 Lc 34.26N 70.28 E
Jalālah al Baḥrīyah, Jabal al- 24 Eh 29.20N 32.20 E
Jalālah al Qiblīyah, Jabal al- 24 Eh 28.42N 32.22 E
Jalán, Río- 49 Df 15.43N 87.34W
Jalandhar 22 Jf 31.19N 75.34 E
Jalapa [3] 49 Cf 14.35N 89.55W
Jalapa [Guat.] 47 Gf 14.38N 89.59W
Jalapa [Mex.] 48 Mi 17.43N 92.49W
Jalapa [Nic.] 47 Gf 13.55N 86.08W
Jalapa Enriquez 39 Jh 19.32N 96.55W
Jalasjarvi 7 Fe 62.30N 22.45 E
Jales 55 Ge 20.16S 50.33W
Jālgaon 25 Fd 21.01N 75.34 E
Jalhay 12 Hd 50.34N 5.58 E
Jalībah 24 Lg 30.35N 46.32 E
Jalib Shahab 24 Lg 30.23N 46.09 E
Jalingo 34 Hd 8.53N 11.22 E
Jalisco [2] 47 Dd 20.20N 103.40W
Jāliṭah=La Galite (EN) 30 He 37.32N 8.56 E
Jāliṭah, Canal de- 14 Cm 37.20N 9.00 E
Jallas 13 Cb 42.54N 9.08W
Jālna 25 Fe 19.50N 75.53 E
Jalón 13 Kc 41.47N 1.04W
Jalostotitlán 48 Hg 21.12N 102.28W
Jalpa 48 Hg 21.38N 102.58W
Jalpaiguri 25 Hc 26.31N 88.44 E
Jalpan 48 Jg 21.14N 99.29W
Jalpug, Ozero- 16 Fg 45.25N 28.40 E
Jalta 19 Dg 44.30N 34.10 E
Jaltepec, Rio- 48 Li 17.26N 94.59W
Jālū 34 Dd 28.30N 21.05 E
Jālū, Wāḥāt-=Gialo Oasis (EN) 30 Jf 29.00N 21.20 E
Jaluit Atoll 57 Hd 6.00N 169.35 E
Jalūlā' 24 Ke 34.16N 45.10 E
Jalutorovsk 19 Gd 56.40N 66.18 E
Jam [Iran] 24 Pe 35.45N 55.02 E
Jam [Iran] 24 Oi 27.50N 52.22 E
Jama/Jaama 8 Lf 58.59N 27.45 E
Jamaari 30 Ig 12.06N 10.14 E
Jamaica 49 Jc 20.12N 75.09W
Jamaica 38 Lh 18.15N 77.30W
Jamaica [1] 39 Lh 18.15N 77.30W
Jamaica Channel 47 Ie 18.00N 75.30W
Jamaica Channel (EN)=Jamaïque, Canal de- 49 Jd 18.00N 75.30W
Jamaïque, Canal de-=Jamaica Channel (EN) 49 Jd 18.00N 75.30W
Jamal, Poluostrov-=Yamal Peninsula (EN) 21 Ib 70.00N 70.00 E
Jamalo-Nenecki Nacionalny okrug [3] 20 Cc 67.00N 75.00 E
Jamālpur 25 Hd 24.55N 89.56 E
Jamāme 31 Lh 0.04N 42.46 E
Jamantau, Gora- 5 Le 54.15N 58.06 E
Jamanxim, Rio- 52 Kf 4.43S 56.18W
Jamari, Rio- 54 Fe 8.27S 63.30W
Jamarovka 20 Gf 50.38N 110.16 E
Jambi 22 Oj 1.38S 123.42 E
Jambi [3] 26 Dg 1.36S 103.37 E
Jambol [2] 15 Jg 42.15N 26.35 E
Jambol 15 Jg 42.29N 26.30 E
Jambongan, Pulau- 26 Ge 6.41N 117.25 E
Jambuair, Tanjung- 26 Ce 5.16N 97.30 E
Jambusar 25 Ed 22.03N 72.48 E
James Bay 38 Kd 51.00N 80.30W
Jameson Land 41 Jd 70.45N 23.45W
James River [U.S.] 38 Je 42.52N 97.18W
James River [U.S.] 44 Ig 36.56N 76.27W
James Ross 66 Re 64.15S 57.45W
James Ross Strait 42 Hc 69.50N 96.30W
Jamestown [Austl.] 59 Hf 33.12S 138.36 E
Jamestown [N.D.-U.S.] 43 Hb 46.54N 98.42W
Jamestown [N.Y.-U.S.] 43 Lc 42.05N 79.15W
Jamestown [St.Hel.] 31 Gj 15.56S 5.43W
Jamestown Reservoir 45 Gc 47.15N 98.40W
Jamm 8 Mf 58.24N 28.15 E
Jammer Bugt 7 Bh 57.20N 9.30 E
Jammu 22 Jf 32.44N 74.52 E
Jammu and Kashmir [3] 25 Fb 34.00N 76.00 E
Jāmnagar 22 Jg 22.28N 70.04 E
Jamno, Jezioro- 10 Mb 54.15N 16.10 E
Jampol 16 Fe 48.16N 28.17 E
Jämsä 7 Ff 61.52N 25.12 E
Jamsah 24 Ei 27.38N 33.35 E
Jämsänkoski 8 Kc 61.55N 25.11 E
Jamshedpur 22 Kg 22.48N 86.11 E
Jamsk 20 Ke 59.37N 154.10 E
Jämtland [2] 7 De 63.00N 14.40 E
Jämtland 8 Fa 63.25N 14.05 E
Janā 24 Mi 27.22N 49.54 E
Jana 21 Pb 71.31N 136.32 E
Janakpur 25 Hc 26.42N 85.55 E
Janaucu, Ilha- 54 Hc 0.30N 50.10W
Janaul 17 Gh 56.16N 54.59 E
Janda, Laguna de la- 13 Gh 36.15N 5.51W
Jandaia 55 Gc 17.06S 50.07W
Jandaq 24 Pe 34.02N 54.26 E
Jandiatuba, Rio- 54 Ed 3.28S 68.42W
Jandowae 59 Ke 26.47S 151.06 E
Jandula 13 Hf 38.03N 4.06W
Jane Peak 62 Cf 45.20S 168.19 E
Janesville 43 Jc 42.41N 89.01W
Jangada 55 Db 15.14S 56.29W
Jangada, Rio- 55 Db 15.12S 56.24W
Jangao Shan 27 Gf 25.31N 98.08 E
Jange 27 Ie 31.59N 105.28 E
Jangijer 18 Gd 40.18N 68.50 E
Jangijul 19 Gg 41.07N 69.03 E
Jangirabad 18 Ed 40.03N 65.59 E
Jango 55 Ee 20.27S 55.29W
Jangxi Sheng (Chiang-hsi Sheng)=Kiangsi (EN) [2] 27 Kf 28.00N 116.00 E
Jangy-Bazar 18 Hd 41.40N 70.52 E
Janikowo 10 Od 52.45N 18.07 E
Janīn 24 Ff 32.28N 35.18 E
Janisjarvi, Ozero- 7 He 62.00N 31.00 E
Janja 14 Nf 44.40N 19.19 E
Jan Mayen 5 Fa 71.00N 8.30W
Jan Mayen Ridge (EN) 5 Fb 69.00N 8.00W
Jano-Indigirskaja Nizmennost 20 Ib 71.00N 139.30 E
Janos 47 Cb 30.56N 108.08W
Jánoshalma 10 Pj 46.18N 19.20 E
Jánosháza 10 Ni 47.07N 17.10 E
Janów Lubelski 10 Sf 50.43N 22.24 E
Janów Podlaski 10 Td 52.11N 23.11 E
Jansenville 37 Cf 32.56S 24.40 E
Jansha Jang 21 Mg 28.46N 104.38 E
Janski Zaliv 21 Pb 72.00N 136.00 E
Jantarny 8 Hj 54.53N 19.55 E
Jantra 15 If 43.38N 25.34 E
Januária 54 Jg 15.29S 44.22W
Janūbīyah, Aṣ Ṣaḥrā' al-=Southern Desert (EN) 30 Jf 24.00N 30.00 E
Janykurgan 19 Gg 43.55N 67.14 E
Janzhang Ansha 27 Ke 9.30N 116.59 E
Japan (EN) 21 Pf 35.00N 135.00 E
Japan (EN)=Nippon [1] 22 Pf 38.00N 137.00 E
Japan, Sea of- (EN)=Japonskoje More 21 Pf 40.00N 134.00 E
Japan, Sea of- (EN)=Nippon Kai 21 Pf 40.00N 134.00 E
Japan, Sea of- (EN)=Tong-Hae 21 Pf 40.00N 134.00 E
Japan Basin (EN) 27 Nc 40.00N 135.00 E
Japan Trench (EN) 3 If 37.00N 143.00 E
Japiim 54 De 7.37S 72.54W
Japonskoje More=Japan, Sea of- (EN) 21 Pf 40.00N 134.00 E
Jäppilä 8 Lb 62.23N 27.26 E
Japtiksale 17 Pb 69.25N 72.29 E
Japurá 54 Ed 1.24S 69.25W
Japurá, Rio- 52 Jf 3.08S 64.46W
Jaqué 49 Hj 7.31N 78.10W
Jaquet, Point- 51g Ba 15.38N 61.26W
Jaquirana 55 Gi 28.54S 50.23W
Jar 7 Mg 58.17N 52.06 E
Jarabub Oasis (EN)=Jaghbūb, Wāḥāt al- 30 Jf 29.41N 24.43 E
Jarābulus 24 Hd 36.49N 38.01 E
Jaraguá [Braz.] 55 Hb 15.45S 49.20W
Jaraguá [Braz.] 55 Hh 26.29S 49.04W
Jaraguá, Serra do- 55 Hh 26.40S 49.15W
Jaraguari 55 Ee 20.09S 54.25W
Jaraiz de la Vera 13 Gd 40.04N 5.45W
Jarama 13 Id 40.02N 3.39W
Jaramillo 56 Gg 47.11S 67.09W
Jarandilla 13 Gd 40.08N 5.39W
Jaransk 19 Ed 57.18N 47.55 E
Jarānwāla 25 Eb 31.20N 73.26 E
Jarash 24 Ff 32.17N 35.54 E
Jarau, Cêrro do- 55 Dj 30.18S 56.32W
Jarbah 30 Ie 33.48N 10.54 E
Järbo 7 Df 60.43N 16.36 E
Jarcevo [R.S.F.S.R.] 16 Hb 55.05N 32.45 E
Jarcevo [R.S.F.S.R.] 20 Ed 60.15N 90.10 E
Jardāwīyah 24 Jj 25.24N 42.42 E
Jardim 54 Gh 21.28S 56.09W
Jardine River 59 Ib 11.10S 142.30 E
Jardines de la Reina, Archipiélago de los- 47 Id 20.50N 78.55W
Jardinópolis 55 Ie 21.02S 47.46W
Jarega 17 Fe 63.27N 53.31 E
Jaremča 16 De 48.31N 24.33 E
Jarenga 7 Le 62.08N 49.03 E
Jarez de Garcias Salinas 47 Dd 22.39N 103.00W
Järfälla 8 Ge 59.24N 17.50 E
Jargava 15 Lc 46.27N 28.27 E
Jari, Rio- 52 Kf 1.09S 51.54W
Jarīd, Shaṭṭ al- 30 He 33.42N 8.26 E
Jarīr, Wādī- 24 Jj 25.38N 42.30 E
Jarjīs 32 Jc 33.30N 11.07 E
Jarkovo 17 Mh 57.26N 67.05 E
Jarmah 33 Bd 26.32N 13.04 E
Järna 8 Ge 59.06N 17.34 E
Jarnac 11 Fi 45.41N 0.10W
Järnlunden 8 Ff 58.10N 15.40 E
Jarny 11 Le 49.09N 5.53 E
Jarocin 10 Ne 51.59N 17.31 E
Jaroměř 10 Lf 50.21N 15.55 E
Jaroměřice nad Rokytnou 10 Lg 49.06N 15.54 E
Jaroslavl 6 Jd 57.37N 39.52 E
Jaroslavskaja Oblast [3] 19 Dd 57.45N 39.15 E
Jaroslavski 28 Lb 44.10N 132.13 E
Jarosław 10 Sf 50.02N 22.42 E
Järpen 8 Ea 63.21N 13.29 E
Jarrāḥī 24 Mg 30.44N 48.46 E
Jarroto, Ozero- 17 Oc 67.55N 71.40 E
Jar-Sale 20 Cc 66.50N 70.50 E
Jartai 27 Id 39.45N 105.46 E
Jartai Yanchi 27 Id 39.45N 105.40 E
Jarudej 17 Od 65.50N 71.50 E
Jarud Qi (Lubei) 27 Lc 44.30N 120.55 E
Järva-Jaani/Järva-Jani 8 Ke 59.00N 25.49 E
Järva-Jani/Järva-Jaani 8 Ke 59.00N 25.49 E
Järvakandbi/Järvakandi 8 Kf 58.45N 24.44 E
Järvakandi/Järvakandbi 8 Kf 58.45N 24.44 E
Järvenpää 7 Ff 60.28N 25.06 E
Jarvis Island 57 Ke 0.23S 160.01W
Järvsö 7 Df 61.43N 16.10 E
Jaščera 8 Ne 59.05N 30.00 E
Jaselda 16 Ec 52.07N 26.29 E
Jasień 10 Le 51.46N 15.01 E
Jasikan 34 Fd 7.24N 0.28 E
Jasinja 10 Uh 48.14N 24.31 E
Jasinovataja 16 Je 48.05N 37.57 E
Jasiołka 10 Rg 49.47N 21.30 E
Jasīra 35 He 1.57N 45.16 E
Jasīred Mayd 35 Hc 11.12N 47.14 E
Jāsk 23 Id 25.38N 57.46 E
Jaškul 16 Nf 46.17N 45.10 E
Jaškul 16 Nf 46.11N 45.17 E
Jasło 10 Rg 49.45N 21.29 E
Jasmund 10 Jb 54.32N 13.35 E
Jasnogorsk 16 Jb 54.29N 37.42 E
Jasny [R.S.F.S.R.] 19 Fe 51.01N 59.59 E
Jasny [R.S.F.S.R.] 20 Hf 53.18N 128.03 E
Jason Islands 56 Hh 51.00S 61.00W
Jasper [Alta.-Can.] 39 Hd 52.53N 118.05W
Jasper [Al.-U.S.] 43 Je 33.50N 87.17W
Jasper [Fl.-U.S.] 44 Fj 30.31N 82.57W
Jasper [In.-U.S.] 44 Df 38.24N 86.56W
Jasper [Tn.-U.S.] 44 Eh 35.04N 85.38W
Jasper [Tx.-U.S.] 45 Jk 30.55N 93.59W
Jasper Seamount (EN) 38 Gf 30.32N 122.42W
Jaşşān 24 Kf 32.58N 45.53 E
Jastrebarsko 14 Je 45.40N 15.39 E
Jastrowie 10 Mc 53.26N 16.49 E
Jastrzebie Zdrój 10 Og 49.58N 18.34 E
Jászapáti 10 Qi 47.31N 20.09 E
Jászárokszállás 10 Pi 47.38N 19.59 E
Jászberény 10 Pi 47.30N 19.55 E
Jászság 10 Pi 47.25N 20.00 E
Jat, Uad el- 30 Ff 26.47N 13.03W
Jatai 53 Kg 17.53S 51.43W
Jatapu, Rio- 54 Gd 2.30S 58.17W
Játiva/Xátiva 13 Lf 38.59N 0.31W
Jatobá, Rio- 55 Ea 12.23S 54.07W
Jaú 56 Kb 22.18S 48.33W
Jaú, Rio- 54 Fd 1.55S 61.25W
Jaua, Cerro- 54 Fc 4.48N 64.26W
Jauaperi, Rio- 54 Fd 1.26S 61.35W
Jauja 54 Cf 11.48S 75.30W
Jaumave 48 Jf 23.25N 99.23W
Jaunanna 8 Lg 57.13N 27.10 E
Jaunelgava/Jaunjelgava 7 Fh 56.37N 25.06 E
Jaunfeld 14 Id 46.35N 14.45 E
Jaungulbene 8 Lh 57.00N 26.42 E
Jaunjelgava/Jaunelgava 7 Fh 56.37N 25.06 E
Jaunpiebalga 8 Lg 57.05N 26.03 E
Jaunpur 25 Gc 25.44N 82.41 E
Jauru 55 Ed 18.35S 54.17W
Jauru, Rio- [Braz.] 54 Hg 18.40S 54.36W
Jauru, Rio- [Braz.] 55 Dc 16.22S 57.46W
Java (EN)=Jawa 21 Mj 7.20S 110.00 E
Javalambre 13 Ld 40.06N 1.00W
Javalambre, Sierra de- 13 Ld 40.05N 1.00W
Javan 18 Ge 38.19N 69.01 E
Javānrūd 24 Le 34.48N 46.30 E
Javari, Rio- 52 If 4.21S 70.02W
Java Sea (EN)=Jawa, Laut- 21 Mj 5.00S 110.00 E
Java Trench (EN) 3 Hk 10.30S 110.00 E
Jávea 13 Mf 38.47N 0.10 E
Javier 13 Kb 42.36N 1.13W
Javor 14 Mf 44.07N 18.59 E
Javorie 10 Ph 48.27N 19.18 E
Javornik 10 Jh 48.10N 13.35 E
Javorníky 10 Og 49.20N 18.20 E
Javorov 16 Cd 50.00N 23.27 E
Javorová skála 10 Kg 49.31N 14.30 E
Jävre 7 Ed 65.09N 21.29 E
Jawa=Java (EN) 21 Mj 7.20S 110.00 E
Jawa, Laut-=Java Sea (EN) 21 Mj 5.00S 110.00 E
Jawa Barat [3] 26 Eh 7.00S 107.00 E
Jawa Tengah [3] 26 Eh 7.30S 110.00 E
Jawa Timur [3] 26 Fh 8.00S 113.00 E
Jawf, Wādī- 33 If 15.50N 45.30 E
Jawor 10 Me 51.03N 16.11 E
Jaworzno 10 Pf 50.13N 19.15 E
Jaya, Puncak- 57 Ee 4.10S 137.00 E
Jayapura 58 Fe 2.32S 140.42 E
Jayawijaya, Pegunungan- 26 Kg 4.30S 139.30 E
Jāyezān 24 Mg 30.50N 49.52 E
Jaypur 25 He 18.51N 82.35 E
Jazāyer va Banāder-e Khalīj-e Fārs va Daryā-ye Omān → Hormozgān 23 Id 27.30N 56.00 E
Jaz Mūriān, Hāmūn-e- 23 Id 27.20N 58.55 E
Jazva 17 Hf 60.23N 56.50 E
Jazvān 24 Md 36.58N 48.40 E
Jazykovo 7 Li 54.20N 47.22 E
Jazzīn 24 Ff 33.32N 35.34 E
Jdiouia 13 Mi 35.56N 0.50 E
Jeannetty, Ostrov- 20 Ka 76.45N 158.25 E
Jean-Rabel 49 Kd 19.52N 73.11W
Jebala 13 Gi 35.25N 5.30W
Jebal Bārez, Kūh-e- 23 Id 28.30N 58.20 E
Jebba 34 Fd 9.08N 4.50 E
Jebel 15 Ed 45.33N 21.14 E
Jebha 13 Hi 35.13N 4.40W
Jedincy 16 Ee 48.06N 27.19 E
Jedisa 16 Nh 42.32N 44.14 E
Jędrzejów 10 Qf 50.39N 20.18 E
Jeetze 10 Hc 53.09N 11.04 E
Jefferson 45 Ie 42.01N 94.23W
Jefferson, Mount- [Nv.-U.S.] 43 Dd 38.46N 116.55W
Jefferson, Mount- [Or.-U.S.] 46 Ed 44.40N 121.47W
Jefferson City 39 Jf 38.34N 92.10W
Jefferson River 46 Jd 45.56N 111.30W
Jeffersonville 44 Ef 38.17N 85.44W
Jef-Jef el Kebir 35 Ca 20.30N 21.25 E
Jefremov 16 Jc 53.11N 38.07 E
Jega 34 Fc 12.13N 4.23 E
Jegersfontein 37 De 29.44S 25.29 E
Jegorjevsk 7 Ji 55.25N 39.07 E
Jegorlyk 16 Lf 46.34N 41.52 E
Jegorlykskaja 16 Lf 46.34N 40.44 E
Jehegnadzor 16 Nj 39.47N 45.18 E
Jeja 16 Kf 46.39N 38.36 E
Jejsk 19 Df 46.40N 38.15 E
Jejuí Guazú, Río- 55 Dg 24.13S 57.09W
Jēkabpils/Jekabpils 19 Cd 56.30N 25.59 E
Jekaterinovka 16 Nc 52.04N 44.30 E
Jekkevarre 7 Eb 69.28N 20.00 E
Jelabuga 19 Fd 55.48N 52.05 E
Jelai 26 Fg 2.59S 110.45 E
Jelan 16 Md 50.57N 43.43 E
Jelancy 20 Ff 52.44N 106.27 E
Jelanec 16 Gf 47.42N 31.50 E
Jelcz 10 Ne 51.01N 17.18 E
Jelec 6 Je 52.37N 38.30 E
Jeleckij 17 Lc 67.03N 64.15 E
Jelenia Góra 10 Lf 50.55N 15.46 E
Jelenia Góra [2] 10 Lf 50.55N 15.45 E
Jelgava 19 Cd 56.39N 23.41 E
Jelica 15 Df 43.47N 20.20 E
Jelin vrh 15 Cf 43.02N 19.27 E
Jelizavety, Mys- 5 Qd 54.30N 142.40 E
Jelizovo [Bye.-U.S.S.R.] 16 Fc 53.24N 29.00 E
Jelizovo [R.S.F.S.R.] 20 Kf 53.06N 158.20 E
Jelling 8 Ci 55.45N 9.26 E
Jelnja 16 Hb 54.35N 33.12 E
Jeloguj 20 Dd 63.10N 87.45 E
Jelow Gīr 24 Lf 32.58N 47.48 E
Jeløy 8 De 58.30N 10.40 E
Jelsk 16 Fd 51.49N 29.13 E
Jelva 17 Ee 63.05N 50.50 E
Jemaja, Pulau- 26 Ef 2.55N 105.45 E
Jemanželinsk 19 Ge 54.45N 61.20 E
Jember 26 Fh 8.10S 113.42 E
Jemca 7 Je 63.32N 41.56 E
Jemca 7 Je 63.04N 40.18 E
Jemeppe-sur-Sambre 12 Gd 50.28N 4.40 E
Jeminay 27 Eb 47.28N 85.48 E
Jemnice 10 Lg 49.01N 15.35 E
Jena 10 Hf 50.56N 11.35 E
Jenakijevo 16 Ke 48.12N 38.18 E
Jenašimski Polkan, Gora- 20 Ee 59.50N 92.45 E
Jendyr 17 Mf 61.38N 67.20 E
Jeneponto 26 Gh 5.41S 119.42 E
Jenisej=Yenisey (EN) 21 Kb 71.50N 82.40 E
Jenisejsk 20 Ee 58.27N 92.10 E
Jenisejski Krjaž=Yenisey Ridge (EN) 21 Ld 59.00N 92.30 E
Jenisejski Zaliv=Yenisey Bay (EN) 20 Db 72.00N 81.00 E
Jennersdorf 14 Kd 46.56N 16.08 E
Jennings 45 Jk 30.13N 92.39W
Jenny Lind 42 Hc 68.50N 101.30W
Jenny Point 51g Bb 15.28N 61.15W
Jensen 46 Kf 40.22N 109.17W
Jens Munk 42 Jc 69.40N 79.40W
Jequié 53 Lg 13.51S 40.05W
Jequitai 55 Jc 17.15S 44.28W
Jequitai, Rio 55 Jc 17.04S 44.50W
Jequitinhonha, Rio- 52 Mg 15.51S 38.53W
Jerada 32 Gc 34.19N 2.09W
Jeralijev 19 Fg 43.12N 51.43 E
Jerbogačen 20 Fd 61.15N 107.57 E
Jérémie 47 Je 18.39N 74.08W
Jeremoabo 54 Kf 10.04S 38.21W
Jerer 35 Gd 7.40N 43.48 E
Jerevan 6 Kg 40.11N 44.30 E
Jerez, Punta- 48 Kf 22.54N 97.46W
Jerez de la Frontera 13 Fh 36.41N 6.08W
Jerez de los Caballeros 13 Ff 38.19N 6.46W
Jergeni 5 Kf 47.00N 44.00 E
Jericho 59 Jd 23.36S 146.08 E
Jermak 19 He 52.02N 76.55 E
Jermakovskoje 20 Ef 53.16N 92.24 E
Jermentau 19 He 51.38N 73.10 E
Jermolajevo 17 Gj 52.43N 55.48 E
Jeroaquara 55 Gb 15.23S 50.25W
Jerofej Pavlovič 20 Hf 53.58N 121.57 E
Jerome 46 He 42.43N 114.31W
Jersa 17 Fc 66.19N 52.32 E
Jersey 9 Kl 49.15N 2.10W
Jersey City 43 Mc 40.44N 74.04W
Jerseyville 45 Kg 39.07N 90.20W
Jeršov 19 Ee 51.20N 48.17 E
Jertarski 17 Lh 56.47N 64.25 E
Jerte 13 Fe 39.58N 6.17W
Jerusalem (EN)=Yerushalayim 22 Ff 31.46N 35.14 E
Jeruslan 16 Od 50.20N 46.25 E
Jervis Bay 59 Kg 35.05S 150.44 E
Jerzu 14 Dk 39.47N 9.31 E
Jesberg 12 Lc 51.00N 9.09 E
Jesenice [Yugo.] 14 Jf 44.14N 15.34 E
Jesenice [Yugo.] 14 Id 46.27N 14.04 E
Jeseník 10 Nf 50.14N 17.12 E
Jesi 14 Hg 43.31N 13.14 E
Jesil 19 Ge 51.58N 66.24 E
Jeskianhor, Kanal- 18 Fe 39.15N 66.00 E
Jessej 20 Fc 68.29N 102.10 E
Jessentuki 16 Mg 44.03N 42.51 E
Jessheim 7 Cf 60.09N 11.11 E
Jessore 25 Hd 23.10N 89.13 E
Ještěd 10 Kf 50.42N 14.59 E
Jestro, Wabe- 30 Lh 4.11N 42.09 E
Jesup 43 Ke 31.36N 81.53W
Jesús Carranza 48 Li 17.26N 95.02W
Jesús María 56 Hd 30.59S 64.06W
Jesús María, Boca de- 48 Ke 24.29N 97.40W
Jesús María, Rio- 48 Gg 21.55N 104.30W
Jetmore 45 Gg 38.03N 99.54W
Jever 10 Dc 53.35N 7.54 E
Jevgenjevka 18 Kc 43.27N 77.40 E
Jevišovka 10 Mh 48.52N 16.36 E
Jevlah 19 Eg 40.35N 47.10 E
Jevnaker 7 Cf 60.15N 10.28 E
Jevpatorija 19 Df 45.12N 33.18 E
Jevrejskaja Avtonomnaja Oblast 20 Ig 48.30N 132.00 E
Jeyḥūn 24 Pi 27.16N 55.12 E
Jeypore → Jaypur 25 He 18.51N 82.35 E
Jezercës 5 Hg 42.26N 19.49 E
Jezero 14 Lf 44.21N 17.10 E
Jeziorak, Jezioro- 10 Pc 53.50N 19.35 E
Jeziorany 10 Qc 53.58N 20.46 E
Jeziorka 10 Rd 52.10N 21.06 E
Jhang Sadar 25 Eb 31.16N 72.19 E
Jhānsi 22 Jg 25.26N 78.35 E
Jhelum 25 Eb 32.56N 73.44 E
Jhelum 21 Jf 31.12N 72.08 E
Jiaji → Qionghai 27 Jh 19.25N 110.28 E
Jialing Jiang 21 Mg 29.34N 106.35 E
Jiamusi 22 Pe 46.49N 130.21 E
Ji'an [China] 27 Mc 41.08N 126.10 E
Ji'an [China] 22 Ng 27.12N 114.59 E
Jianchang 28 Ed 40.49N 119.46 E
Jianchuan 27 Gf 26.32N 99.53 E
Jiande (Baisha) 27 Kf 29.31N 119.17 E
Jiang'an 27 If 28.40N 105.07 E
Jiangao Shan 27 Gf 25.31N 98.08 E
Jiangbiancun 27 Kf 27.13N 115.57 E
Jiangcheng 27 Hg 22.37N 101.48 E
Jiangdu (Xiannümiao) 28 Eh 32.30N 119.33 E
Jianghua (Shuikou) 27 Jg 24.58N 111.56 E
Jiangjin 27 If 29.15N 106.18 E
Jiangle 27 Kf 26.48N 117.29 E
Jiangling (Jingzhou) 27 Je 30.21N 112.10 E
Jiangmen 27 Jg 22.35N 113.02 E
Jiangpu 28 Eh 32.03N 118.37 E
Jiangshan 28 Ej 28.45N 118.37 E
Jiangsu Sheng (Chiang-su Sheng)=Kiangsu (EN) [2] 27 Ke 33.00N 120.00 E
Jiangyou (Zhongba) 27 He 31.48N 104.39 E
Jianhu 28 Eh 33.28N 119.47 E
Jianli 27 Jf 29.50N 112.55 E
Jian'ou 27 Kf 27.08N 118.20 E
Jianping (Yebaishou) 27 Kc 41.55N 119.37 E
Jianshi 27 Ie 30.32N 109.43 E
Jianshui 27 Hg 23.39N 102.46 E
Jianyang 27 Kf 27.23N 118.03 E
Jiaocheng 27 Jd 37.32N 112.09 E
Jiaoding Shan 27 Lc 41.11N 120.01 E
Jiaohe [China] 27 Mc 43.43N 127.20 E
Jiaohe [China] 28 De 38.01N 116.17 E
Jiaolai He [China] 28 Ef 37.07N 119.35 E
Jiaolai He [China] 28 Fc 43.02N 120.48 E
Jiaoliu He 28 Gb 45.21N 122.48 E
Jiaonan (Wanggezhuang) 28 Eg 35.53N 119.58 E

Index Symbols

- [1] Independent Nation
- [2] State, Region
- [3] District, County
- [4] Municipality
- [5] Colony, Dependency
- Continent
- Physical Region
- Historical or Cultural Region
- Mount, Mountain
- Volcano
- Hill
- Mountains, Mountain Range
- Hills, Escarpment
- Plateau, Upland
- Pass, Gap
- Plain, Lowland
- Delta
- Salt Flat
- Valley, Canyon
- Crater, Cave
- Karst Features
- Depression
- Polder
- Desert, Dunes
- Forest, Woods
- Heath, Steppe
- Oasis
- Cape, Point
- Coast, Beach
- Cliff
- Peninsula
- Isthmus
- Sandbank
- Island
- Atoll
- Rock, Reef
- Islands, Archipelago
- Rocks, Reefs
- Coral Reef
- Well, Spring
- Geyser
- River, Stream
- Waterfall Rapids
- River Mouth, Estuary
- Lake
- Salt Lake
- Intermittent Lake
- Reservoir
- Swamp, Pond
- Canal
- Glacier
- Ice Shelf, Pack Ice
- Ocean
- Sea
- Gulf, Bay
- Strait, Fjord
- Lagoon
- Bank
- Seamount
- Tablemount
- Ridge
- Shelf
- Basin
- Escarpment, Sea Scarp
- Fracture
- Trench, Abyss
- National Park, Reserve
- Point of Interest
- Recreation Site
- Cave, Cavern
- Historic Site
- Ruins
- Wall, Walls
- Church, Abbey
- Temple
- Scientific Station
- Airport
- Port
- Lighthouse
- Mine
- Tunnel
- Dam, Bridge

Jiaoxian	27	Kd	36.20N	120.00 E
Jiaozhou-Wan	28	Ff	36.10N	120.15 E
Jiaozuo	22	Nf	35.15N	113.18 E
Jiashan	28	Fi	30.51N	120.54 E
Jiashan (Mingguang)	28	Dh	32.47N	118.00 E
Jiashi/Payzawat	27	Cd	39.29N	76.39 E
Jiawang	28	Dg	34.27N	117.26 E
Jiaxian	28	Bh	33.58N	113.13 E
Jiaxing	27	Le	30.44N	120.46 E
Jiayin (Chaoyang)	27	Nb	48.52N	130.21 E
Jiayu	27	Jf	30.00N	113.57 E
Jiayuguan	27	Gd	39.49N	98.18 E
Jibalei	35	Ic	10.07N	50.47 E
Jibão, Serra do-	55	Jb	14.48S	45.15W
Jibiya	34	Gc	13.06N	7.14 E
Jibou	15	Gb	47.16N	23.15 E
Jicarón, Isla-	49	Gj	7.16N	81.47W
Jičín	10	Lf	50.26N	15.22 E
Jiddah	22	Fg	21.29N	39.12 E
Jiddat al Ḩarāsīs	23	Ie	20.05N	56.00 E
Jiehu → Yinan	28	Eg	35.33N	118.27 E
Jieshou	28	Ch	33.17N	115.22 E
Jiesjjavrre	7	Fb	69.40N	24.12 E
Jiexiu	27	Jd	37.00N	112.00 E
Jieyang	27	Kg	23.32N	116.25 E
Jieznas/Eznas	8	Kj	54.34N	24.17 E
Jifn, Wādī al-	24	Jj	25.48N	42.15 E
Jiftūn, Jazā'ir-	24	Ei	27.13N	33.56 E
Jigley	35	He	4.25N	45.22 E
Jiguaní	49	Ic	20.22N	76.26W
Jigüey, Bahía de-	49	Hb	22.08N	78.05W
Jigzhi	27	He	33.28N	101.29 E
Jihlava	10	Mh	48.55N	16.37 E
Jihlava	10	Lg	49.24N	15.34 E
Jihlavské vrchy	10	Lg	49.15N	15.20 E
Jihočeský kraj [3]	10	Kg	49.05N	14.30 E
Jihomoravský kraj [3]	10	Mg	49.10N	16.40 E
Jijel	32	Ib	36.48N	5.46 E
Jijel [3]	32	Ib	36.45N	5.45 E
Jijia	15	Lc	46.54N	28.05 E
Jijiga	35	Gd	9.21N	42.48 E
Jijona	13	Lf	38.32N	0.30W
Jikharrah	33	Dd	29.17N	21.38 E
Jilava	15	Je	44.20N	26.05 E
Jilf al Kabīr, Haḑabat al-	33	Ee	23.30N	26.00 E
Jilib	31	Lh	0.29N	42.47 E
Jilin	27	Mc	43.51N	126.33 E
Jilin Sheng (Chi-lin Sheng) =Kirin (EN) [2]	27	Mc	43.00N	126.00 E
Jiliu He	27	La	52.02N	120.41 E
Jiloca	13	Kc	41.21N	1.39W
Jima=Jimma (EN)	31	Kh	7.39N	36.49 E
Jimāl, Wādī-	24	Fj	24.40N	35.06 E
Jimani	49	Ld	18.28N	71.51W
Jimbe	36	De	11.05S	24.00 E
Jimbolia	15	Dd	45.48N	20.43 E
Jimena	13	Ig	37.50N	3.28W
Jimena de la Frontera	13	Gh	36.26N	5.27W
Jiménez	47	Dc	27.08N	104.55W
Jiménez del Teul	48	Gf	23.10N	104.05W
Jimma (EN)=Jima	31	Kh	7.39N	36.49 E
Jimo	28	Ff	36.24N	120.27 E
Jimsar	27	Ec	43.59N	89.04 E
Jimulco	48	He	25.20N	103.10W
Jināh	24	Dj	25.20N	30.31 E
Jinan=Tsinan (EN)	22	Nf	36.35N	117.00 E
Jincheng [China]	27	Jd	35.32N	112.53 E
Jincheng [China]	28	Fd	41.12N	121.25 E
Jinchuan /Quqên	27	He	31.02N	102.02 E
Jind	25	Fc	29.19N	76.19 E
Jindřichův Hradec	10	Kg	49.09N	15.00 E
Jinfo Shan	27	If	29.01N	107.14 E
Jing/Jinghe	27	Dc	44.39N	82.50 E
Jing'an	28	Cj	28.51N	115.21 E
Jingbian (Zhangjiapan)	27	Id	37.32N	108.45 E
Jingde	28	Ei	30.18N	118.30 E
Jingdezhen	22	Ng	29.18N	117.18 E
Jingfeng → Hexigten Qi	27	Kc	43.15N	117.31 E
Jinggang Shan	27	Jf	26.42N	114.07 E
Jinggu	27	Hg	23.28N	100.39 E
Jinghai	28	De	38.57N	116.56 E
Jinghe/Jing	27	Dc	44.39N	82.50 E
Jinghong (Yunjinghong)	27	Hg	21.59N	100.48 E
Jinghong Dao	27	Je	9.45N	114.28 E
Jingjiang	28	Fh	32.01N	120.15 E
Jingle	28	Ae	38.22N	111.56 E
Jingmen	27	Je	31.00N	112.11 E
Jingning	27	Id	35.30N	105.45 E
Jingping → Pinglu	28	Be	39.32N	112.14 E
Jingpo Hu	28	Jc	43.50N	128.53 E
Jingshan	28	Bi	31.04N	113.08 E
Jingtai	27	Hd	37.10N	104.08 E
Jingxian [China]	27	If	26.40N	109.37 E
Jingxian [China]	27	Ke	30.41N	118.29 E
Jingxing (Weishui)	28	Ce	38.03N	114.09 E
Jingyu	28	Ic	42.25N	126.48 E
Jingyuan	27	Hd	36.35N	104.40 E
Jingzhi	28	Ef	36.18N	119.22 E
Jingzhou→Jiangling	27	Je	30.21N	112.10 E
Jinhu (Licheng)	28	Eh	33.01N	119.01 E
Jinhua	27	Kf	29.09N	119.38 E
Jining [China]	22	Nf	37.26N	116.36 E
Jining [China]	22	Ne	41.02N	113.07 E
Jinja	31	Kh	0.26N	33.13 E
Jin Jiang	28	Cj	28.23N	115.48 E
Jinkou	28	Ci	30.20N	114.07 E
Jinotega [3]	49	Eg	14.00N	85.25W
Jinotega	47	Gf	13.06N	86.00W
Jinotepe	47	Gf	11.51N	86.12W
Jinping	27	Hg	22.45N	103.15 E
Jinsha	27	If	27.18N	106.16 E
Jinsha→Nantong	28	Fh	32.06N	120.52 E
Jinshan	28	Fi	30.54N	121.09 E
Jinshan → Harqin Qi	28	Ed	41.57N	118.40 E
Jinshi	28	Aj	29.03N	111.52 E
Jinta	27	Gc	40.00N	99.00 E
Jintan	28	Ei	31.45N	119.34 E
Jinxi	27	Lc	40.46N	120.50 E
Jinxian [China]	27	Ld	39.06N	121.44 E
Jinxian [China]	28	Dj	28.21N	116.16 E
Jinxiang	28	Dg	35.04N	116.19 E
Jinyang	27	Hf	27.39N	103.12 E
Jinyun	28	Fj	28.39N	120.05 E
Jinzhai (Meishan)	28	Ci	31.40N	115.52 E
Jinzhou	22	Oe	41.09N	121.08 E
Jinzū-Gawa	29	Ec	36.45N	137.13 E
Jiparaná, Rio-	52	Jf	8.03S	62.52W
Jipijapa	54	Bd	1.22S	80.34W
Jiquilisco	49	Cg	13.19N	88.35W
Jiquilisco, Bahia de-	49	Cg	13.10N	88.28W
Jirjā	33	Fd	26.20N	31.53 E
Jishou	27	If	28.18N	109.43 E
Jishu	28	Ib	44.16N	126.50 E
Jisr ash Shughur	24	Ge	35.48N	36.19 E
Jiu	15	Gd	43.47N	23.48 E
Jiucai Ling	27	Jf	25.33N	111.18 E
Jiucheng → Wucheng	28	Df	37.12N	116.04 E
Jiujiang	22	Ng	29.39N	116.00 E
Jiuling Shan	27	Jf	28.55N	114.50 E
Jiulong/Gyaisi	27	Hf	28.58N	101.33 E
Jiuquan (Suzhou)	22	Lf	39.46N	98.34 E
Jiurongcheng	28	Gf	37.22N	122.33 E
Jiutai	27	Mc	44.10N	125.50 E
Jiwani, Rās-	25	Cc	25.01N	61.44 E
Jixi [China]	28	Ei	30.04N	118.36 E
Jixi [China]	22	Pe	45.15N	130.55 E
Jixian [China]	28	Cg	35.23N	114.04 E
Jixian [China]	28	Cf	37.34N	115.34 E
Jixian [China]	28	Dd	40.03N	117.24 E
Jiyang	28	Df	36.59N	117.11 E
Jiyuan	28	Bg	35.06N	112.35 E
Jiyun He	28	De	39.05N	117.45 E
Jiz, Wādī al-	35	Ib	16.12N	52.14 E
Jīzān	22	Gh	16.54N	42.32 E
Jize	28	Cf	36.54N	114.52 E
Jizera	10	Kf	50.10N	14.43 E
Jizerské Hory	10	Lf	50.50N	15.13 E
Jizl, Wādī al-	24	Hj	25.39N	38.25 E
Jizō-Zaki	28	Lg	35.33N	133.18 E
Jmbe	36	De	10.20S	16.40 E
Jnchengjiang → Hechi	27	Ig	24.44N	108.02 E
Joaçaba	55	Gh	27.10S	51.30W
Joal-Fadiout	34	Bc	14.10N	16.51W
João Câmara	54	Ke	5.32S	35.48W
João Monlevade	55	Kd	19.50S	43.08W
João Pessoa	53	Mf	7.07S	34.52W
João Pinheiro	54	Ig	17.45S	46.10W
Joaquin V. González	56	Hb	25.00S	64.11W
Jobado	49	Ic	20.54N	77.17W
Jódar	13	Ig	37.50N	3.21W
Jodhpur	22	Jg	26.17N	73.02 E
Jodoigne/Geldenaken	12	Gd	50.43N	4.52 E
Joensuu	6	Ic	62.36N	29.46 E
Joerg Plateau	66	Qf	75.00S	69.30W
Joes Hill	64g	Bb	1.48N	157.19W
Jōetsu	27	Od	37.06N	138.15 E
Joeuf	12	He	49.14N	6.01 E
Jôf di Montasio	14	Hd	46.26N	13.26 E
Joffre, Mount-	46	Ha	50.32N	115.13W
Jogbani	25	Hc	26.25N	87.15 E
Jõgeva/Jygeva	7	Gg	58.46N	26.26 E
Joghatāy	24	Qd	36.36N	57.01 E
Joghatāy, Kūh-e-	24	Qd	36.30N	57.00 E
Jōhana	29	Ec	36.31N	136.54 E
Johannesburg	31	Jk	26.15S	28.00 E
Jōhen	29	Ce	32.57N	132.35 E
John Day	46	Fd	44.25N	118.57W
John Day River	43	Cb	45.44N	120.39W
John H. Kerr Reservoir	44	Hg	36.31N	78.18W
John Martin Reservoir	45	Eg	38.05N	103.02W
John o' Groat's	9	Jc	58.38N	3.05W
Johnson	45	Fh	37.34N	101.45W
Johnson, Pico de-	48	Cc	29.13N	112.07W
Johnson City [Tn.-U.S.]	43	Kd	36.19N	82.21W
Johnson City [Tx.-U.S.]	45	Gk	30.17N	98.25W
Johnsons Crossing	42	Ed	60.29N	133.17W
Johnsons Point	51d	Bb	17.02N	61.53W
Johnstone, Lake-	59	Ef	32.25S	120.40 E
Johnstone Strait	46	Ca	50.25N	126.00W
Johnston Island	57	Kc	17.00N	168.30W
Johnston Island [5]	58	Kc	17.00N	168.30W
Johnstown [N.Y.-U.S.]	44	Jd	43.01N	74.22W
Johnstown [Pa.-U.S.]	43	Lc	40.20N	78.56W
Johor Baharu	22	Mi	1.28N	103.45 E
Joia	55	Ei	28.39S	54.08W
Joigny	11	Jg	47.59N	3.24 E
Joinvile	53	Lh	26.18S	48.50W
Joinville	11	Lf	48.27N	5.08 E
Joinville Island	66	Re	63.15S	55.45W
Jokau	35	Ed	8.24N	33.49 E
Jokela	8	Kd	60.33N	24.59 E
Jokelbugten	41	Kc	78.25N	19.00W
Jokioinen	8	Jd	60.49N	23.28 E
Jokkmokk	7	Ec	66.36N	19.51 E
Jøkuleggi	8	Cc	61.03N	8.12 E
Jolfā	24	Kc	38.57N	45.38 E
Joliet	43	Jc	41.32N	88.05W
Joliette	42	Kg	46.01N	73.26W
Jolo	26	He	6.00N	121.00 E
Jolo Group	21	Oi	6.00N	121.09 E
Jølstravatnet	8	Bc	61.30N	6.15 E
Jomala	8	Hd	60.09N	19.58 E
Jombang	26	Fh	7.33S	112.14 E
Jomda	27	Ge	31.37N	98.20 E
Jönåker	8	Gf	58.44N	16.40 E
Jonava/Ionava	7	Fi	55.05N	24.17 E
Jonê	27	He	34.35N	103.32 E
Jones Bank	9	Fl	49.50N	8.00W
Jonesboro [Ar.-U.S.]	43	Id	35.50N	90.42W
Jonesboro [La.-U.S.]	45	Jj	32.15N	92.43W
Jones Mountains	66	Pf	73.32S	94.00W
Jones Sound	38	Kb	76.00N	85.00W
Jonesville	44	Fg	36.41N	83.06W
Jonglei [3]	35	Ed	7.20N	32.00 E
Jonglei	35	Ed	6.50N	31.18 E
Jonglei, Tur'ah- = Jonglei Canal (EN)	35	Ed	9.22N	31.30 E
Jonglei Canal (EN)=Jonglei, Tur'ah-	35	Ed	9.22N	31.30 E
Joniškėlis/Ioniškelis	8	Ki	56.00N	24.14 E
Joniškis/Ioniškis	7	Fh	56.16N	23.37 E
Jönköping	6	Hd	57.47N	14.11 E
Jönköping [2]	7	Dh	57.30N	14.30 E
Jonquière	42	Kg	48.25N	71.15W
Jonuta	48	Mh	18.05N	92.08W
Jonzac	11	Fi	45.27N	0.26W
Joplin	39	Jf	37.06N	94.31W
Jordan	43	Fb	47.19N	106.55W
Jordan	23	Ec	31.46N	35.33 E
Jordan (EN)=Al Urdun [1]	22	Ff	31.00N	36.00 E
Jordan Valley	46	Ge	42.58N	117.03W
Jordão, Rio-	55	Fg	25.46S	52.07W
Jorhāt	22	Lg	26.45N	94.13 E
Jörn	7	Ed	65.04N	20.02 E
Joroinen	7	Ge	62.11N	27.50 E
Jørpeland	7	Bg	59.01N	6.03 E
Jos	31	Hh	9.55N	8.54 E
José A. Guisasola	55	Bn	38.40S	61.05W
José Battle y Ordóñez	55	Ek	33.28S	55.07W
José Bonifácio	55	He	21.03S	49.41W
José de San Martín	56	Ff	44.02S	70.29W
Joselandia	55	Dc	16.32S	56.12W
José Otávio	55	Ej	31.17S	54.07W
José Pedro Varela	55	Ek	33.27S	54.32W
Joseph, Lake-	44	Hc	45.14N	79.45W
Joseph Bonaparte Gulf	57	Df	14.55S	128.15 E
Josephine Seamount (EN)	5	Eh	36.52N	14.20W
Joseph Lake	42	Kf	52.48N	65.17W
Joshimath	25	Fb	30.34N	79.34 E
Joškar-Ola	6	Kd	56.40N	47.55 E
Jos Plateau	30	Hh	10.00N	9.30 E
Josselin	11	Dg	47.57N	2.33W
Jostedalen	8	Bc	61.35N	7.20 E
Jostedalsbreen	7	Bf	61.40N	7.00 E
Jostefonn	8	Bc	61.26N	6.33 E
Jost Van Dyke	51a	Db	18.28N	64.45W
Jotunheimen	5	Gc	61.40N	8.20 E
Joubertberge	37	Ac	18.45S	13.55 E
Joué-lès-Tours	11	Gg	47.21N	0.40 E
Jouquara, Rio-	55	Db	15.06S	57.06W
Joure, Haskerland-	12	Hb	52.58N	5.47 E
Joutsa	7	Gf	61.44N	26.07 E
Joutseno	7	Gf	61.06N	28.30 E
Jovan, Deli-	15	Fe	44.15N	22.13 E
Jovellanos	49	Gb	22.48N	81.12W
Joviânia	55	Hc	17.49S	49.30W
Jowhar	31	Lh	2.46N	45.32 E
Jow Kār	24	Me	34.26N	48.42 E
Jowzjān [3]	23	Kb	36.30N	66.00 E
Joya, Laguna de la-	48	Mj	15.55N	93.40W
Jreïda	32	Df	18.19N	16.03W
Jrian Jaya [3]	26	Kg	3.55S	138.00 E
Juan Aldama	47	Dd	24.19N	103.21W
Juana Ramírez, Isla-	48	Kg	21.50N	97.40W
Juan Blanquier	55	Cl	35.46S	59.18W
Juancheng	28	Cg	35.33N	115.30 E
Juan de Fuca, Strait of-	38	Ge	48.20N	124.00W
Juan de Nova, Ile-	30	Lj	17.03S	42.45 E
Juan E. Barra	55	Bm	37.48S	60.29W
Juan Fernández, Archipielago-=Juan Fernández, Islands (EN)	52	Ii	33.00S	80.00W
Juan Fernandez Islands (EN)=Juan Fernández, Archipielago-	52	Ii	33.00S	80.00W
Juan G. Bazán	55	Bg	24.33S	60.50W
Juangriego	50	Eg	11.05N	63.57W
Juanjuy	54	Ce	7.11S	76.45W
Juan L. Lacaze	55	Dl	34.26S	57.27W
Juárez [Arg.]	56	Ie	37.40S	59.48W
Juárez [Mex.]	48	Id	27.37N	100.44W
Juárez, Sierra de-	48	Bb	32.00N	115.50W
Juarzohn	34	Dd	5.20N	8.58W
Juàzeirinho	54	Ke	7.04S	36.35W
Juàzeiro	53	Lf	9.25S	40.30W
Juàzeiro do Norte	53	Mf	7.12S	39.20W
Jūbā	31	Kh	4.51N	31.37 E
Juba (EN)=Ganāne, Webi-	30	Lh	0.15S	42.38 E
Juba, Rio-	55	Db	14.59S	57.44W
Jūbāl, Maḑīq-	24	Ei	27.40N	33.55 E
Jubaland (EN)	30	Lh	1.00N	42.00 E
Jubayl [Eg.]	24	Eh	28.12N	33.38 E
Jubayl [Leb.]	24	Fe	34.07N	35.39 E
Jubayt [Sud.]	35	Fb	18.57N	36.50 E
Jubayt [Sud.]	35	Fa	20.59N	36.18 E
Jubbada Dhexe [3]	35	Ge	1.15N	42.30 E
Jubbada Hoose [3]	35	Gf	0.30S	42.00 E
Jubbah	24	Ih	28.02N	40.56 E
Jubilee Lake	59	Fe	29.10S	126.40 E
Juby, Cap-	30	Ff	27.57N	12.55W
Júcar/Xúquer	5	Fh	39.09N	0.14W
Juçara	55	Gb	15.53S	50.51W
Jucaro	49	Hc	21.37N	78.51W
Jüchen	12	Ic	51.06N	6.30 E
Juchipila	48	Hg	21.25N	103.07W
Juchipila, Rio-	48	Hg	21.03N	103.25W
Juchitán de Zaragoza	39	Jh	16.26N	95.01W
Jučjugej	20	Jd	63.20N	142.15 E
Judas, Punta-	49	Ei	9.31N	84.32W
Judayyidat 'Ar'ar	23	Fc	31.22N	41.26 E
Judenburg	14	Ic	47.10N	14.40 E
Juding Shan	27	He	31.30N	104.00 E
Judith Mountains	46	Kc	47.12N	109.15W
Judith River	46	Kc	47.44N	109.38W
Judoma	20	Ie	59.20N	135.03 E
Judomski Hrebet	20	Jd	61.05N	141.30 E
Juegang→Rudong	28	Fh	32.19N	121.11 E
Juelsminde	8	Di	55.43N	10.01 E
Jufrah, Wāḩāt al-=Giofra Oasis (EN)	30	If	29.10N	16.00 E
Jug	5	Kc	60.45N	46.20 E
Jug	17	Hh	57.43N	56.12 E
Jugo-Osetinskaja Avtonomnaja Oblast [3]	19	Eg	42.20N	44.05 E
Jugorski Poluostrov	17	Kb	69.30N	62.30 E
Jugorski Šar, Proliv-	19	Gb	69.45N	60.35 E
Jugoslavija = Yugoslavia (EN) [1]	6	Hg	44.00N	19.00 E
Jugo-Tala	20	Kc	66.03N	151.05 E
Jugydjan	17	Gf	61.42N	54.58 E
Juhaym	24	Kh	29.36N	45.24 E
Juhnov	16	Ib	54.43N	35.12 E
Juhor	15	Ef	43.50N	21.15 E
Juhoslovenská nížina	10	Ph	48.10N	19.40 E
Juhua Dao	28	Fd	40.32N	120.48 E
Juigalpa	49	Eg	12.05N	85.24W
Juina, Rio-	55	Ca	12.36S	58.57W
Juine	11	If	48.32N	2.23 E
Juininha, Rio-	55	Ca	12.55S	59.13W
Juist	10	Cc	53.40N	7.00 E
Juiz de Fora	53	Lh	21.45S	43.20W
Jujuy [2]	56	Gb	23.00S	66.00W
Jukagirskoje Ploskogorje	20	Kc	66.00N	155.30 E
Jukonda	17	Mg	59.38N	67.20 E
Juksejevo	17	Gg	59.52N	54.16 E
Jula	7	Ke	63.48N	44.44 E
Juldybajevo	17	Hj	52.20N	57.52 E
Julesburg	45	Ef	40.59N	102.16W
Juli	54	Eg	16.13S	69.27W
Juliaca	54	Dg	15.30S	70.08W
Julia Creek	59	Id	20.39S	141.45 E
Julian Alps (EN)=Julijske Alpe	14	Hd	46.20N	13.45 E
Juliana Top	54	Gc	3.41N	56.32W
Julianehåb/Qaqortoq	67	Nc	60.50N	46.10W
Jülich	10	Cf	50.56N	6.22 E
Jülicher Borde	12	Id	50.50N	6.30 E
Julijske Alpe=Julian Alps (EN)	14	Hd	46.20N	13.45 E
Julimes	48	Gc	28.25N	105.27W
Júlio de Castilhos	55	Fi	29.14S	53.41W
Jullundur → Jalandhar	22	Jf	31.19N	75.34 E
Julong/New Kowloon	22	Ng	22.20N	114.09 E
Julu	28	Cf	37.13N	115.02 E
Juma	7	Hd	65.05N	33.13 E
Juma He	28	De	39.31N	116.08 E
Jumet, Charleroi-	11	Kd	50.27N	4.26 E
Jumièges	12	Ce	49.26N	0.49 E
Jumilla	13	Kf	38.29N	1.17W
Jümme	12	Ja	53.13N	7.31 E
Junāgadh	25	Ed	21.31N	70.28 E
Junan (Shizilu)	28	Eg	35.10N	118.50 E
Junaynah, Ra's al-	24	Eh	29.01N	33.58 E
Juncal	48	De	24.50N	111.47W
Juncos	51a	Cb	18.13N	65.55W
Junction [Tx.-U.S.]	45	Gk	30.29N	99.46W
Junction [Ut.-U.S.]	46	Ig	38.14N	112.13W
Junction City	43	Hd	39.02N	96.50W
Jundiai	56	Kb	23.11S	46.52W
Jundiai do Sul	55	Gf	23.27S	50.17W
Jundūbah	32	Ib	36.30N	8.45 E
Jundūbah [3]	32	Ib	36.28N	8.41 E
Juneau	39	Fd	57.20N	134.27W
Junee	59	Jf	34.52S	147.35 E
Jungar Qi (Shagedu)	27	Jd	39.37N	110.58 E
Jungfrau	14	Bd	46.32N	7.58 E
Junggar Pendi=Dzungarian Basin	21	Ke	45.00N	88.00 E
Junín [2]	54	Df	11.30S	75.00W
Junín [Arg.]	53	Ji	34.35S	60.57W
Junín [Peru]	54	Cf	11.10S	76.00W
Junín, Lago de-	54	Cf	11.02S	76.05W
Junín de los Andes	56	Fe	39.56S	71.05W
Juniville	12	Ge	49.24N	4.23 E
Jūniyah	24	Ff	33.59N	35.38 E
Junjaha	17	Jc	66.25N	62.00 E
Junlian	27	Hf	28.12N	104.34 E
Junsele	7	De	63.41N	16.54 E
Juntura	46	Fe	43.45N	118.05W
Junxian (Danjiang)	27	Je	32.31N	111.32 E
Juodupé	8	Kh	56.03N	25.44 E
Juojärvi	8	Mb	62.45N	28.35 E
Juoksengi	7	Fc	66.34N	23.51 E
Jupiá, Reprêsa de-	56	Jb	20.47S	51.39W
Juquiá	55	Ig	24.19S	47.38W
Juquiá, Rio-	55	Ig	24.22S	47.49W
Juquiá, Serra do-	55	Gg	25.10S	52.00W
Jur	20	Ie	59.48N	137.29 E
Jur	30	Jh	8.39N	29.18 E
Jura [2]	14	Ac	47.25N	6.15 E
Jura	5	Gf	46.45N	6.30 E
Jura [3]	11	Lh	46.50N	5.50 E
Jura	9	Hf	56.00N	5.50W
Jura/Jūra	7	Fi	55.03N	22.10 E
Jūra/Jura	7	Fi	55.03N	22.10 E
Jura, Sound of-	9	Hf	55.55N	5.22W
Juradó	54	Cb	7.07N	77.46W
Juratiški	8	Kj	54.02N	26.00 E
Jurayb'īt	24	Lh	29.50N	46.03 E
Juraybī'āt	24	Kh	29.08N	45.30 E
Jurbarkas	7	Fi	55.08N	22.47 E
Jurdī, Wādī-	24	Ei	26.33N	32.44 E
Jurga	20	De	55.42N	84.55 E
Jurgamyš	17	Li	55.25N	64.28 E
Juribej	17	Nb	68.55N	69.05 E
Jurien Bay	59	Cf	30.15S	115.00 E
Jurigue, Rio-	55	Ec	16.29S	54.37W
Jurilovca	15	Le	44.46N	28.52 E
Jurja	7	Lg	59.03N	49.20 E
Jurjaha	17	Gc	66.42N	56.00 E
Jurjevec	7	Kh	57.22N	43.06 E
Jurjev-Polski	7	Jh	56.31N	39.44 E
Jurjuzan	17	Hi	55.43N	56.57 E
Jurjuzan	17	Ii	54.52N	58.28 E
Jurla	17	Gg	59.20N	54.16 E
Jurmala/Jūrmala	19	Cd	56.59N	23.38 E
Jūrmala/Jurmala	19	Cd	56.59N	23.38 E
Jurmo	8	Ie	59.50N	21.35 E
Jurong	28	Ei	31.56N	119.10 E
Juruá	54	Ed	3.27S	66.03W
Juruá, Rio-	52	Jf	2.37S	65.44W
Juruena, Rio-	52	Kf	7.20S	58.03W
Jurumirim, Reprêsa de-	56	Kb	23.20S	49.00W
Juruti	54	Gd	2.09S	56.04W
Jurva	8	Ib	62.41N	21.59 E
Jusan-Kō	29a	Bc	41.00N	140.20 E
Jusayrah	24	Nj	25.53N	50.36 E
Jusheng	27	Mb	48.44N	126.37 E
Ju Shui	28	Ci	31.09N	114.52 E
Juškozero	19	Dc	64.45N	32.08 E
Jussarö	8	Je	59.50N	23.35 E
Justo Daract	56	Gd	33.52S	65.11W
Jusva	17	Gg	58.59N	54.57 E
Jutai	54	Ee	5.11S	68.54W
Jutai, Rio-	52	Jf	2.43S	66.57W
Jüterbg	10	Je	51.59N	13.05 E
Juti	55	Ef	22.52S	54.37W
Jutiapa [3]	49	Bf	14.10N	89.50W
Jutiapa [Guat.]	47	Gf	14.17N	89.54W
Jutiapa [Hond.]	49	Df	15.46N	86.34W
Juticalpa	47	Gf	14.42N	86.15W
Jutland (EN)=Jylland	5	Gd	56.00N	9.15 E
Juuka	7	Ge	63.14N	29.15 E
Juva	7	Gf	61.54N	27.51 E
Juventud, Isla de la-=Pines, Isle of- (EN)	38	Kg	21.40N	82.50W
Juxian	27	Kd	35.33N	118.45 E
Jūybār	24	Od	36.38N	52.53 E
Juye	28	Dg	35.23N	116.05 E
Jüyom	24	Oh	28.10N	54.02 E
Juža	7	Kh	56.36N	42.01 E
Južnaja Keltma	17	Gf	60.30N	55.40 E
Južna Morava	15	Ef	43.41N	21.24 E
Južni Rodopi	15	Ih	41.15N	25.30 E
Južnoje	20	Jg	46.13N	143.27 E
Južno-Jenisejski	20	Ee	58.48N	94.45 E
Južno-Kurilsk	20	Jh	44.05N	145.52 E
Južno-Sahalinsk	22	Qe	46.58N	142.42 E
Južno-Uralsk	19	Ge	54.26N	61.15 E
Južny, Mys-	20	Ke	57.42N	156.55 E
Južny Bug	5	Jf	46.59N	31.58 E
Južny Ural=Southern Urals (EN)	5	Le	54.00N	58.30 E
Jygeva/Jõgeva	7	Gg	58.46N	26.26 E
Jylland=Jutland (EN)	5	Gd	56.00N	9.15 E
Jylland Bank	8	Bh	56.55N	7.20 E
Jyske Ås	8	Dg	57.15N	10.14 E
Jyväskylä	6	Ic	62.14N	25.44 E

K

K2=Godwin Austen (EN)	21	Jf	35.53N	76.30 E
Ka	34	Fc	11.39N	4.11 E
Kaabong	36	Fb	3.31N	34.09 E
Kaahka	19	Fh	37.21N	59.36 E
Kaala	65a	Cb	21.31N	158.09W
Kaala-Gomén	63b	Be	20.40S	164.24 E
Kaalualu Bay	65a	Fe	18.58N	155.37W
Kaamanen	7	Gb	69.06N	27.12 E
Kaap Kruis	37	Ad	21.46S	13.58 E
Kaap Plateau (EN)=Kaapplato	30	Jk	27.30S	23.45 E
Kaapplato=Kaap Plateau (EN)	30	Jk	27.30S	23.45 E
Kaapprovinsie/Cape Province [2]	37	Cf	32.00S	22.00 E
Kaapstad / Cape Town	31	Il	33.55S	18.22 E
Kaarst	12	Ic	51.15N	6.37 E
Kaarta	34	Cc	14.35N	10.00W
Kaba/Habahe	27	Eb	47.53N	86.12 E
Kabaena, Pulau-	26	Hh	5.15S	121.55 E
Kabah	48	Og	20.07N	89.29W
Kabala	34	Cd	9.35N	11.33W
Kabale	36	Ec	1.15S	29.59 E
Kabalega Falls	36	Fb	2.17N	31.41 E
Kabalo	31	Ji	6.03S	26.55 E
Kabaman	63a	Aa	4.38S	152.42 E
Kabambare	36	Ec	4.16S	27.07 E
Kabamet	36	Gb	0.30N	35.45 E
Kabanjahe	26	Cf	3.06N	98.30 E
Kabardino-Balkarskaja ASSR [3]	19	Eg	43.30N	43.30 E
Kabare	36	Ec	2.29S	28.48 E
Kabasalan	26	He	7.48N	122.45 E
Kaba-Shima [Jap.]	29	Ae	32.45N	129.00 E
Kaba-Shima [Jap.]	29	Ae	32.34N	129.47 E
Kabba	34	Gd	7.50N	6.04 E
Kåbdalis	7	Ec	66.09N	20.00 E
Kaberamaido	36	Fb	1.45N	33.10 E
Kabetogama Lake	45	Jb	48.28N	92.59W
Kabhegy	10	Ni	47.03N	17.39 E
Kabinakagami Lake	44	Ea	48.58N	84.25W
Kabinda	31	Ji	6.08S	24.29 E
Kabīr, Wādī al-	14	Dn	36.23N	9.52 E
Kabīr Kūh	24	Lf	33.25N	46.45 E
Kabkābīyah	35	Cc	13.39N	24.05 E
Kableškovo	15	Kg	42.39N	27.34 E
Kabna	35	Eb	19.10N	32.41 E
Kabo	35	Bd	7.35N	18.38 E
Kābol	22	If	34.31N	69.12 E
Kābol	23	Kc	34.30N	69.00 E
Kabompo	36	De	13.36S	24.12 E
Kabompo	30	Jj	14.11S	23.11 E
Kabondo Dianda	36	Ed	8.53S	25.40 E
Kabongo	36	Ed	7.19S	25.35 E
Kabou	34	Fd	9.27N	0.49 E
Kabūdiyāh, Ra's-	32	Jb	35.14N	11.10 E
Kabūd Rāhang	24	Me	35.12N	48.44 E
Kābul	21	Jf	34.33N	69.12 E
Kabunda	36	Ee	12.13S	29.23 E

Index Symbols

[1] Independent Nation
[2] State, Region
[3] District, County
[4] Municipality
[5] Colony, Dependency
Continent
Physical Region

Historical or Cultural Region
Mount, Mountain
Volcano
Hill
Mountains, Mountain Range
Hills, Escarpment
Plateau, Upland

Pass, Gap
Plain, Lowland
Delta
Salt Flat
Valley, Canyon
Crater, Cave
Karst Features

Depression
Polder
Desert, Dunes
Forest, Woods
Heath, Steppe
Oasis
Cape, Point

Coast, Beach
Cliff
Peninsula
Isthmus
Sandbank
Island
Atoll

Rock, Reef
Islands, Archipelago
Rocks, Reefs
Coral Reef
Well, Spring
Geyser
River, Stream

Waterfall Rapids
River Mouth, Estuary
Lake
Salt Lake
Intermittent Lake
Reservoir
Swamp, Pond

Canal
Glacier
Ice Shelf, Pack Ice
Ocean
Sea
Gulf, Bay
Strait, Fjord

Lagoon
Bank
Seamount
Tablemount
Ridge
Shelf
Basin

Escarpment, Sea Scarp
Fracture
Trench, Abyss
National Park, Reserve
Point of Interest
Recreation Site
Cave, Cavern

Historic Site
Ruins
Wall, Walls
Church, Abbey
Temple
Scientific Station
Airport

Port
Lighthouse
Mine
Tunnel
Dam, Bridge

Kabunga 36 Ec 1.42S 28.08 E
Kaburuang, Pulau- 26 If 3.48N 126.48 E
Kabwe 31 Jj 14.27S 28.27 E
Kača 16 Hg 44.44N 33.32 E
Kačanik 15 Eg 42.14N 21.15 E
Kačanovo 8 Lg 57.24N 27.53 E
Kačergine 8 Jj 54.53N 23.49 E
Kachchh, Gulf of 21 Ig 22.36N 69.30 E
Kachchh, Rann of 25 Dd 23.51N 70.30 E
Kachia 34 Gd 9.52N 7.57 E
Kachikau 37 Cc 18.09S 24.29 E
Kachin 25 Jc 26.00N 97.30 E
Kačiry 19 He 53.04N 76.07 E
Kačkanar 19 Fd 58.42N 59.35 E
Kačug 20 Ff 54.00N 105.52 E
Kaczawa 10 Me 51.18N 16.27 E
Kadada 16 Oc 53.09N 46.01 E
Kadaň 10 Jf 50.23N 13.16 E
Kadan Kyun 25 Jf 12.30N 98.22 E
Kadei 30 Ih 3.31N 16.03 E
Kadijevka 19 Df 48.32N 38.40 E
Kadiköy 24 Bb 40.51N 26.50 E
Kadıköy, İstanbul 15 Mi 40.59N 29.01 E
Kadina 59 Hf 33.58S 137.43 E
Kadınhanı 24 Ec 38.15N 32.14 E
Kadiolo 34 Dc 10.34N 5.45W
Kadiri 25 Ff 14.07N 78.10 E
Kadirli 23 Eb 37.23N 36.05 E
Kadja 35 Cc 12.02N 22.28 E
Kadmat Island 25 Ef 11.14N 72.47 E
Kadnikov 7 Jg 59.30N 40.24 E
Kadoka 45 Fe 43.50N 101.31W
Kaduj 7 Ig 59.14N 37.09 E
Kaduna 34 Gc 11.00N 7.30 E
Kaduna 30 Hh 8.45N 5.48 E
Kaduna 31 Hg 10.31N 7.26 E
Kâduqlî 31 Jg 11.01N 29.43 E
Kadykčan 20 Jd 63.05N 146.58 E
Kadžaran 16 Oj 39.11N 46.10 E
Kadžerom 17 Gd 64.41N 55.54 E
Kadži-Saj 18 Kc 42.08N 77.10 E
Kaech'ŏn 28 He 39.42N 125.53 E
Kaédi 31 Fg 16.08N 13.31W
Kaélé 34 Hc 10.07N 14.27 E
Kaena Point 65a Cb 21.35N 158.17W
Kaeo 62 Ea 35.06S 173.47 E
Kaesŏng 22 Of 37.58N 126.33 E
Kaesŏng Si 28 Ie 38.05N 126.30 E
Kāf 24 Gg 31.24N 37.29 E
Kafakumba 36 Dd 9.41S 23.44 E
Kafan 19 Eh 39.12N 46.28 E
Kafanchan 34 Gd 9.35N 8.18 E
Kaffrine 34 Bc 14.06N 15.33W
Kafia Kingi 35 Cd 9.16N 24.25 E
Kafiréos, Dhiékplous- 15 Hl 38.00N 24.40 E
Kafirévs, Ákra- 15 Hk 38.10N 24.35 E
Kafr ad Dawwār 24 Dg 31.08N 30.07 E
Kafr ash Shaykh 33 Fc 31.07N 30.56 E
Kafta 35 Fc 13.54N 37.11 E
Kafu 36 Fb 1.39N 32.05 E
Kafue 30 Ef 15.56S 28.55 E
Kafue 31 Jj 15.47S 28.11 E
Kafue Dam 36 Ef 15.45S 28.28 E
Kafue Flats 36 Ef 15.40S 26.25 E
Kafufu 36 Fd 7.12S 31.31 E
Kaga 28 Nf 36.18N 136.18 E
Kaga Bandoro 35 Bd 7.02N 19.13 E
Kagalaska 40a Cb 51.47N 176.23W
Kagalnik 16 Kf 47.04N 39.18 E
Kagami 29 Be 32.34N 130.40 E
Kagan 19 Gh 39.43N 64.32 E
Kagarlyk 16 Ge 49.53N 30.56 E
Kagawa Ken 28 Mg 34.15N 134.15 E
Kagera 30 Ki 0.57S 31.47 E
Kağızman 24 Jb 40.09N 43.07 E
Kagoshima 22 Pf 31.36N 130.33 E
Kagoshima Bay (EN) =
Kagoshima-Wan 28 Ki 31.27N 130.40 E
Kagoshima Ken 28 Ki 31.45N 130.40 E
Kagoshima-Taniyama 29 Bf 31.31N 130.31 E
Kagoshima-Wan =
Kagoshima Bay (EN) 28 Ki 31.27N 130.40 E
Kagul 15 Ld 45.32N 28.27 E
Kagul 19 Cf 45.53N 28.14 E
Kahal Tabelbala 32 Gd 28.45N 2.15W
Kahama 36 Fc 3.50S 32.36 E
Kahemba 31 Ii 7.17S 19.00 E
Kahi 16 Oi 41.23N 46.59 E
Kahiu Point 65a Eb 21.13N 156.58W
Kahler Asten 10 Ee 51.11N 8.29 E
Kahnūj 24 Qi 27.58N 57.47 E
Kahoku 29 Gb 38.30N 141.20 E
Kahoku-Gata 29 Ec 36.40N 136.40 E
Kahoolawe Island 57 Lb 20.33N 156.35W
Kahouanne, Ilet à- 51e Ab 16.22N 61.47W
Kahovka 19 Df 46.47N 33.32 E
Kahovskoje Vodohranilišče
=Kakhovka Reservoir (EN)
5 Jf 47.25N 34.10 E
Kahramanmaraş 23 Eb 37.36N 36.55 E
Kahrūyeh 24 Ng 31.43N 51.48 E
Kāhta 24 Hd 37.46N 38.36 E
Kahuku 65a Db 21.41N 157.57W
Kahuku Point 65a Db 21.43N 157.59W
Kahului 65a Ec 20.53N 156.27W
Kahului Bay 65a Ec 20.55N 156.30W
Kahurangi Point 62 Ed 40.46S 172.13 E
Kai, Kepulauan- 57 Ee 5.35S 132.45 E
Kaiama 34 Fd 9.36N 3.57 E
Kaiapoi 62 Ee 43.23S 172.39 E
Kaibab Plateau 46 Ih 36.30N 112.15W
Kai Besar 26 Jh 5.35S 133.00 E
Kaidu He/Karaxabar He 27 Ec 41.55N 86.38 E
Kaieteur Falls 54 Gc 5.10N 59.28W
Kaifeng 22 Nf 34.45N 114.25 E
Kaihua 28 Ej 29.10N 118.24 E
Kai Kecil 26 Jh 5.45S 132.40 E
Kaikohe 62 Ea 35.24S 173.48 E
Kaikoura 61 Dh 42.25S 173.41 E
Kaili 27 If 26.35N 107.59 E
Kailu 27 Lc 43.37N 121.19 E
Kailua [Hi.-U.S.] 65a Fd 19.39N 155.59W
Kailua [Hi.-U.S.] 65a Db 21.23N 157.44W
Kaimana 26 Jg 3.39S 133.45 E
Kaimanawa Mountains 62 Fc 39.15S 176.00 E
Kaimon-Dake 29 Bf 31.10N 130.32 E
Kain, Tournai- 12 Fd 50.38N 3.22 E
Kainach 14 Jd 46.54N 15.31 E
Kainan [Jap.] 29 Dd 34.09N 135.12 E
Kainan [Jap.] 29 De 33.36N 134.22 E
Kainantu 60 Di 6.15S 145.53 E
Kainji Dam 34 Fd 9.55N 4.40 E
Kainji Reservoir 34 Fc 10.30N 4.35 E
Kaipara Harbour 62 Fb 36.25S 174.15 E
Kaiparowits Plateau 46 Jh 37.20N 111.15W
Kaiser Franz Josephs
Fjord 41 Jd 73.30N 24.00W
Kaisersesch 12 Jd 50.13N 7.09 E
Kaiserslautern 10 Dg 49.27N 7.45 E
Kaiserstuhl 10 Dh 48.06N 7.40 E
Kaishantun 27 Mc 42.43N 129.37 E
Kaišiadorys/Kajšjadoris 7 Fi 54.53N 24.31 E
Kaita 29 Cd 34.20N 132.32 E
Kaitaia 62 Ea 35.07S 173.14 E
Kaitangata 62 Cg 46.17S 169.51 E
Kaithal 25 Fc 29.48N 76.23 E
Kaitong → Tongyu 27 Lc 44.47N 123.05 E
Kaituma River 50 Gh 8.11N 59.41W
Kaiwaka 61 Dg 36.10S 174.26 E
Kaiwi Channel 60 Oc 21.13N 157.30W
Kaixian 27 Ie 31.10N 108.25 E
Kaiyuan [China] 27 Lc 42.33N 124.04 E
Kaiyuan [China] 27 Hg 23.47N 103.15 E
Kaiyuh Mountains 40 Hd 64.00N 158.00W
Kaja 30 Jg 12.02N 22.28 E
Kajaani 6 Ic 64.14N 27.41 E
Kajaapu 26 Dh 5.26S 102.24 E
Kajabbi 58 Fg 20.02S 140.02 E
Kajak 20 Fb 71.30N 103.15 E
Kajang 26 Df 2.59N 101.47 E
Kajdak, Sor- 16 Rg 44.40N 53.30 E
Kajerkan 20 Dc 69.25N 87.30 E
Kajiado 36 Gc 1.51S 36.47 E
Kajiki 29 Bf 31.44N 130.40 E
Kajmakčalan 15 Ei 40.58N 21.48 E
Kajnar 15 Lb 47.50N 28.06 E
Kajo Kaji 35 Ee 3.53N 31.40 E
Kajrakkumskoje
Vodohranilišče 18 Hd 40.20N 70.05 E
Kajrakty 19 Hf 48.31N 73.14 E
Kajšjadoris/Kaišiadorys 7 Fi 54.53N 24.31 E
Kajuru 34 Gc 10.19N 7.41 E
Kaka 35 Fd 7.28N 39.06 E
Kākā 35 Ec 10.36N 32.11 E
Kakagi Lake 45 Jb 49.13N 93.52W
Kakamas 37 Ce 28.45S 20.33 E
Kakamega 36 Fb 0.17N 34.45 E
Kakamigahara 29 Ed 35.25N 136.50 E
Kakanj 14 Mf 44.08N 18.05 E
Kaka Point 65a Ec 20.32N 156.33W
Kakata 34 Cd 6.32N 10.21W
Kake 29 Cd 34.36N 132.19 E
Kakegawa 29 Ed 34.46N 138.00 E
Kakenge 36 Dc 4.51S 21.55 E
Kakeroma-Jima 29b Ba 28.08N 129.15 E
Kakhovka Reservoir (EN) =
Kahovskoje
Vodohranilišče 5 Jf 47.25N 34.10 E
Kākī 24 Nh 28.19N 51.34 E
Kākināda 22 Kh 16.56N 82.13 E
Kakisa Lake 42 Fd 60.55N 117.40W
Kakizaki 29 Fc 37.16N 138.22 E
Kaklkan 24 Cd 36.15N 29.24 E
Kakogawa 29 Dd 34.46N 134.51 E
Kakpin 34 Ed 8.39N 3.48W
Kaktovik 40 Kb 70.08N 143.37W
Kakuda 29 Gc 37.58N 140.47 E
Kakuma 36 Fb 3.43N 34.52 E
Kakunodate 28 Pe 39.40N 140.32 E
Kakva 17 Jg 59.37N 60.50 E
Kakya 36 Gc 1.36S 39.02 E
Kalaa 13 Mi 35.35N 0.20 E
Kalaa Khasba 14 Co 35.38N 8.36 E
Kalaallit Nunaat/Grønland =
Greenland (EN) 39 Pb 70.00N 40.00W
Kalaallit Nunaat/Grønland =
Greenland (EN) 38 Pb 70.00N 40.00W
Kalabahi 26 Hh 8.13S 124.31 E
Kalabáka 15 Ej 39.42N 21.38 E
Kalabera 64b Ba 15.14N 145.48 E
Kalabo 36 De 14.58S 22.41 E
Kalâbsha 33 Fe 23.33N 32.50 E
Kalač 19 Ee 50.23N 41.01 E
Kalačinsk 19 Hd 55.03N 74.34 E
Kalač-na-Donu 19 Ef 48.43N 43.32 E
Kaladan 25 Id 20.09N 92.57 E
Ka Lae 60 Od 18.55N 155.41W
Kalahari Desert 30 Jk 23.00S 22.00 E
Kalaheo 65a Bb 21.56N 159.32W
Kalai-Mor 19 Gh 35.37N 62.31 E
Kalaj Humo 18 He 38.25N 70.47 E
Kalajoki 7 Fd 64.15N 23.57 E
Kalakan 20 Ge 55.10N 116.45 E
Kalaldi 34 Hd 6.30N 14.04 E
Kaläleh 24 Pd 37.25N 55.40 E
Kalámai 6 Ih 37.02N 22.07 E
Kalamákion 15 Gl 37.55N 23.43 E
Kalamazoo 43 Jc 42.17N 85.32W
Kalambo Falls 36 Fd 8.36S 31.14 E
Kalamitski Zaliv 16 Hg 45.00N 33.25 E
Kálamos 15 Dk 38.37N 20.55 E
Kalamunda,
Perth- 59 Df 31.57S 116.03 E
Kalan 23 Eb 39.07N 39.32 E
Kalanshiyū, Sarīr- 30 Jf 27.00N 21.30 E
Kalao, Pulau- 26 Hh 7.18S 120.58 E
Kalaotoa, Pulau- 26 Hh 7.22S 121.47 E
Kalapana 65a Gd 19.21N 154.59W
Kalaraš 16 Ff 47.16N 28.16 E
Kälarne 8 Gb 62.59N 16.05 E
Kalarski Hrebet 20 Ge 56.30N 118.50 E
Kalasin [Indon.] 26 Ff 0.12N 114.16 E
Kalasin [Thai.] 25 Ke 16.29N 103.31 E
Kalāt 25 Dc 29.02N 66.35 E
Kalāteh 24 Pd 36.29N 54.10 E
Kalau 65b Bc 21.28S 174.57W
Kalaupapa 65a Eb 21.12N 156.59W
Kalaus 16 Ng 45.43N 44.07 E
Kalavárdha 15 Km 36.20N 27.57 E
Kálavrita 15 Fk 38.02N 22.07 E
Kalbā' 24 Qj 25.03N 56.21 E
Kalbīyah, Sabkhat al- 14 Eo 35.51N 10.17 E
Kaldbakur 7a Ab 65.49N 23.39W
Kaldygajty 16 Re 49.20N 52.38 E
Kale [Tur.] 24 Cd 37.26N 28.51 E
Kale [Tur.] 24 Cd 36.14N 29.59 E
Kalecik 24 Eb 40.06N 33.25 E
Kalehe 36 Ec 2.06S 28.55 E
Kalemie 31 Ji 5.56S 29.12 E
Kāl-e Shur 23 Jb 35.05N 60.59 E
Kalevala 19 Db 65.12N 31.10 E
Kalewa 25 Id 23.12N 94.18 E
Kaleybar 24 Lc 38.47N 47.02 E
Kalgoorlie 58 Dh 30.45S 121.28 E
Kaliakoúdha 15 Ek 38.48N 21.46 E
Kaliakra, Nos- 15 Lf 43.18N 28.30 E
Kalibo 26 Hd 11.43N 122.22 E
Kali Limni 15 Kn 35.35N 27.08 E
Kalima 31 Ji 2.34S 26.37 E
Kalimantan/Borneo 21 Ni 1.00N 114.00 E
Kalimantan Barat 26 Ff 0.01N 110.30 E
Kalimantan Selatan 26 Gg 2.30S 115.30 E
Kalimantan Tengah 26 Fg 2.00S 113.30 E
Kalimantan Timur 26 Gf 1.30N 116.30 E
Kálimnos 15 Jm 36.57N 26.59 E
Kálimnos 15 Jl 37.00N 27.00 E
Kalinin [R.S.F.S.R.] 6 Jd 56.52N 35.55 E
Kalinin [Tur.-U.S.S.R.] 19 Fg 42.07N 59.40 E
Kalininabad 18 Gf 37.53N 68.57 E
Kaliningrad [R.S.F.S.R.] 6 Ie 54.43N 20.30 E
Kaliningrad [R.S.F.S.R.] 7 Ii 55.55N 37.57 E
Kaliningradskaja Oblast 19 Ce 54.45N 21.20 E
Kalinino [Arm.-U.S.S.R.] 16 Ni 41.08N 44.14 E
Kalinino [R.S.F.S.R.] 16 Kg 45.05N 38.59 E
Kalininsk [Mold.-U.S.S.R.] 15 Ka 48.07N 27.16 E
Kalininsk [R.S.F.S.R.] 16 Nd 51.30N 44.30 E
Kalininskaja Oblast 19 Dd 57.20N 34.40 E
Kalinkoviči 19 Ce 52.07N 29.23 E
Kalino 17 Hg 58.15N 57.35 E
Kalinovik 14 Mg 43.31N 18.26 E
Kalinovka 16 Fe 49.29N 28.32 E
Kaliro 36 Fb 0.54N 33.30 E
Kalispell 39 He 48.12N 114.19W
Kalisz 10 Of 51.45N 18.05 E
Kalisz 10 Oe 51.46N 18.06 E
Kalisz Pomorski 10 Lc 53.19N 15.54 E
Kalitva 16 Le 48.10N 40.46 E
Kaliua 36 Fd 5.04S 31.48 E
Kalix 7 Fd 65.51N 23.08 E
Kalixälven 7 Fd 65.47N 23.13 E
Kalja 17 Jf 60.20N 60.01 E
Kaljazin 19 Dd 57.15N 37.55 E
Kalkandere 24 Ib 40.55N 40.28 E
Kalkar 12 Ic 51.44N 6.18 E
Kalkaska 44 Ec 44.44N 85.11W
Kalkfeld 37 Bd 20.53S 16.11 E
Kalkfontein 37 Cd 22.07S 20.54 E
Kalkim 15 Kj 39.48N 27.13 E
Kalkrand 37 Bd 24.03S 17.33 E
Kall 7 Ce 63.28N 13.15 E
Kållands Halvö 8 Ef 58.35N 13.05 E
Kållandsö 8 Ef 58.40N 13.10 E
Kallaste 7 Gg 58.41N 27.08 E
Kallavesi 5 Ic 62.50N 27.45 E
Kalletal 12 Kb 52.08N 8.57 E
Kallhäll 8 Ge 59.27N 17.48 E
Kallidhromon Óros 15 Fk 38.44N 22.34 E
Kallinge 7 Dh 56.14N 15.17 E
Kallonis, Kolpos- 15 Jj 39.07N 26.08 E
Kallsjön 7 Ce 63.35N 13.00 E
Kalmar 6 Hd 56.40N 16.22 E
Kalmar 7 Dh 57.20N 16.00 E
Kalmarsund 7 Dh 56.40N 16.25 E
Kalmit 12 Ke 49.19N 8.05 E
Kalmius 16 Jf 47.03N 37.34 E
Kalmthout 12 Gc 51.23N 4.28 E
Kalmyckaja ASSR 19 Ef 46.30N 45.30 E
Kalmykovo 16 Qe 49.05N 51.47 E
Kalnciems 8 Jh 56.48N 23.34 E
Kalnik 14 Kd 46.10N 16.30 E
Kalocsa 10 Oj 46.32N 19.00 E
Kalofer 15 Hg 42.37N 24.59 E
Kalohi Channel 65a Ec 21.00N 156.56W
Kaloko 36 Ed 6.47S 25.47 E
Kalole 36 Ec 3.42S 27.22 E
Kaloli Point 65a Gd 19.37N 154.57W
Kalomo 36 Ef 17.02S 26.30 E
Kalpa 25 Fb 31.37N 78.10 E
Kalpákion 15 Dj 39.53N 20.35 E
Kalpeni Island 25 Ef 10.05N 73.38 E
Kalpin 27 Cc 40.31N 79.03 E
Kalsūbai 21 Jh 19.36N 73.43 E
Kaltern/Caldaro 14 Fd 46.25N 11.14 E
Kaltungo 34 Hd 9.49N 11.19 E
Kaluga 6 Je 54.31N 36.16 E
Kalulushi 36 Ee 12.50S 28.05 E
Kalumburu Mission 59 Fb 14.18S 126.39 E
Kalundborg 7 Ci 55.41N 11.06 E
Kaluš 19 Cf 49.03N 24.23 E
Kałuszyn 10 Rd 52.13N 21.49 E
Kalužskaja Oblast 19 De 54.20N 35.30 E
Kalvåg 8 Ac 61.46N 4.53 E
Kalvarija 7 Fi 54.27N 23.14 E
Kalya 36 Fd 6.28S 30.03 E
Kalyān 25 Ee 19.15N 73.09 E
Kám 10 Mi 47.06N 16.53 E
Kama 36 Ec 3.32S 27.07 E
Kama [R.S.F.S.R.] 17 Nf 60.27N 69.00 E
Kama [U.S.S.R.] 5 Ld 55.45N 52.00 E
Kamae 29 Be 32.48N 131.56 E
Kamaï 35 Ba 21.12N 17.30 E
Kamaing 25 Jc 25.31N 96.44 E
Kamaishi 28 Pe 39.16N 141.53 E
Kamakou 65a Eb 21.07N 156.52W
Kamakura 29 Fd 35.19N 139.32 E
Kamālia 25 Eb 30.44N 72.39 E
Kamalo 65a Eb 21.03N 156.53W
Kaman 24 Ec 39.25N 33.45 E
Kamand, Āb-e- 24 Mf 33.28N 49.04 E
Kamanjab 37 Ac 19.35S 14.51 E
Kamanyola 36 Ec 2.46S 29.00 E
Kamaran 23 Ff 15.12N 42.35 E
Kamarang 54 Fb 5.53N 60.35W
Kama Reservoir (EN) =
Kamskoje
Vodohranilišče 5 Ld 58.50N 56.15 E
Kamaši 19 Gh 38.48N 66.29 E
Kamativi 37 Dc 18.19S 27.03 E
Kambalda 59 Ef 31.10S 121.37 E
Kambalnaja Sopka, Vulkan-
20 Kf 51.17N 156.57 E
Kambara 29 Fd 35.07N 138.36 E
Kambara 63d Cc 18.57S 178.57W
Kambarka 7 Nh 56.18N 54.14 E
Kambia 34 Cd 9.07N 12.55W
Kambja 8 Lf 58.11N 26.43 E
Kambove 36 Ee 10.52S 26.35 E
Kamčatka 20 Le 56.10N 162.30 E
Kamčatka, Poluostrov- =
Kamchatka Peninsula (EN)
21 Rd 56.00N 160.00 E
Kamčatskaja Oblast 20 Kf 54.50N 159.00 E
Kamčatskij Zaliv 20 Le 55.30N 163.00 E
Kamchatka Peninsula (EN)
=Kamčatka, Poluostrov-
21 Rd 56.00N 160.00 E
Kamčija 15 Kf 43.02N 27.53 E
Kamčijska Plato 15 Kg 42.56N 27.32 E
Kameda [Jap.] 29 Fc 37.52N 139.06 E
Kameda [Jap.] 29a Bc 41.49N 140.46 E
Kameda-Hantō 29a Bc 41.45N 141.00 E
Kámeiros 15 Km 36.18N 27.56 E
Kamelik 16 Pc 52.06N 49.30 E
Kamen 12 Jc 51.36N 7.40 E
Kaménai 15 Im 36.25N 25.25 E
Kamende 36 Dd 6.28S 24.33 E
Kamenec 10 Td 52.23N 23.49 E
Kamenec-Podolski 19 Cf 48.39N 26.33 E
Kamenjak, Rt- 14 Hf 44.46N 13.56 E
Kamenka [Kaz.-U.S.S.R.] 16 Qd 51.07N 50.20 E
Kamenka [Mold.-U.S.S.R.] 16 Fe 48.03N 28.45 E
Kamenka [R.S.F.S.R.] 16 Kd 50.43N 39.25 E
Kamenka [R.S.F.S.R.] 19 Ee 53.13N 44.03 E
Kamenka [R.S.F.S.R.] 7 Kd 65.54N 44.04 E
Kamenka [R.S.F.S.R.] 28 Nb 44.28N 136.01 E
Kamenka [Ukr.-U.S.S.R.] 19 Df 49.03N 32.06 E
Kamenka-Bugskaja 10 Uf 50.01N 24.25 E
Kamenka-Dneprovskaja 16 If 47.29N 34.29 E
Kamen-Kaširski 16 Dd 51.36N 24.59 E
Kamen-na-Obi 20 Df 53.47N 81.20 E
Kamennogorsk 7 Gf 60.59N 29.12 E
Kamennoje, Ozero- 7 Hd 64.30N 30.15 E
Kamennomostski 16 Lg 44.17N 40.12 E
Kamen-Rybolov 28 Kb 44.45N 132.04 E
Kamenskoje 20 Ld 62.30N 166.12 E
Kamensk-Šahtinski 16 Le 48.18N 40.16 E
Kamensk-Uralski 22 Id 56.28N 61.54 E
Kamenz/Kamjenc 10 Ke 51.16N 14.06 E
Kameoka 29 Dd 35.00N 135.35 E
Kameškovo 7 Jh 56.22N 41.01 E
Kamet 25 Fd 30.55N 79.35 E
Kameyama 29 Ed 34.51N 136.27 E
Kami-Agata 29 Ad 34.38N 129.25 E
Kamiah 46 Gc 46.14N 116.02W
Kamicharo 29a Cb 43.11N 143.52 E
Kamienna 10 Re 51.06N 21.47 E
Kamienna Góra 10 Mf 50.47N 16.01 E
Kamień Pomorski 10 Kc 53.58N 14.46 E
Kamieńsk 10 Pe 51.12N 19.30 E
Kamieskroon 37 Bf 30.09S 17.56 E
Kami-furano 29a Cb 43.29N 142.27 E
Kamiiso 28 Pd 41.49N 140.39 E
Kamiita 29 Dd 34.08N 134.24 E
Kamiji 36 Dd 6.39S 23.17 E
Kamikawa 29a Cb 43.50N 142.47 E
Kami-Koshiki-Jima 29 Af 31.50N 129.55 E
Kamina 31 Ji 8.44S 24.59 E
Kaminak Lake 42 Id 62.13N 95.00W
Kaminokuni 29a Bc 41.48N 140.05 E
Kamino-Shima 29 Ad 34.30N 129.25 E
Kaminoyama 28 Pe 38.09N 140.17 E
Kaminuriak Lake 42 Hd 63.00N 95.45W
Kamioka 28 Nf 36.16N 137.18 E
Kami-shihoro 29a Cb 43.13N 143.16 E
Kamisunagawa 29a Bb 43.28N 141.58 E
Kamitsushima 29 Ad 34.39N 129.28 E
Kamituga 36 Ec 3.04S 28.11 E
Kamiyama 29 De 33.58N 134.21 E
Kami-yūbetsu 29a Ca 44.11N 143.34 E
Kamjenc/Kamenz 10 Ke 51.16N 14.06 E
Kamloops 39 Gd 50.40N 120.20W
Kamloops Plateau 46 Ea 50.10N 120.35W
Kamnik 14 Id 46.14N 14.37 E
Kamo [Arm.-U.S.S.R.] 16 Ni 40.22N 45.05 E
Kamo [Jap.] 29 Fc 37.39N 139.03 E
Kamo [N.Z.] 62 Fa 35.41S 174.17 E
Kamōda-Misaki 29 De 33.50N 134.45 E
Kamogawa 29 Gd 35.06N 140.05 E
Kamp 14 Jb 48.23N 15.48 E
Kampala 31 Kh 0.19N 32.35 E
Kampar 26 Df 4.18N 101.09 E
Kampar 26 Mi 0.32N 103.08 E
Kampen 11 Lb 52.33N 5.54 E
Kampene 36 Ec 3.36S 26.40 E
Kamphaeng Phet 25 Je 16.26N 99.33 E
Kamp-Lintfort 12 Ic 51.30N 6.32 E
Kamp'o 28 Jg 35.48N 129.30 E
Kâmpóng Cham 22 Mh 12.00N 105.27 E
Kâmpóng Chhnâng 25 Kf 12.15N 104.40 E
Kâmpóng Saôm 22 Mh 10.38N 103.30 E
Kâmpóng Saôm, Chhâk- 25 Kf 10.50N 103.32 E
Kâmpóng Thum 25 Kf 12.42N 104.54 E
Kâmpôt 25 Kf 10.37N 104.11 E
Kampti 34 Ec 10.08N 3.27W
Kampuchea → Cambodia 22 Mh 13.00N 105.00 E
Kamrau, Teluk- 26 Jg 3.32S 133.37 E
Kamsack 42 Hf 51.34N 101.54W
Kamsar 34 Cc 10.40N 14.36W
Kamskoje Ustje 7 Li 55.14N 49.16 E
Kamskoje Vodohranilišče =
Kama Reservoir (EN) 5 Ld 58.50N 56.15 E
Kam Summa 35 Ge 0.21N 42.44 E
Kamuenai 29a Bb 43.08N 140.26 E
Kamui-Dake 29a Cb 42.25N 142.52 E
Kamui-Misaki 27 Pc 43.20N 140.20 E
Kámuk, Cerro- 49 Fi 9.17N 83.04W
Kamvoúnia Óri 15 Ei 40.00N 21.52 E
Kāmyārān 24 Le 34.47N 46.56 E
Kamyšin 6 Ke 50.06N 45.24 E
Kamyšlov 19 Gd 56.52N 62.43 E
Kamyšovaja Buhta 16 Hg 44.31N 33.33 E
Kamysty-Ajat 17 Jj 53.01N 61.35 E
Kamyzjak 19 Ef 46.06N 48.05 E
Kan 24 Ne 35.45N 51.16 E
Kan 20 Ee 56.31N 93.47 E
Kana 37 Dc 18.32S 27.24 E
Kanaaupscow 42 Jf 54.01N 76.32W
Kanaaupscow 42 Jf 53.40N 77.08W
Kanab 43 Ed 37.03N 112.32W
Kanab Creek 46 Ih 36.24N 112.38W
Kanaga 40a Cb 51.45N 177.10W
Kanagawa Ken 28 Og 35.30N 139.10 E
Kanaliasem 26 Dg 1.44S 103.35 E
Kanami-Zaki 29b Bb 27.53N 128.58 E
Kananga 31 Ji 5.54S 22.25 E
Kanariktok 42 Le 55.03N 60.10W
Kanaš 7 Li 55.31N 47.31 E
Kanathea 63d Cb 17.16S 179.09W
Kanaya 29 Fd 34.48N 138.07 E
Kanayama 29 Ed 35.39N 137.09 E
Kanazawa 22 Pf 36.34N 136.39 E
Kanbalu 25 Jd 23.12N 95.31 E
Kanbe 25 Je 16.42N 96.01 E
Kanchanaburi 25 Jf 14.02N 99.33 E
Känchenjunga 21 Kg 27.42N 88.08 E
Kānchipuram 25 Ff 12.50N 79.43 E
Kandalakša 6 Jb 67.09N 32.21 E
Kandalaksha, Gulf of- (EN)
=Kandalakšski Zaliv
5 Jb 66.35N 32.45 E
Kandalakšski Zaliv =
Kandalaksha, Gulf of- (EN)
5 Jb 66.35N 32.45 E
Kandangan 26 Gg 2.47S 115.16 E
Kándanos 15 Gn 35.20N 23.44 E
Kandava 7 Fh 57.03N 22.46 E
Kandavu Island 57 If 19.00S 178.13 E
Kandavu Passage 63d Ac 18.45S 178.00 E
Kandel 12 Ke 49.05N 8.12 E
Kandel 10 Eh 48.04N 8.01 E
Kandhelioúsa 15 Jm 36.30N 26.58 E
Kandi 31 Hg 11.08N 2.56 E
Kandıra 24 Db 41.04N 30.09 E
Kandla 25 Ed 23.02N 70.14 E
Kando-Gawa 29 Cd 35.22N 132.40 E
Kandovān, Gardaneh-ye- 24 Nd 36.09N 51.18 E
Kandrian 60 Di 6.13S 149.33 E
Kandry 17 Gi 54.34N 54.10 E
Kandy 22 Ki 7.18N 80.38 E
Kane 44 He 41.40N 78.48W
Kane Bassin 67 Od 79.35N 67.00W
Kaneh 24 Pi 27.04N 54.18 E
Kanem 35 Bc 15.00N 16.00 E
Kanem 30 Ig 14.45N 15.30 E
Kaneohe 60 Oc 21.25N 157.48W
Kaneohe Bay 65a Db 21.28N 157.48W
Kanéstron, Ákra- 15 Gj 39.56N 23.45 E
Kanev 16 Ge 49.42N 31.29 E
Kanevskaja 19 Df 46.06N 38.58 E
Kaneyama 29 Fc 37.27N 139.30 E
Kang 37 Cd 23.44S 22.50 E
Kangaba 34 Dc 11.56N 8.25W
Kangal 24 Gc 39.15N 37.24 E
Kangalassy 20 Hd 62.17N 129.58 E
Kangâmiut 41 Ge 65.39N 53.55W
Kangān [Iran] 24 Oi 27.50N 52.03 E
Kangān [Iran] 24 Qj 25.48N 57.28 E
Kangar 26 De 6.26N 100.12 E
Kangaré 34 Dc 11.37N 8.08W
Kangaroo Island 57 Eh 35.50S 137.05 E
Kangasala 8 Kc 61.28N 24.05 E
Kangasniemi 7 Gf 61.59N 26.38 E
Kangâtsiaq 41 Ge 68.20N 53.18W
Kangāvar 24 Le 34.30N 47.58 E
Kangbao 28 Cd 41.51N 114.37 E
Kangding/Dardo 27 He 30.01N 101.58 E
Kangean, Kepulauan- =
Kangean Islands (EN) 26 Gh 6.55S 115.30 E
Kangean, Pulau- 26 Gh 6.54S 115.20 E
Kangean Islands (EN) =
Kangean, Kepulauan- 26 Gh 6.55S 115.30 E
Kangeeak Point 42 Lc 68.01N 64.45W
Kangen 30 Kh 6.47N 33.09 E
Kangerdlugssuaq 41 Ie 68.20N 31.40W
Kangetet 36 Gb 1.58N 36.06 E

Index Symbols

Independent Nation
State, Region
District, County
Municipality
Colony, Dependency
Continent
Physical Region
Historical or Cultural Region
Mount, Mountain
Volcano
Hill
Mountains, Mountain Range
Hills, Escarpment
Plateau, Upland
Pass, Gap
Plain, Lowland
Delta
Salt Flat
Valley, Canyon
Crater, Cave
Karst Features
Depression
Polder
Desert, Dunes
Forest, Woods
Heath, Steppe
Oasis
Cape, Point
Coast, Beach
Cliff
Peninsula
Isthmus
Sandbank
Island
Atoll
Rock, Reef
Islands, Archipelago
Rocks, Reefs
Coral Reef
Well, Spring
Geyser
River, Stream
Waterfall Rapids
River Mouth, Estuary
Lake
Salt Lake
Intermittent Lake
Reservoir
Swamp, Pond
Canal
Glacier
Ice Shelf, Pack Ice
Ocean
Sea
Gulf, Bay
Strait, Fjord
Lagoon
Bank
Seamount
Tablemount
Ridge
Shelf
Basin
Escarpment, Sea Scarp
Fracture
Trench, Abyss
National Park, Reserve
Point of Interest
Recreation Site
Cave, Cavern
Historic Site
Ruins
Wall, Walls
Church, Abbey
Temple
Scientific Station
Airport
Port
Lighthouse
Mine
Tunnel
Dam, Bridge

Kanggup'o	28	Id	41.07N	127.31 E
Kanggye	27	Mc	40.58N	126.36 E
Kangi	35	Dd	8.10N	27.39 E
Kangjin	28	Ig	34.38N	126.46 E
Kangiqsualujjuaq	39	Md	58.35N	65.59W
Kangiqsujuaq	42	Kd	61.36N	71.57W
Kangirsuk	39	Lc	60.00N	70.01W
Kangmar	27	Ef	28.32N	89.43 E
Kangnŭng	27	Md	37.44N	128.54 E
Kango	36	Bb	0.09N	10.08 E
Kangondu	36	Gc	1.06 S	37.42 E
Kangping	28	Gc	42.45N	123.20 E
Kangrinboqê Feng	27	De	31.04N	81.30 E
Kangto	25	Ic	27.52N	92.30 E
Kangwŏn-Do [N.Kor.] [2]	28	Ie	38.45N	127.35 E
Kangwŏn-Do [S.Kor.] [2]	28	Jf	37.45N	128.15 E
Kani	34	Dd	8.29N	6.36W
Kaniama	36	Dd	7.31 S	24.11 E
Kanibadam	18	Hd	40.17N	70.25 E
Kaniet Islands	57	Fe	0.53 S	145.30 E
Kanija	15	Lc	46.16N	28.13 E
Kanimeh	18	Ed	40.18N	65.09 E
Kanina	15	Ci	40.26N	19.31 E
Kanin Kamen	17	Bb	68.15N	45.15 E
Kanin Nos	19	Eb	68.39N	43.14 E
Kanin Nos, Mys-	5	Kb	68.39N	43.16 E
Kanin Peninsula (EN)= Kanin Poluostrov	5	Kb	68.00N	45.00 E
Kanin Poluostrov=Kanin Peninsula (EN)	5	Kb	68.00N	45.00 E
Kanioumé	34	Eb	15.46N	3.09W
Kanita	29a	Bc	41.02N	140.38 E
Kanjiža	15	Dc	46.04N	20.03 E
Kankaanpää	7	Ff	61.48N	22.25 E
Kankakee	43	Jc	41.07 N	87.52 W
Kankakee River	45	Lf	41.23N	88.16W
Kankalabé	34	Cc	11.00N	12.00W
Kankan	31	Gg	10.23N	9.18W
Kanker	25	Gd	20.17N	81.29 E
Kankesanturai	25	Gg	9.49N	80.02 E
Kankossa	32	Ef	15.55N	11.31W
Kankunski	20	He	57.39N	126.25 E
Kanla	10	Hf	50.48N	11.35 E
Kanmav Kyun	25	Jf	11.40N	98.28 E
Kanmon-Kaikyō	29	Bd	33.56N	130.57 E
Kanmuri-Yama	29	Cd	34.28N	132.05 E
Kannapolis	43	Kd	35.30N	80.37W
Kannone-Jima	28	Jj	28.51N	128.58 E
Kannonkoski	8	Kb	62.58N	25.15 E
Kannus	7	Fe	63.54N	23.54 E
Kano [2]	34	Gc	12.00N	9.00 E
Kano	31	Hg	12.00N	8.31 E
Kanona	36	Fe	13.04 S	30.38 E
Kan'onji	28	Lg	34.07N	133.39 E
Kanoya	28	Ki	31.23N	130.51 E
Kanozero, Ozero-	7	Ic	67.00N	34.05 E
Kānpur	22	Kg	26.28N	80.21 E
Kansas	38	Jf	39.07N	94.36W
Kansas [2]	43	Hd	38.45N	98.15W
Kansas City [Ks.-U.S.]	39	Jf	39.07N	94.39W
Kansas City [Mo.-U.S.]	39	Jf	39.05N	94.35W
Kanshi	27	Kg	24.57N	116.52 E
Kansk	22	Ld	56.13N	95.41 E
Kansŏng	28	Je	38.22N	128.28 E
Kansu (EN)=Gansu Sheng (Kan-sụ Sheng) [2]	27	Hd	38.00N	102.00 E
Kansu (EN)=Kan-su Sheng→Gansu Sheng [2]	27	Hd	38.00N	102.00 E
Kan-su Sheng→Gansu Sheng=Kansu (EN) [2]	27	Hd	38.00N	102.00 E
Kansyat	26	Kg	2.15 S	138.51 E
Kant	18	Jc	42.52N	74.50 E
Kantang	25	Jg	7.23N	99.32 E
Kantchari	34	Fc	12.29N	1.31 E
Kanté	34	Fd	9.57N	1.03 E
Kantemirovka	19	Df	49.45N	39.53 E
Kantō-Heiya	29	Fc	36.00N	139.30 E
Kanton Atoll	57	Je	2.50 S	171.41W
Kantō-Sanchi	29	Fc	36.00N	138.45 E
Kantubek	18	Bb	45.06N	59.16 E
Kanturk/Ceann Toirc	9	Ei	52.10N	8.55W
Kanuma	29	Fc	36.34N	139.45 E
Kanye	31	Jk	24.58 S	25.21 E
Kanyu	37	Cd	20.04 S	24.36 E
Kanzenze	36	Ee	10.31 S	25.12 E
Kao	65b	Aa	19.40 S	175.01W
Kaohsiung	22	Og	22.38N	120.17 E
Kaôk Nhêk	25	Lf	13.05N	107.04 E
Kaoko Otavi	37	Ac	18.15 S	13.37 E
Kaokoveld [3]	37	Ac	18.00 S	13.00 E
Kaokoveld	30	Ij	19.30 S	13.30 E
Kaolack	31	Fg	14.09N	16.04W
Kao Neua, Col de-	25	Le	18.23N	105.10 E
Kaouadja	35	Cd	8.00N	23.14 E
Kaouar	34	Hb	19.05N	12.52 E
Kapaa	65a	Ba	22.05N	159.19W
Kapanga	31	Ji	8.21 S	22.35 E
Kapar	24	Ld	36.32N	47.30 E
Kapčagaj	19	Hg	43.52N	77.03 E
Kapčagajskoje Vodohranilišče	19	Hg	43.45N	78.00 E
Kapchorwa	36	Fb	1.24N	34.27 E
Kap Dan	41	Ie	65.32N	37.30W
Kapelle	12	Fc	51.39N	3.57 E
Kapellskär	8	He	59.43N	19.04 E
Kapena	36	Ee	10.47 S	28.20 E
Kapenguria	36	Gb	1.14N	35.07 E
Kapfenberg	14	Jc	47.26N	15.18 E
Kapidaği Yarimadası	15	Ki	40.28N	27.50 E
Kapiri Mposhi	36	Ee	13.58 S	28.41 E
Kāpīsā [3]	23	Kc	34.45N	69.30 E
Kapit	26	Ff	2.01N	112.56 E
Kapiti Island	62	Fd	40.50 S	174.55 E
Kapka, Massif du-	35	Cb	15.07N	21.45 E
Kapoeta	31	Kh	4.47N	33.35 E
Kapona	36	Ed	7.11 S	29.09 E
Kapos	10	Oj	46.44N	18.29 E
Kaposvár	10	Nj	46.22N	17.48 E
Kapp	8	Dd	60.42N	10.52 E
Kappeln	10	Fb	54.40N	9.56 E
Kapša	7	Hg	59.52N	33.45 E
Kapsan	28	Jd	41.05N	128.18 E
Kapsukas	7	Fi	54.33N	23.23 E
Kapuas [Indon.]	26	Mj	0.25 S	109.40 E
Kapuas [Indon.]	26	Fg	3.01 S	114.20 E
Kapuas Hulu, Pegunungan- =Kapuas Mountains (EN)	26	Ff	1.25N	113.15 E
Kapuas Mountains (EN)= Kapuas Hulu, Pegunungan	26	Ff	1.25N	113.15 E
Kapugargin	15	Lm	36.40N	28.50 E
Kapušany	10	Rg	49.03N	21.21 E
Kapuskasing	39	Ke	49.25N	82.26W
Kapustin Jar	16	Ne	48.35N	45.45 E
Kapustoje	7	Ic	67.17N	34.12 E
Kaputdžuh, Gora-	16	Oj	39.12N	46.01 E
Kapuvár	10	Ni	47.36N	17.02 E
Kara	17	Lb	69.10N	64.45 E
Kara	34	Fd	9.33N	1.12 E
Kara [3]	34	Fd	9.35N	1.05 E
Kara Ada [Tur.]	15	Km	36.58N	27.28 E
Kara Ada [Tur.]	15	Jk	38.25N	26.20 E
Kara-Balta	19	Hg	42.49N	73.57 E
Karabas	19	Hf	49.30N	73.00 E
Karabaš	17	Ji	55.29N	60.13 E
Karabekaul	19	Gh	38.28N	64.10 E
Karabiga	15	Ki	40.24N	27.18 E
Karabil, Vozvyšennost-	18	Df	36.20N	63.30 E
Kara-Bogaz-Gol	19	Fg	41.01N	52:59 E
Kara-Bogaz-Gol, proliv-	16	Ri	41.04N	52.59 E
Kara-Bogaz-Gol, Zaliv-	5	Lg	41.00N	53.15 E
Karabuk	23	Da	41.12N	32.37 E
Karabulak [Kaz.-U.S.S.R.]	18	Lb	44.54N	78.29 E
Karabulak [Kaz.-U.S.S.R.]	19	Gg	42.31N	69.47 E
Kara Burun	15	Km	36.32N	27.58 E
Karaburun [Tur.]	24	Cb	41.21N	28.40 E
Karaburun [Tur.]	24	Bc	38.37N	26.31 E
Karabutak	19	Gf	49.57N	60.08 E
Karacabey	24	Cb	40.13N	28.21 E
Karaca Dağ	24	Hd	37.40N	39.50 E
Karačajevo-Čerkessakaja Avtonomnaja Oblast [3]	19	Eg	43.45N	41.45 E
Karačajevsk	16	Lh	43.44N	41.58 E
Karacaköy	24	Cb	41.22N	28.30 E
Karacaoğlan	15	Kh	41.32N	27.04 E
Karacasu	24	Cd	37.43N	28.37 E
Karačev	19	De	53.04N	34.59 E
Karāchi	22	Ig	24.52N	67.03 E
Kara Dağ [Tur.]	24	Jd	37.40N	43.42 E
Kara Dağ [Tur.]	24	Ed	37.23N	33.10 E
Karadah	16	Oh	42.29N	46.54 E
Karadeniz=Black Sea (EN)	5	Jg	43.00N	35.00 E
Kara Dong	27	Dd	38.26N	81.50 E
Karagajly	19	Hf	49.20N	75.48 E
Karaganda	22	Je	49.50N	73.10 E
Karagandinskaja Oblast [3]	19	Hf	50.00N	74.00 E
Karaginski, Ostrov-	21	Sd	58.48N	164.05 E
Karaginski Zaliv	21	Sd	58.50N	164.00 E
Kara Gölü	15	Mm	36.42N	29.50 E
Karagoš, Gora-	20	Df	51.44N	89.24 E
Karahalli	15	Mk	38.20N	29.32 E
Karaidelski	17	Hi	55.49N	57.05 E
Kara-Irtyš	21	Ke	47.52N	84.16 E
Karaisali	24	Fd	37.16N	35.03 E
Karaj	24	Ne	35.48N	50.59 E
Karaj	24	Ne	35.07N	51.35 E
Karak, Gora-	19	Gg	44.59N	63.05 E
Kara-Kala	19	Fh	38.28N	56.18 E
Karakalpak ASSR (EN)= Karakalpakskaja ASSR [3]	19	Fg	43.30N	59.00 E
Karakalpakskaja ASSR= Karakalpak ASSR (EN) [3]	19	Fg	43.30N	59.00 E
Karakax/Moyu	27	Cd	37.17N	79.42 E
Karakax He	27	Dd	38.06N	80.24 E
Karakaya Barajı	24	Hc	38.25N	38.45 E
Karakeçi	24	Hd	37.26N	39.26 E
Karakelong, Pulau-	26	If	4.15N	126.48 E
Karakoçan	24	Ic	38.02N	40.07 E
Karakoin, Ozero-	18	Ga	46.10N	68.40 E
Karakojsu	16	Oh	42.30N	47.05 E
Karakolka	18	Kd	41.29N	77.24 E
Karakoram	21	Jf	34.00N	78.00 E
Karakoram Pass	21	Jf	35.30N	77.50 E
Karakore	35	Gc	10.25N	40.01 E
Karakoro	34	Cc	14.43N	12.03 E
Karakorum Shan	27	Cd	36.00N	76.00 E
Karakorum Shankou	27	Cd	35.30N	77.50 E
Karaköy	24	Ic	39.04N	41.42 E
Kara-Kul	18	Id	41.34N	72.47 E
Karakul, Ozero-	19	Hh	39.05N	73.25 E
Karakumski kanal imeni V.I. Lenina	19	Gh	37.42N	64.20 E
Karakumy	21	Hf	39.00N	60.00 E
Karakuwisa	37	Bc	18.56 S	19.40 E
Karam	20	Fe	55.09N	107.37 E
Karama	26	Gg	2.18 S	119.06 E
Karaman	23	Db	37.11N	33.14 E
Karamanli	15	Ml	37.22N	29.49 E
Karamay	22	Ke	45.30N	84.55 E
Karamea	61	Dh	41.15 S	172.06 E
Karamea Bight	62	Dd	41.25 S	171.50 E
Karamet-Nijaz	19	Gh	37.43N	64.31 E
Karamiran He	27	Dd	37.50N	84.35 E
Karamiran Shankou	27	Ed	36.15N	87.05 E
Karamiševo	8	Mg	57.44N	28.50 E
Karamoja [3]	36	Fb	2.45N	34.15 E
Karamürsel	15	Mi	40.42N	29.36 E
Kara-myk	19	Hh	39.30N	71.51 E
Karamyš	16	Nd	51.18N	45.00 E
Karān	24	Mi	27.43N	49.49 E
Karaova	15	Kl	37.05N	27.40 E
Karapınar	24	Ed	37.43N	33.33 E
Kara-Saki	29	Ad	34.40N	129.29 E
Kara-Sal	16	Mf	47.18N	43.36 E
Karasay	27	Dd	36:48N	83.48 E
Karasburg	31	Ik	28.00 S	18.43 E
Kara Sea (EN)=Karskoje More	67	Hd	76.00N	80.00 E
Karašica	14	Me	45.36N	18.36 E
Karasjok	7	Fb	69.27N	25.30 E
Kara Strait (EN)=Karskije Vorota, Proliv-	21	Hb	70.30N	58.00 E
Karasu	24	Db	41.04N	30.47 E
Karasu [Tur.]	21	Ff	38.52N	38.48 E
Karasu [Tur.]	24	Ic	38.49N	41.28 E
Karasu [Tur.]	24	Jc	38.32N	43.10 E
Karasu Dağları	24	Ic	39.30N	40.45 E
Karasuk	20	Cf	53.44N	78.08 E
Karasuk	20	Cf	53.35N	77.30 E
Karasuyama	29	Gc	36.39N	140.08 E
Karatá, Laguna-	49	Fg	13.56N	83.30W
Karatal	19	Hf	46.26N	77.10 E
Karataş [Tur.]	24	Fd	36.36N	35.21 E
Karataş [Tur.]	15	Lk	38.34N	28.17 E
Karataş Burun	24	Fb	36.35N	35.22 E
Karatau	19	Hg	43.10N	70.29 E
Karatau, Hrebet-	21	Ie	43.40N	69.00 E
Karatj	7	Ec	66.43N	18.33 E
Karatobe	16	Re	49.42N	53.33 E
Karaton	19	Ff	46.25N	53.34 E
Karatsu	28	Jh	33.26N	130.00 E
Karatsu-Wan	29	Be	33.30N	130.00 E
Kara-Turgaj	21	Ie	48.01N	62.45 E
Karaul [Kaz.-U.S.S.R.]	19	Hf	49.00N	79.20 E
Karaul [R.S.F.S.R.]	20	Db	70.10N	83.08 E
Karaulbazar	18	Ee	39.29N	64.47 E
Karaulkala	18	Bc	42.18N	58.41 E
Karáva	15	Ej	39.19N	21.36 E
Karavanke	14	Id	46.25N	14.25 E
Karavastase, Gjiri i-	15	Ci	40.55N	19.30 E
Karavastase, Laguna e-	15	Ci	40.55N	19.30 E
Karávi	15	Gm	36.45N	23.35 E
Karavonísia	15	Jn	35.59N	26.26 E
Karawa	36	Db	3.20N	20.18 E
Karaxabar He/Kaidu He	27	Ec	41.55N	86.38 E
Karažal	19	Hf	47.59N	70.53 E
Karbalā'	22	Gf	32.36N	44.02 E
Karbalā [3]	24	Jf	32.30N	43.45 E
Kårbole	7	Df	61.59N	15.19 E
Karcag	10	Qi	47.19N	20.56 E
Kardhámaina	15	Km	36.47N	27.09 E
Kardhámila	15	Jk	38.31N	26.06 E
Kardhiótissa	15	Im	36.38N	25.01 E
Kardhítsa	15	Ej	39.22N	21.55 E
Kärdla/Kjardla	7	Fg	59.01N	22.42 E
Kărdžali	15	Ih	41.39N	25.22 E
Kărdžali [2]	15	Ih	41.30N	25.30 E
Kareha, Jbel-	13	Gi	35.15N	5.30W
Karelia (EN)	5	Jc	64.00N	32.00 E
Karelskaja ASSR [3]	19	Dc	63.30N	33.30 E
Karema	36	Fd	6.49S	30.26 E
Karen → Kayin	25	Je	17.30N	97.45 E
Karen	25	If	12.51N	92.53 E
Karesuando	7	Fb	68.27N	22.29 E
Karêt	30	Gf	24.00N	7.30W
Kärevere/Kjarevere	8	Lf	58.23N	26.30 E
Kargala	16	Sd	51.59N	55.10 E
Kargapazarı Dağı	24	Ib	40.07N	41.35 E
Kargapolje	17	Li	55.57N	64.27 E
Kargasok	20	De	59.07N	81.01 E
Kargat	20	De	55.10N	80.17 E
Kargı	24	Fb	41.08N	34.30 E
Kargil	25	Fb	34.34N	76.06 E
Kargilik/Yecheng	22	Jf	37.54N	77.26 E
Kargopol	19	Dc	61.32N	38.58 E
Karhula	7	Gf	60.31N	26.57 E
Kari	34	Hc	11.14N	10.34 E
Kariaí	6	Ig	40.15N	24.15 E
Kariba	31	Jj	16.30 S	28.45 E
Kariba, Lake-	30	Jj	17.00 S	28.00 E
Kariba-Dake	29a	Ab	42.37N	139.56 E
Kariba Dam	37	Dc	16.30 S	28.50 E
Karibib	31	Ik	21.58 S	15.51 E
Karibib [3]	37	Bd	22.00 S	16.00 E
Kariet-Arkmane	13	Ji	35.06N	2.45W
Karigasniemi	7	Fb	69.24N	25.50 E
Karijärvi	8	Jc	61.35N	22.30 E
Karikachi Tōge	29a	Cb	43.10N	142.40 E
Kārikāl	25	Ff	10.55N	79.50 E
Karikari, Cape-	62	Ea	34.47 S	173.24 E
Karima (EN)=Kuraymah	31	Kg	18.33N	31.51 E
Karimama	34	Fc	12.04N	3.11 E
Karimata, Kepulauan-= Karimata Islands (EN)	26	Eg	1.25 S	109.05 E
Karimata, Pulau-	26	Eg	1.36 S	108.55 E
Karimata, Selat-=Karimata Strait (EN)	21	Mj	2.05 S	108.40 E
Karimata Islands (EN)= Karimata, Kepulauan-	26	Eg	1.25 S	109.05 E
Karimata Strait (EN)= Karimata, Selat-	21	Mj	2.05 S	108.40 E
Karīmganj	25	Id	24.42N	92.33 E
Karīmnagar	25	Fe	18.26N	79.09 E
Karimunjawa, Kepulauan-= Karimunjawa Islands (EN)	26	Fh	5.50 S	110.25 E
Karimunjawa Islands (EN)= Karimunjawa, Kepulauan-	26	Fh	5.50 S	110.25 E
Karin [Som.]	35	Hc	10.59N	49.13 E
Karin [Som.]	35	Hc	10.51N	45.45 E
Karis/Karjaa	7	Ff	60.05N	23.40 E
Karisimbi	30	Ji	1.30 S	29.27 E
Káristos	15	Hk	38.01N	24.25 E
Karjaa/Karis	7	Ff	60.05N	23.40 E
Karkār	35	Hd	9.57N	49.20 E
Karkaralinsk	19	Hf	49.23N	75.31 E
Karkar Island	57	Fe	4.40 S	146.00 E
Karkas, Kūh-e	24	Nf	33.27N	51.48 E
Karkheh	23	Gc	31.31N	47.55 E
Karkinitski zaliv	5	Jf	45.55N	33.00 E
Karkkila/Högfors	7	Ff	60.32N	24.11 E
Karkku	8	Jc	61.25N	23.01 E
Kärkölä	8	Kd	60.55N	25.15 E
Kärla/Kjarla	8	Jf	58.16N	22.05 E
Karlholm	8	Gd	60.31N	17.37 E
Karlik Shan	21	Le	43.00N	94.30 E
Karlino	10	Lb	54.03N	15.51 E
Karliova	24	Ic	39.18N	41.01 E
Karl Marx, Pik-	19	Hh	37.08N	72.29 E
Karl-Marx-Stadt	6	He	50.50N	12.55 E
Karl-Marx-Stadt [2]	10	If	50.45N	12.50 E
Karlö/Hailuoto	5	Ib	65.02N	24.42 E
Karlobag	14	Jf	44.32N	15.05 E
Karlovac	14	Je	45.29N	15.33 E
Karlovka	16	Ie	49.28N	35.08 E
Karlovo	15	Hg	42.38N	24.48 E
Karlovy Vary	10	If	50.14N	12.52 E
Karlsbad	12	Kf	48.55N	8.35 E,
Karlsborg	7	Df	58.32N	14.31 E
Karlshamn	7	Dh	56.10N	14.51 E
Karlskoga	7	Dg	59.20N	14.31 E
Karlskrona	6	Hd	56.10N	15.35 E
Karlsöarna	8	Gg	57.15N	18.00 E
Karlsruhe	10	Eg	49.01N	8.24 E
Karlstad [Mn.-U.S.]	45	Hb	48.35N	96.31W
Karlstad [Swe.]	6	Hd	59.22N	13.30 E
Karluk	40	Ie	57.34N	154.28W
Karmah=Kerma (EN)	35	Eb	19.38N	30.25 E
Karmana	18	Ed	40.09N	65.15 E
Karmøy	7	Ag	59.15N	5.15 E
Karnāli	25	Gc	28.45N	81.16 E
Karnataka (Mysore) [3]	25	Ff	13.30N	76.00 E
Karnobat	15	Jg	42.39N	26.59 E
Kärnten = Carinthia (EN) [2]	14	Hd	46.45N	14.00 E
Kärnten = Carinthia (EN)	14	Hd	46.45N	14.00 E
Karoi	37	Dc	16.50 S	29.40 E
Karonga	31	Ki	9.56 S	33.56 E
Karora	35	Fb	17.39N	38.22 E
Káros	15	Im	36.53N	25.39 E
Kárpathos	15	Kn	35.30N	27.14 E
Kárpathos=Karpathos (EN)	5	Ih	35.40N	27.10 E
Karpathos (EN)= Kárpathos	5	Ih	35.40N	27.10 E
Karpáthou, Stenón-	15	Kn	35.50N	27.30 E
Karpenision	15	Ek	38.55N	21.47 E
Karpinsk	17	Jg	59.45N	60.01 E
Karpuzlu	15	Kl	37.33N	27.50 E
Kars	23	Fa	40.37N	43.05 E
Karsakpaj	19	Gf	47.48N	66.45 E
Kärsämäki	7	Fe	64.00N	25.46 E
Karsava/Kārsava	7	Gh	56.47N	27.42 E
Kārsava/Karsava	7	Gh	56.47N	27.42 E
Karši	22	If	38.53N	65.48 E
Karşiyaka	15	Ki	40.26N	28.00 E
Karsiyaka	15	Kk	38.27N	27.07 E
Karskije Vorota, Proliv-= Kara Strait (EN)	21	Hb	70.30N	58.00 E
Karskoje More=Kara Sea (EN)	67	Hd	76.00N	80.00 E
Kars Platosu	24	Jb	40.40N	43.07 E
Karst (EN)=Kras	5	Hf	45.48N	14.00 E
Kårsta	8	He	59.39N	18.14 E
Karstula	7	Fe	62.52N	24.47 E
Kartal	24	Cb	40.53N	29.10 E
Kartaly	19	Ge	53.03N	60.40 E
Kartaly-Ajat	17	Jj	53.01N	61.50 E
Karttula	8	Lb	62.53N	26.58 E
Kartuzy	10	Ob	54.20N	18.12 E
Karumai	29	Ga	40.20N	141.28 E
Karumba	59	Ic	17.29 S	140.50 E
Karūn	21	Gf	30.25N	48.12 E
Karungi	7	Fc	66.03N	23.57 E
Karungu	36	Fc	0.51 S	34.09 E
Karunki	7	Fc	66.02N	24.01 E
Karūr	25	Ff	10.57N	78.05 E
Karvia	7	Fe	62.08N	22.34 E
Karviná	10	Og	49.51N	18.32 E
Kārwār	25	Ef	14.48N	74.08 E
Karwendel Gebirge	14	Fc	47.28N	11.20 E
Karymskoje	20	Gf	51.37N	114.21 E
Kas	35	Cc	12.34N	24.14 E
Kaş	24	Cd	36.12N	29.38 E
Kasaba [Tur.]	15	Mm	36.18N	29.44 E
Kasaba [Zam.]	36	Ee	10.44 S	29.43 E
Kasado-Shima	29	Be	33.57N	131.50 E
Kasah	16	Mi	40.03N	43.52 E
Kasai	29	Dd	34.56N	134.49 E
Kasai	30	Ii	3.02 S	16.57 E
Kasai Occidental [2]	36	Dc	5.00 S	21.30 E
Kasai Oriental [2]	36	Dc	3.00 S	23.00 E
Kasaji	36	De	10.22 S	23.27 E
Kasaku	36	Ec	1.55 S	25.50 E
Kasama [Jap.]	29	Gc	36.22N	140.16 E
Kasama [Zam.]	31	Kj	10.13 S	31.12 E
Kasan	18	Ee	39.01N	65.35 E
Kasane	31	Jj	17.48 S	25.09 E
Kasanga	36	Fd	8.28 S	31.09 E
Kasangulu	36	Bc	4.36 S	15.10 E
Kasansaj	18	Hd	41.10N	71.32 E
Kasaoka	29	Cd	34.30N	133.29 E
Kāsaragod	25	Ef	12.30N	75.00 E
Kasari	29b	Ba	28.27N	129.41 E
Kašary	16	Le	49.02N	41.03 E
Kasatori-Yama	29	Ce	33.33N	132.55 E
Kasba Lake	42	Hd	60.20N	102.10W
Kasba Tatla	32	Fc	32.36N	6.16W
Kaseda	28	Ki	31.25N	130.19 E
Kasempa	36	Ee	13.27 S	25.50 E
Kasenga	31	Jj	10.22 S	28.37 E
Kasenye	36	Fb	1.24N	30.26 E
Kasese [Ug.]	36	Fb	0.10N	30.05 E
Kasese [Zaire]	36	Ec	1.38 S	27.07 E
Kashaf	23	Jb	35.58N	61.07 E
Kāshān	22	Hf	33.59N	51.29 E
Kashi	22	Jf	39.29N	75.58 E
Kashihara	29	Dd	34.31N	135.47 E
Kashima [Jap.]	29	Cd	35.31N	132.59 E
Kashima [Jap.]	29	Gd	35.58N	140.38 E
Kashima [Jap.]	29	Be	33.07N	130.07 E
Kashima-Nada	29	Gc	36.30N	140.45 E
Kashiobwe	36	Ed	9.39 S	28.37 E
Kashiwazaki	28	Of	37.25N	138.30 E
Kashkū'īyeh	24	Qh	28.58N	56.37 E
Kāshmar	23	Ib	35.12N	58.27 E
Kashmir	21	Jf	34.00N	76.00 E
Kashmor	25	Dc	28.26N	69.35 E
Kasimov	19	Ee	54.59N	41.28 E
Kašin	19	Dd	57.23N	37.37 E
Kasindi	36	Eb	0.02N	29.43 E
Kašira	7	Ji	54.52N	38.11 E
Kasiruta, Pulau-	26	Ig	0.25 S	127.12 E
Kasisty	20	Fb	73.40N	109.45 E
Kaškadarinskaja Oblast [3]	19	Gh	38.50N	66.10 E
Kaškadarja	18	Ee	39.35N	64.38 E
Kaskaskia River	45	Lh	37.59N	89.56W
Kaskelen	19	Hg	43.09N	76.37 E
Kaskö/Kaskinen	7	Ee	62.23N	21.13 E
Kasli	17	Ji	55.53N	60.48 E
Kaslo	46	Gb	49.55N	116.55W
Kasongo	31	Ji	4.27 S	26.40 E
Kasongo-Lunda	36	Cd	6.28 S	16.49 E
Kásos	15	Jn	35.25N	26.55 E
Kásou, Stenón-	15	Jn	35.25N	26.35 E
Kaspi	16	Ni	41.58N	44.25 E
Kaspičan	15	Kf	43.18N	27.11 E
Kaspijsk	19	Eg	42.57N	47.35 E
Kaspijski	19	Ef	45.25N	47.22 E
Kaspijskoje More=Caspian Sea (EN)	5	Lg	42.00N	50.30 E
Kasplja	16	Gb	55.24N	30.43 E
Kasr, Ra's-	35	Fb	18.04N	38.33 E
Kassaar/Kassar	8	Jf	58.47N	22.40 E
Kassalā	31	Kg	15.28N	36.24 E
Kassalā [3]	35	Fc	14.40N	35.30 E
Kassándra	15	Gi	40.00N	23.30 E
Kassandra, Gulf of- (EN) = Kassándras, Kólpos-	15	Gi	40.05N	23.30 E
Kassándras, Ákra-	15	Gj	39.57N	23.21 E
Kassándras, Kólpos- = Kassandra, Gulf of- (EN)	15	Gi	40.05N	23.30 E
Kassel	10	Fe	51.19N	9.30 E
Kassiópi	15	Cj	39.47N	19.55 E
Kastamonu	23	Da	41.22N	33.47 E
Kastanéai	15	Jh	41.39N	26.28 E
Kastellaun	12	Jd	50.04N	7.27 E
Kastéllion [Grc.]	15	In	35.12N	25.20 E
Kastéllion [Grc.]	15	Gn	35.30N	23.39 E
Kastéllos, Ákra-	15	Kn	35.23N	27.09 E
Kasterlee	12	Gc	51.15N	4.57 E
Kastlösa	8	Gh	56.28N	16.25 E
Kastoría	15	Ei	40.31N	21.16 E
Kastorias, Límni-	15	Ei	40.31N	21.18 E
Kastornoje	16	Kd	51.51N	38.07 E
Kastós	15	Dk	38.35N	20.55 E
Kasuga	29	Be	33.32N	130.27 E
Kasugai	29	Ed	35.14N	136.58 E
Kasulu	36	Fc	4.34 S	30.06 E
Kasumbalesa	36	Ee	12.13 S	27.48 E
Kasumi	29	Dd	35.38N	134.38 E
Kasumi-ga-Ura	28	Pf	36.00N	140.25 E
Kasumkent	16	Pi	41.42N	48.10 E
Kasungan	26	Fg	1.58 S	113.24 E
Kasungu	36	Fe	13.02 S	33.29 E
Kasupe	36	Gf	15.10 S	35.18 E
Kasūr	25	Eb	31.07N	74.27 E
Kaszuby	10	Ob	54.10N	18.15 E
Kataba	31	Jj	16.05 S	25.10 E
Katahdin, Mount-	43	Nb	45.55N	68.55W
Katajsk	17	Kh	56.18N	62.35 E
Katako-Kombe	36	Dc	3.24 S	24.25 E
Katanga	36	Ed	10.00 S	25.30 E
Katanga	20	Fd	60.10N	102.10 E
Katangli	20	Jf	51.43N	143.16 E
Katanning	59	Df	33.42 S	117.33 E
Katav-Ivanovsk	17	Ii	54.47N	58.15 E
Katchall	25	Ig	7.57N	93.22 E
Katchi	32	Ef	17.00N	13.55W
Katende, Chutes de-	36	Dd	6.30 S	22.10 E
Katerini	15	Fi	40.16N	22.30 E
Katesh	36	Gc	4.31 S	35.23 E
Katete	36	Fe	14.06 S	32.05 E
Katha	25	Jd	24.11N	96.21 E
Katherine	58	Ef	14.28 S	132.16 E
Katherine River	59	Gb	14.39 S	131.42 E
Kāthiāwār	21	Jg	21.58N	70.30 E
Kāṭhmāṇḍãũ = Kathmandu (EN)	22	Kg	27.43N	85.19 E
Kathmandu → Kāṭhmāṇḍãũ	22	Kg	27.43N	85.19 E
Kathua	36	Gc	1.17 S	39.03 E
Kati	34	Dc	12.43N	8.05W
Katihār	25	Hc	25.32N	87.35 E
Katiki, Volcán-	65d	Bb	27.06 S	109.16W
Katima Mulilo	36	Df	17.28 S	24.14 E
Katiola	34	Dd	8.08N	5.06W
Katiola [3]	34	Dd	8.13N	5.02W
Katiu Atoll	61	Mc	16.26 S	144.22W
Katla	7a	Bc	63.36N	18.58W
Katlabuh, Ozero-	15	Ld	45.25N	29.00 E
Katlanovo	15	Eh	41.54N	21.41 E
Katmai, Mount-	40	Ie	58.17N	154.56W
Káto Akhaía	15	Ek	38.09N	21.33 E
Katofio	36	Ee	11.02 S	28.01 E
Katompi	36	Ed	6.11 S	26.20 E
Katonga	36	Fb	0.10N	30.40 E
Katon-Karagaj	19	If	49.11N	85.37 E
Káto Ólimbos	15	Fj	39.55N	22.28 E
Katoomba	59	Kf	33.42 S	150.18 E
Katopasa, Gunung-	26	Hg	1.14 S	121.25 E

Index Symbols

[1] Independent Nation
[2] State, Region
[3] District, County
Municipality
Colony, Dependency
Continent
Physical Region
Historical or Cultural Region
Mount, Mountain
Volcano
Hill
Mountains, Mountain Range
Hills, Escarpment
Plateau, Upland
Pass, Gap
Plain, Lowland
Delta
Salt Flat
Valley, Canyon
Crater, Cave
Karst Features
Depression
Polder
Desert, Dunes
Forest, Woods
Heath, Steppe
Oasis
Cape, Point
Coast, Beach
Cliff
Peninsula
Isthmus
Sandbank
Island
Atoll
Rock, Reef
Islands, Archipelago
Rocks, Reefs
Coral Reef
Well, Spring
Geyser
River, Stream
Waterfall Rapids
River Mouth, Estuary
Lake
Salt Lake
Intermittent Lake
Reservoir
Swamp, Pond
Canal
Glacier
Ice Shelf, Pack Ice
Ocean
Sea
Gulf, Bay
Strait, Fjord
Lagoon
Bank
Seamount
Tablemount
Ridge
Shelf
Basin
Escarpment, Sea Scarp
Fracture
Trench, Abyss
National Park, Reserve
Point of Interest
Recreation Site
Cave, Cavern
Historic Site
Ruins
Wall, Walls
Church, Abbey
Temple
Scientific Station
Airport
Port
Lighthouse
Mine
Tunnel
Dam, Bridge

Katowice [2] 10 Of 50.15N 19.00 E
Katowice 6 He 50.16N 19.00 E
Katrancık Dağı 24 Dd 37.27N 30.25 E
Kātrīnā, Jabal- 30 Kf 28.31N 33.57 E
Katrineholm 7 Dg 59.00N 16.12 E
Katsina 31 Hg 13.00N 7.36 E
Katsina Ala 34 Gd 7.48N 8.52 E
Katsumoto 28 Jh 33.51N 129.42 E
Katsuta 28 Pf 36.24N 140.32 E
Katsuura 28 Pg 35.08N 140.18 E
Katsuyama [Jap.] 28 Nf 36.03N 136.30 E
Katsuyama [Jap.] 29 Cd 35.06N 133.41 E
Kattakurgan 19 Gh 39.55N 66.15 E
Kattavía 15 Kn 35.57N 27.46 E
Kattegat 5 Hd 57.00N 11.00 E
Katthammarsvik 8 Hg 57.26N 18.50 E
Katulo, Lagh- 36 Hb 2.08N 40.56 E
Katumbi 36 Fe 10.49S 33.32 E
Katun 21 Kd 52.25N 85.05 E
Katwijk aan Zee 11 Kb 52.13N 4.24 E
Katwijk aan Zee, Katwijk- 12 Gb 52.12N 4.25 E
Katwijk-Katwijk aan Zee 12 Gb 52.12N 4.25 E
Katzenelnbogen 12 Jd 50.17N 7.57 E
Kau 26 If 1.11N 127.54 E
Kauai Channel 60 Oc 21.45N 158.50W
Kauai Island 57 Lb 22.03N 159.30W
Kaub 12 Jd 50.05N 7.46 E
Kauehi Atoll 61 Lc 15.51S 145.09W
Kaufbeuren 10 Gi 47.53N 10.37 E
Kauhajoki 7 Fe 62.26N 22.11 E
Kauhava 7 Fe 63.06N 23.05 E
Kauiki Head 60 Oc 20.46N 155.59W
Kaukauna 45 Ld 44.17N 88.17W
Kaukauveld 30 Jk 20.00S 21.50 E
Kaukonen 7 Fc 67.29N 24.54 E
Kaukura Atoll 57 Mf 15.45S 146.42W
Kaula Island 57 Kb 21.40N 160.32W
Kaulakahi Channel 65a Bb 22.02N 159.53W
Kaumalapau 65a Ec 20.47N 156.59W
Kaunakakai 60 Oc 21.05N 157.02W
Kaunas 6 Ie 54.54N 23.54 E
Kaunasskoje Vodohranilišče /Kauno Marios 8 Kj 54.50N 24.15 E
Kauniainen/Grankulla 8 Kd 60.13N 24.45 E
Kauno Marios/Kaunasskoje Vodohranilišče 8 Kj 54.50N 24.15 E
Kaunos 15 Lm 36.50N 28.35 E
Kaupanger 7 Bf 61.11N 7.14 E
Kau Paulatmada, Gunung- 26 Ig 3.15S 126.09 E
Kaura Namoda 34 Gc 12.36N 6.35 E
Kauriāla Ghāt 25 Gc 28.27N 80.59 E
Kaušany 16 Ff 46.39N 29.25 E
Kaustinen 7 Fe 63.32N 23.42 E
Kautokeino 7 Fb 68.59N 23.08 E
Kavacik 15 Lj 39.40N 28.30 E
Kavadarci 15 Fh 41.26N 22.01 E
Kavaja 15 Ch 41.11N 19.33 E
Kavak [Tur.] 15 Ji 40.36N 26.54 E
Kavak [Tur.] 24 Gb 41.05N 36.03 E
Kavaklidere 15 Ll 37.26N 28.22 E
Kavála 6 Ig 40.56N 24.25 E
Kaválas, Kólpos- 15 Hi 40.52N 24.25 E
Kavalerovo 20 Ih 44.19N 135.05 E
Kavali 25 Ff 14.55N 79.59 E
Kavār 24 Oh 29.11N 52.44 E
Kavaratti 22 Jh 10.33N 72.38 E
Kavaratti Island 25 Ef 10.33N 72.38 E
Kavarna 15 Lf 43.25N 28.20 E
Kavarskas/Kovarskas 8 Ki 55.24N 25.03 E
Kavendou, Mont- 30 Fg 10.41N 12.12W
Kavieng 60 Eh 2.34S 150.48 E
Kavīr, Dasht-e- 21 Hf 34.40N 54.30 E
Kavkaz 16 Jg 45.21N 36.12 E
Kavkaz, Bolšoj-=Caucasus (EN) 5 Kg 42.30N 45.00 E
Kävlinge 8 Ei 55.48N 13.06 E
Kävlingeån 8 Ei 55.47N 13.06 E
Kawa 35 Eb 19.10N 30.39 E
Kawabe 29 Gb 39.39N 140.15 E
Kawachi-nagano 29 Dd 34.27N 135.34 E
Kawagoe 29 Fd 35.55N 139.28 E
Kawaguchi 29 Fd 35.48N 139.42 E
Kawaihae Bay 65a Fc 20.02N 155.51W
Kawaihoa Point 65a Ab 21.47N 160.12W
Kawakawa 62 Fa 35.23S 174.04 E
Kawalusu, Pulau- 26 If 4.15N 125.19 E
Kawamata 29 Gc 37.40N 140.36 E
Kawambwa 36 Ed 9.47S 29.05 E
Kawaminami 29 Be 32.12N 131.32 E
Kawamoto 29 Cd 34.59N 132.29 E
Kawanishi 29 Gc 37.59N 140.03 E
Kawanoe 29 Cd 34.01N 133.34 E
Kawartha Lakes 44 Hc 44.32N 78.30W
Kawasaki [Jap.] 29 Gb 38.10N 140.38 E
Kawasaki [Jap.] 28 Og 35.32N 139.43 E
Kawashiri-Misaki 29 Bd 34.26N 130.58 E
Kawauchi 29a Bc 41.12N 141.00 E
Kawau Island 62 Fb 36.25S 174.50 E
Kawaura 29 Be 32.21N 130.05 E
Kawerau 62 Gc 38.05S 176.42 E
Kawhia 62 Fc 38.04S 174.49 E
Kawich Range 46 Gh 37.40N 116.30W
Kawio, Kepulauan- 26 If 4.30N 125.30 E
Kawkareik 25 Je 16.33N 98.14 E
Kawm Umbū 33 Fe 24.28N 32.57 E
Kawthaung 25 Jg 9.59N 98.33 E
Kaxgar He 21 Jf 39.46N 78.15 E
Kax He 27 Dc 43.37N 81.48 E
Kaya 34 Ec 13.05N 1.05W
Kayah [2] 25 Je 19.15N 97.30 E
Kayak 40 Ke 59.52N 144.30W
Kayali Daği 15 Jj 39.58N 26.38 E
Kayan 21 Ni 2.55N 117.35 E
Kayanga 34 Bc 11.58N 15.00W
Kayangel Islands 57 Ed 8.04N 134.43 E
Kayangel Passage 64a Ba 8.01N 134.42 E
Kaycee 46 Le 43.43N 106.38W
Kayenta 46 Jh 36.44N 110.17W
Kayes [3] 34 Cc 14.00N 11.00W
Kayes 31 Fg 14.26N 11.27W
Kayin 25 Je 17.30N 97.45 E
Kayoa, Pulau- 26 Ig 0.05S 127.25 E
Kayseri 22 Ff 38.43N 35.30 E
Kayuagung 26 Dg 3.24S 104.50 E
Kayu Ara, Pulau- 26 Ef 1.31N 106.26 E
Kazačje 20 Ib 70.40N 136.13 E
Kazah 16 Ni 41.05N 45.22 E
Kazahskaja Sovetskaja Socialističeskaja Respublika [2] 19 Gf 48.00N 68.00 E
Kazahskaja SSR/Kazak Sovettik Socialistik Respublikasy [2] 19 Gf 48.00N 68.00 E
Kazahskaja SSR=Kazakh SSR (EN) [2] 19 Gf 48.00N 68.00 E
Kazahski Melkosopočnik=Kazakh Hills (EN) 21 Je 49.00N 73.00 E
Kazahski Zaliv 16 Rh 42.40N 52.25 E
Kazakh Hills (EN)=Kazahski Melkosopočnik 21 Je 49.00N 73.00 E
Kazakh SSR (EN)=Kazahskaja SSR [2] 19 Gf 48.00N 68.00 E
Kazakhstan (EN) 21 Hd 51.11N 52.52 E
Kazaklija 15 Lc 46.05N 28.38 E
Kazak Sovettik Socialistik Respublikasy [2] 19 Gf 48.00N 68.00 E
Kazalak 15 Ke 44.03N 27.24 E
Kazalinsk 19 Gf 45.46N 62.07 E
Kazan 6 Kd 55.45N 49.08 E
Kazan 38 Jc 64.02N 95.30W
Kazandžik 19 Fh 39.17N 55.34 E
Kazanka 7 Li 55.48N 49.05 E
Kazanka 16 Hf 47.50N 32.49 E
Kazanlăk 15 Ig 42.37N 25.24 E
Kazan-Rettō/Iō=Volcano Islands (EN) 21 Qg 25.00N 141.00 E
Kazanskoje 19 Gd 55.38N 69.14 E
Kazarman 19 Hg 41.20N 74.02 E
Kazatin 19 Cf 49.43N 28.50 E
Kazbek, Gora- 16 Nh 42.42N 44.31 E
Kaz Daği 23 Cb 39.42N 26.50 E
Kaz Daği 15 Mk 38.35N 29.15 E
Kāzerūn 22 Hg 29.37N 51.38 E
Kažim 17 Ef 60.20N 51.32 E
Kazi-Magomed 16 Pi 40.02N 48.56 E
Kazimierza Wielka 10 Qf 50.16N 20.30 E
Kāzımkarabekir 24 Ed 37.14N 32.59 E
Kazincbarcika 10 Qh 48.15N 20.38 E
Kazinga Channel 36 Ec 0.13S 29.53 E
Kazlų-Rūda/Kazlu-Ruda 8 Jj 54.42N 23.32 E
Kazo 29 Fc 36.08N 139.36 E
Kaztalovka 16 Pe 49.46N 48.44 E
Kazumba 36 Dd 6.25S 22.02 E
Kazuno 28 Pd 40.14N 140.48 E
Kazym 19 Gc 63.54N 65.50 E
Kazyr 20 Ef 53.50N 92.53 E
Kcynia 10 Nd 53.00N 17.30 E
Kdyně 10 Jg 49.24N 13.02 E
Ké 35 Bb 18.32N 17.55 E
Kéa 15 Hl 37.37N 24.20 E
Kéa 15 Hl 37.39N 24.20 E
Keaau 65a Fd 19.37N 155.03W
Keahole Point 65a Ed 19.44N 156.04W
Kealaikahiki Channel 65a Ec 20.37N 156.50W
Kealaikahiki Point 65a Ec 20.32N 156.42W
Kealakekua Bay 65a Fd 19.28N 155.56W
Keams Canyon 46 Ji 35.49N 110.12W
Keanae 65a Ec 20.52N 156.09W
Keanapapa Point 65a Dc 20.54N 157.04W
Kearney 43 Hc 40.42N 99.05W
Kearns 46 Jf 40.39N 111.59W
Kéas, Stenón- 15 Hl 37.40N 24.12 E
Keats Bank (EN) 57 Id 5.23N 173.28 E
Keb 8 Mg 57.44N 28.38 E
Keban Baraji 24 Hc 38.53N 39.00 E
Kébémer 34 Bb 15.22N 16.27W
Kebir, Oued el- 14 Bn 36.51N 7.57 E
Kebnekaise 7 Eb 67.53N 18.33 E
Kebri Dehar 31 Lh 6.45N 44.17 E
Kebumen 26 Eh 7.40S 109.39 E
Kecel 10 Pj 46.32N 19.16 E
Kechika 42 Ee 59.38N 127.09W
Kecskemét 10 Pj 46.54N 19.42 E
Kédainiai/Kedajnjaj 7 Fi 55.18N 23.59 E
Kedajnjaj/Kédainiai 7 Fi 55.18N 23.59 E
Kedgwick 44 Nb 47.39N 67.21W
Kediri 22 Nj 7.49S 112.01 E
Kédougou 34 Cc 12.33N 12.11W
Kedva 17 Fd 64.14N 53.30 E
Kędzierzyn-Koźle 10 Of 50.20N 18.10 E
Keele 42 Fd 64.24N 124.47W
Keele Peak 38 Fc 63.26N 130.19W
Keeling Islands→Cocos Islands 21 Lk 12.10S 96.55 E
Keeling Islands→Cocos Islands [5] 22 Lk 12.10S 96.55 E
Keelung 22 Og 25.08N 121.44 E
Keene 44 Kd 42.55N 72.17W
Keer-Weer, Cape- 59 Ib 13.58S 141.30 E
Keetmanshoop 31 Ik 26.36S 18.08 E
Keetmanshoop [3] 37 Be 26.30S 18.30 E
Keewatin 42 Ig 49.46N 94.34W
Keewatin, District of- [3] 42 Hd 64.00N 96.00W
Kefa [3] 35 Fd 7.00N 36.00 E
Kefallinía=Cephalonia (EN) 5 Ih 38.15N 20.35 E
Kefamenanu 26 Hh 9.27S 124.29 E
Kefar Sava 24 Ff 32.10N 34.54 E
Keffi 34 Gd 8.51N 7.52 E
Keflavík 7a Ab 64.01N 22.34W
Kegen 19 Hg 42.58N 79.12 E
Kegums 8 Kh 56.41N 24.44 E
Kehdingen 10 Fc 53.45N 9.20 E
Kehl 10 Dh 48.35N 7.49 E
Kehra 7 Fg 59.19N 25.18 E
Keighley 9 Lh 53.52N 1.54W
Keila/Kejla 7 Fg 59.19N 24.27 E
Keila Jõgi/Kejla 8 Ke 59.25N 24.15 E
Keimoes 37 Ce 28.41S 21.00 E
Keipel Bank (EN) 59 Le 25.15S 159.30 E
Keïta 34 Gc 14.46N 5.46 E
Kéita, Bahr- 35 Bd 9.14N 18.21 E
Keitele 5 Ic 62.55N 26.00 E
Keith [Austl.] 59 Ig 36.06S 140.21 E
Keith [Scot.-U.K.] 9 Kd 57.32N 2.57W
Keith Arm 42 Fc 65.20N 122.00W
Keiyasi 63d Ab 17.53S 177.45 E
Kejla/Keila 7 Fg 59.19N 24.27 E
Kejla/Keila Jõgi 8 Ke 59.25N 24.15 E
Kejvy 7 Ic 67.30N 37.45 E
Kekaha 65a Bb 21.58N 159.43W
Kekerengu 62 Ee 42.00S 174.00 E
Kékes 10 Qi 47.52N 20.01 E
Keklau 64a Bb 7.35N 134.39 E
Kelafo 35 Gd 5.37N 44.13 E
Kelakam 34 Hc 13.35N 11.44 E
Kela Met 35 Fb 15.50N 38.23 E
Kelan 27 Jd 38.44N 111.34 E
Kelang 22 Mi 3.02N 101.27 E
Kelasa, Selat-=Gaspar Strait (EN) 26 Eg 2.40S 107.15 E
Kelberg 12 Id 50.18N 6.55 E
Kelcyra 15 Di 40.19N 20.11 E
Kelefesia 65b Bb 20.30S 174.44W
Kelekçi 15 Ml 37.14N 29.28 E
Kelem 35 Fe 4.49N 35.59 E
Keles 15 Mj 39.55N 29.14 E
Keles 18 Gd 41.02N 68.37 E
Kelheim 10 Hh 48.55N 11.52 E
Kelifely, Causse du- 37 Hc 17.15S 45.30 E
Kelifski Uzboj 18 Ef 37.45N 64.40 E
Keli Hāji Ibrāhīm 24 Kd 36.42N 45.00 E
Kelkheim 12 Kd 50.08N 8.27 E
Kelkit 23 Ea 40.46N 36.32 E
Kelkit 24 Hb 40.08N 39.27 E
Kellé 36 Bc 0.06S 14.33 E
Kellerberrin 59 Df 31.38S 117.43 E
Kellerwald 12 Lc 51.03N 9.10 E
Kellett, Cape- 42 Eb 72.57N 125.27W
Kellett Strait 42 Fa 75.50N 117.40W
Kellog 20 Dd 62.27N 86.35 E
Kellogg 43 Db 47.32N 116.07W
Kelloselkä 7 Gc 66.56N 29.00 E
Kells/Ceanannas Mór 9 Gh 53.44N 6.53W
Kelmė/Kelme 7 Fi 55.39N 22.58 E
Kelme/Kelmė 7 Fi 55.39N 22.58 E
Kelmency 15 Ja 48.27N 26.47 E
Kelmis/La Calamine 12 Hd 50.43N 6.00 E
Kélo 35 Bd 9.15N 15.48 E
Kelowna 39 He 49.53N 119.29W
Kelsey 42 He 56.00N 97.00W
Kelsey Bay 42 Ef 50.24N 125.57W
Kelso 46 Dc 46.09N 122.54W
Kelso Bank 59 Ld 24.10S 159.10 E
Kelso Bank (EN) 59 Ld 24.10S 159.30 E
Kel Tepe [Tur.] 24 Eb 41.05N 32.27 E
Kel Tepe [Tur.] 15 Ni 40.39N 30.06 E
Keltie, Mount- 66 Jf 79.15S 159.00 E
Keluang 26 Df 2.02N 103.19 E
Kelvin Seamount (EN) 43 Od 38.50N 64.00W
Kelyeḫed 35 Hd 8.44N 49.10 E
Kem 19 Dc 64.57N 34.31 E
Kema 7 If 60.19N 37.15 E
Ké Macina 34 Dc 13.57N 5.23W
Kemah 24 Hc 39.36N 39.02 E
Kemaliye 24 Hc 39.16N 38.29 E
Kemalpaşa 24 Cc 40.00N 28.20 E
Kemalpaşa 15 Kk 38.25N 27.26 E
Kembé 35 Ce 4.36N 21.54 E
Kemer [Tur.] 15 Mm 36.28N 29.21 E
Kemer [Tur.] 24 Dd 36.36N 30.34 E
Kemer Baraji 15 Ll 37.30N 28.35 E
Kemeri/Ķemeri 8 Jh 56.56N 23.25 E
Ķemeri/Kemeri 8 Jh 56.56N 23.25 E
Kemerovo 22 Kd 55.20N 86.05 E
Kemerovskaja Oblast [3] 20 De 55.00N 87.00 E
Kemi 6 Ib 65.44N 24.34 E
Kemijärvi 7 Gc 66.40N 27.25 E
Kemijärvi=Kenni, Lake- (EN) 7 Gc 66.36N 27.24 E
Kemijoki 5 Ib 65.47N 24.30 E
Kemiö 8 Jd 60.10N 22.40 E
Kemiö/Kimito 8 Jd 60.10N 22.40 E
Kemlja 7 Ki 54.43N 45.15 E
Kemmerer 46 Jf 41.48N 110.32W
Kémo-Gribingui [3] 35 Bd 6.00N 19.00 E
Kemp, Lake- 45 Gj 33.45N 99.13W
Kempaž 17 Jd 64.03N 61.02 E
Kempele 7 Fd 64.55N 25.30 E
Kempen 12 Ic 51.22N 6.25 E
Kempen/Campine 11 Lc 51.10N 5.20 E
Kempendjaj 20 Gd 62.02N 118.42 E
Kempenich 12 Jd 50.25N 7.08 E
Kemp Land 66 Ee 67.10S 58.00 E
Kemps Bay 49 Ia 24.02N 77.33W
Kempsey 59 Kf 31.05S 152.50 E
Kempston 12 Bb 52.06N 0.29W
Kempt, Lac- 44 Kg 47.25N 74.15W
Kempten 10 Gi 47.43N 10.19 E
Ken 25 Hc 25.46N 80.31 E
Ken, Loch- 9 If 55.02N 4.02W
Kena 7 Je 62.06N 39.05 E
Kenadsa 32 Gc 31.34N 2.26W
Kenai 39 Dc 60.33N 151.15W
Kenai Mountains 40 Ie 60.00N 150.00W
Kenai Peninsula 38 Ed 60.10N 150.00W
Kendal 9 Kg 54.20N 2.45W
Kendall 44 Gm 25.41N 80.19W
Kendall, Cape- 42 Id 63.36N 87.13W
Kendallville 44 Ee 41.27N 85.16W
Kendari 22 Oj 3.57S 122.35 E
Kendawangan 26 Fg 2.32S 110.12 E
Kenema 31 Fh 7.52N 11.12W
Kenge 31 Ii 4.52S 16.59 E
Kengere 36 Ee 11.10S 25.28 E
Keng Tung 25 Jd 21.17N 99.36 E
Kenhardt 37 Ce 29.19S 21.12 E
Kéniéba 34 Cc 12.50N 11.14W
Keningau 26 Ge 5.20N 116.10 E
Kenitra 31 Ge 34.16N 6.36W
Kenitra [3] 32 Fc 34.00N 6.00W
Kenli (Xishuanghe) 28 Ef 37.35N 118.30 E
Kenmare 43 Gb 48.40N 102.05W
Kenmare/Neidin 9 Dj 51.53N 9.35W
Kenmare River/An Ribhéar 9 Dj 51.50N 9.50W
Kennebunk 44 Ld 43.23N 70.33W
Kennedy Peak 25 Id 23.19N 93.46 E
Kennedy Range 59 Cd 24.30S 115.00 E
Kenner 45 Ki 29.59N 90.15W
Kennet 9 Mj 51.28N 0.57W
Kennett 45 Kh 36.14N 90.03W
Kennewick 46 Fc 46.12N 119.07W
Kenni, Lake- (EN)=Kemijärvi 7 Gc 66.36N 27.24 E
Kennington 12 Cc 51.09N 0.53 E
Kenn Reef 57 Gg 21.10S 155.50 E
Kénogami 44 La 48.26N 71.14W
Kénogami, Lac- 44 La 48.21N 71.28W
Kenogami River 42 Jf 51.06N 84.29W
Keno Hill 42 Dd 63.54N 135.18W
Kenora 39 Je 49.47N 94.29W
Kenosha 43 Jc 42.35N 87.49W
Kent 9 Nj 51.10N 0.55 E
Kent [3] 9 Nj 51.20N 0.55 E
Kent [S.L.] 34 Cd 8.10N 13.10W
Kent [Wa.-U.S.] 46 Dc 47.23N 122.14W
Kent, Vale of- 9 Nj 51.10N 0.30 E
Kentau 19 Gg 43.32N 68.33 E
Kent Group 59 Jg 39.30S 147.20 E
Kenton 44 Fe 40.38N 83.38W
Kent Peninsula 42 Gc 68.30N 107.00W
Kentucky [2] 43 Jd 37.30N 85.15W
Kentucky Lake 43 Jd 36.25N 88.05W
Kentucky River 44 Ef 38.41N 85.11W
Kenya [1] 31 Kh 1.00N 38.00 E
Kenya, Mount-/Kirinyaga 30 Ki 0.10S 37.20 E
Keokea 65a Ec 20.42N 156.21W
Keokuk 43 Ic 40.24N 91.24W
Keonjhargarh 25 Hd 21.38N 85.35 E
Keowee, Lake- 44 Fh 34.55N 82.50W
Kepe 7 Hd 65.09N 32.08 E
Kepi 26 Kh 6.32S 139.19 E
Kępno 10 Ne 51.17N 17.59 E
Kepsut 24 Cc 39.41N 28.09 E
Kerala [3] 25 Ff 11.00N 76.30 E
Kerama-Rettō 29b Ab 26.10N 127.15 E
Kerang 59 Ig 35.44S 143.55 E
Keratéa 15 Gl 37.48N 23.59 E
Kerava/Kervo 8 Kd 60.24N 25.07 E
Kerč 6 Jf 45.22N 36.27 E
Kerčenski Poluostrov 16 Ig 45.15N 36.00 E
Kerčenski Proliv 5 Jf 45.22N 36.38 E
Kerdhílion Óros 15 Gi 40.47N 23.39 E
Kerema 60 Di 7.58S 145.46 E
Keren 35 Fb 15.47N 38.27 E
Keret, Ozero- 7 Hd 65.50N 32.50 E
Kerewan 34 Bc 13.29N 16.06W
Kerguélen 30 Nm 49.20S 69.30 E
Kerguélen, Iles- 30 Nm 49.15S 69.10 E
Kerguelen Plateau (EN) 3 Go 55.00S 75.00 E
Kericho 36 Gc 0.22S 35.17 E
Keri Kera 35 Ec 12.21N 32.46 E
Kerimäki 8 Mc 61.55N 29.17 E
Kerinci, Gunung- 21 Mj 1.42S 101.16 E
Kerio 30 Kh 2.59N 36.07 E
Kerion 15 Dl 37.40N 20.49 E
Keriya/Yutian 22 Kf 36.52N 81.42 E
Keriya He 27 Dd 38.30N 82.10 E
Keriya Shankou 27 Dd 35.12N 81.44 E
Kerka 10 Mj 46.28N 16.36 E
Kerken 12 Ic 51.27N 6.26 E
Kerkennah Islands (EN)=Qarqannah, Juzur- 30 Ie 34.44N 11.12 E
Kerketevs Óros 15 Jl 37.44N 26.38 E
Kerki 19 Gh 37.50N 65.13 E
Kerkíni Óros 15 Fh 41.21N 22.50 E
Kérkira 15 Cj 39.36N 19.55 E
Kérkira=Corfu (EN) 5 Hh 39.40N 19.45 E
Kerkíras, Stenón- = Corfu, Strait of- (EN) 15 Dj 39.35N 20.05 E
Kerkrade 12 Id 50.52N 6.04 E
Kerma (EN)=Karmah 35 Eb 19.38N 30.25 E
Kermadec Islands 57 Jh 30.00S 178.30W
Kermadec Ridge (EN) 57 Jh 30.30S 178.30W
Kermadec Trench (EN) 3 Km 30.00S 177.00W
Kermajarvi 8 Mb 62.30N 28.40 E
Kermān [3] 23 Ic 30.50N 57.50 E
Kermān 22 Hf 30.17N 57.05 E
Kermānshāh→Bakhtarān 22 Gf 34.19N 47.04 E
Kermānshāhān 24 Pg 31.17N 54.55 E
Kerme 15 Kl 37.02N 28.00 E
Kerme Körfezi 24 Bd 36.50N 28.00 E
Kermit 45 Ek 31.51N 103.06W
Kern River 46 Fi 35.13N 119.17W
Kérouané 34 Dd 9.16N 9.01W
Kerpen 12 Id 50.52N 6.41 E
Kerrobert 42 Gf 51.55N 109.08W
Kerrville 43 He 30.03N 99.08W
Kerry/Ciarraí [2] 9 Di 52.10N 9.30W
Kerry, Mountains of- 9 Dj 51.58N 9.50W
Kertamulya 26 Eg 0.23N 109.09 E
Kerteh 26 Df 4.31N 103.27 E
Kerteminde 8 Di 55.27N 10.40 E
Kerulen (Cherlen) 21 Ne 48.48N 117.00 E
Kervo/Kerava 8 Kd 60.24N 25.07 E
Kerzaz 32 Gd 29.27N 1.25W
Kerženec 7 Kh 56.04N 45.01 E
Kesagami Lake 42 Jf 50.23N 80.10W
Kesälahti 8 Mc 61.54N 29.50 E
Keşan 23 Ca 40.51N 26.37 E
Keşap 24 Hb 40.55N 38.31 E
Kesen'numa 28 Pe 38.54N 141.35 E
Kesen'numa-Wan 29 Gb 38.50N 141.35 E
Keshan 27 Mb 48.04N 125.51 E
Keskastel 12 Jf 48.58N 7.02 E
Keskin 24 Ec 39.41N 33.37 E
Keski-Suomi [2] 7 Fe 62.30N 25.30 E
Kestenga 7 Hd 65.53N 31.45 E
Keswick 9 Jg 54.37N 3.08W
Keszthely 10 Nj 46.46N 17.15 E
Ket 21 Kd 58.55N 81.32 E
Keta 34 Fd 5.55N 0.59 E
Keta, Ozero- 20 Dc 68.45N 90.00 E
Ketanda 20 Jd 60.38N 141.30 E
Ketapang 22 Mj 1.52S 109.59 E
Ketchikan 39 Fd 55.21N 131.35W
Ketchum 43 Ec 43.41N 114.22W
Ketchum Mountain 45 Fk 31.15N 101.00W
Kete Krachi 34 Ed 7.46N 0.03W
Ketelmeer 12 Hb 52.35N 5.45 E
Ketlī, Jbel- 13 Gi 35.22N 5.17W
Ketmen, Hrebet- 18 Lc 43.20N 80.00 E
Kétou 34 Fd 7.22N 2.36 E
Kętrzyn 10 Rb 54.06N 21.23 E
Kettering [Eng.-U.K.] 9 Mi 52.24N 0.44W
Kettering [Oh.-U.S.] 44 Ef 39.41N 84.10W
Kettle River 46 Fb 48.42N 118.07W
Kettle River Range 46 Fb 48.30N 118.40W
Keuka Lake 44 Id 42.27N 77.10W
Keur Massène 32 Df 16.33N 16.14W
Keuruu 7 Fe 62.16N 24.42 E
Keuruunselkä 8 Kb 62.10N 24.40 E
Kevelaer 12 Ic 51.35N 6.15 E
Kew 49 Kc 21.54N 72.02W
Kewanee 45 Jc 41.14N 89.56W
Keweenaw Bay 44 Cb 46.56N 88.23W
Keweenaw Peninsula 43 Jb 47.12N 88.25W
Key, Lough-/Loch Ce 9 Eg 54.00N 8.15W
Keya Paha River 45 Ge 42.54N 99.00W
Keyhole Reservoir 46 Md 44.21N 104.51W
Key Largo 44 Gm 25.04N 80.28W
Keypel Bank (EN) 59 Le 25.15S 159.30 E
Keystone Lake 45 Hh 36.15N 96.25W
Key West 39 Kg 24.33N 81.48W
Kez 7 Mh 57.56N 53.43 E
Kezi 37 Dd 20.55S 28.29 E
Kežma 20 Fe 59.02N 101.09 E
Kežmarok 10 Qg 49.08N 20.25 E
Kgalagadi [3] 37 Ce 25.00S 22.00 E
Kgatleng [3] 37 Dd 24.28S 26.05 E
Kghoti 37 Cd 24.55S 21.59 E
Khabr, Kūh-e- 23 Id 28.50N 56.26 E
Khābūr, Nahr al- 24 Ie 35.08N 40.26 E
Khadari, Wādī al- 35 Dc 10.29N 27.00 E
Khādim, Shūshat al- 24 Bh 28.35N 27.43 E
Khadki (Kirkee) 25 Ee 18.34N 73.52 E
Khadra 13 Mh 36.15N 0.35 E
Khafs Banbān 24 Lj 25.31N 46.27 E
Khairónia 15 Fk 38.30N 22.51 E
Khairpur 25 Dc 27.32N 68.46 E
Khāīz, Kūh-e- 24 Ng 30.27N 50.55 E
Khakhea 37 Cd 24.42S 23.30 E
Khalatse 25 Fb 34.20N 76.49 E
Khalīj-e Fārs=Persian Gulf (EN) 21 Hg 27.00N 51.00 E
Khálki 15 Km 36.13N 27.37 E
Khálki 15 Km 36.14N 27.36 E
Khalkidhikí=Chalcidice (EN) 5 Ig 40.25N 23.25 E
Khalkís 15 Gk 38.28N 23.36 E
Khaluf 23 Ie 20.29N 57.59 E
Khambhāt 25 Ed 22.18N 72.37 E
Khambhāt, Gulf of- 21 Jg 21.00N 72.30 E
Khāmgaon 25 Fd 20.41N 76.34 E
Khamílí 15 Jn 35.52N 26.14 E
Khamir 23 Ff 15.59N 43.57 E
Khāmis, Ash Shallāl al-=Fifth Cataract (EN) 30 Kg 18.23N 33.47 E
Khamīs Mushayţ 23 Ff 18.18N 42.44 E
Khammam 25 Ge 17.15N 80.09 E
Khamseh 24 Md 36.40N 48.50 E
Khan 37 Ad 22.42S 14.54 E
Khān 24 Qj 24.13N 56.20 E
Khānābād 23 Kb 36.41N 69.07 E
Khān al Baghdādī 24 Jf 33.51N 42.33 E
Khān al Hammād 24 Kf 32.19N 44.17 E
Khānaqīn 23 Gc 34.21N 45.22 E
Khān az Zabīb 24 Gg 31.28N 36.06 E
Khandwa 25 Fd 21.50N 76.20 E
Khāneh Sorkh, Gardaneh-ye- 24 Qh 29.49N 56.06 E
Khānewāl 25 Eb 30.18N 71.56 E
Khangai Mountains (EN)=Changajn Nuruu→Hangaj, Hrebet- 21 Le 47.30N 100.00 E
Khangai Mountains (EN)=Hangaj, Hrebet- (Changajn Nuruu) 21 Le 47.30N 100.00 E
Khánia 6 Ih 35.31N 24.02 E
Khanion, Kólpos- 15 Gn 35.35N 23.50 E
Khanka, Lake- (EN)=Hanka, Ozero- 21 Pe 45.00N 132.24 E
Khanka Lake (EN)=Xingkai Hu 21 Pe 45.00N 132.24 E
Khānpur 25 Ec 28.39N 70.39 E
Khān Shaykhūn 24 Ge 35.26N 36.38 E
Khan Takhtī 24 Kc 38.09N 44.55 E
Khān Yūnus 24 Fg 31.21N 34.19 E
Khānzīr, Rās- 35 Hc 10.50N 45.50 E

Index Symbols

[1] Independent Nation
[2] State, Region
[3] District, County
[4] Municipality
[5] Colony, Dependency
Continent
Physical Region
Historical or Cultural Region
Mount, Mountain
Volcano
Hill
Mountains, Mountain Range
Hills, Escarpment
Plateau, Upland
Pass, Gap
Plain, Lowland
Delta
Salt Flat
Valley, Canyon
Crater, Cave
Karst Features
Depression
Polder
Desert, Dunes
Forest, Woods
Heath, Steppe
Oasis
Cape, Point
Coast, beach
Cliff
Peninsula
Isthmus
Sandbank
Island
Atoll
Rock, Reef
Islands, Archipelago
Rocks, Reefs
Coral Reef
Well, Spring
Geyser
River, Stream
Waterfall Rapids
River Mouth, Estuary
Lake
Salt Lake
Intermittent Lake
Reservoir
Swamp, Pond
Canal
Glacier
Ice Shelf, Pack Ice
Ocean
Sea
Gulf, Bay
Strait, Fjord
Lagoon
Bank
Seamount
Tablemount
Ridge
Shelf
Basin
Escarpment, Sea Scarp
Fracture
Trench, Abyss
National Park, Reserve
Point of Interest
Recreation Site
Cave, Cavern
Historic Site
Ruins
Wall, Walls
Church, Abbey
Temple
Scientific Station
Airport
Port
Lighthouse
Mine
Tunnel
Dam, Bridge

Khao Laem	25	Kf	14.19N	101.11 E
Khao Miang	25	Ke	17.42N	101.01 E
Khao Mokochu	25	Je	15.56N	99.06 E
Khao Saming	25	Kf	12.16N	102.26 E
Khar	24	Me	35.53N	48.55 E
Kharagpur	22	Kg	22.20N	87.20 E
Khárakas	15	In	35.01N	25.07 E
Khārān	24	Qh	28.55N	57.09 E
Kharānaq	24	Pf	32.20N	54.39 E
Kharānaq, Kūh-e-	24	Pf	32.10N	54.39 E
Kharga Oasis (EN)= Khārijah, Waḩāt al-	30	Kf	25.20N	30.35 E
Khārijah, Wāḩāt al-= Kharga Oasis (EN)	30	Kf	25.20N	30.35 E
Kharīţ, Wādī al-	24	Ej	24.26N	33.03 E
Kharīţah, Shiqqat al-	33	If	17.10N	47.50 E
Khārk	24	Nh	29.15N	50.20 E
Khārk, Jazīreh-ye-	23	Hd	29.15N	50.20 E
Khār Khū	24	Og	31.39N	53.46 E
Kharmān, Kūh-e-	23	Hd	29.13N	53.35 E
Kharshah, Qārat al-	24	Bg	30.35N	27.25 E
Khartoum (EN)=Al Kharţūm [3]	35	Eb	15.50N	33.00 E
Khartoum (EN)=Al Kharţūm	31	Kg	15.36N	32.32 E
Khartoum North (EN)=Al Kharţūm Baḩrī	31	Kg	15.38N	32.33 E
Khāsh	23	Jc	31.31N	62.52 E
Khāsh	23	Jc	31.11N	62.05 E
Khashm al Qirbah	35	Fc	14.58N	35.55 E
Khāsi Jaintia	21	Lg	25.35N	91.38 E
Khatikhon, Yam-= Mediterranean Sea (EN)	5	Hh	35.00N	20.00 E
Khaţţ	33	Dd	28.40N	22.40 E
Khātūn, Kūh-e-	24	Og	30.25N	53.38 E
Khawr al Fakkān	24	Qk	25.21N	56.22 E
Khawr āl Juḩaysh	35	Ia	20.36N	50.59 E
Khawr al Mufattaḩ	24	Mh	28.40N	48.25 E
Khawr Umm Qasr	24	Lg	30.02N	47.56 E
Khay'	23	Ff	18.45N	41.24 E
Khaybar	23	Ed	25.42N	39.31 E
Khaybar, Ḩarrat-	24	Hj	25.30N	39.45 E
Khazzī, Qārat-	30	Jf	21.26N	24.30 E
Khemis	13	Qh	36.10N	4.04 E
Khemis Anjra	13	Gi	35.41N	5.32W
Khémis Beni Arouss	13	Gi	35.19N	5.38W
Khemis Miliana	32	Hb	36.16N	2.13 E
Khemissat	32	Fc	33.49N	6.04W
Khemisset [3]	32	Fc	33.49N	6.00W
Khemmarat	25	Ke	16.03N	105.11 E
Khenchela	32	Ib	35.26N	7.08 E
Khenifra	32	Fc	32.56N	5.40W
Khenifra [3]	32	Fc	33.00N	5.08W
Kherāmeh	24	Oh	29.32N	53.21 E
Khersan	24	Ng	31.33N	50.22 E
Khersónisos Akrotíri	15	Hn	35.35N	24.10 E
Kheyrābād [Iran]	24	Mg	31.49N	48.23 E
Kheyrābād [Iran]	24	Ph	29.26N	55.19 E
Khionótripa	15	Hh	41.18N	24.05 E
Khios	15	Jk	38.22N	26.08 E
Khios=Chios (EN)	5	Ih	38.22N	26.00 E
Khirbat Isrīyah	24	Ge	35.21N	37.46 E
Khirr, Nahr al-	24	Kf	33.17N	44.21 E
Khlomón Óros	15	Fk	38.36N	23.00 E
Khlong Yai	25	Kf	11.46N	102.53 E
Khokhropār	25	Ec	25.42N	70.12 E
Khok Kloi	25	Jg	8.17N	98.19 E
Khok Samrong	25	Ke	15.03N	100.44 E
Kholm	23	Kb	36.42N	67.41 E
Khomām	24	Md	37.22N	49.40 E
Khomas Highland (EN)= Khomas Hochland	30	Ik	22.40 S	16.20 E
Khomas Hochland=Khomas Highland (EN)	30	Ik	22.40 S	16.20 E
Khomeyn	24	Nf	33.38N	50.04 E
Khomeynīshahr	23	Hc	32.42N	51.27 E
Khon Kaen	25	Ke	16.26N	102.50 E
Khonsār	24	Nf	33.21N	50.19 E
Khóra	15	El	37.03N	21.43 E
Khor Anghar	35	Gc	12.27N	43.18 E
Khorāsān	21	Hf	34.00N	56.00 E
Khorāsān [3]	23	Ic	35.00N	58.00 E
Khorāsānī, Godār-e	24	Qg	30.44N	57.03 E
Khóra Sfakion	15	Hn	35.12N	24.09 E
Khormūj, Kūh-e-	23	Hd	28.43N	51.22 E
Khorof Harar	36	Hb	2.14N	40.44 E
Khorramābād	23	Gc	33.30N	48.20 E
Khorramshahr	23	Gc	30.25N	48.11 E
Khorsābād	24	Jd	36.38N	43.17 E
Khoshyeylāq	24	Pd	36.53N	55.15 E
Khosrowābād	24	Mg	30.00N	48.25 E
Khosrowshah	24	Ld	37.57N	46.03 E
Khouribga [3]	32	Fc	32.56N	6.36W
Khouribga	32	Fc	32.53N	6.54W
Khowst	23	Kc	33.22N	69.57 E
Khrisi	15	Io	34.52N	25.42 E
Khrisoúpolis	15	Hi	40.59N	24.42 E
Khristianá	15	Im	36.14N	25.13 E
Khu Dağı	24	Jc	38.35N	43.40 E
Khuff [Lib.]	33	Cd	28.17N	18.20 E
Khuff [Sau.Ar.]	23	Ed	25.20N	37.20 E
Khulna	22	Kg	22.48N	89.33 E
Khūrān	24	Pi	26.50N	55.40 E
Khurayş	23	Gd	25.05N	48.02 E
Khurayt	35	Dc	13.57N	26.02 E
Khurīyā Murīyā, Jazā'ir-= Kuria Muria Islands (EN)	21	Hh	17.30N	56.00 E
Khurr, Wādī al-	24	Jg	30.52N	42.10 E
Khursanīyah	24	Mi	27.18N	49.16 E
Khūshābar	24	Md	37.59N	48.54 E
Khutse	37	Cd	23.20 S	24.34 E
Khuwayy	35	Dc	13.05N	29.14 E
Khuzdār	25	Dc	27.48N	66.37 E
Khūzestān [3]	23	Gc	32.00N	48.30 E
Khūzestan	21	Gf	30.33N	50.00 E
Khvojeh Lāk, Kūh-e-	24	Le	35.43N	46.29 E
Khvor	24	Pf	33.47N	55.03 E
Khvorāsgān	24	Nf	32.39N	51.45 E
Khvormūj	24	Nh	28.39N	51.23 E
Khvoshkūh	24	Qi	27.37N	56.41 E
Khvoy	24	Kc	38.33N	44.58 E
Khyber Pass	25	Eb	34.05N	71.10 E
Kia	63a	Db	7.32 S	158.26 E
Kia	63d	Bb	16.14 S	179.05 E
Kiamba	26	He	5.59N	124.37 E
Kiambi	36	Ed	7.20 S	28.01 E
Kiamichi River	45	Ij	33.57N	95.14W
Kiangarow, Mount-	59	Ke	26.49 S	151.33 E
Kiangsi (EN)=Chiang-hsi Sheng→Jangxi Sheng [2]	27	Kf	28.00N	116.00 E
Kiangsi (EN)=Jangxi Sheng (Chiang-hsi Sheng) [2]	27	Kf	28.00N	116.00 E
Kiangsu (EN)=Chiang-su Sheng→Jiangsu Sheng [2]	27	Ke	33.00N	120.00 E
Kiangsu (EN)=Jiangsu Sheng (Chiang-su Sheng) [2]	27	Ke	33.00N	120.00 E
Kiantajärvi	7	Gd	65.03N	29.07 E
Kiáton	15	Fk	38.01N	22.45 E
Kibali	36	Eb	3.37N	28.34 E
Kibangou	36	Bc	3.27 S	12.21 E
Kibartaj/Kybartai	8	Jj	54.38N	22.44 E
Kibasira Swamp	36	Gd	8.20 S	36.18 E
Kibau	36	Gd	8.35 S	35.17 E
Kibaya	36	Gd	5.18 S	36.34 E
Kibbish	35	Fe	4.40N	35.53 E
Kiberg	7	Ha	70.17N	31.00 E
Kibikogen	29	Cd	34.45N	133.15 E
Kiboko	36	Gc	2.15 S	37.42 E
Kibombo	36	Ec	3.54 S	25.55 E
Kibondo	36	Fc	3.35 S	30.42 E
Kibre Mengist	35	Fd	5.58N	39.00 E
Kıbrıs/Kypros=Cyprus (EN) [1]	22	Ff	35.00N	33.00 E
Kıbrıs/Kypros=Cyprus (EN)	21	Ff	35.00N	33.00 E
Kibungo	36	Fc	2.10 S	30.32 E
Kibuye	36	Ec	2.03 S	29.21 E
Kibwezi	36	Gc	2.25 S	37.58 E
Kičevo	15	Dh	41.31N	20.58 E
Kichi Kichi	35	Bb	17.36N	17.19 E
Kicking Horse Pass	42	Ff	51.50N	116.30W
Kidal	31	Hg	18.26N	1.24 E
Kidapawan	26	Ie	7.01N	125.03 E
Kidatu	36	Gd	7.42 S	36.57 E
Kidira	34	Cc	14.28N	12.13W
Kidnappers, Cape-	62	Gc	39.38 S	177.06 E
Kiekie	65a	Ab	21.53N	160.13W
Kiel	6	He	54.20N	10.08 E
Kiel Canal (EN)=Nord-Ostsee Kanal	5	Ge	53.53N	9.08 E
Kielce	6	Ie	50.52N	20.37 E
Kielce [2]	10	Qf	50.50N	20.35 E
Kieler Bucht	10	Gb	54.35N	10.35 E
Kienge	36	Ee	10.33 S	27.33 E
Kierspe	12	Jc	51.08N	7.35 E
Kieta	58	Ge	6.15 S	155.37 E
Kietrz	10	Of	50.05N	18.01 E
Kiev (EN)=Kijev	6	Je	50.26N	30.31 E
Kiev Reservoir (EN)= Kijevskoje Vodohranilišče	5	Je	51.00N	30.25 E
Kiffa	31	Fg	16.36N	11.23W
Kifisiá	15	Gk	38.04N	23.49 E
Kifisós	15	Gk	38.26N	23.15 E
Kifrī	24	Ke	34.42N	44.58 E
Kigač	16	Pf	46.28N	49.08 E
Kigali	31	Ki	1.57 S	30.04 E
Kiğı	24	Ic	39.19N	40.21 E
Kigille	35	Ed	8.40N	34.02 E
Kigoma	31	Ji	4.52 S	29.38 E
Kigoma [3]	36	Fc	4.50 S	30.05 E
Kigosi	36	Fc	4.40 S	31.27 E
Kihelkonna	8	If	58.20N	21.54 E
Kihniö	8	Jb	62.12N	23.11 E
Kihnu	7	Fg	58.10N	24.00 E
Kiholo	65a	Fd	19.51N	155.55W
Kiholo Bay	65a	Fd	19.52N	155.56W
Kihti/Skiftet	8	Id	60.15N	21.05 E
Kii-Hantō	27	Oe	34.00N	135.45 E
Kiikka	8	Jc	61.20N	22.46 E
Kiil	16	Se	49.27N	54.50 E
Kiiminki	7	Fd	65.08N	25.44 E
Kii-Sanchi	29	Dd	34.15N	135.50 E
Kii-Suido	28	Mh	34.00N	134.55 E
Kija	20	De	56.52N	86.40 E
Kijev=Kiev (EN)	6	Je	50.26N	30.31 E
Kijevka	19	He	50.16N	71.34 E
Kijevskaja Oblast [3]	19	De	50.20N	30.45 E
Kijevskoje Vodohranilišče= Kiev Reservoir (EN)	5	Je	51.00N	30.25 E
Kijma	19	Ge	51.35N	67.34 E
Kikai-Jima	27	Mf	28.15N	130.00 E
Kikerino	8	Me	59.23N	29.38 E
Kikinda	15	Dd	45.50N	20.29 E
Kikládhes = Cyclades (EN)	5	Ih	37.00N	25.10 E
Kikonai	28	Pd	41.40N	140.26 E
Kikori	58	Fe	7.25 S	144.13 E
Kikori River	57	Fe	7.23 S	144.16 E
Kikuchi	29	Be	32.59N	130.49 E
Kikuma	29	Cd	34.03N	132.51 E
Kikvidze	16	Md	50.44N	43.03 E
Kikwit	31	Ii	5.02 S	18.49 E
Kil [Nor.]	8	Cf	58.52N	9.19 E
Kil [Swe.]	7	Cg	59.30N	13.19 E
Kilafors	7	Df	61.15N	16.33 E
Kilambé, Cerro-	49	Eg	13.34N	85.42W
Kilauea	65a	Ba	22.13N	159.25W
Kilauea Crater	65a	Fd	19.24N	155.17W
Kilauea Point	65a	Ba	22.14N	159.24W
Kilbrannan Sound	9	Hf	55.40N	5.25W
Kilbuck Mountains	40	Hd	60.30N	159.45W
Kilchu	27	Mc	40.58N	129.20 E
Kilcoy	59	Ke	26.57 S	152.33 E
Kildare/Cill Dara [2]	9	Gh	53.15N	6.45W
Kildare/Cill Dara	9	Gh	53.10N	6.55W
Kildin, Ostrov-	7	Ib	69.20N	34.10 E
Kilembe	36	Cd	5.42 S	19.55 E
Kilgore	45	Ij	32.23N	94.53W
Kilgoris	36	Fc	1.00 S	34.53 E
Kiliao He	21	Oe	43.24N	123.42 E
Kiliç	15	Mi	40.40N	29.23 E
Kilifi	36	Gc	3.38 S	39.51 E
Kili Island	57	Hd	5.39N	169.04 E
Kilija	19	Cf	45.27N	29.14 E
Kilijskoje girlo	15	Md	45.13N	29.43 E
Kilimanjaro [3]	36	Gc	4.00 S	37.40 E
Kilimanjaro, Mount-	30	Ki	3.04 S	37.22 E
Kilimli	24	Db	41.29N	31.50 E
Kilinailau Islands	60	Fh	4.45 S	155.20 E
Kilindoni	31	Ki	7.55 S	39.39 E
Kilingi-Nõmme/Kilingi-Nymme	7	Fg	58.08N	24.59 E
Kilingi-Nymme/Kilingi-Nõmme	7	Fg	58.08N	24.59 E
Kilis	23	Eb	36.44N	37.05 E
Kilitbahir	24	Bb	40.12N	26.20 E
Kilkee/Cill Chaoi	9	Di	52.41N	9.38W
Kilkenny/Cill Chainnigh	9	Fi	52.39N	7.15W
Kilkenny/Cill Chainnigh [2]	9	Fi	52.40N	7.20W
Kilkieran Bay	9	Dh	53.15N	9.45W
Kilkis	15	Fi	41.00N	22.52 E
Killala Bay/Cuan Chill Ala	9	Dg	54.15N	9.10W
Killarney/Cill Airne	9	Di	52.03N	9.30W
Killary Harbour/An Caoláire Rua	9	Dh	53.38N	9.55W
Killdeer	45	Ec	47.22N	102.45W
Killeen	43	He	31.08N	97.44W
Killinck	42	Ld	60.25N	64.40W
Killíni	15	El	37.56N	21.09 E
Killíni Óros	15	Fl	37.55N	22.26 E
Kilmallock/Cill Mocheallóg	9	Ei	52.25N	8.35W
Kilmarnock	9	If	55.37N	4.30W
Kilmez	7	Mh	56.58N	50.29 E
Kilmez	7	Mh	57.03N	51.24 E
Kilmore	59	Ig	37.18 S	144.57 E
Kilombero	36	Gd	8.31 S	37.22 E
Kilosa	31	Ki	6.50 S	36.59 E
Kilpisjärvi	7	Eb	69.03N	20.48 E
Kilp-Javr	7	Hb	69.07N	32.28 E
Kilrush/Cill Rois	9	Di	52.39N	9.29W
Kilsbergen	8	Fe	59.20N	14.45 E
Kiltān Island	25	Ef	11.29N	73.00 E
Kilwa	36	Ed	9.17 S	28.20 E
Kilwa Kisiwani	31	Ki	8.58 S	39.30 E
Kilwa Kivinje	36	Gd	8.45 S	39.24 E
Kilwa Masoko	36	Gd	8.56 S	39.31 E
Kilyos → Kumköy	15	Mh	41.15N	29.02 E
Kim	45	Eh	37.15N	103.21W
Kimamba	36	Gd	6.47 S	37.08 E
Kimba	59	Hf	33.09 S	136.25 E
Kimball [Nb.-U.S.]	45	Ef	41.14N	103.40W
Kimball [S.D.-U.S.]	45	Ge	43.45N	98.57W
Kimball, Mount-	40	Kd	63.14N	144.39W
Kimbe	59	Ka	5.31 S	150.12 E
Kimbe Bay	60	Ei	5.30 S	150.30 E
Kimberley	57	Df	16.00 S	126.00 E
Kimberley [B.C.-Can.]	42	Fg	49.41N	115.59W
Kimberley [S.Afr.]	31	Jk	28.43 S	24.46 E
Kimberley Plateau	59	Fc	17.00 S	127.00 E
Kimch'aek (Sŏngjin)	27	Mc	40.41N	129.12 E
Kimch'ŏn	27	Md	36.07N	128.07 E
Kimhandu	30	Ki	7.05 S	37.35 E
Kimi	15	Hk	38.38N	24.06 E
Kimito	8	Jd	60.10N	22.40 E
Kimito/Kemiö	8	Jd	60.10N	22.40 E
Kimje	28	Ig	35.48N	126.53 E
Kimobetsu	29a	Bb	42.47N	140.56 E
Kímolos	15	Hm	36.48N	24.34 E
Kimongo	36	Bc	4.29 S	12.58 E
Kimovsk	19	De	54.01N	38.36 E
Kimpu-San	29	Fd	35.52N	138.37 E
Kimry	19	Dd	56.52N	37.24 E
Kimvula	36	Cd	5.44 S	15.58 E
Kinabalu, Gunong-	21	Ni	6.05N	116.33 E
Kinabatangan	26	Ge	5.42N	118.23 E
Kinango	36	Gc	4.08 S	39.19 E
Kínaros	15	Jm	36.59N	26.17 E
Kincardine	42	Jh	44.11N	81.38W
Kind	8	Eg	57.35N	13.25 E
Kinda	36	Ed	9.18 S	25.04 E
Kinda	8	Ff	58.05N	15.40 E
Kindamba	36	Bc	3.44 S	14.31 E
Kinder	45	Jk	30.29N	92.51W
Kinder Scout	9	Lh	53.23N	1.52W
Kindersley	42	Gf	51.27N	109.10W
Kindi	34	Ec	12.26N	2.01W
Kindia	31	Fg	10.04N	12.51W
Kindu	31	Ji	2.57 S	25.56 E
Kinel	7	Mj	53.14N	50.40 E
Kinesi	36	Fc	1.28 S	33.52 E
Kinešma	19	Ed	57.28N	42.16 E
King	63a	Aa	4.24 S	152.43 E
King, Cayos-	49	Fg	12.45N	83.20W
Kingaroy	59	Ke	26.33 S	151.50 E
King Christian	42	Ha	77.45N	102.00W
King Christian IX Land (EN) = Kong Christian IX Land	67	Mc	68.00N	36.30W
King Christian X Land (EN) = Kong Christian X Land	67	Md	72.20N	32.30W
King City	43	Cd	36.13N	121.08W
King Edward River	59	Fb	14.14 S	126.35 E
Kingfisher	45	Hi	35.52N	97.56W
King Frederik VI Coast (EN) =Kong Frederik VI Kyst	67	Nc	63.00N	43.30W
King Frederik VIII Land (EN) = Kong Frederik VIII Land	67	Md	78.30N	28.00W
King George Island	66	Re	62.00 S	58.15W
King George Islands	42	Je	57.15N	78.30W
King George Sound	59	Dg	35.10 S	118.10 E
Kingisepp	7	Gg	59.23N	28.37 E
Kingisepp/Kingissepp	19	Cd	58.17N	22.29 E
King Island	57	Fh	39.50 S	144.00 E
Kingissepp/Kingisepp	19	Cd	58.17N	22.29 E
King Lear Peak	46	Ff	41.12N	118.34W
King Leopold Ranges	59	Fc	17.30 S	125.45 E
Kingman [Az.-U.S.]	43	Ed	35.12N	114.04W
Kingman [Ks.-U.S.]	45	Gh	37.39N	98.07W
Kingman Reef	57	Kd	6.19N	162.28W
Kingombe [Zaire]	36	Ec	2.35 S	26.37 E
Kingombe [Zaire]	36	Ec	3.52 S	26.35 E
Kingoome Inlet	46	Ba	50.49N	126.13W
Kingoonya	58	Eh	30.54 S	135.18 E
King Peninsula	66	Of	73.12 S	101.00W
Kingsclere	12	Ac	51.19N	1.15W
Kingscote	59	Hg	35.40 S	137.38 E
King's Lynn	9	Ni	52.45N	0.24 E
King Sound	57	Df	17.00 S	123.30 E
Kings Peak [Ca.-U.S.]	46	Cf	40.10N	124.08W
Kings Peak [U.S.]	38	He	40.46N	110.22W
Kingsport	43	Kd	36.32N	82.33W
Kings River	46	Fh	36.03N	119.49W
Kingston [Jam.]	39	Lh	18.00N	76.50W
Kingston [Nor.I.]	58	Hg	29.04 S	167.58 E
Kingston [N.Y.-U.S.]	43	Mc	41.55N	74.00W
Kingston [N.Z.]	61	Ci	45.20 S	168.43 E
Kingston [Ont.-Can.]	39	Le	44.14N	76.30W
Kingston Peak	46	Hi	35.42N	115.52W
Kingston South East	58	Eh	36.50 S	139.51 E
Kingston-upon-Hull (Hull)	6	Fe	53.45N	0.20W
Kingston-upon-Thames, London-	9	Mj	51.28N	0.19W
Kingstown	39	Mh	13.09N	61.14W
Kingsville	43	Hf	27.31N	97.52W
Kings Worthy	12	Ac	51.05N	1.18W
Kingussie	9	Id	57.05N	4.04W
King William	38	Jc	69.00N	97.30W
King William's Town	31	Jl	32.51 S	27.22 E
Kiniama	36	Ee	11.26 S	28.19 E
Kınık	24	Bc	39.05N	27.23 E
Kinkala	36	Bc	4.22 S	14.46 E
Kinlochleven	9	Ie	56.43N	4.58W
Kinna	8	Eg	57.30N	12.41 E
Kinnairds Head	9	Ld	57.42N	2.00W
Kinnared	8	Eg	57.02N	13.06 E
Kinnekulle	8	Ef	58.35N	13.23 E
Kinneret, Yam-	24	Ff	32.48N	35.35 E
Kino-Kawa	29	Dd	34.13N	135.08 E
Kinomoto	29	Ed	35.31N	136.13 E
Kinoosao	42	He	57.06N	102.01W
Kinós Kefalai	15	Fj	39.25N	22.34 E
Kinross	9	Je	56.13N	3.27W
Kinsale/cionn tSáile	9	Ej	51.42N	8.32W
Kinsale, Old Head of-/An Seancheann	9	Ej	51.36N	8.32W
Kinsangire	36	Gd	7.26 S	38.35 E
Kinsarvik	7	Bf	60.23N	6.43 E
Kinshasa [2]	36	Cc	4.00 S	16.00 E
Kinshasa (Leopoldville)	31	Ii	4.18 S	15.18 E
Kinsley	45	Gh	37.55N	99.25W
Kinston	43	Ld	35.16N	77.35W
Kintampo	34	Ed	8.03N	1.43W
Kintap	26	Gg	3.51 S	115.13 E
Kintyre	9	Hf	55.32N	5.35W
Kin-Wan	29b	Ab	26.25N	127.54 E
Kinyan	34	Dc	11.51N	6.01W
Kinyeti	30	Kh	3.57N	32.54 E
Kinzig [Eur.]	10	Dh	48.37N	7.49 E
Kinzig [F.R.G.]	10	Ef	50.08N	8.54 E
Kioa	63d	Bb	16.39 S	179.55 E
Kipaka	36	Ec	4.09 S	26.30 E
Kiparissia	15	El	37.15N	21.40 E
Kiparissia, Gulf of- (EN) = Kiparissiakós Kólpos	15	El	37.30N	21.25 E
Kiparissiakós Kólpos = Kiparissia, Gulf of- (EN)	15	El	37.30N	21.25 E
Kipawa, Lac-	42	Jg	46.55N	79.00W
Kipembawe	36	Fd	7.39 S	33.24 E
Kipengere Range	30	Ki	9.10 S	34.15 E
Kiperčeny	15	Lb	47.32N	28.40 E
Kipili	36	Fd	7.26 S	30.36 E
Kipini	36	Hc	2.32 S	40.31 E
Kipling	45	Ea	50.10N	102.38W
Kippure	9	Gh	53.11N	6.20W
Kiprarenukk, Mys-/Undva Neem	8	If	58.25N	21.45 E
Kípros = Cyprus (EN)	23	Db	35.01N	33.00 E
Kipushi	36	Ee	11.46S	27.14 E
Kirakira	58	Hf	10.27S	161.56 E
Kiraz	24	Cc	39.21N	27.25 E
Kirazlı	24	Bb	40.01N	26.40 E
Kirbla	8	Jf	58.42N	23.49 E
Kircasalih	15	Jh	41.23N	26.48 E
Kirchberg (Hunsrüch)	12	Je	49.57N	7.24 E
Kirchhain	12	Kd	50.49N	8.58 E
Kirchheimbolanden	12	Ke	49.40N	8.01 E
Kirchheim unter Teck	10	Fh	48.39N	9.27 E
Kirchhundem	12	Kc	51.06N	8.06 E
Kirchhundem-Rahrbach	12	Jc	51.02N	7.59 E
Kirchlengern	12	Kb	52.12N	8.38 E
Kirdimi	35	Bb	18.11N	18.38 E
Kireç	15	Lj	39.33N	28.22 E
Kirenga	21	Md	57.47N	107.59 E
Kirensk	22	Md	57.46N	108.08 E
Kirghiz SSR (EN)= Kirgizskaja SSR [2]	19	Hg	41.30N	75.00 E
Kirghiz Steppe (EN)	5	Lf	49.30N	50.30 E
Kirgizskaja Sovetskaja Socialističeskaja Respublika [2]	19	Hg	41.30N	75.00 E
Kirgizskaja SSR/Kyrgyz Sovetik Socialistik Respublikasy [2]	19	Hg	41.30N	75.00 E
Kirgizskaja SSR=Kirghiz SSR (EN) [2]	19	Hg	41.30N	75.00 E
Kirgizski Hrebet	19	Hg	42.30N	74.00 E
Kiri	36	Cc	1.27 S	19.00 E
Kiribati [1]	58	Je	0.01 S	174.00 E
Kirikhan	24	Gd	36.32N	36.19 E
Kırıkkale	23	Db	39.50N	33.31 E
Kirillov	7	Jg	59.54N	38.27 E
Kirillovskoje	8	Md	60.28N	29.28 E
Kirin (EN)=Chi-lin Sheng→Jilin Sheng [2]	27	Mc	43.00N	126.00 E
Kirin (EN)=Jilin Sheng (Chi-lin Sheng) [2]	27	Mc	43.00N	126.00 E
Kirinyaga/Kenya, Mount-	30	Ki	0.10 S	37.20 E
Kirishima-Yama	29	Bf	31.56N	130.52 E
Kiriši	19	Dd	59.27N	32.02 E
Kiritimati Atoll (Christmas)	57	Ld	1.52N	157.20W
Kirja	7	Li	55.05N	46.52 E
Kirkağaç	24	Bc	39.06N	27.40 E
Kirkby Lonsdale	9	Kg	54.13N	2.36W
Kirkcaldy	9	Je	56.07N	3.10W
Kirkcudbright	9	Ig	54.50N	4.03W
Kirkee→Khadki	25	Ee	18.34N	73.52 E
Kirkenær	7	Cf	60.28N	12.03 E
Kirkenes	6	Jb	69.43N	30.03 E
Kirkjubæjarklaustur	7a	Bc	63.47N	18.04W
Kirkkonummi/Kyrkslätt	8	Kd	60.07N	24.26 E
Kirkland	46	Dc	47.41N	122.12W
Kirkland Lake	39	Ke	48.09N	80.02W
Kırklareli	23	Ca	41.44N	27.12 E
Kirkpatrick, Mont-	66	Kg	84.20 S	166.19 E
Kırkpınar Dağı	24	Fd	37.14N	34.15 E
Kirksville	43	Ic	40.12N	92.35W
Kirkūk	22	Gf	35.28N	44.23 E
Kirkwall	9	Kc	58.59N	2.58W
Kirkwood [Mo.-U.S.]	45	Kg	38.35N	90.24W
Kirkwood [S.Afr.]	37	Df	33.22S	25.15 E
Kırlangıç Burun	24	Dd	36.13N	30.25 E
Kirn	10	Dg	49.47N	7.27 E
Kirobasi	24	Ed	36.43N	33.52 E
Kirov [R.S.F.S.R.]	19	De	54.03N	34.21 E
Kirov [R.S.F.S.R.]	6	Kd	58.33N	49.42 E
Kirova, Zaliv-	16	Pj	39.05N	49.05 E
Kirovabad	6	Kg	40.40N	46.22 E
Kirovakan	19	Eg	40.48N	44.28 E
Kirovgrad	17	Jh	57.26N	60.04 E
Kirovo	18	Hd	40.28N	70.34 E
Kirovo-Čepeck	19	Fd	58.35N	50.03 E
Kirovograd	6	Jf	48.30N	32.18 E
Kirovogradskaja Oblast [3]	19	Df	48.20N	31.50 E
Kirovsk [R.S.F.S.R.]	19	Db	67.37N	33.37 E
Kirovsk [R.S.F.S.R.]	7	Hg	59.53N	31.01 E
Kirovsk [Tur.-U.S.S.R.]	18	Cf	37.43N	60.24 E
Kirovskaja Oblast [3]	19	Ed	58.30N	50.00 E
Kirovski [Kaz.-U.S.S.R.]	19	Hg	44.53N	78.12 E
Kirovski [R.S.F.S.R.]	20	Ig	45.05N	133.27 E
Kirovski [R.S.F.S.R.]	16	Pg	45.48N	48.08 E
Kirovski [R.S.F.S.R.]	20	Kf	54.25N	155.37 E
Kirovski [R.S.F.S.R.]	20	Hf	54.26N	127.00 E
Kirovskoje	18	Hc	42.39N	71.35 E
Kirpilski Liman	16	Kg	45.50N	38.05 E
Kirriemuir	9	Je	56.41N	3.01W
Kirs	19	Fd	59.21N	52.18 E
Kirsanov	16	Mc	52.41N	42.45 E
Kırşehir	23	Db	39.09N	34.10 E
Kīrthar Range	21	Ig	27.00N	67.20 E
Kirton	12	Bb	52.55N	0.03W
Kiruna	6	Ib	67.51N	20.13 E
Kirundu	36	Ec	0.44 S	25.32 E
Kiryū	29	Fc	36.25N	139.20 E
Kiržač	7	Jh	56.11N	38.53 E
Kisa	7	Dh	57.59N	15.37 E
Kisabi	36	Ed	8.03 S	29.11 E
Kisač	15	Cd	45.21N	19.44 E
Kisakata	29	Fb	39.14N	139.54 E
Kisaki	36	Gd	7.28 S	37.36 E
Kisalföld	10	Mi	47.30N	17.00 E
Kisangani	31	Jh	0.25N	25.12 E
Kisarazu	29	Fd	35.23N	139.55 E
Kisbér	10	Oi	47.30N	18.02 E
Kiselevsk	20	Df	54.03N	86.49 E
Kiserawe	36	Gd	6.54 S	39.05 E
Kishangarh	25	Ec	26.34N	74.52 E
Kishb, Harraţ al-	33	He	22.47N	41.30 E
Kishi	34	Fd	9.05N	3.51 E
Kishiwada	28	Mg	34.28N	135.22 E
Kisii	36	Fc	0.41 S	34.46 E
Kisiju	36	Gd	7.24 S	39.20 E
Kišinev	6	If	46.59N	28.52 E
Kısır Dağı	24	Jb	40.58N	43.04 E
Kiska	40a	Bb	52.00N	177.30 E
Kiska Volcano	40a	Bb	52.07N	177.36 E
Kisko	8	Jd	60.14N	23.29 E
Kiskörei Víztároló	10	Qi	47.44N	20.40 E
Kiskőrös	10	Pj	46.37N	19.18 E
Kiskunfélegyháza	10	Pj	46.33N	19.51 E
Kiskunhalas	10	Pj	46.26N	19.30 E
Kiskunmajsa	10	Pj	46.29N	19.45 E
Kiskunság	10	Pj	46.35N	19.15 E
Kislovodsk	19	Eg	43.54N	42.42 E
Kismanyo	31	Li	0.22 S	42.32 E
Kisofukushima	29	Ed	35.51N	137.41 E
Kiso-Gawa	28	Ng	35.05N	136.45 E
Kisoro	36	Ec	1.17 S	29.41 E
Kiso-Sanmyaku	29	Ed	35.45N	137.45 E
Kisria, Daiet el-	13	Oi	35.44N	2.47 E
Kissámou, Kólpos-	15	Gn	35.35N	23.40 E
Kissidougou	34	Cd	9.11N	10.06W
Kissimmee	44	Gk	28.18N	81.24W
Kissimmee, Lake-	44	Gl	27.55N	81.16W
Kissū, Jabal-	35	Da	21.35N	25.09 E
Kistelek	10	Pj	46.28N	19.59 E
Kisterenye	10	Ph	48.01N	19.50 E

Index Symbols

- [1] Independent Nation
- [2] State, Region
- [3] District, County
- [4] Municipality
- [5] Colony, Dependency
- Continent
- Physical Region
- Historical or Cultural Region
- Mount, Mountain
- Volcano
- Hill
- Mountains, Mountain Range
- Hills, Escarpment
- Plateau, Upland
- Pass, Gap
- Plain, Lowland
- Delta
- Salt Flat
- Valley, Canyon
- Crater, Cave
- Karst Features
- Depression
- Polder
- Desert, Dunes
- Forest, Woods
- Heath, Steppe
- Oasis
- Cape, Point
- Coast, Beach
- Cliff
- Peninsula
- Isthmus
- Sandbank
- Island
- Atoll
- Rock, Reef
- Islands, Archipelago
- Rocks, Reefs
- Coral Reef
- Well, Spring
- Geyser
- River, Stream
- Waterfall Rapids
- River Mouth, Estuary
- Lake
- Salt Lake
- Intermittent Lake
- Reservoir
- Swamp, Pond
- Canal
- Glacier
- Ice Shelf, Pack Ice
- Ocean
- Sea
- Gulf, Bay
- Strait, Fjord
- Lagoon
- Bank
- Seamount
- Tablemount
- Ridge
- Shelf
- Basin
- Escarpment, Sea Scarp
- Fracture
- Trench, Abyss
- National Park, Reserve
- Point of Interest
- Recreation Site
- Cave, Cavern
- Historic Site
- Ruins
- Wall, Walls
- Church, Abbey
- Temple
- Scientific Station
- Airport
- Port
- Lighthouse
- Mine
- Tunnel
- Dam, Bridge

Kisújszállás 10 Qi 47.13N 20.46 E
Kisuki 29 Cd 35.17N 132.54 E
Kisumu 31 Ki 0.06S 34.45 E
Kisvárda 10 Sh 48.13N 22.05 E
Kita 31 Gg 13.03N 9.30W
Kitab 19 Gh 39.08N 66.54 E
Kita-Daitō-Jima 27 Nf 25.55N 131.20 E
Kitaibaraki 28 Pf 36.48N 140.45 E
Kita-Iō-Jima 60 Cb 25.26N 141.17 E
Kitaj, Ozero- 15 Md 45.35N 29.15 E
Kitakami 27 Pd 39.30N 141.10 E
Kitakami-Gawa 29 Gb 38.25N 141.19 E
Kitakami-Sanchi 29 Gb 39.30N 141.30 E
Kitakata 28 Of 37.39N 139.52 E
Kitakyushū 22 Pf 33.53N 130.50 E
Kitale 31 Kh 1.01N 35.00 E
Kitamaiaioi 29a Cb 43.33N 143.57 E
Kitami 27 Pc 43.48N 143.54 E
Kitami-Fuji 29a Cb 43.42N 143.14 E
Kitami-Sanchi 28 Qb 44.30N 142.30 E
Kitami Tōge 29a Cb 43.55N 142.55 E
Kitan-Kaikyō 29 Dd 34.15N 135.00 E
Kita-Taiheyō=Pacific Ocean (EN) 60 Ch 22.00N 167.00 E
Kita-Ura 29 Gc 36.00N 140.34 E
Kit Carson 45 Eg 38.46N 102.48W
Kitchener 42 Jh 43.27N 80.29W
Kitee 7 He 62.06N 30.09 E
Kitessa 35 Dd 5.22N 25.22 E
Kitgum 36 Fb 3.19N 32.53 E
Kithira=Cythera (EN) 15 Fm 36.09N 23.00 E
Kithira=Kythera (EN) 5 Ih 36.15N 23.00 E
Kithira Channel (EN)= Kithiron Dhiékplous 15 Fm 36.00N 23.00 E
Kithiron, Dhiékplous-= Kithira Channel (EN) 15 Fm 36.00N 23.00 E
Kithnos 15 Hl 37.25N 24.26 E
Kithnos 15 Hl 37.23N 24.25 E
Kithnou, Stenón- 15 Hl 37.25N 24.30 E
Kitimat 39 Gd 54.05N 128.38W
Kitimat Ranges 42 Ef 53.58N 128.39W
Kitoushi-Yama 29a Cb 43.27N 143.25 E
Kitriani 15 Hm 36.54N 24.44 E
Kitridge Point 51q Bb 13.09N 59.25W
Kitros 15 Fi 40.22N 22.35 E
Kitsuki 29 Be 33.25N 131.37 E
Kittanning 44 He 40.49N 79.31W
Kittery 44 Ld 43.05N 70.45W
Kittilä 7 Fc 67.40N 24.54 E
Kitui 31 Ki 1.22S 38.01 E
Kitunda 36 Fd 6.48S 33.13 E
Kitutu 36 Ec 3.17S 28.05 E
Kitwe-Nkana 31 Jj 12.49S 28.13 E
Kitzbühel 14 Gc 47.27N 12.23 E
Kitzbüheler Alpen 14 Gc 47.20N 12.20 E
Kitzingen 10 Gg 49.44N 10.10 E
Kiunga [Kenya] 36 Hc 1.45S 41.29 E
Kiunga [Pap.N.Gui.] 60 Ci 6.07S 141.18 E
Kiuruvesi 7 Ge 63.39N 26.37 E
Kivalina 40 Gc 67.59N 164.33W
Kivercy 16 Dd 50.50N 25.31 E
Kivijärvi [Fin.] 8 Ld 60.55N 27.40 E
Kivijärvi [Fin.] 7 Fe 63.10N 25.09 E
Kivik 7 Di 55.41N 14.15 E
Kiviõli/Kiviyli 7 Gg 59.23N 26.59 E
Kiviyli/Kiviõli 7 Gg 59.23N 26.59 E
Kivu [2] 36 Ec 2.30S 27.30 E
Kivu, Lac-=Kivu, Lake- (EN) 30 Ii 2.00S 29.10 E
Kivu, Lake- (EN)=Kivu, Lac- 30 Ii 2.00S 29.10 E
Kiwai Island 60 Ci 8.30S 143.25 E
Kiyamaki Dağh 24 Kc 38.47N 45.51 E
Kıyıköy 24 Cb 41.25N 28.01 E
Kiyosato 29a Db 43.51N 144.35 E
Kizel 19 Fd 59.03N 57.40 E
Kizema 7 Kf 61.09N 44.46 E
Kizilcabölük 15 Ml 37.37N 29.01 E
Kızılca Dağı 24 Cd 36.55N 29.52 E
Kızılcahamam 24 Eb 40.28N 32.39 E
Kızıl Dağ 24 Ed 36.25N 32.42 E
Kizilhisar 15 Ml 37.33N 29.18 E
Kızılırmak 21 Fe 41.45N 35.59 E
Kızılırmak 24 Eb 40.22N 33.59 E
Kiziljurt 16 Oh 43.13N 46.55 E
Kizilskoje 17 Ij 52.44N 58.54 E
Kızıltepe 24 Id 37.12N 40.36 E
Kizimen, Vulkan- 20 Le 55.03N 160.27 E
Kižinga 20 Ff 51.51N 109.55 E
Kizir 20 Ef 54.10N 93.30 E
Kizljar 19 Eg 43.50N 46.42 E
Kizljarski Zaliv 16 Og 44.35N 46.55 E
Kizukuri 29a Bc 40.48N 140.22 E
Kizyl-Arvat 19 Fh 39.01N 56.20 E
Kizyl-Atrek 19 Fh 37.38N 54.47 E
Kizyl-Su 19 Fh 39.46N 53.01 E
Kjahta 20 Ff 50.26N 106.25 E
Kjalvaz 16 Pj 38.38N 48.20 E
Kjardla/Kärdla 7 Fg 59.01N 22.42 E
Kjarevere/Kärevere 8 Lf 58.23N 26.30 E
Kjarla/Kärla 8 Jf 58.16N 22.05 E
Kjellerup 8 Ch 56.17N 9.26 E
Kjøllefjord 7 Ga 70.56N 27.27 E
Kjölur 7a Bb 64.50N 19.25W
Kjøpsvik 7 Db 68.06N 16.21 E
Kjubjume 20 Jd 63.28N 140.30 E
Kjurdamir 19 Eg 40.20N 48.07 E
Kjusjur 20 Hb 70.35N 127.45 E
Kjustendil 15 Fg 42.17N 22.41 E
Kjustendil [2] 15 Fg 42.17N 22.41 E
Kjyosumi-Yama 29 Gd 35.10N 140.09 E
Klabat, Gunung- 26 If 1.28N 125.02 E
Kladanj 23 Gf 44.14N 18.42 E
Kladno 10 Kf 50.09N 14.07 E
Kladovo 15 Fe 44.37N 22.37 E
Klagenfurt 6 Hf 46.38N 14.18 E
Klaipėda/Klajpeda 6 Id 55.43N 21.07 E
Klajpeda/Klaipėda 6 Id 55.43N 21.07 E
Klamath 46 Cf 41.32N 124.02W
Klamath Falls 39 Ge 42.13N 121.46W
Klamath Mountains 43 Cc 41.40N 123.20W
Klamath River 46 Cf 41.33N 124.04W
Klamono 26 Jg 1.08S 131.30 E
Klarälven 5 Hd 59.23N 13.32 E
Klaten 26 Fh 7.42S 110.35 E
Klatovy 10 Jg 49.24N 13.19 E
Klavreström 8 Fg 57.08N 15.08 E
Klawer 37 Bf 31.44S 18.36 E
Klazienaveen, Emmen- 12 Jb 52.44N 7.01 E
Kleck 16 Ec 53.03N 26.40 E
Kłecko 10 Nd 52.38N 17.26 E
Kleinblittersdorf 12 Je 49.09N 7.02 E
Kleine Nete 12 Gc 51.08N 4.34 E
Kleine Sluis, Anna Paulowna- 12 Gb 52.52N 4.52 E
Klein-Karoo=Little Karroo (EN) 37 Cf 33.42S 21.20 E
Kleinsee 37 Be 29.40S 17.05 E
Klekovača 14 Kf 44.26N 16.31 E
Kléla 34 Dc 11.40N 5.40W
Kleppe 8 Af 58.46N 5.40 E
Klerksdorp 37 De 26.58S 26.39 E
Kletnja 19 De 53.27N 33.17 E
Kletski 16 Me 49.19N 43.04 E
Kleve 10 Ce 51.47N 6.09 E
Klibreck, Ben- 9 Ic 58.19N 4.30W
Klička 20 Gf 50.24N 118.01 E
Klimoviči 19 De 53.37N 32.01 E
Klimovo 16 Hc 52.23N 32.16 E
Klin 19 Dd 56.20N 36.42 E
Klina 15 Dg 42.37N 20.35 E
Klincy 19 De 52.46N 32.17 E
Klingbach 12 Ke 49.11N 8.24 E
Klingenthal 10 If 50.22N 12.28 E
Klinovec 10 If 50.24N 12.58 E
Klintehamn 7 Eh 57.24N 18.12 E
Klippan 8 Eh 56.08N 13.06 E
Klipplaat 37 Cf 33.02S 24.21 E
Kliškovcy 15 Ja 48.23N 26.13 E
Klisura 15 Hg 42.42N 24.27 E
Klitmøller 8 Cg 57.02N 8.31 E
Kljazma 5 Kd 56.10N 42.58 E
Ključevskaja Sopka, Vulkan- 21 Sd 56.04N 160.38 E
Kljuci 20 Le 56.14N 160.58 E
Kłobuck 10 Of 50.55N 18.57 E
Kłodawa 10 Od 52.16N 18.55 E
Kłodzka, Kotlina- 10 Mf 50.30N 16.35 E
Kłodzko 10 Mf 50.28N 16.40 E
Kløfta 8 Dd 60.04N 11.09 E
Kloga/Klooga 8 Ke 59.24N 24.10 E
Kłomnice 10 Pf 50.56N 19.21 E
Klondike Plateau 42 Dd 63.10N 139.55W
Klondike River 42 Dd 64.03N 139.26W
Klooga/Kloga 8 Ke 59.24N 24.10 E
Kloosteezande, Hontenisse- 12 Gc 51.23N 4.00 E
Klosi 15 Dh 41.29N 20.06 E
Klosterneuburg 14 Kb 48.18N 16.19 E
Klosters/Claustra 14 Dd 46.52N 9.52 E
Kloten 14 Cc 47.27N 8.35 E
Klotz, Lac- 42 Kd 60.40N 73.00W
Kluane Lake 42 Dd 61.15N 138.40W
Kluczbork 10 Of 50.59N 18.13 E
Knaben 8 Bf 58.39N 7.04 E
Knäred 8 Eh 56.32N 13.19 E
Kneža 15 Hf 43.30N 24.05 E
Knife River 45 Fc 47.20N 101.23W
Knin 14 Kf 44.02N 16.12 E
Knislinge 8 Fh 56.11N 14.05 E
Knittelfeld 14 Ic 47.13N 14.49 E
Knivsta 8 Ge 59.43N 17.48 E
Knjaževac 15 Ff 43.34N 22.15 E
Knobly Mountain 44 Hf 39.15N 79.05W
Knockmealdown Mountains/ Cnoc Mhaoldonn 9 Fi 52.15N 8.00W
Knokke-Heist [Bel.] 12 Fc 51.21N 3.15 E
Knokke-Heist [Bel.] 11 Jc 51.21N 3.17 E
Knokke-Westkapelle 12 Fc 51.19N 3.18 E
Knolls grund 8 Gg 57.30N 17.30 E
Knøsen 8 Dg 57.12N 10.18 E
Knosós=Cnossus (EN) 15 In 35.18N 25.10 E
Knox, Cape- 42 Ef 54.11N 133.05W
Knox Coast 66 He 66.30S 105.00 E
Knoxville [Ia.-U.S.] 45 Jf 41.19N 93.06W
Knoxville [Tn.-U.S.] 39 Kf 35.58N 83.56W
Knud Rasmussen Land 67 Nd 80.00N 55.00W
Knüllgebirge 10 Ff 50.50N 9.30 E
Knutsholstind 8 Cc 61.26N 8.34 E
Knysna 31 Jl 34.02S 23.02 E
Ko, Kut 25 Kf 11.40N 102.35 E
Koartac 42 Kd 60.50N 69.30W
Koba 26 Eg 2.29S 106.24 E
Koba, Pulau- 26 Jh 6.25S 134.28 E
Kobar Sink 35 Gc 14.00N 40.30 E
Kobayashi 28 Ki 31.59N 130.59 E
Kobdo 22 Le 48.01N 91.38 E
Kobdo (Chovd) 27 Fb 48.06N 92.11 E
Kōbe 22 Pf 34.41N 135.10 E
Kobeljaki 16 Ie 49.08N 34.12 E
København [2] 8 Ei 55.40N 12.10 E
København=Copenhagen (EN) 6 Hi 55.40N 12.35 E
Kobenni 32 Ff 15.55N 9.05W
Kobern-Gondorf 12 Jd 50.19N 7.28 E
Kobjaj 20 Hd 63.30N 126.26 E
Koblenz 10 Df 50.21N 7.36 E
Kobo 35 Fc 12.09N 39.39 E
Koboldo 20 If 52.58N 132.42 E
Kobra 7 Mg 59.19N 50.54 E
Kobrin 19 Ce 52.13N 24.23 E
Kobrinskoje 8 Ne 59.22N 30.14 E
Kobroor, Pulau- 26 Jh 6.12S 134.32 E
Kobuk 38 Cc 66.45N 161.00W
Kobuleti 16 Li 41.47N 41.45 E
Koca 24 Eb 41.41N 32.15 E
Kocabaş 24 Bb 40.22N 27.19 E
Koca Çay 15 Lj 38.43N 28.03 E
Koca Çay [Tur.] 24 Bb 40.08N 27.57 E
Koca Çay [Tur.] 24 Cd 36.17N 29.16 E
Koca Çay/Orhaneli 15 Lj 39.56N 28.32 E
Kočani 15 Fh 41.55N 22.25 E
Kocasu 15 Mj 39.42N 29.31 E
Kočečum 20 Fd 64.17N 100.10 E
Kočetovka 16 Lc 53.01N 40.31 E
Kočevje 14 Ie 45.39N 14.51 E
Kočevski rog 14 Ie 45.41N 15.00 E
Koch 42 Jc 69.35N 78.20W
Kŏch'ang 28 Ig 35.41N 127.55 E
Ko Chang 25 Kf 12.00N 102.23 E
Koch Bihār 25 Hc 26.19N 89.26 E
Kochi 27 Ne 33.33N 133.33 E
Kōchi Ken [2] 28 Lh 33.20N 133.30 E
Kochisar Ovası 24 Ec 38.50N 33.30 E
Kock 10 Se 51.39N 22.27 E
Kočkorka 18 Jc 42.11N 75.45 E
Kočmar 15 Kf 43.41N 27.28 E
Kočubej 19 Eg 44.23N 46.31 E
Kočubejevskoje 16 Lg 44.41N 41.50 E
Kodiak 39 Dd 57.48N 152.23W
Kodiak 38 Dd 57.30N 153.30W
Kodino 7 Je 63.44N 39.40 E
Kodok 35 Ed 9.53N 32.07 E
Kodomari 29a Bc 41.08N 140.18 E
Kodori 16 Lh 42.49N 41.10 E
Kodry 15 Lb 47.15N 28.15 E
Kodyma 16 Ge 48.01N 30.48 E
Kodža Balkan 15 Jg 42.50N 27.00 E
Koekenaap 37 Bf 31.29S 18.19 E
Koes 37 Be 25.59S 19.08 E
Kofa Mountains 46 Ij 33.20N 114.00W
Koçarli 15 Kl 37.45N 27.42 E
Kofaz 24 Bb 41.58N 27.12 E
Koffiefontein 37 Ce 29.30S 25.00 E
Kofiau, Pulau- 26 Ig 1.11S 129.50 E
Köflach 14 Jc 47.04N 15.05 E
Koforidua 31 Gh 6.05N 0.15W
Kōfu [Jap.] 29 Cd 35.18N 133.29 E
Kōfu [Jap.] 27 Od 35.39N 138.35 E
Koga 29 Fc 36.12N 139.42 E
Kogaluc 42 Je 59.38N 77.30W
Kōge 29 Dd 35.24N 134.15 E
Køge 7 Ci 55.27N 12.11 E
Køge Bugt 8 Ei 55.30N 12.20 E
Kogel 17 He 62.38N 57.07 E
Kogilnik 15 Md 45.51N 29.38 E
Kogilnik (Kunduk) 15 Md 45.51N 29.38 E
Kogon 34 Cc 11.09N 14.42W
Kogota 29 Gb 38.32N 141.01 E
Kohala Mountains 65a Fc 20.05N 155.43W
Kohāt 25 Eb 33.35N 71.26 E
Kohila 8 Ke 59.11N 24.40 E
Kohima 25 Ic 25.40N 94.07 E
Koh-i Mārān 25 Dc 29.05N 66.50 E
Kohinggo 63a Cc 8.13S 157.10 E
Kohma 7 Jh 56.57N 41.07 E
Kohtla-Jarve/Kohtla-Järve 19 Cd 59.25N 27.14 E
Kohu Dağı 15 Mm 36.30N 29.50 E
Kohunlich 48 Oh 18.30N 88.55W
Koide 29 Fc 37.14N 138.57 E
Koigi/Kojgi 8 Kf 58.49N 25.40 E
Koin 17 Ee 63.10N 51.15 E
Koindu 34 Cd 8.28N 10.20W
Koitere 7 He 62.58N 30.45 E
Kojā 23 Jd 25.34N 61.13 E
Kojandytau 18 Lb 44.20N 78.45 E
Kojda 7 Kc 66.23N 42.31 E
Koje-Do 28 Jg 34.52N 128.37 E
Kojetín 10 Ng 49.21N 17.20 E
Kojgi/Koigi 8 Kf 58.49N 25.40 E
Ko-Jima [Jap.] 29 Fe 33.07N 139.40 E
Ko-Jima [Jap.] 28 Od 41.22N 139.47 E
Kojō 27 Md 38.57N 127.52 E
Kojonup 59 Df 33.50S 117.09 E
Kojtaš 18 Fd 40.14N 67.22 E
Kojtezek, Pereval- 18 If 37.29N 72.45 E
Kojur 24 Nd 36.23N 51.43 E
Kojva 17 Ig 58.15N 58.14 E
Kokab 35 Cc 10.03N 22.04 E
Kokai-Gawa 29 Gd 35.52N 140.08 E
Kokand 22 Je 40.33N 70.57 E
Kökar 7 Eg 59.55N 20.55 E
Kökarsfjärden 8 Ie 59.55N 20.45 E
Kokas 26 Jg 2.42S 132.26 E
Kokava nad Rimavicou 10 Ph 48.34N 19.50 E
Kokawa 29 Dd 34.17N 135.26 E
Kokčetav 22 Id 53.17N 69.25 E
Kokčetavskaja Oblast [3] 19 Ge 53.30N 70.00 E
Kokemäenjoki 8 Ic 61.33N 21.42 E
Kokemäki/Kumo 7 Ff 61.15N 22.21 E
Kok-Jangak 19 Hg 40.59N 73.15 E
Kokkina 24 Ee 35.10N 32.36 E
Kokkola/Gamlakarleby 6 Ic 63.50N 23.07 E
Koko [Eth.] 35 Fc 10.20N 36.04 E
Koko [Nig.] 34 Fc 11.26N 4.30 E
Kokomo 43 Jc 40.29N 86.08W
Kokonau 26 Kg 4.43S 136.26 E
Kokong 37 Cd 24.27S 23.03 E
Koko Nor (EN)=Qinghai Hu 21 Mf 37.00N 100.20 E
Kokpekty 19 If 48.45N 82.24 E
Kokšaal-Tau, Hrebet- 19 Hg 41.00N 78.00 E
Kokšenga 7 Kf 61.27N 42.38 E
Koksijde 12 Ec 51.06N 2.39 E
Koksoak 42 Ke 58.31N 68.11W
Kokstad 31 Jl 30.32S 29.29 E
Koktal 18 Lb 44.05N 79.44 E
Koktokay/Fuyun 22 Ke 47.13N 89.39 E
Kokubu 28 Ki 31.44N 130.46 E
Kola 19 Db 68.53N 33.01 E
Kola, Pulau- 26 Jh 5.30S 134.35 E
Kolahun 34 Cd 8.17N 10.05W
Kolaka 26 Hg 4.03S 121.36 E
Kolamadulu Atoll 25a Bb 2.25N 73.10 E
Kola Peninsula (EN)=Kolski Poluostrov 5 Jb 67.30N 37.00 E
Kolār Gold Fields 25 Ff 12.55N 78.17 E
Kolari 7 Fc 67.20N 23.48 E
Kolárovo 10 Ni 47.55N 18.00 E
Kolašin 15 Cg 42.49N 19.32 E
Kolbäck 8 Ge 59.34N 16.15 E
Kolbäcksån 8 Ge 59.32N 16.16 E
Kolbio 36 Hc 1.09S 41.12 E
Kolbuszowa 10 Rf 50.15N 21.47 E
Kolby 8 Di 55.48N 10.33 E
Kolčugino 7 Jh 56.16N 39.23 E
Kolda 34 Cc 12.53N 14.57W
Kolding 6 Gd 55.31N 9.29 E
Kole [Zaire] 36 Dc 3.31S 22.27 E
Kole [Zaire] 36 Eb 2.07N 25.26 E
Koléa 13 Oh 36.38N 2.46 E
Kolendo 20 Jf 53.43N 142.57 E
Kolente 34 Cd 8.55N 13.08W
Kolesnoje 15 Mc 46.04N 29.45 E
Kolga 8 Ke 59.28N 25.29 E
Kolga, Zaliv-/Kolga Laht 8 Ke 59.30N 25.15 E
Kolga Laht/Kolga, Zaliv- 8 Ke 59.30N 25.15 E
Kolgompja, Mys- 8 Me 59.44N 28.35 E
Kolgujev, Ostrov- 5 Kb 69.05N 49.15 E
Kolhāpur 22 Jh 16.42N 74.13 E
Kolhozabad 18 Gf 37.35N 68.39 E
Kolhozbentskoje, Vodohranilišče- 18 Df 37.10N 62.30 E
Koli 7 Ge 63.06N 29.53 E
Kolimbine 34 Cc 14.45N 11.00 E
Kolín 10 Lf 50.02N 15.13 E
Kolito 35 Fd 7.25N 38.07 E
Koljučinskaja Guba 20 Nc 66.50N 174.30W
Kolka 8 Jg 57.44N 22.27 E
Kolkasrags 7 Fh 57.46N 22.37 E
Kolki 16 Dd 51.07N 25.42 E
Kollínai 15 Fl 37.17N 22.22 E
Kollumúli 7a Cb 65.47N 14.21W
Kolmården 8 Gf 58.41N 16.35 E
Köln=Cologne (EN) 6 Ge 50.56N 6.57 E
Köln-Lövenich 12 Id 50.57N 6.50 E
Kolno 10 Rc 53.25N 21.56 E
Köln-Porz 10 Df 50.53N 7.03 E
Koło 10 Od 52.12N 18.38 E
Koloa 65a Bb 21.54N 159.28W
Kołobrzeg 10 Lb 54.12N 15.33 E
Kolodnja 16 Hb 54.49N 32.11 E
Kologriv 7 Kg 58.51N 44.17 E
Kolokani 34 Dc 13.34N 8.03W
Koloko 34 Dc 11.05N 5.19W
Kolokolkova Guba 17 Fb 68.30N 52.30 E
Kolomna 6 Jd 55.05N 38.49 E
Kolombangara Island 60 Fi 8.00S 157.05 E
Kolomyja 19 Cf 48.32N 25.01 E
Kolondiéba 34 Dc 11.06N 6.53W
Kolonga 65b Ac 21.08S 175.04W
Kolonodale 26 Hg 2.00S 121.19 E
Kolosovka 19 Hd 56.28N 73.36 E
Kolossa 34 Dc 13.52N 7.35W
Kolovai 65b Ac 21.06S 175.20W
Kolozero, Ozero- 7 Hb 68.15N 33.15 E
Kolp 7 Ig 59.20N 36.50 E
Kolpaševo 22 Kd 58.20N 82.50 E
Kolpino 7 Hg 59.45N 30.33 E
Kolpny 16 Jc 52.16N 37.00 E
Kolski Poluostrov=Kola Peninsula (EN) 5 Jb 67.30N 37.00 E
Koltubanovski 16 Rc 52.57N 52.02 E
Kolubara 15 De 44.40N 20.15 E
Koluszki 10 Pe 51.44N 19.49 E
Koluton 19 Ge 51.42N 69.25 E
Kolva [R.S.F.S.R.] 19 Fb 65.55N 57.20 E
Kolva [R.S.F.S.R.] 17 Hf 60.22N 56.33 E
Kolvickoje, Ozero- 7 Hc 67.05N 33.30 E
Kølvrå 8 Ch 56.18N 9.08 E
Kolwezi 31 Jj 10.43S 25.28 E
Kolyma 21 Sc 69.30N 161.00 E
Kolyma Plain (EN)= Kolymskaja Nizmennost 21 Rc 68.30N 154.00 E
Kolyma Range (EN)= Kolymskoje Nagorje 21 Rc 62.30N 155.00 E
Kolymskaja Nizmennost= Kolyma Plain (EN) 21 Rc 68.30N 154.00 E
Kolymskoje Nagorje= Kolyma Range (EN) 21 Rc 62.30N 155.00 E
Kolyšlej 16 Nc 52.40N 44.31 E
Kolžat 19 Ig 43.29N 80.37 E
Kom 15 Gf 43.10N 23.03 E
Kom 36 Gb 1.05N 38.02 E
Komádi 10 Rj 47.00N 21.30 E
Komadugu Gana 34 Hc 13.05N 12.24 E
Komadugu Yobe 30 Ig 13.42N 13.24 E
Komagane 29 Ed 35.43N 137.54 E
Koma-ga-Take [Jap.] 27 Fd 35.45N 138.13 E
Koma-ga-Take [Jap.] 29 Gb 39.47N 140.50 E
Koma-ga-Take [Jap.] 29a Bb 42.04N 140.40 E
Komandorskie Islands (EN) =Komandorskije Ostrova 21 Sd 55.00N 167.00 E
Komandorskije Ostrova= Komandorski Islands (EN) 21 Sd 55.00N 167.00 E
Komandorskiye Basin (EN) 20 Le 57.00N 168.00 E
Komarin 16 Gd 51.27N 30.32 E
Komarno 10 Tg 49.34N 23.43 E
Komárno 10 Oi 47.46N 18.09 E
Komárom [2] 10 Oi 47.40N 18.15 E
Komárom 10 Oi 47.44N 18.07 E
Komatipoort 37 Ee 25.25S 31.55 E
Komatsu 27 Od 36.24N 136.37 E
Komatsujima 29 Dd 34.01N 134.35 E
Komba, Pulau- 26 Hh 7.47S 123.35 E
Kombissiri 34 Ec 12.04N 1.20W
Kombolcha 35 Fc 11.05N 39.45 E
Komebail Lagoon 64a Ac 7.24N 134.27 E
Komen/Comines 12 Ed 50.46N 2.59 E
Komi ASSR [3] 19 Fc 64.00N 55.00 E
Komi-Permjacki Nacionalny Okrug [3] 19 Fd 60.00N 54.30 E
Komló 10 Oj 46.12N 18.16 E
Kommunarsk 16 Ke 48.27N 38.52 E
Kommunary 8 Nd 60.55N 30.10 E
Kommunizma, Pik-= Communism Peak (EN) 21 Jf 38.57N 72.08 E
Komodo, Pulau- 26 Gh 8.36S 119.30 E
Komoé 30 Gh 5.12N 3.44W
Komoé [3] 34 Ec 10.25N 4.20W
Komono 36 Bc 3.15S 13.14 E
Komoran, Pulau- 26 Kh 8.18S 138.45 E
Komoro 29 Fc 36.19N 138.24 E
Komotini 15 Ih 41.07N 25.24 E
Komovi 15 Cg 42.41N 19.39 E
Kompasberg 30 Jl 31.46S 24.32 E
Komrat 16 Ff 46.17N 28.38 E
Komsa 20 Dd 61.40N 89.25 E
Komsomolec 17 Kj 53.45N 62.02 E
Komsomolec, Ostrov- 21 La 80.30N 95.00 E
Komsomolec, Zaliv- 16 Rg 45.30N 52.45 E
Komsomolsk [R.S.F.S.R.] 7 Jh 57.02N 40.22 E
Komsomolsk [R.S.F.S.R.] 20 De 57.25N 86.02 E
Komsomolsk [Tur.-U.S.S.R.] 19 Gh 39.02N 63.36 E
Komsomolski [Kaz.-U.S.S.R.] 19 Ff 47.20N 53.44 E
Komsomolski [R.S.F.S.R.] 16 Og 45.22N 46.01 E
Komsomolski [R.S.F.S.R.] 7 Ki 54.27N 45.45 E
Komsomolski [R.S.F.S.R.] 19 Gb 67.35N 63.47 E
Komsomolski [R.S.F.S.R.] 17 Kf 61.20N 63.15 E
Komsomolski [R.S.F.S.R.] 20 Mc 69.12N 172.55 E
Komsomolsk-na-Amure 22 Pd 50.36N 137.02 E
Komsomolsk-na-Ustjurte 19 Fg 44.07N 58.17 E
Komsomolskoje [Ukr.-U.S.S.R.] 16 Je 49.36N 36.33 E
Komsomolskoje [Ukr.-U.S.S.R.] 16 Kf 47.37N 38.05 E
Komsomolskoj Pravdy, Ostrova- 20 Fa 77.15N 107.30 E
Kŏmun-Do 28 Ig 34.02N 127.19 E
Kömür Burun 15 Jk 38.39N 26.25 E
Komusan 27 Mc 42.07N 129.42 E
Kona 34 Ec 14.57N 3.53W
Kona Coast 65a Fd 19.35N 155.56W
Konakovo 19 Dd 56.42N 36.46 E
Konar 23 Lc 34.25N 70.32 E
Konārak 25 Hh 19.54N 86.07 E
Konarha [3] 23 Lb 35.15N 71.00 E
Konda 19 Gc 60.40N 69.46 E
Kondagaon 25 Ge 19.36N 81.40 E
Kondinin 59 Df 32.30S 118.16 E
Kondinskoje 17 Mg 59.40N 67.25 E
Kondoa 31 Ki 4.54S 35.47 E
Kondopoga 6 Jc 62.13N 34.17 E
Kondratjevo 8 Md 60.36N 28.02 E
Kondrovo 16 Je 54.49N 35.55 E
Kondurča 7 Mj 53.31N 50.24 E
Koné 61 Bd 21.04S 164.52 E
Konečnaja 19 He 50.45N 78.27 E
Konevic, Ostrov- 8 Nd 60.50N 30.45 E
Kong 34 Ed 9.09N 4.37W
Kŏng 25 Lf 13.32N 105.58 E
Kŏng, Kaôh- 25 Kf 11.20N 103.00 E
Konga/Koonga 8 Jf 58.34N 24.00 E
Kongauru 64a Ac 7.04N 134.17 E
Kong Christian IX Land = King Christian IX Land (EN) 67 Mc 68.00N 36.30W
Kong Christian X Land = King Christian X Land (EN) 67 Md 72.20N 32.30W
Kongeå 8 Ci 55.23N 8.39 E
Kong Frederik VIII Land = King Frederik VIII Land (EN) 67 Md 78.30N 28.00W
Kong Frederik VI Kyst = King Frederik VI Coast (EN) 67 Nc 63.00N 43.30W
Konginkangas 8 Kb 62.46N 25.48 E
Kongju 28 If 36.27N 127.08 E
Kong Karls Land 41 Oc 78.50N 28.00 E
Kong Kong 35 Ed 7.26N 33.14 E
Kongolo 31 Ji 5.23S 27.00 E
Kongor 35 Ed 7.10N 31.21 E
Kong Oscars Fjord 67 Md 72.20N 23.00W
Kongoussi 34 Ec 13.19N 1.32W
Kongsberg 7 Bg 59.39N 9.39 E
Kongsøya 41 Oc 78.55N 28.40 E
Kongsvinger 7 Cf 60.12N 12.00 E
Kongur Shan 21 Jf 38.40N 75.21 E
Kongwa 36 Gd 6.12S 36.25 E
Kong Wilhelms Land 41 Jc 75.48N 23.15W
Koniecpol 10 Pf 50.48N 19.41 E
Königslutter am Elm 10 Gd 52.15N 10.49 E
Königswinter 12 Jd 50.41N 7.11 E
Königs Wusterhausen 10 Jd 52.17N 13.37 E
Konin 10 Od 52.13N 18.16 E
Konin [2] 10 Od 52.15N 18.15 E
Konispoli 15 Dj 39.39N 20.10 E
Kónitsa 15 Di 40.03N 20.45 E
Konj 14 Kg 43.43N 16.55 E
Konjed Jān 24 Nf 33.30N 50.27 E
Konjic 14 Lg 43.39N 17.58 E
Konjuh 14 Mf 44.18N 18.33 E
Konkan 25 Ee 18.05N 73.25 E
Konkiep 37 Be 28.00S 17.23 E
Konko 36 Ed 10.12S 27.27 E
Konkouré 34 Cd 9.58N 13.42W
Konnevesi 8 Lb 62.40N 26.35 E
Konnevesi 8 Lb 62.37N 26.19 E
Konnivesi 8 Lc 61.10N 26.10 E
Konoša 6 Kc 60.58N 40.15 E

Index Symbols

[1] Independent Nation
[2] State, Region
[3] District, County
[4] Municipality
[5] Colony, Dependency
Continent
Physical Region
Historical or Cultural Region
Mount, Mountain
Volcano
Hill
Mountains, Mountain Range
Hills, Escarpment
Plateau, Upland
Pass, Gap
Plain, Lowland
Delta
Salt Flat
Valley, Canyon
Crater, Cave
Karst Features
Depression
Polder
Desert, Dunes
Forest, Woods
Heath, Steppe
Oasis
Cape, Point
Coast, Beach
Cliff
Peninsula
Isthmus
Sandbank
Island
Atoll
Rock, Reef
Islands, Archipelago
Rocks, Reefs
Coral Reef
Well, Spring
Geyser
River, Stream
Waterfall Rapids
River Mouth, Estuary
Lake
Salt Lake
Intermittent Lake
Reservoir
Swamp, Pond
Canal
Glacier
Ice Shelf, Pack Ice
Ocean
Sea
Gulf, Bay
Strait, Fjord
Lagoon
Bank
Seamount
Tablemount
Ridge
Shelf
Basin
Escarpment, Sea Scarp
Fracture
Trench, Abyss
National Park, Reserve
Point of Interest
Recreation Site
Cave, Cavern
Historic Site
Ruins
Wall, Walls
Church, Abbey
Temple
Scientific Station
Airport
Port
Lighthouse
Mine
Tunnel
Dam, Bridge

Kōnosu	29	Fc	36.04N	139.30 E
Konotop	6	Je	51.14N	33.12 E
Konqi He	21	Ke	41.48N	86.47 E
Konrei	64a	Bb	7.43N	134.37 E
Konsei-Tōge	29	Fc	36.52N	139.22 E
Konsen-Daichi	29a	Db	43.20N	144.50 E
Końskie	10	Qe	51.12N	20.26 E
Konstantinovka	16	Je	48.29N	37.43 E
Konstantinovsk	16	Lf	47.35N	41.05 E
Konstanz	10	Fi	47.40N	9.11 E
Kontagora	31	Hg	10.24N	5.29 E
Kontcha	34	Hd	7.58N	12.14 E
Kontich	12	Gc	51.08N	4.27 E
Kontiolahti	7	Ge	62.46N	29.51 E
Kontiomäki	7	Gd	64.21N	28.09 E
Kontum	25	Lf	14.21N	108.00 E
Kontum, Plateau de-	25	Lf	13.55N	108.05 E
Konusin, Mys-	7	Kc	67.10N	43.50 E
Konya	22	Ff	37.52N	32.31 E
Konya Ovası	24	Ed	37.30N	33.20 E
Konz	12	Ie	49.42N	6.35 E
Konza	36	Gc	1.45S	37.07 E
Konžakovski Kamen, Gora-	5	Ld	59.38N	59.08 E
Koocanusa, Lake-	46	Hb	48.45N	115.15W
Kook, Punta-	65d	Ab	27.08S	109.26W
Koolau Range	65a	Db	21.21N	157.47W
Koonga/Konga	8	Jf	58.34N	24.00 E
Koorda	59	Df	30.50S	117.29 E
Koosa	8	Lf	58.33N	27.07 E
Kootenay Lake	46	Gb	49.35N	116.50W
Kootenay River	38	He	49.15N	117.39W
Kopa	18	Jc	43.31N	75.48 E
Kopaonik	15	Df	43.15N	20.50 E
Kópasker	7a	Ca	66.18N	16.27W
Kópavogur	7a	Bb	64.06N	21.55W
Kopejsk	19	Gd	55.08N	61.39 E
Koper	14	He	45.33N	13.44 E
Kopervik	7	Ag	59.17N	5.18 E
Kopetdag, Hrebet-	21	Hf	37.45N	58.15 E
Kop Geçidi	24	Ib	40.01N	40.28 E
Ko Phangan	25	Jg	9.45N	100.00 E
Köping	7	Dg	59.31N	16.00 E
Köpingsvik	8	Gh	56.53N	16.43 E
Kopjevo	20	Df	54.59N	89.55 E
Kopliku	15	Cg	42.13N	19.26 E
Köpmanholmen	7	Ee	63.10N	18.34 E
Koporje	8	Me	59.40N	29.08 E
Koporski Zaliv	8	Me	59.45N	28.45 E
Koppal	25	Fe	15.21N	76.09 E
Koppang	7	Cf	61.34N	11.04 E
Koppány	10	Oj	46.35N	18.26 E
Kopparberg	8	Fe	59.52N	14.59 E
Kopparberg [2]	7	Df	61.00N	14.30 E
Kopparstenarna	8	Hf	58.32N	19.20 E
Koppom	8	Ee	59.43N	12.09 E
Koprivnica	14	Kd	46.10N	16.50 E
Kopru	24	Dd	36.49N	31.10 E
Köprüören	15	Mj	39.30N	29.47 E
Korab	5	Ig	41.44N	20.32 E
Korablino	7	Jj	53.57N	40.00 E
Korahe	35	Gd	6.36N	44.16 E
Korak	64a	Bc	7.21N	134.34 E
Koralpe	14	Id	46.45N	15.00 E
Koramlik	27	Ed	37.32N	85.42 E
Korana	14	Je	45.30N	15.35 E
Korangi	25	Dd	24.47N	67.08 E
Koraput	25	Ge	18.49N	82.43 E
Korba	25	Gd	22.21N	82.41 E
Korbach	10	Ee	51.17N	8.52 E
Körby	8	Ei	55.51N	13.39 E
Korça	15	Di	40.37N	20.46 E
Korčula	14	Kh	42.57N	16.55 E
Korčula	14	Lh	42.58N	17.08 E
Korčulanski Kanal	14	Kg	43.03N	16.40 E
Kordān	24	Ne	35.56N	50.50 E
Kordel	12	Ie	49.50N	6.38 E
Kordestān [3]	23	Gb	35.30N	47.00 E
Kord Küy	23	Hb	36.48N	54.07 E
Kordun	14	Je	45.10N	15.35 E
Korea Bay (EN)=Sŏjosŏn-man	21	Of	39.15N	125.00 E
Korean Peninsula (EN)	21	Of	35.30N	125.30 E
Korea Strait (EN)=Taehan-Haehyŏp	21	Of	34.40N	129.00 E
Korea Strait (EN)=Tsushima-Kaikyō	21	Of	34.40N	129.00 E
Korec	16	Ed	50.37N	27.10 E
Korem	35	Fc	12.30N	39.32 E
Korenovsk	19	Df	45.28N	39.28 E
Korf	20	Ld	60.18N	166.01 E
Korfovski	20	Ig	48.11N	135.04 E
Korgen	7	Cc	66.05N	13.50 E
Kõrgesaare/Kyrgesare	8	Je	59.00N	22.25 E
Korhogo	31	Gh	9.27N	5.38W
Korhogo [3]	34	Dd	9.35N	5.55W
Koribundu	34	Cd	7.43N	11.42W
Korienzé	34	Eb	15.24N	3.47W
Korinthiakós Kólpos=Corinth, Gulf of- (EN)	5	Ih	38.12N	22.30 E
Kórinthos	15	Fl	37.55N	22.53 E
Kórinthos = Corinth (EN)	15	Fl	37.55N	22.53 E
Korínthou, Dhiórix- = Corinth Canal (EN)	15	Fl	37.57N	22.58 E
Koriolei	31	Lh	1.48N	44.30 E
Kőrishegy	10	Ni	47.12N	17.49 E
Koritnik	15	Dg	42.05N	20.34 E
Kōriyama	27	Pd	37.24N	140.23 E
Korjakskaja Sopka, Vulkan-	21	Rd	53.20N	158.47 E
Korjakski Nacionalny okrug [3]	20	Le	60.00N	163.00 E
Korjakskoje Nagorje=Koryak Range (EN)	21	Tc	62.30N	172.00 E
Korjažma	19	Ec	61.18N	47.07 E
Korjukovka	16	Hd	51.47N	32.17 E
Korkino	17	Ji	54.54N	61.25 E

Korkodon	20	Kd	64.43N	154.05 E
Korkuteli	24	Dd	37.04N	30.13 E
Korla	22	Ke	41.44N	86.09 E
Körmend	10	Mi	47.01N	16.36 E
Kormy, Gora-	20	Fd	62.15N	106.08 E
Kornati	14	Jg	43.49N	15.20 E
Kornejevka	17	Ni	54.01N	68.27 E
Kornešty	15	Kb	47.23N	28.00 E
Korneuburg	14	Kb	48.21N	16.20 E
Kórnik	10	Nd	52.17N	17.04 E
Kornsjø	7	Cg	58.57N	11.39 E
Koro	34	Ec	14.05N	3.04W
Koroba	59	Ia	5.40S	142.45 E
Koroča	16	Jd	50.50N	37.13 E
Köroğlu Dağları	23	Da	40.40N	32.35 E
Köroğlu Tepe	24	Db	40.31N	31.53 E
Korogwe	36	Gd	5.09S	38.29 E
Koro Island	57	If	17.32S	179.42 E
Koroit	59	Ig	38.17S	142.22 E
Korolevo	10	Th	48.08N	23.07 E
Korolevu	63d	Ac	18.12S	177.53 E
Korom, Bahr	35	Bc	10.35N	19.45 E
Koromiri	64p	Cc	21.15S	159.43W
Koronadal	26	He	6.12N	125.01 E
Korónia, Limni-	15	Gi	40.40N	23.10 E
Koronowo	10	Nc	53.19N	17.57 E
Koronowski e, Jezioro-	10	Nc	53.22N	17.55 E
Koror	57	Ed	7.20N	134.30 E
Koror	58	Ed	7.20N	134.29 E
Körös	10	Qj	46.43N	20.12 E
Koro Sea	61	Ec	18.00S	180.00
Korosten	6	Ie	50.57N	28.39 E
Korostyšev	16	Fd	50.18N	29.05 E
Korotaiha	17	Jb	68.55N	60.55 E
Koro Toro	31	Ig	16.05N	18.30 E
Korovin Volcano	40a	Db	52.22N	174.10W
Korpijärvi	8	Lc	61.15N	27.10 E
Korpilahti	7	Fe	62.01N	25.33 E
Korpo/Korppoo	8	Id	60.10N	21.35 E
Korppoo/Korpo	8	Id	60.10N	21.35 E
Korsakov	20	Jg	46.37N	142.51 E
Korshäs	7	Ee	62.47N	21.12 E
Korsholm/Mustasaari	8	Ia	63.05N	21.43 E
Korso	8	Kd	60.21N	25.06 E
Korsør	7	Ci	55.20N	11.09 E
Korsun-Ševčenkovski	16	Ge	49.26N	31.18 E
Korsze	10	Rb	54.10N	21.09 E
Kortemark	12	Fc	51.02N	3.02 E
Kortrijk/Courtrai	11	Jd	50.50N	3.16 E
Koruçam Burnu	24	Ee	35.24N	32.56 E
Korucu	15	Kj	39.28N	27.22 E
Koru Dağ	15	Ji	40.42N	26.45 E
Koryak Range (EN)=Korjakskoje Nagorje	21	Tc	62.30N	172.00 E
Korzybie	10	Mb	54.18N	16.50 E
Kos	15	Km	36.53N	27.18 E
Kos	15	Km	36.50N	27.10 E
Kosa	17	Gg	59.56N	55.01 E
Kosa	17	Gf	60.11N	55.10 E
Kosai	29	Ed	34.43N	137.30 E
Kosaja Gora	16	Jb	54.09N	37.31 E
Kosaka	29	Ga	40.20N	140.44 E
Kō-Saki	29	Ad	34.05N	129.13 E
Ko Samui	25	Jg	9.30N	99.58 E
Kosan-ūp	27	Md	38.51N	127.25 E
Koščagyl	16	Rf	46.52N	53.47 E
Kościan	10	Md	52.06N	16.38 E
Kościerzyna	10	Nb	54.08N	18.00 E
Kosciusko	45	Lj	32.58N	89.35W
Kosciusko, Mount-	57	Fg	36.27S	148.16 E
Kose/Koze	8	Ke	59.11N	25.05 E
Köse Dağ	24	Gb	40.06N	37.58 E
Kosha	35	Ea	20.49N	30.32 E
Koshigaya	29	Fd	35.55N	139.45 E
Koshiji	29	Fc	37.24N	138.45 E
Koshiki-Kaikyō	29	Bf	31.45N	130.05 E
Koshiki Rettō	27	Me	31.45N	129.45 E
Koshimizu	29a	Db	43.51N	144.25 E
Kōshoku	28	Of	36.38N	138.06 E
Kōshyū Seamount (EN)	29	Df	31.35N	135.50 E
Košice	6	If	48.43N	21.15 E
Kosjerić	15	Cf	44.00N	19.55 E
Kosju	17	Ic	66.18N	59.53 E
Kosju	17	Id	65.38N	58.59 E
Köşk	15	Ll	37.51N	28.03 E
Koski	8	Jd	60.39N	23.09 E
Koskolovo	8	Me	59.34N	28.30 E
Koslan	19	Ec	63.29N	48.52 E
Kosma	17	Dd	65.43N	49.50 E
Kosmaj	15	De	44.28N	20.33 E
Kosŏng	27	Md	38.40N	128.19 E
Kosov	15	Ia	48.15N	25.08 E
Kosovo	15	Eg	42.40N	21.05 E
Kosovo [3]	15	Dg	42.35N	21.00 E
Kosovska Mitrovica	15	Dg	42.53N	20.52 E
Kosrae (Kusaie)	57	Hd	5.19N	162.59 E
Kossol Passage	64a	Bb	7.52N	134.36 E
Kossol Reef	64a	Bb	7.57N	134.41 E
Kossou, Barrage de-	34	Dd	7.01N	5.29W
Kossovo	16	Dc	52.47N	25.10 E
Kostajnica	14	Ke	45.13N	16.33 E
Kostenec	15	Gg	42.16N	23.49 E
Koster	37	De	25.57S	26.42 E
Kosteröarna	8	Df	58.55N	11.05 E
Kostjukoviči	16	Hc	53.23N	32.06 E
Kostjukovka	16	Gc	52.32N	30.58 E
Kostolac	15	Ee	44.44N	21.12 E
Kostopol	16	Ed	50.53N	26.29 E
Kostriževka	15	Ia	48.31N	25.45 E
Kostroma	6	Kd	57.47N	40.59 E
Kostromskaja Oblast [3]	19	Ed	58.30N	44.00 E
Kostrzyń	10	Nd	52.25N	17.14 E
Kostrzyn	10	Kd	52.37N	14.39 E
Kosva	17	Hg	58.50N	56.45 E
Koszalin	10	Mb	54.12N	16.09 E
Koszalin [2]	10	Mb	54.10N	16.10 E
Kőszeg	10	Mi	47.23N	16.33 E

Kota	22	Jg	25.16N	75.55 E
Kotaagung	26	Dh	5.30S	104.38 E
Kota Baharu	22	Mi	6.08N	102.15 E
Kotabaru	26	Gg	3.14S	116.13 E
Kotabumi	22	Mj	4.50S	104.54 E
Kotadabok	26	Dg	0.30S	104.33 E
Kota Kinabalu	22	Ni	5.59N	116.04 E
Kotamobagu	26	Hf	0.46N	124.19 E
Ko Tao	25	Jf	10.05N	99.52 E
Kotari	14	Jf	44.05N	15.30 E
Ko Tarutau	25	Jg	6.35N	99.40 E
Kota Tinggi	26	Df	1.44N	103.54 E
Kotel	15	Jg	42.53N	26.27 E
Kotelnič	19	Ed	58.20N	48.20 E
Kotelnikovo	16	Mf	47.38N	43.09 E
Kotelny, Ostrov-	21	Pb	75.45N	138.44 E
Kotelva	16	Id	50.03N	34.45 E
Köthen	10	He	51.45N	11.58 E
Kotido	36	Fb	3.00N	34.09 E
Kotjužany	29	Gb	47.50N	28.27 E
Kotka	7	Gf	60.28N	26.55 E
Kot Kapūra	25	Eb	30.35N	74.54 E
Kotlas	6	Kc	61.16N	46.35 E
Kotlenik	15	Df	43.51N	20.42 E
Kotlenski prohod	15	Jg	42.53N	26.27 E
Kotlik	40	Gd	63.02N	163.33W
Kotlin, Ostrov-	8	Md	60.00N	29.45 E
Kotly	8	Me	59.30N	28.48 E
Kotobi	34	Ed	6.42N	4.08W
Kotohira	29	Cd	34.11N	133.48 E
Koton Karifi	34	Gd	8.06N	6.48 E
Kotor	15	Bg	42.25N	18.46 E
Kotorosl	7	Jh	57.38N	39.57 E
Kotorska, Boka-	15	Bg	42.25N	18.40 E
Kotor Varoš	14	Lf	44.37N	17.22 E
Kotouba	34	Ed	8.41N	3.12W
Kotovo	19	Ee	50.18N	44.48 E
Kotovsk [Mold.-U.S.S.R.]	16	Ff	46.49N	28.33 E
Kotovsk [R.S.F.S.R.]	19	Ee	52.35N	41.32 E
Kotovsk [Ukr.-U.S.S.R.]	19	Cf	47.43N	29.33 E
Kotra	10	Uc	53.32N	24.17 E
Kotri	25	Dc	25.22N	68.18 E
Kötschach	14	Gd	46.40N	13.00 E
Kottayam	25	Fg	9.35N	76.31 E
Kotto	30	Jh	4.14N	22.02 E
Kotton	35	Id	9.37N	50.32 E
Kotu	65b	Ba	19.57S	174.48W
Kotu Group	57	Jg	20.00S	174.45W
Kotuj	21	Mb	71.55N	102.05 E
Kotujkan	20	Fb	70.40N	103.25 E
Koturdepe	16	Rj	39.26N	53.40 E
Kotzebue	39	Cc	66.53N	162.39W
Kotzebue Sound	38	Cc	66.20N	163.00W
Kouandé	34	Fc	10.20N	1.42 E
Kouango	35	Be	4.58N	19.59 E
Kouba Modounga	35	Bb	15.40N	18.15 E
Koudougou	31	Gg	11.44N	4.31W
Kouéré	34	Ec	10.27N	3.59W
Koufália	15	Fi	40.47N	22.35 E
Koufonísion [Grc.]	15	Jo	34.56N	26.10 E
Koufonísion [Grc.]	15	Im	36.55N	25.35 E
Koufonísiou, Stenón-	15	Jo	35.00N	26.10 E
Kouilou [3]	36	Bc	4.00S	12.00 E
Kouilou	30	Ii	4.28S	11.41 E
Koukdjuak	42	Kc	66.47N	73.10W
Kouki	35	Bd	7.10N	17.18 E
Koukourou	35	Cd	7.12N	20.02 E
Koulamoutou	36	Bc	1.08S	12.29 E
Koulikoro	34	Dc	12.51N	7.34W
Koulountou	34	Cc	13.15N	13.37W
Koumac	58	Hg	20.30S	164.12 E
Koumac, Grand Récif de-	63b	Be	20.32S	164.04 E
Koumbi-Saleh	32	Ff	15.47N	7.58W
Koumi	29	Fc	36.05N	138.28 E
Koumpentoum	34	Cc	13.59N	14.34W
Koumra	35	Bd	8.55N	17.33 E
Koundara	31	Fg	12.29N	13.18W
Koundian	34	Cc	13.08N	10.42W
Kounoúpoi	15	Jm	36.32N	26.27 E
Kounradski	19	Hf	46.57N	75.01 E
Kounta	34	Eb	17.30N	0.40W
Koupéla	34	Ec	12.11N	0.21W
Kouqian → Yongji	28	Ic	43.40N	126.30 E
Kourou	54	Hb	5.09N	52.39W
Kouroussa	34	Dc	10.39N	9.53W
Koury	34	Ec	12.10N	4.48W
Koussané	34	Cc	14.52N	11.15W
Kousséri	34	Ic	12.05N	15.02 E
Koussi, Emi-	30	Ig	19.55N	18.30 E
Koutiala	31	Gg	12.23N	5.27W
Koutoumo	63b	Cf	22.40S	167.32 E
Koutous	34	Hc	14.30N	10.00 E
Kouvola	7	Gf	60.52N	26.42 E
Kouyou	36	Cc	0.45S	16.38 E
Kova	20	Fe	58.20N	100.20 E
Kovač	15	Cf	43.31N	19.07 E
Kovačica	15	Dd	45.06N	20.38 E
Koval	10	Pd	52.31N	19.10 E
Kovalevka	15	Nc	46.42N	30.31 E
Kovarskas/Kavarskas	8	Ki	55.24N	25.03 E
Kovdor	19	Db	67.33N	30.25 E
Kovdozero, Ozero-	7	Hc	66.47N	32.00 E
Kovel	19	Ce	51.13N	24.43 E
Kovenskaja	17	Mf	61.24N	67.39 E
Kovin	15	De	44.45N	20.59 E
Kovinskaja Grjada	20	Fe	57.15N	101.00 E
Kovrov	19	Ed	56.24N	41.20 E
Kovylkino	7	Ki	54.02N	43.58 E
Kowŏn	27	Md	39.26N	127.15 E
Kowtal-e Do Rāh	23	Lb	36.07N	71.15 E
Kowt-e 'Ashrow	23	Kc	34.27N	68.48 E
Kōyama	29	Bf	31.19N	130.57 E
Köyceğiz	24	Cd	36.55N	28.43 E
Köycegiz Gölü	15	Lm	36.55N	28.40 E
Koyoshi-Gawa	29	Gb	39.24N	140.01 E
Koyuk	40	Gd	64.56N	161.08W

Koyukuk	38	Dc	64.56N	157.30W
Kozaklı	24	Fc	39.13N	34.49 E
Kozan	24	Fd	37.27N	35.49 E
Kozáni	15	Ei	40.18N	21.47 E
Kozara	14	Ke	45.00N	16.55 E
Kozawa	29a	Bb	42.58N	140.40 E
Koze/Kose	8	Ke	59.11N	25.05 E
Kozelsk	19	De	54.01N	35.46 E
Koževnikovo	20	De	56.18N	84.00 E
Kozhikode → Calicut	22	Jh	11.19N	75.46 E
Kozienice	10	Re	51.35N	21.33 E
Kožim	17	Id	65.43N	59.31 E
Kožim	17	Id	65.45N	59.15 E
Kozima	14	He	45.37N	13.56 E
Kozjak	15	Eh	41.06N	21.54 E
Kozloduj	15	Gf	43.47N	23.44 E
Kozlovka	7	Li	55.52N	48.13 E
Kozlovščina	10	Vc	53.14N	25.20 E
Kozlu	24	Db	41.25N	31.46 E
Kozluk	24	Ic	38.11N	41.29 E
Koźmin	10	Ne	51.50N	17.28 E
Kozmodemjansk	7	Lh	56.20N	46.36 E
Kožozero, Ozero-	7	Je	63.05N	38.05 E
Kożuchów	10	Le	51.45N	15.35 E
Kožuf	15	Fh	41.09N	22.10 E
Kōzu-Shima	27	Oe	34.15N	139.10 E
Kožva	17	Hd	65.07N	56.57 E
Kožva	17	Hd	65.10N	57.00 E
Kozyrevsk	20	Ke	55.59N	159.59 E
Kpalimé	34	Fd	6.54N	0.38 E
Kpandu	34	Fd	7.00N	0.18 E
Kpessi	34	Fd	8.04N	1.16 E
Kra, Isthmus of- (EN)=Kra, Khokhok-	21	Lh	10.20N	99.00 E
Kra, Khokhok-=Kra, Isthmus of- (EN)	21	Lh	10.20N	99.00 E
Kraba	15	Ch	41.12N	19.59 E
Krabbfjärden	8	Gf	58.45N	17.40 E
Krabi	25	Jg	8.05N	98.53 E
Krabit, Mali i-	15	Cg	42.07N	19.59 E
Kra Buri	25	Jf	10.24N	98.47 E
Krâchéh	22	Mh	12.29N	106.01 E
Kragerø	7	Bg	58.52N	9.25 E
Kragujevac	15	De	44.01N	20.55 E
Kraichbach	12	Ke	49.22N	8.31 E
Kraichgau	10	Eg	49.10N	8.50 E
Kraichtal	12	Ke	49.07N	8.46 E
Krajina	14	Kf	44.45N	16.35 E
Krajina	15	Fe	44.10N	22.30 E
Krajište	15	Fg	42.35N	22.25 E
Krajnovka	16	Oh	43.57N	47.24 E
Kråka	8	Ca	63.28N	9.00 E
Krakatau, Gunung-	21	Mj	6.07S	105.24 E
Krak des Chevaliers	24	Ge	34.46N	36.19 E
Krakovec	10	Tg	49.56N	23.13 E
Kraków [2]	10	Pf	50.05N	20.00 E
Kraków	6	He	50.03N	19.58 E
Kraków-Nowa Huta	10	Qf	50.04N	20.05 E
Krakowsko-Częstochowska, Wyżyna-	10	Pf	50.50N	19.15 E
Kralendijk	50	Bf	12.10N	68.16W
Kraljevica	14	Ie	45.16N	14.34 E
Kraljevo	15	Df	43.44N	20.43 E
Kralupy nad Vltavou	10	Kf	50.14N	14.19 E
Kramatorsk	16	Je	48.43N	37.32 E
Kramfors	7	De	62.56N	17.47 E
Krammer	12	Gc	51.38N	4.15 E
Kranenburg	12	Ic	51.47N	6.01 E
Kranídhion	15	Gl	37.23N	23.09 E
Kranj	14	Id	46.14N	14.22 E
Krapina	14	Jd	46.10N	15.53 E
Krapkowice	10	Nf	50.29N	17.56 E
Kras=Karst (EN)	5	Hf	45.48N	14.00 E
Krasavino	19	Ec	60.59N	46.28 E
Krasiczyn	10	Sg	49.48N	22.39 E
Krasilov	16	Ee	49.37N	26.59 E
Kraskino	28	Kc	42.44N	130.48 E
Kraslava/Krāslava	7	Gi	55.54N	27.10 E
Krāslava/Kraslava	7	Gi	55.54N	27.10 E
Krasnaja Poljana	16	Lh	43.40N	40.12 E
Kraśnik	10	Sf	50.56N	22.13 E
Kraśnik Fabryczny, Kraśnik-	10	Sf	50.58N	22.12 E
Kraśnik-Kraśnik Fabryczny	10	Sf	50.58N	22.12 E
Krasnoarmejsk [Kaz.-U.S.S.R.]	19	Ge	53.57N	69.43 E
Krasnoarmejsk [R.S.F.S.R.]	19	Ee	51.02N	45.42 E
Krasnoarmejsk [Ukr.-U.S.S.R.]	16	Je	48.11N	37.12 E
Krasnoarmejski	20	Mc	69.37N	172.02 E
Krasnodar	6	Jf	45.02N	39.00 E
Krasnodarski Kraj [3]	19	Df	45.20N	39.30 E
Krasnodon	16	Ke	48.17N	39.44 E
Krasnogorodskoje	8	Mh	56.47N	28.18 E
Krasnogorsk [R.S.F.S.R.]	20	Jg	48.26N	142.10 E
Krasnogorsk [R.S.F.S.R.]	7	Ii	55.51N	37.20 E
Krasnogorski	17	Ji	54.36N	61.15 E
Krasnograd	19	Df	49.22N	35.27 E
Krasnogvardejsk	18	Fe	39.45N	67.16 E
Krasnogvardejskoje	16	Lg	45.49N	41.31 E
Krasnoholmski	17	Gh	56.02N	55.05 E
Krasnoilsk	15	Ia	48.02N	25.48 E
Krasnojarsk	22	Ld	56.01N	92.50 E
Krasnojarski	17	Ij	51.58N	59.57 E
Krasnojarski Kraj [3]	20	Ee	57.30N	95.00 E
Krasnojarskoje Vodohranilišče	20	Ee	55.05N	91.30 E
Krasnoje	10	Ug	49.49N	24.39 E
Krasnoje Selo	7	Hg	59.43N	30.03 E
Krasnoje Znamja	18	Df	36.50N	62.29 E
Krasnokamensk	20	Gf	50.00N	118.05 E
Krasnokamsk	19	Fd	58.04N	55.45 E
Krasnokutsk	19	He	52.59N	75.59 E
Krasnolesje	8	Jj	54.23N	22.25 E
Krasnolesny	16	Kd	51.52N	39.35 E
Krasnooktjabrski [Kirg.-U.S.S.R.]	18	Jc	42.45N	74.20 E

Krasnooktjabrski [R.S.F.S.R.]	7	Lh	56.43N	47.37 E
Krasnooskolskoje Vodohranilišče	16	Je	49.25N	37.35 E
Krasnoostrovski	8	Md	60.12N	28.39 E
Krasnoperekopsk	19	Df	45.57N	33.47 E
Krasnorečenski	28	Mb	44.38N	135.15 E
Krasnoščelje	7	Ic	67.23N	37.02 E
Krasnoselki	10	Uc	53.14N	24.30 E
Krasnoselkup	20	Dc	65.41N	82.28 E
Krasnoslobodsk [R.S.F.S.R.]	16	Ne	48.40N	44.31 E
Krasnoslobodsk [R.S.F.S.R.]	7	Ki	54.27N	43.47 E
Krasnoturinsk	19	Gd	59.46N	60.18 E
Krasnoufimsk	19	Fd	56.37N	57.46 E
Krasnouralsk	19	Gd	58.24N	60.03 E
Krasnousolski	19	Fe	53.54N	56.29 E
Krasnovišersk	19	Fc	60.23N	57.03 E
Krasnovodsk	22	He	40.00N	53.00 E
Krasnovodskaja Oblast [3]	19	Fh	39.50N	55.00 E
Krasnovodski Poluostrov	16	Rc	40.30N	53.15 E
Krasnovodski Zaliv	16	Rj	39.50N	53.15 E
Krasnozatonski	19	Fc	61.41N	51.01 E
Krasnozavodsk	7	Jh	56.29N	38.13 E
Krasnoznamensk [Kaz.-U.S.S.R.]	19	Ge	51.03N	69.30 E
Krasnoznamensk [R.S.F.S.R.]	8	Jj	54.52N	22.27 E
Krasny Čikoj	20	Ff	50.25N	108.45 E
Krasny Holm	7	Ig	58.04N	37.09 E
Krasny Jar [R.S.F.S.R.]	20	De	57.07N	84.40 E
Krasny Jar [R.S.F.S.R.]	19	Hd	55.14N	72.56 E
Krasnyje Barrikady	16	Of	46.13N	47.50 E
Krasnyje Okny	15	Mb	47.34N	29.23 E
Krasny Kut	19	Ee	50.58N	46.58 E
Krasny Liman	16	Je	48.59N	37.47 E
Krasny Luč	16	Ke	48.09N	38.57 E
Krasny Oktjabr	19	Gd	55.37N	64.48 E
Krasny Profintern	7	Jh	57.47N	40.29 E
Krasnystaw	10	Tf	50.59N	23.10 E
Krasny Sulin	16	Lf	47.53N	40.09 E
Kratovo	15	Fg	42.05N	22.12 E
Kraulshavn	41	Gd	74.10N	57.00W
Krâvanh, Chuŏr Phnum-	21	Mh	12.00N	103.15 E
Krawang	26	Eh	6.19S	107.17 E
Krefeld	10	Ce	51.20N	6.34 E
Krefeld-Hüls	12	Ic	51.22N	6.31 E
Kremastá, Limni-	15	Ek	38.50N	21.30 E
Kremenchug Reservoir (EN) =Kremenčugskoje Vodohranilišče	5	Jf	49.20N	32.30 E
Kremenčug	6	Jf	49.04N	33.25 E
Kremenčugskoje Vodohranilišče=Kremenchug Reservoir (EN)	5	Jf	49.20N	32.30 E
Kremenec	16	Dd	50.06N	25.43 E
Kremennaja	16	Ke	49.03N	38.14 E
Kremmling	45	Cf	40.03N	106.24W
Krems	14	Jb	48.25N	15.36 E
Krems an der Donau	14	Jb	48.25N	15.36 E
Kremsmünster	14	Ib	48.03N	14.08 E
Krenitzin Islands	40a	Eb	54.08N	166.00W
Kresta, Zaliv-	20	Nc	65.30N	179.00W
Krestcy	7	Hg	58.15N	32.31 E
Krestovy, Pereval-	16	Nh	42.32N	44.30 E
Kretek	26	Fh	7.59S	110.19 E
Kretinga	7	Ei	55.55N	21.17 E
Kreuzau	12	Id	50.45N	6.29 E
Kreuzberg	10	Ff	50.22N	9.58 E
Kreuzlingen	14	Dc	47.39N	9.10 E
Kreuztal	10	Df	50.58N	7.59 E
Kría Vrísi	15	Fi	40.41N	22.18 E
Kribi	31	Hh	2.57N	9.55 E
Kričev	19	De	53.43N	31.43 E
Kričim	15	Hg	42.08N	24.31 E
Krim	14	Ie	45.56N	14.28 E
Krimml	14	Gc	47.13N	12.11 E
Krimpen aan den IJssel	12	Gc	51.55N	4.35 E
Kriós, Ákra-	5	Ih	35.14N	23.35 E
Krishna	21	Kh	15.57N	80.59 E
Krishnanagar	25	Hd	23.24N	88.30 E
Kristdala	8	Gg	57.24N	16.11 E
Kristiansand	6	Gd	58.10N	8.00 E
Kristianstad	7	Dh	56.02N	14.08 E
Kristianstad [2]	7	Ch	56.15N	14.00 E
Kristiansund	6	Gc	63.07N	7.45 E
Kristiinankaupunki/Kristinestad	7	Ee	62.17N	21.23 E
Kristineberg	7	Ed	65.04N	18.35 E
Kristinehamn	7	Dg	59.20N	14.07 E
Kristinestad/Kristiinankaupunki	7	Ee	62.17N	21.23 E
Kriti = Crete (EN)	5	Ih	35.15N	24.45 E
Kriti = Crete (EN) [2]	15	Hn	35.35N	25.00 E
Kritikón Pélagos = Crete, Sea of- (EN)	15	Hn	36.00N	25.00 E
Krivaja	14	Mf	44.27N	18.10 E
Kriva Palanka	15	Fg	42.12N	22.21 E
Kriviči	8	Lj	54.44N	27.20 E
Krivodol	15	Gf	43.23N	23.29 E
Krivoje Ozero	16	Gf	47.57N	30.21 E
Krivoj Rog	6	Jf	47.54N	33.21 E
Križevci	14	Kd	46.02N	16.32 E
Krk	14	Ie	45.05N	14.35 E
Krk	14	Ie	45.02N	14.35 E
Krka [Yugo.]	14	Jg	43.43N	15.51 E
Krka [Yugo.]	14	Je	45.53N	15.36 E
Krkonoše	10	Lf	50.46N	15.35 E
Krn	14	Hd	46.16N	13.40 E
Krndija	14	Le	45.27N	17.55 E
Krnjača, Beograd-	15	De	44.52N	20.28 E
Krnov	10	Nf	50.05N	17.41 E
Krobia	10	Me	51.47N	16.58 E
Krøderen	8	Cd	60.15N	9.40 E
Krokeaí	15	Fm	36.53N	22.33 E
Krokek	8	Gf	58.40N	16.24 E
Kroken	7	Dd	65.22N	14.16 E

Index Symbols

[1] Independent Nation
[2] State, Region
[3] District, County
Municipality
Colony, Dependency
Continent
Physical Region
Historical or Cultural Region
Mount, Mountain
Volcano
Hill
Mountains, Mountain Range
Hills, Escarpment
Plateau, Upland
Pass, Gap
Plain, Lowland
Delta
Salt Flat
Valley, Canyon
Crater, Cave
Karst Features
Depression
Polder
Desert, Dunes
Forest, Woods
Heath, Steppe
Oasis
Cape, Point
Coast, Beach
Cliff
Peninsula
Isthmus
Sandbank
Island
Atoll
Rock, Reef
Islands, Archipelago
Rocks, Reefs
Coral Reef
Well, Spring
Geyser
River, Stream
Waterfall Rapids
River Mouth, Estuary
Lake
Salt Lake
Intermittent Lake
Reservoir
Swamp, Pond
Canal
Glacier
Ice Shelf, Pack Ice
Ocean
Sea
Gulf, Bay
Strait, Fjord
Lagoon
Bank
Seamount
Tablemount
Ridge
Shelf
Basin
Escarpment, Sea Scarp
Fracture
Trench, Abyss
National Park, Reserve
Point of Interest
Recreation Site
Cave, Cavern
Historic Site
Ruins
Wall, Walls
Church, Abbey
Temple
Scientific Station
Airport
Port
Lighthouse
Mine
Tunnel
Dam, Bridge

Krokom 7 De 63.20N 14.28 E
Krolevec 16 Hd 51.32N 33.30 E
Kroměříž 10 Ng 49.18N 17.22 E
Krompachy 10 Qh 48.56N 20.52 E
Kronach 10 Hf 50.14N 11.19 E
Krŏng Kaôh Kŏng 25 Kf 11.37N 102.59 E
Kronoberg [2] 7 Dh 56.40N 14.40 E
Kronockaja Sopka, Vulkan- 20 Lf 54.47N 160.35 E
Kronocki, Mys- 20 Lf 54.43N 162.07 E
Kronocki Zaliv 20 Lf 54.00N 161.00 E
Kronoki 20 Lf 54.33N 161.14 E
Kronprins Christian Land 41 Jb 80.45N 22.00W
Kronprinsesse Mærtha Kyst 66 Bf 72.00S 7.30W
Kronprins Frederiks Bjerge 41 Ie 67.20N 34.00W
Kronprins Olav Kyst 66 Ee 68.30S 42.30 E
Kronštadt 19 Cc 60.01N 29.44 E
Kroonstad 31 Jk 27.46S 27.12 E
Kropotkin [R.S.F.S.R.] 19 Ef 45.26N 40.34 E
Kropotkin [R.S.F.S.R.] 20 Ge 58.36N 115.27 E
Kroppefjäll 8 Ef 58.40N 12.13 E
Krośniewice 10 Pd 52.16N 19.10 E
Krosno 10 Rg 49.42N 21.46 E
Krosno [2] 10 Rg 49.40N 21.45 E
Krosno Odrzańskie 10 Ld 52.04N 15.05 E
Krossfjorden 8 Ad 60.10N 5.05 E
Krotoszyn 10 Ne 51.42N 17.26 E
Kroviga, Gora- 20 Ed 60.40N 91.30 E
Krško 14 Je 45.58N 15.28 E
Krstača 15 Dg 42.58N 20.08 E
Krugersdorp 31 Jk 26.05S 27.35 E
Krui 26 Dh 5.11S 103.56 E
Kruibeke 12 Gc 50.10N 4.19 E
Kruiningen 12 Gc 51.27N 4.02 E
Kruja 15 Ch 41.30N 19.48 E
Krulevščina 8 Li 55.03N 27.52 E
Krumbach 10 Gh 48.15N 10.22 E
Krumovgrad 15 Ih 41.28N 25.39 E
Krung Thep=Bangkok (EN) 22 Mh 13.45N 100.31 E
Krupanj 15 Ce 44.22N 19.22 E
Krupinica 10 Oh 48.05N 18.54 E
Krupinská vrchovina 10 Ph 48.20N 19.15 E
Kruså 8 Cj 54.50N 9.25 E
Krušedol 15 Cd 45.07N 19.57 E
Kruševac 15 Ef 43.35N 21.20 E
Kruševo 15 Eh 41.22N 21.15 E
Krušné Hory=Ore Mountains (EN) 5 He 50.30N 13.15 E
Krustpils 8 Lh 56.29N 26.00 E
Kruzof 40 Le 57.10N 135.40W
Krym 16 Jg 45.23N 36.36 E
Krymsk 19 Dg 44.54N 37.57 E
Krymskaja Oblast [3] 19 Dg 45.15N 34.20 E
Krymskije Gory=Crimean Mountains (EN) 5 Jg 44.45N 34.30 E
Krymski Poluostrov=Crimea (EN) 5 Jf 45.00N 34.00 E
Krynica 10 Qg 49.25N 20.56 E
Krzemieniucha 10 Sb 54.12N 22.54 E
Krzepice 10 Of 50.58N 18.44 E
Krzna 10 Td 52.08N 23.31 E
Krzywiń 10 Me 51.58N 16.49 E
Krzyż 10 Md 52.53N 16.01 E
Ksar el Boukhari 32 Hb 35.53N 2.45 E
Ksar el Kebir 32 Fc 35.00N 5.59W
Ksar es Srhir 13 Gi 35.51N 5.34W
Ksenjevka 20 Gf 53.34N 118.44 E
Kšenski 16 Jd 51.52N 37.44 E
Ksour, Monts des- 32 Gc 32.45N 0.10W
Kstovo 7 Kh 56.12N 44.11 E
Kū', Wādī al- 35 Dc 12.12N 25.43 E
Kuai He 28 Dh 33.09N 117.32 E
Kuala Belait 26 Ff 4.35N 114.11 E
Kuala Dungun 26 Df 4.47N 103.26 E
Kuala Kangsar 26 Df 4.46N 100.56 E
Kualakapuas 26 Fg 3.01S 114.21 E
Kuala Kerai 26 De 5.32N 102.12 E
Kualakurun 26 Fg 1.07S 113.53 E
Kualalangsa 26 Cf 4.32N 98.01 E
Kuala Lipis 26 Df 4.11N 102.03 E
Kuala Lumpur 22 Mi 3.10N 101.42 E
Kuala Pilah 26 Df 2.44N 102.15 E
Kuala Rompin 26 Df 2.49N 103.29 E
Kuala Terengganu 22 Mi 5.20N 103.08 E
Kuancheng 28 Ed 40.37N 118.31 E
Kuandang 26 Hf 0.52N 122.55 E
Kuandian 27 Lc 40.45N 124.48 E
Kuang-hsi-chuang-tsu Tzu-chih-ch'ü → Guangxi Zhuangzu Zizhiqu=Kwangsi Chuang (EN) [2] 27 Ig 24.00N 109.00 E
Kuang-tun Sheng → Guangdong Sheng =Kwangtung (EN) [2] 27 Jg 23.00N 113.00 E
Kuantan 26 Df 3.48N 103.20 E
Kuba 19 Eg 41.20N 48.35 E
Kuban 5 Jf 45.20N 37.30 E
Kuba-Shima 29b Ab 26.10N 127.15 E
Kubaysah 24 Jf 33.35N 42.37 E
Kubbum 35 Cc 11.47N 23.47 E
Kubena 7 Jg 59.37N 39.48 E
Kubenskoje, Ozero- 7 Jg 59.40N 39.30 E
Kubnja 7 Li 55.32N 48.28 E
Kubokawa 28 Lh 33.12N 133.08 E
Kubolta 15 Lb 47.48N 28.03 E
Kubrat 15 Jf 43.48N 26.30 E
Kubumesaai 26 Gf 1.31N 115.06 E
Kučaj 15 Ef 43.53N 21.44 E
Kučevo 15 Ee 44.29N 21.41 E
Kuching 22 Ni 1.33N 110.20 E
Kuchinoerabu-Shima 28 Ki 30.28N 130.10 E
Kuchinotsu 29 Be 32.36N 130.12 E
Kuçukçekmece 15 Li 40.59N 28.46 E
Küçükerenköy 24 Ee 35.22N 33.45 E
Küçükkuyu 15 Jj 39.32N 26.36 E
Küçuk Menderes 15 Kl 37.57N 27.16 E
Kučurgan 15 Mc 46.35N 29.55 E
Kudaka-Jima 29b Ab 26.10N 127.54 E
Kudamatsu 29 Bd 34.01N 131.53 E
Kudat 26 Ge 6.53N 116.50 E
Kudeb 8 Mg 57.30N 28.16 E
Kudirkos-Naumestis 8 Jj 54.43N 22.49 E
Kudowa-Zdrój 10 Mf 50.27N 16.20 E
Kudremukh 25 Ff 13.08N 75.16 E
Kudus 26 Fh 6.48S 110.50 E
Kudymkar 19 Fd 59.01N 54.37 E
Kuee Ruins 65a Fd 19.12N 155.23W
Kuei-chou Sheng → Guizhou Sheng=Kweichow (EN) [2] 27 If 27.00N 107.00 E
Kufi 24 Cc 38.10N 29.43 E
Kufrah, Wāḩāt al-=Kufra Oasis (EN) 30 Jf 24.10N 23.15 E
Kufra Oasis (EN)=Kufrah, Wāḩāt al- 30 Jf 24.10N 23.15 E
Kufstein 14 Gc 47.35N 12.10 E
Kuganavolok 7 Ie 62.16N 36.55 E
Kugmallit Bay 42 Ek 69.30N 133.20W
Kugojeja 16 Kf 46.33N 39.38 E
Kūh, Ra's al- 23 Id 25.48N 57.19 E
Kuḩaylī 35 Eb 19.29N 32.49 E
Kūhbonān 24 Qg 31.23N 56.19 E
Kūhdasht 24 Lf 33.32N 47.36 E
Kūh-e Būrh 24 Pi 27.22N 54.40 E
Kūh-e Gāvbūs 24 Oi 27.10N 54.00 E
Kūh-e Karkas 24 Nf 33.27N 51.48 E
Kūh-e Kārūn 24 Ng 31.27N 50.18 E
Kūhestak 24 Qi 26.47N 57.02 E
Kūhīn, Gardaneh-ye- 24 Md 36.23N 49.37 E
Kühlungsborn 10 Hb 54.09N 11.43 E
Kuhmo 7 Gd 64.08N 29.31 E
Kuhmoinen 8 Kc 61.34N 25.11 E
Kuhn 41 Kd 74.45N 19.45W
Kūhpāyeh 23 Ic 30.35N 57.15 E
Kūhpāyeh [Iran] 24 Of 32.43N 52.26 E
Kūhpāyeh [Iran] 24 Qg 30.43N 57.30 E
Kūhrān, Kūh-e- 23 Id 26.46N 58.12 E
Kuhtuj 20 Je 59.23N 143.10 E
Kuhva 8 Mg 57.17N 28.17 E
Kuiseb 37 Ad 23.00S 14.33 E
Kuishan Ding 27 Ig 22.32N 109.52 E
Kuito 31 Ij 12.23S 16.56 E
Kuiu 40 Me 57.45N 134.10W
Kuivaniemi 7 Fd 65.35N 25.11 E
Kujang 27 Md 39.52N 126.01 E
Kujawy 10 Od 52.45N 18.30 E
Kujawy 10 Od 52.45N 18.35 E
Kujbyšev 6 Le 53.12N 50.09 E
Kujbyšev [R.S.F.S.R.] 7 Li 55.01N 49.06 E
Kujbyšev [R.S.F.S.R.] 20 Ce 55.27N 78.29 E
Kujbyševskaja Oblast [3] 19 Fe 53.20N 50.30 E
Kujbyševski [Kaz.-U.S.S.R.] 19 Ge 53.15N 66.51 E
Kujbyševski [Tad.-U.S.S.R.] 18 Gf 37.53N 68.44 E
Kujbyševskoje Vodohranilišče=Kuybyshev Reservoir (EN) 5 Ke 53.50N 49.00 E
Kujeda 17 Gh 56.26N 55.35 E
Kujgan 19 Hf 45.22N 74.10 E
Kuji 28 Pd 40.11N 141.46 E
Kuji-Gawa 29 Gc 36.30N 140.37 E
Kujtun 20 Ff 54.21N 101.35 E
Kujūkuri-Hama 29 Gd 35.40N 140.30 E
Kujū-San 28 Kh 33.09N 131.15 E
Kūkalār, Kūh-e- 24 Ng 31.50N 50.53 E
Kukalaya, Río- 49 Fg 13.39N 83.37W
Kukësi 15 Dg 42.05N 20.24 E
Kukkia 8 Kc 61.20N 24.40 E
Kukmor 7 Mh 56.13N 50.52 E
Kükürt Dağı 24 Ib 41.07N 41.27 E
Kula [Bul.] 15 Ff 43.53N 22.31 E
Kula [Tur.] 24 Cc 38.30N 28.40 E
Kula [Yugo.] 15 Cd 45.37N 19.32 E
Kulai 26 Df 1.40N 103.36 E
Kulanak 18 Jd 41.18N 75.34 E
Kulandy 19 Ff 46.08N 59.31 E
Kular 20 Ib 70.32N 134.26 E
Kular, Hrebet- 20 Ic 69.00N 133.30 E
Kulata 15 Gh 41.23N 23.22 E
Kulautuva 8 Jj 54.55N 23.43 E
Kulbus 35 Cc 14.24N 22.31 E
Kuldiga/Kuldīga 19 Cd 56.59N 21.59 E
Kuldīga/Kuldiga 19 Cd 56.59N 21.59 E
Kuldur 20 Ig 49.10N 131.40 E
Kulebaki 7 Ki 55.26N 42.32 E
Kulenjin 24 Me 35.40N 49.30 E
Kulen Vakuf 14 Kf 44.33N 16.06 E
Kulgera 58 Eg 25.50S 133.18 E
Kulikov 10 Ug 49.55N 24.06 E
Kulim 26 De 5.22N 100.34 E
Kuljab 19 Gh 37.55N 69.47 E
Kuljabskaja Oblast [3] 19 Gh 38.00N 69.40 E
Kullaa 8 Jc 61.28N 22.10 E
Kullen 7 Ch 56.18N 12.26 E
Kulmasa 34 Ed 9.35N 2.27W
Kulmbach 10 Hf 50.06N 11.27 E
Kuloj 7 Kf 61.03N 42.30 E
Kuloj [R.S.F.S.R.] 19 Eb 66.00N 43.30 E
Kuloj [R.S.F.S.R.] 7 Kf 61.01N 42.12 E
Kulp 24 Ic 38.30N 41.02 E
Kulsary 19 Ff 46.57N 54.02 E
Kultuk 20 Ff 51.44N 103.42 E
Kulu 20 Jd 62.15N 147.45 E
Kulu [India] 25 Fb 31.58N 77.06 E
Kulu [Tur.] 24 Ec 39.06N 33.05 E
Kulumadau 63a Ac 9.03S 152.43 E
Kulunda 20 Cf 52.35N 78.57 E
Kulundinskaja Step 20 Cf 52.45N 79.00 E
Kulundinskoje, Ozero- 20 Cf 53.00N 79.30 E
Kum 24 Bc 38.38N 27.32 E
Kum, Kūh-e- 24 Oh 29.55N 53.45 E
Kuma 29 Ce 33.39N 132.54 E
Kuma [R.S.F.S.R.] 17 Mg 59.33N 66.40 E
Kuma [R.S.F.S.R.] 7 Hc 66.15N 31.02 E
Kuma [U.S.S.R.] 5 Kg 44.56N 47.00 E
Kumagaya 28 Of 36.08N 139.23 E
Kumai [Indon.] 26 Fg 2.44S 111.43 E
Kumai [Indon.] 26 Fg 3.23S 112.33 E
Kumaishi 29a Ab 42.08N 139.59 E
Kumak 16 Vd 51.13N 60.08 E
Kumamoto 22 Pf 32.48N 130.43 E
Kumamoto Ken [2] 28 Kh 32.30N 130.50 E
Kumano 28 Nh 33.54N 136.05 E
Kumano-Gawa 29 De 33.45N 135.59 E
Kumano-Nada 29 Ee 34.00N 136.30 E
Kumanovo 15 Eg 42.08N 21.43 E
Kumara [N.Z.] 62 De 42.38S 171.11 E
Kumara [R.S.F.S.R.] 20 Hf 51.35N 126.45 E
Kumasi 31 Gh 6.41N 1.37W
Kumba 34 Ge 4.38N 9.25 E
Kumbakonam 25 Ff 10.58N 79.23 E
Kumbe 26 Lh 8.21S 140.13 E
Kumbo 34 Hd 6.12N 10.40 E
Kumboro Cape 63a Cb 7.18S 157.32 E
Kümch'ŏn 28 Ie 38.10N 126.30 E
Kum-Dag 19 Fh 39.13N 54.40 E
Kumdah 33 Ie 20.23N 45.05 E
Kume-Jima [Jap.] 27 Mf 26.20N 126.45 E
Kumertau 19 Fe 52.46N 55.47 E
Kumhwa 28 Ie 38.17N 127.28 E
Kumihama 29 Dd 35.36N 134.54 E
Kuminski 19 Gd 58.40N 65.55 E
Kumköy (Kilyos) 15 Mh 41.15N 29.02 E
Kumkuduk 27 Fc 40.15N 91.55 E
Kumkurgan 18 Ff 37.50N 67.35 E
Kumla 7 Dg 59.08N 15.08 E
Kumlinge 8 Id 60.15N 20.45 E
Kumluca 24 Dd 36.22N 30.18 E
Kummerower See 10 Ic 53.49N 12.52 E
Kumo/Kokemäki 7 Ff 61.15N 22.21 E
Kumo-Manyčski Kanal 16 Ng 45.27N 44.38 E
Kumon Taung 21 Lg 26.30N 96.50 E
Kumora 20 Ge 55.56N 111.13 E
Kumru 24 Gb 40.53N 37.17 E
Kumu 36 Eb 3.04N 25.09 E
Kumuh 16 Oh 42.11N 47.07 E
Kumukahi, Cape- 60 Od 19.31N 154.49W
Kumul/Hami 22 Le 42.48N 93.27 E
Kümüx 27 Ec 42.15N 88.10 E
Kumzār 24 Qj 26.20N 56.25 E
Kunashiri-Tō/Kunašir, Ostrov- 21 Qe 44.05N 145.51 E
Kunašir, Ostrov-/Kunashiri-Tō 21 Qe 44.05N 145.51 E
Kunaširski Proliv=Nemuro Strait (EN) 20 Jh 43.50N 145.30 E
Kunchaung 25 Jd 23.50N 96.35 E
Kunda 7 Gg 59.30N 26.30 E
Kunda Jõgi 8 Le 59.25N 26.27 E
Kundelungu, Monts- 36 Ed 9.30S 28.00 E
Kundiawa 59 Ia 6.00S 145.00 E
Kunduchi 36 Gd 6.40S 39.13 E
Kunduk 15 Md 45.51N 29.38 E
Kunduk → Kogilnik 15 Md 45.51N 29.38 E
Kunduk → Sasyk, Ozero- 16 Fg 45.45N 29.40 E
Kunene 30 Ij 17.20S 11.50 E
Kunene (EN)=Cunene 30 Ij 17.20S 11.50 E
Künes/Xinyuan 27 Dc 43.24N 83.18 E
Künes He 27 Dc 43.32N 82.29 E
Kungälv 7 Ch 57.52N 11.58 E
Kungej-Alatau, Hrebet- 19 Hg 42.50N 77.15 E
Kûngmiut 41 Ie 65.50N 36.45W
Kungrad 19 Fg 43.06N 58.54 E
Kungsbacka 7 Ch 57.29N 12.04 E
Kungsbackafjorden 8 Eg 57.25N 12.04 E
Kungshamn 8 Df 58.21N 11.15 E
Kungsör 8 Ge 59.25N 16.05 E
Kungu 36 Cb 2.47N 19.12 E
Kungur 19 Fd 57.25N 56.57 E
Kunhegyes 10 Qi 47.22N 20.38 E
Kunhing 25 Jd 21.18N 98.26 E
Kunigami 29b Bb 26.45N 128.11 E
Kunigami-Misaki 29b Bb 27.26N 128.43 E
Kunimi-Dake 29 Be 32.33N 131.01 E
Kunisaki 29 Be 33.34N 131.45 E
Kunisaki-Hantō 29 Be 33.30N 131.40 E
Kunja 7 Hh 57.09N 31.10 E
Kunja-Urgenč 19 Fg 42.20N 59.12 E
Kunlong 25 Jd 23.25N 98.39 E
Kunlun Guan 27 Ig 23.06N 108.40 E
Kunlun Shan 21 Kf 36.00N 84.00 E
Kunlun Shankou 27 Fd 35.40N 94.03 E
Kunming 22 Mg 25.08N 102.43 E
Kunnui 29a Bb 42.26N 140.19 E
Kunovat 17 Ld 64.59N 65.35 E
Kunsan 27 Md 35.59N 126.43 E
Kunshan 28 Fi 31.22N 120.57 E
Kuntaur 34 Cc 13.40N 14.53W
Kununurra 59 Fc 15.47S 128.44 E
Kunyao 36 Gb 1.47N 35.03 E
Kunyu Shan 28 Ff 37.15N 121.46 E
Künzelsau 10 Fg 49.17N 9.41 E
Kuohijärvi 8 Kc 61.15N 24.55 E
Kuolimo 8 Lc 61.15N 27.35 E
Kuop Atoll 64d Bb 7.03N 151.56 E
Kuopio [2] 7 Ge 63.20N 27.35 E
Kuopio 6 Ic 62.54N 27.41 E
Kuorboaivi 7 Gb 69.41N 27.45 E
Kuortane 8 Jb 62.48N 23.30 E
Kupa 14 Ke 45.28N 16.24 E
Kupang 22 Ok 10.10S 123.35 E
Kupiano 60 Dj 10.10S 148.02 E
Kupičev 10 Uf 50.58N 24.52 E
Kupino 20 Cf 54.22N 77.18 E
Kupiškis 7 Fi 55.49N 25.01 E
Kupjansk 19 Df 49.42N 37.37 E
Kupjansk-Uzlovoj 16 Je 49.39N 37.45 E
Küplü [Tur.] 15 Jh 4..07N 26.21 E
Küplü [Tur.] 15 Mi 40.06N 30.00 E
Kuppenheim 12 Kf 48.50N 8.15 E
Kupreanof 40 Me 56.50N 133.30W
Kuqa 22 Ke 41.43N 82.57 E
Kura [R.S.F.S.R.] 16 Mh 44.05N 44.45 E
Kura [U.S.S.R.] 5 Kh 39.20N 49.25 E
Kuragaty 18 Ic 43.55N 73.34 E
Kuragino 20 Ef 53.53N 92.40 E
Kurahashi-Jima 29 Cd 34.08N 132.31 E
Kuraminski Hrebet 18 Hd 40.50N 70.30 E
Kurashiki 28 Lg 34.35N 133.46 E
Kurashiki-Kojima 29 Cd 34.28N 133.48 E
Kurashiki-Tamashima 29 Cd 34.33N 133.40 E
Kura-Take 29 Be 32.27N 130.20 E
Kuraymah=Karima (EN) 31 Kg 18.33N 31.51 E
Kurayoshi 28 Lg 35.28N 133.49 E
Kurbneshi 15 Dh 41.47N 20.05 E
Kurčatov 16 Id 51.41N 35.42 E
Kurdaj 18 Jc 43.18N 74.59 E
Kurdistan 21 Gf 37.00N 44.00 E
Kurdistan 23 Fb 37.00N 44.00 E
Kurdufān 30 Jg 13.00N 30.00 E
Kurdufān al Janūbīyah [3] 35 Dc 11.00N 29.30 E
Kurdufān ash Shamālīyah [3] 35 Dc 14.50N 29.40 E
Kure 28 Lg 34.14N 132.34 E
Küre 24 Eb 41.48N 33.43 E
Kure Island 57 Jb 28.25N 178.25W
Kurejka 21 Kc 66.25N 87.12 E
Kurgaldžinski 19 He 50.30N 70.03 E
Kurgalski, Mys- 8 Me 59.39N 28.03 E
Kurgan 22 Id 55.26N 65.18 E
Kurganinsk 16 Lg 44.57N 40.35 E
Kurganskaja Oblast [3] 19 Gd 55.00N 65.00 E
Kurgan-Tjube 19 Gh 37.51N 68.46 E
Kurgan-Tjubinskaja Oblast [3] 19 Gh 37.30N 68.30 E
Kuria Island 57 Id 0.14N 173.25 E
Kuria Muria Islands (EN)=Khurīyā Murīyā, Jazā'ir 21 Hh 17.30N 56.00 E
Kuri Bay 59 Ec 15.35S 124.50 E
Kurikka 7 Fe 62.37N 22.25 E
Kurikoma 29 Gb 38.50N 140.59 E
Kurikoma-Yama 29 Gb 38.57N 140.47 E
Kuril Basin (EN) 20 Jg 47.00N 150.00 E
Kuril Islands (EN)=Kurilskije Ostrova 21 Re 46.10N 152.00 E
Kurilo 15 Gg 42.49N 23.21 E
Kurilsk 20 Jg 45.16N 147.58 E
Kurilskije Ostrova=Kuril Islands (EN) 21 Re 46.10N 152.00 E
Kuril Trench (EN) 3 Je 47.00N 155.00 E
Kuring Kuru 37 Bc 17.38S 18.33 E
Kurino 29 Bf 31.57N 130.43 E
Kurinskaja Kosa 16 Pj 39.05N 49.10 E
Kurinwás, Río- 49 Fg 12.49N 83.41W
Kuriyama 29a Bb 43.03N 141.45 E
Kūrkhūd, Kūh-e- 24 Qd 37.15N 56.30 E
Kurkosa 16 Pj 38.59N 49.08 E
Kurkūmā, Ra's- 24 Gj 25.51N 36.39 E
Kurkur 24 Ek 23.54N 32.19 E
Kurlovski 7 Ji 55.29N 40.39 E
Kurmuk 35 Ec 10.33N 34.17 E
Kurnool 22 Jh 15.50N 78.03 E
Kurobe 28 Nf 36.51N 137.26 E
Kurobe-Gawa 29 Ec 36.55N 137.26 E
Kurogi 29 Be 33.14N 130.40 E
Kuroishi 28 Pd 40.38N 140.36 E
Kuroiso 28 Pf 36.58N 140.03 E
Kuromatsunai 28 Pc 42.43N 140.20 E
Kurono-Seto 29 Be 32.05N 130.10 E
Kurort Družba 15 Kf 43.12N 28.00 E
Kurort Slănčev brjag 15 Kg 42.40N 27.42 E
Kurort Zlatni pjasăci 15 Lf 43.16N 28.02 E
Kuro-Shima 28 Ji 31.52N 129.58 E
Kurovskoje 7 Ji 55.35N 38.59 E
Kurow 61 Dh 44.44S 170.28 E
Kurów 10 Se 51.25N 22.10 E
Kurpiowska, Puszcza- 10 Rc 53.20N 21.30 E
Kuršėnai/Kuršenaj 19 Cd 56.03N 22.58 E
Kuršenaj/Kuršėnai 19 Cd 56.03N 22.58 E
Kuršiu užūrekis 8 Ii 55.05N 21.00 E
Kursk 6 Je 51.42N 36.12 E
Kurskaja Kosa 7 Ei 55.18N 21.00 E
Kurskaja Oblast [3] 19 De 51.45N 36.15 E
Kurski zaliv 7 Ei 55.05N 21.00 E
Kuršumlija 15 Ef 43.09N 21.16 E
Kurtalan 24 Id 37.57N 41.42 E
Kurtamyš 19 Ge 54.55N 64.27 E
Kürtī 31 Kg 18.07N 31.33 E
Kurtistown 65 Fd 19.36N 155.04W
Kurty 18 Kb 44.19N 76.42 E
Kuru 8 Jc 61.52N 23.44 E
Kuru 35 Dd 9.08N 26.57 E
Kuruąsile 24 Eb 41.51N 32.43 E
Kuruktag 27 Ec 41.30N 89.00 E
Kuruman 30 Jk 26.56S 20.39 E
Kuruman 31 Jk 27.28S 23.28 E
Kurume 28 Kh 33.19N 130.31 E
Kurunegala 25 Gg 7.29N 80.22 E
Kurur, Jabal- 35 Ea 20.31N 31.32 E
Kurzeme=Courland (EN) 8 Ih 56.50N 22.00 E
Kurzemes Augstiene/Kurzemskaja Vozvyšennost 8 Jh 56.45N 22.15 E
Kurzemskaja Vozvyšennost/Kurzemes Augstiene 8 Jh 56.45N 22.15 E
Kusa 17 Ii 55.20N 59.29 E
Kuşada Körfezi 15 Kl 37.50N 27.08 E
Kuşadasi 24 Bd 37.51N 27.15 E
Kusagaki-Guntō 27 Me 31.00N 129.00 E
Kusaie → Kosrae 57 Hd 5.19N 162.59 E
Kusalu/Kuusalu 8 Ke 59.23N 25.25 E
Kusary 16 Pi 41.24N 48.29 E
Kusatsu [Jap.] 29 Fc 36.37N 138.35 E
Kusatsu [Jap.] 29 Dd 35.03N 135.59 E
Kuščevskaja 16 Kf 46.33N 39.37 E
Kuščinski 16 Oi 40.33N 46.06 E
Kusel 12 Je 49.33N 7.24 E
Kuş Gölü 24 Bb 40.10N 27.59 E
Kushida-Gawa 29 Ed 34.36N 136.34 E
Kushikino 28 Ki 31.44N 130.16 E
Kushima 28 Ki 31.29N 131.14 E
Kushimoto 28 Mh 33.28N 135.47 E
Kushiro 22 Qe 42.58N 144.23 E
Kushiro-Gawa 29a Db 42.59N 144.23 E
Kushtia 25 Hd 23.55N 89.07 E
Kuška 18 Dg 35.16N 62.18 E
Kuskokwim 38 Cc 60.17N 162.27W
Kuskokwim Bay 38 Cd 59.45N 162.25W
Kuskokwim Mountains 38 Dc 62.30N 156.00W
Kušmurun 19 Ge 52.27N 64.40 E
Kušmurun, Ozero- 19 Ge 52.40N 64.45 E
Kušnarenkovo 17 Gi 55.06N 55.22 E
Kušnica 16 Ce 48.29N 23.20 E
Kusŏng 27 Md 39.59N 125.16 E
Kussharo Ko 28 Rc 43.35N 144.15 E
Kustanaj 22 Id 53.10N 63.35 E
Kustanajskaja Oblast [3] 19 Ge 53.00N 64.00 E
Kustavi 8 Id 60.30N 21.25 E
Kustavi/Gustavs 8 Id 60.30N 21.25 E
Küstenkanal 10 Dd 52.57N 7.18 E
Kūstī 31 Kg 13.10N 32.40 E
Kustvlakte=Coast Plain (EN) 11 Ic 51.00N 2.30 E
Kusu 29 Be 33.16N 131.09 E
Kušva 19 Fd 58.18N 59.45 E
Kut, Ko- 25 Kf 11.40N 102.35 E
Kūt 'Abdollāh 24 Mg 31.13N 48.39 E
Kutacane 26 Cf 3.30N 97.48 E
Kutahya 23 Cb 39.25N 29.59 E
Kutaisi 6 Kg 42.15N 42.40 E
Kutch, Gulf of- → Kachchh, Gulf of 21 Ig 22.36N 60.30 E
Kutch, Rann of- 25 Ed 24.05N 70.10 E
Kutchan 28 Pc 42.54N 140.45 E
Kutcharo-Ko 29a Ca 45.10N 142.20 E
Kutina 14 Ke 45.29N 16.47 E
Kutkai 25 Jd 23.27N 97.56 E
Kutkašen 16 Oi 40.58N 47.52 E
Kutná Hora 10 Lg 49.57N 15.16 E
Kutno 10 Pd 52.15N 19.23 E
Kutse, Gora-/Kuutse Mägi 8 Lg 57.58N 26.24 E
Kuttara-Ko 29a Bb 42.30N 141.10 E
Kutu 31 Ii 2.44S 18.09 E
Kutum 35 Cc 14.12N 24.40 E
Kúty 10 Nh 48.40N 17.01 E
Kuty 15 Ia 48.13N 25.15 E
Kuujjuaq 39 Md 58.10N 68.30W
Kuujjuarapik 42 Je 55.20N 76.50W
Kuuli-Majak 19 Fg 40.16N 52.45 E
Kuurne 12 Fd 50.51N 3.17 E
Kuusalu/Kusalu 8 Ke 59.23N 25.25 E
Kuusamo 6 Ib 66.00N 29.11 E
Kuusankoski 8 Ld 60.54N 26.38 E
Kuutse Mägi/Kutse, Gora- 8 Lg 57.58N 26.24 E
Kuvandyk 16 Td 51.29N 57.28 E
Kuvdlorssuaq 41 Gd 74.38N 56.40W
Kuvšinovo 7 Ih 57.03N 34.13 E
Kuwait (EN)=Al Kuwayt [1] 22 Gg 29.30N 47.45 E
Kuwait (EN)=Al Kuwayt 22 Gg 29.20N 47.59 E
Kuwana 29 Ed 35.04N 136.39 E
Kuybyshev Reservoir (EN)=Kujbyševskoje Vodohranilišče 5 Ke 53.50N 49.00 E
Kūysanjaq 24 Kd 36.05N 44.38 E
Kuytun 27 Dc 44.25N 84.58 E
Kuyucak 15 Ll 37.55N 28.28 E
Kuzey Kibris = North Cyprus 23 Db 35.15N 33.40 E
Kuzneck 19 Ee 53.07N 46.36 E
Kuznecki Alatau 21 Kd 54.45N 88.00 E
Kuznečnoje 8 Mc 61.04N 29.58 E
Kuźnia Raciborska 10 Of 50.11N 18.15 E
Kuzomen 19 Db 66.18N 36.49 E
Kuzovatovo 7 Lj 53.33N 47.41 E
Kuzumaki 29 Ga 40.02N 141.26 E
Kuzuryū-Gawa 29 Ec 36.13N 136.08 E
Kvænangen 7 Ea 70.05N 21.13 E
Kvaløy 7 Eb 69.40N 18.30 E
Kvaløya 7 Fa 70.37N 23.52 E
Kvalsund 7 Fa 70.30N 24.00 E
Kvam 8 Cc 61.40N 9.42 E
Kvareli 16 Ni 41.57N 45.47 E
Kvarkeno 17 Ij 52.05N 59.40 E
Kvarnbergsvattnet 7 Dd 64.36N 14.03 E
Kvarner 14 If 44.45N 14.15 E
Kvarnerić 14 If 44.45N 14.35 E
Kvichak Bay 40 He 58.48N 157.30W
Kvemo-Kedi 16 Oi 41.22N 46.31 E
Kvenna 8 Bd 60.01N 7.56 E
Kvichak 40 He 59.10N 156.40W
Kvikkjokk 7 Dc 66.57N 17.47 E
Kvina 8 Bf 58.17N 6.56 E
Kvinesdal 7 Bg 58.19N 6.57 E
Kvissleby 8 Gb 62.17N 17.21 E
Kviteggia 8 Bb 62.05N 6.40 E
Kviteseid 8 Ce 59.24N 8.30 E
Kvitøya 67 Je 80.08N 32.35 E
Kwa 30 Ii 3.10S 16.11 E
Kwahu Plateau 34 Ed 6.30N 0.30W
Kwailibesi 63a Ec 8.20S 160.40 E
Kwajalein Atoll 57 Hd 9.05N 167.20 E
Kwakoegron 54 Gb 5.15N 55.20W
Kwale [Kenya] 36 Gc 4.11S 39.27 E
Kwale [Nig.] 34 Gd 5.45N 6.25 E
Kwamouth 36 Cc 3.10S 16.12 E
Kwa Mtoro 36 Gd 5.14S 35.26 E
Kwando 36 Df 18.27S 23.32 E
Kwangdae-ri 27 Mc 40.34N 127.33 E
Kwangju 22 Of 35.09N 126.55 E
Kwango 30 Ii 3.14S 17.22 E

Index Symbols

[1] Independent Nation
[2] State, Region
[3] District, County
[4] Municipality
[5] Colony, Dependency
Continent
Physical Region
Historical or Cultural Region
Mount, Mountain
Volcano
Hill
Mountains, Mountain Range
Hills, Escarpment
Plateau, Upland
Pass, Gap
Plain, Lowland
Delta
Salt Flat
Valley, Canyon
Crater, Cave
Karst Features
Depression
Polder
Desert, Dunes
Forest, Woods
Heath, Steppe
Oasis
Cape, Point
Coast, Beach
Cliff
Peninsula
Isthmus
Sandbank
Island
Atoll
Rock, Reef
Islands, Archipelago
Rocks, Reefs
Coral Reef
Well, Spring
Geyser
River, Stream
Waterfall Rapids
River Mouth, Estuary
Lake
Salt Lake
Intermittent Lake
Reservoir
Swamp, Pond
Canal
Glacier
Ice Shelf, Pack Ice
Ocean
Sea
Gulf, Bay
Strait, Fjord
Lagoon
Bank
Seamount
Tablemount
Ridge
Shelf
Basin
Escarpment, Sea Scarp
Fracture
Trench, Abyss
National Park, Reserve
Point of Interest
Recreation Site
Cave, Cavern
Historic Site
Ruins
Wall, Walls
Temple
Scientific Station
Airport
Port
Lighthouse
Mine
Tunnel
Dam, Bridge

L

Index Symbols

[1] Independent Nation
[2] State, Region
[3] District, County
[4] Municipality
[5] Colony, Dependency
Continent
Physical Region
Historical or Cultural Region
Mount, Mountain
Volcano
Hill
Mountains, Mountain Range
Hills, Escarpment
Plateau, Upland
Pass, Gap
Plain, Lowland
Delta
Salt Flat
Valley, Canyon
Crater, Cave
Karst Features
Depression
Polder
Desert, Dunes
Forest, Woods
Heath, Steppe
Oasis
Cape, Point
Coast, Beach
Cliff
Peninsula
Isthmus
Sandbank
Island
Atoll
Rock, Reef
Islands, Archipelago
Rocks, Reefs
Coral Reef
Well, Spring
Geyser
River, Stream
Waterfall Rapids
River Mouth, Estuary
Lake
Salt Lake
Intermittent Lake
Reservoir
Swamp, Pond
Canal
Glacier
Ice Shelf, Pack Ice
Ocean
Sea
Gulf, Bay
Strait, Fjord
Lagoon
Bank
Seamount
Tablemount
Ridge
Shelf
Basin
Escarpment, Sea Scarp
Fracture
Trench, Abyss
National Park, Reserve
Point of Interest
Recreation Site
Cave, Cavern
Historic Site
Ruins
Wall, Walls
Church, Abbey
Temple
Scientific Station
Airport
Port
Lighthouse
Mine
Tunnel
Dam, Bridge

Name	Page	Grid	Lat.	Long.
Lamotte-Beuvron	11	Ig	47.36N	2.01 E
La Moure	45	Gc	46.21N	98.18W
Lampang	25	Je	18.16N	99.34 E
Lampasas	45	Gk	31.03N	98.12W
Lampazos de Naranjo	48	Id	27.01N	100.31W
Lampedusa	14	Go	35.30N	12.35 E
Lampertheim	10	Eg	49.36N	8.28 E
Lampeter	9	Ii	52.07N	4.05W
Lamphun	25	Je	18.35N	99.00 E
Lampione	14	Go	35.35N	12.20 E
Lampung [3]	26	Dg	5.00S	105.00 E
Lamu	31	Li	2.16S	40.54 E
Lamud	54	Ce	6.09S	77.55W
La Mure	11	Lj	44.54N	5.47 E
Lan	16	Ec	52.09N	27.18 E
Lana	14	Fd	46.37N	11.09 E
Lana, Rio de la-	48	Li	17.49N	95.09W
Lanai City	65a	Ec	20.50N	156.55W
Lanaihale	65a	Ec	20.49N	156.52W
Lanai Island	57	Lb	20.50N	156.55W
Lanaken	12	Hd	50.53N	5.39 E
Lanark	9	Jf	55.41N	3.48W
Lanbi Kyun	25	Jf	10.50N	98.15 E
Lancang (Menglangba)	27	Gg	22.37N	99.57 E
Lancang Jiang=Mekong (EN)	21	Mh	10.15N	105.55 E
Lancashire [3]	9	Kh	53.55N	2.40W
Lancashire Plain	9	Kh	53.40N	2.45W
Lancaster	9	Kh	53.45N	2.50W
Lancaster [Ca.-U.S.]	43	De	34.42N	118.08W
Lancaster [Eng.-U.K.]	9	Kg	54.03N	2.48W
Lancaster [Mo.-U.S.]	45	Jf	40.31N	92.32W
Lancaster [N.H.-U.S.]	44	Lc	44.29N	71.34W
Lancaster [Oh.-U.S.]	44	Ff	39.43N	82.37W
Lancaster [Ont.-Can.]	44	Jc	45.12N	74.30W
Lancaster [Pa.-U.S.]	43	Lc	40.01N	76.19W
Lancaster [S.C.-U.S.]	44	Gh	34.43N	80.47W
Lancaster Sound	38	Kb	74.13N	84.00W
Lançeiro	55	Fe	20.59S	53.43W
Lancelin	59	Df	31.01S	115.19 E
Lanciano	14	Ih	42.14N	14.23 E
Lančin	15	Ha	48.31N	24.49 E
Lancun	28	Ff	36.25N	120.11 E
Łańcut	10	Sf	50.05N	22.13 E
Land	8	Cd	60.45N	10.00 E
Lândana	36	Bd	5.15S	12.10 E
Landau an der Isar	10	Ih	48.41N	12.41 E
Landau in der Pfalz	10	Eg	49.12N	8.07 E
Land Bay	66	Mf	75.25S	141.45W
Landeck	14	Ec	47.08N	10.34 E
Landen	12	Hd	50.45N	5.05 E
Lander	43	Fc	42.50N	108.44W
Landerneau	11	Bf	48.27N	4.15W
Lander River	59	Gd	20.25S	132.00 E
Landeryd	8	Eg	57.05N	13.16 E
Landes	11	Fj	44.15N	1.00W
Landes [3]	11	Fj	44.00N	0.50W
Landesbergen	12	Lb	52.34N	9.08 E
Landeta	55	Ak	32.01S	62.04W
Landete	13	Ke	39.54N	1.22W
Landfallis	25	If	13.40N	93.02 E
Land Glacier	66	Mf	75.40S	141.45W
Landi Kotal	25	Eb	34.06N	71.09 E
Landless Corner	36	Ee	14.53S	28.04 E
Landrecies	12	Fd	50.08N	3.42 E
Landsberg am Lech	10	Gh	48.03N	10.52 E
Landsbro	8	Fg	57.22N	14.54 E
Land's End	5	Fe	50.03N	5.44W
Lands End	42	Fa	76.25N	122.45W
Landshut	10	Ih	48.32N	12.09 E
Landskrona	8	Ei	55.52N	12.50 E
Landsort	8	Gf	58.45N	17.50 E
Landsortsdjupet	8	Hf	58.40N	18.30 E
Landstuhl	12	Je	49.25N	7.34 E
Landusky	46	Kc	47.54N	108.37W
La Neuve-Lyre	12	Cf	48.54N	0.45 E
Lanfeng → Lankao	28	Cg	34.49N	114.48 E
Lang	46	Mb	49.56N	104.23W
La'nga Co	27	De	30.41N	81.17 E
Langadhás	15	Gi	40.45N	23.04 E
Langádhia	15	Fl	37.39N	22.03 E
Långan	7	De	63.19N	14.44 E
Langano, Lake-	35	Fd	7.36N	38.43 E
Langao	27	Ie	32.20N	108.53 E
Langara	26	Hg	4.02S	123.00 E
Langarfoss	7a	Cb	65.35N	14.15W
Langasian	26	Ie	8.16N	125.39 E
Langdon	45	Gb	48.46N	98.22W
Langeac	11	Ji	45.06N	3.29 E
Langeais	11	Gg	47.20N	0.24 E
Langeb	35	Fb	17.46N	36.41 E
Langebaan	37	Bf	33.06S	18.02 E
Langeberg	37	Cf	33.56S	20.45 E
Langedijk	12	Gb	52.42N	4.48 E
Langeland	7	Ci	55.00N	10.50 E
Langelands Bælt	8	Dj	54.50N	10.55 E
Längelmävesi	8	Kc	61.30N	24.20 E
Langen	12	Ke	49.59N	8.40 E
Langenberg	12	Kc	51.17N	8.34 E
Langenburg	45	Fa	50.50N	101.43W
Langenfeld (Rheinland)	12	Ic	51.06N	6.57 E
Langenhagen	10	Fd	52.27N	9.45 E
Langenselbold	12	Ld	50.11N	9.02 E
Langenthal	14	Bc	47.13N	7.49 E
Langeoog	10	Dc	53.46N	7.32 E
Langeri	20	Jf	50.08N	143.20 E
Langesund	8	Ce	59.00N	9.45 E
Langesundsfjorden	8	Cf	59.00N	9.48 E
Langevåg	8	Bb	62.27N	6.12 E
Langfang → Anci	27	Kd	39.29N	116.40 E
Långfjället	8	Eb	62.10N	12.20 E
Langfjorden	8	Bb	62.45N	7.30 E
Langhe	14	Bf	44.30N	8.00 E
Langholm	9	Kf	55.09N	3.00W
Langjökull	5	Ec	64.39N	20.00W
Langkawi, Pulau-	26	Ce	6.22N	99.48 E
Langkon	26	Ge	6.32N	116.42 E
Langlade	44	Ja	48.12N	75.57W
Langnau im Emmental	14	Bd	46.56N	7.46 E
Langogne	11	Jj	44.43N	3.51 E
Langon	11	Fj	44.33N	0.15W
Langorūd	24	Md	37.11N	50.10 E
Langøya	7	Db	68.44N	14.50 E
Langreo	13	Ga	43.18N	5.41W
Langres	11	Lg	47.52N	5.20 E
Langres, Plateau de-	5	Gf	47.41N	5.03 E
Langrune-sur-Mer	12	Be	49.19N	0.22W
Langsa	22	Li	4.28N	97.58 E
Långsele	8	Ga	63.11N	17.04 E
Långshyttan	8	Gd	60.27N	16.01 E
Lang Son	25	Ld	21.50N	106.44 E
Lang Suan	25	Jg	9.55N	99.07 E
Languedoc	5	Gg	44.00N	4.00 E
Languedoc	11	Jj	44.00N	4.00 E
Langueyú, Arroyo-	55	Cm	36.39S	58.27W
Langwedel	12	Lb	52.58N	9.13 E
Langxi	28	Ei	31.08N	119.11 E
Langzhong	27	Ie	31.40N	106.04 E
Lan Hsu	27	Lg	22.00N	121.30 E
Laniel	44	Hb	47.06N	79.15W
Lanin, Volcán-	52	Ii	39.38S	71.30W
Lankao	27	Cd	35.12N	79.50 E
Lankao (Lanfeng)	27	Kg	21.00N	116.00 E
Lankao (Lanfeng)	28	Cg	34.49N	114.48 E
Länkipohja	8	Kc	61.44N	24.48 E
Lannemezan	11	Gk	43.08N	0.23 E
Lannemezan, Plateau de-	11	Gk	43.09N	0.27 E
Lannion	11	Cf	48.44N	3.28W
Lannion, Baie de-	11	Cf	48.43N	3.34W
La Noria	56	Gb	20.23S	69.53W
Lansdowne House	42	If	52.13N	87.53W
L'Anse	44	Cb	46.45N	88.27W
Lansing [Ia.-U.S.]	45	Ke	43.22N	91.13W
Lansing [Mi.-U.S.]	39	Ke	42.43N	84.34W
Lansjärv	7	Fc	66.39N	22.12 E
Łańskie, Jezioro-	10	Qc	53.33N	20.30 E
Lantar	20	Ie	56.05N	137.35 E
Lanta Yai, Ko-	25	Jg	7.35N	99.03 E
Lanteri	55	Ci	28.50S	59.39W
Lanterne	11	Mg	47.44N	6.03 E
Lanús	55	Cl	34.43S	58.24W
Lanusei	14	Dk	39.53N	9.32 E
Lanvaux, Landes de-	11	Dg	47.47N	2.36W
Lanxi [China]	28	Ej	29.13N	119.28 E
Lanxi [China]	28	Ha	46.15N	126.16 E
Lanxian (Dongcun)	28	Ae	38.17N	111.38 E
Lanyi He	28	Ae	38.40N	110.53 E
Lanzarote	30	Ff	29.00N	13.40W
Lanzhou	22	Mf	36.03N	103.41 E
Lanzo Torinese	14	Be	45.16N	7.28 E
Lao	14	Jk	39.47N	15.48 E
Laoag	22	Oh	18.12N	120.36 E
Laoang	26	Id	12.34N	125.00 E
Lao Cai	22	Mg	22.30N	103.57 E
Laocheng	28	Hc	42.37N	124.04 E
Laoha He	27	Lc	43.24N	120.39 E
Lao He	28	Cj	29.02N	115.47 E
Laohuanghe Kou	28	Ef	37.39N	119.02 E
Laois [2]	9	Fi	53.00N	7.30W
Laojunmiao → Yumen	22	Lf	39.50N	97.44 E
Laojun Shan	27	Je	33.45N	111.38 E
Lao Ling	28	Id	41.24N	126.10 E
Laon	11	Je	49.34N	3.37 E
Laona	45	Ld	45.34N	88.40W
Laonnois	12	Fe	49.35N	3.40 E
La Orchila, Isla-	54	Ea	11.48N	66.10W
La Oroya	53	Ig	11.32S	75.57W
Laos [1]	22	Mh	18.00N	105.00 E
Laoshan (Licun)	28	Ff	36.10N	120.25 E
Laotougou	28	Jc	42.54N	129.09 E
Laou	13	Gi	35.26N	5.05W
Laoye Ling	28	Kb	44.50N	130.10 E
Lapa	56	Kc	25.45S	49.42W
Lapai	34	Gd	9.03N	6.43 E
Lapalisse	11	Jh	46.15N	3.38 E
La Palma	30	Ff	28.40N	17.52W
La Palma [ElSal.]	49	Cf	14.19N	89.11W
La Palma [Pan.]	47	Ig	8.25N	78.09W
La Palma del Condado	13	Fg	37.23N	6.33W
La Paloma	55	El	34.40S	54.10W
La Pampa [2]	56	Ge	37.00S	66.00W
La Panne/De Panne	12	Ec	51.06N	2.35 E
La Paragua	54	Fb	6.50N	63.20W
La Partida, Isla-	48	De	24.30N	110.25W
La Paz [3]	49	Df	14.15N	87.50W
La Paz [2]	54	Eg	15.00S	68.00W
La Paz [Arg.]	56	Id	30.45S	59.39W
La Paz [Arg.]	56	Gd	33.28S	67.33W
La Paz [Bol.]	53	Jg	16.30S	68.09W
La Paz [Col.]	49	Kh	10.23N	73.10W
La Paz [Hond.]	47	Gf	14.16N	87.40W
La Paz [Mex.]	39	Hg	24.10N	110.18W
La Paz [Ur.]	55	Dl	34.46S	56.13W
La Paz [Ven.]	49	Lh	10.41N	72.00W
La Paz, Bahia de-	47	Bd	24.09N	110.25W
La Paz, Llano de-	48	De	24.00N	110.30W
La Paz Centro	49	Dg	12.20N	86.41W
La Pedrera	54	Ed	1.18S	69.40W
Lapeer	44	Fd	43.03N	83.19W
La Pelada	55	Bj	30.52S	60.59W
La Pérouse, Bahía-	65d	Bb	27.04S	109.18W
La Perouse Strait (EN)= Laperuza, Proliv-	21	Qe	45.30N	142.00 E
La Perouse Strait (EN)= Sōya-Kaikyō	21	Qe	45.30N	142.00 E
Laperuza, Proliv-=La Perouse Strait (EN)	21	Qe	45.30N	142.00 E
La Pesca	47	Ed	23.47N	97.47W
La Petite Pierre	12	Jf	48.52N	7.19 E
La Picasa, Laguna-	55	Al	34.20S	62.14W
La Piedad Cavadas	48	Hg	20.21N	102.00W
La Pine	46	Ee	43.40N	121.30W
Lapinjärvi/Lappträsk	8	Ld	60.36N	26.09 E
Lapinlahti	7	Ge	63.22N	27.30 E
La Plaine	51g	Bb	15.20N	61.15W
La Plana	13	Ld	40.00N	0.05W
Lapland (EN)=Lappi	5	Ib	66.50N	22.00 E
Lapland (EN)=Lappland	5	Ib	66.50N	22.00 E
La Plant	45	Fd	45.10N	100.38W
La Plata	53	Ki	34.55S	57.57W
La Pobla de Lillet	13	Nb	42.15N	1.59 E
La Pobla de Segur/Pobla de Segur	13	Mb	42.15N	0.58 E
La Pocatièr	44	Lb	47.21N	70.02W
La Porte	44	De	41.36N	86.43W
Lapovo	15	Ee	44.11N	21.06 E
Lappajärvi	7	Fe	63.08N	23.40 E
Lappeenranta/Villmanstrand	6	Ic	61.04N	28.11 E
Lappfjärd/Lapväärtti	8	Ib	62.15N	21.32 E
Lappi [2]	7	Gc	67.40N	26.30 E
Lappi	8	Ic	61.06N	21.50 E
Lappi=Lapland (EN)	5	Ib	66.50N	22.00 E
Lappo/Lapua	7	Fe	62.57N	23.00 E
Lappträsk/Lapinjärvi	8	Ld	60.36N	26.09 E
Lapri	20	He	55.45N	124.59 E
Laprida	56	He	37.33S	60.49W
Lâpseki	24	Bb	40.20N	26.31 E
Lapta	24	Ee	35.20N	33.10 E
Laptev Sea (EN)=Laptevyh, More-	67	Fd	76.00N	126.00 E
Laptevyh, More-=Laptev Sea (EN)	67	Fd	76.00N	126.00 E
Lapua/Lappo	7	Fe	62.57N	23.00 E
La Puebla	13	Pe	39.46N	3.01 E
La Puebla de Cazalla	13	Gg	37.14N	5.19W
Lapuna	55	Ba	13.19S	60.28W
La Puntilla	52	Hf	2.11S	81.01W
La Purisima	48	Cd	26.10N	112.04W
Lăpuş	15	Hb	47.30N	24.01 E
Lăpuş	15	Gb	47.39N	23.24 E
La Push	46	Cc	47.55N	124.38W
Lapväärtti/Lappfjärd	8	Ib	62.15N	21.32 E
Łapy	10	Sd	53.00N	22.53 E
Laqīyat al Arba'in	35	Da	20.03N	28.02 E
La Quemada	48	Hf	22.27N	102.45W
La Quiaca	56	Gb	22.06S	65.37W
L'Aquila	6	Hg	42.22N	13.22 E
Lar	23	Hd	27.41N	54.17 E
Lara [2]	54	Ea	10.10N	69.50W
Larache	32	Fb	35.12N	6.09W
Laragne-Montéglin	11	Lj	44.19N	5.49 E
Lårak	23	Id	26.52N	56.22 E
La Rambla	13	Hg	37.36N	4.44W
Laramie	39	Ie	41.19N	105.35W
Laramie Mountains	43	Fc	42.00N	105.40W
Laramie Peak	46	Me	42.17N	105.27W
Laramie River	46	Me	42.12N	104.32W
Laranjal, Rio-	55	Ff	23.12S	53.45W
Laranjeiras do Sul	56	Jc	25.25S	52.25W
Larantuka	26	Hh	8.21S	122.59 E
Larat	26	Jh	7.09S	131.45 E
Larat, Pulau-	26	Jh	7.10S	131.50 E
La Raya	49	Ji	8.20N	74.34W
L'Arba	13	Ph	36.34N	3.09 E
L'Arbaa-Naït-Irathen	13	Qh	36.38N	4.12 E
L'Arbresle	11	Ki	45.50N	4.37 E
Lärbro	7	Eh	57.47N	18.47 E
Larche, Col de-	11	Mj	44.25N	6.53 E
Larde	37	Fc	16.28S	39.43 E
Larderello	14	Eg	43.14N	10.53 E
La Réale	11	Fj	44.35N	0.02W
Laredo [Sp.]	13	Ia	43.24N	3.25W
Laredo [Tx.-U.S.]	39	Jg	27.31N	99.30W
Laren	12	Hb	52.16N	5.16 E
Lārestān	21	Hg	27.00N	55.30 E
Larestan	24	Pi	27.00N	55.30 E
Large Island	51p	Cb	12.24N	61.30W
Largentière	11	Kj	44.32N	4.18 E
L'Argentière-la-Bessée	11	Mj	44.47N	6.33 E
Largo, Cayo-	49	Gc	21.38N	81.28W
Largs	9	If	55.48N	4.52W
La Ribagorça/Ribagorza	13	Mb	42.15N	0.30 E
La Ribera	13	Kb	42.30N	2.00W
Larimore	45	Hc	47.54N	97.38W
Larino	14	Ii	41.48N	14.54 E
La Rioja [2]	56	Gc	30.00S	67.30W
La Rioja	13	Jb	42.20N	2.20W
La Rioja	53	Jh	29.25S	66.50W
Lárisa	6	Ih	39.38N	22.25 E
La Rivière-Thibouville, Nassandres-	12	Ce	49.07N	0.44 E
Lārkāna	25	Dc	27.33N	68.13 E
Larmor-Plage	11	Cg	47.42N	3.23W
Larnaka/Lárnax	23	Dc	34.55N	33.38 E
Lárnax/Larnaka	23	Dc	34.55N	33.38 E
Larne/Latharna	9	Hg	54.51N	5.49W
Larned	45	Gg	38.11N	99.06W
La Robla	13	Gb	42.48N	5.37W
La Roche	63b	De	21.28S	168.02 E
La Roche-en-Ardenne	11	Ld	50.11N	5.35 E
La Rochefoucauld	11	Gi	45.44N	0.23 E
La Roche-Guyon	12	De	49.05N	1.38 E
La Rochelle	6	Ff	46.10N	1.09W
La Roche-sur-Yon	11	Eh	46.40N	1.26W
La Roda	13	Je	39.13N	2.09W
La Romana	47	Ke	18.25N	68.58W
La Ronge	42	Ge	55.06N	105.17W
La Ronge, Lac-	38	Id	55.05N	104.59W
Larose	45	Kl	29.35N	90.23W
La Rosita	48	Ic	28.24N	101.43W
Larouco	13	Ec	41.56N	7.40W
Larreynaga	49	Dg	12.40N	86.34W
Larrey Point	59	Dc	20.00S	119.10 E
Larrimah	58	Ef	15.35S	133.12 E
Larsa	24	Kg	31.16N	45.49 E
Lars Christensen Kyst	66	Fe	69.30S	68.00 E
Larsen, Mount-	66	Kf	74.51S	162.12 E
Larsen Ice Shelf	66	Qe	68.30S	62.30W
Lartijas Padomju Socialistiska Respublika/ Latvijskaja SSR [2]	19	Cd	57.00N	25.00 E
La Rumorosa	48	Aa	32.34N	116.06W
Laruns	11	Fk	43.00N	0.25W
Larvik	7	Bg	59.04N	10.00 E
La Sabana [Arg.]	55	Ch	27.52S	59.57W
La Sabana [Col.]	54	Ec	2.20N	68.32W
Las Adjuntas, Presa de-	48	Jf	23.55N	98.45W
La Sagra	13	Id	40.05N	4.00W
La Sagra	13	Jg	37.57N	2.34W
La Salle	45	Lf	41.20N	89.06W
La Salle, Pic-	47	Je	18.22N	71.59W
La Sal Mountains	46	Kg	38.30N	109.10W
Las Alpujarras	13	Ih	36.50N	3.25W
La Sanabria	13	Fb	42.08N	6.30W
Las Animas	45	Eg	38.04N	103.13W
Lās 'ānōd	35	Hd	8.26N	47.24 E
La Sarre	42	Jg	48.48N	79.12W
Las Aves, Islas-	54	Ea	11.58N	67.33W
Las Avispas	55	Bi	29.53S	61.18W
Las Bardenas	13	Kb	42.10N	1.25W
Las Bonitas	50	Di	7.52N	65.40W
Las Breñas	56	Hc	27.05S	61.05W
Las Cabezas de San Juan	13	Gh	36.59N	5.56W
Lascahobas	49	Ld	18.50N	71.56W
Lascano	55	Ek	33.40S	54.12W
Las Casitas, Cerro-	47	Cd	23.31N	109.53W
Lascaux, Grotte de-	11	Hi	45.03N	1.11 E
Las Cejas	56	Hc	26.53S	64.44W
Las Chilcas, Arroyo-	55	Cm	37.16S	58.26W
Las Choapas	47	Fe	17.55N	94.05W
Las Cinco Villas	13	Kb	42.05N	1.07W
Las Cruces	43	Fe	32.23N	106.29W
Läsdäred	35	Hc	10.10N	46.01 E
Lās Dawa'o	35	Hc	10.22N	49.03 E
La Segarra	13	Nc	41.30N	1.10 E
La Selva	13	Oc	41.40N	2.50 E
La Serena	13	Gf	38.45N	5.30W
La Serena	53	Ih	29.54S	71.16W
La Seu d'Urgell/Seo de Urgel	13	Nb	42.21N	1.28 E
La-Seyne-sur-Mer	11	Lk	43.06N	5.53 E
Las Flores	56	Ie	36.03S	59.07W
Lāsh-e Joveyn	23	Jc	31.43N	61.37 E
Las Heras	56	Gd	32.51S	68.49W
Lashkar Gāh	22	If	31.35N	64.21 E
Las Hurdes	13	Fd	40.20N	6.20W
La Sila	5	Hh	39.15N	16.30 E
Łasin	10	Pc	53.32N	19.05 E
Łask	10	Pe	51.36N	19.07 E
Las Lajas	56	Fe	38.31S	70.22W
Las Lomitas	56	Hb	24.42S	60.36W
Las Margaritas	48	Ni	16.19N	91.59W
Las Mariñas	13	Da	43.20N	8.15W
Las Marismas	13	Fg	37.00N	6.15W
Las Mercedes	54	Eb	9.07N	66.24W
Las Mestenas	48	Gc	28.13N	104.35W
Las Minas, Cerro-	47	Gf	14.33N	88.39W
Las Minas, Sierra de-	47	Ge	15.05N	90.00W
Las Mixtecas, Sierra del-	48	Ki	17.45N	97.15W
La Sola, Isla-	54	Fa	11.20N	63.34W
La Solana	13	If	38.56N	3.14W
Lasolo	26	Hg	3.29S	122.04 E
La Sorcière	51k	Bb	13.59N	60.56W
La Souterraine	11	Hh	46.14N	1.29 E
Las Palmas [3]	32	Ed	28.20N	14.20W
Las Palmas de Gran Canaria	31	Ff	28.06N	15.24W
Las Petas	55	Cc	16.23S	59.11W
La Spezia	6	Gg	44.07N	9.50 E
Las Piedras	56	Id	34.45S	56.13W
Las Plumas	53	Jj	43.40S	67.15W
Lās Qoray	35	Hc	11.15N	48.22 E
Las Rosas	55	Bk	32.28S	61.34W
Lassen Peak	43	Cc	40.29N	121.31W
Lassigny	12	Ee	49.35N	2.51 E
Laßnitz	14	Jd	46.46N	15.32 E
Lasso	64b	Ba	15.02N	145.38 E
Las Tablas	49	Gj	7.46N	80.17W
Last Mountain Lake	42	Gf	51.10N	105.15W
Las Toscas	55	Ci	28.21S	59.17W
Lastoursville	36	Bc	0.49S	12.42 E
Lastovo	14	Kh	42.46N	16.55 E
Lastovo	14	Kh	42.45N	16.50 E
Lastovski kanal	14	Kh	42.50N	16.59 E
Las Tres Virgenes, Volcán-	47	Bc	27.27N	112.34W
Las Tunas [3]	49	Ic	21.00N	77.00W
Las Tunas, Punta-	51a	Bb	18.30N	66.37W
Las Varillas	56	Hd	31.52S	62.43W
Las Vegas [N.M.-U.S.]	43	Fd	35.36N	105.13W
Las Vegas [Nv.-U.S.]	39	Hf	36.11N	115.08W
Las Villuercas	13	Ge	39.33N	5.27W
Łaszczów	10	Tf	50.32N	23.40 E
Lata	65c	Db	14.14S	169.29W
Latacunga	54	Cd	0.55S	78.37W
La Tagua	54	Dd	0.03S	74.40W
Latakia (EN)=Al Lādhiqīyah	22	Ff	35.31N	35.07 E
Latarc, Causse du-	11	Jk	43.57N	3.11 E
Late Island	61	Gc	18.48S	174.39W
Laterza	14	Kj	40.37N	16.48 E
La Teste	11	Ej	44.38N	1.09W
Latgale	8	Lh	56.45N	27.30 E
Latgales Augstiene/ Latgalskaja Vozvyšennost	8	Lh	56.10N	27.30 E
Latgalskaja Vozvyšennost/ Latgales Augstiene	8	Lh	56.10N	27.30 E
Latharna/Larne	9	Hg	54.51N	5.49W
Lathen	12	Jb	52.52N	7.19 E
La Tigra	55	Bh	27.06S	60.34W
Latina	14	Gi	41.28N	12.52 E
Latisana	14	Ge	45.47N	13.00 E
Latium (EN) = Lazio [2]	14	Gh	42.02N	12.23 E
La Toja	13	Db	42.27N	8.50W
La Toma	56	Gd	33.03S	65.37W
La Tontouta	63b	Ce	22.00S	166.15 E
Latorica	10	Rh	48.28N	21.50 E
La Tortuga, Isla-	54	Ea	10.56N	65.20W
La-Tour-du-Pin	11	Li	45.34N	5.27 E
La Trimouille	11	Hh	46.28N	1.03 E
La Trinidad	49	Dg	12.58N	86.14W
La Trinidad de Orichuna	50	Bi	7.07N	69.45W
La Trinité	50	Fe	14.44N	60.58W
Latronico	14	Kj	40.05N	16.01 E
Lattari, Monti-	14	Ij	40.40N	14.30 E
La Tuque	42	Kg	47.27N	72.47W
Lātūr	25	Fe	18.24N	76.35 E
Latvian SSR (EN)=Latvijas PSR [2]	19	Cd	57.00N	25.00 E
Latvijas PSR=Latvian SSR (EN) [2]	19	Cd	57.00N	25.00 E
Latvijskaja Sovetskaja Socialističeskaja Respublika [2]	19	Cd	57.00N	25.00 E
Latvijskaja SSR/Latvijas Padomju Socialistiska Respublika [2]	19	Cd	57.00N	25.00 E
Lau	30	Kh	6.56N	30.16 E
Laubach	12	Kd	50.33N	8.59 E
Lauchert	10	Fh	48.05N	9.15 E
Lauchhammer	10	Je	51.30N	13.48 E
Lauenburg	10	Gc	53.22N	10.34 E
Lauf an der Pegnitz	10	Hg	49.31N	11.17 E
Laughlan Islands	63a	Ac	9.15S	153.40 E
Laughlin Peak	45	Dh	36.38N	104.12W
Lau Group	57	Jf	18.20S	178.30W
Lauhanvuori	8	Jb	62.10N	22.10 E
Laujar de Andarax	13	Jh	36.59N	2.51W
Laukaa	7	Fe	62.25N	25.57 E
Laukuva	8	Ji	55.35N	22.08 E
Laulau, Bahia-	64b	Ba	15.08N	145.46 E
Launceston [Austl.]	58	Fi	41.26S	147.08 E
Launceston [Eng.-U.K.]	9	Ik	50.38N	4.21W
La Unión [Bol.]	55	Bb	15.18S	61.05W
La Unión [Chile]	56	Ff	40.17S	73.05W
La Unión [Col.]	54	Cc	1.37N	77.08W
La Unión [ElSal.]	47	Gf	13.20N	87.51W
La Unión [Mex.]	48	Ii	17.58N	101.49W
La Unión [Peru]	54	Ce	9.46S	76.48W
La Unión [Sp.]	13	Lg	37.37N	0.52W
La Unión [Ven.]	49	Ni	8.13N	67.46W
Laura	59	Ic	15.34S	144.28 E
La Urbana	50	Ci	7.08N	66.56W
Laurel [Ms.-U.S.]	43	Je	31.42N	89.08W
Laurel [Mt.-U.S.]	43	Fb	45.40N	108.46W
Laureles	55	Ej	31.23S	55.52W
Laurel Hill	44	He	40.02N	79.17W
Laurel Mountain	44	Hf	39.20N	79.50W
Laurens	44	Fh	34.30N	82.01W
Laurentian Plateau (EN)= Laurentien, Plateau-	38	Md	50.00N	70.00W
Laurentian Scarp	44	Ic	45.50N	76.15W
Laurentide Scarp	44	Kb	46.38N	73.00W
Laurentien, Plateau-= Laurentian Plateau (EN)	38	Md	50.00N	70.00W
Lauria	14	Jj	40.02N	15.50 E
Lau Ridge (EN)	3	Kl	25.00S	179.00 E
Laurie River	42	He	56.00N	100.58W
Laurinburg	44	Hh	34.47N	79.27W
Laurium	44	Cb	47.14N	88.26W
Lauro Muller	55	Hi	28.24S	49.23W
Lausanne	6	Gf	46.30N	6.40 E
Lausitzer Gebirge	10	Kf	50.48N	14.40 E
Lausitzer Neiße	10	Kd	52.04N	14.46 E
Laut, Pulau-	26	Ef	4.43N	107.59 E
Laut, Pulau-	21	Nj	3.40S	116.10 E
Lautaret, Col du-	11	Mi	45.02N	6.24 E
Lautaro	56	Fe	38.31S	72.27W
Lautém	26	Ih	8.22S	126.54 E
Lauter	10	Eg	48.58N	8.11 E
Lauterbach	10	Ff	50.38N	9.24 E
Lauterbourg	12	Kf	48.59N	8.11 E
Lauterecken	12	Je	49.39N	7.36 E
Lauthala	63d	Cb	16.45S	179.41W
Laut Kecil, Kepulauan-	26	Gg	4.50S	115.45 E
Lautoka	61	Ec	17.37S	177.27 E
Lauvergne Island	64d	Cb	7.00N	152.00 E
Lauwersmeer	12	Ia	53.25N	6.15 E
Lauzerte	11	Hj	44.15N	1.08 E
Lauzon	44	Lb	46.50N	71.10W
Lauzoue	11	Gj	44.03N	0.15 E
Lava	10	Rb	54.37N	21.14 E
Lava, Nosy- [Mad.]	37	Hb	12.49S	48.41 E
Lava, Nosy- [Mad.]	37	Hb	14.33S	47.36 E
Lavaca River	45	Hl	28.50N	96.36W
Lava Flow	45	Bi	34.45N	108.20W
Laval	11	Ff	48.01N	0.46W
Lavalle	55	Ci	29.01S	59.11W
Lavalleja [2]	55	El	34.00S	55.00W
Lāvān, Jazīreh-ye-	23	Hd	26.48N	53.00 E
Lavanggu	63a	Ed	11.37S	160.15 E
Lavant	14	Id	46.38N	14.56 E
Lavapié, Punta-	52	Ii	37.09S	73.35W
Lāvar Meydān	24	Pg	30.20N	54.30 E
Lavassaare	8	Kf	58.29N	24.16 E
Lavaur	11	Hk	43.42N	1.49 E
La Vecilla	13	Gb	42.51N	5.24W
La Vega	47	Je	19.13N	70.31W
La Vela de Coro	49	Mh	11.27N	69.34W
Lavelanet	11	Hl	42.56N	1.51 E
Lavello	14	Ji	41.03N	15.48 E
La Venta	47	Fe	18.08N	94.03W
Laventie	12	Ed	50.38N	2.46 E
La Ventura	48	Ie	24.37N	100.54W
La Vera	13	Gd	40.05N	5.30W
L'Averdy, Cape-	63a	Ba	5.33S	155.04 E
Laverton	59	Ee	28.38S	122.25 E
Lavia	7	Ff	61.36N	22.36 E
La Victoria	54	Ea	10.14N	67.20W
La Vila Jojosa/Villajoyosa	13	Lf	38.30N	0.14W
La Villita, Presa-	48	Hh	18.05N	102.05W
La Viña	54	Ce	6.54S	79.28W

Index Symbols

- [1] Independent Nation
- [2] State, Region
- [3] District, County
- Municipality
- Colony, Dependency
- Continent
- Physical Region
- Historical or Cultural Region
- Mount, Mountain
- Volcano
- Hill
- Mountains, Mountain Range
- Hills, Escarpment
- Plateau, Upland
- Pass, Gap
- Plain, Lowland
- Delta
- Salt Flat
- Valley, Canyon
- Crater, Cave
- Karst Features
- Depression
- Polder
- Desert, Dunes
- Forest, Woods
- Heath, Steppe
- Oasis
- Cape, Point
- Coast, Beach
- Cliff
- Peninsula
- Isthmus
- Sandbank
- Island
- Atoll
- Rock, Reef
- Islands, Archipelago
- Rocks, Reefs
- Coral Reef
- Well, Spring
- Geyser
- River, Stream
- Waterfall Rapids
- River Mouth, Estuary
- Lake
- Salt Lake
- Intermittent Lake
- Reservoir
- Swamp, Pond
- Canal
- Glacier
- Ice Shelf, Pack Ice
- Ocean
- Sea
- Gulf, Bay
- Strait, Fjord
- Lagoon
- Bank
- Seamount
- Tablemount
- Ridge
- Shelf
- Basin
- Escarpment, Sea Scarp
- Fracture
- Trench, Abyss
- National Park, Reserve
- Point of Interest
- Recreation Site
- Cave, Cavern
- Historic Site
- Ruins
- Wall, Walls
- Church, Abbey
- Temple
- Scientific Station
- Airport
- Port
- Lighthouse
- Mine
- Tunnel
- Dam, Bridge

La Vôge 11 Mf 48.05N 6.05 E
Lavoisier Island 66 Qe 66.12S 66.44W
Lavougba 35 Cd 5.37N 23.19 E
La Voulte-sur-Rhône 11 Kj 44.48N 4.47 E
Lavouras 55 Db 14.59S 56.47W
Lavras 54 Jh 21.14S 45.00W
Lavras do Sul 55 Fj 30.49S 53.55W
Lavrentija 20 Nc 65.33N 171.02W
Lávrion 15 Hl 37.43N 24.03 E
Lavumisa 37 Ee 27.15S 31.55 E
Lawas 26 Gf 4.51N 115.24 E
Lawdar 23 Gg 13.53N 45.52 E
Lawe 12 Ed 50.38N 2.42 E
Lawers, Ben- 9 Ie 56.33N 4.15W
Lawit, Gunong- 26 Ff 1.23N 112.55 E
Lawqah 24 Jh 29.49N 42.45 E
Lawra 34 Ec 10.39N 2.52W
Lawrence [Ks.-U.S.] 43 Hd 38.58N 95.14W
Lawrence [Ma.-U.S.] 43 Mc 42.42N 71.09W
Lawrence [N.Z.] 62 Cf 45.55S 169.42 E
Lawrenceburg [Ky.-U.S.] 44 Ef 38.02N 84.54W
Lawrenceburg [Tn.-U.S.] 44 Dh 35.15N 87.20W
Lawson, Mount- 59 Ja 7.44S 146.37 E
Lawton 39 Jf 34.37N 98.25W
Lawu, Gunung- 21 Nj 7.38S 111.11 E
Lawz, Jabal al- 24 Fh 28.41N 35.18 E
Laxå 7 Dg 58.59N 14.37 E
Lay 11 Eh 46.18N 1.17W
Laylá 23 Ge 22.17N 46.45 E
Layon 11 Fg 47.20N 0.45W
Layou 51g Bb 15.23N 61.26W
Layou 51n Ba 13.12N 61.17W
Laysan Island 57 Jb 25.50N 171.50W
Layton 46 Jf 41.04N 111.58W
La Zarca 48 Ge 25.50N 104.44W
Lazarev 20 Jf 52.13N 141.35 E
Lazarevac 15 De 44.23N 20.16 E
Lázaro Cárdenas, Presa- 48 Ge 25.35N 105.05W
Lazdijai/Lazdijaj 7 Fi 54.13N 23.33 E
Lazdijaj/Lazdijai 7 Fi 54.13N 23.33 E
Lāzeh 24 Oi 26.48N 53.22 E
Lazio = Latium (EN) 14 Gh 42.02N 12.23 E
Lazo 28 Mc 43.25N 134.01 E
Lazovsk 16 Ff 47.38N 28.12 E
Łazy 10 Pf 50.27N 19.26 E
Lea 9 Nj 51.30N 0.01 E
Lead 43 Gc 44.21N 103.46W
Leader 46 Ka 50.53N 109.31W
Lead Hill 45 Jh 37.06N 92.38W
Leadville 43 Fd 39.15N 106.20W
Leaf River 45 Lk 31.00N 88.45W
League City 45 Il 29.31N 95.05W
Leamington 44 Fd 42.03N 82.36W
Leandro N. Alem 55 Bl 34.30S 61.24W
Leane, Lough-/Loch Léin 9 Di 52.05N 9.35W
Le'an Jiang 28 Dj 28.58N 116.41 E
Learmonth 59 Cd 22.13S 114.04 E
Leavenworth [Ks.-U.S.] 45 Ig 39.19N 94.55W
Leavenworth [Wa.-U.S.] 46 Ec 47.36N 120.40W
Łeba 10 Nb 54.47N 17.33 E
Łeba 10 Nb 54.43N 17.25 E
Lebach 12 Ie 49.24N 6.55 E
Lébamba 36 Bc 2.12S 11.30 E
Lebanon [In.-U.S.] 44 De 40.03N 86.28W
Lebanon [Ky.-U.S.] 44 Eg 37.34N 85.15W
Lebanon [Mo.-U.S.] 45 Jh 37.41N 92.40W
Lebanon [N.H.-U.S.] 44 Kd 43.38N 72.15W
Lebanon [Or.-U.S.] 46 Dd 44.32N 122.54W
Lebanon [Pa.-U.S.] 44 Ie 40.21N 76.25W
Lebanon [Tn.-U.S.] 44 Dg 36.12N 86.18W
Lebanon (EN)=Lubnān 22 Ff 33.50N 35.50 E
Lebanon Mountains (EN)= Lubnān, Jabal- 23 Ec 34.00N 36.30 E
Lebap 18 Cd 41.02N 61.54 E
Le Bec-Hellouin 12 Ce 49.14N 0.43 E
Lebedin 19 De 50.36N 34.30 E
Lebediny 20 He 58.25N 125.58 E
Lebedjan 19 De 53.02N 39.07 E
Le Bény-Bocage 12 Bf 48.56N 0.50W
Lebjažje [Kaz.-U.S.S.R.] 19 He 51.28N 77.46 E
Lebjažje [R.S.F.S.R.] 17 Mi 55.16N 66.29 E
Le Blanc 11 Hh 46.38N 1.04 E
Lebo 36 Db 4.29N 23.57 E
Lebomboberge 30 Kk 26.15S 32.00 E
Lebombo Mountains 30 Kk 26.15S 32.00 E
Łebork 10 Nb 54.33N 17.44 E
Le Bourget 12 Ef 48.56N 2.25 E
Lebrija 13 Fh 36.55N 6.04W
Łebsko, Jezioro- 10 Nb 54.44N 17.24 E
Lebu 56 Fe 37.37S 73.39W
Le Carbet 51h Ab 14.43N 61.11W
Le Cateau 12 Fd 50.06N 3.33 E
Le Catelet 12 Fd 50.01N 3.15 E
Lecce 6 Hg 40.23N 18.11 E
Lecco 14 De 45.51N 9.23 E
Lech 10 Gh 48.44N 10.56 E
Lech 14 Ec 47.12N 10.09 E
Le Champ du Feu 11 Nf 48.24N 7.15 E
Lechang 27 Jf 25.15N 113.25 E
Le Château-d'Oléron 11 Ei 45.54N 1.12W
Le Chesne 11 Ke 49.31N 4.46 E
Le Cheylard 11 Kj 44.54N 4.25 E
Lechfeld 10 Gh 48.10N 10.50 E
Lechiguiri, Cerro- 48 Li 16.43N 95.30W
Lechtaler Alpen 14 Ec 47.15N 10.30 E
Léconi 36 Bc 1.11S 13.16 E
Léconi 36 Bc 1.35S 14.14 E
Le Cornate 14 Eg 43.10N 10.58 E
Le Coudray-Saint-Germer 12 De 49.25N 1.50 E
Le Creusot 11 Kh 46.48N 4.26 E
Le Croisic 11 Dg 47.18N 2.30W
Le Crotoy 12 Dd 50.13N 1.37 E
Łęczna 10 Se 51.19N 22.52 E
Łęczyca 10 Pd 52.04N 19.13 E
Led 7 Ke 62.20N 43.00 E
Lede 12 Fd 50.57N 3.59 E
Ledesma 13 Gc 41.05N 6.00W
Le Diamant 51h Ac 14.29N 61.02W
Ledjanaja, Gora- [R.S.F.S.R.] 21 Tc 61.45N 171.15 E
Ledjanaja, Gora- [R.S.F.S.R.] 21 Qe 49.28N 142.45 E
Lednik Entuziastov 66 Cf 70.30S 16.00 E
Lednik Mušketova 66 Cf 72.00S 14.00 E
Ledo, Cabo- 36 Bd 9.41S 13.12 E
Ledolom Tajmyrski 66 Ge 66.00S 83.00 E
Le Donjon 11 Jh 46.21N 3.48 E
Le Dorat 11 Hh 46.13N 1.05 E
Lędyczek 10 Mc 53.33N 16.58 E
Lee/An Laoi 9 Ej 51.55N 8.30W
Leech Lake 43 Ib 47.09N 94.23W
Leeds [Al.-U.S.] 44 Di 33.33N 86.33W
Leeds [Eng.-U.K.] 6 Fe 53.50N 1.35W
Leeds [N.D.-U.S.] 45 Gb 48.17N 99.27W
Leek 12 Ia 53.10N 6.24 E
Leer 10 Dc 53.14N 7.26 E
Leer (Ostfriesland) 10 Dc 53.14N 7.26 E
Leerdam 12 Hc 51.53N 5.06 E
Lées 11 Fk 43.38N 0.14W
Leesburg 43 Kf 29.49N 81.53W
Leeste, Weyhe- 12 Kb 52.59N 8.50 E
Leesville 45 Jk 31.08N 93.16W
Leeuwarden 11 La 53.12N 5.46 E
Leeuwarderadeel 12 Ha 53.16N 5.46 E
Leeuwarderadeel-Stiens 12 Ha 53.16N 5.46 E
Leeuwin, Cape- 59 Cf 34.25S 115.00 E
Leeward Islands 47 Le 17.00N 63.00W
Leeward Islands (EN)=Sous le Vent, Iles- 57 Lf 16.38S 151.30W
Léfini 36 Cc 2.57S 16.10 E
Lefka 15 Jh 41.52N 26.16 E
Lefke 24 Ee 35.07N 32.51 E
Lefkoşa/Levkosia = Nicosia (EN) 22 Ff 35.10N 33.22 E
Le François 51h Bb 14.37N 60.54W
Lefroy, Lake- 59 Ef 31.15S 121.40 E
Łeg 10 Rf 50.38N 21.49 E
Leganés 13 Id 40.19N 3.45W
Legazpi 22 Oh 13.09N 123.44 E
Legden 12 Jb 52.02N 7.06 E
Legges Tor 59 Jh 41.32S 147.40 E
Leggett 46 Dg 39.52N 123.43W
Leghorn (EN)=Livorno 6 Hg 43.33N 10.19 E
Legionowo 10 Qd 52.25N 20.56 E
Léglise 12 He 49.48N 5.32 E
Legnago 14 Fe 45.11N 11.18 E
Legnano 14 Ce 45.36N 8.54 E
Legnica 10 Me 51.15N 16.10 E
Legnica 10 Me 51.13N 16.09 E
Le Grand-Quevilly 12 De 49.25N 1.02 E
Le Grand Veymont 11 Lj 44.52N 5.32 E
Le Grau-du-Roi 11 Kk 43.32N 4.08 E
Léguer 11 Cf 48.44N 3.32W
Leh 25 Fb 34.10N 77.35 E
Le Havre 6 Gf 49.30N 0.08 E
Lehi 46 Jf 40.24N 111.51W
Lehmann 55 Bj 31.08S 61.27W
Le Hohneck 11 Nf 48.02N 7.01 E
Le Houlme 12 De 49.31N 1.02 E
Lehrte 10 Fd 52.23N 9.58 E
Lehtimäki 8 Jb 62.47N 23.55 E
Lehua Island 65a Aa 22.01N 160.06W
Lehututu 37 Cd 23.53S 21.49 E
Leibnitz 14 Jd 46.46N 15.32 E
Leibo 27 Hf 28.13N 103.34 E
Leicester 6 Fe 52.38N 1.05W
Leicester 9 Mi 52.40N 1.00W
Leicestershire 9 Mi 52.38N 1.00W
Leichhardt Range 59 Jd 20.40S 147.05 E
Leichhardt River 59 Hc 17.35S 139.48 E
Leiden 11 Kb 52.09N 4.30 E
Leidschendam 12 Gb 52.05N 4.26 E
Leie 11 Jc 51.03N 3.43 E
Leifear/Lifford 9 Fg 54.50N 7.29W
Leigh Creek 58 Eh 30.28S 138.25 E
Leighton Buzzard 12 Bc 51.55N 0.39W
Leigong Shan 27 If 26.23N 108.15 E
Leikanger 7 Ae 62.07N 5.20 E
Léim an Mhadaidh/Limavady 9 Gf 55.03N 6.57W
Leimen 12 Ke 49.21N 8.41 E
Leimus 49 Ef 14.44N 84.07W
Leine 10 Fd 52.40N 9.40 E
Leinster/Laighean 9 Gh 53.00N 7.00W
Leipzig 6 He 51.18N 12.20 E
Leipzig 10 Ie 51.20N 12.20 E
Leira 8 Cd 60.58N 9.18 E
Leiria 13 De 39.40N 8.50W
Leiria 13 De 39.45N 8.48W
Leirvik 7 Ag 59.47N 5.30 E
Leisi/Lejsi 8 Jf 58.33N 22.30 E
Leisler, Mount- 59 Fd 23.30S 129.20 E
Leiston 12 Db 52.12N 1.34 E
Leitariegos, Puerto de- 13 Fa 43.00N 6.25W
Leitha 14 Lc 47.52N 17.18 E
Leithagebirge 14 Kc 47.58N 16.40 E
Leitir Ceanainn/Letterkenny 9 Fg 54.57N 7.44W
Leitrim/Liatroim 9 Eg 54.20N 8.20W
Leiva, Cerro- 54 Dc 2.54N 74.48W
Leiyang 27 Jf 26.30N 112.57 E
Leizhou → Haikang 27 Jg 20.56N 110.06 E
Leizhou Bandao 21 Ng 20.40N 110.05 E
Lejasciems 8 Lg 57.08N 26.36 E
Lejsi/Leisi 8 Jf 58.33N 22.30 E
Lek 11 Lc 52.00N 6.00 E
Leka 7 Cd 65.05N 11.37 E
Lékana 36 Cc 2.19S 14.36 E
Leketi, Monts de la- 30 Ii 2.34S 14.17 E
Lekhainá 15 El 37.56N 21.16 E
Lekhal 13 Ph 36.20N 3.51 E
Lekitobi 26 Hg 1.58S 124.33 E
Lekki Lagoon 34 Fd 6.30N 4.07 E
Leknes 7 Cb 68.10N 13.42 E
Łęknica 10 Ke 51.32N 14.48 E
Lékoumou 36 Bc 3.00S 13.50 E
Leksand 7 Df 60.44N 15.01 E
Leksozero, Ozero- 7 He 63.45N 31.00 E
Leksula 26 Ig 3.46S 126.31 E
Leksvik 7 Ce 63.40N 10.37 E
Le Lamentin 50 Fe 14.37N 61.01W
Leland 45 Kj 33.24N 90.54W
Lelång 8 Ee 59.10N 12.10 E
Le Lavandou 11 Mk 43.08N 6.22 E
Lelčicy 16 Fd 51.49N 28.21 E
Leleiwi Point 65a Gd 19.44N 155.00W
Lelepa 63b Dc 17.36S 168.13 E
Leleque 56 Ff 42.23S 71.03W
Leli 63a Ec 8.45S 161.02 E
Leli → Tianlin 27 Ig 24.22N 106.11 E
Lelija 14 Mg 43.26N 18.29 E
Leling 28 Df 37.44N 117.13 E
Léliogat 63b Ce 21.18S 167.35 E
Lelle 7 Fg 58.53N 25.00 E
Le Locle 14 Ac 47.05N 6.45 E
Le Lorrain 51h Ab 14.50N 61.04W
Lelystad 11 Lb 52.31N 5.27 E
Le Madonie 14 Hm 37.50N 14.00 E
Le Maire, Estrecho de- 56 Hh 54.50S 65.00W
Léman, Lac-=Geneva, Lake- (EN) 5 Gf 46.25N 6.30 E
Leman Bank 9 Oh 53.10N 1.58 E
Lemankoa 63a Ba 5.03S 154.34 E
Le Mans 6 Gf 48.00N 0.12 E
Le Marin 51h Bc 14.28N 60.52W
Le Mars 45 He 42.47N 96.10W
Le Mas-d'Azil 11 Hk 43.05N 1.22 E
Lembach 12 Je 49.00N 7.48 E
Lembeck 12 Ic 51.44N 6.59 E
Lemberg 12 Je 49.00N 7.23 E
Lembolovskaja Vozvyšennost 8 Md 60.50N 30.15 E
Lembruch 12 Kb 52.32N 8.21 E
Leme 55 If 22.12S 47.24W
Lemelerberg 12 Ib 52.29N 6.23 E
Lemesós/Limassol 23 Dc 34.40N 33.02 E
Lemgo 10 Ed 52.02N 8.54 E
Lemhi Range 46 Id 44.30N 113.25W
Lemieux Islands 42 Ld 64.00N 64.20W
Lemju 17 He 63.50N 56.57 E
Lemland 8 Id 60.05N 20.10 E
Lemmer, Lemsterland- 12 Hb 52.51N 5.42 E
Lemmon 43 Gb 45.56N 102.10W
Lemmon, Mount- 46 Jj 32.26N 110.47W
Lemnos (EN)=Limnos 5 Ih 39.55N 25.15 E
Le-Molay-Littry 12 Be 49.15N 0.53W
Le-Mont-Saint-Michel 11 Ef 48.38N 1.30W
Le Morne Rouge 51h Ab 14.46N 61.08W
Lemotol Bay 64d Bb 7.21N 151.35 E
Le Moyne, Lac- 42 Ke 57.00N 68.00W
Lempa, Rio- 47 Gf 13.14N 88.49W
Lempäälä 8 Jd 61.19N 23.45 E
Lempira 49 Cf 14.20N 88.40W
L'Empordà/Ampurdán 13 Ob 42.12N 2.45 E
Lemro 25 Id 20.25N 93.20 E
Lemsid 32 Ed 26.33N 13.51W
Lemsterland 12 Hb 52.51N 5.42 E
Lemsterland-Lemmer 12 Hb 52.51N 5.42 E
Le Murge 5 Hg 40.50N 16.40 E
Le Muy 11 Mk 43.28N 6.33 E
Lemvig 8 Ch 56.32N 8.18 E
Lemya 17 Jc 66.30N 62.00 E
Lena 21 Ob 72.25N 126.40 E
Lena, Mount- 46 Kf 40.50N 109.27W
Lénakel 63b Dd 19.32S 169.16 E
Lena Mountains (EN) = Prilenskoje Plato 21 Oc 60.45N 125.00 E
Lena Tablemount (EN) 30 Ln 53.00S 45.00 E
Lençóis Paulista 55 Hf 22.36S 48.47W
Lendava 14 Kd 46.34N 16.27 E
Lendery 7 He 63.26N 31.12 E
Lendinara 14 Fe 45.05N 11.36 E
Le Neubourg 12 Ce 49.09N 0.55 E
Lenger 19 Gg 42.10N 69.55 E
Lengerich 10 Dd 52.11N 7.52 E
Lengoué 36 Cb 0.49N 15.47 E
Lengshuijiang 27 Jf 27.41N 111.28 E
Lengua de Vaca, Punta- 56 Fd 30.14S 71.38W
Lengulu 36 Eb 3.15N 26.30 E
Lenhovda 7 Dh 57.00N 15.17 E
Lenina, Pik-=Lenin Peak (EN) 21 Jf 39.19N 73.01 E
Leninabad 22 Ie 40.17N 69.37 E
Leninabadskaja Oblast 19 Gh 40.00N 69.10 E
Leninakan 6 Kg 40.47N 43.50 E
Lenin Canal (EN)=Volgo-Donskoj sudohodny kanal imeni V. I. Lenina 5 Kf 48.40N 43.37 E
Leningrad 6 Jc 59.55N 30.15 E
Leningradskaja 66 Je 69.30S 159.23 E
Leningradskaja 16 Kf 46.17N 39.25 E
Leningradskaja Oblast 19 Dd 60.00N 31.40 E
Leningradski [R.S.F.S.R.] 20 Mc 69.17N 178.10 E
Leningradski [Tad.-U.S.S.R.] 19 Hh 38.09N 70.01 E
Lenino 16 Ig 45.17N 35.44 E
Leninogorsk [Kaz.-U.S.S.R.] 22 Kd 50.27N 83.32 E
Leninogorsk [R.S.F.S.R.] 19 Fe 54.38N 52.30 E
Lenin Peak (EN)=Lenina, Pik- 21 Jf 39.19N 73.01 E
Leninsk [R.S.F.S.R.] 16 Ne 48.42N 45.11 E
Leninsk [Tur.-U.S.S.R.] 18 Bc 42.04N 59.24 E
Leninsk [Uzb.-U.S.S.R.] 18 Id 40.40N 72.20 E
Leninski [Kaz.-U.S.S.R.] 19 He 52.13N 76.50 E
Leninski [Mold.-U.S.S.R.] 15 Lb 47.50N 28.16 E
Leninski [R.S.F.S.R.] 20 He 58.32N 125.58 E
Leninsk-Kuznecki 22 Kd 54.38N 86.10 E
Leninskoje [Kaz.-U.S.S.R.] 19 Ge 54.05N 65.23 E
Leninskoje [R.S.F.S.R.] 7 Lg 58.21N 47.07 E
Leninskoje [R.S.F.S.R.] 20 Ig 47.59N 132.38 E
Leninváros 10 Ri 47.56N 21.05 E
Lenkoran 6 Kh 38.44N 48.50 E
Lenne 10 De 51.25N 7.30 E
Lenne 12 Jc 51.15N 7.50 E
Lennestadt 12 Kc 51.08N 8.01 E
Lennestadt-Grevenbrück 12 Kc 51.08N 8.01 E
Lennox Hills 9 Ie 56.05N 4.10W
Leno-Angarskoje Plato 20 Fe 55.00N 104.30 E
Lenoir 44 Gh 35.55N 81.32W
Le Nouvion-en-Thiérache 12 Fd 50.01N 3.47 E
Lens 11 Id 50.26N 2.50 E
Lensk 22 Nc 61.00N 114.50 E
Lenti 10 Mj 46.37N 16.33 E
Lentiira 7 Gd 64.21N 29.50 E
Lentini 14 Jm 37.17N 15.01 E
Lentua 7 Gd 64.14N 29.36 E
Lentvaris 8 Kj 54.38N 25.13 E
Léo 34 Ec 11.06N 2.06W
Leoben 14 Jc 47.23N 15.06 E
Léogâne 49 Kd 18.31N 72.38W
Leok 26 Hf 1.11N 121.26 E
Leola 45 Gd 45.43N 98.56W
Leominster 9 Ki 52.14N 2.45W
León 13 Gc 42.00N 6.00W
Léon 11 Ek 43.53N 1.18W
León [Mex.] 39 Ig 21.10N 101.42W
León [Nic.] 49 Dg 12.35N 86.35W
León [Nic.] 39 Kh 12.26N 86.54W
León [Sp.] 6 Fg 42.36N 5.34W
León [Sp.] 13 Gb 42.40N 6.00W
León, Montes de- 13 Fb 42.30N 6.20W
León, Puerto del- 13 Hh 36.50N 4.21W
Leonardville 37 Bd 23.29S 18.49 E
Leonberg 12 Kf 48.48N 9.01 E
Leone, Monte- 14 Cd 46.15N 8.10 E
Leones 55 Ak 32.39S 62.18W
Leonessa 14 Gh 42.34N 12.58 E
Leonforte 14 Im 37.38N 14.23 E
Leonídhion 15 Fl 37.10N 22.52 E
Leonora 58 Dg 28.53S 121.20 E
Leon River 45 Hk 30.59N 97.24W
Leopold and Astrid Coast 66 Ge 67.10S 84.10 E
Leopoldina 54 Jh 21.32S 42.38W
Leopold McClintock, Cape- 42 Fa 77.38N 116.20W
Leopoldo de Bulhões 55 Hc 16.37S 48.46W
Leopoldsburg 12 Hc 51.07N 5.15 E
Leopoldville → Kinshasa 31 Ii 4.18S 15.18 E
Leovo 16 Ff 46.29N 28.15 E
Lepa 65c Bb 14.01S 171.28W
Le Palais 11 Cg 47.21N 3.09W
Lepar, Pulau- 26 Eg 2.57S 106.50 E
Le Parcq 12 Ed 50.23N 2.06 E
Lepaterique 49 Df 14.02N 87.27W
Lepe 13 Eg 37.15N 7.12W
Lepel 19 Ce 54.53N 28.46 E
Lepenica 15 Ee 44.10N 21.08 E
Le Petit Caux 12 De 49.55N 1.20 E
Le Petit-Couronne 12 De 49.23N 1.01 E
Le Petit-Quevilly 12 De 49.26N 1.02 E
Lephepe 37 Dd 23.22S 25.52 E
Leping 27 Kf 28.59N 117.07 E
Lepini, Monti- 14 Gi 41.35N 13.00 E
Le Plessis-Belleville 12 Ee 49.06N 2.46 E
Le Pont-de-Claix 11 Li 45.07N 5.42 E
Le Portel 12 Dd 50.42N 1.34 E
Leppävesi 8 Kb 62.15N 25.55 E
Leppävirta 8 Lb 62.29N 27.47 E
Le Prêcheur 51h Ab 14.48N 61.14W
Lepsøya 8 Bb 62.35N 6.10 E
Lepsy 18 La 46.18N 78.20 E
Lepsy 19 Hf 46.12N 78.55 E
Leptis Magna 33 Bc 32.38N 14.18 E
Le Puy 11 Ji 45.02N 3.53 E
Leqemt (EN)=Nekemt 31 Kh 9.05N 36.33 E
Le Quesnoy 12 Fd 50.15N 3.38 E
Lercara Friddi 14 Hm 37.45N 13.36 E
Lerchenfeld Glacier 66 Af 77.50S 34.50W
Lere 34 Gc 10.23N 8.35 E
Léré 35 Ad 9.39N 14.13 E
Lérida 54 Dc 0.06N 70.43W
Lérida 13 Nc 42.00N 1.10 E
Lérida/Lleida 13 Mc 41.37N 0.37 E
Lérins, Iles de- 11 Nk 43.31N 7.03 E
Lerma 13 Ib 42.02N 3.45W
Lerma, Río- 48 Hg 20.13N 102.46W
Lermontov 16 Mg 44.06N 42.45 E
Le Robert 51h Bb 14.41N 60.57W
Léros 15 Jl 37.08N 26.50 E
Lerum 7 Ch 57.46N 12.16 E
Lerwick 9 La 60.09N 1.09W
Léry 12 De 49.17N 1.13 E
Les Abrets 11 Li 45.32N 5.35 E
Le Saint-Esprit 51h Bb 14.34N 60.57W
Les Alberes/Albères, Montes- 11 In 42.28N 2.56 E
Les Allobroges 63b Dc 16.47S 168.09 E
Les Andelys 11 He 49.15N 1.25 E
Les Anses-d'Arlets 51h Ac 14.29N 61.05W
Les-Baux-de-Provence 11 Kk 43.45N 4.48 E
Les Borges Blanques/Borjas Blancas 13 Mc 41.31N 0.52 E
Lesbos (EN)=Lésvos 5 Ih 39.10N 26.32 E
L'Escala/La Escala 13 Pb 42.07N 3.08 E
Les Cayes 47 Je 18.12N 73.45W
Les Coëvrons 11 Ff 48.12N 0.10W
Le Serre 14 Kl 38.30N 16.30 E
Les Escoumins 44 Ma 48.25N 69.29W
Les Eyzies-de-Tayac 11 Hj 44.56N 1.01 E
Les Falaises 12 Ce 49.44N 0.21 E
Leshan 27 Hf 29.34N 103.45 E
Les Herbiers 11 Eh 46.52N 1.01W
Lesina, Lago di- 14 Ji 41.55N 15.25 E
Lesja 8 Cb 62.07N 8.52 E
Lesjöfors 7 Dg 59.59N 14.11 E
Leskino 20 Cb 72.25N 79.40 E
Lesko 10 Sg 49.29N 22.21 E
Leskov 66 Ad 56.40S 28.10W
Leskovac 15 Eg 42.59N 21.57 E
Leskoviku 15 Di 40.09N 20.35 E
Les Mangles 51e Ab 16.23N 61.27W
Les Mauges 11 Fg 47.10N 1.00W
Les Minquiers 9 Km 48.58N 2.08W
Les Monédières 11 Hi 45.30N 1.52 E
Les Mureaux 12 Df 49.00N 1.55 E
Lesnaja 10 Vd 52.55N 25.52 E
Lesnaja 16 Cc 52.11N 23.30 E
Lesneven 11 Bf 48.34N 4.19W
Lešnica 15 Ce 44.39N 19.19 E
Lesnoj [R.S.F.S.R.] 19 Gd 57.01N 67.50 E
Lesnoj [R.S.F.S.R.] 19 Fd 59.49N 52.10 E
Lesnoj, Ostrov- 8 Md 60.02N 28.20 E
Lesný 10 If 50.02N 12.37 E
Lesogorski 8 Mc 61.01N 28.51 E
Lesosibirsk 22 Ld 58.15N 92.30 E
Lesotho 31 Jk 29.30S 28.30 E
Lesozavodsk 20 Ig 45.26N 133.25 E
Lesozavodski 7 Hc 66.45N 32.50 E
Lesparre-Médoc 11 Fi 45.18N 0.56W
L'Espérance Rock 57 Jh 31.26S 178.54W
Les Ponts-de-Cé 11 Fg 47.25N 0.31W
Les Posets 13 Mb 42.39N 0.25 E
Les Sables-d'Olonne 11 Eh 46.30N 1.47W
Lessay 11 Ee 49.13N 1.32W
Lesse 11 Kd 50.14N 4.54 E
Lessebo 7 Dh 56.45N 15.16 E
Lessen/Lessines 12 Fd 50.43N 3.50 E
Les Sept Iles 11 Cf 48.53N 3.28W
Lesser Antilles (EN)= Antillas Menores 38 Mh 15.00N 61.00W
Lesser Caucasus (EN)= Maly Kavkaz 5 Kg 41.00N 44.35 E
Lesser Khingan Range (EN)= Xiao Hinggan Ling 21 Oe 48.45N 127.00 E
Lesser Slave Lake 38 Hd 55.25N 115.30W
Lesser Sunda Islands (EN) 21 Oj 9.13S 121.12 E
Lessines/Lessen 12 Fd 50.43N 3.50 E
Lessini 14 Fe 45.41N 11.13 E
Les Tantes 51p Bb 12.19N 61.33W
Les Thilliers-en-Vexin 12 De 49.14N 1.36 E
Les Triagoz 11 Cf 48.53N 3.40W
Les Trois-Ilets 51h Ab 14.33N 61.03W
Lešukonskoje 7 Kd 64.52N 45.40 E
Lésvos=Lesbos (EN) 5 Ih 39.10N 26.32 E
Leszno 10 Me 51.50N 16.35 E
Leszno 10 Me 51.51N 16.35 E
Letälven 8 Fe 59.05N 14.20 E
Le Tanargue 11 Kj 44.37N 4.09 E
Letchworth 12 Bc 51.58N 0.13W
Letea, Ostrovul- 15 Md 45.20N 29.20 E
Le Teil 11 Kj 44.33N 4.41 E
Letenye 10 Mj 46.26N 16.44 E
Lethbridge 39 He 49.42N 110.50W
Lethem 53 Ke 3.20N 59.50W
Le Thillot 11 Mg 47.53N 6.46 E
Leti, Kepulauan-=Leti Islands (EN) 26 Ih 8.13S 127.50 E
Letiahau 30 Jk 21.04S 24.25 E
Leticia 53 Jf 4.09S 69.57W
Leti Islands (EN)=Leti, Kepulauan- 26 Ih 8.13S 127.50 E
Leting 28 Ee 39.25N 118.55 E
Letka 7 Mg 58.59N 50.14 E
Letlhakane 37 Dd 21.25S 25.36 E
Letnerečenski 7 Id 64.19N 34.25 E
Letni Bereg 7 Jd 64.50N 38.20 E
Letohrad 10 Mf 50.03N 16.31 E
Le Touquet-Paris-Plage 12 Hd 50.31N 1.35 E
Letovice 10 Mg 49.33N 16.36 E
Letpadan 25 Je 17.47N 95.45 E
Le Translay 12 De 49.58N 1.41 E
Le Tréport 11 Hd 50.04N 1.22 E
Letsôk-aw Kyun 25 Jf 11.37N 98.15 E
Letterkenny/Leitir Ceanainn 9 Fg 54.57N 7.44W
Leu 15 Ge 44.11N 24.00 E
Leuca 14 Mk 39.48N 18.21 E
Leucas (EN) = Levkás 15 Dk 38.43N 20.38 E
Leucate 11 Jl 42.55N 3.02 E
Leucate, Étang de- 11 Il 42.51N 3.00 E
Leuk 14 Bd 46.20N 7.38 E
Leukónoikon 24 Ee 35.15N 33.42 E
Leulumoega 65c Ba 13.49S 171.55W
Leuna 10 Ie 51.19N 12.01 E
Leušeny 15 Lc 46.51N 28.11 E
Leuser, Gunung- 21 Li 3.45N 97.11 E
Leutkirch im Allgäu 10 Gi 47.50N 10.02 E
Leuven/Louvain 11 Kd 50.53N 4.42 E
Leuze-en-Hainaut 12 Fd 50.36N 3.36 E
Levádhia 15 Fk 38.26N 22.53 E
Levaja Hetta 20 Cc 65.15N 73.20 E
Levanger 7 Ce 63.45N 11.18 E
Levante, Riviera di- 14 Df 44.15N 9.30 E
Levanzo 14 Gm 38.00N 12.20 E
Levaši 16 Oh 42.27N 47.20 E
Le Vauclin 51h Bb 14.33N 60.51W
Levelland 45 Ej 33.35N 102.23W
Lévêque, Cape- 59 Ec 16.25S 122.55 E
Le Verdon-sur-Mer 11 Ei 45.33N 1.04W
Leverkusen 10 Ce 51.01N 6.59 E
Leverkusen-Opladen 10 De 51.04N 7.01 E
Lévézou 11 Ij 44.09N 2.53 E
Levice 10 Oh 48.13N 18.37 E
Levico Terme 14 Fd 46.01N 11.18 E
Le Vigan 11 Jk 43.59N 3.36 E
Levin 61 Eh 40.37S 175.17 E
Lévis 42 Kg 46.48N 71.10W
Levisa Fork 44 Ff 38.06N 82.37W
Levitha 15 Jm 37.00N 26.28 E
Levittown 44 Je 40.09N 74.50W
Levká Óri 15 Gn 35.20N 24.00 E
Levkás 15 Dk 38.50N 20.42 E
Levkás = Leucas (EN) 15 Dk 38.43N 20.38 E

Index Symbols

- Independent Nation
- State, Region
- District, County
- Municipality
- Colony, Dependency
- Continent
- Physical Region
- Historical or Cultural Region
- Mount, Mountain
- Volcano
- Hill
- Mountains, Mountain Range
- Hills, Escarpment
- Plateau, Upland
- Pass, Gap
- Plain, Lowland
- Delta
- Salt Flat
- Valley, Canyon
- Crater, Cave
- Karst Features
- Depression
- Polder
- Desert, Dunes
- Forest, Woods
- Heath, Steppe
- Oasis
- Cape, Point
- Coast, Beach
- Cliff
- Peninsula
- Isthmus
- Sandbank
- Island
- Atoll
- Rock, Reef
- Islands, Archipelago
- Rocks, Reefs
- Coral Reef
- Well, Spring
- Geyser
- River, Stream
- Waterfall Rapids
- River Mouth, Estuary
- Lake
- Salt Lake
- Intermittent Lake
- Reservoir
- Swamp, Pond
- Canal
- Glacier
- Ice Shelf, Pack Ice
- Ocean
- Sea
- Gulf, Bay
- Strait, Fjord
- Lagoon
- Bank
- Seamount
- Tablemount
- Ridge
- Shelf
- Basin
- Escarpment, Sea Scarp
- Fracture
- Trench, Abyss
- National Park, Reserve
- Point of Interest
- Recreation Site
- Cave, Cavern
- Historic Site
- Ruins
- Wall, Walls
- Church, Abbey
- Temple
- Scientific Station
- Airport
- Port
- Lighthouse
- Mine
- Tunnel
- Dam, Bridge

Levkôsia/Lefkosa=Nicosia (EN) 22 Ff 35.10N 33.22 E
Levoča 10 Qg 49.02N 20.35 E
Levroux 11 Hh 46.59N 1.37 E
Levski 15 If 43.22N 25.08 E
Lev Tolstoj 16 Kc 53.12N 39.28 E
Levuka 63d Bb 17.41S 178.50 E
Levuo/Lévuo 8 Kh 56.02N 24.28 E
Lévuo/Levuo 8 Kh 56.02N 24.28 E
Lewes [De.-U.S.] 44 Jf 38.47N 75.08W
Lewes [Eng.-U.K.] 9 Nk 50.52N 0.01 E
Lewin Brzeski 10 Nf 50.46N 17.37 E
Lewis, Butt of- 9 Gc 58.31N 6.15W
Lewis, Isle of- 5 Fd 58.10N 6.40W
Lewis and Clark Lake 45 He 42.50N 97.45W
Lewisburg 44 Gg 37.49N 80.28W
Lewis Pass 62 Ee 42.24S 172.24 E
Lewis Range 38 He 48.30N 113.15W
Lewis River 46 Dd 45.51N 122.48W
Lewis Smith Lake 44 Dh 34.00N 87.07W
Lewiston [Id.-U.S.] 39 He 46.25N 117.01W
Lewiston [Me.-U.S.] 43 Mc 44.06N 70.13W
Lewistown [Mt.-U.S.] 43 Fb 47.04N 109.26W
Lewistown [Pa.-U.S.] 44 Ie 40.37N 77.36W
Lewisville 45 Jj 33.22N 93.35W
Lexington [Ky.-U.S.] 39 Kf 38.03N 84.30W
Lexington [Nb.-U.S.] 43 Hc 40.47N 99.45W
Lexington [N.C.-U.S.] 44 Gh 35.49N 80.15W
Lexington [Ok.-U.S.] 45 Hi 35.01N 97.20W
Lexington [Va.-U.S.] 44 Hg 37.47N 79.27W
Leygues, Iles- 30 Nm 48.45S 69.30 E
Leyre 11 Ej 44.39N 1.01W
Leysdown-on-Sea 12 Cc 51.23N 0.55 E
Leyte 21 Oh 10.50N 124.50 E
Lez 11 Kj 44.13N 4.43 E
Ležajsk 10 Sf 50.16N 22.24 E
Lézard, Pointe à- 51e Ab 16.08N 61.47W
Lézarde, Rivière- 51h Ab 14.36N 61.01W
Lezha 15 Ch 41.47N 19.39 E
Lézignan-Corbières 11 Ik 43.12N 2.46 E
Lgov 19 De 51.41N 35.17 E
Lhari 27 Fe 30.48N 93.25 E
Lhasa 22 Lg 29.42N 91.07 E
Lhazê 27 Ef 29.13N 87.44 E
Lhazhong 27 Ee 31.28N 86.36 E
Lhokseumawe 26 Ce 5.10N 97.08 E
Lhoksukon 26 Ce 5.03N 97.19 E
L'Hôpital 12 Ie 49.10N 6.44 E
Lhorong 27 Ge 30.45N 95.48 E
L'Hospitalet de l'Infant/Hospitalet del Infante 13 Md 40.59N 0.56 E
Lhozhag 27 Ff 28.18N 90.51 E
Lhünzhub (Poindo) 27 Fe 30.17N 91.20 E
Liádhi 15 Jm 36.55N 26.10 E
Liákoura 15 Fk 38.32N 22.37 E
Liamone 11a Aa 42.04N 8.43 E
Liancheng 27 Kf 25.48N 116.48 E
Liancourt 12 Ee 49.20N 2.28 E
Liane 12 Dd 50.43N 1.36 E
Liangcheng 28 Bd 40.32N 112.28 E
Liangpran, Gunung- 26 Ff 1.04N 114.23 E
Liangshan (Houji) 28 Dg 35.48N 116.07 E
Liangzhou→Wuwei 22 Mf 37.58N 102.48 E
Liangzi Hu 27 Je 30.15N 114.32 E
Lianjiang 27 Jg 21.42N 110.14 E
Lianshui 28 Eh 33.47N 119.16 E
Lianxian 27 Jg 24.48N 112.26 E
Lianyin 27 La 53.26N 123.50 E
Lianyungang 27 Ke 34.38N 119.27 E
Lianyungang (Xinpu) 22 Nf 34.34N 119.15 E
Lianzhou → Hepu 27 Ig 21.40N 109.12 E
Lianzhushan 28 Kb 45.28N 131.45 E
Liaocheng 27 Kd 36.27N 115.58 E
Liaodong Bandao=Liaotung Peninsula (EN) 21 Of 40.00N 122.20 E
Liaodong Wan=Liaotung, Gulf of- (EN) 27 Lc 40.00N 121.30 E
Liao He 21 Oe 40.39N 122.12 E
Liaoning Sheng (Liao-ning Sheng) [2] 27 Lc 41.00N 123.00 E
Liao-ning Sheng→Liaoning Sheng [2] 27 Lc 41.00N 123.00 E
Liaotung, Gulf of- (EN)=Liaodong Wan 27 Lc 40.00N 121.30 E
Liaotung Peninsula (EN)=Liaodong Bandao 21 Of 40.00N 122.20 E
Liaoyang 27 Lc 41.16N 123.10 E
Liaoyuan 22 Oe 42.55N 125.09 E
Liaozhong 28 Gd 41.30N 122.42 E
Liard 38 Gc 61.52N 121.18W
Liard River 42 Ee 59.15N 126.09W
Liat, Pulau- 26 Eg 2.53S 107.05 E
Liatorp 7 Fh 56.40N 14.16 E
Liatroim/Leitrim [2] 9 Eg 54.20N 8.20W
Liban 30 Lh 5.05N 40.05 E
Libano 55 Bm 37.32S 61.18W
Libby 46 Hb 48.23N 115.33W
Libenge 31 Ih 3.39N 18.38 E
Libengé 36 Cb 3.39N 18.38 E
Liberal 43 Gd 37.02N 100.55W
Liberec 10 Lf 50.46N 15.03 E
Liberia 47 Gf 10.38N 85.27W
Liberia [1] 31 Fh 6.00N 10.00W
Libertad [Ur.] 55 Dl 34.38S 56.39W
Libertad [Ven.] 49 Li 8.08N 71.28W
Libertad [Ven.] 54 Eb 8.20N 69.37W
Libertade, Rio- 54 He 9.35S 52.17W
Libertador General Bernardo O'Higgins [2] 56 Fd 33.35S 70.45W
Libertador Gen. San Martin 56 Hb 23.48S 64.48W
Libertador General San Martin, Cumbre del- 52 Jh 24.55S 66.40W
Liberty [Mo.-U.S.] 45 Ig 39.15N 94.25W
Liberty [Tx.-U.S.] 45 Ik 30.03N 94.47W
Lībiyā=Libya (EN) [1] 31 If 27.00N 17.00 E
Lībīyah, Aş Şaḩrā' al-=Libyan Desert (EN) 30 Jf 24.00N 25.00 E
Libo 27 If 25.28N 107.52 E
Libobo, Tanjung- 26 Ig 0.54S 128.28 E
Liboi 36 Hb 0.24N 40.57 E
Libourne 11 Fj 44.55N 0.14W
Libramont-Chevigny 12 He 49.55N 5.23 E
Librazhdi 15 Dh 41.11N 20.19 E
Libreville 31 Hh 0.23N 9.27 E
Libro Point 26 Gd 11.26N 119.29 E
Libya (EN)=Lībiyā [1] 31 If 27.00N 17.00 E
Libyan Desert (EN)=Lībīyah, Aş Şaḩrā' al- 30 Jf 24.00N 25.00 E
Licantén 56 Fe 34.59S 72.00W
Licata 14 Hm 37.06N 13.56 E
Lice 24 Ic 38.28N 40.39 E
Licenciado Matienzo 55 Cm 37.55S 58.54W
Lich 12 Kd 50.31N 8.50 E
Licheng → Jinhu 28 Eh 33.01N 119.01 E
Lichfield 9 Li 52.42N 1.48W
Lichinga 31 Kj 13.20S 35.20 E
Lichtenau 12 Kc 51.37N 8.54 E
Lichtenburg 37 De 26.08S 26.08 E
Lichtenfels 10 Hf 50.09N 11.04 E
Lichtenvoorde 12 Ic 51.59N 6.34 E
Licking River 44 Ff 39.06N 84.30W
Licosa, Punta- 14 Ij 40.15N 14.54 E
Licuare 37 Fc 17.54S 36.49 E
Licun → Laoshan 28 Ff 36.10N 120.25 E
Licungo 37 Fc 17.40S 37.22 E
Lida 19 Ce 53.56N 25.18 E
Lidan 8 Ef 58.31N 13.09 E
Liddel 9 Kf 55.04N 2.57W
Liddon Gulf 42 Gb 75.00N 113.30W
Liden 7 De 62.42N 16.48 E
Lidhorikion 15 Fk 38.32N 22.12 E
Lidhult 8 Eh 56.50N 13.26 E
Lidingö 7 Eg 59.22N 18.08 E
Lidköping 7 Cg 58.30N 13.10 E
Lido 34 Fc 12.54N 3.44 E
Lido, Venezia- 14 Ge 45.25N 12.22 E
Lido di Ostia 14 Gi 41.44N 12.16 E
Lidzbark 10 Pc 53.17N 19.49 E
Lidzbark Warmiński 10 Qb 54.09N 20.35 E
Lié 11 Df 48.00N 2.40W
Liebenau 12 Lb 52.36N 9.06 E
Liebig, Mount- 59 Gd 23.15S 131.20 E
Liechtenstein [1] 6 Gf 47.10N 9.30 E
Liège [3] 12 Hd 50.30N 5.40 E
Liège/Luik 6 Ge 50.38N 5.34 E
Lieksa 7 He 63.19N 30.01 E
Lielupe 7 Fh 57.03N 23.56 E
Lielvarde/Lielvārde 8 Kh 56.40N 24.49 E
Lielvārde/Lielvarde 8 Kh 56.40N 24.49 E
Lienen 12 Jb 52.09N 7.59 E
Lienz 14 Gd 46.50N 12.47 E
Liepaja/Liepāja 6 Id 56.35N 21.01 E
Liepāja/Liepaja 6 Id 56.35N 21.01 E
Liepajas, Ozero-/Liepājas Ezers 8 Ih 56.35N 20.35 E
Liepājas ezers/Liepaja, Ozero- 8 Ih 56.35N 20.35 E
Liepna 8 Lg 57.16N 27.35 E
Liepupe 8 Kg 57.22N 24.22 E
Lier/Lierre 11 Kc 51.08N 4.34 E
Lierbyen 8 De 59.47N 10.14 E
Lierneux 12 Hd 50.17N 5.48 E
Lierre/Lier 11 Kc 51.08N 4.34 E
Liesborn, Wadersloh- 12 Kc 51.43N 8.16 E
Lieser 10 Dg 49.55N 7.01 E
Liesing 14 Jc 47.20N 15.02 E
Liestal 14 Bc 47.29N 7.44 E
Lieşti 15 Kd 45.37N 27.31 E
Lieto 8 Jd 60.30N 22.27 E
Lietuvos Tarybu Socialistine Respublika/Litovskaja SSR [2] 19 Cd 56.00N 24.00 E
Lietuvos TSR=Lithuanian SSR (EN) [2] 19 Cd 56.00N 24.00 E
Lietvesi 8 Lc 61.30N 28.00 E
Lieurey 12 Ce 49.14N 0.29 E
Lieuvin 11 Ge 49.10N 0.30 E
Lievestuoreenjärvi 8 Lb 62.20N 26.10 E
Liévin 11 Id 50.25N 2.46 E
Lievre, Rivière du- 44 Jc 45.35N 75.25W
Liezen 14 Ic 47.34N 14.14 E
Lifford/Leifear 9 Fg 54.50N 7.29W
Li Fiord 42 Ia 80.17N 94.35W
Lifjell 8 Ce 59.30N 8.52 E
Lifou, Ile- 57 Hg 20.53S 167.13 E
Lifuka 65b Ba 19.48S 174.21W
Ligatne/Līgatne 8 Kg 57.07N 25.00 E
Līgatne/Ligatne 8 Kg 57.07N 25.00 E
Lighthouse Reef 49 De 17.20N 87.32W
Lignano Sabbiadoro 14 He 45.42N 13.09 E
Lignières 11 Ih 46.45N 2.10 E
Lignon 11 Ki 45.44N 4.08 E
Ligny-en-Barrois 11 Lf 48.41N 5.20 E
Ligonha 37 Fc 16.51S 39.09 E
Ligure, Mar-=Ligurian Sea (EN) 5 Gg 43.30N 9.00 E
Liguria [2] 14 Cf 44.30N 8.50 E
Ligurian Sea (EN)=Ligure, Mar- 5 Gg 43.30N 9.00 E
Lihir Group 57 Ge 3.05S 152.40 E
Lihme 8 Ch 56.36N 8.44 E
Lihoslavl 7 Ih 57.09N 35.29 E
Lihou Reefs and Cays 57 Gf 17.25S 151.40 E
Lihue 60 Oc 21.59N 159.22W
Lihula 7 Fg 58.44N 23.49 E
Liinahamari 7 Hb 69.40N 31.22 E
Lijiang (Dayan) 22 Mg 26.56N 100.15 E
Lijin 28 Ef 37.29N 118.15 E
Lika 14 Jf 44.46N 15.10 E
Lika 14 Jf 44.30N 15.30 E
Likasi 31 Jj 10.59S 26.43 E
Likati 36 Db 2.53N 24.03 E
Likati 36 Db 3.21N 23.53 E
Likénai/Likenaj 8 Kh 56.11N 24.42 E
Likenaj/Likėnai 8 Kh 56.11N 24.42 E
Likenäs 8 Ed 60.37N 13.02 E
Likhapani 25 Jc 27.19N 95.54 E
Likiep Atoll 57 Hc 9.53N 169.09 E
Likolo 36 Cc 0.43S 19.40 E
Likoma Island 36 Fe 12.04S 34.44 E
Likoto 36 Dc 1.10S 24.45 E
Likouala [3] 36 Cb 2.00N 17.30 E
Likouala 36 Cc 1.13S 16.48 E
Likouala aux Herbes 36 Cc 0.50S 17.11 E
Liku 64k Bb 19.02S 169.47W
L'Ile Rousse 11a Aa 42.38N 8.56 E
Lilibeo, Capo-→Boeo, Capo- 14 Gm 37.34N 12.41 E
Lilienfeld 14 Jb 48.01N 15.38 E
Lilienthal 12 Ka 53.08N 8.55 E
Lilla Edet 7 Cg 58.08N 12.08 E
Lille [Bel.] 12 Gc 51.14N 4.50 E
Lille [Fr.] 6 Ge 50.38N 3.04 E
Lille Bælt=Little Belt (EN) 5 Gd 55.20N 9.45 E
Lillebonne 11 Ge 49.31N 0.33 E
Lille Fiskebanke 8 Bh 56.56N 6.20 E
Lillehammer 7 Cf 61.08N 10.30 E
Lille Hellefiske Bank (EN) 41 Ge 65.05N 54.00W
Lillers 11 Id 50.34N 2.29 E
Lillesand 7 Bg 58.15N 8.24 E
Lillestrøm 8 De 59.57N 11.05 E
Lillhärdal 7 Df 61.51N 14.04 E
Lillie Glacier 66 Kf 70.45S 163.55 E
Lillo 13 Ie 39.43N 3.18W
Lillooet 42 Ff 50.42N 121.56W
Lillooet Range 46 Eb 50.00N 121.45W
Lillooet River 42 Fg 49.45N 122.10W
Lilongwe 31 Kj 13.59S 33.47 E
Liloy 26 He 8.08N 122.40 E
Lim [Afr.] 35 Bd 7.54N 15.46 E
Lim [Yugo.] 14 Ng 43.45N 19.13 E
Lima 13 Dc 41.41N 8.50W
Lima [2] 54 Cf 12.00S 76.35W
Lima [Mt.-U.S.] 46 Id 44.38N 112.36W
Lima [Oh.-U.S.] 43 Kc 40.43N 84.06W
Lima [Par.] 55 Df 23.54S 56.20W
Lima [Peru] 53 Ig 12.03S 77.03W
Lima [Swe.] 8 Ed 60.56N 13.21 E
Lima, Pulau-Pulau- 26 Gg 3.03S 107.24 E
Limagne 11 Jh 46.00N 3.20 E
Limah 24 Qj 25.56N 56.25 E
Liman [R.S.F.S.R.] 16 Oj 45.45N 47.14 E
Liman [Ukr.-U.S.S.R.] 15 Md 45.42N 29.46 E
Limanskoje 15 Mc 46.38N 29.54 E
Limari, Rio- 56 Fd 30.44S 71.43W
Limassol/Lemesós 23 Dc 34.40N 33.02 E
Limavady/Léim an Mhadaidh 9 Gf 55.03N 6.57W
Limay 12 Df 48.59N 1.44 E
Limay, Rio- 52 Ji 38.59S 68.00W
Limbara 14 Dj 40.51N 9.10 E
Limbaži 7 Fh 57.31N 24.47 E
Limbé 49 Kd 19.42N 72.24W
Limbe, Blantyre- 36 Gf 15.49S 35.03 E
Limbot 63b Cb 14.12S 167.34 E
Limboto 26 Hf 0.37N 122.57 E
Limbourg 12 Hd 50.37N 5.56 E
Limbourg/Limburg 11 Lc 51.05N 5.40 E
Limburg [Bel.] [3] 12 Hc 51.00N 5.30 E
Limburg [Neth.] [3] 12 Hc 51.14N 5.50 E
Limburg/Limbourg 11 Lc 51.05N 5.40 E
Limburg an der Lahn 10 Ef 50.23N 8.03 E
Limedsforsen 8 Ed 60.54N 13.23 E
Limeira 56 Kb 22.34S 47.24W
Limerick/Luimneach [2] 9 Ei 52.30N 9.00W
Limerick/Luimneach 6 Fe 52.40N 8.38W
Limestone, Haḑabat- 33 Fe 24.50N 32.00 E
Limfjorden 5 Gd 56.55N 9.10 E
Limia 13 Dc 41.41N 8.50W
Limingen 7 Cd 64.47N 13.36 E
Liminka 7 Fd 64.49N 25.29 E
Limmat 14 Cc 47.30N 8.15 E
Limmen Bight 59 Hb 14.45S 135.40 E
Limmen Bight River 59 Hc 15.15S 135.30 E
Limni 15 Gk 38.46N 23.19 E
Limnos=Lemnos (EN) 5 Ih 39.55N 25.15 E
Limoeiro 54 Ke 7.52S 35.27W
Limoges 6 Gf 45.51N 1.15 E
Limogne, Causse de- 11 Hj 44.20N 1.55 E
Limon 43 Gd 39.16N 103.41W
Limón [3] 49 Fi 10.00N 83.15W
Limón [C.R.] 39 Kh 10.00N 83.02W
Limón [Hond.] 49 Ef 15.52N 85.33W
Limone Piemonte 14 Bf 44.12N 7.34 E
Limousin 11 Hi 45.30N 1.50 E
Limousin, Plateau du- 11 Hi 45.50N 1.10 E
Limoux 11 Ik 43.04N 2.14 E
Limpopo 30 Jk 25.12S 33.32 E
Limu Ling 27 Ie 19.02N 109.43 E
Limuru 36 Gc 1.06S 36.39 E
Līnah 24 Jh 28.42N 43.48 E
Lin'an 27 Ke 30.14N 119.39 E
Linapacan 26 Gd 11.27N 119.49 E
Linares [Chile] 53 Ii 35.51S 71.36W
Linares [Mex.] 47 Ed 24.52N 99.34W
Linares [Sp.] 13 If 38.05N 3.38W
Linares Viejo 55 Bf 23.09S 61.46W
Linaro, Capo- 14 Fh 42.02N 11.50 E
Lincang 22 Mg 23.48N 100.04 E
Lincheng 28 Cf 37.26N 114.34 E
Lincheng→Xuecheng 28 Dg 34.48N 117.14 E
Lincoln [3] 9 Mh 53.20N 0.30W
Lincoln [Arg.] 56 Hd 34.52S 61.32W
Lincoln [Eng.-U.K.] 9 Mh 53.14N 0.33W
Lincoln [Il.-U.S.] 45 Lf 40.09N 89.22W
Lincoln [Nb.-U.S.] 39 Je 40.48N 96.42W
Lincoln [N.Z.] 62 Ee 43.38S 172.29 E
Lincoln, Mount- 45 Cg 39.21N 106.07W
Lincoln City 46 Cd 44.59N 124.01W
Lincoln Sea 67 Ne 83.00N 56.00W
Lincolnshire [3] 9 Mh 53.00N 0.10W
Lindashalvøya 8 Ad 60.40N 5.15 E
Lindau 10 Fi 47.33N 9.41 E
Linde [Neth.] 12 Hb 52.49N 5.52 E
Linde [R.S.F.S.R.] 20 Hd 64.59N 124.36 E
Linden [Guy.] 54 Gb 6.00N 58.18W
Linden [Tn.-U.S.] 44 Dh 35.37N 87.50W
Lindenows Fjord 41 Hf 60.25N 43.00W
Linderödsåsen 8 Ei 55.53N 13.56 E
Lindesberg 7 Dg 59.35N 15.15 E
Lindesnes 5 Gd 58.00N 7.02 E
Lindhorst 12 Lb 52.22N 9.17 E
Lindhos 15 Lm 36.06N 28.04 E
Lindi [3] 36 Gd 9.30S 38.20 E
Lindi 31 Ki 10.00S 39.43 E
Lindi 30 Jh 0.33N 25.05 E
Lindis Pass 62 Cf 44.35S 169.39 E
Lindlar 12 Jc 51.01N 7.23 E
Lindome 8 Eg 57.34N 12.05 E
Lindong→Bairin Zuoqi 27 Kc 43.59N 119.22 E
Lindsay [Ca.-U.S.] 46 Fh 36.12N 119.05W
Lindsay [Ont.-Can.] 44 Hc 44.21N 78.44W
Lindsdal 8 Gh 56.44N 16.18 E
Line Islands 57 Le 0.01S 157.00W
Linfen 27 Jd 36.03N 111.32 E
Lingayen 22 Oh 16.01N 120.14 E
Lingayen Gulf 26 Hc 16.15N 120.14 E
Lingbi 28 Dh 33.33N 117.33 E
Lingbo 7 Df 61.03N 16.41 E
Lingchuan 28 Bg 35.46N 113.16 E
Lingen (Ems) 10 Dd 52.31N 7.19 E
Lingfield 12 Bc 51.10N 0.01W
Lingga, Kepulauan-=Lingga Archipelago (EN) 21 Mj 0.02S 104.35 E
Lingga, Pulau- 26 Dg 0.12S 104.35 E
Lingga Archipelago (EN)=Lingga, Kepulauan- 21 Mj 0.02S 104.35 E
Linghed 8 Fd 60.47N 15.51 E
Lingling 27 Jf 26.24N 111.41 E
Lingomo 36 Db 0.38N 21.59 E
Lingqiu 28 Ce 39.26N 114.14 E
Lingshan 27 Ig 22.30N 109.17 E
Lingshan Dao 28 Fg 35.45N 120.10 E
Lingshi 28 Af 36.50N 111.46 E
Lingshou 28 Ce 38.18N 114.22 E
Linguère 31 Fg 15.24N 15.07W
Lingwu 27 Id 38.05N 106.20 E
Lingxian 28 Df 37.20N 116.35 E
Lingyuan 28 Ed 41.15N 119.23 E
Linh, Ngoc- 21 Mh 15.04N 107.59 E
Linhai 27 La 51.36N 124.22 E
Linhai (Taizhou) 27 Lf 28.52N 121.08 E
Linhares 54 Jg 19.25S 40.04W
Linhe 27 Ic 40.49N 107.28 E
Linhuaiguan 28 Dh 32.54N 117.39 E
Linjiang 28 Id 41.49N 126.55 E
Linköping 6 Hd 58.25N 15.37 E
Linkou 27 Nb 45.18N 130.18 E
Linkuva 8 Jh 56.02N 23.58 E
Linlü Shan 28 Bf 36.02N 113.42 E
Linn, Mount- 46 Df 40.03N 122.48W
Linneryd 8 Fh 56.40N 15.07 E
Linnhe, Loch- 9 He 56.37N 5.25W
Linnich 12 Id 50.59N 6.16 E
Linosa 14 Go 35.50N 12.50 E
Linovo 10 Ud 52.28N 24.35 E
Linqing 27 Kd 36.48N 115.49 E
Linqu 28 Ef 36.31N 118.32 E
Linquan 28 Ch 33.04N 115.16 E
Linru 28 Bg 34.10N 112.51 E
Lins 56 Kb 21.40S 49.45W
Linsell 8 Eb 62.09N 13.53 E
Linshu (Xiazhuang) 28 Eg 34.56N 118.38 E
Linslade 12 Bc 51.55N 0.40W
Linta 37 Ge 25.02S 44.05 E
Lintao 27 Hd 35.20N 104.00 E
Linthal 14 Cd 46.55N 9.00 E
Linton [Eng.-U.K.] 12 Cb 52.06N 0.16 E
Linton [N.D.-U.S.] 45 Fc 46.16N 100.14W
Linxi [China] 22 Ne 43.36N 118.02 E
Linxi [China] 28 Ee 39.42N 118.26 E
Linxia 22 Mf 35.28N 102.59 E
Linxian 27 Jd 37.57N 111.00 E
Linxiang 28 Bj 29.29N 113.28 E
Linyi [China] 28 Df 37.11N 116.51 E
Linyi [China]' 27 Kd 35.09N 118.15 E
Linz 6 Hf 48.18N 14.18 E
Linze (Shahezhen) 27 Hd 39.10N 100.21 E
Lion, Golfe du-=Lion, Gulf of- (EN) 5 Gg 43.00N 4.00 E
Lion, Gulf of- (EN)=Lion, Golfe du- 5 Gg 43.00N 4.00 E
Lions Den 37 Ec 17.16S 30.02 E
Lion-sur-Mer 12 Be 49.18N 0.19W
Lioppa 26 Ih 7.40S 126.00 E
Lios Mór/Lismore 9 Fi 52.08N 7.55W
Lios na gCearrbhach/Lisburn 9 Gg 54.31N 6.03W
Lios Tuathail/Listovel 9 Di 52.27N 9.29W
Liouesso 36 Cb 1.02N 15.43 E
Lipa 26 Hd 13.57N 121.10 E
Lipany 10 Qg 49.10N 20.58 E
Lipari 14 Il 38.30N 14.55 E
Lipari 14 Il 38.28N 14.57 E
Lipari Islands (EN)=Eolie o Lipari, Isole- 5 Hh 38.35N 14.55 E
Lipeck 6 Je 52.37N 39.35 E
Lipeckaja Oblast [3] 19 De 52.45N 39.10 E
Lipenská přehradní nádrž 10 Kh 48.45N 14.05 E
Liperi 7 Ge 62.32N 29.22 E
Lipez, Cordillera de- 54 Eh 22.00S 66.45W
Liphook 12 Bc 51.04N 0.48W
Lipkani 15 Ja 48.13N 26.48 E
Lipljan 15 Eg 42.32N 21.08 E
Lipno 10 Pd 52.51N 19.10 E
Lipova 15 Ec 46.05N 21.42 E
Lipovcy 20 Ih 44.15N 131.45 E
Lippborg, Lippetal- 12 Kc 51.40N 8.02 E
Lippe 10 Ce 51.39N 6.38 E
Lipper Bergland 12 Kb 52.05N 8.57 E
Lippetal 12 Kc 51.40N 8.13 E
Lippetal-Eickelborn 12 Kc 51.39N 8.13 E
Lippetal-Lippborg 12 Kc 51.40N 8.02 E
Lippischer Wald 12 Kc 51.56N 8.45 E
Lippstadt 10 Ee 51.40N 8.21 E
Lipsko 10 Re 51.09N 21.39 E
Lipsoi 15 Jl 37.20N 26.45 E
Liptako 30 Hg 14.15N 0.02 E
Liptovský Mikuláš 10 Pg 49.05N 19.38 E
Lira 36 Fb 2.15N 32.54 E
Liranga 36 Cc 0.40S 17.36 E
Liri 14 Hi 41.25N 13.52 E
Liria 13 Le 39.38N 0.36W
Lis 13 De 39.53N 8.58W
Lisa 15 Cf 43.08N 19.42 E
Lisac 15 Eg 42.45N 21.56 E
Lisakovsk 19 Ge 52.33N 62.28 E
Lisala 31 Jh 2.09N 21.31 E
Lisboa [2] 13 Ce 39.00N 9.08W
Lisboa=Lisbon (EN) 6 Fh 38.43N 9.08W
Lisbon 45 Hc 46.27N 97.41W
Lisbon (EN)=Lisboa 6 Fh 38.43N 9.08W
Lisbon Canyon (EN) 13 Cf 38.20N 9.20W
Lisburn/Lios na gCearrbhach 9 Gg 54.31N 6.03W
Lisburne, Cape- 40 Fc 68.52N 166.14W
Liscannor Bay/Bá Thuath Reanna 9 Di 52.55N 9.25W
Lisec 10 Uh 48.48N 24.45 E
Li Shan 28 Ag 35.25N 111.58 E
Lishi 27 Jd 37.29N 111.08 E
Lishu 28 Hc 43.19N 124.20 E
Lishui 27 Kf 28.30N 119.55 E
Lisianski Island 57 Jb 26.02N 174.00W
Lisičansk 19 Df 48.53N 38.28 E
Lisieux 11 Ge 49.09N 0.14 E
Liska 15 Dh 41.19N 20.58 E
L'Isle-Adam 12 Ee 49.07N 2.14 E
L'Isle-Jourdain 11 Hk 43.37N 1.05 E
L'Isle sur-la-Sorgue 11 Lk 43.55N 5.03 E
Lismore 58 Gg 28.48S 153.17 E
Lismore/Lios Mór 9 Fi 52.08N 7.55W
Liss 24 Hg 31.14N 38.31 E
Liss 12 Bc 51.02N 0.54W
List 10 Ea 55.01N 8.26 E
Lista 8 Bf 58.10N 6.40 E
Listafjorden 8 Bf 58.10N 6.35 E
Lister, Mount- 66 Kf 78.04S 162.41 E
Lištica 14 Lg 43.23N 17.39 E
Listovel/Lios Tuathail 9 Di 52.27N 9.29W
Listowel 44 Gd 43.44N 80.57W
Liswarta 10 Pe 51.06N 19.01 E
Lit 8 Fa 63.19N 14.49 E
Litang [China] 27 Ig 23.12N 109.05 E
Litang [China] 27 He 30.02N 100.18 E
Litani Rivier 54 Hc 3.18N 54.06W
Litchfield 45 Id 45.08N 94.31W
Lithgow 58 Gh 33.29S 150.09 E
Lithinon, Ákra- 15 Ho 34.55N 24.44 E
Lithuania (EN) 5 Id 56.00N 24.00 E
Lithuanian SSR (EN)=Lietuvos TSR [2] 19 Cd 56.00N 24.00 E
Litókhoron 15 Fi 40.06N 22.30 E
Litoměřice 10 Kf 50.32N 14.08 E
Litovel 10 Ng 49.43N 17.05 E
Litovko 20 Ig 49.17N 135.10 E
Litovskaja Sovetskaja Socialističeskaja Respublika [2] 19 Cd 56.00N 24.00 E
Litovskaja SSR/Lietuvos Tarybu Socialistine Respublika [2] 19 Cd 56.00N 24.00 E
Little Abaco Island 47 Ic 26.53N 77.43W
Little Abitibi River 44 Ha 49.29N 79.32W
Little Aden 23 Fg 12.45N 44.52 E
Little America 46 Kf 41.32N 109.47W
Little Andaman 21 Lh 10.45N 92.30 E
Little Bahama Bank (EN) 47 Ic 26.30N 78.00W
Little Barrier Island 62 Fb 36.10S 175.05 E
Little Beaver Creek 45 Ec 46.17N 103.56W
Little Belt (EN)=Lille Bælt 5 Gd 55.20N 9.45 E
Little Belt Mountains 46 Jc 46.45N 110.35W
Little Blue River 45 Hg 39.41N 96.40W
Little Bow River 46 Ib 49.53N 112.29W
Little Carpathians (EN)=Malé Karpaty 10 Nh 48.30N 17.20 E
Little Cayman 47 He 19.41N 80.03W
Little Colorado River 38 Hc 36.11N 111.48W
Little Current 42 Jg 45.58N 81.56W
Little Current 42 Jf 50.57N 84.36W
Little Dry Creek 46 Lc 47.21N 106.22W
Little Exuma Island 49 Jb 23.27N 75.37W
Little Falls 43 Ib 45.59N 94.21W
Littlefield 45 Ej 33.55N 102.20W
Little Fort 46 Ea 51.25N 120.12W
Little Grand Rapids 42 Hf 52.02N 95.25W
Little Halibut Bank 9 Lc 58.20N 1.15W
Littlehampton 12 Bd 50.48N 0.32W
Little Inagua Island 47 Jd 21.30N 73.00W
Little Karroo (EN)=Klein-Karoo 37 Cf 33.42S 21.20 E
Little Missouri 38 Ie 47.30N 102.25W
Little Namaland (EN)=Namakwaland 37 Be 29.00S 17.00 E
Little Nicobar 25 Ig 7.20N 93.40 E
Little Ouse 9 Ni 52.30N 0.22 E
Littleport 12 Cb 52.27N 0.18 E
Little Powder River 46 Md 45.28N 105.20W
Little Quill Lake 46 Ma 51.55N 104.05W
Little River 62 Ee 43.46S 172.47 E
Little Rock 39 Jf 34.44N 92.15W
Little Rocky Mountains 46 Kb 48.00N 108.45W

Index Symbols

- [1] Independent Nation
- [2] State, Region
- [3] District, County
- [4] Municipality
- [5] Colony, Dependency
- Continent
- Physical Region
- Historical or Cultural Region
- Mount, Mountain
- Volcano
- Hill
- Mountains, Mountain Range
- Hills, Escarpment
- Plateau, Upland
- Pass, Gap
- Plain, Lowland
- Delta
- Salt Flat
- Valley, Canyon
- Crater, Cave
- Karst Features
- Depression
- Polder
- Desert, Dunes
- Forest, Woods
- Heath, Steppe
- Oasis
- Cape, Point
- Coast, Beach
- Cliff
- Peninsula
- Isthmus
- Sandbank
- Island
- Atoll
- Rock, Reef
- Islands, Archipelago
- Rocks, Reefs
- Coral Reef
- Well, Spring
- Geyser
- River, Stream
- Waterfall Rapids
- River Mouth, Estuary
- Lake
- Salt Lake
- Intermittent Lake
- Reservoir
- Swamp, Pond
- Canal
- Glacier
- Ice Shelf, Pack Ice
- Ocean
- Sea
- Gulf, Bay
- Strait, Fjord
- Lagoon
- Bank
- Seamount
- Tablemount
- Ridge
- Shelf
- Basin
- Escarpment, Sea Scarp
- Fracture
- Trench, Abyss
- National Park, Reserve
- Point of Interest
- Recreation Site
- Cave, Cavern
- Historic Site
- Ruins
- Wall, Walls
- Church, Abbey
- Temple
- Scientific Station
- Airport
- Port
- Lighthouse
- Mine
- Tunnel
- Dam, Bridge

Little Scarcies	34	Cd	8.51N	13.09W
Little Sioux River	45	Hf	41.49N	96.04W
Little Sitkin	40a	Cb	51.55N	178.30 E
Little Smoky	42	Fe	55.39N	117.37W
Little Snake River	45	Bf	40.27N	108.26W
Littleton [Co.-U.S.]	45	Dg	39.37N	105.01W
Littleton [N.H.-U.S.]	44	Lc	44.18N	71.46W
Little White River [Ont.-Can.]	44	Fb	46.15N	83.00W
Little White River [S.D.-U.S.]	45	Fe	43.44N	100.40W
Littoral	34	He	4.30N	10.00 E
Litvínov	10	Jf	50.36N	13.36 E
Liuba	27	Ie	33.39N	106.53 E
Liuhe	27	Mc	42.16N	125.45 E
Liu He [China]	28	Gd	41.48N	122.43 E
Liu He [China]	28	Ic	42.46N	126.13 E
Liuheng Dao	28	Gj	29.43N	122.08 E
Liujia Xia	27	Hd	35.50N	103.00 E
Liukang Tenggaja, Kepulauan-	26	Gh	6.45 S	118.50 E
Liupai → Tian'e	27	If	25.05N	107.12 E
Liupan Shan	27	Id	35.40N	106.15 E
Liuqu He	28	Fd	40.10N	120.15 E
Liuwa Plain	36	De	14.27 S	22.25 E
Liuyang	28	Bj	28.09N	113.38 E
Liuzhangzhen → Yuanqu	27	Jd	35.19N	111.44 E
Liuzhou	22	Mg	24.22N	109.20 E
Līvāni/Livány	7	Gh	56.22N	26.12 E
Livanjsko Polje	14	Kg	43.51N	16.50 E
Livany/Līvāni	7	Gh	56.22N	26.12 E
Livarot	12	Ce	49.01N	0.09 E
Livengood	40	Jc	65.32N	148.33W
Livenza	14	Ge	45.35N	12.51 E
Livenzi	15	Ge	44.14N	23.47 E
Live Oak	44	Fj	30.18N	82.59W
Livermore	46	Eh	37.41N	121.46W
Livermore, Mount-	45	Dk	30.37N	104.08W
Liverpool [Eng.-U.K.]	6	Fe	53.25N	2.55W
Liverpool [N.S.-Can.]	42	Lh	44.02N	64.43W
Liverpool, Cape -	42	Jb	73.38N	78.05W
Liverpool Bay [Can.]	42	Ec	70.00N	129.00W
Liverpool Bay [Eng.-U.K.]	9	Jh	53.30N	3.16W
Liverpool Range	59	Kf	31.40 S	150.30 E
Liverpool River	59	Gb	12.00 S	134.00 E
Livigno	14	Ed	46.32N	10.04 E
Livingston [Guat.]	49	Cf	15.50N	88.45W
Livingston [Mt.-U.S.]	43	Eb	45.40N	110.34W
Livingston [Newf.-Can.]	42	Kf	53.40N	66.10W
Livingston [Tn.-U.S.]	44	Eg	36.23N	85.19W
Livingston [Tx.-U.S.]	45	Ik	30.43N	94.56W
Livingston, Lake-	45	Ik	30.45N	95.15W
Livingstone, Chutes de- = Livingstone Falls (EN)	30	Ii	4.50 S	14.30 E
Livingstone Falls (EN) = Livingstone, Chutes de-	30	Ii	4.50 S	14.30 E
Livingstone Memorial	36	Fe	12.19 S	30.18 E
Livingstone Mountains	36	Fd	9.45 S	34.20 E
Livingstonia	36	Fe	10.36 S	34.07 E
Livingston Island	66	Qe	62.36 S	60.30W
Livno	14	Lg	43.50N	17.01 E
Livny	19	De	52.28N	37.37 E
Livonia	44	Fd	42.25N	83.23W
Livonia (EN)=Livonija	5	Id	58.50N	27.30 E
Livonija=Livonia (EN)	5	Id	58.50N	27.30 E
Livorno=Leghorn (EN)	6	Hg	43.33N	10.19 E
Livradois, Monts du-	11	Ji	45.30N	3.33 E
Livramento do Brumado	54	Jf	13.39 S	41.50W
Livron-sur-Drôme	11	Kj	44.46N	4.51 E
Liwale	36	Gd	9.46 S	37.56 E
Liwiec	10	Rd	52.35N	21.33 E
Liwonde	36	Gf	15.01 S	35.13 E
Lixi	27	Hf	26.21N	102.03 E
Lixian [China]	27	Ie	34.11N	105.02 E
Lixian [China]	27	Jf	29.40N	111.45 E
Lixian [China]	28	Ce	38.29N	115.34 E
Lixin	28	Dh	33.09N	116.12 E
Lixoúrion	15	Dk	38.12N	20.26 E
Liyang	28	Ei	31.26N	119.29 E
Lizard	9	Hl	49.57N	5.13W
Lizard Point	5	Ff	49.56N	5.13W
Lizhu	28	Fj	29.58N	120.26 E
Lizy sur Ourcq	12	Fe	49.01N	3.02 E
Ljady	8	Mf	58.35N	28.55 E
Ljahoviči	16	Ec	53.04N	26.15 E
Ljahovskije Ostrova = Lyakhov Islands (EN)	21	Qb	73.30N	141.00 E
Ljalja	17	Jg	59.10N	61.30 E
Ljamin	17	Of	61.18N	71.45 E
Ljangar	18	Ed	40.23N	65.59 E
Ljangasovo	7	Lg	58.33N	49.29 E
Ljapin	17	Je	63.38N	61.58 E
Ljaskelja	8	Nc	61.39N	31.03 E
Ljaskovec	15	If	43.06N	25.43 E
Ljig	15	De	44.14N	20.15 E
Ljuban [Bye.-U.S.S.R.]	16	Ec	52.48N	27.59 E
Ljuban [R.S.F.S.R.]	7	Hg	59.22N	31.13 E
Ljubar	16	Ee	49.55N	27.44 E
Ljubašcevka	15	Nb	47.50N	30.07 E
Ljubelj	14	Id	46.26N	14.16 E
Ljubercy	19	Dd	55.40N	37.55 E
Ljubesŏv	10	Ve	51.45N	25.37 E
Ljubim	7	Jg	58.22N	40.41 E
Ljubimec	15	Jh	41.50N	26.05 E
Ljubinje	14	Mh	42.57N	18.06 E
Ljubišnja	15	Cf	43.20N	19.07 E
Ljubljana	6	Hf	46.02N	14.30 E
Ljuboml	16	Cd	51.15N	23.59 E
Ljubotin	16	Ie	49.59N	35.55 E
Ljubovija	15	Ce	44.12N	19.22 E
Ljubuški	14	Lg	43.12N	17.33 E
Ljubytino	7	Hg	58.50N	33.25 E
Ljudinovo	19	De	53.51N	34.28 E
Ljugarn	7	Eh	57.19N	18.42 E
Ljungan	5	Hc	62.19N	17.23 E
Ljungaverk	8	Gb	62.29N	16.03 E
Ljungby	7	Ch	56.50N	13.56 E
Ljungbyholm	8	Gh	56.38N	16.10 E
Ljungdalen	7	Ce	62.51N	12.47 E
Ljungsbro	8	Ff	58.31N	15.30 E
Ljungskile	8	Df	58.14N	11.55 E
Ljusdal	7	Df	61.50N	16.05 E
Ljusnan	5	Hc	61.12N	17.08 E
Ljusne	7	Df	61.13N	17.08 E
Ljusterö	8	He	59.30N	18.35 E
Ljuta	8	Mf	58.33N	28.45 E
Llandilo	9	Jj	51.53N	3.59W
Llandovery	9	Jj	51.59N	3.48W
Llandrindod Wells	9	Ji	52.15N	3.23W
Llandudno	9	Jh	53.19N	3.49W
Llanelli	9	Ij	51.42N	4.10W
Llanes	13	Ha	43.25N	4.45W
Llangefni	9	Ih	53.16N	4.18W
Llangollen	9	Ji	52.58N	3.10W
Llano	45	Gk	30.45N	98.41W
Llano Estacado	38	If	33.30N	102.40W
Llano River	45	Gk	30.35N	98.25W
Llanos	52	Je	5.00N	70.00W
Llanos de Sonora	47	Bc	28.20N	111.00W
Llanquihue, Lago-	56	Ff	41.08 S	72.48W
Llata	54	Ce	9.25 S	76.47W
Lleida/Lérida	13	Mc	41.37N	0.37 E
Llerena	13	Ff	38.14N	6.01W
Lleyn	9	Ii	52.54N	4.30W
Llica	54	Eg	19.52 S	68.16W
Llivia	13	Nb	42.28N	1.59 E
Llobregat	13	Oc	41.19N	2.09 E
Lloret de Mar	13	Oc	41.42N	2.51 E
Llorona, Punta-	49	Fi	8.37N	83.44W
Llorri/Orri, Pic d'-	13	Nb	42.23N	1.12 E
Lloydminster	42	Gf	53.17N	110.00W
Lluchmayor	13	Oe	39.29N	2.54 E
Llullaillaco, Volcán-	52	Jh	24.43 S	68.33W
Lo	63b	Ca	13.21 S	166.38 E
Loa	46	Jg	38.24N	111.38W
Loa, Río-	56	Fb	21.26 S	70.04W
Loanatit, Pointe-	63b	Dd	19.21 S	169.14 E
Loange	30	Ji	4.17 S	20.02 E
Loango	36	Bc	4.39 S	11.48 E
Loano	14	Cf	44.08N	8.15 E
Loban	7	Mh	56.59N	51.12 E
Lobatse	31	Jk	25.13 S	25.41 E
Löbau/Lubij	10	Ke	51.06N	14.40 E
Lobaye	30	Ih	3.41N	18.35 E
Lobaye	35	Be	4.00N	17.40 E
Lobenstein	10	Hf	50.27N	11.39 E
Lobería	56	Ie	38.09 S	58.47W
Łobez	10	Lc	53.39N	15.36 E
Lobito	31	Ij	12.22 S	13.34 E
Lobo	34	Dd	6.02N	6.47W
Lobos	56	Ie	35.11 S	59.06W
Lobos	32	Ed	28.45N	13.49W
Lobos, Cabo-	48	Cc	29.55N	112.45W
Lobos, Cay-	49	Ib	22.24N	77.32W
Lobos, Cayo-	48	Ph	18.22N	87.24W
Lobos, Isla-	48	Dd	27.20N	110.36W
Lobos, Islas de-	48	Kg	21.27N	97.15W
Lobos de Afuera, Islas-	54	Be	6.57 S	80.42W
Lobos de Tierra, Isla-	54	Be	6.27 S	80.52W
Lobva	19	Gd	59.12N	60.30 E
Łobżonka	10	Nc	53.07N	17.18 E
Locana	14	Be	45.25N	7.27 E
Locarno	14	Cd	46.10N	8.48 E
Loch Aillionn/Allen, Lough-	9	Eg	54.08N	8.08W
Loch Arabhach/Arrow, Lough-	9	Eg	54.05N	8.20W
Lochboisdale	9	Fd	57.09N	7.19W
Loch Cairlinn/Carlingford Lough	9	Gg	54.05N	6.14W
Loch Ce/Key, Lough-	9	Eg	54.00N	8.15W
Loch Coirib/Corrib, Lought	9	Dh	53.05N	9.10W
Loch Con/Conn, Lough-	9	Dg	54.04N	9.20W
Loch Cuan/Strangford Lough	9	Hg	54.26N	5.36W
Loch Deirgeirt/Derg, Lough-	9	Ei	53.00N	8.20W
Lochearnhead	9	Ie	56.23N	4.18W
Loch Éirne Iochtair/Lower Lough Erne	9	Fg	54.30N	7.50W
Loch Éirne Uachtair/Upper Lough Erne	9	Fg	54.20N	7.30W
Lochem	12	Ib	52.10N	6.25 E
Loches	11	Gg	47.08N	1.00 E
Loch Feabhail/Foyle, Lough-	9	Ff	55.05N	7.10W
Loch Garman/Wexford	6	Fe	52.20N	6.27W
Loch Garman/Wexford	9	Gi	52.20N	6.40W
Lochgilphead	9	He	56.03N	5.26W
Loch Hinninn/Ennell, Lough-	9	Fh	53.28N	7.24W
Lochinver	9	Hc	58.09N	5.15W
Loch Lao/Belfast Lough	9	Hg	54.40N	5.50W
Loch Léin/Leane, Lough-	9	Di	52.05N	9.35W
Loch Leven	9	Je	56.13N	3.10W
Loch Long	9	Ie	56.04N	4.50W
Lochmaddy	9	Fd	57.36N	7.10W
Loch Measca/Mask, Lough-	9	Dh	53.35N	9.20W
Lochnagar	9	Je	56.55N	3.10W
Loch nEathach/Neagh, Lough-	5	Fe	54.38N	6.24W
Loch Ness	9	Id	57.15N	4.30W
Łochów	10	Rd	52.32N	21.48 E
Loch Pholl an Phúca/Poulaphuca Reservoir	9	Gh	53.10N	6.30W
Loch Rí/Ree, Lough-	9	Fh	53.35N	8.00W
Lochsa River	46	Hc	46.08N	115.36W
Loch Síleann/Sheelin, Lough-	9	Fh	53.48N	7.20W
Loch Suili/Swilly, Lough-	9	Ff	55.10N	7.38W
Loch Uí Ghadra/Gara, Lough-	9	Eh	53.55N	8.30W
Lochy	9	He	56.49N	5.06W
Lochy, Loch-	9	Ie	56.55N	4.55W
Lockerbie	9	Jf	55.07N	3.22W
Lockhart	45	Hl	29.53N	97.41W
Lock Haven	44	Ie	41.09N	77.28W
Löcknitz	10	Hc	53.07N	11.16 E
Lockport	44	Hd	43.11N	78.39W
Locminé	11	Dg	47.53N	2.50W
Locri	14	Kl	38.14N	16.16 E
Lod	24	Fg	31.58N	34.54 E
Lodalskåpa	7	Bf	61.47N	7.12 E
Loddon	12	Db	52.32N	1.29 E
Loddon River	59	Ig	36.41 S	143.55 E
Lodejnoje Pole	19	Dc	60.44N	33.33 E
Lodève	11	Jk	43.43N	3.19 E
Lodi [Ca.-U.S.]	46	Eg	38.08N	121.16W
Lodi [It.]	14	De	45.19N	9.30 E
Lødingen	7	Db	68.25N	16.00 E
Lodja	31	Ji	3.29 S	23.26 E
Lodosa	13	Jb	42.25N	2.05W
Lödöse	8	Ef	58.02N	12.08 E
Lodwar	31	Kh	3.07N	35.36 E
Łódź	6	He	51.46N	19.30 E
Łódź	10	Pe	51.45N	19.30 E
Loei	25	Ke	17.32N	101.34 E
Loeriesfontein	37	Bf	30.56 S	19.26 E
Lofanga	65b	Ba	19.50 S	174.33W
Loffa	30	Fh	6.36N	11.05W
Loffa	34	Dd	7.45N	10.00W
Lofoten	5	Hb	68.30N	15.00 E
Lofoten Basin (EN)	5	Ga	70.00N	4.00 E
Lofsdalen	8	Eb	62.07N	13.16 E
Loftahammar	8	Gg	57.52N	16.40 E
Loga	34	Fc	13.37N	3.14 E
Logan [N.M.-U.S.]	45	Ei	35.22N	103.25W
Logan [Oh.-U.S.]	44	Ff	39.32N	82.24W
Logan [Ut.-U.S.]	43	Ec	41.44N	111.50W
Logan [W.V.-U.S.]	44	Gg	37.52N	81.58W
Logan, Mount- [Can.]	38	Ec	60.34N	140.24W
Logan, Mount- [Wa.-U.S.]	46	Eb	48.32N	120.57W
Logan Martin Lake	44	Di	33.40N	86.15W
Logan Mountains	42	Ed	61.00N	128.00W
Logansport	44	De	40.45N	86.21W
Loge	30	Ii	7.49 S	13.06 E
Logojsk	8	Lj	54.12N	27.57 E
Logone	30	Ig	12.06N	15.02 E
Logone Birni	34	Ic	11.47N	15.06 E
Logone Occidental	35	Bd	8.40N	16.00 E
Logone Occidental	35	Bd	9.07N	16.26 E
Logone Oriental	35	Bd	8.20N	16.30 E
Logone Oriental	35	Bd	9.07N	16.26 E
Logroño	13	Jb	42.15N	2.30W
Logroño [Arg.]	55	Bi	29.30 S	61.42W
Logroño [Sp.]	13	Jb	42.28N	2.27W
Logrosán	13	Ge	39.20N	5.29W
Løgstør	7	Bh	56.58N	9.15 E
Logudoro	14	Cj	40.35N	8.40 E
Løgumkloster	8	Ci	55.03N	8.57 E
Lögurinn	7a	Cb	65.15N	14.30W
Lohja/Lojo	7	Ff	60.15N	24.05 E
Lohjanjärvi	8	Jd	60.15N	23.55 E
Lohjanselkä/Lojo åsen	8	Kd	60.15N	24.10 E
Löhme	12	Kc	51.41N	8.42 E
Löhne	10	Ed	52.11N	8.41 E
Lohne	12	Kb	52.40N	8.14 E
Lohra	12	Kd	50.44N	8.38 E
Lohr am Main	10	Ff	49.59N	9.35 E
Lohusuu/Lokusu	8	Lf	58.53N	27.01 E
Lohvica	16	Hd	50.22N	33.15 E
Loi, Phou-	25	Kd	20.16N	103.12 E
Loi-Kaw	25	Je	19.41N	97.13 E
Loile	36	Dc	0.52 S	20.12 E
Loimaa	7	Ff	60.51N	23.03 E
Loimijoki	8	Jc	61.13N	22.38 E
Loing	11	If	48.23N	2.48 E
Loir	11	Fg	47.33N	0.32W
Loir, Vaux du-	11	Gg	47.45N	0.25 E
Loire	11	Ji	45.30N	4.00 E
Loire	5	Ff	47.16N	2.11W
Loire, Canal latéral à la-	11	Jh	46.29N	3.59 E
Loire, Val de-	11	Hg	47.40N	1.35 E
Loire-Atlantique	11	Eg	47.15N	1.50W
Loiret	11	Ig	47.55N	2.20 E
Loir-et-Cher	11	Hg	47.30N	1.30 E
Loisach	10	Hi	47.56N	11.27 E
Loison	12	He	49.30N	5.17 E
Loja [Ec.]	53	If	4.00 S	79.13W
Loja [Sp.]	13	Hg	37.10N	4.09W
Lojo/Lohja	7	Ff	60.15N	24.05 E
Lojo åsen/Lohjanselkä	8	Kd	60.15N	24.10 E
Loka	35	Ee	4.16N	31.01 E
Lokači	10	Uf	50.43N	24.44 E
Lokalahti	8	Id	60.41N	21.28 E
Lokandu	36	Ec	2.31 S	25.47 E
Lokantekojärvi	7	Gc	68.56N	27.40 E
Lokbatan	16	Pi	40.21N	49.42 E
Lokčim	17	Ef	61.48N	51.45 E
Løken	8	De	59.48N	11.29 E
Lokeren	11	Jc	51.06N	4.00 E
Lokichar	36	Gb	2.23N	35.39 E
Lokichokio	36	Fb	4.12N	34.21 E
Lokitaung	36	Gb	4.16N	35.45 E
Løkken [Den.]	8	Cg	57.22N	9.43 E
Løkken [Nor.]	7	Be	63.05N	9.36 E
Loknja	7	Hh	56.49N	30.09 E
Loko	34	Gd	8.00N	7.50 E
Lokoja	34	Gd	7.48N	6.44 E
Lokomo	34	Ie	2.41N	15.19 E
Lokoro	36	Cc	1.43 S	18.23 E
Lokossa	34	Fd	6.38N	1.43 E
Lokot	16	Ic	52.33N	34.31 E
Lokoti	34	Hd	6.22N	14.20 E
Loksa	7	Fg	59.34N	25.44 E
Loks Land	42	Ld	62.27N	64.30W
Lokuru	63a	Cc	8.35 S	157.20 E
Lokusu/Lohusuu	8	Lf	58.53N	27.01 E
Lokwa Kangole	36	Gb	3.32N	35.54 E
Lol	30	Jh	9.13N	28.59 E
Lola	34	Dd	7.48N	8.32W
Lolimi	35	Ee	4.35N	33.59 E
Loliondo	36	Gc	2.03 S	35.37 E
Lolland	5	He	54.45N	11.30 E
Lollar	12	Kd	50.38N	8.42 E
Lolo	36	Db	2.13N	23.00 E
Lolo	36	Bc	0.40 S	12.28 E
Lolodorf	34	He	3.14N	10.44 E
Lolo Pass	46	Hc	46.40N	114.33W
Loloway	63b	Cb	15.17 S	167.58 E
Lom	15	Gf	43.49N	23.14 E
Lom [Afr.]	34	Hd	5.20N	13.24 E
Lom [Bul.]	15	Gf	43.50N	23.15 E
Loma Bonita	48	Lh	18.07N	95.53W
Lomaloma	63d	Cb	17.17 S	178.59W
Lomami	30	Jh	0.46N	24.16 E
Loma Mountains	30	Fh	9.10N	11.07W
Lomas de Vallejos	55	Dh	27.44 S	57.56W
Loma Verde	55	Cl	35.16 S	58.24W
Lomba	36	Df	15.36 S	21.32 E
Lombarda, Serra-	54	Hc	2.50N	51.50W
Lombarde, Prealpi-	14	De	46.00N	9.30 E
Lombardia = Lombardy (EN)	14	De	45.40N	9.30 E
Lombardy (EN) = Lombardia	14	De	45.40N	9.30 E
Lomblen, Pulau-	21	Oj	8.25 S	123.30 E
Lombok, Pulau-	21	Nj	8.45 S	116.30 E
Lombok, Selat-	26	Gh	8.30 S	115.50 E
Lomé	31	Hh	6.08N	1.13 E
Lomela	31	Ji	2.18 S	23.17 E
Lomela	30	Ji	0.14 S	20.42 E
Lomellina	14	Ce	45.15N	8.45 E
Loméméti	63b	Dd	19.30 S	169.27 E
Lomié	34	He	3.10N	13.37 E
Lomlom	63c	Bb	10.19 S	166.16 E
Lomma	8	Ei	55.41N	13.05 E
Lomme	12	Hd	50.08N	5.10 E
Lommel	11	Lc	51.14N	5.18 E
Lomnica	10	Ug	49.02N	24.47 E
Lomond, Loch-	9	Ie	56.08N	4.38W
Lomonosov	19	Cd	59.55N	29.40 E
Lomonosovki	19	Ge	52.50N	66.28 E
Lomonosov Ridge (EN)	67	De	88.00N	140.00 E
Lomont	11	Mg	47.21N	6.36 E
Lompobatang, Gunung-	26	Gh	5.20 S	119.55 E
Lompoc	43	Ce	34.38N	120.27W
Lomsegga	8	Cc	61.49N	8.22 E
Łomża	10	Sc	53.11N	22.05 E
Łomża	10	Sc	53.10N	22.05 E
Lønahorg	8	Bd	60.42N	6.25 E
Loncoche	56	Fe	39.22 S	72.38W
Londa	25	Ee	15.28N	74.31 E
Londerzeel	12	Gc	51.01N	4.18 E
Londiani	36	Gc	0.10 S	35.36 E
Londinières	12	De	49.50N	1.24 E
London [Eng.-U.K.]	6	Fe	51.30N	0.10W
London [Kir.]	64g	Bb	1.58N	157.29W
London [Ky.-U.S.]	44	Eg	37.08N	84.05W
London [Ont.-Can.]	39	Ke	42.59N	81.14W
London-Barnet	12	Bc	51.39N	0.12W
London-Bexley	12	Cc	51.26N	0.09 E
London Bridge	51p	Bb	12.17N	61.35W
London-Bromley	12	Cc	51.25N	0.01 E
London-Croydon	9	Mj	51.23N	0.07W
Londonderry/Doire	6	Fd	55.00N	7.19W
Londonderry, Cape-	59	Fb	13.45 S	126.55 E
London-Ealing	12	Bc	51.30N	0.19W
London-Enfield	12	Bc	51.40N	0.04W
London-Greenwich	9	Mj	51.28N	0.00
London-Haringey	12	Bc	51.36N	0.06W
London-Harrow	12	Bc	51.36N	0.20W
London-Havering	12	Cc	51.36N	0.11 E
London-Hillingdon	12	Bc	51.31N	0.27W
London-Kingston-upon-Thames	9	Mj	51.28N	0.19W
London-Redbridge	12	Cc	51.35N	0.08 E
London-Sutton	12	Bc	51.21N	0.12W
London-Wandsworth	12	Bc	51.27N	0.12W
London-Westminster	12	Bc	51.30N	0.07W
Londrina	53	Kh	23.18 S	51.09W
Lone Pine	46	Fh	36.36N	118.04W
Longa	36	Ce	14.41 S	18.29 E
Longa [Ang.]	36	Cf	16.25 S	19.04 E
Longa [Ang.]	36	Be	10.15 S	13.30 E
Longa, Proliv- = De Long Strait (EN)	21	Tb	70.20N	178.00 E
Longá, Rio-	54	Jd	3.09 S	41.56W
Long Akah	26	Ff	3.19N	114.47 E
Longarone	14	Gd	46.16N	12.18 E
Longbangun	26	Gf	0.36N	115.11 E
Long Bay [Bar.]	51q	Bb	13.04N	59.29W
Long Bay [S.C.-U.S.]	43	Le	33.35N	78.45W
Long Beach [Ca.-U.S.]	39	Hf	33.46N	118.11W
Long Beach [N.Y.-U.S.]	44	Ke	40.35N	73.40W
Long Beach [Wa.-U.S.]	46	Cc	46.21N	124.03W
Long Branch	43	Mc	40.17N	73.59W
Long Buckby	12	Ab	52.18N	1.04W
Long Cay	49	Jb	22.37N	74.20W
Longchuan	27	Kg	24.10N	115.17 E
Long Creek	46	Nb	49.07N	103.00W
Long Eaton	12	Ab	52.54N	1.16W
Longfeng	28	Ha	46.31N	125.02 E
Longford/An Longfort	9	Fh	53.40N	7.40W
Longford/An Longfort	9	Fh	53.44N	7.47W
Long Forties	9	Nd	57.10N	0.05 E
Long Hu	28	Dj	29.37N	116.12 E
Longhua	28	Dd	41.18N	117.44 E
Longido	36	Gc	2.44 S	36.41 E
Long Island [Atg.]	51d	Bb	17.08N	61.45W
Long Island [Bah.]	38	Lg	23.10N	75.10W
Long Island [Can.]	42	Jf	54.50N	79.20W
Long Island [Can.]	44	Nc	44.20N	66.15W
Long Island [Pap.N.Gui.]	57	Fe	5.36 S	148.00 E
Long Island [U.S.]	38	Le	40.50N	73.00W
Long Island Sound	44	Ke	41.05N	72.58W
Longjiang	27	Lb	47.20N	123.09 E
Longjuzhai → Danfeng	27	Je	33.44N	110.22 E
Longkou	27	Ld	37.39N	120.20 E
Longlac	42	Ig	49.50N	86.32W
Long Lake [N.D.-U.S.]	45	Fc	46.43N	100.07W
Long Lake [Ont.-Can.]	45	Mb	49.32N	86.45W
Longmalinau	26	Gf	3.30N	116.31 E
Long Men	27	Je	34.40N	110.30 E
Longmont	45	Df	40.10N	105.06W
Longnan	27	Jg	24.54N	114.48 E
Longobucco	14	Kk	39.27N	16.37 E
Longoz	15	Kf	43.02N	27.41 E
Longping → Luodian	27	If	25.26N	106.47 E
Long Point	44	Gd	42.34N	80.15W
Long Point Bay	44	Gd	42.40N	80.14W
Longpujungan	26	Gf	2.34N	115.40 E
Longquan	27	Kf	28.06N	119.05 E
Long Range Mountains	42	Lg	48.00N	58.30W
Longreach	58	Fg	23.26 S	144.15 E
Long Sand	12	Dc	51.37N	1.10 E
Longs Peak	38	Ie	40.15N	105.37W
Long Sutton	12	Cb	52.47N	0.08 E
Longtan	28	Eh	32.10N	119.03 E
Longtown	9	Kf	55.01N	2.58W
Longué	11	Fg	47.23N	0.07W
Longueau	12	Ee	49.52N	2.21 E
Longueville-sur-Scie	12	De	49.48N	1.06 E
Longuyon	11	Le	49.26N	5.36 E
Long Valley	46	Ji	34.37N	111.16W
Longview [Tx.-U.S.]	43	Ie	32.30N	94.44W
Longview [Wa.-U.S.]	43	Cb	46.08N	122.57W
Longwu	27	Hg	24.07N	102.18 E
Longwy	11	Le	49.31N	5.46 E
Longxi	27	Hd	35.01N	104.38 E
Longxian	27	Id	35.00N	106.53 E
Longxian → Wengyuan	27	Jg	24.21N	114.13 E
Longxi Shan	27	Kf	26.35N	117.17 E
Long Xuyen	25	Lf	10.23N	105.25 E
Longyan	27	Kf	25.06N	117.01 E
Longyao	28	Cf	37.21N	114.46 E
Longyearbyen	67	Kd	78.13N	15.38 E
Longyou	28	Ej	29.01N	119.10 E
Longzhou	27	Ig	22.23N	106.49 E
Lonigo	14	Fe	45.23N	11.23 E
Löningen	10	Dd	52.44N	7.46 E
Lonja	14	Ke	45.27N	16.41 E
Lonjsko Polje	14	Ke	45.24N	16.42 E
Lönsboda	8	Fh	56.24N	14.19 E
Lons-le-Saunier	11	Lh	46.40N	5.33 E
Lontra, Ribeirão-	55	Fe	21.28 S	53.37W
Lookout, Cape- [N.C.-U.S.]	43	Le	34.35N	76.32W
Lookout, Cape- [Or.-U.S.]	46	Dd	45.20N	124.00W
Lookout Mountain	44	Eh	34.40N	85.20W
Lookout Pass	43	Db	47.27N	115.42W
Loolmalasin	36	Gc	3.03 S	35.49 E
Loop Head/Ceann Léime	9	Di	52.34N	9.56W
Loosdrechtse Plassen	12	Hb	52.10N	5.08 E
Lop	27	Dd	37.01N	80.16 E
Lopatina, Gora-	21	Qd	50.52N	143.10 E
Lopatino	16	Nc	52.37N	45.47 E
Lopatka, Mys-	21	Rd	50.52N	156.40 E
Lop Buri	25	Kf	14.48N	100.37 E
Lopča	20	He	55.44N	122.45 E
Lopévi	63b	Dc	16.30 S	168.21 E
Lopez, Cap- = Lopez, Cape- (EN)	30	Hi	0.37 S	8.43 E
Lopez, Cape- (EN) = Lopez, Cap-	30	Hi	0.37 S	8.43 E
Lop Nur	21	Le	40.30N	90.30 E
Lopnur/Yuli	27	Ec	41.22N	86.09 E
Lopori	30	Ih	1.14N	19.49 E
Loppersum	12	Ia	53.19N	6.45 E
Lopphavet	7	Ea	70.25N	22.00 E
Loppi	8	Kd	60.43N	24.27 E
Lopud	14	Lh	42.41N	17.57 E
Łopuszno	10	Qf	50.57N	20.15 E
Lora del Río	13	Gg	37.39N	5.32W
Lorain	43	Kc	41.28N	82.11W
Lorán, Boca-	54	Fb	9.00N	60.45W
Lorca	13	Kg	37.40N	1.42W
Lorch	12	Jd	50.03N	7.49 E
Lord Howe Island	57	Gh	31.35 S	159.05 E
Lord Howe Rise (EN)	3	Jm	32.00 S	162.00 E
Lord Mayor Bay	42	Ic	69.45N	92.00W
Lordsburg	45	Bj	32.21N	108.43W
Loreley	12	Jd	50.08N	7.43 E
Lorena	55	Jf	22.44 S	45.08W
Lorengau	60	Dh	2.01 S	147.17 E
Lorestān	23	Gc	33.30N	48.40 E
Loreto	54	Dd	5.00 S	75.00W
Loreto [Arg.]	55	Dh	27.46 S	57.17W
Loreto [Bol.]	54	Fg	15.13 S	64.40W
Loreto [Braz.]	54	Ie	7.05 S	45.09W
Loreto [It.]	14	Hg	43.26N	13.36 E
Loreto [Mex.]	48	If	22.16N	101.58W
Loreto [Mex.]	47	Bc	26.01N	111.21W
Loreto [Par.]	56	Ib	23.16 S	57.11W
Loreto Aprutino	14	Hh	42.26N	13.59 E
Lorica	54	Cb	9.14N	75.49W
Lorient	6	Ff	47.45N	3.22W
Lőrinci	10	Pi	47.44N	19.41 E
Lorn, Firth of-	9	He	56.20N	5.40W
Lorne	59	Ig	38.33 S	143.59 E
Lörrach	10	Di	47.37N	7.40 E
Lorrain, Plateau-	11	Me	49.00N	6.30 E
Lorrain, Rivière du-	51h	Ab	14.50N	61.03W
Lorraine	11	Lf	49.00N	6.00 E
Lorraine, Plaine-	11	Lf	48.10N	5.50 E
Lorsch	12	Ke	49.39N	8.34 E
Los	7	Df	61.44N	15.10 E
Los, Iles de- = Los Islands (EN)	34	Cd	9.30N	13.48W

Index Symbols

- 1 Independent Nation
- 2 State, Region
- 3 District, County
- 4 Municipality
- 5 Colony, Dependency
- Continent
- Physical Region
- Historical or Cultural Region
- Mount, Mountain
- Volcano
- Hill
- Mountains, Mountain Range
- Hills, Escarpment
- Plateau, Upland
- Pass, Gap
- Plain, Lowland
- Delta
- Salt Flat
- Valley, Canyon
- Crater, Cave
- Karst Features
- Depression
- Polder
- Desert, Dunes
- Forest, Woods
- Heath, Steppe
- Oasis
- Cape, Point
- Coast, Beach
- Cliff
- Peninsula
- Isthmus
- Sandbank
- Island
- Atoll
- Rock, Reef
- Islands, Archipelago
- Rocks, Reefs
- Coral Reef
- Well, Spring
- Geyser
- River, Stream
- Waterfall Rapids
- River Mouth, Estuary
- Lake
- Salt Lake
- Intermittent Lake
- Reservoir
- Swamp, Pond
- Canal
- Glacier
- Ice Shelf, Pack Ice
- Ocean
- Sea
- Gulf, Bay
- Strait, Fjord
- Lagoon
- Bank
- Seamount
- Tablemount
- Ridge
- Shelf
- Basin
- Escarpment, Sea Scarp
- Fracture
- Trench, Abyss
- National Park, Reserve
- Point of Interest
- Recreation Site
- Cave, Cavern
- Historic Site
- Ruins
- Wall, Walls
- Church, Abbey
- Temple
- Scientific Station
- Airport
- Port
- Lighthouse
- Mine
- Tunnel
- Dam, Bridge

Los Alamos 39 If 35.53N 106.19W
Los Amates 49 Cf 15.16N 89.06W
Los Amores 55 Ci 28.06S 59.59W
Los Angeles 39 Hf 34.03N 118.15W
Los Ángeles 53 Ii 37.28S 72.21W
Los Angeles Aqueduct 46 Fi 35.22N 118.05W
Losap Atoll 57 Gd 6.54N 152.44 E
Los Banos 46 Eh 37.04N 120.51W
Los Blancos 56 Hb 23.36S 62.36W
Los Charrúas 55 Cj 31.10S 58.11W
Los Chiles 49 Eh 11.02N 84.43W
Los Conquistadores 55 Cj 30.36S 58.28W
Los Frailes, Islas- 50 Eg 11.12N 63.45W
Los Frentones 55 Bh 26.25S 61.25W
Los Gatos 46 Eh 37.14N 121.59W
Losheim 12 Ie 49.31N 6.45 E
Los Hermanos, Islas- 54 Fa 11.45N 64.25W
Łosice 10 Sd 52.14N 22.43 E
Lošinj 14 If 44.35N 14.28 E
Los Islands (EN)=Los, Iles de- 34 Cd 9.30N 13.48W
Los Juries 55 Ai 28.28S 62.06W
Los Lagos 56 Fe 39.51S 72.50W
Los Lagos [2] 56 Ff 41.20S 73.00W
Los Llanos de Aridane 32 Dd 28.39N 17.54W
Los Médanos, Istmo de- 49 Mh 11.35N 69.45W
Los Mochis 39 Ig 25.45N 108.53W
Los Monegros 13 Lc 41.29N 0.03W
Los Monjes, Islas- 54 Da 12.25N 70.55W
Los Navalmorales 13 He 39.43N 4.38W
Loso 36 Ec 1.10S 27.10 E
Los Palacios 49 Fb 22.35N 83.12W
Los Palacios y Villafranca 13 Gg 37.10N 5.56W
Los Pedroches 13 Hf 38.27N 4.45W
Los Pirpintos 55 Ah 26.08S 62.05W
Los Remedios, Rio de- 48 Fe 24.41N 106.28W
Los Reyes de Salgado 48 Hh 19.35N 102.29W
Los Roques, Islas- 54 Ea 11.50N 66.45W
Los Roques Basin (EN) 50 Cf 12.20N 67.40W
Los Santos [3] 49 Gj 7.45N 80.30W
Los Santos 49 Gj 7.56N 80.25W
Losser 12 Jb 52.16N 7.01 E
Lossiemouth 9 Jd 57.43N 3.18W
Lossnen 8 Eb 62.30N 12.50 E
Los Taques 49 Lh 11.50N 70.16W
Los Telares 56 Hc 28.59S 63.26W
Los Teques 54 Ea 10.21N 67.02W
Los Testigos, Islas- 54 Fa 11.23N 63.06W
Lost River 46 Ef 41.56N 121.30W
Lost River Range 46 Id 44.10N 113.35W
Lost Trail Pass 43 Eb 45.41N 113.57W
Los Vilos 56 Fd 31.55S 71.31W
Lot 5 Gg 44.18N 0.20 E
Lot [3] 11 Hj 44.30N 1.30 E
Lota 56 Fe 37.05S 73.10W
Lotagipi Swamp 35 Ee 4.36N 34.55 E
Løten 8 Dd 60.49N 11.19 E
Lot-et-Garonne [3] 11 Gj 44.20N 0.30 E
Lothair 37 Ee 26.26S 30.27 E
Lothian [3] 9 Jf 55.55N 3.30W
Lothian 9 Jf 55.55N 3.05W
Loto 36 Dc 2.47S 22.30 E
Lotofaga 65c Ba 13.59S 171.50W
Lotoi 36 Cc 1.35S 18.30 E
Lotru 15 Hd 45.20N 24.16 E
Lotrului, Munţii- 15 Gd 45.30N 23.52 E
Lotta 7 Hb 68.39N 30.20 E
Lottefors 8 Gc 61.25N 16.24 E
Löttorp 8 Gg 57.10N 16.59 E
Lotuke, Jabal- 35 Ee 4.07N 33.48 E
Louang Namtha 25 Kd 20.57N 101.25 E
Louangphrabang 22 Mh 19.52N 102.08 E
Loubomo 31 Ii 4.12S 12.41 E
Loučná 10 Lf 50.06N 15.48 E
Loudéac 11 Df 48.10N 2.45W
Loudima 36 Bc 4.07S 13.04 E
Loudon 44 Eh 35.44N 84.20W
Loudun 11 Gh 47.00N 0.04 E
Loué 11 Fg 48.00N 0.09W
Loue 11 Lg 47.01N 5.27 E
Loufan 28 Ae 38.04N 111.47 E
Louga 34 Bb 15.37N 16.13W
Louga [3] 34 Bb 15.00N 15.30W
Louge 11 Hk 43.27N 1.20 E
Loughborough 9 Li 52.47N 1.11W
Lougheed 42 Ha 77.30N 105.00W
Loughrea/Baile Locha Riach 9 Eh 53.12N 8.34W
Louhans 11 Lh 46.38N 5.13 E
Louhi 19 Db 66.04N 33.01 E
Louisa 44 Ff 38.07N 82.36W
Louiseville 44 Kb 46.16N 72.57W
Louisiade Archipelago 57 Gf 11.00S 153.00 E
Louisiana 45 Kg 39.27N 91.03W
Louisiana [2] 43 Ie 31.15N 92.15W
Louis Trichardt 37 Dd 23.01S 29.43 E
Louisville [Ky.-U.S.] 39 Kf 38.16N 85.45W
Louisville [Ms.-U.S.] 45 Lj 33.07N 89.03W
Louis-XIV, Pointe - 42 Jf 54.50N 79.30W
Loukoléla 36 Cc 1.02S 17.07 E
Loulan Yiji 27 Ec 40.32N 89.50 E
Loulé 13 Dg 37.08N 8.02W
Loum 34 Ge 4.43N 9.44 E
Lount Lake 45 Ia 50.10N 94.20W
Louny 10 Jf 50.22N 13.49 E
Loup City 45 Gf 41.17N 98.58W
Loup River 45 Hc 41.24N 97.19W
Loups Marins, Lacs des - 42 Ke 56.40N 74.00W
Lourdes 11 Fk 43.06N 0.03W
Lourenço Marques→Maputo 31 Kk 25.58S 32.34 E
Lousa, Serra da- 13 Dd 40.04N 8.13W
Loushan Guan 27 If 28.02N 106.51 E
Louštin 10 Jf 50.12N 13.48 E
Louth [Austl.] 59 Jf 30.32S 145.07 E
Louth [Eng.-U.K.] 9 Mh 53.22N 0.01W
Louth/Lú [2] 9 Gh 53.55N 6.30W
Loutrá Aidhipsoú 15 Gk 38.51N 23.03 E
Loutrá Killinís 15 El 37.52N 21.07 E
Loutrákion 15 Fl 37.59N 23.00 E
Louvain/Leuven 11 Kd 50.53N 4.42 E
Louvet Point 51k Bb 13.58N 60.53W
Louviers 11 He 49.13N 1.10 E
Lövånger 7 Ed 64.22N 21.18 E
Lovászi 10 Mj 46.33N 16.34 E
Lovat 5 Jd 58.14N 31.28 E
Lovćen 15 Bg 42.24N 18.49 E
Loveč [2] 15 Hf 43.08N 24.43 E
Loveč 15 Hf 43.08N 24.43 E
Loveland 45 Df 40.24N 105.05W
Lovell 43 Fc 44.50N 108.24W
Lovelock 43 Dc 40.11N 118.28W
Lövenich, Köln- 12 Id 50.57N 6.50 E
Lovenske Gorice 14 Jd 46.40N 16.00 E
Lovere 14 Ee 45.49N 10.04 E
Loviisa 7 Gf 60.27N 26.14 E
Loviisa/Lovisa 7 Gf 60.27N 26.14 E
Loving 45 Dj 32.17N 104.06W
Lovington 43 Ge 33.27N 103.21W
Lovisa 7 Gf 60.27N 26.14 E
Lovisa/Loviisa 7 Gf 60.27N 26.14 E
Lovoi 36 Ed 8.05S 26.40 E
Lovosice 10 Kf 50.31N 14.03 E
Lovozero 7 Ib 68.01N 35.01 E
Lovozero, Ozero- 7 Ic 67.50N 35.10 E
Lövstabruk 8 Gd 60.24N 17.53 E
Lövstabukten 8 Gd 60.35N 17.45 E
Lovua 36 Dd 6.07S 20.35 E
Lovua 36 De 11.31S 23.35 E
Low, Cape - 42 Id 63.06N 85.18W
Lowa 30 Ji 1.24S 25.52 E
Lowell 43 Mc 42.39N 71.18W
Löwenberg in der Mark 10 Jd 52.53N 13.09 E
Lower Arrow Lake 46 Fb 49.40N 118.08W
Lower Austria (EN) = Niederösterreich [2] 14 Jb 48.30N 15.45 E
Lower California (EN)=Baja California 38 Hg 28.00N 112.00W
Lower Hutt 62 Fd 41.13S 174.55 E
Lower Lake 46 Ef 41.15N 120.02W
Lower Lake 46 Dg 38.55N 122.36W
Lower Lough Erne/Loch Éirne Íochtair 9 Fg 54.30N 7.50W
Lower Post 42 Ee 59.55N 128.30W
Lower Red Lake 45 Ic 48.00N 94.50W
Lower Rhine (EN) = Neder-Rijn 11 Mc 51.59N 6.20 E
Lower Saxony (EN)= Niedersachsen [2] 10 Fd 52.00N 10.00 E
Lower Trajan's Wall (EN)= Nižni Trajanov Val 15 Ld 45.45N 28.30 E
Lower Tunguska (EN)= Nižnjaja Tunguska 21 Kc 65.48N 88.04 E
Lowestoft 9 Oi 52.29N 1.45 E
Lowestoft Ness 9 Oi 52.28N 1.44 E
Lowgar [3] 23 Kc 33.50N 69.00 E
Łowicz 10 Pd 52.07N 19.56 E
Lowlands 9 Jf 56.00N 4.00W
Lowrah 21 If 31.33N 66.33 E
Lowshān 24 Md 36.39N 49.32 E
Low Tatra (EN) = Nízke Tatry 10 Ph 48.54N 19.40 E
Lowther 42 Hb 74.35N 97.40W
Lowville 44 Jd 43.47N 75.30W
Loxton [Austl.] 59 If 34.27S 140.35 E
Loxton [S.Afr.] 37 Cf 31.30S 22.22 E
Loyalty Islands (EN)= Loyauté, Iles- 57 Hg 21.00S 167.00 E
Loyauté, Iles-=Loyalty Islands (EN) 57 Hg 21.00S 167.00 E
Loyoro 36 Fb 3.21N 34.17 E
Lozère [3] 11 Jj 44.30N 3.30 E
Lozère, Mont- 11 Jj 44.25N 3.46 E
Loznica 15 Ce 44.32N 19.13 E
Lozovaja 19 Df 48.53N 36.15 E
Lozva 19 Gd 59.36N 62.20 E
Lú/Louth [2] 9 Gh 53.55N 6.30W
Lua 36 Cb 2.46N 18.26 E
Luacano 36 De 11.16S 21.38 E
Luachimo 36 Dd 6.33S 20.59 E
Luaha-Sibuha 26 Cg 0.31S 98.28 E
Luahoko 65b Ba 19.40S 174.24W
Luala 37 Fc 17.57S 36.30 E
Lualaba 29 Jh 0.26N 25.20 E
Luama 36 Ec 4.46S 26.53 E
Lua Makika 65a Ec 20.35N 156.34W
Luampa 36 De 14.32S 24.10 E
Lu'an 27 Ke 31.44N 116.30 E
Luanda 31 Ii 8.50S 13.15 E
Luanda [3] 36 Bd 8.30S 13.20 E
Luando 30 Ij 10.19S 16.40 E
Luang, Khao- 25 Jg 8.31N 99.47 E
Luang, Thale- 25 Kg 7.30N 100.15 E
Luang Chiang Dao, Doi- 25 Je 19.23N 98.54 E
Luanginga 30 Jj 15.11S 22.55 E
Luang Prabang Range 25 Ke 18.30N 101.15 E
Luangue 36 Dc 4.17S 20.01 E
Luangwa 30 Kj 15.36S 30.25 E
Luan He 21 Nf 39.20N 119.10 E
Luaniva 64h Bb 13.16S 176.07W
Luannan (Bencheng) 28 Ee 39.30N 118.42 E
Luanping (Anjiangying) 28 Dd 40.55N 117.19 E
Luanshya 31 Jj 13.08S 28.25 E
Luanxian 27 Kd 39.45N 118.44 E
Luanza 36 Ed 8.40S 28.40 E
Luapula 30 Ji 9.26S 28.33 E
Luapula [3] 36 Ee 10.40S 29.15 E
Luarca 13 Fa 43.32N 6.32W
Luashi 36 De 10.56S 23.37 E
Luba 34 Ge 3.28N 8.40 E
Lubaantum 49 Ce 16.17N 88.58W
Lubaczów 10 Tf 50.10N 23.07 E
Lubaczówka 10 Sf 50.08N 22.35 E
Lubalo 36 Cd 7.22S 19.20 E
Lubalo 36 Cd 9.07S 19.15 E
Lubamba 36 Ed 5.14S 26.02 E
Lubań 10 Le 51.08N 15.18 E
Lubāna/Lubana 8 Lh 56.49N 26.49 E
Lubana/Lubāna 8 Lh 56.49N 26.49 E
Lubanas, Ozero-/Lubānas Ezers 8 Lh 56.40N 27.00 E
Lubānas Ezers/Lubanas, Ozero- 8 Lh 56.40N 27.00 E
Lubang Islands 26 Hd 13.45N 120.15 E
Lubango 31 Ij 14.55S 13.28 E
Lubao 31 Ji 5.22S 25.45 E
Lubartów 10 Se 51.28N 22.46 E
Lubawa 10 Pc 53.30N 19.45 E
Lübbecke 10 Ed 52.18N 8.37 E
Lubbeek 12 Gd 50.53N 4.50 E
Lübben/Lubin 10 Je 51.57N 13.54 E
Lübbenau/Lubnjow 10 Je 51.52N 13.58 E
Lubbock 39 If 33.35N 101.51W
Lübeck 6 He 53.52N 10.42 E
Lübecker Bucht 10 Gb 54.00N 10.55 E
Lübeck-Travemünde 10 Gc 53.57N 10.52 E
Lubefu 36 Dc 4.10S 23.00 E
Lubefu 36 Dc 4.43S 24.25 E
Lubei→Jarud Qi 27 Lc 44.30N 120.55 E
Lubelska, Wyżyna- 10 Sf 51.00N 23.00 E
Lubenec 10 Jf 50.08N 13.20 E
Lubenka 16 Sd 50.28N 54.06 E
Lubero 36 Ec 0.06S 29.06 E
Lubéron, Montagne du- 11 Lk 43.48N 5.22 E
Lubi 36 Dc 4.59S 23.26 E
Lubie, Jezioro- 10 Lc 53.30N 15.50 E
Lubień Kujawski 10 Pd 52.25N 19.10 E
Lubij/Löbau 10 Ke 51.06N 14.40 E
Lubilash 29 Ji 6.02S 23.45 E
Lubin 10 Me 51.24N 16.13 E
Lubin/Lübben 10 Je 51.57N 13.54 E
Lublin 6 Ie 51.15N 22.35 E
Lublin [2] 10 Se 51.15N 22.35 E
Lubliniec 10 Of 50.40N 18.41 E
Lubnān=Lebanon (EN) [1] 22 Ff 33.50N 35.50 E
Lubnān, Jabal-=Lebanon Mountains (EN) 23 Ec 34.00N 36.30 E
Lubnjow/Lübbenau 10 Je 51.52N 13.58 E
Lubny 19 De 50.01N 33.00 E
Luboń 10 Md 52.23N 16.54 E
Lubraniec 10 Od 52.33N 18.50 E
Lubsko 10 Ke 51.46N 14.59 E
Lubsza 10 Ke 51.55N 14.45 E
Lubudi 29 Ji 9.13S 25.38 E
Lubudi 36 Ed 9.57S 25.58 E
Lubue 36 Cc 4.10S 19.53 E
Lubukinggau 26 Dg 3.10S 102.52 E
Lubuksikaping 26 Df 0.08N 100.10 E
Lubumba 36 Ec 3.58S 29.06 E
Lubumbashi 31 Jj 11.40S 27.30 E
Lubuskie, Pojezierze- 10 Ld 52.18N 15.20 E
Lubutu 31 Ji 0.44S 26.35 E
Lucala 36 Bd 6.38S 12.34 E
Lucala 36 Cd 9.16S 15.16 E
Lucania, Mount- 42 Dd 61.01N 140.29W
Lucas 55 Ea 13.05S 55.56W
Lucca 14 Eg 43.50N 10.29 E
Lucea 49 Hd 18.27N 78.10W
Luce Bay 9 Ig 54.47N 4.50W
Lucedale 45 Lk 30.55N 88.35W
Lučegorsk 20 Ig 46.25N 134.20 E
Lucélia 55 Ge 21.44S 51.01W
Lucena [Phil.] 26 Hd 13.56N 121.37 E
Lucena [Sp.] 13 Hg 37.24N 4.29W
Lucena del Cid 13 Ld 40.08N 0.17W
Luc-en-Diois 11 Lj 44.37N 5.27 E
Lučenec 10 Ph 48.20N 19.41 E
Lucera 14 Ji 41.30N 15.20 E
Lucerne (EN) = Luzern 14 Cc 47.05N 8.20 E
Lucerne, Lake- (EN) = Vierwaldstätter-See 14 Cc 47.00N 8.30 E
Lucero 48 Fb 30.49N 106.30W
Lucheng 28 Bf 36.18N 113.15 E
Lucheringo 37 Fb 11.43S 36.15 E
Lucheux 12 Ed 50.12N 2.25 E
Luchico 30 Ij 12.15S 44.25 E
Luchico 36 Cd 6.12S 19.42 E
Lüchow 10 Hd 52.58N 11.09 E
Lüchun 27 Hg 23.02N 102.19 E
Lucipara, Kepulauan- 26 Ih 5.30S 127.33 E
Lucira 36 Be 13.52S 12.32 E
Luck 19 Ce 50.47N 25.20 E
Luckau 10 Je 51.51N 13.43 E
Luckenwalde 10 Jd 52.05N 13.10 E
Lucknow 22 Kg 26.51N 80.55 E
Luçon 11 Eh 46.27N 1.10W
Lucrecia, Cabo- 49 Jc 21.04N 75.37W
Luc-sur-Mer 12 Be 49.18N 0.21W
Lucunga 36 Bd 6.49S 14.35 E
Lucusse 36 De 12.33S 20.51 E
Lüda→Dalian=Dairan (EN) 22 Of 38.55N 121.39 E
Luda Kamčija 15 Kg 43.03N 27.29 E
Ludbreg 14 Kd 46.15N 16.37 E
Lüdenscheid 10 De 51.13N 7.37 E
Lüderitz 31 Ik 26.38S 15.10 E
Lüderitz [3] 37 Be 26.00S 15.00 E
Lüderitz Bay 37 Be 26.35S 15.10 E
Ludhiāna 22 Jf 30.54N 75.51 E
Ludinghausen 10 De 51.46N 7.28 E
Ludington 43 Jc 43.57N 86.27W
Ludlow 9 Ki 52.22N 2.43W
Ludogorije 15 Jf 43.46N 26.56 E
Ludogorsko Plato 15 Kf 43.35N 27.03 E
Luduş 15 Hc 46.29N 24.06 E
Ludvika 7 Df 60.09N 15.11 E
Ludwigsburg 10 Fh 48.54N 9.11 E
Ludwigshafen am Rhein 10 Eg 49.29N 8.27 E
Ludwigslust 10 Hc 53.19N 11.30 E
Ludza 7 Gh 56.32N 27.45 E
Luebo 31 Ji 5.21S 21.25 E
Lueki 36 Ec 3.24S 25.57 E
Lueki 36 Ec 3.22S 25.51 E
Luele 36 Dd 7.55S 20.00 E
Luembé 36 Dd 6.43S 24.11 E
Luembe 36 Dd 6.37S 21.06 E
Luena [Ang.] 36 De 12.31S 22.34 E
Luena [Ang.] 31 Ij 11.48S 19.55 E
Luena [Zaire] 36 Ed 9.27S 25.47 E
Luena [Zam.] 36 Df 15.20S 23.30 E
Luengué 36 Df 16.54S 21.52 E
Luenha 37 Ec 16.24S 33.48 E
Luera Peak 45 Cj 33.47N 107.49W
Lueta 36 Dd 7.04S 21.40 E
Lueyang 27 Ie 33.25N 106.14 E
Lufeng 27 Kg 22.57N 115.41 E
Lufico 36 Bd 6.22S 13.30 E
Lufira 29 Ji 8.16S 26.27 E
Lufira, Chutes de la- 36 Ed 9.50S 27.30 E
Lufkin 43 Ie 31.20N 94.44W
Lug 15 De 44.23N 20.45 E
Luga 19 Cd 59.43N 28.18 E
Luga 19 Cd 58.44N 29.50 E
Lugano 14 Cd 46.00N 8.57 E
Lugano, Lago di- 14 Cd 46.00N 9.00 E
Luganville 58 Hf 15.32S 167.10 E
Lugards Falls 30 Ki 3.03S 38.42 E
Lügde 12 Lc 51.57N 9.15 E
Lugela 37 Fc 16.26S 36.39 E
Lugenda 30 Kj 11.26S 38.33 E
Lugnaquillia 9 Gi 52.58N 6.27W
Lugo [3] 13 Eb 43.00N 7.30W
Lugo [It.] 14 Ff 44.25N 11.54 E
Lugo [Sp.] 13 Ea 43.00N 7.34W
Lugoj 15 Ed 45.41N 21.55 E
Lugovoj [Kaz.-U.S.S.R.] 19 Hg 42.55N 72.47 E
Lugovoj [R.S.F.S.R.] 19 Gd 59.44N 65.55 E
Lugovski 20 Ge 58.05N 112.55 E
Lugulu 36 Ec 2.17S 26.32 E
Luh 7 Kh 56.14N 42.28 E
Luhe 10 Gc 53.18N 10.11 E
Luhe 28 Eh 32.21N 118.50 E
Luhin Sum 27 Kb 46.41N 118.38 E
Luhit 25 Jc 27.48N 95.28 E
Luhovicy 7 Ji 54.59N 39.02 E
Luhuo 27 He 31.21N 100.41 E
Lui 36 Cd 8.41S 17.56 E
Luia 36 Dd 8.26S 21.45 E
Luiana 36 Df 17.22S 22.59 E
Luiana 30 Jj 17.27S 23.14 E
Luie 36 Cc 4.33S 17.41 E
Luik/Liège 6 Ge 50.38N 5.34 E
Luilaka 30 Ji 0.52S 20.12 E
Luilu 36 Dd 6.22S 23.50 E
Luimneach/Limerick 6 Fe 52.40N 8.38W
Luimneach/Limerick [2] 9 Ei 52.30N 9.00W
Luing 9 He 56.13N 5.39W
Luino 14 Cd 46.00N 8.44 E
Luio 36 De 13.15S 21.39 E
Lui Pătru, Virful- 15 Gd 45.30N 23.30 E
Luis Correia 54 Jd 2.53S 41.40W
Luishia 36 Ee 11.13S 27.07 E
Luitpold Coast 66 Af 78.30S 32.00W
Luiza 36 Dd 7.12S 22.25 E
Luján [Arg.] 56 Gd 32.22S 65.57W
Luján [Arg.] 56 Id 34.34S 59.07W
Lujiang 28 Di 31.15N 117.17 E
Lukafu 36 Ee 10.30S 27.33 E
Lukanga Swamp 36 Ee 14.25S 27.45 E
Lukavac 14 Mf 44.33N 18.32 E
Lukenge 36 Ed 5.46S 29.06 E
Lukenie 30 Ii 2.44S 18.09 E
Lukeville 46 Ik 31.57N 112.50W
Lukojanov 19 Ed 55.02N 44.30 E
Lukolela 36 Cc 1.03S 17.12 E
Lukonzolwa 36 Ed 8.47S 28.39 E
Lukov 10 Ue 51.14N 24.25 E
Lukovit 15 Hf 43.12N 24.10 E
Łuków 10 Se 51.56N 22.23 E
Lukuga 30 Ji 5.40S 26.55 E
Lukula 36 Bd 5.23S 12.57 E
Lukulu 36 De 14.23S 23.15 E
Lukusashi 36 Fe 14.38S 30.00 E
Luleå 6 Ib 65.34N 22.10 E
Luleälven 5 Ib 65.35N 22.03 E
Lüleburgaz 23 Ca 41.24N 27.21 E
Lüliang Shan 21 Nf 37.45N 111.25 E
Lulimba 36 Ec 4.42S 28.38 E
Luling 45 Hl 29.41N 97.39W
Lulong 28 Ee 39.53N 118.52 E
Lulonga 36 Cb 0.37N 18.23 E
Lulonga 30 Ih 0.43N 18.23 E
Lulua 30 Ji 5.02S 21.07 E
Lulu Fakahega, Mount- 64h Bb 13.16S 176.10W
Luma 65c Db 14.14S 169.32W
Lumajang 26 Fh 8.08S 113.13 E
Lumajangdong Co 27 De 34.00N 81.37 E
Lumbala Kaquengue 31 Jj 14.06S 21.25 E
Lumbala N'guimbo 36 De 12.39S 22.32 E
Lumberton 43 Le 34.37N 79.00W
Lumbo 37 Gc 15.00S 40.44 E
Lumbrales 13 Fd 40.56N 6.43W
Lumbres 12 Ed 50.42N 2.08 E
Lumby 46 Fa 50.15N 118.58W
Lumding 25 Ic 25.45N 93.10 E
Lumege 36 De 11.34S 20.48 E
Lumesule 36 Ge 11.14S 38.06 E
Lumi 60 Ch 3.29S 142.03 E
Lummen 12 Hd 50.59N 5.15 E
Lumparland 8 Id 60.10N 20.15 E
Lumphăt 25 Lf 13.30N 106.59 E
Lumsden [N.Z.] 62 Cf 45.44S 168.26 E
Lumsden [Sask.-Can.] 46 Ma 50.34N 104.53W
Lumuna 36 Ec 3.46S 26.24 E
Lumut 26 Df 4.14N 100.38 E
Luna 13 Gb 42.40N 5.49W
Luna, Laguna de- 55 Di 28.06S 56.46W
Lunan Shan 27 Hf 27.00N 102.30 E
Lunayyr, Harrat- 24 Gj 25.10N 37.50 E
Lunca Ilvei 15 Hb 47.22N 24.59 E
Lund 7 Ci 55.42N 13.11 E
Lunda [3] 36 Cd 9.30S 20.00 E
Lundazi 31 Kj 12.19S 33.13 E
Lunde 8 Gb 62.53N 17.51 E
Lundevatn 8 Bf 58.20N 6.35 E
Lundi 30 Kk 21.19S 32.24 E
Lundu 26 Ef 1.40N 109.51 E
Lundy Island 9 Ij 51.10N 4.40W
Lüneburg 10 Gc 53.15N 10.24 E
Lüneburger Heide 10 Gc 53.10N 10.20 E
Lunel 11 Kk 43.41N 4.08 E
Lünen 10 De 51.37N 7.31 E
Lunéville 11 Mf 48.36N 6.30 E
Lunga 30 Jj 14.34S 26.26 E
Lungué-Bungo 37 Jj 28.38S 16.27 E
Lungwebungu 36 De 14.19S 23.14 E
Lūni 25 Ed 24.41N 71.14 E
Lūni 25 Ec 26.00N 73.00 E
Lunigiana 14 Df 44.20N 9.55 E
Luninec 19 Ce 52.16N 26.50 E
Lunino 16 Nc 53.35N 45.14 E
Lunsemfwa 36 Fe 14.54S 30.12 E
Luntai/Bügür 27 Dc 41.46N 84.10 E
Luobei (Fengxiang) 27 Nb 47.36N 130.58 E
Luobuzhuang 27 Ed 39.30N 88.15 E
Luocheng 27 Ig 24.51N 108.53 E
Luodian (Longping) 27 If 25.26N 106.47 E
Luoding 27 Jg 22.43N 111.33 E
Luohe 27 Je 33.30N 114.08 E
Luo He 27 Id 32.18N 109.12 E
Luoma Hu 28 Eg 34.10N 118.12 E
Luonteri 8 Lc 61.35N 27.45 E
Luoping 27 Hg 24.58N 104.19 E
Luopioinen 8 Kc 61.22N 24.40 E
Luoshan 28 Ch 32.13N 114.32 E
Luotian 28 Ci 30.48N 115.23 E
Luoxiao Shan 27 Jf 26.35N 114.00 E
Luoyang 22 Nf 34.41N 112.25 E
Luoyuan 27 Kf 26.31N 119.32 E
Luozi 36 Bc 4.57S 14.08 E
Lupa 36 Fd 8.39S 33.12 E
Lupane 37 Dc 18.56S 27.48 E
Łupawa 10 Nb 54.42N 17.07 E
Lupeni 15 Gd 45.21N 23.14 E
Luperón 49 Ld 19.54N 70.57W
Łupków 10 Sg 49.12N 22.06 E
Luputa 36 Dd 7.10S 23.42 E
Lüq 31 Lh 3.56N 42.32 E
Luqiao 28 Fj 28.39N 120.05 E
Luqu 27 He 34.36N 102.30 E
Luque 56 Ic 25.16S 57.34W
Luquillo 51a Cb 18.22N 65.43W
Luray 44 Hf 38.40N 78.28W
Lure 11 Mg 47.41N 6.30 E
Lure, Montagne de- 11 Lj 44.07N 5.47 E
Luremo 36 Cd 8.30S 17.51 E
Lurgan/An Lorgain 9 Gg 54.28N 6.20W
Lurín 54 Cf 12.17S 76.52W
Lúrio 37 Gb 13.32S 40.30 E
Lúrio 30 Lj 13.31S 40.42 E
Lusaka 31 Jj 15.25S 28.17 E
Lusambo 31 Ji 4.58S 23.27 E
Lusanga 36 Cc 4.44S 18.58 E
Lusangi 36 Ec 4.37S 27.08 E
Lu Shan 27 Kf 29.30N 115.55 E
Lushan [China] 28 Cj 29.33N 115.58 E
Lushan [China] 28 Bh 33.44N 112.54 E
Lushi 27 Je 34.04N 111.02 E
Lushiko 36 Cd 6.12S 19.42 E
Lushnja 15 Ci 40.56N 19.42 E
Lushoto 36 Gc 4.47S 38.17 E
Lu Shui 28 Bj 29.54N 113.39 E
Lushui (Luzhangjie) 27 Gf 26.00N 98.50 E
Lüshun=Port Arthur (EN) 27 Ld 38.50N 121.13 E
Lusignan 11 Gh 46.26N 0.07 E
Lusk 43 Gc 42.46N 104.27W
Lussac-les-Châteaux 11 Gh 46.24N 0.43 E
Lustrafjorden 8 Bc 61.20N 7.20 E
Lūt, Dasht-e-=Lut, Dasht-i- (EN) 21 Hf 33.00N 57.00 E
Lut, Dasht-i- (EN)=Lūt, Dasht-e- 21 Hf 33.00N 57.00 E
Lu Tao 27 Lg 22.35N 121.30 E
Lutembo 36 De 13.28S 21.22 E
Luti 63a Cb 7.14S 157.00 E
Lütjenburg 10 Gb 54.17N 10.35 E
Luton 9 Mj 51.53N 0.25W
Luton Airport 12 Bc 51.50N 0.22W
Lutong 26 Ff 4.28N 114.00 E
Lutshima 36 Cd 5.22S 18.59 E
Lutshima 36 Cd 5.22S 18.59 E
Lutterworth 12 Ab 52.27N 1.12W
Lutuai 36 De 12.40S 20.12 E
Lutugino 16 Ke 48.23N 39.13 E
Lützow-Holmbukta 66 De 69.10S 37.30 E
Lutzputs 37 Ce 28.22S 20.37 E
Luuk 26 He 5.58N 121.18 E
Luverne 45 He 43.39N 96.13W
Luvidjo 36 Ed 6.26S 26.59 E
Luvua 30 Ji 6.46S 26.58 E
Luvuei 36 De 13.06S 21.12 E
Luwegu 30 Ki 8.31S 37.23 E
Luwingu 36 Ee 10.15S 29.54 E
Luwuk 26 Hg 0.56S 122.47 E
Luxembourg [3] 12 He 50.00N 5.30 E
Luxembourg/Luxemburg [1] 6 Gf 49.45N 6.05 E
Luxembourg/Luxemburg 6 Gf 49.45N 6.05 E
Luxemburg/Luxembourg 6 Gf 49.45N 6.05 E
Luxemburg/Luxembourg [1] 6 Gf 49.45N 6.05 E
Luxeuil-les-Bains 11 Mg 47.49N 6.23 E
Luxi 22 Mg 24.34N 103.44 E
Luxi (Mangshi) 27 Gg 24.29N 98.40 E
Luxor (EN)=Al Uqşur 33 Fd 25.41N 32.39 E
Luy 11 Ek 43.39N 1.08W
Luy de Béarn 11 Fk 43.38N 0.47W

Index Symbols

[1] Independent Nation
[2] State, Region
[3] District, County
[4] Municipality
[5] Colony, Dependency
Continent
Physical Region
Historical or Cultural Region
Mount, Mountain
Volcano
Hill
Mountains, Mountain Range
Hills, Escarpment
Plateau, Upland
Pass, Gap
Plain, Lowland
Delta
Salt Flat
Valley, Canyon
Crater, Cave
Karst Features
Depression
Polder
Desert, Dunes
Forest, Woods
Heath, Steppe
Oasis
Cape, Point
Coast, Beach
Cliff
Peninsula
Isthmus
Sandbank
Island
Atoll
Rock, Reef
Islands, Archipelago
Rocks, Reefs
Coral Reef
Well, Spring
Geyser
River, Stream
Waterfall Rapids
River Mouth, Estuary
Lake
Salt Lake
Intermittent Lake
Reservoir
Swamp, Pond
Canal
Glacier
Ice Shelf, Pack Ice
Ocean
Sea
Gulf, Bay
Strait, Fjord
Lagoon
Bank
Seamount
Tablemount
Ridge
Shelf
Basin
Escarpment, Sea Scarp
Fracture
Trench, Abyss
National Park, Reserve
Point of Interest
Recreation Site
Cave, Cavern
Historic Site
Ruins
Wall, Walls
Church, Abbey
Temple
Scientific Station
Airport
Port
Lighthouse
Mine
Tunnel
Dam, Bridge

Luy de France 11 Fk 43.38N 0.47W
Luyi 28 Ch 33.51N 115.28 E
Luz 55 Jd 19.48S 45.41W
Luz, Costa de la- 13 Fh 36.40N 6.20W
Luza 19 Ec 60.39N 47.15 E
Luza 5 Kc 60.40N 46.25 E
Luzarches 12 Ee 49.07N 2.25 E
Luzern [2] 14 Cc 47.05N 8.10 E
Luzern = Lucerne (EN) 14 Cc 47.05N 8.20 E
Luzhai 27 Ig 24.31N 109.46 E
Luzhangjie → Lushui 27 Gf 26.00N 98.50 E
Luzhou 22 Mg 28.55N 105.20 E
Luziânia 54 Ig 16.15S 47.56W
Lužická Nisa 10 Kd 52.04N 14.46 E
Luzilândia 54 Jd 3.28S 42.22W
Lužnice 10 Kg 49.16N 14.25 E
Luzon 21 Oh 16.00N 121.00 E
Luzon Sea 26 Gd 12.30N 119.00 E
Luzon Strait (EN) 21 Og 21.00N 122.00 E
Luz-Saint-Sauveur 11 Gl 42.52N 0.01 E
Lužskaja Guba 8 Me 59.35N 28.25 E
Lužskaja Vozvyšennost 8 Mf 58.15N 28.45 E
Luzy 11 Jh 46.47N 3.58 E
Łużyca 10 Oe 51.33N 18.15 E
Lvov 6 If 49.50N 24.00 E
Lvovskaja Oblast [3] 19 Cf 49.45N 24.00 E
Lwowa 60 Hj 10.44S 165.45 E
Lwówek 10 Md 52.28N 16.10 E
Lwówek Śląski 10 Le 51.07N 15.35 E
Lyakhov Islands (EN)= Ljahovskije Ostrova 21 Qb 73.30N 141.00 E
Lyall, Mount- 62 Bf 45.17S 167.33 E
Lyallpur 22 Jf 31.25N 73.05 E
Lychsele 7 Ed 64.36N 18.40 E
Lycia 15 Mm 36.30N 29.30 E
Lyckeby 8 Fh 56.12N 15.39 E
Lyckebyån 8 Fh 56.11N 15.40 E
Lyčkovo 7 Hh 57.57N 32.24 E
Lydd 9 Nk 50.57N 0.55 E
Lydd Airport 12 Cd 50.58N 0.56 E
Lydenburg 37 Ee 25.10S 30.29 E
Lydia 15 Lk 38.35N 28.30 E
Lygna 8 Bf 58.10N 7.02 E
Lygnern 8 Eg 57.29N 12.20 E
Lyme Bay 9 Kk 50.38N 3.00W
Lyminge 12 Dc 51.07N 1.05 E
Lymington 9 Lk 50.46N 1.33W
Łyna 10 Rb 54.37N 21.14 E
Lynchburg 43 Ld 37.24N 79.09W
Lynd 58 Ff 18.56S 144.30 E
Lynden 46 Db 48.57N 122.27W
Lyndon River 59 Cd 23.29S 114.06 E
Lyngdal 7 Bg 58.08N 7.05 E
Lyngen 7 Eb 69.58N 20.30 E
Lyngør 8 Cf 58.38N 9.10 E
Lyngseidet 7 Eb 69.35N 20.13 E
Lynn 44 Ld 42.28N 70.57W
Lynnaj, Gora- 20 Ld 62.55N 163.58 E
Lynn Canal 40 Le 58.50N 135.15W
Lynn Deeps 12 Cb 52.58N 0.20 E
Lynn Lake 39 Id 56.51N 101.03W
Lyntupy 8 Li 55.02N 26.27 E
Lynx Lake 42 Gd 62.25N 106.20W
Lyon 6 Gf 45.45N 4.51 E
Lyon Inlet 42 Jc 66.20N 83.40W
Lyonnais, Monts du- 11 Ki 45.40N 4.30 E
Lyon River 59 De 25.00S 115.20 E
Lyons [Ga.-U.S.] 44 Fi 32.12N 82.19W
Lyons [Ks.-U.S.] 45 Gg 38.21N 98.12W
Lyons, Forêt de- 12 De 49.25N 1.30 E
Lyons-la-Forêt 12 De 49.24N 1.28 E
Lyra Reef 60 Eh 1.50S 153.35 E
Lys 11 Jc 51.03N 3.43 E
Łysa Góra 10 Nd 52.07N 17.33 E
Lysaja, Gora- 8 Lj 54.12N 27.40 E
Lysá nad Labem 10 Kf 50.12N 14.50 E
Lysefjorden 8 Be 59.00N 6.14 E
Lysekil 7 Cf 58.16N 11.26 E
Lyskovo 19 Ed 56.03N 45.03 E
Lyss 14 Bc 47.04N 7.37 E
Lysva 19 Fd 58.07N 57.47 E
Lytham Saint Anne's 9 Jh 53.45N 3.01W
Lyttelton 62 Ee 43.36S 172.43 E
Lytton 46 Ea 50.14N 121.34W
Lyža 17 Hd 65.42N 56.40 E

M

Ma, Oued el- 32 Fe 24.03N 9.10W
Ma, Song 25 Le 19.45N 105.55 E
Maâdis, Djebel- 13 Qi 35.52N 4.44 E
Maalaea Bay 65a Ec 20.47N 156.29W
Ma'āmir 24 Mg 30.04N 48.20 E
Ma'ān 23 Ec 30.12N 35.44 E
Ma'āniyah 24 Jg 30.44N 43.00 E
Maanselkä 5 Ib 68.07N 28.29 E
Maanselka 7 Ge 63.54N 28.30 E
Ma'anshan 27 Ke 31.38N 118.30 E
Maardu 8 Ke 59.28N 24.56 E
Maarianhamina/Mariehamn 7 Ef 60.06N 19.57 E
Ma 'arrat an Nu 'mān 24 Ge 35.38N 36.40 E
Maarssen 12 Hb 52.08N 5.03 E
Maas=Meuse (EN) 5 Ge 51.49N 5.01 E
Maaseik 11 Lc 51.06N 5.48 E
Maaseik-Neeroeteren 12 Hc 51.05N 5.42 E
Maasin 26 Hd 10.08N 124.50 E
Maasmechelen/Mechelen 12 Hd 50.57N 5.40 E
Maassluis 12 Gc 51.55N 4.17 E
Maastricht 11 Ld 50.52N 5.43 E
Maasupa 63a Ec 9.18S 161.15 E
Ma'āzah, Al Hadabat al- 33 Fd 27.44N 31.44 E
Mabalane 37 Ed 23.38S 32.31 E
Mabaruma 50 Gh 8.12N 59.47W
Mabechi-Gawa 29 Ga 40.31N 141.31 E
Mabella 45 Lb 48.37N 89.58W
Mabel Lake 46 Fa 50.35N 118.44W
Mablethorpe 9 Nh 53.21N 0.15 E
Mabote 37 Ed 22.03S 34.08 E
Ma'būs Yūsuf 31 Jf 25.45N 21.00 E
Maçaão 13 Ee 39.33N 8.00W
McAdam 42 Kg 45.36N 67.20W
Macajaí, Rio- 54 Fc 2.25N 60.50W
McAllen 43 Hf 26.12N 98.15W
Macaloge 37 Fb 12.25S 35.25 E
Mac Alpine Lake 42 Hc 66.40N 102.50W
Macambará 55 Di 29.08S 56.03W
Macamic 44 Ha 48.48N 79.01W
Macamic, Lac- 44 Ha 48.46N 79.00W
Macao (EN)=Aomen/Macau [5] 22 Ng 22.10N 113.33 E
Macao (EN)=Aomen/Macau 27 Jg 22.12N 113.33 E
Macao (EN)=Macau/Aomen [5] 22 Ng 22.10N 113.33 E
Macao (EN)=Macau/Aomen 27 Jg 22.12N 113.33 E
Macapá 53 Ke 0.02N 51.03W
Macará 54 Cd 4.21S 79.56W
Macaracas 49 Gj 7.44N 80.33W
Macareo, Caño- 54 Fb 9.47N 61.36W
McArthur 44 Ff 39.14N 82.29W
Mc Arthur River 59 Hc 15.54S 136.40 E
Maçãs 13 Fc 41.29N 6.39W
Macas 54 Cd 2.18S 78.06W
Macatete, Sierra de- 48 Dd 28.00N 110.05W
Macau 53 Mf 5.07S 36.38W
Macau/Aomen=Macao (EN) 27 Jg 22.12N 113.33 E
Macau/Aomen=Macao (EN) [5] 22 Ng 22.10N 113.33 E
Macaúbas 54 Jf 13.02S 42.42W
Macauley Island 57 Ih 30.13S 178.33W
Macaya, Pic de- 47 Je 18.23N 74.02W
McBeth Fiord 42 Kc 69.43N 69.20W
McCamey 45 Ek 31.08N 102.13W
McCammon 46 Ie 42.39N 112.12W
Mc Carthy 40 Kd 61.26N 142.55W
McClellanville 44 Hi 33.06N 79.28W
MacClenny 44 Fj 30.18N 82.07W
Macclesfield 9 Kh 53.16N 2.07W
Macclesfield Bank (EN) 26 Fc 15.50N 114.20 E
McClintock 42 Ie 57.48N 94.12W
McClintock, Mount- 66 Jg 80.13S 157.26 E
Mc Clintock Channel 38 Ib 71.00N 101.00W
McCluer Gulf (EN)=Berau, Teluk- 26 Jg 2.30S 132.30 E
Mc Clure Strait 38 Hb 74.30N 116.00W
McClusky 45 Fc 47.29N 100.27W
McComb 43 Ie 31.14N 90.27W
McConaughy, Lake- 45 Ff 41.18N 101.46W
McConnelsville 44 Gf 39.39N 81.51W
McCook 43 Gc 40.12N 100.38W
McCormick 44 Fi 33.55N 82.19W
McDame 42 Ee 59.13N 129.14W
McDermitt 46 Gf 41.59N 117.36W
Macdhui, Ben- 9 Jd 57.04N 3.40W
Macdonald, Lake- 59 Fd 23.30S 129.00 E
Mc Donald Islands 30 On 52.59S 72.50 E
McDonald Peak [Ca.-U.S.] 46 Ef 40.58N 120.26W
McDonald Peak [Mt.-U.S.] 46 Ic 47.29N 113.46W
Macdonald Range 46 Hb 49.12N 114.46W
Macdonnell Ranges 57 Eg 23.45S 132.20 E
McDouglas Sound 42 Hd 75.15N 97.30W
Macduff 9 Kd 57.40N 2.29W
Macedo de Cavaleiros 13 Fc 41.32N 6.58W
Macedonia (EN)= Makedhonia 5 Ig 41.00N 23.00 E
Macedonia (EN)= Makedhonia 15 Fh 41.00N 23.00 E
Macedonia (EN)= Makedonija [2] 15 Eh 41.50N 22.00 E
Macedonia (EN)= Makedonija 5 Ig 41.00N 23.00 E
Macedonia (EN)= Makedonija 15 Fh 41.00N 23.00 E
Maceió 53 Mf 9.40S 35.43W
Macenta 34 Dd 8.33N 9.28W
Macerata 14 Hg 43.18N 13.27 E
McGehee 45 Kj 33.38N 91.24W
McGill 46 Hg 39.23N 114.47W
Macgillycuddy's Reeks/Na Cruacha Dubha 9 Di 52.00N 9.50W
McGrath 40 Hd 62.58N 155.38W
MacGregor 45 Gb 49.57N 98.49W
McGregor 45 Jc 46.36N 93.19W
McGregor Lake 46 Ia 50.31N 112.53W
Mc Gregor Range 59 Ie 26.40S 142.45 E
McGuire, Mount- 46 Hd 45.10N 114.36W
Machachi 54 Cd 0.30S 78.34W
Machado 55 Je 21.41S 45.56W
Machagai 56 Hc 26.56S 60.03W
Machaila 37 Ed 22.15S 32.58 E
Machaire na Mumhan/Golden Vale 9 Fi 52.30N 8.00W
Machaire Rátha/Maghera 9 Gg 54.51N 6.40W
Machakos 36 Gc 1.31S 37.16 E
Machala 54 Cd 3.16S 79.58W
Machaneng 37 Dd 23.12S 27.30 E
Machareti 54 Fh 20.49S 63.24W
Machar Marshes 35 Ed 9.20N 33.10 E
Machattie, Lake- 59 Hd 24.50S 139.48 E
Machault 12 Ge 49.21N 4.30 E
Macheke 37 Ec 18.05S 31.51 E
Macheng 27 Je 31.10N 115.00 E
Machias 44 Nc 44.43N 67.28W
Machida 29 Fd 35.32N 139.27 E
Machilipatnam (Bandar) 25 Ge 16.10N 81.08 E
Machiques 54 Da 10.04N 72.34W
Machona, Laguna- 48 Mh 18.20N 93.40W
Machów 10 Rf 50.34N 21.40 E
Machupicchu 53 Ig 13.07S 72.34W
Macia 37 Ef 25.02S 33.06 E
Mc Ilwraith Range 59 Ib 13.45S 143.20 E
Măcin 15 Ld 45.15N 28.09 E
Macina 30 Gg 14.30N 5.00W
McIntosh 45 Fd 45.55N 101.21W
Macintyre River 59 Je 29.25S 148.45 E
Maçka 24 Hb 40.50N 39.38 E
Mackay [Austl.] 58 Fg 21.09S 149.11 E
Mackay [Id.-U.S.] 46 Ie 43.55N 113.37W
Mackay, Lake- 57 Dg 22.30S 129.00 E
McKay Lake 45 Mb 49.35N 86.22W
McKean Atoll 57 Je 3.36S 174.08W
McKeand 42 Kd 63.00N 65.05W
McKeesport 44 He 40.21N 79.52W
Mackenzie 38 Fc 69.15N 134.08W
McKenzie 44 Cg 36.08N 88.31W
Mackenzie, District of- [3] 42 Gd 65.00N 115.00W
Mackenzie Bay [Ant.] 66 Fe 68.20S 71.15 E
Mackenzie Bay [Can.] 38 Fc 69.00N 136.30W
McKenzie Island 42 If 51.05N 93.48W
Mackenzie King 38 Hb 77.45N 111.00W
Mackenzie Mountains 38 Gc 64.00N 130.00W
McKenzie River 46 Dd 44.07N 123.06W
Mackenzie River 59 Jd 24.00S 149.55 E
McKerrow, Lake- 62 Cf 44.30S 168.05 E
Mackinac, Straits of- 43 Kb 45.49N 82.45W
Mackinaw City 44 Ec 45.47N 84.44W
McKinley, Mount- 38 Dc 63.30N 151.00W
McKinley Park 40 Jd 63.44N 148.54W
McKinney 45 Hj 33.12N 96.37W
Mackinnon Road 36 Gc 3.44S 39.03 E
McLaughlin 45 Fd 45.49N 100.49W
McLean 45 Fi 35.14N 100.36W
McLeans Town 44 Il 26.39N 77.59W
Maclean Strait 42 Ha 77.30N 103.10W
Maclear 37 Df 31.02S 28.23 E
Macleay River 59 Kf 30.52S 153.01 E
Mc Leod, Lake- 57 Cg 24.10S 113.35 E
McLeod Bay 42 Gd 62.53N 110.15W
McLeod Lake 42 Ff 54.59N 123.02W
McLoughlin, Mount- 46 De 42.27N 122.19W
McLure 46 Ea 51.03N 120.14W
Macmillan 42 Dd 62.52N 135.55W
McMillan, Lake- 45 Dj 32.40N 104.20W
McMillan Pass 42 Ed 63.00N 130.00W
McMinnville [Or.-U.S.] 46 Dd 45.13N 123.12W
McMinnville [Tn.-U.S.] 44 Eh 35.41N 85.46W
McMurdo 66 Kf 77.51S 166.37 E
McNaughton Lake 42 Ff 52.40N 117.50W
Macomb 45 Kf 40.27N 90.40W
Macomer 14 Cj 40.16N 8.47 E
Macomia 37 Gb 12.15S 40.08 E
Mâcon 11 Kh 46.18N 4.50 E
Macon [Ga.-U.S.] 39 Kf 32.50N 83.38W
Macon [Mo.-U.S.] 45 Jg 39.44N 92.28W
Macon [Ms.-U.S.] 45 Lj 33.07N 88.34W
Macondo 36 De 12.36S 23.43 E
Mâconnais, Monts du- 11 Kh 46.18N 4.45 E
Macoris, Cabo- 49 Ld 19.47N 70.28W
Macouba 51h Ab 14.52N 61.09W
McPherson 43 Hd 38.22N 97.40W
Mc Pherson Range 59 Ke 28.20S 153.00 E
Macquarie 66 Jd 54.30S 158.30 E
Macquarie Harbour 59 Jh 42.20S 145.25 E
Macquarie Ridge (EN) 3 Jo 57.00S 159.00 E
Macquarie River 57 Fh 30.07S 147.24 E
Mac Robertson Land 66 Fe 70.00S 65.00 E
Macroom/Maigh Chromtha 9 Ej 51.54N 8.57W
Macugnaga 14 Be 45.58N 7.58 E
Macujer 54 Dc 0.24N 73.07W
Macuro 50 Fg 10.39N 61.56W
Macusani 54 Df 14.05S 70.26W
Macuspana 48 Mi 17.48N 92.36W
Mačva 15 Ce 44.49N 19.30 E
McVicar Arm 42 Fc 65.10N 120.30W
Ma'dabā 24 Fg 31.43N 35.48 E
Madagali 34 Hc 10.53N 13.38 E
Madagascar 30 Lj 20.00S 47.00 E
Madagascar (EN)= Madagasikara [1] 31 Lj 19.00S 46.00 E
Madagascar Basin (EN) 3 Fl 27.00S 53.00 E
Madagascar Plateau (EN) 3 Fm 30.00S 45.00 E
Madagasikara=Madagascar (EN) [1] 31 Lj 19.00S 46.00 E
Madā'in Şāliḩ 24 Gi 26.48N 37.53 E
Madalai 64a Ac 7.20N 134.28 E
Madama 34 Ha 21.58N 13.39 E
Madan 15 Hh 41.30N 24.57 E
Madang 58 Fe 5.13S 145.48 E
Madanīyīn 31 Ie 33.21N 10.30 E
Madanīyīn [3] 32 Jc 33.00N 10.45 E
Madaoua 34 Gc 14.05N 5.58 E
Madara 15 Kf 43.17N 27.06 E
Madara-Shima 29 Ae 33.35N 129.45 E
Madaroumfa 34 Gc 13.18N 7.09 E
Madau 63a Ac 9.00S 152.26 E
Madawaska Highlands 44 Hc 45.20N 78.15W
Maddalena 14 Di 41.15N 9.25 E
Maddalena, Colle della- 11 Mj 44.25N 6.53 E
Maddaloni 14 Ii 41.02N 14.23 E
Made, Made en Drimmelen- 12 Gc 51.41N 4.48 E
Made en Drimmelen 12 Gc 51.41N 4.48 E
Made en Drimmelen-Made 12 Gc 51.41N 4.48 E
Madeir 35 Dd 7.50N 29.12 E
Madeira [5] 31 Fe 32.40N 16.45W
Madeira 30 Fe 32.44N 17.00W
Madeira, Arquipélago da-= Madeira Islands (EN) 30 Fe 32.40N 16.45W
Madeira, Rio- 52 Kf 3.22S 58.45W
Madeira Islands (EN)= Madeira, Arquipélago da- 30 Fe 32.40N 16.45W
Madeleine, Ile de la - 42 Lg 47.26N 61.44W
Madeleine, Monts de la- 11 Jh 46.03N 3.50 E
Maden 24 Hc 38.23N 39.40 E
Madenassa Veld 30 Jj 19.00N 25.30 E
Madera [Ca.-U.S.] 46 Eh 36.57N 120.03W
Madera [Mex.] 47 Cc 29.12N 108.07W
Mader-Chih 13 Ri 35.26N 5.07 E
Madero, Puerto del- 13 Jc 41.48N 2.05W
Madesimo 14 Dd 46.26N 9.21 E
Madgaon 25 Ee 15.22N 73.49 E
Madhya Pradesh [3] 25 Fd 22.00N 79.00 E
Madimba 36 Cc 4.58S 15.08 E
Madina do Boé 34 Cc 11.45N 14.13W
Madinani 34 Dd 9.37N 6.57W
Madīnat al Abyār 33 Dc 32.11N 20.36 E
Madīnat ash Sha'b 22 Gh 12.50N 44.56 E
Madingo-Kayes 36 Bc 4.10S 12.18 E
Madingou 36 Bc 4.09S 13.34 E
Madirovalo 37 Hc 16.29S 46.30 E
Madison [Fl.-U.S.] 44 Fj 30.28N 83.25W
Madison [In.-U.S.] 44 Ef 38.44N 85.23W
Madison [Mn.-U.S.] 45 Hd 45.01N 96.11W
Madison [S.D.-U.S.] 45 He 44.00N 97.07W
Madison [Wi.-U.S.] 39 Ke 43.05N 89.22W
Madison [W.V.-U.S.] 44 Gf 38.03N 81.50W
Madison Range 46 Jd 45.15N 111.20W
Madison River 46 Jd 45.56N 111.30W
Madisonville 43 Jd 37.20N 87.30W
Madiun 26 Fh 7.37S 111.31 E
Mado Gashi 36 Gb 0.44N 39.10 E
Madoi (Huangheyan) 22 Lf 35.00N 98.56 E
Madon 11 Mf 48.36N 6.06 E
Madona 7 Gh 56.53N 26.20 E
Madra Dağı 15 Kj 39.23N 27.12 E
Madrakah, Ra's al- 23 If 18.59N 57.45 E
Madranbaba Dağı 15 Ll 37.38N 28.12 E
Madras [India] 22 Kh 13.05N 80.17 E
Madras [Or.-U.S.] 46 Ed 44.38N 121.08W
Madre, Laguna- [Mex.] 47 Ed 25.00N 97.40W
Madre, Laguna- [Tx.-U.S.] 43 Hf 27.00N 97.35W
Madre, Sierra- 38 Jh 15.20N 92.20W
Madre de Dios [2] 54 Df 12.00S 70.15W
Madre de Dios 54 Df 12.36S 69.59W
Madre de Dios, Isla- 52 Ik 50.15S 75.05W
Madre de Dios, Rio- 52 Jg 10.59S 66.08W
Madre del Sur, Sierra-= Southern Sierra Madre (EN) 38 Jj 17.00N 100.00W
Madre Occidental, Sierra-= Western Sierra Madre (EN) 38 Ig 25.00N 105.00W
Madre Oriental, Sierra-= Eastern Sierra Madre (EN) 38 Jg 22.00N 99.30W
Madrid [3] 13 Id 40.30N 3.40W
Madrid 6 Fg 40.24N 3.41W
Madrid-Aravaca 13 Id 40.27N 3.47W
Madridejos 13 Ie 39.28N 3.32W
Madrid-El Pardo 13 Id 40.32N 3.46W
Madrid-Vallecas 13 Id 40.23N 3.37W
Madrid-Villaverde 13 Id 40.21N 3.42W
Madrigal de las Altas Torres 13 Hc 41.05N 5.00W
Mad River 46 Cf 40.57N 124.07W
Madriz [3] 49 Dg 13.30N 86.30W
Madrona, Sierra- 13 Hf 38.25N 4.10W
Madula 36 Eb 0.28N 25.23 E
Madura, Palau- 21 Nj 7.00S 113.20 E
Madurai 22 Ji 9.56N 78.07 E
Madvār, Kūh-e- 23 Hc 30.36N 54.52 E
Madwīn 33 Cd 28.42N 17.31 E
Madyan 21 Fg 27.40N 35.35 E
Madžalis 16 Oh 42.08N 47.50 E
Maebara 28 Be 33.34N 130.13 E
Maebashi 27 Od 36.23N 139.04 E
Mae Hong Son 25 Je 19.16N 97.56 E
Mæl 8 Ce 59.56N 8.48 E
Mae Nam Khong=Mekong (EN) 21 Mh 10.15N 105.55 E
Maesawa 29 Gb 39.03N 141.07 E
Mae Sot 25 Je 16.40N 98.35 E
Maestra, Sierra- 38 Lh 20.00N 76.45W
Maevatanana 37 Hc 16.56S 46.49 E
Maéwo, Ile- 57 Hf 15.10S 168.10 E
Mafeteng 37 De 29.45S 27.18 E
Mafia Channel 36 Gd 7.50S 39.35 E
Mafia Island 30 Ki 7.50S 39.50 E
Mafikeng 31 Jk 25.53S 25.39 E
Mafra [Braz.] 56 Kc 26.07S 49.49W
Mafra [Port.] 13 Cf 38.56N 9.20W
Magadan 22 Rd 59.34N 150.48 E
Magadanskaja Oblast [3] 20 Kd 62.30N 154.00 E
Magadi 36 Gc 1.54S 36.17 E
Magallanes, Estrecho de-= Magellan, Strait of- (EN) 52 Ik 54.00S 71.00W
Magallanes y Antártica Chilena [2] 56 Fh 51.30S 73.30W
Magangué 54 Db 9.14N 74.46W
Maganik 15 Cg 42.44N 19.16 E
Maganoy 26 He 6.51N 124.31 E
Magaria 34 Gc 12.59N 8.50 E
Magazine Mountain 45 Ji 35.10N 93.38W
Magdagači 20 Hf 53.29N 125.55 E
Magdala 55 Bm 36.06S 61.42W
Magdalena [2] 54 Db 10.00N 74.15W
Magdalena [Arg.] 55 Dl 35.04S 57.32W
Magdalena [Bol.] 54 Ff 13.20S 64.08W
Magdalena [Mex.] 47 Bb 30.38N 110.57W
Magdalena [N.M.-U.S.] 45 Ci 34.07N 107.14W
Magdalena, Bahía- 48 Ce 24.35N 112.00W
Magdalena, Isla- 47 Bd 24.55N 112.15W
Magdalena, Llano de la- 47 Bd 24.30N 111.40W
Magdalena, Rio- [Col.] 52 Id 11.06N 74.51W
Magdalena, Rio- [Mex.] 48 Cb 30.48N 112.32W
Magda Plateau 42 Jb 72.18N 82.55W
Magdeburg 6 He 52.10N 11.40 E
Magdeburg [2] 10 Hd 52.15N 11.35 E
Magdeburger Börde 10 Hd 52.00N 11.30 E
Magdelaine Cays 57 Gf 16.35S 150.15 E
Magee 45 Lk 31.52N 89.44W
Magee, Island-/Oileán Mhic Aodha 9 Hg 54.50N 5.50W
Magelang 26 Fh 7.28S 110.13 E
Magellan, Strait of- (EN) = Magallanes, Estrecho de- 52 Ik 54.00S 71.00W
Magellan Seamounts (EN) 57 Gc 17.30N 152.00 E
Magenta 14 Ce 45.28N 8.53 E
Magerøya 7 Fa 71.03N 25.45 E
Magetan 26 Fh 7.39S 111.20 E
Maggiorasca 14 Df 44.33N 9.29 E
Maggiore, Lago- 14 Ce 45.55N 8.40 E
Maghāghah 33 Fd 28.39N 30.50 E
Maghama 32 Ef 15.31N 12.50W
Maghera/Machaire Rátha 9 Gg 54.51N 6.40W
Maghnia 32 Gc 34.51N 1.44W
Magic Reservoir 46 He 43.20N 114.18W
Mágina, Sierra- 13 Ig 37.45N 3.30W
Magistralny 20 Fe 56.03N 107.35 E
Maglaj 14 Mf 44.33N 18.06 E
Măglenik 15 Ih 41.20N 25.45 E
Maglie 14 Mj 40.07N 18.18 E
Măgliž 15 Ig 42.36N 25.33 E
Magnetawan River 44 Gc 45.46N 80.37W
Magnetic Island 59 Jc 19.10S 146.50 E
Magnitka 17 Ii 55.21N 59.43 E
Magnitnaja, Gora- 17 Ij 53.10N 59.10 E
Magnitogorsk 6 Le 53.27N 59.04 E
Magnolia 45 Jj 33.16N 93.14W
Magnor 7 Cg 59.57N 12.12 E
Magny-en-Vexin 11 He 49.09N 1.47 E
Mago 20 Jf 53.18N 140.20 E
Magoé 37 Ec 15.48S 31.43 E
Magoebaskloof 37 Ed 23.51S 30.02 E
Magog 44 Kc 45.16N 72.09W
Magosa=Famagusta (EN) 23 Dc 35.07N 33.57 E
Magra [Alg.] 13 Qi 35.29N 4.58 E
Magra [It.] 14 Df 44.03N 9.58 E
Magtá Lahjar 32 Ef 17.50N 13.20W
Maguarinho, Cabo- 54 Id 0.20S 48.20W
Magude 37 Ee 25.02S 32.40 E
Magumeri 34 Hc 12.07N 12.49 E
Magura, Gora- 10 Th 48.50N 23.44 E
Magway 25 Jd 20.00N 95.00 E
Magway 22 Lg 20.09N 94.55 E
Magyarország = Hungary (EN) [1] 6 Hf 47.00N 20.00 E
Mahābād 23 Gb 36.45N 45.53 E
Mahabalipuram 25 Gf 12.37N 80.12 E
Mahabe 37 Hc 17.05S 45.20 E
Mahabo 37 Gd 20.21S 44.39 E
Mahačkala 6 Kg 42.58N 47.30 E
Mahadday Wēyne 35 He 3.00N 45.32 E
Mahādeo Range 25 Ee 17.50N 74.15 E
Mahafaly, Plateau- 37 Gd 24.30S 44.00 E
Mahagi 36 Fb 2.18N 30.59 E
Mahajamba 37 Hc 15.33S 47.08 E
Mahājan 25 Ec 28.47N 73.50 E
Mahajanga 31 Lj 15.17S 46.43 E
Mahajanga [3] 37 Hc 16.30S 47.00 E
Mahajilo 37 Hc 19.42S 45.22 E
Mahakam 21 Nj 0.35S 117.17 E
Mahalapye 37 Dd 23.07S 26.46 E
Mahalevona 37 Hc 15.26S 49.55 E
Mahallāt 24 Nf 33.55N 50.27 E
Mahamid 35 Cb 15.09N 20.25 E
Māhān 24 Qg 30.05N 57.19 E
Mahānadi 21 Kg 20.19N 86.45 E
Mahanoro 37 Hc 19.53S 48.49 E
Maharadze 19 Eg 41.53N 42.01 E
Mahārāshtra [3] 25 Ee 18.00N 75.00 E
Mahārlū, Daryācheh-ye- 24 Oh 29.25N 52.50 E
Mahās 35 He 4.24N 46.07 E
Maha Sarakham 25 Ke 16.12N 103.16 E
Mahavavy 30 Lj 15.57S 45.54 E
Mahbés 32 Dd 27.10N 9.50W
Maḩḑah 24 Pj 24.24N 55.59 E
Mahdia 54 Gb 5.16N 59.09W
Mahe 25 Ff 11.42N 75.32 E
Mahébourg 37a Bb 20.24S 57.42 E
Mahé Island 30 Mi 4.40S 55.28 E
Mahendra Giri 25 Ge 18.58N 84.21 E
Mahenge 31 Ki 8.41S 36.43W
Maheno 62 Df 45.10S 170.50 E
Mahesāna 25 Ed 23.36N 72.24 E
Mahi 25 Ed 22.16N 72.58 E
Mahia Peninsula 61 Eg 39.10S 177.55 E
Mahmudābād 24 Lc 39.25N 47.15 E
Mahmūdābād 24 Od 36.38N 52.15 E
Mahmūd-e 'Erāqī 23 Kb 35.01N 69.20 E
Mahmudiye 24 Dc 39.30N 31.00 E
Mahmutşevketpaşa 15 Mh 41.09N 29.11 E
Māhneshān 24 Ld 36.45N 47.38 E
Mahnevo 17 Jg 58.27N 61.42 E
Mahnomen 45 Ic 47.19N 95.59W
Mahón/Mao 13 Qe 39.53N 4.15 E
Mahoré/Mayotte 30 Lj 12.50S 45.10 E
Mahrāt, Jabal- 35 Ib 17.00N 52.20 E
Mahuan Dao 27 Kd 10.50N 115.47 E
Mahua Point 63a Fd 10.28S 162.05 E
Maiana Atoll 57 Id 0.55N 173.00 E
Maïao, Ile- (Tubai-Manu) 57 Lf 17.34S 150.35W
Maicao 54 Da 11.23N 72.15W
Maicasagi, Lac- 44 Ia 49.52N 76.48W
Maîche 11 Mg 47.15N 6.48 E
Maicuru, Rio- 54 Hd 2.10S 54.17W
Maidenhead 12 Bc 51.31N 0.42W
Maidstone 9 Nj 51.17N 0.32 E
Maiduguri 31 Ig 11.51N 13.09 E
Maigh Chromtha/Macroom 9 Ej 51.54N 8.57W
Maigudo 35 Fd 7.26N 37.10 E
Maihara 29 Ed 35.20N 136.18 E
Maikala Range 25 Gd 22.30N 81.30 E
Maiko 36 Eb 0.14N 25.33 E
Maikona 36 Gb 2.56N 37.38 E
Maikoor, Pulau- 26 Jh 6.15S 134.15 E
Main 10 Ef 50.00N 8.18 E
Mainalon Óros 15 Fl 37.40N 22.15 E

Index Symbols

[1] Independent Nation
[2] State, Region
[3] District, County
[4] Municipality
[5] Colony, Dependency
Continent
Physical Region
Historical or Cultural Region
Mount, Mountain
Volcano
Hill
Mountains, Mountain Range
Hills, Escarpment
Plateau, Upland
Pass, Gap
Plain, Lowland
Delta
Salt Flat
Valley, Canyon
Crater, Cave
Karst Features
Depression
Polder
Desert, Dunes
Forest, Woods
Heath, Steppe
Oasis
Cape, Point
Coast, Beach
Cliff
Peninsula
Isthmus
Sandbank
Island
Atoll
Rock, Reef
Islands, Archipelago
Rocks, Reefs
Coral Reef
Well, Spring
Geyser
River, Stream
Waterfall Rapids
River Mouth, Estuary
Lake
Salt Lake
Intermittent Lake
Reservoir
Swamp, Pond
Canal
Glacier
Ice Shelf, Pack Ice
Ocean
Sea
Gulf, Bay
Strait, Fjord
Lagoon
Bank
Seamount
Tablemount
Ridge
Shelf
Basin
Escarpment, Sea Scarp
Fracture
Trench, Abyss
National Park, Reserve
Point of Interest
Recreation Site
Cave, Cavern
Historic Site
Ruins
Wall, Walls
Church, Abbey
Temple
Scientific Station
Airport
Port
Lighthouse
Mine
Tunnel
Dam, Bridge

Main Barrier Range	59	If	31.25 S	141.25 E
Mainburg	10	Hh	48.39 N	11.47 E
Main Camp	64g	Ba	2.01 N	157.25 W
Main Channel	44	Gc	45.22 N	81.50 W
Mai-Ndombe, Lac-	30	Ii	2.10 S	18.15 E
Main-Donau-Kanal	10	Gg	49.55 N	10.50 E
Maindong → Coqên	27	Ee	31.15 N	85.13 E
Maine	11	Ff	48.15 N	0.10 W
Maine [2]	43	Nb	45.15 N	69.15 W
Maine [Fr.]	11	Fg	47.25 N	0.37 W
Maine [Fr.]	11	Eg	47.09 N	1.27 W
Maine, Gulf of-	38	Me	43.00 N	68.00 W
Maine-et-Loire [3]	11	Fg	47.30 N	0.20 W
Mainé-Soroa	34	Hc	13.18 N	12.02 E
Mainistir Fhear Mai/Fermoy	9	Ei	52.08 N	8.16 W
Mainistir na Búille/Boyle	9	Eh	53.58 N	8.18 W
Mainistir na Corann/ Midleton	9	Ej	51.55 N	8.10 W
Mainistir na Féile/ Abbeyfeale	9	Di	52.24 N	9.18 W
Mainit, Lake-	26	Ie	9.26 N	125.32 E
Mainland [Scot.-U.K.]	5	Fc	60.20 N	1.22 W
Mainland [Scot.-U.K.]	5	Fd	59.00 N	3.10 W
Maintal	12	Kd	50.08 N	8.51 E
Maintenon	11	Hf	48.35 N	1.35 E
Maintirano	31	Lj	18.03 S	44.03 E
Mainz	10	Eg	50.00 N	8.15 E
Maio	32	Cf	23.10 N	15.10 W
Maio	30	Eg	15.15 N	23.10 W
Maipo, Volcán-	52	Ji	34.10 S	69.50 W
Maipú	56	Ie	36.52 S	57.52 W
Maiquetia	54	Ea	10.36 N	66.57 W
Maira	14	Bf	44.49 N	7.38 E
Mairi	54	Jf	11.43 S	40.08 W
Mairipotaba	55	Hc	17.21 S	49.31 W
Maisān [3]	24	Lg	32.00 N	47.00 E
Maisí, Punta-	47	Jd	20.15 N	74.09 W
Maišiagala/Maišjagala	8	Kj	54.51 N	25.14 E
Maišjagala/Maišiagala	8	Kj	54.51 N	25.14 E
Maîter	13	Qi	35.23 N	4.17 E
Maitland [Austl.]	59	Hf	34.22 S	137.40 E
Maitland [Austl.]	58	Gh	32.44 S	151.33 E
Maíz, Isla Grande del-	49	Fg	12.10 N	83.03 W
Maíz, Isla Pequeña del-	49	Fg	12.18 N	82.59 W
Maíz, Islas del-	47	Hf	12.15 N	83.00 W
Maizhokunggar	27	Ff	29.50 N	91.40 E
Maizières-lès-Metz	12	Ie	49.13 N	6.09 E
Maizuru	28	Mg	35.27 N	135.20 E
Maizuru-Nishimaizuru	29	Dd	35.28 N	135.19 E
Maizuru-Wan	29	Dd	35.30 N	135.20 E
Maja	21	Pd	60.17 N	134.41 E
Majagual	49	Ji	8.35 N	74.37 W
Majakovski	16	Mh	42.02 N	42.47 E
Majangat	27	Fb	48.20 N	91.58 E
Majardah, Wādī-	14	Em	37.07 N	10.13 E
Majāz al Bāb	14	Dn	36.39 N	9.37 E
Majdanpek	15	Ee	44.25 N	21.56 E
Majene	22	Nj	3.33 S	118.57 E
Majërtēn = Mijirtein (EN)	30	Lh	9.00 N	50.00 E
Majevica	14	Mf	44.40 N	18.40 E
Maji	35	Fd	6.10 N	35.35 E
Majia He	27	Kd	38.09 N	117.53 E
Majja	20	Id	61.38 N	130.25 E
Majkain	19	He	51.27 N	75.52 E
Majkamys	18	Ka	46.34 N	77.37 E
Majkop	6	Kg	44.35 N	40.07 E
Majli-Saj	18	Id	41.15 N	72.30 E
Majma'ah	24	Kj	25.54 N	45.20 E
Majmak	19	Hg	42.40 N	71.14 E
Majmakan	20	Ie	57.30 N	135.23 E
Majmeča	20	Fb	71.20 N	104.15 E
Majn	20	Mc	65.03 N	172.10 E
Majna [R.S.F.S.R.]	20	Ef	53.00 N	91.28 E
Majna [R.S.F.S.R.]	7	Li	54.09 N	47.37 E
Major, Puig-	13	Oe	39.48 N	2.48 E
Major, Puig-/Mayor, Puig-	13	Oe	39.48 N	2.48 E
Majorca (EN) = Mallorca	5	Gh	39.30 N	3.00 E
Majrur	35	Db	16.40 N	26.53 E
Majski [R.S.F.S.R.]	16	Nh	43.36 N	44.03 E
Majski [R.S.F.S.R.]	20	Hf	52.18 N	129.38 E
Maju, Pulau	26	If	1.20 N	126.25 E
Majuro Atoll	57	Id	7.09 N	171.12 E
Makabana	31	Ii	3.28 S	12.36 E
Makaha	65a	Cb	21.29 N	158.13 W
Makahuena Point	65a	Bb	21.52 N	159.27 W
Makalamabedi	37	Cd	20.20 S	23.53 E
Makale	26	Gg	3.06 S	119.51 E
Makallè	56	Ic	27.13 S	59.17 W
Makalondi	34	Fc	12.50 N	1.41 E
Makamby, Nosy-	37	Hc	15.42 S	45.54 E
Makanči	19	If	46.51 N	81.57 E
Makanza	36	Cb	1.36 N	19.07 E
Makapala	65a	Fc	20.13 N	155.45 W
Makapu Point	64k	Ba	18.59 S	169.55 W
Makapuu Head	65a	Db	21.18 N	157.39 W
Makara, Prohod-	15	Ih	41.16 N	25.26 E
Makares	15	Il	37.05 N	25.42 E
Makarfi	34	Gc	11.23 N	7.53 E
Makari	34	Ic	12.35 N	14.28 E
Makari Mountains	36	Ed	6.05 S	29.50 E
Makarjev	7	Kh	57.57 N	43.49 E
Makarov	20	Jg	48.39 N	142.51 E
Makarov Basin (EN)	67	Ce	87.00 N	170.00 E
Makarov Seamount (EN)	57	Gb	29.30 N	153.30 E
Makarska	14	Lg	43.18 N	17.02 E
Makā Rūd	24	Nd	36.21 N	51.16 E
Makasar → Ujung Pandang	22	Nj	5.07 S	119.24 E
Makasar, Selat- = Makassar Strait (EN)	21	Nj	2.00 S	117.30 E
Makassar Strait (EN) = Makasar, Selat-	21	Nj	2.00 S	117.30 E
Makat	6	Lf	47.40 N	53.28 E
Makatea, Ile-	57	Mf	15.50 S	148.15 W
Makaw	25	Jc	26.27 N	96.42 E
Makawao	65a	Ec	20.51 N	156.19 W
Makay, Massif du-	37	Hd	21.15 S	45.15 E
Makedhonia [2]	15	Fi	40.40 N	22.30 E
Makedhonia = Macedonia (EN)	15	Fh	41.00 N	23.00 E
Makedhonia = Macedonia (EN)	5	Ig	41.00 N	23.00 E
Makedonija = Macedonia (EN)	5	Ig	41.00 N	23.00 E
Makedonija = Macedonia (EN) [2]	15	Eh	41.50 N	22.00 E
Makedonija = Macedonia (EN)	15	Fh	41.00 N	23.00 E
Makejevka	16	Jf	48.00 N	37.58 E
Makelulu, Mount-	64a	Bb	7.34 N	134.35 E
Makemo Atoll	57	Mf	16.35 S	143.40 W
Makeni	31	Fh	8.53 N	12.03 W
Makgadikgadi Pans	30	Jk	20.50 S	25.30 E
Makhfar al Buşayyah	24	Lg	30.08 N	46.07 E
Makhfar al Hammām	24	He	35.51 N	38.45 E
Makhmūr	24	Je	35.46 N	43.35 E
Makhyah, Wādī-	23	Gf	17.40 N	49.01 E
Maki	29	Fc	37.45 N	138.52 E
Makian, Pulau-	26	If	0.20 N	127.25 E
Makikihi	62	Df	44.38 S	171.09 E
Makinsk	19	He	52.40 N	70.26 E
Makkah = Mecca (EN)	22	Fg	21.27 N	39.49 E
Makkovik	42	Le	55.05 N	59.11 W
Maknassy	32	Ic	34.37 N	9.36 E
Makó	10	Qj	46.13 N	20.29 E
Makokou	31	Ih	0.34 N	12.52 E
Makongai	63d	Bb	17.27 S	178.58 E
Makongolosi	36	Fd	8.24 S	33.09 E
Makorako	62	Gc	39.09 S	176.03 E
Makoua	31	Ih	0.01 N	15.39 E
Makoura	63b	Dc	17.08 S	168.26 E
Makov	10	Og	49.22 N	18.29 E
Maków Mazowiecki	10	Rd	52.52 N	21.06 E
Makrā	15	Im	36.16 N	25.53 E
Makrān	21	Hg	26.00 N	60.00 E
Makrónisos	15	Hl	37.42 N	24.07 E
Maksatiha	7	Ih	57.48 N	35.55 E
Makteir	30	Ff	21.50 N	11.40 W
Makthar	14	Do	35.50 N	9.13 E
Makthar	32	Ib	35.51 N	9.12 E
Makū	23	Hd	27.52 N	52.26 E
Mākū	24	Kc	39.17 N	44.31 E
Makubetsu	29a	Cb	42.54 N	143.19 E
Makumbato	36	Fd	8.51 S	34.50 E
Makumbi	36	Dd	5.51 S	20.41 E
Makunduchi	36	Gd	6.25 S	39.33 E
Makung	27	Kg	23.35 N	119.35 E
Makurazaki	28	Ki	31.16 N	139.19 E
Makurdi	31	Hh	7.44 N	8.32 E
Makushin Volcano	40a	Eb	53.53 N	166.50 W
Makušino	19	Gd	55.13 N	67.13 E
Makuyuni	36	Gc	3.33 S	36.06 E
Malå	7	Ed	65.11 N	18.44 E
Mala/Mallow	9	Ei	52.08 N	8.39 W
Mala, Punta-	47	Ig	7.28 N	80.00 W
Malabang	26	He	7.38 N	124.03 E
Malabar Coast	21	Jh	10.00 N	76.15 E
Malabo	31	Hh	3.45 N	8.47 E
Malabrigo	55	Ci	29.20 S	59.58 W
Malacca, Strait of- (EN) = Melaka, Selat-	21	Mi	2.30 N	101.20 E
Malacky	10	Nh	48.27 N	17.01 E
Malad City	46	Ie	42.12 N	112.15 W
Malá Fatra	10	Og	49.08 N	18.50 E
Málaga [3]	13	Hh	36.48 N	4.45 W
Málaga [Col.]	54	Db	6.42 N	72.44 W
Málaga [Sp.]	6	Fh	36.43 N	4.25 W
Malagarasi	30	Ji	5.12 S	29.47 E
Malagón	13	Ie	39.10 N	3.51 W
Malaimbandi	37	Hd	20.20 S	45.36 E
Malaita Island	57	He	9.00 S	161.00 E
Malaja Kuonamka	20	Gb	70.50 N	113.20 E
Malaja Ob	20	Bc	66.08 N	65.50 E
Malaja Sosva	19	Gc	63.10 N	64.22 E
Malaja Višera	19	Dd	58.52 N	32.14 E
Malaja Viska	16	Ge	48.39 N	31.38 E
Malakāl	31	Kh	9.31 N	31.39 E
Malakal Harbor	64a	Ac	7.20 N	134.26 E
Malakal Pass	64a	Ac	7.17 N	134.28 E
Mala Kapela	14	Jf	44.55 N	15.28 E
Malakobi	63a	Db	7.19 S	158.07 E
Mallamalla Range	25	Fe	16.17 N	79.29 E
Malang	22	Nj	7.59 S	112.37 E
Malangen	7	Eb	69.30 N	18.20 E
Malanje	36	Cd	9.30 S	16.30 E
Malanje	31	Ii	9.33 S	16.22 E
Malanville	34	Fc	11.52 N	3.23 E
Malao	63b	Cb	15.10 S	166.51 E
Mała Panew	10	Nf	50.44 N	17.52 E
Mälaren	5	Hd	59.30 N	17.15 E
Malargüe	56	Ge	35.28 S	69.35 W
Malartic, Lac-	44	Ha	48.15 N	78.05 W
Malaspina Glacier	40	Ke	59.50 N	140.30 W
Malatya	22	Ff	38.21 N	38.19 E
Malāvi	24	Lf	33.10 N	47.50 E
Malawi [1]	31	Kj	13.30 S	34.00 E
Malawi, Lake-	30	Kj	12.00 S	34.30 E
Malaya	26	Df	4.00 N	102.00 E
Malaybalay	26	Ie	8.09 N	125.05 E
Malāyer	24	Me	34.16 N	48.12 E
Malāyer	23	Gc	34.17 N	48.50 E
Malay Peninsula (EN)	21	Mi	6.00 N	102.00 E
Malaysia [1]	22	Mi	4.00 N	102.00 E
Malaysia, Semenanjung- [2]	26	Df	4.00 N	102.00 E
Malazgirt	24	Jc	39.09 N	42.31 E
Malberg	12	Id	50.03 N	6.35 E
Mālbor	24	Og	30.45 N	52.05 E
Malbork	10	Pb	54.02 N	19.01 E
Malbrán	56	Hc	29.21 S	62.27 W
Malchin	10	Ic	53.44 N	12.47 E
Maldegem	12	Fc	51.13 N	3.27 E
Malden	45	Lh	36.34 N	89.57 W
Malden Island	57	Le	4.03 S	154.59 W
Malditos, Montes-/La Maladeta	13	Mb	42.40 N	0.50 E
Maldive Islands	21	Ji	3.15 N	73.00 E
Mal di Ventre	14	Ck	40.00 N	8.20 E
Maldives [1]	22	Ji	3.15 N	73.00 E
Maldon	9	Nj	51.45 N	0.40 E
Maldonado [2]	55	El	34.40 S	54.55 W
Maldonado	56	Jd	34.54 S	54.57 W
Maldonado, Punta-	48	Ji	16.20 N	98.35 W
Male	22	Ji	4.10 N	73.30 E
Malé	14	Ed	46.21 N	10.55 E
Mâle, Lac du-	44	Ja	48.30 N	75.30 W
Malea, Cape- (EN) = Maléas, Ákra-	15	Gm	36.26 N	23.12 E
Maléas, Ákra- = Malea, Cape- (EN)	15	Gm	36.26 N	23.12 E
Male Atoll	21	Ji	4.29 N	73.30 E
Malebo, Pool-	30	Ii	4.17 S	15.20 E
Mālegaon	25	Ed	20.33 N	74.32 E
Maléha	34	Dc	11.48 N	9.43 W
Malek	35	Ed	6.04 N	31.36 E
Malé Karpaty = Little Carpathians (EN)	10	Nh	48.30 N	17.20 E
Malek Kandī	24	Ld	37.09 N	46.06 E
Malékoula, Ile	57	Hf	16.15 S	167.30 E
Malema	37	Fb	14.57 S	37.25 E
Malemba Nkulu	36	Ed	8.02 S	26.48 E
Malenga	7	Ie	63.50 N	36.25 E
Măleruş	15	Id	45.54 N	25.32 E
Malesherbes	11	If	48.18 N	2.25 E
Malgobek	16	Nh	43.32 N	44.34 E
Malgomaj	7	Dd	64.47 N	16.12 E
Malhada	55	Kb	14.21 S	43.47 W
Malhanski Hrebet	20	Ff	50.30 N	109.00 E
Malhão da Estrêla	13	Ed	40.19 N	7.37 W
Malha Wells	35	Db	15.08 N	26.12 E
Malheur Lake	43	Dc	43.20 N	118.45 W
Malheur River	46	Gd	44.03 N	116.59 W
Mali [1]	31	Gg	17.00 N	4.00 W
Mali	34	Cc	12.05 N	12.18 W
Mali	25	Jc	25.42 N	97.30 E
Mali	63d	Bb	16.20 S	179.21 E
Mália	15	In	35.17 N	25.28 E
Maliakós Kólpos	15	Fk	38.52 N	22.38 E
Malik, Wādī al-	30	Kg	18.02 N	30.58 E
Mali kanal	15	Cd	45.42 N	19.19 E
Malik Sīah, Kūh-i-	23	Jd	29.51 N	60.52 E
Målilla	8	Fg	57.23 N	15.48 E
Mali Lošinj	14	If	44.32 N	14.28 E
Malimba, Monts-	36	Ed	7.32 S	29.30 E
Malin	16	Fd	50.46 N	29.14 E
Malinalco	48	Jh	18.57 N	99.30 W
Malinaltepec	48	Ji	17.03 N	98.40 W
Malindi	31	Li	3.13 S	40.07 E
Malines/Mechelen	11	Kc	51.02 N	4.29 E
Malin Head/Cionn Mhálanna	5	Fd	55.23 N	7.24 W
Malino, Bukit-	26	Hf	0.45 N	120.47 E
Malinovoje Ozero	20	Cf	51.40 N	79.55 E
Malinyi	36	Gd	8.56 S	36.08 E
Malipo	27	Hg	23.07 N	104.42 E
Maliqi	15	Di	40.43 N	20.41 E
Malita	26	Ie	6.25 N	125.36 E
Maljen	15	De	44.07 N	20.03 E
Maljovica	15	Gg	42.11 N	23.22 E
Malka	16	Nh	43.44 N	44.15 E
Malkara	24	Bb	40.53 N	26.54 E
Malki Lom	15	Jf	43.39 N	26.04 E
Malko Tărnovo	15	Kh	41.59 N	27.32 E
Mallacoota	59	Jg	37.30 S	149.50 E
Mallaig	9	Hd	57.00 N	5.50 W
Mallāq, Wādī-	14	Cn	36.32 N	8.51 E
Mallawī	33	Fd	27.44 N	30.50 E
Mallery Lake	42	Hd	64.00 N	98.00 W
Malles Venosta / Mals	14	Ed	46.41 N	10.32 E
Mallet	55	Gg	25.55 S	50.50 W
Mallorca = Majorca (EN)	5	Gh	39.30 N	3.00 E
Mallow/Mala	9	Ei	52.08 N	8.39 W
Malm	7	Cd	64.04 N	11.13 E
Malmbäck	8	Fg	57.35 N	14.28 E
Malmberget	7	Ec	67.10 N	20.40 E
Malmédy	11	Md	50.26 N	6.02 E
Malmesbury	37	Bf	33.28 S	18.44 E
Malmö	6	Hd	55.36 N	13.00 E
Malmöhus [2]	7	Ci	55.45 N	13.30 E
Malmön	8	Df	58.21 N	11.20 E
Malmslätt	8	Ff	58.25 N	15.30 E
Malmyž	19	Fd	56.31 N	50.41 E
Malo	63b	Cb	15.41 S	167.10 E
Maloarhangelsk	16	Jc	52.26 N	36.29 E
Maloelap	57	Id	8.45 N	171.03 E
Maloggia/Malojapaß	14	Dd	46.24 N	9.41 E
Malojapaß/Maloggia	14	Dd	46.24 N	9.41 E
Malojaroslavec	16	Jb	55.02 N	36.28 E
Maloje Polesje	10	Jf	50.10 N	24.30 E
Malolo	63d	Ab	17.45 S	177.10 E
Malolos	26	Hd	14.51 N	120.49 E
Malombe, Lake-	36	Ge	14.38 S	35.12 E
Malone	44	Jc	44.52 N	74.19 W
Malonga	36	De	10.24 S	23.10 E
Małopolska	10	Pf	50.45 N	20.00 E
Malorita	16	Dd	51.48 N	24.05 E
Malošujka	7	Ie	63.47 N	37.22 E
Måløy	7	Af	61.56 N	5.07 E
Malozemelskaja Tundra	17	Ec	68.00 N	52.00 E
Malpaso	48	Mi	17.20 N	93.30 W
Malpelo, Isla de-	52	He	3.59 N	81.35 W
Malprabha	25	Fe	16.12 N	76.03 E
Mals / Malles Venosta	14	Ed	46.41 N	10.32 E
Malsch	12	Kf	48.53 N	8.20 E
Malše	10	Kh	48.59 N	14.29 E
Malta	5	Hh	35.54 N	14.31 E
Malta [1]	6	Hh	35.50 N	14.30 E
Malta [Lat.-U.S.S.R.]	8	Lh	56.18 N	27.15 E
Malta [Mt.-U.S.]	43	Fb	48.21 N	107.52 W
Malta, Canale di- [Eur.] = Malta Channel (EN)	14	In	36.30 N	14.30 E
Malta Channel (EN) = Malta, Canale di- [Eur.]	14	In	36.30 N	14.30 E
Maltahöhe [3]	37	Bd	25.00 S	16.30 E
Maltahöhe	31	Ik	24.50 S	17.00 E
Maltepe	15	Mi	40.55 N	29.08 E
Malton	9	Mg	54.08 N	0.48 W
Maluku [3]	26	Ig	4.00 S	128.00 E
Maluku, Kepulauan- = Moluccas (EN)	57	De	2.00 S	128.00 E
Maluku, Laut- = Molucca Sea (EN)	21	Oj	0.05 S	125.00 E
Malumfashi	34	Gc	11.48 N	7.37 E
Malunda	26	Gg	3.00 S	118.50 E
Malung	7	Cf	60.40 N	13.44 E
Malungsfors	8	Ed	60.44 N	13.33 E
Malūţ	35	Ec	10.26 N	32.12 E
Maluu	63a	Ec	8.21 S	160.38 E
Malvern [Ar.-U.S.]	45	Ji	34.22 N	92.49 W
Malvern [Eng.-U.K.]	9	Ki	52.07 N	2.19 W
Malvinas	55	Ci	29.37 S	58.59 W
Malvinas, Islas-/Falkland Islands [5]	53	Kk	51.45 S	59.00 W
Malvinas, Islas-/Falkland Islands	52	Kk	51.45 S	59.00 W
Maly, Ostrov-	8	Ld	60.02 N	27.58 E
Malya	36	Fc	2.59 S	33.31 E
Maly Anjuj	20	Lc	68.35 N	161.03 E
Maly Čeremšan	7	Mi	54.20 N	50.01 E
Malý Dunaj	10	Nh	48.08 N	17.09 E
Malygina, Proliv-	20	Cb	73.00 N	70.30 E
Maly Jenisej	20	Ef	51.40 N	94.26 E
Maly Kavkaz = Lesser Caucasus (EN)	5	Kg	41.00 N	44.35 E
Maly Ljahovski, Ostrov-	20	Jb	74.07 N	140.36 E
Maly Tajmyr, Ostrov-	20	Fa	78.08 N	107.08 E
Maly Uzen	5	Kf	48.50 N	49.38 E
Mama	20	Ge	58.20 N	112.54 E
Mamadyš	7	Mi	55.45 N	51.24 E
Mamagota	63a	Bb	6.46 S	155.24 E
Mamaia	15	Le	44.17 N	28.37 E
Mamakan	20	Ge	57.48 N	114.05 E
Mamantel	48	Nh	18.33 N	91.05 W
Mamanutha Group	63d	Ab	17.34 S	177.04 E
Mamaqān	24	Kd	37.51 N	45.59 E
Mambaj	55	Ib	14.28 S	46.07 W
Mambajao	26	He	9.15 N	124.43 E
Mambasa	36	Eb	1.21 N	29.03 E
Mambéré	35	Be	3.31 N	16.03 E
Mambili	36	Cb	0.07 N	16.08 E
Mamborê	55	Fg	24.18 S	52.32 W
Mambova	36	Ef	17.44 S	25.11 E
Mambrui	36	Hc	3.07 S	40.09 E
Mamburao	26	Hd	13.14 N	120.35 E
Mamedkala	16	Ph	42.12 N	48.06 E
Mamer	12	Ie	49.38 N	6.02 E
Mamers	11	Gf	48.21 N	0.23 E
Mamfe	34	Gd	5.46 N	9.17 E
Mamiá, Lago-	54	Fd	4.15 S	63.05 W
Mamisonski, Pereval-	16	Mh	42.43 N	43.45 E
Mamljutka	19	Ge	54.57 N	68.35 E
Mammoth Cave	44	Dg	37.10 N	86.08 W
Mammoth Hot Springs	46	Jd	44.59 N	110.43 W
Mamoré, Rio-	52	Jg	10.23 S	65.53 W
Mamou	31	Fg	10.23 N	12.05 W
Mampikony	37	Hc	16.05 S	47.37 E
Mampodre, Picos de-	13	Ga	43.02 N	5.12 W
Mampong	34	Ed	7.04 N	1.24 W
Mamry, Jezioro-	10	Rb	54.08 N	21.42 E
Mamuju	26	Gg	2.41 S	118.54 E
Mamuno	37	Cd	22.17 S	20.02 E
Ma'mūrah, Ra's al-	14	En	36.27 N	10.49 E
Mamurokawa	29	Gb	38.54 N	140.15 E
Mamutzu	37	Hb	12.47 S	45.14 E
Man	31	Gh	7.24 N	7.33 W
Man [3]	34	Dd	7.13 N	7.41 W
Man, Calf of-	9	Ig	54.03 N	4.48 W
Man, Isle of-	5	Fe	54.15 N	4.30 W
Mana	60	Oc	22.02 N	159.46 W
Mana	20	Ee	55.57 N	92.28 E
Manacapuru	54	Fd	3.18 S	60.37 W
Manacor	13	Pe	39.34 N	3.12 E
Manado	22	Oi	1.29 N	124.51 E
Managua	39	Kh	12.09 N	86.17 W
Managua [3]	49	Dg	12.05 N	86.20 W
Managua, Lago de-	47	Gf	12.20 N	86.20 W
Manakara	31	Lk	22.07 S	48.00 E
Manama (EN) = Al Manāmah	22	Hg	26.13 N	50.35 E
Manambolo	37	Gc	19.19 S	44.17 E
Manam Island	57	Fe	4.05 S	145.03 E
Manamo, Caño-	54	Fb	9.55 N	62.16 W
Mananara	37	Hd	16.10 S	49.45 E
Mananara	37	Hd	23.21 S	47.42 E
Mananjary	31	Lk	21.14 S	48.17 E
Manankoro	34	Dc	10.28 N	7.25 W
Manantenina	37	Hd	24.17 S	47.18 E
Manaoba	63a	Ec	8.19 S	160.47 E
Manapire, Rio-	50	Ci	7.42 N	66.07 W
Manapouri	58	Hi	45.34 S	167.36 E
Manapouri, Lake-	62	Bf	45.30 S	167.30 E
Manār, Jabal-	33	Hg	14.10 N	44.17 E
Manas	22	Ke	44.18 N	86.13 E
Manas, Gora-	18	Hc	42.18 N	71.06 E
Manas He	27	Eb	45.38 N	85.12 E
Manas Hu	27	Eb	45.45 N	85.55 E
Manasija, Manastir-	15	Ee	44.06 N	21.28 E
Manati	49	Ic	21.19 N	76.56 W
Manati	49	Nd	18.26 N	66.29 W
Manatuto	26	Ih	8.30 S	126.01 E
Manaure	49	Kh	11.46 N	72.28 W
Manaus	53	Jf	3.08 S	60.01 W
Manavgat	24	Dd	36.47 N	31.26 E
Manbij	24	Gd	36.31 N	37.57 E
Manbūbnagar	25	Fe	16.44 N	77.59 E
Mancelona	44	Ec	44.54 N	85.04 W
Mancha Real	13	Ig	37.47 N	3.37 W
Manche [3]	11	Ee	49.00 N	1.10 W
Mancheng	28	Ce	38.57 N	115.19 E
Manchester [Ct.-U.S.]	44	Ke	41.47 N	72.31 W
Manchester [Eng.-U.K.]	6	Fe	53.30 N	2.15 W
Manchester [Ia.-U.S.]	45	Ke	42.29 N	91.27 W
Manchester [Ky.-U.S.]	44	Fg	37.09 N	83.46 W
Manchester [N.H.-U.S.]	43	Mc	42.59 N	71.28 W
Manchester [Tn.-U.S.]	44	Dh	35.29 N	86.05 W
Manchok	34	Gd	9.40 N	8.31 E
Manchuria (EN)	22	Oe	47.00 N	125.00 E
Manciano	14	Fh	42.35 N	11.31 E
Mand	23	Hd	28.11 N	51.17 E
Manda [Chad]	35	Bd	9.11 N	18.13 E
Manda [Tan.]	36	Fe	10.28 S	34.35 E
Manda, Jabal-	35	Cd	8.39 N	24.27 E
Mandabe	37	Gd	21.02 S	44.56 E
Mandaguari	56	Jb	23.32 S	51.42 W
Manda Island	36	Hc	2.17 S	40.57 E
Mandal	7	Bg	58.02 N	7.27 E
Mandalay [3]	25	Jd	21.00 N	96.00 E
Mandalay	22	Lg	22.00 N	96.05 E
Mandal-Gobi	27	Ib	45.45 N	106.12 E
Mandalī	24	Kf	33.45 N	45.32 E
Mandalselva	8	Bf	58.02 N	7.28 E
Mandalt → Sonid Zuoqi	27	Kc	43.50 N	116.45 E
Mandalya körfezi	24	Bd	37.12 N	27.20 E
Mandan	43	Gb	46.50 N	100.54 W
Mandaon	26	Hd	12.13 N	123.17 E
Mandara, Monts- = Mandara Mountains (EN)	34	Hc	10.45 N	13.40 E
Mandara Mountains (EN) = Mandara, Monts-	34	Hc	10.45 N	13.40 E
Mandas	14	Dk	39.38 N	9.07 E
Mandasor	25	Fd	24.04 N	75.04 E
Mandera	31	Lh	3.56 N	41.52 E
Manderscheid	12	Id	50.06 N	6.49 E
Mandeville	49	Id	18.02 N	77.30 W
Mandi	25	Fb	31.43 N	76.55 E
Mandiana	34	Dc	10.38 N	8.41 W
Mandimba	37	Fb	14.21 S	35.39 E
Mandingues, Monts-	34	Cc	13.00 N	11.00 W
Mandioli, Pulau-	26	Ig	0.44 S	127.14 E
Mandioré, Laguna-	55	Dd	18.08 S	57.33 W
Mandirituba	55	Hg	25.46 S	49.19 W
Mandji	36	Bc	1.42 S	10.24 E
Mandla	25	Gd	22.36 N	80.23 E
Mandø	8	Ci	55.15 N	8.35 E
Mandoúdhion	15	Gk	38.48 N	23.29 E
Mandrákion	15	Km	36.36 N	27.08 E
Mandritsara	37	Hc	15.49 S	48.48 E
Mandurah	59	Df	32.32 S	115.43 E
Manduria	14	Lj	40.24 N	17.38 E
Māndvi	25	Dd	22.50 N	69.22 E
Mandya	25	Ff	12.33 N	76.54 E
Måne	8	Ce	59.56 N	8.48 E
Măneciu Ungureni	15	Id	45.19 N	25.59 E
Manendragarh	25	Gd	23.10 N	82.35 E
Maneromango	36	Gd	7.16 S	38.46 E
Maneviči	16	Dd	51.19 N	25.33 E
Manfalūţ	33	Fd	27.19 N	30.58 E
Manfredonia	14	Ji	41.38 N	15.55 E
Manfredonia, Golfo di-	14	Ki	41.35 N	16.05 E
Manga [Afr.]	30	Ig	15.00 N	14.00 E
Manga [Braz.]	54	Jf	14.46 S	43.56 W
Mangabeiras, Chapada das-	52	Lg	10.00 S	46.30 W
Mangai	36	Cc	4.03 S	19.35 E
Mangaia Island	57	Lg	21.55 S	157.55 W
Mangakino	62	Fc	38.22 S	175.46 E
Mangalia	15	Lf	43.48 N	28.35 E
Mangalmé	35	Bc	12.21 N	19.37 E
Mangalore	22	Jh	12.52 N	74.53 E
Mangareva, Ile-	57	Ng	23.07 S	134.57 W
Mangfall	10	Ii	47.51 N	12.08 E
Manggar	26	Eg	2.53 S	108.16 E
Manggautu	63a	Dd	11.30 S	159.59 E
Mangin Yoma	25	Jd	24.20 N	95.42 E
Mangistau	16	Qg	44.03 N	51.57 E
Mangit	19	Gg	42.07 N	60.01 E
Mangkalihat, Tanjung-	26	Gf	1.02 N	118.59 E
Manglares, Cabo-	54	Cc	1.36 N	79.02 W
Mangnai	27	Fd	37.48 N	91.55 E
Mangniu He	28	Ib	45.10 N	126.58 E
Mango [Fiji]	63d	Cb	17.27 S	179.09 W
Mango [Ton.]	65b	Bb	20.20 S	174.43 W
Mangoche	36	Ge	14.28 S	35.16 E
Mangoky [Mad.]	37	Hd	23.27 S	45.13 E
Mangoky [Mad.]	30	Lk	21.29 S	43.41 E
Mangole, Pulau-	26	Ig	1.53 S	125.50 E
Mangonui	62	Ea	34.59 S	173.32 E
Mangrove Cay	49	Ia	24.51 N	76.14 W
Mangrullo, Cuchilla-	55	Fk	32.27 S	53.50 W
Mangshi → Luxi	27	Gg	24.29 N	98.40 E
Mangualde	13	Ed	40.36 N	7.46 W
Mangueira, Lagoa-	56	Jd	33.06 S	52.48 W
Mangueni, Plateau de-	30	If	22.35 N	12.40 E
Mangui	27	La	52.03 N	122.09 E
Mangula	37	Ec	16.52 S	30.08 E
Mangum	45	Gi	34.53 N	99.30 W
Manguredjipa	36	Eb	0.21 N	28.44 E
Mangyšlak	19	Fg	43.40 N	51.15 E
Mangyšlak, Plato-	19	Fg	43.25 N	53.00 E
Mangyšlakskaja Oblast [3]	19	Fg	44.00 N	53.30 E
Mangyšlakski Zaliv	16	Qg	44.45 N	51.00 E
Manhattan	43	Hd	39.11 N	96.35 W
Manhica	37	Ee	25.24 S	32.48 E
Mani	36	Ed	6.27 S	25.20 E
Mani	54	Dc	4.49 N	72.17 W
Mānī', Wādī al-	24	Ie	34.16 N	41.02 E
Mania	37	Hc	19.42 S	45.22 E
Maniago	14	Gd	46.10 N	12.43 E
Manica [3]	37	Ec	19.00 S	33.20 E
Manica	37	Ec	18.56 S	32.53 E
Manicaland [3]	37	Ec	19.00 S	32.30 E
Manicoré	53	Jf	5.49 S	61.17 W

Index Symbols

[1] Independent Nation
[2] State, Region
[3] District, County
[4] Municipality
[5] Colony, Dependency
Continent
Physical Region
Historical or Cultural Region
Mount, Mountain
Volcano
Hill
Mountains, Mountain Range
Hills, Escarpment
Plateau, Upland
Pass, Gap
Plain, Lowland
Delta
Salt Flat
Valley, Canyon
Crater, Cave
Karst Features
Depression
Polder
Desert, Dunes
Forest, Woods
Heath, Steppe
Oasis
Cape, Point
Coast, Beach
Cliff
Peninsula
Isthmus
Sandbank
Island
Atoll
Rock, Reef
Islands, Archipelago
Rocks, Reefs
Coral Reef
Well, Spring
Geyser
River, Stream
Waterfall Rapids
River Mouth, Estuary
Lake
Salt Lake
Intermittent Lake
Reservoir
Swamp, Pond
Canal
Glacier
Ice Shelf, Pack Ice
Ocean
Sea
Gulf, Bay
Strait, Fjord
Lagoon
Bank
Seamount
Tablemount
Ridge
Shelf
Basin
Escarpment, Sea Scarp
Fracture
Trench, Abyss
National Park, Reserve
Point of Interest
Recreation Site
Cave, Cavern
Historic Site
Ruins
Wall, Walls
Church, Abbey
Temple
Scientific Station
Airport
Port
Lighthouse
Mine
Tunnel
Dam, Bridge

Name	Page	Grid	Lat.	Long.
Manicoré, Rio-	54	Fe	5.51S	61.19W
Manicouagan	42	Kg	49.10N	68.15W
Manicouagan	42	Kf	51.00N	68.20W
Manicouagan, Réservoir-	38	Md	51.30N	68.19W
Manigotagan	45	Ha	51.06N	96.18W
Manihi Atoll	57	Mf	14.24S	145.56W
Manihiki Anchorage	64n	Ab	10.23S	161.03W
Manihiki Atoll	57	Kf	10.24S	161.01W
Manika, Plateau de la-	36	Ed	10.00S	26.00 E
Manila [Phil.]	22	Oh	14.35N	121.00 E
Manila [Ut.-U.S.]	46	Kf	40.59N	109.43W
Manila Bay	21	Oh	14.30N	120.45 E
Manilaid/Manilajd	8	Kf	58.08N	24.03 E
Manilajd/Manilaid	8	Kf	58.08N	24.03 E
Manily	20	Ld	62.30N	165.20 E
Maningrida Settlement	59	Gb	12.05S	134.10 E
Maniouro, Pointe-	63b	Dc	17.41S	168.35 E
Manipa, Selat-	26	Ig	3.20S	127.23 E
Manipur [3]	25	Id	25.00N	94.00 E
Manipur	25	Id	22.52N	94.05 E
Manisa	23	Cb	38.36N	27.26 E
Manisa Dağı	15	Kk	38.33N	27.28 E
Manises	13	Le	39.29N	0.27W
Manissau a-Missu, Rio-	54	Hf	10.58S	53.20W
Manistee	44	Dc	44.15N	86.18W
Manistee River	44	Dc	44.15N	86.21W
Manistique	43	Jb	45.57N	86.15W
Manitique Lake	44	Eb	46.15N	85.45W
Manitoba [3]	42	Hf	55.00N	97.00W
Manitoba, Lake-	38	Jd	51.00N	98.45W
Manitou Islands	44	Ec	45.10N	86.00W
Manitou Lake	44	Gc	45.48N	82.00W
Manitoulin Island	42	Jg	45.45N	82.30W
Manitou Springs	45	Dg	38.52N	104.55W
Manitouwadge	45	Nb	49.08N	85.47W
Manitowoc	43	Jc	44.06N	87.40W
Manitsoq/Sukkertoppen	41	Ge	65.25N	53.00W
Maniwaki	42	Jg	46.23N	75.58W
Manizales	53	Ie	5.05N	75.32W
Manja	17	Jd	64.23N	60.50 E
Manja	37	Gd	21.23S	44.20 E
Manjača	14	Lf	44.35N	17.05 E
Manjacaze	37	Ed	24.42S	33.33 E
Manjakandriana	37	Hc	18.55S	47.47 E
Manji	29a	Bb	43.09N	141.59 E
Manjimup	59	Df	34.14S	116.09 E
Mānjra	25	Fe	18.49N	77.52 E
Män Kät	25	Jd	22.05N	98.01 E
Mankato [Ks.-U.S.]	45	Gg	39.47N	98.12W
Mankato [Mn.-U.S.]	43	Ic	44.10N	94.01W
Mankono	34	Dd	8.04N	6.12W
Mankono [3]	34	Dd	7.58N	6.02W
Mankoya	31	Jj	14.50S	25.00 E
Manley Hot Springs	40	Ic	65.00N	150.37W
Manlleu	13	Ob	42.00N	2.17 E
Manmād	25	Ed	20.15N	74.27 E
Manmanoc, Mount-	26	Hc	17.40N	121.06 E
Manna	26	Dh	4.27S	102.55 E
Mannahill	59	Hf	32.26S	139.59 E
Mannar	25	Fg	8.59N	79.54 E
Mannar, Gulf of-	21	Ji	8.30N	79.00 E
Mannheim	6	Gf	49.29N	8.28 E
Manning [Alta.-Can.]	42	Fe	56.55N	117.33W
Manning [S.C.-U.S.]	44	Gi	33.42N	80.12W
Manning, Cape-	64g	Ba	2.02N	157.26W
Manning Strait	63a	Db	7.24S	158.04 E
Manningtree	12	Dc	51.57N	1.04 E
Mann Ranges	59	Fe	26.00S	129.30 E
Mann River	59	Gb	12.20S	134.07 E
Mannu, Capo-	14	Cj	40.02N	8.22 E
Mannu, Rio- [It.]	14	Cj	40.50N	8.23 E
Mannu, Rio- [It.]	14	Cj	40.41N	8.59 E
Mano	34	Cd	6.56N	11.31W
Mano [Jap.]	29	Fc	37.58N	138.20 E
Mano [S.L.]	34	Cd	7.55N	12.00W
Manoa	54	Ee	9.40S	65.27W
Man of War, Cayos-	49	Fg	13.02N	83.22W
Manokwari	58	Ee	2.30S	134.36 E
Manombo	37	Gd	22.55S	43.28 E
Manompana	37	Hc	16.41S	49.45 E
Manonga	36	Fc	4.08S	34.12 E
Manono	31	Ji	7.18S	27.25 E
Manono	65c	Aa	13.50S	172.05W
Manosque	11	Lk	43.50N	5.47 E
Manouane, Lac-	42	Kf	50.40N	70.45W
Mano-Wan	29	Fc	37.55N	138.15 E
Manp'ojin	28	Id	41.09N	126.17 E
Manra Atoll (Sydney)	57	Je	4.27S	171.15W
Manresa	13	Nc	41.44N	1.50 E
Mansa	31	Jj	11.12S	28.53 E
Mansa Konko	34	Bc	13.28N	15.33W
Mansel	38	Lc	62.00N	79.50W
Mansfield [Austl.]	59	Jg	37.03S	146.05 E
Mansfield [Eng.-U.K.]	9	Lh	53.09N	1.11W
Mansfield [La.-U.S.]	45	Jj	32.02N	93.43W
Mansfield [Oh.-U.S.]	43	Kc	40.46N	82.31W
Mansfield [Pa.-U.S.]	44	Ie	41.47N	77.05W
Mansfield, Mount-	44	Kc	44.33N	72.49W
Mansle	11	Gi	45.52N	0.11 E
Manso, Rio-	55	Db	14.42S	56.16W
Manso, Rio- ou Mortes, Rio das-	52	Kg	11.45S	50.44W
Mansôa	34	Bc	12.04N	15.19W
Mansourah	13	Qh	36.04N	4.28 E
Mansourah, Djebel-	13	Qh	36.02N	4.28 E
Manta	54	Bd	0.57S	80.42W
Manta, Bahia de-	54	Bd	0.50S	80.40W
Mantalingajan, Mount-	26	Ge	8.48N	117.40 E
Manteca	46	Eh	37.48N	121.13W
Mantecal [Ven.]	50	Di	6.52N	65.38W
Mantecal [Ven.]	50	Bi	7.33N	69.09W
Manteigas	13	Ed	40.24N	7.32W
Manteo	44	Jh	35.55N	75.40W
Mantes-la-Jolie	11	Hf	48.59N	1.43 E
Manti	46	Jg	39.16N	111.38W
Mantiqueira, Serra da-	52	Lh	22.00S	44.45W
Manto	49	Df	14.55N	86.23W
Manton	44	Ec	44.24N	85.24W
Mantova	14	Ee	45.09N	10.48 E
Mäntsälä	8	Kd	60.38N	25.20 E
Mänttä	7	Fe	62.02N	24.38 E
Mantua	49	Eb	22.17N	84.17W
Manturovo	19	Ed	58.22N	44.44 E
Mäntyharju	7	Gf	61.25N	26.53 E
Mäntyluoto	8	Ic	61.35N	21.29 E
Manu	54	Df	12.15S	70.50W
Manuae Atoll	57	Lf	19.21S	158.56W
Manua Islands	57	Kf	14.13S	169.35W
Manuangi Atoll	57	Mf	19.12S	141.16W
Manūbah	14	En	36.48N	10.06 E
Manuel	48	Jf	22.44N	98.19W
Manuel Alves, Rio-	54	If	11.19S	48.28W
Manuel Bonavides	48	Hc	29.05N	103.55W
Manuel Derqui	55	Ch	27.50S	58.48W
Manuel J. Cobo	55	Dl	35.49S	57.54W
Manuel Ocampo	55	Bk	33.46S	60.39W
Manuga Reefs	63a	Ad	11.00S	153.21 E
Manui, Pulau-	26	Hg	3.35S	123.08 E
Manujān	24	Qi	27.24N	57.32 E
Mānūk, Tell-	24	Hf	33.10N	38.50 E
Manukau	58	Ih	36.56S	174.56 E
Manulu Lagoon	64g	Bb	1.56N	157.20W
Manus Island	57	Fe	2.05S	147.00 E
Many	45	Jk	31.34N	93.29W
Manyara, Lake-	36	Gc	3.35S	35.50 E
Manyas	24	Bb	40.02N	27.58 E
Manyč	5	Kf	47.15N	40.00 E
Manyč-Gudilo, Ozero-	5	Kf	46.25N	42.35 E
Manyoni	36	Fd	5.45S	34.50 E
Manzanal, Puerto del-	13	Fb	42.32N	6.10W
Manzanares	13	Ie	39.00N	3.22W
Manzaneda, Cabeza de-	13	Eb	42.20N	7.15W
Manzanilla	13	Fg	37.23N	6.25W
Manzanillo [Cuba]	39	Lg	20.21N	77.07W
Manzanillo [Mex.]	39	Ih	19.03N	104.20W
Manzanillo, Bahia de- [Dom.Rep.]	49	Ld	19.45N	71.46W
Manzanillo, Bahía de- [Mex.]	48	Gh	19.04N	104.25W
Manzanillo, Punta-	49	Hi	9.38N	79.32W
Manzano Mountains	45	Ci	34.45N	106.20W
Manzhouli	22	Ne	49.33N	117.28 E
Manzilah, Buḩayrat al-	24	Eg	31.15N	32.00 E
Manzil Bū Ruqaybah	32	Ib	37.10N	9.48 E
Manzil bū Zalafah	14	En	36.41N	10.35 E
Manzil Tamīn	14	En	36.47N	10.59 E
Manzini	37	Ee	26.29S	31.22 E
Mao	63b	Dc	17.29S	168.29 E
Mao [Chad]	31	Ig	14.07N	15.19 E
Mao [Dom.Rep.]	47	Je	19.34N	71.05W
Mao/Mahón	13	Qe	39.53N	4.15 E
Maoke, Pegunungan-	57	Ee	4.00S	138.00 E
Maomao Shan	27	Hd	37.12N	103.10 E
Maoming	22	Ng	21.41N	110.52 E
Maoniu Shan	27	He	32.50N	104.12 E
Maotou Shan	27	Hg	24.31N	100.38 E
Maouri, Dallol-	34	Fc	12.05N	3.32 E
Mapai	37	Ed	22.51S	31.58 E
Mapanda	36	Dd	9.32S	24.16 E
Mapati	36	Bc	3.38S	13.21 E
Mapi	58	Ee	7.05S	139.23 E
Mapi	26	Kh	7.00S	139.16 E
Mapia, Kepulauan-	26	Jf	0.50N	134.20 E
Mapimi, Bolsón de-	38	Ig	27.30N	103.15W
Mapinhane	37	Fd	22.15S	35.07 E
Mapire	50	Di	7.45N	64.42W
Mapiri	54	Eg	15.15S	68.10W
Maple Creek	42	Gg	49.55N	109.27W
Maprik	60	Ch	3.38S	143.03 E
Mapuera, Rio-	54	Gd	1.05S	57.02W
Maputo [3]	37	Ee	26.00S	32.30 E
Maputo (Lourenço Marques)	31	Kk	25.58S	32.34 E
Maputo, Baia de-	30	Kk	26.05S	33.00 E
Maqên (Dawu)	27	He	34.29N	100.01 E
Maqran, Wādī al-	33	Ie	20.55N	47.12 E
Maqu	27	He	34.05N	101.45 E
Maquan He/Damqog Kanbab	27	Df	29.36N	84.09 E
Maquela do Zombo	31	Ii	6.03S	15.08 E
Maquinchao	56	Gf	41.15S	68.44W
Maquoketa	45	Ke	42.04N	90.40W
Mar, Serra do-	52	Lh	25.00S	48.00W
Mara	36	Fc	1.31S	33.56 E
Mara [3]	36	Fc	2.30S	34.00 E
Maraã	54	Ed	1.50S	65.22W
Marab	35	Fc	14.54N	37.55 E
Marabá	52	Lf	5.21S	49.07W
Marabahan	26	Fg	3.00S	114.45 E
Marabá Paulista	55	Gf	22.06S	51.56W
Maraca, Ilha de-	54	Hc	2.05N	50.25W
Maracaibo	53	Id	10.40N	71.37W
Maracaibo, Lago de- = Maracaibo, Lake- (EN)	52	Ie	9.50N	71.30W
Maracaibo, Lake- (EN) = Maracaibo, Lago de-	52	Ie	9.50N	71.30W
Maracaju	54	Gh	21.38S	55.09W
Maracaju, Serra de- [Braz.]	52	Kh	21.00S	55.00W
Maracaju, Serra de- [S.Amer.]	55	Ef	23.57S	55.01W
Maracanã	54	Id	0.46S	47.27W
Maracás	54	Jf	13.26S	40.27W
Maracay	53	Jd	10.15N	67.36W
Marādah	33	Cd	29.14N	19.13 E
Maradi	31	Hg	13.29N	7.06 E
Maradi [2]	34	Gc	14.15N	7.15 E
Marāgheh	23	Gb	37.23N	46.40 E
Marāh	23	Gd	25.04N	45.28 E
Maraho	35	Bb	18.21N	17.28 E
Marahuaca, Cerro-	52	Je	3.34N	65.27W
Marajó, Baia de-	52	Lf	1.00S	48.30W
Marajó, Ilha de-	52	Lf	1.00S	49.30W
Marakei Atoll	57	Id	1.58N	173.25 E
Maralal	36	Gb	1.06N	36.42 E
Maralinga	59	Gf	30.13S	131.35 E
Maralwexi/Bachu	27	Cd	39.46N	78.15 E
Maramag	26	He	7.46N	125.00 E
Maramasike Island	60	Gi	9.30S	161.25 E
Maramba	31	Jj	17.51S	25.52 E
Marampa	34	Cd	8.41N	12.28W
Maramureş [2]	15	Gb	47.40N	24.00 E
Maranchón	13	Jc	41.03N	2.12W
Marānd	23	Gb	38.26N	45.46 E
Marang	26	De	5.12N	103.13 E
Maranhão [2]	54	Je	5.00S	45.00W
Maranhão, Rio-	54	If	14.34S	49.02W
Marano, Laguna di-	14	He	45.44N	13.10 E
Maranoa River	59	Je	27.50S	148.37 E
Marañón, Rio-	52	If	4.30S	73.35W
Marans	11	Fh	46.18N	1.00W
Marão	37	Ed	24.18S	34.07 E
Marão, Serra do-	13	Ec	41.15N	7.55W
Maraoué	34	Dd	6.54N	5.31W
Marapanim	54	Id	0.42S	47.42W
Marapi, Gunung-	26	Dg	0.23S	100.28 E
Marargiu, Capo-	14	Cj	40.20N	8.23 E
Marari, Serra do-	55	Gh	27.30S	51.00W
Mara Rosa	55	Ha	13.58S	49.09W
Mărăşeşti	15	Kd	45.53N	27.14 E
Maratea	14	Jk	39.59N	15.43 E
Marathón	15	Gk	38.09N	23.58 E
Marathon	45	Ek	30.12N	103.15W
Marathon	42	Ig	48.46N	86.26W
Maratua, Pulau-	26	Gf	2.15N	118.36 E
Marau	55	Fi	28.27S	52.12W
Maravari	63a	Cb	7.54S	156.44 E
Marāveh Tappeh	24	Pd	37.55N	55.57 E
Maravilha	55	Fh	26.47S	53.09W
Maravillas Creek	45	El	29.34N	102.47W
Maravovo	63a	Dc	9.17S	159.38 E
Marāwah	33	Dc	32.29N	21.25 E
Marawi	26	He	8.13N	124.15 E
Marawī	35	Eb	18.29N	31.49 E
Marāwiḩ	24	Oj	24.18N	53.18 E
Marayes	56	Gd	31.29S	67.20W
Marbella	13	Hh	36.31N	4.53W
Marble Bar	59	Dd	21.11S	119.44 E
Marble Canyon	46	Jh	36.30N	111.50W
Marble Falls	45	Gk	30.34N	98.17W
Marble Hall	37	Dd	24.57S	29.13 E
Marburg an der Lahn	10	Ef	50.49N	8.46 E
Marca, Ponta da-	30	Ij	16.31S	11.42 E
Marcal	10	Ni	47.38N	17.32 E
Marcala	49	Df	14.07N	88.00W
Marçal Dağlari	15	Kl	37.09N	28.00 E
Marcali	10	Nj	46.35N	17.25 E
March	10	Mh	48.10N	16.59 E
March	9	Ni	52.33N	0.06 E
Marche	11	Hh	46.10N	1.30 E
Marche = Marches (EN) [2]	14	Hh	43.30N	13.15 E
Marche, Plateau de la-	11	Hh	46.10N	1.30 E
Marche-en-Famenne	11	Ld	50.14N	5.20 E
Marchena	13	Gg	37.20N	5.24W
Marchena, Isla-	54a	Aa	0.20N	90.30W
Marches (EN) = Marche [2]	14	Hh	43.30N	13.15 E
Marchesato	14	Kk	39.05N	17.00 E
Marchfeld	14	Kb	48.15N	16.40 E
Mar Chiquita, Laguna-	55	Dm	37.37S	57.24W
Mar Chiquita, Laguna-	52	Ji	30.42S	62.36W
Marciana Marina	14	Eh	42.48N	10.12 E
Marcigny	11	Kh	46.16N	4.02 E
Marcilly-sur-Eure	12	Df	48.49N	1.21 E
Marcinelle, Charleroi-	12	Gd	50.25N	4.28 E
Marck	12	Dd	50.57N	1.57 E
Marcoing	12	Fd	50.07N	3.11 E
Marcos Juaréz	56	Hd	32.42S	62.06W
Marcus Baker, Mount-	40	Jd	61.26N	147.45W
Marcus Island (EN) = Minami-Tori-Shima	57	Gb	26.32N	142.09 E
Marcy, Mount-	43	Mc	44.07N	73.56W
Mardakert	16	Oi	40.12N	46.52 E
Mardakjan	16	Qi	40.29N	50.12 E
Mardān	25	Eb	34.09N	71.52 E
Mardarovka	15	Mb	47.30N	29.40 E
Mar del Plata	53	Ki	38.01S	57.35W
Marden	12	Cc	51.10N	0.30 E
Mardin	23	Fb	37.18N	40.44 E
Mardın Dağları	24	Id	37.20N	41.00 E
Maré, Ile-	57	Hg	21.30S	168.00 E
Mare, Muntele-	15	Gc	46.29N	23.14 E
Marechal Cândido Rondon	55	Eg	24.34S	54.04W
Maree, Loch-	9	Hd	57.40N	5.30W
Mareeba	59	Jc	17.00S	145.26 E
Mārēg	35	He	3.47N	47.18 E
Maremma	14	Fh	42.30N	11.30 E
Marennes	11	Ei	45.49N	1.07W
Marettimo	14	Gm	37.56N	12.05 E
Mareuil-en-Brie	12	Ff	48.57N	3.45 E
Marfa	43	Ge	30.18N	104.01W
Marfil, Laguna-	55	Bb	15.30S	60.20W
Margai Caka	27	Ed	35.10N	86.55 E
Marganec	19	Df	47.38N	34.40 E
Margaret River	59	Df	33.57S	115.04 E
Margarida	55	De	21.41S	56.44W
Margarita, Isla de-	54	Fa	11.00N	64.00W
Margarita Belén	55	Ch	27.16S	58.58W
Margarition	15	Dj	39.21N	20.26 E
Margate [Eng.-U.K.]	9	Oj	51.24N	1.24 E
Margate [S.Afr.]	37	Ef	30.55S	30.15 E
Marghera, Venezia-	14	Ge	45.28N	12.44 E
Margherita	30	Jh	0.23N	29.54 E
Margherita di Savoia	14	Ki	41.22N	16.09 E
Marghine, Catena del-	14	Cj	40.20N	8.50 E
Marghita	15	Fb	47.21N	22.20 E
Marghūb, Kūh-e-	24	Qf	33.06N	57.30 E
Margilan	19	Hg	40.28N	71.46 E
Margina	15	Fd	45.51N	22.16 E
Marguerite Bay	66	Qe	68.30S	68.30W
Margut	12	He	49.35N	5.16 E
Marha	20	Hd	60.35N	123.10 E
Marha	21	Nc	63.20N	118.50 E
Mari	24	Ie	34.39N	40.53 E
Mari	24	Ee	34.44N	33.18 E
Maria Atoll [W.F.]	57	Ng	22.00S	136.10W
Maria Atoll [W.F.]	57	Lg	21.48S	154.41W
Maria Cleofas, Isla-	48	Fg	21.16N	106.14W
Maria Elena	56	Gb	22.21S	69.40W
Mariager	8	Ch	56.39N	10.00 E
Mariager Fjord	8	Dh	56.40N	10.20 E
Maria Grande, Arroyo-	55	Ci	29.21S	58.45W
Maria Ignacia	55	Cm	37.24S	59.30W
Maria Island [Austl.]	59	Jh	42.40S	148.05 E
Maria Island [Austl.]	59	Hb	14.55S	135.40 E
Maria Island [St.Luc.]	51k	Bb	13.44N	60.56W
Mariakani	36	Gc	3.52S	39.28 E
Maria Laach	12	Jd	50.25N	7.15 E
Maria Madre, Isla-	48	Fg	21.35N	106.33W
Maria Magdalena, Isla-	48	Fg	21.25N	106.25W
Mariana Islands	57	Fc	16.00N	145.30 E
Marianao	47	Hd	23.05N	82.26W
Mariana Trench (EN)	3	Ih	14.00N	147.30 E
Marianna [Ar.-U.S.]	45	Ki	34.46N	90.46W
Marianna [Fl.-U.S.]	44	Ej	30.47N	85.14W
Mariannelund	8	Fg	57.37N	15.34 E
Mariano I. Loza	55	Ci	29.22S	58.12W
Mariánské Lázně	10	Ig	49.58N	12.43 E
Marías, Islas-	38	Ig	21.25N	106.28W
Marias Pass	46	Ib	48.19N	113.21W
Marias River	43	Eb	47.56N	110.30W
Maria Theresa Reef	57	Lh	36.58S	151.23W
Mariato, Punta-	47	Hg	7.13N	80.53W
Maria van Diemen, Cape-	62	Ea	34.29S	172.39 E
Mariazell	14	Jc	47.46N	15.19 E
Ma'rib	23	Gf	15.30N	45.21 E
Maribo	8	Dj	54.46N	11.31 E
Maribor	14	Jd	46.33N	15.39 E
Marica	5	Ig	40.52N	26.12 E
Marica	15	Ig	42.02N	25.50 E
Maricao	51a	Bb	18.10N	66.58W
Maricopa	46	Ij	33.04N	112.03W
Maridi	35	Dd	6.05N	29.24 E
Maridī	35	De	4.55N	29.28 E
Marié, Rio-	54	Ed	0.25S	66.26W
Marie Byrd Land (EN)	66	Nf	80.00S	120.00W
Mariec	7	Lh	56.31N	49.51 E
Marie Galante	47	Le	15.56N	61.16W
Marie-Galante, Canal de-	51e	Bc	15.55N	61.25W
Mariehamn/Maarianhamina	7	Ef	60.06N	19.57 E
Marie Louise Island	37b	Bb	6.11S	53.09 E
Mariembourg, Couvin-	12	Gd	50.06N	4.31 E
Marienburg	12	Jd	50.04N	7.08 E
Marienmünster	12	Lc	51.50N	9.13 E
Marienstatt	12	Jd	50.40N	7.49 E
Mariental	31	Ik	24.36S	17.59 E
Mariestad	7	Cg	58.43N	13.51 E
Marietta [Ga.-U.S.]	43	Ke	33.57N	84.33W
Marietta [Oh.-U.S.]	44	Gf	39.26N	81.27W
Mariga	34	Gd	9.36N	5.57 E
Marignac	11	Gl	42.55N	0.39 E
Marignane	11	Lk	43.25N	5.13 E
Marigot [Dom.]	50	Fe	15.32N	61.18W
Marigot [Guad.]	50	Ec	18.04N	63.06W
Marigot [Haiti]	49	Kd	18.14N	72.19W
Marigot [Mart.]	51h	Ab	14.49N	61.02W
Marigot [St.Luc.]	51k	Ab	13.58N	61.02W
Mariinsk	20	De	56.13N	87.45 E
Mariinski Posad	7	Lh	56.08N	47.48 E
Mariinskoje	20	Jf	51.43N	140.19 E
Marijovo	15	Eh	41.04N	21.45 E
Marijskaja ASSR [3]	19	Ed	56.40N	48.00 E
Marília	56	Jb	22.13S	50.01W
Mariluz	55	Fg	24.02S	53.13W
Marimba	36	Cd	8.22S	17.02 E
Marimbondo, Cachoeira do-	55	He	20.18S	49.10W
Marin	13	Db	42.23N	8.42W
Marin, Cul-de-Sac du-	51h	Bc	14.27N	60.53W
Marina di Catanzaro	14	Kl	38.49N	16.36 E
Marina di Gioiosa Ionica	14	Kl	38.18N	16.20 E
Marina di Pisa	14	Eg	43.40N	10.16 E
Marina di Ravenna	14	Gf	44.29N	12.17 E
Marina Gorka	19	Ce	53.31N	28.12 E
Marinduque	26	Hd	13.24N	121.58 E
Marineland	44	Gk	29.43N	81.12W
Marines	12	De	49.09N	1.59 E
Marinette	43	Jb	45.06N	87.38W
Maringá	53	Kh	23.25S	51.55W
Maringa	30	Ih	1.14N	19.48 E
Marinha Grande	13	De	39.45N	8.56W
Marino [It.]	14	Gi	41.46N	12.39 E
Marino [Van.]	63b	Db	14.59S	168.03 E
Marins, Pico dos-	55	Jf	22.27S	45.10W
Marinsko	8	Mf	58.46N	28.39 E
Marion	30	Km	46.36S	37.55 E
Marion [Al.-U.S.]	44	Di	32.32N	87.26W
Marion [Ia.-U.S.]	45	Ke	42.02N	91.36W
Marion [Il.-U.S.]	45	Lh	37.44N	88.56W
Marion [In.-U.S.]	44	Ee	40.33N	85.40W
Marion [Oh.-U.S.]	43	Kc	40.35N	83.08W
Marion [S.C.-U.S.]	44	Hh	34.11N	79.23W
Marion [Va.-U.S.]	44	Gg	36.51N	81.30W
Marion, Lake-	44	Gi	33.30N	80.25W
Marion Reefs	57	Gf	19.10S	152.20 E
Maripa	54	Ea	7.26N	65.09W
Mariposa	46	Fh	37.29N	119.58W
Mariquita, Cerro-	48	Jf	23.13N	98.22W
Marisa	26	Hf	0.28N	121.56 E
Mariscala	55	El	34.03S	54.47W
Mariscal Estigarribia	56	Hb	22.02S	60.38W
Mariupol'	6	Jf	47.06N	37.33 E
Mariusa, Caño	50	Fh	9.43N	61.26W
Mariusa, Isla-	50	Fh	9.39N	61.19W
Marivan	24	Le	35.31N	46.10 E
Märjamaa/Marjamaa	8	Kf	58.54N	24.21 E
Marjamaa/Märjamaa	8	Kf	58.54N	24.21 E
Marjanovka [R.S.F.S.R.]	19	He	54.58N	72.38 E
Marjanovka [Ukr.-U.S.S.R.]	10	Uf	50.23N	24.55 E
Mark	12	Gc	51.39N	4.39 E
Mark [F.R.G.]	12	Jc	51.13N	7.36 E
Mark [Swe.]	8	Eg	57.35N	12.35 E
Marka	31	Lh	1.43N	44.46 E
Markako, Ozero-	19	If	48.45N	85.50 E
Markam (Gartog)	27	Gf	29.32N	98.33 E
Markaryd	7	Ch	56.26N	13.36 E
Markazi [3]	23	Hb	35.30N	51.30 E
Marken	12	Hb	52.27N	5.05 E
Markerwaard	12	Hb	52.31N	5.15 E
Market Deeping	12	Bb	52.40N	0.18W
Market Harborough	9	Mi	52.29N	0.55W
Markham, Mount-	66	Kg	82.51S	161.21 E
Markham Bay	42	Kd	63.30N	71.40W
Markham River	59	Ja	6.35S	146.25 E
Marki	10	Rd	52.20N	21.07 E
Märkische Schweiz	10	Jd	52.35N	14.00 E
Markit	27	Cd	38.53N	77.35 E
Markounda	35	Bd	7.37N	16.59 E
Markovac	15	Ee	44.14N	21.06 E
Markovka	16	Ke	49.31N	39.32 E
Markovo	22	Tc	64.40N	170.25 E
Markoye	34	Fc	14.39N	0.02 E
Marksburg	12	Jd	50.16N	7.40 E
Marksville	45	Jk	31.08N	92.04W
Marktoberdorf	10	Gi	47.47N	10.37 E
Marktredwitz	10	If	50.00N	12.05 E
Markulešty	15	Lb	47.51N	28.07 E
Marl	10	De	51.39N	7.05 E
Marlagne	12	Gd	50.25N	4.40 E
Marlborough [2]	62	Ed	41.50S	173.40 E
Marlborough [Austl.]	59	Jd	22.49S	149.53 E
Marlborough [Guy.]	50	Gi	7.29N	58.38W
Marle	11	Je	49.44N	3.46 E
Marlin	45	Hk	31.18N	96.53W
Marlinton	44	Gf	38.14N	80.06W
Marlow [Eng.-U.K.]	12	Bc	51.34N	0.46W
Marlow [Ok.-U.S.]	45	Hi	34.39N	97.57W
Marmande	11	Gj	44.30N	0.10 E
Marmara	24	Bb	40.35N	27.33 E
Marmara, Sea of- (EN) = Marmara Denizi	5	Ig	40.40N	28.15 E
Marmara Adasi	24	Bb	40.38N	27.37 E
Marmara Denizi = Marmara, Sea of- (EN)	5	Ig	40.40N	28.15 E
Marmara Ereğlisi	15	Ki	40.58N	27.57 E
Marmara Gölü	15	Lk	38.37N	28.02 E
Marmarica (EN) = Barqah al Bahrīyah	30	Je	31.40N	24.30 E
Marmaris	23	Cb	36.51N	28.16 E
Marmelos, Rio-	54	Fe	6.08S	61.47W
Marmion Lake	45	Kb	48.54N	91.30W
Marmolada	14	Fd	46.26N	11.51 E
Marmora	44	Ic	44.29N	77.41W
Marmore, Cascata delle-	14	Gh	42.35N	12.45 E
Marne	10	Ec	53.57N	9.00 E
Marne	5	Gf	48.49N	2.24 E
Marne [3]	11	Kf	48.55N	4.10 E
Marne à la Saône, Canal de la-	11	Kf	48.44N	4.36 E
Marne au Rhin, Canal de la-	11	Nf	48.35N	7.47 E
Mårnes	7	Dc	67.09N	14.06 E
Marneuli	16	Ni	41.29N	44.45 E
Maro	35	Bd	8.25N	18.46 E
Maro	35	Bb	19.23N	16.38 E
Maroa	54	Ec	2.43N	67.33W
Maroantsetra	31	Lj	15.27S	49.44 E
Marokau Atoll	61	Mc	18.02S	142.17W
Marolambo	37	Hd	20.04S	48.08 E
Maromandia	37	Hb	14.11S	48.06 E
Maromme	11	He	49.28N	1.02 E
Maromokotro	37	Hb	14.01S	48.58 E
Maroni, Fleuve-	52	Ke	5.45N	53.58W
Marónia	15	Ii	40.55N	25.31 E
Maronne	11	Hi	45.04N	1.56 E
Maroochydore	59	Ke	26.39S	153.06 E
Maro Reef	57	Jb	25.25N	170.35W
Maros	15	Dc	46.15N	20.12 E
Maros	26	Gg	5.00S	119.34 E
Maroua	31	Ig	10.36N	14.20 E
Marovoay	37	Hc	16.06S	46.37 E
Marowijne River	54	Hb	5.45N	53.58W
Marqādah	24	Ie	35.44N	40.46 E
Mar Qu	27	He	31.58N	101.54 E
Marquard	37	De	28.54S	27.28 E
Marquenterre	12	Dd	50.20N	1.41 E
Marquesas Islands (EN) = Marquises, Iles-	57	Ne	9.00S	139.30W
Marquette	43	Jb	46.33N	87.24W
Marquion	12	Fd	50.13N	3.05 E
Marquis [Gren.]	51p	Bb	12.06N	61.37W
Marquis [St.Luc.]	51k	Ba	14.02N	60.55W
Marquis, Cape-	51k	Ba	14.03N	60.54W
Marquise	12	Dd	50.49N	1.42 E
Marquises, Iles- = Marquesas Islands (EN)	57	Ne	9.00S	139.30W
Marracuene	37	Ee	25.44S	32.41 E
Marradi	14	Ff	44.04N	11.37 E
Marrah, Jabal-	30	Jg	13.04N	24.21 E
Marrak	33	Hf	16.26N	41.54 E
Marrakech	31	Ge	31.38N	8.00W
Marrakech [3]	32	Fc	32.00N	8.00W
Marrawah	59	Ih	40.56S	144.41 E
Marree	58	Eg	29.39S	138.04 E
Marreh, Kūh-e-	24	Oh	29.15N	52.20 E
Marrero	45	Kl	29.54N	90.07W
Marresalja	17	Mb	69.44N	66.59 E
Marresalskije Koški, Ostrova-	17	Mb	69.30N	67.10 E
Marromeu	37	Fc	18.17S	35.56 E
Marrti	7	Gc	67.28N	28.22 E
Marrupa	37	Fb	13.12S	37.30 E
Marsá al 'Alam	33	Fd	25.05N	34.54 E
Marsá al Burayqah	33	Cc	30.25N	19.35 E

Index Symbols

- [1] Independent Nation
- [2] State, Region
- [3] District, County
- [4] Municipality
- [5] Colony, Dependency
- Continent
- Physical Region
- Historical or Cultural Region
- Mount, Mountain
- Volcano
- Hill
- Mountains, Mountain Range
- Hills, Escarpment
- Plateau, Upland
- Pass, Gap
- Plain, Lowland
- Delta
- Salt Flat
- Valley, Canyon
- Crater, Cave
- Karst Features
- Depression
- Polder
- Desert, Dunes
- Forest, Woods
- Heath, Steppe
- Oasis
- Cape, Point
- Coast, Beach
- Cliff
- Peninsula
- Isthmus
- Sandbank
- Island
- Atoll
- Rock, Reef
- Islands, Archipelago
- Rocks, Reefs
- Coral Reef
- Well, Spring
- Geyser
- River, Stream
- Waterfall Rapids
- River Mouth, Estuary
- Lake
- Salt Lake
- Intermittent Lake
- Reservoir
- Swamp, Pond
- Canal
- Glacier
- Ice Shelf, Pack Ice
- Ocean
- Sea
- Gulf, Bay
- Strait, Fjord
- Lagoon
- Bank
- Seamount
- Tablemount
- Ridge
- Shelf
- Basin
- Escarpment, Sea Scarp
- Fracture
- Trench, Abyss
- National Park, Reserve
- Point of Interest
- Recreation Site
- Cave, Cavern
- Historic Site
- Ruins
- Wall, Walls
- Church, Abbey
- Temple
- Scientific Station
- Airport
- Port
- Lighthouse
- Mine
- Tunnel
- Dam, Bridge

Marsá al Uwayjah 33 Cc 30.55N 17.52 E
Marsa Ben Mehidi 13 Ji 35.05N 2.11W
Marsabit 31 Kh 2.20N 37.59 E
Marsala 14 Gm 37.48N 12.26 E
Marsá Sha'b 35 Fa 22.52N 35.47 E
Marsá Umm Ghayj 24 Fj 25.38N 34.30 E
Marsberg 10 Ee 51.27N 8.51 E
Marsciano 14 Gh 42.54N 12.20 E
Marsdiep 12 Gb 52.58N 4.45 E
Marseille = Marseilles (EN) 6 Gg 43.18N 5.24 E
Marseille-en-Beauvaisis 11 He 49.35N 1.57 E
Marseilles (EN) = Marseille 6 Gg 43.18N 5.24 E
Marshall [Ak.-U.S.] 40 Gd 61.52N 162.04W
Marshall [Ar.-U.S.] 45 Ji 35.55N 92.38W
Marshall [Il.-U.S.] 45 Mg 39.23N 87.42W
Marshall [Lbr.] 34 Cd 6.09N 10.23W
Marshall [Mn.-U.S.] 43 Hc 44.27N 95.47W
Marshall [Mo.-U.S.] 45 Jg 39.07N 93.12W
Marshall [Tx.-U.S.] 43 Ie 32.33N 94.23W
Marshall Islands [5] 58 Hd 9.00N 168.00 E
Marshall Islands 57 Hd 9.00N 168.00 E
Marshall River 59 Hd 22.59S 136.59 E
Marshalltown 43 Ic 42.03N 92.54W
Marshfield 45 Kd 44.40N 90.10W
Marsh Harbour 47 Ic 26.33N 77.03W
Mārshinān, Kūh-e- 24 Of 32.53N 52.24 E
Marsh Island 45 Kl 29.35N 91.53W
Marsica 14 Hi 41.55N 13.35 E
Marsico Nuovo 14 Jj 40.25N 15.44 E
Marsjaty 17 Jf 60.05N 60.29 E
Marsland 45 Ee 42.29N 103.16W
Mars-la-Tour 12 He 49.06N 5.54 E
Marson 12 Gf 48.55N 4.32 E
Märsta 8 Ge 59.37N 17.51 E
Marstal 8 Dj 54.51N 10.31 E
Marstrand 8 Dg 57.53N 11.35 E
Marta 14 Fh 42.14N 11.42 E
Martaban 25 Je 16.32N 97.37 E
Martaban, Gulf of- (EN) 21 Lh 16.30N 97.00 E
Martap 34 Hd 6.54N 13.03 E
Martapura [Indon.] 26 Dg 4.19S 104.22 E
Martapura [Indon.] 26 Fg 3.25S 114.51 E
Martelange/Martelingen 12 He 49.50N 5.44 E
Martelingen/Martelange 12 He 49.50N 5.44 E
Martés, Sierra de- 13 Le 39.20N 0.57W
Martha's Vineyard 43 Mc 41.25N 70.40W
Martigny 14 Bd 46.06N 7.05 E
Martigues 11 Lk 43.24N 5.03 E
Martil 13 Gi 35.37N 5.17W
Martim Vaz, Ilhas- 52 Nh 20.30S 28.51W
Martin 12 Lc 41.18N 0.19W
Martin [Czech.] 10 Og 49.04N 18.55 E
Martin [S.D.-U.S.] 43 Gc 43.10N 101.44W
Martin [Tn.-U.S.] 44 Cg 36.21N 88.51W
Martina Franca 14 Lj 40.42N 17.20 E
Martinez de Hoz 55 Bl 35.19S 61.37W
Martinez de la Torre 48 Kg 20.04N 97.03W
Martin García, Isla- 55 Cl 34.11S 58.15W
Martin Hills 66 Pg 82.04S 88.01W
Martinho Campos 55 Jd 19.20S 45.13W
Martinique 38 Mh 14.40N 61.00W
Martinique [5] 39 Mh 14.40N 61.00W
Martinique, Canal de la- = Martinique Passage (EN) 47 Le 15.10N 61.20W
Martinique Passage 50 Fe 15.10N 61.20W
Martinique Passage (EN) = Martinique, Canal de la- 47 Le 15.10N 61.20W
Martin Lake 44 Ei 32.50N 85.55W
Martin Peninsula 66 Of 74.25S 114.10W
Martinsburg 44 If 39.28N 77.59W
Martins Ferry 44 Ge 40.07N 80.45W
Martinsville [In.-U.S.] 44 Df 39.26N 86.25W
Martinsville [Va.-U.S.] 43 Ld 36.43N 79.53W
Marton 62 Fd 40.05S 175.23 E
Martos 13 Ig 37.43N 3.58W
Martre, Lac la- 42 Fd 63.20N 118.00W
Martuk 19 Fe 50.47N 56.31 E
Martuni 16 Ni 40.06N 45.18 E
Maru 34 Gc 12.21N 6.24 E
Marud 25 Ee 18.19N 72.58 E
Marudi 26 Ff 4.11N 114.19 E
Marudu, Teluk- 26 Ge 6.45N 116.55 E
Marugame 29 Cd 34.18N 133.47 E
Maruko 29 Fc 36.19N 138.15 E
Mārūn 24 Mg 31.02N 49.36 E
Marungu, Monts- 30 Ji 7.42S 30.00 E
Maruoka 29 Ec 36.09N 136.16 E
Maruseppu 29a Ca 44.01N 143.19 E
Marutea Atoll [W.F.] 57 Ng 21.30S 135.34W
Marutea Atoll [W.F.] 57 Mf 17.00S 143.10W
Maruyama-Gawa 29 Dd 35.40N 134.50 E
Marvão 13 Ee 39.24N 7.23W
Marvast 24 Pg 30.30N 54.15 E
Marvast, Kavīr-e- 24 Pg 30.20N 54.25 E
Mårvatn 8 Cd 60.10N 8.15 E
Marv-Dasht 23 Hd 29.50N 52.40 E
Marvejols 11 Jj 44.33N 3.17 E
Marvine, Mount- 46 Jg 38.40N 111.39W
Marx 16 Od 51.42N 46.46 E
Mary 22 If 37.36N 61.50 E
Maryborough [Austl.] 58 Gg 25.32S 152.42 E
Maryborough [Austl.] 59 Ig 37.03S 143.45 E
Marydale 37 Ce 29.23S 22.05 E
Maryjskaja Oblast [3] 19 Gh 37.15N 62.30 E
Maryland [2] 43 Ld 39.00N 76.45W
Maryland [3] 34 De 4.45N 8.00W
Maryport 9 Jg 54.43N 3.30W
Mary River 59 Gb 12.53S 131.38 E
Marysville [Ca.-U.S.] 43 Eg 39.09N 121.35W
Marysville [Ks.-U.S.] 45 Hg 39.51N 96.39W
Marysville [N.B.-Can.] 44 Nc 45.59N 66.35W
Marysville [Oh.-U.S.] 44 Fe 40.13N 83.22W
Marysville [Wa.-U.S.] 46 Db 48.03N 122.11W
Maryville [Mo.-U.S.] 43 Ic 40.21N 94.52W
Maryville [Tn.-U.S.] 44 Fh 35.46N 83.58W
Marzūq 31 If 25.55N 13.55 E
Marzūq, Ḩamādat- 33 Bd 26.00N 12.30 E
Marzuq, Şaḩrā'- 30 If 24.30N 13.00 E
Masachapa 49 Dh 11.47N 86.31W
Masāhim, Kūh-e- 24 Pg 30.21N 55.20 E
Masai Steppe 30 Ki 4.45S 37.00 E
Masaka 36 Fc 0.20S 31.44 E
Masākin 32 Jb 35.44N 10.35 E
Masalembo, Kepulauan- 26 Fh 5.30S 114.26 E
Masally 19 Eh 39.01N 48.40 E
Masalog, Puntan- 64b Ba 15.01N 145.41 E
Masan 27 Md 35.11N 128.24 E
Masasi 31 Kj 10.43S 38.48 E
Masaya [3] 49 Dh 12.00N 86.10W
Masaya 47 Gf 11.58N 86.06W
Masbate 21 Oh 12.15N 123.30 E
Masbate 26 Hd 12.10N 123.35 E
Mascara 32 Hb 35.24N 0.08 E
Mascara [3] 32 Hb 35.30N 0.15 E
Mascareignes, Iles-/Mascarene Islands 30 Mk 21.00S 57.00 E
Mascarene Basin (EN) 3 Fk 15.00S 56.00 E
Mascarene Islands/Mascareignes, Iles- 30 Mk 21.00S 57.00 E
Mascarene Plateau (EN) 3 Gk 10.00S 60.00 E
Mascota 48 Gg 20.32N 104.49W
Masela, Pulau- 26 Ih 8.09S 129.50 E
Maseru 31 Jk 29.28S 27.29 E
Maşfūţ 24 Qk 24.48N 56.06 E
Mashābih 24 Gj 25.37N 36.32 E
Mashan 28 Kb 45.12N 130.32 E
Mashava 37 Ed 20.02S 30.29 E
Mashhad 22 Hf 36.18N 59.36 E
Mashike 28 Pc 43.51N 141.31 E
Mashiki 29 Be 32.47N 130.50 E
Mashīz 24 Qh 29.56N 56.37 E
Mashkel 21 Ig 28.02N 63.25 E
Mashonaland North [3] 37 Ec 17.00S 31.00 E
Mashonaland South [3] 37 Ec 18.00S 31.00 E
Mashra' ar Raqq 35 Dd 8.25N 29.16 E
Mashū-Ko 29a Db 43.35N 144.30 E
Masiaca 48 Ed 26.45N 109.18W
Masīlah, Wādī al- 21 Hh 15.10N 51.08 E
Masi-Manimba 36 Cc 4.46S 17.55 E
Masindi 36 Fb 1.42N 31.43 E
Maşīrah, Jazīrat- 21 Hg 20.29N 58.33 E
Maşīrah, Khalīj- 21 Hg 20.15N 57.40 E
Masisi 36 Ec 1.24S 28.49 E
Masjed-Soleymān 23 Gc 31.58N 49.18 E
Mask, Lough-/Loch Measca 9 Dh 53.35N 9.20W
Maskanah 24 Hd 36.01N 38.05 E
Maskelynes, Iles- 63b Cc 16.32S 167.49 E
Maslovare 14 Lf 44.34N 17.33 E
Masoala, Cap- 30 Mj 15.59S 50.13 E
Masoala, Presqu'île de- 37 Ic 15.40S 50.12 E
Mason 45 Gk 30.45N 99.14W
Mason Bay 62 Bg 46.55S 167.45 E
Mason City 39 Je 43.09N 93.12W
Masovia (EN) = Mazowsze 5 Ie 52.40N 20.20 E
Masparro, Rio- 49 Mi 8.04N 69.26W
Masqaţ = Muscat (EN) 22 Hg 23.29N 58.33 E
Massa 14 Ef 44.01N 10.09 E
Massachusetts [2] 43 Mc 42.15N 71.50W
Massachusetts Bay 44 Ld 42.20N 70.50W
Massaciuccoli, Lago di- 14 Eg 43.50N 10.20 E
Massafra 14 Lj 40.35N 17.07 E
Massaguet 35 Bc 12.28N 15.26 E
Massakori 35 Bc 13.00N 15.44 E
Massa Marittima 14 Eg 43.03N 10.53 E
Massangano 36 Bd 9.37S 14.17 E
Massangena 37 Ed 21.32S 32.57 E
Massapê 54 Jd 3.31S 40.19W
Massawa (EN) = Mitsiwa 31 Kg 15.37N 39.39 E
Massena 43 Mc 44.56N 74.57W
Masséna 35 Bc 11.24N 16.10 E
Masset 42 Ef 54.02N 132.09W
Masseube 11 Gk 43.26N 0.35 E
Massey Sound 42 Ia 78.00N 94.00W
Massiac 11 Ji 45.15N 3.13 E
Massiaru 8 Kg 57.52N 24.27 E
Massillon 44 Ge 40.48N 81.32W
Massinga 37 Fd 23.20S 35.22 E
Masson Island 66 Ge 66.08S 96.34 E
Massuma 36 De 14.05S 22.00 E
Mastābah 33 Ge 20.49N 39.26 E
Maštaga 16 Pi 40.32N 49.59 E
Masterton 61 Eh 40.57S 175.39 E
Mastūrah 33 Ge 23.06N 38.50 E
Mastuj 24 Ne 34.40N 131.51 E
Masturah 36 Hd 37.10N 48.59 E
Māsūleh 24 Mc 37.10N 48.59 E
Masurai, Gunung- 26 Dg 2.30S 101.51 E
Masuria (EN) 5 Ie 53.50N 21.30 E
Masurian Lakes (EN) 5 Ie 53.45N 21.45 E
Maşyāf 24 Ge 35.03N 36.21 E
Maszewo 10 Lc 53.29N 15.02 E
Mataabé, Cap- 63b Cb 15.38S 166.46 E
Matabeleland North [3] 37 Dc 19.00S 27.30 E
Matabeleland South [3] 37 Dd 21.00S 29.30 E
Matachel 13 Ff 38.50N 6.17W
Matachewan 42 Jg 47.56N 80.39W
Matacu 55 Bc 17.21S 61.28W
Matadi 31 Ii 5.49S 13.27 E
Matador 45 Fi 34.01N 100.49W
Matagalpa [3] 49 Eg 13.00N 85.30W
Matagalpa 39 Kh 12.53N 85.57W
Matagami 42 Jg 49.45N 77.35W
Matagami, Lac- 44 Ia 49.54N 77.32W
Mata Gassile 35 Ge 2.30N 42.16 E
Matagorda Bay 45 Hl 28.35N 96.20W
Matagorda Island 43 Hf 28.15N 96.30W
Matagorda Peninsula 45 Hl 28.32N 96.07W
Mataiea 65e Fc 17.46S 149.25W
Mataiva Atoll 57 Mf 14.53S 148.40W
Mataj 19 Hf 45.51N 78.43 E
Matak, Pulau- 26 Ef 3.18N 106.16 E
Matakana Island 62 Gb 37.35S 176.05 E
Matala 36 Ce 14.43S 15.02 E
Matalaa, Pointe- 64h Bc 13.20S 176.08W
Matale 25 Gg 7.28N 80.37 E
Mataliele 37 Df 30.24S 28.43 E
Matam 34 Cb 15.40N 13.15W
Matamey 34 Gc 13.26N 8.28 E
Matamoros [Mex.] 47 Dc 25.32N 103.15W
Matamoros [Mex.] 39 Jg 25.53N 97.30W
Matana, Danau- 26 Hg 2.28S 121.20 E
Ma'ţan as Sarra 33 De 21.41N 21.52 E
Matancita 48 De 25.09N 111.59W
Matane 42 Kg 48.51N 67.32W
Matankari 34 Fc 13.46N 4.01 E
Matanza 55 Cl 34.33S 58.35W
Matanzas 39 Kg 23.03N 81.35W
Matanzas [3] 49 Gb 22.40N 81.10W
Matão 55 He 21.35S 48.22W
Matapalo, Cabo- 49 Fi 8.23N 83.19W
Matapan, Cape- (EN) = Tainaron, Ákra- 5 Ih 36.23N 22.29 E
Matape, Rio- 48 Dc 28.17N 110.41W
Mata Point 64k Bb 19.07S 169.50W
Matara 35 Fc 14.35N 39.28 E
Matara 25 Gg 5.56N 80.33 E
Mataram 22 Nj 8.35S 116.07 E
Mataranka 59 Gb 14.56S 133.07 E
Mataró 13 Oc 41.32N 2.27 E
Matarraña/Matarranya 13 Mc 41.14N 0.22 E
Matarranya/Matarraña 13 Mc 41.14N 0.22 E
Mataso 63b Dc 17.15S 168.25 E
Matatula, Cape- 65c Cb 14.15S 170.34W
Mataura 62 Cg 46.34S 168.44 E
Mataura 62 Cg 46.12S 168.52 E
Mata-Utu 58 Jf 13.17S 176.08W
Mata-Utu, Baie de- 64h Bb 13.19S 176.07W
Matavai 61 Gb 13.28S 172.35W
Matavera 64p Cb 21.13S 159.44W
Mataveri 65d Ab 27.10S 109.27W
Matawai 62 Gc 38.21S 177.32 E
Matawin, Réservoir- 44 Kb 46.45N 73.50W
Matawin, Rivière- 44 Kb 46.55N 72.55W
Maţāy 24 Dh 28.25N 30.46 E
Maţbakhayn 33 Hf 17.29N 41.48 E
Matca 15 Kd 45.51N 27.32 E
Matemo, Ilha- 37 Gb 12.13S 40.36 E
Matera 14 Kj 40.40N 16.36 E
Matese 14 Ii 41.25N 14.20 E
Mátészalka 10 Si 47.57N 22.20 E
Matfors 7 De 62.21N 17.02 E
Matha 11 Fi 45.52N 0.19W
Mathematicians Seamounts (EN) 47 Be 15.30N 111.00W
Matheson 44 Ga 48.32N 80.28W
Mathis 45 Hl 28.06N 97.50W
Mathrákion 15 Cj 39.46N 19.31 E
Mathura 25 Fc 27.30N 77.41 E
Mati 15 Ch 41.39N 19.34 E
Mati 26 Ie 6.57N 126.13 E
Matias Cardoso 55 Kb 14.52S 43.56W
Matias Romero 47 Ee 16.53N 95.02W
Maticora, Rio- 49 Lh 11.01N 71.09W
Matina 49 Fh 10.05N 83.17W
Matinha 54 Id 3.06S 45.02W
Māţir 32 Ib 37.03N 9.40 E
Matiyure, Rio- 50 Ci 7.36N 67.39W
Matkaselkja 8 Nc 61.57N 30.33 E
Mātmāţah 32 Ic 33.33N 9.58 E
Matnog 26 Hd 12.35N 124.05 E
Mato, Cerro- 50 Di 7.15N 65.14W
Mato, Rio- 50 Di 7.09N 65.07W
Matočkin Šar, Proliv- 19 Fa 73.30N 54.55 E
Mato Grosso 54 Gf 14.00S 56.00W
Mato Grosso [Braz.] 55 Dd 18.18S 57.20W
Mato Grosso [Braz.] 53 Kg 15.00S 59.57W
Mato Grosso, Planalto do- = Mato Grosso, Plateau of- (EN) 52 Kg 15.30S 56.00W
Mato Grosso, Plateau of- (EN) = Mato Grosso, Planalto do- 52 Kg 15.30S 56.00W
Mato Grosso do Sul [2] 54 Hg 20.00S 55.00W
Matos Costa 55 Gh 26.27S 51.09W
Matosinhos 13 Dc 41.11N 8.42W
Matou 28 Cj 29.50N 115.32 E
Matou → Qiuxian 28 Cf 36.47N 114.30 E
Mátra 5 Hf 47.55N 19.57 E
Maţraḩ 23 Ie 23.29N 58.31 E
Matrei in Osttirol 14 Gc 47.00N 12.32 E
Maţrūḩ 31 Je 31.21N 27.14 E
Matsiatra 37 Hd 21.25S 45.33 E
Matsudo 28 Og 35.48N 139.55 E
Matsue 27 Nd 35.28N 133.04 E
Matsukawa [Jap.] 29 Gc 37.40N 140.28 E
Matsukawa [Jap.] 29 Ed 35.36N 137.53 E
Matsu Liehtao 27 Kf 26.05N 119.56 E
Matsumae 29a Bc 41.26N 140.07 E
Matsumae-Hantō 29a Bc 41.40N 140.15 E
Matsumoto 27 Od 36.14N 137.58 E
Matsuo 29 Gb 39.58N 141.02 E
Matsu-Ōminato 29a Bc 41.16N 141.09 E
Matsusaka 28 Ng 34.34N 136.32 E
Matsushima 29 Gb 38.22N 141.04 E
Matsutō 29 Ec 36.31N 136.33 E
Matsuura 29 Ae 33.22N 129.42 E
Matsuyama 22 Pf 33.50N 132.45 E
Matsuzaki 29 Fd 34.44N 138.45 E
Mattagami Lake 44 Gb 47.57N 81.35W
Mattagami River 42 Jf 50.43N 81.30W
Mattawa 42 Jg 46.19N 78.42W
Matterhorn [Eur.] 14 Be 45.58N 7.39 E
Matterhorn [Nv.-U.S.] 46 Hf 41.49N 115.23W
Matthew, Ile- 57 Ig 22.20S 171.20 E
Matthews Ridge 54 Fb 7.30N 60.10W
Matthew Town 47 Jd 20.57N 73.40W
Maţţī, Sabkhat- 35 Ia 23.30N 52.00 E
Mattighofen 14 Hb 48.06N 13.09 E
Mattoon 45 Lg 39.29N 88.22W
Matua, Ostrov- 20 Kg 48.00N 153.10 E
Matucana 54 Cf 11.51S 76.24W
Matuku Island 61 Ec 19.10S 179.46 E
Matundu 36 Db 4.21N 23.40 E
Matundu 36 Gd 8.50S 39.30 E
Maturin 53 Je 9.45N 63.11W
Matvejev Kurgan 16 Kf 47.34N 38.55 E
Maùa 37 Fb 13.52S 37.09 E
Maubeuge 11 Jd 50.17N 3.58 E
Ma-ubin 25 Je 16.44N 95.39 E
Maudheimvidda 66 Bf 74.00S 8.00W
Maud Seamount (EN) 66 Ce 65.00S 2.35 E
Maués 54 Gd 3.24S 57.42W
Maués, Rio- 54 Gd 3.22S 57.44W
Mau Escarpment 36 Gc 0.40S 36.02 E
Maug Islands 57 Fb 20.01N 145.13 E
Maui Island 57 Lb 20.45N 156.20W
Mauke Island 57 Lg 20.09S 157.23W
Mau Kyun 25 Jf 12.45N 98.20 E
Mauldre 12 Df 48.59N 1.49 E
Maule [2] 56 Fe 35.45S 72.15W
Mauléon 11 Fh 46.55N 0.45W
Mauléon-Licharre 11 Fk 43.14N 0.53W
Maullin 56 Ff 41.38S 73.37W
Maumee 44 Fe 41.35N 83.40W
Maumere 26 Hh 8.37S 122.14 E
Maun 31 Jj 19.58S 23.26 E
Maun 14 If 44.26N 14.55 E
Mauna Kea 57 Lc 19.50N 155.28W
Maunaloa 65a Db 21.08N 157.13W
Mauna Loa 65a Fd 19.28N 155.36W
Maunath 25 Gc 25.40N 82.38 E
Maunawili 65a Db 21.21N 157.47W
Maunga Roa 64p Bb 21.13S 159.48W
Maungdaw 25 Id 20.49N 92.22 E
Maunoir, Lac - 42 Fc 67.30N 125.00W
Maupihaa Atoll (Mopelia, Atoll-) 57 Lf 16.50S 153.55W
Maupin 46 Ed 45.11N 121.05W
Maupiti, Ile- 57 Lf 16.27S 152.15W
Maurepas, Lake- 45 Kk 30.15N 90.30W
Maures 11 Mk 43.16N 6.23 E
Mauriac 11 Ii 45.13N 2.20 E
Maurice, Lake- 59 Ge 29.30S 131.00 E
Maurienne 11 Mi 45.13N 6.30 E
Mauritania (EN) = Mūrītāniyā [1] 31 Fg 20.00N 12.00W
Mauriti 54 Ke 7.23S 38.46W
Mauritius 30 Mk 20.17S 57.33 E
Mauritius [1] 31 Mj 18.00S 57.40 E
Mauron 11 Df 48.05N 2.18W
Maurs 11 Ij 44.43N 2.12 E
Mauston 45 Ke 43.48N 90.05W
Mauthausen 14 Ib 48.14N 14.31 E
Mauzé-sur-le-Mignon 11 Fh 46.12N 0.40W
Mavinga 36 Df 15.47S 20.24 E
Mavita 37 Ec 19.32S 33.09 E
Mavrovoúni [Grc.] 15 Fj 39.37N 22.47 E
Mavrovoúni [Grc.] 15 Gh 41.07N 23.08 E
Mawchi 25 Je 18.49N 97.09 E
Mawei 27 Kf 26.02N 119.30 E
Mawlaik 25 Id 23.38N 94.25 E
Mawlamyine 22 Le 16.30N 97.38 E
Mawqaq 24 Ii 27.25N 41.08 E
Mawr, Wādī- 23 Ff 15.41N 42.42 E
Mawson 66 Fe 67.36S 62.53 E
Mawson Coast 66 Fe 67.40S 63.30 E
Mawson Escarpment 66 Ff 73.05S 68.10 E
Maxcanú 47 Fd 20.35N 90.01W
Maxixe 37 Fd 23.51S 35.21 E
Maxwell Bay 42 Ib 74.32N 89.00W
May, Isle of- 9 Ke 56.10N 2.30W
Maya, Pulau- 26 Eg 1.10S 109.35 E
Mayaguana Island 47 Jd 22.23N 72.57W
Mayaguana Passage 49 Kb 22.32N 73.15W
Mayagüez 47 Ke 18.12N 67.09W
Mayahi 34 Gc 13.58N 7.40 E
Mayama 36 Bc 3.51S 14.54 E
Mayāmey 24 Pd 36.24N 55.42 E
Maya Mountains 47 Ge 16.40N 88.50W
Mayapan 47 Gd 20.38N 89.27W
Mayari 49 Jc 20.40N 75.41W
Maybell 45 Bf 40.31N 108.05W
Maychew 35 Fc 12.46N 39.34 E
Mayd 35 Hc 10.57N 47.06 E
Maydān 24 Ke 34.55N 45.37 E
Maydena 59 Jh 42.55S 146.30 E
Maydī 23 Ff 16.18N 42.48 E
Mayen 10 Df 50.20N 7.13 E
Mayenne 11 Ff 48.18N 0.37W
Mayenne 11 Fg 47.30N 0.32W
Mayenne [3] 11 Ff 48.05N 0.40W
Mayfa'ah 35 Hc 14.16N 47.35 E
Mayfield 44 Cg 36.44N 88.38W
May Glacier 66 Ie 67.00S 130.00 E
Mayi He 28 Jb 45.52N 128.46 E
Maymyo 25 Jd 22.02N 96.28 E
Maynas 54 Dd 3.00S 75.00W
Mayo 39 Fc 63.35N 135.54W
Mayo/Muigheo [2] 9 Dh 53.50N 9.30W
Mayo, Mountains of- 9 Dg 54.05N 9.30W
Mayo, Rio- 48 Ed 26.45N 109.47W
Mayo Darlé 34 Hd 6.30N 11.55 E
Mayo-Kébbi 35 Ad 9.18N 13.33 E
Mayo-Kébbi [3] 35 Bd 10.00N 15.30 E
Mayoko 36 Bc 2.18S 12.49 E
Mayon, Mount- 21 Oh 13.15N 123.41 E
Mayor, Puig-/Major, Puig- 13 Oe 39.48N 2.48 E
Mayor Island 62 Gb 37.15S 176.15 E
Mayor Pablo Lagerenza 56 Ha 19.58S 60.45W
Mayotte 31 Lj 12.50S 45.10 E
Mayotte/Mahoré 30 Lj 12.50S 45.10 E
May Pen 47 Ie 17.58N 77.14W
Mayraira Point 26 Hc 18.39N 120.51 E
Mayran, Laguna de- 48 He 25.45N 102.45W
Mayreau Island 51n Bb 12.39N 61.23W
May-sur-Orne 12 Be 49.06N 0.22W
Maysville 44 Ff 38.39N 83.46W
Mayumba [Gabon] 31 Ii 3.25S 10.39 E
Mayumba [Zaire] 36 Ed 7.16S 27.03 E
Mayum La 27 De 30.35N 82.27 E
Mayville 44 Hd 42.15N 79.32W
Mayyit, Al Baḩr al- = Dead Sea (EN) 21 Ff 31.30N 35.30 E
Mazabuka 36 Ef 15.51S 27.46 E
Mazagão 54 Hd 0.07S 51.17W
Mazamet 11 Ik 43.30N 2.24 E
Māzandarān [3] 23 Hb 36.00N 54.00 E
Māzandarān, Daryā-ye- = Caspian Sea (EN) 5 Lg 42.00N 50.30 E
Mazar 27 Cd 36.27N 77.03 E
Mazara del Vallo 14 Gm 37.39N 12.35 E
Mazār-e Sharīf 22 If 36.42N 67.06 E
Mazarrón, Golfo de- 13 Kg 37.30N 1.18W
Mazartag 27 Dd 38.29N 80.50 E
Mazaruni River 54 Gb 6.25N 58.38W
Mazatenango 47 Ff 14.32N 91.30W
Mazatlán 39 Ig 23.13N 106.25W
Mažeikiai/Mažejkjaj 7 Fh 56.20N 22.22 E
Mažejkjaj/Mažeikiai 7 Fh 56.20N 22.22 E
Mazhafah, Jabal- 24 Fh 28.48N 34.57 E
Mazhūr, 'Irq al- 24 Ji 27.25N 43.55 E
Mazinga 51c Ab 17.29N 62.58W
Mazirbe 8 Jg 57.40N 22.10 E
Mazoe 37 Ec 17.30S 30.58 E
Mazoe 37 Kj 16.32S 33.25 E
Mazomeno 36 Ec 4.55S 27.13 E
Mazong Shan 27 Gc 41.33N 97.10 E
Mazowsze 10 Qd 52.40N 20.20 E
Mazowsze = Masovia (EN) 5 Ie 52.40N 20.20 E
Mazsalaca 8 Kg 57.45N 24.59 E
Mazunga 37 Dd 21.44S 29.52 E
Mazurskie, Pojezierze- 10 Qc 53.40N 21.00 E
Mazzarino 14 Im 37.18N 14.13 E
Mba 63d Ab 17.32S 177.42 E
Mbabane 31 Kk 26.18S 31.07 E
Mbabo, Tchabal- 34 Hd 7.16N 12.09 E
Mbacké 34 Bc 14.48N 15.55W
Mbaéré 35 Be 3.47N 17.31 E
Mbaïki 31 Ih 3.53N 18.00 E
Mbakaou 34 Hd 6.19N 12.49 E
Mbakaou, Barrage de- 34 Hd 6.25N 13.00 E
Mbala 31 Ki 8.50S 31.22 E
Mbalam 34 He 2.13N 13.49 E
Mbale 31 Kh 1.05N 34.10 E
Mbali 35 Be 4.27N 18.20 E
Mbalmayo 34 He 3.31N 11.30 E
Mbam 30 Ih 4.24N 11.17 E
Mbamba Bay 36 Fe 11.17S 34.46 E
Mbandaka 31 Ih 0.04N 18.16 E
Mbanga 34 Ge 4.30N 9.34 E
Mbanika 63a Dc 9.05S 159.12 E
M'banza Congo 36 Bd 6.16S 14.15 E
Mbanza-Ngungu 31 Ii 5.35S 14.47 E
Mbarangandu 36 Gd 8.57S 37.24 E
Mbarara 36 Fc 0.36S 30.38 E
Mbari 35 Ce 4.34N 22.43 E
Mbatiki 63d Bb 17.46S 179.08 E
Mbava 63a Cb 7.49S 156.37 E
Mbé 34 Hd 7.51N 13.36 E
Mbengga 63d Bc 18.23S 178.08 E
Mbengwi 34 Hd 6.01N 10.00 E
Mbéré 35 Bd 9.07N 16.26 E
Mbeya 31 Ki 8.54S 33.27 E
Mbeya [3] 36 Fd 8.00S 33.30 E
Mbi 35 Be 4.28N 18.07 E
Mbigou 36 Bc 1.53S 11.56 E
Mbinda 31 Ii 2.07S 12.52 E
Mbinga 36 Ge 10.56S 35.01 E
Mbingué 34 Dc 10.00N 5.54W
Mbini 34 Ge 1.34N 9.37 E
Mbini [3] 34 He 1.30N 10.00 E
Mbini 30 Ih 1.30N 10.30 E
Mboki 35 Dd 5.19N 25.58 E
Mbokonimbeti 63a Ec 8.57S 160.05 E
Mbomo 36 Bb 0.24N 14.44 E
Mbomou = Bomu (EN) [3] 35 Cd 5.30N 23.30 E
Mbomou = Bomu (EN) 30 Jh 4.08N 22.26 E
Mborokua 63a Dc 9.02S 158.44 E
Mbour 34 Bc 14.24N 16.58W
Mbout 32 Ef 16.01N 12.35W
Mbozi 36 Fd 9.02S 32.56 E
Mbrés 35 Bd 6.40N 19.48 E
M'Bridge 36 Bd 7.14S 12.52 E
Mbua 63d Bb 16.48S 178.37 E
Mbuji-Mayi 31 Ji 6.09S 23.33 E
Mbulo 63a Dc 8.46S 158.21 E
Mbulu 36 Gc 3.51S 35.32 E
Mburucuyá 55 Ci 28.03S 58.14W
Mbutha 63d Bb 16.39S 179.51 E
Mbuyuni 36 Gd 7.23S 36.32 E
Mbwemburu 36 Gd 9.29S 39.39 E
Mcalester 43 He 34.56N 95.46W
Mcensk 19 De 53.17N 36.32 E
M'Chedallah 13 Qh 36.22N 4.16 E
Mcherrah 32 Gd 27.00N 4.30W
Mchinga 36 Gd 9.44S 39.42 E
Mchinji 36 Fe 13.48S 32.54 E
Mdandu 36 Fd 9.09S 34.42 E
M'Daourouch 14 Bn 36.05N 7.49 E
Mdennah 32 Gd 25.00N 4.50W
Mdiq 13 Gi 35.41N 5.19W
Mead 44 Fa 49.29N 83.50W
Mead, Lake- 43 Ed 36.05N 114.25W
Meade 40 Hb 70.50N 156.25W
Meade 45 Fh 37.17N 100.20W
Meade Peak 46 Je 42.30N 111.15W
Meadow Lake 42 Gf 54.07N 108.20W
Meadville 44 Ge 41.38N 80.10W
Me-akan-Dake 29a Cb 43.23N 143.59 E
Mealhada 13 Dd 40.22N 8.27W

Index Symbols

[1] Independent Nation; [2] State, Region; [3] District, County; [4] Municipality; [5] Colony, Dependency; Continent; Physical Region; Historical or Cultural Region; Mount, Mountain; Volcano; Hill; Mountains, Mountain Range; Hills, Escarpment; Plateau, Upland; Pass, Gap; Plain, Lowland; Delta; Salt Flat; Valley, Canyon; Crater, Cave; Karst Features; Depression; Polder; Desert, Dunes; Forest, Woods; Heath, Steppe; Oasis; Cape, Point; Coast, Beach; Cliff; Peninsula; Isthmus; Sandbank; Island; Atoll; Rock, Reef; Islands, Archipelago; Rocks, Reefs; Coral Reef; Well, Spring; Geyser; River, Stream; Waterfall Rapids; River Mouth, Estuary; Lake; Salt Lake; Intermittent Lake; Reservoir; Swamp, Pond; Canal; Glacier; Ice Shelf, Pack Ice; Ocean; Sea; Gulf, Bay; Strait, Fjord; Lagoon; Bank; Seamount; Tablemount; Ridge; Shelf; Basin; Escarpment, Sea Scarp; Fracture; Trench, Abyss; National Park, Reserve; Point of Interest; Recreation Site; Cave, Cavern; Historic Site; Ruins; Wall, Walls; Church, Abbey; Temple; Scientific Station; Airport; Port; Lighthouse; Mine; Tunnel; Dam, Bridge

Mealy Mountains 42 Lf 53.20N 59.30W
Meama 65b Ba 19.45S 174.34W
Méan, Havelange- 12 Hd 50.22N 5.20 E
Meander Reef 26 Ge 8.09N 119.14 E
Meander River 42 Fe 59.02N 117.42W
Meanguera, Isla- 49 Dg 13.12N 87.43W
Mearim, Rio- 52 Lf 3.04S 44.35W
Meath/An Mhí [2] 9 Gh 53.35N 6.40W
Meaux 11 If 48.57N 2.52 E
Mecca (EN)=Makkah 22 Fg 21.27N 39.49 E
Mechara 35 Gd 8.34N 40.28 E
Mechelen/Maasmechelen 12 Hd 50.57N 5.40 E
Mechelen/Malines 11 Kc 51.02N 4.29 E
Mecheraa-Asfa 13 Ni 35.24N 1.03 E
Mecheria 32 Gc 33.33N 0.17W
Mechernich 12 Id 50.36N 6.39 E
Mechongué 55 Cn 38.09S 58.13W
Mecidiye 15 Ji 40.38N 26.32 E
Mecitözü 24 Fb 40.31N 35.19 E
Mecklemburgischer Höhenrücken 10 Ic 53.40N 12.10 E
Mecklenburg 10 Hc 53.30N 12.00 E
Mecklenburger Bucht 10 Hb 54.20N 11.40 E
Mecklenburger Schweiz 10 Ic 53.45N 12.35 E
Mecoacán, Laguna- 48 Mh 18.20N 93.10W
Meconta 37 Fb 14.59S 39.50 E
Mecsek 10 Oj 46.10N 18.18 E
Mecubúri 37 Gb 14.10S 40.31 E
Mecúfi 37 Gb 13.17S 40.33 E
Mecula 37 Fb 12.05S 37.39 E
Médala 32 Ff 15.30N 5.37W
Medan 22 Li 3.35N 98.40 E
Médanos [Arg.] 56 He 38.50S 62.41W
Médanos [Arg.] 55 Ck 33.24S 59.05W
Medanosa, Punta- 56 Gg 48.06S 65.55W
Mede 14 Ce 45.06N 8.44 E
Médéa 32 Hb 36.16N 2.45 E
Médéa [3] 32 Hb 36.20N 3.25 E
Medebach 12 Kc 51.12N 8.43 E
Medellín 26 Hd 11.08N 123.58 E
Medellín 53 Ie 6.15N 75.35W
Medelpad 8 Gb 62.35N 16.15 E
Medemblik 12 Hb 52.46N 5.06 E
Medenica 10 Tg 49.21N 23.45 E
Mederdra 32 Df 16.54N 15.40W
Medetzız 24 Fd 37.25N 34.40 E
Medford [Or.-U.S.] 39 Ge 42.19N 122.52W
Medford [Wi.-U.S.] 45 Kd 45.09N 90.20W
Medgidia 15 Le 44.15N 28.17 E
Medi 35 Ed 5.06N 30.44 E
Media Luna, Arrecife de la- 49 Ff 15.13N 82.36W
Medianeira 55 Eg 25.17S 54.05W
Mediaş 15 Hc 46.10N 24.21 E
Medical Lake 46 Gc 47.34N 117.41W
Medicine Bow 46 Lf 41.54N 106.12W
Medicine Bow Mountains 46 Lf 41.10N 106.25W
Medicine Butte 46 Jf 41.29N 110.48W
Medicine Hat 39 Hd 50.03N 110.40W
Medicine Lake 46 Mb 48.28N 104.24W
Medicine Lodge 45 Gh 37.17N 98.35W
Međimurje 14 Kd 46.25N 16.30 E
Medina (EN)=Al Madīnah [Sau.Ar.] 22 Fg 24.28N 39.36 E
Medina Az-Zahra 13 Hg 37.52N 4.50W
Medinaceli 13 Jc 41.10N 2.26W
Medina del Campo 13 Hc 41.18N 4.55W
Medina de Rioseco 13 Gc 41.53N 5.02W
Medina-Sidonia 13 Gh 36.27N 5.55W
Medininkai/Medinikaj 8 Kj 54.32N 25.46 E
Medinīpur 25 Hd 22.26N 87.20 E
Medio, Arroyo del- 55 Bk 33.16S 60.15W
Mediterranean Sea (EN)= Akdeniz 5 Hh 35.00N 20.00 E
Mediterranean Sea (EN)= Khatikhon, Yam- 5 Hh 35.00N 20.00 E
Mediterranean Sea (EN)= Méditerranée, Mer- 5 Hh 35.00N 20.00 E
Mediterranean Sea (EN)= Mediterraneo, Mar- 5 Hh 35.00N 20.00 E
Mediterranean Sea (EN)= Mediterráneo, Mar- 5 Hh 35.00N 20.00 E
Mediterranean Sea (EN)= Mesoyéios Thálassa 5 Hh 35.00N 20.00 E
Mediterranean Sea (EN)= Mutawassiţ, Al Baḩr al- 5 Hh 35.00N 20.00 E
Méditerranée, Mer-= Mediterranean Sea (EN) 5 Hh 35.00N 20.00 E
Mediterráneo, Mar-= Mediterranean Sea (EN) 5 Hh 35.00N 20.00 E
Mediterraneo, Mar-= Mediterranean Sea (EN) 5 Hh 35.00N 20.00 E
Medje 36 Eb 2.25N 27.18 E
Medjerda, Monts de la- 32 Ib 36.35N 8.15 E
Mednogorsk 19 Fe 51.26N 57.40 E
Medny, Ostrov- 20 Lf 54.40N 167.50 E
Médoc 11 Fi 45.00N 1.00W
Mêdog 27 Gf 29.18N 95.27 E
Médouneu 36 Bb 1.01N 10.48 E
Medveđa 15 Eg 42.51N 21.36 E
Medvedica [R.S.F.S.R.] 5 Kf 49.35N 42.41 E
Medvedica [R.S.F.S.R.] 7 Ih 57.05N 37.31 E
Medvednica 14 Je 45.55N 15.58 E
Medvedok 7 Mh 57.24N 50.06 E
Medvenka 16 Jd 51.27N 36.08 E
Medveži, Ostrova-=Bear Islands (EN) 21 Sb 70.52N 161.26 E
Medvežjegorsk 19 Dc 62.56N 34.29 E
Medway 12 Cc 51.23N 0.31 E
Medzilaborce 10 Rg 49.16N 21.55 E
Meekatharra 58 Cg 26.36S 118.29 E
Meeker 45 Cf 40.02N 107.55W
Meerane 10 If 50.51N 12.28 E
Meerbusch 12 Ic 51.16N 6.40 E
Meerut 25 Fc 28.59N 77.42 E
Meeteetse 46 Kd 44.09N 108.52W
Mefarlane, Lake- 59 Hf 32.00S 136.40 E
Mega [Eth.] 31 Kh 4.03N 38.20 E
Mega [Indon.] 26 Jg 0.41S 131.53 E
Mega, Pulau- 26 Dg 4.00S 101.02 E
Megalo 35 Gd 6.52N 40.47 E
Megálon Khorion 15 Km 36.27N 27.21 E
Megalópolis 15 Fl 37.24N 22.08 E
Megálo Sofráno 15 Jm 36.04N 26.25 E
Meganision 15 Dk 38.38N 20.43 E
Meganom, Mys- 16 Ig 44.48N 35.05 E
Mégara 15 Gk 38.00N 23.21 E
Megève 11 Mi 45.52N 6.37 E
Meghalaya [3] 25 Ic 26.00N 91.00 E
Megid 33 Dd 28.35N 22.10 E
Megion 19 Hc 61.00N 76.15 E
Megiscane, Lac- 44 Ia 48.30N 76.04W
Megri 16 Oj 38.55N 46.15 E
Mehadia 15 Fe 44.54N 22.22 E
Mehaigne 12 Hd 50.32N 5.13 E
Meharry, Mount- 59 Dd 23.00S 118.35 E
Mehdia 13 Ni 35.25N 1.45 E
Mehdīshahr 24 Oe 35.44N 53.22 E
Mehedinţi [2] 15 Fe 44.30N 23.00 E
Mehetia, Ile- 61 Lc 17.52S 148.03W
Mehrabān 24 Lc 38.05N 47.08 E
Mehrān 24 Pi 26.52N 55.24 E
Mehrān 24 Lf 33.07N 46.10 E
Mehrenga 7 Je 63.17N 41.20 E
Mehrīz 24 Pg 31.35N 54.28 E
Mehtar Lām 23 Lc 34.39N 70.10 E
Mehun-sur-Yèvre 11 Ig 47.09N 2.13 E
Meia Meia 36 Gd 5.49S 35.48 E
Meia Ponte, Rio- 54 Ig 18.32S 49.36W
Meiganga 34 Hd 6.31N 14.18 E
Meighen 42 Ha 79.55N 99.00W
Meihekou→Hailong 27 Mc 42.32N 125.37 E
Meiktila 25 Jd 20.52N 95.52 E
Meilü→Wuchuan 27 Jg 21.28N 110.44 E
Meinerzhagen 12 Jc 51.07N 7.39 E
Meiningen 10 Gf 50.33N 10.25 E
Meio, Rio do- 55 Ja 13.20S 44.34W
Meisenheim 12 Je 49.43N 7.40 E
Meishan [China] 27 He 30.05N 103.48 E
Meishan [China] 28 Ei 31.06N 119.43 E
Meishan → Jinzhai 28 Ci 31.40N 115.52 E
Meißen 10 Je 51.09N 13.29 E
Meißner 10 Fe 51.12N 9.50 E
Meitan (Yiquan) 27 If 27.48N 107.32 E
Meixian 27 Kg 24.21N 116.07 E
Meiyukou 28 Bd 40.01N 113.08 E
Méjean, Causse- 11 Jj 44.16N 3.22 E
Mejillones 56 Fb 23.06S 70.27W
Mékambo 36 Bb 1.01N 13.56 E
Mekdela 35 Fc 11.28N 39.20 E
Mekele=Meqele (EN) 31 Kg 13.30N 39.28 E
Mékhé 34 Bb 15.07N 16.38W
Mekherrhane, Sebkha- 30 Hf 26.22N 1.20 E
Meknès [3] 32 Fc 33.00N 5.30W
Meknès 31 Ge 33.54N 5.32W
Mekong (EN)=Lancang Jiang 21 Mh 10.15N 105.55 E
Mekong (EN)=Mae Nam Khong 21 Mh 10.15N 105.55 E
Mekong (EN)=Mékôngk 21 Mh 10.15N 105.55 E
Mekong (EN)=Mènam Khong 21 Mh 10.15N 105.55 E
Mekong Delta (EN) 21 Mi 10.20N 106.40 E
Mekongga, Gunung- 26 Hg 3.35S 121.15 E
Mékôngk=Mekong (EN) 21 Mh 10.15N 105.55 E
Mekoryuk 40 Fd 60.23N 166.12W
Mékrou 34 Fc 12.24N 2.49 E
Mel, Ilha do- 55 Hg 25.31S 48.20W
Melaab 13 Ni 35.43N 1.20 E
Mēlādēn 35 Hc 10.25N 49.52 E
Melaka 22 Mi 2.12N 102.15 E
Melaka, Selat-=Malacca, Strait of- (EN) 21 Mi 2.30N 101.20 E
Melamo, Cabo- 30 Lj 14.24S 40.49 E
Melanesia 57 Hf 13.00S 164.00 E
Melanesian Basin (EN) 3 Jj 0.05S 160.35 E
Melawi 26 Ff 0.05N 111.29 E
Melbourne [Ar.-U.S.] 45 Kh 36.04N 91.54W
Melbourne [Austl.] 58 Fh 37.49S 144.58 E
Melbourne [Eng.-U.K.] 12 Ab 52.49N 1.26W
Melbourne [Fl.-U.S.] 43 Kf 28.05N 80.37W
Melbourne-Dandenong 59 Jg 37.59S 145.12 E
Melchor Múzquiz 47 Dc 27.53N 101.31W
Melchor Ocampo 48 Hi 17.59N 102.11W
Meldorf 10 Fb 54.05N 9.05 E
Mele, Capo- 14 Cg 43.57N 8.10 E
Melekeiok 64a Bc 7.29N 134.38 E
Melela 37 Fc 17.04S 38.36 E
Melenci 15 Dd 45.31N 20.19 E
Melenki 18 Ed 55.23N 41.42 E
Meleto Dağı 24 Ic 38.35N 41.32 E
Meleuz 19 Fe 52.58N 55.59 E
Mélèzes, Rivière aux- 42 Ke 57.00N 69.00W
Melfa 14 Hi 41.30N 13.35 E
Melfi [Chad] 35 Bc 11.04N 17.56 E
Melfi [It.] 14 Jj 41.00N 15.39 E
Melfort 42 Hf 52.52N 104.36W
Melgaço 54 Hd 1.47S 50.44W
Melibocus 10 Eg 49.42N 8.40 E
Melilla [5] 32 Ge 35.19N 2.58W
Melincué, Laguna- 55 Bk 33.42S 61.28W
Melipilla 56 Fd 33.42S 71.13W
Melita 45 Fb 49.16N 101.00W
Meliti 15 Ei 40.50N 21.35 E
Melito di Porto Salvo 14 Jm 37.55N 15.47 E
Melito di Porto Salvo, Punta di- 14 Jm 37.57N 15.45 E
Melitopol 6 Jf 46.50N 35.22 E
Melk 14 Jb 48.13N 15.19 E
Mella 14 Ee 45.13N 10.13 E
Mellakou 13 Ni 35.15N 1.14 E
Mellanfryken 8 Ee 59.40N 13.15 E
Melle [Fr.] 11 Fh 46.13N 0.08W
Melle [F.R.G.] 12 Kb 52.12N 8.21 E
Mellen 45 Kc 46.20N 90.40W
Mellerud 7 Cg 58.42N 12.28 E
Mellish Reef 59 Lc 17.25S 155.50 E
Mellish Seamount (EN) 57 Ia 34.00N 178.15 E
Mellit 35 Dc 14.08N 25.33 E
Mělník 10 Kf 50.21N 14.30 E
Melnik 15 Gh 41.31N 23.24 E
Melo 53 Ki 32.22S 54.11W
Melo, Rio- 55 De 21.25S 57.55W
Melrhir, Chott- 30 He 34.20N 6.20 E
Melrose 46 Id 45.38N 112.40W
Melsungen 10 Fe 51.08N 9.33 E
Meltaus 7 Fc 66.54N 25.22 E
Melton Constable 12 Db 52.51N 1.02 E
Melton Mowbray 9 Mi 52.46N 0.53W
Meluco 37 Fb 12.33S 39.37 E
Meluli 37 Fc 16.28S 39.44 E
Melun 11 If 48.32N 2.40 E
Melville 38 Ib 75.15N 110.00W
Melville 46 Na 50.55N 102.48W
Melville, Cape- 59 Ib 14.10S 144.30 E
Melville, Lake- 42 Lf 53.42N 59.30W
Melville Bay 59 Hb 12.05S 136.45 E
Melville Bay (EN)=Melville Bugt 67 Od 75.35N 62.30W
Melville Bugt=Melville Bay (EN) 67 Od 75.35N 62.30W
Melville Hills 42 Fc 69.20N 123.00W
Melville Island 57 Ef 11.40S 131.00 E
Melville Peninsula 38 Kc 68.00N 84.00W
Melville Sound 42 Gc 68.05N 107.30W
Melvin, Lough- 9 Eg 54.25N 8.10W
Mélykút 10 Pj 46.13N 19.23 E
Memaliaj 15 Ci 40.20N 19.58 E
Memambetsu 29a Db 43.55N 144.11 E
Memba, Baia de- 37 Gb 14.11S 40.35 E
Memberamo 26 Kg 1.28S 137.52 E
Memboro 26 Gh 9.22S 119.32 E
Mēmele 8 Kh 56.24N 24.10 E
Memmert 10 Cc 53.39N 6.53 E
Memmingen 10 Gi 47.59N 10.10 E
Mempawan 26 Ef 0.22N 108.58 E
Memphis 33 Fd 29.52N 31.15 E
Memphis [Mo.-U.S.] 45 Jf 40.28N 92.10W
Memphis [Tn.-U.S.] 39 Jf 35.08N 90.03W
Memphis [Tx.-U.S.] 45 Fi 34.44N 100.32W
Memrut Dağı 24 Jc 38.40N 42.12 E
Memuro 29 Qc 42.55N 143.03 E
Memuro-Dake 29a Cb 42.52N 142.45 E
Mena 35 Gd 5.30N 41.06 E
Mena [Ar.-U.S.] 45 Ii 34.35N 94.15W
Mena [Ukr.-U.S.S.R.] 19 De 51.33N 32.14 E
Menabe 30 Lk 20.00S 44.40 E
Menai Strait 9 Ih 53.12N 4.12W
Ménaka 31 Hg 15.55N 2.26 E
Mènam Khong=Mekong (EN) 21 Mh 10.15N 105.55 E
Menangalaku 26 Gh 9.36S 119.01 E
Menard 45 Gk 30.55N 99.47W
Menawashei 35 Dc 12.40N 25.01 E
Menčul, Gora- 10 Th 48.16N 23.49 E
Mendala, Puncak- 26 Lg 4.44S 140.20 E
Mendanau, Pulau- 26 Eg 2.51S 107.26 E
Mendanha 55 Kd 18.06S 43.30W
Mende 11 Jj 44.31N 3.30 E
Mendebo 30 Kh 6.50N 39.40 E
Mendelejevsk 7 Mi 55.57N 52.22 E
Menden (Sauerland) 10 De 51.26N 7.48 E
Mendes 13 Mi 35.39N 0.52 E
Méndez 48 Je 25.07N 98.34W
Mendi [Eth.] 35 Fd 9.48N 35.05 E
Mendi [Pap.N.Gui.] 60 Ci 6.10S 143.40 E
Mendig 12 Jd 50.22N 7.16 E
Mendip Hills 9 Kj 51.15N 2.40W
Mendocino 46 Dg 39.19N 123.48W
Mendocino, Cape- 38 Ge 40.25N 124.25W
Mendocino Fracture Zone (EN) 3 Lf 40.00N 145.00W
Mendota [Ca.-U.S.] 46 Eh 36.45N 120.23W
Mendota [Il.-U.S.] 45 Lf 41.33N 89.07W
Mendoza 53 Ji 32.54S 68.50W
Mendoza [2] 56 Gd 34.30S 68.30W
Mené, Landes du- 11 Df 48.15N 2.32W
Mene de Mauroa 49 Lh 10.43N 71.01W
Mene Grande 54 Db 9.49S 70.56W
Menemen 24 Bc 38.36N 27.04 E
Menen/Menin 11 Jd 50.48N 3.07 E
Meneng Point 64e Bb 0.33S 166.57 E
Meneses 55 Dj 30.53S 56.30W
Ménez Hom 11 Bf 48.13N 4.16W
Menfi 14 Gm 37.36N 12.58 E
Mengcheng 27 Ke 33.11N 116.30 E
Mengdingjie 27 Gg 23.31N 99.07 E
Menggala 26 Eg 4.28S 105.17 E
Mengibar 13 Ig 37.58N 3.48W
Mengjin 28 Bg 34.50N 112.26 E
Mengla 27 Hg 21.30N 101.35 E
Menglangba→Lancang 27 Gg 22.37N 99.57 E
Menglian 27 Gg 22.20N 99.27 E
Mengoun Huizu Zizhixian 28 De 38.04N 117.06 E
Mengyin 28 Dg 35.42N 117.56 E
Mengzi 22 Mg 23.23N 103.34 E
Menihek Lakes 42 Kf 54.00N 66.30W
Menin/Menen 11 Jd 50.48N 3.07 E
Menindee 59 If 32.24S 142.25 E
Menindee Lake 59 If 32.00S 142.23 E
Meningie 59 Hg 35.42S 139.20 E
Menjapa, Gunung- 26 Gf 1.05N 116.05 E
Menno 45 He 43.14N 97.34W
Menoikion Óros 15 Gh 41.11N 23.48 E
Menominee 44 Dc 45.07N 87.39W
Menongue 31 Ij 14.40S 17.39 E
Menor, Mar- 13 Lg 37.43N 0.48W
Menorca=Minorca (EN) 5 Gg 40.00N 4.00 E
Menor do Araguaia, Braço- ou Javaes 54 He 9.50S 50.12W
Mentana 14 Gh 42.02N 12.38 E
Mentasta Lake 40 Kd 62.55N 143.45W
Mentawai, Kepulauan-=Mentawai Islands (EN) 21 Lj 2.00S 99.30 E
Mentawai, Selat- 21 Lj 2.00S 99.30 E
Mentawai Islands (EN)= Mentawai, Kepulauan- 21 Lj 2.00S 99.30 E
Menton 11 Nk 43.47N 7.30 E
Mentougou 28 De 39.56N 116.02 E
Menyuan 27 Hd 37.30N 101.35 E
Menzelinsk 7 Mi 55.45N 53.09 E
Menzies 59 Ee 29.41S 121.02 E
Menzies, Mount- 66 Ff 73.30S 61.50 E
Meon 12 Ad 50.49N 1.15W
Meoqui 47 Cc 28.17N 105.29W
Meponda 37 Eb 13.25S 34.52 E
Meppel 11 Mb 52.42N 6.11 E
Meppen 10 Dd 52.41N 7.19 E
Meqele(EN)=Mekele 31 Kg 13.30N 39.28 E
Mê Qu 27 He 33.58N 102.10 E
Mequinensa, Pantà de-/ Mequinenza, Embalse de- 13 Lc 41.15N 0.02W
Mequinenza, Embalse de-/ Mequinensa, Pantà de- 13 Lc 41.15N 0.02W
Mera 14 Dd 46.11N 9.25 E
Merabello, Gulf of- (EN) = Merabéllou, Kólpos- 15 In 35.14N 25.47 E
Merabéllou, Kólpos- = Merabello, Gulf of- (EN) 15 In 35.14N 25.47 E
Merak 26 Eh 5.56S 106.00 E
Meråker 7 Ce 63.26N 11.45 E
Méralab 63b Db 14.27S 168.03 E
Meramangye, Lake- 59 Ge 28.25S 132.15 E
Meran / Merano 14 Fd 46.40N 11.09 E
Merano / Meran 14 Fd 46.40N 11.09 E
Meratus, Pegunungan- 26 Gg 2.45S 115.40 E
Merauke 58 Fe 8.28S 140.20 E
Mercadal 13 Qe 39.59N 4.05 E
Mercato Saraceno 14 Gg 43.57N 12.12 E
Merced 43 Cd 37.18N 120.29W
Mercedario, Cerro- 52 Ii 31.59S 70.14W
Mercedes [Arg.] 56 Id 34.39S 59.27W
Mercedes [Arg.] 56 Ic 29.12S 58.05W
Mercedes [Arg.] 53 Ji 33.40S 65.30W
Mercedes [Ur.] 53 Ki 33.16S 58.01W
Merchants Bay 42 Lc 67.10N 62.50W
Merchtem 12 Gd 50.58N 4.14 E
Mercury Islands 62 Fb 36.35S 175.50 E
Mercy, Cape- 42 Ld 64.56N 63.40W
Mercy Bay 42 Fb 74.15N 118.10W
Meredith, Cape- 56 Hh 52.15S 60.38W
Meredith, Lake- 45 Fi 35.36N 101.42W
Meredoua 32 Hd 25.20N 2.05 E
Merefa 19 Df 49.51N 36.00 E
Merelbeke 12 Fd 51.00N 3.45 E
Merenga 20 Kd 61.43N 156.05 E
Mergui 25 Jf 12.26N 98.36 E
Mergui Archipelago 21 Lh 12.00N 98.00 E
Méri 34 Hc 10.47N 14.06 E
Meriç 15 Jh 41.11N 26.25 E
Meriç 24 Bb 40.52N 26.12 E
Mérida [2] 54 Db 8.30N 71.10W
Mérida [Mex.] 39 Kg 20.58N 89.37W
Mérida [Sp.] 13 Ff 38.55N 6.20W
Mérida [Ven.] 53 Ie 8.36N 71.08W
Merida, Cordillera de- 52 Ie 8.40N 71.00W
Meridian 39 Kf 32.22N 88.42W
Mérig 63b Cb 14.19S 167.48 E
Mérignac 11 Fj 44.50N 0.38W
Merikarvia 7 Ef 61.51N 21.30 E
Merín, Laguna- 56 Jd 32.45S 52.50W
Meringur 59 If 34.24S 141.29 E
Merir Island 57 Ed 4.19N 132.19 E
Merizo 64c Bb 13.16N 144.40 E
Merke 18 Ic 42.52N 73.12 E
Merkem, Houthulst- 12 Ed 50.57N 2.51 E
Merkine/Merkinė 8 Kj 54.07N 24.20 E
Merkinė/Merkine 8 Kj 54.07N 24.20 E
Merkis/Merkys 7 Fi 54.10N 24.11 E
Merksem, Antwerpen- 12 Gc 51.15N 4.27 E
Merksplas 12 Gc 51.22N 4.52 E
Merkys/Merkis 7 Fi 54.10N 24.11 E
Meroe 35 Eb 16.56N 33.59 E
Meroe 35 Eb 16.05N 33.55 E
Merouane, Chott- 32 Ic 34.00N 6.02 E
Merredin 59 Df 31.29S 118.16 E
Merrick 9 If 55.08N 4.29W
Merrill 43 Jb 45.11N 89.41W
Merriman 45 Fe 42.55N 101.42W
Merritt 42 Ff 50.07N 120.47W
Merritt Island 43 Kf 28.21N 80.42W
Merritt Reservoir 45 Fe 42.35N 100.55W
Mersa Fatma 35 Gc 14.53N 40.19 E
Mersa Teklay 35 Fb 17.25N 38.45 E
Mersea Island 12 Cc 51.47N 0.57 E
Merseburg 10 He 51.22N 12.00 E
Mers el Kebir 13 Li 35.44N 0.43W
Mersey 9 Kh 53.25N 3.00W
Merseyside [3] 9 Kh 53.30N 3.00W
Mersin → İçel 23 Db 36.48N 34.38 E
Mersing 26 Df 2.26N 103.50 E
Mers-les-Bains 12 Dd 50.04N 1.23 E
Mērsrags/Mersrags 8 Jg 57.19N 23.01 E
Mersrags/Mērsrags 8 Jg 57.19N 23.01 E
Merta 25 Ec 26.39N 74.02 E
Merta Road 25 Ec 26.43N 73.55 E
Mertert 12 Ie 49.42N 6.29 E
Merthyr Tydfil 9 Jj 51.46N 3.23W
Merti 36 Gb 1.04N 38.40 E
Mértola 13 Eg 37.38N 7.40W
Mertule Maryam 35 Fc 10.50N 38.15 E
Mertvyj Kultuk, Sor- 16 Rg 45.30N 53.40 E
Mertz Glacier 66 Je 67.40S 144.45 E
Meru 36 Gb 0.03N 37.39 E
Méru 11 Ie 49.14N 2.08 E
Meru, Mount- 36 Gc 3.14S 36.45 E
Merure 55 Fb 15.33S 53.05W
Merville 12 Ed 50.38N 2.38 E
Merzifon 23 Ea 40.53N 35.29 E
Merzig 10 Cg 49.27N 6.38 E
Meša 7 Li 55.34N 49.24 E
Mesa [Az.-U.S.] 39 Hf 33.25N 111.50W
Mesa [Co.-U.S.] 45 Bg 39.14N 108.08W
Mesabi Range 45 Jc 47.30N 92.50W
Mesagne 14 Lj 40.34N 17.48 E
Mescalero 45 Dj 33.09N 105.46W
Meščera=Moscow Basin 5 Kd 55.00N 40.30 E
Meschede 10 Ee 51.21N 8.17 E
Mescit Dağı 24 Ib 40.22N 41.11 E
Meščovsk 16 Ib 54.19N 35.18 E
Mesegon 64d Bb 7.09N 151.55 E
Mesfinto 35 Fc 13.28N 37.23 E
Me-Shima 28 Jh 32.01N 128.25 E
Meshkīnshahr 24 Lc 38.24N 47.40 E
Mesima 14 Jl 38.30N 15.55 E
Mesjagutovo 17 Ii 55.35N 58.20 E
Meskiana 14 Bo 35.38N 7.40 E
Meskiana, Oued- 14 Bo 35.48N 7.53 E
Meslo 35 Fd 6.22N 39.50 E
Mesnil-Val, Criel-sur-Mer- 12 Dd 50.03N 1.20 E
Mesola 14 Gf 44.55N 12.14 E
Mesolóngion 15 Ek 38.21N 21.26 E
Mesopotamia 52 Kh 30.00S 58.00W
Mesopotamia (EN) 23 Fc 34.00N 44.00 E
Mesoyéios Thálassa= Mediterranean Sea (EN) 5 Hh 35.00N 20.00 E
Mesquite [Nv.-U.S.] 46 Hh 36.48N 114.04W
Mesquite [Tx.-U.S.] 45 Hj 32.46N 96.36W
Mesra 13 Mi 35.50N 0.10 E
Messaad 32 Hc 34.10N 3.30 E
Messalo 30 Lj 11.40S 40.46 E
Messará, Órmos- 15 Ho 35.00N 24.40 E
Messina [It.] 6 Hh 38.11N 15.34 E
Messina [S.Afr.] 31 Kk 22.23S 30.00 E
Messina, Strait of- (EN) = Messina, Stretto di- 5 Hh 38.15N 15.35 E
Messina, Stretto di- = Messina, Strait of- (EN) 5 Hh 38.15N 15.35 E
Messíni 15 El 37.15N 21.50 E
Messíni 15 Fl 37.03N 22.01 E
Messiniakós Kólpos 15 Fm 36.45N 22.10 E
Messojaha 20 Cc 67.52N 77.27 E
Mesta 15 Hi 40.51N 24.44 E
Mestecăniş, Pasul- 15 Ib 47.28N 25.20 E
Mesters Vig 41 Jd 72.15N 24.20W
Mestia 16 Mh 43.03N 42.43 E
Mestre, Espigão- 54 If 12.30S 46.00W
Mestre, Venezia- 14 Ge 45.29N 12.14 E
Mesuji 26 Eg 4.08S 105.52 E
Meta [2] 54 Dc 3.30N 73.00W
Meta, Rio- 52 Je 6.12N 67.28W
Meta Incognita Peninsula 38 Mc 62.40N 68.00W
Metairie 45 Kl 29.59N 90.09W
Metaliferi, Munţii- 15 Fc 46.10N 22.50 E
Metallifere, Colline- 14 Eg 43.10N 10.55 E
Metán 56 Hc 25.29S 64.57W
Metangula 37 Eb 12.43S 34.49 E
Metaponto 14 Kj 40.20N 16.50 E
Metauro 14 Hg 43.50N 13.03 E
Metautu 65c Ba 13.57S 171.54W
Meteghan 44 Nc 44.11N 66.10W
Metelen 12 Jb 52.09N 7.12 E
Metéora 15 Ej 39.43N 21.40 E
Meteor Seamount (EN) 30 Hm 48.00S 8.30 E
Meteor Trench (EN) 3 Do 55.00S 27.00 E
Méthana 15 Gl 37.35N 23.23 E
Methánon, Khersónisos- 15 Gl 37.36N 23.22 E
Methven 62 De 43.38S 171.38 E
Methwold 12 Cb 52.31N 0.33 E
Metković 14 Lg 43.03N 17.39 E
Metlakatla 40 Me 55.08N 131.35W
Metlika 14 Je 45.39N 15.19 E
Metlili Chaamba 32 Hc 32.16N 3.38 E
Metmårfag 32 Ed 26.26N 13.26W
Metohija 15 Dg 42.40N 20.27 E
Metro 26 Eh 5.05S 105.20 E
Metropolis 45 Lh 37.09N 88.44W
Métsovon 15 Ej 39.46N 21.11 E
Métsovon, Zigós- = Métsovon Pass (EN) 15 Ej 39.47N 21.15 E
Métsovon Pass (EN) = Métsovon, Zigós- 15 Ej 39.47N 21.15 E
Mettet 12 Gd 50.19N 4.40 E
Mettingen 12 Jb 52.19N 7.47 E
Mettlach 12 Ie 49.30N 6.36 E
Mettmann 12 Ic 51.15N 6.58 E
Metu 31 Kh 8.20N 35.38 E
Metuje 10 Lf 50.20N 15.55 E
Metz 6 Gf 49.08N 6.10 E
Metzervisse 12 Ie 49.19N 6.17 E
Meu 11 Ef 48.02N 1.47W
Meulaboh 26 Cf 4.09N 96.08 E
Meulan 12 De 49.01N 1.54 E
Meulebeke 12 Fd 50.57N 3.17 E
Meureudu 26 Ce 5.16N 96.16 E
Meurthe 11 Mf 48.47N 6.09 E
Meurthe-et-Moselle [3] 11 Mf 48.35N 6.10 E
Meuse [3] 11 Lf 49.00N 5.30 E
Meuse 5 Ge 51.49N 5.01 E
Meuse (EN)=Maas 5 Ge 51.49N 5.01 E
Meuse, Côtes de- 11 Le 49.10N 5.30 E
Meuzenti 35 Bb 18.14N 17.06 E
Mexia 45 Hk 31.41N 96.29W
Mexiana, Ilha 54 Ic 0.00 49.35W
Mexicali 39 Hf 32.40N 115.29W
Mexicana, Altiplanicie-= Mexico, Plateau of- (EN) 38 Ig 25.30N 104.00W
Mexican Hat 46 Kh 37.09N 109.52W
Mexicanos, Laguna de los- 48 Fc 28.09N 106.57W
Mexico 45 Kg 39.10N 91.53W
México [1] 39 Ig 23.00N 102.00W

Index Symbols

[1] Independent Nation
[2] State, Region
[3] District, County
[5] Municipality
Colony, Dependency
Continent
Physical Region
Historical or Cultural Region
Mount, Mountain
Volcano
Hill
Mountains, Mountain Range
Hills, Escarpment
Plateau, Upland
Pass, Gap
Plain, Lowland
Delta
Salt Flat
Valley, Canyon
Crater, Cave
Karst Features
Depression
Polder
Desert, Dunes
Forest, Woods
Heath, Steppe
Oasis
Cape, Point
Coast, Beach
Cliff
Peninsula
Isthmus
Sandbank
Island
Atoll
Rock, Reef
Islands, Archipelago
Rocks, Reefs
Coral Reef
Well, Spring
Geyser
River, Stream
Waterfall Rapids
River Mouth, Estuary
Lake
Salt Lake
Intermittent Lake
Reservoir
Swamp, Pond
Canal
Glacier
Ice Shelf, Pack Ice
Ocean
Sea
Gulf, Bay
Strait, Fjord
Lagoon
Bank
Seamount
Tablemount
Ridge
Shelf
Basin
Escarpment, Sea Scarp
Fracture
Trench, Abyss
National Park, Reserve
Point of Interest
Recreation Site
Cave, Cavern
Historic Site
Ruins
Wall, Walls
Church, Abbey
Temple
Scientific Station
Airport
Port
Lighthouse
Mine
Tunnel
Dam, Bridge

Index Symbols

[1] Independent Nation	≈ Historical or Cultural Region	) (Pass, Gap	▱ Depression	▱ Coast, Beach	▱ Rock, Reef
[2] State, Region	▲ Mount, Mountain	▱ Plain, Lowland	▱ Polder	▱ Cliff	▱ Islands, Archipelago
[3] District, County	▲ Volcano	▱ Delta	▱ Desert, Dunes	▱ Peninsula	▱ Rocks, Reefs
[4] Municipality	● Hill	▱ Salt Flat	▱ Forest, Woods	▱ Isthmus	▱ Coral Reef
[5] Colony, Dependency	▲ Mountains, Mountain Range	▱ Valley, Canyon	▱ Heath, Steppe	▱ Island	▱ Well, Spring
■ Continent	▲ Hills, Escarpment	◡ Crater, Cave	▱ Oasis	◡ Atoll	▱ Geyser
◨ Physical Region	▱ Plateau, Upland	◡ Karst Features	▱ Cape, Point		≈ River, Stream

≈ Waterfall Rapids	▱ Canal	▱ Lagoon	▱ Escarpment, Sea Scarp	▲ Historic Site	▱ Port
≈ River Mouth, Estuary	▱ Glacier	▱ Bank	▱ Fracture	▱ Ruins	▱ Lighthouse
≈ Lake	▱ Ice Shelf, Pack Ice	▱ Seamount	▱ Trench, Abyss	▱ Wall, Walls	▱ Mine
≈ Salt Lake	▱ Ocean	▱ Tablemount	▱ National Park, Reserve	▱ Church, Abbey	▱ Tunnel
▱ Intermittent Lake	▱ Sea	▱ Ridge	▱ Point of Interest	▱ Temple	▱ Dam, Bridge
▱ Reservoir	▱ Gulf, Bay	▱ Shelf	▱ Recreation Site	▱ Scientific Station	
≈ Swamp, Pond	▱ Strait, Fjord	▱ Basin	▱ Cave, Cavern	▱ Airport	

Index Symbols

[1] Independent Nation
[2] State, Region
[3] District, County
[4] Municipality
[5] Colony, Dependency
■ Continent
□ Physical Region
Historical or Cultural Region
Mount, Mountain
Volcano
Hill
Mountains, Mountain Range
Hills, Escarpment
Plateau, Upland
Pass, Gap
Plain, Lowland
Delta
Salt Flat
Valley, Canyon
Crater, Cave
Karst Features
Depression
Polder
Desert, Dunes
Forest, Woods
Heath, Steppe
Oasis
Cape, Point
Coast, Beach
Cliff
Peninsula
Isthmus
Sandbank
Island
Islands, Archipelago
Atoll
Rock, Reef
Rocks, Reefs
Coral Reef
Well, Spring
Geyser
River, Stream
Waterfall Rapids
River Mouth, Estuary
Lake
Salt Lake
Intermittent Lake
Reservoir
Swamp, Pond
Canal
Glacier
Ice Shelf, Pack Ice
Ocean
Sea
Gulf, Bay
Strait, Fjord
Lagoon
Bank
Seamount
Tablemount
Ridge
Shelf
Basin
Escarpment, Sea Scarp
Trench, Abyss
Fracture
National Park, Reserve
Point of Interest
Recreation Site
Cave, Cavern
Historic Site
Ruins
Wall, Walls
Church, Abbey
Temple
Scientific Station
Airport
Port
Lighthouse
Mine
Tunnel
Dam, Bridge

Name	Page	Ref	Lat	Long
Monte Lindo Grande, Riacho-	55	Cg	25.45 S	58.06W
Montello [Nv.-U.S.]	46	Hf	41.16N	114.12W
Montello [Wi.-U.S.]	45	Le	43.48N	89.20W
Montemorelos	47	Ec	25.12N	99.49W
Montemor-o-Novo	13	Df	38.39N	8.13W
Montemor-o-Velho	13	Dd	40.10N	8.41W
Montemuro, Serra de-	13	Dc	40.58N	8.01W
Montenegro	56	Jc	29.42 S	51.28W
Montenegro (EN) = Crna Gora [2]	15	Cg	42.30N	19.18 E
Montenegro (EN)=Crna Gora	15	Cg	42.30N	19.18 E
Monte Plata	49	Md	18.48N	69.47W
Montepuez	37	Gb	12.32 S	40.27 E
Montepuez	37	Fb	13.07 S	39.00 E
Montepulciano	14	Fg	43.05N	11.47 E
Monte Quemado	56	Hc	25.48 S	62.52W
Monte Real	13	De	39.51N	8.52W
Montereale, Passo di-	14	Hh	42.31N	13.13 E
Montereau-Faut-Yonne	11	If	48.23N	2.57 E
Monterey	43	Cd	36.37N	121.55W
Monterey Bay	43	Cd	36.45N	121.55W
Monteria	53	Ie	8.46N	75.53W
Montero	54	Fg	17.20 S	63.15W
Monteros	56	Gc	27.10 S	65.30W
Monterotondo	14	Gh	42.03N	12.37 E
Monterrey	39	Ig	25.40N	100.19W
Montesano	46	Dc	46.59N	123.36W
Monte San Savino	14	Fg	43.20N	11.43 E
Monte Sant'Angelo	14	Ji	41.42N	15.57 E
Monte Santu, Capo di-	14	Dj	45.05N	9.44 E
Montes Claros	53	Lg	16.43 S	43.52W
Montes Claros de Goiás	55	Gb	15.54 S	51.13W
Montesilvano	14	Ih	42.31N	14.09 E
Montevarchi	14	Fg	43.31N	11.34 E
Montevideo [2]	55	Dl	34.50 S	56.10W
Montevideo [Mn.-U.S.]	45	Id	44.57N	95.43W
Montevideo [Ur.]	53	Ki	34.53 S	56.11W
Monte Vista	45	Ch	37.35N	106.09W
Montfaucon	12	He	49.17N	5.08 E
Montfort-l'Amaury	12	Df	48.47N	1.49 E
Montfort-sur-Risle	12	Ce	49.18N	0.40 E
Montgenèvre, Col de-	11	Mj	44.56N	6.44 E
Montgomery	39	Kf	32.23N	86.18W
Montgomery Pass	46	Fh	38.00N	118.20W
Montguyon	11	Fi	45.13N	0.11W
Monthermé	12	Ge	49.53N	4.44 E
Monthey	14	Ad	46.15N	6.56 E
Monthois	12	Ge	49.19N	4.43 E
Monticello [Ar.-U.S.]	45	Kj	33.38N	91.47W
Monticello [Fl.-U.S.]	44	Fj	30.33N	83.52W
Monticello [Ia.-U.S.]	45	Ke	42.15N	91.12W
Monticello [In.-U.S.]	44	De	40.45N	86.46W
Monticello [Ky.-U.S.]	44	Eg	36.50N	84.51W
Monticello [N.Y.-U.S.]	44	Je	41.39N	74.41W
Monticello [Ut.-U.S.]	43	Fd	37.52N	109.21W
Montiel	13	Jf	38.42N	2.52W
Montiel, Campo de-	13	Jf	38.46N	2.44W
Montiel, Cuchilla de-	55	Cj	31.05 S	59.10W
Montignac	11	Hi	45.04N	1.10 E
Montigny-le-Roi	11	Lf	48.00N	5.30 E
Montigny-les-Metz	11	Me	49.06N	6.09 E
Montigny-le-Tilleul	12	Gd	50.23N	4.22 E
Montijo [Pan.]	49	Gj	7.59N	81.03W
Montijo [Port.]	13	Df	38.42N	8.58W
Montijo [Sp.]	13	Ff	38.55N	6.37W
Montijo, Golfo de-	49	Gj	7.40N	81.07W
Montilla	13	Hg	37.35N	4.38W
Montividiu	55	Gc	17.24 S	51.14W
Montivilliers	11	Ge	49.33N	0.12 E
Mont Joli	42	Kg	48.35N	68.11W
Mont-Laurier	42	Jg	46.33N	75.30W
Mont Louis	44	Oa	49.15N	65.43W
Mont-Louis	11	Il	42.31N	2.07 E
Montluçon	11	Ih	46.20N	2.36 E
Montmagny	42	Kg	46.59N	70.33W
Montmarault	11	Ih	46.19N	2.57 E
Montmédy	11	Le	49.31N	5.22 E
Montmirail	11	Jf	48.52N	3.32 E
Montmorency	12	Ef	49.00N	2.20 E
Montmorillon	11	Gh	46.26N	0.52 E
Montmort-Lucy	12	Ff	48.55N	3.49 E
Monto	59	Kd	24.52 S	151.07 E
Montoire-sur-le-Loir	11	Gg	47.45N	0.52 E
Montone	14	Gf	44.24N	12.14 E
Montoro	13	Hf	38.01N	4.23W
Montpelier [Id.-U.S.]	43	Ec	42.19N	111.18W
Montpelier [Vt.-U.S.]	39	Le	44.16N	72.35W
Montpellier	6	Gg	43.36N	3.53 E
Montpon-Ménestérol	11	Gi	45.01N	0.10 E
Montréal	39	Le	45.31N	73.34W
Montreal Lake	42	Gf	54.20N	105.40W
Montreal River	44	Hb	47.08N	79.27W
Montréjeau	11	Gk	43.05N	0.35 E
Montreuil [Fr.]	11	Hd	50.28N	1.46 E
Montreuil [Fr.]	12	Ef	48.52N	2.26 E
Montreuil-l'Argillé	12	Cf	48.56N	0.29 E
Montreux	14	Ad	46.26N	6.55 E
Montrose [Co.-U.S.]	43	Fd	38.29N	107.53W
Montrose [Scot.-U.K.]	9	Ke	56.43N	2.29W
Monts, Pointe des-	44	Na	49.19N	67.23W
Mont-Saint-Aignan	12	De	49.28N	1.05 E
Mont-Saint-Michel, Baie du-	11	Ef	48.40N	1.40W
Montsalvy	11	Ij	44.42N	2.30 E
Montsant, Serra del-/ Montsant, Sierra de-	13	Mc	41.17N	0.50 E
Montsant, Sierra de-/ Montsant, Serra del-	13	Mc	41.17N	0.50 E
Montsec, Serra del-/ Montsech, Sierra del-	13	Mb	42.02N	0.50 E
Montsech, Sierra del-/ Montsec, Serra del-	13	Mb	42.02N	0.50 E
Montseny/Pallars, Montsent de-	13	Nb	42.29N	1.02 E
Montseny, Sierra de-	13	Oc	41.48N	2.24 E
Montserrado [3]	34	Cd	6.35N	10.35W
Montserrat [5]	39	Mh	16.45N	62.12W
Montserrat, Monasterio de-	13	Nc	41.35N	1.49 E
Montserrat, Monasterio de-/ Montserrat, Monèstir de-	13	Nc	41.35N	1.49 E
Montserrat, Monèstir de-	13	Nc	41.35N	1.49 E
Montserrat, Monèstir de-/ Montserrat, Monasterio de-	13	Nc	41.35N	1.49 E
Montuosa, Isla-	49	Fj	7.28N	82.14W
Montville	12	De	49.33N	1.07 E
Monument Peak	46	He	42.07N	114.14W
Monument Valley	46	Jh	36.50N	110.20W
Monveda	36	Db	2.57N	21.27 E
Monviso	5	Gg	44.40N	7.07 E
Monywa	25	Jd	22.07N	95.08 E
Monza	14	De	45.35N	9.16 E
Monze	36	Ef	16.16 S	27.29 E
Monzen	29	Ec	37.17N	136.46 E
Monzón	13	Mc	41.55N	0.12 E
Mo'oka	29	Fc	36.27N	139.59 E
Moonbeam	44	Fa	49.25N	82.11W
Moonie	59	Ke	27.40 S	150.19 E
Moonie River	59	Je	29.19 S	148.43 E
Moonta	59	Hf	34.04 S	137.35 E
Moora	58	Ch	30.39 S	116.00 E
Moorcroft	46	Md	44.16N	104.57W
Moore	45	Hi	35.20N	97.29W
Moore, Lake-	57	Cg	29.50 S	117.35 E
Moorea, Ile-	57	Mf	17.32 S	149.50W
Moore's Island	44	Il	26.18N	77.33W
Moorhead	43	Hb	46.53N	96.45W
Moormerland	12	Ja	53.18N	7.26 E
Moormerland-Neermoor	12	Ja	53.18N	7.26 E
Moorreesburg	37	Bf	33.09 S	18.40 E
Moosburg an der Isar	10	Hh	48.28N	11.56 E
Moose	38	Kd	50.48N	81.18W
Moosehead Lake	43	Nb	45.40N	69.40W
Moose Jaw	39	Id	50.23N	105.32W
Moose Jaw River	46	Ma	50.34N	105.17W
Moose Lake	45	Jc	46.25N	92.45W
Mooselookmeguntic Lake	44	Lc	44.53N	70.48W
Moose Mountain	45	Eb	49.45N	102.37W
Moose Mountain Creek	45	Eb	49.12N	102.10W
Moosomin	42	Hf	50.09N	101.40W
Moosonee	42	Jf	51.17N	80.39W
Mopeia	37	Fc	17.59 S	35.43 E
Mopelia, Atoll- → Maupihaa Atoll	57	Lf	16.50 S	153.55W
Mopti	31	Gg	14.30N	4.12W
Mopti [3]	34	Ec	14.40N	4.15W
Moqokorei	35	He	4.04N	46.08 E
Moquegua [2]	54	Dg	16.50 S	70.55W
Moquegua	54	Dg	17.12 S	70.56W
Mór	10	Oi	47.23N	18.12 E
Mor, Glen-	9	Id	57.10N	4.40W
Mora [Cam.]	34	Hc	11.03N	14.09 E
Mora [Port.]	13	Df	38.56N	8.10W
Mora [Sp.]	13	Ie	39.41N	3.46W
Mora [Swe.]	7	Df	61.00N	14.33 E
Morača	15	Cg	42.16N	19.09 E
Morača, Manastir-	15	Cg	42.46N	19.24 E
Morādābād	22	Jg	28.50N	78.47 E
Morada Nova de Minas	55	Jd	18.25 S	45.22W
Móra d'Ebre/Mora de Ebro	13	Mc	41.05N	0.38 E
Mora de Ebro/Móra d'Ebre	13	Mc	41.05N	0.38 E
Mora de Rubielos	13	Ld	40.15N	0.45W
Morafenobe	37	Gc	17.49 S	44.55 E
Morag	10	Pc	53.56N	19.56 E
Mórahalom	10	Pj	46.13N	19.53 E
Moraleda, Canal-	56	Ff	44.30 S	73.30W
Moraleja	13	Fd	40.04N	6.39W
Morales [Col.]	49	Ki	8.17N	73.52W
Morales [Guat.]	49	Cf	15.29N	88.49W
Morales, Laguna-	48	Kf	23.35N	97.45W
Moramanga	37	Hc	18.57 S	48.11 E
Moran	46	Je	43.50N	110.28W
Morane Atoll	57	Ng	23.10 S	137.07W
Morangas, Ribeirão-	55	Fd	19.39 S	52.19W
Morant Bay	49	Ie	17.53N	76.25W
Morant Cays	47	Ie	17.24N	75.59W
Morant Point	49	Ie	17.55N	76.10W
Morar, Loch-	9	He	56.58N	5.45W
Morarano	37	Hc	17.46 S	48.10 E
Mora River	45	Di	35.44N	104.23W
Moraska, Góra-	10	Md	52.30N	16.52 E
Morat/Murten	14	Bd	46.56N	7.08 E
Morata, Puerto de-	13	Kc	41.29N	1.31W
Moratalla	13	Kf	38.12N	1.53W
Moratuwa	25	Fg	6.46N	79.53 E
Morava	5	Hf	48.10N	16.59 E
Morava=Moravia (EN)	5	Hf	49.30N	17.00 E
Morava=Moravia (EN)	10	Mg	49.30N	17.00 E
Moravia (EN)=Morava	5	Hf	49.30N	17.00 E
Moravia (EN)=Morava	10	Mg	49.30N	17.00 E
Moravian Gate (EN)= Moravská Brána	5	Hf	49.33N	17.42 E
Moravian Upland (EN)= Českomoravská Vrchovina	5	Hf	49.20N	15.30 E
Moravica	15	Df	43.51N	20.05 E
Moravská Brána=Moravian Gate(EN)	5	Hf	49.33N	17.42 E
Moravské Budějovice	10	Lg	49.03N	15.49 E
Morawa	59	De	29.13 S	116.00 E
Morawhanna	54	Gb	8.16N	59.45W
Moray Firth	5	Fd	57.50N	3.30W
Morbach	12	Je	49.49N	7.07 E
Morbihan [3]	11	Dg	47.55N	2.50W
Morbihan	11	Dg	47.35N	2.48W
Morbylånga	7	Dh	56.31N	16.23 E
Morcenx	11	Fj	44.02N	0.55W
Mordāb	24	Md	37.26N	49.25 E
Mordaga	27	La	51.14N	120.43 E
Morden	42	Hg	49.11N	98.05W
Mordovo	16	Lc	52.05N	40.46 E
Mordovskaja ASSR [3]	19	Ee	54.20N	44.30 E
Möre	8	Fh	56.25N	15.55 E
More, Ben-	9	Ie	56.23N	4.31W
Morea	37	Bd	22.41 S	15.54 E
More Assynt, Ben-	9	Ic	58.07N	4.51W
Moreau River	43	Gb	45.18N	100.43W
Morecambe	9	Kg	54.04N	2.53W
Morecambe Bay	9	Kg	54.07N	3.00W
Moree	58	Fg	29.28 S	149.51 E
Morehead [Ky.-U.S.]	44	Ff	38.11N	83.25W
Morehead [Pap.N.Gui.]	60	Ci	8.50 S	141.57 E
Morehead City	43	Le	34.43N	76.43W
Moreiz, Gora-	19	Gb	69.30N	62.05 E
Moreju	17	Ib	68.20N	59.45 E
Morelia	39	Ih	19.42N	101.07W
Morella	13	Ld	40.37N	0.06W
Morelos	48	Ic	28.25N	100.53W
Morelos [2]	47	Ee	18.45N	99.00W
Morena, Sierra-	5	Fh	38.00N	5.00W
Moreni	15	Ie	44.59N	25.39 E
Møre og Romsdal [2]	7	Be	62.40N	7.50 E
Moresby	42	Ef	52.45N	131.50W
Moreton Bay	59	Ke	27.20 S	153.15 E
Moreton Island	59	Ke	27.10 S	153.25 E
Moret-sur-Loing	11	If	48.22N	2.49 E
Moreuil	12	Ee	49.46N	2.29 E
Morez	11	Mh	46.31N	6.02 E
Morezu	15	Hd	45.09N	24.01 E
Mörfelden	12	Ke	49.59N	8.34 E
Morgan City	45	Kl	29.42N	91.12W
Morganfield	44	Dg	37.41N	87.55W
Morganton	44	Gh	35.45N	81.41W
Morgantown [Ky.-U.S.]	44	Dg	37.14N	86.41W
Morgantown [W.V.-U.S.]	44	Hf	39.38N	79.57W
Morges	14	Ad	46.31N	6.30 E
Morghāb	23	Jb	38.18N	61.12 E
Morhange	11	Mf	48.55N	6.38 E
Mori [China]	27	Fc	43.49N	90.11 E
Mori [Jap.]	28	Pc	42.06N	140.35 E
Moriarty	45	Ci	34.59N	106.03W
Morichal Largo, Rio-	50	Eh	9.27N	62.25W
Moriguchi	29	Dd	34.44N	135.34 E
Morin Dawa (Nirji)	27	Lb	48.30N	124.28 E
Morioka	22	Qf	39.42N	141.09 E
Moriyoshi	29	Ga	40.07N	140.22 E
Moriyoshi-Yama	29	Gb	39.59N	140.33 E
Morjärv	7	Fc	66.04N	22.43 E
Morki	7	Lh	56.28N	49.00 E
Morko	8	Gf	59.00N	17.40 E
Morkoka	20	Gc	65.03N	115.40 E
Morkøv	8	Di	55.40N	11.32 E
Morlaix	11	Cf	48.35N	3.50W
Morlanwelz	12	Gd	50.27N	4.14 E
Mörlunda	8	Fg	57.19N	15.51 E
Mormanno	14	Jk	39.53N	15.59 E
Morne-à-l'Eau	50	Fd	16.21N	61.31W
Morne Diablotin	47	Le	15.30N	61.24W
Mornington, Isla-	56	Eg	49.45 S	75.23W
Mornington Island	59	Hc	16.35 S	139.24 E
Moro	46	Ed	45.29N	120.44W
Morobe	58	Fe	7.45 S	147.37 E
Morocco (EN)=Al Maghrib [1]	31	Ge	32.00N	5.50W
Morogoro	31	Ki	6.49 S	37.40 E
Morogoro [3]	36	Gd	8.20 S	37.00 E
Moro Gulf	26	He	6.51N	123.00 E
Moroleón	48	Ig	20.08N	101.12W
Morombe	31	Lk	21.44 S	43.23 E
Morón [Arg.]	55	Cl	34.39 S	58.37W
Morón [Cuba]	47	Id	22.06N	78.38W
Morón [Ven.]	54	Ea	10.29N	68.11W
Morona, Rio-	54	Cd	4.45 S	77.04W
Morondava	31	Lk	20.15 S	44.17 E
Morón de la Frontera	13	Gg	37.08N	5.27W
Morones, Sierra-	48	Hg	21.55N	103.05W
Moroni	31	Lj	11.41 S	43.16 E
Moron Us He	21	Lf	34.42N	94.50 E
Morotai, Pulau-	57	Dd	2.20N	128.25 E
Moroto	31	Kh	2.32N	34.39 E
Morovița	15	Ed	45.16N	21.16 E
Morozov	15	Ig	42.30N	25.10 E
Morozovsk	19	Ef	48.20N	41.50 E
Morpeth	9	Lf	55.10N	1.41W
Morphou → Güzelyurt	24	Ee	35.12N	32.59 E
Morrilton	45	Ji	35.09N	92.45W
Morrinhos	54	Ig	17.44 S	49.07W
Morrinsville	62	Fb	37.39 S	175.32 E
Morris [Il.-U.S.]	45	Lf	41.22N	88.26W
Morris [Man.-Can.]	42	Hg	49.21N	97.22W
Morris [Mn.-U.S.]	45	Id	45.35N	95.55W
Morris, Mount-	59	Ge	26.09 S	131.04 E
Morrisburg	44	Jc	44.54N	75.11W
Morris Jesup, Kap-	67	Me	83.45N	35.50W
Morrison Dennis Cays	49	Ff	14.28N	82.53W
Morristown	44	Fg	36.13N	83.18W
Morrito	49	Eh	11.37N	85.05W
Morro, Punta del-	48	Kh	19.51N	96.27W
Morro Bay	43	Cd	35.22N	120.51W
Morro do Chapéu	54	Jf	11.33 S	41.09W
Morrosquillo, Golfo de-	49	Ji	9.35N	75.40W
Morro Vermelho, Serra do-	55	Jc	17.45 S	45.20W
Mörrum	8	Fh	56.11N	14.45 E
Morrumbala	37	Fc	17.20 S	35.35 E
Morrumbene	37	Fd	23.39 S	35.20 E
Mörrumsån	8	Fh	56.09N	14.44 E
Mors	8	Ch	56.50N	8.45 E
Moršansk	19	Ee	53.26N	41.49 E
Morsbach	12	Jd	50.52N	7.45 E
Morsberg	12	Ke	49.43N	8.54 E
Mörsil	7	Ce	63.19N	13.38 E
Mörskom/Myrskylä	8	Kd	60.40N	25.51 E
Morsott	14	Co	35.40N	8.01 E
Mortagne	11	Mf	48.33N	6.27 E
Mortagne-au-Perche	11	Gf	48.31N	0.33 E
Mortagne-sur-Sèvre	11	Fg	47.00N	0.57W
Mortain	11	Ff	48.39N	0.56W
Mortara	14	Ce	45.15N	8.44 E
Mortcha	30	Jg	16.00N	21.10 E
Morteau	11	Mg	47.04N	6.37 E
Morteaux-Couliboeuf	12	Bf	48.56N	0.04W
Morteros	56	Hd	30.42 S	62.00W
Mortes, Rio das-	55	Je	21.09 S	44.53W
Mortesoro	35	Ec	10.12N	34.09 E
Mortlock Islands	57	Gd	5.27N	153.40 E
Morton	46	Dc	46.33N	122.17W
Mortsel	12	Gc	51.10N	4.28 E
Morumbi	55	Ef	23.46 S	54.06W
Morvan	11	Jg	47.05N	4.00 E
Morven	59	Je	26.25 S	147.07 E
Morvern	9	He	56.35N	5.50W
Morvi	25	Ed	22.49N	70.50 E
Morwell	58	Fh	38.14 S	146.24 E
Morzine	11	Mh	46.11N	6.43 E
Moržovec, Ostrov-	7	Kc	66.45N	42.35 E
Moša	7	Je	62.25N	39.48 E
Mosbach	10	Fg	49.21N	9.09 E
Mosby	8	Bf	58.14N	7.54 E
Mošćny, Ostrov-	7	Gg	60.00N	27.50 E
Mosconi	55	Bl	35.44 S	60.34W
Moscos Islands	25	Jf	14.00N	97.45 E
Moscow [Id.-U.S.]	43	Db	46.44N	116.59W
Moscow (EN)=Moskva	5	Jd	55.08N	38.50 E
Moscow (EN)=Moskva [R.S.F.S.R.]	6	Jd	55.45N	37.35 E
Moscow Basin (EN)= Meščera	5	Kd	55.00N	40.30 E
Moscow Canal (EN)= Moskvy, kanal imeni-	5	Jd	56.43N	37.08 E
Moscow Upland (EN)= Moskovskaja Vozvyšennost	5	Jd	56.30N	37.30 E
Mosel=Moselle (EN)	5	Ge	50.22N	7.36 E
Moselberge	12	Ie	49.57N	6.56 E
Moselle [3]	11	Me	49.00N	6.30 E
Moselle	5	Ge	50.22N	7.36 E
Moselle (EN)=Mosel	5	Ge	50.22N	7.36 E
Moses Lake	43	Db	47.08N	119.17W
Mosgiel	61	Di	45.53 S	170.22 E
Moshi	31	Ki	3.21 S	37.20 E
Mosina	10	Md	52.16N	16.51 E
Mosjøen	7	Cd	65.50N	13.12 E
Moskalvo	20	Jf	53.39N	142.37 E
Moskenesøy	7	Cc	67.59N	13.00 E
Moskovskaja Oblast [3]	19	Dd	55.45N	37.45 E
Moskovskaja Vozvyšennost =Moscow Upland (EN)	5	Jd	56.30N	37.30 E
Moskovski	18	Gf	37.40N	69.39 E
Moskva [R.S.F.S.R.] = Moscow (EN)	6	Jd	55.45N	37.35 E
Moskva [Tur.-U.S.S.R.]	18	Ee	38.27N	64.24 E
Moskva=Moscow (EN)	5	Jd	55.08N	38.50 E
Moskva, Pik-	18	He	38.55N	71.52 E
Moskvy, kanal imeni-= Moscow Canal (EN)	5	Jd	56.43N	37.08 E
Moslavačka Gora	14	Ke	45.38N	16.42 E
Moso	63b	Dc	17.32 S	168.15 E
Mosomane	37	Dd	24.01 S	26.19 E
Mosoni-Duna	10	Ni	47.44N	17.47 E
Mosonmagyaróvár	10	Ni	47.52N	17.17 E
Mosor	14	Kg	43.30N	16.40 E
Mosquero	45	Ei	35.47N	103.58W
Mosquito, Baie -	42	Jd	60.40N	78.00W
Mosquito Coast (EN)= Mosquitos, Costa de-	38	Kh	13.00N	83.45W
Mosquito, Riacho-	55	Cf	22.12 S	57.57W
Mosquitos, Costa de-= Mosquito Coast (EN)	38	Kh	13.00N	83.45W
Mosquitos, Golfo de los-	38	Ki	9.00N	81.20W
Moss	6	Hd	59.26N	10.42 E
Mossaka	36	Cc	1.13 S	16.48 E
Mossâmedes	55	Gc	16.07 S	50.11W
Mossbank	46	Mb	49.55N	105.59W
Mossburn	61	Ci	45.41 S	168.15 E
Mosselbaai	31	Jl	34.11 S	22.08 E
Mossendjo	36	Bc	2.57 S	12.44 E
Mossman	58	Ff	16.28 S	145.22 E
Mossø	8	Ch	56.05N	9.50 E
Mossoró	53	Mf	5.11 S	37.20W
Moss Point	45	Lk	30.25N	88.29W
Mossuril	37	Gb	14.58 S	40.40 E
Most	10	Jf	50.32N	13.39 E
Mostaganem [3]	32	Hb	35.40N	0.30 E
Mostaganem	31	He	35.56N	0.05 E
Mostar	14	Lg	43.21N	17.49 E
Mostardas	55	Gj	31.06 S	50.57W
Møsting, Kap-	41	Hf	63.45N	41.00W
Mostiska	16	Ce	49.48N	23.09 E
Mostiștea	15	Je	44.15N	26.54 E
Most na Soci	14	Hd	46.09N	13.45 E
Mostovskoj	16	Lg	44.22N	40.48 E
Mosty	19	Ce	53.27N	24.33 E
Mosul (EN)=Al Mawșil	22	Gf	36.20N	43.08 E
Møsvatn	7	Bg	59.50N	8.05 E
Mota	63b	Ca	13.40 S	167.42 E
Mota	35	Fc	11.05N	37.53 E
Motaba	36	Cb	2.03N	18.03 E
Motacusito	55	Bd	17.35 S	61.31W
Mota del Marques	13	Gc	41.38N	5.10W
Motagua	38	Kh	15.44N	88.14W
Motajica	14	Le	45.04N	17.40 E
Motala	7	Dg	58.33N	15.03 E
Motala ström	8	Gf	58.38N	16.10 E
Motatán	49	Li	9.24N	70.36W
Motatán, Rio-	49	Li	9.32N	71.02W
Motegi	29	Gc	36.32N	140.10 E
Motehuala	47	Dd	23.39N	100.39W
Mothe	63d	Cc	18.40 S	178.30W
Motherwell	9	Jf	55.48N	4.00W
Motīhāri	25	Gc	26.39N	84.55 E
Motilla del Palancar	13	Ke	39.34N	1.53W
Motiti Island	62	Gb	37.40 S	176.25 E
Motlav	63b	Ca	13.40 S	167.40 E
Motobu	29b	Ab	26.40N	127.55 E
Motol	10	Vd	52.17N	25.40 E
Motovski Zaliv	7	Hb	69.30N	32.30 E
Motoyoshi	29	Gb	38.48N	141.31 E
Motozintla de Mendoza	48	Mj	15.22N	92.14W
Motril	13	Ih	36.45N	3.31W
Motru	15	Ge	44.33N	23.27 E
Motru	15	Fe	44.48N	23.00 E
Motsuta-Misaki	29a	Ab	42.36N	139.49 E
Mott	45	Ec	46.22N	102.20W
Motteville	12	Ce	49.38N	0.51 E
Motu	62	Gb	37.51 S	177.35 E
Motueka	62	Ed	41.07 S	173.01 E
Motuhora Island	62	Gb	37.50 S	177.00 E
Motu-Iti	65d	Ac	27.11 S	109.27W
Motu-Iti → Tupai Atoll	61	Kc	16.17 S	151.50W
Motul	47	Gd	21.06N	89.17W
Motu-Nui	65d	Ac	27.12 S	109.28W
Motu One Atoll	57	Lf	15.48 S	154.33W
Motupae	64n	Ac	10.27 S	161.02W
Motupena Point	63a	Bb	6.32 S	155.09 E
Moturiki	63d	Bb	17.46 S	178.45 E
Motutapu	64p	Cb	21.14 S	159.43W
Motu Tautara	65d	Ab	27.05 S	109.26W
Motutunga Atoll	57	Mf	17.06 S	144.22W
Moubray Bay	66	Kf	72.11 S	170.15 E
Mouchard	11	Lh	46.58N	5.48 E
Mouchoir Bank (EN)	47	Jd	20.57N	70.42W
Mouchoir Passage	49	Lc	21.10N	71.00W
Moudjéria	32	Ef	17.52N	12.20W
Mouila	31	Ii	1.52 S	11.01 E
Mouka	35	Cd	7.16N	21.52 E
Moul	34	Hb	15.03N	13.18 E
Mould Bay	39	Hb	76.15N	119.30W
Moule	50	Fd	16.20N	61.21W
Moule à Chique, Cap-	51k	Bb	13.43N	60.57W
Moulins	11	Jh	46.34N	3.20 E
Moulmein → Mawlamyine	22	Le	16.30N	97.38 E
Moulouya	30	Ge	35.06N	2.20W
Moult	12	Be	49.07N	0.10W
Moultrie	44	Fj	31.11N	83.47W
Moultrie, Lake-	44	Gi	33.20N	80.05W
Mouly, Pointe de-	63b	Ce	20.43 S	166.23 E
Moúnda, Ákra-	15	Dk	38.03N	20.47 E
Moundou	31	Ih	8.34N	16.05 E
Moundsville	44	Gf	39.54N	80.44W
Mo'unga'one	65b	Ba	19.38 S	174.29W
Moungoudou	36	Bc	2.40 S	12.41 E
Mountainair	45	Ci	34.31N	106.15W
Mountain Grove	45	Jh	37.08N	92.16W
Mountain Home [Ar.-U.S.]	45	Jh	36.21N	92.23W
Mountain Home [Id.-U.S.]	43	Dc	43.08N	115.41W
Mountain Nile (EN)=Jabal, Baḩr al-	30	Kh	9.30N	30.30 E
Mountain Village	40	Gd	62.05N	163.44W
Mount Airy	44	Gg	36.31N	80.37W
Mount Barker	59	Df	34.38 S	117.40 E
Mount Carmel	45	Mf	38.25N	87.46W
Mount Desert Island	44	Mc	44.20N	68.20W
Mount Douglas	58	Fg	21.30 S	146.50 E
Mount Eba	59	Hf	30.12 S	135.40 E
Mount Forest	44	Gd	43.59N	80.44W
Mount Frere	37	Df	31.00 S	28.58 E
Mount Gambier	58	Fh	37.50 S	140.46 E
Mount Hagen	60	Ci	5.52 S	144.13 E
Mount Hope	59	Hf	34.07 S	135.23 E
Mount Isa	58	Eg	20.44 S	139.30 E
Mountlake Terrace	46	Dc	47.47N	122.18W
Mount Lebanon	44	Ge	40.23N	80.03W
Mount Lofty Ranges	59	Hg	35.15 S	138.50 E
Mount Magnet	58	Cg	28.04 S	117.49 E
Mount Maunganui	61	Eg	37.38 S	176.12 E
Mount Morgan	59	Kd	23.39 S	150.23 E
Mountnorris Bay	59	Gb	11.20 S	132.45 E
Mount Peck	46	Ha	50.10N	115.02W
Mount Pleasant [Ia.-U.S.]	45	Kf	40.58N	91.33W
Mount Pleasant [Mi.-U.S.]	44	Ed	43.35N	84.47W
Mount Pleasant [S.C.-U.S.]	44	Hi	32.47N	79.52W
Mount Pleasant [Tx.-U.S.]	45	Ij	33.09N	94.58W
Mount Pleasant [Ut.-U.S.]	46	Jg	39.33N	111.27W
Mount's Bay	9	Hk	50.03N	5.25W
Mount Somers	62	De	43.42 S	171.25 E
Mount Sterling [Il.-U.S.]	45	Kg	39.59N	90.45W
Mount Sterling [Ky.-U.S.]	44	Ff	38.04N	83.56W
Mount Vancouver	42	Dd	60.20N	139.41W
Mount Vernon [Al.-U.S.]	44	Cj	31.05N	88.01W
Mount Vernon [Austl.]	59	Dd	24.13 S	118.14 E
Mount Vernon [Il.-U.S.]	43	Jd	38.19N	88.55W
Mount Vernon [In.-U.S.]	44	Dg	37.56N	87.54W
Mount Vernon [Ky.-U.S.]	44	Eg	37.21N	84.20W
Mount Vernon [Oh.-U.S.]	44	Fe	40.23N	82.30W
Mount Vernon [Wa.-U.S.]	43	Cb	48.25N	122.20W
Moura [Austl.]	59	Jd	24.35 S	150.00 E
Moura [Port.]	13	Ef	38.08N	7.27W
Mourão	13	Ef	38.23N	7.21W
Mourdi	35	Cb	17.50N	22.25 E
Mourdi, Dépression du-= Mourdi Depression (EN)	30	Jg	18.10N	23.00 E
Mourdiah	34	Dc	14.26N	7.31W
Mourdi Depression (EN)= Mourdi, Dépression du-	30	Jg	18.10N	23.00 E
Mourmelon-le-Grand	12	Ge	49.08N	4.22 E
Mourne Mountains/Beanna Boirche	9	Gg	54.10N	6.04W
Mouscron/Moeskroen	11	Jd	50.44N	3.13 E
Moussoro	31	Ig	13.39N	16.29 E
Moustiers-Sainte-Marie	11	Mk	43.51N	6.13 E
Moutier/Münster	14	Bc	47.16N	7.22 E
Moutiers	11	Mi	45.29N	6.32 E
Moutong	26	Hf	0.28N	121.13 E
Mouy	12	Ee	49.19N	2.19 E
Mouydir	30	Hf	25.00N	4.10 E
Mouyondzi	36	Bc	3.58 S	13.57 E
Mouzaia	13	Oh	36.28N	2.41 E
Mouzon	12	He	49.36N	5.05 E
Movas	48	Ec	28.10N	109.25W

Index Symbols

- [1] Independent Nation
- [2] State, Region
- [3] District, County
- [4] Municipality
- [5] Colony, Dependency
- Continent
- Physical Region
- Historical or Cultural Region
- Mount, Mountain
- Volcano
- Hill
- Mountains, Mountain Range
- Hills, Escarpment
- Plateau, Upland
- Pass, Gap
- Plain, Lowland
- Delta
- Salt Flat
- Valley, Canyon
- Crater, Cave
- Karst Features
- Depression
- Polder
- Desert, Dunes
- Forest, Woods
- Heath, Steppe
- Oasis
- Cape, Point
- Coast, Beach
- Cliff
- Peninsula
- Isthmus
- Sandbank
- Island
- Atoll
- Rock, Reef
- Islands, Archipelago
- Rocks, Reefs
- Coral Reef
- Well, Spring
- Geyser
- River, Stream
- Waterfall Rapids
- River Mouth, Estuary
- Lake
- Salt Lake
- Intermittent Lake
- Reservoir
- Swamp, Pond
- Canal
- Glacier
- Ice Shelf, Pack Ice
- Ocean
- Sea
- Gulf, Bay
- Strait, Fjord
- Lagoon
- Bank
- Seamount
- Tablemount
- Ridge
- Shelf
- Basin
- Escarpment, Sea Scarp
- Fracture
- Trench, Abyss
- National Park, Reserve
- Point of Interest
- Recreation Site
- Cave, Cavern
- Historic Site
- Ruins
- Wall, Walls
- Church, Abbey
- Temple
- Scientific Station
- Airport
- Port
- Lighthouse
- Mine
- Tunnel
- Dam, Bridge

Moxico [3]	36	De	12.00 S	20.00 E
Moxico	36	De	11.51 S	20.01 E
Moy/An Mhuaidh	9	Dg	54.12N	9.08W
Moyahua	48	Hg	21.16N	103.10W
Moyale [Eth.]	31	Kh	3.32N	39.04 E
Moyale [Kenya]	36	Gb	3.32N	39.03 E
Moyamba	34	Cd	8.10N	12.26W
Moÿ-de-l'Aisne	12	Fe	49.45N	3.22 E
Moyen Atlas=Middle Atlas (EN)	30	Ge	33.30N	4.30W
Moyen-Chari [3]	35	Bd	9.00N	18.00 E
Moyenne Guinée [3]	34	Cc	11.15N	12.30W
Moyenneville	12	Dd	50.04N	1.45 E
Moyen-Ogooué [3]	36	Bc	0.30 S	10.30 E
Moyeuvre-Grande	12	Ie	49.15N	6.02 E
Moyo	36	Fb	3.40N	31.43 E
Moyo, Pulau-	26	Gh	8.15 S	117.34 E
Moyobamba	53	If	6.02 S	76.58W
Moyowosi	36	Fc	4.50 S	31.24 E
Moyto	35	Bc	12.35N	16.33 E
Moyu/Karakax	27	Cd	37.17N	79.42 E
Možajsk	7	Ii	55.32N	36.02 E
Mozambique (EN)= Moçambique [1]	31	Kj	18.15 S	35.00 E
Mozambique (EN)= Moçambique	31	Lk	15.03 S	40.45 E
Mozambique, Canal de-= Mozambique Channel (EN)	30	Lk	20.00 S	43.00 E
Mozambique Channel (EN) =Moçambique, Canal de-	30	Lk	20.00 S	43.00 E
Mozambique Channel (EN) =Mozambique, Canal de-	30	Lk	20.00 S	43.00 E
Mozambique Plateau (EN)	30	Kl	32.00 S	35.00 E
Mozdok	19	Eg	43.44N	44.38 E
Možga	19	Fd	56.28N	52.13 E
Mozuli	8	Mh	56.32N	28.14 E
Mozyr	19	Ce	52.02N	29.16 E
Mpala	36	Ed	6.45 S	29.31 E
Mpanda	31	Ki	6.22 S	31.02 E
Mpigi	36	Fb	0.15N	32.20 E
Mpika	31	Kj	11.50 S	31.27 E
Mpoko	35	Be	4.19N	18.33 E
Mporokoso	36	Fd	9.23 S	30.08 E
Mpouia	36	Cc	2.37 S	16.13 E
Mpui	36	Fd	8.21 S	31.50 E
Mpulungu	36	Fd	8.46 S	31.07 E
Mpwapwa	36	Gd	6.21 S	36.29 E
Mrągowo	10	Rc	53.52N	21.19 E
Mrakovo	17	Hj	52.43N	56.38 E
Mrkonjić Grad	14	Lf	44.25N	17.06 E
Mrocza	10	Nc	53.14N	17.36 E
Mroga	10	Pd	52.09N	19.42 E
Msangesi	36	Ge	11.40 S	36.45 E
Msid, Djebel-	14	Cn	36.25N	8.04 E
Msif	13	Qi	35.23N	4.45 E
M'Sila	13	Qi	35.31N	4.30 E
M'Sila [3]	32	Hb	35.00N	4.30 E
M'Sila	32	Hb	35.42N	4.33 E
Mšinskaja	8	Nf	58.55N	30.03 E
Msta	5	Jd	58.25N	31.20 E
Mstislavl	16	Gc	53.59N	31.45 E
Mszana Dolna	10	Qg	49.42N	20.05 E
Mtakuja	36	Fd	7.22 S	30.37 E
Mtama	36	Ge	10.18 S	39.22 E
Mtelo	36	Gb	1.39N	35.23 E
Mtera Reservoir	36	Gd	7.01 S	35.55 E
Mtito Andei	36	Gc	2.41 S	38.10 E
Mtubatuba	37	Ee	28.30 S	32.08 E
Mtwara [3]	36	Ge	10.40 S	39.00 E
Mtwara	31	Lj	10.16 S	40.11 E
Mu, Cerro-	49	Ki	9.29N	73.07W
Mua	64h	Ac	13.21 S	176.10W
Mu'a	65b	Ac	21.11 S	175.07W
Mua, Baie de-	64h	Bc	13.23 S	176.09W
Muaná	54	Id	1.32 S	49.13W
Muang Huon	25	Kd	20.09N	101.27 E
Muang Khammouan	25	Ke	17.24N	104.48 E
Muang Không	25	Lf	14.07N	105.51 E
Muang Khôngxédôn	25	Le	15.34N	105.49 E
Muang Khoua	25	Kd	21.05N	102.31 E
Muang Pak Lay	25	Ke	18.12N	101.25 E
Muang Pakxan	25	Ke	18.22N	103.39 E
Muang Pakxong	25	Le	15.11N	106.14 E
Muang Sing	25	Kd	21.11N	101.09 E
Muang Tahoi	25	Le	16.10N	106.38 E
Muang Thai=Thailand (EN) [1]	22	Lh	15.00N	100.00 E
Muang Vangviang	25	Ke	18.56N	102.27 E
Muang Xaignabouri	25	Ke	19.15N	101.45 E
Muang Xay	25	Kd	20.42N	101.59 E
Muang Xépôn	25	Le	16.41N	106.14 E
Muanzanza	36	Dd	6.32 S	20.51 E
Muar	26	Df	2.02N	102.34 E
Muaraaman	26	Dg	3.07 S	102.12 E
Muarabungo	26	Dg	1.28 S	102.07 E
Muaraenim	26	Dg	3.39 S	103.48 E
Muaralasan	26	Gf	1.48N	117.12 E
Muarapajang	26	Gg	1.32 S	115.48 E
Muarasiberut	26	Cg	1.36 S	99.11 E
Muarasiram	26	Gg	0.46 S	116.11 E
Muaratebo	26	Dg	1.30 S	102.26 E
Muaratewe	26	Fg	0.57 S	114.53 E
Muarawahau	26	Gf	1.02N	116.52 E
Mubarek	18	Ee	39.16N	65.07 E
Mubende	36	Fb	0.35N	31.23 E
Mubi	31	Ig	10.16N	13.16 E
Much	12	Jd	50.55N	7.24 E
Muchinga Escarpment	36	Fe	13.40S	34.00 E
Muchinga Mountains	30	Kj	12.00S	31.45 E
Muck	9	Ge	56.50N	6.14W
Mücke	12	Ld	50.37N	9.02 E
Mucojo	37	Gb	12.04 S	40.28 E
Muconda	36	De	10.34 S	21.20 E
Mucua	37	Ec	18.09 S	34.58 E
Mucubela	37	Fc	16.54 S	37.49 E
Mucuchies	49	Li	8.45N	70.55W
Mucumbura	37	Ec	16.10 S	31.42 E
Mucur	24	Fc	39.04N	34.23 E
Mucusso	36	Df	18.00 S	21.25 E
Mudan Jang	21	Oe	46.18N	129.31 E
Mudanjiang	22	Oe	44.35N	129.34 E
Mudanya	24	Cb	40.22N	28.52 E
Muddy Gap	46	Le	42.22N	107.27W
Mudgee	59	Jf	32.36 S	149.35 E
Mud Lake	46	Ie	43.53N	112.24W
Mud Lake	46	Gh	37.55N	117.05W
Mudon	25	Je	16.15N	97.44 E
Mudug [3]	35	Hd	6.30N	48.00 E
Mudug	35	Hd	6.20N	47.00 E
Mudurnu	24	Db	40.28N	31.13 E
Muecate	37	Fb	14.53 S	39.38 E
Mueda	37	Fb	11.39 S	39.33 E
Muerto, Cayo-	49	Ff	14.34N	82.44W
Muerto, Mar-	48	Li	16.10N	94.10W
Mufulira	31	Jj	12.33 S	28.14 E
Mufu Shan	27	Jf	29.15N	114.20 E
Mufu Shan	27	Jf	29.00N	113.50 E
Mugello	14	Fg	43.55N	11.25 E
Múggia	14	He	45.36N	13.46 E
Mughshin, Wādī-	35	Ib	19.44N	55.00 E
Mugi	29	De	33.40N	134.25 E
Mu Gia, Deo-	25	Le	17.40N	105.47 E
Mugila, Monts-	36	Ed	6.49 S	29.08 E
Muğla	23	Cb	37.12N	28.22 E
Mugodžary	21	He	49.00N	58.40 E
Mugur an Na'ām	24	Ig	31.56N	40.30 E
Muhaiwir	24	If	33.28N	40.59 E
Muḩammad, Ra's-	33	Fd	27.42N	34.13 E
Muḩammad Oawl	35	Fa	20.54N	37.05 E
Muhen	20	Ig	48.10N	136.08 E
Muheza	36	Gd	5.10 S	38.47 E
Muhīt, Al Baḩr al-=Atlantic Ocean (EN)	3	Di	2.00N	25.00W
Mühlacker	10	Eh	48.57N	8.50 E
Mühldorf am Inn	10	Ih	48.15N	12.32 E
Mühlhausen in Thüringen	10	Ge	51.13N	10.27 E
Mühlig-Hofmann Gebirge	66	Cf	72.00 S	5.20 E
Mühlviertel	14	Ib	48.30N	14.10 E
Muhoršibir	20	Ff	51.01N	107.50 E
Muhos	7	Gd	64.50N	26.01 E
Muhu	7	Fg	58.35N	23.15 E
Muhu	8	Jf	58.37N	23.05 E
Muhu, Proliv-/Muhu Väin	8	Jf	58.45N	23.15 E
Muhulu	36	Ec	1.03 S	27.17 E
Muhu Väin/Muhu, Proliv-	8	Jf	58.45N	23.15 E
Muhuwesi	36	Ge	11.16 S	37.58 E
Muiderslot	12	Hb	52.20N	5.06 E
Muigheo/Mayo [2]	9	Dh	53.50N	9.30W
Muikamachi	28	Of	37.04N	138.53 E
Muineachán/Monaghan [2]	9	Gg	54.10N	7.00W
Muineachán/Monaghan	9	Gg	54.15N	6.58W
Muine Bheag	9	Gi	52.42N	6.57W
Muir Bhreatan=Saint George's Channel (EN)	5	Fe	52.00N	6.00W
Muir Eireann=Irish Sea (EN)	5	Fe	53.30N	5.20W
Muiron Islands	59	Cd	21.35 S	114.20 E
Muir Seamount (EN)	38	Mf	33.41N	63.32W
Muíte	37	Fb	14.02 S	39.02 E
Mujeres, Isla-	48	Pg	21.13N	86.43W
Mujezerski	7	He	63.57N	32.01 E
Muji	27	Cd	37.27N	78.33 E
Mujnak	19	Fg	43.44N	59.02 E
Mujnakski Zaliv	18	Bc	43.50N	58.40 E
Mujunkum, Peski-	21	Je	44.00N	70.30 E
Mukačevo	19	Cf	48.26N	22.45 E
Mukah	26	Ff	2.54N	112.06 E
Mukawa	29a	Bb	42.35N	141.55 E
Mu-Kawa	29a	Bb	42.33N	141.53 E
Mukâwwar	35	Fa	20.48N	37.13 E
Mukdahan	25	Ke	16.31N	104.42 E
Mukden → Shenyang	22	Oe	41.48N	123.24 E
Mukeru	64a	Bc	7.25N	134.30 E
Mukho	28	Jf	37.33N	129.07 E
Mukinbudin	59	Df	30.54 S	118.13 E
Mukojima-Rettō	60	Cb	27.37N	142.10 E
Mukomuko	26	Dg	2.35 S	101.07 E
Muksu	18	He	39.17N	71.25 E
Mula	25	Dc	27.57N	67.36 E
Mula	13	Kf	38.03N	1.30W
Mulainagiri	25	Ff	13.24N	75.43 E
Mulaku Atoll	25a	Bb	2.57N	73.34 E
Mulaly	19	Hf	45.27N	78.20 E
Mulan	27	Mb	46.00N	128.02 E
Mulanje	30	Kj	16.03 S	35.31 E
Mulanje	36	Gf	16.02 S	35.30 E
Mulatre, Point-	51g	Bb	15.17N	61.15W
Mulatupo Sasardí	49	Ii	8.57N	77.45W
Mulchatna	40	Hd	59.39N	157.08W
Mulchén	56	Fe	37.34 S	72.14W
Mulda	17	Kc	67.28N	63.34 E
Mulde	10	Ie	51.48N	12.10 E
Mulebreen	66	Ee	67.28 S	59.21 E
Mulegé	47	Bc	26.53N	112.01W
Mulegé, Sierra de-	47	Bc	37.30N	112.40W
Mulenda	36	Dc	4.18 S	24.58 E
Muleshoe	45	Ei	34.13N	102.43W
Mulgrave Island	59	Ib	10.05 S	142.10 E
Mulhacén	5	Fh	37.03N	3.19W
Mülheim an der Ruhr	12	Ic	51.26N	6.53 E
Mülheim-Kärlich	12	Jd	50.23N	7.30 E
Mulhouse	6	Gf	47.45N	7.20 E
Muli (Bowa)	27	Hf	27.55N	101.13 E
Mulifanua	65c	Aa	13.50 S	172.02W
Muling	28	Kb	44.34N	130.12 E
Muling (Bamiantong)	28	Kb	44.55N	130.32 E
Muling Guan	28	Ef	36.10N	118.46 E
Muling He	28	Lb	45.53N	133.30 E
Mull, Island of-	5	Fd	56.27N	6.00W
Mull, Sound of-	9	He	56.35N	5.50W
Mullen	45	Fe	42.03N	101.01W
Mullens	44	Gg	37.35N	81.25W
Muller, Pegunungan-	26	Ff	0.40N	113.50 E
Mullet Peninsula/An Muirthead	9	Cg	54.15N	10.04W
Mullett Lake	44	Ec	45.30N	84.30W
Mullewa	59	De	28.33 S	115.31 E
Müllheim	10	Di	47.48N	7.38 E
Mullingar/An Muileann gCearr	9	Fh	53.32N	7.20W
Mullsjö	8	Eg	57.55N	13.53 E
Mulobezi	36	Ef	16.47 S	25.10 E
Mulock Glacier	66	Jf	79.03 S	159.10 E
Mulongo	36	Ed	7.50 S	26.57 E
Multān	22	Jf	30.11N	71.29 E
Multé	48	Ni	17.41N	91.24W
Multia	8	Kb	62.25N	24.47 E
Multien	12	Ee	49.05N	2.55 E
Mulu, Gunong-	26	Ff	4.03N	114.56 E
Mulvane	45	Hh	37.29N	97.14W
Mulymja	17	Lf	60.12N	64.32 E
Mumbué	36	Ce	13.53 S	17.19 E
Mumbwa	36	Ee	14.59 S	27.04 E
Mumhan/Munster	9	Ei	52.30N	9.00W
Mumra	16	Og	45.43N	47.41 E
Mun	21	Mh	15.19N	105.30 E
Muna	48	Og	20.29N	89.43W
Muna	21	Oc	67.52N	123.10 E
Muna, Pulau-	26	Hg	5.00 S	122.30 E
Munābāo	25	Ec	25.45N	70.17 E
Munamägi/Munamjagi	8	Lg	57.38N	27.10 E
Munaybarah, Sharm-	24	Gi	26.04N	36.38 E
Muncar	26	Fh	8.29 S	114.21 E
Münchberg	10	Hf	50.12N	11.47 E
München=Munich (EN)	6	Hf	48.09N	11.35 E
Münchhausen	12	Kd	50.57N	8.43 E
Muncho Lake	42	Ee	58.56N	125.46W
Munch'ŏn	28	Ie	39.14N	127.22 E
Muncie	43	Jc	40.11N	85.23W
Munda	63a	Cc	8.19 S	157.15 E
Mundaring, Perth-	59	Df	31.54 S	116.10 E
Munday	45	Gj	33.27N	99.38W
Mundemba	34	Ge	4.59N	8.40 E
Münden	10	Fe	51.25N	9.41 E
Mundesley	12	Db	52.52N	1.25 E
Mundford	12	Cb	52.30N	0.39 E
Mundiwindi	58	Dg	23.52 S	120.09 E
Mundo	13	Kf	38.19N	1.40W
Mundo Novo	54	Jf	11.52 S	40.28W
Munellës, Mali i-	15	Dh	41.58N	20.06 E
Munera	13	Je	39.02N	2.28W
Mungana	59	Ic	17.07 S	144.24 E
Mungbere	31	Jh	2.38N	28.30 E
Munger	25	Hc	25.23N	86.28 E
Mungindi	59	Je	28.58S	148.59 E
Munhango	36	Ce	12.10 S	18.34 E
Munh-Hajrhan-Ula	21	Le	46.40N	91.30 E
Munich (EN)=München	6	Hf	48.09N	11.35 E
Muniesa	13	Lc	41.02N	0.48W
Munīfah	23	Gd	27.38N	49.00 E
Munising	44	Db	46.25N	86.40W
Munkedal	7	Cg	58.29N	11.41 E
Munkfors	7	Cg	59.50N	13.32 E
Munku Sardik, Gora-	21	Md	51.45N	100.20 E
Muñoz Gamero, Peninsula-	56	Fh	52.30 S	73.10W
Munsan	28	If	37.55N	126.22 E
Münsingen	10	Fh	48.25N	9.30 E
Munster	11	Nf	48.03N	7.08 E
Münster [F.R.G.]	12	Ke	49.55N	8.52 E
Münster [F.R.G.]	10	De	51.58N	7.38 E
Münster/Moutier	14	Bc	47.16N	7.22 E
Munster/Mumhan	9	Ei	52.30N	9.00W
Münster-Hiltrup	12	Jc	51.54N	7.38 E
Münsterland [F.R.G.]	12	Kb	52.45N	8.10 E
Münsterland [F.R.G.]	10	De	52.00N	7.30 E
Münstermaifeld	12	Jd	50.15N	7.22 E
Muntenia	15	Ie	44.00N	26.00 E
Munteni Buzău	15	Je	44.38N	26.59 E
Muntok	26	Eg	2.04 S	105.11 E
Munzur Dağları	24	Hc	39.30N	39.10 E
Muojärvi	7	Gd	65.56N	28.36 E
Muong Sen	25	Ke	19.24N	104.08 E
Muonio	6	Ib	67.57N	23.42 E
Muonioälven Muonionijoki	5	Ib	67.11N	23.34 E
Muping	28	Ff	37.23N	121.36 E
Muqaddam	35	Eb	18.04N	31.30 E
Muqayshiţ	24	Oj	24.10N	53.45 E
Muqdisho=Mogadishu (EN)	31	Lh	2.03N	45.22 E
Mur	5	Hf	46.18N	16.55 E
Mura	5	Hf	46.18N	16.55 E
Muradiye [Tur.]	15	Kk	38.39N	27.24 E
Muradiye [Tur.]	24	Jc	39.00N	43.43 E
Murafa	16	Fe	48.13N	28.14 E
Murakami	28	Oe	38.14N	139.29 E
Murallón, Cerro-	52	Ij	49.48 S	73.25W
Muráň	10	Qh	48.45N	20.02 E
Mur'aňyo	35	Ic	11.41N	50.27 E
Muraši	19	Ed	59.24N	48.59 E
Murat	21	Ff	38.52N	38.48 E
Murat	11	Ii	45.07N	2.52 E
Murat Dağı	23	Cb	38.55N	29.43 E
Muratlı [Tur.]	24	Ib	41.29N	41.41 E
Muratlı [Tur.]	15	Kh	41.10N	27.30 E
Murau	14	Ic	47.06N	14.10 E
Muravera	14	Dk	39.25N	9.34 E
Murayama	29	Gb	38.29N	140.23 E
Mūrchen Khvort	24	Nf	33.06N	51.30 E
Murchison	62	Ed	41.48 S	172.20 E
Murchison, Mount- [Austl.]	59	De	26.46 S	116.25 E
Murchison, Mount- [N.Z.]	62	De	43.01 S	171.17 E
Murchison River	57	Cg	27.50 S	114.00 E
Murcia	6	Fh	37.59N	1.07W
Murcia [3]	13	Kg	38.00N	1.30W
Murcia	13	Kf	38.30N	1.45W
Mur-de-Barrez	11	Ij	44.51N	2.39 E
Murdo	45	Fe	43.53N	100.43W
Mürefte	15	Ki	40.40N	27.14 E
Muren	22	Me	49.38N	100.10 E
Mureş	5	If	46.15N	20.12 E
Mureş [2]	15	Hc	46.30N	24.40 E
Muret	11	Hk	43.28N	1.21 E
Murfreesboro	43	Jd	35.51N	86.23W
Murg	10	Eh	48.55N	8.10 E
Murgab	21	If	38.18N	61.12 E
Murgab [Tad.-U.S.S.R.]	19	Hh	38.10N	73.59 E
Murgab [Tur.-U.S.S.R.]	18	Df	37.32N	62.01 E
Murgaš	15	Gg	42.50N	23.40 E
Murgeni	15	Lc	46.12N	28.01 E
Murgon	59	Ke	26.15 S	151.57 E
Muri	64p	Cc	21.15 S	159.43W
Muriaé	54	Jh	21.08 S	42.22W
Murici	54	Ke	9.19 S	35.56W
Muriege	36	Dd	9.53 S	21.13 E
Murihiti	64n	Ab	10.23 S	161.02W
Murilo Atoll	57	Gd	8.40N	152.11 E
Mūrītāniyā=Mauritania (EN) [1]	31	Fg	20.00N	12.00W
Müritz	10	Ic	53.25N	12.43 E
Murkong Selek	25	Jc	27.44N	95.18 E
Murmansk	6	Jb	68.58N	33.05 E
Murmanskaja Oblast [3]	19	Db	68.00N	35.30 E
Murmaši	19	Db	68.49N	32.49 E
Murnau	10	Hi	47.41N	11.12 E
Muro	13	Pe	39.44N	3.03 E
Muro, Capo di-	11a	Ab	41.44N	8.40 E
Muro Lucano	14	Jj	40.45N	15.29 E
Murom	6	Kd	55.34N	42.02 E
Muromcevo	19	Hd	56.23N	75.14 E
Muroran	22	Qe	42.18N	140.59 E
Muros	13	Cb	42.47N	9.02W
Muros y Noya, Ría de-	13	Db	42.45N	9.00W
Muroto	27	Ne	33.18N	134.09 E
Muroto Zaki	28	Mh	33.16N	134.10 E
Murowana Goślina	10	Nd	52.35N	17.01 E
Murphy [Id.-U.S.]	46	Ge	43.13N	116.33W
Murphy [N.C.-U.S.]	44	Eh	35.05N	84.01W
Murphysboro	45	Lh	37.46N	89.20W
Murrah al Kubrá, Al Buḩayrah al-	24	Eg	30.20N	32.23 E
Murray [Ky.-U.S.]	44	Cg	36.37N	88.19W
Murray [Ut.-U.S.]	46	Jf	40.40N	111.53W
Murray, Lake- [Pap.N.Gui.]	60	Ci	7.00 S	141.30 E
Murray, Lake- [S.C.-U.S.]	44	Gh	34.04N	81.23W
Murray Bridge	59	Hg	35.07 S	139.17 E
Murray Fracture zone (EN)	3	Lf	34.00N	135.00W
Murray Islands	59	Ia	9.55 S	144.05 E
Murray Ridge (EN)	3	Gg	21.00N	61.50 E
Murray River	57	Eh	35.22 S	139.22 E
Murraysburg	37	Cf	31.58 S	23.47 E
Murro di Porco, Capo-	14	Jm	37.00N	15.20 E
Murrumbidgee River	57	Fh	34.43 S	143.12 E
Murrupula	37	Fc	15.27 S	38.47 E
Murska Sobota	14	Kd	46.40N	16.10 E
Murten/Morat	14	Bd	46.56N	7.08 E
Murter	14	Jg	43.47N	15.37 E
Murtle Lake	46	Fa	52.08N	119.38W
Murud, Gunong-	26	Gf	3.52N	115.30 E
Murupara	62	Gc	38.27 S	176.42 E
Mururoa Atoll	57	Ng	21.52 S	138.55W
Murwāra	25	Gd	23.51N	80.24 E
Murwillumbah	59	Ke	28.19 S	153.24 E
Mürz	14	Jc	47.24N	15.17 E
Mürzzuschlag	14	Jc	47.36N	15.41 E
Muş	23	Fb	38.44N	41.30 E
Muša/Mūša	7	Fh	56.24N	24.12 E
Mūša/Muša	7	Fh	56.24N	24.12 E
Mūsa, Jabal-=Sinai, Mount- (EN)	24	Eh	28.32N	33.59 E
Musa Ali	35	Gc	12.30N	42.27 E
Musāfī	24	Qk	25.18N	56.10 E
Musā'id	33	Ed	31.36N	25.03 E
Musala	5	Ig	42.11N	23.34 E
Musallam	24	Lg	31.53N	46.56 E
Musan	27	Mc	42.14N	129.13 E
Musandam Peninsula	24	Qi	26.18N	56.24 E
Musay'īd	24	Nj	25.00N	51.33 E
Musaymir	33	Hg	13.27N	44.37 E
Muscat (EN)=Masqaţ	22	Hg	23.29N	58.33 E
Muscat and Oman (EN) → Oman (EN) [1]	22	Hg	21.00N	57.00 E
Muscatine	45	Kf	41.25N	91.03W
Musgrave	58	Ff	14.47 S	143.30 E
Musgrave Ranges	57	Eg	26.10 S	131.50 E
Mūshā	24	Di	27.07N	31.14 E
Mus-Haja, Gora-	21	Qc	62.35N	140.50 E
Mushāsh al 'Ashawī	24	Mj	24.12N	48.50 E
Mushāsh Ramlān	24	Mj	24.25N	49.15 E
Mushayrib, Ra's-	24	Nj	24.18N	51.44 E
Mushie	36	Cc	3.01 S	16.54 E
Mūsi	25	Ge	15.20N	80.06 E
Musi	21	Mj	2.20 S	104.56 E
Mūsiān	24	Lf	32.28N	47.26 E
Musicians Seamounts (EN)	57	Kb	29.00N	162.00W
Muskegon	43	Jc	43.14N	86.16W
Muskegon Heights	44	Dd	43.12N	86.12W
Muskegon River	44	Dd	43.14N	86.20W
Muskö	8	He	59.00N	18.05 E
Muskogee	43	Hd	35.45N	95.22W
Muskoka, Lake-	44	Hc	45.00N	79.25W
Musoma	31	Ki	1.30 S	33.48 E
Musone	14	Hg	43.28N	13.38 E
Mussaţţaḩah, Al Jazīrah al-	14	Em	37.11N	10.20 E
Mussau Island	60	Dh	1.25 S	149.38 E
Musselkanaal, Stadskanaal-	12	Jb	52.56N	7.02 E
Musselshell River	43	Fb	47.21N	107.58W
Mussende	36	Ce	10.31 S	16.02 E
Mussidan	11	Gi	45.02N	0.22 E
Mussòmeli	14	Hm	37.35N	13.45 E
Must	27	Fb	46.40N	92.40 E
Muşţafá, Ra's-	14	Fn	36.50N	11.07 E
Mustafakemalpaşa	24	Cb	40.02N	28.24 E
Mustahil	35	Gd	5.15N	44.44 E
Mustāng	25	Gc	29.11N	83.58 E
Mustang Draw	45	Fj	32.00N	101.40W
Mustang Island	45	Hm	28.00N	96.55W
Mustasaari/Korsholm	8	Ia	63.05N	21.43 E
Musters, Lago-	56	Gg	45.27 S	69.13W
Mustique Island	50	Ff	12.39N	61.15W
Mustjala	8	Jf	58.25N	22.04 E
Mustla	7	Fg	58.14N	25.52 E
Mustvee	7	Gg	58.52N	26.59 E
Musu-dan	28	Jd	40.50N	129.43 E
Muswellbrook	59	Kf	32.16 S	150.53 E
Muszyna	10	Qg	49.21N	20.54 E
Mut	24	Ed	36.39N	33.27 E
Mūţ	33	Ed	25.29N	28.59 E
Mūtaf, Ra's al-	23	Hd	27.41N	51.27 E
Mutalau	64k	Ba	18.56 S	169.50W
Mutarara	31	Kj	17.27 S	35.04 E
Mutatá	54	Cb	7.16N	76.32W
Mutawassiţ, Al Baḩr al-= Mediterranean Sea (EN)	5	Hh	35.00N	20.00 E
Mutha	36	Gc	1.48 S	38.26 E
Muting	26	Lh	7.23 S	140.20 E
Mutis, Gunung-	26	Hh	9.34 S	124.14 E
Mutoraj	20	Fd	61.20N	100.20 E
Mutsamudu	31	Lj	12.09 S	44.25 E
Mutshatsha	36	De	10.39 S	24.27 E
Mutsu	27	Pc	41.05N	140.55 E
Mutsu-Wan	28	Pd	41.10N	140.55 E
Muttaburra	59	Id	22.36 S	144.33 E
Mutterstadt	12	Ke	49.27N	8.21 E
Mutton/Oiléan Coarach	9	Di	52.49N	9.31W
Mutton Bird Islands	62	Bg	47.15 S	167.25 E
Mutuali	37	Fb	14.53 S	37.00 E
Mutún	55	Dd	19.10 S	57.54W
Mutunópolis	55	Ha	13.40 S	49.15W
Mutusjärvi	7	Gb	69.31N	26.57 E
Muurame	8	Kb	62.08N	25.40 E
Mu Us Shamo=Ordos Desert (EN)	21	Mf	38.45N	109.10 E
Muxima	36	Bd	9.32 S	13.57 E
Muyinga	36	Fc	2.51 S	30.20 E
Muy Muy	49	Eg	12.46N	85.38W
Muzaffarābād	25	Eb	34.22N	73.28 E
Muzaffargarh	25	Eb	30.04N	71.12 E
Muzaffarnagar	25	Fc	29.28N	77.41 E
Muzaffarpur	25	Hc	26.07N	85.24 E
Muzambinho	55	Ie	21.22 S	46.32W
Muzat He	27	Dc	41.15N	83.27 E
Muži	20	Bc	65.27N	64.40 E
Muzillac	11	Dg	47.33N	2.29W
Mužlja	15	Dd	45.21N	20.25 E
Muztag [China]	21	Kf	35.55N	80.20 E
Muztag [China]	21	Kf	36.25N	87.25 E
Muztagata	27	Cd	38.17N	75.07 E
Mvolo	35	Dd	6.03N	29.56 E
Mvomero	36	Gd	6.20 S	37.25 E
Mvoung	36	Bb	0.04N	12.18 E
Mwadingusha	36	Ee	10.45 S	27.15 E
Mwali	30	Lj	12.15 S	43.45 E
Mwanza [3]	36	Fc	2.30 S	32.30 E
Mwanza [Mwi.]	36	Ff	15.37 S	34.31 E
Mwanza [Tan.]	31	Ki	2.31 S	32.54 E
Mwanza [Zaire]	36	Ed	7.54 S	26.45 E
Mwatate	36	Gc	3.30 S	38.23 E
Mweelrea	9	Dh	53.38N	9.50W
Mweka	31	Ji	4.51 S	21.34 E
Mwene Ditu	31	Ji	7.03 S	23.27 E
Mwenga	36	Ec	3.02 S	28.26 E
Mweru, Lake-	30	Ji	9.00 S	28.45 E
Mweru Wantipa, Lake-	36	Ed	8.42 S	29.46 E
Mwimbi	36	Fd	8.39 S	31.40 E
Mwinilunga	36	De	11.44 S	24.26 E
Mya	30	He	31.40N	5.15 E
Myaing	25	Id	21.37N	94.51 E
Myanaung	25	Je	18.17N	95.19 E
Myanmar-Nainggan-Daw → Burma [1]	22	Lg	22.00N	98.00 E
Myaungmya	25	Ie	16.36N	94.56 E
Mycenae (EN) = Mikínai	15	Fl	37.43N	22.45 E
Myebon	25	Id	20.03N	93.22 E
Myingyan	22	Lg	21.28N	95.23 E
Myinmoletkat Taung	25	Jf	13.28N	98.48 E
Myitta	25	Jf	14.10N	98.31 E
Myjava	10	Mh	48.33N	16.58 E
Myjzakjula/Mõisaküla	7	Fg	58.07N	25.10 E
Mykulkin, Mys-	17	Cc	67.48N	46.40 E
Mylius Erichsens Land	41	Jb	81.40N	24.00W
Myltkyinā	22	Lg	25.23N	97.24 E
Mymensingh	25	Id	24.45N	90.24 E
Mynämäki	7	Ef	60.40N	22.00 E
Mynaral	19	Hf	45.22N	73.39 E
Myōkō-Zan	29	Fc	36.52N	138.06 E
Mýrdalsjökull	7a	Bc	63.40N	19.06W
Myre	7	Db	68.51N	15.05 E
Myrskylä/Mörskom	8	Kd	60.40N	25.51 E
Myrtle Beach	43	Le	33.42N	78.54W
Myrtle Point	46	Ce	43.04N	124.08W
Mysen	7	Cg	59.33N	11.20 E
Mysia	15	Kj	39.30N	28.00 E
Myśla	10	Kd	52.40N	14.29 E
Myślenice	10	Pg	49.51N	19.56 E
Myślibórz	10	Kd	52.55N	14.52 E
Mysore	22	Jh	12.18N	76.39 E
Mysore → Karnataka [3]	25	Ff	13.30N	76.00 E
Mys Saryč	16	Hg	44.23N	33.45 E
Myszków	10	Pf	50.36N	19.20 E
Myszyniec	10	Rc	53.24N	21.21 E
My Tho	22	Mh	10.21N	106.21 E
Mytišči	7	Ii	55.56N	37.46 E
Mývatn	7a	Cb	65.36N	17.00W

Index Symbols

[1] Independent Nation; [2] State, Region; [3] District, County; [4] Municipality; [5] Colony, Dependency; Continent; Physical Region; Historical or Cultural Region; Mount, Mountain; Volcano; Hill; Mountains, Mountain Range; Hills, Escarpment; Plateau, Upland; Pass, Gap; Plain, Lowland; Delta; Salt Flat; Valley, Canyon; Crater, Cave; Karst Features; Depression; Polder; Desert, Dunes; Forest, Woods; Heath, Steppe; Oasis; Cape, Point; Coast, Beach; Cliff; Peninsula; Isthmus; Sandbank; Island; Atoll; Rock, Reef; Islands, Archipelago; Rocks, Reefs; Coral Reef; Well, Spring; Geyser; River, Stream; Waterfall Rapids; River Mouth, Estuary; Lake; Salt Lake; Intermittent Lake; Reservoir; Swamp, Pond; Canal; Glacier; Ice Shelf, Pack Ice; Ocean; Sea; Gulf, Bay; Strait, Fjord; Lagoon; Bank; Seamount; Tablemount; Ridge; Shelf; Basin; Escarpment, Sea Scarp; Fracture; Trench, Abyss; National Park, Reserve; Point of Interest; Recreation Site; Cave, Cavern; Historic Site; Ruins; Wall, Walls; Church, Abbey; Temple; Scientific Station; Airport; Port; Lighthouse; Mine; Tunnel; Dam, Bridge

Myzeqeja 15 Ci 41.01N 19.36 E
M'Zab 32 Hc 32.35N 3.20 E
Mže 10 Jg 49.46N 13.24 E
Mziha 36 Gd 5.54S 37.47 E
Mzimba 36 Fe 11.54S 33.36 E
Mzuzu 31 Kj 11.27S 33.55 E

N

Naab 10 Ig 49.01N 12.02 E
Naaldwijk 12 Gc 51.59N 4.12 E
Naalehu 65a Fd 19.04N 155.35W
Naantali/Nådendal 7 Ff 60.27N 22.02 E
Naarden 12 Hb 52.18N 5.10 E
Naas/An Nás 9 Gh 53.13N 6.39W
Nabadid 35 Gd 9.38N 43.29 E
Nabão 13 De 39.31N 8.21W
Nabari 29 Ed 34.37N 136.05 E
Naberera 36 Gc 4.12S 38.56 E
Naberežnyje Čelny 6 Ld 55.42N 52.19 E
Nabileque, Rio- 55 De 20.55S 57.49W
Nabire 58 Ee 3.22S 135.29 E
Nabī Shu'ayb, Jabal an- 21 Gh 15.17N 43.59 E
Nabq 24 Fh 28.04N 34.25 E
Nābul 31 Ie 36.27N 10.44 E
Nābul [3] 32 Jb 36.45N 10.45 E
Nābulus 24 Ff 32.13N 35.16 E
Nabusanke 36 Fb 0.01N 32.03 E
Nacala 37 Gb 14.33S 40.40 E
Nacala-a-Velha 31 Lj 14.33S 40.36 E
Nacaome 49 Dg 13.31N 87.30W
Nacaroa 37 Fb 14.23S 39.55 E
Nacereddine 13 Ph 36.08N 3.26 E
Nachikatsuura 29 De 33.39N 135.55 E
Nachingwea 36 Ge 10.23S 38.46 E
Nachi-San 29 De 33.42N 135.51 E
Náchod 10 Mf 50.26N 16.10 E
Nachuge 25 If 10.35N 92.28 E
Nachvak Fiord 42 Le 59.03N 63.45W
Nacka 7 Ee 59.18N 18.10 E
Ná Clocha Liatha/ Greystones 9 Gh 53.09N 6.04W
Nacogdoches 45 Ik 31.36N 94.39W
Na Comaraigh/Comeragh Mountains 9 Fi 52.13N 7.35W
Nacori, Sierra- 48 Ec 29.50N 108.50W
Nacozari, Rio- 48 Ec 29.48N 109.42W
Nacozari de Garcia 47 Cb 30.24N 109.39W
Na Cruacha/Blue Stack 9 Eg 54.45N 8.06W
Na Cruacha Dubha/ Macgillycuddy's Reeks 9 Di 52.00N 9.50W
Nacunday, Rio- 55 Eh 26.03S 54.45W
Nada → Danxian 21 Ih 19.38N 109.32 E
Nådendal/Naantali 7 Ff 60.27N 22.02 E
Nadiād 25 Ed 22.42N 72.52 E
Nădlac 15 Dc 46.10N 20.45 E
Nador [3] 32 Gb 35.00N 3.00W
Nador 32 Gb 35.11N 2.56W
Nádusa 15 Fi 40.38N 22.04 E
Nadvoicy 19 Dc 63.52N 34.20 E
Nadvornaja 16 De 48.38N 24.34 E
Nadym 22 Jc 65.35N 72.42 E
Naeba-San 29 Fc 36.51N 138.41 E
Nærbø 8 Af 58.40N 5.39 E
Næstved 7 Ci 55.14N 11.46 E
Nafada 34 Hc 11.06N 11.20 E
Näfels 14 Dc 47.06N 9.04 E
Naftah 14 Dn 36.57N 9.04 E
Naftan Rock 64b Bb 14.50N 145.32 E
Naft-e-Safid 24 Mg 31.40N 49.17 E
Naft-e-Shāh 24 Kf 33.59N 45.30 E
Naft Khāneh 24 Ke 34.02N 45.28 E
Nafūsah, Jabal- 30 Ie 31.50N 12.00 E
Nāg 25 Dc 27.24N 65.08 E
Naga 22 Oh 13.28N 123.39 E
Nāga, Kreb en- 32 Fe 24.00N 6.00W
Nagagami Lake 44 Ea 49.28N 85.02W
Nagagami River 45 Na 50.25N 84.20W
Nagahama [Jap.] 27 Ed 35.23N 136.16 E
Nagahama [Jap.] 29 Ce 33.36N 132.29 E
Nagai 29 Gb 38.06N 140.02 E
Nagai 40 Ge 55.11N 159.55W
Na Gaibhlte/Galty Mountains 9 Ei 52.23N 8.11W
Nāgāland [3] 25 Ic 26.30N 94.00 E
Nagano 22 Pf 36.39N 138.11 E
Nagano Ken [2] 28 Nf 36.10N 138.00 E
Nagano-Matsushiro 29 Fc 36.34N 138.10 E
Nagano-Shinonoi 29 Fc 36.35N 138.06 E
Nagaoka 27 Od 37.27N 138.51 E
Nāgappattinam 25 Ff 10.46N 79.50 E
Nagara-Gawa 29 Ed 35.02N 136.43 E
Nagarote 49 Dg 12.16N 86.34W
Nagarzê 27 Ff 28.59N 90.28 E
Nagasaki 22 Of 32.47N 129.56 E
Nagasaki-Hantō 29 Ae 32.40N 129.45 E
Nagasaki Ken [2] 28 Jh 33.00N 129.50 E
Naga-Shima 29 Ce 33.50N 132.05 E
Nagashima 29 Ed 34.12N 136.19 E
Nagashima 29 Be 32.10N 130.10 E
Naga-Shima-Kaikyō 29 Be 32.15N 130.10 E
Nagato 28 Kg 34.21N 131.10 E
Nagayo 29 Ae 32.50N 129.52 E
Nāgda 25 Fd 23.27N 75.25 E
Nāgercoil 25 Fg 8.10N 77.26 E
Naghora Point 60 Gj 10.50S 162.24 E
Nagichot 35 Ee 4.16N 33.34 E
Nagi-San 29 Dd 35.10N 134.10 E
Nagiso 29 Ed 35.36N 137.36 E
Nago 27 Mf 26.35N 128.01 E
Nagold 10 Eh 48.52N 8.42 E
Nagorno-Karabahskaja Avtonomnaja Oblast [3] 19 Eh 39.55N 46.45 E
Nagorny [R.S.F.S.R.] 20 He 55.45N 124.58 E
Nagorny [R.S.F.S.R.] 20 Md 63.10N 179.05 E
Nagorsk 7 Mg 59.21N 50.48 E
Nago-Wan 29b Ab 26.35N 127.55 E
Nagoya 22 Pf 35.10N 136.55 E
Nāgpur 22 Jg 21.09N 79.06 E
Nagqu 22 Lf 31.30N 92.00 E
Nag's Head 51c Ab 17.13N 62.38W
Nagua 49 Md 19.23N 69.50W
Naguabo 51a Cb 18.13N 65.44W
Nagyatád 10 Nj 46.13N 17.22 E
Nagybajom 10 Mj 46.23N 16.31 E
Nagyecsed 10 Si 47.52N 22.24 E
Nagyhalász 10 Rh 48.08N 21.46 E
Nagykálló 10 Ri 47.53N 21.51 E
Nagykanizsa 10 Mj 46.27N 16.59 E
Nagykáta 10 Pi 47.25N 19.45 E
Nagykőrös 10 Pi 47.02N 19.47 E
Nagykunság 10 Qj 46.55N 20.15 E
Nagy-Milic 10 Rh 48.35N 21.28 E
Naha 22 Og 26.13N 127.40 E
Nahanni Butte 42 Fd 61.04N 123.24W
Nahari 29 De 33.25N 134.01 E
Naharyya 24 Ff 33.00N 35.05 E
Nahāvand 23 Gc 34.12N 48.22 E
Nahe 10 Dg 49.58N 7.57 E
Nahičevan 6 Kh 39.13N 45.27 E
Nahičevanskaja ASSR [3] 19 Eh 39.15N 45.35 E
Na'hīmābād 24 Qg 30.51N 56.31 E
Nahodka 22 Pe 42.48N 132.52 E
Nahr al 'Āṣī=Orontes (EN) 23 Eb 36.02N 35.58 E
Nahr Quassel 13 Oi 35.45N 2.46 E
Nahuala, Laguna- 48 Ji 16.50N 99.40W
Nahuel Huapi, Lago- 56 Ff 40.58S 71.30W
Nahunta 44 Gj 31.12N 81.59W
Naie 29a Bb 43.24N 141.52 E
Naiguatá, Pico- 54 Ea 10.33N 66.46W
Naila 10 Hf 50.19N 11.42 E
Naiman Qi (Daqin Tal) 27 Lc 42.49N 120.38 E
Nain 39 Md 57.00N 61.40W
Nā'īn 24 Of 32.52N 53.05 E
Na'īnābād 24 Pd 36.14N 54.39 E
Nairai 63d Bb 17.49S 179.24 E
Nairn 9 Jd 57.35N 3.53W
Nairobi 31 Kf 1.17S 36.49 E
Nairobi [3] 36 Gc 1.17S 36.50 E
Naissaar/Najssar 8 Ke 59.35N 24.25 E
Naitamba 63d Cb 17.01S 179.17W
Naizishan 28 Ic 43.41N 127.27 E
Najafābād 23 Hc 32.37N 51.21 E
Najd 23 Fe 25.00N 44.30 E
Najd 21 Gg 25.00N 44.30 E
Nájera 13 Jb 42.25N 2.44W
Najerilla 13 Jb 42.31N 2.42W
Naj' Ḩammādī 33 Fd 26.03N 32.15 E
Najibābād 25 Fc 29.58N 78.10 E
Najin 27 Nc 42.15N 130.18 E
Najō 29 Ec 35.47N 136.12 E
Najrān 33 Hf 17.30N 44.10 E
Najrān 33 Hf 17.30N 44.10 E
Najssar/Naissaar 8 Ke 59.35N 24.25 E
Najstenjarvi 7 He 62.18N 32.42 E
Naju 28 Ig 35.02N 126.43 E
Najzataš, Pereval- 18 If 37.52N 73.46 E
Nakadōri-Jima 28 Jh 32.58N 129.05 E
Nakagawa 29a Ca 44.47N 142.05 E
Naka-Gawa [Jap.] 29 Gc 36.20N 140.36 E
Naka-Gawa [Jap.] 29 De 33.56N 134.42 E
Nakagusuku-Wan 29b Ab 26.15N 127.50 E
Nakahechi 29 De 33.47N 135.29 E
Naka-lō-Jima 60 Cc 24.47N 141.20 E
Naka-Jima 29 Ce 33.58N 132.37 E
Nakajō 28 Oe 38.03N 139.24 E
Naka-Koshiki-Jima 29 Af 31.48N 129.50 E
Nakalele Point 65a Eb 21.02N 156.35W
Nakama 29 Be 33.50N 130.43 E
Nakaminato 29 Gc 36.22N 140.36 E
Nakamura 28 Lh 32.59N 132.56 E
Nakanai Mountains 59 Ka 5.35S 151.10 E
Nakano 29 Fc 36.45N 138.22 E
Naka-no-Dake 29 Fc 37.04N 139.06 E
Nakanojō 29 Fc 36.35N 138.51 E
Naka-no-Shima 28 Lf 36.05N 133.04 E
Naka-no- Shima 27 Mf 29.50N 129.50 E
Nakasato 29a Bc 40.58N 140.26 E
Naka-satsunai 29a Cb 42.42N 143.08 E
Nakashibetsu 29a Db 43.33N 144.58 E
Nakasongola 36 Fb 1.19N 32.28 E
Nakatonbetsu 29a Ca 44.58N 142.17 E
Nakatsu 28 Kh 33.34N 131.13 E
Nakatsugawa 28 Ng 35.29N 137.30 E
Nakfa 35 Fb 16.40N 38.30 E
Nakhon Pathom 25 Kf 13.49N 100.06 E
Nakhon Phanom 25 Mh 17.22N 104.46 E
Nakhon Ratchasima 22 Mh 14.57N 102.09 E
Nakhon Sawan 22 Mh 15.42N 100.06 E
Nakhon Si Thammarat 22 Li 8.26N 99.58 E
Nakijin 29b Ab 26.42N 127.59 E
Nakina 39 Kd 50.10N 86.42W
Nakkila 8 Ic 61.22N 22.00 E
Nakło nad Notecia 10 Nc 53.08N 17.35 E
Naknek 40 He 58.44N 157.02W
Nakonde 36 Fd 9.19S 32.46 E
Nakskov 7 Ci 54.50N 11.09 E
Näkten 8 Fb 62.50N 14.40 E
Naktong-gang 28 Jg 35.07N 128.57 E
Nakuru 31 Ki 0.20S 35.56 E
Nakusp 46 Ga 50.15N 117.48W
Nāl 25 Dc 26.02N 65.29 E
Nalajch → Nalajha 27 Ib 47.45N 107.16 E
Nalajha (Nalajch) 27 Ib 47.45N 107.16 E
Nalčik 6 Kg 43.29N 43.37 E
Nallıhan 24 Db 40.11N 31.21 E
Nalón 13 Fa 43.32N 6.04W
Nālūt 31 Ie 31.52N 10.59 E
Nalwasha 36 Gc 0.43S 36.26 E
Na Machairi/Brandon Head 9 Ci 52.16N 10.15W
Namacurra 37 Fc 17.29S 37.01 E
Namai Bay 64a Bb 7.32N 134.39 E
Namak, Daryācheh-ye- = Namak Lake (EN) 21 Hf 34.45N 51.36 E
Namak Lake (EN)= Namak, Daryācheh-ye- 21 Hf 34.45N 51.36 E
Namakan Lake 45 Jb 48.27N 92.35W
Namak-e Mighān, Kavīr-e- 24 Me 34.13N 49.49 E
Namakia 37 Hc 15.56S 45.48 E
Namakwaland=Little Namamland (EN) 37 Be 29.00S 17.00 E
Namanga 36 Gc 2.33S 36.47 E
Namangan 22 Je 41.00N 71.40 E
Namanganskaja Oblast [3] 19 Hg 41.00N 71.20 E
Namanyere 36 Fd 7.31S 31.03 E
Namapa 37 Fb 13.43S 39.50 E
Namaqua Seamount (EN) 37 Af 31.30S 11.20 E
Namarrói 37 Fc 15.57S 36.51 E
Namasagali 36 Fb 1.01N 32.57 E
Namasale 36 Fb 1.30N 32.37 E
Namatanai 60 Eh 3.40S 152.27 E
Namathu 63d Bb 17.21S 179.26 E
Nambavatu 63d Bb 16.36S 178.55 E
Namber 26 Jg 1.04S 134.49 E
Nambour 59 Ke 26.38S 152.58 E
Nambouwalu 61 Ec 16.59S 178.42 E
Nam Can 25 Kg 8.46N 104.59 E
Namche Bazar 25 Hc 27.49N 86.43 E
Nam Co 21 Lf 30.45N 90.35 E
Namčy 20 Hd 62.35N 129.40 E
Namdalen 7 Cd 64.38N 12.35 E
Nam Dinh 22 Mg 20.25N 106.10 E
Nämdö 8 He 59.10N 18.40 E
Nam Du, Quan Dao- 25 Kg 9.42N 104.22 E
Namêche, Andenne- 12 Hd 50.28N 5.00 E
Namelakl Passage 64a Bc 7.24N 134.38 E
Namen/Namur 11 Kd 50.28N 4.52 E
Namerikawa 29 Ec 36.45N 137.20 E
Náměšt nad Oslavou 10 Mg 49.12N 16.09 E
Nametil 37 Fc 15.43S 39.21 E
Namib Desert/ Namibwoestyn 30 Ik 23.00S 15.00 E
Namibia (South West Africa) 31 Ik 22.00S 17.00 E
Namibe 31 Ij 15.12S 12.10 E
Namibe 36 Bf 15.20S 12.30 E
Namie 28 Pf 37.29N 140.59 E
Namīn 24 Mc 38.25N 48.30 E
Namioka 29 Ga 40.42N 140.35 E
Namiquipa 48 Fc 29.15N 107.40W
Namiranga 37 Gb 10.33S 40.30 E
Namjagbarwa Feng 21 Lg 29.38N 95.04 E
Namja La 27 Df 29.58N 82.34 E
Namkham 25 Jd 23.50N 97.41 E
Namlea 26 Ig 3.18S 127.06 E
Namling 27 Ef 29.44N 89.05 E
Namnoi, Khao- 25 Jf 10.36N 98.38 E
Namoi River 59 Je 30.00S 148.07 E
Namoluk Island 57 Gd 5.55N 153.08 E
Namonuito Atoll 57 Gd 8.46N 150.02 E
Namorik Atoll 57 Hd 5.36N 168.07 E
Namous 32 Gc 30.28N 0.14W
Nampa 43 Dc 43.34N 116.34W
Nampala 34 Db 15.17N 5.33W
Nam Phan=Cochin China (EN) 21 Mg 11.00N 107.00 E
Nam Phong 25 Ke 16.45N 102.52 E
Nampi 28 De 38.02N 116.42 E
Namp'o 27 Md 38.44N 125.25 E
Nampula [3] 37 Fb 15.00S 39.30 E
Nampula 31 Kj 15.07S 39.15 E
Namsê Shankou 27 Df 29.58N 82.34 E
Namsos 6 Hc 64.30N 11.30 E
Namtu 25 Jd 23.05N 97.24 E
Namu 46 Ba 51.49N 127.52W
Namu Atoll 57 Hd 8.00N 168.10 E
Namuka-I-Lau 63d Cc 18.51S 178.38W
Namúli, Serra- 30 Kj 15.21S 37.00 E
Namuno 37 Fb 13.37S 38.48 E
Namur [3] 12 Gd 50.20N 4.50 E
Namur/Namen 11 Kd 50.28N 4.52 E
Namur-Saint Servais 12 Gd 50.28N 4.50 E
Namuruputh 36 Gb 4.34N 35.57 E
Namur-Wépion 12 Gd 50.25N 4.52 E
Namutoni 37 Bc 18.30S 17.55 E
Namwala 36 Ef 15.45S 26.26 E
Namwŏn 28 Ig 35.24N 127.23 E
Namysłów 10 Ne 51.05N 17.42 E
Nan 21 Mh 15.42N 100.09 E
Nan 25 Ke 18.48N 100.46 E
Nana 35 Bd 5.00N 15.50 E
Nana Barya 35 Bd 7.59N 17.43 E
Nanae 29a Bc 41.53N 140.41 E
Nanaimo 42 Fg 49.10N 123.56W
Nanakuli 65a Cb 21.23N 158.08W
Nana-Mambéré [3] 35 Bd 6.00N 16.00 E
Nanango 59 Ke 26.40S 152.00 E
Nanao 27 Od 37.03N 136.58 E
Nanao-Wan 29 Ec 37.10N 137.00 E
Nanatsu-Shima 29 Ec 37.35N 136.50 E
Nancha 27 Mb 47.08N 129.09 E
Nanchang 22 Ng 28.40N 115.58 E
Nancheng 27 Kf 27.32N 116.36 E
Nanchong 22 Mf 30.47N 106.03 E
Nancowry 25 Ig 7.59N 93.32 E
Nancy 6 Gf 48.41N 6.12 E
Nanda Devi 21 Jf 30.23N 79.59 E
Nandaime 49 Dh 11.46N 86.03W
Nandan [China] 27 Ig 24.59N 107.31 E
Nandan [Jap.] 28 Mg 34.15N 134.43 E
Nandaran → Qingyuan 28 Ce 38.46N 115.29 E
Nanded 22 Jh 19.09N 77.20 E
Nandewar Range 59 Kf 30.40S 151.10 E
Nandi 61 Ec 17.48S 177.25 E
Nandu Jiang 27 Jg 20.04N 110.22 E
Nanduri 63d Bb 16.27S 179.09 E
Nandyāl 25 Fe 15.29N 78.29 E
Nanfen 28 Gd 41.06N 123.45 E
Nanfeng 27 Kf 27.15N 116.30 E
Nanga-Eboko 34 He 4.41N 12.22 E
Nanga Parbat 21 Jf 35.15N 74.36 E
Nangapinoh 26 Fg 0.20S 111.44 E
Nangarhār [3] 23 Lc 34.15N 70.30 E
Nangatayap 26 Fg 1.32S 110.34 E
Nangis 11 If 48.33N 3.00 E
Nangnim-san 28 Id 40.21N 126.55 E
Nangnim-Sanmaek 28 Id 40.30N 127.00 E
Nangong 27 Kd 37.22N 115.23 E
Nangqên 27 Ge 32.15N 96.13 E
Nanguan 28 Af 36.42N 111.41 E
Nanguantao → Guantao 28 Cf 36.33N 115.18 E
Nangweshi 36 Df 16.26S 23.20 E
Nan Hai=South China Sea (EN) 21 Ni 10.00N 113.00 E
Nanhaoqian → Shangyi 28 Bd 41.06N 113.58 E
Nanhe 28 Cf 36.58N 114.41 E
Nanhua 27 Hf 25.16N 101.18 E
Nanhui 28 Fi 31.03N 121.46 E
Nan Hulsan Hu 27 Gd 36.45N 95.45 E
Nanjian 27 Hf 25.05N 100.32 E
Nanjiang 27 Ie 32.22N 106.45 E
Nanjing=Nanking (EN) 22 Nf 31.59N 118.51 E
Nankai Trough (EN) 27 Ne 32.00N 135.00 E
Nanking (EN)=Nanjing 22 Nf 31.59N 118.51 E
Nankoku 28 Lh 33.39N 133.44 E
Nanle 28 Cf 36.06N 115.12 E
Nanling 28 Ei 30.55N 118.19 E
Nan Ling 21 Ng 25.00N 112.00 E
Nanlou Shan 28 Ic 43.24N 126.40 E
Nanma → Yiyuan 28 Ef 36.11N 118.10 E
Nanning 22 Mg 22.50N 108.18 E
Nannup 59 Df 33.59S 115.45 E
Nanortalik 41 Hf 60.32N 45.45W
Nanpan Jiang 27 Ig 24.56N 106.12 E
Nānpāra 25 Gc 27.52N 81.30 E
Nanping [China] 22 Ng 26.42N 118.09 E
Nanping [China] 27 He 33.15N 104.13 E
Nanpu 28 Ee 39.16N 118.12 E
Nanqiao → Fengxian 28 Fi 30.55N 121.27 E
Nansei-Shotō=Ryukyu Islands (EN) 21 Og 26.30N 128.00 E
Nansen Cordillera (EN) 67 Ge 87.00N 90.00 E
Nansen Land 41 Hb 83.20N 46.00W
Nanshan Islands (EN)= Nansha Qundao 21 Ni 9.40N 113.30 E
Nansha Qundao= Nanshan Islands (EN) 21 Ni 9.40N 113.30 E
Nansio 36 Fc 2.08S 33.03 E
Nant 11 Jj 44.01N 3.18 E
Nantais, Lac- 42 Kd 61.00N 73.50W
Nanterre 11 If 48.54N 2.12 E
Nantes 6 Ff 47.13N 1.33W
Nantes à Brest, Can. de- 11 Bf 48.12N 4.06W
Nanteuil-le-Haudouin 12 Ee 49.08N 2.48 E
Nanticoke 44 Je 41.13N 76.00W
Nantō 29 Ed 34.17N 136.29 E
Nantong 27 Le 32.00N 120.52 E
Nantong (Jinsha) 28 Fh 32.06N 120.52 E
Nantou 27 Lg 23.54N 120.51 E
Nantua 11 Lh 46.09N 5.37 E
Nantucket 44 Le 41.17N 70.06W
Nantucket Island 43 Mc 41.16N 70.03W
Nantucket Sound 44 Le 41.30N 70.15W
Nanuku Passage 63d Cb 16.45S 179.15W
Nanuku Reef 63d Cb 16.40S 179.26W
Nanumanga Island 57 Ie 6.18S 176.20 E
Nanumea Atoll 57 Ie 5.43S 176.00 E
Nanuque 54 Jg 17.50S 40.21W
Nanusa, Pulau-Pulau- 26 If 4.42N 127.06 E
Nanwan Shuiku 28 Bh 32.02N 113.57 E
Nanwei Dao 27 Je 8.42N 111.40 E
Nanweng He 27 Ma 51.10N 125.59 E
Nanxian 28 Bj 29.22N 112.25 E
Nanxiang 28 Fi 31.18N 121.17 E
Nanxiong 27 Jf 25.13N 114.18 E
Nanxun 28 Fi 30.53N 120.26 E
Nanyandang Shan 27 Lf 27.37N 120.06 E
Nanyang 22 Nf 32.56N 112.32 E
Nanyang Hu 28 Dg 35.15N 116.39 E
Nanyō 28 Pe 38.03N 140.10 E
Nanyuki 31 Kh 0.01N 37.04 E
Nanzhang 27 Je 31.45N 111.53 E
Nanzhao 27 Je 33.28N 112.29 E
Nao, Cabo de la- 5 Gh 38.44N 0.14 E
Naococane, Lac- 42 Kf 52.50N 70.40W
Naoero/Nauru [1] 58 He 0.31S 166.56 E
Naoetsu 29 Fc 37.11N 138.14 E
Não-me-Toque 55 Fi 28.28S 52.49W
Naours, Souterrains de- 12 Ed 50.05N 2.17 E
Napa 46 Dg 38.18N 122.17W
Napanee 44 Ic 44.15N 76.57W
Napassoq 41 Ge 65.45N 52.30W
Napata 35 Eb 18.29N 31.51 E
Na-Peng 25 Lg 23.10N 98.26 E
Napf 14 Bc 47.01N 7.57 E
Napier 58 Ih 39.30S 176.54 E
Napier, Mount- 59 Fc 17.32S 129.10 E
Napier Mountains 66 Ee 66.30S 53.40 E
Naples [Fl.-U.S.] 43 Kf 26.08N 81.48W
Naples [Id.-U.S.] 46 Gb 48.34N 116.24W
Naples (EN) = Napoli 6 Hg 40.50N 14.15 E
Naples, Gulf of- (EN) = Napoli, Golfo di- 14 Ij 40.45N 14.10 E
Napo 27 Ig 23.25N 105.49 E
Napo, Río- 52 If 3.20S 72.40W
Napoleon 45 Gc 46.30N 99.46W
Napoli = Naples (EN) 6 Hg 40.50N 14.15 E
Napoli, Golfo di- = Naples, Gulf of- (EN) 14 Ij 40.45N 14.10 E
Napostá 55 An 38.26S 62.15W
Napuka, Ile- 57 Mf 14.12S 141.15W
Naqa 35 Eb 16.16N 33.17 E
Naqadeh 23 Gb 36.57N 45.23 E
Naqsh-e-Rostam 24 Og 30.01N 52.50 E
Nar 9 Ni 52.45N 0.24 E
Nāra 25 Dc 24.07N 69.07 E
Nara [Jap.] 27 Oe 34.41N 135.50 E
Nara [Mali] 34 Db 15.11N 7.15W
Naračenskibani 15 Hh 41.54N 24.45 E
Naracoorte 59 Ig 36.58S 140.44 E
Nara-Ken [2] 28 Mg 34.20N 135.55 E
Naranjo 48 Ee 25.48N 108.31W
Naranjos [Bol.] 55 Cd 18.38S 59.09W
Naranjos [Mex.] 48 Kg 21.21N 97.41W
Narao 29 Ae 32.52N 129.04 E
Narathiwat 25 Kg 6.25N 101.48 E
Nārāyanganj 25 Id 23.37N 90.30 E
Narbonne 11 Ik 43.11N 3.00 E
Narca, Ponta da- 36 Bd 6.07S 12.16 E
Narcea 13 Fa 43.28N 6.06W
Narcondam 25 If 13.15N 94.30 E
Nardò 14 Mj 40.11N 18.02 E
Naré 55 Bj 30.58S 60.28W
Nares Land 41 Hb 82.25N 47.30W
Nares Strait 38 Lb 78.50N 73.00W
Narew 10 Td 52.55N 23.29 E
Narew 10 Qd 52.26N 20.42 E
Narian, Pointe- 63b Be 20.05S 164.00 E
Narin Gol 27 Fd 36.54N 92.51 E
Nariño [2] 54 Cc 1.30N 78.00W
Narita 29 Gd 35.47N 140.18 E
Narjan-Mar 6 Lb 67.39N 53.00 E
Närke 8 Ff 59.05N 15.05 E
Narlı 24 Gd 37.27N 37.09 E
Narmada 21 Jg 21.38N 72.36 E
Narman 24 Ib 40.21N 41.52 E
Nārnaul 25 Fc 28.03N 76.06 E
Narni 14 Gh 42.31N 12.31 E
Naroč 8 Lj 54.27N 26.45 E
Naroč 8 Lj 54.57N 26.49 E
Naroč, Ozero- 16 Eb 54.50N 26.45 E
Naroda 17 Jd 64.15N 61.00 E
Narodnaja, Gora- 5 Mb 65.04N 60.09 E
Naro-Fominsk 19 Dd 55.24N 36.43 E
Narok 36 Gc 1.05S 35.52 E
Narovlja 16 Fd 51.48N 29.31 E
Närpes/Närpio 8 Ib 62.28N 21.20 E
Närpio/Närpes 8 Ib 62.28N 21.20 E
Narrabri 59 Jf 30.19S 149.47 E
Narrandera 59 Jf 34.45S 146.33 E
Narrogin 59 Df 32.56S 117.10 E
Narromine 59 Jf 32.14S 148.15 E
Narrows, The- 51c Ab 17.12N 62.38W
Narryer, Mount- 59 De 26.30S 116.25 E
Narsimhapur 25 Fd 22.57N 79.12 E
Narssalik 41 Hf 61.42N 49.11W
Narssaq [Grld.] 41 Hf 61.00N 46.00W
Narssaq [Grld.] 41 Gf 64.00N 51.33W
Narssarssuaq 41 Hf 61.10N 45.15W
Narthákion 15 Fj 39.14N 22.22 E
Nartkala 16 Mh 43.32N 43.47 E
Narubis 37 Be 26.55S 18.35 E
Narugo 29 Gb 38.44N 140.43 E
Năruja 15 Jd 45.50N 26.47 E
Naru-Shima 29 Ae 32.50N 128.56 E
Naruto 28 Mg 34.11N 134.37 E
Naruto-Kaikyō 29 Dd 34.15N 134.40 E
Narva 7 Gg 59.29N 28.02 E
Narva 6 Id 59.23N 28.11 E
Narva Jõesuu/Narva-Jyesuu 8 Me 59.21N 28.04 E
Narva-Jyesuu/Narva Jõesuu 8 Me 59.21N 28.04 E
Narva laht 7 Gg 59.30N 27.40 E
Narvik 6 Hb 68.26N 17.25 E
Narvski Zaliv 7 Gg 59.30N 27.40 E
Narvskoje Vodohranilišče 8 Me 59.10N 28.30 E
Narym 20 De 58.58N 81.40 E
Naryn 21 Je 40.54N 71.45 E
Naryn 22 Je 41.26N 75.59 E
Naryncol 19 Ig 42.43N 80.08 E
Narynskaja Oblast [3] 19 Hg 41.20N 75.40 E
Nås 7 Df 60.27N 14.29 E
Na Sailti/Saltee Islands 9 Gi 52.07N 6.36W
Nåsåker 7 De 63.23N 16.54 E
Nasarawa 34 Gd 8.32N 7.43 E
Năsăud 15 Hb 47.17N 24.24 E
Nasawa 63b Db 15.12S 168.06 E
Na Sceiri/Skerries 9 Gh 53.35N 6.07W
Nāshik 22 Jg 20.05N 73.48 E
Nash Point 9 Jj 51.24N 3.27W
Nashtārud 24 Nd 36.45N 51.02 E
Nashua 44 Ld 42.44N 71.28W
Nashville [Ar.-U.S.] 45 Jj 33.57N 93.51W
Nashville [Ga.-U.S.] 44 Fj 31.12N 83.15W
Nashville [Il.-U.S.] 45 Lg 38.21N 89.23W
Nashville [In.-U.S.] 44 Df 39.12N 86.15W
Nashville [Tn.-U.S.] 39 Kf 36.09N 86.48W
Nashville Seamount (EN) 38 Nf 35.00N 57.20W
Našice 14 Me 45.30N 18.06 E
Nasielsk 10 Qd 52.36N 20.48 E
Näsijärvi 5 Ic 61.35N 23.40 E
Nāşir 35 Ed 8.36N 33.04 E
Naskaupi 42 Lf 53.45N 60.51W
Nasorolevu 63d Bb 16.38S 179.24 E
Naşr [Eg.] 24 Dg 30.36N 30.23 E
Naşr [Lib.] 33 Dd 28.59N 21.13 E
Naşrābād 24 Of 32.09N 52.08 E
Nass 42 Ee 55.00N 129.50W
Nassandres 12 Ce 49.07N 0.44 E
Nassandres-La Rivière Thibouville 12 Ce 49.07N 0.44 E
Nassau [Bah.] 39 Lg 25.05N 77.21W
Nassau [F.R.G.] 12 Jd 50.19N 7.48 E
Nassau, Bahia- 56 Gi 55.25S 67.40W
Nassau Island 57 Kf 11.33S 165.25W
Nassau River 59 Ic 15.58S 141.30 E
Nasser, Birkat- = Nasser, Lake-(EN) 30 Kf 22.40N 32.00 E

Index Symbols

[1] Independent Nation
[2] State, Region
[3] District, County
[4] Municipality
[5] Colony, Dependency
Continent
Physical Region
Historical or Cultural Region
Mount, Mountain
Volcano
Hill
Mountains, Mountain Range
Hills, Escarpment
Plateau, Upland
Pass, Gap
Plain, Lowland
Delta
Salt Flat
Valley, Canyon
Crater, Cave
Karst Features
Depression
Polder
Desert, Dunes
Forest, Woods
Heath, Steppe
Oasis
Cape, Point
Coast, Beach
Cliff
Peninsula
Isthmus
Sandbank
Island
Atoll
Rock, Reef
Islands, Archipelago
Rocks, Reefs
Coral Reef
Well, Spring
Geyser
River, Stream
Waterfall Rapids
River Mouth, Estuary
Lake
Salt Lake
Intermittent Lake
Reservoir
Swamp, Pond
Canal
Glacier
Ice Shelf, Pack Ice
Ocean
Sea
Gulf, Bay
Strait, Fjord
Lagoon
Bank
Seamount
Tablemount
Ridge
Shelf
Basin
Escarpment, Sea Scarp
Fracture
Trench, Abyss
National Park, Reserve
Point of Interest
Recreation Site
Cave, Cavern
Historic Site
Ruins
Wall, Walls
Church, Abbey
Temple
Scientific Station
Airport
Port
Lighthouse
Mine
Tunnel
Dam, Bridge

Nasser, Lake-(EN)=Nasser, Birkat- 30 Kf 22.40N 32.00 E
Nassian 34 Ed 9.24N 4.29W
Nässjö 7 Dh 57.39N 14.41 E
Nassogne 12 Hd 50.08N 5.21 E
Na Staighri Dubha/Blackstairs Mountains 9 Gi 52.33N 6.49W
Nastapoka Islands 42 Je 56.50N 76.50W
Nastätten 12 Jd 50.12N 7.52 E
Nastola 8 Kd 60.57N 25.56 E
Nasu 29 Gc 37.02N 140.06 E
Nasu-Dake 29 Fc 37.07N 139.58 E
Näsviken 8 Gc 61.45N 16.52 E
Natá 49 Gi 8.20N 80.31W
Nata 30 Jk 20.14S 26.10 E
Nata 37 Dd 20.13S 26.11 E
Natal [2] 37 Ee 29.00S 30.00 E
Natal [B.C.-Can.] 46 Hb 49.44N 114.50W
Natal [Braz.] 53 Mf 5.47S 35.13W
Natal [Indon.] 26 Cf 0.33N 99.07 E
Natal Basin (EN) 3 Fm 30.00S 40.00 E
Natanz 24 Nf 33.31N 51.54 E
Natashquan 42 Lf 50.09N 61.37W
Natashquan 42 Lf 50.11N 61.49W
Natchez 43 Ie 31.34N 91.23W
Natchitoches 43 Ie 31.46N 93.05W
Natewa Bay 63d Bb 16.35S 179.40 E
Nathorsts Land 41 Jd 72.20N 27.00W
Nathula 63d Ab 16.53S 177.25 E
Natitingou 31 Hg 10.19N 1.22 E
Natityāy, Jabal- 33 Fe 23.01N 34.22 E
Natividad, Isla- 48 Bd 27.55N 115.10W
Natividade 54 If 11.43S 47.47W
Natori 28 Pe 38.11N 140.58 E
Natron, Lake- 30 Ki 2.25S 36.00 E
Naṭrūn, Wādī an- 24 Dg 30.25N 30.13 E
Natsudomari-Zaki 29a Bc 41.00N 140.53 E
Nättarö 8 Hf 58.50N 18.10 E
Nättraby 8 Fh 56.12N 15.31 E
Natuna Besar, Pulau- 26 Ef 4.00N 108.15 E
Natuna Islands (EN)= Bunguran, Kepulauan- 21 Mi 2.45N 109.00 E
Naturaliste, Cape- 57 Ch 33.32S 115.01 E
Naturaliste Channel 59 Ce 25.25S 113.00 E
Naturita 45 Bg 38.14N 108.34W
Naturno / Naturns 14 Ed 46.39N 11.00 E
Naturns / Naturno 14 Ed 46.39N 11.00 E
Nau 18 Gd 40.09N 69.22 E
Nau, Cap de la-/Nao, Cabo de la- 5 Gh 38.44N 0.14 E
Naucelle 11 Ij 44.12N 2.21 E
Nauēji-Akmjane/Naujoji-Akmenė 7 Fh 56.21N 22.50 E
Naugo/Nauvo 8 Id 60.10N 21.50 E
Nauhcampatépetl→ Cofre de Perote, Cerro- 48 Kh 19.29N 97.08W
Nauja Bay 42 Kc 68.58N 75.00W
Naujamiestis/Naujamiestis 8 Ki 55.41N 24.09 E
Naujamiestis/Naujamiestis 8 Ki 55.41N 24.09 E
Naujoji-Akmenė/Nauēji-Akmjane 7 Fh 56.21N 22.50 E
Naukluft 37 Bd 24.10S 16.10 E
Naumburg [F.R.G.] 12 Lc 51.15N 9.10 E
Naumburg [G.D.R.] 10 He 51.09N 11.49 E
Nā'ūr 24 Fg 31.53N 35.50 E
Nauru 57 He 0.31S 166.56 E
Nauru/Naoero [1] 58 He 0.31S 166.56 E
Nauški 20 Ff 50.28N 106.07 E
Nausori 61 Ec 18.02S 178.32 E
Nauta 54 Dd 4.32S 73.33W
Nautanwa 25 Gc 27.26N 83.25 E
Nautla 48 Kg 20.13N 96.47W
Nauvo/Naugo 8 Id 60.10N 21.50 E
Nava 48 Ic 28.25N 100.45W
Navacerrada, Puerto de- 13 Id 40.47N 4.00W
Nava del Rey 13 Gc 41.20N 5.05W
Navahermosa 13 He 39.38N 4.28W
Navajo Mountain 46 Jh 37.02N 110.52W
Navajo Reservoir 45 Ch 36.55N 107.30W
Navalmoral de la Mata 13 Ge 39.54N 5.32W
Navan/An Uaimh 9 Gh 53.39N 6.41W
Navarin, Mys- 21 Tc 62.16N 179.10 E
Navarino, Isla- 52 Jk 55.05S 67.40W
Navarra [3] 13 Kb 42.45N 1.40W
Navarra = Navarre (EN) 13 Kb 43.00N 1.30W
Navarre (EN) = Navarra 13 Kb 43.00N 1.30W
Navarro 55 Cl 35.01S 59.16W
Navarro Mills Lake 45 Hk 31.56N 96.45W
Navašino 7 Ki 55.33N 42.12 E
Navasota 45 Hk 30.23N 96.05W
Navasota River 45 Hk 30.20N 96.09W
Navassa 47 Ie 18.24N 75.01W
Navaste Jõgi/Navesti 8 Kf 58.56N 24.58 E
Nävekvarn 8 Gf 58.38N 16.49 E
Naver 9 Ic 58.30N 4.15W
Navesti/Navaste Jõgi 8 Kf 58.56N 24.58 E
Navia 13 Fa 43.32N 6.43W
Navia 13 Fa 43.33N 6.44W
Navidad, Bahía de- 48 Gh 19.10N 104.45W
Navidad Bank (EN) 49 Mc 20.00N 68.50W
Naviti 63d Ab 17.07S 177.15 E
Navlja 16 Ic 52.42N 34.03 E
Navlja 19 De 52.50N 34.31 E
Năvodari 15 Le 44.19N 28.36 E
Navoi 19 Gg 40.10N 65.15 E
Navoja 47 Cc 27.06N 109.26W
Navolato 48 Fe 24.47N 107.42W
Navoloki 7 Jh 57.28N 41.59 E
Návpaktos 15 Ek 38.24N 21.50 E
Návplion 15 Fl 37.34N 22.48 E
Navrongo 34 Ec 10.54N 1.06W
Navsāri 25 Ed 20.55N 72.55 E
Navtilos 15 Gn 35.57N 23.13 E
Navua 63d Bc 18.13S 178.10 E
Navy Board Inlet 42 Jb 73.30N 81.00W
Nawa 24 Gf 32.53N 36.03 E
Nawābshāh 25 Dc 26.15N 68.25 E
Nawāşif, Ḩarrat- 33 He 21.20N 42.10 E
Ņaws, Ra's- 23 If 17.18N 55.16 E
Náxos 15 Il 37.06N 25.23 E
Naxos 14 Jm 37.49N 15.15 E
Náxos=Naxos (EN) 5 Ih 37.02N 25.35 E
Naxos (EN)=Náxos 5 Ih 37.02N 25.35 E
Nayarit [2] 47 Cd 22.00N 105.00W
Nayarit, Sierra- 47 Dd 22.00N 103.50W
Nayau 63d Cb 17.58S 179.03W
Nāy Band [Iran] 24 Oi 27.23N 52.38 E
Nāy Band [Iran] 24 Qf 32.20N 57.34 E
Nāy Band, Ra's-e- 24 Oi 27.23N 52.34 E
Nayoro 27 Pc 44.21N 142.28 E
Nazaré [Braz.] 54 Kf 13.02S 39.00W
Nazaré [Port.] 13 Ce 39.36N 9.04W
Nazareth (EN)=Nazerat 24 Ff 32.42N 35.18 E
Nazarovo 20 Ee 56.01N 90.36 E
Nazas 48 Ge 25.14N 104.08W
Nazas, Rio- 38 Ig 25.35N 105.00W
Nazca 53 Ig 14.50S 74.55W
Nazca Ridge (EN) 3 Nl 22.00S 82.00W
Naze 27 Mf 28.23N 129.30 E
Nazerat=Nazareth (EN) 24 Ff 32.42N 35.18 E
Nazilli 23 Cb 37.55N 28.21 E
Nazimiye 24 Hc 39.11N 39.50 E
Nazimovo 20 Ee 59.30N 90.58 E
Nazino 20 Cd 60.15N 78.58 E
Nazlū 24 Kd 37.42N 45.16 E
Nazran 16 Nh 43.15N 44.46 E
Nazret 35 Fd 8.34N 39.18 E
Nazw'a 23 Ie 22.54N 57.31 E
Nazym 17 Nf 61.12N 68.57 E
Nazyvajevsk 19 Hd 55.34N 71.21 E
Nbâk 32 Ef 17.15N 14.59W
Nchanga 36 Ee 12.31S 27.52 E
Ncheu 36 Fe 14.49S 34.38 E
Ndala 36 Fc 4.46S 33.16 E
N'dalatando 36 Bd 9.18S 14.54 E
Ndali 34 Fd 9.51N 2.43 E
Ndélé 31 Jh 8.24N 20.39 E
Ndélélé 34 He 4.02N 14.56 E
Ndendé 36 Bc 2.23S 11.23 E
Ndindi 36 Bc 3.46S 11.09 E
N'Djamena (Fort-Lamy) 31 Ig 12.07N 15.03 E
Ndola 31 Jj 12.58S 28.38 E
Ndouana, Pointe- 63b Dc 16.35S 168.09 E
Ndrhamcha, Sebkha de- 32 Df 18.45N 15.48W
Nduindui 60 Fi 9.48S 159.58 E
Ndui Ndui 63b Cb 15.24S 167.46 E
Né 11 Fi 45.40N 0.23W
Nea 63c Ab 10.51S 165.47 E
Nea 7 Ce 63.13N 11.02 E
Néa Alikarnassós 15 In 35.20N 25.09 E
Néa Artáki 15 Gk 38.31N 23.38 E
Neagari 29 Ec 36.26N 136.26 E
Neagh, Lough-/Loch nEathach 5 Fe 54.38N 6.24W
Neagră, Marea-=Black Sea (EN) 5 Jg 43.00N 35.00 E
Neah Bay 46 Cb 48.22N 124.37W
Néa Ionía 15 Fj 39.23N 22.56 E
Neajlov 15 Je 44.11N 26.12 E
Neale, Lake- 59 Fd 24.20S 130.00 E
Neamț [2] 15 Jb 47.00N 26.20 E
Neápolis [Grc.] 15 In 35.15N 25.37 E
Neápolis [Grc.] 15 Ei 40.19N 21.23 E
Neápolis [Grc.] 15 Gm 36.31N 23.04 E
Near Islands 38 Bd 52.40N 173.30W
Neath 9 Jj 51.37N 3.50W
Neath 9 Jj 51.40N 3.48W
Néa Zíkhni 15 Gh 41.02N 23.50 E
Néba 63b Ae 20.09S 163.55 E
Nebaj 49 Bf 15.24N 91.08W
Nebbou 34 Ec 11.18N 1.53W
Nebit-Dag 22 Hf 39.30N 54.22 E
Neblina, Pico da- 52 Je 1.08N 66.10W
Nebo 59 Jd 21.40S 148.39 E
Nebo, Mount- 46 Jg 39.49N 111.46W
Nebolči 7 Hg 59.08N 33.21 E
Nebraska [2] 43 Gc 41.30N 100.00W
Nebraska City 43 Hc 40.41N 95.52W
Nebrodi (Caronie) 14 Im 37.55N 14.35 E
Necedah 45 Kd 44.02N 90.03W
Nechako 42 Ff 53.55N 122.44W
Nechako Reservoir 42 Ef 53.00N 126.10W
Nechar, Djebel- 13 Qi 35.52N 4.59 E
Neches River 45 Jl 29.55N 93.52W
Nechí 49 Ji 8.07N 74.46W
Nechí, Rio- 49 Ji 8.08N 74.46W
Neckako Plateau 42 Ff 53.25N 124.40W
Neckar 10 Eg 49.31N 8.26 E
Neckarsulm 10 Fg 49.11N 9.14 E
Necker Island 57 Kb 23.35N 164.42W
Necochea 53 Ki 38.34S 58.45W
Necy 12 Bf 48.50N 0.07W
Nedeley 35 Bb 15.34N 18.10 E
Nederland 45 Jl 29.58N 93.59W
Nederland=Netherlands (EN) [1] 6 Ge 52.15N 5.30 E
Nederlandse Antillen [5] 50 Ec 18.06N 63.10W
Nederlandse Antillen = Netherlands Antilles (EN) [5] 53 Jd 12.15N 69.00W
Neder-Rijn = Lower Rhine (EN) 11 Mc 51.59N 6.20 E
Nêdong 22 Lg 29.14N 91.46 E
Nedstrand 8 Ae 59.21N 5.51 E
Nedstrandefjorden 8 Ae 59.20N 5.50 E
Neede 12 Ib 52.08N 6.37 E
Needham Market 12 Db 52.09N 1.02 E
Needham's Point 51q Ab 13.05N 59.36W
Needles 43 Ee 34.51N 114.37W
Neembucú [3] 55 Dh 27.00S 58.00W
Neenah 45 Ld 44.11N 88.28W
Neepawa 45 Ga 50.13N 99.29W
Neermoor, Moormerland- 12 Ja 53.18N 7.26 E
Neeroeteren, Maaseik- 12 Hc 51.05N 5.42 E
Neerpelt 12 Hc 51.13N 5.25 E
Nefasit 35 Fb 15.18N 39.04 E
Nefedova 19 Hd 58.48N 72.34 E
Né Finn/Nephin 9 Dg 54.01N 9.22W
Neftah 32 Ic 33.52N 7.53 E
Neftečala 16 Pj 39.19N 49.13 E
Neftegorsk [R.S.F.S.R.] 16 Kg 44.22N 39.42 E
Neftegorsk [R.S.F.S.R.] 20 Jf 53.00N 143.00 E
Neftegorsk [R.S.F.S.R.] 19 Fe 52.45N 51.13 E
Neftejugansk 19 Hc 61.05N 72.45 E
Neftekamsk 19 Fd 56.06N 54.17 E
Neftekumsk 19 Eg 44.43N 44.59 E
Neftjanyje Kamin 16 Qi 40.15N 50.49 E
Negage 36 Cd 7.46S 15.18 E
Negara 26 Fh 8.22S 114.37 E
Negele=Neghelle (EN) 31 Kh 5.20N 39.37 E
Negev Desert (EN)= Ha̱negev 24 Fg 30.30N 34.55 E
Neghelle (EN)=Negele 31 Kh 5.20N 39.37 E
Negla, Arroyo- 55 Df 22.52S 56.41W
Negola 36 Be 14.10S 14.30 E
Negomano 37 Fb 11.26S 38.33 E
Negombo 25 Fg 7.13N 79.50 E
Negonego Atoll 57 Mf 18.47S 141.48W
Negotin 15 Fe 44.13N 22.32 E
Negotino 15 Fh 41.29N 22.06 E
Negra, Cordillera- 54 Ce 9.25S 77.40W
Negra, Coxilha- 55 Ej 31.02S 55.45W
Negra, Peña- 13 Fb 42.11N 6.30W
Negra, Ponta- 55 Jf 23.21S 44.36W
Negra, Punta- 52 Hf 6.06S 81.10W
Negra, Serra- 55 Fc 16.30S 52.10W
Negra o de los Difuntos, Laguna- 55 Fl 34.03S 53.40W
Negreira 13 Db 42.54N 8.44W
Negreni 15 He 44.34N 24.36 E
Negreşti 15 Gb 47.52N 23.26 E
Negrine 32 Ic 34.29N 7.31 E
Negrinho, Rio- 55 Ed 19.20S 55.05W
Negro, Cerro- 13 Gi 35.41N 5.17W
Negro, Rio- [Arg.] 55 Ch 27.27S 58.54W
Negro, Rio- [Arg.] 52 Jj 41.02S 62.47W
Negro, Rio- [Bol.] 54 Ff 14.11S 63.07W
Negro, Rio- [Braz.] 54 Gg 19.13S 57.17W
Negro, Rio- [Braz.] 56 Jc 26.01S 50.30W
Negro, Rio- [Par.] 56 Ib 24.23S 57.11W
Negro, Rio- [S.Amer.] 52 Kf 3.08S 59.55W
Negro, Rio- [S.Amer.] 55 Ce 20.11S 58.10W
Negro, Rio- [Ur.] 52 Ki 33.24S 58.22W
Negros 21 Oi 10.00N 123.00 E
Negru, Rîu- 15 Id 45.45N 25.46 E
Negru Vodă 15 Lf 43.49N 28.12 E
Nehajevski 16 Ld 50.27N 41.46 E
Nehalem River 46 Dd 45.40N 123.56W
Nehāvand 24 Me 35.56N 49.31 E
Nehe 27 Lb 48.28N 124.53 E
Nehoiu 15 Jd 45.26N 26.17 E
Néhoué, Baie de- 63b Be 20.21S 164.09 E
Neiba 49 Ld 18.28N 71.25W
Neiba, Bahía de- 49 Ld 18.15N 71.02W
Neidín/Kenmare 9 Dj 51.53N 9.35W
Neige, Crêt de la- 11 Lh 46.16N 5.56 E
Neiges, Piton des- 30 Mk 21.05S 55.29 E
Neijiang 22 Mg 29.38N 104.58 E
Neilton 46 Dc 47.25N 123.52W
Nei-meng-ku Tzu-chih-ch'ü→ Nei Monggol Zizhiqu [2] 27 Jc 44.00N 112.00 E
Nei Monggol Gaoyuan 21 Ne 42.00N 111.00 E
Nei Monggol Zizhiqu (Nei-meng-ku Tzu-chih-ch'ü)=Inner Mongolia (EN) [2] 27 Jc 44.00N 112.00 E
Neiqiu 28 Cf 37.17N 114.30 E
Neiva 53 Ie 2.56N 75.18W
Neja 19 Ed 58.19N 43.52 E
Nejanilini Lake 42 He 59.30N 97.50W
Nejdek 10 If 50.19N 12.44 E
Nejo 35 Fd 9.30N 35.32 E
Nejva 17 Kh 57.54N 62.18 E
Nekemt=Leqemt (EN) 31 Kh 9.05N 36.33 E
Neksø 8 Fi 55.04N 15.09 E
Nelemnoje 20 Kc 65.23N 151.08 E
Nelgese 20 Ic 66.40N 136.30 E
Nelichu 35 Ed 6.08N 34.25 E
Nelidovo 19 Dd 56.13N 32.50 E
Neligh 45 Ge 42.08N 98.02W
Neljaty 20 Ge 56.29N 115.50 E
Nelkan 20 Jd 64.15N 143.03 E
Nellore 22 Jh 12.56N 79.08 E
Nelma 20 Ig 47.40N 139.08 E
Nelson [2] 62 Ed 41.45S 172.30 E
Nelson 38 Jd 57.04N 92.30W
Nelson [B.C.-Can.] 42 Fg 49.29N 117.17W
Nelson [N.Z.] 58 Ii 41.16S 173.15 E
Nelson, Cape- [Austl.] 57 Fh 38.26S 141.33 E
Nelson, Cape- [Pap.N.Gui.] 59 Ja 9.00S 149.15 E
Nelson Island 40 Gd 60.35N 164.45W
Nelson's Dockyard 51d Bb 17.00N 61.46W
Nelspruit 31 Kk 25.30S 30.58 E
Néma 31 Gg 16.36N 7.15W
Néma, Dahr- 32 Ff 16.14N 7.30W
Neman 5 Id 55.18N 21.23 E
Neman 7 Fi 55.03N 22.01 E
Nembrala 26 Hi 10.53S 122.50 E
Nemda 7 Kh 57.31N 43.15 E
Neméa 15 Fl 37.49N 22.39 E
Neméa 15 Fl 37.49N 22.40 E
Nëmëçkes, Mali i- 15 Di 40.08N 20.24 E
Nemenčiné 8 Kj 54.50N 25.29 E
Nëmërçkes, Mali i- 15 Di 40.08N 20.24 E
Nemira, Virful- 15 Jc 46.15N 26.19 E
Nemirov [Ukr.-U.S.S.R.] 10 Tf 50.08N 23.28 E
Nemirov [Ukr.-U.S.S.R.] 16 Fe 48.59N 28.50 E
Némiscau 42 Jf 51.30N 77.00W
Nemjuga 7 Kd 65.29N 43.40 E
Nemours 11 If 48.16N 2.42 E
Nemunas 5 Id 55.18N 21.23 E
Nemunėlis 8 Kh 56.24N 24.10 E
Nemuro 27 Qc 43.20N 145.35 E
Nemuro-Hantō 29a Db 43.20N 145.35 E
Nemuro-Kaikyō=Nemuro Strait (EN) 20 Jh 43.50N 145.30 E
Nemuro Strait (EN)= Kunašírski Proliv 20 Jh 43.50N 145.30 E
Nemuro Strait (EN)= Nemuro-Kaikyō 20 Jh 43.50N 145.30 E
Nemuro-Wan 29a Db 43.25N 145.25 E
Nenagh/An tAonach 9 Ei 52.52N 8.12W
Nenana 40 Jd 64.30N 149.00W
Nenana 40 Jd 64.34N 149.07W
Nendo Island 57 Hf 10.40S 165.54 E
Nene 9 Ni 52.48N 0.13 E
Nenecki Nacionalny Okrug [3] 19 Fb 67.30N 54.00 E
Nenjiang 22 Oe 49.10N 125.12 E
Nen Jiang 21 Oe 45.26N 124.39 E
Neo 29 Ed 35.38N 136.37 E
Neodesha 45 Ih 37.25N 95.41W
Néon Karlovásion 15 Jl 37.47N 26.42 E
Neosho 45 Ih 36.52N 94.22W
Neosho River 45 Ih 35.48N 95.18W
Néouvielle, Massif de- 11 Gl 42.51N 0.07 E
Nepal [1] 22 Kg 28.00N 84.00 E
Nepalganj 25 Gc 28.03N 81.37 E
Nephi 43 Ed 39.43N 111.50W
Nephin/Né Finn 9 Dg 54.01N 9.22W
Nepisiguit River 44 Ob 47.37N 65.38W
Nepoko 30 Jh 1.40N 27.01 E
Nepomuk 10 Jg 49.29N 13.34 E
Ner 10 Od 52.10N 18.40 E
Nera [It.] 14 Gh 42.26N 12.24 E
Nera [Rom.] 15 Ee 44.49N 21.22 E
Nérac 11 Gj 44.08N 0.21 E
Neratovice 10 Kf 50.16N 14.31 E
Nerău 15 Dd 45.58N 20.34 E
Nerča 20 Gf 51.54N 116.30 E
Nerčinsk 20 Gf 51.58N 116.35 E
Nerčinski Zavod 20 Gf 51.17N 119.30 E
Nerehta 19 Ed 57.28N 40.34 E
Nereju 15 Jd 45.42N 26.43 E
Nereta 8 Kh 56.12N 25.24 E
Neretva 14 Lg 43.02N 17.27 E
Neretvanski kanal 14 Lg 43.03N 17.11 E
Nerica 17 Fd 65.20N 52.45 E
Neringa 7 Ei 55.24N 21.05 E
Neringa 7 Ei 55.18N 21.00 E
Neringa-Juodkrante/Neringa-Juodkrantė 8 Ii 55.35N 21.01 E
Neringa-Juodkrantė/Neringa-Juodkrante 8 Ii 55.35N 21.01 E
Neringa-Nida 8 Ii 55.18N 20.53 E
Neringa-Preila/Neringa-Prejla 8 Ii 55.20N 20.59 E
Neringa-Prejla/Neringa-Preila 8 Ii 55.20N 20.59 E
Neriquinha 36 Df 15.45S 21.33 E
Neris/Njaris 8 Kj 54.55N 25.45 E
Nerja 13 Ih 36.44N 3.52W
Nerjungri 20 He 56.40N 124.47 E
Nerl [R.S.F.S.R.] 7 Jh 56.11N 40.34 E
Nerl [R.S.F.S.R.] 7 Ih 57.07N 37.39 E
Nerpio 13 Jf 38.09N 2.18W
Nerussa 16 Hc 52.33N 33.47 E
Nerva 13 Fg 37.42N 6.32W
Nervi, Genova- 14 Df 44.23N 9.02 E
Nervión 13 Ja 43.14N 2.53W
Nes 8 Cd 60.34N 9.59 E
Nes, Ameland- 12 Ha 53.26N 5.48 E
Nesbyen 7 Bf 60.34N 9.06 E
Nesebăr 15 Kg 42.39N 27.44 E
Nesjøen 8 Db 63.00N 12.00 E
Neskaupstaður 7a Db 65.09N 13.42W
Nesle 12 Ee 49.46N 2.45 E
Nesna 7 Cc 66.12N 13.02 E
Ness City 45 Gg 38.27N 99.54W
Nesterov [R.S.F.S.R.] 7 Fi 54.42N 22.34 E
Nesterov [Ukr.-U.S.S.R.] 16 Cd 50.03N 24.00 E
Néstos 15 Hi 40.51N 24.44 E
Nesttun 8 Ad 60.19N 5.20 E
Nesviž 16 Ec 53.13N 26.39 E
Netanya 24 Ff 32.20N 34.51 E
Netcong 44 Je 40.54N 74.43W
Nete 11 Kc 51.10N 4.15 E
Nethe 12 Lc 51.44N 9.23 E
Netherdale 59 Jd 21.08S 148.32 E
Netherlands (EN)= Nederland [1] 6 Ge 52.15N 5.30 E
Netherlands Antilles (EN) = Nederlandse Antillen [5] 53 Jd 12.15N 69.00W
Neto 14 Lk 39.12N 17.09 E
Netphen 12 Kd 50.55N 8.06 E
Nettebach 12 Jd 50.26N 7.28 E
Nettersheim 12 Id 50.30N 6.38 E
Nettetal 12 Ic 51.18N 6.12 E
Nettilling Lake 38 Lc 66.30N 70.40W
Nettuno 14 Gi 41.27N 12.39 E
Netzahualcóyotl, Presa- 48 Mi 17.00N 93.30W
Neubourg, Campagne du- 11 Ge 49.08N 1.00 E
Neubrandenburg 10 Jc 53.34N 13.16 E
Neubrandenburg [2] 10 Jc 53.35N 13.15 E
Neuburg an der Donau 10 Hh 48.44N 11.11 E
Neuchâtel [2] 14 Ac 47.05N 6.50 E
Neuchâtel/Neuenburg 14 Ad 46.59N 6.56 E
Neuchâtel, Lac de-/Neuenburger See 14 Ad 46.55N 6.55 E
Neuenbürg 12 Kf 48.50N 8.35 E
Neuenburg/Neuchâtel 14 Ad 46.59N 6.56 E
Neuenburger See/Neuchâtel, Lac de- 14 Ad 46.55N 6.55 E
Neuenhaus 12 Ib 52.30N 6.58 E
Neuenkirchen 12 Jb 52.15N 7.22 E
Neuerburg 12 Id 50.01N 6.18 E
Neufchâteau [Bel.] 11 Le 49.51N 5.26 E
Neufchâteau [Fr.] 11 Lf 48.21N 5.42 E
Neufchâtel-en-Bray 11 He 49.44N 1.27 E
Neufchâtel-Hardelot 12 Dd 50.37N 1.38 E
Neufchâtel Hardelot-Hardelot Plage 12 Dd 50.38N 1.35 E
Neufchâtel-sur-Aisne 12 Ge 49.26N 4.02 E
Neuffossé, Canal de- 12 Ed 50.45N 2.15 E
Neuhaus am Rennweg 10 Hf 50.31N 11.09 E
Neuilly-en-Thelle 12 Ee 49.13N 2.17 E
Neuilly-Saint-Front 12 Fe 49.10N 3.16 E
Neu-Isenburg 12 Kd 50.03N 8.42 E
Neukirchen-Vluyn 12 Ic 51.27N 6.35 E
Neum 14 Lh 42.55N 17.38 E
Neumagen Dhron 12 Ie 49.51N 6.54 E
Neumarkter Sattel 14 Id 47.06N 14.22 E
Neumarkt in der Oberpfalz 10 Hg 49.17N 11.28 E
Neumünster 10 Fb 54.04N 9.59 E
Neunkirchen [Aus.] 14 Kc 47.43N 16.05 E
Neunkirchen [F.R.G.] 10 Dg 49.21N 7.11 E
Neunkirchen [F.R.G.] 12 Jd 50.51N 7.20 E
Neunkirchen [F.R.G.] 12 Kd 50.48N 8.00 E
Neuquén 53 Ji 39.00S 68.05W
Neuquén [2] 56 Ge 39.00S 70.00W
Neuquén, Rio- 52 Ji 38.59S 68.00W
Neuruppin 10 Id 52.56N 12.48 E
Neuse River 44 Ih 35.06N 76.30W
Neusiedl am See 14 Kc 47.56N 16.50 E
Neusiedler See (Fertő) 10 Mi 47.50N 16.45 E
Neuß 10 Ce 51.12N 6.42 E
Neustadt (Hessen) 12 Ld 50.51N 9.07 E
Neustadt am Rübenberge 10 Fd 52.30N 9.28 E
Neustadt an der Aisch 10 Gg 49.35N 10.36 E
Neustadt an der Orla 10 Hf 50.44N 11.45 E
Neustadt an der Weinstraße 10 Eg 49.21N 8.09 E
Neustadt bei Coburg 10 Hf 50.19N 11.07 E
Neustadt in Holstein 10 Gb 54.06N 10.49 E
Neustrelitz 10 Jc 53.22N 13.05 E
Neu-Ulm 10 Gh 48.24N 10.01 E
Neuville-les-Dieppe 12 De 49.55N 1.06 E
Neuville-sur-Saône 11 Ki 45.52N 4.51 E
Neuwerk 10 Ec 53.55N 8.30 E
Neuwied 10 Df 50.26N 7.28 E
Neva 5 Jd 59.55N 30.15 E
Nevada [2] 43 Dd 39.00N 117.00W
Nevada [Ia.-U.S.] 45 Je 42.01N 93.27W
Nevada [Mo.-U.S.] 43 Id 37.51N 94.22W
Nevada, Sierra- [Sp.] 5 Fh 37.05N 3.10W
Nevada, Sierra- [U.S.] 38 Hf 38.00N 119.15W
Nevada del Cocuy, Sierra- 52 Ie 6.10N 72.15W
Nevada de Santa Marta, Sierra- 52 Id 10.50N 73.40W
Nevado, Cerro- 52 Ie 3.59N 74.04W
Nevado de Ampato 52 Ig 15.50S 71.52W
Neve, Serra da- 30 Ij 13.52S 13.26 E
Nevel 19 Cd 56.02N 29.55 E
Nevele 12 Fc 51.02N 3.33 E
Nevelsk 20 Jg 46.37N 141.57 E
Neverkino 16 Oc 52.47N 46.48 E
Nevers 11 Jg 46.59N 3.10 E
Nevesinje 14 Mg 43.16N 18.07 E
Nevinnomyssk 19 Eg 44.38N 41.58 E
Nevis 47 Le 17.10N 62.34W
Nevis, Ben- 5 Fd 56.48N 5.01W
Nevis Peak 51c Ab 17.10N 62.34W
Nevjansk 19 Gd 57.32N 60.13 E
Nevşehir 23 Db 38.38N 34.43 E
Nevskoje 28 Lb 45.42N 133.40 E
Newala 36 Ge 10.56S 39.18 E
New Albany [In.-U.S.] 43 Jd 38.18N 85.49W
New Albany [Ms.-U.S.] 45 Li 34.29N 89.00W
New Alresford 12 Ac 51.05N 1.10W
New Amsterdam 53 Ke 6.17N 57.36W
Newark [De.-U.S.] 44 Jf 39.41N 75.45W
Newark [N.J.-U.S.] 43 Mc 40.44N 74.11W
Newark [N.Y.-U.S.] 44 Id 43.03N 77.06W
Newark [Oh.-U.S.] 43 Kc 40.03N 82.25W
Newark-on-Trent 9 Mh 53.05N 0.49W
New Bedford 43 Mc 41.38N 70.56W
New Bern 43 Ld 35.07N 77.03W
Newberry [Mi.-U.S.] 44 Eb 46.21N 85.30W
Newberry [S.C.-U.S.] 44 Gh 34.17N 81.37W
New Braunfels 43 Hf 29.42N 98.08W
New Britain 44 Ke 41.40N 72.47W
New Britain Island 57 Ge 5.40S 151.00 E
New Britain Trench (EN) 60 Ei 6.00S 153.00 E
New Brunswick 44 Je 40.29N 74.27W
New Brunswick [3] 42 Kg 46.30N 66.45W
New Buckenham 12 Db 52.28N 1.05 E
New Buffalo 44 De 41.47N 86.45W
Newburgh 43 Mc 41.30N 74.00W
Newbury 9 Lj 51.25N 1.20W
New Caledonia (EN) = Nouvelle-Calédonie [5] 58 Hg 21.30S 165.30 E
New Caledonia (EN)= Nouvelle-Calédonie 57 Hg 21.30S 165.30 E
New Caledonia Basin (EN) 3 Jm 30.00S 165.00 E
New Carlisle 44 Oa 48.01N 65.20W
New Castile (EN)=Castilla la Nueva 13 Id 40.00N 3.45W
New Castle [In.-U.S.] 44 Ef 39.55N 85.22W
New Castle [Pa.-U.S.] 43 Kc 41.00N 80.22W
Newcastle [Austl.] 58 Gh 32.56S 151.46 E
Newcastle [N.B.-Can.] 42 Kg 47.00N 65.34W
Newcastle [N.Ire.-U.K.] 9 Hg 54.12N 5.54W
Newcastle [S.Afr.] 37 De 27.49S 29.55 E
Newcastle [St.C.N.] 51c Ab 17.13N 62.35W
Newcastle/An Caisleán Nua 9 Hg 54.12N 5.54W
Newcastle Creek 59 Gc 17.20S 133.23 E
Newcastle-under-Lyme 9 Kh 53.00N 2.14W

Index Symbols

[1] Independent Nation
[2] State, Region
[3] District, County
[4] Municipality
[5] Colony, Dependency
Continent
Physical Region
Historical or Cultural Region
Mount, Mountain
Volcano
Hill
Mountains, Mountain Range
Hills, Escarpment
Plateau, Upland
Pass, Gap
Plain, Lowland
Delta
Salt Flat
Valley, Canyon
Crater, Cave
Karst Features
Depression
Polder
Desert, Dunes
Forest, Woods
Heath, Steppe
Oasis
Cape, Point
Coast, Beach
Cliff
Peninsula
Isthmus
Sandbank
Island
Atoll
Rock, Reef
Islands, Archipelago
Rocks, Reefs
Coral Reef
Well, Spring
Geyser
River, Stream
Waterfall Rapids
River Mouth, Estuary
Lake
Salt Lake
Intermittent Lake
Reservoir
Swamp, Pond
Canal
Glacier
Ice Shelf, Pack Ice
Ocean
Sea
Gulf, Bay
Strait, Fjord
Lagoon
Bank
Seamount
Tablemount
Ridge
Shelf
Basin
Escarpment, Sea Scarp
Fracture
Trench, Abyss
National Park, Reserve
Point of Interest
Recreation Site
Cave, Cavern
Historic Site
Ruins
Wall, Walls
Church, Abbey
Temple
Scientific Station
Airport
Port
Lighthouse
Mine
Tunnel
Dam, Bridge

Name	Page	Grid	Lat.	Long.
Newcastle-upon-Tyne	6	Fd	54.59N	1.35W
Newcastle Waters	58	Ef	17.24S	133.24 E
Newcastle West/An Caisleán Nua	9	Di	52.27N	9.03W
New Delhi	22	Jg	28.36N	77.12 E
New Denver	46	Ga	50.00N	117.22W
Newell	45	Ed	44.43N	103.25W
Newell, Lake-	46	Ja	50.25N	111.56W
New England	38	Le	44.00N	71.20W
New England Range	57	Gh	30.00S	151.50 E
New England Seamounts (EN)	38	Mf	38.00N	61.00W
Newenham, Cape-	40	Ge	58.37N	162.12W
New Forest	9	Lk	50.55N	1.35W
Newfoundland [3]	42	Lf	52.00N	56.00W
Newfoundland, Island of-	38	Ne	48.30N	56.00W
Newfoundland Basin (EN)	3	De	45.00N	40.00W
New Galloway	9	If	55.05N	4.10W
New Georgia	57	Ge	8.30S	157.20 E
New Georgia Island	60	Fi	8.15S	157.30 E
New Georgia Sound (The Slot)	60	Fi	8.00S	158.10 E
New Glasgow	42	Lg	45.35N	62.39W
New Guinea/Pulau Irian	57	Fe	5.00S	140.00 E
New Guinea Trench (EN)	60	Bg	0.05N	135.50 E
New Hampshire [2]	43	Mc	43.35N	71.40W
New Hampton	45	Je	43.03N	92.19W
New Hanover Island	57	Ge	2.30S	150.15 E
New Harmony	44	Df	38.08N	87.56W
New Haven	39	Le	41.18N	72.56W
Newhaven	9	Nk	50.47N	0.03 E
New Hebrides/Nouvelles Hébrides	57	Hf	16.01S	167.01 E
New Hebrides Trench (EN)	3	Jl	20.00S	168.00 E
New Iberia	43	If	30.00N	91.49W
New Ireland Island	57	Ge	3.20S	152.00 E
New Jersey [2]	43	Mc	40.15N	74.30W
New Kowloon/Julong	22	Ng	22.20N	114.09 E
New Liskeard	42	Jg	47.30N	79.40W
New London	43	Mc	41.21N	72.07W
New Madrid	45	Lh	36.36N	89.32W
Newman	59	Dd	23.15S	119.35 E
Newmarket [Eng.-U.K.]	9	Ni	52.15N	0.25 E
Newmarket [Ont.-Can.]	44	Hc	44.03N	79.28W
New Martinsville	44	Gf	39.39N	80.52W
New Meadows	46	Gd	44.58N	116.32W
New Mexico [2]	43	Fe	34.30N	106.00W
Newnan	44	Ei	33.23N	84.48W
New Norfolk	59	Jh	42.47S	147.03 E
New Orleans	39	Jg	29.58N	90.07W
New Philadelphia	44	Ge	40.30N	81.27W
New Pine Creek	46	Ee	42.01N	120.18W
New-Plymouth	58	Ih	39.04S	174.04 E
Newport [Ar.-U.S.]	45	Ki	35.37N	91.17W
Newport [Eng.-U.K.]	12	Cc	51.59N	0.15 E
Newport [Eng.-U.K.]	9	Lk	50.42N	1.18W
Newport [Fl.-U.S.]	44	Ej	30.14N	84.12W
Newport [Or.-U.S.]	43	Cc	44.38N	124.03W
Newport [R.I.-U.S.]	44	Le	41.30N	71.19W
Newport [Tn.-U.S.]	44	Fh	35.58N	83.11W
Newport [Vt.-U.S.]	44	Kc	44.56N	72.13W
Newport [Wales-U.K.]	9	Kj	51.35N	3.00W
Newport [Wa.-U.S.]	46	Gb	48.11N	117.03W
Newport Beach	43	De	33.37N	117.54W
Newport News	39	Lf	37.04N	76.28W
Newport Pagnell	12	Bb	52.05N	0.43W
New Providence Island	47	Ic	25.02N	77.24W
Newquay	9	Hk	50.25N	5.05W
New Quebec Crater (EN) = Nouveau-Québec, Cratère du-	42	Kd	61.30N	73.55W
New Richmond [Oh.-U.S.]	44	Ef	38.57N	84.16W
New Richmond [Que.-Can.]	44	Oa	48.10N	65.52W
New River [Blz.]	49	Cd	18.22N	88.24W
New River [Guy.]	54	Gc	3.23N	57.36W
New River [U.S.]	44	Ff	38.50N	82.06W
New Rockford	45	Gc	47.41N	99.15W
New Romney	12	Cd	50.59N	0.56 E
New Ross/Ros Mhic Thriúin	9	Gi	52.24N	6.56W
Newry/an t-lúr	9	Gg	54.11N	6.20W
New Salem	45	Fc	46.51N	101.25W
New Sandy Bay	51n	Ba	13.20N	61.08W
New Schwabenland (EN)	66	Cf	72.30S	1.00 E
New Siberia (EN)=Novaja Sibir, Ostrov-	21	Qb	75.00N	149.00 E
New Siberian Islands (EN) =Novosibirskije Ostrova	21	Qb	75.00N	142.00 E
New Smyrna Beach	44	Gk	29.02N	80.56W
New South Wales	59	Jf	33.00S	146.00 E
Newton [Ia.-U.S.]	45	Jf	41.42N	93.03W
Newton [Il.-U.S.]	45	Lg	38.59N	88.10W
Newton [Ks.-U.S.]	43	Hd	38.03N	97.21W
Newton [Ma.-U.S.]	44	Ld	42.21N	71.13W
Newton [Ms.-U.S.]	45	Lj	32.19N	89.10W
Newton [N.J.-U.S.]	44	Je	41.03N	74.45W
Newton Abbot	9	Jk	50.32N	3.36W
Newton Stewart	9	Ig	54.57N	4.29W
Newtontoppen	67	Kd	72.02N	17.30 E
New Town	45	Ec	47.59N	102.30W
Newtown	9	Ji	52.32N	3.19W
Newtownabbey/Baile na Mainistreach	9	Hg	54.42N	5.54W
Newtownards/Baile Nua na hArda	9	Hg	54.36N	5.41W
New Ulm	43	Ic	44.19N	94.28W
New Westminster	42	Fg	49.12N	122.55W
New York	39	Le	40.43N	74.01W
New York [2]	43	Lc	43.00N	75.00W
New York State Barge Canal	44	Hd	43.05N	78.43W
New Zealand [1]	58	Ii	41.00S	174.00 E
New Zealand	57	Ii	41.00S	174.00 E
Nexpa, Río-	48	Hh	18.05N	102.46W
Neyagawa	29	Dd	34.46N	135.36 E
Neyrīz	24	Ph	29.12N	54.19 E
Neyshābūr	23	Ib	36.12N	58.50 E
Nežárka	10	Kg	49.11N	14.43 E
Nežin	19	De	51.02N	31.57 E
Ngabé	36	Cc	3.12S	16.11 E
Ngahere	62	De	42.24S	171.26 E
Ngajangel	64a	Ba	8.05N	134.43 E
Ngala	34	Hc	12.20N	14.11 E
Ngaliema, Chutes-=Stanley Falls (EN)	30	Jh	0.30N	25.30 E
Ngamegei Passage	64a	Bb	7.44N	134.34 E
Ngami, Lake-	37	Cd	20.37S	22.40 E
Ngamiland [3]	37	Cc	19.09S	22.47 E
Ngamring	27	Ef	29.14N	87.12 E
Ngangala	35	Ee	4.42N	31.55 E
Ngangerabeli Plain	36	Hc	1.30S	40.15 E
Ngangla Ringco	27	De	31.40N	83.00 E
Nganglong Kangri	27	De	32.45N	81.12 E
Nganglong Kangri	21	Kf	32.00N	83.00 E
Ngangzê Co	27	Ee	31.00N	86.55 E
Ngao	25	Je	18.45N	99.59 E
Ngaoundéré	31	Ih	7.19N	13.35 E
Ngapara	62	Df	44.57S	170.45 E
Ngara	36	Fc	2.28S	30.39 E
Ngardmau	64a	Bb	7.37N	134.35 E
Ngardmau Bay	64a	Bb	7.39N	134.35 E
Ngardololok	64a	Ac	7.00N	134.16 E
Ngaregur	64a	Bb	7.45N	134.38 E
Ngarekeukl	64a	Ac	7.00N	134.14 E
Ngariungs	64a	Ba	8.03N	134.43 E
Ngaruangl	64a	Ba	8.10N	134.39 E
Ngaruangl Passage	64a	Ba	8.07N	134.40 E
Ngaruawahia	62	Fb	37.40S	175.09 E
Ngaruroro	62	Gc	39.34S	176.55 E
Ngatangiia	64p	Cb	21.14S	159.43W
Ngatangiia Harbour	64p	Cb	21.14S	159.43W
Ngateguil, Point-	64a	Bc	7.26N	134.37 E
Ngatik Atoll	57	Gd	5.51N	157.16 E
Ngatpang	64a	Bc	7.28N	134.32 E
Ngau Island	63d	Bc	18.02S	179.18 E
Ngauruhoe	62	Fc	39.09S	175.38 E
Ngawa/Aba	27	He	32.55N	101.45 E
Ngayu	36	Eb	1.35N	27.13 E
Ngemelis Islands	64a	Ac	7.07N	134.15 E
Ngeregong	64a	Ac	7.07N	134.22 E
Ngergoi	64a	Ac	7.05N	134.17 E
Ngesebus	64a	Ac	7.03N	134.16 E
Nggamea	63d	Cb	16.46S	179.46W
Nggatokae	63a	Dc	8.46S	158.11 E
Nggela Pile	63a	Ec	9.08S	160.20 E
Nggela Sule	63a	Ec	9.03S	160.12 E
Nggelelevu	63d	Cb	16.05S	179.09W
Ngidinga	36	Cd	5.37S	15.17 E
Ngiro, Ewaso-	36	Gb	0.28N	39.55 E
Ngo	36	Cc	2.29S	15.45 E
Ngoangoa	35	Dd	5.58N	25.10 E
Ngobasangel	64a	Ac	7.16N	134.20 E
Ngoko	36	Cb	1.40N	16.03 E
Ngola Shankou	27	Gd	35.30N	99.36 E
Ngoma	36	Ef	15.58S	25.56 E
Ngoring Hu	27	Gd	35.00N	97.30 E
Ngorongoro Crater	30	Ki	3.10S	35.35 E
Ngoui	34	Cb	16.09N	13.55W
Ngouna	63b	Dc	17.26S	168.21 E
Ngounié [3]	36	Bc	2.00S	11.00 E
Ngounié	36	Bc	0.37S	10.18 E
Ngoura	35	Bc	12.52N	16.27 E
Ngouri	35	Bc	13.38N	15.22 E
Ngourti	34	Hb	15.19N	13.12 E
Ngousouboot, Pointe-	63b	Ca	13.58S	167.27 E
Ngudu	36	Fc	2.58S	33.20 E
Nguigmi	31	Ig	14.15N	13.07 E
Ngulu Atoll	57	Ed	8.18N	137.29 E
Nguni	36	Gc	0.50S	38.20 E
Nguru	31	Ig	12.53N	10.28 E
Ngwaketse	37	Cd	24.50S	24.00 E
Nhachengue	37	Fd	22.51S	35.11 E
Nhamundá	54	Gd	2.14S	56.43W
Nhamundá, Rio-	54	Gd	2.12S	56.41W
Nhandeara	55	Ge	20.40S	50.02W
Nhandutiba	55	Jb	14.37S	44.12W
Nharea	36	Ce	11.28S	16.53 E
Nha Trang	22	Mh	12.15N	109.11 E
Nhecolândia	55	Dd	19.16S	57.04W
Nhia	36	Be	10.15S	14.12 E
Nhulunbuy	58	Ef	12.00S	35.58 E
Niafounké	34	Eb	15.56N	4.00W
Niagara Escarpment	44	Gc	44.30N	80.35W
Niagara Falls	38	Le	43.05N	79.04W
Niagara Falls [N.Y.-U.S.]	43	Lc	43.06N	79.02W
Niagara Falls [Ont.-Can.]	42	Jh	43.06N	79.04W
Niagara River	44	Hd	43.15N	79.04W
Niagassola	34	Dc	12.19N	9.07W
Niah	26	Ff	3.52N	113.44 E
Niakaramandougou	34	Dd	8.40N	5.17W
Niamey	31	Hg	13.31N	2.07 E
Niamey [2]	34	Fc	14.00N	2.00 E
Niandan	34	Dc	10.35N	9.45W
Niangara	31	Jh	3.42N	27.52 E
Niangay, Lac-	34	Eb	15.50N	3.00W
Niangoloko	34	Ec	10.17N	4.55W
Nia-Nia	36	Eb	1.24N	27.36 E
Nianzishan	27	Lb	47.31N	122.50 E
Niao Dao	27	Gd	37.20N	99.50 E
Niaoshu Shan	27	He	34.54N	104.04 E
Niari [3]	36	Bc	4.30S	13.00 E
Niari	36	Bc	3.56S	12.12 E
Nias, Palau-	21	Li	1.05N	97.35 E
Niassa [3]	37	Fb	13.00S	36.00 E
Niassa, Lago-=Nyasa, Lake- (EN)	30	Kj	12.00S	34.30 E
Niau, Ile-	57	Mf	16.09S	146.21W
Nibāk	24	Nj	24.24N	50.50 E
Nibe	8	Ch	56.59N	9.38 E
Nica	17	Lh	57.29N	64.33 E
Nīca/Nica	8	Ih	56.25N	20.56 E
Nica/Nīca	8	Ih	56.25N	20.56 E
Nicanor Olivera	55	Cn	38.17S	59.12W
Nicaragua [1]	39	Kh	13.00N	85.00W
Nicaragua, Lago de-= Nicaragua, Lake- (EN)	38	Kh	11.35N	85.25W
Nicaragua, Lake- (EN)= Nicaragua, Lago de-	38	Kh	11.35N	85.25W
Nicastro	14	Kl	38.59N	16.19 E
Nice	6	Gg	43.42N	7.15 E
Niceville	44	Dj	30.31N	86.29W
Nichicum, Lac-	42	Kf	53.08N	70.55W
Nichinan [Jap.]	29	Cd	35.10N	133.16 E
Nichinan [Jap.]	28	Ki	31.36N	131.23 E
Nicholas Channel	49	Gb	23.25N	80.05W
Nicholas Channel (EN)= Nicolás, Canal-	47	Hd	23.25N	80.05W
Nicholasville	44	Eg	37.53N	84.34W
Nicholls Town	49	Ia	25.08N	78.00W
Nicholson Range	59	De	27.15S	116.45 E
Nicholson River	57	Ef	17.31S	139.36 E
Nickerson Ice Shelf	66	Mf	75.45S	145.00W
Nickol Bay	59	Dd	20.40S	116.50 E
Nicobar Islands	21	Li	8.00N	93.30 E
Nicoclí	49	Ii	8.26N	76.48W
Nicolajevka	15	Nb	47.33N	30.41 E
Nicola River	46	Ea	50.25N	121.18W
Nicolás, Canal-=Nicholas Channel (EN)	47	Hd	23.25N	80.05W
Nicolet	44	Kb	46.14N	72.37W
Nicopolis (EN) = Nikópolis	15	Dj	39.00N	20.45 E
Nicosia	14	Im	37.45N	14.24 E
Nicosia (EN)=Lefkosa/ Levkōsia	22	Ff	35.10N	33.22 E
Nicosia (EN)=Levkōsia/ Lefkosa	22	Ff	35.10N	33.22 E
Nicotera	14	Jl	38.33N	15.56 E
Nicoya	47	Gf	10.09N	85.27W
Nicoya, Golfo de-	47	Hg	9.47N	84.48W
Nicoya, Peninsula de-= Nicoya Peninsula (EN)	38	Ki	10.00N	85.25W
Nicoya Peninsula (EN)= Nicoya, Peninsula de-	38	Ki	10.00N	85.25W
Nicuadala	37	Fc	17.37S	36.50 E
Niculiţel	15	Ld	45.11N	28.29 E
Nida	10	Qf	50.18N	20.52 E
Nidda	12	Ld	50.25N	9.00 E
Nidda	10	Ef	50.06N	8.34 E
Nidder	12	Kd	50.12N	8.47 E
Nideggen	12	Id	50.42N	6.29 E
Nidelva [Nor.]	8	Cf	58.24N	8.48 E
Nidelva [Nor.]	8	Da	63.26N	10.25 E
Nido, Sierra del-	48	Fc	29.30N	106.45W
Nidže	15	Ei	41.00N	21.50 E
Nidzica	10	Qf	50.12N	20.40 E
Nidzica	10	Qc	53.22N	20.26 E
Nidzkie, Jezioro-	10	Rc	53.37N	21.30 E
Niebüll	10	Eb	54.48N	8.50 E
Nied	12	Ie	49.23N	6.40 E
Nieddu	14	Dj	40.44N	9.34 E
Niederbayern	10	Ih	48.35N	12.30 E
Niederbronn-les-Bains	11	Nf	48.58N	7.38 E
Niedere Tauern	14	Hc	47.20N	14.00 E
Niederlausitz	10	Ke	51.40N	14.15 E
Nieder-Olm	12	Ke	49.54N	8.13 E
Niederösterreich = Lower Austria (EN) [2]	14	Jb	48.30N	15.45 E
Niedersachsen=Lower Saxony (EN) [2]	10	Fd	52.00N	10.00 E
Niederwald	10	Df	50.10N	8.00 E
Niederzier	12	Id	50.53N	6.28 E
Niefang	34	He	1.50N	10.14 E
Niegocin, Jezioro-	10	Rb	54.00N	21.50 E
Niel	12	Gc	51.07N	4.20 E
Nielfa, Puerto de-	13	Hf	38.32N	4.23W
Niéllé	34	Dc	10.12N	5.38W
Niellim	35	Bd	9.42N	17.49 E
Niemba	36	Ed	5.57S	28.26 E
Niemba	36	Ed	5.57S	28.26 E
Niemodlin	10	Nf	50.39N	17.37 E
Niéna	34	Dc	11.25N	6.20W
Nienburg (Weser)	10	Fd	52.38N	9.13 E
Niepołomice	10	Qf	50.03N	20.13 E
Niermalak, Pointe-	63b	Cb	14.21S	167.24 E
Niers	10	Be	51.43N	5.57 E
Nierstein	12	Ke	49.53N	8.20 E
Niesky/Niska	10	Ke	51.18N	14.49 E
Nieszawa	10	Od	52.50N	18.55 E
Nieuport/Nieuwpoort	11	Ic	51.08N	2.45 E
Nieuw Amsterdam	54	Gb	5.53N	55.05W
Nieuwe-Pekela	12	Ia	53.04N	6.59 E
Nieuweschans	12	Ja	53.11N	7.15 E
Nieuw Milligen, Apeldoorn-	12	Hb	52.14N	5.45 E
Nieuw Nickerie	53	Ke	5.57N	56.59W
Nieuwolda	12	Ia	53.14N	6.59 E
Nieuwoudtville	37	Bf	31.22S	19.06 E
Nieuwpoort/Nieuport	11	Ic	51.08N	2.45 E
Nieuw Weerdinge, Emmen-	12	Jb	52.52N	7.01 E
Nieves	48	He	24.00N	103.01W
Nièvre [3]	11	Jg	47.05N	3.30 E
Nièvre	11	Jh	46.59N	3.10 E
Nigata	28	Lg	34.13N	132.29 E
Niğde	23	Db	37.59N	34.42 E
Nigenān	24	Qe	34.13N	57.19 E
Niger [1]	31	Hg	16.00N	8.00 E
Niger	30	Hh	5.33N	6.33 E
Niger [2]	34	Gd	9.40N	6.00 E
Niger Basin (EN)	30	Gg	15.00N	2.00 E
Niger Delta	30	Hh	4.50N	6.00 E
Nigeria [1]	31	Hh	10.00N	8.00 E
Night Hawk Lake	44	Ga	48.28N	81.00W
Nightingale Island	30	Fi	37.24S	12.28W
Nigrita	15	Gi	40.54N	23.30 E
Nihiru Atoll	57	Mf	16.42S	142.50W
Nihoa Island	57	Kb	23.06N	161.58W
Nihonmatsu	28	Pf	37.35N	140.26 E
Nihuil, Embalse del-	56	Ge	35.05S	68.45W
Niigata	22	Pf	37.55N	139.03 E
Niigata Ken [2]	28	Of	37.30N	138.50 E
Niihama	28	Lh	33.58N	133.16 E
Niihau Island	57	Kb	21.55N	160.10W
Nii-Jima	27	Oe	34.20N	139.15 E
Niikappu-Gawa	29a	Cb	42.22N	142.16 E
Niimi	28	Lg	34.59N	133.28 E
Niisato	29	Gb	39.36N	141.49 E
Niitsu	28	Of	37.48N	139.07 E
Nijar	13	Jh	36.58N	2.12W
Nijkerk	12	Hb	52.14N	5.29 E
Nijlen	12	Gc	51.10N	4.39 E
Nijmegen	11	Lc	51.50N	5.50 E
Nijvel/Nivelles	11	Kd	50.36N	4.20 E
Nijverdal, Hellendoorn-	12	Ib	52.22N	6.27 E
Nikel	19	Db	69.24N	30.13 E
Níki	15	Ei	40.55N	21.25 E
Nikitin Seamount (EN)	21	Kj	3.00S	83.00 E
Nikki	34	Fd	9.56N	3.12 E
Nikkō	29	Fc	36.44N	139.35 E
Nikolajev [Ukr.-U.S.S.R.]	16	Ce	49.32N	23.58 E
Nikolajev [Ukr.-U.S.S.R.]	6	Jf	46.58N	32.00 E
Nikolajevka	18	Kc	43.37N	77.01 E
Nikolajevo	8	Mf	58.14N	29.32 E
Nikolajevsk	19	Ee	50.02N	45.31 E
Nikolajevskaja Oblast [3]	19	Df	47.20N	32.00 E
Nikolajevski	20	Hf	54.50N	129.25 E
Nikolajevsk-na-Amure	22	Qd	53.08N	140.44 E
Nikolsk [R.S.F.S.R.]	19	Ee	53.42N	46.03 E
Nikolsk [R.S.F.S.R.]	19	Ed	59.33N	45.31 E
Nikolski [Ak.-U.S.]	40a	Eb	53.15N	168.22W
Nikolski [Kaz.-U.S.S.R.]	19	Gf	47.55N	67.33 E
Nikonga	36	Fc	4.40S	31.28 E
Nikopol [Bul.]	15	Hf	43.42N	24.54 E
Nikopol [Ukr.-U.S.S.R.]	19	Df	47.35N	34.25 E
Nikópolis = Nicopolis (EN)	15	Dj	39.00N	20.45 E
Nīkpey	24	Md	36.50N	48.10 E
Niksar	24	Gb	40.36N	36.58 E
Nikšić	15	Bg	42.46N	18.58 E
Nikumaroro Atoll (Gardner)	57	Je	4.40S	174.32W
Nikunau Island	57	Ie	1.23S	176.26 E
Nīl, Kūh-e-	24	Ng	30.52N	50.49 E
Nīl, Nahr an-=Nile (EN)	30	Ke	30.10N	31.06 E
Nila, Pulau-	26	Ih	6.44S	129.31 E
Nilakka	7	Ge	63.07N	26.33 E
Niland	46	Hj	33.14N	115.31W
Nilandu Atoll	25a	Bb	3.00N	72.55 E
Nile [3]	36	Fb	3.00N	31.30 E
Nile (EN)=Nīl, Nahr an-	30	Ke	30.10N	31.06 E
Nile Delta (EN)	30	Ke	31.20N	31.00 E
Nīleh, Kūh-e-	24	Nf	32.59N	50.32 E
Niles	44	De	41.50N	86.15W
Nilka	27	Dc	43.47N	82.20 E
Nīl Kowtal	23	Kc	34.48N	67.22 E
Nilsiä	7	Ge	63.12N	28.05 E
Nilüfer	15	Li	40.18N	28.27 E
Nimba [3]	34	Dd	6.45N	8.45W
Nimba, Monts-=Nimba Mountains (EN)	30	Gh	7.35N	8.28W
Nimba Mountains (EN)= Nimba, Monts-	30	Gh	7.35N	8.28W
Nîmes	6	Gg	43.50N	4.21 E
Nimjad	32	Df	17.25N	15.41W
Nimmitabel	59	Jg	36.31S	149.16 E
Nimpkish River	46	Ba	50.32N	126.59W
Nimrode Glacier	66	Kg	82.27S	161.00 E
Nimrud	24	Jd	36.06N	43.20 E
Nīmrūz [3]	23	Jc	30.30N	62.00 E
Nims	12	Ie	49.51N	6.28 E
Nimule	31	Kh	3.36N	32.03 E
Nimún, Punta-	48	Ng	20.46N	90.25W
Nin	14	Jf	44.14N	15.11 E
Nina	37	Bd	22.57S	18.14 E
Nīnawā [3]	24	Je	35.45N	42.45 E
Nīnawā=Nineveh (EN)	23	Fb	36.22N	43.09 E
Nine Degree Channel	21	Ji	9.00N	73.00 E
Ninetyeast Ridge (EN)	3	Gj	10.00S	90.00 E
Ninety Mile Beach [Austl.]	59	Jg	38.15S	147.25 E
Ninety Mile Beach [N.Z.]	62	Ea	34.45S	173.00 E
Nineveh (EN)=Nīnawā	23	Fb	36.22N	43.09 E
Ning'an	27	Mc	44.22N	129.23 E
Ningbo	22	Og	29.55N	121.28 E
Ningcheng (Tianyi)	27	Kc	41.34N	119.25 E
Ningde	27	Kf	26.44N	119.29 E
Ningdu	27	Kf	26.31N	115.59 E
Ningguo	28	Ei	30.39N	119.00 E
Ninghai	28	Fj	29.19N	121.26 E
Ning-hsia-hui-tsu Tzu-chih-ch'ü → Ningxia Huizu Zizhiqu=Ningsia Hui (EN) [2]	27	Id	37.00N	106.00 E
Ningjin [China]	28	Df	37.39N	116.48 E
Ningjin [China]	28	Cf	37.37N	114.55 E
Ningjing Shan	27	Ge	31.45N	97.15 E
Ninglang	27	Hf	27.17N	100.52 E
Ningling	28	Cg	34.27N	115.18 E
Ningnan	27	Hf	27.05N	102.44 E
Ningqiang	27	Ie	32.48N	106.15 E
Ningsia Hui (EN)=Ning-hsia-hui-tsu Tzu-chih-ch'ü → Ningxia Huizu Zizhiqu [2]	27	Id	37.00N	106.00 E
Ningsia Hui (EN)=Ningxia Huizu Zizhiqu (Ning-hsia-hui-tsu Tzu-chih-ch'ü) [2]	27	Id	37.00N	106.00 E
Ningwu	27	Jd	38.59N	112.14 E
Ningxia Huizu Zizhiqu (Ning-hsia-hui-tsu Tzu-chih-ch'ü)=Ningsia Hui (EN) [2]	27	Id	37.00N	106.00 E
Ningxian	27	Id	35.27N	107.50 E
Ningxiang	28	Bj	28.16N	112.33 E
Ningyang	28	Dg	35.45N	116.48 E
Ningyō-Tōge	29	Cd	35.19N	133.56 E
Ninh Binh	25	Ld	20.15N	105.59 E
Ninh Hoa	25	Lf	12.29N	109.08 E
Ninigo Group	57	Fe	1.15S	144.15 E
Niniva	65b	Ba	19.46S	174.38W
Ninnis Glacier	66	Je	68.12S	147.12 E
Ninohe	27	Pc	40.16N	141.18 E
Ninove	12	Fd	50.50N	4.00 E
Nioaque	54	Gh	21.08S	55.48W
Niobrara	38	Je	42.45N	98.00W
Niobrara	45	He	42.25N	98.00W
Nioghalvfjerdsfjorden	41	Kc	79.30N	18.45W
Nioki	36	Cc	2.43S	17.41 E
Niono	34	Dc	14.15N	6.00W
Nioro du Rip	34	Bc	13.45N	15.48W
Nioro du Sahel	31	Gg	15.14N	9.37W
Niort	11	Fh	46.19N	0.28W
Nipawin	42	Hf	53.22N	104.00W
Nipe, Bahía de-	49	Jc	20.47N	75.42W
Nipesotsu-Yama	29a	Cb	43.27N	143.02 E
Nipigon	39	Ke	49.01N	88.16W
Nipigon, Lake-	38	Ke	49.50N	88.30W
Nipigon Bay	45	Mb	48.53N	87.50W
Nipissing, Lake-	38	Le	46.17N	80.00W
Nippon=Japan (EN) [1]	22	Pf	38.00N	137.00 E
Nippon-Kai=Japan, Sea of- (EN)	21	Pf	40.00N	134.00 E
Nippur	24	Kf	32.10N	45.10 E
Niquelândia	54	If	14.27S	48.27W
Niquero	49	Ic	20.03N	77.35W
Niquitao, Teta de-	49	Li	9.07N	70.30W
Niquivil	56	Gd	30.25S	68.42W
Nīr	24	Lc	38.02N	47.59 E
Nirasaki	29	Fd	35.43N	138.27 E
Nirji → Morin Dawa	27	Lb	48.30N	124.28 E
Nirmal	25	Fe	19.06N	78.21 E
Niš	6	Ig	43.19N	21.54 E
Nisa	13	Ee	39.31N	7.39W
Nīşāb	23	Gg	14.24N	46.38 E
Nisāh, Sha'īb-	24	Lj	24.11N	47.11 E
Nišava	15	Ef	43.22N	21.46 E
Niscemi	14	Im	37.09N	14.23 E
Nishibetsu-Gawa	29a	Db	43.23N	145.17 E
Nishikawa	29	Gb	38.26N	140.08 E
Nishiki	29	Bd	34.16N	131.57 E
Nishinomiya	29	Dd	34.43N	135.20 E
Nishino'omote	27	Ne	30.44N	131.00 E
Nishino-Shima	60	Cb	27.30N	140.53 E
Nishi-No-Shima	28	Lf	36.06N	133.00 E
Nishiokoppe	29a	Ca	44.20N	142.57 E
Nishi-Sonogi-Hantō	29	Ae	32.55N	129.45 E
Nishiwaki	29	Dd	34.59N	134.58 E
Nísiros	15	Km	36.35N	27.10 E
Niska/Niesky	10	Ke	51.18N	14.49 E
Niška Banja	15	Ff	43.18N	22.01 E
Nisko	10	Sf	50.31N	22.09 E
Nismes, Viroinval-	12	Gd	50.05N	4.33 E
Nísoi Aiyaíou [2]	15	Il	37.40N	25.40 E
Nisporeny	16	Ff	47.06N	28.10 E
Nissan	8	Eh	56.40N	12.51 E
Nissan	63a	Ba	4.30S	154.14 E
Nisser	8	Ce	59.10N	8.30 E
Nissum Bredning	8	Ch	56.40N	8.20 E
Nissum Fjord	8	Ch	56.20N	8.15 E
Nita	29	Cd	35.12N	133.00 E
Nitchequon	42	Kf	53.15N	70.44W
Niterói	53	Lh	22.53S	43.07W
Nith	9	Jf	55.00N	3.35W
Nitra	10	Oi	47.46N	18.10 E
Nitra	10	Oh	48.19N	18.05 E
Niuafo'ou Island	57	Jf	15.35S	175.38W
Niuatoputapu Island	57	Jf	15.57S	173.45W
Niue [5]	58	Kf	19.02S	169.55W
Niue Island	57	Kf	19.02S	169.55W
Niu'erhe	27	La	51.30N	121.40 E
Niufu	29a	Ca	44.35N	142.35 E
Niulakita Island	57	If	10.45S	179.30 E
Niutaca, Corrente-	55	De	20.42S	57.37W
Niutao Island	57	Ie	6.06S	177.16 E
Niutg, Gunung-	26	Ef	1.00N	109.55 E
Niutoushan	27	Ke	31.00N	119.35 E
Niuzhuang	28	Gd	40.57N	122.30 E
Nivala	7	Fe	63.58N	25.01 E
Nive	11	Ek	43.30N	1.29W
Nivelles/Nijvel	11	Kd	50.36N	4.20 E
Nivernais	11	Jg	47.00N	3.30 E
Nivernais, Canal du-	11	Jg	47.40N	3.40 E
Nivernais, Côtes du-	11	Jg	47.10N	3.30 E
Nivillers	12	Ee	49.28N	2.10 E
Nixon	45	Hl	29.16N	97.46W
Niya/Minfeng	27	Dd	37.04N	82.46 E
Nīyābād	24	Le	35.12N	46.20 E
Niyodo-Gawa	29	Ce	33.28N	133.29 E
Nīza	24	Ph	28.25N	55.55 E
Nizāmābad	25	Fe	18.40N	78.07 E
Nižankoviči	10	Sg	49.40N	22.48 E
Nizip	23	Eb	37.01N	37.46 E
Nízke Tatry = Low Tatra (EN)	10	Ph	48.54N	19.40 E
Nízký-Jeseník	10	Ng	49.50N	17.30 E
Nižná	10	Pg	49.19N	19.32 E
Nižneangarsk	22	Md	55.47N	109.33 E
Nižnegorski	16	Ig	45.27N	34.44 E
Nižnejansk	20	Ib	71.24N	136.00 E
Nižnekamsk	19	Fd	55.38N	51.49 E
Nižnekolymsk	20	Lc	68.38N	160.56 E
Nižnetroicki	17	Fi	54.20N	53.41 E
Nižneudinsk	20	Ef	54.54N	99.03 E
Nižnevartovsk	22	Jc	61.00N	77.00 E
Nižni Baskunčak	19	Ef	48.13N	46.50 E
Nižni Bestjah	20	Hd	61.48N	129.55 E
Nižni Casučej	20	Gf	50.27N	115.08 E
Nižnije Serogozy	16	If	46.49N	34.24 E
Nižni Kuranah	20	He	58.40N	125.48 E
Nižni Lomov	19	Ee	53.32N	43.41 E
Nižni Odes	17	Ge	63.40N	54.52 E

Index Symbols

- [1] Independent Nation
- [2] State, Region
- [3] District, County
- [4] Municipality
- [5] Colony, Dependency
- Continent
- Physical Region
- Historical or Cultural Region
- Mount, Mountain
- Volcano
- Hill
- Mountains, Mountain Range
- Hills, Escarpment
- Plateau, Upland
- Pass, Gap
- Plain, Lowland
- Delta
- Salt Flat
- Valley, Canyon
- Crater, Cave
- Karst Features
- Depression
- Polder
- Desert, Dunes
- Forest, Woods
- Heath, Steppe
- Oasis
- Cape, Point
- Coast, Beach
- Cliff
- Peninsula
- Isthmus
- Sandbank
- Island
- Atoll
- Rock, Reef
- Islands, Archipelago
- Rocks, Reefs
- Coral Reef
- Well, Spring
- Geyser
- River, Stream
- Waterfall Rapids
- River Mouth, Estuary
- Lake
- Salt Lake
- Intermittent Lake
- Reservoir
- Swamp, Pond
- Canal
- Glacier
- Ice Shelf, Pack Ice
- Ocean
- Sea
- Gulf, Bay
- Strait, Fjord
- Lagoon
- Bank
- Seamount
- Tablemount
- Ridge
- Shelf
- Basin
- Escarpment, Sea Scarp
- Fracture
- Trench, Abyss
- National Park, Reserve
- Point of Interest
- Recreation Site
- Cave, Cavern
- Historic Site
- Ruins
- Wall, Walls
- Church, Abbey
- Temple
- Scientific Station
- Airport
- Port
- Lighthouse
- Mine
- Tunnel
- Dam, Bridge

Nižni Oseredok, Ostrov- 16 Pg 45.45N 48.35 E
Nižni Tagil 6 Ld 57.55N 59.57 E
Nižni Trajanov Val = Lower Trajan's Wall (EN) 15 Ld 45.45N 28.30 E
Nižnjaja Omra 17 Ge 62.46N 55.46 E
Nižnjaja Peša 19 Eb 66.43N 47.36 E
Nižnjaja Pojma 20 Ee 56.08N 97.18 E
Nižnjaja Salda 17 Jg 58.05N 60.48 E
Nižnjaja Tavda 19 Gd 57.40N 66.12 E
Nižnjaja Tojma 7 Ke 62.22N 44.15 E
Nižnjaja Tunguska = Lower Tunguska (EN) 21 Kc 65.48N 88.04 E
Nižnjaja Tura 17 Ig 58.37N 59.49 E
Nižnjaja Zolotica 7 Jd 65.41N 40.13 E
Nižny Pjandž 18 Gf 37.14N 68.35 E
Nizza Monferrato 14 Cf 44.46N 8.21 E
Njajs 17 Je 62.25N 60.47 E
Njamunas 5 Id 55.18N 21.23 E
Njandoma 19 Ec 61.43N 40.12 E
Njaris/Neris 8 Kj 54.55N 25.45 E
Njazepetrovsk 17 Ih 56.03N 59.38 E
Njazidja 30 Lj 11.35S 43.20 E
Njegoš 15 Bg 42.53N 18.45 E
Njinjo 36 Gd 8.48S 38.54 E
Njombe 30 Ki 6.56S 35.06 E
Njombe 31 Ki 9.20S 34.46 E
Njudung 8 Fg 57.25N 14.50 E
Njuja 20 Gd 60.32N 116.25 E
Njuk, Ozero- 7 Hd 64.25N 31.45 E
Njuksenica 7 Kf 60.28N 44.15 E
Njukža 20 He 56.30N 121.40 E
Njunes 7 Eb 68.45N 19.30 E
Njurba 22 Nc 63.17N 118.20 E
Njurundabommen 7 De 62.16N 17.22 E
Njutånger 8 Gc 61.37N 17.03 E
Njuvčim 17 Ef 61.22N 50.42 E
Nkambe 34 Hd 6.38N 10.40 E
Nkawkaw 34 Ed 6.33N 0.46W
Nkayi [Con.] 31 Ii 4.05S 13.18 E
Nkayi [Zimb.] 37 Dc 19.00S 28.54 E
Nkhata Bay 36 Fe 11.36S 34.18 E
Nkongsamba 31 Hh 4.57N 9.56 E
Nkota Kota 31 Kj 12.55S 34.18 E
Nkululu 36 Fd 6.26S 32.49 E
Nkusi 36 Fb 1.07N 30.40 E
Nkwalini 37 Ee 28.45S 31.30 E
'Nmai 25 Jc 25.42N 97.30 E
Nmaki 24 Pg 31.16N 55.29 E
Nnewi 34 Gd 6.01N 6.55 E
Nō 29 Ec 37.05N 137.59 E
Noailles 12 Ee 49.20N 2.12 E
Noākhāli 25 Id 22.49N 91.06 E
Noatak 40 Gc 67.34N 162.59W
Nobel 44 Gc 45.25N 80.06W
Nobeoka 27 Ne 32.35N 131.40 E
Noblesville 44 Ee 40.03N 86.00W
Noboribetsu 28 Pc 42.25N 141.11 E
Noce 14 Fd 46.09N 11.04 E
Nocra 35 Fc 15.40N 39.55 E
Nodaway River 45 Ig 39.54N 94.58W
Noēn 27 Hc 43.15N 102.20 E
Noeuf, Ile des- 37b Bb 6.14S 53.03 E
Noeux-les-Mines 12 Ed 50.29N 2.40 E
Nogajskaja Step 16 Ng 44.15N 46.00 E
Nogales [Az.-U.S.] 43 Ee 31.21N 110.55W
Nogales [Mex.] 39 Hf 31.20N 110.56W
Nogaro 11 Fk 43.46N 0.02W
Nogat 10 Pb 54.11N 19.15 E
Nōgata 29 Be 33.44N 130.44 E
Nogent-le-Rotrou 11 Gf 48.19N 0.50 E
Nogent-sur-Marne 12 Ef 48.50N 2.29 E
Nogent-sur-Oise 12 Ee 49.16N 2.28 E
Nogent-sur-Seine 11 Jf 48.29N 3.30 E
Noginsk [R.S.F.S.R.] 20 Ed 64.25N 91.10 E
Noginsk [R.S.F.S.R.] 19 Dd 55.54N 38.28 E
Nogliki 20 Jf 51.45N 143.15 E
Nōgō-Hakusan 29 Ed 35.46N 136.31 E
Nogoyá 56 Id 32.24S 59.48W
Nogoya, Arroyo- 55 Ck 32.55S 59.59W
Nógrád 10 Ph 48.00N 19.35 E
Nogueira, Serra da- 13 Fc 41.42N 6.52W
Noguera Pallaresa 13 Mb 42.15N 0.54 E
Noguera Ribagorçana/ Noguera Ribagorzana 13 Mc 41.40N 0.43 E
Noguera Ribagorzana/ Noguera Ribagorçana 13 Mc 41.40N 0.43 E
Noh, Laguna- 48 Nh 18.40N 90.20W
Nohain 11 Ig 47.24N 2.55 E
Noheji 28 Pd 40.52N 141.08 E
Nohfelden 12 Je 49.35N 7.09 E
Noidore, Rio- 55 Fb 14.50S 52.34W
Noir, Causse- 11 Jj 44.09N 3.15 E
Noire, Montagne- 11 Ik 43.28N 2.18 E
Noires, Montagnes- 11 Cf 48.09N 3.40W
Noirétable 11 Ji 45.49N 3.46 E
Noirmoutier, Ile de- 11 Dh 46.58N 2.12W
Noirmoutier-en-l'Ile 11 Dg 47.00N 2.15W
Nojima-Zaki 29 Fd 34.54N 139.50 E
Nojiri-Ko 29 Fc 36.49N 138.13 E
Noka 63c Bb 10.40S 166.03 E
Nokaneng 37 Cc 19.40S 22.12 E
Nokia 7 Ff 61.28N 23.30 E
Nok Kundi 25 Cc 28.48N 62.46 E
Nokomis 46 Ma 51.30N 105.00W
Nokou 35 Ac 14.35N 14.47 E
Nokra 35 Fb 15.42N 39.56 E
Nol 8 Eg 57.55N 12.03 E
Nola [C.A.R.] 35 Be 3.32N 16.04 E
Nola [It.] 14 Ij 40.55N 14.33 E
Nolin Lake 44 Dg 37.20N 86.10W
Nolinsk 19 Ed 57.33N 50.00 E
Nomad 58 Fe 6.21S 142.12 E
Noma Omuramba 37 Cc 19.10S 22.16 E
Noma-Zaki 29 Bf 31.25N 130.06 E
Nombre de Dios 48 Gf 23.51N 104.14W
Nome 39 Cc 64.30N 165.24W
Nomeny 12 If 48.54N 6.14 E
Nomo-Saki 29 Ae 32.35N 129.45 E
Nomozaki 29 Ae 32.35N 129.45 E
Nomuka 65b Bb 20.15S 174.48W
Nomuka Group 57 Jg 20.20S 174.45W
Nomuka Iki 65b Bb 20.17S 174.49W
Nomwin Atoll 57 Gd 8.32N 151.47 E
Nonacho Lake 42 Gd 62.40N 109.30W
Nonancourt 12 Df 48.46N 1.12 E
Nonette 12 Ee 49.12N 2.24 E
Nong'an 27 Mc 44.24N 125.08 E
Nong Han 25 Ke 17.21N 103.06 E
Nong Khai 22 Mh 17.52N 102.45 E
Nongoma 37 Ee 27.53S 31.38 E
Nonoava 48 Fd 27.28N 106.44W
Nonouti Atoll 57 Ie 0.40S 174.21 E
Nonsan 28 If 36.12N 127.05 E
Nonsuch Bay 51d Bb 17.03N 61.42W
Nontron 11 Gi 45.32N 0.40 E
Noord-Beveland 12 Fc 51.35N 3.45 E
Noord-Brabant 12 Gc 51.30N 5.00 E
Noord-Holland 12 Gb 52.40N 4.50 E
Noordhollandskanaal 11 Kb 52.55N 4.50 E
Noordoewer 37 Be 28.45S 17.37 E
Noordoostpolder 11 Lb 52.42N 5.45 E
Noordoostpolder 12 Hb 52.42N 5.44 E
Noordoostpolder-Emmeloord 12 Hb 52.42N 5.44 E
Noordwijk aan Zee 11 Kb 52.14N 4.26 E
Noordwijk aan Zee, Noordwijk- 12 Gb 52.14N 4.26 E
Noordwijk-Noordwijk aan Zee 12 Gb 52.14N 4.26 E
Noordzee = North Sea (EN) 5 Gd 55.20N 3.00 E
Noordzeekanaal 11 Kb 52.30N 4.35 E
Noormarkku/Norrmark 8 Ic 61.35N 21.52 E
Noorvik 40 Gc 66.50N 161.12W
Nootka Island 46 Bb 49.32N 126.42W
Nootka Sound 46 Bb 49.33N 126.38W
Nóqui 36 Bd 5.50S 13.27 E
Nora [It.] 14 Dk 39.00N 9.02 E
Nora [Swe.] 7 Dg 59.31N 15.02 E
Noraskog 8 Fe 59.40N 14.50 E
Norberg 8 Fd 60.04N 15.56 E
Norcia 14 Hh 42.48N 13.05 E
Nord 41 Kb 81.45N 17.30W
Nord [Cam.] 34 Hd 9.00N 13.50 E
Nord [Fr.] 11 Jd 50.20N 3.40 E
Nord [U.V.] 34 Ec 13.40N 2.50W
Nord, Canal du- 11 Id 49.57N 2.55 E
Nord, Mer du- = North Sea (EN) 5 Gd 55.20N 3.00 E
Nordausques 12 Ed 50.49N 2.05 E
Nordaustlandet 67 Jd 79.48N 22.24 E
Nordborg 8 Ci 55.03N 9.45 E
Nordby 8 Ci 55.27N 8.25 E
Norddeutsches Tiefland = North German Plain (EN) 5 He 53.00N 11.00 E
Norden 10 Dc 53.36N 7.12 E
Nordenham 10 Ec 53.39N 8.29 E
Nordenskjölda, Ostrova- = Nordenskjöld, Archipelago (EN) 20 Ea 76.50N 96.00 E
Nordenskjöld Archipelago (EN) = Nordenskjölda, Ostrova- 20 Ea 76.50N 96.00 E
Norderney 10 Dc 53.42N 7.10 E
Norderstedt 10 Fc 53.41N 9.58 E
Nordfjord 8 Bc 61.50N 6.15 E
Nordfjord 7 Af 61.55N 5.10 E
Nordfjordeid 7 Af 61.54N 6.00 E
Nordfold 7 Dc 67.46N 15.12 E
Nordfriesische Inseln = North Frisian Islands (EN) 10 Ea 54.50N 8.30 E
Nordfriesland 10 Eb 54.40N 8.55 E
Nordgau 10 Hg 49.15N 11.50 E
Nordgrønland = North Greenland (EN) 41 Gc 79.30N 50.00W
Nordhausen 10 Ge 51.31N 10.48 E
Nordhordland 8 Ad 60.50N 5.50 E
Nordhorn 10 Dd 52.26N 7.05 E
Nord-Jylland 8 Cg 57.15N 10.00 E
Nordkapp [Nor.] = North Cape (EN) 5 Ia 71.11N 25.48 E
Nordkapp [Sval.] 41 Nb 80.31N 20.00 E
Nordkinn 5 Ia 71.08N 27.39 E
Nordkinnhalvøya 7 Ga 70.55N 27.45 E
Nord-Kvaløy 7 Ea 70.10N 19.11 E
Nordland 7 Cc 67.06N 13.20 E
Nördlingen 10 Gh 48.51N 10.30 E
Nordloher Tief 12 Ja 53.10N 7.45 E
Nordmark 8 Fe 59.50N 14.06 E
Nordmøre 8 Ca 63.00N 8.30 E
Nordostrundingen 67 Le 81.30N 11.00W
Nord-Ostsee Kanal = Kiel Canal (EN) 5 Ge 53.53N 9.08 E
Nord-Ouest 34 Hd 6.30N 10.30 E
Nordøyane 8 Bb 62.40N 6.15 E
Nordreisa 7 Eb 69.46N 21.03 E
Nordre Rønner 8 Dg 57.22N 10.56 E
Nordrhein-Westfalen = North Rhine-Westphalia (EN) 10 De 51.30N 7.30 E
Nordsee = North Sea (EN) 5 Gd 55.20N 3.00 E
Nordsjøen = North Sea (EN) 5 Gd 55.20N 3.00 E
Nordskjobotn 7 Eb 69.13N 19.34 E
Nordsøen = North Sea (EN) 5 Gd 55.20N 3.00 E
Nord Strand 10 Eb 54.30N 8.55 E
Nordtiroler Kalkalpen 14 Fc 47.30N 11.30 E
Nord-Trøndelag 7 Cd 64.25N 12.00 E
Nordwestfjord 41 Jd 71.30N 26.30W
Nore/An Fheoir 9 Gi 52.25N 6.58W
Norefjell 8 Cd 60.16N 9.29 E
Norefjorden 8 Cd 60.10N 9.00 E
Norfolk 9 Oi 52.40N 1.05 E
Norfolk 9 Mi 52.45N 0.40W
Norfolk [Nb.-U.S.] 43 Hc 42.02N 97.25W
Norfolk [Va.-U.S.] 39 Lf 38.40N 76.14W
Norfolk Island 58 Hg 29.05S 167.59 E
Norfolk Island 57 Hg 29.05S 167.59 E
Norfolk Ridge (EN) 57 Hg 29.00S 168.00 E
Norfork Lake 45 Jh 36.25N 92.10W
Norg 12 Ia 53.04N 6.32 E
Norge = Norway (EN) 6 Gc 62.00N 10.00 E
Norheimsund 7 Bf 60.22N 6.08 E
Norikura-Dake 29 Ec 36.06N 137.33 E
Norilsk 22 Kc 69.20N 88.06 E
Normal 45 Lf 40.31N 88.59W
Norman 43 Hd 35.15N 97.26W
Norman, Lake- 44 Gh 35.35N 81.00W
Normanby Island 60 Ej 10.00S 151.00 E
Normanby River 59 Ib 14.25S 144.08 E
Normand, Bocage- 11 Ef 49.00N 1.10W
Normandie = Normandy (EN) 11 Gf 49.00N 0.10 E
Normandie = Normandy (EN) 5 Gf 49.00N 0.10 E
Normandie, Collines de- = Normandy Hills (EN) 5 Ff 48.50N 0.40W
Normandin 44 Ka 48.52N 72.30W
Normandy (EN) = Normandie 11 Gf 49.00N 0.10 E
Normandy (EN) = Normandie 5 Gf 49.00N 0.10 E
Normandy Hills (EN) = Normandie, Collines de- 5 Ff 48.50N 0.40W
Norman Island 51a Db 18.20N 64.37W
Norman River 59 Ic 17.28S 140.39 E
Normanton 58 Ff 17.40S 141.05 E
Norman Wells 39 Gc 65.17N 126.51W
Norquinco 56 Ff 41.51S 70.54W
Norra Dellen 8 Gc 61.55N 16.40 E
Norrahammar 8 Fg 57.42N 14.06 E
Norrala 8 Gc 61.22N 16.59 E
Norra Midsjöbanken 8 Gh 56.10N 17.30 E
Norra Ny 7 Cf 60.24N 13.15 E
Norra Storfjället 7 Dd 65.53N 15.14 E
Norrbotten 7 Ec 67.26N 19.35 E
Nørre Åby 8 Ci 55.27N 9.54 E
Nørre Alslev 8 Dj 54.54N 11.54 E
Nørre-Nebel 8 Ci 55.47N 8.18 E
Norrent-Fontes 12 Ed 50.35N 2.24 E
Nørresundby 7 Bh 57.04N 9.55 E
Norrhult 7 Dh 57.08N 15.10 E
Norris Lake 44 Fg 36.20N 83.55W
Norristown 44 Je 40.07N 75.20W
Norrköping 6 Hd 58.36N 16.11 E
Norrland 5 Hc 64.27N 17.20 E
Norrland 7 Dd 65.00N 18.00 E
Norrmark/Noormarkku 8 Ic 61.35N 21.52 E
Norrsundet 8 Gd 60.56N 17.08 E
Norrtälje 7 Eg 59.46N 18.42 E
Norseman 58 Dh 32.12S 121.46 E
Norsewood 62 Gd 40.04S 176.13 E
Norsjö 7 Ed 64.55N 19.29 E
Norsjø 8 Ce 59.20N 9.20 E
Norsk 20 Hf 52.20N 129.59 E
Norske Havet = Norwegian Sea (EN) 5 Gc 70.00N 2.00 E
Norske Øer 41 Kc 79.00N 18.00W
Norsoup 63b Cc 16.04S 167.23 E
Norte, Baía- 55 Hh 27.30S 48.35W
Norte, Cabo- [Braz.] 54 Ic 1.40N 50.00W
Norte, Cabo- [Pas.] 65d Ab 27.03S 109.24W
Norte, Canal do- 54 Hc 0.30N 50.30W
Norte, Punta- 56 Hf 42.04S 63.45W
Norte, Serra do- 54 Gf 11.00S 59.00W
Norte del Cabo San Antonio, Punta- 56 Ie 36.17S 56.47W
Norte de Santander 54 Db 8.00N 73.00W
Nortelândia 54 Gf 14.25S 56.48W
North, Cape - 42 Lg 47.02N 60.25W
North Adams 44 Kd 42.42N 73.02W
Northallerton 9 Lg 54.20N 1.26W
Northam [Austl.] 58 Ch 31.39S 116.40 E
Northam [S.Afr.] 37 Dd 24.58S 27.11 E
North America 38 Jf 40.00N 95.00W
North American Basin (EN) 3 Cf 30.00N 60.00W
Northampton 9 Mi 52.30N 1.00W
Northampton [Austl.] 59 Ce 28.21S 114.37 E
Northampton [Eng.-U.K.] 9 Mi 52.14N 0.54W
Northampton [Ma.-U.S.] 44 Kd 42.19N 72.38W
Northampton Seamounts (EN) 57 Jb 25.20N 172.04W
Northamptonshire 9 Mi 52.25N 0.55W
North Andaman 25 If 13.15N 92.55 E
North Arm 42 Gd 62.00N 114.30W
North Astrolabe Reef 63d Bc 18.39S 178.32 E
North Augusta 44 Gi 33.30N 81.58W
North Aulatsivik 42 Le 59.45N 64.04W
North Australian Basin (EN) 3 Hk 14.30S 116.30 E
North Battleford 39 Id 52.47N 108.17W
North Bay 39 Le 46.19N 79.28W
North Belcher Islands 42 Je 56.45N 79.45W
North Berwick 9 Ke 56.04N 2.44W
North Buganda 36 Fb 0.50N 32.10 E
North Caicos 49 Lc 21.56N 71.59W
North Canadian River 43 Hd 35.17N 95.31W
North Cape 57 Ih 34.25S 173.03 E
North Cape (EN) = Nordkapp [Nor.] 5 Ia 71.11N 25.48 E
North Caribou Lake 42 If 52.48N 90.45W
North Carolina 43 Ld 35.30N 80.00W
North Channel 42 Jg 46.02N 82.50W
North Channel/Sruth na Maoile 5 Fd 55.10N 5.40W
Northchapel 12 Bc 51.03N 0.38W
North Charleston 44 Hi 32.53N 80.00W
North Chicago 45 Me 42.20N 87.51W
North Cove 46 Cc 46.47N 124.06W
North Cyprus 22 Ff 35.15N 33.40 E
North Dakota 43 Gb 47.30N 100.15W
North Downs 9 Nj 51.20N 0.10 E
North East 44 Hd 42.13N 79.51W
North-East 37 Dd 21.00S 27.30 E
Northeast Cape 40 Fd 63.18N 168.42W
North-Eastern 36 Hb 1.00N 40.15 E
Northeast Islands 64d Ba 7.36N 151.57 E
Northeast Pacific Basin (EN) 3 Lg 20.00N 140.00W
Northeast Pass 64d Ba 7.30N 151.59 E
North East Point 64g Bb 1.57N 157.16W
Northeast Point [Bah.] 49 Kc 21.18N 72.54W
Northeast Point [Bah.] 49 Kb 22.43N 73.50W
Northeast Providence Channel 47 Ic 25.40N 77.09W
Northeim 10 Fe 51.42N 10.00 E
North Entrance 64a Bb 7.59N 134.37 E
Northern [Ghana] 34 Ed 9.30N 1.00W
Northern [Mwi.] 36 Fe 11.00S 34.00 E
Northern [S.L.] 34 Cd 9.15N 11.45W
Northern [Ug.] 36 Fb 2.45N 32.45 E
Northern [Zam.] 36 Fe 11.00S 31.00 E
Northern Cay 49 De 17.27N 87.28W
Northern Cook Islands 57 Kf 10.00S 161.00W
Northern Dvina (EN) = Severnaja Dvina 5 Kc 64.32N 40.30 E
Northern Guinea 30 Gh 8.30N 1.00W
Northern Indian Lake 42 He 57.20N 97.17W
Northern Ireland 9 Gg 54.40N 6.45W
Northern Mariana Islands 58 Fc 16.00N 145.30 E
Northern Sporades (EN) = Vórioi Sporádhes, Nisoi- 5 Ih 39.15N 23.55 E
Northern Territory 59 Gc 20.00S 134.00 E
Northern Urals (EN) = Severny Ural 5 Lc 62.00N 59.00 E
Northern Uvals (EN) = Severnyje Uvaly 5 Kd 59.30N 49.00 E
Northfield 45 Jd 44.27N 93.09W
North Fiji Basin (EN) 3 Jk 16.00S 174.00 E
North Foreland 9 Oj 51.23N 1.27 E
North Fork Grand River 45 Ed 45.47N 102.16W
North Fork John Day River 46 Fd 44.45N 119.38W
North Fork Moreau River 45 Ed 45.09N 102.50W
North Fork Pass 42 Dd 64.00N 138.00W
North Fork Powder River 46 Le 43.40N 106.30W
North Fork Red 45 Gi 34.25N 99.14W
North Fort Myers 44 Gl 26.40N 81.54W
North Frisian Islands (EN) = Nordfriesische Inseln 10 Ea 54.50N 8.30 E
North German Plain (EN) = Norddeutsches Tiefland 5 He 53.00N 11.00 E
North Greenland (EN) = Nordgrønland 41 Gc 79.30N 50.00W
North Highlands 46 Eg 38.40N 121.23W
North Horr 36 Gb 3.19N 37.04 E
North Island [N.Z.] 57 Ih 39.00S 176.00 E
North Island [Sey.] 37b Bc 10.07S 51.11 E
North Kent 42 Ia 76.40N 90.15W
North Korea (EN) = Chosŏn M.I.K. 22 Oe 40.00N 127.30 E
North Lakhimpur 25 Ic 27.14N 94.07 E
Northland 62 Ea 35.30S 173.40 E
North Las Vegas 46 Hh 36.12N 115.07W
North Lincoln Land 42 Ja 76.15N 80.00W
North Little Rock 43 Ie 34.46N 92.14W
North Loup River 45 Gf 41.17N 98.23W
North Magnetic Pole (1980) 67 Qd 77.03N 101.08W
North Malosmadulu Atoll 25a Ba 5.35N 72.55 E
North Mamm Peak 45 Cg 39.23N 107.52W
North Mayreau Channel 51n Bb 12.41N 61.20W
North Miami 44 Gm 25.56N 80.09W
North Minch 5 Fd 58.05N 5.55W
North Palisade 46 Fh 37.10N 118.38W
North Pass [F.S.M.] 64d Ba 7.41N 151.48 E
North Pass [U.S.] 45 Ll 29.10N 89.15W
North Platte 43 Gc 41.08N 100.46W
North Platte 38 Ie 41.15N 100.45W
North Point 64n Ab 10.22S 161.02W
North Point [Bar.] 51q Ab 13.20N 59.36W
North Pole 67 Ge 90.00N 0.00
Northport 44 Di 33.14N 87.35W
North Powder 46 Gd 45.03N 117.55W
North Raccoon River 45 Jf 41.35N 93.31W
North Reef 63a Ee 12.13S 160.04 E
North Rhine-Westphalia (EN) = Nordrhein-Westfalen 10 De 51.30N 7.30 E
North Rim 46 Ih 36.12N 112.03W
North River 42 Ie 58.53N 94.42W
North Rona 9 Hb 59.10N 5.40W
North Ronaldsay 9 Kb 59.25N 2.30W
North Saskatchewan 38 Id 53.15N 105.06W
North Sea 5 Gd 55.20N 3.00 E
North Sea (EN) = Noordzee 5 Gd 55.20N 3.00 E
North Sea (EN) = Nord, Mer du- 5 Gd 55.20N 3.00 E
North Sea (EN) = Nordsee 5 Gd 55.20N 3.00 E
North Sea (EN) = Nordsjøen 5 Gd 55.20N 3.00 E
North Sea (EN) = Nordsøen 5 Gd 55.20N 3.00 E
North Sentinel 25 If 11.33N 92.15 E
North Shoshone Peak 46 Gg 39.10N 117.29W
North Siberian Plain (EN) = Severo-Sibirskaja Niz. 21 Mb 72.00N 104.00 E
North Sound 51d Bb 17.07N 61.45W
North Sound 49 Gd 19.25N 81.26W
North Stradbroke Island 59 Ke 27.35S 153.30 E
North Taranaki Bight 62 Fc 38.50S 174.25 E
North Thompson 42 Ff 50.41N 120.11W
North Tokelau Trough (EN) 3 Kj 3.00S 165.00W
North Tonawanda 44 Hd 43.02N 78.54W
North Trap 62 Bg 47.20S 167.55 E
North Tyne 9 Kg 54.59N 2.08W
North Uist 9 Fd 57.37N 7.22W
Northumberland 9 Kf 55.15N 2.10W
Northumberland 9 Kf 55.15N 2.05W
Northumberland Islands 57 Gg 21.40S 150.00 E
Northumberland Strait 42 Lg 46.00N 63.30W
North Umpqua River 46 De 43.16N 123.27W
North Vancouver 46 Db 49.19N 123.04W
North Walsham 12 Db 52.49N 1.23 E
Northway 40 Kd 62.59N 141.43W
North West Bluff 51c Bc 16.49N 62.12W
North West Cape 57 Cg 21.45S 114.10 E
North-Western 36 Ee 13.00S 25.00 E
Northwest Frontier 25 Eb 33.00N 70.30 E
North West Highlands 5 Fd 57.30N 5.00W
Northwest Pacific Basin (EN) 3 Je 40.00N 155.00 E
North West Point 64g Ab 2.02N 157.30W
Northwest Providence Channel 44 Hl 26.10N 78.20W
Northwest Reef 64a Bb 7.59N 134.33 E
North West River 42 Lf 53.32N 60.09W
Northwest Territories 42 Hc 66.00N 102.00W
Northwich 9 Kh 53.16N 2.32W
North York Moors 9 Mg 54.25N 0.50W
North Yorkshire 9 Lg 54.15N 1.40W
Norton [Ks.-U.S.] 43 Gd 39.50N 100.01W
Norton [Va.-U.S.] 44 Fg 36.56N 82.37W
Norton [Zimb.] 37 Ec 17.53S 30.41 E
Norton Bay 40 Gd 64.45N 161.15W
Norton Sound 38 Cc 64.45N 161.15W
Norvegia, Kapp- 66 Bf 71.25S 12.18W
Norwalk [Ct.-U.S.] 44 Ke 41.07N 73.27W
Norwalk [Oh.-U.S.] 44 Fe 41.14N 82.37W
Norway 44 Dc 45.47N 87.55W
Norway (EN) = Norge 6 Gc 62.00N 10.00 E
Norway Bay 42 Hb 71.00N 104.35W
Norway House 42 Hf 53.58N 97.50W
Norwegian Basin (EN) 3 Dc 68.00N 2.00W
Norwegian Bay 42 Ij 77.45N 90.30W
Norwegian Sea (EN) = Norske Havet 5 Gc 70.00N 2.00 E
Norwegian Trench (EN) 5 Gd 59.00N 4.30 E
Norwich [Ct.-U.S.] 44 Ke 41.32N 72.05W
Norwich [Eng.-U.K.] 6 Ge 52.38N 1.18 E
Norwich [N.Y.-U.S.] 44 Jd 42.33N 75.33W
Norwich Airport 12 Db 52.40N 1.18 E
Norwood 44 Ef 39.10N 84.28W
Nosappu-Misaki 29a Db 43.23N 145.47 E
Noshappu-Misaki 29a Ba 45.27N 141.39 E
Noshiro 27 Pc 40.12N 140.02 E
Nosovaja 19 Fb 68.15N 54.31 E
Nosovka 19 De 50.54N 31.37 E
Nosratābād 23 Id 29.54N 59.59 E
Nossa Senhora das Candeias 54 Kf 12.40S 38.33W
Nossa Senhora do Livramento 55 Db 15.48S 56.22W
Noss Head 9 Jc 58.30N 3.05W
Nossob 30 Jk 26.55S 20.40 E
Nossop 37 Ce 26.55S 20.40 E
Nosy-Be 30 Lj 13.20S 48.15 E
Nosy-Be 31 Lj 13.22S 48.16 E
Nosy-Varika 37 Hd 20.35S 48.30 E
Nota 7 Hb 68.07N 30.10 E
Notch Peak 46 Ig 39.08N 113.24W
Noteć 10 Ld 52.44N 15.26 E
Notecka, Puszcza- 10 Ld 52.45N 16.00 E
Note Kemopla 63c b 10.55S 165.51 E
Notengo, Laguna de- 48 Ji 16.15N 98.10W
Notia Pindhos 15 Ej 39.30N 21.20 E
Nótioi Sporádhes = Dodecanese (EN) 5 Ih 36.00N 27.00 E
Nótios Evvoikós Kólpos 15 Gk 38.20N 23.50 E
Nötö 8 Ie 60.00N 21.45 E
Noto [It.] 14 Jn 36.53N 15.04 E
Noto [Jap.] 28 Nf 37.18N 137.09 E
Noto, Golfo di- 14 Jn 36.50N 15.10 E
Notodden 7 Bg 59.34N 9.17 E
Noto-Hantō 27 Od 37.20N 137.00 E
Noto-Jima 29 Ec 37.07N 137.00 E
Notoro-Ko 29a Da 44.05N 144.10 E
Notoro-Misaki 29a Da 44.07N 144.15 E
Notranjsko 14 Ie 45.46N 14.26 E
Notre-Dame, Monts- 38 Me 48.00N 69.00W
Notre Dame Bay 42 Mg 49.50N 55.00W
Notre-Dame-de-Courson 12 Cf 48.59N 0.16 E
Notre-Dame-de-Gravenchon 12 Ce 49.29N 0.35 E
Notre Dame-du-Lac 44 Mb 47.38N 68.49W
Notre-Dame-du-Nord 44 Hb 47.36N 79.29W
Notsé 34 Fd 6.59N 1.12 E
Notsuke-Zaki 29a Db 43.34N 145.19 E
Nottawasaga Bay 44 Gc 44.40N 80.30W
Nottaway 38 Ld 51.25N 79.50W
Notterøy 8 De 59.15N 10.25 E
Nottingham 6 Fe 52.58N 1.10W
Nottingham 42 Jd 63.20N 78.00W
Nottingham 9 Mh 53.05N 1.00W
Nottinghamshire 9 Mh 53.10N 0.55W
Nottoway River 44 Ig 36.33N 76.55W
Nottuln 12 Jc 51.56N 7.21 E
Notukeu Creek 46 Lb 49.55N 106.30W
Nouâdhibou 31 Ff 20.54N 17.01W
Nouâdhibou, Dahklet- 32 De 21.00N 16.50W
Nouâdhibou, Râs- = Blanc Cape- (EN) 30 Ff 20.46N 17.03W
Nouakchott 31 Fg 18.07N 15.59W
Nouakchott, District de- 32 Df 18.06N 15.57W
Nouamrhar 32 Df 19.22N 16.31W
Nouméa 58 Hg 22.16S 166.26 E
Nouna 34 Ec 12.44N 3.52W
Noupoort 37 Cf 31.10S 24.57 E

Index Symbols

1 Independent Nation
2 State, Region
3 District, County
4 Municipality
5 Colony, Dependency
Continent
Physical Region
Historical or Cultural Region
Mount, Mountain
Volcano
Hill
Mountains, Mountain Range
Hills, Escarpment
Plateau, Upland
Pass, Gap
Plain, Lowland
Delta
Salt Flat
Valley, Canyon
Crater, Cave
Karst Features
Depression
Polder
Desert, Dunes
Forest, Woods
Heath, Steppe
Oasis
Cape, Point
Coast, Beach
Cliff
Peninsula
Isthmus
Sandbank
Island
Atoll
Rock, Reef
Islands, Archipelago
Rocks, Reefs
Coral Reef
Well, Spring
Geyser
River, Stream
Waterfall Rapids
River Mouth, Estuary
Lake
Salt Lake
Intermittent Lake
Reservoir
Swamp, Pond
Canal
Glacier
Ice Shelf, Pack Ice
Ocean
Sea
Gulf, Bay
Strait, Fjord
Lagoon
Bank
Seamount
Tablemount
Ridge
Shelf
Basin
Escarpment, Sea Scarp
Fracture
Trench, Abyss
National Park, Reserve
Point of Interest
Recreation Site
Cave, Cavern
Historic Site
Ruins
Wall, Walls
Church, Abbey
Temple
Scientific Station
Airport
Port
Lighthouse
Mine
Tunnel
Dam, Bridge

Name	Map	Grid	Lat.	Long.
Nouveau-Comptoir	42	Jf	52.35N	78.40W
Nouveau-Québec, Cratère du- = New Quebec Crater (EN)	42	Kd	61.30N	73.55W
Nouvelle-Calédonie = New Caledonia (EN) [5]	58	Hg	21.30S	165.30 E
Nouvelle-Calédonie=New Caledonia (EN)	57	Hg	21.30S	165.30 E
Nouvelle-France, Cap de -	42	Kd	62.33N	73.35W
Nouvelles Hébrides/New Hebrides	57	Hf	16.01S	167.01 E
Nouvion	12	Dd	50.12N	1.47 E
Nouzonville	11	Ke	49.49N	4.45 E
Novabad	18	He	39.01N	70.09 E
Nová Baňa	10	Oh	48.26N	18.39 E
Nová Bystřice	10	Lg	49.02N	15.06 E
Nova Cruz	54	Ke	6.28S	35.26W
Nova Esperança	55	Ff	23.08S	52.13W
Nova Friburgo	54	Jh	22.16S	42.32W
Nova Gaia	36	Ce	10.05S	17.32 E
Nova Gorica	14	He	45.57N	13.39 E
Nova Gradiška	14	Le	45.16N	17.23 E
Nova Granada	55	He	20.29S	49.19W
Nova Iguaçu	53	Lh	22.45S	43.27W
Novaja Igirma	20	Fe	57.10N	103.55 E
Novaja-Ivanovka	15	Md	45.59N	29.04 E
Novaja Kahovka	16	Hf	46.43N	33.23 E
Novaja Kazanka	16	Pe	48.58N	49.37 E
Novaja Ladoga	7	Hf	60.05N	32.16 E
Novaja Ljalja	19	Gd	59.03N	60.36 E
Novaja Odessa	16	Gf	47.18N	31.47 E
Novaja Sibir, Ostrov-=New Siberia (EN)	21	Qb	75.00N	149.00 E
Novaja Vodolaga	16	Ie	49.45N	35.52 E
Novaja Zemlja=Novaya Zemlya (EN)	21	Hb	74.00N	57.00 E
Nova Lamego	34	Cc	12.17N	14.13W
Nova Lima	54	Jh	19.59S	43.51W
Nova Londrina	55	Ff	22.45S	53.00W
Nova Mambone	37	Fd	20.58S	35.00 E
Nova Olinda do Norte	54	Gd	3.45S	59.03W
Nová Paka	10	Lf	50.29N	15.31 E
Nova Prata	55	Gi	28.47S	51.36W
Novara	14	Ce	45.28N	8.38 E
Nova Roma	55	Ia	13.51S	46.57W
Nova Russas	54	Jd	4.42S	40.34W
Nova Scotia [3]	42	Lh	45.00N	63.00W
Nova Scotia	38	Me	45.00N	63.00W
Nova Sintra	32	Cf	14.54N	24.40W
Nova Sofala	37	Ed	20.10S	34.44 E
Novato	46	Dg	38.06N	122.34W
Nova Varoš	15	Cf	43.28N	19.49 E
Nova Venécia	54	Jg	18.43S	40.24W
Novaya Zemlya (EN)= Novaja Zemlja	21	Hb	74.00N	57.00 E
Nova Zagora	15	Jg	42.29N	26.01 E
Novelda	13	Lf	38.23N	0.46W
Novellara	14	Ef	44.51N	10.44 E
Nové Mesto nad Váhom	10	Nh	48.46N	17.50 E
Nové Zámky	10	Oi	47.59N	18.11 E
Novgorod	6	Jd	58.31N	31.17 E
Novgorodka	8	Mg	57.00N	28.37 E
Novgorod-Severski	19	De	52.01N	33.16 E
Novgorodskaja Oblast [3]	19	Dd	58.20N	32.40 E
Novi Bečej	15	Dd	45.36N	20.08 E
Novigrad [Yugo.]	14	He	45.19N	13.34 E
Novigrad [Yugo.]	14	Jf	44.11N	15.33 E
Novi Kričim	15	Hg	42.03N	24.28 E
Novi Ligure	14	Cf	44.46N	8.47 E
Novillero	48	Gf	22.21N	105.39W
Novion-Porcien	12	Ge	49.36N	4.25 E
Novi Pazar [Bul.]	15	Kf	43.21N	27.12 E
Novi Pazar [Yugo.]	15	Df	43.08N	20.31 E
Novi Sad	6	Hf	45.15N	19.50 E
Novi Travnik	14	Lf	44.10N	17.39 E
Novi Vinodolski	14	Ie	45.08N	14.47 E
Novoaleksandrovsk	16	Lg	45.24N	41.14 E
Novoaleksejevka [Kaz.-U.S.S.R.]	16	Sd	50.08N	55.42 E
Novoaleksejevka [Ukr.-U.S.S.R.]	16	If	46.16N	34.39 E
Novoaltajsk	20	Df	53.24N	83.58 E
Novoanninski	19	Ee	50.31N	42.45 E
Novoarhangelsk	16	Ge	48.39N	30.50 E
Novo Aripuanã	54	Fe	5.08S	60.22W
Novoazovsk	16	Kf	47.05N	38.05 E
Novobirjusinski	20	Ee	56.58N	97.55 E
Novobogdanovka	16	If	47.05N	35.18 E
Novočeboksarsk	7	Lh	56.08N	47.29 E
Novočeremšansk	7	Mi	54.23N	50.10 E
Novočerkassk	19	Ef	47.25N	40.03 E
Novodevičje	7	Lj	53.35N	48.51 E
Novograd-Volynski	19	Ce	50.36N	27.36 E
Novogrudok	16	Dc	53.37N	25.50 E
Nôvo Hamburgo	56	Jc	29.41S	51.08W
Novohopërsk	16	Ld	51.06N	41.37 E
Novo Horizonte	55	He	21.28S	49.13W
Novoizborsk	8	Mg	57.43N	28.05 E
Novojenisejsk	20	Ee	58.19N	92.27 E
Novojerudinski	20	Ee	59.47N	93.30 E
Novokačalinsk	20	Ig	45.05N	131.59 E
Novokazalinsk	22	Ie	45.50N	62.10 E
Novokubansk	16	Lg	45.06N	41.01 E
Novokujbyševsk	19	Ee	53.08N	49.58 E
Novokuzneck	22	Kd	53.45N	87.06 E
Novolazarevskaja	66	Cf	70.46S	11.50 E
Novolukoml	7	Gi	54.38N	29.07 E
Novo Mesto	14	Je	45.48N	15.10 E
Novomičurinsk	7	Ji	54.02N	39.48 E
Novomihajlovka	20	Ih	44.17N	133.50 E
Novo Miloševo	15	Dd	45.43N	20.18 E
Novomirgorod	16	Ge	48.45N	31.39 E
Novomoskovsk [R.S.F.S.R.]	6	Je	54.05N	38.13 E
Novomoskovsk [Ukr.-U.S.S.R.]	19	Df	48.37N	35.16 E
Novonikolajevski	16	Md	50.55N	42.24 E
Novoorsk	19	Fe	51.24N	58.59 E
Novopokrovskaja	16	Lg	45.56N	40.42 E
Novopolock	19	Cd	55.31N	28.40 E
Novorossijsk	6	Jg	44.45N	37.45 E
Novorybnaja	20	Fb	72.50N	105.45 E
Novoržev	19	Cd	57.02N	29.20 E
Novo-Šahtinsk	19	Df	47.47N	39.54 E
Novoselica	15	Ja	48.13N	26.17 E
Novoselje	8	Mf	58.05N	29.00 E
Novoselki	10	Ud	52.04N	24.25 E
Novoselovo	20	Ef	54.55N	91.00 E
Novosergijevka	19	Fe	52.03N	53.39 E
Novosibirsk	22	Kd	55.02N	82.55 E
Novosibirskaja Oblast [3]	20	Ce	55.30N	80.00 E
Novosibirskije Ostrova= New Siberian Islands (EN)	21	Qb	75.00N	142.00 E
Novosibirskoje Vodohranilišče	20	Df	54.40N	82.35 E
Novosil	16	Jc	52.59N	37.01 E
Novosineglazovski	17	Ji	55.05N	61.25 E
Novosokolniki	19	Dd	56.19N	30.12 E
Novospasskoje	7	Lj	53.09N	47.44 E
Novotroick	19	Fe	51.12N	58.35 E
Novotroickoje	19	Hg	43.39N	73.45 E
Novoukrainka	16	Ge	48.19N	31.32 E
Novouljanovsk	7	Li	54.10N	48.23 E
Novouzensk	19	Ee	50.29N	48.08 E
Novovjatsk	7	Lg	58.31N	49.43 E
Novovolynsk	19	Ce	50.46N	24.09 E
Novovoronežski	16	Kd	51.17N	39.16 E
Novozybkov	19	De	52.32N	32.00 E
Novska	14	Ke	45.20N	16.59 E
Novy Bug	16	Hf	47.43N	32.29 E
Nový Bydžov	10	Lf	50.15N	15.29 E
Novy Jaričev	10	Ug	49.50N	24.21 E
Novyje Aneny	15	Mc	46.53N	29.13 E
Novyje Burasy	16	Oc	52.06N	46.06 E
Nový Jičín	10	Og	49.36N	18.01 E
Novy Oskol	19	De	50.43N	37.54 E
Novy Pogost	8	Li	55.30N	27.32 E
Novy Port	22	Jc	67.40N	72.52 E
Novy Tap	17	Mh	56.55N	67.15 E
Novy Terek	16	Oh	43.37N	47.25 E
Novy Uzen	19	Fg	43.19N	52.55 E
Novy Vasjugan	20	Ce	58.34N	76.29 E
Novy Zaj	7	Mi	55.17N	52.02 E
Nowa Dęba	10	Rf	50.26N	21.46 E
Nowa Huta, Kraków-	10	Qf	50.04N	20.05 E
Nowa Ruda	10	Mf	50.35N	16.31 E
Nowa Sarzyna	10	Sf	50.23N	22.22 E
Nowa Sól	10	Le	51.48N	15.44 E
Now Bandegān	24	Oh	28.52N	53.53 E
Nowbarān	24	Me	35.08N	49.42 E
Nowdesheh	24	Le	35.11N	46.15 E
Nowe	10	Oc	53.40N	18.43 E
Nowe Miasto Lubawskie	10	Pc	53.27N	19.35 E
Nowe Miasto-nad-Pilicą	10	Qe	51.38N	20.35 E
Nowe Warpno	10	Kc	53.44N	14.20 E
Nowfel low Shātow	24	Ne	34.27N	50.55 E
Nowgong	25	Ic	26.21N	92.40 E
Nowogard	10	Lc	53.40N	15.08 E
Nowogród	10	Rc	53.15N	21.53 E
Nowood River	46	Ld	44.17N	107.58W
Nowra	59	Kf	34.53S	150.36 E
Nowshahr	24	Nd	36.39N	51.31 E
Nowy Dwór Gdański	10	Pb	54.13N	19.06 E
Nowy Dwór Mazowiecki	10	Qd	52.26N	20.43 E
Nowy Korczyn	10	Qf	50.20N	20.50 E
Nowy Sącz [2]	10	Qg	49.40N	20.40 E
Nowy Sącz	10	Qg	49.38N	20.42 E
Nowy Targ	10	Qg	49.29N	20.02 E
Nowy Tomyśl	10	Md	52.20N	16.07 E
Noya	13	Db	42.47N	8.53W
Noya/Anoia	13	Nc	41.28N	1.56 E
Noyant	11	Gg	47.31N	0.08 E
Noyon	11	Ie	49.35N	3.00 E
Nozaki-Jima	29	Ae	33.11N	129.08 E
Nozay	11	Eg	47.34N	1.38W
Nsanje	36	Gf	16.55S	35.16 E
Nsawan	34	Ed	5.48N	0.21W
Nschodnia	10	Rf	50.30N	21.18 E
Nsefu	36	Fe	13.03S	32.07 E
Nsukka	34	Gd	6.52N	7.23 E
Ntadembele	36	Cc	2.11S	17.08 E
Ntchisi	36	Fe	13.22S	34.00 E
Ntem	30	Hh	2.10N	9.57 E
Ntoum	36	Ab	0.22N	9.47 E
Ntui	34	He	4.27N	11.38 E
Ntusi	36	Fb	0.03N	31.13 E
Nuageuses, Iles-	30	Nm	48.40S	68.58 E
Nuanetsi	30	Kk	22.40S	31.49 E
Nūbah, Jibāl an-	30	Kg	12.00N	30.45 E
Nubian Desert (EN)= Nūbiyah, Aş Şaḩrā' an-	30	Kf	20.30N	33.00 E
Nūbiyah, Aş Şaḩrā' an-= Nubian Desert (EN)	30	Kf	20.30N	33.00 E
Nudha	63a	Ec	9.32S	160.48 E
Nueces Plain	43	Hf	28.30N	99.15W
Nueces River	43	Hf	27.50N	97.30W
Nueltin Lake	38	Jc	60.50N	99.30W
Nü'er He	28	Fd	41.06N	121.09 E
Nueva Asunción [3]	55	Be	21.00S	60.20W
Nueva Ciudad Guerrero	48	Jd	26.35N	99.15W
Nueva Esparta [2]	54	Fa	11.00N	64.00W
Nueva Germania	55	Df	23.54S	56.34W
Nueva Gerona	47	Hd	21.53N	82.48W
Nueva Imperial	56	Fe	38.44S	72.57W
Nueva Italia de Ruiz	48	Hh	19.01N	102.06W
Nueva Ocotepeque	49	Cf	14.24N	89.13W
Nueva Palmira	55	Ck	33.53S	58.25W
Nueva Rosita	39	Ig	27.57N	101.13W
Nueva San Salvador	47	Gf	13.41N	89.17W
Nueva Segovia [3]	49	Dg	13.40N	86.10W
Nueve de Julio	56	He	35.27S	60.52W
Nuevitas	47	Id	21.33N	77.16W
Nuevitas, Bahia de-	49	Ic	21.30N	77.12W
Nuevo, Cayo-	48	Mg	21.51N	92.05W
Nuevo, Golfo-	52	Jj	42.42S	64.36W
Nuevo Berlín	55	Ck	32.59S	58.03W
Nuevo Casas Grandes	39	If	30.25N	107.55W
Nuevo Laredo	39	Jg	27.30N	99.31W
Nuevo León [2]	47	Ec	25.40N	100.00W
Nuevo Mundo, Cerro-	54	Eh	21.55S	66.53W
Nuevo Rocafuerte	54	Cd	0.56S	75.25W
Nugaal [3]	35	Hd	8.30N	48.00 E
Nugālēd, Dēḥ-	30	Lh	7.58N	49.51 E
Nugālēd, Dōḥo-	35	Hd	8.35N	48.35 E
Nûgâtsiaq	41	Gd	71.39N	53.45W
Nugget Point	62	Cg	46.27S	169.49 E
Nûgssuaq	41	Gd	70.30N	51.30W
Nuguria Islands	57	Ge	3.20S	154.45 E
Nuguš	17	Gj	53.05N	56.00 E
Nuhaka	62	Gc	39.02S	177.45 E
Nui Atoll	57	Ie	7.15S	177.10 E
Nuijama	8	Md	60.58N	28.32 E
Nuiqsut	40	Ib	70.20N	151.00W
Nu Jang	21	Lh	16.31N	97.37 E
Nûk/Godthåb	67	Nc	64.15N	51.40W
Nukapu	63c	Ab	10.07S	165.59 E
Nukey Bluff	59	Hf	32.35S	135.40 E
Nukhayb	23	Fc	32.02N	42.15 E
Nukhaylak	31	Jg	19.08N	26.20 E
Nukiki	63a	Cb	6.45S	156.29 E
Nukuaéta	64h	Ac	13.22S	176.11W
Nuku'alofa	58	Jg	21.08S	175.12W
Nukufetau Atoll	57	Ie	8.00S	178.22 E
Nukufotu	64h	Bb	13.11S	176.10W
Nukuhifala	64h	Bb	13.17S	176.05W
Nukuhione	64h	Bb	13.16S	176.06W
Nuku Hiva, Ile-	57	Me	8.54S	140.06W
Nukulaelae Atoll	57	Ie	9.23S	179.52 E
Nukuloa	64h	Bb	13.11S	176.09W
Nukumanu Islands	57	Ge	4.30S	159.30 E
Nukumbasanga	63d	Cb	16.18S	179.15W
Nukunonu Atoll	57	Je	9.10S	171.53W
Nukuoro Atoll	57	Gd	3.51N	154.58 E
Nukus	22	He	42.50N	59.29 E
Nukutapu	64h	Bb	13.13S	176.08W
Nukuteatea	64h	Bb	13.12S	176.08W
Nulato	40	Hd	64.43N	158.06W
Nules	13	Le	39.51N	0.09W
Nullagine	58	Dg	21.53S	120.06 E
Nullagine River	59	Ed	20.43S	120.33 E
Nullarbor	59	Gf	31.26S	130.55 E
Nullarbor Plain	57	Dh	31.00S	129.00 E
Nulu'erhu Shan	27	Kc	41.40N	119.50 E
Numakawa	29a	Ba	45.15N	141.51 E
Numan	34	Hd	9.28N	12.02 E
Numancia [Phil.]	26	Ie	9.52N	125.58 E
Numancia [Sp.]	13	Jc	41.47N	2.30W
Numanohata	29a	Bb	42.40N	141.41 E
Numata [Jap.]	29a	Bb	43.49N	141.55 E
Numata [Jap.]	28	Of	36.38N	139.03 E
Numatinna	35	Dd	7.14N	27.37 E
Numazu	28	Og	35.06N	138.52 E
Nümbrecht	12	Jd	50.54N	7.33 E
Numedal	7	Bf	60.05N	9.05 E
Numena	36	Ee	11.46S	26.31 E
Número Cinco, Canal-	55	Cm	37.14S	58.06W
Número Doce, Canal-	55	Cm	36.30S	59.08W
Número Dos, Canal-	55	Cm	36.51S	58.03W
Número Nueve, Canal-	55	Cm	36.08S	58.36W
Número Once, Canal-	55	Bm	36.28S	60.01W
Número Quince, Canal-	55	Dl	35.55S	57.45W
Número Uno, Canal-	55	Cm	36.40S	58.35W
Numfoor, Pulau-	26	Jg	1.03S	134.54 E
Nuneaton	9	Li	52.32N	1.28W
Nungarin	59	Df	31.11S	118.06 E
Nungnain Sum	27	Kb	45.45N	118.56 E
Nungo	37	Fb	13.25S	37.46 E
Nunivak	38	Cd	60.00N	166.30W
Nunkirchen, Wadern-	12	Ie	49.32N	6.53 E
Nunn	45	Df	40.45N	104.46W
Nunspeet	12	Hb	52.22N	5.46 E
Nunukan Timur, Pulau-	26	Gf	4.05N	117.40 E
Nuomin He	27	Lb	48.21N	124.32 E
Nuorgam	7	Ga	70.05N	27.51 E
Nuoro	6	Gg	40.19N	9.20 E
Nupani	63c	Ab	10.04S	165.40 E
Nūq	24	Pg	30.55N	55.35 E
Nuqayr	24	Mi	27.48N	48.21 E
Nuqrah	24	Ij	25.34N	41.24 E
Nuqruş, Jabal-	33	Fe	24.49N	34.36 E
Nuquí	54	Cb	5.43N	77.16W
Nūr	24	Od	36.15N	52.20 E
Nūr	24	Pg	31.25N	54.20 E
Nura	19	Gf	48.57N	62.20 E
Nura	21	Id	50.30N	69.59 E
Nūrābād	24	Ng	30.48N	51.27 E
Nuraghe Santu Antine	14	Cj	40.29N	8.45 E
Nurata	19	Gg	40.34N	65.35 E
Nur Dağları	24	Gd	36.45N	36.20 E
Nure	14	De	45.03N	9.49 E
Nurek	19	Gh	38.25N	69.20 E
Nurhak Dağı	23	Eb	38.04N	37.29 E
Nūrī	35	Eb	18.30N	32.02 E
Nurki	20	Ie	56.42N	138.28 E
Nurlat	19	Fe	54.28N	50.48 E
Nurlati	7	Li	55.38N	48.17 E
Nurmes	7	Ge	63.33N	29.07 E
Nurmijärvi	8	Kd	60.28N	24.48 E
Nurmo	8	Jb	62.50N	22.54 E
Nürnberg	6	Hf	49.27N	11.05 E
Nurra	14	Cj	40.45N	8.15 E
Nurri, Mount-	59	Jf	31.42S	146.02 E
Nurugas	37	Bc	19.11S	18.54 E
Nurzec	10	Sd	52.33N	22.28 E
Nusa Tenggara Barat [3]	26	Gh	8.50S	117.30 E
Nusa Tenggara Timur [3]	26	Hh	9.30S	122.00 E
Nusaybin	24	Id	37.03N	41.13 E
Nushagak	40	He	58.57N	158.29W
Nushan	27	Gf	25.00N	99.00 E
Nu-Shima	29	Dd	34.10N	134.50 E
Nutak	42	Le	57.31N	62.00W
Nuttal	25	Dc	28.45N	68.08 E
Nuutele	65c	Bb	14.02S	171.22W
Nuwākot	25	Gc	28.08N	83.53 E
Nuwara	25	Gg	6.58N	80.46 E
Nuwaybi 'al Muzayyinah	33	Fd	28.58N	34.39 E
Nyabing	59	Df	33.32S	118.09 E
Nyagquka/Yajiang	27	He	30.07N	100.58 E
Nyagrong/Xinlong	27	He	30.57N	100.12 E
Nyahanga	36	Fc	2.23S	33.33 E
Nyahua	36	Fc	4.58S	33.34 E
Nyainqêntanglha Feng	27	Fe	30.12N	90.33 E
Nyainqêntanglha Shan	21	Kf	30.10N	90.00 E
Nyakanazi	36	Fc	3.00S	31.15 E
Nyala	31	Jg	12.03N	24.53 E
Nyalam	27	Ef	28.15N	85.55 E
Ny-Ålesund	41	Nc	78.56N	11.57 E
Nyalikungu	36	Fc	3.11S	33.47 E
Nyamandhlovu	37	Dc	19.51S	28.16 E
Nyamapanda	37	Ec	16.55S	32.52 E
Nyamlell	35	Dd	9.07N	26.58 E
Nyamtumbo	36	Ge	10.30S	36.06 E
Nyanding	35	Ed	8.40N	32.41 E
Nyanga	30	Ii	2.58S	10.15 E
Nyanga [3]	36	Bc	3.00S	11.00 E
Nyanza [3]	36	Fc	0.30S	34.30 E
Nyanza-Lac	36	Ec	4.21S	29.36 E
Nyasa, Lake- (EN)=Niassa, Lago-	30	Kj	12.00S	34.30 E
Nyaunglebin	25	Je	17.57N	96.44 E
Nyborg	7	Ci	55.19N	10.48 E
Nybro	7	Dh	56.45N	15.54 E
Nyda	17	Pc	66.40N	72.50 E
Nyda	20	Cc	66.36N	72.54 E
Nyeboe Land	41	Gb	81.45N	56.40W
Nyêmo	27	Ff	29.30N	90.07 E
Nyeri	36	Gc	0.25S	36.57 E
Nyerol	35	Ed	8.41N	32.02 E
Ny Friesland	41	Nc	79.30N	17.00 E
Nyhammar	8	Fd	60.17N	14.58 E
Nyhem	8	Fb	62.54N	15.40 E
Nyika	30	Ki	2.37S	38.44 E
Nyika Plateau	30	Kj	10.40S	33.50 E
Nyikog Qu	27	He	30.24N	100.40 E
Nyimba	36	Fe	14.33S	30.48 E
Nyingchi	27	Ff	29.38N	94.23 E
Nyírbátor	10	Si	47.50N	22.08 E
Nyíregyháza	10	Ri	47.57N	21.43 E
Nyiri Desert	36	Gc	2.20S	37.20 E
Nyiro, Mount-	36	Gb	2.08N	36.51 E
Nyírség	10	Ri	47.50N	21.55 E
Nykøbing [Den.]	7	Ci	54.46N	11.53 E
Nykøbing [Den.]	7	Ci	55.55N	11.41 E
Nykøbing [Den.]	8	Ch	56.48N	8.52 E
Nyköping	7	Dg	58.45N	17.00 E
Nyköpingsån	8	Gf	58.45N	17.01 E
Nykroppa	8	Fe	59.38N	14.18 E
Nyland	8	Ga	63.00N	17.46 E
Nylstroom	37	Dd	24.42S	28.20 E
Nymburk	10	Lf	50.11N	15.03 E
Nymphe Bank (EN)	9	Fj	51.30N	7.05W
Nynäshamn	7	Dg	58.54N	17.57 E
Nyngan	58	Fh	31.34S	147.11 E
Nyon	14	Ad	46.23N	6.15 E
Nyong	30	Hh	3.17N	9.54 E
Nyonga	36	Fd	6.43S	32.04 E
Nyons	11	Lj	44.22N	5.08 E
Nýřany	10	Jg	49.43N	13.13 E
Nyrob	17	Hf	60.42N	56.45 E
Nyš	20	Jf	51.30N	142.49 E
Nysa	10	Nf	50.29N	17.20 E
Nysa Kłodzka	10	Nf	50.49N	17.50 E
Nysa Łuzycka	10	Kd	52.04N	14.46 E
Nyslott/Savonlinna	7	Gf	61.52N	28.53 E
Nyssa	46	Ge	43.53N	117.00W
Nystad/Uusikaupunki	7	Ef	60.48N	21.25 E
Nysted	8	Dj	54.40N	11.45 E
Nytva	19	Fd	57.56N	55.20 E
Nyūdō-Zaki	28	Od	40.00N	139.35 E
Nyunzu	36	Ed	5.57S	28.01 E
Nyūzen	29	Ec	36.56N	137.30 E
Nzambi	36	Bc	3.58S	11.16 E
Nzara	35	De	4.40N	28.14 E
Nzega	36	Fc	4.13S	33.11 E
Nzérékoré	31	Gh	7.45N	8.49W
N'zeto	36	Bd	7.05S	12.50 E
Nzi	30	Gh	5.57N	4.50W
Nzilo, Barrage de-	36	Ee	10.35S	25.30 E
Nzo	34	Dd	6.16N	7.03W
Nzoro	36	Eb	3.18N	29.26 E
Nzwani	30	Lj	12.15S	44.25 E

O

Name	Map	Grid	Lat.	Long.
Oa, Mull of-	9	Gf	55.35N	6.20W
Oahe, Lake-	38	Ie	45.30N	100.25W
Oahu Island	57	Lb	21.30N	158.00W
O-akan-Dake	29a	Db	43.27N	144.10 E
Oakdale [Ca.-U.S.]	46	Eh	37.46N	120.51W
Oakdale [La.-U.S.]	45	Jk	30.49N	92.40W
Oakham	9	Mi	52.40N	0.44W
Oak Harbor	46	Db	48.18N	122.39W
Oak Lake	45	Fb	49.40N	100.45W
Oakland [Ca.-U.S.]	39	Gf	37.47N	122.13W
Oakland [Md.-U.S.]	44	Hf	39.25N	79.24W
Oakley [Id.-U.S.]	46	Ie	42.15N	113.53W
Oakley [Ks.-U.S.]	43	Gd	39.08N	100.51W
Oak Park	45	Mf	41.53N	87.48W
Oak Ridge	43	Kd	36.01N	84.16W
Oakridge	46	De	43.45N	122.28W
Oakville	44	Hd	43.27N	79.41W
Oamaru	61	Di	45.05S	170.59 E
Oancea	15	Ld	45.55N	28.06 E
Oani-Gawa	29	Ga	40.12N	140.16 E
Ōarai	29	Gc	36.18N	140.33 E
Oaro	62	Ee	42.31S	173.30 E
Oasis	46	Hf	41.01N	114.37W
Oasis	32	Hd	26.00N	5.00 E
Oates Coast	66	Jf	70.00S	160.00 E
Oaxaca [2]	47	Ee	17.00N	96.30W
Oaxaca, Sierra Madre de-	48	Ki	17.30N	96.30W
Oaxaca de Juárez	39	Jh	17.03N	96.43W
Ob	21	Ic	66.45N	69.30 E
Oba	42	Jg	48.55N	84.17W
Obala	34	He	4.10N	11.32 E
Obama [Jap.]	28	Mg	35.30N	135.45 E
Obama [Jap.]	29	Be	32.43N	130.13 E
Obama-Wan	29	Dd	35.30N	135.40 E
Oban [N.Z.]	61	Ci	46.52S	168.10 E
Oban [Scot.-U.K.]	9	He	56.25N	5.29W
Obanazawa	28	Pe	38.36N	140.24 E
Obando	53	Je	4.07N	67.45W
Oban Hills	34	Gd	5.30N	8.35 E
Obeliai/Obeljaj	8	Ki	55.58N	25.59 E
Obeljaj/Obeliai	8	Ki	55.58N	25.59 E
Oberá	56	Ic	27.29S	55.08W
Oberbayern	10	Hi	47.50N	11.50 E
Oberderdingen	12	Ke	49.04N	8.48 E
Oberfranken	10	Hf	50.10N	11.30 E
Oberhausen	10	Ce	51.28N	6.51 E
Oberkirchen, Schmallenberg-	12	Kc	51.09N	8.18 E
Oberland [Switz.]	14	Bd	46.35N	7.30 E
Oberland [Switz.]	14	Dd	46.45N	9.05 E
Oberlausitz	10	Ke	51.15N	14.30 E
Oberlin	45	Fg	39.49N	100.32W
Obermoschel	12	Je	49.44N	7.46 E
Obernkirchen	12	Lb	52.16N	9.08 E
Oberösterreich=Upper Austria (EN) [2]	14	Hb	48.15N	14.00 E
Oberpfalz	10	Ig	49.30N	12.10 E
Oberpfälzer Wald= Bohemian Forest (EN)	10	Ig	49.50N	12.30 E
Oberpullendorf	14	Kc	47.30N	16.31 E
Ober-Ramstadt	12	Ke	49.50N	8.45 E
Oberstdorf	10	Gi	47.24N	10.16 E
Oberursel (Taunus)	12	Kd	50.12N	8.35 E
Obervellach	14	Hd	46.56N	13.12 E
Oberwesel	12	Jd	50.06N	7.44 E
Ob Gulf (EN)=Obskaja Guba	21	Jc	69.00N	73.00 E
Obi, Kepulauan-	26	Ig	1.30S	127.45 E
Obi, Pulau-	57	De	1.30S	127.45 E
Obi, Selat-	26	Ig	0.52S	127.33 E
Óbidos [Braz.]	53	Kf	1.55S	55.31W
Óbidos [Port.]	13	Ce	39.22N	9.09W
Obihiro	27	Pc	42.55N	143.12 E
Obilić	15	Eg	42.41N	21.05 E
Obira	29a	Ba	44.01N	141.38 E
Obispos	49	Li	8.36N	70.05W
Obispo Trejo	56	Hd	30.46S	63.25W
Obitočnaja Kosa	16	Jf	46.35N	36.15 E
Oblučje	20	Ig	48.59N	131.05 E
Obninsk	19	Dd	55.05N	36.37 E
Obo	31	Jh	5.24N	26.30 E
Obock	35	Gc	11.57N	43.17 E
Obojan	19	De	51.13N	36.16 E
Obokote	36	Ec	0.52S	26.19 E
Obol	7	Gi	55.24N	29.01 E
Oborniki	10	Md	52.39N	16.51 E
Obouya	36	Cc	0.56S	15.43 E
Obozerski	19	Ec	63.28N	40.20 E
Obra	10	Ld	52.36N	15.28 E
Obrenovac	15	De	44.39N	20.12 E
Obrovac	14	Jf	44.12N	15.41 E
Obrovo	10	Vd	52.27N	25.43 E
Obruchev Rise (EN)	20	Lf	52.30N	166.00 E
Obruk Platosu	24	Ec	38.02N	33.30 E
Obšči Syrt	5	Le	51.50N	51.00 E
Obskaja Guba=Ob Gulf (EN)	21	Jc	69.00N	73.00 E
Ob' Tablemount (EN)	30	Ln	52.30S	42.00 E
Ōbu	29	Ed	35.01N	136.58 E
Obuasi	34	Ed	6.12N	1.40W
Obudu	34	Gd	6.40N	9.10 E
Obuhov	16	Gd	50.07N	30.37 E
Obva	17	Gg	58.35N	55.25 E
Obzor	15	Kg	42.49N	27.53 E
Oca	13	Ib	42.46N	3.26W
Oca, Montes de-	13	Ib	42.20N	3.15W
Očakov	19	Df	46.38N	31.33 E
Ocala	43	Kf	29.11N	82.07W
Očamcira	16	Lh	42.46N	41.27 E
Ocampo [Mex.]	48	Hd	27.20N	102.21W
Ocampo [Mex.]	48	Ec	28.11N	108.23W
Ocaña [Col.]	54	Db	8.15N	73.20W
Ocaña [Sp.]	13	Ie	39.56N	3.31W
Occhito, Lago di-	14	Ii	41.35N	14.55 E
Ocean Bight	49	Kc	21.15N	73.15W
Ocean City [Md.-U.S.]	43	Ld	38.20N	75.05W
Ocean City [N.J.-U.S.]	44	Jf	39.16N	74.35W
Ocean Falls	42	Ef	52.21N	127.40W
Oceania	57	Ie	5.00S	175.00 E
Ocean Point	44	Il	26.16N	77.03W
Oceanside	43	De	33.12N	117.23W
Ocean Springs	45	Lk	30.25N	88.50W
Ocejón, Pico-	13	Ic	41.07N	3.15W
Očenyrd, Gora-	17	Mb	68.05N	66.20 E
Očer	19	Fd	57.53N	54.45 E
Ochagavia	13	Kb	42.55N	1.05W
Ochiai	29	Cd	35.02N	133.45 E
Ochi-Gata	29	Ec	36.55N	136.48 E
Ochiishi-Misaki	29a	Db	43.10N	145.28 E
Ochil Hills	9	Je	56.23N	3.35W
Och'onjang	28	Jd	40.55N	128.50 E
Ocho Rios	49	Id	18.25N	77.07W
Ochsenfurt	10	Gg	49.39N	10.05 E
Ochtrup	12	Jb	52.13N	7.11 E
Ockelbo	7	Dd	60.53N	16.43 E
Öckerö	8	Dg	57.43N	11.39 E
Ocmulgee River	44	Fj	31.58N	82.32W
Ocna Mureş	15	Gc	46.23N	23.51 E

Index Symbols

[1] Independent Nation
[2] State, Region
[3] District, County
[4] Municipality
[5] Colony, Dependency
Continent
Physical Region
Historical or Cultural Region
Mount, Mountain
Volcano
Hill
Mountains, Mountain Range
Hills, Escarpment
Plateau, Upland
Pass, Gap
Plain, Lowland
Delta
Salt Flat
Valley, Canyon
Crater, Cave
Karst Features
Depression
Polder
Desert, Dunes
Forest, Woods
Heath, Steppe
Oasis
Cape, Point
Coast, Beach
Cliff
Peninsula
Isthmus
Sandbank
Island
Atoll
Rock, Reef
Islands, Archipelago
Rocks, Reefs
Coral Reef
Well, Spring
Geyser
River, Stream
Waterfall Rapids
River Mouth, Estuary
Lake
Salt Lake
Intermittent Lake
Reservoir
Swamp, Pond
Canal
Glacier
Ice Shelf, Pack Ice
Ocean
Sea
Gulf, Bay
Strait, Fjord
Lagoon
Bank
Seamount
Tablemount
Ridge
Shelf
Basin
Escarpment, Sea Scarp
Fracture
Trench, Abyss
National Park, Reserve
Point of Interest
Recreation Site
Cave, Cavern
Historic Site
Ruins
Wall, Walls
Church, Abbey
Temple
Scientific Station
Airport
Port
Lighthouse
Mine
Tunnel
Dam, Bridge

Ocna Sibiului	15	Hc	45.53N	24.03 E
Ocoa, Bahía de-	49	Ld	18.22N	70.39W
Oconee River	44	Fj	31.58N	82.32W
Oconto	45	Md	44.55N	87.52W
Ocosingo	48	Mi	17.04N	92.15W
Ocotal	49	Dg	13.38N	86.29W
Ocotepeque [3]	49	Cf	14.30N	89.00W
Ocotlán	47	Dd	20.21N	102.46W
Ocotlán de Morelos	48	Ki	16.48N	96.43W
Ocracoke Inlet	44	Ih	35.10N	76.05W
Ocracoke Island	44	Jh	35.09N	75.53W
Ocreza	13	Ee	39.32N	7.50W
Octeville-sur-Mer	12	Ce	49.33N	0.07 E
October Revolution Island (EN)=Oktjabrskoj Revoljuci, Ostrov-	21	Lb	79.30N	97.00 E
Ocú	49	Gj	7.57N	80.47W
Ocumare del Tuy	50	Cg	10.07N	66.46W
Oda [Ghana]	34	Ed	5.55N	0.59W
Oda [Jap.]	29	Ce	33.34N	132.48 E
Ōda	28	Lg	35.11N	132.30 E
Oda, Jabal-	35	Fa	20.21N	36.39 E
Ódáđahraun	7a	Cb	65.09N	17.00W
Ōdai	29	Ed	34.24N	136.24 E
Odaigahara-San	29	Ed	34.11N	136.06 E
Odalen	8	Dd	60.15N	11.40 E
Ōdate	28	Pd	40.16N	140.34 E
Odawara	28	Og	35.15N	139.10 E
Odda	7	Bf	60.04N	6.33 E
Odder	8	Di	55.58N	10.10 E
Odeleite	13	Eg	37.21N	7.27W
Odemira	13	Dg	37.36N	8.38W
Ödemiş	24	Bc	38.13N	27.59 E
Odendaalsrus	37	De	27.48S	26.45 E
Odense	6	Hd	55.24N	10.23 E
Odenthal	12	Jc	51.02N	7.07 E
Odenwald	10	Eg	49.40N	9.00 E
Oder [Eur.]	5	He	53.40N	14.33 E
Oder [F.R.G.]	10	Ge	51.40N	10.02 E
Oderbruch	10	Kd	52.40N	14.15 E
Oderské vrchy	10	Ng	49.40N	17.45 E
Oderzo	14	Ge	45.47N	12.29 E
Ödeshög	7	Dg	58.14N	14.39 E
Odessa [Tx.-U.S.]	39	If	31.51N	102.22W
Odessa [Ukr.-U.S.S.R.]	6	Jf	46.28N	30.44 E
Odessa [Wa.-U.S.]	46	Fc	47.20N	118.41W
Odesskaja Oblast [3]	19	Df	46.45N	30.30 E
Odet	11	Bg	47.52N	4.06W
Odiel	13	Fg	37.10N	6.54W
Odienné	31	Gh	9.30N	7.34W
Odienné [3]	34	Dd	9.45N	7.45W
Odivelas	13	Df	38.12N	8.18W
Ödmården	8	Gc	61.05N	16.40 E
Odobeşti	15	Kd	45.46N	27.03 E
Ŏdŏngk	25	Kf	11.48N	104.45 E
Odoorn	12	Ib	52.51N	6.50 E
Odorheiu Secuiesc	15	Ic	46.18N	25.18 E
Ōdose-Zaki	29a	Bc	40.46N	140.03 E
Odra	5	He	53.40N	14.33 E
Ōdwēyne	35	Hd	9.23N	45.04 E
Odžaci	15	Cd	45.31N	19.16 E
Odžak	14	Me	45.01N	18.18 E
Odzi	37	Ec	19.47S	32.24 E
Oeiras	13	Eg	37.38N	7.40W
Oeiras [Braz.]	54	Je	7.01S	42.08W
Oeiras [Port.]	13	Cf	38.41N	9.19W
Oelde	12	Kc	51.49N	8.09 E
Oelerbeek	12	Ib	52.21N	6.38 E
Oelrichs	45	Ee	43.15N	103.10W
Oelsnitz	10	If	50.25N	12.10 E
Oelwein	45	Ke	42.41N	91.55W
Oeno Island	57	Ng	23.56S	130.44W
Oer-Erkenschwick	12	Jc	51.38N	7.15 E
Oeste, Punta-	51a	Ab	18.05N	67.57W
Oeventrop, Arnsberg-	12	Kc	51.24N	8.08 E
Ōe-Yama	29	Dd	35.27N	135.06 E
Of	24	Ib	40.57N	40.16 E
O'Fallon Creek	46	Mc	46.50N	105.09W
Ofanto	14	Ki	41.21N	16.13 E
Ofaqim	24	Fg	31.17N	34.37 E
Offa	34	Fd	8.09N	4.43 E
Offaly/Uíbh Fhailí [2]	9	Fh	53.20N	7.30W
Offenbach am Main	10	Ef	50.06N	8.46 E
Offenbach-Hundheim	12	Je	49.37N	7.33 E
Offenburg	10	Dh	48.29N	7.56 E
Offida	14	Hh	42.56N	13.41 E
Offoué	36	Bc	0.04S	11.44 E
Offranville	12	De	49.52N	1.03 E
Ofidhoúsa	15	Jm	36.33N	26.09 E
Ofolanga	65b	Ba	19.36S	174.27W
Ofu	65c	Db	14.11S	169.42W
Ōfunato	28	Pe	39.04N	141.43 E
Oga	28	Oe	40.43N	141.18 E
Ogachi	29	Gb	39.05N	140.28 E
Ogaden	30	Lh	7.30N	45.00 E
Oga-Hantō	28	Oe	39.55N	139.50 E
Ōgaki	28	Ng	35.21N	136.37 E
Ogallala	43	Gc	41.08N	101.43W
Ogasawara-Shotō=Bonin Islands (EN)	21	Qg	27.00N	142.10 E
Ogawara-Ko	29a	Bc	40.45N	141.20 E
Ogbomosho	31	Hh	8.08N	4.16 E
Ogden	39	He	41.14N	111.58W
Ogdensburg	44	Jc	44.42N	75.31W
Ogeechee River	44	Gj	31.51N	81.06W
Oghāsh	24	Lc	39.10N	46.55 E
Ogi	29	Fc	37.50N	138.16 E
Ogilvie Mountains	42	Dc	65.00N	140.00W
Ogi-no-Sen	29	Dd	35.26N	134.26 E
Oginski Kanal	16	Dc	52.20N	25.55 E
Oglanly	16	Sj	39.50N	54.33 E
Oglethorpe	44	Ei	31.28N	84.04W
Ogliastra	14	Dk	39.55N	9.35 E
Oglio	14	Ee	45.02N	10.39 E
Ognon	11	Lg	47.20N	5.29 E
Ogo	35	Hd	9.48N	45.35 E
Ogoamas, Bulu-	26	Hf	0.40N	120.12 E
Ogodža	20	If	52.48N	132.40 E
Ogoja	34	Gd	6.40N	8.48 E
Ogoki	42	If	51.38N	85.56W
Ogoki	42	If	51.38N	85.55W
Ogoki Reservoir	42	If	51.35N	86.00W
Ogonëk	20	Ie	59.40N	138.01 E
Ogooué	30	Hi	0.49S	9.00 E
Ogooué-Ivindo [3]	36	Bb	0.30N	13.00 E
Ogooué-Lolo [3]	36	Bc	1.00S	13.00 E
Ogooué-Maritime [3]	36	Ac	2.00S	9.30 E
Ogōri [Jap.]	29	Bd	34.06N	131.25 E
Ogōri [Jap.]	29	Be	33.24N	130.34 E
Ogosta	15	Gf	43.45N	23.51 E
Ogražden	15	Fh	41.30N	22.55 E
Ogre	8	Kh	56.42N	24.33 E
Ogre	7	Fh	56.50N	24.39 E
Ogulin	14	Je	45.16N	15.14 E
Ogun [2]	34	Fd	7.00N	3.40 E
Oguni [Jap.]	29	Fb	38.04N	139.45 E
Oguni [Jap.]	29	Be	33.07N	131.04 E
Ogurčinski, Ostrov-	16	Rj	38.55N	53.05 E
Oğuzeli	24	Gd	37.00N	37.30 E
Oha	22	Qd	53.34N	142.56 E
Ohai	62	Bf	45.56S	167.57 E
Ohakune	62	Fc	39.25S	175.25 E
Ohanet	32	Id	28.40N	8.50 E
Ohansk	17	Gh	57.42N	55.25 E
Ōhara	29	Gd	35.15N	140.23 E
Ōhasama	29	Gb	39.28N	141.17 E
Ohata	20	Je	59.20N	143.05 E
Ōhata	28	Pd	41.24N	141.10 E
Ohau, Lake-	62	Cf	44.15S	169.50 E
Ohey	12	Hd	50.26N	5.08 E
O'Higgins, Cabo-	65d	Bb	27.05S	109.15W
Ohio	38	Kf	36.59N	89.08W
Ohio [2]	43	Kc	40.15N	82.45W
Ohm	10	Ef	50.51N	8.48 E
Ohmberge	10	Ge	51.30N	10.28 E
'Ohonua	65b	Bc	21.20S	174.57W
Ohopoho	31	Ij	18.03S	13.45 E
Ohotsk	22	Qd	59.23N	143.18 E
Ohotskoje More=Okhotsk, Sea of- (EN)	21	Qd	53.00N	150.00 E
Ohre	10	Hd	52.18N	11.47 E
Ohře	10	Kf	50.32N	14.08 E
Ohrid	15	Dh	41.07N	20.48 E
Ohrid, Lake- (EN) = Ohridsko Jezero	5	Ig	41.00N	20.45 E
Ohrid, Lake- (EN) = Ohrit, Liqen i-	5	Ig	41.00N	20.45 E
Ohridsko Jezero=Ohrid, Lake- (EN)	5	Ig	41.00N	20.45 E
Öhringen	10	Fg	49.12N	9.30 E
Ohrit, Liqen i- = Ohrid, Lake- (EN)	5	Ig	41.00N	20.45 E
Ohura	62	Fc	38.51S	174.59 E
Oiapoque	54	Hc	3.50N	51.50W
Oich	9	Id	57.10N	4.45W
Oi-Gawa	29	Fd	34.46N	138.17 E
Oil City	44	He	41.26N	79.44W
Oildale	46	Fi	35.25N	119.01W
Oiléan Baoi/Dursey	9	Cj	51.36N	10.12W
Oileán Ciarraí/Castleisland	9	Di	52.14N	9.27W
Oileán Coarach/Mutton	9	Di	52.49N	9.31W
Oileán Mhic Aodha/Magee, Island-	9	Hg	54.50N	5.50W
Oinoúsai	15	Jk	38.32N	26.13 E
Oinoúsai, Nísoi-	15	Jk	38.31N	26.14 E
Oirschot	12	Hc	51.30N	5.18 E
Oisans	11	Mi	45.02N	6.02 E
Oise [3]	11	Ie	49.30N	2.30 E
Oise	11	Ie	49.00N	2.04 E
Oise à l'Aisne, Canal de l'-	11	Je	49.36N	3.11 E
Oisemont	12	De	49.57N	1.46 E
Oissel	12	De	49.20N	1.06 E
Oisterwijk	12	Hc	51.35N	5.11 E
Oistins	51q	Ab	13.04N	59.32W
Oistins Bay	51q	Ab	13.03N	59.33W
Ōita	27	Ne	33.14N	131.36 E
Ōita Ken [2]	28	Kh	33.15N	131.20 E
Oíti Óros	15	Fk	38.49N	22.17 E
Oituz, Pasul-	15	Jc	46.03N	26.23 E
Oiwake	29a	Bb	42.52N	141.48 E
Ojat	7	Hf	60.31N	33.05 E
Öje	8	Ed	60.49N	13.51 E
Ojestos de Jalisco	48	Ig	21.50N	101.35W
Ojika-Jima	29	Ae	33.13N	129.03 E
O-Jima	29	Be	34.00N	130.45 E
Ojinaga	47	Dc	29.34N	104.25W
Ojiya	28	Of	37.18N	138.48 E
Ojmjakon	20	Jd	63.28N	142.49 E
Ojocaliente	48	Hf	22.34N	102.15W
Ojo Caliente	48	Fb	30.25N	106.33W
Ojos del Salado, Nevado-	52	Jh	27.06S	68.32W
Ojos Negros	13	Kd	40.44N	1.30W
Ojtal	19	Hg	42.54N	73.21 E
Oka [R.S.F.S.R.]	21	Md	55.00N	102.03 E
Oka [U.S.S.R.]	5	Kd	56.20N	43.59 E
Okaba	26	Kh	8.06S	139.42 E
Okahandja [3]	37	Bd	21.30S	17.30 E
Okahandja	31	Ik	21.59S	16.58 E
Okahukura	62	Fc	38.47S	175.14 E
Okaihau	62	Ea	35.19S	173.46 E
Okak Islands	42	Le	57.28N	61.48W
Okanagan Lake	42	Fg	49.55N	119.30W
Okano	36	Bc	0.05S	10.57 E
Okanogan River	43	Db	48.06N	119.43W
Okapa	59	Ja	6.31S	145.32 E
Okāra	25	Eb	30.49N	73.27 E
Okarem	19	Fh	38.07N	54.05 E
Okato	62	Ec	39.12S	173.53 E
Okaukuejo	37	Bc	19.10S	15.54 E
Okavango	30	Jj	18.53N	22.24 E
Okavango [3]	37	Cc	18.00S	21.00 E
Okavango Swamp	30	Jj	19.30S	23.00 E
Ōkawa	29	Be	33.12N	130.23 E
Okaya	28	Of	36.03N	138.03 E
Okayama	22	Pf	34.39N	133.55 E
Okayama Ken [2]	28	Lg	34.50N	133.45 E
Okazaki	28	Ng	34.57N	137.10 E
Okeechobee	44	Gl	27.15N	80.50W
Okeechobee, Lake-	38	Kg	26.55N	80.45W
Okefenokee Swamp	44	Fj	30.42N	82.20W
Okehampton	9	Jk	50.44N	4.00W
Okene	34	Gd	7.33N	6.14 E
Oker	10	Gd	52.30N	10.22 E
Oketo	29a	Cb	43.41N	143.32 E
Okha	25	Dd	22.27N	69.04 E
Ókhi Óros	15	Hk	38.04N	24.28 E
Okhotsk, Sea of- (EN)= Hok-Kai	21	Qd	53.00N	150.00 E
Okhotsk, Sea of- (EN)= Ohotskoje More	21	Qd	53.00N	150.00 E
Okhthonía, Ákra-	15	Hk	38.32N	24.14 E
Oki-Daitō-Jima	27	Ng	24.30N	131.00 E
Okiep	37	Be	29.39S	17.53 E
Okinawa	29b	Ab	26.20N	127.47 E
Okinawa Islands (EN)= Okinawa-Shotō	21	Og	26.40N	128.00 E
Okinawa-Jima	27	Mf	26.40N	128.20 E
Okinawa Ken [2]	29b	Ab	26.31N	127.59 E
Okinawa-Shotō=Okinawa Islands (EN)	21	Og	26.40N	128.00 E
Okinoerabu-Jima	27	Mf	27.20N	128.35 E
Okino-Shima [Jap.]	29	Ce	32.44N	132.33 E
Okino-Shima [Jap.]	29	Bd	34.15N	130.08 E
Okino-Tori-Shima	21	Pg	20.25N	136.00 E
Oki Ridge (EN)	28	Mf	37.00N	135.00 E
Oki-Shotō	27	Nd	36.00N	132.50 E
Okitipupa	34	Fd	6.30N	4.48 E
Oki Trench (EN)	29	Dc	37.00N	135.30 E
Oklahoma [2]	43	Hd	35.30N	98.00W
Oklahoma City	39	Jf	35.28N	97.32W
Okmulgee	45	Ii	35.37N	95.58W
Oknica	15	Ka	48.22N	27.24 E
Oko	35	Fa	22.20N	35.56 E
Okoko	36	Fb	2.06N	33.53 E
Okolo	36	Fb	2.40N	31.09 E
Okolona	44	Ef	38.08N	85.41W
Okondja	36	Bc	0.41S	13.47 E
Okonek	10	Mc	53.33N	16.50 E
Okoppe	28	Qb	44.28N	143.08 E
Okotoks	46	Ia	50.44N	113.59W
Okoyo	36	Cc	1.28S	15.04 E
Okrzeika	10	Re	51.40N	21.30 E
Øksfjord	7	Fa	70.14N	22.22 E
Oksino	17	Fc	67.33N	52.10 E
Okstindane	5	Hb	66.02N	14.10 E
Oktemberjan	16	Ni	40.09N	44.03 E
Oktjabrsk [Kaz.-U.S.S.R.]	6	Lf	48.40N	57.11 E
Oktjabrsk [R.S.F.S.R.]	7	Lj	53.13N	48.40 E
Oktjabrski [Bye.-U.S.S.R.]	16	Fc	52.38N	28.54 E
Oktjabrski [Kaz.-U.S.S.R.]	17	Kj	52.37N	62.43 E
Oktjabrski [R.S.F.S.R.]	20	Ee	56.05N	99.25 E
Oktjabrski [R.S.F.S.R.]	19	Fe	54.31N	53.28 E
Oktjabrski [R.S.F.S.R.]	17	Hh	56.31N	57.12 E
Oktjabrski [R.S.F.S.R.]	7	Kf	61.05N	43.08 E
Oktjabrski [R.S.F.S.R.]	20	Hf	53.00N	128.42 E
Oktjabrski [R.S.F.S.R.]	20	Kf	52.38N	156.15 E
Oktjabrski [R.S.F.S.R.]	16	Mf	47.56N	43.38 E
Oktjabrskoje	19	Gc	62.28N	66.01 E
Oktjabrskoj Revoljuci, Ostrov-=October Revolution Island (EN)	21	Lb	79.30N	97.00 E
Oku	29b	Bb	26.50N	128.17 E
Ōkuchi	28	Kh	32.04N	130.37 E
Okulovka	7	Hg	58.24N	33.18 E
Okushiri	28	Oc	42.09N	139.29 E
Okushiri-Kaikyō	29a	Ab	42.15N	139.40 E
Okushiri-Tō	27	Oc	42.10N	139.25 E
Okuta	34	Fd	9.13N	3.11 E
Oku Tango-Hantō	29	Dd	35.40N	135.10 E
Okwa	30	Jk	22.26S	22.58 E
Ola	20	Ke	59.37N	151.20 E
Ólafsfjördur	7a	Ba	66.04N	18.39W
Ólafsvík	7a	Ab	64.53N	23.43W
Ola Grande, Punta-	51a	Bc	17.55N	66.08W
Olaiņe/Olajne	7	Fh	56.49N	23.59 E
Olajne/Olaiņe	7	Fh	56.49N	23.59 E
Olancha	46	Gh	36.17N	117.59W
Olanchito	49	Df	15.30N	86.35W
Olancho [3]	49	Ef	14.45N	86.00W
Öland	5	Hd	56.45N	16.40 E
Ölands norra udde	8	Gg	57.22N	17.05 E
Ölands södra grund	8	Gh	55.40N	17.25 E
Ölands södra udde	8	Gh	56.11N	16.24 E
Olanga	7	Hc	66.08N	30.38 E
Olathe	45	Ig	38.53N	94.49W
Olavarría	53	Ji	36.53S	60.20W
Oława	10	Nf	50.57N	17.17 E
Oława	10	Nf	50.57N	17.17 E
Olbernhau	10	Jf	50.40N	13.20 E
Olbia	6	Gg	40.55N	9.31 E
Olbia, Golfo di-	14	Dj	40.55N	9.40 E
Old Bahama Channel	49	Ib	22.30N	78.05W
Old Bahama Channel (EN)= Bahamas, Canal Viejo de-	49	Ib	22.30N	78.05W
Old Castile (EN)=Castilla la Vieja	13	Ic	41.30N	4.00W
Old Crow	39	Fc	67.35N	139.50W
Oldeani	36	Gc	3.21S	35.33 E
Oldebroek	12	Hb	52.26N	5.53 E
Oldenburg	10	Ec	53.10N	8.12 E
Oldenburg in Holstein	10	Gb	54.18N	10.53 E
Oldenzaal	11	Mb	52.19N	6.56 E
Old Faithful Geyser	46	Jd	44.30N	110.45W
Old Fletton	12	Bb	52.34N	0.15W
Oldham	9	Kh	53.33N	2.07W
Old Hickory Lake	44	Dg	36.18N	86.30W
Oldman River	46	Jb	49.56N	111.42W
Old Marsh Bed	59	Gd	20.55S	130.30 E
Old Mkuski	36	Ee	14.22S	29.22 E
Old Road	51d	Bb	17.01N	61.50W
Old Road Town	51c	Ab	17.19N	62.48W
Olds	42	Gf	51.47N	114.06W
Old Town	44	Mc	44.56N	68.39W
Old Wives Lake	46	Ma	50.06N	106.00W
Olean	44	Hd	42.05N	78.26W
Olecko	10	Sb	54.03N	22.30 E
Oleiros	13	Ee	39.55N	7.55W
Olëkma	21	Oc	60.22N	120.42 E
Olëkminsk	22	Oc	60.30N	120.15 E
Olëkminski Stanovik	20	Gf	54.00N	119.00 E
Ølen	7	Ag	59.36N	5.48 E
Olenegorsk	19	Db	68.10N	33.13 E
Olenëk	21	Nb	73.00N	119.55 E
Olenëkski Zaliv	20	Hb	73.10N	121.00 E
Olenica	7	Ic	66.29N	35.19 E
Olenj, Ostrov-	20	Cb	72.25N	77.45 E
Olenty	16	Re	49.45N	52.10 E
Oléron, Ile d'-	5	Ff	45.56N	1.18W
Olesko	10	Ug	49.53N	24.58 E
Oleśnica	10	Ne	51.13N	17.23 E
Olesno	10	Of	50.53N	18.25 E
Olevsk	16	Ed	51.13N	27.41 E
Olga	20	Ih	43.46N	135.21 E
Olga, Mount-	59	Ge	25.19S	130.46 E
Olgastretet	41	Oc	78.30N	24.00 E
Ølgod	8	Ci	55.49N	8.37 E
Olhão	13	Eg	37.02N	7.50W
Olhovatka	16	Kd	50.17N	39.17 E
Oli	34	Fd	9.40N	4.29 E
Oliana	13	Nb	42.04N	1.19 E
Olib	14	If	44.23N	14.47 E
Oliena	14	Dj	40.16N	9.24 E
Olifants [Afr.]	30	Kk	24.03S	32.40 E
Olifants [Nam.]	37	Be	25.30S	19.30 E
Olifantshoek	37	Ce	27.57S	22.42 E
Olimarao Atoll	57	Fd	7.42N	145.53 E
Olimbía	15	El	37.39N	21.38 E
Ólimbos	15	Kn	35.44N	27.13 E
Ólimbos, Óros-=Olympus, Mount- (EN)	5	Ig	40.05N	22.21 E
Ólimbos Óros	15	Jj	39.05N	26.20 E
Olímpia	55	He	20.44S	48.54W
Olinda	54	Le	8.01S	34.51W
Olite	13	Kb	42.29N	1.39W
Oliva [Arg.]	56	Hd	32.03S	63.34W
Oliva [Sp.]	13	Lf	38.55N	0.07W
Oliva, Monasterio de la-	13	Kb	42.20N	1.25W
Oliva de la Frontera	13	Ff	38.16N	6.55W
Oliveira	55	Je	20.41S	44.49W
Oliveira dos Brejinhos	54	Jf	12.19S	42.54W
Olivença	37	Fb	11.46S	35.13 E
Olivenza	13	Ef	38.41N	7.06W
Oliver	46	Fb	49.11N	119.33W
Olivet	11	Hg	47.52N	1.54 E
Olivia	45	Id	44.46N	94.59W
Olja	16	Og	45.47N	47.35 E
Olji Moron He	28	Fb	44.16N	121.42 E
Oljutorski, Mys-	21	Td	59.55N	170.25 E
Oljutorski Zaliv	20	Ld	60.00N	168.00 E
Olkusz	10	Pf	50.17N	19.35 E
Ollan	64d	Bb	7.14N	151.38 E
Ollerton	12	Aa	53.13N	1.01W
Olmedo	13	Hc	41.17N	4.41W
Olmos	54	Ce	5.59S	79.46W
Olney [Eng.-U.K.]	12	Bb	52.09N	0.42W
Olney [Il.-U.S.]	45	Lg	38.44N	88.05W
Olney [Tx.-U.S.]	45	Gj	33.22N	98.45W
Oloči	20	Gf	51.20N	119.53 E
Olofström	7	Dh	56.16N	14.30 E
Oloitokitok	36	Gc	2.56S	37.30 E
Oloj	20	Kc	66.20N	159.29 E
Olojski Hrebet	20	Lc	65.50N	162.30 E
Olombo	36	Cc	1.18S	15.53 E
Ólomburi	63a	Ec	8.59S	161.09 E
Olomouc	6	Hf	49.36N	17.16 E
Olona	14	De	45.06N	9.21 E
Olonec	19	Dc	61.01N	32.58 E
Olonešty	15	Mc	46.29N	29.52 E
Olongapo	22	Oh	14.50N	120.16 E
Oloron, Gave d'-	11	Ek	43.33N	1.05W
Oloron-Sainte-Marie	11	Fk	43.12N	0.36W
Olosega	65c	Db	14.11S	169.39W
Olot	13	Ob	42.11N	2.29 E
Olovjannaja	20	Gf	50.56N	115.35 E
Olovo	14	Mf	44.07N	18.35 E
Olpe	10	De	51.02N	7.51 E
Olpoy	63b	Cb	14.52S	166.33 E
Olroyd River	59	Ib	14.10S	141.50 E
Olsberg	12	Kc	51.21N	8.30 E
Olshammar	8	Ff	58.45N	14.48 E
Olst	12	Ib	52.20N	6.08 E
Olsztyn	6	Ie	53.48N	20.29 E
Olsztyn [2]	10	Qc	53.50N	20.30 E
Olsztynek	10	Qc	53.36N	20.17 E
Olt [2]	15	He	44.25N	24.30 E
Olt	5	If	43.43N	24.51 E
Oltedal	8	Bf	58.50N	6.02 E
Olten	14	Bc	47.22N	7.55 E
Olteni	15	Ie	44.11N	25.17 E
Oltenia	15	Ge	44.30N	23.30 E
Olteniţa	15	Je	44.05N	26.38 E
Olteţ	15	He	44.14N	24.27 E
Oltu	24	Ib	40.33N	41.59 E
Oluanpi	21	Og	21.54N	120.51 E
Olutanga	26	He	7.22N	122.52 E
Olvera	13	Gh	36.56N	5.16W
Olym	16	Kc	52.27N	38.05 E
Olympia	39	Ge	47.03N	122.53W
Olympic Mountains	46	Dc	47.50N	123.45W
Olympus, Mount-	38	Ge	47.48N	123.43W
Olympus, Mount- (EN)= Ólimbos, Óros-	5	Ig	40.05N	22.21 E
Om	20	Cf	54.59N	73.22 E
Ōma	29a	Bc	41.30N	140.55 E
Oma	17	Cc	66.45N	46.20 E
Ōmachi	28	Nf	36.30N	137.52 E
Omae-Zaki	29	Fd	34.36N	138.14 E
Ōmagari	28	Pe	39.27N	140.29 E
Omagh/An Ómaigh	9	Fg	54.36N	7.18W
Omaha	39	Je	41.16N	95.57W
Omak	46	Fb	48.24N	119.31W
Omakau	62	Cf	45.06S	169.36 E
Omak Lake	46	Fb	48.16N	119.23W
Oman (EN)='Umān [1]	22	Hg	21.00N	57.00 E
Oman, Gulf of- (EN)= 'Umān, Khalīj-	21	Hg	25.00N	58.00 E
Omarama	61	Ch	44.29S	169.58 E
Omar Gambon	35	He	3.10N	45.47 E
Omaru-Gawa	29	Be	32.07N	131.34 E
Omaruru	37	Bd	21.28S	15.56 E
Omaruru [3]	37	Bd	21.30S	15.00 E
Omatako	37	Bd	21.07S	16.43 E
Omatako, Omuramba-	30	Jj	17.57S	20.25 E
Omate	54	Dg	16.41S	70.59W
Ōma-Zaki	29a	Bc	41.32N	140.55 E
Ombai, Selat-	26	Hh	8.30S	125.00 E
Ombella-Mpoko [3]	35	Bd	5.00N	18.00 E
Omberg	8	Ff	58.20N	14.39 E
Ombo	8	Ae	59.15N	6.00 E
Omboué	36	Ac	1.34S	9.15 E
Ombrone	14	Fh	42.39N	11.01 E
Ombu	27	Ee	31.18N	86.33 E
Omčak	20	Jd	61.38N	147.55 E
Omdurman (EN)=Umm Durmān	31	Kg	15.38N	32.30 E
Ōme	29	Fd	35.47N	139.15 E
Omegna	14	Ce	45.53N	8.24 E
Omeo	59	Jg	37.06S	147.36 E
Ömerköy	15	Lj	39.50N	28.04 E
Ometepe, Isla de-	47	Gf	11.30N	85.35W
Ometepec	47	Ee	16.41N	98.25W
Omhajer	35	Fc	14.19N	36.40 E
Ōmihachiman	29	Ed	35.08N	136.05 E
Omihi	62	Ee	43.01S	172.51 E
Omineca	42	Fe	56.05N	124.05W
Omineca Mountains	42	Ee	56.35N	125.55W
Omiš	14	Kg	43.27N	16.42 E
Ōmi-Shima [Jap.]	29	Bd	34.25N	131.15 E
Ōmi-Shima [Jap.]	29	Cd	34.15N	133.00 E
Omitara	37	Bd	22.18S	18.01 E
Ōmiya	27	Od	35.54N	139.38 E
Ommanney Bay	42	Hb	73.00N	101.00W
Omme Å	8	Ci	55.55N	8.25 E
Ommen	12	Ib	52.31N	6.25 E
Omo	30	Kh	4.32N	36.04 E
Omø	8	Di	55.10N	11.10 E
Omoa, Bahía de-	49	Cf	15.50N	88.10W
Omodeo, Lago-	14	Cj	40.10N	8.55 E
Omoloj	20	Ib	71.08N	132.01 E
Omolon	21	Rc	68.42N	158.36 E
Omolon	20	Lc	65.12N	160.27 E
Omono-Gawa	29	Gb	39.44N	140.04 E
Omont	12	Ge	49.36N	4.44 E
Omoto-Gawa	29	Gb	39.51N	141.58 E
Omsk	22	Jd	55.00N	73.24 E
Omskaja Oblast [3]	19	Hd	56.00N	72.30 E
Omsukčan	20	Kd	62.27N	155.50 E
Omsukčanski Hrebet	20	Kd	63.00N	155.10 E
Ōmu	28	Qb	44.34N	142.58 E
Omu, Vîrful-	15	Id	45.26N	25.25 E
Omulew	10	Rc	53.05N	21.32 E
Ōmura	28	Jh	32.54N	129.57 E
Ōmura-Wan	29	Ae	33.00N	129.50 E
Omurtag	15	Jf	43.06N	26.25 E
Ōmuta	28	Kh	33.02N	130.27 E
Omutinski	19	Gd	56.31N	67.45 E
Omutninsk	19	Fd	58.43N	52.12 E
Oña	13	Ib	42.44N	3.24W
Onagawa	29	Gb	38.26N	141.27 E
Onakayale	37	Bc	17.30S	15.01 E
Onaman Lake	45	Ma	50.00N	87.29W
Onamia	45	Jc	46.04N	93.40W
Onamue	64d	Bb	7.21N	151.31 E
Onaping Lake	44	Gb	46.57N	81.30W
Onatchiway, Lac-	44	La	49.03N	71.03W
Onawa	45	He	42.02N	96.06W
Onch'ŏn	28	He	38.49N	125.13 E
Oncócua	36	Bf	16.40S	13.24 E
Onda	13	Le	39.58N	0.15W
Ondangua	31	Ij	17.55S	16.00 E
Ondàrroa	13	Ja	43.19N	2.25W
Ondava	10	Rh	48.27N	21.48 E
Ondo [2]	34	Gd	7.00N	5.00 E
Ondo [Jap.]	29	Cd	34.12N	132.32 E
Ondo [Nig.]	34	Fd	7.06N	4.50 E
Ondor Sum	28	Bc	42.30N	113.00 E
Ondozero, Ozero-	7	He	63.40N	33.15 E
One and Half Degree Channel	21	Ji	1.30N	73.10 E
Oneata	63d	Cc	18.27S	178.29W
Oneata Passage	63d	Cc	18.32S	178.28W
Onega	6	Jc	63.57N	38.05 E
Onega	5	Jc	63.58N	37.55 E
Onega, Lake- (EN)= Onežskoje Ozero	5	Jc	61.30N	35.45 E
Onega Peninsula (EN)= Onežski Poluostrov	5	Jc	64.35N	38.00 E
One Hundred Mile House	42	Ff	51.38N	121.16W
Oneida	44	Jd	43.04N	75.40W
Oneida Lake	44	Jd	43.13N	76.00W
O'Neil	43	Hc	42.27N	98.39W
Ōnejime	29	Bf	31.14N	130.47 E
Onekotan, Ostrov-	21	Re	49.25N	154.45 E
Oneonta [Al.-U.S.]	44	Di	33.57N	86.29W
Oneonta [N.Y.-U.S.]	44	Jd	42.28N	75.04W
Oneroa	64p	Cb	21.15S	159.43W
Onežskaja Guba	5	Jc	64.20N	36.30 E
Onežski Poluostrov=Onega Peninsula (EN)	5	Jc	64.35N	38.00 E
Onežskoje Ozero=Onega, Lake- (EN)	5	Jc	61.30N	35.45 E
Ongea Levu	63d	Cc	19.08S	178.24W

Index Symbols

[1] Independent Nation · [2] State, Region · [3] District, County · [4] Municipality · [5] Colony, Dependency · Continent · Physical Region

Historical or Cultural Region · Mount, Mountain · Volcano · Hill · Mountains, Mountain Range · Hills, Escarpment · Plateau, Upland

Pass, Gap · Plain, Lowland · Delta · Salt Flat · Valley, Canyon · Crater, Cave · Karst Features

Depression · Polder · Desert, Dunes · Forest, Woods · Heath, Steppe · Oasis · Cape, Point

Coast, Beach · Cliff · Peninsula · Isthmus · Sandbank · Island · Atoll

Rock, Reef · Islands, Archipelago · Rocks, Reefs · Coral Reef · Well, Spring · Geyser · River, Stream

Waterfall Rapids · River Mouth, Estuary · Lake · Salt Lake · Intermittent Lake · Reservoir · Swamp, Pond

Canal · Glacier · Ice Shelf, Pack Ice · Ocean · Sea · Gulf, Bay · Strait, Fjord

Lagoon · Bank · Seamount · Tablemount · Ridge · Shelf · Basin

Escarpment, Sea Scarp · Fracture · Trench, Abyss · National Park, Reserve · Point of Interest · Recreation Site · Cave, Cavern

Historic Site · Ruins · Wall, Walls · Church, Abbey · Temple · Scientific Station · Airport

Port · Lighthouse · Mine · Tunnel · Dam, Bridge

Ongijn-Gol	27	Hc	44.30N	103.40 E
Ongjin	27	Md	37.56N	125.22 E
Ongniud Qi (Wudan)	27	Kc	42.58N	119.01 E
Ongole	25	Ge	15.30N	80.03 E
Ongon	27	Jb	45.49N	113.08 E
Onhaye	12	Gd	50.15N	4.50 E
Oni	16	Mh	42.35N	43.27 E
Onigajō-Yama	29	Ce	33.07N	132.41 E
Onilany	30	Lk	23.34S	43.45 E
Onishibetsu	29a	Ca	45.21N	142.06 E
Onitsha	31	Hh	6.10N	6.47 E
Ono	29	Dd	34.51N	134.57 E
Ono	63d	Bc	18.54S	178.29 E
Ōno [Jap.]	28	Ng	35.59N	136.29 E
Ōno [Jap.]	29	Cd	34.18N	132.17 E
Onoda	29	Be	33.59N	131.11 E
Ōno-Gawa	29	Be	33.15N	131.43 E
Ōnohara-Jima	29	Fd	34.02N	139.23 E
Onohoj	20	Ff	51.55N	108.01 E
Ono-i-Lau Islands	57	Jg	20.39S	178.42W
Onojō	29	Be	33.34N	130.29 E
Onomichi	28	Lg	34.25N	133.12 E
Onon	21	Nd	51.42N	115.50 E
Onoto	50	Dh	9.36N	65.12W
Onotoa Atoll	57	Ie	1.52S	175.34 E
Ons, Isla de-	13	Db	42.23N	8.56W
Onsala	7	Ch	57.25N	12.01 E
Onseepkans	37	Be	28.45S	19.17 E
Onslow	58	Cg	21.39S	115.06 E
Onslow Bay	43	Le	34.20N	77.20W
On-Take	29	Bf	31.35N	130.39 E
Ontake-San	29	Ed	35.53N	137.29 E
Ontario [3]	42	If	50.00N	86.00W
Ontario [Ca.-U.S.]	46	Gi	34.04N	117.39W
Ontario [Or.-U.S.]	43	Dc	44.02N	116.58W
Ontario, Lake-	38	Le	43.40N	78.00W
Ontario Peninsula	38	Ke	43.50N	81.00W
Onteniente/Ontinyent	13	Lf	38.49N	0.37W
Ontinyent/Onteniente	13	Lf	38.49N	0.37W
Ontojärvi	7	Gd	64.08N	29.09 E
Ontonagon	44	Cb	46.52N	89.19W
Ontong Java Atoll	57	Ge	5.20S	159.30 E
Ō-Numa	29a	Bc	41.59N	140.41 E
Oodnadatta	58	Eg	27.33S	135.28 E
Ooidonk	12	Fc	51.01N	3.35 E
Ookala	65a	Fc	20.01N	155.17W
Ooldea	58	Eh	30.27S	131.50 E
Oologah Lake	45	Ih	36.39N	95.36W
Ooltgensplaat, Oostflakkee-	12	Gc	51.41N	4.21 E
Oostburg	12	Fc	51.20N	3.30 E
Oostelijk Flevoland	12	Hb	52.30N	5.40 E
Oostende/Ostende	11	Ic	51.14N	2.55 E
Oosterhout	11	Kc	51.38N	4.51 E
Oosterschelde=East Schelde (EN)	11	Jc	51.30N	4.00 E
Oosterwolde, Ooststellingwerf-	12	Ha	53.00N	6.18 E
Oosterzele	12	Fd	50.57N	3.48 E
Oostflakkee	12	Gc	51.41N	4.21 E
Oostflakkee-Ooltgensplaat	12	Gc	51.41N	4.21 E
Oostkamp	12	Fc	51.09N	3.14 E
Oost-Souburg, Vlissingen-	12	Fc	51.28N	3.36 E
Ooststellingwerf	12	Ib	53.00N	6.18 E
Ooststellingwerf-Oosterwolde	12	Ha	53.00N	6.18 E
Oost Vieland, Vieland-	12	Ha	53.17N	5.06 E
Oost-Vlaanderen [3]	12	Fc	51.00N	3.40 E
Ootmarsum	12	Ib	52.25N	6.54 E
Opala	36	Dc	0.37S	24.21 E
Opalenica	10	Md	52.19N	16.23 E
Opanake	25	Gg	6.36N	80.37 E
Opari	35	Ee	3.56N	32.03 E
Oparino	7	Lg	59.53N	48.25 E
Opasatika	44	Fa	49.31N	82.58W
Opasatika Lake	44	Fa	49.06N	83.08W
Opasatika River	44	Fa	50.15N	82.25W
Opatija	14	Ie	45.20N	14.19 E
Opatów	10	Rf	50.49N	21.26 E
Opatówka	10	Rf	50.42N	21.50 E
Opava	10	Ng	49.57N	17.54 E
Opava	10	Og	49.51N	18.17 E
Opelika	43	Je	32.39N	85.23W
Opelousas	45	Jk	30.32N	92.05W
Opémisca, Lac-	44	Ja	49.58N	74.57W
Opheim	46	Lb	48.51N	106.24W
Ophir	40	Hd	63.10N	156.31W
Ophthalmia Range	59	Dd	23.15S	119.30 E
Opienge	36	Eb	0.12N	27.30 E
Opihikao	65a	Gd	19.26N	154.53W
Opinaca	42	Jf	52.14N	78.02W
Opiscotéo, Lac-	42	Kf	53.09N	68.10W
Opladen, Leverkusen-	10	De	51.04N	7.01 E
Opobo	34	Ge	4.34N	7.27 E
Opočka	19	Cd	56.42N	28.41 E
Opoczno	10	Qe	51.23N	20.17 E
Opole [2]	10	Nf	50.40N	17.55 E
Opole	10	Nf	50.41N	17.55 E
Opole Lubelskie	10	Re	51.09N	21.58 E
Oporny	19	Ff	46.13N	54.29 E
Opotiki	62	Gc	38.01S	177.17 E
Opp	44	Dj	31.17N	86.22W
Oppa-Wan	29	Gb	38.35N	141.30 E
Oppdal	7	Be	62.36N	9.40 E
Oppenheim	10	Eg	49.51N	8.21 E
Oppland [2]	7	Bf	61.10N	9.40 E
Opportunity	46	Gc	47.39N	117.15W
Opsa	8	Li	55.31N	26.54 E
Opsterland	12	Ia	53.03N	6.04 E
Opsterland-Beetsterzwaag	12	Ia	53.03N	6.04 E
Opua	61	Dg	35.18S	174.07 E
Opunake	62	Ec	39.27S	173.51 E
Oputo	48	Eb	30.03N	109.20W
Oquossoc	44	Lc	45.04N	70.44W
Or	16	Ud	51.12N	58.33 E
Ōra	33	Cd	28.20N	19.35 E
Oradea	6	If	47.04N	21.56 E
Orahovac	15	Dg	42.24N	20.40 E
Orahovica	14	Le	45.32N	17.53 E
Orai	25	Fc	25.59N	79.28 E
Oraibi Wash	46	Ji	35.26N	110.49W
Oran	31	Ge	35.42N	0.38W
Oran [3]	32	Gb	36.00N	0.35W
Orange [Austl.]	58	Fh	33.17S	149.06 E
Orange [Fr.]	11	Kj	44.08N	4.48 E
Orange [Tx.-U.S.]	43	Ie	30.01N	93.44W
Orange [Va.-U.S.]	44	Hf	38.14N	78.07W
Orange/Oranje	30	Ik	28.38S	16.27 E
Orange, Cabo-	52	Ke	4.24N	51.33W
Orangeburg	43	Ke	33.30N	80.52W
Orange Free State/Oranje Vrystaat [2]	37	De	29.00S	26.00 E
Orange Lake	44	Fk	29.25N	82.13W
Orange Park	44	Gj	30.10N	81.42W
Orangeville	44	Gd	43.55N	80.06W
Orange Walk	47	Ge	18.06N	88.33W
Orango	30	Fg	11.05N	16.08W
Oranienburg	10	Jd	52.45N	13.14 E
Oranje/Orange	30	Ik	28.38S	16.27 E
Oranje Gebergte	54	Hc	3.00N	55.00W
Oranjemund	37	Be	28.38S	16.24 E
Oranjestad	54	Da	12.33N	70.06W
Oranje Vrystaat/Orange Free State [2]	37	De	29.00S	26.00 E
Oranžerei	16	Og	45.50N	47.36 E
Orapa	37	Dd	21.16S	25.22 E
Orăștie	15	Gd	45.50N	23.12 E
Orava	10	Pg	49.08N	19.10 E
Oravița	15	Ed	45.02N	21.42 E
Oravská Priehradní Nádrž	10	Pg	49.20N	19.35 E
Orb	11	Jk	43.15N	3.18 E
Orba	14	Cf	44.53N	8.37 E
Orba Co	27	De	34.33N	81.06 E
Ørbæk	8	Di	55.16N	10.41 E
Orbec	12	Ce	49.01N	0.25 E
Orbetello	14	Fh	42.27N	11.13 E
Orbetello, Laguna di-	14	Fh	42.25N	11.15 E
Orbigo	13	Gc	41.58N	5.40W
Orbiquet	12	Ce	49.09N	0.14 E
Orbost	59	Jg	37.42S	148.27 E
Örbyhus	8	Gd	60.14N	17.42 E
Orcadas	66	Re	60.40S	44.30W
Orcas Island	46	Db	48.39N	122.55W
Orchies	12	Fd	50.28N	3.14 E
Orchon → Orhon	21	Md	50.21N	106.05 E
Orcia	14	Fh	42.58N	11.21 E
Orco	14	Be	45.10N	7.52 E
Ord, Mount-	59	Fc	17.20S	125.35 E
Ördenes	13	Da	43.04N	8.24W
Ordos Desert (EN)=Mu Us Shamo	21	Mf	38.45N	109.10 E
Ord River	57	Df	15.30S	128.21 E
Ordu	23	Ea	41.00N	37.53 E
Ordubad	16	Oj	38.55N	46.01 E
Ordynskoje	20	Df	54.22N	81.58 E
Ordžonikidze [Ukr.-U.S.S.R.]	16	If	47.40N	34.04 E
Ordžonikidze [Kaz.-U.S.S.R.]	17	Jj	52.25N	61.45 E
Ordžonikidze [R.S.F.S.R.]	6	Kg	43.03N	44.40 E
Ordžonikidzeabad	19	Gh	38.34N	69.02 E
Ore älv	8	Fc	61.08N	14.35 E
Orebić	14	Lh	42.58N	17.11 E
Örebro	6	Hd	59.17N	15.13 E
Örebro [2]	7	Dg	59.30N	15.00 E
Oredež	8	Nf	58.50N	30.13 E
Oregon	44	Fe	41.38N	83.28W
Oregon [2]	43	Cc	44.00N	121.00W
Oregon City	43	Cb	45.21N	122.36W
Oregon Inlet	44	Jh	35.50N	75.35W
Öregrund	8	Hd	60.20N	18.26 E
Orehov	16	If	47.34N	35.47 E
Orehovo-Zujevo	6	Jd	55.49N	38.59 E
Orel	6	Je	52.59N	36.05 E
Orel	16	Ie	48.31N	34.55 E
Orel, Gora-	20	Jf	53.55N	140.01 E
Orellana [Peru]	54	Ce	6.54S	75.04W
Orellana [Peru]	54	Cd	4.40S	78.10W
Orem	43	Ec	40.19N	111.42W
Ore Mountains (EN)=Erzgebirge	5	He	50.30N	13.15 E
Ore Mountains (EN)=Krušné Hory	5	He	50.30N	13.15 E
Ören	24	Bd	37.18N	27.29 E
Orenbel	24	Hb	40.00N	39.10 E
Orenburg	6	Le	51.54N	55.06 E
Orenburgskaja Oblast [3]	19	Fe	52.00N	55.00 E
Örencik	24	Cc	39.16N	29.34 E
Orense [3]	13	Eb	42.10N	7.30W
Orense [Arg.]	56	Ie	38.40S	59.47W
Orense [Sp.]	13	Eb	42.20N	7.51W
Oreón, Dhíavlos-	15	Fk	38.54N	22.55 E
Orepuki	62	Bg	46.17S	167.44 E
Orestiás	15	Jh	41.30N	26.31 E
Øresund	5	Hd	55.50N	12.40 E
Oreti	62	Cg	46.28S	168.17 E
Orewa	62	Fb	36.35S	174.42 E
Orford	12	Db	52.05N	1.32 E
Orford Ness	9	Oi	52.05N	1.34 E
Orgañá/Organyà	13	Nb	42.13N	1.20 E
Organ Needle	45	Cj	32.21N	106.33W
Organyà/Orgañá	13	Nb	42.13N	1.20 E
Orgaz	13	Ie	39.39N	3.54W
Orgejev	19	Cf	47.23N	28.50 E
Orgelet	11	Lh	46.31N	5.37 E
Orgon Tal	28	Bc	43.20N	112.40 E
Orgosolo	14	Dj	40.12N	9.21 E
Orgün	23	Kc	32.57N	69.11 E
Orhaneli	15	Lj	39.54N	29.00 E
Orhaneli/Koca Çay	15	Lj	39.56N	28.32 E
Orhangazi	15	Mi	40.30N	29.18 E
Orhomenós	15	Fk	38.35N	22.54 E
Orhon (Orchon)	21	Md	50.21N	106.05 E
Orhy, Pico de-	13	La	42.59N	1.00W
Oria	13	Ja	43.17N	2.08W
Orichuna, Río-	50	Bi	7.30N	68.13W
Orick	46	Cf	41.17N	124.04W
Oriental	48	Kh	19.22N	97.37W
Oriental, Cordillera-	49	Md	18.55N	69.15W
Oriente	56	He	38.44S	60.37W
Orihuela	13	Lf	38.05N	0.57W
Oriku	15	Ci	40.17N	19.25 E
Óri Lekánis	15	Hh	41.08N	24.33 E
Orillia	42	Jh	44.37N	79.25W
Orimattila	7	Ff	60.48N	25.45 E
Orinoco, Río-	52	Je	8.37N	62.15W
Oripää	8	Jd	60.51N	22.41 E
Orissa [3]	25	Gd	21.00N	84.00 E
Orissaare/Orissare	7	Fg	58.34N	23.05 E
Orissare/Orissaare	7	Fg	58.34N	23.05 E
Oristano	14	Ck	39.54N	8.36 E
Oristano, Golfo di-	14	Ck	39.50N	8.30 E
Orituco, Río-	50	Ch	8.45N	67.27W
Orivesi	5	Ic	62.15N	29.25 E
Orivesi	7	Ff	61.41N	24.21 E
Oriximiná	54	Gd	1.45S	55.52W
Orizaba	39	Jh	18.51N	97.06W
Orizaba, Pico de- (Citlaltépetl, Volcán-)	38	Jh	19.01N	97.16W
Orizona	55	Hc	17.03S	48.18W
Orjahovo	15	Gf	43.44N	23.58 E
Ørje	8	De	59.29N	11.39 E
Orjen	15	Bg	42.34N	18.33 E
Orjiva	13	Ih	36.54N	3.25W
Orkanger	7	Be	63.19N	9.52 E
Orkdalen	8	Ca	63.15N	9.50 E
Örkelljunga	8	Eh	56.17N	13.17 E
Orkla	8	Ca	63.18N	9.50 E
Orkney	37	De	27.00S	26.39 E
Orkney [3]	9	Kb	59.00N	3.00W
Orkney Islands	5	Fd	59.00N	3.00W
Orlândia	55	Ie	20.43S	47.53W
Orlando	39	Kg	28.32N	81.23W
Orlando, Capo d'-	14	Il	38.10N	14.45 E
Orlanka	10	Td	52.52N	23.12 E
Orléanais	11	Hf	48.40N	1.20 E
Orléans	6	Gf	47.55N	1.54 E
Orlice	10	Lf	50.12N	15.49 E
Orlické Hory	10	Mf	50.10N	16.30 E
Orlik	20	Ef	52.30N	99.55 E
Orlovskaja Oblast [3]	19	De	52.45N	36.30 E
Orlovski	16	Mf	46.52N	42.06 E
Orlovski, mys-	7	Jc	67.16N	41.18 E
Orly	11	If	48.45N	2.24 E
Ormāra	25	Cc	25.12N	64.38 E
Ormes	12	Ce	49.03N	0.59 E
Ormoc	26	Hd	11.00N	124.37 E
Ormond	62	Gc	38.33S	177.55 E
Ormond Beach	44	Gk	29.17N	81.02W
Ornain	11	Kf	48.46N	4.47 E
Ornans	11	Mg	47.06N	6.09 E
Ornäs	8	Fd	60.31N	15.32 E
Orne [3]	11	Gf	48.40N	0.05 E
Orne [Fr.]	11	Ie	49.17N	6.11 E
Orne [Fr.]	11	Be	49.19N	0.14W
Orne Seamount (EN)	61	Je	27.30S	157.30W
Orneta	10	Qb	54.08N	20.08 E
Ornö	7	Eg	59.05N	18.25 E
Örnsköldsvik	7	Ee	63.18N	18.43 E
Oro	28	Id	40.01N	127.27 E
Oro, Rio de-	55	Ch	27.04S	58.34W
Oro, Rio del-	48	Ge	25.35N	105.03W
Orocué	54	Dc	4.48N	71.20W
Orodara	34	Ec	10.59N	4.55W
Orofino	46	Gc	46.29N	116.15W
Orogrande	45	Cj	32.23N	106.08W
Orohena, Mont-	65e	Fc	17.31S	149.28W
Oroluk Atoll	57	Gd	7.32N	155.18 E
Orom	36	Fb	3.20N	33.40 E
Oromocto	42	Kg	45.51N	66.29W
Oron	34	Ge	4.50N	8.14 E
Orona Atoll (Hull)	57	Je	4.29S	172.10W
Orongo	65d	Ac	27.10S	109.26W
Oronsay	9	Ge	56.01N	6.14W
Orontes (EN)=Nahr al 'Āṣī	23	Eb	36.02N	35.58 E
Oropesa [Sp.]	13	Ge	39.55N	5.10W
Oropesa [Sp.]	13	Ld	40.06N	0.09W
Oroqen Zizhiqi (Alihe)	27	La	50.35N	123.42 E
Oroquieta	26	He	8.29N	123.48 E
Orós	54	Ke	6.15S	38.55W
Orós, Açude-	54	Ke	6.15S	39.05W
Orosei	14	Dj	40.23N	9.42 E
Orosei, Golfo di-	14	Dj	40.15N	9.45 E
Orosháza	10	Qj	46.34N	20.40 E
Oro-Shima	29	Be	33.52N	130.02 E
Oroszlány	10	Oi	47.29N	18.19 E
Orote Peninsula	64c	Bb	13.26N	144.38 E
Orote Point	64c	Bb	13.27N	144.37 E
Orotukan	20	Kd	62.17N	151.50 E
Oroville [Ca.-U.S.]	46	Eg	39.31N	121.33W
Oroville [Wa.-U.S.]	46	Fb	48.56N	119.26W
Orp-Jauche	12	Gd	50.40N	4.57 E
Orqohan	27	Lb	49.36N	121.23 E
Orr	45	Jb	48.03N	92.50W
Orrefors	8	Fh	56.50N	15.45 E
Orri, Pic d'-/Llorri	13	Nb	42.23N	1.12 E
Orša	6	Je	54.30N	30.24 E
Orsa	7	Df	61.07N	14.37 E
Orsasjön	8	Fc	61.05N	14.35 E
Orsay	12	Ef	48.42N	2.11 E
Orsjön	8	Gc	61.35N	16.20 E
Orsk	6	Le	51.12N	58.34 E
Orşova	15	Fe	44.42N	22.25 E
Ørsta	7	Be	62.12N	6.09 E
Örsundsbro	8	Ge	59.44N	17.18 E
Orta, Lago d'-	14	Ce	45.50N	8.25 E
Ortaca	24	Cd	36.49N	28.47 E
Ortakent	15	Kl	37.02N	27.21 E
Ortaklar	15	Kl	37.53N	27.30 E
Orta Nova	14	Ji	41.19N	15.42 E
Orte	14	Gh	42.27N	12.23 E
Ortegal, Cabo-	13	Ea	43.45N	7.53W
Ortenberg	12	Ld	50.21N	9.03 E
Orthez	11	Fk	43.29N	0.46W
Orthon, Río-	54	Ef	10.50S	66.04W
Ortigueira [Braz.]	56	Jb	24.12S	50.55W
Ortigueira [Sp.]	13	Fa	43.34N	6.44W
Ortisei / Sankt Ulrich	14	Fd	46.34N	11.40 E
Ortiz [Mex.]	48	Dc	28.15N	110.43W
Ortiz [Ven.]	50	Ch	9.37N	67.17W
Ortlergruppe/Ortles	14	Ed	46.30N	10.40 E
Ortles/Ortlergruppe	14	Ed	46.30N	10.40 E
Ortolo	11a	Ab	41.30N	8.55 E
Ortona	14	Ih	42.21N	14.24 E
Ortonville	45	Hd	45.19N	96.27W
Orto-Tokoj	18	Kc	42.20N	76.02 E
Örtze	10	Fd	52.40N	9.57 E
Orukuizu	64a	Ac	7.10N	134.17 E
Orūmīyeh	22	Gf	37.33N	45.04 E
Orūmīyeh, Daryācheh-ye-=Urmia, Lake- (EN)	21	Gf	37.40N	45.30 E
Oruro [2]	54	Eg	18.40S	67.30W
Oruro	53	Jg	17.59S	67.09W
Orust	8	Df	58.10N	11.38 E
Orūzgān [3]	23	Kc	33.15N	66.00 E
Orūzgān	23	Kc	32.56N	66.38 E
Orval, Abbaye d'-	12	He	49.38N	5.22 E
Orvault	11	Eg	47.16N	1.37W
Orvieto	14	Gh	42.43N	12.07 E
Orville Escarpment	66	Qf	75.45S	65.30W
Orvílos, Óros-	15	Gh	41.23N	23.36 E
Orwell	12	Dc	51.58N	1.18 E
Orxois	12	Fe	49.08N	3.12 E
Orz	10	Rd	52.50N	21.30 E
Orzinuovi	14	De	45.24N	9.55 E
Orzyc	10	Rd	52.47N	21.13 E
Orzysz	10	Rc	53.49N	21.56 E
Oš	19	Hg	40.32N	72.50 E
Os	7	Ce	62.30N	11.12 E
Osa	19	Fd	57.17N	55.26 E
Oša	8	Lh	56.21N	26.29 E
Osa	10	Oc	53.33N	18.45 E
Osa, Peninsula de-	47	Hg	8.35N	83.33W
Osage	45	Je	43.17N	92.49W
Osage River	43	Id	38.35N	91.57W
Osaka	29	Ed	35.57N	137.14 E
Ōsaka	22	Pf	34.40N	135.30 E
Osaka Bay (EN)=Ōsaka-Wan	28	Mg	34.36N	135.27 E
Ōsaka-Fu [2]	28	Mg	34.45N	135.35 E
Osakarovka	19	He	50.32N	72.39 E
Ōsaka-Wan=Osaka Bay (EN)	28	Mg	34.36N	135.27 E
Osām	15	Hf	43.42N	24.51 E
Osan	28	If	37.09N	127.04 E
Osasco	55	If	23.32S	46.46W
Osat	14	Nf	44.02N	19.20 E
Osawatomie	45	Ig	38.31N	94.57W
Osborne	45	Gg	39.26N	98.42W
Osburger Hochwald	12	Ie	49.40N	6.50 E
Osby	7	Ch	56.22N	13.59 E
Osceola [Ar.-U.S.]	45	Li	35.42N	89.58W
Osceola [Ia.-U.S.]	45	Ic	41.02N	93.46W
Osceola [Mo.-U.S.]	45	Jh	38.03N	93.42W
Oschatz	10	Je	51.18N	13.07 E
Oschersleben	10	Hd	52.02N	11.15 E
Oschiri	14	Dj	40.43N	9.06 E
Osen	7	Cd	64.18N	10.31 E
Osered	16	Ld	50.01N	40.48 E
Osetr	16	Kb	55.00N	38.45 E
Ōse-Zaki	28	Jh	32.38N	128.42 E
Oshamanbe	28	Pc	42.30N	140.22 E
Oshawa	42	Jh	43.54N	78.51W
Oshekehia Lake	37	Bc	18.08S	15.45 E
Oshika	29	Gb	38.17N	141.31 E
Oshika-Hantō	28	Pe	38.22N	141.27 E
Oshikango	37	Bc	17.22S	15.55 E
Oshima	29	Ce	33.55N	132.11 E
Ō-Shima [Jap.]	29	De	33.28N	135.50 E
Ō-Shima [Jap.]	29	Ae	33.30N	129.33 E
Ō-Shima [Jap.]	29	Ae	32.34N	128.54 E
Ō-Shima [Jap.]	29	Be	33.54N	130.27 E
Ō-Shima [Jap.]	27	Oe	34.45N	139.30 E
Ōshima [Jap.]	29	Fd	34.44N	139.20 E
Ō-Shima [Jap.]	29	Bf	31.32N	131.25 E
Ō-Shima [Jap.]	29	De	33.38N	134.30 E
Ō-Shima [Jap.]	29	Cd	34.10N	133.05 E
Ōshima [Jap.]	29	Ae	33.04N	129.36 E
Ō-Shima [Jap.]	28	Od	41.30N	139.15 E
Ō-Shima [Jap.]	28	Jh	32.04N	128.26 E
Oshima-Hantō	28	Pd	41.40N	140.30 E
Ōshima-Kaikyō	29b	Ba	28.10N	129.15 E
Oshkosh [Nb.-U.S.]	45	Ef	41.24N	102.21W
Oshkosh [Wi.-U.S.]	43	Jc	44.01N	88.33W
Oshnavīyeh	24	Kd	37.02N	45.06 E
Oshogbo	31	Hh	7.46N	4.34 E
Oshtorān Kūh	23	Gc	33.20N	49.16 E
Oshtorīnān	24	Me	34.01N	48.38 E
Oshwe	36	Cc	3.24S	19.30 E
Osich'ŏn-ni	28	Jd	41.25N	128.16 E
Osijek	6	Hf	45.33N	18.42 E
Osilo	14	Cj	40.45N	8.40 E
Osimo	14	Hg	43.28N	13.29 E
Osinki	7	Lj	52.52N	49.31 E
Osinniki	20	Df	53.37N	87.31 E
Osipaonica	15	Ee	44.33N	21.04 E
Osipoviči	16	Fc	53.19N	28.40 E
Osječenica	14	Kf	44.29N	16.17 E
Oskaloosa	45	Jf	41.18N	92.39W
Oskarshamn	7	Dh	57.16N	16.26 E
Oskarström	8	Eh	56.48N	12.58 E
Oskélanéo	44	Ja	48.08N	75.05W
Oskino	20	Fd	60.48N	107.58 E
Öskjuvatn	7a	Cb	65.02N	16.45W
Oskol	16	Je	49.06N	37.25 E
Oskü	24	Ld	37.55N	46.06 E
Oslava	10	Mg	49.05N	16.22 E
Ösling	11	Le	49.55N	6.00 E
Osljanka, Gora-	17	Ig	59.10N	58.33 E
Oslo [2]	7	Cg	59.55N	10.45 E
Oslo	6	Hd	59.55N	10.45 E
Oslofjorden	5	Hd	59.20N	10.35 E
Osmānābād	25	Fe	18.10N	76.03 E
Osmancık	24	Fb	40.59N	34.49 E
Osmaneli	15	Ni	40.22N	30.01 E
Osmaniye	23	Eb	37.05N	36.14 E
Osmino	8	Mf	58.54N	29.15 E
Ošmjanskaja Vozvyšennost	8	Kj	54.30N	26.00 E
Ošmjany	16	Db	54.27N	25.57 E
Ösmo	8	Gf	58.59N	17.54 E
Osmussaar/Osmussar	8	Je	59.20N	23.15 E
Osmussar/Osmussaar	8	Je	59.20N	23.15 E
Osnabrück	6	Ge	52.16N	8.03 E
Osning	12	Kb	52.10N	8.05 E
Oso, Sierra del-	48	Gd	26.00N	105.25W
Osobłoga	10	Nf	50.27N	17.58 E
Osogovske Planine	15	Fg	42.10N	22.30 E
Osor	14	If	44.42N	14.24 E
Osório	56	Jc	29.54S	50.16W
Osorno	53	Ij	40.34S	73.09W
Osoyoos	42	Fg	49.02N	119.28W
Osøyra	7	Af	60.11N	5.28 E
Ospino	50	Bh	9.18N	69.27W
Osprey Reef	57	Ff	13.55S	146.40 E
Oss	11	Lc	51.46N	5.31 E
Ossa, Mount-	57	Fi	41.54S	146.01 E
Óssa, Óros-	15	Fj	39.49N	22.40 E
Ossabaw Island	44	Gj	31.47N	81.06W
Ossa de Montiel	13	Jf	38.58N	2.45W
Osse	11	Gj	44.07N	0.17 E
Ossining	44	Ke	41.10N	73.52W
Ossjøen	8	Dc	61.15N	11.55 E
Oškaja Oblast [3]	19	Hg	40.45N	73.20 E
Ossora	20	Le	59.15N	163.02 E
Östanvik	8	Fc	61.10N	15.13 E
Ostaškov	19	Dd	57.09N	33.07 E
Ostbevern	12	Jb	52.03N	7.51 E
Oste	10	Fc	53.33N	9.10 E
Ostende/Oostende	11	Ic	51.14N	2.55 E
Oster	16	Gd	50.55N	30.57 E
Oster [Ukr.-U.S.S.R.]	16	Gd	50.53N	30.55 E
Oster [U.S.S.R.]	16	Gc	53.47N	31.45 E
Osterburg in der Altmark	10	Hd	52.47N	11.44 E
Österbybruk	8	Gd	60.12N	17.54 E
Österdalälven	7	Df	60.33N	15.08 E
Østerdalen	7	Cf	62.00N	10.40 E
Österfjorden	8	Ad	60.30N	5.20 E
Österforse	8	Ga	63.09N	17.01 E
Östergarnsholm	8	Hg	57.25N	19.00 E
Östergötland	8	Ff	58.25N	15.35 E
Östergötland [2]	7	Dg	58.25N	15.45 E
Osterholz Scharmbeck	10	Ec	53.14N	8.48 E
Österlen	8	Fi	55.30N	14.10 E
Ostermark/Teuva	7	Ee	62.29N	21.44 E
Osterode am Harz	10	Ge	51.44N	10.11 E
Osterøya	7	Af	60.35N	5.35 E
Österreich = Austria (EN) [1]	6	Hf	47.30N	14.00 E
Östersjön=Baltic Sea (EN)	5	Hd	57.00N	19.00 E
Østersøen=Baltic Sea (EN)	5	Hd	57.00N	19.00 E
Östersund	6	Hc	63.11N	14.39 E
Osterwick, Rosendahl-	12	Jb	52.01N	7.12 E
Østfold [2]	7	Cg	59.20N	11.30 E
Ostfriesische Inseln=East Frisian Islands (EN)	10	Dc	53.45N	7.25 E
Ostfriesland=East Friesland (EN)	10	Dc	53.20N	7.40 E
Østgrønland=East Greenland (EN) [2]	41	Id	72.00N	35.00W
Östhammar	7	Ed	60.16N	18.22 E
Osthofen	12	Ke	49.42N	8.20 E
Östmark	8	Ed	60.17N	12.45 E
Ostrach	10	Fh	48.05N	9.25 E
Östra Silen	8	Ee	59.15N	12.20 E
Ostrava	6	Hf	49.50N	18.17 E
Ostrhauderfehn	12	Ja	53.08N	7.37 E
Ostróda	10	Pc	53.43N	19.59 E
Ostrog	16	Ed	50.19N	26.32 E
Ostrogožsk	16	Jd	50.52N	39.05 E
Ostrołęka [2]	10	Rc	53.05N	21.35 E
Ostrołęka	10	Rc	53.06N	21.34 E
Ostrošicki Gorodok	8	Lj	54.03N	27.46 E
Ostrov [Bye.-U.S.S.R.]	10	Vd	52.48N	26.01 E
Ostrov [Czech.]	10	If	50.18N	12.57 E
Ostrov [Rom.]	15	Ke	44.07N	27.22 E
Ostrov [R.S.F.S.R.]	19	Cd	57.23N	28.22 E
Ostrov [R.S.F.S.R.]	8	Mf	58.28N	28.44 E
Ostrovec	8	Lj	54.38N	26.06 E
Ostrovicës, Mali i-	15	Di	40.34N	20.27 E
Ostrovskoje	7	Kh	57.50N	42.13 E
Ostrov Zmeiny	16	Gg	45.15N	30.12 E
Ostrowiec Świętokrzyski	10	Rf	50.57N	21.23 E
Ostrów Lubelski	10	Se	51.30N	22.52 E
Ostrów Mazowiecka	10	Rd	52.49N	21.54 E
Ostrów Wielkopolski	10	Ne	51.39N	17.49 E
Ostryna	10	Uc	53.41N	24.37 E
Ostrzeszów	10	Ne	51.25N	17.57 E
Ostsee=Baltic Sea (EN)	5	Hd	57.00N	19.00 E
Oststeirisches Hügelland	14	Jd	47.00N	15.45 E
Osttirol	14	Gd	46.55N	12.30 E
Ostuni	14	Lj	40.44N	17.35 E
Osumi	15	Ci	40.48N	19.52 E
Ōsumi	29	Bf	31.36N	130.59 E
Ōsumi-Hantō	29	Bf	31.15N	130.50 E
Osumi Islands (EN)=Ōsumi-Shotō	21	Pf	30.35N	130.59 E
Ōsumi-Shotō=Osumi Islands (EN)	21	Pf	30.35N	130.59 E
Osuna	13	Gg	37.14N	5.07W
Osveja	8	Mi	55.59N	28.10 E
Osvejskoje, Ozero-	8	Mh	56.00N	28.15 E
Oswego	43	Lc	43.27N	76.31W
Oswestry	9	Ji	52.52N	3.04W

Index Symbols

[1] Independent Nation
[2] State, Region
[3] District, County
[4] Municipality
[5] Colony, Dependency
Continent
Physical Region
Historical or Cultural Region
Mount, Mountain
Volcano
Hill
Mountains, Mountain Range
Hills, Escarpment
Plateau, Upland
Pass, Gap
Plain, Lowland
Delta
Salt Flat
Valley, Canyon
Crater, Cave
Karst Features
Depression
Polder
Desert, Dunes
Forest, Woods
Heath, Steppe
Oasis
Cape, Point
Coast, Beach
Cliff
Peninsula
Isthmus
Sandbank
Island
Atoll
Rock, Reef
Islands, Archipelago
Rocks, Reefs
Coral Reef
Well, Spring
Geyser
River, Stream
Waterfall Rapids
River Mouth, Estuary
Lake
Salt Lake
Intermittent Lake
Reservoir
Swamp, Pond
Canal
Glacier
Ice Shelf, Pack Ice
Ocean
Sea
Gulf, Bay
Strait, Fjord
Lagoon
Bank
Seamount
Tablemount
Ridge
Shelf
Basin
Escarpment, Sea Scarp
Fracture
Trench, Abyss
National Park, Reserve
Point of Interest
Recreation Site
Cave, Cavern
Historic Site
Ruins
Wall, Walls
Church, Abbey
Temple
Scientific Station
Airport
Port
Lighthouse
Mine
Tunnel
Dam, Bridge

Oświęcim 10 Pf 50.03N 19.12 E
Osyka 45 Kk 31.00N 90.28W
Ōta 29 Fc 36.18N 139.22 E
Ota 29 Ec 35.56N 136.03 E
Otago [2] 62 Cf 45.00S 169.10 E
Otago Peninsula 62 Df 45.50S 170.45 E
Ōtake 28 Lg 34.12N 132.13 E
Otakeho 62 Fc 39.33S 174.03 E
Otaki 62 Fd 40.45S 175.08 E
Ōtakime-Yama 29 Gc 37.22N 140.42 E
Otanoshike 29a Db 43.01N 144.16 E
Otar 19 Hg 43.31N 75.12 E
Otaru 27 Pc 43.13N 141.00 E
Otautau 62 Bg 46.09S 168.00 E
Otava 10 Kg 49.26N 14.12 E
Otava 8 Lc 61.39N 27.04 E
Otavi 37 Bc 19.39S 17.20 E
Ōtawara 28 Pf 36.52N 140.02 E
Otelu Roşu 15 Fd 45.32N 22.22 E
Otematata 62 Df 44.37S 170.11 E
Otepää/Otepja 7 Gg 58.03N 26.30 E
Otepää, Vozvyšennost-/
Otepää Kõrgustik 8 Lf 58.00N 26.40 E
Otepää Kõrgustik/Otepää,
Vozvyšennost- 8 Lf 58.00N 26.40 E
Otepja/Otepää 7 Gg 58.03N 26.30 E
Oteros 47 Cc 26.55N 108.30W
Othain 12 He 49.31N 5.23 E
Othello 46 Fc 46.50N 119.10W
Othonoi 15 Cj 39.50N 19.25 E
Óthris Óros 15 Fj 39.02N 22.37 E
Oti 30 Hh 7.48N 0.08 E
Otira 62 De 42.51S 171.33 E
Otish, Monts- 38 Md 52.45N 69.15W
Otjikondo 37 Bc 19.50S 15.23 E
Otjimbingwe 37 Bd 22.21S 16.08 E
Otjiwarongo 31 Ik 20.29S 16.36 E
Otjiwarongo [3] 37 Bd 20.30S 17.30 E
Otjosondjou, Omuramba- 30 Ij 19.55S 20.00 E
Otjosondu 37 Bd 21.12S 17.58 E
Otmuchowskie, Jezioro- 10 Nf 50.27N 17.15 E
Otnes 7 Cf 61.46N 11.12 E
Otobe 29a Bc 41.57N 140.08 E
Otočac 14 Jf 44.52N 15.14 E
Otofuke 29a Cb 42.59N 143.10 E
Otofuke-Gawa 29a Cb 42.56N 143.12 E
Otog Qi (Ulan) 27 Id 39.07N 108.00 E
Otoineppu 29a Ca 44.43N 142.16 E
Otok 14 Me 45.09N 18.53 E
Otopeni 15 Je 44.33N 26.04 E
Otorohanga 62 Fc 38.11S 175.12 E
Otorten, Gora- 17 If 61.50N 59.13 E
Ōtoyo 29 Ce 33.46N 133.40 E
Otra 5 Gd 58.09N 8.00 E
Otradnaja 16 Lg 44.23N 41.31 E
Otradnoje, Ozero- 8 Nd 60.50N 30.25 E
Otradny 7 Mj 53.23N 51.24 E
Otranto 14 Mj 40.09N 18.30 E
Otranto, Canale d'-=
Otranto, Strait of- (EN) 5 Hg 40.00N 19.00 E
Otranto, Capo d'- 14 Mj 40.06N 18.31 E
Otranto, Strait of- (EN)=
Otranto, Canale d'- 5 Hg 40.00N 19.00 E
Otranto, Strait of- (EN)=
Otrantos, Kanali i- 15 Bi 40.00N 19.00 E
Otranto, Terra d'- 14 Mj 40.20N 18.15 E
Otrantos, Kanali i-=Otranto,
Strait of- (EN) 15 Bi 40.00N 19.00 E
Ötscher 14 Jc 47.51N 15.12 E
Ōtsu 28 Mg 35.00N 135.52 E
Ōtsuchi 28 Pe 39.21N 141.54 E
Ōtsuki [Jap.] 29 Fd 35.36N 138.54 E
Ōtsuki [Jap.] 29 Ce 32.50N 132.41 E
Otta 8 Cc 61.46N 9.31 E
Otta 7 Bf 61.46N 9.32 E
Otta 64d Bb 7.09N 151.54 E
Ottadalen 8 Bc 61.55N 8.00 E
Ottana 14 Dj 40.15N 9.05 E
Otta Pass 64d Bb 7.09N 151.53 E
Ottawa [Il.-U.S.] 45 Lf 41.21N 88.51W
Ottawa [Ks.-U.S.] 43 Hd 38.37N 95.16W
Ottawa [Oh.-U.S.] 44 Ee 41.02N 84.03W
Ottawa [Ont.-Can.] 39 Le 45.25N 75.42W
Ottawa Islands 42 Kd 59.30N 80.10W
Ottawa River 38 Le 45.20N 73.58W
Ottemby 7 Dh 56.16N 16.24 E
Otterberg 12 Je 49.30N 7.46 E
Otter Creek 44 Fk 29.19N 82.48W
Otterndorf 10 Ec 53.48N 8.54 E
Otteroy 8 Bb 62.40N 6.50 E
Otter Rapids 44 Ga 50.15N 81.45W
Otterup 8 Di 55.31N 10.24 E
Ottumwa 43 Ic 41.01N 92.25W
Ottweiler 12 Je 49.23N 7.10 E
Otukpa 34 Gd 7.05N 7.40 E
Otumpa 55 Ah 27.19S 62.13W
Otuquis, Bañados de- 54 Gg 19.20S 58.30W
Otuquis, Rio- 55 Cd 19.41S 58.20W
Oturkpo 34 Gd 7.13N 8.09 E
Otu Tolu Group 65b Bb 20.21S 174.32W
Otuzco 54 Ce 7.54S 78.35W
Otway, Cape- 59 Ig 38.52S 143.31 E
Otwock 10 Rd 52.07N 21.16 E
Otynja 10 Uh 48.40N 24.57 E
Ötz 14 Ec 47.12N 10.54 E
Ötztaler Ache 14 Ec 47.14N 10.50 E
Ötztaler Alpen 10 Gi 46.45N 10.55 E
Ou 25 Kd 20.04N 102.13 E
'O'ua 65b Bb 20.02S 174.41W
Oua 63b Ce 21.14S 167.05 E
Ouachita, Lake- 45 Ji 34.40N 93.25W
Ouachita Mountains 38 Jf 34.40N 94.25W
Ouachita River 43 Ie 31.38N 91.49W
Ouadane 31 Ff 20.57N 11.35W
Ouaddai [3] 35 Cc 13.00N 21.00 E
Ouaddai 30 Jg 13.00N 21.00 E
Ouagadougou 31 Gg 12.22N 1.31W
Ouahigouya 31 Gg 13.35N 2.25W
Ouaka [3] 35 Cd 6.00N 21.00 E
Ouaka 30 Ih 4.59N 19.56 E
Oualata 32 Ff 17.18N 7.00W
Oualata, Dahr- 32 Ff 17.48N 7.24W
Oualidia 32 Fc 32.44N 9.02W
Ouallam 34 Fc 14.19N 2.05 E
Ouallene 32 He 24.35N 1.17 E
Ouanda-Djallé 35 Cd 8.54N 22.48 E
Ouandja 35 Cd 8.35N 23.12 E
Ouandjia 35 Cd 9.35N 21.43 E
Ouango 35 Ce 4.19N 22.33 E
Ouangolodougou 34 Dd 9.58N 5.09W
Ouanne 11 Ig 47.57N 2.47 E
Ouarane 30 Ff 21.00N 10.00W
Ouargaye 34 Fc 11.32N 0.01 E
Ouargla 31 He 31.57N 5.20 E
Ouargla [3] 32 Id 30.00N 6.30 E
Ouarkziz, Jbel- 30 Gf 28.00N 8.20W
Ouarra 30 Jh 5.05N 24.26 E
Ouarsenis, Djebel- 13 Ni 35.53N 1.38 E
Ouarsenis, Massif de l'- 32 Hb 35.50N 2.05 E
Ouarzazate [3] 32 Fc 31.00N 6.30W
Ouarzazate 32 Fc 30.55N 6.55W
Oubangui 30 Ii 0.30S 17.42 E
Ouborré, Pointe- 63b Dd 18.47S 169.16 E
Ouche, Pays d'- 11 Gf 48.55N 0.45 E
Ōuchi 29 Gb 39.27N 140.06 E
Oud Beijerland 12 Gc 51.50N 4.26 E
Oude IJssel 12 Ic 52.00N 6.10 E
Oudenaarde/Audenarde 11 Jd 50.51N 3.36 E
Oudenbosch 12 Gc 51.35N 4.34 E
Oude Rijn 11 Kb 52.05N 4.20 E
Oudon 11 Fg 47.37N 0.42W
Oudtshoorn 31 Jl 33.35S 22.14 E
Oued Ben Tili 32 Fd 25.48N 9.32W
Oued el Abtal 13 Mi 35.27N 0.41 E
Oued Fodda 13 Nh 36.11N 1.32 E
Oued Lili 13 Ni 35.31N 1.16 E
Oued Rhiou 32 Hb 35.58N 0.55 E
Oued-Taria 13 Mi 35.07N 0.05 E
Oued Tlelat 13 Li 35.33N 0.27W
Oued Zem 31 Ge 32.52N 6.34W
Ouégoa 63b Be 20.21S 164.26 E
Ouéllé 34 Ed 7.18N 4.01W
Ouémé 30 Hh 6.29N 2.32 E
Ouémé [3] 34 Fd 7.00N 2.35 E
Ouen 63b Cf 22.26S 166.48 E
Ouenza 32 Ib 35.57N 8.07 E
Ouenza, Djebel- 14 Co 35.57N 8.05 E
Ouessa 34 Ec 11.03N 2.47W
Ouessant, Ile d'- 11 Af 48.28N 5.05W
Ouesso 31 Ih 1.37N 16.04 E
Ouest [3] 34 Hd 5.20N 10.30 E
Ouest, Baie de l'- 64h Ab 13.15S 176.13W
Ouezzane 32 Fc 34.48N 5.36W
Oughter, Lough- 9 Fg 54.00N 7.29W
Ouham [3] 35 Bd 7.00N 18.00 E
Ouham 30 Ih 9.18N 18.14 E
Ouham-Pendé [3] 35 Bd 7.00N 16.00 E
Ouidah 34 Fd 6.22N 2.05 E
Ouistreham 11 Fe 49.17N 0.15W
Ouistreham-Riva Bella 12 Be 49.17N 0.16W
Oujda [3] 32 Gc 33.00N 2.00W
Oujda 31 Ge 34.40N 1.54W
Oujeft 32 Ee 20.02N 13.03W
Oulainen 7 Fd 64.16N 24.57 E
Oulchy-le-Château 12 Fe 49.12N 3.21 E
Ouled Djellal 32 Ic 34.25N 5.04 E
Ouled Naïl, Monts des-
32 Hc 34.40N 3.25 E
Oulou, Bahr- 35 Cd 9.48N 21.32 E
Oulu [2] 7 Gd 65.00N 27.00 E
Oulu/Uleåborg 6 Ib 65.01N 25.30 E
Oulu, Lake- (EN)=
Oulujärvi 5 Ic 64.20N 27.15 E
Oulujärvi=Oulu, Lake- (EN)
5 Ic 64.20N 27.15 E
Oulujoki 5 Ib 65.01N 25.25 E
Oum Chalouba 31 Jg 15.48N 20.46 E
Oumé [3] 34 Dd 6.25N 5.30W
Oumé 34 Dd 6.23N 5.25W
Oum el Bouaghi [3] 32 Ib 35.30N 7.10 E
Oum el Bouaghi 32 Ib 35.53N 7.07 E
Oum er Rbia 30 Ge 33.19N 8.20W
Oum Hadjer 35 Bc 13.18N 19.41 E
Oumm ed Droûs Guebli,
Sebkhet- 32 Ee 24.03N 11.45W
Oumm ed Droûs Telli,
Sebkhet- 32 Ee 24.20N 11.30W
Ounasjoki 5 Ib 66.30N 25.45 E
Oundle 12 Bb 52.29N 0.28W
Ounianga 35 Cb 19.10N 20.30 E
Ounianga Kébir 31 Jg 19.04N 20.29 E
Ountivou 34 Fd 7.21N 1.34 E
Ouolossébougou 34 Dc 12.00N 7.55W
Oupeye 12 Hd 50.42N 5.39 E
Oupu 27 Ma 52.45N 126.00 E
Our 12 Ie 49.53N 6.18 E
Ouray 45 Cg 38.01N 107.40W
Ouray, Mount- 45 Cg 38.25N 106.14W
Ource 11 Kf 48.06N 4.23 E
Ourcq 11 Je 49.01N 3.01 E
Ourcq, Canal de l'- 11 If 48.51N 2.22 E
Ourém 54 Id 1.33S 47.06W
Ouricuri 54 Je 7.35S 40.05W
Ourinhos 53 Lh 22.59S 49.52W
Ouro, Rio do- 55 Ha 13.20S 48.59W
Ouro Fino 55 If 22.17S 46.22W
Ouro Prêto 54 Jh 20.23S 43.30W
Ourthe [Bel.] 11 Ld 50.38N 5.35 E
Ourville-en-Caux 12 Ce 49.44N 0.36 E
Ous 19 Gc 60.55N 61.31 E
Ōu-Sanmyaku 28 Pe 39.00N 141.00 E
Ouse [Eng.-U.K.] 9 Nk 50.47N 0.03 E
Ouse [Eng.-U.K.] 9 Mh 53.42N 0.41W
Oust 11 Dg 47.35N 2.06W
Outagouna 34 Fb 15.11N 0.43 E
Outaouais, Rivière- 38 Le 45.20N 73.58W
Outardes, Rivière aux-
42 Kg 49.05N 68.23W
Outat Oulad El Hajj 32 Gc 33.21N 3.42W
Outer Dowsing 9 Oh 53.25N 1.05 E
Outer Hebrides 9 Fd 57.50N 7.32W
Outer Santa Barbara
Passage 46 Fj 33.10N 118.30W
Outer Silver Pit 9 Og 54.05N 2.00 E
Outjo 31 Ik 20.08S 16.08 E
Outjo [3] 37 Ac 19.30S 14.30 E
Outlook 46 La 51.30N 107.03W
Outokumpu 7 Ge 62.44N 29.01 E
Outram Mountain 46 Eb 49.19N 121.05W
Outreau 12 Dd 50.42N 1.35 E
Out Skerries 9 Ma 60.30N 0.50W
Outwell 12 Cb 52.37N 0.14 E
Ouvéa, Ile- 57 Hg 20.35S 166.35 E
Ouvèze 11 Kk 43.59N 4.51 E
Ouxian 28 Ej 28.58N 118.53 E
Ouyen 59 Ig 35.04S 142.20 E
Ouyou Bézédinga 34 Hb 16.32N 13.15 E
Ouzera 13 Oh 36.15N 2.51 E
Ovacık [Tur.] 24 Ed 36.11N 33.40 E
Ovacık [Tur.] 24 Hc 39.22N 39.13 E
Ovada 14 Cf 44.38N 8.38 E
Ova Gölü 15 Mm 36.16N 29.22 E
Ovakent 15 Lk 38.06N 28.02 E
Ovalau Island 63d Bb 17.40S 178.48 E
Ovalle 53 Ii 30.36S 71.12W
Oval Peak 46 Eb 48.15N 120.25W
Ovamboland 37 Bc 18.30S 16.00 E
Ovamboland [3] 37 Bc 18.00S 16.00 E
Ovan 36 Bb 0.30N 12.10 E
Ovanåker 7 Df 61.21N 15.54 E
Ovar 13 Dd 40.52N 8.38W
Ovau 63a Cb 6.48S 156.02 E
Ovejas 49 Ji 9.32N 75.14W
Overath 12 Jd 50.57N 7.18 E
Øverbygd 7 Eb 69.01N 19.18 E
Overflakkee 11 Kc 51.45N 4.10 E
Overhalla 7 Cd 64.30N 12.00 E
Overijse 12 Gd 50.46N 4.32 E
Overijssel [3] 12 Ib 52.25N 6.30 E
Överkalix 7 Fc 66.19N 22.50 E
Overland Park 45 Ig 38.59N 94.40W
Övermark/Ylimarkku 8 Ib 62.37N 21.28 E
Overpelt 12 Hc 51.12N 5.25 E
Overri 34 Gd 5.29N 7.02 E
Overton 46 Hh 36.33N 114.27W
Övertorneå 7 Fc 66.23N 23.40 E
Överum 8 Gg 57.59N 16.19 E
Ovidiu 15 Le 44.16N 28.34 E
Oviedo [3] 13 Ga 43.20N 6.00W
Oviedo [Dom.Rep.] 49 Le 17.47N 71.22W
Oviedo [Sp.] 6 Fg 43.22N 5.50W
Oviši 8 Ig 57.34N 21.35 E
Ovo, Capo dell'- 14 Lj 40.18N 17.30 E
Övre Årdal 7 Bf 61.19N 7.48 E
Övre Fryken 8 Ed 60.00N 13.05 E
Övre Soppero 7 Eb 68.05N 21.41 E
Ovruč 19 Ce 51.19N 28.50 E
Ovsjanka 20 Hf 53.32N 126.58 E
Owaka 62 Cg 46.27S 169.40 E
Owando 31 Ii 0.29S 15.55 E
Ōwani 28 Pd 40.31N 140.35 E
Owase 28 Ng 34.04N 136.12 E
Owatonna 43 Ic 44.05N 93.14W
Owego 44 Id 42.06N 76.16W
Owen, Mount- 62 Ed 41.33S 172.32 E
Owendo 36 Ab 0.17N 9.30 E
Owen Falls Dam 36 Fb 0.24N 33.11 E
Owensboro 43 Jd 37.46N 87.07W
Owens Lake 46 Gh 36.25N 117.56W
Owen Sound 42 Jh 44.34N 80.56W
Owens River 46 Gh 36.31N 117.57W
Owen Stanley Range 57 Fe 9.20S 148.00 E
Owl Creek Mountains
46 Ke 43.30N 108.35W
Ownay, Kowlal-e- 23 Kc 34.27N 68.22 E
Owo 34 Gd 7.11N 5.35 E
Owosso 44 Ed 43.00N 84.10W
Owyhee 46 Gf 41.57N 116.06W
Owyhee, Lake- 46 Ge 43.28N 117.20W
Owyhee Mountains 46 Ge 43.00N 116.45W
Owyhee River [U.S.] 46 Ge 43.40N 117.16W
Owyhee River [U.S.] 43 Dc 43.46N 117.02W
Oxberg 8 Fc 61.07N 14.10 E
Oxbow 45 Eb 49.14N 102.11W
Oxelösund 7 Dg 58.40N 17.06 E
Oxford 9 Lj 51.50N 1.30W
Oxford [Eng.-U.K.] 6 Fe 51.46N 1.15W
Oxford [Ms.-U.S.] 45 Li 34.22N 89.32W
Oxford [N.C.-U.S.] 44 Hg 36.19N 78.35W
Oxford [N.Z.] 62 Ee 43.17S 172.11 E
Oxford Lake 42 Hf 54.50N 95.35W
Oxfordshire [3] 9 Lj 51.50N 1.20W
Oxia 15 Ek 38.18N 21.06 E
Oxkutzcab 48 Og 20.18N 89.25W
Oxnard 43 De 34.12N 119.11W
Ox or Slieve Gamph
Mountains/Sliabh
Gamh 9 Eg 54.10N 8.50W
Oxted 12 Bc 51.14N 0.01W
Oyabe 29 Ec 36.40N 136.52 E
Oyahue 53 Jh 21.08S 68.45W
O-Yama 29 Fd 34.04N 139.31 E
Oyama 28 Of 36.21N 139.50 E
Ōyama 29 Ec 36.35N 137.18 E
Ōyano 29 Be 32.35N 130.27 E
Oyapock, Fleuve- 52 Ke 4.08N 51.40W
Oyem 31 Ih 1.37N 11.35 E
Oyen 46 Ja 51.22N 110.28W
Øyeren 8 De 59.50N 11.14 E
Oykel 9 Id 57.50N 4.25W
Oyo [2] 34 Fd 8.00N 3.50 E
Oyo [Nig.] 34 Fd 7.51N 3.56 E
Oyo [Sud.] 35 Fa 21.55N 36.06 E
Oyodo-Gawa 29 Bf 31.55N 131.28 E
Oyonnax 11 Lh 46.15N 5.40 E
Oyster Bay 59 Jh 42.10S 148.10 E
Øystese 8 Bd 60.23N 6.13 E
Özalp 24 Jc 38.39N 43.59 E
Ozamiz 26 He 8.08N 123.50 E
Ozark 44 Ej 31.28N 85.38W
Ozark Plateau 38 Jf 37.00N 93.00W
Ozark Reservoir 45 Ii 35.25N 94.05W
Ozarks, Lake of the- 43 Id 37.39N 92.50W
Ózd 10 Qh 48.13N 20.18 E
Ozeblin 14 Jf 44.35N 15.53 E
Ozernoj, Zaliv- 20 Le 57.00N 163.20 E
Ozernovski 20 Kf 51.21N 156.32 E
Ozerny 16 Vd 51.08N 60.55 E
Ozersk 8 Ij 54.24N 21.59 E
Ozery [Bye.-U.S.S.R.] 10 Uc 53.38N 24.18 E
Ozery [R.S.F.S.R.] 7 Ji 54.54N 38.32 E
Ožezdy 19 Gf 48.03N 67.09 E
Ozieri 14 Cj 40.35N 9.00 E
Ozinki 19 Ee 51.12N 49.47 E
Ožogina 20 Kc 66.12N 151.05 E
Ozona 43 Ge 30.43N 101.12W
Ozorków 10 Pe 51.58N 19.19 E
Ozouri 36 Ac 0.55S 8.55 E
Ozren [Yugo.] 14 Mf 44.37N 18.15 E
Ozren [Yugo.] 14 Mg 43.59N 18.30 E
Ozren [Yugo.] 15 Ef 43.36N 21.54 E
Ōzu [Jap.] 29 Be 32.52N 130.52 E
Ōzu [Jap.] 28 Lh 33.30N 132.23 E

P

Pääjärvi 8 Kb 62.50N 24.45 E
Paama 63b Dc 16.28S 168.13 E
Pa-an → Pha-an 25 Je 16.53N 97.38 E
Paar 10 Hh 48.45N 11.35 E
Paarl 31 Il 33.45S 18.56 E
Paauilo 65a Fc 20.03N 155.22W
Paavola 7 Fd 64.36N 25.12 E
Pabbay 9 Fd 57.47N 7.20W
Pabellón, Ensenada del-
48 Fe 24.27N 107.36W
Pabianice 10 Pe 51.40N 19.22 E
Pābna 25 Hd 24.00N 89.15 E
Pabradė/Pabrade 7 Fi 54.59N 25.50 E
Pabrade/Pabradė 7 Fi 54.59N 25.50 E
Pacaás Novos, Serra dos-
54 Ff 10.50S 64.00W
Pacajá, Rio- 54 Hd 1.56S 50.55W
Pacajus 54 Kd 4.10S 38.28W
Pacaraima, Serra-
52 Je 4.30N 60.40W
Pacasmayo 54 Ce 7.24S 79.34W
Paceco 14 Gm 37.59N 12.33 E
Pachala 35 Ed 7.10N 34.06 E
Pacheco 48 Eb 30.06N 108.21W
Pachino 14 Jn 36.43N 15.05 E
Pachitea, Río- 54 De 8.46S 74.32W
Pachuca de Soto 47 Ed 20.07N 98.44W
Pacific-Antarctic Ridge (EN)
3 Kp 62.00S 157.00W
Pacific City 46 Dd 45.12N 123.57W
Pacific Grove 46 Eh 36.38N 121.56W
Pacific Islands, Trust
Territory of the- 58 Ed 7.30N 134.30 E
Pacífico, Océano- = Pacific
Ocean (EN) 3 Ki 5.00N 155.00W
Pacific Ocean 3 Ki 5.00N 155.00W
Pacific Ocean (EN)=Kita-
Taiheiyō 60 Ch 22.00N 167.00 E
Pacific Ocean (EN)=
Pacífico, Océano- 3 Ki 5.00N 155.00W
Pacific Ocean (EN)=
Pacifique, Océan- 3 Ki 5.00N 155.00W
Pacific Ocean (EN)=
Taiheiyō 3 Ki 5.00N 155.00W
Pacific Ocean (EN)=Tihi
Okean 3 Ki 5.00N 155.00W
Pacific Ranges 42 Ef 50.55N 125.10W
Pacifique, Océan-=Pacific
Ocean (EN) 3 Ki 5.00N 155.00W
Packsattel 14 Id 46.58N 14.58 E
Pacuí, Rio- 55 Jc 16.46S 45.01W
Pacuneiro, Rio- 55 Fa 13.02S 53.25W
Pacy-sur-Eure 12 De 49.01N 1.23 E
Paczków 10 Mf 50.27N 17.00 E
Padana, Pianura-=Po
Valley (EN) 5 Gf 45.20N 10.00 E
Padang 22 Mj 0.57S 100.21 E
Padangsidempuan 26 Cf 1.22N 99.16 E
Padangtikar, Pulau- 26 Eg 0.50S 109.30 E
Padany 7 He 63.19N 33.25 E
Padasjoki 8 Kc 61.21N 25.17 E
Padauiri, Rio- 54 Fd 0.15S 64.05W
Paddle Prairie 42 Fe 58.02N 117.50W
Paderborn 10 Ee 51.43N 8.46 E
Paderborn-Elsen 12 Kc 51.44N 8.41 E
Paderborn-Schloß Neuhaus 12 Kc 51.44N 8.42 E
Padeş, Vîrful- 15 Fd 45.40N 22.20 E
Padilla 54 Fg 19.19S 64.20W
Padina 15 Ke 44.50N 27.07 E
Padornelo, Portillo del-
13 Fb 42.03N 6.50W
Padova = Padua (EN) 14 Fe 45.25N 11.53 E
Padre, Morro do- 55 Ic 16.48S 47.35W
Padre Bernardo 55 Hb 15.21S 48.30W
Padre Island 43 Hf 27.00N 97.15W
Padrón 13 Db 42.44N 8.40W
Padua (EN) = Padova 14 Fe 45.25N 11.53 E
Paducah [Ky.-U.S.] 39 Kf 37.05N 88.36W
Paducah [Tx.-U.S.] 45 Fi 34.01N 100.18W
Padula 14 Jj 40.20N 15.39 E
Paea 65e Fc 17.41S 149.35W
Paegam-san 28 Id 40.35N 126.15 E
Paengnyong-Do 27 Ld 38.00N 124.40 E
Paeroa 61 Eg 37.23S 175.41 E
Paestum 14 Jj 40.25N 15.01 E
Paeu 63c Bb 11.22S 166.50 E
Pafuri 37 Ed 22.26S 31.20 E
Pag 14 Jf 44.27N 15.03 E
Pag 14 If 44.30N 15.00 E
Pagadian 26 He 7.49N 123.25 E
Pagai, Kepulauan-=Pagi
Islands (EN) 21 Lj 2.45S 100.00 E
Pagai Selatan 26 Dg 3.00S 100.20 E
Pagai Utara 26 Cg 2.42S 100.07 E
Pagan Island 57 Fc 18.07N 145.46 E
Pagasitikós Kólpos 15 Fj 39.15N 23.00 E
Pagatan 26 Gg 3.36S 115.56 E
Pagat Point 64c Bb 13.30N 144.53 E
Page 46 Jh 36.57N 111.27W
Pagėgiai 8 Ii 55.09N 21.54 E
Paget, Mount- 66 Ad 54.26S 36.33W
Pagi Islands (EN)=Pagai,
Kepulauan- 21 Lj 2.45S 100.00 E
Paglia 14 Gh 42.42N 12.11 E
Pago Bay 64c Bb 13.25N 144.48 E
Pagoda Point 21 Lh 15.57N 94.15 E
Pāgodār 24 Qh 28.10N 57.22 E
Pago Pago 58 Jf 14.16S 170.42W
Pago Pago Harbor 65c Cb 14.17S 170.40W
Pago Redondo 55 Ci 29.35S 59.13W
Pagosa Springs 45 Ch 37.16N 107.01W
Pagoua Bay 51g Ba 15.32N 61.17W
Pagwa River 45 Na 50.01N 85.10W
Pahači 20 Ld 60.30N 169.00 E
Pahala 65a Fd 19.12N 155.29W
Pāhara, Laguna- 49 Ff 14.18N 83.15W
Pahiatua 62 Fd 40.27S 175.50 E
Pahkaing Bum 21 Lg 26.00N 95.30 E
Pahoa 65a Gd 19.30N 154.57W
Pahokee 44 Gl 26.49N 80.40W
Pahtakor 18 Fd 40.16N 67.55 E
Pahute Mesa 46 Gh 37.20N 116.40W
Paia 63b Dc 16.35S 168.12 E
Paide/Pajde 7 Fg 58.57N 25.35 E
Paignton 9 Jk 50.28N 3.30W
Päijänne 5 Ic 61.35N 23.30 E
Páikon Óros 15 Fi 40.56N 22.21 E
Paila 48 He 25.39N 102.07W
Pailín 25 Kf 12.51N 102.36 E
Pailitas 49 Ki 8.58N 73.38W
Pailolo Channel 65a Eb 21.05N 156.42W
Paimio/Pemar 8 Jd 60.27N 22.42 E
Paimionjoki 8 Jd 60.25N 22.40 E
Paimpol 11 Cf 48.46N 3.03W
Painan 26 Dg 1.21S 100.34 E
Paine, Mount- 66 Mg 86.46S 147.32W
Painel 55 Gh 27.55S 50.06W
Painesville 44 Ge 41.43N 81.15W
Painted Desert 43 Ed 36.00N 111.20W
Paintsville 44 Fg 37.49N 82.48W
Pais do Vinho 13 Ec 41.15N 7.55W
Paisley 9 If 55.50N 4.26W
Paita 54 Be 5.06S 81.07W
Paita 63b Cf 22.08S 166.22 E
Paiva 13 Dc 41.04N 8.16W
Paj 7 If 61.43N 34.28 E
Pajala 7 Fc 67.12N 23.22 E
Pajares, Puerto de- 13 Ga 43.00N 5.46W
Pajaros, Punta- 48 Ph 19.36N 87.25W
Pajaros Point 51a Db 18.31N 64.18W
Pajatén 54 Ce 7.29S 77.22W
Pajde/Paide 7 Fg 58.57N 25.35 E
Pajęczno 10 Oe 51.09N 19.00 E
Pajer, Gora- 19 Gb 66.40N 64.20 E
Paj-Hoj 5 Mb 69.00N 62.30 E
Pajule 36 Fb 2.58N 32.56 E
Pakanbaru 22 Mi 0.32N 101.27 E
Pakaraima Mountains 54 Fb 4.05N 61.30W
Pakch'on 28 He 39.44N 125.35 E
Pakhiá 15 Im 36.16N 25.50 E
Pakhna 24 Ee 34.46N 32.48 E
Pákhnes 15 Gn 35.18N 23.58 E
Paki 34 Gc 11.30N 8.09 E
Pakima 36 Dc 3.21S 24.06 E
Pakin Atoll 57 Gd 7.04N 157.48 E
Pakistan [1] 22 Ig 30.00N 70.00 E
Pakleni Otoci 14 Kg 43.10N 16.23 E
Pakokku 25 Jd 21.17N 95.06 E
Pakowki Lake 46 Jb 49.22N 110.57W
Pak Phanang 25 Kg 8.21N 100.12 E
Pakrac 14 Le 45.26N 17.12 E
Pakruois/Pakruojis 7 Fi 55.57N 23.50 E
Pakruojis/Pakruois 7 Fi 55.57N 23.50 E
Paks 10 Oj 46.38N 18.52 E
Paktiā [3] 23 Kc 33.30N 69.30 E
Pakwach 36 Fb 2.28N 31.30 E
Pakxé 22 Mh 15.07N 105.47 E
Pakxèng 25 Kd 20.10N 102.40 E
Pala 35 Ad 9.22N 14.54 E
Palacca Point 49 Kc 21.15N 73.26W
Palacios [Arg.] 55 Bj 30.43S 61.37W
Palacios [Tx.-U.S.] 45 Hl 28.42N 96.13W
Palafrugell 13 Pc 41.55N 3.10 E
Palagruža 14 Kh 42.24N 16.15 E
Palaiokastritsa 15 Cj 39.40N 19.41 E
Palaiokhóra 15 Gn 35.14N 23.41 E
Palaiseau 12 Ef 48.43N 2.15 E
Palamás 15 Fj 39.28N 22.05 E
Palamós 13 Pc 41.51N 3.08 E
Palamuse/Palamuze 8 Lf 58.39N 26.35 E
Palamut 15 Kk 38.59N 27.41 E
Palamuze/Palamuse 8 Lf 58.39N 26.35 E
Palana 22 Rd 59.07N 159.58 E
Palancia 13 Le 39.40N 0.12W
Palanga 19 Cd 55.57N 21.05 E
Palangkaraya 26 Fg 2.16S 113.56 E
Pālanpur 25 Ed 24.10N 72.26 E

Index Symbols

[1] Independent Nation
[2] State, Region
[3] District, County
[4] Municipality
[5] Colony, Dependency
Continent
Physical Region
Historical or Cultural Region
Mount, Mountain
Volcano
Hill
Mountains, Mountain Range
Hills, Escarpment
Plateau, Upland
Pass, Gap
Plain, Lowland
Delta
Salt Flat
Valley, Canyon
Crater, Cave
Karst Features
Depression
Polder
Desert, Dunes
Forest, Woods
Heath, Steppe
Oasis
Cape, Point
Coast, Beach
Cliff
Peninsula
Isthmus
Sandbank
Island
Atoll
Rock, Reef
Islands, Archipelago
Rocks, Reefs
Coral Reef
Well, Spring
Geyser
River, Stream
Waterfall Rapids
River Mouth, Estuary
Lake
Salt Lake
Intermittent Lake
Reservoir
Swamp, Pond
Canal
Glacier
Ice Shelf, Pack Ice
Ocean
Sea
Gulf, Bay
Strait, Fjord
Lagoon
Bank
Seamount
Tablemount
Ridge
Shelf
Basin
Escarpment, Sea Scarp
Fracture
Trench, Abyss
National Park, Reserve
Point of Interest
Recreation Site
Cave, Cavern
Historic Site
Ruins
Wall, Walls
Church, Abbey
Temple
Scientific Station
Airport
Port
Lighthouse
Mine
Tunnel
Dam, Bridge

Palaoa Point 65a Ec 20.44N 156.58W
Palapye 31 Jk 22.33S 27.08 E
Palasa 26 Hf 0.29N 120.24 E
Palatka [Fl.-U.S.] 43 Kf 29.39N 81.38W
Palatka [R.S.F.S.R.] 20 Kd 60.05N 151.00 E
Palau (EN) = Belau 14 Di 41.11N 9.23 E
Palau [5] 58 Ed 7.30N 134.30 E
Palau Islands 57 Ed 7.30N 134.30 E
Palauli 65c Aa 13.44S 172.16W
Palauli Bay 65c Aa 13.47S 172.14W
Palau Trench (EN) 60 Af 6.30N 134.30 E
Palavas-les-Flots 11 Jk 43.32N 3.56 E
Palaw 25 Jf 12.58N 98.39 E
Palawan 21 Ni 9.30N 118.30 E
Palawan Passage 26 Gd 10.00N 118.00 E
Palayan 26 Hc 15.33N 121.06 E
Pālayankottai 25 Fg 8.43N 77.44 E
Palazzo, Punta- 11a Aa 42.22N 8.33 E
Palazzolo Acreide 14 Im 37.04N 14.54 E
Palazzolo sull'Oglio 14 De 45.36N 9.53 E
Paldiski 19 Cd 59.20N 24.06 E
Pale di San Martino 14 Fd 46.14N 11.53 E
Paleleh 26 Hf 1.04N 121.57 E
Palembang 22 Mj 2.55S 104.45 E
Palena 14 Ii 41.59N 14.08 E
Palencia [3] 13 Hb 42.25N 4.30W
Palencia 13 Hb 42.01N 4.32W
Palen Lake 46 Hj 33.46N 115.12W
Palenque 39 Jh 17.30N 92.00W
Palenque [Mex.] 48 Ni 17.31N 91.58W
Palenque [Pan.] 49 Hi 9.13N 79.41W
Palenque, Punta- 49 Ld 18.14N 70.09W
Palermo 6 Hh 38.07N 13.22 E
Palermo, Golfo di- 14 Hl 38.10N 13.25 E
Palestine 43 He 31.46N 95.38W
Palestine (EN) 23 Dc 32.15N 34.47 E
Palestrina 14 Gi 41.50N 12.53 E
Pālghāt 25 Ff 10.47N 76.39 E
Palgrave Point 37 Ad 20.28S 13.16 E
Palhoça 55 Hh 27.38S 48.40W
Pāli 25 Ec 25.46N 73.20 E
Palinuro 14 Jj 40.02N 15.17 E
Palinuro, Capo- 14 Jj 40.02N 15.16 E
Palisades Reservoir 46 Je 43.04N 111.26W
Paliseul 12 He 49.54N 5.08 E
Palivere 8 Jf 59.00N 23.45 E
Palizada 48 Mh 18.15N 92.05W
Paljakka 7 Gd 64.45N 28.07 E
Paljavaam 20 Mc 68.50N 170.50 E
Paljenik 5 Hg 44.15N 17.36 E
Pälkäne 8 Kc 61.20N 24.16 E
Palkino 8 Mg 57.29N 28.10 E
Palk Strait 21 Ji 10.00N 79.45 E
Palla Bianca/Weißkugel 14 Ed 46.48N 10.44 E
Pallars 13 Mb 42.25N 0.55 E
Pallars, Montsent de-/Montseny 13 Nb 42.29N 1.02 E
Pallasovka 19 Ee 50.03N 46.55 E
Pallastunturi 7 Fb 68.06N 24.02 E
Palliser, Cape- 61 Eh 41.37S 175.16 E
Palliser, Iles- 57 Mf 15.30S 146.30W
Palma [Moz.] 37 Gb 10.46S 40.28 E
Palma [Sp.] 6 Gh 39.34N 2.39 E
Palma, Badia de-/Palma, Bahia de- 13 Oe 39.27N 2.35 E
Palma, Bahia de-/Palma, Badia de- 13 Oe 39.27N 2.35 E
Palma, Rio- 54 If 12.33S 47.52W
Palma, Sierra de la- 48 Id 26.00N 101.35W
Palma del Rio 13 Gg 37.42N 5.17W
Palma di Montechiaro 14 Hm 37.11N 13.46 E
Palmar, Laguna del- 55 Bi 29.35S 60.42W
Palmar, Rio- 49 Lh 10.11N 71.52W
Palmar, Salto- 55 Cg 24.18S 59.18W
Palmares 54 Ke 8.41S 35.36W
Palmares do Sul 55 Gj 30.16S 50.31W
Palmarito 54 Db 7.37N 70.10W
Palmarola 14 Gj 40.55N 12.50 E
Palmar Sur 47 Hg 8.58N 83.29W
Palmas 56 Jc 26.30S 52.00W
Palmas, Cape- 30 Gh 4.22N 7.44W
Palmas, Golfo di- 14 Cl 39.00N 8.30 E
Palmas Bellas 49 Gi 9.14N 80.05W
Palma Soriano 47 Id 20.13N 76.00W
Palm Bay 44 Gk 28.01N 80.35W
Palm Beach 43 Kf 26.42N 80.02W
Palmdale 46 Fi 34.35N 118.07W
Palmeira 55 Gg 25.25S 50.00W
Palmeira das Missões 56 Jc 27.55S 53.17W
Palmeira dos Indios 54 Ke 9.25S 36.37W
Palmeirais 54 Je 5.58S 43.04W
Palmeiras, Rio- 55 Gb 15.25S 51.10W
Palmeiras de Goiás 55 Hc 16.47S 49.53W
Palmeirinhas, Ponta das- 30 Ii 9.05S 13.00 E
Palmela 13 Df 38.34N 8.54W
Palmer 40 Jd 61.36N 149.07W
Palmer Archipelago 66 Qe 64.10S 62.00W
Palmer Land (EN) 66 Qf 71.30S 65.00W
Palmer Station 66 Qe 64.46S 64.05W
Palmerston 62 Df 45.29S 170.43 E
Palmerston Atoll 57 Kf 18.04S 163.10W
Palmerston North 58 Ii 40.28S 175.17 E
Palmetto Point 51d Ba 17.35N 61.52W
Palmi 14 Jl 38.21N 15.51 E
Palmira [Col.] 53 Ie 3.32N 76.16W
Palmira [Cuba] 49 Gb 22.14N 80.23W
Palm Islands 59 Jc 18.40S 146.30 E
Palmital 55 Fg 24.39S 52.16W
Palmitas 55 Dk 33.27S 57.48W
Palmito 55 Cd 18.53S 58.22W
Palmitos 55 Fh 27.05S 53.08W
Palm Springs 43 De 33.50N 116.33W
Palmyra 23 Ec 34.33N 38.17 E
Palmyra Atoll 57 Kd 5.52N 162.06W
Palo Alto 43 Cd 37.27N 122.09W
Paloh 26 Ef 1.43N 109.18 E
Paloich 35 Ec 10.28N 32.32 E
Palomani, Nevado- 52 Jg 14.38S 69.14W
Palomar Mountain 43 De 33.22N 116.50W
Palomera, Sierra- 13 Kd 40.40N 1.12W
Palopo 22 Oj 3.00S 120.12 E
Palos, Cabo de- 5 Fh 37.38N 0.41W
Palo Santo 55 Cg 25.34S 59.21W
Palotina 55 Fg 24.17S 53.50W
Palouse River 46 Fc 46.35N 118.13W
Palpa 54 Cf 14.32S 75.11W
Palsa 8 Lg 57.23N 26.24 E
Pålsboda 8 Fe 59.04N 15.20 E
Paltamo 7 Gd 64.25N 27.50 E
Palu [Indon.] 22 Nj 0.53S 119.53 E
Palu [Tur.] 24 Hc 38.42N 39.57 E
Palu, Pulau- 26 Hh 8.20S 121.43 E
Pam 63b Be 20.15S 164.17 E
Pama 34 Fc 11.15N 0.42 E
Påmark/Pomarkku 8 Ic 61.42N 22.00 E
Pambarra 37 Fd 21.56S 35.06 E
Pambeguwa 34 Gc 10.40N 8.17 E
Pamekasan 26 Fh 7.10S 113.28 E
Pamiers 11 Hk 43.07N 1.36 E
Pamir 21 Jf 38.00N 73.00 E
Pamir 19 Hh 37.01N 72.41 E
Påmiut/Frederikshåb 41 Hf 62.00N 49.45W
Pamlico Sound 43 Ld 35.20N 75.55W
Pampa 43 Gd 35.32N 100.58W
Pampa del Indio 55 Ch 26.02S 59.55W
Pampa del Infierno 55 Bh 26.31S 61.10W
Pampa de los Guanacos 56 Hc 26.14S 61.51W
Pampas 54 Df 12.24S 74.54W
Pampas 52 Ji 35.00S 63.00W
Pampeiro 55 Ej 30.38S 55.16W
Pamplona [Col.] 54 Db 7.23N 72.38W
Pamplona [Sp.] 6 Fg 42.49N 1.38W
Pamukkale 15 Ml 37.47N 29.04 E
Pamukova 15 Ni 40.31N 30.09 E
Pamunkey River 44 Ig 37.32N 76.48W
Pan, Tierra del- 13 Gc 41.50N 6.00W
Pana 36 Bc 1.41S 12.39 E
Panagjurište 15 Hg 42.30N 24.11 E
Panaitan, Pulau- 26 Eh 6.36S 105.12 E
Panaitolikón Óros 15 Ek 38.43N 21.39 E
Panaji (Panjim) 22 Jh 15.29N 73.50 E
Panakhaïkón Óros 15 Ek 38.12N 21.54 E
Panamá [1] 39 Li 9.00N 80.00W
Panamá = Panama (EN) [3] 49 Hi 9.00N 79.00W
Panamá = Panama City (EN) 49 Hi 8.58N 79.31W
Panama (EN) = Panamá [3] 49 Hi 9.00N 79.00W
Panamá, Bahía de- 49 Hi 8.50N 79.15W
Panamá, Canal de- = Panama Canal (EN) 47 Ig 9.20N 79.55W
Panamá, Golfo de- = Panama, Gulf of- (EN) 38 Li 8.00N 79.10W
Panama, Gulf of- (EN) = Panamá, Golfo de- 38 Li 8.00N 79.10W
Panama, Isthmus of- (EN) = Panamá, Istmo de- 38 Li 9.20N 79.30W
Panamá, Istmo de- = Panama, Isthmus of- (EN) 38 Li 9.20N 79.30W
Panama Canal (EN) = Panamá, Canal de- 47 Ig 9.20N 79.55W
Panama City [La.-U.S.] 39 Kf 30.10N 85.41W
Panama City (EN) = Panamá 39 Li 8.58N 79.31W
Panamá La Vieja 49 Hi 9.00N 79.29W
Panambi 55 Fi 28.18S 53.30W
Panamint Range 46 Gh 36.30N 117.20W
Panao 54 Ce 9.49S 76.00W
Panarea 14 Jl 38.40N 15.05 E
Panaro 14 Ff 44.55N 11.25 E
Pana Tinai 63a Ad 11.14S 153.10 E
Pana-Wina 63a Ad 11.11S 153.01 E
Panay 21 Oh 11.15N 122.30 E
Pancake Range 46 Hg 39.00N 115.45W
Pančevo 15 De 44.52N 20.39 E
Pančićev vrh 15 Df 43.15N 20.45 E
Panciu 15 Kd 45.54N 27.05 E
Pancros 63b Db 15.58S 168.12 E
Panda 37 Ed 24.03S 34.43 E
Panda ma Tenga 37 Dc 18.32S 25.38 E
Pandan 26 Hd 11.43N 122.06 E
Pan de Azúcar 55 El 34.48S 55.14W
Pandeiros, Ribeirão- 55 Jb 15.42S 44.36W
Pandelis/Pandėlys 8 Kh 56.01N 25.21 E
Pandėlys/Pandelis 8 Kh 56.01N 25.21 E
Pandharpur 25 Fe 17.40N 75.20 E
Pándheon 15 Fi 40.05N 22.20 E
Pāndhurna 25 Fd 21.36N 78.31 E
Pandivere Kõrgustik/Pandivere Vozvyšennost 8 Le 59.00N 26.15 E
Pandivere Vozvyšennost/Pandivere Kõrgustik 8 Le 59.00N 26.15 E
Pando 56 Id 34.43S 55.57W
Pando [2] 54 Ef 11.20S 67.40W
Pandokrátor 15 Cj 39.45N 19.52 E
Pandora 49 Fi 9.45N 82.57W
Pandrup 8 Cg 57.14N 9.41 E
Pandu 36 Cb 4.59N 19.16 E
Panevežis/Panevėžys 19 Cd 55.44N 24.22 E
Panevėžys/Panevežis 19 Cd 55.44N 24.22 E
Panfilov 19 Ig 44.08N 80.01 E
Panga 36 Eb 1.51N 26.25 E
Pangai 65b Ba 19.48S 174.21W
Pangaion Óros 15 Hi 40.50N 24.05 E
Pangalanes, Canal de- 30 Lk 22.48S 47.50 E
Pangani 36 Gd 5.26S 38.58 E
Pangani or Ruvu 36 Gc 5.26S 38.58 E
Pange 12 Ie 49.05N 6.22 E
Panggoe 58 Ge 7.01S 157.05 E
Pangi 36 Ec 3.11S 26.38 E
Pangkajene 26 Gg 4.50S 119.32 E
Pangkalanberandan 26 Cf 4.01N 98.17 E
Pangkalanbuun 26 Fg 2.41S 111.37 E
Pangkalaseang, Tanjung- 26 Hg 0.42S 123.26 E
Pangkalpinang 26 Eg 2.08S 106.08 E
Pangnirtung 39 Mc 66.08N 65.44W
Pang-Pang 63b Dc 17.41S 168.32 E
Panguitch 43 Ed 37.49N 112.26W
Panguma 34 Cd 8.24N 11.13W
Pangutaran Group 26 He 6.15N 120.30 E
Panhandle 45 Fi 35.21N 101.23W
Pania Mutombo 36 Dd 5.11S 23.51 E
Paniau 65a Ab 21.57N 160.05W
Panié, Mont- 61 Bd 20.36S 164.46 E
Pānīpat 25 Fc 29.23N 76.58 E
Paniza, Puerto de- 13 Kc 41.15N 1.20W
Panjang 26 Eh 5.29S 105.18 E
Panjang, Pulau- 26 Ef 2.44N 108.55 E
Panjgūr 25 Cc 26.58N 64.06 E
Panjim → Panaji 22 Jh 15.29N 73.50 E
Panjwīn 24 Ke 35.36N 45.58 E
Pankow, Berlin- 10 Jd 52.34N 13.24 E
Pankshin 34 Gd 9.20N 9.27 E
P'anmunjŏm 28 If 37.57N 126.40 E
Panopah 26 Fg 1.56S 111.11 E
Panorama 56 Jb 21.21S 51.51W
Panshan 28 Gd 41.12N 122.03 E
Panshi 27 Mc 42.56N 126.02 E
Pant 12 Cc 51.53N 0.39 E
Pantanal 52 Kg 18.00S 56.00W
Pantar, Pulau- 26 Hh 8.25S 124.07 E
Pantego 44 Ih 35.34N 76.36W
Pantelleria 14 Fn 36.50N 11.57 E
Pantelleria 5 Hh 36.45N 12.00 E
Pantelleria, Canale di- 14 Fn 36.40N 11.45 E
Pante Makassar 26 Hh 9.12S 124.23 E
Pantoja 54 Cd 0.58S 75.10W
Pánuco 48 Jf 22.03N 98.10W
Pánuco 38 Jg 22.16N 97.47W
Panxian 27 Hf 25.45N 104.39 E
Panyam 34 Gd 9.25N 9.13 E
Panzi 36 Cd 7.13S 17.58 E
Panzós 49 Cf 15.24N 89.40W
Pao, Rio- [Ven.] 50 Bh 8.33N 68.01W
Pao, Rio- [Ven.] 50 Dh 8.06N 64.17W
Paola [It.] 14 Kk 39.21N 16.03 E
Paola [Ks.-U.S.] 45 Ig 38.35N 94.53W
Paoli 44 Df 38.33N 86.28W
Paopao 65e Fc 17.30S 149.49W
Paoua 35 Bd 7.15N 16.26 E
Pápa 10 Ni 47.20N 17.28 E
Papa 65a Fd 19.13N 155.52W
Papaaloa 65a Fd 19.59N 155.13W
Papagaios 55 Jd 19.32S 44.45W
Papagayo, Golfo del- 47 Gf 10.45N 85.45W
Papaikou 65a Fd 19.47N 155.06W
Papakura 62 Fb 37.03S 174.57 E
Papaloapan, Rio- 48 Lh 18.42N 95.38W
Papanduva 55 Gh 26.25S 50.09W
Papangpanjang 26 Dg 0.27S 100.25 E
Papantla de Olarte 47 Ed 20.27N 97.19W
Papar 26 Ge 5.44N 115.56 E
Paparoa Range 62 De 42.05S 171.35 E
Papa Stour 9 La 60.30N 1.40W
Papa Westray 9 Kb 59.22N 2.54W
Papeete 58 Mf 17.32S 149.34W
Papenburg 10 Dc 53.04N 7.24 E
Papenburg-Aschendorf (Ems) 12 Ja 53.04N 7.22 E
Papenoo 65e Fc 17.30S 149.25W
Papes Ezers/Papes Ozero 8 Ih 56.15N 20.55 E
Papes Ozero/Papes Ezers 8 Ih 56.15N 20.55 E
Papetoai 65e Fc 17.30S 149.52W
Papey 7a Cb 64.36N 14.11W
Paphos/Baf 24 Ee 34.50N 32.35 E
Papija 15 Kg 42.07N 27.51 E
Papíkion Óros 15 Ih 41.15N 25.18 E
Papilė/Papile 8 Jh 56.09N 22.45 E
Papile/Papilė 8 Jh 56.09N 22.45 E
Papillion 45 Hf 41.09N 96.03W
Papua, Gulf of- 57 Fe 8.32S 145.00 E
Papua New Guinea [1] 58 Fe 6.00S 150.00 E
Papua Passage 64p Bc 21.15S 159.47W
Papuk 14 Le 45.31N 17.39 E
Papun 25 Je 18.04N 97.27 E
Para 7 Ji 54.23N 40.53 E
Pará [2] 54 Hd 4.00S 53.00W
Pará, Rio- 55 Jd 19.13S 45.07W
Para, Rio- 52 Lf 1.30S 48.55W
Parabel 20 De 58.40N 81.30 E
Parabel 20 De 58.43N 81.31 E
Paraburdoo 59 Dd 23.15S 117.45 E
Paracas 54 Cf 13.49S 76.16W
Paracatu 54 Ig 17.13S 46.52W
Paracatu, Rio- [Braz.] 55 Ic 17.30S 46.32W
Paracatu, Rio- [Braz.] 55 Jc 16.30S 45.04W
Paracel Islands (EN) = Xisha Qundao 21 Nh 16.30N 112.15 E
Pārachinār 25 Eb 33.54N 70.06 E
Paraćin 15 Ef 43.52N 21.25 E
Paracuru 54 Kd 3.24S 39.04W
Parada Km 329 55 Ek 32.30S 55.25W
Paradip 25 Hd 20.19N 86.42 E
Paradise [Ca.-U.S.] 46 Eg 39.46N 121.37W
Paradise [Mi.-U.S.] 44 Eb 46.38N 85.03W
Paragould 45 Kh 36.03N 90.29W
Paragua, Rio- 54 Fb 6.55N 62.55W
Paraguá, Rio- 54 Ff 13.34S 61.53W
Paraguaçu, Rio- 52 Mg 12.45S 38.54W
Paraguaçu Paulista 55 Gf 22.25S 50.34W
Paraguai, Rio- 52 Kh 27.18S 58.38W
Paraguaipoa 49 Lh 11.21N 71.57W
Paraguaná, Peninsula de- 52 Jd 11.55N 70.00W
Paraguari [3] 55 Dg 26.00S 57.10W
Paraguari 56 Ic 25.38S 57.09W
Paraguay [1] 53 Kh 23.00S 58.00W
Paraguay, Rio- 52 Kh 27.18S 58.38W
Paraiba [2] 54 Ke 7.10S 36.30W
Paraiba do Sul, Rio- 52 Lh 21.37S 41.03W
Paraibuna, Represa do- 55 Jf 23.25S 45.35W
Paraibuna, Rio- 55 Jf 23.22S 45.40W
Parainen/Pargas 7 Ff 60.18N 22.18 E
Paraíso [Braz.] 55 Fd 19.03S 52.59W
Paraiso [Mex.] 48 Mh 18.24N 93.14W
Paraiso, Rio- 55 Bb 15.08S 61.52W
Parakou 31 Hh 9.21N 2.37 E
Param 64d Bb 7.22N 151.48 E
Paramaribo 53 Ke 5.50N 55.10W
Paramera, Sierra de la- 13 Hd 40.30N 4.46W
Paramithiá 15 Dj 39.28N 20.31 E
Paramušir, Ostrov- 21 Rd 50.25N 155.50 E
Paraná 53 Ji 31.45S 60.30W
Paraná [2] 56 Jb 24.00S 51.00W
Paraná, Pico- 55 Hg 25.14S 48.48W
Paraná, Rio- 52 Ki 33.43S 59.15W
Paranã, Rio- 52 Lg 12.30S 48.14W
Paraná de las Palmas, Rio- 55 Cl 34.18S 58.33W
Paranaguá 53 Lh 25.31S 48.30W
Paraná-Guazú, Rio- 55 Ck 34.00S 58.25W
Paranaíba 54 Hg 19.40S 51.11W
Paranaíba, Rio- 52 Kh 20.07S 51.05W
Paranaiguara 55 Gd 18.53S 50.28W
Paranapanema, Rio- 52 Kh 22.40S 53.09W
Paranapiacaba, Serra do- 52 Lh 24.20S 49.00W
Paranapuã-Guaçu, Ponta do- 55 Ig 24.24S 47.00W
Paranavai 56 Jb 23.04S 52.28W
Parandak 24 Ne 35.21N 50.42 E
Paranéstion 15 Hh 41.16N 24.30 E
Paranhos 55 Ef 23.55S 55.25W
Paraoa Atoll 57 Mf 19.09S 140.43W
Paraopeba 55 Jd 19.18S 44.25W
Paraopeba, Rio- 55 Jd 18.50S 45.11W
Parapara 63b Ca 13.32S 167.20 E
Paraparaumu 62 Fd 40.55S 175.00 E
Paraspóri 15 Kn 35.54N 27.14 E
Parati 55 Jf 23.13S 44.43W
Paratodos, Serra- 55 Jb 14.40S 44.50W
Paratunka 20 Kf 52.52N 158.12 E
Pārāu, Kūh-e- 24 Le 34.37N 47.05 E
Paraúna 55 Gc 17.02S 50.26W
Paravae 64n Bc 10.27S 160.58W
Paray-le-Monial 11 Kh 46.27N 4.07 E
Parbati 25 Fc 25.51N 76.36 E
Parbhani 25 Fe 19.16N 76.47 E
Parchim 10 Hc 53.26N 11.51 E
Parczew 10 Se 51.39N 22.54 E
Pardo 55 Cm 36.15S 59.22W
Pardo, Rio- [Braz.] 55 Fi 29.59S 52.23W
Pardo, Rio- [Braz.] 55 Hh 21.46S 52.09W
Pardo, Rio- [Braz.] 55 He 20.10S 48.38W
Pardo, Rio- [Braz.] 55 Hf 22.55S 49.58W
Pardo, Rio- [Braz.] 55 Jb 15.48S 44.48W
Pardo, Rio- [Braz.] 54 Kg 15.39S 38.57W
Pardubice 10 Lf 50.02N 15.45 E
Parea 65e Eb 16.49S 150.58W
Parecis, Chapada dos- 52 Kg 13.00S 60.00W
Parecis, Rio- 55 Da 12.56S 56.43W
Paredes de Nava 13 Hb 42.09N 4.41W
Parelhas 54 Ke 6.41S 36.39W
Paren 20 Ld 62.28N 163.05 E
Parent 42 Kg 47.55N 74.37W
Parentis-en-Born 11 Ej 44.21N 1.04W
Pareora 62 Df 44.29S 171.13 E
Parepare 22 Nj 4.01S 119.38 E
Párga 15 Dj 39.17N 20.24 E
Pargas/Parainen 7 Ff 60.18N 22.18 E
Pargolovo 8 Nd 60.03N 30.30 E
Parham 51d Bb 17.05N 61.46W
Parhar 19 Gh 37.31N 69.23 E
Pari, Rio- 55 Db 15.36S 56.08W
Paria, Golfo de-/Paria, Gulf of- 54 Fa 10.20N 62.00W
Paria, Gulf of-/Paria, Golfo de- 54 Fa 10.20N 62.00W
Paria, Peninsula de- 50 Eg 10.40N 62.30W
Pariaguán 54 Fb 8.51N 64.43W
Pariaman 26 Dg 0.38S 100.08 E
Paria River 46 Jh 36.52N 111.36W
Paricutin, Volcán- 48 Hh 19.28N 102.15W
Parida, Isla- 49 Fi 8.07N 82.20W
Pari das Pedras 55 Ja 12.45S 44.47W
Parigi 26 Hg 0.48S 120.10 E
Parika 54 Gb 6.52N 58.25W
Parikkala 7 Gf 61.33N 29.30 E
Parima, Serra- 52 Je 3.00N 64.20W
Parinacota 56 Ga 18.12S 69.16W
Pariñas, Punta- 52 Hf 4.40S 81.20W
Paringul Mare, Vîrful- 15 Gd 45.20N 23.30 E
Parintins 53 Kf 2.36S 56.44W
Paris [Fr.] 6 Gf 48.52N 2.20 E
Paris [Il.-U.S.] 45 Mg 39.36N 87.42W
Paris [Kir.] 64g Ab 1.56N 157.31W
Paris [Ky.-U.S.] 44 Ef 38.13N 84.14W
Paris [Tn.-U.S.] 44 Cg 36.19N 88.20W
Paris [Tx.-U.S.] 43 He 33.40N 95.33W
Paris Basin (EN) = Parisien, Bassin- 5 Gf 49.00N 2.00 E
Parisien, Bassin- = Paris Basin (EN) 5 Gf 49.00N 2.00 E
Parita 49 Gi 8.00N 80.31W
Parita, Bahía de- 49 Gi 8.08N 80.24W
Parit Buntar 26 De 5.07N 100.30 E
Parkano 7 Fe 62.01N 23.01 E
Parkent 18 Gd 41.18N 69.40 E
Parker 46 Hi 34.09N 114.17W
Parker, Mount- 59 Fc 17.10S 128.20 E
Parkersburg 43 Kd 39.17N 81.33W
Parker Seamount (EN) 40 Ef 52.35N 151.15W
Parkes 58 Fh 33.08S 148.11 E
Park Falls 45 Kd 45.56N 90.32W
Parkland 46 Dc 47.09N 122.26W
Park Range 43 Fc 40.00N 106.30W
Park Rapids 45 Ic 46.55N 95.04W
Park River 45 Hb 48.24N 97.45W
Park Valley 46 If 41.50N 113.21W
Parma 14 Ef 44.56N 10.26 E
Parma [It.] 6 Hg 44.48N 10.20 E
Parma [Oh.-U.S.] 44 Ge 41.24N 81.44W
Parnaguá 54 Jf 10.13S 44.38W
Parnaiba 53 Lf 2.54S 41.47W
Parnaiba, Rio- 52 Lf 3.00S 41.50W
Parnamirim [Braz.] 54 Ke 8.05S 39.34W
Parnamirim [Braz.] 54 Ke 5.55S 35.15W
Parnarama 54 Je 5.41S 43.06W
Parnassós Óros = Parnassus (EN) 5 Ih 38.30N 22.37 E
Parnassus 62 Ee 42.43S 173.17 E
Parnassus (EN) = Parnassós Óros 5 Ih 38.30N 22.37 E
Párnis Óros 15 Gk 38.10N 23.40 E
Párnon Óros 15 Fl 37.12N 22.38 E
Pärnu/Pjarnu 6 Id 58.24N 24.32 E
Pärnu-Jaagupi/Pjarnu-Jagupi 8 Kf 58.36N 24.25 E
Pärnu Jõgi/Pjarnu 7 Fg 58.23N 24.34 E
Pärnu Laht/Pjarnu, Zaliv- 7 Fg 58.15N 24.25 E
Parola 8 Kc 61.03N 24.22 E
Paroo River 57 Fh 31.28S 143.32 E
Paropamisus/Salseleh-ye Safid Kūh 21 If 34.30N 63.30 E
Páros 15 Il 37.05N 25.09 E
Páros 15 Il 37.06N 25.12 E
Parowan 46 Ih 37.51N 112.57W
Parpaillon 11 Mj 44.35N 6.40 E
Parque Industrial 55 Jd 19.57S 44.01W
Parral 56 Fe 36.09S 71.50W
Parral, Rio- 48 Gd 27.35N 105.25W
Parras, Sierra de- 48 He 25.25N 102.00W
Parras de la Fuente 47 Dc 25.25N 102.11W
Parravicini 55 Dm 36.27S 57.46W
Parrett 9 Jj 51.13N 3.01W
Parrita 49 Ei 9.30N 84.19W
Parry, Cape- 42 Fb 70.12N 124.35W
Parry, Kap- [Grld.] 41 Jd 72.28N 22.00W
Parry, Kap- [Grld.] 41 Ec 77.00N 71.00W
Parry Bay 42 Jc 68.00N 82.00W
Parry Islands 38 Ib 76.00N 110.00W
Parry Peninsula 42 Fc 69.45N 124.35W
Parry Sound 42 Jg 45.21N 80.02W
Parsęta 10 Lb 54.12N 15.33 E
Parsons [Ks.-U.S.] 43 Hd 37.20N 95.16W
Parsons [W.V.-U.S.] 44 Hf 39.06N 79.43W
Parsons Range 59 Hb 13.30S 135.15 E
Partanna 14 Gm 37.43N 12.53 E
Parthenay 11 Fh 46.39N 0.15W
Partille 8 Eg 57.44N 12.07 E
Partinico 14 Hl 38.03N 13.07 E
Partizansk 20 Ih 43.13N 133.05 E
Partizánske 10 Oh 48.38N 18.23 E
Partizanskoje 20 Ee 55.30N 94.30 E
Paru, Rio- 52 Kf 1.33S 52.38W
Paru de Este, Rio- 54 Hc 1.10N 54.40W
Paru de Oeste, Rio- 52 Kf 1.30S 56.00W
Paruru 63a Ec 9.51S 160.49 E
Parvān [3] 23 Kb 35.15N 69.30 E
Pǎrvomaj 15 Ig 42.06N 25.13 E
Parys 37 De 27.04S 27.16 E
Paša 7 Hf 60.28N 32.55 E
Pasadena [Ca.-U.S.] 39 Hf 34.09N 118.09W
Pasadena [Tx.-U.S.] 45 Il 29.42N 95.13W
Paşaeli Yarimadası 15 Lh 41.20N 28.25 E
Paşalimani Adası 15 Ki 40.28N 27.37 E
Pasangkaju 26 Gg 1.10S 119.20 E
Pāsārgād 24 Og 30.17N 52.55 E
Pasarwajo 26 Hh 5.29S 122.50 E
Pascagoula 43 Je 30.23N 88.31W
Paşcani 15 Jb 47.15N 26.44 E
Pasco 43 Db 46.14N 119.06W
Pasco [2] 54 Cf 10.30S 75.15W
Pascoal 55 Ba 13.38S 61.06W
Pascoal, Monte- 54 Kg 16.54S 39.24W
Pascua, Isla de-/Rapa Nui = Easter Island (EN) 57 Qg 27.07S 109.22W
Pas-de-Calais [3] 11 Id 50.30N 2.20 E
Pas-en-Artois 12 Ed 50.09N 2.30 E
Pasewalk 10 Jc 53.31N 13.59 E
Pasinler 24 Ib 40.00N 41.41 E
Pašino 20 De 55.11N 83.02 E
Pasión, Rio de la- 49 Be 16.28N 90.33W
Pasir Mas 26 De 6.02N 102.08 E
Pasirpengarayan 26 Df 0.51N 100.16 E
Pasir Puteh 26 De 5.50N 102.24 E
Påskallavik 8 Gg 57.10N 16.27 E
Paškovski 16 Kg 45.01N 39.05 E
Pasłęk 10 Pb 54.05N 19.39 E
Pasłęka 10 Pb 54.25N 19.50 E
Pašman 14 Jg 43.57N 15.21 E
Pasni 22 Ig 25.16N 63.28 E
Paso de Indios 56 Gf 43.52S 69.06W
Paso del Cerro 55 Ej 31.31S 55.46W
Paso de los Libres 56 Ic 29.43S 57.05W
Paso de los Toros 56 Id 32.49S 56.31W
Paso Tranqueras 55 Ej 31.12S 55.45W
Passamaquoddy Bay 44 Nc 45.06N 66.59W
Passa Três, Serra- 55 Hb 14.40S 49.30W
Passau 10 Jh 48.35N 13.29 E
Passero, Capo- 14 Jn 36.40N 15.10 E
Passo Fundo 53 Kh 28.15S 52.24W
Passo Fundo, Rio- 55 Fh 27.16S 52.42W
Passos 54 Ig 20.43S 46.37W
Pastaza, Rio- 52 If 4.50S 76.25W
Pasteur 56 He 35.08S 62.14W
Pasto 53 Ie 1.13N 77.17W
Pastora Peak 46 Kh 36.47N 109.10W
Pastoria, Laguna de- 48 Ki 16.00N 97.40W
Pastos Bons 54 Je 6.36S 44.05W
Pastrana 13 Jd 40.25N 2.55W
Paštrik 15 Dg 42.14N 20.32 E
Pasubio 14 Fe 45.47N 11.10 E
Pasvalis/Pasvalys 7 Fh 56.02N 24.28 E
Pasvalys/Pasvalis 7 Fh 56.02N 24.28 E
Pásztó 10 Pi 47.55N 19.42 E

Index Symbols

[1] Independent Nation
[2] State, Region
[3] District, County
[4] Municipality
[5] Colony, Dependency
Continent
Physical Region
Historical or Cultural Region
Mount, Mountain
Volcano
Hill
Mountains, Mountain Range
Hills, Escarpment
Plateau, Upland
Pass, Gap
Plain, Lowland
Delta
Salt Flat
Valley, Canyon
Crater, Cave
Karst Features
Depression
Polder
Desert, Dunes
Forest, Woods
Heath, Steppe
Oasis
Cape, Point
Coast, Beach
Cliff
Peninsula
Isthmus
Sandbank
Island
Atoll
Rock, Reef
Islands, Archipelago
Rocks, Reefs
Coral Reef
Well, Spring
Geyser
River, Stream
Waterfall Rapids
River Mouth, Estuary
Lake
Salt Lake
Intermittent Lake
Reservoir
Swamp, Pond
Canal
Glacier
Ice Shelf, Pack Ice
Ocean
Sea
Gulf, Bay
Strait, Fjord
Lagoon
Bank
Seamount
Tablemount
Ridge
Shelf
Basin
Escarpment, Sea Scarp
Fracture
Trench, Abyss
National Park, Reserve
Point of Interest
Recreation Site
Cave, Cavern
Historic Site
Ruins
Wall, Walls
Church, Abbey
Temple
Scientific Station
Airport
Port
Lighthouse
Mine
Tunnel
Dam, Bridge

Patagonia	52	Jj	44.00S	68.00W
Patagonica, Cordillera-	52	Ij	46.00S	71.30W
Patan	25	Hc	27.40N	85.20 E
Pātan	25	Ed	23.50N	72.07 E
Patani	26	If	0.18N	128.48 E
Pata Peninsula	64d	Bb	7.23N	151.35 E
Patchogue	44	Ke	40.46N	73.01W
Pate	36	Hc	2.08S	41.00 E
Patea	62	Fc	39.46S	174.29 E
Patea	62	Fc	39.46S	174.30 E
Pategi	34	Gd	8.44N	5.45 E
Patensie	37	Cf	33.46S	24.49 E
Paternò	14	Jm	37.34N	15.54 E
Paterson	43	Mc	40.55N	74.10W
Paterson Inlet	62	Bg	46.55S	168.00 E
Paterson Range	59	Ed	21.45S	122.05 E
Pathānkot	25	Fb	32.17N	75.39 E
Pathein	22	Lh	16.47N	94.44 E
Pathfinder Reservoir	46	Le	42.30N	106.50W
Pathfinder Seamount (EN)	40	Kf	50.55N	143.15W
Pathiu	25	Jf	10.41N	99.20 E
Patia, Río-	54	Cc	2.13N	78.40W
Patiāla	25	Fb	30.19N	76.24 E
Patiño, Estero-	55	Cg	24.05S	59.55W
Patio	65e	Db	16.35S	151.29W
Pati Point	64c	Ba	13.36N	144.57 E
Pātîrlagele	15	Jd	45.19N	26.21 E
Pativilca	54	Cf	10.42S	77.47W
Pátmos	15	Jl	37.19N	26.34 E
Pátmos	15	Jl	37.20N	26.33 E
Patna	22	Kg	25.36N	85.07 E
Patnos	24	Jc	39.14N	42.52 E
Pato Branco	56	Jc	26.13S	52.40W
Patom Plateau (EN) = Patomskoje Nagorje	20	Ge	59.00N	115.30 E
Patomskoje Nagorje = Patom Plateau (EN)	20	Ge	59.00N	115.30 E
Patos	53	Mf	7.01S	37.16W
Patos, Isla de-	50	Fg	10.38N	61.52W
Patos, Lagoa dos-	52	Ki	31.06S	51.15W
Patos, Laguna de los-	55	Aj	30.25S	62.15W
Patos, Ribeirão dos-	55	Gd	18.58S	50.30W
Patos, Rio dos- [Braz.]	55	Da	13.33S	56.29W
Patos, Rio dos- [Braz.]	55	Hb	14.59S	48.46W
Patos de Minas	53	Lg	18.35S	46.32W
Patosi	15	Ci	40.38N	19.39 E
Patquía	56	Gd	30.03S	66.53W
Pátrai	6	Ih	38.15N	21.44 E
Patrai, Gulf of- (EN) = Patraïkós Kólpos	15	Ek	38.15N	21.30 E
Patraïkós Kólpos = Patrai, Gulf of- (EN)	15	Ek	38.15N	21.30 E
Patricio Lynch, Isla-	56	Eg	48.36S	75.26W
Patricios	55	Bl	35.27S	60.42W
Patrocínio	54	Ig	18.57S	46.59W
Patta Island	30	Li	2.07S	41.03 E
Pattani	25	Kg	6.51N	101.16 E
Patteson, Passage-	63b	Db	15.26S	168.09 E
Patti	14	Il	38.08N	14.58 E
Patti, Golfo di-	14	Jl	38.10N	15.05 E
Patton Seamount (EN)	38	Dd	54.40N	150.30W
Pattullo, Mount-	42	Ee	56.14N	129.39W
Patu	54	Ke	6.06S	37.38W
Patuākhāli	25	Id	22.16N	90.18 E
Patuca, Punta-	49	Ef	15.51N	84.18W
Patuca, Río-	47	He	15.50N	84.18W
Pătulele	15	Fe	44.21N	22.47 E
Patutahi	62	Gc	38.37S	177.53 E
Patuxent Range	66	Qg	84.43S	64.30W
Pátzcuaro	48	Ih	19.31N	101.36W
Pau	11	Fk	43.18N	0.22W
Pau, Gave de-	11	Ek	43.33N	1.12W
Paucartambo	54	Df	13.18S	71.40W
Paucerne, Rio-	55	Ba	13.34S	61.14W
Pau dos Ferros	54	Ke	6.07S	38.10W
Pauillac	11	Fi	45.12N	0.45W
Pauini	54	Ee	7.40S	66.58W
Pauini, Rio-	54	Ee	7.47S	67.15W
Pauksa Taung	25	Ie	19.55N	94.18 E
Paulatuk	39	Gc	69.23N	124.00W
Paulaya, Rio-	49	Ef	15.51N	85.06W
Paulding Bay	66	Ie	66.35S	123.00 E
Paulina Peak	46	Ee	43.41N	121.15W
Păuliş	15	Ec	46.07N	21.35 E
Paulistana	54	Je	8.09S	41.09W
Paulo Afonso	53	Mf	9.21S	38.14W
Paulo Afonso, Cachoeira de-	52	Mf	9.24S	38.12W
Pauls Valley	45	Hi	34.44N	97.13W
Paungde	25	Je	18.29N	95.30 E
Pavant Range	46	Ig	39.00N	112.15W
Pāveh	24	Le	35.03N	46.22 E
Pavia	14	De	45.10N	9.10 E
Pavilly	12	Ce	49.34N	0.58 E
Pāvilosta/Pavilosta	7	Eh	56.55N	21.13 E
Pavilosta/Pāvilosta	7	Eh	56.55N	21.13 E
Pavlikeni	15	If	43.14N	25.18 E
Pavlodar	22	Jd	52.18N	76.57 E
Pavlodarskaja Oblast [3]	19	He	52.00N	76.30 E
Pavlof Islands	40	Ge	55.15N	161.20W
Pavlof Volcano	40	Ge	55.24N	161.55W
Pavlograd	16	Ie	48.32N	35.53 E
Pavlovka	17	Hi	55.25N	56.33 E
Pavlovo	19	Ed	55.58N	43.04 E
Pavlov Seamount (EN)	20	Lf	50.40N	162.00 E
Pavlovsk	16	Ld	50.27N	40.08 E
Pavlovskaja	19	Df	46.06N	39.48 E
Pavullo nel Frignano	14	Ef	44.20N	10.50 E
Pavuvu	63a	Dc	9.04S	159.08 E
Pawa	63a	Ed	10.15S	161.44 E
Pawhuska	45	Hh	36.40N	96.20W
Pawnee	45	Hh	36.20N	96.48W
Pawnee River	45	Gg	38.10N	99.06W
Pawtucket	44	Le	41.53N	71.23W
Paximádhia, Nisídhes-	15	Ho	35.00N	24.35 E
Paxoí	15	Dj	39.12N	20.10 E
Paxson	40	Jd	63.02N	145.30W
Payakumbuk	26	Dg	0.14S	100.38 E
Payas, Cerro-	49	Ef	15.50N	85.00W
Payerne	14	Ad	46.49N	6.58 E
Payette	46	Gd	44.05N	116.57W
Payette	43	Dc	44.05N	116.56W
Payne, Baie-	42	Ke	59.55N	69.35W
Payne, Lac-	42	Ke	59.30N	74.00W
Paysandú [2]	55	Dk	32.00S	57.15W
Paysandú	53	Ki	32.19S	58.05W
Pays de Léon	11	Bf	48.28N	4.30W
Pays d'Othe	11	Jf	48.06N	3.37 E
Payson [Az.-U.S.]	46	Ji	34.14N	111.20W
Payson [Ut.-U.S.]	46	Jf	40.03N	111.44W
Payzawat/Jiashi	27	Cd	39.29N	76.39 E
Pazanān	24	Mg	30.35N	49.59 E
Pazar	24	Ib	41.11N	40.53 E
Pazarbası Burun	24	Db	41.13N	30.17 E
Pazarcık	24	Gd	37.31N	37.19 E
Pazardžik	15	Hg	42.12N	24.20 E
Pazardžik [2]	15	Hg	42.12N	24.20 E
Pazarköy	15	Kj	39.51N	27.24 E
Pazaryeri	24	Cc	40.00N	29.54 E
Pazin	14	He	45.14N	13.56 E
Pčinja	15	Eh	41.49N	21.40 E
Pea	65b	Ac	21.11S	175.14W
Peabirú	55	Ff	23.54S	52.20W
Peace Point	42	Ge	59.12N	112.33W
Peace River	39	Hd	56.14N	117.17W
Peace River [Can.]	38	Hd	56.14N	117.17W
Peace River [Fl.-U.S.]	44	Fl	26.55N	82.05W
Peachland	46	Fb	49.46N	119.44W
Peach Springs	46	Ii	35.32N	113.25W
Peacock Hills	42	Gc	66.05N	110.00W
Peak District	9	Lh	53.17N	1.45W
Peake Creek	59	He	28.05S	136.07 E
Peaked Mountain	44	Mb	46.34N	68.49W
Peale, Mount-	43	Fd	38.26N	109.14W
Pearl	45	Lb	48.42N	88.44W
Pearland	45	Il	29.34N	95.17W
Pearl and Hermes Reef	57	Jb	27.55N	175.45W
Pearl City	65a	Db	21.23N	157.58W
Pearl Harbor	65a	Cb	21.20N	158.00W
Pearl River	43	Je	30.11N	89.32W
Pearsall	45	Gl	28.53N	99.06W
Pearsoll Peak	46	De	42.18N	123.50W
Peary Channel	42	Ha	79.25N	101.00W
Peary Land	67	Me	82.40N	30.00W
Pease River	45	Gi	34.12N	99.07W
Pebane	37	Fc	17.14S	38.10 E
Pebas	54	Dd	3.20S	71.49W
Peć	15	Dg	42.39N	20.18 E
Peca	14	Id	46.29N	14.48 E
Peças, Ilha das-	55	Hg	25.26S	48.19W
Pecatonica River	45	Le	42.29N	89.03W
Pečeneżskoje Vodohranilišče	16	Jd	50.05N	36.50 E
Pečenga	6	Jb	69.33N	31.07 E
Pečenga	7	Hb	69.39N	31.27 E
Pechea	15	Kd	45.38N	27.48 E
Pechora (EN) = Pečora	6	Lb	68.13N	54.10 E
Pechora (EN) = Pečora	5	Lb	65.10N	57.11 E
Pechora Bay (EN) = Pečorskaja Guba	19	Fb	68.40N	54.45 E
Pechora Sea (EN) = Pečorskoje More	19	Fb	69.45N	54.30 E
Pecica	15	Ec	46.10N	21.04 E
Peçin	15	Kl	37.19N	27.45 E
Peckelsheim, Willebadessen-	12	Lc	51.36N	9.08 E
Pečora = Pechora (EN)	6	Lb	65.10N	57.11 E
Pečora = Pechora (EN)	5	Lb	68.13N	54.10 E
Pecora, Capo-	14	Ck	39.27N	8.23 E
Pečorskaja Guba = Pechora Bay (EN)	19	Fb	68.40N	54.45 E
Pečorskoje More = Pechora Sea (EN)	19	Fb	69.45N	54.30 E
Pečory	7	Gh	57.49N	27.38 E
Pecos	43	Ge	31.25N	103.30W
Pecos	38	Ig	29.42N	101.22W
Pecos Plain	43	Ge	33.20N	104.30W
Pécs	6	Hf	46.05N	18.14 E
Pécs [2]	10	Oj	46.06N	18.15 E
Pedasí	49	Gj	7.32N	80.02W
Pedder, Lake-	59	Jh	43.00S	146.15 E
Peddie	37	Dl	33.14S	27.07 E
Pededze	8	Lh	56.53N	27.01 E
Pedernales [Dom.Rep.]	49	Ld	18.02N	71.45W
Pedernales [Ven.]	50	Eh	9.58N	62.16W
Pedernales, Salar de-	56	Gc	26.15S	69.10W
Pedja Jõgi	8	Lf	58.20N	26.10 E
Pêdo Shankou	27	Df	29.12N	83.26 E
Pedra Azul	54	Jg	16.01S	41.16W
Pedra Branca	54	Ke	5.27S	39.43W
Pedra do Sino	55	Kf	22.27S	43.03W
Pedra Lume	32	Cf	16.46N	22.54W
Pedras, Rio das-	55	Ia	13.30S	47.09W
Pedras Altas, Coxilha-	55	Fj	31.45S	53.35W
Pedregal	54	Da	11.01N	70.08W
Pedreiras	54	Jd	4.34S	44.39W
Pedriceña	48	He	25.06N	103.47W
Pedrizas, Puerto de las-	13	Hh	36.55N	4.30W
Pedro Afonso	54	Ie	8.59S	48.11W
Pedro Bank (EN)	49	He	17.00N	78.30W
Pedro Betancourt	49	Gb	22.44N	81.17W
Pedro Cays	47	Ie	17.00N	77.50W
Pedro de Valdivia	56	Gb	22.37S	69.38W
Pedro Gomes	55	Ed	18.05S	54.32W
Pedro Gonzáles, Isla-	49	Hi	8.24N	79.06W
Pedro II	54	Jd	4.25S	41.28W
Pedro II, Ilha-	54	Ec	1.10N	66.44W
Pedro Juan Caballero	56	Ib	22.34S	55.37W
Pedro Leopoldo	55	Jd	19.38S	44.03W
Pedro Luro	56	He	39.29S	62.41W
Pedro Lustoza	55	Gg	25.49S	51.51W
Pedro Montoya	48	Jg	21.38N	99.49W
Pedro Osorio	56	Jd	31.51S	52.45W
Pedro R. Fernández	55	Ci	28.45S	58.39W
Pedro Severo	55	Ec	17.40S	54.02W
Pedroso, Sierra del-	13	Gf	38.35N	5.35W
Peebles	9	Jf	55.39N	3.12W
Pee Dee River	38	Lf	33.21N	79.16W
Peekskill	44	Ke	41.18N	73.56W
Peel	38	Fc	67.37N	134.40W
Peel	11	Lc	51.25N	5.50 E
Peel	9	Ig	54.13N	4.40W
Peel Sound	42	Hb	73.00N	96.00W
Peene	10	Jb	54.09N	13.46 E
Peer	12	Hc	51.08N	5.28 E
Peera Peera Poolanna Lake	59	He	26.30S	138.00 E
Peetz	45	Ef	40.58N	103.07W
Pegasus, Port-	62	Bg	47.10S	167.40 E
Pegasus Bay	61	Dh	43.20S	172.50 E
Pegnitz	10	Gg	49.29N	11.00 E
Pegnitz	10	Hg	49.45N	11.33 E
Pego	13	Lf	38.51N	0.07W
Pegtymel	20	Mc	69.47N	174.00 E
Pegu → Bago	22	Lh	17.30N	96.30 E
Pegu Yoma	21	Lh	19.00N	95.50 E
Pegwell Bay	12	Dc	51.18N	1.23 E
Pehčevo	15	Fh	41.46N	22.54 E
Pehlivanköy	15	Jh	41.21N	26.55 E
Pehuajó	56	He	35.48S	61.53W
Pei-ching Shih → Beijing Shi	27	Kc	40.15N	116.30 E
Peine	10	Gd	52.19N	10.14 E
Peipsi järv = Peipus, Lake- (EN)	5	Id	58.45N	27.30 E
Peipus, Lake- (EN) = Čudskoje Ozero	5	Id	58.45N	27.30 E
Peipus, Lake- (EN) = Peipsi järv	5	Id	58.45N	27.30 E
Peixe	54	If	12.03S	48.32W
Peixe, Lagoa do-	55	Gj	31.18S	51.00W
Peixe, Rio do- [Braz.]	55	Ge	21.31S	51.58W
Peixe, Rio do- [Braz.]	55	Gb	14.06S	50.51W
Peixe, Rio do- [Braz.]	55	Hc	17.37S	48.29W
Peixe, Rio do- [Braz.]	55	Fc	16.32S	52.38W
Peixe, Rio do- [Braz.]	55	Gh	27.27S	51.54W
Peixe de Couro, Rio-	55	Ec	17.21S	55.29W
Peixes, Rio dos-	55	Hb	15.10S	49.30W
Peixian (Yunhe)	28	Dg	34.44N	116.56 E
Peixoto, Reprêsa de-	54	Ih	20.30S	46.30W
Pejantan, Pulau-	26	Ef	0.07N	107.14 E
Pējde/Pōide	8	Jf	58.30N	22.50 E
Pek	15	Ee	44.46N	21.33 E
Pekalongan	26	Eh	6.53S	109.40 E
Pekan	26	Df	3.30N	103.25 E
Pekin	43	Jc	40.35N	89.40W
Peking (EN) = Beijing	22	Nf	39.55N	116.23 E
Pekulnei, Hrebet-	20	Mc	66.30N	176.00 E
Pelabuhanratu	26	Eh	6.59S	106.33 E
Pelagie, Isole-	5	Hh	35.40N	12.40 E
Pelagonija	15	Eh	41.05N	21.30 E
Pélagos	15	Hj	39.20N	24.05 E
Pelaihari	26	Fg	3.48S	114.45 E
Pelat, Mont-	11	Mj	44.16N	6.42 E
Pelawanbesar	26	Gf	1.10N	117.54 E
Pélé	63b	Dc	17.30S	168.24 E
Peleaga, Vîrful-	15	Fd	45.22N	22.53 E
Peleduj	20	Ge	59.40N	112.38 E
Pelée, Montagne-	47	Le	14.48N	61.10W
Pelee, Point-	44	Fe	41.54N	82.30W
Pelee Island	44	Fe	41.46N	82.39W
Peleliu Island	57	Ed	7.01N	134.15 E
Peleng, Pulau-	26	Hg	1.20S	123.10 E
Pelhřimov	10	Lg	49.26N	15.13 E
Pelican Lake	45	Gb	49.20N	99.35W
Pelicanpunt	37	Ad	22.54S	14.26 E
Peligre, Lac de-	49	Ld	18.52N	71.56W
Pelinaion Óros	15	Ik	38.32N	26.00 E
Pelješac	14	Lh	42.55N	17.25 E
Pelkosenniemi	7	Gc	67.07N	27.30 E
Pella	45	Jf	41.25N	92.55W
Pélla	15	Fi	40.46N	22.34 E
Pellegrini	56	He	36.16S	63.09W
Pellice	14	Bf	44.50N	7.38 E
Pellinge/Pellinki	8	Kd	60.15N	25.50 E
Pellinki/Pellinge	8	Kd	60.15N	25.50 E
Pello	7	Fc	66.47N	24.01 E
Pellworm	10	Eb	54.30N	8.40 E
Pelly	38	Fc	62.47N	137.19W
Pelly Bay	42	Ic	68.50N	90.10W
Pelly Bay	39	Kc	68.52N	89.55W
Pelly Crossing	42	Dd	62.50N	136.35W
Pelly Mountains	42	Ed	61.30N	132.00W
Peloncillo Mountains	46	Kj	32.15N	109.10W
Pelón de Nado, Cerro-	48	Jg	20.05N	99.55W
Peloponnesus (EN) = Pelopónnisos	5	Ih	37.40N	22.00 E
Peloponnesus (EN) = Pelopónnisos	15	El	37.40N	22.00 E
Pelopónnisos [2]	15	El	37.40N	22.00 E
Pelopónnisos = Peloponnesus (EN)	15	El	37.40N	22.00 E
Pelopónnisos = Peloponnesus (EN)	5	Ih	37.40N	22.00 E
Peloritani	14	Jl	38.05N	15.20 E
Peloro, Capo- o Faro, Punta del-	14	Jl	38.16N	15.39 E
Pelotas	53	Ki	31.46S	52.20W
Pelotas, Rio-	56	Jc	27.28S	51.55W
Pelplin	10	Oc	53.56N	18.42 E
Pelvoux, Massif du-	5	Gg	44.55N	6.20 E
Pelym	19	Gd	59.40N	63.05 E
Pelymski Tuman, Ozero-	17	Kf	60.05N	63.05 E
Pemalang	26	Eh	6.54S	109.22 E
Pemar/Paimio	8	Jd	60.27N	22.42 E
Pematangsiantar	22	Li	2.57N	99.03 E
Pemba	36	Hd	5.02S	40.00 E
Pemba [Moz.]	31	Lj	12.57S	40.30 E
Pemba [Zam.]	36	Ef	16.31S	27.22 E
Pemba Channel	36	Gd	5.10S	39.20 E
Pemba Island	30	Ki	5.10S	39.48 E
Pemberton [Austl.]	59	Df	34.28S	116.01 E
Pemberton [B.C.-Can.]	46	Da	50.20N	122.48W
Pembina	42	Gf	54.45N	114.17W
Pembina	43	Hb	48.58N	97.15W
Pembina River	43	Hb	48.56N	97.15W
Pembroke [Ont.-Can.]	42	Jg	45.49N	77.07W
Pembroke [Wales-U.K.]	9	Ij	51.41N	4.55W
Pembuang	26	Fg	3.24S	112.33 E
Peña, Sierra de la-	13	Lb	42.31N	0.38W
Peñafiel	13	Dc	41.12N	8.17W
Peñafiel	13	Hc	41.36N	4.07W
Peñagolosa/Penyagolosa	13	Ld	40.13N	0.21W
Peña Gorda, Cerro-	48	Gg	20.40N	104.55W
Peñalara	13	Id	40.51N	3.57W
Penalva	54	Id	3.18S	45.10W
Penamacor	13	Ed	40.10N	7.10W
Peña Nevada, Cerro-	38	Jg	23.46N	99.52W
Penápolis	55	Ge	21.24S	50.04W
Peñaranda de Bracamonte	13	Gd	40.54N	5.12W
Peñarroya	13	Ld	40.28N	0.43W
Peñarroya-Pueblonuevo	13	Gf	38.18N	5.16W
Peñas, Cabo de-	5	Fg	43.39N	5.51W
Penas, Golfo de-	52	Ij	47.22S	74.50W
Peñas, Punta-	54	Fa	10.44N	61.51W
Peñasco, Rio-	45	Dj	32.45N	104.19W
Pendé	35	Ad	9.07N	16.26 E
Pendembu [S.L.]	34	Cd	9.06N	12.12W
Pendembu [S.L.]	34	Cd	8.06N	10.42W
Pendik	15	Mi	40.53N	29.13 E
Pendjari	34	Fc	10.54N	0.51 E
Pendle Hill	9	Kh	53.52N	2.17W
Pendleton	39	He	45.40N	118.47W
Pendolo	26	Hg	2.05S	120.42 E
Pend Oreille Lake	43	Db	48.10N	116.11W
Pend Oreille River	43	Db	49.04N	117.37W
Pendžikent	19	Gh	39.29N	67.38 E
Peneda	13	Dc	41.58N	8.15W
Penedo	54	Kf	10.17S	36.36W
Penetanguishene	44	Hc	44.47N	79.55W
Penganga	25	Fe	19.53N	79.09 E
Pengcheng	27	Jd	36.25N	114.08 E
Penge	36	Dd	5.31S	24.37 E
Pengho Jiao	27	Jc	16.03N	112.35 E
Penghu Liehtao = Pescadores (EN)	27	Kg	23.30N	119.30 E
Penglai (Dengzhou)	27	Ld	37.44N	120.45 E
Pengshui	27	If	29.17N	108.13 E
Pengze	27	Kf	29.52N	116.34 E
Penha	55	Hh	26.46S	48.39W
Penhalonga	37	Ec	18.54S	32.40 E
Penibético, Sistema-	13	Ig	37.00N	3.30W
Peniche	13	Ce	39.21N	9.23W
Penicuik	9	Jf	55.50N	3.14W
Penida, Nusa-	26	Gh	8.44S	115.32 E
Península Ibérica = Iberian Peninsula (EN)	5	Fg	40.00N	4.00W
Peñíscola	13	Md	40.21N	0.25 E
Penisola Salentina = Salentine Peninsula (EN)	5	Hg	40.30N	18.00 E
Penitente, Serra do-	54	Ie	8.45S	46.20W
Pénjamo	48	Ig	20.26N	101.44W
Penju, Kepulauan-	26	Ih	5.22S	127.46 E
Penmarch, Pointe de-	11	Bg	47.48N	4.22W
Penne	14	Hh	42.27N	13.55 E
Penne, Punta-	14	Lj	40.41N	17.56 E
Pennell Coast	66	Kf	71.00S	167.00 E
Penner	21	Kh	14.35N	80.10 E
Penn Hills	44	He	40.28N	79.53W
Pennines	5	Fe	54.10N	2.05W
Pennsylvania [2]	43	Lc	40.45N	77.30W
Penn Yan	44	Id	42.41N	77.03W
Penny Ice Cap	42	Kc	67.00N	65.10W
Penny Strait	42	Ha	76.35N	97.10W
Peno	7	Hh	56.57N	32.45 E
Penobscot Bay	44	Mc	44.15N	68.52W
Penobscot River	43	Nc	44.30N	68.50W
Penola	59	Ig	37.23S	140.50 E
Peñón del Rosario, Cerro-	48	Jh	19.40N	98.12W
Penong	58	Eh	31.55S	133.01 E
Penonomé	47	Hg	8.31N	80.22W
Pénot, Mont-	63b	Cc	16.20S	167.31 E
Penrhyn Atoll	57	Le	9.00S	158.00W
Penrith	9	Kg	54.40N	2.44W
Penrith, Sydney-	59	Kf	33.45S	150.42 E
Pensacola	39	Kf	30.25N	87.13W
Pensacola Mountains	66	Rg	83.45S	55.00W
Pensacola Seamount (EN)	57	Lc	18.17N	157.20W
Pensamiento	55	Bb	14.44S	61.35W
Pensiangan	26	Gf	4.33N	116.19 E
Pentecôte, Ile-	57	Hf	15.45S	168.10 E
Penticton	42	Fg	49.30N	119.35W
Pentland	59	Jd	20.32S	145.24 E
Pentland Firth	9	Jc	58.44N	3.13W
Pentland Hills	9	Jf	55.48N	3.23W
Penwith	9	Hk	50.13N	5.40W
Penyagolosa/Peñagolosa	13	Ld	40.13N	0.21W
Penza	6	Ke	53.13N	45.00 E
Penzance	6	Ff	50.07N	5.33W
Penzenskaja Oblast [3]	19	Ee	53.15N	44.40 E
Penzhina Bay (EN) = Penžinskaja Guba	20	Ld	61.00N	163.00 E
Penžina	21	Sc	62.28N	165.18 E
Penžinskaja Guba = Penzhina Bay (EN)	20	Ld	61.00N	163.00 E
Penžinski Hrebet	20	Ld	62.15N	166.35 E
Peoples Creek	46	Kb	48.24N	108.19W
Peoria	39	Ke	40.42N	89.36W
Peoúia	24	Ee	34.53N	32.23 E
Pepa	36	Ed	7.42S	29.47 E
Pepel	34	Cd	8.35N	13.03W
Peperiguaçu, Rio-	55	Fh	27.10S	53.50W
Peqini	15	Ch	41.03N	19.45 E
Pequena, Lagoa-	55	Fj	31.36S	52.04W
Pequiri, Rio-	54	Gg	17.23S	55.38W
Perabumulih	26	Dg	3.27S	104.15 E
Perälä	8	Ib	62.28N	21.36 E
Perales, Puerto de-	13	Fd	40.15N	6.41W
Pérama	15	Hn	35.22N	24.42 E
Peräseinäjoki	8	Jb	62.34N	23.04 E
Perche, Col de la-	11	Il	42.30N	2.06 E
Perche, Collines du-	11	Gf	48.25N	0.40 E
Percival Lakes	59	Ed	21.25S	125.00 E
Percy Islands	59	Kd	21.40S	150.15 E
Perdasdefogu	14	Dk	39.41N	9.26 E
Perdida, Sierra-	48	Hd	27.30N	103.30W
Perdido, Monte-	5	Gg	42.40N	0.05 E
Perdido, Rio-	55	Df	22.10S	57.33W
Perdizes	55	Id	19.21S	47.17W
Perečin	10	Sh	48.44N	22.29 E
Pereginskoje	16	De	48.49N	24.12 E
Pereira	54	Cc	4.48N	75.42W
Pereira Barreto	56	Jb	20.38S	51.07W
Perejaslav-Hmelnicki	16	Gd	50.04N	31.27 E
Perejil, Isla de-	13	Gi	35.55N	5.26W
Pereljub	16	Qd	51.52N	50.20 E
Peremennyj, Cape-	66	He	66.08S	105.30 E
Peremyšliany	10	Ug	49.38N	24.35 E
Perenjori	59	De	29.26S	116.17 E
Pereščepino	16	Ie	48.59N	35.22 E
Pereslavl-Zalesski	7	Jh	56.45N	38.55 E
Peretu	15	Ie	44.03N	25.05 E
Peretyčiha	20	Ig	47.10N	138.35 E
Perevolocki	16	Sd	51.51N	54.15 E
Pergamino	56	Hd	33.53S	60.35W
Pergamon	15	Kj	39.08N	27.13 E
Perge	24	Dd	37.00N	30.10 E
Pergine Valsugana	14	Fd	46.04N	11.14 E
Pergola	14	Gg	43.34N	12.50 E
Perham	45	Ic	46.36N	95.34W
Perho	7	Fe	63.13N	24.25 E
Periam	15	Dc	46.03N	20.52 E
Péribonca, Rivière-	42	Kg	48.44N	72.06W
Perico	56	Hb	24.23S	65.00W
Pericos	48	Fe	25.03N	107.42W
Périgord	11	Gi	45.00N	0.30 E
Perigoso, Canal-	54	Ic	0.05N	49.40W
Périgueux	11	Gi	45.11N	0.43 E
Perijá, Sierra de-	52	Ie	10.00N	73.00W
Peristerá	15	Gj	39.12N	23.59 E
Perito Moreno	53	Ij	46.36S	70.56W
Perkam, Tanjung- = Urville, Cape d'- (EN)	26	Kg	1.28S	137.54 E
Perković	14	Kg	43.41N	16.06 E
Perlas, Archipiélago de las-	47	Ig	8.25N	79.00W
Perlas, Cayos de-	49	Fg	12.28N	83.28W
Perlas, Laguna de-	49	Fg	12.30N	83.40W
Perlas, Punta de-	49	Fg	12.23N	83.30W
Perleberg	10	Hc	53.04N	11.52 E
Perlez	15	Dd	45.12N	20.23 E
Perm	6	Ld	58.00N	56.15 E
Përmeti	15	Di	40.14N	20.21 E
Permskaja Oblast [3]	19	Fd	59.00N	57.00 E
Pernambuco [2]	54	Ke	8.30S	37.30W
Pernik	15	Gg	42.36N	23.02 E
Pernik [2]	15	Fg	42.35N	22.50 E
Perniö/Bjärna	7	Ff	60.12N	23.08 E
Péronne	11	Ie	49.56N	2.56 E
Perote	48	Kh	19.34N	97.14W
Perpignan	6	Gg	42.41N	2.53 E
Perro, Laguna del-	45	Di	34.40N	105.57W
Perros-Guirec	11	Cf	48.49N	3.27W
Perry [Fl.-U.S.]	44	Fj	30.07N	83.35W
Perry [Ga.-U.S.]	44	Fi	32.27N	83.44W
Perry [Ia.-U.S.]	45	If	41.50N	94.06W
Perry [Ok.-U.S.]	45	Hh	36.17N	97.17W
Perry Lake	45	Ig	39.20N	95.30W
Perryton	45	Fh	36.24N	100.48W
Perryville	40	He	55.54N	159.10W
Persan	12	Ee	49.09N	2.16 E
Perşani, Munţii-	15	Id	45.40N	25.15 E
Persberg	8	Fe	59.45N	14.15 E
Persembe	24	Gb	41.04N	37.46 E
Persepolis	24	Oh	29.57N	52.52 E
Perseverancia	54	Ff	14.44S	62.48W
Persian Gulf (EN) = Al-Khalīj al-'Arabī	21	Hg	27.00N	51.00 E
Persian Gulf (EN) = Khalīj-e Fārs	21	Hg	27.00N	51.00 E
Perstorp	8	Eh	56.08N	13.23 E
Pertek	24	Hc	38.50N	39.22 E
Perth [Austl.]	58	Ch	31.56S	115.50 E
Perth [Ont.-Can.]	44	Ic	44.54N	76.15W
Perth [Scot.-U.K.]	9	Je	56.24N	3.28W
Perth Amboy	44	Je	40.32N	74.17W
Perth-Andover	44	Nb	46.44N	67.42W
Perth-Armadale	59	Df	32.09S	116.00 E
Perth-Fremantle	59	Df	32.03S	115.45 E
Perth-Kalamunda	59	Df	31.57S	116.03 E
Perth-Mundaring	59	Df	31.54S	116.10 E
Perthus, Col de-/Portús, Coll del-	13	Ob	42.28N	2.51 E
Perthus, Col du-	13	Ob	42.28N	2.51 E
Pertuis	11	Lk	43.41N	5.30 E
Pertusato, Capo-	11a	Bb	41.21N	9.11 E
Perú [1]	53	Ig	10.00S	76.00W
Peru [Il.-U.S.]	45	Lf	41.20N	89.08W
Peru [In.-U.S.]	44	De	40.45N	86.04W
Perú, Altiplano del-	54	Df	15.00S	72.00W
Peruaçu, Rio-	55	Jb	15.11S	44.07W
Peru Basin (EN)	3	Mk	17.00S	90.00W
Peru-Chile Trench (EN)	3	Nl	20.00S	73.00W
Perugia	6	Hg	43.08N	12.22 E
Perugorria	55	Ci	29.20S	58.37W
Peruíbe	55	Ig	24.19S	47.00W
Perušić	14	Jf	44.39N	15.22 E
Péruwelz	12	Fd	50.31N	3.35 E

Index Symbols

- [1] Independent Nation
- [2] State, Region
- [3] District, County
- [4] Municipality
- [5] Colony, Dependency
- Continent
- Physical Region
- Historical or Cultural Region
- Mount, Mountain
- Volcano
- Hill
- Mountains, Mountain Range
- Hills, Escarpment
- Plateau, Upland
- Pass, Gap
- Plain, Lowland
- Delta
- Salt Flat
- Valley, Canyon
- Crater, Cave
- Karst Features
- Depression
- Polder
- Desert, Dunes
- Forest, Woods
- Heath, Steppe
- Oasis
- Cape, Point
- Coast, Beach
- Cliff
- Peninsula
- Isthmus
- Sandbank
- Island
- Atoll
- Rock, Reef
- Islands, Archipelago
- Rocks, Reefs
- Coral Reef
- Well, Spring
- Geyser
- River, Stream
- Waterfall Rapids
- River Mouth, Estuary
- Lake
- Salt Lake
- Intermittent Lake
- Reservoir
- Swamp, Pond
- Canal
- Glacier
- Ice Shelf, Pack Ice
- Ocean
- Sea
- Gulf, Bay
- Strait, Fjord
- Lagoon
- Bank
- Seamount
- Tablemount
- Ridge
- Shelf
- Basin
- Escarpment, Sea Scarp
- Fracture
- Trench, Abyss
- National Park, Reserve
- Point of Interest
- Recreation Site
- Cave, Cavern
- Historic Site
- Ruins
- Wall, Walls
- Church, Abbey
- Temple
- Scientific Station
- Airport
- Port
- Lighthouse
- Mine
- Tunnel
- Dam, Bridge

Pervari	24	Jd	37.54N	42.36 E
Pervomajsk [R.S.F.S.R.]	19	Ee	54.52N	43.48 E
Pervomajsk [Ukr.-U.S.S.R.]	16	Ke	48.36N	38.32 E
Pervomajsk [Ukr.-U.S.S.R.]	19	Df	48.03N	30.52 E
Pervomajski [Bye.-U.S.S.R.]	10	Vc	53.52N	25.33 E
Pervomajski [Kaz.-U.S.S.R.]	19	Ie	50.15N	81.59 E
Pervomajski [R.S.F.S.R.]	16	Lc	53.18N	40.15 E
Pervomajski [R.S.F.S.R.]	19	Ec	64.26N	40.48 E
Pervomajski [R.S.F.S.R.]	17	Ji	54.52N	61.08 E
Pervomajski [R.S.F.S.R.]	16	Sd	51.34N	54.59 E
Pervomajski [Ukr.-U.S.S.R.]	16	Je	49.24N	36.15 E
Pervouralsk	19	Fd	57.00N	60.00 E
Pervy Kurilski Proliv ≍	20	Kf	50.50N	156.50 E
Perwez/Perwijs	12	Gd	50.37N	4.49 E
Perwijs/Perwez	12	Gd	50.37N	4.49 E
Pes ∿	7	Ig	59.10N	35.18 E
Peša ∿	17	Cc	66.50N	47.32 E
Pesaro	14	Gg	43.54N	12.55 E
Pescadores (EN)=Penghu Liehtao ❖	27	Kg	23.30N	119.30 E
Pescadores, Punta- ▶	48	Ef	23.45N	109.45W
Pesčany, Mys- ▶	16	Qh	43.10N	51.18 E
Pesčany, Ostrov ◆	20	Gb	74.20N	115.55 E
Pescara ∿	14	Ih	42.28N	14.13 E
Pescara	6	Hg	42.28N	14.13 E
Pescasseroli	14	Hi	41.48N	13.47 E
Peschici	14	Ki	41.57N	16.01 E
Pescia	14	Eg	43.54N	10.41 E
Pescocostanzo	14	Ii	41.53N	14.04 E
Peshāwar	22	Jf	34.01N	71.33 E
Peshkopia	15	Dh	41.41N	20.26 E
Pesio ∿	14	Bf	44.28N	7.53 E
Peskovka	7	Mg	59.03N	52.22 E
Pesmes	11	Lg	47.17N	5.34 E
Pesočny	8	Nd	60.05N	30.20 E
Peso da Régua	13	Ec	41.10N	7.47W
Pesqueira	54	Ke	8.22S	36.42W
Pesqueria, Rio- ∿	48	Je	25.54N	99.11W
Pessac	11	Fj	44.48N	0.37W
Pest [2]	10	Pi	47.25N	19.20 E
Pešter ⊠	15	Df	43.05N	20.02 E
Peštera	15	Hg	42.02N	24.18 E
Pestovo	19	Dd	58.36N	35.47 E
Petacalco, Bahía de- ◐	47	De	17.57N	102.05W
Petaḥ Tiqwa	24	Ff	32.05N	34.53 E
Petäjävesi	8	Kb	62.15N	25.12 E
Petal	45	Lk	31.21N	89.17W
Petalioí ◆	15	Hl	38.01N	24.17 E
Petalioi, Gulf of- (EN) = Petalión, Kólpos- ◐	15	Hk	38.00N	24.05 E
Petalión, Kólpos- = Petalioi, Gulf of- (EN) ◐	15	Hk	38.00N	24.05 E
Petaluma	46	Dg	38.14N	122.39W
Pétange/Petingen	12	He	49.33N	5.53 E
Petare	54	Ea	10.29N	66.49W
Petatlán	48	Ii	17.31N	101.16W
Petatlán, Río- ∿	48	Fd	26.09N	107.45W
Petauke	36	Fe	14.15S	31.20 E
Petén ⊠	47	Fe	16.15N	89.50W
Petén [3]	49	Be	16.50N	90.00W
Petén Itzá, Lago- ◍	49	Ce	16.59N	89.50W
Petenwell Lake ◍	45	Ld	44.05N	89.45W
Peterborough [Austl.]	59	Hf	32.58S	138.50 E
Peterborough [Eng.-U.K.]	9	Mi	52.35N	0.15W
Peterborough [Ont.-Can.]	42	Jh	44.18N	78 19W
Peterhead	9	Ld	57.30N	1.46W
Peter I, Oy- ◆	66	Pe	68.47S	90.35W
Peter Island ◆	51a	Db	18.22N	64.35W
Peterlee	9	Lg	54.46N	1.19W
Petermann Gletscher ❄	41	Fb	80.45N	61.00W
Petermann Ranges ⛰	59	Fd	25.00S	129.45 E
Petermanns Bjerg ▲	67	Md	73.10N	28.00W
Peter Pond Lake ◍	42	Ge	55.55N	108.40W
Petersberg ▲	10	He	51.35N	11.57 E
Petersburg [Ak.-U.S.]	40	Me	56.49N	132.57W
Petersburg [In.-U.S.]	44	Df	38.30N	87.16W
Petersburg [Va.-U.S.]	43	Ld	37.14N	77.24W
Petersburg [W.V.-U.S.]	44	Hf	39.01N	79.09W
Petersfield	9	Mk	51.00N	0.56W
Petershagen	12	Kb	52.23N	8.58 E
Peter the Great Bay (EN)= Petra Velikogo, Zaliv- ◐	21	Pe	42.40N	132.00 E
Petilia Policastro	14	Kk	39.07N	16.47 E
Petingen/Pétange	12	He	49.33N	5.53 E
Petit-Bourg	51e	Ab	16.12N	61.36W
Petit-Canal	51e	Bb	16.23N	61.29W
Petit Canouan ◆	51n	Bb	12.47N	61.17W
Petit Cul-de-Sac Marin ◐	51e	Ab	16.12N	61.33W
Petite Kabylie ⊠	13	Rh	36.35N	5.25 E
Petite Rivière de l'Artibonite	49	Kd	19.08N	72.29W
Petites Pyrénées ⛰	11	Hk	43.05N	1.10 E
Petite-Terre, Iles de la- ❖	51e	Bb	16.10N	61.07W
Petit-Goâve	49	Kd	18.26N	72.52W
Petit Martinique Island ◆	51p	Ca	12.32N	61.22W
Petit-Mécatina, Rivière du- ∿	42	Lf	50.39N	59.25W
Petit Morin ∿	11	Jf	48.56N	3.07 E
Petit Mustique Island ◆	51n	Bb	12.51N	61.13W
Petit Nevis Island ◆	51n	Bb	12.58N	61.15W
Petitot ∿	42	Fd	60.14N	123.29W
Petit Saint-Bernard, Col du- ⌒	14	Ae	45.40N	6.55 E
Petit Saint Vincent Island ◆	51n	Bb	12.33N	61.23W
Petit Savanne ▶	51g	Bb	15.15N	61.17W
Petitsikapau Lake ◍	42	Kf	54.40N	66.25W
Petkula	7	Gc	67.40N	26.41 E
Petlalcingo	48	Kh	18.05N	97.54W
Peto	47	Gd	20.08N	88.55W
Petorca	56	Fd	32.15S	71.00W
Petoskey	44	Ec	45.22N	84.57W
Petra ⁘	24	Fg	30.19N	35.29 E
Petralia Soprana	14	Im	37.47N	14.06 E
Petra Pervogo, Hrebet- ⛰	18	He	39.00N	71.10 E
Petra Velikogo, Zaliv-= Peter the Great Bay (EN) ◐	21	Pe	42.40N	132.00 E
Petre, Point- ▶	44	Id	43.50N	77.09W
Petre Bay ◐	62	Je	43.55S	176.40W
Petrel ✱	66	Re	63.28S	56.17W
Petrela	15	Ch	41.15N	19.51 E
Petrella Tifernina	14	Ii	41.41N	14.42 E
Petrič	15	Gh	41.24N	23.13 E
Pétrie, Récif- ✿	61	Bc	18.30S	164.20 E
Petrikov	16	Fc	52.08N	28.31 E
Petrila	15	Gd	45.27N	23.25 E
Petrinja	14	Ke	45.27N	16.17 E
Petrodvorec	7	Gg	59.53N	29.50 E
Petrólea	54	Db	8.30N	72.35W
Petrolia	44	Fd	42.52N	82.09W
Petrolina	54	Je	9.24S	40.30W
Petrolina de Goiás	55	Hc	16.06S	49.20W
Petronanski prohod ⌒	15	Gf	43.08N	23.08 E
Petronell	14	Kb	48.07N	16.51 E
Petropavlovka	20	Ff	50.38N	105.19 E
Petropavlovsk	22	Id	54.54N	69.06 E
Petropavlovsk-Kamčatski	22	Rd	53.01N	158.39 E
Petrópolis	53	Lh	22.31S	43.10W
Petroşani	15	Gd	45.25N	23.22 E
Petrovac [Yugo.]	15	Bg	42.12N	18.57 E
Petrovac [Yugo.]	15	Ee	44.22N	21.25 E
Petrova Gora ⛰	14	Je	45.17N	15.47 E
Petrovaradin	15	Cd	45.15N	19.53 E
Petrovka	15	Nc	46.55N	30.40 E
Petrovsk	19	Ee	52.18N	45.23 E
Petrovski Jam	7	Ie	63.18N	35.15 E
Petrovsk-Zabajkalski	22	Md	51.17N	108.50 E
Petrov Val	16	Nd	50.10N	45.12 E
Petrozavodsk	6	Jc	61.47N	34.20 E
Petuhovo	19	Gd	55.06N	67.58 E
Petuški	7	Ji	55.59N	39.28 E
Petworth	12	Bd	50.59N	0.36W
Peuetsagoe, Gunung- ▲	26	Cf	4.55N	96.20 E
Peumo	56	Fd	34.24S	71.10W
Peureulak	26	Cf	4.48N	97.53 E
Pevek	22	Tc	69.42N	170.17 E
Pevensey	12	Cd	50.48N	0.21 E
Pevensey Bay ◐	12	Cd	50.48N	0.22 E
Peza ∿	7	Kd	65.34N	44.33 E
Pézenas	11	Jk	43.27N	3.25 E
Pezinok	10	Nh	48.18N	17.16 E
Pfaffenhofen an der Ilm	10	Hh	48.32N	11.31 E
Pfaffenhoffen	12	Jf	48.51N	7.37 E
Pfalz ⊟	12	Je	49.20N	7.57 E
Pfalzel, Trier-	12	Ie	49.46N	6.41 E
Pfälzer Bergland ⛰	10	Dg	49.35N	7.30 E
Pfälzer Wald ⛰	10	Dg	49.15N	7.50 E
Pfarrkirchen	10	Ih	48.26N	12.52 E
Pfinz ∿	12	Ke	49.11N	8.25 E
Pfinztal	12	Ke	49.02N	8.30 E
Pforzheim an der Enz	10	Eh	48.53N	8.42 E
Pfrimm ∿	12	Ke	49.39N	8.22 E
Pfullendorf	10	Fi	47.55N	9.15 E
Pfunds	14	Ed	46.58N	10.33 E
Pfungstadt	12	Ke	49.48N	8.36 E
Phalaborwa	37	Ed	23.55S	31.13 E
Phalodi	25	Ec	27.08N	72.22 E
Pha-an	25	Je	16.53N	97.38 E
Phangnga	25	Jg	8.28N	98.32 E
Phan Ly Cham	25	Lf	11.13N	108.31 E
Phanom	25	Jg	8.49N	98.50 E
Phan Rang	25	Lf	11.34N	108.59 E
Phan Thiet	25	Lf	10.56N	108.06 E
Pharr	45	Gm	26.12N	98.11W
Phatthalung	25	Kg	7.38N	100.04 E
Phayao	25	Ke	18.07N	100.11 E
Phenix City	43	Je	32.29N	85.01W
Phet Buri	25	Jf	13.06N	99.56 E
Phetchabun, Thiu Khao- ⛰	25	Ke	16.20N	100.55 E
Phichit	25	Ke	16.24N	100.21 E
Philadelphia [Ms.-U.S.]	45	Lj	32.46N	89.07W
Philadelphia [Pa.-U.S.]	39	Lf	39.57N	75.07W
Philae ⁘	33	Fe	23.35N	32.52 E
Philip	45	Fd	44.02N	101.40W
Philippeville	11	Kd	50.12N	4.33 E
Philippi	44	Gf	39.08N	80.03W
Philippi (EN) = Filippoi ⁘	15	Hh	41.02N	24.18 E
Philippi, Lake- ◍	59	Hd	24.20S	139.00 E
Philippi Glacier ❄	66	Ge	66.45S	88.20 E
Philippine Basin (EN) ⌣	3	Ih	17.00N	132.00 E
Philippine Islands (EN)= Pilipinas ❖	21	Oh	13.00N	122.00 E
Philippines (EN)=Pilipinas [1]	22	Oh	13.00N	122.00 E
Philippine Sea (EN) ≈	21	Oh	20.00N	130.00 E
Philippine Trench (EN) ⩡	3	Ii	9.00N	127.00 E
Philippsburg	12	Ke	49.14N	8.27 E
Philipsburg [Mt.-U.S.]	46	Ic	46.20N	113.08W
Philipsburg [Neth.Ant.]	50	Ec	18.01N	63.04W
Philip Smith Mountains ⛰	40	Jc	68.30N	148.00W
Philipstown	37	Cf	30.26S	24.29 E
Phillipsburg	45	Gg	39.45N	99.19W
Philpots ◆	42	Jb	74.55N	80.00W
Phitsanulok	22	Mh	16.49N	100.15 E
Phnom Penh (EN)=Phnum Pénh	22	Mh	11.33N	104.55 E
Phnum Penh=Phnom Penh (EN)	22	Mh	11.33N	104.55 E
Phoenix	39	Hf	33.27N	112.05W
Phoenix → Rawaki Atoll ⊙	57	Je	3.43S	170.43W
Phoenix Islands ❖	57	Je	4.00S	172.00W
Phôngsali	25	Kd	21.41N	102.06 E
Phrae	25	Ke	18.07N	100.11 E
Phra Nakhom Si Ayutthaya	22	Mh	14.21N	100.33 E
Phrygia ⊟	15	Mk	38.30N	29.50 E
Phu Cuong	25	Lf	10.58N	106.39 E
Phuket	22	Li	7.54N	98.24 E
Phuket, Ko- ◆	21	Li	8.00N	98.20 E
Phulbani	25	Gd	20.28N	84.14 E
Phumĭ Mlu Prey	25	Lf	13.48N	105.16 E
Phumĭ Sâmraông	25	Kf	14.11N	103.31 E
Phu My	25	Lf	14.10N	109.03 E
Phuoc Binh	25	Lf	11.50N	106.58 E
Phu Quoc, Dao- ◆	25	Kf	10.12N	104.00 E
Phu Tho	25	Ld	21.24N	105.13 E
Phu Vinh → Tra Vinh	25	Lg	9.56N	106.20 E
Piaanu Pass ≍	64d	Ab	7.20N	151.26 E
Piacenza	14	De	45.01N	9.40 E
Piana degli Albanesi	14	Hm	37.59N	13.17 E
Piana Mwanga	36	Ed	7.40S	28.10 E
Piancó	54	Ke	7.12S	37.57W
Pianguan	27	Jd	39.28N	111.32 E
Pianosa [It.] ◆	14	Jh	42.15N	15.45 E
Pianosa [It.] ◆	14	Eh	42.35N	10.05 E
Piaseczno	10	Rd	52.05N	21.01 E
Piaski	10	Se	51.08N	22.51 E
Piątek	10	Pd	52.05N	19.28 E
Piatra	15	If	43.49N	25.10 E
Piatra Neamţ	15	Jc	46.55N	26.20 E
Piatra Olt	15	He	44.22N	24.16 E
Piauí [2]	54	Je	7.00S	43.00W
Piauí, Rio- ∿	52	Lf	6.38S	42.42W
Piave ∿	5	Hf	45.32N	12.44 E
Piaxtla, Punta- ▶	48	Ff	23.38N	106.50W
Piaxtla, Río- ∿	48	Ff	23.42N	106.49W
Piazza Armerina	14	Im	37.23N	14.22 E
Pibor ∿	35	Ed	8.26N	33.13 E
Pibor Post	35	Ed	6.48N	33.08 E
Pica	56	Gb	20.30S	69.21W
Picachos, Cerro dos- ▲	48	Bc	29.25N	114.10W
Picardie = Picardy (EN) ⊟	11	Je	50.00N	3.30 E
Picardy (EN) = Picardie ⊟	11	Je	50.00N	3.30 E
Picayune	45	Lk	30.26N	89.41W
Picentini, Monti- ⛰	14	Jj	40.45N	15.10 E
Pichanal	53	Jh	23.20S	64.15W
Pichilemu	56	Fd	34.23S	72.00W
Pichilingue	48	De	24.20N	110.20W
Pichna ∿	10	Oe	51.50N	18.40 E
Pichones, Cayos- ❖	49	Ff	15.45N	82.55W
Pichucalco	48	Mi	17.31N	93.04W
Pickering	9	Mg	54.14N	0.46W
Pickering, Vale of- ⋁	9	Mg	54.10N	0.45W
Pickle Lake	42	If	51.29N	90.10W
Pickwick Lake ◍	44	Ch	34.55N	88.10W
Pico ◆	30	Ee	38.28N	28.20W
Picos	53	Lf	7.05S	41.28W
Pico Truncado	56	Gg	46.48S	67.58W
Picquigny	11	Ie	49.57N	2.09 E
Picton	61	Dh	41.18S	174.00 E
Pictou	42	Lg	45.41N	62.43W
Picunda	16	Lh	43.12N	40.21 E
Pidurutalagala ▲	21	Ki	7.00N	80.46 E
Piedecuesta	54	Db	6.59N	73.03W
Piedimonte Matese	14	Ii	41.20N	14.22 E
Piedmont [Al.-U.S.]	44	Ei	33.55N	85.37W
Piedmont [Mo.-U.S.]	45	Kh	37.09N	90.42W
Piedmont (EN) = Piemonte [2]	14	Be	45.00N	8.00 E
Piedmont Plateau ⊠	38	Kf	35.00N	81.00W
Piedra ∿	13	Kc	41.19N	1.48W
Piedra, Monasterio de- ✝	13	Kc	41.10N	1.50W
Piedrabuena	13	He	39.02N	4.10W
Piedrafita, Puerto de- ⌒	13	Fb	42.36N	6.57W
Piedrahita	13	Gd	40.28N	5.19W
Piedras	54	Cd	3.38S	79.54W
Piedras, Punta- ▶	56	Ie	35.25S	57.08W
Piedras, Río de las- ∿	54	Ef	12.30S	69.14W
Piedras Negras	39	Ig	28.42N	100.31W
Piedras Negras ⁘	49	Be	17.12N	91.15W
Piedra Sola	56	Id	32.04S	56.21W
Piekary Śląskie	10	Of	50.24N	18.58 E
Pieksämäki	7	Ge	62.18N	27.08 E
Pielach ∿	14	Jb	48.15N	15.22 E
Pielavesi	7	Ge	63.14N	26.45 E
Pielinen ◍	5	Ic	63.15N	29.40 E
Piemonte = Piedmont (EN) [2]	14	Be	45.00N	8.00 E
Pieniężno	10	Qb	54.15N	20.08 E
Pieni Salpausselkä ◬	8	Lc	61.10N	27.20 E
Piennes	12	He	49.19N	5.47 E
Pienza	14	Fg	43.04N	11.41 E
Pierce	46	Hc	46.29N	115.48W
Piéria Óri ▲	15	Fi	40.12N	22.07 E
Pierre	39	Ie	44.22N	100.21W
Pierrefitte-sur-Aire	12	Hf	48.54N	5.20 E
Pierrefonds	12	Ee	49.21N	2.59 E
Pierrelatte	11	Kj	44.23N	4.42 E
Pieskehaure ◍	7	Dc	66.57N	16.30 E
Piešťany	10	Nh	48.36N	17.50 E
Pietarsaari/Jakobstad	7	Fe	63.40N	22.42 E
Pietermaritzburg	31	Kk	29.37S	30.16 E
Pietersburg	31	Jk	23.54S	29.25 E
Pietraperzia	14	Im	37.25N	14.08 E
Pietrasanta	14	Eg	43.57N	10.14 E
Piet Retief	37	Ee	27.01S	30.50 E
Pietrii, Vîrful- ▲	15	Fd	45.23N	22.40 E
Pietroşani	15	If	43.43N	25.38 E
Pietrosu, Vîrful- [Rom.] ▲	15	Ib	47.08N	25.11 E
Pietrosu, Vîrful- [Rom.] ▲	5	If	47.23N	25.33 E
Pieve di Cadore	14	Gd	46.26N	12.22 E
Pigeon Island ◆	51k	Ba	14.06N	60.58W
Pigeon River	45	Lb	48.02N	89.41W
Piggott	45	Kh	36.23N	90.11W
Pigg's Peak	37	Ee	25.58S	31.15 E
Pigs, Bay of- (EN)= Cochinos, Bahia de- ◐	49	Gb	22.07N	81.10W
Pigüé	55	Am	37.37S	62.25W
Pi He ∿	28	Dh	32.26N	116.34 E
Pihkva järv=Pskov, Lake- (EN) ◍	7	Gg	58.00N	28.00 E
Pihlajavesi ◍	7	Gf	61.45N	28.45 E
Pihlava	8	Ic	61.33N	21.36 E
Pihtipudas	7	Fe	63.23N	25.34 E
Piikkiö	8	Jd	60.26N	22.31 E
Piirisaar/Pirissar ◆	8	Lf	58.23N	27.40 E
Pijijiapan	48	Mj	15.42N	93.14W
Pijol, Pico- ▲	49	Df	15.06N	87.35W
Pikalevo	7	Ig	59.32N	34.03 E
Pikangikum	42	If	51.49N	94.00W
Pikelot Island ◆	57	Fd	8.05N	147.38 E
Pikes Peak ▲	43	Fd	38.51N	105.03W
Piketberg	37	Bf	32.54S	18.46 E
Pikiutdleq ◐	41	Hf	64.45N	40.10W
Pikou	28	Ge	39.24N	122.21 E
Pikounda	36	Cb	0.33N	16.42 E
Piła	10	Mc	53.10N	16.44 E
Piła [2]	10	Mc	53.10N	16.45 E
Pila	55	Cm	36.01S	58.08W
Pila, Sierra de la- ⛰	13	Kf	38.16N	1.11W
Pilar [Arg.]	55	Bj	31.27S	61.15W
Pilar [Braz.]	54	Ke	9.36S	35.56W
Pilar [Par.]	56	Ic	26.52S	58.23W
Pilas Group ❖	26	He	6.45N	121.35 E
Pilat, Mont- ▲	11	Ki	45.23N	4.35 E
Pílatus ▲	14	Cd	46.59N	8.20 E
Pilaya, Río- ∿	54	Fh	20.55S	64.04W
Pilcaniyeu	56	Ff	41.08S	70.40W
Pilcomayo, Río- ∿	52	Kh	25.21S	57.42W
Pile, Jezioro- ◍	10	Mc	53.35N	16.30 E
Píli	15	Ej	39.28N	21.37 E
Pilībhīt	25	Fc	28.38N	79.48 E
Pilica ∿	10	Re	51.52N	21.17 E
Pílion Óros ▲	15	Gj	39.24N	23.05 E
Pilipinas=Philippine Islands (EN) ❖	21	Oh	13.00N	122.00 E
Pilipinas=Philippines (EN) [1]	22	Oh	13.00N	122.00 E
Pilis ▲	10	Oi	47.41N	18.53 E
Pillahuincó, Sierra de- ⛰	55	Bn	38.18S	60.45W
Pillar, Cape- ▶	59	Jh	43.15S	148.00 E
Pilna	7	Ki	55.33N	45.55 E
Pilões, Rio- ∿	55	Gc	16.14S	50.54W
Pilões, Serra dos- ⛰	55	Ic	17.50S	47.13W
Pilón, Río- ∿	48	Je	25.32N	99.32W
Pílos	15	Em	36.55N	21.42 E
Pílos = Pylos (EN) ⁘	15	Em	36.56N	21.40 E
Pilot Peak ▲	46	Hf	41.02N	114.06W
Pilot Rock	46	Fd	45.29N	118.50W
Pilsen (EN)=Plzeň	6	Hf	49.45N	13.24 E
Piltene	7	Eh	57.15N	21.42 E
Pilzno	10	Rg	49.59N	21.17 E
Pim ∿	19	Hc	61.18N	71.57 E
Pimba	59	Hf	31.15S	136.47 E
Pimenteiras	54	Je	6.14S	41.25W
Pimža Jõgi ∿	8	Lg	57.57N	27.59 E
Pina	13	Lc	41.29N	0.32W
Pinacate, Cerro- ▲	48	Cb	31.45N	113.31W
Pinaki Atoll ⊙	57	Nf	19.22S	138.44W
Pinamar	55	Dm	37.07S	56.50W
Piñami, Arroyo- ∿	48	Cd	27.44N	113.47W
Pinar ▲	13	Gh	36.46N	5.26W
Pinarbaşi	24	Gc	38.50N	36.30 E
Pınar del Río	39	Kg	22.25N	83.42W
Pinar del Río [3]	49	Eb	22.35N	83.40W
Pinarello	11a	Bb	41.41N	9.22 E
Pinarhisar	15	Kh	41.37N	27.30 E
Pinchbeck	12	Bb	52.48N	0.09W
Pincher Creek	42	Gg	49.30N	113.48W
Pinçon, Mont- ▲	11	Ff	48.58N	0.37W
Pîncota	15	Ec	46.20N	21.42 E
Pindaíba, Ribeirão ∿	55	Gb	14.48S	52.00W
Pindaré, Rio- ∿	54	Jd	3.17S	44.47W
Pindaré-Mirim	54	Id	3.37S	45.21W
Pindaval	55	Dc	17.08S	56.09W
Píndhos Óros=Pindus Mountains (EN) ⛰	5	Ih	39.45N	21.30 E
Pindus Mountains (EN)= Píndhos Óros ⛰	5	Ih	39.45N	21.30 E
Pine Bluff	43	Ie	34.13N	92.01W
Pine Bluffs	46	Mf	41.11N	104.04W
Pine Creek	59	Gb	13.49S	131.49 E
Pine Falls	42	Hf	50.35N	96.15W
Pinega	19	Ec	64.42N	43.22 E
Pinega ∿	5	Kc	64.08N	41.54 E
Pine Island Glacier ❄	66	Of	75.00S	101.00W
Pineland	45	Jk	31.15N	93.58W
Pine Mountain [Ga.-U.S.] ⛰	44	Ei	32.51N	84.47W
Pine Mountain [U.S.] ⛰	44	Fg	36.55N	83.20W
Pine Pass ⌒	42	Fe	55.50N	122.30W
Pine Point	39	Hc	61.01N	114.15W
Pine Ridge	45	Ee	43.02N	102.33W
Pinerolo	14	Bf	44.53N	7.21 E
Pines, Isle of- (EN)= Juventud, Isla de la- ◆	38	Kg	21.40N	82.50W
Pines, Isle of- (EN)=Pins, Ile des- ◆	57	Hg	22.37S	167.30 E
Pines, Lake O' The ◍	45	Ij	32.46N	94.35W
Pinetown	37	Ee	29.52S	30.46 E
Ping ∿	21	Mh	15.42N	100.09 E
Pingbian	27	Hg	22.56N	103.46 E
Pingchang	27	Ie	31.38N	107.06 E
Pingding	28	Bf	37.48N	113.37 E
Pingdingbu → Guyuan	28	Cd	41.40N	115.41 E
Pingding Shan ⛰	27	Mb	46.39N	128.30 E
Pingdingshan	27	Je	33.41N	113.27 E
Pingdu	28	Ef	36.47N	119.57 E
Pingelap Atoll ⊙	57	Hd	6.13N	160.42 E
Pingelly	59	Df	32.32S	117.05 E
Pinggu	28	Dd	40.08N	117.07 E
Pingguo	27	Ig	23.21N	107.34 E
Pinghu	28	Fi	30.42N	121.02 E
Pingjiang	28	Bj	28.45N	113.37 E
Pingle	27	Jg	24.43N	110.42 E
Pingli	27	Ie	32.27N	109.21 E
Pingliang	22	Mf	35.32N	106.41 E
Pinglu (Jingping)	28	Be	39.32N	112.14 E
Pingluo	22	Mf	38.56N	106.34 E
Pingma → Tiandong	27	Ig	23.40N	107.09 E
Pingnan	27	Jg	23.38N	110.23 E
Pingouins, Ile des- ◆	30	Mm	46.25S	50.19 E
Pingquan	27	Kc	41.00N	118.36 E
Pingshan	28	Ce	38.21N	114.01 E
Pingshun	28	Bf	36.12N	113.26 E
Pingtan	27	Kf	25.31N	119.48 E
Pingtung	27	Lg	22.40N	120.29 E
Pingüicas, Cerro- ▲	48	Jg	21.10N	99.42W
Pingvallavatn ◍	7a	Bb	64.15N	21.09W
Pingvellir	7a	Bb	64.17N	21.03W
Pingwu	27	He	32.27N	104.35 E
Pingxiang [China]	27	Ig	22.11N	106.46 E
Pingxiang [China]	27	Jf	27.43N	113.48 E
Pingyang	27	Lf	27.40N	120.30 E
Pingyao	27	Jd	37.12N	112.13 E
Pingyi	28	Dg	35.30N	117.38 E
Pingyin	28	Df	36.17N	116.26 E
Pingyu	28	Ci	32.58N	114.36 E
Pingyuan	28	Df	37.10N	116.25 E
Pinhal	55	If	22.12S	46.45W
Pinhão	55	Gg	25.43S	51.38W
Pinheir Machado	55	Fj	31.34S	53.23W
Pinhel	13	Ed	40.46N	7.04W
Pini, Pulau- ◆	26	Cf	0.08N	98.40 E
Piniós [Grc.] ∿	15	Fj	39.53N	22.44 E
Piniós [Grc.] ∿	15	El	37.48N	21.14 E
Pinipel ◆	63a	Ba	4.24S	154.08 E
Pinjug	7	Lf	60.16N	47.54 E
Pinka ∿	10	Mi	47.00N	16.35 E
Pink Mountain	42	Fe	56.06N	122.35W
Pinnaroo	59	Ig	35.16S	140.55 E
Pinneberg	10	Fc	53.39N	9.48 E
Pínnes, Ákra- ▶	15	Hi	40.07N	24.18 E
Pinolosean	26	Hf	0.23N	124.07 E
Pinos	48	If	22.18N	101.34W
Pinos, Mount- ▲	38	Hf	34.50N	119.09W
Pinos-Puente	13	Ig	37.15N	3.45W
Pinrang	26	Gg	3.48S	119.38 E
Pins, Cap des- ▶	63b	Ce	21.04S	167.28 E
Pins, Ile des-=Pines, Isle of- (EN) ◆	57	Hg	22.37S	167.30 E
Pins, Pointe aux- ▶	44	Gd	42.15N	81.51W
Pinsk	19	Ce	52.08N	26.06 E
Pinta, Isla- ◆	54a	Aa	0.35N	90.44W
Pintas, Sierra de las- ⛰	48	Bb	31.40N	115.10W
Pinto [Arg.]	56	Hc	29.09S	62.39W
Pinto [Sp.]	13	Id	40.14N	3.41W
Pintwater Range ⛰	46	Hh	36.55N	115.30W
Pio ◆	63a	Ed	10.12S	161.42 E
Pioche	46	Hh	37.56N	114.27W
Piombino	14	Eh	42.55N	10.32 E
Piombino, Canale di- ≍	14	Eh	42.55N	10.30 E
Pioneer Mountains ⛰	46	Id	45.40N	113.00W
Pioner, Ostrov- ◆	21	Lb	79.50N	92.30 E
Pionerski [R.S.F.S.R.]	19	Gc	61.12N	62.57 E
Pionerski [R.S.F.S.R.]	7	Ei	54.57N	20.13 E
Pionki	10	Re	51.30N	21.27 E
Piorini, Lago- ◍	54	Fd	3.35S	63.15W
Piorini, Rio- ∿	54	Fd	3.23S	63.30W
Piotrków [2]	10	Pe	51.25N	19.40 E
Piotrków Trybunalski	10	Pe	51.25N	19.42 E
Piove di Sacco	14	Ge	45.18N	12.02 E
Pipa Dingzi ▲	27	Mc	43.57N	128.14 E
Pipéri ◆	15	Hj	39.19N	24.21 E
Pipestone	45	Hd	44.01N	96.19W
Pipestone Creek ∿	45	Fb	49.42N	100.45W
Pipi ∿	35	Cd	7.27N	22.48 E
Pipinas	55	Dl	35.32S	57.20W
Pipmouacan, Réservoir - ⊞	42	Kg	49.40N	70.20W
Piqan → Shanshan	27	Fc	42.52N	90.10 E
Piqua	44	Ee	40.08N	84.14W
Piqueras, Puerto de- ⌒	13	Jb	42.03N	2.32W
Piquiri, Rio- ∿	56	Jb	24.03S	54.14W
Piquiri, Serra do- ⛰	55	Fg	24.53S	52.25W
Piracanjuba	55	Hc	17.18S	49.01W
Piracanjuba, Rio- [Braz.] ∿	55	Hd	18.14S	48.48W
Piracanjuba, Rio- [Braz.] ∿	55	Hc	17.18S	48.13W
Piracema	55	Je	20.31S	44.29W
Piracicaba	56	Kb	22.43S	47.38W
Piracicaba, Rio- ∿	55	Hf	22.36S	48.19W
Piraçununga	55	Ie	21.59S	47.25W
Piracuruca	54	Jd	3.56S	41.42W
Piraeus (EN) = Piraiévs	6	Ih	37.57N	23.38 E
Pirai do Sul	55	Hg	24.31S	49.56W
Piraiévs = Piraeus (EN)	6	Ih	37.57N	23.38 E
Piraju	55	Hf	23.12S	49.23W
Pirajuí	55	He	21.59S	49.29W
Piramide, Cerro- ▲	52	Ij	49.01S	73.32W
Piran	14	He	45.32N	13.34 E
Pirané	56	Ic	25.43S	59.06W
Piranhas	55	Gc	16.31S	51.51W
Piranhas, Rio- ∿	55	Gc	16.01S	51.52W
Pīrān Shahr	24	Kd	36.40N	45.05 E
Pirapora	53	Lg	17.21S	44.56W
Pirarajá	56	Jd	33.44S	54.45W
Pirate Well	49	Kb	22.26N	73.04W
Piratini	55	Fj	31.27S	53.06W
Piratini, Rio- ∿	55	Fk	32.01S	52.25W
Piratinim, Rio- ∿	55	Ei	28.06S	55.27W
Pirdop	15	Hg	42.42N	24.11 E
Pirenópolis	55	Hb	15.51S	48.57W
Pires do Rio	54	Ig	17.18S	48.17W
Pírgos	15	El	37.41N	21.27 E
Pirgós	15	Fi	40.38N	22.44 E
Piriápolis	55	El	34.54S	55.17W
Pirin ⛰	15	Gh	41.40N	23.30 E
Pirineos=Pyrenees (EN) ⛰	5	Gg	42.40N	1.00 E
Pirineus, Serra dos- ⛰	55	Hc	16.15S	49.10W
Piripiri	54	Jd	4.16S	41.47W
Pirissar/Piirisaar ◆	8	Lf	58.23N	27.40 E
Píritu	50	Bh	9.23N	69.12W
Piritu, Islas- ❖	50	Dg	10.10N	64.56W
Pirizal	55	Dc	16.16S	56.23W
Pirjatin	16	Hd	50.14N	32.30 E
Pirmasens	10	Dg	49.12N	7.36 E
Pirna	10	Jf	50.58N	13.56 E
Piron ◆	63a	Ad	11.20S	153.27 E
Pirón ∿	13	Hc	41.23N	4.31W
Pirot	15	Ff	43.09N	22.36 E
Pirre, Cerro- ◭	49	Ij	7.49N	77.43W
Pirrit Hills ◬	66	Pg	81.17S	85.21W
Pirsagat ∿	16	Pj	39.53N	49.19 E
Pīr Tāj	24	Me	35.45N	48.07 E
Pirttikyla/Pörtom	8	Ib	62.42N	21.37 E
Piru	26	Ig	3.04S	128.12 E
Pis ◆	64d	Ba	7.41N	151.46 E
Pisa	14	Eg	43.43N	10.23 E
Pisa ∿	10	Rc	53.15N	21.52 E
Pisagua	56	Fa	19.36S	70.13W

Index Symbols

[1] Independent Nation
[2] State, Region
[3] District, County
[4] Municipality
[5] Colony, Dependency
■ Continent
⊠ Physical Region
⊟ Historical or Cultural Region
▲ Mount, Mountain
△ Volcano
◭ Hill
⛰ Mountains, Mountain Range
◬ Hills, Escarpment
⏢ Plateau, Upland
⌒ Pass, Gap
▭ Plain, Lowland
◺ Delta
▦ Salt Flat
⋁ Valley, Canyon
◠ Crater, Cave
✺ Karst Features
⊔ Depression
⊓ Polder
∴ Desert, Dunes
♣ Forest, Woods
⁑ Heath, Steppe
❀ Oasis
▶ Cape, Point
⌇ Coast, Beach
◧ Cliff
⊏ Peninsula
⧓ Isthmus
⋯ Sandbank
◆ Island
⊙ Atoll
✱ Rock, Reef
❖ Islands, Archipelago
✲ Rocks, Reefs
✿ Coral Reef
⊚ Well, Spring
⛲ Geyser
∿ River, Stream
≋ Waterfall Rapids
⩤ River Mouth, Estuary
◍ Lake
◎ Salt Lake
◌ Intermittent Lake
⊞ Reservoir
⩨ Swamp, Pond
═ Canal
❄ Glacier
❅ Ice Shelf, Pack Ice
〰 Ocean
≈ Sea
◐ Gulf, Bay
≍ Strait, Fjord
◯ Lagoon
▥ Bank
⩙ Seamount
⊼ Tablemount
⩞ Ridge
▬ Shelf
⌣ Basin
⟋ Escarpment, Sea Scarp
⚡ Fracture
⩡ Trench, Abyss
⚑ National Park, Reserve
★ Point of Interest
✚ Recreation Site
⌓ Cave, Cavern
⌂ Historic Site
⁘ Ruins
▙ Wall, Walls
✝ Church, Abbey
⛩ Temple
⚗ Scientific Station
✈ Airport
⚓ Port
⛯ Lighthouse
⚒ Mine
⋂ Tunnel
⌿ Dam, Bridge

Pisano 14 Eg 43.46N 10.33 E
Pisar 64d Cb 7.19N 152.01 E
Pisciotta 14 Jj 40.06N 15.14 E
Pisco 53 Ig 13.42S 76.13W
Pişcolt 15 Fb 47.35N 22.18 E
Písek 10 Kg 49.19N 14.10 E
Pishan/Guma 27 Cd 37.38N 78.19 E
Pīsh Qal'eh 24 Qd 37.35N 57.05 E
Pīshvā 24 Ne 35.18N 51.44 E
Piso Firme 55 Ba 13.41S 61.52W
Pissa 7 Ei 54.39N 21.50 E
Pisshiri-Dake 29a Ba 44.20N 141.55 E
Pista 7 Hd 65.28N 30.45 E
Pisticci 14 Kj 40.23N 16.33 E
Pistoia 14 Eg 43.55N 10.54 E
Pisuerga 13 Hc 41.33N 4.52W
Pisz 10 Rc 53.38N 21.49 E
Pita 34 Cc 11.05N 12.24W
Pitalito 54 Cc 1.53N 76.02W
Pitanga 56 Jb 24.46S 51.44W
Pitanga, Serra da- 55 Gg 24.52S 51.48W
Pitangui 55 Jd 19.40S 44.54W
Pitcairn [5] 58 Og 24.00S 129.00W
Pitcairn Island 57 Ng 25.04S 130.05W
Piteå 7 Ed 65.20N 21.30 E
Piteälven 5 Ib 65.14N 21.32 E
Piteşti 6 Ig 44.51N 24.52 E
Pithiviers 11 If 48.10N 2.15 E
Pithorāgarh 25 Gc 29.35N 80.13 E
Piti 36 Fd 7.00S 32.44 E
Piti 64c Bb 13.28N 144.41 E
Pitiquito 48 Cb 30.42N 112.02W
Pitkjaranta 19 Dc 61.35N 31.31 E
Pitkkala 8 Jc 61.28N 23.34 E
Pitljar 20 Bc 65.52N 65.55 E
Pitlochry 9 Je 56.43N 3.45W
Pitomača 14 Le 45.57N 17.14 E
Piton, Pointe du- 51e Ba 16.30N 61.27W
Pit River 43 Cc 40.45N 122.22W
Pitrufquén 56 Fe 38.59S 72.39W
Pitt 42 Ef 53.40N 129.50W
Pitt Island 57 Ji 44.20S 176.10W
Pittsburg 43 Id 37.25N 94.42W
Pittsburgh 39 Le 40.26N 80.00W
Pittsfield [Il.-U.S.] 45 Kg 39.36N 90.48W
Pittsfield [Ma.-U.S.] 44 Kd 42.27N 73.15W
Pittsfield [Me.-U.S.] 44 Mc 44.47N 69.23W
Pitt Strait 62 Jf 44.10S 176.20W
Pitu 26 If 1.41N 128.01 E
Piũi 55 Je 20.28S 45.58W
Piura 53 Hf 5.12S 80.38W
Piura [2] 54 Be 5.00S 80.20W
Piuthān 25 Gc 28.06N 82.52 E
Piva 15 Bf 43.21N 18.51 E
Pivan 20 If 50.27N 137.05 E
Pivijay 49 Jh 10.28N 74.38W
Pižma [R.S.F.S.R.] 7 Lh 57.36N 48.58 E
Pižma [R.S.F.S.R.] 17 Fd 65.24N 52.05 E
Pizzo 14 Kl 38.44N 16.40 E
Pjakupur 20 Cd 65.00N 77.48 E
Pjalica 7 Jc 66.12N 39.32 E
Pjalma 19 Dc 62.27N 35.53 E
Pjana 7 Ki 55.37N 45.58 E
Pjandž 19 Gh 37.15N 69.07 E
Pjandž 21 If 37.06N 68.20 E
Pjaozero, Ozero- 5 Jb 66.05N 30.55 E
Pjarnu/Pärnu 6 Id 58.24N 24.32 E
Pjarnu/Pärnu Jõgi 7 Fg 58.23N 24.34 E
Pjarnu, Zaliv-/Pärnu Laht 7 Fg 58.15N 24.25 E
Pjarnu-Jagupi/Pärnu-Jaagupi 8 Kf 58.36N 24.25 E
Pjasina 21 Kb 73.47N 87.01 E
Pjasino, Ozero- 20 Dc 69.45N 87.30 E
Pjasinski Zaliv 20 Db 74.00N 85.00 E
Pjatigorsk 6 Kg 44.03N 43.04 E
Pjatihatki 16 He 48.27N 33.40 E
Pjórsá 5 Dc 63.45N 20.50W
Pjussi/Püssi 8 Le 59.17N 26.57 E
Pkulagalid 64a Bb 7.36N 134.33 E
Pkulagasemieg 64a Ac 7.08N 134.23 E
Pkurengel 64a Ac 7.27N 134.28 E
Plá 55 Bl 35.07S 60.13W
Placentia 42 Mg 47.14N 53.58W
Placentia Bay 38 Ne 47.15N 54.30W
Placer 26 Hd 11.52N 123.55 E
Placerville 46 Eg 38.43N 120.48W
Placetas 47 Id 22.19N 79.40W
Plácido Rosas 55 Fk 32.45S 53.44W
Plačkovci 15 Ig 42.49N 25.28 E
Plačkovica 15 Fh 41.46N 22.32 E
Plainfield 44 Je 40.37N 74.25W
Plains [Mt.-U.S.] 46 Hc 47.27N 114.53W
Plains [Tx.-U.S.] 45 Ej 33.11N 102.50W
Plainview [Nb.-U.S.] 45 He 42.21N 97.47W
Plainview [Tx.-U.S.] 43 Ge 34.11N 101.43W
Plainville 45 Gg 39.14N 99.18W
Pláka, Ákra- 15 Ii 40.02N 25.25 E
Plake 15 Eh 41.14N 21.02 E
Plampang 26 Gh 8.48S 117.48 E
Planá 10 Ig 49.52N 12.44 E
Plana Cays 49 Kb 22.37N 73.33W
Plana o Nueva Tabarca, Isla- 13 Lf 38.10N 0.28W
Planco, Peñón- 48 Ge 24.35N 104.15W
Plane, Ile- 13 Li 35.46N 0.54W
Planeta Rica 54 Cb 8.25N 75.35W
Planet Depth (EN) 3 Hi 10.20S 110.30 E
Planézes 11 Ij 45.00N 2.50 E
Plankinton 45 Ge 43.43N 98.29W
Plantation 44 Gl 26.05N 80.14W
Plantaurel 11 Hk 43.04N 1.30 E
Plant City 44 Fk 28.01N 82.08W
Plasencia 13 Fd 40.02N 6.05W
Plast 19 Ge 54.22N 60.55 E
Plaster Rock 44 Nb 46.54N 67.24W
Plastun 20 Ih 44.48N 136.17 E
Plasy 10 Jg 49.56N 13.24 E
Plata, Rio de la- [P.R.] 51a Bb 18.30N 66.14W
Plata, Rio de la- [S.Amer.] 52 Ki 35.00S 57.00W
Plataiai 15 Gk 38.13N 23.16 E
Platani 14 Hm 37.24N 13.16 E
Plateau [2] 34 Gd 8.50N 9.00 E
Plateau [3] 36 Cc 2.10S 15.00 E
Plateau, Khorat- 21 Mh 15.30N 102.50 E
Plateaux [3] 34 Fd 7.30N 1.10 E
Platen, Kapp- 41 Ob 80.31N 22.48 E
Plati 15 Fi 40.39N 22.32 E
Plato 54 Db 9.47N 74.47W
Platte 45 Ge 43.23N 98.51W
Platte 38 Je 43.23N 98.51W
Platte Island 30 Mi 5.52S 55.23 E
Platte River 45 Ig 39.16N 94.50W
Platteville 45 Ke 42.44N 90.29W
Plattsburgh 43 Mc 44.42N 73.29W
Plattsmouth 45 If 41.01N 95.53W
Plau 10 Ic 53.27N 12.16 E
Plauen 10 If 50.30N 12.08 E
Plauer See 10 Ic 53.30N 12.20 E
Plav 15 Cg 42.36N 19.57 E
Plavecký Mikuláš 10 Nh 48.30N 17.18 E
Pļaviņas/Pljavinjas 7 Fh 56.38N 25.46 E
Plavsk 16 Jc 53.43N 37.18 E
Playa Azul 47 De 17.59N 102.24W
Playa Noriega, Laguna- 48 Dc 29.10N 111.50W
Playa Vicente 48 Li 17.50N 95.49W
Playón Chico 49 Hi 9.18N 78.14W
Pleasanton [Ks.-U.S.] 45 Ig 38.11N 94.43W
Pleasanton [Tx.-U.S.] 45 Gl 28.58N 98.29W
Pleasant Point 62 Df 44.16S 171.08 E
Pleasant Valley 45 Fi 35.15N 101.48W
Plechý 10 Jh 48.49N 13.53 E
Pleiku 25 Lf 13.59N 108.00 E
Pleiße 10 Ie 51.20N 12.22 E
Plekinge 8 Fh 56.20N 15.05 E
Plenița 15 Ge 44.13N 23.11 E
Plenty, Bay of- 57 Ih 37.45S 177.10 E
Plentywood 43 Gb 48.47N 104.34W
Pleščenicy 16 Eb 54.29N 27.55 E
Pleseck 19 Ec 62.44N 40.18 E
Plešivec 10 Qh 48.33N 20.25 E
Pleșu, Vîrful- 15 Fc 46.32N 22.11 E
Pleszew 10 Ne 51.54N 17.48 E
Plétipi, Lac- 42 Kf 51.42N 70.08W
Plettenberg 12 Jc 51.13N 7.53 E
Plettenbergbaai 37 Cf 34.03S 23.22 E
Pleven [2] 15 Hf 43.25N 24.37 E
Pleven 6 Ig 43.25N 24.37 E
Plibo 34 De 4.35N 7.40W
Pliska 15 Kf 43.22N 27.07 E
Pliszka 10 Kd 52.15N 14.40 E
Plitvice 14 Jf 44.54N 15.36 E
Pljavinjas/Pļaviņas 7 Fh 56.38N 25.46 E
Plješevica 14 Jf 44.45N 15.45 E
Pljevlja 15 Cf 43.21N 19.21 E
Pljusa 7 Gg 58.25N 29.20 E
Pljusa 7 Gg 59.13N 28.11 E
Ploča, Rt- 14 Jg 43.30N 15.58 E
Ploče 14 Lg 43.04N 17.26 E
Płock [2] 10 Pd 52.35N 19.45 E
Płock 10 Pd 52.33N 19.43 E
Ploërmel 11 Dg 47.56N 2.24W
Ploiești 6 Ig 44.57N 26.01 E
Plomárion 15 Jk 38.59N 26.22 E
Plomb du Cantal 11 Ii 45.03N 2.46 E
Plön 10 Gb 54.10N 10.26 E
Płonia 10 Kc 53.25N 14.36 E
Płonka 10 Qd 52.37N 20.30 E
Płońsk 10 Qd 52.38N 20.23 E
Plopana 15 Kc 46.41N 27.13 E
Płoty 10 Lc 53.50N 15.16 E
Plouguerneau 11 Bf 48.36N 4.30W
Plovdiv [2] 15 Hg 42.09N 24.45 E
Plovdiv 6 Ig 42.09N 24.45 E
Plummer 46 Gc 47.20N 116.53W
Plumridge Lakes 59 Fe 29.30S 125.25 E
Plumtree 37 Dd 20.31S 27.48 E
Plungė/Plunge 7 Ei 55.56N 21.48 E
Plunge/Plungė 7 Ei 55.56N 21.48 E
Plymouth [Eng.-U.K.] 6 Fe 50.23N 4.10W
Plymouth [In.-U.S.] 44 De 41.21N 86.19W
Plymouth [Ma.-U.S.] 44 Le 41.58N 70.41W
Plymouth [Mont.] 47 Le 16.42N 62.13W
Plymouth Sound 9 Ik 50.25N 4.05W
Plzeň=Pilsen (EN) 6 Hf 49.45N 13.24 E
Plzeňská pahorkatina 10 Jg 49.50N 13.15 E
Pniewy 10 Md 52.31N 16.15 E
Pô 34 Ec 11.10N 1.09W
Po 5 Hg 44.57N 12.05 E
Po, Colline del- 14 Be 45.05N 7.50 E
Po, Foci del-=Po, Mouths of the- (EN) 14 Gf 44.52N 12.30 E
Po, Mouths of the- (EN)=Po, Foci del- 14 Gf 44.52N 12.30 E
Poarta de Fier a Transilvaniei, Pasul- 15 Fd 45.25N 22.40 E
Poarta Orientală, Pasul- 15 Fd 45.08N 22.20 E
Poás, Volcán- 49 Eh 10.11N 84.13W
Pobé 34 Fd 6.58N 2.41 E
Pobeda, Gora- 21 Qc 65.12N 146.12 E
Pobeda Ice Island 66 Ge 64.30S 97.00 E
Pobedy, Pik- 21 Ke 42.02N 80.05 E
Pobla de Segur/La Pobla de Segur 13 Mb 42.15N 0.58 E
Poblet, Monasterio de-/Poblet, Monèstir de- 13 Nc 41.20N 1.05 E
Poblet, Monèstir de-/Poblet, Monasterio de- 13 Nc 41.20N 1.05 E
Pobrežije 15 Jf 43.56N 26.21 E
Pocahontas 45 Kh 36.16N 90.58W
Pocatello 39 He 42.52N 112.27W
Počep 16 Hc 52.57N 33.28 E
Pocerina 15 Ce 44.38N 19.35 E
Počinok 19 De 54.23N 32.29 E
Počitelj 14 Lg 43.08N 17.44 E
Pocito, Sierra del- 13 He 39.20N 4.05W
Pocito Casas 48 Dc 28.32N 111.06W
Pocklington Reef 60 Fj 11.00S 155.00 E
Poções 54 Jf 14.31S 40.21W
Poço Fundo, Cachoeira- 55 Jc 16.10S 45.51W
Poconé 54 Gg 16.15S 56.37W
Pocono Mountains 44 Je 41.10N 75.20W
Poços de Caldas 54 Ih 21.48S 46.34W
Pocri 49 Gj 7.40N 80.07W
Podborovje [R.S.F.S.R.] 8 Mg 57.51N 28.46 E
Podborovje [R.S.F.S.R.] 7 Ig 59.32N 35.01 E
Podbrezová 10 Ph 48.49N 19.31 E
Podčerje 17 He 63.55N 57.30 E
Poděbrady 10 Lf 50.09N 15.07 E
Podgajcy 10 Vg 49.12N 25.12 E
Podgorina 15 Ce 44.15N 19.56 E
Po di Volano 14 Gf 44.49N 12.15 E
Podjuga 7 Jf 61.07N 40.54 E
Podkamennaja Tunguska=Stony Tunguska (EN) 21 Lc 61.36N 90.18 E
Podlasie 10 Sd 52.30N 23.00 E
Podlaska, Nizina- 10 Sc 53.00N 22.45 E
Podlužje 15 Ce 44.45N 19.55 E
Podolia (EN)=Podolskaja Vozvyšennost 5 If 49.00N 28.00 E
Podolsk 19 Dd 55.27N 37.33 E
Podolskaja Vozvyšennost=Podolia (EN) 5 If 49.00N 28.00 E
Podor 34 Cb 16.40N 14.57W
Podporožje 19 Dc 60.54N 34.09 E
Podravina 14 Le 45.40N 17.40 E
Podravska Slatina 14 Le 45.42N 17.42 E
Podrima 15 Dg 42.24N 20.33 E
Podromanija 14 Mg 43.54N 18.46 E
Podsvilje 8 Mi 55.09N 28.01 E
Podujevo 15 Eg 42.55N 21.12 E
Podunajská nížina 10 Nh 48.00N 17.40 E
Podvološino 20 Fe 58.15N 108.25 E
Poel 10 Hb 54.00N 11.26 E
Poenița, Vîrful- 15 Gc 46.15N 23.20 E
Pofadder 37 Be 29.10S 19.22 E
Pogăniș 15 Ed 45.41N 21.21 E
Pogar 16 Hc 52.33N 33.16 E
Poggibonsi 14 Fg 43.28N 11.09 E
Pöggstall 14 Jb 48.19N 15.11 E
Pogibi 20 Jf 52.15N 141.45 E
Pogny 12 Gf 48.52N 4.29 E
Pogoanele 15 Je 44.55N 27.00 E
Pogórze Karpackie 10 Qg 49.52N 21.00 E
Pogradeci 15 Di 40.54N 20.39 E
Pograničny 20 Ih 44.26N 131.20 E
Pogrebišče 16 Fe 49.29N 29.14 E
Poguba Xoréu, Rio- 55 Ec 16.29S 54.58W
P'ohang 27 Md 36.02N 129.22 E
Pohja/Pojo 8 Jd 60.06N 23.31 E
Pohjankangas 8 Jc 62.00N 22.30 E
Pohjanlahti=Bothnia, Gulf of- (EN) 5 Hc 63.00N 20.00 E
Pohjanmaa 8 Jb 63.00N 22.30 E
Pohjois-Karjala [2] 7 Ge 63.00N 30.00 E
Pohlheim 12 Kd 50.32N 8.42 E
Pohorje 14 Jd 46.32N 15.28 E
Po Hu 28 Di 30.15N 116.32 E
Pohue Bay 65a Fd 19.01N 155.48W
Pohvistnevo 19 Fe 53.40N 52.08 E
Poiana Mare 15 Gf 43.55N 23.04 E
Poiana Ruscă, Munții 15 Fd 45.41N 22.30 E
Pöide/Pejde 8 Jf 58.30N 22.50 E
Poie 36 Dc 2.55S 23.10 E
Poindimié 61 Cd 20.56S 165.20 E
Poindo → Lhünzhub 27 Fe 30.17N 91.20 E
Poinsett, Cape- 66 He 65.42S 113.18 E
Poinsett, Lake- 45 Hd 44.34N 97.05W
Point Arena 46 Dg 38.55N 123.41W
Point au Fer Island 45 Kl 29.15N 91.15W
Pointe-à-Pitre 47 Le 16.14N 61.32W
Pointe Duble 51e Bb 16.20N 61.00W
Pointe-Noire 51e Ab 16.14N 61.47W
Pointe Noire 31 Ii 4.48S 11.51 E
Point Hope 40 Fc 68.21N 166.41W
Point Lake 42 Gc 65.15N 113.00W
Point Lay 40 Gc 69.45N 163.03W
Point Pleasant [N.J.-U.S.] 44 Je 40.06N 74.02W
Point Pleasant [W.V.-U.S.] 44 Ff 38.53N 82.07W
Poisson-Blanc, Lac- 44 Jc 46.00N 75.44W
Poissonnier Point 59 Dc 20.00S 119.10 E
Poissy 11 If 48.56N 2.03 E
Poitevin, Marais- 11 Eh 46.22N 1.06W
Poitiers 6 Gf 46.35N 0.20 E
Poitou 11 Fh 46.40N 0.30W
Poitou, Plaines et Seuil du- 11 Gh 46.26N 0.17 E
Poivre Islands 37b Bb 5.46S 53.19 E
Poix-de-Picardie 11 He 49.47N 1.59 E
Poix-Terron 12 Ge 49.39N 4.39 E
Pojarkovo 20 Hg 49.42N 128.50 E
Pojkovski 19 Hc 60.59N 72.00 E
Pojo/Pohja 8 Jd 60.06N 23.31 E
Pojuba, Rio- 55 Ec 16.30S 54.59W
Pokaran 25 Ec 26.55N 71.55 E
Pokhara 25 Gc 28.14N 83.59 E
Poko 36 Eb 3.09N 26.53 E
Pokoinu 64p Bb 21.12S 159.49W
Pokój 10 Nf 50.56N 17.50 E
Pokrovka 18 Lc 42.19N 78.01 E
Pokrovsk 20 Hd 61.29N 129.10 E
Pokrovskoje [R.S.F.S.R.] 16 Jc 52.38N 36.51 E
Pokrovskoje [Ukr.-U.S.S.R.] 16 Jf 47.59N 36.13 E
Pokšenga 7 Kd 64.01N 44.15 E
Pokutje 15 Ia 48.20N 25.05 E
Pola 7 Hg 58.05N 31.40 E
Polabí 10 Lf 50.10N 15.10 E
Polacca 46 Ji 35.50N 110.23W
Pola de Laviana 13 Ga 43.15N 5.34W
Pola de Lena 13 Ga 43.10N 5.49W
Pola de Siero 13 Ga 43.23N 5.40W
Polanco 55 Ek 33.54S 55.09W
Poland 64g Ab 1.52N 157.33W
Poland (EN)=Polska [1] 6 He 52.00N 19.00 E
Polanów 10 Mb 54.08N 16.39 E
Polar Plateau 66 Cg 90.00S 0.00
Polar Urals (EN)=Poljarny Ural 5 Mb 66.55N 64.30 E
Polatlı 23 Db 39.36N 32.09 E
Polch 12 Jd 50.18N 7.19 E
Połczyn Zdrój 10 Mc 53.46N 16.06 E
Pol-e Khomrī 23 Kb 35.56N 68.43 E
Pole of Inaccessibility (EN) 66 Eg 82.06S 54.58 E
Pol-e-Safid 24 Od 36.06N 53.01 E
Polesella 14 Ff 44.58N 11.45 E
Polesie Lubelskie 10 Te 51.30N 23.20 E
Polesine 14 Fe 45.00N 11.45 E
Polesje=Polesye (EN) 5 Ie 52.00N 27.00 E
Polessk 8 Ij 54.51N 21.02 E
Polesskoje 16 Fd 51.16N 29.27 E
Polesye (EN)=Polesje 5 Ie 52.00N 27.00 E
Polevskoj 19 Gd 56.28N 60.11 E
Polewali 26 Gg 3.25S 119.20 E
Poležan 15 Gh 41.43N 23.30 E
Polgár 10 Ri 47.52N 21.07 E
Pŏlgyo 28 Ig 34.51N 127.21 E
Poli 34 Hd 8.29N 13.15 E
Poliaigos 15 Hm 36.46N 24.38 E
Poliçani 15 Di 40.08N 20.21 E
Policastro, Golfo di- 14 Jk 40.00N 15.35 E
Police 10 Kc 53.33N 14.35 E
Policoro 14 Kj 40.13N 16.41 E
Poligny 11 Lh 46.50N 5.43 E
Poligus 20 Ed 61.58N 94.40 E
Polikastron 15 Fh 41.00N 22.34 E
Polikhnitos 15 Jj 39.05N 26.11 E
Polillo Islands 21 Oh 14.50N 122.05 E
Pólis 24 Ee 35.02N 32.25 E
Polist 7 Hg 58.07N 31.32 E
Polistena 14 Kl 38.24N 16.04 E
Políyiros 15 Gi 40.23N 23.27 E
Poljarny [R.S.F.S.R.] 19 Db 69.13N 33.28 E
Poljarny [R.S.F.S.R.] 20 Mc 69.01N 178.45 E
Poljarny Ural=Polar Urals (EN) 5 Mb 66.55N 64.30 E
Polkowice 10 Me 51.32N 16.06 E
Pöllau 14 Jc 47.18N 15.50 E
Polle 64d Bb 7.20N 151.15 E
Pollença/Pollensa 13 Pe 39.53N 3.01 E
Pollensa/Pollença 13 Pe 39.53N 3.01 E
Pollino 5 Hh 39.55N 16.10 E
Polochic, Rio- 49 Cf 15.28N 89.22W
Polock 19 Cd 55.29N 28.52 E
Polog 15 Dh 42.00N 21.00 E
Pologi 19 Df 47.28N 36.15 E
Polonina 10 Jh 48.30N 23.30 E
Polonnaruwa 25 Gg 7.56N 81.00 E
Polonnoje 16 Ed 50.06N 27.29 E
Polousny Krjaž 20 Jc 69.30N 144.00 E
Polska=Poland (EN) [1] 6 He 52.00N 19.00 E
Polski Gradec 15 Jg 42.11N 26.06 E
Polski Trămbeš 15 If 43.22N 25.38 E
Polson 46 Hc 47.41N 114.09W
Poltár 10 Ph 48.27N 19.48 E
Poltava 6 Jf 49.35N 34.34 E
Poltavka 19 He 54.22N 71.45 E
Poltavskaja Oblast [3] 19 Df 49.45N 33.50 E
Põltsamaa/Pyltsamaa 8 Lf 58.23N 26.08 E
Põltsamaa/Pyltsamaa 7 Fg 58.39N 25.59 E
Poluj 20 Bc 66.30N 66.31 E
Polunočnoje 19 Gc 60.52N 60.25 E
Polūr 24 Oe 35.52N 52.03 E
Põlva/Pylva 7 Gg 58.04N 27.06 E
Polvijärvi 7 Ge 62.51N 29.22 E
Polynesia 57 Le 4.00S 156.00W
Polynésie Française=French Polynesia (EN) [5] 58 Mf 16.00S 145.00W
Pom, Laguna de- 48 Mh 18.35N 92.15W
Pomarance 14 Eg 43.18N 10.52 E
Pomarkku/Påmark 8 Ic 61.42N 22.00 E
Pombal [Braz.] 54 Ke 6.46S 37.47W
Pombal [Port.] 13 De 39.55N 8.38W
Pombo, Rio- 55 Fe 20.53S 52.23W
Pomerania (EN)=Pommern 5 He 54.00N 16.00 E
Pomerania (EN)=Pommern 10 Lc 54.00N 16.00 E
Pomeranian Bay (EN)=Pommersche Bucht 10 Kb 54.20N 14.20 E
Pomeranian Bay (EN)=Pomorska, Zatoka- 10 Kb 54.20N 14.20 E
Pomeroy 44 Ff 39.03N 82.03W
Pomio 58 Ge 5.32S 151.30 E
Pomme de Terre Reservoir 45 Jh 37.51N 93.19W
Pommern=Pomerania (EN) 10 Lc 54.00N 16.00 E
Pommern=Pomerania (EN) 5 He 54.00N 16.00 E
Pommersche Bucht=Pomeranian Bay (EN) 10 Kb 54.20N 14.20 E
Pommersfelden 10 Gg 49.46N 10.49 E
Pomona 46 Gi 34.04N 117.45W
Pomona Lake 45 Ig 38.40N 95.35W
Pomorije 15 Kg 42.33N 27.39 E
Pomorska, Zatoka-=Pomeranian Bay (EN) 10 Kb 54.20N 14.20 E
Pomorski Bereg 7 Id 64.00N 36.15 E
Pomorskie, Pojezierze- 10 Mc 53.30N 16.30 E
Pomorski Proliv 19 Eb 68.40N 50.00 E
Pomošnaja 16 Ge 48.14N 31.29 E
Pompano Beach 44 Gl 26.15N 80.07W
Pompei 14 Ij 40.45N 14.30 E
Pompeu 55 Jd 19.12S 44.59W
Ponape 58 Gd 6.52N 158.15 E
Ponape Island 57 Gd 6.55N 158.15 E
Ponca City 43 Hd 36.42N 97.05W
Ponce 39 Mh 18.01N 66.37W
Poncheville, Lac- 44 Ia 50.12N 76.55W
Pondcreek 45 Hh 36.40N 97.48W
Pondicherry 25 Ff 11.56N 79.53 E
Pondicherry [3] 25 Ff 11.55N 79.45 E
Pond Inlet 39 Lb 72.48N 78.00W
Pond Inlet 42 Jb 72.41N 77.00W
Ponea 64n Ac 10.28S 161.01W
Ponente, Riviera di- 14 Cf 44.10N 8.20 E
Ponérihouen 63b Be 21.05S 165.24 E
Pones 64d Bb 7.12N 151.59 E
Ponferrada 13 Fb 42.33N 6.35W
Pongaroa 62 Gd 40.33S 176.11 E
Pongo 30 Jh 8.42N 27.40 E
Pongola 37 Ee 26.52S 32.20 E
Pong Qu 27 Ef 26.49N 87.09 E
Poniatowa 10 Se 51.11N 22.05 E
Ponoj 6 Kb 67.05N 41.07 E
Ponoj 5 Kb 66.59N 41.10 E
Ponomarevka 16 Sc 53.09N 54.12 E
Ponorogo 26 Fh 7.52S 111.27 E
Pons 11 Fi 45.35N 0.33W
Pons/Ponts 13 Nc 41.55N 1.12 E
Ponsul 13 Ee 39.40N 7.31W
Pont-à-Celles 12 Gd 50.30N 4.21 E
Ponta Delgada 31 Ee 37.44N 25.40W
Ponta Delgada [3] 32 Bb 37.48N 25.30W
Ponta Grossa 53 Kh 25.05S 50.09W
Pont-à-Mousson 11 Mf 48.54N 6.04 E
Ponta Porã 53 Kh 22.32S 55.43W
Pontarlier 11 Mh 46.54N 6.22 E
Pontassieve 14 Fg 43.46N 11.26 E
Pont-Audemer 11 Ge 49.21N 0.31 E
Pontaut 55 Bm 37.44S 61.20W
Pontávert 12 Fe 49.25N 3.49 E
Pontchartrain, Lake- 43 Ie 30.10N 90.10W
Pontchâteau 11 Dg 47.26N 2.05W
Pont-de-l'Arche 12 De 49.18N 1.10 E
Pont de Suert 13 Mb 42.24N 0.45 E
Pont-de-Vaux 11 Kh 46.26N 4.56 E
Ponte Alta 55 Gh 27.29S 50.23W
Ponte Alta, Serra da- 55 Id 19.42S 47.40W
Ponte Branca 55 Fc 16.27S 52.40W
Pontecorvo 14 Hi 42.27N 13.40 E
Ponte de Lima 13 Dc 41.46N 8.35W
Ponte de Pedra 55 Ec 17.06S 54.23W
Ponte de Pedrã 55 Da 13.35S 57.21W
Pontedera 14 Eg 43.40N 10.38 E
Ponte de Sor 13 De 39.15N 8.01W
Ponte Firme, Chapada da- 55 Id 18.05S 46.25W
Ponteix 46 Lb 49.49N 107.30W
Ponte Nova 54 Jh 20.24S 42.54W
Pontes e Lacerda 55 Cb 15.11S 59.21W
Pontevedra [3] 13 Db 42.30N 8.30W
Pontevedra 13 Db 42.26N 8.38W
Pontevedra, Ria de- 13 Db 42.22N 8.45W
Ponte Vermelha 55 Ed 19.29S 54.25W
Pont-Farcy 12 Af 48.56N 1.02W
Pontfaverger-Moronvilliers 12 Ge 49.18N 4.19 E
Ponthieu 11 Hd 50.10N 1.55 E
Pontiac [Il.-U.S.] 45 Lf 40.53N 88.38W
Pontiac [Mi.-U.S.] 44 Fd 42.37N 83.18W
Pontianak 22 Mj 0.02S 109.20 E
Pontian Kechil 26 Df 1.29N 103.23 E
Pontine Islands (EN)=Ponziane, Isole- 14 Gj 40.55N 13.00 E
Pontivy 11 Df 48.04N 2.59W
Pontivy, Pays de- 11 Dg 48.00N 3.00W
Pont-l'Abbé 11 Bg 47.52N 4.13W
Pont-l'Evêque 12 Ce 49.18N 0.11 E
Pontoise 11 Ie 49.03N 2.06 E
Pontorson 11 Ef 48.33N 1.31W
Pontremoli 14 Df 44.22N 9.53 E
Pontresina 14 Dd 46.28N 9.53 E
Ponts/Pons 13 Nc 41.55N 1.12 E
Pont-Sainte-Maxence 12 Ee 49.18N 2.36 E
Pont-Saint-Esprit 11 Kj 44.15N 4.39 E
Pontypool 9 Jj 51.43N 3.02W
Ponza 14 Gj 40.54N 12.58 E
Ponza 14 Gj 40.55N 12.55 E
Ponziane, Isole-=Pontine Islands (EN) 14 Gj 40.55N 13.00 E
Pool [3] 36 Bc 3.30S 15.00 E
Poole 9 Lk 50.43N 1.59W
Poona → Pune 22 Jh 18.32N 73.52 E
Poopó 54 Eg 18.23S 66.59W
Poopó, Lago de-=Poopó, Lake- (EN) 52 Jg 18.45S 67.07W
Poopó, Lake- (EN)=Poopó, Lago de- 52 Jg 18.45S 67.07W
Poor Knights Islands 62 Fa 35.30S 174.45 E
Pōōsaspea Neem/Pyzaspea Neem 8 Je 59.15N 23.25 E
Popakai 54 Gc 3.22N 55.25W
Popayán 53 Ie 2.27N 76.36W
Poperinge 11 Id 50.51N 2.43 E
Poperinge-Watou 12 Ed 50.51N 2.37 E
Popigaj 20 Gb 71.55N 110.47 E
Popigaj 20 Fb 72.55N 106.00 E
Poplar 46 Mb 48.07N 105.12W
Poplar 42 Hf 53.00N 97.18W
Poplar Bluff 43 Id 36.45N 90.24W
Poplar River 46 Mb 48.05N 105.11W
Popocatépetl, Volcán- 38 Jh 19.02N 98.38W
Popokabaka 36 Cd 5.42S 16.35 E
Popoli 14 Hh 42.10N 13.50 E
Popomanaseu, Mount- 63a Ec 9.42S 160.03 E
Popondetta 60 Di 8.46S 148.14 E
Popovo 15 Jf 43.21N 26.14 E
Poppberg 10 Hg 49.20N 11.45 E
Poppel, Ravels- 12 Hc 51.27N 5.02 E
Poprad 10 Qg 49.38N 20.42 E
Poprad 6 If 49.03N 20.19 E
Poptún 49 Ce 16.21N 89.26W
Por 10 Tf 50.48N 23.01 E
Porangahau 62 Gd 40.18S 176.38 E

Index Symbols

[1] Independent Nation
[2] State, Region
[3] District, County
[4] Municipality
[5] Colony, Dependency
Continent
Physical Region
Historical or Cultural Region
Mount, Mountain
Volcano
Hill
Mountains, Mountain Range
Hills, Escarpment
Plateau, Upland
Pass, Gap
Plain, Lowland
Delta
Salt Flat
Valley, Canyon
Crater, Cave
Karst Features
Depression
Polder
Desert, Dunes
Forest, Woods
Heath, Steppe
Oasis
Cape, Point
Coast, Beach
Cliff
Peninsula
Isthmus
Sandbank
Island
Atoll
Rock, Reef
Islands, Archipelago
Rocks, Reefs
Coral Reef
Well, Spring
Geyser
River, Stream
Waterfall Rapids
River Mouth, Estuary
Lake
Salt Lake
Intermittent Lake
Reservoir
Swamp, Pond
Canal
Glacier
Ice Shelf, Pack Ice
Ocean
Sea
Gulf, Bay
Strait, Fjord
Lagoon
Bank
Seamount
Tablemount
Ridge
Shelf
Basin
Escarpment, Sea Scarp
Fracture
Trench, Abyss
National Park, Reserve
Point of Interest
Recreation Site
Cave, Cavern
Historic Site
Ruins
Wall, Walls
Church, Abbey
Temple
Scientific Station
Airport
Port
Lighthouse
Mine
Tunnel
Dam, Bridge

Porangatu 55 Ha 13.26S 49.10W
Porbandar 25 Dd 21.38N 69.36 E
Porcien 12 Ge 49.40N 4.20 E
Porcos, Rio dos- 55 Ja 12.42S 45.07W
Porcuna 13 Hg 37.52N 4.11W
Porcupine 38 Ec 66.35N 145.15W
Porcupine 44 Ga 48.32N 81.10W
Porcupine Bank (EN) 5 Ee 53.20N 13.30W
Porcupine Hills 46 Ha 50.05N 114.10W
Porcupine Plain 42 Dc 67.30N 137.30W
Pordenone 14 Ge 45.57N 12.39 E
Poreč 14 He 45.13N 13.37 E
Poreč 15 Fe 44.20N 22.05 E
Porecatu 55 Gf 22.43S 51.24W
Porećje 8 Kk 53.53N 24.08 E
Poreckoje 7 Li 55.13N 46.19 E
Porhov 19 Cd 57.45N 29.32 E
Pori/Björneborg 6 Ic 61.29N 21.47 E
Porion 15 Gn 35.58N 23.16 E
Porirua 61 Dh 41.08S 174.50 E
Pórisvatn 7a Bb 64.20N 18.55W
Porjus 7 Ec 66.57N 19.49 E
Porkkala 8 Ke 59.55N 24.25 E
Porlamar 54 Fa 10.57N 63.51W
Porma 13 Gb 42.29N 5.28W
Pornic 11 Dg 47.07N 2.06W
Poronajsk 22 Qe 49.14N 143.04 E
Poronin 10 Qg 49.20N 20.04 E
Póros 15 Gl 37.30N 23.31 E
Póros 15 Gl 37.30N 23.27 E
Poroshiri-Dake 28 Qc 42.42N 142.35 E
Porosozero 7 He 62.44N 32.42 E
Porozovo 10 Ud 52.54N 24.27 E
Porpoise Bay 66 Ie 66.30S 128.30 E
Porquis Junction 44 Ga 48.43N 80.52W
Porrentruy 14 Bc 47.25N 7.10 E
Porreras 13 Oe 39.31N 3.00 E
Porretta, Passo della- 14 Ef 44.02N 10.56 E
Porretta Terme 14 Ef 44.09N 10.59 E
Porsangen 5 Ia 70.50N 26.00 E
Porsangerhalvøya 7 Fa 70.50N 25.00 E
Porsgrunn 7 Bg 59.09N 9.40 E
Pórshöfn 7a Ca 66.10N 15.20W
Porsuk 24 Dc 39.42N 31.59 E
Portachuelo 54 Fg 17.21S 63.24W
Portadown/Port an Dúnáin 9 Gg 54.26N 6.27W
Portage 45 Le 43.33N 89.28W
Portage la Prairie 42 Hg 49.57N 98.18W
Port Alberni 42 Fg 49.14N 124.48W
Portalegre 13 Ee 39.17N 7.26W
Portalegre [2] 13 Ee 39.15N 7.35W
Portales 43 Ge 34.11N 103.20W
Port-Alfred 42 Kg 48.20N 70.53W
Port Alfred 37 Df 33.36S 26.55 E
Port Alice 42 Ef 50.23N 127.27W
Port Allegany 44 He 41.48N 78.18W
Port an Dúnáin/Portadown 9 Gg 54.26N 6.27W
Port Angeles 43 Cb 48.07N 123.27W
Port Antonio 47 Ie 18.11N 76.28W
Port Arthur [Austl.] 59 Jh 43.09S 147.51 E
Port Arthur [Tx.-U.S.] 39 Jg 29.55N 93.55W
Port Arthur (EN)=Lüshun 27 Ld 38.50N 121.13 E
Port Augusta 58 Eh 32.30S 137.46 E
Port-Au-Prince 39 Lh 18.32N 72.20W
Port-au-Prince, Baie de- 49 Kd 18.40N 72.30W
Port Austin 44 Fc 44.03N 83.01W
Port aux Français 31 Om 49.25S 70.10 E
Porta Westfalica 12 Kb 52.15N 8.56 E
Port-Bergé-Vao Vao 37 Hc 15.33S 47.38 E
Port Blair 22 Lh 11.36N 92.45 E
Port-Bou/Portbou 13 Pb 42.25N 3.10 E
Portbou/Port-Bou 13 Pb 42.25N 3.10 E
Port Burwell [Newf.-Can.] 39 Mc 60.25N 64.49W
Port Burwell [Ont.-Can.] 44 Gd 42.39N 80.49W
Port-Cartier 42 Kf 50.01N 66.53W
Port Chalmers 62 Df 45.49S 170.37 E
Port Charlotte 43 Kf 26.59N 82.06W
Port Clinton 44 Fe 41.30N 82.58W
Port Coquitlam 46 Db 49.16N 122.46W
Port-de-Bouc 11 Kk 43.24N 4.59 E
Port-de-Paix 49 Kd 19.57N 72.50W
Port Dickson 26 Df 2.31N 101.48 E
Port Edward 37 Ef 31.03S 30.13 E
Portel [Braz.] 54 Hd 1.57S 50.49W
Portel [Port.] 13 Ef 38.18N 7.42W
Port Elgin 44 Gc 44.26N 81.24W
Port Elizabeth [S.Afr.] 31 Jl 33.58S 25.40 E
Port Elizabeth [St.Vin.] 51n Ba 13.00N 61.16W
Port Ellen 9 Gf 55.39N 6.12W
Port-en-Bessin-Huppain 11 Fe 49.21N 0.45W
Port Erin 9 Ig 54.05N 4.43W
Porter Point 51n Ba 13.23N 61.11W
Porterville [Ca.-U.S.] 43 Dd 36.04N 119.01W
Porterville [S.Afr.] 37 Bf 33.00S 19.00 E
Portete, Bahia de- 49 Lg 12.13N 71.55W
Port Fairy 59 Ig 38.23S 142.14 E
Port Fitzroy 62 Fb 36.10S 175.21 E
Port-Gentil 31 Hi 0.43S 8.47 E
Port Gibson 45 Kk 31.58N 90.58W
Port Harcourt 31 Hh 4.46N 7.01 E
Port Hardy 42 Ef 50.43N 127.29W
Port Hawkesbury 42 Lg 45.37N 61.21W
Porthcawl 9 Jj 51.29N 3.43W
Port Hedland 58 Cg 20.19S 118.34 E
Port Heiden 40 He 56.55N 158.41W
Port Hope Simpson 42 Lf 52.30N 56.17W
Port Huron 43 Kc 42.58N 82.27W
Portile de Fier = Iron Gate (EN) 5 Ig 44.41N 22.31 E
Port-Ilič 16 Pj 38.53N 48.51 E
Portimão 13 Dg 37.08N 8.32W
Port Isabel 45 Hm 26.04N 97.13W
Portița 15 Le 44.41N 29.00 E
Port Láirge/Waterford [2] 9 Fi 52.10N 7.40W
Port Láirge/Waterford 6 Fe 52.15N 7.06W
Portland [Austl.] 59 Ig 38.21S 141.36 E
Portland [Eng.-U.K.] 9 Kk 50.33N 2.27W
Portland [In.-U.S.] 44 Ee 40.26N 84.59W
Portland [Me.-U.S.] 39 Le 43.39N 70.17W
Portland [N.D.-U.S.] 45 Hc 47.30N 97.22W
Portland [N.Z.] 62 Fa 35.48S 174.20 E
Portland [Or.-U.S.] 39 Ge 45.33N 122.36W
Portland [Tx.-U.S.] 45 Hm 27.53N 97.20W
Portland, Bill of- 9 Kk 50.31N 2.28W
Portland, Promontoire - 42 Je 58.41N 78.33W
Portland Bight 49 Ie 17.57N 77.08W
Portland Island 62 Gc 39.20S 177.50 E
Portland Point 49 Ie 17.42N 77.11W
Port-la-Nouvelle 11 Jk 43.01N 3.03 E
Portlaoise/Port Laoise 9 Fh 53.02N 7.17W
Port Laoise/Portlaoise 9 Fh 53.02N 7.17W
Port Lavaca 43 Hf 28.37N 96.38W
Port Lincoln 58 Eh 34.44S 135.52 E
Port Loko 34 Cd 8.46N 12.47W
Port Louis 50 Fd 16.25N 61.32W
Port-Louis 31 Mk 20.10S 57.30 E
Port Macquarie 59 Kf 31.26S 152.44 E
Portmadoc 9 Ii 52.55N 4.08W
Port Maria 49 Id 18.22N 76.54W
Port-Menier 42 Lg 49.49N 64.20W
Port Moller 40 Ge 55.59N 160.34W
Port Moody 46 Db 49.17N 122.51W
Port Moresby 58 Fe 9.30S 147.07 E
Port Nelson 42 Ie 57.04N 92.30W
Portneuf, Rivière- 44 Ma 48.37N 69.05W
Port Nolloth 31 Ik 29.17S 16.51 E
Porto [2] 13 Dc 41.11N 8.20W
Porto [Fr.] 11a Aa 42.16N 8.42 E
Porto [Port.] 6 Fg 41.09N 8.37W
Porto, Golfe de- 11a Aa 42.16N 8.37 E
Pôrto Acre 54 Ee 9.34S 67.31W
Porto Alegre [Braz.] 53 Ki 30.04S 51.11W
Porto Alegre [SaoT.P.] 34 Ge 0.02N 6.32 E
Porto Amboim 31 Ij 10.44S 13.45 E
Porto Azzurro 14 Eh 42.46N 10.24 E
Portobelo 49 Hi 9.33N 79.39W
Pôrto Cedro 55 Ed 18.17S 55.02W
Porto Cervo 14 Di 41.08N 9.35 E
Porto Curupai 55 Ff 22.50S 53.53W
Porto de Moz 53 Kf 1.45S 52.14W
Porto Empedocle 14 Hm 37.17N 13.32 E
Porto Esperança [Braz.] 55 Dd 19.37S 57.27W
Porto Esperança [Braz.] 55 Db 14.02S 56.06W
Porto Esperança [Braz.] 55 Dc 17.47S 57.07W
Porto Esperidião 55 Cb 15.51S 58.28W
Porto Estrêla 55 Db 15.20S 57.14W
Portoferraio 14 Eh 42.49N 10.19 E
Port of Ness 9 Gc 58.30N 6.15W
Porto Franco 54 Ie 6.20S 47.24W
Port of Spain 53 Jd 10.39N 61.31W
Porto Fundação 55 Ea 13.39S 55.18W
Portogruaro 14 Ge 45.47N 12.50 E
Porto Lucena 55 Eh 27.51S 55.01W
Pörtom/Pirttikylä 8 Ib 62.42N 21.37 E
Portomaggiore 14 Ff 44.42N 11.48 E
Porto Mendes 55 Eg 24.30S 54.20W
Porto Moniz 32 Dc 32.51N 17.10W
Porto Moroco 55 Ea 13.24S 55.35W
Porto Morrinho 55 Dc 16.38S 57.49W
Porto Murtinho 53 Kh 21.42S 57.52W
Porto Novo [Ben.] 31 Hh 6.29N 2.37 E
Porto Novo [C.V.] 32 Bf 17.07N 25.04W
Port Orford 46 Ce 42.45N 124.30W
Porto San Giorgio 14 Hg 43.11N 13.48 E
Pôrto Santana 54 Hd 0.03S 51.11W
Porto Sant'Elpidio 14 Hg 43.15N 13.45 E
Porto Santo 30 Fe 33.04N 16.20W
Porto Santo Stefano 14 Fh 42.26N 11.07 E
Portoscuso 14 Ck 39.12N 8.23 E
Pôrto Seguro 54 Kg 16.26S 39.05W
Porto Tolle 14 Gf 44.56N 12.22 E
Porto Torres 14 Cj 40.50N 8.24 E
Porto União 55 Gh 26.15S 51.05W
Pôrto Válter 54 De 8.15S 72.45W
Porto Vecchio 11a Bb 41.35N 9.17 E
Porto Velho 53 Jf 8.46S 63.54W
Portoviejo 53 Hf 1.03S 80.27W
Porto Xavier 55 Eh 27.54S 55.08W
Port Phillip Bay 59 Ig 38.05S 144.50 E
Port Pirie 58 Eh 33.11S 138.01 E
Portree 9 Gd 57.24N 6.12W
Port Renfrew 46 Cb 48.33N 124.25W
Port Rois/Portrush 9 Gf 55.12N 6.40W
Port Royal 47 If 38.10N 77.12W
Portrush/Port Rois 9 Gf 55.12N 6.40W
Port Said (EN)=Būr Saʽīd 31 Ke 31.16N 32.18 E
Port Saint Joe 43 Jf 29.49N 85.18W
Port Saint Johns 37 Df 31.38S 29.33 E
Port-Saint-Louis-du-Rhône 11 Kk 43.23N 4.48 E
Port-Salut 49 Kd 18.05N 73.55W
Port Saunders 42 Lf 50.39N 57.18W
Port Shepstone 31 Kl 30.46S 30.22 E
Portsmouth [Dom.] 50 Fe 15.35N 61.28W
Portsmouth [Eng.-U.K.] 9 Lk 50.48N 1.05W
Portsmouth [N.H.-U.S.] 43 Mc 43.03N 70.47W
Portsmouth [Oh.-U.S.] 43 Kd 38.45N 82.59W
Portsmouth [Va.-U.S.] 43 Ld 36.50N 76.26W
Portsmouth City Airport 12 Ad 50.46N 1.04W
Port Sudan (EN)=Būr Sūdān 31 Kg 19.37N 37.14 E
Port Sulphur 45 Ll 29.29N 89.42W
Port Talbot 9 Jj 51.36N 3.47W
Porttipahdantekojärvi 7 Gb 68.06N 26.33 E
Port Townsend 46 Db 48.07N 122.46W
Portugal [1] 6 Fh 39.30N 8.00W
Portugalete 13 Ia 43.19N 3.01W
Portuguesa [2] 54 Eb 9.10N 69.15W
Portuguesa, Rio- 54 Eb 7.57N 67.32W
Portuguesa, Sierra de- 50 Bh 9.35N 69.45W
Portuguese Guinea (EN) → Guinea Bissau (EN) [1] 31 Fg 12.00N 15.00W
Portús, Coll del-/Perthus, Col de- 13 Ob 42.28N 2.51 E
Port-Vendres 11 Jl 42.31N 3.07 E
Port-Vila 58 Hf 17.44S 168.19 E
Port Wakefield 59 Hf 34.11S 138.09 E
Port Washington 45 Me 43.23N 87.53W
Porvenir [Bol.] 54 Ef 11.15S 68.41W
Porvenir [Bol.] 55 Ba 13.59S 61.39W
Porvenir [Chile] 56 Fh 53.18S 70.22W
Porvenir [Ur.] 55 Dk 32.23S 57.59W
Porvoo/Borgå 7 Ff 60.24N 25.40 E
Porvoonjoki 8 Kd 60.23N 25.40 E
Porz, Köln- 10 Df 50.53N 7.03 E
Posada, Fiume di- 14 Dj 40.39N 9.45 E
Posadas [Arg.] 53 Kh 27.25S 55.50W
Posadas [Sp.] 13 Gg 37.48N 5.06W
Posavina 15 De 44.33N 20.04 E
Poschiavo 14 Ed 46.20N 10.04 E
Pošehonje-Volodarsk 7 Jg 58.30N 39.08 E
Posht-e Bādām 24 Pf 33.02N 55.23 E
Posio 7 Gc 66.06N 28.09 E
Posjet 28 Kc 42.39N 130.48 E
Poskam/Zepu 27 Cd 38.12N 77.18 E
Poso 22 Oj 1.23S 120.44 E
Poso, Danau- 26 Hg 1.52S 120.35 E
Posof 24 Jb 41.31N 42.42 E
Posŏng 28 Ig 34.46N 127.05 E
Pospeliha 20 Df 52.02N 81.56 E
Posse 54 If 14.05S 46.22W
Possession, Ile de la- 30 Mm 46.14S 49.55 E
Possession Island 37 Be 27.01S 15.30 E
Pößneck 10 Hf 50.42N 11.36 E
Post 45 Fj 33.12N 101.23W
Posta de San Martín 55 Bk 33.09S 60.31W
Postavy 19 Cd 55.07N 26.50 E
Poste Maurice Cortier/Bidon V 32 He 22.18N 1.05 E
Poste Weygand 32 He 24.29N 0.40 E
Postmasburg 37 Ce 28.18S 23.05 E
Postojna 14 Ie 45.47N 14.14 E
Posto Simões Lopes 55 Eb 14.14S 54.41W
Postville [Ia.-U.S.] 45 Ke 43.05N 91.34W
Postville [Newf.-Can.] 42 Lf 54.55N 59.58W
Potchefstroom 37 De 26.46S 27.01 E
Poteau 45 Ii 35.03N 94.37W
Potenza 14 Hg 43.25N 13.40 E
Potenza 14 Jj 40.38N 15.48 E
Poteriteri, Lake- 62 Bg 46.05S 167.05 E
Potes 13 Ha 43.09N 4.37W
Potgietersrus 37 Dd 24.15S 28.55 E
Potholes Reservoir 46 Fc 47.01N 119.19W
Poti 6 Kg 42.08N 41.39 E
Poti, Rio- 54 Je 5.02S 42.50W
Potigny 12 Bf 48.58N 0.14W
Potiskum 31 Ig 11.43N 11.04 E
Potnarhvin 63b Dd 18.45S 169.12 E
Potomac 38 Lf 38.00N 76.18W
Potosí [2] 54 Eh 20.40S 67.00W
Potosí [Bol.] 53 Jg 19.35S 65.45W
Potosí [Mex.] 47 Dd 24.51N 100.19W
Potosi, Bahía- 48 Ii 17.35N 101.30W
Potosi, Cerro- 48 Ie 24.52N 100.13W
Pototan 26 Hd 10.55N 122.40 E
Potrerillos 56 Gc 26.26S 69.29W
Potrero, Rio- 55 Bc 17.32S 61.35W
Potsdam [2] 10 Id 52.30N 13.00 E
Potsdam [G.D.R.] 10 Jd 52.24N 13.04 E
Potsdam [N.Y.-U.S.] 44 Jc 44.40N 75.01W
Pott 63b Ad 19.35S 163.36 E
Potters Bar 12 Bc 51.41N 0.10W
Pottstown 44 Je 40.15N 75.38W
Pottsville 44 Ie 40.42N 76.13W
Pouancé 11 Eg 47.45N 1.10W
Pouébo 63b Be 20.24S 164.34 E
Pouembout 63b Be 21.08S 164.54 E
Poughkeepsie 44 Ke 41.43N 73.56W
Poulaphuca Reservoir/Loch Pholl an Phúca 9 Gh 53.10N 6.30W
Poum 63b Be 20.14S 164.01 E
Pourtalé 55 Bm 37.02S 60.36W
Pouso Alegre 54 Ih 22.13S 45.56W
Pouss 34 Ic 10.51N 15.03 E
Poutasi 65c Bb 14.01S 171.41W
Poŭthĭsăt 25 Kf 12.32N 103.55 E
Poutrincourt, Lac- 44 Ja 49.13N 74.04W
Po Valley (EN)=Padana, Pianura- 5 Gf 45.20N 10.00 E
Považská Bystrica 10 Og 49.07N 18.28 E
Považský Inovec 10 Nh 48.35N 18.00 E
Povenec 7 Ie 62.51N 34.45 E
Poverty Bay 62 Gc 38.45S 178.00 E
Povlen 15 Ce 44.09N 19.44 E
Póvoa de Varzim 13 Dc 41.23N 8.46W
Povorino 16 Md 51.12N 42.17 E
Povungnituk 42 Jd 60.03N 77.16W
Povungnituk 39 Lc 60.02N 77.10W
Powassan 44 Hb 46.05N 79.22W
Powder River [U.S.] 43 Fb 46.44N 105.26W
Powder River [Or.-U.S.] 46 Gd 44.45N 117.03W
Powell 46 Kd 44.45N 108.46W
Powell, Lake- [U.S.] 43 Ed 37.25N 110.45W
Powell Lake [Can.] 46 Ca 50.11N 124.24W
Powell River 42 Fg 49.52N 124.33W
Powers 44 Dc 45.39N 87.32W
Powers Lake 45 Eb 48.34N 102.39W
Powidzkie, Jezioro- 10 Nc 52.24N 17.57 E
Powys [3] 9 Ji 52.25N 3.20W
Poxoréu 54 Hg 15.50S 54.23W
Poxoréu, Rio- [Braz.] 55 Ec 16.32S 54.46W
Poxoréu, Rio- [Braz.] 55 Ec 16.08S 54.14W
Poya 63b Be 21.21S 165.09 E
Poyang Hu 21 Ng 29.00N 116.25 E
Poza de la Sal 13 Ib 42.40N 3.30W
Pozanti 24 Fd 37.25N 34.52 E
Požarevac 15 Ee 44.37N 21.12 E
Poza Rica de Hidalgo 39 Jg 20.33N 97.27W
Požarskoje 28 Ma 46.16N 134.04 E
Požega 15 Df 43.51N 20.02 E
Poznań [2] 10 Pd 52.25N 19.55 E
Poznań 6 He 52.25N 16.55 E
Pozoblanco 13 Hf 38.22N 4.51W
Pozo Borrado 55 Bi 28.56S 61.41W
Pozo Colorado 55 Cf 23.22S 58.55W
Pozo del Mortero 55 Bg 24.24S 61.02W
Pozo del Tigre 55 Bc 17.34S 61.59W
Pozo Dulce 55 Ai 29.04S 62.02W
Pozos, Punta- 56 Gg 47.57S 65.47W
Pozuelos 54 Fa 10.11N 64.39W
Pozzallo 14 In 36.43N 14.51 E
Pozzuoli 14 Ij 40.49N 14.07 E
Pra [Ghana] 34 Ed 6.27N 1.47W
Pra [R.S.F.S.R.] 7 Ji 54.45N 41.01 E
Prabuty 10 Pc 53.46N 19.10 E
Prachatice 10 Jg 49.01N 14.00 E
Prachin Buri 25 Kf 14.02N 101.22 E
Prachuap Khiri Khan 25 Jf 11.48N 99.47 E
Praděd 10 Nf 50.06N 17.14 E
Prades 11 Il 42.37N 2.26 E
Prado 54 Kg 17.21S 39.13W
Præstø 8 Ei 55.07N 12.03 E
Prague (EN)=Praha 6 He 50.05N 14.26 E
Praha=Prague (EN) 6 He 50.05N 14.26 E
Prahova [2] 15 Id 45.10N 26.00 E
Praia 31 Eg 14.55N 23.31W
Praia a Mare 14 Jk 39.54N 15.47 E
Praia da Rocha 13 Dg 37.07N 8.32W
Praia Rica 55 Eb 14.51S 55.33W
Praid 15 Ic 46.33N 25.08 E
Prainha 54 Hd 1.48S 53.29W
Prairie Dog Town Fork 45 Gi 34.26N 99.21W
Prairie du Chien 45 Ke 43.03N 91.09W
Prangli 8 Ke 59.38N 24.50 E
Prānhita 25 Fe 18.49N 79.55 E
Prapat 26 Cf 2.40N 98.56 E
Prasat 25 Kf 14.38N 103.24 E
Praslin 51k Bb 13.53N 60.54W
Praslin, Port- 51k Bb 13.53N 60.54W
Praslin Island 37b Ca 4.19S 55.44 E
Prasonisíon 15 Kn 35.52N 27.46 E
Prat, Isla- 56 Fg 48.15S 75.00W
Prata 54 Ig 19.18S 48.55W
Prata, Rio da- 55 Hd 18.49S 49.54W
Pratapgarh 25 Ed 24.02N 74.47 E
Prat de Llobregat/El Prat de Llobregat 13 Oc 41.20N 2.06 E
Prato 14 Fg 43.53N 11.06 E
Pratomagno 14 Fg 43.40N 11.40 E
Pratt 43 Hd 37.39N 98.44W
Prättigau 14 Dd 46.55N 9.40 E
Pratt Seamount (EN) 40 Ke 56.10N 142.30W
Prattville 44 Di 32.28N 86.29W
Pratudinho, Rio- 55 Ja 13.58S 45.10W
Pravda 18 Cf 36.50N 60.33 E
Pravda Coast 66 Ge 67.00S 94.00 E
Pravdinsk [R.S.F.S.R.] 8 Ij 54.28N 21.00 E
Pravdinsk [R.S.F.S.R.] 7 Kh 56.33N 43.33 E
Pravia 13 Fa 43.29N 6.07W
Praxedis G. Guerrero 48 Gb 31.22N 106.00W
Praya 26 Gh 8.42S 116.17 E
Prealpi Venete 14 Fd 46.25N 11.50 E
Predazzo 14 Fd 46.19N 11.36 E
Predeal 15 Id 45.30N 25.34 E
Predeal, Pasul- 15 Id 45.28N 25.36 E
Predel 14 Hd 46.25N 13.35 E
Predivinsk 20 Ee 57.04N 93.37 E
Predporožny 20 Jd 65.00N 143.20 E
Pré-en-Pail 11 Ff 48.27N 0.12W
Preetz 10 Gb 54.14N 10.17 E
Pregolia 7 Ei 54.42N 20.24 E
Pregradnaja 16 Lh 43.58N 41.12 E
Preilj/Prejli 7 Gh 56.19N 26.48 E
Preissac, Lac- 44 Ha 48.25N 78.28W
Prejli/Preilj 7 Gh 56.19N 26.48 E
Prekmurje 14 Kd 46.45N 16.15 E
Prekornica 15 Cg 42.40N 19.12 E
Prekule/Priekule 8 Ii 55.36N 21.12 E
Přelouč 10 Lf 50.02N 15.33 E
Premià de Mar/Premiá de Mar 13 Oc 41.29N 2.22 E
Premiá de Mar/Premià de Mar 13 Oc 41.29N 2.22 E
Premnitz 10 Id 52.32N 12.20 E
Premuda 14 If 44.21N 14.37 E
Prenaj/Prienai 7 Fi 54.39N 23.59 E
Prenj 14 Lg 43.32N 17.52 E
Prenjasi 15 Dh 41.04N 20.32 E
Prentice 45 Kd 45.33N 90.17W
Prentiss 45 Lk 31.36N 89.52W
Prenzlau 10 Jc 53.19N 13.52 E
Preobraženije 20 Ih 42.58N 133.55 E
Preobraženka 20 Fd 60.04N 107.58 E
Preparis Island 25 If 14.52N 93.41 E
Preparis North Channel 25 Ie 15.27N 94.05 E
Preparis South Channel 25 If 14.45N 94.05 E
Přerov 10 Ng 49.27N 17.27 E
Prescelly, Mynydd- 9 Ij 51.58N 4.42W
Prescott [Ar.-U.S.] 45 Jj 33.48N 93.23W
Prescott [Az.-U.S.] 43 Ee 34.33N 112.28W
Preševo 15 Eg 42.19N 21.39 E
Presho 45 Fe 43.53N 100.04W
Presicce 14 Mk 39.54N 18.16 E
Presidencia Roque Sáenz Peña 53 Jh 26.50S 60.30W
Presidente Epitácio 56 Jb 21.46S 52.06W
Presidente Frei 66 Re 62.12S 58.55W
Presidente Hayes [3] 55 Cf 24.00S 59.00W
Presidente Juscelino 55 Jd 18.39S 44.05W
Presidente Murtinho 55 Fb 15.39S 53.54W
Presidente Olegário 55 Id 18.25S 46.25W
Presidente Prudente 56 Jb 22.07S 51.22W
Presidente Venceslau 55 Ge 21.52S 51.50W
President Thiers Seamount (EN) 57 Lg 24.39S 145.51W
Presidio 43 Gf 29.33N 104.23W
Presidio, Rio del- 48 Ff 23.06N 106.17W
Preslav 15 Jf 43.10N 26.49 E
Presnovka 17 Mi 54.40N 67.09 E
Prešov 10 Rh 49.00N 21.14 E
Prespa 15 Hh 41.43N 24.53 E
Prespa, Lake- (EN)=Prespansko jezero 5 Ig 40.55N 21.00 E
Prespansko jezero=Prespa, Lake- (EN) 5 Ig 40.55N 21.00 E
Presque Isle 43 Nb 46.41N 68.01W
Prestea 34 Ed 5.26N 2.09W
Přeštice 10 Jg 49.35N 13.21 E
Preston [Eng.-U.K.] 9 Kh 53.46N 2.42W
Preston [Id.-U.S.] 43 Ec 42.06N 111.53W
Preston [Ont.-Can.] 44 Gd 43.23N 80.21W
Prestonsburg 44 Fg 37.40N 82.46W
Preststranda 8 Ce 59.06N 9.04 E
Prestwick 9 If 55.30N 4.37W
Prêto, Rio- [Braz.] 54 Jf 11.21S 43.52W
Prêto, Rio- [Braz.] 55 Gd 18.44S 50.23W
Prêto, Rio- [Braz.] 55 Ic 17.00S 46.12W
Prêto, Rio- [Braz.] 55 Ha 13.37S 48.06W
Preto do Igapó Açu, Rio- 54 Fd 4.26S 59.48W
Pretoria 31 Jk 25.45S 28.10 E
Pretty Rock Butte 45 Fc 46.10N 101.42W
Preußisch-Oldendorf 12 Kb 52.18N 8.30 E
Préveza 15 Dk 38.57N 20.45 E
Prey 12 Df 48.52N 1.13 E
Prey Vêng 25 Lf 11.29N 105.19 E
Priangarskoje Plato 20 Ee 57.30N 97.00 E
Priargunsk 20 Gf 50.27N 119.00 E
Pribelski 17 Hi 54.24N 56.29 E
Pribilof Islands 38 Cd 57.00N 170.00W
Priboj 15 Cf 43.35N 19.32 E
Příbram 10 Kg 49.42N 14.01 E
Price [Que.-Can.] 44 Ma 48.39N 68.12W
Price [Ut.-U.S.] 46 Jg 39.36N 110.48W
Price River 46 Jg 39.10N 110.06W
Prichard 44 Cj 30.44N 88.05W
Prickly Pear Cays 51b Ab 18.16N 63.11W
Prickly Point 51p Bc 11.59N 61.45W
Pridneprovskaja Vozvyšennost=Dnepr Upland (EN) 5 Jf 49.00N 32.00 E
Priego 13 Jd 40.27N 2.18W
Priego de Córdoba 13 Hg 37.26N 4.11W
Priei, Măgura- 15 Fc 46.58N 22.50 E
Priekule 7 Eh 56.29N 21.37 E
Priekulė/Prekule 8 Ii 55.36N 21.12 E
Prienai/Prenaj 7 Fi 54.39N 23.59 E
Priene 24 Bd 37.40N 27.13 E
Prieska 31 Jk 29.40S 22.42 E
Priest Lake 46 Gb 48.34N 116.52W
Prieta, Peña- 13 Ha 43.01N 4.44W
Prieta, Sierra- 48 Cb 31.15N 112.55W
Prievidza 10 Oh 48.46N 18.39 E
Prignitz 10 Hc 53.00N 12.00 E
Prijedor 14 Kf 44.59N 16.42 E
Prijepolje 15 Cf 43.24N 19.39 E
Prijutovo 19 Fe 53.58N 53.58 E
Prikaspijskaja Nizmennost=Caspian Depression (EN) 5 Lf 48.00N 52.00 E
Prilenskoje Plato = Lena Mountains (EN) 21 Oc 60.45N 125.00 E
Prilep 15 Eh 41.21N 21.34 E
Priluki 19 De 50.36N 32.24 E
Primavera 66 Qe 64.09S 60.57W
Primeira Cruz 54 Jd 2.30S 43.26W
Primorje 8 Hj 54.56N 20.00 E
Primorsk [R.S.F.S.R.] 7 Gf 60.22N 28.36 E
Primorsk [Ukr.-U.S.S.R.] 16 Jf 46.43N 36.22 E
Primorski Hrebet 20 Ff 52.30N 106.00 E
Primorski Kraj [3] 20 Ig 45.30N 135.30 E
Primorsko 15 Kg 42.16N 27.46 E
Primorsko-Ahtarsk 19 Df 46.03N 38.11 E
Primorskoje [R.S.F.S.R.] 8 Ld 60.32N 27.56 E
Primorskoje [Ukr.-U.S.S.R.] 15 Nd 45.59N 30.15 E
Primošten 14 Jg 43.36N 15.55 E
Primrose Lake 42 Gf 54.55N 109.45W
Prims 10 Cg 49.20N 6.44 E
Prince Albert 39 Id 53.12N 104.46W
Prince Albert Mountains 66 Jf 76.00S 161.30 E
Prince Albert Peninsula 42 Fb 72.30N 116.00W
Prince Albert Road 37 Cf 33.13S 22.02 E
Prince Albert Sound 42 Gb 70.25N 115.00W
Prince Alfred, Cape - 42 Fb 74.05N 124.29W
Prince Charles 38 Lc 67.50N 76.00W
Prince Charles Mountains 66 Ff 72.00S 67.00 E
Prince-de-Galles, Cap - 42 Kd 61.36N 71.30W
Prince Edward 30 Km 46.33S 37.57 E
Prince Edward Island [3] 42 Lg 46.30N 63.00W
Prince Edward Island 38 Me 46.30N 63.00W
Prince Edward Islands 30 Km 46.35S 37.56 E
Prince George 39 Gd 53.55N 122.49W
Prince Gustaf Adolf Sea 38 Ib 78.30N 107.00W
Prince of Wales [Ak.-U.S.] 40 Me 55.47N 132.50W
Prince of Wales [Can.] 38 Jb 72.40N 99.00W
Prince of Wales, Cape- 38 Cc 65.40N 168.05W
Prince of Wales Island 59 Ib 10.40S 142.10 E
Prince of Wales Mountains 42 Ja 77.45N 78.00W
Prince of Wales Strait 42 Fb 72.45N 118.00W
Prince Patrick 38 Hb 76.45N 119.30W
Prince Regent Inlet 42 Ib 72.45N 90.30W
Prince Rupert 39 Fd 54.19N 130.19W
Prince Rupert Bay 51g Ba 15.34N 61.29W
Prince Rupert Bluff 51g Ba 15.35N 61.29W
Princes Risborough 12 Bc 51.43N 0.49W
Princess Anne 44 Jf 38.12N 75.41W
Princess Charlotte Bay 59 Ib 14.25S 144.00 E
Princess Elizabeth Land 66 Ff 70.00S 80.00 E

Index Symbols

[1] Independent Nation
[2] State, Region
[3] District, County
[4] Municipality
[5] Colony, Dependency
Continent
Physical Region
Historical or Cultural Region
Mount, Mountain
Volcano
Hill
Mountains, Mountain Range
Hills, Escarpment
Plateau, Upland
Pass, Gap
Plain, Lowland
Delta
Salt Flat
Valley, Canyon
Crater, Cave
Karst Features
Depression
Polder
Desert, Dunes
Forest, Woods
Heath, Steppe
Oasis
Cape, Point
Coast, Beach
Cliff
Peninsula
Isthmus
Sandbank
Island
Atoll
Rock, Reef
Islands, Archipelago
Rocks, Reefs
Coral Reef
Well, Spring
Geyser
River, Stream
Waterfall Rapids
River Mouth, Estuary
Lake
Salt Lake
Intermittent Lake
Reservoir
Swamp, Pond
Canal
Glacier
Ice Shelf, Pack Ice
Ocean
Sea
Gulf, Bay
Strait, Fjord
Lagoon
Bank
Seamount
Tablemount
Ridge
Shelf
Basin
Escarpment, Sea Scarp
Fracture
Trench, Abyss
National Park, Reserve
Point of Interest
Recreation Site
Cave, Cavern
Historic Site
Ruins
Wall, Walls
Church, Abbey
Temple
Scientific Station
Airport
Port
Lighthouse
Mine
Tunnel
Dam, Bridge

Index Symbols

[1] Independent Nation	Historical or Cultural Region
[2] State, Region	Mount, Mountain
[3] District, County	Volcano
[4] Municipality	Hill
[5] Colony, Dependency	Mountains, Mountain Range
Continent	Hills, Escarpment
Physical Region	Plateau, Upland

Pass, Gap	Depression
Plain, Lowland	Polder
Delta	Desert, Dunes
Salt Flat	Forest, Woods
Valley, Canyon	Heath, Steppe
Crater, Cave	Oasis
Karst Features	Cape, Point

Coast, Beach	Rock, Reef
Cliff	Islands, Archipelago
Peninsula	Rocks, Reefs
Isthmus	Coral Reef
Sandbank	Well, Spring
Island	Geyser
Atoll	River, Stream

Waterfall Rapids	Canal
River Mouth, Estuary	Glacier
Lake	Ice Shelf, Pack Ice
Salt Lake	Ocean
Intermittent Lake	Sea
Reservoir	Gulf, Bay
Swamp, Pond	Strait, Fjord

Lagoon	Escarpment, Sea Scarp
Bank	Fracture
Seamount	Trench, Abyss
Tablemount	National Park, Reserve
Ridge	Point of Interest
Shelf	Recreation Site
Basin	Cave, Cavern

Historic Site	Port
Ruins	Lighthouse
Wall, Walls	Mine
Church, Abbey	Tunnel
Temple	Dam, Bridge
Scientific Station	
Airport	

Princess Margaret Range 42 Ia 79.00N 88.30W
Princess Royal 42 Ef 52.55N 128.50W
Princeton [B.C.-Can.] 42 Fg 49.27N 120.31W
Princeton [Il.-U.S.] 45 Lf 41.23N 89.28W
Princeton [In.-U.S.] 44 Df 38.21N 87.34W
Princeton [Ky.-U.S.] 44 Dg 37.07N 87.53W
Princeton [Mo.-U.S.] 45 Jf 40.24N 93.35W
Prince William Sound 38 Ec 60.40N 147.00W
Principe 30 Hh 1.37N 7.25 E
Prineville 46 Ed 44.18N 120.51W
Prineville Reservoir 46 Ed 44.08N 120.42W
Prins Christians Sund 41 Hf 60.00N 43.10W
Prinsesse Astrid Kyst 66 Cf 70.45S 12.30 E
Prinsesse Ragnhild Kyst 66 Df 70.15S 27.30 E
Prins Harald Kyst 66 De 69.30S 36.00 E
Prins Karls Forland 41 Nc 78.32N 11.10 E
Prinzapolka 47 Hf 13.24N 83.34W
Prinzapolka, Río- 49 Fg 13.24N 83.34W
Priora, Mount- 59 Ja 6.51S 145.58 E
Priozersk 19 Dc 61.04N 30.07 E
Pripet Marshes (EN) 5 Ie 52.00N 27.00 E
Pripjat 5 Je 51.21N 30.09 E
Pripoljarny Ural=Subpolar
Urals (EN) 5 Lb 65.00N 60.00 E
Prirečny 19 Db 69.02N 30.15 E
Prišib 16 Pj 39.06N 48.38 E
Prislop, Pasul- 15 Hb 47.37N 24.55 E
Pristan-Prževalsk 18 Lc 42.33N 78.18 E
Pristen 16 Jd 51.15N 36.42 E
Priština 15 Eg 42.40N 21.10 E
Pritzwalk 10 Ic 53.09N 12.11 E
Privas 11 Kj 44.44N 4.36 E
Priverno 14 Hi 41.28N 13.11 E
Privolžskaja Vozvyšennost=
Volga Hills (EN) 5 Ke 52.00N 46.00 E
Privolžsk 7 Jh 57.27N 41.16 E
Privolžski 16 Od 51.23N 46.02 E
Prizren 15 Dg 42.13N 20.45 E
Prizzi 14 Hm 37.43N 13.26 E
Prjaža 7 Hf 61.43N 33.37 E
Prnjavor 14 Lf 44.52N 17.40 E
Probolinggo 26 Fh 7.45S 113.13 E
Prochowice 10 Me 51.17N 16.22 E
Procida 14 Hj 40.45N 14.00 E
Proctor Reservoir 45 Gj 32.02N 98.32W
Proddatur 25 Ff 14.44N 78.33 E
Profitis Ilias [Grc.] 15 Fm 36.53N 22.22 E
Profitis Ilias [Grc.] 15 Fj 39.50N 22.38 E
Profondeville 12 Gd 50.23N 4.52 E
Progonati 15 Ci 40.13N 19.56 E
Prograničnik 18 Dg 35.43N 63.12 E
Progreso [Mex.] 39 Kg 21.17N 89.40W
Progreso [Mex.] 48 Id 27.28N 101.04W
Progress 20 Hg 49.41N 129.40 E
Prohladny 16 Nh 43.45N 44.01 E
Prohorovka 16 Jd 51.02N 36.42 E
Prokopjevsk 22 Kd 53.53N 86.45 E
Prokuplje 15 Ef 43.15N 21.36 E
Proletari 7 Hg 58.26N 31.43 E
Proletarsk [R.S.F.S.R.] 19 Ef 46.41N 41.44 E
Proletarsk [Tad.-U.S.S.R.] 18 Gd 40.10N 69.31 E
Proletarski 16 Id 50.51N 35.46 E
Proletarskoje
Vodohranilišče 16 Mf 46.30N 42.10 E
Proliv Soela/Soela Väin 8 Jf 58.40N 22.30 E
Prome 22 Lh 18.49N 95.13 E
Promissão, Represa- 56 Kb 21.32S 49.52W
Promissão 55 He 21.32S 49.52W
Promyšlenny 17 Kc 67.35N 63.55 E
Pronja [Bye.-U.S.S.R.] 16 Gc 53.27N 31.03 E
Pronja [U.S.S.R.] 16 Lb 54.21N 40.24 E
Pronsfeld 12 Id 50.10N 6.20 E
Prophet 42 Fe 58.46N 122.45W
Propriá 54 Kf 10.13S 36.51W
Propriano 11a Ab 41.40N 8.54 E
Prorva 16 Rg 45.57N 53.15 E
Proserpine 59 Jd 20.24S 148.34 E
Prosna 10 Nd 52.10N 17.39 E
Prosotsáni 15 Gh 41.11N 23.59 E
Prosperidad 26 Ie 8.34N 125.52 E
Prospihino 20 Ee 58.37N 99.20 E
Prosser 46 Fc 46.12N 119.46W
Prostějov 10 Ng 49.29N 17.07 E
Proszowice 10 Qf 50.12N 20.18 E
Próti 15 El 37.03N 21.33 E
Protoka 16 Jg 45.43N 37.46 E
Protva 7 Ii 54.51N 37.16 E
Provadija 15 Kf 43.11N 27.26 E
Prøven 41 Gd 72.15N 55.40W
Provence 11 Lk 44.00N 6.00 E
Provence 5 Gg 44.00N 6.00 E
Providence [Ky.-U.S.] 44 Dg 37.24N 87.39W
Providence [R.I.-U.S.] 39 Le 41.50N 71.25W
Providence, Cape- 62 Bg 46.01S 166.28 E
Providence Bay 44 Fc 45.44N 82.18W
Providence Island 30 Mi 9.14S 51.02 E
Providencia, Isla de- 47 Hf 13.21N 81.22W
Providenciales 49 Kc 21.49N 72.15W
Provideniya 22 Uc 64.23N 173.18W
Provincetown 44 Ld 42.03N 70.11W
Provins 11 Jf 48.33N 3.18 E
Provo 39 He 40.14N 111.39W
Prozor 14 Lg 43.49N 17.37 E
Prudentópolis 55 Gg 25.12S 50.57W
Prudhoe Bay 39 Eb 70.20N 148.25W
Prudnik 10 Nf 50.19N 17.34 E
Prüm 12 Ie 49.49N 6.28 E
Prüm 10 Cf 50.13N 6.25 E
Prune Island 51n Bb 12.35N 61.24W
Prussia (EN) 10 Pc 53.45N 20.00 E
Pruszcz Gdański 10 Ob 54.16N 18.36 E
Pruszków 10 Qd 52.11N 20.48 E
Prut 5 If 45.28N 28.14 E
Pružany 19 Ce 52.36N 24.28 E
Prvić 14 If 44.54N 14.48 E
Prydz Bay 66 Fe 69.00S 76.00 E
Pryor 45 Ih 36.19N 95.19W
Przasnysz 10 Qc 53.01N 20.55 E
Przedbórz 10 Pe 51.06N 19.53 E
Przemyśl [2] 10 Sg 49.45N 22.45 E
Przemyśl 10 Sg 49.47N 22.47 E
Prževalsk 22 Je 42.29N 78.24 E
Przeworsk 10 Sf 50.05N 22.29 E
Przysucha 10 Qe 51.22N 20.38 E
Psakhná 15 Gk 38.35N 23.38 E
Psará 15 Ik 38.35N 25.37 E
Psathoúra 15 Hj 39.30N 24.11 E
Pščiš 16 Kg 45.03N 39.25 E
Psebaj 16 Lg 44.07N 40.47 E
Psël 5 Jf 49.05N 33.30 E
Psérimos 15 Km 36.56N 27.09 E
Psina 10 Of 50.02N 18.16 E
Pšiš, Gora- 16 Lh 43.24N 41.14 E
Pskem 18 Hd 41.38N 70.01 E
Pskent 18 Gd 40.54N 69.23 E
Pskov 6 Id 57.50N 28.20 E
Pskov, Lake- (EN)=Pihkva
järv 7 Gg 58.00N 28.00 E
Pskov, Lake- (EN)=
Pskovskoje Ozero 5 Id 58.00N 28.00 E
Pskova 8 Mg 57.47N 28.30 E
Pskovskaja Oblast [3] 19 Cd 57.20N 29.20 E
Pskovskoje Ozero=Pskov,
Lake- (EN) 5 Id 58.00N 28.00 E
Psunj 14 Le 45.24N 17.20 E
Ptič 16 Fc 52.09N 28.52 E
Ptolemais 15 Ei 40.31N 21.41 E
Ptuj 14 Jd 46.25N 15.52 E
Pua-a, Cape- 65c Aa 13.26S 172.43W
Puah, Pulau- 26 Hg 0.30S 122.34 E
Puapua 65c Aa 13.34S 172.09W
Pucallpa 53 If 8.20S 74.30W
Pučež 7 Kh 56.59N 43.11 E
Pucheng [China] 27 Kf 27.55N 118.30 E
Pucheng [China] 27 Id 35.00N 109.38 E
Pucho 36 Cf 17.35S 16.30 E
Pucioasa 15 Id 45.05N 25.25 E
Pučišća 14 Kg 43.21N 16.44 E
Puck 10 Ob 54.44N 18.27 E
Pucka, Zatoka- 10 Ob 54.40N 18.35 E
Pudasjärvi 7 Gd 65.23N 27.00 E
Pudož 19 Dc 61.50N 36.32 E
Pudukkottai 25 Ff 10.23N 78.49 E
Puebla [2] 47 Ee 18.50N 98.00W
Puebla, Sierra de- 48 Kh 19.50N 97.00W
Puebla de Alcocer 13 Gf 38.59N 5.15W
Puebla de Don Fabrique 13 Jg 37.58N 2.26W
Puebla de Guzmán 13 Eg 37.37N 7.15W
Puebla de Sanabria 13 Fb 42.03N 6.38W
Puebla de Trives 13 Eb 42.20N 7.15W
Puebla de Zaragoza 39 Jh 19.03N 98.12W
Pueblo 39 If 38.16N 104.37W
Pueblo Libertador 55 Cj 30.13S 59.23W
Pueblo Nuevo [Mex.] 48 Gf 23.23N 105.23W
Pueblo Nuevo [Ven.] 49 Mh 11.58N 69.55W
Pueblo Nuevo Tiquisate 49 Bf 14.17N 91.22W
Pueblo Viejo, Laguna de- 48 Kf 22.10N 97.55W
Puelches 56 Ge 38.09S 65.55W
Puenteáreas 13 Db 42.11N 8.30W
Puente de la Reina 13 Kb 42.40N 1.49W
Puentedeume 13 Da 43.24N 8.10W
Puente-Genil 13 Hg 37.23N 4.47W
Puentelarrá 13 Ib 42.45N 3.03W
Pueo Point 65a Ab 21.54N 160.04W
Pu'er 27 Hg 23.00N 101.00 E
Puerca, Punta- 51a Cb 18.15N 65.35W
Puerco, Rio- 45 Ci 34.22N 107.50W
Puerco River 46 Ji 34.52N 110.05W
Puerto Abente 55 Df 22.55S 57.43W
Puerto Acosta 54 Eg 15.32S 69.15W
Puerto Adela 55 Eg 24.33S 54.22W
Puerto Aisén 53 Ij 45.24S 72.42W
Puerto Alegre 54 Ff 13.53S 61.36W
Puerto Ángel 47 Ee 15.40N 96.29W
Puerto Arista 48 Mj 15.56N 93.48W
Puerto Armuelles 49 Hg 8.17N 82.52W
Puerto Asis 54 Cc 0.29N 76.32W
Puerto Ayacucho 53 Je 5.40N 67.35W
Puerto Ayora 54a Ab 0.45S 90.23W
Puerto Barrios 39 Kh 15.43N 88.36W
Puerto Bermejo 55 Ch 26.56S 58.30W
Puerto Berrio 54 Db 6.30N 74.25W
Puerto Boyacá 54 Db 5.45N 74.29W
Puerto Caballo 55 Ce 20.12S 58.12W
Puerto Cabello 53 Jd 10.28N 68.01W
Puerto Cabezas 47 Hf 14.02N 83.23W
Puerto Carreño 53 Je 6.12N 67.22W
Puerto Casado 56 Ib 20.20S 57.55W
Puerto Colombia 49 Jh 10.59N 74.57W
Puerto Colón 55 Df 23.11S 57.33W
Puerto Constanza 55 Ck 33.50S 59.03W
Puerto Cooper 56 Ib 23.03S 57.43W
Puerto Cortés [C.R.] 49 Fi 8.58N 83.32W
Puerto Cortés [Hond.] 39 Kh 15.48N 87.56W
Puerto Cumarebo 54 Ea 11.29N 69.21W
Puerto de Eten 54 Ce 6.56S 79.52W
Puerto de la Cruz 32 Dd 28.23N 16.33W
Puerto de Lajas, Cerro- 47 Cc 28.59N 107.02W
Puerto del Rosario 32 Ed 28.30N 13.52W
Puerto de Mazarrón 13 Kg 37.34N 1.15W
Puerto de San José 47 Ff 13.55N 90.49W
Puerto Deseado 53 Jj 47.45S 65.55W
Puerto de Sóller 13 Oe 39.48N 2.41 E
Puerto Escondido [Mex.] 47 Ee 15.48N 96.57W
Puerto Escondido [Mex.] 48 De 25.48N 111.20W
Puerto Esperanza [Arg.] 55 Eh 26.01S 54.39W
Puerto Esperanza [Par.] 55 Ce 20.26S 58.06W
Puerto Estrella 49 Lg 12.14N 71.13W
Puerto Fonciere 55 Df 22.29S 57.48W
Puerto Francisco de
Orellana 54 Cd 0.27S 76.57W
Puerto Frey 55 Bb 14.42S 61.10W
Puerto Gaitán 54 Dc 4.20N 72.10W
Puerto General Diaz 55 Eg 25.12S 54.32W
Puerto Goya 55 Ci 29.09S 59.20W
Puerto Grether 54 Fg 17.12S 64.21W
Puerto Guarani 55 De 21.18S 57.55W
Puerto Heath 54 Ef 12.30S 68.40W
Puerto Huasco 56 Fc 28.28S 71.14W
Puerto Huitoto 54 Dc 0.18N 74.03W
Puerto Iguazú 56 Jc 25.34S 54.34W
Puerto Indio 55 Eg 24.52S 54.29W
Puerto Ingeniero Ibañez 56 Fg 46.18S 71.56W
Puerto Isabel 55 Dd 18.11S 57.37W
Puerto Jesús 49 Eh 10.07N 85.16W
Puerto Juárez 39 Kg 21.11N 86.49W
Puerto la Concordia 54 Dc 2.38N 72.47W
Puerto la Cruz 53 Jd 10.13N 64.38W
Puerto Leguízamo 53 If 0.12S 74.46W
Puerto Lempira 49 Ff 15.15N 83.46W
Puerto Libertad 47 Bc 29.55N 112.43W
Puerto Limón [Col.] 54 Cc 1.02N 76.32W
Puerto Limón [Col.] 54 Dc 3.23N 73.30W
Puertollano 13 Hf 38.41N 4.07W
Puerto Lopez 54 Dc 4.06N 72.58W
Puerto López 49 Lh 11.56N 71.17W
Puerto Lumbreras 13 Kg 37.34N 1.49W
Puerto Madero 48 Mj 14.44N 92.25W
Puerto Madryn 56 Gf 42.46S 65.03W
Puerto Magdalena 48 Ce 24.35N 112.05W
Puerto Maldonado 53 Jg 12.36S 69.11W
Puerto Marangatú 55 Eg 24.39S 54.21W
Puerto Mayor Otaño 55 Eh 26.19S 54.44W
Puerto Mihanovich 55 De 20.52S 57.59W
Puerto Monte Lindo 55 Df 23.57S 57.12W
Puerto Montt 53 Ij 41.28S 72.57W
Puerto Morelos 48 Pg 20.50N 86.52W
Puerto Mutis 54 Cb 6.14N 77.25W
Puerto Naranjito 55 Eh 26.57S 55.18W
Puerto Nariño 54 Ec 4.56N 67.48W
Puerto Natales 53 Ik 51.44S 72.31W
Puerto Nuevo 55 Ce 20.33S 58.03W
Puerto Nuevo, Punta- 51a Bb 18.30N 66.21W
Puerto Ordaz 54 Fb 8.22N 62.41W
Puerto Padre 49 Ic 21.12N 76.36W
Puerto Páez 54 Eb 6.13N 67.28W
Puerto Peñasco 47 Bb 31.20N 113.33W
Puerto Piña 49 Hj 7.35N 78.10W
Puerto Pinasco 56 Ib 22.43S 57.50W
Puerto Píritu 50 Dg 10.04N 65.03W
Puerto Plata 47 Je 19.48N 70.41W
Puerto Presidente
Stroessner 55 Eg 25.33S 54.39W
Puerto Princesa 22 Ni 9.44N 118.44 E
Puerto Quijarro 55 Dc 17.47S 57.46W
Puerto Real 13 Fh 36.32N 6.11W
Puerto Rico [5] 39 Mh 18.15N 66.30W
Puerto Rico 38 Mh 18.15N 66.30W
Puerto Rico [Arg.] 56 Jc 26.48S 54.59W
Puerto Rico [Bol.] 54 Ef 11.05S 67.38W
Puerto Rico [Col.] 54 Cc 1.54N 75.10W
Puerto Rico Trench (EN) 3 Bg 20.00N 66.00W
Puerto Rondón 54 Db 6.18N 71.06W
Puerto San José 55 Eg 26.32S 54.50W
Puerto Santa Cruz 53 Jk 50.09S 68.30W
Puerto Sastre 56 Ib 22.06S 57.59W
Puerto Siles 54 Ef 12.48S 65.05W
Puerto Suárez 53 Kg 18.57S 57.51W
Puerto Tacurú Pytá 55 Df 23.49S 57.09W
Puerto Tirol 55 Ch 27.23S 59.05W
Puerto Tres Palmas 55 De 21.43S 57.58W
Puerto Triunfo 55 Eg 26.45S 55.06W
Puerto Vallarta 47 Cd 20.37N 105.15W
Puerto Varas 56 Ff 41.19S 72.59W
Puerto Victoria 55 Eh 26.20S 54.39W
Puerto Viejo 49 Eh 10.26N 83.59W
Puerto Villamizar 49 Ki 8.19N 72.26W
Puerto Villazón 55 Ba 13.32S 61.57W
Puerto Wilches 54 Db 7.20N 73.54W
Puerto Ybapobó 55 Df 23.42S 57.12W
Pueu 65e Fc 17.44S 149.13W
Pugačev 19 Ee 52.03N 48.48 E
Puget Sound 46 Dc 48.00N 122.30W
Puglia=Apulia (EN) [2] 14 Ki 41.15N 16.15 E
Pu He 28 Gd 41.21N 122.47 E
Puhja 8 Lf 58.13N 26.17 E
Puigcerdá 13 Nb 42.26N 1.56 E
Puigmal 13 Ob 42.23N 2.07 E
Puir 20 Jf 53.10N 141.25 E
Puisaye, Collines de la- 11 Jg 47.35N 3.18 E
Puisieux 12 Ed 50.07N 2.42 E
Pujehun 34 Cd 7.21N 11.42W
Pujești 15 Kc 46.25N 27.29 E
Puji → Wugong 27 Ie 34.15N 108.14 E
Pujiang 28 Ei 29.28N 119.53 E
Pujili 54 Cd 0.57S 78.42W
Puka 15 Cg 42.03N 19.54 E
Pukaki, Lake- 62 Df 44.05S 170.10 E
Pukalani 65a Ec 20.50N 156.21W
Pukapuka Atoll 57 Kf 10.53S 165.49W
Pukapuka Atoll [W.F.] 57 Nf 14.49S 138.48W
Pukaruha Atoll 57 Nf 18.20S 137.02W
Pukatawagan 42 He 55.44N 101.19W
Pukchin 28 Hd 40.12N 125.45 E
Pukch'ŏng 27 Mc 40.14N 128.19 E
Pukega, Pointe- 64h Ab 13.17S 176.13W
Pukekohe 62 Fb 37.12S 174.54 E
Pukemiro 62 Fb 37.37S 175.01 E
Pukeuri Junction 62 Df 45.02S 171.02 E
Pukšenga 7 Je 63.36N 41.55 E
Puksoozero 19 Ec 62.38N 40.32 E
Puksubaek-san 28 Id 40.42N 127.15 E
Pula [It.] 14 Ck 39.01N 9.00 E
Pula [Yugo.] 14 Hf 44.52N 13.50 E
Pula, Capo di- 14 Dl 38.59N 9.01 E
Pulandian → Xinjin 27 Ld 39.24N 121.59 E
Pulap Atoll 57 Fd 7.39N 149.25 E
Pulaski [Tn.-U.S.] 44 Dh 35.12N 87.02W
Pulaski [Va.-U.S.] 44 Gg 37.03N 80.47W
Pulau 26 Kh 5.50S 138.15 E
Pulau Halura 26 Hi 10.19S 120.11 E
Pulau Irian/New Guinea 57 Fe 5.00S 140.00 E
Pulau Sapudi 26 Fh 7.06S 114.20 E
Puławy 10 Re 51.25N 21.57 E
Pulborough 12 Bd 50.57N 0.31W
Pulheim 12 Ic 51.00N 6.48 E
Pulkau 14 Kb 48.43N 16.21 E
Pulkkila 7 Fd 64.16N 25.52 E
Pullman 43 Db 46.44N 117.10W
Pulo Anna Island 57 Ed 4.40N 131.58 E
Pulog, Mount- 21 Oh 16.36N 120.54 E
Pulpito, Punta- 48 Dd 26.30N 111.30W
Pulsano 14 Lj 40.23N 17.21 E
Pułtusk 10 Rd 52.43N 21.05 E
Pülümür 24 Hc 39.30N 39.54 E
Pulusuk Island 57 Fd 6.42N 149.19 E
Puluwat Atoll 57 Fd 7.22N 149.11 E
Puma Yumco 27 Ff 28.35N 90.20 E
Pumpénai/Pumpenaj 8 Ki 55.53N 24.25 E
Pumpenaj/Pumpénai 8 Ki 55.53N 24.25 E
Pumpkin Creek 46 Mc 46.15N 105.45W
Puná, Isla- 54 Bd 2.50S 80.10W
Punākha 25 Hc 27.37N 89.52 E
Punaluu 65a Fd 19.08N 155.30W
Pūnch 25 Eb 33.46N 74.06 E
Punda Milia 37 Ed 22.40S 31.05 E
Pune (Poona) 22 Jh 18.32N 73.52 E
Pūnel 24 Md 37.33N 49.07 E
Pungan 18 Hd 40.45N 70.50 E
P'unggi 28 Jf 36.52N 128.32 E
Púngoè 37 Ec 19.50S 34.48 E
P'ungsan 28 Jd 40.40N 128.05 E
Punia 36 Ec 1.28S 26.27 E
Punitaqui 56 Fd 30.50S 71.16W
Punjab [3] 25 Fb 31.00N 76.00 E
Punjab 21 Jf 30.00N 74.00 E
Punjad [3] 25 Eb 30.00N 74.00 E
Punkaharju 8 Mc 61.48N 29.24 E
Punkalaidun 8 Jc 61.07N 23.06 E
Puno 53 Ig 15.50S 70.02W
Puno [2] 54 Ef 15.00S 70.00W
Punta, Cerro de- 47 Ke 18.10N 66.36W
Punta Alta 53 Ji 38.53S 62.04W
Punta Arenas 53 Ik 53.09S 70.55W
Punta Cardón 54 Da 11.38N 70.14W
Punta de Mata 50 Eh 9.43N 63.38W
Punta Gorda [Blz.] 47 Ge 16.07N 88.48W
Punta Gorda [Fl.-U.S.] 44 Fl 26.56N 82.03W
Punta Gorda [Nic.] 49 Fh 11.31N 83.47W
Punta Gorda, Bahía de- 49 Fh 11.15N 83.45W
Punta Gorda, Río- 49 Fh 11.30N 83.47W
Punta Indio 55 Dl 35.16S 57.14W
Punta Prieta 47 Bc 28.58N 114.17W
Puntarenas [3] 49 Ei 9.00N 83.15W
Puntarenas 39 Ki 9.58N 84.50W
Punta Róbalo 49 Fi 9.02N 82.15W
Punto Fijo 54 Da 11.42N 70.13W
Puolanka 7 Gd 64.52N 27.40 E
Puolo Point 65a Bb 21.54N 159.36W
Puqi 27 Jf 29.43N 113.52 E
Puquio 54 Df 14.42S 74.08W
Purace, Volcán- 54 Cc 2.21N 76.23W
Purari 60 Ci 7.52S 145.10 E
Purcell Mountains 42 Fg 49.55N 116.15W
Purdy Islands 57 Fe 2.53S 146.20 E
Purgatoire River 45 Eg 38.04N 103.10W
Puri 25 He 19.48N 85.51 E
Purificación 47 Ed 23.58N 98.42W
Purikari Neem/
Purikarinem 8 Ke 59.36N 25.35 E
Purikarinem/Purikari
Neem 8 Ke 59.36N 25.35 E
Purmani/Puurmani 8 Lf 58.30N 26.14 E
Purmerend 11 Kb 52.31N 4.57 E
Purna [India] 25 Fe 19.07N 77.02 E
Purna [India] 25 Fd 21.05N 76.00 E
Purnač 7 Jc 67.00N 40.15 E
Pūrnia 25 Hc 25.47N 87.28 E
Purukcahu 26 Fg 0.35S 114.35 E
Puruliya 25 Hd 23.20N 86.22 E
Puruni River 50 Gi 6.00N 59.12W
Purus, Rio- 52 Jf 3.42S 61.28W
Puruvesi 7 Gf 61.50N 29.25 E
Purwakarta 26 Eh 6.34S 107.26 E
Purwokerto 26 Eh 7.25S 109.14 E
Pusala Dağı 24 Ed 37.12N 32.54 E
Pusan 22 Of 35.06N 129.03 E
Pusan Si [2] 28 Jg 35.10N 129.05 E
Pushi He 28 Hd 40.17N 124.43 E
Puškin 19 Dd 59.43N 30.24 E
Puškino [Abz.-U.S.S.R.] 16 Pj 39.28N 48.33 E
Puškino [R.S.F.S.R.] 16 Od 51.14N 46.59 E
Puškino [R.S.F.S.R.] 7 Ih 56.02N 37.53 E
Puškinskije Gory 8 Mh 56.59N 28.59 E
Pušlahta 7 Id 64.48N 36.33 E
Püspökladány 10 Ri 47.19N 21.07 E
Püssi/Pjussi 8 Le 59.17N 26.57 E
Pusteci 15 Di 40.47N 20.54 E
Pusteria, Val-/Pustertal 14 Gd 46.45N 12.20 E
Pustertal/Pusteria, Val- 14 Gd 46.45N 12.20 E
Pustomyty 10 Tg 49.37N 23.59 E
Pustoška 7 Gh 56.20N 29.22 E
Putao 25 Jc 27.21N 97.24 E
Putaruru 62 Fc 38.03S 175.47 E
Putian 27 Kf 25.32N 119.01 E
Putignano 14 Lj 40.51N 17.07 E
Putila 15 Ip 48.00N 25.07 E
Putivl 16 Hd 51.22N 33.55 E
Putjatin 28 Lc 42.52N 132.25 E
Putla de Guerrero 48 Ki 17.02N 97.56W
Putna 15 Kd 45.34N 27.30 E
Putna 15 Ib 47.52N 25.37 E
Putnok 10 Qh 48.18N 20.26 E
Puto 63a Ba 5.41S 154.43 E
Putorana, Plato-=Putoran
Mountains (EN) 21 Lc 69.00N 95.00 E
Putoran Mountains (EN)=
Putorana, Plato- 21 Lc 69.00N 95.00 E
Puttalam 25 Fg 8.02N 79.49 E
Putte 12 Gc 51.04N 4.38 E
Puttelange-aux-Lacs 12 Ie 49.03N 6.56 E
Putten 12 Hb 52.16N 5.35 E
Putten 12 Gc 51.50N 4.15 E
Puttgarden, Burg auf
Fehmarn- 10 Hb 54.30N 11.13 E
Püttlingen 12 Ie 49.17N 6.53 E
Putumayo [2] 54 Cc 0.30N 76.00W
Putumayo, Rio- 52 Jf 3.07S 67.58W
Putuo (Shenjiamen) 28 Gj 29.57N 122.18 E
Putussibau 26 Ff 0.50N 112.56 E
Puu Kukui 65a Ec 20.54N 156.35W
Puulavesi 5 Ic 61.50N 26.40 E
Puumala 7 Gf 61.32N 28.11 E
Puu o Umi 65a Fc 20.05N 155.42W
Puurmani/Purmani 8 Lf 58.30N 26.14 E
Puurs 12 Gc 51.05N 4.17 E
Puuwai 65a Ab 21.54N 160.12W
Puyallup 46 Dc 47.11N 122.18W
Puyang 27 Jd 35.41N 115.00 E
Puy-de-Dôme [3] 11 Ii 45.40N 3.00 E
Puy-l'Evêque 11 Hj 44.30N 1.08 E
Puymorens, Col de- 11 Hl 42.34N 1.49 E
Puyo 54 Cd 1.29S 77.58W
Puysegur Point 62 Bg 46.10S 166.37 E
Pwani [3] 36 Gd 7.30S 39.00 E
Pweto 31 Ji 8.28S 28.54 E
Pwllheli 9 Ii 52.53N 4.25W
Pyapon 25 Je 16.17N 95.41 E
Pyhäjärvi 7 Fe 63.40N 25.59 E
Pyhäjärvi [Fin.] 7 Ff 61.00N 22.20 E
Pyhäjärvi [Fin.] 7 Fe 63.35N 25.57 E
Pyhäjärvi [Fin.] 8 Kc 62.45N 25.25 E
Pyhäjärvi [Fin.] 8 Jc 61.30N 23.35 E
Pyhäjoki 7 Fd 64.28N 24.13 E
Pyhäjoki 7 Fd 64.28N 24.14 E
Pyhäntä 7 Gd 64.06N 26.19 E
Pyhäranta 8 Id 60.57N 21.27 E
Pyhäselkä 7 Ge 62.30N 29.40 E
Pyhäselkä 8 Mb 62.26N 29.58 E
Pyhätunturi 7 Gc 67.01N 27.09 E
Pyhävesi 8 Lc 61.25N 26.35 E
Pyhävuori 8 Ib 62.17N 21.38 E
Pyhrnpaß 14 Ic 47.38N 14.18 E
Pyhtää/Pyttis 7 Gf 60.29N 26.32 E
Pyinmana 22 Lh 19.44N 96.13 E
Pylos (EN) = Pilos 15 Em 36.56N 21.40 E
Pyltsamaa/Põltsamaa 8 Lf 58.23N 26.08 E
Pyltsamaa/Põltsamaa 7 Fg 58.39N 25.59 E
Pylva/Põlva 7 Gg 58.04N 27.06 E
Pymatuning Reservoir 44 Ge 41.37N 80.30W
P'yŏngan-Namdo [2] 28 Ie 39.20N 126.00 E
P'yŏngan-Pukto [2] 28 Hd 40.00N 125.15 E
P'yŏnggang 27 Md 38.25N 127.17 E
P'yŏngsan 27 Md 38.20N 126.24 E
P'yongt'aek 28 If 36.59N 127.05 E
P'yŏngyang 22 Of 39.01N 125.45 E
P'yŏngyang Si [2] 28 He 39.04N 125.50 E
Pyramiden 41 Nc 77.54N 16.41 E
Pyramid Lake 43 Dc 40.00N 119.35W
Pyramid Mountains 45 Bj 32.00N 108.30W
Pyrénées=Pyrenees (EN)
5 Gg 42.40N 1.00 E
Pyrenees (EN)=Pirineos 5 Gg 42.40N 1.00 E
Pyrenees (EN)=
Pyrénées 5 Gg 42.40N 1.00 E
Pyrenees (EN)=Serralada
Pirinenca 5 Gg 42.40N 1.00 E
Pyrénées-Atlantiques [3] 11 Fk 43.15N 0.50W
Pyrénées-Orientales [3] 11 Il 42.30N 2.20 E
Pyrzyce 10 Kc 53.10N 14.55 E
Pyšma 19 Gd 57.08N 66.18 E
Pytalovo 7 Gh 57.06N 27.59 E
Pyttegga 8 Bb 62.13N 7.42 E
Pyttis/Pyhtää 7 Gf 60.29N 26.32 E
Pyu 25 Je 18.29N 96.26 E
Pyzaspea/Pöösaspea
Neem 8 Je 59.15N 23.25 E
Pyzdry 10 Nd 52.11N 17.41 E

Q

Qā', Wādī al- 24 Hi 27.04N 38.34 E
Qābis [3] 32 Ic 33.00N 9.30 E
Qābis 31 Ie 33.53N 10.07 E
Qābis, Khalīj-=Gabès, Gulf
of-(EN) 30 Ie 34.00N 10.25 E
Qabr Hūd 35 Hb 16.09N 49.34 E
Qāderābād 24 Og 30.17N 53.16 E
Qādir Karam 24 Ke 35.12N 44.53 E
Qāḑub 23 Hg 12.38N 53.57 E
Qa'emshahr 24 Od 36.30N 52.55 E
Qafṣah 31 He 34.25N 8.48 E
Qafṣah [3] 32 Ic 34.30N 9.00 E
Qa'fūr 14 Dn 36.20N 9.19 E
Qagan 27 Kb 49.16N 118.04 E
Qagan Moron He 28 Ec 43.13N 119.02 E
Qagan Nur 27 Jc 43.20N 112.58 E
Qagan Nur [China] 28 Bd 41.33N 113.48 E
Qagan Nur [China] 27 Jc 43.25N 114.50 E
Qagan Nur [China] 28 Hb 45.14N 124.17 E
Qagan Nur → Zhengxiangbai
Qi 27 Jc 42.16N 114.59 E
Qagan Us → Dulan 27 Gd 36.29N 98.29 E
Qagchêng/Xiangcheng 27 Gf 28.56N 99.46 E
Qahar Youyi Houqi (Bayan
Qagan) 28 Bd 41.28N 113.10 E
Qahar Youyi Qianqi (Togrog
Ul) 28 Bd 40.46N 113.13 E
Qahar Youyi Zhongqi 28 Bd 41.15N 112.36 E
Qahd, Wādī- 24 Ii 26.13N 40.49 E
Qaidam He 27 Gd 36.48N 95.50 E
Qaidam Pendi=Tsaidam
Basin (EN) 27 Fd 37.00N 95.00 E

Index Symbols

[1] Independent Nation
[2] State, Region
[3] District, County
[4] Municipality
[5] Colony, Dependency
Continent
Physical Region
Historical or Cultural Region
Mount, Mountain
Volcano
Hill
Mountains, Mountain Range
Hills, Escarpment
Plateau, Upland
Pass, Gap
Plain, Lowland
Delta
Salt Flat
Valley, Canyon
Crater, Cave
Karst Features
Depression
Polder
Desert, Dunes
Forest, Woods
Heath, Steppe
Oasis
Cape, Point
Coast, Beach
Cliff
Peninsula
Isthmus
Sandbank
Island
Atoll
Rock, Reef
Islands, Archipelago
Rocks, Reefs
Coral Reef
Well, Spring
Geyser
River, Stream
Waterfall Rapids
River Mouth, Estuary
Lake
Salt Lake
Intermittent Lake
Reservoir
Swamp, Pond
Canal
Glacier
Ice Shelf, Pack Ice
Ocean
Sea
Gulf, Bay
Strait, Fjord
Lagoon
Bank
Seamount
Tablemount
Ridge
Shelf
Basin
Escarpment, Sea Scarp
Fracture
Trench, Abyss
National Park, Reserve
Point of Interest
Recreation Site
Cave, Cavern
Historic Site
Ruins
Wall, Walls
Church, Abbey
Temple
Scientific Station
Airport
Port
Lighthouse
Mine
Tunnel
Dam, Bridge

Index Symbols

① Independent Nation	⬙ Historical or Cultural Region
② State, Region	⬙ Mount, Mountain
③ District, County	⬙ Volcano
④ Municipality	⬙ Hill
⑤ Colony, Dependency	⬙ Mountains, Mountain Range
■ Continent	⬙ Hills, Escarpment
⬙ Physical Region	⬙ Plateau, Upland

▸ Pass, Gap	⬙ Depression
⬙ Plain, Lowland	⬙ Polder
⬙ Delta	⬙ Desert, Dunes
⬙ Salt Flat	⬙ Forest, Woods
⬙ Valley, Canyon	⬙ Heath, Steppe
⬙ Crater, Cave	⬙ Oasis
⬙ Karst Features	⬙ Island
⬙ Cape, Point	⬙ Atoll

⬙ Coast, Beach	⬙ Rock, Reef
⬙ Cliff	⬙ Islands, Archipelago
⬙ Peninsula	⬙ Rocks, Reefs
⬙ Isthmus	⬙ Coral Reef
⬙ Sandbank	⬙ Well, Spring
⬙ Island	⬙ Geyser
⬙ River, Stream	

⬙ Waterfall Rapids	⬙ Canal
⬙ River Mouth, Estuary	⬙ Glacier
⬙ Lake	⬙ Ice Shelf, Pack Ice
⬙ Salt Lake	⬙ Ocean
⬙ Intermittent Lake	⬙ Sea
⬙ Reservoir	⬙ Gulf, Bay
⬙ Swamp, Pond	⬙ Strait, Fjord

⬙ Lagoon	⬙ Escarpment, Sea Scarp
⬙ Bank	⬙ Fracture
⬙ Seamount	⬙ Trench, Abyss
⬙ Tablemount	⬙ National Park, Reserve
⬙ Ridge	⬙ Point of Interest
⬙ Shelf	⬙ Recreation Site
⬙ Basin	⬙ Cave, Cavern

⬙ Historic Site	⬙ Port
⬙ Ruins	⬙ Lighthouse
⬙ Wall, Walls	⬙ Mine
⬙ Church, Abbey	⬙ Tunnel
⬙ Temple	⬙ Dam, Bridge
⬙ Scientific Station	
⬙ Airport	

Rājshāhi	25	Hd	24.22N	88.36 E
Rakahanga Atoll	57	Kl	10.02S	161.05W
Rakaia	62	Ee	43.54S	172.13 E
Rakaia	62	Ee	43.45S	172.01 E
Rakan, Ra's-	24	Ni	26.10N	51.13 E
Rakata, Pulau-	26	Eh	6.10S	105.26 E
Raka Zangbo	27	Ef	29.24N	87.58 E
Rakhawt, Wādī-	35	Ib	18.16N	51.50 E
Rakht-e Shāh	24	Mf	33.17N	49.23 E
Rakitnoje	28	Mb	45.36N	134.17 E
Rakitovo	15	Hh	41.59N	24.05 E
Rakkestad	8	De	59.26N	11.21 E
Rakoniewice	10	Md	52.10N	16.16 E
Rakops	37	Cd	21.01S	24.20 E
Rakovnicka panev	10	Jf	50.10N	13.30 E
Rakovník	10	Jf	50.06N	13.43 E
Rakovski	15	Hg	42.18N	24.58 E
Raków	10	Rf	50.42N	21.03 E
Rakušečny, Mys-	16	Qh	42.52N	51.55 E
Råkvåg	7	Ce	63.46N	10.05 E
Rakvere	7	Gg	59.22N	26.22 E
Raleigh [N.C.-U.S.]	39	Lf	35.47N	78.39W
Raleigh [Ont.-Can.]	45	Kb	49.31N	91.56W
Raleigh Bay	44	Ih	35.00N	76.20W
Ralik Chain	57	Hd	8.00N	167.00 E
Rama	47	Hf	12.09N	84.15W
Rama, Río-	49	Eg	12.08N	84.13W
Ramādah	32	Jc	32.19N	10.24 E
Ramağin, Wādī-	24	Ej	24.57N	32.34 E
Ramales de la Victoria	13	Ia	43.15N	3.27W
Ramalho, Serra do-	55	Ja	13.45S	44.00W
Ramapo Bank (EN)	57	Fb	27.15N	145.10 E
Ramatlabama	37	De	25.37S	25.30 E
Ramberg	10	He	51.45N	11.05 E
Rambervillers	11	Mf	48.21N	6.38 E
Rambi	63d	Cb	16.30S	179.59W
Rambouillet	11	Hf	48.39N	1.50 E
Rambutyo Island	57	Fe	2.18S	147.48 E
Rāmhormoz	24	Mg	31.16N	49.36 E
Ramigala/Ramygala	8	Ki	55.28N	24.23 E
Ramis	35	Gd	8.02N	41.36 E
Ramla	24	Fg	31.55N	34.52 E
Ramlīyah, 'Aqabat ar-	24	Di	26.01N	30.42 E
Ramlu	35	Gc	13.20N	41.45 E
Ramm, Jabal-	24	Fh	29.35N	35.24 E
Rammāk, Ghurd ar-	24	Ch	29.40N	29.20 E
Rāmnagar	25	Fc	29.24N	79.07 E
Ramnäs	8	Ge	59.46N	16.12 E
Ramón Santamarina	55	Cn	38.26S	59.20W
Ramos	63a	Ec	8.16S	160.11 E
Ramos, Río-	48	Ge	25.35N	105.03W
Ramotswa	37	Dd	24.52S	25.50 E
Rāmpur	25	Fc	28.49N	79.02 E
Ramree	25	Ie	19.06N	93.48 E
Rams	24	Qj	25.53N	56.02 E
Ramsele	7	De	63.33N	16.29 E
Ramsey [Eng.-U.K.]	12	Bb	52.27N	0.07W
Ramsey [Ont.-Can.]	44	Fb	47.29N	82.24W
Ramsey [U.K.]	9	Ig	54.20N	4.21W
Ramsey Lake	42	Jg	47.20N	83.00W
Ramsgate	9	Oj	51.20N	1.25 E
Rāmshīr	24	Mg	30.50N	49.30 E
Ramsjö	7	De	62.11N	15.39 E
Ramstein-Miesenbach	12	Je	49.27N	7.32 E
Ramsund	7	Db	68.29N	16.32 E
Ramu	60	Di	4.02S	144.41 E
Ramu	36	Hb	3.56N	41.13 E
Ramvik	7	De	62.49N	17.51 E
Ramville, Ilet-	51h	Bb	14.42N	60.53W
Ramygala/Ramigala	8	Ki	55.28N	24.23 E
Rana	7	Dc	66.20N	14.08 E
Rañadoiro, Sierra del-	13	Fa	43.20N	6.45W
Ranai	26	Ef	3.55N	108.23 E
Ranakah, Potjo-	26	Hh	8.38S	120.31 E
Rana Kao, Volcán-	65d	Ac	27.11S	109.27W
Rana Roi, Volcán-	65d	Ab	27.05S	109.23W
Rana Roraka, Volcán-	65d	Bb	27.07S	109.18W
Ranau	26	Ge	5.58N	116.41 E
Ranča	14	Lf	44.24N	17.22 E
Rancagua	53	Ii	34.10S	70.45W
Rance	11	Ef	48.31N	1.59W
Rance, Sivry-Rance-	12	Gd	50.09N	4.16 E
Rancharia	55	Gf	22.15S	50.55W
Rancheria, Río-	49	Kh	11.34N	72.54W
Rānchī	22	Kg	23.21N	85.20 E
Ranchos	55	Cl	35.32S	58.22W
Ranco, Lago-	56	Ff	40.14S	72.24W
Randa	35	Gc	11.51N	42.40 E
Randaberg	8	Ae	59.00N	5.36 E
Randazzo	14	Im	37.53N	14.57 E
Randers	7	Ch	56.28N	10.03 E
Randers Fjord	8	Dh	56.35N	10.20 E
Randijaure	7	Ec	66.42N	19.18 E
Randow	10	Kc	53.41N	14.04 E
Randsfjorden	7	Cf	60.25N	10.25 E
Ranérou	34	Cb	15.18N	13.58W
Ranfurly	62	Df	45.08S	170.06 E
Rangasa, Tanjung-	26	Gg	3.33S	118.56 E
Ranger	45	Gj	32.28N	98.41W
Rangiora	62	Ee	43.18S	172.36 E
Rangiroa Atoll	57	Mf	15.10S	147.35W
Rangitaiki	62	Gb	37.55S	176.53 E
Rangitata	62	Df	44.05S	171.30 E
Rangitikei	62	Fd	40.17S	175.13 E
Rangkasbitung	26	Eh	6.21S	106.15 E
Rangoon (EN) = Yangon	22	Lh	16.47N	96.10 E
Rangpur	25	Hc	25.44N	89.16 E
Rāniyah	24	Kd	36.15N	44.53 E
Rankin Inlet	39	Jc	62.45N	92.10W
Rankoshi	29a	Bb	42.47N	140.31 E
Rannoch, Loch-	9	Ie	56.41N	4.20W
Ranobe	37	Gc	17.10S	44.08 E
Ranon	63b	Dc	16.09S	168.07 E
Ranong	25	Jg	9.59N	98.40 E
Ranongga Island	60	Fi	8.05S	156.34 E
Ranova	16	Lb	54.07N	40.14 E
Ransaren	7	Dd	65.14N	14.59 E
Rantabe	37	Hc	15.42S	49.39 E
Rantasalmi	8	Mb	62.04N	28.18 E
Rantaupanjang	26	Fg	1.23S	112.04 E
Rantauprapat	26	Cf	2.06N	99.50 E
Rantekombola, Bulu-	21	Oj	3.21S	120.01 E
Rantoul	45	Lf	40.19N	88.09W
Ranua	7	Gd	65.55N	26.32 E
Ranyah, Wādī-	33	He	21.18N	43.20 E
Raohe	27	Nb	46.48N	133.58 E
Raon-l'Étape	11	Mf	48.24N	6.51 E
Raoui, Erg er-	32	Gd	29.15N	2.45W
Raoul Island	57	Jg	29.15S	177.52W
Raoyang	28	Ce	38.14N	115.44 E
Raoyang He	28	Gd	41.13N	122.12 E
Rapa, Ile-	57	Mg	27.36S	144.20W
Rapallo	14	Df	44.21N	9.14 E
Rapang	26	Gg	3.50S	119.48 E
Rapa Nui/Pascua, Isla de- = Easter Island (EN)	57	Qg	27.07S	109.22W
Raper, Cape-	42	Kc	69.41N	67.24W
Rapid City	39	Ie	44.05N	103.14W
Rapid Creek	45	Ee	43.54N	102.37W
Rapid River	44	Dc	45.58N	86.59W
Räpina/Rjapina	8	Lf	58.03N	27.35 E
Rapla	7	Fg	59.02N	24.47 E
Rappahannock River	44	Ig	37.34N	76.18W
Rápulo, Río-	52	Jg	13.43S	65.32W
Rāqūbah	31	If	28.58N	19.02 E
Raraka Atoll	57	Mf	16.10S	144.54W
Raroia Atoll	57	Mf	16.05S	142.26W
Rarotonga Island	57	Lg	21.14S	159.46W
Rasa, Punta-	52	Jj	40.51S	62.19W
Ra's Abū Daraj	24	Eh	29.23N	32.33 E
Ra's Abū Rudays	24	Eh	28.53N	33.11 E
Ra's Abū Shajarah	35	Fa	21.04N	37.14 E
Ra's Ajdīr	33	Bc	33.09N	11.34 E
Ra's al 'Ayn	24	Id	36.51N	40.04 E
Ra's al-Barr	24	Dg	31.31N	31.50 E
Ra's al Ḥikmah	24	Bg	31.08N	27.50 E
Ra's al Jabal	14	Em	37.13N	10.08 E
Ra's al Khafjī	24	Mh	28.25N	48.30 E
Ra's al Khaymah	23	Id	25.47N	55.57 E
Ra's al Mish'āb	24	Mh	28.12N	48.37 E
Ra's al Unūf	33	Cc	30.31N	18.34 E
Ra's an Naqb	24	Fh	30.00N	35.29 E
Ra's as Sidr	24	Eh	29.36N	32.40 E
Ra's at Tannūrah	24	Ni	26.42N	50.10 E
Ras Beddouza	30	Ge	32.22N	9.18W
Ras Dashan	30	Kg	13.19N	38.20 E
Raseiniai/Rasejnjaj	7	Fi	55.23N	23.07 E
Rasejnjaj/Raseiniai	7	Fi	55.23N	23.07 E
Râs el Mâ	34	Eb	16.37N	4.27W
Ras-el-Ma	13	Ji	35.08N	2.29W
Ras el Oued	13	Ri	35.57N	5.02 E
Ra's Ghārib	33	Fd	28.21N	33.06 E
Rashād	35	Ec	11.51N	31.04 E
Rāshayyā	24	Ff	33.30N	35.51 E
Rashīd = Rosetta (EN)	33	Fc	31.24N	30.25 E
Rashīd, Maṣabb-	24	Dg	31.30N	30.20 E
Rasht	22	Gf	37.16N	49.36 E
Rāsiga 'Alūla	35	Ic	11.59N	50.50 E
Rās Jumbo	35	Gf	1.37S	41.31 E
Raška	15	Df	43.18N	20.38 E
Ra's Madhar, Jabal-	24	Gj	25.46N	37.32 E
Ra's Matārimah	24	Eh	29.27N	32.43 E
Rasmussen Basin	42	Hc	67.56N	95.15W
Rason Lake	59	Ee	28.45S	124.20 E
Rasskazovo	19	Ee	52.39N	41.57 E
Rassūa, Ostrov-	20	Kg	47.40N	153.00 E
Rassvet	20	Ee	57.00N	91.32 E
Ras-Tarf, Cap-	13	Ii	35.17N	3.41W
Rastatt	10	Eh	48.51N	8.12 E
Rastede	12	Ka	53.15N	8.12 E
Rastigaissa	7	Ga	70.03N	26.18 E
Råstojaure	7	Eb	68.45N	20.30 E
Ra's Ṭurunbī	24	Fj	25.40N	34.35 E
Rasūl	24	Pi	27.10N	55.30 E
Ra's Zayt	33	Fd	27.56N	33.31 E
Rat	40a	Bb	51.55N	178.20 E
Ratak Chain	57	Id	9.00N	171.00 E
Ratangarh	25	Ec	28.05N	74.36 E
Rätansbyn	7	De	62.29N	14.32 E
Rat Buri	25	Jf	13.32N	99.49 E
Rathbun Lake	45	Jf	40.54N	93.05W
Ráth Droma/Rathdrum	9	Gi	52.56N	6.13W
Rathdrum/Ráth Droma	9	Gi	52.56N	6.13W
Rathenow	10	Id	52.36N	12.20 E
Rathlin Island/Reachlainn	9	Gf	55.18N	6.13W
Ráth Luirc/An Ráth	9	Ei	52.21N	8.41W
Rathor, Pik-	18	If	37.55N	72.14 E
Rätikon	14	Dc	47.03N	9.40 E
Ratingen	12	Ic	51.18N	6.51 E
Rätische Alpen = Rhaetian Alps (EN)	14	Dd	46.30N	10.00 E
Rat Islands	38	Ad	52.00N	178.00 E
Ratlām	25	Fd	23.19N	75.04 E
Ratmanova, Ostrov-	20	Lc	35.45N	169.00W
Ratnāgiri	25	Ee	16.59N	73.18 E
Ratnapura	25	Gg	6.41N	80.24 E
Ratno	16	Dd	51.42N	24.31 E
Raton	43	Gd	36.54N	104.24W
Ratqh, Wādī ar-	24	Ie	34.25N	40.55 E
Ratta	20	Dd	63.35N	84.05 E
Rattlesnake Hills	46	Le	42.45N	107.10W
Rattray Head	9	Ld	57.38N	1.46W
Rättvik	7	Df	60.53N	15.06 E
Ratz, Mount-	38	Fd	57.23N	132.19W
Ratzeburg	10	Gc	53.42N	10.46 E
Raub	26	Df	3.48N	101.52 E
Rauch	56	Ie	36.46S	59.06W
Raucourt-et-Flaba	12	Ge	49.36N	4.57 E
Raudeberg	8	Ab	61.59N	5.09 E
Rauer Islands	66	Fe	68.51S	77.50 E
Raufarhöfn	7a	Ca	66.27N	15.57W
Raufjellet	8	Dc	61.15N	11.00 E
Raufoss	7	Cf	60.43N	10.37 E
Raukotaha	64n	Ac	10.28S	161.01W
Raukumara Range	62	Gc	38.00S	178.00 E
Rauland	8	Be	59.44N	8.00 E
Raúl Leoni, Represa- (Guri)	54	Fb	7.30N	63.00W
Rauma	7	Be	62.33N	7.43 E
Rauma/Raumo	7	Ef	61.08N	21.30 E
Raumo/Rauma	7	Ef	61.08N	21.30 E
Rauna	8	Kg	57.14N	25.39 E
Raunds	12	Bb	52.20N	0.32W
Raurimu	62	Fc	39.07S	175.24 E
Raurkela	22	Kg	22.13N	84.53 E
Rausu	28	Rb	44.01N	145.12 E
Rausu-Dake	29a	Da	44.06N	145.07 E
Rautalampi	8	Lb	62.38N	26.50 E
Ravahere Atoll	57	Mf	18.14S	142.09W
Ravan	14	Mf	44.15N	18.16 E
Ravanica, Manastir-	15	Ef	43.58N	21.30 E
Ravānsar	24	Le	34.43N	46.40 E
Ravanusa	14	Hm	37.16N	13.58 E
Rāvar	24	Qg	31.12N	56.53 E
Rava-Russkaja	16	Cd	50.13N	23.37 E
Ravels	12	Gc	51.22N	4.59 E
Ravelsbach	14	Jb	48.30N	15.50 E
Ravels-Poppel	12	Hc	51.27N	5.02 E
Ravenna [It.]	14	Gf	44.25N	12.12 E
Ravenna [Nb.-U.S.]	45	Gf	41.02N	98.55W
Ravensburg	10	Fi	47.47N	9.37 E
Ravenshoe	58	Ff	17.37S	145.29 E
Ravensthorpe	59	Ef	33.35S	120.02 E
Ravi	21	Jf	30.35N	71.49 E
Ravnina	19	Gh	37.57N	62.42 E
Rawaki Atoll (Phoenix)	57	Je	3.43S	170.43W
Rāwalpindi	22	Jf	33.35N	73.03 E
Rawa Mazowiecka	10	Qe	51.46N	20.16 E
Rawāndūz	24	Kd	36.37N	44.31 E
Rawdah	24	Ie	35.15N	41.05 E
Rawene	62	Ea	35.24S	173.30 E
Rawicz	10	Me	51.37N	16.52 E
Rawka	10	Qd	52.07N	20.08 E
Rawlinna	58	Dh	31.01S	125.20 E
Rawlins	43	Fc	41.47N	107.14W
Rawlinson Range	59	Fd	24.50S	128.00 E
Rawson [Arg.]	55	Bl	34.36S	60.04W
Rawson [Arg.]	53	Jj	43.18S	65.06W
Rawura, Ras-	36	He	10.20S	40.30 E
Raxaul	25	Gc	26.59N	84.51 E
Ray, Cape-	42	Lg	47.37N	59.19W
Raya, Bukit-	21	Nj	1.32S	111.05 E
Rayadrug	25	Ff	14.42N	76.52 E
Rayāt	24	Kd	36.40N	44.58 E
Rayleigh	12	Cc	51.35N	0.37 E
Raymond [Alta.-Can.]	46	Ib	49.27N	112.39W
Raymond [Wa.-U.S.]	46	Dc	46.41N	123.44W
Raymondville	43	Hf	26.29N	97.47W
Rayne	45	Jk	30.14N	92.16W
Rayón [Mex.]	48	Jg	21.51N	99.40W
Rayón [Mex.]	48	Dc	29.43N	110.35W
Rayones	48	Ie	25.01N	100.05W
Rayong	25	Kf	12.40N	101.17 E
Raysūt	23	Hf	16.54N	54.02 E
Raytown	45	Ig	39.00N	94.28W
Raz, Pointe du-	11	Bf	48.02N	4.44W
Razan	24	Me	35.23N	49.02 E
Razdan	16	Ni	40.28N	44.43 E
Razdelnaja	16	Gf	46.50N	30.05 E
Razdolinsk	20	Ee	58.25N	94.44 E
Razdolnaja	28	Kc	43.20N	131.49 E
Razdolnoje [R.S.F.S.R.]	28	Kc	43.33N	131.55 E
Razdolnoje [Ukr.-U.S.S.R.]	16	Hg	45.47N	33.30 E
Razgrad	15	Jf	43.32N	26.31 E
Razgrad [2]	15	Jf	43.32N	26.31 E
Razī	24	Mc	38.32N	48.08 E
Raziku/Raasiku	8	Ke	59.22N	25.11 E
Razlog	15	Gh	41.53N	23.28 E
Razo	32	Cf	16.37N	24.36W
Ré, Ile de-	5	Ff	46.12N	1.25W
Reachlainn	9	Gf	55.18N	6.13W
Reachlainn/Rathlin Island	9	Gf	55.18N	6.13W
Reachrainn/Lambay	9	Gh	53.29N	6.01W
Read	42	Gc	69.12N	114.30W
Reading [Eng.-U.K.]	9	Mj	51.28N	0.59W
Reading [Pa.-U.S.]	43	Lc	40.20N	75.55W
Real, Cordillera- [Bol.]	54	Eg	16.30S	68.30W
Real, Cordillera- [Ec.]	52	If	3.00S	78.00W
Real Audiencia	55	Cm	36.11S	58.35W
Real del Castillo	48	Aa	31.58N	116.19W
Realicó	56	He	35.02S	64.15W
Réalmont	11	Ik	43.47N	2.12 E
Reao Atoll	57	Nf	18.31S	136.23W
Reatini, Monti-	14	Gh	42.35N	12.50 E
Rebais	12	Ff	48.51N	3.14 E
Rebecca, Lake-	59	Ee	29.55S	122.10 E
Rebiana Oasis (EN) = Rabyānah, Wāḥāt al-	33	De	24.14N	21.59 E
Rebollera	13	Hf	38.25N	4.02W
Reboly	7	He	63.52N	30.47 E
Rebord Manamblen	37	Hd	24.05S	46.30 E
Rebun	28	Pb	45.23N	141.02 E
Rebun-Dake	29a	Ba	45.23N	141.01 E
Rebun-Suidō	29a	Ba	45.15N	141.05 E
Rebun-Tō	27	Pb	45.23N	141.10 E
Recalde	55	Bm	36.39S	61.05W
Recanati	14	Hg	43.24N	13.32 E
Recaş	15	Ed	45.48N	21.30 E
Recherche, Archipelago of the-	57	Dh	34.06S	122.45 E
Rečica	19	De	52.22N	30.25 E
Recife	53	Mf	8.03S	34.54W
Recife, Cape-	30	Jl	34.02S	25.45 E
Recke	12	Jb	52.23N	7.43 E
Recklinghausen	10	De	51.37N	7.12 E
Recknitz	10	Ib	54.14N	12.28 E
Recoaro Terme	14	Fe	45.42N	11.13 E
Reconquista	56	Ic	29.09S	59.39W
Recovery Glacier	66	Ag	81.10S	28.00W
Recreo	56	Gc	29.16S	65.04W
Recz	10	Lc	53.16N	15.33 E
Reda	10	Ob	54.38N	18.30 E
Redange	12	He	49.46N	5.54 E
Red Bank	44	Eh	35.07N	85.17W
Red Bay	42	Lf	51.44N	56.25W
Red Bluff	43	Cc	40.11N	122.15W
Red Bluff Reservoir	45	Ek	31.57N	103.56W
Redbridge, London-	12	Cc	51.35N	0.08 E
Red Butte	46	Ii	35.55N	112.03W
Redcar	9	Lg	54.37N	1.04W
Red Cliff	51c	Ab	17.05N	62.32W
Redcliff	37	Dc	19.02S	29.50 E
Redcliffe, Mount-	59	Ee	28.25S	121.32 E
Red Cloud	45	Gf	40.05N	98.32W
Red Deer	39	Hd	52.16N	113.48W
Red Deer [Can.]	42	Hf	52.55N	101.27W
Red Deer [Can.]	38	Id	50.56N	109.54W
Redding	39	Ge	40.35N	122.24W
Redditch	9	Li	52.19N	1.56W
Rede	9	Kf	55.08N	2.13W
Redenção	54	Kd	4.13S	38.43W
Redfield	43	Hc	44.53N	98.31W
Red Hill	65a	Ec	20.43N	156.15W
Red Hills	45	Gh	37.25N	99.25W
Redkino	7	Ih	56.40N	36.19 E
Red Lake	42	If	51.05N	93.55W
Red Lake	42	If	51.03N	93.49W
Red Lake River	45	Hc	47.55N	97.01W
Red Lakes	43	Ib	48.05N	94.45W
Redlands	46	Gi	34.03N	117.11W
Red Lodge	46	Kd	45.11N	109.15W
Redmond	43	Cc	44.17N	121.11W
Red Mountain [Ca.-U.S.]	46	Df	41.35N	123.06W
Red Mountain [Mt.-U.S.]	46	Ic	47.07N	112.44W
Red Oak	45	If	41.01N	95.14W
Redon	11	Dg	47.39N	2.05W
Redonda	50	Ed	16.55N	62.19W
Redondela	13	Db	42.17N	8.36W
Redondo	13	Ef	38.39N	7.33W
Redondo Beach	46	Fj	33.51N	118.23W
Redoubt Volcano	38	Dc	60.29N	152.45W
Red River [N.Amer.]	38	Jd	50.24N	96.48W
Red River [U.S.]	38	Jf	31.00N	91.40W
Red River (EN) = Hóng, Sông-	21	Mg	20.17N	106.34 E
Red River (EN) = Yuan Jiang [Asia]	21	Mg	20.17N	106.34 E
Red Rock, Lake-	45	Jf	41.30N	93.20W
Red Rock River	46	Id	44.59N	112.52W
Redruth	9	Hk	50.13N	5.14W
Red Sea (EN) = Aḥmar, Al Baḥr al-	30	Kf	25.00N	38.00 E
Redstone	42	Fd	64.17N	124.33W
Redstone	46	Da	52.08N	123.42W
Red Volta (EN) = Volta Rouge	30	Gh	10.34N	0.30W
Redwater Creek	46	Mb	48.03N	105.13W
Red Wing	43	Ic	44.34N	92.31W
Redwood City	46	Dh	37.29N	122.13W
Redwood Falls	45	Id	44.32N	95.07W
Ree, Lough-/Loch Rí	9	Fh	53.35N	8.00W
Reed City	44	Ed	43.53N	85.31W
Reedley	46	Fh	36.24N	119.37W
Reeds Peak	45	Cj	33.09N	107.51W
Reedsport	43	Cc	43.42N	124.06W
Reedy Glacier	66	Ng	85.30S	134.00W
Reef Islands	57	Hf	10.15S	166.10 E
Reefton	62	De	42.07S	171.52 E
Reepham	12	Db	52.45N	1.07 E
Rees	12	Ic	51.46N	6.24 E
Reese River	46	Gf	40.39N	116.54W
Refahiye	24	Hc	39.54N	38.46 E
Reforma, Río-	48	Ed	26.56N	108.12W
Reftele	8	Eg	57.11N	13.35 E
Reftinski	17	Jh	57.10N	61.43 E
Refugio	45	Hl	28.18N	97.17W
Refugio, Punta-	48	Cc	29.30N	113.30W
Rega	10	Lb	54.10N	15.18 E
Regar	19	Gh	38.34N	68.13 E
Regen	10	Jh	48.58N	13.08 E
Regen	10	Ig	49.01N	12.06 E
Regensburg	6	Hf	49.01N	12.06 E
Reggane	31	Hf	26.42N	0.10 E
Regge	12	Ib	52.26N	6.29 E
Reggio di Calabria	6	Hh	38.06N	15.39 E
Reggio nell'Emilia	14	Ef	44.43N	10.36 E
Reghin	15	Hc	46.46N	24.42 E
Regina [Fr.Gui.]	54	Hc	4.19N	52.08W
Regina [Sask.-Can.]	39	Id	50.25N	104.39W
Registan (EN) = Rīgestān	21	If	31.00N	65.00 E
Registro	55	Ig	24.30S	47.50W
Registro do Araguaia	55	Gb	15.44S	51.50W
Regnitz	10	Gg	49.54N	10.49 E
Regocijo	48	Gf	23.35N	105.11W
Reguengos de Monsaraz	13	Ef	38.25N	7.32W
Rehburg-Loccum	12	Lb	52.28N	9.14 E
Rehoboth [3]	37	Bd	23.50S	17.00 E
Rehoboth	37	Bd	23.18S	17.03 E
Reḥovot	24	Fg	31.54N	34.49 E
Reichelsheim (Odenwald)	12	Ke	49.43N	8.51 E
Reichenbach	10	If	50.37N	12.18 E
Reichshoffen	12	Jf	48.56N	7.40 E
Reichshoft	12	Jd	50.55N	7.39 E
Reichshoft-Denklingen	12	Jd	50.55N	7.39 E
Reidsville	44	Hg	36.21N	79.40W
Reigate	9	Mj	51.14N	0.13W
Reims	6	Gf	49.15N	4.02 E
Rein = Rhine (EN)	5	Ge	51.52N	6.02 E
Reina Adelaida, Archipiélago-	52	Ik	52.10S	74.25W
Reindeer	42	He	55.34N	103.10W
Reindeer Bank (EN)	51p	Ac	11.50N	62.05W
Reindeer Lake	38	Id	57.15N	102.40W
Reineskarvet	8	Cd	60.47N	8.13 E
Reinga, Cape-	62	Ea	34.25S	172.41 E
Reinhardswald	10	Fe	51.30N	9.30 E
Reinheim	12	Je	49.08N	7.11 E
Reinosa	13	Ha	43.00N	4.08W
Reisa	7	Eb	69.48N	21.00 E
Reitoru Atoll	57	Mf	17.52S	143.05W
Reitz	37	De	27.53S	28.31 E
Rejmyra	8	Ff	58.50N	15.55 E
Rejowiec Fabryczny	10	Te	51.08N	23.13 E
Reka Devnja	15	Kf	43.13N	27.36 E
Rekarne	8	Ge	59.20N	16.25 E
Reken	12	Jc	51.48N	7.03 E
Reliance	39	Ic	62.42N	109.08W
Relizane	32	Hb	35.45N	0.33 E
Remagen	12	Jd	50.34N	7.14 E
Remarkable, Mount-	59	Hf	32.48S	138.10 E
Rembang	26	Fh	6.42S	111.20 E
Remedios	49	Gi	8.14N	81.51W
Remedios, Punta-	49	Cg	13.31N	89.49W
Remedios, Río-	49	Mh	11.01N	69.15W
Remich	12	Ie	49.32N	6.22 E
Rémire	54	Hc	4.53N	52.17W
Remiremont	11	Mf	48.01N	6.35 E
Remire Reef	37b	Bb	5.05S	53.22 E
Remontnoje	16	Mf	46.33N	43.40 E
Remoulins	11	Kk	43.56N	4.34 E
Remscheid	10	De	51.11N	7.12 E
Rena	7	Cf	61.08N	11.22 E
Rena	8	Dc	61.08N	11.23 E
Renaix/Ronse	11	Jd	50.45N	3.36 E
Renana, Fossa-	5	Gf	48.40N	7.50 E
Renard Islands	63a	Ad	10.50S	153.00 E
Renaud Island	66	Qe	65.40S	66.00W
Rende	14	Kk	39.20N	16.11 E
Rendezvous Bay	51b	Ab	18.10N	63.07W
Rend Lake	45	Lg	38.05N	88.58W
Rendova Island	60	Fi	8.32S	157.20 E
Rendsburg	10	Fb	54.18N	9.40 E
Renfrew	42	Jg	45.28N	76.41W
Rengat	26	Dg	0.24S	102.33 E
Rengo	56	Fd	34.25S	70.52W
Reni	16	Fg	45.29N	28.18 E
Renko	8	Kd	60.54N	24.17 E
Renkum	12	Hc	51.58N	5.45 E
Renland	41	Jd	71.15N	27.20W
Renmark	58	Fh	34.11S	140.45 E
Rennell, Islas-	56	Fh	52.00S	74.00W
Rennell Island	57	Hf	11.40S	160.10 E
Rennes	6	Ff	48.05N	1.41W
Rennes, Bassin de-	11	Ef	48.05N	1.40W
Rennesøy	8	Ae	59.05N	5.40 E
Rennick Glacier	66	Kf	70.30S	161.45 E
Rennie Lake	42	Gd	61.10N	105.30W
Reno	39	Hf	39.31N	119.48W
Reno	14	Gf	44.38N	12.16 E
Renqiu	28	De	38.42N	116.06 E
Rensselaer [In.-U.S.]	44	De	40.57N	87.09W
Rensselaer [N.Y.-U.S.]	44	Kd	42.37N	73.44W
Renterria	13	Ka	43.19N	1.54W
Renton	46	Dc	47.30N	122.11W
Renwez	12	Ge	49.50N	4.36 E
Renxian	28	Cf	37.07N	114.41 E
Reo	26	Hh	8.19S	120.30 E
Repartimento, Serra do-	55	Jc	17.40S	44.50W
Répce	10	Ni	47.41N	17.02 E
Repino	8	Md	60.10N	29.58 E
Repong, Pulau-	26	Ef	2.22N	105.53 E
Reposaari/Räfsö	8	Ic	61.37N	21.27 E
Republic	46	Fb	48.39N	118.44W
Republican	38	Jf	39.03N	96.48W
Repulse Bay	39	Kc	66.32N	86.15W
Repulse Bay [Austl.]	59	Jd	20.35S	148.45 E
Repulse Bay [Can.]	42	Ic	66.20N	86.00W
Repvåg	7	Fa	70.45N	25.41 E
Requena [Peru]	54	Dd	5.00S	73.50W
Requena [Sp.]	13	Ke	39.29N	1.06W
Requin Bay	51p	Bb	12.02N	61.38W
Réquista	11	Ij	44.02N	2.32 E
Reşadiye Yarimadası	15	Km	36.40N	27.45 E
Reschenpass/Resia, Passo di-	14	Ed	46.50N	10.30 E
Resen	15	Eh	41.05N	21.01 E
Reserva	55	Gg	24.38S	50.52W
Reserve	45	Bj	33.43N	108.45W
Reševilovka	16	Ie	49.33N	34.05 E
Reshui	27	Hd	37.38N	100.30 E
Resia, Passo di-/Reschenpass	14	Ed	46.50N	10.30 E
Resistencia	53	Kh	27.30S	58.59W
Reşiţa	15	Ed	45.18N	21.55 E
Resko	10	Lc	53.47N	15.25 E
Reso/Raisio	7	Ff	60.29N	22.11 E
Resolute	39	Jb	74.41N	94.54W
Resolution	38	Mc	61.30N	65.00W
Resolution Island	42	Ld	61.35N	64.39W
Resolution Island	62	Bf	45.40S	166.35 E
Respublikai Soveth Socialisti Todžikiston/Tadžikskaja SSR [2]	19	Hh	39.00N	71.00 E
Respublika Sovetike Socialiste Moldovenjaske/Moldavskaja SSR [2]	19	Cf	47.00N	29.00 E
Ressa	16	Ib	54.45N	35.10 E
Ressons-sur-Matz	12	Ee	49.33N	2.45 E
Restigouche River	44	Na	48.04N	66.20W
Restinga de Sefton, Isla-	52	Hi	37.00S	83.50W
Restinga Sêca	55	Fi	29.49S	53.23W
Reszel	10	Rb	54.04N	21.09 E
Retalhuleu [3]	49	Bf	14.20N	91.50W
Retalhuleu	47	Ff	14.32N	91.41W
Retavas/Rietavas	8	Ii	55.43N	21.49 E
Retezatului, Munţii-	15	Fd	45.25N	23.00 E
Rethel	11	Ke	49.31N	4.22 E
Rethem (Aller)	12	Lb	52.47N	9.23 E
Réthinnon	15	Hn	35.22N	24.28 E
Retie	12	Hc	51.17N	5.05 E

Index Symbols

[1] Independent Nation
[2] State, Region
[3] District, County
[4] Municipality
[5] Colony, Dependency
Continent
Physical Region
Historical or Cultural Region
Mount, Mountain
Volcano
Hill
Mountains, Mountain Range
Hills, Escarpment
Plateau, Upland
Pass, Gap
Plain, Lowland
Delta
Salt Flat
Valley, Canyon
Crater, Cave
Karst Features
Depression
Polder
Desert, Dunes
Forest, Woods
Heath, Steppe
Oasis
Cape, Point
Coast, Beach
Cliff
Peninsula
Isthmus
Sandbank
Island
Atoll
Rock, Reef
Islands, Archipelago
Rocks, Reefs
Coral Reef
Well, Spring
Geyser
River, Stream
Waterfall Rapids
River Mouth, Estuary
Lake
Salt Lake
Intermittent Lake
Reservoir
Swamp, Pond
Canal
Glacier
Ice Shelf, Pack Ice
Ocean
Sea
Gulf, Bay
Strait, Fjord
Lagoon
Bank
Seamount
Tablemount
Ridge
Shelf
Basin
Escarpment, Sea Scarp
Fracture
Trench, Abyss
National Park, Reserve
Point of Interest
Recreation Site
Cave, Cavern
Historic Site
Ruins
Wall, Walls
Church, Abbey
Temple
Scientific Station
Airport
Port
Lighthouse
Mine
Tunnel
Dam, Bridge

Retourne 12 Ge 49.26N 4.02 E
Rétság 10 Pi 47.56N 19.08 E
Rettihovka 28 Lb 44.10N 132.45 E
Retz 14 Jc 48.45N 15.57 E
Retz, Pays de- 11 Eg 47.07N 1.58W
Réunion=Reunion (EN) 30 Mk 21.06S 55.36 E
Réunion=Reunion (EN) [5] 31 Mk 21.06S 55.36 E
Reunion (EN)=Réunion 30 Mk 21.06S 55.36 E
Reunion (EN)=Réunion [5] 31 Mk 21.06S 55.36 E
Reus 13 Nc 41.09N 1.07 E
Reusel 12 Hc 51.22N 5.10 E
Reuss 14 Cc 47.28N 8.14 E
Reut 16 Ff 47.15N 29.09 E
Reutlingen 10 Fh 48.29N 9.13 E
Reutte 14 Ec 47.29N 10.43 E
Revda [R.S.F.S.R.] 17 Ih 56.48N 59.57 E
Revda [R.S.F.S.R.] 7 Ic 67.57N 34.32 E
Revel 11 Hk 43.28N 2.00 E
Revelstoke 42 Ff 50.59N 118.12W
Revermont 11 Lh 46.27N 5.25 E
Revillagigedo 40 Me 55.35N 131.23W
Revillagigedo, Islas- 38 Hh 19.00N 111.30W
Revin 11 Ke 49.56N 4.38 E
Revoljucii, Pik- 18 Ie 38.33N 72.28 E
Revsundssjön 8 Fb 62.50N 15.15 E
Rewa 63d Bc 18.08S 178.33 E
Rewa 25 Gd 24.32N 81.18 E
Rewāri 25 Fc 28.11N 76.37 E
Rex, Mount- 66 Qf 74.54S 75.57W
Rexburg 43 Je 43.49N 111.47W
Rexpoëde 12 Ed 50.56N 2.32 E
Rey 23 Hb 35.35N 51.25 E
Rey, Arroyo del- 55 Ci 29.12S 59.36W
Rey, Isla del- 47 Ig 8.22N 78.55W
Rey, Laguna del- 48 Hd 27.00N 103.25W
Rey Bouba 34 Hd 8.40N 14.11 E
Reyes, Point- 46 Dg 38.00N 123.01W
Reyhanli 24 Gd 36.18N 36.32 E
Reykjalid 7a Cb 65.39N 16.55W
Reykjanes 5 Dc 63.49N 22.43W
Reykjanes Ridge (EN) 3 Dc 62.00N 27.00W
Reykjavik 6 Dc 64.09N 21.57W
Reynolds Range 59 Gd 22.20S 132.50 E
Reynosa 39 Jg 26.07N 98.18W
Reyssouze 11 Kh 46.27N 4.54 E
Rež 17 Kh 57.54N 62.20 E
Rež 17 Jh 57.23N 61.24 E
Rezé 11 Eg 47.12N 1.34W
Rezekne/Rēzekne 6 Id 56.30N 27.19 E
Rēzekne/Rezekne 6 Id 56.30N 27.19 E
Rezelm, Lacul- 15 Le 44.54N 28.57 E
Rezina 16 Ff 47.43N 28.58 E
Reznas, Ozero-/Rēznas Ezers 8 Lh 56.20N 27.30 E
Rēznas Ezers/Reznas, Ozero- 8 Lh 56.20N 27.30 E
Rezovo 15 Lh 41.59N 28.02 E
Rezvān 24 Qi 27.34N 56.06 E
Rezve 15 Lh 41.59N 28.01 E
Rgotina 15 Fe 44.01N 22.17 E
Rhaetian Alps (EN)=Alpi Retiche 14 Dd 46.30N 10.00 E
Rhaetian Alps (EN)= Rätische Alpen 14 Dd 46.30N 10.00 E
Rhallamane 30 Ff 23.15N 10.00W
Rhauderfehn 12 Ja 53.08N 7.34 E
Rhaunen 12 Je 49.51N 7.21 E
Rheda-Wiedenbrück 10 Ee 51.51N 8.18 E
Rheden 12 Ib 52.01N 6.01 E
Rheden-Dieren 12 Ib 52.03N 6.08 E
Rheider Land 12 Ja 53.13N 7.18 E
Rhein 12 Ke 49.52N 8.07 E
Rhein=Rhine (EN) 5 Ge 51.52N 6.02 E
Rheinberg 12 Ic 51.33N 6.36 E
Rheine 10 Dd 52.17N 7.27 E
Rheinfall 14 Cc 47.41N 8.38 E
Rheinfelden 10 Di 47.34N 7.48 E
Rheingaugebirge 12 Jd 50.05N 8.00 E
Rheinisches Schiefergebirge =Rhenish Slate Mountains (EN) 5 Ge 50.25N 7.10 E
Rheinland-Pfalz=Rhineland-Palatinate (EN) [2] 10 Cf 50.00N 7.00 E
Rheinsberg 10 Ic 53.06N 12.53 E
Rheinstetten 12 Kf 48.58N 8.18 E
Rhenen 12 Hc 51.58N 5.35 E
Rhenish Slate Mountains (EN)=Rheinisches Schiefergebirge 5 Ge 50.25N 7.10 E
Rheris 32 Gc 30.41N 4.57W
Rheydt, Mönchengladbach- 12 Ic 51.10N 6.27 E
Rhin=Rhine (EN) 5 Ge 51.52N 6.02 E
Rhine (EN)=Rein 5 Ge 51.52N 6.02 E
Rhine (EN)=Rhein 5 Ge 51.52N 6.02 E
Rhine (EN)=Rhin 5 Ge 51.52N 6.02 E
Rhine (EN)=Rijn 5 Ge 51.52N 6.02 E
Rhine Bank (EN) 56 Ji 50.30S 53.30W
Rhineland-Palatinate (EN)= Rheinland Pfalz [2] 10 Cf 50.00N 7.00 E
Rhinelander 43 Jb 45.38N 89.25W
Rhinluch 10 Id 52.50N 12.50 E
Rhino Camp 36 Fb 2.58N 31.24 E
Rhiou 13 Mi 35.59N 0.53 E
Rhir, Cap- 32 Fc 30.38N 9.54W
Rho 14 De 45.32N 9.02 E
Rhode Island [2] 43 Mc 41.40N 71.30W
Rhode Island Sound 44 Le 41.25N 71.15W
Rhodes (EN)=Ródhos 6 Ih 36.26N 28.13 E
Rhodes (EN)=Ródhos 5 Ih 36.10N 28.00 E
Rhodesia→Zimbabwe [1] 31 Jj 20.00S 30.00 E
Rhodes Peak 46 Hc 46.41N 114.47W
Rhodope Mountains (EN)= Rodopi 5 Ig 41.30N 24.30 E
Rhomara 13 Hi 35.10N 4.57W
Rhön 10 Gf 50.25N 10.05 E
Rhondda 9 Jj 51.40N 3.30W
Rhône 5 Gg 43.20N 4.50 E
Rhône [3] 11 Ki 46.00N 4.30 E
Rhône au Rhin, Canal du- 11 Lg 47.06N 5.19 E
Rhourd el Baguel 32 Ic 31.24N 6.57 E
Rhue 11 Ii 45.23N 2.29 E
Rhum 9 Ge 57.00N 6.20W
Rhyl 9 Jh 53.19N 3.29W
Riaba 34 Ge 3.24N 8.42 E
Riacho de Santana 54 Jf 13.37S 42.57W
Riangnom 35 Ed 9.55N 30.01 E
Riaño 13 Gb 42.58N 5.01W
Riánsares 13 Ie 39.32N 3.18W
Říčany 10 Kg 50.00N 14.39 E
Rias Altas 13 Da 43.30N 8.30W
Rias Bajas 13 Db 42.30N 9.00W
Riau [3] 26 Df 1.00N 102.00 E
Riau Archipelago (EN)= Riau, Kepulauan- 21 Mi 1.00N 104.30 E
Riau Kepulauan-=Riau Archipelago (EN) 21 Mi 1.00N 104.30 E
Riaza 13 Ic 41.17N 3.28W
Riaza 13 Ic 41.42N 3.25W
Ribadavia 13 Db 42.17N 8.08W
Ribadeo 13 Ea 43.32N 7.02W
Ribadesella 13 Ga 43.28N 5.04W
Ribagorza/La Ribagorça 13 Mb 42.15N 0.30 E
Ribamar 54 Jd 2.33S 44.03W
Ribas do Rio Pardo 55 Fe 20.27S 53.46W
Ribatejo 13 De 39.15N 8.30W
Ribáuè 37 Fb 14.57S 38.17 E
Ribble 9 Kh 53.44N 2.50W
Ribe 7 Bi 55.21N 8.46 E
Ribe [2] 8 Ci 55.35N 8.45 E
Ribécourt-Dreslincourt 12 Ee 49.31N 2.55 E
Ribeira [Braz.] 55 Hg 24.39S 49.00W
Ribeira [Sp.] 13 Db 42.33N 9.00W
Ribeira, Rio- 55 Ig 24.40S 47.24W
Ribeira Brava 32 Cf 16.37N 24.18W
Ribeira Grande 32 Bf 17.11N 25.04W
Ribeirão Prêto 53 Lh 21.10S 47.48W
Ribeirãozinho 55 Fc 16.22S 52.36W
Ribeiro Gonçalves 54 Ie 7.32S 45.14W
Ribemont 12 Fe 49.48N 3.28 E
Ribera 14 Hm 37.30N 13.16 E
Ribérac 11 Gi 45.15N 0.20 E
Riberalta 53 Jg 10.59S 66.06W
Ribnica 14 Ie 45.44N 14.44 E
Ribnitz-Damgarten 10 Ib 54.15N 12.28 E
Ricardo Flores Magón 48 Fc 29.58N 106.58W
Riccia 14 Ii 41.29N 14.50 E
Riccione 14 Gg 43.59N 12.39 E
Rice Lake 44 Hc 44.08N 78.13W
Rich 32 Gc 32.15N 4.30W
Richan 45 Jb 49.59N 92.49W
Richard Collinson Inlet 42 Gb 72.45N 113.00W
Richards 42 Ec 69.20N 134.35W
Richard's Bay 31 Kk 28.47S 32.06 E
Richardson 45 Hj 32.57N 96.44W
Richardson Mountains 38 Fc 66.00N 135.20W
Richard Toll 34 Bb 16.28N 15.41W
Richât, Guel er- 32 Ee 21.07N 11.24W
Richel 12 Ha 53.18N 5.10 E
Richel Griend 12 Ha 53.18N 5.15 E
Richelieu 11 Gg 47.01N 0.19 E
Richer 45 Hb 49.39N 96.28W
Richey 46 Mc 47.39N 105.04W
Richfield 43 Ed 38.46N 112.05W
Richibucto 44 Ob 46.41N 64.52W
Richland 43 Db 46.17N 119.18W
Richland Center 45 Ke 43.22N 90.21W
Richmond [Austl.] 59 Id 20.44S 143.08 E
Richmond [Ca.-U.S.] 43 Cd 37.57N 122.22W
Richmond [Eng.-U.K.] 9 Lg 54.24N 1.44W
Richmond [In.-U.S.] 43 Kd 39.50N 84.54W
Richmond [Ky.-U.S.] 43 Kd 37.45N 84.18W
Richmond [N.Z.] 62 Ed 41.21S 173.11 E
Richmond [S.Afr.] 37 Cf 31.23S 23.56 E
Richmond [Tx.-U.S.] 45 Il 29.35N 95.46W
Richmond [Va.-U.S.] 43 Lf 37.30N 77.28W
Richmond, Mount- 62 Ed 41.28S 173.24 E
Richmond Hill 44 Hd 43.52N 79.27W
Richmond Peak 51n Ba 13.17N 61.13W
Richthofen, Mount- 45 Df 40.29N 105.57W
Rickmansworth 12 Bc 51.38N 0.28W
Ricobayo, Embalse de- 13 Gc 41.35N 5.50W
Ridā' 33 Hg 14.25N 44.50 E
Ridderkerk 12 Gc 51.52N 4.36 E
Ridgecrest 46 Gi 35.38N 117.36W
Ridgway 44 He 41.25N 78.45W
Riding Mountain 45 Fa 50.55N 100.25W
Riecito, Rio- 50 Bi 6.50N 68.51W
Ried 12 Ke 49.50N 8.25 E
Ried im Innkreis 14 Hb 48.13N 13.30 E
Riedlingen 10 Fh 48.09N 9.28 E
Riemst 12 Hd 50.48N 5.36 E
Ries 10 Gh 48.55N 10.40 E
Riesa 10 Je 51.18N 13.18 E
Riesco, Isla- 56 Fh 53.00S 72.30W
Riesi 14 Im 37.17N 14.05 E
Riet 30 Jk 29.00S 23.53 E
Rietavas/Retavas 8 Ii 55.43N 21.49 E
Rietberg 12 Kc 51.48N 8.26 E
Rietbron 37 Cf 32.54S 23.09 E
Rietfontein [Nam.] 37 Cd 21.58S 20.58 E
Rietfontein [S.Afr.] 37 Ce 26.44S 20.01 E
Rieti 14 Gh 42.24N 12.51 E
Rif 30 Ge 35.00N 4.00W
Rifle 45 Cg 39.32N 107.47W
Rifstangi 7a Cb 66.32N 16.12W
Rift Valley [3] 36 Gb 0.30N 36.00 E
Rift Valley 30 Kh 0.30N 36.00 E
Riga/Rīga 6 Id 56.57N 24.06 E
Rīga/Riga 6 Id 56.57N 24.06 E
Riga, Gulf of- (EN)=Rīgas Jūras Līcis 5 Id 57.30N 23.35 E
Riga, Gulf of- (EN)=Riia Laht 5 Id 57.30N 23.35 E
Riga, Gulf of- (EN)=Rižski Zaliv 5 Id 57.30N 23.35 E
Rigachikum 34 Gc 10.38N 7.28 E
Rīgas Jūras Līcis=Riga, Gulf of- (EN) 5 Id 57.30N 23.35 E
Rigestān=Registan (EN) 21 If 31.00N 65.00 E
Riggins 46 Gd 45.25N 116.19W
Rigolet 42 Lf 54.10N 58.26W
Rig-Rig 35 Ac 14.16N 14.21 E
Rihand Sagar 25 Hd 24.05N 83.05 E
Riia Laht=Riga, Gulf of- (EN) 5 Id 57.30N 23.35 E
Riihimäki 7 Ff 60.45N 24.46 E
Riiser-Larsen-Halvøya 66 De 68.55S 34.00 E
Riito 48 Ba 32.10N 114.45W
Riječki zaljev = Rijeka, Gulf of- (EN) 14 Ie 45.15N 14.25 E
Rijeka 6 Hf 45.21N 14.24 E
Rijeka, Gulf of- (EN)= Riječki zaljev 14 Ie 45.15N 14.25 E
Rijksmuseum Kröller-Müller 12 Hb 52.06N 5.47 E
Rijn=Rhine (EN) 5 Ge 51.52N 6.02 E
Rijssen 12 Ib 52.18N 6.37 E
Rijswijk 12 Gb 52.03N 4.21 E
Rika 10 Th 48.08N 23.22 E
Rikā, Wādī ar- 33 He 22.25N 44.50 E
Rikubetsu 29a Cb 43.28N 143.43 E
Rikuzentakada 28 Pe 39.01N 141.38 E
Rila 15 Gh 42.08N 23.33 E
Rila 15 Gg 42.08N 23.08 E
Riley 46 Fe 43.32N 119.29W
Riley, Mount- 45 Ck 31.58N 107.05W
Rilski Manastir 15 Gg 42.08N 23.20 E
Rima 30 Hg 13.04N 5.10 E
Rimatara, Ile- 57 Lg 22.38S 152.51W
Rimava 10 Qh 48.15N 20.21 E
Rimavská Sobota 10 Qh 48.23N 20.01 E
Rimbo 7 Eg 59.45N 18.22 E
Rimé 35 Bc 14.02N 18.03 E
Rimforsa 8 Ff 58.08N 15.40 E
Rimini 14 Gf 44.04N 12.34 E
Rimito/Rymättylä 8 Jd 60.25N 21.55 E
Rîmnic 15 Kd 45.32N 27.31 E
Rîmnicu Sărat 15 Kd 45.23N 27.03 E
Rîmnicu Vîlcea 15 Hd 45.06N 24.22 E
Rimouski 39 Me 48.27N 68.32W
Rimše/Rimšė 8 Li 55.30N 26.33 E
Rimšė/Rimše 8 Li 55.30N 26.33 E
Rinbung 27 Ef 29.15N 89.52 E
Rincon 51 Bf 12.14N 68.20W
Rincón 51a Ab 18.21N 67.16W
Rincón, Bahia de- 51a Bc 17.57N 66.19W
Rincón del Bonete, Lago Artificial de- 56 Id 32.45S 56.00W
Rincón de Romos 48 Hf 22.14N 102.18W
Rindal 7 Be 63.03N 9.13 E
Ringe 8 Di 55.14N 10.29 E
Ringebu 8 Dc 61.31N 10.10 E
Ringerike 8 Dd 60.05N 10.15 E
Ringgold Isles 57 Jf 16.15S 179.25W
Ringim 34 Gc 12.09N 9.10 E
Ringkøbing [2] 8 Ch 56.10N 8.45 E
Ringkøbing 7 Bh 56.05N 8.15 E
Ringkøbing Fjord 7 Bi 56.00N 8.15 E
Ringládes 15 Dj 39.25N 20.04 E
Ringsjön 8 Ei 55.50N 13.30 E
Ringsted 7 Ci 55.27N 11.49 E
Ringvassøy 7 Eb 69.55N 19.15 E
Rinia 15 Ii 37.25N 25.13 E
Rinjani, Gunung- 26 Gh 8.24S 116.28 E
Rinn Chathóir/Cahore Point 9 Gi 52.34N 6.11W
Rinn Dúain/Hook Head 9 Gi 52.07N 6.55W
Rinteln 10 Fd 52.11N 9.05 E
Rinya 10 Nk 45.57N 17.27 E
Rio Azul 55 Gg 25.43S 50.47W
Riobamba 53 If 1.40S 78.38W
Rio Branco 53 Jf 9.58S 67.48W
Rio Branco 55 Fk 32.34S 53.25W
Rio Branco do Sul 55 Hg 25.10S 49.18W
Rio Brilhante 54 Hh 21.48S 54.33W
Rio Bueno 56 Ff 40.19S 72.58W
Rio Caribe 54 Fa 10.42N 63.07W
Rio Chico 50 Dg 10.19N 65.59W
Rio Claro [Braz.] 55 If 22.24S 47.33W
Rio Claro [Trin.] 50 Fg 10.18N 61.11W
Rio Colorado 56 He 39.01S 64.05W
Rio Cuarto 53 Ji 33.08S 64.20W
Rio de Janeiro 53 Lh 22.54S 43.15W
Rio de Janeiro [2] 54 Jh 22.30S 42.30W
Rio de Jesús 49 Gj 7.59N 81.10W
Rio de Oro 52 Ee 24.00N 14.00W
Rio de Oro 49 Ki 8.57N 73.23W
Rio de Oro, Bahia de- 32 De 23.45N 15.50W
Rio do Sul 56 Kc 27.13S 49.39W
Rio Fortuna 55 Hi 28.06S 49.07W
Rio Gallegos 53 Jk 51.37S 69.10W
Rio Grande 53 Ki 32.02S 52.05W
Rio Grande [Arg.] 56 Gh 53.47S 67.42W
Rio Grande [Nic.] 49 Dg 12.59N 86.34W
Rio Grande [P.R.] 51a Cb 18.23N 65.50W
Rio Grande City 45 Gm 26.23N 98.49W
Rio Grande de Añasco 51a Ab 18.17N 67.10W
Rio Grande de Manati 51a Bb 18.29N 66.32W
Rio Grande de Matagalpa 47 Hf 12.54N 83.32W
Rio Grande do Norte [2] 54 Ke 5.40S 36.00W
Rio Grande do Sul [2] 56 Jc 30.00S 54.00W
Rio Grande Rise (EN) 3 Cm 31.00S 35.00W
Riohacha 54 Dd 11.32N 72.54W
Rio Hato 49 Gi 8.23N 80.10W
Rio Lagartos 48 Og 21.36N 88.10W
Rio Largo 54 Ke 9.29S 35.51W
Riom 11 Ji 45.54N 3.07 E
Rio Maior 13 De 39.20N 8.56W
Rio Mayo 56 Fg 45.41S 70.16W
Riom-ès-Montagnes 11 Ii 45.17N 2.40 E
Rio Miranda 54 Gg 19.25S 57.20W
Rio Mulatos 54 Eg 19.42S 66.47W
Rion 15 Ek 38.18N 21.47 E
Rio Negro [Chile] 56 Ff 40.47S 73.14W
Rio Negro [Arg.] [2] 56 Gf 40.00S 67.00W
Rio Negro [Braz.] 56 Kc 26.06S 49.48W
Rio Negro [Braz.] 55 Dd 19.33S 56.32W
Rio Negro [Ur.] [2] 55 Dk 32.45S 57.20W
Rio Negro, Pantanal do- 54 Gg 18.50S 56.00W
Rionero in Vulture 14 Jj 40.56N 15.40 E
Rioni 16 Lh 42.10N 41.38 E
Rio Novo 55 Dc 16.28S 56.30W
Rio Pardo 56 Jc 29.59S 52.22W
Rio Prêto, Serra do- 55 Gd 18.18S 50.42W
Rio San Juan [3] 49 Eh 11.10N 84.30W
Rio Segundo 56 Hd 31.40S 63.55W
Riosucio 54 Cb 7.27N 77.07W
Rio Tercero 56 Hd 32.11S 64.06W
Rio Tinto 54 Ke 6.48S 35.05W
Rioverde 47 Dd 21.56N 100.01W
Rio Verde 54 Hg 17.43S 50.56W
Rio Verde, Serra do- 55 Fc 17.32S 52.25W
Rio Verde de Mato Grosso 54 Hg 18.56S 54.52W
Rio Verde do Sul 55 Ef 22.54S 55.27W
Rioz 11 Mg 47.25N 6.04 E
Řip 10 Kf 50.24N 14.18 E
Ripanj 15 De 44.38N 20.32 E
Ripley [Eng.-U.K.] 12 Aa 53.02N 1.24W
Ripley [Tn.-U.S.] 44 Ch 35.44N 89.33W
Ripley [W.V.-U.S.] 44 Gf 38.49N 81.44W
Ripoll 13 Ob 42.12N 2.12 E
Ripon 9 Lg 54.08N 1.31W
Riposto 14 Jm 37.44N 15.12 E
Ripple Mountain 46 Gb 49.02N 117.05W
Risan 15 Bg 42.31N 18.42 E
Risaralda [2] 54 Cb 5.00N 75.45W
Risbäck 7 Dd 64.42N 15.32 E
Rīshah, Wādī- 24 Kj 25.33N 44.05 E
Rī Shahr 24 Nh 28.55N 50.50 E
Rishiri 28 Pb 45.11N 141.15 E
Rishiri-Suidō 29a Ba 45.10N 141.30 E
Rishiri-Tō 27 Pb 45.11N 141.15 E
Rishiri-Yama 29a Ba 45.11N 141.15 E
Rishmūk 24 Ng 31.15N 50.20 E
Rishon Leziyyon 24 Fg 31.58N 34.48 E
Rising Star 45 Gj 32.06N 98.58W
Risle 11 Ge 49.26N 0.23 E
Risnjak 14 Ie 45.26N 14.37 E
Rišnov 15 Id 45.35N 25.27 E
Risør 7 Bg 58.43N 9.14 E
Risoux, Mont- 11 Mh 46.36N 6.10 E
Risøyhamn 7 Db 69.00N 15.45 E
Riß 10 Fh 48.17N 9.49 E
Risti 7 Fg 59.03N 24.01 E
Ristiina 8 Lc 61.30N 27.16 E
Ristijärvi 7 Gd 64.30N 28.13 E
Ristna, Mys-/Ristna Neem 8 If 58.55N 21.55 E
Ristna Neem/Ristna, Mys- 8 If 58.55N 21.55 E
Risū 24 Qf 33.52N 57.28 E
Ritchie's Archipelago 25 If 12.14N 93.10 E
Ritidian Point 64c Ba 13.39N 144.51 E
Ritscher-Hochland 66 Bf 73.20S 9.30W
Ritter, Mount- 43 Dd 37.42N 119.20W
Ritterhude 12 Ka 53.11N 8.45 E
Rituerto 13 Jc 41.36N 2.22W
Ritzville 46 Fc 47.08N 118.23W
Riva-Bella, Ouistreham- 12 Be 49.17N 0.16W
Rivadavia [Arg.] 56 Hb 24.11S 62.53W
Rivadavia [Arg.] 56 Gd 33.11S 68.28W
Riva del Garda 14 Ee 45.53N 10.50 E
Rivas 39 Kh 11.26N 85.51W
Rivas [3] 49 Eh 11.25N 85.50W
Rive-de-Gier 11 Ki 45.22N 4.37 E
Rivellata, Punta di a- 11a Aa 42.35N 8.40 E
Rivera [2] 55 Ej 31.30S 55.15W
Rivera [Arg.] 56 He 37.12S 63.14W
Rivera [Ur.] 53 Ki 30.54S 55.31W
River Cess 34 Dd 5.27N 9.35W
Riverdale 45 Fc 47.30N 101.22W
Riverina 59 Jg 35.25S 145.30 E
River Inlet 42 Ef 51.41N 127.15W
Rivers [2] 34 Ge 4.50N 6.30 E
Rivers, Lake of the- 46 Mb 49.45N 105.45W
Riversdale [N.Z.] 62 Cf 45.54S 168.44 E
Riversdale [S.Afr.] 37 Cf 34.07S 21.15 E
Riverside 43 De 33.59N 117.22W
Riverton [N.Z.] 62 Bg 46.21S 168.00 E
Riverton [Wy.-U.S.] 43 Fc 43.02N 108.23W
Rivesaltes 11 Il 42.46N 2.52 E
Riviera Beach 44 Ge 26.47N 80.04W
Rivière-à-Pierre 44 Kb 46.58N 72.11W
Rivière-du-Loup 42 Kg 47.50N 69.32W
Rivière-Pilote 51h Bc 14.29N 60.54W
Rivière-Salée 51h Bb 14.32N 60.59W
Rivoli 14 Be 45.04N 7.31 E
Rivungo 36 Df 16.15S 22.00 E
Riwaka 62 Ed 41.05S 173.00 E
Riwoqê 27 Ge 31.13N 96.29 E
Rixensart 12 Gd 50.43N 4.35 E
Riyadh (EN)=Ar Riyāḍ 22 Gg 24.38N 46.43 E
Rize 23 Fa 41.02N 40.31 E
Rize, Gora- 18 Bf 37.48N 58.13 E
Rize Dağları 24 Ib 40.30N 40.50 E
Rizhao 27 Kd 35.27N 119.28 E
Rizokarpásso → Dipkarpas 24 Fe 35.36N 34.23 E
Rižski Zaliv = Riga, Gulf of- (EN) 5 Id 57.30N 23.35 E
Rizzuto, Capo- 14 Ll 38.53N 17.05 E
Rjabovo 8 Md 60.17N 29.01 E
Rjapina/Räpina 8 Lf 58.03N 27.35 E
Rjazan 6 Je 54.38N 39.44 E
Rjazanovski 7 Ji 55.08N 39.35 E
Rjazanskaja Oblast [3] 19 Ee 54.30N 40.40 E
Rjažsk 6 Ke 53.43N 40.04 E
Rjukan 7 Bg 59.52N 8.34 E
Rjuven 8 Be 59.13N 7.10 E
Rkiz 32 Df 16.50N 15.20W
Rldal 8 Be 59.49N 6.48 E
Roa [Nor.] 8 Dd 60.17N 10.37 E
Roa [Sp.] 13 Ic 41.42N 3.55W
Road Town 47 Le 18.27N 64.37W
Roag, Loch- 9 Gc 58.16N 6.50W
Roan Antelope 36 Ee 13.08S 28.24 E
Roannais 11 Kh 46.05N 4.10 E
Roanne 11 Kh 46.02N 4.04 E
Roanoke 38 Lf 35.56N 76.43W
Roanoke [Al.-U.S.] 44 Ei 33.09N 85.22W
Roanoke [Va.-U.S.] 39 Lf 37.16N 79.57W
Roanoke Rapids 44 Ig 36.28N 77.40W
Roan Plateau 46 Kg 39.35N 108.55W
Roaringwater Bay 9 Dj 51.25N 9.30W
Roatán 49 De 16.18N 86.35W
Roatán, Isla de- 49 De 16.23N 86.30W
Robāṭ [Iran] 24 Qd 37.55N 57.42 E
Robāṭ [Iran] 24 Pg 30.04N 54.49 E
Robāṭ-e-Khān 23 Ic 33.21N 56.02 E
Robāṭ-e-Kord 24 Qf 33.45N 56.37 E
Robāṭ Karīm 24 Ne 35.28N 51.05 E
Robbie Bank (EN) 61 Fb 11.03S 176.53W
Robe, Mount- 59 If 31.40S 141.20 E
Röbel 10 Ic 53.23N 12.36 E
Robert Lee 45 Fk 31.54N 100.29W
Roberts 55 Bl 35.09S 61.57W
Roberts, Mount- 59 Ke 28.13S 152.28 E
Roberts Creek Mountain 46 Gg 39.52N 116.18W
Robertsfors 7 Ed 64.11N 20.51 E
Robert S. Kerr Lake 45 Ii 35.25N 95.00W
Robertson 37 Bf 33.46S 19.50 E
Robertson Bay 66 Kf 71.25S 170.00 E
Robertson Range 59 Ed 23.10S 121.00 E
Robertsport 34 Cd 6.45N 11.22W
Roberval 42 Kg 48.31N 72.13W
Robi 35 Fd 7.38N 39.52 E
Robinson Crusoe (EN) = Robinson Crusoe, Isla- 52 Ii 33.38S 78.52W
Robinson Crusoe, Isla- = Robinson Crusoe (EN) 52 Ii 33.38S 78.52W
Robinson Range 59 De 25.45S 119.00 E
Robinson River 59 Hc 16.03S 137.16 E
Roboré 53 Kg 18.20S 59.45W
Rob Roy 63a Cb 7.23S 157.36 E
Robson, Mount- 38 Hd 53.07N 119.09W
Robstown 45 Hm 27.27N 97.40W
Roby 45 Fj 32.45N 100.23W
Roca, Cabo da- 5 Fh 38.47N 9.30W
Rocamadour 11 Hj 44.48N 1.38 E
Roca Partida, Isla- 47 Be 19.01N 112.02W
Roca Partida, Punta- 48 Lh 18.42N 95.10W
Rocas, Atol das- 52 Mf 3.52S 33.49W
Roccaraso 14 Ii 41.51N 14.05 E
Ročegda 19 Ec 62.42N 43.23 E
Rocha [2] 55 Fk 34.00S 54.00W
Rocha 56 Jd 34.29S 54.20W
Rochdale 9 Kh 53.38N 2.09W
Rochechouart 11 Gi 45.49N 0.49 E
Rochedo 55 Ed 19.57S 54.52W
Rochefort [Bel.] 11 Ld 50.10N 5.13 E
Rochefort [Fr.] 11 Fi 45.56N 0.59W
Rochefort-Han-sur-Lesse 12 Hd 50.08N 5.11 E
Rochelle 45 Lf 41.56N 89.04W
Rocher River 42 Gd 61.23N 112.45W
Roche's Bluff 51c c 16.42N 62.09W
Rochester [Eng.-U.K.] 9 Nj 51.24N 0.30 E
Rochester [In.-U.S.] 44 De 41.04N 86.13W
Rochester [Mn.-U.S.] 43 Ic 44.02N 92.29W
Rochester [N.H.-U.S.] 44 Ld 43.18N 70.59W
Rochester [N.Y.-U.S.] 39 Le 43.10N 77.36W
Rochlitzer Berg 10 Ie 51.05N 12.48 E
Rocigalgo 13 He 39.35N 4.35W
Rockall 5 Ed 57.35N 13.48W
Rockall Rise (EN) 5 Ed 57.00N 14.00W
Rock Creek Butte 46 Fd 44.49N 118.07W
Rockefeller Plateau 66 Ng 80.00S 135.00W
Rockenhausen 12 Je 49.38N 7.50 E
Rockford 43 Jc 42.17N 89.06W
Rockglen 46 Mb 49.10N 105.57W
Rockhampton 58 Gg 23.23S 150.31 E
Rock Hill 43 Ke 34.55N 81.01W
Rockingham [Austl.] 59 Df 32.17S 115.44 E
Rockingham [N.C.-U.S.] 44 Hh 34.56N 79.46W
Rock Island 43 Ic 41.30N 90.34W
Rockland 43 Nc 44.06N 69.06W
Rocklands Reservoir 59 Ig 37.15S 142.00 E
Rockledge 44 Gk 28.20N 80.43W
Rockneby 8 Gh 56.49N 16.20 E
Rockport 45 Hl 28.01N 97.04W
Rock River 45 Kf 41.29N 90.37W
Rock Sound 44 Im 24.53N 76.09W
Rock Spring 44 Fc 41.35N 109.13W
Rocksprings 45 Fk 30.01N 100.13W
Rockville [In.-U.S.] 44 Df 39.45N 87.15W
Rockville [Md.-U.S.] 44 If 39.05N 77.09W
Rockwood 44 Eh 35.52N 84.41W
Rocky Ford 45 Eg 38.03N 103.43W
Rocky Island Lake 44 Fb 46.56N 83.04W
Rocky Mount 43 Ld 35.56N 77.48W
Rocky Mountain 43 Eb 47.49N 112.49W
Rocky Mountain House 42 Gf 52.22N 114.55W
Rocky Mountains 38 He 48.00N 116.00W
Rocky Point [Blz.] 49 Cd 18.22N 88.06W
Rocky Point [Nam.] 37 Ac 19.01S 12.29 E
Rocroi 12 Ge 49.55N 4.31 E
Rodach 10 Gf 50.08N 10.52 E
Rodalben 12 Je 49.14N 7.38 E
Roda Velha, Rio- 55 Ja 12.27S 45.33W
Rødberg 8 Cd 60.16N 8.58 E
Rødby 8 Dj 54.42N 11.24 E
Rødby Havn, Rødby- 7 Ck 54.39N 11.21 E
Rødby-Rødby Havn 7 Ci 54.39N 11.21 E
Roddickton 42 Lf 50.51N 56.07W
Rødding 8 Ci 55.22N 9.04 E

Index Symbols

[1] Independent Nation
[2] State, Region
[3] District, County
[4] Municipality
[5] Colony, Dependency
Continent
Physical Region
Historical or Cultural Region
Mount, Mountain
Volcano
Hill
Mountains, Mountain Range
Hills, Escarpment
Plateau, Upland
Pass, Gap
Plain, Lowland
Delta
Salt Flat
Valley, Canyon
Crater, Cave
Karst Features
Depression
Polder
Desert, Dunes
Forest, Woods
Heath, Steppe
Oasis
Cape, Point
Coast, Beach
Cliff
Peninsula
Isthmus
Sandbank
Island
Atoll
Rock, Reef
Islands, Archipelago
Rocks, Reefs
Coral Reef
Well, Spring
Geyser
River, Stream
Waterfall Rapids
River Mouth, Estuary
Lake
Salt Lake
Intermittent Lake
Reservoir
Swamp, Pond
Canal
Glacier
Ice Shelf, Pack Ice
Ocean
Sea
Gulf, Bay
Strait, Fjord
Lagoon
Bank
Seamount
Tablemount
Ridge
Shelf
Basin
Escarpment, Sea Scarp
Fracture
Trench, Abyss
National Park, Reserve
Point of Interest
Recreation Site
Cave, Cavern
Historic Site
Ruins
Wall, Walls
Church, Abbey
Temple
Scientific Station
Airport
Port
Lighthouse
Mine
Tunnel
Dam, Bridge

Rödeby 8 Fh 56.15N 15.36 E
Rodeio Bonito 55 Fh 27.28S 53.10W
Roden 12 Ia 53.09N 6.26 E
Rodeo [Arg.] 56 Gd 30.12S 69.06W
Rodeo [Mex.] 48 Ge 25.11N 104.34W
Rodeo [N.M.-U.S.] 45 Bk 31.50N 109.02W
Röder 10 Je 51.30N 13.25 E
Rodez 11 Ij 44.20N 2.34 E
Rodgau 12 Kd 50.01N 8.53 E
Rodholivos 15 Gi 40.56N 23.59 E
Ródhos = Rhodes (EN) 6 Ih 36.26N 28.13 E
Ródhos = Rhodes (EN) 5 Ih 36.10N 28.00 E
Rodi Garganico 14 Ji 41.55N 15.53 E
Roding 9 Nj 51.31N 0.06 E
Rodna 15 Hb 47.25N 24.49 E
Rodnei, Munţii- 15 Hb 47.35N 24.40 E
Rodney, Cape- 40 Fd 64.39N 166.24W
Rodniki 7 Jh 57.07N 41.48 E
Rodonit, Gjiri i- 15 Ch 41.35N 19.30 E
Rodonit, Kep i- 15 Ch 41.35N 19.27 E
Rodopi=Rhodope
Mountains (EN) 5 Ig 41.30N 24.30 E
Rodrigues Island 30 Nj 19.42S 63.25 E
Roebourne 59 Dd 20.47S 117.09 E
Roebuck Bay 59 Ec 18.04S 122.15 E
Roer 10 Be 51.12N 5.59 E
Roermond 11 Lc 51.12N 6.00 E
Roeselare/Roulers 11 Jd 50.57N 3.08 E
Roes Welcome Sound 42 Id 64.30N 86.45W
Roetgen 12 Id 50.39N 6.12 E
Rogačev 16 Gc 53.09N 30.06 E
Rogačevka 16 Kd 51.31N 39.34 E
Rogagua, Laguna- 54 Ef 13.45S 66.55W
Rogaguado, Laguna- 54 Ef 12.55S 65.45W
Rogaland [2] 7 Bg 59.00N 6.15 E
Rogaška Slatina 14 Jd 46.15N 15.38 E
Rogatica 14 Ng 43.48N 19.01 E
Rogatin 10 Ug 49.19N 24.40 E
Rogers 45 Ih 36.20N 94.07W
Rogers, Mount- 44 Gg 36.39N 81.33W
Rogers City 44 Fc 45.25N 83.49W
Rogers Lake 46 Gi 34.52N 117.51W
Rogers Peak 46 Jg 38.04N 111.32W
Rogersville 44 Fg 36.25N 82.59W
Roggan 42 Jf 54.24N 79.30W
Roggeveldberge 37 Bf 31.50S 19.50 E
Roggewein, Cabo- 65d Bb 27.07S 109.15W
Rognan 7 Dc 67.06N 15.23 E
Rogozhina 15 Ch 41.05N 19.40 E
Rogozna 15 Df 43.04N 20.40 E
Rogoźno 10 Md 52.46N 17.00 E
Rogue River 46 Ce 42.26N 124.25W
Rohan, Plateau de- 11 Df 48.10N 3.00W
Rohl 35 Dd 7.05N 29.46 E
Rohrbach in Oberösterreich 14 Hb 48.34N 13.59 E
Rohrbach-lès-Bitche 12 Je 49.03N 7.16 E
Rohri 25 Dc 27.41N 68.54 E
Rohtak 25 Fc 28.54N 76.34 E
Roi, Le Bois du- 11 Kh 46.59N 4.02 E
Roi Et 25 Ke 16.05N 103.42 E
Roi Georges, Iles du- 57 Mf 14.32S 145.08W
Roine 8 Kc 61.25N 24.05 E
Roisel 12 Fe 49.57N 3.06 E
Roja 7 Fh 57.30N 22.51 E
Rojas 56 Hd 34.12S 60.44W
Rojo, Cabo- [Mex.] 47 Ed 21.33N 97.20W
Rojo, Cabo- [P.R.] 49 Nd 18.01N 67.15W
Rokan 26 Df 2.00N 100.52 E
Rokiškis 7 Fi 55.59N 25.37 E
Rokitnoje 16 Ed 51.21N 27.14 E
Rokkasho 29a Bc 40.58N 141.21 E
Rokycany 10 Jg 49.45N 13.36 E
Rokytná 10 Mg 49.05N 16.21 E
Rola Co 27 Ed 35.25N 88.25 E
Rolândia 55 Gf 23.18S 51.22W
Rolla [Mo.-U.S.] 43 Id 37.57N 91.46W
Rolla [N.D.-U.S.] 45 Gb 48.52N 99.37W
Rolleston 62 Ee 43.35S 172.23 E
Rolvsøya 7 Fa 71.00N 24.00 E
Roma [Austl.] 58 Fg 26.35S 148.47 E
Roma [It.] = Rome (EN) 6 Hg 41.54N 12.29 E
Roma [Swe.] 7 Eh 57.32N 18.26 E
Romagna 14 Gf 44.30N 12.15 E
Romaine 42 Lf 50.18N 63.48W
Roman 15 Jc 46.55N 26.55 E
Romanche 11 Li 45.05N 5.43 E
Romanche Gap (EN) 3 Dj 0.10S 18.15W
Romang 55 Ci 29.30S 59.46W
Romang, Pulau- 26 Ih 7.35S 127.26 E
România=Romania (EN) [1] 6 If 46.00N 25.30 E
Romania (EN)=România [1] 6 If 46.00N 25.30 E
Romanija 14 Mg 43.51N 18.43 E
Roman Koš, Gora- 19 Dg 44.36N 34.16 E
Romano, Cayo- 49 Ib 22.04N 77.50W
Romanovka 20 Gf 53.14N 112.46 E
Romans-sur-Isère 11 Li 45.03N 5.03 E
Romanzof, Cape- 38 Cc 61.49N 166.09W
Romanzof Mountains 40 Kc 69.00N 144.00W
Rombas 12 Ie 49.15N 6.05 E
Romblon 26 Hd 12.35N 122.15 E
Rome [Ga.-U.S.] 43 Je 34.16N 85.11W
Rome [N.Y.-U.S.] 43 Lc 43.13N 75.28W
Rome [Or.-U.S.] 46 Ge 42.50N 117.37W
Rome (EN) = Roma [It.] 6 Hg 41.54N 12.29 E
Romeleåsen 8 Ei 55.34N 13.33 E
Romerike 8 Dd 60.05N 11.10 E
Romilly-sur-Seine 11 Jf 48.31N 3.43 E
Rommani 32 Fc 33.32N 6.36W
Romme 8 Fd 60.26N 15.30 E
Rommerskirchen 12 Ic 51.02N 6.41 E
Romney Marsh 12 Cc 51.02N 0.55 E
Romny 19 De 50.45N 33.29 E
Rømø 7 Bi 55.10N 8.30 E
Romodanovo 7 Ki 54.28N 45.18 E
Romont 14 Ad 46.42N 6.55 E
Romorantin-Lanthenay 11 Hg 47.22N 1.45 E
Romsdal 8 Bb 62.35N 7.50 E
Romsdalen 8 Bb 62.30N 7.55 E
Romsdalsfjorden 8 Bb 62.40N 7.15 E
Romsdalshorn 8 Bd 62.29N 7.50 E
Romsey 9 Lk 50.59N 1.30W
Ronas Hill 9 La 60.38N 1.20W
Ronave 64e Ba 0.29S 166.56 E
Roncador, Cayos de- 47 Hf 13.32N 80.03W
Roncador, Serra do- 52 Kg 13.00S 51.50W
Roncador Reef 57 Ge 6.13S 159.22 E
Roncesvalles 13 Ka 43.01N 1.19W
Roncesvalles o Ibañeta,
Puerto de- 13 Ka 43.01N 1.19W
Ronciglione 14 Gh 42.17N 12.13 E
Ronco 14 Gf 44.24N 12.12 E
Ronda 13 Gh 36.44N 5.10W
Ronda, Serrania de- 13 Gh 36.45N 5.05W
Ronda do Sul 55 Cb 15.57S 59.42W
Rondane 7 Bf 61.55N 9.45 E
Rønde 7 Ch 56.18N 10.29 E
Ronde, Point- 51g Ba 15.33N 61.29W
Ronde Island 50 Ff 12.18N 61.31W
Rondeslottet 8 Cc 61.55N 9.46 E
Rondon 55 Ff 23.23S 52.48W
Rondón, Pico- 54 Fc 1.36N 63.08W
Rondônia 53 Jg 10.52S 61.57W
Rondônia, Território de- [2] 54 Ff 11.00S 63.00W
Rondonópolis 53 Kg 16.28S 54.38W
Rong'an (Chang'an) 27 If 25.16N 109.23 E
Rongcheng 28 Ce 39.03N 115.52 E
Rongcheng (Yatou) 28 Gf 37.10N 122.25 E
Rongelap Atoll 57 Hc 11.09N 166.50 E
Rongerik Atoll 57 Hc 11.21N 167.26 E
Rongjiang (Guzhou) 27 If 25.58N 108.30 E
Rongxian 27 Jg 22.48N 110.30 E
Rongzhag/Danba 27 He 30.48N 101.54 E
Rønne 7 Di 55.06N 14.42 E
Ronne Bay 66 Qf 72.30S 74.00W
Ronneby 7 Dh 56.12N 15.18 E
Ronnebyån 8 Fh 56.10N 15.18 E
Ronne Ice Shelf 66 Qf 78.30S 61.00W
Ronse/Renaix 11 Jd 50.45N 3.36 E
Ronuro, Rio- 52 Kg 11.56S 53.33W
Roodepoort 37 De 26.11S 27.54 E
Roof Butte 43 Fd 36.28N 109.05W
Rooiboklaagte 37 Cd 20.20S 21.15 E
Roon, Pulau- 26 Jg 2.23S 134.33 E
Rooniu, Mont- 65e c 17.49S 149.12W
Roorkee 25 Fc 29.52N 77.53 E
Roosendaal 11 Kc 51.32N 4.28 E
Roosevelt [Az.-U.S.] 46 Jj 33.40N 111.09W
Roosevelt [Ut.-U.S.] 46 Kf 40.18N 109.59W
Roosevelt, Mount- 42 Ee 58.23N 125.04W
Roosevelt, Rio- 52 Jf 7.35S 60.20W
Roosevelt Island 66 Lf 79.30S 162.00W
Root Portage 45 Ka 50.53N 91.18W
Ropa 10 Rg 49.46N 21.29 E
Ropar 25 Fb 30.58N 76.20 E
Ropaži 8 Kh 56.58N 24.26 E
Ropczyce 10 Rf 50.03N 21.37 E
Rope, The- 64q Ab 25.04S 130.05W
Roper River 57 Ef 14.43S 135.27 E
Roquefort 11 Fj 44.02N 0.19W
Roque Pérez 55 Cl 35.25S 59.20W
Roquetas de Mar 13 Jh 36.46N 2.36W
Roraima, Monte- 52 Je 5.12N 60.44W
Roraima, Território de- [2] 54 Fc 1.30N 61.00W
Røros 7 Ce 62.35N 11.24 E
Rorschach 14 Dc 47.30N 9.30 E
Rørvik 7 Cd 64.51N 11.14 E
Ros 16 Ge 49.39N 31.35 E
Rosa, Cap- 14 Cn 36.57N 8.14 E
Rosa, Lake- 49 Kc 20.55N 73.20W
Rosa, Monte- 5 Gf 45.55N 7.53 E
Rošal 7 Ji 55.41N 39.55 E
Rosala 8 Je 59.50N 22.25 E
Rosalia 46 Gc 47.14N 117.22W
Rosalia, Punta- 65d Bb 27.03S 109.19W
Rosalie 51g Bb 15.22N 61.16W
Rosalind Bank (EN) 49 Ge 16.30N 80.30W
Rosamond Lake 46 Fi 34.50N 118.04W
Rosamorada 48 Gf 22.08N 105.12W
Rosana 55 Ff 22.36S 53.01W
Rosario [Arg.] 53 Ji 32.57S 60.40W
Rosario [Braz.] 54 Jd 2.57S 44.14W
Rosario [Mex.] 48 Dd 26.27N 111.38W
Rosario [Mex.] 47 Cd 23.00N 105.52W
Rosario [Par.] 56 Ib 24.27S 57.03W
Rosario [Ven.] 49 Kh 10.19N 72.19W
Rosario, Arroyo- 48 Bb 30.03N 115.45W
Rosario, Bahía- 48 Bc 29.50N 115.45W
Rosario, Cayo del- 49 Gc 21.38N 81.53W
Rosario, Islas de- 49 Jh 10.10N 75.46W
Rosario, Sierra del- 48 He 25.35N 103.50W
Rosario de Arriba 47 Ab 30.01N 115.40W
Rosario de la Frontera 56 Hc 25.48S 64.58W
Rosario de Lerma 56 Gb 24.59S 65.35W
Rosario del Tala 55 Ck 32.18S 59.09W
Rosario do Sul 56 Jd 30.15S 54.55W
Rosário Oeste 54 Gf 14.50S 56.25W
Rosarito 48 Bc 28.38N 114.04W
Rosarno 14 Jl 38.29N 15.58 E
Rosas/Roses 13 Pb 42.16N 3.11 E
Rosas, Golfo de-/Roses,
Golf de- 13 Pb 42.10N 3.15 E
Rosa Seamount (EN) 47 Bc 26.12N 114.58W
Rosa Zarate 54 Cc 0.18N 79.27W
Roščino 8 Md 60.13N 29.43 E
Roscoe Glacier 66 Ge 66.30S 95.20 E
Ros Comáin/Roscommon [2] 9 Eh 53.40N 8.30W
Ros Comáin/Roscommon 9 Eh 53.38N 8.11W
Roscommon 44 Ec 44.30N 84.35W
Roscommon/Ros Comáin 9 Eh 53.38N 8.11W
Roscommon/Ros Comáin [2] 9 Eh 53.40N 8.30W
Ros Cré/Roscrea 9 Fi 52.57N 7.47W
Roscrea/Ros Cré 9 Fi 52.57N 7.47W
Rose, Pointe de la- 51h Bb 14.33N 61.03W
Roseau [Dom.] 39 Mh 15.18N 61.24W
Roseau [Dom.] 51g Bb 15.18N 61.24W
Roseau [Mn.-U.S.] 45 Ib 48.51N 95.46W
Roseau [St.Luc.] 51k Ab 13.58N 61.06W
Roseau River 45 Hb 49.08N 97.14W
Rosebery 59 Jh 41.46S 145.32 E
Rosebud 46 Lc 46.16N 106.27W
Rosebud Creek 46 Lc 46.16N 106.28W
Rosebud River 46 Ia 51.25N 112.37W
Roseburg 43 Cc 43.13N 123.20W
Rosemary Bank (EN) 9 Cb 59.15N 10.10W
Rosenberg 43 Hf 29.33N 95.48W
Rosendahl 12 Jb 52.01N 7.12 E
Rosendahl-Osterwick 12 Jb 52.01N 7.12 E
Rosendal 7 Bf 59.59N 6.01 E
Rosenheim 10 Ii 47.51N 12.08 E
Rosental 14 Id 46.33N 14.15 E
Roses/Rosas 13 Pb 42.16N 3.11 E
Roses, Golf de-/Rosas,
Golfo de- 13 Pb 42.10N 3.15 E
Roseţi 15 Ke 44.13N 27.26 E
Roseto degli Abruzzi 14 Ih 42.41N 14.01 E
Rosetown 42 Gf 51.33N 108.00W
Rosetta (EN) = Rashid 33 Fc 31.24N 30.25 E
Roseville 46 Eg 38.45N 121.17W
Roshage 7 Bh 57.07N 8.38 E
Rosica 15 If 43.15N 25.42 E
Rosières-en-Santerre 12 Ee 49.49N 2.43 E
Rosignano Solvay 14 Eg 43.23N 10.26 E
Rosignol 54 Gb 6.17N 57.32W
Roşiori de Vede 15 He 44.07N 24.59 E
Roskilde [2] 8 Ei 55.35N 12.10 E
Roskilde 7 Ci 55.39N 12.05 E
Roslagen 8 He 59.30N 18.40 E
Ros Láir/Rosslare 9 Gi 52.17N 6.23W
Roslavl 19 De 53.58N 32.53 E
Roslyn 46 Ec 47.13N 120.59W
Ros Mhic Thriúin/New Ross 9 Gi 52.24N 6.56W
Røsnæs 8 Di 55.45N 10.55 E
Rosny-sur-Seine 12 Df 49.00N 1.38 E
Rösrath 12 Jd 50.54N 7.12 E
Ross 42 Ed 62.00N 132.25W
Ross [Austl.] 59 Jh 42.02S 147.29 E
Ross [Bye.-U.S.S.R.] 10 Uc 53.16N 24.29 E
Ross [N.Z.] 62 De 42.54S 170.49 E
Ross, Cape- 26 Gd 10.56N 119.13 E
Ross, Mount- 30 Nm 49.25S 69.08 E
Rossano 14 Kk 39.34N 16.38 E
Rossan Point/Ceann Ros
Eoghain 9 Eg 54.42N 8.48W
Ross Barnett Reservoir 45 Lj 32.30N 90.00W
Rosseau Lake 44 Hc 45.10N 79.35W
Rossel Island 57 Gf 11.26S 154.07 E
Rossell, Cap- 63b Ce 20.23S 166.36 E
Ross Ice Shelf 66 Lg 81.30S 175.00W
Rossijskaja Sovetskaja
Federativnaja
Socialističeskaja
Respublika (RSFSR) [2] 19 Jc 60.00N 100.00 E
Ross Island 66 Kf 77.30S 168.00 E
Ross Lake 46 Eb 48.53N 121.04W
Rossland 46 Gb 49.05N 117.48W
Rosslare/Ros Láir 9 Gi 52.17N 6.23W
Roßlau 10 Ie 51.53N 12.15 E
Rosso 31 Fg 16.31N 15.49W
Ross-on-Wye 9 Kj 51.55N 2.35W
Rossony 8 Mi 55.53N 28.49 E
Rossoš 19 De 50.11N 39.39 E
Ross River 42 Ed 61.59N 132.27W
Ross Sea (EN) 66 Lf 76.00S 175.00W
Røssvatn 7 Cd 65.45N 14.00 E
Røst 7 Cc 67.31N 12.07 E
Rosta 7 Eb 69.02N 18.40 E
Rostamī 24 Nh 28.52N 51.02 E
Rostan Kalā 24 Od 36.42N 53.27 E
Rösterkopf 12 Ie 49.40N 6.50 E
Rosthern 42 Gf 52.40N 106.20W
Rostock 6 He 54.05N 12.08 E
Rostock [2] 10 Ib 54.10N 12.10 E
Rostock-Warnemünde 10 Ib 54.10N 12.05 E
Rostov 19 Dd 57.13N 39.25 E
Rostov-na-Donu 6 Jf 47.14N 39.42 E
Rostovskaja Oblast [3] 19 Ef 47.45N 41.15 E
Roswell [Ga.-U.S.] 44 Eh 34.03N 84.22W
Roswell [N.M.-U.S.] 39 If 33.24N 104.32W
Rot 8 Fc 61.15N 14.02 E
Rota 13 Fh 36.37N 6.21W
Rota Island 57 Fc 14.10N 145.12 E
Rotenburg (Wümme) 10 Fc 53.07N 9.24 E
Rotenburg an der Fulda 10 Ff 50.59N 9.43 E
Roter Main 10 Hf 50.03N 11.27 E
Roth 10 Hg 49.15N 11.06 E
Rothaargebirge 10 Ee 51.05N 8.15 E
Rothenburg ob der Tauber 10 Gg 49.23N 10.11 E
Rother [Eng.-U.K.] 9 Nk 50.57N 0.45 E
Rother [Eng.-U.K.] 12 Bd 50.57N 0.22W
Rothera 66 Qe 67.46S 68.54W
Rotherham 9 Lh 53.26N 1.20W
Rothesay 9 Hf 55.51N 5.03W
Rothorn 14 Cd 46.47N 8.03 E
Rothschild Island 66 Qe 69.25S 72.30W
Rothwell 12 Bb 52.25N 0.48W
Roti, Pulau- 21 Ok 10.45S 123.10 E
Roti, Selat- 26 Hi 10.25S 123.25 E
Rotja, Punta- 13 Nf 38.38N 1.34 E
Rotnes 8 Dd 60.04N 10.53 E
Roto 59 Jf 33.03S 145.29 E
Rotoiti, Lake- 62 Ed 41.50S 172.50 E
Rotondella 14 Kj 40.10N 16.31 E
Rotondo, Monte- 11a Ba 42.13N 9.03 E
Rotoroa, Lake- 62 Ed 41.50S 172.40 E
Rotorua 61 Eg 38.09S 176.15 E
Rotorua, Lake- 62 Gc 38.05S 176.15 E
Rotselaar 12 Gd 50.57N 4.43 E
Rott 10 Jh 48.25N 13.20 E
Rottenburg am Neckar 10 Eh 48.28N 8.56 E
Rotterdam 6 Ge 51.55N 4.28 E
Rottnaälven 8 Ed 59.48N 13.07 E
Rottnen 8 Fh 56.45N 15.05 E
Rottneros 8 Ee 59.48N 13.07 E
Rottnest Island 59 Df 32.00S 115.30 E
Rottumerplaat 11 Ma 53.35N 6.30 E
Rottweil 10 Eh 48.10N 8.37 E
Rotuma Island 57 If 12.30S 177.05 E
Roubaix 11 Jd 50.42N 3.10 E
Roubion 11 Kj 44.31N 4.42 E
Roudnice nad Labem 10 Kf 50.26N 14.16 E
Rouen 6 Gf 49.26N 1.05 E
Rouergue 11 Ij 44.30N 2.56 E
Rouge, Rivière- 44 Jc 45.38N 74.42W
Rouillac 11 Fi 45.47N 0.04W
Roulers/Roeselare 11 Jd 50.57N 3.08 E
Roumois 11 Ge 49.30N 0.30 E
Roundup 43 Fb 46.27N 108.33W
Rousay 9 Jb 59.01N 3.02W
Roussillon 11 Ki 45.22N 4.49 E
Roussillon 11 Il 42.30N 2.30 E
Roussin, Cap- 63b Ce 21.21S 167.59 E
Routot 12 Ce 49.23N 0.44 E
Rouyn-Noranda 39 Le 48.14N 79.01W
Rovaniemi 6 Ib 66.30N 25.43 E
Rovenskaja Oblast [3] 19 Ce 51.00N 26.30 E
Rovereto 14 Fe 45.53N 11.02 E
Rovigo 14 Fe 45.04N 11.47 E
Rovinari 15 Ge 44.55N 23.11 E
Rovinj 14 He 45.05N 13.38 E
Rovkulskoje, Ozero- 7 Hd 64.00N 31.00 E
Rovno 6 Ie 50.37N 26.15 E
Rovnoje 16 Od 50.47N 46.05 E
Rovuma=Ruvuma (EN) 30 Lj 10.29S 40.28 E
Rowa, Iles- 63b Ca 13.37S 167.32 E
Rowley 42 Jc 69.05N 78.55W
Rowley Shoals 57 Cf 17.30S 119.00 E
Roxas [Phil.] 26 Gd 10.28N 119.30 E
Roxas [Phil.] 26 Hd 11.35N 122.45 E
Roxboro 44 Hg 36.24N 78.59W
Roxburgh 62 Cf 45.33S 169.19 E
Roxen 8 Ff 58.30N 15.40 E
Roxo, Cap- 30 Fg 12.20N 16.43W
Roy [N.M.-U.S.] 45 Di 35.57N 104.12W
Roy [Ut.-U.S.] 46 If 41.10N 112.02W
Roya 11 Nk 43.48N 7.35 E
Royal Canal 9 Gh 53.21N 6.15W
Royale, Isle- 43 Jb 48.00N 89.00W
Royal Leamington Spa 9 Li 52.18N 1.31W
Royal Society Range 66 Jf 78.10S 162.36 E
Royal Tunbridge Wells 9 Nj 51.08N 0.16 E
Royan 11 Ei 45.38N 1.02W
Royat 11 Ji 45.46N 3.03 E
Royaumont, Abbaye de- 12 Ee 49.17N 2.28 E
Roye 11 Ie 49.42N 2.48 E
Roy Hill 59 Dd 22.38S 119.57 E
Røyken 8 De 59.45N 10.23 E
Royston 9 Mi 52.03N 0.01W
Rožaj 15 Dg 42.51N 20.10 E
Rožan 10 Rd 52.53N 21.25 E
Rozdol 10 Ug 49.24N 24.08 E
Rozewie, Przylądek- 10 Ob 54.51N 18.21 E
Rožišče 16 Dd 50.54N 25.19 E
Rožňava 10 Qh 48.40N 20.32 E
Rožniatov 10 Uh 48.51N 24.14 E
Roznov 15 Jc 46.50N 26.31 E
Rožnov pod Radhoštěm 10 Og 49.28N 18.09 E
Rožnów 10 Qg 49.46N 20.42 E
Rožnowskie, Jezioro- 10 Qg 49.48N 20.45 E
Rozoy-sur-Serre 12 Ge 49.43N 4.08 E
Roztocze 5 Ie 50.30N 23.20 E
Rrësheni 15 Ch 41.47N 19.54 E
RSFSR=Russian SFSR (EN)
[2] 19 Jc 60.00N 100.00 E
RSFSR→Rossijskaja
Sovetskaja Federativnaja
Socialističeskaja
Respublika [2] 19 Jc 60.00N 100.00 E
Rtanj 15 Ef 43.47N 21.54 E
Rtiščevo 19 Ee 52.16N 43.52 E
Ruacana, Quedas- 30 Jj 17.23S 14.15 E
Ruahine Range 62 Gc 39.50S 176.05 E
Ruapehu 57 Ih 39.17S 175.34 E
Ruapuke Island 61 Ci 46.45S 168.30 E
Rua Sura 63a Ec 9.30S 160.36 E
Ruatahuna 62 Gc 38.38S 176.58 E
Rubbestadneset 8 Ae 59.49N 5.17 E
Rubcovsk 22 Kd 51.33N 81.10 E
Rubeho Mountains 36 Gd 6.55S 36.30 E
Rubeshibe 28 Qc 43.47N 143.38 E
Rubežnoje 16 Ke 48.59N 38.26 E
Rubi 36 Db 2.48N 23.54 E
Rubiataba 55 Hb 15.08S 49.48W
Rubiku 15 Ch 41.46N 19.45 E
Rubio 54 Db 7.43N 72.22W
Rubio 13 Ic 41.26N 3.47W
Ruby 40 Hd 64.44N 155.30W
Ruby Lake 46 Hf 40.15N 115.30W
Ruby Mountains 46 Hf 40.25N 115.35W
Ruby Range 46 Id 45.15N 112.15W
Rucăr 15 Id 45.24N 25.10 E
Rucava 8 Ih 56.10N 21.00 E
Ruciane Nida 10 Rc 53.39N 21.35 E
Ruda 10 Of 50.10N 18.18 E
Rudabánya 10 Qh 48.23N 20.38 E
Rūdak 24 Nh 35.51N 51.33 E
Rūdān 24 Qi 27.17N 57.13 E
Ruda Śląska 10 Of 50.18N 18.51 E
Rūdbār [Afg.] 23 Jc 30.09N 62.36 E
Rūdbār [Iran] 24 Md 36.48N 49.24 E
Rüdersdorf bei Berlin 10 Jd 52.27N 13.47 E
Rudesheim am Rhein 12 Je 49.59N 7.55 E
Rudiškes/Rūdiškės 8 Kj 54.30N 24.58 E
Rūdiškės/Rudiškes 8 Kj 54.30N 24.58 E
Rudki 10 Tg 49.34N 23.30 E
Rudkøbing 7 Ci 54.56N 10.43 E
Rudnaja-Pristan 20 Ih 44.25N 135.49 E
Rudničny 7 Mg 59.38N 52.29 E
Rudnik 15 De 44.08N 20.30 E
Rudnik [Bul.] 15 Kg 42.57N 27.46 E
Rudnik [Pol.] 10 Sf 50.28N 22.15 E
Rudnik [Yugo.] 15 De 44.08N 20.31 E
Rudnja [R.S.F.S.R.] 16 Nd 50.49N 44.36 E
Rudnja [R.S.F.S.R.] 19 De 54.57N 31.07 E
Rudno 10 Tg 49.44N 23.57 E
Rudny [Kaz.-U.S.S.R.] 19 Ge 52.57N 63.07 E
Rudny [R.S.F.S.R.] 28 Mb 44.28N 135.00 E
Rudolf, Lake-/Turkana,
Lake- 30 Kh 3.30N 36.00 E
Rudolstadt 10 Hf 50.43N 11.20 E
Rudong (Juegang) 28 Fh 32.19N 121.11 E
Rudozem 15 Hh 41.29N 24.51 E
Rūd Sar 23 Hb 37.08N 50.18 E
Rudyard 46 Jb 48.34N 110.33W
Rue 11 Hd 50.16N 1.40 E
Ruecas 13 Ge 39.00N 5.55W
Ruelle-sur-Touvre 11 Gi 45.41N 0.14 E
Rufā'ah 35 Ec 14.46N 33.22 E
Ruffec 11 Gh 46.01N 0.12 E
Ruffing Point 51a Db 18.45N 64.25W
Rufiji 30 Ki 8.00S 39.20 E
Rufino 56 Hd 34.16S 62.42W
Rufisque 34 Bc 14.43N 17.17W
Rufunsa 36 Ef 15.05S 29.40 E
Rugao 28 Fh 32.24N 120.34 E
Rugby [Eng.-U.K.] 9 Li 52.23N 1.15W
Rugby [N.D.-U.S.] 43 Gb 48.22N 99.59W
Rügen 5 He 54.25N 13.24 E
Rugles 12 Cf 48.49N 0.42 E
Ru He 28 Ch 32.55N 114.24 E
Ruhea 25 Hc 26.10N 88.25 E
Ruhengeri 36 Ec 1.30S 29.38 E
Rühlertwist 12 Jb 52.39N 7.06 E
Ruhner Berge 10 Hc 53.17N 11.55 E
Ruhnu, Ostrov-/Ruhnu
Saar 7 Fh 57.50N 23.15 E
Ruhnu Saar/Ruhnu, Ostrov- 7 Fh 57.50N 23.15 E
Ruhr 10 Ce 51.27N 6.44 E
Rui'an 27 Lf 27.48N 120.38 E
Ruichang 28 Cj 29.41N 115.38 E
Ruiena/Rūjiena 7 Fh 57.54N 25.17 E
Ruijin 27 Kf 25.59N 116.03 E
Ruili 27 Gg 24.03N 97.46 E
Ruiselede 12 Fc 51.03N 3.24 E
Ruiz 48 Gg 21.57N 105.09W
Ruiz, Nevado del- 54 Cc 4.54N 75.18W
Ruj 15 Fg 42.51N 22.35 E
Ruja/Rūja 8 Kg 57.38N 25.10 E
Rūja/Ruja 8 Kg 57.38N 25.10 E
Rujan 15 Eg 42.23N 21.49 E
Rujen 15 Fg 42.10N 22.31 E
Rūjiena/Ruiena 7 Fh 57.54N 25.17 E
Ruki 30 Ih 0.05N 18.17 E
Rukwa [3] 36 Fd 7.00S 31.20 E
Rukwa, Lake- 30 Ki 8.00S 32.15 E
Rūl Dadnah 24 Qk 25.33N 56.21 E
Rülzheim 12 Ke 49.10N 8.18 E
Ruma 15 Cd 45.01N 19.49 E
Rumaylah 35 Fc 12.57N 35.02 E
Rumbek 31 Jh 6.48N 29.41 E
Rumberpon, Pulau- 26 Jg 1.50S 134.15 E
Rum Cay 47 Jd 23.40N 74.53W
Rumes 12 Fd 50.33N 3.18 E
Rumford 44 Lc 44.33N 70.33W
Rumia 10 Ob 54.35N 18.25 E
Rumigny 12 Ge 49.48N 4.16 E
Rumija 15 Cg 42.06N 19.12 E
Rumilly 11 Li 45.52N 5.57 E
Rum Jungle 59 Gb 13.01S 131.00 E
Rummah, Wādī ar- 24 Ki 26.38N 44.18 E
Rumoi 27 Pc 43.56N 141.39 E
Rumphi 36 Fe 11.01S 33.52 E
Run 12 Hc 51.40N 5.20 E
Runan 28 Ci 33.00N 114.21 E
Runanga 62 De 42.24S 171.15 E
Runaway, Cape- 62 Gb 37.32S 177.59 E
Rundēni/Rundeni 8 Lh 56.14N 27.52 E
Rundeni/Rundēni 8 Lh 56.14N 27.52 E
Rundu 31 Ij 17.55S 19.45 E
Rungu 36 Eb 3.11N 27.52 E
Rungwa 31 Ki 6.57S 33.31 E
Rungwa 36 Fd 7.36S 31.50 E
Runmarö 8 He 59.15N 18.45 E
Runn 8 Fd 60.35N 15.40 E
Ruokolahti 7 Gf 61.17N 28.50 E
Ruoqiang/Qarkilik 22 Kf 39.02N 88.00 E
Ruo Shui 21 Le 40.20N 99.40 E
Ruotsalainen 8 Kc 61.15N 25.55 E
Ruotsinpyhtää/Strömfors 8 Ld 60.32N 26.27 E
Ruovesi 7 Ff 61.59N 24.05 E
Ruovesi 8 Kc 61.55N 24.10 E
Rupanco 56 Ff 40.46S 72.42W
Rupea 15 Ic 46.02N 25.13 E
Rupel 12 Gc 51.07N 4.19 E
Rupert 42 Jf 51.30N 78.48W
Rupert 46 Ie 42.37N 113.41W
Rupert, Baie de- 42 Jf 51.35N 79.00W
Rupert Coast 66 Mf 75.45S 141.00W
Rur 10 Be 51.12N 5.59 E
Rurrenabaque 53 Jg 14.28S 67.34W
Rurstausee 12 Id 50.38N 6.24 E
Rurutu, Ile- 57 Lg 22.26S 151.20W
Rušan 19 Hh 37.57N 71.31 E
Rusape 37 Ec 18.32S 32.07 E
Ruşayriş, Khazzān ar-=
Rusayris, Lake- (EN) 35 Ec 11.40N 34.20 E
Rusayris, Lake- (EN)=
Ruşayriş, Khazzān ar- 35 Ec 11.40N 34.20 E
Ruse 6 Ig 43.50N 25.57 E
Ruse [2] 15 If 43.50N 25.57 E
Ruşeţu 15 Ke 44.57N 27.13 E
Rushan (Xiacun) 28 Ff 36.55N 121.30 E
Rushden 12 Bb 52.17N 0.35W
Rushville 45 Kf 40.07N 90.34W
Rusk 45 Ik 31.48N 95.09W

Index Symbols

[1] Independent Nation
[2] State, Region
[3] District, County
[4] Municipality
[5] Colony, Dependency
Continent
Physical Region
Historical or Cultural Region
Mount, Mountain
Volcano
Hill
Mountains, Mountain Range
Hills, Escarpment
Plateau, Upland
Pass, Gap
Plain, Lowland
Delta
Salt Flat
Valley, Canyon
Crater, Cave
Karst Features
Depression
Polder
Desert, Dunes
Forest, Woods
Heath, Steppe
Oasis
Cape, Point
Coast, Beach
Cliff
Peninsula
Isthmus
Sandbank
Island
Atoll
Rock, Reef
Islands, Archipelago
Rocks, Reefs
Coral Reef
Well, Spring
Geyser
River, Stream
Waterfall Rapids
River Mouth, Estuary
Lake
Salt Lake
Intermittent Lake
Reservoir
Swamp, Pond
Canal
Glacier
Ice Shelf, Pack Ice
Ocean
Sea
Gulf, Bay
Strait, Fjord
Lagoon
Bank
Seamount
Tablemount
Ridge
Shelf
Basin
Escarpment, Sea Scarp
Fracture
Trench, Abyss
National Park, Reserve
Point of Interest
Recreation Site
Cave, Cavern
Historic Site
Ruins
Wall, Walls
Church, Abbey
Temple
Scientific Station
Airport
Port
Lighthouse
Mine
Tunnel
Dam, Bridge

Rusken 8 Fg 57.17N 14.20 E
Rusne/Rusnė 8 Ii 55.19N 21.16 E
Rusnė/Rusne 8 Ii 55.19N 21.16 E
Russel 42 Hb 73.55N 98.35W
Russell [Man. Can.] 42 Hf 50.47N 101.15W
Russell [Ks.-U.S.] 45 Gg 38.54N 98.52W
Russell [N.Z.] 62 Fa 35.16S 174.08 E
Russell Islands 60 Fi 9.04S 159.12 E
Russellville [Al.-U.S.] 44 Dh 34.30N 87.44W
Russellville [Ar.-U.S.] 45 Ji 35.17N 93.08W
Russellville [Ky.-U.S.] 44 Dg 36.51N 86.53W
Russel Range 59 Ef 33.25S 123.30 E
Rüsselsheim 10 Eg 50.00N 8.25 E
Russian River 46 Dg 38.27N 123.08W
Russian SFSR (EN) = RSFSR [2] 19 Jc 60.00N 100.00 E
Rust 14 Kc 47.48N 16.40 E
Rustavi 19 Eg 41.33N 45.02 E
Rustenburg 37 De 25.37S 27.08 E
Ruston 45 Je 32.32N 92.38W
Rutaki Passage 64p Bc 21.15S 159.48W
Rutana 36 Fc 3.55S 30.00 E
Rutanzige, Lac- = Edward, Lake- (EN) 30 Ji 0.25S 29.30 E
Rute 13 Hg 37.19N 4.22W
Ruteng 26 Hh 8.36S 120.27 E
Rutenga 37 Ed 21.15S 30.44 E
Rüthen 12 Kc 51.29N 8.27 E
Rutherfordton 44 Gh 35.22N 81.57W
Ruthin 9 Jh 53.07N 3.18W
Rutland 9 Mi 52.40N 0.40W
Rutland 44 Kd 43.37N 72.59W
Rutland 25 If 11.25N 92.10 E
Rutog 22 Jf 33.29N 79.42 E
Rutshuru 36 Ec 1.11S 29.27 E
Rutter 44 Gb 46.06N 80.40W
Rutul 16 Oi 41.33N 47.29 E
Ruutana 8 Kc 61.31N 24.02 E
Ruvo di Puglia 14 Ki 41.09N 16.29 E
Ruvu 36 Gd 6.48S 38.39 E
Ruvuma [3] 36 Ge 10.30S 35.50 E
Ruvuma 30 Lj 10.29S 40.28 E
Ruvuma (EN) = Rovuma 30 Lj 10.29S 40.28 E
Ruwayshid, Wādī 24 Hf 32.41N 38.04 E
Ruwer 12 Ie 49.47N 6.42 E
Ruya 37 Ec 16.34S 33.12 E
Ruyang 28 Bg 34.10N 112.28 E
Ru'yas, Wādī ar- 33 Cd 27.06N 19.24 E
Ruyigi 36 Fc 3.29S 30.15 E
Ruza 7 Ii 55.39N 36.18 E
Ruzajevka [Kaz.-U.S.S.R.] 17 Mj 52.49N 67.01 E
Ruzajevka [R.S.F.S.R.] 19 Ee 54.05N 44.54 E
Ružany 10 Ud 52.48N 24.58 E
Ružomberok 10 Pg 49.05N 19.18 E
Rwanda [1] 31 Ji 2.30S 30.00 E
Ry 8 Ch 56.05N 9.46 E
Ryan 45 Hi 34.01N 97.57W
Rybachi Peninsula (EN) = Rybači, Poluostrov- 5 Jb 69.45N 32.35 E
Rybači 8 Ii 55.09N 20.45 E
Rybači, Poluostrov- = Rybachi Peninsula (EN) 5 Jb 69.45N 32.35 E
Rybačje 19 Hg 42.28N 76.11 E
Rybinsk 6 Jd 58.03N 38.52 E
Rybinskoje Vodohranilišče = Rybinsk Reservoir (EN) 5 Jd 58.30N 38.25 E
Rybinsk Reservoir (EN) = Rybinskoje Vodohranilišče 5 Jd 58.30N 38.25 E
Rybnica 16 Ff 47.45N 29.01 E
Rybnik 10 Of 50.06N 18.32 E
Rybnoje 19 De 54.46N 39.33 E
Rybnovsk 20 Jf 53.15N 141.55 E
Rychnov nad Kněžnou 10 Mf 50.10N 16.17 E
Rychwał 10 Od 52.05N 18.09 E
Ryd 8 Fh 56.28N 14.41 E
Rydaholm 8 Fh 56.59N 14.16 E
Ryde 12 Ad 50.43N 1.10W
Rye 9 Mg 54.10N 0.45W
Rye 9 Nk 50.57N 0.44 E
Rye Bay 12 Cd 50.55N 0.48 E
Ryegate 46 Kc 46.18N 109.15W
Rye Patch Reservoir 46 Ff 40.38N 118.18W
Ryes 12 Be 49.19N 0.37W
Ryfylke 8 Be 59.30N 6.30 E
Ryki 10 Re 51.39N 21.56 E
Rylsk 19 De 51.36N 34.43 E
Rymanów 10 Rg 49.34N 21.53 E
Rymättylä/Rimito 8 Jd 60.25N 21.55 E
Ryn 10 Rc 53.56N 21.33 E
Ryńskie, Jezioro- 10 Rc 53.53N 21.30 E
Ryōhaku-Sanchi 29 Ec 36.05N 136.45 E
Ryōsō-Yosui 29 Gd 35.22N 140.25 E
Ryōtsu 28 Oe 38.05N 138.26 E
Ryōtsu-Wan 29 Fb 38.10N 138.30 E
Ryō-Zen 29 Gc 37.46N 140.41 E
Rypin 10 Pc 53.05N 19.25 E
Ryškany 16 Ef 47.57N 27.32 E
Ryssby 8 Fh 56.52N 14.10 E
Rytterknægten 8 Fi 55.06N 14.54 E
Ryūgasaki 29 Gd 35.54N 140.10 E
Ryukyu Islands (EN) = Nansei-Shotō 21 Og 26.30N 128.00 E
Ryūkyū-Shotō 27 Mf 25.30N 126.30 E
Ryukyu Trench (EN) 3 Ig 25.45N 128.00 E
Rzepin 10 Kd 52.22N 14.50 E
Rzeszów 6 Ie 50.03N 22.00 E
Rzeszów [2] 10 Rf 50.05N 22.00 E
Ržev 6 Jd 56.16N 34.20 E

S

Šaa, Gora- 16 Nh 42.39N 44.43 E
Sa'ādatābād [Iran] 24 Ph 28.02N 55.50 E
Sa'ādatābād [Iran] 24 Og 30.08N 52.38 E
Sa'ādatābād [Iran] 24 Og 30.06N 53.08 E
Sääksjarvi 8 Jc 61.24N 22.24 E
Saalbach 12 Ke 49.15N 8.27 E
Saale 10 He 51.57N 11.55 E
Saaler Bodden 10 Ib 54.20N 12.28 E
Saalfeld 10 Hf 50.39N 11.22 E
Saalfelden am Steinernen Meer 14 Gc 47.25N 12.51 E
Saaminki 8 Mc 61.52N 28.50 E
Saâne 12 Ce 49.54N 0.56 E
Saane 14 Bd 46.59N 7.16 E
Saanen 14 Bd 46.30N 7.15 E
Saar 10 Cg 49.42N 6.34 E
Saar-Bergland 12 Ie 49.27N 6.45 E
Saarbrücken 6 Gf 49.14N 7.00 E
Saarbrücken-Dudweiler 12 Je 49.17N 7.02 E
Saarburg 10 Cg 49.36N 6.33 E
Sääre/Sjare 8 Ig 57.57N 21.53 E
Saaremaa/Sarema 5 Id 58.25N 22.30 E
Saarijärvi 7 Fe 62.43N 25.16 E
Saaristomeri 8 Id 60.20N 21.10 E
Saarland [2] 10 Cg 49.20N 7.00 E
Saarlouis 10 Cg 49.19N 6.45 E
Šaartuz 19 Gh 37.16N 68.06 E
Saarwellingen 12 Ie 49.21N 6.49 E
Saas Fee 14 Bd 46.07N 7.55 E
Saatly 16 Pj 39.57N 48.26 E
Saavedra 55 Am 37.45S 62.22W
Sab, Tônlé- 25 Kf 11.34N 104.57 E
Saba 47 Le 17.38N 63.10W
Saba 8 Me 59.05N 29.10 E
Saba Bank (EN) 50 Ed 17.30N 63.30W
Šabac 15 Ce 44.45N 19.43 E
Sabadell 13 Oc 41.33N 2.06 E
Sabae 28 Ng 35.57N 136.11 E
Sabah [2] 26 Ge 5.30N 117.00 E
Sab'ah, Qārat as- 33 Cd 27.20N 17.10 E
Sabak Bernam 26 Df 3.46N 100.59 E
Sabalān, Kūhhā-ye- 21 Gf 38.15N 47.49 E
Sab'ān 24 Ii 27.04N 41.58 E
Sabana, Archipiélago de- 49 Hb 22.30N 79.00W
Sabana de la Mar 49 Md 19.04N 69.23W
Sabanagrande 49 Dg 13.50N 87.15W
Sabanalarga 54 Da 10.38N 74.56W
Sabancuy 48 Nh 18.58N 91.11W
Sabaneta 49 Ld 19.12N 70.58W
Sabaneta, Puntan- 64b Ba 15.17N 145.49 E
Sabang [Indon.] 26 Gf 0.11N 119.51 E
Sabang [Indon.] 26 Ce 5.55N 95.19 E
Şabanözü 24 Eb 40.29N 33.18 E
Săbăoani 15 Jb 47.01N 26.51 E
Sabarei 36 Gb 4.20N 36.55 E
Sab'Atayn, Ramlat as- 33 If 15.30N 46.10 E
Sabatini, Monti- 14 Gh 42.10N 12.15 E
Sabaudia 14 Hi 41.18N 13.01 E
Sabaudia, Lago di- 14 Hi 41.15N 13.05 E
Şabbāgh, Jabal- 24 Fh 28.12N 34.04 E
Sab 'Bi 'Ār 24 Gf 33.46N 37.41 E
Sabbioneta 14 Ee 45.00N 10.39 E
Sa Bec 25 Lf 10.18N 105.46 E
Sabhā [3] 33 Bd 26.00N 14.00 E
Sabhā 31 If 27.02N 14.26 E
Şabḥā 24 Gf 32.20N 36.30 E
Sābhā, Wāḥāt- = Sebha Oasis (EN) 30 If 27.00N 14.25 E
Sabi 30 Kk 21.00S 35.02 E
Sabidana, Jabal- 35 Fb 18.04N 36.50 E
Sabile 8 Jg 57.05N 22.29 E
Sabina 14 Gh 42.20N 12.45 E
Sabinal 48 Fb 30.57N 107.30W
Sabinal, Peninsula de- 49 Ic 21.40N 77.18W
Sabiñánigo 13 Lb 42.31N 0.22W
Sabinas 47 Dc 27.51N 101.07W
Sabinas, Rio- 48 Id 27.37N 100.42W
Sabinas Hidalgo 47 Dc 26.30N 100.10W
Sabine Lake 45 Jl 29.50N 93.50W
Sabine Pass 45 Jl 29.44N 93.52W
Sabine Peninsula 42 Ga 76.25N 109.50W
Sabine River 43 Ie 30.00N 93.45W
Sabini, Monti- 14 Gh 42.15N 12.50 E
Şabir, Jabal- 23 Fg 13.30N 44.03 E
Sabirabad 16 Pj 39.59N 48.29 E
Šabla 15 Lf 43.32N 28.32 E
Sable, Anse de- 51e b 16.07N 61.34W
Sable, Cape- [Can.] 38 Me 43.25N 65.35W
Sable, Cape- [U.S.] 38 Kg 25.12N 81.05W
Sable, Ile de- 57 Gf 19.15S 159.56 E
Sable Island 38 Ne 43.55N 59.55W
Sablé-sur-Sarthe 11 Fg 47.50N 0.20W
Sablūkah, Ash Shallāl as- = Sixth Cataract (EN) 30 Kg 16.20N 32.42 E
Sabonetau, Serra da- 55 Kb 15.20S 43.50W
Sabonkafi 34 Gc 14.38N 8.45 E
Sabór 13 Ec 41.10N 7.07W
Şabrātah 33 Bc 32.47N 12.29 E
Sabres 11 Fj 44.09N 0.44W
Sabrina Coast 66 He 67.00S 119.30 E
Sabtang 26 Hb 20.19N 121.52 E
Sabunči 16 Pi 40.27N 49.57 E
Şabyā 23 Ff 17.09N 42.37 E
Sabzevār 22 Hf 36.13N 57.42 E
Saca, Vîrful- 15 Ic 46.30N 25.15 E
Sacajawea Peak 43 Db 45.15N 117.17W
Sacalin, Insula- 15 Me 44.50N 29.39 E
Sacandica 36 Cd 5.58S 15.56 E
Sacatepéquez [3] 49 Bf 14.35N 90.45W
Sacavém 13 Cf 38.46N 9.05W
Sac City 45 Ie 42.25N 95.00W
Sacco 14 Hi 41.31N 13.32 E
Sacedón 13 Jd 40.29N 2.43W
Săcel 15 Hb 47.38N 24.26 E
Săcele 15 Id 45.37N 25.41 E
Sachayoj 55 Bh 26.41S 61.50W
Sačhere 16 Mh 42.20N 43.22 E
Sachigo 42 Ie 55.05N 89.00W
Sachsen = Saxony (EN) 10 Jf 51.00N 13.30 E
Sachsenhagen 12 Lb 52.24N 9.16 E
Sachs Harbour 42 Eb 72.00N 125.08W
Šack [R.S.F.S.R.] 7 Ji 54.04N 41.42 E
Šack [Ukr.-U.S.S.R.] 10 Je 51.30N 24.00 E
Sackets Harbor 44 Id 43.57N 76.07W
Saco [Me.-U.S.] 44 Ld 43.29N 70.28W
Saco [Mt.-U.S.] 46 Lb 48.28N 107.21W
Sacramento 38 Gf 38.03N 121.56W
Sacramento [Braz.] 54 Ig 19.53S 47.27W
Sacramento [Ca.-U.S.] 39 Gf 38.35N 121.30W
Sacramento, Pampa del- 54 Ce 8.00S 75.50W
Sacramento Mountains 38 If 33.10N 105.50W
Sacramento Valley 43 Cd 39.15N 122.00W
Sacre ou Timalacia, Rio- 55 Ca 13.55S 58.02W
Săcueni 15 Fb 47.21N 22.06 E
Sacuriuiná ou Ponte de Pedra, Rio- 55 Da 13.58S 57.18W
Sádaba 13 Kb 42.17N 1.16W
Sa'dābād 24 Nh 29.23N 51.07 E
Şa'dah 22 Gh 16.57N 43.44 E
Sada-Misaki 29b Ce 33.22N 132.01 E
Sada-Misaki-Hantō 29 Ce 33.25N 132.15 E
Sadani 36 Gd 6.03S 38.47 E
Sadao 25 Kg 6.39N 100.31 E
Sadd al 'Ālī 33 Fe 23.54N 32.52 E
Saddle Mountains 46 Fc 46.50N 119.55W
Saddle Peak [India] 25 If 13.09N 93.01 E
Saddle Peak [Mt.-U.S.] 46 Jd 45.57N 110.58W
Sad-e Eskandar 24 Pd 37.10N 55.00 E
Sadiya 25 Jc 27.50N 95.40 E
Sa'diyah, Hawr as- 24 Lf 32.00N 46.45 E
Sad Kharv 24 Qd 36.19N 57.05 E
Sado 13 Df 38.29N 8.55W
Sado-Kaikyō 29 Fc 37.55N 138.40 E
Sado-Shima 21 Pf 38.00N 138.25 E
Sadowara 29 Be 32.04N 131.26 E
Šadrinsk 19 Gd 56.05N 63.38 E
Saeby 7 Ch 57.20N 10.32 E
Saeh, Teluk- 26 Gh 8.00S 117.30 E
Saengcheon 28 Ie 39.55N 126.34 E
Saerbeck 12 Jb 52.11N 7.38 E
Şafājah 24 Hi 26.30N 39.30 E
Safājah, Jazīrat- 24 Ei 26.45N 33.59 E
Safané 34 Ec 12.08N 3.13W
Şafāqis = Sfax (EN) [3] 32 Jc 34.30N 10.30 E
Şafāqis = Sfax (EN) 31 Ie 34.44N 10.46 E
Safata Harbour 65c Bb 14.00S 171.50W
Saffānīyah, Ra's as- 23 Gd 27.59N 48.37 E
Säffle 7 Cg 59.08N 12.56 E
Safford 43 Fe 32.50N 109.43W
Saffron Walden 9 Ni 52.01N 0.15 E
Safi 31 Ge 32.18N 9.14W
Safi [3] 32 Fc 31.55N 9.00W
Safia, Hamâda- 34 Ea 23.10N 4.15W
Şafīābād 24 Qd 36.45N 57.58 E
Safid 23 Hb 37.23N 50.11 E
Safid, Kūh-e 24 Lf 33.55N 47.30 E
Safid Kūh, Salseleh-ye- 21 Jc 34.30N 63.30 E
Safonovo [R.S.F.S.R.] 19 Dd 55.06N 33.14 E
Safonovo [R.S.F.S.R.] 7 Ld 65.41N 47.43 E
Şafrā' al Asyāḥ 24 Ji 26.50N 43.57 E
Şafrā' as Sark 24 Kj 25.25N 44.20 E
Safranbolu 24 Eb 41.15N 32.42 E
Şafwān 24 Lg 30.07N 47.43 E
Saga [Jap.] 27 Ne 33.15N 130.18 E
Saga [Jap.] 29 Ce 33.05N 133.06 E
Saga [Kaz.-U.S.S.R.] 19 Fe 50.30N 64.14 E
Saga (Gya'gya) 27 Ef 29.22N 85.15 E
Sagae 29 Gb 38.22N 140.17 E
Sagaing [3] 25 Jd 23.30N 95.30 E
Sagaing 25 Jd 21.52N 95.59 E
Saga Ken [2] 28 Kh 33.15N 130.15 E
Sagamihara 29 Fd 35.34N 139.22 E
Sagami-Nada 29 Fd 35.00N 139.30 E
Sagami-Wan 29 Fd 35.15N 139.20 E
Sagan 35 Fd 5.17N 36.57 E
Saganaga Lake 45 Kb 48.14N 90.52W
Saganoseki 29 Be 33.15N 131.53 E
Šagany, Ozero- 15 Md 45.45N 29.55 E
Sāgar [India] 25 Ff 14.10N 75.02 E
Sāgar [India] 22 Jg 23.50N 78.42 E
Sagara 29 Fd 34.40N 138.12 E
Sagaredžo 16 Ni 41.43N 45.16 E
Sagavanirktok 40 Jb 70.20N 148.00W
Sagawa 29 Ce 33.29N 133.16 E
Sage 46 Jf 41.50N 110.56W
Saghād 24 Og 31.12N 52.30 E
Saginaw 43 Kc 43.25N 83.58W
Saginaw Bay 43 Kc 43.50N 83.40W
Sagiz 19 Ff 47.32N 53.45 E
Sagiz [Kaz.-U.S.S.R.] 19 Ff 48.12N 54.56 E
Sagiz [Kaz.-U.S.S.R.] 16 Rf 47.32N 53.27 E
Saglek Bay 42 Le 58.30N 63.00W
Saglouc → Salluit 39 Lc 62.12N 75.38W
Šagonar 20 Ef 51.32N 92.51 E
Sagone, Golfe de- 11a Aa 42.06N 8.41 E
Sagres 13 Dg 37.01N 8.56W
Sagres, Ponta de- 13 Dh 37.00N 8.57W
Sagter Ems 12 Ja 53.10N 7.40 E
Şagu 15 Ec 46.03N 21.17 E
Sagu/Sauvo 8 Jd 60.21N 22.42 E
Saguache 45 Cg 38.05N 106.08W
Sagua de Tánamo 49 Jc 20.35N 75.14W
Sagua la Grande 47 Hd 22.49N 80.05W
Saguenay 38 Me 48.10N 69.45W
Saguia el-Hamra 32 Ed 26.50N 12.00W
Sagunt/Sagunto 13 Le 39.41N 0.16W
Sagunto/Sagunt 13 Le 39.41N 0.16W
Sagunto-Grao de Sagunto 13 Le 39.40N 0.16W
Sa'gya 27 Ef 28.53N 88.10 E
Sahagún [Col.] 54 Cb 8.57N 75.27W
Sahagún [Sp.] 13 Gb 42.22N 5.02W
Sahalin, Ostrov- = Sakhalin (EN) 21 Qd 51.00N 143.00 E
Sahalinskaja Oblast [3] 20 Jf 50.00N 143.00 E
Sahalinski Zaliv 20 Jf 53.45N 141.30 E
Sahara 30 Hf 21.00N 6.00 E
Saharan Atlas (EN) = Atlas Saharien 30 He 34.00N 2.00 E
Sahāranpur 22 Jg 29.58N 77.23 E
Sahel 34 Ec 14.10N 0.50W
Sahel 30 Gg 15.40N 8.30W
Şahin 15 Jh 41.01N 26.50 E
Sāhīwāl [Pak.] 25 Eb 30.41N 72.57 E
Sāhīwāl [Pak.] 25 Eb 31.58N 72.20 E
Sahlābād 23 Ic 32.10N 59.51 E
Sahneh 24 Le 34.29N 47.41 E
Sahnovščina 16 Ie 49.09N 35.57 E
Šahova Kosa, Mys- 16 Qi 40.13N 50.22 E
Šahrihan 18 Id 40.40N 72.03 E
Šahrisabz 19 Gh 39.03N 66.41 E
Šahristan, Pereval- 18 Ge 39.35N 68.38 E
Šahtersk [R.S.F.S.R.] 20 Jg 49.13N 142.09 E
Šahtersk [Ukr.-U.S.S.R.] 16 Ke 48.01N 38.32 E
Šahterski 20 Md 64.46N 177.47 E
Šahtinsk 19 Hf 49.40N 72.37 E
Šahty 19 Ef 47.42N 40.13 E
Sahuaripa 47 Cc 29.03N 109.14W
Sahuayo de Diaz 47 Dd 20.04N 102.43W
Šahunja 19 Ed 57.43N 46.35 E
Saḥūq, Wādī- 24 Jj 25.18N 42.20 E
Šahy 10 Oh 48.05N 18.58 E
Sahyadri/Western Ghats 21 Jh 14.00N 75.00 E
Sai Buri 25 Kg 6.42N 101.37 E
Saïda [3] 32 Hc 33.35N 0.30 E
Saïda 31 He 34.50N 0.09 E
Saïda, Monts de- 13 Mi 35.10N 0.30 E
Sa'īdābād 23 Id 29.28N 55.42 E
Saidaiji 29 Dd 34.39N 134.02 E
Said Bundas 35 Cd 8.35N 24.30 E
Saidia 13 Ji 35.04N 2.13W
Saidor 60 Di 5.37S 146.28 E
Saidu 25 Eb 34.45N 72.21 E
Saigō 29 Cc 36.13N 133.20 E
Saigon → Ho Chi Minh 22 Mh 10.45N 106.40 E
Saihan Tal → Sonid Youqi 27 Jc 42.45N 112.36 E
Saihan Toroi 27 Hc 41.54N 100.24 E
Saijō 29 Ce 33.55N 133.10 E
Saikai 29 Ae 33.03N 129.44 E
Sai-Kawa 29 Fc 36.37N 138.14 E
Saiki, 28 Kh 32.57N 131.54 E
Saiki-Wan 29 Be 33.00N 131.55 E
Sail Rock 51n Bb 12.37N 61.16W
Saimaa 5 Ic 61.15N 28.15 E
Saimaa Canal (EN) = Sajmenski Kanal 8 Mc 61.05N 28.18 E
Sain Alto 48 Hf 23.35N 103.15W
Sā in Dezh 24 Ld 36.40N 46.33 E
Sains-Richaumont 12 Fe 49.49N 3.42 E
Saint Abb's Head 9 Kf 55.54N 2.09W
Saint-Affrique 11 Ik 43.57N 2.53 E
Saint Agnes Head 9 Hk 50.23N 5.07W
Saint-Agrève 11 Ki 45.01N 4.24 E
Saint Albans [Eng.-U.K.] 9 Mj 51.46N 0.21W
Saint Albans [Vt.-U.S.] 44 Kc 44.49N 73.05W
Saint Albans [W.V.-U.S.] 44 Gf 38.24N 81.53W
Saint Alban's Head 9 Kk 50.34N 2.04W
Saint Albert 42 Gf 53.38N 113.38W
Saint-Amand-les-Eaux 11 Jd 50.26N 3.26 E
Saint-Amand-Mont-Rond 11 Ih 46.43N 2.31 E
Saint-André, Cap- 30 Lj 16.11S 44.27 E
Saint-André, Plaine de- 11 Hf 48.55N 1.10 E
Saint-André-de-Cubzac 11 Fi 45.00N 0.27W
Saint-André-de-l'Eure 12 Df 48.54N 1.17 E
Saint-André-sur-Cailly 12 De 49.33N 1.13 E
Saint Andrews [N.B.-Can.] 44 Nc 45.06N 67.02W
Saint Andrews [Scot.-U.K.] 9 Ke 56.20N 2.48W
Saint Anne 9 Kl 49.40N 2.10W
Saint Ann's Bay 49 Id 18.26N 77.16W
Saint Ann's Head 9 Hj 51.41N 5.10W
Saint Anthony [Id.-U.S.] 46 Je 43.58N 111.41W
Saint Anthony [Newf.-Can.] 42 Lf 51.22N 55.35W
Saint Arnaud 59 Ig 36.37S 143.15 E
Saint-Aubert 44 Lb 47.14N 70.15W
Saint-Aubin-sur-Mer 12 Be 49.20N 0.24W
Saint Augustine 43 Kf 29.51N 81.25W
Saint-Augustin-Saguenay 42 Lf 51.14N 58.39W
Saint Austell 9 Ik 50.20N 4.48W
Saint-Avold 11 Me 49.06N 6.42 E
Saint Barthélemy 47 Le 17.55N 62.50W
Saint-Barthélemy 11 Hl 42.49N 1.45 E
Saint Barthélemy, Canal de- 51b Bb 18.00N 63.00W
Saint Barthélemy, Kanaal Van- 51b Bb 18.00N 63.00W
Saint Bees Head 9 Jg 54.32N 3.38W
Saint-Benoît 37a b 21.02S 55.43 E
Saint-Benoît-sur-Loire 11 Ig 47.49N 2.18 E
Saint-Bonnet 11 Mj 44.41N 6.05 E
Saint-Brévin-les-Pins 11 Dg 47.15N 2.10W
Saint Brides Bay 9 Hj 51.48N 5.15W
Saint-Brieuc 11 Df 48.31N 2.47W
Saint-Brieuc, Baie de- 11 Df 48.38N 2.40W
Saint-Calais 11 Gg 47.55N 0.45 E
Saint-Camille 44 Lb 46.29N 70.12W
Saint Catharines 42 Jh 43.10N 79.15W
Saint Catherine, Monastery of- (EN) = Dayr Kātrīnā 33 Fd 28.31N 33.57 E
Saint Catherine, Mount- 51p Bb 12.10N 61.40W
Saint Catherines Island 44 Gj 31.38N 81.10W
Saint Catherine's Point 9 Lk 50.34N 1.15W
Saint-Céré 11 Hj 44.52N 1.54 E
Saint-Chamond 11 Ki 45.28N 4.30 E
Saint Charles 43 Id 38.47N 90.29W
Saint-Chély-d'Apcher 11 Jj 44.48N 3.17 E
Saint-Christol, Plateau de- 11 Lj 44.00N 5.50 E
Saint Christopher/Saint Kitts 38 Mh 17.21N 62.48W
Saint Christopher-Nevis [5] 39 Mh 17.21N 62.48W
Saint-Cirq-Lapopie 11 Hj 44.28N 1.40 E
Saint Clair, Lake- 38 Ke 42.25N 82.41W
Saint Clair River 44 Fd 42.37N 82.31W
Saint Clair Shores 44 Fd 42.30N 82.54W
Saint-Clair-sur-l'Elle 12 Ae 49.12N 1.02W
Saint-Claud 11 Gi 45.54N 0.28 E
Saint-Claude [Fr.] 11 Lh 46.23N 5.52 E
Saint Claude 45 Gb 49.40N 98.22W
Saint-Claude [Guad.] 51e Ab 16.02N 61.42W
Saint Cloud 39 Je 45.33N 94.10W
Saint Croix 47 Le 17.45N 64.45W
Saint Croix Falls 45 Jd 45.24N 92.38W
Saint Croix River 43 Ic 44.45N 92.49W
Saint-Cyr-l'Ecole 12 Ef 48.48N 2.04 E
Saint-Cyr-sur-Loire 11 Gg 47.24N 0.40 E
Saint David Bay 51g Bb 15.26N 61.15W
Saint David's [Gren.] 51p Bb 12.04N 61.39W
Saint David's [Wales-U.K.] 9 Hj 51.54N 5.16W
Saint David's Head 9 Hj 51.55N 5.19W
Saint David's Point 51p Bb 12.01N 61.40W
Saint-Denis [Fr.] 11 If 48.56N 2.22 E
Saint-Denis [May.] 31 Mk 20.52S 55.28 E
Saint-Dié 11 Mf 48.17N 6.57 E
Saint-Dizier 11 Kf 48.38N 4.57 E
Sainte-Adresse 12 Ce 49.30N 0.05 E
Sainte-Anne [Guad.] 51e Bb 16.14N 61.23W
Sainte-Anne [Mart.] 51h Bc 14.26N 60.53W
Sainte-Anne-des-Monts 44 Na 49.07N 66.29W
Sainte Baume, Chaîne de la- 11 Lk 43.20N 5.45 E
Sainte-Énimie 11 Jj 44.22N 3.25 E
Sainte Genevieve 45 Kh 37.59N 90.03W
Sainte-Geneviève 12 Ee 49.17N 2.12 E
Saint Elias, Mount- 38 Ec 60.18N 140.55W
Saint Elias Mountains 38 Fc 60.30N 139.30W
Saint-Elie 54 Hc 4.50N 53.17W
Sainte-Livrade-sur-Lot 11 Gj 44.24N 0.36 E
Sainte-Eloy-les-Mines 11 Ih 46.09N 2.50 E
Sainte Luce 37 Hd 24.46S 47.12 E
Sainte-Luce 51h Bc 14.28N 60.56W
Sainte-Lucie, Canal de- = Saint Lucia Channel (EN) 50 Fe 14.09N 60.57W
Sainte-Marcellin 11 Li 45.09N 5.19 E
Sainte-Marie [Guad.] 51e Ab 16.06N 61.34W
Sainte-Marie [Mart.] 51h Ab 14.47N 61.00W
Sainte-Marie, Cap- = Sainte-Marie, Cape- (EN) 30 Lk 25.36S 45.08 E
Sainte-Marie, Cape-(EN) = Sainte-Marie, Cap- 30 Lk 25.36S 45.08 E
Sainte-Marie, Ile- 30 Lj 16.50S 49.55 E
Sainte-Marie-aux-Mines 11 Nf 48.15N 7.11 E
Sainte-Maure-de-Touraine 11 Gg 47.06N 0.37 E
Sainte-Maxime 11 Mk 43.18N 6.38 E
Sainte-Menehould 11 Ke 49.05N 4.54 E
Sainte-Rose 51e Ab 16.20N 61.42W
Sainte-Rose-du-Dégelé 44 Mb 47.33N 68.39W
Sainte Rose du Lac 45 Ga 51.03N 99.32W
Saintes 11 Fi 45.45N 0.38W
Saintes, Canal des- 51e Ac 15.55N 61.40W
Saintes, Iles des- 50 Fe 15.52N 61.37W
Sainte-Savine 11 Kf 48.18N 4.03 E
Saintes-Maries-de-la-Mer 11 Kk 43.27N 4.26 E
Sainte-Thérèse 44 Kc 45.22N 73.15W
Saint-Étienne 6 Gf 45.26N 4.24 E
Saint-Étienne-du-Rouvray 11 He 49.23N 1.06 E
Sainte Victoire, Montagne- 11 Lk 43.32N 5.39 E
Saint-Félicien 44 Ka 48.39N 72.28W
Saint-Florent 11a Ba 42.41N 9.18 E
Saint-Florent, Golfe de- 11a Ba 42.45N 9.16 E
Saint-Florentin 11 Jf 48.00N 3.44 E
Saint-Florent-sur-Cher 11 Ih 46.59N 2.15 E
Saint-Flour 11 Ji 45.02N 3.05 E
Saint Francis 45 Fg 39.46N 101.48W
Saint Francis River 45 Ki 34.38N 90.35W
Saint Francisville 45 Kk 30.47N 91.23W
Saint-François 51e Bb 16.15N 61.17W
Saint François Island 37b Bb 7.10S 52.44 E
Saint Francois Mountains 45 Kh 37.30N 90.35W
Saint-Gaudens 11 Gk 43.07N 0.44 E
Saint George 40 Fe 56.35N 169.35W
Saint George [Austl.] 59 Je 28.02S 148.35 E
Saint George [N.B.-Can.] 44 Nc 45.10N 66.48W
Saint George [Ut.-U.S.] 43 Ed 37.06N 113.35W
Saint George, Cape - [Newf.-Can.] 42 Lm 48.28N 59.16W
Saint George, Cape- [Pap.N.Gui.] 60 Eh 4.52S 152.52 E
Saint George, Point- 46 Cf 41.47N 124.15W
Saint George Harbour 44 Nd 43.15N 66.10W
Saint George Island 44 Ek 29.39N 84.55W
Saint George's 39 Mh 12.03N 61.45W
Saint-Georges 44 Lb 46.10N 70.38W
Saint George's Bay 42 Lg 48.20N 59.00W
Saint George's Channel 5 Fe 52.00N 6.00W
Saint George's Channel (EN) = Muir Bhreatan 5 Fe 52.00N 6.00W
Saint-Georges-du-Vièvre 12 Ce 49.15N 0.35 E
Saint-Germain-en-Laye 12 Ef 48.54N 2.05 E
Saint-Gervais-d'Auvergne 11 Ih 46.02N 2.49 E
Saint-Gervais-les-Bains 11 Mi 45.54N 6.43 E
Saint-Ghislain 12 Fd 50.27N 3.49 E
Saint-Ghislain-Baudour 12 Fd 50.29N 3.49 E
Saint-Gildas, Pointe de- 11 Dg 47.08N 2.15W
Saint-Gilles 11 Kk 43.41N 4.26 E
Saint-Gilles-Croix-de-Vie 11 Eh 46.41N 1.55W
Saint-Girons 11 Hl 42.59N 1.09 E
Saint-Gobain 12 Fe 49.36N 3.23 E
Saint Gotthard Pass (EN) = San Gottardo/Sankt Gotthard 5 Gf 46.30N 8.30 E
Saint Gotthard Pass (EN) = Sankt Gotthard/San Gottardo 5 Gf 46.30N 8.30 E
Saint Govan's Head 9 Ij 51.36N 4.55W
Saint Helena [5] 31 Gj 15.57S 5.42W
Saint Helena 30 Gj 15.57S 5.42W
Saint Helena Bay 30 Il 32.45S 18.05 E
Saint Helena Island 44 Gi 32.30N 80.30W

Index Symbols

[1] Independent Nation
[2] State, Region
[3] District, County
[4] Municipality
[5] Colony, Dependency
Continent
Physical Region
Historical or Cultural Region
Mount, Mountain
Volcano
Hill
Mountains, Mountain Range
Hills, Escarpment
Plateau, Upland
Pass, Gap
Plain, Lowland
Delta
Salt Flat
Valley, Canyon
Crater, Cave
Karst Features
Depression
Polder
Desert, Dunes
Forest, Woods
Heath, Steppe
Oasis
Cape, Point
Coast, Beach
Cliff
Peninsula
Isthmus
Sandbank
Island
Atoll
Rock, Reef
Islands, Archipelago
Rocks, Reefs
Coral Reef
Well, Spring
Geyser
River, Stream
Waterfall Rapids
River Mouth, Estuary
Lake
Salt Lake
Intermittent Lake
Reservoir
Swamp, Pond
Canal
Glacier
Ice Shelf, Pack Ice
Ocean
Sea
Gulf, Bay
Strait, Fjord
Lagoon
Bank
Seamount
Tablemount
Ridge
Shelf
Basin
Escarpment, Sea Scarp
Fracture
Trench, Abyss
National Park, Reserve
Point of Interest
Recreation Site
Cave, Cavern
Historic Site
Ruins
Wall, Walls
Church, Abbey
Temple
Scientific Station
Airport
Port
Lighthouse
Mine
Tunnel
Dam, Bridge

Saint Helena Sound 44 Gi 32.27N 80.25W
Saint Helens [Austl.] 59 Jh 41.20S 148.15 E
Saint Helens [Eng.-U.K.] 9 Kh 53.28N 2.44W
Saint Helens [Or.-U.S.] 46 Dd 45.52N 122.48W
Saint Helens, Mount- 46 Dc 46.12N 122.11W
Saint Helier 9 Kl 49.12N 2.07W
Saint-Hubert 12 Hd 50.03N 5.23 E
Saint-Hyacinthe 44 Kc 45.38N 72.57W
Saint Ignace Island 45 Mb 48.48N 87.55W
Saint Ignatius 46 Hc 47.19N 114.06W
Saint Ives [Eng.-U.K.] 9 Hk 50.12N 5.29W
Saint Ives [Eng.-U.K.] 12 Bb 52.18N 0.04W
Saint James 45 Ie 43.59N 94.38W
Saint James, Cape - 42 Ef 51.57N 131.01W
Saint-Jean 42 Kg 45.13N 73.15W
Saint-Jean, Baie de- 51b Bc 17.55N 62.51W
Saint-Jean, Lac- 38 Le 48.35N 72.00W
Saint-Jean-d'Angély 11 Fi 45.57N 0.31W
Saint-Jean-de-Luz 11 Ek 43.23N 1.40W
Saint-Jean-de-Maurienne 11 Mi 45.17N 6.21 E
Saint-Jean-de-Monts 11 Dh 46.47N 2.04W
Saint-Jean-du-Gard 11 Jj 44.06N 3.53 E
Saint-Jean-Pied-de-Port 11 Ek 43.10N 1.14W
Saint-Jérôme [Que.-Can.] 42 Kg 45.46N 74.00W
Saint-Jérôme [Que.-Can.] 44 La 48.26N 71.52W
Saint Joe River 46 Gc 47.21N 116.42W
Saint John 50 Dc 18.20N 64.42W
Saint John [Can.] 38 Me 45.15N 66.04W
Saint John [Ks.-U.S.] 45 Gh 38.00N 98.46W
Saint John [Lbr.] 34 Cd 5.55N 10.05W
Saint John [N.B.-Can.] 39 Me 45.16N 66.03W
Saint John's [Atg.] 47 Le 17.06N 61.51W
Saint Johns [Az.-U.S.] 46 Ki 34.30N 109.22W
Saint Johns [Mi.-U.S.] 44 Ed 43.00N 84.33W
Saint John's [Mont.] 51c Bc 16.48N 62.11W
Saint John's [Newf.-Can.] 39 Ne 47.34N 52.43W
Saint Johnsbury 44 Kc 44.25N 72.01W
Saint Johns River 44 Gj 30.24N 81.24W
Saint Joseph [Dom.] 51g Bb 15.24N 61.26W
Saint Joseph [La.-U.S.] 45 Kk 31.55N 91.14W
Saint-Joseph [Mart.] 51h Ab 14.40N 61.03W
Saint Joseph [Mi.-U.S.] 44 Dd 42.06N 86.29W
Saint Joseph [Mo.-U.S.] 43 Id 39.46N 94.51W
Saint-Joseph [New Caledonia] 63b Ce 20.27S 166.36 E
Saint-Joseph [Reu.] 37a Bb 21.22S 55.37 E
Saint Joseph, Lake- 42 If 51.06N 90.36W
Saint Joseph Island 44 Fb 46.13N 83.57W
Saint Joseph River 44 Dd 42.06N 86.29W
Saint-Junien 11 Gi 45.53N 0.54 E
Saint-Just-en-Chaussée 12 Ee 49.30N 2.26 E
Saint Kilda 9 Ed 57.49N 8.36W
Saint Kitts/Saint Christopher 38 Mh 17.21N 62.48W
Saint-Lary-Soulan 11 Gl 42.49N 0.19 E
Saint Laurent 53 Ke 5.30N 54.02W
Saint Laurent = Saint Lawrence (EN) 38 Me 49.15N 67.00W
Saint Lawrence 38 Bc 63.30N 170.30W
Saint Lawrence 38 Me 49.15N 67.00W
Saint Lawrence (EN) = Saint Laurent 38 Me 49.15N 67.00W
Saint Lawrence, Gulf of- 38 Me 48.00N 62.00W
Saint-Léger-en-Yvelines 12 Df 48.43N 1.46 E
Saint-Léonard 44 Nb 47.10N 67.56W
Saint-Léonard-de-Noblat 11 Hi 45.50N 1.29 E
Saint-Lewis 42 Lf 52.22N 55.58W
Saint-Lô 11 Ee 49.07N 1.05W
Saint Louis 39 Jf 38.38N 90.11W
Saint-Louis [Guad.] 51e Bc 15.57N 61.20W
Saint-Louis [Sen.] 31 Fg 16.02N 16.30W
Saint-Loup-sur-Semouse 11 Mg 47.53N 6.16 E
Saint Lucia 37 Ee 28.23S 32.25 E
Saint Lucia [1] 39 Mh 13.53N 60.58W
Saint Lucia 38 Mh 13.53N 60.58W
Saint Lucia, Cape- 30 Kk 28.32S 32.24 E
Saint Lucia, Lake- 37 Ee 28.00S 32.30 E
Saint Lucia Channel 50 Fe 14.09N 60.57W
Saint Lucia Channel (EN) = Sainte-Lucie, Canal de- 50 Fe 14.09N 60.57W
Saint Magnus Bay 9 La 60.25N 1.35W
Saint-Maixent-l'École 11 Fh 46.25N 0.12W
Saint-Malo 6 Ff 48.39N 2.01W
Saint-Malo, Golfe de- 5 Ff 48.45N 2.00W
Saint-Marc 47 Je 19.06N 72.43W
Saint-Marc, Canal de- 49 Kd 18.50N 72.45W
Saint Margaret's at Cliffe 12 Dc 51.09N 1.19 E
Saint Margaret's Hope 9 Kc 58.49N 2.57W
Saint Maries 46 Gc 47.19N 116.35W
Saint Martin 47 Le 18.04N 63.04W
Saint Martin, Cap- 51h Ab 14.52N 61.13W
Saint-Martin-Boulogne 12 Dd 50.43N 1.40 E
Saint-Martin-de-Ré 11 Eh 46.12N 1.22W
Saint-Martin-des-Besaces 12 Be 49.01N 0.51W
Saint Martins 44 Oc 45.21N 65.32W
Saint-Martin-Vésubie 11 Nj 44.04N 7.15 E
Saint Mary, Cape- 44 Nc 44.05N 66.13W
Saint Mary Peak [Austl.] 59 Hf 31.30S 138.35 E
Saint Mary Peak [U.S.] 46 Hc 46.40N 114.20W
Saint Mary's 9 Gl 49.55N 6.20W
Saint Marys [Austl.] 59 Jh 41.35S 148.10 E
Saint Marys [Oh.-U.S.] 44 Ee 40.32N 84.22W
Saint Marys [W.V.-U.S.] 44 Gf 39.24N 81.13W
Saint Mary's, Cape - 42 Mg 46.49N 54.12W
Saint Mary's Bay [N.S.-Can.] 44 Nc 44.25N 66.10W
Saint Mary's Bay [N.W.T.-Can.] 42 Mg 46.50N 53.47W
Saint Marys River 44 Gj 30.45N 81.30W
Saint-Mathieu, Pointe de- 5 Ff 48.20N 4.46W
Saint Matthew 38 Bb 60.30N 172.45W
Saint Matthias Group 57 Fe 1.30S 149.48 E
Saint-Maur-des-Fossés 11 If 48.48N 2.30 E
Saint-Maurice, Rivière- 42 Kg 46.21N 72.31W
Saint Michael 40 Gd 63.29N 162.02W
Saint Michaels 46 Ki 35.46N 109.04W
Saint-Michel 12 Ge 49.55N 4.08 E
Saint-Mihiel 11 Lf 48.54N 5.33 E
Saint-Nazaire 11 Dg 47.17N 2.12W
Saint Neots 12 Bb 52.13N 0.16W
Saint-Nicolas/Sint Niklaas 11 Kc 51.10N 4.08 E
Saint-Nicolas-d'Aliermont 12 De 49.53N 1.13 E
Saint-Nicolas-de-Port 11 Mf 48.38N 6.18 E
Saint-Omer 11 Id 50.45N 2.15 E
Saintonge 11 Fi 45.50N 0.30W
Saint Patrick's 51c Bc 16.41N 62.12W
Saint Paul 34 Cd 6.23N 10.48W
Saint-Paul 37a Bb 21.00S 55.16 E
Saint Paul 30 Ol 38.55S 77.41 E
Saint Paul [Ak.-U.S.] 40 Ee 57.07N 170.17W
Saint Paul [Alta.-Can.] 42 Gf 53.59N 111.17W
Saint Paul [Mn.-U.S.] 39 Je 44.58N 93.07W
Saint Paul [Nb.-U.S.] 45 Gf 41.13N 98.27W
Saint Paul, Cape- 34 Fd 5.49N 0.57 E
Saint-Paul-lès-Dax 11 Ek 43.44N 1.03W
Saint Paul's 51c Ab 17.24N 62.49W
Saint Paul's Point 64q Ab 25.04S 130.05W
Saint-Péray 11 Kj 44.57N 4.50 E
Saint Peter 45 Jd 44.17N 93.57W
Saint Peter Port 9 Kl 49.27N 2.32W
Saint Peter's 51c Bc 16.46N 62.12W
Saint Petersburg 39 Kg 27.46N 82.38W
Saint Petersburg Beach 44 Fl 27.45N 82.45W
Saint-Pierre [Mart.] 50 Fe 14.45N 61.11W
Saint-Pierre [May.] 31 Mk 21.19S 55.29 E
Saint-Pierre [St.P.M.] 42 Lg 46.46N 56.12W
Saint-Pierre, Lac- 44 Kb 46.10N 72.50W
Saint Pierre and Miquelon (EN)=Saint-Pierre et Miquelon [5] 39 Ne 46.55N 56.10W
Saint-Pierre-en-Port 12 Ce 49.48N 0.29 E
Saint-Pierre et Miquelon 38 Ne 46.55N 56.10W
Saint-Pierre et Miquelon = Saint Pierre and Miquelon (EN) [5] 39 Ne 46.55N 56.10W
Saint Pierre Island 37b Bb 9.19S 50.43 E
Saint-Pierre-sur-Dives 12 Be 49.01N 0.02W
Saint-Pol-de-Léon 11 Cf 48.41N 3.59W
Saint-Pol-sur-Mer 12 Ec 51.02N 2.21 E
Saint-Pol-sur-Ternoise 11 Id 50.23N 2.20 E
Saint-Pons 11 Ik 43.29N 2.46 E
Saint-Pourçain-sur-Sioule 11 Jh 46.18N 3.17 E
Saint-Quentin 11 Je 49.51N 3.17 E
Saint-Quentin, Canal de- 12 Fe 49.36N 3.11 E
Saint-Raphaël 11 Mk 43.25N 6.46 E
Saint-Rémy-de-Provence 11 Kk 43.47N 4.50 E
Saint-Rigaux, Mont- 11 Kh 46.12N 4.29 E
Saint-Riquier 12 Dd 50.08N 1.57 E
Saint Roch Basin 42 Ic 68.50N 95.00W
Saint Rogatien Bank (EN) 60 Mc 24.40N 167.10W
Saint-Romain-de-Colbosc 12 Ce 49.32N 0.22 E
Saint-Saëns 12 De 49.40N 1.17 E
Saint Sauflieu 12 Ee 49.47N 2.15 E
Saint-Savin 11 Gh 46.34N 0.52 E
Saint-Sébastien, Cap- 37 Hb 12.26S 48.44 E
Saint-Seine-l'Abbaye 11 Kg 47.26N 4.47 E
Saint-Servais, Namur- 12 Gd 50.28N 4.50 E
Saint Simon 12 Fe 49.45N 3.10 E
Saint Simons Island 44 Gj 31.14N 81.21W
Saint Stanislas Bay 64g Bb 1.53N 157.30W
Saint Stephen 42 Kg 45.12N 67.17W
Saint-Sylvain 12 Be 49.03N 0.13W
Saint Teresa Beach 44 Ek 29.58N 84.28W
Saint Thomas 42 Gd 42.47N 81.12W
Saint Thomas 47 Le 18.21N 64.55W
Saint-Trond/Sint-Truiden 11 Ld 50.49N 5.12 E
Saint-Tropez 11 Mk 43.16N 6.38 E
Saint-Tropez, Golfe de- 11 Mk 43.17N 6.38 E
Saint-Valéry-en-Caux 11 Ge 49.52N 0.44 E
Saint-Valery-sur-Somme 11 Hd 50.11N 1.38 E
Saint-Vallier 11 Ki 45.10N 4.49 E
Saint-Venant 12 Ed 50.37N 2.33 E
Saint Vincent 14 Be 45.45N 7.39 E
Saint Vincent 38 Mh 13.15N 61.12W
Saint-Vincent, Baie de- 63b Cf 22.00S 166.05 E
Saint Vincent, Cap- 30 Lk 21.57S 43.16 E
Saint Vincent, Gulf- 59 Hf 35.00S 138.05 E
Saint Vincent and the Grenadines [1] 39 Mh 13.15N 61.12W
Saint-Vincent-de-Tyrosse 11 Ek 43.40N 1.18W
Saint Vincent Island 44 Ek 29.40N 85.07W
Saint Vincent Passage 50 Ff 13.30N 61.00W
Saint-Wandrille-Rançon 12 Ce 49.32N 0.46 E
Saint-Yrieix-la-Perche 11 Hi 45.31N 1.12 E
Saipan 64a Ad 6.54N 134.08 E
Saipan Channel 64b Ba 15.05N 145.41 E
Saipan Island 57 Fc 15.12N 145.45 E
Saira 55 Ak 32.24S 62.06W
Sairecabur, Cerro- 54 Eh 22.43S 67.54W
Saitama Ken [2] 28 Of 36.00N 139.50 E
Saito 28 Kh 32.06N 131.24 E
Sajak 19 Hf 46.55N 77.22 E
Sajama 54 Eg 18.07S 69.00W
Sajama, Nevado de- 52 Jg 18.06S 68.54W
Sajānan 14 Dm 37.03N 9.14 E
Sajat 18 De 38.49N 63.51 E
Sajid 18 Hf 16.52N 41.55 E
Sajir, Ra's- 35 Ib 16.45N 53.35 E
Sajmenski Kanal = Saimaa Canal (EN) 8 Mc 61.05N 28.18 E
Sajn-Sand 22 Ne 44.55N 110.11 E
Sajó 10 Ri 47.56N 21.08 E
Sajószentpéter 10 Qh 48.13N 20.43 E
Sajram 18 Gc 42.18N 69.45 E
Sajzī 24 Of 32.41N 52.07 E
Saka 36 Gc 0.09S 39.20 E
Sakai 28 Mg 34.35N 135.28 E
Sakaide 29 Cd 34.19N 133.51 E
Sakaiminato 29 Cd 35.33N 133.15 E
Sakākah 23 Fd 29.59N 40.06 E
Sakakawea, Lake- 43 Gb 47.50N 102.20W
Sakala, Vozvyšennost-/Sakala Kõrgustik 8 Kf 58.00N 25.30 E
Sakala Kõrgustik/Sakala, Vozvyšennost- 8 Kf 58.00N 25.30 E
Sakami 42 Jf 53.18N 76.45W
Sakami, lac- 42 Jf 53.15N 76.45W
Sâkâne, 'Erg i-n- 34 Ea 20.40N 0.51W
Sakania 36 Ee 12.43S 28.33 E
Sakao 63b Cb 14.58S 167.07 E
Sakar 15 Jh 41.59N 26.16 E
Sakar 18 De 38.59N 63.45 E
Sakaraha 37 Gd 22.54S 44.32 E
Sakar-Čaga 18 Cf 37.39N 61.40 E
Sakārinah, Jabal as- 14 Do 35.45N 9.05 E
Sakartvelos Sabčata Socialisturi Respublica/Gruzinskaja SSR [2] 19 Eg 42.00N 44.00 E
Sakarya 23 Da 41.07N 30.39 E
Sakata 27 Od 38.55N 139.50 E
Sakchu 28 Hd 40.23N 125.02 E
Sakhalin (EN) = Sahalin, Ostrov- 21 Qd 51.00N 143.00 E
Saki 16 Hg 45.07N 33.37 E
Šakiai/Šakjaj 7 Fi 54.57N 23.01 E
Sakishima Islands (EN) = Sakishima-Shotō 21 Og 24.30N 125.00 E
Sakishima-Shotō = Sakishima Islands (EN) 21 Og 24.30N 125.00 E
Sakito 29 Ae 33.02N 129.34 E
Sakız Boğazı 15 Jk 38.20N 26.12 E
Šakjaj/Šakiai 7 Fi 54.57N 23.01 E
Sakmara 5 Le 51.46N 55.01 E
Sakon Nakhon 25 Ke 17.10N 104.01 E
Sakrivier 37 Cf 30.54S 20.28 E
Šakša 17 Hi 54.47N 56.15 E
Saksaulski 19 Gf 47.05N 61.13 E
Sakskøbing 8 Dj 54.48N 11.39 E
Saku 28 Of 36.09N 138.26 E
Sakuma 29 Ed 35.05N 137.47 E
Sakura 29 Gd 35.43N 140.13 E
Sakurai 29 Dd 34.31N 135.50 E
Sakura-Jima 29 Bf 31.35N 130.40 E
Säkylä 8 Jc 61.02N 22.20 E
Sal 30 Eg 16.45N 22.55W
Sal 19 Ef 47.31N 40.45 E
Sal, Cay- 49 Gb 23.42N 80.24W
Sal, Punta- 49 Df 15.53N 87.37W
Sala 35 Cb 17.00N 20.53 E
Šalá 10 Nh 48.09N 17.53 E
Sala 7 Dg 59.55N 16.36 E
Salabangka, Kepulauan- 26 Hg 3.02S 122.25 E
Salacca 8 Kg 57.39N 24.15 E
Salacgriva/Salacgrīva 7 Fh 57.46N 24.27 E
Salacgrīva/Salacgriva 7 Fh 57.46N 24.27 E
Sala Consilina 14 Jj 40.23N 15.36 E
Salada 48 Hc 28.36N 103.28W
Salada, Laguna- 48 Ba 32.20N 115.40W
Saladas 56 Ic 28.15S 58.38W
Saladillo 56 Ie 35.38S 59.46W
Saladillo, Arroyo- 55 Bj 31.22S 60.30W
Saladillo Amargo, Arroyo- 55 Ci 31.01S 60.19W
Saladillo Dulce, Arroyo- 55 Bj 31.01S 60.19W
Salado, Arroyo- [Arg.] 55 Bm 36.27S 61.06W
Salado, Arroyo- [Mex.] 48 De 24.25N 111.30W
Salado, Riacho- 55 Ch 26.30S 58.18W
Salado, Rio- 45 Ci 34.16N 106.52W
Salado, Rio- 47 Ec 26.52N 99.19W
Salado, Rio- [Arg.] 52 Ji 31.42S 60.44W
Salado, Rio- [Arg.] 56 Ee 38.49S 64.57W
Salado, Rio- [Arg.] 52 Ki 35.44S 57.21W
Salado, Valle- 48 He 24.47N 102.50W
Salaga 34 Ed 8.33N 0.31W
Salagle 35 Ge 1.50N 42.18 E
Salāhuddīn [3] 24 Je 34.40N 44.00 E
Salailua 65c Aa 13.41S 172.34W
Salairski Krjaž 20 Df 54.00N 85.00 E
Sălaj [2] 15 Fb 47.10N 23.00 E
Salakuša 7 Je 62.15N 40.18 E
Salal 35 Bc 14.51N 17.13 E
Salālah [Oman] 22 Hh 17.05N 54.10 E
Salālah [Sud.] 35 Fa 21.19N 36.13 E
Salamá 49 Bf 15.06N 90.16W
Salamanca [3] 13 Gd 40.50N 6.00W
Salamanca [Chile] 56 Fd 31.47S 70.58W
Salamanca [Mex.] 47 Dd 20.34N 101.12W
Salamanca [N.Y.-U.S.] 44 Hd 42.11N 78.43W
Salamanca [Sp.] 6 Fg 40.58N 5.39W
Salamat [3] 35 Cc 11.00N 20.30 E
Salamat, Bahr- 35 Bd 9.27N 18.06 E
Salamina 49 Jh 10.30N 74.48W
Salamis 15 Gl 37.58N 23.29 E
Salamis 24 Ee 35.10N 33.54 E
Salamis 15 Gl 37.55N 23.30 E
Salang, Tūnel-e- 23 Kb 35.19N 69.02 E
Salani 65c Bb 14.00S 171.34W
Salantai/Salantaj 8 Ih 56.05N 21.30 E
Salantaj/Salantai 8 Ih 56.05N 21.30 E
Salas 13 Fa 43.24N 6.16W
Salas de los Infant 13 Ib 42.01N 3.17W
Salat 64d Cb 7.14N 152.01 E
Salat 11 Gk 43.10N 0.58 E
Salatiga 26 Fh 7.19S 110.30 E
Salavat 6 Le 53.25N 55.58 E
Salawati, Pulau- 26 Jg 1.07S 130.52 E
Sala y Gómez 57 Qg 26.28S 105.28W
Sala y Gómez Ridge (EN) 3 Ml 25.00S 98.00W
Salazar 55 Am 36.18S 62.12W
Salbris 11 Ig 47.26N 2.03 E
Salcantay, Nevado de- 52 Ig 13.22S 72.34W
Šalčininkai/Šalčininkaj 8 Kj 54.18N 25.30 E
Šalčininkaj/Šalčininkai 8 Kj 54.18N 25.30 E
Salda Gölü 15 Ml 37.33N 29.42 E
Saldaña 13 Hb 42.31N 4.44W
Saldanha 31 Il 33.00S 17.56 E
Saldungaray 55 Bn 38.12S 61.47W
Saldus 19 Cd 56.40N 22.31 E
Sale 59 Jg 38.06S 147.04 E
Salé 32 Fc 34.04N 6.48W
Salebabu, Pulau- 26 If 3.55N 126.40 E
Şāleḩābād 24 Me 34.56N 48.20 E
Salehard 22 Ic 66.33N 66.40 E
Saleimoa 65c Ba 13.48S 171.52W
Saleloloa 65c Aa 13.44S 172.10W
Salem [Fl.-U.S.] 44 Fk 29.58N 83.28W
Salem [Il.-U.S.] 45 Lg 38.38N 88.57W
Salem [India] 22 Jh 11.39N 78.10 E
Salem [In.-U.S.] 44 Df 38.36N 86.06W
Salem [Ma.-U.S.] 44 Ld 42.31N 70.55W
Salem [Mont.] 51c Bc 16.45N 62.13W
Salem [Mo.-U.S.] 45 Kh 37.39N 91.32W
Salem [N.J.-U.S.] 44 Jf 39.35N 75.28W
Salem [Oh.-U.S.] 44 Ge 40.54N 80.52W
Salem [Or.-U.S.] 39 Ge 44.57N 123.01W
Salem [S.D.-U.S.] 45 He 43.44N 97.23W
Salem [Va.-U.S.] 44 Gg 37.17N 80.03W
Salemi 14 Gm 37.49N 12.48 E
Sälen 8 Ec 61.10N 13.16 E
Salentine Peninsula (EN) = Penisola Salentina 5 Hg 40.30N 18.00 E
Sale Pit 9 Oh 53.40N 1.30 E
Salerno 6 Hg 40.41N 14.47 E
Salerno, Golfo di- 14 Ij 40.30N 14.40 E
Salers 11 Ii 45.08N 2.30 E
Salève, Mont- 11 Mh 46.07N 6.10 E
Salgir 16 Ig 45.38N 35.01 E
Salgótarján 10 Ph 48.07N 19.49 E
Salgueiro 54 Ke 8.04S 39.06W
Salher 25 Ed 20.41N 73.52 E
Salhus 7 Af 60.30N 5.16 E
Sali 14 Jg 43.56N 15.10 E
Šali 16 Nh 43.06N 45.56 E
Salice Terme 14 Df 44.55N 9.01 E
Salida 43 Fd 38.32N 106.00W
Salies-de-Béarn 11 Fk 43.29N 0.55W
Salihli 23 Cb 38.29N 28.09 E
Salima 36 Fe 13.47S 34.26 E
Salīma, Wāḩāt- = Salimah Oasis (EN) 31 Jf 21.22N 29.19 E
Salimah Oasis (EN) = Salīma, Wāḩāt- 31 Jf 21.22N 29.19 E
Salina 14 Il 38.35N 14.50 E
Salina [Ks.-U.S.] 39 Jf 38.50N 97.37W
Salina [Ut.-U.S.] 46 Jg 38.58N 111.51W
Salina Cruz 47 Ee 16.10N 95.12W
Salinas [Ca.-U.S.] 39 Gf 36.40N 121.38W
Salinas [Ec.] 54 Bd 2.13S 80.58W
Salinas [P.R.] 51a Bc 17.59N 66.17W
Salinas, Bahia de- 49 Eh 11.03N 85.43W
Salinas, Cabo de-/Ses Salines, Cap de- 13 Pe 39.16N 3.03 E
Salinas, Punta- [Dom.Rep.] 49 Ld 18.12N 70.34W
Salinas, Punta- [P.R.] 51a Bb 18.29N 66.10W
Salinas, Rio- 49 Be 16.28N 90.33W
Salinas de Hidalgo 48 If 22.38N 101.43W
Salinas Peak 45 Cj 33.18N 106.31W
Saline, Point- 50 Fg 12.00N 61.48W
Saline Island 51p Cb 12.26N 61.29W
Saline River [Ks.-U.S.] 45 Hg 38.51N 97.30W
Saline River [U.S.] 45 Jj 33.10N 92.08W
Salines, Pointe des- 51h Bc 14.24N 60.53W
Salinópolis 54 Id 0.37S 47.20W
Salins-les-Bains 11 Lh 46.57N 5.53 E
Salisbury 42 Jd 63.35N 77.00W
Salisbury [Dom.] 51g Bb 15.26N 61.27W
Salisbury [Eng.-U.K.] 9 Lj 51.05N 1.48W
Salisbury [Md.-U.S.] 43 Ld 38.22N 75.36W
Salisbury [N.C.-U.S.] 44 Gh 35.40N 80.29W
Salisbury Plain 9 Lj 51.15N 1.55W
Săliște 15 Gd 45.47N 23.53 E
Šalja 19 Fd 57.15N 58.43 E
Saljany 19 Eh 39.35N 48.59 E
Šalkar, Ozero- 16 Qd 50.35N 51.40 E
Šalkar-Jega-Kara, Ozero- 16 Vd 50.45N 60.55 E
Salkhad 24 Gf 32.29N 36.43 E
Salla 7 Gc 66.50N 28.40 E
Sallent de Gállego 13 Lb 42.46N 0.20W
Salling 8 Ch 56.40N 9.00 E
Salliqueló 56 He 36.45S 62.56W
Sallisaw 45 Ii 35.28N 94.47W
Salluit 39 Lc 62.12N 75.38W
Sallūm, Khalīj as- = Salum, Gulf of- (EN) 33 Ec 31.40N 25.20 E
Sallyana 25 Gc 28.22N 82.10 E
Salm 12 Ie 49.51N 6.51 E
Salmās 23 Fb 38.11N 44.47 E
Salmi 7 Hf 61.24N 31.54 E
Salmo 46 Gb 49.12N 117.17W
Salmon 43 Eb 45.11N 113.54W
Salmon Arm 42 Ff 50.42N 119.16W
Salmon Bank (EN) 60 Kb 26.56N 176.28W
Salmon Falls Creek Reservoir 46 He 42.05N 114.45W
Salmon Mountain 46 Hd 45.38N 114.50W
Salmon Mountains 46 Df 41.00N 123.00W
Salmon River 38 He 45.51N 116.46W
Salmon River Mountains 43 Dc 44.45N 115.30W
Salmtal 12 Ie 49.56N 6.48 E
Salmyš 16 Sc 52.01N 55.21 E
Salò 14 Ee 45.36N 10.31 E
Salo [C.A.R.] 35 Be 3.12N 16.07 E
Salo [Fin.] 7 Ff 60.23N 23.08 E
Salobra, Rio- 55 De 20.12S 56.29W
Salobreña 13 Ih 36.44N 3.35W
Salomon, Cap- 51h Ab 14.30N 61.06W
Salon-de-Provence 11 Lk 43.38N 5.06 E
Salonga 30 Ji 0.10S 19.50 E
Salonika (EN) = Thessaloníki 6 Ig 40.38N 22.56 E
Salonika, Gulf of- (EN) = Thermaïkós Kólpos 5 Ig 40.20N 22.45 E
Salonta 15 Ec 46.48N 21.39 E
Salop [3] 9 Ki 52.40N 2.50W
Salop 9 Ki 52.40N 2.50W
Salor 13 Ee 39.39N 7.03W
Salou 13 Nc 41.04N 1.08 E
Salouël 12 Ee 49.52N 2.15 E
Saloum 34 Bc 13.50N 16.45W
Salpausselkä 5 Ic 61.00N 26.30 E
Sal-Rei 32 Cf 16.11N 22.55W
Salsbruket 7 Cd 64.48N 11.52 E
Salseleh-ye Safīd Kūh/Paropamisus 21 If 34.30N 63.30 E
Salsipuedes, Canal de- 48 Cc 28.40N 113.00W
Salsipuedes, Punta- 49 Fi 8.28N 83.37W
Salsk 19 Ef 46.28N 41.29 E
Šalški 7 If 61.48N 36.03 E
Salso [It.] 14 Hm 37.06N 13.57 E
Salso [It.] 14 Im 37.39N 14.49 E
Salsola 14 Ji 41.37N 15.40 E
Salsomaggiore Terme 14 Df 44.49N 9.59 E
Salt 13 Oc 41.59N 2.47 E
Salta [2] 56 Hb 25.00S 64.30W
Salta 53 Jh 24.47S 65.24W
Saltash 9 Ik 50.24N 4.12W
Salt Basin 45 Dk 31.50N 105.00W
Saltburn by the Sea 9 Mg 54.35N 0.58W
Salt Cay 49 Lc 21.20N 71.11W
Salt Creek 46 Gh 36.15N 116.49W
Salt Draw 45 Ek 31.19N 103.28W
Saltee Islands/Na Sailti 9 Gi 52.07N 6.36W
Salten 7 Dc 67.45N 15.31 E
Salt Fork Arkansas River 45 Hh 36.36N 97.03W
Salt Fork Brazos 45 Gj 33.15N 100.00W
Salt Fork Red 45 Gi 34.30N 99.22W
Saltholm 8 Ei 55.40N 12.45 E
Saltillo 39 Ig 25.25N 101.01W
Salt Lake City 39 He 40.46N 111.53W
Salto [2] 55 Dj 31.25S 57.00W
Salto 14 Gh 42.23N 12.54 E
Salto [Arg.] 56 Hd 34.17S 60.15W
Salto [Ur.] 53 Ki 31.23S 57.58W
Salto da Divisa 54 Kg 16.00S 39.57W
Salto Grande 55 Hf 22.54S 49.59W
Salton Sea 38 Hf 33.20N 115.50W
Salt River 43 Ee 33.23N 112.18W
Saltsjöbaden 8 He 59.17N 18.18 E
Saltvik 7 Ef 60.17N 20.03 E
Saluafata Harbour 65c Ba 13.55S 171.38W
Saluda 44 Ig 37.36N 76.36W
Salum, Gulf of-(EN) = Sallūm, Khalīj as- 33 Ec 31.40N 25.20 E
Saluzzo 14 Bf 44.39N 7.29 E
Salvación, Bahía- 56 Eh 50.55S 75.05W
Salvador [Braz.] 53 Mg 12.59S 38.31W
Salvador [Niger] 34 Ha 23.14N 12.05 E
Salvador, Lake- 45 Kl 29.45N 90.15W
Salvador Maza 56 Hb 22.10S 63.43W
Salvaterra de Magos 13 De 39.01N 8.48W
Salvatierra [Mex.] 48 Ig 20.13N 100.53W
Salvatierra [Sp.] 13 Jb 42.51N 2.23W
Salwa, Dawḩat as- 24 Nj 25.30N 50.40 E
Salwā Baḩrī 33 Fe 24.44N 32.56 E
Salween (EN) = Thanlwin 21 Lg 16.31N 97.37 E
Salyersville 44 Fg 37.45N 83.04W
Salza 14 Ic 47.40N 14.43 E
Salzach 10 Ih 48.12N 12.56 E
Salzburg 6 Hf 47.48N 13.02 E
Salzburg [2] 14 Gc 47.20N 13.00 E
Salzburger Kalkalpen 14 Gc 47.35N 12.55 E
Salzgitter 10 Gd 52.05N 10.20 E
Salzkammergut 14 Hc 47.45N 13.30 E
Salzkotten 12 Kc 51.40N 8.36 E
Salzwedel 10 Hd 52.51N 11.09 E
Samadāy, Ra's- 24 Fj 25.00N 34.56 E
Samagaltaj 20 Ef 50.36N 95.03 E
Samaḩ [Lib.] 33 Cd 28.10N 19.10 E
Samaḩ [Sau.Ar.] 24 Kh 28.52N 45.30 E
Samaipata 54 Fg 18.09S 63.52W
Samalayuca 48 Fb 31.21N 106.28W
Samales Group 26 He 6.00N 121.45 E
Samalga Pass 40a Eb 52.48N 169.25W
Samālūt 33 Fd 28.18N 30.42 E
Samambaia, Rio- 55 Ff 22.45S 53.21W
Samaná 49 Md 19.13N 69.19W
Samaná, Bahia de- 47 Ke 19.10N 69.25W
Samaná, Cabo- 49 Md 19.18N 69.09W
Samana Cay 49 Kb 23.06N 73.42W
Samandağı 24 Fd 36.07N 35.56 E
Samangān [3] 23 Kb 36.15N 67.40 E
Samani 27 Pc 42.07N 142.56 E
Samanli Dağlari 15 Mi 40.32N 29.10 E
Samar 21 Oh 12.00N 125.00 E
Samara [R.S.F.S.R.] 5 Le 53.10N 50.04 E
Samara [Ukr.-U.S.S.R.] 16 Ie 48.33N 35.12 E
Samarai 58 Gf 10.36S 150.39 E
Samarinda 22 Nj 0.30S 117.09 E
Samarkand 22 If 39.40N 66.58 E
Samarkandskaja Oblast [3] 19 Gg 40.10N 66.20 E
Sāmarrā' 23 Fc 34.12N 43.52 E
Samar Sea 26 Hd 11.50N 124.32 E
Samaru 34 Gc 11.10N 7.38 E
Samatan 11 Gk 43.30N 0.56 E
Samate 26 Jg 0.58S 131.04 E
Samba [Zaire] 36 Ec 4.38S 26.22 E
Samba [Zaire] 36 Db 0.14N 21.19 E
Samba Caju 36 Cd 8.45S 15.25 E
Sambalpur 25 Gd 21.27N 83.58 E
Sambar, Tanjung- 26 Fg 2.59S 110.19 E
Sambas 26 Ef 1.20N 109.15 E
Sambava 37 Ib 14.15S 50.10 E
Samber 11 Kd 50.28N 4.52 E
Sāmbhar 25 Fc 26.55N 75.12 E
Sambiase 14 Kl 38.58N 16.17 E
Samboja 26 Gg 1.02S 117.02 E
Sambor 19 Cf 49.32N 23.11 E
Samborombón, Bahía- 56 Ie 36.00S 57.12W
Samborombón, Río- 55 Dl 35.43S 57.20W
Sambre 11 Kd 50.28N 4.52 E
Sambre à l'Oise, Canal de la- 11 Je 49.39N 3.20 E
Samburg 20 Cc 67.00N 78.25 E

Index Symbols

[1] Independent Nation
[2] State, Region
[3] District, County
[4] Municipality
[5] Colony, Dependency
Continent
Physical Region
Historical or Cultural Region
Mount, Mountain
Volcano
Hill
Mountains, Mountain Range
Hills, Escarpment
Plateau, Upland
Pass, Gap
Plain, Lowland
Delta
Salt Flat
Valley, Canyon
Crater, Cave
Karst Features
Depression
Polder
Desert, Dunes
Forest, Woods
Heath, Steppe
Oasis
Cape, Point
Coast, Beach
Cliff
Peninsula
Isthmus
Sandbank
Island
Atoll
Rock, Reef
Islands, Archipelago
Rocks, Reefs
Coral Reef
Well, Spring
Geyser
River, Stream
Waterfall Rapids
River Mouth, Estuary
Lake
Salt Lake
Intermittent Lake
Reservoir
Swamp, Pond
Canal
Glacier
Ice Shelf, Pack Ice
Ocean
Sea
Gulf, Bay
Strait, Fjord
Lagoon
Bank
Seamount
Tablemount
Ridge
Shelf
Basin
Escarpment, Sea Scarp
Fracture
Trench, Abyss
National Park, Reserve
Point of Interest
Recreation Site
Cave, Cavern
Historic Site
Ruins
Wall, Walls
Church, Abbey
Temple
Scientific Station
Airport
Port
Lighthouse
Mine
Tunnel
Dam, Bridge

Samch'ŏk 27 Md 37.27N 129.10 E
Samch'ŏnp'o 27 Me 34.55N 128.04 E
Samdi Dağı 24 Kd 37.19N 44.15 E
Samdŏng-ni 28 Ie 39.21N 126.14 E
Samdŭng 28 Ie 38.59N 126.11 E
Same [Indon.] 26 Ih 8.59 S 125.40 E
Same [Tan.] 36 Gc 4.04 S 37.44 E
Samer 12 Dd 50.38N 1.45 E
Sam Ford Fiord 42 Kb 70.40N 70.35W
Samfya 36 Ee 11.20 S 29.32 E
Šamhor 16 Oi 40.48N 46.01 E
Sâmi 15 Dk 38.15N 20.39 E
Sāmī Ghar 23 Kc 31.43N 67.01 E
Samīrah 24 Ji 26.18N 42.05 E
Samisu-Jima 27 Oe 31.40N 140.00 E
Şamli 15 Kj 39.48N 27.51 E
Samnah, Jabal- 24 Ei 26.26N 33.34 E
Samoa I Sisifo=Western Samoa (EN) [1] 58 Jf 13.40 S 172.30W
Samoa Islands 57 Jf 14.00 S 171.00W
Samobor 14 Je 45.48N 15.43 E
Samojlovka 16 Md 51.10N 43.43 E
Samokov 15 Gg 42.20N 23.33 E
Samolva 8 Lf 58.16N 27.45 E
Sámos 15 Jl 37.45N 26.58 E
Sámos 5 Ih 37.45N 26.48 E
Samosir, Pulau- 26 Cf 2.35N 98.50 E
Samothrace (EN) = Samothráki 15 Ii 40.27N 25.35 E
Samothráki 15 Ii 40.29N 25.31 E
Samothráki = Samothrace (EN) 15 Ii 40.27N 25.35 E
Sampacho 56 Hd 33.23 S 64.43W
Sampaga 26 Gg 2.19 S 119.07 E
Sampit 26 Fg 3.00 S 113.03 E
Sampit 22 Nj 2.32 S 112.57 E
Sampoku 29 Fb 38.30N 139.30 E
Sampwe 36 Ed 9.20 S 27.23 E
Sam Rayburn Reservoir 45 Ik 31.27N 94.37W
Samro, Ozero- 8 Mf 58.55N 28.50 E
Samsjøen 8 Da 63.05N 10.40 E
Samsø 7 Ci 55.50N 10.35 E
Samsø Bælt 8 Di 55.50N 10.45 E
Sam Son 25 Ld 19.44N 105.54 E
Samsun 22 Fe 41.17N 36.20 E
Samsun Dağı 15 Kl 37.40N 27.15 E
Samtredia 16 Mh 42.11N 42.17 E
Samuel, Mount- 59 Gc 19.41 S 134.09 E
Samuhú 55 Bh 27.31 S 60.24W
Samui, Ko- 21 Li 9.30N 100.00 E
Samur 16 Pi 41.53N 48.32 E
Samur-Apšeronski Kanal 16 Pi 40.35N 49.35 E
Samus 20 De 56.46N 84.44 E
Samut Prakan 25 Kf 13.36N 100.36 E
Samut Sakhon 25 Kf 13.31N 100.15 E
San 31 Gg 13.08N 4.53W
San [Asia] 21 Ff 13.32N 105.57 E
San [Pol.] 10 Rf 50.45N 21.51 E
San'ā' 22 Gh 15.23N 44.12 E
Sana 14 Ke 45.03N 16.23 E
Sanaag [3] 35 Hc 10.10N 47.50 E
Şanabū 24 Di 27.30N 30.47 E
Sanae 66 Bf 70.18 S 2.22W
Sanāfir 24 Fi 27.55N 34.42 E
Sanāg 35 Hd 7.45N 48.00 E
Sanaga 30 Hh 3.35N 9.38 E
San Agustín 55 Cn 38.01 S 58.21W
San Agustin, Cabo- 48 Bc 28.05N 115.20W
San Agustin, Cape- 26 Ie 6.16N 126.11 E
Sanak Islands 40 Gf 54.25N 162.35W
Sanalona, Presa- 47 Fe 24.53N 107.00W
San Ambrosio, Isla- 56 Ec 26.21 S 79.52W
Sanana 26 Ig 2.04 S 125.08 E
Sanana, Pulau- 26 Ig 2.12 S 125.55 E
Sanandaj 23 Gb 35.19N 47.00 E
San Andreas 46 Eg 38.12N 120.41W
San Andrés [3] 47 Hf 12.35N 81.42W
San Andres, Cerro- 48 Ih 19.48N 100.36W
San Andres, Isla de- 52 Hd 12.32N 81.42W
San Andrés, Laguna de- 48 Kf 22.40N 97.50W
San Andrés de Giles 55 Cl 34.27 S 59.27W
San Andrés del Rabanedo 13 Gb 42.37N 5.36W
San Andres Mountains 45 Fe 32.55N 106.45W
San Andres Peak 45 Cj 32.43N 106.30W
San Andrés Tuxtla 47 Ee 18.27N 95.13W
San Andrés y Providencia [2] 54 Ba 12.30N 81.45W
Sananduva 55 Gh 27.57 S 51.48W
San Angelo 43 Ge 31.28N 100.26W
San Antonio [Blz.] 49 Ce 16.30N 89.02W
San Antonio [Chile] 56 Fd 33.35 S 71.38W
San Antonio [Tx.-U.S.] 39 Jg 29.28N 98.31W
San Antonio [Ur.] 55 Dj 31.20 S 57.45W
San Antonio, Cabo- [Arg.] 52 Ki 36.40 S 56.42W
San Antonio, Cabo- [Cuba] 38 Kg 21.52N 84.57W
San Antonio, Cabo de-/Sant Antoni, Cap- 13 Mf 38.48N 0.12 E
San Antonio, Canal- 55 Aj 31.42 S 62.15W
San Antonio, Punta- 48 Bc 29.45N 115.45W
San Antonio, Sierra de- 48 Db 30.00N 110.20W
San Antonio Abad 13 Nf 38.58N 1.18 E
San Antonio Bay 45 Hl 28.20N 96.45W
San Antonio de Caparo 49 Lj 7.35N 71.27W
San Antonio de Cortés 49 Cf 15.05N 88.04W
San Antonio de los Baños 49 Fb 22.53N 82.30W
San Antonio de los Cobres 56 Gb 24.11 S 66.21W
San Antonio del Táchira 54 Db 7.50N 72.27W
San Antonio de Tamanaco 50 Ch 9.14N 66.03W
San Antonio Oeste 53 Jj 40.44 S 64.57W
San Antonio River 43 Hf 28.30N 96.50W
Sanare 49 Mi 9.45N 69.39W
Sanary-sur-Mer 11 Lk 43.07N 5.48 E
San Augustin 53 Ie 1.53N 76.16W
San Augustine 45 Ik 31.32N 94.07W
Sanāw 35 Ib 17.50N 51.05 E
San Bartolomeo in Galdo 14 Ji 41.24N 15.01 E
San Baudilio de Llobregat/Sant Boi de Llobregat 13 Oc 41.21N 2.03 E
San Benedetto del Tronto 14 Hh 42.57N 13.53 E
San Benedetto Po 14 Ee 45.02N 10.55 E
San Benedicto, Isla- 47 Be 19.18N 110.49W
San Benito [Guat.] 49 Ce 16.55N 89.54W
San Benito [Tx.-U.S.] 45 Hm 26.08N 97.38W
San Benito, Islas- 48 Bc 28.20N 115.35W
San Benito Abad 49 Ji 8.56N 75.02W
San Benito Mountain 46 Eh 36.22N 120.38W
San Bernardino 39 Hf 34.06N 117.17W
San Bernardino, Passo del-/Sankt Bernardin Paß 14 Dd 46.30N 9.10 E
San Bernardino Mountains 46 Gi 34.10N 117.00W
San Bernardino Strait 26 Hd 12.32N 124.10 E
San Bernardo [Arg.] 55 Bh 27.17 S 60.42W
San Bernardo [Chile] 56 Fd 33.36 S 70.43W
San Bernardo [Mex.] 48 De 25.32N 111.45W
San Bernardo, Islas de- 49 Ji 9.45N 75.50W
San Bernardo, Punta de- 49 Ji 9.42N 75.42W
San Bernardo del Viento 54 Cb 9.22N 75.57W
San Blas 49 Hi 7.50N 81.10W
San Blas [Mex.] 47 Cd 21.31N 105.16W
San Blas [Mex.] 47 Cc 26.05N 108.46W
San Blas [Mex.] 48 Id 27.25N 101.40W
San Blas, Archipiélago de- 49 Hi 9.30N 78.30W
San Blas, Cape- 43 Jf 29.40N 85.22W
San Blas, Cordillera de- 49 Hi 9.18N 79.00W
San Blas, Golfo de- 49 Hi 9.30N 79.00W
San Blas, Punta- 49 Hi 9.34N 78.58W
San Borja 54 Ef 14.49 S 66.51W
San Borjas, Sierra de- 48 Cc 28.40N 113.45W
San Buenaventura 48 Id 27.05N 101.32W
Sancai 35 Fc 10.43N 35.40 E
San Carlos [Arg.] 55 Eh 27.45 S 55.54W
San Carlos [Chile] 56 Fe 36.25 S 71.58W
San Carlos [Mex.] 48 Je 24.35N 98.56W
San Carlos [Mex.] 48 Ic 29.01N 100.51W
San Carlos [Nic.] 49 Eh 11.07N 84.47W
San Carlos [Pan.] 49 Hi 8.29N 79.57W
San Carlos [Par.] 55 Df 22.16 S 57.18W
San Carlos [Phil.] 26 Hd 10.30N 123.25 E
San Carlos [Phil.] 26 Hc 15.55N 120.20 E
San Carlos [Ur.] 56 Jd 34.48 S 54.55W
San Carlos [Ven.] 54 Eb 9.40N 68.39W
San Carlos, Bahía- 48 Cd 27.55N 112.45W
San Carlos, Mesa de- 48 Bc 29.40N 115.25W
San Carlos, Punta- 48 Cc 28.00N 112.45W
San Carlos, Riacho- 55 Df 22.49 S 57.53W
San Carlos, Rio- [C.R.] 49 Eh 10.47N 84.12W
San Carlos, Rio- [Ven.] 50 Bh 9.07N 68.25W
San Carlos de Bariloche 53 Ij 41.08 S 71.15W
San Carlos de Bolívar 56 He 36.15 S 61.06W
San Carlos de la Rápita/Sant Carles de la Ràpita 13 Md 40.37N 0.36 E
San Carlos del Zulia 54 Db 9.01N 71.55W
San Carlos de Rio Negro 54 Ec 1.55N 67.04W
San Carlos Reservoir 46 Jj 33.13N 110.24W
San Cataldo [It.] 14 Mj 40.23N 18.18 E
San Cataldo [It.] 14 Hm 37.29N 13.59 E
San Cayetano 55 Cn 38.20 S 59.37W
Sancerre 11 Ig 47.20N 2.50 E
Sancerrois, Collines du- 11 Ig 47.20N 2.30 E
Sanchahe 28 Ib 44.59N 126.03 E
Sánchez 49 Md 19.14N 69.36W
Sánchez Magallanes 48 Mh 18.17N 93.59W
San Clemente [Ca.-U.S.] 43 De 33.26N 117.37W
San Clemente [Sp.] 13 Je 39.24N 2.26W
San Clemente del Tuyú 55 Dm 36.22 S 56.43W
San Clemente Island 46 Fj 32.55N 118.30W
Sancois 11 Ih 46.50N 2.55 E
San Cosme 55 Ch 27.22 S 58.31W
San Cristóbal [Arg.] 56 Hd 30.19 S 61.14W
San Cristóbal [Bol.] 55 Ba 13.56 S 61.50W
San Cristóbal [Cuba] 49 Fb 22.43N 83.03W
San Cristóbal [Dom.Rep.] 49 Ld 18.25N 70.06W
San Cristóbal [Mex.] 48 Li 17.49N 94.32W
San Cristóbal [Ven.] 53 Ie 7.46N 72.14W
San Cristobal, Baia de- 48 Bd 27.25N 114.40W
San Cristóbal, Isla- 54 b 0.50 S 89.26W
San Cristóbal de las Casas 47 Fe 16.45N 92.38W
San Cristóbal Island 57 Hf 10.36 S 161.45 E
San Cristóbal Verapaz 49 Bf 15.23N 90.24W
Sancti Spiritus 47 Id 21.56N 79.27W
Sancti Spiritus [3] 49 Hb 22.00N 79.30W
Sancy, Puy de- 11 Ii 45.32N 2.50 E
Sand 7 Bg 59.29N 6.15 E
Sand 37 Ed 22.25 S 30.05 E
Sanda 29 Dd 34.53N 135.14 E
Sandai 26 Fg 1.15 S 110.31 E
Sandakan 22 Ni 5.50N 118.07 E
Sandal, Baie de- 63b Ce 20.49 S 167.10 E
Sandal, Ozero- 7 Ie 62.25N 34.10 E
Sandane 7 Bf 61.46N 6.13 E
Sandanski 15 Gh 41.34N 23.17 E
Sandaré 34 Cc 14.42N 10.18W
Sandared 8 Eg 57.43N 12.47 E
Sandarne 8 Gc 61.16N 17.10 E
Sanday 9 Kb 59.15N 2.30W
Sande 8 De 59.36N 10.12 E
Sandefjord 7 Cg 59.08N 10.14 E
Sandégué 34 Ed 7.59N 3.33W
Sandeid 7 Ag 59.33N 5.50 E
Sanders 46 Ki 35.13N 109.20W
Sanderson 43 Ge 30.09N 102.24W
Sandersville 44 Fi 32.59N 82.48W
Sandfontein 37 Bd 22.11 S 19.58 E
Sandgate 12 Dc 51.04N 1.09 E
Sandhammaren 8 Fi 55.23N 14.12 E
Sandhamn 8 He 59.17N 18.55 E
Sand Hills 45 Ff 42.10N 101.30W
Sandia 54 Ef 14.17 S 69.26W
Sandia Crest 45 Ci 35.13N 106.27W
San Diego [Bol.] 55 Bc 16.04 S 60.28W
San Diego [Ca.-U.S.] 39 Hf 32.43N 117.09W
San Diego, Cabo- 52 Jk 54.38 S 65.07W
Sandıklı 24 Dc 38.28N 30.17 E
San Dimitri Point 14 In 36.05N 14.05 E
Sand in Taufers / Campo Tures 14 Fd 46.55N 11.57 E
Sand Lake 45 Ia 50.05N 94.39W
Sand Mountain 44 Dh 34.20N 86.02W
Sandnes 7 Ag 58.51N 5.44 E
Sandnessjøen 7 Cc 66.01N 12.38 E
Sandoa 31 Ji 9.41 S 22.52 E
Sandö bank 8 Hf 58.10N 19.15 E
Sandomierska, Kotlina- 10 Rf 50.30N 22.00 E
Sandomierz 10 Rf 50.41N 21.45 E
San Domino 14 Jh 42.05N 15.30 E
Sandoná 54 Cc 1.18N 77.28W
San Donà di Piave 14 Ge 45.38N 12.34 E
Sandoval, Boca de- 48 Ke 24.58N 97.32W
Sandover River 59 Hd 21.43 S 136.32 E
Sandoway 25 Ie 18.28N 94.22 E
Sandown 9 Lk 50.39N 1.09W
Sand Point 40 Ge 55.20N 160.30W
Sandpoint 43 Db 48.16N 116.33W
Sandras Dağı 15 Ll 37.04N 28.51 E
Sandray 9 Fe 56.54N 7.25W
Sandspit 42 Ef 53.15N 131.50W
Sand Springs [Mt.-U.S.] 46 Lc 47.09N 107.27W
Sand Springs [Ok.-U.S.] 45 Hh 36.09N 96.07W
Sandstone [Austl.] 59 De 27.59 S 119.17 E
Sandstone [Mn.-U.S.] 45 Jc 46.08N 92.52W
Sandu 27 Jf 26.08N 113.16 E
Sandusky [Mi.-U.S.] 44 Fd 43.25N 82.50W
Sandusky [Oh.-U.S.] 43 Kc 41.27N 82.42W
Sandveld 37 Cd 21.20 S 20.10 E
Sandvig-Allinge 7 Di 55.15N 14.49 E
Sandvika 8 De 59.54N 10.31 E
Sandviken 7 Df 60.37N 16.46 E
Sandwich 9 Oj 51.17N 1.20 E
Sandwich Bay 42 Lf 53.35N 57.15W
Sandy 12 Bb 52.07N 0.17W
Sandy Cape [Austl.] 59 Ih 41.25 S 144.45 E
Sandy Cape [Austl.] 57 Gg 24.40 S 153.15 E
Sandy Desert 25 Cc 28.46N 62.30 E
Sandykači 19 Gh 36.32N 62.35 E
Sandy Lake 42 If 53.02N 92.55W
Sandy Lake 42 If 53.02N 93.14W
Sandy Point 44 Il 26.01N 77.24W
Sandy Point Town 50 Ed 17.22N 62.50W
Sandžak 15 Cf 43.10N 20.00 E
Sanem 12 He 49.33N 5.56 E
San Estanislao 56 Ib 24.39 S 56.26W
San Esteban 49 Ef 15.17N 85.52W
San Esteban, Bahía de- 48 Ee 25.40N 109.15W
San Esteban, Isla- 48 Cc 28.42N 112.36W
San Esteban de Gormaz 13 Ic 41.35N 3.12W
San Felice Circeo 14 Hi 41.14N 13.05 E
San Felipe [Chile] 56 Fd 32.45 S 70.44W
San Felipe [Col.] 54 Ec 1.55N 67.06W
San Felipe [Mex.] 47 Bb 31.00N 114.52W
San Felipe [Mex.] 48 Ig 21.29N 101.13W
San Felipe [Ven.] 54 Ea 10.20N 68.44W
San Felipe, Cayos de- 49 Fc 21.58N 83.30W
San Felipe, Cerro de- 13 Kd 40.24N 1.51W
San Felipe Creek 46 Hj 33.09N 115.46W
San Feliu de Guixols 13 Pc 41.47N 3.02 E
San Feliu de Llobregat/Sant Feliu de Llobregat 13 Oc 41.23N 2.03 E
San Felix, Isla- 56 Dc 26.17 S 80.05W
San Fermin, Punta- 48 Bb 30.25N 114.40W
San Fernando [Chile] 56 Fd 34.35 S 71.00W
San Fernando [Mex.] 48 Bb 29.59N 115.17W
San Fernando [Mex.] 47 Ed 24.51N 98.10W
San Fernando [Phil.] 26 Hc 16.37N 120.19 E
San Fernando [Phil.] 26 Hc 15.01N 120.41 E
San Fernando [Sp.] 13 Fh 36.28N 6.12W
San Fernando [Trin.] 54 Fa 10.17N 61.28W
San Fernando, Rio- [Bol.] 55 Cc 17.13 S 58.23W
San Fernando, Rio- [Mex.] 48 Ke 24.55N 97.40W
San Fernando de Apure 53 Je 7.54N 67.28W
San Fernando de Atabapo 54 Ec 4.03N 67.42W
Sanford [Fl.-U.S.] 43 Kf 28.48N 81.16W
Sanford [Me.-U.S.] 44 Ld 43.26N 70.46W
Sanford [N.C.-U.S.] 44 Hh 35.29N 79.10W
Sanford, Mount- 40 Kd 62.13N 144.09W
San Francisco [Arg.] 56 Hd 31.26 S 62.05W
San Francisco [Bol.] 55 Cc 17.42 S 59.38W
San Francisco [Ca.-U.S.] 39 Gf 37.48N 122.24W
San Francisco [Pan.] 49 Gi 8.15N 80.58W
San Francisco, Isla- 48 De 24.50N 110.35W
San Francisco Bay 38 Gf 37.43N 122.17W
San Francisco Creek 45 El 29.53N 102.19W
San Francisco de Arriba 48 Hd 26.15N 102.50W
San Francisco de Bellocq 55 Bn 38.42 S 60.01W
San Francisco de la Paz 49 Df 14.55N 86.14W
San Francisco del Laishi 55 Ch 26.14 S 58.38W
San Francisco del Oro 47 Cc 26.52N 105.51W
San Francisco del Rincón 48 Ig 21.01N 101.51W
San Francisco de Macoris 47 Je 19.18N 70.15W
San Francisco Gotera 49 Cg 13.42N 88.06W
San Francisco Javier 13 Nf 38.42N 1.25 E
San Francisco Mountains 46 Kj 33.45N 109.00W
San Francisco River 46 Kj 32.59N 109.22W
San Fratello 14 Il 38.01N 14.36 E
San Gabriel 55 Di 28.58 S 58.12W
San Gabriel, Punta- 48 Cc 28.25N 112.50W
San Gabriel Mountains 46 Gi 34.20N 117.45W
San Gallán, Isla- 54 Cf 13.50 S 76.28W
Sangamon River 45 Kf 40.07N 90.20W
Sangar [Iran] 24 Md 37.08N 49.02 E
Sangar [R.S.F.S.R.] 22 Oc 63.55N 127.31 E
Sangatte 12 Dd 50.56N 1.45 E
San Gavino Monreale 14 Ck 39.33N 8.47 E
Sangay, Volcán- 52 If 2.00 S 78.20W
Sange 36 Ed 7.02 S 28.21 E
Sangeang, Pulau- 26 Gh 8.12 S 119.04 E
San Gemini 14 Gh 42.37N 12.33 E
Sanger 46 Fh 36.42N 119.27W
Sangerhausen 10 He 51.28N 11.18 E
San Germán [Cuba] 49 Ic 20.36N 76.08W
San Germán [P.R.] 49 Nd 18.05N 67.03W
Sanggan He 28 Cd 40.24N 115.18 E
Sanggau 26 Ff 0.08N 110.36 E
Sangha 30 Ii 1.13 S 16.49 E
Sangha [C.A.R.] [3] 35 Be 3.30N 16.00 E
Sangha [Con.] [3] 36 Cb 2.00N 15.00 E
Sangihe, Kepulauan-=Sangihe Islands (EN) 21 Oi 3.00N 125.30 E
Sangihe, Pulau- 26 If 3.35N 125.32 E
Sangihe Islands (EN)=Sangihe, Kepulauan- 21 Oi 3.00N 125.30 E
San Gil 54 Db 6.32N 73.08W
San Gimignano 14 Fg 43.28N 11.02 E
San Giovanni in Fiore 14 Kk 39.15N 16.42 E
San Giovanni in Persiceto 14 Ff 44.38N 11.11 E
San Giovanni Rotondo 14 Ji 41.42N 15.44 E
San Giovanni Valdarno 14 Fg 43.34N 11.32 E
Sangju 28 Jf 36.25N 128.10 E
Sāngli 22 Jh 16.52N 74.34 E
Sangmélima 34 He 2.56N 11.59 E
Sangoli 24 Pd 37.25N 54.35 E
San Gorgonio 38 Hf 34.05N 116.50W
San Gottardo/Sankt Gotthard=Saint Gotthard Pass (EN) 5 Gf 46.30N 8.30 E
Sangradouro Grande, Rio- 55 Dc 16.24 S 57.10W
Sangre de Cristo Mountains 38 If 37.30N 105.15W
San Gregorio 55 Al 34.19 S 62.02W
Sangre Grande 50 Fg 10.35N 61.07W
Sangri 27 Ff 29.20N 92.15 E
Sangro 14 Ih 42.14N 14.32 E
Sangue, Rio- 54 Gf 11.00 S 58.40W
Sangüesa 13 Kb 42.35N 1.17W
Sanguinaires, Iles- 11 Ab 41.53N 8.35 E
San Gustavo 55 Cj 30.41 S 59.23W
Sangyuan → Wuqiao 28 Df 37.38N 116.23 E
Sangzhi 27 Jf 29.23N 110.11 E
Sanhe [China] 28 Dd 40.00N 117.01 E
Sanhe [China] 27 La 50.30N 120.04 E
Sanhe-San 29 Cd 35.08N 132.37 E
Sanhezhen 28 Di 31.30N 117.15 E
San Hilario [Arg.] 55 Ch 26.02 S 58.39W
San Hilario [Mex.] 48 De 24.22N 110.59W
San Hipolito, Bahía- 48 Cd 26.55N 113.55W
San Ignacio [Arg.] 55 Eh 27.16 S 55.32W
San Ignacio [Blz.] 49 Ge 17.10N 89.04W
San Ignacio [Bol.] 54 Ef 14.53 S 65.36W
San Ignacio [Bol.] 54 Fg 16.23 S 60.59W
San Ignacio [Mex.] 48 Ff 25.55N 106.25W
San Ignacio [Mex.] 47 Bc 27.27N 112.51W
San Ignacio [Par.] 56 Ic 26.52 S 57.03W
San Ignacio, Isla de- 48 Ee 25.25N 108.55W
San Ignacio, Laguna- 48 Cd 26.55N 113.15W
San Ildefonso, Cape- 26 Hc 16.02N 121.59 E
San Ildefonso, Cerro- 49 Cf 15.31N 88.17W
San Ildefonso o La Granja 13 Id 40.54N 4.00W
Saniquellie 34 Dd 7.22N 8.43W
San Isidro [Arg.] 56 Id 34.27 S 58.30W
San Isidro [Phil.] 26 Hd 11.24N 124.21 E
San Isidro de El General 47 Hg 9.22N 83.42W
Saniyah 24 If 33.49N 42.43 E
San Jacinto 49 Ji 9.50N 75.07W
San Jacinto Peak 46 Gj 33.49N 116.41W
San Jaime 55 Cj 30.20 S 58.19W
San Javier [Arg.] 56 Id 30.35 S 59.57W
San Javier [Chile] 56 Fe 35.36 S 71.45W
San Javier [Sp.] 13 Lg 37.48N 0.51W
San Javier [Ur.] 55 Ck 32.41 S 58.08W
San Javier, Rio- 55 Bj 31.30 S 60.20W
San Jerónimo Taviche 48 Ki 16.44N 96.35W
Sanjiachang 27 Hg 24.45N 101.53 E
Sanjiaocheng → Haiyan 27 Hd 36.58N 100.50 E
Sanjō 28 Of 37.37N 138.57 E
San Joaquin 54 Ff 13.04 S 64.49W
San Joaquín, Rio- 54 Ff 13.08 S 63.41W
San Joaquín, Sierra de- 55 Eg 24.48 S 56.00W
San Joaquin River 46 Eh 36.43N 121.50W
San Joaquin Valley 38 Gf 36.50N 120.10W
San Jon 45 Ei 35.06N 103.20W
San Jorge 56 Hd 31.54 S 61.52W
San Jorge, Bahía de- 48 Cb 31.10N 113.15W
San Jorge, Golfe de-/Sant Jordi, Golf de- 13 Md 40.53N 1.00 E
San Jorge, Golfo- 52 Jj 46.00 S 67.00W
San Jorge, Rio- 49 Ji 9.07N 74.44W
San Jorge, Serrania- 55 Be 20.21 S 60.59W
San Jorge Island 63a Dc 8.27 S 159.35 E
San José 55 Dl 34.15 S 56.45W
San José [3] 49 Ei 9.40N 84.00W
San José [Arg.] 55 Eh 27.46 S 55.47W
San José [Ca.-U.S.] 39 Gf 37.20N 121.53W
San José [C.R.] 39 Ki 9.56N 84.05W
San José [Mex.] 48 Dd 27.32N 110.09W
San José [Par.] 55 Dg 25.33 S 56.45W
San Jose [Phil.] 26 Hc 15.48N 121.00 E
San Jose [Phil.] 26 Hd 12.21N 121.04 E
San José, Isla- [Mex.] 47 Bc 25.00N 110.38W
San José, Isla- [Pan.] 49 Hi 8.15N 79.07W
San José, Salinas de- 55 Bd 19.07 S 60.54W
San José, Serrania de- 55 Bc 17.52 S 60.49W
San José de Buenavista 26 Hd 10.46N 121.56 E
San José de Chiquitos 54 Fg 17.51 S 60.47W
San José de Feliciano 55 Cj 30.23 S 58.45W
San José de Gracia 48 Fd 26.08N 107.58W
San José de Guanipa 54 Fb 8.54N 64.09W
San José de Jachal 56 Gd 30.14 S 68.45W
San José de las Lajas 49 Fb 22.58N 82.09W
San José del Cabo 47 Cd 23.03N 109.41W
San José del Guaviare 53 Ie 2.35N 72.38W
San José del Rosario 55 Dg 24.12 S 56.48W
San José de Mayo 56 Id 34.20 S 56.42W
San José de Ocuné 54 Dc 4.15N 70.20W
San José de Tiznados 50 Ch 9.23N 67.33W
San Juan [2] 56 Gd 31.00 S 69.00W
San Juan [Arg.] 53 Ji 31.30 S 68.30W
San Juán [Bol.] 55 Cc 17.52 S 59.59W
San Juán [Bol.] 55 Bd 18.08 S 60.08W
San Juan [C.Amer.] 38 Kh 10.56N 83.42W
San Juan [Dom.Rep.] 47 Je 18.48N 71.14W
San Juan [P.R.] 39 Mh 18.28N 66.07W
San Juan [U.S.] 38 Hf 37.18N 110.28W
San Juan, Cabezas de- 51a Cb 18.23N 65.36W
San Juan, Cabo- 30 Hh 1.10N 9.21 E
San Juan, Muela de- 13 Kd 40.26N 1.44W
San Juan, Pico- 47 Hd 21.59N 80.09W
San Juan, Punta- 65d Ab 27.03 S 109.22W
San Juan, Rio- [Arg.] 56 Gd 32.17 S 67.22W
San Juan, Rio- [Mex.] 48 Jd 26.10N 99.00W
San Juan, Rio- [Mex.] 48 Lh 18.36N 95.40W
San Juan, Rio- [Ven.] 50 Eg 10.14N 62.39W
San Juan, Volcán- 48 Gg 21.30N 104.57W
San Juan Bautista [Par.] 56 Ic 26.38 S 57.10W
San Juan Bautista [Sp.] 13 Ne 39.05N 1.30 E
San Juan Bautista Tuxtepec 48 Kh 18.06N 96.07W
San Juan de Colón 49 Ki 8.02N 72.16W
San Juan de Guadalupe 48 He 24.38N 102.44W
San Juan del César 49 Kh 10.46N 72.59W
San Juan de Lima, Punta- 48 Hh 18.36N 103.42W
San Juan del Norte 47 Hf 10.55N 83.42W
San Juan de los Cayos 54 Ea 11.10N 68.25W
San Juan de los Lagos 48 Hg 21.15N 102.14W
San Juan de los Morros 54 Ea 9.55N 67.21W
San Juan del Rio [Mex.] 48 Jg 20.29N 100.00W
San Juan del Rio [Mex.] 48 Ge 24.47N 104.27W
San Juan del Sur 47 Gf 11.15N 85.52W
San Juan de Payara 50 Ci 7.39N 67.36W
San Juanico, Isla- 48 Fg 21.55N 106.40W
San Juanico, Punta- 48 Cd 26.05N 112.15W
San Juan Island 46 Db 48.32N 123.05W
San Juan Mountains 43 Fd 37.35N 107.10W
San Juan Neembucú 55 Dh 26.39 S 57.56W
San Juan Nepomuceno [Col.] 54 Cb 9.57N 75.05W
San Juan Nepomuceno [Par.] 55 Eh 26.06 S 55.58W
San Juan y Martinez 49 Fb 22.16N 83.50W
San Julián 53 Jj 49.19 S 67.40W
San Just, Sierra de- 13 Ld 40.46N 0.48W
San Justo 56 Hd 30.47 S 60.35W
Sankarani 30 Gg 12.01N 8.19W
Sankt Anton am Arlberg 14 Ec 47.08N 10.16 E
Sankt Augustin 12 Jd 50.47N 7.11 E
Sankt Bernardin Paß/San Bernardino, Passo del- 14 Dd 46.30N 9.10 E
Sankt Gallen 14 Dc 47.25N 9.25 E
Sankt Gallen [2] 14 Dc 47.20N 9.10 E
Sankt Goar 10 Df 50.09N 7.43 E
Sankt Goarshausen 12 Jd 50.09N 7.44 E
Sankt Gotthard/San Gottardo=Saint Gotthard Pass (EN) 5 Gf 46.30N 8.30 E
Sankt Ingbert 10 Dg 49.17N 7.07 E
Sankt Johann im Pongau 14 Hc 47.21N 13.12 E
Sankt Michael im Lungau 14 Hc 47.06N 13.38 E
Sankt Michel/Mikkeli 6 If 61.41N 27.15 E
Sankt Moritz 14 Dd 46.30N 9.52 E
Sankt Peter-Ording 10 Eb 54.18N 8.38 E
Sankt Pölten 14 Jb 48.12N 15.38 E
Sankt Ulrich / Ortisei 14 Fd 46.34N 11.40 E
Sankt Veit an der Glan 14 Id 46.46N 14.22 E
Sankt-Vith 11 Md 50.17N 6.08 E
Sankt Wendel 10 Dg 49.28N 7.10 E
Sankt Wolfang im Salzkammergut 14 Hc 47.44N 13.27 E
Sankuru 30 Ji 4.17 S 20.25 E
San Lázaro 56 Ib 22.10 S 57.55W
San Lázaro, Cabo- 47 Bd 24.48N 112.19W
San Lazaro, Sierra de- 48 Df 23.25N 110.00W
San Leandro 46 Dh 37.43N 122.09W
San Lorenzo 47 Fe 17.44N 94.45W
San Lorenzo [Arg.] 55 Bk 32.45 S 60.44W
San Lorenzo [Ec.] 53 Ie 1.17N 78.50W
San Lorenzo [Hond.] 49 Dg 13.25N 87.27W
San Lorenzo, Isla- [Mex.] 48 Cc 28.38N 112.51W
San Lorenzo, Isla- [Peru] 54 Cf 12.05 S 77.15W
San Lorenzo, Rio- [Mex.] 48 Je 25.07N 98.32W
San Lorenzo, Rio- [Mex.] 48 Fe 24.15N 107.24W
San Lorenzo de El Escorial 13 Hd 40.35N 4.09W
San Louis Potosi [2] 47 Dd 22.30N 100.30W
Sanlúcar de Barrameda 13 Fh 36.47N 6.21W
Sanlúcar la Mayor 13 Fg 37.23N 6.12W
San Lucas [Mex.] 48 Gf 22.33N 104.24W
San Lucas [Mex.] 47 Cd 22.53N 109.54W
San Lucas, Cabo- 38 Ig 22.50N 109.55W
San Lucas, Serrania de- 54 Db 8.00N 74.20W
San Lucido 14 Kk 39.18N 16.03 E
San Luis [Arg.] 53 Ji 33.20 S 66.20W
San Luis [2] 56 Gd 34.00 S 66.00W
San Luis [Bol.] 55 Cc 17.39 S 58.42W
San Luis [Cuba] 49 Jc 20.12N 75.51W
San Luis [Guat.] 49 Ce 16.14N 89.27W
San Luis [Mex.] 48 Dc 29.33N 111.05W
San Luis, Isla- 48 Bb 29.58N 114.26W
San Luis, Sierra de- 49 Mh 11.11N 69.42W
San Luis de la Paz 48 Ig 21.18N 100.31W
San Luis del Palmar 55 Ch 27.31 S 58.34W
San Luis de Palenque 54 Db 5.25N 71.40W
San Luis Gonzaga, Bahía- 48 Bc 30.00N 114.25W
San Luis Obispo 39 Gf 35.17N 120.40W
San Luis Pass 45 Il 29.05N 95.08W
San Luis Peak 45 Ch 37.59N 106.56W
San Luis Potosi 39 Ig 22.09N 100.59W
San Luis Rio Colorado 47 Bb 32.29N 114.48W
San Luis Valley 43 Fd 37.25N 106.00W
Sanluri 14 Ck 39.34N 8.54 E
San Manuel [Arg.] 55 Cm 37.47 S 58.50W
San Manuel [Az.-U.S.] 46 Jj 32.36N 110.38W

Index Symbols

[1] Independent Nation
[2] State, Region
[3] District, County
[4] Municipality
[5] Colony, Dependency
Continent
Physical Region
Historical or Cultural Region
Mount, Mountain
Volcano
Hill
Mountains, Mountain Range
Hills, Escarpment
Plateau, Upland
Pass, Gap
Plain, Lowland
Delta
Salt Flat
Valley, Canyon
Crater, Cave
Karst Features
Depression
Polder
Desert, Dunes
Forest, Woods
Heath, Steppe
Oasis
Cape, Point
Coast, Beach
Cliff
Peninsula
Isthmus
Sandbank
Island
Atoll
Rock, Reef
Islands, Archipelago
Rocks, Reefs
Coral Reef
Well, Spring
Geyser
River, Stream
Waterfall Rapids
River Mouth, Estuary
Lake
Salt Lake
Intermittent Lake
Reservoir
Swamp, Pond
Canal
Glacier
Ice Shelf, Pack Ice
Ocean
Sea
Gulf, Bay
Strait, Fjord
Lagoon
Bank
Seamount
Tablemount
Ridge
Shelf
Basin
Escarpment, Sea Scarp
Fracture
Trench, Abyss
National Park, Reserve
Point of Interest
Recreation Site
Cave, Cavern
Historic Site
Ruins
Wall, Walls
Church, Abbey
Temple
Scientific Station
Airport
Port
Lighthouse
Mine
Tunnel
Dam, Bridge

Index Symbols

① Independent Nation
② State, Region
③ District, County
④ Municipality
⑤ Colony, Dependency
■ Continent
▣ Physical Region

▨ Historical or Cultural Region
▲ Mount, Mountain
▲ Volcano
▲ Hill
▣ Mountains, Mountain Range
▣ Hills, Escarpment
▣ Plateau, Upland

▭ Pass, Gap
▭ Plain, Lowland
▭ Delta
▭ Salt Flat
▭ Valley, Canyon
▣ Crater, Cave
▣ Karst Features

▨ Depression
▨ Polder
▨ Desert, Dunes
▨ Forest, Woods
▨ Heath, Steppe
▨ Oasis
▨ Cape, Point

▨ Coast, Beach
▨ Cliff
▨ Peninsula
▨ Isthmus
▨ Sandbank
▨ Island
▣ Atoll

▨▨ Rock, Reef
▨ Islands, Archipelago
▨ Rocks, Reefs
▨ Coral Reef
▨ Well, Spring
▨ Geyser
▨ River, Stream

▨ Waterfall Rapids
▨ River Mouth, Estuary
▨ Lake
▨ Salt Lake
▨ Intermittent Lake
▨ Reservoir
▨ Swamp, Pond

▨ Canal
▨ Glacier
▨ Ice Shelf, Pack Ice
▨ Ocean
▨ Sea
▨ Gulf, Bay
▨ Strait, Fjord

▨ Lagoon
▨ Bank
▨ Seamount
▨ Tablemount
▨ Ridge
▨ Shelf
▨ Basin

▨ Escarpment, Sea Scarp
▨ Fracture
▨ Trench, Abyss
▨ National Park, Reserve
▨ Point of Interest
▨ Recreation Site
▨ Cave, Cavern

▨ Historic Site
▨ Ruins
▨ Wall, Walls
▨ Church, Abbey
▨ Temple
▨ Scientific Station
▨ Airport

▨ Port
▨ Lighthouse
▨ Mine
▨ Tunnel
▨ Dam, Bridge

São Mateus, Rio-	55	Ia	13.48S	46.54W
São Miguel	30	Ee	37.47N	25.30W
São Miguel, Rio-	55	Ic	16.03S	46.07W
São Miguel do Araguaia	55	Ga	13.19S	50.13W
São Miguel d'Oeste	55	Fh	26.45S	53.34W
Saona, Isla-	49	Md	18.09N	68.40W
Saône	5	Gf	45.44N	4.50 E
Saône-et-Loire [3]	11	Kh	46.40N	4.30 E
Saonek	26	Jg	0.28S	130.47 E
São Nicolau	30	Eg	16.35N	24.15W
São Nicolau [Braz.]	55	Ei	28.11S	55.16W
São Patricio, Rio-	55	Hb	15.02S	49.15W
São Paulo	53	Lh	23.32S	46.37W
São Paulo [2]	56	Kb	22.00S	49.00W
São Paulo de Olivença	54	Ed	3.27S	68.48W
São Pedro, Ribeirão	55	Ic	16.54S	46.32W
São Pedro do Sul [Braz.]	55	Ei	29.37S	54.10W
São Pedro do Sul [Port.]	13	Dd	40.45N	8.04W
São Pedro e São Paulo, Penedos de-	52	Ne	0.56N	29.22W
São Raimundo Nonato	54	Je	9.01S	42.42W
São Romão [Braz.]	55	Ed	18.33S	54.27W
São Romão [Braz.]	54	Ig	16.22S	45.04W
São Roque	55	De	21.43S	57.46W
São Roque, Cabo de-	52	Mf	5.29S	35.16W
São Roque, Serra de-	55	Ib	14.40S	46.50W
São Sebastião	55	Jf	23.48S	45.25W
São Sebastião, Ilha de-	52	Lh	23.50S	45.18W
São Sebastião, Ponta-	30	Kk	22.05S	35.24 E
São Sebastião da Boa Vista	54	Id	1.42S	49.31W
São Sebastião do Paraiso	54	Ih	20.55S	47.00W
São Sepé	55	Fj	30.10S	53.34W
São Simão	54	Hg	18.56S	50.30W
São Tiago	30	Eg	15.05N	23.40W
São Tomé	30	Hh	0.12N	6.39 E
São Tomé	31	Hh	0.20N	6.44 E
São Tomé, Cabo de-	54	Jh	22.00S	40.59W
Sao Tome and Principe (EN) = São Tomé e Principe [1]	31	Hh	1.00N	7.00 E
São Tomé e Principe = Sao Tome and Principe (EN) [1]	31	Hh	1.00N	7.00 E
Saoura	32	Gd	27.50N	2.50W
Saoura	30	Gf	28.48N	0.50W
São Vicente	30	Eg	16.50N	25.00W
São Vicente [Braz.]	55	Ia	13.38S	46.31W
São Vicente [Braz.]	56	Kb	23.58S	46.23W
São Vicente, Cabo de-	5	Fh	37.01N	9.00W
São Xavier, Serra de-	55	Ei	29.15S	54.15W
Sápai	15	Ih	41.02N	25.42 E
Sapanca	15	Ni	40.41N	30.16 E
Sapanca Gölü	15	Ni	40.43N	30.15 E
Sape [Braz.]	54	Ke	7.06S	35.13W
Sape [Indon.]	26	Gh	8.34S	118.59 E
Sape, Selat-	26	Gh	8.39S	119.18 E
Sapele	34	Gd	5.55N	5.42 E
Sapelo Island	44	Gj	31.28N	81.15W
Şaphane	15	Mj	39.01N	29.14 E
Şaphane Daği	15	Mj	39.03N	29.16 E
Sapiéntza	15	Em	36.45N	21.42 E
Šapkina	17	Fc	66.44N	52.25 E
Sapo, Serranía del-	49	Hi	7.50N	78.17W
Saponé	34	Ec	12.03N	1.36W
Sapopema	55	Gf	23.55S	50.35W
Saposoa	54	Ce	6.56S	76.48W
Sapphire Mountains	46	Ic	46.20N	113.45W
Sapporo	22	Qe	43.03N	141.21 E
Sapri	14	Jj	40.04N	15.38 E
Sapucaí, Rio-	55	He	20.08S	48.27W
Sapulpa	43	Hd	36.00N	96.06W
Sapulut	26	Gf	4.42N	116.29 E
Sāqiyat Sīdī Yūsuf	14	Cn	36.13N	8.21 E
Saqqez	23	Gb	36.14N	46.16 E
Sarāb	23	Gb	37.56N	47.32 E
Saraburi	25	Kf	14.30N	100.55 E
Saraf Doungous	35	Bc	12.33N	19.42 E
Sarafjagān	24	Ne	34.28N	50.28 E
Saragmatha = Everest, Mount- (EN)	21	Kg	27.59N	86.56 E
Saragossa (EN) = Zaragoza [Sp.]	6	Fg	41.38N	0.53W
Sarai	7	Jj	53.44N	41.03 E
Sarajevo	6	Hg	43.50N	18.25 E
Saraji Mine	59	Jd	22.30S	148.20 E
Sarakhs	23	Jb	36.32N	61.11 E
Sarakiná	15	Hk	38.40N	24.37 E
Šarakol	17	Kj	52.03N	62.47 E
Saraktaš	19	Fe	51.47N	56.18 E
Saraland	44	Cj	30.49N	88.02W
Saramati	25	Jc	25.44N	95.02 E
Saran	19	Hf	49.46N	72.52 E
Saran, Gunung-	26	Fg	0.25S	111.18 E
Saranac Lake	44	Jc	44.20N	74.08W
Saranci	15	Gg	42.43N	23.46 E
Saranda	15	Cj	39.52N	20.00 E
Sarandi	55	Fh	27.56S	52.55W
Sarandí, Arroyo-	55	Cj	30.13S	59.19W
Sarandí del Yí	55	Ek	33.21S	55.38W
Sarandí Grande	55	Dk	33.44S	56.20W
Šaranga	7	Lh	57.12N	46.34 E
Sarangani Bay	26	Ie	5.57N	125.11 E
Sarangani Islands	26	Ie	5.25N	125.26 E
Saranley	35	Ge	2.23N	42.16 E
Saransk	6	Ke	54.11N	45.11 E
Sarapul	6	Ld	56.28N	53.48 E
Sarapulskoje	20	Ig	48.50N	135.58 E
Sarare	49	Mi	9.47N	69.10W
Sararé, Rio-	55	Cb	14.51S	59.58W
Sarasota	43	Kf	27.20N	82.34W
Sarata	16	Ff	46.01N	29.41 E
Sărăţel	15	Kb	47.03N	27.25 E
Saratoga	46	Lf	41.27N	106.48W
Saratoga Springs	43	Mc	43.04N	73.47W
Saratok	26	Ff	1.24N	111.31 E
Saratov	6	Ke	51.34N	46.02 E
Saratov Reservoir (EN) = Saratovskoje Vodohranilišče	5	Ke	52.50N	47.50 E
Saratovskaja Oblast [3]	19	Ee	51.30N	47.00 E
Saratovskoje Vodohranilišče = Saratov Reservoir (EN)	5	Ke	52.50N	47.50 E
Saravan	25	Le	15.43N	106.25 E
Sarawak [2]	26	Ff	2.30N	113.30 E
Saray	24	Bb	41.26N	27.55 E
Saraya	34	Cc	12.50N	11.45W
Sarāyā	24	Fe	35.47N	35.58 E
Sarayköy	24	Cd	37.55N	28.56 E
Sarbāz	23	Jd	26.39N	61.15 E
Sárbogárd	10	Oj	46.53N	18.38 E
Sarca	14	Ee	45.52N	10.52 E
Sarcelle, Passe de la-	63b	Cf	22.28S	167.13 E
Sarcelles	12	Ef	49.00N	2.23 E
Sarcidano	14	Dk	39.40N	9.15 E
Sardara	14	Ck	39.37N	8.49 E
Sar Dasht [Iran]	24	Mf	32.32N	48.52 E
Sar Dasht [Iran]	24	Kd	36.09N	45.28 E
Sardegna [2]	14	Cj	40.00N	9.00 E
Sardegna = Sardinia (EN)	5	Gh	40.00N	9.00 E
Sardegna, Mar di-	14	Bk	40.00N	7.30 E
Sardes	15	Lk	38.29N	28.03 E
Sardinal	49	Eh	10.31N	85.39W
Sardinata	54	Db	8.07N	72.48W
Sardinia (EN) = Sardegna	5	Gh	40.00N	9.00 E
Sardis Lake	45	Li	34.27N	89.43W
Sarektjåkkå	7	Dc	67.25N	17.46 E
Sarema/Saaremaa	5	Id	58.25N	22.30 E
Sar-e Pol	23	Kb	36.14N	65.55 E
Sar Eskand Khān	24	Ld	37.29N	47.04 E
Sar-e Yazd	24	Pg	31.36N	54.35 E
Sargasso Sea	38	Mg	29.00N	65.00W
Sargatskoje	19	Hd	55.37N	73.30 E
Sargodha	25	Eb	32.05N	72.40 E
Šargun	18	Fe	38.31N	67.59 E
Sarh	31	Ih	9.09N	18.23 E
Sarhe	11	Fg	47.30N	0.32W
Sarhro, Jebel-	32	Fc	31.00N	6.00W
Sāri [Iran]	22	Hf	36.34N	53.04 E
Sāri [Iraq]	24	Je	34.42N	42.44 E
Sariá	15	Kn	35.50N	27.15 E
Sariçakaya	24	Db	40.02N	30.31 E
Sarigan Island	57	Fc	16.42N	145.47 E
Sarigöl	24	Cc	38.14N	28.43 E
Sarıkamış	24	Jb	40.15N	42.35 E
Sarıkaya	24	Fc	39.48N	35.24 E
Sarikei	26	Ff	2.07N	111.31 E
Sariköy	15	Ki	40.12N	27.36 E
Sarina	59	Jd	21.26S	149.13 E
Sarine	14	Bd	46.59N	7.16 E
Sariñena	13	Lc	41.48N	0.10W
Sarıoğlan	24	Fc	39.05N	35.59 E
Sarīr	33	Dd	27.30N	22.30 E
Sariwŏn	27	Md	38.30N	125.45 E
Sarıyer	24	Cb	41.10N	29.03 E
Sarj, Jabal as-	14	Do	35.56N	9.32 E
Šarja	6	Kd	58.24N	45.30 E
Sark	9	Kl	49.26N	2.21W
Sarkad	10	Rj	46.45N	21.23 E
Sarkand	19	Hf	45.25N	79.54 E
Şarkikaraağaç	24	Dc	38.04N	31.23 E
Sarkışla	24	Gc	39.21N	36.26 E
Šarkovščina	8	Li	55.22N	27.32 E
Sarköy	24	Bb	40.37N	27.06 E
Sarlat-la-Canéda	11	Hj	44.53N	1.13 E
Šarlyk	16	Sc	52.54N	54.42 E
Sarmi	58	Ee	1.51S	138.44 E
Sarmiento	53	Jj	45.35S	69.05W
Sarmizegetuza	15	Fd	45.31N	22.47 E
Särna	8	Ec	61.41N	13.08 E
Sarnen	14	Cd	46.54N	8.15 E
Sărnena Gora	15	Ig	42.35N	25.30 E
Sarnia	42	Jh	42.58N	82.23W
Sarny	19	Ce	51.21N	26.36 E
Saroako	26	Hg	2.31S	121.22 E
Sarolangun	26	Dg	2.18S	102.42 E
Saroma	29a	Ca	44.02N	143.45 E
Saroma-Ko	28	Qb	44.10N	143.40 E
Šaromy	20	Kf	54.23N	158.14 E
Saronic Gulf (EN) = Saronikós Kólpos	15	Gl	37.45N	23.30 E
Saronikós Kólpos = Saronic Gulf (EN)	15	Gl	37.45N	23.30 E
Saronno	14	De	45.38N	9.02 E
Saros, Gulf of- (EN) = Saros Körfezi	24	Bb	40.30N	26.20 E
Saros Körfezi = Saros, Gulf of- (EN)	24	Bb	40.30N	26.20 E
Sárospatak	10	Rh	48.19N	21.35 E
Sar Passage	64a	Ac	7.12N	134.23 E
Sarpinskije Ozera	16	Nf	47.45N	45.00 E
Šar Planina	15	Dg	42.05N	20.50 E
Sarpsborg	8	De	59.17N	11.07 E
Sarqaq	41	Gd	70.00N	51.39W
Sarrabus	14	Dk	39.20N	9.30 E
Sarralbe	11	Ne	49.00N	7.01 E
Sarrāt, Wādī-	14	Co	35.59N	8.23 E
Sarre	10	Cg	49.42N	6.34 E
Sarrebourg	11	Nf	48.44N	7.03 E
Sarreguemines	11	Ne	49.06N	7.03 E
Sarre-Union	12	Jf	48.56N	7.05 E
Sarria	13	Eb	42.47N	7.24W
Sarstún, Río-	49	Cf	15.54N	88.54W
Sartang	20	Ic	67.30N	133.20 E
Sartène	11a	Ab	41.37N	8.59 E
Sarthe [3]	11	Gf	48.00N	0.05 E
Sartu → Anda	28	Ha	46.35N	125.00 E
Sarufutsu	29a	Ca	45.18N	142.13 E
Saru-Gawa	29a	Cb	42.30N	142.00 E
Saruhanlı	24	Bc	38.44N	27.34 E
Šarukaishi-Gawa	29	Gb	39.25N	141.08 E
Sārūq	24	Me	34.25N	49.30 E
Saruyama-Misaki	29	Ec	37.18N	136.43 E
Sárvár	10	Mi	47.15N	16.56 E
Sarvestān	24	Oh	29.16N	53.13 E
Sárvíz	10	Oj	46.22N	18.48 E
Saryagač	18	Gd	41.28N	69.11 E
Sarybarak	18	Hc	43.24N	71.29 E
Sary-Bulak	18	Jd	41.54N	75.47 E
Saryč, Mys-	5	Jg	44.23N	33.45 E
Saryg-Sep	20	Ef	51.30N	95.40 E
Sary-Išikotrau	18	Kb	45.15N	76.25 E
Sarykamys	19	Ff	46.00N	53.41 E
Sarykamyšskoje, Ozero-	19	Fg	41.58N	57.58 E
Sarykolski Hrebet	18	Je	38.30N	74.15 E
Šaryn-Gol	27	Ib	49.20N	106.30 E
Saryozek	19	Hg	44.22N	77.54 E
Saryšagan	19	Hf	46.05N	73.38 E
Saryšiganak, Zaliv-	18	Ca	46.35N	61.25 E
Sarysu	21	Ie	45.12N	66.36 E
Sary-Taš	19	Hh	39.44N	73.16 E
Saryžaz	18	Lc	42.54N	79.31 E
Sarzana	14	Df	44.07N	9.58 E
Sasabe	48	Db	31.27N	111.31W
Sasabeneh	35	Gd	8.00N	43.44 E
Sasa-ga-Mine	29	Ce	33.49N	133.17 E
Sasago-Tōge	29	Fd	35.37N	138.45 E
Sasamungga	63a	Cb	7.02S	156.47 E
Sasarām	25	Gd	24.57N	84.02 E
Sasari, Mount-	63a	Dc	8.11S	159.33 E
Sascut	15	Kc	46.11N	27.04 E
Sásd	10	Oj	46.15N	18.07 E
Sasebo	27	Me	33.12N	129.44 E
Saseginaga, Lac-	44	Hb	47.05N	78.34W
Saskatchewan [3]	42	Gf	54.00N	106.00W
Saskatchewan	38	Jd	53.12N	99.16W
Saskatoon	39	Id	52.07N	106.38W
Saskylah	20	Gb	72.00N	114.00 E
Saslaya, Cerro-	49	Eg	13.45N	85.03W
Sasovo	19	Ee	54.22N	41.54 E
Sassafras Mountain	44	Fh	35.03N	82.48W
Sassandra	30	Gh	4.58N	6.05W
Sassandra [3]	34	Dd	5.20N	6.10W
Sassandra	31	Gh	4.57N	6.05W
Sassari	6	Gg	40.43N	8.34 E
Sassenberg	12	Kc	51.59N	8.03 E
Sassenheim	12	Gb	52.14N	4.33 E
Sassetot-le-Mauconduit	12	Ce	49.48N	0.32 E
Saßnitz	10	Jb	54.31N	13.39 E
Sasso Marconi	14	Ff	44.24N	11.15 E
Sassuolo	14	Ef	44.33N	10.47 E
Sastobe	18	Hc	42.34N	70.03 E
Sastre	55	Bj	31.45S	61.50W
Sasyk, Ozero- (Kunduk)	16	Fg	45.45N	29.40 E
Sasykkol, Ozero-	19	If	46.40N	81.00 E
Sata	29	Bf	31.04N	130.42 E
Sata, Cape- (EN) = Sata Misaki	21	Pf	30.59N	130.37 E
Satakunta	8	Jc	61.30N	23.00 E
Sata-Misaki = Sata, Cape- (EN)	21	Pf	30.59N	130.37 E
Satan, Pointe de-	63b	Dd	19.00S	169.17 E
Sātāra	25	Ee	17.41N	73.59 E
Sataua	65c	Aa	13.28S	172.40W
Satawal Island	57	Fd	7.21N	147.02 E
Satawan Atoll	57	Gd	5.25N	153.35 E
Satellite Bay	42	Fa	77.25N	117.15W
Säter	7	Df	60.21N	15.45 E
Satihaure	7	Ec	67.30N	18.45 E
Satipo	54	Df	11.16S	74.37W
Satīt	35	Fc	14.20N	35.50 E
Satka	19	Fd	55.03N	59.01 E
Šatki	7	Ki	55.11N	44.08 E
Sātmāla Range	25	Fe	19.30N	78.45 E
Satna	25	Gd	24.35N	80.50 E
Šator	14	Kf	44.09N	16.37 E
Sátoraljaújhely	10	Rh	48.24N	21.40 E
Sātpura Range	21	Jg	21.25N	76.10 E
Satsuma-Hantō	29	Bf	31.25N	130.25 E
Satsunai-Gawa	29a	Cb	42.55N	143.15 E
Satsunan-Shotō	27	Mf	29.00N	130.00 E
Sattahip	25	Kf	12.39N	100.54 E
Satulung	15	Gb	47.34N	23.26 E
Satu Mare	15	Fb	47.48N	22.53 E
Satu Mare [2]	15	Fb	47.46N	22.56 E
Satun	25	Kg	6.39N	100.03 E
Saturniná ou Papagaio, Rio-	55	Ca	13.55S	58.18W
Saualpe	14	Id	46.50N	14.40 E
Sauce	56	Ic	30.00S	58.46W
Sauce Corto, Arroyo-	55	Bm	36.55S	61.48W
Sauceda Mountains	46	Ij	32.30N	112.30W
Sauce Grande, Río-	55	Bn	38.59S	61.07W
Saucillo	47	Cc	28.01N	105.17W
Sauda	8	Be	59.39N	6.20 E
Saudade, Serra da- [Braz.]	55	Jd	19.20S	45.50W
Saudade, Serra da- [Braz.]	55	Fc	16.20S	53.53W
Saudarkrókur	7a	Bb	65.45N	19.39W
Saudi Arabia (EN) = Al 'Arabīyah As-Su'ūdīyah [1]	22	Gg	25.00N	45.00 E
Sauer [Eur.]	10	Cg	49.44N	6.31 E
Sauer [Fr.]	12	Kf	48.55N	8.10 E
Sauerland	10	De	51.10N	8.00 E
Sauêruiná, Rio-	54	Gf	12.00S	58.40W
Sauga Jõgi	8	Kf	58.19N	24.25 E
Saugatuck	44	Dd	42.40N	86.12W
Saugues	11	Jj	44.58N	3.33 E
Sauk Centre	45	Id	45.44N	94.57W
Sauk Rapids	45	Id	45.34N	94.09W
Saül	54	Hc	3.37N	53.12W
Šaulder	18	Gc	42.47N	68.24 E
Sauldre	11	Hg	47.16N	1.30 E
Saulieu	11	Kg	47.16N	4.14 E
Saulkrasti/Saulkrasty	7	Fh	57.17N	24.29 E
Saulkrasty/Saulkrasti	7	Fh	57.17N	24.29 E
Saulnois	12	If	48.52N	6.30 E
Sault	11	Lj	44.05N	5.25 E
Sault Sainte Marie [Mi.-U.S.]	43	Kb	46.30N	84.21W
Sault Sainte Marie [Ont.-Can.]	39	Ke	46.31N	84.20W
Saumarez Reefs	57	Gg	21.50S	153.40 E
Saumâtre, Étang-	49	Kd	18.35N	72.00W
Saumlaki	26	Jh	7.57S	131.19 E
Saumur	11	Fg	47.16N	0.05W
Saunders	66	Ad	57.47S	26.27W
Saunders Coast	66	Mf	77.45S	150.00W
Saurimo	31	Ji	9.38S	20.24 E
Sauro	14	Kj	40.18N	16.21 E
Sautar	36	Ce	11.09S	18.25 E
Sauteurs	51p	Bb	12.14N	61.38W
Sauveterre, Causse de-	11	Jj	44.22N	3.17 E
Sauveterre-de-Guyenne	11	Fj	44.42N	0.05W
Sauvo/Sagu	8	Jd	60.21N	22.42 E
Sauwald	14	Hb	48.28N	13.40 E
Sava	5	Ig	44.50N	20.28 E
Savage River	59	Jh	41.33S	145.09 E
Savai'i Island	57	Jf	13.35S	172.25W
Savala	16	Ld	51.06N	41.29 E
Savalou	34	Fd	7.56N	1.58 E
Savanes [3]	34	Fc	10.30N	0.30 E
Savan Island	51n	Bb	12.48N	61.12W
Savanna	45	Ke	42.05N	90.08W
Savannah	38	Kf	32.02N	80.53W
Savannah [Ga.-U.S.]	39	Kf	32.04N	81.05W
Savannah [Tn.-U.S.]	44	Ch	35.14N	88.14W
Savannah Beach	44	Gi	32.01N	80.51W
Savannakhét	22	Mh	16.33N	104.45 E
Savanna-la-Mar	47	Ie	18.13N	78.08W
Savanne	45	Kb	48.59N	90.12W
Savannes Bay	51k	Bb	13.45N	60.56W
Savant Lake	42	If	50.15N	90.42W
Savant Lake	45	Ka	50.30N	90.20W
Savaştepe	24	Bc	39.22N	27.40 E
Savdirī	35	Dc	14.25N	29.05 E
Savé	31	Hh	8.02N	2.29 E
Save [Afr.]	30	Kk	21.00S	35.02 E
Save [Fr.]	11	Hk	43.47N	1.17 E
Saveån	8	Dg	57.43N	11.59 E
Sāveh	23	Hb	35.01N	50.20 E
Săveni	15	Jb	47.57N	26.52 E
Saverdun	11	Hk	43.14N	1.35 E
Saverne	11	Nf	48.44N	7.22 E
Savigliano	14	Bf	44.38N	7.40 E
Savigsivik	41	Fc	76.00N	64.45W
Săvineşti	15	Jc	46.51N	26.28 E
Savinjske Alpe	14	Id	46.20N	14.30 E
Savinski	19	Ec	62.57N	40.13 E
Savio	14	Gf	44.19N	12.20 E
Săvîrşin	15	Fc	46.01N	22.14 E
Savitaipale	7	Gf	61.12N	27.42 E
Šavnik	15	Cg	42.57N	19.06 E
Savo	63a	Dc	9.08S	159.48 E
Savo	8	Lb	62.30N	27.30 E
Savoie [3]	11	Mi	45.30N	6.25 E
Savoie = Savoy (EN)	11	Mi	45.24N	6.30 E
Savona	14	Cf	44.17N	8.30 E
Savonlinna/Nyslott	7	Gf	61.52N	28.53 E
Savonranta	7	Ge	62.11N	29.12 E
Savonselkä	8	Lb	62.05N	27.20 E
Savoonga	40	Ed	63.42N	170.27W
Savoy (EN) = Savoie	11	Mi	45.24N	6.30 E
Şavşat	24	Jb	41.15N	42.20 E
Savsjö	7	Dh	57.25N	14.40 E
Savudrija, Rt-	14	He	45.30N	13.31 E
Savukoski	7	Gc	67.17N	28.10 E
Savur	24	Id	37.33N	40.53 E
Savusavu	61	Ec	17.34S	178.15 E
Savusavu Bay	63d	Bb	16.45S	179.15 E
Savu Sea (EN) = Sawu, Laut-	21	Oj	9.40S	122.00 E
Savuto	14	Kk	39.02N	16.06 E
Sawahlunto	26	Dg	0.40S	100.47 E
Sawai Mādhopur	25	Fc	25.59N	76.22 E
Sawākin	31	Kg	19.07N	37.20 E
Sawākin, Jazā'ir- = Suakin Archipelago (EN)	30	Kg	19.07N	37.20 E
Sawankhalok	25	Je	17.19N	99.54 E
Sawara	29	Gd	35.53N	140.29 E
Sawasaki-Hana	28	Of	37.47N	138.12 E
Sawatch Range	45	Cg	39.10N	106.25W
Sawbā = Sobat (EN)	30	Kh	9.45N	31.45 E
Sawbridgeworth	12	Cc	51.49N	0.09 E
Sawdā', Jabal as-	33	Cd	28.40N	15.30 E
Sawfajjīn	33	Cc	31.54N	15.07 E
Sawhāj = Sohag (EN)	31	Kf	26.33N	31.42 E
Sawkanah	33	Cd	29.04N	15.47 E
Sawla	34	Ed	9.17N	2.25W
Sawqirah	23	If	18.10N	56.30 E
Şawqirah, Ghubbat-	23	If	18.35N	56.45 E
Sawtooth Mountains	46	He	44.00N	115.00W
Sawu, Kepulauan-	26	Hi	10.30S	121.50 E
Sawu, Laut- = Savu Sea (EN)	21	Oj	9.40S	122.00 E
Sawu, Pulau-	21	Ok	10.30S	121.54 E
Şawwān, Ard as-	24	Gg	31.00N	37.00 E
Sax	13	Lf	38.32N	0.49W
Saxby River	59	Ic	18.25S	140.53 E
Saxmundham	12	Db	52.13N	1.30 E
Saxony (EN) = Sachsen	10	Jf	51.00N	13.30 E
Say	34	Fc	13.07N	2.21 E
Sayabec	44	Na	48.36N	67.37W
Saya de Malha Bank (EN)	30	Nj	11.00S	61.00 E
Sayago	13	Fc	41.20N	6.10W
Sayan	54	Cf	11.08S	77.12W
Sayang, Pulau-	26	If	0.18N	129.54 E
Sayaxché	49	Be	16.31N	90.10W
Saydā	23	Ec	33.33N	35.22 E
Sayḩūt	22	Hh	15.12N	51.14 E
Saylorville Lake	45	Jf	41.48N	93.46W
Säynätsalo	8	Kb	62.08N	25.46 E
Sayō	29	Dd	35.01N	134.22 E
Sayram Hu	27	Dc	44.35N	81.10 E
Sayula	48	Hh	19.52N	103.37W
Saywūn	35	Hb	15.56N	48.47 E
Sazanit, Ishull i-	15	Ci	40.30N	19.16 E
Sázava	10	Kg	49.53N	14.24 E
Sázava	10	Kg	49.52N	14.54 E
Sbaa	32	Gd	28.13N	0.10W
Sbisseb	13	Pi	35.42N	3.51 E
Sbruč	16	Ee	48.32N	26.25 E
Scaër	11	Cf	48.02N	3.42W
Scafell Pike	9	Jg	54.27N	3.12W
Scalea	14	Jk	39.49N	15.47 E
Scalone, Passo dello-	14	Jk	39.38N	15.57 E
Scammon, Laguna-	48	Bd	27.45N	114.15W
Scammon Bay	40	Fd	61.53N	165.38W
Scandinavia (EN)	5	Hc	65.00N	16.00 E
Scanno	14	Hi	41.54N	13.53 E
Scansano	14	Fh	42.41N	11.20 E
Scapa Flow	9	Jc	58.54N	3.05W
Scapegoat Mountain	46	Ic	47.19N	112.50W
Ščapino	20	Ke	55.15N	159.25 E
Ščara	16	Dc	53.27N	24.44 E
Scaramia, Capo-	14	In	36.47N	14.29 E
Scarba	9	He	56.11N	5.42W
Scarborough [Eng.-U.K.]	9	Mg	54.17N	0.24W
Scarborough [Trin.]	54	Fa	11.11N	60.44W
Scarpe	11	Jd	50.30N	3.27 E
Sčastje	16	Ke	48.44N	39.14 E
Sceaux	12	Ef	48.47N	2.17 E
Ščekino	16	Jb	54.01N	37.29 E
Ščekurja	17	Jd	64.15N	60.52 E
Ščeljajur	19	Fb	65.21N	53.25 E
Scenic	45	Ee	43.47N	102.30W
Ščerbakty	19	He	52.29N	78.14 E
Schaalsee	10	Gc	53.35N	10.57 E
Schaarbeek/Schaerbeek	12	Gd	50.51N	4.23 E
Schaerbeek/Schaarbeek	12	Gd	50.51N	4.23 E
Schaffhausen [2]	14	Cc	47.45N	8.40 E
Schaffhausen	14	Cc	47.40N	8.40 E
Schagen	12	Gb	52.48N	4.48 E
Schärding	14	Hb	48.27N	13.26 E
Scharmützelsee	10	Kd	52.15N	14.03 E
Scharnhörn	10	Ec	53.57N	8.25 E
Scheeßel	12	La	53.10N	9.29 E
Schefferville	39	Md	54.47N	64.49W
Scheibbs	14	Jb	48.00N	15.10 E
Schela	15	Gd	45.10N	23.18 E
Schelde	11	Kc	51.22N	4.15 E
Schelde (EN) = Escaut	11	Kc	51.22N	4.15 E
Schell Creek Range	43	Ed	39.10N	114.40W
Schenectady	43	Mc	42.48N	73.57W
Scheno	35	Fd	9.35N	39.25 E
Scherfede, Warburg-	12	Lc	51.32N	9.02 E
Scherpenheuvel-Zichem	12	Gd	50.59N	4.59 E
Scheveningen, 's-Gravenhage-	11	Kb	52.06N	4.18 E
Schiedam	11	Kc	51.55N	4.24 E
Schiermonnikoog	11	Ma	53.28N	6.15 E
Schifferstadt	12	Ke	49.23N	8.22 E
Schiffgraben	10	Hd	52.02N	11.10 E
Schifflange	12	Ie	49.30N	6.01 E
Schijndel	12	Hc	51.37N	5.28 E
Schiltigheim	11	Nf	48.36N	7.45 E
Schio	14	Fe	45.43N	11.21 E
Schipbeek	12	Ib	52.15N	6.14 E
Schladming	14	Hc	47.23N	13.41 E
Schlei	10	Fb	54.35N	9.50 E
Schleiden	10	Cf	50.32N	6.28 E
Schleiz	10	Hf	50.35N	11.49 E
Schleswig	10	Fb	54.31N	9.33 E
Schleswig Holstein [2]	10	Gb	54.00N	10.30 E
Schlitz	10	Ff	50.40N	9.34 E
Schloß Holte-Stukenbrock	12	Kc	51.55N	8.38 E
Schloß Neuhaus, Paderborn-	12	Kc	51.44N	8.42 E
Schluchsee	10	Ei	47.49N	8.10 E
Schlüchtern	10	Ff	50.21N	9.31 E
Schmallenberg	12	Kc	51.09N	8.18 E
Schmallenberg-Bödefeld-Freiheit	12	Kc	51.15N	8.24 E
Schmallenberg-Oberkirchen	12	Kc	51.09N	8.18 E
Schmelz	12	Ie	49.26N	6.51 E
Schmida	14	Kb	48.20N	16.14 E
Schneeberg	10	If	50.36N	12.38 E
Schneeberg [Aus.]	14	Jc	47.46N	15.52 E
Schneeberg [F.R.G.]	10	Hf	50.00N	11.51 E
Schneifel	12	Id	50.16N	6.23 E
Schoberpaß	14	Ic	47.27N	14.40 E
Schoberspitze	14	Ic	47.17N	14.09 E
Schœlcher	51h	Ab	14.37N	61.06W
Schönebeck	10	Hd	52.01N	11.45 E
Schönecken	12	Id	50.10N	6.28 E
Schongau	10	Gi	47.49N	10.54 E
Schöningen	10	Gd	52.08N	10.57 E
Schoondijke	12	Fc	51.21N	3.33 E
Schoonebeek	12	Ib	52.40N	6.53 E
Schoonhoven	12	Gc	51.55N	4.51 E
Schorfheide	10	Jd	52.55N	13.35 E
Schoten	12	Gc	51.15N	4.30 E
Schotten	12	Ld	50.30N	9.08 E
Schouten Islands	57	Fe	3.30S	144.30 E
Schouwen	11	Jc	51.43N	3.50 E
Schramberg	10	Eh	48.14N	8.23 E
Schreiber	42	Ig	48.48N	87.15W
Schriesheim	12	Ke	49.29N	8.40 E
Schrobenhausen	10	Hh	48.33N	11.16 E
Schruns	14	Dc	47.04N	9.55 E
Schuls / Scuol	14	Ed	46.48N	10.17 E
Schultz Lake	42	Hd	64.45N	97.30W
Schurz	46	Fg	38.58N	118.46W
Schussen	10	Fi	47.37N	9.32 E
Schüttorf	12	Jb	52.19N	7.14 E
Schwabach	10	Hg	49.20N	11.02 E
Schwaben = Swabia (EN)	10	Gh	48.20N	10.30 E
Schwäbisch-Bayerisches Alpenvorland = Swabian-Bavarian Plateau (EN)	5	Hf	48.15N	10.30 E
Schwäbische Alb = Swabian Jura (EN)	5	Gf	48.25N	9.30 E

Index Symbols

[1] Independent Nation; [2] State, Region; [3] District, County; [4] Municipality; [5] Colony, Dependency; Continent; Physical Region; Historical or Cultural Region; Mount, Mountain; Volcano; Hill; Mountains, Mountain Range; Hills, Escarpment; Plateau, Upland; Pass, Gap; Plain, Lowland; Delta; Salt Flat; Valley, Canyon; Crater, Cave; Karst Features; Depression; Polder; Desert, Dunes; Forest, Woods; Heath, Steppe; Oasis; Cape, Point; Coast, Beach; Cliff; Peninsula; Isthmus; Sandbank; Island; Atoll; Rock, Reef; Islands, Archipelago; Rocks, Reefs; Coral Reef; Well, Spring; Geyser; River, Stream; Waterfall Rapids; River Mouth, Estuary; Lake; Salt Lake; Intermittent Lake; Reservoir; Swamp, Pond; Canal; Glacier; Ice Shelf, Pack Ice; Ocean; Sea; Gulf, Bay; Strait, Fjord; Lagoon; Bank; Seamount; Tablemount; Ridge; Shelf; Basin; Escarpment, Sea Scarp; Fracture; Trench, Abyss; National Park, Reserve; Point of Interest; Recreation Site; Cave, Cavern; Historic Site; Ruins; Wall, Walls; Church, Abbey; Temple; Scientific Station; Airport; Port; Lighthouse; Mine; Tunnel; Dam, Bridge

Name	Map	Grid	Lat	Long
Schwäbisch Gmünd	10	Fh	48.48N	9.47 E
Schwäbisch Hall	10	Fg	49.06N	9.44 E
Schwalbach (Saar)	12	Ie	49.18N	6.49 E
Schwalm	12	Lc	51.07N	9.24 E
Schwalm	10	Ff	50.45N	9.25 E
Schwalmstadt	10	Ff	50.55N	9.12 E
Schwalmtal	12	Ic	51.15N	6.15 E
Schwandorf	10	Ig	49.20N	12.07 E
Schwaner, Pegunungan-	26	Fg	0.40S	112.40 E
Schwanewede	12	Ka	53.14N	8.36 E
Schwarzach	10	Ig	49.30N	12.10 E
Schwarzbach	12	Je	49.17N	7.40 E
Schwarze Elster	10	Ie	51.49N	12.51 E
Schwarzer Mann	12	Id	50.15N	6.22 E
Schwarzrand	37	Be	26.00S	17.10 E
Schwarzwald=Black Forest (EN)	5	Gf	48.00N	8.15 E
Schwarzwalder Hochwald	12	Ie	49.39N	6.55 E
Schwatka Mountains	40	Hc	67.25N	157.00W
Schwaz	14	Fc	47.20N	11.42 E
Schwechat	14	Kb	48.08N	16.28 E
Schwechat	14	Kb	48.08N	16.28 E
Schwedt	10	Kc	53.04N	14.18 E
Schweich	12	Ie	49.49N	6.45 E
Schweinfurt	10	Gf	50.03N	10.14 E
Schweiz / Suisse / Svizra / Svizzera = Switzerland (EN) [1]	6	Gf	46.00N	8.30 E
Schweizer-Reneke	37	De	27.11S	25.18 E
Schwelm	12	Jc	51.17N	7.17 E
Schwerin [2]	10	Hc	53.35N	11.25 E
Schwerin	10	Hc	53.38N	11.23 E
Schweriner See	10	Hc	53.45N	11.28 E
Schwerte	12	Jc	51.27N	7.34 E
Schwetzingen	12	Ke	49.23N	8.34 E
Schwielochsee	10	Kd	52.03N	14.12 E
Schwyz [2]	14	Cc	47.10N	8.50 E
Schwyz	14	Cc	47.03N	8.40 E
Sciacca	14	Hm	37.31N	13.03 E
Scicli	14	In	36.47N	14.42 E
Ščigry	19	De	51.53N	36.55 E
Scilly, Isles of-	5	Ff	49.57N	6.15W
Scioto River	44	Ff	38.44N	83.01W
Ščirec	10	Tg	49.34N	23.54 E
Scobey	46	Mb	48.47N	105.25W
Scordia	14	Im	37.18N	14.51 E
Scoresby Land	41	Jd	71.45N	26.30W
Scoresbysund	67	Md	70.35N	21.40W
Scoresby Sund	67	Md	70.20N	23.30W
Scorff	11	Cg	47.46N	3.21W
Ščors	19	De	51.48N	31.59 E
Scotia Ridge (EN)	3	Co	57.00S	45.00W
Scotia Sea (EN)	52	Mk	57.00S	40.00W
Scotland [2]	9	Ie	56.30N	4.30W
Scotland	5	Fd	56.30N	4.30W
Scotlandville	45	Kk	30.31N	91.11W
Scotstown	44	Lc	45.31N	71.17W
Scott	42	Gf	52.27N	108.23W
Scott, Cape- [Austl.]	59	Fb	13.30S	129.50 E
Scott, Cape - [B.C.-Can.]	42	Ef	50.47N	128.25W
Scott, Mount-	46	De	42.56N	122.01W
Scott Base	66	Kf	77.51S	166.46 E
Scottburgh	37	Ef	30.19S	30.40 E
Scott Channel	46	Aa	50.45N	128.30W
Scott City	45	Fg	38.29N	100.54W
Scott Coast	66	Kf	76.30S	162.30 E
Scott Glacier [Ant.]	66	He	66.15S	100.05 E
Scott Glacier [Ant.]	66	Mg	85.45S	153.00W
Scott Inlet	42	Kb	71.05N	71.05W
Scott Island	66	Le	67.24S	179.55W
Scott Islands	46	Aa	50.48N	128.40W
Scott Peak	46	Id	44.21N	112.50W
Scott Reef	59	Eb	14.00S	121.50 E
Scottsbluff	39	Ie	41.52N	103.40W
Scottsboro	44	Dh	34.40N	86.01W
Scottsburg	44	Ef	38.41N	85.46W
Scottsdale [Austl.]	59	Jh	41.10S	147.31 E
Scottsdale [Az.-U.S.]	43	Ee	33.30N	111.56W
Scotts Head	51g	Bb	15.13N	61.23W
Scottsville	44	Dg	36.45N	86.11W
Scottville	44	Dd	43.59N	86.17W
Scranton	39	Le	41.24N	75.40W
Scrivia	14	Ce	45.03N	8.54 E
Scrub Cays	49	Ia	24.07N	76.55W
Scrub Island	51b	Bb	18.17N	62.57W
Ščučin	16	Dc	53.39N	24.48 E
Ščučinsk	19	He	53.00N	70.11 E
Ščučja	17	Nc	66.45N	68.20 E
Ščučje	19	Gd	55.15N	62.43 E
Scugog, Lake-	44	Hc	44.10N	78.51W
Ščugor	17	Hd	64.12N	57.32 E
Scunthorpe	9	Mh	53.36N	0.38W
Scuol / Schuls	14	Ed	46.48N	10.17 E
Scutari, Lake- (EN)= Shkodrës, Liqen i-	5	Hg	42.10N	19.20 E
Scutari, Lake- (EN)= Skadarsko Jezero	5	Hg	42.10N	19.20 E
Seaford	9	Nk	50.46N	0.06 E
Seahorse Point	42	Jd	63.47N	80.10W
Sea Islands	43	Ke	31.20N	81.20W
Seal	42	Ie	59.04N	94.47W
Seal Island	44	Nd	43.30N	66.01W
Sealpunt	30	Jl	34.06S	23.24 E
Searcy	45	Ki	35.15N	91.44W
Searles Lake	46	Gi	35.43N	117.20W
Seaside [Ca.-U.S.]	46	Eh	36.37N	121.50W
Seaside [Or.-U.S.]	46	Dc	46.01N	123.55W
Seattle	39	Ge	47.36N	122.20W
Seaward Kaikoura Range	62	Ee	42.15S	173.35 E
Seba	26	Hi	10.29S	121.50 E
Sébaco	49	Dg	12.51N	86.06W
Sebago Lake	44	Ld	43.50N	70.35W
Sebaiera	32	Ee	24.51N	13.02W
Sebaou	13	Ph	36.55N	3.51 E
Sebastian, Cape-	46	Ce	42.19N	124.26W
Sebastián Vizcaíno, Bahía-	38	Hg	28.00N	114.30W
Sebastopol	46	Dg	38.24N	122.49W
Sebatik, Pulau-	26	Gf	4.10N	117.45 E
Sebba	34	Fc	13.26N	0.32 E
Sebderat	35	Fb	15.27N	36.39 E
Sébé	36	Bc	1.02S	13.06 E
Šebekino	19	De	50.27N	37.00 E
Sébékoro	34	Dc	12.49N	8.50W
Seberi	55	Fh	27.29S	53.24W
Sebeş	15	Gd	45.58N	23.34 E
Sebeş	15	Gd	46.00N	23.34 E
Sebes-Körös	15	Dc	46.55N	20.59 E
Sebeşului, Munţii-	15	Gd	45.38N	23.27 E
Sebewaing	44	Fd	43.44N	83.27W
Sebež	19	Cd	56.19N	28.31 E
Sebha Oasis (EN)=Sabhā, Wāḩāt	30	If	27.00N	14.25 E
Şebinkarahisar	24	Hb	40.18N	38.26 E
Sebiş	15	Fc	46.22N	22.07 E
Sebou	30	Ge	34.16N	6.41W
Sebring	44	Gl	27.30N	81.26W
Sebugal	13	Ed	40.21N	7.05W
Sebuku, Pulau-	26	Gg	3.30S	116.22 E
Šebunino	20	Jg	46.24N	141.56 E
Secas, Islas-	49	Gi	7.58N	82.02W
Secchia	14	Ee	45.04N	11.00 E
Sechura	54	Be	5.33S	80.51W
Sechura, Bahía de-	54	Be	5.40S	81.00W
Sechura, Desierto de-	54	Be	6.00S	80.30W
Seckau	14	Ic	47.16N	14.47 E
Seclin	12	Fd	50.33N	3.02 E
Secondigny	11	Fh	46.37N	0.25W
Secos, Ilhéus-	32	Cf	14.58N	24.40W
Secretary Island	62	Bf	45.15S	166.55 E
Sécure, Rio-	54	Fg	15.10S	64.52W
Seda	8	Kg	57.38N	25.12 E
Sêda	13	Df	38.56N	8.03W
Seda [Lat.-U.S.S.R.]	8	Kg	57.32N	25.43 E
Seda [Lith.-U.S.S.R.]	8	Jh	56.10N	22.00 E
Sedalia	43	Id	38.42N	93.14W
Sedan	11	Ke	49.42N	4.57 E
Sedanka	40a	Eb	53.50N	166.10W
Sedano	13	Ib	42.43N	3.45W
Sedbergh	9	Kg	54.20N	2.31W
Seddenga	35	Ea	20.33N	30.18 E
Seddon	62	Fd	41.40S	174.04 E
Seddon, Kap-	41	Gc	75.20N	58.45W
Seddonville	62	Dd	41.33S	171.59 E
Seddülbahir	15	Ji	40.03N	26.10 E
Sedelnikovo	19	Hd	56.57N	75.18 E
Séderon	11	Lj	44.12N	5.32 E
Sédhiou	34	Bc	12.44N	15.33W
Sedini	14	Ci	40.51N	8.49 E
Šedok	16	Lg	44.13N	40.52 E
Sedom	24	Fg	31.04N	35.24 E
Sedona	46	Ji	34.52N	111.46W
Sedrada	14	Bn	36.08N	7.32 E
Šédro	14	Kg	43.05N	16.42 E
Sedro Woolley	46	Db	48.30N	122.14W
Šeduva	7	Fi	55.48N	23.45 E
Sée	11	Ef	48.39N	1.26W
Seeheim [F.R.G.]	12	Ke	49.46N	8.40 E
Seeheim [Nam.]	37	Be	26.50S	17.45 E
Seeis	37	Bd	22.29S	17.39 E
Seeland	14	Bc	47.05N	7.05 E
Seeling, Mount-	66	Og	82.28S	103.00W
Seelow	10	Kd	52.31N	14.23 E
Sées	11	Gf	48.36N	0.10 E
Seesen	10	Ge	51.54N	10.11 E
Seewarte Seamounts (EN)	30	Ee	33.00N	28.30W
Şefaatli	24	Fc	39.31N	34.46 E
Sefadu	34	Cd	8.39N	10.59W
Seferihisar	24	Bc	38.11N	26.51 E
Séféto	34	Dc	14.08N	9.51W
Sefid Dasht	24	Nf	32.09N	51.10 E
Sefrou	32	Gc	33.50N	4.50W
Sefuri-San	29	Be	33.26N	130.22 E
Segaf, Kepulauan-	26	Jg	2.10S	130.28 E
Ségalas	11	Ij	44.09N	2.30 E
Segamat	26	Df	2.30N	102.49 E
Segangane	13	Ii	35.10N	3.01W
Şegarcea	15	Ge	44.06N	23.45 E
Šegarka	20	De	57.16N	84.02 E
Segbana	34	Fc	10.56N	3.42 E
Segeg	35	Gd	7.40N	42.50 E
Segesta	14	Gm	37.55N	12.50 E
Segeža	6	Jc	63.44N	34.19 E
Seghe	63a	Cc	8.25S	157.51 E
Seglinge	8	Id	60.15N	20.40 E
Segmon	8	Ee	59.17N	13.01 E
Segorbe	13	Le	39.51N	0.29W
Ségou [3]	34	Dc	14.00N	6.20W
Ségou	31	Gg	13.27N	6.15W
Segovia	13	Hd	40.57N	4.07W
Segovia [3]	13	Ic	41.10N	4.00W
Segozero, Ozero-	5	Jc	63.18N	33.45 E
Segré	11	Fg	47.41N	0.52W
Segre	13	Mc	41.40N	0.43 E
Seguam	40a	Db	52.17N	172.30W
Séguédine	34	Ha	20.12N	12.59 E
Séguéla	34	Dd	7.57N	6.40W
Séguéla [3]	34	Dd	8.05N	6.32W
Seguin	43	Hf	29.34N	97.58W
Segula	40a	Bb	52.01N	178.07 E
Segura	13	Lf	38.06N	0.38W
Segura, Sierra de-	13	Jf	38.00N	2.45W
Segura de la Sierra	13	Jf	38.18N	2.39W
Sehithwa	37	Cd	20.27S	22.42 E
Seia	13	Ed	40.25N	7.42W
Seibal	49	Be	16.27N	90.05W
Seiche	11	Eg	48.00N	1.46W
Seiland	7	Fa	70.25N	23.15 E
Seiling	45	Gh	36.09N	98.56W
Seille [Fr.]	11	Me	49.07N	6.11 E
Seille [Fr.]	11	Kh	46.31N	4.56 E
Sein, Ile de-	11	Bf	48.02N	4.51W
Seinäjoki	7	Fe	62.47N	22.50 E
Seine	5	Gf	49.26N	0.26 E
Seine, Baie de la-=Seine, Bay of the- (EN)	5	Ff	49.30N	0.30W
Seine, Bay of the- (EN)= Seine, Baie de la-	5	Ff	49.30N	0.30W
Seine, Val de-	11	Jf	48.30N	3.20 E
Seine-et-Marne [3]	11	If	48.30N	3.00 E
Seine-Maritime [3]	11	Ge	49.45N	1.00 E
Seine-Saint-Denis [3]	11	If	48.55N	2.30 E
Seine Seamount (EN)	5	Ei	33.45N	14.25W
Seini	15	Gb	47.45N	23.17 E
Seistan (EN)=Sīstān	21	If	30.30N	62.00 E
Seixal	13	Cf	38.38N	9.06W
Sëjaha	20	Cb	70.10N	72.30 E
Sejerø	8	Di	55.55N	11.10 E
Sejerø Bugt	8	Di	55.50N	11.15 E
Sejm	5	Je	51.27N	32.34 E
Sejmčan	20	Kd	62.52N	152.27 E
Sejny	10	Tb	54.07N	23.20 E
Sekakes	37	Df	30.04S	28.21 E
Sekenke	36	Fc	4.16S	34.10 E
Šeki	19	Eg	41.10N	47.11 E
Seki [Jap.]	29	Ed	35.28N	136.54 E
Seki [Tur.]	24	Cd	36.44N	29.33 E
Sekincau, Gunung-	26	Dh	5.05S	104.18 E
Seki-Zaki	29b	Be	33.16N	131.54 E
Sekoma	37	Cd	24.36S	23.58 E
Sekondi-Takoradi	31	Gh	4.53N	1.45W
Sekota	35	Fc	12.37N	39.03 E
Šeksna	19	Dd	59.13N	38.32 E
Šelagski, Mys-	20	Mb	70.10N	170.45 E
Selah	46	Ec	46.39N	120.32W
Selajar, Pulau-	26	Hh	6.05S	120.30 E
Selajar, Selat-	26	Hh	5.42S	120.28 E
Selaön	8	Ge	59.25N	17.10 E
Selaru, Pulau-	26	Jh	8.09S	131.00 E
Selatan, Cape- (EN)= Selatan, Tanjung-	21	Nj	4.10S	113.48 E
Selaṭan, Tanjung-=Selatan, Cape- (EN)	21	Nj	4.10S	113.48 E
Selawik	40	Gc	66.37N	160.03W
Selawik Lake	40	Hc	66.30N	160.40W
Selb	10	If	50.10N	12.08 E
Selbjørn	8	Ae	60.00N	5.10 E
Selbjørnsfjorden	8	Ae	59.55N	5.10 E
Selbu	8	Da	63.13N	11.02 E
Selbukta	66	Bf	71.40S	12.25W
Selbusjøen	8	Da	63.15N	10.55 E
Selby [Eng.-U.K.]	9	Lh	53.48N	1.04W
Selby [S.D.-U.S.]	45	Fd	45.31N	100.02W
Selco	16	Ic	53.23N	34.05 E
Selçuk	24	Bd	37.56N	27.22 E
Seldovia	40	Ie	59.27N	151.43W
Sele	14	Ij	40.29N	14.56 E
Sele, Piana del-	14	Ij	40.30N	14.55 E
Selebi-Pikwe	31	Jk	22.13S	27.58 E
Selečka Planina	15	Eh	41.05N	21.35 E
Šelehov	20	Ff	52.10N	104.01 E
Selemdža	21	Od	51.49N	128.53 E
Selencia	24	Kf	33.04N	44.33 E
Selendi	15	Lk	38.40N	28.41 E
Selendi	15	Lk	38.45N	28.53 E
Selenduma	20	Ff	50.55N	106.10 E
Selenga (Selenge)	21	Md	52.16N	106.16 E
Selenge [Mong.]	27	Hb	49.25N	103.59 E
Selenge [Zaire]	36	Cc	1.58S	18.11 E
Selenge → Selenga	21	Md	52.16N	106.16 E
Selenginsk	20	Ff	51.59N	106.57 E
Selenica	15	Ci	40.32N	19.38 E
Selennjah	20	Jc	67.55N	145.00 E
Sélestat	11	Nf	48.16N	7.27 E
Selety	19	He	53.06N	73.00 E
Seletyteniz, Ozero-	19	He	53.15N	73.15 E
Selevac	15	De	44.30N	20.53 E
Seleznevo	8	Md	60.44N	28.37 E
Selfoss	7a	Bc	63.56N	21.00W
Seli	34	Cd	8.33N	12.48W
Sélibabi	32	Ef	15.10N	12.11W
Seliger, Ozero-	19	Dd	57.20N	33.05 E
Seligman	46	Ii	35.20N	112.53W
Šelihova, Zaliv-=Shelikhov Gulf (EN)	21	Rc	60.00N	158.00 E
Selimağa	15	Lj	39.35N	28.33 E
Selimiye	24	Bd	37.24N	27.40 E
Selingenstadt	12	Kd	50.03N	8.59 E
Selinunte	14	Gm	37.35N	12.48 E
Seližarovo	7	Hh	56.51N	33.29 E
Seljatin	15	Ib	47.52N	25.14 E
Selje	8	Ab	62.03N	5.22 E
Seljord	7	Bg	59.29N	8.37 E
Selkirk [Man.-Can.]	45	Ha	50.09N	96.52W
Selkirk [Scot.-U.K.]	9	Kf	55.33N	2.50W
Selkirk Mountains	42	Ff	50.00N	117.00W
Sella	13	Ga	43.28N	5.04W
Sellasia	15	Fl	37.10N	22.25 E
Selle	12	Fd	50.19N	3.23 E
Selles-sur-Cher	11	Hg	47.16N	1.33 E
Sells	46	Jk	31.55N	111.53W
Selm	12	Jc	51.42N	7.28 E
Selma [Al.-U.S.]	43	Je	32.25N	87.01W
Selma [Ca.-U.S.]	46	Fh	36.34N	119.37W
Selmer	44	Ch	35.11N	88.36W
Selmeţ Wielki, Jezioro-	10	Sc	53.50N	22.30 E
Šelon	7	Hg	58.14N	30.50 E
Selong	26	Gh	8.39S	116.32 E
Selsey	12	Bd	50.44N	0.47W
Selsey Bill	9	Mk	50.43N	0.48W
Seltz	12	Kf	48.53N	8.06 E
Selu, Pulau-	26	Jh	7.32S	130.54 E
Sélune	11	Ef	48.39N	1.26W
Selva	55	Ai	29.46S	62.03W
Selvagens, Ilhas-	30	Fe	30.05N	15.55W
Selvānā	24	Kd	37.25N	44.51 E
Selvas	52	Jf	5.00S	68.00W
Selway River	46	Hc	46.08N	115.36W
Selwyn, Détroit de-	63b	Dc	16.04S	168.11 E
Selwyn Lake	42	He	60.00N	104.30W
Selwyn Mountains	38	Fc	63.10N	130.20W
Selwyn Range	57	Fg	21.35S	140.35 E
Selz	12	Ke	49.59N	8.02 E
Šemaha	16	Pi	40.39N	48.38 E
Semani	15	Ci	40.54N	19.26 E
Semara	31	Ff	26.44N	11.41W
Semarang	22	Nj	6.58S	110.25 E
Sematan	26	Ef	1.48N	109.46 E
Semau, Pulau-	26	Hi	10.13S	123.22 E
Sembakung	26	Gf	3.47N	117.30 E
Sembé	36	Bb	1.39N	14.36 E
Semberija	14	Nf	44.45N	19.10 E
Sembuan	26	Gg	0.19S	115.30 E
Semenicului, Munţii-	15	Fd	45.05N	22.05 E
Semenov	7	Kh	56.49N	44.29 E
Semenovka	16	Hc	52.11N	32.40 E
Semeru, Gunung-	21	Nj	7.58S	113.35 E
Semichi Islands	40a	Db	52.42N	174.00 E
Semidi Islands	40	He	56.07N	156.44W
Semiluki	19	De	51.43N	39.02 E
Semily	10	Lf	50.36N	15.20 E
Seminoe Reservoir	46	Le	42.00N	106.50W
Seminole [Ok.-U.S.]	45	Hi	35.14N	96.14W
Seminole [Tx.-U.S.]	45	Ej	32.43N	102.39W
Seminole, Lake-	43	Ke	30.46N	84.50W
Semipalatinsk	22	Kd	50.28N	80.13 E
Semipalatinskaja Oblast [3]	19	If	48.30N	80.10 E
Semirara Islands	26	Hd	11.57N	121.27 E
Semīrom	24	Ng	31.22N	51.47 E
Semisopochnoi	40a	Cb	52.00N	179.35 E
Semitau	26	Ff	0.33N	111.58 E
Semiun, Pulau-	26	Ef	4.31N	107.44 E
Semizbugy	19	He	50.12N	74.48 E
Semliki	30	Kh	1.14N	30.28 E
Semmering	14	Jc	47.38N	15.49 E
Semnām [3]	23	Hb	35.00N	53.30 E
Semnān	22	Hf	35.33N	53.24 E
Semnon	11	Eg	47.54N	1.45W
Semois	11	Ke	49.53N	4.45 E
Šemonaiha	19	Ie	50.39N	81.54 E
Semporna	26	Gf	4.28N	118.36 E
Semuda	26	Fg	2.51S	112.58 E
Semur-en-Auxois	11	Kg	47.29N	4.20 E
Sên	25	Kf	12.32N	104.28 E
Senador Mourão	55	Kc	17.51S	43.22W
Senador Pompeu	54	Ke	5.35S	39.22W
Senaja	26	Ge	6.45N	117.03 E
Sena Madureira	54	Ee	9.04S	68.40W
Senanga	36	Df	16.07S	23.16 E
Senarpont	12	De	49.53N	1.43 E
Senatobia	45	Li	34.39N	89.58W
Sendai [Jap.]	28	Ki	31.49N	130.18 E
Sendai [Jap.]	22	Qf	38.15N	140.53 E
Sendai-Gawa [Jap.]	29	Bf	31.51N	130.12 E
Sendai-Gawa [Jap.]	29	Dd	35.34N	134.11 E
Sendai-Wan	28	Pe	38.10N	141.15 E
Senden	12	Jc	51.51N	7.30 E
Sendenhorst	12	Jc	51.50N	7.50 E
Senderg	24	Qi	26.52N	57.37 E
Seneca	45	Hg	39.50N	96.04W
Seneca Lake	44	Id	42.40N	76.57W
Sénégal=Senegal (EN)	30	Fg	15.48N	16.32W
Sénégal=Senegal (EN) [1]	31	Fg	14.00N	14.00W
Senegal (EN)=Sénégal [1]	31	Fg	14.00N	14.00W
Senegal (EN)=Sénégal	30	Fg	15.48N	16.32W
Sénégal Oriental [3]	34	Cc	13.30N	13.00W
Senekal	37	De	28.30S	27.32 E
Senetosa, Punta di-	11a	Ab	41.33N	8.47 E
Seney	44	Eb	46.21N	85.56W
Senftenberg/Zły Komorow	10	Ke	51.31N	14.01 E
Sengata	22	Ni	0.28N	117.33 E
Sengilej	7	Lj	53.58N	48.46 E
Senguerr, Río-	56	Gg	45.32S	68.54W
Sengwa	37	Dc	17.05S	28.03 E
Senhor do Bonfim	53	Lg	10.27S	40.11W
Senica	10	Nh	48.41N	17.23 E
Senigallia	14	Hg	43.43N	13.13 E
Senirkent	24	Dc	38.07N	30.33 E
Senj	14	If	45.00N	14.54 E
Senja	5	Hb	69.20N	17.30 E
Senjsko Bilo	14	Jf	44.55N	15.03 E
Senkaku-Shotō	27	Lf	25.45N	124.00 E
Şenkaya	24	Jb	40.35N	42.21 E
Senkevičevka	10	Vf	50.29N	25.05 E
Šenkursk	19	Ec	62.08N	42.53 E
Senlin Shan	28	Kc	43.12N	130.38 E
Senlis	11	Ie	49.12N	2.35 E
Senmonorom	25	Lf	12.27N	107.12 E
Senn, Dahr Ou-	32	Ef	17.55N	11.00W
Sennestadt, Bielefeld-	12	Kc	51.57N	8.35 E
Senneterre	42	Jg	48.24N	77.14W
Senno	7	Gi	54.47N	29.41 E
Sennoj	16	Oc	52.07N	46.59 E
Senorbì	14	Dk	39.32N	9.08 E
Senqu	37	Be	28.38S	16.27 E
Sens	11	Jf	48.12N	3.17 E
Sensée	12	Fd	50.16N	3.06 E
Sensuntepeque	49	Cg	13.52N	88.38W
Senta	15	Dd	45.56N	20.05 E
Sentinel Peak	42	Ff	54.58N	122.00W
Sentinel Range	66	Pf	78.10S	85.30W
Senyavin Islands	57	Gd	6.55N	158.00 E
Şenyurt	24	Id	37.06N	40.40 E
Senzaki-Wan	29	Bd	34.25N	131.20 E
Senžarka	17	Mi	54.45N	67.50 E
Seo de Urgel/La Seu d'Urgell	13	Nb	42.21N	1.28 E
Seoni	25	Fd	22.05N	79.32 E
Seoul (EN)=Sŏul	22	Of	37.34N	127.00 E
Séoune	11	Gj	44.10N	0.41 E
Sepanjang, Pulau-	26	Gh	7.10S	115.50 E
Separation Point	62	Ed	40.47S	173.00 E
Sepetovka	19	Ce	50.12N	27.04 E
Sepik River	57	Fe	3.51S	144.34 E
Sępólno Krajeńskie	10	Nc	53.28N	17.32 E
Sępopol	10	Qb	54.15N	21.00 E
Sępopolska, Nizina-	10	Rb	54.15N	21.10 E
Septemvri	15	Hg	42.13N	24.06 E
Septentrional, Cordillera-	49	Ld	19.35N	70.45W
Septeuil	12	Df	48.54N	1.41 E
Sept-Iles	39	Md	50.12N	66.23W
Sepúlveda	13	Ic	41.18N	3.45W
Sequeros	13	Fd	40.31N	6.01W
Sequillo	13	Gc	41.45N	5.30W
Sera	29	Cd	34.36N	133.01 E
Sera, Pulau-	26	Jh	7.40S	131.05 E
Šerabad	19	Gh	37.43N	66.59 E
Šerabad	18	Ff	37.22N	67.03 E
Serafettın Dağları	24	Ic	39.05N	41.10 E
Serafimovič	16	Me	49.36N	42.47 E
Serahs	19	Gh	36.30N	61.13 E
Seraidi	14	Bn	36.55N	7.40 E
Seraing	11	Ld	50.36N	5.31 E
Seram	57	De	3.00S	129.00 E
Seram, Laut-=Ceram Sea (EN)	57	De	2.30S	128.00 E
Serang	26	Eh	6.07S	106.09 E
Serasan, Pulau-	26	Ef	2.30N	109.03 E
Serasan, Selat-	26	Ef	2.20S	109.00 E
Serbia (EN) = Srbija [2]	15	Df	44.00N	21.00 E
Serbia (EN) = Srbija	5	Ig	43.00N	21.00 E
Serbia (EN)=Srbija	15	Df	44.00N	21.00 E
Şercaia	15	Id	45.50N	25.08 E
Serchio	14	Eg	43.47N	10.16 E
Serdo	35	Gc	11.58N	41.18 E
Serdoba	16	Nc	52.34N	44.01 E
Serdobsk	19	Ee	52.29N	44.16 E
Sereba	35	Gc	13.12N	40.32 E
Serebrjansk	19	If	49.43N	83.20 E
Serebrjanski	7	Ib	68.52N	35.32 E
Sered'	10	Nh	48.17N	17.45 E
Seredka	8	Mf	58.10N	28.25 E
Şereflikoçhisar	24	Ec	38.56N	33.33 E
Serein	11	Jg	47.55N	3.31 E
Seremban	26	Df	2.43N	101.56 E
Serengeti Plain	36	Fc	2.50S	35.00 E
Serenje	36	Fe	13.14S	30.14 E
Šereševo	10	Ud	52.31N	24.19 E
Seret	16	De	48.38N	25.52 E
Serfopoúla	15	Hl	37.15N	24.36 E
Sergač	19	Ed	55.33N	45.28 E
Sergeievka	28	Lc	43.23N	133.22 E
Sergeja Kirova, Ostrova-	20	Da	77.10N	90.00 E
Sergejevka [Kaz.-U.S.S.R.]	19	Ge	53.51N	67.28 E
Sergejevka [R.S.F.S.R.]	28	Kb	44.20N	131.40 E
Sergino	22	Ic	62.30N	65.40 E
Sergipe [2]	54	Kf	10.30S	37.10W
Sergokala	16	Oh	42.30N	47.40 E
Sergozero, Ozero-	7	Ic	66.45N	36.50 E
Seria	26	Ff	4.37N	114.19 E
Serian	26	Ff	1.10N	110.34 E
Seriana, Val-	14	De	45.50N	9.50 E
Seribu, Kepulauan-	26	Fh	5.36S	106.33 E
Sérifontaine	12	De	49.21N	1.46 E
Sérifos	15	Hl	37.09N	24.30 E
Sérifos	15	Hl	37.10N	24.30 E
Serifou, Stenón-	15	Hl	37.15N	24.30 E
Serik	24	Dd	36.55N	31.06 E
Seringapatam Reef	59	Eb	13.40S	122.05 E
Serio	14	De	45.16N	9.45 E
Šerlovaja Gora	20	Gf	50.34N	116.18 E
Sermata, Kepulauan-	26	Ih	8.10S	128.40 E
Sermilik	41	Ie	66.00N	38.45W
Sernovodsk	7	Mj	53.54N	51.09 E
Sernur	7	Lh	56.57N	49.11 E
Sernyje Vody	7	Mj	53.53N	50.59 E
Sero	24	Kd	37.33N	44.40 E
Serock	10	Rd	52.31N	21.03 E
Serodino	55	Bk	32.37S	60.57W
Serov	22	Id	59.29N	60.31 E
Serowe	31	Jk	22.23S	26.43 E
Serpa	13	Eg	37.56N	7.36W
Serpent, Vallée du-	34	Dc	14.50N	8.00W
Serpentine Lakes	59	Fe	28.30S	129.10 E
Serpent's Mouth/Serpiente, Boca de la-	54	Fa	10.10N	61.58W
Serpiente, Boca de la-/ Serpent's Mouth	54	Fa	10.10N	61.58W
Serpis	13	Lf	38.59N	0.09W
Serpnevoje	15	Lc	46.23N	28.59 E
Serpuhov	6	Je	54.55N	37.25 E
Serra, Aparados da-	55	Hi	28.45S	49.45W
Serra Bonita	55	Ib	15.13S	46.49W
Serra das Araras	55	Jb	15.30S	45.21W
Serra do Navio	53	Ke	0.59N	52.03W
Serra do Salitre	55	Id	19.06S	46.41W
Serra Dourada	55	Ka	12.50S	43.56W
Sérrai	15	Gh	41.05N	23.33 E
Serralada Litoral Catalana/ Cadena Costero Catalana= Catalan Coastal Range (EN)	5	Gg	41.35N	1.40 E
Serralada Pirinenca= Pyrenees (EN)	5	Gg	42.40N	1.00 E
Serrana Bank	47	Hf	14.23N	80.12W
Serranilla Bank	47	Ie	15.50N	79.50W
Serranópolis	55	Fd	18.16S	52.00W
Serra San Bruno	14	Kl	38.35N	16.20 E
Serrat, Cap-	32	Ib	37.14N	9.13 E
Serra Talhada	54	Ke	7.59S	38.18W
Serre	11	Je	49.41N	3.23 E
Serre, Massif de la-	11	Lg	47.10N	5.35 E
Serre-Ponçon, Réservoir de-	11	Mj	44.27N	6.16 E
Serres	11	Lj	44.26N	5.43 E
Serrezuela	56	Gd	30.38S	65.23W
Serrinha	54	Kf	11.39S	39.00W
Serriola, Bocca-	14	Gg	43.31N	12.21 E
Serro	55	Kd	18.37S	43.23W
Serrota	13	Gd	40.30N	5.04W
Serrote, Rio-	55	Ee	21.27S	54.40W

Index Symbols

[1] Independent Nation
[2] State, Region
[3] District, County
Municipality
Colony, Dependency
Continent
Physical Region
Historical or Cultural Region
Mount, Mountain
Volcano
Hill
Mountains, Mountain Range
Hills, Escarpment
Plateau, Upland
Pass, Gap
Plain, Lowland
Delta
Salt Flat
Valley, Canyon
Crater, Cave
Karst Features
Depression
Polder
Desert, Dunes
Forest, Woods
Heath, Steppe
Oasis
Cape, Point
Coast, Beach
Cliff
Peninsula
Isthmus
Sandbank
Island
Atoll
Rock, Reef
Islands, Archipelago
Rocks, Reefs
Coral Reef
Well, Spring
Geyser
River, Stream
Waterfall Rapids
River Mouth, Estuary
Lake
Salt Lake
Intermittent Lake
Reservoir
Swamp, Pond
Canal
Glacier
Ice Shelf, Pack Ice
Ocean
Sea
Gulf, Bay
Strait, Fjord
Lagoon
Bank
Seamount
Tablemount
Ridge
Shelf
Basin
Escarpment, Sea Scarp
Fracture
Trench, Abyss
National Park, Reserve
Point of Interest
Recreation Site
Cave, Cavern
Historic Site
Ruins
Wall, Walls
Church, Abbey
Temple
Scientific Station
Airport
Port
Lighthouse
Mine
Tunnel
Dam, Bridge

Sersou, Plateau du- ◠	13	Ni	35.30N	2.00 E
Sertã	13	De	39.48N	8.06W
Sertão ψ	52	Lg	10.00S	41.00W
Sertãozinho	55	Ie	21.08S	47.59W
Sêrtar	27	He	32.20N	100.20 E
Serti	34	Hd	7.30N	11.22 E
Serua, Pulau- ◆	26	Jh	6.18S	130.01 E
Serui	26	Kg	1.53S	136.14 E
Serule	37	Dd	21.55S	27.19 E
Sérvia	15	Ei	40.11N	22.00 E
Sêrxü	27	Ge	32.56N	98.02 E
Seryítsi ◆	15	Ii	40.00N	25.10 E
Seryševo	20	Hf	51.02N	128.25 E
Sesayap ≈	26	Gf	3.36N	117.15 E
Sese	36	Eb	2.11N	25.47 E
Seseganaga Lake ⌓	45	Ka	50.10N	90.15W
Sese Islands ◈	36	Fc	0.20S	32.20 E
Sesfontein	37	Ac	19.07S	13.39 E
Sesheke	36	Df	17.29S	24.18 E
Sesia ≈	14	Ce	45.05N	8.37 E
Sesibi ⁖	35	Ea	20.05N	30.31 E
Sesimbra	13	Cf	38.26N	9.06W
Šešma ≈	7	Mi	55.20N	51.12 E
Sesnut ▲	8	Be	59.42N	7.21 E
Sessa Aurunca	14	Hi	41.14N	13.56 E
Ses Salines, Cap de-/ Salinas, Cabo de- ►	13	Pe	39.16N	3.03 E
Sestao	13	Ja	43.18N	3.00W
Sesto Fiorentino	14	Fg	43.50N	11.12 E
Sesto San Giovanni	14	De	45.32N	9.14 E
Sestriere	14	Af	44.57N	6.53 E
Sestri Levante	14	Df	44.16N	9.24 E
Sestroreck	7	Gf	60.06N	29.59 E
Šešupė ≈	7	Fi	55.00N	22.10 E
Šešuvis ≈	8	Ji	55.12N	22.31 E
Sesvenna, Piz- ▲	14	Ed	46.42N	10.25 E
Sesvete	14	Ke	45.50N	16.07 E
Šeta/Šėta	8	Ki	55.14N	24.18 E
Šėta/Šeta	8	Ki	55.14N	24.18 E
Setaka	29	Be	33.09N	130.28 E
Setana	28	Oc	42.26N	139.51 E
Sète	11	Jk	43.24N	3.41 E
Sete de Setembro, Rio- ≈	55	Fa	12.56S	52.51W
Sete Lagoas	54	Jg	19.27S	44.14W
Setenil	13	Gh	36.51N	5.11W
Sete Quedas, Saltos das- = Guaira Falls (EN) ⥥	56	Jb	24.02S	54.16W
Setermoen	7	Eb	68.52N	18.28 E
Setesdal ⌧	7	Bg	59.05N	7.35 E
Setesdalsheiane ▲	8	Be	59.30N	7.10 E
Seti ≈	25	Gc	28.58N	81.06 E
Sétif ③	32	Ib	36.05N	5.00 E
Sétif	31	He	36.12N	5.24 E
Seto	29	Ed	35.13N	137.05 E
Setonaikai = Inland Sea (EN) ▦	21	Pf	34.10N	133.00 E
Setouchi	29b	Ba	28.08N	129.20 E
Šetpe	19	Fg	44.06N	52.02 E
Settat	32	Fc	33.00N	7.37W
Settat ③	32	Fc	33.00N	7.30W
Setté Cama	36	Ac	2.32S	9.45 E
Sette-Daban, Hrebet- ⛰	20	Id	62.00N	138.00 E
Settle	9	Kg	54.04N	2.16W
Setúbal ②	13	Df	38.20N	8.30W
Setúbal	6	Fh	38.32N	8.54W
Setúbal, Baia de- ◧	13	Df	38.27N	8.53W
Setúbal o de Guadalupe, Laguna- ⌓	55	Bj	31.33S	60.35W
Seudre ≈	11	Ei	45.48N	1.09W
Seugne ≈	11	Fi	45.42N	0.32W
Seui	14	Dk	39.50N	9.19 E
Seuil-d'Argonne	12	Hf	48.58N	5.03 E
Seul, Lac- ⌓	38	Jd	50.20N	92.30W
Seulles ≈	12	Be	49.20N	0.27W
Seurre	11	Lg	47.00N	5.09 E
Sevan	19	Eg	40.32N	44.57 E
Sevan, Lake- (EN) = Sevan, Ozero- ⌓	5	Kg	40.20N	45.20 E
Sevan, Ozero- = Sevan, Lake- (EN) ⌓	5	Kg	40.20N	45.20 E
Sévaré	34	Ec	14.32N	4.06W
Sevastopol	6	Jg	44.36N	33.32 E
Ševčenko	22	He	43.35N	51.05 E
Ševčenko, Zaliv- ◧	18	Ca	46.30N	60.15 E
Sevenoaks	9	Nj	51.16N	0.12 E
Sever ≈	13	Ee	39.40N	7.32W
Sévérac-le-Château	11	Jj	44.19N	3.04 E
Severn ▬	9	Kj	51.20N	3.10W
Severn [Can.] ≈	38	Kd	56.02N	87.36W
Severn [U.K.] ≈	9	Kj	51.35N	2.40W
Severnaja Dvina = Northern Dvina (EN) ≈	5	Kc	64.32N	40.30 E
Severnaja Keltma ≈	17	Ff	61.30N	54.00 E
Severnaja Pseašho, Gora- ▲	16	Lh	43.47N	40.30 E
Severnaja Sosva ≈	19	Gc	64.10N	65.28 E
Severnaja Zemlja = Severnaya Zemlya (EN) ◈	21	Lb	79.30N	98.00 E
Severnaya Zemlya (EN) = Severnaja Zemlja ◈	21	Lb	79.30N	98.00 E
Severn Lake ⌓	42	If	53.52N	90.58W
Severnoje [R.S.F.S.R.]	16	Rb	54.05N	52.32 E
Severnoje [R.S.F.S.R.]	20	Ce	56.21N	78.23 E
Severny	19	Gb	67.38N	64.06 E
Severnyje Uvaly = Northern Uvals (EN) ⌒	5	Kd	59.30N	49.00 E
Severny Kommunar	17	Gg	58.23N	54.02 E
Severny Ledovity Okean = Arctic Ocean (EN) ▤	67	Be	85.00N	170.00 E
Severny Ural = Northern Urals (EN) ⛰	5	Lc	62.00N	59.00 E
Severobajkalsk	20	Fe	55.40N	109.25 E
Severočeský kraj ③	10	Kf	50.35N	14.15 E
Severodoneck	16	Ke	48.57N	38.31 E
Severodvinsk	6	Jc	64.34N	39.50 E
Severo-Jenisejski	20	Ed	60.28N	93.01 E
Severo-Kazahstanskaja Oblast ③	19	Ge	54.30N	68.00 E
Severo-Krymski Kanal ═	16	Ig	45.30N	34.35 E
Severo-Kurilsk	22	Rd	50.40N	156.08 E
Severomoravský kraj ③	10	Ng	49.45N	17.50 E
Severomorsk	19	Db	69.04N	33.24 E
Severo-Osetinskaja ASSR ③	19	Eg	43.00N	44.10 E
Severo-Sibirskaja Nizmennost = North Siberian Plain (EN) ▭	21	Mb	72.00N	104.00 E
Severouralsk	19	Gc	60.09N	60.01 E
Sevier	46	Ig	38.35N	112.14W
Sevier Bridge Reservoir ◎	46	Jg	39.21N	111.57W
Sevier Desert ◢	46	Ig	39.25N	112.50W
Sevier Lake □	43	Ed	38.55N	113.09W
Sevier River ≈	43	Ed	39.04N	113.06W
Sevilla ③	13	Gg	37.30N	5.30W
Sevilla [Col.]	54	Cc	4.16N	75.53W
Sevilla [Sp.] = Seville (EN)	6	Fh	37.23N	5.59W
Sevilla, Isla- ◆	49	Fi	8.14N	82.24W
Seville (EN) = Sevilla [Sp.]	6	Fh	37.23N	5.59W
Sevlijevo	15	If	43.01N	25.06 E
Sèvre Nantaise ≈	11	Eg	47.12N	1.33W
Sèvre Niortaise ≈	11	Eh	46.18N	1.08W
Sevron ≈	11	Lh	46.32N	5.16 E
Sevsk	16	Ic	52.08N	34.30 E
Sewa ≈	34	Cd	7.18N	12.08W
Seward [Ak.-U.S.]	39	Ec	60.06N	149.26W
Seward [Nb.-U.S.]	45	Hf	40.55N	97.06W
Seward Peninsula ▰	38	Cc	65.00N	164.00W
Sewell	56	Fd	34.05S	70.21W
Seyāhkal	24	Md	37.09N	49.52 E
Seybaplaya	48	Nh	19.39N	90.40W
Seybaplaya, Punta- ►	48	Nh	19.45N	90.42W
Seybouse, Oued- ≈	14	Bn	36.53N	7.46 E
Seychelles ①	31	Mi	8.00S	55.00 E
Seychelles Islands ◈	30	Mi	4.35S	55.40 E
Seydān	24	Og	30.01N	53.01 E
Seydişehir	24	Dd	37.25N	31.51 E
Seyðisfjörður	6	Eb	65.16N	14.00W
Seyfe Gölü ⌓	24	Fc	39.13N	34.23 E
Seyf Ţāleh	24	Le	35.57N	46.19 E
Seyhan ≈	23	Db	36.43N	34.53 E
Seyitgazi	24	Dc	39.27N	30.43 E
Seyitömer	15	Mj	39.34N	29.52 E
Seyla'	35	Gc	11.21N	43.30 E
Seymour [Austl.]	59	Jg	37.02S	145.08 E
Seymour [In.-U.S.]	44	Ef	38.58N	85.53W
Seymour [Mo.-U.S.]	45	Jh	37.09N	92.46W
Seymour [S.Afr.]	37	Df	32.33S	26.46 E
Seymour [Tx.-U.S.]	43	He	33.35N	99.16W
Sezana	14	He	45.42N	13.52 E
Sézanne	11	Jf	48.43N	3.43 E
Sfaktiria ◆	15	Em	36.56N	21.40 E
Sfax (EN) = Şafāqis ③	32	Jc	34.30N	10.30 E
Sfax (EN) = Şafāqis	31	Ie	34.44N	10.46 E
Sferracavallo, Capo- ►	14	Dk	39.43N	9.40 E
Sfîntu Gheorghe [Rom.]	15	Me	44.53N	29.26 E
Sfîntu Gheorghe [Rom.]	15	Id	45.52N	25.47 E
Sfîntu Gheorghe, Braţul- ≈	15	Me	44.53N	29.36 E
Sfîntu Gheorghe, Ostrovul- ◆	15	Md	45.07N	29.22 E
Sfizef	13	Li	35.14N	0.15W
's-Gravenhage/Den Haag = The Hague (EN)	6	Ge	52.06N	4.18 E
's-Gravenhage-Scheveningen	11	Kb	52.06N	4.18 E
Shaan-hsi Sheng → Shaanxi Sheng = Shensi (EN) ②	27	Id	36.00N	109.00 E
Shaanxi Sheng (Shaan-hsi Sheng) = Shensi (EN) ②	27	Id	36.00N	109.00 E
Shaba ②	36	Ed	8.30S	25.00 E
Sha'bah, Wādī ash- ≈	24	Ij	25.59N	41.55 E
Shabeellaha Dhexe ③	35	He	3.00N	46.00 E
Shabellaha Hoose ③	35	Ge	2.00N	44.40 E
Shabēlle, Webi- = Shebeli Webi (EN) ≈	30	Lh	0.12S	42.45 E
Shabestar	24	Kc	38.11N	45.42 E
Shabunda	36	Ec	2.42S	27.20 E
Shache/Yarkant	27	Cd	38.24N	77.15 E
Shacheng → Huailai	27	Kc	40.29N	115.30 E
Shackleton Coast ▥	66	Kg	82.00S	162.00 E
Shackleton Glacier ❄	66	Lg	84.35S	176.15W
Shackleton Ice Shelf ❅	66	He	66.00S	101.00 E
Shackleton Range ⛰	66	Ag	80.40S	26.00W
Shaddādī	24	Id	36.02N	40.45 E
Shādegān	24	Mg	30.40N	48.38 E
Shadwān, Jazīrat- ◆	33	Fd	27.30N	33.55 E
Shaftesbury	9	Kk	51.01N	2.12W
Shagedu → Jungar Qi	27	Jd	39.37N	110.58 E
Shāghir Bazar	24	Id	36.52N	40.53 E
Shag Rocks ⁑	66	Rd	54.26S	36.33W
Shāh'Abbās	24	Oe	34.44N	52.10 E
Shah Alam	26	Df	3.05N	101.29 E
Shahdol	25	Gd	23.13N	81.18 E
Sha He [China] ≈	28	Ch	33.39N	114.38 E
Sha He [China] ≈	28	Cf	37.09N	114.46 E
Shahezhen → Linze	27	Hd	39.10N	100.21 E
Shah Jahān, Kūh-e- ▲	24	Qd	37.02N	57.54 E
Shahjahānpur	25	Fc	27.53N	79.55 E
Shah Kūh ▲	23	Hb	36.35N	54.31 E
Shahmīrzād	24	Oe	35.47N	53.20 E
Shāhpūr ⁖	24	Nh	32.50N	51.45 E
Shāhpūr ≈	24	Nh	29.39N	51.03 E
Shahrak	24	Nd	36.14N	50.40 E
Shahr-e-Bābak	24	Pg	30.10N	55.09 E
Shahr-e Khafr	24	Oh	28.56N	53.14 E
Shahr Kord	23	Hc	32.19N	50.50 E
Shāhrūd ≈	24	Md	37.17N	48.43 E
Shahu, Kūh-e- ⛰	24	Le	34.45N	46.30 E
Shāh Zeyd	24	Od	36.13N	52.22 E
Shā'ib al Banāt, Jabal- ▲	30	Kf	26.59N	33.29 E
Sha'īt, Wādī- ≈	24	Ej	24.33N	33.01 E
Shakaga-Dake ▲	29	Be	33.11N	130.53 E
Shakawe	31	Ji	18.23S	21.51 E
Shak Bay (Denham)	59	Ce	25.55S	113.32 E
Shaker Heights	44	Ge	41.29N	81.36W
Shaki	34	Fd	8.40N	3.23 E
Shakotan-Dake ▲	29a	Bb	43.16N	140.26 E
Shakotan-Hantō ▰	29a	Bb	43.15N	140.30 E
Shakotan-Misaki ►	29a	Bb	43.23N	140.28 E
Shaktoolik	40	Gd	64.20N	161.09W
Shāl	24	Me	35.54N	49.46 E
Shala, Lake- ⌓	35	Fd	7.29N	38.32 E
Shalamzār	24	Nf	32.02N	50.49 E
Shalānbōd	35	Ge	1.40N	44.42 E
Shaler Mountains ⛰	42	Gb	71.45N	111.00W
Shaliuhe → Gangca	27	Hd	37.30N	100.14 E
Shaluli Shan ⛰	21	Lf	30.45N	99.45 E
Shām, Bādiyat ash- = Syrian Desert (EN) ◢	21	Ff	32.00N	40.00 E
Shām, Jabal ash- ▲	21	Hg	23.10N	57.20 E
Shamattawa	42	Ie	55.52N	92.05W
Shambe	35	Ed	7.07N	30.46 E
Shambu	35	Fd	9.33N	37.07 E
Shamīl	24	Qi	27.30N	56.53 E
Shāmīyah ⌧	21	Ff	34.00N	39.59 E
Shammar, Jabal- ⛰	21	Gg	27.20N	41.45 E
Shamo, Lake- ⌓	35	Fd	5.50N	37.40 E
Shamokin	44	Ie	40.47N	76.34W
Shamrock	45	Fi	35.13N	100.15W
Shams	24	Pg	31.04N	55.02 E
Shamsī	35	Db	19.03N	29.54 E
Shamwa	37	Ec	17.18S	31.34 E
Shan ②	25	Jd	22.00N	98.00 E
Shandī	31	Kg	16.42N	33.26 E
Shandian He ≈	28	Dc	42.20N	116.20 E
Shandong Bandao = Shantung Peninsula (EN) ▰	21	Of	37.00N	121.00 E
Shandong Sheng (Shan-tung Sheng) = Shantung (EN) ②	27	Kd	36.00N	119.00 E
Shandūr Pass ⌵	25	Ea	36.04N	72.31 E
Shangani	37	Dc	19.42S	29.22 E
Shangani ≈	37	Dc	18.30S	27.11 E
Shangbahe	28	Ci	30.39N	115.06 E
Shangcai	28	Ch	33.16N	114.15 E
Shangcheng	28	Ci	31.49N	115.24 E
Shangdu	27	Jc	41.31N	113.32 E
Shanggao	28	Cj	28.15N	114.55 E
Shanghai	22	Of	31.14N	121.28 E
Shanghai Shi (Shang-hai Shih) ④	27	Le	31.14N	121.28 E
Shang-hai Shih → Shanghai Shi ④	27	Le	31.14N	121.28 E
Shanghang	27	Kf	25.04N	116.21 E
Shanghe	28	Df	37.19N	117.09 E
Shanghekou	27	Lc	40.26N	124.51 E
Shangpaihe → Feixi	28	Di	31.42N	117.09 E
Shangqiu (Zhuji)	27	Ke	34.24N	115.37 E
Shangrao	27	Kf	28.29N	117.59 E
Shan Guan ⌵	27	Kf	27.28N	117.05 E
Shangxian	27	Ie	33.55N	109.57 E
Shangyi (Nanhaoqian)	28	Bd	41.06N	113.58 E
Shangyu (Baiguan)	28	Fi	30.01N	120.53 E
Shangzhi	27	Mb	45.13N	127.55 E
Shanhaiguan	28	Ed	40.01N	119.45 E
Shanhetun	28	Ib	44.43N	127.14 E
Shan-hsi Sheng → Shanxi Sheng = Shansi (EN) ②	27	Jd	37.00N	112.00 E
Shanklin	12	Ad	50.37N	1.11W
Shanmatang Ding ▲	27	Jg	24.45N	111.50 E
Shannon ◆	41	Kc	75.20N	18.10W
Shannon	62	Fd	40.33S	175.25 E
Shannon/Aerfort na Sionainne ✈	9	Ei	52.42N	8.57W
Shannon/An tSionainn ≈	5	Fe	52.36N	9.41W
Shannon, Mount- ▲	59	Ie	29.58S	141.30 E
Shannon, Mouth of the- ◁	9	Di	52.30N	9.53W
Shanshan (Piqan)	27	Fc	42.52N	90.10 E
Shansi (EN) = Shan-hsi Sheng → Shanxi Sheng ②	27	Jd	37.00N	112.00 E
Shansi (EN) = Shanxi Sheng (Shan-hsi Sheng) ②	27	Jd	37.00N	112.00 E
Shansonggang	28	Ic	42.30N	126.13 E
Shanţah, Ra's- ►	24	Qi	26.22N	56.26 E
Shantar Islands (EN) = Šantarskije Ostrova ◈	21	Pd	55.00N	137.36 E
Shantou	22	Ng	23.26N	116.42 E
Shantung (EN) = Shandong Sheng (Shan-tung Sheng) ②	27	Kd	36.00N	119.00 E
Shantung (EN) = Shan-tung Sheng → Shandong Sheng ②	27	Kd	36.00N	119.00 E
Shantung Peninsula (EN) = Shandong Bandao ▰	21	Of	37.00N	121.00 E
Shan-tung Sheng → Shandong Sheng = Shantung (EN) ②	27	Kd	36.00N	119.00 E
Shanxian	28	Dg	34.47N	116.05 E
Shanxi Sheng (Shan-hsi Sheng) = Shansi (EN) ②	27	Jd	37.00N	112.00 E
Shanyin (Daiyue)	28	Be	39.30N	112.48 E
Shanyincheng	28	Be	39.27N	112.56 E
Shaoguan	22	Ng	24.57N	113.34 E
Shaoshan	27	Jf	27.55N	112.32 E
Shaowu	27	Kf	27.21N	117.29 E
Shaoxing	22	Og	30.00N	120.30 E
Shaoyang	22	Ng	27.13N	111.31 E
Shapinsay ◆	9	Kb	59.03N	2.51W
Shaqlāwah	24	Kd	36.23N	44.18 E
Shaqq al Ju'ayfir ≈	35	Db	15.16N	26.00 E
Shaqrā'	23	Gg	13.21N	45.42 E
Shaqū	24	Qi	27.14N	56.22 E
Sharāf	24	Jg	30.37N	43.45 E
Sharafah	35	Dc	12.04N	27.07 E
Sharafkhāneh	24	Kc	38.11N	45.29 E
Sharāh, Jibāl ash- ⛰	24	Fg	30.10N	35.30 E
Sharā 'Iwah ◆	24	Oj	25.02N	52.14 E
Shareh	24	Kd	37.38N	44.50 E
Shari	27	Pc	43.55N	144.40 E
Shārī, Buḩayrat- ⌓	24	Ke	34.23N	44.07 E
Shari-Dake ▲	29a	Db	43.46N	144.43 E
Sharifābād [Iran]	24	Nd	36.12N	50.08 E
Sharifābād [Iran]	24	Ne	35.25N	51.47 E
Shark Bay ◧	57	Cg	25.30S	113.30 E
Sharm ash Shaykh	33	Fd	27.50N	34.16 E
Sharon	44	Ge	41.16N	80.30W
Sharon Springs	45	Fg	38.54N	101.45W
Sharp ◆	9	Fc	58.05N	7.05W
Sharqīyah, Aş Şaḩrā' ash- = Arabian Desert (EN) ◢	30	Kf	28.00N	32.00 E
Sharshar, Jabal- ▲	24	Dk	23.52N	30.20 E
Shary	23	Fd	27.15N	43.27 E
Shashe	37	Dd	21.24S	27.27 E
Shashemene	35	Fd	7.13N	38.36 E
Shashi	22	Nf	30.22N	112.11 E
Shashi ≈	30	Jk	22.12S	29.21 E
Shasta, Mount- ▲	38	Ge	41.20N	122.20W
Shasta Lake ⌓	43	Cc	40.50N	122.25W
Shāţi', Wādī ash- ≈	33	Bd	27.10N	13.25 E
Shattuck	45	Gh	36.16N	99.53W
Shaunavon	42	Gg	49.40N	108.25W
Shawan	27	Ec	44.21N	85.37 E
Shawano	45	Ld	44.47N	88.36W
Shawinigan	42	Kg	46.33N	72.45W
Shawnee	43	Hd	35.20N	96.55W
Shawneetown	45	Lh	37.42N	88.08W
Shaw River ≈	59	Dd	20.20S	119.17 E
Shāwshāw, Jabal- ▲	24	Ci	26.03N	28.56 E
Shayang	28	Bi	30.42N	112.34 E
Shaybārā ◆	24	Gj	25.25N	36.51 E
Shaykh Aḩmad	24	Lf	32.53N	46.26 E
Shaykh Fāris	24	Lf	32.05N	47.36 E
Shaykh Sa'd	24	Lf	32.34N	46.17 E
Shaykh 'Uthmān	23	Fg	12.52N	44.59 E
Shebar, Kowtal-e- ▲	23	Kc	34.54N	68.14 E
Shebele, Wabe- = Shebeli Webi (EN) ≈	30	Lh	0.12S	42.45 E
Shebeli Webi (EN) = Shabēlle, Webi- ≈	30	Lh	0.12S	42.45 E
Shebeli Webi (EN) = Shebele, Wabe- ≈	30	Lh	0.12S	42.45 E
Sheberghān	22	If	36.41N	65.45 E
Sheboygan	45	Me	43.46N	87.44W
Shebshi Mountains ⛰	30	Ih	8.30N	11.45 E
Shedin Peak ▲	42	Ee	55.50N	127.00W
Sheelin, Lough-/Loch Síleann ⌓	9	Fh	53.48N	7.20W
Sheenjek ≈	40	Kc	66.45N	144.33W
Sheep Haven/Cuan na gCaorach ◧	9	Ff	55.10N	7.52W
Sheep Mountain ▲	46	Hj	32.32N	114.14W
Sheep Range ⛰	46	Hh	36.45N	115.05W
s'Heerenberg, Bergh-	12	Ic	51.53N	6.16 E
Sheerness	9	Nj	51.27N	0.45 E
Sheffield [Al.-U.S.]	44	Dh	34.46N	87.40W
Sheffield [Eng.-U.K.]	6	Fe	53.23N	1.30W
Sheffield [Tx.-U.S.]	45	Fk	30.43N	101.50W
Shefford	12	Bb	52.02N	0.20W
Shek Hasan	35	Fc	12.04N	35.53 E
Shek Husen	35	Gd	7.45N	40.42 E
Shelburne [N.S.-Can.]	42	Kh	43.46N	65.19W
Shelburne [Ont.-Can.]	44	Gc	44.04N	80.12W
Shelby [Mt.-U.S.]	43	Eb	48.30N	111.51W
Shelby [N.C.-U.S.]	44	Gh	35.17N	81.32W
Shelbyville [Il.-U.S.]	45	Lg	39.24N	88.48W
Shelbyville [In.-U.S.]	44	Ef	39.31N	85.47W
Shelbyville [Tn.-U.S.]	44	Dh	35.29N	86.27W
Shelbyville, Lake- ⌓	45	Lg	39.30N	88.40W
Sheldon	45	Ie	43.11N	95.51W
Sheldon Point	40	Gd	63.32N	164.52W
Shelikhov Gulf (EN) = Şelihova, Zaliv- ◧	21	Rc	60.00N	158.00 E
Shelikof Strait ▬	40	Ie	57.30N	155.00W
Shell	46	Ld	44.33N	107.44W
Shellbrook	42	Gf	53.13N	106.24W
Shellharbour	58	Gh	34.35S	150.52 E
Shelter Point ►	62	Cg	47.06S	168.13 E
Shelton	46	Dc	47.13N	123.06W
Shenandoah	45	If	40.46N	95.22W
Shenandoah Mountain ⛰	44	Hf	38.58N	79.00W
Shenandoah Valley ∨	44	Hf	38.45N	78.45W
Shenchi	28	Be	39.05N	112.11 E
Shendam	34	Gd	8.53N	9.32 E
Shending Shan ▲	27	Nb	46.34N	133.27 E
Shenge	34	Cd	7.55N	12.57W
Shëngjini	15	Ch	41.49N	19.35 E
Shengsi (Caiyuanzhen)	28	Gi	30.42N	122.29 E
Shengsi Liedao ◈	27	Le	30.45N	122.40 E
Shengxian	27	Lf	29.35N	120.45 E
Shengze	28	Fi	30.55N	120.39 E
Shenjiamen → Putuo	28	Gj	29.57N	122.18 E
Shenmu	27	Jd	38.52N	110.35 E
Shenqiu (Huaidian)	27	Ke	33.27N	115.05 E
Shensi (EN) = Shaan-hsi Sheng → Shaanxi Sheng ②	27	Id	36.00N	109.00 E
Shensi (EN) = Shaanxi Sheng (Shaan-hsi Sheng) ②	27	Id	36.00N	109.00 E
Shenton, Mount- ▲	59	Ee	28.00S	123.22 E
Shenxian	28	Ce	38.01N	115.33 E
Shenyang (Mukden)	22	Oe	41.48N	123.24 E
Shenze	28	Ce	38.11N	115.11 E
Shepherd, Iles- = Shepherd Islands (EN) ◈	63b	Dc	16.55S	168.35 E
Shepherd Islands (EN) = Shepherd, Iles- ◈	63b	Dc	16.55S	168.35 E
Shepparton	58	Fh	36.23S	145.25 E
Sheppey ◆	9	Nj	51.24N	0.50 E
Shepshed	12	Ab	52.45N	1.17W
Sheqi	28	Bh	33.04N	112.56 E
Sherard, Cape - ►	42	Jb	74.36N	80.10W
Sherard Osborn Fjord ▬	41	Gb	82.10N	51.30W
Sherborne	9	Kk	50.57N	2.31W
Sherbro Island ◆	30	Fh	7.33N	12.42W
Sherbrooke	39	Le	45.24N	71.54W
Sherda	35	Ba	20.08N	16.45 E
Shere Hill ▲	34	Gd	9.57N	9.03 E
Sheridan [Mt.-U.S.]	46	Id	45.27N	112.12W
Sheridan [Wy.-U.S.]	39	Ie	44.48N	106.58W
Sheridan Lake	45	Eg	38.30N	102.15W
Sheringham	9	Oi	52.57N	1.12 E
Sherman	43	He	33.38N	96.36W
Sherman Station	44	Mc	45.54N	68.26W
Sherridon	42	He	55.07N	101.05W
's-Hertogenbosch/Den Bosch	11	Lc	51.41N	5.19 E
Sherwood Forest ♣	9	Lh	53.10N	1.10W
She Shui ≈	28	Ci	30.52N	114.22 E
Shetland ③	9	La	60.30N	1.30W
Shetland Islands (Zetland) ◈	5	Fc	60.30N	1.30W
Shewa ③	35	Fd	9.20N	38.55 E
Shewa Gimira	35	Fd	7.00N	35.50 E
Shexian	28	Bf	36.33N	113.40 E
Shexian (Huicheng)	28	Ej	29.53N	118.27 E
Sheyang (Hede)	28	Fh	33.47N	120.15 E
Sheyenne River ≈	43	Hb	47.05N	96.50W
Shiant Islands ◈	9	Gd	57.54N	6.30W
Shibām	35	Hb	15.56N	48.38 E
Shibamīnah, Wādī- ≈	23	Ie	22.12N	55.30 E
Shibata [Jap.]	28	Of	37.57N	139.20 E
Shibata [Jap.]	29	Gb	38.05N	140.50 E
Shibayama-Gata ⌓	29	Ec	36.21N	136.23 E
Shibazhan	27	Ma	42.28N	125.20 E
Shibecha	28	Rc	43.17N	144.36 E
Shibetsu [Jap.]	28	Rc	43.40N	145.08 E
Shibetsu [Jap.]	27	Pc	44.10N	142.23 E
Shibetsu-Gawa ≈	29a	Db	43.40N	145.06 E
Shibīn al Kawm	33	Fc	30.33N	31.01 E
Shibiutan	29a	Ca	44.47N	142.35 E
Shibi-Zan ▲	29	Bf	31.59N	130.22 E
Shīb Kūh ⛰	23	Hd	27.20N	52.40 E
Shibukawa	28	Of	36.29N	139.00 E
Shibushi	29	Bf	31.28N	131.07 E
Shibushi-Wan ◧	28	Ki	31.25N	131.12 E
Shichinohe	29	Ga	40.41N	141.10 E
Shichiyo Islands ◈	64d	Bb	7.23N	151.40 E
Shidao	27	Ld	36.51N	122.18 E
Shido	29	Dd	34.19N	134.10 E
Shidongsi → Gaolan	27	Hd	36.23N	103.55 E
Shiel, Loch- ▬	9	He	56.50N	5.50W
Shiga Ken ②	28	Ng	35.15N	136.10 E
Shigu	27	Gf	26.54N	99.44 E
Shi He ≈	28	Ch	32.32N	115.52 E
Shihezi	27	Ec	44.18N	86.02 E
Shiiba	29	Be	32.28N	131.09 E
Shijaku	15	Ch	41.20N	19.34 E
Shijiazhuang	22	Nf	38.00N	114.30 E
Shijiusuo	28	Eg	35.24N	119.32 E
Shika	29	Ec	37.01N	136.46 E
Shikabe	29a	Bb	42.02N	140.47 E
Shikārpur	25	Dc	27.57N	68.38 E
Shiki Islands ◈	64d	Bb	7.24N	151.53 E
Shikine-Jima ◆	29	Fd	34.19N	139.13 E
Shikoku ◆	21	Pf	33.30N	133.30 E
Shikoku Basin (EN) ◡	27	Oe	30.00N	135.30 E
Shikoku-Sanchi ⛰	29	Ce	33.45N	133.35 E
Shilabo	35	Gd	6.05N	44.45 E
Shiliguri	22	Kg	26.42N	88.26 E
Shiliu → Changjiang	27	Ih	19.20N	109.03 E
Shilla ▲	25	Fb	32.24N	78.12 E
Shillong	22	Lg	25.34N	91.53 E
Shimabara	28	Kh	32.47N	130.22 E
Shimabara-Hantō ▰	29	Be	32.45N	130.15 E
Shimabara-Wan ◧	29	Be	32.50N	130.30 E
Shimada	29	Fd	34.49N	138.09 E
Shima-Hantō ▰	29	Ed	34.25N	136.45 E
Shimane-Hantō ▰	29	Cd	35.30N	133.00 E
Shimane Ken ②	28	Lg	35.00N	132.20 E
Shimanto-Gawa ≈	29	Ce	32.56N	133.00 E
Shimaura-Tō ◆	29	Bd	34.50N	131.50 E
Shimian	27	Hf	29.10N	102.26 E
Shimizu [Jap.]	29a	Cb	43.01N	142.51 E
Shimizu [Jap.]	28	Og	35.01N	138.29 E
Shimla	22	Jf	31.06N	77.10 E
Shimoda	28	Og	34.40N	138.57 E
Shimodate	29	Fc	36.19N	139.58 E
Shimoga	22	Jh	13.55N	75.34 E
Shimo-Jima ◆	29	Be	32.25N	130.05 E
Shimokawa	29a	Ca	44.18N	142.38 E
Shimokita-Hantō ▰	29a	Bc	41.15N	141.05 E
Shimo-Koshiki-Jima ◆	29	Af	31.40N	129.40 E
Shimo la Tewa	36	Gc	3.57S	39.44 E
Shimoni	36	Gc	4.39S	39.23 E
Shimonoseki	27	Ne	33.57N	130.57 E
Shimono-Shima ◆	29	Ad	34.15N	129.15 E
Shimotsu	29	Dd	34.07N	135.08 E
Shimotsuma	29	Fc	36.11N	139.58 E
Shin, Loch- ⌓	9	Ic	58.07N	4.32W
Shinano	29	Fc	36.47N	138.10 E
Shinano-Gawa ≈	29	Fc	37.57N	139.04 E
Shināş	24	Qj	24.43N	56.27 E
Shindand	23	Jc	33.18N	62.08 E
Shinga	36	Dc	3.16S	24.38 E
Shingbwiyang	25	Jc	26.41N	96.13 E
Shingū	27	Oe	33.44N	135.59 E
Shingwidzi	37	Ed	23.01S	30.43 E
Shinji	29	Cd	35.24N	132.54 E
Shinji-Ko ⌓	28	Lg	35.27N	133.02 E
Shinjō	27	Pd	38.46N	140.18 E
Shinkafe	34	Gc	13.05N	6.31 E
Shinminato	29	Ec	36.47N	137.04 E
Shinnanyō	29	Bd	34.05N	131.45 E
Shinshiro	29	Ed	34.53N	137.30 E
Shintoku	28	Qc	43.12N	142.55 E
Shintotsugawa	29a	Bb	43.32N	141.40 E
Shinyanga	31	Ki	3.40S	33.26 E
Shinyanga ③	36	Fc	3.30S	33.00 E
Shiogama	29	Gb	38.19N	141.01 E
Shiojiri	28	Nf	36.06N	137.58 E
Shiokubi-Misaki ►	29a	Bc	41.43N	140.57 E
Shio-no-Misaki ►	27	Oe	33.25N	135.45 E
Shipai → Huaining	28	Di	30.25N	116.39 E

Index Symbols

① Independent Nation
② State, Region
③ District, County
④ Municipality
⑤ Colony, Dependency
■ Continent
⌧ Physical Region
▣ Historical or Cultural Region
▲ Mount, Mountain
△ Volcano
∩ Hill
⛰ Mountains, Mountain Range
⌒ Hills, Escarpment
◠ Plateau, Upland
⌵ Pass, Gap
▭ Plain, Lowland
◣ Delta
▱ Salt Flat
∨ Valley, Canyon
◉ Crater, Cave
✲ Karst Features
⊔ Depression
⊓ Polder
◢ Desert, Dunes
♣ Forest, Woods
ψ Heath, Steppe
✿ Oasis
► Cape, Point
▥ Coast, Beach
▌ Cliff
▰ Peninsula
⧖ Isthmus
⋯ Sandbank
◆ Island
⊙ Atoll
✱ Rock, Reef
◈ Islands, Archipelago
⁑ Rocks, Reefs
✺ Coral Reef
⊚ Well, Spring
⇞ Geyser
≈ River, Stream
⥥ Waterfall Rapids
◁ River Mouth, Estuary
⌓ Lake
⍜ Salt Lake
□ Intermittent Lake
◎ Reservoir
⩪ Swamp, Pond
═ Canal
❄ Glacier
❅ Ice Shelf, Pack Ice
▤ Ocean
▦ Sea
◧ Gulf, Bay
▬ Strait, Fjord
◌ Lagoon
▧ Bank
⩙ Seamount
⊼ Tablemount
⋀ Ridge
▁ Shelf
◡ Basin
⟋ Escarpment, Sea Scarp
⚡ Fracture
⩡ Trench, Abyss
✦ National Park, Reserve
✚ Point of Interest
☼ Recreation Site
◓ Cave, Cavern
♜ Historic Site
⁖ Ruins
▙ Wall, Walls
✝ Church, Abbey
⛩ Temple
⚗ Scientific Station
✈ Airport
⚓ Port
⚑ Lighthouse
⚒ Mine
⊃ Tunnel
⌇ Dam, Bridge

Index Symbols

[1] Independent Nation
[2] State, Region
[3] District, County
[4] Municipality
[5] Colony, Dependency
Continent
Physical Region

Historical or Cultural Region
Mount, Mountain
Volcano
Hill
Mountains, Mountain Range
Hills, Escarpment
Plateau, Upland

Pass, Gap
Plain, Lowland
Delta
Salt Flat
Valley, Canyon
Crater, Cave
Karst Features

Depression
Polder
Desert, Dunes
Forest, Woods
Heath, Steppe
Oasis
Cape, Point

Coast, Beach
Cliff
Peninsula
Isthmus
Sandbank
Island
Atoll

Rock, Reef
Islands, Archipelago
Rocks, Reefs
Coral Reef
Well, Spring
Geyser
River, Stream

Waterfall Rapids
River Mouth, Estuary
Lake
Salt Lake
Intermittent Lake
Reservoir
Swamp, Pond

Canal
Glacier
Bank
Ice Shelf, Pack Ice
Ocean
Sea
Gulf, Bay
Strait, Fjord

Lagoon
Bank
Seamount
Tablemount
Ridge
Shelf
Basin

Escarpment, Sea Scarp
Fracture
Trench, Abyss
National Park, Reserve
Point of Interest
Recreation Site
Cave, Cavern

Historic Site
Ruins
Wall, Walls
Church, Abbey
Temple
Scientific Station
Airport

Port
Lighthouse
Mine
Tunnel
Dam, Bridge

Sion/Sitten	14	Bd	46.15N	7.20 E
Siorapaluk	41	Ec	77.39N	71.00W
Sioule	11	Jh	46.22N	3.19 E
Sioux City	39	Je	42.30N	96.23W
Sioux Falls	39	Je	43.32N	96.44W
Sioux Lookout	42	If	50.06N	91.55W
Sipalay	26	He	9.45N	122.24 E
Šipan	14	Lh	42.43N	17.54 E
Siparia	50	Fg	10.08N	61.30W
Šipčenski prohod	15	Ig	42.46N	25.19 E
Siping	22	Oe	43.11N	124.24 E
Sipiwesk	42	He	55.27N	97.24W
Sipiwesk Lake	42	He	55.05N	97.35W
Siple, Mount-	66	Nf	73.15S	126.06W
Siple Coast	66	Mg	82.00S	153.00W
Siple Island	66	Nf	73.39S	125.00W
Siple Station	66	Pf	75.55S	83.55W
Sipora, Pulau-	26	Cg	2.12S	99.40 E
Sippola	8	Ld	60.44N	27.00 E
Siqueira Campos	55	Hf	23.42S	49.50W
Siquia, Río-	49	Eg	12.09N	84.13W
Siquijor	26	He	9.13N	123.31 E
Siquisique	54	Ea	10.34N	69.42W
Šira	20	Ef	54.29N	90.02 E
Sira	8	Be	58.17N	6.24 E
Sira	7	Bg	58.25N	6.38 E
Şīr Abū Nu'Ayr	24	Pj	25.13N	54.13 E
Si Racha	25	Kf	13.10N	100.57 E
Siracusa=Syracuse (EN)	6	Hh	37.04N	15.18 E
Sir Alexander, Mount -	42	Ff	53.56N	120.23W
Sirasso	34	Dd	9.16N	6.06W
Şirāţ, Jabal-	33	Hf	17.00N	43.50 E
Sirba	34	Fc	13.46N	1.40 E
Şīr Banī Yās	24	Oj	24.19N	52.37 E
Sirdalen	8	Bf	58.50N	6.40 E
Sirdalsvatn	8	Bf	58.35N	6.40 E
Sire [Eth.]	35	Fd	8.58N	37.00 E
Sire [Eth.]	35	Fd	8.16N	39.30 E
Sir Edward Pellew Group	59	Hc	15.40S	136.50 E
Siret	5	If	45.24N	28.01 E
Siret	15	Jb	47.57N	26.04 E
Sirevåg	7	Ag	58.30N	5.47 E
Sīrīk	23	Id	26.29N	57.09 E
Sirik, Tanjong-	26	Ff	2.46N	111.19 E
Sirina	15	Jm	36.21N	26.41 E
Sirino	14	Jj	40.07N	15.50 E
Sirius Seamount (EN)	40	Gf	52.00N	160.50W
Širjajevo	16	Gf	47.24N	30.13 E
Sir James Mac Brian, Mount-	42	Ed	62.08N	127.40W
Sirjān, Kavīr-e-	24	Ph	29.30N	55.30 E
Sirmione	14	Ee	45.29N	10.36 E
Şırnak	24	Jd	37.32N	42.28 E
Širokaja Pad	20	Jf	50.15N	142.11 E
Široki	20	Jd	63.04N	148.01 E
Širokoje	16	Hf	47.38N	33.14 E
Sironcha	25	Fe	18.50N	79.58 E
Síros	15	Hl	37.26N	24.55 E
Sirpsindiği	15	Jh	41.50N	26.29 E
Sirr, Nafūd as-	24	Kj	25.15N	44.45 E
Sirrayn	33	Hf	19.38N	40.36 E
Sirretta Peak	46	Fi	35.59N	118.20W
Sīrrī, Jazīreh-ye-	24	Pj	25.55N	54.32 E
Sirsa	25	Fc	29.32N	75.01 E
Sir Sandford, Mount-	46	Ga	51.40N	117.52W
Sirte Desert (EN)=As Sidrah	30	Ie	30.30N	17.30 E
Sir Thomas, Mount-	59	Fe	27.11S	129.46 E
Širvintos	7	Fi	55.03N	25.01 E
Sir Wilfrid Laurier, Mount -	42	Ff	52.48N	119.45W
Sisak	14	Ke	45.29N	16.22 E
Si Sa Ket	25	Ke	15.07N	104.19 E
Sīsakht	24	Ng	30.47N	51.33 E
Sisal	48	Ng	21.10N	90.02W
Sisante	13	Je	39.25N	2.13W
Sisargas, Islas-	13	Da	43.22N	8.50W
Šišchid-Gol	27	Ga	51.30N	97.10 E
Sishen	37	Ce	27.55S	22.59 E
Sishui	28	Dg	35.40N	117.17 E
Sisian	16	Oj	39.31N	46.03 E
Sisili	34	Ec	10.16N	1.15W
Sisimiut/Holsteinsborg	67	Nc	67.05N	53.45W
Siskiyou Mountains	46	Df	41.55N	123.15W
Sisŏphŏn	25	Kf	13.35N	102.59 E
Sissano	60	Ch	3.00S	142.03 E
Sisseton	45	Hd	45.40N	97.03W
Sissonne	12	Fe	49.34N	3.54 E
Sīstān=Seistan (EN)	21	If	30.30N	62.00 E
Sistema Central	5	Fg	40.30N	5.00W
Sistema Ibérico=Iberian Mountains (EN)	5	Fg	41.30N	2.30W
Sistemas Béticos	5	Fh	37.35N	3.30W
Sisteron	11	Lj	44.12N	5.56 E
Sisters	46	Ed	44.17N	121.33W
Sistranda	7	Be	63.43N	8.50 E
Sitāpur	25	Gc	27.34N	80.41 E
Sitasjaure	7	Dc	68.00N	17.25 E
Siteki	37	Ee	26.27S	31.57 E
Sitges	13	Nc	41.14N	1.49 E
Sithonia	15	Gi	40.05N	23.55 E
Sitía	15	Jn	35.12N	26.07 E
Sitio d'Abadia	55	Ib	14.48S	46.16W
Sitio Nuevo	49	Jh	10.46N	74.43W
Sitka	39	Fd	57.03N	135.14W
Sitkalidak	40	Ie	57.10N	153.14W
Sitna	15	Kb	47.30N	27.10 E
Sitnica	15	Dg	42.53N	20.52 E
Sitona	35	Fc	14.23N	37.22 E
Sitrah [Bhr.]	24	Ni	26.10N	50.40 E
Sitrah [Eg.]	24	Bh	28.42N	26.54 E
Sittard	11	Ld	51.00N	5.53 E
Sittee Point	49	Ce	16.48N	88.15W
Sitten/Sion	14	Bd	46.15N	7.20 E
Sittingbourne	12	Cc	51.20N	0.45 E
Sittoung	25	Je	17.10N	96.58 E
Sittwe (Akyab)	22	Lg	20.09N	92.54 E
Siuna	49	Eg	13.44N	84.46W
Siuslaw River	46	Cd	44.01N	124.08W
Siva	7	Mh	56.49N	53.55 E
Sivac	15	Cd	45.42N	19.23 E
Sivaki	20	Hf	52.38N	126.45 E
Sivas	22	Ff	39.50N	37.03 E
Sivaš, Ozero-	16	Ig	45.50N	34.40 E
Sivasli	15	Mk	38.30N	29.42 E
Šiveluč, Vulkan-	20	Le	56.33N	161.25 E
Sivera, Ozero-/Sivera Ezers	8	Li	55.58N	27.25 E
Sivera Ezers/Sivera, Ozero-	8	Li	55.58N	27.25 E
Siverek	23	Eb	37.45N	39.19 E
Siverski	7	Hg	59.22N	30.02 E
Sivomaskinski	17	Kc	66.40N	62.31 E
Sivrice	24	Hc	38.27N	39.19 E
Sivrihisar	24	Dc	39.27N	31.34 E
Sivry-Rance	12	Gd	50.10N	4.16 E
Sivry Rance-Rance	12	Gd	50.09N	4.16 E
Sivry-sur-Meuse	12	He	49.19N	5.16 E
Sīwah	31	Jf	29.12N	25.31 E
Sīwah, Wāḩāt-=Siwa Oasis (EN)	30	Jf	29.10N	25.40 E
Siwalik Range	21	Jg	29.00N	80.00 E
Siwān	25	Gc	26.13N	84.22 E
Siwa Oasis (EN)=Sīwah, Wāḩāt-	30	Jf	29.10N	25.40 E
Sixaola, Río-	49	Fi	9.35N	82.34W
Six Cross Road	51q	Bb	13.07N	59.28W
Six-Fours-la-Plage	11	Lk	43.06N	5.51 E
Sixian	28	Dh	33.29N	117.53 E
Six Men's Bay	51q	Ab	13.16N	59.38W
Sixth Cataract (EN)=Sablūkah, Ash Shallāl as-	30	Kg	16.20N	32.42 E
Siyah-Chaman	24	Ld	37.35N	47.10 E
Siyang (Zhongxing)	28	Eh	33.43N	118.40 E
Siziwang Qi (Ulan Hua)	28	Ad	41.31N	111.41 E
Sjaelland=Zealand (EN)	5	Hd	55.30N	11.45 E
Sjamozero, Ozero-	7	Hf	61.55N	33.15 E
Sjare/Sääre	8	Ig	57.57N	21.53 E
Sjas	7	Hf	60.10N	32.31 E
Sjasstroj	7	Hf	60.09N	32.36 E
Šjašupe	7	Fi	55.00N	22.10 E
Šjauljaj/Šiauliai	6	Id	55.53N	23.19 E
Sjenica	15	Cf	43.16N	20.00 E
Sjnjaja	20	Hd	61.00N	126.57 E
Sjoa	8	Cc	61.41N	9.33 E
Sjöbo	8	Ei	55.38N	13.42 E
Sjøholt	7	Be	62.29N	6.50 E
Sjujutlijka	15	Ig	42.17N	25.55 E
Sjun	17	Gi	55.43N	54.17 E
Sjuøyane	41	Ob	80.43N	20.45 E
Skadarsko Jezero=Scutari, Lake- (EN)	5	Hg	42.10N	19.20 E
Skadovsk	19	Df	46.07N	32.56 E
Skælskør	8	Di	55.15N	11.19 E
Skærbæk	8	Ci	55.09N	8.46 E
Skagatá	7a	Ba	66.07N	20.06W
Skagen	7	Ch	57.44N	10.36 E
Skagern	8	Ff	59.00N	14.15 E
Skagerrak	5	Gd	57.45N	9.00 E
Skaget	8	Cc	61.17N	9.12 E
Skagit River	46	Db	48.20N	122.25W
Skagway	39	Fd	59.28N	135.19W
Skaidi	7	Fa	70.26N	24.30 E
Skaland	7	Db	69.27N	17.18 E
Skälderviken	8	Eh	56.20N	12.40 E
Skålevik	8	Bf	58.04N	8.00 E
Skalisty Golec, Gora- [R.S.F.S.R.]	20	Ge	56.20N	119.10 E
Skalisty Golec, Gora- [R.S.F.S.R.]	20	Ie	55.55N	130.35 E
Skanderborg	7	Bh	56.02N	9.56 E
Skåne	5	Hd	56.00N	13.30 E
Skånevik	8	Ae	59.44N	5.59 E
Skänninge	8	Ff	58.24N	15.05 E
Skanör	8	Ei	55.25N	12.52 E
Skántzoura	15	Hj	39.05N	24.07 E
Skara	7	Cg	58.22N	13.25 E
Skaraborg [2]	7	Cg	58.20N	13.30 E
Skärblacka	8	Ff	58.34N	15.54 E
Skārdu	25	Fa	35.18N	75.37 E
Skärhamn	8	Dg	57.59N	11.33 E
Skarnes	8	Dd	60.15N	11.41 E
Skarsstind	8	Cb	62.03N	8.35 E
Skarsvåg	7	Fa	71.06N	25.56 E
Skarszewy	10	Ob	54.05N	18.27 E
Skarvdalsegga	8	Cb	62.09N	8.03 E
Skaryszew	10	Re	51.19N	21.15 E
Skarżysko-Kamienna	10	Qe	51.08N	20.53 E
Skasøy	8	Ca	63.20N	8.35 E
Şkăt	15	Gf	43.44N	23.51 E
Skattkärr	8	Ee	59.25N	13.41 E
Skattungbyn	8	Fc	61.12N	14.52 E
Skaudvile/Skaudvilė	7	Fi	55.27N	22.33 E
Skaudvilė/Skaudvile	7	Fi	55.27N	22.33 E
Skaulen	8	Be	59.38N	6.35 E
Skawa	10	Pf	50.02N	19.26 E
Skawina	10	Pg	49.59N	19.49 E
Skee	8	Df	58.56N	11.19 E
Skeena	38	Fd	54.09N	130.02W
Skeena Mountains	42	Ee	56.45N	128.40W
Skegness	9	Nh	53.10N	0.21 E
Skeidararsandur	7a	Cc	63.54N	17.14W
Skeldon	54	Gb	5.53N	57.08W
Skeleton Coast	37	Ac	17.50S	12.45 E
Skellefteå	6	Ic	64.46N	20.57 E
Skellefteälven	5	Ic	64.42N	21.06 E
Skelleftehamn	7	Ed	64.41N	21.14 E
Skëndërbeut, Mali i-	15	Ch	41.35N	19.50 E
Skene	8	Eg	57.29N	12.38 E
Skerki Bank (EN)	32	Jb	37.45N	10.50 E
Skerries/Na Sceirí	9	Gh	53.35N	6.07W
Skerryvore	9	Fe	56.20N	7.05W
Skhíza	15	Em	36.44N	21.46 E
Skhoinoúsa	15	Im	36.50N	25.30 E
Ski	7	Cg	59.43N	10.50 E
Skiathos	15	Gj	39.10N	23.28 E
Skíathos	15	Gj	39.10N	23.29 E
Skibbereen/An Sciobairín	9	Dj	51.33N	9.15W
Skibotn	7	Eb	69.24N	20.16 E
Skidel	16	Dc	53.38N	24.17 E
Skien	6	Gd	59.12N	9.36 E
Skierniewice	10	Qe	51.58N	20.08 E
Skierniewice [2]	10	Qe	52.00N	20.10 E
Skiftet/Kihti	8	Id	60.15N	21.05 E
Skikda	31	He	36.52N	6.54 E
Skikda [3]	32	Ib	36.45N	6.50 E
Skillet Fork	45	Lg	38.08N	88.07W
Skillingaryd	8	Fg	57.26N	14.05 E
Skinári, Ákra-	15	Dl	37.56N	20.42 E
Skinnskatteberg	8	Fe	59.50N	15.41 E
Skipton	9	Kh	53.58N	2.01W
Skiptvet	8	De	59.28N	11.11 E
Skiropoúla	15	Hk	38.50N	24.21 E
Skíros	15	Hk	38.54N	24.34 E
Skiros	15	Hk	38.53N	24.32 E
Skive	7	Bh	56.34N	9.02 E
Skive Å	8	Ch	56.34N	9.04 E
Skjærhalden	8	De	59.02N	11.02 E
Skjåk	8	Cc	61.52N	8.22 E
Skjálfandafljót	7a	Cb	65.59N	17.38W
Skjeberg	8	De	59.14N	11.12 E
Skjern	7	Bi	55.57N	8.30 E
Skjern Å	7	Bi	55.55N	8.24 E
Skjervøy	7	Ea	70.02N	20.59 E
Skjoldungen	41	Hf	63.20N	41.20W
Sklad	20	Hb	71.52N	123.35 E
Šklov	16	Gb	54.14N	30.18 E
Skobeleva, Pik-	18	Ie	39.51N	72.47 E
Skœrfjorden	41	Kc	77.30N	19.10W
Škofja Loka	14	Id	46.10N	14.18 E
Skog	8	Gc	61.10N	16.55 E
Skógafoss	7a	Bc	63.32N	19.31W
Skoghall	8	Ee	59.19N	13.26 E
Skogshorn	8	Cd	60.53N	8.42 E
Skokie	45	Me	42.02N	87.46W
Skole	10	Th	48.58N	23.32 E
Skópelos	15	Gj	39.07N	23.44 E
Skópelos	15	Gj	39.10N	23.40 E
Skopí	15	Jn	35.11N	26.02 E
Skopin	7	Jj	53.52N	39.37 E
Skopje	6	Ig	42.00N	21.29 E
Skórcz	10	Oc	53.48N	18.32 E
Skorovatn	7	Cd	64.39N	13.07 E
Skorpa	8	Ac	61.35N	4.50 E
Skørping	8	Ch	56.50N	9.53 E
Skorpiós	15	Dk	38.42N	20.45 E
Škotovo	28	Lc	43.20N	132.21 E
Skotselv	8	Ce	59.51N	9.53 E
Skoura	32	Fc	31.04N	6.43W
Skövde	7	Cg	58.24N	13.50 E
Skovorodino	22	Od	53.59N	123.55 E
Skowhegan	44	Mc	44.46N	69.43W
Skradin	14	Jg	43.49N	15.56 E
Skreia	8	Dd	60.34N	11.04 E
Skreia	8	Dd	60.39N	10.56 E
Skrekken	8	Bd	60.13N	7.49 E
Skridulaupen	8	Bc	61.55N	7.35 E
Skrimkolla	8	Cb	62.23N	9.04 E
Skrīveri/Skriveri	8	Kh	56.37N	25.10 E
Skriveri/Skrīveri	8	Kh	56.37N	25.10 E
Skrunda	7	Eh	56.41N	22.00 E
Skrwa	10	Pd	52.33N	19.32 E
Skudenesfjorden	8	Ae	59.05N	5.20 E
Skudeneshavn	7	Ag	59.09N	5.17 E
Skuodas	7	Eh	56.17N	21.31 E
Skurup	8	Ei	55.28N	13.30 E
Skutskär	8	Gd	60.38N	17.25 E
Skvira	16	Fe	49.44N	29.42 E
Skwierzyna	10	Ld	52.35N	15.30 E
Skye, Island of-	5	Fd	57.15N	6.10W
Slagelse	7	Ci	55.24N	11.22 E
Slagnäs	7	Ed	65.36N	18.10 E
Slamet, Gunung-	21	Mj	7.14S	109.12 E
Slaná	10	Ri	47.56N	21.08 E
Slancy	19	Cd	59.08N	28.02 E
Slaney/An tSláine	9	Gi	52.21N	6.30W
Slănic	15	Id	45.15N	25.56 E
Slănic Moldova	15	Jc	46.12N	26.26 E
Slannik	15	Jf	43.06N	26.13 E
Slano	14	Lh	42.47N	17.54 E
Slaný	10	Kf	50.14N	14.06 E
Śląsk=Silesia (EN)	10	Me	51.00N	16.45 E
Śląsk=Silesia (EN)	5	He	51.00N	16.45 E
Śląska, Wyżyna-	10	Of	50.28N	18.40 E
Slate Islands	45	Mb	48.34N	86.45W
Slatina	15	He	44.26N	24.22 E
Slatina	10	Ph	48.32N	19.10 E
Slaton	45	Fj	33.26N	101.39W
Slave Coast	30	Hh	6.00N	3.30 E
Slave Lake	42	Ge	55.17N	114.46W
Slave River	38	Hc	61.18N	113.39W
Slavgorod [Bye.-U.S.S.R.]	16	Gc	53.27N	31.01 E
Slavgorod [R.S.F.S.R.]	20	Cf	53.03N	78.48 E
Slavičin	10	Ng	49.06N	17.53 E
Slavjanka	20	Ih	42.55N	131.20 E
Slavjanka	15	Gh	41.23N	23.36 E
Slavjansk	6	Jf	48.52N	37.37 E
Slavjansk-na-Kubani	19	Df	45.15N	38.08 E
Slavkoje	10	Th	48.45N	23.31 E
Slavkoviči	8	Mg	57.37N	29.10 E
Slavonia (EN) = Slavonija	5	Hf	45.00N	18.00 E
Slavonia (EN)=Slavonija	14	Le	45.00N	18.00 E
Slavonija=Slavonia (EN)	14	Le	45.00N	18.00 E
Slavonija = Slavonia (EN)	5	Hf	45.00N	18.00 E
Slavonska Požega	14	Le	45.20N	17.41 E
Slavonski Brod	14	Me	45.09N	18.02 E
Slavsk	8	Ii	55.01N	21.37 E
Slavuta	19	Ce	50.18N	26.52 E
Sława	10	Me	51.53N	16.04 E
Sławatycze	10	Te	51.43N	23.30 E
Sławno	10	Mb	54.22N	16.40 E
Slayton	45	Id	44.01N	95.45W
Sleaford	9	Mh	53.00N	0.24W
Slea Head/Ceann Sléibhe	9	Ci	52.06N	10.27W
Sleat, Sound of-	9	Hd	57.10N	5.50W
Sleen	12	Ib	52.47N	6.49 E
Sleeper Islands	42	Je	57.25N	79.50W
Sléibhte Chill Mhantáin/Wicklow Mountains	9	Gh	53.02N	6.24W
Sleidinge, Evergem-	12	Fc	51.08N	3.41 E
Slesin	10	Od	52.23N	18.19 E
Slessor Glacier	66	Af	79.50S	28.30W
Slessor Peak	66	Qe	66.31S	64.58W
Slettefjell	8	Cc	61.13N	8.44 E
Sletterhage	8	Dh	56.06N	10.31 E
Ślęża	10	Me	51.10N	16.58 E
Ślęża	10	Mf	50.52N	16.45 E
Sliabh Bearnach/Slieve Bernagh	9	Ei	52.50N	8.35W
Sliabh Bladhma/Slieve Bloom	9	Fh	53.10N	7.35W
Sliabh Eachtaí/Slieve Aughty	9	Eh	53.10N	8.30W
Sliabh Gamh/Ox or Slieve Gamph Mountains	9	Eg	54.10N	8.50W
Sliabh Mis/Slieve Mish	9	Di	52.10N	9.50W
Sliabh Speirín/Sperrin Mountains	9	Fg	54.50N	7.05W
Slidell	45	Lk	30.17N	89.47W
Slide Mountain	44	Jd	42.00N	74.23W
Slidre	8	Cc	61.10N	9.00 E
Sliedrecht	12	Gc	51.50N	4.46 E
Slieve Aughty/Sliabh Eachtaí	9	Eh	53.10N	8.30W
Slieve Bernagh/Sliabh Bearnach	9	Ei	52.50N	8.35W
Slieve Bloom/Sliabh Bladhma	9	Fh	53.10N	7.35W
Slievefelim Mountains	9	Ei	52.45N	8.15W
Slieve Mish/Sliabh Mis	9	Di	52.10N	9.50W
Sligeach/Sligo [2]	9	Eg	54.10N	8.40W
Sligeach/Sligo	6	Fe	54.17N	8.28W
Sligo/Sligeach [2]	9	Eg	54.10N	8.40W
Sligo/Sligeach	6	Fe	54.17N	8.28W
Sligo Bay/Cuan Shligigh	9	Eg	54.20N	8.40W
Slinge	12	Ib	52.08N	6.31 E
Slingebeek	12	Ic	51.59N	6.18 E
Slite	8	Hg	57.43N	18.48 E
Sliven	15	Jg	42.40N	26.19 E
Sliven [2]	15	Jg	42.40N	26.19 E
Slivnica	15	Gg	42.51N	23.02 E
Sljudjanka	20	Ff	51.38N	103.40 E
Slobodka	15	Mb	47.54N	29.12 E
Slobodskoj	19	Fd	58.47N	50.12 E
Slobodzeja	16	Ff	46.43N	29.43 E
Slobozia [Rom.]	15	Ke	44.34N	27.22 E
Slobozia [Rom.]	15	Ie	44.30N	25.11 E
Slochteren	12	Ia	53.12N	6.50 E
Slocum Mountain	46	Gi	35.18N	117.13W
Slonim	19	Ce	53.05N	25.18 E
Sloten	12	Hb	52.54N	5.40 E
Slotermeer	12	Hb	52.55N	5.40 E
Slough	9	Mj	51.31N	0.36W
Slovakia (EN)=Slovensko	10	Ph	48.45N	19.30 E
Slovakia (EN)=Slovensko	5	Hf	48.45N	19.30 E
Slovečna	16	Fd	51.41N	29.42 E
Slovenia (EN) = Slovenija	5	Hf	46.00N	15.00 E
Slovenia (EN) = Slovenija	14	Id	46.00N	15.00 E
Slovenia (EN) = Slovenija [2]	14	Id	46.00N	15.00 E
Slovenija=Slovenia (EN) [2]	14	Id	46.00N	15.00 E
Slovenija = Slovenia (EN)	14	Id	46.00N	15.00 E
Slovenija = Slovenia (EN)	5	Hf	46.00N	15.00 E
Slovenska Bistrica	14	Jd	46.24N	15.34 E
Slovenske Gorice	14	Jd	46.35N	15.55 E
Slovenské rudohorie	10	Ph	48.45N	20.00 E
Slovensko [2]	10	Ph	48.45N	19.30 E
Slovensko=Slovakia (EN)	5	Hf	48.45N	19.30 E
Slovensko=Slovakia (EN)	10	Ph	48.45N	19.30 E
Slovenský kras	10	Qh	48.35N	20.40 E
Słubice	10	Kd	52.20N	14.35 E
Sluč [Bye.-U.S.S.R.]	16	Ec	52.08N	27.32 E
Sluč [Ukr.-U.S.S.R.]	16	Ed	51.37N	26.38 E
Sluck	19	Ce	53.02N	27.31 E
Slunj	14	Je	45.07N	15.35 E
Słupca	10	Nd	52.19N	17.52 E
Słupia	10	Mb	54.35N	16.50 E
Słupsk	10	Nb	54.28N	17.01 E
Słupsk [2]	10	Mb	54.30N	17.00 E
Slyne Head/Ceann Gólaim	9	Ch	53.24N	10.13W
Småland	7	Dh	57.20N	15.05 E
Smålandsfarvandet	8	Di	55.06N	11.20 E
Smålandsstenar	8	Eg	57.10N	13.24 E
Smalininkai/Smalininkaj	8	Ji	55.01N	22.32 E
Smalininkaj/Smalininkai	8	Ji	55.01N	22.32 E
Smallingerland-Drachten	11	Ma	53.06N	6.05 E
Smallwood Reservoir	38	Md	54.00N	64.30W
Smederevo	15	De	44.39N	20.56 E
Smederevska Palanka	15	De	44.22N	20.58 E
Smedjebacken	7	Df	60.08N	15.25 E
Smela	19	Df	49.13N	31.53 E
Smidovič	20	Ig	48.36N	133.50 E
Šmidta, Mys-	20	Nc	68.45N	178.40W
Šmidta, Ostrov-	21	La	81.08N	90.48 E
Šmidta, Poluostrov-	20	Jf	54.15N	142.40 E
Śmigiel	10	Md	52.01N	16.32 E
Smilde	12	Ib	52.56N	6.28 E
Smiltene	7	Fh	57.28N	25.56 E
Smirnovo	17	Ni	54.31N	69.28 E
Smirnyh	20	Jg	49.45N	142.53 E
Smith	55	Bl	35.30S	61.36W
Smith Arm	42	Fc	66.15N	124.00W
Smith Bay [Ak.-U.S.]	40	Ib	70.51N	154.25W
Smith Bay [Can.]	42	Ja	77.15N	79.00W
Smith Center	45	Gg	39.47N	98.47W
Smithers	42	Ef	54.47N	127.10W
Smithfield [S.Afr.]	37	Df	30.09S	26.30 E
Smithfield [Ut.-U.S.]	46	Jf	41.50N	111.50W
Smith Knoll	9	Pi	52.50N	2.10 E
Smith Mountain Lake	44	Hg	37.10N	79.40W
Smith Peak	46	Gb	48.50N	116.39W
Smith River	46	Jc	47.25N	111.29W
Smiths Falls	42	Jh	44.54N	76.01W
Smith Sound	46	Ba	51.18N	127.48W
Smithton	58	Fi	40.51S	145.07 E
Smjadovo	15	Kf	43.04N	27.01 E
Smjörfjoll	7a	Cb	65.35N	14.46W
Smögen	8	Df	58.21N	11.13 E
Smoke Creek Desert	46	Ff	40.30N	119.40W
Smokey Dome	46	He	43.29N	114.56W
Smoky Bay	59	Gf	32.20S	133.45 E
Smoky Cape	59	Kf	30.56S	153.05 E
Smoky Falls	42	Jf	50.03N	82.10W
Smoky Hill	38	Jf	39.03N	96.48W
Smoky Hills	45	Gg	39.15N	99.00W
Smoky River	42	Fe	56.11N	117.19W
Smøla	7	Be	63.25N	8.00 E
Smolensk	6	Je	54.47N	32.03 E
Smolenskaja Oblast [3]	19	De	55.00N	33.00 E
Smolenskaja Vozvyšennost =Smolensk Upland (EN)	5	Je	54.40N	33.00 E
Smolensk Upland (EN)= Smolenskaja Vozvyšennost	5	Je	54.40N	33.00 E
Smoleviči	16	Fb	54.03N	28.02 E
Smolianica	10	Ud	52.40N	24.40 E
Smólikas Óros	5	Ig	40.06N	20.55 E
Smoljan	15	Hh	41.35N	24.41 E
Smoljan [2]	15	Hh	41.40N	24.40 E
Smooth Rock Falls	44	Ga	49.20N	81.39W
Smorgon	19	Ce	54.31N	26.23 E
Smørstabbren	8	Cc	61.32N	8.06 E
Smrdeš	15	Fh	41.34N	22.28 E
Smygehamn	8	Ei	55.21N	13.22 E
Smygehuk	8	Ei	55.21N	13.23 E
Smyley, Cape-	66	Qf	72.00S	78.50W
Smyrna	44	Ei	33.53N	84.31W
Smyrna (EN)=İzmir	22	Ef	38.25N	27.09 E
Smyšljajevka	7	Mj	53.17N	50.24 E
Smythe, Mount-	38	Gd	57.50N	124.59W
Snacke Point	51b	Bb	18.17N	62.58W
Snæfell	7a	Cb	64.48N	15.34W
Snaefell	9	Ig	54.16N	4.27W
Snæfellsjökull	7a	Ab	64.49N	23.46W
Snag	42	Dd	62.23N	140.22W
Snake Bay Settlement	59	Gb	11.25S	130.40 E
Snake Range	46	Hg	39.00N	114.15W
Snake River [Can.]	42	Ec	65.57N	134.13W
Snake River [U.S.]	38	He	46.12N	119.02W
Snake River Plain	43	Ec	42.45N	114.30W
Snare	42	Fd	63.15N	116.08W
Snares Islands	61	Ci	48.00S	166.35 E
Snarumselva	8	Cc	59.57N	9.58 E
Snåsa	7	Cd	64.15N	12.22 E
Sneek	11	La	53.02N	5.40 E
Snekermeer	11	La	52.59N	5.40 E
Snežnaja, Gora-	20	Lc	65.18N	165.30 E
Snežnik	14	Ie	45.26N	14.36 E
Snežnogorsk	20	Dc	68.15N	87.35 E
Šnežnoje	16	Kf	47.59N	38.50 E
Śniardwy, Jezioro-	10	Rc	53.46N	21.44 E
Śnieżka	5	He	50.45N	15.43 E
Śnieżnik	10	Mf	50.12N	16.50 E
Snigirevka	16	Hf	47.04N	32.45 E
Snillfjord	8	Ca	63.24N	9.30 E
Snina	10	Sh	48.59N	22.08 E
Snizort, Loch-	9	Gd	57.30N	6.25W
Snjatyn	16	De	48.29N	25.34 E
Snøhetta	5	Gc	62.20N	9.17 E
Snohomish	46	Dc	47.55N	122.06W
Snønuten	8	Be	59.31N	6.54 E
Snøonipa	8	Bc	61.42N	6.41 E
Snota	8	Cb	62.51N	9.06 E
Snov	16	Gd	51.32N	31.33 E
Snowbird Lake	42	Hd	60.40N	102.50W
Snowdon	5	Fe	53.04N	4.05W
Snowdonia	9	Jh	53.05N	3.55W
Snowdrift	42	Gd	62.23N	110.47W
Snowflake	46	Ji	34.30N	110.05W
Snow Hill	44	Jf	38.11N	75.24W
Snow Lake	42	Hf	54.53N	100.02W
Snow Mountain	43	Cd	39.23N	122.46W
Snowshoe Peak	46	Hb	48.13N	115.41W
Snowville	46	If	41.58N	112.43W
Snowy Mountain [B.C.-Can.]	46	Fb	49.02N	119.57W
Snowy Mountain [N.Y.-U.S.]	44	Jd	43.42N	74.23W
Snowy Mountains	59	Jg	36.30S	148.20 E
Snowy River	59	Jg	37.48S	148.32 E
Snudy, Ozero-	8	Li	55.40N	27.15 E
Snug Corner	49	Kb	22.32N	73.53W
Snuŏl	25	Lf	12.04N	106.26 E
Snyder	43	Ge	32.44N	100.55W
Soalala	37	Hc	16.07S	45.21 E
Soalara	37	Gd	23.35S	43.44 E
Soanierana-Ivongo	37	Hc	16.54S	49.34 E
Soar	12	Ab	52.52N	1.17W
Şoarş	15	Hd	45.56N	24.55 E
Soavinandriana	37	Hc	19.10S	46.43 E
Sob [R.S.F.S.R.]	17	Mc	66.20N	66.02 E

Index Symbols

[1] Independent Nation
[2] State, Region
[3] District, County
[4] Municipality
[5] Colony, Dependency
Continent
Physical Region
Historical or Cultural Region
Mount, Mountain
Volcano
Hill
Mountains, Mountain Range
Hills, Escarpment
Plateau, Upland
Pass, Gap
Plain, Lowland
Delta
Salt Flat
Valley, Canyon
Crater, Cave
Karst Features
Depression
Polder
Desert, Dunes
Forest, Woods
Heath, Steppe
Oasis
Cape, Point
Coast, Beach
Cliff
Peninsula
Isthmus
Sandbank
Island
Atoll
Rock, Reef
Islands, Archipelago
Rocks, Reefs
Coral Reef
Well, Spring
Geyser
River, Stream
Waterfall Rapids
River Mouth, Estuary
Lake
Salt Lake
Intermittent Lake
Reservoir
Swamp, Pond
Canal
Glacier
Ice Shelf, Pack Ice
Ocean
Sea
Gulf, Bay
Strait, Fjord
Lagoon
Bank
Seamount
Tablemount
Ridge
Shelf
Basin
Escarpment, Sea Scarp
Fracture
Trench, Abyss
National Park, Reserve
Point of Interest
Recreation Site
Cave, Cavern
Historic Site
Ruins
Wall, Walls
Church, Abbey
Temple
Scientific Station
Airport
Port
Lighthouse
Mine
Tunnel
Dam, Bridge

Index Symbols

Symbol group	Symbol group	Symbol group	Symbol group
[1] Independent Nation	Depression	Rock, Reef	Lagoon
[2] State, Province	Polder	Islands, Archipelago	Glacier
[3] District, County	Desert, Dunes	Rocks, Reefs	Ice Shelf, Pack Ice
[4] Municipality	Forest, Woods	Coral Reef	Tablemount
[5] Colony, Dependency	Heath, Steppe	Well, Spring	Gulf, Bay
Continent	Oasis	Geyser	
Physical Region	Cape, Point	River, Stream	

Historical or Cultural Region	Pass, Gap	Coast, Beach	Waterfall Rapids	Canal	Escarpment, Sea Scarp	Historic Site	Port
Mount, Mountain	Plain, Lowland	Cliff	River Mouth, Estuary	Bank	Fracture	Ruins	Lighthouse
Volcano	Delta	Peninsula	Lake	Seamount	Trench, Abyss	Wall, Walls	Mine
Hill	Salt Flat	Isthmus	Salt Lake	Ocean	National Park, Reserve	Church, Abbey	Tunnel
Mountains, Mountain Range	Valley, Canyon	Sandbank	Intermittent Lake	Sea	Point of Interest	Temple	Dam, Bridge
Hills, Escarpment	Crater, Cave	Island	Reservoir	Shelf	Recreation Site	Scientific Station	
Plateau, Upland	Karst Features	Atoll	Swamp, Pond	Strait, Fjord	Cave, Cavern	Airport	
				Basin			

Index Symbols

[1] Independent Nation	Pass, Gap
[2] State, Region	Plain, Lowland
[3] District, County	Delta
[4] Municipality	Salt Flat
[5] Colony, Dependency	Valley, Canyon
Continent	Crater, Cave
Physical Region	Karst Features
Historical or Cultural Region	Depression
Mount, Mountain	Polder
Volcano	Desert, Dunes
Hill	Forest, Woods
Mountains, Mountain Range	Heath, Steppe
Hills, Escarpment	Oasis
Plateau, Upland	Cape, Point

Coast, Beach	Waterfall Rapids	Canal	Escarpment, Sea Scarp	Historic Site	Port
Cliff	River Mouth, Estuary	Glacier	Fracture	Ruins	Lighthouse
Peninsula	Lake	Ice Shelf, Pack Ice	Trench, Abyss	Wall, Walls	Mine
Isthmus	Salt Lake	Ocean	National Park, Reserve	Church, Abbey	Tunnel
Sandbank	Intermittent Lake	Sea	Point of Interest	Temple	Dam, Bridge
Island	Reservoir	Gulf, Bay	Recreation Site	Scientific Station	
Atoll	Swamp, Pond	Strait, Fjord	Cave, Cavern	Airport	

Rock, Reef
Islands, Archipelago
Rocks, Reefs
Coral Reef
Well, Spring
Geyser
River, Stream

Lagoon
Bank
Seamount
Tablemount
Ridge
Shelf
Basin

Index Symbols

- [1] Independent Nation
- [2] State, Region
- [3] District, County
- [4] Municipality
- [5] Colony, Dependency
- Continent
- Physical Region
- Historical or Cultural Region
- Mount, Mountain
- Volcano
- Hill
- Mountains, Mountain Range
- Hills, Escarpment
- Plateau, Upland
- Pass, Gap
- Plain, Lowland
- Delta
- Salt Flat
- Valley, Canyon
- Crater, Cave
- Karst Features
- Depression
- Polder
- Desert, Dunes
- Forest, Woods
- Heath, Steppe
- Oasis
- Cape, Point
- Coast, Beach
- Cliff
- Peninsula
- Isthmus
- Sandbank
- Island
- Atoll
- Rock, Reef
- Islands, Archipelago
- Rocks, Reefs
- Coral Reef
- Well, Spring
- Geyser
- River, Stream
- Waterfall Rapids
- River Mouth, Estuary
- Lake
- Salt Lake
- Intermittent Lake
- Reservoir
- Swamp, Pond
- Canal
- Glacier
- Ice Shelf, Pack Ice
- Ocean
- Sea
- Gulf, Bay
- Strait, Fjord
- Lagoon
- Bank
- Seamount
- Tableland
- Ridge
- Shelf
- Basin
- Escarpment, Sea Scarp
- Fracture
- Trench, Abyss
- National Park, Reserve
- Point of Interest
- Recreation Site
- Cave, Cavern
- Historic Site
- Ruins
- Wall, Walls
- Church, Abbey
- Temple
- Scientific Station
- Airport
- Port
- Lighthouse
- Mine
- Tunnel
- Dam, Bridge

Surahammar	8	Ge	59.43N	16.13 E
Sūrak	23	Id	25.43N	58.48 E
Surakarta	22	Nj	7.35 S	110.50 E
Şūrān	24	Ge	35.17N	36.45 E
Šurany	10	Oh	48.06N	18.11 E
Surar	35	Gd	7.29N	40.54 E
Surat	22	Jg	21.10N	72.50 E
Surat Thani	22	Li	9.06N	99.20 E
Suraž [Bye.-U.S.S.R.]	7	Hi	55.26N	30.43 E
Suraž [R.S.F.S.R.]	19	De	53.02N	32.29 E
Surčin	15	De	44.47N	20.17 E
Sur del Cabo San Antonio, Punta-	56	Ie	36.52 S	56.40W
Surduc	15	Gb	47.15N	23.21 E
Sûre	10	Cg	49.44N	6.31 E
Surendranagar	25	Ed	22.42N	71.41 E
Surgères	11	Fh	46.06N	0.45W
Surgut	22	Jc	61.14N	73.20 E
Surgutiha	20	Dd	63.47N	87.20 E
Surhandarinskaja Oblast [3]	19	Gh	38.00N	67.30 E
Surhandarja	18	Ff	37.14N	67.20 E
Surhob	19	Hh	38.54N	70.04 E
Surigao	26	Ie	9.45N	125.30 E
Surin	25	Kf	14.53N	103.30 E
Suriname [1]	53	Ke	4.00N	56.00W
Suripá, Río-	49	Mj	7.47N	69.53W
Sūrīyah = Syria (EN) [1]	22	Ff	35.00N	38.00 E
Sūrmaq	24	Og	31.03N	52.48 E
Surmelin	12	Fe	49.04N	3.31 E
Sürmene	24	Ib	40.55N	40.07 E
Surna	8	Cb	62.59N	8.40 E
Surnadalsøra	8	Cb	62.59N	8.39 E
Surovikino	19	Ef	48.36N	42.54 E
Surovo	20	Fe	55.39N	105.36 E
Sur-Pakri/Suur-Pakri	8	Je	59.50N	23.45 E
Surprise, Ile-	63b	Ad	18.32 S	163.02 E
Surprise, Lac-	44	Ja	49.20N	74.57W
Surrey [3]	9	Mj	51.25N	0.30W
Surrey	9	Mj	51.20N	0.05W
Sursee	14	Cc	47.10N	8.07 E
Sursk	16	Nc	53.04N	45.42 E
Surskoje	7	Li	54.31N	46.44 E
Surt	31	Ie	31.13N	16.35 E
Surt, Khalīj- = Sidra, Gulf of-(EN)	30	Ie	31.30N	18.00 E
Surte	8	Eg	57.49N	12.01 E
Surtsey	7a	Bc	63.20N	20.38W
Sürüç	24	Hd	36.58N	38.24 E
Surud Ad	30	Lg	10.42N	47.09 E
Suruga-Wan	28	Og	34.55N	138.35 E
Surulangun	26	Dg	2.37 S	102.45 E
Survey Pass	40	Ic	67.52N	154.10W
Sur-Vjajn/Suur Väin	8	Jf	58.30N	23.20 E
Surwold	12	Jb	52.57N	7.31 E
Suså	8	Di	55.11N	11.46 E
Šuša	16	Oj	39.43N	46.44 E
Susa [It.]	14	Be	45.08N	7.03 E
Susa [Jap.]	29	Bd	34.37N	131.36 E
Susa, Val di-	14	Be	45.10N	7.10 E
Sušac	14	Kh	42.46N	16.30 E
Sūsah [Lib.]	33	Dc	32.54N	21.58 E
Sūsah [Tun.] = Sousse (EN)	31	Ie	35.49N	10.38 E
Sūsah = Sousse (EN) [3]	32	Jb	35.45N	10.30 E
Susak	14	If	44.31N	14.18 E
Susaki	27	Ne	33.22N	133.17 E
Susami	29	De	33.33N	135.29 E
Susamyr	18	Ic	42.09N	73.59 E
Susanville	43	Cc	40.25N	120.39W
Suşehri	24	Hb	40.11N	38.06 E
Suseja	8	Kh	56.23N	25.00 E
Šušenskoje	20	Ef	53.19N	92.01 E
Sušice	10	Jg	49.14N	13.30 E
Susitna	40	Id	61.16N	150.30W
Suslonger	7	Lh	56.18N	48.12 E
Susoh	26	Cf	3.43N	96.50 E
Susong	28	Di	30.10N	116.06 E
Suspiro	55	Ej	30.38 S	54.22W
Suspiro del Moro, Puerto del-	13	Ig	37.08N	3.40W
Susquehanna River	43	Ld	39.33N	76.05W
Susques	56	Gb	23.25 S	66.29W
Sussex	9	Mk	50.55N	0.30W
Sussex	44	Oc	45.43N	65.31W
Sussex, Vale of-	9	Mk	51.00N	0.15W
Susubona	63a	Dc	8.19 S	159.27 E
Susuman	22	Qc	62.47N	148.10 E
Susurluk	24	Cc	39.54N	28.10 E
Susuzmüsellim	15	Kh	41.06N	27.03 E
Šušvė	8	Ji	55.08N	23.53 E
Susz	10	Pc	53.44N	19.20 E
Suţeşti	15	Kd	45.13N	27.26 E
Sutherland	37	Cf	32.24 S	20.40 E
Sutherland Falls	62	Bf	44.48 S	167.44 E
Sutherlin	46	De	43.25N	123.19W
Sutla	14	Je	45.51N	15.41 E
Sutlej	21	Jg	29.23N	71.02 E
Sutton	44	Gf	38.41N	80.43W
Sutton, London-	12	Bc	51.21N	0.12W
Sutton Bridge	12	Cb	52.46N	0.11 E
Sutton in Ashfield	12	Aa	53.07N	1.16W
Sutton Scotney	12	Ac	51.09N	1.20W
Suttor River	59	Jd	21.25 S	147.45 E
Suttsu	28	Pc	42.48N	140.14 E
Sütüler	24	Dd	37.30N	30.59 E
Sutwik	40	He	56.34N	157.05W
Su'uholo	63a	Ec	9.46 S	161.58 E
Suunduk	16	Ud	51.46N	58.46 E
Suure-Jaani	7	Fg	58.31N	25.29 E
Suur-Pakri/Sur-Pakri	8	Je	59.50N	23.45 E
Suur Väin/Sur-Vjajn	8	Jf	58.30N	23.20 E
Suva	58	If	18.08 S	178.25 E
Suvadiva Atoll	21	Ji	0.30N	73.13 E
Suva Gora	15	Eh	41.51N	21.03 E
Suva Planina	15	Ff	43.08N	22.13 E
Suvasvesi	7	Ge	62.40N	28.10 E
Suvorov	16	Jb	54.08N	36.32 E
Suvorovo [Mold.-U.S.S.R.]	15	Mc	46.33N	29.35 E
Suvorovo [Ukr.-U.S.S.R.]	15	Ld	45.35N	29.00 E
Suvorovskaja	16	Mg	44.10N	42.38 E
Suwa	28	Of	36.02N	138.08 E
Suwa-Ko	29	Fc	36.03N	138.05 E
Suwałki	10	Sb	54.07N	22.56 E
Suwałki [2]	10	Sb	54.05N	22.55 E
Suwalskie, Pojezierze-	10	Sb	54.15N	23.00 E
Suwannee River	44	Fk	29.18N	83.09W
Suwanose-Jima	27	Mf	29.40N	129.45 E
Suwarrow Atoll	57	Kf	13.15 S	163.05W
Suwayqīyah, Hawr as-	24	Lf	32.40N	46.03 E
Suways, Khalīj as- = Suez, Gulf of-(EN)	30	Kf	28.10N	33.27 E
Suways, Qanāt as- = Suez Canal (EN)	30	Ke	29.55N	32.33 E
Suwŏn	27	Md	37.16N	127.01 E
Suxian	27	Ke	33.36N	116.58 E
Suzaka	29	Fc	36.39N	138.18 E
Suzdal	7	Jh	56.28N	40.27 E
Suzhou	22	Of	31.16N	120.37 E
Suzhou/Jiuquan	22	Lf	39.46N	98.34 E
Suzi He	28	Hd	41.56N	124.20 E
Suzu	27	Od	37.25N	137.17 E
Suzuka	29	Ed	34.51N	136.35 E
Suzuka-Sanmyaku	29	Ed	35.10N	136.20 E
Suzu-Misaki	28	Nf	37.28N	137.20 E
Suzun	20	Df	53.47N	82.19 E
Suzzara	14	Ef	45.00N	10.45 E
Sværholthalvøya	7	Ga	70.30N	26.05 E
Svågan	8	Gc	61.54N	16.33 E
Svalbard [5]	67	Kd	78.00N	20.00 E
Svaljava	16	Ce	48.32N	22.59 E
Svalöv	8	Ei	55.55N	13.06 E
Svaneholm	8	Ee	59.11N	12.33 E
Svaneke	7	Di	55.08N	15.09 E
Svängsta	8	Fh	56.16N	14.46 E
Svanøy	8	Ac	61.30N	5.05 E
Svapa	16	Id	51.44N	34.59 E
Svappavaara	7	Ec	67.39N	21.04 E
Svärdsjö	8	Fd	60.45N	15.55 E
Svartå	8	Fe	59.08N	14.31 E
Svartälven	8	Fe	59.20N	14.35 E
Svartån [Swe.]	8	Fe	59.17N	15.15 E
Svartån [Swe.]	8	Ff	58.28N	15.33 E
Svartån [Swe.]	8	Ge	59.37N	16.33 E
Svartenhuk Halvø = Svartenhuk Peninsula (EN)	41	Gd	71.30N	55.20W
Svartenhuk Peninsula (EN) = Svartenhuk, Halvø	41	Gd	71.30N	55.20W
Svartisen	7	Cc	66.38N	13.58 E
Svatoj Nos, Mys-	20	Jb	72.45N	140.45 E
Svatovo	19	Df	49.24N	38.13 E
Svay Riĕng	25	Lf	11.05N	105.48 E
Sveabreen	66	Cf	72.08 S	1.53 E
Sveagruva	41	Nc	78.39N	16.25 E
Svealand	7	Dd	60.30N	15.30 E
Svealand	5	Hc	60.30N	15.30 E
Svedala	8	Ei	55.30N	13.14 E
Sveg	7	De	62.02N	14.21 E
Švėkšna	8	Ii	55.32N	21.30 E
Svelgen	7	Af	61.45N	5.18 E
Svelvik	8	De	59.37N	10.24 E
Švenčėneljaj/Švenčioneliai	7	Gi	55.09N	26.02 E
Švenčėnis/Švenčionys	7	Gi	55.07N	26.12 E
Švenčioneliai/Švenčėneljaj	7	Gi	55.09N	26.02 E
Švenčionys/Švenčėnis	7	Gi	55.07N	26.12 E
Svendborg	7	Ci	55.03N	10.37 E
Svendsen Peninsula	42	Ja	77.50N	84.00W
Svenljunga	7	Ch	57.30N	13.07 E
Svenska högarna	8	He	59.35N	19.35 E
Svenskøya	41	Oc	78.43N	26.30 E
Svenstavik	7	De	62.46N	14.27 E
Šventoj/Šventoji	8	Ih	56.04N	20.59 E
Šventoji	7	Fi	55.05N	24.24 E
Šventoji/Šventoj	8	Ih	56.04N	20.59 E
Sverdlovsk	22	Id	56.51N	60.36 E
Sverdlovskaja Oblast [3]	19	Gd	59.00N	62.00 E
Sverdrup, Ostrov-	20	Cb	74.30N	79.35 E
Sverdrup Channel	42	Ha	80.00N	96.30W
Sverdrup Islands	38	Jb	79.00N	98.00W
Sverige = Sweden (EN) [1]	6	Hc	62.00N	15.00 E
Svetac	14	Jg	43.02N	15.45 E
Svēte/Svete	8	Jh	56.40N	23.38 E
Svete/Svēte	8	Jh	56.40N	23.38 E
Sveti Naum	15	Di	40.55N	20.45 E
Sveti Nikola, Prohod-	15	Ff	43.27N	22.36 E
Sveti Nikole	15	Eh	41.52N	21.57 E
Sveti Stefan	15	Bg	42.16N	18.54 E
Svetlaja	20	Ig	46.31N	138.18 E
Svetli	20	Ge	58.34N	116.00 E
Svetlogorsk [Bye.-U.S.S.R.]	19	Ce	52.38N	29.42 E
Svetlogorsk [R.S.F.S.R.]	8	Ij	54.55N	20.08 E
Svetlograd	19	Ef	45.19N	42.40 E
Svetlovodsk	16	He	49.02N	33.15 E
Svetly [R.S.F.S.R.]	19	Ge	50.51N	60.53 E
Svetly [R.S.F.S.R.]	7	Ei	54.41N	20.08 E
Svetly Jar	16	Ne	48.29N	44.46 E
Svetogorsk	7	Gf	61.07N	28.58 E
Svetozarevo	15	Ef	43.59N	21.15 E
Sviča	10	Ug	49.04N	24.06 E
Svid	7	Jf	61.13N	38.45 E
Svidník	10	Rg	49.18N	21.35 E
Svidník	10	Kg	49.23N	14.58 E
Svijaga	19	Ed	55.39N	48.28 E
Svilaja	14	Kg	43.50N	16.26 E
Svilengrad	15	Jh	41.46N	26.12 E
Svincovy Rudnik	18	Ff	37.52N	66.28 E
Svinecea Mare, Vîrful-	15	Fe	44.48N	22.09 E
Svir	5	Jc	60.30N	32.48 E
Svir	8	Lj	54.50N	26.34 E
Svirica	7	Hf	60.30N	32.54 E
Svirsk	20	Ff	53.04N	103.18 E
Svisloč	16	Fc	53.27N	28.59 E
Svisloč	16	Dc	53.03N	24.07 E
Svištov	15	If	43.37N	25.20 E
Svit	10	Qg	49.03N	20.12 E
Svitava	10	Mg	49.11N	16.38 E
Svitavy	10	Mg	49.46N	16.27 E
Svizra / Svizzera / Schweiz / Suisse = Switzerland (EN) [1]	6	Gf	46.00N	8.30 E
Svizzera / Schweiz / Suisse / Svizra = Switzerland (EN) [1]	6	Gf	46.00N	8.30 E
Svjatoj Nos, Mys-	5	Jb	68.10N	39.43 E
Svobodny	22	Od	51.24N	128.07 E
Svoge	15	Gg	42.58N	23.21 E
Svolvær	7	Db	68.14N	14.34 E
Svratka	10	Mh	48.52N	16.38 E
Svrljig	15	Ff	43.25N	22.08 E
Svulrya	8	Ed	60.25N	12.24 E
Svytaya Anna Trough (EN)	67	He	80.00N	70.00 E
Swabia (EN) = Schwaben	10	Gh	48.20N	10.30 E
Swabian-Bavarian Plateau (EN) = Schwäbisch-Bayerisches Alpenvorland	5	Hf	48.15N	10.30 E
Swabian Jura (EN) = Schwäbische Alb	5	Gf	48.25N	9.30 E
Swaffham	12	Cb	52.39N	0.41 E
Swain Reefs	57	Gg	21.40 S	152.15 E
Swains Atoll	57	Jf	11.03 S	171.05W
Swainsboro	44	Fi	32.36N	82.20W
Swakop	37	Ad	22.41 S	14.31 E
Swakopmund [3]	37	Ad	22.30 S	15.00 E
Swakopmund	31	Ik	22.41 S	14.34 E
Swale	9	Lg	54.06N	1.20W
Swalmen	12	Ic	51.14N	6.02 E
Swanage	9	Lk	50.37N	1.58W
Swan Hill	59	Ig	35.21 S	143.34 E
Swan Range	46	Ic	47.50N	113.40W
Swan River	42	Hf	52.06N	101.16W
Swansboro	44	Ih	34.36N	77.07W
Swansea [Austl.]	59	Jh	42.08 S	148.04 E
Swansea [Wales-U.K.]	6	Fe	51.38N	3.57W
Swansea Bay	9	Jj	51.35N	3.52W
Swans Island	44	Mc	44.10N	68.25W
Swanson Lake	45	Ff	40.09N	101.06W
Swan Valley	46	Je	43.28N	111.20W
Swartberge	30	Jl	33.23 S	21.48 E
Swarzędz	10	Nd	52.26N	17.05 E
Swastika	44	Ga	48.07N	80.12W
Swaziland [1]	31	Kk	26.30 S	31.10 E
Sweden (EN) = Sverige [1]	6	Hc	62.00N	15.00 E
Swedru	34	Ed	5.32N	0.42W
Sweet Grass Hills	46	Jb	48.55N	111.30W
Sweet Home	46	Dd	44.24N	122.44W
Sweetwater	43	Ge	32.28N	100.25W
Sweetwater River	43	Fc	42.31N	107.02W
Swellendam	37	Cf	34.02 S	20.26 E
Świder	10	Rd	52.08N	21.12 E
Świdnica	10	Mf	50.51N	16.29 E
Świdnik	10	Se	51.14N	22.41 E
Świdwin	10	Lc	53.47N	15.47 E
Świebodzin	10	Ld	52.15N	15.32 E
Świecie	10	Oc	53.25N	18.28 E
Świętej Anny, Góra-	10	Of	50.28N	18.13 E
Świętokrzyskie, Góry-	10	Qf	50.55N	21.00 E
Swift Current	42	Gf	50.17N	107.50W
Swift Current Creek	46	La	50.40N	107.44W
Swift River	42	Ed	60.05N	131.11W
Swilly, Lough-/Loch Suili	9	Ff	55.10N	7.38W
Swinburne, Cape -	42	Hb	71.14N	98.33W
Swindon	9	Lj	51.34N	1.47W
Swinford/Béal Átha na Muice	9	Eh	53.57N	8.57W
Świnoujście	10	Kc	53.53N	14.14 E
Swischenahner Meer	12	Ka	53.12N	8.01 E
Swisttal	12	Id	50.44N	6.54 E
Switzerland (EN) = Schweiz / Suisse / Svizra / Svizzera [1]	6	Gf	46.00N	8.30 E
Switzerland (EN) = Suisse / Svizra / Svizzera / Schweiz [1]	6	Gf	46.00N	8.30 E
Switzerland (EN) = Svizra / Svizzera / Schweiz / Suisse [1]	6	Gf	46.00N	8.30 E
Switzerland (EN) = Svizzera / Schweiz / Suisse / Svizra [1]	6	Gf	46.00N	8.30 E
Syčevka	16	Ib	55.51N	34.15 E
Syców	10	Ne	51.19N	17.43 E
Sydfalster-Gedser	7	Ci	54.35N	11.57 E
Sydkap Ice Cap	42	Ja	76.30N	85.00W
Sydney [Austl.]	58	Gh	33.52 S	151.13 E
Sydney [N.S.-Can.]	39	Me	46.09N	60.11W
Sydney → Manra Atoll	57	Je	4.27 S	171.15W
Sydney-Campbelltown	59	Kf	34.04 S	150.49 E
Sydney Lake	45	Ia	50.40N	94.24W
Sydney Mines	42	Lg	46.14N	60.12W
Sydney-Penrith	59	Kf	33.45 S	150.42 E
Syktyvkar	6	Lc	61.40N	50.46 E
Sylacauga	44	Di	33.10N	86.15W
Sylane	7	Ce	63.02N	12.13 E
Sylarna	7	Ce	63.02N	12.13 E
Sylhet	25	Id	24.54N	91.52 E
Sylling	8	De	59.54N	10.17 E
Sylt	10	Eb	54.55N	8.20 E
Sylva	17	Hh	57.40N	56.57 E
Sylvania	44	Gi	32.45N	81.38W
Sylvania Tablemount (EN)	60	Ge	11.58N	165.00 E
Sylvan Pass	43	Ec	44.28N	110.08W
Sylvester	44	Fj	31.32N	83.49W
Sylvester, Lake-	59	Hc	18.50 S	135.50 E
Sym	20	Ed	60.15N	90.02 E
Syndassko	20	Fb	73.14N	108.05 E
Synja	17	Ld	65.12N	64.45 E
Synnfjell	8	Cc	61.05N	9.45 E
Syowa	66	De	69.00 S	39.35 E
Syracuse [Ks.-U.S.]	45	Fh	37.59N	101.45W
Syracuse [N.Y.-U.S.]	39	Le	43.03N	76.09W
Syracuse (EN) = Siracusa	6	Hh	37.04N	15.18 E
Syrdarinskaja Oblast [3]	19	Gg	40.30N	68.40 E
Syrdarja	19	Gg	40.52N	68.38 E
Syrdarja = Syr Darya (EN)	21	Ie	46.03N	61.00 E
Syr Darya (EN) = Syrdarja	21	Ie	46.03N	61.00 E
Syria (EN)	21	Ff	35.00N	38.00 E
Syria (EN) = Sūrīyah [1]	22	Ff	35.00N	38.00 E
Syriam	25	Je	16.46N	96.15 E
Syrian Desert- (EN) = Shām, Bādiyat ash-	21	Ff	32.00N	40.00 E
Syrkovoje, Ozero-	17	Lf	60.40N	65.00 E
Syrski	16	Kc	52.36N	39.28 E
Sysert	17	Jh	56.31N	60.49 E
Sysmä	7	Ff	61.30N	25.41 E
Sysola	19	Fc	61.42N	50.58 E
Sysslebäck	8	Ed	60.44N	12.52 E
Sysulp, Gora-	15	Ha	48.29N	24.17 E
Syverma, Plato-	21	Lc	67.00N	99.00 E
Syzran	6	Ke	53.09N	48.27 E
Szabolcs-Szatmár [2]	10	Sh	48.00N	22.10 E
Szamocin	10	Nc	53.02N	17.08 E
Szamos	15	Fa	48.07N	22.20 E
Szamotuły	10	Md	52.37N	16.35 E
Szarvas	10	Qj	46.52N	20.33 E
Szczawnica Krościenko	10	Qg	49.26N	20.30 E
Szczebrzeszyn	10	Sf	50.42N	22.59 E
Szczecin [2]	10	Kc	52.35N	14.30 E
Szczecin = Stettin (EN)	6	He	53.24N	14.32 E
Szczecinek	10	Mc	53.43N	16.42 E
Szczeciński, Zalew-	10	Kc	53.46N	14.14 E
Szczekociny	10	Pf	50.38N	19.50 E
Szczerców	10	Pe	51.18N	19.09 E
Szczucin	10	Rf	50.18N	21.04 E
Szczuczyn	10	Sc	53.34N	22.18 E
Szczytno	10	Qc	53.34N	21.00 E
Szechwan (EN) = Sichuan Sheng (Ssu-ch'uan Sheng) [2]	27	He	30.00N	103.00 E
Szechwan (EN) = Ssu-ch'uan Sheng → Sichuan Sheng [2]	27	He	30.00N	103.00 E
Szécsény	10	Ph	48.05N	19.31 E
Szeged	6	If	46.15N	20.10 E
Szeged [2]	10	Qj	46.16N	20.08 E
Szeghalom	10	Ri	47.02N	21.10 E
Székesfehérvár	6	Hf	47.12N	18.25 E
Szekszárd	10	Oj	46.21N	18.43 E
Szendrő	10	Qh	48.24N	20.44 E
Szentendre	10	Pi	47.40N	19.05 E
Szentes	10	Qj	46.39N	20.16 E
Szentgotthárd	10	Mj	46.57N	16.17 E
Szérencs	10	Rh	48.10N	21.12 E
Szeskie Wzgórza	10	Sb	54.14N	22.22 E
Szigetvár	10	Nj	46.03N	17.48 E
Szkwa	10	Rc	53.10N	21.45 E
Szlichtyngowa	10	Me	51.43N	16.15 E
Szob	10	Oi	47.49N	18.52 E
Szolnok	10	Qi	47.11N	20.12 E
Szolnok [2]	10	Qi	47.15N	20.30 E
Szombathely	10	Mi	47.14N	16.37 E
Szprotawa	10	Le	51.34N	15.33 E
Szreniawa	10	Qf	50.10N	20.35 E
Sztum	10	Pc	53.56N	19.01 E
Szubin	10	Nc	53.00N	17.44 E
Szydłów	10	Rf	50.35N	21.01 E
Szydłowiec	10	Qe	51.14N	20.51 E

T

Taakoka	64p	Cc	21.15 S	159.43W
Taalintendas/Dalsbruk	8	Jd	60.02N	22.31 E
Taavetti	8	Ld	60.55N	27.34 E
Tab	10	Oj	46.44N	18.02 E
Tabacal	56	Hb	23.16 S	64.15W
Ţābah	24	Ji	27.02N	42.08 E
Tabaqah	24	He	35.52N	38.34 E
Tabar Islands	57	Ge	2.50 S	152.00 E
Ţabarqah	32	Ib	36.57N	8.45 E
Ţabas	24	Qf	33.36N	56.54 E
Tabasará, Serranía de-	49	Gi	8.33N	81.40W
Tabasco [2]	47	Fe	18.00N	92.40W
Tabasco y Campeche, Llanos de-	47	Fe	18.15N	91.00W
Tabašino	7	Lh	56.59N	47.43 E
Tābask, Kūh-e-	24	Nh	29.52N	51.49 E
Tabay	55	Ci	28.18 S	58.17W
Tabelbala	32	Gd	29.24N	3.15W
Taber	42	Gg	49.47N	112.08W
Taberg	8	Fg	57.41N	14.05 E
Taberg	8	Fg	57.41N	14.05 E
Tabernacle	51c	Ab	17.23N	62.46W
Tabernas	13	Jg	37.03N	2.23W
Tabernes de Valldigna	13	Le	39.04N	0.16W
Tabiteuea Atoll	57	Ie	1.20 S	174.50 E
Tabla	34	Fc	13.46N	3.01 E
Tablas	26	Hd	12.24N	122.02 E
Tablas Strait	26	Hd	12.40N	121.48 E
Tablat	13	Ph	36.25N	3.19 E
Tablazo, Bahía del-	49	Lh	10.52N	71.35W
Table Cape	62	Gc	39.06 S	178.00 E
Table Rock Lake	45	Jh	36.35N	93.30W
Tabocas	55	Jb	14.39 S	45.28W
Taboco, Rio-	55	Ed	19.53 S	55.58W
Tabola	16	Pg	45.53N	48.20 E
Tábor	10	Kg	49.25N	14.41 E
Tabora	31	Ki	5.01 S	32.48 E
Tabora [3]	36	Fd	5.20 S	32.30 E
Tabory	17	Lg	58.31N	64.33 E
Tabou	31	Gh	4.25N	7.21W
Tabrīz	22	Gf	38.05N	46.18 E
Tábua	13	Dd	40.21N	8.02W
Tabuaeran Atoll (Fanning)	57	Ld	3.52N	159.20W
Tabūk	22	Fg	28.23N	36.35 E
Tabuk	26	Hc	17.24N	121.25 E
Ţaburbah	14	Dn	36.50N	9.50 E
Tabursuq	14	Dn	36.28N	9.15 E
Tabursuq, Monts de-	14	Dn	36.25N	9.05 E
Tabusintac	44	Ob	47.24N	65.02W
Tabwemasana	63b	Cb	15.22 S	166.45 E
Täby	7	Eg	59.30N	18.03 E
Tacámbaro de Codallos	48	Ih	19.14N	101.28W
Tacarcuna, Cerro-	49	Ij	8.05N	77.17W
Tacarigua, Laguna de-	50	Dg	10.15N	65.50W
Tacheng/Qoqek	22	Ke	46.45N	82.57 E
Tachibana-Wan	29	Be	32.45N	130.05 E
Tachichilte, Isla de-	48	Ee	24.59N	108.04W
Tachikawa [Jap.]	29	Fd	35.42N	139.23 E
Tachikawa [Jap.]	29	Fb	38.48N	139.58 E
Táchira [2]	54	Db	7.50N	72.05W
Tachiumet	33	Bd	26.19N	10.03 E
Tachov	10	Ig	49.48N	12.40 E
Tachungnya	64b	Bb	14.58N	145.36 E
Tacinski	16	Le	48.13N	41.17 E
Tacir	15	Mi	40.32N	29.44 E
Tacloban	22	Oh	11.15N	125.00 E
Tacna	53	Ig	18.01 S	70.15W
Tacna [2]	54	Dg	17.40 S	70.20W
Tacoma	39	Ge	47.15N	122.27W
Tacotalpa, Río-	48	Mi	17.50N	92.52W
Tacuaral	55	Cd	18.59 S	58.07W
Tacuarembó [2]	55	Ek	32.10 S	55.30W
Tacuarembó, Río-	55	Ek	32.25 S	55.29W
Tacuarí, Río-	55	Fk	32.46 S	53.18W
Tacuati	55	Df	23.27 S	56.35W
Tadami	29	Fc	37.21N	139.17 E
Tadami-Gawa	29	Fc	37.38N	139.45 E
Tadarimana, Rio-	55	Ec	16.29 S	54.31W
Tademaït, Plateau du-	30	Hf	28.30N	2.15 E
Tadine	63b	Ce	21.33 S	167.53 E
Tadjeraout	32	He	21.17N	1.20 E
Tadjetaret	32	Ie	22.00N	7.30 E
Tadjourah	35	Gc	11.45N	42.54 E
Tadjourah, Golfe de-	35	Gc	11.45N	43.00 E
Tadoule Lake	42	He	58.35N	98.20W
Tadoussac	44	Ma	48.09N	69.43W
Tadžikskaja Sovetskaja Socialističeskaja Respublika [2]	19	Hh	39.00N	71.00 E
Tadžikskaja SSR/ Respublikai Soveth Socialisti Todžikiston	19	Hh	39.00N	71.00 E
Tadžikskaja SSR = Tajik SSR (EN) [2]	19	Hh	39.00N	71.00 E
T'aebaek-Sanmaek	21	Of	37.40N	128.50 E
Taechon	28	If	36.21N	126.36 E
T'aech'on	28	He	39.55N	125.30 E
Taedong-gang	28	He	38.42N	125.15 E
Taegu	22	Of	35.52N	128.36 E
Taeha-dong	28	Kf	37.31N	130.48 E
Taehan-Haehyŏp = Korea Strait (EN)	21	Of	34.40N	129.00 E
Taehan-Min' guk = South Korea (EN) [1]	22	Of	38.00N	127.30 E
Taehuksan-Do	28	Hg	34.40N	125.25 E
Taejŏn	22	Of	36.20N	127.26 E
Tafahi Island	57	Jf	15.52 S	173.55W
Tafalla	13	Kb	42.31N	1.40W
Tafassasset	30	If	21.56N	10.12 E
Tafassasset, Ténéré du-	34	Ha	21.20N	11.00 E
Taff	9	Jj	51.27N	3.09W
Tafilalt	32	Gc	31.18N	4.18W
Tafiré	34	Dd	9.04N	5.10W
Tafi Viejo	56	Gc	26.44 S	65.16W
Taflan	24	Gb	41.25N	36.09 E
Tafna	13	Ki	35.18N	1.28W
Tafraout	32	Fd	29.43N	9.00W
Tafresh	24	Ne	34.41N	50.01 E
Taft	24	Pg	31.45N	54.14 E
Taftān, Kuh-e-	21	Ig	28.36N	61.06 E
Taftanāz	24	Ge	35.59N	36.47 E
Taga	65c	Aa	13.46 S	172.28W
Taga Dzong	25	Hc	27.04N	89.53 E
Tagajō	29	Gb	38.18N	140.58 E
Tagama	30	Hg	15.50N	8.12 E
Taganrog	6	Jf	47.12N	38.56 E
Taganrogski Zaliv	16	Kf	46.50N	38.25 E
Tagant [3]	32	Ef	18.30N	10.30W
Tagant	30	Fg	17.31N	12.07W
Tagarev, Gora-	18	Ae	38.19N	57.18 E
Tagawa	29	Be	33.39N	130.48 E
Tagbilaran	26	He	9.39N	123.51 E
Tageru, Jabal-	35	Db	16.25N	27.10 E
Taggia	14	Bg	43.52N	7.51 E
Taghit	32	Gc	30.55N	2.02W
Tagil	17	Kg	58.33N	62.30 E
Tagish Lake	42	Ed	60.00N	134.00W
Tagliamento	14	He	45.38N	13.06 E
Taglio di Po	14	Ge	45.00N	12.12 E
Tagomago, Isla de-	13	Ne	39.02N	1.39 E
Tagounit	32	Fd	29.58N	5.35W
Tagpochau, Ogso-	64b	Ba	15.11N	145.45 E
Tāgrīfat	33	Cd	29.12N	17.21 E
Taguatinga	54	If	12.25 S	46.26W
Taguersimet	32	De	24.09N	15.07W
Tagula	63a	Ad	11.20 S	153.00 E
Tagula Island	57	Gf	11.30 S	153.30 E
Tagum	26	Ie	7.21N	125.50 E
Tagus (EN) = Tajo	5	Fh	38.40N	9.24W
Tagus (EN) = Tejo	5	Fh	38.40N	9.24W
Tah	32	Ed	27.37N	12.50W
Tahaa, Ile-	61	Kc	16.38 S	151.30W
Tahakopa	62	Cg	46.31 S	169.23 E
Tahan, Gunong-	21	Mi	4.39N	102.14 E
Tahanea Atoll	57	Mf	16.52 S	144.45W

Index Symbols

[1] Independent Nation
[2] State, Region
[3] District, County
[4] Municipality
[5] Colony, Dependency
Continent
Physical Region
Historical or Cultural Region
Mount, Mountain
Volcano
Hill
Mountains, Mountain Range
Hills, Escarpment
Plateau, Upland
Pass, Gap
Plain, Lowland
Delta
Salt Flat
Valley, Canyon
Crater, Cave
Karst Features
Depression
Polder
Desert, Dunes
Forest, Woods
Heath, Steppe
Oasis
Cape, Point
Coast, Beach
Cliff
Peninsula
Isthmus
Sandbank
Island
Atoll
Rock, Reef
Islands, Archipelago
Rocks, Reefs
Coral Reef
Well, Spring
Geyser
River, Stream
Waterfall Rapids
River Mouth, Estuary
Lake
Salt Lake
Intermittent Lake
Reservoir
Swamp, Pond
Canal
Glacier
Ice Shelf, Pack Ice
Ocean
Sea
Gulf, Bay
Strait, Fjord
Lagoon
Bank
Seamount
Tablemount
Ridge
Shelf
Basin
Escarpment, Sea Scarp
Fracture
Trench, Abyss
National Park, Reserve
Point of Interest
Recreation Site
Cave, Cavern
Historic Site
Ruins
Wall, Walls
Church, Abbey
Temple
Scientific Station
Airport
Port
Lighthouse
Mine
Tunnel
Dam, Bridge

Tahat 30 Hf 23.18N 5.32 E
Tahe 27 La 52.22N 124.48 E
Ţāherī 24 Oi 27.42N 52.21 E
Tahgong, Puntan- 64b Ba 15.06N 145.39 E
Tahiataš 18 Bc 42.20N 59.33 E
Tahifet 32 Ie 22.56N 5.59 E
Tahir Geçidi 24 Jc 39.52N 42.20 E
Tahiti, Île- 57 Mf 17.37S 149.27W
Tahkuna Neem/Takuna, Mys- 8 Je 59.05N 22.30 E
Tahlequah 45 Ii 35.55N 94.58W
Tahoe, Lake- 46 Fg 38.54N 120.00W
Tahoua [2] 34 Gb 16.00N 5.30 E
Tahoua 31 Hg 14.54N 5.16 E
Ţahţā 33 Fd 26.46N 31.28 E
Tahta-Bazar 18 Dg 35.55N 62.55 E
Tahtabrod 19 Ge 52.40N 67.35 E
Tahtakarača Pereval 18 Fe 39.17N 66.55 E
Tahtaköprü 15 Mj 39.57N 29.39 E
Tahtakupyr 19 Gg 43.01N 60.22 E
Tahtali Dağları 24 Gc 38.46N 36.47 E
Tahtamygda 20 Hf 54.09N 123.38 E
Tahuata, Île- 57 Ne 9.57S 139.05W
Tahulandang, Pulau- 26 If 2.20N 125.25 E
Tahuna 26 If 3.37N 125.29 E
Taï 34 Dd 5.52N 7.27W
Tai'an [China] 28 Gd 41.24N 122.27 E
Tai'an [China] 27 Kd 36.09N 117.05 E
Taiarapu, Presqu'île de- 65e Fc 17.47S 149.14W
Taibai Shan 27 Ie 33.57N 107.40 E
Taibilla, Canal del- 13 Kg 37.43N 1.22W
Taibilla, Sierra de- 13 Jf 38.10N 2.10W
Taibus Qi (Baochang) 27 Kc 41.55N 115.22 E
Taicang 28 Fi 31.26N 121.06 E
Taichung 22 Og 24.09N 120.41 E
Taieri 62 Dg 46.03S 170.12 E
Taiga 20 De 56.04N 85.37 E
Taigonos Peninsula (EN) = Tajgonos, Poluostrov- 20 Ld 61.35N 161.00 E
Taigu 28 Bf 37.26N 112.33 E
Taihang Shan 21 Nf 37.00N 114.00 E
Taihape 62 Fc 39.41S 175.48 E
Taihe [China] 28 Ch 33.11N 115.38 E
Taihe [China] 27 Jf 26.50N 114.52 E
Taiheiyō = Pacific Ocean (EN) 3 Ki 5.00N 155.00W
Tai Hu 21 Of 31.15N 120.10 E
Taihu 27 Ke 30.26N 116.10 E
Taikang 27 Je 34.00N 114.56 E
Taiki 29a Cb 42.30N 143.16 E
Tailai 27 Lb 46.24N 123.26 E
Tailles, Plateau des- 12 Hd 50.15N 5.45 E
Taim 55 Fk 32.30S 52.35W
Tain 9 Id 57.48N 4.04W
Tainan 22 Og 23.00N 120.11 E
Tainaron, Ákra- = Matapan, Cape- (EN) 5 Ih 36.23N 22.29 E
Taiof 63a Ba 5.31S 154.39 E
Taipei 22 Og 25.03N 121.30 E
Taiping 26 Df 4.51N 100.44 E
Taiping (Gantang) 28 Ei 30.18N 118.07 E
Taipingchuan 28 Gb 44.24N 123.11 E
Taiping Dao 27 Jd 10.15N 113.42 E
Taiping Ling 27 Lb 47.36N 120.12 E
Tairadate 29a Bc 41.09N 140.38 E
Tairadate-Kaikyō 29a Bc 41.10N 140.40 E
Taisei 29a Ab 42.14N 139.49 E
Taisetsu-Zan 21 Qe 43.40N 142.48 E
Taisha 29 Cd 35.24N 132.40 E
Taishaku-San 29 Fc 36.58N 139.28 E
Tai Shan 21 Nf 36.30N 117.20 E
Taishō 29 Ce 33.12N 132.57 E
Taitao Peninsula (EN) = Taitao, Peninsula de- 52 Ij 46.30S 74.25W
Taitung 27 Lg 22.45N 121.09 E
Taiwa 29 Gb 38.26N 140.52 E
Taiwan [1] 22 Og 23.30N 121.00 E
Taiwan Haixia = Taiwan Strait (EN) 21 Ng 24.00N 119.00 E
Taixian 28 Fh 32.31N 120.08 E
Taixing 28 Fh 32.10N 120.00 E
Taiyang Shan 27 Ie 33.37N 106.26 E
Taiyetos Óros- 15 Fl 37.06N 22.18 E
Taiyuan 22 Nf 37.50N 112.37 E
Taiyue Shan 28 Bf 36.48N 112.00 E
Taizhou 28 Eh 32.29N 119.55 E
Taizhou → Linhai 27 Lf 28.52N 121.08 E
Taizhou Wan 28 Fj 28.40N 121.37 E
Taizi He 28 Gd 41.00N 122.23 E
Ta'izz 22 Gh 13.38N 44.02 E
Tājābād 24 Pg 30.02N 54.24 E
Tajarḩī 33 Be 24.21N 14.28 E
Tajgonos, Mys- 20 Ld 60.35N 160.10 E
Tajgonos, Poluostrov- = Taigonos Peninsula (EN) 20 Ld 61.35N 161.00 E
Tajik SSR (EN) = Tadžikskaja SSR 19 Hh 39.00N 71.00 E
Tajima 28 Of 37.12N 139.46 E
Tajimi 29 Ed 35.19N 137.08 E
Tājirwin 14 Co 35.54N 8.33 E
Tajito 48 Cb 30.58N 112.18W
Tajmba 20 Ed 60.22N 98.50 E
Tajmyr 20 Ea 76.05N 98.55 E
Tajmyr, Ozero- 21 Mb 74.30N 102.30 E
Tajmyr, Poluostrov- = Taymyr Peninsula (EN) 21 Mb 76.00N 104.00 E
Tajmyra 21 Lb 76.00N 99.40 E
Tajmyrlur 20 Hb 72.30N 121.39 E
Tajmyrski (Dolgano-Nenecki) Nacionalny okrug [3] 20 Eb 72.00N 95.00 E
Tajo = Tagus (EN) 5 Fh 38.40N 9.24W
Tajo-Segura, Canal de Trasvase- 13 Je 39.30N 2.05W
Tajrish 23 Hb 38.48N 51.25 E
Tajšet 22 Ld 55.57N 98.00 E
Tajumulco, Volcán- 38 Jh 15.02N 91.54W
Tajuña 13 Id 40.07N 3.35W
Tak 25 Je 16.52N 99.08 E
Taka Atoll 3 Ii 4.00N 146.45 E
Takāb 24 Ld 36.24N 47.07 E
Takaba 36 Hb 3.27N 40.14 E
Takahagi 28 Pf 36.42N 140.41 E
Takahama 29 Dd 35.29N 135.33 E
Takahara-Gawa 29 Ec 36.27N 137.15 E
Takaharu 29 Bf 31.55N 130.59 E
Takahashi 28 Lg 34.47N 133.37 E
Takahashi-Gawa 29 Cd 34.32N 133.42 E
Takahata 29 Gc 38.00N 140.12 E
Takahe, Mount- 66 Of 76.17S 112.05W
Takaka 62 Ed 40.51S 172.48 E
Takakuma-Yama 29 Bf 31.28N 130.49 E
Takalar 26 Gh 5.28S 119.24 E
Takalous 32 Ie 23.25N 7.02 E
Takamatsu 27 Ne 34.21N 134.03 E
Takamori 29 Be 32.48N 131.08 E
Takanabe 29 Be 32.08N 131.31 E
Takanawa-Hantō 29 Ce 34.00N 132.55 E
Takanawa-San 29 Ce 33.57N 132.50 E
Takanosu 29 Ga 40.14N 140.22 E
Takaoka [Jap.] 28 Nf 36.45N 137.01 E
Takaoka [Jap.] 29 Bf 31.57N 131.17 E
Takapoto Atoll 61 Lb 15.00S 148.10W
Takapuna 62 Fb 36.48S 174.47 E
Takara-Jima 27 Mf 29.10N 129.05 E
Takarazuka 29 Dd 34.49N 135.21 E
Takaroa Atoll 61 Mb 14.28S 144.58W
Takasaki 28 Of 36.20N 139.01 E
Taka-Shima [Jap.] 29 Be 32.40N 131.50 E
Taka-Shima [Jap.] 29 Af 31.26N 129.45 E
Takatshwane 37 Cd 22.36S 21.55 E
Takatsu-Gawa 29 Bd 34.42N 131.49 E
Takatsuki 28 Mg 34.51N 135.37 E
Takayama 28 Nf 36.08N 137.15 E
Takebe 29 Cd 34.53N 133.54 E
Takefu 28 Ng 35.54N 136.10 E
Takehara 29 Cd 34.21N 132.54 E
Takeo 29 Ae 33.12N 130.00 E
Tåkern 8 Ff 58.20N 14.50 E
Take-Shima 28 Kf 37.22N 131.58 E
Tåkestān 23 Gb 36.05N 49.14 E
Taketa 29 Be 32.58N 131.24 E
Takêv 25 Kf 10.59N 104.47 E
Takhādīd 24 Kh 29.59N 44.30 E
Takhār [3] 23 Kb 36.30N 69.30 E
Takhmaret 13 Mi 35.06N 0.41 E
Takht-e Soleimān 24 Nd 36.20N 51.00 E
Taki [Jap.] 29 Cd 35.16N 132.38 E
Taki [Pap.N.Gui.] 63a Bb 6.29S 155.50 E
Takijuq Lake 42 Gc 66.05N 113.00W
Takikawa 28 Pc 43.33N 141.54 E
Takingeun 26 Cf 4.38N 96.50 E
Takinoue 29a Ca 44.13N 143.03 E
Takko 29 Ga 40.20N 141.09 E
Takla Lake 42 Ee 55.30N 126.00W
Takla Landing 42 Ee 55.29N 125.58W
Takla Makan (EN) = Taklimakan Shamo 21 Kf 39.00N 83.00 E
Taklimakan Shamo = Takla Makan (EN) 21 Kf 39.00N 83.00 E
Takob 18 Ge 38.51N 69.00 E
Tako-Bana 29 Cd 35.35N 133.05 E
Takolokouzet, Massif de- 34 Gb 18.40N 9.30 E
Taku 29 Be 33.19N 130.06 E
Takuan, Mount- 63a Bb 6.27S 155.36 E
Takua Pa 25 Jg 8.52N 98.21 E
Takum 34 Gd 7.16N 9.59 E
Takuma 29 Cd 34.14N 133.40 E
Takume Atoll 57 Mf 15.49S 142.12W
Takuna, Mys-/Tahkuna Neem 8 Je 59.05N 22.30 E
Takutea Island 57 Lf 19.49S 158.19W
Tala 48 Hg 20.40N 103.42W
Talāh 32 Ib 35.35N 8.40 E
Talaimmannar 25 Fg 9.05N 79.44 E
Talāīyeh 24 Kd 37.50N 45.00 E
Talaja 20 Kd 61.03N 152.30 E
Talak 30 Hg 18.20N 6.00 E
Talamanca, Cordillera de- 49 Fi 9.30N 83.40W
Talara 53 Hf 4.35S 81.25W
Talas 19 Hg 42.29N 72.14 E
Talas 18 Ic 44.05N 70.20 E
Talasea 59 Ka 5.20S 150.05 E
Talasski Alatau, Hrebet- 18 Hc 42.10N 72.00 E
Talata Mafara 34 Gc 12.34N 6.04 E
Talaud, Kepulauan- = Talaud Islands (EN) 21 Oi 4.20N 126.50 E
Talaud Islands (EN) = Talaud, Kepulauan- 21 Oi 4.20N 126.50 E
Talavera, Isla- 55 Dh 27.32S 56.26W
Talavera de la Reina 13 He 39.57N 4.50W
Talawdī 35 Ec 10.38N 30.23 E
Talbot Inlet 42 Ja 77.55N 77.35W
Talca 53 Ii 35.26S 71.40W
Talcahuano 53 Ii 36.43S 73.07W
Tälcher 25 Hd 20.57N 85.13 E
Taldom 7 Ih 56.45N 37.32 E
Taldy-Kurgan 22 Je 44.59N 78.23 E
Taldy-Kurganskaja Oblast [3] 19 Hf 44.00N 78.00 E
Taleh 35 Hd 9.09N 48.26 E
Tal-e Khosravī 24 Ng 30.47N 51.29 E
Talence 11 Fj 44.49N 0.36W
Ţalesh, Kūhhā-Ye- 24 Md 37.35N 48.38 E
Talgar 19 Hg 43.18N 77.13 E
Taliabu, Pulau- 26 Hg 1.48S 124.48 E
Talica 19 Gd 57.01N 63.43 E
Talimardžan 19 Gh 38.21N 65.31 E
Tali Post 35 Ed 5.54N 30.47 E
Talisajan 22 Ni 1.37N 118.11 E
Taliwang 26 Gh 8.44S 116.52 E
Talkeetna 40 Id 62.20N 150.07W
Talkeetna Mountains 40 Jd 62.10N 148.15W
Talkheh 24 Kd 37.40N 45.46 E
Talladega 44 Di 33.26N 86.06W
Tall 'Afar 23 Fb 36.22N 42.27 E
Tallah 24 Dh 28.05N 30.44 E
Tallahassee 39 Kf 30.25N 84.16W
Tallahatchie River 45 Kj 33.33N 90.10W
Tall al Abyaḑ 24 Hd 36.41N 38.57 E
Tallapoosa River 44 Di 32.30N 86.16W
Tallard 11 Mj 44.28N 6.03 E
Tällberg 8 Fd 60.49N 15.00 E
Tall Birāk at Taḩtānī 24 Id 36.38N 41.05 E
Tallinn 6 Id 59.25N 24.45 E
Tall Kayf 24 Jd 36.29N 43.08 E
Tall Kūshik 24 Jd 36.48N 42.04 E
Tallulah 45 Kj 32.25N 91.11W
Tălmaciu 15 Hd 45.39N 24.16 E
Talmenka 20 Df 53.51N 83.45 E
Talmest 32 Fc 31.09N 9.00W
Talnah 20 Dc 69.30N 88.15 E
Talnoje 16 Ge 48.53N 30.42 E
Talo 30 Kg 10.44N 37.55 E
Talofofo 64c Bb 13.20N 144.46 E
Talon 20 Je 59.48N 148.50 E
Tāloqān 23 Kb 36.44N 69.33 E
Talovaja 16 Ld 51.06N 40.48 E
Talpa de Allende 48 Gg 20.23N 104.51W
Talsi 7 Fh 57.17N 22.37 E
Taltal 53 Ih 25.24S 70.29W
Taltson 42 Gd 61.24N 112.45W
Taluk 26 Dg 0.32S 101.35 E
Talvik 7 Fa 70.03N 22.58 E
Talwār 24 Md 36.00N 48.00 E
Tama 35 Cc 14.45N 22.25 E
Tamaghzah 32 Ic 34.23N 7.57 E
Tamala 16 Mc 52.33N 43.18 E
Tamalameque 49 Ki 8.52N 73.38W
Tamale 31 Gh 9.24N 0.50W
Tamames 13 Fd 40.39N 6.06W
Tamana 29 Be 32.55N 130.33 E
Tamanaco, Río- 50 Dh 9.25N 65.23W
Tamana Island 57 Ie 2.29S 175.59 E
Tamano 28 Lg 34.30N 133.56 E
Tamanoura 29 Ae 32.38N 128.37 E
Tamanrasset 30 Hf 22.03N 0.10 E
Tamanrasset 31 Hf 22.47N 5.31 E
Tamanrasset [3] 32 Ie 23.00N 5.30 E
Tamar 9 Ik 50.22N 4.10W
Tamara 15 Cg 42.27N 19.33 E
Támara 54 Db 5.50N 72.10W
Tamarit de Llitera/Tamarite de Litera 13 Mc 41.52N 0.26 E
Tamarite de Litera/Tamarit de Llitera 13 Mc 41.52N 0.26 E
Tamarro 14 Ii 41.09N 14.50 E
Tamarugal, Pampa del- 56 Gb 21.00S 69.25W
Tamási 10 Oj 46.38N 18.17 E
Tamassoumit 32 Ef 18.35N 12.39W
Tamaulipas [2] 47 Ed 24.00N 98.45W
Tamaulipas, Llanos de- 47 Ed 25.00N 98.25W
Tamaulipas, Sierra de- 48 Jf 23.30N 98.20W
Tamayama 29 Gb 39.50N 141.11 E
Tamazula de Gordiano 48 Hh 19.38N 103.15W
Tamazunchale 47 Ed 21.16N 98.47W
Tambach 36 Gb 0.36N 35.31 E
Tambacounda 31 Fg 13.12N 15.48W
Tambara 37 Ec 16.44S 34.15 E
Tambelan, Kepulauan- = Tambelan Islands (EN) 26 Ef 1.00N 107.30 E
Tambelan, Pulau- 26 Ef 0.58N 107.34 E
Tambelan Islands (EN) = Tambelan, Kepulauan- 26 Ef 1.00N 107.30 E
Tambo 59 Jd 24.53S 146.15 E
Tambohorano 37 Gc 17.29S 43.58 E
Tambora, Gunung- 26 Gh 8.14S 117.55 E
Tambores 55 Dj 31.52S 56.16W
Tambov 6 Ke 52.43N 41.27 E
Tambovskaja Oblast [3] 19 Ee 52.45N 41.40 E
Tambre 13 Db 42.49N 8.53W
Tambunan 26 Ge 5.40N 116.22 E
Tambura 31 Jh 5.36N 27.28 E
Tamchaket 32 Ef 17.20N 10.40W
Tame 54 Db 6.27N 71.45W
Tâmega 13 Dc 41.05N 8.21W
Tâmega 13 Dc 41.05N 8.21W
Tamel Aike 56 Fg 48.19S 70.58W
Tamesi 47 Ed 22.13N 97.52W
Tamesnar 30 Hg 18.25N 3.33 E
Tamgak, Monts- 30 Hg 19.11N 8.42 E
Tamgue, Massif du- 30 Fg 12.00N 12.18W
Tamiahua 48 Kg 21.16N 97.27W
Tamiahua, Laguna de- 47 Ed 21.35N 97.35W
Tamianglajang 26 Gg 2.07S 115.10 E
Tamil Nādu [3] 25 Ff 11.00N 78.00 E
Tamiš 15 De 44.51N 20.39 E
Tamise/Temise 12 Gc 51.08N 4.13 E
Tamitatoala, Rio- 54 Hf 11.56S 53.36W
Ţāmiyah 24 Dh 29.29N 30.58 E
Tam Ky 25 Le 15.34N 108.29 E
Tammela 8 Jd 60.48N 23.46 E
Tammerfors/Tampere 6 Ic 61.30N 23.45 E
Tammisaari/Ekenäs 7 Fg 59.58N 23.26 E
Tämnaren 8 Gd 60.10N 17.20 E
Tamnava 15 De 44.25N 20.05 E
Tamou 34 Fc 12.45N 2.11 E
Tampa 39 Kg 27.57N 82.27W
Tampa Bay 43 Kf 27.45N 82.35W
Tampake-Misaki 29a Bb 43.43N 141.20 E
Tampere/Tammerfors 6 Ic 61.30N 23.45 E
Tampico 39 Jg 22.13N 97.51W
Tampin 26 Df 2.28N 102.14 E
Tamri 32 Fc 30.43N 9.50 E
Tamsag-Bulak 27 Kb 47.14N 117.21 E
Tamsalu 7 Gg 59.10N 26.07 E
Tamsweg 14 Hc 47.08N 13.48 E
Tamu 25 Id 24.13N 94.19 E
Tamuín 48 Jg 21.59N 98.45W
Tamuín 47 Ed 22.00N 98.44W
Tamuín, Río- 48 Jg 21.47N 98.28W
Tamworth [Austl.] 58 Gh 31.05S 150.55 E
Tamworth [Eng.-U.K.] 9 Li 52.39N 1.40W
Tamyang 28 Ig 35.19N 126.59 E
Tana [Eur.] 5 Ia 70.28N 28.18 E
Tana [Kenya] 30 Li 2.32S 40.31 E
Tana, Lake- 30 Kg 12.00N 37.20 E
Tanabe 28 Mh 33.42N 135.44 E
Tana bru 7 Ga 70.16N 28.10 E
Tanacross 40 Kd 63.23N 143.21W
Tanafjorden 7 Ga 70.54N 28.40 E
Tanaga 40a Cb 51.50N 178.00W
Tanagro 14 Jj 40.38N 15.14 E
Tanagura 29 Gc 37.02N 140.23 E
Tanahbala, Pulau- 26 Cg 0.25S 98.25 E
Tanahgrogot 26 Gg 1.55S 116.12 E
Tanahjampea, Pulau- 26 Hh 7.05S 120.42 E
Tanahmasa, Pulau- 26 Cg 0.12S 98.27 E
Tanah Merah 26 De 5.48N 102.09 E
Tanahmerah 26 Lh 6.05S 140.17 E
Tanakpur 25 Gc 29.05N 80.07 E
Tanalyk 17 Ij 51.46N 58.45 E
Tanami 59 Fc 19.59S 129.43 E
Tanami Desert 57 Eg 20.00S 132.00 E
Tan An 25 Lf 10.32N 106.25 E
Tanana 40 Ic 65.10N 152.05W
Tanana 38 Dc 65.09N 151.55W
Tanapag 64b Ba 15.14N 145.45 E
Tanapag, Puetton- 64b Ba 15.14N 145.44 E
Tanāqib, Ra's at- 24 Mi 27.50N 48.53 E
Tanaro 14 Ce 45.01N 8.47 E
Tanba-Sanchi 29 Dd 35.15N 135.35 E
Tancheng 28 Eg 34.37N 118.20 E
Tanch'ŏn 27 Mc 40.25N 128.57 E
Tancítaro, Pico de- 47 De 19.26N 102.19W
Tanda 34 Ed 7.48N 3.10W
Tanda, Lac- 34 Eb 15.45N 4.42W
Tandag 26 Ie 9.04N 126.12 E
Tandaltī 35 Ec 13.01N 31.52 E
Tăndărei 15 Ke 44.39N 27.40 E
Tandijungbalai 26 Cf 2.58N 99.48 E
Tandil 53 Ki 37.20S 59.05W
Tandil, Sierras del- 55 Cm 37.24S 59.06W
Tandjilé [3] 35 Bd 9.30N 16.30 E
Tando Ādam 25 Dc 25.46N 68.40 E
Tandsjöborg 7 Df 61.42N 14.43 E
Tanḑubāyah 35 Db 18.40N 28.37 E
Taneatua 62 Gc 38.04S 177.00 E
Tane-Ga-Shima 27 Ne 30.40N 131.00 E
Taneichi 29 Ga 40.24N 141.43 E
Tan Emellel 32 Id 27.28N 9.45 E
Tanew 10 Sf 50.27N 22.16 E
Tanezrouft 30 Gf 24.00N 0.45W
Tanezzuft 33 Bd 25.51N 10.19 E
Tanf, Jabal at- 24 Hf 33.30N 38.42 E
Tanga [3] 36 Gd 5.30S 38.00 E
Tanga 31 Ki 5.04S 39.06 E
Tangail 25 Hd 24.15N 89.55 E
Tanga Islands 57 Ge 3.30S 153.15 E
Tangalla 25 Gg 6.01N 80.48 E
Tanganyika [2] 36 Fd 6.00S 35.00 E
Tanganyika, Lac- = Tanganyika, Lake- (EN) 30 Ji 6.00S 29.30 E
Tanganyika, Lake- 30 Ji 6.00S 29.30 E
Tanganyika, Lake- (EN) = Tanganyika, Lac- 30 Ji 6.00S 29.30 E
Tangará 54 Ke 6.11S 35.49W
Tangarare 63a Dc 9.35S 159.39 E
Tangdan → Dongchuan 27 Hf 26.07N 103.05 E
Tanghegol 24 Pd 37.25N 55.50 E
Tanger = Tangier (EN) [3] 32 Fb 35.45N 5.45W
Tanger = Tangier (EN) 31 Ge 35.48N 5.48W
Tangerang 26 Eh 6.11S 106.37 E
Tangermünde 10 Hd 52.33N 11.57 E
Tanggu 27 Kd 39.00N 117.36 E
Tanggula Shan (Dangla Shan) 21 Lf 33.00N 92.00 E
Tanggula Shankou 27 Fe 32.42N 92.27 E
Tanggulashanqu/Tuotuohe 22 Lf 34.15N 92.29 E
Tang He 28 Bh 32.10N 112.20 E
Tanghe 27 Je 32.37N 112.57 E
Tangier (EN) = Tanger 31 Ge 35.48N 5.48W
Tang La 21 Kg 28.00N 89.15 E
Tango 29 Dd 35.44N 135.05 E
Tangra Yumco 21 Kf 31.00N 86.25 E
Tangshan 22 Nf 39.35N 118.09 E
Tanguiéta 34 Fc 10.37N 1.16 E
Tanguro, Rio- 55 Fa 12.36S 52.56W
Tangxian 28 Ce 38.46N 114.58 E
Tangyin 28 Cg 35.54N 114.21 E
Tangyuan 27 Mb 46.45N 129.53 E
Tanhoj 20 Ff 51.33N 105.07 E
Tanhuijo, Arrecife- 48 Kg 21.07N 97.17W
Taniantaweng Shan 27 Ge 30.00N 98.00 E
Tanimbar, Kepulauan- = Tanimbar Islands (EN) 57 Ee 7.30S 131.30 E
Tanimbar Islands (EN) = Tanimbar, Kepulauan- 57 Ee 7.30S 131.30 E
Tanintharyi 25 Jf 13.00N 99.00 E
Tanjung [Indon.] 26 Gg 2.11S 115.23 E
Tanjung [Indon.] 26 Dg 1.23S 103.58 E
Tanjungpandan 26 Eg 2.45S 107.39 E
Tanjungpinang 26 Df 0.55N 104.27 E
Tanjungredep 26 Gf 2.09N 117.29 E
Tanjungselor 26 Gf 2.51N 117.22 E
Tankenberg 12 Ib 52.21N 6.58 E
Tanna, Île- 57 Hf 19.30S 169.20 E
Tännäs 7 Ce 62.27N 12.40 E
Tanner, Mount- 46 Fb 49.40N 118.34W
Tannis Bugt 8 Dg 57.40N 10.15 E
Tannu-Ola 21 Ld 51.00N 94.00 E
Tano 34 Ed 5.07N 2.56W
Tanout 31 Hg 14.58N 8.53 E
Ţanţā 31 Ke 30.47N 31.00 E
Tan Tan 32 Ed 28.30N 11.02W
Tan-Tan [3] 32 Ed 28.30N 11.00W
Tan Tan Plage 32 Ed 28.26N 11.15W
Tantoyuca 48 Jg 21.21N 98.14W
Tanum 7 Cg 58.43N 11.20 E
Tanzania [1] 31 Ki 6.00S 35.00 E
Tao, Ko- 25 Jf 10.05N 99.52 E
Tao'an (Taonan) 27 Lb 45.20N 122.46 E
Tao'er He 21 Oe 45.42N 124.05 E
Taoghe 37 Cd 20.37S 22.35 E
Tao He 27 Hd 35.50N 103.20 E
Taojiang 28 Bj 28.33N 112.05 E
Taonan → Tao'an 27 Lb 45.20N 122.46 E
Taongi Atoll 57 Hc 14.37N 168.56 E
Taormina 14 Jm 37.51N 15.17 E
Taos 43 Fd 36.24N 105.24W
Taoudenni 31 Gf 22.42N 3.56W
Taougrite 13 Mh 36.15N 0.55 E
Taounate 32 Gc 34.33N 4.39W
Taounate [3] 32 Gc 34.04N 4.06W
Taoura 14 Cn 36.10N 8.02 E
Taourirt 32 Gc 34.25N 2.54W
Taouz 32 Gc 31.00N 4.00W
Taoyuan 27 Lg 25.00N 121.18 E
Tapa 19 Cd 59.15N 25.59 E
Tapachula 39 Jh 14.54N 92.17W
Tapaga, Cape- 65c Bb 14.01S 171.23W
Tapah 26 Df 4.11N 101.16 E
Tapajera 55 Fi 28.09S 52.01W
Tapajós, Rio- 52 Kf 2.24S 54.41W
Tapaktuan 26 Cf 3.16N 97.11 E
Tapalqué 55 Bm 36.21S 60.01W
Tapan 26 Dg 2.10S 101.04 E
Tapanahoni Rivier 54 Hc 4.22N 54.27W
Tapanlieh 27 Lg 21.58N 120.47 E
Tapanui 62 Cf 45.57S 169.16 E
Tapauá 54 Fe 5.45S 64.23W
Tapauá, Rio- 52 Jf 5.40S 64.21W
Tapenagá, Rio- 55 Ci 28.04S 59.10W
Taperas 55 Bc 17.54S 60.23W
Tapes 56 Jd 30.40S 51.23W
Tapes, Serra do- 55 Fj 30.25S 51.55W
Tapeta 34 Dd 6.29N 8.51W
Taphan Hin 25 Ke 16.12N 100.26 E
Tapili 36 Eb 3.25N 27.40 E
Tapini 60 Di 8.19S 146.59 E
Tapiola, Espoo- 8 Kd 60.11N 24.49 E
Tapirai 55 Id 19.52S 46.01W
Tapirapuã 55 Db 14.51S 57.45W
Tapolca 10 Nj 46.53N 17.26 E
Tappahannock 44 Ig 37.55N 76.54W
Tappi-Zaki 28 Pd 41.18N 140.22 E
Tappu 29a Ba 44.04N 141.52 E
Tapsuj 17 Je 62.20N 61.30 E
Tāpti 21 Jg 21.06N 72.41 E
Tapul Group 26 He 5.30N 121.00 E
Tapurucuara 54 Ed 0.24S 65.02W
Taputapu, Cape- 65c Cb 14.19S 170.50W
Tāqbostān 24 Le 34.30N 46.58 E
Ţaqţaq 24 Ke 35.53N 44.35 E
Taquara 56 Jc 29.39S 50.47W
Taquaral, Serra do- 55 Fb 15.42S 52.30W
Taquari 55 Fc 17.50S 53.17W
Taquari, Pantanal de- 54 Gg 18.10S 56.30W
Taquari, Rio- [Braz.] 55 Gi 29.56S 51.44W
Taquari, Rio- [Braz.] 55 Hf 23.16S 49.12W
Taquari, Rio- [Braz.] 52 Kg 19.15S 57.17W
Taquari, Serra do- 55 Fd 18.18S 53.49W
Taquaritinga 55 He 21.24S 48.30W
Taquarituba 55 Hf 23.31S 49.15W
Taquaruçu, Rio- 55 Fe 21.35S 52.08W
Tar 18 Id 40.38N 73.26 E
Tara 15 Cf 43.55N 19.25 E
Tara 9 Gh 53.34N 6.35W
Tara [Austl.] 59 Ke 27.17S 150.28 E
Tara [Jap.] 29 Be 33.02N 130.11 E
Tara [R.S.F.S.R.] 20 Ce 56.40N 74.50 E
Tara [R.S.F.S.R.] 19 Hd 56.54N 74.22 E
Tara [Yugo.] 15 Bf 43.21N 18.51 E
Taraba 34 Hd 8.34N 10.15 E
Tarabuco 54 Fg 19.10S 64.57W
Ţarābulus = Tripoli (EN) [3] 33 Bc 32.40N 13.15 E
Ţarābulus [Leb.] = Tripoli (EN) 23 Ec 34.26N 35.51 E
Ţarābulus [Lib.] = Tripoli (EN) 31 Ie 32.54N 13.11 E
Ţarābulus = Tripolitania (EN) 30 Ie 31.00N 14.00 E
Ţarābulus = Tripolitania (EN) 33 Bc 30.00N 15.00 E
Taradale 62 Gc 39.32S 176.51 E
Tarāghin 33 Bd 25.59N 14.26 E
Tarahumara, Sierra- 47 Cc 28.26N 106.50W
Tarakan 22 Ni 3.18N 117.38 E
Tarakan, Pulau- 26 Gf 3.21N 117.36 E
Taraklija 16 Fg 45.57N 28.41 E
Tarama Jima 27 Lg 24.40N 124.40 E
Taran, Mys- 7 Ei 54.57N 19.59 E
Taranaki [2] 62 Fc 39.10S 174.40 E
Tarancón 13 Jd 40.01N 3.00W
Taranga Island 62 Fa 36.00S 174.45 E
Taransay 9 Fd 57.55N 7.10W
Taranto 6 Hg 40.28N 17.14 E
Taranto, Golfo di- = Taranto, Gulf of- (EN) 5 Hg 40.10N 17.20 E
Taranto, Gulf of- (EN) = Taranto, Golfo di- 5 Hg 40.10N 17.20 E
Tarapacá [2] 56 Ga 20.00S 69.20W
Tarapacá 56 Ga 19.55S 69.31W
Tarapaina 63a Ec 9.23S 161.24 E
Tarapoto 54 Ce 6.30S 76.25W
Taraquá 54 Ec 0.06N 68.28W
Tarara 63a Bb 6.02S 155.24 E
Tarare 11 Kk 45.54N 4.26 E
Tararua Range 62 Fd 40.45S 175.25 E
Tarašča 16 Ge 49.34N 30.31 E
Tarascon 11 Kk 43.48N 4.40 E
Tarascon-sur-Ariège 11 Hl 42.51N 1.36 E
Tarat 32 Id 26.08N 9.21 E
Tarata 54 Dg 17.27S 70.02W

Index Symbols

[1] Independent Nation
[2] State, Region
[3] District, County
[4] Municipality
[5] Colony, Dependency
Continent
Physical Region
Historical or Cultural Region
Mount, Mountain
Volcano
Hill
Mountains, Mountain Range
Hills, Escarpment
Plateau, Upland
Pass, Gap
Plain, Lowland
Delta
Salt Flat
Valley, Canyon
Crater, Cave
Karst Features
Depression
Polder
Desert, Dunes
Forest, Woods
Heath, Steppe
Oasis
Cape, Point
Coast, Beach
Cliff
Peninsula
Isthmus
Sandbank
Island
Atoll
Rock, Reef
Islands, Archipelago
Rocks, Reefs
Coral Reef
Well, Spring
Geyser
River, Stream
Waterfall Rapids
River Mouth, Estuary
Lake
Salt Lake
Intermittent Lake
Reservoir
Swamp, Pond
Canal
Glacier
Ice Shelf, Pack Ice
Ocean
Sea
Gulf, Bay
Strait, Fjord
Lagoon
Bank
Seamount
Tablemount
Ridge
Shelf
Basin
Escarpment, Sea Scarp
Fracture
Trench, Abyss
National Park, Reserve
Point of Interest
Recreation Site
Cave, Cavern
Historic Site
Ruins
Wall, Walls
Church, Abbey
Temple
Scientific Station
Airport
Port
Lighthouse
Mine
Tunnel
Dam, Bridge

Index Symbols

[1] Independent Nation	⊟ Historical or Cultural Region	◻ Pass, Gap
[2] State, Region	▲ Mount, Mountain	◻ Plain, Lowland
[3] District, County	▲ Volcano	◻ Delta
[4] Municipality	▲ Hill	◻ Salt Flat
[5] Colony, Dependency	⌐ Mountains, Mountain Range	◻ Valley, Canyon
■ Continent	⌐ Hills, Escarpment	◻ Crater, Cave
⊠ Physical Region	⌐ Plateau, Upland	◻ Karst Features

◻ Depression	⊟ Coast, Beach	⊞ Rock, Reef
◻ Polder	◻ Cliff	⊞ Islands, Archipelago
◻ Desert, Dunes	⊢ Peninsula	⊞ Rocks, Reefs
◻ Forest, Woods	⊠ Isthmus	⊞ Coral Reef
◻ Heath, Steppe	⊟ Sandbank	◻ Well, Spring
◻ Oasis	⊞ Island	⊟ Intermittent Lake
⊢ Cape, Point	⊡ Atoll	⊟ Reservoir
		⌐ River, Stream

⌐ Waterfall Rapids	⌐ Canal	◖ Lagoon
◖ River Mouth, Estuary	⌐ Glacier	⊟ Bank
⌐ Lake	⌐ Ice Shelf, Pack Ice	⌐ Fracture
⌐ Salt Lake	⌐ Seamount	⌐ Trench, Abyss
⊟ Ocean	⌐ Tablemount	⊞ National Park, Reserve
⊟ Sea	⌐ Ridge	⊟ Point of Interest
◖ Gulf, Bay	⌐ Shelf	⊟ Recreation Site
⊟ Strait, Fjord	⌐ Basin	⌐ Cave, Cavern

⌐ Escarpment, Sea Scarp	⊞ Port
⊟ Historic Site	⊞ Lighthouse
⊟ Ruins	⊞ Mine
⊞ Wall, Walls	⊟ Tunnel
⊟ Church, Abbey	⊠ Dam, Bridge
⊟ Temple	
⊞ Scientific Station	
⊞ Airport	

Tenterfield 59 Ke 29.03S 152.01 E
Tenuku 25 Ge 81.40N 16.45 E
Tenuze/Teenuse Jõgi 7 Jf 58.44N 23.58 E
Ten-Zan 29 Be 33.20N 130.08 E
Teocaltiche 48 Hg 21.26N 102.35W
Teodelina 55 Bl 34.11S 61.32W
Teodoro Sampaio 55 Ff 22.31S 52.10W
Teófilo Otoni 53 Lg 17.51S 41.30W
Teotepec, Cerro- 38 Ih 16.50N 100.50W
Teotihuacan 47 Ee 19.44N 98.50W
Teotilán del Camino 48 Kh 18.08N 97.05W
Tepa [Indon.] 26 Ih 7.52S 129.31 E
Tepa [W.F.] 64h Bb 13.19S 176.09W
Te Pae Roa Ngake o Tuko 64n Bb 10.23S 161.00W
Tepako, Pointe- 64h Bb 13.16S 176.08W
Tepalcatepec, Río- 48 Ih 18.35N 101.59W
Tepa Point 64k Bb 19.07S 169.56W
Tepatitlán de Morelos 48 Hg 20.49N 102.44W
Tepehuanes 47 Cc 25.21N 105.44W
Tepehuanes, Río- 48 Ge 25.11N 105.26W
Tepehuanes, Sierra de- 47 Cc 25.00N 105.40W
Tepelenë 15 Di 40.18N 20.01 E
Tepi 35 Fd 7.03N 35.30 E
Tepic 39 Ig 21.30N 104.54W
Teplá 10 Ig 49.59N 12.52 E
Teplá 10 If 50.14N 12.52 E
Teplice 10 Jf 50.39N 13.50 E
Tepoca, Bahía de- 48 Cb 30.15N 112.50W
Tepopa, Cabo- 48 Cc 29.20N 112.25W
Te Puka 64n Ac 10.26S 161.02W
Te Puke 62 Gb 37.47S 176.20 E
Tequepa, Bahía de- 48 Ii 17.17N 101.05W
Tequila 48 Hg 20.54N 103.47W
Tequisquiapan 48 Jg 20.31N 99.52W
Ter 13 Pb 42.01N 3.12 E
Téra 13 Hg 14.01N 0.45 E
Tera [Port.] 13 Df 38.56N 8.03W
Tera [Sp.] 13 Gc 41.54N 5.44W
Teradomari 29 Fc 37.38N 138.45 E
Terai 21 Kg 26.30N 85.15 E
Teraina Island (Washington) 57 Kd 4.43N 160.24W
Terakeka 35 Ed 5.26N 31.45 E
Teramo 14 Hh 42.39N 13.42 E
Terampa 26 Ef 3.14N 106.14 E
Ter Apel, Vlagtwedde- 12 Jb 52.52N 7.06 E
Terborg, Wisch- 12 Ic 51.55N 6.22 E
Tercan 24 Ic 39.47N 40.24 E
Terceira 30 Ee 38.43N 27.13W
Tercero, Río- 56 Hd 32.55S 62.19W
Terebovlja 16 De 49.18N 25.42 E
Terehovka 28 Kc 43.38N 131.55 E
Terek 16 Nh 43.29N 44.08 E
Terek 5 Kg 43.44N 47.30 E
Térékolé 34 Cb 15.07N 10.53W
Terek-Saj 18 Hd 41.29N 71.13 E
Terenos 55 Ee 20.26S 54.50W
Teresa Cristina 55 Gg 24.48S 51.07W
Teresina 53 Lf 5.05S 42.49W
Teresinha 54 Hc 0.58N 52.02W
Tereška 16 Od 51.50N 46.45 E
Terespol 10 Td 52.05N 23.36 E
Teressa 25 Ig 8.15N 93.10 E
Teresva 16 Cf 47.59N 23.15 E
Terevaka, Cerro- 65d Ab 27.05S 109.23W
Tergnier 11 Je 49.39N 3.18 E
Terhazza 34 Ea 23.36N 4.56W
Teriberka 7 Ib 69.10N 35.10 E
Teriberka 7 Ib 69.09N 35.08 E
Terlingua Creek 45 El 29.10N 103.36W
Termas de Río Hondo 56 Hc 27.29S 64.52W
Terme 24 Gb 41.12N 36.59 E
Termez 22 If 37.14N 67.16 E
Termini Imerese 14 Hm 37.59N 13.42 E
Termini Imerese, Golfo di- 14 Hl 38.00N 13.45 E
Terminillo 14 Hh 42.28N 13.01 E
Términos, Laguna de- 47 Fe 18.37N 91.33W
Termit, Massif de- 34 Hb 16.15N 11.17 E
Termit-Kaoboul 34 Hb 15.43N 11.37 E
Termoli 14 Ii 42.00N 15.00 E
Termonde/Dendermonde 12 Gc 51.02N 4.07 E
Ternaard, Westdongeradeel- 12 Ha 53.23N 5.58 E
Ternate 25 If 0.48N 127.24 E
Ternej 20 Ig 45.05N 136.35 E
Terneuzen 11 Jc 51.20N 3.50 E
Terni 14 Gh 42.34N 12.37 E
Ternitz 14 Kc 47.43N 16.02 E
Ternois 12 Ed 50.25N 2.19 E
Ternopol 6 If 49.34N 25.38 E
Ternopolskaja Oblast [3] 19 Cf 49.20N 25.35 E
Terpenija, Mys- 20 Jg 48.38N 144.40 E
Terpenija, Zaliv- 21 Qe 49.00N 143.30 E
Terrace 42 Ef 54.31N 128.35W
Terrace Bay 45 Mb 48.47N 87.09W
Terracina 14 Hi 41.17N 13.15 E
Terra de Basto 13 Ec 41.25N 8.00W
Terra Firma 37 Ce 25.36S 23.24 E
Terråk 7 Cd 65.05N 12.25 E
Terralba 14 Ck 39.43N 8.39 E
Terra Rica 55 Ff 22.43S 52.38W
Terrebonne Bay 45 Kl 29.09N 90.35W
Terre-de-Bas 51e Ac 15.51N 61.39W
Terre-de-Haut 51e Ac 15.58N 61.35W
Terre Froides 11 Li 45.30N 5.30 E
Terre Haute 43 Jd 39.28N 87.24W
Terrell 45 Hj 32.44N 96.17W
Terre Plaine 11 Jg 47.25N 4.00 E
Terril 13 Gh 37.00N 5.11W
Territoire de Belfort [3] 11 Mg 47.45N 7.00 E
Terruca 13 Fc 41.45N 6.25W
Terry 46 Mc 46.47N 105.19W
Tersa 16 Nd 50.46N 44.42 E
Terschelling 12 Ha 53.21N 5.13 E
Terschelling 11 La 53.24N 5.20 E
Terschelling-West-Terschelling 12 Ha 53.21N 5.13 E
Tersef 35 Bc 12.55N 16.49 E
Terskej-Alatau, Hrebet- 19 Hg 42.10N 78.45 E
Terski Bereg 7 Jc 66.10N 39.30 E
Tersko-Kumski Kanal 16 Ng 44.47N 44.37 E
Terter 16 Oi 40.27N 47.16 E
Teruel 13 Kd 40.21N 1.06W
Teruel [3] 13 Ld 40.40N 0.40W
Tervakoski 8 Kd 60.48N 24.37 E
Tervel 15 Kf 43.45N 27.24 E
Tervo 8 Lb 62.57N 26.45 E
Tervola 7 Fc 66.05N 24.48 E
Tes 27 Fa 50.27N 93.30 E
Teša 7 Ki 55.38N 42.10 E
Tesalia 54 Cc 2.29N 75.44W
Tesaret 32 Hd 25.40N 2.43 E
Tesdrero, Cerro- 48 Hf 22.47N 103.04W
Teseney 35 Fb 15.07N 36.40 E
Teshekpuk Lake 40 Ib 70.35N 153.30W
Teshikaga 28 Rc 43.29N 144.28 E
Teshio 28 Pb 44.53N 141.44 E
Teshio-Dake 28 Qc 43.58N 142.50 E
Teshio-Gawa 28 Pb 44.53N 141.44 E
Teshio-Sanchi 29a Ba 44.20N 142.00 E
Tesijn → Tesijn Gol 21 Ld 50.28N 93.04 E
Tesijn Gol (Tesijn) 21 Ld 50.28N 93.04 E
Teslić 14 Lf 44.37N 17.52 E
Teslin 42 Ed 61.34N 134.50W
Teslin 42 Ed 60.09N 132.45W
Teslin Lake 42 Ed 60.00N 132.30W
Teslui 15 He 44.09N 24.29 E
Tesocoma 48 Ed 27.41N 109.16W
Tesouras, Rio- 55 Gb 14.36S 50.51W
Tesouro 55 Fc 16.04S 53.34W
Tessala, Monts du- 13 Li 35.15N 0.45W
Tessalit 31 Hf 20.14N 0.59 E
Tessaoua 34 Gc 13.45N 7.59 E
Tessenderlo 12 Hc 51.04N 5.05 E
Test 9 Lk 50.55N 1.29W
Test, Tizi n'- 32 Fc 30.50N 8.20W
Testa, Capo- 14 Di 41.14N 9.08 E
Têt 11 Jl 42.44N 3.02 E
Tetari, Cerro- 49 Ki 9.59N 72.55W
Tetas, Punta- 56 Fc 23.31S 70.38W
Tete 31 Kj 16.10S 33.36 E
Tete [3] 37 Ec 15.30S 33.00 E
Te Teko 62 Gc 38.02S 176.48 E
Tetepare Island 63a Cc 8.45S 157.35 E
Tetérchen 12 Ie 49.14N 6.34 E
Tetere 63a Ec 9.25S 160.15 E
Teterev 16 Gd 51.01N 30.08 E
Teterow 10 Ic 53.47N 12.34 E
Teteven 15 Hg 42.55N 24.16 E
Tetiaroa Atoll 57 Mf 17.05S 149.32W
Tetijev 16 Fe 49.23N 29.41 E
Tetjuši 7 Li 54.57N 48.49 E
Teton Peak 46 Ic 47.55N 112.48W
Teton Range 46 Je 43.50N 110.55W
Teton River 46 Jc 47.56N 110.31W
Tétouan 31 Ge 35.34N 5.22W
Tétouan [3] 32 Fb 35.35N 5.30W
Tetovo 15 Dg 42.01N 20.59 E
Tetri-Ckaro 16 Ni 41.33N 44.27 E
Teuco, Río- 55 Bg 25.38S 60.12W
Teufelskopf 12 Ie 49.36N 6.49 E
Teulada 14 Cl 38.58N 8.46 E
Teulada, Capo- 5 Gh 38.52N 8.38 E
Téul de Gonzales Ortega 48 Hg 21.28N 103.29W
Teun, Pulau- 26 Ih 6.59S 129.08 E
Teupasenti 49 Df 14.13N 86.42W
Teuquito, Río- 55 Bg 24.22S 61.09W
Teuri-Tō 29a Ba 44.25N 141.20 E
Teutoburger Wald 10 Ee 52.10N 8.15 E
Teuva/Ostermark 7 Ee 62.29N 21.44 E
Teuz 15 Ec 46.39N 21.33 E
Tevai 63c Bb 11.37S 166.55 E
Tevaïtoa 65e Db 16.46S 151.28W
Tevere = Tiber (EN) 5 Hg 41.44N 12.14 E
Teverya 24 Ff 32.47N 35.32 E
Teviot 9 Kf 55.36N 2.26W
Tevli 10 Ud 52.19N 24.23 E
Tevriz 19 Hd 57.34N 72.24 E
Tevšruleh 27 Hb 47.25N 101.55 E
Te Waewae Bay 62 Bg 46.15S 167.30 E
Tewkesbury 9 Kj 51.59N 2.09W
Têwo (Dêngkagoin) 27 He 34.03N 103.21 E
Texada Island 46 Cb 49.40N 124.24W
Texarkana [Ar.-U.S.] 43 Ie 33.26N 94.02W
Texarkana [Tx.-U.S.] 39 Jf 33.26N 94.03W
Texas 59 Ke 28.51S 151.11 E
Texas [2] 43 He 31.30N 99.00W
Texas City 43 If 29.23N 94.54W
Texcoco 48 Jh 19.31N 98.53W
Texel 12 Ga 53.03N 4.47 E
Texel 11 Ka 53.05N 4.45 E
Texel-De Koog 12 Ga 53.07N 4.46 E
Texel-Den Burg 12 Ga 53.03N 4.47 E
Texoma, Lake- 43 He 33.55N 96.37W
Teyéa = Tegea (EN) 15 Fl 37.27N 22.25 E
Teza 17 Jh 56.32N 41.57 E
Teze-Jel 19 Gh 37.55N 60.22 E
Teziutlán 47 Ee 19.49N 97.21W
Tezpur 25 Ic 26.38N 92.48 E
Tha-anne 42 Id 60.31N 94.37W
Thabana Ntlenyana 30 Jk 29.30S 29.15 E
Thabazimbi 37 Dd 24.41S 27.21 E
Thai, Ao- = Thailand, Gulf of- (EN) 21 Mh 10.00N 102.00 E
Thai Binh 25 Ld 20.27N 106.20 E
Thailand (EN) = Muang Thai [1] 22 Mh 15.00N 100.00 E
Thailand, Gulf of- (EN) = Thai, Ao- 21 Mh 10.00N 102.00 E
Thai Nguyen 25 Ld 21.36N 105.50 E
Thal 25 Eb 31.30N 71.40 E
Thālith, Ash Shallāl ath- = Third Cataract (EN) 30 Kg 19.49N 30.19 E
Thamad Bū Ḩashīshah 33 Cd 25.50N 18.05 E
Thamarīd 35 Ib 17.39N 54.02 E
Thame 12 Bc 51.45N 0.59W
Thames 61 Eg 37.08S 175.33 E
Thames 5 Ge 51.28N 0.43 E
Thames River 44 Fd 42.19N 82.28W
Thamūd 23 Gf 17.15N 49.54 E
Thāna 22 Jh 19.12N 72.58 E
Thandaung 25 Je 19.04N 96.41 E
Thanh Hoa 22 Mh 19.48N 105.46 E
Thanh Pho Ho Chi Minh (Saigon) 22 Mh 10.45N 106.40 E
Thanjāvūr 25 Ff 10.48N 79.08 E
Thanlwin = Salween (EN) 21 Lg 16.31N 97.37 E
Thann 11 Ng 47.49N 7.05 E
Thaon-les-Vosges 11 Mf 48.15N 6.25 E
Thap Sakae 25 Jf 11.14N 99.31 E
Thar/Great Indian Desert 21 Ig 27.00N 70.00 E
Thargomindah 59 Ie 28.00S 143.49 E
Tharrawaddy 25 Je 17.39N 95.48 E
Tharros 14 Ck 39.54N 8.28 E
Tharthār, Baḩr ath- 23 Fc 33.59N 43.12 E
Tharthār, Wādī ath- 23 Fc 33.59N 43.12 E
Thasi Gang Dzong 25 Ic 27.19N 91.34 E
Thásos 5 Ig 40.49N 24.42 E
Thásos 15 Hi 40.47N 24.43 E
Thásou, Dhíavlos- 15 Hi 40.49N 24.42 E
Thathlīth, Wādī- 33 He 20.25N 44.55 E
Thau, Bassin de- 11 Jk 43.23N 3.36 E
Thaxted 12 Cc 51.57N 0.22 E
Thaya 10 Mh 48.37N 16.56 E
Thayetchaung 25 Jf 13.52N 98.16 E
Thayetmyo 25 Je 19.19N 95.11 E
Thaywthadangyi Kyun 25 Jf 12.20N 98.00 E
The Alberga River 59 He 27.06S 135.33 E
The Aldermen Islands 62 Gb 37.00S 176.05 E
Thebai = Thebes (EN) 33 Fd 25.43N 32.35 E
Thebes (EN) = Thebai 33 Fd 25.43N 32.35 E
Thebes (EN) = Thivai 15 Gk 38.19N 23.19 E
The Black Sugarloaf 59 Kf 31.20S 151.33 E
The Borders 9 Kf 55.35N 2.50W
The Bottom 50 Ed 17.38N 63.15W
The Broads 9 Oi 52.40N 1.30 E
The Cheviot 9 Kf 55.28N 2.09W
The Cheviot Hills 9 Kf 55.30N 2.10W
The Crane 51q Bb 13.06N 59.26W
The Dalles 43 Cb 45.36N 121.10W
Thedford 43 Gc 41.59N 100.35W
The Entrance 59 Kf 33.21S 151.30 E
The Everglades 43 Kf 26.00N 81.00W
The Fens 9 Mi 5.24N 0.02W
The Gap 46 Jh 36.25N 111.30W
The Granites 59 Gd 20.35S 130.21 E
The Hague (EN) = Den Haag/'s-Gravenhage 6 Ge 52.06N 4.18 E
The Little Minch 9 Gd 57.35N 6.55W
Thelle 12 De 49.23N 1.51 E
Thelon 38 Jc 64.16N 96.05W
The Macumba River 57 Eg 27.45S 136.50 E
The Merse 9 Kf 55.50N 2.10W
The Naze 12 Dc 51.42N 1.47 E
The Neales River 59 He 28.08S 136.47 E
The Needles 9 Lk 50.39N 1.34W
Theniet el Had 13 Oi 35.32N 2.01 E
Theodore 59 Kd 24.57S 150.05 E
Theológos 15 Hi 40.40N 24.42 E
The Pas 39 Id 53.50N 101.15W
The Pillories 51n Bb 12.54N 61.12W
Thérain 11 Ie 49.15N 2.27 E
Thermaïkós Kólpos = Salonika, Gulf of- (EN) 5 Ig 40.20N 22.45 E
Thermopílai = Thermopylae (EN) 15 Fk 38.48N 22.32 E
Thermopolis 43 Fc 43.39N 108.13W
Thermopylae (EN) = Thermopílai 15 Fk 38.48N 22.32 E
Thérouanne 12 Ed 50.38N 2.15 E
The Round Mountain 59 Kf 30.27S 152.16 E
The Sandlings 9 Oi 52.10N 1.30 E
Thesiger Bay 42 Fb 71.30N 124.00W
The Slot → New Georgia Sound 60 Fi 8.00S 158.10 E
The Solent Spithead 9 Lk 50.46N 1.20W
Thessalia [2] 15 Fj 39.30N 22.10 E
Thessalia = Thessaly (EN) 5 Ih 39.30N 22.10 E
Thessalia = Thessaly (EN) 15 Fj 39.30N 22.10 E
Thessalon 44 Fb 46.15N 83.34W
Thessaloníki = Salonika (EN) 6 Ig 40.38N 22.56 E
Thessaly (EN) = Thessalia 15 Fj 39.30N 22.10 E
Thessaly (EN) = Thessalia 5 Ih 39.30N 22.10 E
The Stevenson River 59 He 27.06S 135.33 E
Thet 12 Cb 52.24N 0.45 E
Thetford 9 Ni 52.25N 0.45 E
Thetford Mines 44 Lb 46.05N 71.18W
The Twins 62 Ed 41.14S 172.40 E
Theux 12 Hd 50.33N 5.49 E
The Valley 47 Le 18.03N 63.04W
The Warburton River 59 He 27.55S 137.28 E
The Wash 5 Ge 52.55N 0.15 E
The Weald 9 Nj 51.05N 0.05 E
The Witties 49 Ff 14.10N 82.45W
The Wolds 9 Mh 53.20N 0.10W
Thiaucourt-Regniéville 12 Hf 48.57N 5.52 E
Thiberville 12 Ce 49.08N 0.27 E
Thibodaux 45 Kl 29.48N 90.49W
Thief River Falls 43 Hb 48.07N 96.10W
Thiel Mountains 66 Pg 85.15S 91.00W
Thiene 14 Fe 45.42N 11.29 E
Thiérache, Collines de la- 12 Je 49.48N 3.55 E
Thiers 11 Ji 45.51N 3.34 E
Thiès 31 Fg 14.48N 16.56W
Thiès [3] 34 Bc 14.45N 16.50W
Thiesi 14 Cj 40.31N 8.43 E
Thika 36 Gc 1.03S 37.05 E
Thikombia 61 Fc 15.44S 179.55W
Thimerais 11 Hf 48.40N 1.20 E
Thimphu 22 Kg 27.28N 89.39 E
Thio 61 Cd 21.37S 166.14 E
Thionville 11 Me 49.22N 6.10 E
Thiou 34 Ec 13.48N 2.40W
Thira 15 Im 36.25N 25.26 E
Thira = Thira (EN) 15 Im 36.24N 25.26 E
Thira (EN) = Thira 15 Im 36.24N 25.26 E
Thirasia 15 Im 36.25N 25.20 E
Third Cataract (EN) = Thālith, Ash Shallāl ath- 30 Kg 19.49N 30.19 E
Thirsk 9 Lg 54.14N 1.20W
Thisted 7 Bh 56.57N 8.42 E
Thíthia 63d Cb 17.45S 179.18W
Thiu Khao Phetchabun 25 Ke 16.20N 100.55 E
Thivai = Thebes (EN) 15 Gk 38.19N 23.19 E
Thiviers 11 Gi 45.25N 0.55 E
Thlewiaza 42 Id 60.28N 94.42W
Thoa 42 Gd 60.31N 109.45W
Tho Chu, Dao- 25 Kg 9.00N 103.50 E
Thoen 25 Je 17.41N 99.14 E
Tholen 12 Gc 51.32N 4.13 E
Tholen 11 Kc 51.35N 4.05 E
Tholey 12 Je 49.29N 7.04 E
Thomasset, Rocher- 57 Nf 10.21S 138.25W
Thomaston 44 Ei 32.54N 84.20W
Thomasville [Al.-U.S.] 44 Dj 32.18N 87.47W
Thomasville [Ga.-U.S.] 43 Ke 30.50N 83.59W
Thomasville [N.C.-U.S.] 44 Gh 35.53N 80.05W
Thompson 42 He 55.45N 97.45W
Thompson Falls 46 Hc 47.36N 115.21W
Thompson River 45 Jg 39.45N 93.36W
Thompson Sound 62 Bf 45.10S 167.00 E
Thomsen 42 Fb 73.40N 119.30W
Thomson 44 Fi 33.28N 82.30W
Thomson River 59 Ie 25.11S 142.53 E
Thomson's Falls 36 Gb 0.02N 36.22 E
Thon 12 Fe 49.53N 3.55 E
Thon Buri 22 Mh 13.43N 100.29 E
Thong Pha Phum 25 Jf 14.44N 98.38 E
Thongwa 25 Je 16.46N 96.32 E
Thonon-les-Bains 11 Mh 46.22N 6.29 E
Thoreau 45 Bi 35.24N 108.13W
Thornaby-on-Tees 9 Lg 54.34N 1.18W
Thornbury 61 Ci 46.17S 168.06 E
Thorney 12 Bb 52.37N 0.06W
Thornhill 9 Jf 55.18N 3.40W
Thorshavn 6 Fc 62.01N 6.46W
Thouars 11 Fh 46.58N 0.13W
Thouet 11 Fg 47.17N 0.06W
Thrace (EN) = Thráki 15 Jh 41.20N 26.45 E
Thrace (EN) = Thráki 5 Ig 41.20N 26.45 E
Thrace (EN) = Trakya 15 Jh 41.20N 26.45 E
Thrace (EN) = Trakya 5 Ig 41.20N 26.45 E
Thráki [2] 15 Ih 41.10N 25.30 E
Thráki = Thrace (EN) 5 Ig 41.20N 26.45 E
Thráki = Thrace (EN) 15 Jh 41.20N 26.45 E
Thrakikón Pélagos 15 Hi 40.30N 25.00 E
Thrapston 12 Bb 52.24N 0.32W
Three Forks 43 Eb 45.54N 111.33W
Three Kings Islands 57 Ih 34.10S 172.10 E
Three Kings Trough (EN) 3 Jm 32.00S 170.30 E
Three Points, Cape- 30 Gh 4.45N 2.06W
Three Rivers 44 Ee 41.57N 85.38W
Three Sisters Islands 63a Ed 10.10S 161.57 E
Throckmorton 45 Gj 33.11N 99.11W
Throssel, Lake- 59 Ee 27.25S 124.15 E
Thua 36 Gc 1.17S 40.00 E
Thuin 11 Kd 50.20N 4.17 E
Thule 66 Ad 59.27S 27.19W
Thule/Qânâq 67 Od 77.35N 69.40W
Thule, Mount- 42 Jb 73.00N 78.27W
Thun 14 Bd 46.45N 7.40 E
Thunder Bay 39 Ke 48.23N 89.15W
Thunder Bay [Mi.-U.S.] 44 Fc 45.04N 83.25W
Thunder Bay [Ont.-Can.] 45 Lb 48.24N 89.00W
Thunder Butte 45 Fd 45.19N 101.53W
Thuner See 14 Bd 46.40N 7.45 E
Thung Song 25 Jg 8.11N 99.41 E
Thur 14 Cc 47.36N 8.35 E
Thurgau [2] 14 Dc 47.40N 9.10 E
Thüringen 10 Gf 50.40N 11.00 E
Thüringer Wald = Thuringian Forest (EN) 5 He 50.30N 11.00 E
Thuringian Forest (EN) = Thüringer Wald 5 He 50.30N 11.00 E
Thurles/Durlas 9 Fi 52.41N 7.49W
Thurrock 9 Nj 51.28N 0.20 E
Thursday Island 59 Ib 10.35S 142.13 E
Thurso 6 Fd 58.35N 3.32W
Thurso 9 Jc 58.35N 3.30W
Thurston Island 66 Pf 72.06S 99.00W
Thury-Harcourt 12 Bf 48.59N 0.29W
Thusis/Tusaun 14 Dd 46.42N 9.26 E
Thuwayrāt, Nafūd ath- 24 Kj 26.00N 44.50 E
Thuy Phong 25 Lf 11.14N 108.43 E
Thwaites Iceberg Tongue 66 Of 74.00S 108.30W
Thy 8 Ch 57.00N 8.30 E
Thyborøn 8 Ch 56.42N 8.13 E
Tianbaoshan 28 Jc 42.57N 128.57 E
Tianchang 27 Ke 32.37N 119.00 E
Tiandong (Pingma) 27 Ig 23.40N 107.09 E
Tian'e (Liupai) 27 If 25.05N 107.12 E
Tianguá 54 Jd 3.44S 40.59W
Tianjin = Tientsin (EN) 22 Nf 39.08N 117.12 E
Tianjin Shi (T'ien-chin Shih) [4] 27 Kd 39.08N 117.12 E
Tianjun (Xinyuan) 22 Lf 37.18N 99.15 E
Tianlin (Leli) 27 Ig 24.22N 106.11 E
Tian Ling 28 Kb 44.24N 130.10 E
Tianmen 27 Je 30.40N 113.10 E
Tianmu Shan 28 Ei 30.31N 119.36 E
Tianmu Xi 28 Ej 29.59N 119.24 E
Tianqiaoling 27 Mc 43.35N 129.35 E
Tian Shan 21 Ke 42.00N 80.01 E
Tianshan → Ar Horqin Qi 27 Lc 43.55N 120.05 E
Tianshifu 27 Lc 41.15N 124.20 E
Tianshui 22 Mf 34.35N 105.43 E
Tiantai 28 Fj 29.08N 121.00 E
Tianwangsi 28 Ei 31.45N 119.12 E
Tianyi → Ningcheng 27 Kc 41.34N 119.25 E
Tianzhen 28 Cd 40.24N 114.05 E
Tianzhen → Gaoqing 28 Df 37.10N 117.50 E
Tianzhuangtai 28 Gd 40.49N 122.06 E
Tiaraju 55 Ej 30.15S 54.23W
Tiarei 65e Fc 17.32S 149.20W
Tiaret [3] 32 Hc 34.50N 1.30 E
Tiaret 31 He 35.20N 1.14 E
Tiaret, Monts de- 13 Ni 35.26N 1.15 E
Tiassalé 34 Ed 5.54N 4.50W
Tiavea 65c Ba 13.57S 171.24W
Ṭīb, Ra's At- = Bon, Cape- (EN) 30 Ie 37.05N 11.03 E
Tibaji 55 Gg 24.30S 50.24W
Tibaji, Rio- 55 Gf 22.47S 51.01W
Tibasti, Sarīr- 30 If 24.00N 17.00 E
Tibati 31 Ih 6.28N 12.38 E
Tiber (EN) = Tevere 5 Hg 41.44N 12.14 E
Tiberina, Val- 14 Gg 43.30N 12.10 E
Tibesti 30 If 21.30N 17.30 E
Tibet (EN) = Xizang Zizhiqu (Hsi-tsang Tzu-chih-ch'ü) [2] 27 Ee 32.00N 90.00 E
Tibet, Plateau of- (EN) = Qing Zang Gaoyuan 21 Kf 32.30N 87.00 E
Tibidabo 13 Oc 41.25N 2.07 E
Tibni 24 He 35.35N 30.49 E
Tibro 8 Ff 58.26N 14.10 E
Tibú 49 Ki 8.40N 72.42W
Tibugà, Golfo de- 54 Cb 5.45N 77.20W
Tiburón, Capo- 49 Ii 8.42N 77.21W
Tiburon, Isla- 47 Bc 29.00N 112.25W
Ticao 26 Hd 12.31N 123.42 E
Tice 44 Gl 26.41N 81.49W
Tichá Orlice 10 Mf 50.09N 16.05 E
Tichît 31 Gg 18.26N 9.31W
Tichît, Dahr- 32 Ff 18.30N 9.25W
Tichka, Tizi n'- 32 Fc 31.17N 7.21W
Tichla 32 Ee 21.36N 14.58W
Ticino [2] 14 Cd 46.20N 9.00 E
Ticino 14 De 45.09N 9.14 E
Ticul 47 Gd 20.24N 89.32W
Tidaholm 7 Cg 58.11N 13.57 E
Tidan 8 Ef 58.42N 13.48 E
Tiddim 25 Id 23.22N 93.40 E
Tidikelt, Plaine du- 30 Hf 27.00N 1.30 E
Tidirhine 32 Gc 34.51N 4.31W
Tidjikja 31 Fg 18.32N 11.27W
Tidore 26 If 0.40N 127.26 E
Tidra, Ile- 30 Fg 19.44N 16.24W
Tiebissou 34 Dd 7.10N 5.13W
Tiechang 28 Id 41.40N 126.12 E
Tiel 11 Lc 51.54N 5.25 E
Tieli 27 Mb 47.04N 128.02 E
Tieling 28 Gc 42.18N 123.51 E
Tielt 11 Jc 51.00N 3.20 E
Tienba 34 Dd 8.30N 7.10W
T'ien-chin Shih → Tianjin Shi [4] 27 Kd 39.08N 117.12 E
Tienen/Tirlemont 12 Gd 50.48N 4.57 E
Tiengemeten 12 Gc 51.45N 5.20 E
Tientsin (EN) = Tianjin 22 Nf 39.08N 117.12 E
Tieroko, Tarso- 35 Ba 20.45N 17.52 E
Tierp 7 Df 60.20N 17.30 E
Tierra Amarilla [Chile] 56 Fc 27.29S 70.17W
Tierra Amarilla [N.M.-U.S.] 45 Ch 36.42N 106.33W
Tierra Blanca 47 Ee 18.27N 96.21W
Tierra Colorada 48 Ji 17.10N 99.35W
Tierra del Fuego [2] 56 Gh 54.00S 67.00W
Tierra del Fuego (EN) = Tierra del Fuego, Isla Grande de- 52 Jk 54.00S 69.00W
Tierra del Fuego, Isla Grande de- = Tierra del Fuego (EN) 52 Jk 54.00S 69.00W
Tierralta 54 Cb 8.10N 76.04W
Tiétar 13 Fe 39.50N 6.01W
Tietê, Rio- 52 Kh 20.40S 51.35W
Tietjerksteradeel 12 Ia 53.12N 6.00 E
Tietjerksteradeel-Bergum 12 Hb 52.17N 5.58 E
Tifariti 32 Ed 26.09N 10.33W
Tiffany Mountain 46 Fb 48.40N 119.56W
Tiffin 44 Fe 41.07N 83.11W
Tifton 43 Ke 31.27N 83.31W
Tiga 63b Ce 21.08S 167.49 E
Tigalda 40a Fb 54.05N 165.05W
Tigănești 15 If 43.54N 25.22 E
Tighennif 13 Mi 35.25N 0.15 E
Tigil 20 Ke 57.57N 158.20 E
Tigil 20 Ke 57.48N 158.40 E
Tignère 34 Hd 7.22N 12.39 E
Tigray [3] 35 Fc 14.00N 39.00 E
Tigre 48 Hh 19.53N 102.59W
Tigre, Cerro del- 48 Jf 23.03N 99.16W
Tigre, Rio- [S.Amer.] 52 If 4.30S 74.10W
Tigre, Rio- [Ven.] 50 Eh 9.20N 62.30W
Tigris (EN) = Dicle 21 Gf 31.00N 47.25 E
Tigris (EN) = Dijlah 21 Gf 31.00N 47.25 E
Tigrovy Hvost, Mys- 18 Bc 43.57N 58.45 E
Tiguent 32 Df 17.15N 16.00W
Tiguentourine 32 Id 27.43N 9.33 E
Tigui 35 Bb 18.38N 18.47 E
Tigzirt 13 Qh 36.54N 4.07 E
Tīh, Jabal at- 33 Fd 29.35N 34.00 E
Tīh, Ṣaḥrā' at- = At Tih Desert (EN) 33 Fc 30.05N 34.00 E
Tihāmat 23 Ff 18.30N 41.30 E
Tihāmat Ash Shām 33 Hf 19.15N 41.10 E

Index Symbols

[1] Independent Nation
[2] State, Region
[3] District, County
[4] Municipality
[5] Colony, Dependency
Continent
Physical Region
Historical or Cultural Region
Mount, Mountain
Volcano
Hill
Mountains, Mountain Range
Hills, Escarpment
Plateau, Upland
Pass, Gap
Plain, Lowland
Delta
Salt Flat
Valley, Canyon
Crater, Cave
Karst Features
Depression
Polder
Desert, Dunes
Forest, Woods
Heath, Steppe
Oasis
Cape, Point
Coast, Beach
Cliff
Peninsula
Isthmus
Sandbank
Island
Atoll
Rock, Reef
Islands, Archipelago
Rocks, Reefs
Coral Reef
Well, Spring
Geyser
River, Stream
Waterfall Rapids
River Mouth, Estuary
Lake
Salt Lake
Intermittent Lake
Reservoir
Swamp, Pond
Canal
Glacier
Ice Shelf, Pack Ice
Ocean
Sea
Gulf, Bay
Strait, Fjord
Lagoon
Bank
Seamount
Tablemount
Ridge
Shelf
Basin
Escarpment, Sea Scarp
Fracture
Trench, Abyss
National Park, Reserve
Point of Interest
Recreation Site
Cave, Cavern
Historic Site
Ruins
Wall, Walls
Church, Abbey
Temple
Scientific Station
Airport
Port
Lighthouse
Mine
Tunnel
Dam, Bridge

Index Symbols

- [1] Independent Nation
- [2] State, Region
- [3] District, County
- [4] Municipality
- [5] Colony, Dependency
- ■ Continent
- ▭ Physical Region

- Historical or Cultural Region
- Mount, Mountain
- Volcano
- Hill
- Mountains, Mountain Range
- Hills, Escarpment
- Plateau, Upland

- Pass, Gap
- Plain, Lowland
- Delta
- Valley, Canyon
- Crater, Cave
- Karst Features

- Depression
- Polder
- Desert, Dunes
- Salt Flat
- Forest, Woods
- Heath, Steppe
- Oasis
- Cape, Point

- Coast, Beach
- Cliff
- Peninsula
- Isthmus
- Sandbank
- Island
- Islands, Archipelago
- Atoll

- Rock, Reef
- Rocks, Reefs
- Coral Reef
- Well, Spring
- Geyser
- River, Stream

- Waterfall Rapids
- River Mouth, Estuary
- Lake
- Salt Lake
- Intermittent Lake
- Sea
- Gulf, Bay
- Strait, Fjord

- Canal
- Glacier
- Ice Shelf, Pack Ice
- Ocean
- Reservoir
- Shelf
- Ridge
- Basin

- Lagoon
- Bank
- Seamount
- Tablemount
- Sea
- Slope

- Escarpment, Sea Scarp
- Fracture
- Trench, Abyss
- National Park, Reserve
- Point of Interest
- Recreation Site
- Cave, Cavern

- Historic Site
- Ruins
- Wall, Walls
- Church, Abbey
- Temple
- Scientific Station
- Airport

- Port
- Lighthouse
- Mine
- Tunnel
- Dam, Bridge

Tongaat 37 Ee 29.37S 31.03 E
Tonga Islands 57 Jf 20.00S 175.00W
Tonga Ridge (EN) 57 Jg 21.00S 175.00W
Tongariki 63b Dc 17.01S 168.37 E
Tongatapu Group 57 Jg 21.10S 175.10W
Tongatapu Island 61 Fd 21.10S 175.10W
Tonga Trench (EN) 3 Kl 20.00S 173.00W
Tongbai 28 Bh 32.21N 113.24 E
Tongbai Shan 27 Je 32.20N 113.14 E
Tongcheng [China] 28 Bj 29.15N 113.49 E
Tongcheng [China] 28 Di 31.04N 116.56 E
Tongcheng → Dong'e 28 Df 36.19N 116.14 E
Tongchuan 27 Id 35.10N 109.03 E
Tongdao (Shuangjiang) 27 If 26.14N 109.45 E
Tongde 27 Hd 35.29N 100.32 E
Tongeren/Tongres 11 Ld 50.47N 5.28 E
Tonggu 28 Cj 28.33N 114.21 E
Tongguzbasti 27 Dd 38.23N 82.00 E
Tonggu Zhang 27 Kg 24.12N 116.22 E
Tong-Hae = Japan, Sea of- (EN) 21 Pf 40.00N 134.00 E
Tonghai 22 Mg 24.15N 102.45 E
Tonghe 27 Mb 46.01N 128.42 E
Tonghua 22 Oe 41.43N 125.55 E
Tongjiang 27 Nb 47.39N 132.30 E
Tongjosŏn-man 21 Of 39.30N 128.00 E
Tongliao 22 Oe 43.37N 122.15 E
Tongling 27 Ke 30.49N 117.47 E
Tonglu 28 Ej 29.48N 119.39 E
Tongmun'gŏ-ri 27 Mc 40.58N 127.08 E
Tongoa 63b Dc 16.54S 168.33 E
Tongoy 56 Fd 30.15S 71.30W
Tongren [China] 27 If 27.45N 109.09 E
Tongren [China] 27 Hd 35.40N 102.07 E
Tongres/Tongeren 11 Ld 50.47N 5.28 E
Tongsa Dzong 25 Ic 27.31N 90.30 E
Tongshan 28 Cj 29.36N 114.30 E
Tongta 25 Jd 21.20N 99.16 E
Tongtian He/Zhi Qu 21 Lf 33.26N 96.36 E
Tongue 9 Ic 58.28N 4.25W
Tongue of the Ocean 49 Ia 24.12N 77.10W
Tongue River 43 Fb 46.24N 105.52W
Tongxian 27 Kd 39.52N 116.38 E
Tongxin 27 Id 36.59N 105.50 E
Tongxu 28 Cg 34.29N 114.27 E
Tongyu (Kaitong) 27 Lc 44.47N 123.05 E
Tongyu Yunhe 28 Eg 34.46N 119.51 E
Tongzi 27 If 28.09N 106.50 E
Tonichi 48 Ec 28.35N 109.34W
Tönisvorst 12 Ic 51.19N 6.28 E
Tonj 35 Dd 7.17N 28.45 E
Tonj 30 Jh 7.31N 29.25 E
Tonk 25 Fc 26.10N 75.47 E
Tonkin (EN) = Bac-Phan 21 Mg 22.00N 105.00 E
Tonkin, Gulf of- (EN) = Beibu Wan 21 Mh 20.00N 108.00 E
Tonkin, Gulf of- (EN) = Vinh Bac Phan 21 Mh 20.00N 108.00 E
Tônlé Sab, Bœng- = Tonle Sap (EN) 21 Mh 13.00N 104.00 E
Tonle Sap (EN) = Tônlé Sab, Bœng- 21 Mh 13.00N 104.00 E
Tonnay-Charente 11 Fi 45.57N 0.54W
Tonneins 11 Gj 44.23N 0.19 E
Tönning 10 Eb 54.19N 8.57 E
Tōno 28 Pe 39.19N 141.32 E
Tonopah 43 Dd 38.04N 117.14W
Tonoshō 29 Dd 34.29N 134.11 E
Tonosí 49 Gj 7.24N 80.27W
Tønsberg 7 Cg 59.17N 10.25 E
Tonstad 7 Bg 58.40N 6.43 E
Tonumeia 65b Bb 20.28S 174.46W
Tonya 24 Hb 40.53N 39.16 E
Tooele 43 Ec 40.32N 112.18W
Toora-Hem 20 Ef 52.28N 96.22 E
Tootsi 8 Kf 58.34N 24.43 E
Toovoomba 58 Gg 27.33S 151.57 E
Topalu 15 Le 44.33N 28.03 E
Topa Taung 25 Jd 21.08N 95.12 E
Topeka 39 Jf 39.03N 95.41W
Topki 20 De 55.18N 85.40 E
Topko, Gora- 20 Ie 57.00N 137.23 E
Topl'a 10 Rh 48.45N 21.45 E
Topleţ 15 Fe 44.48N 22.24 E
Toplica 15 Ef 43.13N 21.51 E
Topliţa 15 Ic 46.55N 25.20 E
Topola 15 De 44.16N 20.42 E
Topol'čany 10 Oh 48.34N 18.10 E
Topolnica 15 Hg 42.11N 24.18 E
Topolobampo 47 Cc 25.36N 109.03W
Topolobampo, Bahía de- 48 Ee 25.30N 109.05W
Topolog 15 Hd 44.56N 24.16 E
Topolovgrad 15 Jg 42.05N 26.20 E
Topozero, Ozero- 5 Jb 65.40N 32.00 E
Toppenish 46 Ec 46.23N 120.19W
Toprakkale 24 Gd 37.06N 36.07 E
Top Springs 59 Gc 16.38S 131.50 E
Toquepala 54 Eg 17.38S 69.56W
Tor 35 Ed 7.51N 33.36 E
Tora 64d Ba 7.39N 151.53 E
Toraigh/Tory Island 9 Ef 55.16N 8.13W
Tora Island Pass 64d Ba 7.39N 151.53 E
Toråker 8 Gd 60.31N 16.29 E
Torbalı 24 Bc 38.10N 27.21 E
Torbat-e Heydarīyeh 22 Hf 35.16N 59.13 E
Torbat-e Jam 23 Jb 35.14N 60.36 E
Torbay 9 Jk 50.28N 3.30W
Torbert, Mount- 40 Id 61.25N 152.24W
Torch Lake 44 Ec 45.00N 85.19W
Torčin 10 Vf 50.44N 25.05 E
Tordesillas 13 Hc 41.30N 5.00W
Tordino 14 Hh 42.44N 13.59 E
Töre 7 Fd 65.54N 22.39 E
Töreboda 7 Dg 58.43N 14.08 E
Torekov 8 Eh 56.26N 12.37 E
Torenberg 11 Lb 52.15N 5.55 E
Torez 16 Kf 47.59N 38.41 E
Torgau 10 Ie 51.34N 13.00 E
Torgelow 10 Kc 53.38N 14.01 E
Torgun 16 Od 50.10N 46.20 E
Torhamn 8 Fh 56.05N 15.50 E
Torhout 11 Jc 51.04N 3.06 E
Toribulu 26 Hg 0.19S 120.01 E
Torigni-sur-Vire 12 Be 49.05N 0.59W
Torii-Tōge 29 Ed 35.59N 137.49 E
Tori-Jima 29b Ab 26.35N 126.50 E
Torino = Turin (EN) 6 Gf 45.03N 7.40 E
Toriparu 55 Fc 16.20S 53.55W
Tori-Shima [Jap.] 27 Pe 30.25N 140.15 E
Tori-Shima [Jap.] 29b Bb 27.52N 128.14 E
Torit 35 Ee 4.24N 32.34 E
Torixoreu 54 Hg 16.15S 52.26W
Torkoviči 7 Hg 58.53N 30.20 E
Törmänen 7 Gb 68.36N 27.29 E
Tormes 13 Fc 41.18N 6.29W
Tornado Mountain 46 Hb 49.58N 114.39W
Tornavacas, Puerto de- 13 Gd 40.16N 5.37W
Torneå/Tornio 7 Fd 65.51N 24.08 E
Torneälven 5 Ib 65.48N 24.08 E
Torneträsk 7 Eb 68.22N 19.06 E
Torngat Mountains 38 Md 59.00N 64.00W
Tornio/Torneå 7 Fd 65.51N 24.08 E
Tornionjoki 5 Ib 65.48N 24.08 E
Tornquist 55 An 38.06S 62.14W
Toro 13 Gc 41.31N 5.24W
Toro 8 Gf 58.50N 17.50 E
Toro, Cerro del- 52 Jh 29.08S 69.48W
Toro, Isla del- 48 Kg 21.35N 97.32W
Toro, Monte- 13 Qe 39.59N 4.07 E
Toroiaga, Vîrful- 15 Hb 47.44N 24.43 E
Torokina 63a Bb 6.14S 155.03 E
Tōro-Ko 29a Db 43.08N 144.30 E
Törökszentmiklós 10 Qi 47.11N 20.25 E
Torola, Río- 49 Cg 13.52N 88.30W
Toronto 39 Le 43.39N 79.23W
Toropec 19 Dd 56.31N 31.39 E
Tororo 36 Fb 0.41N 34.11 E
Toros Dağları = Taurus Mountains (EN) 21 Ff 37.00N 33.00 E
Torquato Severo 55 Ej 31.02S 54.11W
Torquay 9 Jk 50.29N 3.29W
Torrá, Cerro- 52 Ie 4.38N 76.15W
Torrance 46 Fj 33.50N 118.19W
Torre Annunziata 14 Ij 40.45N 14.27 E
Torreblanca 13 Md 40.13N 0.12 E
Torrecilla 13 Hh 36.41N 5.00W
Torrecilla en Cameros 13 Jb 42.16N 2.37W
Torre del Greco 14 Ij 40.47N 14.22 E
Torre del Mar 13 Hh 36.44N 4.06W
Torredembarra 13 Nc 41.09N 1.24 E
Torre de Moncorvo 13 Ec 41.10N 7.03W
Torre de' Passeri 14 Hh 42.14N 13.56 E
Torredonjimeno 13 Ig 37.46N 3.57W
Torrejón de Ardoz 13 Id 40.27N 3.29W
Torrelaguna 13 Id 40.50N 3.32W
Torrelavega 13 Ha 43.21N 4.03W
Torre Miró, Puerto de- 13 Ld 40.42N 0.05W
Torremolinos 13 Hh 36.37N 4.30W
Torrens, Lake- 57 Eh 31.00S 137.50 E
Torrens Creek 59 Jd 20.46S 145.02 E
Torrent de l'Horta/Torrente 13 Le 39.26N 0.28W
Torrente/Torrent de l'Horta 13 Le 39.26N 0.28W
Torrenueva 13 If 38.38N 3.22W
Torreón 39 Ig 25.33N 103.26W
Torre-Pacheco 13 Lg 37.44N 0.57W
Torre Pellice 14 Bf 44.49N 7.13 E
Torres 64d Ab 7.19N 151.27 E
Tôrres 56 Kc 29.21S 49.44W
Torrès, Iles- = Torres Islands (EN) 57 Hf 13.15S 166.37 E
Torres Islands (EN) = Torrès, Iles- 57 Hf 13.15S 166.37 E
Torres Novas 13 De 39.29N 8.32W
Torres Strait 57 Ff 10.25S 142.10 E
Torres Vedras 13 Ce 39.06N 9.16W
Torrevieja 13 Lg 37.59N 0.41W
Torridon, Loch- 9 Hd 57.35N 5.50W
Torriglia 14 Df 44.31N 9.10 E
Torrijos 13 He 39.59N 4.17W
Torrington [Ct.-U.S.] 44 Ke 41.48N 73.08W
Torrington [Wy.-U.S.] 43 Gc 42.04N 104.11W
Torroella de Montgri 13 Pb 42.02N 3.08 E
Torröjen 7 Cf 63.55N 12.56 E
Torrox 13 Ih 36.46N 3.58W
Torsås 7 Dh 56.24N 16.00 E
Torsby 7 Cf 60.08N 13.00 E
Torshälla 8 Ge 59.25N 16.28 E
Torsken 7 Db 69.20N 17.06 E
Torsö 7 Cg 58.50N 13.50 E
Torto 14 Hm 37.58N 13.46 E
Tortola 47 Le 18.27N 64.36W
Tortoli 14 Dk 39.55N 9.39 E
Tortona 14 Cf 44.54N 8.52 E
Tortorici 14 Il 38.02N 14.49 E
Tortosa 13 Md 40.48N 0.31 E
Tortosa, Cabo de-/Tortosa, Cap de- 13 Md 40.43N 0.55 E
Tortosa, Cap de-/Tortosa, Cabo de- 13 Md 40.43N 0.55 E
Tortue, Ile de la- 47 Jd 20.04N 72.49W
Tortuga, Isla- 48 Dd 27.26N 111.55W
Tortum 24 Ib 40.19N 41.35 E
Torud 24 Pe 35.26N 55.07 E
Torugart, Pereval- 21 Je 40.32N 75.24 E
Torul 24 Hb 40.35N 39.18 E
Toruń 10 Oc 53.00N 18.35 E
Toruń 10 Oc 53.02N 18.35 E
Torunos 49 Li 8.30N 70.04W
Toruńska, Kotlina- 10 Oc 53.00N 18.30 E
Torup 7 Ch 56.58N 13.05 E
Tōrva/Tyrva 7 Fg 58.01N 25.59 E
Tory Island/Toraigh 9 Ef 55.16N 8.13W
Torysa 10 Rh 48.39N 21.21 E
Toržok 19 Dd 57.03N 35.01 E
Tosa 28 Lh 33.29N 133.25 E
Tosas, Puerto de-/Toses, Port de- 13 Ob 42.20N 2.01 E
Tosashimizu 28 Lh 32.46N 132.57 E
Tosa-Wan 28 Lh 33.25N 133.35 E
Tosa-yamada 29 Ce 33.36N 133.40 E
Toscana = Tuscany (EN) 14 Eg 43.25N 11.00 E
Toses, Port de-/Tosas, Puerto de- 13 Ob 42.20N 2.01 E
Toshibetsu-Gawa [Jap.] 29a Cb 42.54N 143.25 E
Toshibetsu-Gawa [Jap.] 29a Ab 42.25N 139.48 E
Tōshi-Jima 29 Ed 34.31N 136.52 E
To-Shima 29 Fd 34.31N 139.17 E
Tosno 7 Hg 59.34N 30.50 E
Toson-Cengel 27 Gb 48.47N 98.15 E
Toson Hu 27 Gd 37.08N 96.52 E
Töss 14 Cc 47.33N 8.33 E
Tossa de Mar 13 Oc 41.43N 2.56 E
Tostado 56 Hc 29.14S 61.46W
Tōstamaa/Tystama 8 Jf 58.17N 23.52 E
Tosu 29 Be 33.22N 130.30 E
Tosya 24 Fb 41.01N 34.02 E
Totak 8 Be 59.40N 7.55 E
Totana 13 Kg 37.46N 1.30W
Toten 8 Dd 60.40N 10.50 E
Toteng 37 Cd 20.23S 22.59 E
Tôtes 11 He 49.41N 1.03 E
Totes Gebirge 14 Hc 47.42N 13.55 E
Tōtias 35 Ge 3.57N 43.58 E
Totland 12 Ad 50.40N 1.32W
Totma 19 Ed 60.00N 42.45 E
Totness 54 Gb 5.53N 56.19W
Toto 36 Bd 7.10S 14.25 E
Totonicapán 49 Bf 15.00N 91.20W
Totonicapán 47 Ff 14.55N 91.22W
Totora 54 Eg 17.42S 65.09W
Totoras 55 Bk 32.35S 61.11W
Totota 34 Dd 6.49N 9.56W
Totoya 63d Cc 18.57S 179.50W
Totten Glacier 66 He 66.45S 116.10 E
Totton 12 Ad 50.55N 1.29W
Tottori 27 Nd 35.30N 134.14 E
Tottori Ken 28 Lg 35.25N 133.50 E
Tou, Motu- 64p Bb 21.11S 159.48W
Touâjil 32 Ee 21.45N 12.35W
Touat 30 Gf 27.40N 0.01W
Touba 34 Dd 8.15N 7.45W
Touba 34 Dd 8.17N 7.41W
Toubkal, Jebel- 30 Ge 31.03N 7.55W
Touch 11 Hk 43.38N 1.24 E
Toucy 11 Jg 47.44N 3.18 E
Tougan 34 Ec 13.04N 3.04W
Touggourt 31 He 33.06N 6.04 E
Tougué 34 Cc 11.27N 11.41W
Touho 63b Be 20.47S 165.14 E
Touil 32 Hb 35.33N 2.36 E
Toûîl 13 Oi 35.33N 2.36 E
Toukoto 34 Dc 13.28N 9.52W
Toul 11 Lf 48.41N 5.54 E
Toulépleu 34 Dd 6.35N 8.25W
Toulon 6 Gg 43.07N 5.56 E
Toulouse 6 Gg 43.36N 1.26 E
Toulumne River 46 Eh 37.36N 121.10W
Toumodi 34 Dd 6.33N 5.01W
Tounassine, Hamada- 32 Fd 28.36N 5.10W
Toungo 34 Hd 8.07N 12.03 E
Toungoo 22 Lh 18.56N 96.26 E
Touques 11 Ge 49.22N 0.06 E
Toura 35 Bc 10.30N 15.19 E
Touraine 11 Hg 47.12N 1.30 E
Touraine, Val de- 11 Hg 47.20N 1.30 E
Tourcoing 11 Jd 50.43N 3.09 E
Touriñan, Cabo de- 13 Ca 43.03N 9.18W
Tourine 32 Ee 22.00N 12.15W
Tournai/Doornik 11 Jd 50.36N 3.23 E
Tournai-Kain 12 Fd 50.38N 3.22 E
Tournon 11 Ki 45.04N 4.50 E
Tournus 11 Kh 46.34N 4.54 E
Touros 54 Ke 5.12S 35.28W
Tours 6 Gf 47.23N 0.41 E
Tourteron 12 Ge 49.32N 4.39 E
Toury 11 Hf 48.12N 1.56 E
Touside, Pic- 35 Ba 21.02N 16.25 E
Toussoro 35 Cd 9.02N 23.55 E
Toutouba 63b Cb 15.34S 167.16 E
Touwsrivier 37 Cf 33.20S 20.00 E
Toužim 10 If 50.04N 12.59 E
Tovar 49 Li 8.20N 71.46W
Tovarkovski 16 Kc 53.43N 38.13 E
Tovdalselva 8 Cf 58.12N 8.06 E
Tove 12 Bb 52.04N 0.50W
Tōwa 29 Gb 39.23N 141.15 E
Towada 28 Pd 40.35N 141.13 E
Towada-Kō 29 Ga 40.28N 140.55 E
Towanda 44 Ie 41.46N 76.27W
Tower 45 Jc 47.48N 92.17W
Towner 45 Fb 48.21N 100.25W
Townsend 46 Jc 46.19N 111.31W
Townshend, Cape- 59 Kd 22.15S 150.30 E
Townsville 58 Ff 19.16S 146.48 E
Towot 35 Ed 6.12N 34.25 E
Towson 44 If 39.24N 76.36W
Towuti, Danau- 26 Hg 2.45S 121.32 E
Toxkan He 27 Dc 41.08N 80.11 E
Tōya 29a Bb 42.39N 140.48 E
Toyah Creek 45 Ek 31.18N 103.27W
Tōya-Ko 28 Pc 42.33N 140.50 E
Toyama 22 Pf 36.41N 137.13 E
Toyama Ken 28 Nf 30.40N 137.10 E
Toyama Trench (EN) 29 Ec 38.00N 138.00 E
Toyama-Wan 28 Nf 37.00N 137.15 E
Tōyō 28 Mh 33.22N 134.18 E
Toyohashi 27 Oe 34.46N 137.23 E
Toyokoro 29a Cb 42.48N 143.28 E
Toyonaka 29 Dd 34.47N 135.28 E
Toyo'oka 27 Od 35.33N 137.54 E
Toyosaka 29 Fc 37.55N 139.12 E
Toyota 28 Ng 35.05N 137.09 E
Toyotama 29 Ad 34.27N 129.19 E
Toyotomi 29a Ba 45.08N 141.47 E
Toyoura 29 Bd 34.10N 130.55 E
Trabancos 13 Gc 41.27N 5.11W
Traben Trabach 12 Je 49.57N 7.07 E
Trabzon 22 Fe 40.59N 39.43 E
Traer 45 Je 42.12N 92.28W
Trafalgar, Cabo- 13 Fh 36.11N 6.02W
Tragacete 13 Kd 40.21N 1.51W
Traiguén 56 Fe 38.15S 72.41W
Trail 39 He 49.06N 117.43W
Traill 41 Jd 72.45N 24.00W
Traíras, Rio- 55 Hb 14.07S 48.31W
Trairi 54 Kd 3.17S 39.15W
Traisen 14 Jb 48.22N 15.46 E
Trakai/Trakaj 7 Fi 54.38N 24.57 E
Trakaj/Trakai 7 Fi 54.38N 24.57 E
Trakt 17 Ee 62.44N 51.11 E
Trakya = Thrace (EN) 15 Jh 41.20N 26.45 E
Trakya = Thrace (EN) 5 Ig 41.20N 26.45 E
Tralee/Trá Lí 9 Di 52.16N 9.42W
Tralee Bay/Bá Thrá Lí 9 Di 52.15N 9.59W
Trá Lí/Tralee 9 Di 52.16N 9.42W
Trá Mhór/Tramore 9 Fi 52.10N 7.10W
Tramore/Trá Mhór 9 Fi 52.10N 7.10W
Tramping Lake 46 Ka 52.10N 108.48W
Trăn 15 Fg 42.50N 22.39 E
Tranås 7 Dg 58.03N 14.59 E
Trancoso 13 Ed 40.47N 7.21W
Tranebjerg 8 Di 55.50N 10.36 E
Tranemo 8 Eg 57.29N 13.21 E
Trang 22 Li 7.33N 99.36 E
Trani 14 Ki 41.17N 16.25 E
Transantarctic Mountains (EN) 66 Lg 85.00S 175.00W
Transcaucasia (EN) 5 Kg 41.00N 45.00 E
Transilvania = Transylvania (EN) 15 Hc 46.30N 25.00 E
Transilvania = Transylvania (EN) 5 If 46.30N 25.00 E
Transkei 30 Jl 31.30S 29.00 E
Transkei 37 Df 32.45S 28.30 E
Transtrand 8 Ec 61.05N 13.19 E
Transtrandsfjällen 8 Ec 61.15N 12.58 E
Transvaal 37 Dd 25.00S 30.00 E
Transylvania (EN) = Transilvania 15 Hc 46.30N 25.00 E
Transylvania (EN) = Transilvania 5 If 46.30N 25.00 E
Transylvanian Alps (EN) = Carpâţii Meridionali 5 If 45.30N 24.15 E
Trants Bay 51c Bc 16.46N 62.09W
Trapani 6 Hh 38.01N 12.29 E
Trapper Peak 46 Hd 45.54N 114.18W
Trappes 12 Ef 48.47N 2.01 E
Traralgon 59 Jg 38.12S 146.32 E
Trarza 32 Ef 18.00N 15.00W
Trarza 30 Fg 17.20N 14.40W
Traşcăului, Munţii- 15 Gc 46.23N 23.33 E
Trasimeno, Lago- 14 Gg 43.10N 12.05 E
Träslövsläge 8 Eg 57.04N 12.16 E
Trás os Montes e Alto Douro 13 Ec 41.30N 7.15W
Trat 25 Kf 12.13N 102.16 E
Traun 14 Ib 48.13N 14.14 E
Traun 14 Ib 48.16N 14.22 E
Traunsee 14 Hc 47.52N 13.48 E
Traunstein 10 Ii 47.53N 12.39 E
Trave 10 Gc 53.54N 10.50 E
Travemünde, Lübeck- 10 Gc 53.57N 10.52 E
Travers, Mount- 61 Dh 42.01S 172.44 E
Traverse, Lake- 45 Hd 45.43N 96.40W
Traverse City 43 Jc 44.46N 85.37W
Traverse Islands 66 Ad 56.36S 27.43W
Travers Reservoir 46 Ia 50.14N 112.51W
Tra Vinh 25 Lg 9.56N 106.20 E
Travis, Lake- 45 Hk 30.27N 98.00W
Travnik 23 Ff 44.14N 17.40 E
Travo 11a Bb 41.54N 9.24 E
Trbovlje 14 Jd 46.10N 15.03 E
Treasurers 63c Ba 9.53S 167.09 E
Treasury Islands 63a Bb 7.22S 155.37 E
Trebbia 14 De 45.04N 9.41 E
Třebíč 10 Lg 49.13N 15.53 E
Trebinje 14 Mh 42.43N 18.21 E
Trebisacce 14 Kk 39.52N 16.32 E
Trebišnjica 14 Lg 43.01N 17.47 E
Trebišov 10 Rh 48.40N 21.43 E
Treblinka 10 Sd 52.40N 22.03 E
Trebnje 14 Je 45.54N 15.01 E
Třeboň 10 Kg 49.01N 14.48 E
Třeboňska pánev 10 Kg 49.00N 14.50 E
Trégorrois 11 Cf 48.45N 3.15W
Tregrosse Islets 57 Gf 17.40S 150.45 E
Tréguier 11 Cf 48.47N 3.14W
Treherne 45 Gb 49.38N 98.41W
Treignac 11 Hi 45.32N 1.48 E
Treinta y Tres 55 Ek 33.00S 54.15W
Treinta y Tres 56 Jd 33.14S 54.23W
Treis-Karden 12 Jd 50.11N 7.17 E
Trélazé 11 Fg 47.27N 0.28W
Trelew 56 Gf 43.15S 65.18W
Trelleborg 6 Hd 55.22N 13.10 E
Trélon 12 Gd 50.04N 4.06 E
Tremadoc Bay 9 Ii 52.40N 4.10W
Tremblant, Mount- 38 Le 46.15N 74.34W
Tremiti, Isole- = Tremiti Islands (EN) 5 Hg 42.10N 15.30 E
Tremiti Islands (EN) = Tremiti, Isole- 5 Hg 42.10N 15.30 E
Tremonton 46 If 41.43N 112.10W
Tremp 13 Mb 42.10N 0.54 E
Třemšín 10 Jg 49.33N 13.48 E
Trenche, Rivière- 44 Kb 47.35N 72.58W
Trenčín 10 Oh 48.54N 18.04 E
Trenque Lauguen 56 He 35.58S 62.42W
Trent 9 Mh 53.42N 0.41W
Trent, Vale of- 9 Li 52.45N 1.50W
Trentino-Alto Adige / Südtirol 14 Fd 46.30N 11.20 E
Trento 14 Fd 46.04N 11.08 E
Trenton [Mo.-U.S.] 45 Jf 40.05N 93.37W
Trenton [N.J.-U.S.] 39 Le 40.13N 74.45W
Trenton [Ont.-Can.] 44 Ic 44.06N 77.35W
Tréon 12 Df 48.41N 1.20 E
Trepassey 42 Mg 46.44N 53.22W
Tres Arboles [Ur.] 56 Id 32.24S 56.43W
Tres Arroyos 53 Ji 38.22S 60.15W
Tres Bocas 55 Ck 32.44S 59.45W
Tres Carações 54 Ih 21.42S 45.16W
Tres Cruces, Cerro- 48 Mj 15.28N 92.24W
Três de Maio 55 Eh 27.47S 54.14W
Tres Esquinas 54 Cc 0.43N 75.15W
Tres Isletas 55 Bh 26.21S 60.26W
Treska 15 Eh 41.59N 21.19 E
Treskavica 14 Mg 43.35N 18.24 E
Três Lagoas 53 Kh 20.48S 51.43W
Três Marias, Reprêsa- 54 Ig 18.15S 45.15W
Tres Montes, Peninsula- 56 Eg 46.50S 75.30W
Três Passos 56 Jc 27.27S 53.56W
Tres Picos, Cerro- [Arg.] 52 Ji 38.09S 61.57W
Tres Picos, Cerro- [Mex.] 48 Li 16.36N 94.13W
Três Pontas 55 Je 21.22S 45.31W
Tres Puntas, Cabo- [Arg.] 52 Jj 47.06S 65.53W
Tres Puntas, Cabo- [Guat.] 49 Cf 15.58N 88.37W
Três Ranchos 55 Id 18.22S 47.47W
Três Rios 55 Kf 22.07S 43.12W
Třešť 10 Lg 49.18N 15.28 E
Tres Valles 48 Kh 18.15N 96.08W
Tres Zapotes 47 Ee 18.28N 95.24W
Tretten 7 Cf 61.19N 10.19 E
Treuer Range 59 Gd 22.15S 130.50 E
Treungen 8 Ce 59.02N 8.33 E
Trêve, Lac la- 44 Ja 49.58N 75.31W
Trevi 14 Gh 42.52N 12.45 E
Trévières 12 Be 49.19N 0.54W
Treviglio 14 De 45.31N 9.35 E
Trevinca, Peña- 13 Fb 42.15N 6.46W
Treviño 13 Jb 42.44N 2.45W
Treviso 14 Ge 45.40N 12.15 E
Trevose Head 9 Hk 50.33N 5.01W
Trgovište 15 Fg 42.21N 22.06 E
Triánda 15 Lm 36.24N 28.10 E
Triangle 37 Ed 21.02S 31.28 E
Triángulos, Arrecifes- 48 Mg 20.57N 92.16W
Trianísia 15 Jm 36.18N 26.45 E
Tribeč 10 Oh 48.27N 18.15 E
Tribune 45 Fg 38.28N 101.45W
Tricarico 14 Kj 40.37N 16.09 E
Tricase 14 Mk 39.56N 18.22 E
Trichūr 25 Ff 10.31N 76.13 E
Tri City 46 De 43.02N 123.15W
Trie-Château 12 De 49.17N 1.50 E
Triel-sur-Seine 12 Ef 48.59N 2.01 E
Trier 10 Cg 49.45N 6.38 E
Trier-Ehrang 12 Ie 49.49N 6.41 E
Trier-Pfalzel 12 Ie 49.46N 6.41 E
Trieste 6 Hf 45.40N 13.46 E
Trieste, Golfo di- 14 He 45.40N 13.30 E
Trieux 11 Cf 48.50N 3.03W
Trifels 12 Je 49.11N 7.59 E
Triglav 5 Hf 46.23N 13.50 E
Trigno 14 Ih 42.04N 14.48 E
Trikala 15 Ej 39.33N 21.46 E
Trikhonis, Límni- 15 Ek 38.34N 21.30 E
Trikomo → Yeniboğaziçi 24 Ee 35.17N 33.52 E
Trikomon → Yeniboğaziçi 24 Ee 35.17N 33.52 E
Trikora, Puncak- 26 Kg 4.15S 138.45 E
Trilport 12 Ef 48.57N 2.57 E
Trim/Baile Átha Troim 9 Gh 53.34N 6.47W
Trincheras 48 Gc 28.55N 104.18W
Trincomalee 22 Ki 8.34N 81.14 E
Trindade 54 Ig 16.40S 49.30W
Trindade, Ilha da- 52 Nh 20.31S 29.19W
Třinec 10 Og 49.41N 18.42 E
Tring 12 Bc 51.47N 0.39W
Tringia 15 Ej 39.38N 21.25 E
Trinidad 52 Jd 10.30N 61.15W
Trinidad [Bol.] 53 Jg 14.47S 64.47W
Trinidad [Ca.-U.S.] 46 Cf 41.07N 124.07W
Trinidad [Co.-U.S.] 39 If 37.10N 104.31W
Trinidad [Cuba] 47 Id 21.48N 79.59W
Trinidad [Mex.] 48 Ec 28.25N 109.06W
Trinidad [Ur.] 56 Id 33.32S 56.54W
Trinidad, Golfo- 56 Eg 49.55S 75.25W
Trinidad, Isla- 55 Bn 39.08S 61.58W
Trinidad, Laguna- 55 Be 20.21S 61.35W
Trinidad and Tobago 53 Jd 11.00N 61.00W
Trinidade Spur (EN) 3 Cl 21.00S 35.00W
Trinitapoli 14 Ki 41.21N 16.05 E
Trinity 45 Ik 30.57N 95.22W
Trinity 38 Jg 29.47N 94.42W
Trinity Bay [Austl.] 59 Jc 16.25S 145.35 E
Trinity Bay [Can.] 42 Mg 48.15N 53.10W
Trinity Islands 40 Ie 56.33N 154.25W
Trinity Range 46 Ff 40.20N 118.45W
Trinity River 46 Df 41.11N 123.42W
Trinkitat 35 Fb 18.41N 37.43 E
Trino 14 Ce 45.12N 8.18 E
Trionto 14 Kk 39.37N 16.45 E
Trionto, Capo- 14 Kk 39.37N 16.45 E
Triora 14 Bf 43.59N 7.46 E
Tripoli (EN) = Ţarābulus 33 Bc 32.40N 13.15 E
Tripoli (EN) = Ţarābulus [Leb.] 23 Ec 34.26N 35.51 E
Tripoli (EN) = Ţarābulus [Lib.] 31 Ie 32.54N 13.11 E
Trípolis 15 Fl 37.31N 22.22 E
Tripolitania (EN) = Tarabulus 30 Ie 31.00N 14.00 E
Tripolitania (EN) = Ţarābulus 33 Bc 30.00N 15.00 E

Index Symbols

1 Independent Nation
2 State, Region
3 District, County
4 Municipality
5 Colony, Dependency
Continent
Physical Region
Historical or Cultural Region
Mount, Mountain
Volcano
Hill
Mountains, Mountain Range
Hills, Escarpment
Plateau, Upland
Pass, Gap
Plain, Lowland
Delta
Salt Flat
Valley, Canyon
Crater, Cave
Karst Features
Depression
Polder
Desert, Dunes
Forest, Woods
Heath, Steppe
Oasis
Cape, Point
Coast, Beach
Cliff
Peninsula
Isthmus
Sandbank
Island
Atoll
Rock, Reef
Islands, Archipelago
Rocks, Reefs
Coral Reef
Well, Spring
Geyser
River, Stream
Waterfall Rapids
River Mouth, Estuary
Lake
Salt Lake
Intermittent Lake
Reservoir
Swamp, Pond
Canal
Glacier
Ice Shelf, Pack Ice
Ocean
Sea
Gulf, Bay
Strait, Fjord
Lagoon
Bank
Seamount
Tablemount
Ridge
Shelf
Basin
Escarpment, Sea Scarp
Fracture
Trench, Abyss
National Park, Reserve
Point of Interest
Recreation Site
Cave, Cavern
Historic Site
Ruins
Wall, Walls
Church, Abbey
Temple
Scientific Station
Airport
Port
Lighthouse
Mine
Tunnel
Dam, Bridge

Tripura [3] 25 Id 24.00N 92.00 E
Trisanna 14 Ec 47.07N 10.30 E
Tristan da Cunha 30 Fi 37.05S 12.17W
Tristan da Cunha Group 30 Fi 37.15S 12.30W
Triste, Golfo- 50 Bg 10.40N 68.10W
Triunfo 55 Ee 20.46S 55.47W
Trivandrum 22 Ji 8.29N 76.55 E
Trivento 14 Ii 41.47N 14.33 E
Trjavna 15 Ig 42.52N 25.30 E
Trnava 10 Nh 48.22N 17.35 E
Troarn 12 Be 49.11N 0.11W
Trobriand Islands 57 Ge 8.30S 151.05 E
Trödje 8 Gd 60.49N 17.12 E
Trofors 7 Cd 65.34N 13.25 E
Trögd 8 Ge 59.30N 17.15 E
Trogir 14 Kg 43.32N 16.15 E
Troglav [Yugo.] 14 Kg 43.58N 16.36 E
Troglav [Yugo.] 14 Mg 43.02N 18.33 E
Trøgstad 8 De 59.38N 11.18 E
Troia 14 Ji 41.22N 15.18 E
Troick [R.S.F.S.R.] 22 Id 54.06N 61.35 E
Troick [R.S.F.S.R.] 20 Ee 57.23N 94.55 E
Troickoje [R.S.F.S.R.] 20 Df 52.58N 84.45 E
Troickoje [R.S.F.S.R.] 20 Ig 49.30N 136.32 E
Troickoje [Ukr.-U.S.S.R.] 15 Nb 47.38N 30.12 E
Troicko Pečorsk 19 Fc 62.44N 56.06 E
Troina 14 Im 37.47N 14.36 E
Troisdorf 12 Jd 50.49N 7.10 E
Trois Fourches, Cap des- 32 Gb 35.26N 2.58W
Trois-Pistoles 44 Ma 48.07N 69.10W
Trois Pitons, Morne- 51g Bb 15.22N 61.20W
Trois-Ponts 12 Hd 50.22N 5.52 E
Trois-Rivières [Guad.] 51e Ac 15.59N 61.39W
Trois-Rivières [Que.-Can.] 39 Le 46.21N 72.33W
Troissereux 12 Ee 49.29N 2.03 E
Troisvierges/Ulflingen 12 Hd 50.07N 6.00 E
Trojah 15 Hg 42.53N 24.43 E
Trojanovka 10 Ve 51.21N 25.25 E
Trojanski Manastir 15 Hg 42.53N 24.48 E
Trojanski prohod 15 Hg 42.48N 24.40 E
Trojebratski 19 Ge 54.25N 66.03 E
Trollhättan 7 Cg 58.16N 12.18 E
Trollheimen 7 Be 62.50N 9.05 E
Trollhetta 8 Cb 62.51N 9.19 E
Trolltindane 8 Bd 62.29N 7.43 E
Tromba 55 Ha 13.28S 48.45W
Trombetas, Rio- 52 Kf 1.55S 55.35W
Tromelin 30 Mj 15.52S 54.25 E
Tromøya 8 Cf 58.30N 8.50 E
Troms [3] 7 Eb 69.07N 19.15 E
Tromsø 6 Hb 69.40N 19.00 E
Tron 8 Db 62.10N 10.43 E
Tronador, Monte- 52 Ij 41.10S 71.54W
Trondheim 6 Hc 63.25N 10.25 E
Trondheimsfjorden 5 Hc 63.40N 10.50 E
Tronto 14 Hh 42.54N 13.55 E
Tropea 14 Jl 38.41N 15.54 E
Tropeiros, Serra dos- 55 Jb 14.43S 44.33W
Tropoja 15 Dg 42.24N 20.10 E
Trosa 7 Dg 58.54N 17.33 E
Troškūnai/Troškunaj 8 Ki 55.32N 24.59 E
Troškunaj/Troškūnai 8 Ki 55.32N 24.59 E
Trostberg 10 Ih 48.02N 12.33 E
Trostjanec 16 Id 50.29N 34.59 E
Trotuş 15 Kc 46.03N 27.14 E
Trou Gras Point 51k Bb 13.52N 60.53W
Troumasse 51k Bb 13.49N 60.54W
Trout Lake [Mi.-U.S.] 44 Eb 46.12N 85.01W
Trout Lake [N.W.T.-Can.] 42 Fd 60.35N 121.10W
Trout Lake [Ont.-Can.] 42 If 51.12N 93.19W
Trout Lake [Ont.-Can.] 42 If 53.54N 89.56W
Trout Peak 46 Kd 44.36N 109.32W
Trout River 42 Lg 49.29N 58.08W
Trouville-sur-Mer 11 Ge 49.22N 0.05 E
Trowbridge 9 Kj 51.20N 2.13W
Troy [Al.-U.S.] 43 Je 31.48N 85.58W
Troy [Mo.-U.S.] 45 Kg 38.59N 90.59W
Troy [Mt.-U.S.] 46 Hb 48.28N 115.53W
Troy [N.Y.-U.S.] 43 Mc 42.43N 73.40W
Troy [Oh.-U.S.] 44 Ee 40.02N 84.12W
Troy (EN)=Truva 24 Bc 39.57N 26.15 E
Troyes 6 Gf 48.18N 4.05 E
Troy Peak 43 Dd 38.19N 115.30W
Trstenik 15 Df 43.37N 21.00 E
Trubčevsk 19 De 52.36N 33.46 E
Truc Giang 25 Lf 10.14N 106.23 E
Truchas Peak 45 Di 35.58N 105.39W
Trucial Coast (EN) 21 Hg 24.00N 53.00 E
Trucial States (EN) → United Arab Emirates (EN) [1] 22 Hg 24.00N 54.00 E
Truckee 46 Eg 39.20N 120.11W
Trudfront 16 Og 45.56N 47.41 E
Trudovoje 20 Ih 43.18N 132.05 E
Trufanova 7 Kd 64.29N 44.05 E
Trujillo [2] 54 Db 9.25N 70.30W
Trujillo [Hond.] 47 Ge 15.55N 86.00W
Trujillo [Peru] 53 If 8.10S 79.02W
Trujillo [Sp.] 13 Ge 39.28N 5.53W
Trujillo [Ven.] 54 Db 9.22N 70.26W
Trujillo, Río- 48 Hf 23.39N 103.08W
Truk Islands 57 Gd 7.25N 151.47 E
Trumann 45 Ki 35.41N 90.31W
Trumbull, Mount- 43 Ed 36.25N 113.10W
Trun 12 Gf 48.51N 0.02 E
Trung Phan=Annam (EN) 21 Me 15.00N 108.00 E
Truro [Eng.-U.K.] 9 Hk 50.16N 5.03W
Truro [N.S.-Can.] 39 Me 45.22N 63.16W
Truskavec 16 Ce 49.17N 23.34 E
Truth or Consequences (Hot Springs) 43 Fe 33.08N 107.15W
Trutnov 10 Lf 50.34N 15.54 E
Truva=Troy (EN) 24 Bc 39.57N 26.15 E
Truyère 11 Ij 44.38N 2.34 E
Trysil 8 Ec 61.25N 12.25 E
Trysil 7 Cf 61.18N 12.16 E
Trysilelva 5 Hd 59.23N 13.32 E
Trysilfjellet 8 Ec 61.18N 12.11 E
Trzcianka 10 Mc 53.03N 16.28 E
Trzcińsko Zdrój 10 Kd 52.58N 14.35 E
Trzebiatów 10 Lb 54.04N 15.14 E
Trzebież 10 Kc 53.42N 14.31 E
Trzebinia-Siersza 10 Pf 50.11N 19.25 E
Trzebnica 10 Ne 51.19N 17.03 E
Trzebnicki, Wał- 10 Me 51.30N 16.20 E
Trzebnickie, Wzgórza- 10 Me 51.15N 17.00 E
Trzemeszno 10 Nd 52.35N 17.50 E
Tsaidam Basin (EN)= Qaidam Pendi 27 Fd 37.00N 95.00 E
Tsamandá, Óri- 15 Dj 39.48N 20.21 E
Tsarap 25 Fb 33.31N 76.56 E
Tsaratanana 37 Hc 16.46S 47.38 E
Tsaratanana (EN)= Tsaratanana, Massif du- 30 Lj 14.00S 49.00 E
Tsaratanana, Massif du-= Tsaratanana (EN) 30 Lj 14.00S 49.00 E
Tsau 37 Cd 20.10S 22.27 E
Tsavo 36 Gc 2.59S 38.28 E
Tses 37 Be 25.58S 18.08 E
Tsévié 34 Fd 6.25N 1.13 E
Tshabong 31 Jk 26.02S 22.06 E
Tshane 31 Jk 24.01S 21.43 E
Tshangalele, Lac- 36 Ee 10.55S 27.03 E
Tshela 31 Ii 4.59S 12.56 E
Tshesebe 37 Dd 20.43S 27.37 E
Tshibala 36 Dd 6.56S 21.28 E
Tshibamba 36 Dd 9.06S 22.34 E
Tshikapa 31 Ji 6.25S 20.48 E
Tshilenge 36 Dd 6.15S 23.46 E
Tshimbalanga 36 Dd 9.43S 23.06 E
Tshimbulu 36 Dd 6.29S 22.51 E
Tshinsenda 36 Ee 12.16S 27.55 E
Tshofa 36 Ed 5.14S 25.15 E
Tshopo 36 Eb 0.33N 25.07 E
Tshuapa 30 Ji 0.14S 20.42 E
Tshwaane 37 Cd 22.38S 22.05 E
Tsiafajavona 37 Hc 19.21S 47.15 E
Tsihombe 37 He 25.17S 45.30 E
Tsimlyansk Reservoir (EN)= Cimljanskoje Vodohranilišče 5 Kf 48.00N 43.00 E
Tsinan (EN)=Jinan 22 Nf 36.35N 117.00 E
Tsinghai (EN)=Ch'ing-hai Sheng → Qinghai Sheng [2] 27 Gd 36.00N 96.00 E
Tsinghai (EN)=Qinghai Sheng (Ch'ing-hai Sheng) [2] 27 Gd 36.00N 96.00 E
Tsingtao (EN)=Qingdao 22 Of 36.05N 120.21 E
Tsiribihina 37 Gc 19.42S 44.31 E
Tsiroanomandidy 37 Hc 18.50S 46.00 E
Tsis 64d Bb 7.18N 151.50 E
Tsjokkarassa 7 Fb 69.59N 24.32 E
Tsodilo Hill 37 Cc 18.50S 21.45 E
Tsu 27 Oe 34.43N 136.31 E
Tsubame 29 Fc 37.39N 138.56 E
Tsubata 28 Nf 36.40N 136.44 E
Tsubetsu 29a Db 43.43N 144.01 E
Tsuchiura 28 Pf 36.05N 140.12 E
Tsugaru-Hantō 29a Bc 41.00N 140.30 E
Tsugaru-Kaikyō=Tsugaru Strait (EN) 21 Qe 41.40N 140.55 E
Tsugaru Strait (EN)= Tsugaru-Kaikyō 21 Qe 41.40N 140.55 E
Tsuken-Jima 29b Ab 26.15N 127.57 E
Tsukidate 29 Gb 38.44N 141.01 E
Tsukigata 29a Bb 43.20N 141.39 E
Tsukuba-San 29 Gc 36.13N 140.06 E
Tsukumi 29 Be 33.04N 131.52 E
Tsukura-Se 29 Af 31.18N 129.47 E
Tsukushi-Sanchi 29 Be 33.25N 130.30 E
Tsumeb 31 Ij 19.13S 17.42 E
Tsumeb [3] 37 Bc 19.00S 17.30 E
Tsumkwe 37 Cc 19.32S 20.30 E
Tsuna 29 Dd 34.26N 134.54 E
Tsuno-Shima 29 Bd 34.22N 130.52 E
Tsuru 29 Fd 35.35N 138.50 E
Tsuruga 27 Od 35.39N 136.04 E
Tsuruga-Wan 29 Ed 35.45N 136.05 E
Tsurugi 29 Ec 36.26N 136.37 E
Tsurugi-San 29 De 33.51N 134.03 E
Tsurui 29a Db 43.14N 144.21 E
Tsurumi-Dake 29 Be 33.18N 131.27 E
Tsurumi-Saki 29 Ce 32.56N 132.05 E
Tsuruoka 28 Oe 38.44N 139.50 E
Tsuruta 29 Ga 40.44N 140.26 E
Tsushima 21 Of 34.30N 129.20 E
Tsushima [Jap.] 29 Ce 33.07N 132.30 E
Tsushima [Jap.] 29 Ed 35.10N 136.43 E
Tsushima-Kaikyō=Korea, Strait (EN) 21 Of 34.40N 129.00 E
Tsuwano 29 Bd 34.28N 131.46 E
Tsuyama 28 Lg 35.03N 134.00 E
Tua 13 Ec 41.13N 7.26W
Tuai 62 Gc 38.49S 177.08 E
Tuaim/Tuam 9 Eh 53.31N 8.50W
Tuakau 62 Fb 37.15S 174.57 E
Tual 26 Jh 5.40S 132.45 E
Tuam/Tuaim 9 Eh 53.31N 8.50W
Tuamotu, Iles-=Tuamotu Archipelago (EN) 57 Mf 19.00S 142.00W
Tuamotu Archipelago (EN) =Tuamotu, Iles- 57 Mf 19.00S 142.00W
Tuamotu Ridge (EN) 3 Ll 20.00S 145.00W
Tuapa 64k Ba 18.57S 169.54W
Tuapse 6 Jg 44.07N 39.05 E
Tuaran 26 Ge 6.11N 116.14 E
Tuasivi 65c Aa 13.40S 172.07W
Tuasivi, Cape- 65c Aa 13.40S 172.07W
Tuatapere 61 Ci 46.08S 167.41 E
Tuba 20 Ef 54.00N 91.40 E
Tuba City 46 Jh 36.08N 111.14W
Tubaï, Ile- 57 Mg 23.18S 149.30W
Tubai-Manu → Maïao, Ile- 57 Lf 17.34S 150.35W
Tubal, Wādī at- 24 Jf 32.19N 42.13 E
Tuban 26 Fh 6.54S 112.03 E
Tubarão 56 Kc 28.30S 49.01W
Ţubayq, Jabal at- 24 Gh 29.32N 37.30 E
Tubbataha Reefs 26 Ge 8.51N 119.56 E
Tubeke/Tubize 12 Gd 50.41N 4.12 E
Tübingen 10 Fh 48.32N 9.03 E
Tubize/Tubeke 12 Gd 50.41N 4.12 E
Ţubruq=Tobruk (EN) 31 Je 32.05N 23.59 E
Tubuaï, Iles-/Australes, Iles- =Tubuai Islands (EN) 57 Lg 23.00S 150.00W
Tubuai Islands (EN)= Australes, Iles-/Tubuaï, Iles- 57 Lg 23.00S 150.00W
Tubuai Islands (EN)= Tubuaï, Iles-/Australes, Iles- 57 Lg 23.00S 150.00W
Tubutama 48 Db 30.53N 111.29W
Tucacas 54 Ea 10.48N 68.19W
Tucacas, Punta- 49 Mh 10.52N 68.13W
Tucavaca 55 Cd 18.36S 58.55W
Tucavaca, Río- 55 Cd 18.37S 58.59W
Tuchola 10 Nc 53.35N 17.50 E
Tucholska, Równina- 10 Oc 53.40N 18.30 E
Tuchów 10 Rg 49.54N 21.03 E
Tucker Glacier 66 Kf 72.35S 169.20 E
Tucson 39 Hf 32.13N 110.58W
Tucuarembó 56 Id 31.44S 55.59W
Tucumán [2] 56 Gc 27.00S 65.30W
Tucumcari 43 Gd 35.10N 103.44W
Tucunuí 54 Id 3.42S 49.27W
Tucupido 54 Eb 9.17N 65.47W
Tucupita 54 Fb 9.04N 62.03W
Tudela 13 Kb 42.05N 1.36W
Tudía, Sierra de- 13 Ff 38.05N 6.20W
Tudmur 23 Ec 34.33N 38.17 E
Tudora 15 Jb 47.31N 26.38 E
Tuela 13 Ec 41.30N 7.12W
Tuensang 25 Ic 26.17N 94.40 E
Tuerto 13 Gb 42.18N 5.53W
Tufanbeyli 24 Gc 38.18N 36.11 E
Tufi 58 Fe 9.08S 149.20 E
Tugela 30 Kk 29.14S 31.30 E
Tug Fork 44 Ff 38.25N 82.35W
Tuguegarao 26 Hc 17.37N 121.44 E
Tugulym 17 Lh 57.04N 64.39 E
Tugur 20 If 53.51N 136.52 E
Tuhai He 28 Ee 38.05N 118.13 E
Tujiabu → Yongxiu 27 Kf 29.05N 115.49 E
Tujmazy 19 Fe 54.36N 53.42 E
Tukan 17 Hj 53.50N 57.31 E
Tukangbesi, Kepulauan-= Tukangbesi Islands (EN) 26 Hh 5.40S 123.50 E
Tukangbesi Islands (EN)= Tukangbesi, Kepulauan- 26 Hh 5.40S 123.50 E
Tukayel 35 Hd 8.05N 45.20 E
Tukayyid 24 Kh 29.47N 45.36 E
Tukituki 62 Gc 39.36S 176.56 E
Tuko Village 64n Ab 10.22S 161.02W
Tūkrah 33 Dc 32.32N 20.34 E
Tuktoyaktuk 39 Fc 69.27N 133.02W
Tukums 7 Fh 56.59N 23.10 E
Tukuringra, Hrebet- 20 Hf 54.30N 126.00 E
Tukuyu 36 Fd 9.15S 33.39 E
Tula 47 Ed 20.06N 99.19W
Tula 36 Gc 0.50S 39.51 E
Tula [Mex.] 48 Jf 23.00N 99.43W
Tula [R.S.F.S.R.] 6 Je 54.12N 37.37 E
Tula de Allende 48 Jg 20.03N 99.21W
Tula Mountains 66 Ee 66.54S 51.06 E
Tulancingo 47 Ed 20.05N 98.22W
Tulare 46 Fh 36.13N 119.21W
Tulare Lake Bed 46 Fh 36.03N 119.49W
Tularosa 45 Cj 33.04N 106.01W
Tularosa Valley 45 Cj 32.45N 106.10W
Tulcán 54 Cc 0.48N 77.43W
Tulcea [2] 15 Md 45.12N 29.10 E
Tulcea 15 Ld 45.10N 28.48 E
Tulčin 16 Fe 48.39N 28.52 E
Tulelake 46 Ef 41.57N 121.29W
Tulemalu Lake 42 Hd 62.55N 99.25W
Tulgheş 15 Ic 46.57N 25.46 E
Tuli 37 Dd 21.55S 29.12 E
Tuli 37 Dd 21.48S 29.04 E
Tulia 45 Fi 34.32N 101.46W
Tulihe 27 La 50.30N 121.51 E
Tullahoma 44 Dh 35.22N 86.11W
Tullamore/An Tulach Mhór 9 Fh 53.16N 7.30W
Tulle 11 Hi 45.16N 1.46 E
Tulln 14 Kb 48.22N 16.03 E
Tulln 14 Kb 48.20N 16.03 E
Tullner Becken 14 Jb 48.25N 15.55 E
Tullow/An Tulach 9 Gi 52.48N 6.44W
Tullus 35 Cc 11.03N 24.33 E
Tully 59 Jc 17.56S 145.56 E
Ţulmaythah 33 Dc 32.43N 20.57 E
Tuloma 5 Jb 68.52N 32.49 E
Tulos, Ozero- 7 He 63.35N 30.35 E
Tulsa 39 Jf 36.09N 95.58W
Tulskaja Oblast [3] 19 De 54.00N 37.30 E
Tuluá 54 Cc 4.05N 76.12W
Tuluksak 40 Gd 61.06N 160.58W
Tulum 47 Gd 20.15N 87.27W
Tulum 48 Pg 20.13N 87.28W
Tulun 22 Md 54.35N 100.33 E
Tulungagung 26 Fh 8.04S 111.54 E
Tuma 7 Ji 55.10N 40.36 E
Tuma, Río- 49 Eg 13.03N 84.44W
Tumaco 53 Ie 1.49N 78.46W
Tumaco, Rada de- 54 Cc 1.50N 78.40W
Tumacuarí, Pico- 54 Fc 1.15N 64.40W
Tuman-gang 28 Kc 42.18N 130.41 E
Tumba 8 Ge 59.12N 17.49 E
Tumbarumba 59 Jg 35.47S 148.01 E
Tumbes [2] 54 Bd 3.50S 80.30W
Tumbes 53 Hf 4.05S 80.35W
Tumča 7 Hc 66.35N 31.45 E
Tumd Youqi 27 Jc 40.33N 110.32 E
Tumd Zuoqi 27 Jc 40.43N 111.06 E
Tumen 22 Oe 42.58N 129.49 E
Tumen Jiang 28 Kc 42.18N 130.41 E
Tumeremo 54 Fb 7.18N 61.30W
Tumkur 25 Ff 13.21N 77.05 E
Tummel 9 Je 56.43N 3.44W
Tummo 33 Be 23.00N 14.10 E
Tumon Bay 64c Ba 13.31N 144.48 E
Tumpat 26 De 6.12N 102.10 E
Tumu 34 Ec 10.52N 1.59W
Tumucumaque, Serra- 52 Ke 2.20N 55.00W
Tumwater 46 Dc 47.01N 122.54W
Tuna, Punta- 51a Cc 18.00N 65.52W
Tunapuna 50 Fg 10.38N 61.23W
Tunas 55 Hg 24.58S 49.06W
Tunas, Sierra de las- 48 Fc 29.40N 107.15W
Tunas Chicas, Laguna- 55 Am 36.01S 62.20W
Tunaydah 24 Cj 25.31N 29.21 E
Tunçbilek 15 Mj 39.37N 29.29 E
Tunduma 36 Fd 9.18S 32.46 E
Tunduru 36 Ge 11.07S 37.21 E
Tundža 15 Jh 41.40N 26.34 E
Tunga 34 Gd 8.07N 9.12 E
Tungabhadra 25 Fe 15.57N 78.15 E
Tungaru 35 Ec 10.14N 30.42 E
Tungnaá 7a Bb 64.10N 19.34W
Tungokočen 20 Gf 53.33N 115.34 E
Tungsten 42 Ed 62.05N 127.42W
Tungua 65b Bb 20.01S 174.46W
Tuni 25 Ge 17.21N 82.33 E
Tūnis=Tunis (EN) [3] 32 Jb 36.30N 10.00 E
Tūnis=Tunis (EN) 31 Ie 36.48N 10.11 E
Tūnis=Tunisia (EN) [1] 31 He 34.00N 9.00 E
Tunis (EN)=Tūnis 31 Ie 36.48N 10.11 E
Tunis (EN)=Tūnis [3] 32 Jb 36.30N 10.00 E
Tūnis, Canal de-=Sicily, Strait of- (EN) 5 Hh 37.20N 11.20 E
Tūnis, Khalīj- 32 Jb 37.00N 10.30 E
Tunisia (EN)=Tūnis [1] 31 He 34.00N 9.00 E
Tunja 53 Ie 5.31N 73.22W
Tunkhannock 44 Je 41.32N 75.57W
Tunliu 28 Bf 36.18N 112.53 E
Tunnhovdfjorden 8 Cd 60.25N 8.55 E
Tunø 8 Di 55.55N 10.25 E
Tunumuk 42 Ec 69.00N 134.57W
Tununak 40 Fd 60.35N 165.16W
Tunungayualok 42 Le 56.05N 61.05W
Tunxi 27 Kf 29.45N 118.15 E
Tuo He 28 Dh 33.16N 117.45 E
Tuo Jang 27 If 28.55N 105.26 E
Tuostah 20 Ic 67.50N 135.40 E
Tuotuo He 27 Fe 34.03N 92.46 E
Tuotuohe/Tanggulashanqu 22 Lf 34.15N 92.29 E
Tupã 56 Jb 21.56S 50.30W
Tupaciguara 55 Hd 18.35S 48.42W
Tupai Atoll (Motu-Iti) 61 Kc 16.17S 151.50W
Tupanciretã 56 Jc 29.05S 53.51W
Tupelo 43 Je 34.16N 88.43W
Tupik 20 Gf 54.28N 119.57 E
Tupinambarana, Ilha- 54 Gd 3.00S 58.00W
Tupiraçaba 55 Hb 14.29S 48.34W
Tupper Lake 44 Jc 44.13N 74.29W
Tupungato, Cerro- 56 Gd 33.22S 69.47W
Tuquan 27 Lb 45.22N 121.33 E
Túquerres 54 Cc 1.06N 77.37W
Tur 15 Fa 48.04N 22.33 E
Tura 19 Gd 57.12N 66.56 E
Tura [India] 25 Ic 25.31N 90.13 E
Tura [R.S.F.S.R.] 22 Mc 64.17N 100.15 E
Turabah [Sau.Ar.] 23 Fe 21.13N 41.39 E
Turabah [Sau.Ar.] 23 Fd 28.13N 42.59 E
Turagua, Serranías- 50 Di 7.20N 64.35W
Turakina 62 Fd 40.02S 175.13 E
Turān 24 Qe 35.40N 56.50 E
Turan 20 Ef 52.08N 93.55 E
Turana, Hrebet- 20 If 51.30N 132.00 E
Turangi 62 Fc 38.59S 175.48 E
Turano 14 Gh 42.26N 12.47 E
Turanskaja Nizmennost 21 Ie 44.30N 63.00 E
Turawa 10 Of 50.45N 18.05 E
Turawskie, Jezioro- 10 Of 50.43N 18.10 E
Turbaco 49 Jh 10.19N 75.25W
Turbat 25 Cc 25.59N 63.04 E
Turbo 53 Ie 8.06N 76.43W
Turcoaia 15 Ld 45.07N 28.11 E
Turda 15 Gc 46.34N 23.47 E
Tūreh 24 Me 34.02N 49.17 E
Tureia Atoll 57 Ng 20.50S 138.32W
Turek 10 Od 52.02N 18.30 E
Turenki 8 Kd 60.55N 24.38 E
Turfan Depression (EN)= Turpan Pendi 21 Ke 42.30N 89.30 E
Turgai Gates (EN)= Turgajskaja Ložbina 21 Id 51.00N 64.30 E
Turgai Upland (EN)= Turgajskoje Plato 21 Id 51.00N 64.00 E
Turgaj [Kaz.-U.S.S.R.] 19 Gf 49.38N 63.28 E
Turgaj [U.S.S.R.] 21 Ie 48.01N 62.45 E
Turgajskaja Ložbina=Turgai Gates (EN) 21 Id 51.00N 64.30 E
Turgajskaja Oblast [3] 19 Ge 50.30N 66.00 E
Turgajskoje Plato=Turgai Upland (EN) 21 Id 51.00N 64.00 E
Turgeon, Rivière- 44 Ha 50.00N 78.55W
Turgutlu 24 Bc 38.30N 27.50 E
Turhal 24 Gb 40.24N 36.06 E
Türi/Tjuri 7 Fg 58.50N 25.27 E
Turia 13 Le 39.27N 0.19W
Turiaçu, Baia de- 54 Id 1.30S 45.15W
Turiec 10 Og 49.06N 18.52 E
Turijsk 10 Ue 51.10N 24.37 E
Turimiquire, Cerro- 54 Fa 10.03N 64.00W
Turin (EN) = Torino 6 Gf 45.03N 7.40 E
Turinsk 19 Gd 58.03N 63.42 E
Turja 16 Dd 51.48N 24.52 E
Turka [R.S.F.S.R.] 20 Ff 52.57N 108.13 E
Turka [Ukr.-U.S.S.R.] 10 Tg 49.07N 23.01 E
Turkana 36 Gb 4.00N 35.30 E
Turkana, Lake-/Rudolf, Lake- 30 Kh 3.30N 36.00 E
Türkeli 24 Fb 41.57N 34.21 E
Turkenstanski Hrebet 19 Gh 39.35N 69.00 E
Turkestan 22 Ie 43.18N 68.15 E
Túrkeve 10 Qi 47.06N 20.45 E
Turkey (EN)=Türkiye [1] 22 Fg 39.00N 35.00 E
Turkey Creek 59 Fc 17.02S 128.12 E
Turki 16 Mc 52.01N 43.16 E
Türkiye=Turkey (EN) [1] 22 Fg 39.00N 35.00 E
Turkmenistan Sovet Socialistik Respublikasy/ Turkmenskaja SSR [2] 19 Fh 40.00N 60.00 E
Turkmen-Kala 18 Df 37.26N 62.19 E
Turkmenskaja Sovetskaja Socialističeskaja Respublika [2] 19 Fh 40.00N 60.00 E
Turkmenskaja SSR/ Turkmenistan Sovet Socialistik Respublikasy [2] 19 Fh 40.00N 60.00 E
Turkmenskaja SSR= Turkmen SSR (EN) [2] 19 Fh 40.00N 60.00 E
Turkmenski Zaliv 16 Ff 39.00N 53.30 E
Turkmen SSR (EN)= Turkmenskaja SSR [2] 19 Fh 40.00N 60.00 E
Türkoğlu 24 Gd 37.31N 36.49 E
Turks and Caicos Islands [5] 39 Ff 21.45N 71.35W
Turks Island Passage 49 Lc 21.25N 71.19W
Turks Islands 47 Jd 21.24N 71.07W
Turku/Åbo 6 Ic 60.27N 22.17 E
Turku-Pori [2] 7 Ff 61.00N 22.30 E
Turkwel 36 Gb 3.06N 36.06 E
Turlock 46 Eh 37.30N 120.51W
Turmantas 8 Li 55.42N 26.34 E
Turnagain, Cape- 62 Gd 40.30S 176.37 E
Turneffe Islands 47 Ge 17.22N 87.51W
Turnhout 11 Kc 51.19N 4.57 E
Turnov 10 Lf 50.35N 15.09 E
Turnu Roşu, Pasul- 15 Hd 45.33N 24.16 E
Turnu Măgurele 15 Hf 43.45N 24.52 E
Turočak 20 Df 52.16N 87.05 E
Turó de L'Home 13 Oc 41.45N 2.25 E
Turopolje 14 Ke 45.38N 16.07 E
Turpan 22 Ke 42.56N 89.10 E
Turpan Pendi=Turfan Depression 21 Ke 42.30N 89.30 E
Turquino, Pico- 47 Ie 19.59N 76.51W
Turrialba 49 Fi 9.54N 83.41W
Tursuntski Tuman, Ozero- 17 Kf 60.35N 63.55 E
Turtas 17 Ng 58.57N 69.10 E
Turtas 17 Ng 59.06N 68.50 E
Turtkul 19 Gg 41.35N 61.00 E
Turtle Mountain 45 Fb 49.05N 100.15W
Turugart Shankou 21 Je 40.32N 75.24 E
Turuhan 20 Dc 65.56N 87.42 E
Turuhansk 20 Dc 65.49N 87.59 E
Turvânia 55 Gc 16.39S 50.09W
Turvo 55 Hi 28.56S 49.41W
Turvo, Rio- [Braz.] 55 Hd 19.56S 49.55W
Turvo, Rio- [Braz.] 55 Gc 17.46S 50.12W
Tusaun/Thusis 14 Dd 46.42N 9.26 E
Tuscaloosa 43 Je 33.13N 87.33W
Tuscan Archipelago (EN)= Arcipelago Toscano 5 Hg 42.45N 10.20 E
Tuscania 14 Fh 42.25N 11.52 E
Tuscany (EN) = Toscana [2] 14 Eg 43.25N 11.00 E
Tuscarora Mountain 44 Ie 40.10N 77.45W
Tuscarora Mountains 46 Gf 41.00N 116.20W
Tuščibas, Zaliv- 18 Ba 46.10N 59.45 E
Tuscola 45 Lg 39.48N 88.17W
Tusenøyane 41 Oc 77.05N 22.00 E
Tuskar 16 Jd 51.40N 36.15 E
Tuskegee 44 Ei 32.26N 85.42W
Tuşnad Băi 15 Ic 46.09N 25.51 E
Tustna 8 Ca 63.10N 8.05 E
Tuszymka 10 Rf 50.09N 21.30 E
Tuszyn 10 Pe 51.37N 19.34 E
Tutajev 19 Dd 57.52N 39.32 E
Tutak 24 Jc 39.32N 42.46 E
Tuticorin 25 Fg 8.47N 78.08 E
Tutira 62 Gc 39.12S 176.53 E
Tutóia 54 Jd 2.45S 42.16W
Tutoko Peak 62 Bf 44.36S 167.58 E
Tutončana 20 Ed 64.05N 93.50 E
Tutova 15 Kc 46.06N 27.32 E
Tutrakan 15 Je 44.03N 26.37 E
Tuttle Creek Lake 45 Hg 39.22N 96.40W
Tuttlingen 10 Ei 47.59N 8.49 E
Tutuala 26 Ih 8.24S 127.15 E
Tutuila Island 57 Jf 14.18S 170.42W
Tutupaca, Volcán- 54 Dg 17.01S 70.22W
Tuupovaara 8 Nb 62.29N 30.36 E
Tuusniemi 7 Ge 62.49N 28.30 E
Tuvalu (Ellice Islands) [1] 58 Ie 8.00S 178.00 E
Tuvalu Islands 57 Ie 8.00S 178.00 E
Tuvana-i-Ra Island 61 Fd 21.00S 178.43W
Tuvana-i-Tholo Island 57 Ig 21.02S 178.49W
Tuvinskaja ASSR [3] 20 Ef 51.30N 94.00 E
Tuvutha 63d Cb 17.40S 178.48W
Tuwayq, Jabal- 21 Gg 25.30N 46.20 E
Tuxer Alpen 14 Fc 47.10N 11.45 E
Tuxford 12 Ba 53.13N 0.53W
Tuxpan 48 Hh 19.33N 103.24W
Tuxpán 47 Cd 21.57N 105.18W
Tuxpan, Arrecife- 48 Kg 21.02N 97.13W
Tuxpan, Rio- 48 Kg 20.53N 97.18W
Tuxpán de Rodríguez Cano 47 Ed 20.57N 97.24W
Tuxtla Gutiérrez 39 Jh 16.45N 93.07W
Túy 13 Db 42.03N 8.38W
Tuy, Río- 50 Dg 10.24N 65.59W
Tuy An 25 Lf 13.17N 109.16 E

Index Symbols

[1] Independent Nation
[2] State, Region
[3] District, County
[4] Municipality
[5] Colony, Dependency
Continent
Physical Region
Historical or Cultural Region
Mount, Mountain
Volcano
Hill
Mountains, Mountain Range
Hills, Escarpment
Plateau, Upland
Pass, Gap
Plain, Lowland
Delta
Salt Flat
Valley, Canyon
Crater, Cave
Karst Features
Depression
Polder
Desert, Dunes
Forest, Woods
Heath, Steppe
Oasis
Cape, Point
Coast, Beach
Cliff
Peninsula
Isthmus
Sandbank
Island
Atoll
Rock, Reef
Islands, Archipelago
Rocks, Reefs
Coral Reef
Well, Spring
Geyser
River, Stream
Waterfall Rapids
River Mouth, Estuary
Lake
Salt Lake
Intermittent Lake
Reservoir
Swamp, Pond
Canal
Glacier
Ice Shelf, Pack Ice
Ocean
Sea
Gulf, Bay
Strait, Fjord
Lagoon
Bank
Seamount
Tablemount
Ridge
Shelf
Basin
Escarpment, Sea Scarp
Fracture
Trench, Abyss
National Park, Reserve
Point of Interest
Recreation Site
Cave, Cavern
Historic Site
Ruins
Wall, Walls
Church, Abbey
Temple
Scientific Station
Airport
Port
Lighthouse
Mine
Tunnel
Dam, Bridge

Name	Page	Grid	Lat.	Long.
Tuy Hoa	25	Lf	13.05N	109.18 E
Tüyserkān	24	Me	34.33N	48.27 E
Tuz, Lake- (EN)=Tuz Gölü	21	Ff	38.45N	33.25 E
Tuz Gölü=Tuz, Lake- (EN)	21	Ff	38.45N	33.25 E
Tuzkan, Ozero-	18	Fd	40.35N	67.30 E
Tūz Khurmātū	23	Fc	34.53N	44.38 E
Tuzla	14	Mf	44.33N	18.41 E
Tuzlov	16	Lf	47.23N	40.08 E
Tuzluca	24	Jb	40.03N	43.39 E
Tuzly	15	Nd	45.56N	30.05 E
Tvååker	8	Eg	57.03N	12.24 E
Tvărdica	15	Ig	42.42N	25.54 E
Tvedestrand	7	Bg	58.37N	8.55 E
Tverca	7	Ih	56.52N	35.59 E
Tweed	9	Lf	55.46N	2.00W
Tweedsmuir Hills	9	Jf	55.30N	3.22W
Tweerivier	37	Be	25.35S	19.37 E
Twello, Voorst-	12	Ib	52.14N	6.07 E
Twente	11	Mb	52.17N	6.40 E
Twentekanaal	12	Ib	52.13N	6.53 E
Twilight Cove	59	Ff	32.20S	126.00 E
Twin Buttes Reservoir	45	Fk	31.20N	100.35W
Twin Falls	39	He	42.34N	114.28W
Twin Islands	42	Jf	53.50N	80.00W
Twin Peaks	46	Hd	44.35N	114.29W
Twisp	46	Eb	48.22N	120.07W
Twiste	12	Lc	51.29N	9.09 E
Twistringen	10	Ed	52.48N	8.39 E
Two Butte Creek	45	Eg	38.02N	102.08W
Two Harbors	45	Kc	47.01N	91.40W
Two Rivers	45	Md	44.09N	87.34W
Two Thumb Range	62	De	43.45S	170.40 E
Tychy	10	Of	50.09N	18.59 E
Tyczyn	10	Sg	49.58N	22.02 E
Tydal	7	Ce	63.04N	11.34 E
Tygda	20	Hf	53.07N	126.20 E
Tyin	8	Cc	61.15N	8.15 E
Tyin	8	Cc	61.14N	8.14 E
Tyler	43	He	32.21N	95.18W
Tylertown	45	Kk	31.07N	90.09W
Tylösand	8	Eh	56.39N	12.44 E
Tylöskog	8	Ff	58.40N	15.10 E
Tym	20	De	59.30N	80.07 E
Tymovskoje	20	Jf	50.50N	142.41 E
Tympákion	15	Hn	35.06N	24.45 E
Tynda	22	Od	53.07N	126.20 E
Tyne	9	Lf	55.01N	1.26W
Tyne and Wear [3]	9	Lg	55.00N	1.35W
Tynemouth	9	Lf	55.01N	1.24W
Týn nad Vltavou	10	Kg	49.14N	14.26 E
Tynset	7	Ce	62.17N	10.47 E
Tyra, Cayos-	49	Fg	12.50N	83.20W
Tyrifjorden	8	De	60.05N	10.10 E
Tyringe	8	Eh	56.10N	13.35 E
Tyrma	20	If	50.01N	132.10 E
Tyrnyauz	16	Mh	43.23N	42.56 E
Tyrol (EN)=Tirol [2]	14	Fc	47.10N	11.25 E
Tyrol (EN)=Tirol/Tirolo	14	Fd	47.00N	11.20 E
Tyrol (EN)=Tirolo/Tirol	14	Fd	47.00N	11.20 E
Tyrone	44	He	40.41N	78.15W
Tyrrell, Lake-	59	Ig	35.20S	142.50 E
Tyrrel Lake	42	Gd	63.05N	105.30W
Tyrrhenian Basin (EN)	5	Hh	40.00N	13.00 E
Tyrrhenian Sea (EN)=Tirreno, Mar-	5	Hh	40.00N	12.00 E
Tyrva/Tõrva	7	Fg	58.01N	25.59 E
Tyrvää	8	Jc	61.21N	22.53 E
Tysmenica	10	Uh	48.49N	24.56 E
Tyśmienica	10	Se	51.33N	22.30 E
Tysnesøy	7	Af	60.00N	5.35 E
Tysse	8	Ad	60.22N	5.45 E
Tyssedal	8	Bd	60.07N	6.34 E
Tystama/Tõstamaa	8	Jf	58.17N	23.52 E
Tystberga	8	Gf	58.52N	17.15 E
Tyszowce	10	Tf	50.36N	23.41 E
Tytuvėnai/Tituvenaj	8	Ji	55.33N	23.09 E
Tywyn	9	Ii	52.35N	4.05W
Tzanconeja, Río-	48	Ni	16.51N	91.47W
Tzaneen	37	Ed	23.50S	30.09 E
Tzintzuntzan	48	Ih	19.38N	101.34W
Tzucacab	48	Og	20.04N	89.05W
U				
Uaboe	64e	Ab	0.31S	166.54 E
Uacurizal, Ilha do-	55	Dc	16.25S	56.05W
Ua Huka, Ile-	57	Ne	8.54S	139.33W
Uanukuhahaki	65b	Ba	19.58S	174.29W
Ua Pou, Ile-	57	Me	9.23S	140.03W
Uaroo	59	Dd	23.00S	115.10 E
Uatumã, Rio-	52	Kf	2.26S	57.37W
Uaupés	53	Jf	0.08S	67.05W
Uaupés, Rio-	52	Je	0.02N	67.16W
Uaxactún	47	Ge	17.25N	89.29W
Ub	15	De	44.27N	20.05 E
Ubá	54	Jh	21.07S	42.56W
Übach-Palenberg [F.R.G.]	10	Cf	50.56N	6.05 E
Ubagan	19	Ge	54.23N	64.40 E
Ubaila	24	If	33.06N	40.15 E
Ubaitaba	54	Kf	14.18S	39.20W
Ubajay	55	Cj	31.47S	58.18W
Ubangi	30	Ii	0.30S	17.42 E
Ubatuba	55	Jf	23.26S	45.04W
Ubay	26	Hd	10.03N	124.28 E
Ubaye	11	Mj	44.28N	6.18 E
Ubayyiḍ, Wādī al-	24	Fc	32.34N	43.48 E
Ube	28	Kh	33.56N	131.15 E
Ubeda	13	If	38.01N	3.22W
Ubekendt Ejland	41	Gd	71.10N	53.45W
Uberaba	53	Lg	19.45S	47.55W
Uberaba, Lagoa-	55	Dc	17.30S	57.45W
Uberlândia	53	Lg	18.56S	48.18W
Überlingen	10	Fi	47.46N	9.10 E
Ubiaja	34	Gd	6.39N	6.23 E
Ubiña, Peña-	13	Ga	43.01N	5.57W
Ubiratã	55	Fg	24.32S	52.56W
Ubon Ratchathani	22	Mh	15.15N	104.54 E
Ubort	16	Fc	52.06N	28.30 E
Ubrique	13	Gh	36.41N	5.27W
Ubsu-Nur (Uvs nuur)	21	Ld	50.20N	92.45 E
Ubundu	31	Ji	0.21S	25.29 E
Učaly	19	Fe	54.20N	59.31 E
Učami	20	Ed	63.50N	96.39 E
Učaral	19	If	46.08N	80.52 E
Ucayali, Río-	52	If	4.30S	73.30W
Uccle/Ukkel	12	Gd	50.48N	4.19 E
Üçdoruk Tepe	24	Ib	40.45N	41.05 E
Ucero	13	Ic	41.31N	3.04W
Uchiko	29	Ce	33.34N	132.38 E
Uchi Lake	45	Ja	51.05N	92.35W
Uchinomi	29	Dd	34.30N	134.19 E
Uchinoura	29	Bf	31.16N	131.05 E
Uchiura-Wan	28	Pc	42.18N	140.35 E
Uchte	12	Ed	52.30N	8.55 E
Učka	14	Ie	45.17N	14.12 E
Uckange	12	Ie	49.18N	6.09 E
Uckermark	10	Jc	53.10N	13.35 E
Uckfield	12	Cd	50.58N	0.06 E
Učkuduk	19	Gg	42.10N	63.30 E
Učkurgan	18	Id	41.01N	72.04 E
Ucrainskaja Sovetskaja Socialističeskaja Respublika [2]	19	Df	49.00N	32.00 E
Ucross	46	Ld	44.33N	106.31W
Ucua	36	Bd	8.40S	14.12 E
Učur	21	Pd	58.48N	130.35 E
Uda [R.S.F.S.R.]	21	Pd	54.42N	135.14 E
Uda [R.S.F.S.R.]	20	Ff	51.45N	107.25 E
Uda [R.S.F.S.R.]	20	Ee	56.05N	99.34 E
Udačny	22	Gc	66.25N	112.20 E
Udaipur	22	Jg	24.35N	73.41 E
Udaj	16	Hd	50.05N	33.07 E
Udaquiola	55	Cm	36.34S	58.31W
Udbina	14	Jf	44.32N	15.46 E
Uddevalla	7	Cg	58.21N	11.55 E
Uddjaure	5	Hb	65.58N	17.50 E
Uden	12	Hc	51.40N	5.37 E
Udgīr	25	Fe	18.23N	77.07 E
Udhampur	25	Fb	32.56N	75.08 E
Udimski	7	Kf	61.09N	45.52 E
Udine	14	Hd	46.03N	13.14 E
Udipi	25	Ef	13.21N	74.45 E
Udmurtskaja ASSR [3]	19	Fd	57.20N	52.50 E
Udoha	8	Mg	57.58N	29.50 E
Udomlja	7	Ih	57.56N	35.02 E
Udone-Jima	29	Fd	34.28N	139.17 E
Udon Thani	25	Ke	17.25N	102.48 E
Udot	64d	Bb	7.23N	151.43 E
Udskaja Guba	21	Pd	55.00N	136.00 E
Udskoje	20	If	54.36N	134.30 E
Udy	16	Je	49.47N	36.35 E
Udžary	16	Oi	40.31N	47.40 E
Udzungwa Range	36	Gd	8.05S	35.50 E
Uebonti	26	Hg	0.55S	121.38 E
Uecker	10	Kc	53.45N	14.04 E
Ueckermünde	10	Kc	53.44N	14.03 E
Ueda	27	Od	36.24N	138.16 E
Uele	30	Jh	4.09N	22.26 E
Uelen	20	Oc	66.13N	169.48W
Uelzen	10	Gd	52.58N	10.34 E
Ueno	29	Ed	34.46N	136.06 E
Uere	30	Jh	3.42N	25.24 E
Ufa	5	Le	54.40N	56.00 E
Ufa	6	Le	54.44N	55.56 E
Uftjuga	7	Lf	61.28N	46.12 E
Ugab	30	Ik	21.12S	13.38 E
Ugale/Ugāle	8	Ig	57.19N	21.52 E
Ugāle/Ugale	8	Ig	57.19N	21.52 E
Ugalla	36	Fd	5.08S	30.42 E
Uganda [1]	31	Kh	1.00N	32.00 E
Ugărčin	15	Hf	43.06N	24.25 E
Ugashik	40	He	57.32N	157.25W
Ughelli	34	Gd	5.30N	5.59 E
Ugijar	13	Ih	36.57N	3.03W
Uglegorsk	20	Jg	49.05N	142.06 E
Uglekamensk	20	Ih	43.18N	133.08 E
Ugleuralski	17	Hg	58.59N	57.38 E
Uglič	19	Dd	57.33N	38.23 E
Ugljan	14	Jf	44.05N	15.10 E
Uglovoje	28	Lc	43.20N	132.06 E
Ugnev	10	Tf	50.20N	23.45 E
Ugo	29	Gb	39.13N	140.23 E
Ugolnyje Kopi	20	Md	64.42N	177.50 E
Ugoma	36	Ec	4.55S	26.50 E
Ugra	19	De	54.30N	36.07 E
Ugtal-Cajdam	27	Ib	48.25N	105.30 E
Uh	10	Rh	48.33N	22.00 E
Uherské Hradiště	10	Ng	49.04N	17.27 E
Úhlava	10	Jg	49.45N	13.23 E
Uhlenhorst	37	Bd	23.45S	17.55 E
Uhta	6	Lc	63.33N	53.40 E
Uibh Fhaili/Offaly [2]	9	Fh	53.20N	7.30W
Uig	9	Gd	57.30N	6.20W
Uige	31	Ii	7.35S	15.04 E
Uige [3]	36	Cd	7.00S	15.30 E
'Uiha	65b	Ba	19.54S	174.25W
Uijec	64d	Bb	7.10N	151.57 E
Üijŏngbu	28	If	37.44N	127.02 E
Uiju	28	Hd	40.12N	124.32 E
Uil	17	Ff	48.36N	52.30 E
Uil	19	Ff	49.04N	54.42 E
Uilpata, Gora-	16	Mh	42.47N	43.44 E
Uinta Mountains	43	Ec	40.45N	110.05W
Uinta River	46	Kf	40.14N	109.51W
Uis	37	Ad	21.08S	14.49 E
Üisŏng	28	Jf	36.21N	128.42 E
Uitenhage	31	Jl	33.40S	25.28 E
Uithoorn	12	Gb	52.14N	4.52 E
Uithuizen	12	Ia	53.25N	6.42 E
Uithuizerwaad	12	Ia	53.30N	6.40 E
Ujae Atoll	57	Hd	9.05N	165.40 E
Ūjān	24	Og	30.45N	52.05 E
Ujandina	20	Jc	68.23N	145.50 E
Ujar	20	Ee	55.48N	94.20 E
Ujarrás	49	Fi	9.50N	83.40W
Ujedinenija, Ostrov-	20	Da	77.30N	82.30 E
Ujelang Atoll	57	Hd	9.49N	160.55 E
Újfehértó	10	Ri	47.48N	21.41 E
Uji	29	Dd	34.53N	135.47 E
Uji	19	Ge	54.20N	63.58 E
Uji-Guntō	28	Ji	31.10N	129.28 E
Ujiie	29	Fc	36.41N	139.57 E
Ujiji	31	Ji	4.55S	29.41 E
Ujjain	22	Jg	23.11N	75.46 E
Ujunglamuru	26	Gg	4.40S	119.58 E
Ujung Pandang (Makasar)	22	Nj	5.07S	119.24 E
Uk	20	Ee	55.04N	98.52 E
Ukata	34	Gc	10.50N	5.50 E
Ukeng, Bukit-	26	Gf	1.45N	115.08 E
Ukerewe Island	36	Fc	2.03S	33.00 E
Uke-Shima	29b	Ba	28.02N	129.15 E
Ukhayḍir	24	Jf	32.26N	43.36 E
Ukiah [Ca.-U.S.]	43	Cd	39.09N	123.13W
Ukiah [Or.-U.S.]	46	Fd	45.08N	118.56W
Uki Ni Masi	63a	Ed	10.15S	161.44 E
Ukkel/Uccle	12	Gd	50.48N	4.19 E
Ukmerge/Ukmergė	7	Fi	55.14N	24.47 E
Ukmergė/Ukmerge	7	Fi	55.14N	24.47 E
Ukraine (EN)	5	Jf	49.00N	32.00 E
Ukrainian SSR (EN)=Ukrainskaja SSR [2]	19	Df	49.00N	32.00 E
Ukrainskaja SSR/Ukrainska Radyanska Socialistična Respublika [2]	19	Df	49.00N	32.00 E
Ukrainskaja SSR=Ukrainian SSR (EN) [2]	19	Df	49.00N	32.00 E
Ukrainska Radyanska Socialistična Respublika/Ukrainskaja SSR [2]	19	Df	49.00N	32.00 E
Ukrina	14	Le	45.05N	17.56 E
Uku-Jima	29	Ae	33.16N	129.07 E
Ula	24	Cd	37.05N	28.26 E
Ulah Lake	45	Hh	36.58N	96.10W
Ulaidh/Ulster	9	Gg	54.30N	7.00W
Ulalu	64d	Bb	7.25N	151.40 E
Ulan (Xiligou)	27	Gd	36.55N	98.16 E
Ulan → Otog Qi	27	Id	39.07N	108.00 E
Ulanbaatar → Ulan-Bator	22	Me	47.55N	106.53 E
Ulan-Badrah	28	Ac	43.58N	110.37 E
Ulan-Bator (Ulaanbaatar)	22	Me	47.55N	106.53 E
Ulanbel	19	Hg	44.49N	71.10 E
Ulan-Burgasy, Hrebet-	20	Ff	52.30N	108.30 E
Ulangom	22	Le	49.58N	92.02 E
Ulanhad/Chifeng	27	Kc	42.16N	118.57 E
Ulan Hol	19	Ef	45.27N	46.46 E
Ulan Hot/Horqin Youyi Qianqi	22	Oe	46.04N	122.00 E
Ulan Hua → Siziwang Qi	28	Ad	41.31N	111.41 E
Ulan-Hus	27	Eb	49.02N	89.23 E
Ulanów	10	Sf	50.30N	22.16 E
Ulansuhai Nur	27	Ic	40.56N	108.49 E
Ulan-Tajga	27	Ga	50.45N	98.30 E
Ulan-Ude	22	Md	51.50N	107.37 E
Ulan Ul Hu	27	Fe	34.45N	90.25 E
Ulas	24	Gc	39.27N	37.03 E
Ulawa Island	60	Gi	9.46S	161.57 E
Ulbeja	20	Je	59.20N	144.25 E
Ulchin	28	Jf	36.59N	129.24 E
Ulcinj	15	Ch	41.56N	19.13 E
Uleåborg/Oulu	6	Ib	65.01N	25.30 E
Ulefoss	7	Bg	59.17N	9.16 E
Ulegej	22	Ke	48.56N	89.57 E
Ulety	20	Gf	51.22N	112.30 E
Uleza	15	Ch	41.40N	19.53 E
Ulfborg	8	Ch	56.16N	8.20 E
Ulflingen/Troisvierges	12	Hd	50.07N	6.00 E
Ulft, Gendringen-	12	Ic	51.54N	6.24 E
Ulgain Gol	27	Kb	45.31N	117.50 E
Ulhāsnagar	25	Ee	19.10N	73.07 E
Uliastai → Dong Ujimqin Qi	27	Kc	45.31N	116.58 E
Uliga	58	Id	7.09N	171.13 E
Ulindi	30	Ji	1.40S	25.52 E
Ulithi Atoll	57	Ed	9.58N	139.40 E
Ulja	20	Je	58.48N	141.40 E
Uljanovka [R.S.F.S.R.]	8	Ne	59.37N	30.55 E
Uljanovka [Ukr.-U.S.S.R.]	16	Ge	48.20N	30.13 E
Uljanovsk	6	Ke	54.20N	48.24 E
Uljanovskaja Oblast [3]	19	Ee	54.00N	48.00 E
Uljanovski	19	He	50.05N	73.45 E
Uljasutaj	22	Le	47.45N	96.49 E
Ulkan	20	Fe	55.55N	107.55 E
Ulla	13	Db	42.39N	8.44W
Ullapool	9	Hd	57.54N	5.10W
Ullared	7	Ch	57.08N	12.43 E
Ulldecona	13	Md	40.36N	0.27 E
Ullsfjorden	7	Eb	69.58N	20.00 E
Ullswater	9	Kg	54.34N	2.54W
Ullŭng-Do	28	Kf	37.29N	130.52 E
Ullvettern	8	Fe	59.25N	14.15 E
Ulm	10	Fh	48.25N	10.00 E
Ulmen	12	Id	50.13N	6.59 E
Ulmeni	15	Jd	45.04N	26.39 E
Ulmu	15	Je	44.16N	26.55 E
Ulongwé	37	Eb	14.43S	34.21 E
Ulricehamn	7	Ch	57.47N	13.25 E
Ulrichstein	12	Ld	50.35N	9.12 E
Ulrum	12	Ia	53.22N	6.20 E
Ulrum-Zoutkamp	12	Ia	53.20N	6.18 E
Ulsan	27	Md	35.33N	129.19 E
Ulsteinvik	7	Ae	62.20N	5.53 E
Ulster	10	Ff	50.51N	9.59 E
Ulster/Ulaidh	9	Gg	54.30N	7.00W
Ulster Canal	9	Gg	54.27N	6.40W
Ulu	35	Ec	10.43N	33.29 E
Ulu/Uulu	8	Kf	58.13N	24.29 E
Ulúa, Río-	47	Ge	15.56N	87.43W
Ulubat Gölü	24	Cb	40.10N	28.35 E
Ulubey	24	Cc	38.09N	29.33 E
Uludağ	23	Ca	40.04N	29.13 E
Uludere	24	Jd	37.27N	42.51 E
Ulugqat/Wuqia	27	Cd	39.40N	75.07 E
Ulukışla	24	Fd	37.33N	34.30 E
Ulungur He	21	Ke	46.58N	87.28 E
Ulungur Hu	27	Eb	47.20N	87.10 E
Ulus	24	Eb	41.35N	32.39 E
Ulus Dağ	15	Lj	39.18N	28.24 E
Ulva	9	Ge	56.28N	6.12W
Ulverston	9	Jg	54.12N	3.06W
Ulverstone	59	Jh	41.09S	146.10 E
Ulvik	8	Bd	60.34N	6.54 E
Ulvön	8	Ha	63.05N	18.40 E
Ulysses	45	Fh	37.35N	101.22W
Ulytau	19	Gf	48.35N	67.05 E
Ulytau, Gora-	19	Gf	48.45N	67.00 E
Uly-Žilanšik	19	Gf	48.51N	63.47 E
Uma	27	La	52.36N	120.38 E
Umag	14	He	45.25N	13.32 E
Umala	54	Eg	17.24S	67.58W
Umán	48	Og	20.53N	89.45W
Uman	64d	Bb	7.18N	151.53 E
Uman	19	Df	48.47N	30.09 E
'Umān	21	Hg	22.10N	58.00 E
'Umān=Oman (EN) [1]	22	Hg	21.00N	57.00 E
'Umān, Khalīj-=Oman, Gulf of- (EN)	21	Hg	25.00N	58.00 E
Umanak	41	Gd	70.36N	52.15W
Ūmánarssuaq/Farvel, Kap-	67	Nb	59.50N	43.50W
Umatac	64c	Bb	13.18N	144.40 E
Umba	19	Db	66.41N	34.17 E
Umbelasha	35	Cd	9.51N	24.50 E
Umbertide	14	Gg	43.18N	12.20 E
Umberto de Campos	54	Jd	2.37S	43.27W
Umboi Island	57	Fe	5.36S	148.00 E
Umbozero, Ozero-	7	Ic	67.45N	34.20 E
Umbria [2]	14	Gh	43.00N	12.30 E
Ume	37	Dc	17.15S	28.20 E
Umeå	6	Ic	63.50N	20.15 E
Umeälven	5	Ic	63.47N	20.16 E
Umm al Arānib	33	Bd	26.08N	14.45 E
Umm al Hayf, Wādī-	23	Hf	18.37N	53.59 E
Umm al Jamaājim	24	Ki	26.59N	45.19 E
Umm al Qaywayn	23	Id	25.35N	55.34 E
Ummanz	10	Jb	54.30N	13.10 E
Umm ar Rizam	33	Dc	32.32N	23.00 E
Umm as Samīm	23	Ie	21.30N	56.45 E
Umm Bāb	24	Nj	25.12N	50.48 E
Umm Bel	35	Dc	13.32N	28.04 E
Umm Buru	35	Cb	15.01N	23.36 E
Umm Dhibbān	35	Dc	14.14N	29.37 E
Umm Durmān=Omdurman (EN)	31	Kg	15.38N	32.30 E
Umm Inderaba	35	Eb	15.12N	31.54 E
Umm Kaddādah	35	Dc	13.36N	26.42 E
Umm Lajj	23	Ed	25.04N	37.13 E
Umm Naqqāṭ, Jabal-	24	Fj	25.30N	34.14 E
Umm Qam'ul	24	Pj	24.47N	54.42 E
Umm Ruwābah	31	Kg	12.54N	31.13 E
Umm Sayyālah	35	Ec	14.25N	31.00 E
Umm Urūmah	24	Gj	25.46N	36.33 E
Umnak	38	Cd	58.25N	168.10W
Umne-Gobi	27	Fb	49.06N	91.43 E
Umpqua River	46	Ce	43.42N	124.03W
Umpulu	36	Ce	12.42S	17.40 E
Umsini, Gunung-	26	Jg	1.35S	133.30 E
Umtata	31	Jl	31.35S	28.47 E
Umuarama	56	Jb	23.45S	53.20W
Umurbey	15	Ji	40.14N	26.36 E
Umvukwes	37	Ec	17.01S	30.52 E
Umvuma	37	Ec	19.19S	30.35 E
Umzingwani	37	Dd	22.12S	29.56 E
Una	14	Ke	45.16N	16.55 E
Unabetsu-Dake	29a	Db	43.52N	144.51 E
Unac	14	Kf	44.29N	16.08 E
Unaí	54	Ig	16.23S	46.53W
Unalakleet	40	Gd	63.53N	160.47W
Unalaska	38	Cd	53.45N	166.45W
Unare, Río-	50	Dg	10.06N	65.12W
Unauna, Pulau-	26	Hg	0.10S	121.35 E
'Unayzah [Jor.]	24	Fg	30.29N	35.48 E
'Unayzah [Sau. Ar.]	22	Gg	26.06N	43.56 E
Uncia	54	Eg	18.27S	66.37W
Uncompahgre Peak	43	Fd	38.04N	107.28W
Uncompahgre Plateau	45	Bg	38.30N	108.25W
Unden	8	Ff	58.45N	14.25 E
Underberg	37	De	29.50S	29.22 E
Under-Han	22	Ne	47.19N	110.39 E
Undjuljung	20	Hc	66.20N	124.40 E
Undu Point	63d	Cb	16.08S	179.57W
Undva Neem/Kiprarenukk, Mys-	8	If	58.25N	21.45 E
Uneča	16	Hc	52.50N	32.44 E
'Ung, Jabal al-	14	Dn	36.45N	9.35 E
Unga	40	Ge	55.15N	160.45W
Ungava, Péninsule d'-=Ungava Peninsula (EN)	38	Lc	60.00N	74.00W
Ungava Bay	38	Md	59.30N	67.30W
Ungava Peninsula (EN)=Ungava, Péninsule d'-	38	Lc	60.00N	74.00W
Ungeny	16	Ef	47.13N	27.50 E
Unggi	28	Kc	42.21N	130.23 E
Ungureni	15	Jb	47.53N	26.47 E
Ungwatiri	35	Fb	16.55N	36.05 E
União	54	Jd	4.35S	42.52W
União da Vitória	56	Jc	26.13S	51.05W
União dos Palmares	54	Ke	9.10S	36.02W
Uničov	10	Ng	49.49N	17.07 E
Uniejów	10	Oe	51.58N	18.49 E
Unije	14	If	44.38N	14.15 E
Unimak	38	Cd	54.50N	164.00W
Unimak Pass	40	Gf	54.35N	164.43W
Unini, Rio-	54	Fd	1.41S	61.30W
Union [Mo.-U.S.]	45	Kg	38.27N	91.00W
Union [S.C.-U.S.]	44	Gh	34.43N	81.37W
Union City	44	Cg	36.26N	89.03W
Uniondale	37	Cf	33.40S	23.08 E
Unión de Reyes	49	Gb	22.48N	81.32W
Unión de Tula	48	Gh	19.58N	104.16W
Union Island	50	Ff	12.36N	61.26W
Union Islands/Tokelau	57	Je	9.00S	171.45W
Union of Soviet Socialist Republics (USSR) (EN)=SSSR [1]	22	Jd	60.00N	80.00 E
Union Seamount (EN)	42	Eg	49.35N	132.45W
Union Springs	44	Ei	32.09N	85.49W
Uniontown	44	Hf	39.54N	79.44W
Unionville	45	Jf	40.29N	93.01W
United Arab Emirates (EN)=Al Imārāt al 'Arabīyah al Muttaḥidah [1]	22	Hg	24.00N	54.00 E
United Arab Republic (EN) → Egypt (EN) [1]	31	Jf	27.00N	30.00 E
United Kingdom [1]	6	Fe	54.00N	2.00W
United Kingdom of Great Britain and Northern Ireland [1]	6	Fe	54.00N	2.00W
United States [1]	39	Jf	38.00N	97.00W
United States of America [1]	39	Jf	38.00N	97.00W
Unity [Or.-U.S.]	46	Fd	44.29N	118.13W
Unity [Sask.-Can.]	42	Gf	52.27N	109.10W
Universales, Montes-	13	Kd	40.18N	1.33W
University City	45	Kg	38.39N	90.19W
Unna	10	De	51.32N	7.41 E
Unnāb, Wādī al-	24	Gg	30.11N	36.39 E
Unnukka	8	Lb	62.25N	27.55 E
Unst	5	Fc	60.45N	0.55W
Unstrut	10	He	51.10N	11.48 E
Unterfranken	10	Fg	50.00N	10.00 E
Unterwalden-Nidwalden [2]	14	Cd	46.55N	8.30 E
Unterwalden-Obwalden [2]	14	Cd	46.50N	8.20 E
Unuli Horog	27	Fd	35.12N	91.58 E
Ünye	23	Ea	41.08N	37.17 E
Unža	5	Kd	57.20N	43.08 E
Unzen-Dake	29	Be	32.45N	130.17 E
Uoleva	65b	Ba	19.51S	174.24W
Uozu	28	Nf	36.48N	137.24 E
Úpa	10	Lf	50.22N	15.54 E
Upata	54	Fb	8.01N	62.24W
Upemba, Lac-	36	Ed	8.36S	26.26 E
Upernavik	41	Gd	72.20N	56.00W
Upin	26	Ig	2.56S	129.11 E
Upington	31	Jk	28.25S	21.15 E
Upland	12	Kc	51.18N	8.42 E
Upolu Island	57	Jf	13.55S	171.45W
Upolu Point	60	Oc	20.16N	155.52W
Upper [3]	34	Ec	10.30N	1.30W
Upper Arlington	44	Fe	40.01N	83.03W
Upper Arrow Lake	46	Ga	50.30N	117.55W
Upper Austria (EN)=Oberösterreich [2]	14	Hb	48.15N	14.00 E
Upper Hutt	62	Fd	41.07S	175.04 E
Upper Klamath Lake	43	Cc	42.23N	122.00W
Upper Lake	46	Ef	41.44N	120.08W
Upper Lough Erne/Loch Éirne Uachtair	9	Fg	54.20N	7.30W
Upper Red Lake	45	Ib	48.10N	94.40W
Upper Sandusky	44	Fe	40.48N	83.17W
Upper Sheik	35	Hd	9.57N	45.09 E
Upper Thames Valley	9	Lj	51.40N	1.40W
Upper Trajan's Wall (EN)=Verhni Traijanov Val	15	Lc	46.40N	29.00 E
Upper Volta→Burkina Faso [1]	31	Gg	13.00N	2.00W
Uppingham	12	Bb	52.35N	0.43W
Uppland	8	Gd	60.00N	17.50 E
Upplands Väsby	8	Ge	59.31N	17.54 E
Uppsala [2]	7	Df	60.00N	17.45 E
Uppsala	6	Hd	59.52N	17.38 E
Upsala	45	Kb	49.02N	90.29W
Upshi	25	Fb	33.50N	77.49 E
Upton	46	Md	44.06N	104.38W
Uqbān	33	Hf	15.30N	42.23 E
'Uqlat aş Şuqūr	24	Jj	25.53N	42.15 E
Uqturpan/Wushi	27	Cc	41.10N	79.16 E
Ur	23	Gc	30.58N	46.06 E
Urabá, Golfo de-	54	Cb	8.25N	77.00W
Uracoa	50	Eh	9.00N	62.21W
Uracoa, Rio-	50	Eh	9.08N	62.20W
Uradarja	18	Fe	38.51N	66.02 E
Urad Qianqi	27	Ic	40.49N	108.37 E
Urad Zhonghou Lianheqi (Haliut)	27	Ic	41.34N	108.32 E
Uraga-Suido	29	Fd	35.15N	139.45 E
Ura-Guba	7	Hb	69.18N	32.48 E
Urahoro	29a	Cb	42.48N	143.38 E
Urahoro-Gawa	29a	Cb	42.44N	143.40 E
Uraj	19	Gc	60.08N	64.40 E
Urakawa	28	Qc	42.09N	142.47 E
Ural	5	Lf	47.00N	51.48 E
Ural Mountains (EN)=Uralskije Gory	5	Ld	57.00N	60.00 E
Uralsk	6	Le	51.14N	51.22 E
Uralskaja Oblast [3]	19	Ff	49.45N	51.00 E
Uralskije Gory=Ural Mountains (EN)	5	Ld	57.00N	60.00 E
Urambo	36	Fd	5.04S	32.03 E
Uranium City	39	Id	59.34N	108.36W
Uraricoera	54	Fc	3.27N	60.59W
Uraricoera, Rio-	52	Je	3.02N	60.30W
Ura-Tjube	19	Gh	39.53N	69.01 E
Urawa	28	Og	35.51N	139.39 E
'Uray'irah	24	Mj	25.57N	48.53 E
Urayq, Nafūd al-	24	Jj	25.17N	42.25 E
Urbana [Il.-U.S.]	45	Lf	40.07N	88.12W
Urbana [Oh.-U.S.]	44	Fe	40.06N	83.45W
Urbandale	45	Jf	41.38N	93.48W
Urbania	14	Gg	43.40N	12.31 E

Index Symbols

[1] Independent Nation
[2] State, Region
[3] District, County
[4] Municipality
[5] Colony, Dependency
Continent
Physical Region
Historical or Cultural Region
Mount, Mountain
Volcano
Hill
Mountains, Mountain Range
Hills, Escarpment
Plateau, Upland
Pass, Gap
Plain, Lowland
Delta
Salt Flat
Valley, Canyon
Crater, Cave
Karst Features
Depression
Polder
Desert, Dunes
Forest, Woods
Heath, Steppe
Oasis
Cape, Point
Coast, Beach
Cliff
Peninsula
Isthmus
Sandbank
Island
Atoll
Rock, Reef
Islands, Archipelago
Rocks, Reefs
Coral Reef
Well, Spring
Geyser
River, Stream
Waterfall Rapids
River Mouth, Estuary
Lake
Salt Lake
Intermittent Lake
Reservoir
Swamp, Pond
Canal
Glacier
Ice Shelf, Pack Ice
Ocean
Sea
Gulf, Bay
Strait, Fjord
Lagoon
Bank
Seamount
Tablemount
Ridge
Shelf
Basin
Escarpment, Sea Scarp
Fracture
Trench, Abyss
National Park, Reserve
Point of Interest
Recreation Site
Cave, Cavern
Historic Site
Ruins
Wall, Walls
Church, Abbey
Temple
Scientific Station
Airport
Port
Lighthouse
Mine
Tunnel
Dam, Bridge

Index Symbols

[1] Independent Nation	◫ Historical or Cultural Region	⌂ Pass, Gap	▭ Depression	⊞ Coast, Beach
[2] State, Region	▲ Mount, Mountain	▭ Plain, Lowland	▭ Polder	▭ Cliff
[3] District, County	▲ Volcano	▭ Delta	▭ Desert, Dunes	▭ Peninsula
[4] Municipality	▲ Hill	▭ Salt Flat	▭ Forest, Woods	▭ Isthmus
[5] Colony, Dependency	▲ Mountains, Mountain Range	～ Valley, Canyon	▭ Heath, Steppe	▭ Sandbank
■ Continent	▬ Hills, Escarpment	▭ Crater, Cave	▭ Oasis	▭ Island
◫ Physical Region	▭ Plateau, Upland	⌘ Karst Features	▸ Cape, Point	⊙ Atoll

◨ Rock, Reef	～ Waterfall Rapids	⊞ Canal	▭ Lagoon	▬ Escarpment, Sea Scarp
⊞ Islands, Archipelago	◨ River Mouth, Estuary	▭ Glacier	▭ Bank	▭ Fracture
◨ Rocks, Reefs	▣ Lake	▭ Ice Shelf, Pack Ice	▭ Seamount	▭ Trench, Abyss
◨ Coral Reef	▣ Salt Lake	▭ Ocean	▭ Tableland	▭ National Park, Reserve
▭ Well, Spring	▣ Intermittent Lake	▭ Sea	▭ Ridge	▭ Point of Interest
▭ Geyser	▣ Reservoir	◨ Gulf, Bay	▭ Shelf	▭ Recreation Site
～ River, Stream	▣ Swamp, Pond	◨ Strait, Fjord	▭ Basin	▭ Cave, Cavern

⌂ Historic Site	⌂ Port
⌂ Ruins	⌂ Lighthouse
⌂ Wall, Walls	⌂ Mine
⌂ Church, Abbey	⌂ Tunnel
⌂ Temple	⌂ Dam, Bridge
⊠ Scientific Station	
⌂ Airport	

Vang 8 Cc 61.08N 8.35 E
Vangaindrano 37 Hd 23.23S 47.33 E
Van Gölü = Van, Lake- (EN) 21 Gf 38.33N 42.46 E
Vangunu Island 57 Ge 8.40S 158.05 E
Van Horn 43 Ge 31.03N 104.50W
Vanick, Rio- 55 Fa 13.06S 52.52W
Vanier 42 Ha 76.00N 103.50W
Vanikolo 63c Bb 11.37S 166.58 E
Vanikolo Islands 57 Hf 11.37S 167.03 E
Vanimo 60 Ch 2.40S 141.18 E
Vanino 20 Jg 49.11N 140.19 E
Vankavesi 8 Jc 61.50N 23.50 E
Vanna 7 Ea 70.09N 19.51 E
Vännäs 7 Ee 63.55N 19.45 E
Vanne 11 Jf 48.12N 3.16 E
Vannes 11 Dg 47.40N 2.45W
Van Ninh 25 Lf 12.42N 109.14 E
Vannsjø 8 De 59.25N 10.50 E
Vanoise, Massif de la- 11 Mi 45.20N 6.40 E
Vanona Lava, Ile- 57 Hf 14.00S 167.30 E
Van Phong, Vung- 25 Lf 12.33N 109.18 E
Van Rees, Pegunungan- 26 Kg 2.35S 138.15 E
Vanrhynsdorp 37 Bf 31.36S 18.44 E
Vansbro 7 Df 60.31N 14.13 E
Vanse 8 Bf 58.07N 6.42 E
Vansittart 42 Jc 65.50N 84.00W
Vantaa 8 Kd 60.13N 24.59 E
Vänte Litets grund 8 Hb 62.35N 18.12 E
Vanua Levu 57 If 17.28S 177.03 E
Vanua Mbalavu 61 Fc 17.14S 178.57W
Vanuatu [1] 58 Hf 16.00S 167.00 E
Vanua Vatu 63d Cc 18.22S 179.16W
Van Wert 44 Ee 40.53N 84.36W
Van Wyksvlei 37 Cf 30.18S 21.49 E
Vanzylsrus 37 Ce 26.52S 22.04 E
Vao 63b Cf 22.40S 167.29 E
Vao, Nosy- 37 Gc 17.30S 43.45 E
Vão das Almas 55 Ia 13.42S 47.27W
Vapnjarka 16 Fe 48.32N 28.46 E
Var [3] 11 Mk 43.30N 6.20 E
Var 11 Nk 43.39N 7.12 E
Vara 14 Df 44.09N 9.53 E
Vara 8 Ef 58.16N 12.57 E
Varaita 14 Bf 44.49N 7.36 E
Varakļāni/Varakljany 7 Gh 56.36N 26.48 E
Varakljany/Varakļāni 7 Gh 56.36N 26.48 E
Varaldsøy 8 Ad 60.10N 6.00 E
Varalé 34 Ed 9.40N 3.17W
Varallo 14 Ce 45.49N 8.15 E
Varāmīn 24 Ne 35.20N 51.39 E
Vārānasi (Benares) 22 Kg 25.20N 83.00 E
Varangerfjorden 5 Ia 70.00N 30.00 E
Varangerhalvøya = Varanger Peninsula (EN) 5 Ia 70.25N 29.30 E
Varanger Peninsula (EN) = Varangerhalvøya 5 Ia 70.25N 29.30 E
Varano, Lago di- 14 Ji 41.53N 15.45 E
Varāvī 24 Oi 27.25N 53.06 E
Varaždin 14 Kd 46.18N 16.20 E
Varazze 14 Cf 44.22N 8.34 E
Varberg 7 Ch 57.06N 12.15 E
Vardak [3] 23 Kc 34.15N 68.00 E
Vardar 5 Ig 40.35N 22.50 E
Varde 7 Bi 55.38N 8.29 E
Varde Å 8 Ci 55.35N 8.20 E
Vardhoúsia Óri 15 Fk 38.40N 22.10 E
Vårdö 8 Id 60.15N 20.20 E
Vardø 7 Ha 70.22N 31.06 E
Varel 10 Ec 53.24N 8.08 E
Varėna/Varena 7 Fi 54.15N 24.39 E
Varena/Varėna 7 Fi 54.15N 24.39 E
Värend 8 Fh 56.45N 14.55 E
Varengeville-sur-Mer 12 Ce 49.55N 0.59 E
Varenikovskaja 16 Jg 45.06N 37.37 E
Varenne 11 Ff 48.24N 0.39W
Varennes-en-Argonne 12 He 49.14N 5.02 E
Varennes-sur-Allier 11 Jh 46.19N 3.24 E
Vareš 14 Mf 44.10N 18.20 E
Varese 14 Ce 45.48N 8.50 E
Varese, Lago di- 14 Ce 45.50N 8.45 E
Vårgårda 8 Ef 58.02N 12.48 E
Vargaši 19 Gd 55.23N 65.48 E
Vargem Grande 54 Jd 3.33S 43.56W
Varginha 54 Ih 21.33S 45.26W
Vargön 8 Ef 58.21N 12.22 E
Varhaug 8 Af 58.37N 5.39 E
Varjão 55 Hc 17.03S 49.37W
Varkaus 6 Ic 62.19N 27.55 E
Värmdö 8 He 59.20N 18.35 E
Värmeln 8 Ee 59.30N 12.55 E
Värmland 8 Ee 59.50N 13.05 E
Värmland [2] 7 Cg 59.45N 13.15 E
Värmlandsnäs 8 Ee 59.00N 13.10 E
Varna [2] 15 Kf 43.10N 27.35 E
Varna [Bul.] 6 Ig 43.13N 27.55 E
Varna [R.S.F.S.R.] 17 Jj 53.24N 60.58 E
Värnamo 7 Dh 57.11N 14.02 E
Varnenski Zaliv 15 Kf 43.11N 27.56 E
Varniai/Varnjaj 8 Ji 55.44N 22.17 E
Varnjaj/Varniai 8 Ji 55.44N 22.17 E
Varnsdorf 10 Kf 50.54N 14.38 E
Várpalota 10 Oi 47.12N 18.08 E
Varšec 15 Gf 43.12N 23.17 E
Varsinais-Suomi/Egentliga Finland 8 Jd 60.40N 22.30 E
Värska 8 Lg 57.58N 27.38 E
Vartašen 16 Oi 41.05N 47.29 E
Varto 24 Ic 39.10N 41.28 E
Vartofta 8 Ef 58.06N 13.38 E
Värtsilä 8 Nb 62.15N 30.40 E
Varzaneh 24 Of 32.25N 52.39 E
Varzaqān 24 Lc 38.31N 46.39 E
Varzarīn, Kūh-e- 24 Gc 33.24N 46.48 E
Várzea, Rio da- 55 Fh 27.13S 53.19W
Várzea da Palma 55 Jc 17.36S 44.44W
Varzea Grande 54 Gg 15.39S 56.08W
Varzelândia 55 Jb 15.42S 44.02W
Varzi 14 Df 44.49N 9.12 E
Varzuga 7 Ic 66.17N 36.50 E
Varzy 11 Jg 47.22N 3.23 E
Vas [2] 10 Mi 47.10N 16.45 E
Vasa/Vaasa 6 Ic 63.06N 21.36 E
Vasai (Bassein) 25 Ee 19.21N 72.48 E
Vasalemma/Vazalemma 8 Ke 59.15N 24.11 E
Vásárosnamény 10 Sh 48.08N 22.19 E
Vascão 13 Eg 37.31N 7.31W
Vaşcău 15 Fc 46.28N 22.28 E
Vascoeuil 12 De 49.27N 1.23 E
Vascongadas/Euzkadi = Basque Provinces (EN) 13 Ja 43.00N 2.30W
Vascos, Montes- 13 Jb 42.50N 2.10W
Vasgün 24 Qe 34.55N 56.30 E
Vasileviči 16 Fc 52.14N 29.47 E
Vasiliká 15 Gi 40.28N 23.08 E
Vasiljevka 16 If 47.23N 35.18 E
Vasilkov 19 De 50.12N 30.22 E
Vasilkovka 16 Je 48.13N 36.03 E
Vasiss 19 Hd 57.30N 74.55 E
Vasjugan 20 De 59.10N 80.50 E
Vasjuganje 21 Jd 58.00N 77.00 E
Vaška 19 Ec 64.53N 45.47 E
Vaškovcy 15 Ia 48.16N 25.34 E
Vaslui 15 Kc 46.38N 27.44 E
Vaslui 15 Kc 46.37N 27.44 E
Vaslui [2] 15 Kc 46.41N 27.43 E
Väsman 8 Fd 60.11N 15.04 E
Vassako 35 Bd 8.36N 19.07 E
Vassdalsegga 7 Bg 59.46N 7.07 E
Vassy 12 Bf 48.51N 0.40W
Västeras 6 Hd 59.37N 16.33 E
Västerbotten [2] 7 Dd 64.58N 17.28 E
Västerdalälven 7 Df 60.33N 15.08 E
Västergötland 8 Eg 58.00N 13.05 E
Västerhaninge 8 He 59.07N 18.06 E
Västernorrland [2] 7 De 63.00N 17.30 E
Västervik 7 Dh 57.45N 16.38 E
Västmanland 8 Fe 59.40N 15.15 E
Västmanland [2] 7 Dg 59.45N 16.20 E
Vasto 14 Ih 42.07N 14.42 E
Västra Silen 8 Ee 59.15N 12.10 E
Vasvár 10 Mi 47.03N 16.48 E
Vatan 11 Hg 47.04N 1.49 E
Vatersay 9 Fe 56.53N 7.28W
Vatican City (EN) = Città del Vaticano [1] 6 Hg 41.54N 12.27 E
Vaticano, Capo- 14 Jl 38.37N 15.50 E
Vatilau 63a Ec 8.53S 160.01 E
Vatnajökull 5 Ec 64.24N 16.48W
Vatneyri 7a Ab 65.35N 24.00W
Vatoa Island 57 Jf 19.50S 178.13W
Vatomandry 37 Hc 19.20S 48.59 E
Vatra Dornei 15 Ib 47.21N 25.22 E
Vättern 5 Hd 58.25N 14.35 E
Vatu-i-Ra Channel 63d Bb 17.24S 178.29 E
Vatulele 63d Ac 18.33S 177.38 E
Vatutino 16 Ge 49.02N 31.09 E
Vatu Vara 61 Fc 17.26S 179.32W
Vaubecourt 12 Hf 48.56N 5.07 E
Vauclin, Pointe du- 51h Bb 14.34N 60.50W
Vaucluse [3] 11 Lj 44.00N 5.10 E
Vaucluse, Montagne du- 11 Lk 44.32N 5.11 E
Vaucouleurs 11 Lf 48.36N 5.40 E
Vaud [2] 14 Ad 46.35N 6.30 E
Vaudemont, Butte de- 11 Lf 48.25N 6.00 E
Vaughn 43 Fe 34.36N 105.13W
Vaupés [2] 54 Dc 1.00N 71.00W
Vaupés, Rio- 52 Je 0.02N 67.16W
Vauvilliers 63b Ce 21.09S 167.35 E
Vaux 12 Ce 49.31N 4.17 E
Vaux-le-Vicomte 11 If 48.34N 2.43 E
Vavatenina 37 Hc 17.26S 49.22 E
Vava'u Group 57 Jf 18.40S 174.00W
Vava'u Island 61 Gc 18.36S 174.00W
Vavoua 34 Dd 7.23N 6.29W
Vavuniya 25 Gg 8.45N 80.30 E
Vaxholm 8 He 59.24N 18.20 E
Växjö 6 Hd 56.53N 14.49 E
Vaza-Barris, Rio- 54 Kf 11.10S 37.10W
Vazalemma/Vasalemma 8 Ke 59.15N 24.11 E
Vazante 54 Ig 18.00S 46.54W
Vazuza 16 Ia 56.10N 34.35 E
Vding Skovhøj 8 Ch 56.01N 9.48 E
Veadeiros, Chapada dos- 54 If 14.05S 47.28W
Vecht 10 Cd 52.35N 6.05 E
Vechta 10 Ed 52.43N 8.17 E
Vechte 10 Cd 52.35N 6.05 E
Vecpiebalga 8 Kh 56.57N 25.50 E
Vecsés 10 Pi 47.24N 19.17 E
Vedavågen 8 Ae 59.19N 5.12 E
Veddige 8 Eg 57.16N 12.19 E
Vedea 15 He 44.47N 24.37 E
Vedea 15 Ie 43.59N 25.59 E
Vedeno 16 Oh 42.57N 46.05 E
Vedia 55 Bl 34.30S 61.32W
Vedrá Isla- 13 Nf 38.52N 1.12 E
Veendam 11 Ma 53.06N 6.58 E
Veenendaal 12 Hb 52.02N 5.35 E
Veere 12 Fc 51.33N 3.40 E
Vega 7 Cd 65.39N 11.50 E
Vega 45 Ei 35.15N 102.26W
Vega Baja 51a Bb 18.25N 66.23W
Veganj 14 Kg 43.50N 16.45 E
Vegår 8 Cf 58.48N 8.47 E
Vegårshei 8 Cf 58.46N 8.48 E
Veghel 12 Hc 51.37N 5.32 E
Veglie 14 Lj 40.20N 17.58 E
Vegorritis, Limni- 15 Ei 40.45N 21.48 E
Vègre 11 Fg 47.51N 0.14W
Vegreville 42 Gf 53.30N 112.03W
Vehmersalmi 8 Mb 62.46N 28.02 E
Vehnemoor 12 Ka 53.04N 8.02 E
Veinge 8 Eh 56.34N 13.05 E
Veinticinco de Mayo [Arg.] 56 He 35.26S 60.10W
Veinticinco de Mayo [Ur.] 55 Dl 34.12S 56.22W
Veio 14 Gh 42.02N 12.23 E
Veisiejai/Vejsejaj 8 Jj 54.03N 23.46 E
Vejen 7 Bi 55.29N 9.09 E
Vejer de la Frontera 13 Gh 36.15N 5.58W
Vejle [2] 8 Ci 55.45N 9.20 E
Vejle 7 Bi 55.42N 9.32 E
Vejsejaj/Veisiejai 8 Jj 54.03N 23.46 E
Vel 7 Kf 61.06N 42.10 E
Vela, Cabo de la- 49 Kg 12.13N 72.11W
Vela Luka 14 Kh 42.58N 16.44 E
Velas 32 Bb 38.41N 28.13W
Velas, Cabo- 49 Eh 10.22N 85.53W
Velásquez 55 El 34.02S 54.17W
Velay, Plateaux du- 11 Ji 45.10N 3.50 E
Velaz 55 Ch 26.42S 58.40W
Velbăždski prohod 15 Fg 42.14N 22.28 E
Velbert 10 De 51.20N 7.02 E
Velddrif 37 Bf 32.47S 18.10 E
Velden am Wörthersee 14 Id 46.37N 14.03 E
Veldhoven 12 Hc 51.24N 5.24 E
Velebit 5 Hg 44.17N 15.12 E
Velebitski kanal 14 If 44.45N 14.50 E
Veleka 15 Kg 42.04N 27.58 E
Velencei-tó 10 Oi 47.13N 18.36 E
Velenje 14 Jd 46.22N 15.07 E
Velestinon 15 Fj 39.23N 22.45 E
Veleta 13 Ig 37.04N 3.22W
Velež 14 Lg 43.20N 18.00 E
Vélez Blanco 13 Jg 37.41N 2.05W
Vélez de La Gomera, Peñón de- 13 Hi 35.11N 4.54W
Vélez-Málaga 13 Hh 36.47N 4.06W
Vélez Rubio 13 Jg 37.39N 2.04W
Velhas, Rio das- 52 Lg 17.13S 44.49W
Velika Gorica 14 Ke 45.44N 16.04 E
Velikaja 20 Md 64.35N 176.03 E
Velikaja-Gluša 10 Ve 51.49N 25.11 E
Velikaja Guba 7 Ie 62.17N 35.06 E
Velikaja Kema 20 Ig 45.29N 137.08 E
Velikaja Lepetiha 16 Hf 47.09N 33.59 E
Velikaja Mihajlovka 16 Ff 47.04N 29.52 E
Velika Kapela 14 Je 45.13N 15.02 E
Velika Kladuša 14 Je 45.11N 15.49 E
Velika Morava 15 Ee 44.43N 21.03 E
Velika Plana 15 Ee 44.20N 21.05 E
Veliki Berezny 10 Sh 48.54N 22.30 E
Veliki Byčkov 10 Ui 47.58N 24.04 E
Veliki Drvenik 14 Kg 43.27N 16.09 E
Veliki Jastrebac 15 Ef 43.24N 21.26 E
Velikije Luki 6 Jd 56.20N 30.32 E
Velikije Mosty 10 Uf 50.10N 24.12 E
Veliki kanal 15 Bd 45.52N 18.52 E
Veliki Ljuben 10 Tg 49.37N 23.45 E
Veliki Trnovac 15 Eg 42.29N 21.45 E
Veliki Ustjug 6 Kc 60.46N 46.20 E
Velikodolinskoje 15 Nc 46.20N 30.29 E
Veliko Gradište 15 Ee 44.46N 21.32 E
Veliko Tărnovo [2] 15 If 43.04N 25.39 E
Veliko Tărnovo 6 Ig 43.04N 25.39 E
Velikovisočnoje 19 Fb 67.16N 52.01 E
Veli Lošinj 14 If 44.31N 14.31 E
Vélingara 34 Cc 13.09N 14.07W
Velingrad 15 Gg 42.01N 24.00 E
Velino 14 Hh 42.09N 13.23 E
Velino 14 Gh 42.33N 12.43 E
Veliž 16 Gb 55.36N 31.12 E
Vel'ká Fatra 10 Ph 49.00N 19.05 E
Velké Meziříčí 10 Lg 49.21N 16.00 E
Vel'ký Krtiš 10 Ph 48.13N 19.20 E
Vella Lavella Island 57 Ge 7.45S 156.40 E
Velletri 14 Gi 41.41N 12.47 E
Vellinge 8 Ei 55.28N 13.01 E
Vellore 22 Jh 14.26N 79.58 E
Velmerstot 12 Kc 51.50N 9.00 E
Velmo 20 Ed 61.43N 92.25 E
Velopoúla 15 Gm 36.55N 23.28 E
Vels 17 Hf 60.45N 58.45 E
Velsen-IJmuiden [Neth.] 11 Kb 52.27N 4.39 E
Velsen-IJmuiden [Neth.] 12 Gb 52.28N 4.35 E
Velsk 19 Ec 61.05N 42.05 E
Veluwe 11 Lb 52.20N 5.50 E
Veluwemeer 12 Hb 52.23N 5.40 E
Velva 45 Fb 48.04N 100.56W
Velvendós 15 Fi 40.15N 22.04 E
Veman 8 Fb 62.02N 14.16 E
Vema Seamount (EN) 30 Hl 31.38S 8.19 E
Vemdalen 8 Eb 62.27N 13.52 E
Ven 8 Ei 55.55N 12.40 E
Venable Ice Shelf 66 Pf 73.03S 87.20W
Venado 48 If 22.56N 101.05W
Venado, Cerro- 50 Ei 6.17N 62.45W
Venado Tuerto 56 Hd 33.45S 61.58W
Venafro 14 Ii 41.29N 14.02 E
Venamo, Rio- 50 Fi 6.43N 61.07W
Vence 11 Nk 43.43N 7.07 E
Venceslau Brás 55 Hf 23.51S 49.48W
Venda 37 Ed 22.35S 30.45 E
Venda Nova 54 Jg 19.45S 43.50W
Vendas Novas 13 Df 38.41N 8.27W
Vendée [3] 11 Eh 46.40N 1.20W
Vendée 11 Hh 46.40N 1.10 E
Vendée 11 Fh 46.19N 0.58W
Vendéen, Bocage- 11 Eh 46.50N 1.20W
Vendéenne, Plaine- 11 Eh 46.40N 1.20W
Vendel 8 Gd 60.10N 17.36 E
Vendeuvre-sur-Barse 11 Kf 48.14N 4.29 E
Vendôme 11 Hg 47.48N 1.04 E
Vendrell/El Vendrell 13 Nc 41.13N 1.32 E
Vendsyssel 8 Cg 57.20N 10.00 E
Venetia (EN) = Veneto [2] 14 Fe 45.30N 12.00 E
Venétiko [Grc.] 15 Jk 38.08N 26.01 E
Venétiko [Grc.] 15 Em 36.42N 21.53 E
Veneto = Venetia (EN) [2] 14 Fe 45.30N 12.00 E
Venev 16 Kb 54.22N 38.18 E
Venezia = Venice (EN) 6 Hf 45.27N 12.21 E
Venezia, Golfo di- = Venice, Gulf of- (EN) 5 Hf 45.15N 13.00 E
Venezia-Lido 14 Ge 45.25N 12.22 E
Venezia-Marghera 14 Ge 45.28N 12.44 E
Venezia-Mestre 14 Ge 45.29N 12.14 E
Venezuela [1] 53 Je 8.00N 65.00W
Venezuela, Golfo de- = Venezuela, Gulf of- (EN) 52 Id 11.30N 71.00W
Venezuela, Gulf of- (EN) = Venezuela, Golfo de- 52 Id 11.30N 71.00W
Venezuelan Basin (EN) 38 Mh 15.00N 68.00W
Vengerovo 20 Ce 55.41N 76.55 E
Veniaminof, Mount- 40 He 56.13N 159.18W
Venice 44 Fl 27.06N 82.27W
Venice (EN) = Venezia 6 Hf 45.27N 12.21 E
Venice, Gulf of- (EN) = Venezia, Golfo di- 5 Hf 45.15N 13.00 E
Vénissieux 11 Ki 45.41N 4.53 E
Venjan 8 Ed 60.57N 13.55 E
Venjansjön 8 Ed 60.55N 14.00 E
Venlo 11 Mc 51.24N 6.10 E
Venlock River 59 Ib 12.15S 142.00 E
Vennesla 7 Bg 58.17N 7.59 E
Venosa 14 Jj 40.58N 15.49 E
Venosta, Val-/Vintschgau 14 Ed 46.40N 10.35 E
Venraij 11 Lc 51.32N 5.59 E
Vent, Canal du- = Windward Passage (EN) 49 Lh 20.00N 73.50W
Vent, Iles du- = Windward Islands (EN) 57 Mf 17.30S 149.30W
Venta 7 Eh 57.23N 21.32 E
Venta de Baños 13 Hc 41.55N 4.30W
Ventana, Cerro- 48 Fe 24.15N 106.20W
Ventersdorp 37 De 26.17S 26.48 E
Venterstad 37 Df 30.47S 25.48 E
Venticinco de Diciembre 55 Dg 24.42S 56.33W
Ventimiglia 14 Bg 43.47N 7.36 E
Ventnor 12 Ad 50.36N 1.11W
Ventotene 14 Hj 40.45N 13.25 E
Ventoux, Mont- 11 Lj 44.10N 5.17 E
Ventspils 19 Cd 57.24N 21.33 E
Ventuari, Rio- 52 Je 3.58N 67.02W
Ventura 43 De 34.17N 119.18W
Vénus, Pointe- 65e Fc 17.29S 149.29W
Venus Bay 59 Jg 38.40S 145.45 E
Venustiano Carranza 48 Mi 16.21N 92.33W
Venustiano Carranza, Presa- 48 Id 27.30N 100.40W
Ver 8 Bc 51.31N 0.27W
Vera [Arg.] 56 Hc 29.28S 60.13W
Vera [Sp.] 13 Kg 37.15N 1.52W
Verá, Laguna- 55 Dh 26.05S 57.39W
Veracruz [2] 47 Ee 19.20N 96.40W
Veracruz Llave 39 Jh 19.12N 96.08W
Veraguas [3] 49 Gj 8.30N 81.00W
Verāval 22 Ed 20.54N 70.22 E
Vera y Pintado 55 Bj 30.09S 60.21W
Verbania 14 Ce 45.56N 8.33 E
Verbovski 7 Ji 55.29N 41.59 E
Vercelli 14 Ce 45.19N 8.25 E
Vercors 11 Lj 44.57N 5.25 E
Verdalsøra 7 Ce 63.48N 11.29 E
Verde, Cape- 49 Jb 22.50N 74.52W
Verde, Cay- 49 Jb 22.02N 75.12W
Verde, Costa- 13 Ga 43.40N 5.40W
Verde, Rio- 52 Kh 23.09S 57.37W
Verde, Rio- [Braz.] 54 Hh 21.12S 51.53W
Verde, Rio- [Braz.] 55 Hb 15.07S 48.40W
Verde, Rio- [Braz.] 55 Hd 19.50S 49.45W
Verde, Rio- [Braz.] 55 Ge 21.12S 51.53W
Verde, Rio- [Braz.] 55 Gd 18.01S 50.14W
Verde, Rio- [Braz.] 55 Je 21.27S 45.40W
Verde, Rio- [Braz.] 55 Ca 13.33S 58.01W
Verde, Rio- [Braz.] 54 Gf 11.54S 55.50W
Verde, Rio- [Braz.] 54 Hg 19.11S 50.44W
Verde, Rio- [Mex.] 48 Jg 21.37N 99.15W
Verde, Rio- [Mex.] 48 Hg 20.42N 103.14W
Verde, Rio- [S.Amer.] 55 Ba 13.59S 60.20W
Verde Grande, Rio- 55 Kb 14.35S 43.53W
Verden (Aller) 10 Fd 52.55N 9.14 E
Verde River 43 Ee 33.33N 111.40W
Verdigris River 45 Ii 35.48N 95.18W
Verdinho, Rio- 55 Gc 17.29S 50.27W
Verdon 11 Lk 43.43N 5.46 E
Verdun [Fr.] 11 Le 49.10N 5.23 E
Verdun [Que.-Can.] 44 Kc 45.28N 73.34W
Verdura 14 Hm 37.28N 13.12 E
Vereeniging 37 De 26.38S 27.57 E
Vereščagino 19 Fd 58.05N 54.40 E
Verga, Cap- 34 Cc 10.12N 14.27W
Vergara [Arg.] 55 Dl 35.23S 57.48W
Vergara [Sp.] 13 Ja 43.07N 2.25W
Vergara [Ur.] 55 Fk 32.56S 53.57W
Vergato 14 Ff 44.17N 11.07 E
Verhnedneprovsk 16 Ie 48.39N 34.21 E
Verhnedneprovski 16 Hb 55.01N 33.21 E
Verhnedvinsk 7 Gi 55.46N 27.59 E
Verhneimbatsk 20 Dd 63.09N 88.00 E
Verhne-Karabahski Kanal 16 Oj 39.44N 47.57 E
Verhnespasskoje 7 Kg 58.45N 45.28 E
Verhnetulomski 7 Hb 68.38N 31.48 E
Verhnetulomskoje Vodohranilišče 7 Hb 68.35N 31.00 E
Verhneuralsk 17 Ij 53.53N 59.13 E
Verhneviljujsk 20 Hd 63.20N 120.25 E
Verhni At-Urjah 20 Kd 62.38N 150.03 E
Verhni Avzjan 17 Hj 53.32N 57.33 E
Verhni Kujto, Ozero- 7 Hd 65.00N 30.40 E
Verhni Most 8 Mg 57.29N 29.00 E
Verhni Tagil 17 Jh 57.22N 60.01 E
Verhni Trajanov Val = Upper Trajan's Wall (EN) 15 Lc 46.40N 29.00 E
Verhni Ufalej 19 Gd 56.04N 60.14 E
Verhnjaja Inta 17 Jd 65.59N 60.29 E
Verhnjaja Pyšma 17 Jh 56.59N 60.37 E
Verhnjaja Salda 17 Jg 58.02N 60.33 E
Verhnjaja Tojma 19 Ec 62.13N 45.01 E
Verhnjaja Tura 17 Ig 58.22N 59.49 E
Verhnj Uslon 7 Li 55.47N 48.58 E
Verhnoje Sinevidnoje 10 Tg 49.02N 23.36 E
Verhojansk 22 Pc 67.35N 133.27 E
Verhojanski Hrebet = Verhoyansk Mountains (EN) 21 Oc 67.00N 129.00 E
Verhoturje 17 Jg 58.52N 60.48 E
Verhovcevo 16 Ie 48.31N 34.12 E
Verhovina 15 Ha 48.08N 24.48 E
Verhovje 16 Jc 52.49N 37.14 E
Verhoyansk Mountains (EN) = Verhojanski Hrebet 21 Oc 67.00N 129.00 E
Verin 13 Ec 41.56N 7.26W
Veriora 8 Lg 58.00N 27.21 E
Verissimo, Rio- 55 Hd 18.23S 48.20W
Verissimo, Serra do- 55 Hd 19.33S 48.25W
Verl 12 Kc 51.53N 8.31 E
Vermand 12 Fe 49.52N 3.09 E
Vermeille, Côte- 11 Jl 42.30N 3.20 E
Vermelho, Rio- [Braz.] 55 Ib 14.26S 46.26W
Vermelho, Rio- [Braz.] 55 Ed 19.36S 55.58W
Vermelho, Rio- [Braz.] 55 Gb 14.54S 51.06W
Vermenton 11 Jg 47.40N 3.44 E
Vermilion Bay 42 Ig 49.51N 93.24W
Vermilion Cliffs 46 Ih 37.10N 112.35W
Vermilion Lake 45 Jc 47.53N 92.25W
Vermilion River 44 Gb 46.16N 81.41W
Vermillion 45 He 42.47N 96.56W
Vermillion River 45 He 42.44N 96.53W
Vermillon, Rivière- 44 Kb 47.38N 72.59W
Vérmion Óros 15 Ei 40.30N 22.00 E
Vermont [2] 43 Mc 43.50N 72.45W
Vernal 43 Fc 40.27N 109.32W
Verneuil-sur-Avre 11 Gf 48.44N 0.56 E
Vernhi Barskunčak 16 Oe 48.14N 46.42 E
Vernon [B.C.-Can.] 42 Ff 50.16N 119.16W
Vernon [Fr.] 11 He 49.05N 1.29 E
Vernon [Tx.-U.S.] 43 He 34.09N 99.17W
Vérnon Óros 15 Ei 40.39N 21.22 E
Vernou 51e Ab 16.11N 61.39W
Verny 12 Ie 49.01N 6.12 E
Vero 13 Mb 42.00N 0.10 E
Vero Beach 43 Kf 27.38N 80.24W
Véroia 15 Fi 40.31N 22.12 E
Verona 6 Hf 45.27N 11.00 E
Verónica 56 Ie 35.22S 57.20W
Versailles [Fr.] 11 If 48.48N 2.08 E
Versailles [In.-U.S.] 44 Ef 39.04N 85.15W
Versilia 14 Eg 43.55N 10.15 E
Veršino-Darasunski 20 Gf 52.18N 115.32 E
Veršino-Šahtaminski 20 Gf 51.16N 117.55 E
Versmold 12 Kb 52.03N 8.09 E
Verson 12 Be 49.09N 0.27W
Vert, Cap- = Vert, Cape- (EN) 30 Fg 14.43N 17.30W
Vert, Cape- (EN) = Vert, Cap- 30 Fg 14.43N 17.30W
Vertentes, Serra das- 55 Je 20.56S 44.00W
Vértes 10 Oi 47.25N 18.20 E
Vertientes 49 Hc 21.16N 78.09W
Vertiskos Óros 15 Gi 40.50N 23.19 E
Verviers 11 Ld 50.36N 5.52 E
Vervins 12 Fe 49.50N 3.54 E
Vesanto 8 Lb 62.56N 26.25 E
Vescovato 11a Ba 42.29N 9.26 E
Vesder/Vesdre 12 Hd 50.37N 5.37 E
Vesdre/Vesder 12 Hd 50.37N 5.37 E
Veselí nad Lužnicí 10 Kg 49.11N 14.43 E
Veselovskoje Vodohranilišče 16 Lf 47.00N 41.15 E
Vešenskaja 19 Ef 49.38N 41.46 E
Vesgre 12 Df 48.53N 1.28 E
Vesijarvi 8 Kc 61.05N 25.30 E
Vesjegonsk 7 Ig 58.41N 37.16 E
Veškajma 7 Li 54.03N 47.08 E
Vesle 11 Je 49.23N 3.28 E
Vesljana 17 Gf 60.20N 54.03 E
Vesoul 11 Mg 47.38N 6.10 E
Vessigebro 8 Eh 56.59N 12.39 E
Vest-Agder [2] 7 Bg 58.30N 7.10 E
Vestbygd 7 Bg 58.06N 6.35 E
Vesterålen 5 Hb 68.45N 15.00 E
Vesterhavn 8 Dg 57.18N 10.56 E
Vestfjorden 5 Hb 68.35N 14.30 E
Vestfold [2] 7 Cg 59.15N 10.10 E
Vestfonna 41 Oc 79.58N 20.15 E
Vestgrønland = West Greenland (EN) [2] 41 He 69.00N 49.30W
Véstia 55 Ge 20.23S 51.25W
Vestmannæyjar 7a Bc 63.26N 20.16W
Vestnes 8 Bb 62.38N 7.06 E
Vestre Jakobselv 7 Ga 70.07N 29.25 E
Vestsjælland [2] 8 Di 55.30N 11.30 E
Vestvågøy 7 Cb 68.15N 13.50 E
Vésubie 11 Nk 43.52N 7.12 E
Vesuvio = Vesuvius (EN) 5 Hg 40.49N 14.26 E
Vesuvius (EN) = Vesuvio 5 Hg 40.49N 14.26 E
Veszprém [2] 10 Ni 47.10N 17.40 E
Veszprém 10 Ni 47.06N 17.55 E
Vészto 10 Rj 46.55N 21.16 E
Vétaoundé, Ile- 57 Hf 13.15S 167.38 E
Vetauua 63d Ca 15.57S 179.24W
Vété, Pointe- 63b Ca 13.27S 166.41 E
Vetka 16 Gc 52.34N 31.13 E
Vetlanda 7 Dh 57.26N 15.04 E
Vetljanka 7 Mj 52.52N 51.09 E
Vetluga 5 Kd 56.18N 46.24 E
Vetluga 7 Kh 57.52N 45.46 E

Index Symbols

- [1] Independent Nation
- [2] State, Region
- [3] District, County
- [4] Municipality
- [5] Colony, Dependency
- Continent
- Physical Region
- Historical or Cultural Region
- Mount, Mountain
- Volcano
- Hill
- Mountains, Mountain Range
- Hills, Escarpment
- Plateau, Upland
- Pass, Gap
- Plain, Lowland
- Delta
- Salt Flat
- Valley, Canyon
- Crater, Cave
- Karst Features
- Depression
- Polder
- Desert, Dunes
- Forest, Woods
- Heath, Steppe
- Oasis
- Cape, Point
- Coast, Beach
- Cliff
- Peninsula
- Isthmus
- Sandbank
- Island
- Atoll
- Rock, Reef
- Islands, Archipelago
- Rocks, Reefs
- Coral Reef
- Well, Spring
- Geyser
- River, Stream
- Waterfall Rapids
- River Mouth, Estuary
- Lake
- Salt Lake
- Intermittent Lake
- Reservoir
- Swamp, Pond
- Canal
- Glacier
- Ice Shelf, Pack Ice
- Ocean
- Sea
- Gulf, Bay
- Strait, Fjord
- Lagoon
- Bank
- Seamount
- Tablemount
- Ridge
- Shelf
- Basin
- Escarpment, Sea Scarp
- Fracture
- Trench, Abyss
- National Park, Reserve
- Point of Interest
- Recreation Site
- Cave, Cavern
- Historic Site
- Ruins
- Wall, Walls
- Church, Abbey
- Temple
- Scientific Station
- Airport
- Port
- Lighthouse
- Mine
- Tunnel
- Dam, Bridge

Index Symbols

[1] Independent Nation · [2] State, Region · [3] District, County · [4] Municipality · [5] Colony, Dependency · Continent · Physical Region

Historical or Cultural Region · Mount, Mountain · Volcano · Hill · Mountains, Mountain Range · Hills, Escarpment · Plateau, Upland

Pass, Gap · Plain, Lowland · Delta · Salt Flat · Valley, Canyon · Crater, Cave · Karst Features

Depression · Polder · Desert, Dunes · Forest, Woods · Heath, Steppe · Oasis · Cape, Point

Coast, Beach · Cliff · Peninsula · Isthmus · Sandbank · Island · Atoll

Rock, Reef · Islands, Archipelago · Rocks, Reefs · Coral Reef · Well, Spring · Geyser · River, Stream

Waterfall Rapids · River Mouth, Estuary · Lake · Salt Lake · Intermittent Lake · Reservoir · Swamp, Pond

Canal · Glacier · Ice Shelf, Pack Ice · Ocean · Sea · Gulf, Bay · Strait, Fjord

Lagoon · Bank · Seamount · Tablemount · Ridge · Shelf · Basin

Escarpment, Sea Scarp · Trench, Abyss · Fracture · National Park, Reserve · Point of Interest · Recreation Site · Cave, Cavern

Historic Site · Ruins · Wall, Walls · Church, Abbey · Temple · Scientific Station · Airport

Port · Lighthouse · Mine · Tunnel · Dam, Bridge

Vittangi 7 Ec 67.41N 21.39 E
Vitteaux 11 Kg 47.24N 4.32 E
Vittel 11 Lf 48.12N 5.57 E
Vittinge 8 Ge 59.54N 17.04 E
Vittoria 14 In 36.57N 14.32 E
Vittorio Veneto 14 Ge 45.59N 12.18 E
Vityaz Depth (EN) 3 Je 44.00N 151.00 E
Vityaz ı Depth (EN) 3 Ih 11.20N 141.30 E
Vityaz II Depth (EN) 3 Ki 23.27 S 175.00W
Vityaz III Depth (EN) 3 Km 32.00 S 178.00W
Vityaz Seamount (EN) 57 Jc 13.30N 173.15W
Vityaz Trench (EN) 3 Jj 10.00 S 170.00 E
Vivarais, Monts du- 11 Ki 44.55N 4.15 E
Vivarais, Plateaux du- 11 Kj 44.50N 4.45 E
Viver 13 Le 39.55N 0.36W
Vivero 13 Ea 43.40N 7.35W
Viverone, Lago di- 14 Ce 45.25N 8.05 E
Vivi 20 Ed 63.52N 97.50 E
Vivian 45 Jj 32.53N 93.59W
Viviers 11 Kj 44.29N 4.41 E
Vivo 37 Dd 23.03 S 29.17 E
Vivoratá 55 Dm 37.40 S 57.39W
Vivorillo, Cayos- 49 Ff 15.50N 83.18W
Viwa 63d Ab 17.08 S 176.56 E
Vizcaíno, Desierto de- 47 Bc 27.40N 114.40W
Vizcaíno, Sierra- 48 Bd 27.20N 114.00W
Vizcaya [3] 13 Ja 43.15N 2.55W
Vizcaya, Golfo de- 5 Fg 44.00N 4.00W
Vize 15 Kh 41.34N 27.45 E
Vize, Ostrov 21 Jb 79.30N 77.00 E
Vizianagaram 25 Ge 18.07N 83.25 E
Vizille 11 Li 45.05N 5.46 E
Vizinga 19 Fc 61.05N 50.10 E
Viziru 15 Kd 45.00N 27.42 E
Vižnica 16 De 48.14N 25.12 E
Vizzini 14 Im 37.10N 14.45 E
Vjajke-Maarja/Väike-Maarja 8 Le 59.04N 26.12 E
Vjajke-Pakri/Väike-Pakri 8 Je 59.50N 23.50 E
Vjajke-Vjajn/Väik Vain 8 Jf 58.30N 23.10 E
Vjalje, Ozero- 8 Ne 59.00N 30.20 E
Vjalozero, Ozero- 7 Ic 66.50N 35.10 E
Vjandra/Vändra 7 Fg 58.40N 25.01 E
Vjartsilja 7 He 62.10N 30.48 E
Vjatka 5 Ld 55.36N 51.30 E
Vjatskije Poljany 19 Fd 56.14N 51.04 E
Vjatski Uval 7 Lg 58.00N 49.45 E
Vjazemski 20 Ig 47.31N 134.45 E
Vjazma 6 Jd 55.13N 34.18 E
Vjazniki 7 Kh 56.15N 42.12 E
Vjeio, Rio- 49 Dg 12.17N 86.54W
Vjosa 15 Ci 40.37N 19.20 E
Vlaamse Banken 12 Ec 51.15N 2.30 E
Vlaanderen/Flandres= Flanders (EN) 5 Ge 51.00N 3.20 E
Vlaanderen/Flandres= Flanders (EN) 11 Jc 51.00N 3.20 E
Vlaardingen 11 Kc 51.54N 4.21 E
Vlădeasa, Vîrful- 15 Fc 46.45N 22.48 E
Vlădeni 15 Kb 47.25N 27.20 E
Vladičin Han 15 Fg 42.43N 22.04 E
Vladimir 6 Kd 56.10N 40.25 E
Vladimirskaja Oblast [3] 19 Ed 56.00N 40.40 E
Vladimirski Tupik 16 Hb 55.42N 33.18 E
Vladimir-Volynski 19 Ce 50.51N 24.22 E
Vladivostok 22 Pe 43.10N 131.56 E
Vlad Ţepeş 15 Ke 44.21N 27.05 E
Vlagtwedde 12 Ja 53.02N 7.08 E
Vlagtwedde-Ter Apel 12 Jb 52.52N 7.06 E
Vlahina 15 Fi 41.54N 22.52 E
Vlăhiţa 15 Ic 46.21N 25.31 E
Vlamse Vlakte=Flanders Plain (EN) 11 Id 50.40N 2.50 E
Vlasenica 14 Mf 44.11N 18.57 E
Vlašic [Yugo.] 14 Lf 44.19N 17.40 E
Vlašim 10 Kg 49.42N 14.54 E
Vlasotince 15 Fg 42.58N 22.08 E
Vlasovo 20 Ib 70.40N 134.35 E
Vlieland 11 Ka 53.15N 5.00 E
Vlieland 12 Ha 53.17N 5.06 E
Vlieland-Oost Vlieland 12 Ha 53.17N 5.06E
Vliestroom 12 Ha 53.17N 5.10 E
Vlissingen 11 Jc 51.26N 3.35 E
Vlissingen-Oost-Souburg 12 Fc 51.28N 3.36 E
Vloesberg/Flobecq 12 Fd 50.44N 3.44 E
Vlora 6 Hg 40.27N 19.30 E
Vlorës, Gjiri i- 15 Ci 40.25N 19.25 E
Vlotho 12 Kb 52.10N 8.51 E
Vltava=Moldau (EN) 5 He 50.21N 14.30 E
Vöcklabruck 14 Hb 48.01N 13.39 E
Vodice 14 Jg 43.46N 15.47 E
Vodla 7 If 61.49N 36.00 E
Vodlozero, Ozero- 7 Ie 62.20N 37.00 E
Vodňany 10 Kg 49.09N 14.11 E
Vodnjan 14 Hf 44.57N 13.51 E
Vodny 17 Fe 63.32N 53.20 E
Voerde (Niederrhein) 10 Ce 51.35N 6.41 E
Voeren/Fouron 12 Hd 50.45N 5.48 E
Vogel Peak 34 Hd 8.24N 11.47 E
Vogelsberg 10 Ff 50.30N 9.15 E
Voghera 14 Df 44.59N 9.01 E
Vogtland 10 If 50.30N 12.05 E
Voh 63b Be 20.58 S 164.42 E
Võhandu Jõgi/Vyhandu 8 Lf 58.03N 27.40 E
Vohémar 37 Ib 13.22 S 50.00 E
Vohipeno 37 Hd 22.20 S 47.52 E
Vöhl 12 Kc 51.12N 8.56 E
Vohma 7 Lg 58.45N 46.36 E
Vohma 19 Ed 58.58N 46.45 E
Voi 31 Ki 3.23 S 38.34 E
Voikoski 8 Lc 61.16N 26.48 E
Voinjama 31 Gh 8.25N 9.45W
Vóïon Óros 15 Ei 40.15N 21.03 E
Voire 11 Kf 48.27N 4.25 E
Voiron 11 Li 45.22N 5.35 E
Voitsberg 14 Jc 47.02N 15.09 E
Võiviis, Limni- 15 Fj 39.32N 22.45 E
Vojens 8 Ci 55.15N 9.19 E
Vojkar 17 Ld 65.38N 64.40 E
Vojmsjön 7 Dd 65.00N 16.24 E
Vojnić 14 Je 45.19N 15.42 E
Vojnilov 10 Ug 49.04N 24.33 E
Vojvodina [3] 15 Cd 45.00N 20.00 E
Voj-Vož 19 Fc 62.56N 54.59 E
Voknavolok 7 Hd 64.57N 30.31 E
Vokré, Hoséré- 30 Ih 8.21N 13.15 E
Volary 10 Jh 48.55N 13.54 E
Volcán 49 Fi 8.46N 82.38W
Volcanica, Cordillera- 38 Ih 18.00N 101.00W
Volcano 65a Fd 19.26N 155.20W
Volcano Islands (EN)=lō/ Kazan-Rettō 21 Qg 25.00N 141.00 E
Volcano Islands (EN)= Kazan-Rettō/lō 21 Qg 25.00N 141.00 E
Volcán Rana Roi 65d Ab 27.05 S 109.23W
Volčansk [R.S.F.S.R.] 17 Jg 59.59N 60.04 E
Volčansk [Ukr.-U.S.S.R.] 16 Jd 50.16N 37.01 E
Volčiha 20 Df 52.02N 80.23 E
Volda 7 Be 62.09N 6.06 E
Voldafjorden 8 Ab 62.10N 6.00 E
Volga 5 Kf 45.55N 47.52 E
Volga 7 Jh 57.57N 38.25 E
Volga-Baltic Canal (EN)= Volgo-Baltijski vodny put imeni V. I. Lenina 5 Jd 59.58N 37.10 E
Volga Delta (EN) 5 Kf 46.30N 47.00 E
Volga Hills (EN)= Privolžkaja Vozvyšennost 5 Ke 52.00N 46.00 E
Volgo-Baltijski vodny put imeni V.I. Lenina=Volga-Baltic Canal (EN) 5 Jd 59.58N 37.10 E
Volgodonsk 19 Ef 47.33N 42.08 E
Volgo-Donskoj sudohodny kanal imeni V. I. Lenina= Lenin Canal (EN) 5 Kf 48.40N 43.37 E
Volgograd (Stalingrad) 6 Kf 48.44N 44.25 E
Volgograd Reservoir (EN)= Volgogradskoje Vodohranilišče 5 Kf 49.20N 45.00 E
Volgogradskaja Oblast [3] 19 Ef 49.30N 44.30 E
Volgogradskoje Vodohranilišče=Volgograd Reservoir (EN) 5 Kf 49.20N 45.00 E
Volhov 5 Jc 60.08N 32.20 E
Volhov 6 Jd 59.55N 32.20 E
Volhynia 5 Ie 51.00N 25.00 E
Volissós 15 Ik 38.29N 25.55 E
Volja 17 Je 63.11N 61.16 E
Volka 10 Vd 52.43N 25.43 E
Völkermarkt 14 Id 46.39N 14.38 E
Völklingen 10 Cg 49.15N 6.51 E
Volkmarsen 12 Lc 51.24N 9.07 E
Volkovysk 16 Dc 53.10N 24.31 E
Volkovysskaja Vozvyšennost 10 Kc 53.10N 24.30 E
Volksrust 37 De 27.24 S 29.53 E
Vollenhove 12 Hb 52.40N 5.57 E
Vollsjö 8 Ei 55.42N 13.46 E
Volme 12 Jc 51.24N 7.27 E
Volmunster 12 Je 49.07N 7.21 E
Volna, Gora- 20 Kd 63.30N 154.57 E
Volnjansk 16 If 47.54N 35.29 E
Volnovaha 16 Jf 47.37N 37.36 E
Voločajevka 2-ja 20 Ig 48.36N 134.36 E
Voločisk 16 Ee 49.31N 26.13 E
Volodarsk 7 Kh 56.14N 43.13 E
Volodarski 16 Pf 46.26N 48.31 E
Volodarskoje 19 Ge 53.18N 68.08 E
Vologda 6 Jd 59.12N 39.55 E
Vologodskaja Oblast [3] 19 Ed 60.00N 41.00 E
Volokolamsk 7 Ih 56.03N 35.58 E
Volokonovka 16 Jd 50.29N 37.52 E
Vólos 6 Ih 39.22N 22.57 E
Vološka 7 Jf 61.42N 39.15 E
Vološka 7 Jf 61.21N 40.03 E
Volosovo 7 Gg 59.28N 29.31 E
Volovec 10 Th 48.42N 23.17 E
Volovo 16 Kc 53.35N 38.01 E
Vološin 16 Eb 54.06N 26.32 E
Volquart Boons Kyst 41 Jd 70.20N 24.20W
Volsini, Monti- 14 Fh 42.40N 11.55 E
Volsk 19 Ee 52.02N 47.23 E
Volta 30 Hh 5.46N 0.41 E
Volta [3] 34 Fd 7.00N 0.30 E
Volta Blanche=White Volta (EN) 30 Gh 8.38N 0.59W
Volta Lake 30 Hh 7.30N 0.15 E
Volta Noire=Black Volta (EN) 30 Gh 8.38N 1.30W
Volta Noire=Black Volta (EN) [3] 34 Ec 12.30N 4.00W
Volta Redonda 53 Lh 22.32 S 44.07W
Volta Rouge=Red Volta (EN) 30 Gh 10.34N 0.30W
Volterra 14 Eg 43.24N 10.51 E
Voltoya 13 Hc 41.13N 4.31W
Voltri, Genova- 14 Cf 44.26N 8.45 E
Volturino 14 Jj 40.25N 15.48 E
Volturno 14 Hi 41.01N 13.55 E
Volubilis 32 Fc 34.04N 5.33W
Vólvi, Limni- 15 Gi 40.41N 23.28 E
Volynskaja Grjada 10 Ue 51.05N 25.00 E
Volynskaja Oblast [3] 19 Ce 51.10N 25.00 E
Volynskaja Vozvyšennost 16 Dd 50.30N 25.00 E
Volžsk 19 Ed 55.55N 48.19 E
Volžski [R.S.F.S.R.] 6 Kf 48.48N 44.44 E
Volžski [R.S.F.S.R.] 7 Mj 53.28N 50.08 E
Voma 63d Bc 18.00 S 178.08 E
Vomano 14 Ih 42.39N 14.02 E
Vonavona 63a Cc 8.12 S 157.05 E
Vondrozo 37 Hd 22.47 S 47.17 E
Von Frank Mountain 40 Id 63.33N 154.20W
Vónitsa 15 Dk 38.55N 20.53 E
Vonne 11 Gh 46.25N 0.15 E
Võnnu/Vynnu 8 Lf 58.15N 27.10 E
Voorne 12 Gc 51.52N 4.05 E
Voorschoten 12 Gb 52.08N 4.28 E
Voorst 12 Ib 52.10N 6.09 E
Voorst-Twello 12 Ib 52.14N 6.07 E
Vop 16 Hb 54.56N 32.44 E
Vopnafjördur 7a Cb 65.45N 14.50W
Vora 15 Ch 41.23N 19.40 E
Vörå/Vöyri 8 Ja 63.09N 22.15 E
Vorarlberg [2] 14 Dc 47.15N 9.50 E
Vóras Óros 15 Ei 41.00N 21.50 E
Vorau 14 Jc 47.24N 15.53 E
Vorden 12 Ib 52.06N 6.20 E
Vorderrhein 14 Dd 46.49N 9.26 E
Vordingborg 7 Ci 55.01N 11.55 E
Voreifel 12 Jd 50.10N 7.00 E
Vorga Šor 17 Kc 67.35N 63.40 E
Voria Pindhos 15 Dj 40.20N 20.55 E
Vórioi Sporádhes, Nisoi-= Northern Sporades (EN) 5 Ih 39.15N 23.55 E
Vórios Evvoïkós Kólpos= Évvoia, Gulf of- (EN) 15 Gk 38.45N 23.10 E
Vorkuta 6 Mb 67.27N 63.58 E
Vorma 7 Cf 60.09N 11.27 E
Vormsi 8 Je 59.02N 23.05 E
Vormsi 7 Fg 59.00N 23.15 E
Vorniceni 15 Jb 47.59N 26.40 E
Vorogovo 20 Dd 60.58N 89.28 E
Vorona 16 Md 51.22N 42.03 E
Voroncovo [R.S.F.S.R.] 20 Db 71.40N 83.40 E
Voroncovo [R.S.F.S.R.] 8 Mg 57.15N 28.49 E
Voronež 6 Je 51.40N 39.10 E
Voronež 16 Kd 51.31N 39.05 E
Voronežskaja Oblast [3] 19 Ee 51.00N 40.15 E
Voronin Trough (EN) 67 Ge 80.00N 85.00 E
Voronja 7 Ib 69.09N 35.47 E
Voronovo 8 Kj 54.09N 25.19 E
Voropajevo 8 Li 55.07N 27.19 E
Vorošilovgrad 6 Jf 48.34N 39.20 E
Vorošilovgradskaja Oblast [3] 19 Df 49.00N 39.10 E
Vorotan 16 Oj 39.15N 46.43 E
Vorotynec 7 Kh 56.02N 45.52 E
Vorožba 16 Id 51.10N 34.11 E
Vorskla 16 Ie 48.52N 34.05 E
Vorsma 7 Ki 55.58N 43.17 E
Vörts Järv/Vyrtsjarv, Ozero- 7 Gg 58.15N 26.05 E
Võru/Vyru 19 Cd 57.52N 27.05 E
Voruh 18 He 39.52N 70.35 E
Vosges 5 Gf 48.30N 7.10 E
Vosges [3] 11 Mf 48.10N 6.20 E
Voskresensk 7 Ji 55.22N 38.42 E
Voskresenskoje 7 Kh 56.51N 45.27 E
Voss 8 Bd 60.40N 6.30 E
Vossa 8 Ad 60.39N 5.42 E
Vossevangen 7 Bd 60.39N 6.26 E
Vostočno-Kazahstanskaja Oblast [3] 19 If 49.00N 84.00 E
Vostočno-Kounradski 19 Hf 46.58N 75.07 E
Vostočno Sibirskoje More= East Siberian Sea (EN) 67 Cd 74.00N 166.00 E
Vostočny [R.S.F.S.R.] 20 Jg 48.19N 142.40 E
Vostočny [R.S.F.S.R.] 17 Jg 58.48N 61.52 E
Vostočny, Hrebet- 20 Lf 55.00N 160.30 E
Vostočny Sajan=Eastern Sayans (EN) 21 Ld 53.00N 97.00 E
Vostok 66 Hf 78.28 S 106.48 E
Vostok Island 57 Lf 10.06 S 152.23W
Vostrecovo 20 Ig 45.56N 134.59 E
Vošu/Vyzu 8 Ke 59.30N 25.50 E
Votkinsk 19 Fd 57.05N 53.59 E
Votkinskoje Vodohranilišče = Votkinsk Reservoir (EN) 5 Ld 57.30N 55.10 E
Votkinsk Reservoir (EN) = Votkinskoje Vodohranilišče 5 Ld 57.30N 55.10 E
Votuporanga 55 He 20.24 S 49.59W
Vouga 13 Dd 40.41N 8.40W
Vouillé 11 Gh 46.38N 0.10 E
Voulgára 15 Ej 39.06N 21.54 E
Vouliagméni 15 Gl 37.49N 23.47 E
Voúrinos Óros 15 Ei 40.11N 21.40 E
Voúxa, Ákra- 15 Gn 35.38N 23.36 E
Vouziers 11 Ke 49.24N 4.42 E
Voves 11 Hf 48.16N 1.38 E
Vovodo 35 Cd 5.40N 24.21 E
Voxna 8 Fc 61.21N 15.34 E
Voxnan 8 Gc 61.17N 16.26 E
Voyeykov Ice Shelf 66 Ie 66.20 S 124.38 E
Vöyri/Vörå 8 Ja 63.09N 22.15 E
Vože, Ozero- 7 Jf 60.35N 39.05 E
Vožega 7 Jf 60.33N 39.13 E
Vožega 7 Jf 60.30N 40.12 E
Voznesenje 7 If 61.01N 35.27 E
Voznesensk 19 Df 47.35N 31.20 E
Vozroždenija, Ostrov- 18 Bb 45.05N 59.15 E
Vraca [2] 15 Gf 43.12N 23.33 E
Vraca 15 Dh 41.54N 20.45 E
Vraca 15 Gf 43.12N 23.33 E
Vradijevka 16 Gf 47.51N 30.34 E
Vrakhiónas 15 Dl 37.48N 20.45 E
Vran 14 Lg 43.39N 17.27 E
Vrancea [2] 15 Jd 45.50N 26.42 E
Vranica 14 Lg 43.57N 17.44 E
Vranje 15 Eg 42.33N 21.54 E
Vranov nad Topľou 10 Rh 48.54N 21.41 E
Vrăška čuka, Prohod- 15 Ff 43.50N 22.23 E
Vratnica 15 Eg 42.08N 21.07 E
Vratnik, prohod- 15 Jg 42.49N 26.10 E
Vrbas 14 Le 45.07N 17.31 E
Vrbas 15 Cd 45.34N 19.39 E
Vrbno pod Pradědem 10 Nf 50.08N 17.23 E
Vrbovsko 14 Je 45.22N 15.05 E
Vrchlabí 10 Lf 50.38N 15.37 E
Vrede 37 De 27.30 S 29.06 E
Vreden 12 Ib 52.02N 6.50 E
Vredenburg 37 Bf 32.54 S 17.59 E
Vredendal 37 Bf 31.41 S 18.35 E
Vresse, Vresse-sur-Semois- 12 Ge 49.52N 4.56 E
Vresse-sur-Semois 12 Ge 49.52N 4.56 E
Vresse-sur-Semois-Vresse 12 Ge 49.52N 4.56 E
Vretstorp 8 Fe 59.02N 14.52 E
Vrhnika 14 Ie 45.58N 14.18 E
Vries 12 Ia 53.05N 6.36 E
Vriezenveen 12 Ib 52.26N 6.36 E
Vrigstad 8 Fg 57.21N 14.28 E
Vron 12 Dd 50.19N 1.45 E
Vršac 15 Ed 45.07N 21.18 E
Vryburg 31 Jk 26.55 S 24.45 E
Vryheid 37 Ee 27.52 S 30.38 E
Vsetín 10 Ng 49.21N 18.00 E
Vsevidof, Mount- 40a Eb 53.07N 168.43W
Vsevoložsk 7 Hf 60.04N 30.41 E
Vstrečny 20 Lc 68.00N 165.58 E
Vtačnik 10 Oh 48.42N 18.37 E
Vuanggava 63d Cc 18.52 S 178.54W
Vučitrn 15 Dg 42.49N 20.58 E
Vučjak 15 Fh 41.28N 22.20 E
Vuka 14 Me 45.21N 19.00 E
Vukovar 14 Me 45.21N 19.00 E
Vuktyl 19 Fc 63.50N 57.25 E
Vulavu 63a Dc 8.31 S 159.48 E
Vulcan 15 Gd 45.23N 23.16 E
Vulcan, Vîrful- 15 Fc 46.14N 22.58 E
Vulcano 14 Il 38.25N 15.00 E
Vulkanešty 16 Fg 45.38N 28.27 E
Vulture 14 Jj 40.57N 15.38 E
Vung Tau 25 Lf 10.21N 107.04 E
Vunindawa 63d Bb 17.49 S 178.19 E
Vunisea Station 61 Ec 19.03 S 178.09 E
Vuohijarvi 8 Lc 61.10N 26.40 E
Vuoksa 8 Nd 60.35N 30.42 E
Vuoksa, Ozero- [R.S.F.S.R.] 8 Mc 61.00N 30.00 E
Vuoksa, Ozero- [R.S.F.S.R.] 8 Md 60.38N 29.55 E
Vuollerim 7 Ec 66.25N 20.36 E
Vuosjärvi 8 Ka 63.00N 25.30 E
Vuotso 7 Gb 68.06N 27.08 E
Vuranimala 63a Ec 9.05 S 160.51 E
Vyborg 6 Ic 60.42N 28.45 E
Vyčegda 5 Kc 61.18N 46.36 E
Vyčegodski 7 Lf 61.17N 46.48 E
Východočeský kraj [3] 10 Lf 50.10N 16.00 E
Východoslovenská nižina 10 Rh 48.35N 21.50 E
Východoslovenský kraj [3] 10 Rg 49.00N 21.15 E
Vyg 7 Ie 63.17N 35.17 E
Vygoda [Ukr.-U.S.S.R.] 15 Nc 46.38N 30.24 E
Vygoda [Ukr.-U.S.S.R.] 10 Uh 48.52N 24.01 E
Vygozero, Ozero- 5 Jc 63.35N 34.45 E
Vyhandu/Võhandu Jõgi 8 Lf 58.03N 27.40 E
Vyja 7 Le 62.57N 46.42 E
Vyksa 19 Ed 55.20N 42.12 E
Vym 19 Fc 62.13N 50.25 E
Vynnu/Võnnu 8 Lf 58.15N 27.10 E
Vyrica 19 Dd 59.24N 30.19 E
Vyrnwy 9 Ki 52.45N 2.50W
Vyrtsjarv, Ozero-/Vörts Järv 7 Gg 58.15N 26.05 E
Vyru/Võru 19 Cd 57.52N 27.05 E
Vyša 16 Mb 54.03N 42.06 E
Vyšgorod 16 Gd 50.38N 30.29 E
Vyšgorodok 8 Mh 56.55N 28.05 E
Vyškov 10 Mg 49.17N 17.00 E
Vyškovsk, pereval 10 Th 48.38N 23.45 E
Vyšni Voloček 19 Dd 57.37N 34.32 E
Vysock 7 Gf 60.36N 28.36 E
Vysoké Tatry=High Tatra (EN) 10 Pg 49.10N 20.00 E
Vysokogorny 20 If 50.07N 139.10 E
Vysokogorsk 28 Mh 44.23N 135.23 E
Vysokoje 10 Td 52.22N 23.26 E
Vysokovsk 7 Ih 56.21N 36.29 E
Vyšši Brod 10 Kh 48.37N 14.18 E
Vytebet 16 Ic 53.53N 35.38 E
Vytegra 19 Dc 61.01N 36.28 E
Vyvenka 20 Ld 60.10N 165.20 E
Vyzu/Vošu 8 Ke 59.30N 25.50 E
Vzmorje 20 Jg 47.45N 142.30 E

W

Wa 34 Ec 10.03N 2.29W
Waal 11 Kc 51.55N 4.30 E
Waalre 12 Hc 51.23N 5.27 E
Waalwijk 12 Hc 51.41N 5.04 E
Waar, Meos- 26 Jg 2.05 S 134.23 E
Waardgronden 12 Ha 53.12N 5.05 E
Waarschoot 12 Fc 51.09N 3.36 E
Wabana 42 Mg 47.38N 52.57W
Wabao, Cap- 63b Ce 21.36 S 167.51 E
Wabasca 42 Ge 56.00N 113.53W
Wabasca 42 Fe 58.21N 115.20W
Wabash 38 Kf 37.46N 88.02W
Wabash 44 Ee 40.48N 85.49W
Wabasha 45 Jd 44.23N 92.02W
Wabash River 45 Lh 37.46N 88.02W
Wabowden 42 Hf 54.55N 98.38W
Wąbrzeźno 10 Oc 53.17N 18.57 E
Wabu Hu 27 Ke 32.20N 116.55 E
Wachau 14 Jb 48.20N 15.25 E
Wachile 35 Fe 4.33N 39.03 E
Wachusett Seamount (EN) 57 Lh 32.00 S 151.20W
Waco 39 Jf 31.55N 97.08W
Waconda Lake 45 Gg 39.30N 98.30W
Wadayama 29 Dd 35.20N 134.51 E
Wad Bandah 35 Dc 13.06N 27.57 E
Waddān 33 Cd 29.10N 16.08 E
Waddān, Jabal- 33 Cd 29.20N 16.20 E
Waddeneilanden=West Frisian Islands (EN) 11 Ka 53.30N 5.00 E
Waddenzee 11 Ha 53.20N 5.30 E
Waddington, Mount- 38 Gd 51.23N 125.15W
Wadena 45 Ic 46.26N 95.08W
Wadern 12 Ie 49.32N 6.53 E
Wadern-Nunkirchen 12 Ie 49.32N 6.53 E
Wadersloh 12 Kc 51.44N 8.15 E
Wadersloh-Liesborn 12 Kc 51.43N 8.16 E
Wadesboro 44 Gh 34.58N 80.04W
Wadhams 46 Ba 51.30N 127.31W
Wādī Bīshah 23 Fe 21.24N 43.26 E
Wādī Fajr 23 Ec 30.17N 38.18 E
Wādī Ḩalfā' 31 Kf 21.56N 31.20 E
Wādī Jimāl, Jazīrat- 24 Fj 24.40N 35.10 E
Wādī Mūsá 24 Fg 30.19N 35.29 E
Wādī Shiḩan 35 Ib 18.10N 52.57 E
Wad Madanī 31 Kg 14.24N 33.32 E
Wad Nimr 35 Ec 14.32N 32.08 E
Wadowice 10 Pg 49.53N 19.30 E
Wadsworth 46 Fg 39.38N 119.17W
Wafangdian → Fuxian 27 Ld 39.38N 121.59 E
Wafrah 23 Gd 28.25N 47.56 E
Waga-Gawa 29 Gb 39.18N 141.07 E
Wagenfeld 12 Kb 52.33N 8.35 E
Wagenfeld-Ströhen 12 Kb 52.32N 8.39 E
Wageningen 12 Hc 51.57N 5.41 E
Wager, Qar- 35 Hc 10.01N 45.30 E
Wager Bay 38 Kc 65.26N 88.40W
Wagga Wagga 58 Fh 35.07 S 147.22 E
Waghäusel 12 Ke 49.15N 8.30 E
Wagin 58 Ch 33.18 S 117.21 E
Waginger See 10 Ii 47.58N 12.50 E
Wagoner 45 Ii 35.58N 95.22W
Wagon Mound 45 Dh 36.01N 104.42W
Wagontire Mountain 46 Fe 43.21N 119.53W
Wagrien 10 Gb 54.15N 10.45 E
Wągrowiec 10 Nd 52.49N 17.11 E
Wah 25 Eb 33.48N 72.42 E
Waha 31 If 28.10N 19.57 E
Wahai 26 Ig 2.48 S 129.30 E
Wahiawa 60 Oc 21.30N 158.02W
Wahoo 45 Hf 41.13N 96.37W
Wahpeton 43 Hb 46.16N 96.36W
Waialeale, Mount- 65a Ba 22.04N 159.30W
Waialua 65a Cb 21.35N 158.08W
Waianae 65a Cb 21.27N 158.12W
Waiau 62 Ee 42.47 S 173.22 E
Waiau 61 Dh 42.39 S 173.03 E
Waiblingen 10 Fh 48.50N 9.18 E
Waibstadt 12 Ke 49.18N 8.56 E
Waidhofen an der Thaya 14 Jb 48.49N 15.17 E
Waidhofen an der Ybbs 14 Ic 47.58N 14.46 E
Waigame 26 Ig 1.50 S 129.49 E
Waigeo, Pulau- 57 Ee 0.14 S 130.45 E
Waihi 62 Fb 37.24 S 175.50 E
Waihou 62 Fb 37.10 S 175.33 E
Waikabubak 26 Gh 9.38 S 119.25 E
Waikare, Lake- 62 Fb 37.25 S 175.10 E
Waikaremoana, Lake- 61 Eg 38.45 S 177.05 E
Waikato 62 Fb 37.23 S 174.43 E
Waikawa 62 Cg 46.38 S 169.08 E
Waikouaiti 62 Df 45.36 S 170.41 E
Waikangilala 63d Cb 16.45 S 179.06W
Wailua 65a Ba 22.03N 159.20W
Wailuku 60 Oc 20.53N 156.30W
Waimamaku 62 Ea 35.34 S 173.29 E
Waimanalo Beach 65a Db 21.20N 157.42W
Waimangaroa 62 Dd 41.43 S 171.46 E
Waimate 62 Df 44.45 S 171.03 E
Waimea 65a Fc 20.02N 155.40W
Waimes 12 Id 50.25N 6.07 E
Wainfleet All Saints 12 Ca 53.06N 0.15 E
Wainganga 21 Jh 19.36N 79.48 E
Waingapu 26 Hh 9.39 S 120.16 E
Waini Point 50 Gh 8.24N 59.49W
Waini River 50 Gh 8.24N 59.51W
Wainwright [Ak.-U.S.] 40 Gb 70.38N 160.01W
Wainwright [Alta.-Can.] 42 Gf 52.49N 110.52W
Waiouru 62 Fb 39.29 S 175.40 E
Waipahu 65a Cb 21.23N 158.01W
Waipara 62 Ee 43.03 S 172.45 E
Waipawa 62 Gc 39.56 S 176.35 E
Waipiro 62 Hc 38.02 S 178.20 E
Waipu 62 Fa 35.59 S 174.26 E
Waipukurau 62 Gd 40.00 S 176.33 E
Wairakei 62 Gc 38.37 S 176.05 E
Wairarapa, Lake- 62 Fd 41.15 S 175.15 E
Wairau 62 Fd 41.31 S 174.03 E
Wairoa 61 Eg 39.03 S 177.26 E
Wairoa 62 Fb 36.11 S 174.02 E
Waitaki 62 Df 44.56 S 171.09 E
Waitangi 61 Fh 43.56 S 176.34W
Waitara 61 Dg 39.00 S 174.14 E
Waitati 62 Df 45.45 S 170.34 E
Waitemata 62 Fb 36.50 S 174.40 E
Waitotara 62 Fc 39.48 S 174.44 E
Waiuku 62 Fb 37.15 S 174.44 E
Waiwerang 26 Hh 8.23 S 123.09 E
Waiyevo 61 Fc 16.48 S 179.59W
Wājid 35 Ge 3.50N 43.14 E
Wajima 28 Nf 37.24N 136.54 E
Wajir 31 Ih 1.42N 40.04 E
Waka [Eth.] 35 Fd 7.09N 37.19 E
Waka [Zaire] 36 Db 1.01N 20.13 E
Wakamatsu-Shima 29 Ae 32.54N 129.00 E
Wakasa-Wan 27 Od 35.45N 135.40 E
Wakatipu, Lake- 61 Ci 45.05 S 168.35 E
Wakaya 63d Bb 17.37 S 179.00 E
Wakayama 22 Pf 34.13N 135.11 E
Wakayama Ken [2] 28 Mh 33.55N 135.20 E
Wake 29 Dd 34.48N 134.08 E
Wa Keeney 45 Gg 39.01N 99.53W
Wakefield [Eng.-U.K.] 9 Lh 53.42N 1.29W
Wakefield [N.Z.] 62 Ed 41.24 S 173.03 E

Index Symbols

[1] Independent Nation
[2] State, Region
[3] District, County
[4] Municipality
[5] Colony, Dependency
Continent
Physical Region
Historical or Cultural Region
Mount, Mountain
Volcano
Hill
Mountains, Mountain Range
Hills, Escarpment
Plateau, Upland
Pass, Gap
Plain, Lowland
Delta
Salt Flat
Valley, Canyon
Crater, Cave
Karst Features
Depression
Polder
Desert, Dunes
Forest, Woods
Heath, Steppe
Oasis
Cape, Point
Coast, Beach
Cliff
Peninsula
Isthmus
Sandbank
Island
Atoll
Rock, Reef
Islands, Archipelago
Rocks, Reefs
Coral Reef
Well, Spring
Geyser
River, Stream
Waterfall Rapids
River Mouth, Estuary
Lake
Salt Lake
Intermittent Lake
Reservoir
Swamp, Pond
Canal
Glacier
Ice Shelf, Pack Ice
Ocean
Sea
Gulf, Bay
Strait, Fjord
Lagoon
Bank
Seamount
Tablemount
Ridge
Shelf
Basin
Escarpment, Sea Scarp
Fracture
Trench, Abyss
National Park, Reserve
Point of Interest
Recreation Site
Cave, Cavern
Historic Site
Ruins
Wall, Walls
Church, Abbey
Temple
Scientific Station
Airport
Port
Lighthouse
Mine
Tunnel
Dam, Bridge

Index Symbols

[1] Independent Nation
[2] State, Region
[3] District, County
[4] Municipality
[5] Colony, Dependency
Continent
Physical Region

Historical or Cultural Region
Mount, Mountain
Volcano
Hill
Mountains, Mountain Range
Hills, Escarpment
Plateau, Upland

Pass, Gap
Plain, Lowland
Delta
Salt Flat
Valley, Canyon
Crater, Cave
Karst Features

Depression
Polder
Desert, Dunes
Forest, Woods
Heath, Steppe
Oasis
Cape, Point

Coast, Beach
Cliff
Peninsula
Isthmus
Sandbank
Island
Atoll

Rock, Reef
Islands, Archipelago
Rocks, Reefs
Coral Reef
Well, Spring
Geyser
River, Stream

Waterfall Rapids
River Mouth, Estuary
Lake
Salt Lake
Intermittent Lake
Reservoir
Swamp, Pond

Canal
Glacier
Ice Shelf, Pack Ice
Ocean
Sea
Gulf, Bay
Strait, Fjord

Lagoon
Bank
Seamount
Tablemount
Ridge
Shelf
Basin

Escarpment, Sea Scarp
Fracture
Trench, Abyss
National Park, Reserve
Point of Interest
Recreation Site
Cave, Cavern

Historic Site
Ruins
Wall, Walls
Church, Abbey
Temple
Scientific Station
Airport

Port
Lighthouse
Mine
Tunnel
Dam, Bridge

Wolseley 42 Hf 50.25N 103.19W
Wolstenholme, Cap - 42 Jd 62.34N 77.30W
Wolstenholme Fjord 41 Ec 76.40N 69.45W
Wolsztyn 10 Md 52.08N 16.06 E
Wolvega, Weststellingwerf- 12 Ib 52.53N 6.00 E
Wolverhampton 9 Ki 52.36N 2.08W
Wolverton 9 Mi 52.04N 0.50W
Wŏnju 27 Md 37.21N 127.58 E
Wŏnsan 22 Of 39.10N 127.26 E
Wonseradeel 12 Ha 53.06N 5.28 E
Wonseradeel-Witmarsum 12 Ha 53.06N 5.28 E
Wonthaggi 59 Jg 38.36S 145.35 E
Woodall Mountain 45 Li 34.45N 88.11W
Woodbridge 9 Oi 52.06N 1.19 E
Woodbridge Bay 51g Bb 15.19N 61.25W
Woodhall Spa 12 Ba 53.09N 0.13W
Woodland [Ca.-U.S.] 46 Eg 38.41N 121.46W
Woodland [Wa.-U.S.] 46 Dd 45.54N 122.45W
Woodlark Island 57 Ge 9.05S 152.50 E
Wood Mountain 46 Lb 49.14N 106.20W
Woodridge 45 Hb 49.17N 96.09W
Wood River 46 Lb 50.08N 106.10W
Wood River Lakes 40 He 59.30N 158.45W
Woodroffe, Mount- 59 Ge 26.20S 131.45 E
Woods, Lake- 59 Gc 17.50S 133.30 E
Woods, Lake of the- 38 Je 49.15N 94.45W
Woods Hole 44 Le 41.31N 70.40W
Woodside 46 Jg 39.21N 110.18W
Woodstock [Eng.-U.K.] 9 Lj 51.52N 1.21W
Woodstock [N.B.-Can.] 42 Kg 46.09N 67.34W
Woodstock [Ont.-Can.] 44 Gd 43.08N 80.45W
Woodstock [Vt.-U.S.] 44 Kd 43.37N 72.31W
Woodville [Ms.-U.S.] 45 Kk 31.01N 91.18W
Woodville [N.Z.] 62 Fd 40.20S 175.52 E
Woodville [Tx.-U.S.] 45 Ik 30.46N 94.25W
Woodward 43 Hd 36.26N 99.24W
Wooler 9 Kf 55.33N 2.01W
Woomera 59 Hf 31.11S 137.10 E
Wooramel River 59 Ce 25.47S 114.10 E
Wooster 44 Ge 40.46N 81.57W
Worcester 9 Ki 52.15N 2.10W
Worcester [Eng.-U.K.] 9 Ki 52.11N 2.13W
Worcester [Ma.-U.S.] 43 Mc 42.16N 71.48W
Worcester [S.Afr.] 31 Il 33.39S 19.27 E
Worcester Range 66 Jf 78.50S 161.00 E
Wörgl 14 Gc 47.29N 12.04 E
Workai, Pulau- 26 Jh 6.40S 134.40 E
Workington 9 Jg 54.39N 3.33W
Worksop 9 Lh 53.18N 1.07W
Workum 12 Hb 52.59N 5.27 E
Worland 43 Fc 44.01N 107.57W
Wormer 12 Gb 52.30N 4.52 E
Wormhout 12 Ed 50.53N 2.28 E
Worms 10 Eg 49.38N 8.21 E
Worms Head 9 Ij 51.34N 4.20W
Wörrstadt 12 Ke 49.50N 8.06 E
Wörth am Rhein 12 Ke 49.03N 8.16 E
Wörther-See 14 Id 46.37N 14.10 E
Worthing 9 Mk 50.48N 0.23W
Worthington 43 Hc 43.37N 95.36W
Wosi 26 Ig 0.11S 127.58 E
Wotho Atoll 57 Hc 10.06N 165.59 E
Wotje Atoll 57 Id 9.27N 170.02 E
Woudenberg 12 Hb 52.05N 5.25 E
Wounnioné, Pointe- 63b Db 14.54S 168.02 E
Wounta, Laguna de- 49 Fg 13.38N 83.34W
Wour 35 Ba 21.21N 15.57 E
Wousi 63b Cb 15.22S 166.39 E
Wowoni, Pulau- 26 Hg 4.08S 123.06 E
Woy Woy 59 Kf 33.30S 151.20 E
Wrangel, Ostrov-=Wrangel Island (EN) 21 Tb 71.00N 179.30 E
Wrangel Island (EN)= Wrangel, Ostrov- 21 Tb 71.00N 179.30 E
Wrangell 39 Fd 56.28N 132.23W
Wrangell, Cape- 40a Ab 52.50N 172.26 E
Wrangell Mountains 38 Ec 62.00N 143.00W
Wrath, Cape- 5 Fd 58.37N 5.01W
Wray 43 Gc 40.05N 102.13W
Wreake 12 Ab 52.41N 1.05W
Wreck Reef 57 Gg 22.15S 155.10 E
Wrecks, Bay of- 64g Bb 1.52N 157.17W
Wrexham 9 Kh 53.03N 3.00W
Wright Island 66 Of 74.03S 116.45W
Wright Patman Lake 45 Ij 33.16N 94.14W
Wrightson, Mount- 46 Jk 31.42N 110.50W
Wrigley 42 Fd 63.19N 123.38W
Wrigley Gulf 66 Nf 74.00S 129.00W
Wrocław 10 Me 51.05N 17.00 E
Wrocław=Breslau (EN) 6 He 51.06N 17.00 E
Wronki 10 Md 52.43N 16.23 E
Wrotham 12 Cc 51.18N 0.19 E
Wroxham 12 Db 52.42N 1.24 E
Września 10 Nd 52.20N 17.34 E
Wschowa 10 Me 51.48N 16.19 E
Wu'an 28 Cf 36.42N 114.12 E
Wuchale 35 Fc 11.31N 39.37 E
Wuchang 28 Ib 44.55N 127.11 E
Wuchang, Wuhan- 28 Ci 30.32N 114.18 E
Wucheng (Jiucheng) 28 Df 37.12N 116.04 E
Wuchiu Hsu 27 Kg 25.00N 119.27 E
Wuchuan 28 Ad 41.08N 111.25 E
Wuchuan (Duru) 27 If 28.28N 107.57 E
Wuchuan (Meilü) 27 Jg 21.28N 110.44 E
Wuda 27 Id 39.30N 106.33 E
Wudan → Ongniud Qi 27 Kc 42.58N 119.01 E
Wudao 27 Ld 39.28N 121.30 E
Wudaoliang 27 Fd 35.15N 93.14 E
Wudi 28 Df 37.44N 117.36 E
Wudil 34 Gc 11.49N 8.51 E
Wuding 27 Hf 25.36N 102.27 E
Wudu 27 He 33.24N 105.00 E
Wugang 27 Jf 26.48N 110.32 E
Wugong (Puji) 27 Ie 34.15N 108.14 E
Wuhai 27 Id 39.32N 106.55 E
Wuhan 22 Nf 30.30N 114.20 E
Wuhan-Hankou 28 Ci 30.35N 114.16 E
Wuhan-Hanyang 28 Ci 30.33N 114.16 E
Wuhan- Wuchang 28 Ci 30.32N 114.18 E
Wuhe 27 Ke 33.08N 117.51 E
Wuhu 22 Nf 31.18N 118.27 E
Wuhu (Wanzhi) 28 Ei 31.21N 118.23 E
Wujia He 27 Ic 40.56N 108.52 E
Wu Jiang 21 Mg 29.43N 107.24 E
Wujiang 28 Fi 31.09N 120.38 E
Wukari 31 Hh 7.51N 9.47 E
Wukro 35 Fc 13.48N 39.37 E
Wular 25 Eb 34.30N 74.30 E
Wulff Land 41 Hb 82.19N 50.00W
Wulian (Hongning) 28 Eg 35.45N 119.13 E
Wuliang Shan 27 Hg 24.00N 101.00 E
Wuliaru, Pulau- 26 Jh 7.27S 131.04 E
Wuling Shan 21 Mg 28.20N 110.00 E
Wulongbei 28 Hd 40.15N 124.16 E
Wulongji → Huaibin 28 Ci 32.27N 115.23 E
Wulur 26 Ih 7.09S 128.39 E
Wum 34 Hd 6.23N 10.04 E
Wumei Shan 28 Cj 28.47N 114.50 E
Wümme 12 Ka 53.10N 8.40 E
Wuning 28 Cj 29.17N 115.05 E
Wünnenberg 12 Kc 51.31N 8.42 E
Wünnenberg-Haaren 12 Kc 51.34N 8.44 E
Wunnummin Lake 42 If 52.55N 89.10W
Wun Rog 35 Dd 9.00N 28.21 E
Wunstrof 10 Fd 52.26N 9.25 E
Wuntho 25 Jd 23.54N 95.41 E
Wupper 10 Ce 51.05N 7.00 E
Wuppertal 10 De 51.16N 7.11 E
Wuqi 27 Id 36.57N 108.15 E
Wuqia/Ulugqat 27 Cd 39.40N 75.07 E
Wuqiao (Sangyuan) 28 Df 37.38N 116.23 E
Wuqing (Yangcun) 28 De 39.23N 117.04 E
Würm 12 Kf 48.53N 8.42 E
Wurno 34 Gc 13.18N 5.26 E
Würselen 12 Id 50.49N 6.08 E
Würzburg 6 Gf 49.48N 9.56 E
Wurzen 10 Ie 51.22N 12.44 E
Wu Shan 27 Ie 31.00N 110.00 E
Wushaoling 27 Hd 37.15N 102.50 E
Wuski/Uqturpan 27 Cc 41.10N 79.16 E
Wusong 28 Fi 31.23N 121.29 E
Wüst Seamount (EN) 30 Gl 34.00S 3.40W
Wusuli Jiang 27 Ob 48.28N 135.02 E
Wutach 10 Ei 47.37N 8.15 E
Wutai [China] 28 Be 38.43N 113.14 E
Wutai [China] 27 Dc 44.38N 82.06 E
Wutai Shan 27 Jd 39.04N 113.28 E
Wuustwezel 12 Gc 51.23N 4.36 E
Wuvulu Island 57 Fe 1.43S 142.50 E
Wuwei 28 Di 31.17N 117.54 E
Wuwei (Liangzhou) 22 Mf 37.58N 102.48 E
Wuxi [China] 22 Of 31.32N 120.18 E
Wuxi [China] 27 Ie 31.27N 109.34 E
Wu Xia 27 Je 31.02N 110.10 E
Wuxiang (Duancun) 28 Bf 36.50N 112.51 E
Wuxing (Huzhou) 27 Le 30.47N 120.07 E
Wuxue→Guangji 27 Kf 29.58N 115.32 E
Wuyang [China] 28 Bh 33.26N 113.35 E
Wuyang [China] 27 Jd 36.29N 113.07 E
Wuyang → Zhenyuan 27 If 27.05N 108.26 E
Wuyi [China] 28 Cf 37.49N 115.54 E
Wuyi [China] 28 Ej 28.54N 119.50 E
Wuyiling 27 Mb 48.37N 129.20 E
Wuyi Shan 21 Ng 27.00N 117.00 E
Wuyuan [China] 22 Me 41.08N 108.17 E
Wuyuan [China] 28 Dj 29.15N 117.52 E
Wuyuanzhen→Haiyan 28 Fi 30.31N 120.56 E
Wuzhai 28 Ae 38.54N 111.49 E
Wuzhen 28 Ai 31.42N 112.00 E
Wuzhi Shan [China] 28 Ed 40.31N 118.02 E
Wuzhi Shan [China] 21 Mh 18.54N 109.40 E
Wuzhong 27 Id 38.00N 106.10 E
Wuzhou 22 Ng 23.32N 111.21 E
Wyalkatchem 59 Df 31.10S 117.22 E
Wyandotte 44 Fd 42.12N 83.10W
Wyandra 59 Je 27.15S 145.59 E
Wye 9 Kj 51.37N 2.39W
Wye 12 Cc 51.11N 0.56 E
Wyemandoo, Mount- 59 De 28.31S 118.32 E
Wyk auf Föhr 10 Eb 54.42N 8.34 E
Wylie, Lake- 44 Gh 35.07N 81.02W
Wymondham 9 Oi 52.34N 1.07 E
Wyndham [Austl.] 58 Df 15.28S 128.06 E
Wyndham [N.Z.] 62 Cg 46.20S 168.51 E
Wyndmere 45 Hc 46.16N 97.08W
Wynne 45 Ki 35.14N 90.47W
Wynniatt Bay 42 Gb 72.50N 111.00W
Wynyard [Austl.] 59 Jh 40.59S 145.41 E
Wynyard [Sask.-Can.] 42 Hf 51.47N 104.10W
Wyoming 44 Ed 42.54N 85.42W
Wyoming 43 Fc 43.00N 107.30W
Wyoming Peak 43 Ec 42.36N 110.37W
Wyśmierzyce 10 Qe 51.38N 20.49 E
Wysoka 10 Nc 53.11N 17.05 E
Wysokie Mazowieckie 10 Sd 52.56N 22.32 E
Wyszków 10 Rd 52.36N 21.28 E
Wyszogród 10 Qd 52.23N 20.11 E
Wytheville 44 Gg 36.57N 81.07W
Wyville Thomson Ridge (EN) 9 Fa 60.10N 8.00W
Wyvis, Ben- 9 Id 57.42N 4.30W

X

Xaintrie 11 Ii 45.00N 2.10 E
Xainza 27 Ee 30.50N 88.37 E
Xaitongmoin 27 Ef 29.26N 88.08 E
Xai-Xai 31 Kk 25.04S 33.39 E
Xamba→Hanggin Houqi 27 Ic 40.59N 107.07 E
Xam Nua 25 Kd 20.25N 104.02 E
Xangongo 31 Ij 16.46S 14.59 E
Xang Qu 27 Ef 29.22N 89.09 E
Xanten 10 Ce 51.40N 6.27 E
Xánthi 15 Hh 41.08N 24.53 E
Xanthos 24 Cd 36.20N 29.20 E
Xanxerê 56 Jc 26.53S 52.23W
Xapuri 54 Ef 10.39S 68.31W
Xar Hudag 27 Jb 45.06N 114.30 E
Xar Moron 28 Ac 42.37N 111.02 E
Xar Moron He 27 Lc 43.24N 120.39 E
Xarrama 13 Df 38.14N 8.20W
Xátiva/Játiva 13 Lf 38.59N 0.31W
Xau, Lake- 37 Cd 21.15S 24.44 E
Xavantes, Represa de- 55 Hf 23.20S 49.35W
Xavantina 55 Fe 21.15S 52.48W
Xayar 27 Dc 41.15N 82.50 E
Xebert 28 Fc 44.00N 122.00 E
Xêgar → Tingri 27 Ef 28.41N 87.00 E
Xenia 44 Ff 39.41N 83.56W
Xiabin Ansha 27 Ke 9.48N 116.38 E
Xiachengzi 28 Kb 44.41N 130.26 E
Xiacun → Rushan 28 Ff 36.55N 121.30 E
Xiaguan 27 Hf 25.32N 100.12 E
Xiahe (Labrang) 27 Hd 35.18N 102.30 E
Xiajin 28 Cf 36.57N 116.00 E
Xiamen 22 Ng 24.32N 118.06 E
Xi'an 22 Mf 34.15N 108.50 E
Xianfeng 27 If 29.41N 109.09 E
Xiangcheng 28 Bh 33.51N 113.29 E
Xiangcheng/Qagchêng 27 Gf 28.56N 99.46 E
Xiangcheng (Shuizhai) 28 Ch 33.27N 114.53 E
Xiangfan 22 Nf 32.03N 112.05 E
Xianggang/Hong Kong 22 Ng 22.15N 114.10 E
Xianghua Ling 27 Jf 25.26N 112.32 E
Xianghuang Qi (Xin Bulag) 27 Jc 42.12N 113.59 E
Xiang Jiang 21 Ng 29.26N 113.08 E
Xiangkhoang 25 Ke 19.20N 103.22 E
Xiangkhoang, Plateau de- 25 Ke 19.30N 103.10 E
Xiangquan He 27 Ce 32.05N 79.20 E
Xiangshan (Dancheng) 27 Lf 29.29N 121.52 E
Xiangshan Gang 28 Fj 29.35N 121.38 E
Xiangtan 22 Ng 27.54N 112.55 E
Xiangtang 28 Cj 28.26N 115.59 E
Xiangyin 28 Bj 28.41N 112.53 E
Xiangyuan 28 Bf 36.32N 113.02 E
Xianju 27 Lf 28.50N 120.42 E
Xianning 28 Cj 29.52N 114.17 E
Xiannümiao→Jiangdu 28 Eh 32.30N 119.33 E
Xiantaozhen → Mianyang 28 Bi 30.22N 113.27 E
Xianxia Ling 27 Kf 28.24N 118.40 E
Xianxian 28 De 38.12N 116.07 E
Xianyang 27 Ie 34.26N 108.40 E
Xiaobole Shan 27 La 51.46N 124.09 E
Xiao'ergou 27 Lb 49.10N 123.43 E
Xiaogan 27 Je 30.52N 113.58 E
Xiao He 28 Bf 37.38N 112.24 E
Xiao Hinggan Ling=Lesser Khingan Range (EN) 21 Oe 48.45N 127.00 E
Xiaoling He 28 Fd 40.55N 121.12 E
Xiaoluan He 28 Dd 41.36N 117.05 E
Xiaoqing He 28 Ef 37.19N 118.59 E
Xiaowutai Shan 28 Ce 39.57N 114.59 E
Xiaoxian 28 Dg 34.11N 116.56 E
Xiaoyi 28 Af 37.07N 111.48 E
Xiaoyi → Gongxian 28 Bg 34.46N 112.57 E
Xiapu 27 Kf 26.57N 119.59 E
Xiawa 28 Fc 42.36N 120.33 E
Xiayi 28 Dg 34.14N 116.07 E
Xiazhuang → Linshu 28 Eg 34.56N 118.38 E
Xicalango, Punta- 48 Nh 19.41N 92.00W
Xichang 22 Mg 27.52N 102.15 E
Xicheng → Yangyuan 28 Cd 40.08N 114.10 E
Xicoténcatl 48 Jf 23.00N 98.56W
Xicotepec de Juárez 48 Kg 20.17N 97.57W
Xiejiaji → Qingyun 28 Df 37.46N 117.22 E
Xifei He 28 Dh 32.38N 116.39 E
Xifeng 28 Hc 42.45N 124.44 E
Xifengzhen 27 Id 35.40N 107.42 E
Xigazê 22 Kg 29.15N 88.52 E
Xi He [China] 27 Hc 42.23N 101.03 E
Xi He [China] 28 Dj 29.38N 116.53 E
Xiheying 28 Ce 39.53N 114.42 E
Xihua 28 Ch 33.48N 114.31 E
Xi Jang 21 Ng 23.05N 114.23 E
Xiji [China] 27 Id 35.52N 105.35 E
Xiji [China] 28 Ia 46.09N 127.08 E
Xi Jiang 27 Jg 23.05N 114.23 E
Xijir Ulan Hu 27 Fd 35.12N 90.18 E
Xikouzi 27 La 42.58N 120.29 E
Xiligou → Ulan 27 Gd 36.55N 98.16 E
Xilin 27 Ig 24.30N 105.05 E
Xilin Gol 28 Dc 43.55N 116.05 E
Xilin Hot→Abagnar Qi 22 Ne 43.58N 116.08 E
Xilitla 48 Jg 21.20N 98.58W
Xilókastron 15 Fk 38.05N 22.38 E
Ximiao 27 Hc 41.04N 100.14 E
Xin'an 28 Bg 34.43N 112.09 E
Xin'anjiang 28 Ei 29.27N 119.15 E
Xin'anjiang Shuiku 27 Kf 29.25N 119.05 E
Xin'anzhen → Guannan 28 Eg 34.04N 119.21 E
Xin'anzhen → Xinyi 27 Ke 34.17N 118.14 E
Xin Barag Youqi (Altan-Emel) 27 Kb 48.41N 116.47 E
Xin Barag Zuoqi (Amgalang) 27 Kb 48.13N 118.14 E
Xinbin 28 Hd 41.44N 125.02 E
Xin Bulag→Xianghuang Qi 27 Jc 42.12N 113.59 E
Xincai 27 Je 32.40N 114.57 E
Xinchang 28 Fj 29.30N 120.54 E
Xincheng [China] 28 Bf 37.57N 112.33 E
Xincheng [China] 27 Ig 24.04N 108.39 E
Xincheng [China] 27 Id 38.33N 106.10 E
Xincheng (Gaobeidian) 28 Ce 39.20N 115.50 E
Xindi → Honghu 28 Bj 29.50N 113.28 E
Xing'an→Ankang 22 Mf 32.37N 109.03 E
Xingcheng 28 Fd 40.38N 120.43 E
Xingguo 27 Kf 26.22N 115.21 E
Xinghai 27 Gd 35.45N 99.59 E
Xinghe 27 Jc 40.52N 113.56 E
Xinghua 28 Eh 32.56N 119.49 E
Xingkai Hu=Khanka Lake (EN) 21 Pe 45.00N 132.24 E
Xinglong 28 Dd 40.25N 117.31 E
Xinglongzhen 28 Ia 46.26N 127.03 E
Xingren 27 If 25.26N 105.08 E
Xingtai 22 Nf 37.00N 114.30 E
Xingtang 28 Ce 38.26N 114.33 E
Xingu, Rio- 52 Kf 1.30S 51.53W
Xingxingxia 27 Gc 41.47N 95.07 E
Xingyang 28 Bg 34.47N 113.21 E
Xinryi (Huangcaoba) 27 Hf 25.03N 104.55 E
Xingzi 28 Dj 29.28N 116.03 E
Xinhe 28 Cf 37.32N 115.14 E
Xinhe/Toksu 27 Dc 41.34N 82.38 E
Xin Hot→Abag Qi 27 Jc 44.01N 114.59 E
Xinhuai He 28 Fg 34.23N 120.05 E
Xinhui → Aohan Qi 28 Ec 42.18N 119.53 E
Xining 22 Mf 36.37N 101.46 E
Xinji → Shulu 28 Cf 37.56N 115.14 E
Xinjian 28 Cj 28.41N 115.50 E
Xin Jiang 28 Dj 28.37N 116.40 E
Xinjiangkou → Songzi 28 Ai 30.10N 116.46 E
Xinjiang Uygur Zizhiqu (Hsin-chiang-wei-wu-erh Tzu-chih-ch'ü)=Sinkiang (EN) 27 Ec 42.00N 86.00 E
Xinjin 27 He 30.25N 103.46 E
Xinjin (Pulandian) 27 Ld 39.24N 121.59 E
Xinkai He 28 Gc 43.36N 122.31 E
Xinle 28 Ce 38.15N 114.40 E
Xinlin 28 Ec 43.58N 118.03 E
Xinlitun [China] 27 Ma 50.58N 126.39 E
Xinlitun [China] 28 Gc 42.01N 122.11 E
Xinlong/Nyagrong 27 He 30.57N 100.12 E
Xinmin 28 Gc 42.00N 122.50 E
Xinpu→Lianyungang 22 Nf 34.34N 119.15 E
Xinqing 27 Mb 48.15N 129.31 E
Xintai 28 Dg 35.54N 117.44 E
Xinwen (Suncun) 27 Kd 35.49N 117.38 E
Xinxian [China] 27 Jd 38.24N 112.43 E
Xinxian [China] 28 Ci 31.42N 114.50 E
Xinxiang 22 Nf 35.17N 113.50 E
Xinyang 27 Je 32.05N 114.07 E
Xinye 28 Bh 32.30N 112.22 E
Xinyi (Xin'anzhen) 27 Ke 34.17N 118.14 E
Xinyi He 28 Eg 34.29N 119.49 E
Xinyuan/Künes 27 Dc 43.24N 83.18 E
Xinyuan→Tianjun 22 Lf 37.18N 99.15 E
Xinzhan 28 Ic 43.52N 127.20 E
Xin Zhen→Hanggin Qi 27 Id 39.54N 108.55 E
Xinzheng 28 Bg 34.25N 113.46 E
Xinzhou 28 Ci 30.51N 114.49 E
Xioashan 28 Fi 30.10N 120.16 E
Xiong Xian 28 De 38.59N 116.06 E
Xionyuecheng 28 Gd 40.12N 122.08 E
Xiping [China] 28 Ej 28.27N 119.29 E
Xiping [China] 28 Bh 33.22N 114.00 E
Xisha Qundao=Paracel Islands (EN) 21 Nh 16.30N 112.15 E
Xishuangbanna 27 Gg 22.15N 100.00 E
Xishuanghe → Kenli 28 Ef 37.35N 118.30 E
Xishui 28 Ci 30.28N 115.15 E
Xitianmu Shan 27 Ke 30.21N 119.25 E
Xiuanzi → Chongli 28 Cd 40.57N 115.12 E
Xi Ujimqin Qi (Bayan Ul Hot) 27 Kc 44.31N 117.33 E
Xiuning 28 Ej 29.47N 118.11 E
Xiushan 27 If 28.29N 108.58 E
Xiu Shui 28 Cj 29.13N 116.00 E
Xiushui 27 Jf 29.02N 114.33 E
Xiuwu 28 Bg 35.13N 113.27 E
Xiuyan 27 Lc 40.18N 123.10 E
Xiwanzi→Chongli 28 Cf 36.50N 115.10 E
Xixabangma Feng 27 Ef 28.21N 85.47 E
Xixian 28 Ch 32.21N 114.43 E
Xixiang 27 Ie 32.58N 107.45 E
Xiyang 28 Bf 37.38N 113.41 E
Xizang Zizhiqu (Hsi-tsang Tzu-chih-ch'ü)=Tibet (EN) 27 Ee 32.00N 90.00 E
Xizhong Dao 28 Fe 39.25N 121.18 E
Xi Taijnar Hu 27 Fd 37.15N 93.30 E
Xochicalco 48 Jh 18.45N 99.20W
Xochimilco 48 Jh 19.16N 99.06W
Xorkol 27 Fd 39.04N 91.05 E
Xpujil 48 Oh 18.35N 89.25W
Xuancheng 28 Ei 30.56N 118.44 E
Xuande Qundao 26 Fc 17.08N 111.30 E
Xuan'en 27 Ie 30.02N 109.30 E
Xuanhan 27 Ie 31.23N 107.39 E
Xuanhua 27 Kc 40.39N 115.05 E
Xuanwei 27 Hf 26.19N 104.05 E
Xuchang 22 Nf 34.00N 113.58 E
Xuecheng (Lincheng) 28 Dg 34.38N 117.14 E
Xuefeng Shan 27 Jf 27.35N 110.50 E
Xue Shan 27 Gf 27.30N 99.55 E
Xugezhuang → Fengnan 28 Ee 39.34N 118.05 E
Xugou 28 Eg 34.37N 119.08 E
Xugui 27 Gd 35.45N 96.08 E
Xuguit Qi (Yakeshi) 27 Lb 49.16N 120.41 E
Xümatang 27 Ge 33.57N 97.00 E
Xun Jiang 23 Hf 23.28N 111.18 E
Xunke (Qike) 27 Mb 49.34N 128.28 E
Xunwu 27 Kg 24.59N 115.33 E
Xunxian 28 Cg 35.40N 114.33 E
Xupu 27 Jf 27.54N 110.35 E
Xúquer/Júcar 5 Fh 39.09N 0.14W
Xushui 28 Ce 39.02N 115.40 E
Xuwen 27 Jg 20.22N 110.10 E
Xuyi 27 Ke 32.58N 118.33 E
Xuyong (Yongning) 27 If 28.13N 105.26 E
Xuzhou 22 Nf 34.12N 117.13 E

Y

Ya'an 22 Mg 30.00N 102.57 E
Yabassi 34 Ge 4.28N 9.58 E
Yabe 29 Be 32.42N 130.59 E
Yabebyry 55 Dh 27.24S 57.11W
Yabelo 35 Fe 4.53N 38.07 E
Yablonovy Range (EN)= Jablonovy Hrebet 21 Nd 53.30N 115.00 E
Yabrai Shan 27 Hc 40.00N 103.10 E
Yabrīn 35 Ha 23.15N 48.59 E
Yabrūd 24 Gf 33.58N 36.40 E
Yabucoa 51a Cb 18.03N 65.53W
Yabuli 27 Mc 44.56N 128.37 E
Yabulu 59 Jc 19.00S 146.40 E
Yacaré Cururú, Cuchilla- 55 Dj 30.30S 56.33W
Yacaré Norte, Riacho- 55 Cf 22.43S 58.14W
Yacaré Sur, Riacho- 55 Cf 22.43S 58.15W
Yachats 46 Cd 44.20N 124.03W
Yacuma, Rio- 54 Ef 13.38S 65.23W
Yacyretá, Isla- 55 Dh 27.25S 56.30W
Yadé, Massif du- 35 Bd 7.00N 15.30 E
Yādgīr 25 Fe 16.46N 77.08 E
Yadong/Chomo 27 Ef 27.38N 89.03 E
Yae-Dake 29b Ab 26.38N 127.56 E
Yaeyama-Rettō 27 Lg 24.20N 124.00 E
Yafran 33 Bc 32.04N 12.31 E
Yağcilar 15 Lj 39.25N 28.23 E
Yagishiri-Tō 29a Ba 44.26N 141.25 E
Yagoua 34 Ic 10.20N 15.14 E
Yagradagzê Shan 27 Gd 35.09N 95.39 E
Yaguajay 49 Hb 22.19N 79.14W
Yaguari 55 Ej 31.31S 54.58W
Yaguari, Arroyo- 55 Di 29.44S 57.37W
Yahalica de Gonzáles Gallo 48 Hg 21.08N 102.51W
Yahuma 36 Db 1.06N 23.10 E
Yaita 29 Fc 36.50N 139.55 E
Yaizu 29 Fd 34.51N 138.19 E
Yajiang/Nyagquka 27 He 30.07N 100.58 E
Yakacik 24 Ed 36.05N 32.45 E
Yake-Dake 29 Ec 36.14N 137.35 E
Yakeishi-Dake 29 Gb 39.10N 140.50 E
Yakeshi → Xuguit Qi 27 Lb 49.16N 120.41 E
Yake-Yama 29 Gb 39.58N 140.48 E
Yakima 39 Ge 46.36N 120.31W
Yakima River 46 Fc 46.15N 119.02W
Yako 34 Ec 12.58N 2.16W
Yakumo 27 Pc 42.15N 140.16 E
Yaku-Shima 27 Ne 30.20N 130.30 E
Yakutat 40 Le 59.33N 139.44W
Yakutat Bay 40 Ke 59.45N 140.45W
Yala 25 Kg 6.32N 101.19 E
Yalahán, Laguna de- 48 Pg 21.30N 87.15W
Yalcubul, Punta- 48 Og 21.35N 88.35W
Yale Point 46 Kh 36.25N 109.48W
Yalewa Kalou 63d Ab 16.40S 177.46 E
Yalgoo 59 De 28.20S 116.41 E
Yalikavak 15 Kl 37.06N 27.18 E
Yaliköy 15 Lh 41.29N 28.17 E
Yalinga 35 Cd 6.31N 23.13 E
Yaloké 35 Bd 5.19N 17.05 E
Yalong Jiang 21 Mg 26.37N 101.48 E
Yalova 24 Cb 40.39N 29.15 E
Yalu Jiang 21 Of 39.55N 124.20 E
Yalvaç 24 Dc 38.17N 31.11 E
Yām, Ramlat- 33 If 17.42N 45.09 E
Yamada [Jap.] 28 Pe 39.28N 141.57 E
Yamada [Jap.] 29 Be 33.33N 130.45 E
Yamada-Wan 29 Hb 39.30N 142.00 E
Yamaga 29 Be 33.01N 130.41 E
Yamagata 27 Pd 38.15N 140.15 E
Yamagata Ken 28 Pe 38.30N 140.00 E
Yamagawa 29 Bf 31.12N 130.39 E
Yamaguchi 27 Ne 34.10N 131.29 E
Yamaguchi Ken 28 Kh 34.10N 131.30 E
Yamakuni 29 Be 33.24N 131.02 E
Yamal Peninsula (EN)= Jamal, Poluostrov- 21 Ib 70.00N 70.00 E
Yamamoto 29 Ga 40.06N 140.03 E
Yamanaka 29 Ec 36.15N 136.22 E
Yamanashi Ken 28 Og 35.30N 138.45 E
Yamashiro 29 Ce 33.57N 133.43 E
Yamato Rise (EN) 28 Me 39.30N 134.30 E
Yamatsuri 29 Gc 36.53N 140.25 E
Yamazaki 29 Dd 35.00N 134.33 E
Yambi, Mesa de- 54 Dc 1.30N 71.20W
Yambio 31 Jh 4.34N 28.23 E
Yambo 35 Fd 8.25N 36.00 E
Yambu Head 51n Ba 13.09N 61.09W
Yambuya 36 Db 1.16N 24.33 E
Yame 29 Be 33.13N 130.34 E
Yamethin 25 Jd 20.26N 96.09 E
Yamma Yamma, Lake- 59 Ie 26.20S 141.25 E
Yamoto 29 Gb 38.25N 141.13 E
Yamoussoukro 34 Dd 6.49N 5.17W
Yampa River 43 Fc 40.32N 108.59W
Yampi Sound 59 Ec 16.11S 123.40 E
Yamuna 21 Kg 25.30N 81.53 E
Yamunanagar 25 Fb 30.08N 76.59 E
Yamzho Yumco 27 Ff 29.00N 90.40 E
Yanagawa 29 Be 33.10N 130.24 E
Yanahara 29 Dd 34.57N 134.05 E
Yanahuanca 54 Cf 10.30S 76.30W
Yanai 29 Ce 33.58N 132.07 E
Yanam 25 Ge 16.51N 82.15 E
Yan'an 22 Mf 36.36N 109.30 E
Yanaoca 54 Df 14.13S 71.26W
Yanbian 27 Hf 26.51N 101.32 E
Yanbu' 23 Ee 24.05N 38.03 E
Yanchang 27 Jd 36.39N 110.03 E
Yancheng [China] 28 Bh 33.35N 114.00 E
Yancheng [China] 27 Le 33.28N 120.10 E
Yanchi 27 Id 37.47N 107.24 E
Yandé 63b Ae 20.03S 163.48 E
Yandina 63a Dc 9.07S 159.13 E
Yandja 36 Cc 1.41S 17.43 E

Index Symbols

Independent Nation
State, Region
District, County
Municipality
Colony, Dependency
Continent
Physical Region
Historical or Cultural Region
Mount, Mountain
Volcano
Hill
Mountains, Mountain Range
Hills, Escarpment
Plateau, Upland
Pass, Gap
Plain, Lowland
Delta
Salt Flat
Valley, Canyon
Crater, Cave
Karst Features
Depression
Polder
Desert, Dunes
Forest, Woods
Heath, Steppe
Oasis
Cape, Point
Coast, Beach
Cliff
Peninsula
Isthmus
Sandbank
Island
Atoll
Rock, Reef
Islands, Archipelago
Rocks, Reefs
Coral Reef
Well, Spring
Geyser
River, Stream
Waterfall Rapids
River Mouth, Estuary
Lake
Salt Lake
Intermittent Lake
Reservoir
Swamp, Pond
Canal
Glacier
Ice Shelf, Pack Ice
Ocean
Sea
Gulf, Bay
Strait, Fjord
Lagoon
Bank
Seamount
Tablemount
Ridge
Shelf
Basin
Escarpment, Sea Scarp
Fracture
Trench, Abyss
National Park, Reserve
Point of Interest
Recreation Site
Cave, Cavern
Historic Site
Ruins
Wall, Walls
Church, Abbey
Temple
Scientific Station
Airport
Port
Lighthouse
Mine
Tunnel
Dam, Bridge

Index Symbols

- ⊡ Independent Nation
- ⊡ State, Region
- ⊡ District, County
- ⊡ Municipality
- ⊡ Colony, Dependency
- ■ Continent
- ⊡ Physical Region
- ⊞ Historical or Cultural Region
- ⊠ Mount, Mountain
- ⊠ Volcano
- ⊠ Hill
- ⊠ Mountains, Mountain Range
- ⊠ Hills, Escarpment
- ⊠ Plateau, Upland
- ⊠ Pass, Gap
- ⊠ Plain, Lowland
- ⊠ Delta
- ⊠ Salt Flat
- ⊠ Valley, Canyon
- ⊠ Crater, Cave
- ⊠ Karst Features
- ⊠ Depression
- ⊠ Polder
- ⊠ Desert, Dunes
- ⊠ Forest, Woods
- ⊠ Heath, Steppe
- ⊠ Oasis
- ⊠ Cape, Point
- ⊠ Coast, Beach
- ⊠ Cliff
- ⊠ Peninsula
- ⊠ Isthmus
- ⊠ Sandbank
- ⊠ Island
- ⊠ Atoll
- ⊠ Rock, Reef
- ⊠ Islands, Archipelago
- ⊠ Rocks, Reefs
- ⊠ Coral Reef
- ⊠ Well, Spring
- ⊠ Geyser
- ⊠ River, Stream
- ⊠ Waterfall Rapids
- ⊠ River Mouth, Estuary
- ⊠ Lake
- ⊠ Salt Lake
- ⊠ Intermittent Lake
- ⊠ Reservoir
- ⊠ Swamp, Pond
- ⊠ Canal
- ⊠ Glacier
- ⊠ Ice Shelf, Pack Ice
- ⊠ Ocean
- ⊠ Sea
- ⊠ Strait, Fjord
- ⊠ Gulf, Bay
- ⊠ Lagoon
- ⊠ Bank
- ⊠ Seamount
- ⊠ Tablemount
- ⊠ Ridge
- ⊠ Shelf
- ⊠ Basin
- ⊠ Escarpment, Sea Scarp
- ⊠ Fracture
- ⊠ Trench, Abyss
- ⊠ National Park, Reserve
- ⊠ Point of Interest
- ⊠ Recreation Site
- ⊠ Cave, Cavern
- ⊠ Historic Site
- ⊠ Ruins
- ⊠ Wall, Walls
- ⊠ Church, Abbey
- ⊠ Temple
- ⊠ Scientific Station
- ⊠ Airport
- ⊠ Port
- ⊠ Lighthouse
- ⊠ Mine
- ⊠ Tunnel
- ⊠ Dam, Bridge

Index Symbols

[1] Independent Nation — [2] State, Region — [3] District, County — [4] Municipality — [5] Colony, Dependency — Continent — Physical Region — Historical or Cultural Region — Mount, Mountain — Volcano — Hill — Mountains, Mountain Range — Hills, Escarpment — Plateau, Upland — Pass, Gap — Plain, Lowland — Delta — Salt Flat — Valley, Canyon — Crater, Cave — Karst Features — Depression — Polder — Desert, Dunes — Forest, Woods — Heath, Steppe — Oasis — Cape, Point — Coast, Beach — Cliff — Peninsula — Isthmus — Sandbank — Island — Atoll — Rock, Reef — Islands, Archipelago — Rocks, Reefs — Coral Reef — Well, Spring — Geyser — River, Stream — Waterfall Rapids — River Mouth, Estuary — Lake — Salt Lake — Intermittent Lake — Reservoir — Swamp, Pond — Canal — Glacier — Ice Shelf, Pack Ice — Ocean — Sea — Gulf, Bay — Strait, Fjord — Lagoon — Bank — Seamount — Tablemount — Ridge — Shelf — Basin — Escarpment, Sea Scarp — Fracture — Trench, Abyss — National Park, Reserve — Point of Interest — Recreation Site — Cave, Cavern — Historic Site — Ruins — Wall, Walls — Church, Abbey — Temple — Scientific Station — Airport — Port — Lighthouse — Mine — Tunnel — Dam, Bridge

Index Symbols

[1] Independent Nation	Historical or Cultural Region	Pass, Gap	Depression	Coast, Beach	Rock, Reef
[2] State, Region	Mount, Mountain	Plain, Lowland	Polder	Cliff	Islands, Archipelago
[3] District, County	Volcano	Delta	Desert, Dunes	Peninsula	Rocks, Reefs
[4] Municipality	Hill	Salt Flat	Forest, Woods	Isthmus	Coral Reef
[5] Colony, Dependency	Mountains, Mountain Range	Valley, Canyon	Heath, Steppe	Sandbank	Well, Spring
Continent	Hills, Escarpment	Crater, Cave	Oasis	Island	Geyser
Physical Region	Plateau, Upland	Karst Features	Cape, Point	Atoll	River, Stream

Waterfall Rapids	Canal	Lagoon	Escarpment, Sea Scarp	Historic Site
River Mouth, Estuary	Glacier	Bank	Fracture	Ruins
Lake	Ice Shelf, Pack Ice	Seamount	Trench, Abyss	Wall, Walls
Salt Lake	Ocean	Tablemount	National Park, Reserve	Church, Abbey
Intermittent Lake	Sea	Shelf	Point of Interest	Temple
Reservoir	Ridge	Basin	Recreation Site	Scientific Station
Swamp, Pond	Strait, Fjord		Cave, Cavern	Airport

Port
Lighthouse
Mine
Tunnel
Dam, Bridge